The Oxford Companion
—TO THE—
Mind

The Oxford Companion

—— TO THE ——

Mind

Second Edition

EDITED BY

RICHARD L. GREGORY

OXFORD

UNIVERSITY PRESS

OXFORD

UNIVERSITY PRESS

Great Clarendon Street, Oxford OX2 6DP

Oxford University Press is a department of the University of Oxford.
It furthers the University's objective of excellence in research, scholarship,
and education by publishing worldwide in

Oxford New York

Auckland Bangkok Buenos Aires Cape Town Chennai
Dar es Salaam Delhi Hong Kong Istanbul Karachi Kolkata
Kuala Lumpur Madrid Melbourne Mexico City Mumbai Nairobi
São Paulo Shanghai Taipei Tokyo Toronto

Oxford is a registered trade mark of Oxford University Press
in the UK and in certain other countries

Published in the United States
by Oxford University Press Inc., New York

© Oxford University Press 2004

Database right Oxford University Press (maker)

First edition published 1987
Second edition published 2004

British Library Cataloguing in Publication Data
Data available

Library of Congress Cataloging in Publication Data
Data available

ISBN 0–19–866224–6

1 3 5 7 9 10 8 6 4 2

Typeset in Pondicherry, India,
by Alliance Interactive Technology
Printed in Great Britain
on acid-free paper
by Biddles Ltd
King's Lynn, Norfolk

Preface

The mind is the universe in our heads—reaching out to explore physical reality, creating myths and music, arts and sciences—struggling to understand the world out there and itself. This book is about the last: the mind seeking to understand itself. Here in this volume, written by many talented people, is something of what minds have so far discovered of mind.

It was a rare strange honour, nearly thirty years ago, to be invited to edit the first edition of this book. It meant reviewing a wide range of subjects, and persuading friends and colleagues to express their thoughts with brief, telling clarity. Its reception marked their skill in communicating sometimes complicated, though fortunately almost always interesting topics. Undertaking this new updated edition has been somewhat less daunting, as being now officially retired I have more time and possibly more wisdom, though studies of mind and brain have moved on so fast it is difficult to keep up. These developments are of course the spur to this new edition, as the wealth of new facts demands revisions, with accounts of recent discoveries and new ideas. These have, indeed, forced major changes of balance and of what should be included or left out—they have even changed what we mean by 'mind'.

As in practically any science, new techniques and technologies have profound effects. Attempts to make intelligent—and even conscious—machines reveal the powers and limitations of computers; the limitations telling us just how amazing the brain is, and how much we still have to learn. Artificial Intelligence (AI) is technically difficult, and was not appropriate to present in detail in this book, which is not generally aimed at the specialist. However essential concepts, and successes of AI such as in chess, and also the doubts of philosophers about the possibility of artificial minds like ours, will be found here, presented from a variety of viewpoints.

When the first edition appeared nearly twenty years ago, brain imaging or 'scanning' had only just become available. In fact, publication was held up to include the article by Marcus Raichle, a classic account of this wonderful new technology—revealing where the brain is especially active when we see, or think, or imagine, or experience emotion. These new technologies for seeing structures and functions of the living brain reveal more of how mind is related to brain than dreamed of by philosophers. For, by letting us see *where* activity occurs, it becomes possible to appreciate what brain functions are doing, as we learn more of how the brain works, and so what processes are involved. This requires related observations and experiments from the brain and mind sciences, which may help clinicians in their work. This updated edition includes a mini-symposium on brain imaging, organized by Professor Chris Frith FRS (Deputy Director of the Leopold Müller Functional Imaging Laboratory of the Wellcome Department of Neurology in University College London).

Another topic that has taken off recently is consciousness. Why are we *aware* of the world around us, with *feelings* of bodily and emotional states? What have we got that robots haven't? As we think of the brain as an amazing machine, couldn't a computer–robot ever be conscious much as we are? A score of the most distinguished writers on consciousness have been invited to focus their thoughts in short essays on this most puzzling, most teasing topic, in a mini-symposium on consciousness. Much of this book impinges in various ways on consciousness and—what can be almost as puzzling—unconsciousness, because we are entirely unaware of almost everything going on in our active, incredibly complex brains or our minds. What is so special about conscious processes?

In order to keep this volume to a reasonable length (about 20 per cent longer than the original) much has had to be abandoned, or occasionally compressed. Sometimes this improves the presentation, as essentials can be lost in details, and no doubt readers have become more knowledgeable over the last decade or so, as so much is discussed in the media. The original, very long 'tutorial' on the nervous system has been abandoned, though it was an excellent account, as there are now several readable books on the brain and nervous system, and detailed texts are readily available for more technical information.

Where old ideas have changed with new knowledge, it is fairly safe to cut down on some of the classical topics and accounts. The immense contribution of Freud's ideas may, and in our judgement should, be revised and looked at critically in the light of later discoveries. Although we follow Freud in thinking of much of the mind as unconscious, perhaps the Unconscious he described should now be thought of quite simply as brain processes that are not in consciousness. This is a significant change, which raises new questions. Yet consciousness is only part of mind.

Over recent years, much powerful international research has focused on investigating the brain with a multitude of physiological and clinical techniques. Ancient questions of how memory, perception, and creative intelligence work are exposed to experimental methods, while still being discussed by philosophers. There is a new race of philosophers combining powers of questioning via logic and precise formulations with knowledge of experimental findings. Such changes of emphasis since the first edition have led to corresponding changes in the balance of this book. Having cut down quite drastically on Freudian ideas and claims, we have tried to represent the current technically sophisticated 'brain sciences' as they relate to mind. Some readers may see this as a loss, no doubt others as a gain. One can't win them all!

Although this Companion is useful for students, its readership is seen as much wider. Some contributions should be helpful for people and families with problems, perhaps especially of education and of mental illnesses of various kinds. It is hoped that the insights and advice of the experts here may be of practical use, while also illuminating general and personal questions that we may all ask from time to time. Answers come not only from psychologists, or from other mind or brain scientists, but from creative thinkers and writers and artists. So we find in these pages writing by all manner of people who have illuminated life with various kinds of understanding, contributing questions and answers that challenge, and with beauty and humour that fill our minds with pleasure.

As in the first edition, the brief Lives are confined to those no longer alive. It would have been too hard to explain to friends left out why they failed to be immortalized. Also as in the first edition, authorship of each entry is given with initials, with a master list that indicates who they are. Entries without initials are written by the Editor (RLG), thus explicitly admitting authorship only of those he liked, or which express more-or-less personal opinions. New to this edition is a short Glossary. This includes not only unusual or technical words, but perhaps more important, familiar words used in special ways, by those who stray into the fascinating, dangerous territory of the mind.

An issue throughout has been the 'level' to aim at, for the book to be useful for students and interesting and entertaining for the general reader. Much recent research on the mindful-brain consists of detailed anatomical descriptions, with strange names given to structures that are not generally familiar. Though this is very important for scientific and medical research, it reads like a telephone directory in a foreign language for the uninitiated. How much of such detail to include has no simple answer. It is for readers to judge whether we have got it about right. Extensive references lead to more specialized sources and further discussions.

Some readers may question why they are being introduced to such detailed accounts of structures, especially where brain–mind processes take place. Here one might draw analogy with the functioning of a city. It is useful to know where important buildings are, and it can be useful to know that they are made of stones or bricks, or of wood. For getting around, it is essential to observe rights of way, and obstructions that may be physical or symbolic, such as traffic lights. It may also be useful and add interest to know the history of the city, and how it is developing into the future. How does it compare with other cities? In what ways, and how, might it be improved? For 'cities', read the brains we live in with our minds.

The physical architectures of cities and of brains are vital to their functioning, which can go wrong for 'physical' or 'psychological' reasons. Their structures allow what is possible, and set limits of impossibility, that may be shifted once understood. Not only an architect will gain from appreciation of the structure and functioning of their city. Everyone living or visiting or communicating will be enriched by knowledge of its origins and what goes on in it—how it works and why it sometimes goes wrong.

As cities have theatres and art and games, and are fun in many light-hearted ways, so we have allowed space here for art and music, creative writing, and humour. There are also temptations of sin. These also are challenging and delightful in a city, lifting mind above the mundane of mere survival.

There is a danger with experts, and this book is written by experts. Get an enthusiastic architect to show you his city: the danger is, the expert will spend hours on features of special interest to architects, or historians or whatever, and pass over the obvious but immediately interesting that may be found in a small guide book. Yet not only the Devil is in the details, details are where the action and the interest lie. So this book must be more than a cursory guide, to reveal wonders of the mind and how it lives in the brain; details that are, in the long run, deeply entertaining.

Thanks for making this book possible are due especially to the Oxford University Press. Its Editor responsible for the first edition was Michael Rodgers. We had many ambulatory lunches at the Trout, just outside Oxford, discussing the Grand Plan, and details, as the original book grew. Pam Coote took over the first edition from Michael Rodgers, about halfway through. It was she, with immense tact and skill, who brought it to fruition.

Michael Rodgers again took up the reigns for this new edition, until his retirement from the Press in 2003. The onerous task of completing the work for the Press was then undertaken by Joanna Harris, who has done a wonderful job. Indeed, halfway through the proofs, I named her a 'galley-slave': she steered and rowed with Trojan grace and power, bethumped by a million words. She in turn was assisted by a strong team in house and out, especially Edwin Pritchard, Jane Sugarman, John Mackrell, Nick Clarke, the illustrator, Paul Simmons, and finally the indexer, Susan Leech.

My Emeritus position as Senior Research Fellow in the University of Bristol, in the Department of Psychology, has made this possible with a grant from the Gatsby Foundation. I am extremely grateful to Lord Sainsbury for his remarkable generosity over the years, which has benefited so many people, and made possible so many enterprises, of which this is just one small example.

It has been my good fortune to work with wonderful, patient, and highly intelligent secretaries. For many years Janet John devoted much of her time to this book, gradually weaning it, as technology advanced, from scissors and sticky tape to computers and fax and email. These advances have made a tremendous difference to the speed and pleasure of this, as of so much other creative work. Upon Janet's retirement, Susan Szafarz took over, with care and attention beyond normal, continually repairing my characteristic chaos. Then, upon Susan's retirement, Sally Haseman has recently taken over, with a quickness of finger on the keys and of mind that is a delight.

There has been a wealth of advice and creative criticism. For the first edition, the late Professor Oliver Zangwill FRS, then Professor of Psychology at Cambridge, advised on clinical psychology for which I have no special knowledge. Sadly, Oliver, who was my respected boss for sixteen years at Cambridge, died in 1987 after a long illness. Another much respected teacher was the late Professor Derek Russell-Davis, who contributed much-to-the-point articles in the first edition, almost all retained here. Professor Sir Martin Roth FRS (Emeritus Professor of Psychiatry at Cambridge) took over from Oliver Zangwill to advise on clinical issues, contributing his immense knowledge and experience, for which I am extremely grateful. A recent graduate of this Department, Katriina Burnet, helped with references and gave useful suggestions and advice from her fresh knowledge, and not over-convoluted cortex.

Lastly for thanks—the contributors—whose work speaks for itself in these pages. May I echo, as I much hope, your thanks for their efforts to interest and instruct, and also to entertain, as this book sets out to be a friendly companion to the mind.

RICHARD LANGTON GREGORY, CBE, MA (Cantab), DSc., LLD, FRS

Contents

Editors and Contributors

Richard L. Gregory, CBE, FRS,
Emeritus Professor of Neuropsychology at the University of Bristol, UK

CONSULTANT EDITORS
John Marshall, Professor of Neuropsychology,
Department of Clinical Neurology, Radcliffe Infirmary, Oxford, UK
Sir Martin Roth, FRS, Professor of Psychiatry, Trinity College,
University of Cambridge, UK

KEY TO CONTRIBUTOR INITIALS
The names in **bold** are those of contributors to the present edition; their biographies follow on pages xiii–xv.

AC	Alan Cowey	BH	Beate Hermelin	CSC	Claudia Schmölders
ACH	Anya C. Hurlbert	BJ	Bela Julesz	**CSH**	**Carol Haywood**
ACha	Abhijit Chauduri	**BJR**	**Brian Rogers**	**CT**	**Colwyn Trevarthen**
AD	A. Dickinson	BL	Brian Lake	CW	Colin Wilson
ADB	Alan Baddeley	BLB	Brian Lewis	**DaC**	**David Chalmers**
ADM	**A. D. Milner**		Butterworth	DAGC	David Angus Graham
AH	Atiya Hakeem	**BMH**	**Bruce Hood**		Cook
AI	Ainsley Iggo	**BP**	**Brian Pippard**	**DAO**	**David A. Oakley**
AJA	Sir Alfred Ayer	BS	Barbara J. Sahakian	DC	David Cohen
AJC	Anthony J. Chapman	BSE	Ben Semeonoff	**DCD**	**Daniel C. Dennett**
AJW	**Arnold J. Wilkins**	**BSh**	**Ben Shephard**	DD	Diana Deutsch
AKJ	**Anil K. Jain**	CE	Christopher Evans	DDH	Deborah Duncan
AKS	**Annette Karmiloff-**	CF	Colin Fraser		Honoré
	Smith	**CFr**	**Chris Frith**	**DDS**	**Doron Swade**
ALB	Ann Low-Beer	CH	Charles Hannam	**DE**	**Dylan Evans**
AMH	A. M. Halliday	**ChK**	**Christof Koch**	DEB	D. E. Blackman
AML	Alan M. Leslie	**ChT**	**Chris Tyler**	**DF**	**Deborah H. Fouts**
AMS	A. M. Sillito	CHU	Corinne Hutt	DFP	David Pears
AO	Andrew Ortony	**ChW**	**Chongwei Wang**	DH	David Howard
ARL	A. R. Luria	**CJ**	**C. Jarrold**	**DHH**	**Dorothy H. Heard**
ARVC	Arthur Cooper	CK	C. Kennard	DJM	D. J. McFarland
AS	**Andrew Sims**	CM	Colin McGinn	DJS	D. J. Satterly
ATW	A. T. Welford	CMP	Colin Murray Parkes	DLC	Dorothy L. Cheney
AWH	Alice W. Heim	**CMW**	**Claude M. Wischik**	**DM**	**Donald Michie**
BB	**Beryl Bainbridge**	CP	Colin Patterson	DMA	D. M. Armstrong
BCJM	Brian C. J. Moore	CR	Charles Rycroft	**DMB**	**David Buss**
BFS	B. F. Skinner	**CRH**	**Charles R. Harrington**	**DMBe**	**Daniel M. Bernstein**

DMM	Donald MacKay
DNC	**David N. Caplan**
DP	**David Papineau**
DR	**David Rosenbluth**
DRD	Derek Russell Davis
DRJL	Donald R. J. Laming
DRR	**Diane Rogers-Ramachandran**
DRS	**David Shank**
ECP	E. C. Poulton
EdeB	Edward de Bono
EFL	**Elizabeth F. Loftus**
ENAM	**Elvidina N. Adamson-Macedo**
ERL	Sir Edmund Leach
ETR	**Edmund T. Rolls**
EWFT	E. W. F. Tomlin
FAW	F. A. Whitlock
FCTM	Francis Charles Timothy Moore
FFRHA	Richard H. Adrian
FGR	Graham Rooth
FHCC	**Francis Crick**
FHG	Frank George
FJF	F. J. Fitzpatrick
FNJ	F. Nowell Jones
FS	Francis Schiller
GB	**Geoffrey Beattie**
GBE	Glin Bennet
GE	G. Ettlinger
GERL	Geoffrey Ernest Richard Lloyd
GFR	Graham F. Reed
GG	**Giorgio Ganis**
GGa	**Giorgio Gabella**
GJW	Sir Geoffrey Warnock
GM	George Mandler
GNAV	Godfrey N. A. Vesey
GR	**Geraint Rees**
GT	Georges Thinès
GW	Gerald Westheimer
GWB	**George Brandt**
HA	Hans Ågren
HBB	**Horace B. Barlow**
HER	**Helen E. Ross**
HFB	**H. F. Bradford**
HJE	Hans J. Eysenck
HK	Harry Kay
HKS	**Heather Shovelton**
HRR	H. R. Rollin

HW	**Harvey Wickham**
IA	**Igor Aleksander**
IBW	Ivan Bodis-Wollner
ID	**Ian Deary**
IDG	**Iain D. Gilchrist**
IG	**Ian Glynn**
IMLH	Ian M. L. Hunter
IO	Ian Oswald
IPH	**Ian P. Howard**
IR	**Ilona Roth**
IRH	**Inman Harvey**
IS	The Sayed Idries Shah
IWPP	I. W. Pleydell-Pearce
JA	**Jonathan Ashmore**
JAD	J. A. Deutsch
JAl	**John Allman**
JAn	**John Annett**
JB	John Brown
JBA	Jonathan Barnes
JBD	J. B. Deregowski
JBE	John Beloff
JBO	John Bowlby
JCH	John C. Haugeland
JCO	J. Cohen
JCP	**John Polkinghorne**
JD	**James Dalgety**
JEL	**Joseph LeDoux**
JET	J. E. Tiles
JFS	**J. F. Stein**
JGC	John G. Cottingham
JH	Julian Hochberg
JHI	John Hick
JHP	John Hunter Padel
JHW	John Wolstencroft
JJMcC	J. J. McCann
JMA	John M. Allman
JMC	June Crown
JMO	John Oxbury
JN	Joanna North
JPH	John Harris
JR	**John Rust**
JRU	Julian R. Ullman
JSH	**Joan Stevenson-Hinde**
JSHT	Jeremy S. H. Taylor
JZY	J. Z. Young
KAF	**K. A. Flowers**
KAT	**Kathleen Turano**
KD	Kurt Danziger
KJC	Kevin J. Connolly
KP	Klaus Poeck

LAI	Lawrence Alfred Ives.
LH	Liam Hudson
LLI	**Les Iverson**
LSH	Leslie S. Hearnshaw
LW	**L. Weiskrantz**
MA	Michael Argyle
MAA	**Michael A. Arbib**
MAB	**Margaret A. Boden**
MAG	**Melvyn A. Goodale**
MAJ	Malcolm A. Jeeves
MAn	**Michael Anderson**
MAP	M. A. Preece
MaR	**Martin Roth**
MB	**Mark Blagrove**
MC	**Martin A. Conway**
MD	Margaret Donaldson
MER	Marcus E. Raichle
MET	Mary Elizabeth Tiles
MF	Marianne Frankenhaeuser
MH	**M. Hammerton**
MHU	Miranda Hughes
MJM	M. J. Morgan
MJW	Martin John Wells
MK	**Morten L. Kringelbach**
MM	Michel Millodot
MMcD	**Michael McDonough**
MNH	**Mary N. Haslum**
MOM	Michael O'Mahoney
MR	Mark Ridley
MW	Baroness Warnock
MWI	Moyra Williams
NB	**Ned Block**
NC	A. Noam Chomsky
NDW	Nigel D. Walker
NFD	N. F. Dixon
NG	Norman Geschwind
NHF	**Norman H. Freeman**
NK	N. Kreitman
NKH	**Nicholas Humphrey**
NM	Neville Moray
NN	Nigel Nicholson
NOC	Neil O'Connor
NPS	Noel P. Sheehy
NS	Norman Stephenson
NSP	Lady Natasha Spender
NSS	Stuart Sutherland
OA	**Osi Audu**
OH	**Oliver Howes**

OJWH	The Revd. O. J. W. Hunkin	RCTP	R. C. T. Parker	**SBC**	**Simon Baron-Cohen**
OLZ	O. L. Zangwill	RDL	R. D. Laing	**SBl**	**Sarah-Jayne Blakemore**
OS	Oliver Sacks	RE	Robert Epstein		
OTP	O. T. Phillipson	REK	R. E. Kendell	**SBu**	**Stuart Butler**
PA	Peter Alexander	RHM	R. H. McCleery	SC	Steven Collins
PAK	Paul A. Kolers	RJ	Richard Jung	SCR	Sidney Crown
PAM	P. A. Merton	**RJL**	**Roy J. Lewicki**	**SJB**	**Susan J. Blackmore**
PBW	Peter B. Warr	RJS	Robert J. Sternberg	SM	Stanley Milgram
PCW	Peter Cathcart Wason	RJW	Roger J. Watt	**SMH**	**Susan M. Heidenreich**
PEV	Philip E. Vernon	**RL**	**Richard Lynn**	**SMK**	**Stephen M. Kosslyn**
PFS	Sir Peter Strawson	RLG	Richard L. Gregory	**SPRR**	**Steven Rose**
PH	Peter Herriot	RLH	Richard Langton-Hewer	SR	S. Rachman
PHV	Peter H. Venables			**SS**	**Sean Spence**
PJR	**Peter Rogers**	RME	Ronald Melzack	TEP	Theodore E. Parks
PM	**Patrick Moore**	**RMG**	**R. M. Gaze**	**TH**	**Ted Honderich**
PMa	**Pierre Macquet**	**RMM**	**Robin M. Murray**	**THJ**	**Tina Hamilton-James**
PMC	**Paul Churchland**	RMS	Robert M. Seyfarth	**TR**	**Thomas P. Reilly**
PMcG	Peter McGuffin	RNG	R. N. Gooderson	TRM	T. R. Miles
PMH	Pam Hannam	**RoC**	**Ron Chrisley**	**TT**	**Tom Troscianko**
PMM	Peter M. Milner	**RP**	**Raj Persaud**	**TZA**	**T. Z. Aziz**
PP	Philip Pettit	**RPe**	**Roger Penrose**	**UF**	**Uta Frith**
PPGB	P. P. G. Bateson	**RPl**	**Robert Plomin**	**VB**	**Vicki Bruce**
PR	P. A. M. Rabbitt	**RPWD**	**Robert P. W. Duin**	VH	Volker Henn
PRo	**Peter Robinson**	**RSF**	**Roger S. Fouts**	**VN**	**Victor Nell**
PS	**Paola Sandroni**	RTM	Raymond T. McNally	**VR**	**V. S. Ramachandran**
PSM	**Paul S. MacDonald**	**RW**	**Richard Wiseman**	VS	Vieda Skultans
PTB	P. T. Brown	RWD	Robert William Ditchburn	WAHR	William Rushton
PWN	Peter W. Nathan			WCM	W. Cheyne McCallum
RA	Rudolf Arnheim	RWO	Ronald W. Oppenheim	WDMP	Sir William Paton
RAH	**Robert A. Hinde**	RWP	R. W. Pickford	**WLT**	**William L. Thompson**
RC	Ray Cooper	RWS	Roger Walcott Sperry	WVQ	Willard V. Quine
RCSW	Ralph C. S. Walker	**SA**	**Stuart Anstis**	YZ	Y. Zotterman
		SB	**Simon Blackburn**	ZP	Zenon Pylyshyn

Contributors to the present edition

Listed in order of surname.

Elvidina N. Adamson-Macedo, Senior Lecturer in Psychology, University of Wolverhampton, UK

Igor Aleksander, Professor of Neural Systems Engineering and Gabor Chair of Electrical Engineering, Imperial College, London, UK

John Allman, Hixon Professor of Psychobiology, California Institute of Technology, San Francisco, California, USA

Michael Anderson, Department of Psychology, University College London, UK

John Annett, Emeritus Professor, Department of Psychology, University of Warwick, UK

Stuart Anstis, Professor of Psychology, University of California at San Diego, La Jolla, USA

Michael A. Arbib, Professor of Computer Science, Neurobiology and Physiology, and of Biomedical Engineering, Electrical Engineering, and Psychology at the University of Southern California, Los Angeles, USA

Jonathan Ashmore, Professor of Physiology, University College London, UK

Osi Audu, British and African artist

T. Z. Aziz, Department of Neurosurgery, Radcliffe Infirmary, Oxford, UK

Dame Beryl Bainbridge, writer, UK

Horace B. Barlow, Royal Society Research Professor of Physiology, Cambridge, UK

Simon Baron-Cohen, Director of the Autism Research Centre, Cambridge University, UK

Geoffrey Beattie, Professor of Psychology, University of Manchester, UK

Daniel M. Bernstein, Post-Doctoral Fellow, University of Washington, USA

Simon Blackburn FBA, Professor of Philosophy, University of Cambridge, UK

Susan J. Blackmore, freelance writer, lecturer, and broadcaster, and Visiting Lecturer at the University of the West of England, Bristol, UK

Mark Blagrove, Reader in Psychology, University of Wales, UK

Sarah-Jayne Blakemore, Royal Society Dorothy Hodgkin Fellow, Institute of Cognitive Neuroscience, University College London, UK

Ned Block, Professor of Philosophy and Psychology, Department of Philosophy, New York University, USA

Margaret A. Boden, Professor of Philosophy and Psychology, School of Cognitive Sciences, University of Sussex, UK

H. F. Bradford, Emeritus Professor of Neurochemistry and Senior Research Fellow, Royal College of Science, Imperial College of Science and Technology, London, UK

George Brandt, Emeritus Professor of Film and Television Studies and former Head of Department of Drama, University of Bristol, UK

Vicki Bruce, Professor of Psychology, University of Stirling, UK

David Buss, Professor of Psychology, University of Texas, Austin, USA

Stuart Butler, Burden Institute, Department of Experimental Psychology, University of Bristol, UK

David N. Caplan, Professor of Neurology, Neuropsychology Laboratory, Massachusetts General Hospital, USA

David Chalmers, Professor of Philosophy, University of Arizona, Tuscon, Arizona, USA

Abhijit Chauduri, Senior Lecturer in Clinical Neurosciences, University of Glasgow, and Consultant Neurologist, Institute of Neurological Sciences, Glasgow, UK

Ron Chrisley, Senior Lecturer, School of Cognitive and Computing Sciences, University of Sussex, UK

Paul Churchland, Professor of Philosophy, University of Southern California, La Jolla, California, USA

Martin A. Conway, Professor of Psychology, University of Durham, UK

Alan Cowey, Emeritus Professor of Physiological Psychology, Lincoln College, University of Oxford, UK

Francis Crick formerly J. W. Kieckhefer Distinguished Research Professor at the Salk Institute for Biological Studies, and Adjunct Professor of Psychology, University of California at San Diego, USA

James Dalgety, The Puzzle Museum, www.puzzle-museum.com

Ian Deary, Professor of Differential Psychology, Department of Psychology, University of Edinburgh, UK

Daniel C. Dennett, Director and Professor of Philosophy, Center for Cognitive Studies, Tufts University, Medford, Massachusetts, USA

Robert P. W. Duin, Associate Professor, Delft University of Technology, The Netherlands

Dylan Evans, Senior Lecturer in Intelligent Autonomous Systems, Faculty of Computing, Engineering and Mathematical Sciences, University of the West of England, UK

K. A. Flowers, Senior Lecturer in Psychology, University of Hull, UK

Deborah H. Fouts, Co-Director of the Chimpanzee and Human Communication Institute, Central Washington University, Ellensburg, Washington, USA

Roger. S. Fouts, Co-Director and Professor of Psychology, the Chimpanzee and Human Communication Institute, Central Washington University, Ellensburg, Washington, USA

Norman H. Freeman, Professor of Psychology, Department of Experimental Psychology, University of Bristol, UK

Chris Frith FRS, Professor of Neuropsychology, Wellcome Department, Cognitive Neurology, University College London, UK

Uta Frith, Professor and Deputy Director, Institute of Cognitive Neuroscience and Department of Psychology, University College London, UK

Giorgio Gabella, Emeritus Professor, Department of Anatomy and Developmental Biology, University College London, UK

Giorgio Ganis, Professor of Radiology, Harvard Medical School, Harvard University, USA

Iain D. Gilchrist, Reader in Neuropsychology, Department of Experimental Psychology, University of Bristol, UK

Ian Glynn FRS, Emeritus Professor of Physiology, University of Cambridge, UK

Melvyn A. Goodale, Canada Research Professor in Visual Neuroscience, University of Western Ontario, Canada

Richard L. Gregory, CBE, FRS, Emeritus Professor of Neuropsychology, University of Bristol, UK

Atiya Hakeem, Post-Doctoral Scholar, Allman Laboratory, California Institute of Technology, San Francisco, California, USA

Tina Hamilton-James, Certified Transactional Analyst and Psychotherapist, Child and Adolescent Mental Health, Bristol Royal Hospital for Children, Bristol, UK

M. Hammerton, Emeritus Professor of Psychology, University of Newcastle upon Tyne, UK

Charles R. Harrington, Senior Research Fellow, Department of Mental Health, Institute of Medical Sciences, University of Aberdeen, UK

Inman Harvey, Senior Research Fellow, Centre for Computational Neuroscience and Robotics and Evolutionary and Adaptive Systems Group, University of Sussex, Brighton, UK

Mary N. Haslum, Reader in Psychology at the University of the West of England, Bristol, UK

Carol Haywood, sculptor and physiotherapist, Bristol, UK

Dorothy H. Heard, Honorary Lecturer, Department of Psychology, University of Leeds, UK

Susan M. Heidenreich, Department of Psychology, University of San Francisco, California, USA

Robert A. Hinde, Emeritus Professor, Department of Zoology, Cambridge, UK

Ted Honderich, Emeritus Professor, Department of Philosophy, University College London, UK

Bruce Hood, Professor of Experimental Psychology, University of Bristol, UK

Ian P. Howard, Emeritus Professor of Psychology, York University, Downsview, Ontario, Canada

Oliver Howes, Institute of Psychiatry, King's College, London, UK

Nicholas Humphrey, Professor, Centre for Philosophy of the Natural and Social Sciences, London School of Economics, UK, and Department of Psychology, New School for Social Research, New York, USA

Anya C. Hurlbert, Lecturer in Biology, University of Newcastle upon Tyne, UK

Ainsley Iggo, Professor of Veterinary Physiology, University of Edinburgh, UK

Les Iversen, Department of Pharmacology, University of Oxford, UK

Anil K. Jain, Distinguished Professor, Michigan State University, Michigan, USA

C. Jarrold, Reader in Cognitive Development, Department of Experimental Psychology, University of Bristol, UK

Annette Karmiloff-Smith FBA, Professor of Neurocognitive Development and Head of Unit, Neurocognitive Development Unit, Institute of Child Health, Great Ormond Street Hospital, London, UK

Christof Koch, Lois and Victor Troendle Professor of Cognitive and Behavioral Biology and Executive Officer of Computation and Neural Systems, California Institute of Technology, USA

Stephen M. Kosslyn, Professor of Psychology, Harvard University, USA

Morten L. Kringelbach, Junior Research Fellow, The Queen's College, University of Oxford, UK

Joseph LeDoux, Henry and Lucy Moses Professor of Science and Professor of Neural Science and Psychology, Center for Neural Science, New York University, USA

Roy J. Lewicki, Professor of Management and Human Resources, Fisher College of Business, Ohio State University, USA

Elizabeth F. Loftus, Professor of Psychology, University of Washington, USA

Richard Lynn, Emeritus Professor, Department of Psychology, University of Ulster, UK

Paul S. MacDonald, Professor of Philosophy, Murdoch University, Perth, Australia

Michael McDonough, Specialist Registrar in Psychiatry at the Maudsley Hospital and the Institute of Psychiatry, London, UK

Pierre Macquet, Cyclotron Research Centre, University of Liège, Belgium

Donald Michie, Senior Fellow, The Turing Institute, Glasgow, and Emeritus Professor of Machine Intelligence, University of Edinburgh, UK

A. D. Milner, Professor of Psychology, University of Durham, UK

Patrick Moore, astronomer, West Sussex, UK

Robin M. Murray, Professor of Psychiatry, Maudsley Hospital, London, UK

Victor Nell, Visiting Fellow, Department of Experimental Psychology, University of Bristol, UK

David A. Oakley, Director, Hypnosis Unit, Department of Psychology, University College London, UK

David Papineau, Professor of Philosophy, King's College, London, UK

Roger Penrose, Rouse Ball Professor of Mathematics, Mathematical Institute, University of Oxford, UK

Raj Persaud, Consultant Psychiatrist and Senior Lecturer, Maudsley Hospital, London, UK

Sir Brian Pippard FRS, Emeritus Professor of the History of Physics, Cavendish Laboratory, University of Cambridge, UK

Robert Plomin, MRC Research Professor in Behavioural Genetics and Deputy Director of the Social, Genetic, and Developmental Psychiatry Research Centre, Institute of Psychiatry, King's College, London, UK

Revd Dr John Charlton Polkinghorne KBE, FRS, Queen's College, Cambridge, UK

Zenon Pylyshyn, Department of Psychology, Rutgers University Center for Cognitive Science, New Jersey, USA

V. S. Ramachandran, Director of the Center for Brain and Cognition and Professor with the Psychology Department and the Neurosciences Program, University of California, San Diego, La Jolla, USA

Geraint Rees, Wellcome Advanced Fellow, Division of Biology, California Institute of Technology, San Francisco, California, USA

Thomas P. Reilly, Professor and Director of Research, Institute for Sport and Exercise Studies, Liverpool John Moores University, UK

Peter Robinson, Emeritus Professor, Department of Experimental Psychology, University of Bristol, UK

Brian Rogers, Professor of Experimental Psychology, University of Oxford, UK

Peter Rogers, Professor and Head of Department, Department of Experimental Psychology, University of Bristol, UK

Diane Rogers-Ramachandran, Center for Brain and Cognition, University of California, San Diego, La Jolla California, USA

Edmund T. Rolls, Professor of Experimental Psychology, University of Oxford, UK

Steven Rose, Professor of Biology and Director of the Brain and Behaviour Research Group, The Open University, Milton Keynes, UK

David Rosenbluth, Allman Laboratory, California Institute of Technology, San Francisco, California, USA

Helen E. Ross, Honorary Reader in Psychology, University of Stirling, UK

Ilona Roth, Senior Lecturer in Psychology, Open University, UK

Sir Martin Roth FRS, Professor of Psychiatry, Trinity College, University of Cambridge, UK

John Rust, Professor of Psychometrics, City University, London, UK

Paola Sandroni, Department of Neurology, Mayo Clinic, Rochester, Minnesota, USA

David Shank, Professor of Psychology and Head of the Department of Psychology, University College London, UK

Ben Shephard, historian and journalist, Bristol, UK

Heather Shovelton, Research Fellow, University of Manchester, UK

Andrew Sims, Professor of Psychiatry, St James's Hospital, Leeds, UK

Sean Spence, Reader in General Adult Psychiatry, Academic Clinical Psychiatry, University of Sheffield, UK

John Stein, Professor of Physiology, Laboratory of Physiology, University of Oxford, UK

Joan Stevenson-Hinde, Senior Research Fellow, Department of Zoology, University of Cambridge, UK

Doron Swade, Assistant Director and Head of Collections, Science Museum, London, UK

William L. Thompson, Department of Psychology, Harvard University, USA

Colwyn Trevarthen, Professor of Child Psychology and Psychobiology, University of Edinburgh, UK

Tom Troscianko, Professor, Department of Experimental Psychology, University of Bristol, UK

Kathleen Turano, Associate Professor of Ophthalmology, the Wilmer Eye Institute, Johns Hopkins University, Baltimore, USA

Chris Tyler, Associate Director, Smith-Kettlewell Eye Research Institute, San Franscisco, USA

Chongwei Wang, postgraduate student, Department of Organizational Behavior and Human Resource Management, Ohio State University, USA

Larry Weiskrantz, Professor of Psychology, Department of Experimental Psychology, University of Oxford, UK

Harvey Wickham, Research Associate, Division of Psychological Medicine, Institute of Psychiatry, London, UK

Arnold J. Wilkins, Professor, Department of Psychology, University of Essex, Colchester, UK

Claude M. Wischik, Professor of Gerontology and Old Age Psychiatry, Aberdeen University, UK

Richard Wiseman, Professor in Public Understanding of Psychology, University of Hertfordshire, UK

Glossary

acetylcholine (Ach) a major neurotransmitter, released at neuromuscular junctions, allowing neural signals to produce movements for behaviour

action potentials brief spikes of electricity propagated along afferent and efferent axons, conveying information by their frequency

afferent incoming sensory signals, or nerves

agonist a drug which stimulates or enhances a particular neurotransmitter

Alzheimer's disease degenerative disorder associated with ageing, affecting especially memory

ambiguity the word is ambiguous, having two very different meanings: (1) *confusing* or confounding different stimuli or objects; (2) creating different perceptions (or meanings) from one stimulus, or object, or picture or word. 'Ambiguous figures' such as the Necker cube are 'flipping' not 'confounded' visual illusions

amnesia loss of memory

amygdala nuclei in the anterior temporal lobe, associated with emotion and memory

antagonist a drug that inhibits the effect of a neurotransmitter

anterograde amnesia inability to store new memories since the onset of amnesia, as following a brain-damaging accident

aphasias disorders of language

a postiori (Latin) 'what comes after'. Propositions deriving from observations or empirical evidence, e.g. smoking causes lung cancer

apraxia loss of function due to (usually left hemisphere) brain damage

a priori (Latin) 'what comes before'. Propositions or beliefs accepted as true before empirical evidence, e.g. $2 + 3 = 5$ or (according to Euclid) parallel lines never meet

association cortex areas linking sources of sensory information and motor (muscle) commands

associative learning responses built from relationships between stimuli or events, especially when occurring closely spaced in time. Hence Pavlovian conditioning and instrumental learning (q.v.)

auditory cortex area in the upper surface of the temporal lobe, in the Sylvian fissure, receiving information from the ears

automatism behaviour without awareness, or consciousness, such as sleepwalking

autonomic nervous system controls the inner workings of the body, with the sympathetic and the parasympathetic systems (q.v.)

axons long nerve fibres

basal ganglia brain systems controlling voluntary movement; damage can cause Parkinson's disease

basilar membrane its hair cells transmit (or rather transduce) air vibrations to neural signals for hearing (the physics for allocating frequencies to hair cells is still not fully understood)

Betz cells in motor cortex: the largest cells in the brain's cortex. Also known as 'pyramidal' cells

binocular vision the two eyes giving stereo depth, when the eye fields overlap, and there are small horizontal differences ('disparity') in their images from parallax

brain the human brain is the most complicated object known in the universe; a concentration of about 100 million neurons in the head, weighing about 3 pounds, it is divided into various regions according to structures and functions

Broca's speech area in lateral frontal cortex, usually in the left hemisphere; damage gives Broca's *aphasia

cell body contains the nucleus of nerves, the 'soma'

cerebellum important for coordinated movements of skills, situated at the back of the brain, above the pons. Sometimes known as the 'little brain'

cerebral cortex the brain's outer layers of cells; the seat of cognition

cerebrum mass of structures above the brain stem

CNS central nervous system

cognition knowledge-based perception and behaviour. Cognitive psychology has replaced behaviourism, which held that behaviour is controlled by stimuli, in favour of brain representations being perceptions, and controlling behaviour predictively

consciousness awareness. Most mysterious (see the mini symposium in this volume for various accounts)

deduction logical argument from premises to conclusion, such that the conclusion must be true if the premises are valid, e.g. Aristotelian syllogism: 'All men are mortal, Socrates is a man, therefore Socrates is mortal.' Why deductions are certain is controversial; one account being that the meaning of the conclusion is contained in the premises. (For mathematics: $2 + 3 = 5$, because $2 + 3$ is another way of writing 5)

diplopia double vision, usually from failure to converge the eyes appropriately; associated with alcohol

efferent signals and nerve fibres controlling movements

eidetic image extraordinarily vivid mental image, experienced especially when half-awake

emergence surprising properties arising from combining simpler elements, e.g combining atoms of the gases oxygen and hydrogen producing very different liquid water. It is controversial whether the apparent jumps or gaps of emergence are in the structure of reality, or whether they are symptoms of our ignorance through lack of adequate explanations. Mind, and consciousness, are sometimes said to be *emergent* from brain functions or from its unique complexity

emotion short-term state of mind or mood, such as joy or grief; associated with directed, and with thwarted actions

endocrine the ductless glands, including the adrenal glands, ovaries and testes, and pituitary—signalling independently of the nervous system, by introducing chemical signals into the bloodstream

evolution doctrine that plants and animals are not pre-designed, by God, but change through the generations. Darwinian evolution by natural selection works by inheriting genes (though not known to Darwin) as successful chance changes (mutations) tend to be perpetuated in off-spring

explicit memory awareness of stored information, especially with speech

fovea centre of the retina, where the receptors are most closely packed and acuity is highest

free will supposed human ability to make choices 'autonomously' and so to escape some physical restraints. Not the same as random; for believed to be intentional, and so to justify blame or praise

GABA main inhibitory neurotransmitter

ganglia groups of nerve cells outside the CNS

ganglion simple brain (concentration of neurons) in a primitive creature

gene a molecule of DNA, encoding physical and (some) mental characteristics. As potential characteristics may be inherited from genes, environment is (with exceptions such as eye colour which are purely genetic) also important

glia small brain cells, not neuronal, believed to serve ancillary functions such as cleaning up

Golgi staining for selectively showing a proportion of nerve cells for light microscopy

Golgi stretch receptors signal force, in tendons

grey matter brain areas of mainly cell bodies

habituation decrease of response with repeated stimulation

hair cells in the inner ear, signal vibrations for hearing; also for balance

hippocampus named 'sea horse' from its shape; structure in the limbic system associated with spatial perception and memory

homeostasis maintaining body states (temperature etc.) at optimal levels by feedback

hormones substances released into the blood, usually by endocrine glands, affecting various organs and often modifying psychological states; dramatic at puberty

hypothalamus master control system for the autonomic and endocrine systems

iconic memory short-term visual memory

implicit memory memory without awareness

induction arguing from several instances to a more general conclusion, which is only probably true: 'all swans I have seen are white, so the next swan will be white.' (When black swans were discovered in Australia, they might have been rejected as swans—if white was a defining characteristic, then swans would *have* to be white, deductively. As it was decided that white is not a defining property, this is an induction!)

inhibition reduction of conditioned reflexes when stimuli are presented without reward; restraint of especially anti-social behaviour or thoughts

instrumental learning associative learning where the subject can control later stimuli by his/her responses

intelligence has two meanings: (1) knowledge or information (such as military intelligence) and (2) ability to solve problems. These may be called 'potential' and 'kinetic' intelligence respectively, by analogy with storing potential and using kinetic energy

intension technical word in linguistics. Broadly the meaning of a word or phrase; used to be called 'comprehension'

intention deliberate aimed-to-a-goal behaviour

James–Langer theory of emotion: that the body reacts 'automatically' to, for example, danger, and the body changes are then sensed as emotions

kinaesthesis sense of bodily movement

Lamarckianism from French naturalist, Jean Baptiste Pierre Antoine de Monet Lamarck, who held a theory of evolution that characteristics or knowledge acquired in life could be inherited.

limen a sensory threshold

machine a physical system that is designed to serve some purpose and achieve some result. For theology the designer might be God. But modern biology rejects any such pre-design in favour of continuous designing by natural selection. The brain is seen as a machine working on physical principles, though in later versions, especially ours, including cognitive processes based on evolutionarily inherited and learned knowledge. (This bears analogy with computer hardware supporting cognitive software)

masking blocking perception with a stimulus such as random 'noise'

memory from Latin *memor* 'mindfull'. Storing brain-accounts of past events (declarative memory) and skills (procedural memory), with short-term 'note pad' for tasks such as speaking and arithmetic. How the brain changes to encode memories is not at all fully known. As suggested by F. C. Bartlett, in the 1930s, memory is not passive but rather active constructions from limited stored data

mind a vague term, covering control of intentional behaviour and awareness; but 'unconscious mind' is not an oxymoron, as not all accepted as 'mind' is conscious. Covers learning, memory, perception, emotion, intention, aesthetics, and much more; but automatism and reflex responses are 'mindless'

model (1) a relatively simple biological example, or preparation, for studying complicated functions or processes; (2) a working representation, such as the brain-modelling aspects of the external world

modularity derived from early nineteenth-century phrenologists' Faculties, revived by the American psychologist Gerry Fodor, suggesting many specialized brain regions and appropriate processes for various kinds of problem solving, for perception and other cognitive activities.

neural net interconnected neurons, capable of learning; may be artificial, or in biological nervous systems

neuron the unit components of the nervous system. Specialized cell bodies which receive (by their branching dendrites) and transmit (with their long axons) information, with trains of action potentials

noise technically, random activity that masks signals. All detectors are noise limited for sensitivity. (Loss of memory and perception etc. in ageing may be due to increased neural noise)

occipital back of the head and brain

ontology theories of knowledge and truth

operant conditioning responses increasing with rewards

operationalism a theory in early logical positivism suggesting that concepts derive from procedures of observations and experiments. No longer held in an extreme form, this anticipated Karl Popper's plea that hypotheses should be framed to be vulnerable to empirical tests

paradigm (shift) implicitly accepted general concepts, which when they change, affect how experiments and observations are interpreted

paranormal supposed perception or behaviour beyond physical possibilities; if true, would have immensely significant implications for considering mind

parasympathetic nervous system one of the two major divisions of the autonomic nervous system (q.v.), mainly optimizing metabolic activity

Pavlovian conditioning classical conditioning, named after the Russian physiologist Ivan Petrovich Pavlov (1849–1936)

perception sensory knowledge and experience of states of the external world, and the owner's body

Perceptual illusions errors of perception, especially systematic errors giving interesting phenomena of physiology and mind

peripheral nervous system the senses and their afferent nerves, and efferent nerves to the muscles

proprioception largely unconscious sense of limb movements and positions

prosopagnosia inability to recognize faces

qualia philosophers' term for sensations, such as red, and pain; regarded as the Ultimate Mystery of mind

reaction time neural delay from stimuli to responses, due to slow conduction rate of nerves and brain-processing time; discovered and measured by Hermann von Helmholtz in 1850

reflex stimulus-response arc; may be given innately, or learned by conditioning

schema supposed brain structures representing memories dynamically

scotoma blind region of the retina, e.g. the 'blind spot' where the optic nerve leaves for the brain. Small scotomas are generally not noticed, or 'seen', either because they are ignored or are actively filled in by the brain

semantic memory long-term memory for facts, other than autobiographical

semiotics study of symbols and language

stimulus patterns in space and time of physical events, received by sense organs and coded into neural signals

strong AI the notion that mental acts and skill can in principle be carried out by man-made robotic machines

sympathetic nervous system part of the autonomic nervous system (q.v.), involved in arousal

synapse connection between nerves; function with neurotransmitter chemicals

tactile sense of touch

thought experiment (*Gedanken experiment*) imaginary experiment, which may lead to actual experiments, as when technology becomes available

tinnitus annoying sounds generated within the ear

Turing machine basic concept of computers; named after Alan Turing (1912–54)

Turing test that intelligent AI machines should be indistinguishable from (suitably hidden) intelligent humans, to be called 'intelligent'

unconditioned response response to e.g. food, or mate, which has not been learned, so is innate

universal grammar supposed underlying structure of all natural languages. Inherited, so making language learning by infants possible; associated with Noam Chomsky

ventral for brain, the bottom or lower part (also means, near the front of an organism)

vergence inward pointing of the eyes, signalling distance

Weber's law the ratio for discrimination of signal intensity against background remains constant over a very wide range ($\Delta I / I = C$)

working memory supposed 'scratch pad' for holding currently important facts in store

X chromosome sex chromosome present in pairs in females and present singly with a Y chromosome in males

Y chromosome sex chromosome in all diploid cells of males, paired with an X chromosome

zygote a fertilized ovum or egg

Note to the Reader

Entries are arranged in strict alphabetical order of their headword, although names beginning with Mc are ordered as if they were spelt Mac. **Cross-references** between entries are indicated either by an asterisk (*) in front of the word to be looked up, or by 'See' or 'See also' followed by the entry title in SMALL CAPITALS. Cross-references are discretionary, and are given only when the entry indicated will provide further information relevant to the subject under discussion. **Contributor initials** are given at the end of entries; a key to these is provided on pages x–xxii, followed by details of contributors to this edition on pages xiii–xv. Those entries that are not signed are by the editor. The **Glossary** on pages xvi–xix provides accessible definitions of terms that appear frequently in the Companion. A comprehensive **Index** on pages 961–1002 includes not only the subjects discussed within entries but also the names of the contributors.

A

abacus. Ancient calculating instrument in which numbers and operations (especially adding) are represented by the numbers and positions of pebbles or (later) beads on strings or wooden rods; it may be regarded as an early form of *digital computer. Although it originated in prehistoric times, the abacus is still widely used especially in China and Japan. The fact that this 'mind tool' can vastly improve mental arithmetic might suggest that the unaided mind functions on very different principles (perhaps that thinking is an analogical rather than a digital process). Just as, if fingers were like screwdrivers, we would not need screwdrivers, so, if the brain worked like an abacus, bead-counters would not be so helpful. But perhaps the abacus serves as a memory.

Our language reflects the importance of the abacus throughout history. The word 'calculate' comes from the Latin word for a pebble, and the term 'Exchequer' derives from the chequered table on which counters or jettons were moved to reckon the nation's accounts (the abacus continued to be used for British governmental accounting into the 18th century). The mechanical calculating machine with geared wheels (invented by Blaise *Pascal in 1642) is a direct development of the abacus, and this in turn led to Charles *Babbage's programmable wheeled calculator and, eventually, to today's electronic computers.   RLG

Pullan, J. M. (1969). *The History of the Abacus.*

abnormal. 'Abnormal' has richer meanings than 'unusual'. Its meanings depend very much on context. In clinical medicine, and psychology, abnormal states or symptoms are often warnings of possible trouble. They may be readings (of blood pressure, blood sugar, personality variables) outside the normal range. In research science abnormal suggests questions to ask, and may point to new discoveries.

abreaction. A recalling or re-experiencing of stressful or disturbing situations or events which appear to have precipitated a neurosis. During the recalling the patient is encouraged to give an uninhibited display of emotion and afterwards it is hoped that the neurosis will have vanished. Abreaction was used by Joseph *Breuer in the treatment of patients with *hysteria; in a modified form, it still finds some applications in modern psychiatry, especially in the treatment of battle stress.

acceleration. Acceleration of the body is sensed in the inner ear by the otoliths, small weights of calcium carbonate suspended on stalks. Accelerated movements of the head produce deflections of the stalks, since the otoliths do not respond immediately to movement because of their inertia. Unaccelerated motion cannot be sensed intrinsically by any sense or by any physical instrument, but only by reference to external objects that may themselves be moving. So there is ambiguity, such as occurs when a stationary train appears, to one who is in it, to move when a neighbouring train moves past it. Here the visual sense of movement dominates the sensing of acceleration—or rather the lack of acceleration—for the observer in the stationary train.

accidental property. See CONTINGENT PROPERTY.

accident proneness. Accident proneness is a deceptively easy term. We all know what it means but we do not all mean the same thing. Since the ambiguities arise partly because of the way we speak about accidents, it may be helpful to clarify this term.

An accident refers to the results of an action, generally to an unplanned, even an unexpected result. It has been described as 'an error with sad consequences', but the relationship between the preceding behaviour and the consequences is not at all simple. A time-honoured example of an accident is a person falling flat as he slips on a banana skin—an act, incidentally, that few have ever witnessed and which conveys the impression that the world at one time must have been littered with banana skins. In such an example the person who slips has the accident for which he was partly responsible. But we also speak of someone having an accident when something falls on him. *A* spills a cup of tea over *B* and we say that *B* has suffered an accident. To add to the confusion, different kinds of action result in similar accidents, while the same act often has very different results. Hence, if we are to understand accidents we need to understand the preceding behaviour. But accident data are usually only records of the outcome of actions.

There is a further complication. It is a feature of accident statistics that the more severe the accident

1

(particularly a fatal injury), the more accurate is the record. But the majority of accidents are relatively trivial, and in our society the greatest number occur in the home and often go unrecorded. The basis for extrapolation, therefore, is somewhat shaky. Nevertheless we can be confident that over the years the trend of incidence in different kinds of activities has shifted. Industrial accidents are no longer the major component; rather, the home and transport make up the bulk of the total. This shift is important, for a quick inspection of a nation's annual accident data shows such regularity from year to year that it might be concluded that accidents were an inevitable consequence of man's mobility. Closer scrutiny reveals that within the total of accidents the pattern has shifted from one class of accidents to another.

Within this general framework, it is accepted that the risks inherent in some activities are greater than in others and that the chances of accident also fluctuate with varying environmental conditions: changes in lighting, humidity, temperature, for example. The behaviour of the individual is the common factor, and inevitably explanation has been sought for accident proneness. The direct question has been asked: in the same circumstances, do individuals differ in their liability to accident? In everyday thinking about skilled actions, some individuals would be more proficient than others; conversely, some individuals would be less so, and to that extent they would have more accidents. This straightforward and rather simple line of thought presumed that a single measure of overall performance provided a reliable index of the skill of a performer. But a performer's degree of skill is not necessarily an index to his liability to accident. A palpably poor driver of a car may be aware of his fallibility and drive more cautiously, with the result that he has fewer accidents than a skilful but overconfident driver. It is necessary to analyse the skill in some detail if it is to provide a guide to accident liability.

Even so, accepting for the moment that we may use an overall measure, it is easy enough to demonstrate by statistical data that some individuals over a limited time period incur more accidents than others. It is tempting to infer that this identifies those who are more liable to have accidents—the accident prone. But, of course, such an inference is not necessarily justified. In a normal distribution of random events over a sample time period, some will occur more frequently than others.

Early research workers, such as Greenwood and Yule (1920), were well aware of statistically attractive fallacies and, though their data indicated that some individuals had incurred a high proportion of the accidents in situations where other factors were equal, they stressed the need for caution. But in 1926 Farmer and Chambers suggested the term 'accident proneness' for this liability to incur accidents, and such is the power of an attractive label that it

was universally accepted, not as a tentative guess to be examined by further research, as they proposed, but as an established fact. The concept of accident proneness was taken a stage further by Flanders Dunbar in America who claimed that a personality trait of accident proneness was proven fact. She gave psychodynamic interpretations which claimed that persons involved in repeated accidents had some unconscious need for physical trauma. Later she had to modify her original views about accident proneness being an enduring personality trait when it was pointed out that some of these so-called accident-prone personalities ceased to have accidents as they grew older.

The history is typical of what happens when scientific ideas are accepted on too little evidence. For a time accident proneness became the major explanatory concept in its field; then in the 1940s doubts began to creep in and by the 1950s careful assessments were pointing out that the evidence was insufficient. Soon opposition swung well beyond this point, as in the highly critical major review of Haddon, Suchman, and Klein (1964). During the 1960s, the fact that the statistical evidence failed to demonstrate the existence of accident proneness was interpreted as a refutation of all hypotheses relating to it. The pendulum had to swing back, and in 1971 Shaw published her comprehensive analysis of accident proneness. She avoided an extreme position. She conceded that many characteristics of behaviour change with age and that it is not true that most accidents are sustained by a small number of people. But she examined in detail earlier studies and demonstrated the importance of certain factors such as *attention (defined as the ability to choose quickly and perform a correct response to a sudden stimulus), the stability of behaviour, and the involuntary control of motor behaviour. She supported the study of car drivers—'a man drives as he lives'—and the finding that a bad civil record tends to indicate a bad accident risk.

Where does this leave accident proneness? In spite of, perhaps because of, much contentious writing, the problem is still with us and becoming of increasing importance as accidents assume an ever-greater significance in mortality rates. Now, if accident data are not recording behaviour directly but its consequences, then the less the probability of an accident following an action, the more insensitive the data as an index of behaviour. Little can be inferred about, say, the behaviour of pedestrians at railway level crossings from accident data for, fortunately, there is little data—but what if behaviour could be recorded directly? In general the problem would be lessened, given guidance on the kinds of behaviour that cause accidents, or if the number of situations that have to be studied were reduced. Some beginnings have been made with detailed examinations of the behaviour of drivers on the roads, and these should be extended into the home and to other everyday situations. An understanding is required of the basis of human skills, and fortunately advances have now been made in this field of study. When a human operator is carrying out a skill, he is receiving signals from several sensory modalities and initiating responses to them. The whole process is conceived as an information loop. The operator is in the centre and the information is measured statistically in terms of the probability of the signals. Though this concept may seem at first sight a little removed from everyday thinking, a moment's reflection will show that it is not. We expect to see certain things under certain conditions and we know how we shall respond. For example, it is no surprise to drive round a corner and see another car; it would be to see an elephant. And evidence shows we respond more quickly to the car than we would to the elephant, or, to put it another way, the more certain the signal, the less information in a statistical sense it carries. If, then, we conceive of a skill as processing information, one essential is for the operator to reduce the amount of information by anticipating the probability of different signals. It is a truism to say that accidents occur when the operator has too much information to process in too little time. One way to handle such situations is to know which events are likely to occur. See INFORMATION THEORY.

But although a sensitive analysis may be made of human skills, and insight gained into how a person's propensities vary with different tasks and at different stages of his life, knowledge of how performance is affected by the personality of the individual is still sketchy. Over and above the psychomotor skill itself, there is a further influence reflecting the personal qualities of the performer, but exactly how this affects accident proneness is not known. The influence differs according to the state of fatigue or the vigilance of the operator, to the difficulty or length of the task, to the importance of the occasion, and so forth. This area requires much more study. We see its importance exemplified in the case of age. It is often said, 'Tell me a person's age and I will tell you what accidents he may have.' The under-25s contribute disproportionately to road accidents the world over (seen even when experience is held constant over different age groups). Similarly the over-65s contribute a large proportion of the psychomotor accidents in the home, which are generally due to falls as control deteriorates. It is a question of coming to terms with the varying skills we possess as life advances. Finally, there is the puzzling and recurring example of accidents that turn out to be anything but accidental. Investigation into the antecedent history of the individual in these cases suggests that the behaviour causing the accident was highly predictable and that the accident had the inevitability of Greek tragedy. It was fitting that Michael Ayrton (the English cartoonist, 1921–75) added a new dimension to the classical myth of Daedalus and his son Icarus; under his interpretation it was no mischance that Icarus flew too

close to the sun god, Apollo, and thereby caused the wax of his wings to melt: it was his act of challenge and defiance. HK

Dunbar, F. (1954). *Emotions and Bodily Changes* (4th edn. 1976).
Farmer, E., and Chambers, E. G. (1926). *A Psychological Study of Individual Differences in Accident Rate*. Industrial Health Research Board, report no. 38.
Greenwood, M., and Yule, C. V. (1920). 'An enquiry into the nature of frequency distribution in repeated accidents'. *Journal of the Royal Statistical Society*, 83.
Haddon, W., Suchman, E. A., and Klein, D. (1964). *Accident Research*.
Shaw, L., and Sichel, H. S. (1971). *Accident Proneness*.

accommodation (of the eye). The lens in the eye of land-living vertebrates focuses by changing the curvature of its surface, a process known as 'accommodation'. In fish the rigid spherical lens moves backwards and forwards as in a camera. Accommodation brings objects of interest, when fixated on the centre of the retinas in animals that have foveae, into sharp focus. This is achieved by 'hunting' for the sharpest image (or highest spatial frequency response of the eye), as there is no available signal indicating whether accommodation is set too *far* (insufficient curvature of the lens) or too *near* (too much curvature). Spectacles can correct for too great or too small a curvature of the lens, to give focused images when the eye's accommodation is incorrect or, as almost invariably happens in middle age, when the lens of the eye becomes too inflexible to change its shape to keep the image in focus for a wide range of distances of objects. Spectacles were invented in the 13th century in the West, and earlier in China. Several inventors have been suggested, especially Salvino d'Armato (d. 1312), and Roger Bacon (?1214–94), who also described the magnifying glass.

acetylcholine (ACh). An important *neurotransmitter, liberated at nerve endings, that transmits nervous impulses to muscles or to other nerve cells. Once released, acetylcholine has a very short existence as it is quickly broken down by the enzyme cholinesterase.

acupuncture. See PAIN.

addiction. For most people the concept of drug addiction is dominated by images of physical and mental degradation brought about by the use of heroin and cocaine. It is generally forgotten that the most widely used *drugs are *caffeine (in tea and coffee), nicotine, and alcohol, and that the most successful drug 'pushers' are tobacconists and publicans. Of course the great majority of those who enjoy these drugs are not necessarily addicted, if addiction means a tendency to excessive use of the drug, a craving for it when it is not available, and the development of a variety of physical and psychological symptoms when it is suddenly withdrawn.

Addiction is a difficult word to define, and a World Health Organization expert committee in 1970 substituted the words 'drug dependence'. This is characterized by psychological symptoms such as craving and a compulsion to take the drug on a continuous or periodic basis, and physical effects developing when the drug is withheld or is unavailable. Although many drugs will meet these criteria, those of overriding concern are the opiates, alcohol, and the sedatives, particularly barbiturates, all of which cause both physical and psychological symptoms of dependence. Other drugs of significance are stimulants such as cocaine and the amphetamines, the hallucinogens, of which mescaline and lysergic acid diethylamide (LSD) are examples, and cannabis. Most of these drugs do not induce the symptoms of physical dependence associated with abrupt discontinuance, and it is their psychological effects that are the main driving forces behind their continued use. Glue sniffing and the inhalation of volatile solvents by children are probably increased by publicity. None of these substances can be regarded as addictive; apart from the risk of liver damage from the solvents, the chief danger is from asphyxia, should the user place the glue in a plastic bag and pull it over his head. Glue sniffing is a form of behaviour that usually ceases with adolescence—and possibly with legal access to alcoholic drinks.

Although government concern centres principally on the illegal use of heroin, the number of known 'addicts' is relatively small in comparison with the very large number of people who have become dependent on alcohol. Precise figures are impossible to obtain but, as the purchase of alcoholic drinks has increased considerably over the past few decades, so has the number of alcoholics. A well-known formula has related the estimated number of alcoholics in a community to the annual consumption of liquor calculated as pure ethanol per head of population. In Great Britain the overall consumption of alcohol between 1950 and 1976 increased by 87 per cent, and it was estimated that in 1979 there were at least 300,000 alcoholics in the country. Whereas in the past alcoholism and excessive drinking were mainly male attributes, over the past few decades there has been a sharp increase in the number of women damaged by intemperance, a phenomenon which is probably related to the ease of purchase of liquor from supermarkets and other retail outlets, and of its concealment.

The problem of addiction to alcohol is not peculiar to the present. The Romans passed laws to control drunken charioteers and Victorian philanthropy was well acquainted with the evils of drink. Now, as then, excessive drinking results in medical and social damage. Research in Great Britain and Australia has shown that 15–20 per cent of hospital beds are occupied by patients suffering from diseases or injuries directly or indirectly brought about by excessive indulgence in alcohol. As its consumption has increased, so have deaths from cirrhosis of the liver and the other diseases it causes, while psychiatric hospitals are familiar with the acute and chronic psychoses due to it. The social damage is not always recognized or acknowledged. In Great Britain, Australia, and the USA, for example, some 50 per cent of deaths and injuries from car crashes and 20–40 per cent of other accidental deaths such as falls, drowning, and incineration can be attributed to the effects of alcohol. It is impossible to obtain accurate figures on the role of alcohol in occupational accidents but there is a striking correlation between the numbers of patients admitted to hospital with alcoholism and those of patients undergoing treatment for injuries sustained at work. The contribution of alcohol to antisocial behaviour is well known: violence in the streets, at football matches, and in the home, and the battering of women and of babies, are all familiar examples of the phenomenon. Criminal behaviour such as rape and homicide can often be attributed to intoxication of the aggressor and, in some cases, of the victim as well. Yet in the West it continues to be a widely advertised drug; the British government reaped tax of £3,900 million from it in 1983–4. As for nicotine, in recent years much publicity has been given to the contribution of tobacco to diseases of the heart and lungs to whose aetiology heavy smoking is an important contributor. Following the introduction of tobacco into England in 1565, James I wrote his trenchant 'Counterblaste to Tobacco' (1604). Wiser than some other rulers, however, he did not attempt to ban its use but placed a tax on it; and governments ever since have found it a singularly lucrative source of revenue.

The reputation of heroin, with its addictive properties, may mislead some people into thinking that other drugs are relatively trouble free. But in the case of sedative drugs, the widespread use of barbiturates—predominantly by middle-aged women—in the 1960s was an epidemic which caused considerable ill health and an increase in the rates of suicide and attempted suicide. For therapeutic use they have been largely superseded by the safer benzodiazepines (Valium, Mogadon, etc.—see PSYCHOPHARMACOLOGY), though these are not so free from addictive potential as was believed initially. Sudden cessation of their regular use by an individual accustomed to them can cause a drug-withdrawal syndrome with both physical and psychological symptoms (Ashton 1984). While their popularity for the control of anxiety, insomnia, and a variety of psychosomatic symptoms is testified to by Tyrer's estimate (1980) that some 40 billion doses were being consumed each day throughout the world, the publicity given to benzodiazepine dependence in recent years has probably influenced doctors towards greater caution in prescribing them for long periods of time. The greater the dose and duration of consumption, the greater is the risk of dependence developing.

Cannabis (also known as marijuana, pot, and hashish) grows wild as hemp in many parts of the world. It was used medicinally in China as long ago as 2737 BC, Herodotus (c.484–425 BC) mentions its being inhaled by Scythians as part of a funeral ritual, and the physician *Galen says that it was customary to give hemp to guests at feasts to promote hilarity and happiness. In recent times every kind of evil has been attributed to smokers of marijuana (see Schofield 1971), but the evidence for these baneful effects is far from satisfactory and there are singularly few dangers to health that can be attributed to cannabis alone—though anyone driving while affected by cannabis is at risk, and even more so if alcohol has also been consumed. Few addicts confine their intake to a single substance, and interactions are often more hazardous than the effects of single substances; even so, the cultivation and possession of hemp products are generally prohibited by law. Whether such laws should continue has become a matter for continued debate.

The control of drug trafficking and misuse is based on the United Nations Single Convention on Narcotic Drugs (1961), to which most countries are signatories. This instrument wholly restricts the use of a wide range of substances and requires governments to enforce by punishment its regulations on the cultivation, manufacture, and sale of the drugs listed. Unfortunately, total prohibition of the recreational use of drugs which users are determined to obtain appears to be a singularly unsuccessful policy, as the USA discovered when alcoholic drinks were forbidden for nearly fourteen years from 1919. Attempts by governments to prevent their citizens from smoking tobacco have been equally futile: suppliers were liable to decapitation in ancient China; smokers were tortured to death or exiled to Siberia in tsarist Russia, and had molten lead poured down their throats in Persia; and the popes from time to time threatened excommunication. Similarly, with suppliers and users of opiates and cannabis, the draconian laws of some countries seem not to inhibit those who are prepared to risk apprehension.

In the United Kingdom great emphasis is placed on the control of opiates. In many cities heroin addicts can be treated in special centres, where the main task of the therapist is to wean the addict off the heroin by reducing his daily intake or else to substitute a long-acting opiate, such as methadone, that will block the action of heroin if this continues to be used. In addition, much attention is paid to the addict's life circumstances, with counselling offered by social workers, psychologists, and other members of the centre's staff. Whereas withdrawal of the drug is comparatively easy, the task of ensuring continued abstinence is decidedly difficult, and relapses are commonplace. It is

questionable whether young addicts 'mature out' of dependence on reaching an age even of 30–35, yet it is possible that a change in circumstances coupled with a desire to be free from the constant need for opiates and money for their purchase may persuade a sufferer to find other satisfactions in life.

The treatment of alcoholism is scarcely easier, largely because of the ready availability of alcoholic drink: a person persuaded to give up the drink habit in the clinic may suffer immediate relapse on returning to former surroundings. Yet there is evidence to show that some alcoholics can abstain sufficiently to permit a return to 'normal social drinking', an elastic-sided term that depends on the attitudes of a society to drinking behaviour.   FAW

Ashton, H. (1984). 'Benzodiazepine withdrawal: an unfinished story'. *British Medical Journal*, 1.

Davies, D. L. (1962). 'Normal drinking in recovered alcohol addicts'. *Quarterly Journal of Studies of Alcohol*, 23.

Schofield, M. (1971). *The Strange Case of Pot.*

Tyrer, P. (1980). 'Dependence on benzodiazepines'. *British Journal of Psychiatry*, 137.

Adler, Alfred (1870–1937). Founder of the School of Individual Psychology. He was born in Vienna, and qualified in medicine in 1895. He spent his early years in medical practice, and became increasingly interested in the environmental and psychological aspects of physical disorders. In 1902, Sigmund *Freud invited Adler and three other colleagues to discuss the psychology of the *neuroses. The group was later to become the Vienna Psychoanalytic Society, with Adler as a president and co-editor of its journal. During this period he developed the theory of organ inferiority and compensation, based on his observation of the effects of different environments on the outcome of developmentally retarded organs. The purpose of compensation, either organic or psychological, was seen to make up a deficiency by increasing development or function. Compensation, which could be favourable or unfavourable, might, for example, in good enough circumstances bring about normal speech in cases of retarded speech development; while overcompensation in particular cases might lead a stutterer like Demosthenes to brilliant oratory. The theory led to the development of Adler's view that feelings of inferiority (determined by genetic, organic, or situational factors) were of fundamental importance in provoking the small, weak, and dependent child to conceive of weakness as analogous to both inferiority and femininity. The 'masculine protest' and the striving for power and superiority were thus the predictable outcome of compensation in a male-dominated society.

In 1911 Adler's theoretical divergence from Freud's views was forcefully expressed in his papers given to the Psychoanalytic Congress at Weimar. He disagreed with

Freud's view of the sex instinct as the pre-eminent motivational drive and pertinently questioned whether *ego drives did not have a libidinal character: a position that Freud was later to entertain, and one that Carl *Jung regarded as a 'rather poky corner' in Freud's psychology. Adler criticized Freud's concept of repression, replacing it by ego-defensive safeguarding tendencies, and asserted that the neurotic's value system resulted from increased feelings of inferiority and the subsequent unfavourable overcompensation of the masculine protest, of which the *Oedipus complex represented a comparatively insignificant stage. Freud in his reply recognized this presentation as 'ego psychology deepened by knowledge of the unconscious', but saw it as an impediment to his development of an instinct and impulse psychology. Only one helmsman was required, and Adler left to form a society with the rebuking title of 'The Society of Free Analytic Research', which was, within the year, significantly renamed 'The Society of Individual Psychology'.

In 1911 Adler was profoundly influenced by Vaihinger's concept of 'fictions', i.e. mental constructs or early conceptions of what might now be called working models. This led him, in his first and essentially most significant book, *The Neurotic Character* (1912), to insist that human character and actions must be explained teleologically, separate goals coming under the dominance of, and oriented towards, the final purpose. This guiding fiction or purpose, developed by the age of 5 years, was to move feelings of inferiority to those of superiority—under the direction of the individual's unconscious but uniquely created self-ideal—as a constellation of wishful thoughts and imaginings of being and becoming strong and powerful; or, if overcompensation was present, in fantasies of godlike immutable supremacy. 'Counter-fiction forces', Adler's name for the correcting factors of social and ethical demand on the self-ideal, led to mental health if mutual compatibility with the self-ideal was achieved. However, devaluation of corrective factors (later seen to be the patient's overt or covert mode of dealing with the therapist), when combined with a high level of unfavourable overcompensation, led to the development of the more extreme personality traits and psychological disorders.

A major period of expansion in the influence of Individual Psychology took place between 1920 and 1935. Adler, whose work had been restricted during his service as a physician in the Austrian army in the First World War, was to extend and consolidate both his theory and his practice. In 1927 he established 22 child guidance clinics in Austria, a number that increased to 30 before they were closed down in 1933. He became a regular visitor to, and frequent lecturer in, the United States, where, as in Europe, Individual Psychology Societies increased in number, activities, and influence.

Freud was correct in thinking that Adlerian doctrines would 'make a great impression'. Adler's understandable, rational, and optimistic approach to interpersonal and social problems contrasted favourably with Freud's psychobiological, more mechanistic, pessimistic concepts, and with the more mystical and esoteric ingredients of Jung's theory. Later developments of Adler's theory of personality included his concept of the 'style of life', which comprised not only the person's 'fictive' goal but his plans and schemes to achieve it, including self-evaluation. He came to regard the origin of a neurotic disposition or style of life as the result of: the overburdening of the child with physical disorders and illness; pampering (his wishes being treated as laws); neglect (not knowing what love and cooperation can be); marital disharmony; and certain dispositions of sibling arrangements. Mental disorders of every sort were conceived as having a common cause, constructed by individuals who determine themselves by the meaning they give to situations.

Adler's therapeutic method avoided, as he stated, 'tedious excursions into the mysterious regions of the *psyche'. It was sensibly concerned with the prevention of adult maladjustment by the early correction of the mistakes of the child, a task which he attempted to accomplish through the training of teachers. It was their duty to see that children were not discouraged at school but were put in a position, by being given tasks which they could accomplish, to gain faith in themselves. His own therapy, based on his understanding of the symptoms, problems, and the specific lifestyle of the patient, insisted on explanations to the patient of the predictable effects of his lifestyle, and an encouragement and strengthening of his social interest, which was Adler's criterion of mental health. This was done in a relationship in which blame was excluded, and resistance (the depreciation tendency) reduced by repeatedly drawing the patient's attention to the similarity of all his behaviour, and disarming him by refusing to adopt a superior role or engage in a fight. Devices included what are now called paradoxical injunctions and the use of humorous models and historical instances. *Transference was recognized but avoided by teaching the patient to take full responsibility for his conduct. Aggression was recognized behind the patient's attempts to devalue the therapist, and blame others before himself. Narcissism resulted from the exclusion of obviously given social relationships or from not having found them. Symptoms were seen as attempts to safeguard self-esteem and the current lifestyle.

In 1935 Adler was appointed professor in medical psychology at the Long Island College of Medicine, and died in Aberdeen two years later, on the last day of a course of lectures given at the university. The influence of the School of Individual Psychology receded after his death. Many of his ideas, however, while rarely attributed to him, became common currency in the so-called neo-Freudian group of Sullivan, Horney, and Fromm, and are clearly recognizable in contemporary cognitive, problem-solving, and existential therapies.

Adler's writings are intuitively penetrating and frequently inspirational, but are at times confusing and lacking in objective rigour and refinement. It is a matter of regret that he took insufficient time to argue his ideas more closely and present them as a fully coherent alternative to those of Freud and Jung, although the Ansbachers' work (1956) has helped to correct this. It leaves him open to the criticism that while helping to lay the foundations of contemporary ego and social psychology his theories oversimplified the inherent complexity of their subject.   BL

Adler, A. (1929). *Individual Psychology* (rev. edn.).
——(1935). 'The structure of neurosis'. *International Journal of Industrial Psychology*, 3–12.
Ansbacher, H. L. (1985). 'The significance of Alfred Adler for the concept of narcissism'. *American Journal of Psychiatry*, 142/2.
—— and Ansbacher, R. R. (1956). *The Individual Psychology of Alfred Adler*.
Bottome, P. (1939). *Alfred Adler: Apostle of Freedom*.
Freud, S. (1957). *On the History of the Psychoanalytic Movement*. Standard edition of *Complete Psychological Works*, vol. xiv (1914–16).
Guntrip, H. (1968). *Personality Structure and Human Interaction*.
Jung, C. G. (1953). *Two Essays on Analytical Psychology*. Collected *Works*, vol. vii (Bollingen series 20), first essay, ch. 3.

adolescence. See HUMAN GROWTH; SEXUAL DEVELOPMENT.

adrenaline (epinephrine). One of the two main hormones released by the medulla of the adrenal gland, the other being the related noradrenaline. It produces effects similar to the stimulation of the sympathetic nervous system, increasing heart activity and muscular action, generally preparing the body for 'fright, flight, or fight', hence the oft-quoted need for sportsmen 'to get their adrenaline going'.

See NEUROTRANSMITTERS AND NEUROMODULATORS.

Adrian, Edgar Douglas, 1st Baron Adrian (1889–1977). Adrian was born in London and educated at Westminster School, where he became a King's Scholar at the end of his first term. Like his mentor at Cambridge, Keith Lucas (1879–1916), he at first studied classics but went over to science in his last year. He went up to Cambridge as a scholar of Trinity College, where he read medicine, and became a Fellow in 1913. On the outbreak of war in 1914, he completed his medical studies at St Bartholomew's Hospital, London. After qualifying, he obtained a resident appointment at the National Hospital for Nervous Diseases, Queen Square, London, following which he became

medical officer at the Connaught Military Hospital at Aldershot. After the war he returned to the Cambridge Physiological Laboratory to continue the work he had started in association with Keith Lucas, who had died as the result of a flying accident in 1916. Keith Lucas's interest had centred on 'all-or-nothing' activity in skeletal muscle and in motor nerves, and there is no doubt that Adrian conceived it to be a pious duty to carry on and complete his work.

In November 1925 he succeeded in recording with Lucas's capillary electrometer the impulse traffic in a single afferent nerve fibre. He wrote of the experiment in this way:

At all events the great simplicity of the discharge from the sensory end organ came as an exciting and welcome surprise. Bitter experience does not encourage physiologists to suppose that their material will give predictable reactions except under the most rigorously controlled conditions, but the stretch receptors in the frog's muscle did not merely give a discharge which could be reproduced many times without variation, there was the added pleasure of finding that the discharge from each unit was a simple series of impulses varying only in frequency in accordance with the strength of the stimulus. It cannot be often that a general principle like this is as plainly revealed in the course of a single experiment.

This experiment finally proved that Lucas and Adrian's conception of the 'all-or-nothing' character of the propagated nervous impulse, based on indirect evidence, was true. The transmission in the nerve fibre occurs according to what today would be called impulse frequency modulation.

Adrian was always hunting big game: 'the unsatisfactory gap between two such events as the sticking of a pin into my finger and the appearance of pain in my consciousness', as he wrote in *Basis of Sensation* (1928). In this book he gives a summary of the experiments on the muscle spindle, on the cutaneous senses (touch, pressure, and pain), and on the optic nerve, which he performed within the course of only two years.

It is amazing to read today how at that early date he had arrived at the following fundamental view on the relation between the sensation and the impulse frequency in sensory nerve fibres:

The simplicity of the relation is at once very natural and very surprising. It means that our mind receives all the information which can be got out of the messages from those receptors which are in touch with it, but it means also that the mental correlate is a very close copy of the physical events in the sensory nerves. The only kind of distortion which takes place in the transference from body to mind (or in the parallelism of the bodily and mental events) is that the sensations rise and fall smoothly, whereas the nervous message consists of a series of discrete impulses with pauses in between. Somewhere on the way between the two there must be a smoothing process which converts the disconnected impulses into a change of much slower period.

Adrian's study of the adaptation in various sensory receptors led him further to the suggestion, seen in Fig. 1, that the excitatory state in the receptor consists of a slow potential, the peak height of which varies with the strength of the stimulus. This receptor potential modulates the impulse frequency transmitted in the nerve fibre via relay stations (synapses) to the cerebral cortex, inducing there the '*evoked potential' which integrates the series of impulses into a 'quasi-steady effect', as Adrian suggested in 1928. 'The diagram [Fig. 1] does not bridge the gap between stimulus and sensation,' he concludes in *Basis of Sensation*, 'but at least it shows that the gap is a little narrower than it was before.' This was typical of his modesty. Recent parallel recordings in humans of the neural and perceptual responses to sensory stimuli have proved that there is a close linear relation between the two events, thus definitely confirming Adrian's pioneer conception of 1928.

From these early recordings followed a quick development. Adrian's simple amplifier and Keith Lucas's capillary electrometer and camera were gradually exchanged

Stimulus (change in environment)

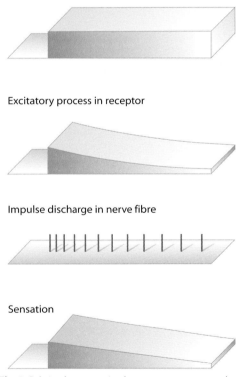

Excitatory process in receptor

Impulse discharge in nerve fibre

Sensation

Fig. 1. Relation between stimulus, sensory message, and sensation.

for new inventions—Matthews's iron-tongue oscillograph, cathode ray oscillographs, etc.—which enabled Adrian and the hundreds of his followers all over the world to study the inflow and outflow of nerve impulses and to record the bio-electrical events within the whole nervous system. In nearly all these fields Adrian was the leader who opened the field or who made the proper analysis and interpretation of bio-electrical phenomena: for instance, the cochlear microphonics first described by Wever and Bray, and the *electroencephalogram discovered by Hans *Berger in Germany.

Adrian used to work alone and had not more than a dozen co-workers through all his active period in the famous basement room of the Cambridge Physiology Laboratory, which covered nearly 60 years. He was Foulerton Research Professor of the Royal Society from 1929 to 1937, when he succeeded Joseph Barcroft as professor of physiology at Cambridge. In 1951 he was appointed master of Trinity College, and from 1950 to 1955 he was president of the Royal Society. He shared the Nobel Prize in physiology or medicine with Sir Charles Scott *Sherrington in 1932, received the Order of Merit in 1942, and delivered the Waynflete Lectures at Magdalen College, Oxford, in 1946. These lectures were published by the Clarendon Press in the following year under the title *The Physical Background of Perception*.

Although Adrian never thought of himself as a psychologist, he was a founder member of the British Psychological Society and greatly encouraged the growth of experimental psychology in the University of Cambridge; in particular, he held the young Cambridge psychologist Kenneth *Craik in high regard and commented on his achievement in the Waynflete Lectures. Adrian was by no means unsympathetic to psychoanalysis in spite of his firm belief that psychology should develop on the model of the biological sciences.

In 1955 he was created Baron Adrian, and in 1967 was elected chancellor of Cambridge University. He died in his eighty-eighth year, in August 1977. At his funeral, the master of Selwyn College, Professor Owen Chadwick, said: 'I am not sure what wisdom is, but whatever it is, Adrian had it'.   YZ / OLZ

aesthetics. Derived from the Greek verb *aesthanesthai* (to perceive), the term 'aesthetic' was until fairly recently used in connection with the philosophy of sensation and *perception. The present use of the label 'aesthetics' to refer to the study of criticism and taste in the arts is due to the German philosopher A. G. Baumgarten, whose *Aesthetica* (1750) dealt with art and the nature of beauty.

The earliest and still probably the most influential discussions of aesthetics, embracing the beautiful and the good, are in *Plato's Socratic dialogues. In the *Hippias* *major* a distinction is drawn between what *appears* beautiful and what *is* beautiful. It is almost accepted that the beautiful is whatever is useful or powerful; but Socrates objects that power may be used for evil, which is not beautiful, so power and beauty cannot be the same. One may reply by making a qualification (e.g. power when used for good is beautiful), but this implies that the good and the beautiful are cause and effect and therefore different things. Yet this is absurd, given the ancient and long accepted identification of the beautiful and the good. It is then suggested that the beautiful is a particular species of the agreeable or pleasurable—comprising all things that give pleasure through the senses of sight and hearing. Socrates questions, though, why these pleasures should be so special compared with other pleasures, and, finding no answer, he rejects this account.

In the *Republic* Plato reveals his more metaphysical thinking, as he describes the beautiful as seen as approximating to the ideal forms of the timeless perfect reality of the universe hidden from mortal view. For Plato, the world as perceived is a rough and imperfect model of the hidden ideal world of the gods, as fully described in the early part of the *Timaeus*. In the *Republic*, Plato describes how works of art, and especially paintings, are at a still further remove from the ideal reality than are the objects of sense—which are but semblances of his perfect universe from which somehow spring truth and beauty. Thus:

. . . you may look at a bed or any other object from straight in front or slantwise or at any angle. Is there then any difference in the bed itself, or does it merely look different?

It only looks different.

Well, that is the point. Does painting aim at reproducing any actual object as it is, or the appearance of it as it looks? In other words, is it a representation of the truth or of a semblance?

Of a semblance [i.e. of the sensed object world].

The art of representation, then, is a long way from reality; and apparently the reason why there is nothing it cannot reproduce is that it grasps only a small part of any object, and that only an image. (*Republic*, Book X, 598)

Plato goes on to deny that artists or poets convey reliable truth, as they have neither knowledge nor correct belief, and he argues that the errors of the artist, at this third remove from reality, are somewhat similar to perceptual errors caused by optical illusions that distance the perceiver from reality.

Only the intellect of philosophers can, for Plato, correct the errors of art and poetry, and the errors of perception. Here geometry is especially important, for the diagrams of geometry most nearly represent the mathematically elegant and unchanging underlying forms, which are true, good, and beautiful. This is still echoed by physicists and mathematicians who seek and find mathematical elegance in nature—for example, the Cambridge mathematician G. H. Hardy in *A Mathematician's Apology* (1941):

'Beauty is the first test; there is no permanent place in the world for ugly mathematics.'

Plato's account of aesthetics has had the most profound effects on art and architecture, and perhaps on music. The close association between the beautiful and the morally good, together with his rejection of action and change in the ideal world, promoted distrust and even distaste for the living body and its normal activities, which is a basis of puritanism.

A worldly kind of Platonism was developed by the English painter Sir Joshua Reynolds (1723–92), who held that beauty is given by the central idea, or by representative examples of classes of things, including faces and the human figure, while the deformed is what is uncommon. Thus beauty is above singular forms, local customs, particularities, and details of every kind. It was objected to this idea that in fact there are many different particular forms and examples of beauty in each species, including man. Reynolds replied that individuals can represent subclasses, which can have distinct forms of beauty, and that 'perfect beauty in any species must combine all the characters which are beautiful in that species'. He thus tried to bring Plato's ideal forms down to earth.

A theory entirely different from Plato's—based firmly on our bodily characteristics and sensations rather than on hidden ideal forms of the structure of the universe or the averages of classes—is the *empathy theory. An early exponent was the artist William Hogarth (1697–1764), who in his *Analysis of Beauty* (1753) suggests that twisted columns are elegant (he prefers waving lines because they are more varied) but they displease when they are required to bear a great weight. The notion is that we identify ourselves with the columns: when thin they look inadequate, as we, if thin, would be too weak to support a great weight; and when too thick they look clumsy, as we feel clumsy when too large for delicate work. This notion is no doubt related directly to the muscle sense of required effort. A golfer driving a ball high and long identifies himself with its flight by an empathy perhaps not so different from the power of art to take us out of this world.

The philosophers of mind of the 18th and 19th centuries, holding associationist theories, tended to believe that the beautiful is not intrinsic in the nature of things, or related to empathy, or to the muscle sense, but that it is given by associations with objects or concepts, such as whiteness associated with purity, or the grandeur of mountains with their creation by the superhuman power of gods or the magnificent forces of nature. On this account, what is associated determines what is seen as beautiful. So, there is a related fear that if belief, for example in gods, is abandoned the world will lose its beauty, and be drab and meaningless. No doubt scientific understanding imparts new beauties to the world, but this is surely no reason for it to destroy our appreciation of art, though it changes associations and the meaning of things so that we develop new appreciations.

Certain proportions have been regarded as intrinsically beautiful—that is, apart from associations with objects or concepts. This is especially so of the Golden Mean or Golden Section, the name given to a division of a line or figure in which the ratio of the smaller section to the larger section is the same as the ratio of the larger section to the whole. The notion can be traced back to Plato's obsession with the regular solids—cube, tetrahedron, octahedron, icosahedron—and their supposed association with the four elements. It is the root of much misty mysticism. There is no clear experimental evidence that the Golden Section is an aesthetically unique or specially preferred proportion; and it is suggestive that it is rarely found in the proportions of artists' pictures, or frames. Aesthetic proportions are often supposed to be based on the human form, as in the *Divina proportione* of Luca Pacioli (*c*.1445–*c*.1514), who was a Franciscan, a celebrated mathematician, and a friend of *Leonardo and of Leon Battista Alberti (1404–72). Pacioli tries to relate Euclidean geometry to Christianity, and describes the sacred ratio as 'occult and secret'—the three-in-one proportion of the Holy Trinity.

There are several biologically based theories of aesthetics, with various emphases on innate properties of mind (perhaps derived from ancient experience) and associations with things and situations that give individual pleasure in life or are important for survival. A subtle notion is that repetitions and symmetries, which are characteristics of all decoration, are appealing because we have had to search out repetitions and symmetries in nature in order to predict, control, and survive by intelligence. The Austrian physicist Ernst *Mach points out the biological importance of discovering order, in a lecture 'On symmetry' (reprinted in his *Popular Scientific Lectures* 1894). This general view is developed in detail by Sir Ernst Gombrich (1979).

In *Art and Illusion* (1960), Gombrich relates processes of perception and representative art. He is, however, concerned here not so much with theories of beauty as with issues of the cultural basis of the visual arts. He takes 'illusion' to mean the techniques and aims of the artist in representing reality rather than the sense of misleading error that the word usually suggests. (See ILLUSIONS.)

Is beauty objective, or is it in the eye of the beholder? The notion that the universe is beautiful apart from man, and so objectively beautiful as well as good, was an essential of Platonism. But how can beauty be objective? Agreement of aesthetic practice and judgement between different societies and over long intervals of time may be taken as evidence of some kind of objectivity, but it must be remembered that all human environments, and the human form itself, have much in common in all societies throughout history, so commonality of experience might be responsible for similarities of art forms. Also, there was a surprising amount of trade (by the Beaker people, for instance) with dissemination of artefacts over Europe and Asia even in neolithic times. This, indeed, works against C. G. *Jung's argument (*Psychology and Alchemy*, 1944; *Man and his Symbols*, 1964) that the spontaneous emergence of 'archetypal' forms is evidence for the existence of innate symbols universally accepted as beautiful, and especially significant, although not representational.

When Jung was writing, the extent of prehistoric and ancient trade routes was not appreciated. In addition, there is, perhaps, only a limited number of simple symmetrical shapes to choose from. What seems at least as remarkable as the frequent occurrence of certain formal designs is the local individuality and gradual changes of aesthetically accepted forms in particular communities, making it possible to date pottery and other artefacts with astonishing accuracy. Why should the craftsmen of a community or region accept current aesthetic standards or conventions? Why is art and design not a free-for-all—the individual expressing himself as he wishes? It has been suggested (Gregory 1981) that there is a technological need for agreement over non-functional features of artefacts if they are to be made cooperatively, without endless arguments and disagreements, that cannot be resolved or decided on functional grounds. Thus the slope of a roof is, within limits, determined by the available building materials and by the climate (for example roofs for heavy snow are steep so that it slides off), but the proportion (if not the size) of windows is largely arbitrary. There are many features of boats, tools, pots, and other useful artefacts that may be varied over wide limits with no loss of function, but these have fixed conventional forms at certain times in society. Could it be that social leaders and artists set accepted forms where discussion leads merely to argumentative waste of time and effort? Could this be so important that the aesthetic sense has developed as man has learned to make and use tools and undertake cooperative projects? Could aesthetics be a by-product of tool using? This seems a far cry from the beauty of pictures and music, but possibly the roots of style and fashion lie in ancient technology, rather than in pictorial and decorative art. From this humble start it may have grown to evoke the range of human experience; to lift us beyond Nature, while revealing our own natures, such is the power of art.   RLG

Gombrich, E. H. (1960). *Art and Illusion*.
—— (1979). *The Sense of Order: A Study in the Psychology of Decorative Art*.
Gregory, R. L. (1981). *Mind in Science*.
Mach, E. (1894). *Popular Scientific Lectures*. Trans. T. J. McCormack.
Plato (1941). *Republic*. Trans. F. M. Cornford.

aesthetics: some psychological approaches. There are five main ways in which psychological approaches are made to visual *aesthetics. First, there is the use of special experimental methods of dealing with judgements about art and aesthetic feelings and attitudes. Next there is the application of existing psychological facts and theories—for instance, as formulated in the psychology of perception—to illuminate problems of art and aesthetics. Thirdly, there is the study of cross-cultural and racial differences and similarities in aesthetic judgements and preferences. Fourthly, there is the study of the influences on the development of artistic styles and cultural changes in art exerted by the interaction of social groups. And fifthly, there is the approach to aesthetics and the understanding of art through the study of the lives of artists, and any influences which are due to personality qualities and psychiatric factors. These different approaches have been reviewed by Pickford (1972, 1976). The many aspects of psychology and the arts are discussed in O'Hare (1981). There has been an almost equally varied and extensive development in the psychology of musical aesthetics—as seen, for example, in the writings of Francès (1973) and Imberty (1976).

G. T. *Fechner (*Vorschule der Aesthetik*, 1876) is generally regarded as the founder of experimental aesthetics, and he established the first method of approach mentioned above. He put forward a number of principles on which aesthetics could be approached as an experimental science 'from below', in contrast to the philosophical approaches 'from above'. He was a major contributor to the development of psychophysical methods in experimental psychology, and he argued that such methods, especially the method of paired comparisons, could be used to measure preferences for colours, colour combinations, figures, shapes, proportions, and actual works of visual art or musical composition. The essential foundations of aesthetics could thereby be established on a factual basis. He cast a wide net, with five main and seven subordinate principles (Pickford 1972: 18), and was not as restrictive as is often supposed.

For about 50 years after Fechner's work only a small number of researches based on it were published, but by the 1930s it had begun to become popular among experimental psychologists, and the study of aesthetic judgements and preferences was introduced into laboratory courses on experimental psychology. Since then experimental aesthetics, although not always tied strictly to Fechner's concepts, has expanded rapidly. Now it is a major branch of experimental psychology, applying itself not only to the visual arts but also to auditory and musical problems, and using factor analysis, the analysis of variance, the semantic differential and other statistical techniques, and *information theory (Moles 1966).

With regard to the second method of approach

mentioned at the start, it is clear that a very large part of visual art depends on (i) the representation of three-dimensional scenes and objects, viewed in perspective, upon two-dimensional surfaces; and (ii) the construction of solid shapes, in sculpture or architecture, in such a way that they create the best aesthetic impression when seen from one or even from many points of view. The representation of three-dimensional scenes and objects on flat surfaces has presented complex and interesting problems for artists, and, in turn, for psychologists in understanding and explaining how they worked. After the accurate handling of the geometry of perspective became important in Renaissance art, these problems came to be of outstanding interest (see Osborne 1970).

Apparent depth perception in flat pictures is essentially monocular, and viewing is assumed to be from a particular point. Viewing flat pictures with two eyes, and from all sorts of positions and distances, tends to be a disadvantage. All distances or positions except one are unrelated to the perspective construction of the picture, and two eyes commit us to two viewing points, which, because the picture is flat, cannot contribute to stereoscopic vision. Monocular depth perception depends on shadows, the overlapping of distant by near objects, decrease in precision of outline as distance increases, changes of colour, usually towards less saturation and more blue-grey or purplish hues in the distance, the recession of parallel lines towards vanishing points, and on the automatic variation in focusing of the eye in spite of the picture being flat. When two eyes are used there is also a tendency to variation of convergence when looking at near or distant objects in a flat picture.

The branch of psychology which has given most illumination to aesthetics is *Gestalt psychology. Its phenomenological principles are almost a practical guide for the artist and the viewer. The first of its four basic principles is that of 'figure and ground', according to which every form or object perceived is experienced as a figure standing out against a ground or background. The second principle is that of 'differentiation' or 'segregation', by which presentations tend to organize themselves into perceptual structures. The third is that of 'closure', by which incomplete or partly occluded figures or objects tend to be perceived or experienced as wholes. (Thus a face partly occluded by shadow is seen as a full face, as every artist knows.) And the fourth principle is that of the 'good Gestalt', according to which a strongly emphasized or more complete or adequate pattern or configuration will take precedence over weaker or less adequate patterns. These principles operate phenomenologically even though the physiological theory of 'isomorphism' (that the excitations in the brain's visual area are the same as those in outward experience) cannot be supported. Indeed few people would suspect that it could be supported, or that it would clarify perceptual theory even if it were supported, by experimentally established fact. After all, even if a solid stimulus object when perceived were known to be represented in the brain by a solid pattern of neurological excitations, we should be no nearer to understanding how such a solid neurological pattern would give rise to the perception of the stimulus object as a three-dimensional solid. The gap between neurology and experience cannot be bridged so easily.

Turning to the third psychological principle or approach, which deals with cross-cultural and allied matters, there have been numerous experimental researches on colour preferences, preferences for figures, shapes, and complete works of art such as pictures, sculptures including African masks, and musical works. The central aim of these researches has been to test the hypothesis that there are cultural or racial differences in aesthetic preferences. In the field of colour preferences, Eysenck (1941) showed that in sixteen studies of white people's colour choices and ten of choices by non-whites, there was a surprising degree of conformity. The average order for six saturated colours among the whites was blue first, then red, green, violet, yellow, and finally orange. The order for non-whites differed only in that yellow and orange changed places. Child and Siroto (1965), for instance, showed that, when American art experts' judgements of BaKwele ceremonial masks were compared with choices by BaKwele judges, the least degree of agreement was found with tribesmen, most agreement with those who actually carved the masks, and an intermediate degree of agreement with the ceremonial leaders who used the masks. Similar results were found in other experiments, and it seems that, when competent judges of art are used, there is more cross-cultural agreement than is often supposed. Differences of material, style, subject matter, or intention of the works of art do not necessarily imply basic differences of aesthetic evaluation (Pickford 1972, 1976). A significant contribution to cross-cultural studies has been made by Segall (1976). (See also PERCEPTION: CULTURAL DIFFERENCES.)

The fourth approach of psychology to aesthetics is based on study of the interactions of groups and of individuals with groups in the history of art. F. C. *Bartlett's interesting and stimulating book *Psychology and Primitive Culture* (1923) was based largely on the study of folk tales and their changes and vicissitudes under varying cultural conditions. Sayce followed this with a study of primitive arts and crafts (1933), and Pickford attempted to apply a similar approach to movements in the history of painting (1943). Very interesting studies have been made by Brothwell (1976).

The fifth approach has been biographical and in the study of the relation of personality factors and differences to aesthetic judgements and preferences. Burt (1939) showed a relation between *extroversion/introversion on the one hand, and instability/stability of personality on the other, in aesthetic preferences for pictures. Unstable extroverts tended to prefer romantic art, while stable extroverts preferred realistic art; unstable introverts tended to prefer impressionistic whereas stable introverts preferred classical art. Eysenck (1940) showed a connection between introversion and liking for classical art, and between extroversion and liking for modern and colourful art. Many other researches have been carried out, and some of them are summarized by Pickford (1972).

The relations between various mental or psychiatric disturbances and aesthetic preferences have been studied experimentally, as by Katz (1931), Warner (1949), and Robertson (1952). Blue was the most preferred colour among mental hospital patients, as among normal people, but in one study male patients put green second while females put red in that position. Manic–depressives liked red, orange, and yellow more than did schizophrenics, who preferred green. Another study showed that anxiety neurotics preferred green to yellow, and also liked lighter colours. Male patients preferred cool hues more than did females. Robertson's study of paintings made by patients showed that red was more used by male than by female schizophrenics. It was also found that schizophrenics tended to be less aroused by colours than were psychopaths, depressives, and psychoneurotics, and that the difference probably lay in a diminished reactivity to colour in the more seriously disturbed patients.   RWP

Bartlett, F. C. (1923). *Psychology and Primitive Culture*.
Brothwell, D. R. (1976). 'Visual art, evolution and environment'. In Brothwell, D. R. (ed.), *Beyond Aesthetics*.
Burt, C. (1939). 'Factorial analysis of emotional traits, II'. *Character and Personality*, 7.
Child, I. L., and Siroto, L. (1965). 'BaKwele and American esthetic evaluations compared'. *Ethnology*, 4.
Eysenck, H. J. (1940). 'The general factor in aesthetic judgements'. *British Journal of Psychology*, 31.
—— (1941). 'A critical and experimental study of colour preference'. *American Journal of Psychology*, 54.
Francès, R. (1958). *La Perception de la musique*.
Imberty, M. (1976). *Signification and Meaning in Music*.
Katz, S. E. (1931). 'Colour preference in the insane'. *Journal of Abnormal and Social Psychology*, 26.
Moles, A. (1966). *Information Theory and Esthetic Perception*.
O'Hare, D. (1981). *Psychology and the Arts*.
Osborne, H. (ed.) (1970). *The Oxford Companion to Art*.
Pickford, R. W. (1943). 'The psychology of cultural change in painting'. *British Journal of Psychology*, Monograph Supplement 26.
—— (1972). *Psychology and Visual Aesthetics*.
—— (1976). 'Psychology, culture and visual art'. In Brothwell, D. R. (ed.), *Beyond Aesthetics*.
Robertson, J. D. S. (1952). 'The use of colour in paintings by psychotics'. *Mental Science*, 98.
Sayce, R. N. (1933). *Primitive Arts and Crafts*.

Segall, M. H. (1976). 'Visual art: some perspectives from cross-cultural psychology'. In Brothwell, D. R. (ed.), *Beyond Aesthetics*.

Warner, S. J. (1949). 'The color preferences of psychiatric groups'. *Psychological Monographs*, 301.

affect. A term used in psychology for a feeling or emotion, particularly one leading to action.

afferent. A word pertaining to the sensory neural inputs to the nervous system—the nerves and their signals (action potentials) running from the senses to the brain. See also EFFERENT.

after-effect, perceptual. A distortion occurring after prolonged sensory stimulation by alternating patterns. While there are early reports of effects which with hindsight we can see were contingent after-effects, there has been a growth in interest due to a paper published by Celeste McCollough in 1965. She presented human subjects with two alternating visual patterns: a grating of blue and black vertical stripes, and a grating of orange and black horizontal stripes. After her subjects had gazed at these alternating, adapting patterns for a few minutes (and so adapted to them), they were shown a test field of black and white stripes of the same size. In one part of the field the stripes were vertical, in the other horizontal. However, to the subjects the stripes did not appear black and white: where vertical they appeared pinkish and where horizontal they appeared bluish. This is now called the 'McCollough effect'.

Such effects are different from simple *after-images produced by staring at a bright, coloured surface. If one looks for half a minute or so at an unpatterned red field, for a few moments all subsequently viewed white objects will appear tinged with green. But in the McCollough effect, although the perceived colours are also the approximate complementaries of the adapting colours, they depend (or are contingent) upon the orientation of the stripes of the adapting and test fields. It is the orientation with respect to the retina that is important. McCollough's subjects were adapted and tested with their heads upright, but if while looking at the test field they tilted their heads sideways, by 45 degrees, the apparent colours disappeared, even though the stripes in the test field still looked horizontal and vertical. If they tilted their heads through 90 degrees the effects reappeared, though now the stripes that had appeared pinkish with the head vertical appeared bluish, and vice versa.

Interest in the McCollough effect, and related effects, has generated a large volume of research. It is worth asking why. The original interpretation of the effects seems to have been right for the *Zeitgeist* of the late 1960s. It was becoming clear from the discoveries of the neurophysiologists that cells in the visual cortex of the brains of cats and monkeys are specialized to respond to rather specific features of the sensory input. After-effects seemed to suggest a similar organization in man. For example, the movement after-effect (apparent motion of a stationary field in one direction, following prolonged viewing of real motion in the other) is consistent with the idea that there are specific *channels sensitive to particular directions of motion, whose outputs are reduced by prolonged stimulation and are compared to give perceived motion. The McCollough effect, as a complicated after-effect, might reveal how the human brain processes more complex patterns. This hope has, however, not been realized. Contingent after-effects have revealed little about how a face is recognized. Like other after-effects they seem to tell us only about the organization of early stages of visual processing.

Many other contingent after-effects (or CAEs) have been discovered since Celeste McCollough's original report. For example, coloured after-effects can be made contingent on the width of stripes, as well as on their orientation. Another effect, reported by H. J. Wyatt, is the size of after-effect contingent upon orientation. After adaptation to coarse horizontal stripes, alternating with fine vertical stripes, medium stripes appear fine when horizontal and coarse when vertical.

There are several ways for finding out where in the brain a particular effect is occurring (see Julesz 1971 for a discussion of them). One trick is to induce a visual effect with one eye, and then see if it can be obtained with the other eye. For example, for the after-effect of movement: if one gazes for a time with one eye at a moving display, which is then stopped, the now stationary display will appear to move in the opposite direction—and this apparent motion can be seen not only with the eye that inspected the moving display but also with the other eye, when the adapted eye is closed. This phenomenon is known as interocular transfer. It implies (provided there is no activity from the closed eye) that the anatomical site of the after-effect lies at a point at or after the combination of the two optic tracts. Some CAEs transfer between the eyes—for example, the movement after-effect contingent on the orientation of a superimposed grating. However, the McCollough effect exhibits little, if any, transfer. It used to be thought that it was a purely monocular effect, whose site lay peripheral to binocular combination, but more recent studies have found evidence for binocular effects. One way to do this is to divide up colour and pattern information between the eyes so that, instead of coloured gratings, the subject sees a plain coloured field with, say, his left eye, and a black and white grating with his right eye. The alternate adapting stimulus used is another colour, seen by his left eye, and a grating at 90 degrees to the first, seen by his right eye. (These adapting conditions are shown diagrammatically in Fig. 1.)

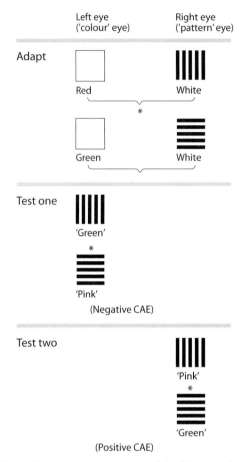

Left eye
('colour' eye)

Right eye
('pattern' eye)

Adapt

Red

White

*

Green

White

Test one

'Green'

*

'Pink'

(Negative CAE)

Test two

'Pink'

*

'Green'

(Positive CAE)

Fig. 1. Diagrammatic representation of the dichoptic induction of the McCollough effect, reported by D. M. and V. MacKay. During adaptation, the subject's left eye always sees colour and his right eye always sees black-and-white stripes. The colour and stripe orientations are systematically paired so that, say, red and vertical are always seen together, though by different eyes, and similarly green and horizontal. The pairs of stimuli alternate every 10 seconds or so during adaptation. To test for an after-effect, the subject views a black-and-white grating with one eye. If this is the eye that is adapted to colour, the after-effects are negative, but if it is the eye that is adapted to the gratings the after-effects are positive.

McCollough effects are then found, but they are of opposite sign in each eye. So when the subject views the test field with the eye that has seen colour, the perceived colours are the complementary colours to those paired with a particular orientation during adaptation. This is the normal relationship between the colours seen during adaptation and those that appear during testing. But, when the eye that has adapted to black and white stripes is tested, the perceived colours are the same as those with which that orientation was paired during the adaptation. Here the normal relationship is reversed. Perhaps when the left eye is flooded with green light while the right sees a black and white grating, the visual system treats the colour input as 'left eye greener than right'. At any rate, the apparently simple scheme suggested by the early interocular transfer results has now been complicated by such later work.

Although most work on contingent after-effects has been done in vision, they can be found in other sensory modalities such as touch. For example, contingent tactile adaptation can be obtained with a wedge-shaped block of wood, held with the tips of the forefinger and thumb. If your hand moves from left to right as the finger and thumb slide from the thick to the thin end of the wedge, then, after some moments of sliding the hand right to left and left to right, a rectangular block of wood will feel deformed. As the finger and thumb of the adapted hand are moved from left to right the block will feel to be getting thicker, and for the reverse direction of movement it will seem to be getting thinner. Here the tactile adaptation is dependent upon the direction of movement of the hand.

Although it is easy to generate CAEs within several (perhaps all) sensory modalities, no one has succeeded in generating CAEs across modalities. For example, the author failed to find a coloured after-effect contingent upon the frequency of sound, after staring at a red field while listening to a high tone, and alternating with a green field accompanied by a low tone. Absence of cross-modal links suggests that the underlying mechanisms lie peripheral to the site(s) where information from different modalities is combined. However, although vision and hearing have not been linked, different parts of the visual field will cooperate to give CAEs. For example, Michael Potts and the author found that a movement after-effect contingent on colour can be obtained when the coloured adapting stimuli are not superimposed on, but surround, the moving stimuli, so that no area of retina sees coloured moving patterns. This suggests some spatial spread of the mechanism linking colour and motion.

What do these striking and robust effects tell us about the brain? At present, there is still no generally accepted explanation for CAEs, but current theories are of two main types. One view likens CAEs to other after-effects supposed to result from adaptation in overlapping sensory channels. So, orientation would be coded by a number of neural channels: some tuned preferentially to vertical, some to, say, 10 degrees from vertical, and so on round the clock. Each group of channels tuned to a particular orientation would have members also tuned for red as well as vertical; others for green and vertical, and so on. During McCollough-type adaptation, gazing at a red vertical grating would reduce to below normal the output of channels tuned for both red and vertical. When the test grating is presented, channels tuned for vertical and other colours would give their usual output, but the red/vertical channels would be less active than normal. This imbalance in favour of the other channels would add an apparent green tinge to the vertical stripes. This is sometimes called a 'built-in' theory, since the mechanism producing the CAE is supposed already to exist in the subject's visual system before adaptation. It can be contrasted with a group of 'built-up' theories which propose that some kind of link is forged during the adaptation period, between previously separate mechanisms for processing colour and orientation. Different kinds of link have been proposed: some authors have suggested that an association is made like that in classical (Pavlovian) *conditioning (in which, after a bell has been presented together with food on several occasions, the bell alone comes to elicit salivation); others that a neural inhibitory link is formed, so that activity in, say, the orientation system reduces activity in the colour system. However, despite numerous attempts, no experiment has yet been reported which convincingly decides between 'built-in' and 'built-up' theories.

There are several important characteristics of CAEs which a successful theory will have to explain. First, the effects are usually 'negative'. That is, the value taken by a sensory quality in the after-effect is opposite to or shifted further away from the value of that quality during adaptation. So, in the McCollough effect the colour seen on a particular orientation (say, red) in the test field is the complementary one to that viewed on that orientation during adaptation (in this case, green). Second, CAEs can be very long-lived. McCollough effects have been reported six weeks after adaptation, and reports that they can be re-evoked days after adaptation are common in the literature. Third, they do not decay during sleep. Indeed, there is some evidence that to remove the effects one has to look at the usual test field.

It is interesting to ask what the role is in normal perception of the mechanisms that produce the McCollough effect. Presumably, they do not exist simply to provide amusing perceptual demonstrations! One possibility is that, if indeed the initial stages of human perception consist of banks of filters tuned to particular features of the sensory input, then there will be a need to keep the outputs of these filter channels calibrated. For example, the gain of a particular sensory channel (that is, how much output it produces for a given input) might be subject to unwanted drifts, or fluctuations, as, say, a blood vessel narrowed which supplied that area of cortex. The brain could attempt to distinguish between such internal changes and those introduced by stimuli in the external world, by sampling over time the outputs of all channels. On the assumption that red vertical stimuli are about as likely to

occur on average as green vertical stimuli, it would turn down the gain of a channel whose output was abnormally high for a long period, or turn up the gain of one that was correspondingly low. Such an automatic gain control system would act to keep the gains of sensory channels roughly equal despite biological drift. It could also remove from the neural image false signals—such as colour fringes introduced by chromatic aberration in the optics of the eye—since these constant errors would be treated in the same way as the unvarying colour/orientation combination in the McCollough effect. But such a system would be misled by prolonged exposure to stimuli exciting only very few channels. It would surely mistake the activity in these channels for internal drift, rather than external stimulation, and turn down their gain. This would give negative after-effects, since these channels would contribute less than their appropriate share to the final percept. The system would also require evidence that the gains of the adapted channels were too low before readjusting them. The best evidence of this would be for the subject to inspect (in the case of the McCollough effect) black and white gratings. Thus presenting the test field should cause CAEs to decay, but withholding it should produce long-lasting after-effects, as is found. CAEs may, therefore, reflect the brain's usually efficient but sometimes erroneous attempts at self-calibration.

See also VISUAL ADAPTATION.   JPH

Dodwell, P. C., and Humphrey, G. K. (1990). 'A functional theory of the McCollough effect'. *Psychological Review*, 97/1.

Humphrey, G. K. (1998). 'The McCollough effect: misperception and reality'. In Walsh, V. (ed.), *Perceptual Constancy: Why Things Look as They Do*.

Julesz, B. (1971). *Foundations of Cyclopean Perception*.

McCollough, C. M. (1965). 'Color adaptation of edge-detectors in the human visual system'. *Science*, 149.

Potts, M. J., and Harris, J. P. (1975). 'Movement after-effects contingent on the colour or pattern of a stationary surround'. *Vision Research*, 15.

Skowbo, D., Timney, B. N., Gentry, T. A., and Morant, R. B. (1975). 'McCollough effects: experimental findings and theoretical accounts'. *Psychological Bulletin*, 82.

Vladusich, T., and Broerse, J. (2002). 'Color constancy and the functional significance of McCollough effects'. *Neural Networks*, 15/7.

after-image. An image seen immediately after the intense stimulation of the eye by light has ceased. For about a second, the after-image is 'positive', and then it turns to 'negative', often with fleeting colours. The positive phase is due to after-discharge of the receptors of the retina (see COLOUR VISION: EYE MECHANISMS); the negative phase is caused by loss of sensitivity of the receptors as a result of bleaching of the photo-pigments by the intense light. After-images can be annoying, but they are usually ignored or suppressed. They are technically useful for visual experiments as they are precisely fixed on the retina. They are seen to move with the eyes during normal eye movement. See also AFTER-EFFECT, PERCEPTUAL; VISUAL ADAPTATION.

ageing. Performance at many types of task studied in the laboratory rises to a peak somewhere between the late teens and late thirties, and then gradually declines into old age. It used to be assumed that the declines were due either to age effects in sense organs, muscles, and joints, or to older people being uninterested in, or out of practice at, the kinds of tasks set by laboratory experiments. Research since the 1940s has shown that, while peripheral changes may be important in later old age, central brain functions account for the main trends of performance in middle and early old age. The trends are by no means all adverse: certain kinds of 'mental agility', such as indicated by scores on typical *intelligence tests, decline from the early twenties—it has been estimated that by the age of 60 they have returned to their level at the age of 10—but the decline is offset, at least partly and sometimes more than fully, by increased knowledge gained in the course of experience. The age of peak performance is thus usually in the thirties, forties, or fifties rather than in the twenties, and varies with the balance between demands for 'mental agility' and for knowledge: for example, it comes relatively early among mathematicians, and relatively late among historians and philosophers.

It must be emphasized that these statements are of *average* trends and that some individuals achieve their peak performance much earlier or later than the majority. Indeed, the extent and rate of changes differ widely between individuals, so that performances tend to become more variable with age—some people in their seventies or eighties perform some tasks in a manner similar to that of people half a century younger, whereas others show profound differences. It is thus all too easy for ideas about old age to be coloured, for better or worse, by a few striking examples who are not typical of their contemporaries.

Psychological studies of ageing made during the last thirty years or so may be broadly divided into three areas:

1. Speed of performance
2. Memory and learning
3. Personality

1. Speed of performance
Perhaps the most characteristic age change is that performance becomes slower. The extent to which it does so is not, however, uniform for all tasks. For simple, aimed movements the change is comparatively slight—a loss of less than 10 per cent between the twenties and seventies. Slowing in sensory motor tasks is mainly in the making of decisions about what action to take—in other words, in cognitive and intellectual rather than in motor functions.

When the relationships between signals for action and the corresponding responses are straightforward, as, for example, when the signals are a row of lights and response is by pressing a button under whichever comes on, the time to react increases typically by about 25 per cent from the twenties to the seventies. When the relationships are more complex, as, for instance, when lights on the right have to be responded to by pressing buttons on the left, and vice versa, increases of 50 per cent or more have been found between these ages. Slowing with age is also greater in continuous tasks, where each response immediately brings on the signal for the next, than in discontinuous tasks, where responses and ensuing signals are separated by an interval of a second or more. The reason appears to be that older people tend more than younger to have their attention diverted to monitoring the response they have just made, so that they cannot attend immediately to any fresh signal.

Much if not all slowing with age can be explained by the fact that signals from the sense organs to the brain and from one part of the brain to another become weaker, while at the same time random neural activity in the brain tends to increase. The latter blurs the former and leads to errors. The blurring can, however, be at least partly overcome by taking a longer time. This allows data to be accumulated, making the signals stronger and averaging out some of the random activity. As a result, older people, although slower, may be as accurate or more so than younger people. With some highly complex tasks, however, such compensation is incomplete, so that older people tend not only to be slower but also to make more errors.

The laboratory findings accord well with studies of real-life situations. In industry, operatives tend to move before retiring age not only from physically strenuous work such as coal mining, but also from lighter jobs where there is pressure for speed, such as on assembly lines. Industrial accidents sustained by older people tend to involve either being hit by moving objects or tripping and falling—in other words, slowness either in getting out of the way or in recovering balance—whereas younger people's accidents tend to be the result of either rashness or lack of experience. The same is true of road accidents and traffic offences: older people fail to react in time to rapidly changing situations, while younger people take undue risks. The problem of complexity is shown in difficulties often found by older industrial operatives with complex machinery and elaborate working drawings. It is also epitomized in the finding that some older people can no longer read a map while travelling south without turning it upside down.

2. Memory and learning
A six- or seven-digit number heard once can be recalled immediately about equally well by people of all ages from

the twenties to the sixties. With more items than this, older people recall less than younger. The reason appears to be that they have difficulty in transferring material from a limited and ephemeral *short-term memory to a more enduring long-term memory: some of the material is lost, and the traces of what is transferred are weaker. The strength of the traces can be increased by repetition, and with enough additional practice recall by older people can equal that by younger. Once material has been learnt, older people do not forget more rapidly than younger. Well-learnt facts, familiar events, and thoroughly practised motor skills such as riding a bicycle or driving a car are, therefore, retained well in old age even if there is difficulty in learning new facts and acquiring new skills.

Failure to register material in long-term memory probably accounts for many difficulties in *problem-solving and other tasks in which data have to be 'held in mind' while other data are gathered: for example, when multiplying, say, 57 by 38, the product $57 \times 3 \times 10$ has to be held while 57×8 is obtained. Calculating the second product will destroy the short-term memory of the first, so that it will be lost unless it has been transferred to long-term memory.

Probably the most successful method of training older people in industry has been the 'discovery method' whereby the trainee is given just enough information to enable him to discover accurately for himself how to perform his task. The active decisions required have the effect of facilitating registration in long-term memory, and the fact that the trainee can learn at his own pace means that he has time to sort out difficulties. It is fair to suggest that insufficient time devoted to mastering new facts and ideas is a reason why thinking often becomes hidebound in later middle age among those hard pressed by day-to-day activities and responsibilities, and that time set aside to acquaint themselves with new developments would be well repaid.

3. Personality

This often appears to change with age, yet scores on personality tests show small, if any, trends. The apparent changes seem instead to represent reactions to altered circumstances in old age which are not measured by the usual tests. For example, on the one hand, retirement brings increased leisure and opportunities, while, on the other, changing capacities may restrict interests and activities and in extreme cases lead to dependency. The ways in which individuals adjust to these circumstances vary greatly. Some welcome the new opportunities and accept the restrictions. Others find little use for leisure, resent restrictions, and become self-centred. This last reaction is well illustrated in many who complain of being lonely. Older people are understandably lonely for a time following *bereavement: however, complaint typically comes from those who are surrounded by relatives, neighbours, and others, but whose self-centredness makes normal social intercourse unrewarding. In all cases the manner of adjustment seems to have little relation to economic or material circumstances or, within limits, to health: it depends upon personality traits that have been present throughout life but which may not have had the opportunity to show earlier because of the exigencies of work or bringing up a family.

The changes in personality can perhaps be summed up by saying that old age is a revealing time, when the best and worst in us stand out in bold relief. As a recipe for contentment, we may cite a remark by Maurice Chevalier: 'Growing old is inevitable for all of us. The clever thing is to accept it and always plan your next move well in advance.'

See also AGEING: SENSORY AND PERCEPTUAL CHANGES.

ATW

Birren, J. E., and Schaie, K. W. (eds.) (1977). *Handbook of the Psychology of Aging.*
Bromley, D. B. (1974). *The Psychology of Human Ageing* (2nd edn.).
Charness, N. (ed.) (1985). *Aging and Human Performance.*
Welford, A. T. (1958). *Ageing and Human Skill.*

ageing: sensory and perceptual changes. Since a person can deal efficiently with his social and physical environment only if his sensory and perceptual processes are not unduly impaired or distorted, changes which might be attributable to the inevitable process of ageing assume considerable importance. In briefly reviewing this topic, two generalizations need to be kept in mind. First, it is not always clear that a given impairment is a natural result of advancing age rather than the result of disease, trauma, or disuse. Secondly, individual differences in general become more pronounced with age, so that some elderly people may exceed the norms in a particular function.

Certain reductions in the efficiency of seeing appear to be inevitable with advancing age, although there are, of course, individual differences. Most obvious is the change in ability to focus on nearby objects, and the use of reading spectacles or bifocals is commonplace. To understand the importance of this change, consider the plight of an artisan doing fine work before the advent of spectacles! Fig. 1 shows the approximate distance from the eyes of the limit of clear focus for 'normal' eyes—or eyes corrected to normal by spectacles—as a function of age. Other apparently 'normal' changes are ordinarily not so obvious to the individual. These include a reduction in resting pupil size, an increase in yellow pigment in the eye media, some reduction in overall acuity, a slight narrowing of the visual field, some loss of colour discrimination, and increased susceptibility to glare. It can readily be appreciated that in our modern society these changes might have serious consequences for the automobile driver or pedestrian.

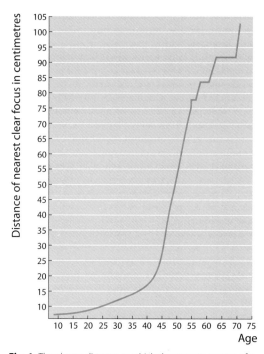

Fig. 1. The closest distance at which the average person of a given age can see clearly. There are no significant sex differences.

However, tests of visual *efficiency* show that many of the old surpass many of the young, so that knowing a person's age does not permit us automatically to assume that he is visually inefficient. It is also true that we cannot be certain how much effect training might have on the maintenance of visual skills, nor has our physiological knowledge so far led to any great advance in the treatment of the ageing eye.

Although the changes in seeing are, barring some actual disease process, rather generally regarded as 'normal' effects of age, the case for hearing is not at all decided. Fig. 2 illustrates the results of hearing surveys which find a progressive decline in the ability to hear the higher frequencies ('pitches') of sound. Fortunately, until the impairment involves frequencies below about 1,800 hertz (about three octaves above middle C), ability to comprehend speech, that basic ingredient of interpersonal interaction, is not significantly reduced. Of course we know that exposure to loud sounds will adversely affect the sensitivity of hearing, whether the exposure be in the boiler factory or the rock concert hall. The modern environment is rather noisy, and most if not all hearing loss is traumatically caused. In fact one investigator has found that persons living in a quiet, remote environment showed little or no loss. In any event, there are most certainly pathological causes of hearing loss or deafness, some of which (those involving conduction of sound to the inner ear) can be helped by 'hearing aids'. Also, lip reading and other

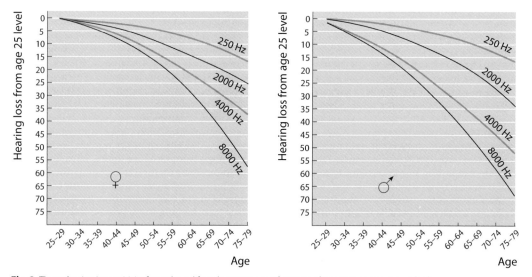

Fig. 2. The reduction in sensitivity for male and female persons as a function of age. Curves are shown for four sound frequencies.

skills can partially compensate for any kind of loss, provided that the perceptual inefficiency is not of cerebral origin.

When we consider 'bodily sensibility'—the skin senses, position sense, and internal sensations—the picture becomes very blurred by the effects of vascular and nervous disorders. Reported changes in some persons in sensitivity to touch and temperature are rendered ambiguous by these possible disorders. Even so, there does seem, with age, to be a reduction in sensitivity to vibration and to pain, and some loss of sensitivity to the detection of fine movements of various joints, although the practical implications of these results have not been fully explored. Indeed, here lies a rich field for research.

Since dietary problems can be important in the elderly, changes in tasting and smelling that might affect the choice or enjoyment of food are of potential importance. It appears that loss of sensitivity does occur, although, especially in the case of smelling, pathological processes as simple as the common cold may also affect sensitivity. In recognition of this decline, especially of smell sensitivity, flavour enhancers have been tried, with some degree of success. Also of considerable interest is the danger that loss of smell sensitivity may cause in the detection of warning agents such as the odorous agents added to domestic gas. Although some persons at any age are not sensitive to at least some of these agents, it has been shown that the elderly are particularly at risk.

It should be noted that demonstrably pathological states, such as senile *dementia, which affect sensory and perceptual processes, have not been considered. Although such conditions are relatively rare, they may affect 10 per cent of persons aged over 65, with the frequency increasing to 22 per cent among those aged 80 and over. Nevertheless, to reiterate a previously made point, it is entirely possible that many sensory losses now considered to be 'normal' decline may be found to result from exogenous influences, or to loss of perceptual skill through disuse.

See also AGEING.   FNJ

Corso, J. L. (1981). Aging Sensory Systems and Perception.

Ordy, J. M., and Brizzee, K. R. (eds.) (1979). Sensory Systems in the Elderly.

Sekuler, R., Kline, D., and Dismukes, K. (eds.) (1982). Aging and Human Visual Function.

Thomas, A. J. (1984). Acquired Hearing Loss.

Van Toller, C., Dodd, G. H., and Billing, A. (1985). Ageing and the Sense of Smell.

Verillo, R. T., and Verillo, V. (1985). 'Sensory and perceptual performance'. In Charness, N. (ed.), Aging and Human Performance.

aggressive behaviour. Behaviour directed towards causing physical injury to another person must clearly be labelled as aggressive, but beyond that hard core the boundaries of aggressive behaviour or aggression are shady. Behaviour causing psychological harm to another is usually included, but the question of intent is crucial: accidental injury is not usually considered aggressive. However even here there is room for latitude: driving a car which causes injury to others may be described as aggressive driving. But aggressive behaviour should not be used as a synonym for assertive behaviour, as in the popular misnomer 'assertive salesman'. Although assertiveness may have causal factors in common with aggressiveness, it is best not to confuse the two. The term 'aggressiveness' is usually used to refer to a propensity to behave aggressively. Not all aggressive behaviour depends on aggressiveness (see discussion of violence in war, below).

Since attack on another individual usually involves risk of injury for the attacker, aggression is often associated with elements of self-protection and withdrawal. Many animal threat postures consist of a mosaic of elements of attack and withdrawal. Attack, threat, submission, and fleeing are often lumped together as 'agonistic behaviour'.

1. Heterogeneity of aggression
2. Motivational complexity
3. Proximate factors relating to aggression
4. Ultimate causes of aggressive behaviour
5. Aggression between groups
6. Morality
7. War

1. Heterogeneity of aggression

The category of aggressive behaviour inevitably conceals considerable heterogeneity, and there are numerous schemes for subdividing it. In studies of children, four categories have been useful (Manning, Heron, and Marshall 1978): (i) Instrumental aggression, concerned with obtaining or maintaining particular objects, positions, or access to situations. (ii) Teasing or hostile aggression, directed towards annoying or injuring another individual, without regard to any object or situation. (iii) Games aggression, escalating out of playful fighting. (iv) Defensive aggression, provoked by the actions of others.

One scheme for subdividing aggressive behaviour in adults involves categorization according to whether it is motivated by a conscious desire to eliminate the victim, performed in extreme rage or anger, committed in the course of another crime, or can be regarded as psychopathic. In addition, violent acts that gain approbation from the reference group are distinguished as 'dyssocial' (Tinklenberg and Ochberg 1981).

Many other schemes have been proposed, but intermediates between the categories are nearly always to be found.

2. Motivational complexity

Confronted with the astonishing range and diversity of aggressive behaviour in many non-human species, *ethologists came to realize that the relations between the categories could be understood in terms of hypothesized variables—aggressiveness involving motivation specific to a particular context (e.g. over food, territory, etc.; see Moyer 1968) and conflicting tendencies to attack, flee, and stay put. These hypothesized motivations could be assessed by a number of methods, including analysis of the behaviour shown and of that which immediately preceded and followed the attack. The diversity of the behaviour could be understood in terms of variations in the absolute and relative levels of the several motivations (Baerends 1975). Human aggression may involve not only aggressiveness, but also assertiveness (attempts to elevate one's status or push oneself forwards), acquisitiveness (attempts to acquire objects or situations), and fear. A study of youth groups who used violence in apartheid South Africa revealed a number of personality types, including genuine idealists, those who were trying to achieve an ego ideal as warrior heroes, those who sought a sense of self, social conformists, and near-psychopaths with antisocial motivation (Straker 1992; Hinde 1997).

3. Proximate factors relating to aggression

The 'causes' of aggressive behaviour stretch far back in time, and may be divided into developmental, predisposing, and eliciting factors.

Developmental factors are those that predispose individuals towards aggressiveness. They involve both genetic and experiential factors. Physical aggressiveness tends to be higher in boys than in girls, and to increase with age up to late adolescence or early adulthood, and then to decline. In our own culture, attention has been focused on the roles of classical conditioning, operant conditioning, social learning, and on social relationships in the genesis of aggressive tendencies. These affect both motivation and the acquisition of cognitive capacities, the latter including capacities for conflict resolution. Parental techniques involving warmth coupled with firm but reasoned and sensitive control tend to promote low aggressiveness (Baumrind 1971). Physical punishment tends to be counter-productive. Individuals outside the family are also likely to be important, including especially those who serve as role models and the peer group with its norms. Television violence and violence in video games can also enhance aggressiveness, especially in susceptible individuals.

The behaviour of the socializing agent, whether intra- or extra-familial, will be influenced by the norms and values incorporated into the sociocultural structure of the group or society, and these may differ with the nature of the targeted individual: thus norms may be different for boys and girls, for first-borns and later-borns, as well as differing between social classes, groups, etc. Thus the development of the aggressive propensities of individuals

can be fully understood only through the two-way influences between factors internal to the individual, the individual and his or her behaviour, relationships and group memberships, and the sociocultural structure (see Fig. 1).

Predisposing factors. The view that aggression depends on spontaneously generated energy which must be dissipated in action rests on an outdated model of motivation and lacks consistent empirical support (Berkowitz 1993). There are circumstances in which behaving aggressively or watching aggression can enhance aggressiveness, and others in which they decrease it. The display of aggression does depend on the hormonal state, though the action of hormonal factors is less easy to specify in apes and humans than in other species. In humans social factors are crucial. Across societies, violence is more frequent in those that tolerate or extol violent acts by individuals or the state, those with marked wealth differentials, and those that lack social and political institutions linking their members in networks of communal obligation (Gartner 1996). However the issues here are complex. While political violence may provide a context for an increase in criminal violence (e.g Liddell, Kemp, and Moema 1991), homicide rates tend to decrease in countries actually at

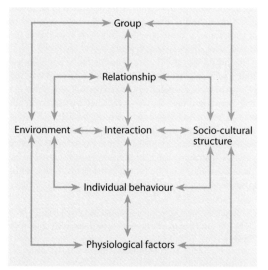

Fig. 1. The understanding of aggressive behaviour requires analysis at a number of levels of complexity which mutually influence each other. Each level, and the sociocultural structure with its norms and values, continually affects and is affected by others. The mutual influences involve behavioural, cognitive, and affective processes in the individuals concerned, mediated by the meanings ascribed to events and situations. Each level is thus to be seen as involving processes of continuous creation, change, or degradation through the dialectical processes between levels.

war, perhaps because of the increased integration. After the war, however, they tend to increase. In addition the propensity for aggressiveness may be influenced by a variety of contextual factors, including the current social situation and its attendant norms, the presence and density of other individuals, the temperature, and so on.

Eliciting factors. The elicitation of an aggressive act used to be ascribed to frustration, but this is not very helpful since a source of frustration can usually be postulated for every aggressive situation. Pain, fear, frustration, the availability of a weapon, the nature of the victim, social influences, and many other contextual factors can play a role (Berkowitz 1993).

4. Ultimate causes of aggressive behaviour

Biologists distinguish between the proximate causes (ontogenetic, predisposing, and eliciting factors) of behaviour and the ultimate factors through which natural selection has acted to maintain the behaviour in the potential repertoire of individuals. Ultimate factors involve the consequences of the behaviour which augment the chances of surviving and reproducing successfully for the individual or his or her close relatives. In general, the ultimate factors in the case of aggressive behaviour involve the acquisition or retention of resources and defence of self or of relatives. But beyond that, the propensity for aggressive behaviour has been fine-tuned so that the extent to which aggression is shown varies with the situation. The data comes mostly from animals, but there is growing evidence that the principles apply also to humans.

In the first place, threat postures have been elaborated or 'ritualized' in the course of evolution to make them more effective as signals. Their effectiveness depends in part on their not being easy to fake, and that in turn on their cost to the actor: signals that are costly to the actor are unlikely to be fakes. At the same time, selection has modified the responsiveness of other individuals to the signals. The selection pressures on actor and reactor are of course distinct, as their interests are not the same.

The principles involved can be explored by modelling the situation. Suppose the population consists of two types of individuals, one that tends to retreat from a situation if there is any sign of danger ('doves') and the other being vicious fighters ('hawks'). If the population consisted largely of doves, a hawk would clearly be at an advantage, because every individual he or she encountered would be likely to be a dove, and so he or she would win every encounter. At the other extreme, if the population consisted mainly of hawks, each hawk would be likely to encounter another, and someone would be likely to get hurt. If the gains of winning were less or doubtfully greater than the costs of losing (in terms of the survival and reproduction of the actor and his close relatives), it

might be better not to be a hawk: a dove could retreat and obtain needed resources in some other way. John Maynard Smith (1976) has shown that, given certain assumptions, a stable situation would arise when there was a particular ratio of hawks to doves, or when each individual adopted each strategy for a particular proportion of the time. This is an example of an 'evolutionary stable state'.

The advantage to an individual of winning an encounter depends on the value of the resource over which the encounter takes place and on the costs of being involved (benefits and costs being reckoned in evolutionary terms). Therefore the difference between costs and benefits will vary between individuals and classes of individuals. One issue here concerns the differences between the sexes. Human sex differences, interpreted in the light of data on other species (e.g. Short 1979), suggest that in the environments in which humans evolved males competed for females. Selection would then have enhanced aggressiveness in males more than in females. It is still the case that men tend to be more physically violent than women, though women may use more verbal aggression than men. This in itself says nothing about the way in which this difference in physical aggressiveness came about. For instance, selection (natural and/or cultural) could have acted so that males were inherently more aggressive than females, or to make parents encourage aggressiveness more in boys than in girls, or promote cultural values to the same end, or any combination of these.

Consideration of costs and benefits (in either evolutionary or more immediate terms) should warn us against expecting any simple relation between the conditions of development and socialization, on the one hand, and aggressiveness in adulthood, because the costs and benefits of aggressiveness vary with the probability of meeting other aggressive individuals and with the scarcity of resources. In a population with few hawks and plentiful resources the advantages to individuals of cooperating in group living may detract from the advantages of being an egotistical hawk. In a population containing a moderate number of hawks and few resources it may be necessary to be a hawk or succumb. But if the population consists very largely of hawks, so that the costs of encounters are certain to be great, it may be better to contract out and find some other way of obtaining resources. These speculations about crude caricatures of 'hawks' and 'doves' are, of course, gross simplifications of reality, but they provide a route towards general principles and sound a warning against expectations of simple monotonic relations between childhood experiences and later psychological characteristics.

5. Aggression between groups

Most of the above concerns aggression between individuals. Aggression between groups involves a number of additional factors, including the factors conducive to group integration. Members of a social group see themselves as interdependent and as more similar to each other than they are to members of other groups. Since an individual's self-image involves both personal identity and social identity, and since individuals in general like to think well of themselves, members of a group tend to see their group as superior to other groups. Furthermore members of the in-group tend to be treated as heterogeneous differentiated individuals, members of the out-group as undifferentiated. The sharing of beliefs with like-minded individuals helps to support the individual's own beliefs, and this contributes to the integrity of the group. Group leaders may foster group integrity by their example, and by using group activities and symbols (flags, mottoes, etc). Loyalty to the group can be a critical element in inter-group conflict, overriding personal interests. The initiation of violence is sometimes due to the assertiveness of one individual wishing to show off to his peers. (See also below.)

6. Morality

As mentioned above, aggressive behaviour cannot be understood solely in terms of ontogenetic, predisposing, and eliciting factors, since all of these are influenced by cultural norms (see Fig. 1). The acceptability of physical violence differs between societies and with the context. Thus while homicide is a criminal offence in peacetime, the killing of enemies is a desired goal in war. The moral code and norms of a society are influenced by and influence the behaviour of individuals in that society. In addition it may be influenced by those in power so as to maintain the status quo—for instance, by extolling the virtue of humility and condemning violence.

7. War

Aggressive acts in war require special consideration. Wars are diverse, and involve raiding parties, conflicts between small parties, larger-scale conflicts involving semi-autonomous groups on both sides, and major international conflicts such as the Second World War. While in every war individuals harm other individuals, the extent to which aggressiveness (in the sense of aggressive motivation) is involved tends to decrease with the complexity of the conflict. Here it is helpful to see war as an institution with a number of constituent roles, each with its specific rights and duties. In major wars those involved are motivated primarily by the duty inherent in the role that they occupy in the institution of war. Major wars involve many different roles, each involving specific duties. The munition workers are motivated by the duty associated with the role that they occupy, the medics with that associated with theirs, the politicians by that associated with theirs, and the combatants by their duty to attack the enemy. In major wars it is closer to the truth to

say that wars cause aggression than that aggressiveness causes war.

To understand why people are willing to go to war, therefore, it is necessary to ask what factors support the institution. These can be categorized into three groups. First, certain everyday factors contribute. These include the warisms current in everyday speech; the sanitization of war in books and films; the war toys that exploit boys' fascination with mechanical devices and cause them to see war as a normal part of life; male chauvinism and the macho ideal; and the failure of most countries to reform their education system in accordance with the UNESCO recommendation of 1974 and institute a programme of peace education. The second category includes a number of pervasive cultural factors, such as national traditions of belligerence and the promotion of nationalism; religions that condone or even promote war, or which lend themselves to its support—as when death in war is glorified by equating it with Christ's death on the cross in war propaganda or war memorials; racism; and propaganda that denigrates other people, making potential enemies seem evil and even subhuman and bestial. Finally, the complex of the arms industries, the military, and scientists play a major part in the institution of war. Each member of this triad depends on and supports the others. Each can be seen as a sub-institution, spawning further sub-institutions, such as the arms trade, in its turn. And each of these constituent sub-institutions is supported in large measure by the ambitions and assertiveness of those within its system (Hinde 1997).   RAH

Azrin, N. H., Hutchinson, R. R., and Hake, D. F. (1966). 'Extinction induced aggression'. *Journal of Experimental Animal Behavior*, 9.

Baerends, G. P. (1975). 'An evaluation of the conflict hypothesis as an explanatory principle for the evolution of displays'. In Baerends, G. P., Beer, C., and Manning, A. (eds.), *Essays on Form and Function in Behaviour*.

Baumrind, D. (1971). 'Current patterns of parental authority'. *Developmental Psychology Monographs*, 4/1 and 2.

Berkowitz, L. (1993). *Aggression*.

Gartner, R. (1996). 'Cross-cultural aspects of violence'. In Grisolia, J. S., et al. (eds.), *Violence: From Biology to Society*.

Hinde, R. A. (1997). 'War: some psychological causes and consequences'. *Interdisciplinary Science Reviews*, 22.

—— (2002). *Why Good is Good*.

Liddell, C., Kemp, J., and Moema, M. (1991). 'The young lions: South African children and youth in political struggle'. In Leavitt, L. A., and Fox, N. A. (eds.), *The Psychological Effects of War and Violence on Children*.

Manning, M., Heron, J., and Marshall, T. (1978). 'Styles of hostility and social interactions at nursery, at school, and at home'. In Hersov, L. A., and Berger, M. (eds.), *Aggression and Anti-social Behaviour in Childhood and Adolescence*.

Maynard Smith, J. (1976). 'Evolution and the theory of games'. *American Scientist*, 64.

Moyer, K. E. (1968). 'Kinds of aggression and their physiological basis'. *Communications in Behavioral Biology*, 2.

Short, R. (1979). 'Sexual selection and its component parts, somatic and genital selection, as illustrated by man and the great apes'. *Advances in the Study of Behaviour*, 9.

Straker, J. (1992). *Faces in the Revolution*.

Tinklenberg, J. R., and Ochberg, F. M. (1981). 'Patterns of adolescent violence'. In Hamburg, D., and Trudeau, M. B. (eds.), *Biobehavioral Aspects of Aggression*.

agnosia. Originally Sigmund *Freud used the term agnosia to mean loss of perception. It is now applied to disorders whereby the patient cannot interpret sensory information correctly even though the sense organs and the nerves leading to the brain are operating normally. Thus in auditory agnosia, the patient can hear but he cannot interpret sounds, including speech.

agoraphobia. See PHOBIAS.

agraphia. The loss of the ability to write, which may or may not be connected with alexia, the loss of ability to comprehend the written or printed word. It is thought to be caused by a lesion in the cerebral cortex or by more generalized cerebral dysfunction.

akinesia. The severe reduction or absence of spontaneous movement, characteristic of the later stages of *Parkinsonism.

alcoholism. See ADDICTION.

alexia (or word-blindness). Inability to read the printed or written word, usually caused by cerebral hemisphere damage. See DYSLEXIA.

Al-Farabi (Muhammad Ibn-Muhammad Ibn-Tarkhan Ibn-Uzlagh Abu-Nasr Al-Farabi, or Alpharabius) (870–950). The first great Turkic exponent of *Islamic philosophy. Born in Farab, Sughd, now in Uzbekistan, he studied at Baghdad and taught as a *Sufi at Aleppo, now in Syria. He states that he read *Aristotle's *De anima* 200 times; he was certainly so well versed in it that he gained the Arabic title of *Al-Mu'allim al-Thani*—the Second Teacher (after Aristotle). The author of over a hundred volumes, he lived simply, taking employment as a night watchman so that he could work by the light of the lantern provided.

He harmonized Greek philosophy with Islamic thinking, thus continuing the work of *Al-Kindi and preceding *Avicenna; his considerations covered logic and rhetoric, geometry, psychology, and politics. Baron Carra de Vaux and others state that the logic of Farabi had a permanent effect upon the thought of the Latin Schoolmen.

Farabi believed that God exists as the only ultimate reality and unity, intermediary agencies successively producing the world as we know it through conventional avenues of perception. Human society he regards as

emerging through two impulses: a social contract not unlike that later proposed by *Rousseau, and an urge prefiguring the *Nietzschean will to power. Society, for Farabi, realizes its perfection (the Ideal City) through a ruler who has become a divine agent, or alternatively by the administration of a group of wise men, each specializing in one subject. The capacity to be detached from objects and concerns enables a human being to go beyond familiar dimensions, transcending the ignorance produced by regarding secondary phenomena, such as time and space, as primary.   IS

Hammond, R. (1947). *The Philosophy of Alfarabi and its Influence on Medieval Thought*.

Sheikh, M. S. (1982). *Islamic Philosophy*.

Al-Ghazzali (Imam Abu-Hamid Ibn-Muhammad Al-Ghazzali, or Algazel) (1058–1111). Born at Tus, Persia, originally a theologian and scholastic philosopher, and professor at the Nizamiyyah College in Baghdad, Ghazzali is known as *Hujjat al-Islam* (Proof of Islam) and is one of Islam's greatest thinkers. He decided that ultimate truth could not be attained by intellectual means, and became a *Sufi. He influenced all subsequent Sufic thought as well as many Western philosophers and theologians. His *Ihya Ulum al-Din* (Revival of the Sciences of Religion) is a classic which is widely believed to have had a great (some believe determining) effect upon Europe, through Latin and Hebrew translations, especially in his method of criticizing hypotheses and assumptions. Jehuda Halevi (in his *Khazari*) follows the Ghazzalian method as found in the remarkable *Incoherence of the Philosophers*, and the first Hebrew translations of the influential *Maqasid al-Falasifah* (Aims of the Philosophers) were made by Isaac Albalagh, c.1292, and by Judah ben Solomon Nathan, c.1340. The Dominican Raymund Martin (d. 1285) used Ghazzali's arguments in his *Explanatio symboli apostolorum* and *Pugio fidei*, continually quoting the devout Islamic thinker in support of Christian ideas. St Thomas *Aquinas (1225–74) also cites Ghazzali. Blaise *Pascal, writing on belief in God, echoes Ghazzali's *Ihya*, *Kimia*, and other writings, while Pascal's theory of knowledge (in *Pensées sur la religion*) closely follows Ghazzali's book *Al-Munqidh*. Ghazzali's work is as widely studied today as it ever was.   IS

Kamali, S. A. (trans.) (1963). *Tahafat Al-Falasifah*.

Shah, I. (1964). *The Sufis*.

Sheikh, M. S. (1982). *Islamic Philosophy*.

Watt, W. M. (1953). *The Faith and Practice of Al-Ghazzali*.

algorithm. A predetermined procedure or ordered sequence of instructions for carrying out an operation in a finite number of steps. Computer programming involves designing such procedures since computing is precisely the automation and execution of algorithms. Moving the decimal point for multiplication or division by multiples of 10 is a commonly used algorithm. The Euclidean algorithm is a method for finding the greatest common divisor of two numbers by continued subtraction.

The origin of the term is from the name of an Arab mathematician, al-Kuwārizmi (*c*.830), who wrote an extensive account of the Hindu system of numerals and numeration from which our current system evolved. Writing numbers and performing calculations using Hindu numbers became known through his account as 'algorismi', and competitions were held between the abacists, who favoured the abacus for calculations, and the algorists, who preferred pencil-and-paper calculations. To use an algorithm, perhaps as a rule of thumb, need not require an understanding of why it works, and algorithmic thinking can be a term used derogatively. Yet making some mental operations a matter of mechanical routine can free the conscious attention for other more demanding matters. RLG

Alhazen (or Ibn al-Haytham) (*c*.965–1040). An Arab scholar working in Cairo. He wrote his *Optics* in Arabic around 1034, basing it on the works of *Euclid, *Ptolemy, and *Galen, but expanding greatly beyond their ideas. A Latin translation has been available since the Middle Ages, and Book I became well known and formed the basis of many later books on optics, image formation in the eye, and the visual pathways. The recent translation of Books I–III into English has made his other writing on visual perception more widely known. These and other works contain many observations, experiments, and explanations concerning such phenomena as binocular vision and motion perception, size and shape constancy, the *moon illusion, and other illusions. Alhazen clearly stated that visual rays were incoming rather than outgoing, and formed an inverted image within the eye (though he re-inverted them on the back of the eye). This work led to *Kepler's correct analysis of visual images as the first stage of visual perception. Alhazen was aware that incoming rays did not 'know' their own length, so he argued that distance was perceived or inferred by the visual sense through ground cues. Size was perceived by taking account of distance and of angular size, in a geometrical manner. He pre-dated many modern ideas on perception, including that of an 'unconscious inference' which is often attributed to *Helmholtz. HER

Howard, I. P. (1996). 'Alhazen's neglected discoveries of visual phenomena'. *Perception*, 25.

Al-Kindi (Abu-Yusuf Ya'Qub Ibn-Ishaq) (803–73). The first Arab philosopher. Born at Al-Kufah, now in Iraq, of a southern Arabian family, he worked mainly in Baghdad. He attempted to combine the views of *Plato and *Aristotle, and his collation of the *Theologia* ascribed to

Aristotle had considerable influence on philosophy and theology in both East and West until the time of St Thomas *Aquinas.

Al-Kindi was a polymath, like almost all of the major Islamic philosophers: an optician, music theorist, pharmacist, and mathematician; he wrote 265 treatises, most of them now lost. He saw the universe as an architectonic whole, not as something to be observed piecemeal to discover causality. He asserted 'one of the most marked features of Islamic thought—the belief that there was only one active intellect for all humanity, and that every human soul was moved and informed by this separated active intellect' (Leff 1958). More of his work survives in Latin (such as in the translations by Gerard of Cremona) than in Arabic. One of his major scientific contributions was *De aspectibus*, on the *Optics* of *Euclid, which influenced Roger Bacon. His works show that mensural music was studied in his culture centuries before it appeared in the Latin West. IS

Abdulwahab Emiri (1976). *The Scientists of Islam.*
Hitti, P. K. (1951). *History of the Arabs.*
Leff, G. (1958). *Medieval Thought.*
Sheikh, M. S. (1982). *Islamic Philosophy.*

allotropy. Variation of physical properties without change of substance. Thus diamond and graphite are the two allotropes of the element carbon. Both are composed of pure carbon but have different physical forms. In most early philosophy, there was supposed to be underlying substance which maintained the continuity of objects even when they changed. This same idea was often applied to the mind—that the mind of an individual is a continuing substance even though, throughout life, the individual changes in his ideas, *emotions, and behaviour. David *Hume took the opposite view, arguing that the self is no more than a 'bundle of sensations'. See also PERSONAL IDENTITY.

Alzheimer's disease (AD). A progressive neurodegenerative form of dementia. In the early stages it is marked by a memory deficit. Patients have increasing difficulty in learning new information and retaining it over a delay. Patients typically forget recent events and become more repetitive. As the disease progresses, patients experience difficulty with everyday tasks that require concurrent manipulation of information. Subsequently language and spatial difficulties emerge. Behavioural changes, such as apathy, delusions, and agitation, occur often in AD. Ultimately patients are no longer able to manage basic activities of daily living and require total care. The course of the disease from onset to death can be variable but may average 10–12 years.

When Alois Alzheimer described the post-mortem findings on a lady suffering from dementia in 1907, the neuropathology was insufficient to define a distinct disorder. Since that time, clinical criteria have been developed to define groups of elderly patients and these groups have been examined for clinicopathological correlates of dementia. These studies have made it possible to focus on the structure, composition, and molecular biology of the neurofibrillary tangle. The outcome of this research programme has been to identify a normal 'tau protein' that undergoes abnormal processing in AD. This results in aggregates of tau that are harmful to neurons. A therapeutic strategy to prevent this process offers the potential to combat the progression of the disease in patients with Alzheimer's disease.

1. The heterogeneity and pathological basis of dementia
2. Clinical diagnosis
3. Pathology
4. Molecular composition of the PHF
5. Therapeutic potential

1. The heterogeneity and pathological basis of dementia

Dementia has many causes and the neurodegenerative forms of the disease are both clinically and pathologically heterogeneous. The most common form of dementia, AD, can be caused by mutations in a number of proteins. Such cases are largely indistinguishable from the more common, sporadic form of the disease that occurs later in life and as yet have no identified genetic basis. A constant feature of AD is the neurofibrillary, tau protein pathology that is temporally associated with the clinical symptoms of dementia. Since the finding that mutations in the tau protein can cause related forms of dementia, renewed interest in tau pathology has two incentives. First, there is the therapeutic potential for preventing tau aggregation. Second, the mechanism of tau aggregation may be a generic process common to a number of distinct neurodegenerative disorders that are characterized by the aggregation of different proteins.

The progressive increase in the population over the age of 65 relative to the rest of the population is a feature of all industrialized societies. This demographic transformation has resulted, in the main, from increased longevity or life expectancy at birth and reduced fertility. In the UK, for example, there is a projected 80 per cent increase in the over-65 population between 1965 and 2025. The prevalence of dementia increases as an exponential function of age, with a representative estimate of around 8 per cent of the over-65 population.

More than 50 medical, psychiatric, and neurological conditions are associated with dementia. AD is the major cause of dementia in the elderly, although the reported frequency of other types of dementia has increased as the result of improvements in their diagnosis. These include a variety of disorders including: vascular dementias,

dementia with Lewy bodies, Parkinson's disease, Pick's disease, corticobasal degeneration, progressive supranuclear palsy, Huntington's disease, Creutzfeldt–Jakob disease (CJD), and chromosome 17-linked frontotemporal dementias. The delineation and clinical diagnosis of these disorders rest on the presence of a characteristic pattern of deficit that arises from the involvement of particularly vulnerable areas of the cerebral cortex, e.g. the medial temporal lobe and hippocampus to AD and the anterior temporal and frontal lobes to Pick's disease. Diagnostic criteria have been improved in the light of clinicopathological studies and, in the case of CJD, for example, by the identification of specific genetic determinants of the phenotypic variability.

2. Clinical diagnosis

The concept of dementia has evolved in recent years from the rather non-specific notion of an organic brain syndrome to a more specific concept. During the first half of the 20th century, all mental disorders of the elderly were considered as different manifestations of senile degeneration of the brain. At that time, nobody had associated the various symptoms of dementia, depression, and paranoia with any particular brain pathology. To do this, 'operational criteria' were developed to classify elderly people into five clinical groups: affective psychosis, senile dementia (or Alzheimer's disease), late paraphrenia, confusional–delirious states, and vascular dementia. The classification was further enhanced with a range of neuropsychological tests. These studies also defined social and familial problems of the elderly in the community which, in turn, paved the way for the development of domiciliary social services and psychogeriatric assessment units, the first of which was established in Newcastle in the 1970s.

3. Pathology

The relationship between measures of cognitive function and quantitative measures of brain pathology was first examined in Newcastle in the 1960s. The presence of abundant neurofibrillary tangles (NFTs) in the cerebral cortex proved to be diagnostic of AD. Although some NFTs were present in the hippocampus of normal elderly persons, the number in AD was almost twenty times as great. Approaches to prevent the accumulation of insoluble NFTs in the brain are important, as it is this very pathology that is intimately linked with clinical symptoms. These endeavours encouraged molecular biologists into the study of AD, and the discovery of the composition of the pathological hallmarks that underlie the disease, namely NFTs and neuritic senile plaques. The tangles that form within neurons are composed of paired helical elements (PHFs). These PHFs are made up almost entirely of tau protein. Senile plaques are composed of extracellular deposits of amyloid β-protein interspersed with dystrophic neurites packed with tau-containing PHFs.

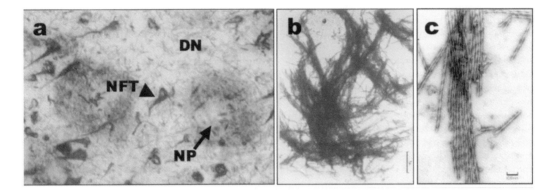

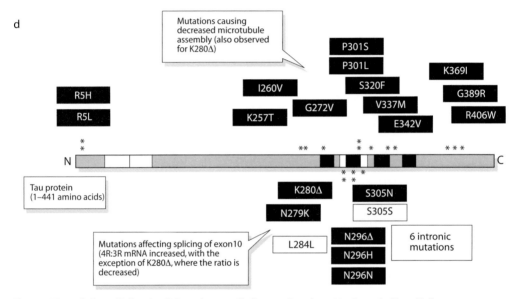

Fig. 1. a. The pathological hallmarks of AD are the neurofibrillary tangle and neuritic plaque. **b.** Neurofibrillary pathology is composed of insoluble, fibrous accumulations of tau protein. **c.** Tau proteins exist as a family of proteins up to 441 amino acids in length. Mutations associated with other tau-based dementias are clustered largely around a repeated domain of the protein that is indicated by four filled boxes.

Factors that predispose individuals to an increased risk of acquiring AD include the following: increased age, family history, head trauma, and Down's syndrome. Mutations in three genes have been identified which co-segregate with disease in families with the less common, early-onset forms of AD: the amyloid β-protein precursor gene and two presenilin protein genes. A genetic factor in as many as half of the early, autosomal-dominant AD cases has yet to be found. A polymorphism in the apolipoprotein E gene can account for as much as 60 per cent of the susceptibility to AD; inheritance of an *APOE* β4 allele, however, does not reliably predict whether or when a carrier will develop AD. While various mutations are associated with slight differences in clinical presentation, the pathological changes at autopsy are relatively insignificant and the neurofibrillary pathology is invariably constant.

4. Molecular composition of the PHF
The clinicopathological findings indicated the importance of the neurofibrillary tangle in the aetiology of Alzheimer's disease and led to a project designed to understand the structure and composition of the tangle. Image reconstruction techniques, developed by Aaron Klug in the MRC Laboratory for Molecular Biology, were applied to tangles purified from Alzheimer brains.

The constituent PHFs are made up of a double-helical stack of subunits with the overall appearance of a ribbon twisted into a left-handed helix, each consisting of two symmetrical C-shaped subunits with three domains.

The core of the PHF consists of short, truncated tau molecules that represent fragments derived by proteolysis of the microtubule-associated tau protein. Tau normally serves in the assembly and stabilization of axonal microtubules that are necessary for the transport of vesicles along axons. In Alzheimer's disease, normal, full-length tau disappears, while aggregates of truncated tau accumulate as PHFs within the neuronal cell bodies and dendrites.

It has also been possible to trace the progressive development of the tangle in the brain by immunohistochemistry. In the first stage, amorphous aggregates of truncated tau assemble in the neuron. As tau molecules become truncated the aggregates that form become increasingly more resistant to degradation and neuronal dysfunction commences. When the expanding tangle bursts through the cell membrane, it becomes a 'ghost' tangle representing the tombstone of a neuron that has been destroyed. These steps arise by aggregation and proteolysis of the tau protein molecules in affected neurons. The extent of tau pathology is intimately correlated with cognitive impairment and commences even before the overt appearance of tangles and plaques.

Recently, mutations in the tau gene have been found that co-segregate with a number of familial dementias associated with a variety of phenotypes that can be broadly categorized as frontotemporal dementias. Although mutations have not been found in AD, the discovery that tau mutations are associated with dementia in the absence of Aβ pathology further asserts the view that tau pathology need not be a secondary consequence of altered APP metabolism. The regional distribution, ultrastructural, and biochemical characteristics of the tau deposits in these frontotemporal dementias differentiate them from those present in AD. In many families no Aβ deposits are present, indicating that FTDP-17 is a disorder distinct from AD. This implies that the tau aggregation in the brain *per se* is not dependent upon prior deposition of Aβ. Conversely, it implies that intraneuronal tauopathy does not necessarily lead to the deposition of Aβ. If tau and amyloid pathologies are linked in AD, then some other factor(s) is required to account for the association between these two deposits in the brain in AD.

5. Therapeutic potential

The shortened fragment of tau protein that accumulates in PHFs in AD neurons is able to capture normal full-length tau *in vitro* and impose upon it a conformational change that enhances the subsequent capture of further tau molecules. This sequence of events bears resemblance to the pathological process demonstrated by Stanley Prusiner for the prion disorders. In Alzheimer's disease, it proceeds in an exponential fashion, leading to the formation of PHFs and thence tangles. The recent identification of diaminophenothiazine compounds that selectively inhibit tau aggregation without affecting the normal tau–tubulin interaction offers great therapeutic potential not only for Alzheimer's disease but also perhaps for other disorders characterized by protein aggregation.

Alzheimer's disease and the related tauopathies constitute a diverse and heterogeneous group of dementing disorders. There is no single pathway that can explain the pathogenesis of all these disorders. Central to all of them is the ability of tau protein to form proteolytically resistant aggregates. Neurodegeneration might arise as a result of cytoskeletal destruction or be due to the toxicity of the aggregated tau. The proof that protein aggregation causes neurodegeneration will be demonstrated if agents that prevent aggregation are able to prevent the progression of these diseases. CMW / CRH / MaR

Blessed, G., Tomlinson, B. E., and Roth, M. (1968). 'The association between quantitative measures of dementia and of senile change in the cerebral grey matter of elderly subjects'. *British Journal of Psychiatry, 114*.

Roth, M. (1955). 'The natural history of mental disorder in old age'. *Journal of Mental Science, 101*.

—— Tomlinson, B. E., and Blessed, G. (1967). 'The relationship between quantitative measures of dementia and the degenerative changes in the cerebral grey matter of elderly subjects'. *Proceedings of The Royal Society of Medicine. 60*.

Wischik, C. M., Novak, M., Thøgersen, H. C., et al. (1988). 'Isolation of a fragment of tau derived from the core of the paired helical filament of Alzheimer disease'. *Proceedings of the National Academy of Sciences of the USA, 85*.

—— Edwards, P. C., Lai, R. Y. K., Roth, M., and Harrington, C. R. (1996). 'Selective inhibition of Alzheimer disease-like tau aggregation by phenothiazines'. *Proceedings of the National Academy of Sciences of the USA, 93*.

amnesia. The popular conception of amnesia is probably typified by the occasional newspaper report of the appearance of someone who has mysteriously lost his *memory. The person has no idea what his name is, where he comes from, or indeed about any of his past. Such cases usually recover their memory within a day or two, and typically turn out to be people attempting to escape from some socially stressful situation by simply opting out through the mechanism of dissociation. The precise nature of their memory defect is variable and seems to depend very much on their own views about how the human memory system works. In this respect they resemble *hysterical patients suffering from glove anaesthesia, numbness in the hand which extends up to the wrist but not beyond and bears no relationship to the underlying pattern of innervation of the hand, indicating that it is of psychogenic origin rather than based on a physiological defect. The extent to which psychogenic amnesia represents genuine inability to recall, as opposed to conscious refusal to remember, is hard to ascertain. For further details see Pratt (in Whitty and Zangwill 1977).

The most extensively studied form of amnesia is that resulting from damage to the *limbic system of the brain, typically involving the temporal lobes, hippocampus, and mamillary bodies. Such damage may occur in people suffering from *Korsakoff syndrome, which results from a prolonged period of drinking too much alcohol and eating too little food, leading to a vitamin deficiency of thiamine (vitamin B₁). Such patients often go through a delirious confused state, before stabilizing. They may then show a range of symptoms extending from considerable general intellectual impairment with relatively little memory decrement to occasional cases in which a relatively pure memory defect occurs. A broadly comparable memory defect occasionally occurs following encephalitis, and may also be produced by other kinds of brain damage such as stroke, tumour, or coal gas poisoning. There is some controversy over whether such a wide range of patients have a common memory defect, or whether subtle differences occur but the broad pattern of symptoms is similar.

Such patients have no difficulty in knowing where they grew up or telling you about their job or family background. In the case of relatively pure amnesics at least, their ability to use language is unimpaired, as is their general knowledge of the world. Their *short-term memory also appears to be intact, at least in many cases. Their ability to repeat back a telephone number is just as good as would be the case in a normal person, and if you present them with a list of words, they show the normal tendency for the last few words presented to be well recalled. Their retention of the earlier words in a list is, however, likely to be very poor indeed.

The amnesic defect in the case of these patients appears to be one of episodic memory. They would be quite unable to tell you what they had for breakfast, and would very probably have no idea where they were or how long they had been there. If you had spent the morning testing them, by the afternoon they would probably fail to recognize you, and if asked for items of current information such as the name of the prime minister, would be likely to come up with a totally inappropriate response, naming a figure from twenty or thirty years ago. They have great difficulty in learning lists of words, whether you test them by recall or recognition, and have similar problems in remembering non-verbal material such as pictures of faces or objects.

There are, however, aspects of long-term memory that seem to be relatively unimpaired. Amnesic patients can learn motor skills, and one case, a pianist who was taught a tune on one day, had no difficulty in reproducing it on another. But characteristically such patients have no idea how or when they acquired the relevant information. A classic example is that cited by the Swiss psychologist *Claparède, who on one occasion secreted a pin in his hand before shaking hands with an amnesic patient. On a subsequent day when he extended his hand the patient withdrew hers. When asked why, she could give no justification other than the general comment that sometimes things were hidden in people's hands. As one would expect from this demonstration, amnesics appear to be quite capable of classical avoidance *conditioning. They are also quite capable of learning verbal materials under certain conditions. For example, Warrington and Weiskrantz used a learning procedure whereby subjects were presented with a series of words, and recall was tested by presenting the first three letters of each word and requiring the subject to produce the whole word. When tested in this way, amnesics were virtually normal.

What characterizes the long-term learning tasks that amnesics can do? This is still a controversial issue, but broadly speaking the tasks seem to be ones in which the patient simply has to use the information available in his memory store, without needing to worry about how it was acquired. The case where he is cued by being presented with the initial letters may be interpreted as simply a problem-solving task where he must find a word that fits these particular constraints. Having recently been presented with the relevant word will in fact make it more available, but he does not need to know this in order to take advantage of such an effect.

While classic amnesics like those just described are theoretically extremely interesting, patients having such a dense amnesia unaccompanied by more general intellectual deterioration are relatively rare. It is much more common for memory disturbance to stem from the aftereffects of a blow on the head, as is often the case in road traffic accidents. Consider, for example, a motorcyclist who is involved in an accident causing a severe head injury. He is likely to lose consciousness for a period which may range from a few seconds to several months; if and when he regains consciousness he is likely to show a range of memory problems. It is usual to distinguish three separate types or aspects of such traumatic amnesia, namely retrograde amnesia, post-traumatic amnesia, and anterograde amnesia.

On recovery there will be evidence of loss of memory extending over the period between the injury and full return of consciousness. Following a head injury there will be a period of confusion characterized by the patient's inability to orient himself in time and place. The duration of post-traumatic amnesia, which will comprise the duration of total and partial loss of consciousness, provides a useful measure of the severity of the patient's injury and so permits some estimate of the extent of probable recovery to be made. On emerging from post-traumatic amnesia the patient is still likely to show considerable retrograde amnesia. This is indicated by an inability to remember events before the accident. In the case of a severe blow the amnesia may extend over a period of several years. Typically this blank period becomes less and less, with earlier memories being recovered first, although the process is far from systematic, with 'islands' of memory cropping up in periods that are otherwise still blank. Typically the retrograde amnesia shrinks up to a point within a few minutes of the accident. These final few moments are seldom ever recovered, possibly because the memory trace was never adequately consolidated. This point was illustrated rather neatly in a study of American football players who had been 'dinged' (concussed) during a game. As they were led off the field they were asked the code name of the play in which they had been engaged when concussed (e.g. 'Thirty-two pop'). Typically they were able to supply this information immediately on leaving the field, but when retested 20 to 30 minutes later they were quite unable to provide it. A subsequent study showed that this was not simply due to normal forgetting, or to the mnemonic limitations of American football players, but suggests that failure of memory traces to consolidate during the concussed state may be an important factor.

The third memory disturbance associated with head injury concerns difficulty in learning and retaining new information. During the process of recovery from a closed head injury, memory problems are commonly reported, together with difficulties in concentrating and a tendency to become fatigued much more rapidly than was previously the case. While the memory problems of patients with head injuries have been rather less extensively investigated than those of the classic amnesic syndrome, we do know that they show some of the same characteristics. Typically short-term memory is not greatly affected, and if one presents an amnesic head-injured patient with a list of words, he is likely to do reasonably well on the last few presented, but relatively poorly on the earlier items in the list. Although not much work has been done in directly comparing such patients with other types of amnesics, it seems likely that the pattern will be somewhat different, since closed head injury appears to cause neuronal and vascular damage in large areas of the brain as opposed to specific subcortical damage in the classic amnesic syndrome. Furthermore, whereas the classic amnesic patient does not completely recover, head-injured patients typically do improve quite substantially from the time when they emerge from their initial period of post-traumatic amnesia. In many cases they return to performing at what appears to be their level before injury.

Amnesia is an important component in senile and pre-senile *dementia. In both these cases intellectual deterioration probably results from a substantial loss of cortical neurons, and in addition to showing memory problems such patients usually show a more general intellectual deterioration. This in turn increases the memory problem, since they seem unable or unwilling to use effective learning strategies.

We have so far discussed patients who have long-term learning problems but normal short-term memory. However, the reverse has also been reported. Tim Shallice and Elizabeth Warrington (1970) describe a patient who had great difficulty in repeating back sequences of numbers, the longest sequence he could repeat back reliably being two digits. He was, however, quite unimpaired in his long-term memory as measured both by his ability to learn word sequences and by his memory for faces and for the events of everyday life. As is suggested in its entry, short-term memory is almost certainly not a single unitary function, and there is some evidence to suggest that there are other patients who have different defects of the short-term memory system.

Theoretical interpretation of the various ways in which memory can break down obviously depends crucially on one's interpretation of normal memory. As such, amnesia presents a theoretically important though difficult question. We have in recent years made progress in exploring and defining more precisely the amnesic syndrome, but are as yet some way from constructing a completely adequate interpretation at a psychological, neurological, or biochemical level.   ADB

Baddeley, A. D. (1982). 'Amnesia as a minimal model and an interpretation'. In Cermak, L. S. (ed.), *Human Memory and Amnesia*.

Shallice, T., and Warrington, E. K. (1970). 'Independent functioning of the verbal memory stores: a neuropsychological study'. *Quarterly Journal of Experimental Psychology*, 22.

Whitty, C. W. M., and Zangwill, O. L. (eds.) (1977). *Amnesia*.

anaesthesia. Anaesthesia may be described as a reversible loss of consciousness produced by a drug, from which arousal does not take place even with painful stimuli such as setting a fracture or surgical operation. In this latter respect it differs from *sleep or the change in consciousness following sensory deprivation, and it is this that made it so revolutionary a discovery, opening the gateway to modern surgery and safer childbirth. The name is not quite exact, since loss of consciousness is not the same as loss of feeling, and a good anaesthetic in clinical practice should exert other actions, such as some analgesia (to diminish reflex responses to what would be very painful stimuli) and muscular relaxation (to facilitate the surgeon's work). When an anaesthetic such as ether or chloroform is given, there is a characteristic progression of effects, first described by Guedel in 1937: first analgesia, some loss of memory, and perhaps euphoria; then consciousness is lost, but the patient may struggle, breathe irregularly, is sweating and flushed; in the third stage, the patient becomes quieter with regular breathing, but the eyeballs move rhythmically and a good many reflexes are still present. As anaesthesia deepens, and the patient passes through the successive planes of the third stage, various reflexes progressively fall away, the breathing becomes shallower, and eventually death may ensue (the fourth stage). In modern practice anaesthesia is induced with a suitable barbiturate (such as thiopentone) injected intravenously: the patient then passes through the early stages within seconds; once 'under', anaesthesia is usually maintained by some other substance.

How do anaesthetics work? It is paradoxical that more is known at the molecular level than at any other. A remarkable feature is the astonishing range of substances that can produce anaesthesia: in addition to the classical anaesthetics and the barbiturates, nitrogen in the air (if given at high pressure) and many other gases, alcohols, dry cleaning fluids (such as trichloroethene), industrial solvents, and certain steroids can all produce typical anaesthesia. There is no common chemical structure such as would suggest a specific action on some particular part of the brain. Instead, as two pharmacologists, Overton and Meyer, pointed out over 80 years ago, anaesthetics all share the property of dissolving in fats and it is remarkable that one can predict the potency of an anaesthetic quite accurately by measuring the pressure of a gas or the concentration of a vapour that will produce a given concentration (about 0.05 moles per litre) of the substance concerned in olive oil. Modern work has revealed the significance of this: the cell membrane, which defines the cell's limits, and across which an electric potential is maintained, consists of an ordered array of fatty molecules (mostly phospholipids and cholesterol); the anaesthetic dissolves in it, and slightly expands and disorders the membrane. Since the membrane also carries large protein molecules (enzymes, ion channels, receptors, transport mechanisms) which mediate its 'traffic' with its environment and with other cells, disturbance of their normal function becomes possible. A fascinating aspect is that very high pressures (which compress and reorder the membrane) cause recovery from anaesthesia. Conversely, a suitable amount of an anaesthetic can be used to neutralize the adverse effects of high pressure. The 'high-pressure nervous syndrome', which includes tremor, bursts of 'micro-sleep', and convulsions, threatened to limit the depth to which *divers could go, but the addition of nitrogen (using it as a small dose of anaesthetic) to the diver's helium–oxygen mixture has extended that limit.

But if one asks, 'On what synapses, or on what cell groups of the brain, is this molecular action particularly exerted?', no satisfactory answer exists. The simple fact of surgical anaesthesia shows that higher brain functions are particularly sensitive, while respiration and simple reflexes, as well as other bodily processes like the heartbeat, are relatively resistant. Detailed analysis yields a bewildering variety of effects, with actions both pre- and post-synaptically, varying with the synapse and with the anaesthetic. A simple view is that the anaesthetic picks out any delicately poised nervous activity, and that the pattern of anaesthetic activity is simply that of reduced activity in the most vulnerable nervous pathways—particularly complex nervous functions rather than (for example) simple reflex movement. Theories include the idea of a specific effect on the 'ascending reticular activating system', in the absence of whose activity the cerebral cortex is believed to relapse into a sleeping state, or on cortical cells generally. Some recent drugs (such as ketamine), which produce the so-called 'dissociative anaesthesia', may help to throw light on the problem; these differ, both in having a specific chemical structure and in producing a rather different pattern of anaesthesia.

There is an abundant literature on the effects of anaesthetics on mental function, short of anaesthesia, and Humphry Davy's description (in 1800) of the effect of nitrous oxide (*laughing gas) on himself and his friends (including Southey, Coleridge, Roget, and Wedgwood) reveals the salient features recorded many times subsequently: considerable variation with the individual; excitement; euphoria or sometimes dysphoria; compulsive movements or laughter; 'thrilling' sensations in the limbs; feelings of deep significance; rush of ideas; *synaesthesiae; drowsiness; warmth, rapid breathing, palpitations, giddiness; and often a strong desire to repeat the performance. This last characteristic brings the risk of *addiction in its train, particularly for those (such as anaesthetists and nurses) with easy access to the drugs; and it shows itself again in 'glue-sniffing' in children, or with workers using some solvents in industry.

An important feature with all these volatile substances is the speed with which effects are produced by inhalation, by which the vapour passes very quickly into the circulation. More familiar to most people will be the effect of anaesthetics such as alcohol or barbiturates taken orally, with an onset delayed by circulatory absorption, and the fact that by this route some of the more dramatic effects are lacking (although euphoria and the risk of addiction remain) suggests that these effects are largely due to especially rapid access to, and uptake by, particular parts of the brain, producing a selective action which fades as distribution of the drug becomes general. With sustained exposure to any anaesthetic, the adaptation known as 'tolerance' develops, by which an increasing dose is required to produce the effect. 'Cross-tolerance' occurs between different anaesthetics—hence the difficulty often encountered of anaesthetizing an alcoholic! When exposure stops and the drug is withdrawn, characteristic symptoms appear: for example, insomnia after a short course of any sleeping pill, or delirium tremens (DTs) after prolonged high exposure to alcohol, or convulsions after chronic barbiturate use. While some of the adaptive changes may be biochemical, some of them certainly represent a change in nerve cell function, and there are interesting indications that the composition of the cell membrane changes so as to reduce the effect of the anaesthetic.

One would like to think that experience with anaesthetics would deepen our understanding of consciousness, mood, sensation, pain, memory. Yet it is still impossible to move convincingly from the subjective phenomena to physiological understanding. Perhaps it is unreasonable to expect to do so until our knowledge of normal neurophysiology is more satisfactory, or perhaps pharmacology and physiology need to proceed, collaboratively, in parallel. Some areas may be picked out as potentially fruitful.

1. The effect on *sense of time*. There is a puzzle here: nitrous oxide and alcohol appear to reduce 'felt' time compared with 'clock' time, whereas ketamine (like cannabis) prolongs it. With the latter drugs, one can readily suggest, as William *James suggested, that 'disinhibition' in the brain, allowing a greater than normal sensory input, could give rise to an experience of more numerous mental impressions than usual per unit of 'clock' time, and hence a greater 'felt' time. But why should other anaesthetics differ?

2. The effect on *pain sense*. There is some evidence that enkephalins or endorphins may play a part in analgesia produced by anaesthetics. (See NEUROPEPTIDES.) But there remain remarkable differences between anaesthetics, some with pronounced analgesic action, some potentiating the response to a painful stimulus. Bearing in mind its practical relevance, as well as the recent advances in our knowledge of the neuroanatomy and neurochemistry of the nociceptive pathways, and the successful application of decision theory to the study of pain, a systematic study of the action of a range of anaesthetics on pain discrimination and pain report seems well worth while.

3. The effect on *sensation generally*. An intriguing but neglected observation is that anaesthetics facilitate the generation of impulses in the vagal nerve fibres registering the inflation of the lung, which accounts for the ability of many anaesthetics to produce what is known as 'rapid shallow breathing'. It is an intriguing action and, exerted peripherally on the proprioceptive endings in muscles, it might account for the 'thrilling' sensation described by Davy. But more generally there might also be an important effect both on the pattern of sensory input to the brain and on subsequent processing.

4. Effect on *memory*. With the recent advances in our knowledge of registration, consolidation, and retrieval, systematic study of the effect of a range of anaesthetics on memory is overdue, although the problem is complicated by 'state dependence'. An old method of anaesthesia for childbirth, 'twilight sleep', exploited the effect of the drug hyoscine on memory, so that, even if pain was felt, it was not remembered. The method has been abandoned because of the effect on the baby, but the approach is still interesting.

5. The concept of *disinhibition* is constantly, and plausibly, invoked to account for phenomena such as the rush of ideas, synaesthesia, and electroencephalographic synchronization. The underlying idea is that the great complexity of mental activity does not merely need some neurons to be active, but also needs others to be actively 'switched off' (inhibited): if the latter process were interfered with (disinhibition), then differential activity and 'gating' of information transfer could become progressively impaired. Simple model systems exist, illustrating how depression of an inhibitory pathway can lead to release phenomena, but no serious attempt has been made to extend the idea to more complex systems. Yet if certain inhibitory mechanisms are particularly vulnerable, it should be possible, by careful choice of systems sharing common elements, to identify them more closely.

6. A tedious but necessary development is that of knowledge about the kinetics of *anaesthetic distribution* in the brain. Some knowledge exists of the rise and fall of the concentration of an anaesthetic during and after an exposure, for samples of brain containing thousands or millions of neurons. But this is merely a gross average, telling us nothing of local concentration in synaptic detail. Equilibrium with an anaesthetic is virtually never reached in clinical practice, and rarely in experimental work, so that (as mentioned earlier) there is ample scope for differential effects arising, not from the properties of the drug itself, but from varying access and uptake. For instance, evidence is accumulating that if any part of the brain becomes particularly active it consumes more energy, with a corresponding increase in blood flow, which would at once open the way to differential access by an anaesthetic.

7. Finally one must recall that, despite all the advances in neuroanatomy, it is only a tiny minority of nervous pathways that can be precisely and completely described in anatomical and neurochemical detail, with the specific neurons and their connections specified. But some beautiful techniques now exist for mapping out these pathways, for recording the activity of single or groups of neurons, and for neurochemical analysis (see NEUROANATOMICAL TECHNIQUES): the new methods of anaesthesia that a deeper understanding will provide are not far away.   WDMP

Miller, K. W. (1986). 'General anaesthetics'. In Feldman, S. A., Scurr, C. F., and Paton, W. D. M. (eds.), *Mechanisms of Action of Drugs in Anaesthetic Practice*.

Paton, W. D. M. (1984). 'How far do we understand the mechanism of anaesthesia?' *European Journal of Anaesthesiology*, 1.

anaglyph. A picture that can be used to create a stereoscopic image. It uses two colours (in practice red and green, or sometimes red and blue) with corresponding colour filters, so that a picture with different colours can be presented to each eye. This method is used for presenting stereoscopic pictures in printed books, instead of using separate pictures that require a stereoscope to present one picture to each eye. See STEREOSCOPIC VISION.

analytic proposition. The idea behind the notion of an analytic proposition is that at least some of our concepts can be represented as complexes of simpler concepts and that a proposition may state nothing more than what an analysis would reveal, namely a relation between a simple concept and a complex concept of which it forms a part. Thus *Kant, taking judgements expressed by propositions to have the form '*A* is *B*', defined an analytic judgement as one where 'the predicate *B* belongs to the subject *A* as something which is (covertly) contained in the concept *A*'. In more linguistic terms, if the criteria for calling something 'a body' include the criterion 'being extended', then the latter is 'contained in' the former and the proposition 'a body is extended' is analytic. An analytic statement thus cannot be denied without contradiction and is a logically necessary possibility. That this necessity can be seen simply from a grasp of the concepts or words involved leads to speaking of analytic propositions as true in virtue of the meanings of words.

Gottlob Frege freed the notion of analytic proposition from the assumption that the logical structure of all concepts is based upon conjunction of criteria, by taking as analytic any proposition whose proof rested only on general logical laws and definitions. This also made clear that whether a proposition is regarded as analytic is relative to what are recognized as legitimate means of definition and what general logical laws are accepted as valid.

A proposition that is not analytic is synthetic. The arguments of W. V. Quine showed that the analytic/synthetic distinction is not as sharp as had previously been assumed, but not that the distinction is wholly without foundation.   JET

Frege, G. (1959). *The Foundations of Arithmetic*. Trans. J. L. Austin, section 3.
Kant, I. (1929). *The Critique of Pure Reason*. Trans. N. Kemp-Smith, Preface and Introduction.
Quine, W. V. (1953). *From a Logical Point of View*, ch. 2.

Angell, James Rowland (1869–1949). American psychologist. He worked at Harvard with William *James, then at Chicago, where he became a founder of the Chicago 'functionalist' school which stressed the importance of physiological processes (see FUNCTIONALISM). This was a direct development of much of Angell's thinking, and led to *behaviourism. The founder of behaviourism, J. B. *Watson, was a student of Angell's.

Angell showed that *reaction times have two components—sensory and muscular—and that unpractised subjects have greater individual differences in reaction time than when they are practised. This raises a curious question. Specially trained or skilled subjects give more reliable results—but they are not typical subjects. So, should subjects be given special training, to get more consistent results which look better on paper; or should relatively naive subjects be used, as they are typical of most people and so represent normality? This is quite a general problem in experimental psychology, even for simple skills or tasks that seem close to basic physiological limits, such as designing and interpreting experiments on reaction time.

Boring, E. G. (1950). *A History of Experimental Psychology* (2nd edn.), ch. 24.

animal. Although in its widest sense the term 'animal', as contrasted with vegetable and mineral, includes mankind, in common usage the term is restricted to 'lower' or non-human animals—the 'brutes' or 'beasts'. For *Descartes (whose *Discourse on Method*, 1637, examines the difference between men and beasts), the crucial point is that animals lack language: their 'utterances' are always elicited by a specific stimulus, and thus can never amount to genuine speech. It follows, on Descartes's view, that animals lack thought, and that their behaviour can be explained on purely mechanical principles—a view that led later Cartesians to the notorious doctrine of the 'bête machine' and that animals are merely mechanical automata. In recent times the linguistic theories of Noam Chomsky have reinforced the view that animals lack genuine (i.e. creative, stimulus-free) language; current empirical research, however, suggests that chimpanzees, at least, may have a degree of linguistic competence. Current work in moral philosophy has stressed the fact that animals, though they may lack thought, are at least sentient, and hence are entitled to moral consideration. (See PRIMATE LANGUAGE.)   JGC

Singer, P. (1977). *Animal Liberation*.
—— and Regan, T. (1976). *Animal Rights and Human Obligations*.

animal behaviour. See ETHOLOGY.

animal–human comparisons. Comparisons of the behaviour or test performance between humans and other species have been used in three main ways, two of which will be discussed only briefly here.

The first involved attempts to construct a phylogeny of animal learning, in some cases with the intention of understanding the evolution of learning abilities. To this end, individuals of diverse and usually distantly related species were faced with comparable problems and their performances compared. Tests of conditioning, maze learning ability, and tool use figured prominently in this work (e.g. Bitterman 1960). Sometimes the emphasis was on similarities across species: thus similarities in the cumulative records obtained in operant conditioning experiments were regarded by, B. F. *Skinner (1938) as indicative of basic principles of learning. In others the emphasis was on differences, T. C. Schneirla (1949) stressing the importance of recognizing differences in the cognitive capacities of animals. However ethologists found that animals showed learning abilities that were specific to particular contexts, and indicated that different species had been adapted to learn in particular contexts relative to their way of life (e.g. N. Tinbergen 1951). This led to research on species-specific constraints on learning and predispositions to learn in some contexts rather than others (Seligman and Hager 1972, Hinde and Stevenson-Hinde 1973), and simple comparisons became unfashionable.

Second, the comparative method has been used to study the evolution of behaviour (by comparing the behaviour of closely related species) and to study the phylogenetic relations between species (by using behavioural similarities/differences to categorize species) (e.g. K. Lorenz 1941). This work is primarily of interest to biologists.

The third and perhaps most important use has involved studying animals as models to facilitate understanding of particular aspects of human behaviour. This has had a long history in psychology, going back at least to William James (1892) and reaching a peak with the learning theorists in the middle of the twentieth century (Skinner 1938, Estes et al. 1954).

Nevertheless it involves certain obvious dangers. The most obvious arises from the very diversity of animal species and of human cultures. It is not difficult to find parallels between animal and human data that will support practically any thesis. Straight comparisons between particular aspects of animal behaviour and particular human characteristics are therefore likely to be misleading. Aggressive behaviour is an obvious example. Most vertebrate species show aggressive behaviour in a variety of contexts—in acquiring food, territory, mates, and so on. The eliciting situation, the motivating conditions, and the movements used differ between contexts. Human aggressive behaviour is even more diverse, and principles drawn from animal studies contribute to its understanding in only limited ways.

A second obvious problem arises from the difference in cognitive abilities. The development of the brain and the longer period of development permit greater behavioural variability, and thus greater ability to adapt to circumstances, in humans as compared with any other species. In addition, human linguistic abilities permit communication about objects distant in space and time, and about the individual's own thoughts and feelings. They also make possible quite different processes of socialization. As a result, behaviour that appears to be similar in animals and humans may depend on quite different causal bases. Again, aggression is a case in point. In wartime, the motivation of a bomb aimer as he presses the bomb release is utterly different from that of a territorial bird, or even a displaying chimpanzee, yet both come within the definition of aggression as behaviour directed towards causing harm to others.

Although the existence of a sort of proto-culture has been described for some apes (De Waal 1996), it has nowhere near the far-reaching influence of human culture. The culture in which a person is reared and lives affects virtually all aspects of behaviour and experience. In particular, our language-based culture permits the existence of a limited set of roles, each with its attendant rights and duties within institutions within each society. Although differences between the behaviour of animals of a given species can sometimes be described in role terms, nothing comparable to the complexity found in humans exists in other species.

In spite of these dangers, much of our understanding of human behaviour has come from studies of animals. The close similarities between the brains of humans and other mammals has meant that it has been possible to investigate brain mechanisms by experimental work with other species, especially monkeys— though in recent years ethical considerations have come properly to limit the use of invasive techniques. Similar considerations apply to the investigation of endocrine effects on behaviour, though humans show less immediate dependence on endocrine factors than other mammals.

A comparative approach can also provide a new perspective on aspects of human behaviour. The fears of darkness, separation from the caregiver, heights, and so on shown by human infants were formerly categorized as 'irrational fears of childhood', to be overcome by appropriate training. However precisely similar behaviours are shown by non-human primate infants and are adaptive in the maintenance of contact with the mother, without which the infant would be very liable to predation. *Bowlby (1969) therefore pointed out that they were a natural part of the human infant's behavioural repertoire, and that child-rearing techniques should be accommodated to take account of them. This approach, based on ethological studies of animals, led to the development of *attachment theory, and thus to important advances in the study of child development with paediatric and clinical implications.

In making animal–human comparisons the key issue is to find the right level of analysis at which comparisons should be made. Some have sought for parallels at a global level, comparing for instance the human propensity to seek for exclusive group or individual rights over a particular area with animal territorial behaviour. Others have worked at a more physiological level, for instance seeking for common mechanisms of depression. The more complex the level at which comparison is made, the greater the probability that there will be differences in the underlying mechanisms.

But in some cases insufficient awareness of the importance of level could lead to the wrong conclusion. For instance, young children remaining at home while their mother goes into hospital for a few weeks tend to be less disturbed than children who go into hospital or other strange place while their mother stays at home (Robertson 1970). In an experiment with rhesus monkeys exactly the opposite was found. Some infants were left in the group pen while their mothers were removed for 10–14 days, whereas in other cases the infant was removed and the mother left in the group cage. Both groups were disturbed by the period of separation. However, while the infant-removed group continued to protest for longer during separation than those whose mothers had been removed, they were (contrary to expectations) less upset after reunion. Thus the monkey and human evidence agree that there can be fairly devastating effects of separation from the mother, but disagree in the type of separation that produces the most marked effects. The explanation lies in the fact that the removed monkey mothers on return to the group spent much time re-establishing their relations with their group companions, and this took some precedence over caring for their demanding infants (Hinde and McGinnis 1977). Thus the principle that temporary deprivation of maternal care is an important issue is general for both monkeys and humans, but the precise independent variables that affect the consequences differ.

In any case, direct comparisons between animals and humans are not always the most useful strategy. *Principles* concerning the evolution of behaviour drawn from studies of animals are often revealing when applied to the human case. The 'irrational fears of childhood', mentioned already, are a case in point. Again, the principle of natural selection would lead one to expect that an individual would be more prepared to make sacrifices for a close relative than for a stranger. Thus it would be predicted that biological parents would lavish more parental care on their children than would step-parents, or that individuals would be more ready to care for relatives than for strangers. Recent work has shown that these and other aspects of human behaviour as diverse as cognitive processes and pregnancy sickness are understandable in terms of evolutionary principles (e.g. Barkow, Cosmides, and Tooby 1999, Betzig 1997). Evolutionary principles drawn from studies of animals are even proving useful

in understanding such peculiarly human phenomena as religion (Hinde 1999).

Finally, comparisons that depend as much on the differences between animal and man may be as useful as those that depend on similarities. The relative simplicity of the animal case facilitates the refining of concepts and the elaboration of principles whose applicability to the human case can then be assessed. The very fact that animals lack verbal language and culture comparable in complexity to our own can help us to assess the impact of language and culture on human cognitive abilities and personal relationships.   RAH

Barkow, J. H., Cosmides, L., and Tooby, J. (1999). *The Adapted Mind*.

Betzig, L. (1997). *Human Nature*.

Bitterman, M. E. (1960). 'Toward a comparative psychology of learning'. *American Psychologist*, 15.

Bowlby, J. (1969). *Attachment and Loss*, vol. i: *Attachment*.

De Waal, F. (1996). *Good Natured*.

Estes, W. K. et al. (1954). *Modern Learning Theory*.

Hinde, R. A. (1999). *Why Gods Persist*.

—— and McGinnis, L. (1977). 'Some factors influencing the effects of temporary mother–infant separation'. *Psychological Medicine*, 7.

—— and Stevenson-Hinde, J. (eds.) (1973). *Constraints on Learning: Limitations and Predispositions*.

James, W, (1892). *Textbook of Psychology*.

Lorenz, K. (1941). 'Vergleichende Bewegungsstudien an Anatinen'. *Suppl. Journal für Ornithologie*, 89.

Robertson, J. (1970). *Young Children in Hospital*.

Schneirla, T. C. (1949). 'Levels in the psychological capacities of animals'. In Sellars, R. W., et al. (eds.), *Philosophy for the Future*.

Seligman, M. E. P., and Hager, J. L. (1972). *Biological Boundaries of Learning*.

Skinner, B. F. (1938). *The Behavior of Organisms: An Experimental Analysis*.

Tinbergen, N. (1951). *The Study of Instinct*.

animal magnetism. See MESMERISM.

animism. 1. The belief, common among primitive peoples, that all things in the world (including stones, plants, the wind, etc.) are imbued with some kind of spiritual or psychological presence; this may imply that things are 'ensouled' or 'animated' by a universal 'world soul', or by individual spirits of various kinds. **2.** The philosophical doctrine, sometimes known as 'panpsychism', that there is some spark or germ of consciousness present in all things. A version of this view was developed by the German philosopher G. W. Leibniz. (See LEIBNIZ'S PHILOSOPHY OF MIND.) For a recent attempt to take panpsychism seriously, see T. Nagel (1980), *Mortal Questions*, ch. 13.

animus. The Greeks lacked our concepts of inertia and frictional loss. For them there had to be an activating animus to initiate and maintain motion. Thus Aristotle supposed that the continuing motion of the projectile was given in puffs of air ('pneuma'), moving from in front and pushing it along from behind. Animals of course, had animus—they were self-motivated. It has been suggested that this conceptual difficulty for the Greeks may have been due to lack of prime movers in their technology. For Aristotle, it was animals' ability to initiate movements that distinguished animals as special, and outside physics. It might be said that how movements are initiated remains the problem of *free will.

It was Galileo, in the 17th century, who realized that objects continue moving forever in the absence of friction, which is a basic concept of Newton's cosmology—which is entirely different from the Greek idea and does not require animus.   RLG

anoesis. Literally, the absence of thought. It seems clear that there can be 'anoetic' mental states—that is, states in which there is some form of consciousness (for example, sensation), but no thought.

Anokhin, Piotre Kuzmich (1897–1974). Soviet psychologist whose work did much to place the work of Ivan *Pavlov and other reflexologists of his time on a broader biological foundation. Anokhin worked first under V. M. Bechterev, the self-styled reflexologist, and later under Pavlov before he became head of the department of physiology in the University of Gorki, where much of his best work was done. He later became a senior professor in the University of Moscow.

Early in his career, Anokhin became convinced that animal behaviour cannot be satisfactorily explained in terms of a mere colligation of discrete unconditioned and conditioned *reflexes. It should be viewed, he contended, as a functional system, in which the separate links are related to a particular biological goal. Such a system plays a decisive role in the organization of behaviour involving the whole organism.

In support of his view, Anokhin devised a series of experiments in which the relations of the central and peripheral portions of a pair of nerves innervating an extremity, e.g. flexors and extensors, were interchanged so that the central parts of the extensors now innervated the flexors and vice versa. This led to a reorganization of the functional system such that its basic biological role was preserved, the new adaptations being executed by novel neural relationships.

These ideas of flexibility in nervous adaptation were followed up in conditioning experiments. Anokhin devised a novel technique which combined salivary and motor responses while allowing the experimental dog freedom of movement. He pointed out that there is a preliminary stage of orientation to the situation before *conditioning begins and that the whole reaction, whether unconditioned or conditioned, does not end with a final reflex. The result of the action has to be evaluated and only if intention and final result are in accord does the action cease. If result and intention do not accord, further trials take place and behaviour continues. Thus the simple concept of a reflex arc is replaced by that of a system regulated by the results of its own actions, showing that functional systems are essentially self-regulating systems, as Norbert Wiener appreciated many years later (see CYBERNETICS, HISTORY OF).

To this formulation, Anokhin later added the idea of 'forward afference' or 'feedforward', i.e. a form of anticipation which serves to prepare the system for action (see FEEDBACK AND FEEDFORWARD). Anokhin later devoted much study to the physiological and biochemical processes which he believed to be involved in the functional systems of the brain that regulate its behaviour. For Anokhin's work on conditioning and its neurology, see his *Biology and Neurophysiology of the Conditioned Reflex and its Role in Adaptive Behaviour* (1974). This brings together 22 papers.   ARL/OLZ

Luria, A. R. (1980). *Higher Cortical Functions in Man.* (For an explanation of Anokhin's concept of functional systems and its application in neurology.)

anorexia nervosa and bulimia nervosa. Many people are now familiar with the disorder of anorexia nervosa, which is diagnosed by the criteria of self-induced weight loss (which may be so severe as to result in amenorrhoea in female patients) coupled with a morbid fear of becoming fat and a relentless pursuit of thinness. Other distinguishing features of the condition include a denial of the subjective feelings of *hunger, a distortion of body image, and a desire to increase energy expenditure by elevated physical activity. It is potentially a fatal disorder, with mortality rates ranging from 5 to 15 per cent, mainly from suicide.

Anorexia nervosa most commonly occurs in middle-class females, although it has also been reported in males. The disorder appears generally during adolescence, though it has been known to begin prior to this period, or even during adulthood. In Britain, the incidence in young women has been estimated to range between 1 and 4 per cent. Many believe that it is a disorder of very recent origin; however, patients with such a disorder have been described by physicians practising from the 17th century onwards.

The related disorder bulimia nervosa is far less well known, perhaps partly because of its antisocial and somewhat shocking symptoms, which may have retarded its identification. Bulimia was not differentiated from anorexia and was not described as a distinct disorder until very recently. Like anorectics, bulimics have a distorted body image, are obsessed with their body weight, and have a tremendous fear of becoming fat. However, bulimics have an overwhelming desire to eat large quantities of food at a single sitting (termed 'compulsive' or 'binge' eating); they then immediately self-induce vomiting, abuse laxatives, or use both these forms of purging before the food has had time to be digested and absorbed. The majority of bulimics induce vomiting by pushing their fingers into the throat, thus producing the gagging reflex. Use of this method frequently results in calluses over the dorsum of the hand caused by its rubbing against the upper teeth (see Russell 1979: Fig. 1). But some bulimics have developed their purging techniques to such a degree that they simply need to stoop over the toilet to vomit.

Thoughts about food and body weight are obsessional, and the behaviour related to food becomes compulsive. For example, some bulimics have as many as 20 or 30 episodes of bingeing and vomiting in a 24-hour period. The energy value of food consumed during frequent binges has been measured, and it was found that a bulimic subject may be eating food with an energy value of at least 26 megajoules (about 6,214 kilocalories) per day. Obviously, much of this energy would never be absorbed, because the partly digested food would be expelled by vomiting immediately following the binge. By contrast, women with no history of eating disorders and with comparable indices of body weight were eating food with an energy value of under 15 megajoules (approximately 2,585 kilocalories) per day.

Many bulimics have never been treated for their disorder, since many retain normal or slightly below normal weight through the use of these bizarre purging methods. Hence, unlike the painfully thin anorectic, whose illness is obvious to both her doctor and others around her, the bulimic may be ill for years without anyone discovering her secret disorder, not even her husband, parents, or friends.

The causes of these two disorders are not known; there is no convincing evidence for either inherited or biologically determining factors. Anorexia nervosa has been viewed in the psychodynamic sense as a struggle towards a self-respecting identity, as a 'defensive, biologically regressed' attitude taken in response to pressures (especially sexual ones) experienced in puberty, and as an attempt to realize society's current view of the ideal feminine figure as sylphlike. Similarly, evidence has been provided that the development of bulimia is related to the struggle to attain a perfect stereotyped female image of beauty, helplessness, and dependence.

Both anorexia nervosa and bulimia nervosa are very resistant to treatment, with a less favourable prognosis for bulimia nervosa than for anorexia nervosa. Thus physical complications, such as potassium depletion, urinary infections, and renal failure, are more frequent and dangerous, and the risk of suicide is greater for those suffering from bulimia.

Pharmacological treatment is possible, and the drugs that have been used exert their behavioural actions through the central monoamine and opiate *neurotransmitter systems. Certain drugs that have been shown to be effective in the treatment of other psychiatric or neurological disorders—for example, chlorpromazine used predominantly in treating *schizophrenia and which appears to have had some success in combating compulsive behaviour—have been used to treat patients with anorexia or bulimia nervosa. In addition, tricyclic antidepressants have been tried in several studies. The results of these drug trials to date have been unconvincing, however, because of the small number of subjects studied and the failure in general to use control procedures. Indeed, in the few studies where the latter procedure has been implemented, pharmacological treatment has *not* been shown to be effective.

It has been reported in one study that in-patient treatment for anorexia nervosa was required in 80 per cent of cases. When the patient was separated from her family, weight was usually restored but only with some difficulty, using a combination of psychotherapy, capable nursing, and, in about half of the cases, treatment with chlorpromazine. Most patients were reported to take between one and five years to stabilize their weight at a reasonable level, to lose their fear of increasing weight, and to be considered fully recovered.

Some success has been reported in treating bulimic patients using a 'cognitive–behavioural' approach. This focuses on increasing the patient's control of eating, eliminating food avoidance, and changing maladaptive attitudes. A recent approach, with some similarities to this, combines dietary and cognitive techniques. The patient is placed on a calorie-controlled diet that allows her to control her weight at an acceptable level while enabling her to eat a balanced diet, including food rich in carbohydrate, which is normally irrationally avoided. This dietary regimen is coupled with behavioural modification techniques, together with cognitive and self-control strategies. *Behaviour therapy is employed to help render normal the patient's eating patterns, while the cognitive techniques enable her to concentrate on other creative, positive aspects of her life, rather than on ruminations about her body weight and feeding behaviour.   BS

Boskind-Lodahl, M., and Sirlin, J. (1977). 'The gorging–purging syndrome'. *Psychology Today*, Mar.

Bruch, H. (1978). *The Golden Cage: The Enigma of Anorexia Nervosa*.

Crisp, A. H. (1977). 'Anorexia nervosa'. *Proceedings of the Royal Society of Medicine*, 70.

Dally, P. (1977). 'Anorexia nervosa: do we need a scape-goat?' *Proceedings of the Royal Society of Medicine*, 70.

Lask, B., and Bryant-Waugh, R. (2000). *Anorexia Nervosa and Related Eating Disorders in Childhood and Adolescence* (2nd edn.).

Minuchin, S., Rosman, B., and Baker, L. (1978), *Psychosomatic Families: Anorexia Nervosa in Context*.

Russell, G. F. M. (1979). 'Bulimia nervosa: an ominous variant of anorexia nervosa'. *Psychological Medicine*, 9.

—— (1983). 'Anorexia nervosa'. In Weatherall, D. J., Ledingham, J. G. G., and Warrell, D. A. (eds.), *Oxford Textbook of Medicine*.

anosmia. The loss of the ability to *smell. It may be congenital but can be caused by a variety of reasons, including the common cold and lesions in the olfactory tract incurred as a result of head injury.

anthropomorphism. Seeing human capacities in 'lower' animals. It is all too easy to 'project' human characteristics into other animals, as we do in pictures, statues, and automata. This can be highly misleading in biology and psychology, but as we are derived from earlier species we should expect similarities—and can learn from them. With the recent dominating respect for evolution and evolutionary explanations of much behaviour, instincts, and emotions, criticisms of anthropomorphist analogies have greatly diminished. This is, indeed, the thrust of evolutionary biology and *evolutionary psychology.

anticipation (or prediction). The development of the *nervous system through the evolution of species is characterized by increasing powers of anticipation—the ability to survive against nature and predators. Anticipatory behaviour is not initiated by stimuli, so a stimulus-response account of the behaviour of higher animals is essentially inadequate. Intelligent anticipation requires stored knowledge, and the ability to draw analogies from past situations, which may be in many ways different from the current situation. This ability is uniquely developed in humans. Its neural localization is essentially in the frontal lobes of the cerebral cortex, but it may be the case that damage to the frontal lobes produces personality changes such that the future is judged less important.

Anticipation allows organisms and societies to avoid danger before disaster strikes; it allows strategies to be devised and individual and communal plans to be made for overcoming nature and enemies, and for achieving goals. Such abilities are quite foreign to inanimate matter, and are beyond the capacity of many living things: anticipation requires a mind. Some would argue, however, that computers may reasonably be said to have the ability to anticipate and warn of situations and events, and hence to be 'mindful'.

anxiety. The characteristics of anxiety as an *emotion are that it is distressing, and that its sources are indefinite. In the latter respect it is unlike *fear, which has reference to a specific aspect of the outside world. Fear with a more or less specific reference but out of proportion to the real danger is a *phobia. Agoraphobia, for instance, is a morbid fear of public places. An anxious person is in suspense, waiting for information to clarify his situation. He is watchful and alert, often excessively alert and overreacting to noise or other stimuli. He may feel helpless in the face of a danger which, although felt to be imminent, cannot be identified or communicated. Hope and despair tend to alternate, whereas *depression describes a prevailing mood of pessimism and discouragement.

With the emotion of anxiety may be associated such bodily symptoms as feelings in the chest of tightness or uneasiness which tend to move upwards into the throat, sinking feelings in the epigastrium, or light feelings in the head which may be described as dizziness. The patient tends to be pale or, less often, flushed. His pulse is rapid, and his heart overacting. He shows effort intolerance, mild exertion producing an undue increase in pulse and respiration rate; he tires rapidly. His posture is tense, his tendon reflexes brisk. Sexual interest tends to be in abeyance. The function of every organ in the body is affected in some degree. Numerous studies have examined physiological changes associated with the experience of anxiety. Among the better known is the change in skin conductivity, the galvanic skin reflex (GSR)—the basis of action of the so-called '*lie detector'. Increased anxiety causes sweating and a sharp drop in the resistance between the two electrodes attached to the subject's finger. In an anxious person, however, spontaneous fluctuations of the GSR will be recorded. Such an individual, when tested by a lie detector, would show even greater fluctuations in the tracing; sufficient, probably, to make an interpretation of the results invalid.

*Freud's psychoanalytic theory offers explanations of anxiety, which occurs to a greater or lesser degree in almost every form of mental disorder. In his earliest formulation, Freud argued that anxiety is a vicarious manifestation or transformation of sexual tension (libido) not discharged through normal sexual activity. It might sometimes be a repetition of the experience of being born. In his later work he wrote of it as reflecting motives which, although excluded from consciousness by repression, threaten the dissolution of the ego. The contemporary explanation, although similar, is expressed in different terms.

Anxiety has also been used in a broader sense as a term for the drive aroused by a danger signal, i.e. a conditioned stimulus associated in previous experience with *pain, physical or psychological. To a danger signal a response is made which has proved effective in avoiding the pain. The pain is not experienced again, but the response is reinforced every time it reduces the anxiety aroused by the danger signal. Responding by avoidance has other consequences. It precludes further exploration of the danger situation, and, not being explored, the sources of the danger remain ill defined, and other ways of coping with them are not learnt. Avoidance responses tend, therefore, to become firmly established.

The emotion of anxiety is felt whenever responses made to a danger signal appear to be ineffective. Because it is frustrated, the behaviour associated with anxiety tends to become vacillating and disorganized; also, destructive impulses occur. The anxiety is then mixed with anger. To these effects are due some of the special qualities of anxiety as an emotion.

The agoraphobic patient does not feel anxious while he succeeds in avoiding whatever dangers public places contain for him; otherwise he would feel helpless in the face of whatever demands being in a public place might make. These demands might represent threats to his conception of himself or to the assumptions he makes about the world. Akin to agoraphobia is 'separation anxiety', which arises when a person faces demands while being denied, as a result of separation, the reassurance and support of a parent or other significant person. Existentialist theory equates anxiety with the dread of being alone or of being nothing; without the reassurance given through a relationship with another person, the sense of self is threatened.   DRD

aphasia. The ability to talk may not, as was once thought, be the crucial factor that distinguishes humans from the animals, but loss of the power of speech is one of the most distressing things that can happen to a human being. Aphasia (the disruption of speech) commonly follows a stroke—especially if the stroke also impairs movement of the right arm or leg. The loss of articulated language is not always or necessarily accompanied by loss of other linguistic functions, like reading and writing. Least of all is it necessarily accompanied by loss of comprehension: a sufferer often knows that the words he is uttering are wrong, but he cannot correct or alter them ('Pass me the bread—no, not the bread the *bread*—no!'). However, where one of the linguistic skills is seriously disturbed, one or more of the others tends to be somewhat reduced as well. Neither does the disruption of speech mean that all aspects of it are obliterated, nor, even if it is seriously reduced in the early stages after the disrupting incident, that it can never be regained. But the recovery of abilities by an aphasic person does not follow the same principles of learning as the acquisition of learning a language by a normal, healthy child or adult. Asking the patient to repeat a word or phrase over and over again is not necessarily going to help him to say it later on; it is more likely merely to make him angry and depressed. Impairment of language does not necessarily imply loss of other faculties, such as intelligence or memory.

The three aspects of aphasia that have been studied most intensively are the manner in which speech breaks down, the causes of the breakdown, and treatment of and recovery from it.

1. The manner of breakdown
2. The causes of breakdown
3. Recovery

1. The manner of breakdown

The different forms of breakdown can be classified in different ways, but most people nowadays consider just two major groups: non-fluent (or *Broca's) and fluent (or *Wernicke's), the names in parentheses being those of the neurologists who first described them. (See LANGUAGE: NEUROPSYCHOLOGY, for a fuller discussion.)

In non-fluent aphasia, the sufferer has difficulty finding words, particularly uncommon ones. He has difficulty naming objects, and his syntax is often faulty. He tends to talk hesitantly and gropingly, although he is often acutely aware of how stupid he sounds. The fluent aphasic, on the other hand, emits a stream of words the intonation of which is perfectly normal. Heard from a distance, they sound obscure or clever, but closer listening reveals meaningless jargon. Unlike the non-fluent aphasic, the fluent one seems undisturbed by, and even unaware of, his poor communication. In each of these conditions, concomitant disorders of reading, writing, and comprehension may be present in some degree, but are usually more severe in fluent than in non-fluent disorders.

2. The causes of breakdown

Aphasia is caused by damage to tissue within the brain. But whether injuries to different areas of the brain cause different types of disorder, and whether the same patterns of disorder occur in all individuals, is less certain. Each hemisphere of the brain not only controls movement and sensation of the opposite side of the body, but seems to specialize in particular mental functions. (See NEUROPSYCHOLOGY.) It is the left hemisphere that seems to be most closely concerned with language, although in left-handed people and those with a family history of left-handedness the association is not so strong. Moreover it is not inevitable. People whose left hemispheres are damaged in early infancy or childhood can 'learn to speak' perfectly adequately with their right. By and large, however, it is damage to the left hemisphere that most commonly causes aphasia, that to the anterior part causing non-fluent disorders, and that to the posterior part causing those of the fluent type. It is sometimes held, though, that in fluent aphasia there is also usually some damage to the right or non-dominant hemisphere as well as to the left.

An important factor relating to breakdown is the degree to which a person made use of language before his injury. Although after breakdown the words and phrases previously used most commonly can usually be found more easily than others, this does not necessarily mean that the first language of a bilingual or polyglot is the one best preserved: it is frequency of usage rather than recency that is important. Even so, there is a tendency for sufferers of non-fluent aphasia to emit swear words and taboo words when searching for those they cannot find. Here it is the words which have *not* been uttered in the past that appear before those which have. The reason for this is probably that inhibition or repression of an act gives it particularly strong emotional force, and the emotional aspects of mental behaviour are not controlled by the same areas of the brain as language. Indeed, they tend to be released when intellectual control is removed.

3. Recovery

The vast majority of aphasic people, especially in the younger age groups, recover a good deal of speech as time goes on; and a few of the more literary ones have written accounts of their experiences. Unfortunately these seldom contain information about how the faculties were regained, probably because such processes—like many other forms of learning and remembering—occur at a level that is not available to normal consciousness. Psychologists who have been able to watch and study these people have, however, identified several factors that seem to be involved, especially in non-fluent aphasia.

(*a*) Arousal of previous or common contexts. In most languages there are words that have different meanings in different contexts. In English, the word *hand* can be applied to a part of the human body, parts of a clock-face, a unit for the measurement of horses, a style of penmanship, a pledge of fidelity, a member of a ship's crew. The first usage here is undoubtedly the commonest, and aphasics can often name the body part when asked to do so, even when they cannot find the word 'hand' in its other contexts. However, once a word has been found in its most common context, it can often be found in others too ('Of course, those are called "hands", aren't they?').

(*b*) Narrowing of syntactical constraints. In most languages, words are uttered and understood in sequences rather than individually, and are controlled by those preceding them. For instance, in the sentence starting 'The man was bitten by—', there is a limit to the choice of words that can follow. Narrowing the field of possibilities by such means seems to be very helpful to the aphasic patient, who can often find words if they form parts of familiar sentences (or song phrases) when not able to do so otherwise.

(*c*) The hesitancy seen in non-fluent aphasia is usually due to the patient's knowledge that the first words which occur to him are wrong and must be corrected. Yet if these words *are* uttered, they are usually far from random. Indeed, they tend to be closely related to the word being sought. They arise from the same semantic field or consist of functional descriptions of the object to be named ('They're the things that point to the time—the fingers—no, the pointers—no!').

Summing up, it seems that in non-fluent aphasia the difficulty is one of having lost not the ability to speak, but only the ability to find the right words at the right moment. Any stimulus that gives a 'lead in' to the general semantic field helps. After this, it is a matter of sifting through the various items until the target is found. (How one recognizes the target is a different problem, and although this ability seems to be intact in the non-fluent aphasic, it seems to be at fault in the fluent one, who does not try to inhibit or correct his 'near misses'.)

Experiments with normal, healthy humans indicate that the processes whereby they find and utter words are very similar to those seen in aphasia, but that the processes take place more quickly and efficiently. But rare words take longer to find than common ones, and if the sorting/sifting/correcting process is impeded by external factors (such as distraction) or internal ones (such as intoxication), 'near misses' of much the same sort as those given by the aphasic may be emitted.   MWI

Basso, A. (2003). *Aphasia and its Therapy*.
Gardner, H. (1977). *The Shattered Mind*.
Luria, A. R. (1970). *Traumatic Aphasia*.
Russell, W. R., and Espir, M. L. E. (1961). *Traumatic Aphasia*.
Spreen, O., and Risser, A. H. (2003). *Assessment of Aphasia*.
Wernicke, C. (1874). *Der Aphasische Symptomkomplex*.

aphrodisiacs. The search for aphrodisiacs dates back millennia. They can be classified by their mode of action into three types: those that increase libido, potency, or sexual pleasure. Various substances of animal and plant origin have been used in folk medicines of different cultures: some have been identified pharmacologically, allowing for understanding of their mechanisms of action.

Substances that increase libido. These aphrodisiacs act at the level of the central nervous system by altering specific neurotransmitter or specific sex hormone levels. Some of them can be effective in both sexes, although most act through an increase in testosterone level and are therefore male specific. Ambrein, a major constituent of Ambra grisea, is used in Arab countries. This tricyclic triterpene alcohol increases the level of several anterior pituitary hormones and serum testosterone. Ambrein also enhances central noradrenergic trafficking, which in turn stimulates sexual arousal, and it can antagonize the contractile action of various agents (acetylcholine, noradrenaline, prostaglandin, oxytocin) on smooth muscles. Various plants purportedly enhance libido, and some animal studies showed their androgenic activity. Bufo toad skin and glands contain bufetanine (and others bufadienolides), a putative hallucinogenic congener of serotonin. It is the active ingredient in West Indian Love Stone and the Chinese medication *Chan Su*. The aphrodisiac properties are probably of central origin, as are other (psychoactive) effects of the drug; hence, it is listed as a hallucinogen.

Substances increasing potency. Panax ginseng, used in traditional Chinese medicine, works as an antioxidant by enhancing nitric oxide synthesis in the endothelium of many organs, including the corpora cavernosa; ginsenosides also enhance acetylcholine-induced and transmural nerve stimulation-activated relaxation associated with increased tissue cGMP, hence the aphrodisiac properties. Sildenafil (Viagra) acts through a similar mechanism. Ginseng's central effect (increase in brain-stem dopamine, noradrenaline (norepinephrine), cortical serotonin, attenuation of monoamine oxidase activity) can explain its memory-enhancing and anti-anxiety properties and contribute to its aphrodisiac effect.

Substances that enhance sensory experience during coitus. The effect of such substances is generally through irritation of the genital mucosa, thus enhancing sensation. They are sold in sex shops and used by both sexes. Not infrequently, they are ingested by an unsuspecting subject through a drink prepared by the (potential) partner. Cantharidin (Spanish fly) is a chemical with vesicant properties derived from blister beetles, which have been used for millennia as a sexual stimulant. Its mode of action is by inhibition of phosphodiesterase and protein phosphatase activity and stimulation of β-receptors, inducing vascular congestion and inflammation. Morbidity from its abuse is significant. The ingestion of live beetles (*Palembus dermestoides*) in South-East Asia and triatomids in Mexico may have a similar basis. Aphrodisiac properties have also been attributed to various foods. Among them are spices (anise, basil, coriander, fennel, sage, ginger, garlic, saffron), vegetables (artichokes, asparagus), oysters, chocolate, and many fruits. In general, many of them contain volatile oils that act as irritants when excreted through the urinary tract, inducing engorgement of the mucosa. There is little pharmacological evidence to support aphrodisiac claims in some of these items.

Physicians should be more aware of their patients' often unspoken concerns. Medications, such as sildenafil, and various devices are available: it is the physician's role to identify the patients who could be helped, depending upon the underlying pathology, and advise them accordingly, also alerting them to the risks of using uncontrolled substances advertised as powerful aphrodisiacs. Newer treatments do not reduce the need for education and counselling for all patients with such problems.   PS

apperception. When experimental psychology became a fact towards the end of the 19th century, the only concepts available to it were those developed in either a philosophical or a biological context. 'Apperception' belongs to the former category, having played an important role in the German philosophical tradition since the beginning of the 18th century. Wilhelm *Wundt, who initiated the first systematic research programme in experimental psychology and trained many of its early practitioners, was steeped in this tradition and actively contributed to it. As a result, the concept of apperception occupied a prominent place in the early literature of experimental psychology.

The term was originally used by G. W. *Leibniz, particularly in his critique of Lockian sensationalism, as a way of emphasizing the distinction between a passive sensation and a mental content self-consciously 'apperceived'. It became the major technical term used by German philosophers to express what they considered to be the two fundamental features of the human mind: the fact that mental experience is not composed of separate bits but forms a unity, and the fact that this unity involves a constructive activity of the mind itself rather than a passive reflection of external events.

This usage is found in the highly influential philosophy of Immanuel *Kant, where a clear distinction is introduced between the empirically observed unity of experience and a *transcendental apperception*, a cognitive act, which makes this unity possible. This distinction devalued the introspective analysis of inner experience as being concerned only with effects and appearances, but it also acted as a challenge for 19th-century psychologists to find a more satisfactory explanation for the empirical unity of experience.

The challenge was taken up by Kant's successor, J. F. *Herbart, whose model of mental functioning involved the notion of ideas combining to form powerful 'masses' that dominated the mental life of the individual. Apperception occurred through the assimilation of new ideas by an existing complex of ideas. Herbart's concepts achieved wide popularity among 19th-century educationists, so that the concept of apperception began to descend from the lofty heights of philosophical speculation.

This process was continued in the work of Wundt, who proposed to subject the process of apperception to experimental investigation in the psychological laboratory. The original vehicle for accomplishing this was provided by *reaction-time experiments which had been developed by physiologists. Wundt conceived the idea of using variations in reaction times that occur with different patterns of stimulus presentation as an empirical index of central apperceptive processes. Responses to sequences of stimuli or to distracting stimuli, for example, had to involve the kind of synthesizing cognitive activity that was traditionally referred to as apperception. These early experiments constituted the first systematic attempt to subject central psychological processes to precise laboratory investigation.

The notion that the process of apperception occupied measurable periods of time implied that it was not transcendental but involved physiological processes of definite physical duration. Wundt speculated that these processes were localized in an 'apperception centre' in the forebrain that coordinated the activity of lower sensory and motor centres.

This was the physical side of Wundt's psychophysical theory of apperception. The more prominent psychological side treated the phenomenon of *attention as the primary subjectively observable expression of the apperceptive process. While this provided further opportunities for experimental study, Wundt also used the theory of apperception to explain the structure of language, developing an early version of psycholinguistics (see NEUROLINGUISTICS, LURIA ON).

Thus, apperception became the major unifying concept in the first important theoretical system of modern psychology, attempting to synthesize evidence from psychophysiology, from laboratory studies of human *cognition, and from comparative studies of symbolic structures. It is noteworthy that, while the *effects* of apperception were generally investigated in the context of cognition, Wundt believed that its psychological *sources* lay in affective processes.

This theoretical *tour de force* proved to be premature. Wundt's successors, including his most prominent students, abandoned the concept of apperception, restricting themselves to observables, like attention. This generation of psychologists was anxious to cut psychology's ties with philosophy, which Wundt had wanted to maintain. Apperception was rejected as excessively metaphysical. Possible practical applications of their findings became more interesting to many empirical psychologists than were broad theoretical syntheses, and from this point of view apperception was a redundant concept. For many years work on central integrative processes was neglected in favour of a more simplistic sensorimotor psychology. Some of the phenomena that apperception had been intended to explain were more effectively reinterpreted in the framework of *Gestalt psychology. Thus the term went out of use rather quickly and permanently. Contemporary cognitive science has revived an interest in many of the problems that the theory of apperception had been concerned with, but the term itself has not been resurrected.   KD

Leahy, T. H. (1980). *A History of Psychology*, ch. 7.
Rieber, R. W. (ed.) (1980). *Wilhelm Wundt and the Making of a Scientific Psychology*, chs. 2–4.
Wundt, W. (1911). *An Introduction to Psychology*, ch. 4. Repr. 1973.

apraxia. The inability to make purposeful skilled movements. Like the *aphasias, the apraxias are classical syndromes in human neuropsychology. Animals do not develop apraxia as a consequence of brain lesions, no matter where the lesion is located. In man, apraxia occurs, as a rule, after a lesion in the hemisphere dominant for language, usually the left hemisphere. In those rare instances where language is processed in the right hemisphere, apraxia might be expected after right-sided brain damage.

This observation might suggest that apraxia should be considered among those neuropsychological symptoms that are language dependent. An inherent relationship between the two syndromes, however, has not been demonstrated. Both aphasia and apraxia vary independently. After left-sided brain damage there can be recovery of language functions in the presence of persisting apraxia, and vice versa.

There are two varieties of apraxia, traditionally termed ideomotor apraxia and ideational apraxia. These terms reflect late 19th-century views on the organization of psychological processes in the brain; in particular, they imply a two-stage model of motor processing, similar to the traditional two-stage model of sensory processing (*perception and *apperception) developed during the same period. Although these models have been abandoned in favour of a multi-step, multi-modal integration model of processing, it is still convenient to adopt the terms ideomotor and ideational in modern research provided they are used as neutral denominators and do not confer a priori theoretical implications.

1. Ideomotor apraxia
2. Ideational apraxia

1. Ideomotor apraxia
This is a common syndrome in which the execution of simple or complex, meaningful (or symbolic), or meaningless (or non-symbolic) movements with the oro-facial musculature and/or with the limbs is impaired in a characteristic way. The paramount feature is not clumsiness of movement or absence of execution, but rather a distortion of movements, which Hugo Liepmann termed parapraxia. Parapraxias are brought about by inadequate selection of the elements that contribute to a motor sequence and/or by impairment in the sequential combination of these elements. Both aspects, impaired selection and sequencing of elements, are of equal importance. In order to arrive at the diagnosis of ideomotor apraxia, one has to make sure that the motor disorder is not explained by paresis, sensory impairment, disturbances in the co-ordination of movements, or problems in understanding a specified task because of either language disturbance or impaired intellectual performance.

A striking feature of ideomotor apraxia is that the execution of movements is impaired only when they are required out of their natural context. Traditionally, the examination is done by making the patient perform certain movements, like whistling, sticking out his tongue, blowing out his cheeks, performing the sign of the cross or a military salute, or placing the back of his hand on his front. These and similar movements are required either on verbal command or by imitation after demonstration by the examiner. It is important to note that a patient with ideomotor apraxia is perfectly able to brush his teeth in the morning, in a natural setting, whereas he performs the same movement in a rather parapraxic way when required to do so in the doctor's examination room. A convincing explanation for this well-recognized feature has not yet been put forward. One could be tempted to entertain a disconnection model, specifying that movements are impaired when they are elicited by input from the language system or from the visual system, but not when the input is generated in the limbic system. The reliance of spontaneous, context-dependent actions on limbic input to the motor system, however, still has to be demonstrated in both physiological and anatomical terms.

The structure of apraxia has been investigated on the basis of qualitative analysis of the parapraxic errors. This analysis was based on studies by David Efron, who was the first to apply sophisticated methods for the description of expressive movements in a study of gestural behaviour. He used the term 'linguistic' to denote the referential aspect of symbolic movements. While his analysis was focused only on movements as a whole, single components of movements were systematically studied by Birdwhistel (1970), who applied the methods of structural linguistics to the study of normal movements. He recognized posture and movement as patterned behaviour, and he developed a notation system which permitted a description of a hierarchy of motor elements similar to the description of speech elements in a linguistic hierarchy.

Stimulated by this research, K. Poeck and M. Kerschensteiner have developed a method permitting the quantitative and qualitative assessment of single components constituting the apraxic movements. A code has been elaborated which enables one to transcribe the characteristics of the single components of the motor sequence. Error analysis showed that the most characteristic behaviour in apraxia is perseveration (the inappropriate repetition of parts of speech or movement). In apraxia it occurs not only as the repetition of a whole movement or motor sequence but also, much more importantly, as the intrusion of motor elements that were part of a movement correctly or incorrectly performed many tasks before. To give an example, the patients not only repeated the military salute when they were asked to touch their chin but they perseverated on the rhythmic elements of the movement 'to show that somebody is crazy' when they performed the static movement of the military salute—i.e. they tapped their temple while their hand was in correct military salute position. The perseveratory tendency is so strong that when asked to imitate a movement, the patients were likely to repeat a movement or an element of a movement carried out earlier in spite of the visual evidence of the correct execution by the examiner.

In a systematic study with 200 apraxia tasks given to 88 patients with left-sided brain damage, 10 patients with right-sided brain damage, and 10 control subjects, no differences between the right and left limbs were found. Meaningful (i.e. practised, easily verbalized) and meaningless (i.e. unpractised and difficult to verbalize) tasks were equally impaired. The aphasic language disturbance did not explain errors on verbal command. No qualitative relation between aphasia and apraxia was detected, nor any subtypes of apraxia characterized by certain patterns of error.

Therapy is not necessary because ideomotor apraxia occurs only under the conditions of examination and does not impair the patient's spontaneous actions.

2. Ideational apraxia

A rare condition, this is observed in patients with lesions in the language-dominant hemisphere. There is only one case on record where the syndrome was the consequence of a right-sided brain lesion. This patient was left-handed and had right-sided or at least bilateral representation of language functions.

Patients with ideational apraxia are seriously impaired when they are about to carry out sequences of actions requiring the use of various objects in the correct way and order necessary to achieve an intended goal. These patients are conspicuous in everyday behaviour because they have problems in, for example, preparing or even eating a meal, or doing some professional routine they have performed for years. The behavioural disturbance of these patients is most frequently misinterpreted as indicating mental confusion—and all the more so since, in addition to ideational apraxia, they are regularly aphasic.

Patients do not fail these tasks because they have problems in the recognition of objects. In spite of their aphasia they frequently give pertinent verbal comments on the task, indicating that the language problem cannot be the determinant factor. Ideational apraxia is not a very severe degree of ideomotor apraxia; although both syndromes may occur in the same patient, they vary independently of each other. On the basis of a small number of observations it is suggested that the ideational apraxia syndrome is due to a disturbance in the associative elaboration of various inputs with motor programmes. This would be in line with modern concepts of the hierarchical organization of the motor system. Ideational apraxia is a great handicap for the patient, and therefore it is necessary to develop appropriate lines of treatment. Such treatment should first attempt to teach the patient to avoid perseverative behaviour. KP

Birdwhistel, R. L. (1970). *Kinesics and Context.*

Geschwind, N. (1974). *Selected Papers on Language and the Brain.*

Poeck, K. (1984). 'Clues to the disruptions to limb praxis: Qualitative studies'. In Roy, E. A. (ed.), *Disruptions to the Sequencing of Actions: Advances in Psychology.*

Rothi, L. J., and Heilman, K. M. (1997). *Apraxia: The Neuropsychology of Action.*

a priori. A term applied to statements to reflect the status of our knowledge of their truth (or falsehood). It means literally 'from what comes before', where the answer to 'before what?' is understood to be 'experience'. Loosely, one may speak of knowing some truth 'a priori' where it is possible to infer the truth without having to experience the state of affairs in virtue of which it is true, but in strict philosophical usage, an a priori truth must be knowable independently of *all* experience. *Kant held that the criteria of a priori knowledge were (i) necessity, for 'experience teaches us that a thing is so and so, but not that it cannot be otherwise', and (ii) universality, for all experience can confer on a judgement is 'assumed and comparative universality through *induction'. Gottlob Frege stressed that the issue was one of justification, and defined an a priori truth as one whose proof rests exclusively on general laws which neither need nor admit of proof, while a truth which cannot be proved without appeal to assertions about particular objects is a posteriori.

Statements such as 'A vixen is a fox', whose truth is *analytic, are accorded a priori status without dispute. Kant held that in addition truths of arithmetic and geometry, and such statements about the natural world as 'Every event has a cause', were not analytic but nevertheless had the hallmarks of being a priori. The central question that his philosophy addressed was how such synthetic a priori truths were possible, whereas the strategy of his 20th-century empiricist critics was to argue that there are no a priori truths that are not analytic.   JET

Frege, G. (1959). *The Foundations of Arithmetic.* Trans. J. L. Austin, section 3.

Kant, I. (1929). *The Critique of Pure Reason.* Trans. N. Kemp-Smith, Preface and Introduction.

Aquinas, St Thomas (1225–74). The greatest of the medieval scholastics. Aquinas was primarily a theologian, but in his theological work he was led to develop a comprehensive treatment of the philosophical issues at stake; hence we can extract from his writings a philosophical psychology which he considered capable of standing on its own feet, without requiring support from Christian revelation.

St Thomas, the seventh son of Landulf, count of Aquino, was born at the family's castle of Roccasecca, near Aquino (about halfway between Rome and Naples). He was educated at the Benedictine abbey of Monte Cassino and at the University of Naples. In 1244 he decided to join the newly established Dominican order, and afterwards studied at the University of Paris and at the Dominicans' institute in Cologne, where one of his teachers was St Albert the Great. Aquinas lectured at various times at the universities of Paris and Naples and at the papal court. He died while on his way to the Fourth Ecumenical Council of Lyon, and was canonized in 1323.

Aquinas rejected much contemporary Christian theorizing about man, based on the thought of St Augustine and, via Augustine, on *Plato and Neoplatonism, and instead took over and developed many of *Aristotle's conclusions. Like Aristotle, he viewed human activity as taking place on three levels: vegetative (comprising the powers of nutrition, growth, and reproduction), sensitive (comprising sensory activity and locomotion), and intellectual (comprising reason and will). Among bodily creatures, only man possesses reason and will, but these powers are found also in angels and, in a very much higher manner which we cannot adequately comprehend, in God; and it is because man shares, to some degree, in these divine attributes of reason and will that the Scriptures speak of man as made in the image and likeness of God (Genesis 1: 26–7).

Aquinas followed Aristotle in defining the soul of a living being as its substantial form, i.e. as that inherent principle by which it is the kind of entity or substance that it is; and he contrasted the soul as form with the matter that it organizes or 'informs': both soul and matter are necessary constituent principles of the living being. So, he believed, all living creatures have souls, but only human beings have spiritual souls. Aquinas rejected the medieval Augustinians' belief that in man there are three distinct souls, vegetative, sensitive, and intellectual, each accounting for human activity at its corresponding level. This view, he said, would destroy man's natural unity by breaking him up into three distinct entities; rather, there is just the one soul, which is responsible for all of a man's activities, regardless of the level to which they belong.

Following Aristotle, Aquinas distinguished the five external senses of sight, hearing, touch, taste, and smell, and four 'internal senses'. These latter are: the 'common sense' by means of which sense impressions or 'phantasms' produced by different external senses are referred to a single entity existing outside the perceiver; secondly, the imagination (*imaginatio* or *phantasia*), which stores sense impressions and can combine them into complex images of hitherto unperceived things and events; thirdly, the 'cogitative power' (*vis cogitativa*), which corresponds to instinct in animals and by which we can apprehend things and events in the world as either beneficial or harmful to us; and finally the sense memory (*vis rememorativa*), in which information gained by the cogitative power is stored.

In sensory cognition we appropriate the sensible forms of objects, that is, their observable characteristics, without the matter of the objects themselves; so (for example) in seeing a silver coin I receive its colour into my sense organ, but not the actual matter of the coin. Likewise, he thinks, the two kinds of human activity at the rational level, thinking and willing, involve receiving into the soul the *intelligible* form of whatever one's thinking or willing is about. For an entity or substance in the external world is made to be the sort of thing that it is by possession of a certain nature or form—the form of oak tree, for example—and we understand and think about things by mentally receiving their forms: in this way, as Aristotle said, 'the mind is in a way all things'. But matter as such, considered in isolation from any determining form, is unintelligible, and so we can 'latch on' to a thing in thought only by mentally disengaging or 'abstracting' its intelligible form from the material conditions of sensation. This process of abstraction, Aquinas said, is carried out by a power called the agent intellect (*intellectus agens*), and another power, the receptive intellect (*intellectus possibilis*), then receives and stores the forms abstracted by the agent intellect. Thus the form of (say) cat which is present in cats themselves, thereby making them the kind of animal they are, is also present in the minds of human beings, thereby making them capable of thinking about cats. In this way Aquinas accounted for the fact of *intentionality, that is, the fact that our thoughts are *about* things. The form of something, as stored in the receptive intellect, is a concept. Unlike sensations, which are particular modifications of the sense powers, concepts are universals because they enable us to think about a potentially indefinite number of things of a given kind, and the receptive intellect employs these concepts in carrying out such intellectual operations as judging, reasoning, and deliberating. A form present in someone's mind as a concept is, Aquinas said, obviously present in a very different way from that of a form present in an external thing, and he called this mental mode of presence 'intentional being' (*esse intentionale*).

Against the Latin Averroism of Siger of Brabant and others, St Thomas denied that the agent intellect is a single entity which is distinct from all human beings but in which the latter somehow participate. Rather, he said, it is a constituent power of each human mind. There are, then, as many agent intellects as there are men.

Because he believed that human beings can acquire concepts only by abstracting forms from sense appearances, Aquinas can be called an empiricist. He insisted that without some sensory input on which the mind's abstractive power could get to work, no concepts would ever be constructed, nor would any rational activity ever take place: there are no 'innate ideas'. Moreover, any actual use of concepts in thinking or willing must—at least in this life, in which the soul is embodied—be constantly referred to sense contents, either of perception or memory or imagination. This necessary human orientation to sensory data is what Aquinas called 'conversion to sense experience' (*conversio ad phantasmata*).

Since concept formation involves the abstraction of intelligible forms from all material conditions, Aquinas concluded that the formation and utilization of concepts are activities that cannot in principle be performed by any physical organ or organism. For, he said, if there were a physical organ of thought it would be unable to do something that it obviously can do, namely, receive the forms of all physical objects, but would be restricted to receiving the forms of only one particular kind of object, as the eye is restricted to receiving colours. Nor would any physical organ be capable of that self-conscious awareness which is so prominent a feature of human thought. Our concepts are, then, present in us in a non-material way; hence that which performs mental acts must be a wholly non-material, that is, spiritual, principle. So the human soul, as well as being the substantial form of the body—that by which the human body *is* a body—must also be a spiritual substance in its own right.

Because man's soul is a spiritual substance, it can survive death. For it is not made up of physical parts and is, therefore, unlike the body, free from corruption and dissolution. Admittedly, since man depends on his sense organs to provide him with appropriate objects of thought—things to think about—it seems that a disembodied soul will be unable to exercise its mental abilities without some special help from God; and in any case, since the human soul is the substantial form of the human body, disembodiment is clearly an unnatural condition for it. Thus, although we can have reason to accept the Christian doctrine of the resurrection of the body only on the basis of God's revelation, that doctrine is entirely appropriate to the human condition. For only if soul and body are eventually reunited will there be a fully constituted human being once more; until then, the souls of the departed will exist in a condition that is abnormal, contrary to nature (*praeter naturam*).

For Aquinas, man is not the highest of all created beings, because angels far exceed him in intellectual power. But he is the highest of all bodily creatures, and as a partly material, partly spiritual being, man forms the bridge, so to speak, between the physical and spiritual realms.

How does a human being come into existence? Is he generated out of physical elements, as is a plant, or is some higher, non-physical agency required? Aquinas replies that since the soul is a purely spiritual entity it must be created directly, out of nothing, by God. But there is no pre-existence of souls: when God creates a soul he immediately infuses it into the appropriate matter which is present in a woman's womb.

Just as man's cognitive powers are present on both sensory and rational levels, so it is with what Aquinas calls man's appetitive or striving functions. The latter include such activities as wishing, willing, desiring, intending, and feeling emotions. Here we shall concentrate on Aquinas's account of the will, which he defines as the rational appetite, that is, the appetite or tendency that belongs to the rational part of the soul. As rational, it is directed not to any particular good, as are the sensory appetitive powers, but rather to goodness as such: it is the power by which man strives towards that which he rationally apprehends as in some way good or desirable. Aquinas analyses the process of deciding to do something into a whole series of 'component' acts, some belonging to the intellect and some to the will. The decisive choice (*electio*) which results in some action's being performed is an act of the will, but the will cannot function without the intellect's aid; we can will something only if we have already recognized it to be good. However, Aquinas also believes that the will very often operates freely, i.e. without being determined to any particular outcome. For, he says, we choose to do one thing rather than another because our intellect apprehends the goodness of what is chosen, but nothing short of the supreme and final good of man (which, for Aquinas, ultimately consists in the vision of God in heaven) can irresistibly attract the human mind; everything other than this will be attractive in some respects but unattractive in others. Hence the will can choose freely among goods which fall short of the complete and ultimate good. This is St Thomas's principal argument for the freedom of the will, or 'free choice' (*liberum arbitrium*), as he calls it; but he also argues that unless man were capable of making free choices, 'advice, exhortations, precepts, prohibitions, rewards, and punishments would be in vain'.

While some of Aquinas's arguments rest upon outdated theses of Aristotelian science, his major conclusions concerning thinking, willing, and the nature and destiny of the human soul escape this limitation and still find defenders today. P. T. Geach's *Mental Acts*, for example, is a particularly interesting analysis of human mental activity that owes much to Aquinas.

Aquinas's account of the nature and workings of the mind is presented, above all, in the *Summa theologiae* (English translation in 60 vols., ed. T. Gilby, 1963–75), especially vols. xi–xiii, and in the *Summa contra Gentiles* (English translation by A. C. Pegis et al., 1955–7), especially vol. ii. A useful selection of readings is A. C. Pegis, (ed.), *Introduction to St Thomas Aquinas* (1948).   FJF

Copleston, F. C. (1955). *Aquinas*.

Geach, P. T. (1957). *Mental Acts*.

Lonergan, B. J. F. (1967). *Verbum: Word and Idea in Aquinas*.

Weisheipl, J. A. (1974). *Friar Thomas D'Aquino*.

Aristotle (384–322 BC). Greek philosopher. Aristotle was born in the obscure Chalcidic village of Stagira, far from the intellectual centre of Greece. His father Nicomachus was court physician to King Amyntas III of Macedon, and it is pleasing to speculate that Nicomachus encouraged his son to take an interest in matters scientific and philosophical. However that may be, in 367 Aristotle migrated to Athens, where he joined the brilliant band of thinkers who studied with *Plato in the Academy. He soon made a name for himself as a student of great intellect, acumen, and originality.

On the death of Plato in 347, Aristotle moved to Asia Minor, where he spent some years devoted principally to the study of biology and zoology. In 343 he moved to Pella, where he served as tutor to King Philip's son, the future Alexander the Great. (What influence Aristotle may have had on that obnoxious young man is uncertain.) After further migrations, Aristotle returned to Athens in 335, and for the next decade engaged in teaching and research in his own school in the Lyceum. He fled from Athens on the death of Alexander in 323, and died a year later in Chalcis. His will, which has survived for us to read, is a humane and touching document.

Aristotle was a polymath: his researches ranged from abstract logic and metaphysics to highly detailed studies in biology and anatomy; with the possible exception of the mathematical sciences, no branch of knowledge was left untouched by him. His contributions were both innovatory and systematic: no one man has achieved more, no one man has had greater influence, and Aristotle remains, in Dante's phrase, 'the master of those who know'.

Aristotle's main contributions to the study of mind are to be found in his treatise *De anima* (On the Soul or Concerning Psyche) and in a series of short papers known collectively as the *Parva naturalia*. He regarded the study of psychology as a part of the general study of animate nature (see PSYCHE): there is no division in his thought between the study of mind and the study of matter, and his psychological writings are continuous with his overtly biological works.

An early work, the *Eudemus* (only fragments of which survive), betrays a juvenile interest in a Platonic account of the psyche: there Aristotle argued that the psyche was independent of the body, pre-existing it and surviving its death. But that separation of mind from body is foreign to Aristotle's mature works: in the *De anima* he defines the psyche as 'the first actuality of a natural organic body'; and he associates psyche with the animate functions of nutrition, perception, thought, and motion. Psychology is thus by definition linked to the biological sciences, and Aristotle explicitly states that the student of the psyche must investigate the behavioural and physiological aspects of his subject—he must know, for example, that anger is the boiling of the blood around the heart.

*Perception receives a lengthy discussion in the *De anima* and in the *De sensu*, a component treatise of the *Parva naturalia*. Aristotle regards perceiving as a special sort of change in the perceiver: objects of perception, acting via some medium of perception, causally affect the perceiver's sensory apparatus; the apparatus changes inasmuch as it 'receives the form of the object without its matter', and that change is perception. For example, if you look at a white piece of paper, your eyes (or some part of them) actually become white: the eyes are made white by the paper, although no material part of the paper enters them. Similar stories are told of the other four senses. (Aristotle thinks he can prove that there can be no more than five senses.) Each sense has its own 'proper objects' (colours for sight, sounds for hearing, etc.), but some objects (for example, shape, size, motion) are 'common' to two or more senses. Other objects (men or trees, say) are perceived only 'accidentally' or indirectly: you see a man by virtue of seeing something white and moving, which happens to be a man.

The different sense modalities are somehow unified by a 'common faculty', sometimes called the 'common sense'; that faculty, which is located in the heart, is employed to explain various perceptual and quasi-perceptual phenomena, the most important of which is the 'unity of consciousness'. Colours are perceived by way of the eyes, sounds by way of the ears; but nevertheless, both perceptions belong to one and the same unitary subject or perceiver, who can compare and associate the data given by the two senses. By my eyes I see the colour and shine of the trumpet; by my ears I hear its tones: but it is a unitary *I* who perceives the trumpet, and I perceive the trumpet as a unitary substance. That task of perceptual unification is performed by the 'common sense'.

Perception is fundamentally a physical change, and it leaves physical traces in the body. Aristotle refers to those traces as 'phantasms', and they constitute the objects of *phantasia* or the faculty of imagination. The imagination is invoked in a number of contexts: thus it has an important role to play in the analysis of memory, which Aristotle discusses in his *De memoria*, and in the account of sleep and dreaming which he gives in the *De somno* and *De somniis*. (All three works are parts of the *Parva naturalia*.) Most importantly, the imagination supplies the link between perception and thought.

Aristotle's account of thought or 'the intellect' (*nous*) is one of the most perplexing aspects of his mental philosophy. On the one hand, he tends to treat thought on the model of perception: thought, like perception, is a change, and in thinking of things the mind somehow 'becomes' what it is thinking of (as the eye becomes what it is seeing, for example, white). Less obscurely, Aristotle holds that thought is dependent on imagination, and hence on perception: phantasms are, or represent, or accompany, the objects of thought, and we cannot think without phantasms. Since phantasms are the traces of perceptions, it follows that we cannot think without having perceived, and that the scope of our thought is determined by the extent of our perceptual experience. On the other hand, that strongly empiricist approach to the prob-

lems of thought seems to be modified by some remarks in one of the most celebrated and painfully difficult chapters in the whole of the Aristotelian corpus: in *De anima*, iii. 5, Aristotle distinguishes between two types of intellect: one, the 'passive' intellect, is securely tied, by way of phantasms, to perception and the body; the other, the 'active' intellect, is pure and unmixed, free from physical trappings, and capable of independent and eternal existence. The 'active' intellect has been discussed for more than 2,000 years, and scholars are no nearer understanding Aristotle's doctrine than was his own first pupil, Theophrastus. It is legitimate to suspect that Aristotle's brief notes on the two varieties of *nous* represent no more than a passing fancy or a temporary aberration; in any event, their presence in the *De anima* should not blind us to the fact that for the most part that treatise is uncompromisingly empiricist and materialist in its doctrines.

Movement is treated in the *De anima*, and also in certain of Aristotle's ethical and biological works. (The short treatise *On the Movement of Animals* is a particularly rich source for Aristotle's views on the subject.) Aristotle's treatment is remarkable for its attempt to combine a physiological explanation of animal locomotion (in terms of 'spirit' or *pneuma*, which runs through the body like current in an electric motor) with a psychological account in terms of desire and thought (imagination and perception). The physiology is inevitably crude, but Aristotle's aim is sophisticated: he thinks it possible to account for animal (and human) movements purely in terms of the physical events taking place in the body, while at the same time he wants to explain action, at a philosophical or analytical level, by way of the interaction of desires and beliefs. The attempt to combine those two approaches raises questions of their mutual consistency: Aristotle did not face up to those questions, but it is fair to observe that the issue is still a central and unresolved problem in the philosophy of the mind.

An outline survey of Aristotle's psychological theories does scant justice to his contributions to the subject; indeed, it may have the unwanted effect of belittling those contributions, since it is bound to stress the more abstract or general elements in Aristotle's thought. It is above all in the detail—both scientific and philosophical—of his account that Aristotle's genius shines out: a single page of his own writings will reveal more clearly than any summary the perspicuity, the intellectual acumen, and the scientific richness which justify his pre-eminence in the history of the study of mind and its place in nature.   JBA

The standard translation of Aristotle, and the only complete English translation, was prepared by several scholars under the general editorship of J. A. Smith and Sir David Ross; usually known as the 'Oxford translation', it is now available in two volumes (revised by Jonathan Barnes) under the title *The Complete Works of Aristotle* (1984).

arousal. Arousal differs from *attention in that it involves a general rather than a particular increase (or decrease) in perceptual or motor activity. There can, however, be quite specific 'arousal', such as sexual arousal. General arousal is mediated by a diffuse neural system, centred in the brain stem, which not only sets a level from *sleep to wakefulness (and sometimes over-arousal) but also provides moment-to-moment changes of arousal which are usually appropriate to the prevailing situation, or task in hand. A great deal is known of the neurology of arousal (Milner 1971), especially in the amygdala.

Subtle moment-to-moment changes of arousal are experienced, for example, while driving a car, arousal immediately increasing with any small unexpected event or situation. It has been suggested that *fatigue results from over-arousal, the blurring of *perception perhaps being due to raised 'neural noise', or increased randomness of neural signals (which may also occur in *ageing) in over-arousal. Experiments conducted on vigilance during the Second World War found that radar operators and others looking out for infrequent signals or events rapidly became inefficient as their level of arousal dropped—errors or misses increasing in as short a time as half an hour. This loss of arousal in repetitive or boring situations (though it also occurs in the stress and danger of battle) can be distinguished experimentally from fatigue.

Arousal has been related to stress; indeed stress may be over-arousal. There is an optimal level of arousal, which has been thought of as following an inverted 'U', for performing a task. But the performance of skills at low arousal differs from that when arousal is 'over the top' of optimal arousal; this suggests that the arousal function is not truly U shaped. Errors under conditions of under-arousal tend to be omissions while over-arousal tends to lead to errors of commission or overcorrection.

Learning is improved with increase of arousal—again up to an optimum level, when over-arousal becomes associated with distractions of various kinds (Bills 1927; Sherwood 1965). There is considerable evidence that long-term but not short-term recall is improved with increased arousal. This is presumably because the laying-down of memory traces is more efficient, perhaps with more cross-associations for future reference, for learning while arousal is high. Many people learn to control and optimize their arousal level when working or studying, by varying the task, or perhaps with the aid of music, or (not to be recommended!) smoking. There is little point in working when arousal falls close to the level of sleep.

Bills, A. G. (1927). 'The influence of muscular tension on the efficiency of mental work'. *American Journal of Psychology*, 38.
Broadbent, D. E. (1971). *Decision and Stress*.
Crawford, A. (1961). 'Fatigue and driving'. *Ergonomics*, 4.
Milner, P. (1971). *Physiological Psychology*.
Sherwood, J. J. (1965). 'A relation between arousal and performance'. *American Journal of Psychology*, 78.
Welford, A. T. (1976). *Skilled Performance: Perceptual and Motor Skills*.

art and visual abstraction. The following attempts to demonstrate the role played by abstractive processes of contour, areal contrast, body axes, and movement in pictorial representation. Some of these abstractions show parallels with physiological mechanisms of the visual brain, as is demonstrated in Fig. 1. The treatment is restricted to the graphic arts in which mostly white–black contrasts are used. Colour effects are not treated, although they, too, may contribute to these abstractive processes.

In drawing, the artist uses a reduction to contours similar to that found in vision. A physiological basis of pattern perception in the visual system is the signalling of outlines signifying the contoured forms of the object seen. The draughtsman usually first sketches these linear outlines and later fills them in with hatching or wash to give the illusion of light, shade, and plastic form. In vision the eye receives the projections of bright and dark areas on the retina, and the neuronal systems code them for relative brightness or darkness respectively, and enhance their linear borders. During the transfer of visual information from the eye to the brain, the contoured borders are accentuated progressively in the retina, the lateral geniculate, and the visual cortex (Jung and Baumgartner 1965). By means of this border contrast enhancement, the neurons of the visual cortex can signal complex patterns with linear contours. Fig. 1 shows the principles of this neurophysiological contour abstraction.

In sketching, the artist acts in accordance with the same visual laws, but proceeds in a direction opposite to the abstractive process of vision. He begins with the linear outlines and ends with a picture showing also the values of light and space (Jung 1971). In addition, he can delineate the structures and movements of the human body graphically, using oriented lines without contours, as is illustrated in Fig. 6.

1. Abstractions of contour, structure, and movement
2. Contour dominance
3. Uncontoured brightness contrast
4. Wash and colour-supplementing contour
5. Linearity, light effects, and style
6. Dynamic linear structures
7. Structural axes and representations of movements
8. Perception of axial clues and motion
9. Conclusion

1. Abstractions of contour, structure, and movement
Three main kinds of linear abstraction can be distinguished in the graphic arts: (i) the enhancement of form and contour by linear outlines; (ii) the emphasis of the

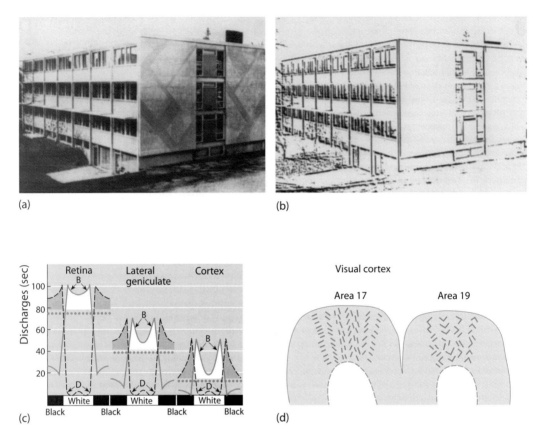

Fig. 1. Contour enhancement in the visual system by progressive effects of simultaneous contrast. The halftone picture (**a**) is transformed into the linear figure (**b**) by neuronal mechanisms of border contrast (**c**). The order of contour-signalling neurons in the visual cortex is shown in **d**.

a, b. Photographic imitation of contour abstraction, obtained by copying from displaced positive and negative photographic plates. **a** may correspond approximately to the retinal image, **b** to the information of the visual cortex. **c.** Neuronal responses to a light bar on black background show progressive contour enhancement from retina to cortex in the brightness system B (on-centre neurons signalling contrast brightness) and the darkness system D (off-centre neurons signalling contrast darkness). A comparison of the discharge rates of diffuse illumination (. . .) with contrast stimulation shows the contrast enhancement in the tinted and white areas for the brightness and darkness systems respectively. **d.** Scheme of neuronal columns in visual cortex areas for information about contours and angles of certain orientations. In the orientation columns the retinal image is abstracted into linear contours similar to **b**.

structural axes of the body, independent of contoured forms; and (iii) the representation of movement by schematic line drawings. To put it simply: outlines determine the form (Fig. 2), axial lines show the structure, and certain relations of structural axes signify a body in motion (Fig. 6).

Only the contour form of linear abstraction (i) can be explained by neurophysiological processes, as is shown in Fig. 1. Although the physiological basis of abstractions (ii) and (iii) is unknown, they may be characterized in *cy-bernetic terms as a reduction in redundant information about visual forms, in favour of information about axial orientation.

Figs. 2–6 show works of art, selected from different ages and cultures, in which the human body is predominantly depicted by linear contours, non-linear brightness contrast, or structural axes for the representation of motion. The figures demonstrate the power of linear expression in the graphic arts and the truth of the ancient saying that drawing is the art of omission. This omission is

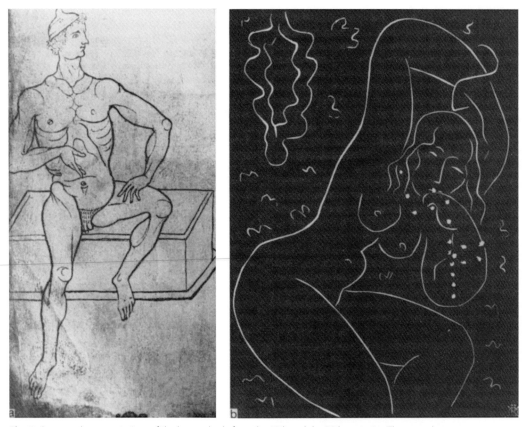

Fig. 2. Contoured representations of the human body from the 13th and the 20th centuries. The examples show opposite contrasts: black on white (**a**) and white on black (**b**). **a.** Medieval drawing of a sitting man in Villard d'Honnecourt's sketch-book (*c*.1230). It is limited mainly to the body contour with a few added lines indicating muscles and ribs. Pen on parchment. Left side, 14 × 7 cm of a 14 × 22 cm page. **b.** Modern contoured print by Matisse in white lines on black background (1944). It shows the essential outlines of a sitting female nude wearing a pearl necklace and surrounded by some background decoration. Linocut. 24·3 × 17·7 cm.

effected by abstractions to the essential values of contour, light, and movement.

2. Contour dominance

Forms and individuals can be recognized from a few contoured lines without other brightness or colour information. The building in Fig. 1*a* is perceived almost as clearly in the linear abstraction of Fig. 1*b*. This linear simplification is used by caricaturists to characterize individuals or constructs. Contoured drawings or prints are examples of this contour dominance. They may provide both form perception and aesthetic value, as in Figs. 2*a* and 2*b*.

Thus it seems to be true that outlines give sufficient information to characterize a form and that areal and colour contrast provide only additional and redundant information. With more radical reduction of redundant information even contours may be renounced, information being limited to the axial lines of body and limbs, as is shown in Fig. 6. The Stone Age pictures of the Franco-Cantabrian group, for example in Lascaux, have mainly contoured outlines in the naturalistic style of 10,000–8,000 years BC, whereas axial line reduction is mainly used in the late Stone Age rock painting of the sixth to fourth millennium BC in eastern Spain.

3. Uncontoured brightness contrast

Physiologists have demonstrated two kinds of visual contrast: one is border contrast, which enhances the contours by the so-called Mach bands (Ratliff 1971); and the other is areal contrast, which exaggerates the brightness differences of large surfaces, as investigated by Ewald *Hering (1878). In Hering's contrast, a bright area is seen brighter in a dark surround, and vice versa: a dark area appears blacker when framed by bright areas relatively independent of contoured borders. Hering's contrast may be seen as non-linear brightness differences. Some artists, such as Seurat and Signac, avoided all linear contours in their drawings and pictures, producing only a pointillistic surface effect (Ratliff 1971). This is demonstrated in Fig. 3, a typical uncontoured drawing by Seurat. Contours may be seen, at the borders of non-linear bright and dark areas, as a linear illusion caused by Mach bands.

The special uncontoured technique of Seurat is exceptional in the art of drawing. Most artists combine lines with areal contrast by supplementing the linear design with added brushwork and wash in different halftone gradations of brightness. In etchings, these halftones may be added by the mezzotint technique as shown in

Fig. 3. Non-linear drawing of a female nude made by G. Seurat in 1887 using pure bright–dark contrast. Light values, atmosphere, plastic form, and contour effects are obtained without lines by more or less dense rubbing of black chalk (*crayon conté*) on granulated paper. The black granules contrast with the white paper. Seurat avoided linear contours with his pointillist technique, both in black–white drawings and in coloured pictures. This sketch for the painting *Poseuses* was preceded by a contoured outline-drawing. 29·7 × 22·5 cm.

Fig. 4. Here Turner designed the original contoured etching (Fig. 4a) and a professional engraver completed it with mezzotint (4b). Linear and areal contrast are also combined in the so-called *Craik illusion, resulting in border-induced brightness and darkness, which Ratliff (1971) discusses for East Asiatic brush paintings. The Craik effect may enhance areal contrasts.

4. Wash and colour-supplementing contour

Visual forms and patterns are most easily reproduced as outline drawings. This linear contour abstraction may remain dominant, as in Fig. 2, or may be supplemented by surface effects adding brightness and colour contrast (Fig. 4b). Both types are found in the pictorial art of all ages. The most ancient examples come from neolithic cave art, which produced many contoured and coloured drawings of animals. In this Stone Age naturalistic style, the first outline sketch either remains linear or is completed in colour. A linear style is also prominent in medieval pen drawings and in the earliest woodcuts. All woodcuts of the 15th century were contoured, before Dürer introduced more or less dense hatchings and cross-hatchings to the woodblock to depict the values of light and shade. The frequent colouring of the early woodcuts and the adding of wash to contoured drawings shows that there was a need for additional colour and surface values. These are often completed by refined brushwork, so that the subjects drawn appear as plastic forms in an envelope of light. Some artists also prefer linearity for light and shade and achieve these effects by the use of hatching and cross-hatching—for example, Dürer and Raphael. Others express non-linear values of light, shade, and colour by additional brushwork (e.g. Tiepolo), or by special techniques with chalk (Seurat, Fig. 3). All variations, including the soft shining surface of the late Nazarene or Pre-Raphaelite drawings of the nude, and the vigorous linear or surface contrasts of modern art (which often deform or destroy the contours), have their special aesthetic appeal. In prints made as reproductions, aquatint and mezzotint techniques are used to represent surface values of bright and dark areas similar to brushwork and wash in the drawings (see Fig. 4b).

5. Linearity, light effects, and style

The linear and non-linear tendencies of the graphic arts vary in different style epochs, often alternating in a process of reaction and counter-reaction (Jung 1971). For example, in the 19th century academic linearization and classicizing contour enhancement provoked the emphasis on light and colour in the Romantic movement and in Turner's aquarelles. Later the rather dry figure drawing of historical painters gave way to the impressionists' turbulent drawing style with dissolution of patterns and dispersed light. This again was followed by the sharply contrasting boundaries seen in art nouveau, the black–white areal

Fig. 4. Linear contours of an etching by J. M. W. Turner (**a**) completed in 1812 as a mezzotint (**b**) in halftones of light and shade. 18·7 × 26·5 cm. **a.** The pure linear etching depicts the landscape mainly by contours, with a few hatchings at the trees and on the human figure. It was sketched by Turner himself and intended to be mezzotinted by a professional engraver. **b.** Completed mezzotint. The engraver, W. Say, has added the halftones, varying from a dark blackish brown in the foreground to light yellowish brown in the buildings of the background. The scraped, smooth parts of the plate ground are seen as light areas in contrast to the dark, roughened, unscraped areas.

contrast of the expressionists' woodcuts, the contour distortions of the fauvists, and the tendency to deformation in many modern artists following Picasso (Jung 1974).

Although the neo-impressionists, such as Seurat, used physiological concepts of colour contrast for their art theories, the influence of these scientific tendencies on the pictorial arts was negligible. Discussions of art on the basis of science are limited to a few aspects of contrast and colour, already mentioned by *Leonardo da Vinci in his treatise on painting written around 1500. Many a limit can be transgressed in free artistic creation, but even the artists followed physiological laws of visual perception when they applied principles of contour and brightness vision almost instinctively in their work, as *Helmholtz remarked as early as 1871. The abstractive processes of vision in art receive little attention in the monographs on art and visual perception. Ratliff (1971) has depicted good examples of contour-induced brightness effects in oriental art.

6. Dynamic linear structures

Many purely contoured drawings from all historical periods—for example, the medieval Fig. 2*a* or the classicizing drawings by Flaxman and others—appear static, dry, and often somewhat boring. To avoid this the artist tends to vivify or dissolve these pure contours by interrupting them or adding a variety of line or light values. Dynamic effects may be obtained by irregular contours and lively hatching without wash and areal brightness contrast. Fig. 5 shows two modern drawings of human figures in which dynamic linear structures are added. In *information theory, these dynamic additions would be called redundant, since they do not supply further information about the forms, but they are aesthetically rewarding.

A vivid drawing technique and a dissolution of contours may depict emotional values or physical movement. However, dynamic lines are not necessarily expressions of lively motion. In Fig. 5 the dynamically drawn women appear to move slowly from a standing or sitting posture, in Fig. 5a bending forward during the act of washing, and in Fig. 5b turning sideways. Slight modifications to this dynamic drawing technique are used to depict moving figures. Motion *per se*, however, can also be expressed without any linear redundancy by very simple drawings of the essential body axes in single lines, as is shown in Fig. 6.

Here the redundancy is reduced, whereas in Fig. 5 it is increased.

In modern art the tendency towards contour distortion and expressionist deformation is counteracted by a tendency in the opposite direction, towards natural contour representation and calm. Matisse is a good example of this predilection for clean, simple, and balanced line drawings, avoiding extreme expression and wild movements or gestures. This return from excessive extravagance to the rules of classic art is marked more in the works of French than German or British artists of recent decades. From his Fauves period (1905), when he used contrasting surfaces or dissolved outlines, Matisse turned to clear and serene contours. The odalisque-like women of his pen drawings, etchings, and linocuts made in 1930–48 show sharp outlines without effects of light or movement. The background is usually formed by decorative additions at a distance from the body, as in Fig. 2b. His contoured bodies signify relaxed rest or perhaps quiet movement. Matisse himself remarked: 'Je veux un art d'équilibre, de pureté, qui n'inquiète ni trouble. Je veux que l'homme fatigué, surmené, éreinté, goûte devant mes peintures le calme et le repos.'

a   b

Fig. 5. Dynamic structures with dissolving contours in modern drawings of female bodies. **a.** Weisgerber's woman standing in front of a dressing-table is drawn with irregular hatching and restless contour lines. Hence body and objects appear more vivid than in pure contour drawings, but the impression of quiet stance bending forward prevails over movement. Pen black. *c.*1913. 20·7 × 15·3 cm. **b.** Friesz's sitting woman turned to the left, and the signature, are drawn in vivid lines. Quick and turbulent hatchings and interrupted contours enhance the impression of a turning movement from a quiet sitting posture. Pencil. *c.*1928. 39·6 × 29·0 cm.

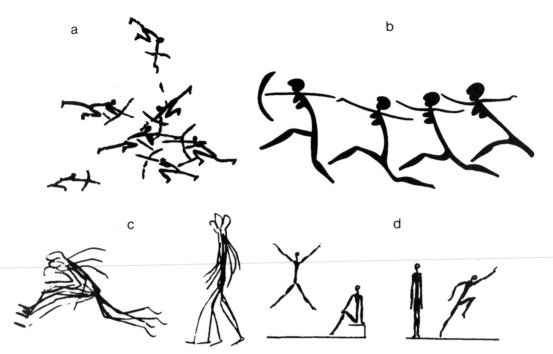

Fig. 6. Human motion depicted by oriented axial line patterns in Stone Age rock paintings and in modern drawings. **a.** A battle of archers (eastern Spain), painted in simple axial lines of limbs and trunk signifying moving and shooting men. Red lines on grey rock. *c*.5000 BC. 10·5 × 12·0 cm. **b.** Running and dancing women drawn in simple line figures by Australian Aborigines. Red paint on grey rock. *c.* AD 1700(?). 50 × 150 cm. **c.** Modern drawing of a running and walking man with multiple axial lines of body and limbs. Pen black. *c*.6 × 10 cm. **d.** Sitting, standing, jumping, and running men, with slightly thickened orientated lines indicating the limb postures. Pen black. *c*.6 × 10 cm.

7. Structural axes and representation of movements

The oriented axis of a body or limb can be drawn in a single line. The combined arrangement of these lines depicts characteristic postures of the human figure that can be recognized at a single glance. These axes are independent of body contours but are related to the position of the joints in various postures. When the limbs are drawn in positions of walking or running, the viewer immediately recognizes these movements in the immobile picture. Fig. 6 shows examples of this depiction of motion in various cultures, from Stone Age rock paintings down to modern art.

Axial structures have been used since prehistoric times to depict men and animals in motion. Linear human figures of this type are typical of the 'Levante' rock paintings in eastern Spain made about 5000 BC (Fig. 6*a*). Similar figures appear in Viking pictures in Scandinavia in the first centuries AD, in the later South African bushman drawings, and in Australian Aboriginal rock pictures (Fig. 6*b*). Their use by these very different populations, who had no cultural relations with each other, demonstrates that the representation of axial structures and movement is a universal feature in the human visual arts. Such linear figures depicting running men are recognizable at a glance and are even understood by children as signifying movement.

8. Perception of axial clues and motion

The neuronal mechanisms of the visual abstraction of body axes are unknown. One can only presume that they may be related to Hubel and Wiesel's orientation columns and direction-specific responses in the visual cortex (Hubel and Wiesel 1959) (see VISUAL SYSTEM: PHYSIOLOGY). The perception of axial clues, however, has been well investigated since Marey began his chronophotographic analyses of body movements marked by axial lines of the limbs. G. Johansson (1973) has shown that we can recognize complex movements of human bodies in a film from a few dots positioned at the limbs. This extremely reduced information on spatio-temporal patterns is integrated into a *Gestalt perception of moving bodies.

9. Conclusion

We have come to the general conclusion that forms are determined by outlines, organic structures by axial lines, and bodies in motion by arrangements of structural axes. These principles of visual abstraction appear to be valid for both visual representation and cognition.

The few examples of visual abstractions in graphic art discussed with Figs. 2–6 show that the artist, albeit dependent on the physiological laws of vision, has some freedom of selection and variation. According to his concepts he can express what he wants to say by different techniques. In spite of these various possibilities, art is not completely autonomous, since its effect on the viewer is processed by the viewer's visual system. The draughtsman can add colour and wash to contour drawings to obtain surface values in an envelope of light, but the effect on the viewer is determined by the mechanisms of contrast vision. The draughtsman can depict motion in a static picture by arranging contours and axial lines, but this is only an illusion of movement. We perceive moving figures in these drawings, although there is, of course, no real movement in them. Visual recognition, trained by experience and memory, helps us to see motion in the simple line figures of Fig. 6. A further information reduction to an immobile pattern of spots positioned at the joints, such as used by Johansson in his experiments, is not seen as moving. Only real motion of these spots, as seen in a film, transforms them into apparently moving bodies.

In general, the significance and the beauty of art are apparent only to those who can see and are trained in viewing. The artist himself is not interested in the process of seeing, and lets the physiologist investigate visual mechanisms. Leonardo, who discovered certain laws of contrast vision, was unique in being both an artist and a scientist. The vain attempts of the neo-impressionists to build a theory of painting on the physiology of colour contrast show the limits of the relation between physiology and art. Modern techniques of Op Art, deliberately using optical illusions to induce stereo-patterns and movement perceptions, are confined to a narrow field.

Although it may be useful for the artist to know some of the principles of vision and their possible applications to the visual arts, the relevance of physiological laws to the visual arts and to *aesthetic values is limited. Art has a greater degree of freedom than science. Even if the scientist elucidates certain principles and limits of the visual perception of form, science cannot dictate to the artist what he should do. The frontiers of the visual arts must be set by the creative artist himself.

See also ART AS PERCEPTUAL EXPERIENCE.   RJ

Arnheim, R. (1956). *Art and Visual Perception*.

Gombrich, E. H. (1962). *Art and Illusion* (2nd edn.).
Helmholtz, H. von (1871–3). *Optisches über Malerei*.
Hering, E. (1878). *Zur Lehre vom Lichtsinne*.
Hubel, D. H., and Wiesel, T. N. (1959). 'Receptive fields of single neurones in the cat's striate cortex'. *Journal of Physiology*, 148.
Johansson, G. (1973). 'Visual perception of biological motion and a model of its analysis'. *Perception and Psychophysics*, 14.
Jung, R. (1974). 'Neuropsychologie und Neurophysiologie des Kontur- und Formsehen in Zeichnung and Malerei'. In Wieck, H. H. (ed.), *Psychopathologie Musischer Gestaltungen*.
——and Baumgartner, G. (1965). 'Neuronenphysiologie der visuellen und paravisuellen Rindenfelder'. *Proceedings of the 8th International Congress of Neurology* (Vienna), vol. iii.
Livingstone, M. (2002), *Vision and Art: The Biology of Seeing*.
Kleint, B. (1969). *Bildlehre, Elemente und Ordnung der Sichtbaren Welt*.
Ratliff, F. (1971). 'Contour and contrast'. *Proceedings of the American Philosophical Society*, 115.

art as perceptual experience.

1. The objectivity of images
2. The perception of images

1. The objectivity of images

For most practical purposes, human beings do not get into much trouble when they base their conduct on the conviction that the world they see is the world as it is. It is a reasonable simplification, and only occasional refinements call for minor corrections. 'This colour looks yellower than it is in the daylight.' 'In this dress she looks taller than she is.' 'The mountains are further away than they look.' Corrections of this kind consist in revising a particular view on the basis of one's total perceptual resources. One may correct, for example, an observed size by comparing it with the length of a yardstick, or test a colour against a sample swatch.

These corrections are necessary as long as we use visual images as intermediary information for the purpose of getting along in what we call the physical world. The physical world, known to us through the totality of our perceptual experiences and the inferences suggested by these experiences, is governed by laws we cannot ignore with impunity. If one builds a house whose walls look vertical but are not, the house may collapse. Hence the need for correcting our images.

In the visual arts such corrections are inappropriate because a painting or piece of sculpture is not a stand-in for physical objects, to be subjected to physical handling. Rather a work of art is a statement *about* such objects and other facts of experience. Being perceptual statements, the images produced by art objects are final in all their properties. A giant in a painting by Goya is as large as he looks. The Rialto bridge in a view of Venice is, rightly or wrongly, as far away as we see it. The weightiness of a wooden figure by Ernst Barlach has little to do with the weight of the wood, and a certain orange in a painting by

Matisse is orange, even though it might look red when put somewhere else. What *looks* vertical *is* vertical.

Are we then to say that the perceptual features of the mental images we call works of art are purely subjective? 'Subjective' is a dangerous term, to be used with caution. Those visual qualities are subjective in the sense that they require a pair of functioning eyes in the observer. Without eyes there is no picture. And yet, images have an objectivity of their own, which we acknowledge when we say that a tired tourist looking at Leonardo's cartoon of the Virgin with St Anne may see something pale, stiff, indifferent, but his image has to be discounted. The tourist has failed to see the picture. The cartoon contains objective qualities of expression and compositional relation that must be fully perceived to be appreciated. Only because art images are objective facts can there be critical dialogue about their nature. Only because images are objective facts can the eyes of a student be opened by a perceptive teacher.

Somebody may assert, 'In this etching by Picasso the head of the Minotaur is much too large in relation to his body', and be told, 'But in relation to all the other small figures in the picture, the large size of the head is exactly right!' The first judge has been convicted of misinterpretation caused by restricted vision. There is no way of avoiding the debate about the true perceptual structure of the picture by insisting on one's right to look subjectively.

The observer, however, has a mental structure of his own. When one of Picasso's paintings is used by psychologists in a personality test—as in fact has been done—someone who is being tested may report that the figures in the painting look at each other with bitter hatred. Such a response cannot be brushed aside as irrelevant. It may not do justice to the picture, but it describes the result of the encounter between two mental structures, namely the perceptual image received and the personal views, needs, and attitudes of the beholder. Such encounters attain more general importance when a historian notes how differently certain cultural periods react to works of a particular style, for example to Gothic architecture, Roman portraiture, or the paintings of El Greco. The interplay between the viewer and the work of art viewed sheds light on the objective structures of both parties. These structures can be extrapolated from the context by a comparison between many different works seen by the same viewer or, vice versa, between many different responses to the same work. If you collect and compare the responses to the Laocoön group in the Vatican over the last 500 years, you will learn something about the work's objective nature and qualities.

2. The perception of images

The ability to see visual representations at all cannot be taken for granted. On closer scrutiny this ability turns out to be a combination of two abilities. (i) The viewer can recognize the subject matter, even though the image varies from the model in size, colour, spatial dimensions, etc. A primitive tribesman, confronted with a photograph for the first time, may see only a flat object with a mottled surface. But the same tribesman may recognize simply shaped outlines of human faces, fishes, or the sun. So may a monkey, looking at similarly simple pictures—a remarkable feat of perceptual abstraction. (ii) The viewer is able to conceive of images as representations of kinds of subjects existing elsewhere. Instead of, or in addition to, responding to a portrait by saying, 'A smiling woman is looking at me'—an experience that can lead in extreme cases to actual delusions—the viewer realizes, 'This picture is meant to look like someone who actually lived in Italy in the past.' A monkey, as far as we know, could not treat a picture in this way as a referential statement.

A picture may be called a *self-image* when it is taken as a visual expression of its own properties, and a *likeness* when it is taken as a statement about other objects, kinds of objects, or properties. The first conception, more elementary, can exist without the second; the second, more sophisticated, combines with the first.

Both abilities to deal with images may occur at various levels of abstraction. Man and animal would be unable to see a simple outline figure as a human face unless perception consisted in the grasping of general structural features rather than in the mechanical recording of all individual detail. In the arts, this fact is demonstrated to us, for example, when we step close to a portrait by Frans Hals and find that the face, moustache, and lace collar disintegrate into a qualitatively different pattern of brushstrokes. With changing distance, the level of abstraction has shifted.

Observe now that the structural features of shape and colour which make us see a Dutch cavalier on the canvas are perceptual generalities. The roundness of a face, the curliness of hair, the whiteness of a collar are examples of very general qualities, found everywhere. Hence, seeing a clearly shaped thing means also seeing a *kind* of structural behaviour. This sort of generality remains subordinated to the objects portrayed in the naturalistic paintings of a Van Eyck or Holbein. It comes increasingly to the fore in highly abstract styles, for example in the arts of our century. In such works the formal features predominate to such an extent that they subdue the vehicle of subject matter. In a reclining woman by Henry Moore the particular shapes of a female body are reduced to very general although characteristic curvatures of surfaces and volumes. Viewed even more abstractly, the sculptor's piece of wood or stone becomes an image of man's relation to the earth, on which his body reposes; and finally one may go beyond the distinction between the organic and the inorganic and see a grouping of masses in which characteristics of living bodies and rolling hills combine indistinguishably in an image of the forms of nature.

When the references to natural subject matter are entirely suppressed and representation is entrusted to purely 'abstract', non-mimetic shapes, colours, and movement, the artist probes the outer limits of the imagery which is accessible to man as a symbolizing animal.

See also ART AND VISUAL ABSTRACTION.   RA

artificial intelligence *(see opposite)*

artificial life. As *artificial intelligence is concerned with understanding rational thought through creating intelligent machines, so artificial life is concerned with understanding the principles underlying life, through synthesizing lifelike properties in computer simulations or in physical implementations. The motivation stretches back at least as far as the 1st century AD, when Hero of Alexandria described working models of animals and humans, using hydraulics and pneumatics. From the Middle Ages on, technological developments in clockwork led to increasingly sophisticated automata that aroused admiration for their lifelike properties. In the late 20th century, technological developments in computing allowed people to attempt to recreate different aspects of the properties of living organisms in simulations. The field of artificial life became identified under that name from a workshop organized by Chris Langton in Los Alamos in 1987, bringing together physicists, computer scientists, complexity theorists, and biologists with a common interest in trying to understand the abstract principles behind the properties of life that might underlie not only carbon-based life as we know it on this planet, but also other possible life forms elsewhere in the universe—including potentially artificially created life forms. A series of conferences and a journal form a focus for a loosely defined field distinguished by its interdisciplinarity.

Among computing pioneers with an interest in artificial life in the 1950s before the term was invented, Alan Turing modelled possible mechanisms for morphogenesis that could produce large-scale patterns through only short-scale local interactions. John von Neumann used cellular automata to describe how a (simulated) physical mechanism could replicate itself; in showing how this could be done with one part of the mechanism both directing the construction of a new version of the remainder and then being copied directly itself, he foreshadowed the later discovery of the role of DNA. Cellular automata were later used by John Horton Conway for the 'Game of Life', where local interactions between neighbouring cells on a two-dimensional lattice (displayable as black and white dots on a screen) can, with the appropriate update rules, lead to global phenomena such as 'gliders' travelling across the screen and interacting with

each other. Artificial life now includes the study of the origin of life, artificial chemistry, self-organization, morphogenesis, evolutionary and adaptive dynamics, robots and autonomous agents, computer viruses, communication, and collective behaviour. Any aspect of living organisms that differentiates them from lifeless matter is a possible topic, from metabolism and self-repair to learning and behaviour. Also included are studies on the origin and evolution of language, though logic and rational thought would be considered to be traditionally the domain of artificial intelligence.

The different disciplines represented cover a range of motivations. Some theoretical biologists seek to understand real life using the new tools afforded by computer simulations, and new ideas from complexity theory. Computational neuroscience, and neuroethology—the relationship between brains and behaviour—are areas where use of computers has yielded new theoretical insights. In contrast, some computer scientists have the different goal of creating 'real artificial life' within a computer (artificial here meaning 'synthesized' rather than 'fake'); this leads to philosophical debates on just what is meant by such terms. There is a further different interest in artificial life that is application driven; designers of complex systems ranging from robots to telecommunication networks recognize that conventional designs have, so far, been lacking the robustness, the adaptivity, and the ability to self-repair that living systems have, and hope to learn practical lessons from this field. Examples where practical insights have resulted from artificial life approaches include the Sojourner Rover robot sent to Mars in 1997, based on ideas from Rodney Brooks's group at the Massachusetts Institute of Technology; evolutionary methods for optimizing the design of aircraft wings by British Aerospace and other manufacturers; the use of algorithms based on models of ant behaviour for dynamic routing; and load balancing by various telecommunication companies.   IRH

Brooks, R. A. (2002). *Robot: The Future of Flesh and Machines.*

Conway, J. H. (2000). *On Numbers and Games* (2nd edn. First published 1976).

astigmatism. Defect of vision due to the radius of curvature of the optics of the eye—especially the cornea—being unequal at different orientations around the visual axis. Lines or bars at different orientations are not all simultaneously in focus, and there can be distortions for some orientations. It is well corrected by suitable spectacles.

astrology. Anyone who has taken even the most casual interest in astrology will have noticed that, contrary to all common sense, it *seems* to work. That is to say, the personal characteristics that are supposed to be governed by

(cont. on page 64)

artificial intelligence (AI)

IGOR ALEXANDER

The process of designing machines with abilities modelled on human thought. While this mostly involves writing computer programs with human-like characteristics, it has implications for the design of robots and raises philosophical questions about machine–human comparisons.

1. Origins and ambitions
2. Knowledge, logic, and learning
3. Evolution, agents, and brain–mind comparisons

1. Origins and ambitions

Artificial intelligence may be said to have begun in 1950 when Claude Shannon of the Bell Telephone Laboratories in the United States wrote an ingenious program that was to be the forerunner of all chess-playing machines. This work drastically changed the accepted perception of stored-program computers which, since their birth in 1947, had been seen just as automatic calculating machines. Shannon's program added the promise of automated intelligent action to the actuality of automated calculation.

In Shannon's program the programmer stores in the computer the value of important features of board positions. A 'checkmate' being a winning position would have the highest value and the capture of more or less important pieces would be given relatively lower values. So, say that the computer is to take the next move, it would (by being programmed to follow the rules of the game) work out all the possible moves that the opponent might take. It could then work out which moves are available to itself at the next playing period and so on for several periods ahead in the search for a winning path through this 'tree' of possibilities. Sadly, the amount of computation needed to evaluate board positions grows prodigiously the further ahead the computer is meant to look. This process of searching through a large number of options became central in AI programs throughout the 1960s and the early 1970s. Other intelligent tasks besides game playing came under scrutiny: general problem solving, the control of robots, computer vision, speech processing, and the understanding of natural language. Solving general problems requires searches that are similar to those in the playing of board games. For example, to work out how to get from an address in London to the Artificial Intelligence laboratory at the University of Edinburgh, the problem can be represented as a search among subgoals (e.g. get to Edinburgh airport) and the use of 'means' such as airlines, taxis, or railways. The paths through the scheme are evaluated in terms of the reduction of cost and/or the reduction of time to the user. Robot control is similar. The physical rearrangement of objects in a space has to follow a strategy that involves the most efficient path between a current arrangement and the desired one, via several intermediate ones.

Computer vision and the recognition of speech required the programmer to determine that some features of the sensory input generated as signals from a video camera or a microphone are important. For example, for face recognition, the program has to identify the central positions of eyes, nose, and mouth and then measure the size of these objects and the distances between them. These measurements for a collection of faces are stored in a database, each together with the identity of the face. So were a face in the known set to be presented to the camera, finding the closest fit to the measurements stored in the database could identify it. Similarly the features of voices and the sound of words could be stored in databases for the purpose of eventual recognition.

Perhaps the most ambitious target for AI designers was the extraction of meaning from language. This goes beyond speech recognition and sentences could be presented in their written form. The difficulty is for the programmer to find rules that distinguish between sentences such as 'he broke the window with a rock' and 'he broke the window with a curtain'. This required a storage of long lists of words indicating whether they were instruments (rock) or embellishments (curtain) so that the correct meaning could be ascribed to them as they appear in a sentence.

However, early enthusiasm that AI computers could perform tasks comparable to those of humans were to be curtailed by the mid-1970s when poignant shortcomings emerged because the techniques used suffered from serious limitations. In 1971, the British mathematician Sir James Lighthill advised the major science-funding agency in the United Kingdom that AI was suffering from something he called the 'combinatorial explosion' which has been mentioned above in the chess-playing example. Every time the computer needs to look a further step ahead, the number of moves to be evaluated is that of the previous level multiplied by a large amount. In 1980, US philosopher John Searle levelled a second criticism at those who had claimed that they had enabled computers to understand natural language. Through his celebrated 'Chinese Room' argument he pointed out that the computer, by stubbornly following rules, was like a non-Chinese speaker using a massive set of rules to match questions expressed in Chinese symbols about a story also written in Chinese symbols. Given the time to examine many rules, the non-Chinese speaker could find the correct answers in Chinese symbols, without there being any understanding in the procedure. According to Searle, understanding requires a feeling of 'aboutness' for words and phrases which computers do not have. Also a third difficulty began to emerge: artificial intelligence depended too heavily on programmers having to work out in detail *how* to specify intelligent tasks. In pattern recognition, for example, ideas about how to recognize faces, scenes, and sounds turned out to be inadequate, particularly with respect to human performance.

2. Knowledge, logic, and learning

These censures had a healthy effect on AI. The 1980s saw a maturing of the field through the appearance of new methodologies dubbed *knowledge-based systems*, *expert systems*, and *artificial neural networks* (or *connectionism*). Effort in knowledge-based systems used formal logic to greater effect than before. The application of the logical rules of inheritance and resolution made more efficient use of knowledge stored in databases. For example, 'Socrates is a man' and 'All men are mortals' could lead to the knowledge that 'Socrates is mortal' by logical inference rather than by explicit storage, thus easing the problem of holding vast amounts of data in databases.

Expert systems was the name given to applications of AI which sought to transfer human expertise into knowledge bases so as to make such knowledge widely available to non-experts. This employed a 'knowledge engineer' who elicited knowledge from the expert and structured it appropriately for inclusion in a database. Facts and rules were clearly distinguished to enable them to be logically manipulated. Typical applications are in engineering design and fault finding, medical diagnosis and advice, and financial advice.

The aim of artificial neural network studies is to simulate mechanisms which, in the brain, are responsible for mind and intelligence. An artificial neuron learns to respond or not to respond ('fire' or not) to a pattern of signals from other neurons to which it is connected. A multi-layered network of such devices can learn (by automatically adjusting the strengths of the interconnections in the network) to classify patterns by learning to extract increasingly telling features of such patterns as data progresses through the layers. The presence of learning overcomes some of the difficulties previously due to the programmer having to decide exactly how to recognize complex visual and speech patterns. Also, a totally different class of artificial neural networks may be used to store and retrieve knowledge. Known as dynamic neural networks, such systems rely on the inputs of neurons being connected to the outputs of other neurons. This allows the net to be taught to keep a pattern of firing activity stable at its outputs. It can also learn to store sequences of patterns. These stable states or sequences are the stored knowledge of the network which may be retrieved in response to some starting state or a set of inputs also connected to the neurons in the net. So in terms of pattern recognition, not only can these networks learn to label patterns, but also 'know' what things look like in terms of neural firing patterns.

3. Evolution, agents, and brain–mind comparisons

Despite the above two major phases in the history of artificial intelligence, the subject is still developing, particularly in three domains: new techniques for creating intelligent programs, using computers to understand the complexities of brain and mind, and, finally, contributing to philosophical debate. The techniques added to the AI repertoire are evolutionary programming, artificial life, and intelligent software agents. Evolutionary programming borrows from human genetic development in the sense that some variants of a program may have a better performance than others. It is possible to represent the design parameters of a system as a sequence of values resembling a chromosome. An evolutionary program tests a range of systems against a performance criterion (the fitness function). It chooses the chromosomes of various system pairs that have good fitness behaviour to combine them and create a new generation of systems. This gives rise to increasingly more able systems even to the extent that their design holds surprises for expert designers. Such mimicking of a major mechanism of biological life leads to the concept of *artificial life*. For example, UK entrepreneur Steve Grand includes in his 'Creatures' game simulations of some biochemical processes to produce societies of virtual (computer-bound but observable) creatures with realistic life cycles and social interactions. This allows the game player to take care of a virtual creature in a game that gets close to the problems of survival in real life. The more general study of intelligent software agents takes virtual creatures into domains where they could perform useful tasks such as finding desired data on the internet. They are little programs that store the needs of a user and trawl the World Wide Web for this desired information. Also a burgeoning interest is in societies of such agents to discover how cooperation between them may lead to the solution of problems in distributed domains. Translated to multiple interacting robots, agent studies lead to a better understanding of flocking behaviour and the way that this achieves goals for the flock.

A better understanding of the brain flows from the study of artificial neural networks (ANNs). Accepting that the brain is the most complex machine in existence, ANNs are now being used to isolate some of its structural features in order to begin to understand their interactions. For example, it has been possible to suggest a theoretical basis for understanding dyslexia, visual hallucinations under the influence of drugs, and the nature of visual awareness in general. The latter and grander ambition feeds a philosophical debate on whether machines could think like humans that has paralleled AI for its entire existence. The question was first raised by British mathematician Alan Turing in 1950. His celebrated test was based on the external behaviour of an AI machine and its ability to fool a human interlocutor into thinking that it too was human. This debate has now moved on to discuss whether a machine could ever be conscious. The main arguments against this come from a belief that consciousness, being a 'first-person' phenomenon, cannot be approached from the 'third-person' position which is inherent in all man-made designs. The contrary arguments are put by those who feel that by simulating with great care the function and structure of the brain it will be possible both to understand the mechanisms of consciousness and to transfer them to a machine.

Aleksander, I. (2001). *How to Build a Mind: Machines with Imagination*.

——and Morton, B. H. (1993). *Neurons and Symbols*.

Boden, M. A. (ed.) (1996). *Artificial Intelligence* (2nd edn.).

Crick, F. (1994). *The Astonishing Hypothesis*.

Grand, S. (2000). *Creation: Life and How to Make it*.

Searle, J. R. (1980). 'Minds brains and programs'. *Behavioural and Brain Sciences*, 3.

Shannon, C. E. (1950). 'Programming a computer for playing chess'. *Phil. Mag.* 4.

Tecuci, G. (1998). *Building Intelligent Agents*.

Turing, A. M. (1950). 'Computing machinery and intelligence'. *Mind*, 59.

MARGARET BODEN

The science of making machines do the sorts of things that are done by human minds. Such things include holding a conversation, answering questions sensibly on the basis of incomplete knowledge, assembling another machine from its components given the blueprint, learning how to do things better, playing *chess, writing or translating stories, understanding analogies, neurotically repressing knowledge that is too threatening to admit consciously, learning to classify visual or auditory patterns, composing a poem or a sonata, and recognizing the various things seen in a room—even an untidy and ill-lit room. AI helps one to realize how enormous is the background knowledge and thinking (computational) power needed to do even these everyday things.

The 'machines' in question are typically digital computers, but AI is not the study of computers. Rather, it is the study of intelligence in thought and action. Computers are its tools, because its theories are expressed as computer programs which are tested by being run on a machine. Some AI programs are lists of symbolic rules (if this is the case then do that, else do another . . .). Others specify 'brainlike' networks made of many simple, interconnected, computational units. These types of AI are called traditional (or classical) and connectionist, respectively. They have differing, and largely complementary, strengths and weaknesses.

Other theories of intelligence are expressed verbally, either as psychological theories of thinking and behaviour, or as philosophical arguments about the nature of knowledge and *purpose and the relation of mind to body (the *mind–body problem). Because it approaches the same subject matter in different ways, AI is relevant to psychology and the philosophy of mind.

Similarly, attempts to write programs that can interpret the two-dimensional image from a TV camera in terms of the three-dimensional objects in the real world (or which can recognize photographs or drawings as representations of solid objects) help make explicit the range and subtlety of knowledge and unconscious inference that underlie our introspectively 'simple' experiences of seeing. Much of this knowledge is tacit (and largely innate) knowledge about the ways in which, given the laws of optics, physical surfaces of various kinds can give rise to specific visual images on a retina (or camera). Highly complex computational processes are needed to infer the nature of the physical object (or of its surfaces), on the basis of the two-dimensional image.

If we think of an AI system as a picture of a part of the mind, we must realize that a functioning program is more like a film of the mind than a portrait of it. Programming one's hunches about how the mind works is helpful in two ways. First, it enables one to express richly structured psychological theories in a rigorous, and testable, fashion. Second, it forces one to suggest specific hypotheses about precisely how a psychological change can come about. Even if (as in connectionist systems: see below) one only provides a learning rule, rather than telling the AI system precisely what to learn, that rule has to be rigorously expressed; a different rule will lead to different performance.

In general, it is easier to model logical and mathematical reasoning (which people find difficult) than to simulate high-level perception or language understanding (which we do more or less effortlessly). Significant progress has been made, for instance, in recognizing keywords and grammatical structure, and AI programs can even come up with respectable, though juvenile, puns and jokes. But many sentences, and jokes, assume a large amount of world knowledge, including culture-specific knowledge about sport, fashion, politics, soap operas . . . the list is literally endless. There is little or no likelihood than an actual AI system could use language as well as we can, because it is too difficult to provide, and to structure, the relevant knowledge (much of it is tacit, and very difficult to bring into consciousness). But this need not matter, if all we want is a psychological theory that explains how these human capacities are possible. Similarly, research in AI has shown that highly complex, and typically unconscious, computational processes are needed to infer the nature of physical objects from the image reaching the retina / camera.

Traditional philosophical puzzles connected with the mind–body problem can often be illuminated by AI, because modelling a psychological phenomenon on a computer is a way of showing that and how it is *possible* for that phenomenon to arise in a physical system. For instance, people often feel that only a spiritual being (as opposed to a bodily one) could have purposes and try to achieve them, and the problem then arises of how the spiritual being, or mind, can possibly tell the body what to do, so that the body's hand can try to achieve the mind's purpose of, say, picking a daisy. It is relevant to ask whether, and how, a program can enable a machine to show the characteristic features of purpose. Is its behaviour guided by its idea of a future state? Is that idea sometimes illusory or mistaken (so that the 'daisy' is made of plastic, or is really a buttercup)? Does it symbolize what it is doing in terms of goals and subgoals (so that the picking of the daisy may be subordinate to the goal of stocking the classroom nature table)? Does it use this representation to help plan its actions (so that the daisies on the path outside the sweetshop are picked, rather than those by the petrol station)? Does it vary its means–end activities so as to achieve its goal in different circumstances (so that buttercups will do for the nature table if all the daisies have died)? Does it learn how to do so better (so that daisies for a daisy-chain are picked with long stalks)? Does it judge which purposes are the more important, or easier to achieve, and behave accordingly (if necessary, abandoning the daisy picking when a swarm of bees appears with an equally strong interest in the daisies)? Questions like these, asked with specific examples of functioning AI systems in mind, cannot fail to clarify the concept of purpose. Likewise, philosophical problems about the nature and criteria of knowledge can be clarified by reference to programs that process and use knowledge, so that AI is relevant to *epistemology.

AI is concerned with mental processing in general, not just with mathematics and logical deduction. It includes computer models of perception, thought, motivation, and emotion. *Emotion, for instance, is not just a feeling: emotions are scheduling mechanisms that have evolved to enable finite creatures with many potentially conflicting motives to choose what to do, when. (No matter how hungry one is, one had better stop eating and run away if faced by a tiger.) So a complex animal is going to need some form of computational interrupt, and some way of 'stacking' and realerting those unfulfilled intentions that shouldn't, or needn't, be abandoned. In human language users, motivational–emotional processing includes deliberately thought–out plans and contingency plans, and anticipation of possible outcomes from the various actions being considered.

One important variety of AI is connectionism, or artificial neural networks. Very few connectionist systems are implemented in fundamentally connectionist hardware. Most are simulated (as virtual machines) in digital computers. That is, the program does not list a sequence of symbolic rules but simulates many interconnected 'neurons', each of which does only very simple things. Connectionism enables a type of learning wherein the 'weights' on individual units in the network are gradually altered until recognition errors are minimized. Unlike learning in classical AI, the unfamiliar pattern need not be specifically described to the system before it can be learnt; however, it must be describable in the 'vocabulary' used for the system's input. Connectionism allows that beliefs and perceptions may be grounded on partly inconsistent evidence, and that most concepts are not strictly defined in terms of necessary and sufficient conditions. Many connectionist systems represent a concept as a pattern of activity across the whole network; the units eventually settle into a state of maximum, though not necessarily perfect, equilibrium. Connectionism is a powerful way of implementing pattern recognition and the 'intuitive' association of ideas. But it is very limited for implementing hierarchical structure of sequential processes, such as are involved in deliberate planning. Some AI research aims to develop 'hybrid' systems combining the strengths of traditional and connectionist AI. Certainly, the full range of adult human psychology cannot be captured by either of these approaches alone.

The main areas of AI include natural language understanding (see SPEECH RECOGNITION BY MACHINE), machine vision (see PATTERN RECOGNITION), problem solving and game playing (see COMPUTER CHESS), robotics, automatic programming, and the development of programming languages. Among the practical applications most recently developed or currently being developed are medical diagnosis and treatment (where a program with specialist knowledge of, say, bacterial infections answers the questions of and elicits further relevant information from a general practitioner who is uncertain which drug to prescribe in a given case); prediction of share prices on the stock exchange; assessment of creditworthiness; speech analysis and speech synthesis; the composition of music, including jazz improvisation; location of mineral deposits, such as gold or oil; continuous route planning for car drivers; programs for playing chess, bridge, or Go, etc.; teaching some subject such as geography, or electronics, to students with differing degrees of understanding of the material to be explored; the automatic assembly of factory-made items, where the parts may have to be inspected first for various types of flaw and where they need not be accurately positioned at a precise point in the assembly line, as is needed for the automation in widespread use today; and the design of complex systems, whether electrical circuits or living spaces or some other, taking into account factors that may interact with each other in complicated ways (so that a mere 'checklist' program would not be adequate to solve the design problem).

An area closely related to AI is artificial life (A-life). This is a form of mathematical biology. It uses computational concepts and models to study (co-)evolution and self-organization, both of which apply to life in general, and to explain specific aspects of living things—such as navigation in insects or flocking in birds. (The dinosaurs in *Jurassic Park* were computer generated using simple A-life algorithms.) One example of A-life is evolutionary robotics, where the robot's neural network 'brain' and/or sensorimotor anatomy is not designed by hand but evolved over thousands of generations. The programs make random changes in their own rules, and a fitness function is applied, either automatically or manually, to select the best from the resulting examples; these are then used to breed the next generation. Some A-life scientists, but not all, accept 'strong' A-life: the view that a virtual creature, defined by computer software, could be genuinely alive. And some believe that A-life could help us to find an agreed definition of what 'life' is. All the minds we know of are embodied in living things, and some people argue that only a living thing could have a mind, or be intelligent. If that is right, then success in AI cannot be achieved without success in A-life. (In both cases, however, 'success' might be interpreted either as merely showing mindlike/lifelike behaviour or as being genuinely intelligent/alive.)

The social implications of AI are various. As with all technologies, there are potential applications which may prove bad, good, or ambiguous in human terms. A competent medical diagnosis program could be very useful, whereas a competent military application would be horrific for those at the receiving end, and a complex data-handling system could be well or ill used in many ways by individuals or governments. Then there is the question of what general implication AI will be seen to have for the commonly held 'image of man'. If it is interpreted by the public as implying that people are 'nothing but clockwork, really', then the indirect effects on self-esteem and social relations could be destructive of many of our most deeply held values. But it could (and should) be interpreted in a radically different and less dehumanizing way, as showing how it is possible for material systems (which, according to the biologist, we are) to possess such characteristic features of human psychology as subjectivity, purpose, freedom, and choice. The central theoretical concept in AI is *representation*, and AI workers ask how a (programmed) system constructs, adapts, and uses its inner representations in interpreting and changing its world. On this view, a programmed computer may be thought of as a subjective system (subject to illusion and error much as we are) functioning by way of its idiosyncratic view of the world. By analogy, then, it is no longer scientifically disreputable, as it has been thought to be for so long, to describe people in these radically subjective terms also. AI can therefore counteract the dehumanizing

influence of the natural sciences that has been part of the mechanization of our world picture since the scientific revolution of the 16th and 17th centuries.

Boden, M. A. (1987). *Artificial Intelligence and Natural Man* (2nd rev. edn.).
——(1990). *The Creative Mind.*
——(ed.) (1990). *The Philosophy of Artificial Intelligence.*
Clark, A. J. (1990). *Associative Engines.*
Cope, D. (2001). *Virtual Music.*
Feigenbaum, E. A., and Feldman, J. (eds.) (1963). *Computers and Thought.*
Jullam, J. (ed.) (1995). *Hybrid Problems, Hybrid Solutions.*
Levy, S. J. (1992). *Artificial Life.*
McClelland, J. L., and Rumelhart, D. E. (eds.) (1986). *Parallel Distributed Processing: Explorations in the Microstructure of Cognition,* 2 vols.
Marr, D. A. (1980). *Vision.*
Minsky, M. L. (1985). *The Society of Mind.*
Whitby, B. (1996). *Reflections on Artificial Intelligence.*
Winograd, T. (1972). *Understanding Natural Language.*

RON CHRISLEY

Researchers in artificial intelligence attempt to design and create artefacts which have, or at least appear to have, mental properties: not just intelligences, but also perception, action, emotion, creativity, and consciousness.

1. Recent developments
2. The relevance of AI to understanding the mind

1. Recent developments

Since the mid-1980s, there has been sustained development of the core ideas of artificial intelligence, e.g. representation, planning, reasoning, natural language processing, machine learning, and perception. In addition, various subfields have emerged, such as research into agents (autonomous, independent systems, whether in hardware or software), distributed or multi-agent systems, coping with uncertainty, affective computing/models of emotion, and ontologies (systems of representing various kinds of entities in the world—achievements that, while new advances, are conceptually and methodologically continuous with the field of artificial intelligence as envisaged at the time of its modern genesis: the Dartmouth conference of 1956.

However, a substantial and growing proportion of research into artificial intelligence, while often building on the foundations just mentioned, has shifted its emphasis. This change in emphasis, inasmuch as it constitutes a conceptual break with those foundations, promises to make substantial contributions to our understanding and concepts of mind. It remains to be seen whether these contributions will replace or (as may seem more likely) merely supplement those already provided by what might be termed the 'Dartmouth approach' and its direct successors.

The new developments, which have their roots in the cybernetics work of the 1940s and 1950s as much as, if not more than, they do in mainstream AI, can be divided into two broad areas: adaptive systems and embodied/ situated approaches. This is not to say that they are exclusive; much promising work, such as the field of evolutionary robotics, combines elements of both areas.

Adaptive systems The 1980s saw a rise in the popularity of both neural networks (sometimes also called connectionist models) and genetic algorithms.

Neural networks are systems comprising thousands or more of (usually simulated) simple processing units; the computational result of the network is determined by the input and the connections between the units, which may vary their ability to pass a signal from one unit to the next. Nearly all of these networks are adaptive in that they can learn. Learning typically consists in finding a set of connections that will make the network give the right output for each input in a given training set.

Genetic algorithms produce systems that perform well on some tasks by emulating natural selection. An initial random population of systems (whose properties are determined by a few parameters) are ranked according to their performance on the task; only the best performers are retained (selection). A new population is created by mutating or combining the parameters of the winners (reproduction and variation). Then the cycle repeats.

Although the importance of learning had been acknowledged since the earliest days of AI, these two approaches, despite their differences, had a common effect of making adaptivity absolutely central to AI.

While machine learning assumed conceptual building blocks with which to build learned structures, neural networks allowed for subsymbolic learning: the acquisition of the conceptual 'blocks' themselves, in a way that cannot be understood in terms of logical inference, and that may involve a continuous change of parameters, rather than discrete steps of accepting or rejecting sentences as being true or false. By allowing systems to construct their own 'take' on the world, AI researchers were able to begin overcoming the obstacles that were thrown up when they attempted to put adult human conceptual structures into systems that were quite different from us.

Standard AI methodology for giving some problem-solving capability to a machine had at first been: think about how you would solve the problem, write down the steps of your solution in a computer language, give the program to the machine to run. This was refined and extended in several ways. For example, the knowledge engineering approach asks an expert about the important facts of the domain, translates these into sentences in a knowledge representation language, gives these sentences to the machine, and lets the machine perform various forms of reasoning by manipulating these sentences. But it remained the case that, in these extensions of the basic AI methodology, the machine was limited to using the programmer's or expert's way of representing the world. By using adaptive approaches like artificial evolution, AI systems are no longer limited to solutions that humans can conceptualize—in fact the evolved or learned solutions are often inscrutable. Our concepts and intuitions might not be of much use in getting a six-legged robot to walk; our introspection might even lead us astray concerning the workings of our own minds. For both reasons, genetic algorithms are an impressive addition to the AI methodological toolbox.

However, along with these advantages come limitations. There is a general consensus that the simple, incremental methods of the adaptive approaches, while giving relatively good results for tasks closely related to perception and action, cannot scale up to tasks that require sophisticated, abstract, and conceptual abilities. Give a system some symbols and some rules for combining them, and it can potentially produce an infinite number of well-formed symbol structures—a feature that parallels human competence. But a neural network that has learned to produce a set of complex structures will usually fail to generalize this into a systematic competence to construct an infinite number of novel combinations. Genetic algorithms have similar limitations to their 'scaling up'. But even if these obstacles are overcome, and systems with advanced forms of mentality are created by these means, the very fact that we shall not have imposed our own concepts on them may render their behaviour itself inexplicable. What we do not need is another mind we cannot understand! With respect to AI's goal of adding to our understanding of the mind, adaptive (especially evolved) systems may be as much a part of the problem as a part of the solution (see section 2). And technological AI is also hindered if the systems it produces cannot be understood well enough to be trusted for use in the real world.

Embodied and situated systems Embodied and situated approaches to AI investigate the role that the *body* and its sensorimotor processes (as opposed to symbols or representations on their own) can and do play in intelligent behaviour. Intelligence is viewed as the capacity for real-time, situated activity, typically inseparable from and often fully interleaved with perception and action. Further, it is by having a body that a system is *situated* in the world, and can thus exploit its relations to things in the world in order to perform tasks that might previously have been thought to require the manipulation of internal representations or data structures.

For an example of embodied intelligence, suppose a child sees something of interest in front of him, points to it, turns his head back to get his mother's attention, and then returns his gaze to the front. He does not need to have some internal representation that stores the eye, neck, torso, etc. positions necessary to gaze on the item of interest; the child's arm itself will indicate where the child should look; the child's exploitation of his own embodiment obviates the need for him to store and access a complex inner symbolic structure. For an example of situated problem solving, suppose another child is solving a jigsaw puzzle. The child does not need to look at each piece intently, forming an internal representation of its shape, and then when all pieces have been examined, close her eyes and solve the puzzle in her head! Rather, the child can manipulate the pieces themselves, making it possible for her to *perceive* whether two of them will fit together. If nature has sometimes used these alternatives to complex inner symbol processing, then AI can (perhaps must) as well.

These are a cluster of other AI approaches that, while properly distinct from embodiment and situatedness, are nevertheless their natural allies. (i) Some researchers have found it useful to turn away from discontinuous, atemporal, logic-based formalisms and instead use the continuous mathematics of change offered by *dynamical systems theory* as a way to characterize and design intelligent systems. (ii) Some researchers have claimed that AI should, whenever possible, build systems working in the *real world*, with, for example, real cameras receiving real light, instead of relying on ray-traced simulations of light; a real-world AI system might exploit aspects of a situation we are not aware of and which we therefore do not incorporate in our simulations. (iii) Some insist that AI should concentrate on building complete working systems, with simple but functioning and interacting perceptual, reasoning, learning, action, etc. systems, rather than working on developed yet isolated competences, as has been the method in the past.

Architectures A change of emphasis common to both the more and less traditional varieties of AI is a move away from a search for specific algorithms and representations, and toward a search for the *architectures* that support various forms of mentality. An architecture specifies how the various components of a system, which may in fact be representations or algorithms, fit together and interact in order to yield a working system. Thus, an architecture-based approach can render irrelevant many debates over which algorithm or representational scheme is 'best'.

2. The relevance of AI to understanding the mind

Why do AI? Of course, there are technological reasons. But are there scientific reasons? Can AI illuminate our understanding of the mind? The acts involved in bringing natural intelligences into the world do not (usually!) confer any insight into the nature of intelligence; why should one think the acts involved in creating artificial intelligence would be any more enlightening?

For one thing, not all AI eschews design to the extent that the genetic algorithm approach (above) does; most approaches involve the designer understanding, in advance, at least roughly how the constructed system works. AI need not got so far as to say 'if you can't build it, you can't understand it', but building an intelligence might at least help.

It is sometimes argued in return that the kind of systems that AI is likely to produce will be so different from naturally intelligent systems (e.g. they are not alive) that (i) they will not shed much light on natural intelligence and (ii) they will not be able to reach the heights that natural intelligence does. Surely, these people conclude, if one is interested in intelligence and the mind, one should instead do neuroscience, or at least psychology?

One can defend the AI methodology for understanding natural intelligence by appealing to the history of understanding flight. Attempts both to achieve artificial flight and to understand natural flight failed as long as scientists tried to reproduce too closely what they saw in nature. It wasn't until scientists looked at simple, synthetic systems (such as Bernoulli's aerofoil), which could be arbitrarily manipulated and studied, that the general aerodynamic principles that underlie both artificial and natural flight could be identified. So also it may be that it is only by creating and interacting with simple (but increasingly complex) artificial systems that we will be able to uncover the general principles that will allow us both to construct artificial intelligence and understand natural intelligence.

Bishop, C. M. (1995). *Neural Networks for Pattern Recognition*.

Brooks, R. (1991). 'Intelligence without representation'. *Artificial Intelligence*, 47.

Chrisley, R. (ed.) (2000). *Artificial Intelligence: Critical Concepts*.

Clark, A. (1997). *Being There: Putting Brain, Body and World Together Again*.

Franklin, S. (1995). *Artificial Minds*.

Goldberg, D. E. (1989). *Genetic Algorithms in Search, Optimization, and Machine Learning*.

Nilsson, N. (1998). *Artificial Intelligence: A New Synthesis*.

Sharples, M., Hogg, D., Hutchison, C., Torrance, S., and Young, D. (1998). *Computers and Thought: A Practical Introduction to Artificial Intelligence*.

Sloman, A. (1997). 'What sort of architecture is required for a human-like agent?' In Wooldridge, M., and Rao, A. (eds.), *Foundations of Rational Agency*.

Smith, B. C. (1991). 'The owl and the electric encyclopedia'. *Artificial Intelligence*.

the 'sun signs' often appear curiously accurate. People born under Aries (between 21 March and 19 April) are supposed to have drive and enterprise; Tauruses are supposed to be practical and stubborn; Geminis clever but changeable; Cancers home-lovers with a tendency to oversensitivity; Leos dominant extroverts with a touch of egoism; Virgos hard workers who are obsessed by detail; Libras charmers who know how to get their own way; and so on. And most of us can, without much trouble, recall acquaintances who are typical Leos, Cancers, Geminis, etc.

Scientifically speaking, of course, this proves nothing; the sceptic can always point to untidy Virgos, modest Leos, timid Aries. Yet it is not difficult to feel that the 'hits' are striking enough to be worth closer investigation. In a case like this, the obviously sensible method is statistical—how many people can be shown to fit their astrological 'type'? In the early years of this century, a Frenchman, Paul Choisnard, tried the statistical approach, and his work inspired a Swiss mathematician, Karl Ernst Krafft, to even more ambitious efforts. Emphasizing his strictly scientific approach, Krafft preferred to call the subject 'astrobiology'; his immense *Traité d'astrobiologie* appeared (in French) in 1939; but the times were unpropitious, and it attracted little attention. It was Krafft who, in a letter of 2 November 1939 (to a member of Himmler's Secret Intelligence Service), predicted that Hitler's life would be in danger between the 7th and 10th of the month—he specifically mentioned 'assassination by explosive material'. When Hitler narrowly escaped death in the Munich beer cellar—he had just left when the bomb exploded— on 8 November 1939, Krafft's prediction was remembered and he was brought to Berlin. For a while he became a kind of semi-official astrologer to Himmler, but soon fell out of favour, and died in a concentration camp.

Krafft had attempted to 'prove' astrology by examining the birth certificates of thousands of professional men—he concentrated on musicians—and trying to show that their temperament corresponded to their sun sign. In 1950, a Sorbonne-trained statistician and psychologist, Michel Gauquelin, became interested in Krafft's *Traité*, and fed its results into a computer. His conclusion was that Krafft was deceiving himself when he believed his figures proved anything—he had allowed himself too much leeway of interpretation. Gauquelin's book, *Songes et mensonges de l'astrologie* (1969), was a scathing attack on astrology, as its title (Dreams and Delusions of Astrology) indicates. Yet the unsatisfactoriness of Krafft's experimental method led Gauquelin to devise a few simple tests of his own.

He concentrated his analysis on two straightforward questions. The first was whether astrologers are correct in stating that people born under 'odd' signs of the zodiac—Aries, Gemini, Leo, Libra, Sagittarius, Aquarius—tend to be extroverts, while those born under even signs—Taurus, Cancer, Virgo, Scorpio, Capricorn, Pisces—are likely to be introverts (see EXTROVERSION/INTROVERSION). The second question was whether a person's choice of profession is in any way governed by the planet that is in the ascendant (coming up over the horizon) at the moment of birth.

Greatly to his surprise, the evidence in both cases was positive. The tests were repeated many times, in four European countries, and the results continued to favour these assertions of astrology. Professor H. J. Eysenck was asked to check the results. He agreed, apparently with the expectation that they would prove to be invalid, and was equally surprised to find that they were positive.

The method used by Gauquelin—and later by Eysenck (and two associates, Jeff Mayo and A. White)—was as follows. Certain professions were chosen—sports champions, actors, scientists—and their birth certificates consulted for the exact time of birth (which is recorded on the Continent, though not in Britain). The subjects were 'famous'—to be found in reference books—and the numbers ran into thousands.

Astrologers believe that the 'rising sign' (the sign coming up over the horizon at the moment of birth) and the rising planet are of basic importance in governing the subject's temperament. Gauquelin's computer analysis seemed to show that three other positions were equally important: directly overhead, sinking below the horizon, and directly underfoot—the four quarters of the heavens, as it were. The findings were perfectly clear. Sportsmen tended to be born when Mars was in one of these critical positions, actors when Jupiter was there, and scientists (and doctors) when Saturn was there. Eysenck (1979) states: 'The results were extremely clear-cut and so significant statistically that there is no question whatsoever that the effects were not produced by chance.' But Eysenck, like Gauquelin, is careful to state that he does not consider these results 'prove' astrology; rather, he says, they should be regarded as the possible foundation of a new science of astrobiology.

Now there can be no possible doubt that astrology, as traditionally practised, is a pseudoscience. Early astrology —as practised by the Sumerians and Babylonians—was a jumble of old wives' tales. 'When a yellow dog enters a palace there will be destruction in its gates,' says a Babylonian text; 'When the planet Mercury approaches Aldebaran the king of Elam will die,' says another; and the two assertions sound equally absurd. But they are no more embarrassingly silly than modern popular books on astrology with titles like *Love Signs* and *The Stars and You*. How, then, is it possible to take seriously any 'science' that asserts a connection between 'the stars' and human destiny?

It must first be noted that the stars, as such, play no part in astrology. Because they are 'fixed', they can be used as reference points for the positions of the planets—that is to say, they could be regarded as the figures around the face of a clock, while the planets are the hands. It is the bodies in our own solar system that are believed to exert forces upon the earth, which, in turn, exerts forces on human beings. How? Astrology has never been concerned with this question, but Gauquelin suggests that the answer lies in the earth's magnetic field. In 1962, Y. Rocard, professor of physics at the Sorbonne, conducted an investigation into the claims of water-diviners, and demonstrated that the dowser's muscles react to weak changes in terrestrial magnetism caused by underground water, and that a capacity for detecting extremely small magnetic gradients is surprisingly common among human beings. It has long been widely accepted that the moon can produce emotional tension—hence 'lunatics'—and the statistical evidence has been documented by Arnold Lieber (1978). Leonard J. Ravitz, of the Virginia Department of Health, investigated the influence of moon cycles on mental patients in the late 1950s and found that the difference in electrical potential between the head and chest is greater in mental patients than in normal people, and increases at the full moon. In the late 1930s, Maki Takata of Tokyo discovered that when there is high sunspot activity, the 'flocculation index'—the rate at which albumin curdles in the blood—rises abruptly. It also rises before dawn, as the blood responds to the rising sun. At about the same time, Harold Burr of Yale observed that the electric field produced by living creatures—trees, for example—varied with the seasons, as well as with the cycles of the moon and sunspot activities.

So the basic medical facts may seem to be fairly well established. It may also be worth mentioning the discovery of John H. Nelson, an electronics engineer, that most magnetic storms (causing radio interference) occur when two or more planets are in conjunction, or at angles of 180 or 90 degrees from the sun. This seems to establish a foundation for a science of astrobiology; what still remains to be discovered is how forces of terrestrial magnetism could influence a human being to the extent of predisposing him to one profession or another—or even what regular monthly cycle could possibly determine whether a person is introverted or extroverted.

I should emphasize that I am not now asserting that the claims of astrology must somehow be 'reduced' to a series of statements about the influence of magnetic fields on animal organisms. Even a sceptical historian of astrology like Ellic Howe (1967) concedes that a 'good astrologer' can produce results of astounding accuracy—describing not only a person's temperament, but the pattern of his life. Similarly, anyone who has ever investigated dowsing will feel that the dowser's powers of detection—of other substances besides water—go far beyond the results obtained by Rocard. When the old wives' tales have been sifted out, there still seems to be more to explain than science is at present willing to admit. Modern computer analysis of structures like Stonehenge, the stones of Karnak, and the Great Pyramid suggests that their original purpose was connected with astronomy, which in turn suggests that our neolithic ancestors (the outer ditch of Stonehenge was constructed about 2900 BC) had a far more precise knowledge of astronomy than we give them credit for. Incised reindeer bones dating back 20,000 years earlier still suggest that Cro-Magnon man went to the trouble of tabulating the phases of the moon. It is difficult to imagine why, unless our ancestors possessed their own primitive science of 'astrobiology'—undoubtedly involved with magic and religious ritual—which later degenerated into traditional astrology.

Eysenck has said: 'At the moment the only feedback that most research workers in the field get is to be shouted down by both sides—by the astrologers for daring to have any doubts, and by the scientists for daring to look at the alleged phenomena of planetary influences on humankind at all.' But this statement in itself indicates that some of the investigations he wishes to see are already beginning to take place.   CW

Burr, H. S. (1972). *Blueprint for Immortality: The Electric Patterns of Life.*

Eysenck, H. J. (1979). 'Astrology—science or superstition?' *Encounter*, December.

Gauquelin, M. (1967). *The Cosmic Clocks.*

Howe, E. (1967). *Urania's Children: The Strange World of the Astrologers.*

Lieber, A. L. (1978). *The Lunar Effect: Biological Tides and Human Emotions.*

Lindsay, J. (1971). *Origins of Astrology.*

Marshack, A. (1972). *The Roots of Civilization.*

asylums: a historical survey. In England the care of the insane in special asylums dates from the 18th century and institutional care on a large scale came to be practised in the 19th century. The origins of the madhouse system are probably to be found in the practice of boarding out lunatics and idiots to private households. This custom persisted until well into the 19th century and was, predictably, much abused. Abuse occurred in two areas: first in the unjust confinement of sane persons, and secondly in the quality of care provided. Illegitimate confinements were already feared in the 18th century. In a *Review of the State of the English Nation* (1706), Defoe described the convenient ploy which alleged insanity provided in the case of unwanted wives or other relatives, particularly where inheritance was at stake. This fear has haunted public imagination ever since the beginnings of confinement and has provided a favourite theme in 19th-century literature. (For example, *Jane Eyre*, *The Woman in White*, *Melmoth the Wanderer*, and *Hard Cash* all deal with unjust or, at least, mysterious confinement.)

The second area of abuse, namely the physical conditions of the insane, was brought to public notice by the vigilant activities of 19th-century philanthropists. Parliamentary reports on the condition of lunacy relied on the evidence of these men and described instances of lunatics kept for many years in chicken pens or coal sheds, and generally under conditions of extreme barbarity and neglect.

The law did not make separate reference to lunatics until 1714. This Act (12 Anne, c. 23) distinguished between lunatics and 'rogues, vagabonds and sturdy beggars and vagrants'. It authorized two or more justices of the peace to detain a lunatic and confine him in a safe place. The cost of the detention was to be borne by the lunatic's parish of settlement. Although the Act did not require treatment to be provided, it at least exempted the lunatic from the customary whipping legally sanctioned for rogues, vagabonds, and vagrants. The Vagrant Act of 1744 (17 Geo. II, c. 5) added the cost of cure to the expenses to be defrayed by the parish.

During the time that separate legal provision was being made for lunatics, private madhouses and asylums grew up to cater for their needs. Evidence from newspaper advertisements and books written by madhouse proprietors suggests that the practice of confining the insane in private madhouses was well established by the beginning of the 18th century and that it grew steadily thereafter. In 1774 an Act (14 Geo. III, c. 49) was passed for the regulation of private madhouses within a 7-mile radius of London. It made obligatory the licensing and inspection of private madhouses by five commissioners to be elected from the Royal College of Physicians. However, the Act was largely ineffective. For example, it had no influence over provincial madhouses, over single lunatics, or over public subscription asylums. The commissioners could refuse to license a house to which they had been denied admission, but ill treatment and neglect were not grounds for refusal. Thus they had no powers to bring about improvements. Nevertheless, the Act marked the beginnings of state control of lunacy.

The illness of George III (1760–1820) played an important part in the development of public awareness and tolerance of insanity. George III suffered from several distinct episodes of what was thought to be insanity, and the state of his health became a matter of grave political consequence and a point of national discussion. (For a fuller discussion, see Macalpine and Hunter (1969), in which they claim that the king was, in fact, suffering from a rare metabolic disorder called porphyria, which is liable to cause phasic attacks of mental disorder.) What is important is that the king was thought to be insane and that the nation was much moved by his sufferings. During the latter part of his reign the lunacy reform movement got under way.

From the beginning of the 19th century parliamentary reports on the condition of lunacy followed one another in steady succession. The establishment of county lunatic asylums was prompted partly by moral outrage felt upon the discovery of the revolting and inhuman conditions of the insane and partly by the newly found faith in the possibility of cure. The committees submitting these reports consisted of well-meaning people who displayed some of the best features of Victorian philanthropy, namely, scrupulous attention to detail and a compassion for the destitute. They took it upon themselves to visit all workhouses and asylums where lunatics were kept. The committee of 1807 concluded that 'the practice of confining such lunatics and other insane persons as are chargeable to their respective parishes in gaols, houses of correction, poor houses and houses of industry is highly dangerous and inconvenient'. They therefore recommended that 'the measure which appears to your committee most adequate to enforce the proper care and management of these unfortunate persons and the most likely to conduce to their perfect cure, is the erection of asylums for their reception in the different parts of the kingdom'. The following year (1808) an Act was passed recommending that each county erect an asylum for the care of the insane. The asylums were to be supported by public funds. The Act was a permissive one, since it had no powers to enforce its regulations. As a result few county asylums were built for the time being.

The following years saw the growth of 'a free market in lunatics' and private madhouses multiplied to cope with increasing demands. Although some asylums provided a high standard of care, many more kept lunatics in dreadful conditions. These were publicized by the reports of 1815 and 1828. In York Asylum, a series of tiny cells was discovered, each housing many filthy and incontinent patients. For example, one cell measuring 3.7 × 2.4 metres (12 feet by 7 feet 10 inches) housed thirteen incontinent women. At Bethlem the case of William Norris, who had been chained by the neck to a stone wall for nine years, was given much publicity. Throughout the 1815 report conditions are described as inhuman and the patients as animal-like. In Bethlem Hospital this was particularly true. For example, the report says, 'the patients in this room were dreadful idiots, their nakedness and their mode of confinement gave this room the appearance of a dog-kennel'. The 1828 committee looked into the conditions within metropolitan madhouses. Their findings include the earlier ingredients of darkness, overcrowding, filth, and stench. They provide a catalogue of abuses and horrors.

The idea of moral management provided theoretical support for asylum-based treatment (see INSANITY: HISTORY). It advocated the abandonment of physical restraint and an appeal to the will of the patient. It aimed to restore the dignity of the patient and to enlist him as an ally in the treatment process. Two requirements of moral management were the early detection of insanity and separation of the patient from the circumstances precipitating his attack, usually his home. Both these requirements, together with claims of a near 100 per cent recovery rate, favoured the growth of the asylum. Moral management also contributed towards the recovery of lunatics from workhouses. The lunacy reformers deplored the indiscriminate intermingling of lunatics with other destitute persons.

By 1844 the abuses within madhouses had been made public and the need for improvement was clearly established. Despite the recommendation of the 1808 Act only twelve county asylums had been built. The 1844 report of the metropolitan commissioners in lunacy provides a landmark. One of the most influential commissioners was Lord Shaftesbury. The report was comprehensive: it included domestic details of the running of asylums, information on the non-restraint system, a discussion of the nature of insanity, and comments on the admission of pauper lunatics from workhouses. It was based on 166 visits to public and private asylums. One of the less well-known themes of the report concerned the dangers of clogging up asylums with incurable patients, thereby 'converting them into a permanent refuge for the insane instead of hospitals for their relief and cure'. By the middle of the 19th century the paradoxical situation had arisen where asylums were not able to cure because of the large numbers of incurable patients. One major reason for the asylums' lack of success was that the problems which confronted them were not specifically medical, but had a large social component. The problems of lunacy were closely related to the problems of pauperism, as 75 per cent of the insane came under poor law authorities. The year following the report two Acts were passed, one making compulsory the erection of county asylums and the other providing a more comprehensive system of asylum inspection. By 1847, 36 of the 52 counties had complied with the Act and built asylums of their own. However, within a short space of time it was found that the demand for asylum beds far exceeded supply. The size of the lunacy problem grew to fit and then exceed the provisions made for it. Interestingly, the vast increases in the lunatic population occurred among pauper and not private patients: between 1844 and 1870 the number of private patients increased by about 100 per cent whereas the number of pauper lunatics increased by about 365 per cent. Alongside this growth in asylums the numbers of curable patients declined. Superintendents of asylums estimated that roughly 90 per cent of their patients were incurable. No matter how many new beds were provided the promised cures never materialized. When the asylum failed to fulfil its initial promise a cheaper asylum system

Table 1. Total number of patients in public asylums in England and Wales

Year	Number	Year	Number
1850	7,140	1954	148,100
1870	27,109	1960	136,200
1890	52,937	1970	103,300
1910	97,580	1980	92,000
1930	119,659		

and a return to the workhouse were advocated, precisely the state of affairs that had earlier aroused so much horror.

Lunatic asylums deteriorated from being small family-based units to becoming large, custodial institutions offering little hope to their inmates. Emphasis moved from early detection and treatment to illegal detention. The next major piece of legislation, the Lunacy Act of 1890, was concerned with protecting the individual against wrongful detention rather than with cure and treatment. Physicians of the period already recognized the bad effects of increasing size and routine on the inhabitants of the asylum: 'In a colossal refuge for the insane, a patient may be said to lose his individuality and to become a member of a machine so put together, as to move with precise regularity, and invariable routine; a triumph of skill adapted to show how such unpromising materials as crazy men and women may be drilled into order and guided by rule, but not an apparatus guided to restore their pristine self-governing existence. In all cases admitting of recovery, or of material amelioration, a gigantic asylum is a gigantic evil and figuratively speaking a manufactory of chronic insanity.' Despite the pessimism which came to surround the asylum, its population continued to grow. Figures show a steady increase in the asylum population (excluding the two world wars) until its peak in 1954, and thereafter a dramatic decline (see Table 1). With the introduction and widespread use of the major tranquillizers from the mid-1950s onwards, the emphasis on community treatment, and the attacks by sociologists on the pernicious effects of institutional care, the asylum population has continued to decrease (see ASYLUMS: ARE THEY REALLY NECESSARY?). By 1980 the total number of beds in England and Wales for the reception and treatment of patients with mental illnesses had declined to about 92,000, of which some 4,360 were in psychiatric units in general hospitals. These beds are intended for short-stay patients, and the majority of psychiatrically ill persons are still admitted to and treated in the old county mental hospitals. The asylum buildings remain as a robust testimony to the Victorian faith in order and progress in the face of unreason and lunacy.   VS

asylums: are they really necessary?

Bynum, W., Porter, R., and Shepherd, M. (1985). *Anatomy of Madness: Essays in the History of Psychiatry, Institutions and Society*.

Donnelly, M. (1983). *Managing the Mind: A Study of Medical Psychology in Early Nineteenth Century Britain*.

Macalpine, I., and Hunter, R. (1969). *George III and the Mad Business*.

Rothman, D. (1971). *The Discovery of the Asylum*.

Scull, A. (1979). *Museums of Madness*.

asylums: are they really necessary? The odium surrounding our mental hospitals, or asylums—a synonym fallen into disrepute but worthy of resurrection in the light of the present situation—is best understood as a chapter in the continuing and complicated history of the care of the mentally disordered (see ASYLUMS: A HISTORICAL SURVEY).

During the 19th and early part of the 20th centuries, Britain's asylums underwent many vicissitudes. From time to time there were scandals leading to inquiries similar in many ways to those that take place all too frequently today and for the very same reasons. However, in the period between the two world wars the trend towards a more liberal approach was established, culminating in the Mental Treatment Act 1930, the outstanding feature of which was the provision made for the admission of voluntary as opposed to certified patients. The same liberalism permeated the hospitals themselves and was reflected in the more imaginative decoration and furnishing of the wards, and an improvement in the clothing and diet of the patients. Of even greater importance was the evolution of the concept of the 'open door', thus acknowledging that the majority of mental patients are not dangerous, and that a prison-like regime is not necessary to contain them. The spirit of enlightenment was crowned with such success that Britain easily led the world. Visitors from far and near came to see what had been achieved.

But the pendulum swung too far. An extraordinary wave of optimism flooded the psychiatric scene in the 1950s, triggered off no doubt by the introduction of the phenothiazines, claimed by some to be as specific for the treatment of the *schizophrenias as, say, insulin is in diabetes or thyroxine in myxoedema. In a way that is difficult to understand, the mental hospitals, so recently declared Good Objects, became, almost overnight, Bad Objects. Consonant with this changed attitude, a most seductive slogan, 'community care', was conjured up; but unfortunately adequate fieldwork had not been done to make quite sure that the community in fact did care. Nevertheless, the policy of 'discharge and be damned' prevailed, a policy that was to be given administrative blessing in the Mental Health Act 1959. Then, stimulated by the statistical forecasts of Tooth and Brook (1961), the Minister of Health, Enoch Powell, in his Hospital Plan (1962), declared that there would be a very substantial reduction in the number of beds in mental hospitals, some of which would be razed to the ground and their function divided between psychiatric units in general hospitals and 'community care'. The local authorities were to provide certain facilities, such as hostels for discharged mental hospital patients, halfway houses, sheltered workshops, home visits, and so on. Unfortunately, no date was given for when these facilities had to be made available, and it is generally accepted that with a very few exceptions the overall response left a great deal to be desired.

The policy of discharge continued, however. In the twenty years 1960–80 there was a reduction of over 44,000 in the number of beds in British mental hospitals. This might in itself be an achievement if it could be guaranteed that the quality of life of those who might have occupied those beds was at least as good as it was when they enjoyed the 'asylum' offered by the hospitals. But is it? An examination of some of the evidence might lead one to believe that it frequently is not.

Failing adequate support in the community in general and from their families (if any) in particular, discharged patients may become vagrants and by one avenue or another return to the mental hospital. Berry and Orwin (1966) report on the steep rise in the number of patients of no fixed address admitted to their hospital in Birmingham since the Mental Health Act came into being. Their summary is worth quoting:

> Their plight is evidence that the initial enthusiasm evoked by the new Act for the discharge of chronic psychotics into community care was premature in view of the resources available and has resulted in the overwhelming of existing community services.

The doss-house is, of course, another alternative focus of redistribution. Edwards et al. (1968), in their study of inmates of Camberwell Reception Centre, London, showed that of a population of 279, 24 per cent had previously been in a mental hospital for reasons other than drinking, and of these 7 per cent had been out of hospital for six months or less. Other studies of 'dossers', for example Lodge-Patch (1970) and Scott, Gaskell, and Morrell (1966), paint equally gloomy pictures.

But of all the foci of redistribution perhaps the most socially undesirable is the exchange of a bed in a mental hospital for a cell in a prison. Mental disorder may and does at times manifest itself in offences against the criminal law. Such offences are for the most part trivial, but they are not necessarily so by any means. Criminal statistics show that the number of cases remanded for psychiatric report rose from 6,366 in 1961 (Home Office Report) to 11,057 in 1976 (Home Office Report), nearly doubling. It is known that 16 per cent at least had been discharged from mental hospitals less than one year before their arrest. Furthermore, it is safe to say that if the period were extended to two years since discharge the number would be in the neighbourhood of 50 per cent.

But of paramount importance in this context is the angry comment contained in the 1976 prison report referring to the growing difficulty in finding accommodation for mentally abnormal offenders in National Health Service psychiatric hospitals: 'mentally ill people are entering prisons and borstals in increasing numbers and people of previous good personality, whose offences frequently stem solely from their illnesses, are now being refused admission to psychiatric hospitals and are, instead, being received and detained in establishments.' Furthermore, the same report refers to an assessment made by prison medical officers of the number of prisoners in custody who were suffering from mental disorder within the meaning of the 1959 Act. It emerged that 'the prison system was then holding some hundreds of offenders who were in need of and capable of gaining benefit from, psychiatric hospital care, management and treatment in psychiatric hospitals'.

Moreover, the official statistics quoted give an account of mentally abnormal offenders dealt with after prosecution (Part V of the Act). But there is also a steep rise in the number admitted, or readmitted, to mental hospitals without prosecution. Of special importance in this respect is the use of Section 136 (Part IV of the Act), a method whereby the police can deal expeditiously with social crises occasioned by the mentally disordered and remove them to a place of safety, in practice almost invariably a mental hospital. For example, in the twelve mental hospitals administered until recently by the South-West Metropolitan Regional Hospital Board the number rose from 308 (1.9 per cent of all admissions) in 1965 to 709 (4 per cent of all admissions) in 1972, an increase of well over 100 per cent. Investigations by the writer indicate that no less than 66 per cent of unprosecuted mentally abnormal offenders have previously been treated in mental hospitals.

From what has been said thus far it would appear that it is those who have no homes, or whose homes are unsatisfactory, who are the ones worst affected by the inadequacies of 'community care'. But are ex-patients who are more fortunate in this respect necessarily better off? A leading article in the *British Medical Journal* (4 May 1974) reads:

As a corollary it might be assumed that a warm, welcoming home would offer optimum conditions for the returning ex-patient. 'No place like home for rehabilitation' could be another seductive slogan and mean as much or as little as its counterpart 'community care'. But even under optimum conditions the major psychoses usually persist in following their predetermined course. Schizophrenia in particular, still one of the major scourges of mankind, characteristically is a chronic disease with alternating remissions and relapses, producing in about half the cases evidence of ever-increasing damage to the personality. The potential for self-sufficiency or 'rehabilitation' will vary inversely with the degree of damage and directly with the support from the family

and the community. If the family burden is too great or the community support inadequate, then not only will the patient suffer but the family may go under too.

Precisely these points have been made with telling and poignant effect in the first report of an organization—the National Schizophrenia Fellowship—which has the support of the Department of Social Psychiatry of the Institute of Psychiatry, London (*Living with Schizophrenia*, 1974). In his foreword John Pringle, the honorary director of the Fellowship, does not pull his punches. He castigates those whose duty it was 'to provide the community support, in replacement for custodial care, which many chronic sufferers [from schizophrenia], unable to fend for themselves, cannot do without'. He goes on: 'The closure of mental hospital wards, which at least provide the basic minimum shelter and life support, goes ruthlessly on, leaving nothing in their place.'

The body of the report contains a series of accounts of relatives, mainly parents, of what it is like to live with schizophrenia. The burning desire to do what is right shines through the pages, but if there is a common theme it is that there are promises and more promises of help from innumerable agencies but in the end the relatives must go it alone. 'The effect of having George at home on our home life has been disastrous' typifies several examples of the way one schizophrenic can wreck the social life of an entire family. 'I do not think "the community" exists' is the sad reflection of a mother whose daughter has encountered 'the sneers, no job, cold shouldering, impatience and general feeling of being out of step'. 'I have found that every hospital wants to discharge my son at the first opportunity' is a wry comment on the administrative policy obtaining in so many mental hospitals today. 'There is, therefore, virtually nothing available in the way of after care, rehabilitation or training for the schizophrenic in this immediate area' is a further caustic statement requiring no further comment.

The Mental Health Act 1983, which consolidated the provisions of the 1959 Act and those of the Mental Health (Amendment) Act 1982, has focused attention even more sharply on the divide between what may be described as the psychosocial as opposed to the medical model. The principal change in the legislation has been new provisions concerning patients' rights, in particular when compulsory detention is involved. The District Health Authority and local social services are charged as a mandatory duty with provision of treatment, care, and support for patients living in the community, employing a cadre of approved social workers with appropriate competence. However, at the time of writing there are few signs that adequate community care under the new Act is likely to be more of a reality than in the past. Isolated experiments, such as those accompanying the closure in

1986 of Digby Hospital, Exeter, may give some cause for hope for the future; but in the main the political will at local level to implement all of the requirements of the Act has been in as short supply as the necessary finance in a time of economic stringency.

It has been necessary to condense a very considerable body of evidence to substantiate the plea made by a not inconsiderable number of psychiatrists that the mental hospital—or asylum in the true meaning of the word—should be retained for the foreseeable future, or at least until satisfactory alternatives for the care of its patients are available. If we go on as we are, sacrificing the well-being of sick people for doctrinaire reasons, or for reasons of economic or political expediency, then we will have turned the wheel full circle and be back where we were at the beginning of the 19th century. There is this difference, however, that in our present industrialized, urbanized, heterogeneous society, the family may not be prepared to shoulder the burden of the psychotic in their midst, nor may the 'community' (analogous to the parish of bygone days) be prepared to shoulder the burden of adequate community services.

As a footnote it could be added that Britain is not alone in reaping the bitter harvest of policies which are both ill considered and precipitate. In Italy, for example, laws were introduced in 1978 which, *inter alia*, forbade the admission of further new patients to mental hospitals which were themselves to be run down and eventually closed. This has led to a new class of vagrants—the *abandonati*—a host of homeless, mentally sick ex-patients who roam the streets and public places. The situation in the USA, where comparable policies have been put into effect, is no better. Dr Alan A. Stone, professor of law and psychiatry at Harvard, wrote in 1984: 'Yet madness has not gone out of the world as was hoped, in fact madness is more visible than ever before in this century. One can see chronic mental patients in the streets of every major city in the United States.'

See also MENTALLY ILL, SERVICE FOR THE.   HRR

Berry, C., and Orwin, A. (1966). 'No fixed abode: a survey of mental hospital admissions'. *British Journal of Psychiatry*, 112.

Edwards, G., Williamson, V., Hawker, A., Hensman, C., and Postoyan, S. (1968). 'Census of a reception centre'. *British Journal of Psychiatry*, 114.

Lodge-Patch, I. C. (1970). 'A London survey'. *Proceedings of the Royal Society of Medicine*, 63.

Scott, R., Gaskell, P. G., and Morrell, D. C. (1966). 'Patients who reside in common lodging houses'. *British Medical Journal*, 2.

Stone, A. A. (1984). *Law, Psychiatry and Morality: Essays and Analysis*.

Tooth, G. C., and Brook, E. M. (1961). 'Trends in the mental hospital population and their effect on future planning'. *Lancet*, 1.

ataxia. The lack of coordination between muscles that causes unsteadiness in body posture and movement and affects eye movement and speech. Sensory (or proprioceptive) ataxia results from an impaired sense of joint position (proprioception). It is aggravated when the patient shuts his eyes, as some of the proprioceptive defect is compensated for visually. Motor ataxia results from cerebellar disorders.

attachment. Attachments within close relationships lie at the heart of our emotional life, and the propensity to form attachments is an integral part of human nature. In the words of John *Bowlby (1907–90), 'It is characteristic of human beings to make strong affectional relationships with each other and for some of their strongest emotions to depend on how these relationships are faring. Whereas stable relationships are a source of enjoyment and security, separation, loss, or threatened loss arouse *anxiety or anger, or else sadness and *depression.' (Bowlby, 1st edition of this Companion, 1987, p. 57).

Bowlby produced a framework for understanding the development and implications of such close relationships, as set out in his trilogy *Attachment and Loss* (1969/82; 1973; 1980). His early clinical observations pointed to the adverse effects of separation or loss of a mother figure, leading him to ask, 'If the disruption of a child's relationship with mother-figure in the early years creates much distress and anxiety, what is so special about the relationship that has been disrupted?' (Bowlby 1991a: 302–3). The prevailing analytical thinking was that a special bond with the mother stemmed from her association with the provision of food. Not convinced by this, Bowlby noted the phenomenon of imprinting in precocial birds such as geese, with a bond developing in its own right, independently of being fed. He therefore turned to the scientific discipline of ethology and the writings of Konrad Lorenz and Niko Tinbergen. Within this framework, the occurrence of species-characteristic behaviour such as following the mother suggests that it may have been selected for in its own right during the course of evolution. Bowlby defined attachment behaviour as any form of behaviour that attains or maintains proximity to a caregiver in times of need or stress. In the environments in which we evolved, individuals who exhibited attachment behaviour would have been more apt to survive and leave offspring, who in turn would reproduce (i.e. would increase their 'inclusive fitness'), compared with those who did not show attachment behaviour. The presumed biological function was protection from harm. Selection for attachment behaviour could not have happened without a similar pressure on its complement, caregiving behaviour. 'During the course of time, the biologically given strategy of attachment in the young has evolved in parallel with the complementary parental strategy of responsive caregiving—the one presumes the other' (Bowlby 1991b: 293).

Bowlby realized that an evolutionary argument could provide insight into behaviour which otherwise appeared abnormal, including the 'irrational fears of childhood'. The tendency to fear unfamiliar situations, darkness, or separation is 'to be regarded as a natural disposition of man . . . that stays with him in some degree from infancy to old age . . . . Thus it is not the presence of this tendency in childhood or later life that is pathological; pathology is indicated either when the tendency is apparently absent or when fear is aroused with unusual readiness and intensity' (Bowlby 1973: 84). In one of his final contributions Bowlby wrote, 'Once we postulate the presence within the organism of an attachment behavioural system regarded as the product of evolution and having protection as its biological function, many of the puzzles that have perplexed students of human relationships are found to be soluble. . . . an urge to keep proximity or accessibility to someone seen as stronger or wiser, and who if responsive is deeply loved, comes to be recognised as an integral part of human nature and as having a vital role to play in life. Not only does its effective operation bring with it a strong feeling of security and contentment, but its temporary or long-term frustration causes acute or chronic anxiety and discontent. When seen in this light, the urge to keep proximity is to be respected, valued, and nurtured as making for potential strength, instead of being looked down upon, as so often hitherto, as a sign of inherent weakness' (Bowlby 1991b: 293).

1. The development of attachment
2. The quality of attachment
3. Implications

1. The development of attachment

As attachment behaviour develops, it forms the basis for an inferred attachment bond. Bowlby described particular phases of its development: pre-attachment (from birth to about 2 months), involving signalling without discriminating one person from another; attachment-in-the-making (2–6 months), where signals become directed to particular persons; clear-cut attachment (0.5–4 years), with locomotion and goal-corrected behaviour; and finally a goal-corrected partnership (4 years onwards) with perspective taking, communication skills, and sharing mutual plans. Although additional attachments may develop throughout life, early attachments endure.

Furthermore, Bowlby (1973) postulated that attachment relationships must become internalized. Internal working models may be defined as ' "operable" models of self and attachment partner, based on their joint relationship history. They serve to regulate, interpret, and predict both the attachment figure's and the self's attachment-related behavior, thoughts, and feelings' (Bretherton and Munholland, in Cassidy and Shaver

1999: 89). This definition reflects Bowlby's view of the complementary nature of an internal working model, representing both sides of the relationship. 'A working model of self as valued and competent, according to this view, is constructed in the context of a working model of parents as emotionally available, but also as supportive of exploratory activities. Conversely, a working model of self as devalued and incompetent is the counterpart of a working model of parents as rejecting or ignoring of attachment behavior and/or interfering with exploration'.

2. The quality of attachment

A wealth of empirical research within Bowlby's attachment theory was enabled by Mary Ainsworth (1913–99). Their friendship and collaboration spanned 40 years, starting from when Ainsworth worked with Bowlby in the early 1950s. Appreciating that assessments of attachment must involve how a child uses the mother (or other caregiver) as a 'secure base' when the attachment behaviour system is activated, Ainsworth developed a laboratory Strange Situation Test for infants (Ainsworth et al. 1978). This is a series of short episodes involving mother and a stranger, in which the child's attachment behaviour system is activated by the unfamiliarity of the situation and by the mother leaving. The return of the mother allows one to see how the child organizes his or her attachment behaviour to her. Ainsworth identified three patterns: Secure, Avoidant, and Ambivalent. A Secure pattern has been associated with antecedent interactions with a 'sensitively responsive' mother, as found in Mary Ainsworth's pioneering Baltimore study and subsequently in other studies (see the meta-analysis by DeWolff and van IJzendoorn 1997). The insecure patterns have been associated with different maternal styles, including Avoidance with rejection, Ambivalence with inconsistency, and a more recently documented pattern—Disorganization with fear (see Cassidy and Shaver 1999).

As for which pattern of attachment is desirable, Bowlby was concerned with what might be called 'psychological desiderata' (Hinde and Stevenson-Hinde 1991). Making an analogy with 'physical well-being', Bowlby argued that 'psychological well-being' had an absolute meaning, involving security of attachment. Research has supported this view, with security associated with self-reliance and efficacy, as opposed to dependency, anxiety, or anger. Insecure patterns are not seen as pathological in themselves, but rather as risk factors for pathology, while security is viewed as a protective factor (reviewed in Weinfield et al. in Cassidy and Shaver 1999).

In addition to behavioural assessments of attachment quality, once children reach Bowlby's 'goal-corrected partnership' stage, their verbal behaviour may be used to index their 'internal working models' of attachment.

Representational methods typically involve a description of separations or other distress-provoking situations, with the child providing narratives around them (see Solomon and George in Cassidy and Shaver 1999).

With adolescents and adults, representations of attachment may be accessed through the Adult Attachment Interview, developed by Mary Main and colleagues in Berkeley (see Hesse in Cassidy and Shaver 1999). This is a semi-structured interview consisting of eighteen basic questions, starting with one's childhood relationships with parents. After providing five adjectives to describe each parent, the interviewee is probed for specific episodic memories to illustrate why each descriptor was chosen. The protocol goes on to explore what happened around physical and emotional upsets, including separation and loss. The final section involves asking in specific ways how this early experience may relate to current feelings and relationships. A verbatim transcript of the interview provides the basis for ratings on continuous scales as well as classifications: Secure/autonomous, Dismissing, Preoccupied, or Unresolved/disorganized. These classifications are related to parenting style and to infants' attachment classification. 'What is most striking about this association is that it suggests that the form in which an individual presents his or her life narrative (regardless of its content) predicts caregiving behavior in highly specific and systematic ways' (Hesse in Cassidy and Shaver 1999: 398).

3. Implications

The fruits of Bowlby and Ainsworth's pioneering work are gathered together in the *Handbook of Attachment* (Cassidy and Shaver 1999), which is suitably dedicated to them and which contains references supporting the following implications of attachment theory:

Normative development and parenting. Attachment research has found patterns in the development and expression of emotions within close relationships, including how patterns may be transmitted across generations. The sense of security which must underlie any appreciation of emotions within one's self and their expression to others depends upon having attachment figures who are sensitively responsive to emotional needs. A number of studies have revealed what types of parental interactions promote security, thereby paving the way for methods of parental guidance and childcare policies in general.

Psychopathology. With children who have already developed disorders, particular patterns of insecure attachment shed light on aspects of parenting that might be modified to promote security. For example, the Disorganized pattern, often seen in clinical samples, appears to be associated with fearfulness in either parent or child or both, thereby suggesting a window for intervention. Additionally, attachment theory has direct implications for

disorders related to separation or loss, such as abnormal grief, depression, or anxiety.

Social policy issues. When a child goes to hospital, we now take it for granted that parents may visit or even live in. However, before Bowlby's influence, hospital practice involved leaving caregiving to the 'experts' and keeping relatives away. Obstetric practice followed similar lines, and Bowlby did not hesitate to challenge this, asking how early separation could possibly promote a close mother–child relationship. His concern over separation from attachment figures remains relevant, including our present provision of care for adults, such as the elderly or mentally ill.

Regarding day care, Bowlby was keen to put right the misinterpretation of what he wrote. In stressing the importance of early caregiving, he did not mean that a parent must be with the child all the time. From the above it will be clear that attachment theory is about the *quality* of a relationship rather than amount of time spent together. Similarly with adoption, attachment theory does not say that caregivers must be biologically related parents, nor that early adversities cannot be overcome. Indeed the implication is that adoptive parents, if sensitively responsive to the child's needs, may do a great deal to set interactions in a cycle that will promote security.

In conclusion, the framework provided by Bowlby has proved to be robust. At the same time, attachment theory continues to grow—not as a closed system, but one that is open to input from many other disciplines, including neuroscience, cognitive psychology, and linguistics.

JSH

Ainsworth, M. D. A., Blehar, M. C., Waters, E., and Wall, S. (1978). *Patterns of Attachment*.

Bowlby, J. (1969/1982). *Attachment and Loss*, i: *Attachment*.

—— (1973). *Attachment and Loss*, ii: *Separation, Anxiety and Anger*.

—— (1980). *Attachment and Loss*, iii: *Loss, Sadness and Depression*.

—— (1991a). 'Ethological light on psychoanalytical problems'. In Bateson, P. (ed.), *Development and Integration of Behaviour*.

—— (1991b). 'Postscript'. In Parkes, C. M., Stevenson-Hinde, J., and Marris, P. (eds.), *Attachment across the Life Cycle*.

Cassidy, J., and Shaver, P. R., (eds.) (1999). *Handbook of Attachment: Theory, Research, and Clinical Applications*.

DeWolff, M. S., and van IJzendoorn, M. H. (1997). 'Sensitivity and attachment: a meta-analysis on parental antecedents of infant attachment'. *Child Development*, 68.

Hinde, R. A., and Stevenson-Hinde, J. (1991). 'Perspectives on attachment'. In Parkes, C. M., Stevenson-Hinde, J., and Marris, P. (eds.), *Attachment across the Life Cycle*.

attachment theory: sustaining exploration. The *Handbook of Attachment* (Cassidy and Shaver 1999) shows how much attachment theory, developed by Bowlby and by Ainsworth, has enlarged and benefited our understanding of human instinctive social behaviour. Despite this, practitioners working primarily with adults rather than with young children find that the difficulties adult clients often present are not included in Bowlby's model. Clients' difficulties frequently relate to relationships with peers, when (i) at work, (ii) at home, and (iii) at leisure, and when they are aroused sexually. To fill this gap, Heard and Lake (1986, 1997) have extended the Bowlby/Ainsworth attachment theory.

The extension gives practitioners a comprehensive model of human instinctive behaviour that takes account of: (i) the way in which the human urge to be creative and enjoy sharing interests with companions can be sustained; (ii) an extended view of caregiving that includes the task of parents, mentors, and other professional carers to promote psychological development (so that children and adolescents can move into the world of their peers safely); (iii) ways in which to conceptualize the variety of sexual relationships that human beings espouse, which range from stable affectional relationships to those that are promiscuous, often violent, and in which sustained long-term affection is lacking; and (iv) the effects on mood and sense of self, which are evoked by the non-verbal signals of body language, leading some people to be described as: 'he is always winding me up'; or 'she is a lovely person to be with, she makes me feel great'; and 'whatever I do, he is always critical so I feel no good'.

The foundations for the extensions lie in the model for instinctive behaviour put forward by Bowlby (1982) as an alternative to the models suggested by Freud. Interestingly Bowlby's model has not been developed sufficiently by attachment researchers to show how exploration may be maintained.

Briefly, Bowlby postulated two complementary instinctive behavioural systems (the attachment system and the complementary caregiving system), which he referred to as goal-corrected systems, making clear that they were governed by servomechanisms. The attachment system is activated by alarming events, the condition of the person, and the behaviour of attachment figures: the small hierarchy of figures to whom a child has become attached, of which the most preferred is 'the person who has looked after you the most', usually the biological mother. Activation of the attachment system leads to behaviour that increases proximity to attachment figures. When increased proximity is attained, the end point or goal of the system is reached and the behaviour of seeking proximity is terminated, but the system remains active, ready to respond when any behaviour-activating events are perceived or felt.

Bowlby saw the attachment, i.e. the careseeking system, as active throughout life. He gave little detail about the attachment figures' caregiving system, beyond stating that its prime function was to provide protection and comfort by attachment figures, who are 'older and wiser'.

Although Bowlby was well aware that feelings are aroused when either of the systems is activated (particularly feelings associated with failure to achieve proximity to the preferred attachment figure) and, although he wrote at some length on information processing, he did not elaborate on the kind of interactions that take place between caregiver and careseeker nor on the subjective experience associated with reaching the goal of either system.

There was at that time no reliable methodology to study subjective experience. Ainsworth's robust Strange Situation Test (Ainsworth et al. 1978) enabled the association to be studied between security in infancy and mothers who were sensitive and attentive. A little later Main recognized the disorganized/disoriented insecure child (Lyons-Ruth and Jacobvitz 1999), and her Adult Attachment Interview (Hesse 1999), showed that insecure relationships are transmitted across generations.

By the 1980s the observations of Trevarthen and of Stern described the reciprocal behaviour seen as people interact with one another. Trevarthen identified primary and secondary intersubjectivity. He expresses his current views in a long article (Trevarthen and Aitken 2001) in which he states that newborn infants, provided they are not motivated to show instinctive behaviours that attract parental care, communicate with adults using expressive forms and rhythms of interest and feelings displayed by other human beings. He considers this purposeful intersubjectivity is fundamental for our understanding of human mental development.

Stern (1985) described the effects of: (i) 'cross modal affect attunement' between infants and mother in which a mother shows her feelings about the exploratory assays being made by her infant; (ii) 'purposeful misattunement' by mother which seems to regulate the infant's level of arousal; and (iii) 'misattunement' which stops the infant exploring. He describes cross-modal affect attunement as a reactive phenomenon, for which empathy is not required; he considers empathy requires information processing at a cognitive level.

Recently McCluskey (2001) described a promising methodology to assess the level of goal-corrected empathic attunement shown to adult clients by counsellors and therapists. She demonstrated that empathic responses to a client's distress, evoked by threat of loss and actual loss of an important relationship, can reawaken the client's ability to explore the situation: that is to say the client begins to face handling the distressing situation. Her methodology is now being replicated and refined to study the elements of non-verbal behaviour governing the degree of closeness or distance kept between client and practitioners during dyadic and group therapeutic encounters.

In extending attachment theory the focus has been on the emotional experience of attaining, or not attaining, the goals of Bowlby's systems and also those of three additional instinctive motivational systems organized on the same principles.

All five systems are now referred to as 'the dynamics of attachment and exploratory collaboration' (Heard and Lake 2002). Together they act as one process that, provided the goals of each of the five systems are sufficiently well met, safeguards the capacity to be collaborative, exploratory, and creative.

The additional systems comprise:

- A system for sharing and extending one's interests with likeminded peers: evidence comes from many observations such as those collected by Hurlock (1972). We consider that the development of social competence (Lake 1985) depends not only on the quality of the relationships individuals have had with attachment figures, but also on the quality of the bonds of companionship made with peers, through sharing a supportive and exploratory pursuit of mutual interests.
- A system for affectional sexuality: evidence comes from the findings of attachment researchers such as Hazen and Shaver (1987), and Hazen and Ziefman (1994). A system for affectional sexuality is distinguished from defensive forms of sexuality.
- A system for personal defence, whose elements are mentioned by many authors: it appears to develop in three forms: maturative, non-maturative stage 1, and non-maturative stage 2.

The maturative form is present in situations in which (1) the individual's internal supportive system (constructed from memories of attachment relationships represented in internal working models of specified relationships) is functional and when it has been possible (2) to construct a personal supportive environment (the style of life individuals construct to provide reminders of attuning relationships with attachment figures (Heard and Lake 1997)). When these two systems are not sufficiently functional, non-maturative forms of the system for personal defence emerge.

The goal of non-maturative stage 1 defence is to reach a form of relating with feared attachment figures in which acceptance and approval can be experienced. When attachment bonds have withered, if ever made, non-maturative stage 2 defence is used. The goal then is to achieve, without concern for others, immediate relief from distress and pleasure. In therapeutic relationships clients usually show non-maturative stage 1 defences.

The caregiving system, renamed the system for promoting growth and development (Heard and Lake 2001), distinguishes two equally essential components: one for caregiving as described by Bowlby, and the second that aids psychological development (previously described as the educative dimension of caregiving). An empathic attachment figure is able to move from one component to the other, keeping in tune with one who is either seeking care and protection or, confident that care will be provided, seeking help to develop interests and skills. The task for attachment figures is not easy. No one will move effortlessly in all contexts from one component to the other. Anecdotal evidence shows that when individuals are demonstrating their non-maturative defences, their capacity to be empathic to the state of someone seeking care or opportunities for development is diminished.

DHH

Ainsworth, M., Bleher, M., Waters, E., and Wall, S. (1978). *Patterns of Attachment: Assessed in the Strange Situation and at Home.*

Bowlby, J. (1982). *Attachment and Loss, i: Attachment.*

——(1988). *A Secure Base: Clinical Applications of Attachment Theory.*

Cassidy, J., and Shaver, P. R. (eds.) (1999). *Handbook of Attachment: Theory, Research, and Clinical Applications.*

Hazen, C., and Shaver, P. (1987). 'Romantic love conceptualised as an attachment process'. *Journal of Personality and Social Psychology*, 52.

—— and Ziefman, D. (1994). 'Sex and the psychological tether'. In Bartholomew, K., and Perlman, D. (eds.), *Attachment Processes in Adulthood.*

Heard, D. H. (1982). 'Family systems and the attachment dynamic'. *British Journal of Family Therapy*, 4.

—— and Lake, B. (1986). 'The attachment dynamic in adult life'. *British Journal of Psychiatry*, 149.

——(1997). *The Challenge of Attachment for Caregiving.*

——(2001). 'Empathic attunement and the attachment system', unpublished paper given to First International Conference of the International Attachment Network.

——(2002). 'The dynamics of attachment and exploratory collaboration', unpublished paper given to the Northern Attachment Seminar.

Hesse, E. (1999). 'The adult attachment interview: historical and current perspectives'. In Cassidy, J., and Shaver, P. (eds.), *Handbook of Attachment.*

Hurlock, E. (1972). *Child Development.*

Lake, B. (1985). 'Concept of ego strength in Psychotherapy'. *British Journal of Psychiatry*, 147.

Lyons-Ruth, K., and Jacobvitz, D. (1999). 'Attachment disorganisation: unresolved loss, relational violence, and lapses in behavioural and attentional strategies'. In Cassidy, J., and Shaver, P. (eds.), *Handbook of Attachment.*

McCluskey, U. (2001). 'A theory of caregiving in adult life: developing and measuring the concept of goal corrected empathic attunement', unpublished Ph.D. thesis, University of York.

Stern, D. (1985). *The Interpersonal World of the Infant.*

Trevarthen, C., and Aitken, K. (2001). 'Infant intersubjectivity: research, theory, and clinical applications'. *Journal of Child Psychology and Psychiatry*, 42.

Attar, Fariduddin (abu-Talib / Abu Hamid Muhammad ibn-Abu-Bakr Ibrahim, ibn-Mustafa ibn-Sha'ban Farid-al-Din Attar, 'The Druggist' (d. 1220/1230). Born at Kadkan, near Nishapur, Persia, one of the major *Sufi teachers, and acknowledged by Jalauddin *Rumi as one of his in-spirers, Attar wrote at least 30 books. The most famous is the classical *Mantiq at-Tair* (The Bird Discourse, or Par-liament), thought by some to have influenced Chaucer in his *Parliament of Fowls*. A major authoritative compilation is his *Tadhkirat al-Awliya* (Recapitulation of the Saints), with biographies of Sufi teachers down the centuries, par-tially translated by A. J. Arberry. Also highly esteemed is his *Pand-Nama* (Book of Counsel) and the *Asrar-Nama* (Book of Secrets). The *Ilahi-Nama* he composed while working at his pharmacy, where he had 500 patients; and it was this work which he presented to Rumi when, as a small boy, he passed through Nishapur with his father in 1212. The *Mantiq* is an allegory of human psychological reactions to the problems encountered on the Sufi way, with each individual bird in turn displaying his hopes, fears, and inadequacies. The birds of the world have elected the hoopoe as their leader in the spiritual quest, and he has to deal with their reactions, in the manner of a Sufi teacher. The purpose of the journey is to seek the king of the birds, the immortal Simurgh (Persian homo-nym for 'thirty birds'). Ultimately the pilgrims reach the throne and find, when a curtain is drawn aside, that they are looking into a mirror: the collective (human) soul is seen to be the divine one, which differentiation conceals from ordinary consciousness.   IS

Arberry, A. J. (trans.) (1966). *Muslim Saints and Mystics: Selections from the Tadhkirat.*

attention. The nervous systems of living creatures are subjected to far more stimulation than can be used. On the one hand, the sense organs receive stimuli of great variety. On the other, memories, images, and ideas arise internally and must be considered from moment to mo-ment. Yet it is a commonplace that we are consciously aware of only a limited amount of this information at any moment. The operation by which a person selects information in attention, and its study, have twice been seen as central to research on our understanding of how information is processed by humans and animals.

The first great period was around 1900, when *James, *Titchener, *Wundt, and W. B. Pillsbury all wrote on at-tention at length. William James, on this as on so many other topics, described the main characteristics of atten-tion with precision. Attention was, for him, 'the taking possession by the mind, in clear and vivid form, of one of what seem simultaneously possible objects or trains of thought'. Titchener and his students, in particular, carried out an extensive experimental programme into such topics as 'prior entry' and the conditions of binocular ri-valry and fluctuations of attention. The first of these was the observation that, of two simultaneous events, the one to which attention was diverted appeared to occur earlier than the other.

The fundamental property of attention was, for those writers, to make the contents of *consciousness appear clearer. It would have made little sense to them to discuss effects of attention of which the observer was not aware. Pillsbury's book *Attention*, published in 1908, contains many observations which modern work has confirmed, and is a remarkably insightful volume in many respects.

With the rise of *behaviourism, attention was rele-gated to the status of a mental function which could not be admitted as a suitable object for research. Indeed, for some 30 years it disappeared from indexes and reviews. The second golden age of attention research dates from the early 1950s, and received a particular impetus with the publication of *Perception and Communication* by Don-ald *Broadbent in 1958. A major reason for the renewed interest was the need for the solution of new practical problems, such as the design of control towers and com-munication networks in the Second World War. A con-troller might receive several messages at once from different aircraft or ships, and be required to make appro-priate responses to each. With an attempt to understand how humans behaved in such situations, modern work on attention began. It was aided by the invention of the tape recorder, which for the first time allowed the ready con-trol and replicability of speech signals, while the phenom-enon of stereophony provided an easy way of varying the content and amount of information in competing mes-sages.

Broadbent's filter theory tried to explain how the brain coped with the information overload caused by having many sense organs receiving information simultaneously. Drawing an analogy with electronic communication, he proposed that there is in the brain a single central infor-mation channel whose rate of information processing is rather limited. This channel could select only one sensory input channel at a time, and could switch no more than about twice a second between input channels. To accept an input was equivalent to paying attention to that source of information, and information on unattended channels could be held in a *short-term memory for a few seconds. Broadbent called the selection mechanism 'the Filter'. While he drew on many fields of research, the most direct line of evidence was the 'split span' experiment. If three digits are read, at a rate of two per second, to the left ear of a listener, and another three to the right ear, so that the listener receives three synchronous pairs, he will recall them ear by ear, not pair by pair. Broadbent interpreted this to mean that the listener attended to one ear first and then switched to the memory trace of material in the other ear. By finding the fastest rate at which the lis-tener could repeat the message as pairs, he believed he had measured the rate of switching of auditory attention. This concept of a single-channel, limited-capacity information-processing system was central to much research in the next 25 years.

From about 1953 to 1963 'speech shadowing' was widely used by Broadbent, Neville Moray, Anne Treisman, and others. This technique had been introduced by Colin Cherry, and required a listener to repeat aloud a prose message in the presence of one or more distracting messages. It was found that major factors which aided selective attention included separation in space of the speakers, difference in voice timbre, and the statistical structure of the messages. In a series of elegant experiments Anne Treisman greatly extended our knowledge. Certain features of a distracting message proved to be potent sources of distraction, including emotional words (such as a listener's own name), contextually probable words, and—for bilingual listeners—the presence of a translation of the message to which they were listening.

However, these experiments also showed that some material, such as emotionally important words and contextually probable words, was perceived even when in the 'rejected' message. This led to a series of modifications to Broadbent's filter theory, notably by Treisman, Anthony Deutsch, and Don Norman. Although differing considerably in detail, they all attempted to account for the fact that the filter apparently did not block all information from the rejected channels, and that selection could be not only of sensory inputs, but of such features as language, class of word, colour (in the case of visual stimuli), and even classes of responses. Attention came to be seen as acting in a variety of ways, at a variety of levels, and on a variety of operations in the nervous system.

By the mid-1960s interest had grown greatly, and a wide variety of experimental techniques was developed. In addition to speech shadowing, simultaneous auditory messages were used, requiring much simpler responses than speech. In a series of studies Moray showed that, contrary to what the early shadowing experiments seemed to indicate, attention acted in the same way on non-linguistic as on linguistic material. Robert Sorkin and his co-workers in America explored attention to non-linguistic auditory material. Others, like Alan Allport and Peter McLeod in Britain, and Richard Shiffrin and Walter Schneider in America, found conditions where little or no interference between two messages occurred. These arose especially when messages were presented in different sensory modalities, where long practice had made performance almost automatic rather than conscious and voluntary, and when no competition between responses was required.

Visual attention was investigated by means of eye movements in such tasks as reading, by Paul Kolers, and in car driving and piloting aircraft, by John Senders. Very spectacular results were found using the 'Stroop test', in which attentional and perceptual conflict is induced by the nature of the stimulus. If the word 'red' is written in green ink, the word 'blue' in yellow ink, and so on, it is possible to read the word rapidly without the colour of the ink causing interference, but almost impossible to name the colour of the ink. Analogues of this effect provide a way of discovering which 'analysers' in the brain can be selectively biased by voluntary attention. (The word 'analyser' originated in a theory of learning and perception due to Deutsch, but its use in attention theory is largely due to Treisman.)

Some attempts were made to investigate the physiological mechanisms underlying attention. For example, the 'Expectancy wave', or CNV, was discovered in *electroencephalographic records, a change in electrical brain activity which appears when the observer is concentrating on the imminent arrival of a signal he knows is probable. In the late 1970s Emmanuel Donchin and his colleagues began work on the 'P-300' component of the brain-evoked potential, and this seems very likely to be intimately connected with attention in the sense of decision making. But to date our understanding of the physiological basis of attention lags a long way behind behavioural research.

More than a dozen theories of attention have been proposed since 1958, most of them strongly influenced by communication theory and computer technology. Their variety to some extent is due to the variety of phenomena which may be subsumed under the heading 'attention'. In addition to our ability to listen selectively to one message and ignore another, or to look at a picture in one colour in the presence of other colours, one may cite *vigilance* (or watch keeping), in which an observer looks for very rare events, such as detecting the presence of a sonar or radar target. Some studies have been made of mental concentration on cognitive problems. The interference between internal images and incoming stimuli has been investigated, as has the ability of the brain of a sleeping person to respond selectively to the sleeper's name, even though the sleeper is not aware of the response.

Although no single theory has emerged as completely dominant, the influence of Broadbent's filter theory remains strong, and what follows is a conflation of theories based on his suggestions. He assumed that an observer can block or weaken the strength of incoming messages to the brain, and there is ample evidence that this can happen. It is not known whether this is done by reducing the intensity of the messages or by switching them on and off rapidly. But some such blocking definitely occurs. In vision it can be done by closing the eyes or averting the gaze. In hearing the mechanism is not so clear. It seems probable that all information which impinges on the receptors of the sense organs reaches the pattern-analysing mechanisms of the brain. The filter perhaps acts to prevent the output of these analysers from reaching consciousness, although behaviour may still be produced, as when we become aware that we have driven for some time 'without being aware of it' (see TIME-GAP EXPERIENCE). It seems likely that information from different sense modalities, or from different dimensions within a modality (such as colour and shape), can be attended to simultaneously, at least after practice, while tasks which are very similar (such as judging the loudness of two tones) cannot. One should note that in making these assertions we are far from James's definition. Very often the observer is conscious of only one message, but it can be shown that the second is producing behaviour simultaneously with that produced consciously. (See also SUBLIMINAL PERCEPTION.)

A second way in which attention can operate is by biasing the interpretation of information proceeding from pattern analysis to consciousness. Thus a person expecting to see a bull in mist will see one, while a person expecting to see a rock will see a rock. This kind of bias is set by the probability of events, their subjectively perceived value, and contextual information derived from recent inputs and from memories. In earlier days this kind of bias was called 'mental set'.

The contents of consciousness as filtered by attention are very limited: attention is frequently modelled as a 'limited-capacity information channel'. But with practice, quite dramatic increases in performance are seen, and some writers, among whom Daniel Kahneman is particularly influential, have proposed a 'parallel processing' model of attention, in which the main limit is on the total effort available, rather than on competition between separate analysers. Such models make extensive use of the concept of *arousal.

Recently, renewed interest in applications of attention has become apparent. Most of the laboratory research has been directed to understanding the internal mechanisms of attention in the brain. But as large and complex man-machine systems appear, and more and more automation is introduced, there is a tremendous need for a good understanding of man as a monitor of complex systems. How should they be designed so as to optimize the use of attention? (It is fairly clear that in real-life tasks attention is never switched more than about twice a second.) How should a man be trained so as to combine to best effect his limited conscious attention with his unconscious control of *skilled behaviour? The solution of such questions is necessary if accidents in power stations, aircraft, and industry are to be avoided. Attention theory has advanced to a point where it can give a real insight into the solution of practical problems, and there is likely to be a third age in which the precise experimental work of the 1950s to the 1970s is extended in more complex ways to solve the problems of man-machine system design. We have come to see attention not merely as a single process concerned with enhancing the clarity of perception. Rather, it is a complex

of skills. These include selecting one from several messages, selecting one from several interpretations of information, selecting one from several plans of action, and selecting one from several actions. But in our interactions with the rich dynamics of the world in which we live and to which we adapt, attention also models that world, and provides us with strategies and high-level control of our tactics of information sampling, optimizing our information processing in the face of our limited processing capacities.   NM

Broadbent, D. (1958). *Perception and Communication*.
James, W. (1890). *Principles of Psychology*.
Kahneman, D. (1973). *Attention and Effort*.
Kanwisher, N., and Wojciulik, E. (2000). 'Visual attention: insights from neuroimaging'. *Nature Reviews Neuroscience*, 1.
Moray, N. (1969). *Listening and Attention*.
Titchener, E. B. (1908). *Lectures on the Elementary Psychology of Feeling and Attention*.
Underwood, G. (1978). *Strategies of Information Processing*.

audiometer. Electronic instrument used for testing *hearing. A simple audiometer is an oscillator having about ten pre-set frequencies in the range 500 to 8,000 hertz, and a stepped attenuator so that tone detection thresholds can be measured in decibels. More elaborate instruments combine noise masking (for measuring recruitment, which is associated with sensory neural deafness). The most sophisticated is the *Békésy audiometer, in which the patient, or subject of an experiment, tracks a continuously changing tone, his responses being recorded with an automatic plotter. Audiometry may test for word recognition, and it may introduce more or less normal confusing sounds. It can be most useful for distinguishing various kinds of hearing impairment.

auditory illusions. Although many visual *illusions were discovered in the 19th century, interest in auditory illusions has developed only recently. Some of these illusions are paradoxical. Apart from their subjective interest they provide valuable information concerning the mechanisms that our auditory system (see HEARING) employs to interpret our environment.

One illusion demonstrates that separate and independent brain mechanisms exist for determining what we hear, and for determining where the sound is coming from. The combined operation of these two mechanisms may lead to the perception of a sound that does not exist, i.e. with its characteristics taken from one source and its location from another.

The configuration that produces this illusion is shown in Fig. 1a. This consists of two tones that are spaced an octave apart and repeatedly presented in alternation. The identical sequence is presented to both ears simultaneously through earphones; however, when the right ear

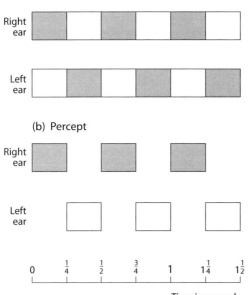

(a) Stimulus

Right ear

Left ear

(b) Percept

Right ear

Left ear

0    $\frac{1}{4}$ $\frac{1}{2}$ $\frac{3}{4}$ 1 $1\frac{1}{4}$ $1\frac{1}{2}$

Time in seconds

Fig. 1. a. Pattern giving rise to the first illusion. Two tones that are spaced an octave apart are repeatedly presented in alternation. When one ear receives the high tone the other ear simultaneously receives the low tone. The filled squares indicate the high tone and the unfilled squares the low tone. **b.** Illusion most commonly obtained. This consists of a high tone in one ear alternating with a low tone in the other ear.

receives the high tone the left ear receives the low tone, and vice versa. So in fact the listener is presented with a single, continuous two-tone chord, but the ear of input for each component switches repeatedly.

It can be imagined how this sequence should sound if perceived correctly. However, with very rare exceptions an illusion is always produced. The type of illusion obtained varies from listener to listener, but the most common one is shown in Fig. 1b. This consists of a single tone that switches from ear to ear; and as it switches its pitch simultaneously shifts back and forth from high to low. That is, the listener hears a single high tone in one ear alternating with a single low tone in the other ear.

There is no simple way to explain this illusion. We can explain the perception of alternating pitches by assuming that the listener processes the input to one ear and ignores the other. But then both of the alternating pitches should appear localized in the same ear. Alternatively, we can explain the alternation of a single tone from ear to ear by supposing that the listener suppresses the input to each ear in turn. But then the pitch of this tone should not change with a change in its apparent location. The

illusion of a single tone that alternates simultaneously both in pitch and in localization is paradoxical.

The illusion is even more surprising when we consider what happens when the listener's earphones are placed in reverse position. Now, most people hear exactly the same thing: that is, the tone that appeared to be in the right ear still appears to be in the right ear, and the tone that appeared to be in the left ear still appears to be in the left ear. So it seems to the listener that the earphone which had been producing the high tone is now producing the low tone, and that the earphone which had been producing the low tone is now producing the high tone!

Experiments have shown that this illusion is based on the operation of two independent mechanisms: one for determining what pitch we hear, and the other for determining where the sound is coming from. To provide the perceived sequence of pitches, those arriving at one ear are heard, and those arriving at the other ear are suppressed. However, each tone is localized in the ear receiving the higher pitch, regardless of whether the higher or the lower is in fact heard. So, given a listener who hears the pitches presented to his right ear when a high tone is delivered to the right ear and a low tone to the left, this listener hears a high tone since this is the tone delivered to his right ear. Further, he localizes the tone in his right ear, since this ear is receiving the higher pitch. However, when a high tone is delivered to the left ear and a low tone to the right, this listener now hears a low tone since this is the tone delivered to his right ear, but he localizes the tone in his left ear, since this ear is receiving the higher pitch. So the entire sequence is heard as a high tone to the right alternating with a low tone to the left. Reversing the position of the earphones would not alter this basic percept (though the identities of the first and last tones in the sequence would reverse); but given a listener who hears the pitches delivered to his left ear instead, keeping the localization rule constant, the same sequence would be perceived as a high tone to the left alternating with a low tone to the right.

Another auditory illusion demonstrates the importance of unconscious inference in auditory perception. This illusion also involves presenting two different tonal sequences through earphones. The configuration consists of a musical scale, presented simultaneously in ascending and descending form. When a tone from the ascending scale is delivered to the left ear, a tone from the descending scale is delivered to the right ear, and successive tones in each scale alternate from ear to ear. This sequence is repetitively presented without pause.

This configuration also produces various illusory percepts, which fall into two main categories. Most listeners perceive the correct set of pitches, but as two melodic lines, one corresponding to the higher tones and the other to the lower tones. Further, the higher tones all appear to be emanating from one earphone and the lower tones from the other. When the earphone positions are reversed there is often no change in what is perceived. So it appears to the listener that the earphone that had been producing the higher tones is now producing the lower tones, and that the earphone that had been producing the lower tones is now producing the higher tones! Other listeners perceive only a single melodic line, which corresponds to the higher tones, and they hear little or nothing of the lower tones.

How can we account for the first type of illusory percept? It must have a different basis from the illusion described earlier, since here all the tones are perceived; they are simply localized incorrectly. There are strong cognitive reasons for expecting such an illusion. In every-day life similar sounds are likely to emanate from the same source, and different sounds from different sources. Our present sequence consists of tones drawn from closely overlapping pitch ranges which are continuously emanating from two specific locations in space. So the best interpretation of this sequence in terms of the real world is that an object which emits sounds in one pitch range is located in one place, and that another object which emits sounds in a different pitch range is located in another place. This inference is here so strong as to over-ride our actual localization cues, so that we perceive the sequence in accordance with this interpretation.   DD

Deutsch, D. (1975). 'Musical illusions'. *Scientific American*, 233.
—— (1983). 'Auditory illusions and audio'. Special issue of the *Journal of the Audio Engineering Society*, 31/9.

authority. See OBEDIENCE, MILGRAM ON.

autism and Asperger syndrome. Autism is a lifelong developmental disorder with multiple biological origins and very heterogeneous behavioural manifestations. Autism is conceptualized as a spectrum defined by core impairments in social communication, with a restricted range of activities and interest that vary with age and ability. The spectrum includes the severely impaired child of low IQ, who may be mute and exhibiting simple motor stereotypies, such as rocking. It includes the classically aloof child with echoed speech and insistence on same-ness who, as well as showing some learning disabilities, shows islets of ability. The spectrum also includes very able and highly verbal individuals with less obvious symptoms. The absence of a delay in language acquisition frequently results in such cases being diagnosed much later in life. Such individuals have the same social communication problems although in a milder form, but retain narrow and obsessively pursued interests. Some of these people may crave social interactions without the understanding or ability to form relationships, have odd speech and body language, and be interested in unusual topics

(e.g. registration numbers on lamp-posts). This latter picture describes the new diagnostic category of Asperger syndrome. The prevalence of autism spectrum disorder is thought to be in the region of 0.6 per cent and possibly up to 0.9 per cent of the population, with approximately three times more males affected than females. There is no evidence for an autism epidemic despite an increase in prevalence. Rather, earlier studies produced much smaller figures but had a very narrow definition of autism that only applies to a small proportion of cases with autism spectrum disorder.

As shown by twin and family studies, genetic causes are most likely to underlie autism and Asperger syndrome. Current genetic studies implicate locations on a number of chromosomes, e.g. 7 and 15. Given the relatively wide criteria of a broader phenotype which includes mild variants, the concordance is 82 per cent in identical twins and 10 per cent in fraternal twins. Non-genetic causes (e.g. viral encephalopathy), toxic influences early in fetal life, or specific neurological conditions (e.g. tuberous sclerosis, fragile X syndrome, Rett's syndrome) have also been implicated. Regardless of aetiology, genetic as well as non-genetic risk factors may adversely affect the development of certain brain systems and consequently the development of certain cognitive systems that are dysfunctional autism.

Because there is currently no biological marker, the diagnosis of autism is by behavioural criteria: qualitative impairments in social interaction and communication and the presence of restricted and repetitive interests and activities. Autism is associated with a variety of neurological signs (epilepsy, EEG abnormalities, mental retardation, motor stereotypies, and impairments). Various types of brain abnormality have been found, e.g. a decrease in Purkinje cells in the cerebellum and brain stem, and decreases as well as increases in various cortical and subcortical regions. However, the specific and defining features of autistic brains have not yet been identified. This is in part due to the heterogeneity of the condition, which makes it problematic to relate physiological and behavioural data.

In contrast, a much better consensus about the nature of the condition has been achieved at the cognitive level. At this level, the multiple biological causes and multiple behavioural consequences can be pulled together by postulating deficits and assets in a small number of cognitive functions. See Fig. 1.

One influential theory, which can be referred to as mind-blindness, has been particularly successful in explaining the very variable core symptoms in social communication in autism. Among the first reliable signs of autism is an absence of joint attention activities, e.g. a lack of spontaneous pointing and a lack of pretend play. These early difficulties signal a failure to attend to the

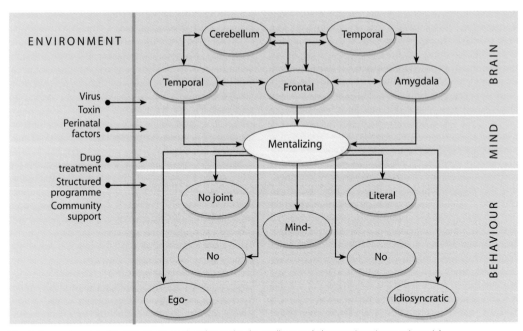

Fig. 1. A causal model of autism spectrum disorder. In the theory illustrated, the core impairments in social interaction and communication are explained by a single cognitive deficit in a mechanism with a complex neural basis. At all levels environmental influences interact with internal factors, either aggravating or ameliorating the condition, and increasing variability. This model can be readily changed to illustrate other theories by adding or substituting other putative cognitive deficits, e.g. theories that explain frequently associated impairments in executive functions, motor functions, and language. The framework can also be used to illustrate theories concerning the coexistence of well-functioning cognitive abilities, e.g. enhanced perceptual processing and high general intelligence.

contents of other minds, or to understand 'make-believe'. This is later manifested in an individual's failure to perform laboratory tasks of false belief, presented in dramatic form, in story form, in pictures or in animations. The crux of these tests is that the child has to understand that another person's behaviour can be predicted from a knowledge of his desires and beliefs. Children with autism, even high-functioning ones, seem unable to pass tests of belief attribution at the appropriate mental and chronological age. This is in contrast to other children with learning disabilities, such as Down's syndrome.

A mentalizing deficit explains the particular social communication difficulties that are typical of children and adults with autism, whilst allowing for a range of social and emotional behaviours which appear to function normally. For instance, children with autism are able to use instrumental gestures (to affect behaviour directly) much better than expressive gestures (to affect inner states). They are able to understand and engage in sabotage (to affect behaviour directly) better than in deception (to alter someone's belief). While able to remember messages

verbatim, to give factual and honest answers to questions, and even to deliver learned speeches, they are curiously unable to respond to hints, to engage in gossip, to keep secrets, and to make confidences.

Faces are arguably some of the most important social cues, and people with autistic disorder have difficulties in remembering individual faces. Brain scans have shown that they do not activate the normal face-processing area. Whether this is a primary or secondary difficulty, arising from a lack of social orientation and a lack of learning about social agents, remains to be seen.

In individuals with Asperger syndrome, verbal ability and social adaptation tend to be higher than in autism. Compensatory learning of social communication skills can occur even in the absence of mentalizing early in life. In a proportion of cases mentalizing abilities are acquired with practice and through the application of logical inference. In a proportion of cases, mentalizing may be merely delayed. However, mentalizing acquired later in life appears to lack an intuitive basis, and tends to be fragile and effortful.

Evidence from neuroimaging has shown that compared to non-autistic individuals, people with autism display a different pattern of activation in the brain structures thought to underlie mentalizing, e.g. the medial frontal cortex, the temporoparietal junction, and the temporal poles adjacent to the amygdala. Some of these structures also show anatomical abnormalities and/or weak connectivity.

A number of other characteristic impairments on psychological tests have been found in autism which appear to be separate from social communication impairments. These notably include repetitiveness and inflexibility, stimulus-driven behaviour, and a lack of foresight and planning. These symptoms have been convincingly linked to frontal lobe dysfunction. People with autism also have unusual abilities, as reflected in a typical profile of intelligence test scores with peaks on tasks that require accurate perception of detail. Hypersensitivity to sensory stimuli and absolute pitch are often reported. In 10 per cent of autism cases, exceptional abilities are shown, most frequently rote memory, but also talents in art, music, language, and number. All these phenomena have been linked to a particular cognitive processing style, labelled weak central coherence, that favours enhanced perception of detail. This processing style appears to be part of the broader phenotype of autism, and deserves fuller investigation. UF

Baron-Cohen, S., Tager-Flusberg, H., and Cohen, D. J. (eds.) (2000). *Understanding Other Minds: Perspectives from Autism* (2nd edn.).

Gillberg, C., and Coleman, M. (2000). *The Biology of the Autistic Syndromes* (3rd edn.).

Happé, F., and Frith, U. (1996). 'The neuropsychology of autism'. *Brain*, 19.

Klin, A., Volkmar, F., and Sparrow, S. (eds.) (2000). *Asperger Syndrome*.

Wing, L. (1996). *The Autistic Spectrum*.

autonomic nervous system. Also known as the involuntary nervous system, it involves the smooth (rather than the striated) muscles, and is essentially the regulatory mechanisms of digestion, respiration, circulation of the blood, and so on. These processes are not normally under voluntary control, though they may be brought under control by *conditioning or by *biofeedback. The fact that much behaviour is involuntary and unconscious raises such questions as: why is some behaviour *voluntary*, and under conscious control? It seems that high rates of information processing in unusual situations require consciousness, and are voluntary. The recent appreciation that many involuntary processes (such as heart rate) can be brought under voluntary control is strengthening the claims and widening the range of *psychosomatic medical practice.

aversion therapy. Applying, or showing, situations or objects that frighten, or disturb, with gradually increasing nearness, or frequency of presentation, as a way of alleviating *phobias by gradually increasing familiarity with the frightening object or situation. See also BEHAVIOUR THERAPY.

Avicenna (Abu 'Ali al-Hussein ibn-'Abdallah ibn-Sina) (980–1037). *Islamic philosopher and eminent physician, born at Afshana, near Bukhara, called by the Arabs *Al-Sheikh al-Rais*, 'Chief and Leader (of thinkers)'. His *Canon of Medicine* was the standard work, in Europe as in the East, until the 17th century. He was a royal physician at the age of 17.

Avicenna's philosophy exercised, through 12th-century translations, a considerable influence upon Western thinkers, his major work being the eighteen-volume *Book of Recovery*, written in eighteen months. He follows *Al-Farabi in ideas, though his work is regarded by scholars as more lucid, dealing with the distinction between necessary and possible being. Among the terms and concepts that he bequeathed to human thought is *intentio (ma 'qulat)*, the intellectually intelligible. His theme is that the entire universe is constituted of *essences: all existing things have specific essences. 'A horse', he says, 'is a horse.' He holds that all the senses are secondary, being divisions of an inner sense, which is common to all. All reality as we know it derives from one ultimate, unitary reality: God—but not directly. There are agencies that, in a series of actions, cause the apparent differences between phenomena. IS

Hitti, P. K. (1951). *History of the Arabs*.

Wickers, G. M. (ed.) (1952). *Avicenna: Scientist and Philosopher*.

axiom. When, in any intellectual discipline, a theory is proposed, there will be some propositions that are regarded as fundamental, or first, principles of the theory. This is in contrast to other propositions which, although part of the theory, are consequences of, or follow from, these fundamental principles. According to *Aristotle, first principles will take the form of either definitions, postulates, or axioms. The Aristotelian definition of an *axiom* is that it is a principle common to all sciences, which is self-evidently true (and thus knowable *a priori) but incapable of proof. Thus we have as one of *Euclid's axioms, or Common Notions, 'The whole is greater than the part'. A *postulate* on the other hand is a principle specific to a given science which is assumed without proof and whose truth may not be self-evident. Thus we have Euclid's postulate that 'if a straight line falling on two straight lines makes the interior angles on the same side less than two right angles, the two straight lines, if produced indefinitely, meet on that side on which the angles are less than the two right angles'. In modern deductive formalizations of theories this distinction between axioms and postulates is retained, but in a slightly modified form as a distinction between logical and non-logical axioms. The non-logical axioms contain terms specific to the science in question. Where these terms are not explicitly defined, the set of axioms adopted is sometimes regarded as providing an implicit definition of the terms involved. Sets of axioms are also used, particularly in mathematics, as ways of characterizing, and hence providing a definition of, a kind of structure. Thus a group is defined as any structure of which a particular set of axioms, the group axioms, are true. (See also DEDUCTION; GEOMETRY) MET

axon. A nerve fibre that transmits signals, sometimes over distances of a metre or more. The signals are action potentials from sense organs (*afferent fibres) to muscle (*efferent fibres). Axons transmit with a wide range of velocities up to about the speed of sound, the largest diameter fibres having the fastest conduction rate. Myelinated axons transmit fastest. The myelin sheathing, formed of the myelin-producing Schwann cells, serves not only to increase the conduction rate but also to isolate fibres from each other. This is important where axons run in bundles, which in the extreme case of the optic nerve contain as many as a million nerve fibres. See NEUROTRANSMITTERS AND NEUROMODULATORS.

B

Babbage, Charles (1791–1871). English mathematician and inventor, widely recognized as the first pioneer of the computer. His conception and design of the Analytical Engine rank among the startling intellectual achievements of the 19th century. Babbage's lifelong efforts to realize a complete physical calculating engine failed despite decades of design and development, massive government funding, 'vision verging on genius', independent means, and the social advantages of a well-heeled gentleman of science.

Babbage went to Trinity College, Cambridge, in 1810 already a precociously accomplished mathematician, largely self-taught. He excelled at mathematics though he graduated without honours from Peterhouse in 1814. He was elected a Fellow of the Royal Society in 1816 and was Lucasian Professor of mathematics at Cambridge from 1828 to 1839. He was presented with the first gold medal of the Astronomical Society in 1823 for his invention of the Difference Engine.

The original motive for the calculating engines was to eliminate human error from the production of printed mathematical tables. The genesis episode occurred in 1821 when Babbage and John Herschel were checking hand-calculated mathematical tables. Dismayed at the errors Babbage exclaimed, 'I wish to God these calculations had been executed by steam'. His first Difference Engine, so called because of the mathematical principle on which it is based (the method of finite differences), was designed to automatically calculate, tabulate, and print numerical tables. The designs call for some 25,000 parts and the machine, if completed, would have been physically massive. By 1833 some 12,000 parts had been made and a small number of these were used to assemble one-seventh of the Engine as a demonstration piece. This 'beautiful fragment' was used by Babbage at his celebrated society soirées to illustrate his theory of miracles. He argued that by analogy with programmed discontinuities in the numerical sequence generated by the machine miracles were explicable not as violations of natural law but as manifestations of higher laws as yet unknown. The 'fragment' is all that was built of the Difference Engine in Babbage's lifetime. It works impeccably and is preserved in the Science Museum in London. The larger construction project was abandoned in 1833 following a dispute with the engineer Joseph Clement.

The connection between mind and machine was not lost on Babbage or his contemporaries. 'We went to see the *thinking* machine, for such it seemed,' wrote Lady Byron in 1833. 'The marvelous pulp and fibre of the brain had been substituted by brass and iron, he [Babbage] had taught wheelwork *to think*, or at least to do the office of thought.' So wrote Harry Wilmot Buxton, a younger contemporary of Babbage, in a posthumous biography.

The attempts to design and construct automatic calculating machines led Babbage from mechanized arithmetic to fully fledged automatic computation, and his Analytical Engine, conceived in 1833, embodies many of the essential logical features of the modern digital computer. The machine had an internal repertoire of operations, was to be programmable using punched cards, had a separate 'Store' (memory) and 'Mill' (central processor), was capable of conditional branching (IF . . . THEN . . . instructions), and featured 'microprogramming', 'looping' (iteration), and 'pipelining' (preparation of a result ahead of need). The major design work was completed by 1840 though Babbage tinkered with improvements till his death. Neither the Engine nor its many variants were built though some small experimental pieces survive. Valuable insights into contemporary thinking are provided by Ada Lovelace, the daughter of Byron, who met Babbage at a party in 1833 and wrote about the Analytical Engine in presciently far-sighted terms.

Babbage was an inveterate inventor and devised contrivances, instruments, and devices in profusion, though he opposed patents on the grounds that profit restricted the wider benefit of invention. He suffered from a vision impairment (bilateral monocular diplopia) in which there are two foci in the same eye, resulting in double vision when looking through either eye singly. He constructed the first ophthalmoscope in 1847, possibly in an attempt at self-diagnosis, though the invention was credited 4 years later to *Helmholtz.

A prevailing theme in his mathematical work as well as in his engine designs is the value of notation as a representational language to assist the manipulation of concepts. The intricacy of the mechanisms he designed 'baffled the most tenacious memory'. To aid visualization of the complex trains of interrelated parts, he developed Mechanical Notation, an elaborate system of signs and symbols, to describe the manner in which parts are intended to interact.

Fig. 1. Difference Engine No. 2. Designed by Charles Babbage between 1846 and 1849. Built at the Science Museum in London to original designs. Completed April 2002. The Engine consists of 8,000 parts, weighs 5 tonnes and measures 3.3 metres (11 feet) long and 2 metres (7 feet) high. Printer and stereotyping apparatus (foreground); calculating section (rear). The machine calculates and tabulates any seventh-order polynomial, prints and stereotypes results automatically to 30 decimal places.

One form of the Notation consists of timing diagrams which show how different motions are phased and harmonized. Another form closely resembles what would now be called flow diagrams. Yet a third form, used extensively to annotate his design drawings, uses a letter to identify a part and numerous subscripts and superscripts to indicate the type of motion (reciprocating, circular, continuous, intermittent, for example) and the relationship to other connected parts whether driving or driven. As many as six alphabets are used. Babbage regarded the Mechanical Notation as a universal language of interaction applicable equally to the circulation of blood, animal respiration, clockwork, and combat. He wrote of the Notation as 'one of the most important additions [he had] made to human knowledge'. He used the Notation extensively in the design and optimization of his machines, but it was largely ignored by others then and since.

In all he published six books and nearly 90 articles. The range of his works is polymathically broad even by the generous standards of the times. In addition to works on mathematics and calculating engines his output includes writings on chess, lock picking, taxation, submersibles, geology, life assurance, philosophy, cryptanalysis, politics, electricity and magnetism, statistics, machine tools, political economics, industrial arts and manufacture, machine tools, astronomy, lighthouses, ordnance, and archaeology. He was a vigorous reformer, proud, touchy, and fiercely principled. In his campaigning writing he preferred protest to persuasion and his first published biographer called him, in 1963, the 'irascible genius', which remains a sharp and durable image. He died disappointed, unacknowledged, and aggrieved. DDS

Campbell-Kelly, M. (ed.) (1989). *The Works of Charles Babbage*, 11 vols.

Hyman, A. (1984). *Charles Babbage: Pioneer of the Computer*.

Swade, D. (2000). *The Cogwheel Brain: Charles Babbage and the Quest to Build the First Computer*.

babbling. The utterance or hearing of incoherent speech sounds. It is thought that the Greeks heard all other languages as 'babble', giving the word an onomatopoeic origin. Indeed unfamiliar languages do sound formless, with no clear demarcation between words. In a familiar language, word units are identified not by breaks in speech but from the continuous 'babble' of speech, much as separate objects are seen from the mosaic pattern of stimulation of the eyes.

It is believed that babies produce all the speech sounds of any language in their babbling, and that speech sounds or phonemes of the language of their environment are gradually selected, according to use (see LANGUAGE DEVELOPMENT IN CHILDREN).

Babinski reflex. The involuntary raising of the big toe upon stroking the side of the foot. The *reflex is present in adult apes and in human infants, but disappears in humans at about 18 months, when it is inhibited by higher centres. The inhibition is lost in tabes dorsalis (the degeneration of the posterior ascending fibres of the spinal cord that occurs in tertiary syphilis) and in other diseases of the brain and spinal cord. It is believed that the reflex is useful for grasping the branches of trees with the toes, and that the inhibitory mechanism was developed late in primate evolution, when apes forsook the trees to walk on the ground. It is a useful diagnostic reflex, and was discovered by the French neurologist Joseph Babinski (1857–1932).

Bacon, Francis (1561–1626). British statesman and philosopher, born at York House in the Strand, London, the younger son of Sir Nicholas Bacon (1509–79), who was Queen Elizabeth's Keeper of the Great Seal—which office Francis later held. He became Baron Verulam, Viscount St Albans, a mark of his highly distinguished legal career culminating in his appointment as Lord High Chancellor in 1618. His public career ended sadly in 1621 when he was convicted on charges of bribery, charges that were probably unfair, given the contemporary professional morality.

Bacon is distinguished for setting out what was to be considered the technique and philosophy of modern science. He developed, from *Aristotelian beginnings, *inductive principles for amassing and interpreting data—especially for establishing *causes. Whereas Aristotle saw causes as the *essence of things, to be discovered by descriptive analysis, Bacon stressed the importance of enumerating instances where characteristics and events occur, or do not occur, in association. By setting out methods of induction, which included looking for exceptions and refutations of hypotheses, he separated science from philosophy. He saw his inductive methods as instruments for generating knowledge. The Royal Society was founded in London in 1660, essentially on the basis of Bacon's *The Advancement of Learning* (1605) and *Novum organum* (1620). In his *Essays*, written throughout his life, Bacon appears as a highly literate and wise man. He was thus a philosopher in the fullest sense of the word, as well as having the vision to set out principles that greatly influenced the development of modern science. RLG

Bacon, F. (1857). *Works*. Eds. J. Spedding, R. L. Ellis, and D. D. Heath.

Quinton, A. (1980). *Francis Bacon*.

Bain, Alexander (1818–1903). British psychologist, born in Aberdeen, where he spent most of his life. His books *The Senses and the Intellect* (1855) and *The Emotions and the Will* (1859) remained, with revisions, standard texts of psychology for half a century. They are still useful reference sources for their historical comments, and their structure remains as the skeleton of modern textbooks of psychology. Bain linked psychology with physiology, paid attention to reflexes, and discussed instinct and belief. Most important, he developed sophisticated views on the still difficult questions of voluntary action, or the will. His discussions of this topic are still worth reading.

Bajjah, Ibn. See IBN BAJJAH.

Bartlett, Sir Frederic Charles (1886–1969). Highly significant British psychologist, born at Stow-on-the-Wold, Gloucestershire: he became the first professor of Psychology at Cambridge University. A world leader with a lasting reputation for originality, and theoretical insights that remain important.

He was an undergraduate at St John's College, Cambridge, where he met the philosopher James *Ward (whose article on 'Psychology' in the *Encyclopaedia Britannica* (1886) had a great influence on British psychologists and influenced Bartlett) and also met C. S. *Myers and W. H. R. *Rivers. In his account of the development of psychology in Cambridge from 1887 to 1937 (Bartlett 1937), he gives an interesting account of these three men and of their influence on him and on psychology in Cambridge.

At first Bartlett had wanted to work on social anthropology with Rivers; but then joined with him, and with Ward and Myers, to establish a laboratory for experimental psychology at 16 Mill Lane, Cambridge. Cyril Burt (1883–1971) assisted Myers with the laboratory work, and when Burt left, Bartlett took his place. Rivers, who had done extensive pioneering work on sensory measurements in the course of his anthropological studies, considered that experience with psychophysical methods would be an advantage to Bartlett if he should do social anthropology in the field. In due course, though, the development of the Cambridge University psychological laboratory became Bartlett's life work, as he became the first occupant of the chair in 1931. He left detailed psychophysics and statistical analysis to others, whom he supported and inspired with remarkably prescient ideas.

Ward's opposition to atomistic–associationist psychologies, such as that of Herbert *Spencer, must have strengthened Bartlett's discontent with prevailing associationist theories of sensation, *perception, learning, memory, and thinking—as with later *behaviourism, which he did a great deal to demolish. He chimed in which William *James, and the Würzberg school, in their different ways. He particularly criticized Hermann Ebbinhaus's, then popular, Nonsense Syllables, saying that meaningless stimuli may give impressively smooth graphs, but the results are also meaningless, as the individual spends his or her life seeking meaning in learning and perception. 'Effort after meaning' was a Bartlettian slogan.

For his quite informal but conceptually significant

experiments, Bartlett used pictures and stories from folk tales. The outcome of many years of research was published in his celebrated book *Remembering* (1932), which remains important. In this book he shows that perceiving, recognition, imaging, and recall are to be understood as the expression of active dynamic processes, dealing with the current situation of the organism and its current needs, based on and related to its past experience. He adopted and adapted Henry *Head's 'schemas', which live on now as active brain traces in connectionist paradigms. ('Schemas', rather than the correct 'schemata', was used as being less clumsy.)

The influence of Myers, apart from in experimental psychology itself, may be seen in Bartlett's keen interest in applied and industrial psychology. This was apparent in his studies during the First World War, when submarine warfare was of paramount significance, especially the problems of perceiving changes in underwater sounds which might indicate the presence of an enemy submarine approaching a ship.

During the 1920s and 1930s Bartlett worked largely on social psychology. His book *Psychology and Primitive Culture* (1923) was an interesting and original work. This and *The Study of Society* (1939) which was compiled during meetings of an informal group of which he was the mainspring and leader, never gained the attention they deserved. The Second World War, with its demand for better understanding of man–machine interaction, and especially for guidance and tracking, and aircraft control and instrument design, found Bartlett the ideal leader. He chaired important war-time research committees.

Important nationally, and for Bartlett, was the coming to Cambridge of Kenneth *Craik, Bartlett's most outstanding pupil. Craik became a legend, combining exceptional gifts for theoretical work—seen for instance in his concept of the human operator viewed as a link in a control system, and his work on vision—with astonishing skill in experimentation, and designing apparatus. He and Bartlett fused their powers in a way that made the applied psychology of wartime problems a major force for success. Craik's sudden death, at the end of the war in 1945, was a severe blow to Bartlett, from which he never fully recovered.

In 1944 the Medical Research Council established an Applied Psychology Unit in Cambridge under Craik's direction, and Bartlett continued his association with it after his retirement. In later years, he extended his earlier work on perceiving and remembering to the psychology of thinking, with the production of a book (Bartlett 1958) in which he showed that the thinker, whether by interpolation or by extrapolation, deals with a present problem in terms of his past experience, and by a flexible activity brings about the completion of an open-ended situation. So thinking is a kind of skill, comparable with the skills seen, for instance, in ball games (which had always interested Bartlett); and it was thus brought into line with perceiving and remembering, which can also be regarded as kinds of skill.

Bartlett had very exceptional intellectual powers. Students felt that he treated them as equals, just as he tells us Rivers treated him. He received numerous honours, including Fellowship of the Royal Society in 1922, and a Knighthood.   RWP/RLG

Bartlett, F. C. (1923). *Psychology and Primitive Culture.*
—— (1932). *Remembering: A Study in Experimental and Social Psychology.*
—— (1937). 'Cambridge, England, 1887–1937'. *American Journal of Psychology,* 50.
—— (1958). *Thinking: An Experimental and Social Study.*
—— Ginsberg, M., Lindgren, E. J., and Thouless, R. H. (eds.) (1939). *The Study of Society: Methods and Problems.*
Oldfield, R. C. (1972). 'Frederic Charles Bartlett, 1886–1969'. *American Journal of Psychology,* 85.
Zangwill, O. L. (1970). 'Sir Frederic Bartlett (1886–1969): Obituary'. *Quarterly Journal of Experimental Psychology,* 22.

basal ganglia. Large masses of grey matter embedded deep in the white matter of the cerebral hemispheres and the midbrain. The basal ganglia have very complicated connections with the central nervous system and are concerned with the control of movement. Degeneration of the basal ganglia can disturb the motor function of the body, as occurs, for example, in *Parkinsonism and *Huntington's disease.

bedlam. A term used initially to describe a lunatic *asylum or madhouse, but now used figuratively to describe a general state of uproar. The word is derived from the Hospital of St Mary of Bethlehem (later the Bethlem Royal Hospital), which was founded in London in 1247 as a priory and which became a hospital specifically for the mentally ill in 1402. In the 18th century, the public, as an entertainment, could view the inmates, and the use of the word bedlam (from Bethlem) arose at this time.

behaviourism. The central tenet of behaviourism is that thoughts, feelings, and intentions, all mental processes, do not determine what we do. Our behaviour is the product of our conditioning. We are biological machines and do not consciously act; rather we *react* to stimuli.

In 1913, John B. *Watson argued that human psychology could do without the concept of *consciousness and the technique of *introspection. Instead, people could be studied objectively, as are cats, monkeys, and rats, by observing their behaviour. Watson claimed that research on consciousness had led nowhere because investigators who contemplated consciousness could never really agree about what was going on 'in the mind'. Behaviour was public. Two scientists could time how long it takes a rat to get to the end of a maze or how much of an evening John spends dancing with Jane. This approach came as a shock because, in its early days, psychology was linked closely to philosophy. The assertion that human beings were observable like animals jolted many pioneers who assumed that humankind was a cut above the rest of nature. Watson, furthermore, did not want behaviourism to be just an academic theory. Its goal ought to be 'the control and prediction of behaviour'. If you could predict behaviour, it would show psychology was a science, just like physics, and if you could control behaviour, you could improve life.

The history of behaviourism has had its ironies. Though Watson was forced out of psychology because of a divorce scandal and temporarily reduced to selling rubber boots, behaviourism came to dominate Anglo-American psychology from the early 1920s to the mid-1950s. Moreover, though it came under increasing attack for neglecting not just consciousness but feelings, it shaped much of psychology in the 20th century. Even a psychoanalyst, Anna *Freud, explained in a late interview that it was well worth observing how children used toys, responded to tests, or ate meals. 'The analyst as behaviourist', she pointed out, 'can use pieces of behaviour to infer for example how a child deals with anxiety or frustration.' It is a mark of the success of behaviourism that even those who were radically opposed to it conceded that psychology has to involve studying actual behaviour. Watson and his followers were remarkable in claiming that psychology should study nothing else. Watson himself, however, did not quite stick to this extreme position: he was always willing to listen to what people said about what they did and, in *A Balance Sheet of the Self,* he suggested that psychology students ought first to analyse their own behaviour, reactions, and fears before being allowed to practise on anyone else.

Behaviourism has featured in political literature. Two nightmares and one Utopia were inspired by the notion that it is possible to condition people's behaviour. Aldous Huxley's *Brave New World* and George Orwell's *1984* both feared that advances in psychology had given the state the technology with which to control individuals. In B. F. Skinner's *Walden Two,* psychology is also in power. But Skinner, a behaviourist, firmly believed that its insights could be used to make people better and happier. In his community there is harmony, love, cooperation, and creativity, because human beings have been reinforced to behave that way to each other. Many critics of behaviourism have argued that *Walden Two* is, in its cloying, apple-pie harmony, just as oppressive as the Orwell and Huxley nightmares. Be that as it may, these three books bear witness to the cultural importance of behaviourism. The only other school of psychology to have impressed the 20th century as much was *psychoanalysis.

Watson was very much responsible for the initial success of behaviourism. He was born in Greenville, South Carolina, in 1878. His mother Emma was a zealous Baptist; his father Pickens was a misfit who enjoyed bourbon whiskey and eventually ran away from his pious wife to live with two Indian women. Religious Greenville was shocked and vitriolic; this helped make Watson detest religion, and was to prove important in his development—and that of behaviourism. After a difficult adolescence during which he was arrested for 'nigger bashing' and for firing a gun in the middle of Greenville, Watson went to Furman University; there 'I cut my teeth on metaphysics'. Having graduated, he went to the University of Chicago to study under the philosopher John *Dewey. But Watson soon became disillusioned with Dewey and turned to the study of animal behaviour. His doctoral thesis, 'Animal learning', looked not at how rats run mazes but at how they learn a variety of tricks including getting out of a box and opening a drawbridge.

In 1903, psychology was very young. Before the start of its first laboratories in 1879, it had often been called experimental philosophy, and in many universities psychologists still worked under the department of philosophy. It is not surprising that much of the discipline was rather abstract. Much effort was devoted to introspection and the unravelling of consciousness. In 1903, introspecting did not mean brooding on one's *psyche but rather trying to dissect what was going on inside one's mind. Psychologists believed that a trained observer could report on what was going on in his consciousness when he saw dots, waited for a tone, or was asked to respond to a picture by pressing a button. Taking their models from chemistry and physics, they hoped to work out what were the 'atoms' of consciousness, but different subjects reported very different mental processes.

Introspection made Watson acerbic. 'I hated to serve as a subject,' he wrote in an autobiographical note in 1936; 'I didn't like the stuffy artificial instructions given to subjects. I always was uncomfortable and acted unnaturally. . . . More and more the thought presented itself. Can't I find out by watching their behaviour everything the other students are finding out by using O's.' O's were introspective observers. Evidence that he began to be highly critical of orthodox ideas does not depend only on his memory. He raised the possibility of studying humans like animals with James *Angell, his doctoral supervisor. Angell told him to stick to animals. This dismayed Watson and, with the pressure of finishing his doctorate, it led to a short breakdown. But he did not abandon his critique. He vowed to a friend that he would remodel psychology.

By 1908, Watson had a national reputation as 'an animal man'. He took the professorship of psychology at Johns Hopkins University and began to read widely in human psychology. He tested some of his ideas in letters to Robert Yerkes, an animal psychologist. Yerkes warned that Watson was too extreme; yet, in 1912, in a series of summer lectures at Columbia University, Watson outlined his critique. The lectures were well attended, and Watson, given the radical nature of his ideas, was nervous about how they would be received. Angell, he had heard, 'thinks I am crazy. I should not be surprised if that is the general consensus of opinion'.

The lectures, published in 1913, remain the text for behaviourism. Psychology 'as the behaviourist views it is a purely objective branch of natural science. Its theoretical goal is the control and prediction of behaviour'. Introspection was no help and psychologists should not judge the value of their data by whether it shed any light on the intricacies of consciousness. The behaviourist 'recognises no dividing line between man and brute.' Watson's dislike of religion, learned in Greenville, made him hostile to the idea that human beings were superior organisms with souls.

He made much fun of the failure of introspection. 'If you can't observe 3–9 states of clearness in attention, your introspection is poor. If, on the other hand, a feeling seems reasonably clear to you, your introspection is again faulty.' Sweeping such mystical nonsense away would enable psychology to become a proper science linked to biology rather than to metaphysics.

Rejecting introspection was easy; developing a coherent theory of how human beings behaved was rather harder. Watson drew heavily on the work of *Pavlov, who had shown that you could condition dogs to salivate not just at the sight of food but at the sound of a bell that preceded food. A reflex like salivation was malleable. Watson argued that human behaviour is built on just such conditioning. He claimed that almost all behaviour is learnt: if one gets up every time a lady enters the room, one is acting not out of politeness but because behaviour is a chain of well-set reflexes. Watson claimed that what determined the next item of behaviour a person 'emitted' was *recency* and *frequency*—what had occurred just before and what, in the past, had been the response a person made to that particular stimulus: if one usually gets up when a lady enters the room, one is very likely, if a lady enters the room now, to get up again. The behaviour may be explained as a polite action, but it is a reaction that could have been predicted. In Watson's scheme, rewards and punishments were not crucial.

In 1916, Watson began to study how children develop. He wanted to isolate the most important early reflexes on which conditioning could build. He also examined the idea of applying such ideas to psychiatry. In the early 1920s, he reported a study of Little Albert, a child who was taught to fear rats and then not to fear them entirely through manipulating. This paper (whose integrity has been disputed) was an inspiration to behaviour therapists who aim to train people out of their phobias and neuroses.

The historian John Burnham has warned against being romantic about Watson. Other psychologists were inching towards behaviourism, too. Burnham stressed T. S. Kuhn's theory of scientific revolutions which states that scientific revolutions occur when the field is ripe for a new paradigm. According to this view, Watson prevailed because the prevailing mood was right. But Kuhn's theory may not fit psychology too well. In arguing for behaviourism, Watson was not so much making a new discovery as offering a new philosophy and methodology. Behaviourism was a self-conscious revolution against consciousness. Some traditional psychologists grasped its dangers very well and reacted with hostility: James Angell said privately that Watson should be 'spanked', while Watson said of E. B. Titchener that he 'roasted me'. There is some dispute about how quickly behaviourist ideas spread through American psychology, but by 1920 Watson was recognized as one of the leading American psychologists.

In the 1930s and 1940s, behaviourism became very much laboratory based. B. F. Skinner (see BEHAVIOURISM, B. F. SKINNER ON and SKINNER BOX) made his name through his studies of how to reward pigeons and other creatures; Clark *Hull, perhaps the leading behaviourist of the 1940s, devised immensely complicated models of animal behaviour. These developments make it easy to imagine that Watson was bent not only on making psychology scientific but on imprisoning it in the laboratory. Nothing could be further from the truth.

In *Psychology from the Standpoint of a Behaviorist* (1919), Watson argued passionately that psychology should be relevant to real life. Scientists should analyse what people did in the factory, the office, the home, and even the bedroom. He initiated studies on subjects as varied as how well one can throw darts while drunk and the effects of anti-venereal disease propaganda on the sex lives of GIs. Behaviourism was to be a psychology of real life. But after the divorce scandal he had to resign from Johns Hopkins and could not see his programme through. Following his job as a travelling salesman, the advertising firm J. Walter Thompson employed him. Advertising was to benefit from his psychological skills—he pioneered many modern advertising techniques—but he was lost to serious psychology. He was only 42 at the time of his divorce, an age at which many psychologists begin doing their best work.

Behaviourism as it developed between 1913 and 1920 had many problems. It was a fluid theory. Watson tended to ignore the power of reinforcement. There was no convincing account of language, let alone of thought. Skinner later attempted to remedy this with his *Verbal Behavior* (1957); further research showed conclusively, however, that we do not just learn language but that we are innately 'wired' to speak. Then, from 1920 and into the 1930s, American universities expanded quickly and many new departments of psychology were set up. Behaviourism was in an attractive position because it seemed to ensure that psychology could be scientific. Most psychologists accepted Watson's methods though not his vision of applying psychology objectively to all of life. Behaviourism became narrower than it might have been if he had remained active.

The three major figures among those who developed behaviourism through the 1930s and 1940s were Edward Guthrie (1886–1959), Clark Hull, and Skinner. Guthrie followed Watson most closely but dropped frequency as an important determinant of behaviour. For Guthrie, 'a combination of stimuli which has accompanied a movement will on its recurrence tend to be followed by that movement'. He tried to show that all learning could be explained on this principle, ignoring how it might explain novel combinations of movements.

Hull proposed a more systematic total behaviourist theory. He tried to link the external circumstances (such as the intensity of a pain stimulus or the size of a reward) with internal body states (hunger and thirst) and with specific behaviours such as the speed with which an animal will run a maze for a food reward. Hull wanted a theory of behaviour as formal as Euclid's theory of geometry, and he introduced theorems and postulates which could account for all behaviour. The scheme was a grand one, and defined precisely some internal states such as drive, and strength of habit. For example, a rat who had been deprived of food for seven hours was likely to be hungrier than a rat deprived of food for three hours, unless the seven-hour rat had been used to going without food for longer. Hull perfected his system over some twenty years, but it had its problems. First, some experiments had inconvenient results. For example, Hull argued that habit strength built up slowly. It could therefore be expected that, for an animal used to doing X for reward Y, if the reward was reduced it would still tend to do X because of the habit strength attached to X. In fact, diminishing rewards reduced the behaviour fast. Then, as Hull tried to accommodate such results, internal inconsistencies in the theory began to creep in. He succeeded in offering a very grand vision of a theory that was precise and quantifiable. His books are full of equations. But by 1952, the year of his death, he knew that he had not quite succeeded, and it may be that his failure to make his system convince affected the ambitions of psychology. Perhaps it was too soon to attempt a comprehensive theory of behaviour.

Skinner now became the leading exponent of behaviourism. His first major theoretical contribution had tended to go against Watson's ideas. Arriving at Harvard in 1929 to work for his doctorate, Skinner was committed to a scientific and practical psychology. But he grew dissatisfied with basing everything on the reflex. It seemed to him not only that people respond to the environment but also that 'behaviour operates on the environment to generate consequences'. If a rat gets food every time it presses a lever, it is operating on the environment. Skinner argued, therefore, that most behaviour involves operant conditioning. We behave the way we do because of the consequences our past behaviour has generated. If every time a man takes his wife out to dinner, she is very loving, he is likely to learn to take her out to dinner if he wants her to be loving. Though this example (like many of Skinner's) involves description of behaviour in which motives, feelings, and intents appear to matter, Skinner himself was always scathing about what he described as 'the mentalists'. For Skinner, it is the history of reinforcements that determines behaviour. Consciousness is just an epiphenomenon, and feelings are not causes of actions but consequences. Behaviour can be predicted and controlled without reference to them.

Skinner made famous the notion of *shaping*. By controlling the rewards and punishments the environment offers in response to particular behaviours, you can shape behaviour. Pigeons can be 'shaped' even to play ping-pong. Psychiatric patients can be 'shaped' to behave in less anxious and more socially acceptable ways. Much of Skinner's detailed technical work was aimed at discovering the different effects of different schedules of reinforcement. Which are most effective: regular rewards, irregular rewards, or a mixture of the two?

The controversies Skinner has fuelled arise largely because, like Watson, he was not content to see behaviourism merely as a scientific method; rather it offers a way of organizing our lives better. Skinner has been accused of helping to perfect technologies of control, but the truth is more prosaic. In the 1950s and 1960s, there was a vogue for trying out 'token economies' in penal and psychiatric institutions. Professionals tried to 'shape' the behaviour of inmates by giving them rewards for behaviour that was deemed good or appropriate. Usually, the inmates were not punished, a point Skinner liked to stress. But though some institutions continue to use such methods of 'behaviour modification', as it has been called, it would be an exaggeration to say they are widespread or entirely successful. The individual histories of human beings are too complex for their behaviour to be shaped like that of laboratory-reared birds. Moreover, Skinner claimed, human beings cling to illusions of being free to act because they think, wrongly, that without them they will lose all dignity. We are, in fact, controlled by our past and controlled by our environment. The more we realize that—the more we analyse the nature of that control—the better our situation. Herein there is a paradox that Skinner does not really explore in his enthusiasm to go

against the importance of thoughts, intentions, and feelings. Skinner has certainly attracted much respect and fame but his form of classic behaviourism is now less and less in vogue especially as cognitive psychology has, since the late 1960s, suggested that it is possible to be objective about studying mental processes.

Behaviourism has been seen in different lights by different observers. The British psychologist Donald *Broadbent argued (1961) that it offers the best method for rational advance in psychology, allowing one to weed out facts from fantasy and to replace armchair speculation about the nature of the soul or the mysteries of consciousness with repeatable results. In contrast, Nehemiah Jorden asked the question (1968), 'can one positive contribution towards any increased knowledge of man be pointed to since Watson wrote his famous paper?' And answered it: 'None such can be found.' Any assessment of behaviourism has to recognize such different opinions, but almost all psychologists and psychiatrists see merit in some of Watson's ideas, while very few are strict behaviourists. One needs to study behaviour objectively. There are close links between human and animal behaviour, and conditioning does play an important part in human development. Many would also applaud the original aim of establishing a scientific psychology of life in the factory, the office, and the home. On the other hand, 70 years of research have shown that consciousness cannot be dismissed as uninteresting in human psychology and that even introspection has its uses, as one tool among many.

DC

Broadbent, D. (1961). *Behaviour*.
Cohen, D. (1979). *J. B. Watson, the Founder of Behaviourism*.
Jorden, N. (1968). *Themes in Speculative Psychology*.
Skinner, B. F. (1961). *Walden Two*.
Watson, J. B. (1919). *Psychology from the Standpoint of a Behaviorist*.

behaviourism, B. F. Skinner on. The scientific study of behaviour covers many fields, including ethology, psychology, sociology, anthropology, economics, and political science. Behaviourism is not one of these fields; it is a consideration of certain problems which arise in all of them. Behaviour is most effectively studied in relation to the environment—the environment in which the species evolved and the physical and social environments in which the individual lives. It has been traditionally viewed, however, in other ways—for example, as the expression of feelings or states of mind, as the role played by a personality, or as the symptom of mental illness. Behaviourism is in part an attack upon these traditional interpretations. It is a philosophy of behavioural science, the roots of which are to be traced through the writings of J. B. *Watson and I. P. *Pavlov to Ernst *Mach, Jules Henri *Poincaré, and Auguste *Comte, among others.

'Methodological' behaviourists often accept the existence of feelings and states of mind, but do not deal with them because they are not public and hence statements about them are not subject to confirmation by more than one person. 'Radical' behaviourists, on the other hand, recognize the role of private events (accessible in varying degrees to self-observation and physiological research), but contend that so-called mental activities are metaphors or explanatory fictions and that behaviour attributed to them can be more effectively explained in other ways. A few examples will be considered here to illustrate the latter position.

Purpose, intention, expectation. Most behaviour is selected by its consequences. For example, we tend to do the things we have successfully done in the past. Although it is the product only of past consequences, behaviour is useful because it may have similar consequences in the future. We refer indirectly to that future when we say that we act with a *purpose, intention, or expectation. Such 'states of mind' are not, however, the causes of our behaviour. We do not act because we have a purpose, we act because of past consequences, the very consequences that generate the condition of our bodies which we observe introspectively and call felt purpose. Natural selection raised the same issues. Has life a purpose? Is a given species the result of an intentional design? (See EVOLUTION: HAS IT A PURPOSE?) These concepts can be abandoned in both fields when the principle of selection by consequences is understood.

Mental processes. Many aspects of mental life are modelled upon the physical environment. The smell of a rose is said to 'remind us of' or 'bring to mind' the visual appearance of a rose because we associate one with the other. But the odour and the visual properties are associated in the rose. When we have been exposed to two physically associated stimuli, we may subsequently respond to one as we responded to the other, but the environmental association is enough to account for our behaviour. We have no introspective evidence of any internal process of association. Abstraction, concept formation, and many other so-called mental processes are also modelled upon complex arrangements of stimuli, and again the arrangements suffice to explain the behaviour without appeal to mental duplicates.

Sensations, perceptions, and images. Most people believe that when they look at a rose they construct an internal copy, called a sensation or perception, and that later, when they are reminded of a rose, they reconstruct that copy, now called a mental image, and look at it again. They do not observe themselves doing so; they simply see a rose. Under special circumstances, they may, in addition, observe that they are seeing one, but even so there is no evidence, introspective or physiological, of an internal copy. If seeing were simply constructing a copy of the thing seen, we should have to make another copy to see the copy, and then another copy to see that. At some point we must 'see a rose' in some other sense. What that means is not well understood—by anyone. Rather than look for internal representations, we should examine the ways in which a person learns to see things, in both the presence and absence of the things seen.

Reasons and reasoning. Three things must be taken into account in the study of behaviour: the situation in which behaviour occurs, the behaviour itself, and the consequences that follow. The relations among these things can be very complex, and only a careful scientific analysis will then untangle them. For practical purposes, however, we describe many of them with reasonable accuracy. When we give someone advice, for example, we specify a situation ('When you have a headache . . .'), an act ('take an aspirin . . .'), and (possibly only by implication) a consequence ('and you will feel better').

People profit from advice because by following it they can behave in ways which, without help, they would have to learn through a possibly long exposure to the conditions described. The social environment called a culture offers a vast store of rules, maxims, and governmental and scientific laws describing relations among situations, behaviour, and consequences, which enable people to acquire much more extensive repertoires than would otherwise be possible.

In taking advice or following rules we can be said to behave because of reasons rather than causes, and in what is called reasoning we formulate rules for our own use. Rather than explore a situation and allow our behaviour to be changed directly by it, we analyse the situation and extract a rule which we then follow. We sometimes extract rules from other rules, as in logic and mathematics.

Introspection. The world within a human skin is part of the physical world. It may seem that we should know it better because we are close to it, and we do, indeed, respond to private events with great precision in the normal functioning of our bodies. But *knowing* about our bodies, in the same sense in which we *know* about the world around us, depends upon conditions which cannot easily be arranged with respect to a private world. We learn to tell *P* from *Q* because other people respond appropriately when we say 'P' or 'Q' when looking at a letter. Unfortunately they cannot respond as precisely when we name or describe a private event (such as those we call feelings or states of mind), because they lack the necessary contact. As a result, we never know our own bodies with any great accuracy. Moreover, we cannot know much about many important parts of them (for example, the physiological processes that mediate the complex behaviour called thinking) because we simply do not have nerves going to relevant places.

Behaviourism criticizes mentalistic explanations of behaviour in this way only to promote a more effective analysis. By dismissing mental states and processes as metaphors or fictions, it directs attention to the genetic and personal histories of the individual and to the current environment, where the real causes of behaviour are to be found. It also clarifies the assignment of the neurosciences, saving the time that would otherwise be wasted in searching for the neurological counterparts of sensations, stored memories, and thought processes. Behaviour is simply part of the biology of the organism and can be integrated with the rest of that field when described in appropriate physical dimensions.

At the same time behaviourism provides an overview which is particularly helpful in the social sciences. The experimental analysis of behaviour has led to an effective technology, applicable to education, psychotherapy, and the design of cultural practices in general, which will be more effective when it is not competing with practices that have had the unwarranted support of mentalistic theories.   BFS

Skinner, B. F. (1974). *About Behaviorism*.

behaviour therapy. The term 'behaviour therapy' was coined towards the end of the 1950s by H. J. Eysenck to denote a method of treatment of neurotic disorders that was based on laboratory studies of *conditioning, and on modern *learning theory. Behaviour therapy is derived from a general theory of neurotic disorder which differs profoundly from psychoanalytic or orthodox psychiatric theories. Before presenting this theory (which is basic to the therapeutic application of the various methods comprised under the general term 'behaviour therapy'), it may be useful to distinguish behaviour therapy from *psychotherapy* and from *behaviour modification*, two terms that partly overlap with behaviour therapy, and are partly contrasted with it.

Psychotherapy denotes the use of psychological theories and methods in the treatment of psychiatric disorders; in its generic sense it therefore includes behaviour therapy as one of the methods used by psychologists and psychiatrists, and is partly synonymous with it. However, psychotherapy also has a narrower meaning, namely the use of interpretative (mostly *Freudian) methods of therapy; in this sense psychotherapy and behaviour therapy are antonyms, the former relying on verbal and symbolic methods, the latter on the direct manipulation of motor and autonomic behaviours. Thus psychotherapy in the wider sense can be usefully divided into psychotherapy in the narrower sense and behaviour therapy. Both psychotherapy and behaviour therapy refer to a whole set of methods; they are not confined to one single method, as the terms used might suggest.

The terms behaviour therapy and behaviour modification are also partly synonymous, partly antonymous. In the United States, particularly, both terms are used indiscriminately to refer to two sets of rather different theories and methods. Both these sets do, indeed, make use of psychological theories of learning and conditioning, and to that extent there is some overlap. However, psychologists make a fairly clear (although probably not absolute) distinction between two kinds of conditioning: *Pavlovian or classical, and instrumental or operant. Behaviour therapy in the narrower sense is concerned with Pavlovian conditioning, behaviour modification with instrumental conditioning. In this sense these methods and theories are antonymous, and we may say that behaviour therapy in the wider sense can be usefully subdivided into behaviour therapy in the narrower sense and behaviour modification. These complications of nomenclature are bothersome and annoying, but they have become so firmly entrenched that they have to be dealt with; clearly anyone writing about these various therapies should indicate in which sense the terms are being used.

Pavlovian conditioning forms associations between conditioned stimuli (neutral before conditioning) and unconditioned stimuli and responses by simple pairing: the animal or human being conditioned does not perform any act that would affect the outcome. Thus a dog may be conditioned to lift his paw upon a signal by fixing to his foot a device that delivers an electric shock and activating it shortly after giving a signal (the conditioned stimulus). The shock makes the dog lift his leg and, although this movement does not enable the dog to escape from the shock, nevertheless the movement becomes conditioned. Instrumental conditioning, pioneered by Pavlov's rival Bekhterev, is based on similar associations, but in this case the action performed by the animal or human is the crucial factor. Thus the shock to the leg of the dog may be delivered through a grid on which the foot of the animal rests; if he lifts his foot in response to the conditioned stimulus he avoids the shock. This is a profound difference, and E. L. *Thorndike, B. F. Skinner (see BEHAVIOURISM, B. F. SKINNER ON), and other American psychologists have elaborated practical methods of using positive and negative reinforcements (rewards and punishments) in order to modify behaviour. These are usually related to explicit behaviour patterns: for instance they may be used to make schoolchildren less boisterous, criminals better behaved, or psychotic in-patients more responsive to the demands of society. In each case the stress is on segments of large-scale behaviour: the child may be required to learn to sit quietly for certain periods of time, the criminal to carry out a series of acts such as making his own bed, keeping his room clean, and working adequately for a certain period of time. The psychotic may be required to come to meals punctually, keep himself tidy, work in the laundry, associate with other people, and so on. Methods have been worked out for the optimum use of rewards ('token economies') according to the laws of operant conditioning, and many practical applications of these methods have been developed, particularly in the treatment of deteriorated psychotics. But little attempt has been made to use these methods in connection with the treatment of the far more widespread neurotic disorders, and in clinical practice there is little doubt that Pavlovian methods are much more frequently used, and much more efficacious.

Operant conditioning applies, for the most part, to motor activities and the performance of integrated activities. Pavlovian conditioning applies, for the most part, to the activity of the autonomic system, i.e. to emotions; thus it is no accident that neurotic behaviour, which is largely characterized by emotional upsets and difficulties, is more closely related to Pavlovian conditioning. (This distinction is not an absolute one, but it is very useful and far-reaching; most human activities, as well as most animal activities studied in the laboratory, partake of both operant and classical conditioning, and complex methods of analysis are required to sort out the respective contributions of these two processes.) The theory of neurosis from which behaviour therapy derives states that neurotic disorders are essentially *conditioned emotional responses*; they are acquired through some traumatic emotional event, or a series of subtraumatic emotional events, in which some previously neutral conditioned stimulus becomes linked (perhaps quite accidentally) with a fear-producing unconditioned stimulus. This theory is clearly different from psychoanalytic and other psychiatric theories according to which the observed signs of the disorder are merely symptoms of some underlying 'complex'; according to Freud and his followers, this 'complex' must be eliminated before any permanent cure is possible. Behaviour therapists deny the existence of these alleged 'complexes', and they assert that the putative 'symptoms' are not in fact symptoms of anything—they *are* the disorder. The aim of behaviour therapy is to eliminate these 'symptoms'; if this can be accomplished, then no 'disease' or 'complex' will remain. Freud predicted that 'purely symptomatic treatment', which did not eliminate the '*complex' allegedly underlying the outward manifestations of the disorder, would lead to relapse or to symptom substitution, i.e. either the 'symptom' would return, or else another one would arise in its place. Behaviour therapists have been on the lookout for such effects, but although they have succeeded much more completely than others in eliminating the 'symptoms', relapse and symptom substitution have been notable mainly by their failure to occur.

The methods of behaviour therapy (in the narrower sense) derive from this general theory. If the manifest-ations of neurotic disorder are conditioned emotional responses, then a cure must consist in the *extinction* of these conditioned responses. Fortunately experimental psychologists, following the lead of Pavlov, have elaborated many different methods for attaining this aim, and these have been tried out very successfully in neurotic patients. The methods include *desensitization* or counter-conditioning (in which the conditioned stimulus that produces fear/anxiety responses in the patient is conditioned by the therapist to more positive anti-anxiety-producing unconditioned stimuli, such as relaxation or self-assertion); *flooding* (in which the patient is exposed for a lengthy period to the conditioned stimulus that produces fear/anxiety responses; by preventing the usual reactions of flight or whatever, the therapist forces the patient to face his fears, which then disappear quickly); and *modelling* (in which the patient is shown a 'model' who copes properly with his own difficulties and fears, and thus learns the absurdity of his conditioned responses). The effectiveness of these, and many other similar methods, is no longer in question; indeed, empirical evidence from clinical and experimental studies has shown that for no other therapy is there anything like as good evidence for speed and efficacy of cure.   HJE

Eysenck, H. J. (ed.) (1973). *Handbook of Abnormal Psychology*.
—— and Rachman, S. (1964). *Causes and Cures of Neurosis*.
Kazdin, A. E. (1978). *History of Behavior Modification*.
—— and Wilson, T. (1978). *Evaluation of Behavior Therapy*.
Rachman, S. (1971). *The Effects of Psychotherapy*.
Ullmann, L. P., and Krasner, L. (1975). *A Psychological Approach to Abnormal Behavior*. (For a presentation of the theories and methods of behaviour modification.)

Békésy, Georg von (1899–1972). Hungarian physicist and physiologist, the son of a Hungarian diplomat. He spent his early years in Munich, Constantinople, Zurich, and Bern. He received his Ph.D. in physics from the University of Budapest, and remained in Budapest until 1946. After a year in Stockholm he moved to the psychoacoustic laboratory in Harvard, where he remained until 1966. He then moved to Honolulu to become professor of sensory sciences at the University of Hawaii. He continued in active research there until shortly before his death.

Békésy is most famous for his work on the inner ear or cochlea. He was the first to observe directly the patterns of vibration on the basilar membrane inside the cochlea. He found that sound evoked a pattern of wave motion which travelled from one end of the membrane towards the other, increasing in amplitude up to a certain point, and then decreasing. He found that the position of maximum vibration varied systematically with the frequency of the sound, thus providing the basis for the frequency-analysing power of the ear. He carried out this work first on models of the cochlea, and later on preparations of human temporal bones and on the cochleas of living animals. Most of his work in this field was carried out in Hungary. (See also HEARING.)

In Stockholm Békésy invented a new method for measuring thresholds of hearing, and devised a new *audiometer to go with it. The Békésy audiometer is still widely used in clinical hearing testing and in auditory research.

At Harvard the emphasis of his work shifted from the mechanics of the ear to biophysics, and particularly the mechanism by which mechanical vibration on the basilar membrane is transformed into neural impulses. Later still he conducted perceptual experiments on a number of different senses, including hearing, sight, smell, and taste.

Békésy's work on hearing is summarized in his fine book *Experiments in Hearing* (1962). The quality of his work was recognized by the award of the Nobel Prize for physiology or medicine in 1961, for 'discoveries concerning the physical mechanisms of excitation in the cochlea'. The award was celebrated by a special issue of the *Journal of the Acoustical Society of America* in 1962.   BCJM

Bell, Sir Charles (1774–1842). British anatomist and surgeon, born in Edinburgh, the son of a Scottish Episcopalian clergyman. He was taught anatomy by his brother and was admitted to membership of the Royal College of Surgeons of Edinburgh in 1799, followed shortly by his appointment as a surgeon at the Edinburgh Royal Infirmary. In 1806 he moved to London, where he taught anatomy and surgery to his house pupils and, from 1811, at the Great Windmill Street School of Anatomy. From 1812 to 1836 he acted as surgeon at the Middlesex Hospital. In 1824 he accepted the senior professorship of anatomy and surgery at the Royal College of Surgeons of London, his lectures there forming the text of a book entitled *Animal Mechanics, or Proofs of Design in the Animal Frame* (1828) (see CYBERNETICS, HISTORY OF). In 1826 he was elected a Fellow of the Royal Society, and in 1828, on the founding of the University of London, he accepted the chair of anatomy and physiology, but after two years he resigned. On the accession of William IV he was knighted, and in 1836 he became professor of surgery at Edinburgh, where he remained until he died, while on a journey to London.

Bell's first claim to fame rests on his contributions to physiological psychology, of which the law bearing his name is the cornerstone. Throughout his published work he has much to say about the mind, and especially in his two favourite books, *The Hand* and *The Anatomy and Philosophy of Expression as Connected with the Fine Arts*, which testify to his capacity for shrewd observation. He delved into the art of antiquity, examined theories of the beauty of the human form, and critically studied the laws governing the expression of feeling, emotion, and passion in the movements of face and figure.

For nearly 2,000 years no one had seriously ventured to question *Galen's conception of brain and nerves. Many anatomists, it is true, had suspected that the nerve fibres serving sensation and movement, though joined in the same sheath, might be distinct, and Thomas Willis (1621–75) had stated that some nerves were exclusively sensory and others exclusively motor. But, as Bell says in his preface to *The Nervous System of the Human Body* (1830), 'the (ancient) hypothesis that a nervous fluid was derived from the brain, and transmitted by nervous tubes, was deemed consistent with anatomical demonstration'. Furthermore, his contemporaries took it for granted that one and the same nerve fibre could serve the twofold function of conducting sensory messages and of transmitting the 'mandate of the will'.

Why, Bell asked himself, should sensation remain entire in a limb when all voluntary power over the action of the muscle is lost? And why should muscular power remain when feeling is gone? In seeking to answer these questions, he demonstrated the separate functions of the anterior and posterior roots of the spinal nerves. Some time between 1812 and 1821, his surgical and clinical 'experiments' led him to believe that movement is served by the anterior or ventral, and sensation by the posterior or dorsal, roots of the spinal nerves (Bell–*Magendie law); the respective fibres are distinct but bound within the same trunks, and terminate separately, both centrally and peripherally.

From this discovery, Bell moved to the suggestion that sensory and motor functions might be served by different parts of the brain. He recognized (before Johannes *Müller) the specificity of sensory nerves, identified (before C. S. *Sherrington) the muscle sense, and understood the facts of reciprocal innervation (relaxation of extensor muscle while the flexor contracts). No one before him had acquired such an understanding of the human hand, and of the manner in which it reveals its superiority over the homologous organs of other animals. By dwelling on the delicate musculature of the fingers, and on the sensibility of the skin, he came to see the hand as the special organ of the sense of *touch, while in the 'muscular sense' he detected a sixth sense which we now recognize as that which serves our powers of *haptic perception. He saw the function of the hand as adapted to the arm and shoulder. In studying their comparative anatomy, he drew striking comparisons with the shoulder of the horse, elephant, and camel, and with corresponding organs of the mole, the bat, the anteater, and other species, including many now extinct.

Bell felt that he was continuing in the tradition of what he called 'the English School of Physiology', in contrast to the French School, which represented life as 'the mere physical result of certain combinations and actions of parts by them termed Organization'. This was an oblique reference to the Cartesian conception of 'animal as machine' (see DESCARTES, RENÉ), which culminated in *La Mettrie's *L'Homme machine*.

A simple principle governed his work, namely 'that design and benevolence were everywhere visible in the natural world'. The 'different affections of the nerves of the outward senses' were, for him, 'the signals which the Author of nature has willed to be the means by which correspondence is held with the realities'. Perfect symmetry of form and function, continuous renewal of the 'material particles', and the integrity of the body amidst the ceaseless changes to which it is subject convinced him of the existence of a 'principle of life' which governed bodily structure and change.

Charles Bell must be counted among the leading men of science of the 19th century, and the most versatile of that illustrious group of men who raised Scottish medicine to pre-eminence. He combined a surgeon's intimacy with the human body with a profound understanding of its anatomy and physiology. To all this he brought considerable gifts as a writer and as a consummate medical artist.   JCO

Boring, E. G. (1926). *A History of Experimental Psychology*.
Carmichael, L. (1926). 'Sir Charles Bell: a contribution to the history of physiological psychology'. *Psychological Review*, 33.
Cole, F. J. (1955). 'Bell's law'. *Notes of the Royal Society of London*, 11.
Cranefield, P. (1974). *The Way In and the Way Out*.
Gordon-Taylor, G., and Walls, E. W. (1958). *Sir Charles Bell: His Life and Times*.
Le Fanu, W. R. (1961). 'Charles Bell and William Cheselden'. *Medical History*, 5.

Benham's top. Quite intense colours can be produced by pulsing coloured or white light. Flashing coloured lights can produce other colours: for example, flashing monochromatic sodium yellow light may produce any spectral hue (and brown, which is not in the spectrum), though not usually with very high saturation. These phenomena are most easily seen with a spinning disc, or top, having black and white sector rings (as in Fig. 1). This gives intermittent stimulation to retinal regions as it is rotated, quite slowly, to give a flicker rate below the fusion frequency. The colours seen depend on the widths and arrangement of the black sectors and the rate of rotation. There are considerable individual differences for what is seen under given conditions.

Although generally called 'Benham's top', after C. E. Benham (1894), the basic effect goes back to a French monk, Benedict Prévost, who, in 1826, observed colours —like a heavenly light on his fingers—when he waved his hands about in the cloisters. Finding that this also happened with white cardboard, he realized that it has a physiological origin, in the eye, and attributed it to different rates of action of specific colour mechanisms of the retina. He was essentially correct. It is remarkable that

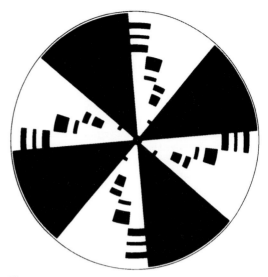

Fig. 1

Prévost's discovery was forgotten, and the effect was rediscovered no less than twelve times: by Gustav *Fechner in 1838 and then by others. John Smith, in 1859, thought that the effects were 'objective' by changing the light itself, and so he (incorrectly) challenged *Newton's account of light and colour. The third rediscovery was made by Sir David *Brewster in 1861. (The history is given fully in Cohen and Gordon 1949.) Hermann von *Helmholtz carried out systematic observations, noting that a white rotating sector is red on the leading edge and blue on the trailing edge, and in dim light the red becomes yellow and the blue violet. In very bright light the red becomes pinker and the blue greenish. Further observations were made by S. *Bidwell, who discovered a related effect, Bidwell's ghost.

These subjective colours have been shown successfully on black and white television, but they are a little too weak for commercial uses. They are due to different time constants of the colour receptor systems of the eye, but they are rather too variable for precise measurements. The effects are interesting but not particularly useful.   RLG

Benham, C. E. (1894). 'The artificial spectrum top'. *Nature*, 51.
Bidwell, S. (1896). 'On subjective colour phenomena attending sudden changes in illumination'. *Proceedings of the Royal Society*, 60.
Cohen, J., and Gordon, D. A. (1949). 'The Prévost–Fechner–Benham subjective colours'. *Psychological Bulletin*, 46.

Bentham, Jeremy (1748–1832). Born in London and educated at Westminster School, he entered the Queen's College, Oxford, at the age of 12. Although he studied law at Lincoln's Inn and was called to the Bar in 1772, he never practised law, but he wrote on its theory. He held that laws should be socially useful and should not merely reflect custom, that men are hedonists (pursuing pleasure and avoiding pain), and that desires may be classified into self- and other-regarding: the function of law is to provide punishments and rewards to maintain a just balance between them. His famous dictum is that all actions are right and good which promote 'the greatest happiness of the greatest number', this principle being the basis of utilitarianism.

Bentham was a founder of University College London, where his mummified body may still be seen, dressed in his own clothes. He collaborated closely with James *Mill, whom he met in 1808. He also founded the *Westminster Review*.

bereavement. Common cause of grief, that 'fierce or violent sorrow' which Robert *Burton in his *Anatomy of Melancholy* referred to as 'the epitome, symptom and chief cause of melancholy'. The relationship between mourning and melancholia was explored in more detail by Sigmund *Freud who, in 1917, suggested that depressive illness (melancholia) differs from grief in the prominent part played by feelings of guilt and in the symbolic significance of the loss that preceded it. Subsequent research has confirmed the frequency of guilt and self-reproach among those who develop depressive illnesses after bereavement.

Despite Freud's claims, little attention was paid to bereavement by psychiatrists until Eric Lindemann described the symptomatology and management of acute grief following the Coconut Grove nightclub fire in Boston, Massachusetts, in 1944. Lindemann showed that people who do not 'break down' and express feelings appropriate to a bereavement may suffer from delayed or distorted grief. Such pathological forms of grief, said Lindemann, could be restored to a more normal form in the course of six to eight weekly interviews in which the bereaved person was encouraged to give vent to the feelings of sadness, anger, or guilt which they had repressed. A recent development of this approach has been the use of 'flooding', a technique derived from *behaviour therapy in which bereaved people are pressed to vivid recollection of the sight, smell, sounds, and feelings associated with the dead person. R. W. Ramsay (1977, 1979), the originator of this method of treatment, has subsequently toned down the intensity of the approach, which, in its original form, could only be safely carried out in a psychiatric in-patient setting.

While there is now much agreement regarding the efficacy of Lindemann's approaches to delayed or avoided grief, their use in the treatment of the severe and protracted grief which sometimes follows the dissolution of relationships characterized by ambivalence or dependency is more controversial. Alternative strategies have been developed by C. M. Parkes, who has also advocated

the introduction of bereavement counselling during the early phases of grief as a means of preventing later difficulties in those who are thought to be at risk. Recent random-allocation studies have confirmed the effectiveness of some counselling services of this kind (Raphael 1984).

The application of Freud's libido theory to grief has been challenged by John Bowlby (1969), whose studies of the development of *attachment between mother and child led him to explain the intense pining or yearning of acute grief as a frustrated form of the urge to search for any loved person from whom one has become separated. This urge to search is thought to be an instinctually derived behaviour pattern which conflicts with the awareness of the older child or adult so that such a search is useless and bound to disappointment. Consequently attempts to avoid reminders of the loss, seek distraction, and inhibit thoughts of loss coexist alongside contrary impulses to cry aloud, to drop everything, and to focus one's mind upon the search for the lost person. Individuals, families, and cultures vary in the extent to which one or other aspect of the conflict is permitted, but some form of expression of sorrow is allowed for in the religious ceremonials of all cultures which have been studied (Rosenblatt, Walsh, and Jackson, 1976). G. Gorer (1965) has claimed that the decline in ritual aspects of mourning which has taken place in industrialized countries since the First World War has removed an important source of support for the bereaved and encouraged pathological reactions to bereavement.

In most bereaved people the urge to search for the lost person is reflected in thoughts, actions, and perceptions. Thoughts about the dead person return repeatedly, and the bereaved tend to pine intensely and to go over in the mind the events leading up to the death as if, even at this time, they could find out what has gone wrong and put it right again. The search is reflected in acts concerned to 'keep alive' the memories of the dead, to visit graves or places associated with them, and to treasure possessions which will act as reminders. Clear visual memories of the dead person are kept in mind, and sights and sounds are commonly misperceived as evidence of his or her return.

In the normal course of events the intensity and duration of episodes of pining (the so-called 'pangs' of grief) grow gradually less, and attachment behaviour is extinguished. As this happens, people become more fully aware of the extent to which their basic assumptions about themselves and the world will have to change. The psychosocial transition which results necessitates lengthy revision of the individual's view of the world (world model), and, in the interim, the bereaved remain insecure and relatively helpless. Many withdraw from social relationships and become disengaged from their wider circle of interests and acquaintances. The elderly bereaved may never become re-engaged with the outside world. Younger people more often find their way through to a new identity which may be more mature than the one that preceded it.

Factors which predispose to a successful outcome of this transition include appropriate anticipation and preparation for bereavement, emotional support from friends and others (permitting expression of grief), psychological resilience and confidence in oneself, opportunities for personal growth, and faith in a religious or philosophical system of belief that gives meaning to death. Conversely the process of grieving may be impaired by sudden, unexpected, and untimely deaths, by the dissolution of relationships characterized by ambivalence or dependence, by social isolation or the presence of others who will block attempts to grieve or distract the griever, by the failure of previous attempts to cope with major loss (particularly in childhood), by lack of self-confidence, by physical or other obstacles to self-fulfilment, and by the absence of a system of belief that gives meaning to death.

Although bereavements are commonest in old age, their frequency and predictability reduce the chance that the bereaved will be unprepared for them. Also there is less need for old people to compete for a place in the world that remains to them, and many come through the stress of bereavement without experiencing the lasting distress which characterizes younger bereaved people.

Although most of the published work on bereavement has focused on bereavement by death, the phenomenon of grief follows many of the 'slings and arrows of outrageous fortune'. Hence an understanding of the psychology of bereavement is important to all those involved in the care of people who are undergoing psychosocial transitions.   CMP

Bowlby, J. (1969, 1973, 1980). *Attachment and Loss*, 3 vols.
Gorer, G. (1965). *Death, Grief, and Mourning in Contemporary Britain*.
Lindemann, E. (1944). 'Symptomatology and management of acute grief'. *American Journal of Psychiatry*, 101.
Parkes, C. M. (1986). *Bereavement: Studies of Grief in Adult Life* (2nd edn.).
—— (2001). *Bereavement* (3rd edn.).
Ramsay, R. W. (1977). 'Behavioural approaches to bereavement'. *Behaviour Research and Therapy*, 15.
—— (1979). 'Bereavement: a behavioural treatment of pathological grief'. In Sjöden, P. (ed.), *Trends in Behaviour Therapy*.
Raphael, B. (1984). *The Anatomy of Bereavement*.
Rosenblatt, P. C., Walsh, R. P., and Jackson, D. A. (1976). *Grief and Mourning in Cross-cultural Perspective*.

Berger, Hans (1873–1941). German psychiatrist who spent most of his career at the University of Jena where, in 1929, he discovered the human *electroencephalogram. Influenced by his father, a physician, and his mother, the daughter of the poet Friedrich Rückert, Berger's interests spanned medicine, science, and philosophy. He sustained a lifelong preoccupation with the *mind–body problem and saw the electrical activity of the brain as a means of clarifying that relationship.

After a brief study of astronomy and an equally brief time in the German army he studied medicine. In 1897 he received his doctorate at Jena and was subsequently appointed to the university psychiatric clinic there. During the period up to 1910 he published work on the spinal cord, cranial blood flow, and brain temperature changes. Underlying the physiological investigations were always questions of psychological state. He had also in this period attempted, less successfully, to record electrical activity from the cerebral cortex of a dog. In 1911 he married his technical assistant, Baroness Ursula von Bülow, with whom he had carried out work on the psychogalvanic reflex (see ELECTRODERMAL ACTIVITY).

During the First World War, Berger served on the Western Front as an army psychiatrist. On his return to Jena after the war he was appointed professor of psychiatry at the university and director of the clinic, where his duties also encompassed neurology. He resumed his research, but not until 1924 did time permit him to begin in earnest his search for cortical currents in the human brain which might relate to consciousness. In that year he observed from the head of a patient very small oscillations on his string galvanometer, although for a long time he retained serious doubts about their cerebral origins. However, by painstaking research he systematically eliminated most of the possibilities that they were due to extra-cerebral artefact. In 1929 he was sufficiently satisfied with their authenticity to publish his first paper 'On the electroencephalogram in man' in the *Archiv für Psychiatrie und Nervenkrankheiten*.

The world of neurophysiology remained unimpressed by the claims of this little known professor of psychiatry, who had only begun his serious investigations at the age of 51 and who seemed more at home in philosophy than in electrophysiology. Contemporary animal evidence provided little support for the human findings. It was not until 1934, when *Adrian and Matthews published their replication of Berger's findings, that neurophysiologists felt obliged to take account of their significance.

Once Berger had satisfied himself that the electroencephalogram (EEG) was a genuine brain phenomenon, he used it as a tool to study psychophysical relationships. The two main features of the EEG were termed 'alpha' and 'beta' waves. The former were represented by regular oscillations of about 10 hertz, seen when the eyes were closed and in states of relaxation. The latter were less synchronous forms of faster activity which replaced the alpha waves when the eyes were open or when the individual was engaged in mental activity such as arithmetic calculations.

For Berger, alpha waves represented a form of automatic brain functioning, a state of electrical readiness which exists when the individual is conscious, but inattentive. The desynchronous blocking of this activity was held to occur when attention was focused on one idea or sensory input. This was considered to result in a localized activation of the specific sensory-receiving area in the brain, coupled with a more generalized inhibition of the surrounding areas, manifesting itself as a blocking of the alpha waves. He postulated that consciousness depended upon the potential gradient between the localized active area and the surrounding area of inhibition. Although he made little attempt to utilize his findings in clinical contexts, he described abnormal patterns of EEG activity in a number of pathological conditions, most notably in epilepsy.

In his thinking Berger was much influenced by the notion of the conservation of energy. He regarded *dualism as inconsistent with that principle, but could not reconcile its alternative, materialism, with his belief in volition. His solution was a form of psychophysical parallelism which accepted transformation of physical energy to 'psychic energy' and vice versa, thus permitting causal interaction between the physical and mental domains.

He retired in 1938 at the age of 65. During his last years in Thuringia he developed a severe depression, and in May 1941 he took his own life.   WCM

Bergson, Henri (1859–1941). French philosopher, born in Paris and educated at the Lycée Condorcet and the École Normale Supérieure. After a teaching career as a schoolmaster in various secondary schools, Bergson was appointed to the École Normale Supérieure in 1898 and, from 1900 to 1921, held the chair of philosophy at the Collège de France. He received the highest honours that France could offer him, including membership of the Académie Française. He was awarded the Nobel Prize for literature in 1927.

In his *Essai sur les données immédiates de la conscience* (1889) (Time and Free Will), Bergson offered an interpretation of consciousness as existing on two levels, the first to be reached by deep introspection, the second an external projection of the first. The deeper self is the seat of creative becoming and of free will. The method of intuitive introspection is developed further in his *Introduction à la métaphysique* (1903; An Introduction to Metaphysics). In *Matière et mémoire* (1896; Matter and Memory), Bergson once again took up the study of consciousness, turning his attention to the relation of mind to body. He argued that this distinction is one of degree, not of kind. In *L'Évolution créatrice* (1907; Creative Evolution), Bergson developed his theory of time. In *Les Deux Sources de la morale et de la religion* (1932; The Two Sources of Morality and Religion), he explored the moral implications of his theory

of freedom. In *Le Rire* (1900; Laughter) he suggests that all humour has human associations, especially with surprise.

Chevalier, J. (1977). *Henri Bergson*.
Herman, D. J. (1979). *The Philosophy of Henri Bergson*.

Berkeley, George (1685–1753). Idealist philosopher. He was born in Ireland, went to school at Kilkenny College, and in 1700 proceeded to Trinity College, Dublin, where he graduated in 1704 and became a Fellow in 1707. He retained his Fellowship, though with long periods of absence, until 1724, in which year he became Dean of Derry.

His intellectual development was strikingly precocious, and he was fortunate in his education. In 1700, although Ireland had so recently been the scene of prolonged turmoil and civil war, the state of learning at Trinity College was much livelier and more progressive than at either of the English universities at that time. It is clear that Berkeley was early and thoroughly acquainted with John *Locke's *Essay Concerning Human Understanding* (published in 1690) and with the physical theories of Isaac *Newton and others which underlay that work. He learned much also—perhaps more than he afterwards cared to admit—from Malebranche's *Recherche de la vérité*. His own first book, *An Essay towards a New Theory of Vision*, was published in Dublin in 1709, when he was 24, and his most important work, *A Treatise Concerning the Principles of Human Knowledge*, followed in 1710. He first visited England in 1713, and the third major work of his youth, the *Three Dialogues between Hylas and Philonous*, was published in London in that year. These are the works on which his fame securely rests, all written and well established before he was 30.

Berkeley was, with the zeal and confidence of youth, in a sense a reactionary figure. He rightly discerned, in the writings of Locke and his scientific mentors, the steady progress towards general acceptance of a certain scientific 'world-view', which he hated and believed that he could utterly confute. This was the idea that mathematics and mechanics are the keys to the understanding of nature—that all matter is fundamentally atomic, or 'corpuscular', in structure, and that its properties, on both the largest and the smallest scale, are ultimately a matter of mechanical interactions. Berkeley believed this idea to be fatal to religion and dangerous to morality; he thought also that he could show it to be philosophically absurd and untenable. His own sweeping solution, by which he believed that all could be set right at a stroke, was his denial of the existence of matter. For if there is no matter, there is nothing that mechanistic materialism can even pretend to be true *of*, and the pretensions of the physical scientist are completely undermined. Not surprisingly, a major theme of Berkeley's writings is his struggle to persuade his readers that, by the denial of the existence of matter, no one—other than the sinister physicist—need be surprised or disturbed. At no time was this struggle particularly successful. Berkeley's contemporary readers, to his chagrin and surprise, were inclined to praise him for his dialectical ingenuity, but to dismiss his conclusions as the paradoxes of an amusing Irishman.

Berkeley's middle years, from about 1722 until late in 1731, were almost wholly given over to a project for founding a college in Bermuda, intended for both indigenous and white colonial Americans. For this project he secured a charter from the king, the promise of a large grant from the public revenues, and wide support from individuals—on this topic at least, his powers of persuasion, supported by what all observers agree to have been great personal charm, proved most efficacious. In September 1728 he set sail for Newport, Rhode Island, where he built himself a house (which still stands) and waited for his project to mature. But he was disappointed. The pragmatic Sir Robert Walpole had always regarded the scheme as visionary, and, once Berkeley's persuasive presence was withdrawn, he worked quietly against it. The crucial grant was found at last not to 'suit with public convenience', and after 3 years in America Berkeley returned, empty-handed, to London.

In 1734—in spite of having, as it appears, never once visited the deanery he had held for 10 years—he was appointed Bishop of Cloyne, in the extreme south of Ireland. Here in 1744 he published his strange work *Siris*, a disquisition on the supposed medicinal virtues of 'tar-water', decked out—in a manner astonishingly unlike that of his graceful, rapid, and lucid early writings—with an oppressive bulk of miscellaneous scientific, medical, and philosophical learning. It has been held that his enthusiasm for tar-water was eccentric enough to catch the professional eye of the psychoanalyst, but it must be remembered that, if Berkeley's medical opinions were somewhat wild and uncritical, they differed little in that respect from those of many of his contemporaries.

Berkeley died in January 1753, while visiting Oxford to supervise his second son's entry to Christ Church. The memorial tablet erected in the cathedral there is noteworthy in that, presumably on his widow's authority, it records his date of birth as six years earlier than it actually was.

See also BERKELEY ON PERCEPTION; BERKELEY ON THE MIND. GJW

The complete and definitive modern edition is *The Works of George Berkeley* (eds. A. A. Luce and T. E. Jessop) (1949–57), 9 vols. The authoritative biography is Luce, A. A. (1949), *Life of George Berkeley*, published uniformly with the *Works*.

Bennett, J. (1971). *Locke, Berkeley, Hume*. (An able, selective commentary on 'central themes'.)

Foster, J., and Robinson, H. (eds.) (1985). *Essays on Berkeley: A Tercentennial Celebration*. (A valuable collection, issued to mark the tercentenary of Berkeley's birth.)

Luce, A. A. (1945). *Berkeley's Immaterialism*. (The work of a learned but somewhat uncritical partisan.)

Pitcher, G. W. (1977). *Berkeley*. (An unusually detailed scrutiny, step by step, of the particular arguments by which Berkeley sought to support his conclusions.)

Tipton, I. C. (1974). *Berkeley: The Philosophy of Immaterialism*. (A notably careful and scholarly work, particularly useful on those topics, for instance Berkeley's theory of the mind, which other commentators have tended to neglect.)

Warnock, G. J. (1969). *Berkeley* (2nd edn.). (A general analytical survey, perhaps over-stressing Berkeley's 'defence of common sense' and underplaying his very curious metaphysical and religious views.)

Berkeley on perception. The principal sources for Berkeley's views on *perception are *An Essay towards a New Theory of Vision* (1709) and *A Treatise Concerning the Principles of Human Knowledge* (1710). The doctrines set out in these two works are not the same. But the explanation of that, according to Berkeley's own statement in the *Principles*, is not that he had changed his mind, but that in the *Essay*, the topic of which was specifically vision, he had deliberately suppressed—even misrepresented—his views on other matters, so as to avoid introducing too many novel doctrines all at once. The explanation seems odd, but there is no good ground for not accepting it.

In the *Essay* Berkeley has two principal aims. The first is negative. Raising the question how and why we make by vision—as on the whole we make pretty successfully—our everyday judgements of the sizes, distances, and positions of objects, Berkeley first contends—contrary to much current theorizing of his day—that such judgements are not made on the basis of a knowledge of optics. It may for example be true that, as an object recedes from us, the angle at which the optic axes converge upon it decreases; but since we do not see those axes or the angle at which they converge, that cannot explain why we judge the object to be receding. His point here, surely a correct one, is that the everyday visual judgements we all make of distance and size must be in some way based on how things look to us, not on theorems of optics which, however sound in their own sphere, cannot constitute direct visual evidence and for that matter are often totally unknown to persons of perfectly sound visual competence.

Berkeley then turns to the question of how it comes about that 'how things look' does enable us to make, on the whole, reliable judgements as to how things are. And here he offers the double contention that the connection between visual 'clues' and actual states of affairs; first is learned only by experience, not calculable *a priori, and second, is completely *contingent, and indeed arbitrary. In support of this contention he argues that objects are, strictly speaking, tangible objects only; they are not, strictly, literally seen—or, for that matter, heard. The 'proper objects' of hearing are sounds, and only indirectly or by inference the things that make sounds. Similarly, he holds, there are purely visual 'proper objects' of vision; and we learn only by experience to make inferences from these 'proper objects' to states of (tangible) things. States of things are, as we learn by experience, fairly reliably correlated with the occurrence of distinctive purely visual objects, but these correlations, however reliable, are fundamentally quite arbitrary—like, for instance, the link between the word 'red' and the colour red. God maintains these correlations for the benefit of his creatures, so that the objects of vision can be said to constitute a 'divine visual language' by which, once we have learned it, we are 'told' about the tangible things in our environment.

Readers of the *Essay* must have been struck, even in 1709, by one conspicuous omission from it. John *Locke's many admirers, for example, would have agreed with Berkeley that the direct objects of vision were purely visual 'ideas', and that these were properly quite distinct from what they would have called 'external bodies'. But why say that the connection between visual ideas and states of things is *arbitrary*, maintained purely at God's pleasure? For surely it is *causal*. Was there not a well-established, or at any rate widely accepted, theory as to the causation of perception, according to which visual ideas, and for that matter all 'ideas of sensation', were the causal products of states of things and of their action upon our sense organs? Why is this theory, which at least appears to offer a unified, non-arbitrary explanation of the connections between our ideas of sensation, not even mentioned by Berkeley?

Berkeley's total rejection of that theory—Locke's so-called 'causal' or 'representational' theory of perception—is made clear in the *Principles*. The theory was that the universe is, fundamentally, a system of solid bodies in mechanical interaction; that the objects of everyday experience are themselves systems of 'corpuscles', 'insensible particles', in mechanical interaction; and that, in perception, these bodies act mechanically upon our various sense organs, causing ultimately, by way of causal chains in the nervous system and brain, 'ideas of sensation' to occur 'in the mind'. Such ideas are the 'immediate objects' of perception, and inform us—or, so Locke held, in some cases *mis*inform us—as to the existence and character of the 'external' bodies that are their originating causes.

Berkeley's chief grounds for rejecting this theory were these. First, he took it to be self-defeating—if true, it could not be known to be true. For if the contents, the 'immediate objects', of perception are all, and only, *ideas*, what ground could there be in perception for supposing the existence of anything else? Second, and for much the same reason, he regarded the theory as ontologically redundant. Given observers ('spirits') and the ideas that they have, which actually constitute their experience, why add

a supposedly distinct 'external' world which forms no actual part of anyone's experience at all? *Experience* would be just the same if no such world existed: why, then, suppose that it does exist? Now the answer to that question was supposed to be that the existence of 'external bodies' *causes* and therefore *explains* the occurrence of ideas in our experience; but Berkeley's third contention is that that cannot be so. For, he asserts, only an active, animate being can be a cause; the only true case of causation is volition, intelligent agency, so that the mere mechanical happenings postulated in Locke's theory could in principle neither cause nor explain anything.

Berkeley's own views in the *Principles* could be said to take the form of a generalization, to all sensory modes, of the account of vision put forward in his *Essay*. He had held there that the 'proper objects' of vision are purely visual ideas 'in the mind', generated by the direct action of God so as to 'tell' us about tangible objects 'in circumambient space'. In the *Principles* he dispenses with those objects. Every sense, he now holds, even the sense of touch, has its own 'proper objects', all 'ideas', all 'in the mind'; there are (besides minds or 'spirits') *only* ideas; and God's work is now said to be, not merely that of informing his creatures by 'visual language' of independent things, but of so maintaining the complex correlations between *all* ideas, of *all* the senses, as to sustain in the experience of us all the apparent unity, continuity, and coherence of a common world. He claims for this extraordinary doctrine, first—surprisingly enough—that it accords with common sense. Locke, with his 'scientific' theory, had been obliged to shock us by concluding that the world is in many ways not as it appears; Berkeley holds that, on his view, the world is exactly as it appears—for, in fact, it *is* 'what appears', no more and no less. Then his doctrine is also, he claims, ontologically economical, non-redundant: to describe our experience we need nothing more than 'spirits' and 'ideas'; and Berkeley makes no further, gratuitous existential assumptions. Then, since the cause of ideas, in Berkeley's doctrine, is the will of God, he has, he claims, a real cause, a truly explanatory agency—and, last but for Berkeley not least, one that firmly entrenches theism in the nature of things, as the ground of all being.

What then of the 'scientific' theory of perception, according to which 'particles' acted on sense organs to cause sensation? Berkeley was at first inclined to dismiss all such talk as mere rubbish, to be simply abandoned. But later he contrived to accommodate this theory also, as not a genuinely causal theory, not really explanatory, and indeed not true, but a possibly *useful* purely theoretical construct to assist us in predicting how the true cause—God's will—was likely to operate in our experience. This was, indeed, his general account of all scientific theories that postulated entities not accessible to direct observation.

GJW

Berkeley on the mind. The task of outlining Berkeley's theory of the mind is complicated by the fact that the work in which he was to treat this topic at length was never published. His major work, *A Treatise Concerning the Principles of Human Knowledge*, as we now have it, was issued in 1710 as 'Part I'. Apparently its account of perception and our knowledge of the external world was to be followed by a second and even a third volume, one dealing with the mind and another with the principles of morality. It seems that the second volume was at least partly written, for in a letter of 1729 Berkeley says that 'the manuscript was lost about fourteen years ago, during my travels in Italy'. But that manuscript was never rewritten, and Berkeley's views on the mind have consequently to be collected, partly from brief passages in his published works, and partly also from his surviving private notebooks of 1707–8, which give many clues to what 'Part II' of his *Principles* was intended to contain.

We may consider first a certain view of the mind by which Berkeley was, not surprisingly, tempted, though he eventually rejects it. His term—shared with John *Locke—for the successive actual contents of experience is, of course, 'ideas', and early in his notebook he had laid down (with his theory of perception in mind) the general principle that 'Language and knowledge are all about ideas, words stand for nothing else'. If so, then clearly language and knowledge about the mind must be 'about ideas', and accordingly in later entries we find Berkeley saying that 'the very existence of Ideas constitutes the soul. . . . Mind is a congeries of Perceptions. . . . Say you the Mind is not the Perceptions but that thing wch. perceives. I answer you are abus'd by the words that & thing: these are vague empty words without a meaning.' These remarks of course suggest a theory of the mind resembling that later put forward by David *Hume—and much later by William *James and Bertrand *Russell—in which the mind is, not a persistent entity distinct from the contents of experience, but a 'logical construction' out of those contents themselves. Such a view, however, is directly and flatly contradicted in the second paragraph of the *Principles*, where Berkeley writes: 'But, besides all that endless variety of ideas or objects of knowledge, there is likewise something which knows or perceives them; and exercises divers operations, as willing, imagining, remembering, about them. This perceiving, active being is what I call MIND, SPIRIT, SOUL, OR MYSELF. By which words I do not denote any one of my ideas, but a thing entirely distinct from them, wherein they exist, or, which is the same thing, whereby they are perceived.'

It is perhaps clearer why Berkeley rejected the Humean 'logical construction' view than what the view actually was with which he sought to replace it. He held—and this was indeed crucial in his criticism of Locke's 'causal' theory of perception—that ideas, and indeed any other non-animate entities if any others exist, are essentially 'inert', inactive, incapable of *doing* anything; and he no doubt took it, reasonably enough, that a 'congeries' of such inactive elements could not but be itself inactive. He came to regard it, by contrast, as the fundamental truth about the mind that it is essentially active—and uniquely as well as essentially so, for he came to hold that mental agency was in fact the *only* case of real activity, of actual doing. That is why, in the passage quoted above, he was careful to speak of MIND as 'this perceiving, active being', and it follows of course that he must regard such 'active beings' as 'entirely distinct' from ideas or any other inanimate items. It should be added that he does not mean to say that mind is active in addition to perceiving, for he came to hold that perceiving, 'taking notice', is itself an act, not merely passive receptiveness. In one notebook entry he goes so far as to say, 'The soul is the will properly speaking', and in another asks 'Whether Identity of Person consists not in the Will'.

Since Berkeley held without question that we could speak intelligibly about, and have knowledge of, minds, then, since minds are 'entirely distinct' from ideas, he naturally had to modify his simple empiricist's maxim that 'language and knowledge are all about ideas'. He does little more, however, than concede that the case of minds is an evident exception to that principle. Though we have no idea of the mind, he says, we have—from our own case—a 'notion' of it; but what it is to have a 'notion' of the mind he then elucidates no further than to insist that 'we understand the meaning of the word'—which, though doubtless true, is unilluminating.

There is one further point, however, on which Berkeley is clear and explicit. While insisting that the mind is 'entirely distinct' from its ideas, he insists no less that it is *not* distinct from its 'acts'. Just as the existence of an inanimate thing consists in, *is*, its being perceived—just as its being perceived and its existing are not to be distinguished—so the existence of 'mind, soul, or spirit' is its acting, and so its acting and its existing are not to be distinguished. Hence Berkeley boldly asserts in the *Principles*, as if it were the most natural thing in the world, that 'it is a plain consequence that *the soul always thinks*'. Since the very existence of 'the soul' is thinking, the very notion of a mind not thinking, not active, is self-contradictory.

Now this conclusion, as Berkeley was of course aware, appears to fly in the face of very obvious facts: for it at least seems to be a fact of common experience that, in the history of 'myself', there are intervals of complete unconsciousness in which the mind is inactive. Remarkably, of the possible ways of attempting to get round this difficulty Berkeley seems quite deliberately to choose the most extraordinary of all. In theory, he might have argued that, while my mind does not exist continuously through periods of complete unconsciousness, *I* do; it is, however, not realistic to suppose that Berkeley could have taken that line, since it requires a distinction between 'myself' and 'my mind' which (however wrongly) he would never have thought of making—like *Descartes, he took it for granted that a person is, and is only, a mind or 'spirit', a 'thinking thing'. Again, he might have argued that, through periods of what is commonly called unconsciousness, the mind is really in some way active after all; but that line has a decidedly ad hoc, unempirical look about it, and Berkeley seems never to have found it tempting. What he held at one time, boldly embracing the paradox, was that persons actually do not exist continuously; since the mind is active only intermittently, 'men die or are in state of annihilation oft in a day'. But that too he rejects, and the doctrine he finally adopts is the very extraordinary one that there can be in a person's life no periods of unconsciousness, since the passage of time itself is nothing but the succession of his 'perceptions'; we cannot ask what the position is *during* the mind's unconsciousness, for if the mind is not active there is no duration. It is clear that, in this strange doctrine of 'private times', with its evident rejection of any public, objective time ordering, desperate paradoxes lurk, and one can only speculate how Berkeley might have tried to deal with them, or alternatively how he might have so modified his theory of the mind as to avoid them, if his projected second volume of the *Principles* had ever been completed.

See also LOCKE ON THE MIND. GJW

'beside oneself' (with anger, grief, etc.). An English phrase suggesting that the individual is temporarily not, or is separated from, his usual self. The implication is that there are limits to how far the self can be different from or change from its usual character—before another self takes over. This is a possible basis for the notion of being *possessed*; and also of multiple personalities, as in the remarkable case of Sally Beauchamp, who was supposed to have several alternating selves or personalities. See DISSOCIATION OF THE PERSONALITY.

Bidwell, Shelford (1848–1909). British physicist and barrister, born at Thetford, Norfolk, and educated at Cambridge. After practising as a barrister for a number of years he devoted himself to scientific research, especially in electricity and magnetism and physiological optics. He was elected a Fellow of the Royal Society in 1888 and was president of the Physical Society (1897–9). In 1899 he published *Curiosities of Light and Vision*, enlarging a series of lectures he gave at the Royal Institution. The so-called Bidwell's ghost is a visual phenomenon associated with *afterimages produced by alternating flashing lights.

bilingualism (or polyglossia). A term that refers to a person's ability to communicate in two or more languages.

The phenomenon is found commonly in border regions, especially in those whose geographical boundaries change from time to time. South-eastern Poland, for example, was formerly part of the Austro-Hungarian Empire, making Austrian the official language for a population whose native language was Polish but which was in contact with neighbouring Ukrainian, Belorussian, and Slovakian communities, and whose religious groups included Orthodox, Roman Catholic, and Jewish. Thus church Slavonic, Greek, Latin, Hebrew, and Yiddish were all likely to be used to varying degrees by inhabitants of the region, in addition to the Slavic languages. The phenomenon is also found in small countries that participate extensively in international relations: the Netherlands and Switzerland are especially well-known examples. In the Netherlands, children characteristically have instruction in Dutch as a first language, begin a second, third, and fourth (English, French, or German) within a few years of each other, and, if they plan to go to university, add several years of Latin and perhaps some Greek. Most high-school graduates can manage to communicate in two foreign languages; fluency in three or four is common among university graduates. Bilingualism is encountered also in small countries experiencing substantial immigration or made up of disparate groups. It is estimated that peoples from more than 90 different language communities have emigrated to Israel since the 1930s. It is encountered in large countries also. In the Soviet Union, as in Iran, China, and India—countries comprising people of many different ethnic, linguistic, and religious backgrounds—a single 'national' language is inculcated as a unifying device, while the separate groups use their own languages for local communication. Even in a country where the languages share a common root, such as Italy, the regional variants may be almost mutually unintelligible. In all of these cases people who wish to communicate with others not in their immediate linguistic community are obliged to learn another language. The fact of two languages in a single person is commonplace in most parts of the world, but is still thought of as an oddity in many others. Most English-speaking countries seem to be among the latter group.

Bilingualism is actively studied by linguists who are interested in the way that speakers of one language accommodate the impact of another on their own; by sociologists and sociolinguists who trace change in social custom as a function of change in language; by teachers concerned to minimize the interfering effects of one language upon the learning of another; by psychologists who are interested in bilingualism as a natural laboratory for the study of the way the mind represents its knowledge; and of course by many others. The psychological issues are the most pertinent here.

One long-standing query has been whether instruction in a second language helps or hinders the student. The question seems not to have been asked when several years of Greek and Latin were customary constituents of the young scholar's programme. It has come to be asked largely following the development of linguistic nationalism. Although first undertaken in the context of educating children in Welsh or Irish, the studies have been extended to the education of many groups in their native language. The findings have been that educating a child in one language interferes with his or her ability to pass examinations in a second, and the interference is greater the more 'minor' the one language and the more elaborate the second. Initially interpreted as evidence that bilingualism interfered with or lessened intellectual capability, the data are now seen as supporting the view that particular skills acquired through one language may not be wholly available for transfer to a second, especially if the two languages are quite different. No evidence has been accumulated to suggest that intelligence is lessened or heightened by instruction in one language or another; what has been shown is that skill in manipulating the dominant symbols of the culture is better acquired one way than another.

Languages are said to differ in their ability to express information in one or another area or on one or another topic. The classic examples have to do with the vocabulary for varieties of snow among some Eskimo, and for varieties of camel in Arabic. A considerable philosophy has been built on related observations. The term 'linguistic relativity' marks the view of the linguists E. Sapir and his student B. L. Whorf, which in its dogmatic form is called the Sapir–Whorf hypothesis: the language one uses controls the way one thinks about the world. This extends well beyond differences in vocabulary items of Eskimo and Arab—or of a vintner for wines, or a perfumer for smells, or any other specialized terms or jargon: the claim is that the mind works differently. In this claim Whorf seemed to identify language with thought—an equation few linguists, psychologists, or philosophers accept at present—and went on to confuse the ability to learn to make a discrimination with the readiness with which it is made. That is, Whorf used lexical and syntactic aspects of a language as evidence for procedures of mind, and in so doing seems to have used faulty reasoning to arrive at a plausible conclusion. The conclusion is that the *symbols the mind uses in its activities actually affect the way the mind works. The interaction of symbol systems and mental operations is under present active study.

Languages do seem to differ in the ease with which they lend themselves to certain topical areas. Italian and French are rich and subtle in the areas of interpersonal relations, German lends itself easily to metaphysics, English dominates modern science—to name a few related languages. The structure of language, it has sometimes been suggested, also influences the way the mind works,

perhaps in the way that speaking a particular language tends to shape the face. Whether a language requires many qualifications of the action before the action is named, or whether it is named first and then qualified; whether disparate items are stuck together to make new composites or whether features are analysed out and put into contrast; whether word order is a fixed or a free variable—these and other questions have been related to 'national character' and to mental activity. The topics are rich in speculation and poor in data.

They attract the psychologist's attention because of their relation to the topic of representation. Psychologists not only study the fact of behavioural change as a function of experience, but also try to give a plausible account of the means by which behaviour is controlled. Since what a person knows somehow affects what he or she does, some formalism is sought by the psychologist to accommodate the knowledge. That is, how knowledge is represented in mind and how best to represent it can be taken as important aspects of the psychologist's study. In this respect bilingual individuals are interesting test cases, for they can learn something through one of their languages and be tested for the knowledge through another; changes in performance as a function of changes in language can then sometimes be used to make plausible inferences about the mental operations underlying the behaviour. The findings suggest that knowledge is often situational and specific and that something learned through one language is not known to the person generally but is available to him or her only through that language. Recent evidence on the effects of stroke and related cerebral accidents upon language performance tends to bear out the supposition that knowledge and skill may be interfered with selectively, according to interference with the means by which the knowledge or skill were acquired.   PAK

Albert, M. L. and Obler, L. K. (1978). *The Bilingual Brain*.
Haugen, E. (1974). 'Bilingualism, language contact, and immigrant languages in the United States: a research report, 1956–1970'. In Sebok, T. A. (ed.), *Current Trends in Linguistics*, vol. x.
Kolers, P. A. (1978). 'On the representations of experience'. In Gerver, D., and Sinaiko, W. (eds.), *Language Interpretation and Communication*.
Weinreich, U. (1953). *Languages in Contact: Findings and Problems*.

Recent research in bilingualism makes use of brain imaging techniques to investigate the cerebral representation of more than one language in the brain. Different areas are used for languages learned after the age of 4 or so years. For recent reviews see:

Fabbro, F. (2001). 'The bilingual brain: cerebral representation of languages'. *Brain and Language*, 79/2.
Fornells, R. A., Rotte, M., Heinze, H. J., Noesselt, T., and Muente, T. F. (2002). 'Brain potential and functional MRI evidence for how to handle two languages with one brain'. *Nature* 6875.

binaural hearing. The use of both ears in order to locate the direction of sound sources. For frequencies lower than about 1,500 hertz the location is given by phase, or time, differences between the ears. For higher frequencies it is given by the different amplitudes of sound in the ears, as the head masks high-frequency sound from the further ear (see HEARING). (It is remarkable that the low-frequency phase detector resolves time differences between the ears of only a few microseconds.) The use of the two ears is important for understanding speech where there is an echo, as there is even in a normal room, the echo being suppressed by some unknown mechanism depending on binaural signals. For this and other reasons, binaural hearing aids can be significantly better than the more usual monaural aids, and are especially useful for blind people with impaired hearing, who make much use of binaural location of the direction of sounds. (See also AUDITORY ILLUSIONS.)

Blauert, J. (1997). 'An Introduction to binaural technology'. In Gilkey, R. H. (ed.), *Binaural and Spatial Hearing in Real and Virtual Environments*.

Binet, Alfred (1857–1911). French psychologist, born at Nice. He became director of the department of physiological psychology at the Sorbonne in 1892. With Theodore Simon, he was responsible for the design and standardization of the first formal *intelligence tests—the 'Binet scale'—originally devised at the request of the French government in order to establish which children were or were not worthy to benefit from education.

He instigated the concept of intelligence quotient (IQ), i.e. chronological age divided by mental age, multiplied by 100, which has been widely used ever since to 'measure' the intelligence of children and, in somewhat modified form, that of adults too. Indeed, the notion that individuals are born with all potential ability assessed along a single continuum is widely regarded as one of the most notable achievements of modern psychology; and yet it may be both conceptually and socially misguided and has led to race and sex rivalries. In spite of extensive research, it still remains unclear how far the IQ score represents actual ability and whether it is genuinely predictive of intellectual accomplishment. At all events, the recent tendency is to interpret the results of intelligence tests only with extreme caution.

Binet's most important book was *L'Étude experimentale de l'intelligence* (1903). But he also wrote books on many other psychological subjects, including hypnosis and suggestibility, and the psychic life of micro-organisms.

OLZ

biological clock. Anybody who has crossed the Atlantic in an aeroplane knows about '*jet lag'. After a journey from London to New York it is difficult to stay awake, while after the return journey one tends to wake up late. Man's body is intolerant of changes in clock time and it takes several days to readjust to a new local time.

The same is true of practically all other animals, not very surprisingly, because we all live on the same planet and experience the same 24-hour cycle as the earth rotates. Mice, birds, and men eat and sleep at particular times of day, depending on their species, and if they are placed (or choose to place themselves) in unvarying habitats such as laboratories or down a mine they will generally retain these regular habits. The cycle tends to drift a little, with waking a few minutes earlier or later on each succeeding day, but it remains amazingly constant in duration. The rhythm of the body's activities can be reset by a new time of sunrise, or by a series of night shifts at a factory, but it cannot be substantially altered: man can be induced to live on a 23- or 25-hour cycle (by speeding up or slowing down his watch), but a 12- or 18-hour day seems impossible.

Shore-living invertebrates typically show an additional 'tidal' cycle, which has obvious adaptive significance, and many also show longer-term rhythms, coincident with the phases of the moon; species may spawn only at spring tides, or even only at spring tides at a particular time of year. Even annual rhythms may persist in constant conditions: weaver-birds, for instance, build nests and lay eggs at the 'correct' time of year for at least two years when deprived of day-length or temperature clues to the time of year.

There are also much shorter cycles—activities that are repeated every few seconds or minutes. Many sessile, burrowing, and boring animals lead monotonous lives in almost constant conditions and show these shorter rhythms very clearly. As with the circadian (*circa diem*, almost 24-hour) cycles, the rhythms tend to persist when all obvious sources of stimulation (even food) have been eliminated; they seem to be generated from within, rather than caused from outside.

The conclusion is that an animal contains one or more 'biological clock' (but the existence of several different rhythms in one animal does not necessarily imply several clocks—it could be a matter of gearing), and a great deal of research has gone into establishing the whereabouts of the mainsprings. A recurrent problem is that, because a body's various activities are interrelated, most if not all of its tissues operate to a cycle, and how does one distinguish between the mainspring and the rest of the clockwork? One approach is to determine which of the tissues will continue to perform rhythmically in isolation, although it is difficult to keep most tissues alive in a test tube, and even if one succeeds it is impossible to be certain that the tissue is behaving normally. The method is useful in the study of short-term cycles, however, and there are now a number of well-documented cases in which individual nerve cells have repeated regular patterns of electrical discharge over periods of hours or even days. The matter can be followed further into the cell, which may show cyclic changes in ribonucleic acid (RNA) content.

But where and how does the timing originate? Some argue that there is no endogenous clock and that the rhythms observed are driven from outside. It is impossible to disprove this, although in laboratories it is relatively easy to screen animals and plants (even potatoes show rhythmic cycles in respiration rates) from changes in lighting, temperature, and vibration. It is difficult, however, to screen them from daily changes in weak magnetic fields (and many are known to respond to these) and quite impossible to screen them from cyclic geophysical events such as the varying pull of the moon. Eventually the use of orbiting laboratories may help; in the meantime conventional wisdom holds that truly endogenous clocks are likely, even though it can offer no convincing models of how they may be engineered.   MJW

Moore-Ede, M. C., Sulzman, F. M., and Fuller, C. A. (1982). *The Clocks that Time Us*.

Biran, Maine de. See MAINE DE BIRAN.

bit. The binary digit, or 'bit' as it is termed, is the primary unit for measuring information and uncertainty. The bit is a yes/no decision, which may be represented in an information system, or computer, by the two positions of a simple on–off switch. *Digital systems are based on 'bits', and their speed may be specified as their maximum 'bit rate'.

The 'Dictionary Game' illustrates very clearly how dividing a set of possibilities into two, and then this set into two again, then again, can lead very quickly to finding a particular item. Any word can usually be located with a dozen questions of the form: 'Is the word before "G"?' or 'Is it after "D"?' . . . But this works only when the items are arranged in some kind of order, such as alphabetical, or numerical. It is, however, just possible that at least some memories may be selected or accessed in this kind of way, by branching search strategies.

In *information theory (Shannon and Weaver 1949), information is related mathematically to uncertainty, for it takes more information to specify a particular specific alternative item from many possibilities than from few possibilities. As the number of alternatives increases, so more bits are needed to select one of them. The number of bits required is the logarithm, to the base 2, of the number of alternatives. So for dice, there are six possibilities for a die, and the uncertainty for each face or number on the die is $\log 6 = 2.58$. For drawing a card from a pack of 52 cards, $\log 52 = 5.70$. Thus, for the die two or three questions will determine the number, and five or six questions will identify a card.

Many experiments have been aimed at measuring the 'bit rate' for human performance, first defined by W. H. Hake and W. R. Garner in 1951. Their subjects identified positions of a pointer on a linear scale, with various possible positions for the pointer. With five positions the subjects lost no information, but with 10, 20, or 50 alternatives the transmitted information was effectively constant, at about 3.0 bits. People can only identify about nine points on a line; increasing the number of alternatives does not increase the amount of information transmitted. The human bit rate for choices along a single dimension is about 3.0 bits, but this rises with more dimensions (for example, recognizing positions of a dot on a square, with a short exposure time) up to about 8 bits. Long practice may raise the bit rate somewhat.

H. Quastler and V. J. Wulff (cited in Attneave 1959) have estimated bit rates for various human skills. For a pianist playing random notes, the bit rate may be as high as 22 bits per second. The skilled pianist learns to '*chunk' notes into familiar chords—each being a single selection—so his effective performance may be much better. Typing is limited to about 15 bits per second. Speech can be as high as 26 bits per second, though around 18 is normal. It has been estimated that silent reading may be as high as 44 bits per second. Mental arithmetic by a 'lightning calculator' was estimated at about 24 bits per second: about the same as that of a pianist.

The pioneering experiment by Edmund Hick (1952), which measured the 'rate of gain of information' by getting subjects to press a key corresponding to a light, with various numbers of keys and lights, showed that *reaction time increases logarithmically as the number of choices (the number of lights and keys, one for each finger) increases. There is, however, a deep problem for this or any other technique for measuring the bit rate for the human nervous system—for we are never quite limited to the alternatives provided by the experimenter. Thus, the subject in Hick's experiment (actually the editor of this *Companion*!) was not deaf, or blind, to everything except the lights to which he was responding, so that his range of possibilities was always greater than the experimenter knew, or could take into account. Possibly *attention serves, consciously or unconsciously, to limit accepted possibilities, to make best use of our limited human bit rate.   RLG

Attneave, F. (1959). *Applications of Information Theory to Psychology*.
Gregory, R. L. (1986). 'Whatever happened to information theory?' In *Odd Perceptions*.
Hick, W. E. (1952). 'On the rate of gain of information'. *Quarterly Journal of Experimental Psychology*, 4.
Shannon, C. E., and Weaver, W. (1949). *The Mathematical Theory of Communication*.

black. The visual sensation associated with lack of, or sudden reduction in, light. Black is not absence of visual sensation but is sensationally a colour. If we think of what is behind the head, we experience *nothing*—which is very different from black. (See NOTHINGNESS.)

blindness, recovery from. What would an adult who had been blind all his life be able to see if the cause of his blindness was suddenly removed? This question was asked by several empiricist philosophers in the 18th century. John *Locke considered the possibilities of such a case in 1690, following the question posed in a letter from his friend William Molyneux:

Suppose a man born blind, and now adult, and taught by his touch to distinguish between a cube and a sphere of the same metal. Suppose then the cube and the sphere were placed on a table, and the blind man made to see: query, whether by his sight, before he touched them, could he distinguish and tell which was the globe and which the cube? . . . The acute and judicious proposer answers: not. For though he has obtained the experience of how the globe, how the cube, affects his touch, yet he has not yet attained the experience that what affects his touch so or so, must affect his sight, so or so. . . .

Locke comments in the *Essay Concerning Human Understanding* (1690), Book II, ch. 9, sect. 8:

I agree with this thinking gentleman, whom I am pleased to call my friend, in his answer to this problem; and am of the opinion that the blind man, at first, would not be able with certainty to say which was the globe, which the cube. . . .

René *Descartes, in a passage in the *Dioptrics* (1637), considers how a blind man might build up a perceptual world by tapping around him with a stick. He first considers a sighted person using a stick in darkness. Descartes must surely have tried this for himself, and perhaps actually tested blind people. He says, of this experiment:

. . . without long practice this kind of sensation is rather confused and dim; but if you take men born blind, who have made use of such sensations all their life, you will find they feel things with such perfect exactness that one might almost say that they see with their hands. . . .

Descartes goes on to suggest that normal vision resembles a blind man exploring and building up his sense world by successive probes with a stick.

George *Berkeley, in *A New Theory of Vision* (1709), sect. 85, stresses the importance of touch for seeing by considering that a microscope, by so changing the scale of things that touch no longer corresponds to vision, is of little use; and so, if our eyes were 'turned into the nature of microscopes, we should not be much benefited by the change . . . and (we would be) left only with the empty amusement of seeing, without any other benefit arising from it' (sect. 86). Berkeley goes on to say that we should expect a blind man who recovered sight not to know visually whether anything was:

. . . high or low, erect or inverted . . . for the objects to which he had hitherto used to apply the terms up and down, high and low, were such as only affected or were in some way perceived by touch; but the proper objects of vision make a new set of ideas, perfectly distinct and different from the former, and which can in no sort make themselves perceived by touch (sect. 95).

These remained interesting speculations, until in 1728 an unusually expert and thoughtful surgeon, William *Cheselden, reported such a clinical case. Though generally distinguished as a surgeon his achievements were especially ophthalmic operations for cataract (Cope 1953). In a celebrated case Cheselden gave sight to a boy aged 13 or 14 who was born with highly opaque cataracts. Cheselden reported that:

When he first saw, he was so far from making any judgment of distances, that he thought all object whatever touched his eyes (as he expressed it) as what he felt did his skin, and thought no object so agreeable as those which were smooth and regular, though he could form no judgment of their shape, or guess what it was in any object that was pleasing to him: he knew not the shape of anything, nor any one thing from another, however different in shape or magnitude; but upon being told what things were, whose form he knew before from feeling, he would carefully observe, that he might know them again; and (as he said) at first learned to know, and again forgot a thousand things in a day. One particular only, though it might appear trifling, I will relate: Having often forgot which was the cat, and which the dog, he was ashamed to ask; but catching the cat, which he knew by feeling, he was observed to look at her steadfastly, and then, setting her down, said, So, puss, I shall know you another time. He was very much surprised, that those things which he had liked best, did not appear most agreeable to his eyes, expecting those persons would appear most beautiful that he loved most, and such things to be most agreeable to his sight, that were so to his taste. We thought he soon knew what pictures represented, which were shewed to him, but we found afterwards we were mistaken; for about two months after he was couched, he discovered at once they represented solid bodies, when to that time he considered them only as party-coloured planes, or surfaces diversified with variety of paint; but even then he was no less surprised, expecting the pictures would feel like the things they represented, and was amazed when he found those parts, which by their light and shadow appeared now round and uneven, felt only flat like the rest, and asked which was the lying sense, feeling or seeing?

Being shewn his father's picture in a locket at his mother's watch, and told what it was, he acknowledged the likeness, but was vastly surprised; asking, how it could be, that a large face could be expressed in so little room, saying, it should have seemed as impossible for him, as to put a bushel of anything into a pint. At first he could bear but very little light, and the things he saw, he thought extremely large; but upon seeing things larger, those first seen he conceived less, never being able to imagine any lines beyond the bounds he saw; the room he was in, he said, he knew to be but part of the house, yet he could not conceive that the whole house could look bigger. Before he was couched, he expected little advantage from seeing, worth undergoing an operation for, except reading and writing; for he said, he thought he could have no more pleasure in walking abroad than he had in the garden, which he could do safely and readily. And even blindness, he observed, had this advantage, that he could go anywhere in the dark, much better than those who can see; and after he had seen, he did not soon lose this quality, nor desire a light to go about the house in the night. He said, every new object was a new delight; and the pleasure was so great, that he wanted words to express it; but his gratitude to his operator he could not conceal, never seeing him for some time without tears of joy in his eyes, and other marks of affection. . . . A year after first seeing, being carried upon Epsom Downs, and observing a large prospect, he was exceedingly delighted with it, and called it a new kind of seeing. And now being couched in his other eye, he says, that objects at first appeared large to this eye, but not so large as they did at first to the other; and looking upon the same object with both eyes, he thought it looked about twice as large as with the first couched eye only, but not double, that we can in any ways discover.

Evidently the sensory worlds of touch and vision were not so separate as at least Berkeley imagined they would be, and visual perception developed remarkably rapidly. This was discussed in terms of the Cheselden case by the materialist philosopher Julien Offray de *La Mettrie, in his dangerously challenging book *Natural History of the Soul* (1745), where he argues that only education received through the senses makes man man, and gives him what we call a soul, while no development of the mind outwards ever takes place. A few years later, in his better-known *Man a Machine* (1748), he says:

Nothing, as any one can see, is so simple as the mechanism of our education. Everything may be reduced to sounds or words that pass from the mouth of one through the ears of another into his brain. At the same moment, he perceives through his eyes the shape of the bodies of which these words are arbitrary signs.

The findings of the Cheselden case (which, though by no means the first, is the first at all adequately reported) are confirmed by some later cases, though in others the development of perception is painfully slow. R. Latta described a case of a successful operation for congenital cataract in 1904, which was broadly similar with almost immediately useful vision; but very often the eye takes a long time to settle down after a cataract operation. This may explain why so many of the historical cases described by M. von Senden showed such slow development.

The case of a man who received corneal grafts when aged 52 (Gregory and Wallace 1963) has the advantage over previous cases that a good retinal image is immediately available after corneal grafts, as the eye is far less disturbed than by a cataract operation. The study started in the hospital a day or so after the first operation, and continued for the rest of his life. In this case the patient, 'S.B.', could see virtually immediately things he already knew by touch; though for objects or features where touch had not been available a long, slow learning process

was required, and in fact he never became perceptually normal. It was striking that he had immediate visual perception for things that must have been learned while he was blind, and could not have been known innately. Thus, from extensive experience of feeling the hands of his pocket watch, he was able, immediately, to tell the time visually. Perhaps even more striking, as a boy at the blind school S.B. had been taught to recognize by touch capital letters which were inscribed on special wooden plates. This was useful for reading street names, brass plates, and so on. Now it turned out that he could immediately read capital letters visually, though not lower-case letters, which he had not been taught by touch. These took months to learn to see. The general finding of this case was dramatic transfer of knowledge from touch to vision. So S.B. was not like a baby learning to see: he already knew a great deal from touch, and this was available for his newly functioning vision.

He had difficulties with shadows. When walking on steps on a sunny day he would quite often step on the shadow, sometimes falling. He was remarkably good at judging horizontal though not vertical distances. Thus, while still in the hospital, he could give the distance of chairs or tables almost normally, but when looking down from the window he thought the ground was at touching distance though the ward was several storeys high. When he was shown various distortion *illusions it was found that he was hardly affected by them: they were almost undistorted. And he did not experience the usual spontaneous depth reversals of the *Necker cube—which appeared to him flat. Indeed, like the Cheselden case, he had great difficulty seeing objects in pictures. Cartoons of faces meant nothing to him. He also found some things he loved ugly (including his wife, and himself!) and he was frequently upset by the blemishes and imperfections of the visible world. He was fascinated by mirrors: they remained wonderful to the end of his life. As for most of the cases, though, S.B. became severely depressed, and felt more handicapped with his vision than when blind.

A dramatic and revealing episode occurred when he was first shown a lathe, at the London Science Museum, shortly after he left hospital. He had a long-standing interest in tools, and he particularly wanted to be able to use a lathe.

We led him to the glass case, and asked him to tell us what was in it. He was quite unable to say anything about it, except he thought the nearest part was a handle. (He pointed to the handle of the transverse feed.) He complained that he could not see the cutting edge, or the metal being worked, or anything else about it, and appeared rather agitated. We then asked the Museum Attendant for the case to be opened, and S.B. was allowed to touch the lathe. The result was startling; he ran his hands deftly over the machine, touching first the transverse feed handle and confidently naming it 'a handle', and then on to the saddle, the bed and the head-stock of the lathe. He ran his hands eagerly over the lathe, with his eyes shut. Then he stood back a little and opened his eyes and said: 'Now that I've felt it I can see.' He then named many of the parts correctly and explained how they would work, though he could not understand the chain of four gears driving the lead screw.

Many of these observations have been confirmed by Valvo (1971) in half a dozen cases of recovery from blindness by a remarkable operation: fitting acrylic lenses to eyes that never formed completely. Tissue rejection of the artificial lenses was prevented by placing them in a tooth, which was implanted as a buffer in the eye. One of these Italian patients, wearing a lens in a tooth in his eye, is a philosopher! It is now possible to implant artificial lenses without tissue rejection, so perhaps more cases of adult recovery from infant blindness will now appear.   RLG

Berkeley, G. (1709). *A New Theory of Vision*. Ed. A. D. Lindsay, (1910).

Cope, Z. (1953). *William Cheselden*.

Descartes, R. (1637). *Discourse on Method*. Trans. E. S. Haldane and G. R. T. Ross, in *The Philosophical Works of Descartes* (2 vols., 1967).

Gregory, R. L., and Wallace, J. G. (1963). *Recovery from Early Blindness: A Case Study*.

Hebb, D. O. (1949). *The Organization of Behaviour*.

La Mettrie, J. O. de (1748). *L'Homme*. Trans. G. C. Bussey, in *Man a Machine* (1953). (The *Natural History of the Soul* (1745) is well discussed by F. A. Langer in his *The History of Materialism*, 1925.)

Latta, R. (1904). 'Notes on a successful operation for congenital cataract in an adult'. *British Journal of Psychology*, 1.

Locke, J. (1690). *Essay Concerning Human Understanding*. Ed. P. H. Nidditch (1975).

Senden, M. von (1932). *Space and Sight: The Perception of Space and Shape in the Congenitally Blind before and after Operation*. Trans. P. Heath (1960).

Valvo, A. (1971). *Sight Restoration after Long-Term Blindness: The Problems and Behaviour Patterns of Visual Rehabilitation*.

blindsight. The term is defined by the *Oxford Concise Dictionary* as '*Medicine*: a condition in which the sufferer responds to visual stimuli without consciously perceiving them.' It is associated with damage to human primary visual cortex (V1), which causes 'blindness' in corresponding parts of the affected visual fields, the field defect having a size and shape to be expected from the classical retino-cortical maps (Holmes 1918) (see VISUAL SYSTEM: ORGANIZATION). Nevertheless, when subjects are required to 'guess' about stimuli in their blind fields, they may be able to discriminate them from each other or locate them in space, even though they say they do not see them and have no awareness of them. When a stimulus contains rapid transient onsets and offsets, or moves very rapidly, blindsight subjects may say they are 'aware' that something is happening, they may 'feel' it, although they do not 'see' it as such. This has been called 'Blindsight Type 2' in contrast to 'Blindsight Type 1', when discriminations

occur in the total absence of any acknowledged awareness.

The historical origins stem from animal research and neuroanatomy. The primate retina, including that of humans, sends its major nerve tract (after a relay in the thalamus) to the visual cortex ('V1', 'striate cortex'). When the striate cortex is damaged or removed or blocked in monkeys, the animals can still carry out visual discriminations although their capacity changes in certain ways. That they can still make such discriminations is, in itself, not surprising because the retinal output also reaches a number of other brain targets, located mainly in the midbrain and thalamus. These routes remain intact even when V1 is entirely removed or damaged, and from these non-striate targets information can be relayed widely to a number of other regions in the brain. The 'extra-striate' tracts from the eye contain fewer nerve fibres than those in the pathway reaching V1, only about one-fifth as many, but this smaller number is not trivial—it amounts to about five times as many fibres as are in the whole auditory nerve. And so the surprise is not that animals can make visual discriminations in the absence of V1: it is that human subjects with damage to V1 claim they are blind. (Because damage to V1 is rarely complete, and is typically confined to one cerebral hemisphere, the region of blindness in most patients is confined to no more than one-half of the visual field, situated contralateral to the damaged hemisphere, although with bilateral cortical damage the blindness covers the entire visual field.)

The surprising discrepancy reflects the fact that the method of testing for visual capacity is usually deeply different in humans and in other animals, rather than there being differences in their brains as such. Humans are typically asked to give verbal descriptions or to comment on visual appearances and differences, whereas animals are trained to make alternative choices for which they are usually rewarded, devoid of any commentary. Even when a human subject is asked to make a discrimination between, say, two colours, he is usually explicitly instructed verbally as to what attribute he should be responding to, and more importantly there is an important implicit assumption that he will be aware of that attribute, or will tell us if he is not. But when the human subject is tested in a manner that is closer to animal methodology, being asked simply to make a forced-choice 'guess' about the visual stimuli whether or not he cannot 'see' them, e.g. whether a visual event is located at *A* or *B*, or whether it is colour *A* or colour *B*, or falls in one temporal interval or a second temporal interval, or whether its shape, or colour, or brightness is different in one or the other interval— in other words, tested in the same forced-choice discriminative way as animals are (but without peanut rewards!)—human subjects can match the performance of animals with visual cortex damage even though they may lack any acknowledged awareness of them. Hence, the term 'blindsight'. It is one example of a dissociation in brain-damage patients between an intact capacity and the commentaries about the contents of the capacity (see BRAIN FUNCTION AND AWARENESS).

Given the counter-intuitive nature of blindsight, early scepticism abounded and questions have been raised about its validity (as was true for earlier examples of implicit processing in neuropsychology). It has been suggested, for example, that there may be stray light falling in the intact visual field, or that the cortical lesion in particular cases is incomplete and patchy, or that subjects really 'see' but deny this, perhaps because of a very conservative criterion, or that their vision is really essentially normal but the percepts are rendered very faint because of the brain damage. All of these alternatives have been roundly and directly addressed in various reviews and experimental analyses; the subject continues to provoke lively discussion not only among neuroscientists but also among philosophers and others interested in the nature of conscious awareness.

Attributes of vision that can be discriminated by blindsight subjects in the absence of their experience of the stimuli include colour, different orientation of lines or gratings, simple shapes, motion, onset and termination of visual events. Interestingly, the emotional expression of unseen faces in the blind field can be 'guessed' at better than chance levels. There are, however, changes in relation to normal vision. By altering the spacing of bars on a sine wave until it can no longer be discriminated from a homogeneous patch, one can measure the subjects' acuity. It is reduced, relative to their normal seeing fields, but is still creditable. Motion perception is retained for simple displacement of a bar or a spot, but more complex motion patterns ('third order motion') seem to be seriously affected. Good colour discrimination remains (again, in the absence of any experience of colour *per se*,) but there is a shift towards a relative increase in sensitivity of long wavelengths (red) and a decrease of middle wavelengths (green). Otherwise the spectral sensitivity curve, and its change under dark adaptation, is relatively normal.

Because it is rare that damage to the visual cortex occurs in isolation in clinical cases, relatively 'pure' examples of blindsight may be rare. It is known from animal work that, if the damage extends very far outside the visual cortex, the residual visual capacity is reduced. It is for this reason that most human blindsight research has concentrated on a small number of well-chosen subjects. However, it now appears that this self-imposed restriction may be too conservative. Residual visual function has been reported to occur in the majority of cases of visual cortical damage if additional damage is only moderate.

The distinction between blindsight Type 1 and Type 2

has allowed us to carry out functional brain imaging contrasting states *with* awareness and *without* awareness, in both conditions using simple movement discriminations, which can be carried out at a high level of success —90 per cent or better. In the unawareness condition, but not the aware condition, activity is seen in the superior colliculus of the midbrain. This also is active for red stimuli but not for equiluminant green. In contrast, in the aware state, dorsal cortical areas, including foci in the right prefrontal cortex, are active. Such research reflects one of the strong interests of neuroscientists in blindsight and other perceptual phenomena in helping to unravel the neural mechanisms that may underlie conscious awareness.

Because of the difficulty subjects may have in being asked to discriminate stimuli they cannot see, other methods of assessing residual function commend themselves, especially for screening of brain-damaged subjects for possible rehabilitation. Some of these methods depend upon asking the subject to discriminate stimuli lying entirely in their intact, seeing hemifields, but showing that their performance can be altered by the presentation of stimuli in their blind fields, which may enhance or interfere. By far the most quantitatively sensitive method depends upon changes in the diameter of the pupil, which constricts not only to increase in light energy, but to a wide variety of stimuli without any energy change. These include sine-wave gratings, movement, and colour. The acuity of the blind field can be accurately measured by pupillometry, as well as the sensitivity to colour and colour after-images, which appear to mirror the blindsight capacity as measured by forced-choice guessing. The pupil can also be used to measure similar capacities in animals or in human infants, where verbal report of course is impossible.

Finally, given that the existence of residual visual capacity was first demonstrated in animals with visual cortex lesions, the question arises as to whether they too show blindsight for the discriminations they can perform. Ingenious experiments appear to show a positive answer. They can detect and locate light stimuli with impressive sensitivity. They can also readily be trained to make differential responses in their normal visual fields for lights versus non-lights ('blanks'). But when the same lights are projected into their affected field, the monkeys reliably treat them as 'blanks', that is, the very stimuli that they can detect with impressive sensitivity are classified by them as being 'blanks', as 'non-lights'—just as a human blindsight subject does. Thus, the contribution made by the visual cortex to visual awareness appears to be similar in humans and other primates. LW

Cowey, A., and Stoerig, P. (1995). 'Blindsight in monkeys'. *Nature*, 373.

Holmes, G. (1918). 'Disturbances of vision by cerebral lesions'. *British Journal of Ophthalmology*. 2.

Pöppel, E., Held, R., and Frost, D. (1974). 'Residual visual function after brain wounds involving the central visual pathways in man'. *Nature*, 243.

Sahraie, A., Weiskrantz, L., Barbur, J. L., Simmons, A., Williams, S. C. R., and Brammer, M. L. (1997). 'Pattern of neuronal activity associated with conscious and unconscious processing of visual signals'. *Proceedings of the National Academy of Sciences of the USA*, 94.

Weiskrantz, L. (1990). 'Outlooks for blindsight: explicit methodologies for implicit processes. The Ferrier Lecture'. *Proceedings of the Royal Society Biological Sciences*, B series, 239.

—— (1997). *Consciousness Lost and Found: A Neuropsychological Exploration*.

—— (1986). *A Case Study and Implications* (new edn. 1998).

blinking. When the eye is irritated by a foreign body, such as grit or a fly, we blink to remove it. This is a *reflex, and there is also reflex closing of the eyes to prevent damage when we sneeze; but everyday blinking is not a reflex activity. A reflex needs an initiating signal; but if, for example, the eyes had to dry up to initiate blink signals, the blink would follow the beginnings of damage, due to the eyes drying, but it would be too late to protect the delicate corneas with a film of tears.

Normal blinking is given by signals initiating in the brain, probably from the *basal ganglia. Rather surprisingly, the rate of blinking is a useful index of general attention, as it tends to increase markedly when anticipating *stress, and it falls below the normal rate during periods of high concentration. This is possibly related to its early use in conditions such as hunting, when the eye needs to be cleared and the fluid on the cornea smoothed out for maximum visual acuity. During a prolonged task, however, the eyes need to remain open for long periods. Blinking can then be so reduced that damage may result as the eyes dry. This is a hazard in some occupations: draughtsmen, for example, are apt to suffer from inflammation of the eyes, and over time from clinical problems with their corneas if they continue to concentrate for prolonged periods without blinking.

It is interesting that the rate of blinking is similarly affected by non-visual tasks. Most curiously, we are not normally aware of blinking, though the eyes are closed every few seconds. One might have thought that blinking would occur in one eye at a time so that we are not intermittently blinded, but it turns out that this seldom matters, as blinking is normally inhibited just prior to important anticipated events. It has been suggested that people having unusually high blink rates may be unsuitable as pilots, or be dangerous drivers, but experiments have shown that high individual blink rates are not a significant hazard for skills where short-term prediction of dangerous events is possible.   RLG

Ponder, E., and Kennedy, W. P. (1928). 'On the act of blinking'. *Quarterly Journal of Experimental Physiology*, 18.

Poulton, E. C. and Gregory, R. L. (1952). 'Blinking during visual tracking'. *Quarterly Journal of Experimental Psychology*, 4.

blushing. Uncontrollable reddening of the cheeks, and sometimes the ears and neck, is associated with embarrassment and guilt. Charles *Darwin made the most interesting suggestion: that blushing is a warning that the individual who is blushing is not to be trusted, as he or she has violated the mores of the group or has committed some crime. This notion that blushing is a visible warning sign that an individual is not to be trusted Darwin puts forward in *Expression of the Emotions in Man and Animals* (1872). Part of his evidence is that children before the age of understanding social rules do not blush, for 'the mental powers of infants are not yet sufficiently developed to allow of their blushing. Hence, also, it is that idiots rarely blush.' Blushing (and also weeping and sobbing) is found only in man and not in other primates, who are generally supposed (in spite of some recent contrary evidence) not to have cognitive understanding of social mores or their violation. This is not to say that only humans have social mores, only that we alone appreciate and evaluate them, and act on our assessments of social situations, and monitor our successes and failures and the appropriateness of our behaviour in situations that had no precedence earlier in evolution. It seems that only humans have the understanding to be embarrassed—and so to blush.

For Darwin 'blushing is the most peculiar and the most human of all expressions'. He goes on to suggest a psychosomatic origin: 'we cannot cause a blush by any physical means. . . . It is the mind which must be affected.' But this is not the *conscious* mind, for (writing nearly twenty years before Sigmund *Freud was born) Darwin points out that blushing is not under control and that, further: 'Blushing is not only involuntary; but the wish to restrain it, by leading to self-attention, actually increases the tendency.' That it is an innate sign of mental states is confirmed by blushing in blind people.

Women blush more than men. Darwin wished to discover how far down the body blushes extend, so he adopted the ingenious notion of asking his medical friends 'who necessarily had frequent opportunities for observation'. His friend Sir James Paget (1814–99, who wrote the standard texts, *Lectures on Surgical Pathology* and *Clinical Lectures*) reported that: 'with women who blush intensely on the face, ears, nape of the neck, the blush does not commonly extend any lower down the body'. He never saw an instance in which it extended below the upper part of the chest. Darwin considers whether it is the exposure of the face to temperature changes that makes the capillaries specially labile; but decides, rather, that the face is intimately associated with the brain and that the blushing is primarily facial, at least in English women, because of the 'attention of the mind having been directed more frequently and earnestly to the face than any other part of the body'.

What we would now call the psychosomatic basis of blushing was pondered in astonishing depth by Darwin, as he considered that its mental effects may be *reversible*. He refers to the observation that when patients are given nitrite of amyl they blush in the same restricted regions as with embarrassment. 'The patients are at first pleasantly stimulated but, as the flushing increases, they become confused and bewildered. One woman to whom the vapour had been administered asserted that, as soon as she grew hot, she grew *muddled.*' Although all this was said well over a century ago there is little to add now, apart from its detailed physiology, to Darwin's comments on blushing. RLG

body language. The traditional theory of body language, originating with *Wundt in 1921, is that it is quite separate from verbal language in terms of both form and function. This theory holds that verbal language in the form of words and sentences is used primarily to convey factual or semantic information about the world whereas body language, in the form of facial expression, eye gaze, posture, gesture, head movement, and foot movement, is used to convey information about emotional states and to communicate information about interpersonal attitudes, crucial to the formation and maintenance of interpersonal relationships. Verbal language articulates thought; body language, on the other hand, communicates emotion and especially about relationships. Intuitively this latter proposition makes some sense. One advantage of interpersonal matters being dealt with non-verbally, is that the expression of such attitudes can be kept vague and flexible. According to Michael Argyle (1972), 'People need not reveal clearly nor commit themselves to what they think about each other.' Once we start using language to communicate our attitudes to another person then we are publicly committed to what we have said and therefore accountable. 'You said that you loved me' would be a perfectly reasonable retort. 'You acted like you loved me, there was just something momentary in your eyes' is much weaker somehow. Clearly body language has some advantages when it comes to the communication of emotion and interpersonal attitudes.

The anthropologist Gregory Bateson (1968) highlighted another possible advantage of using body language to communicate interpersonal attitudes when he wrote that 'It seems that the discourse of nonverbal communication is precisely concerned with matters of relationship. . . . From an adaptive point of view, it is therefore important that this discourse be carried on by techniques which are relatively unconscious and only imperfectly subject to voluntary control.' He implied that it was unconscious body language that was primarily involved in these 'matters of

relationship'. We can all say 'I love you', some rather too easily; it is quite a different matter to fake love nonverbally, or so Gregory Bateson seemed to think.

This is the traditional theory of body language, partly based on reasoning of the sort that we have just outlined but partly based on a set of core studies by Mehrabian in the 1960s and Argyle in the 1970s, which compare the impact of body language to verbal language in the communication of interpersonal attitudes. The problem with these seminal studies is that they are all flawed in one way or another (see Beattie 2003). They all apparently demonstrate that, in the communication of interpersonal attitudes, body language is much more powerful than verbal language, with the facial channel alone estimated to be more than five times as powerful as the verbal channel. These studies were all based around a simple paradigm, the construction of consistent or inconsistent verbal language/body language combinations that were rated by participants. But the problem with these studies is that they underestimate the power of language in the expression of interpersonal attitudes. Mehrabian restricted his analysis to individual words such as 'honey', 'maybe', and 'brute'. But the problem is that no one talks in individual words in the real world if they can help it. Michael Argyle used sentences in his studies but these were extremely explicit and therefore rather unreal sentences, which failed to take into account the great subtlety of language for the communication of interpersonal attitudes in everyday life. So how might verbal language be used to convey interpersonal attitudes? Opening up a conversation, the use of first names, compliments, disclosure, reciprocated disclosure, the asking of personal questions, verbal engagement, shared perspectives, the sharing of childhood memories, offers of help, offers of support are all likely to play some vital role in such communication. Language is almost certainly as crucial to conveying interpersonal attitudes as body language and classic studies, which suggest otherwise, are themselves fundamentally flawed.

But some psychologists have argued that the other half of the traditional theory about language and body language is also incorrect, namely that half which states that only verbal language conveys factual or semantic information. Wundt, the originator of the traditional theory, wrote in 1921 that 'the primary cause of natural gestures does not lie in the motivation to communicate a concept, but rather in the expression of an emotion'. But consider the following extract produced when a participant was narrating a cartoon story:

'she [chases him out again]'
Hand, gripping an object, swings from left to right.

McNeill (1992) pointed out that the speech conveys pursuit and repetition but does not indicate the weapon (an umbrella)—the iconic gesture (the spontaneous hand movement accompanying the speech) conveys this. McNeill emphasized that the sentence is well formed and not in need of repair and that the gesture (whose start point and end point are indicated by the square brackets) is perfectly temporally coordinated with the speech, and therefore the speech and gesture are generated by the brain at exactly the same time. Gesture and speech, McNeill concluded, cooperate to present 'a single cognitive representation' and to get the complete message you need both speech and gesture. This division of meaning between speech and iconic gesture generalizes across different languages. In fact, differences in iconic gesture use in different cultures are relatively trivial compared to the underlying similarities in their use. There are also striking similarities in the form of iconic gestures used to represent core semantic dimensions in different languages (see Beattie 2003).

Other psychologists have recognized that iconic gestures are common in speech but claim that they are too 'imprecise and unreliable' to be of any value in the communication of meaning (Krauss, Morrel-Samuels, and Colasante 1991) on the basis that individuals find it quite difficult to match gestures with the speech they accompany. However, Beattie and Shovelton (1999, 2001) argued that this is the wrong way of investigating the possible communicational function of these gestures. They maintained that if gestures are designed to communicate then they should provide critical information about the semantic domain to be encoded, the world out there or that part of it involved in the experiment, rather than about the accompanying speech.

Beattie and Shovelton video recorded participants narrating cartoon stories and then played just the speech segments or the gesture–speech combinations to another set of participants who were questioned about the original stories. They demonstrated that participants who received gesture–speech combinations recalled significantly more information than those who heard only the speech (60 per cent more specific information, 10 per cent in terms of overall message). The extra information included the speed and direction of the action, whether or not the action involved rotation or upward movement, and the relative position, size, and shape of the people and objects depicted, among other things. This research suggests that the iconic gestures that accompany talk are highly communicative and convey particular semantic aspects of a message. The fact that people gesture on the telephone (but less frequently on the telephone or on an intercom than in face-to-face communication, see Cohen and Harrison 1973) does not disprove this theory. People gesture when they speak, but the brain mechanisms that mediate gesturing are far older than mechanical artefacts like the telephone—on the telephone they simply

cannot inhibit this natural and primitive form of communication.

In conclusion, body language is not separate functionally from verbal language in the way that Wundt, the founder of modern psychology, thought. They both work together to communicate interpersonal relationships and both work together to convey semantic information. However, although some forms of body language like iconic gesture do communicate semantic information they do so in a different fashion from verbal language. Speakers spontaneously create images for the listener with their hands, but unlike verbal language, they do not use a pre-selected lexicon of individual items to do this. It has been argued that in some forms of body language one can see the unconstrained human mind in action, working alongside verbal language to communicate meaning in its own unique way, in everyday talk.   GB/HKS

Argyle, M. (1972). *The Psychology of Interpersonal Behaviour* (2nd edn.).

Bateson, G. (1968). 'Redundancy and coding'. In Sebeok, T. (ed.), *Animal Communication*.

Beattie, G. (2003). *Visible Thoughts: The New Psychology of Body Language*.

——and Shovelton, H. (1999). 'Do iconic hand gestures really contribute anything to the semantic information conveyed by speech? An experimental investigation'. *Semiotica*, 123.

——— (2001). 'An experimental investigation of the role of different types of iconic gesture in communication: a semantic feature approach'. *Gesture*, 1.

Cohen, A., and Harrison, R. (1973). 'Intentionality in the use of hand illustrators in face-to-face communicative situations'. *Journal of Personality and Social Psychology*, 28.

Krauss, R., Morrel-Samuels, P., and Colasante, C. (1991). 'Do conversational hand gestures communicate?' *Journal of Personality and Social Psychology*, 61.

McNeill, D. (1992). *Hand and Mind: What Gestures Reveal about Thought*.

Wundt, W. (1921). *The Language of Gestures* (repr. 1973).

body–mind problem. See MIND AND BODY; MIND–BODY PROBLEM; CONSCIOUSNESS AND CAUSALITY.

boggle. It is said that 'the mind boggles' (meaning an extreme state of incredulity, or rejection of a situation or idea). Nothing but minds can boggle—except computers? Perhaps this depends on whether computers are accepted as having, or not having, minds.

Boole, George (1815–64). English mathematician, born in Lincoln. Boole was mainly self-educated and did not gain an academic degree. He began teaching at the age of 16 while continuing to study on his own. He studied the works of Laplace and Lagrange, making notes that would later be the basis for his first mathematics paper. He received encouragement from Duncan Gregory, who at this time was in Cambridge and the editor of the recently founded *Cambridge Mathematical Journal*.

Boole was unable to take Duncan Gregory's advice and study courses at Cambridge as he required the income from his school to look after his parents. However, he began publishing in the *Cambridge Mathematical Journal*. An application of algebraic methods to the solution of differential equations was published by Boole in the *Transactions of the Royal Society*, and for this work he received the Society's Royal Medal.

In 1849 he was appointed to the chair of mathematics at Queen's College, Cork. He taught there for the rest of his life, gaining a reputation as an outstanding and dedicated teacher.

Boole's first book, *Mathematical Analysis of Logic* (1847), argued that logic is a branch of mathematics rather than metaphysics. In his principal work, *An Investigation of the Laws of Thought on Which Are Founded the Mathematical Theories of Logic and Probabilities* (1854), Boole established a new branch of mathematics, symbolic logic, in which symbols are used to represent logical operations. In this book, Boole proposed a calculus—the Boolean algebra—that he claimed was based on the nature of human logical thought. He saw his project as an attempt to translate thought into mathematical symbols. Boole showed that the symbols of his calculus could be made to take on only two values, 0 and 1, to perform all the necessary operations. This two-valued algebra is used today in computers, which employ the binary system to perform logical operations. His work greatly influenced *Shannon's pioneering work within *information theory.

Boole also worked on differential equations (the influential *Treatise on Differential Equations* appeared in 1859), the calculus of finite differences (*Treatise on the Calculus of Finite Differences*, 1860), and general methods in probability. He published around 50 papers and was one of the first to investigate the basic properties of numbers and how mathematics is related to logic. RLG

Harley, R. (1866). *George Boole: An Essay, Biographical and Expository*.

Kneale, W. (1948). 'Boole and the revival of logic', *Mind*, 57.

MacHale, D. (1985). *George Boole: His Life and Work*.

Taylor, G. (1955). 'George Boole, 1815–1864', *Proceedings of the Royal Irish Academy Section A*, 57.

Boring, Edwin Garrigues (1886–1968). American psychologist, who became Edgar Pierce Professor of Psychology at Harvard. He won distinction for his *History of Experimental Psychology* (1929; revised edition 1942), which traces the genesis of experimental psychology from its origins in early 19th-century philosophy and physiology to its general acceptance as an autonomous academic discipline a century later. While placing the

major stress on its German origins—more particularly the massive contribution of Wilhelm *Wundt—Boring was fair to the claims of the United States and Britain to have developed important brands of experimental psychology in which introspective analysis was less strongly represented and greater emphasis was placed on objective studies of behaviour in both animals and man. There was also wide recognition of the practical applications of psychological enquiry. Boring's book was, however, criticized in some quarters for its identification of scientific with experimental psychology and its correlated neglect of psychological medicine, in particular the work of Sigmund *Freud and his school (remedied, however, in the 1942 edition). None the less, in spite of some noteworthy limitations, Boring's *History* remains a scholarly record of the early days of experimental psychology.

Boring later published *Sensation and Perception in the History of Experimental Psychology*, a less ambitious though perhaps more satisfactory account of its subject viewed in historical perspective. It is fittingly dedicated to the memory of Hermann von *Helmholtz. A slighter book, owing much to its author's mentor, E. B. *Titchener, is the *Physical Dimensions of Consciousness*, which, though dated, is still of some importance. OLZ

Bowlby, John (1907–90). Psychiatrist and founder of *attachment theory.

The son of Sir Anthony and Lady Bowlby, Edward John Mostyn Bowlby was born in London on 26 February 1907, the fourth of six children. It was customary then for an upper-class mother to hand over her children to a nanny and nursemaids. A particular nursemaid took care of John on a daily basis, but she left when he was about 4. The effect of this on Bowlby is unknown, as he never discussed it (van Dijken 1998). The Bowlby children saw their mother for a short time each day and their father, who was a surgeon, on Sundays. He was absent even more during the First World War. However, there were long family holidays in the country—to the New Forest in July and to Scotland in late summer. This remained a family tradition—with Bowlby, his wife Ursula, their four children, and later their grandchildren retreating to the Isle of Skye each summer. Bowlby did much of his writing there, as well as walking and enjoying the 'season', including the Skye Ball with its Scottish reels. Skye is where Bowlby died on 2 September 1990, and where he is buried, on a remote hillside overlooking the cliffs and sea.

When Bowlby was 11, he and his elder brother were sent off to boarding school. From there he went to the Royal Naval College, Dartmouth. But at 17, Bowlby decided that the navy was not for him, writing to his mother that he wanted a job which would 'improve the community as a whole' (van Dijken 1998). At Trinity College, Cambridge, he followed his father by studying medicine, with a departure into psychology in his final year, graduating in 1928. Rather than going straight into clinical school, he spent a year teaching in two boarding schools, including one for disturbed children. Their early disrupted childhoods impressed Bowlby, and he decided to combine his medical training with psychoanalytic training. After becoming medically qualified at University College Hospital in 1933, he went to the Maudsley to train in adult psychiatry, and then to the London Child Guidance Clinic in 1936. He became an army psychiatrist in 1940, and after the war he went to the Tavistock Clinic, where he remained as director of the Department for Children and Parents (Holmes 1993).

At the Institute of Psycho-Analysis, Bowlby was assigned to Joan Riviere and then Melanie *Klein, who supervised him after his analytical qualification in 1937. Differences grew between Bowlby and Klein concerning the importance of real-life experiences vs. unconscious fantasies. For example, when treating a hyperactive and anxious 3-year-old boy, Bowlby noted that the boy's mother had been admitted to a mental hospital and was having another breakdown. Klein, however, did not allow Bowlby to treat the mother, devaluing what was actually happening in real life.

Bowlby was particularly interested in what happened around separation. This interest may have sprung from his own childhood experiences, as well as later when working with maladjusted children. He was struck by the high incidence of severely disrupted relationships with mother figures in the early histories of children and adolescents who had been referred to the clinic on account of repeated and apparently incorrigible stealing. This led to the publication in 1944 of *Forty-Four Juvenile Thieves: Their Characters and Home Life*. His seminal WHO monograph, *Maternal Care and Mental Health*, appeared in 1951, followed by *Child Care and the Growth of Love* in 1953. Around this time Bowlby and his colleagues the Robertsons observed young children in hospital, noting their intense and prolonged distress when not visited by parents. Moreover, home visits afterwards showed that the child's relationship with the mother was seriously disturbed for weeks or longer. Also in 1950, a Canadian woman called Mary Ainsworth (1913–99) joined Bowlby at the Tavistock, and she was to remain a close and influential colleague throughout his life. After her longitudinal study of mother–infant behaviour in Uganda, Ainsworth joined the faculty at the Johns Hopkins University in 1955, where she devised a strange situation procedure for assessing an infant's quality of attachment (Ainsworth et al. 1978). This identification of different 'patterns of attachment' enriched the theory and enabled research into the antecedents and consequences of security vs. insecurity.

During the 1950s, Bowlby's eclecticism was evidenced by his 'weekly workshop in a dingy room in the old Tavi, in Beaumont Street. The group was entirely heterogeneous—a Freudian and a Kleinian analyst, a Hullian and a Skinnerian learning theorist, a Piagetian, an ethologist, sometimes an anti-psychiatrist, psychiatric social workers—having in common only an interest in parent–child relations. . . . John Bowlby's intellectual dynamism and judicious enthusiasm held the group together. . . . During that period Bowlby formulated his ideas on "the child's tie to his mother" and "separation anxiety" . . . with inputs from ethology and systems theory' (Hinde 1991: 216). He came to the view that a child's attachment behaviour to the mother does not depend upon prior association with other behaviour such as feeding, but rather it evolved in its own right through natural selection, with a presumed function of protection from harm. The essence of his theory was set out in 'The nature of a child's tie to his mother' (1958) followed by his trilogy *Attachment and Loss* (1969/82, 1973, 1980). The thesis is that attachment behaviour is shown from birth onwards, leading to the formation over the first year of life of an enduring attachment bond. The quality of this bond, as secure or insecure, plays a key role in our view of ourselves and others, and in what Bowlby called our 'psychological well-being' (further described in the entry ATTACHMENT).

One reason for the power of attachment theory is that it lies at the heart of our emotional life. In one of his final papers Bowlby wrote, 'Many of the most intense emotions arise during the formation, the maintenance, the disruption and the renewal of attachment relationships. The formation of a bond is described as falling in love, maintaining a bond as loving someone, and losing a partner as grieving over someone. Similarly, threat of loss arouses anxiety and actual loss gives rise to sorrow; while each of these situations is likely to arouse anger. The unchallenged maintenance of a bond is experienced as a source of security and the renewal of a bond as a source of joy' (1991: 306).   JSH

Ainsworth, M. D. A., Blehar, M. C., Waters, E., and Wall, S. (1978). *Patterns of Attachment*.

Bowlby, J. (1951). *Maternal Care and Mental Health*.

——(1953). *Child Care and the Growth of Love*.

——(1958). 'The nature of a child's tie to his mother'. *International Journal of Psycho-Analysis*, 39.

——(1969/1982). *Attachment and Loss*, i: *Attachment*.

——(1973). *Attachment and Loss*, ii: *Separation, Anxiety and Anger*.

——(1980). *Attachment and Loss*, iii: *Loss, Sadness and Depression*.

——(1990). *Charles Darwin: A New Biography*.

——(1991). 'Ethological light on psychoanalytical problems'. In Bateson, P. (ed.), *Development and Integration of Behaviour*.

Hinde, R. A. (1991). 'Obituary: John Bowlby'. *Journal of Child Psychology & Psychiatry*, 32.

Holmes, J. (1993). *John Bowlby and Attachment Theory*.

van Dijken, S. (1998). *John Bowlby: His Early Life*.

Bradley, Francis Herbert (1846–1924). English *idealist Oxford philosopher. He followed *Hegel in his ethics, and developed a metaphysics, based on a principle of monism, that truth must always be the whole truth. Bertrand *Russell's logical atomism has been described as 'Bradley turned upside down'. His chief works are: *Ethical Studies* (1876), *Principles of Logic* (1883), and especially *Appearance and Reality* (1893).

Wollheim, R. (1959). *F. H. Bradley*.

Braille. A system by which the blind read from patterns of raised dots. The basic 'cell' consists of six dots in two vertical lines of three, from which can be derived letters, numerals, and punctuation marks (see Fig. 1). Most experienced Braille readers use their left index finger rather than their right to read Braille (see HANDEDNESS). The system was developed by Louis Braille (1809–52), simplifying the system of the army officer Charles Barbier, who wanted to use his system to pass messages silently. Braille became blind at the age of 3 and at 10 became a student at the Institution Nationale des Jeunes Aveugles in Paris, where he was later appointed a professor.

It has recently been found that there is activation of the visual area VI during Braille reading. This has implications for the neuroplasticity of the brain. Would VI become active with meaningless (as for an unknown language) Braille? The answer is not yet known but is being studied.

Burton, H., Synder, A. Z., Diamond, J. B., and Raichle, M. E. (2002). 'Adaptive changes in early and late blind: a fMRI study of verb generation to heard nouns'. *Journal of Neurophysiology*, 88/6.

Hamilton, R., and Pascual-Leone, A. (1998). 'Cortical plasticity associated with Braille learning'. *Trends in Cognitive Sciences*, 2/5.

brain and soul. Mechanistic brain science proceeds on the working assumption that every bodily event has a physical cause in the prior state of the central nervous system. Traditional moral and religious thought, on the other hand, has always presupposed that some at least of our behaviour is determined by our thinking and deciding. This apparent conflict has given rise to suggestions that unless some parts of our nervous system are found to be open to non-physical influences, brain science will effectively debunk all talk of man as a spiritual being, and oblige us to accept a purely materialistic view of our nature. Many people seem to expect a battle to be fought between religion and the neurosciences like that waged by some theologians in the 19th century against evolutionary biology.

How justified is this impression? It is true that the 17th-century French philosopher–mathematician René *Descartes held that the mind or soul would be powerless to influence bodily action unless some part of the brain could act as a transmitter–receiver for its controlling signals. He considered that the pineal gland, in the middle of the head, was ideally suited to the purpose. 'In man', he says,

the brain is also acted on by the soul which has some power to change cerebral impressions just as those impressions in their turn have the power to arouse thoughts which do not depend on the will. . . . Only [figures of excitation] traced in spirits on the surface of [the pineal] gland, where the seat of imagination and common sense [the coming together of the senses] is . . . should

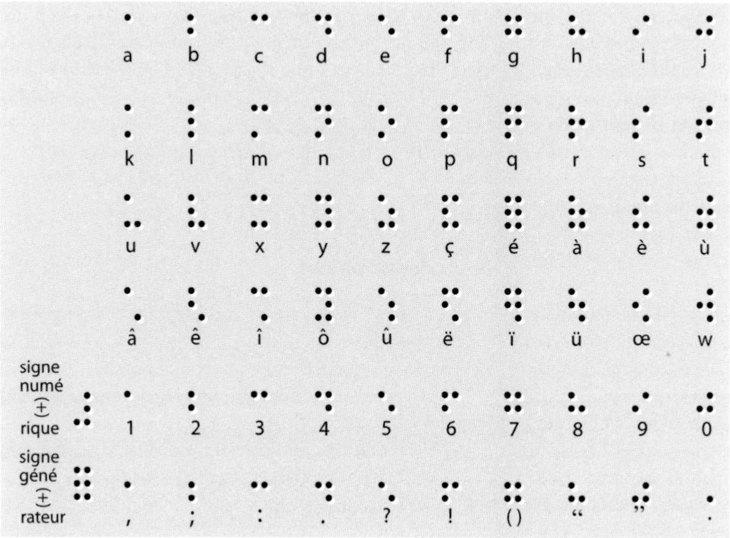

Fig. 1. A Braille alphabet.

be taken to be . . . the forms or images that the rational soul will consider directly when, being united to this machine, it will imagine or will sense any object.

In recent years the neurophysiologist Sir John Eccles and the philosopher Sir Karl Popper have advanced theories of the 'interaction' of mind and brain, which, though they differ in important respects from that of Descartes, agree with him that the brain must be open to non-physical influences if mental activity is to be effective.

At first sight this might indeed seem obvious common sense, but a simple counter-example throws some doubt on the logic of the argument. We are nowadays accustomed to the idea that a computer can be set up to solve a mathematical equation. The mathematician means by this that the behaviour of the computer is *determined* by the equation he wants to solve; were it not so, it would be of no interest to him. On the other hand, if we were to ask a computer engineer to explain what is happening in the computer, he could easily demonstrate that every physical event in it was fully *determined* (same word) by the laws of physics as applied to the physical components. Any appearance of conflict here would be quite illusory. There is no need for a computer to be 'open to non-physical influences' in order that its behaviour may be determined by a (non-physical) equation *as well as* by the laws of physics. The two 'claims to determination' here are not mutually exclusive; rather they are *complementary*.

The analogy is of course a limited one. We (unlike our computing machines) are conscious agents. The data of our conscious experience have first priority among the facts about our world, since it is only through our conscious experience that we learn about anything else. Our consciousness is thus not a matter of convention (like the mathematical significance of the computer's activity) but a matter of fact which we would be lying to deny. Nevertheless the logical point still holds. If we think of our mental activity as embodied in our brain activity, in the sense in which the solving of an equation can be embodied in the workings of a computer, then there is a clear parallel sense in which our behaviour can be determined by that mental activity, regardless of the extent to which our brain activity is determined by physical laws. The two explanations, in mental and in physical terms, are not rivals but complementary.

Note that we are here thinking of mental activity as *embodied in* brain activity rather than *identical with* brain activity. The latter is a notion favoured by what is called 'materialist monism', at the opposite extreme from the 'interactionism' of Eccles and Popper. This would simply identify 'mind' and 'brain', and would go so far as to attribute 'thinking' and other mental activities to the matter of which the brain is composed. The objection to this extreme view can be understood by once again considering the example of a computer. It is true that the solving of an equation is not a separate series of events, running in parallel with the physical happenings in the machine. It is rather the mathematical significance of one and the same series of events, whose physical aspect is well explained by the engineer. On the other hand, it would be nonsensical on these grounds to identify equations with computers as physical objects, or to attribute mathematical properties (such as 'convergence' or 'being quadratic') to the physical matter in which the equation is embodied.

By the same token, even if we regard our thinking and deciding as a 'mental' or 'inner' aspect of one and the same (mysterious) activity that the neuroscientist can study from the outside as brain activity, this gives no rational grounds for taking the material aspect as more 'real' than the mental, still less for identifying the two and speaking of thinking and deciding as attributes of matter. This would be a confusion of categories belonging to different logical levels, for which nothing in brain science offers any justification.

It might appear that thinking of our conscious experience as 'embodied' in our brains would still be incompatible with the Christian concept of 'life after death'. What we have seen in the case of the computer, however, shows that there need be no conflict. The physical destruction of a computer is certainly the end of *that particular embodiment* of the equation it was solving. But it leaves entirely open the possibility that the same equation could be re-embodied, perhaps in a quite different medium, if the mathematician so desires. By the same logic, mechanistic brain science would seem to raise equally little objection to the hope of eternal life expressed in biblical Christian doctrine, with its characteristic emphasis on the 'resurrection' (not to be confused with resuscitation) of the body. The destruction of our present embodiment sets no logical barrier to *our* being re-embodied, perhaps in a quite different medium.   DMM

Dennett, D. (2003). *Freedom Evolves*.
MacKay, D. M. (1979). *Human Science and Human Dignity*.
Popper, K. R., and Eccles, J. C. (1977). *The Self and its Brain*.

brain development.

1. The human brain: adapted for learning meanings from other people
2. What brain science can and cannot explain
3. Discovery of how neurons link up to make mental activity
4. Reflexes, motives, and consciousness: what develops?
5. The embryo brain (conception to 8 weeks)
6. The fetal brain (8 to 40 weeks)
7. The newborn infant's brain

8. Age-related changes in functions of cortex in different lobes of the hemispheres

9. How language and other meanings fit in: a brain with personality and for all cultures

1. The human brain: adapted for learning meanings from other people

Compared to brains of other mammals, the brain of a newborn human infant has two remarkable features. First, it already has uniquely complex anatomy. All major systems are present, in various states of immaturity. It has core mechanisms of motor coordination that are adapted for peculiarly human behaviours: walking with an agile bipedal body; clever manipulation of objects within many senses; and intimate communication with other minds by facial, vocal, and gestural expression of emotions, interests, and purposes. Second, in line with the principle that the longer a mammal species lives and learns from experience the larger is its forebrain cerebral cortex, the human cortex is extremely large, even in its half-developed stage at birth. Moreover, it matures very slowly. For a few months after birth its networks are being transformed, and some of its tissues and axon pathways develop over decades, responding to exercise and education. The baby's cerebellum (hind brain), which contains more neurons than all the rest of the brain, is also exceedingly complex, large, very immature at birth, and slow developing. Its intricate circuits set the timing for sensory control of rapid and skilled movement sequences of an agile body that walks, talks, and has two clever hands. It grows as the body grows in size and power.

The complexity of parts of the baby's brain underneath the cerebral cortex includes neurochemical 'activating', or modulating, systems of the brain stem that have already guided the multiplication, migration, and growth of cortical neurons in fetal stages. These same neural systems generate emotional expressions after birth. The subcortical emotional brain and the limbic cortex most closely connected with it motivate a child's learning, much of which will depend on communicating with other people and with the interests and feelings in their brains. Throughout an infant's cortex, new synaptically connected neuron systems that are essential for planning action and for coordinating the senses are being assembled. These developments both refine perception of objects and increase the precision of movements to manipulate them.

In ways that science is just beginning to comprehend, the human brain is born prepared for awareness of people and for sharing their actions and consciousness. Recently, imitative or sympathetic 'mirror neuron' systems have been discovered in the infant's cortex soon after birth. For example, territories known from neuropsychology of adults and physiological research on monkeys to be critical for recognizing other individuals and perceiving their actions and expressions, and for sympathizing with their motives and emotions, become active in a 2-month-old's brain when the baby is looking at a woman's face. This 'mother/teacher-perceiving system' of a human baby is essential for the education of speech and all other cultural skills, including arts and sciences, technologies, social manners, beliefs, and philosophical explanations, too. Our brains have to learn a distributed consciousness or community wisdom. Our efforts to share this knowledge are driven by powerful emotions of pride and shame, emotions that are expressed to their companions and teachers by infants long before they can speak.

2. What brain science can and cannot explain

Up to a point, functional imaging techniques—tracking local blood flow or electroencephalic activity in brains—enable responses to stimuli, and even the presence though not details of spontaneous thoughts, intentions, or memories, to be detected and mapped in living, thinking persons. How different lobes of the brain and the two cerebral hemispheres become activated for different kinds of mental activity can be observed. But only part of widely distributed and fast-changing brain effects can be imaged, and it is rarely possible to sample what goes on in a freely moving subject. Research in brain genetics, neurochemistry, physiological activity, and plastic developmental change is filling in details. In spite of these advances, however, we still depend on descriptions of brain anatomy and growth built up over more than 100 years. Some who have been trying to find evidence on natural processes of, say, interpersonal recognition or language conclude that neuroscientists must take a wider view of human mental life, incorporating insights from social sciences, anthropology, and philosophy, as well as comparisons with the neuropsychology of other species. And claims that psychologically and culturally important abilities, such as 'music' or 'language', have been 'located' in one or other structure by functional imaging of brain activity are not to be trusted. They depend on artificial testing conditions and selective sampling. They need relating to 'whole person' experience in a mobile body, where consciously intended actions, intuitions, and emotional states, especially those sensed between people, condition awareness, communication, and learning. These are the factors that determine developments in the brain of a child.

Changes in the distribution of cortical activity following regimes of training or exercise, or exposure to highly stressful situations that interfere with normal rest and recuperation, prove that the intercellular connections of cortical tissue can be changed and functions can be increased, relocated, or weakened. People who rely on different senses for communicating, or who have practised different skills, have different functional brain maps. The brains of those who have suffered abuse or extreme lack of sympathetic company may also be irreversibly changed. The diversity of brains due to experience is clear, but internal factors of intention, attention, and emotion that direct changes in the brain in different persons, and that determine temperament and personality differences, are not well understood. Age-related events of brain growth and behaviour in early childhood reflect developments in subcortical mechanisms that have evolved to generate adaptive body–brain relations in this period of accelerating growth and adaptive response to the environment. Advances in our understanding of the psychological abilities of infants and how a child's mind grows help build a natural foundation for explanations from neuroscience about how different adult brains work (see INFANCY, MIND IN).

3. Discovery of how neurons link up to make mental activity

The composition of nerve tissues has been discovered only within the last 150 years. In Charles *Darwin's day, neurons and their delicate connections were almost unknown, and Darwin wisely said little of the brain, though he assumed it to be the evolved organ of the mind.

About 1870 an Italian psychiatrist, Camillo *Golgi, discovered that single nerve cells could be stained black with silver or gold particles, so that their fine receptor branches (*dendrites) and output fibres (*axons) could be seen in brain slices under the microscope. In Spain, Santiago *Ramón y Cajal used silver staining to lay the foundations of modern neuroanatomy. Cajal pioneered microscope studies of how the brain develops. He imagined the growing tip of each new nerve fibre probing its way with delicate filaments, 'a sort of battering ram, possessing an exquisite chemical sensitivity, rapid amoeboid movements and a certain driving force that permits it to push aside, or cross, objects in its way'. He concluded that formation of the right patterns of connections depends upon how this 'growth cone' chooses a path through the densely packed tissues of brain and body. He also saw that developing nerve cells could move in groups to change their location in the brain. He drew remarkably accurate conclusions about mature brain anatomy by studying the forms and connections of neurons in the relatively uncluttered tissues of fetal mice and birds.

In the 19th century, surgical experiments with animals located regions in the cortex necessary for perception in different modalities, and mapped territories from which movements could be elicited. Sensory and motor 'images' of the body were found, and it was noted that the amount of nerve tissue on the surface of the brain in these maps was related to detail of experience and skill in moving. Then, about 1900, methods were developed for amplifying the minute electrical impulses by which neurons

excite one another. Electrodes were used to record nerve discharges, or to stimulate, and connections were followed with new precision. The tissues of the brains of many animals were mapped, showing in outline how the main parts had evolved. A common plan, evidence for common evolved principles of growth and function, became clear.

During the 1960s and 1970s, closer inspections of the complex arrangements of brain tissues were made by staining and by microelectrode techniques capable of identifying inputs to a single cell and of following its projections to the furthest tips. (See NEUROANATOMICAL TECHNIQUES.) It became possible to trace where a cell at one point projects to, and backwards, to locate cell bodies that send axons to that point. With the electron microscope, nerve-cell membranes and the specialized contact points (*synapses), by which selective chemical communication is established from cell to cell, can be seen. The electron microscope can also reveal the intricately folded macromolecular membranes that control nerve-cell biochemistry: the synthesis of protein or of transmitter chemicals, and other processes. Biochemical and immunohistochemical methods show up chemical differences between nerve cells and reveal the location of chemical communication points on the cell surface. The anatomical patterns revealed by these methods testify to the formation of organized cell systems by a process of development and differentiation more complex than in any other tissue. This is the classical picture of an organ designed by evolution for psychological functions that control behaviour. We are more aware now that the human brain maps are changed by environmental stimuli, and that the brain's organization is particularly sensitive to the social or interpersonal environment, especially in early childhood. The task now is to find out how the innate structure guides this education, and what factors are responsible for pathologies of development in essential parts of the brain and for psychological disorders. The brain is not a passive or 'plastic' network of interacting cells excited by stimuli.

4. Reflexes, motives, and consciousness: what develops?

For most of the modern scientific era, descriptions of the human brain have been dualistic or Cartesian (see DESCARTES, RENÉ). One set of conduction pathways is imagined to be prewired innately, before birth. These govern essential 'biological', mindless, or machine-like functions. Somehow, inside these pathways, probably at junctions between nerve cells, changes in transmission of excitation allow use and disuse to modify function. New connections make up new combinations of reflexes by *conditioning, and create purposeful and conscious psychological states. This is the theory of *Pavlov, based on his experiments on the formation of new connections between stimulus effects and movements or gland secretions in restrained dogs. His work gave the physiological foundation to *behaviourism, the belief that the higher mental, moral, and cultural attributes of a human being are added by learning to the reflex sensorimotor biology of the brain.

But this theory does not accord with how brains actually develop. First, sensory and motor nerve cells are in a minority, even in the spinal cord. Interneurons that link input to output, and determine how such links will be grouped into coordinating systems, are hundreds of times more numerous, and they develop first. Everywhere in the brain these intermediate integrative cells, some small, some reaching far in the brain, form systems that can generate states of intention, attention, and emotional feeling. Interneurons are capable of discharging impulses spontaneously that may be transmitted widely through the nerve net. This is not an automatic sensorimotor reflex system.

In fetal birds and mammals, flexibly coordinated movements and rhythmic sequences of action occur before sensory cells are connected to the brain, or in pieces of the central nervous system that have been cut off from sensory nerves by surgery. Rhythmic movement programmes are set up among the interneurons, largely in the brain stem. On the input side, too, the axons of sense cells—from the retina, from the touch cells of the skin, etc.—grow millions of fine branches that end among already organized and active central networks. These afferent terminals segregate themselves in such a way that they map the body and the outside world into the prewired systems of the brain. How the human brain parts grow before birth suggests that the interacting nerve cells make up and coordinate basic rules for object perception, for purposeful movement patterns, and for motive states that construct time and space for action, and that might become conscious of other bodies and their behaviours, without benefit of experience. This is confirmed by detailed analysis of what infants can do shortly after they are born.

In the 1940s, Roger *Sperry proved that surgically rearranged nerve networks of growing fish and amphibia could re-form well-ordered contacts, without benefit of learning. He ruled out 'contact guidance' and 'electrical field' hypotheses, and concluded, as Cajal had done, that some unknown chemical 'landmarks' guided the nerve fibre tips to the right location. This 'chemoaffinity' theory has been upheld by subsequent studies, but no gene code can possibly specify, on its own, this cell-to-cell precision of nerve mappings in such well-ordered arrays as the projections of the visual field. Ordering processes must involve intercellular effects that 'emerge' in the activity traffic of the growing brain and body.

In 1949, Donald *Hebb identified a fundamental principle governing the acquisition of adaptive cell assemblies in impressionable brain tissues, such as the cerebral cortex. Cells that fire together wire together. Synchrony of excitation strengthens synaptic connections and connects cells in new functional groups. As a result, a given cell with its synapse-carrying dendrites can participate in a number of assemblies and perform in different functions, for example making representations of the meanings of different words. There is now much direct evidence of the formation of neuronal assemblies that store skills and experiences by changes in the wiring of the brain caused by use, but guided by motivated 'interests' of the mind.

5. The embryo brain (conception to 8 weeks)

The human brain starts as a slab of identical-looking blocklike cells in the upper layer of a disclike embryo one millimetre long (Fig. 1a, 16 days). These cells become irreversibly different from other cells about 3 weeks after gestation. Different parts are already designated to form specific relations in the future with sense organs and muscles in the body. Brain and body of the embryo have bilateral symmetry, but hidden differences exist between the chemistry of left and right halves. Brain and spinal cord roll into a hollow cylinder (Fig. 1a, 22 days), then, in a few days, cell multiplication occurs round the central cavity, and cells migrate outwards to form rudimentary brain nuclei or cell colonies in the wall of the tube. Some cells become neurons and others change into non-neural support cells (glia). At about 4 weeks, ventral cells in brain stem and cord grow axons out to the muscles of the trunk, limbs, and viscera, the anterior-most motor cells terminating in muscles of the eyes, face, and mouth. Sensory cells grow shortly after motor cells, projecting their input to the dorsal half of the central nervous system (Fig. 1c).

As embryo nerve cells migrate and form patterned aggregates to make up functional circuits, they communicate by biochemical expressions of regulator genes that can switch on other genes governing nerve-cell development. There are message-emitting and message-receiving loci on the cell surfaces. These respond to hormones and growth substances that are produced by cells in many parts of the body. Once the network of nerve connections is formed, conduction of nerve impulses adds power and precision to this cell-to-cell communication. The electrical excitation of nerve-cell membranes causes adjustments in their biochemistry as intercellular chemical messages are turned off or on, and this builds the adaptive organization of primary brain systems.

In this way, the intricate interconnected anatomy of the brain is formed as a result of the multiplying effects of many choices in cell differentiation that are governed by genes acting in the context of development. To effect this, there is much negotiation—an editing of connections,

brain development

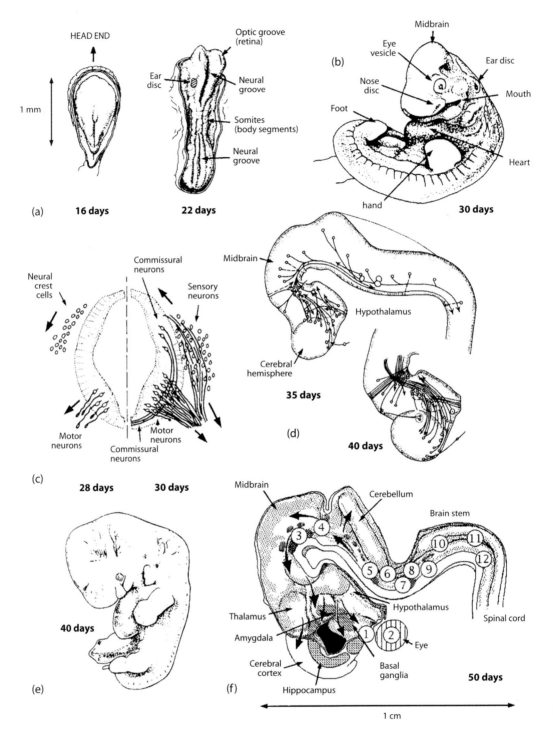

(a)

HEAD END

1 mm

16 days

Optic groove (retina)

Ear disc

Neural groove

Somites (body segments)

Neural groove

22 days

(b)

Midbrain

Eye vesicle

Nose disc

Foot

Ear disc

Mouth

Heart

hand

30 days

(c)

Neural crest cells

Commissural neurons

Sensory neurons

Motor neurons

Motor neurons

Commissural neurons

28 days   **30 days**

(d)

Midbrain

Hypothalamus

Cerebral hemisphere

35 days

40 days

(e)

40 days

(f)

Midbrain

Cerebellum

Brain stem

Thalamus

Amygdala

Cerebral cortex

Hippocampus

Hypothalamus

Spinal cord

Eye

Basal ganglia

50 days

1 cm

with removal of many, so that the remainder establish functional relations inside an overall array oriented approximately by chemical field markers of the body set out early in the embryo period. The multiplication, migration, and survival of neuroblasts, the growth and pruning away of axons, and the reinforcement or suppression of synapses are decided by the molecular compositions of the surrounding media and nerve-cell membranes. Trophic or inhibitory factors are produced by many types of cell, including non-neural supporting cells (glia) in the central nervous system. The glia make up a scaffold that guides migrating neuroblasts and the creeping of axon growth cones, and they assist in the maturation of axons and synapses. Within this tapestry of interacting elements, nerve cells take many forms and become differentiated chemically. They come to contribute different patterns of electrical and chemical activity to the system. This is how the brain begins its 'self-formation' or 'autopoiesis'.

Soon the brain is much larger than the cord, its conspicuous dorsal lobes receiving axons from the nose, eyes, ears, and mouth (Fig. 1b and e). The hypothalamus, the foremost ventral component of the brain stem, is the 'head ganglion' of the viscera (Fig. 1d and f). It will control appetites and aversions, and will act as a coordinator between activities of the central nervous system and the endocrine glands that secrete hormones controlling growth, metabolic activity, and *sexual development. Among the first neurons inside the brain to send axons down to the cord and upward to the forebrain hemispheres are the core interneurons of the 'affective nervous system', which will transmit a spectrum of messenger chemicals to other neurons and maintain the balance of integrative states in the brain throughout its development (Fig. 1d and f). By the end of the embryo period (eight weeks), when the cells of the future neocortex of the cerebral hemispheres first appear, the brain stem has

Fig. 1. The human embryo and its nervous system. **a.** The first 3 weeks. The neural tube closes and the brain end enlarges. **b.** The body, with head and sense organs, is clear at 4 weeks. **c.** The first axons grow from the spinal cord, and bipolar sensory cells grow axons into the cord and dendrites to receptive endings. **d.** After 5 weeks integrative pathways fill the brain stem, while the cerebral hemispheres are rudimentary. **e.** At the end of the embryo period, the body is still like that of other vertebrates. **f.** The advanced embryo brain has an identifiable core reticular system and cranial nerve nuclei (here numbered). Basic elements of the visceral brain, motive systems, special senses, and the emotional motor system are present: smelling and tasting (1); seeing (2); looking and focusing vision, crying (3, 4, 6); face expressions, vocalizing, speech, facial feeling (5, 7); hearing (8); vocalizing, chewing, breathing, gasping, coughing, licking, sucking, expressions of voice, speaking (9, 10, 11, 12).

an elaborate system of projections that will influence the migration and differentiation of cortical neurons (Fig. 1f). Neurochemicals regulate nerve-cell growth and differentiation everywhere in the young brain. They become the media of dynamic emotional states, which will be expressed in special movements, innervated by the cranial nerves (Fig. 1f). In the mature brain, the affective nervous system modulates perception, the formation and recall of memories, and motor coordination.

6. The fetal brain (8 to 40 weeks)
By two months after gestation, the developing human fetus has elaborately adapted special sense organs in the form of eyes, face with nose and mouth, vestibular semicircular canals and cochlea, hands, and feet (Fig. 2a). The cerebral hemispheres appear in the early fetus and increase rapidly in size in mid-fetal stages as nerve cells multiply in the cortex of the hemispheres, which are at this stage thin membranous sacs distended by liquid (Fig. 2b). A second fourfold increase in bulk of the cortex takes place in the last two months of gestation and continues into the first few months of infancy (Fig. 2c). This is due, not to multiplication of cortical neurons, but to their branching and to the formation of the connections that integrate the experience-sensitive cortical tissues with the rest of the brain to make conscious perception, voluntary action, and intelligent learning possible.

The cells of the neocortex, generated round the cavities of the cerebral hemispheres (ventricles), enter the cortex between 15 and 25 weeks after gestation (Fig. 2c). Immature cells (neuroblasts) migrate in waves to make a layer called the 'cortical plate', later arrivals passing through earlier migrants so that the youngest cells are in layers towards the outside of the hemispheres. This flow of neuroblasts into the cortical plate proceeds at different rates in different areas, the last territories to receive a full complement of potential neurons, at six months (25 weeks) after gestation, being areas that will attain mature tissue structure years later, towards adolescence. Cells in cortex and subcortex that are dedicated to one psychological role start as neighbours in the periventicular germ layer, or derive from the same stem neuroblast cell.

Late migrating components of the hemispheres tend to left–right asymmetry (see Fig. 4). How hemispheric asymmetry begins and how it relates to gene-controlled asymmetries in the chemistry and immunological properties of cells widespread in the brain remains to be worked out. It is known that abnormal migration, in the left hemisphere, of one late contingent of cortical and thalamic neurons related to the perisylvian area, where temporal and parietal lobes meet, can lead to language disorders, including *dyslexia, which makes it very difficult for a person of otherwise normal intelligence to learn to generate the high-speed processes required for reading and writing.

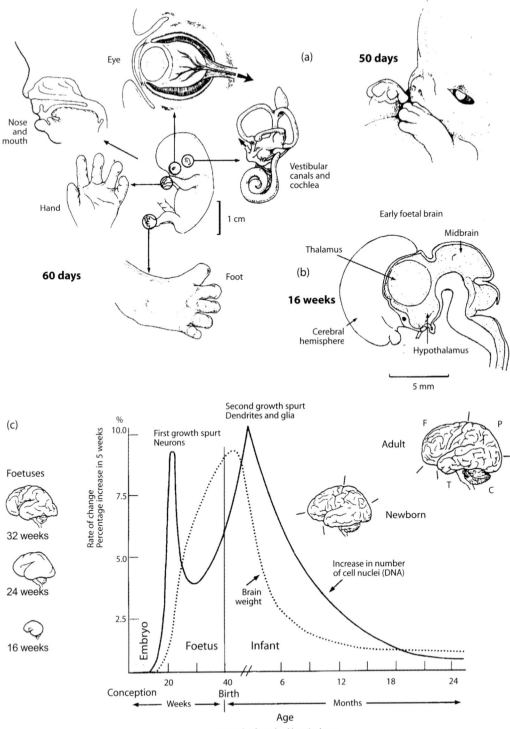

(a)

Eye

50 days

Nose and mouth

Hand

1 cm

Vestibular canals and cochlea

60 days

Foot

Early foetal brain

Midbrain

Thalamus

(b)

16 weeks

Cerebral hemisphere

Hypothalamus

5 mm

(c)

Foetuses

32 weeks

24 weeks

16 weeks

%

Rate of change
Percentage increase in 5 weeks

10.0

First growth spurt
Neurons

Second growth spurt
Dendrites and glia

7.5

5.0

2.5

Embryo

Foetus

Infant

Brain weight

Increase in number
of cell nuclei (DNA)

Adult

Newborn

F

P

T

C

20

40

6

12

18

24

Conception

Birth

Weeks

Months

Age

Growth of cerebral hemispheres

This is an example of a brain development long before birth that shows up only years later, in school performance.

In the 40 weeks of gestation a human brain grows to a two-thirds-sized likeness of the adult brain (Figs. 2c and 3b). At birth all the typically human cortical areas and nuclear masses of the brain stem are there, containing a million million (1,000,000,000,000) nerve cells in total. But this amazing fact is misleading in one important respect. The formation of intercellular connections, which take up little extra space but upon which the function of the brain depends, is far from complete, especially in the neocortex. There is a huge post-natal manufacture of fine branches as nerve cells form effective contacts (synapses) with dendrites of other cells (Fig. 2c). Each mature cortical cell is estimated to have, on average, about 10,000 synapses, the greater part of which develop a few months after birth. The total number of synapses in the cortex of one person (10^{15}) is about 200,000 times the population of humans on earth. Prolific branching of dendrites and formation of synaptic contacts can be seen in microscope slides of the cerebral cortex from infants, and comparable developments occur in the even more intricate anatomy of the cerebellum of toddlers and young children.

How might specific connections be selected accurately to govern mental processes in this teeming array of minute living elements? On the selection of the right connections depends the development of skill in motor coordination, refinement of perception, retention of memories of all kinds, formation of vocabulary, and development of increasingly critical and precise patterns of thought. The facts of brain growth do not imply that mental and physical abilities governed by the brain simply expand and elaborate independently of stimuli. Nor do they give the brain a passive submissiveness to experience and diffuse response to exercise. True, the environment matters.

Even in fetal stages the selection of nerve connections depends upon stimuli from the intra-uterine environment. Serious mental difficulties in childhood can arise if the mother is severely undernourished or under extreme mental stress during critical brain growth periods in gestation. But the process of gaining experience is at all

Fig. 2. In the fetus, the cerebral hemispheres and cerebellum form. **a.** By 2 months all the special senses of the head, and the face, hands, and feet are well formed and clearly human. **b.** At 4 months the cerebral hemispheres and thalamus are swelling rapidly, but cortical cells are undeveloped. **c.** In the mid-fetal period (20 weeks) there is a great production of neurons in the cortex. After birth there is a multiplication of glia cells as dendrites grow. The newborn brain has proportionally small parietal (P), frontal (F), and temporal (T) lobes, and cerebellum (C), compared to the adult.

stages an active one that the growing brain acts to direct. Chemical communication of the fetus's body with the mother's through the placenta affects brain development, and refinement of brain structures responds to gustatory, mechanical, touch, and auditory stimulation. The fetus begins to contribute to this stimulation by moving to change posture, to displace limbs, and to swallow amniotic fluid, but it is vulnerable, and may be permanently damaged by infection, or by the mother taking drugs or alcohol while she is pregnant.

In the last 3 months of gestation, a fetus has a well-developed subcortical auditory system that can hear and learn to recognize the expressive rhythms and tones of the mother's voice. After birth, stimuli that identify her by sight and communicate her feelings are sought and actively taken up by a baby (Fig. 3b). Those stimuli that are assimilated, especially those that come from the mother and other caregiving companions, cause selections to be made from among rival adaptive alternatives in brain structure. The ground rules for recognizing other persons and for sympathizing with their emotions and interests from their expressions are innate in the sense that they are formulated earlier, before stimuli have any effect. The learning takes place as part of a developmental strategy that must be ascribed to a continuous regulated unfolding of nerve-cell interactions from the embryo to the adult. While there is a huge excess of nerve cells and connections in the newborn brain, it is not chaotic, and the elimination to create adaptive systems is neither random nor the statistical consequence of emerging patterns of relative 'use' by stimulation.

7. The newborn infant's brain
At birth the human being enters a new world. New forces on a body no longer floating, new levels and qualities of sound, new material taken in by mouth, air breathed by the lungs and bringing in new substances and microorganisms, new stimulation of the surface of the body, and the immense range of new visual information; all these give the unfinished circuits of the cortex a fresh set of criteria for selective retention of functional nerve connections. More changes occur in the cellular structure of the cortex in the first six months after birth than at any other time in development. Dendrites branch out from large cortical cells and receive astronomical numbers of synapses (Fig. 3a).

Stimuli to the infant are regulated both by the infant's movements and by the behaviour of caretakers who mediate between the environment and the infant, and the immature brain has powerful control of this caretaker behaviour, especially through emotional expression. Indeed, the most precociously mature functions of a young child's brain are those that communicate needs, feelings, and motives to other persons, and that lead them to

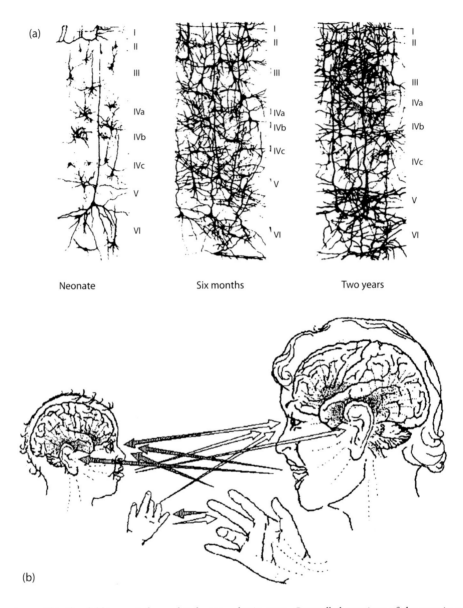

(a)

Neonate   Six months   Two years

(b)

present the world to the child in precisely regulated ways (Fig. 3b).

The brain seeks stimulation of particular kinds that will facilitate developing circuitry in the brain. For example, selection of the circuits necessary for binocular stereoptic perception of depth, which happens in a human baby about six months after birth, depends both on the coincidence of stimulus patterns from the two eyes on cells in layer 4 of the visual cortex, and on activation of these cells by inputs to the cortex from the reticular formation of the brain stem. Controlled rotations of the eyes in precise unison bring corresponding stimuli in register. The visual cortex of girl babies gains binocular discrimination about two weeks ahead of boy babies, which suggests that sex hormones have an influence on the readying of these areas for visual information—possibly it is testosterone, produced in male infants for a few weeks after birth, that delays the process of cortical cell maturation.

In the mature brain, the cortical sheet is composed of columnar territories of uniform size. Interconnections

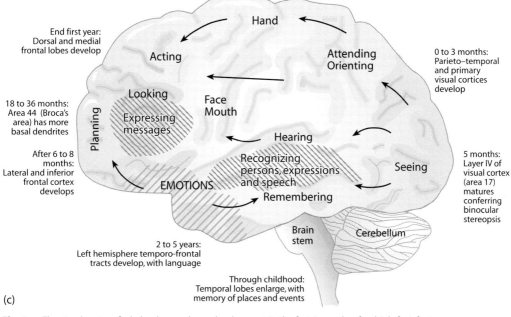

End first year:
Dorsal and medial
frontal lobes develop

Acting

Hand

Attending
Orienting

0 to 3 months:
Parieto–temporal
and primary
visual cortices
develop

18 to 36 months:
Area 44 (Broca's
area) has more
basal dendrites

Looking

Planning

Expressing
messages

Face
Mouth

Hearing

After 6 to 8
months:
Lateral and inferior
frontal cortex
develops

EMOTIONS

Recognizing
persons, expressions
and speech

Remembering

Seeing

5 months:
Layer IV of
visual cortex
(area 17)
matures
conferring
binocular
stereopsis

Brain
stem

Cerebellum

2 to 5 years:
Left hemisphere temporo-frontal
tracts develop, with language

Through childhood:
Temporal lobes enlarge, with
memory of places and events

(c)

Fig. 3. a. The visual cortex of a baby shows a huge development in the first 6 months after birth. **b.** Infants are ready to communicate with other persons by a multi-channel system of senses and expressions. This links the baby's brain activities to those of the adult expressed in touches, vocalizations, face expressions, and gestures. **c.** The functions and memories of the cerebral cortex develop over many years, all learning of knowledge and skills being regulated by emotions and in communication.

between its parts, and with structures deeper in the brain, are arranged so they link columns into ordered systems (Fig 3c). This ordered anatomy becomes clear in infancy, when redundant axons are eliminated and synaptic fields are sorted out, a process that forms the basis for sharp perceptions and precisely skilled movements. From four months after birth the massive interhemispheric bridge (corpus callosum) gains in bulk as its fibres receive a sheath of myelin (see SPLIT-BRAIN AND THE MIND). Interhemispheric communication matures in step with the development of mature synaptic arrays in different cortical areas over the first decade or so of childhood.

8. Age-related changes in functions of cortex in different lobes of the hemispheres

Different parts of a child's brain mature at different times and have different 'sensitive periods' when they are dependent on appropriate stimulation. The biggest developments in perception and in the formation of cognitive strategies occur in infancy or early childhood (Fig. 3c). That is the time when serious deprivation, such as that due to blindness, deafness, limblessness, or lack of affectionate care, can distort the growth of the brain most seriously. For example, defects in the optics or motor con-

trol of an eye (as in squint) cause the cortical connections of that eye to be pushed out of action by the more coherent and regulated input of the other eye. Deprivation of all humane care and emotional support may cause mental deformity—reflected in anatomical abnormalities in the brain.

The cerebral cortex has different relations with sense organs and the muscles of the body in different regions (Fig. 3c). The greater part of all main lobes, frontal, parietal, and temporal, has strong reciprocal connections with subcortical motivating systems that determine exploratory activities, planning of complex sequences of action, and integration of awareness for all the senses and the whole body.

Appearance of new functions at particular ages continues throughout life, along with maturation and ageing in the rest of the body, but at a slowing pace. Temporal, parietal, and frontal lobes of the brain grow disproportionately after infancy, changing the shape of the brain (Fig. 3c). Their surges of development correlate with changes in motivation for social life and for seeking experience; they are centres of desire and curiosity for knowledge and for relationships. In early infancy the right hemisphere and orbitofrontal and inferior temporal

125

cortices develop in relation to the affective regulation of the mother–child relationship and developments in communication with other partners. The lateral prefrontal cortex expands conspicuously in the last months of the first year and into the second year with developments both in intelligence for exploration and combining of objects, and in protolanguage (the use of gesture and voice to make preverbal utterances or 'acts of meaning'). Developments in superior temporal and prefrontal cortex are both significant during the first weeks as the child's social understanding increases and recognition of others' states of mind increases (Fig. 3c).

Changes are observed at the end of infancy, in middle childhood, in adolescence, in middle life, and in old age. The developmental programme of the brain expresses changes in motivation, and this affects who is communicated with, and what is experienced, learned, and remembered. Transformation of psychological processes as new brain parts arrive at functional maturity confers a plasticity of function so that a child can partly recover from loss of brain tissue by injury or disease (see PLASTICITY IN THE NERVOUS SYSTEM). The developments also explain why injury of a given part of the cortex can have different effects in children and adults.

9. How language and other meanings fit in: a brain with personality and for all cultures

Anthropologists and psychologists consider language the hallmark of humankind. It permits symbolic communication without which traditions of belief and understanding could not be built up. It powerfully aids processes of thought and reasoning. There was, therefore, some surprise when brain scientists discovered that territories of the left temporal and parietal lobes, which are essential for language understanding in the great majority of adult humans (Fig. 4), are already asymmetrical in a human fetus of 24 weeks gestational age—4 months before birth. Although quite indeterminate as to which language it will learn, the human brain is set to acquire *some* language long before it hears a single word. Structures anticipating functions in consciousness and communication are seen in various cortical regions of the right hemisphere, which seems, indeed, to be slightly ahead of the left hemisphere in development during fetal stages. These underlie this hemisphere's subsequent superiority in perception of form, in visuo-constructive skills, and in other schematic processes that are of obvious importance in the development of technology and habits of interpersonal and cooperative life. These 'non-verbal' kinds of human mental ability may be more directly related to whole body awareness and self-related conceptions of the world than the more calculating, logically programmed 'propositional' skills of the left hemisphere. The right hemisphere starts life in infancy ahead of the left and it plays a lead role in the development of an affectionate attachment between the infant and caregiver. It is more sensitive to emotion in the voice and apparently to the expression of song and music, and it may recognize the affection of a caregiver more strongly.

It is now clear that the anatomy and function of human cerebral cortices are very variable. People differ in the pattern of their mental abilities because their brains grow in different forms. Males tend to differ from females, left-handers from right-handers, and architects from psychologists or lawyers. Some of this diversity of human minds, and their temperaments and aptitudes, will be 'preprogrammed' in a great variety of outcomes of gene expression in nerve-tissue development, but the same processes are set to respond to intra-uterine and postnatal environments. Among the influential factors are hormones, especially sex hormones, nutrition, and state of health of the mother during pregnancy, chemical and immunological factors, viral infections, epilepsy, and trauma. A pregnant woman who takes psychoactive drugs or alcohol or who smokes heavily can be changing the development of her child's brain. Particular risks are associated with birth—the brain of a fetus or premature infant is sensitive to its chemical and physical environment, which must be regulated inside narrow limits. On the other hand, a premature newborn's state of body and brain benefits from the holding, touching, and affectionate musical speech of 'intuitive parenting'.

Brains grow in conversation and in emotion. Throughout a long life, growing and learning human brains require, and care about, cultivation by intimate and morally regulated communication. Thus are built personal and family histories, and the fellow feeling, rivalry, and powerful collaborations and conflicts of human society.

CT

Damasio, A. R., and Damasio, H. (1992). 'Brain and language'. *Scientific American* 267/3.

Freeman, W. J. (1999). *How Brains Make up their Minds*.

Holowka, S., and Petitto, L. A. (2002). 'Left hemisphere cerebral specialization for babies while babbling'. *Science*, 297.

O'Rahilly, R., and Müller, F. (1994). *The Embryonic Human Brain: An Atlas of Developmental Stages*.

Rizzolatti, G., and Arbib, M. A. (1998). 'Language within our grasp'. *Trends in Neuroscience*, 21.

—— and Gallese, V. (2003). 'Mirror neurons'. In Nadel L. (ed.), *Encyclopedia of Cognitive Science*.

Trevarthen, C. (1996). 'Lateral asymmetries in infancy: implications for the development of the hemispheres'. *Neuroscience and Biobehavioral Reviews*, 20.

——(2001). 'The neurobiology of early communication: intersubjective regulations in human brain development'. In Kalverboer, A. F. and Gramsbergen, A. (eds.), *Handbook on Brain and Behaviour in Human Development*.

—— and Aitken, K. J. (1994). 'Brain development, infant communication, and empathy disorders: intrinsic factors in child mental health'. *Development and Psychopathology*, 6.

——————(2003). 'Regulation of brain development and age-related changes in infants' motives: the developmental function of "regressive" periods'. In Heimann, M., and Plooij, F. (eds.), *Regression Periods in Human Infancy*.

Tucker, D. M. (1992). 'Developing emotions and cortical networks'. In Gunnar, M. R., and Nelson, C. A. (eds.), *Minnesota Symposium on Child Psychology*, xxiv: *Developmental Behavioural Neuroscience*.

Tzourio-Mazoyer, N., De Schonen, S., Crivello, F., Reutter, B., Aujard, Y., and Mazoyer, B. (2002). 'Neural correlates of woman face processing by 2-month-old infants'. *NeuroImage*, 15.

brain function and awareness. It is something of a paradox that the most exacting studies of brain function came from research on animals, whose behaviour can be studied with increasing sophistication but who cannot communicate with us very fluently. In contrast, studies of human brain function derived from the clinic are apt to depend on just those methods of communication that we are precluded from using with animals. That is, most clinical tests of psychological capacity of human patients involve considerable verbal interchange between the patient and the examiner, often expressed in a form intended directly to reveal the patient's disorders. So, in a classical and routine examination of visual capacity, the patient is asked, 'Tell me what you see', 'How many spots do you see?', 'What letters are on the bottom line of the chart?', and so forth. Or the patient with a memory disorder is asked, 'Tell me what you can remember from your trip last week', 'What did you have for breakfast this morning?', 'Do you recognize me?', or 'What words can you recall from the list you just read?'.

In studying animals' memory, vision, or other capacities, it is often assumed that we are simply transforming the questions we usually ask of human patients into an equivalent form, albeit one that is rather more cumbersome to transmit. Examined more closely, however, the resemblance is less than close. Animals reveal their capacity by performing a discrimination between stimuli or events, which they have usually been trained to demonstrate by following some particular rule, and for which they are rewarded. The human subject also discriminates between stimuli and events, of course, but often the clinician does not study the discrimination as such, but rather the subject's commentary upon it, such as 'Yes, now I see the flash', or 'I can see the letter A in the bottom line'. Even when the verbal response appears to be just an embellishment on, or a shortcut to, the discriminative response, serious problems can arise if the subject is unable to render a commentary but nevertheless is capable of making the relevant discrimination. We refer here not to the relatively trivial difficulty when a subject has, say, an impairment in the mechanics of organization of speech. Even if a human subject is able to communicate freely and efficiently they may nevertheless be unaware of their own discriminative capacities and hence have nothing to communicate as a commentary.

It is only recently that this distinction, between a capacity and subject's commentary upon it, has been recognized, and it has thrown light not only on some persistent puzzles in the comparative study of brain function, but also in drawing a contrast between explicit and implicit knowledge. Two examples can be given. In both instances the differences between the results of research on humans and on other animals appeared to be so great that it was argued that the brains of animals must be organized in a qualitatively different way from human brains, despite their very close anatomical similarity.

First, if the region of cerebral cortex to which one of the nerve tracts from the eye ultimately projects is removed or blocked, animals (unlike humans) can still discriminate visual events, although not as well as normally. This in itself is not surprising, because the eye sends information not only to the so-called 'visual cortex' but also directly to a variety of other structures in the midbrain and elsewhere. Indeed, the way in which vision is altered after damage to one route helps one to infer the type of capacity that the remaining targets must have. This residual visual capacity of animals has been studied over several decades. The paradox is that the damage to the human brain, while organized anatomically in a way that appears closely similar to the brains of other primates, is said nevertheless to yield a condition of blindness after removal of the 'visual cortex'. (Because the visual field projects upon the visual cortex in a well-known retinotopic manner (see VISUAL SYSTEM: ORGANIZATION), blindness is in fact commonly restricted to just a certain portion of the visual field, depending upon which part of the visual cortex is damaged, it being rare for the entire visual cortex in both cerebral hemispheres to be damaged.) For example, when a light is flashed in the blind field of a human patient, and he is asked whether he sees it, he will say 'no'. A monkey, in contrast, if appropriately trained, will reach out to touch a brief visual stimulus, can locate it accurately in space, and can discriminate between lines of different orientation and between simple shapes and between moving versus stationary objects. The monkey will pick up even quite minute specks of food if they contrast well with the background.

The difference in outcome puzzled investigators as long ago as the end of the 19th century. They appealed to a doctrine of 'encephalization of function' to account for it. This doctrine asserted that in evolution visual and other functions somehow migrated to higher and new structures in the brain, so that in man visual function had reached the highest level, namely the visual cortex, whereas in lower animals a greater degree of visual capacity was subserved by lower midbrain or even brain-stem structures. It was a somewhat curious doctrine, because the lower structures do not wither away in man, and therefore one wonders just what role they have after being deprived of their earlier role. Be that as it may, it is only relatively recently that investigators have actually started to ask their human patients the questions in a form in which one is perforce obliged to ask them of animals. That is, regardless of whether the subjects say they can 'see' the stimulus, they are asked to discriminate between them by forced-choice guessing. They are asked to guess, say, whether or not a stimulus has occurred, whether it was located at position A or B, whether it was a cross or a circle, was red or green, and so on. Using this approach it has been found that some human subjects with damage to the visual cortex can perform about as well as animals in the absence of such cortex. This residual capacity is called '*blindsight'.

A second example that was taken to imply a basic difference in the organization of primates' brains comes from the field of memory disorders. Damage to certain structures in the midline of the human brain can yield a persistent state of profound memory failure. Patients apparently cannot remember new experiences for more than a few seconds, or a minute or two at most. Paradoxically, in animals it seemed for a long time that these same midline structures—apparently anatomically identical to those in man—could be dispensed with almost with impunity. No obvious losses of memory or learning capacity appeared to result. The story is similar in some respects to that of blindsight. It has emerged that the sorts of tasks that animals were traditionally taught to test their learning capacity, and which they succeeded in learning and retaining, can also be learned quite well by amnesic patients. Indeed, there is now a large catalogue of tasks that such patients are known to succeed in learning and retaining. They all share one property: in none of them is it necessary actually to ask the patient, 'Do you recognize this?' or 'What do you remember of the task you just saw?'. Indeed a patient may acknowledge no memory for the task successfully stored. For example, if shown a list of words, and later asked what the words were, he may well say he cannot remember even seeing a list of words. But if shown the first few letters of each of the words and asked to guess what words they stand for, he is likely to produce the very words for which he says he has no 'memory', but do so less well for words not shown in the original list. Or, to take another example, a patient will show a benefit of having solved a particular jigsaw puzzle by solving it faster the next day (but not other jigsaws he has not solved before) but, again, deny having ever seen the puzzle. Or learn the solutions to verbal problems that require acquisition of new contextual meanings. Amnesic patients can learn such tasks and show good retention over quite long periods—weeks or even months, in fact—although, again, as with blindsight, the capacity is distinct from any 'explicit' acknowledgement of it by the subject.

Both of these examples have come to light specifically in the context of a paradoxical and deep discrepancy between animal and human clinical research. But there are many other examples of 'implicit' functioning that come directly out of human clinical research. The best known are from work on commissurotomized patients, popularly referred to as 'split-brain' patients. In them, surgeons have severed the connections between the two cerebral hemispheres in order to try to control the spread of uncontrollable epileptic discharges throughout the entire brain. In such patients an investigator is able to direct perceptual information to one other of the two cerebral hemispheres, and thereby to infer what its capacities are in isolation from the other hemisphere. (For example, by projecting a visual image onto the left half of the retina, only the visual cortex of the left hemisphere is stimulated. Because the connections between the hemispheres are severed, the right hemisphere is deprived of an input via a relay from the stimulated hemisphere.) Research with such patients has strongly reinforced an already well-established view, namely that the verbal commentaries typically require the participation of the left hemisphere. But it has also shown, interestingly, that information directly to the right hemisphere can still be used by a patient, even in response to a verbal instruction and even though the patient does not acknowledge his success. Thus, a subject will correctly select an object by touch from an array masked from view with his left hand (controlled by the right hemisphere) if 'instructed' to do so by the flashing of its name on the right side of the retina, so that the right hemisphere has access to the word. The subject neither 'sees' the flashed word nor recognizes his success in linking the word with the object.

In fact, there is no area of cognitive neuropsychology in which such 'implicit' residual functioning fails to be demonstrated. Analogues of blindsight are found in other modalities, for example, 'deaf hearing', and 'numbsense' in the tactile mode. In disorders of attention, as in the syndrome of unilateral neglect associated with right parietal lesions, in which patients ignore the left side of space and of objects, it can be shown that information can still sometimes be detected in the 'neglected' field and resolutely not reported by them. Patients with an agnosia for faces (prosopagnosia) show an enhanced autonomic response to familiar as opposed to unfamiliar faces, despite the failure by subjects to tell the difference. Even in the area of language disorders, *dyslexia and *aphasia, implicit processing has been demonstrated. These disorders are severely disabling. In the absence of awareness of the content of a sensory modality or that a particular cognitive capacity exists, the patients are deprived of the capacity to think about the material in the domain in which their capacity exists. One cannot live by implicit processing alone.

On the other hand, a vast amount of our everyday activity is carried out without direct awareness: indeed, it would be wasteful actually to reflect on processes that can be dealt with in an automatic way, once they become routine—for example, constriction of the pupil or accommodation of the lens of the eye. A great variety of skilled motor acts, some learned and some not, do not warrant introspection or derive any benefit from it, or may even be impeded. It is equally wasteful to reflect on each occasion when we stop at a traffic light that we 'remember' that red means stop, even though our stopping clearly demonstrates the retention of a learned association. The brain may well reserve for itself only a small proportion of its capacity to dedicate to those important mental activities that require planning and reflection. The study of patients with 'blindsight', memory without awareness of 'remembering', of split-brain patients, or any of the other examples of implicit functioning following specific instances of brain damage, not only highlights what regions of perception, memory, and other cognitive capacities can be divorced from awareness, but also may advance an empirical analysis of those brain activities and systems that allow explicit conscious awareness to be sustained.

The examples from human clinical research go beyond anything that can be drawn from comparative research with animals. Of course corresponding regions of the brain can be studied in great detail in animals, but how can one ask an animal not only to discriminate or select a stimulus from an array but to reveal to us whether or not it knows that it can 'recognize' it or 'characterize' or 'see' it? Such a question was raised in the 19th century by some of the pioneers of research on the visual cortex, but then afterwards largely ignored. For a long time it appeared that it could be ignored safely—that it might even be a pseudo-problem. But it is difficult to accept that animals, especially advanced primates, differ so fundamentally from humans that they do not demonstrate the same division between automatic unmonitored acts and those acts and perceptions that are effectively monitored so as to serve as a basis for directed action and reflection. The clinical evidence also makes it clear, in humans and in animals, that one cannot decide whether awareness accompanies an act merely from observing the act itself. To pursue such matters with animals, as with humans, would appear to require not only the standard methods used to study their discriminative, mnemonic, and other cognitive capacities, powerful as they are, but the introduction of a parallel response which could serve as an 'off-line' commentary response to provide information on their status. Some progress along these lines can be seen. Animal investigators in recent years, spurred on in

part by the paradoxical discrepancies between their findings and those from the human clinic, have been able to evolve new methods of testing homologous varieties of memory in animals. And the first convincing counterpart to blindsight in monkeys has also emerged from recent research (see BLINDSIGHT). Perhaps the important contribution that animal research has made towards uncovering unsuspected capacities in human patients will be repaid by the development of techniques that will allow us to ask deeper questions of our animal relations.   LW

Garde, M. M., and Cowey, A. (2000). ' "Deaf hearing": unacknowledged detection of auditory stimuli in a patient with cerebral deafness'. *Cortex*, 36.

Paillard, J., Michel, F., and Stelmach, G. (1983). 'Localization without content: a tactile analogue of "blind sight" '. *Archives of Neurology*, 40.

Ross, S. (1976). *The Conscious Brain*.

Rossetti, Y., Rode, G., and Boisson, D. (1995). 'Implicit processing of somaesthetic information: a dissociation between where and how?' *NeuroReport*, 6.

Sperry, R. W. (1974). 'Lateral specialization in the surgically separated hemispheres'. In Schmitt, F. O., and Worden, F. G. (eds.), *The Neurosciences: Third Study Program*.

Tranel, D., and Damasio, A. R. (1985). 'Knowledge without awareness: an autonomic index of facial recognition by prosopagnosics'. *Science*, 228.

Tyler, L. K. (1988). 'Spoken language comprehension in a fluent aphasic patient'. *Cognitive Neuropsychology*, 5.

Weiskrantz, L. (1980). 'Varieties of residual experience. Eighth Sir Frederick Bartlett Lecture'. *Quarterly Journal of Experimental Psychology*, 32.

——(1997). *Consciousness Lost and Found*.

brain imaging. (*see overleaf*)

brain stimulation. In 1907 Sir Victor Horsley and Edward Clarke at University College London invented the technique of stereotactic neurosurgery in order to target the deep nuclei of the cerebellum in monkeys to see what the effects of destroying them would be. Their basic idea was to be able to define any point deep in the brain in terms of a three-dimensional coordinate system centred on a frame fixed to the skull. Then, knowing the relationships between the skull and cerebellar nuclei and between the skull and the frame, they could advance a lesioning electrode to the nuclei through a small hole in the skull using a triaxial drive referenced to the frame. They found that they could locate any point within the brain to within a few millimetres using this technique. Surprisingly they did not see that it might have any use in human neurosurgery, and it was not until 1947 that Speigel and Wycis adapted the Horsley–Clarke frame for use in humans to target deep brain targets in order to alleviate movement disorders and pain and for psychosurgery. They referenced the frame to the pineal gland rather than to the skull

(*cont. on page 135*)

brain imaging: altered states of consciousness.

In trying to understand consciousness, it is useful to distinguish between the level and the content of consciousness. The level of consciousness is closely related to arousal and determines whether we are awake or asleep. Arousal is essentially maintained by activating structures in the brain stem, the diencephalon, and the basal forebrain. Arousal is a prerequisite for the emergence of any conscious experience. The content of consciousness (what we are conscious of) is thought to rely on the function of thalamocortical and corticocortical networks. Some cortical areas are more closely related to conscious experience than are others. In conscious, resting subjects, the brain is most active in several regions of polymodal association cortex: the prefrontal cortex, inferior parietal cortex, and precuneus/posterior cingulate cortex (Fig. 1).

A number of altered states of consciousness (slow wave sleep, anaesthesia, coma) are associated with low levels of *arousal*, implying modification in the activity of the subcortical structures. Slow wave sleep is an example of decreased level and contents of consciousness. This is characterized by a global decrease in blood flow in the brain, which is particularly prominent in the subcortical activating areas as well as in those cortical areas that are the most active during wakefulness.

More rarely, the *level* of consciousness is preserved but the *content* of consciousness is abolished. For instance,

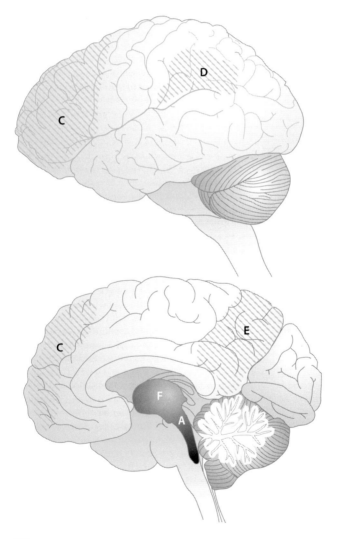

Fig. 1. *Upper panel*, lateral view of the brain. *Lower panel*, medial view of the brain. *In black*, the regions critical for maintaining arousal (A: brain stem, B: basal forebrain). *In grey*, the cortical areas most active in the resting conscious state (C: lateral and medial prefrontal cortex, D: inferior parietal cortex, E: precuneus/ posterior cingulate). In conditions of decreased contents of consciousness (sleep, coma, vegetative state), these areas are relatively quiescent. Note that the thalamus (F) is a crucial interface between structures maintaining arousal and networks supporting the contents of consciousness.

patients in vegetative state look wide awake—they may move, grimace, cry, or laugh—but they are unconscious: as far as we can tell, they have no content of consciousness. In this case, the brain stem is still very active but the cortex is not, especially in the association areas mentioned above.

Of all the altered states of consciousness, rapid eye movement sleep (REM sleep) is probably the most intriguing. During REM sleep we are not fully aware of the environment. On the other hand, our content of consciousness is far from empty. If woken up from REM sleep, we most often report a dream. The distribution of the brain activity in REM sleep is very special. While polymodal association cortex is relatively quiescent (as in the other state of altered consciousness), there is a marked activation of two types of cortical regions: (i) the limbic areas, which are involved in emotion and memory (amygdala, hippocampal formation, anterior cingulate cortex), and (ii) the cortices of the occipital and temporal lobes, concerned with vision and hearing and language. It is tempting to relate this activation to the dream experience. During REM sleep, it is hard to tell whether the level of consciousness is decreased: the brain is as active as during wakefulness. However, the structures that maintain this activation are limited to a small portion of the brain stem, the cholinergic pontine nuclei.

Altered states of consciousness are not only characterized by a change in the distribution of cerebral activity. Interactions between brain areas (*functional and effective connectivity*) are also relevant. The available data stresses the importance of corticocortical and thalamocortical networks involving parietal and prefrontal polymodal association cortex. In the vegetative state, interactions between different regions of polymodal association cortex are reduced. The brain's responses to sound and touch do not go beyond primary sensory cortex. It seems that the primary cortex is disconnected from downstream uni- and polymodal association cortex. It could be argued these alterations in connectivity are the direct result of extensive brain damage. However, this would not explain the resumption of normal interactions between brain regions that has been observed in patients who recover consciousness after a vegetative state.

Finally, although more difficult to assess by functional brain imaging, the *neurochemical modulation* of brain activity by subcortical structures profoundly influences the state of consciousness. Whereas many neurochemical systems are active during wakefulness (histamine, serotonine, noradrenaline (norepinephrine), acetylcholine, orexin, etc.), slow wave sleep is characterized by a decreased firing in most if not all of these systems and the hallmark of REM sleep is a prominent cholinergic drive in the absence of serotonergic and noradrenergic modulation.

CFr/PMa

Frith, C., Perry, R., and Lumer, E. (1999). 'The neural correlates of conscious experience: an experimental framework'. *Trends in Cognitive Sciences*, 3.

Laureys, S., et al. (2000a). 'Auditory processing in vegetative state'. *Brain*, 123.

—— et al. (2000b). 'Restoration of thalamo-cortical connectivity after recovery from persistent vegetative state'. *Lancet*, 355.

Maquet, P. (2000). 'Functional neuroimaging of normal human sleep by positron emission tomography'. *Journal of Sleep Research*, 9.

Plum, F., and Posner, M., (1972). *The Diagnosis of Stupor and Coma.*

Steriade, M., and McCarley, R. W. (1990). *Brainstem Control of Wakefulness and Sleep.*

brain imaging: the methods. It has long been recognized that the brain is the origin of our mental life, but only recently has it become possible to study the relationship between brain and mind in humans in any detail. The change has come about largely through the development of non-invasive brain-imaging techniques in the last quarter of the 20th century. Before these developments our knowledge was either indirect, from experiments in animals, or came from the study of patients who had sustained damage to circumscribed brain regions as result of tumours, strokes, or accidents. Even in these cases it was not easy to know the precise location of this damage prior to examination of the brain after death. The development of computed tomography (CT) scanners in 1972 and magnetic resonance (MR) scanners in 1977 made it possible to locate the damage in exquisite detail (see Fig. 1) (Mansfield 1977). CT scanners use a series of X-rays projected through the skull to reconstruct an image of the brain. MR scanners use a powerful magnet that causes billions of hydrogen atoms (part of molecules throughout the brain) to spin in the same direction. A radio wave is passed through the brain, perturbing these spins, and causing them to emit signals that can be decoded by a computer to produce detailed structural images of the brain.

The brain contains 10 billion nerve cells, which are constantly electrically active. The electrical activity of a single cell, or a small group of cells, can be measured directly by inserting microelectrodes into the brain. However, this technique can only be used in humans if there is a medical reason for the procedure. For about 100 years we have known that electrical activity generated by large populations of nerve cells can also be detected at the surface of the scalp by using electrodes attached to very sensitive amplifiers (see ELECTROENCEPHALOGRAPHY). Such measurements reveal rapid fluctuations in activity known as the electroencephalogram (EEG). Recently, devices have been developed that can measure magnetic activity at the surface of the scalp induced by these changes in electrical activity (MEG). Both techniques give detailed information about the timing of events happening in the brain,

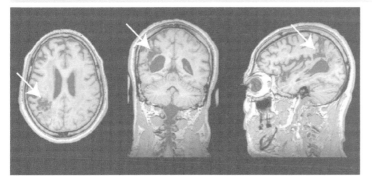

Fig. 1. Structural MRI showing a discrete lesion.

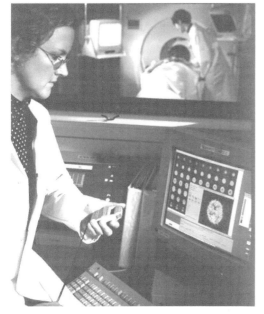

Fig. 2. A PET scanner in use.

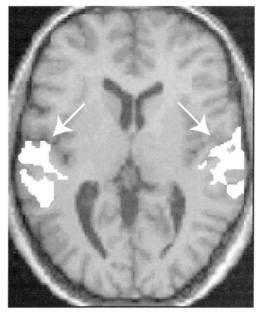

Fig. 3. PET image of auditory stimulation.

but are poor at locating the source of this activity unless it is close to the surface of the brain.

Although the brain accounts for less than 2 per cent of a person's weight, the continuous electrical activity of nerve cells consumes 20 per cent of the body's energy. Energy is supplied, in the form of oxygen and glucose, by a network of blood vessels throughout the brain. It has been known for over 100 years that a local increase in neural activity causes a local increase in blood flow (Roy and Sherrington 1890). It is therefore possible indirectly to measure neural activity by measuring local changes in blood flow (Fulton 1928). Positron emission tomography (PET) was the first technique used to measure blood flow changes by injecting trace amounts of radioactivity into the bloodstream (see Figs. 2 and 3) (Ingvar 1975). More recently it has

proved possible to use MRI (magnetic resonance imaging) to detect changes in blood flow non-invasively, without the need for radioactive injections (Kwong et al. 1992). Oxygen is transported to nerve cells in the bloodstream bound to haemoglobin as oxyhaemoglobin. When the oxygen is released, oxyhaemoglobin becomes deoxyhaemoglobin. Fortuitously, these two molecules differ slightly in their magnetic properties, and so any change in the proportion of oxyhaemoglobin to deoxyhaemoglobin can be detected by MRI. For reasons that are still not clear the local increase in blood flow that is elicited by an increase in neural activity is greater than is needed to replace the oxygen that has been used. As a result there is an increase in the ratio of oxyhaemoglobin and deoxyhaemoglobin, which is detected by MRI as blood oxygenation level dependent (BOLD) contrast (Ogawa et al. 1990). This technique is known as functional MRI (fMRI) and has slightly higher spatial and temporal resolution than PET.

The changes measured by PET and fMRI can be detected throughout the brain, and just as accurately in deep structures as at the surface with a spatial resolution of a few millimetres. However, blood flow measures are far less sensitive to the timing of the neural activity than EEG. Changes in blood flow associated with a brief increase in neural activity do not occur for about five seconds after the onset of the neural activity and carry on for several seconds after the neural activity has ceased. Furthermore the changes in blood flow do not indicate whether the neural activity is excitatory or inhibitory. Nevertheless, blood flow measures can provide important information about neural activity which is entirely consistent with previous work using recordings from single cells in the brains of animals (Posner and Raichle 1994; Frackowiak et al. 1997).   CFr/GR

Frackowiak, R. S. J., Friston, K. J., Frith, C. D., Dolan, R. J., and Mazziotta, J. C. (1997). *Human Brain Function*.

Fulton, J. F. (1928). 'Observations on the vascularity of the human occipital lobe during visual activity'. *Brain*, 51.

Ingvar, D. H. (1975). 'Patterns of brain activity revealed by measurements of regional cerebral blood flow'. In Ingvar, D. H., and Lassen, N. A. (eds.), *Brain Work*.

Kwong, K. K., Belliveau, J. W., Chesler, D. A., et al. (1992). 'Dynamic magnetic resonance imaging of human brain activity during primary sensory stimulation'. *Proceedings of the National Academy of Sciences of the USA*, 89/12.

Mansfield, P. (1977). 'Multiplanar image formation using NMR spin echoes'. *Journal of Physiology*, 10.

Ogawa, S., Lee, T. M., Kay, A. R., and Tank, D. W. (1990). 'Brain magnetic resonance imaging with contrast dependent on blood oxygenation'. *Proceedings of the National Academy of Sciences of the USA*, 87/24.

Posner, M. I., and Raichle, M. E. (1994). *Images of Mind*.

Roy, C. S., and Sherrington, C. S. (1890). 'On the regulation of the blood supply to the brain'. *Journal of Physiology*, 11.

brain imaging: the neural correlates of consciousness. The environment of a brain scanner is extremely restricted. The volunteers must lie flat on their back and move as little as possible. As a result in many early studies volunteers were required to do nothing more than think (e.g. 'Imagine walking through your front door and then turning left at every intersection'). The brain activity associated with such thoughts can easily be detected. More recent studies have shown that the location of the activity relates directly to the content of the thought. If you imagine moving your finger then activity is observed in the brain's motor system. If you imagine seeing a face or a house then activity is seen in the appropriate part of the inferior temporal cortex where objects are represented

(see LOCALIZATION OF BRAIN FUNCTION). Patients with visual disorders who suffer from visual hallucinations of particular objects show similar patterns of activity. These studies show that it is possible to find a localized physiological marker for purely mental activity, that does not result in any observable behaviour. Before the advent of brain imaging we could only know about this mental activity from the subjective report of our volunteer.

The ability to study the relation between mental activity and brain activity has led to a major scientific enterprise of identifying the neural correlates of consciousness (NCC). The ultimate, but far-off aim of this enterprise is to understand how mental activity can emerge from a physical entity such as a brain. So far much of this endeavour has been concerned with identifying neural activity associated with the contents of visual consciousness. In order to identify activity specific to consciousness, situations have been contrasted in which there is a difference in the contents of consciousness, but no difference in the visual signals striking the eye. Such a situation occurs when we view an ambiguous figure such as Rubin's face–vase *illusion. Although the visual input does not change the contents of our consciousness spontaneously switches from a face to a vase and back again. Brain-imaging studies have shown that activity in visual areas of the temporal cortex closely follows what we consciously perceive, while activity at earlier stages of the visual system is less closely correlated. This is consistent with recordings from single neurons in monkeys exposed to similar situations. In addition, brain-imaging studies in humans have shown that there is also activity in frontal and parietal cortex that is time-locked to the occurrence of switches. This activity may represent a mechanism that actively causes the switches between alternative interpretations of the outside world.

A similar strategy can be used to study brain activity associated with unconscious processes. In some situations there can be a change of visual input of which we are not aware, but which still influences our behaviour and therefore must have caused a change in brain activity (see BLINDSIGHT). We can identify this activity by studying situations in which there is a change of visual input, but no change in the contents of consciousness. For example, patients with visual extinction following parietal damage will sometimes fail to report a visual stimulus in the left visual field when it is paired with a second stimulus on the right. Brain imaging has shown that this unseen stimulus in the left visual field nevertheless activates areas of visual cortex in the right hemisphere. Even in normal observers without brain damage, changes in the visual environment that they do not notice can nevertheless produce activity in visual cortex. Similarly, when a word is flashed briefly and immediately followed by a mask it is not seen, but can produce brain activity related to its identity (see SUBLIMINAL PERCEPTION). These studies show that the mere presence of activity in the visual cortex is not sufficient to evoke awareness. Instead, it may be that the level or type of activity is important, or its association with activity in other areas of the brain.

Visual stimuli of which we are not aware can induce emotional responses. Aversive conditioning can be used to elicit an emotional response from a subject when an angry face is presented. If awareness of the angry face is prevented by masking with a neutral, expressionless face, then brain imaging can still detect activity in the amygdala that reflects the learned emotional response to that face. This shows that emotional associations of visual stimuli can be extracted unconsciously by the brain and influence behaviour.

The use of brain imaging to study the NCC is still in its infancy, but has already produced interesting findings. Activity measured with brain imaging in areas of visual cortex may be necessary but not sufficient to result in awareness. In addition, areas outside striate and extra-striate visual cortex, in the parietal and frontal lobes, are consistently associated with visual awareness.   CFr/GR

Dehaene, S., Naccache, L., Cohen, L., (2001). 'Cerebral mechanisms of word masking and unconscious repetition priming'. *Nature and Neuroscience*, 4.

Ffytche, D. H., Howard, R. J., Brammer, M. J., David, A., Woodruff, P., and Williams, S. (1998). 'The anatomy of conscious vision: an fMRI study of visual hallucinations'. *Nature and Neuroscience*, 1.

Frith, C., Perry, R., Lumer, E. (1999), 'The neural correlates of conscious experience: an experimental framework'. *Trends in Cognitive Science*, 3.

Metzinger, T. (ed.) (1999). *Neural Correlates of Consciousness: Empirical and Conceptual Questions*.

Morris, J. S., Ohman, A., and Dolan, R. J. (1998). 'Conscious and unconscious emotional learning in the human amygdala'. *Nature*, 393.

Rees, G. (2001). 'Neuroimaging of visual awareness in patients and normal observers'. *Current Opinion in Neurobiology*, 11.

brain imaging: the neural correlates of will. My voluntary actions, as opposed to my reflexes, are free in the sense that I could have done otherwise. However, in most experimental studies of action the volunteer temporarily gives up this freedom and performs exactly as instructed by the experimenter (e.g. 'lift your finger whenever you hear the tone', 'press the left button when the red light goes on'). A degree of freedom can be introduced into such experiments by giving the volunteer a choice (e.g. 'lift your finger whenever you feel like it', 'whenever you hear the tone lift either your left or your right index finger'). Actions associated with free choices are sometimes referred to as willed actions. Brain regions where activation is associated with willed actions have been identified in a number of neuroimaging studies. These regions

are activated whatever the modality of the action (finger movements, arm movements, speech) and whether the choice concerns the timing or the nature of the action, i.e. *when* to move or *what* to move.

The brain regions most commonly implicated are the dorsolateral prefrontal cortex (DLPFC) and anterior cingulate cortex (ACC), regions on the outer and inner surface of the frontal lobes, respectively. Though these regions appear necessary for willed action they are not (in themselves) sufficient; their 'output' must be relayed through 'lower' brain regions such as the basal ganglia, motor cortex, and thalamus. However, although these lower centres may be sufficient to support stereotypical or learned behaviours, they are supplemented by activity in DLPFC and ACC when *choice* occurs (see Spence and Frith 1999).

Diseases and disorders that impair the execution of wilful actions in humans have been well described: Parkinson's disease, schizophrenia, severe depression, each may be associated with disturbance of DLPFC and ACC function. While patients with these conditions may have difficulty initiating actions, there are also other conditions in which patients are unable to *prevent* their limbs from making superficially 'purposeful' movements. Such patients, exhibiting 'utilization behaviour' or 'alien limbs' often have lesions in orbitofrontal, medial premotor, or callosal regions, giving rise to a failure of response inhibition. People with utilization syndrome, consequent upon bilateral orbitofrontal lesions, seem to be 'driven' by their environments, responding even when they have no desire to do so. Their hands may pick up and grasp objects 'against their will' (Shallice et al. 1989). Hence, there appears to be a tension between the appropriate initiation of an action which the agent wishes to perform, and the inhibition of alternative performances which are inappropriate in the current context. Different neural circuits may be implicated in these complementary functions.

Using EEG it is possible also to look at the *timing* of the brain activity associated with willed actions. Prior to willed action, changes in brain activity (the readiness potential) can be detected up to a second before the action is initiated. These changes probably occur in ACC and in the premotor cortex. In contrast, when we respond as instructed to a stimulus, changes in brain activity are only observed a few hundred milliseconds prior to the action. In a controversial experiment Benjamin Libet asked volunteers to indicate at what time they had the urge to act. This time was typically about 300 milliseconds *after* the first detectable changes in brain activity associated with the ensuing act (Libet et al. 1983). Patrick Haggard has replicated and extended this observation, showing that the timing of the urge to act is correlated with the timing of the onset of the lateralized component of the readiness potential (Haggard and Eimer 1999). Some have argued that these results show that human choices are determined rather than free because changes in brain activity can be observed before the choice has been made. However, we only know about the time of the awareness of the choice. It is still possible that the choice is freely made before we are aware of it (Spence 1996).

Whether or not our actions are determined, we have a strong subjective experience of wilfully choosing courses of action and then initiating them (the experience of agency). In some psychiatric and neurological disorders this experience of agency is compromised. Schizophrenic patients with delusions of control experience their own actions as being made by some alien force. This experience resembles similar experiences reported by people with parietal lobe epilepsy or tumours and is associated with hyperactivity of the right inferior parietal lobe

(Spence et al. 1997). Such hyperactivity has been shown to remit as patients' symptoms resolve.   CFr/ SS

Haggard, P., and Eimer, M. (1999). 'On the relation between brain potentials and awareness of voluntary movements'. *Experimental Brain Research*, 126.

Libet, B., Gleason, C.A., Wright, E.W., et al. (1983). 'Time of conscious intention to act in relation to onset of cerebral activity'. *Brain*, 106.

Shallice, T., Burgess, P. W., Schon, F., and Baxter, D. M. (1989). 'The origins of utilisation behaviour'. *Brain*, 112.

Spence, S.A. (1996). 'Free will in the light of neuropsychiatry'. *Philosophy, Psychiatry and Psychology*, 3.

—— and Frith, C. D. (1999). 'Towards a functional anatomy of volition'. *Journal of Consciousness Studies*, 6.

—— Brooks, D. J., Hirsch, S. R., et al. (1997). 'A PET study of voluntary movement in schizophrenic patients experiencing passivity phenomena (delusions of alien control)'. *Brain*, 120.

---

because the calcified pineal can often be seen in plain X-rays; but nowadays the frame is usually referenced to the anterior and posterior commissures (AC–PC plane) which can be easily identified on computed tomography (CT) and magnetic resonance imaging (MRI).

The main indication for deep brain surgery soon became the alleviation of movement disorders. In 1935 Russell Meyer had discovered that destroying movement centres in and around the basal ganglia, particularly the globus pallidus, could greatly reduce the tremor and rigidity of Parkinson's disease without causing paralysis. However, these open operations killed up to one in five patients (!), and it was soon shown that stereotactic surgery was much safer. Speigel found that most patients who had lost the ability to move after carbon monoxide poisoning showed damage in the globus pallidus. Since he considered most Parkinson's disease symptoms to be caused by uncontrolled release of movements, like Meyer he inferred that destroying the pallidum could help these people. Using his frame to target and destroy the pallidum in Parkinsonian patients that is what he confirmed. Even better, using the stereotactic technique only one in every 100 patients died from complications. Stereotactic lesioning of the globus pallidus or its target in the ventral thalamus became the standard treatment for Parkinson's disease. Various methods were used to destroy the target areas such as passing currents down the electrode to heat the area, injections of pure alcohol into the target, or cutting around it with a wire. Today, very high-frequency currents are used to heat the targets to destroy them in a controlled fashion.

In the 1960s, however, Horniecywicz discovered that Parkinson's disease was due to degeneration of the dopamine-containing cells of the substantia nigra pars

compacta, and soon afterwards it became clear that treatment with the dopamine precursor L-dopa could alleviate all the symptoms of Parkinson's disease without the need for surgery. As a result stereotactic surgery was generally abandoned, even for non-Parkinsonian movement disorders, in the hope that other new drugs were just around the corner.

But a few centres continued to offer such surgery for tremulous disorders and pain. Also the requirement to be able to biopsy deep brain tumours in order to determine their malignancy and susceptibility to cytotoxic drugs and radiotherapy kept stereotactic technology advancing. It was rapidly realized that CT and MRI scans taken with the patient's head in a frame could allow surgeons to directly access tumours using fine cannulae to target and biopsy them via small holes in the skull. Previously surgeons had to use patient symptoms and signs to best guess the location of a brain tumour and then explore a large area of the brain to find it, with predictably high complication rates. Tumour biopsy remained the main indication for stereotactic brain surgery for over a decade. Better imaging technology to study the structure of the brain, beginning with CT scans using X-rays and then MRI using superconducting magnets yielded pictures that provided detail of deep brain structures that could not have been imagined at the birth of stereotactic surgery. Radiolucent and non-magnetic frames were designed to be compatible with CT and MRI imaging, and software was developed to fuse CT and MRI images together to gain the advantages of both. All these were available by the end of the 1980s.

By the 1990s the wheel had turned full circle, however, back to stereotactic surgery for treating movement disorders because it had become clear that long-term L-dopa therapy often has very serious side effects. After about five years' treatment half of all Parkinson's patients develop severe 'dyskinesias' when they take the drug; these are wild flailing involuntary movements, 'chorea', and/or contorted postures, dystonias, that are completely disabling. They are resistant to most drug therapy but can be greatly reduced or even completely eliminated by lesions or high-frequency electrical stimulation in the globus pallidus or subthalamic nucleus of the basal ganglia.

The rationale for these stereotactic treatments of movement disorders derive from the great advances that had been made in our understanding of the neural mechanisms underlying Parkinsonism. This was made possible by the introduction of a good animal model of the disease. In 1978 young drug users in San Francisco unexpectedly began to develop Parkinsonism, which is most unusual under the age of 40. They had been injecting themselves with a home-made recreational drug which was found to be contaminated with a substance, MPTP, that is highly selectively toxic to the dopaminergic neurons in the substantia nigra. Monkeys injected with MPTP develop all the symptoms of Parkinson's disease, so that changes in basal ganglia function in the disease could now be studied in detail using this animal model. This work has revealed that in Parkinson's disease motor control circuits in the basal ganglia get out of control. The subthalamic nucleus (STN) becomes spontaneously overactive and drives the inner half of the pallidum, the medial globus pallidus or GPm, to overinhibit thalamocortical production of motor programmes. This explains why inactivating either the STN or the globus pallidus can reverse most Parkinson's symptoms.

Hence stereotactic lesions of the globus pallidus, pallidotomies, have been reintroduced for the treatment of Parkinsonian dyskinesias, and their success is often dramatic. Many patients who were wheelchair bound and required 24-hour care have been rescued by these operations and restored to useful lives. Lesioning the STN has turned out to be too risky, however, since it is very small and lesions following strokes in this area can cause even worse wild thrashing movements of the whole limb, called hemiballismus. Instead it has been found that electrically stimulating STN neurons at frequencies far higher than their natural rate of discharge, around 100 impulses per second, effectively inactivates them and is comparatively safe. Such stimulation can therefore alleviate all the symptoms of Parkinson's disease with results comparable to those of pallidotomy. Now therefore programmable stimulators connected to electrodes situated in the STN are often implanted subcutaneously, and hundreds of patients have thus been restored to near normal lives.

Thus stereotactic thalamotomy, pallidotomy, or STN stimulation is now routinely used for the treatment of advanced Parkinson's disease. Implantable stimulators in these areas are also increasingly used for other movement disorders that are resistant to drug treatment. These include the ataxic tremors that develop in nearly half of all patients with the demyelinating disease multiple sclerosis. Also childhood contorting body dystonias and the uncontrollable head turning that occurs in 'spasmodic torticollis' are now being treated with stimulators implanted in the basal ganglia.

The alleviation of intractable pain, another of the original indications for stereotactic surgery, is also now being reinvestigated. Many patients, after amputation of a limb, experience severe pain in the absent limb, 'phantom limb pain' that is resistant to all analgesics. Often this is caused by the phantom limb feeling unbearably contorted, and the pain can often be relieved if the patient can gain control over the phantom's movements. This can be achieved by electrically stimulating the contralateral arm area of the motor cortex, and implantable stimulators have been used successfully to relieve the pain.

Phantom limb pain is an example of pain spontaneously generated within the central nervous system, collectively known as 'central' or 'neuropathic' pains. Another way of relieving these is to stimulate the body's own pain control system, which originates in the upper brain-stem periacqueductal grey region. Stimulators are therefore being implanted there with great success at alleviating neuropathic pain. At the same time recording has suggested that the pain is associated with slow frequency spontaneous neuronal activity in the sensory thalamus that correlates with the pain. If the activity is damped down the pain disappears.

Stereotactic surgery is also now being used to implant fetal stem cells, or growth factors into the basal ganglia to attempt to repair the degeneration caused by Parkinson's disease or Huntington's disease. Although even after two decades of experience these procedures have not been very successful, it is clear that this approach offers the best chance of actually curing these diseases. Moreover there is no doubt that stereotactic implantation of repair molecules or stem cells into appropriate sites will become increasingly important for treating a wide range of other diseases, such as Alzheimer's disease, epilepsy, and stroke.

Thus the technique of targeting the deep internal structures of the brain using a stereotactic approach has expanded from a research tool in animals to one with very wide-reaching therapeutic applications in the world of neurology, neurosurgery, and the neurosciences.

See also BRAIN THEORIZING.   TZA/JFS

brain theorizing. Most people working on the brain are experimentalists who think that the only good research is to be conducted in the laboratory but there are quite a few who realize that to understand the complexity of behaviour requires not only experiments on how a human or an animal behaves but also the use of the computer in two very different ways:

- as a tool so that we can store and analyse complex data (neuroinformatics) or explain a complex problem by implementing a model as a computer program, and use that program to explain a body of data and make novel predictions.
- as a metaphor. The brain is in some ways like a computer but it is important to use the computer metaphor without reducing the brain to nothing more than a computer. A brain is attached to a body. A brain has billions of neurons, all active at the same time, in thousands of regions. So instead of thinking of a normal computer which carries out one instruction at a time, doing a problem somebody else has told it to solve, brain theory must understand how a brain in a body with many, many things happening at the same time can see, can act, can learn.

An *artificial intelligence* (AI) scholar might say, 'I don't care very much about what happens inside an animal or human. I want to know how to write a useful program that can transform specific data structures to answer questions, or do pattern recognition for me. This doesn't mean that I think that the wiring of the brain looks like the wiring of the computer'.

A *cognitive psychologist* might say, 'I think you're right that we need to specify precisely how information is stored and transformed. But I want to explain how humans behave; so my model must be successful in the way a human is. It must be slower at things humans are slow at and make the sort of errors a human makes. I want to write a program that makes the machine behave in a way that helps me understand how the human does it'.

But the brain imposes even further constraints. The *brain theorist* says, 'That's all very well. The program may predict the results of experiments on human behavior, but it's *not* a brain model. I want to have the model help me understand information about how brain damage changes behaviour. A neurophysiologist can put an electrode in the brain and check what a few cells are doing in different behaviours. I want my model to show how different cells have different roles in carrying out that behaviour so that I can begin to predict what new cells will do when the animal does something different'.

Experimentalists can now examine single cells in an animal's brain in incredible detail; they can begin to follow patches of activity in the brain of an awake human. Computers enable the brain theorist to make models that represent how different pieces of the brain interact with each other to explain the overall behaviour of the animal or the human. Such models probe systems in which the subsystems have to be mapped to different areas of the brain.

However, the brain is so complicated and has so many different aspects, that it is not going to yield to theory in the same way that 17th-century astronomy did. Newton took Kepler's curve fitting on how the planets move, and Galileo's experiments on a ball rolling, to derive a set of first principles for the subject. But different animals have very different brains; brains have millions and even billions of cells; there are many interesting details below the cellular level, and different brain regions can be characterized at many different levels such as overall patterns of connections, cell morphology, and synaptic neurochemistry. As a result there is an immense diversity of facts to be discovered by pure experiment. This means that many experimentalists will in fact make great contributions without explicit theory. Some such researchers then say, 'Well, I don't need theory so why should we need it at all in neuroscience'. But there are already many successes in brain theory. At the level of how one neuron sends a message to another neuron, Hodgkin and Huxley won a Nobel Prize for coming up with a set of differential equations describing impulse propagation. There begin to be good mathematical descriptions for how rhythms for things like breathing or walking are controlled by neural networks. Computational neuroethologists ask, 'If we have a behaving animal, what is the basic program (in AI terms) that would make it work?'. Because the program is in a brain and not a computer, we think about it as being a parallel program with many things happening at the same time, not a serial program doing one thing at a time, and with all this happening in a body interacting with the world. These ideas have now spread back to AI and cognitive psychology to create the new subfield of Embodied Cognition.

Despite the ascendancy of 'purely symbolic AI' in the 1960s, 1970s, and 1980s, the ideas of 'Embodied Cognition' do themselves have firm roots in the 1960s. Kilmer and *McCulloch showed how an array of modules (each the functional analogue of a cylindrical grouping of cells in the reticular formation) with disparate inputs might be so coupled that they would reach a consensus. The key idea was that this is achieved by *cooperative computation*, each module adjusting its estimate on the basis of input from other modules, without there being any executive control to impose a global solution 'from above'. The concept of an *internal model of the world*, developed in the writings of Richard Gregory, Marvin Minsky, and Donald MacKay, showed us that the brain is to be seen not as a stimulus-response device, but rather as a system whose actions can be chosen in light of the outcomes that they are expected to elicit from the world. Meanwhile, Lettvin, Maturana, McCulloch, and Pitts observed that the frog retina had cells specialized for detecting bugs (the frog's prey) and others for detecting the frog's predators. Such ideas anchored the notion of *action-oriented perception*, grounding perception in the role it plays in supplying the organism with information needed to guide its actions. Moreover, it makes sense to think of the internal representation of the world to consist of units, called *schemas*. Thus, rather than perception having to create a new model with each visual fixation of the eyes, it has the computationally simpler task of updating and tuning perceptual schemas to match changing circumstances, with these schemas giving access to motor schemas to guide interaction with the objects the perceptual schemas represent.

In short, the metaphor 'the brain is a computer' must not be read as reducing the brain to the level of the current technology of serial computers, but rather must expand our concepts of computation to embrace the style of the brain, depending on the constant interaction of many concurrently active systems, many of which express their activity in the interplay of spatio-temporal patterns in manifold layers of neurons. Thus, modern brain theory uses mathematics and the computer to think not only about how one neuron at a time responds when being measured by the experimentalist, but to understand how many neurons interact within the behaving organism. This cannot be done by experiment alone. Experimentalists have long accepted the computer as an invaluable tool for collecting data. Increasingly, they will come to understand that it is also an invaluable tool for using mathematics to understand how behaviour really is mediated by the brain.   MAA

Arbib, M. A. (ed.) (1995). *The Handbook of Brain Theory and Neural Networks* (new edn. 2003).
——Érdi, P., and Szentágothai, J. (1998). *Neural Organization: Structure, Function, and Dynamics.*

brain waves. See ELECTROENCEPHALOGRAPHY.

Brentano, Franz (1838–1917). One of the most original figures in the history of philosophy and psychology. In character he was impressive, courageous, even reckless. He was a Roman Catholic priest, but rejected the Pope's infallibility, and his marriage at the age of 42 meant that he had to resign his professorship at the University of Vienna.

Brentano was a man of broad intellectual interests. He is best known for his work in philosophy and psychology, but he also wrote on theology, ethics, and politics. This, as we shall see, was not foreign to his great endeavour in the field of scientific psychology. Brentano was first interested in Aristotelian metaphysics and, though rejecting *Aristotle's system as a whole, he found in it an important starting point for his later reflections on the value and meaning

of knowledge. But, having done away with Aristotelian philosophy, he was also deeply aware of the weakness of the attempts of the psychologists of his time to develop scientific procedures within the framework of philosophical studies. These circumstances, as well as his personal convictions, led him to consider himself as being charged with the mission of reforming philosophy in a fundamental manner. In his view, this mission assumed an 'almost messianic sense' (Spiegelberg 1960).

This peculiar attitude was ultimately motivated by metaphysical concerns. As a result of his reflections on theology, Brentano developed a basically obsessive anxiety about time and eternity; having rejected his religious faith as far as dogmatic contents were concerned, he nevertheless remained deeply troubled by the problems of human destiny which such teachings necessarily raise. Since he could no longer rely on theology, he was bound to search for another life reference. This he found in *experience*, i.e. in *consciousness. It is therefore not surprising that he should have devoted his main philosophical effort to the epistemological analysis of the foundations of psychology.

The word 'experience' is misleading because it may be understood either as the content of consciousness in the sense of introspective psychology, or as the perceptual phenomena which make up our empirical knowledge of the external world. As a matter of fact, Brentano succeeded in transcending the classical opposition between immanentism and empiricism by developing an original theory of consciousness that allowed him to escape this well-known dualistic conception of the psychological subject. This he achieved by stressing the fact that the fundamental property of consciousness is *intentionality: every subjective experience can only make sense if it is understood as an *act* of consciousness referred to some object, the latter being either some perceptual content, or some mental construct independent of its object but, once again, necessarily referred to some kind of object. Within such a framework, psychological immanentism is condemned at the outset because, though internal *perception* readily exists in subjective experience, internal *observation* of the introspective kind is plainly impossible, since it requires that particular sort of dualism according to which the subject is at the same time an object for himself. If, further, this postulated 'object' is defined as a 'scientific' one, as in early experimental psychology, the study of experience amounts finally to paradoxical realism, because it is a realism devoid of any empirically definable 'reality'.

Given these difficulties, we must now ask ourselves in which sense Brentano claims to be an empiricist, as testified by his well-known contention that experience is his 'only teacher' and by the significant title of his main work, *Psychologie vom empirischen Standpunkt* (Psychology from the Empirical Standpoint) (1874). Empiricism, in this context, carries the meaning of a return to the only unavoidable experience, namely the subjective one as constitutive of a relation to the world. We know from *Descartes's philosophy that his *Cogito ergo sum* led him to a similar attitude regarding the foundations of metaphysics and of science. The basic difference in Brentano's system lies in the fact that, unlike Descartes, he does not discard the relation to experienced objects for the sake of the so-called illusions of the senses but strives on the contrary to establish a firm world reference for every conscious phenomenon. This is the reason why he speaks of *acts* of consciousness, designating thereby not the facts of actual behaviour but the constitutive power of the self as such.

In order to circumscribe the realm of psychic phenomena, empirical psychology must first proceed to a descriptive survey of subjective experience by way of intuition. This first phase is not meant to be introspective; it is in fact an attempt at delineating psychology's own field of investigation, i.e. at a pre-scientific level. This basic task of classifying the 'acts' is ultimately phenomenological and represents the epistemological moment of Brentano's endeavour. In the partial republication of his original work in 1911 under the title *On the Classification of Psychic Phenomena*, Brentano refers to it as 'psychognosis' or 'phenominognosis'. Once this has been completed, the second task of empirical psychology is to establish psychological science as such by evidencing the causal relations between phenomena, eventually up to the physiological level. Brentano refers to this part of his work as 'genetic' psychology. We see therefore that what he is aiming at is finally a kind of experimental psychology epistemologically well founded, i.e. relying firmly on actual subjective experience.

It is worth noting that the publication of *Psychology from the Empirical Standpoint* coincided almost exactly with that of Wilhelm *Wundt's *Grundzüge der physiologischen Psychologie* (Foundations of Physiological Psychology), both works appearing in March 1874. However, of these two founding treatises, for many decades only that of Wundt exerted a wide influence on the developments of psychology as a science. This was most probably due to the fact that in Wundt's system the relation of psychic events to physiological ones was more readily understandable, because Wundt took the existence of phenomena of consciousness for granted, under the form of introspectively accessible 'objects', whereas in Brentano's view the very concept of object could be defined only through the intentional founding acts. Historically speaking, it seems that the positivistic impetus given by Wundt to the new science of consciousness was much stronger than the epistemological warnings of Brentano concerning the *possibility* of a scientific psychology.

More than a century has now elapsed since the birth of experimental psychology, and we are in a better position to appreciate the results. Whatever tendencies made their appearance in psychology during this long period of experimenting and theorizing, we know that the debate is not closed. Brentano's teachings have made their way through the school of Graz and were responsible for the emergence of both *Gestalt psychology and *Husserlian phenomenology. The psychological positivism inherited from Wundt has evolved in its own way; it has not only yielded visible results, but has also given rise to a great deal of methodological and even epistemological reflection. This in itself testifies to the fact that the question of the *essence* of psychic phenomena, to use a phenomenological expression, is an unavoidable one. No doubt it would be careless to consider that a satisfactory answer to it will be found by merely increasing the quantity of factual results, since psychological *data* are the product of intentional acts of scientists. Today's psychologists are therefore indebted to Brentano—be it in an indirect fashion—for his early endeavour to lay the epistemological foundations which psychology needs, in order to exist as an adequate science of man's subjective experience.

See also PHENOMENOLOGY.   GT

Brentano, F. (1874). *Psychologie vom empirischen Standpunkt*, vol. i. Posthumous edn., ed. O. Kraus (1924–8).

Spiegelberg, H. (1960). *The Phenomenological Movement: A Historical Introduction*, 2 vols.

Thinès, G. (1977). *Phenomenology and the Science of Behaviour*.

Breuer, Joseph (1842–1925). Physician and psychiatrist *Freud described his close friend and collaborator Joseph Breuer as 'a man of rich and universal gifts, whose interests extended far beyond his professional activity'. For Breuer's professional activities and achievements extended from being a distinguished physician in Vienna, to discovering the significance of the vagus nerve for controlling breathing, and to establishing the essential functions of the semicircular canals for the sense of balance. He is, however, known best for his work on *hysteria—following the celebrated case of Fräulein Anna O.

During her father's last illness Anna O. developed paralysis of her limbs, and anaesthesias, as well as disturbances of vision and speech. Breuer noted that she had two alternating personality states: one more or less normal, the other that of a naughty child. He found that the symptoms were reduced or disappeared after she described her frequent and terrifying hallucinations. This 'talking cure' or 'chimney sweeping', as they called it, led Breuer to the use of hypnosis to speed things up, and to the concept of catharsis. Anna O.'s true name was Bertha Pappenheim (1859–1936). She was highly intelligent and unusually physically attractive. She became the first social worker in

Germany and founded a journal. She never was entirely cured.

The Anna O. case made a deep impression on Freud, who heard of it shortly after Breuer terminated treatment in June 1882. Discussions of it with Breuer were a formative basis of Freudian theory and psychoanalytic practice, especially the importance of fantasies (in extreme cases, hallucinations), hysteria (which was first fully recognized by *Charcot), and the concept and method of catharsis which were Breuer's major contributions. Breuer also introduced the use of hypnosis as a clinical tool. Freud adopted it for a time but later gave it up in favour of *free association.   OLZ

Jones, E. (1953). *The Life and Work of Sigmund Freud*, 3 vols., Bk. I, ch. 11.

Brewster, Sir David (1781–1868). Scottish physicist, born at Jedburgh and educated at Edinburgh University, of which he became vice-chancellor in 1860. He was elected a Fellow of the Royal Society in 1815 and was active in the foundation of the British Association for the Advancement of Science. His main interest was optics, and in 1816 he invented the kaleidoscope. He also improved Wheatstone's stereoscope (or at least made it more convenient, by introducing lenticular prisms rather than Wheatstone's mirrors) so allowing pairs of large pictures to be presented, one to each eye, in spite of the small interocular distance and the inability of the eyes to diverge for fusion. He also made important discoveries on the polarization of light (notably Brewster's law, that when the polarization is at a maximum the tangent of the angle of polarization—Brewster's angle—is equal to the refractive index of the reflecting medium).   RLG

Wade, N. J. (1984). *Brewster and Wheatstone on Vision*.

brightness. The sensation of light which is roughly associated with the intensity of light at the eye, or its luminance. The sensation of brightness is affected by the adaptation level of the eye and by various contrast phenomena—so brightness cannot be measured simply in physical units.

Broad, Charlie Dunbar (1887–1971). English philosopher, professor of moral philosophy at Cambridge (1933–53). He carried out detailed conceptual analyses of science (*Scientific Thought*, 1923), of mind (*Mind and its Place in Nature*, 1929), and of ethics (*Five Types of Ethical Theory*, 1930). His *Examination of McTaggart's Philosophy* (1933–8) contains interesting discussions on time.

See also `EMERGENCE` AND `REDUCTION` IN EXPLANATIONS; PARANORMAL.

Broadbent, Donald (1926–93). Though born in Birmingham, the distinguished experimental psychologist

Donald Broadbent identified himself, from ancestry and upbringing, as Welsh. Having flown in the RAF, he was drawn to problems of legibility of instruments and confusions of controls. These led him to develop pioneering ideas on information transmission in the nervous system and the role of selective attention. As director of the MRC Applied Psychology Laboratory, he was able to combine work on practical problems while developing theoretical insights of lasting significance, especially in his book *Perception and Communication* (1958), which introduces his notion of limited-capacity information channels and perceptual filters.

Weiskrantz, L. (1994). 'Donald Eric Broadbent'. *Biographical Memoirs of the Royal Society*, 40.

Broca, Paul Pierre (1824–80). French surgeon and anthropologist, professor of surgery and anthropology in Paris. Broca was the only son of a doctor at Sainte-Foy-la-Grande, a small town in the Gascogne, on the river Dordogne, east of Bordeaux. He is remembered chiefly for establishing in 1861 that destruction of an area of grey matter not much larger than 4 square centimetres—'Broca's area'—makes a person unable to speak—Broca's (expressive or motor) *aphasia, by him first called 'aphemia'. In practically all right-handed people this area, he also found, lies in the left hemisphere; hence it is called the 'dominant' hemisphere of the brain. His test case was a patient nicknamed 'Tan', because 'tan-tan' were the only syllables he could produce for an answer. By contrast, Tan's understanding of the spoken word was considered to be intact. For years Tan had also been paralysed on the right side—presumably through a succession of strokes—and had become Broca's surgical patient because of an infected bedsore. He soon died. At autopsy his brain showed the essential lesion situated at the hind end of the third, or inferior, of the three frontal lobe convolutions (or gyri). Here, for the first time, it was demonstrated with fair precision that a small set of muscles as well as a mental function—the expression of ideas through words—could be localized in a fairly circumscribed portion of brain tissue. The observation has been confirmed innumerable times since. (In 1870 Gustav Fritsch and J. L. Hitzig localized motor function, Carl *Wernicke three years later a receptive speech area.) Before Broca established this localization, only a few die-hards had been upholding Franz Joseph *Gall's vague contention of half a century earlier that the frontal lobes generally 'preside over the faculty' of speech.

Broca's other major contribution to understanding the relationship between the structure of the brain and mental function concerns what in the 1950s was revived under the designation of the '*limbic system'. This comprises the convolutions of the inner wall of the cerebral hemispheres and part of the inferior aspect of the frontal lobes.

Broca based his concept of the 'great limbic lobe' on the fact that it is relatively underdeveloped in aquatic mammals and primates, including the human, as compared with lower mammals, which rely to a much greater extent on the sense of smell, and have otherwise less developed hemispheres. On this basis Broca contrasted a 'brute' part with an 'intelligent' part of the brain. Today the limbic (threshold) system is recognized for being concerned with emotion, instinct, and visceral control.

When in 1859—also the year of *Darwin's publication of *The Origin of Species*—Broca was prevented in the Société de Biologie from reading a series of his papers (considered too revolutionary as they negated the permanence of species), he founded the Société d'Anthropologie (the first under this name), and later a laboratory, museum, and institute. One of the papers was based on a study of fertile 'leporids', so called in France because they were a cross between a hare and a female rabbit.

Broca also first described Cro-Magnon and Aurignacian, or palaeolithic, man, developed a large number of instruments for measuring skulls (craniometry), employed the novelty of statistical standardization, and lent the budding science of anthropology his eminently critical spirit. He inaugurated the study of prehistoric trephining of the skull, and exploded the 'Celtic myth' (that the Celts constitute a racial group with inherited characteristics) and other racial prejudices: 'Spread education, and you improve the race,' were his words. In his early years he belonged to a small group who used the microscope to detect cancer cells, and he discovered their spread via the venous system. He published some 500 papers but his only major book was a standard monograph on aneurysms.

He was also active in political life, holding radical views. He was elected to the French Senate in 1879, but died one year later having delivered only one memorandum, which pleaded to grant public high-school education to females. He was sceptical about the prevalent view of equating female inferiority with the female's relatively smaller brain: 'An enlightened person cannot think of measuring intelligence by measuring the brain,' he wrote.   FS

brown. Although perhaps the commonest colour, brown is not in the spectrum: it is not a spectral hue. It cannot normally be produced by a mixture of any three lights—as can the spectral hues (see COLOUR VISION: BRAIN MECHANISMS; COLOUR VISION: EYE MECHANISMS)—and is thus somewhat mysterious. It seems to depend on contrast, and on perceived surface texture, which may also affect other colours.

Brunswik, Egon (1903–55). Austrian–American psychologist, born in Budapest and educated in Vienna.

Brunswik's early interests lay almost exclusively in the field of visual *perception, and he published a scholarly monograph on object constancy based on experiments carried out in Vienna before he emigrated to the USA (*Wahrnehmung und Gegenstandswelt*, 1934). In America he extended and developed his interests in perception, in part as a result of his close friendship with E. C. *Tolman, with whom he published a joint paper on 'The organism and the causal structure of the environment' (*Psychological Review*, **22** (1935)). He also developed a strong interest in the design of psychological experiments, producing an original, though difficult, monograph on *Perception and the Representative Design of Psychological Experiments* (1956). He was also much interested in the philosophy of science and the history of psychology.   OLZ

Hammond, K. R., and Stewart, T. R. (2001). *The Essential Brunswik: Beginnings, Explications, Applications*.

Buddhist ideas of the mind. See INDIAN IDEAS OF THE MIND; CHINESE IDEAS OF THE MIND; JAPANESE CONCEPT OF THE MIND.

Burton, Richard Francis (1821–90). English explorer, writer, and linguist born near Elstree, Hertfordshire. The son of an army colonel, Burton was brought up in France and Italy. He studied for a time at Oxford University but was eventually expelled for attending horse races. At 21 Burton joined the army of the East India Company and was posted to the Sindh, in north-western India (now Pakistan), where he lived with Muslims and learned several Eastern languages and dialects, including Iranian, Hindustani, and Arabic. During this time, Burton became proficient also in Marathi, Sindhi, Punjabi, Telugu, Pashto, and Multani. In his travels in Asia, Africa, and South America, he learned 25 languages, with dialects that brought the number to 40.

After seven years in India working under the direction of the renowned Sir Charles Napier, Burton returned to France. Between 1853 and 1855, Burton visited the Muslim holy cities of Mecca and Medina in disguise and made a dangerous venture to the forbidden city of Harar in eastern Ethiopia, succeeding in being the first white man to enter and leave alive. This is documented in *First Footsteps in East Africa*.

Burton's greatest journey began in 1857, with John Speke, on the coast of what is now eastern Tanzania. Following African paths, they became the first white people in modern times to view Lake Tanganyika. Ill with malaria and in dispute with Speke over the source of the Nile, Burton did not travel north to Lake Victoria. Speke returned as the discoverer of the Nile, which led to a bitter and public dispute between the two men. In 1860 Burton made an overland trip to Utah to visit the Mormons and their leader. This meeting with Brigham Young and extensive reporting on polygamy was recounted in *The City of the Saints* (1861). Shortly after his return from the United States, in January 1861, he secretly married Isabel Arundell, the daughter of an aristocratic Catholic family.

In 1861, Burton joined the British Foreign Office as a consul to Fernando Po, a Spanish island off the coast of West Africa from where he continued to travel to Africa. In the following years, Burton was also posted as consul to Santos, Brazil (1865–9), and then to Damascus in the Middle East. His final post was in Trieste (1872–90), where he continued to write extensively. Burton died in Trieste on 20 October 1890. Following his death, Isabel, his wife, burned his diaries and current manuscripts, providing her own whitewashed version of his life, depicting him as a good Catholic, faithful husband, and wronged and misunderstood adventurer.

His books and translations include the *Kama Sutra* (1883), *The Book of a Thousand Nights and a Night* (1885), the *Ananga Ranga* (1885), and *The Perfumed Garden* (1886). He also published remarkable literal translations of Camões and of the *Arabian Nights* (16 vols., 1885–8).   RLG

Brodie, F. M. (1967). *The Devil Drives: A Life of Sir Richard Burton*.

Edwardes, A. (1963). *Death Rides a Camel*.

Farwell, B. (1990). *Burton: A Biography of Sir Richard Francis Burton*.

Lovell, M. S. (1998). *A Rage to Live: A Biography of Richard & Isabel Burton*.

McLynn, F. (1990). *Of No Country: An Anthology of Richard Burton*.

——(1993). *Burton: Snow on the Desert*.

Ondaatje, C. (1996). *Sindh Revisited: A Journey in the Footsteps of Captain Sir Richard Francis Burton*.

Burton, Robert (1577–1640). English clergyman and Fellow of Christ Church, Oxford. Burton was born at Lindley in Leicestershire and went to Brasenose College, Oxford, in 1593, becoming a student of Christ Church in 1599 and vicar of St Thomas's, Oxford, in 1616. In about 1630 he also became vicar of Seagrave in Leicestershire, but for most of his life he lived a 'silent sedentary, solitary, private life' at Christ Church.

Burton's *The Anatomy of Melancholy* was first published in 1621. Melancholy was, he considered, an 'inbred malady in every one of us' and he wrote on it 'by being busy to avoid melancholy'. The book is divided into three parts: the first deals with the causes and symptoms of melancholy; the second with its cure; and the third with the melancholy of love and the melancholy of religion. He expanded the subject, however, to cover the whole of the life of man, and on every page there are many quotations and paraphrases from a very wide field of literature, giving the book the reputation of a storehouse of miscellaneous learning rather than a medical treatise.

O'Connell, M. (1986). *Robert Burton*.

Butler, Samuel (1835–1902). British author, painter, musician, and eccentric philosopher, born at Langar, Nottinghamshire, where his father was rector. He was a direct descendant of Samuel Butler (1612–80), the author of the satirical poem *Hudibras* (1663), which lampooned puritanism, and the grandson of Samuel Butler (1774–1839), classical scholar and Bishop of Lichfield and Coventry. Educated at Cambridge, he emigrated to New Zealand in 1859, where he ran a successful sheep farm, returning to England in 1865 to concentrate on writing and painting.

Erewhon (1872) is a satirical romance set in the land of Erewhon (roughly nowhere backwards). In chapters 23–5 there is an extended discussion of the effects of machines on people, and of consciousness and intelligence considered in terms of actual or potential machines, as well as animals and plants. Thus:

There is no security against the ultimate development of mechanical consciousness, in the fact of machines possessing little consciousness now . . . who can say that the vapour engine is not a kind of consciousness? Where does consciousness begin and where does it end? The shell of a hen's egg is made of a delicate white ware and is a machine as an egg-cup is; the shell is a device for holding the egg as much as the egg-cup for holding the shell.

And considering fly-eating plants:

When a fly settles upon the blossom, the petals close upon it . . . but they will close on nothing but is good to eat; of a drop of rain or a piece of stick they will take no notice. Curious that so unconscious a thing should have such a keen eye to its own interests! If this is unconsciousness, where is the use of consciousness? . . . Shall we say that the plant does not know what it is doing merely because it has no eyes, or ears, or brains? If we say that it acts mechanically only, shall we not be forced to admit that sundry other and apparently very deliberate actions are also mechanical? If it seems to us that the plant kills and eats a fly mechanically, may it not seem to the plant that a man must kill and eat a sheep mechanically?

There is a prophetic account of *artificial intelligence, as Samuel Butler considers the rapid development, and imagines future machines:

There was a time when it must have seemed highly improbable that machines should learn to make their wants known by sound, even through the ears of man; may we not conceive, then, that a day will come when those ears will be no longer needed, and the hearing will be done by the delicacy of the machine's own construction—when its language shall have developed from the cry of animals to a speech as intricate as our own? . . . We cannot calculate on any corresponding advance in man's intellectual or physical powers which shall be a set-off against the far greater development which seems in store for the machines. Some people may say that man's moral influence will suffice to rule them; but I cannot think it will ever be safe to repose much trust in the moral sense of any machine.

Machines are outlawed in *Erewhon*—as potentially far too dangerous for man to live with.

In *Erewhon* and in some of his other writing, for example *Life and Habit* (1877), *Luck or Cunning* (1886), and in his *Notebooks* (1912, edited by H. Festing Jones), he expressed his views on *Darwinism. Though he accepted natural selection he protested against the banishment of mind from the universe and argued for the inheritance of acquired habits. The novel *The Way of All Flesh* (published posthumously in 1903) is largely autobiographical and explores family strife and morality in ways that affected Shaw and later writers.   RLG

Raby, P. (1991). *Samuel Butler: A Biography.*

C

cafeteria experiments. The self-assessed dietary preferences or needs of animals (and perhaps humans), indicated by free-choice feeding from a large variety of their normal, or sometimes unfamiliar, foods or substances. There is good evidence that animals choose appropriate foods through learning. This involves a combination of learned conditioned preferences based on an association between the taste, flavour, and texture of food and beneficial after-effects and conditioned taste aversions based on the association of these properties and negative after-effects. The effects are often robust and long lasting, presumably so that they provide an adaptive survival function. Evidence with human participants, though harder to obtain due to the natural diversity of our food environment, suggests that a learning mechanism for food choice in the human population also exists (see CAFFEINE: EFFECTS OF).

Rozin, P. (1976). 'The selection of food by rats, humans and other animals'. In Rosenblatt, J., et al. (eds.), *Advances in the Study of Behavior*, vol. vi.

caffeine: effects of. Coffee and tea are the main sources of caffeine, which is consumed daily by some 80 per cent of the world's population. Caffeine's multiple biological effects, including its central nervous system (CNS), cardiovascular, renal, gastrointestinal, and metabolic effects are due to its ability to block adenosine receptors. Adenosine acts on specific cell-surface receptors distributed throughout the body, generally causing inhibition of physiological activity. By blocking adenosine receptors caffeine has broadly stimulant effects. After consuming a caffeine-containing drink, caffeine is fairly rapidly absorbed from the gastrointestinal tract into the bloodstream and then distributed throughout the entire body, including the brain. Caffeine does not accumulate in the body, however, because it and its metabolites are efficiently excreted, mainly in the urine. For adults, the elimination half-life of caffeine (the time it takes for half of the caffeine to be eliminated from the body) is around 3–6 hours. This time is increased during pregnancy and decreased in smokers.

Caffeine is widely regarded as a useful and relatively harmless psychostimulant—a substance that can help, for example, to 'kick-start' the day and counteract sleepiness after lunch, during a long drive, or when working late into the evening. This appears to be confirmed by a large number of experiments showing effects of caffeine on self-rated alertness and sleepiness accompanied by improved concentration, quicker thinking, and shorter reaction times. Indeed, the alerting effects of caffeine are often very obvious to those who consume it.

There is, however, a fundamental and much neglected problem with the interpretation of this evidence, which has to do with the fact that these effects of caffeine are typically measured and experienced in the context of a period of prior caffeine 'withdrawal'. For instance, in the typical placebo-controlled experiment investigating the behavioural effects of caffeine, volunteers with a history of regular caffeine intake are instructed to refrain from consuming caffeine for usually between 10 and 24 hours before being tested. Consequently, there is a question of whether the results obtained are due to beneficial effects of caffeine or to adverse effects of continued caffeine abstinence. That is, lower alertness and poorer psychomotor and cognitive performance on placebo might be due to the fatiguing effects of caffeine withdrawal, which are reversed by caffeine administration, thereby merely reinstating performance to the 'normal' level. This latter interpretation, known as the withdrawal–reversal hypothesis, is consistent with results showing marked negative effects, such as increased headache, drowsiness, and fatigue, even after 10 hours' caffeine abstinence. It is also supported directly by the results of experiments such as those conducted by Goldstein and colleagues (1969). They found that individuals who did not usually consume caffeine-containing drinks were more alert soon after waking in the morning than regular caffeine consumers who had not yet consumed their first caffeine-containing drink of the day. They also found that caffeine subsequently increased alertness only in the caffeine consumers and only to the same level as that reported by the non-consumers. More recent experiments show the same pattern of effects for 'former' caffeine consumers (i.e. individuals who have been withdrawn from caffeine for at least 7–10 days). That is, they were more alert and showed better performance than overnight withdrawn caffeine consumers, and giving them caffeine did not further increase their alertness or performance scores.

It can be argued that pre-existing differences may account for different levels of alertness and different responses to caffeine in caffeine consumers and non-consumers (because these groups are self-selected). This, however, is not a problem for experiments that test 'former' caffeine consumers. Another important feature of these latter experiments is that caffeine was given in several moderate doses across a testing period lasting until early afternoon. This models part of the typical pattern of caffeine intake of regular caffeine consumers, and at the same time rules out the possibility that the failure of caffeine to affect performance of the 'former' caffeine consumers (or to raise performance further in overnight withdrawn consumers) was due to the administration of inadequate amounts of caffeine.

A question left largely unanswered by these experiments investigating the psychostimulant effects of caffeine is: why are caffeine-containing drinks so popular? Based on data on the elimination half-life of caffeine and the results of behavioural experiments such as those described above, it appears that alertness can be maintained (withdrawal effects avoided) by consuming coffee or tea two or perhaps three times a day, yet many individuals consume caffeine far more frequently than this.

Of course, one factor influencing the consumption of caffeine-containing drinks is the expectation of gaining a benefit (increased alertness etc.). However, if people are asked why they drink coffee or other caffeine-containing drinks, they are most likely to say that it is because they like the 'taste' of the drink—people typically do not consume coffee as if it were a medicine, being prepared to tolerate its taste in the expectation of a benefit. At the same time, it is fairly certain that human beings are not born with a liking for the taste and flavour of either coffee or tea, at least partly, because these drinks contain bitter constituents, including caffeine, and bitterness is innately aversive. How, then, do people come to acquire a liking for the sensory qualities of these drinks?

An important way in which liking is modified is through the association of the taste, flavour, etc. of foods and drinks with the after-effects of eating and drinking. The most dramatic example of this is the strong and specific aversions that can develop when consumption of a food is followed by feeling sick and vomiting. Similarly, there is now good evidence that association of a taste or flavour paired with positive after-effects can result in increased liking for that specific taste or flavour. The potent pharmacological activity of certain food and drink constituents might be particularly important in this respect, such that, for example, liking for the initially neutral or even disliked taste of coffee, tea, beer, wine, etc. is reinforced by the psychoactive effects of caffeine and alcohol.

This idea has been tested in experiments in which caffeine ingestion was paired with the consumption of novel-flavoured fruit juices. Caffeine was given in the drink or in some experiments in a capsule swallowed with the drink. A drink of a different flavour was given without caffeine or with a placebo capsule. The results showed that caffeine acted most reliably as a reinforcer in the context of short-term (overnight) caffeine withdrawal, and perhaps when relieving other negative states such as feelings of fatigue and tiredness experienced by some people soon after lunch (the 'post-lunch dip'). In other words, caffeine influenced participants' liking for the drink mainly because it reversed the negative effects arising from withdrawal from the caffeine they had consumed the previous day.

In assessing the psychostimulant effects of caffeine it is important to take into account the impact of caffeine withdrawal. When this is done, the widely held view that caffeine consumption increases alertness and improves psychomotor and cognitive performance is contradicted. The reality is that regular caffeine consumers *experience* a benefit from caffeine, which reinforces their liking for the drink. This is especially noticeable on consuming the first caffeine-containing drink of the day because this typically follows a fairly lengthy period (often at least ten hours) of caffeine withdrawal. In contrast, the *overall* or *net* psychostimulant benefit gained from being a caffeine consumer is small or non-existent.

PJR

Goldstein, A., Kaizer, S., and Whitby, O. (1969). 'Psychotropic effects of caffeine in man. IV. Quantitative and qualitative differences associated with habituation to coffee'. *Clinical Pharmacology and Therapeutics*, 10.

Cajal, Santiago Ramón y. See RAMÓN Y CAJAL.

calculate. To use numerical techniques to find the answer to mathematical problems by formal rules, such as those of arithmetic. The word is derived from the Latin *calculus*, meaning small stone, referring to the ancient, and indeed prehistoric, use of pebbles for counting, later formalized in the *abacus. The first gearwheel calculating machine was built by Blaise *Pascal in the year of Isaac Newton's birth, 1642. It is odd that this and many later demonstrations of the calculations of 'mental arithmetic' being undertaken by machine did not, at once and generally, suggest that human thinking may be carried out by physical brain processes and may be largely or completely unconscious.

RLG

calculating geniuses. The term 'calculating genius' describes anyone strikingly more able than normal to do numerical calculations mentally. Since the term is relative to what is regarded as normal, it is applied to people of three different types. (i) Children whose ability is precocious, i.e. exceptional for their age but not necessarily by comparison with many adults. (ii) Learning disabled people in whom mental calculation is an 'island of ability'. Their ability is not usually outstanding by normal standards but contrasts with their general lack of ability in other respects. (iii) People whose ability is exceptional relative to the adult population at large, and among whom calculating geniuses, in the strict sense, are to be found.

In studying calculating geniuses, four general points merit emphasis. First, the ability rests on the individual's knowledge of numerical facts and short-cut methods. To illustrate, you can multiply by 25 by dividing by 4 and multiplying by 100: for example, 16 times 25 is 4 hundreds. The answer, 400, is attained so rapidly that it seems miraculous to anyone unfamiliar with the short cut. Now, there is literally no end to the numerical facts, interrelations, and short cuts that may be discovered, and when these are deployed in mental calculation, the resulting performances can be impressive, especially to the uninitiated. Mental calculators of high calibre skilfully deploy extensive, recondite knowledge of facts and methods which are largely unknown to, and unsuspected by, most people.

Secondly, people who have acquired a small amount of numerical knowledge can go on by themselves to discover and elaborate new facts and methods, and progressively build calculating ability that is out of the ordinary. Self-taught and with no need for external equipment, they can, unaided and unobtrusively, build an ability which may be well developed before it comes to public notice or before they themselves become aware that they can do something unusual. It may easily be supposed that the ability blossoms abruptly and fully formed. However, there is no evidence that ability develops other than by prolonged, cumulative experience. Furthermore, ability atrophies with disuse.

Thirdly, calculating procedures taught at school are designed for use in conjunction with a written record of the various steps taken, and are not serviceable in mental calculation. To illustrate, multiply 123 by 456 using your accustomed paper-and-pencil method. Now repeat exactly as before but, this time, try to do the entire calculation in your head without writing anything. You lose track, don't you? So would mental calculators. They would use other methods—of which there are many—that lend themselves better to mental working. They would, also, generate the answer (56,088) in natural left-to-right sequence, not right-to-left as happens with your paper-and-pencil procedure. In brief, the numerical language needed for mental calculation is, in many respects, different from that taught in school. This explains why the unschooled are not necessarily disadvantaged in developing talent in mental calculation and why such people often claim, in retrospect, that schooling would have been a positive hindrance.

Fourthly, it is difficult to discover in minute detail how any individual calculates. A certain amount can be inferred from objective characteristics of performance,

but reliance must also be placed on subjective reports which, apart from their inescapable limitations, encounter certain difficulties. When the calculator is highly educated and articulate, he may take his numerical knowledge so much for granted that he neglects to make it explicit, even if able and willing to do so, once the need for communication becomes apparent. When young or uneducated, he may lack vocabulary to describe his self-taught knowledge. George Parker Bidder (1806–78), for example, was a calculating genius who became a distinguished engineer and gave an autobiographical account of his talent. At 6, when he began seriously to calculate, he could not read or write, had no notion of written numbers, and had never heard the word 'multiply'. He remarked, 'The first time I was asked to "multiply" some small affair, say 23 by 27, I did not know what was meant; and it was not until I was told that it meant 23 times 27 that I could comprehend the term.'

The difficulties are worse confounded when the calculator is a public entertainer who contrives theatrical effects and deliberately conceals the tricks of his trade. He may, for example, give the square roots of numbers called out by the audience. His swift, accurate answers are impressive because we all know how cumbersome it is to calculate square roots. What we do not realize is that he has no need to calculate at all. He assumes that the audience will, to save labour and be able to check his answer, take some number, square it, and give him the result. So, assuming a perfect square, he applies special numerical knowledge and, by merely inspecting the number and especially its last two digits, detects what the square root must be. With cube rooting, the inspectional technique is even easier, granted knowledge of certain numerical facts and the assumption that the given number is a perfect cube. Such an entertainer would be embarrassed if given a number that is not a perfect cube and asked to express its cube root to several decimal places.

Fairly full and reliable information exists about the biographies and abilities of several people who properly deserve to be called calculating geniuses. Of these, the ablest and best documented is A. C. Aitken (1895–1967), an outstanding mathematical scholar with exceptional all-round intellectual accomplishments. At the age of 13 he became fascinated by mental calculation, and then spent years exploring numerical facts and calculative methods. In middle age, mental calculation lost its intrinsic appeal, and for certain calculations, such as multiplication by very large numbers, he used electric calculating machines which had, by then, come on the market. However, he still found it convenient, in his mathematical research, to do some calculations mentally, and so he never lost his ability. His nimble deployment of deep numerical knowledge is illustrated by the two following commentaries, both transcribed from a tape-recorded session.

After expressing 1/851 as a decimal, he reported as follows:

The instant observation was that 851 is 23 times 37. I use this fact as follows. 1/37 is 0.027027027, and so on repeated. This I divide mentally by 23. 23 into 0.027 is 0.001 with remainder 4. In a flash I can get that 23 into 4,027 is 175 with remainder 2. And into 2,027 is 88 with remainder 3. And into 3,027 is 131 with remainder 14. And even into 14,027 is 609 with remainder 20. And so on like that. Also, before I even start this . . . I know that there is a recurring period of sixty-six places.

He was asked to multiply 123 by 456, and gave the answer after a pause of two seconds. He then commented as follows:

I see at once that 123 times 450 is 55,350, and that 123 times 6 is 738; I hardly have to think. Then 55,350 plus 738 gives 56,088. Even at the moment of registering 56,088, I have checked it by dividing by 8, so 7,011, and this by 9 gives 779, I recognize 779 as 41 by 19. And 41 by 3 is 123, while 19 by 24 is 456. A check you see; and it passes by in about one second.

The study of calculating geniuses gives insight into how people develop and deploy their varied talents, and how development depends on the interplay of potential ability, interest, and opportunity. It also shows how intellectual skills must be organized differently in order to meet special requirements, such as calculating mentally rather than by using external recording devices. It reminds us that there are many ways of calculating—for example, logarithms, electronic calculating machines, and several forms of *abacus, among which the Japanese *soroban* is especially efficient in expert hands. Each of these calculative systems has its own balance of strengths and weaknesses, and each requires its user to master a distinctive repertoire of skills.

Much of the literature about calculating geniuses is patchy and regrettably unreliable. This is not always because people are inclined to exaggerate, but because it is so easy to gather false impressions when care is not taken to consider each calculator individually and to make precise observations about his ability. We go seriously astray if we assume that every calculator works in exactly the same way, or by conventional procedures that are somehow speeded up. Each uses a knowledge of numerical facts and methods which is, in its details, largely self-taught and uniquely his own.   IMLH

Hunter, I. M. L. (1962). 'An exceptional talent for calculative thinking'. *British Journal of Psychology*, 53.
——(1977). 'Mental calculation'. In Wason, P. C., and Johnson-Laird, P. N. (eds.), *Thinking: Readings in Cognitive Psychology*.
Mitchell, F. D. (1907). 'Mathematical prodigies'. *American Journal of Psychology*, 18.
Smith, S. B. (1983). *The Great Mental Calculators*.

calibrate. To adjust or compare an instrument with a standard, which may be man-made or naturally occurring.

The readings of instruments may be calibrated with correction tables, or curves, so that their errors can be compensated. One can think of much sensory adaptation as setting the calibration of sensory systems—which can be upset by maintained stimuli or by distortions, such as prolonged viewing through deviating prisms or distorting lenses. (See, for instance, AFTER-EFFECT, PERCEPTUAL.)

Cannon, Walter Bradford (1871–1945). American physiologist, born at Praire du Chien, Wisconsin, and educated at Harvard, where he was George Higginson Professor of Physiology at the Harvard Medical School from 1906 until 1945. As a student of medicine he started by studying the phenomenon of swallowing; this led him to observe the motions of the stomach and intestines, and his observations were summarized in *The Mechanical Factors of Digestion* (1911). He gradually moved towards studies of emotion as related to bodily changes, and this resulted in the important book *Bodily Changes in Pain, Hunger, Fear and Rage* (1919; 2nd edn. 1929), and in the work that remains a classic, *The Wisdom of the Body* (1932). For further details, including his critique of the James–Lange theory of emotion, see EMOTION.

Cannon developed the concept of *homeostasis, which in modern terminology is the *feedback control of servo-systems. This concept was not mathematically expressed until the work of Norbert *Wiener in the 1940s, when it became the basis of *cybernetics. Cannon was the first to see the importance of such regulatory mechanisms, which now control complex machines as well as organisms. His work is also a basis of current ideas on *psychosomatic disease.

Capgras's syndrome. This rare and unusual psychological disorder was first described by J. M. J. Capgras (1873–1950) and J. Reboul-Lachaux in 1923 under the title of 'l'illusion des sosies'. The patient comes to believe that familiar persons around him, usually close relatives, have been replaced by impostors who have assumed the exact appearances of those whom they have supplanted. Although this delusional belief has most often been described in patients suffering from schizophrenia or affective psychoses, it can also occur in the presence of organic disease of the brain. The poet Cowper, who suffered from recurrent bouts of manic–depressive psychosis, apparently was suffering from the condition when he came to doubt whether his friend the Revd John Newton was real or some phantom masquerading in his shape (Cecil 1965).

Although 'l'illusion des sosies' is usually translated as 'the illusion of doubles', it is evident that the afflicted person is suffering from a fixed delusional belief and not simply a misinterpretation of appearances. The term 'sosies' derives from the story of Amphitryon and his servant

Socias as recounted in the play by Plautus and later in revivals of the same story by Molière, Dryden, and, most recently, Giraudoux. Robert Graves (1960) recounts how Zeus planned to seduce Alcmene, Amphitryon's beautiful wife, by impersonating him during his absence at the wars. To add verisimilitude to the deception he persuaded Mercury to assume the shape of Socias (Sosie) and pretend that he had been sent ahead to announce Amphitryon's return. To prolong his enjoyment of Alcmene, Zeus arranged that the sun and moon should halt in their courses, so protracting one night to the duration of three. When the real Amphitryon finally returned he was not a little disappointed at Alcmene's lack of enthusiasm for his embraces. Nine months later she gave birth to Heracles.

Related to Capgras's syndrome is the 'illusion de Frégoli', in which the victim claims that persons well known to him are impersonating others, usually individuals said to be persecuting him. Frégoli was a well-known actor, famous for his ability to represent others by changing his facial appearance. The Frégoli phenomenon seems to be even rarer than 'l'illusion des sosies'.

The psychopathology of Capgras's syndrome has been variously interpreted. Some have regarded it as an extreme form of depersonalization. Marked ambivalence towards the person thought to be impersonated allows the patient to project negative feelings on to the impostor while preserving normal feelings of affection towards the one who has been supplanted. Such formulations may serve to explain this phenomenon in persons suffering from one or other of the functional psychoses, but they are inadequate when the delusional belief appears as the result of some physical disease or injury of the brain. In many patients the delusion remains fixed and unchanging but in others the phenomenon may gradually fade, although it is probably true to say that, whatever is done to help the patient, some lingering doubts about the true identity of the alleged impostor will persist. FAW

Cecil, D. (1965). *The Stricken Deer*.

Enoch, M. D., and Trethowan, W. H. (1979). *Uncommon Psychiatric Syndromes* (2nd edn.).

Graves, R. (1960). *The Greek Myths*.

Weston, M. J., and Whitlock, F. A. (1971). 'The Capgras syndrome following head injury'. *British Journal of Psychiatry*, 119.

Carmichael, Leonard (1898–1973). American psychobiologist, educator, and administrator. He was born in Philadelphia, and educated at Tufts University and Harvard.

Beginning in his student days Carmichael was attracted to the fields of animal behaviour, neuroembryology, neuroanatomy, and neurophysiology. These were topics which guided his considerable research efforts early in his career and which remained central to his scientific interests throughout his life. He was the first academic psychologist to study the prenatal origins of behaviour. In a series of now classic experiments begun during his first academic post at Princeton in 1924–5, Carmichael (1926) attempted to determine whether the experimental suppression of all motor behaviour in developing frog embryos, by the use of a paralytic anaesthetic, would impair the normal development and manifestation of swimming in the hatched tadpole. He found that the treatment had little if any effect on later behaviour; the treated tadpoles swam as efficiently as normal frogs. This was one of the first scientific demonstrations that practice, use, or experience during early development is not necessarily critical for normal neurobehavioural development. In subsequent years Carmichael and his students conducted important and extensive pioneering studies on fetal behaviour and physiology in mammals.

In addition to his laboratory research, Carmichael made many scholarly contributions to the field of psychobiology. Paramount among these was his editing of two editions of a fundamental reference work in the field of developmental psychobiology, *The Manual of Child Psychology* (1946, 1954).

Over a period spanning more than 50 years, Carmichael was a strong proponent of a developmental and psychobiological approach to the study of behavioural problems, and as a result he had a vital influence in formulating, and fostering the development of, our modern conceptualization of these problems.

Carmichael was widely honoured during his career, and, in a brief autobiography published in 1967, he noted that 'if I were asked what thread seems to me to have run most consistently through my career, I could answer the question in one word, *Research*'. Despite having stopped his own direct involvement in laboratory research by about 1940, it is therefore fitting that it is his early research contributions that will remain as his most important and lasting legacy. RWO

Carmichael, L. (1926). 'The development of behavior in vertebrates experimentally removed from the influence of external stimulation'. *Psychological Review*, 33.

—— (ed.) (1946, 1954). *The Manual of Child Psychology*.

—— (1967). 'An autobiography'. In Boring, E. G., and Lindzey, L. (eds.), *A History of Psychology in Autobiography*, vol. v.

Carr, Harvey (1873–1954). American psychologist, born in Indiana and educated mainly at the University of Chicago, gaining his doctorate in 1905. He replaced J. B. *Watson as an assistant professor when Watson left for Johns Hopkins in 1904, and remained in Chicago right up to his retirement in 1938, being chairman of his department for much of this period.

Carr's main interests lay in space perception, on which he published a useful book, and comparative psychology, the study of which had always been prominent in the

Chicago laboratory. While Carr held to a *behaviourist line in the case of animal psychology, he remained convinced that human psychology could not be satisfactorily explained without reference to *consciousness. At the same time, he was distinctly sceptical of conventional classification in psychology and always warned his pupils of the hazards of reification. He was even doubtful whether psychology justified its claim to be a fully fledged scientific discipline. OLZ

Carroll, Lewis (pseudonym of Charles Lutwidge Dodgson, 1832–98). British author and logician. He was mathematical lecturer at Christ Church, Oxford (1855–81). *Alice's Adventures in Wonderland* (1865) and *Through the Looking-Glass* (1872) introduced logical puzzles to children and to their parents. He also wrote serious logical and mathematical works: *Euclid and his Modern Rivals* (1879), *Curiosa mathematica* (1888–93), *Symbolic Logic* (1896), and a paper on *Zeno's paradoxes, 'What the tortoise said to Achilles', in *Mind* (1895).

Cohen, M. N. (1996). *Lewis Carroll: A Biography.*

Cartesianism. See DESCARTES, RENÉ.

cartoon. The fact that even very simple drawings convey facial expressions and other rich perceptions is excellent evidence of the creative power of *perception. Cartoonists, by discovering which features of drawings are important, have managed to latch onto the key features for normal perception. There must be a great store of knowledge of perception (if implicit) that artists use. See also ART AND VISUAL ABSTRACTION.

Gombrich, E. H. (2000). *Art and Illusion.*

catecholamines. The principal catecholamines found in the mammalian nervous system are noradrenaline (norepinephrine), *dopamine, and *adrenaline (epinephrine). The adrenal medulla, an endocrine gland which receives innervation from the sympathetic nervous system, contains the largest quantities of catecholamines in the body. This tissue was used in pioneer studies to determine the biosynthetic pathway for the catecholamines. This is as follows: TYROSINE→ DIHYDROXYPHENYLALANINE → DOPAMINE → NORADRENALINE → ADRENALINE.

The ability of cells to synthesize catecholamines depends on the presence of enzymes which catalyse the conversion of tyrosine, taken up from the bloodstream, to dihydroxyphenylalanine, dopamine, noradrenaline, and adrenaline. Noradrenaline and adrenaline in the adrenal medulla function as hormones and are released into the bloodstream in response to activation of the input it receives from the sympathetic nervous system. This occurs during physiological responses to stressful stimuli such as sudden anger, fear, severe cold, or physical exercise.

In the peripheral nervous system, the postganglionic neurons of the sympathetic division of the *autonomic nervous system synthesize and release noradrenaline as a *neurotransmitter, thereby influencing the activity of smooth muscle cells in a wide variety of tissues. For example, they control the diameter of the pupil, the smooth muscle in blood vessels of the salivary glands (thus influencing glandular secretion), the rate of the heartbeat, the diameter of the coronary arteries, the diameter of bronchi in the lungs, the activity of smooth muscle in the bowel (thus influencing movement of intestinal contents), the smooth muscle activity in a variety of pelvic organs, and the diameter of small blood vessels and hence blood flow in large areas of skin and muscle throughout the body. These diverse tissues can thus be influenced by the sympathetic nervous system to respond in a coordinated fashion to stressful stimuli. The well-known cold sweaty hands, fast heartbeat, dilated pupils, and pale complexion produced by fear are explicable in terms of the known hormonal and neurotransmitter actions of the catecholamines.

The brain contains another and separate family of neurons using catecholamines as neurotransmitters. These contain adrenaline, noradrenaline, or dopamine. Adrenaline neurons are few in number and are located in the brain stem. They send their axons down into the spinal cord and into the hypothalamus, as well as to a region of the brain stem known as the nucleus of the tractus solitarius. There is evidence that adrenaline plays a role in this latter nucleus in the control of blood pressure. Abnormally high blood pressure is a common clinical problem, and it is therefore of interest that a genetically distinct strain of laboratory rat has been found in which there are abnormally high quantities of the enzyme that synthesizes adrenaline. These rats suffer from high blood pressure.

Noradrenaline neurons are scattered in small groups throughout the brain stem. The largest of these, the locus ceruleus, contains only a few thousand neurons, but they provide branching axons which together innervate a vast area of the brain and spinal cord. Furthermore, neurons may provide axons to innervate, for example, both cerebellum and cerebral cortex. Therefore these neurons may influence widely separate and functionally distinct brain areas simultaneously (see NEURONAL CONNECTIVITY AND BRAIN FUNCTION). Morphologically these neurons have many similarities to other parts of the brain-stem reticular formation, and make many functional contacts with other divisions of the reticular formation. All the evidence points to the fact that the synaptic actions (see SYNAPSES) of noradrenaline are relatively diffuse (or hormone-like) and act over a relatively slow time course of seconds (compared to a time course of milliseconds for *acetylcholine), while the action of the transmitter is mediated by slow chemical changes rather than fast changes in ionic channels in the nerve-cell membrane. In most cases it seems that the action of the transmitter on single neurons is inhibitory, although it appears to operate without altering the responses of neurons to other specific input stimuli.

As would be expected from the very widespread distribution of noradrenaline fibres in the brain and spinal cord, they appear to influence a correspondingly large number of functions. There seems little doubt that they are involved in the regulation of general brain states such as arousal and sleep, and the coordination of the many brain functions appropriate to these states. It is of interest that drugs which appear to have clinical activity in alleviating depressive illness are able to act by altering the availability of noradrenaline at the receptor level. Noradrenaline fibres may also have a role to play in the establishment and selection of normal synaptic connections during development and in the recovery of function after damage to the nervous system.

The third main group of catecholamine neurons of the brain are those utilizing dopamine as transmitter. These neurons have been the subject of much research, because there are two common clinical conditions alleviated by drugs that interact with dopamine neurons—*Parkinsonism and *schizophrenia.   OTP

Cattell, James McKeen (1860–1944). American psychologist born in Easton, Pennsylvania, the son of the Presbyterian president of a small East Coast university. He studied under Rudolf Lotze (1817–81) at Göttingen, following which he worked for three years with Wilhelm *Wundt at Leipzig and took his doctorate. He then spent a year at St John's College, Cambridge, and at this time made the acquaintance of Francis *Galton, by whom he was immensely impressed. Had he stayed permanently in Cambridge—which at the time he was strongly tempted to do—it is likely that he would have played an important role in the growth and development of experimental psychology in the university.

Cattell's work at Leipzig was largely concerned with measurements of reaction times, which he continued for some time at the University of Pennsylvania after his return to the United States, publishing an important paper with C. S. Fullerton on the perception of small differences. His next move was to Columbia University, where together with E. L. *Thorndike he built up the leading laboratory in America principally concerned with mental tests and the measurement of individual differences. It would thus appear that it was Galton rather than Wundt who had the major influence on his career.   OLZ

Sokal, M. M. (ed.) (1981). *An Education in Psychology: James McKeen Cattell, Journal and Letters from Germany and England 1880–1888.*

causes. The earliest treatments of causality link the concept firmly to that of explanation. Aristotle defines *aitia* (the Latin translation of which is *causa*, from whence our 'cause') as something that answers the question 'why?' (*dia ti?*). Such a question asks for an explanation of some kind, an answer beginning 'because . . .'. If one asks what distinguishes an explanation from other forms of information, such as a mere description, the answer implicit in Aristotle's discussion is that an explanation starts with what is taken to be a correct description of something and indicates what constrained or necessitated that thing to be as it is. An explanation, in other words, shows how the possibilities were restricted so that things *had* to be that way, so that had one known the explanation one would have been justified in expecting things to be that way. This is a task which the citation of a cause is meant to perform. A cause is cited to explain, to show that something is or was in some way necessary.

It is a mark of how the concept of cause has taken on a meaning more specific than simply 'an explanation' or 'what explains' that the so-called 'four Aristotelian causes' are likely to strike a modern mind as having little to do with causes. Regarded as a fourfold classification of explanatory patterns, however, the doctrine is not at all implausible. (The following examples are not Aristotle's, but Aristotelian in spirit.) If one asks why a certain act which resulted in the death of a person counts as murder, one will be referred to an account of what murder is: an Aristotelian *formal* explanation. If one asks 'through what' (a more literal translation of *dia ti?*) means a murder was carried out—was it poison, gunshot, a blow to the head?—one will be referred to an Aristotelian *material* explanation. If one asks why the murderer committed the act, one may be asking for a motive, such as inheriting the victim's money, which is an Aristotelian *final* explanation. Or one may be asking what prompted the murderer to act just then (a short temper and an insult, or greed and the victim's threat to alter his will), i.e. for an Aristotelian *efficient* cause / explanation.

Of the four, it is most natural nowadays to speak of 'cause' in connection with the last of these and then only in connection with a subclass of what Aristotle termed 'a source of change or remaining the same'. For Aristotle gives as examples of such 'causes', human agents, their dispositional states, and also what may be called 'triggering events', i.e. events which set in motion some further event. It is examples of the last sort that set the pattern of contemporary discussions of causality. The historical reason for this lies in a shift in thinking about patterns of explanation which took place in the 17th century.

Aristotelian explanations of natural phenomena ultimately come to rest on the natures (forms, *essences) of things, which are expressed in terms of complexes of active and passive powers. Thus a concept of natural agency is central to Aristotelian explanations of natural phenomena; things cause changes to take place (or fail to take place) by virtue of the powers which constitute them as the sorts of things they are. As a result of developments in the 17th century, explanations came to be thought of as resting on laws rather than on natural agencies. A law is a relationship between quantitative aspects of natural phenomena which can be expressed in the form of a mathematical function. What was explained was no longer the action of one thing on another, but the law-governed interactions which took place between things, such as the motions that resulted when one body collided with another.

But the notion of agency, which is almost certainly modelled on the way we account for the affairs of human beings, is deeply rooted in our thought; and as long as the implications of the shift in explanatory practices were unclear, there was a tendency to look for the powers which had belonged to agents in the events governed by laws, as though an event at the beginning of some law-governed interaction had by itself the power to effect what took place.

The 18th-century philosopher David Hume was able, without any deep familiarity with the science of his day, to reflect in his analysis of causality both the change in forms of explanation to patterns of interaction and the precarious position which the notion of agency had come to occupy. He concluded that a cause was an 'object' (a word which many read in this context as 'event') preceding and spatially adjacent to another (the effect) where we have observed objects resembling the first in 'like relations of precedency and contiguity to those objects that resemble the latter'. As for the limitation of possibility which is the function that cause performs in explanation, Hume dismissed the notion of power as without foundation in experience and concluded that our idea that what we identify as related as cause and effect are in some way necessarily linked is the product of feeling the habit of mind which has been formed by observing so many similar pairs of objects, the one preceding the other.

Hume's analysis does far less justice than does Aristotle's to the variety of forms of explanation which we still use with apparent success every day, and it has not gone unremarked that his approach to *necessity* undermines the hopes of science to establish for us what are the laws of nature. His analysis has, however, had the salutary effect of raising the question of the empirical foundation of our (supposed) knowledge of necessity, and the possibility of our giving explanations. One way of trying not to capitulate to Hume is to pre-empt the question and to argue along the lines suggested by *Kant that experience, i.e. anything that would constitute an empirical foundation for any knowledge, must use, if not the notion

of cause, then that of natural possibility/necessity. There would, if this strategy were successful, be no question of our right to use these notions, only a question of how well we manage to use them.

See also MENTAL CONCEPTS: CAUSAL ANALYSIS.   JET

Harré, R., and Madden, E. H. (1975). *Causal Powers*.
Mackie, J. (1974). *The Cement of the Universe: A Study of Causation*.
Sorabji, R. (1980). *Necessity, Cause and Blame: Perspectives on Aristotle's Theory*.

cerebellum. The region of the brain (posterior below the striate cortex) mainly responsible for coordinating movement.

Highstein, S. M., Thach, W. T., and Nasarina, T. T. (2002). *The Cerebellum: Recent Developments in Cerebellar Research*.

cerebral achromatopsia. By definition, any visual system will respond to the presence of light. Different visual systems vary in their ability to resolve fine detail in the spatial distribution of light, and in their response to rapid changes in the distribution of light. This leads to different acuities and sensitivities to movement.

Many visual systems also have the ability to distinguish between different parts of the visual field on the basis of different distributions of wavelengths of light reaching the eye from various places in the field of view. The perceptual correlate of this ability to distinguish light of different wavelength is called colour vision. Humans are just one of many species which have this ability—so when we see different colours, it is because the eye is viewing a scene which reflects different distributions of wavelengths in the visible spectrum (about 400 to 700 nanometres).

The basis for this ability to see different colours is that we have three different kinds of cone receptor cells in the retina, each responding best to different parts of the visible spectrum. They are often referred to as L, M, and S cones (long-, medium-, and short-wave sensitive). The relationship between the absorption of these cones and human colour vision is well understood and forms the basis of colour reproduction systems such as colour TV. What is less well understood is what happens to the information from the cones once it gets distributed in the visual cortex. Briefly, what seems to be happening is as follows:

- The signals from the three cone types get transmitted as opponent pairs, such as L−M and Y−B where Y = L+M (see Parraga, Troscianko, and Tolhurst 2002 for a description of what this implies for the coding of natural images).
- There is also a luminance (intensity) representation from the combined L+M cone activity.
- There has been debate about the extent to which colour and luminance information is used in the encoding

of visual attributes such as movement—see points below.

- Human vision contains neurons which respond to rapid changes in light and are often assumed to be insensitive to colour (see Troscianko et al. 1996);
- The chromatic pathways mentioned above have a rather sluggish response to rapid changes and are therefore considered to be poor encoders of movement (see Troscianko et al. 1996).

The argument about the above aspects of human vision has been informed as a result of the existence of a rare and highly interesting type of brain damage. Patients suffering from damage to the visual cortex (e.g. as a result of stroke or a blow to the head) occasionally report that they see the world in 'shades of grey' after the damage has occurred. Their retinae are completely unaffected by this, and for at least some of the people it is known that their colour vision was normal before the onset of the damage. The damage is therefore in the brain, not the eye. The condition is called cerebral (or central) achromatopsia, to distinguish it from an inability to see colour because there is only one receptor type in the retina, as can also occur (see Meadows 1974, Mollon et al. 1980).

Various research groups set out to study such individuals, and a curious finding began to emerge. While it seems universally true that the people reported seeing only shades of grey, they could perform above chance in tasks that required some colour discrimination. For example, if two colours of equal luminance were placed side by side, it was found that achromatopsic individuals knew that there was something different about the two halves of the display, without being aware of the colours. Confusingly, some patients were also able to name a few colours correctly, again apparently without 'seeing' them. Thus, evidence was emerging that there was some colour information in the brain, without this information allowing people to have conscious perception of colour (see Heywood, Cowey, and Newcombe 1991, Troscianko et al. 1996, Cavanagh et al. 1998, Heywood, Kentridge, and Cowey 1998).

We were fortunate to be able to study three such patients: HJA, WM, and JPC (Troscianko et al. 1996, Cavanagh et al. 1998). They were all achromatopsic in that they reported seeing the world in 'shades of grey' but they had intact retinae. We devised experiments in which the patients had to respond 'same' or 'different' while looking at a TV display in which the two halves of the screen were either the same or different. The differences could be of luminance, or colour, or both luminance and colour. This allowed us to study the contribution which colour information made to their performance level, without at any point requiring the patient to perceive the colour consciously. As in other such research, we found that performance was better when there was a colour *and* a luminance difference, rather than a colour difference alone.

We were keen to find out how this 'unconscious' colour information was being transmitted in the visual system. We added 'noise' consisting of random variations in luminance which were either unchanging in time (static noise) or alternating 25 times per second (dynamic noise). This noise had a dramatic, but different, effect on the patients. HJA's ability to respond to colour information was unimpaired with dynamic noise but got worse with static noise. This is as expected from what is generally known about colour vision – since colour information is insensitive to rapid change (see above), putting in such rapid change should not impair colour-based performance. However, patient WM showed a very different set of results: his performance dropped to chance with dynamic noise. We were at a loss to understand why this should be, since the noise should not be visible to neurons encoding colour information. We hypothesized that there must be another stream of 'colour' information in vision that responds to rapid changes, but does not reach conscious perception.

What might be the function of such additional information? It seemed likely (given its fast response) that it might be involved in movement perception. We therefore tested WM in a brain-imaging system using functional magnetic resonance imaging (fMRI) (see BRAIN IMAGING: METHODS), expecting to find an augmented response, with colour information present, of the area known as V5 which is known to encode motion signals. We found no such augmented response (Troscianko et al. 1997). However, psychophysical experiments on several achromatopsic patients including WM and JPC showed that their perception of motion was indeed much affected by colour information. Thus, it seemed that we were on the right track but that area V5 was *not* the locus of the effect.

This issue was finally settled by some further fMRI work by a group at Harvard (Hadjikhani et al. 1998). By requiring participants to look at alternating colours, or colours alternating with a grey field and producing coloured after-images, they showed that there may be a separate area of the visual cortex (which they named V8). This area seems to be involved in the conscious perception of colour. So the hypothesis is that this may be the area which is damaged in cerebral achromatopsia. This leaves intact the ability of the 'unconscious' colour information to assist with the encoding of movement, but this is not likely to occur in V5, but rather may occur in a different extra-striate area. Together with the Harvard group, we confirmed that patients WM and JPC had a largely intact contribution of colour to motion perception. Therefore, the function of this unconscious colour information in our cortex is to enhance motion information. To perceive colour consciously, we require another separate cortical area, and it is this which is damaged in cerebral achromatopsia.

The study of individuals who lack colour perception has therefore taught us a surprising amount about the neural basis of colour information.   TT

Cavanagh, P., Henaff, M.-A., Michel, F., Landis, T., Troscianko, T., and Intriligator, J. (1998). 'Complete sparing of high-contrast color input to motion perception in cortical color blindness'. *Nature Neuroscience*, 1.

Hadjikhani, N., Liu, A. K., Dale, A. M., Cavanagh, P., and Tootell, R. B. H. (1998). 'Retinotopy and color sensitivity in human cortical area V8'. *Nature Neuroscience*, 1.

Heywood, C. A., Cowey, A., and Newcombe, F. (1991). 'Chromatic discrimination in a cortically colour blind observer'. *European Journal of Neuroscience*, 3.

—— Kentridge, R. W., and Cowey, A. (1998). 'Form and motion from colour in cerebral achromatopsia'. *Experimental Brain Research*, 123.

Meadows, J. C. (1974). 'Disturbed perception of colours associated with localized cerebral lesions'. *Brain*, 97.

Mollon, J. D., Newcombe, F., Polden, P. G., and Ratcliffe, G. (1980). 'On the presence of three cone mechanisms in a case of total achromatopsia'. In Mollon et al. (eds.), *Colour Vision Deficiencies*, vol v.

Parraga, C. A., Troscianko, T., and Tolhurst, D. J. (2002). 'Spatio-chromatic properties of natural images and human vision'. *Current Biology*, 12.

Troscianko, T., Davidoff, J., Humphreys, G., Landis, T., Fahle, M., Greenlee, M., Brugger, P., and Phillips, W. (1996). 'Human colour discrimination based on a non-parvocellular pathway'. *Current Biology*, 6.

—— Greenlee, M. W., Brugger, P., Freitag, P., Kraemer, F. M., and Radue, E. W. (1997). 'An fMRI investigation of a patient with cerebral achromatopsia: evidence for a role of chromatic extrastriate mechanisms in motion encoding'. *Perception*, 26 (suppl.).

cerebral cortex. The outer layer or 'bark' (from the Greek) of the brain, associated with sensory perception and the higher mental functions. It appeared late in evolution, and is especially developed in man.

cerebral dominance. See HANDEDNESS; NEUROPSYCHOLOGY.

channels, neural. One normally thinks of a channel as a physically existing and easily seen structure, such as a river course. Nerve fibres are, similarly, easily seen courses along which neural signals flow. The situation, however, is not at all simple in neurophysiology because a whole sensory modality, such as vision or hearing, may be called a channel, even though many thousands of nerve fibres comprise these 'channels'. Conversely, and even more tricky, a single physical channel may transmit several channels of information. Thus telephone systems employ a single high-frequency link along which many messages can be simultaneously transmitted, each on its own 'carrier frequency' which is modulated by the channel signals to keep the messages separate. Here the separation is given not in any obvious physical or visible way, but by splitting the very wide frequency range of the carrier into several frequency bands, which provide independent information channels. There seem to be somewhat analogous ways in which different signals are carried separately on shared nerve fibres. Also, by selective attention it is possible to switch from one signal source to another, so that what is effective depends on selection rather than simply on laid down neural channels.

It is now believed that the visual system is organized into many more or less independent channels, not only for colour (which uses three channels) but also, and perhaps more surprisingly, for different orientations of lines or edges, directions of movement, brightness, and texture size. Isolating and studying channel characteristics is an important part of current experimental work on how the senses function. Just how the channels converge to a single unified perception (which used to be called the *common sense) is not yet understood.

What use are channels? If information transmission was the only requirement for designing sensory channels, then just one, covering all the physical information, might suffice. However, the information also has to be analysed and, if there are many different channels, they can sort the information into relevant categories to start the perceptual processing. Many of the objects in the environment are only recognizable in terms of a combination of different physical attributes (think how you would recognize bacon cooking). Likewise many of our actions are determined by the information from various different physical sources. These different physical attributes and sources have therefore to be distinguished and it is convenient to allow the selectivity of channels to make initial distinctions. Conversely, sometimes a particular object can be partially specified by one source of physical information (think how you can search a crowd for a friend wearing a scarlet hat), and in this case a channel more or less specific to that information is very useful.

If I have a private channel from A to B, the receiver at B knows a great deal about the incoming messages in advance, such as their type and range, because these are simply inherent to the channel. The selectivity of a channel is a type of advance knowledge which allows the receiver to correct any systematic errors in the channel. Imagine a channel transmitting edge curvatures, which are physically as often curved one way as any other. If the receiver simply compares each incoming message with the distribution of messages that it has received in the past it will automatically *calibrate the channel for any distortions that it introduces.

All channels have physical limits on the amount of information that they can transmit, but some physical attributes, for example luminance contrast, can take a wide range of values. In such instances, it is useful to be able to split the whole range into a number of separate bands and assign one channel per band. This arrangement allows the transmission of a wide range of values with high accuracy.

Luminance contrast is an interesting case. Imagine a diffuse shadow lying across a finely chequered surface. The luminance contrast between any adjacent black and white squares will always be the same because the shadow will equally affect the two. However, the luminance contrast between a black and a white square that are separated will be affected by the shadow, which may lie over one but not the other. Long-range contrast is different in this case from short-range contrast, even though they physically overlap in space. A channel for contrast must work over some predefined spatial range, and a long-range channel would be indifferent to short-range contrast and vice versa. Therefore it is necessary to have several contrast channels, each selective for a different spatial range.

Many physical aspects of our environment have this complicated overlap property. The wavelength of light is another instance: any physical surface reflects a wide range of different wavelengths. Sound and speech is another interesting case. In a room where several people are speaking at the same time, the air is vibrating in response to all of them together. The perceptual process has a problem, the *'cocktail party problem', because it has to break the air vibrations down in portions that will allow it to select one speaker's message. The hearing system has channels that are selective to frequency of sound and direction and these are thought to provide the basis for this selection.

It is sensible to have many channels for several reasons. They organize the overall sensory information into a structure which is suitable for subsequent cognitive processing. They also allow for automatic calibration and adaptation to prevailing conditions in the physical environment.

Empirically, it has so far proved easier to identify channels than to discover how their outputs are combined or used. Channels can be discovered by seeking interactions between the processing of very similar physical stimuli. Gazing at a periodic pattern of high-contrast black and white stripes will make the visual system less sensitive to very similar patterns, but does not affect sensitivity to patterns where the stripes have a considerably different size or direction (see AFTER-EFFECT, PERCEPTUAL). Similarly, similar patterns will interfere when present simultaneously if they are processed by the same channel. In these observations the important point is the selectivity of the effect for a particular range of physical stimuli, and

this range is thought to correspond to the selectivity of the channel itself.   RLG/RJW

Andrews, D. P. (1964). 'Error-correcting perceptual mechanisms'. *Quarterly Journal of Experimental Psychology*, 16.

Braddick, O., Campbell, F. W., and Atkinson, J. (1978). 'Channels in vision: basic aspects'. In Held, R., Leibowitz, H., and Teuber, H. L. (eds.), *Handbook of Sensory Physiology*, vol. viii.

Charcot, Jean Martin

Charcot, Jean Martin (1825–93). French neurologist, born in Paris, where he qualified in medicine. In 1853 he began to work at the Salpêtrière, becoming physician-in-chief in 1866 and professor of clinical neurology in 1882. He was a brilliant diagnostician and was the first to recognize a number of nervous diseases including multiple sclerosis and the 'lightning pains' of tabes dorsalis. Towards the end of his life, he became much interested in *hysteria and its treatment by *hypnosis, in which he likewise became deeply interested. Among the many who studied with Charcot was Sigmund *Freud, upon whom he made a lasting impression.   OLZ

Guillain, G. (1959). *J. M. Charcot: His Life, his Work.* trans. P. Bailey.

Charles Bonnet syndrome

Charles Bonnet syndrome. Characterized by visual hallucinations, this syndrome was first described in 1780, by the biologist Charles Bonnet (1720–93). Although the condition was known then, it is often goes unrecognized in present clinical practice. This is due partly to the under-reporting of symptoms by patients associating hallucinations with mental illness.

Charles Bonnet syndrome (CBS) occurs in people with visual impairment and is most common in the elderly. Although the aetiology of CBS is unclear, cognitive defects, social isolation, and sensory deprivation have all been implicated. The hallucinations consist of well-defined clear images that are not under the patient's control and may involve a variety of images from simple lines and patterns to complex scenes of fictional and non-fictional characters and places. Images last from seconds through minutes to hours. Patients usually have insight into the unreality of their experience, although those that do not may be distressed by the fear of insanity.

Unfortunately, there is no known cure or treatment for CBS. However, reassurance and explanation that the visions are not real and do not signify mental illness have positive therapeutic effects. Hallucinations may stop following improved visual function or addressing social isolation. Measures such as 'looking' at the images, attempting to approach them, and conversing with them have also been reported to terminate hallucinations. Anticonvulsants may play a limited role in alleviating hallucinations, but the most powerful approaches 'remain empathy sensitivity, communication and reassurance' (Menon et al. 2003).   RLG

Menon, G. J., Rahman, I., Menon, S. J., and Dutton, G. N. (2003). 'Complex visual hallucinations in the visually impaired:

the Charles Bonnet syndrome'. *Survey of Ophthalmology*, 48/1.

Cheselden, William (1688–1752). British surgeon, born near Melton Mowbray in Leicestershire. He became surgeon at St Thomas's Hospital, and later at the Royal Hospital, Chelsea, where he organized the separation of the old Barber-Surgeons' Company, to found the Corporation of Surgeons in 1745 by Act of Parliament. The foremost surgeon of his day, and an excellent anatomist, he was influential also on account of his birth, as his family was entitled to a coat of arms—an unusual advantage, as surgeons of his time were seldom socially acceptable. He was a close friend, among other intellectuals, of the poet Alexander Pope and the painter Jonathan Richardson, whose fine portrait of him hangs in the Council Chamber of the Royal College of Surgeons. Cheselden attended Sir Isaac Newton in his final illness, advising against an operation for stones.

Cheselden was the first to create by operation on the eye an artificial pupil, and he developed improved procedures and instruments for removal of cataract. A case of restoration of sight in 1728 remains famous: the removal of congenital cataracts by 'couching' in a boy 13 or 14 years old who had no previous vision except some indication of the colours of bright lights. (See BLINDNESS, RECOVERY FROM, for a full discussion of this case.)   RLG

Cope, Z. (1953). *William Cheselden.*

chess. See COMPUTER CHESS.

child abuse. Human beings can go to great lengths to care for and to protect children; yet since history began children have been abused. It was not, however, until the 19th century that social reformers in Europe and North America influenced legislation by showing that children employed under conditions accepted as normal were in fact being seriously abused.

Awareness that the two contradictory states, caring for children yet abusing them, could exist side by side was not evident among members of the medical profession and many others caring for children until very recently. Despite a description in 1888 of the signs of child abuse, it was not until Henry Kempe and his associates published in 1962 the now classic paper, emotively entitled 'The Battered Child Syndrome', that professional eyes opened. Shock and initial disbelief were followed by a growing acceptance of Kempe's findings, leading to an extensive literature and registers of children at risk. This sharpening of awareness is illustrated by the paediatrician who, in a recent presidential address, while pointing out clear-cut and unequivocal signs of physical abuse in infants and young children, stated that over a period of seven years

of general paediatric practice he had never seen a case of child abuse because he had not been looking for it.

The term 'child abuse' refers to a number of areas and is usefully considered under three headings. These cover: (i) general neglect, systematic poisoning, and physical violence—which in recent years has been euphemistically relabelled non-accidental injury; (ii) sexual abuse, which since the late 1970s has become increasingly recognized and found to be widespread; and (iii) psychological abuse, a concept that is gaining ground. It is safe to work on the assumption that children subjected to any form of general physical or sexual abuse will also suffer psychological abuse. Moreover, many children who are not physically abused are deliberately made to suffer painful psychological states such as fear, rejection, and loneliness which constitute abuse. The statements that follow refer to findings on non-sexual physical abuse.

All figures on the extent of child abuse are at best imprecise estimates. Furthermore, findings from different studies are not easily compared because workers tend to focus upon different aspects of the subject and to express their findings in different ways. It can however be estimated that in the USA approximately one in every 100 children under 18 is physically abused, sexually molested, or severely neglected; the figure is probably about the same for England and Wales. It is a conservative estimate that up to 10 per cent of abused children die, and that at least 25 per cent suffer serious neurological damage with impairment of intelligence. The epidemiology of child abuse has been reviewed by Jack Oliver (in Smith 1978). Since about 1960 the figures have tended to increase, but it is an unanswerable question whether this reflects greater recognition of the condition or an actual increase in its extent.

Child abuse is not a haphazard occurrence, despite evidence that anyone sufficiently stressed by adversity is liable to abuse a child judged uncooperative. As a group, abusers show certain characteristics, although many people with the same characteristics do not abuse children. For instance, abusers are most frequently parents, stepparents, or others in charge of the child. Parents who abuse tend to be young, unskilled, and often from lower social classes. Criminality, recidivism, and low intelligence are common, whereas mental illness, severe alcoholism, and drug addiction are less frequently found. There is evidence that many abusers show disorders of personality, or neuroses coupled with a sense of low self-esteem, but there is no homogeneous personality profile. They tend to have difficult relationships with their spouses or partners, family, and friends, and consequently have little support or help despite, frequently, suffering hardships such as poor housing and unemployment.

Abusing parents have themselves usually been abused as children. They frequently function at the emotional level of a young child, and the abuse occurs during outbursts of uncontrolled anger. They have, almost always, unrealistic expectations of the abused child, who is expected to be obedient and empathic to the parent's needs, and to have a degree of control over natural functions and behaviour appropriate to a much older child or to an adult. This feature is frequently so marked as to constitute a role reversal: it is as if the child is expected to be the parent of the parent.

There is no one set of characteristics that distinguishes children who are abused, although there is evidence that some groups are especially vulnerable: for instance, the youngest child, any under two years, the premature, and children with congenital deformities. Commonly one child in a family is abused more than the others.

There is now evidence that it is a common human characteristic for parents not to feel love immediately for their newly born offspring and that a loving, protective attitude becomes established as a result of social interaction between infant and parents, in which each plays a part—a process often referred to as 'bonding' (see ATTACHMENT). In many instances of abuse associated with difficult family relationships, the ability of parents to develop their capacities to protect and to care consistently for an infant appears to be limited. In such families particular dynamic patterns can be identified. For example, so long as the infant is an 'easy baby', rewarding to handle and healthy, all may be well, and while this state continues the infant may be protected and loved. Intense anger, associated with irresistible impulses to force the child to comply with the parent's wishes, is, however, aroused whenever the infant's behaviour leads one, or both, parents to feel inadequate (the irritable or sickly baby, the baby who is difficult to feed or to pacify), or to feel rejected by the baby (the unresponsive baby who seldom smiles). In other instances, anger is directed towards the baby because the relationship cannot be isolated from the relationships the parents have with each other or with other members of the family.

Some common examples of family dynamics associated with abuse are: (i) the parents feel they are in some way to blame, because the child is malformed, or because the child's physical attributes or sex do not meet with family or cultural expectations. (ii) One parent, usually the father, or a sibling, feels unloved and jealous because of the attention given to the baby by the other parent. (iii) Anger aroused by someone towards whom a parent cannot show anger is redirected towards the baby, who cannot retaliate. (iv) Abuse is a Medea-like attempt on the part of one spouse to take revenge on the other. The assumption is that it will hurt that spouse if the baby is hurt. (v) A love-hungry parent may demand an unrealistic degree of altruistic devotion, companionship, and love from a child—who is attacked because he or she cannot meet these expectations. An overview of the subject of child abuse has been edited by Ellerstein (1981).

We are still far from constructing a comprehensive theoretical model to explain social behaviour in man, and it may never be possible to explain all instances of child abuse by a single model. For example, abuse by parents who suffer recognizable mental illness—when the abuse is often bizarre—may have a distinctive origin. Nevertheless, many of the characteristics described above are seen frequently enough to suggest that it may be possible to find a theory that will allow useful predictions to be made in many instances of child abuse. The model would have to explain why intensely angry impulses towards a child are regularly aroused whenever the behaviour of the child results in a parent feeling inadequate, lonely, or rejected. Ethologists such as Konrad Lorenz have suggested that harmful behaviour to babies and young animals is inhibited by an innate releasing mechanism which responds to the total configuration characterizing 'babyishness'. For some unknown reason those who abuse their children are apparently not endowed with this innate response to their offspring's behaviour and morphological features. The most comprehensive theory available today postulates that anger as described above is an emotional response to rejection and to a sense of inadequacy. This is attachment theory, formulated by John *Bowlby and elaborated by Mary Ainsworth.

Attachment theory has been described as 'programmatic', in that it acts as a guide to understanding data and to further research. It can be seen as a new paradigm for understanding social development. The theory has integrated several major trends in biological and social science. It is based on the assumptions (i) that behaviour is organized around plans to reach set goals, (ii) that in order to reach goals one has to have internal representations, or working models, of the world in which one acts, and of one's self in action in that world, and (iii) that behaviour is governed by control systems—kinds of mechanisms such that certain behaviour is evoked by specific circumstances and terminated by others. Using these basic assumptions, attachment theory postulates that the infant is born with the potential to develop an internal behavioural system mediating attachment behaviour. The goal of attachment behaviour is to attain physical closeness to and interaction with familiar, more experienced people (attachment figures). Attachment behaviour can be activated at any age, and is aroused whenever strangeness, fear, or physical states such as hunger, fatigue, or malaise are experienced. There is also a complementary inbuilt system, usually fully functional in adults, which mediates parental caregiving. Caregiving behaviour, when effective, terminates attachment behaviour in another person, and restores a child (or indeed another adult) to a state in which he or she is able to explore and to enjoy the surrounding world and relate to others in a caregiving way. Without such experience of caregiving the child, or adult, feels angry and rejected; angry protests then alternate with states of despair.

Child abuse is difficult to treat; but in many instances it is possible, after the first discovery of abuse, to promote the development of effective parental caregiving behaviour, by providing understanding helpers who act, as it were, as surrogate grandparents, taking an active part in supporting and educating parents so that they can achieve a sense of attainment about their lives and parental responsibilities.

Punishment of abusing parents is singularly ineffective. A reason for this can be predicted from attachment theory. Punishment, insofar as it evokes fear and feelings of rejection, arouses the parents' own attachment behaviour and leaves them unassuaged. Moreover, the parents are not helped to develop effective parental behaviour.

It is an important preventive measure to take steps to promote the development of affectionate parent–child relationships, by ensuring that the child and parents have the opportunity to interact right from birth onward, and so build up the new relationships. There is now growing evidence (Bretherton and Waters 1985) that development of harmonious relationships between parents and child is facilitated first by close physical contact between them in a supportive, comforting environment immediately after birth followed by responsive, supportive, and companionable interaction thereafter.

Nevertheless, in some instances it is found that, even with help, a parent's capacity to care for a child reliably and consistently cannot be sufficiently developed. Then a second home, with consistent and loving surrogate parents, has to be found for the child, in order to ensure not only that he survives but that his development in all its aspects proceeds as well as possible. Without such measures an abused child is unlikely to become an effective parent when he grows up, and is liable to continue the tragic tradition of abuse into which he was born.   DHH

Bretherton, I., and Waters, E. (eds.) (1985). *Growing Points of Attachment Theory and Research*.

Ellerstein, N. S. (ed.) (1981). *Child Abuse and Neglect: A Medical Reference*.

Oates, K. (1996). *The Spectrum of Child Abuse: Assessment, Treatment and Prevention*.

Smith, S. M. (ed.) (1978). *The Maltreatment of Children*.

childhood. The way societies treat their children, how they regard them, and how they order their lives reveal a great deal about the values of those societies. In Britain, a curious ambivalence about children has been displayed. Since the end of the First World War, there has been a flood of books on child rearing, much discussion and theorizing about their upbringing and early education, and a plethora of educational toys. The general assumption has been that this is the golden age of childhood, an enormous lollipop that will last for ever. At the same time, though, there is much envy of children and aggression towards them: they are battered, beaten, and sexually exploited (see CHILD ABUSE) and in modern warfare they are killed and injured with impartiality.

In the 20th century it looks as if childhood was celebrated more self-consciously than at other times. As Aries (1973) has pointed out, the concept of childhood as a phase of life existing in its own right is a relatively recent one. Children have always been appreciated as a means of continuing the family line, a way of achieving a kind of immortality, a source of labour, and an investment for the future. But since, in the past, means of contraception were inadequate, more children were born than could possibly be fed in times of food shortage or poverty. They were commonly killed off either by exposure in the open or by being subjected to lethal child-rearing practices. Disease, famine, and war carried off many more and kept the world's population in check. Christian fastidiousness about the preservation of life checked the practice of infanticide in Europe, but unwanted children were left at church doors or outside almshouses. The foundling homes were a response to this practice. If the child was strong enough to survive, he was incorporated into the adult world and put to work as soon as possible. The chief distinction between adult and child was that the child, being smaller and weaker, was worth less and so paid less than the adult in his prime. The appalling incidence of infant mortality set limits to the relationship between parent and child. What was the use of becoming fond of a child who was almost certain to die? The duty of the middle-class parent was to prepare the child for the afterlife, and the possibility of salvation, rather than for the world he was likely to inhabit for so short a time. A look at the readers and grammar of a Puritan family makes this point forcibly: 'Child, you will not live long so prepare to meet your God!' seems to be the predominant message. In an agricultural society where food was produced by labour-intensive methods, there was a place for the labour of those working-class children who survived. If they were set to work at the earliest possible age, this was not merely exploitation: their labour was an important contribution to the needs of the family. The Industrial Revolution too, is often stigmatized as a period of particular horror for children, and our attention is drawn to the small boy sitting for hours opening and shutting a trapdoor in a coal mine, or the half-naked girl dragging a cart full of coal behind her, or to the child mutilated by unprotected machinery. All this happened, and was dreadful, but it must also be remembered the child was contributing to the survival of his family. Working-class families had no alternative and at least the child could take pride in his achievements. The almost desperate resistance to compulsory education when it was first introduced in the 19th century is evidence that many families needed their children's wages and could not afford to lose them to the schoolteachers. Even today many working-class children are eager to leave school as early as possible, in order to earn a living and support themselves. And this is at a time when changes in industrial practice make the employment of the young uneconomic.

The modern child is more likely to survive into adulthood than his predecessors (although the survival rate of working-class children is still lower than that of middle- and upper-class children), and with survival as a probability new attitudes have arisen. Moreover, now parents can control the number of children they have, and can space out pregnancies. Together with children who are 'wanted' comes a belief in the goodness of childhood. Jean-Jacques *Rousseau's conviction that the child is born pure but is ruined by the impositions of civilization which fetter and corrupt, and William Blake's view of the child's innocence and beauty, have powerfully affected society's view of childhood, which has come to be treasured for itself. This new vision was celebrated widely in 19th-century painting and poetry: the innocent child was set alongside the 'noble savage' and onto both were projected society's yearning for a better state. (The strain of maintaining the purity of this image of childhood was perhaps partly responsible for the decline into the sentimentality about children characteristic of middle and late Victorian times.) Then Sigmund *Freud's theories of the powerful (but not specific) sexual drives in the small child undermined this unrealistic view of young innocence. And so two views of childhood have continued to exist side by side in our own time: the child as a beautiful and creative individual in his own right, and as one whose libidinous and chaotic energies must be harnessed and educated.

The 'permissive' view of child rearing has become firmly established both in the USA and in Britain. Beneath the belief that it is wrong to give a firm structure to the life of the child lurks the hope that life will be better for the child than it has been for the parent, even if there is no clear view of what is 'better' in terms of human security and happiness. Sometimes permissiveness has led to a disastrous abandonment of common sense and has caused much unhappiness to both parents and children. Respect for the child has, however, made family life less formal and has made schools happier places to be in; an appreciation of the creative abilities of children and closer attention to their ways of learning have been positive benefits of this new respect.

On the other hand, opposed to this belief in 'freedom' for the child has run an undercurrent of envy, fear of the child's sexuality, and even a hatred, which is expressed in punishment and exploitation. Relegation of the child to the nursery or boarding school, baby batterings and scoldings, the feelings of guilt engendered by the prohibition of masturbation or the insistence of regular bowel movements, have all taken their toll. A. S. *Neill wrote of this 'hatred of children' and insisted that it was the root cause of most of the problems of child rearing—bedwetting, thieving, and the inability to learn. These represented the rebellion of the child against its restrictive upbringing. Life in our large cities brings further restrictions—many children have little mobility, are confined to the upper floors of tower blocks, and have inadequate facilities for play. Often their capacity to understand and to learn are underestimated: they are assumed to be ignorant of the facts of death, sex, or race. It is hard to accept that children, like all human beings, are in their own terms engaged in the task of making sense of the world.

Finding that it is seemingly impossible to bring up children satisfactorily, many in the West have turned to other civilizations for hope and guidance. One thing is certain: the ills of Western civilization have not been cured by changes in child-rearing methods. Truby King's four-hourly feeding schedule did not cause the First World War nor Dr Spock the urban guerrilla!

Dispassionate evaluation of an activity as complex as parenthood is not easy. Children are at once relatively weak and vulnerable and also potentially disruptive of adult peace of mind. There is now a long period during which children have time to become adults; adolescence has been interposed between childhood and adulthood. It used to be that a Jewish boy was told at his bar mitzvah ceremony at the age of 13 that he had become a man; this is still so, but now he must be content, as all youths must be, with the prospect of years at school and possibly, if lucky, professional training before admission to adult society. Girls are in the same predicament: they may secure recognition by early motherhood, otherwise they may have to accept even lower status than boys at school and at work.

The problems associated with adolescence have long been recognized. A society that celebrates childhood, however equivocally, finds it exceedingly difficult to tolerate adolescents. Baby-faced charm gives way to gauche assertiveness, and the object of biologically triggered, parental protectiveness becomes a challenge to authority. Adolescents in Western society have a generally poor image. Aided and abetted by entrepreneurs for commercial gain, they tend to set up what seems to be a separate culture designed to exclude adults. In part this attempt to establish a separate identity is in reaction to a society unable to find a constructive place for them. In dress, in music, and in their general lifestyle, adolescents assert themselves by banding together—though preserving the class distinctions that characterize their parents: the middle-class 'hippy' drop-out is very different from the working-class punk rocker. Their activities are envied and feared. Some adults fear that the young may usurp their rights and privileges; others regret their own lost, though less liberated, youth; many envy the lack of obligations and the freedom of movement and expression that the young seem to enjoy. Adolescents are often the target of the moral panics that sweep society from time to time.

It has to be accepted that there never has been a golden age of childhood when children were cared for without question and when filial duties were carried out without protest. In recent times attitudes to childhood have changed in complex ways. Parents may enjoy their children more positively than those in other centuries have been able to do, but they still have to cope with the envy and inner conflict that is an inevitable part of their relations with the young. A proper balance between the care and the control of children remains difficult to achieve.

CH/NS

Aries, P. (1973). Centuries of Childhood.
Bettelheim, B. (1969). Children of the Dream.
Bronfenbrenner, U. (1974). Two Worlds of Childhood.
de Mause, L. (1974). The History of Childhood.
Erikson, E. H. (1965). Childhood and Society.
Miller, D. (1969). The Age Between.
Newson, J., and Newson, E. (1965). Patterns of Infant Care.
Spock, B. (1969). Baby and Childcare.

children. See BRAIN DEVELOPMENT; CHILD ABUSE; CHILDHOOD; CHILDREN'S DRAWINGS OF HUMAN FIGURES; CHILDREN'S UNDERSTANDING OF THE MENTAL WORLD; HUMAN GROWTH; INFANCY; MIND IN; LANGUAGE DEVELOPMENT IN CHILDREN; REASONING: DEVELOPMENT IN CHILDREN; SEX DIFFERENCES IN CHILDHOOD.

children's drawings of human figures. Children's drawings are often very beautiful. As the article about them in The Oxford Companion to Art says, 'The art of children is not a vehicle for the greatest expression of the human mind, but within its limits it offers a rare perfection of feeling and expression.' Even the collection of decrepit monstrosities shown in Fig. 1 is beautiful. But of course, if these drawings are supposed to be realistic (as we must accept that they are) something is very queer. The realism concerned must be realism in rather a special sense. It results from a sensibility to which, it seems, all children intuitively aspire. The drawings have an undeniable underlying logic: they have been called the products of 'intellectual realism' as opposed to 'visual realism'. The question is precisely what kind of logic they reveal. According to what kind of rules are these children operating? Recent books which discuss the results of detailed experimentation have been written by Cox (1993, 1997), Freeman

Fig. 1. Drawings of people done by nursery-school children, showing their different solutions to the difficult problem.

Fig. 2. The tadpole figure (*homme têtard*). The central one was produced by a severely mentally handicapped adult, the other two by pre-school children. Are the arms really attached to the head?

Fig. 3. Trend towards visually faithful drawings by Helen, between 4 years 6 months and 5 years 6 months, as she develop her characteristic stylization.

(1980), Gardner (1980), Golomb (1974, 1992), Goodnow (1977), and Thomas and Silk (1990).

Without a sophisticated theoretical model of the workings of the child's mind, we shall never know exactly what he or she intends to represent. We cannot rely upon the drawings to give us direct access to the inner world of the child, as though they were faithful reflections of 'body images'. First, it is debatable how far an activity which demands sophisticated motor control can ever be free of planning problems specific to the medium. Secondly, as Neisser (1970) explains, in order to use the concept of a mental image it is necessary to have evidence for its place in a mental system that is independent of the phenomena to be explained. Otherwise one falls into circular

Fig. 4. This pre-school child, who had never produced anything better than a scribble, responds excellently by adding limbs to an incomplete figure pre-drawn on the page.

judgements whereby the form of the mental image is deduced from the drawing and then used to explain it. Thirdly, as Abercrombie and Tyson (1966) point out, it is necessary to have criteria specifying the standard of comparison. If a child who draws a disjointed human figure always draws incoherently, whatever the topic, one would say that the child could not draw adequately rather than that she had a fragmented body image. No research project to date has come near to solving these three linked sets of problems, though Shontz (1969) made a commendable attempt. Therefore, although children's system of thoughts and feelings about themselves and others undoubtedly influences many aspects of their drawings, there is no acceptable evidence that their conceptual system is necessarily the major determinant of the form of any particular drawing.

Faced with these difficulties, some authors have simply attempted to classify drawings. R. Kellogg (1970) produced an elaborate taxonomy of forms based partly on the mandala. Certainly some of the forms are extremely striking in that they seem to conform more to radial symmetry than to the elongated conventional figure whose progression towards visual fidelity is shown in Fig. 3. The ubiquitous 'tadpole' is shown in Fig. 2. But Kellogg's formal scheme does not appear in the development of individual children (Golomb 1981). So if it is unsafe to assume an infantile urge towards radial symmetry, perhaps radial

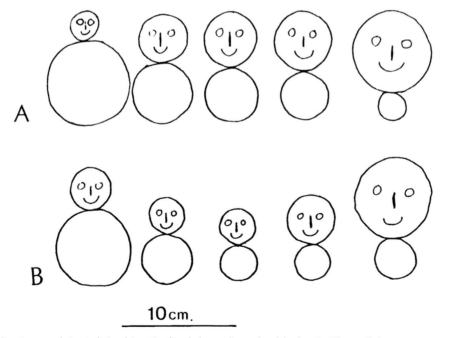

Fig. 5. Drawing-completion tasks involving stimuli scaled according to head–body ratio. Where will the children attach the arms?

161

forms such as the tadpoles represent the solution to a special kind of problem. The child may intend to produce an elongated figure but always slips up in the execution. According to such a view, the drawings would show us more about the child's mastery of spatial relations in laying out lines on a page than about urges governing mental imagery or aesthetic aims. One argument runs as follows.

First, in order to draw body parts and represent the relations between them, the child must have mental representations of them *available*. However, this does not guarantee that the representations will be *accessible* when they are needed. Performance in a task involving the active use of memory can never be assumed to be completely efficient. If one wishes to investigate the contents of memory, it is common practice to 'prompt' the subject, using cues for recall, rather than rely upon unaided performance. So with drawings, if one dictates the parts of the drawing simply by naming them, the child will often produce a vastly improved drawing, showing that she had been aware of the parts but could not call them up for herself. Again, provision of an incomplete drawing often cues the child into producing new parts: even inveterate scribblers may suddenly demonstrate their knowledge, as in Fig. 4. Clearly we ought not to judge the child's ability on the basis of spontaneous drawings without considering the conditions under which she would draw differently.

Secondly, even if the child has access to all the necessary information, she cannot produce it all at once on the page. Drawing is sequential: one can only draw one thing at a time; and there are specific problems inherent in organizing serially ordered behaviour. One problem often manifests itself in a tendency towards end anchoring: the ends of a series can often be recalled or responded to with greater reliability than intermediate items. The phenomenon is most marked with temporal series, but can apply to spatial series too. The end items in the human figure are the head and legs. So we expect them to be produced more reliably than the body or arms. This is indeed the case. When we consider the facial features alone, there is some evidence suggesting that the eyes and mouth are more reliably drawn than the serially intermediate nose.

We can now see how the tadpole figure might be generated. The child might even have available a full body image, but would preferentially access the terminal head and legs. It seems to be the case that most tadpole drawers produce the body parts in the order: head, legs, arms. In such a case the arms are more often put on the head than on the legs. But what kind of rule guides arm positioning here—are the children really aiming for the head? If we were to intervene and draw a body for them, would they then attach the arms to the body?

To put the argument formally, there are two possible responses. One is to attach arms to the head, the other to attach them to the body. The series in Fig. 5 presents two sets of stimuli (*A* and *B*), scaled according to head–body

Fig. 6. Human-figure drawings by Sarah Freeman, aged 3 years 2 months to 3 years 4 months, with spontaneous confident attempts at a cat, *Tyrannosaurus rex*, and a leopard, which are clearly based on her method of drawing the human figure.

Fig. 7. Sarah's drawing of a car with passenger and driver: a first attempt at unification of separate forms, at age 3 years 7 months.

ratio, which might influence the relative strengths of the two response tendencies. Experiment shows that it does so. The majority of tadpole drawers do not consistently go for either the head or the body, but to whichever circle is the larger. The head–body ratio reliably controls the locus of arm attachments: the 'body proportion' effect. So none of the simple accounts based on body image, which children have in their minds as a result of extended sensory experience, can be *quite* right, for they do not predict drawing behaviour associated with the tadpole stage.

The technique opens up the possibility of forcing children to make graphic decisions, in a way that is not possible if one confines oneself to collecting their spontaneous products. This applies most strongly to 2-year-old children who cannot yet draw: they willingly undertake such a drawing-completion game, and it can be shown that they too reliably attach the arms to whichever shape is the larger. Interestingly enough, even when they progress beyond the tadpole stage in their drawings many children show this phenomenon for a time; so the transition from a tadpole to a more conventional figure may not represent a sharp break.

What does the drawing-completion evidence show? It may show that the children simply regard the larger circle as the *real* body, and they know that bodies have arms. However, the basic phenomenon appears even when the children have been asked to draw a nose or a navel immediately prior to attaching the arms. They do so correctly, treating the circles appropriately as head and body, but cannot avoid attaching the arms to the larger circle. Thus the body-proportion effect attests to a graphic production problem: a problem in organizing lines on the page and handling the interactions between what is

Fig. 8. 'Transparency drawings' by two children aged 5 years 6 months, in which a hidden object is shown in its entirety. Perhaps 'superimposition' would be a better term than 'transparency'. The first drawing shows a pirate in a lifeboat, the second shows a house with a bed and a person in it.

already on the page and what is to come. Mastery of this for one topic may be generalized to tackle others (see Fig. 6).

The same approach may be used in analysing the representation of complex scenes involving the combination of separate forms (see Fig. 7). Psychologists are now engaged on research into children's depiction of occlusion (hiding of further by nearer objects), elevation, relative orientation, and perspective. Already one new puzzle has emerged. Given the striking nature of 'transparency representations' (see Fig. 8), which are often held to be the hallmark of 'intellectual realism', why are they so very difficult to obtain under experimental conditions? The status of this indication of drawing ability is one of the topics increasingly questioned as experimenters move away from the 'development of drawings' to the psychological development of the child drawer (Freeman and Cox 1985).   NHF

Abercrombie, M. L. J., and Tyson, M. C. (1966). 'Body image and draw-a-man test in cerebral palsy'. *Developmental Medical Child Neurology*, 8.

Cox, M. V. (1993). *Children's Drawings of the Human Figure.*

——(1997). *Drawings of People by the Under-5's.*

Freeman, N. H. (1975). 'Do children draw men with arms coming out of the head?' *Nature*, 254.

——(1977). 'How young children try to plan drawings'. In Butterworth, G. (ed.), *The Child's Representation of his World.*

——(1980). *Strategies of Representation in Young Children: Analysis of Spatial Skills and Drawing Processes.*

——and Cox, M. V. (1985). *Visual Order: The Nature and Development of Pictorial Representation.*

Gardner, H. (1980). *Artful Scribbles.*

Golomb, C. (1974). *Young Children's Sculpture and Drawing.*

——(1981). 'Representation and reality'. *Review of Research in Visual Art Education*, 14.

——(1992). *The Child's Creation of a Pictorial World.*

Goodnow, J. J. (1977). *Children's Drawing.*

Kellogg, R. (1970). *Analysing Children's Art.*

Neisser, U. (1970). 'Visual imagery as process and experience'. In Antrobus, J. S. (ed.), *Cognition and Affect.*

Osborne, H. (1970). *The Oxford Companion to Art.* (Entries concerning art education, children's art, psychiatric art.)

Shontz, F. C. (1969). *Perceptual and Cognitive Aspects of Body Experience.*

Thomas, G. V., and Silk, A. M. J. (1990). *An Introduction to the Psychology of Children's Drawings.*

children's understanding of the mental world.

One of the most important powers of the human mind is to conceive of and think about itself and other minds. Because the mental states of others (and indeed of ourselves) are completely hidden from the senses, they can only ever be inferred. Thinking about these unobservable states is a subtle business indeed, but in one way or another an essential part of our social life. One could be forgiven therefore for assuming that the deployment of such

a 'theory of mind' must be a very late accomplishment of childhood and that it must require the benefit of education and tutoring. Recent research, however, is beginning to show that this 'theory' emerges during the pre-school years and depends upon specific innate mechanisms.

The most important kinds of mental state that we infer and attribute have a characteristic form. First, they have a *content*—they are about something; second, they take an *attitude* to the content—whether the content is believed, hoped, or desired; and third, they say who is taking this attitude to the content. So, for example, 'John believes it is raining' has John taking the attitude 'believes' to the content 'it is raining'. We use such attributions to explain and to predict behaviour. So, 'John jumped into the doorway *because* he believed it was raining and he will now put up his umbrella *because* he wants to remain dry.'

We can look experimentally to see whether a child can use such attributions in this way. A powerful test of this is when the child can predict someone's behaviour on the basis of an attributed false belief. This attribution will differ from and indeed contradict the child's own beliefs and so provides a stringent test of the child's ability to conceive of beliefs *as* beliefs.

For example, Sally hides a chocolate in a certain box, then goes out for a walk. Meanwhile, someone else, Ann, arrives, finds the chocolate, and transfers it to a basket near by. Ann too then departs. A short time later Sally returns, wanting her chocolate. We can test a child who has been watching these comings and goings, to see if he (or she) understands the various events, and satisfy ourselves that he does. We can then go on to ask the child, 'well, where will Sally look for her chocolate?' If the child understands that Sally will still believe her chocolate to be in the box (while he himself knows it is in the basket), then he will point at the box. If, on the other hand, he cannot work out what Sally will believe, he will predict Sally's behaviour in terms of the actual situation and point to the basket.

Wimmer and Perner (1983) and Baron-Cohen, Leslie, and Frith (1985) found that most 4-year-old children can pass this test. On the other hand, most 3-year-olds will fail. Those who fail consistently point to where the chocolate really is, as if Sally too would know this. One way of understanding the 3-year-olds' failure is in terms of a fundamental logical ability which they, but not the 4-year-old, lack. For example, it may be that, before about 4 years, children are not capable of simultaneously conceiving of and appreciating two alternative and contradictory models of reality.

Thus the very young child can work only with his own model of the situation as he perceives it and not at the same time with Sally's model, which is different from and contradicts his own. By 4 years of age this ability has appeared and the child can now successfully predict Sally's behaviour (where she will look) according to Sally's model of the situation.

Another task requiring appreciation of simultaneously contradictory models of reality occurs when an object appears to be one thing but is really another. For example, a child is shown a sponge which has been cleverly disguised to look like a rock. The child is allowed to discover that really it is a sponge, and is then tested to see if he can appreciate the contrast between what it looks like and what it really is. J. H. Flavell has tested children on this sort of task. Again it appears that most 4-year-olds succeed while most 3-year-olds fail.

Thus it seems that the appreciation that people can have different ideas about a situation develops between 3 and 4 years of age. But is this ability to conceive of alternative realities really absent at 3 years?

Consider what is involved when a 2-year-old child engages in pretend play. Let us suppose that the child sees a banana on a table in front of him. He decides to pretend that the banana is a telephone and accordingly picks it up, holds it at the side of his face, and simulates talking. It is most unlikely that the child has made an error and has wrongly identified the banana as a telephone, for he can see that the banana is a banana. So at one and the same time he is representing the situation as one which contains a banana and one in which the banana is a telephone. Isn't this child appreciating alternative and contradictory models of the same situation?

Consider also what happens when a child watches his mother pretending to take imaginary clothes off a teddy bear and throw them in a pile. She dips the teddy into an imaginary tub, splashes it with imaginary water, and 'soaps' it with a toy brick. What is the child to make of this? What his mother actually does is merely wiggle her fingers in the vicinity of the teddy, put teddy on the floor, accompany more finger wiggling with slurping noises, and rub the teddy with the toy brick. Clearly the child has to infer from this—from what he actually sees and hears—what it is that his mother is pretending.

The price of not being able to infer that someone is pretending something can be very high for a young child. A 2-year-old observing his mother at a telephone is able to acquire useful information about telephones and social practices, even though he does not yet really understand what is going on. But think of the same child seeing his mother pretend that a banana is a telephone. If he interprets this literally he may end up with some very funny ideas about bananas or his mother, or both. Moreover, at the same time as learning about objects and social practices from observing others, children at this age are also learning what words mean. So if a 2-year-old interprets 'Here, take the telephone' literally when what his mother is handing him is in truth a banana, language learning is put in jeopardy as well. The fact that such socially shared

pretence does not have ill effects shows that young children can and do understand the alternative 'reality' of pretence while relating it to the literal reality of what they see before them.

If the 2-year-old is so expert at handling alternative and contradictory models in pretence, then why is the false belief situation (as exemplified in the chocolate box/basket test) so difficult? Why do so many children fail even at 3 years old?

The ability to *conceive* of alternative realities cannot be the breakthrough that brings success in false belief or appearance–reality tasks. But the critical change might be in the child's ability to *handle* such contradictory models—for example, in the ability to work out *precisely* what the alternative should be.

In pretence, the alternative model is essentially merely stipulated or invented. And even where the child has to work out what it is that someone is pretending, it is usually the case (*always* if the child is to succeed?) that the pretence can be read off from, or at least strongly suggested by, what the other person is literally doing. The false belief task, however, differs in both respects, for here there is a right and a wrong answer—it has to be worked out and cannot be read off. In the chocolate test, for example, Sally's belief has to be worked out by the child on the basis of what Sally saw and did not see of the situation. Once that is done the child must deduce what Sally will do on the basis of that belief.

Even so, we may wonder if difficulty in working out the alternative model accounts entirely for the two-year lag in solving the false belief task. In the rock–sponge appearance–reality task, can the child not just 'read off' the appearance of the sponge that looks like a rock? Why is that so much more difficult than 'reading off' what someone is pretending?

Before we try to answer this, let us return to the 2-year-old and pretending. When the child works out that his mother is pretending that the banana is a telephone, he is attributing a mental state to her—the mental state of pretending (attitude) that a banana is a telephone (content). A 2½-year-old girl watches her brother who pretends to fill a cup with water and then turns this cup upside-down over the head of a doll. She reaches for a cloth and pretends to dry the doll, showing that she has worked out the consequences of an attributed pretence. This involves both attributing an alternative model and handling it cognitively.

Furthermore, analysis can show that being able both to pretend and to make attributions of pretence to others requires mastery of exactly the same *logical structures* as understanding mental states in others (Leslie 1986). For a discussion of the peculiar logical properties of things which express mental states—for example, sentences about mental states or thoughts about thoughts—see CONSCIOUSNESS.

So even the very young child can handle the basic logic of mental states. Despite this, most children fail in false belief tasks until about 4 years of age. Our question is, why? So far we have suggested that the failure has something to do with not being able to work out what belief someone with a given exposure to a given situation will have.

Perner, Leekam, and Wimmer (forthcoming) took sixteen 3-year-olds who had failed the false belief task and showed them a Smartie box (for a confection well known to British children), asking them what they thought it contained. The children answered, 'Smarties'. They were then shown that in fact the box contained no Smarties, just a pencil. Nine of the children could tell the experimenter, 'I thought it contained Smarties, but I was wrong.' These children were then asked, 'When we bring your friend in and show him the closed box, what will he think is in it?'. Amazingly enough, they all answered, 'A pencil'!

This shows that these 3-year-olds, despite their ability to model and report a false belief, were unable to understand where the belief came from. Despite the fact that they themselves had just undergone the process of acquiring that false belief, they were quite unable to understand and reconstruct the process, and were thus unable to predict what would happen to their friend.

Adults attribute mental states to machines and plants without actually believing that mental states really exist inside the machines or plants. For example, a person says that his central heating system *knows* when it's cold and *wants* to keep the house warm. He does this to describe its behaviour; but whatever it is that responds to the temperature and makes the heating come on, he never believes that it is a thought or anything like a thought. Can it be in a similar way to this that the young child attributes mental states to people and that, under special circumstances, the child will even attribute mental states in order to understand behaviour, but without regarding them as *things that really exist*?

What would follow from the child's regarding mental states as real? It would allow the build-up of general knowledge to begin, with general knowledge about mental states. If mental states are real, they must exist somewhere (but where?) and, most importantly, they must be part of the *causal* fabric of the world (but how?). It may not even occur to the very young child that mental states are actually caused by other things—by concrete events—and that they are in turn the *cause* of other real things such as behaviour. Without this insight, there is no reason for a child to look closely at situations and people's exposure to them, with mental states in mind. But once a child does, he or she will consider what events lead to what mental states. It seems that these developments begin to take place between 3 and 4 years, culminating in the

cognizance that led to the 4-year-olds' remarkable success in the Wimmer and Perner false belief task reported in 1983.

Wellman (1985, 1986) showed that 3-year-olds have the beginnings of a cohesive and explanatory theory of mind that include ideas about the way mental states exist. For example, they understand quite clearly that while a banana can be eaten, the thought of a banana cannot. When explaining these differences even young children have recourse to mentalistic language and locate states of mind as being in the head. For example, in explanation of whether or not a dream is real, a child might say 'it's in his head, it's only pretend'. Indeed, it is striking how often in these contexts a child qualifies the mental state with 'just', 'just pretending', or 'only', 'only a dream'. Such qualification seems to contrast the mental state with concrete publicly observable objects and events. This focus upon the different reality status of mental events is a perfectly proper emphasis for the child to have and in itself demonstrates the subtlety of early human understanding.

This focus may, however, exact a price in obscuring the fact that mental states are real enough, only in a different way from the concrete world. Again, the crucial step in coming to think of mental states as real will be the linking of them *causally* with the concrete world: if mental states can be both the effect and the cause of something concrete then they must themselves at least be *real*, if not concrete.

The task then for the 4-year-old is to link his developing understanding of causal mechanisms in the physical world with his theory of mind. We know that by 4 years children have a good grasp of the essentials of physical mechanics (Bullock, Gelman, and Baillargeon 1982). One aspect of this has to do with understanding when people are and are not in a position to see and hear things—Level 1 understanding in Flavell's (1978) sense. This then could provide the bridge enabling the 4-year-old to link up his causal understanding of the concrete world with his more abstract understanding of the mental world.

Understanding false belief requires the child to realize that Sally's exposure to the chocolate in the box will *cause* her to believe the chocolate to be in the box, while her non-exposure to its change of location will leave this belief unchanged. Thus when Sally comes back again it is this unchanged belief about the box that will determine her search behaviour. Likewise, in the rock–sponge example, understanding appearance–reality requires the child to figure out what mental state (belief) would result, given exposure to only some of the visual properties of the object. In a sense, the child could indeed just 'read off' the appearance. But what mental state would such an appearance cause in someone who does not know what the object really is (has not been exposed to the other perceptible properties as well)? This may be what provides the insuperable problem for the very young child.

We are suggesting, then, that children start with a causal theory of behaviour which admits only of concrete objects and events as causes of behaviour. Their ability to attribute mental states develops independently and in parallel with this, and is used only in special circumstances—for example, pretence, or reporting the fact of knowledge changes. But at around 4 years of age the two capacities are brought together and the child enlarges its notion of possible causes of behaviour to include mental states. From now on, mental states can cause behaviour, while (perceptual) exposure to situations can cause mental states (which then represent those causing situations). Now it becomes sensible, and indeed natural, for the child to pay attention to the causal relationships between situations, mental states, and behaviour. Mental states become part of the causal fabric of the world and will now therefore be predictable, reliable, and *learnable about*.

Finally, it seems that there are children who do not develop a theory of mind in the normal way. These are children who suffer from the syndrome of childhood *autism. Such children have severe impairments in their social skills. Baron-Cohen, Leslie, and Frith (1985) tested a group of autistic children of high ability with borderline to average intelligence on the false belief task. Their performance was compared with a group of *Down's syndrome children who were more severely retarded and with a group of much younger normal children. The Down's and young normal children performed remarkably similarly, with the vast majority of them passing the false belief task. However, the vast majority of the autistic children failed, pointing consistently to where they themselves knew the object to be.

Subsequently, as a follow-up, these children were tested with a picture-sequencing task (Baron-Cohen, Leslie, and Frith 1986). The pictures depicted various kinds of events. Whereas the autistic children performed very well indeed on picture stories depicting both causal mechanical events and social behavioural events, their performance with regard to events which crucially involved understanding the protagonist's mental state was extremely poor. This pattern of performance was quite different from both the normal and the Down's syndrome children.

The autistic child, then, appears to have a theory of mind impaired in a way that is not accounted for by general learning difficulties. It is too soon to say with confidence precisely what is wrong, but it seems that such children are not simply like very young normal children—for the autistic child appears to show highly abnormal development in pretend play; indeed pretend play may even be entirely absent. Where that is the case it seems likely that the child has suffered a serious neurodevelopmental problem that unfortunately strikes at the innate basis of his theory of mind. AML

Baron-Cohen, S., Leslie, A. M., and Frith, U. (1985). 'Does the autistic child have a "theory of mind"?' *Cognition*, 21.

—— —— —— (1986). 'Mechanical, behavioural and intentional understanding of picture stories in autistic children'. *British Journal of Developmental Psychology*, 4.

Bullock, M., Gelman, R., and Baillargeon, R. (1982). 'The development of causal reasoning'. In Friedman, W. (ed.), *The Developmental Psychology of Time*.

Flavell, J. H. (1978). 'The development of knowledge about visual perception'. In Keasey, C. B. (ed.), *Nebraska Symposium on Motivation*, 25.

—— Flavell, E. R., and Green, F. L. (1983). 'Development of the appearance–reality distinction'. *Cognitive Psychology*, 15.

Leslie, A. M. (1986). 'Some implications of pretence for the child's theory of mind'. Paper presented to the International Conference on Developing Theories of Mind, Toronto, Canada, May 1986.

—— (1987). 'Pretence and representation in infancy: the origins of "theory of mind" '. *Psychological Review*, 94.

Perner, J., Leekam, S. R., and Wimmer, H. (1987). 'Three-year-olds' difficulty with false belief: the case for a conceptual deficit'. *British Journal of Developmental Psychology*, 5.

Wellman, H. M. (1985). 'The child's theory of mind: the development of conceptions of cognition'. In Yussen, S. R. (ed.), *The Growth of Reflection*.

—— (1986). 'First steps in the child's theorizing about the mind'. Paper presented to the International Conference on Developing Theories of Mind, Toronto, Canada, May 1986.

Wimmer, H., and Perner, J. (1983). 'Beliefs about beliefs: representation and constraining function of wrong beliefs in young children's understanding of deception'. *Cognition*, 13.

children's understanding of the physical world.

Most adults take it for granted that the physical world is composed of objects and surfaces that are governed by certain invariant laws. Even the most primitive societies understand some of the most basic aspects of the physical world as a three-dimensional environment occupied by objects with varying attributes. This intuitive understanding has long been the source of philosophical interest (see ARISTOTLE; DESCARTES, RENÉ; BERKELEY, GEORGE; KANT, IMMANUEL) but it was the psychologist *Piaget who first systematically addressed the origin and development of understanding of the physical world in children. Piaget argued that an appreciation of the physical world as enduring and separate from the self was one of the first steps to forming mental pictures or 'representations' of objects no longer available for inspection. For Piaget, representing the physical world was the bedrock for all higher cognition. Once children can think of the physical world as composed of objects as enduring entities, which exist independently of perception, then they have a major tool for reasoning about abstract concepts. Armed with the ability to represent the physical world, the child can start to understand the nature of physical characteristics such as permanence, alterations, transformation, motions, and so forth.

children's understanding of the physical world

Fig. 1. In the tubes task, pre-school children typically search for a dropped ball in the hiding cup below.

In Piaget's view, the origin of mental representation begins in infancy as a direct result of acting upon or playing with objects. Initially, the newborn has no representation of the physical world other than fleeting, uncoordinated perceptions. However, as the sensory and motor systems mature and combine with new experiences to enable more complex interactions with the world, the Piagetian infant gradually builds an understanding of the physical world so that by the end of infancy at around 2 years of age, the child can represent an object and many of its properties. For Piaget, this representation emerges as a consequence of acting on a physical world and experiencing the consequences of those actions.

One physical property that is currently the focus of much experimental interest and debate is the issue of object permanence; namely an appreciation that solid objects continue to exist in the absence of observation. In one of his famous observations, Piaget (1952) noted that, when a toy was covered, infants up to about 7–8 months behaved as if it no longer existed. He interpreted this as evidence for a limited understanding of object permanence. When the toy disappeared, the infant who was not able to form a representation of the toy treated it as if it no longer existed. This is captured in his famous dictum that for the child, the toy is 'out of sight, out of mind'.

The idea that hidden objects cease to exist in the mind of the infant was challenged in the 1980s by a number of infant researchers, including Liz Spelke and Renée Baillargeon (Baillargeon, Spelke, and Wasserman 1985) They argued that the hiding games that Piaget had based his account on were simply too difficult for infants. Infants did not search accurately because the task demands had

overwhelmed their ability to execute the retrieval successfully. These limitations may reflect immaturity of brain structures which support subgoals of complex behaviours necessary for search (see BRAIN DEVELOPMENT).

Spelke and Baillargeon claim that a more accurate evaluation of the infant's understanding of the physical world could be obtained by observing infants' responses to magic tricks. Rather than requiring the infant to act, they simply watch an event sequence involving objects and the amount of time they spend looking at it is measured. The 'violation of expectancy' paradigm, as it has become known, is based on the principle of the conjurer's trick, namely that a trick triggers an increase in the observer's attention because it contravenes an expectancy or belief about the physical world. A simple example is to place an object on a table, cover it with an occluder, and then remove the occluder to reveal either the object (possible condition) or an empty space (impossible condition). If infants understand that the object should continue to exist, then those infants who observe the impossible condition should look significantly longer than those who observe the possible event. Using this simple logic, a large number of studies using the violation of expectancy paradigm have been conducted revealing infant discriminations on an extensive range of physical attributes and properties. Not only do infants understand that objects continue to exist, but they appear to make judgements about the nature of the object's constitution and interactions with other objects. So in the same way that adults reason about the physical world, looking time reveals that infants appreciate that objects continue to exist, retain their spatial and physical properties, and are subject to physical laws when out of sight.

Armed with this paradigm, new accounts of the infant's understanding of the physical world have recently appeared. Both Spelke (1991) and Baillargeon (1995) propose similar accounts with early appreciation of properties of the physical world that are built in at birth and do not need to be learned from experience (see NATIVISM). Baillargeon (1995) argues that experience fine-tunes various physical principles whereas Spelke argues that certain core principles remain constant throughout development.

It may seem that Piaget's account of constructed knowledge can be abandoned following these demonstrations of infant discriminations, but the new accounts of object knowledge are controversial for a number of reasons. To begin, the methodology requires measuring responses to an outcome. While suggestive of an explicit understanding, such measures fall short of the types of behaviour some critics require as evidence for a full appreciation. For example, we may look longer at an outcome without being aware of what is odd. There are many examples of perceptual discriminations in the absence of any awareness.

More importantly, it is not clear that, once the child has overcome the performance limitations of infancy, they are capable of solving the same types of object problems that produce longer looking in infants. For example, one of Spelke's core principles is that two solid objects cannot pass through each other. If infants observe a ball rolling behind a screen from which a solid wall protrudes above and then see the same ball emerge from beyond the other side of the wall, they look significantly longer than other infants observing the same sequence but without a wall in place. In contrast, children who watch the same sequence also look longer but fail to search accurately for the ball in front of the wall. When action is pitted against looking time, these young children seem to have a limited appreciation of the unseen objects. So different methodologies (search versus violation of expectancy) produce different answers to the question, 'What do young children know about unseen physical objects?' While intriguing, the new data from looking time studies is not so devastating to Piaget's action-based account of cognitive development as it would first appear. For Piaget, knowledge derives from action and is substantiated in action. It is not enough to have a good idea; the individual must be able to act upon it.

Despite the controversy surrounding the basis of the mechanisms that support the violation of expectancy, the paradigm reveals a greater sensitivity to and processing of physical attributes within the first year of life than had been generally appreciated. What appears to be in dispute is whether these examples of infant discrimination can be called knowledge. Piaget would probably disagree. Moreover, even though these processes may be operating very early in development, children continue to learn about the physical world, and change in the types of explanation they provide to account for it.

Naive physical theories

Recent research on children's understanding of the physical world has focused on the conceptual frameworks that they spontaneously generate to make explanations and predictions. These are called naive theories to reflect the way that these beliefs are often resistant to counter-evidence. They are similar to formal scientific theories that are initially resistant to counter-evidence prior to a revision or revolution (Kuhn 1962). For example, in the process of discovering how objects balance around the fulcrum, 4-year-olds initially have no appreciation that symmetrical rods should balance in the middle but they discover this by trial and error. Six-year-olds, on the other hand, both predict and understand the relationship between symmetry and balance to the extent that they are unable to balance a symmetrical rod that is secretly weighted at one end (Karmiloff-Smith and Inhelder 1975). Because they are in the grip of theory-like reasoning, they

are unable to accommodate weighted rods into their appreciation of balance and symmetry. Older children initially approach the problem with the symmetry answer but readjust their response when they find that this solution does not work with weighted rods.

Gravity provides another example. Pre-school children believe that falling objects always travel straight down. If asked to find a ball that is dropped down a tube that diverts the ball sideways, children search directly below (see Fig. 1). Even after repeated trials, children continue to search directly below (Hood 1995). This is probably due to extensive experience with falling objects that travel straight down and relatively less experience with tubes. But if the motion is reversed so that the object appears to travel straight up, children solve the task (Hood 1998). Therefore, it is not tubes that confuse children but rather the relative bias to assume that falling, but not levitating, objects move in a straight line. These sorts of observations suggest that understanding the physical world is not simply an accumulation of facts, but rather that facts and observations are organized around naive theories which act to capture the essence of the phenomenon. While naive theories are prevalent in children, it should be noted that formal tuition in science does not always erradicate them. Despite their training in Newtonian principles, 80 per cent of college students still erroneously believed that, all things being equal, the heavier of two identical objects falls faster in spite of *Galileo's demonstrations to the contrary. So rather than being a foible of childhood, naive theories may reflect cognitive mechanisms present throughout development within many domains of reasoning, including reasoning about the physical world.   BMH

Baillargeon, R. (1995). 'A model of physical reasoning in infancy'. In Rovee-Collier, C., and Lipsett, L. (eds.), *Advances in Infancy Research*, vol. ix.

—— Spelke, E. S., and Wasserman, S. (1985). 'Object permanence in 5-month-old infants'. *Cognition*, 20.

Hood, B. M. (1995). 'Gravity rules for 2–4 year-olds?' *Cognitive Development*, 10.

—— (1998). 'Gravity does rule for falling events'. *Developmental Science*, 1.

Karmiloff-Smith, A., and Inhelder, B. (1975). 'If you want to get ahead, get a theory'. *Cognition*, 3.

Kuhn, T. (1962). *The Structure of Scientific Revolutions*.

Piaget, J. (1952). *The Origins of Intelligence in Children*.

Spelke, E. S. (1991). 'Physical knowledge in infancy: reflections on Piaget's theory'. In Carey, S., and Gelman, R. (eds.), *Epigenesis of Mind: Studies in Biology and Cognition*.

Chinese evidence on the evolution of language.
Human language is the unique and most important possession of the human mind, yet thought about it has always proved extraordinarily difficult. It is suggested here that important new light on its evolution is to be found in

an original way of representing it visually, i.e. writing it, developed gradually by the ancient Chinese.

The Chinese script (adopted by the Japanese and Koreans, whose own languages are unrelated to Chinese but who nevertheless use it, especially for the many loanwords they have incorporated from Chinese, much as English has from Latin and Greek, and who eke it out with their own phonetic symbols) differs from all others in wide use today by being logographic: that is, instead of aiming at recording segments of sound that strung together can notate speech, its symbols or characters each represent a *logos* or unit of meaning in the language's construction. In Chinese this is always a grammatically invariable monosyllable, which may be a word used independently, like 'house' or 'boat', or 'man' or 'kind'; or may be combined with other such monosyllables to form polysyllables, like 'houseboat', 'boatman', or 'mankind'. All words of more than one syllable in Chinese were at least originally of this type; word-forming syllables such as '-er' in 'farmer' and so on, which never existed as independent words, did not feature in Chinese word making. Furthermore, grammatical inflexions which also had no independence as words, like our plural '-s' and past tense '-ed', had no place either. Chinese lacks the kind of grammar that makes them necessary: expression of plurality, tense, and the like in Chinese is voluntary, and when necessary is performed by means of independent syllables such as 'two-three', 'some', 'just now', 'long since', and so forth. Otherwise it is left to context. Chinese is therefore described by linguists as an extreme example of the 'analytic' as opposed to the 'synthetic' type (exemplified by Latin and Greek) of human language; and the logographic system of writing invented for it is possible and suits it, as it would not a language of less analytic nature. Because of its analytic nature Chinese has always resisted the importation of foreign words, which would be mere sounds resistant to analysis in Chinese terms, preferring to translate or otherwise find purely Chinese expressions for new ideas from abroad. Etymology, usually a learned subject to those with more synthetic languages and who import foreign words, is to a much greater extent self-evident to the Chinese and is recorded faithfully in their logographic script. The logograms themselves (or ideograms, but this name is ambiguous insofar as it is also used for certain kinds of them only) were devised in several ways. First, there are those most obvious, the *indicative*: for example, one stroke for 'one', two strokes for 'two', a dot above a line for 'above', a dot below a line for 'below', and signs such as 人 'to enter', 'to insert', which, in what became the standard brush-written script, are now respectively 一, 二, 上, 下, and 入. Secondly, there are those that were *pictorial*: for example, like 人 or 人 or 人 for a 'human being, man(kind)', kneeling in a loop 人 for a

'girl', 'young person', 'woman' (one not an adult man), 人 or 人 for a 'child', 田 for 'fields', which are now respectively 人, 大, 女, 子, and 田. In addition, there are characters which, though they depicted things, stood rather for their qualities than for themselves: for example 人, an arm, for 'strength' (the mere cross for the hand showed it was not a focus of attention) is now much changed as 力. Thirdly, there are the characters called by the Chinese *combining meanings*, that showed two or more things together to suggest a meaning: for example, 好, a woman and child, for 'to love; lovely, good' and 男, strength and fields, for '(able-bodied) man, male, masculine'. Each of these logograms was invented to write a monosyllable, with its range of meanings and sometimes minor variations in pronunciation according to usage (for example, as between 'to love' and 'lovely, good'). They were tied to the language for which they were devised as a system of writing it, and did not otherwise depict things or ideas (even though they contained no indication whatever of pronunciation, any more than arabic or roman numerals show how they are pronounced). Finally there is the category, to which the great majority of Chinese characters belong, that does contain some indication of pronunciation. They are divided in two, as the so-called *borrowed characters* (i.e. any symbol belonging originally to any of the above categories but supposedly 'borrowed' only for its sound without respect to its meaning), and the so-called *phonetic compounds*, of which part was a *borrowed character* (called the 'phonetic' by Western scholars) according to traditional descriptions, and part (the 'determinative', 'signific', or 'radical', the latter because of its use as a key in arranging characters in dictionaries) serving to distinguish between words with similar pronunciation. Such words are inevitably legion in a monosyllabic language—like English 'bear', the animal, and 'to bear', to carry, be strong enough, endure. In a phonetic compound, the animal might be distinguished by having 'mammal', and the verb by having 'hand' (which is often used to indicate verbs in Chinese) added to a 'phonetic' which they would share.

In any Chinese text, although many of the characters may be formed by the other methods of character formation (especially those for some common words), the great majority will usually be found to belong to the phonetic compound class, which is even said to account for 95 per cent of the characters listed in Chinese equivalents of the *Oxford English Dictionary*; and each, when etymologies are given, will be described merely as so-and-so 'determinative' with so-and-so 'phonetic'. Such character 'etymologies' do not seem as interesting as the analysis of the other, 'poetic' kinds of character formation, and yet it is these very characters which, when examined afresh with the assistance of newly discovered ancient forms, throw light on the evolution of language. A simply phonetic explanation, though it seems to be universally accepted for most of these so-called phonetic compounds, encounters great difficulties. In the first place, they are by no means truly phonetic but allow extraordinary differences in pronunciation between the supposed phonetic element as a character itself and composite characters containing it: why then were they chosen? Reconstruction of ancient pronunciation, in which the great Swedish phonologist Bernhard Karlgren was a pioneer in the first half of the 20th century, seems to have brought a degree of reason into these anomalies, showing that they were once somewhat *less* unlike than now; but why, if they were intended to represent pronunciation, should they have been unlike at all? As Karlgren said in his seminal *Analytic Dictionary of Chinese and Sino-Japanese* (1923), they cannot, by all experience of phonetic laws, once have been the same and then diverged. Why then should there be such anomalies in this supposed phonetic spelling as mixing *P* with *M*, or *N* with *T*, in characters sharing the same 'phonetic element'? Karlgren could only resort to a theory of 'homorganic spelling', whereby sounds made with the lips or sounds made with the tongue against the teeth could each be treated alike, as *M* and *P*, *N* and *T*, and so on; but why should the ancient Chinese, to whom the differences between these 'homorganic' sounds were as important as to anyone else, have done anything so perverse? Could they have read texts written by such a system? In short, does it make any sense to think of the compound class primarily as a phonetic system of spelling? And if it was not, what was it? There is a vast number of Chinese characters that can be used as supposed 'phonetic elements' in constructing others (much greater than is needed for a simply phonetic function, especially one so imprecise); yet there is remarkable consistency in the choice of one of them, even a very poor phonetic match, for the writing of a given word as a so-called 'phonetic compound'.

There is only one explanation for all this: that the 'phonetic element' also had a *meaning* and that that was even more important than how it was articulated. Let us look again at ∧ 'to enter', now written ⼊ and pronounced *rù* in Modern Standard Chinese but *yap* in Cantonese and reconstructed as **ńiəp** by Karlgren for the language of about 600 BC. The same drawing with a bar or bars behind it, △ or ⍍, is nowadays written ⾦, pronounced *jīn* in Modern Standard Chinese, *kam* in Cantonese, and means 'now'. The reconstructed pronunciation is **kiəm**: 'homorganic' with **ńiəp** because *ń* represents a nasal sound made against the palate, so 'homorganic' with the **k** of **kiəm**, while the **-p** and the **-m** are also 'homorganic', both being

made with the lips. The meaning of ∧ with a bar or bars behind can be seen as 'enclosed', conveyed in speech by the gesture of closing the mouth, hence 'included', 'contained', and so 'present'—used as in English for 'now'. The 'homorganic' qualities of the words ⼊ 'to enter' and ⾦ 'now', in their ancient pronunciations, would have arisen from their being derived from the same *root* which the ∧ represents the differences in pronunciation, from ancient word-forming modifications to that root. When one looks at other characters with ⾦ in them, one finds varying but also 'homorganic' pronunciations for meanings which all clearly relate to ideas of 'included', 'present'. As one example, with determinative ⼼ 'heart, mind', 念 is '(to have) present in mind', 'to think about', 'to remember' (*nian* in Modern Standard Chinese, *nim* in Cantonese. Karlgren did not, in fact, treat these various characters as having the same 'phonetic' although, by his own rules, there was no good reason why he should not have done so).

Another word for 'to have present in mind', 'to think' is written with determinative 'heart, mind' and a different so-called 'phonetic', 隹, which is said in dictionaries to mean 'a short-tailed bird' and, although obsolete now as a character on its own, occurs as the determinative in many characters for the names of birds. There are in fact two characters for 'bird', either of which is used as a determinative in characters for their names: 鳥, said to be a 'long-tailed bird', and this one, but ancient pictograms show them respectively as

and reveal a crowing cock and a squatting hen. Composite characters with the latter as 'phonetic' are used in writing words vaguely related to the hen and to one another phonetically, with a great variety of meanings: 'to be plump', 'isolated', 'stay in one place' (all like a broody hen) and to 'brood', 'think obsessively', as in English. Branching forth, as it were, from some of these ideas, which the hen illustrates, are others (given various determinatives) that can seem exceedingly remote from it: 'high' (of a mountain because isolated by its height) and metaphorical, noble meanings from that; 'moored' (of a boat); 'constant' (of a principle); even a particle with meanings like 'at' a place or time, or isolating a word or phrase for the purpose of drawing attention to it, and so on. The hen, her broodiness and sitting, are put on one side or forgotten, as conscious metaphors must be for language to develop freely from them; but there has to be a conscious metaphor *to start with* for a word to be created, because communication can only take place given a presumption of references shared in common between those endeavouring to communicate. Ultimately, these must be to common observation and experience of the world, and it is therefore not surprising to find close parallels in the etymologies of words in phonetically, grammatically, and historically unrelated languages. And even in cases where there are no such parallels, ultimate etymologies will very seldom not be comprehensible to any human being.

What about the name of the hen herself? In English it was just the feminine gender (something lacking in Chinese) of an old word for a cock, cognate with 'chant' (cf. 'chanticleer'); in Chinese it probably meant 'squatter', also relating it to a verb: in both cases something that could be acted, gestured, before a word was made.

The animal, a 'bear', has been mentioned. Etymologies in dictionaries of English ascribe this word to a root meaning 'brown': as a colour name, an abstraction certainly not amenable to acting. But a Chinese character suggests that it may have been one and the same with the root of the similarly pronounced verb 'to bear'. An early version of the character (on a bronze of the 11th century BC)

$$\text{鮏}$$

is taken now by most scholars as a pictogram, a drawing of a bear, so contradicting the view of an early work (AD 100) on a contemporary version of it, which saw the 〇 in it as the 'phonetic' in a phonetic compound with the rest determinative. The 'phonetic', now ∠, in the modern form 能 of this character representing an old Chinese word for a 'bear', is seen on its own in the earliest, oracle bone script of the second millennium BC as an excellent one-stroke drawing of the profile of a hand in a carrying, *bearing* posture,

$$\text{〇}$$

and meant 'bearing in the hand', hence 'taking with one', 'using as an instrument', and the like (now written with the addition of 'man' determinative as 以 and one of the commonest words in the language). Although this is now pronounced yǐ reconstructed phonology shows that as **diəg** it could well have been the 'phonetic' (or represented the 'root') in 能, which is now pronounced **néng**! It is in fact the 'phonetic' or 'root' in an enormous number of characters with senses of bearing, enduring, being strong; and remarkably like the equally prolific Indo-European base **bher**—from which the English verb 'to bear' is derived, as well as (through Latin) 'fortitude', (through Greek) 'metaphor', and a vast number of other English words. The determinative elements added in the ancient Chinese character for the animal 'bear' were 月: 'flesh, body, physical' (so 'physically strong'), and 匕, which was part of the drawing

$$\text{𢑌}$$

of a stag, to represent a large animal. So 'a physically *strong* (the root of the word) large animal' was the information

conveyed in the Chinese character for a 'bear', which has been too readily supposed a crude and incompetent ('primitive') drawing. Moreover, Indo-European philologists may need to think again about the derivation of our name for the animal. Supposing it just to have meant 'brown', they assume 'beaver' (which was the same root reduplicated) to have meant 'very brown'—as if this were the best name our ancestors managed to think of! Might it not have been a *busy bearer* of materials for its dams? And might not 'brown' itself, certainly from the same root, have implied the colour of strength and health? That is an idea which can be acted, but metaphors do not provide meanings (intentions) in themselves, needing *context*.

This is well illustrated by a Chinese character with meanings now like 'to retire to rest', but in ancient texts also 'to go busily to and fro'. The character 栖, which was 'tree' plus 'bird's nest', illustrated the metaphor lying behind both. Birds 'nest' (go to roost) at sunset and 'nest' (build, go to and from their nests) in spring. Contexts would make it perfectly clear which sense was meant before the notion grew of 'words' possessing meanings in themselves: a notion that has given endless trouble to philosophers since, but which became necessary for human organization, government, and institutions, and for the establishment of laws.

Two Chinese characters for 'words', now 言 and 辭, each reflect this history. Each in early forms of the script contained 辛, which, by studying characters containing it and their meanings, can be identified as 'a crying infant' (cf. 𠃠 for 'child')—whence 'complaint', with legal connotations in these and other characters incorporating it. Though both these characters now have only to do with speech and language, the first, augmented by 'mouth', represented originally *speech about a complaint*, including pronouncement of judgement, while the second, augmented by 'hands unravelling', represented *analysing the complaint*, pleading. (The hands unravelling showed them with a thread between them, on either side of a bar, so could indicate, according to context, *tying* the thread around the bar or *untying* it. In English the verb 'to ravel' can have similar opposing meanings, as will be seen in the *Oxford English Dictionary*. Again an image of an activity was shown, while the specific meaning depended on context.) Pleading is still its sense in ancient texts, whereas now it is like the *lexis* of 'lexicon' and used in the Chinese name for a dictionary.

In the purely metaphorical stage of language, there was no cause to think about its components individually as 'words' with fixed intentions: Chinese characters show legal processes, when they came to be important, as that cause. The revolution then brought about is the reason for misunderstanding now about the original nature of Chinese script; as it is, too, for much of the confusion about the dual nature of human language, both natures vital now to thought and communication. The newer, artificial (logical) language strives for precision, but the original, natural (poetic) language remains necessary for creative thought. ARVC

Chinese ideas of the mind. In traditional Chinese philosophy and science the psychological was almost never regarded separately from the physiological. The stance was holistic, in contrast to common Indo-European thinking stemming from ancient Greece, where *Plato and his school conveniently distinguished matter from ideas, and the soma from the *psyche. Yet the Western tradition in the 20th century gave rise to an array of psychobiological monistic attitudes, which have as their *raison d'être* *idealism, reinforced by Judaeo-Christian tradition. (For further discussion, see MIND AND BODY; MIND–BODY PROBLEM; EVOLUTION: NEO-DARWINIAN THEORY.)

Philosophical anti-dualism in China can be traced to the Warring States period (481–221 BC), to Confucius (Kong Fuzi or Kong Qiu, 551–479 BC), and even earlier. Chinese rationalism of various schools generally opposed supernatural conceptualizations, and an organic outlook on interactions between man, nature, and government became firmly entrenched in the minds of literate people. Religious supernatural thinking nevertheless continued within popular Taoism.

Earlier Chinese sources demonstrate commonly held animistic modes of thinking—devils and spirits were thought to be able to possess the human body and soul and thus produce physical, behavioural, and social disorders. These supernatural factors were soon paralleled by the concept of natural factors such as cold, heat, wind, drought, and humidity affecting the human body in much the same way. Confucians, on the other hand, created a highly rational, though metaphysical, system of thought characterized by numerology and what may be termed 'correlative' thinking. Objects and phenomena in the universe were seen as belonging together in groups and governed by superior principles. Numerological systems were used to analyse the phases of change that these groups, consisting of concrete as well as abstract things, went through, and the changes were believed to occur in resonance, or 'in correlation' with one another. Examples of these numerologies are the well-known yin and yang used in any analysis of paired relationships, the Five Phases (*wu xing*, earlier misleadingly rendered as the Five Elements) used in correlating anything divisible in fives, and the Ten Heavenly Stems and Twelve Earthly Branches used jointly mainly for calendrical purposes. In these contexts, they used terms, more usually applied to the supernatural, in borrowed and natural senses. Supernatural forces were disregarded—there is no way of gaining knowledge about gods, thus they are of no interest. Any dichotomy between the body and an intrapersonal soul was similarly disregarded.

Chinese literate tradition, dominated by Confucian rationalism, thus took a decidedly 'organic' point of view on psychological matters. It did not discriminate among physical, behavioural, emotional, or social cues when incorporating them into more general concepts used in medicine, psychology, or politics. This organic outlook appears to be deeply ingrained in the minds of Chinese, and other East Asians, and helps explain why their attitudes towards psychological explanations of human behaviour differ from those of Westerners. The Chinese never developed any psychology of the *unconscious.

Nevertheless, the history of Chinese philosophy is replete with arguments concerning 'principle' versus 'practicality', and 'idealism' versus 'empiricism'. One finds varying degrees of emphasis on xin ('heart' or 'mind'), as opposed to wu ('things'). For example, the most idealistic school of philosophy in the Song dynasty was that of Lu Xiangshan (1138–91), who wrote: 'Space and time are [in] my mind, and it is my mind which [generates] space and time' (Needham and Wang 1962: 508). A somewhat later but more influential idealist thinker was the neo-Confucian Wang Yangming (1472–1528). Wang's *xin-xue* (study, or school of the mind) emphasized that man should endeavour to become a sage—regarding heaven and earth and all men and things as a unity of close relationship, and relying on (moral) principles (de Bary and Bloom 1979). Wang wrote: 'The master of the body is the Mind; what the Mind develops are Thoughts; the substance of Thought is Knowledge; and those places where the thoughts rest are Things' (Needham and Wang 1962: 509). Confucian *xin-xue* was distinct from its *shi-xue* (real or practical learning). The Japanese Buddhist-turned-neo-Confucian Hayashi Razan (1583–1657), influenced by the Wang school, held that 'principle [li] is prior and material force [qi, often transcribed as ch'i, the Chinese counterpart to the Greek concept of *pneuma* = vitality] posterior', but he came to experience difficulty in sustaining this position:

Principle and material force are one and yet two, two and yet one. This is the view of the Song [neo-]Confucians. However, Wang Yangming claims that principle is the regularity of material force and that material force is the operation of principle. If we follow the latter view, then there is the danger that everything will be chaotic. (de Bary and Bloom 1979)

Buddhism, spreading from India to China in the 2nd century AD onward, held a decidedly idealist position in declaring the visible universe an illusion: the world was nothing but mind, and the individual's mind was part of the universal mind. The Chinese Buddhists substituted xing ([subjective] nature) for qi (material force, or *pneuma*). They came to form one strand in neo-Confucian organic philosophy, but they failed to alter the fundamentally holistic outlook of indigenous Chinese thought patterns. (For further discussion of the Buddhist position, see INDIAN IDEAS OF THE MIND.)

The absence of a mind–body dichotomy is clearly seen in the traditional Chinese medicine of the literate classes. In the rational tradition, supposed pneumatic imbalances between internal organs were analysed in terms of a 'manifestation type' (*zheng*) of a disorder, according to specialized rules for diagnosis, including tongue inspection and pulse palpation. Widely differing disorders ('mental' as well as 'physical') would be shown to have a similar type of manifestation and thus receive similar treatment, such as herbal drugs or acupuncture.

For these reasons, psychiatry has no independent status in traditional Chinese medicine. Instead, concepts with a clearly psychiatric content are found widely dispersed in various fields of medicine. Not surprisingly, therefore, the Chinese word for psychiatry (*jingshenbingxue*: 'mental-disease-study') is a modern translation.

Psychology as a discipline (rendered in Chinese *xinlixue*: 'mind-principle-study') was introduced in Chinese universities around 1915. The subject has had a strongly practical application both before and after 1949. During the 1950s Soviet influence was dominant, with Pavlovianism the leading creed (see PAVLOV, IVAN PETROVICH); a great deal of research attention was devoted to medical, labour, and educational psychology as well as to the development of moral character (Chin and Chin 1969). Psychology, along with sociology, ceased to exist as an academic subject for a decade during the Cultural Revolution but was academically rehabilitated in the subsequent liberalization movement.   HA

de Bary, W. T., and Bloom, I. (eds.) (1979). *Principle and Practicality: Essays in Neo-Confucianism and Practical Learning.*

Chin, R., and Chin, A. L. (1969). *Psychological Research in Communist China, 1949–1966.*

Needham, J., and Wang, L. (1962). *Science and Civilisation in China*, ii: *History of Scientific Thought.*

chunking. The Scottish philosopher Sir William Hamilton (1788–1856), born in Glasgow (where his father and grandfather held the chairs of anatomy and botany), wrote: 'If you throw a handful of marbles on the floor, you will find it difficult to view at once more than six, or seven at most, without confusion.' This was confirmed by the English economist William Stanley Jevons (1835–82), by throwing beans into a box and estimating their number. He found that he never made a mistake with three or four, was sometimes wrong when there were five, was right about half the time with ten beans, and was usually wrong with fifteen. These experiments are cited by the American psychologist George Miller (1956), the author of the famous paper 'The magic number seven, plus or

minus two' (1956). Miller found that more items can be remembered when they are coded, or 'chunked'. Thus, we can remember more numbers or letters when they are in recognized sequences or words. So chunking enormously increases effective memory and perception. One might think of perception of objects as 'chunking' the sensory and stored data into large units—which are objects as perceived.   RLG

Miller, G. (1956a). 'Information theory'. *Scientific American*, August.

——(1956b). 'The magic number seven, plus or minus two'. *Psychological Review*, 63/2

cladistics. A system for classifying organisms. The word 'clade' was coined by Julian Huxley in 1957 to refer to characteristics that can be used as units for setting limits to classes and establishing hierarchies which may or may not be associated with evolutionary sequences. The cladistic system of classification—which, for some reason, arouses heated controversy—has three axioms. (i) Features shared by organisms (homologies) reveal hierarchical ordering in nature. (ii) Hierarchical orderings are economically expressed in branching diagrams, or 'cladograms'. (iii) The nodes in cladograms represent common features (homologies) shared by organisms—so cladograms can be used to represent and suggest biological classifications. The method can be used outside biology—for example, in geology, or linguistics, or wherever homologous characteristics can be recognized and there is no adequate structure of theoretical understanding for classification. The method demands explicit decisions on what are to be accepted as valid homologues, and this can be a useful exercise. Absence of characteristics (such as absence of teeth in birds) may be accepted for cladistic classification.

The current controversy over cladistics and Darwinian evolution seems to be based on the notion that cladistics is somehow opposed to or provides evidence against evolution, but this is mistaken. It can offer classifications which do not assume evolutionary sequences, but this is all to the good, as classifications that assume particular evolutionary sequences can generate vicious circular arguments in biology. See EVOLUTION: NEO-DARWINIAN THEORY.   RLG

Patterson, C. (1980). 'Cladistics'. *Biologist*, 27.

clairvoyance. See EXTRASENSORY PERCEPTION.

Claparède, Édouard (1873–1940). Swiss psychologist and educationalist, who studied at Geneva, Leipzig, and Paris, and with his cousin Flournoy founded the journal *Archives de psychologie* (1901). He became director of the experimental psychology laboratory at Geneva University and later founded the J.-J. Rousseau Institute for Educational Science. He had strong clinical interests and made a number of studies of the psychological sequelae of injury to, and disease of, the human brain, including a seminal study of the partial preservation of recent memory in *amnesic states despite what appears to be total forgetting. He also published, in 1900, an important review on defects in the visual recognition of objects (visual *agnosia) in *L'Année psychologique*, 6. His books include *L'Éducation fonctionelle* (1921).   OLZ

classification of psychiatric disorders.

Historical aspects

Advances in classification have made important contributions to the progress of physical, biological, and even the human sciences. *Kepler, Tycho Brahe, and *Galileo laid the foundations of modern astronomy. Mendeleev, who created the Periodic Table of the Elements, was a pioneer in the development of modern particle physics. *Sydenham's subdivisions of the fevers later proved to have been building blocks of modern medical science. The work of the botanist Linnaeus contributed to the creation by *Darwin and *Wallace of the evolutionary theory. Linnaeus was also a doctor and in his classification of mental disorders melancholia and mania can be identified.

The foundations of modern clinical *psychiatry were laid in the early and middle part of the 19th century. The focus of interest among the 'alienists' responsible at that time for the care of the 'insane', was on persons with mainly psychotic forms of mental disorder who required admission to a mental hospital for treatment. Those with more benign forms of illness rarely came under the observation of the early psychiatrists.

The modern era in the classification of mental diseases began towards the end of the 18th century during the French Revolution with the concepts and humane practices of figures such as Philippe Pinel (1745–1826). William Cullen (1710–90) tried to subsume under the heading of 'neurosis' all forms of mental disorder including such conditions as tetanus, *epilepsy, vesania, and a rough description of *psychosis, but his concepts soon proved over-inclusive.

The term 'psychosis' was first formulated by Ernst von Feuchtersleben (1806–49) in his *Principles of Medical Psychology*. He considered that all psychoses belonged to a single class of mental disorder in which the neuroses were also included. But in German psychiatry of the time neuroses were regarded as non-illnesses and this concept survived during the century that followed.

The concept of unitary psychosis or *Einheitspsychose* arose from another source (Griesinger 1867). This view was challenged by the important contributions of French psychiatrists and at a later stage by the seminal work of *Kraepelin, whose enquiries served to establish the distinct psychotic entities that have survived well into the

modern period. The observations of the French psychiatrist Morel in 1852 were important because he isolated from unitary psychosis a distinct disorder, commencing in the second decade, leading to withdrawal from social contact, odd gestures and delusions, and later to increasing self-neglect and mental deterioration. He named this condition *démence precise*.

Another syndrome, named as 'catatonia', a state of rigid immobility and suspension of speech, was described by Kahlbaum (1863). The condition called 'hebephrenia' by Heller (1871) begins in the teens, marked by incoherence of speech, incongruity of emotion, social withdrawal, hallucinations, and delusions.

Kraepelin came onto the psychiatric scene during the last quarter of the 19th century. The early period of his work with Wilhelm *Wundt had taught him the value of experimental method, and scientific approaches generally, for psychology. These experiences exerted a powerful influence on Kraepelin's later career. The achievements of Kraepelin stemmed from his personal qualities and his disciplined approach to psychiatric theory and practice. He was a painstaking observer and made copious notes on each patient. He attached considerable significance to the course and outcome of specific characteristics of disorders and set down a large corpus of clinical observation.

His account of *dementia praecox* in the fourth edition of his *Textbook* (1893) also appeared in the next edition (1897), as a disorder with features of disorganization of the personality leading to blunting and incongruity of the emotions and impoverishment of volition. The fifth edition of his *Textbook* (1897) included a more extensive account of each of the variants and he later added a fourth ('simple') version of the illness. His talent for identifying both unitary concepts and lines of demarcation enabled him to lay the foundations of the modern syndrome of schizophrenia by uniting three disorders: the catatonic, hebephrenic, and paranoid forms ('simple' schizophrenia was added later), of the disease. Paranoid schizophrenia was dominated by delusions of persecution. In the light of the clinical profile and observations during follow-up studies over long periods, these three syndromes appear to have similar properties in their clinical manifestations and prognosis in the long term.

Kraepelin had first accepted from the French school *dementia praecox*. He later accepted the term 'schizophrenia' as used by Eugen Bleuler (1857–1939), a professor in Zurich, who had been influenced by the teaching of Sigmund *Freud and who spoke of the 'splitting' of mental functions. Bleuler adopted a more psychodynamic approach and a more optimistic view of the outcome of schizophrenia than other psychiatrists. The syndrome of paranoid schizophrenia continues to be unacceptable in France at the present time.

Another original contribution made by Kraepelin was the integration of a number of disorders of mood into a single entity. Some decades previously the French psychiatrist Falret had referred to the most specific psychiatric disorder of mood as 'folie circulaire' (Falret 1854) The central feature of this illness was fluctuation of the emotions, which varied between abnormal elation and sadness, both being of greater severity and depth than normal emotions so named. Pathological elation is associated with explosive anger and irritability and grandiose, paranoid and other delusions (Baillarger 1853). There were intervals between alternations of mood when the mental state returned to its normal form.

There followed a multiplication of disorders. It was Kraepelin who recognized the more attenuated period of affective disorder. He named this as 'cyclothymic temperament', which he regarded as minor mood variations of a single disorder he called 'manic–depressive' illness. The mild forms of 'cyclothymic' states may retain their character as a subclinical fluctuation of mood throughout life which constitutes the soil in which the more severe disorders develop.

A high proportion of those with a 'cyclothymic temperament', as conceived by Kraepelin, continue to have fluctuations of mood throughout their lives without ever crossing the frontier which leads many to develop psychotic illness. The relationship between cyclothymia and manic-depressive disorder closely resembles that between a proportion of those with neuroses such as obsessional or somatoform disorders and anxiety states with disabling hypochondriacal symptoms associated with constant self-scrutiny in seemingly normal subjects.

The main classes of psychiatric disorder and an outline of the hierarchical system The main descriptive classes have been set down in Table 1, which represents the order of precedence of the conditions and the manner in which ambiguities are resolved when there is an overlap between different conditions. The order of precedence in hybrid cases is identified on the basis of the psychiatric clinical features alone. There is insufficient knowledge of causation to create a taxonomy based on established causal factors included in a clinical profile that do not necessarily decide the clinical diagnosis or position of the disorder in the hierarchical system.

Level 1 Organic Syndrome At the head of the hierarchy are disorders that have organic features in clinical manifestations, namely states of 'delirium', 'clouding of consciousness', 'amnestic syndromes' (Korsakow), and 'dementia'. The rationale for placing the organic disorders at the head of the hierarchy is twofold.

The first is that if there is co-morbidity between the organic syndrome features and some features of other personality disorders or other psychiatric entities, the organic part of the total picture will often be the most severe and urgent component and also the one more likely to have a compelling need to be treated first. This refers to cases in which the symptomatology includes features suggestive of a stroke, a haemorrhage, or some cardiovascular emergency.

The second is that some of the organic features co-morbid with the organic disorder (so-called organic syndrome proper), which play a part in causation, might be relieved by treatment administered for alleviation of the organic cluster of features alone, for example paranoid symptoms and psychotic features arising from common independent contributors, and may prove beneficial for the control of one or more co-morbid features.

Level 2 Schizophrenia Second place in the hierarchy is allocated to *schizophrenia, which is thereby given precedence in diagnosis over the clinical profile of the next step in the hierarchical order: the chronic paranoid psychoses (non-schizophrenic).

The clinical profile of schizophrenia represents a qualitative departure from normal mental functioning and in *Jaspers's terms constitutes a break in continuity of psychic life.

The symptomatology comprises delusions, which are persecutory, grandiose, or derived from the realm of religion, or have a sexual content. There are hallucinations usually related to the delusional theme—most commonly auditory or are often visual, olfactory, or tactile. A female patient complained of being sexually violated by strangers working with 'atomic machines' distant from the hospital.

Speech and talk exhibit frequent derailment and incoherence. Negative symptoms include flattening of mood, and mental excitement in which violence to the self or to others nearby may occur. There is poverty of thought and impairment of initiative.

The criteria of Kurt Schneider (1897) are widely regarded, particularly in Europe, as being highly specific for and diagnostic of schizophrenia. They continue to be used and quoted but their value can be realized only in patients in whom a full psychiatric history and examination have been undertaken. Schneider's criteria are listed in Table 1.

Level 3 Chronic paranoid psychoses The next level of disorders are chronic paranoid psychoses (as in the non-schizophrenic form of paranoia) which are separated from schizophrenia by the absence of hallucinations in most cases, the less pervasive nature of this psychosis, and the absence of deterioration of personality manifest in schizophrenia. Some of the forms of paranoid psychoses listed in Table 1 respond to antipsychotic drugs in a manner similar to schizophrenia. In the morbid jealousy syndrome there is serious risk to the life of the married

Table 1. The hierarchical principle in psychiatric diagnosis (schematic and simplified)

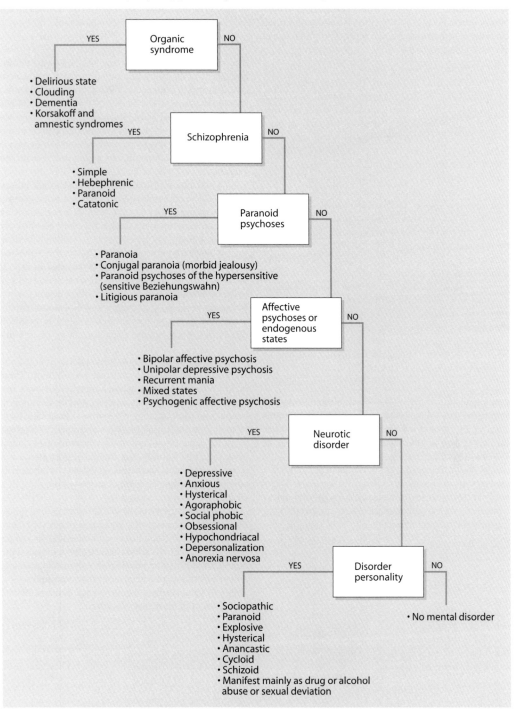

YES — Organic syndrome — NO

- Delirious state
- Clouding
- Dementia
- Korsakoff and amnestic syndromes

YES — Schizophrenia — NO

- Simple
- Hebephrenic
- Paranoid
- Catatonic

YES — Paranoid psychoses — NO

- Paranoia
- Conjugal paranoia (morbid jealousy)
- Paranoid psychoses of the hypersensitive (sensitive Beziehungswahn)
- Litigious paranoia

YES — Affective psychoses or endogenous states — NO

- Bipolar affective psychosis
- Unipolar depressive psychosis
- Recurrent mania
- Mixed states
- Psychogenic affective psychosis

YES — Neurotic disorder — NO

- Depressive
- Anxious
- Hysterical
- Agoraphobic
- Social phobic
- Obsessional
- Hypochondriacal
- Depersonalization
- Anorexia nervosa

YES — Disorder personality — NO

- Sociopathic
- Paranoid
- Explosive
- Hysterical
- Anancastic
- Cycloid
- Schizoid
- Manifest mainly as drug or alcohol abuse or sexual deviation

- No mental disorder

partner (usually female) who may be murdered or violently attacked. In the presence of a colouring of depression or other affective disorder, the paranoid state is given precedence in diagnosis over the depressive component of the total picture.

Level 4 Affective psychoses or endogenous states (The various forms are listed in Table 1.) The symptomatology is not explicable as a variant of normal depression or elation of mood. Its features entail a qualitative departure from normal mental functioning, either in the form of delusional beliefs of guilt and self-reproach and anticipated punishment in the case of depression or, in the case of mania, in elevated mood, grandiose and expansive feelings that represent a stepwise change from the patient's normal behaviour, sexual inhibition, and insightless and ruinous extravagance. The basic personality remains intact during long periods of observation.

In recent years complex syndromes, combining schizophrenic and affective psychotic features, have appeared with greater frequency. The illness is associated in a substantial proportion of cases with an addiction to cocaine, heroin, chronic alcoholism, or other groups of drugs. Criminal and other antisocial behaviour and a steep decline down the social scale or other forms of personality disorder are manifest in some cases.

According to some authorities bipolar disorder should be given precedence in diagnosis as against melancholic and depressive disorders. This may be justified in practice but no evaluation of the proposal has yet been published.

Level 5 Neurotic disorders. (The forms of the disorder are summarized in Table 1.) The psychotic and endogenous affective disorders take precedence in the hierarchy over the depressive and other neurotic disorders. There is an absence of psychotic features such as delusions and of the typical cluster of specific biological changes, such as a tendency to early waking and diurnal variation of depression. Many forms of neurotic disorder respond to treatment with psychotherapy often combined with supervised biological treatments.

Level 6 Personality disorders *Personality disorders are characterized by a lifelong disturbance in behaviour, in personal relationships, social adjustment, and emotionality. The main features of maladjustment can be of disabling severity.

Neurotic disorders frequently appear in a setting of personality disorder. Neurotic breakdown is commonly manifest in the course of those with personality disorder. But those with compensating personality traits or high intelligence frequently respond to behavioural, cognitive, or dynamic therapy. The underlying personality disorder responds less favourably. The presence of alcohol, drug abuse, or unresolved sexual conflicts create further obstacles to improvement. But individuals with assets in the form of positive and constructive features can be helped to achieve a satisfactory adjustment.

Recent developments

The new biological era from the 1950s onwards During the 1950s the discovery of a number of powerful agents which exerted a therapeutic effect in psychiatric disorders marked the onset of the 'biological revolution'. ECT had appeared earlier but it had remained stationary over some decades. Pharmacological studies initiated a succession of significant findings regarding transmission of messages in the brain and the effects on it by a range of *neurotransmitters.

The first discovery was that of lithium by Cade in Australia. This and other discoveries emerged, not as a result of research after a specific hypothesis about causation but as a result of serendipity. Cade's discovery was first observed in animals and proved to have a strikingly mitigating influence upon the alternating manic and depressive symptoms in bipolar disorder. This occurred in 1949. It was not until the long period of obstinate criticism had been overcome that this method of treatment, as described by Mogens Schou, began to spread among psychiatrists and in the process brought to light a wealth of discoveries regarding the phenomenology of this disorder.

Other treatments with the same effects emerged and were used as substitutes in cases inactive to lithium. These included carbamazpine whose effectiveness was discovered by Takasaki et al. and valpromide also used in bipolar disorder, another alternative against this form of mental turmoil. Imipramine was discovered as treatment for depressive illness in the course of open clinical observation by Kuhn in 1957. Within a short period and before clinical trials had firmly established its efficacy, its adoption in practice made rapid progress alongside other treatments for affective disorder.

Other new drugs were capable of inducing total remission in a small proportion of patients with schizophrenia, but induced a remission of a more limited kind in a larger group. These were far from cures but they mitigated the disease and opened up possibilities for rehabilitation and possible discharge of patients into the community.

In addition, advances were recorded in diagnosis and classification of psychiatric disorders.

Progress in the development of classification and diagnosis of psychiatric disorders since 1950: a paradigm shift in the concept and diagnosis of psychiatric disorder One of the most important factors in the revolution of what has come to be called the era of biological psychiatry (in the broad sense of the term) has been the advances achieved in the classification and diagnosis of psychiatric disorders. Surveys undertaken by national and international psychiatric organizations at the beginning of the period reveal wide differences in psychiatric diagnosis reflected in figures of prevalence elicited by epidemiological enquiries and in the results achieved in the treatment of psychiatric disorders since the early 1950s.

Professor Erwin Stengel was invited by the World Health Organization to survey the situation and make recommendations in respect of the unreliability of standardized tests for the examination and diagnosis of psychiatric disorders. This was held up by a grave impediment to the advancement of clinical practice and scientific progress in psychiatry. Professor Stengel had wide-ranging credentials for this task. He had been trained as a clinical psychiatrist by Schulder, also as an immunologist and as a Freudian psychoanalyst in Vienna. He quickly identified the conservatism of the inevitably large international committees, which failed to secure general agreement to all innovations. Their speed was dictated by their slowest members. His second insight would prove a more dynamic one. He met Professor Carl Hempel in the early 1950s, and he recommended the use of 'operational definitions' for all mental syndromes and separate features used to identify them. This proved a fruitful path to follow. Its beneficial effects were manifest in the improvement in the reliability of psychiatric diagnosis in clinical and epidemiological practice that was recorded at an early stage of this period.

These recommendations slowly began to exert a radical influence upon the two main diagnostic scales employed in the classification of psychiatric disorders. In the United States, whose psychiatric populations were the largest and most influential in the world at the time, one scale was the Mental Health Section of the *International Classification of Diseases*. In 1959 Stengel, working for the World Health Organization, reported a poor level of reliability in studies undertaken for the 8th edition of the *International Classification of Diseases*. The second was the *Diagnostic and Statistical Manual of Mental Disorders* of the American Psychiatric Association.

In 1972 Feighner et al. in the United States used operational criteria developed for psychiatric research and applied them in the form of clear, specific inclusion and exclusion criteria for a clinical trial. This study came from the Department of Psychiatry in St. Louis, Mo., which was under the direction of Sam Guze and Eli Robins. The results of this limited study were the first step in the rapid development that led to the American system of diagnostic practice employed by the American Psychiatric Association.

1980 saw publication of the first full edition of the 3rd version of the *Diagnostic and Statistical Manual* (DSM-III). The next stage was to eliminate errors and make other modifications to the script that had not been completed for the 1980 edition. The final completed edition (DSM-IV) appeared in 1994.

An important outcome of the close collaboration on DSM-IV was with the investigators of the 10th edition of the *International Classification of Diseases* (ICD-10), whereby each of the teams appointed representative members of each of their most important working committees to function alongside the corresponding committee of the other organization.

In consequence, DSM-IV and ICD-10 were similar in all essential respects. DSM-IV, with both the teams working on diagnostic problems in the World Health Organization and in the American Psychiatric Association, suddenly acquired access to a greatly expanded potential readership, with opportunities for developing a greater range of joint international enquiries into a range of epidemiological, social, biological, and therapeutic problems.

The hierarchical order of psychiatric clinical syndromes

It was noted that in the disorders described so far and the theoretical disputes about their classification, virtually all the conditions were major psychiatric illnesses, such as schizophrenia or manic-depressive psychosis and disorders related to them. Leading clinicians and investigators who laid the foundations of clinical psychiatry towards the end of the 19th and the beginning of the 20th centuries, in Germany, France, and to some extent the Scandinavian countries, seemed to evince little interest in the neuroses and personality disorders. Their scientific papers were devoted to schizophrenia, paranoid and other delusional states, manic-depressive illness, general paralysis of the insane—their classification, diagnosis, and treatment and the philosophical and legal problems they posed.

One reason for this exclusiveness was that in the mental hospitals in which they conducted their work, the majority of those who had been admitted for psychiatric reasons were suffering from mental disorders that fell into one of the psychotic diagnostic groups cited. A high proportion had been admitted on a compulsory order and had to spend many months or years in hospital. Kraepelin, who was familiar with these disorders and referred to neuroses and personality disorders as 'psychopathies', made it clear in firm sentences that these patients were not suffering from psychiatric illness, or indeed any other medical disorder.

It was well into the modern era, in the 1950s, that Kurt Schneider, the famous German psychiatrist and pupil of Kraepelin, wrote a letter to German psychiatrists stating with a certain emphasis that neurotic and personality disorders did not constitute a medical illness. These patients, he stated, did not require medical treatment although psychotherapy might be useful for them.

However, towards the end of the 19th century a gifted young neurologist named Sigmund Freud moved into a field in which he had already published some works of distinction, to study patients with such conditions as 'hysteria', 'phobias', 'anxiety states', and 'personality disorders'. Moreover, he began to treat these patients at first with *hypnosis and later with the aid of psychoanalysis. He interpreted it as testifying to the consensual correctness of his theories of causation of mental disorders, such as those which emanated from the vicissitudes of unresolved conflicts, generated during the period of development between the early formative years of childhood and the adult mature personality.

Unlike clinical psychiatrists at the beginning of the 19th century, whose work was mainly devoted to the care of chronic psychotic patients and those with organic mental disorder, Freud devoted much of his time to the care of patients suffering from neuroses and personality disorders. They included eating disorders, drug dependence, and some with aggressive behaviour whose symptoms showed paths of continuity with their previous personality traits.

Personality disorder is much more often a predisposing factor in a cluster of psychiatric symptoms and signs rather than the actual cause of the presenting disorder. (In DSM-IV it is classed on Axis II as a concomitant contributory factor.)

By the second half of the 19th century systems of classification had developed to the stage at which classification of psychiatric disorders was already beginning to resemble the psychiatric classifications implemented in our time and used in the majority of countries that provide services for psychiatric patients. There was a variety of causal theories regarding the origin of the different syndromes with little evidence or knowledge. At present, descriptive terms of the phenomena of mental illness fall into six groups of disorder which are shown in Table 1. It will be noted from the ground covered earlier, that most of these groups were already recognized by the last few decades of the 19th century. The two main groups of psychotic disorder were widely accepted and the area of neurotic and personality disorders had been noted.

An early system of classification was that of Philippe Pinel, an intrepid and compassionate psychiatrist who had liberated the insane from their chains. His classification was simple and did not survive, but the force of the example he had set at the Salpetrière had inspired leading psychiatrists in France, where a beginning had been made in defining, for example, the two main groups of psychosis, and provided the early foundations for Kraepelin's major contributions.

The terms used by Jaspers to define the main phenomena of mental disorder were not purely descriptive. He amalgamated aetiological and descriptive criteria and included genuine epilepsy as a major 'functional' psychosis. He was in advance of his time in grouping neuroses with 'abnormal personalities' and combining them under the heading of 'psychopathies'.

Axis classification

A number of modern classifications have included multi-axial sections comprising several headings in respect of which information has to be provided. For example DSM-III and its successors (DSM-III-R, DSM-IV, etc.) include axes under five different headings.

Axis I In both the DSM and ICD systems of classification Axis I is derived from application of the clinical diagnostic criteria to the history and the findings recorded by examination of the patient. The character of the clinical items that have to be provided in relation to Axis II differ from those which have to be specified under Axis I. In the latter all items form part of the clinical profile of the illness under examination and the patient's experience of it. There is no specific link between the items other than the first (which represents the clinical diagnosis derived from Axis I). The items in Axis II relate to associated features that may be relevant for the causation, treatment, and management of the patient and for the prognosis of his condition. They may stem from such items as physical illness due to the age of the patient or his social status, employment, or religious affiliation. They do not necessarily discriminate the patient from other psychiatric disorders and may have no link with any operational inclusion criteria for diagnosis.

The information on the other axes helps to complete the clinical picture and may be relevant for management and prognosis of the patient's illness. But they differentiate the patient less sharply from those with other illnesses than the lists of operational criteria defined within schedules such as DSM-III and IV and ICD-10.

Axis II This is an associated feature only of some 40–45 per cent of those who present with obsessive-compulsive neurotic disorder as recorded on Axis I. But the personality disorder under this heading may occur in depressive, anxious, obsessional, and many other forms of illness. It also occurs as a normal variant that does not call for treatment. It may in fact be one of the patient's most valuable assets as an individual. It may occur in mentally normal individuals.

A similar statement can also be made with regard to schizoid personality. It is a feature in a proportion of those with current or prior schizophrenic illness. Something similar can be found in other disorders, as in obsessive-compulsive neurosis, paranoid psychoses, in socially isolated individuals who are, despite this, not schizophrenic.

Axis III requires specification of a general medical condition. Such information needed to be added and taken into account and set down in the patient's record. Here again physical illness is a common co-morbid condition in psychiatry and gains increasing prevalence with age.

In the treatment programme of psychiatric patients most include a detailed record of physical illness and disability. But it fails to discriminate in the form of disorder diagnosis under Axis I. In dealing with patients in old age it will be found in a high proportion of subjects, either in chronic or acute form. The diffuseness of its prevalence disqualifies it from inclusion among the operational cluster of clinical symptoms and signs which have to be evaluated in order to make a diagnosis.

Axis IV A response to Axis IV calls for information regarding psychosocial and other environmental problems. The information gathered under this heading is clearly of relevance. But there will be considerable variation in prevalence of these psychosocial and environmental problems and it is necessary to make a general statement regarding all psychiatric conditions in respect of this axis. It has no precise diagnostic value except for the genesis of maladjustment and conflict for which certain characteristic features of the patient's basic personality may be manifest.

Axis V Global assessment of function is a basis for assessment of progress or deterioration of the individual's mental health and social achievement. In the course of the disease it may be of crucial importance in accordance with Kraepelinian criteria. The school of Kraepelin which continues to exert a major influence on German psychiatry yields information that makes, as Kraepelin insisted, a specific contribution to diagnosis; in true schizophrenic illness the patient's personality deteriorates according to this school. This is probably the case in a high proportion of patients with hebephrenic schizophrenia or one that arises in a setting of a markedly abnormal personality. Recovery from the illness can be treated, according to some European psychiatrists, as an unequivocal refutation of the diagnosis of schizophrenia.

Neurosis and Psychosis

During the past fifteen years the terms 'psychosis' and 'neurosis', which were previously used in most systems of classification of psychiatric disorder, have been gradually eliminated from the main systems of classification, namely those embodied in ICD-10 and DSM-IV to which reference has been made above.

It has been claimed that use of such words as 'neurosis' and 'psychosis' add little or nothing to the information conveyed by the specific disorder from which the patient is judged to suffer, namely anxiety neurosis or schizophrenia. It is also stated by critics that criteria which are cited as discriminating between these two concepts are vague and unreliable. These views fail to take account of the role played by neurosis and psychosis as organizing concepts in clinical diagnosis and prediction.

The great majority of cases of neurosis can be understood as a quantitative measure of the patient's emotional life, intellectual functioning, confidence, and self-esteem. In psychosis, the contrast changes and qualitative delusions and hallucinations have no antecedents in the patient's premorbid mental life, whereas anxiety, depression, social phobia, agoraphobia, and obsessional neuroses are found to have premorbid antecedents in a circumscribed and non-disabling form. If compelled, the patient seeks help simply because the corresponding traits with which they could cope have undergone an incapacitating change in severity.

When a full history has been taken of the patient's development and adaptation of the premorbid state and an assessment has been made of the personality and the circumstances in which the neurotic disorder evolved, his/her illness can, with the help of empathy, usually be understood. This is not the case in psychotic disorders. There may have been a stepwise experience in the form of adverse circumstances, but the auditory hallucinations, the feelings of passivity, the incongruous emotions, the incoherent speech, have no understandable connection with the appearance of the first symptoms and signs. Jaspers brought these features of schizophrenic psychosis together by referring to them as a break in the continuity of psychic life. There is no such break in cases of neurosis. The continuity of mental life is maintained. With the exercise of empathy it is possible in neurosis to establish contact with the inner life of the patient and a therapeutic relationship can be established with the aid of the contact achieved. In psychotic illness, attempts at empathy usually fail.

Finally, in the great majority of civilized countries and some relatively primitive societies, the law makes a clear distinction between psychotic and neurotic disorder in its attitude towards responsibility for and treatment of those accused of serious offences such as murder. If an individual charged with killing or taking part in the killing of another person had an abnormality of mind which impaired his mental responsibility for his acts, he would not to be convicted of murder. 'Insanity', which invariably refers to psychosis, defends him from conviction of a charge of murder.

Neurosis, no matter how severe, is virtually never accepted as a condition that means an individual is not held to be mentally responsible for an act such as murder, though it might serve to mitigate the sentence. The law therefore recognizes a clear distinction between neurotic and psychotic persons. The abolition of the psychosis/ neurosis dichotomy does nothing to limit the punishment of those with neurosis, and threatens to eliminate the compassion which once protected those who in their mental turmoil can neither form intent nor recognize the difference between right and wrong, from inhumane and unjust punishment.

Summary and conclusions and possible future paths of enquiry

In psychiatry, as in other medical and scientific disciplines, advances in classification have been generally followed by progress in the recognition and treatment of mental disorders. A critical turning point was marked in the 1950s when the unreliability of the existing methods of discriminating between those with psychiatric disorder and those unaffected was recognized.

Erwin Stengel played a leading role at that time. He was quick to identify the defects in the instruments for establishing clinical diagnoses in psychiatry. He recommended the use of operational diagnostic definitions for all psychiatric syndromes and the features of their clinical profile. Each feature of the disorders had to be specified and described in lucid, unambiguous, and consistent language to ensure consistency by different participants.

Increasing expertise in Great Britain and the United States in particular from the 1950s onwards endowed the findings with greater authority. They also gave impetus to psychiatric research into neuropharmacological, biological, neurochemical, and genetic origins of the diseases. The influence of 'biological psychiatry' evolved in an exponential manner.

It is perhaps in the affective disorders that the course of the disease is transformed as compared with what was achieved in the past, for example, the discovery of effective treatments for manic–depressive (bipolar) disorder in the 1950s and drugs which improved the prognosis in schizophrenia. To a more limited extent there were advances in relation to some neurotic disorders, those with predominantly depressive or anxiety symptoms in particular. This ignited scientific enquiries into the mode of action of new pharmacological compounds, research to define the fundamental cerebral mechanisms and the neuronal pathways involved, and the neurotransmitters and their interconnections which mediated them.

Hypotheses were also investigated in attempts to define the normal function of the newly discovered drugs and the role of the underlying cerebral functional systems that came to light in normal mental functioning.

The new knowledge has transformed the chances of relief or recovery in manic depression ('bipolar disorder'), schizophrenia, and paranoid psychoses. Special mention is perhaps deserved by the mental disorders of old age. This area has been transformed during the period from one of general gloom and despondency to one in which a number of disorders formerly regarded as due to 'senile' cerebral degeneration have been shown to respond well to treatment. This has led to scientific developments which show high promise of coming to fruition (Roth and Iversen, 1986, Wischik et al. 1997).

In contrast to these achievements there is a whole range of disorders in psychiatry presenting challenges not only to families but to societies where the progress of enquiry and understanding has stood relatively still. No significant advances have been made in countering the growing problems of addiction to hard drugs such as cocaine, heroin, and dextroamphetamine, established addictions developed against a background of personality disorders.

'Histrionic personality disorder', 'paranoid personality disorder', 'narcissistic personality disorder', 'antisocial personality disorder', 'borderline personality disorder', schizotypal personality, and psychopathic personality with addiction to cocaine and heroin, and personality disorders with chronic alcoholism, are some of the disorders of personality which have become increasingly prominent in psychiatric practice.

Nor has there been progress in research into conditions more in the clinical stream, such as anorexia nervosa, a state of self-induced starvation, often seen in the setting of high intelligence or other gifts, alcoholism, or addiction to hard drugs. There is no decrease either in the number of those who simulate disease in order to gain the comfort they derive from medical care and attention. These are individuals who simulate surgical emergencies or fabricate haemorrhages or other states resembling medical crises to gain admission to hospitals for medical attention. A disturbing aspect of the phenomenon of *Munchausen syndrome by proxy has been the infliction of artefact injuries, or the addition of insulin or other potentially lethal substances into blood or other fluid being administered to patients by intravenous drips, a crime for which several parents and nurses have received sentences of imprisonment.

Jaspers's contribution Long before the concept of phenomenological psychiatry there was theoretical consideration of the relationship between psychotic disorders on the one hand and personality and related disorders on the other. Jaspers, a pioneer of modern psychiatry, had devoted considerable effort to drawing a sharp distinction between the two types of psychiatric disorder. There were those suffering from disorders that could be understood with the aid of empathy into the patient's mental processes and attitudes. The presenting disorder is found to emerge as a result of a continuous 'developmental' process which culminates in the emergence of a neurotic and/or personality disorder in adult life.

On the other hand there were those suffering from disorders that were beyond the reach of comprehension. Insight and understanding into the condition manifest could not be gained by any such effort. Conditions such as schizophrenia and manic-depressive psychosis entailed a break in the continuity of psychic life, to advance beyond comprehension into intervals of illness, or into a state sustained for the rest of the lifespan, even after the patient had suffered and displayed many attacks, and bore no relationship to any progressive, dynamic sequence which could provide an explanation.

The first of the two forms was given the name 'development' by Jaspers. This issued from his observation that these states evolved gradually and continuously to manifest in adolescent or adult life. With the aid of empathy he had achieved entry into the inner life of his subject during years of investigation in attempts to understand how the vulnerable facets in the personality evolved. In contrast, psychotic disorders such as schizophrenia, which he named as 'process', were impervious to enquiry to deepen understanding or attempts at treatment by psychological means.

Jaspers's concept of mental disorder was wide but consistent with his general theory, unlike some psychiatrists who regard anti-social forms of personality disorder as being more a problem for the law and police than psychiatry. Those who covertly inflict injuries on themselves or those who harm or kill others are not psychiatric problems; anorexia nervosa is not a disease, but it has complications of disease and episodes of self-display and narcissistic excess. Eating disorders simply reveal immature or hysterical personalities. The addictive gambler ruins himself and his family and the personality disordered alcoholic dies of liver or cardiac disorders.

With some of the disorders listed here psychiatrists have a compelling duty to collaborate with the police and the law. But they cannot neglect clinical and scientific interests in these phenomena, which cannot be omitted from consideration in attempts to gain insight into the psychopathology of personality disorders.

In recent years cognitive and behavioural therapies have achieved significant results and some significant findings in patients with neuroses have been recorded. These are less expensive, more effective and dynamic than psychoanalytic methods. Very little has been written about phenomenological methods of psychotherapy, which approach the patient through empathy and identification carried out by an experienced and sensitive psychotherapist. This would prove to be a valuable task by trying to map the landscape of inner experiences and observe the results of the course of treatment.

The German psychiatrists who exerted a powerful influence on European clinical and therapeutic psychiatry regarded personality disorders and neuroses as being out of the scope of medical practice. Jaspers's concepts were far wider. He was the first psychiatrist to state boldly that personality disorders, including whatever repugnant offences had been committed by psychopathic criminals, had an important place in psychiatric theory and practice. His writing, as embodied in his classical work (Jaspers 1913), conceived psychiatry in particular terms, enabled to do this by his wide interest in literature and art and his philosophical training and originality. His contributions to philosophy before and after his departure from psychiatry have been widely regarded as original, lucid, and profound.

His views of psychoanalysis took account both of its contributions and shortcomings. His wisdom and compassion for those who suffer in mind and the breadth of his intellect endow his reading with deep interest. His book *General Psychopathology* (1913; trans. into English 1963) was widely acclaimed but very few psychiatrists proceeded to carry his contributions further with the aid of fresh research. There has been only a thin trickle of papers and Jaspers has described the methods in use in empathic approaches to patients as crude. Other contemporary variants of psychotherapy, namely cognitive and behavioural psychotherapy, have failed to make any deep or lasting contribution to those with personality disorder whether anti-social or neurotic in its expression.

As the few cases described by Jaspers and some of his colleagues are stimulating and of profound interest, there is a need to carry his work into contemporary psychiatric research and clinical practice. Initial work would have to be on an individual basis. This would not be scientific in character but would form the basis of a preliminary classification of psychopathology as detected by empathic approaches to the relationship with the patients and to the techniques employed in treatment. There is good reason to anticipate that such studies would bring order and understanding to the personality disorders in particular, and also to neuroses and their relationships to normal states of mental distress and suffering. MaR

Baillarger, J. (1853). 'Note on the type of insanity with attacks characterised by two regular periods, one of depression and one of excitation'. *Bulletin de l'Académie National de Médecine*, 19.

American Psychiatric Association. (1980). *Diagnostic and Statistical Manual of Mental Disorders DSM-III* (3rd edn.), DSM-III-R, 1987, (rev. 3rd edn.), DSM-IV, 1994, (4th edn.).

Falret, J. P. (1854). 'Mémoire sur la folie circulaire'. *Bulletin de l'Académie National de Médecine*, 19. (Trans. into English in M. J. Sedler and E. C. Dessain (1983). 'Falret's discovery: the origin of the concept of bipolar affective illness'. *American Journal of Psychiatry*, 140.

Feighner, J. P., Robins, E., Guze, S. B., et al (1972). 'Diagnostic criteria for use in psychiatric research'. *Archives of General Psychiatry*, 26.

Griesinger, W (1867). *Mental Pathology and Therapeutics* (2nd, edn.).

Jaspers, K. (1913). *Allgemeine Psychopathologie*.

Kahlbaum, K. (1863). *Die Gruppierung der psychischen Krankheiten*.

Kraepelin, E. (1893). *Ein Lehrbuch für Studierende und Aerzt*.

——(1897). 'Dementia praecox'. In *Clinical Roots of Schizophrenia Concept* (ed. J. Cutting and M. Shepherd, 1981).

Schneider, K. (1950). *Psychopathic Personalities* (9th edn.).

World Health Organization (1993). *International Classification of Diseases*, 10th rev. (ICD-10).

Cleomedes. (c.1st–3rd century). Greek philosopher-scientist, author of the *Meteora* (Celestial Bodies), a popular astronomy textbook. Best known for stating the contemporary arguments that the earth was a sphere, and for his estimates of the size of the earth and the sun. As a Stoic he argued against the Epicurean position that we see objects as having their true size, giving the small and variable perceived size of the sun as a counter-example. He explained the small sun by reduced distance perception combined with size–distance invariance (*Emmert's law). He explained the relatively enlarged horizon sun (*moon illusion) in two ways: partly as an angular enlargement caused by atmospheric refraction, similar to enlargement when looking into water; and partly as a linear enlargement caused by increased apparent distance in a misty atmosphere. He attributed these views to Posidonius (c.135–50 BC), but is the earliest extant author to explain the celestial illusion by apparent distance. His explanations remained at the geometrical level, and unlike *Ptolemy (2nd century) he did not speculate on sensory mechanisms.   HER

Ross, H. E. (2000). 'Cleomedes (c.1st century AD) on the celestial illusion, atmospheric enlargement, and size-distance invariance'. *Perception*, 29.

'Clever Hans'. A famous horse once thought to possess powers of telepathy. The horse (of a Russian trotting-horse breed), which lived in Berlin at the beginning of the 20th century, could apparently perform arithmetic in the presence of its owner by tapping a hoof on the ground to count out the answer. Fraud seemed unlikely since the owner and trainer, Herr von Osten, would allow people (free of charge) to watch the animal perform and even to question it themselves.

The phenomenon was investigated in 1904 by O. Pfungst, a student of the psychologist C. Stumpf, and Pfungst subsequently reported his findings in a book, *Clever Hans*. His conclusion was that the horse was receiving clues from *gestures made, probably unwittingly, by the owner and other questioners—an example of non-verbal communication which is easily taken for telepathy.

See also EXTRASENSORY PERCEPTION.

Pfungst, O. (1911). *Clever Hans*. Trans. C. L. Rahn.

'cocktail party' effect. The rejection of unwanted messages by the ears. This rejection depends largely on *binaural hearing, and allows signal sources to be localized. However, the quality of the voice, such as the sex of the speaker, can also be used to accept or reject messages. See ATTENTION; CHANNELS, NEURAL.

Carterette, E. C., and Friedman, M. P. (1978). 'Perceptual processing'. *Handbook of Perception*, 9.

code, coding, and decoding. When physical events or patterns, such as letters and numbers, represent a message, the message is said to be 'encoded' in the marks or events. Thus neural signals (action potentials) are coded activity from the sense organs and must be decoded to be useful. The amount of information that can be transmitted depends not only on the bandwidth (the frequency response) of the *channel but also on the appropriateness of the coding. Morse code is efficient because the most frequent letters are the shortest—they have the fewest dots and dashes—and so occupy least time.

For *cognition—perception or behaviour based on knowledge—neural signals are 'read' on the basis of knowledge or assumptions, which may be false. See INFORMATION THEORY; ILLUSIONS.

cognition. The use or handling of knowledge. Those who stress the role of cognition in *perception underline the importance of knowledge-based processes in making sense of the 'neurally coded' signals from the eye and other sensory organs. It seems that man is different from other animals very largely because of the far greater richness of his cognitive processes. Associated with *memory of individual events and sophisticated generalizations, they allow subtle analogies and explanations—and ability to draw pictures and speak and write. The word 'cognition' is probably related to 'gnomon'—the shadow-casting rod of a sundial—which measures the heavens from shadows.

cognitive modularity. Normal adult patients who sustain some form of sudden brain injury sometimes furnish the field of adult neuropsychology with fascinating cases that yield selective impairment of particular cognitive domains. Thus, after brain insult, prospagnosics suddenly find it impossible to recognize familiar faces, whereas the rest of their spatial processing seems intact. Patients with agrammatism frequently have difficulty using the syntax and morphology of a language, while retaining fluent deployment of vocabulary and other cognitive domains. Acalculic patients display extreme difficulty with some aspects of numerical processing and yet, for instance, their linguistic, spatial, and social cognition reveal scores in the normal range. Such cases have led many neuropsychology theorists to claim that the adult brain is composed of independently functioning cognitive modules that can be selectively spared or impaired. For several decades, such theorizing remained in the form of box-and-arrow models in which one or more boxes in the information flow were crossed through.

It was in 1983 that a much more precise definition of the characteristics of a module were put forward by Jerry Fodor. Fodor divided the human brain into input systems like visual perception and syntax, which were for him the modular part of the mind/brain, and a central, non-modular system that comprised the brain's more cognitive aspects. For Fodor, a module had to meet a number of criteria:

1. Encapsulation: it is impossible to interfere with the inner workings of a module.
2. Unconciousness: it is difficult or impossible to think about or reflect upon the operation of a module.
3. Speed: modules process data in a very fast manner.
4. Shallow outputs: modules provide limited output, without information about the intervening steps that led to that output.
5. Obligatory firing: modules operate reflexively, providing predetermined outputs for predetermined inputs, regardless of the context.
6. Ontogenetic universals: modules develop in a characteristic sequence.
7. Domain specificity: modules deal exclusively with a single information type.
8. Pathological universals: modules break down in a characteristic fashion following some damage to the system.

It was the co-occurrence of these criteria, rather than any single one, that characterized a module for Fodor. Even if subsequently hotly debated, this was a useful model in that it clearly specified what could and could not count as a cerebral module. However, the psychological field was quick to extend the concept of module to cognitive domains such as the lexicon, number, face processing, spatial cognition, and the like. In particular, certain theorists generalized arguments from adult neuropsychology to the developmental case, arguing that evolution had provided the human infant with a number of innately determined modules, each processing proprietary inputs and merely requiring appropriate environmental stimuli to be triggered. In other words, they argued that the infant brain comes pre-specified to process and represent each cognitive domain.

The original data for such arguments emanated from previously normal adult patients, not from infants, but the developmental literature was quick to take on board the notion of a modular mind. Thus, more than two decades of infancy research was to some large degree focused on attempts to validate the modularity thesis. If, for instance, a group of 3-month-old infants was found to be sensitive to changes in, say, the numerosity of displays, the authors tended to claim that the number ability was innate. But it

was the existence of certain types of developmental disorders that, temporarily at least, gave the modularity thesis its real boost and led not merely to the innateness claims but also to the search for a gene or a specific set of genes contributing to each cognitive module.

A number of genetic disorders were pinpointed for modularity theorizing. One of the most cited was that of *autism. Several researchers claimed that people with autism displayed a selective impairment in their so-called 'theory-of-mind module'. Experiments suggested that individuals with autism had particular problems with attributing intentional, mental states to others, while they seemed relatively unimpaired on tasks of equivalent complexity but involving physical objects rather than human beings. Likewise, other researchers hailed certain subgroups of children with so-called specific language impairment as demonstrating that aspects of language develop in isolation of other cognitive skills. Another example came from *Williams syndrome. This rare genetic disorder was upheld by many theorists as demonstrating the independent functioning of language and face processing, alongside seriously impaired spatial cognition. In each of these examples, the (sometimes implicit, sometimes explicit) claim was that the neonate brain is composed of some intact and some deficient or missing cognitive modules, as if the brain developed as a series of isolated components with no effect of the development of any one of them on the development of the others. And, because the disorders were genetic in origin, the search then began for the gene or specific set of genes that codes for such modules. Mouse experiments were soon to corroborate these ideas: the breeding of mice with a single knockout gene in the same chromosomal region as a human disorder revealed impairments of, say, spatial cognition that seemed to resemble the spatial impairments found in the human case.

All of the above approaches look very promising for the modularity thesis and for the notion that cognitive modules are innately specified. But there is a fundamental flaw in the logic of the arguments: there is no mention whatsoever of the process of *ontogenetic development* or self-development. The claim for innately specified modules negates a role for ontogenesis and denies the possibility that, although the *adult* mind/brain may be highly specialized and modular-like, the infant brain does not necessarily begin that way. Rather than generalizing the rather static, adult neuropsychological view to the developmental case, it is vital to consider the possibility that modules are the *end product* of an ontogenetic process, not its starting point. Numerous studies of brain development in human infants have now shown that infants sculpt their own brains as a function of both internal neurocomputational constraints and their active processing of environmental input. Even a domain as crucial to human survival as species recognition, i.e. face processing, takes some twelve months of massive input to progressively reach adult-like brain specialization and localization of function. And the development of face processing continues throughout childhood and puberty. If there is a face-processing module in the adult brain that can be selectively impaired in prosopagnosia, such a module is the result of gradual changes in hemispheric dominance and brain circuitry over the first years of life. And the fact that face processing seems to be intact in a disorder with otherwise low intelligence may turn out to be a myth: the electrophysiological processes underlying equivalent *behavioural* scores in normal controls and adults with Williams syndrome, for example, turn out to be different at the level of the brain.

So, is modularity a useless concept in the cognitive neurosciences? Yes and no. Yes, when theorists focus only on adult end states or when they claim that everything in the brain is modular. In that case, the plethora of tiny modules for each cognitive mechanism makes the concept rather meaningless. But its use in adult cognitive neuroscience can give precision to hypotheses about the relative specialization of brain structure, provided researchers are not seduced by a static view of specific cerebral areas 'lighting up' to specific cognitive inputs and that they always keep in mind that, if modules exist, they are likely to be the result of a lengthy, dynamic developmental process.   AKS

Bellugi, U., Marks, S., Bihrle, A. M., and Sabo, H. (1988). 'Dissociation between language and cognitive functions in Williams syndrome'. In Mogsford, D. B. K. (ed.), *Language Development in Exceptional Circumstances*.

Fodor, J. (1983). *The Modularity of Mind*.

Karmiloff-Smith, A. (1992). *Beyond Modularity: A Developmental Perspective on Cognitive Science*.

——(1998). 'Development itself is the key to understanding developmental disorders'. *Trends in Cognitive Sciences*, 2/10.

Paterson, S. J., Brown, J. H., Gsödl, M. K., Johnson, M. H., and Karmiloff-Smith, A. (1999). 'Cognitive modularity and genetic disorders'. *Science*, 286/5448.

Pinker, S. (1999). *Words and Rules*.

collective unconscious. See JUNG, CARL GUSTAV.

colour-blindness. See COLOUR VISION: EYE MECHANISMS.

colour perception: constancy and contrast. From the time of the ancient Greeks, philosophers have cast doubt on the veracity of the senses, because their reports of the outside world are inherently subjective. Colour is the quintessential *qualia: according to Galileo, it is something that 'resides only in the consciousness' (Gottlieb 2000), not a hard property of real objects.

Perception is remarkable in keeping things appearing much the same in varying conditions. Colours are hardly affected by changes of the ambient light, and sizes remain almost constant for different distances (though this breaks down for large distances, or looking downwards from a considerable height). Evidently there are active scaling processes that make the world appear stable under the ever-changing conditions of perceiving things. When the scaling is not appropriate many *illusions are created.

1. Colour constancy
2. Chromatic adaptation
3. Models of colour constancy
4. Simultaneous colour contrast
5. Colour assimilation
6. Measurements of colour perception

1. Colour constancy
Colour is indeed a construct of the mind, but many modern scientists now believe that it is constructed for a specific purpose: to measure an immutable, physical property, which does exist 'out there'. We possess colour constancy, a fundamental mechanism of vision, which ensures that object colours remain nearly constant even under changing illumination. Thus, a yellow banana stays yellow whether we see it in sunlight or under the glow of a tungsten lamp.

Colour constancy is a remarkable feat, because the light spectrum reflected by the banana changes markedly as the incident light spectrum changes. What remains invariant (until the fruit begins to spoil) is the spectral reflectance of the banana's surface, the physical characteristic that describes the proportion of incident light that it reflects at each wavelength, which is governed largely by the pigment embedded in its skin. Colour constancy enables us to compensate for changes in the spectrum of the illumination, and extract a measure of the banana's surface spectral reflectance from the changing light it reflects. How? We now know that there are several mechanisms that contribute to colour constancy.

2. Chromatic adaptation
At the lowest level of the visual system, chromatic adaptation plays a key role. Each of the three types of cone photoreceptor is responsive to a broad segment of the spectrum (the long- (L), middle- (M), and short- (S) wavelength-selective cones). As the intensity of light in their preferred wavelength band is increased, the sensitivity of the photoreceptors decreases, cancelling out the change in the illumination spectrum. For example, as the sun sets and the long-wavelength light reflected from the scene increases, the sensitivity of the long-wavelength cones decreases, and therefore their excitation tends to remain the same. The notion that the response of each distinct type of receptor may be continually adjusted by a measure of its average stimulation over the whole scene was first proposed by J. von Kries in 1902, before the receptors themselves had been identified.

3. Models of colour constancy

Many theoretical models of colour constancy are based on von Kries-like adaptation of the receptors or the colour-opponent neurons higher in the visual pathway. The question still remains, though, as to how and where—neurally—the necessary sampling of reflected light over the whole scene is performed. It might be that rapid eye movements successively expose the photoreceptors to different parts of the scene, thereby enabling the average to be computed in the retina. Or, it might be that neurons with large receptive fields in the cerebral cortex simultaneously pool information from large regions. In his landmark model, Edwin Land (1964) proposed a specific method for computing the relative reflectance values of a surface in three chromatic channels, by tracking the ratio between the reflected light intensities at nearby points along many random paths starting from the target surface. Land's algorithm was a prescription for a robot, not a description of biology, but in naming it the Retinex, he accorded the retina and cerebral cortex equal probability as sites for similar mechanisms in the human brain. What is known is that chromatic adaptation occurs very quickly, being nearly complete in less than one minute.

The hallmark of von Kries-like models is that they could be implemented at very early levels of the visual pathway, before the brain 'parses' the image into its distinct components. Other mechanisms likely to contribute to colour constancy require more sophisticated image processing: for example, specular highlights (mirror-like reflections of incident light from glossy surfaces) carry direct information about the colour of the illumination. But for this information to be used, bright spots in an image must first be identified for what they are. At an even higher level, cognition may intervene: it may be that we recognize and memorize the colour of familiar objects such as our own hands, and, when the illumination changes, use their colour to calibrate the colours of other objects in the scene.

All modern explanations of colour constancy acknowledge that it can only occur for surfaces in the context of other surfaces: the phenomenon requires comparisons between the light reflected from a surface and its surroundings. Thus, in a seemingly paradoxical way, colour constancy may explain the colour mutability that artists have exploited for centuries: colours depend on the colours we have just seen, nearby in either space or time.

4. Simultaneous colour contrast

This phenomenon is perhaps the most striking example of how colours depend on their context. In the late 19th century, Michel Chevreul, director of dyeing at the Gobelin factory in Paris, observed that the difference between two opposing colours is dramatically enhanced when they are juxtaposed: reds appear redder when placed next to green, blues more blue when placed next to orange, darks darker when surrounded by lights. A small square painted with grey ink will appear pink against a background painted green; it appears greenish when surrounded by red. Chevreul meticulously formulated many such laws of colour contrast, prefiguring the computerized colour appearance models used in today's colour industries.

Recent experiments show that, for simple configurations, the colour appearance of surface may be simply predicted by the ratio between the cone excitations from it and its background. Since changes in natural daylight tend to preserve this ratio, it may be that encoding colours as cone contrasts evolved as a means of achieving colour constancy (Foster and Nascimento 1994).

5. Colour assimilation

In simultaneous contrast, the surrounding colour induces its opponent colour in the target surface. In the lesser-known but equally vivid phenomenon of colour assimilation, the surrounding colour induces the same colour as itself in the target surface. For example, take a chequerboard pattern of alternating green and purple squares. In the centre of the chequerboard, replace a small number of green squares with grey squares. These grey squares will take on a purplish hue, like their immediate surroundings. If the grey squares instead replace the purple squares, they take on a greenish hue.

Why does colour assimilation occur in some patterns, and contrast in others? The full answer is not known, but one rule seems to be: when the surrounding colour is periodically interleaved with the target colour on a fine spatial scale, the colours assimilate. This may be because fine-scale variations in colour are more likely to result from a pattern on a single material than from local changes in illumination; so to estimate any bias induced by the global illumination, these variations must be smoothed, or assimilated. Once assimilated, the common effects of the illumination must be factored out; hence, the need for contrast on a large scale.

Thus, colour contrast and assimilation may both result from a natural striving towards colour constancy in an unnatural situation. The pictures with which we illustrate contextual influences on colour are not like the sunlit vistas in which colour constancy evolved. When the scene does not meet the ancient criteria laid down, constancy mechanisms may fail, with spectacular consequences. Indeed, colour constancy fails under artificial lights (notably, many fluorescent lights) whose energy spectra are not smooth but jagged.

6. Measurements of colour perception

The fact that we can measure the failure of colour constancy does not mean that we can now measure qualia. We can only measure the physical properties of lights and surfaces and record behavioural responses, typically by asking the observer (*a*) to report whether two distinct light spectra appear the same or different, (*b*) to adjust the components of a coloured light to match another, or (*c*) to name the colour.

Matching by adjustment is the technique most often used to demonstrate colour constancy. For example, the observer may be asked to adjust the light reflected from a surface so that it appears 'grey' or 'achromatic' under the particular light source illuminating the scene. If the observer adjusts the light to be the same as that reflected by a true 'grey' surface reflectance (say, if he reproduces the yellowish light that a neutral surface reflects under a yellowish source) then he shows perfect colour constancy. Intriguingly, observers often show relatively poor colour constancy when it is measured with simulated papers and light sources displayed on a computer screen. Yet, measurements under more natural conditions, with real surfaces and lights, reveal almost perfect constancy (Kraft and Brainard 1999). The discrepancy may be because, under natural conditions, all the higher-order clues contribute in full, including those from specular highlights and cognitive factors. None the less, low-level mechanisms of chromatic adaptation and contrast probably do the bulk of the work. This conclusion is supported by the fact that other animals, including goldfish, honeybees, and hens, all show colour constancy when tested with surface identification tasks (Neumeyer 1998).

Colour naming is the least reliable method for measuring perception. Over the past half-century, anthropologists and psychologists have searched for proof that colour is a human universal. In 1969, Berlin and Kay famously argued that all languages develop at least two of the following basic colour terms in the following evolutionary order: white/black, red, green/yellow, blue, brown, purple/pink/orange/grey. The evidence for linguistic universality is shaky (Saunders and van Brakel 1997). Yet, while colour-naming systems vary widely across cultures, basic colour discrimination abilities do not: the Quechi Indians have only one word for blue and green, yet put them in different perceptual categories (Davidoff 1991).

Thus, although no one can experience your perception of yellow, or prove that it is the same as mine, colour scientists can predict which physical and physiological conditions are necessary for you to report the yellow you claimed earlier. In the contextual dependence of colours lies a fundamental similarity between minds—the way in which colours vary·is the same from person to person. Despite their subjectivity, colours are trustworthy measures of real object properties.   ACH

Davidoff, J. (1991). *Cognition through Colour*.

Foster D. H., and Nascimento, S. M. C. (1994). 'Relational colour constancy from invariant cone-excitation ratios'. *Proceedings of the Royal Society of London Series B Biological Sciences*, 257.

Gottlieb, A. (2000). *The Dream of Reason*.

Kraft, J. M., and Brainard, D. H. (1999). 'Mechanisms of color constancy under nearly natural viewing'. *Proceedings of the National Academy of Sciences of the USA*, 96.

Land, E. H. (1964). 'The retinex'. *American Scientist*, 52.

Neumeyer, C. (1998). 'Comparative aspects of colour constancy'. In Walsh, V., and Kulikowski, J. J. (eds.), *Perceptual Constancy: Why Things Look as They Do*.

Saunders, B. A. C., and van Brakel, J. (1997). 'Are there nontrivial constraints on colour categorization?' *Behavioural and Brain Sciences*, 20.

colour vision: brain mechanisms. In *colour vision: eye mechanisms, William Rushton outlines the trichromatic theory that colour vision is mediated by three different kinds of retinal receptor, each responding best to light from a different part of the visible spectrum. The theory is based firmly on the empirically established trichromacy of colour matching: given any four coloured lights, it is always possible to place three of them on one side of a foveal matching field and one on the other, or two on one side and two on the other, and by adjusting the radiances of three of them cause the two sides of the field to match. When the observer makes his adjustment he is thought to be equating, on the two sides of the field, the rates of quantum catch in the three classes of cone. If the two sets of quantum catches are identical, then we may suppose that subsequent neural events are also equivalent and the two sides of the field will look alike to the observer. However, the trichromatic theory limits itself to predicting whether or not two colours will *look alike*; it does not tell us how they will actually look to the observer.

1. Opponent colour theory
2. Electrophysiological studies of opponent processes
3. Psychophysical studies of opponent processes
4. Luminance
5. An analogy with colour television
6. Cortical analysis of colour

1. Opponent colour theory

Historically, a number of rivals to the trichromatic theory have taken as their starting point the phenomenology of colour. The most celebrated of these rivals is the 'opponent colour' or 'tetrachromatic' theory of Ewald *Hering. The trichromatic theory, in the form that it was advanced by Thomas *Young, James Clerk Maxwell, and Hermann von *Helmholtz, does not obviously account for the fact that a mixture of yellowy red and yellowy green can produce a yellow that is without trace of redness or greenness. Hering proposed that colour analysis depends on the action of two types of detector, each having two modes of response: one detector that signals either red or green, and a second that signals either yellow or blue. Finally he supposed that brightness depends on a system that signals white or black. Thus one can see a colour that looks greenish, and bluish, and dark, but not one that is both reddish and greenish, or both light and dark, and so on.

Nowadays it is generally held that a complete theory of colour vision must draw elements from both the trichromatic and the opponent colour theories. Indeed, Helmholtz himself proved that the two theories are not incompatible, since a simple transformation could change the three receptor outputs into two difference signals and one additive signal. Wasserman (1978) gives Helmholtz's argument. Unfortunately, this statement by Helmholtz appeared only in the second edition of his *Handbuch der physiologischen Optik* (1896) and was missing from the third edition (1909), the latter being the one translated into English (by the Optical Society of America, in 1924).

2. Electrophysiological studies of opponent processes

A transformation of the kind considered by Helmholtz probably occurs in the retina itself. In 1958, MacNichol and Svaetichin found that, at the level of the horizontal cells in the goldfish retina, light of one wavelength may depolarize (i.e. excite) a cell, whereas light from a different part of the spectrum may hyperpolarize (i.e. inhibit the cell). In the absence of stimulation the cell's electrical potential has an intermediate value, and this potential can be increased or decreased by stimulating the retina with different colours. Soon afterwards De Valois reported opponent responses in the lateral geniculate nuclei of macaque monkeys, and others have reported such responses at the level of retinal ganglion cells in the monkey, although it has so far proved difficult to obtain recordings from the more distal cells of the primate retina. Thus De Valois was led to propose that colour information is transformed from a 'component' system (three cone types giving responses that increase with increasing intensity of stimulation) to an 'opponent' system in which some wavelengths cause an increase in a given retinal signal and other wavelengths cause a decrease. Such an opponent system effectively transmits colour difference signals: for example, a cell that increases its firing rate as a result of stimulation with red (R) light and decreases its firing rate with green (G) stimulation can be said to be signalling $+R - G$.

If colour difference signals are transmitted, can we tell which combinations of receptor responses are 'differenced'? There is some doubt about this, since the electrophysiological reports are not entirely consistent, but by and large, if we call the three cone types R, G, and B, neural pathways have been found that signal $\pm (R - G)$ and $\pm [(R+G) - B]$. It should be noted that in the second of these expressions, the sum $(R+G)$ may be taken as signalling 'yellow'. This may be the explanation for why yellow is the fourth psychological primary—along with red,

green, and blue. It seems that the responses from the R and G cones are added, thus generating a spare colour (yellow) that looks neither green nor red, and is complementary to blue. For details of the physiological evidence for opponent processing, see De Valois and De Valois (1975).

3. Psychophysical studies of opponent processes

There is good psychophysical evidence that opponent colour channels exist. Thus the efficacy of two adapting fields of different wavelength (or the detectability of two lights of different wavelength) may be less when the two are concurrently presented than when either alone is present (see Mollon 1982). In these experiments the observer is asked only to detect a liminal (difference) stimulus; he is not asked to make subjective judgements about the quality of the colour appearance.

It is currently a controversial question how closely these psychophysically demonstrated opponencies are related to the phenomenological oppositions of red and green and of yellow and blue. The latter oppositions, however, can be systematically measured. This was classically done in the 1950s by Jameson and Hurvich (see Hurvich 1978), using the method of *hue cancellation*: to measure, say, the amount of yellowness in a series of wavelengths from the long-wavelength part of the spectrum, the experimenter adds blue light of a fixed wavelength to each in turn of the long wavelengths. The long wavelengths would range from a slightly yellowish green to a deep red. For each of these test wavelengths, the observer is asked to adjust the added blue light until the mixture looks neither yellowish nor bluish. The amount of blue light required is the dependent variable and is taken as a measure of the yellowness, the 'yellow chromatic valence', of the test wavelength.

4. Luminance

The main tenet of opponent colour theory is that there are two independent '*channels' signalling colour information. One of these signals red or green, the other signals yellow or blue. But from trichromatic theory it is clear that we need three, not two, independent variables to describe colour appearance. Thus, a third channel is necessary. What does this channel signal? The answer is luminance. The signals from the R and G (but probably not B) cones are added, and the information is transmitted as luminance. But again, it is opponent coded. The channel signals 'brighter' or 'darker', but with respect to what? Simply with respect to other parts of the picture, or retinal image. The luminance channel signals comparative information, not about absolute local luminance but about how the local luminance compares with the rest of the scene. Comparisons are made not across colour but across space. The visual system places heavy emphasis on comparison across space. The impressive colour effects demonstrated by Edwin Land (see RETINEX THEORY AND COLOUR CONSTANCY) are a powerful example of long-range interaction in the visual system.

5. An analogy with colour television

Why should opponent coding of colour have evolved? It may be useful to draw analogies with colour television. About 1950, television engineers started looking for a means of transmitting an acceptable colour picture efficiently. This meant transmitting as little information as possible (i.e. keeping the bandwidth low), with a high level of resistance to extraneous noise, and in a way that was compatible with monochrome receivers, i.e. capable of giving an acceptable black-and-white picture.

Obviously this analogy cannot be pursued too far, since colour television aims to provide an image that is a good substitute for the original object; the visual system of each member of the audience must then get to work on the picture. However, the choice of how much importance to attach to different aspects of the information contained in the picture, and how to transmit the information most efficiently, seems to raise interesting questions for visual science.

The simplest system would 'look at' the original scene through three primary filters, transmit the three pictures separately, and recombine them in the receiver. Since the G primary is most similar to the luminance signal, this would be the one that monochrome receivers would receive. But errors would result, reds being too dim and greens too bright. More importantly, three times as much information would have to be transmitted (so the bandwidth would be trebled) in comparison with monochrome transmission. This would be expensive, and impossible where many broadcasts must share a limited range of radio frequencies.

At the time when colour television was being developed, it was known that visual acuity was worse for colour than for brightness contrast. Since it was desirable to separate colour and luminance anyway (to allow monochrome sets to receive a true luminance signal) there now appeared a way of reducing the total transmission bandwidth: give the colour information less bandwidth than the luminance information. But how could colour and luminance be separated? A neat mathematical solution presented itself: opponent coding. If R, G, and B are the signals from the red, green, and blue receivers respectively, then we can define luminance, L, as

$$L = 0.3R + 0.59G + 0.11B \tag{1}$$

The weightings given to the R, G, and B signals are commensurate with the relative contributions of the three primaries to luminance.

We can now derive two 'colour difference equations':

$$R - L = 0.7R - 0.59G - 0.11B \tag{2}$$

and

$$B - L = -0.3R - 0.59G + 0.89B \tag{3}$$

Equations (2) and (3) give 'chrominance' information. If $R = G = B$, then both chrominance signals are zero. Since the viewer's visual acuity is less for colour, less bandwidth need be used to transmit (2) and (3) than (1) (Sims 1969).

There are other consequences of the colour difference operation that hold advantages for both television and the visual system. If three trichromatic signals were transmitted untransformed, then redundant information would be carried in the transmission. For the three signals would be correlated: they would necessarily be correlated because the spectral sensitivities of the three receptors overlap and because objects in the world have broad spectral reflectances. To avoid waste of valuable channel capacity the three signals should be orthogonal, i.e. should not be correlated with each other. By transmitting a luminance signal and two difference signals, visual systems may approach this ideal of communications engineering (Fukurotani 1982).

Another advantage of the difference operation may lie in the preservation of neutral colours. Imagine that a television camera is looking at a neutral object. There will be a luminance signal, but the two chrominance signals will be zero, since the camera is set so that $R = G = B$. The chrominance signals are thus zero: all is well. But now imagine that the gains of the two chrominance channels are altered—that is, the $R - L$ and $G - L$ signals are each multiplied by a different number (as might arise from drift in the electronics). The two channels will still be signalling 'zero' for neutral scenes, since a product of any number and zero is still zero. The resistance of the neutrality of neutral objects to drifts in the gains of opponent channels is likely to be an important consideration in our visual system as well.

6. Cortical analysis of colour

A question of great interest, and still unsettled, is that of the extent to which colour is analysed separately from other attributes of the retinal image, such as form and movement. S. Zeki has identified in the rhesus monkey two adjacent regions of the prestriate cortex that he suggests are specialized for the analysis of colour: these regions (denoted 'V4' and 'V4A') lie on the posterior bank of the lunate sulcus and the anterior bank of the superior temporal sulcus (Zeki 1977). He suggests that colour-specific cells are here more frequent than in other prestriate regions and, most interestingly, that the cells show colour constancy when one patch of a complex, multicoloured array falls within their receptive field; that is to say, they respond to the colour seen by a human observer despite large changes in the local spectral flux that falls on their receptive field. But as yet we have little idea of how the colour constancy is achieved or of how the hue of an object is referred to its other attributes, such as movement, shape, and distance.   TT

De Valois, R. L., and De Valois, K. K. (1975). 'Neural coding of color'. In Carterette, E. C., and Friedman, M. P. (eds.), *Handbook of Perception*, vol. v.

Fukurotani, K. (1982). 'Color information coding of horizontal-cell responses in fish retina'. *Color Research and Application*, 7.

Hurvich, L. M. (1978). 'Two decades of opponent processes'. *Colour*, 77.

Mollon, J. D. (1982). 'Color vision'. *Annual Reviews of Psychology*, 33.

Sims, H. V. (1969). *Principles of PAL Colour Television and Related Systems*.

Wasserman, G. S. (1978). *Color Vision: An Historical Introduction*.

Zeki, S. M. (1977). 'Colour coding in the superior temporal sulcus of the rhesus monkey visual cortex'. *Proceedings of the Royal Society Series B, Biological Sciences*, 197.

colour vision: eye mechanisms. When things are seen, it is usually because light enters the eye and is focused upon the retina, that sensitive membrane at the back. Light consists of electromagnetic vibrations of minute wavelengths—one million waves to the half-metre for green light.

Isaac *Newton, by his famous prism experiment, showed in 1666 that sunlight consists of a mixture of rays, each bent to a different degree in traversing the prism and thus falling at a different place upon the far wall. He showed that each ray was elementary in the sense that it could not be changed into a ray differently bent. Each elementary ray had a different colour, and the colour of objects depended upon the copiousness with which the various coloured rays were reflected or transmitted from the object to the eye.

Newton's conclusions, though true, met with fierce opposition. To *Goethe it was absurd to assert that the mere mixing of all the rainbow colours could appear white since white is without colour. And artists had long known that it was not necessary for them to have a set of seven rainbow paints; a judicious mixture on the palette of a few bright paints—perhaps only three—was sufficient for masterpieces of natural representation.

A person's perception of everything in the world outside him depends upon three factors: (i) the physical stimulus, such as vibrations of light or sound, (ii) the sense organs that respond to particular stimuli in special ways, and send corresponding messages along their nerves to the brain, and (iii) the mind that creates perception out of brain activity. Newton analysed correctly the diversity of light rays that constitute sunlight. But he did not consider the limitations of the eye in responding selectively to these diverse rays. This was done by the physician Thomas *Young in 1801, at St George's Hospital,

London. He saw that human perception of fine detail implies a 'fine grain' of photoreceptors in the retina, and thought it unlikely that each 'grain' would be selectively responsive to every wavelength of light. Nor was this necessary to explain colour discrimination. Young suggested that each grain consisted of a triad of resonators each thrown into vibration by light waves. The 'green receptor' was moved chiefly by waves from the middle of the spectrum (which looks green), though neighbouring spectral waves also acted upon it less vigorously. The 'red receptor' and the 'blue receptor' respond likewise to waves near either end of the spectrum. Thus light of any composition falling upon the eye will throw these three resonators, R, G, and B, into determinate amplitudes of vibration. Their sum, $R + G + B$, defines the brightness, and their ratio, $R : B : B$, defines the colour.

This view, which is essentially what is believed today, is seen not to question Newton's physics but, by taking into account the limited discrimination of the eye, to explain the painter's experience that mixing a few paints will give the whole range of colours. Young's explanation should lead to a simple and striking result. Every colour (including white) should excite the R, G, and B receptors in a characteristic set of ratios. Consequently, a mixture of red + green + blue lights, adjusted to produce this same set of ratios, should appear white, or whatever the initial colour was. In 1854 this was systematically tested by James Clerk Maxwell (1831–79), the great physicist, while a student at Trinity College, Cambridge. He showed that every colour can be matched by a suitable mixture of red + green + blue 'primaries', although sometimes it is necessary for the experimenter to mix one of his three primaries with the colour to be matched rather than with the other primaries. This *trichromacy* of vision was confirmed by Hermann von *Helmholtz in Heidelberg and later measured with spectral lights and great accuracy by W. D. Wright at Imperial College London and independently by W. S. Stiles at the National Physical Laboratory, London.

1. Visual pigments
2. Colour-blindness
3. Adaptation
4. Psychology

1. Visual pigments

What does light do to the photoreceptors of the retina to make them send nerve messages to the brain? Willy Kühne (1837–1900), professor of physiology at Heidelberg, observed in 1877 that a dark-adapted retina removed from a dead frog in dim light and then observed in daylight was initially pink, but bleached to pale yellow upon exposure to light. This showed that the retina contains a photosensitive pigment, i.e. one that changes its chemical constitution on exposure, as does a photographic film. This pigment, 'visual purple' or 'rhodopsin', is present in the photoreceptors called 'rods' that serve deep twilight vision, which is without colour. Therefore the pigments serving colour vision must lie not in the twilight receptors but in the daylight receptors called 'cones'. And Young was correct in supposing that these are of three types.

Researchers in Cambridge were the first to measure the visual pigments in the living human eye, applying the familiar observation that if at night a cat's eye is caught in the beam of a car's headlamps it shines back with reflected light (Rushton 1952). By knowing the incident light and measuring the reflected light, it is found what light has been absorbed in the eye. And if these measurements are made before and after the visual pigment has been bleached away with strong light, the change in absorption, resulting from the change in amount of visual pigment present, is learnt.

The same measurements may be made in human eyes, though here there is a very black surface behind the retina instead of the cat's shining *tapetum lucidum*. Since the measuring light sent in may not be made very strong (or it will bleach away the pigment that is being measured), the great sensitivity of a photomultiplier tube is needed to measure the faint light that emerges from the eye. Using this technique, it has been possible to measure the spectral sensitivity and kinetics of bleaching and regeneration in the living human eye, first of rhodopsin, then of the red and the green cone pigments. There was never sufficient blue light reflected to measure the blue cone pigment.

This work has been confirmed and extended by Marks, Dobelle, and MacNichol at Johns Hopkins University, Baltimore. They used fresh retinas from monkeys' and human eyes removed at operation, and with superb technique measured the visual pigments in single cones. They found Young's three types of cone and specified the visual pigment in each, confirming the measurements made in Cambridge on living colour-blind subjects who possessed only one of the two cone pigments measurable by the Cambridge technique.

2. Colour-blindness

Almost all so-called colour defectives have some appreciation of colour, and generally resent being called colour *blind*. The common defective cannot distinguish well between red and green. This is a hereditary defect, something wrong with a gene carried on one (or rarely both) of the sex chromosomes in the female or on the single active sex chromosome in the male. If in the male the gene is missing or abnormal, colour vision will be defective, and 8 per cent of all males exhibit some defect. But in the female it needs *both* chromosomes to suffer the loss before her defect will show, and of course the probability of the double event is much smaller than that of the single one. In fact only 0.4 per cent of females show some

abnormality. Even so, women who are abnormal in only one chromosome, though showing perfect colour vision themselves, have a 50 per cent chance of transmitting their weakness to their children; and half their sons will be 'colour-blind', since the (normal) father holds his normal gene on the one sex chromosome that will make his child a daughter, and he has none for his sons.

Dichromacy. In the extreme conditions of the red–green defect, the subject cannot tell red from green and can match every colour of the rainbow exactly with a suitable mixture of only *two* coloured lights, for example red and blue. Such subjects are called dichromats, to distinguish them from ordinary people (trichromats) who need also a green primary if every colour is to be matched.

The cone pigments in the red–green spectral range of dichromats have been measured by a reflection technique. It has been shown that instead of the red- *and* green-sensitive cone pigments of normal vision, these subjects have only the red *or* the green. They lack one dimension of colour vision because they lack one kind of cone pigment.

Anomalous trichromacy. The majority of colour defectives are not true dichromats, but anomalous trichromats: like normal subjects, they require three variables in a colour-matching experiment, but the matches they make are different from those of the normal. Thus, in matching a monochromatic yellow with a mixture of red and green, some ('protoanomalous') observers require more red than normal in the match, whereas other ('deuteranomalous') observers need more green. Usually, though not necessarily, the abnormality of matching is associated with a reduced capacity for discriminating colours. It is thought that anomalous trichromacy arises when one of the cone pigments is displaced from its normal position in the spectrum.

3. Adaptation

Newton's physics of colour was inadequate because it did not take into account the selective physiological action of Young's three cone types. We are now on the way to understanding their selectivity and the sort of nerve signals they generate. But though light waves and nerve signals are factors that lead to colour vision, there is still the miracle of how some nerve signals generate a sensation in the mind. This sensation certainly does not depend exclusively upon the $R : G : B$ excitation ratios of the three cone types. We all know how adaptation to any strong-coloured light leaves the eye, as it were, fatigued to the colour so that some extra light of this colour must be added to any presentation if its appearance is to be the same as it was before adaptation. This adaptation is often called 'successive contrast' to distinguish it from the rather similar 'simultaneous contrast', where two different-coloured objects seen close together have their differences enhanced through their proximity. Some of these effects can be objectively measured by recording from nerves in the visual pathways of animals.

4. Psychology

Colours are so gay that those with total colour loss cannot but be pitied, and it must be wondered what it is that makes red produce the wonderful red sensation most people perceive. What has been said here explains only what cannot be discriminated, and nothing has been said about how sensations arise from what is seen. Let it be concluded that Newton ended his first paper with these strong words: 'But to determine . . . by what modes or actions light produceth in our minds the phantasms of colours is not so easie. And I shall not mingle conjectures with certainties.'

WAHR

Boynton, R. M. (1979). *Human Colour Vision*.

Brindley, G. S. (1970). *Physiology of the Retina and the Visual Pathway* (2nd edn.).

Rushton, W. A. H. (1952). 'Apparatus for analysing the light reflected from the eye of a cat'. *Journal of Physiology*, 117.

—— (1975). 'Visual pigments and colour blindness'. *Scientific American*, 232.

common sense. The original meaning is a 'common centre', or neural pool, into which all the five senses were supposed to contribute to give coherent perceptions, though the various senses are so very different. René *Descartes (1596–1650) used the term *le siège du sens commun* in this way. There is indeed still a problem over the coordination of the senses and just how the different sources of information are pooled (see, for example, SPATIAL COORDINATION and CHANNELS, NEURAL).

Nowadays 'common sense' generally refers to practical attitudes and widely accepted beliefs which may be hard to justify but which are generally assumed to be reliable. Extreme deviations from common-sense beliefs may be evidence of psychological disturbance, but may, on the other hand, be the products of genius, sometimes becoming accepted later as common sense. Thus, although it is now common sense that the earth is round, only a few centuries ago a man believing this might have been regarded as mad.

There is indeed a vast body of unquestioned assumptions which is seldom questioned. Common sense is, however, frequently questioned by philosophers—with a curious ambiguity, for at least linguistic philosophy tends to assume that the 'common sense' of normal language is philosophically significant. This is discussed critically by Ernest Gellner (1979).

RLG

Gellner, E. (1979). *Words and Things*.

compassion (from the Latin *compati*, suffer with). To feel another's suffering as keenly as one's own, and be moved to succour. In compassion are subsumed *pity*, the emotion of tenderness aroused by the suffering of another, and *mercy*, the compassion shown to the powerless. Compassion has its evolutionary origin in altruism, doing good to others at some sacrifice to the self, which is an evolved strategy to enhance reproductive success: because kin share genes, helping kin has a fitness advantage. Compassion and pity are intertwined with *empathy*, to understand and enter into another's feelings, a 20th-century coinage from the German *Einfühlung*. Adam Smith's *Theory of Moral Sentiments* held human nature to be fundamentally compassionate:

How selfish soever man may be supposed, there are evidently some principles in his nature, which interest him in the fortunes of others, and render their happiness necessary to him. . . . Of this kind is pity or compassion, the emotion which we feel for the misery of others. . . . This sentiment . . . is by no means confined to the virtuous and humane. . . . By the imagination we place ourselves in his situation, we conceive ourselves enduring all the same torments, we enter as it were into his body. . . . His agonies . . . begin at last to affect us, and we then tremble and shudder at the thought of what he feels. (1759/2002: 11–12)

The view that compassion is a human universal ('the greatest ruffian, the most hardened violator of the laws of society, is not altogether without it': Smith, loc cit.) has ancient origins (Fiering 1976; Clark 1995). But in the history of Western sensibility, felt compassion was until the end of the 18th century no warrant for action; from 1900, compassion for suffering and the drive to succour it had become second nature. Since the 1980s, this humanitarian benevolence has widened to embrace the interrelatedness of all life, and the welfare of the planet itself. These extraordinary transformations in the history of ideas drew on three currents: the 17th-century re-evaluation of the purpose and place of suffering in human life; 19th-century abolitionism; and the extension of compassion to animals. The cumulative effect was in William James's estimation 'a moral transformation [that has] within the past century swept over our western world' (1901). It is a transformation that has profoundly changed literature and politics, helped found settlement houses and create the welfare state, emancipated women, protected children from exploitation and abuse, and reformed the penal system (Turner 1980).

1. Suffering becomes an evil
2. The abolitionist movement
3. Kindness to animals
4. Limitless compassion

1. Suffering becomes an evil

The seeds of change lay in Latitudinarian theology, which from the mid-17th century opposed Puritan predestenarianism, and ranked works above faith in securing salvation: militant benevolence was therefore highly prized, and virtue was identified with universal benevolence.

Emphasis shifted from God the Judge sentencing a depraved humanity to eternal suffering (which was in turn legitimized by the Passion), to God the benevolent father devoted to his children's well-being (Clark 1995). In the latter part of the 18th century, the social and individual relationship to pain thus changed, and suffering was no longer accepted as part of God's plan for which there was no cure, as the lives of the saints and Christ himself showed. But from the 1760s, pain was considered evil, and happiness the absence of pain (Sznaider 1996). By the 19th century, 'most Protestants had come to share a tender-minded distaste for the extravagant agony of the Passion' (Clark 1995: 472), and pain thus became a breach of divinely ordained law.

Serendipitously, it was precisely now that physical pain could be abolished: the 19th century 'opened with the isolation of morphine in 1802 and closed with the introduction of aspirin in 1899' (Turner 1980: 82). Anaesthesia was first demonstrated by William Morton at the Massachusetts General Hospital on 16 October 1846; in Edinburgh in 1847, chloroform was shown to be superior to ether. In 1884, Freud used cocaine to achieve local anaesthesia, and, in 1885, William Halsted demonstrated the nerve block anaesthesia that revolutionized the practice of dentistry. Anaesthesia was hailed as 'the greatest boon ever accorded to the physical welfare of mankind' (Turner 1980: 82). Thus, 'in a convenient sleight of hand, the medical profession assumed epistemological responsibility for pain just as it dropped out as an underpinning of theology' (Clark 1995: 473).

2. The abolitionist movement

Among the secular currents contributing to the general sense that punishments involving bodily pain were objectionable was Cesare Beccaria's 1764 treatise on crimes and punishment, which used utilitarian principles to argue that if government's purpose was to seek the greatest good for the greatest number, the objective of the penal system is to devise the least severe penalties that will achieve social order, since anything more is tyranny. These changing cultural and religious conceptions of pain, compassion, and suffering become visible in the 8th amendment to the US constitution in 1789, banning cruel and unusual punishments, and soon thereafter in the history of the slavery abolition movement in England and the United States: in 1807 the slave trade to the British colonies was abolished, and in 1838 slavery was banned in the British West Indies. In the United States, the northern states had abolished slavery by 1806, and Lincoln's Emancipation Proclamation of 1 January 1863, midway through the Civil War, was followed in 1865 by the 13th amendment to the US constitution that outlawed slavery.

The story of the suffering slave was a fundamental motif in the drive to establish individual human rights;

in the 1830s, accounts of cruel punishments became a staple of antislavery literature. By the later 19th century, legal standards came to incorporate the idea that to be free of physical coercion and deliberately inflicted pain was an essential human right, thus ending legal protection of brutal punishments in the armed forces and in the home (Clark 1995, Sznaider 1996).

3. Kindness to animals

In a related movement that has precise temporal and emotional parallels with abolitionism, compassion began to cross species boundaries. Societies for the prevention of cruelty to animals sprang up on both sides of the Atlantic, first in England, where the SPCA was founded in 1824 at a public house with the unfortunate name of Old Slaughter's (in 1840, by Queen Victoria's warrant, it became the Royal Society for the Prevention of Cruelty to Animals); the American SPCA was incorporated in the state of New York in 1866 (Turner 1980). The huge success of Anna Sewell's *Black Beauty* arose from this new sensibility; in America, it acquired a commercially astute subtitle that linked animal cruelty to the horrors of slavery, The *'Uncle Tom's Cabin' of the Horse* (Clark 1995).

Historically, however, animals had stood 'almost completely outside the emotional walls of premodern Europe' (Turner 1980). Drawing on Stoic teaching, Augustine in *City of God* held that humans had no obligations to animals: 'Since beasts lack reason . . . we need not concern ourselves with their sufferings.' But the most painful outcome of Christian doctrines emerged in the philosophy of Rene *Descartes, who held that because animals have no language, 'they have no reason at all. . . . It would be incredible . . . if their souls were not completely different in nature from ours' (Descartes 1637: i. 140). In a letter to the Cambridge Platonist Henry More in 1649, Descartes wrote, 'It seems reasonable that nature should . . . produce its own automata which are much more splendid than artificial ones—namely the animals. . . . Thus my opinion [that animals are automata] is not so much cruel to animals as indulgent to human beings . . . since it absolves them from the suspicion of crime when they eat or kill animals' (1637: iii. 366).

Conveniently, writes Singer (1975), the physiologists of the period declared themselves Cartesians and mechanists. De Fontenelle wrote of the atmosphere that Descartes's disciple Arnauld created at the Jansenist seminary in Port-Royal-du-Champs:

There was hardly a *solitaire* who did not talk of automata. . . . They administered beatings to dogs with perfect indifference, and made fun of those who pitied the creatures as if they felt pain. They said the animals were clocks; that the cries they emitted when struck were only the noise of a little spring that had been touched, but that the whole body was without feeling. (Rosenfield 1941: 54)

In criticizing William Harvey's 1628 work on the circulation of the blood, Descartes suggests a simple proof of the correctness of his view: 'If you slice off the pointed end of the heart in a live dog, and insert a finger into one of the cavities, you will feel unmistakably that every time the heart gets shorter it presses the finger' (1637: i).

From the mid-19th century, as the animal protection movement gained political power, vivisectionists became their own worst enemy. The RSPCA importuned both the French and Italian authorities to act against vivisection, and in London the physiologist Emanuel Klein unwisely told the Royal Commission on vivisection that he used anaesthesia only as a convenience because he had 'no regard at all' for the suffering of the animals. Turner argues that the scientist–hero of the 20th century emerged from public horror at vivisection: Victorian scientists were as revolted by pain as the public, and appropriated the new humane sensibility, so that the prestige of science became attached to compassion (Turner 1980).

4. Limitless compassion

The final chapter in the history of compassion, which extends to the present and continues to unfold, is the notion that all of nature and the planet itself are bound together in an interdependent balance. This compassionate tender-mindedness is outraged at the deliberate infliction of pain; it extends across national boundaries to the distant and unknown victims of persecution, to all social classes and ethnic groups, to domestic and wild animals, and in the past twenty years to the planet itself: the Gaia hypothesis, named after the Greek goddess of the earth, holds that the earth is a living organism with self-regulating processes that provide for a life-sustaining global climate.

Is contemporary tender-mindedness a unique and precious cultural artefact? Paul MacLean writes that the orientation of the prefrontal lobes away from the present and towards the future has made it possible for family concerns to generalize from one's own children to the national and worldwide human families: 'For the first time in the known history of biology, we are witnessing the evolution of a spirit with a concern for the future suffering and dying of all living things' (1993: 82).

But at a time when the reach of compassion was narrower than it is today, William James prefigured the tension between a kind heart and the exigencies of life in the world:

May not the claims of tender-mindedness go too far? May not the notion of a world saved *in toto* anyhow be too saccharine to stand? May not religious optimism be too idyllic? . . . is *no* price to be paid in the work of salvation? Is the last word sweet? Is all 'yes, yes' in the universe? Doesn't the fact of 'no' stand at the very core of life? Doesn't the very 'seriousness' that we attribute to life mean that ineluctable noes and losses form part of it, that there are genuine sacrifices somewhere, and that something permanently

drastic and bitter always remains at the bottom of its cup? (1907: 141)

VN

Clark, E. B. (1995). ' "The sacred rights of the weak": pain, sympathy, and the culture of individual rights in antebellum America'. *Journal of American History* (Sept.).

Descartes, R. (1637/1985). 'Discourse on method'. In *The Philosophical Writings of Descartes*.

Fiering, N. S. (1976). 'Irresistible compassion: an aspect of 18th century sympathy and humanitarianism'. *Journal of the History of Ideas*, 37.

James, W. (1901/1997). *The Varieties of Religious Experience: A Study in Human Nature*.

——(1907) *Pragmatism: A New Name for some Old Ways of Thinking*. Ed. (1978).

MacLean, P. D. (1993). 'Cerebral evolution of emotion'. In Lewis, M., and Haviland, J. M. (eds.), *Handbook of Emotions*.

Rosenfield, L. C. (1941). *From Beast Machine to Man Machine: Animal Soul in French Letters from Descartes to La Mettrie*.

Singer, P. (1975). *Animal Liberation*.

Smith, A. (1759). *The Theory of Moral Sentiments*. Ed. K. Haakonssen (2002).

Sznaider, N. (1996). 'Pain and cruelty in socio-historical perspective'. *International Journal of Politics, Culture, and Society*, 10.

Turner, J. (1980). *Reckoning with the Beast: Animals, Pain and Humanity in the Victorian Mind*.

compatibilism. Traditionally, those who maintain the truth of determinism and believers in the freedom of the will have been regarded as taking up incompatible positions. Thus from one side it is argued that, since all events, including human actions, are causally determined, the belief that we are free is an illusion; from the other side it is argued that we know we are free, and hence universal determinism must be false. Compatibilists maintain that both these arguments are invalid: since a free action is simply one that is not constrained by external forces, there is a perfectly ordinary and proper sense in which we act freely when we do what we want to do; and the existence of such freedom need not presuppose that determinism is false, or that human beings possess some contra-causal power. Defenders of the compatibilist or 'reconciliationist' position have included Leibniz and Hume.

JGC

complex. A term used in psychoanalysis introduced by Joseph Breuer (1895) in *Studies of Hysteria* and adopted later by Sigmund *Freud and Carl *Jung to mean organized memories, emotions, and fears, which have been pushed down to be largely unconscious, though affecting conscious perception and behaviour.

The term is related to 'complexion', from the humours of medieval physiology and their supposed effects. Thus Chaucer, in the Prologue to the *Canterbury Tales*, writes: 'Of his complexion he was sangwyn.' It might be bilious or phlegmatic—facial complexion revealing underlying complexes of emotions and disturbances though these may be psychological. See EMOTIONS.

compulsions. See OBSESSIVE–COMPULSIVE DISORDER.

computer chess. This is pursued in some cases for sport and in others to deepen scientific understanding of the kinds of knowledge that support mental skills. From specialized activities in both the sport and the science category, *artificial intelligence scientists have obtained insights of general relevance to *cognition and its computer simulation, including topics such as the following. How is a causal model of some problem domain to be exploited in solving particular problems within it? What principles characterize knowledge-based planning? What are the trade-offs between the use of calculation and the use of stored patterns during problem solving? Can the fruits of past calculations be turned into summarizing patterns for future use; and can the fruits of past miscalculations also be utilized, and if so how? What are the limits to human codification of a skill, and can these limits be overcome in any way? What makes a pattern-directed representation intelligible, and what makes such a representation also executable 'in the head'?

The properties of chess which make it especially suitable for computer-based approaches to such questions are that the domain can be fully and exactly defined; it overextends the best human intellects; it demands calculation, learning, concept manipulation, analogical thinking, and long-term judgement. Moreover master skill at chess is measurable on a universal scale, and over the centuries players and scholars have built a vast incremental literature of chess knowledge, as apprehended and improved by each generation.

In the theory of games chess is a two-person game with perfect information: both players have full sight of the board and of every move made. It is also zero-sum, i.e. what is good for one player is bad in precisely equal measure for the other. Further, the rule which declares a draw when 50 moves have passed without castling, captures, or pawn moves ensures that the game is finite. The space of legal positions is, however, rather large, having been estimated as exceeding 10 to the power of 46.

The fraction of these which a chess master would regard as capable of occurrence in serious play, and hence meaningful, is infinitesimal. Yet the number of distinct positions contained in that infinitesimal fraction has been estimated as exceeding 10 to the power of 23. This is still many billion times too many for complete solution by computer search and enumeration. Such an enterprise would also require mechanizable representations of chess meaning, in a language whose most primitive expressions would denote basic features from which the master builds his mental picture of a chess position.

Only a few descriptive clichés of the hypothesized language have been uncovered to date. The '*chunks' involve such relations as mutual defence between pieces, cooperation in attacking a common target, certain types of pawn chain, characteristic castled-king patterns, and the like. Relevant investigations began a century ago with Alfred *Binet's studies of chess memory in simultaneous blindfold chess, and were extended in the 1940s by Adriaan de Groot's analyses of players of varying strengths, including former world champions, 'thinking aloud' about given positions. More recent work by Herbert Simon and by Jorg Nievergeldt has yielded in addition estimates of the number of chunks, or basic patterns, stored by a master in long-term memory. This number, thought to lie between 30,000 and 50,000, corresponds to the size of the vocabulary employed by the hypothesized language. Little use has so far been made of studies of chess cognition by the mechanizers, who have mainly been content to apply brute force along lines mapped out, although not particularly recommended, by Claude Shannon in 1950. Current high-water marks are reviewed below.

1. Brute force: tournament play
2. Brute force: endgame analysis
3. Automation of chess knowledge

1. Brute force: tournament play

The first world computer chess championship in 1974 was won by a program authored by M. Donskoy and V. L. Arlazarov of the USSR. It performed at the level of mediocre club play. Programs for playing under tournament conditions have concentrated on wringing the most out of the concurrent rapid advance of computing technology together with the use of short-cut tricks of programming technique (such as 'alpha-beta'—see below). The Shannon paradigm of searching large trees of possibilities, guided by simplistic but fast means of evaluating each possibility as it is thrown up, has dominated.

The principle of machine search resembles the strenuous 'thinking ahead' of an ambitious beginner, enhanced with miraculous speed, completeness, and accuracy. Tens, or even hundreds, of thousands of variations per second are scored for features generally correlated with a position's strength, such as piece scores, mobility, control of centre, king safety, and pawn structure. From the positions located along the furthermost boundary of the forward search, position values are assessed up the levels of the look-ahead tree, by a method known as minimaxing, until the immediate successors of the position under consideration have received backed-up values. Choice of the highest scoring of these determines the machine move. A refinement of minimax known as alpha-beta pruning almost doubles the depth of analysis obtainable for given computational cost: modern tournament programs regularly search three to four moves ahead (six to eight 'ply'), pursuing capture–recapture or other unstable-looking sequences to as much as twice this depth.

As early established by de Groot, the chess mind follows a diametrically opposite regime. When asked how many moves ahead he looked, the great grandmaster and theorist Richard Reti replied, 'One, the right one.' Even in correspondence chess forward calculations are highly selective, pruned and guided by criteria of strategic meaning not yet seriously addressed by the mechanizers.

In 1985 the strongest programs had reached the borderline of international master strength, as judged by their showing in regular human tournaments. When, however, obliged to play the same opponent repeatedly, they tend to fall to the human's ability to learn his enemy's weak points and exploit them. No tournament program of today has the power to learn from experience. Yet the final of the 1985 North American computer chess championship, in which Hans Berliner's 'Hitech' defeated Robert Hyatt's 'Cray Blitz', was recognizably master level. Both programs searched 20–30 million look-ahead positions per move. The equivalent figure for de Groot's grandmasters was 20–30 positions.

Further annual tournaments led to the creation in 1988 of Deep Thought by a team of Carnegie Mellon University graduate students including Feng-Hsiung Hsu and Murray Campbell. In that same year the program became the first to defeat a grandmaster in a tournament. In the following year, IBM's T. J. Watson Research Center recruited the team's two key members.

The reconstituted team, backed by powerful chess-specific ultra-parallel hardware from IBM, over a period of years developed Deep Blue, Deep Thought's successor. Thousandfold gains of calculating power allowed up to 100 billion positions per move to be evaluated in look-ahead. Additionally a database was incorporated that held the grandmaster games of the past 100 years together with billions of specific endgame scenarios.

In February 1996 Deep Blue met the World Champion Garry Kasparov in the international Association for Computing Machines' six-game Chess Challenge held in Philadelphia, USA. Kasparov was victorious with three wins, one loss and two draws.

The rematch came in May 1997. After a win by each side followed by three draws, all hung on the sixth and final game. To the astonishment of the chess world, Kasparov played a well-known opening blunder and was lost, resigning after the game's nineteenth move. The generally accepted explanation lies in the blow to morale in Game 2, which Kasparov mistakenly resigned in a position that subsequent ultra-deep analysis showed to have been technically drawn.

Well satisfied with the result's public impact, IBM declined Kasparov's immediate request for a rematch, dissolving its winning team and discontinuing significant computer chess work. It was to be five years before his next public opportunity for a challenge match against a reigning world computer champion.

Meanwhile a growing website of chess programs, openings, endgame databases, and computer analyses of past games became accessible at www.chessbase.com. Chessbase has enabled grandmasters not only to train ever harder for combat in human tournaments but also to study the peculiarities and vulnerabilities of computer play. The latter has also strengthened, not least through decreasing costs and increasing speeds of microcircuitry.

2. Brute force: endgame analysis

Given today's fast processors and large computer memories, exhaustive computation can be performed so as fully to solve and tabulate subgames of chess which are not understood by grandmasters, or even (a taller order) by endgame specialists. The first such feat, by T. Strohlein in 1970, fully analysed the four-piece ending king and rook versus king and knight, thought until then to be in the general case a drawn game. Of the 1,347,906 legal rook's-side-to-move positions (neglecting positions equivalent under rotations and reflections of the board), almost half (651,492) turn out to be winnable by correct (though for the most part protracted) play. The two longest wins are represented by positions 27 moves from checkmate or knight capture. Aided by knowledge that it could be done and by samples of the computer-generated material itself, the leading endgame scholar A. J. Roycroft was able to acquire and demonstrate complete mastery of optimal play of positions won for the rook's side (contrast the KBBKN case, below).

Kenneth Thompson has completed exhaustive databases for all the interesting four-piece and five-piece pawnless endings. Of his factual discoveries one of the most spectacular has been the status of king and two bishops versus king and knight (KBBKN), previously believed to be drawable provided that the knight's side can attain the 'Kling & Horwitz' position (Fig. 1a). The position dates from 1851. The verdict that the defending side can draw positions like this (based on the placing of the two black men and largely ignoring the white placement) is repeated in all relevant chess endgame textbooks. In 1983 Thompson's exhaustive solution demonstrated the general win of this endgame in at most 66 moves, and the particular win in Kling & Horwitz positions in about 40–45 moves. Cases of this kind have led to a growing number of ad hoc modifications by the World Chess Federation of the 50-move drawing rule.

Not only does the Thompson database, comprising some 200 million legal positions, show that the bishops' side can win from all but a few freak starting positions, but its manner of doing so passes the comprehension of the ending's dedicated human students. The critical fourth stage of a five-stage win from the starting position shown

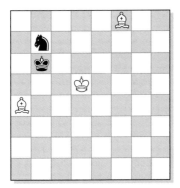

Fig. 1a. Either side to move.

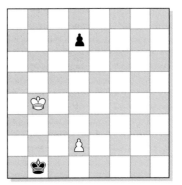

Fig. 2a. White to win.

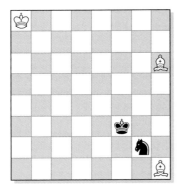

Fig. 1b. White to move.

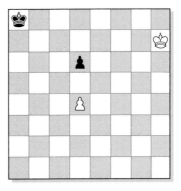

Fig. 2b. White to win.

in Fig. 1b involves a procedure 'not to be found in any book and characterized by excruciating slowness and mystery' (Roycroft). Moreover, following a year's study by Roycroft and others, involving availability of a variety of computer aids, it seems that human mastery (as opposed to machine mastery) of this ending may never be attainable.

Databases generated in this style can also be searched for positions which a master or endgame scholar would recognize as 'studies' or 'compositions'. Here a unique winning (or in appropriate cases drawing) line of play must exist, coupled with properties of elegance, surprise, didactic value, and even wit, not easy to define in programming terms. M. R. B. Clarke has conducted selective trawls with some success: two of his discoveries for king-pawn–king-pawn (KPKP) are shown as Fig. 2a and 2b.

3. Automation of chess knowledge

In addition to purely factual discoveries, computer programs could help the chess expert fill the gaps of which codified chess knowledge is now seen mainly to consist. Knowledge-directed programs can support his endeavours to outline the missing framework and by semi-automatic

Two computer-assisted study compositions in the KPKP domain. The natural-looking Pd4 for Fig. 2a, and Kg6 for Fig. 2b, fail. Correct are Kc3 and Pd5 respectively.

generation of descriptions from expert-supplied examples to fill empty slots in the framework as it takes shape. Using a technique of Alen Shapiro and Timothy Niblett known as 'structured induction', Shapiro was able to generate a complete human-readable codification for adjudicating positions in the king-pawn–king-rook ending (pawn's side to move, pawn on a7) where none pre-existed. A side benefit subsequently extracted from this phenomenon was endowment of the program with the ability to document its own adjudications on demand with explanatory notes.

In the above-mentioned work the induction process was fuelled by hand-supplied examples. In some other cases success has been reported where the examples have been quarried by the program itself from large pre-computed databases. A recent *de novo* synthesis of knowledge in clinical cardiology by Ivan Bratko and colleagues employed just such an alternation between (i) exhaustive derivation of brute facts from a logical model and (ii) induction from these of an operational theory. Sparked initially by the chess work, application is beginning to place emphasis on factual compilations as raw materials for automating the codification of new knowledge as a commercial product. The need to better understand the cognitive invariants with which the designer of codification languages must now come to terms is also leading to closer involvement of professional students of mind.

DM

Binet, A. (1894). *Psychologie des grands calculateurs et des joueurs d'echecs.*

Chase, W. G., and Simon, H. A. (1973). 'Perception in chess'. *Cognitive Psychology*, 4.

de Groot, A. (1965). *Thought and Choice in Chess* (rev. edn.). (For mental representations of chess masters.)

Hayes, J. E., and Levy, D. (1976). *The World Computer Chess Championship, Stockholm 1974*. (For an introduction to chess cognition in relation to artificial intelligence.)

Michie, D., and Shapiro, A. (1986). Several articles in *Advances in Computer Chess*, 4. (For the knowledge-synthesis approach.)

Shannon, C. (1950). 'Programming a computer for playing chess'. *Philosophical Magazine*, 41.

Simon, H. A., and Gilmartin, K. (1973). 'A simulation memory for chess positions'. *Cognitive Psychology*, 5.

Thompson, K. (1986). 'Programs that generate endgame data bases'. *End Game*, 83.

Comte, Auguste (1798–1857). French philosopher and sociologist, and the founder of positivism. His main work is *Philosophie positive* (6 vols., 1830–42), which was freely translated into English and condensed into three volumes by Harriet Martineau: *The Positive Philosophy of Auguste Comte* (1896).

Comte tried to organize knowledge of society and technology into a consistent whole. He argued that all human conceptions pass through a theological and then a metaphysical stage, and then into a positive or experiential form. The abstract sciences form a hierarchy, with mathematics at the top, then astronomy, physics, chemistry, biology, and finally sociology. Sociological development is from militarism to industrialism. Positivism is an expression of *humanism, in which there is no deity and the emphasis is entirely on man and on intellectual conceptions of the world and man's place in it.

concept. An abstraction or general notion that may serve as a unit (or an 'atom') of a theory. Some concepts can be powerful thinking tools even when they are not at all fully understood. Thus even simple concepts or procedures in mathematics (such as 'dividing by x', or 'taking the square root of x') allow problems to be solved even though they, or even the questions addressed, are not understood.

Concepts may be more or less clear, and a major part of philosophy is to clarify them. This can be extremely difficult: what is our concept of time—or of mind?

Perhaps most concepts are components of theories or explanations. At least they seem (though not always correctly) to give fairly direct insight into the nature of things. For example, the astronomer Johannes Kepler's concept of the planets moving in elliptical orbits was essential for *Newton's great synthesis in his *Principia*, which went virtually unchallenged as an account of the universe until Einstein's Special and then General Theory of Relativity. Evidently changes of theory change concepts, and new concepts, or revisions of old ones, can change theories.

In psychology, concepts of mind must be invented or discovered, much as in physics, for we cannot see at all clearly into our own minds by introspection. So we need experiments in psychology; they sometimes suggest concepts far removed from *common sense, or what we *seem* to be like. If we could see 'directly' into our own minds by introspection perhaps we would not need explanatory concepts for understanding at least our own psychologies.

RLG

Boden, M. A. (1972). *Purposive Explanation in Psychology*.

Clark, A. J. (1993). *Associative Engines*.

Fodor, J. A. (1998). *Concepts: Where Cognitive Science Went Wrong*.

Hofstadter, D. R. (1985). *Metamagical Themas*.

concussion. Concussion can be defined as a clinical syndrome characterized by immediate and transient impairment of mental functions such as alteration of *consciousness, and disturbance of vision or equilibrium, due to mechanical forces. Such results follow all but the mildest blows to the head. In the majority of instances loss of consciousness is of short duration, but severe injuries result in periods of unconsciousness varying from hours to weeks or even months. The greater the duration of unconsciousness and the subsequent post-traumatic *amnesia, the greater will be the period of post-concussional disability. Consequently it is important to record the duration of loss of memory following head injuries, not only as an index of severity but also as a guide to ultimate recovery.

It has been estimated that almost one million patients in the UK are admitted to hospital each year following head injuries. The majority of injuries are the consequences of road traffic accidents, which are also often the cause of the most severe injuries. Other causes of head injury include domestic and industrial accidents, sports and recreation, and violent assaults (Teasdale 1995).

The cerebral damage is caused by rotational stresses within the brain, and is likely to be the more severe if the head is in motion at the time of impact. This causes minute haemorrhages and neuronal changes throughout the brain which may be of aetiological importance for the so-called post-concussional syndrome. At the same time it is clear that the principal features of concussion are caused by interference with vital centres in the brain stem. If unconsciousness lasts more than a few hours, it is likely that permanent brain damage has been sustained, with the risk of major psychological disabilities and personality changes that may prevent the patient returning to his former employment or even living equably with his family. The premorbid qualities of the individual will greatly influence his capacity for attaining full recovery, but even the most stable of individuals may suffer to some extent from post-concussional symptoms. These may include headache, dizziness, fatigue, and intolerance of noise, as well as emotional instability and impaired memory and concentration.

Chronic psychological impairment is sometimes seen in professional boxers who have sustained repeated blows to the head without necessarily losing consciousness. In recent times a good deal of attention has been focused on this 'punch-drunk' syndrome, which has led to proposals that boxing should be banned. This is unlikely to happen but greater protection of the head and face of boxers and medical control of those taking part in the sport may do something to minimize the frequency of punch-drunkenness.   FAW

Teasdale, G. M. (1995). 'Head injury'. *Journal of Neurology, Neurosurgery, and Psychiatry*, 58/5.

Condillac, Étienne de (1715–80). Born of an aristocratic family at Grenoble, Condillac was a proponent of the philosophy of sensationalism—that all knowledge is based on the senses. He was also one of the first to realize, after the discovery of the *retinal image (suggested by the astronomer Johannes Kepler in 1604, and observed in the ox eye by C. Scheiner in 1625), that we do not *see* retinal images (as we see pictures): what we see are external objects. Retinal images are just one cross-section of the visual channel, and are not objects of *perception (except for the special case of looking at the image in another's eye with an ophthalmoscope). Condillac concludes that perceptions are inferences from data from retinal images. This is the basis of current representational theories of perception, following Hermann von *Helmholtz, who stressed the importance for perception of 'unconscious inference'.

Condillac, É. de (1754). *Traité des sensations*. Trans. G. Carr (1930), *Treatise on the Sensations*.

Morgan, M. J. (1977). *Molyneux's Question*. (For Condillac's account of perception and comparison with Locke, Berkeley, Diderot, and other earlier and contemporary writers.)

conditioned reflex. See PAVLOV, IVAN PETROVICH.

conditioning. The rudiments of conditioning are familiar to most people. After experiencing a number of pairings of a signal, for example a tone or light, and a reinforcer, in this case food, Ivan *Pavlov's (1927) dogs came to salivate to the signal much as they did to the food. Similarly, B. F. Skinner's (1938) rats (see SKINNER BOX) would readily perform some action, such as pressing a lever, that procured food.

Clearly, both these behaviours depend upon *learning, in that their development requires the animal to experience a relationship or association between the signal and food in the case of Pavlovian or classical conditioning, and between the action and food in instrumental or operant conditioning. Although the empirical phenomena themselves are not a matter of dispute, the significance of this type of learning is contentious. Traditionally, conditioning represented the cornerstone of the *behaviourist's analysis of learning, but with the increasing focus on *cognition and information processing, the study of this form of learning has been consigned to a backwater of psychology.

The current neglect seems to be based largely upon the assumption that conditioning is a simple, automatic, and unconscious form of learning that underlies the acquisition of relatively trivial behaviour. Following a thorough survey of human conditioning studies, W. F. Brewer (1974) concluded that there was no good evidence for conditioning in human beings. This surprising claim was based not on our failure to show the appropriate behavioural changes, but on the observation that whenever conditioning-like effects occur, we are aware of the association between the signal or action and the reinforcer. Underlying this argument there appears to be the assumption that, by definition, conditioning must be an unconscious process. But neither the empirical effect itself nor its associated terminology implies such an assumption. Pavlov referred to the signal and its associated response as a 'conditional stimulus' and a 'conditional response' respectively, simply because the acquisition of this reaction was conditional or dependent upon having experienced the relationship between the signal and the food. Similarly, the food can be identified as a reinforcer because, at an empirical level, it appears to be an important agent for strengthening, or reinforcing, the conditional response. However, this terminology has undergone a subtle change in the West, so that one now finds statements to the effect that people and animals can be 'conditioned' and 'reinforced'. Obviously such statements are a travesty of the Pavlovian terminology: a person cannot be conditioned or strengthened, at least not by a conditioning experience. These distortions are important, however, for they reveal a fundamental and widespread belief about the nature of conditioning, namely that it is a passive process to which a person or animal is subjected.

The origin of this belief lies not in the conditioning phenomenon itself, but rather with the initial behaviourist explanations of this type of learning. For instance, E. L. *Thorndike (1911) in his famous 'law of effect' argued that following an action by a reinforcer simply strengthens a connection between the stimuli present when the action is performed and the action itself, so that the action re-occurs as a response to these stimuli when they are again presented. This stimulus-response theory has at least two features that bolster the idea that conditioning is a simple and passive process. First, the conditions for learning, and by implication the process underlying such learning, appear simple: in essence, successful conditioning depends just upon the temporal contiguity between the response and reinforcer. Secondly, a conditional response occurs because it is automatically elicited by the appropriate conditional stimulus. Thus, a trained rat presses the lever not because it knows about the relationship between its action and the occurrence of the reinforcer, but rather because the sight of the lever automatically triggers lever pressing. Both these claims turn out to be incorrect on further analysis.

It is a relatively easy matter to show that instrumental conditioning does not necessarily establish a simple habit released by the appropriate stimulus. Stimulus-response theory, by denying the animal any knowledge about the consequences of its actions, implies that conditional behaviour, once established, should be insensitive to any subsequent changes in the value of the reinforcer. We can test this claim by training an animal to perform an action for a particular food before devaluing the food, for example, by establishing quite separately an aversion to the food. This is readily done by inducing nausea shortly after consuming the food. If we now give the animal the opportunity to perform the action that had previously procured the food, stimulus-response theory would anticipate that the vigour of the action should be unaffected by the devaluation of the reinforcer. Not surprisingly, however, the animal is reluctant to perform this action (Adams and Dickinson 1981), indicating that simple instrumental conditioning reflects the acquisition of knowledge about the relationship between an action and the occurrence of the reinforcer rather than establishing a reflexively elicited habit. The deployment of this knowledge in controlling behaviour can then be modified by other relevant information, such as the current value of the reinforcer. Given this perspective, instrumental conditioning can be seen to represent a relatively simple procedure for investigating learning about the consequences of our actions and general purposive and goal-directed behaviour.

Just as our view of the knowledge underlying conditioning has changed from that specified by Thorndike's 'law of effect', so have our theories about the conditions for the acquisition of this knowledge. The 'law of effect' states that simple temporal contiguity between an action and a reinforcer is sufficient for instrumental conditioning, and Pavlov himself argued that a classical conditional stimulus also acquires its properties as a result of contiguous pairings with a reinforcer. It has long been recognized that a

system sensitive only to temporal contiguity would often fail to distinguish real causal and predictive relationships from purely fortuitous and coincidental conjunctions, and thus be prone to the development of superstitious beliefs and behaviour. It is now clear, however, that the conditioning mechanisms embody a number of subtle and complex processes designed to counteract the formation of superstitions. For instance, conditioning depends not only upon the temporal relationship between the conditional stimulus or action and the reinforcer, but also upon whether or not the occurrence of the reinforcer is surprising or unexpected. The role of surprise is demonstrated by L. J. Kamin's (1969) 'blocking effect'. If an animal receives conditioning trials in which a conditional stimulus, A, is paired with a reinforcer, it will subsequently show little conditional responding to a second stimulus, X, when a compound of A and X is reinforced. In the initial stage the animal learns to expect the reinforcer following stimulus A, so that its subsequent presentation following the AX compound is fully predicted by stimulus A and hence unsurprising. As a result, minimal conditioning accrues to stimulus X. Conversely, if stimulus A is initially established as a predictor of the non-occurrence of the reinforcer, the presentation of the reinforcer following the AX compound is very surprising and leads to enhanced conditioning to stimulus X (Rescorla 1971). This sensitivity to the surprisingness of the reinforcer will serve to protect us and other animals against the formation of superstitious beliefs and behaviour. Effectively, the conditioning mechanism appears to embody an assumption of minimum sufficient causation; an animal is less likely to attribute the contiguous occurrence of a reinforcer to the presence of a stimulus or the execution of an action if another adequate cause or signal for this reinforcer is also present.

In conclusion, the contemporary view of conditioning is considerably more complex and subtle than that expounded by the early behaviourists. We should not overplay, however, the importance of conditioning as a general model for all learning. There are many examples of non-associative learning that lie outside the scope of conditioning theory. Even so, conditioning studies appear to reveal universal mechanisms by which we and other animals intuitively detect and store information about the causal structure of our environment.   AD

Adams, C. D., and Dickinson, A. (1981). 'Instrumental responding following reinforcer devaluation'. *Quarterly Journal of Experimental Psychology*, 33B.

Brewer, W. F. (1974). 'There is no convincing evidence for operant or classical conditioning in adult humans'. In Weimer, W. B., and Palermo, D. S. (eds.), *Cognition and the Symbolic Processes*.

Kamin, L. J. (1969). 'Predictability, surprise, attention and conditioning'. In Campbell, B. A., and Church, R. M. (eds.), *Punishment and Aversive Behaviour*.

Confucian ideas of the mind

Pavlov, I. P. (1927). *Conditioned Reflexes*.

Rescorla, R. A. (1971). 'Variations in the effectiveness of reinforcement and non-reinforcement following prior inhibitory conditioning'. *Learning and Motivation*, 2.

Skinner, B. F. (1938). *The Behavior of Organisms*.

Thorndike, E. L. (1911). *Animal Intelligence: Experimental Studies*.

Confucian ideas of the mind. See CHINESE IDEAS OF THE MIND.

conjuring. For over 100 years psychologists have been fascinated by the techniques employed by magicians to fool their audiences. In the 1890s both Alfred Binet and Max Dessoir wrote short articles about the ways in which magicians divert attention and use suggestion to accomplish their illusions. In 1896, Joseph Jastrow published an article in *Science* reporting the results of several psychological tests (including, for example, those concerned with reaction time, speed of hand movement, short-term memory, etc.) that he had carried out with two of America's best-known stage magicians. In 1900, Norman Triplett completed the first American Ph.D. in psychology on 'The psychology of conjuring deceptions', and described several experiments investigating the effect of suggestion on the perception and recall of magic tricks (Triplett 1900).

Throughout the last century, a small number of psychologists have continued to investigate the topic, with the most recent work involving experimental investigations into mechanisms that lie behind the stratagems used by magicians (see, for example, Wiseman and Morris 1995).

However, the vast majority of the literature on the psychology of conjuring has been produced by magicians in an attempt to enhance the performance of their art (see, for example, Fitzkee 1945 and Lamont and Wiseman 1999 for a review and bibliography).

This article presents a summary of some of the main topics discussed by those who have attempted to understand the psychology behind this highly unusual, and captivating, form of deception.

1. Effects and methods
2. Misdirection of attention
3. Reducing suspicion
4. Biasing recall
5. Problem solving
6. The psychology of mind-reading
7. Summary

1. Effects and methods

Magicians appear to defy the laws of physics by making rabbits appear, handkerchiefs disappear, and people levitate. These seemingly impossible feats are referred to as 'effects', and are achieved through a wide range of 'methods'. For example, imagine that the magician places a ball into a box, says a few magic words, and opens the box to reveal that the ball has disappeared. The trick could have been accomplished in several ways. For example, the ball may be made of foam and squashed into a small hidden compartment inside the box, or the magician may only appear to place the ball in the box while actually concealing it in his hand. The magician's job is to conceal these methods from the audience, and the psychological techniques used to achieve this are commonly referred to as 'misdirection'. This article will describe some of the main forms of misdirection.

2. Misdirection of attention

Let us imagine that the spectator chooses a playing card, looks at it, and places it into the middle of the deck. The magician intends to perform some simple sleight of hand that will result in the playing card being transferred from the centre to the top of the deck. However, for the secret transfer to go unnoticed, the magician has to direct the audience's attention away from the deck of cards for a few seconds. This could be accomplished in one of several ways. The magician may look at the spectator and ask him to name the card. The few seconds of eye contact between spectator and magician will be enough to hide the sleight of hand involved in the trick. Alternatively, the magician may look at another deck of cards on a table and ask the spectator to pick them up. Again, for a few seconds the spectator's attention will be directed away from the magician's hands and thus he will be able to transfer the position of the chosen card undetected. Both of the strategies described above depend upon the social reciprocation of attention. As John Ramsey, a highly accomplished magician, once remarked, 'If you want somebody to look at something, look at it. If you want somebody to look at you, look at them.'

Another form of misdirecting attention involves exploiting naturally occurring moments when spectators are unlikely to be concentrating on events. One common technique involves the magician carrying out secret preparations for a trick prior to the perceived start of the performance. For example, the magician may look at, and remember, the order of certain cards in a deck while appearing to casually toy with them prior to the start of a trick.

In short, magicians have developed several techniques for manipulating attention and exploiting naturally occurring moments of inattention. Interestingly, for these to be fully effective, the audience must be unaware that their attention has been misdirected, and thus the magician must work without recourse to the types of direct requests (e.g. 'look over there' or 'look at this') used to direct attention during many everyday interactions.

3. Reducing suspicion

Let us imagine that the magician has borrowed a coin, pretended to place it into his left fist, but, in reality, concealing it in his right hand. He now wishes to secretly transfer the coin from his right hand to his inside jacket pocket. Obviously, the magician could simply place his right hand into his pocket and drop the coin. However, most spectators are extremely suspicious of any actions that seem to occur for no apparent reason. To reduce this suspicion, the magician needs to manufacture a reason for placing his hand into his jacket pocket. This could be achieved in several ways. For example, prior to the trick, the magician might place a magic wand into his pocket. During the trick, he could then explain that he now needs the wand, and therefore create a logical reason to place his hand inside his jacket, remove the wand, and, at the same time, drop the coin into his pocket.

Magicians frequently disguise an otherwise suspicious action by creating a 'natural' reason for the action. Such 'naturalness' is central to the performance of magic, and magicians have developed many other stratagems for reducing the amount of suspicion with which spectators view trick objects and deceptive actions. For example, magicians are aware that everyday objects, such as decks of playing cards and coins, are unlikely to arouse suspicion, and thus modify such objects (e.g. creating double headed coins or decks containing 52 identical cards) with little risk of detection.

4. Biasing recall

After a trick has been performed the audience will often try to reconstruct the sequence of events and figure out the secret of the trick. Magicians have developed several stratagems to disrupt this process. During a trick the magician may attempt to influence the spectator's subsequent memory for events. For example, let us imagine that the magician is performing a trick in which a deck of cards has been secretly placed into a known order. The magician will be able to cut the cards without seriously disrupting their order. However, shuffling the cards would result in a completely different order, thus rendering the trick impossible. During the performance the magician may cut the deck of cards. However, a few minutes later he may state that the cards were actually shuffled. After the trick has finished, the audience are likely to incorrectly reconstruct the trick on the basis of the magician's remark, believe that the cards were shuffled, rule out the possibility of the cards being in a certain order, and thus be unable to figure out how the trick was achieved.

5. Problem solving

On occasion, the audience may figure out the correct solution to a trick, but reject it as implausible. For example, the magician may have used a powerful mnemonic technique to quickly remember the entire order of a shuffled deck of cards. However, the audience may believe that such a memory feat is impossible, or that the magician would not go to such lengths to perform the trick, and

thus reject the idea as implausible. At other times the spectator may simply not think of the correct solution in the first place. This might be the case when a trick depends upon clever lateral thinking, or some form of scientific/mathematical principle not known to the spectator. For example, one very simple trick involves a spectator thinking of a number, doubling it, adding four, dividing by two, then subtracting the number he first thought of, and always being left with the number two. A spectator who was unaware of the basic mathematical principles involved in the calculations might be fooled by this trick. Likewise, spectators unaware of mirrors, projections, and esoteric chemical reactions might be fooled by those tricks that rely on such methods.

6. The psychology of mind-reading

All of the above sections refer to magic tricks in which the performer makes objects seem to appear, disappear, transform, etc. However, there is another branch of magic, usually referred to as 'mentalism', in which the performer appears to possess extrasensory perception and thus can read minds, predict the future, and so on. Although some of the principles that have already been discussed are also used in mentalism, other psychological stratagems also come into play. For example, the mentalist may appear to be able to see into the future by predicting the probable. Let us imagine that the performer places four cards, numbered one, two, three, and four, in a row and asks a spectator to select one of them. The spectator selects number two and the mentalist opens his prediction to reveal the statement 'I predict that you will choose number two'. This prediction is likely to be correct as most people will avoid the end positions and choose number two or number three.

At other times, the mentalist will appear to predict the future by making several predictions, but only revealing the one prediction that conforms to some future event. For example, let us imagine that the mentalist asks a spectator to name blue, green, or red. The spectator names 'red', and the mentalist removes a piece of paper from his pocket on which is written 'I predict that you will choose red'. In reality, the mentalist wrote down three statements on three pieces of paper in advance of the trick. Each statement predicted that the spectator would choose a different colour, and each piece of paper was hidden in a different pocket. During the trick, the mentalist simply revealed the prediction that matched the spectator's choice.

7. Summary

Many of the forefathers of modern psychology recognized the potential benefits of studying magic and conjuring. Magicians have classified many different forms of misdirection and have written about the ways in which they can be used to enhance the performance of magic (see e.g. Fitzkee 1945, Tamariz, 1988). Recent investigations by psychologists have provided additional insights into these techniques (see, for example, Wiseman and Morris 1995).

This work has resulted in an understanding of many of the methods used by magicians to deceive their audiences. However, modern experimental tools, such as devices designed to track eye movements and video analysis, could unlock a great deal more information about the ways in which magicians manipulate and misdirect attention, perception, memory, and problem solving. Such information has the potential to inform a wide range of psychological enquiry and may also shed light onto other important areas of deception, including, for example, military deception, financial fraud, and confidence games.

RW

Fitzkee, D. (1945). *Magic by Misdirection*.

Lamont, P., and Wiseman, R. (1999). *Magic In Theory*.

Tamariz, J. (1988). *The Magic Way*.

Triplett, N. (1900). 'The psychology of conjuring deception'. *American Journal of Psychology*, 11/4.

Wiseman, R., and Morris, R. (1995). 'Recalling pseudo-psychic demonstrations'. *British Journal of Psychology*, 86.

consciousness. (*see opposite*)

consciousness and causality. The difference between mind and matter and how the two interrelate has challenged and baffled human understanding ever since man first began to reflect on his nature and the meaning of existence. The common, naive impression that we use the mind to initiate and control our physical actions has long been rejected almost universally in science, following the doctrine of scientific materialism, which predicates that a full account of brain, behaviour, and reality is possible in terms purely physical without reference to conscious, mental, or subjective agents. The more progress neuroscience achieved in explaining the electrophysiology, chemistry, and anatomy of brain activity, the greater became the apparent dichotomy between mind and brain, and the more inconceivable that the course of brain function could be influenced in any way by the subjective qualities of inner experience.

In the 1950s materialistic philosophy was carried to a new extreme in the so-called 'psychophysical (or mind–brain) identity theory'. By involved semantics it was affirmed that no difference exists at all between mind and brain, that they are one and the same, and only seem like two different things because we have used different languages and perspectives in our objective and subjective descriptions. According to this identity theory, there is no mind–brain relation; only a pseudo-problem remains that allegedly can be resolved with a proper linguistic approach. The materialist position as developed through the late 1960s was expressed by D. M. Armstrong, a leading proponent, as 'the view that we can give a complete account of man in purely physico-chemical terms', in a 'purely electrochemical account of the workings of the brain'. 'The mind is nothing but the brain.' 'Life is a purely physico-chemical phenomenon.' 'It seems that man is nothing but a material object having none but physical properties' (Armstrong 1968). The accepted superfluousness of consciousness for neuroscience was expressed by Nobel laureate Sir John Eccles in 1964:

We can, in principle, explain all our input–output performance in terms of activity of neuronal circuits; and consequently, consciousness seems to be absolutely unnecessary! . . . as neurophysiologists we simply have no use for consciousness in our attempts to explain how the nervous system works.

In direct reaction against the materialist view, a modified, mentalistic concept of consciousness and the mind–brain relation emerged in the mid-1960s. In the course of attempts to account for the observed unity and/or duality of conscious experience following surgical disconnection of the cerebral hemispheres (see SPLIT-BRAIN AND THE MIND), favour was given to an interpretation of conscious mind in which subjective unity and subjective meaning generally were conceived to be primarily operational or functional derivatives. It was posited that a brain process acquires subjective meaning by virtue of the way it operates in the context of brain dynamics, not because it is a neural copy, a transform, or an isomorphic or topological representation of the imagined object. This operational concept of subjective meaning necessarily involved a functional, and therefore *causal*, impact of subjective phenomena in the dynamics of brain control. Conscious phenomena were interpreted to be dynamic emergent properties of brain activity. The subjective phenomena by definition were 'different from, more than, and not reducible to' the neural mechanisms of which they are built.

The neural infrastructure of any brain process mediating conscious awareness is composed of elements within elements and forces within forces, ranging from subnuclear and subatomic particles at the lower levels upward through molecular, cellular, and simple-to-complex neural systems. At each level of the hierarchy, elements are bound and controlled by the enveloping organizational properties of the larger systems in which they are embedded. Holistic system properties at each level of organization have their own causal regulatory roles, interacting at their own level and also exerting downward control over their components, as well as determining the properties of the system in which they are embedded. It is postulated that at higher levels in the brain these emergent system properties include the phenomena of inner experience as high-order emergents in the brain's hierarchy of controls.

(*cont. on page 218*)

consciousness.

Michael A. Arbib

Even 'simple' mammals may be aware of the difference between feeling maternal and feeling enraged. Such 'animal awareness' seems to be part of human consciousness but the latter seems qualitatively different in nature. I argue that we are conscious in a fully human sense only because we have language. However, I deny that consciousness is merely a function of language. For example, one may have a vivid, conscious perception of a face yet be unable to put it into words. The argument of this article is further developed in Arbib (2001).

The neurological literature shows that consciousness is not a direct property of having neurons of a particular structure or complexity because the same data can be represented in two networks of comparable neural complexity, yet be accessible to consciousness only when one of the networks rather than the other is intact. In particular, clinical studies show a double dissociation between the 'declarative' ability to communicate the size of an object, whether verbally or by pantomime, and the 'procedural' ability to act upon objects (Goodale et al. 1991, Jeannerod, Decety, and Michel 1994). Since there is no data suggesting that the two regions of the brain involved in the double dissociation contain different microtubules, I think we can reject the space–time geometry view of microtubules in consciousness (Hameroff 2001). Again, since thalamocortical oscillations are equally important for the functioning of these 'conscious' and 'unconscious' regions of cerebral cortex, we must treat Llinás and Ribary's (2001) view of the role of thalamocortical oscillations with care. Perhaps we may see thalamocortical oscillations as the sign that cerebral cortex is 'powered up' into the waking state, without regarding the oscillations as themselves the 'carriers' of consciousness.

Arbib and Hesse (1986) offer a specific account of the co-evolution of human consciousness and language. There are perhaps hundreds of schemas (Arbib et al., 1998: ch. 3) active at any time to subserve the current interaction of the organism with its environment. By contrast, consciousness seems rather focused. But what is the role of consciousness? Wouldn't these schemas do their jobs just as well if there were no such thing as consciousness?

Hughlings Jackson (1878–9) viewed the brain in terms of levels of increasing evolutionary complexity. He argued that damage to a 'higher' level of the brain disinhibited 'older' brain regions from controls evolved later, to reveal evolutionarily more primitive behaviours. But the crucial point is that, once new regions are in place, they provide an enriched environment for the older parts of the brain. These now have new possibilities for further evolution.

Primitive communication subserves primitive coordination of the members of a social group and may not involve consciousness. As communication evolves, the 'instructions' that can be given to other members of the group increase in subtlety. Communication evolves at first purely as a way of coordinating the actions of a group. For this to succeed, the brain of each group member must be able not only to generate such signals, but also to integrate signals from other members of the group into its own ongoing motor planning. The key transition in going from the limited set of vocalizations used in communication by, say, vervet monkeys to the richness of human language came with a *migration in time* from (i) an execution/observation matching system enabling an individual to recognize the action (as distinct from the mere movement) that another individual is making (see MIRROR CELLS), to (ii) the individual becoming able to pantomime 'this is the action I am about to take'. Arbib and Hesse (1986) do not emphasize the external process of 'group selection' which must have evolved in the population as a whole, but rather the changes within the individual brain made possible by the availability of a 'précis'—a gesturable representation—of intended future movements (as distinct from current movements). They use the term *communication plexus* for the circuits involved in generating this representation. The Jacksonian element of their analysis is the suggestion that once the brain has such a communication plexus, then a new process of evolution begins whereby the précis comes to serve not only as a basis for communication between the members of a group, but also as a resource for planning and coordination within the brain itself. This 'communication plexus' thus evolves a crucial role in schema coordination. The thesis is that it is the activity of this co-evolved process that constitutes consciousness. As such it will progress in richness along with the increased richness of communication that culminates as language in the human line.

Arbib and Hesse's thesis, then, is that it is the activity of this communication plexus that constitutes the essentially human dimension of consciousness, i.e. that 'consciousness' is defined by a neurally represented précis of potential behaviour. Such a view does not explain the phenomenology of consciousness—i.e. the way consciousness 'feels' to each of us—but it does accord well with this phenomenology. The fact that lower-level schema activity can often proceed successfully without the high-level coordination afforded by the communication plexus explains why consciousness may sometimes be active as a monitor rather than as a director of action. In other cases, the formation of the précis of schema activity plays the crucial role in determining the future course of schema activity, and thus of action—and this accords with those occasions in which we experience a conscious effort in weighing a number of courses of action before we commit ourselves to behave in a specific way.

Arbib, M.A. (2001). 'Co-evolution of human consciousness and language', *Annals of the New York Academy of Sciences*, 929.

—— and Hesse, M. B. (1986). *The Construction of Reality*.

—— Érdi, P., and Szentágothai, J. (1998). *Neural Organization: Structure, Function, and Dynamics*.

Goodale, M. A., Milner, A. D., Jakobson, L. S., and Carey, D. P. (1991). 'A neurological dissociation between perceiving objects and grasping them'. *Nature*, 349.

Hameroff, S. (2001). 'Consciousness, the brain, and spacetime geometry'. *Annals of the New York Academy of Sciences*, 929.

Jackson, J. H. (1878–9). 'On affections of speech from disease of the brain'. *Brain*, 1, 2.

Jeannerod, M., Decety, J., and Michel, F. (1994). 'Impairment of grasping following a bilateral posterior parietal lesion'. *Neurophysiologia*, 32.

Llinás, R., and Ribary, U. (2001). 'Co-evolution of human consciousness and language'. *Annals of the New York Academy of Sciences*, 929.

Weiskrantz, L. (1974). 'The interaction between occipital and temporal cortex in vision: an overview'. In Schmitt, F. O., and Worden, F. G. (eds.), *The Neurosciences Third Study Program*.

Susan Blackmore

Whenever we ask 'Am I conscious now?' the answer seems to be 'Yes'. We always seem to be consciously feeling, hearing, and seeing something. But how can the existence of millions of interconnected brain cells give rise to this personal, private, ineffable experience? Either we must answer this question, or show why it is the wrong question.

Ever since William James (1890) coined the phrase the 'stream of consciousness', it has seemed indisputable that this rich, flowing succession of thoughts and perceptions is what needs explaining. Research on the 'contents of consciousness', the 'neural correlates of consciousness', and popular global workspace models all depends on distinguishing between what is in and what is out of the conscious stream. But what if it simply is not like that? What if there is no stream and no experiencer?

In experiments on 'change blindness' people look at a picture of a complex scene and, just as they blink or move their eyes, some key feature of the picture is changed. Most of the time they simply do not notice. The effect is very robust and has been shown using cuts in film and video, by making the change just as a 'mud splash' hits the picture, and even in real-life situations. The changes can be very large or right in the centre of the display and still not be noticed.

These surprising results suggest that we do *not* hold in our heads a rich visual image of the world, for if we did we would surely notice the changes. Rather, during each fixation we see only a small area, and when our eyes move that information is lost, leaving at most only a sketchy description. We *think* there is rich detail in our stream of consciousness because if ever we forget something we can look again and there it is. By using the outside world as a memory, we get the illusion of seeing much more than we really do. This alone shows we are wrong about our stream of consciousness. The stream of sounds is peculiar in a different way. The classic example is when the clock chimes several times before you notice. At that point you can distinctly count the number of chimes—chimes you did not consciously hear. With practice it is possible to pull out several such sound threads and, as it were, rehear the past few moments in different ways. Which then was really in the stream of consciousness?

One way of understanding these oddities is to replace the notion of a continuous stream with the idea that much of the time there is no distinction between 'in' and 'out' of consciousness. Then every so often we wonder 'Am I conscious now?' and an answer is concocted, backwards, from memory. A stream of consciousness and a self who observes it, both appear together—and both are illusions.

This may not be how it seems, but then how it seems can change dramatically with a little practice and attention. Perhaps we might even see through the illusion.

Blackmore, S. (2003). *Consciousness: An Introduction*.

Dennett, D. C. (1991). *Consciousness Explained*.

James, W. (1890). *The Principles of Psychology* (2 vols.).

Metzinger., T. (ed.) (2000). *Neural Correlates of Consciousness*.

Nok, A. (ed.) (2002). *Is the Visual World a Grand Illusion?*

Ned Block

There are two broad classes of empirical theories of consciousness, which I will call the *biological* and the *functional*. The biological approach is based on empirical correlations between experience and the brain. For example, there is a great deal of evidence that the neural correlate of visual experience is activity in a set of occipitotemporal pathways, with special emphasis on the inferotemporal cortex.

The functionalist approach is a successor of behaviourism, the view that mentality can be seen as tendencies to emit certain behavioural outputs given certain sensory inputs. The trouble with behaviourism is that it did not allow that mental states were causes and effects, but functionalists do allow this. They characterize consciousness in terms of its causal role: the causal influence on it from inputs and other mental states, and its causal efficacy with respect to other mental states and behaviour. The central idea of functionalism is a proposal about the *concept* of consciousness, but *scientific* functionalists have filled the view in with empirical details—the idea is that a representation is conscious if it is broadcast in a global neuronal workspace. (See the article by S. Dehaene in Dehaene 2001.)

The functional approach says consciousness is a *role*, whereas the biological approach says consciousness is a realizer of that role. For example, one could take solubility to be a role—dissolving in certain circumstances—or, as with the biological view of consciousness, the physico-chemical configuration that has that role.

The key *empirical* difference comes down to the question of whether consciousness might sometimes exist without having its *normal* role or whether something *else* might in some circumstances play that role. There is some evidence for the first possibility. There are unusual circumstances in which the occipitotemporal stream is activated at the level that is correlated with experience but in which the subject says he sees nothing. For example, there is a kind of brain damage in which, if objects are presented on both sides, the subject claims not to see one side, but the part of the occipitotemporal stream stimulated by the 'invisible' object is just as active as when it is seen. (See the articles by Kanwisher and by Driver and Vuillemer, in Dehaene 2001.) It seems *possible* that these patients have a phenomenal representation that they cannot properly access. If so, a phenomenal state needn't always have its characteristic behaviour, and consciousness in one sense of the term—*phenomenality*—would not be captured by the functionalist theory. (See also NEGLECT.)

Liss (1968) presented subjects with four letters in two circumstances, long, e.g. 40 milliseconds followed by a 'mask' known to make stimuli hard to identify, or short, e.g. 9 milliseconds, without a mask. Subjects could identify three of the four letters on average in the short case but said they were weak and fuzzy. In the long case, they could identify only one letter, but said they could see them all and that the letters were sharper, brighter, and higher in contrast. This experiment suggests a *double dissociation*: the short stimuli were phenomenally poor but perceptually and conceptually OK, whereas the long stimuli were phenomenally sharp but perceptually or conceptually poor, as reflected in the low reportability.

The picture that emerges is that phenomenality and accessibility may vary somewhat independently and that there is one concept of consciousness keyed to the former and another keyed to the latter. Phenomenality may be best thought of in biological terms, whereas accessibility is best thought of in terms of global neuronal broadcasting.

Dehaene, S. (ed.) (2001). *The Cognitive Neuroscience of Consciousness*.

Liss, P. (1968). 'Does backward masking by visual noise stop stimulus processing?' *Perception and Psychophysics*, 4.

David Chalmers

The conscious life of a subject comprises all sorts of subjective experiences: visual experiences, other sensory experiences, bodily sensations, mental imagery, and a stream of occurrent thought. There is something it is like to have these experiences, from the subject's point of view. The hard problem of consciousness is that of explaining how it is that physical processes in a brain are associated with experiences of this sort.

The problems of explaining how the brain supports complex behaviour, memory, learning, and language are 'easy' problems in comparison. These problems all concern the objective functioning of the brain, and can be approached by specifying appropriate neural or computational mechanisms. The hard problem, by contrast, concerns the relationship between objective functioning and subjective experience. Even once one has explained all the complex functions above, there may still arise a further question: why is there something it feels like to be a system of this sort? This is the key mystery of consciousness.

The fundamental issue concerns how to integrate two sorts of data about the mind. We have 'third-person data' about the brain and we have 'first-person data' about subjective experiences. Both are equally real, and both need to be explained. The task of a science of consciousness is to integrate them into a single framework.

In my view, we cannot 'reduce' first-person data to third-person data. If one's catalogue of what needs to be explained mentions only third-person data, one is simply overlooking some of the most important data that a science needs to explain. More controversially, I think that we cannot wholly 'explain' first-person data in terms of the third-person data. Third-person data is all data about objective structure and functioning. From this sort of data, one can deduce more third-person data about higher-level structure and functioning. But first-person data is not data about structure and functioning, so the gap is as wide as ever.

Instead, I think a science of consciousness needs to admit both first-person data and third-person data as real and mutually irreducible. The task of a science of consciousness is to investigate the systematic connection between these. First-person data can be gathered directly, through phenomenological methods, or indirectly, by inference from others' verbal reports. Third-person data can be gathered by the usual methods of psychology and neuroscience. One can then find systematic 'correlations' between the two. For example, conscious experiences seem to correlate directly with certain sorts of brain processes. We can eventually hope to find a highly detailed set of correlations between properties of the brain and properties of consciousness. Once this is done, we can attempt to infer a set of underlying 'fundamental principles' connecting physical processes and consciousness. If all goes well, these principles will be simple, basic, and universal.

As I see things, this will not 'reduce' consciousness to a brain process. The fundamental principles here will be analogous in some respects to fundamental laws of nature; on this view, consciousness can itself be seen as fundamental. But importantly, all this is quite compatible with the existence of a science of consciousness. I think that much recent work in the area can be seen as contributing toward a science of the sort I have outlined. There is a long way to go, and we do not yet know if all the obstacles can be overcome. But I think it is reasonable to hope that one day we will have a theory of the fundamental principles that connect physical processes to conscious experience.

PAUL M. CHURCHLAND

This ill-defined topic, which has yet to find a governing research paradigm, is perhaps best defined by a series of unanswered questions. What distinguishes our *waking state* from such diverse states as deep sleep, trauma-induced coma, and the unconscious state induced by anaesthetics? Also, what distinguishes the brain's *conscious* representations and activities from the vast majority of its representational and computational activities that never ascend to that special status? Further, what structural, representational, or dynamical features of the brain are *responsible* for the emergence of conscious activity? And finally, what special *functions* does it perform that made conscious brains worthy of natural selection in the first place?

Aspirant theories are plentiful, as are thought-provoking empirical data, but no success has joined them decisively. Herewith, a critical summary of some popular suggestions.

Special location accounts. Because consciousness is partly or wholly abolished when certain circumscribed brain areas are damaged, it is tempting to identify neuronal activity in those areas as the basis or embodiment of consciousness. For example, unilateral lesions to the thalamic intralaminar nucleus typically produce in the agent a profound hemineglect on the contralateral side, and bilateral lesions yield permanent coma (Bogen 1995). But for any suggested location, we want an *explanation* of what is special about the activities therein. This lacuna leads theorists to a variety of functional accounts.

Self-representation accounts. On these, consciousness is said to occur when the brain perceives, or otherwise represents, some of its own cognitive states and activities. Consciousness is thus a form of *meta*cognition. The favoured subjects of such occasional meta-representations are thereby elevated into consciousness (Armstrong 1981, Lycan 1987, Damasio 1999). A standard objection is that this wrongly conflates one special case of consciousness—awareness-of-*self*—with the more general form of consciousness displayed when any awake, alert creature is selectively aware of some feature of its external environment. That phenomenon, presumably, need require no *self*-representation at all. Also, the brain is massively engaged in 'monitoring' its own states at all times, whereas only a very few of those states are ever present to consciousness.

Self-control accounts. On these, a brain is conscious to the extent that it is modulating, manipulating, and steering its own cognitive activities. Consciousness is thus the mark of an agent that is partly *autonomous* in generating not just its own behaviour, but its own *cognition* as well (Churchland 1995, Damasio 1999, Taylor 2001). Objections parallel those just given for meta-perceptual accounts. An awake, alert agent can be conscious solely by virtue of steering its own gross *motor* behaviour. And a live brain engages in widespread self-modulation as a matter of course, whereas only a few of the activities thus modulated are ever present to consciousness. A deliberate hybrid of views 2 and 3 might alleviate the second of these two problems (states at the focus of *both* self-perception *and* self-modulation might be comparatively rare). But the first problem would remain.

Competition for executive control accounts. These re-address the brain's control of the physical body. Consciousness is here portrayed as the solution to a serious problem confronting any system as complex as the brain, an organ with diverse subsystems devoted to monitoring and controlling a wide range of internal and external phenomena. These subsystems, it is said, are all in competition with one another for here-and-now control of how the body's motor and sensory systems are to be deployed. The current contents of anyone's consciousness are always the current representations of whichever brain subsystem has managed to elbow aside or eclipse the clamouring competition. Those representations are distinguished by their having at least temporary executive control—over our speech mechanisms and over the body as a whole—and also, perhaps, by their being made candidates for storage in long-term memory (Baars 1988, Dennett 1991). In the awake state, this competition is never-ending, and so the contents of consciousness are typically ephemeral.

One wants, of course, an account of the *mechanism* of such selective dominance or focal attention. Here the suggestions diverge. The *global workspace* account posits a distinct brain area to which the unconscious subsystems continually submit information, which information enters consciousness only when it is taken up as somehow relevant to the computational activities already under way in that focal workspace. Another version eschews any special area, and posits a process of *shifting coalitions* of spatially distributed neural activity, coalitions of neurons temporarily united by their mutual interaction, perhaps (Baars 1988, Leopold and Logothetis 1999), or by a temporary *synchrony* in their physiological activities, a synchrony that yields them a temporary collective dominance over non-synchronous neurons (Crick and Koch 1990, Singer 2000).

Special architecture and dynamics accounts. Here we return to the brain's microarchitecture and dynamic profile in search of functional insights. Normal brains display an information-processing ladder that leads ever forward from sensory neuronal populations through many intermediate populations and ultimately to populations of motor neurons. But there are also many axonal *back*-projections from populations higher and later on the ladder to populations lower and earlier. These 'descending' or 'recurrent' pathways introduce an intriguing variety of dynamic possibilities—such as self-modulation, selective attention, and autonomous activity—of interest to *all* of the functional accounts just scouted (Edelman 1993, Churchland 1995).

In particular, such a recurrent network can be configured so as to generate, autonomously, an unfolding trajectory in its neuronal activation space, a trajectory that partially *represents* an unfolding external reality. That trajectory can be continuously steered and edited by sensory input during the awake state; it can be left to wander freely during a disconnected 'dreaming' state, and it can be shut down entirely by the suppression of recurrent activity during 'deep sleep' (Llinás 2001).

These considerations hint that consciousness can come in a wide variety of degrees and flavours, depending on the character, the location, and the extent of such recurrent modulatory activity. Consciousness, some say, is like a light bulb—either it's on or it's off (Searle 1992). But perhaps not. A better analogy might be with light itself—which comes in endlessly different wavelength profiles and radiant intensities. Understanding light is a matter of grasping the relevant dimensions of variation. And just as genuine instances of light can vary widely along such dimensions, perhaps genuine consciousness may vary substantially from one species to another; or from one individual to another; or indeed, within a single individual over time.

Extravagant accounts. These deserve mention for reasons of history and completeness, but they look increasingly barren as sources of fecund research. *Dualism* posits an immaterial substance, distinct from the brain, in which consciousness inheres, forever beyond the explanatory reach of the physical sciences (Popper and Eccles 1978). *Epiphenomenalism* posits, not a substance, but a range of non-physical *properties* of the brain, similarly beyond any physical explanation (Jackson 1982, Chalmers 1996). And a recent suggestion posits *quantum-gravitational coherence* within the microtubules of the brain's axonal fibres as the hallmark or essence of consciousness, on grounds that blocking such coherence may explain how anaesthetics work, while the achievement of such quantum-level coherences may explain the existence of sound but non-algorithmic mathematical knowledge (Penrose 1994). Such options may be discussed in undergraduate classes, or in the media, but they play a negligible role in guiding empirical research.

Armstrong, D. (1981). *The Nature of Mind.*

Baars, B. J. (1988). *A Cognitive Theory of Consciousness.*

Bogen, J. E. (1995). 'On the neurophysiology of consciousness: an overview'. *Consciousness and Cognition*, 4.

Chalmers, D. (1996). *The Conscious Mind.*

Churchland, P. M. (1995). *The Engine of Reason, The Seat of the Soul: A Philosophical Journey into the Brain.*

Crick, F., and Koch, C. (1990). 'Towards a neurobiological theory of consciousness'. *Seminars in the Neurosciences*, 2.

Damasio, A. (1999). *The Feeling of What Happens.*

Dennett, D. C. (1991). *Consciousness Explained.*

Edelman, G. (1993). 'Neural Darwinism: selection and re-entrant signalling in higher brain function'. *Neuron*, 10.

Jackson, F. (1982). 'Epiphenomenal qualia'. *Philosophical Quarterly*, 32.

Leopold, D. A., and Logothetis, N. K. (1999). 'Multistable phenomena: changing views in perception'. *Trends in Cognitive Science*, 3.

Llinás, R. (2001). *I of the Vortex: From Neurons to Self.*

Lycan, W. (1987). *Consciousness.*

Penrose, Roger (1994). *Shadows of the Mind.*

Popper, K., and Eccles, J. (1978). *The Self and its Brain.*

Searle, John (1992). *The Rediscovery of the Mind.*

Singer, W. (2000). 'Phenomenal awareness and consciousness from a neurobiological perspective'. In Metzinger, T. (ed.), *Neural Correlates of Consciousness.*

Taylor, J. G. (2001). 'The central representation: the where, what and how of consciousness'. In Colona, S. (ed.), *The Emergence of Mind.*

Dan Dennett

Consciousness often seems to be utterly mysterious. I suspect that the principal cause of this bafflement is a sort of accounting error that is engendered by a familiar series of challenges and responses. A simplified version of one such path to mysteryland runs as follows:

PHIL. What is consciousness?

SY. Well, some things—such as stones and can-openers—are utterly lacking in any *point of view*, any *subjectivity* at all, while other things—such as you and me—do have points of view: private, perspectival, interior ways of being apprised of some limited aspects of the wider world and our bodies' relations to it. We lead our lives, suffering and enjoying, deciding and choosing our actions, guided by this 'first-person' access that we have. To be conscious is to be an agent with a point of view.

PHIL. But surely there is more to it than that! A cherry tree has limited access to the ambient temperature at its surface, and can be (mis-)guided into blooming inopportunely by unseasonable warm weather; a robot with video camera 'eyes' and microphone 'ears' may discriminate and respond aptly to hundreds of different aspects of its wider world; my own immune system can sense, discriminate, and respond appropriately (for the most part) to millions of different eventualities. Each of these is an agent (of sorts) with a point of view (of sorts) but none of them is conscious.

SY. Yes, indeed; there is more. We conscious beings have capabilities these simpler agents lack. We don't just notice things and respond to them; we *notice* that we notice things. More exactly, among the many discriminative states that our bodies may enter (including the states of our immune systems, our autonomic nervous systems, our digestive systems, and so forth), a subset of them can be discriminated in turn by higher-order discriminations which then become sources of guidance for higher-level control activities. In us, this recursive capacity for self-monitoring exhibits no clear limits—beyond those of available time and energy. If somebody throws a brick at you, you see it coming and duck. But you also discriminate the fact that you *visually* discriminated the projectile, and can then discriminate the further fact that you can tell visual from tactile discriminations (usually), and then go on to reflect on the fact that you are also able to recall recent sensory discriminations in some detail, and that there is a difference between experiencing something and recalling the experience of something, and between thinking about the difference between recollection and experience and thinking about the difference between seeing and hearing, and so forth, till bedtime.

PHIL. But surely there is more to it than that! Although existing robots may have quite paltry provisions for such recursive self-monitoring, I can readily imagine this particular capacity being added to some robot of the future. However deftly it exhibited its capacity to generate and react appropriately to 'reflective' analyses of its underlying discriminative states, it wouldn't be conscious—not the way we are.

SY. Are you sure you can imagine this?

PHIL. Oh yes, absolutely sure. There would be, perhaps, some sort of *executive* point of view definable by analysis of the power such a robot would have to control itself based on these reactive capacities, but this robotic subjectivity would be a pale shadow of ours. When it uttered 'it seems to me . . .' its utterances wouldn't really mean anything—or at least, they wouldn't mean what I mean when I tell you what it's like to be me, how things seem to me.

SY. I don't know how you can be so confident of that, but in any case, you're right that there is more to consciousness than that. Our discriminative states are not just discriminable; they have the power to provoke preferences in us. Given choices between them, we are not indifferent, but these preferences are themselves subtle, variable, and highly dependent on other conditions. There is a time for chocolate and a time for cheese, a time for blue and a time for yellow. In short (and oversimplifying hugely), many if not all of our discriminative states have what might be called a dimension of affective valence. We care which states we are in, and

this caring is reflected in our dispositions to change state.

PHIL. But surely there is more to it than that! When I contemplate the luscious warmth of the sunlight falling on that old brick wall, it's not just that I prefer looking at the bricks to looking down at the dirty pavement beneath them. I can readily imagine outfitting our imaginary robot with built-in preferences for every possible sequence of its internal states, but it would still not have anything like my conscious *appreciation* of the visual poetry of those craggy, rosy bricks.

SY. Yes, I grant it; there is more. For one thing, you have meta-preferences; perhaps you wish you could stop those sexual associations from interfering with your more exalted appreciation of the warmth of that sunlight on the bricks, but at the same time (roughly) you are delighted by the persistence of those saucy intruders, distracting as they are, but . . . what was it you were trying to think about? Your stream of consciousness is replete with an apparently unending supply of associations. As each fleeting occupant of the position of greatest influence gives way to its successors, any attempt to halt this helter-skelter parade and monitor the details of the associations only generates a further flood of evanescent states, and so on. Coalitions of themes and projects may succeed in dominating 'attention' for some useful and highly productive period of time, fending off would-be digressions for quite a while, and creating the sense of an abiding self or ego taking charge of the whole operation. And so on.

PHIL. But surely there is more to it than that! And now I begin to see what is missing from your deliberately evasive list of additions. All these dispositions and meta-dispositions to enter into states and meta-states and meta-meta-states of reflection about reflection could be engineered (I dimly imagine) into some robot. The trajectory of its internal state switching could, I suppose, look strikingly similar to the 'first-person' account I might give of my own stream of consciousness, but those states of the robot would have no actual *feel*, no *phenomenal* properties at all! You're still leaving out what the philosophers call the *qualia*.

SY. Actually, I'm still leaving out *lots* of properties. I've hardly begun acknowledging all the oversimplifications of my story so far, but now you seem to want to preempt any further additions from me by insisting that there are properties of consciousness that are altogether different from the properties I've described so far. I thought I *was* adding 'phenomenal' properties in response to your challenge, but now you tell me I haven't even begun.. Before I can tell if I'm leaving these properties out, I have to know what they are. Can you give me a clear example of a phenomenal property? For instance, if I used to like a particular shade of yellow, but thanks to some traumatic experience (I got struck by a car of that colour, let's suppose), that shade of yellow now makes me very uneasy (whether or not it reminds me explicitly of the accident), would this suffice to change the *phenomenal* properties of my experience of that shade of yellow?

PHIL. Not necessarily. The *dispositional* property of making you uneasy is not itself a phenomenal property. Phenomenal properties are, by definition, not dispositional but rather intrinsic and accessible only from the first-person point of view . . . .

Thus we arrive in mysteryland. If you *define* qualia as *intrinsic properties* of experiences considered in isolation from all their causes and effects, logically independent of all dispositional properties, then they are logically guaranteed to elude all broad functional analysis—but it is an empty victory, since there is no reason to believe such properties exist. To see this, compare the *qualia* of experience to the *value* of money. Some naive Americans cannot get it out of their heads that dollars, unlike francs and marks and yen, have *intrinsic value* ('How much is that in *real* money?'). They are quite content to 'reduce' the value of other currencies in dispositional terms to their exchange rate with dollars (or goods and services), but they have a hunch that dollars are different. Every dollar, they declare, has something logically independent of its functionalistic exchange powers, which we might call its *vim*. So defined, the *vim* of each dollar is guaranteed to elude the theories of economists forever, but we have no reason to believe in it—aside from the heartfelt hunches of those naive Americans, which can be explained without being honoured.

Some participants in the consciousness debates simply demand, flat out, that their intuitions about phenomenal properties are a non-negotiable starting point for any science of consciousness. Such a conviction must be considered an interesting symptom, deserving a diagnosis, a datum that any science of consciousness must account for, in the same spirit that economists and psychologists might set out to explain why it is that so many people succumb to the potent illusion that money has intrinsic value.

There are many properties of conscious states that can and should be subjected to further scientific investigation right now, and once we get accounts of them in place, we may well find that they satisfy us as an explanation of what consciousness is. After all, this is what has happened in the case of the erstwhile mystery of what *life* is. Vitalism—the insistence that there is some big, mysterious, extra ingredient in all living things—turns out to have been not a deep insight but a failure of imagination. Inspired by that happy success story, we can proceed with our scientific exploration of consciousness If the day arrives when all these acknowledged debts are paid and

we plainly see that something big is missing (it should stick out like a sore thumb at some point, if it is really important), those with the unshakeable hunch will get to say they told us so. In the meantime, they can worry about how to fend off the diagnosis that they, like the vitalists before them, have been misled by an illusion.

IAN GLYNN

So far as we can tell, consciousness is always associated with nervous activity in a complex brain, and it is clear that interference with such activity— by changes in sensory input, or injury, or disease, or drugs, or direct electrical stimulation—can alter conscious states. It therefore seems likely that individual conscious states can exist only in the presence of particular patterns of nervous activity, and that the existence of these patterns is always associated with the corresponding conscious states. It is such patterns that are referred to as *the neural correlates of consciousness*. Why certain patterns of nervous activity should be always associated with certain thoughts or feelings is, of course, among the most difficult of all problems, but determining what these patterns are would seem to be a necessary first step—though only a first step— towards solving it.

It is a first step that is surprisingly difficult to take. Stimulating various sense organs is the usual way to produce a variety of sensations, and we know a good deal about many of the neural events that are links in the causative chains involved. A direct approach would therefore be to follow along the chain of events initiated by some sensation- or perception-causing stimulus, in the hope that at some stage it would lead to a pattern of neural events that not only correlated well with the currrent 'contents of consciousness' but which could be shown to be both necessary and sufficient for causing those particular thoughts or feelings. That is a very tall order indeed, not just because of the difficulty of elucidating the neural machinery likely to be involved, but also because of the need to monitor the contents of consciousness during the investigation.

The most successful attempts, so far, have involved *first* exposing a monkey to a stimulus that is ambiguous and can give rise to two different conscious perceptions, *then* training the monkey to indicate which perception it currently has (and when there is a change), *and finally* looking for neurons in the monkey's brain whose behaviour changes when the perception changes. The point of this procedure is that, because the stimulus remains constant, all the early processing should remain constant, and neurons whose behaviour changes when the perception changes are likely (though not certain) to be part of the machinery specifically involved in conscious perception. Ingenious experiments along these lines have been done by Nikos Logothetis and his colleagues, and by others.

Another approach has been to look for neural activity associated with illusory perceptions.

These approaches are, of course, limited to situations in which the contents of consciousness are determined by something in the current environment acting through sensory pathways. Conscious memories must involve the neural machinery in which the memories are stored, and it seems likely that the conscious remembering of a past perception or event involves the partial re-creation, in appropriate areas of the cerebral cortex, of the patterns of activity caused by the perception or event at the time it was experienced. If that is right, the conscious aspect of a memory could depend on the same (unknown) machinery that allows us to be conscious of current perceptions and events.

If individual mental states and processes are inseparable from particular patterns of neural activity, they can have effects in the physical world, and the evolution of consciousness through natural selection is a plausible and attractive hypothesis. There is, though, a difficulty—first pointed out by William *James in 1879. A strong correlation exists between the pleasantness or unpleasantness of sensations and the survival value (or threat to survival) of the situations that engender them. We like eating, drinking, and making love; we dislike hunger, injury, exhaustion. If we believe in old-fashioned, common-sense, interactive dualism, this correlation is to be expected; our mental states influence our behaviour, so, for our ancestors to have survived, their mental preferences must have tended to favour their survival. But once this belief in interactive dualism is relinquished (as it now generally is), and we assume that it is only through their neural correlates that mental events can influence behaviour, the subjective character of mental processes seems irrelevant. Why, then, is there this association between pleasure and situations promoting survival, and between discomfort and situations threatening survival? Whether study of the neural correlates of consciousness will help to solve this problem remains to be seen.

Crick, F., and Koch, C. (2000). 'Some thoughts on consciousness and neuroscience'. In Gazzaniga, M. S. (ed.), *The New Cognitive Neurosciences*.

Glynn, I. (1999). *An Anatomy of Thought: The Origin and Machinery of the Mind*.

RICHARD L. GREGORY

1. Flagging the present
2. Exceptional cases

1. Flagging the present
One can imagine a bunch of interacting robots getting on fine without any awareness, or *qualia, but surely they would not spend hours looking at pictures or listening to Beethoven. This is just how, only a few decades ago,

behaviourist psychologists described us—as lacking qualia of red or pain, or the sound of violins. Why audiences without music qualia would sit through a symphony was hardly questioned. Psychology has now abandoned the behaviourism of J. B. Watson and B. F. Skinner, who tried to make psychology seem more scientific and less whimsical by denying consciousness, though at the cost of throwing out the baby with the bathwater. The situation is indeed reversed, as physicists, especially Roger Penrose, are now asking how the physical world can have consciousness.

Why should consciousness have evolved if it is useless? Yet, if qualia affect the nervous system, how can chemistry and physiology give adequate explanations of how the brain works, to give learning, perception, and behaviour?

We might hazard a guess at what qualia do. As perception depends on rich knowledge from the past, stored in the brain, there must surely be a problem identifying the present moment from past memories. And also from anticipations running into the future. As human perceptions are very largely stored knowledge, the *present moment* needs to be identified, for our behaviour to be appropriate to what is happening now. It is vitally important to recognize the present as special—as the only time that actions can occur. Crossing the road, it is essential to know that the green light is *now*, not in some remembered or anticipated time.

There is no such problem for primitive reflex actions. The present is signalled purely and simply by the onset of stimuli; but with rich memory and imagination, there must be a problem identifying neural activity of present stimuli, from memory and anticipation of other times. Our present, though signalled by stimuli, seems to be marked or 'flagged' by qualia.

Try this simple experiment. Look at the scene around you. Then close your eyes, and imagine it. What happens? Surely the vividness of the scene is lost. Memory and imagination are dim by comparison with the present. To reverse the experiment: imagine the scene, or a particular object known to be out there, then open the eyes and look at it. The qualia of the present visual world are suddenly startlingly vivid. So, perhaps an important role for qualia is to *flag the present*, so we are not confused with remembered past or anticipated future.

2. Exceptional cases
This is not infallible. At least one person with exceptionally vivid memories has been described who confused memories with present reality. This is the remarkable case of Mr S, described by the Russian neuropsychologist Alexander *Luria. Mr S was a professional memory man, with incredibly vast memory and extremely vivid imagination. But he confused his vivid memories with real-time reality, to the point of danger. He would confuse

imagined with real traffic lights. And, as he said, 'I'd look at a clock and for a long while continue to see the hands fixed just as they were, and not realize time had passed . . . That's why I'm often late.'

Another exception is dreams. In dreams vivid qualia unrelated to present sensory signals may be experienced. But in sleep, in a safe place, the present moment has no special significance, as the muscles are inhibited and behaviour is essentially absent.

When sensory inputs are cut off for a long period, perception may become abnormal as in *isolation experiments. In *schizophrenia, and hallucinogenic drug-induced states, vivid qualia are also experienced with no sensory input. We may assume the normal qualia-flagging-the-present system is malfunctioning with sleep, and in schizophrenia and hallucinogens. Then the hypothesis is 'saved', and perhaps we have learned more about these states.

It is reported that in drug-induced states, time may seem to slow or stop. In *Doors of Perception* (1954), Aldous Huxley describes changes of consciousness experienced with mescaline. He ceased to be interested in action, becoming a passive observer—'the will suffers a profound change for the worse'—though his ability to think is little if at all reduced. So he becomes almost a 'not-self'. Most suggestive: 'Visual impressions are greatly intensified', while 'interest in space is diminished and interest in time falls almost to zero'. Huxley emphasizes that colours are immeasurably enhanced in vividness, ordinary objects appearing self-luminous, with the inner fire of jewels, while time essentially stops—becoming 'an indefinite duration alternatively a perpetual present'. With mescaline and other hallucinogenic drugs sensations become enhanced, as super qualia, and the present is emphasized with correspondingly little flow of time.

Although memories usually lack visual or other qualia, sensations are surprisingly vivid in remembered *emotions*, as when an embarrassing situation is recalled years later. With the Danish physician Carl Lange, William James suggested that emotions have a basis in autonomic changes of the body. The *James–Lange theory of the emotions is that the body responds, for example to danger, by unconsciously preparing for action, and these autonomic physiological changes are then sensed as emotions of fear or rage or whatever.

For the emotion of shame, there is autonomic change with visible blushing. Darwin suggested that *blushing is a social signal warning others that this person is not to be trusted. We may blush at the memory of a shame-making deed, experiencing qualia of shame years after the event—presumably when afferent inputs from autonomic bodily changes are evoked by memories. These autonomic changes are in the *present*, so this is not really an exceptional case.

This idea of flagging the present by qualia has implications for consciousness in other animals. As perception evolved, to become more intelligent, it drew away from direct control by stimuli. But as intelligence cannot be tied to the sensed present they can be dangerous. Imagination and intelligence push the mind away from present reality, but nudges of qualia seem to bring us to our senses, to handle the present situation in real time.

Luria, A. (1969). *The Mind of a Mnemonist: A Little Book about a Vast Memory.*

Huxley, A. (1968). *The Complete Works of Aldous Huxley.*

James, W. (1890). *Principles of Psychology.*

Darwin, C. R. (1872). *Expression of the Emotions in Man and Animals.*

Nicholas Humphrey

Fashions change. The problem of consciousness, once banned from serious consideration by psychologists, is again high on the agenda. Yet typically researchers are looking under the lamp that currently shines brightest rather than in the area where the phenomenon went missing. They are identifying consciousness with high-level *thought processes* and seeking to explain it in 'thinking machine' terms, but they are largely ignoring *bodily feeling*.

Yet if we listen to the kinds of questions ordinary people ask—'Are babies conscious?', 'Will I be conscious during the operation?', and so on—it is clear that, again and again, the central issue is not thinking but feeling. People's concern is not with the stream of thoughts that may or may not be running through their heads but with the sense they have of being alive at all—which is to say, alive and *living in the presence of sensation*. The problem, then, is to explain just what these sensations—conscious sensations—are. We want a theory of why it feels to us as it does to taste salt on our tongues, to look at the blue sky with our eyes, to burn our fingers on the stove. But—and here is what is going to make this problem *hard*—the theory must not beg the question by assuming any prior acquaintance with what is being explained: namely, sensory consciousness as such.

Let's stipulate, then, that the theory has to be comprehensible to a scientist from Mars—an individual in many ways not unlike ourselves, highly intelligent, perceptive, and even capable of self-reflection, but who none the less has never evolved into the kind of being who has sensations. Suppose we could explain to this Martian what happens in the brain of a human being who is engaged, say, in smelling a rose. And suppose he could thereby arrive at the entirely novel (to him) conclusion that it must *be like something to be this human being*, and indeed *like this*: 'I am feeling this thick, sweet, olfactory sensation in my nostrils.' It's a tall order, but, still, it is what the theory ought to do.

Is a theory, which could bring this off, a possibility even in principle? Since the theory must employ only such concepts as the Martian can make sense of at the outset, we need to consider what kind of pre-theoretical notions he brings with him. Given that as yet he knows nothing about sensations, will he have other essential concepts on which to build?

We want him to understand that the human being is the *subject of sensations*. Can we assume he will at least have, to start with, the idea of what it is to be a 'subject'? I'd say we can. For presumably the Martian is already himself a subject in the following crucial sense: an autonomous agent *who acts in the world*. Provided he can take himself as a model, he ought already to have the basic concept of an 'I'. Then, can we assume he also understands the idea of being the 'subject of' something? Again, we can. For, as an 'I' who does things with his body, he himself already has this genitive relationship to his own actions: he is the *author of everything he does*. So, will he even have the idea of being the subject of something with some of the peculiar properties of sensations: especially, that (i) they belong to the subject, (ii) they implicate part of his body, (iii) they are present tense, (iv) they have a qualitative modality, (v) their properties are phenomenally immediate? In fact he will: for analysis shows that *bodily actions already have precisely these characteristics (i)–(v)*.

Now, this may not seem much as a basis for understanding sensory consciousness. But I believe that, with the right theory, it will be enough. Suppose we suggest the following theory to the Martian (it is my theory, but others like it might also do the trick).

When a person smells a rose, he responds to what's happening at his nostrils with a 'virtual action pattern': one of a set of action patterns that originated far back in evolutionary history as evaluative responses to various kinds of stimulation at the body surface—wriggles of acceptance or rejection. In modern human beings these responses are still directed to the site of stimulation, and still retain vestiges of their original function and hedonic tone; but today, instead of carrying through into overt behaviour, they have become closed off within internal circuits in the brain; in fact the efferent signals now project only as far as the sensory cortex, where they interact with the incoming signals from the sense organs to create, momentarily, a self-entangling, recursive, loop. The theory is that the person's *sensation*, the way he represents what's happening to him and how he feels about it, *comes through monitoring his own signals for the action pattern*—as extended, by this recursion, into the 'thick moment' of the conscious present.

Then, how will the Martian understand this? Presumably nothing in his own direct experience corresponds to what we have just described to him. But, still, he should be able to work it out. He will be able to grasp the key fact that sensation consists in monitoring commands for action in response to stimulation. He will be able to appreciate the peculiar features of the action pattern that has in fact evolved. And so he will be able to work out that, *if* a subject like himself *were* to get involved in doing what the human being is doing, the result would be that he would have just *these beliefs about it, these attitudes, these things to say, these that he cannot say*, and so on—in short he would experience it *like this*.

But if the Martian can work all this out from the theory, would this mean he actually acquires first-hand experience of sensations in the process? No: no more than someone who works out from physics and chemistry that H_2O makes water gets wet. A theory of consciousness is not a way of conferring consciousness; it is a way of understanding why consciousness-generating brain states have the effects on people's minds they do. The Martian himself may indeed have no sense organ with which to smell the rose at all: and yet, if the theory is right, he will still be able to discover *all* that we ourselves can discover by direct acquaintance. (One day, of course, when *we* get to study Martians, the boot may be on the other foot.)

Humphrey, N. (1992). *A History of the Mind*.

David Papineau

To many it seems obvious that the conscious mind must be distinct from the physical brain. How could mere neural activity possibly constitute the vibrant subjective world of colour experience, pain, and emotion?

However, this dualist intuition should be resisted. The cost of dualism is epiphenomenalism—that is, the doctrine that conscious experiences are mere side effects of brain activity, and do not themselves affect our physical behaviour. This follows because modern physiological science has shown convincingly that all limb movements, muscle contractions, and so on are caused solely by neural and other purely physical antecedents. This leaves no room for a distinct realm of conscious experience to make a difference to what we do.

If we are to avoid this absurd epiphenomenalist conclusion, we therefore have no option but to deny dualism, and identify conscious experiences with the neural causes of behaviour.

But, again, how *could* mere neural activity constitute conscious experience? A first step towards an answer is to admit that, even if the conscious mind is identical to the physical brain, we humans have two quite different ways of thinking about this single realm: we can conceive of it *as physical*, or we can conceive of it *in terms of how it feels*. (Suppose the dentist's drill were to slip on your next visit. You can think of the result in terms of nociceptive-specific neuronal activity. Or you can think of it in terms of how it would feel to you.)

Following David Chalmers (1996), I shall say that the latter mode of thought deploys a 'phenomenal concept', and I shall take the exercise of such phenomenal concepts to involve powers of imagination and introspection. However, as a physicalist, and unlike Chalmers, I take phenomenal concepts to refer to just the selfsame neural items as we refer to using physical concepts of the mind–brain. (When you think of *what the tooth pain would feel like* you refer to just the same thing in reality as when you think of *nociceptive-specific neuronal activity*—just as when you think of *Judy Garland* you refer to just the same person in reality as when you think of *Frances Gumm*.)

Not all physicalists recognize distinct phenomenal concepts. But physicalists are far better off with them than without them. For one thing, phenomenal concepts allow physicalists to explain why mere knowledge of brains as such will never tell you *what some experience feels like*: the point is that 'knowing what it's like' requires phenomenal concepts, and you cannot get these from brain science; rather, you typically need to have had the experience yourself, to develop the requisite powers of imagination and introspection.

In addition, the special structure of phenomenal concepts can help explain why mind–brain identity seems so persistently counter-intuitive (unlike the identity of Judy Garland and Frances Gumm). When we think about conscious items phenomenally, we typically imagine or introspect those same items. Not so when we think about them as physical. So it can strike us that the physical concepts 'leave out' the experiences themselves. And in a sense they do: they do not *activate* those experiences in the way phenomenal concepts do. But it is a fallacy—which elsewhere (2002) I dub 'the antipathetic fallacy'—to conclude that physical concepts do not *refer* to the experiences themselves. After all, most concepts do not activate the things they refer to.

As a physicalist, I hold that phenomenal concepts refer to physical items. But since phenomenal concepts are distinct from physical concepts, it need not be immediately clear which specific physical items they refer to. It is a task for science to identify the physical referents of phenomenal concepts. This is how a physicalist will think of Chalmers's 'hard problem'. The scientific problem of consciousness isn't just the (relatively) easy matter of understanding the brain in physical terms. We also want to know which brain processes are referred to by such phenomenal concepts as *pain*, or *seeing something red*, or indeed *feeling like anything*.

However, once we get this 'hard problem' into proper focus, there is reason to doubt that it will admit of very definite answers. We may be able to identify brain processes that are present in humans whenever they are phenomenally aware of themselves as in *pain*, or *seeing something red*, or *feeling like anything*. But nothing will tell us which specific features of these brain processes are referred to by these phenomenal concepts, nor correspondingly whether non-human creatures, who will share some

of these features but not others, will fall under these concepts.

This doesn't mean that there is some mystery about consciousness that lies beyond science. The trouble is simply that all phenomenal concepts are vague. They offer crude, ancestral ways of thinking about conscious states, and because of this go fuzzy when stretched beyond their normal application to humans.

Chalmers, D. (1996). *The Conscious Mind*.
Papineau, D. (2000). *Introducing Consciousness*.
——(2002). *Thinking about Consciousness*.

ROGER PENROSE

Most scientific discussions concerning the nature of consciousness attempt to find an explanation for this phenomenon in terms of the physical picture of the world that is known today. Particularly popular is *computational functionalism* (or *strong AI*), which asserts that it is entirely the *computational* action of the pattern of neuron firings and synaptic responses that is responsible for our awareness, our feelings of free will, and other aspects of consciousness. Some neurophysiologists argue that the computational model is inadequate and that the detailed *neurochemistry* of the brain must play an essential role in determining consciousness. Still others would claim that the physics of quantum theory is a key ingredient, and that free will is dependent on *quantum indeterminism*.

None of these standpoints demands that we move beyond our present physical world-view, and most of them do not even regard quantum phenomena as having any significant role to play. Yet, quantum theory *is* part of our current world-view and is, by now, extremely well established. No confirmed experiment that has been performed to date contradicts the expectations of quantum theory, and many such experiments clearly demonstrate the physical *need* for this theory. Yet it seems that most neurophysiologists are sceptical that quantum phenomena could have any particular role in brain action beyond determining such things as the rules of chemistry, the physical nature of action potentials, etc.

All this notwithstanding, I believe that there are strong reasons to expect: (*a*) irrespective of any considerations of the nature of consciousness, even existing quantum theory provides an inadequate world-view for physics and will have to be replaced by an ontologically more satisfactory and (ultimately) observationally distinct physical theory; and (*b*) the phenomenon of consciousness must be physically dependent upon the distinctive features of such a yet-to-be-discovered physical theory. What are the reasons for my expectations (*a*) and (*b*)? The reasons behind (*a*) come entirely from within physics itself, as do specific suggestions for moving beyond present-day quantum theory, and they do not call upon any belief in the inadequacy of present-day physics to accommodate the phenomenon of consciousness (cf. Penrose 1994). The reasons behind (*b*) are, on the other hand, largely indirect. They depend upon certain arguments against the computational model of consciousness, coupled with the fact that present-day physics provides us with an essentially computational picture of physical action (cf. Penrose 1994).

This is not the place to expound at length upon (*a*), but the basis of my argument has to do with the *superposition principle* of quantum mechanics, which demands that quantum objects can be put into a state of superposition of two separate locations at the same time. Such superpositions are observed to occur for individual particles such as photons or neutrons, or even complicated molecules such as carbon-60 fullerenes, but they lead to absurdities for genuinely macroscopic objects, such as Schrödinger's (hypothetical) cat, forced into a superposition of death and life. Although there is no consensus as to how to resolve this apparent contradiction—known, generally, as the *measurement paradox*—one school of thought maintains that no adequate resolution is possible without a change in the very structure of quantum mechanics. Within this school, there is a sizeable faction which contends that *gravitational* effects are responsible. According to the most clear-cut scheme along these lines (referred to as gravitational objective reduction or OR), a macroscopic quantum superposition of two distinct stationary states would decay into one or other of these constituent states in a time scale which can be computed knowing the two mass distributions involved (and which would be almost instantaneous for a cat). There are difficult but technically feasible experiments which could settle the correctness of this contention. These are presently in the development stage.

The main arguments behind (*b*) come from the nature of human understanding, particularly mathematical understanding. Understanding is a quality that requires consciousness, and there are reasons, coming from the famous theorem of mathematical logic, known as Gödel's incompleteness theorem, to believe that mathematical understanding cannot be reduced to any purely computational activity. This theorem can be paraphrased as follows: given any (sufficiently broad) computational system *R* of rules of proof which we believe to be *sound* (i.e. to be such that the rigorous following of the rules *R* yields only truths and no falsehoods), then one can construct a clear-cut mathematical statement G(*R*) whose truth can be seen to be a consequence of the soundness of *R*, yet which cannot be deduced by actually *following* the rules of *R*. Thus our belief in G(*R*) cannot be a consequence of our actual use of *R*, but follows from our acceptance of *R* as a valid proof procedure. From this (and some further detailed considerations) it is argued that our access to mathematical truth transcends any purely computational

proof procedure. Accordingly, understanding in general is not simply a matter of computation.

Various suggested counter-arguments have been put forward to circumvent this conclusion; most particularly, human reasoning is subject to error, and there is the possibility that we need not be aware of any particular '*R*' that underlies our thinking. Both these counter-arguments (and numerous others) have been addressed in detail in the literature (see Penrose 1994).

One puzzling feature of conscious perception is what is referred to as the *binding problem*. In the conscious perception of an image, the various ingredients (such as colour, shape, and motion, in a *visual* image) may each be processed in widely separated parts of the brain; yet the image is perceived in its entirety without there being significant direct neural connections between these separate processing regions. In models of perception that depend upon gravitational OR, such non-locality is to be expected, this being a feature of the quantum measurement process. There are characteristically 'quantum' features of this non-locality ('violations of Bell inequalities' cf. Bell 1964, Penrose 1994: 237–49, 287–304) and it may be that these will show up in careful experiments on human perception (A. Duggins, personal communication 1999).

For gravitational OR to have a chance of direct relevance in brain activity, it is necessary for there to be structures in the brain that can support large-scale quantum coherence—without degradation of the quantum state via environmental decoherence—and which can influence synaptic function significantly. This presents severe difficulties, and it is clear that ordinary nerve signalling would not achieve this. The most promising suggestion is that neuronal (A-lattice) microtubules are responsible, and a fairly detailed model, referred to as 'orchestrated objective reduction' (Orch-OR) has been worked out by S. Hameroff and collaborators (Hameroff and Penrose 1996, Hameroff et al. 2002).

Bell, J. S. (1964). 'On the Einstein Podolsky Rosen paradox'. *Physics*, 1. Reprinted in Wheeler, J. A., and Zurek, W. H. (eds.), *Quantum Theory and Measurement*.

Hameroff, S., and Penrose, R. (1996). 'Orchestrated reduction of quantum coherence in brain microtubules: a model for consciousness?' In Hameroff, S. R., Kaszniak, A.W., and Scott, A.C. (eds.), *Toward a Science of Consciousness: The First Tucson Discussions and Debates*.

—— Nip, A., Porter, M., and Tuszynski, J. (2002). 'Conduction pathways in microtubules, biological quantum computation, and consciousness'. *BioSystems*, 64.

Penrose, R. (1994). *Shadows of the Mind: An Approach to the Missing Science of Consciousness*.

Brian Pippard

Nineteenth-century scientists, in their work as in their daily lives, took for granted the reality of the world around them and sought to account for it at every level by the

Newtonian mechanics which, on the human scale, appeared both reasonable and flawless. The forces of gravitation and electromagnetism demanded a medium, the aether—intangible but still Newtonian—by which they could operate across apparently empty space. Failure to invent a plausible model, the advent of Einstein's relativity, and finally quantum mechanics demolished this ideal programme. Action-at-a-distance was restored to the status of an unexplained mathematical rule, as Newton had been forced to leave it, and a succession of new fundamental particles had to be accepted even if their behaviour defied visualization. No longer could we conceive of a definite path connecting one event with the next; indeterminacy was an inevitable consequence of Schrödinger's equation, which gave the right answer to a vast range of problems. Despite many ingenious attempts, which are still being made, no consistent substitute has been found for the early Copenhagen doctrine that limits the scientist's business to the precise description and correlation of observations shared by competent investigators. Ultimate reality, whatever it may be, is a matter for metaphysicians, not scientists.

Within this constraint enormous progress has been made, but the rules of the game, however foreign to everyday intuition, have to be applied with mathematical rigour, even if it means sacrificing ancient beliefs. Thus emergence of life from inert matter can now be accepted as a manifestation of chemical versatility, and replication of the DNA molecule demands no intervention of a vital force. There is indeed a long and barely mapped road to be travelled before we shall appreciate how DNA leads to an undeniably living organism, but no one expects to find a need for new basic laws.

With man, and perhaps before him, what we suppose to be unthinking forms of life evolved to possess the power of thought. Is this also to be seen as a consequence of scientific laws? To be sure, when someone speaks, what he says and the measurable events (chemical, electrical, mechanical) accompanying his statements are public material for use in science; but the relationship between what he says and what he thinks is not, for his thought is private and unshared. My response to Mozart or to the pain in my leg is *my* pleasure or *my* pain; no one else can truly say he feels exactly like that—only, at best, that he would use the same words to describe what he felt. In any case, who can fully express in words his own thoughts and feelings?

Let us suppose we were asked to investigate a black box and analyse its responses. Even if we decided that in every way they matched the responses of a thinking creature, we should still not be justified, as scientists, in concluding 'it thinks', in the sense 'it is conscious of itself'. We might find it convenient to introduce into our calculations symbols representing consciousness, and display them in our answer, but this would be no more meaningful than our forebears' talk of aether, or our own of wave functions and fields. So long as we limit ourselves to observations we cannot go beyond 'as if it thinks'.

The two words 'as if' signal an important change in science since the 19th century. Had the basic laws proved to be intuitively comprehensible, as was once hoped, we might dare to believe that eventually our understanding of the external world—a reality existing independently of observation—might be extended to the point of embracing conscious thought. But now that our only reality is what we ourselves experience, we have no more fundamental terms in which to describe the central experience of conscious thought; we must accept that our science is powerless to make us understand that very faculty without which there would be no science.

STEVEN ROSE

A few years ago I was at a conference at which a bright young Harvard neurophysiologist referred to the study of consciousness as a 'CLM'—a career-limiting move. Today however I fear that the way most neuroscientists approach the matter is itself a CLM—a consciousness-limiting move. The term consciousness has multiple rich meanings. Social and political sciences deal with such concepts as class, race, and gender consciousness. Philosophers may ponder the etymological relationship between consciousness and conscience. Psychoanalysts will contrast consciousness and 'the unconscious', by which they definitely do not mean what an anaesthetist or neurologist might imply. All these rich, social, historical, and personal developmental meanings are lost in the discourse of most neuroscientists. For them, being conscious is merely the antithesis of being asleep or unconscious in the anaesthetist's sense. Thus consciousness reduces to mere 'awareness' and the discussion then focuses on how the multitude of sense data impinging on our brains at any moment becomes ordered and refined into that most relevant for our immediate needs. Francis Crick in his book *The Astonishing Hypothesis* puts this most clearly, following with a further reductionist move: on the basis that more is known about the neurobiology of the visual system than that of any other sensory process, he proposes to exploit the neural mechanisms of perception as a model system, tractable to experiment (and ends the book with an aside locating free will in the anterior cingulate!).

The problem with such ploys is that they empty consciousness out of most of what the computational neuroscientists would doubtless dismiss as its 'folk meanings'. Yet these folk meanings are precisely the important ones if we are concerned with the relevance of neuroscience to an understanding of the human condition. We are not helped either by those philosophers of mind who worry over *qualia, and how the objective becomes subjective.

I have no problem with a two-aspect theory, an ontological unity but epistemological diversity in which brain language and mind language are no more primary and secondary than are English and Italian in referring to the brown furry creature sitting on my desk as I write as 'cat' and 'gatto's. The suggestion that this is the 'hard problem' in Chalmers's sense is simply a category confusion. This does not make me a New Mysterian in the McGinn sense either. It is simply to insist that we be clearer about the nature of the phenomenon or process that we regard as ontologically unitary.

By which I mean that I would argue that (*a*) consciousness is not a thing but a process, and that (*b*) as a process it is essentially social, being constituted in the relationship between a person and his or her social and physical milieu.

This relationship is itself of course shaped by evolution, development, and history. Consciousness then is not simply 'in the brain'. At the very least it is embedded within the brain/body system, being as we know profoundly affected by, for instance, hormonal and immunological status. But far more than that, consciousness is expressible only as a relationship and is thus not physically located within an individual, and certainly not in a specific brain region. The more modest task of neuroscience then becomes not to explain, or worse, explain away, consciousness, nor to translate brain processes into qualia, but rather to look at those aspects of a person's evolved and developed neurobiology which enable them to have conscious experiences in all the multiple rich meanings of the term.

Interpreted as holistic high-level dynamic properties, the mental phenomena are conceived to control their component biophysical, molecular, atomic, and other sub-elements in the same way that the organism as a whole controls the course and fate of its separate organs and cells, or just as the molecule as an entity carries all its component atoms, electrons, and other subatomic and subnuclear parts through a distinctive time–space course in a chemical reaction. As is the rule for part–whole relations, a mutual interaction between the neural and mental events is recognized: the brain physiology determines the mental effects, as generally agreed, but also the neurophysiology, at the same time, is reciprocally governed by the higher subjective properties of the enveloping mental events. These interact at their own level and correspondingly move their subsidiary constituents in brain processing. Although determined in part by the properties of their neural components, the subjective properties are also determined by the spacing and timing of the components. Thus the critical, multinested space–time pattern properties of the neuronal infrastructure, as well as the mass–energy elements, must also be included in the causal account.

The resultant mind–brain model, in which mind acts on brain and brain acts on mind, is classified as being 'interactionist' in contrast to mind–brain 'parallelism' or mind–brain 'identity'. The term 'interaction', however, is not the best for the kind of relationship envisaged, in which mental phenomena are described as primarily *super*vening rather than *inter*vening, in the physiological process. Mind is conceived to move matter in the brain and to govern, rule, and direct neural and chemical events without interacting with the components at the component level, just as an organism may move and govern the time–space course of its atoms and tissues without interacting with them.

In the revised mind–brain model consciousness becomes an integral working component in brain function, an autonomous phenomenon in its own right, not reducible to electrochemical mechanisms. Exerting top-level causal influence in the direction and control of behaviour, the conscious mind is no longer something that can be ignored in objective neuroscience wherever an explanation of conscious activity is concerned. Subjective experience is given a use and reason for being as having a central, ineliminable causal role in brain function. A rationale is thus provided for the evolution of mind in a physical world.

The new mentalist view of consciousness as causal stands in direct opposition to the founding precepts of the behaviourist–materialist philosophy. The two explanatory frameworks are diametrically opposed and mutually exclusive. During the 1970s in the so-called 'consciousness' or 'mentalist' revolution (referred to also as the 'cognitive', 'humanist', or 'third' revolution), the new mentalist interpretation gained acceptance over behaviourism as the dominant paradigm of psychology. The shift from behaviourism to mentalism, or cognitivism, represents a shift to a fundamentally different form of causal determinism. The traditional micro-determinism of the materialist–behaviourist era, emphasizing causal control from below upward, gave way to a paradigm in which primacy is given to emergent top-down control, exerted by the higher, more evolved forces in nature over the less evolved. In the brain this means a downward control of the mental over the neuronal. However, the principle of emergent downward control (referred to also as 'emergent interaction' or 'emergent determinism') applies to all hierarchic systems in all science.

The new mentalism, combining tenets from previously conflicting views, tends to reconcile polar opposites of the past such as mind and matter, the physical and metaphysical, determinism and free choice, as well as 'is' and 'ought' and fact and value, in a unifying view of mind, brain, and man in nature. The new position appears metaphysical in its recognition of mental events as realities existing in their own form different from neural events, in endowing subjective phenomena with causal influence, and in placing mind in a control role above matter in the brain. At the same time, the interpretation appears to be materialistic in defining mental phenomena as being built of physical elements and being inseparable from the neural substrate. Because it is neither traditionally dualistic nor physicalistic, the new mentalist paradigm is taken to represent a distinct third philosophical position. It is emergentist, functionalist, interactionist, and monistic.

In the new mentalist terms, science no longer postulates that all operations of the brain and behaviour are determined mechanistically or physiochemically as in traditional materialist philosophy. Although the neuro-electrochemical mechanisms sustain and help determine any given course of action, the choice of action is determined largely at higher levels by conscious mental events. Willed choice involves the causal influence of subjective value priorities wherein one's personal wishes, feelings, and other *mental* factors override the subsidiary forces of the neural substructure. In other words we do what we *subjectively wish* to do. Free-will decisions are still caused or determined in the new scheme but acquire degrees of freedom and of self-control far above those of classic mechanistic determinism.

The shift of the 1970s in the scientific status and treatment of conscious experience carries far-ranging philosophical and humanistic, as well as scientific, implications. The mind has been restored to the brain of experimental science. The qualitative, colourful, and value-rich world of inner experience, long excluded from the domain of science by behaviourist–materialist doctrine, has been reinstated. The subjective is no longer outside the mainstream of objective science, nor something that will eventually be reducible in principle to neurophysiology. A logical determinist framework is provided for those disciplines that deal directly with subjective experience such as cognitive, clinical, and humanistic psychology. Scientific theory has become squared finally with the impressions of common experience: we do in fact use the mind to initiate and control our physical actions.

See also CONSCIOUSNESS; MIND AND BODY; MIND–BODY PROBLEM: PHILOSOPHICAL THEORIES.   RWS

Armstrong, D. M. (1968). *A Materialist Theory of the Mind.*
Sperry, R. W. (1966). 'Mind, brain and humanist values'. *Bulletin of Atomic Science*, 22.
—— (1976). 'Changing concepts of consciousness and free will'. *Perspectives in Biology and Medicine*, 20.
—— (1983). *Science and Moral Priority.*

consciousness, communication, civilization. Trying to understand the physical relation between the brain and the mind has led many to believe that subjective conscious processes do not really control our behaviour, but are a minor manifestation of neural activity having little importance. For instance T. H. Huxley suggested that each of us is a 'conscious automaton' whose subjective awareness is like the sound of the steam whistle on a locomotive and not like the force of its pistons driving behaviour onwards.

I think this conclusion results from asking an *unproductive question* about an *incomplete system*, and it is not a conclusion one is forced to draw from the belief that neural mechanisms obey normal physical laws.

1. The unproductive question
2. The incomplete system
3. Neural activity can be translated into a shared format
4. Conscious awareness may occur with, and only with, such translation
5. The role of consciously generated reports
6. Take-home messages

1. The unproductive question
When puzzled by something, we tend to ask 'What *is* it?', but it would almost always be more productive to ask 'What *does* it do?' This is the case with conscious awareness, whose nature causes more puzzlement to a modern scientific mind than almost any other question. If one asks 'What can be *done* with conscious experience that cannot be done without it?' one is led to the view that it is indeed concerned with communication, like the sound of the whistle, but that the whole process has a crucial importance, far beyond that implied by Huxley's analogy. You will, however, fail to recognize this aspect of the problem unless you consider all of the relevant system, not just part of it.

2. The incomplete system
We have known for some time that conscious experience is likely to arise in the brain, so it is natural to assume that this is where we shall find the answers to our questions about its nature. But animals, and particularly humans, do not function in isolation, and, if conscious experience is concerned with the relations between a community of animals, confining one's attention to a single brain will prevent one getting the full picture about what consciousness *does*.

3. Neural activity can be translated into a shared format
Since most animals are social, parts of their brains are likely to be devoted to social communications. These can be quite simple and their mechanisms not difficult to understand, as with the alarm signals or mating calls of

birds; even a computer issues some messages that might be considered social, as when it tells you the printer is out of paper, and we can readily understand exactly how that is done.

Now for us social behaviour is very much more important and complicated. The overall evolutionary fitness of a person must depend greatly upon how he or she has managed social relations, for the community has a very large measure of control over the benefits an individual and its offspring receive. These relations are to a large extent managed by the verbal reports we make to other members of our community about the neural activity in certain regions of our brains, and by the similar messages we receive from others. We are consciously aware not only of making, but also of receiving, such reports and of their contents.

4. Conscious awareness may occur with, and only with, such translation

Perhaps conscious awareness occurs when, and only when, regions of the brain capable of dealing with such verbal reports are primed for activity. I shall not justify this in detail, but can anyone suggest any other action that is normally accompanied by conscious experience, and which would not be the same type of action if not so accompanied? An unconscious being could not make reports of this type, and they would not be accepted if they were thought to have been issued in a zombie-like fashion. Perhaps an analogy may clarify.

It is as if we suddenly had a gift-wrapped box of chocolates in our hands, either generated by our own brain, or received from another; the gift-wrapped box corresponds to the conscious awareness, while the contents are verbal translations of neural activity occurring in some region of the originator's brain. We can give a self-generated box to others if we wish, or open a box we have received. If we do so, the contents carry sufficient information to the recipient brain for it to reconstruct to some degree the neural activity in the originator's brain, and the recipient can then discover the implications that activity had about whatever originally caused it.

At first sight this may seem a simple suggestion that assigns a role to conscious experience not too far from the common-sense view. But it brings out the formidable neural computations required by the relevant parts of the brain, and it also clarifies the link between consciousness and language. Suppose you open the front door and are confronted by a lion, so you make one of the suggested reports by shouting up the stairs 'Hey, there's a big furry animal on the front lawn swishing its tail and roaring'. To do this requires effective recognition of objects and actions, together with the ability to express the results in a natural language. This is a horrendously difficult task, obviously very, very much more than

hearing a steam whistle, and although computers are not yet good at doing it, they are good enough to assure us that the job can be done using only well-behaved physical mechanisms.

5. The role of consciously generated reports

Now reports such as that on the lion play a very much more important part in our lives than a simple warning like a bird's alarm call. Of course it does warn the person upstairs of danger, but then this person may shout back 'Sounds like a lion—shut the door at once', so the first report not only had potential survival value for the person upstairs, but the reply brings added information back to the initiator that promotes his survival too. This apparently simple faculty has extraordinary consequences: by translating the visual information received on opening the front door into the common format of a natural language it can create in the recipient's brain a representation in which the new visual information can be combined with stored knowledge about the danger of large furry animals. Furthermore the same faculty in the recipient can then transfer this combined knowledge back to the originator. By translating neural activity into verbal format consciousness has assisted in creating a forum for meaningful communal communication.

One important message from research on sensation and perception over the last half-century is that the quality of decisions depends upon the amount of relevant information that is available for making them: the faculty of generating and receiving reports in a format that is understood by other members of one's community enormously increases the amount of information available for decision making, and if this is what conscious awareness brings to humanity it undoubtedly has the potential for greatly improving individual evolutionary survival. It should be added that it provides access not only to knowledge stored in other brains, but also to knowledge that has passed through other brains but is now stored in books, libraries, and the internet. Civilizations depend upon communal and stored knowledge, and mankind differs from the rest of the animal kingdom in the complexity of the cultures and civilizations it has created. Consciousness has brought the faculty of representing knowledge in a format that is shared among large communities, and it is tempting to suppose that its development was the main factor that led to the extraordinarily rapid evolution of our species.

6. Take-home messages

I started by saying that the physical understanding of the mind had been impeded by asking the *wrong question* about the *wrong system*. I think the *right question* is 'What can we *do* with conscious experience that we could not do without it?' and the important answer is 'It helps us to make reports on our sensory and other subjective experiences in a common language, and to receive and understand such reports from others'. The *right system* is really the whole species that exhibits consciousness, together with its evolutionary history, but considering a community of brains rather than a single isolated brain is a large step in the right direction: only then does the selective advantage of using a common format become evident. Although the survival value of consciousness cannot be understood by considering an isolated brain, these ideas obviously point to the language centres and the parts that feed them as the regions of greatest interest for the neuroscientific analysis of the mechanisms of consciousness.

Several other conclusions have also been reached from this approach:

- Conscious experience is Nature's way of telling us that we have a potential communication to make—it is like the wrapping on a gift.
- Since these gifts can change a recipient's beliefs, and beliefs can modify actions, we need not doubt that conscious experience can be causally effective and has evolutionary survival value.
- Mechanisms associated with consciousness translate neural activity into the common format of a natural language, making possible communal decisions based on far greater knowledge. The improved quality of these decisions can explain why mankind now dominates the earth.   HBB

consciousness, the neural correlates of. Consciousness is a puzzling state-dependent property of certain types of complex, adaptive systems. The best example is a healthy and attentive human brain. If the brain is anaesthetized, consciousness ceases. Small lesions in the midbrain and thalamus of patients can lead to a complete loss of consciousness, while destruction of circumscribed parts of the cerebral cortex of patients can eliminate very specific aspects of consciousness, such as the ability to be aware of motion or to recognize objects as faces, without a concomitant loss of vision in general. Given the similarity in brain structure and behaviour, biologists commonly assume that at least some animals, in particular non-human primates, share certain aspects of consciousness with humans.

The most mysterious aspect of consciousness concerns '*qualia'—the redness of red, or the painfulness of pain. Rather than trying to tackle it directly, it seems more sensible to discover the neural correlates of consciousness (the NCC), that is the minimal brain mechanisms causing any one specific conscious percept, memory, or action, as a preliminary to finding causal explanations, with the hope that when we understand how the brain produces consciousness the problem of qualia may be easier to solve.

Much of the activity of our brain seems to be unconscious. It seems probable that for neural activity to become fully conscious it must both persist for some length of time and interact with a substantial amount of the front of the cerebral cortex, a region that is involved in thinking, planning, and making wilful decisions.

To produce such a big effect a large coalition of active neurons must form. The members of this coalition must each express its own characteristic trigger feature, while at the same time giving support to the other coalition members. It is this widespread, sustained, highly specific activity that corresponds to what we are visually aware of.

In viewing the normal cluttered visual environment the brain must rapidly attend to some salient visual object and segment it from the general background—not an easy task. The visual information coming into the eyes is usually ambiguous, and could be interpreted in more than one way, depending somewhat on our previous experiences. So the winning coalition of active neurons, which represents that object, must compete with other coalitions representing both alternative interpretations and other, unattended parts of the visual scene. The firing of the neurons outside the dominant coalition may represent the unattended parts of the visual field by firing together more locally and more transiently, thus producing a very fleeting form of visual awareness.

The great amount of local mutual excitation between excitatory cortical neurons, and the activity of the many types of inhibitory neurons (which prevent the system going into uncontrolled oscillations, as it does in epilepsy), are all involved in this competition between rival coalitions. Each neuron in the coalition supports its 'friends' (those that support it) and attempts to suppress its 'enemies' (those that would inhibit it). Attention can be thought of as a neural mechanism which biases this competition. One cannot attend to two separate objects simultaneously if they produce strongly overlapping activation in the same local neural network.

The biggest, most powerful coalition will win, and then maintain itself for some time (at least for a few hundred milliseconds) while the unsuccessful neuronal activity, though not negligible, will be fragmented and repressed, at least for the time being.

One has the impression that the activity of the coalition may have to reach a threshold of some sort before it can sustain itself for a reasonable time, possibly with help from feedback loops of one sort or another. It is also possible that the system shows some hysteresis. That is, it will persist even if its support has diminished somewhat.

The activity in the coalition is bound to influence many neurons outside the coalition, but not sufficiently to co-opt them as members. The trigger features of these related neurons would represent the past associations of elements of the coalition, or possible future motor actions. It is these associations that express the meaning of the activity of the coalition members.

Not all our actions are performed consciously. Philosophers have invented a creature they call a zombie who behaves in every way like a normal person but is completely unconscious. There is now highly suggestive evidence that much of our behaviour has this zombie character, as advocated by Milner and Goodale in their book *The Visual Brain in Action* (1995). In brief, there appear to be systems that can respond very rapidly, but in a stereotyped way, to relevant visual inputs, for example in reaching for an object, or grasping it, or moving one's eyes. It is only later that one becomes conscious of such acts. There is much anecdotal evidence that this happens in sports. Additional evidence comes from visual psychology, from sleepwalkers, and also from certain patients with complex partial seizures. Such patients make a series of stereotypical actions, often in a way that repeats from one seizure to the next, but they do not respond to speech or undertake less stereotyped actions. In some cases they have no recollection at all, after they recover, of what happened during their seizure.

Why is our brain not just a whole series of unconscious zombie systems? The answer is that there would have to be a vast number of them to replicate human behaviour unconsciously. It looks as if the function of consciousness is to provide a general-purpose mode of perception that can cope with complicated situations and select one of very many possible reactions, including silent thought. There would be a considerable evolutionary advantage to a creature having these two interacting modes: one, to provide a limited number of rapid, stereotyped unconscious responses, and the other, parallel but slower, for more measured conscious responses to more complex situations. There is evidence that these two modes interact somewhat.

The above account is not a precise explanation of consciousness. It should be regarded as a tentative way of looking at the problem, to help guide more detailed investigations.   FHCC/ChK

Crick, F., and Koch, C. (2000). 'The unconscious homunculus'. *Neuro-Psychoanalysis*, 2/1.

———— (2001). 'Consciousness and neuroscience'. In Bechtel, W., Mandik, P., Mundale, J., and Stufflebeam, R. S. (eds.), *Philosophy and the Neurosciences: A Reader*.

Koch, C., and Crick, F. (2001). 'The zombie within'. *Nature*, 411.

Milner, D., and Goodale, M. (1995). *The Visual Brain in Action*.

construction of fiction. I know nothing of the creative stimulus behind scientific thought, and was brought up to believe that the composition of music owes much to mathematics. The art of painting, it was explained, as exemplified by those masters of a bygone age, achieved perfection through a prolonged apprenticeship in the study of anatomy and nature.

Fiction was different, a latecomer. One could read the work of Cervantes, appreciate the construction of narrative in the novels of Dickens, Stendhal, or Dostoevsky, but the process behind the composing of fiction, particularly in regard to the creation of plot and character, was generally thought to lie in an author's power to form a mental image of something not present to the senses and never before perceived in reality.

This is not an explanation I agree with, for it seems to imply that 'imagination' is an inherited factor, similar to blue eyes or red hair, and one present in a fortunate few at the moment of birth. I hold it to be simply an ability to recall memories: the echoes of voices heard in infancy; words resounding from the wireless; landscapes viewed from trains; recurrent dreams; lines from a poem; emotional experiences little understood at the time but later rising up like bubbles in a glass. We all have such buried recollections, yet only some appear to have a need, a compulsion, to bring the past to the surface.

Novelists, without exception, are egotistical individuals, whose understanding of life has been so shaped, so distorted by events in childhood, good or bad, that it drives them to the exaggeration and drama of storytelling. Think of Dickens, a stupendous spinner of so-called 'fiction', and a man who loved play-acting. Had his father escaped incarceration in a debtors' prison and his mother not taken him out of school and put him to work in a blacking factory, would he have wanted to write? Would he have had anything to write about?

His clinical descriptions of mental and physical symptoms were extremely accurate, and owed as much to personal observation as to the reading of medical books, for his sense of injustice at the casual harm done to his childish self propelled him to examine and analyse the causes. Most writers, faced as they are by physiological puzzles, find the practice of medicine intriguing. The tormented Dr Johnson attended the lectures of the physician John Hunter and, though he shrank from the cruel experiments inflicted upon animals, remained fascinated throughout his life at what he perceived to be the connection of the mind to the workings of the body.

When asked as to how they created character, many writers claim a reliance on 'imagination'. This is often done to avoid possible libel action. For myself, when I make fiction, I always use people I have known. There seems little point in invention, even if that were possible. It is true that sometimes these people become different, but that is because words often interfere with how they really were, or, more accurately, how I saw them. None of us can see anyone clearly; we can only be conscious of ourselves, and even that is suspect, for the long shadows of the past throw up images hard to decipher.

Once only, in writing a novel, did my unconscious, in the true sense of the word, take hold, for I fell off a ladder and was knocked out by cracking my head against the sharp edge of a table. After 30 seconds or so I recovered and rang what I believed to be the telephone number of my mother, who had been dead for twelve years. The male voice of the Speaking Clock answered me—it was 2.36 and 50 seconds into the dawn.

The next morning I rang the archivist of British Telecom and was told that, in my youth in Liverpool, three pennies in the slot gave access to the time told by the voice of a woman always known as the Girl with the Golden Voice. The recording had begun round about the time of my birth and only been replaced some 40 years later. Miss Golden Voice, after attempting to make a career on the stage, emigrated to the United States and 70 years later ended her days in an old people's home in Croydon.

From this information I spun a story about a young girl abandoned when a baby by a mother whom she knows to be the voice of the Speaking Clock. The girl rings her frequently, confides secrets, listens attentively to a response which is nothing more than a detailing of the hour and the minute.

The structure of the novel centres round J. M. Barrie's play *Peter Pan*, in which Tootles, having fired an arrow at Wendy hovering in the skies of Never Never Land, cries out, 'All my life I have wanted a mother, yet when she came I shot her'.

It is my conviction that 'imagination' had little to do with what I wrote. I had hurt my head and wanted my mother; she wasn't there. I had seen a production of *Peter Pan* when a child and never forgotten the tick-tock of the crocodile, nor Captain Hook's horror of the sound, which was surely a fear of time passing, as was mine on hearing the telephone ticking away the seconds.

Barrie's own development as a writer stemmed from the death of a sibling early in childhood and its effect on his mother, an experience he transformed into Lost Boys and a stoppage of time.

Perhaps what we call the creative impulse is not so much an ability to create something from nothing, but rather a need to unravel the anarchic workings of the mind. BB

Bainbridge, B. (1989). *An Awfully Big Adventure*.

contingent property. 'Contingent' (sometimes 'accidental') is applied to certain properties of a thing to suggest that they do not necessarily belong to that thing, either because of their dependence on some further cause, or simply to indicate that the thing need not have those properties to be the thing that it is. Thus a piece of wood may have the contingent property of being stained; however, the property of having been produced from a tree is necessary to its being a piece of wood.

The distinction between contingent and necessary properties is broadly the Aristotelian distinction between what a thing is in virtue of itself (*kath's hauto*) and what it is

by accident (*kata sumbebēkos*). To sustain the distinction requires, on the one hand, a recognition that the very identity of a thing may be bound up with its being of a certain kind, otherwise all its properties are contingent (e.g. it would be thinkable that something that is a piece of wood might not have been a piece of wood). On the other hand, it must be allowed that a thing can alter some of its properties without changing its identity, otherwise all its properties are necessary (e.g. a piece of wood could not be stained without becoming a completely different thing). JET

Kirwan, C. (1971). *Aristotle's Metaphysics Books* Γ, Δ, E (translated with notes).

coordination between different senses. See SPATIAL COORDINATION.

cornea. The transparent window of the eye. It is the main image-forming structure in air-living vertebrates. (In fish, however, the crystalline lens produces the retinal image.) The cornea has no blood vessels, receiving its nutrients by absorption. It is for this reason that corneas can be transplanted without rejection. *Astigmatism is generally due to the cornea having a non-spherical surface.

corpus callosum. The very large bundle of fibres connecting the two cerebral hemispheres in the brain. It is occasionally sectioned as a treatment for *epilepsy, and the results have been used for 'split-brain' experiments, particularly associated with the American neurophysiologist Roger *Sperry, who holds that the patient may then have two minds, or two selves. See SPLIT-BRAIN AND THE MIND.

correlation. An observed association between events (for example, that smoking is associated with lung cancer). It is not possible to assign causes directly from correlations: there must always be an underlying theory, or explicit or implicit assumptions, to set the causal 'arrow'. Discovering correlations is a principal aim of most scientific experiments, and much of learning may also be thought of as discovering correlations, which are useful when predictive.

cortical maps. See LOCALIZATION OF BRAIN FUNCTION AND CORTICAL MAPS.

Coué, Émile (1857–1926). French lay psychotherapist who founded a therapeutic method based on auto-suggestion (self-induced suggestion) that won considerable popularity in its day. He gained fame with his maxim 'day by day and in every way I am getting better and better'.

courage. See FEAR AND COURAGE.

Craik, Kenneth John William (1914–45). British psychologist, educated at the Edinburgh Academy and the University of Edinburgh, where he graduated with first-class honours in philosophy. He then deviated to psychology, working for a year in Edinburgh under Professor James Drever, Sen., before moving on to Cambridge, where he became a research student in the psychological laboratory under Professor F. C. (later Sir Frederic) *Bartlett. Craik was awarded his Ph.D. in 1940 and elected to a fellowship at St John's College, Cambridge, in the following year.

During the Second World War, Craik was heavily engaged in applied research work on behalf of the Medical Research Council and the armed services, especially the Royal Air Force. In 1944 he was appointed the first director of the Medical Research Council's applied psychology unit at Cambridge and seemed well set for an active and productive post-war career. Unfortunately, his premature death in a road accident at the age of 31 deprived British psychology of one of its most promising figures. It can hardly be doubted that had he survived he would have become one of the ablest experimental psychologists of his time.

Craik's early work was concerned almost wholly with problems of vision. He was particularly interested in the adaptation of the eye to changes in the level of illumination and in the effects of such adaptation on visual efficiency. In a series of published papers, he described the effects of various levels of adaptation on differential brightness sensitivity, visual acuity, and subjective brightness, concluding that the efficiency of the eye was highest when at a level of illumination roughly equal to that to which the eye had been pre-adapted. In general, he viewed adaptation as a kind of 'range-setting' adjustment of the visual system and saw in it the first stage of the process whereby a degree of constancy is achieved in the apparent brightness of objects despite wide variations in the general level of illumination. Although he may have underrated the specificity of tuning of the adapted eye, his attempt to establish some general principles of perception on the basis of the simpler mechanisms of physiological response held high promise.

Craik was always much interested in the nature of dark adaptation, and some of his work in this field found important application during the war, particularly in relation to night flying. He also did important work on glare as a factor limiting visual efficiency in locating submarines from the air. On the basis of his impromptu experiments, he was able to evolve a simple experimental law relating intensity of glare to angle of light source and size of target. This led him to suggest a much-improved method of visual scanning which was immediately adopted. Studies of anoxia (oxygen deficiency) in relation to aviation medicine stimulated him to undertake experiments,

with himself as subject, on temporary blindness induced by mechanical pressure on the eyeball. In the course of these somewhat hazardous experiments, he established very convincingly not only that both light and dark adaptation are essentially retinal processes but that visual *after-images are likewise of peripheral origin.

Although vision may well have been Craik's foremost scientific interest, he shook off his earlier preoccupations with philosophy only with difficulty. In 1943 he published *The Nature of Explanation*, his only completed study of any length. Although this was in principle an essay in philosophy, it embodies a highly original attempt to develop a theory of thought along mechanistic lines. His point of departure is that thinking is undeniably predictive and that this predictive capacity is also characteristic of calculating machines, anti-aircraft predictors, and other devices which, at all events to this extent, can be said to operate in essentially the same manner as man himself. Craik therefore postulated that the brain makes use of mechanisms similar in principle to many of the artefacts of modern technology and that these mechanisms can model, or parallel, phenomena in the external world, just as a calculating machine can parallel the development, say, of strains in a bridge of given design and hence predict whether it will stand or fall. On such a view, Craik contends, our thought has objective validity because it is not fundamentally different from external reality and is especially suited to imitating it.

In assessing Craik's theory, it is important to bear in mind that modern computer technology was virtually in its infancy at the time that he was writing and that his model leans heavily on the principles of analogue devices. Had he been alive in the era of digital computers and lived to read A. M. *Turing's famous paper on *Computing Mechanisms and Intelligence*, which appeared five years after Craik's death, he might well have put forward a model of thought more in keeping with the capacity of digital computers to mimic any discrete-state machine. None the less, Craik's theory, and his concept of internal models in the brain, have had considerable influence on psychologists and neurophysiologists seeking mechanical analogues of intelligent behaviour in animals and man (see ARTIFICIAL INTELLIGENCE).

Craik's wide knowledge of general experimental psychology and the physiology of the senses had been appreciably expanded by his wartime work on human factors in tank and anti-aircraft gunnery. This work also fostered a lively interest in servo-mechanisms and automatic control principles, as is well shown in his two posthumous papers (1997–8) on the theory of the human operator in control systems. As the war neared its end, Craik began work on a systematic treatise on the mechanisms of learning and human action. This was never completed, although several chapters survived and have been edited for publication by Stephen Sherwood. They are to be found in a volume of Craik's essays, notes, and papers assembled by Sherwood on the initiative of Warren *McCulloch under the title *The Nature of Psychology* (1966). As Sherwood rightly points out, Craik's draft embodies some of the earliest references to the relationships between learning, cyclical events in the nervous system, and servo-mechanisms. Indeed it foreshadows many of the arguments later developed *in extenso* by the mathematician Norbert *Wiener in his famous book on *Cybernetics* (1948) (see CYBERNETICS, HISTORY OF).

His scientific talents apart, Kenneth Craik was an accomplished designer of technical equipment and derived enormous enjoyment from mechanical invention of all kinds. He was a skilled craftsman, and the set of miniature steam engines, each one smaller than the last, which he made when still a schoolboy are now in the Royal Scottish Museum in Edinburgh. He was also an accomplished amateur violinist and had some talent for poetry.

OLZ

Bartlett, F. C. (1946). 'Obituary notice: K. J. W. Craik'. *British Journal of Psychology*, 36.

Craik, K. J. W. (1943). *The Nature of Explanation*.

——(1947–8). 'Theory of the human operator in control systems', I: 'The operation of the human operator in control systems'; II: 'Man as an element in a control system'. *British Journal of Psychology*, 38.

——(1966). *The Nature of Psychology: A Collection of Papers and Other Writings by the Late Kenneth J. W. Craik.* Ed. S. Sherwood.

Zangwill, O. L. (1980). 'Kenneth Craik: the man and his work'. *British Journal of Psychology*, 71.

creativity. One of those terms (*intelligence is another) that psychologists use as though they refer to single human characteristics, but which direct us in practice to a number of concerns that are rather separate. Some of these, like 'innovation' and 'discovery', have a bearing on the ideas or objects that people produce; some, like 'self-actualization', refer more to the quality of the life an individual leads; and some, like 'imagination' and 'fantasy', point us, in the first instance, to what goes on inside a person's head. Despite its air of vagueness, the notion of 'creativity' has none the less served an important function among psychologists and teachers, acting as a banner under which ideological battles have been fought, and indicating, too, a somewhat disparate body of research, some of which is of real value.

What is now thought of as the 'creativity movement' had its first stirrings in America in the years after the Second World War. At one level, it was psychology's response to the challenge of Sputnik, and to the fact that little of the best space research was being done by home-grown American scientists—the implication being that there was something deadening about the education that clever young American scientists had received. At another level, it represented a liberal reaction, within psychology, against values which were seen as excessively manipulative and bureaucratic. Translated into the classroom, this concern for creativity expressed itself in a desire to shake education free of rote learning and the set syllabus, multiple-choice examinations, and the IQ test, and to give children the opportunity to make discoveries for themselves.

Although hints of its existence were detectable as early as 1950, this movement was not in full swing until the early 1960s. It seems, in other words, to have been a portent of the liberal and anti-authoritarian mood that dominated university life towards the end of the 1960s, and which, in its turn, provoked its own reaction. By the early 1970s, the more self-consciously scientific psychologists had already begun to reassert the virtues of the IQ test, and to argue in favour of genetic rather than cultural explanations of individual and racial differences.

The founding fathers of psychology were keenly interested, Francis *Galton no less than Sigmund *Freud, and research has proceeded quietly for 100 years or more. Two sorts of enquiry have been especially fruitful: straightforwardly descriptive studies of the lives that highly original men and women have led; and research on the processes of thinking itself.

In a sense, the evidence of the biographical studies has been largely negative. It has been found, time and again, that those who display great originality as adults were often, like Charles *Darwin, only mediocre as students. British scientists who become Fellows of the Royal Society show roughly the same distribution of good, mediocre, and poor degree results as do those who go into research but achieve little. The same holds for intelligence-test scores: above a surprisingly low level, there is little or no relationship between IQ and achievement in any sphere of adult endeavour yet studied. As a result, we would expect future Nobel Prize winners to show roughly the same distribution of IQ scores as their fellow students at university. In the American context, the budding scientist of high renown seems typically to be a 'B+' student: one who works hard when a topic captures his or her imagination, but otherwise does the bare minimum. Science springs to life for such individuals when they discover that instead of assimilating knowledge created by others, they can create knowledge for themselves—and are hooked from that moment onwards.

It is the more detailed studies of thinking that indicate the tensions which underlie such creative effort. Some of the most vivid have concerned mathematicians, and a feature of them is the stress they place on the process of 'incubation'. Often, having struggled with a problem and then put it aside, mathematicians find that the solution comes to them quite unexpectedly, in a flash. The clear implication is that our brains are at their most efficient when allowed to switch from phases of intense concentration to ones in which we exert no conscious control at all.

There are many instances of such 'unconscious' work, one of the more dramatic being that of the German poet Rainer Maria Rilke. In 1912, in the midst of a long poem, the *Duino Elegies*, Rilke ran out of inspiration, and lapsed into a long period of frustrated depression. Interrupted in any case by the First World War, he was able to write little for a decade. When 'utterance and release' came to him in 1922, it took the shape of a series of poems, the *Sonnets to Orpheus*, that he had no intention of writing whatever. Eighteen days later, when he had finished both these sonnets and the *Duino Elegies*, he had produced some 1,200 lines of the pithiest and most carefully poised poetry ever written, and had done so largely without correction, as if taking dictation.

Such evidence encourages us to reconsider the popular idea that *genius and madness are closely allied. It is not true, of course, that great poets, painters, scientists, and mathematicians are mad; far from it. On the other hand, it may well be that they work as intensely and imaginatively as they do in order to remain sane; that they have access to aspects of the mind's functioning from which those who live more staid and conventional lives are excluded, and that it is this access which gives their work both its flair and its sense of risk. Rilke's lengthy depression may well have been necessary for the extraordinary burst of creative but also highly disciplined work that followed it.

It is such tensions as these that explain a remark once attributed to Einstein. He suggested that the creative scientists are the ones with access to their *dreams. Occasionally, a dream will actually provide the solution to a problem—as in the case of the chemist August Kekulé and his dream of the snake swallowing its own tail, the clue to the nature of the benzene ring. Einstein's point was less specific, though. As Freud realized, in establishing his distinction between primary and secondary process thought, the mind is capable of functioning both intuitively and according to the dictates of common sense. The implication of Einstein's remark is that, in order to innovate, the scientist, like anyone else, must break the grip on his imagination that our powers of logical-seeming storytelling impose. We must be willing to subvert the conventional wisdom on which our everyday competence depends.

It is here that the research done by the advocates of creativity in the 1960s now seems most relevant. Rather than straining to see whether tests of creativity can be devised, to stand side by side with IQ tests (a largely barren exercise, it seems), we can concentrate on an issue that Francis Galton identified over a century ago: the extent to which each individual can retrieve apparently irrational ideas, sift them, and put them to some constructive use. We know that individuals differ in their ability to *free-associate, to fantasize, and to recall their dreams. We also know that these differences have a bearing on the kinds of work people find it comfortable to do: among the intelligent, it is those who are relatively good at free associating (the 'divergers') who are attracted towards the arts, while those who are relatively weak in this (the 'convergers') are drawn towards science and technology. What we do not yet know is how the abilities to think logically and to free associate combine to produce work of real value: what qualities of mind, for example, a genuinely imaginative solution to an engineering problem demands, or how a sustained contribution to one of the arts is actually achieved.

See also LATERAL THINKING; PROBLEM SOLVING; PROBLEMS: THEIR APPEAL. LH

Getzels, J. W., and Jackson, P. W. (1962). *Creativity and Intelligence*.
Gruber, H. E., et al. (eds.) (1962). *Contemporary Approaches to Creative Thinking*.
Hadamard, J. (1945). *The Psychology of Invention in the Mathematical Field*.
Hudson, L. (1968). *Contrary Imaginations*.
Sternberg, R. (1999). *Handbook of Creativity*.

cretinism. Impaired physical and mental development due to lack of thyroid development. Appearing in early childhood, the problems can be largely avoided by treatment with thyroid extract—if diagnosed and treated sufficiently early in infancy.

criminology. Like medicine, criminology is an amalgam of disciplines. In popular usage it even includes scientific methods of identifying criminals, although nowadays this is distinguished as 'forensic science' or—less elegantly—'criminalistics'. In stricter modern practice criminology comprises four kinds of study: descriptive, explanatory, penological, and nomological.

Descriptive studies are concerned with the frequencies of the various sorts of lawbreaking; the situations in which they are most likely to occur; the kinds of people who are most likely to commit them; and the extent of the harm done. In the past such studies have relied chiefly or entirely on official statistics and police files. More recently, 'self-report' studies, in which samples (usually of teenagers) have told interviewers about their behaviour, have provided less superficial data, as have 'victim surveys'. These studies and surveys have yielded more valid estimates of the real incidence of violence, thefts, robberies, burglaries, and sexual crimes (but not yet of serious traffic offences, or of rare crimes such as homicide). They have shown that victims are selective in what they report to the police; that police are selective in what they regard as worth recording; and that fluctuations in recorded crimes can result from, or be greatly exaggerated by, changes in people's willingness to report them, as well as from variations in the interest which the police take in them.

Explanatory studies need to be subdivided into those that seek to offer explanations of particular breaches of law and those that try to account for especially high (or low) frequencies of lawbreaking (or, better, of certain kinds of lawbreaking), whether in different countries, in different social groups, or during different periods in their histories. Explanations of particular breaches usually attach importance to the disposition of the individual lawbreaker, whether this is attributed to upbringing, to the influence of associates, or—less commonly nowadays —to genetic or perinatal misfortunes. Explanations of differing frequencies emphasize economic conditions, subcultural values that are in conflict with law, or inequalities of opportunity for legitimate acquisition or enjoyment. 'Histories' may figure in both kinds of explanation, whether they take the form of narratives about individuals or trace the origins of, say, violence in a country's past. Most explainers are highly selective, either because they are searching for some factor that can be manipulated so as to reduce the frequency of lawbreaking, or because they want ammunition to support political or moral attacks on the current state of their society. What should not be overlooked, however, is the relevance of explanations when courts are trying to assess the culpability of an individual offender.

Penological research is concerned mainly with the effects of what is officially done to identified offenders, although it has also taken an interest in the social consequences of being labelled as an offender of one kind or another. Until recently most penologists concentrated on assessing the extent to which *desired* effects were achieved: reform, deterrence, rehabilitation, incapacitation. There have always been critics, however, who emphasized the unwanted side effects of sentences, and when it became clear that the wanted effects were confined to a small minority of offenders (who could seldom be identified in advance) the importance of unwanted effects began to be appreciated. These too, however, have been exaggerated, and it is only in the last decade that attempts have been made to define and measure the sorts of damage that incarceration (for example) inflicts, and determine whether it is transient or lasting.

Nomological studies. What can be called 'nomological' studies—for want of a better term—concentrate on law enforcement itself. Some offer answers to the question 'What kinds of conduct should be prohibited by the (criminal) law?' The kinds most frequently discussed are consensual sexual deviations, contraception and abortion, euthanasia, drug abuse, and obscene entertainment. Others are concerned with compulsory benevolence

such as requirements to wear seat belts in motor vehicles. Nomological work is also undertaken into the ways in which the criminal law as it stands is administered. Since police have to be selective—both because of limitations on resources and for the sake of good relations with the public—their selectivity has been subjected to very critical scrutiny in Britain and the USA, though much less in 'police states' for obvious reasons. Public prosecutors, who exercise considerable discretion in bringing people to court and in framing the charges against them, are also a subject of study. Another favourite subject is the criminal courts: chiefly summary courts and appeal courts. Where higher courts are concerned, it has been the jury which has been the focus of the spotlight. The behaviour of prison staff and administrators has also received much attention. Less attention has been paid to the behaviour of probation officers, hostel wardens, and other social workers, chiefly because their roles are seen as less coercive. Furthermore, penologists have interested themselves in 'theories of punishment': more precisely in the differing aims which are held to justify penalizing offenders. Until fairly recently this was regarded as a subject for moral philosophers, but penologists have been able to show that some philosophers' assumptions about the practicability of achieving their aims have been unrealistic.   NDW

Downes, D., and Rock, P. (1982). *Understanding Deviance.*
Floud, J., and Young, W. (1981). *Dangerousness and Criminal Justice.*
Taylor, I., Walton, P., and Young, J. (1973). *The New Criminology.*
Thomas, D. A. (1979 edn.). *Principles of Sentencing.*
Walker, N. D. (1977). *Behaviour and Misbehaviour: Explanations and Non-explanations.*
West, D. J. (1982). *Delinquency: Its Roots, Careers and Prospects.*

critical periods. Walking, language, sensorimotor coordination, and other skills are best learnt at certain 'critical periods' in the development of children, and similarly with other animals. Once the critical period is lost, it may be very difficult or impossible to learn the skill with full effectiveness. (See SPATIAL COORDINATION; VISUAL SYSTEM: ENVIRONMENTAL INFLUENCES.) A major skill in teaching children is to recognize the advent of each critical period. Jerome Bruner speaks of readiness to learn, and Jean *Piaget has attempted to determine the ages at which various lessons are appropriate.

cross-modal sensory integration. To the ordinary observer it is self-evident that an object he perceives remains unchanged even when on different occasions the same object is, say, seen (but not touched, heard, or smelled), or touched (but not seen, heard, or smelled), or heard (but not seen, touched, or smelled). Psychologists have increasingly during the recent past been posing questions with regard to skills of cross-modal recognition.

Were *Berkeley, *Leibniz, and *Piaget correct in their supposition that at birth the perceptual systems relating to each sense modality are independent? Then, during development, do the perceptual systems become integrated, and does the infant learn through the experience of stimulus correlations that equivalences between sensory systems exist? Or, are others (e.g. Werner, Bower) right in arguing that babies have a primitive unity of the senses, so that early perception is 'supramodal' (i.e. the sense modality of the inflow is disregarded)? Then, during development, are the senses increasingly differentiated and does the child learn that the senses are distinct?

In addition, psychologists have been asking questions with regard to special populations. Is cross-modal recognition immediately proficient in patients whose sight has been restored at a later age after being virtually blind from birth on account of cataract (a question first raised by *Locke)? Is there evidence, from neurological patients, of a special brain area that acts as a structural bridge between the separate senses? Does language mediate cross-modal skills, and how do mammals lacking language but with their highly proficient perceptual capacities fare on cross-modal tasks?

Unfortunately, we have no certain answers to most of these questions. The originally posed issue (Piaget versus Bower) seems too broad to answer directly. In accordance with the particular task (which might involve objects or temporal sequences), and depending on the subject's prior experience and individual capacities, codes of processing are flexibly selected, irrespective of modality. Distinctions such as 'separateness' and 'unity' (of the senses) have no general validity: the particular task at a particular time is all important. Moreover, demonstration of certain relatively primitive cross-modal skills in pre-verbal human infants, or in non-human animals, should not imply that symbolic coding is not the normal or preferred human strategy for processing information cross-modally once language has developed. The cross-modal capacities of the human infant (Meltzoff and Borton 1979) and baby monkey (Gunderson 1983) seem extremely crude in comparison with the skills shown (not in all tasks or comparisons, but none the less quite frequently) by children over the age of 8, or by adults.

A broad view of the current evidence suggests that a primitive kind of 'supramodal' perception is structurally given at birth in human infants (and also in apes and monkeys), possibly at a 'low' (subcortical) level of the brain. This system may be involved in stimulus-object identification and re-identification (i.e. recognition), but cannot serve when features of an object, as opposed to the identity of the object *per se*, have to be analysed (i.e. discriminated) and then recognized. Apes and monkeys have not progressed far beyond this stage (so that cross-modal 'transfer of learning' does not occur even in apes capable

of immediate cross-modal 'recognition', and the greater the amount of experience given in the first sense modality, the poorer the cross-modal recognition in the second). With increasing age, the human child resorts to new strategies: he learns from lawful correlations (e.g. bimodal exposure, when the stimuli are perceived simultaneously through different senses, so that feature analyses via different senses become possible); and even physically quite dissimilar properties can be assigned to the same stimulus on a conditional basis (e.g. the sound of the word 'apple' associated with the seen object 'apple'). (Such cross-modal conditional learning is also laboriously possible for non-human animals.) Finally, increasing through childhood, man tends to have recourse to symbolic mediation, where language serves as a cross-modal bridge, allowing for greater flexibility in judging equivalence. This tentative schema may well need to be revised as new evidence becomes available.

See also BLINDNESS, RECOVERY FROM; SPATIAL COORDINATION.
GE

Gunderson, V. M. (1983). *Developmental Psychology*, 19.
Meltzoff, A. N., and Borton, R. W. (1979). *Nature*, 282.

cruelty. From the Latin *crudelem*, morally rough, cruelty is the deliberate—and often joyous—infliction of physical or psychological pain on other living creatures. Cruelty is today, and has throughout human history been, an overwhelming presence in the world; its uses are for punishment, amusement, and social control, and its medium is pain. But despite a vast literature (for example, Edgerton 1985, Scarry 1985, Puppi 1991) on deliberately inflicted pain, there has been scant study of two matters that are fundamental to an an understanding of cruelty's weight in the world: the evidently considerable gratifications of perpetrators and audiences, and the origins of the cruelty impulse in the human psyche.

1. The uses and gratifications of cruelty
2. The origins of cruelty
3. Cultural elaborations of cruelty
4. The problem of prevention

1. The uses and gratifications of cruelty

Punishment. Thoughtlessly or maliciously, the strong punish the weak by the infliction of pain: thus masters with slaves, adults with children, and men with women. When Sarai complained to Abram of Hagar's contempt, he replied, ' "Your slave-girl is in your power, do with her as you please." Then Sarai dealt harshly with her, and she ran away from her' (Genesis 16: 6). Corporal punishment of children and pupils was part of medieval and early modern life. From the 15th century, the birching of school pupils became increasingly common and brutal 'for all offences and all ages' (Aries 1962: 259). Heroard, the physician of King Henri IV of France, kept a diary of the childhood of the king's son who was to become Louis XIII. From 1608, when he was 7, his education was more serious, but, though he had stopped playing with his dolls, 'he was still given a whipping from time to time' (Aries 1962: 66).

Spectacles of pain and death were a fixed part of medieval life, and there is a rich tradition of popular woodcuts of execution scenes (Edgerton 1985, Puppi 1991). The route taken by the procession to the gallows or the wheel was planned so as to draw the whole of the urban fabric into these public demonstrations of the sovereign's power. Great crowds followed the wagon and gathered at the place of execution.

Amusement. Punishment shades over into the most shameful of cruelty's uses, for private pleasure and amusement. The oscillation between the judicial and the personal is detectable in cruelties inflicted by agents of the state when they believe that they will not be held accountable. Thus with the torture and killing of Muslims in Visegrad, eastern Bosnia, reported in the *New York Times* on 25 May 1996. A survivor tells that she crept out of hiding on 19 July 1992, and watched as her mother and sister were made to sit astride the bridge parapet and shot in the stomach by Serb paramilitaries: 'When they fell in the water, the men leaned over and laughed.' Similar scenes of clandestinely videotaped South African police brutality have been widely broadcast—setting dogs on prisoners as a 'training exercise', burning a semi-conscious hijack suspect with a cigarette lighter: the police laugh uproariously at the victims' pain. One of the two British 10-year-olds who abducted, tortured, and killed James Bulger, a baby of 2, said of the other at the trial, 'He probably did it for fun, he was laughing his head off'.

Caligula (AD 12–41) tortured Roman senators, men he knew well, not to extract information, but for amusement. The *Historia Augusta* (c.AD 500) relates that Commodus (AD 177–92) was destructive even in his humorous moments: 'For example, he put a starling on the head of one man who, as he noticed, had a few white hairs, resembling worms, among the black, and caused his head to fester through the continual pecking of the bird's beak.' Ovid (*Art of Love*, 3. 235–8) writes:

> I hate the woman
> who wounds her maid with hairpins, or her nails.
> The poor girl curses every hair she touches
> and weeps and bleeds behind her mistress' back.

Social control. Judicial punishment in order to enforce laws and preserve discipline ranges from verbal reprimand, shaming, and ostracism to execution. Babylonian, Mosaic, and Roman law are founded on the principle of *talion*, retaliation: 'it shall be life for life, eye for eye, tooth for tooth, hand for hand, foot for foot' (Deuteronomy 19: 19–21). The barbarity of the Roman Law of the Twelve

Tables (450 BC)—a parricide was cast into the sea in a sack with a cock, a viper, a dog, and a monkey—led Gibbon to remark that it is 'written in characters of blood'. The worst cruelties were inflicted on slaves and 'inferior races'. Spartan youths killed Helots for sport (Plutarch, c.AD 100, *Lycurgus*, 28); in his Amazon diaries, Roger Casement compiled a report on the fearful atrocities against Indians by rubber traders on the Putamayo River, a tributary of the Amazon.

Cruelty as entertainment, and thus indirectly as an instrument of social control (Coleman 1990), reached its apogee in the late Roman Republic and early Empire. The gladiatorial show was 'the most prominent and most popular spectacle of all', writes Tertullian (*Apologeticum*, AD 197, 12. 1). The sheer extravagance of the arena spectacles attests to their social purpose as an extension of the emperor's power and authority, and a visible manifestation of his benevolence (Coleman 1990). Suetonius (AD 100, *Life of Julius Caesar*, 39.3) records that Caesar, for his triumph in 46 BC, held five days of animal hunts in the arena, and the first *naumachiae* (mock naval battles) in a specially excavated basin near the Tiber with 'biremes, triremes and quadriremes of the Tyrian and Egyptian fleets, manned by a large number of combatants' (loc. cit.). These were mock battles in the sense that they were theatrical—but the deaths were real.

Contemporary accounts attest to the high and delighted arousal of the arena audiences. One cannot attend these shows, writes Tertullian, 'without his mind being aroused and his soul being stirred by some unspoken agitation . . . for even if a man enjoys spectacles modestly and soberly, as befits his rank, age, and natural disposition, he cannot go to them . . . if the passion ceases' (*Apologeticum*, 12.1; 15. 2–6). A platform in the middle of the arena catered to the spectators' fascination with the minutiae of violent death: wounded victims were placed there so that the spectators could more closely observe their death struggle. In his *Confessions*, St Augustine tells of his young friend Alypius, a Christian who had come to Rome to study law. Augustine's account captures the delirious contagion that swept over the Arena audience: 'some man fell; there was a great roar from the whole mass of spectators . . . [Alypius] saw the blood and he gulped savagery . . . he was drunk with the lust of blood' (6. 8).

2. The origins of cruelty

Primatologists, palaeontologists, and evolutionary psychologists have long speculated (see, for example, Dart 1953) about possible continuities between primate, early hominid, and human behaviour. A growing body of field observations (Stanford 1999) suggests that the roots of human cruelty and the gratifications it mediates are to be found in the predatory adaptation.

The first effective predators emerged with the middle Cambrian explosion of animal life, c.540 million years ago, with sense organs to locate prey, and the ability to pursue and overpower it (Brain 2001). But predation (nutritional killing of living creatures by animals) is very hard work: the kill success rate for the wolves on Isle Royale in Lake Superior is under 5 per cent, and the meat yield is 4 kg of meat per wolf per day; for the Gombe chimpanzees, hunting is nutritionally uneconomic: a 1 kg baby monkey is the typical yield for a hunting party of up to 20, so that the effort expended 'is enormously costly relative to the quantity of meat that is usually available' (Stanford 1999: 97).

The costs of hunting (nutritional killing by hominids) in hunter–gatherer societies is equally high: among the Dobe !Kung, 10 hunter-hours yield 1,000 calories of meat, as against 4 hours for 1,000 calories of vegetable foods (Lee 1968: 40); successes for the individual hunter are sparse and unpredictable, with the daily failure rate for individual Hadza hunters at 97 per cent. Hunting thus 'involves a great deal of effort and prestige' (Lee 1968: 40), and a hunter may go days or weeks without a kill; the !Kung hunting yield is 1 hunter-hour/100 calories.

Given these high costs, the predatory and hunting adaptations could not have emerged without massive conditioned reinforcers that derive from the prey's terror and struggles to escape as it is brought down, the shedding of its blood, and its vocalizations as it is wounded and eaten, often while it is still alive (Stanford 1999). In surviving forager societies, killing and butchering game is accompanied by a similar panoply of auditory, visual, olfactory, tactile, gustatory, and visceral stimuli (Lee 1968). A working hypothesis is that it is this stimulus array, tied back to the prey's blood and death, that reinforces and sustains human cruelty and accounts for its high reward value.

3. Cultural elaborations of cruelty

War is the most significant *social* product of the predatory adaptation. In mythology, ethnography, and contemporary culture, there are explicit links between hunting, war, and manhood (Nell 2002). Because of the male gendering of hunting (Lee 1968, Stanford 1999), it becomes an affirmation of manhood: Croesus of Lydia dreamed that his son Atys would die by the blow of an iron weapon, and accordingly forbade him to hunt a huge boar that troubled the people of Mysia. 'What face meanwhile must I wear as I walk to the agora or return from it?' lamented Atys. 'What must . . . my young bride think of me? What sort of man will she suppose her husband to be? . . . I pray you, therefore, let me go with them' (Herodotus, 440 BC, I. 34–9). Reciprocally, the warrior hero is a great predator: Achilles is 'a soaring eagle | launching down from the dark clouds to earth | to snatch some helpless lamb or trembling hare' (Homer, 800 BC, 22. 364–8).

If war is predation's most significant social product, its principle *cultural* product is the emotional weight of blood in mythology, religion, literature, and the graphic arts. A fixed feature of early religions is the gods' thirst for animal and human blood: 'for the life of the flesh is in the blood: . . . for it is the blood that maketh an atonement for the soul' (Leviticus 17: 11). It is the wasting life of the sacrificial victim that gives the words their power: the neo-Platonist Sallustius writes, 'Prayers divorced from sacrifice are only words, prayers with sacrifices are animated words, the word giving power to the life and the life to the word' (361/1926).

The warrior's death is in blood and demands blood. At Patroclus' funeral pyre, Achilles, 'with wild zeal | flung the bodies of four massive stallions onto the pyre . . . and then a dozen brave sons | of the proud Trojans he hacked to pieces' (*Iliad*, 23, 22–6, 35–6, 200–3).

In today's world, Roman and medieval carnivals of death are perpetuated in movies and the electronic media, and in gladiatorial contests—boxing and kickboxing, American football, car and motorcycle racing— that are unwillingly stopped short of frank killing. Violently inflicted cruelty is the coinage of smash-hit novels, films, and TV series. The torture of animals for entertainment, a popular public spectacle until the establishment of humane societies in Europe and the United States in the late 19th century, continues clandestinely. The willingness of military establishments to develop technologies of cruelty as instruments of war flourishes globally, while the coercive forces of the state (and its opponents) use confessional and disciplinary cruelty for political ends.

4. The problem of prevention

For individuals, today as in the past, cruelty continues to serve as a gateway to power and a route to prestige, leadership, and social mastery that entrains survival and reproductive benefits. Thus, despite the human capacity for *compassion, atrocities continue. An essential first step towards more effective prevention of interpersonal, internecine, and international atrocities is to account for the psychological gratifications that perpetrators and audiences derive from inflicting or observing cruelty, which in turn requires an understanding of the deep evolutionary origins of cruelty.   VN

Aries, P. (1962). *Centuries of Childhood: A Social History of Family Life.*

Brain, C. K. (2001). *Do We Owe our Intelligence to a Predatory Past?*

Coleman, K. M. (1990). 'Fatal charades: Roman executions staged as mythological enactments'. *Journal of Roman Studies,* 80.

Dart, R. A. (1953). 'The predatory transition from ape to man'. *International Anthropological and Linguistic Review,* 1.

Edgerton, S. Y. (1985). *Pictures and Punishment: Art and the Criminal Prosecution during the Florentine Renaissance.*

Lee, R. B. (1968). 'What hunters do for a living, or how to make out on scarce resources'. In Lee, R. B., and DeVore, I. (eds.) *Man the Hunter.*

Nell, V. (2002). 'Why young men drive dangerously: implications for injury prevention'. *Current Directions in Psychological Science*, 11.

Puppi, L. (1991). *Torment in Art*.

Scarry, E. (1985). *The Body in Pain: The Making and Unmaking of the World*.

Stanford, C. B. (1999). *The Hunting Apes: Meat Eating and the Origins of Human Behaviour*.

cultural differences in perception. See PERCEPTION: CULTURAL DIFFERENCES.

curiosity. Seeking knowledge without prospect of immediate gain or reward is a characteristic of higher animals, and is most marked by far in man. It implies a degree of risk taking, since the unknown is explored, and is difficult to explain in theories of behaviour based on motivation and drive reduction; but it clearly has survival value, when combined with rapid learning. One might say that man is unique as a species through his extraordinary curiosity.

cybernetics, history of. The word 'cybernetics' was introduced by Norbert *Wiener (1894–1964), the distinguished mathematician. It was the title of a book, *Cybernetics, or Control and Communication in the Animal and the Machine*, published in 1948. The word is formed from the Greek *kubernetes*, 'steersman'. As Wiener explained: 'What recommended the term cybernetics to me was that it was the best word I could find to express the art and science of control over the whole range of fields in which this notion is applicable.' These words can also be used as a definition of cybernetics. It is a theory of *feedback systems, i.e. self-regulating systems, the theory being applicable to machines as well as to living systems. Today, after the introduction of computers, theoretical aspects of control analyses have become so sophisticated and their application to engineering, biomedicine, and economics so firmly rooted and self-evident that it is difficult to recapture the intellectual excitement brought about by Wiener and his publications. The roots of the application of control theory or feedback in engineering reach far back; so too, it was noticed by certain biologists that control or the maintenance of equilibrium is one of the basic properties of life. However, the unifying theory of control and communication as applicable both to living systems and to machines built by man was first generally recognized only in 1948 with the publication of Wiener's book.

It is not certain who was the first person to apply a feedback mechanism to regulate or control a machine. There is evidence that certain kinds of regulating devices, such as for regulating the level of oil in an oil lamp or the outflow of water reservoirs, were already being used more than 2,000 years ago, and were known in the Middle Ages and the Renaissance. However, knowledge was transferred orally from craftsman to craftsman, and only a few written descriptions exist, none of which treats the theoretical aspects of mechanical engineering. In the 17th century, machines that developed great power, like windmills and steam engines, were first used. It then became essential to provide some mechanism to limit or control their power, so that it would not finally destroy the machine which produced it. One of the first patents granted to a feedback mechanism was for a 'whirling regulator' which controlled the speed of rotation in windmills by means of a centrifugal pendulum (T. Mead: Regulator for Wind and Other Mills, patent no. 1628, London 1787). The engineer James Watt (1736–1819) adapted it and used it as a 'governor' to regulate the velocity of rotation in steam engines, where the output (i.e. the velocity of rotation) regulated the input (i.e. the steam). During most of the 19th century, although regulating devices were widely used in engineering, there were no clear concepts of the dimensions and mechanical properties they should have. They were built and simply had to be tried out—and often failed. There was no theoretical framework which allowed the performance of a given regulator to be calculated. Then James Clerk Maxwell (1831–79), a physicist, reduced the problems to mathematical formulae. However, it was not until the end of the 19th century that there became available the mathematical tools for giving easy and practical solutions to the equations suggested by Maxwell. Only then did the theory of feedback regulation become an established discipline that could be applied to all fields of engineering.

Similarly, in biology, the idea of control cannot be traced to a single person. Several steps, each focusing on special aspects, were important and necessary until it became apparent that the theory of feedback as applied to biological systems is structurally and mathematically the same as that used in engineering. Three physiologists of the 19th century deserve to be mentioned, because each of them drew attention to one important aspect of feedback control. The three aspects are the complex organization of organisms, the relative constancy of certain physiological parameters, and the description of animal behaviour using teleological terms.

In 1828 Charles *Bell, the Scottish anatomist and surgeon, published *Animal Mechanics, or Proofs of Design in the Animal Frame*, in which he discussed the complex organization of organisms. He compared the structure which gives stability to bones with elements of architecture and building engineering. Similarly he compared the mechanism and efficiency of the heart and vascular system with pumps and pipes used in engineering. Although he did not go as far as actually to describe feedback mechanisms, by systematically comparing organisms with machines, and by using the same terminology, he was the

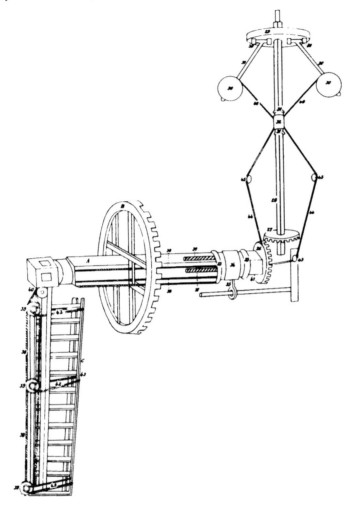

Fig. 1. Original figure from T. Mead, patent no. 1628,1787: 'A regulator on a new principle for wind and other mills, for the better and more regular furling and unfurling of the sails on windmills without the constant attendance of a man, and for grinding corn and other grain, and dressing of flour and meal, superior in quality to the present practice, and for regulating all kind of machinery where the first power is unequal.' Right up one sees a speed regulator. During rotation centrifugal forces will lift the two spherical weights. They pull on strings which then furl the sails so that the effective area exposed to the wind is reduced.

first to widely use the concept of models. Models have since been generally employed, and have become an important element in biological cybernetics. One of their purposes is to isolate certain functional aspects of behaviour and to study their logic and limits of operation in order to better understand the mechanisms of biological design and development.

Claude Bernard (1813–78), a French physiologist, introduced the concept of the constancy of the *milieu intérieur*. By that he understood that within certain limits blood, for example, has a constant composition independent of environmental changes. If the glucose level in the blood falls, animals as well as humans get hungry, eat, and by doing so raise the glucose level again. Bernard saw the results of feedback mechanisms and explored several examples, like the regulation of body temperature as well as glucose levels in the blood. In his book *Lessons on Phenomena of Life in Animals and Plants* (1878) he extended these experimental results and developed a general theory of how animals are able to maintain the constancy of their *milieu intérieur* (see HOMEOSTASIS).

The German physiologist Eduard Pflüger (1829–1910) considered the goal-directed behaviour of feedback mechanisms in biology. In 1877 he published a paper, *The Teleological Mechanics of Nature*. Teleology is defined as the study of final causes. Feedback mechanisms are characterized by the fact that the input is controlled by the output, and thus stabilizes the output, or makes the performance relatively independent from disturbing influences. One can consider the stability of the output as the 'goal' of the system. To turn the argument round, whenever a behaviour in biology is encountered that can be described as goal directed, i.e. teleological, it is very likely that a feedback mechanism is involved.

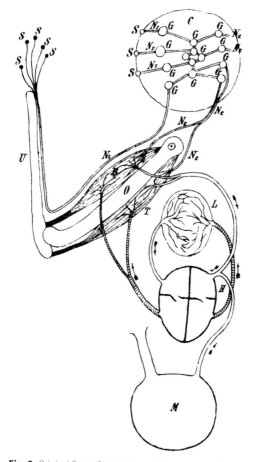

Fig. 2. Original figure from F. Lincke: 'Das mechanische Relais' (the mechanical relay), *VDI Zeitschrift*, 23, 509–24, 577–616 (1879). The 'indicators' are sensory nerves (*S, Ns*), the 'executive' organ (motor nerves *Ne* and muscle *B*), the 'transmitter' (brain with ganglion cells *G*), and the 'motor' (stomach *M*, heart *H*, lung *L*). The activity we use to direct our human "machine" to its goal results from the difference between the will and the observed or imagined reality, i.e. the difference between the intention and the result of the execution.'

The next step in combining biology and technology was taken by Felix Lincke (1840–1917), professor of mechanical engineering at the Institute of Technology in Darmstadt, Germany. He was probably the first who saw the outlines of a unifying theory of feedback control that is applicable to machines as well as to organisms. In 1879 he published a lecture, *The Mechanical Relay*, in which he classified the different feedback mechanisms used in mechanical engineering and listed the necessary elem-

ents of any feedback loop. These are: (i) the 'indicator', which continuously measures the output, (ii) the 'executive' organ, which modifies the input of the feedback loop, (iii) the 'transmitter' which connects the 'indicator' and the 'executive' organ, and (iv) the 'motor', which supplies the energy. Applied to an arm movement, the 'indicator' is the sensory nerve endings that sense the position of the arm, the 'executive organ' is the motor nerves with the muscles that perform the movement, the 'transmitter' is the brain which establishes a connection between the sensory and motor nerves, and the 'motor' is the alimentary tract supplying the energy for the whole system. The action of the indicator, executive organ, transmitter, and motor in a feedback loop can be described in the same way whether they are identified in biological systems or in machines. It is always the difference between the intended goal and the measurement given by the indicator that modifies the input to the feedback loop and thus brings the output of the system nearer to its goal. Although Lincke's paper was published in a widely recognized journal of engineering (*Zeitschrift des VDI*), and also as a book, nobody picked up his ideas and he was virtually unknown until well after Wiener's success in 1948.

In 1940, 60 years after Lincke's lecture, another engineer, Hermann Schmidt (1894–1968), a professor at the Institute of Technology in Berlin, published a series of papers in which he independently developed ideas similar to those of Wiener. Wiener focused his ideas more on the mathematical problems involved, while Schmidt based his theory more on the historical development of engineering. First, with primitive tools like an axe, man determines the exact action. In a second phase, energy is provided, but man still has to control the action by constantly monitoring the state of the machine, as in an automobile. In a third stage, energy *and* control over that energy are provided, as in aeroplanes with automatic landing control. (The pilot approaching the airfield makes only the decision to land; the exact monitoring of height, velocity, etc. is taken over by a computer.) In this third stage of development, energy and the immediate control over it are transferred to a machine, even though man still has to determine the goal of action for the machine. Only in science fiction, like Samuel *Butler's novel *Erewhon* (1872), is a fourth stage envisioned in which machines would develop to such a stage that they would determine their own goals—be it to the benefit of humans or not.

For a discussion of the application of cybernetics to human social behaviour, see also INTERACTIONAL APPROACH.   VH

Mayr, O. (1970). *The Origins of Feedback Control*.

Muses, C. (2002). 'Recollections of Norbert Weiner, Warren McCulloch and Stafford Beer'. *Kybernetes*, 31.

Wiener, N. (1948). *Cybernetics*.

——(1956). *I am a Mathematician*.

D

Dalton, John (1766–1844). British chemist born in Cumberland, the son of a Quaker hand-loom weaver. At the age of 15 he was teaching at the Quaker school in Kendal and in 1793 he moved to Manchester, where he remained for the rest of his life, supporting himself by teaching and tutoring. His atomic theory provided an explanation of the behaviour of elements and compounds and became one of the foundations of modern chemistry. He was also a keen meteorologist (recording over 200,000 observations), and a collector of butterflies and plants.

As a young man he discovered that a geranium appeared to him 'sky blue' by daylight but 'red' by candle-light. Finding that his friends did not experience this striking change (although his brother did), he came to realize that he had unusual colour vision. His detailed observations, reported to the Manchester Literary and Philosophical Society in 1794, suggest that he suffered from the type of dichromacy in which the long-wavelength receptor is missing (see COLOUR VISION). His report excited widespread interest in Daltonism, as colour-blindness came to be known for many years.

Thackray, A. (1972). *John Dalton: Critical Assessments of his Life and Science.*

danger recognition. Recognition of danger in animals requires that they distinguish dangerous stimuli from others, and distinguish among different sorts of danger that may require different escape responses. In many species there is a close relationship between fear and curiosity: confronted with a novel stimulus, or a change in environment, most animals respond first with flight and then with approach and investigation. The degree of novelty is crucial in determining which response will be given: familiar stimuli evoke little response, whereas a moderate degree of novelty elicits curiosity and approach, and fear is shown, by freezing, flight, or alarm signals, when the stimulus is extremely novel. Thus, for a wide variety of stimuli the relation between stimulus novelty and response takes the form of an inverted U: positive interest is high at intermediate levels of stimulation, and fear responses, or the recognition of danger, appear only when stimuli are very unusual.

With many species certain sights, sounds, and smells are particularly effective in eliciting escape behaviour, and different stimuli may elicit different sorts of escape. Many birds and small mammals give acoustically distinct alarm calls when ground or aerial predators appear, and respond differently to each call type. In East Africa, vervet monkeys are preyed upon by leopards, two species of eagle, and pythons. Alarm calls given for leopards cause other monkeys to run up into trees; the different calls given for eagles cause animals to look up into the air or run into bushes; and those for pythons, acoustically distinct from both leopard and eagle alarms, cause animals to stand on their hind legs and peer into the grass around them (Seyfarth, Cheney, and Marler 1980).

In some species, these highly specific responses appear fully formed, even when a stimulus is encountered for the first time: many birds give aerial predator alarm calls on their first encounter with such predators, and chicks of the same species freeze in their nests when they first hear the alarm. In other cases, recognition of specific classes of danger emerges gradually, apparently requiring some experience. While adult vervet monkeys restrict their alarm calling to particular species, infants often make 'mistakes' and give alarms for objects that pose no danger to them. These calls are not entirely undiscriminating, however: leopard alarms are given for many animals other than leopards, but only for terrestrial animals; and eagle alarms are given for many non-predators, such as pigeons and geese, but only for objects flying in the air. Despite such early classification, however, the monkeys' use of warning calls does not emerge fully formed but requires further sharpening with experience.

Parallels in the way humans and other animals recognize danger are most evident in development. Upon first exposure to a novel stimulus, most animals exhibit fear, followed by curiosity and inspection, and then by a loss of interest. For each species some stimuli are particularly alarming, and faced with these an animal readily develops an ability to recognize different kinds of danger. Similarly, human infants are frightened by a variety of general stimuli, such as loud noises, bright lights, and being left alone; later, distress is caused only by more specific stimuli, such as separation from a particular person. Thus children learn to distinguish between different classes of danger.

RMS/DLC

Seyfarth, R. M., Cheney, D. L., and Marler, P. (1980). 'Monkey responses to three different alarm calls: evidence for predator classification and semantic communication'. *Science*, 210.

Darwin, Charles Robert (1809–82). British naturalist, born at Shrewsbury. His grandfather was Erasmus *Darwin, his father, Robert Waring Darwin, was a distinguished physician, and his mother was a daughter of Josiah Wedgwood. Charles studied medicine at Edinburgh, but, finding the operating procedures of that time extremely distasteful, went up to Christ's College, Cambridge, in 1828 in order to enter the Church. However, he was befriended by the botanist Professor J. S. Henslow, and his interests moved to botany and zoology. He graduated in 1831, and with Henslow's recommendation became naturalist to the survey ship HMS *Beagle*, bound on a voyage of scientific discovery. This changed the course of his life and the science of natural history.

Darwin sailed on 27 December 1831, and returned on 2 October 1836, after exploring Tenerife, the Cape Verde Islands, Brazil, Tierra del Fuego, the Galápagos Islands, New Zealand, Tasmania, and the coral reefs of the Keeling Islands. During the voyage he stocked his mind with knowledge, questions, and a hunch that species could not be separately created but must have evolved. He attributed the insight that evolution proceeds by selection of the fittest to reading the *Essay on Population* (1798, 1803) by Thomas *Malthus, which gave the pessimistic prediction that competitive society declines in spite of the individual's struggle for existence. Curiously, this same book later triggered the same concept of evolutionary development by natural selection (a phrase coined by Herbert *Spencer) in the mind of Alfred Russel *Wallace. The theory was presented jointly by Darwin and Wallace (though neither was present) at the Linnean Society in London, on 1 July 1858. It was received in silence, with no questions; and the president of the Linnean summed up 1858 as a year that 'has not been marked by any. . . striking discoveries'. Darwin showed remarkable character in maintaining friendship with Wallace and giving him due credit, though, unlike Wallace, he had spent twenty years collecting notes. He finally published *On the Origin of Species by Means of Natural Selection*, with the spur of Wallace's independent discovery, in November 1859. The entire printing of 1,500 copies was sold out in a day.

It was the science of geology that first cast serious doubt on the biblical account of special creation for each animal species, as it became clear that there had in the past been great changes in rocks, and so in the environment, and yet animals were adapted to the present environment. It also became clear that the age of the earth was very much greater than the biblical account taken literally allows, and, perhaps most important, unknown forms of life were discovered as fossils. These facts were set out in detail by Charles Lyell (1797–1875) in *Principles of Geology* (1830–3). Darwin began to develop an evolutionary theory with such thoughts in mind, and his first theory was very different from natural selection. He first thought (in the

summer of 1837) that species must change in order to remain adapted, and that, as species change, old species must die out, for the number of species to remain nearly constant. He supposed that simple living forms ('monads') appeared through spontaneous generation from inanimate matter, and evolved by direct environmental influences. The monads, he supposed, had a limited lifespan, as do individuals, though presumably for different reasons (see Gruber 1974: ch. 5). Although he soon abandoned this theory, he retained the notion of a continuous branching tree of evolutionary development, with the implication that we should not expect any simple sequence of evolving life forms to be found in the fossil record. There were enormous gaps in the fossil record that was available in his time, and this is still so, with controversial implications (see EVOLUTION: NEO-DARWINIAN THEORY).

Darwin also made specific contributions to human psychology, tracing the origins of emotional responses and *facial expressions from prehuman species, in *The Expression of the Emotions in Man and Animals* (1872). This still unrivalled work contains accounts of the experiments he carried out on his own children, including—in spite of his extreme affection and gentleness—inducing fear to establish their responses.

He studied behaviour not only in animals and man (*The Descent of Man*, 1871, explicitly places man in the evolutionary sequence) but also in plants: *Climbing Plants* (1875), and especially *The Power of Movement in Plants* (1880), which describes not only elaborate movements of tendrils but also their selective sensitivity to appropriate or inappropriate stimuli. Darwin saw this as a precursor to control of animals by the nervous system, an idea yet to be followed up in detail.

Darwin's life after the voyage was spent with his talented family at Downe House, some 30 kilometres (20 miles) south of London, with its splendid garden and greenhouses in which he carried out many experiments while writing his books. Here he worked incessantly though dogged by ill health, possibly sleeping sickness (trypanosomiasis) contracted by an insect bite. The house and garden, with its famous walk, are preserved as a Charles Darwin museum. One can still see the study chair with wheels in which he used to push himself around when too tired to stand among his zoological and botanical specimens and his books.

Darwin's principal regret was the pain his theory caused those of religious persuasion, including his beloved wife Emma. He was personally shy of controversy and debate, and T. H. *Huxley was his champion in public, disarming even the formidable Bishop of Oxford, Samuel Wilberforce, at a celebrated meeting of the British Association for the Advancement of Science, at Oxford, on 30 June 1860, when Wilberforce ('Soapy Sam') asked Huxley: 'Is it on his grandfather's or his grandmother's side that the ape ancestry comes in?' Huxley replied (in a verbal battle during which Lady Brewster fainted) that 'a man has no reason to be ashamed of having an ape for his grandfather', and, 'if there were an ancestor whom I should feel shame in recalling, it would be a man of restless and versatile intellect who . . . plunges into scientific questions with which he has no real acquaintance, only to obscure them by an aimless rhetoric, and distract the attention of his hearers from the point at issue by eloquent digressions and skilled appeals to religious prejudice' (as reported by the historian J. R. Green 22 years later).

In addition to Darwin's books published in his lifetime, there are the notebooks that he kept to record and develop his ideas. Those named 'M' and 'N' record his growing ideas on mind, and man's place in nature. He was well aware that evolutionary accounts implied, or at least strongly suggested, that man's origin is in the animals that one may see in zoos. He ends the *Descent of Man*: 'with all his exalted powers—man still bears in his bodily frame the indelible stamp of his lowly origin'.

Realizing that mental characteristics can be passed on through generations, and assuming that only physical structures can be inherited, Darwin was forced to conclude that mind has a physical basis. On this ground he became a materialist—while aware that this would be painful to his wife Emma, to his friends, and more widely to all he would influence. He postponed for as long as possible his conclusions on the origin of man.

In Notebook 'N', writing at the time of his marriage, Darwin puts forward his theory of *blushing: that it depends on the person's awareness of the thought, or opinion, of another person. It is restricted to humans: 'animals, not being such thinking people, do not blush.' Darwin accepts blushing as evidence of *consciousness, and especially self-consciousness, but he rejects the notion of free will, saying that, although we experience ourselves as causal agents, desires and purposes do not arise from some special endowment but only from natural laws of thought, as we would see if only we could stand outside ourselves. We cannot stand outside ourselves, so, 'on my view of free will, no one could discover he had not it' (N 49). The notebooks are fascinating both for their insights and as documents of the slow, painful development of Darwin's thought: for here are the germs of most of the ideas worked out often much later in his books.   RLG

There is an enormous literature on Darwin's life and work. See his *Life and Letters* (1887) and *More Letters* (1903), edited by his son, Sir Francis Darwin, and his autobiography edited by his granddaughter, Lady Nora Barlow (1958). The voyage of the *Beagle* is described in Darwin's own words in *Charles Darwin and the Voyage of the Beagle*, ed. Nora Barlow (1945), and with many illustrations in Alan Moorhead, *Darwin and the Beagle* (1969). An interesting account of Darwin's mental development (together with the previously unpublished notebooks) is Howard E. Gruber, *Darwin* *on Man: A Psychological Study of Scientific Creativity* (1974). An excellent general study of his work and its implications is Gertrude Himmelfarb, *Darwin and the Darwinian Revolution* (1962). Dennett, D. C. (1995). *Darwin's Dangerous Idea*.

Darwin, Erasmus (1731–1802). British physician and scientist, the grandfather of both Charles *Darwin and Francis *Galton. He was born near Newark in Nottinghamshire, studied at Cambridge and Edinburgh, and became a successful physician at Lichfield in Staffordshire. He was well known for his radical opinions, his 3-hectare (8-acre) botanical garden, and for his books, including the long poem *The Botanic Garden* which appeared in two parts, *The Loves of the Plants* (1789) and *The Economy of Vegetation* (1791). His most important work was *Zoonomia, or The Laws of Organic Life* (1794–6), in which he anticipated *Lamarck's theory of evolution by the inheritance of acquired characteristics, and also, though somewhat vaguely, Charles Darwin's theory of evolution by natural selection. He was a founder member of the Lunar Society of Birmingham, the leading intellectual society of the Midlands, whose members included James Watt and Josiah Wedgwood.

King-Hele, D. (1963). *Erasmus Darwin*.
Krause, E. (1879). *Erasmus Darwin*. (Charles Darwin wrote an account of his grandfather for this volume.)

deduction. In the more general sense any process of reasoning by means of which one draws conclusions from principles or information already known. Thus Isaac Newton talks of making deductions from his experiments with prisms, and G. K. Chesterton's Father Brown, after visiting the scene of the crime, deduces that Flambeau was responsible. But within logic and philosophy deduction is contrasted with *induction. Frequently the contrast is made by use of a directional metaphor: by induction one moves from particular to general and from the less general to the more general, ascending the theoretical ladder which terminates in first principles; by deduction one moves from more general to less general and from general to particular, descending the theoretical ladder which terminates in facts about particular individuals or events. This image of the ascent and descent of reason is to be found in *Plato, *Aristotle, in many medieval treatises on logic, and also in the works of Francis *Bacon.

In the logic of scholastic tradition, deduction is equated with syllogistic inference, for it was by means of the definition and study of syllogisms and their possible forms that Aristotle introduced a framework for both a codification and a theoretical discussion of the principles of valid deductive inference, the kind of inference that can be accepted as providing proofs or demonstrations. The central idea here is that in a valid deductive argument the truth of the premises guarantees the truth of the conclusion; in some sense the conclusion is already contained in the premises. Thus Aristotle defined a syllogism as 'a discourse in which, certain things being stated, something other than what is stated follows of necessity from their being so. I mean by the last phrase that it follows because of them, and by this that no further term is required from without in order to make the consequence necessary' (*Prior Analytics*, 24b 18–23). But the further idea underlying the study of deductive inference, and indeed behind the notion of logic generally, is that this is a study of the principles of correct reasoning and that as such it must be independent of any particular subject matter about which we might want to reason. The laws of logic, if they are to be universally applicable, must thus concern the forms or structures of arguments only, omitting all reference to content. On Aristotle's account, which was dominant for 2,000 years, all deduction is a matter of establishing connections between general terms. He defines a proposition as 'a statement affirming or denying something of something' (24a 16). In other words, a (categorical) proposition is thought of as a statement that a certain relation holds between its subject S and its predicate P. Propositions are then classified according to the relation asserted to hold: Universal Affirmative—'All S are P' (SaP), Universal Negative—'No S are P' (SoP), Particular Affirmative—'Some S are P' (SiP), Particular Negative—'Some S are not P' (SoP). A syllogism is the making of a new connection between terms which goes via a third, or middle term. Syllogisms were traditionally classified into four figures according to the arrangement of their terms (although only the first three of these were recognized by Aristotle, who did not regard the fourth as a distinct figure). The figures are:

(1)	(2)	(3)	(4)
$S - M$	$M - S$	$S - M$	$M - S$
$M - P$	$M - P$	$P - M$	$P - M$
$\therefore S - P$	$\therefore S - P$	$\therefore S - P$	$\therefore S - P$

Thus an example of a valid first-figure syllogism would be:

SaM (All) whales are mammals.
MaP (All) *mammals are warm-blooded.*
$\therefore SaP$ $\therefore$ (All) whales are warm-blooded.

An example of a plausible but invalid first-figure syllogism would be:

SaM (All) larches are conifers.
MiP *Some conifers are deciduous.*
$\therefore SiP$ $\therefore$ Some larches are deciduous.

The invalidity of this form becomes obvious if 'Scots pine' is substituted for 'larch'. Any valid deduction will then be required to be reducible either to a syllogism or to a sequence of syllogisms which traces a chain of connections between the subject and predicate terms of its conclusion.

In the 17th and 18th centuries, partly as a result of the increased hold of nominalism, partly as a result of the dominance of a (Cartesian) thinking-subject-centred approach to philosophy, the Aristotelian view of deductive reasoning was internalized. Instead of referring to classes or to universals, general terms were taken as standing for ideas (mental representations). (Categorical) propositions are thus interpreted as assertions about the relations between ideas, and deductive reasoning becomes a matter of perceiving the relations between ideas. From this perspective the laws of logic become the laws of thought, laws basic to the structure of the human intellect and constitutive of its rationality.

This conception finds perhaps its clearest expression in Immanuel *Kant's *Critique of Pure Reason*. But it is here also that the seeds are sown of the fundamental revisions both in logic and in conceptions of the nature and structure of thought which were brought about as a result of the work of Gottlob Frege and others working in the late 19th and early 20th centuries. For Kant, in spite of his use of a very traditional Aristotelian framework for the construction of his table of judgements, (i) places primary emphasis on judgements as cognitive acts, rather than on ideas as the referents of general terms, and (ii) sees judgement as a matter of the application of a concept to an object according to a rule.

Frege strenuously rejected the idea that laws of logic are laws of thought. It was his view that, if a valid deductive argument is to be one where the *truth* of its premises guarantees the *truth* of its conclusion, the laws of logic must be laws of truth, founded on the way in which language represents reality, not on the nature of the psychological processes by means of which human beings represent reality to themselves and then manipulate these representations. But Frege did retain and build on the Kantian emphasis on judgement which gives logical priority to propositions rather than to terms. Deductive argument is now seen to depend on establishing relations between the possible truth values of propositions (thoughts) expressed by (indicative) sentences; the proposition becomes the basic logical unit and truth the fundamental semantic notion. The simplest (atomic) propositions are regarded as expressing the application of a concept to an object (symbolized as 'Fa'), where there is a fundamental asymmetry at both logical and ontological levels between concepts and objects. Concepts are treated by analogy with mathematical functions. This allowed Frege to develop a logical framework of much greater power and flexibility than Aristotle's. In particular it enabled him to incorporate arguments where the propositions involve relations and where the validity of the argument depends on the characteristics of the relation concerned, as, for example: 'A is heavier than B. B is heavier than C. Therefore A is heavier than C.' In addition, by the device of introducing quantifiers and bound variables, Frege was able to treat such statements as 'Every natural number has a successor' and 'There is no largest natural number'. Present logical systems all exploit the basic Fregean innovations.   MET

Aristotle (1949). *Prior and Posterior Analytics*. Rev. text with introd. and commentary by W. D. Ross.

Frege, G. (1960). *Philosophical Writings*. Sel. and trans. P. Geach and M. Black.

Kant, I. (1929). *The Critique of Pure Reason*. Trans. N. Kemp-Smith.

Kneale, W. and M. (1962). *The Development of Logic*.

déjà vu. 'It happened on my first visit to Paris. I was walking along one of those little streets in Montmartre, when I suddenly had the feeling that I'd been there before. It was all happening again . . . .'

This is a characteristic account of *déjà vu* (literally 'already seen')—the experience that one has witnessed some new situation or episode on a previous occasion. Perception of the scene is accompanied by a compelling sense of familiarity. Usually the sensation lasts only for a few seconds, but in some pathological cases it may be much more prolonged or, indeed, continuous. It is often accompanied by a conviction that one knows what is about to happen next—'When I reached the square, I knew what I was about to see . . . .'

The *déjà vu* experience is often reported by patients suffering from psychiatric disorders. It is known to be associated with temporal lobe lesions, and is one of the 'dreamy state' experiences characteristic of focal *epilepsy. But the phenomenon seems also to be experienced occasionally by the majority of normal people. Most commonly it occurs in youth, or under conditions of fatigue or heightened sensitivity.

Understandably, the sensation of having previously experienced the event in question suggests to the individual that he is recalling a previous occurrence. The present event is taken to be a 'second' occurrence; mystification and interest are thus focused upon the 'first' one. As the crucial aspect of *déjà vu* is that the individual knows that he has not in fact previously experienced the event, lay explanations often posit psychic or magical processes. Such 'explanations' usually attribute unusual talents or powers to the individual concerned. Thus, one obvious 'explanation' is that the event has been 'revealed' to the individual prior to its occurrence. In that case he has demonstrated precognition, and is the fortunate possessor of the 'sixth sense' or the power of prophecy. More commonly, lay explanations make the presumption that the event has, in fact, occurred on a previous occasion, and focus on how the individual could have gained his knowledge of that 'first' occurrence. A common explanation is that the individual experienced the 'first' event in a previous life. His *déjà vu* sensation may thus be taken as evidence for reincarnation. An associated view is that the 'first' event was witnessed by the individual but *through the eyes of another person*. He is therefore taken to possess telepathic gifts. The other witness may be hypothesized to have existed at another period in time. In that case the present individual is presumed to have mediumistic powers. A somewhat more subtle hypothesis is that the 'first' experience took place in a *dream, a proposition that accords well with the dreamlike quality of the *déjà vu* experience itself. The individual himself may feel, not that he has previously witnessed the event, but that he has previously *foretold* it. But there is never any evidence of his actual foretelling, nor does he recall ever having done so. Thus he may speculate that the events were revealed to him in a dream, which would explain his failure to recall consciously his presentiment in the interim. Technically, this feeling is a *pseudo-presentiment*, so termed because the belief is held only at the moment that he witnesses the event. A number of serious writers have maintained this 'dream' hypothesis.

As noted above, the last four explanations presuppose that *déjà vu* is attached to a *second* experiencing of the situation in question—in other words, that the individual is *remembering*. Several psychological and psychiatric authorities have also taken this view, classifying *déjà vu* as an example of paramnesia. For them the question becomes one not of how the individual could remember something that he has not experienced before, but of why he should *think* he has not experienced it before. The obvious assumption is that the original experience aroused distress in the individual, so that its recall would prove painful to him. The standard psychoanalytic explanation of *déjà vu* is that the original experience has been repressed and so, by definition, is no longer accessible to *memory. Any repetition of the experience cannot elicit conscious recall of the original occurrence. But it does constitute a 'reminder' to the ego, and it is this that is reflected in the *déjà vu* feeling.

A more prosaic explanation of *déjà vu* is that, although the overall situation is novel, a number of its component features have in fact been experienced before. For example, the observer may know for certain that he has never walked along this particular street before—indeed, he may never previously have visited the town or even the country in question. But there are many features which all streets have in common, and it is the combination of these specifics which brings some familiarity to this newly visited street. However, this suggestion applies more directly to what has been termed 'restricted paramnesia'. (An everyday example of 'restricted paramnesia' is the frustrating experience of being unable to identify a person whom one knows but in some other context.) There are pronounced phenomenological differences between the preoccupying puzzlement which accompanies a restricted paramnesia and the *déjà vu* experience. In the former, one is well aware of those aspects of the situation which have been experienced previously (such as the other person's facial features, expression, and voice). The perplexity arises from the inability to reconstruct the totality of the previous experience (for example, the circumstances and context of previous encounters). In *déjà vu*, the *whole* of the new experience seems familiar, and so does the ensuing progression of events. Typically, the paramnesia experience is described in terms such as: 'I knew that I had met him before, but for the life of me I couldn't remember who he was . . . .' Whereas *déjà vu* is described as: 'I felt that I had lived through it all before, but knew that I hadn't.'

Two other suggestions should be mentioned. The first one, once held by psychologists, stresses the affective component and classifies *déjà vu* as a paradoxical emotional experience. The argument would be that the sense of familiarity has reference, not to the characteristics of the situation, but to the observer's feelings. It is postulated that these are a carry-over of the emotional state associated with the preceding situation. The second suggestion is of more recent origin and focuses upon neurological function. Here the argument is that the two hemispheres of the brain may temporarily lose synchronicity. Thus the anomalous feeling of familiarity may be due to the fact that one side of the brain is receiving input a fraction of a second after the other.

A more fruitful psychological approach to the consideration of *déjà vu* may be to de-emphasize the recall aspect, with its presumption of a 'previous event', and approach the experience in terms of its other name: *fausse reconnaissance* (false recognition). Instead of 'Why is the observer unable to remember the previous situation?' the question now becomes: 'Why does the observer feel that he recognizes the present situation?' This, indeed, was the approach taken by Pierre *Janet, who was one of the first psychologists to identify, describe, and analyse the experience. He considered *déjà vu* to be one outcome of the obsessional incapacity for active and adequate response to the pressures of reality. The essence of *déjà vu*, he suggested, is not the 'affirmation of the past'; it is the 'negation of the present'. It is not a question of how the observer *remembers* a previous event, but how he *perceives* the present one.

At first sight, the classification of our topic as an anomaly of recognition rather than one of recall does not seem to offer any easier road to explanation. Certainly, conventional laboratory studies of recognition would seem to offer nothing which might throw light upon the *déjà vu* experience. However, consideration of the views of F. C. *Bartlett, as presented in his classic work *Remembering*, may yield some clues. Bartlett's central point, which has been re-emphasized by contemporary cognitive theorists,

was that long-term memory is a dynamic, constructive process. We do not recall an event in its original form, nor even in a merely attenuated version. We *reconstruct* it, drawing upon the *schemata or cognitive structures into which the perceived components of the event were organized. Thus, what is reconstructed during recall or reproduction shows not only omissions and abbreviations but elaborations and distortions.

On each occasion that we recall any given event, further distortions or elaborations are introduced. It could be said that in a series of recollections we are not recalling the original event at all, but our last recollection of it. The longer the series the more the remembered version will differ from the original, because each further recollection will involve distortions of distortions and elaborations of elaborations. If this line of argument (for which there is considerable experimental as well as observational evidence) is applied to the examination of recognition, some interesting implications emerge. Basically, recognition involves the acceptance of a 'good fit' or match of currently perceived material with recalled, imagined material. The better the level of match, the more pronounced will be the accompanying sense of familiarity. In the case of personal experiences, the familiarity includes an added dimension of personal identification. Clearly, the more often an original event has been recalled, the more modifications will have been introduced, and the weaker the subjective fit between our current recollection and any representation of the actual original material. Conversely, the sense of familiarity may now be evoked by the perception of material which differs considerably from the actual original, given that the differences are in line with the distortions and elaborations present in our recollection. If we have good reason to believe that it would be quite impossible for us to have actually experienced this new material previously, then our feeling of familiarity is naturally highly perplexing. It may well be that this perplexity, resulting from the discrepancy between objective knowledge and subjective feeling, constitutes what is termed *déjà vu*.

In that case, why is the experience so rare? Perhaps the problem is not why *déjà vu* occurs, but why it does not occur more frequently. There are several possible answers. One is that perhaps it does occur commonly, but that we register it only under certain conditions. But at the same time, it is probable that there are relatively few occasions when we can be objectively certain that we have not experienced the criterion situation previously. A first visit to a geographic area is one such example. Other cases where the total situation may be labelled emphatically as a personal 'first time' event are often ones of a heightened emotive nature, where we are likely to be more sensitive to our subjective state and more vulnerable to feelings of anxiety and perplexity. It should be noted that while we may be acutely aware that a given situation is a personal 'first', we have almost certainly experienced it at second hand, through descriptions, literary accounts, or films. Perhaps the obvious examples are marriage ceremonies, job interviews, and funerals. And it is of interest that, after the 'strange town' example, these are the very situations in which people most commonly report experiencing *déjà vu*.

Purely psychological explanations of the kind discussed are hardly sufficient when the *déjà vu* experience is part of an epileptic aura. In this situation one might presume that the spontaneous electrical discharge in an area of the brain (the temporal lobe) particularly concerned with memory has reactivated a distant memory from the memory store, which is now perceived as something the patient has previously experienced—as, indeed, he probably has. *Penfield's brain-stimulation studies on patients undergoing neurosurgical operations might be considered as supportive of such an explanation of the *déjà vu* phenomenon, at least in cases when it is associated with temporal lobe epilepsy. GFR

delirium. Delirium has been described as 'An aetiologically non-specific syndrome characterized by concurrent disturbances of consciousness and attention, perception, thinking, memory, psychomotor behaviour, emotion, and the sleep-wake cycle' (World Health Organization, ICD-10).

Delirium was described in *European Psychiatry* by Bonhoeffer (1909) as a syndrome consistently associated with brain failure. He regarded chaotic, incoherent thought as a central feature. Following further investigations Wolff and Curran (1935) confirmed the main features described by Bonhoeffer and others but added that the content of the syndrome had emanated to a considerable extent from previous experience and premorbid personality. Engel and Romano (1959) reported that the EEG showed abnormalities in the form of high-voltage discharges from rhythmic high-voltage delta waves which were in accord with the severity of the physical symptomatology.

At a later stage Lipowski (1990) described two main relatively distinct versions of the clinical picture. In the first, patients were restless, overactive, oversensitive, often with persecutory delusions. In the second the patients tended to be retarded, inactive, silent, and muddled in thought. Visual distortion and hallucinations often of a vivid and terrifying character were a common feature, mainly in the overactive subgroup.

Delirium is a common form of mental illness among aged persons. It is also manifest at earlier stages of the lifespan but its peak prevalence has been found to be at the latter end of life.

In recent decades extensive studies have been devoted to delineating its clinical features, formulating reliable criteria for its diagnosis from other mental disorders of late life, and identifying factors involved in its causation or predisposing individuals to its development. The importance of delirium is derived from a number of different features. In a high proportion of cases the disorder is life threatening, commonly caused by a serious and acute physical illness. The effect of terror and excitement that is manifest at the height of the illness in more than half of cases may cause death by a combination of exhaustion and the effects associated with physical illness. However, in cases where acute disease is benign and there is a response to treatment, the symptoms of delirium subside and recovery from the attack leaves no deficit.

The patient is grossly disoriented in respect of time, date, and place. All aspects of memory function, registration, retention, and recall are severely impaired. He is unable to perceive or to interpret his environment and is incapable of new learning. He cannot explain how and why he has been admitted to hospital. There is impaired awareness and inattention to the outside world. This is associated with disturbing inner experiences dominated by hallucinations and delusions. Speech tends to be more or less incoherent and the capacity to understand communications from others is impaired. Any statement that penetrates into consciousness is rapidly wiped off the slate of memory.

Anxiety and agitation, mounting often into severe and sustained bouts of distress, are the most common and prominent reactions to these symptoms. In the course of long attacks of delirium a strong depressive colouring enters. In other cases, psychotic, depressive illness, or bipolar disorders in a setting of physical illness form the starting point of the delirium and constitute a suicide risk. Treatment with antidepressants and psychotherapy has to be provided in association with management of any concomitant acute physical illness.

Delirium is a many-sided and serious illness particularly in aged persons. The patient has to be kept under close observation in disturbed episodes to provide reassurance and explanation and to protect him from the suicide risk which is manifest in a proportion of cases. However, within a few hours the clinical picture can be entirely transformed. It arises from the marked fluctuation over time in the severity and the clinical profile manifest in the disorder of consciousness suffered by the majority of those affected. A patient who was indubitably delirious during one evening may by noon on the following day appear to be free from symptoms and signs. These phenomena are more fully described below.

Lishman (1987) described the main features of impaired consciousness as slow deterioration of thinking, attending, perceiving, and remembering, a combination that suggests general deterioration of cognitive functions combined with reduced awareness of the environment.

Impairment may be ill considered and it is difficult to establish, with confidence, whether or not consciousness is impaired. Abnormality of the *EEG, which is usual in a high proportion of cases, provides valuable information for the delirious state (Roth and Myers 1962) (Figs. 1 and 2).

The main clinical features have been lucidly and succinctly set out in the fourth edition of the *Diagnostic and Statistical Manual of Mental Disorders* (DSM-IV) of the American Psychiatric Association (1994). The diagnostic criteria are:

(a) Disturbance of consciousness (i.e. reduced clarity of awareness of the environment) with reduced ability to focus, sustain, or shift attention.

(b) A change in cognition (such as memory deficit, disorientation, language disturbance) or the development of a perceptual disturbance that is not better accounted for by pre-existing, established, or evolving dementia.

(c) Disturbance develops over a short period of time (usually hours) and tends to fluctuate during the course of the day.

(d) There is evidence from the history, physical examination, or laboratory findings that the disturbance is caused by the direct physiological consequence of the general medical condition.

1. Related disorders
2. Causation
3. Aspects of treatment
4. Some future perspectives

1. Related disorders

The stages of delirium in which the patient is disoriented, confused, incoherent in speech, deluded, and hallucinating are generally regarded as exhibiting the features of the unconscious phase of delirious phenomena.

There are two syndromes that show that this unconsciousness is unusual, in that it is characterized by perception usually associated with beliefs that have undergone some scrutiny and have been modified by ideas generally associated with consciousness rather than consistent and severe delirious states.

In most cases of anosognosia the patient has suffered hemiplegia and hemi-anaesthesia following a stroke, but in a minority the lesions are in the left, or non-dominant, hemisphere. Most of these patients are left-handed. On examination, if asked to lift his paralysed left arm, the patient will lift his right arm instead. When attention is drawn to his inappropriate response he makes excuses. The left arm has gone to sleep or has been overworked and is too painful to move. In some cases he will insist that the arm in question belongs to the man in the next bed. He may address it by a special name and refer to it in

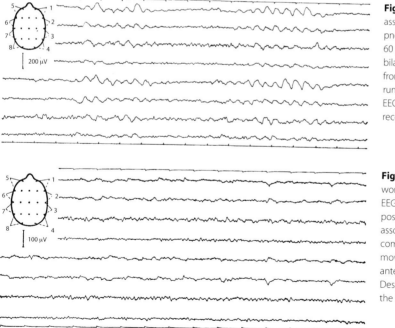

Fig. 1. A severe delirium associated with bronchopneumonia in a woman of 60 years of age. EEG shows bilaterally synchronous frontally predominant 2 c/s runs of delta activity. The EEG returned to normal after recovery.

Fig. 2. Senile dementia in a woman of 80 years of age. EEG shows dominant posterior rhythm at 7–8 c/s associated with irregular theta components, and eye movement artefacts in anteriorly recording channels. Despite advanced dementia, the EEG abnormality is slight.

derisory terms. The patient's posture is characteristic. He lies in bed and is found to pay no attention to the left half of the space and turns towards the right. He is usually in a good, friendly mood and in conversation smiles a great deal in a childish way. The smile and his relative normality of speech in simple conversations may lead to his level of consciousness and mental state as a whole being regarded as normal. Detailed evaluation reveals subtle cognitive deficits.

There are defects of memory for recent events and misinterpretations of his environment, which he may describe as a railway station or as a prison cell, despite being apparently fully alert. Attempts to inform him of the true diagnosis of his condition may be swiftly rejected, sometimes in aggressive tones, and reveal features of dissociation and denial of obvious phenomena. The incongruous, unchanging, smiling face he displays led Paul Schilder (1935) to describe this condition as 'organic hysteria'. The reason is that in this condition a painful truth registered in consciousness is being repressed into the unconscious on account of the patient's inability to assimilate and face up to a threatening piece of reality which he inwardly recognizes as possibly a lasting hemiplegic paralysis and which resembles typical hysterical dissociation and affect.

This interesting hypothesis shows that the vigilance of normal consciousness is not entirely in abeyance even in states of organic separation from normal conscious mental life, and a small element of reality has managed to penetrate the mental curtain of delirium, so creating distortion of reality.

The second variant of consciousness is the phenomenon of double orientation, which is in certain respects similar to anosognosia. A brief account of a case with a typical disorder of this nature was a 58-year-old man with a left hemiparesis who was admitted to hospital in Chichester following a stroke that had supervened after a haemorrhage from an aneurysm on his cerebral artery. When asked to name the city where he was born he said he was born in Edinburgh and added that it was very near Chichester, just outside the walls. He wore a faint smile when he spoke on this subject. As his delirious attack began to improve, the location of his whereabouts began to move north. When questioned about orientation first he mentioned Chichester then London, Stamford, York, Durham, Newcastle, Berwick on Tweed, then Haddington, and finally Edinburgh, this last name when his recovery of his hemiparesis was virtually complete. He had worn the same incongruous smile as a patient with anosognosia and also resisted correction in the same way.

The development and reversal of such chinks of reality with a small part of the truth, which continues to survive in the records that sustain the correct picture of the outside world, are suppressed by intact emotional factors.

2. Causation

The main common causes of delirium are cardiac disorders, such as congestive cardiac failure or dysrhythmia, almost any infection in the elderly, drug intoxication (with benzodiazepines, barbiturates), alcohol (including abrupt withdrawal), anticholinergic drugs, antidepressants, cardiovascular drugs, anti-Parkinsonian agents, metabolic disorders, electrolyte disturbances, liver or renal failure, endocrine factors (myxoedema), sensory deprivation, e.g. with visual and auditory impairment, urinary retention or constipation, central-nervous-system (CNS) disorders, Alzheimer's or multi-infarct dementia, cerebrovascular disease and complications. Loss by death of a member of the family, interconnection with an organic factor, association with a near-threshold level of intoxication with a drug administered over a period may cause delirium of abrupt onset.

After depressive illness delirium is the second most highly prevalent form of mental disorder among aged persons, recorded as being responsible for 15–20 per cent of aged persons admitted to hospital geriatric departments. Early arrival at the correct diagnosis is important for a number of reasons.

In a high proportion the condition is caused by organic factors in the brain or in some non-cerebral organ. The recovery rate following treatment is high and in treatable cases the delirious state is abolished.

A mistaken diagnosis of dementia in severe cases delays prompt treatment. An accurate history helps to establish the correct diagnosis. An important clue is provided by the abrupt development, onset having begun days or weeks previously in dementia, where the history usually extends back months or even years. EEG helps discrimination in difficult cases; high-voltage discharges from rhythmic high-voltage delta waves are characteristic (Engel and Romano 1959).

Symptomatology is abolished in a high proportion of persons but may end in grave illness in a pre-terminal stage. After the first few days of treatment, a fluctuating course is manifest in the patient's mental state and the findings on clinical examination of the mental state have been supported and can receive a definite diagnosis.

Clinical and psychological evaluation shows the patient disoriented, unable to comprehend that he is in hospital and the reasons for his admission. All categories of memory function are impaired and in severe cases in complete abeyance. He is fearful, agitated, and usually deluded and hallucinated. Visual hallucinations are characteristic. The nurse a few yards away is a prison warder or guard in a concentration camp. Irregular cracks in the paintwork are interpreted as writhing snakes. He fails to recognize members of his family paying him a visit and they may be dismissed as impostors. His mood is fearful, agitated to the point of panic, and he may attempt to escape. The consciousness of such a patient in this phase is clouded and impaired in all respects. He is awake but can be regarded as enacting a nightmare, with all mental factors in abeyance, or severely distorted and inadequate so as to falsify his perceptions of the world around him.

There are, however, fluctuations which take the form of intervals of mental lucidity in the mental state lasting a few hours to 1–2 days, during which the features of the phases of impaired consciousness remain in abeyance and a relatively normal mental state is manifest. These phases are the lucid interludes of delirious states. The main features are due to the re-entry of consciousness to mental functioning and the simultaneous elimination of hallucinations, cognitive failure, anxiety, and depression and the revival of speech. That the 'state of impaired consciousness' results essentially from the extinction of the main cognitive, affective, and perceptual abnormalities of limitation of consciousness is confirmed by renewed observations in the late afternoon and evening the same day reveals that the sequence of change that accompanied the lucid reminiscences goes progressively into reverse. The first change is the reappearance of slow activity.

In the first state of impaired consciousness of the delirious state described above, although the patient seems awake, he is in fact virtually unconscious. He is able to remember little or nothing and to register and recall little or nothing.

We can refer to the second state as the 'lucid phase'. In the more normal stages of the delirious state the patient may be regarded as conscious but one would note minor impairments.

The episode of near normality during attacks of delirium occurs regularly but fluctuation is observed in most prolonged delirious states. After sunset, as darkness begins to descend, delirious patients tend to become confused, chaotic in their speech, and fearful. Their hallucinations and delusions are awakened. Their behaviour is restless and they may try to escape. By the following morning clouding begins to recede and by mid-morning or lunchtime the patient's mental functioning has returned to a normal state with only minor impediments. The difference between the two states is that, during the lucid intervals in the morning and early afternoon, the patient's mind is unequivocally in a conscious state. During the clouded phase, at its worst during the night, consciousness is in abeyance. These two states deserve to be compared with each other with the aid of detailed clinical criteria and distinguished by evaluation with standardized psychological tests.

The behaviour of the person during the awake-lucid phases is close to that of his normal self. He is aware from conversation that he has been ill and is able to describe and discuss his symptoms, though his memory is blank for experiences during the clouded phase.

3. Aspects of treatment

As most cases of delirium have a specific physical cause, treatment should be initially focused on elimination of this factor by full investigation and active, specific steps in treatment. Details of nursing care are important. The patient is often confused or ignorant of his whereabouts and repeated explanations have to be given and attempts made to correct his frightening misconceptions by regular, repeated accounts of where he is, banishing beliefs that he is in a prison, a concentration camp, or even a nightclub.

In most specialist centres the patient is treated in a quiet room. But this is not carried to an extreme. Related persons and familiar ones are encouraged to pay him regular visits and are advised to help him comprehend where he is and why he has been sent there and to provide reassurance.

The patient is neither nursed in complete darkness nor exposed to the opposite extreme of bright, intense illumination as both are harmful. In the initial stages sedation should be provided to ensure sleep which has a healing effect. Phenothiazines such as chlorpromazine or haloperidol are usually given. Short-acting benzodiazepines may be needed to ensure sleep. Chlormethazole is generally used in alcoholic cases but its withdrawal requires to be undertaken under close observation in hospital.

4. Some future perspectives

The progress of delirious states deserves to be explored from the beginning to end with the aid of clinical examination with rating scales and standardized cognitive tests and EEGs at regular intervals. The last is valuable in that, during the clouded phase, slow activity at high voltage is manifest at an early stage and gradually declines in parallel with an improvement in symptomatology.

Such enquiries might shed fresh light on the neuropsychological activities underlying delirium. It might also make some contribution to advancing understanding of the contribution of consciousness in mental life as a whole which has baffled clinicians, scientists, and philosophers in their different aspects down the ages. Studies of the phenomenology of the fluctuations between the disturbed and the quiescent phases of delirious illness and their neural correlates would be valuable. There are also related questions that are open to empirical investigation. A systematic comparison of the mental state of patients during the height of delirium and the mental state when normal consciousness has been restored for a period would provide valuable preliminary evidence in an approach to this problem. Comparative studies of the awakened and clouded phases of the delirious states with modern techniques of magnetic resonance imaging (MRI) as well as EEG would be of interest.

It would also require detailed clinical and psychological assessment of each of the cognitive, emotional, perceptual, behavioural, and physiological items. Clinical observations taken over periods of several hours might serve to define a number of deficits and abnormal features and their association with physiological measurements which are manifest during delirious phases but absent during periods of remission.

In this connection the results obtained in a comparative enquiry of patients with dementia and delirium and with schizophrenia of old age and depression is relevant. The data from 50 years ago was obtained with the aid of three standardized scales—the Wechsler–Bellvue Scale, Raven's Progressive Matrices, a special information test, and a diagnostic rating scale.

The distribution of scores of those with Alzheimer's or the vascular form of dementia was quite distinct from patients with depressive and schizophrenic disorders (Hopkins and Roth 1953, Roth and Hopkins 1953). It proved possible to undertake the tests in those with delirious states. The scores overlapped in a striking manner with those recorded in patients with the non-demented state, namely depressive and schizophrenic disorders. But it is plain that a diagnosis of delirious disorder cannot be made on the strength of cognitive tests alone. No attempt has been made to grade, measure, and report on the level of general awareness as inferred from clinical and EEG data. The problem outlined here had not been formulated. It is noteworthy that those with senile dementia who had much more serious physical illness with severe progressive cerebral damage as the main cause but no 'impaired consciousness' were judged to exclude a diagnosis of Alzheimer's disease. None of the cases was complicated by the delirious state. Further enquiries into the questions posed here might shed light on delirious disorder and also serve to define some of the features that separate the seemingly awake and responsive delirious persons from those who are in a fully awake and conscious state.

MaR

American Psychiatric Association (1994). *Diagnostic and Statistical Manual of Mental Disorders*. (DSM-IV) (4th edn.).

Bonhoeffer, K. (1909). 'Exogenous psychoses'. *Zentralblatt für Nervernheilkunde*, 32. Trans. H. Marshall in Hirsch, S. R., and Shepherd, M. (eds.), *Themes and Variations in European Psychiatry* (1974).

Engel, G. L., and Romano, J. (1959). 'Delirium: a syndrome of cerebral insufficiency'. *Journal of Chronic Diseases*, 9.

Hopkins, B., and Roth, M. (1953). 'Psychological test performance in patients over sixty. II: Paraphrenia, arteriosclerotic psychosis and acute confusion'. *Journal of Mental Science*, 99.

Lipowski, Z. J. (1990). *Delirium: Acute Confusional States*.

Lishman, W. A. (1987). *Organic Psychiatry* (2nd edn.).

Roth, M., and Hopkins, B. (1953). 'Psychological test performance in patients over sixty. I: Senile psychoses and the affective disorders of old age'. *Journal of Mental Science*, 99.

—— and Myers, D. H. (1969). 'The diagnosis of dementia'. *British Journal of Hospital Medicine*.

Schilder, P. (1935). *The Image and Appearance of the Human Body*.

Wolff, H. G., and Curran, D. (1935). 'Nature of delirium and allied states'. *Archives of Neurology and Psychiatry*, 35.

World Health Organization (1993). *International Classification of Disease*, 10th revision (ICD-10).

delusion. A delusion is a fixed, idiosyncratic belief, unusual in the culture to which the person belongs. Unlike normal beliefs, which are subject to amendment or correction, a delusion is held to, despite evidence or arguments brought against it. Delusions are usually taken to indicate mental illness, but something akin to them is occasionally to be observed, at a meeting of scientists, for instance, when a person insists on the correctness of an idea he overvalues, and denies any significance to evidence appearing to refute it. There is a difference: usually he gets angry, whereas in mental illness the patient's emotional response when a delusion is challenged tends to be bland or otherwise inappropriate.

Extravagant ideas are relatively common at times of frustration. A driver, frustrated when his car does not start, may allege serious deficiencies in all the cars made in the same country as his. This is to overgeneralize from the particular. Similarly, a student who has failed a test may feel for a while that he has failed as a student or, more generally still, as a person. Such feelings if they persist would amount to a delusion of unworthiness. Or he may conclude that his teachers are hostile to him, or that the world is against him. A persistent idea of this kind, especially if a person believes that there is a conspiracy or concerted action against him, is a delusion of persecution. A fixed belief that he is physically ill or, more extreme, that his organs are rotting or are destroyed, is a hypochondriacal delusion; that he does not exist or is nothing, a nihilistic delusion; that he has an exalted position or powers, a delusion of grandeur.

There is often sense in delusions, although it may be expressed extravagantly or confusingly. A man who declares that his wife is persistently unfaithful to him may be understood to mean that she has had sexual intercourse on many occasions with others. He is deluded if he insists unreasonably that this is so, in which case he is probably an example of the morbid jealousy syndrome; but he may only wish to convey his feelings that she no longer shows love or concern for him, feelings for which there might be some justification.

A delusion may persist because it explains what would otherwise cause *anxiety. Soldiers serving under stressful conditions occasionally express the belief that 'they' are putting bromide into the soup. The meaning of this belief emerges when added to it is the belief that aphrodisiacs are being put into the soup of other units. It serves to explain, for those who hold it, the changes produced by the stressful conditions in the pattern of occurrence of penile erections. Some bizarre delusions are unlabelled metaphors. A mentally ill girl says that she is the Virgin Mary. What perhaps she means is that she feels that she is still a virgin although she fears she is pregnant. The delusion, with its implication of her essential goodness, mitigates the intense anxiety which being seduced and becoming pregnant would otherwise evoke.

Why are delusions resistant to modification in the light of other evidence? In this respect they are similar to the behaviours, characteristic of neurosis, which persist although they appear to be maladaptive. It is supposed that they persist because, being instrumental in reducing anxiety, they are reinforced.

This is only part of an explanation of delusions, which, with *hallucinations, are the cardinal symptoms of some forms of mental illness. In cases of paranoid *schizophrenia, the patient may reveal, as well as hallucinations, a more or less coherent system of delusions of persecution and grandeur, without showing any awareness of how abnormal the ideas he expresses are. In other cases of schizophrenia, the delusions may be contradictory and incoherent. Severely disabling are hypochondriacal delusions, especially when they are associated with symptoms of *depersonalization, the patient then feeling that he has changed in personality with loss of his sense of identity; this may amount to a nihilistic delusion. Delusions of unworthiness occur in depressive illnesses in association with misery and hopelessness.

See also PARANOIA. DRD

dementia. This is defined by W. A. Lishman (1978) as 'an acquired global impairment of intellect, memory, and personality but without impairment of consciousness'. Although often considered to be an irreversible condition, recent studies have shown that about 10 per cent of patients with dementia have conditions for which treatment can reverse the otherwise inexorable decline of mental function. The progressive dementias are most often diagnosed in the elderly under the headings of senile dementia of the Alzheimer type and multi-infarct dementia. The former is caused by widespread degeneration of nerve cells in the brain and their replacement by elements known as plaques and neurofibrillary tangles. Postmortem studies of the brains of patients who have died from senile dementia have enabled correlation of the numbers of these elements with the degree of mental impairment shown by psychometric testing during life. Multi-infarct dementia, which is less common than senile dementia, is caused by loss of brain substance following repeated closure of small or large blood vessels, incidents that cause minor or major strokes. The older term, arteriosclerotic dementia, has now been superseded.

These areas of degeneration may be widespread and scattered, or concentrated in certain areas of the brain. If the latter, the mental changes will be much more severe in some functions than in others. For instance, the person may lose his speech (developing *aphasia) but not his memory, or vice versa. One of the last things usually to be affected is his basic personality, and some of the last skills to be lost are the social ones. Hence some demented persons will retain the major features of personality, remaining well mannered, considerate, and responsive if these were the former characteristics. On the other hand, blunting of emotion and loss of control of social behaviour may lead to episodes of petulant and irritable behaviour or tactless and inappropriate remarks which would not have been uttered before the onset of the illness.

The difference between dementia and the more limited losses of mental ability due to focal injuries is that the demented person can seldom make compensations for his disabilities in the way the others do, and, indeed, very often seems to be unaware of them. He tends to live his life entirely for the present moment, although the present for him may be an era from his own distant past.

Although it is characteristic of the truly demented person that he has little insight into his defects, inability to cope with his environment may make him severely perplexed, or trigger off a condition described by Kurt Goldstein (1878–1965) and called by him the 'catastrophic reaction'. The individual becomes tearful and angry; he may repeat non-adaptive stereotyped movements in a repetitive manner, or start sweating and becoming restless. The 'emotional lability' that accompanies dementia is one of its outstanding characteristics and helps to differentiate it from true *depression, in which the individual remains sad and retarded no matter how his circumstances alter. Dementia must also be differentiated from another, much less common form of emotional disorder: that accompanying bulbar palsy, in which the individual may respond to any sudden stimulus or strong effort by screwing up his face and bursting into tears, without any of the unhappiness that usually causes such outbursts. 'I just can't help crying,' he may be able to tell you between spasms. 'Don't pay any attention to me.' In contrast to both of these, the emotional state of the demented person seems to reflect exactly the situation of the moment. If he is faced with a problem too difficult for him to solve, he shows all the signs of distress, but if this is removed and he is presented with a simpler one, the next moment he will be laughing and cheerful. It follows that even severe dementia may not necessarily cause its sufferer any personal pain, depending on where and how he is cared for. If his environment is simple, cheerful, and constant (i.e. unchanging) he may to all outward appearances (and on his own admission) be perfectly cheerful and contented.

It is important to distinguish dementia from the other disorders which commonly affect the elderly, as, although there is, as yet, no known method of retarding or reversing dementia, many of the other conditions are fully treatable. In the speech disorders of dementia, comprehension is usually just as badly affected as expression, whereas in the aphasia due to focal lesions this is very rare. Moreover, the errors made when trying to name objects are rather different. The aphasic person usually manages to indicate that he knows perfectly well what the object is even though he cannot find its name, but the demented person often seems to fail to recognize the object too. If asked to name different parts of his body, the aphasic person can usually name those parts that are commonly mentioned (such as feet, hands, and arms) but not those less frequently so (knuckles, eyebrows, ankles); in the demented there is seldom any difference.

The failure of memory seen in senile dementia is also different from that seen in normal old age (see AGEING) or in the organic *amnesic conditions. In the latter, cues or prompts very often help, but in the demented they seem rather to do the opposite. If one considers recall as being like searching for an item in a vast territory, a cue for the amnesic narrows the field of search and directs his attention to a specific area; for the demented, it seems to direct him to a new part of the field. For instance, if the target is the word 'cart', a useful cue for an amnesic would be the words 'Horse and——'. A case of senile dementia might respond by saying, 'Horse? Yes, I remember we had many horses when I was a child, one particular one . . .'.

The ability to handle and manipulate objects is usually little impaired in dementia. Those motor skills which were learned in the past are well retained, but since he is inclined to forget what he is aiming to achieve before he has half done it, the demented person gets himself into difficulties. At first appearance he may seem to be suffering from apraxia (the loss of such skills due to focal lesions), but closer study will reveal differences. For example, both apraxic and demented individuals often have difficulty dressing themselves, but in the case of the apraxic the difficulty is due to 'forgetting' how to tie knots, do up buttons, or put an arm into a sleeve; in the demented it is due to forgetting whether he is supposed to be getting dressed or undressed at the time. When preparing meals—even such a simple task as making a pot of tea—the apraxic forgets how to put tea into the pot or stir it with a spoon; the demented can do all these things, if reminded constantly of the task in hand, but if distracted at all is liable to lose track of how far he has got and has to start from the beginning again.

Finally, there are two conditions that may be easily mistaken for dementia. The first is a severe depressive illness which may produce the condition sometimes called pseudodementia which only a skilled psychiatrist can distinguish from true dementia, but which responds to appropriate antidepressant treatment. The second is a delirious state, triggered off in an old person by physical disorder such as pneumonia, a heart attack, or hypothermia. Unlike dementia, which usually comes on slowly over a long period, delirious states are likely to appear suddenly and will be accompanied by severe disorientation and even *hallucinations. These symptoms, however, clear up completely once the underlying physical disorder is rectified, and in former days it was quite common for an old person to 'wake up' after such an illness and find himself in a mental hospital labelled, to his great consternation, a case of senile dementia.   MWI

Lishman, W. A. (1978). *Organic Psychiatry.*
Miller, E. (1977). *Abnormal Ageing.*
Ritchie, K., and Lovestone, S. (2002). 'The dementias'. *Lancet*, 360.
Roth, M., and Iverson, L. L. (eds.) (1986). 'Alzheimer's disease and related disorders'. *British Medical Bulletin*, 42.
Williams, M. (1979). *Brain Damage, Behaviour and the Mind.*

dendrite. One of the branching small neural processes carrying signals to the cell body of a neuron (nerve cell).

denotation. One of several words (the most common alternative is 'reference') used by logicians and philosophers for the relation between a fragment of language and that part or aspect of the world that is used to introduce it into discourse. The paradigm of the relation is that of a proper name to its bearer, but it is a matter of dispute what to say about proper names (and other grammatical subject expressions) which lack a bearer; and it is a matter of dispute whether and how the relationship applies in the case of predicate expressions. It is common to identify the denotation (reference) of a predicate expression with its extension, i.e. the class of all things to which it applies. Those who are prepared to recognize the existence of universals are often inclined to treat predicate expressions as denoting these. For J. S. *Mill a general term like 'man' names the class of men, and denotes the indefinite number of individuals who belong to that class, while it *connotes* the attribute which is signified by 'humanity' (cf. 'white' connotes what 'whiteness' signifies), as well as any attributes implied by this, such as animal life and rationality. All such attributes comprise the connotation of 'man'.

Mill's distinction between denotation and connotation is often confused with Frege's distinction between reference (*Bedeutung*) and sense (*Sinn*); but for Frege the sense of an expression is the manner in which it refers, and this made it possible for him to hold that proper names have a sense, whereas Mill denied that proper names have a connotation.   JET

Frege, G. (1952). 'On sense and reference'. In Geach, P. T., and Black, M., *Translations from the Philosophical Writings of Gottlob Frege*.

Mill, J. S. (1879). *A System of Logic*.

depersonalization. States of depersonalization have been recognized over a long period and there are some eloquent descriptions in the writings of mystics, saints, and poets such as Wordsworth. The condition began to attract the interest of non-medical psychologists towards the end of the 19th century. The modern era began with a number of contributions from Paul Schilder (1928, 1935) and Willy Mayer-Gross (1935).

Depersonalization is a mental state in which the individual perceives himself to be detached and physically separated from his own body and his own mental activities. In this experience the self is felt to be divided into an observed and an observing self. When attacks are consistent or frequent, feelings of unreality and associated experiences cause great distress. Depersonalization may occur in association with a wide range of mental disorders, depression, schizophrenia, obsessive–compulsive neurosis, and a range of organic disorders including temporal lobe epilepsy and other cerebral diseases, taking drugs such as cannabis, LSD, Ecstasy or sudden withdrawal from stimulating drugs such as dextroamphetamine.

Fleeting, short-lived symptoms of depersonalization may also occur in normal subjects. In contemporary usage the secondary disorders are excluded from the illness named as 'primary depersonalization'. This diagnosis is confined to chronic states of unreality. The transient states of normal subjects mentioned above are also excluded since they are neither distressing nor predictive of future breakdown into severe and disabling forms of depersonalization.

Most cases of depersonalization commence in adolescence or under the age of 35 years and usually pursue a chronic course with some measure of fluctuation in severity.

The experience of depersonalization has a number of components which overlap to some extent and interact with each other. A central feature is the patient's complaint that he feels unreal, deprived of his previous traits as a person in a world which appears distant, alien, and dreamlike. He has become a stranger to himself, excluded from his environment and from events in his community. He doubts his own identity. Such experiences are intensified by the patient's reflection in a mirror which seems unfamiliar. When his own name is spoken the sense of unreality intensifies. He fears a sudden failure of memory and lapse into total blankness.

A second prominent feature is the blunting of emotion or its total absence. The patient can experience neither love nor hate, neither pain nor pleasure. He complains of having become a stranger to himself and there are long periods in which he feels dead, loveless, and a mere automaton. Yet emotional responses are preserved and he exhibits natural affective reactions; facial expressions may appear lively and responsive when he is exposed to emotional stimulation.

A third feature is the presence, in a substantial proportion of individuals, of a cluster of changes of perception. Objects in the environment may appear unique, enlarged or minute. Other features include the *déjà vu* phenomenon (the illusory sense of having previously experienced percepts recorded in current experience) and panoramic memory, in which patients report recapitulation in their minds of a succession of, or all of, the experiences in a large part of their lifespan. These features are reminiscent of disturbance in the activity of the limbic system due to a structural lesion such as that in temporal lobe epilepsy and other neurological lesions. Penfield and Jasper (1947) reported that stimulating the exposed temporal lobe during neurosurgery could generate depersonalization, among other effects. But the EEG is almost invariably normal.

These findings have led to a number of hypotheses as possible neurological causes of depersonalization. The best known is the view of Mayer-Gross (1935) that depersonalization is a preformed defensive functional response of the brain which provides protection under circumstances of acute danger. The findings of Noyes et al. (1977), described more fully below, showed that a high proportion of those who narrowly escaped death from drowning, collisions with vehicles, or other perils have reported unreality feelings, *déjà vu*, and panoramic memory and related experiences which are consistent with such a theory.

The detailed investigations of the developmental history of depersonalized patients provide evidence of adverse experiences during maturation and growth to the personality, such as traumas and deprivations experienced, in other words 'meaningful historical connections'. These events and their effects can be interpreted as having contributed to shaping the personality and laying the foundations for the onset of symptoms in adolescence, or later, such that defeats or losses produce Achilles' heels in the personality. However, a proportion of patients with depersonalization disorder appear on investigation to have been of normal premorbid personality. This then is a disorder in which theories of causation have to be formulated with the aid of psychodynamic, as well as organic, causes (Roth and Harper 1962, Roth 1996). We have yet to learn how to combine such seemingly disparate explanations.

Noyes et al. (1977) have published observations of a number of individuals who have escaped death from drowning, collision with other vehicles, or other imminent threats, and their findings have relevance for theories of the nature and significance of depersonalization states. Confronted with imminent destruction the outside world seems unreal and alien; they experience *déjà vu* phenomena and also a rapid succession of vivid memories drawn from several parts of their previous lifespan. Feelings of unreality of the self remain. Emotional responses are displaced in the threatened self to the observing self, leaving the executive self free to engage in cool, prompt, and effective avoidance behaviour. This hypothetical explanation of the findings of Noyes et al. (1977) suggests that the chances of survival of their subjects may have been achieved by protection of the executive self in each case through dissociation from potentially disruptive levels of anxiety.

No information is available about the long-term fate of such persons but some support is provided for the hypothesis that depersonalization disorder is a maladaptive exaggeration and prolongation of a preformed defensive response of the brain to the threat of destructive anxiety caused by sudden danger. Such hypotheses are not necessarily in conflict with theories of causation which include the role of personality factors and the developmental process in the formative years which helped to shape its vulnerable facets.

Depersonalization disorder has in the past proved consistently resistant to both pharmacological and psychological treatments. The situation appears a little more promising in the light of recent investigations. One clinical trial reported six patients with primary depersonalization who were described as having responded with a remission from their distressing symptoms but the long-term outcome has not been reported and double-blind control studies need to be investigated (Hollander et al. 1990). Some success with behavioural therapy has also been reported in some isolated cases of depersonalization.

The phenomenon of depersonalization is of special interest in virtue of a number of its features. It is connected with mental changes associated with defence against sudden danger and threat and dissociation of consciousness. Its features constitute a close opposite of those in ecstasy which involves the expansion and enrichment of self-regard and a passionate enthusiasm which sees the world as apparelled in celestial light.

Fresh creations in the arts and original ideas in science have been described in recent years as occurring in such states of mind. Depersonalization and ecstasy appear to be the product of activity at opposite ends of some functional system in the mind and the brain (Jamison 1993) which might shed light on both, and lead to greater understanding and improved methods of treatment of depersonalization in particular. MaR

Hollander, E., Leibowitz, M. R., DeCaria, C., Fairbanks, J., Fallon, B., and Klein, D. F. (1990). 'Treatment of depersonalization with serotonin reuptake blockers'. *Journal of Clinical Psychopharmacology*, 10.

Jamison, Kay Redfield (1993). *Touched with Fire*.

Mayer-Gross, W. (1935). 'On depersonalisation'. *British Journal of Medical Psychology*, 15.

Noyes, R., Hoenk, P., Kuperman, S., and Slymen, D. J. (1977). 'Depersonalisation in accident victims and psychiatric patients'. *Journal of Nervous and Mental Disorders*, 164.

Penfield, W., and Jasper, H. (1947). 'Highest level seizure'. *Association for Research in Nervous and Mental Diseases Proceedings*, 26.

—— —— (1954). *Epilepsy and the Functional Anatomy of the Human Brain*.

Roth, M. (1996). 'The panic-agoraphobic syndrome: a paradigm of the anxiety group of disorders'. In Andreasen, N. C., and Woods, A. H. (eds.), *John Nemiah Festschrift*, *American Journal of Psychiatry*, 153.

—— and Harper, M. (1962). 'Temporal lobe epilepsy and the phobic anxiety-depersonalization syndrome, part II: practical and theoretical considerations'. *Comprehensive Psychiatry*, 3.

Schilder, P. (1928). 'Depersonalisation'. In *Introduction to Psychoanalytic Psychiatry*.

—— (1935). 'The image and appearance of the human body'. *Psyche. Monograph*, 4.

depression. Depression is a word used to describe a mood, a symptom, and a syndrome as well as a specific group of psychiatric illnesses. The extent to which these symptoms are present and their combination are infinitely variable, and there is no consistent agreement among clinicians about minimal necessary and sufficient criteria for a clinical diagnosis. For this reason depression, like schizophrenia, as a medical label is potentially applicable to two or more patients with no symptoms at all in common.

The diagnosis of the clinical illness of depression, in the absence yet of reliable biological markers, is therefore still based exclusively on symptoms, and not signs. One consequence of this ambiguity is that the dividing line between depression and other kinds of psychological states remains blurred. For example, while some contend depression is a categorical concept, others regard it as existing on a continuum with normal functioning.

To complicate matters even further, cross-cultural specialists have argued that each culture has varying criteria for describing everyday misery, and distinguishing this from abnormal unhappiness. Yet despite the shaky assumptions on which diagnosis and the central concept is built, surveys of depression producing dramatic results have increasingly guided thinking and public policy.

Major depression was cited by the World Health Organization as the fourth main cause of burden of disease in the world in 1990, and it is projected that by 2020 it will then occupy first place in developing countries, and third place in developed ones. Depression is second only to hypertension as the most common chronic condition encountered in Western general medical practice. Despite its prevalence, depression is not taken seriously by governments and health departments, according to campaigners, perhaps because it is seen as relatively innocuous. Yet depression is also a killer, through suicide and other related conditions like alcoholism and drug addiction.

It is estimated that between 40 and 60 per cent of those who commit suicide were suffering from serious clinical depression. Worldwide, suicide is among the top ten causes of death for individuals of all ages, and is the leading cause of death for those under 35.

A very important issue for primary care medicine is that over half of those who commit suicide have seen a physician within the previous 3 months, and 20 per cent of elderly suicides have done so within 24 hours. They may have complained about depression, but more commonly their symptoms (insomnia, weight loss, lack of energy, pain, loss of interest in life, anxiety, irritation, loss of concentration, appetite loss, loss of pleasure, psychomotor retardation) were not seen as part of a psychiatric disturbance, so assessment about suicide was not made. Primary care physicians seem to miss the diagnosis of major clinical depression about 50 per cent of the time. Only 25–30 per cent of those who commit suicide are even under the care of any mental health professional.

So not only is depression common and a killer, it is also frequently missed and misdiagnosed by clinicians. For example, it is estimated that 20–25 per cent of cancer patients suffer often unrecognized and untreated long-term depression, a condition that can make life miserable in the physically unwell. Given that the majority diagnosed with clinical depression can be effectively treated with one form of treatment or another (psychological, pharmacological, or a combination) it is now important that healthcare professionals routinely assess and offer treatment for depression.

Another problem with diagnosis is that there are probably several distinct types of depression, like seasonal affective disorder, where the depression has a strong seasonal component, and atypical depression, where weight gain and increased appetite are a feature. There are also a group of disorders that are commonly thought to be part of the affective spectrum, and include eating disorders, addictions, anxiety problems, obsessive–compulsive disorder, and cycling mood disorder. Another difficulty with the cluster of symptoms used to diagnose depression is that while the 'morning-worse' pattern is commonly mentioned, researchers have, however, also identified an 'evening-worse' pattern of mood. This pattern is sometimes thought to be associated with milder depressive symptoms, and may characterize chronic dysthymia rather than clinical depression.

According to one of the main diagnostic manuals used in psychiatry, the *Diagnostic and Statistical Manual of Mental Disorders*, 4th edn. (DSM-IV) published by the American Psychiatric Association, there are four other symptoms besides depression that must be present before 'major depression' can be diagnosed. So it seems that depression is not simply a state of low mood, but a syndrome comprising mood problems, psychomotor changes, and a variety of bodily and biological disturbances. All of these changes may be present, but none, including oddly enough depressed mood, is essential to the diagnosis.

The dominant paradigm at the moment is to view depression as a biological condition, and accumulating research uncovers strong links with other physical problems. For example, depression significantly increases the risk of mortality following myocardial infarction, and there also appears to be a link between depression and the later onset of dementia. The most likely possibilities for this association are: (i) depression can be an early prodrome of dementia, (ii) depression brings forward the clinical manifestation of dementing diseases, and (iii) depression leads to damage to the hippocampus through a glucocorticoid cascade.

It is this link between depression and structural brain changes that has proved one of the most revolutionary recent findings and current theories focus on the recent discoveries of decreases in various brain structure volumes, including in particular the hippocampus, in depression and anxiety-related conditions. It would now appear that neuron loss is linked to major depression. One theory is that glucocorticoids, the adrenal steroids secreted during stress, may play a contributing role to any such neuron loss.

However, it is also possible that biological differences found in the depressed could be due to genetics, and available data suggests that genes may account for over 50 per cent of the observed correlation between neuroticism and symptoms of anxiety and depression. But little is still known about the genes responsible, though much research activity centres on genes for neurotransmitters implicated in depression like serotonin and noradrenaline. Both the brain serotonergic and noradrenergic systems appear to have a role in suicide, mood disorders, aggression, and alcoholism.

A clear genetic influence in suicide has also been established and appears to operate via mechanisms not necessarily related to the genetics of depression, but implicating impulsivity as a mediating factor.

Yet if depression is common and has a genetic component this has also guided recent thinking towards the idea that it might have played a role in our evolutionary history. Depression may be maladaptive to the individual, but adaptive to the species. For example, it may be that in small bands of ancestral human hunter–gatherers, when a member lost her or his mate, the survival of the tribe was enhanced by the reduced food intake of the remaining member of the pair via depression or death. The genes enhancing a depressive reaction to loss would be carried by close kin of a depressed individual, and the enhanced survival of those kind would promote the increase of the depressogenic genes in the population.

The fact that suicide is partly genetic can also be explained with 'suicide as altruism' reconciling self-destructive behaviour with the 'selfishness' of the gene, thus clearing the way for an evolutionary hypothesis of depression which takes into account the associated increase in mortality. Suicide, paradoxically enough, potentially therefore enhances the likelihood of survival of the individual's genes.

In contrast to these generally currently favoured evolutionary perspectives on depression, psychoanalytic perspectives are less momentarily fashionable, though they continue to play an important role in psychotherapy for depression. Freud noted that the pathological depressed state is always unconscious, summing up his thoughts on depression with the famous sentence: 'The shadow of the object falls over the ego.' Psychodynamic drives involved in depression include, according to Freud, the central importance of aggression turned against the self when intensely ambivalent object investments are lost. Also implicated are the role of the superego in this self-directed aggression, the split in the self revealed in the superego's attack on the ego, and the fusion of another part of the self with an internalized object as the victim of that attack.

More recent psychodynamic formulations emphasize attachment and mourning for loss of major attachment figures perhaps predisposed to by earlier attachment formation difficulties during early childhood. There is an obvious possible convergence between genetic and psychological explanations if attachment difficulties via personality disorder could be shown to have a partial genetic basis.

While it is clear that genes cannot account for the whole story of depression, the relationship between life events and depressed mood is not simple. Though life events account for a reliable and significant portion of the variance of depressed mood, about 10 per cent in some studies, it is not usually large enough to attribute the cause of depressed mood to life events. Another complicating factor is that negative life events themselves seem to be partially heritable, possibly due to passing on poor life management skills within a family.

The latest thinking emphasizes the importance of 'life management' so that it is not what bad things happen to you that predict depression, but how you think about

them, heralding the current dominance of the 'cognitive' approach. Cognitive processes of various types are presumed to represent vulnerabilities to development of depressive symptoms, and the current favourites are the holding of especially high standards, the tendency to be self-critical after failure, plus the tendency to generalize from a single failure to the broader sense of self-worth. There is indeed evidence that cognitive styles like 'generalization' and 'self-criticism' interact with adverse events to predict subsequent depressive symptoms.

These cognitive theories arose out of the Learned Helplessness paradigm, which is one of the few to integrate cognitions, emotions, and biology in depression. The model depended on identifying a particular class of animal behaviours as equivalent to an apparently discrete emotional state in humans. Animals when placed in a situation where they could not escape a negative consequence appear to give up trying and exhibit what looked like an animal equivalent of human depression. Faced by observation that depressed patients often claim excessive responsibility for the misfortunes in life, the theory was then modified to include an attributional component.

According to the revised learned helplessness theory, depression therefore occurs when an individual experiences negative events as uncontrollable, but also attributes them to causes which are internal to the self, stable over time, and global in their impact of areas of the individual's life. Subsequent research indicated that depressed people on the whole did make the expected attributions for negative events, but much less clearly indicated that attributions, especially of internality, were trait vulnerability markers for depression as the theory expected.

However, life event research appears most fruitful when explaining why women are at greater risk of depression, one of the most consistent findings in psychiatric epidemiology. There is little evidence to suggest this is a measurement artefact, or that men develop alternative, more externalizing, disorders to depression. If anything, women are more likely to experience and express anger about life events. Consistent with an explanation based on gender differences of roles, women appear only at greater risk of depression following an event involving children, housing, and reproduction, and then only when there were clear gender differences in associated roles. It seems likely that women's greater risk of depression is a consequence of gender differences in roles, which lead to differences in the experience of life events.

Sociologically inclined researchers have also emphasized the importance of social support as providing a buffer for women when facing stress, and explaining why more isolated women are prone to depression. Men appear on the other hand to be more prone to depression secondary to goal frustration.

However, an alternative to these sociological accounts is a more biological perspective which argues that depression is commoner in women because they are more prone to post-natal depression and menstrual mood problems as a direct result of their hormonal differences to men. It has indeed been found that around 10–20 per cent of women experience an episode of depression during the first 2–3 months after delivery. Maternal depression is important, and vital not to miss, because occurring so early in the infant's life it may affect the child's psychological development, with significant intellectual deficits as a result.

Perhaps the biggest future advance will not need to await the revealing of biological markers for depression, but instead the more widespread teaching of effective coping skills to populations before they experience adverse life events, so heralding an age when depression is prevented rather than merely diagnosed and treated.

RP

Abramson, L.Y., Seligman, M. E. P., and Teasdale, J. D. (1978). 'Learned helplessness in humans: critique and reformulation'. Journal of Abnormal Psychology, 78.
Beck, A. T., Rush, A. J., Shaw, B. F., and Emery, G. (1979). Cognitive Therapy of Depression.
Brown, G. W., and Harris T. (1978). Social Origins of Depression.
Healy, D. (1997). The Anti-Depressant Era.
Mendels, J. (1970). Concepts of Depression.

depth perception. The seeing of objects in three dimensions, although *retinal images are only two dimensional. Depth is seen even with one eye by 'monocular depth cues'. These are the partial hiding of further by nearer objects, loss of fine detail through haze, and the limited resolution of the eye with increasing distance ('aerial perspective'), geometrical perspective (especially the converging of parallel lines as optically projected on the retina), *accommodation of the lens of the eye (the anterior surface of the lens becoming more convex for near vision), and motion parallax (when the observer moves, objects are displaced according to his movements, the visual world rotating round the point of fixation in the direction opposite to his motion). We may say, following Hermann von *Helmholtz, that depth is unconsciously inferred from these cues, or clues, or, following J. J. *Gibson, that we 'pick up' depth information from these features.

*Stereoscopic depth is given by the comparison of 'corresponding points' of the retinal images in the two eyes. This requires remarkably powerful neural computation, which can now be carried out with computer programs, though far more slowly.

When depth cues are misleading, distortions of size can be generated. See ILLUSIONS.

Gibson, J. J. (1950). Perception of the Visual World (repr. 1974).
Gregory, R. L. (1970). The Intelligent Eye.
Howard, I., Rodgers, B. (1995). Binocular Vision and Stereopsis.

Descartes, René (1596–1650). A pivotal figure in the great 17th-century revolution that marked the emergence of modern philosophical and scientific thinking. He was born at La Haye near Tours, and educated at the Jesuit college of La Flèche. He travelled in Germany during 1619, and on the night of 11 November he had a series of dreams which inspired his vision of founding a completely new philosophical and scientific system. In 1628 he moved to Holland, where he lived, with frequent changes of address, for most of the rest of his life. His philosophical masterpiece, the Meditations on First Philosophy, appeared in Latin in 1641, and his Principles of Philosophy, a comprehensive statement of his philosophical and scientific theories, also in Latin, in 1644. He died of pneumonia in Stockholm, where he had gone to act as tutor to Queen Christina of Sweden.

Descartes made important contributions in many areas of human knowledge. His early work was in mathematics, and his Rules for the Direction of the Understanding (1628) provided a general account of scientific knowledge that was strongly influenced by mathematical models. His Geometry (published 1637) lays the foundations for what is now known as analytical *geometry. In the Discourse on Method, a popular introduction to his philosophy, published in French in 1637, Descartes developed his celebrated 'method of doubt': 'I resolved to reject as false everything in which I could imagine the least doubt, in order to see if there afterwards remained anything that was entirely indubitable' (see DOUBTING). This led to the famous affirmation 'I think, therefore I am' (je pense, donc je suis). On the basis of this 'Archimedean point' Descartes erected a comprehensive philosophical and scientific system which was to include both a general theory of the structure and working of the physical universe, and many detailed explanations of particular phenomena, such as the mechanics of human and animal physiology. Although the metaphysical foundations of his system depend heavily on the existence of an omnipotent, benevolent, and non-deceiving God, Descartes aimed, in all areas of natural science, to provide explanations in terms of strictly mechanical models and mathematical principles. All phenomena, whether celestial or terrestrial, were to be explained ultimately by reference to the shapes, sizes, and motions of bits of matter: 'I freely acknowledge that I recognize no matter in corporeal things apart from that which the geometricians call "quantity" and take as the object of their demonstrations' (Principles, pt. ii).

Descartes's theory of the mind stands out as a striking exception to his general insistence on mechanical and mathematical explanations. Mental phenomena, for Descartes, have no place in the quantifiable world of physics, but have a completely autonomous, separate status. 'I am a substance the whole nature or essence of which is to think, and which for its existence does not need any place or depend on any material thing' (*Discourse*, pt. iv). Developing the theory later known as 'Cartesian dualism', Descartes maintains that there are two radically different kinds of substance: physical, extended substance (*res extensa*)—i.e. that which has length, breadth, and depth and can therefore be measured and divided—and thinking substance (*res cogitans*), which is unextended and indivisible. Thus the human body—including the brain and entire nervous system—belongs in the first category, while the mind—including all thoughts, desires, and volitions—belongs in the second.

One of Descartes's reasons for supposing his mind to be essentially non-physical is that in his *Meditations* he found himself able to doubt the existence of all physical objects (including his body), but was unable to doubt the existence of himself as a thinking being. And from this he concluded that having a body was not part of his essential nature. But, as some of his contemporary critics pointed out, this argument seems invalid: ability to doubt that some item *X* possesses some feature *F* does not prove that *X* could in fact exist without *F*. Descartes also argued that the essential indivisibility of the mind proves its noncorporeality, but this seems question begging, since the premiss that the mind is indivisible would be disputed by those who maintain that the mind is some kind of physical system. Despite the shakiness of some of Descartes's arguments, his dualistic approach has continued to exert a dominatingly powerful influence on theories of the mind. As recently as 1977, for example, we find the eminent neurophysiologist Sir John Eccles and the famous philosopher Sir Karl Popper maintaining that Descartes was fundamentally correct. According to Eccles and Popper, the 'self'—the conscious being that is 'me'—is essentially non-physical. The self may make use of the brain in its operations, but its operations have separate and independent status over and above the occurrences in the brain.

As Descartes himself recognized, however, dualism faces considerable philosophical difficulties. The chief of these is the problem of 'causal interaction'. We know from experience that mind and body do not operate in total isolation, but interact with each other: if there is a physical change (e.g. my hand touches a hot stove), a mental change (e.g. pain) results; and, conversely, a mental event (a volition to raise my arm) leads to a physical event (my arm going up). Descartes acknowledges these facts by saying that in many cases mind and body 'intermingle' to form a kind of unit. Thus, sensations like hunger and thirst are, he maintains, 'confused perceptions' resulting from the fact that 'I am not merely lodged with my body, like a sailor in a ship, but am very closely united and as it were intermingled with it' (*Meditations*, pt. vi). But exactly

how there can be such a 'union' or 'intermingling' between two allegedly quite distinct and seemingly incompatible substances is left something of a mystery. Elsewhere (e.g. in the *Passions of the Soul*, 1649), Descartes suggests that the mind or soul, though incorporeal and indivisible, exercises its functions in one particular part of the brain, the *conarion*, or pineal gland. But this manoeuvre seems not to solve but merely to reimport the problem of causal interaction: if there is a problem about how a non-physical soul can cause my arm to go up, there will be no less a problem about how a non-physical soul can cause movements in the brain by acting on the pineal gland.

Although in his psychological and physiological writings Descartes devoted great efforts to the problem of interaction between soul and body, it is worth remembering that in his system there are many areas where such interaction simply does not arise. First, in the case of animal physiology and a great deal of human physiology (e.g. that concerned with digestion, muscular reflexes, etc.), Descartes maintained that the soul is not involved at all: what occurs can be explained purely on mechanical principles. Second, in the case of human beings, though much of our activity (e.g. sense perception) involves complicated transactions between soul and body, there are other mental acts (e.g. purely intellectual thoughts) which, according to Descartes, can occur without any physiological correlates at all; such 'ideas of pure mind' are, in Descartes's view, from start to finish non-corporeal. It must be said that advances in brain science have made this latter part of Descartes's theory increasingly difficult to defend.

Although substantive dualism, the doctrine that the mind is a separate, non-physical entity, now has everfewer supporters, many philosophers have become attracted by a weaker version of Descartes's theory, which has been termed 'attributive dualism'. This is the view that, even if the mind is not a separate entity, there are none the less two distinct sets of properties or attributes that can be ascribed to human beings: psychological properties (thoughts, feelings, volitions) and physical properties (e.g. electrical and chemical properties of the nervous system). Attributive dualists maintain that, even if all human activities must depend on some kind of physical substrate, there is none the less an important sense in which psychological descriptions of those activities cannot be reduced to mere physiological descriptions. This position on the one hand preserves Descartes's insight that what he called 'modes of extension' (size, shape, volume) are fundamentally different from 'modes of thought' (thoughts, feelings, volitions), while on the other hand resisting his conclusion that two separate entities, a 'thinking thing' and an 'extended thing', are involved. This is similar to the hardware and software of a computer.

See also MIND AND BODY; MIND–BODY PROBLEM; PERSONAL
IDENTITY.   JGC

Descartes, R. (1911). *The Philosophical Works of Descartes*. Trans.
E. S. Haldane and G. R. T. Ross (repr. 1969).

Popper, K., and Eccles, J. (1977). *The Self and its Brain*.

Williams, B. (1978). *Descartes: The Project of Pure Enquiry*.

Wilson, M. (1978). *Descartes*.

design, argument from, for the existence of God.

The universe appears designed; a design requires a designer, and so the universe was designed (created) by a
designing intelligence. This of course raises the question:
how was the Designing Intelligence (God) created? Therefore, although the argument by analogy—as human artefacts have human designers, so the universe must have a
superhuman designer—is appealing, it lacks philosophical cogency, because how the Designer was designed remains unanswered. The design of organisms by natural
selection shows that intentional mind is not required for
designing. The most famous critique of the argument
from design is in David *Hume's *Dialogues Concerning Natural Religion*.

design in nature.

Design generally implies the action of
intentional intelligence. The 'design' of organisms is,
however, on the theory of Darwinian evolution, produced
without prior purpose or intention. In this sense evolution is 'blind'. It may be said, though, that random variation and natural selection form a kind of intelligence, as
they produce designs which we would certainly rate as
requiring high intelligence—indeed superhuman intelligence, as they are beyond us to produce or even to understand. See EVOLUTION: NEO-DARWINIAN THEORY; PALEY,
WILLIAM.

Dawkins, R. (1986). *The Blind Watchmaker*.

detection.

In *perception, the term refers to the acceptance of selected patterns of energy by the sense organs—
which are transducers producing neural signals. The retinal receptors can detect illumination down to the theoretical limit of one quantum. The ears detect sound
energies down to the random motion of air molecules
(10^{-16} watts, or 0.00003 dyn/cm^2).

Sensitivity is always limited by the fact that energies
cannot be less than Planck's quantum of action, and because all detectors have residual random activity, or
'noise', against which signals must be discriminated.

Barlow, H. (2001). 'The exploitation of regularities in the environment and the brain'. *Behavioural and Brain Sciences*, 24/4.

Dewey, John

(1859–1952). American philosopher and
educationalist, born at Burlington, Vermont. He went
first to the University of Michigan (1884–94) and then
to the University of Chicago (1894–1904), where he did
much to promote a *functional point of view in psychology. This was well expressed in an influential paper on
the reflex arc concept (1896) in which he laid stress on the
function rather than the structure of *reflexes. In 1904,
Dewey, whose interests had now shifted almost entirely
to the philosophy of education, accepted the chair at
Teachers' College, Columbia, where he remained until
1930. His best-known books are *Democracy and Education*
(1916), *Human Nature and Conduct* (1922), *The Quest for Certainty* (1929), and *Art as Experience* (1934).

diagnosis.

The use of characteristic signs of a generally
established disease or abnormality. This is based on the
notion that diseases and typical abnormalities have
grouped 'syndromes' of characteristics, such that recognition of some enables us to predict the others, and may
also suggest the underlying cause and appropriate treatment. Typical clinical signs or symptoms are, however,
sometimes 'seen' when not present, especially when
they are likely to accord with the prevailing or probable
diagnosis. This can lead to spurious confirmation. The
philosopher Sir Karl Popper has emphasized the importance of looking for *negative* or *disconfirming* evidence to
check diagnoses and to stop the generation of spurious
syndromes when exceptions are overlooked.

dichromatic.

Literally 'two-coloured'. Usually applied
to the (rare cases) of people who have only two, rather
than the normal three, retinal colour channels. They can
match any colour visible to them by adjusting the intensities of only *two* coloured lights, which are mixed.
Thomas *Young showed in 1801 that normally *three* spectral colours (red, green, and blue) are needed to match all
the spectral colours, and white, by adjusting the relative
intensities of the three lights. Normal people are thus
'trichromats'. See COLOUR VISION: EYE MECHANISMS.

digital.

From the Latin for 'finger'—hence 'digital'
counting (on the fingers). 'Digital' essentially means representing states or carrying out mathematical or logical
procedures in steps corresponding to the symbolic operations of a calculus.

A digital computer works in steps representing steps
of logic or computing by means of a formal code. A continuously changing function or signal may be represented
digitally, as in CDs. Because the symbols of logic or arithmetical calculation are discretely different from each
other, digital computers require circuits having discrete
states, which can be selected at great speed. Analogue
computers, on the other hand, manipulate continuous
physical variables, following a change or representing a
function by an equivalent change or function but of a
different physical form (such as a voltage or the line of
a graph).

Digital computers are far more versatile than analogue ones as, in principle, they can be programmed to perform any operation that can be stated. The same mechanism can readily be reprogrammed to perform very different operations, whereas, typically, analogue computers must be virtually rebuilt for different uses. Early analogue computers were relatively fast, because they did not go through many stepped operations, but modern digital computers can carry out up to 10^9 operations per second. A great advantage of digital communication systems is that information is not lost over great distances, or with added noise, especially when 'repeater stations' restore the signals, as for underwater cables.

It is an open question whether the brain is essentially analogue or digital. It is interesting that we are extremely weak at digital operations, such as complicated arithmetical problems, although these are easy to carry out mechanically, or electronically in pocket calculators, which far surpass human accuracy and speed. This may well suggest that the brain works analogically rather than digitally.

diminished responsibility.

1. The McNaghten Rules
2. Doe–Ray tests of insanity
3. Diminished responsibility in Scotland
4. Diminished responsibility in England
5. Proposals for reform

1. The McNaghten Rules

In English law until 1957 there was only one defence based on disease of the mind available to a defendant, that of insanity. In 1843 an authoritative pronouncement by all the judges answered questions put to them by the House of Lords in its legislative capacity. McNaghten had been tried for the murder of Sir Robert Peel's private secretary, Edward Drummond, under the mistaken impression that he was shooting at Sir Robert himself. He was acquitted by the jury on the ground of insanity. The acquittal aroused widespread controversy, and was debated in the House of Lords, with the result that their lordships put abstract questions to the judges. The judges gave their answer to the second question in the following terms:

To establish a defence on the grounds of insanity, it must be clearly proved that, at the time of the committing of the act, the party accused was labouring under such a defect of reason, from disease of the mind, as not to know the nature and quality of the act he was doing, or, if he did know it, that he did not know he was doing what was wrong. (F (1843) 10 Cl. & F. 200)

From the medical standpoint, this all-or-nothing approach to psychological functioning was already obsolete. It had also been shown that inability to distinguish between right and wrong was only one symptom of insanity,

and that many mentally disturbed persons knew the difference between right and wrong. In 1838 Isaac Ray had published in the USA his work *A Treatise on Medical Jurisprudence of Insanity*, described in 1961 by a psychiatrist as the best book in the English language on forensic psychiatry (Diamond (1961) 14 Stan. LR 59). Defence counsel had used this book at the trial of McNaghten, but to no effect.

2. Doe–Ray tests of insanity

In the United States the McNaghten Rules were adopted as the test of insanity in most states, but the state of New Hampshire was an exception. Judge Charles Doe, later chief justice of that state, began to correspond with Isaac Ray, an exchange of letters that continued from 1866 to 1872. One passage from Ray's work may be cited: 'Insanity is a disease, and, as is the case with all other diseases, the fact of its existence is never established by a single diagnostic symptom, but by the whole body of symptoms, no particular one of which is present in every case.'

Convinced of the inadequacy of the McNaghten tests, Doe came to regard the question of insanity as one of fact to be left to the jury, and by 1869 had converted his brother judges in the state to that view (*State* v. *Pike* 49 NH 399). In a letter to Ray he wrote: 'Giving this matter to the jury leaves the way open for the reception of all progress in your science. One jury is not bound by the verdict of another.' Doe and Ray are thus left in harmonious juxtaposition.

3. Diminished responsibility in Scotland

The McNaghten Rules had never been accepted unreservedly in Scotland, and in the very decade in which Charles Doe had wrought a transformation in New Hampshire, Lord Deas initiated a new defence, proof of which led not to an acquittal, but to a verdict of culpable homicide instead of murder. This was in *HMA* v. *Dingwall* 1867 5 Irv. 466. The development did not arise from close contact with medical writing, and seemed out of character for the judge himself, for his general attitude tended towards rigidity and severity. It has even been suggested that his direction to the jury may have sprung from a respect for Hogmanay, as the defendant's fatal attack on his wife had followed bouts of excessive drinking at that season, a time apparently when many a reasonable Scot will consume inordinate quantities of whisky. Whatever the reasons for the new idea, Lord Deas persisted in it. Before his retirement in 1885, he had contributed six of the first nine reported cases embodying the new doctrine. In the third case he instructed the jury that a weak or diseased mind, not amounting to insanity, might competently form an element to be considered in the question between murder and culpable homicide (*HMA* v. *Granger* 1878 4 Coup. 86). In the last of the six, he said that *Dingwall* was now the recognized law of the land (*HMA* v. *Gove* 1882

4 Coup. 598). The new defence received the name of diminished responsibility in *HMA* v. *Edmonstone* 1909 2 SLT 223. In *HMA* v. *Savage* 1923 JC 49 a direction to the jury from Lord Justice-Clerk (Alness) has come to be regarded as a *locus classicus*. He stressed that the doctrine must be applied with care, and that there must be aberration or weakness of the mind, some form of mental unsoundness, a state of mind bordering on insanity, rendering the defendant only partially responsible.

It has been argued by some distinguished writers on the law of Scotland that diminished responsibility operates merely in mitigation of sentence, and does not affect responsibility. Such a view is certainly not tenable in England, where Parliament created the defence in 1957.

4. Diminished responsibility in England

In England the Royal Commission on Capital Punishment, 1949–53, heard much evidence on the operation of the defence of diminished responsibility in Scotland, but made no recommendation for its adoption, regarding the matter as outside its terms of reference. In 1956, however, during a debate in the House of Commons on capital punishment, the Home Secretary undertook to consider the question further. This led to section 2 (1) of the Homicide Act 1957, whereby:

Where a person kills or is a party to the killing of another, he shall not be convicted of murder if he was suffering from such abnormality of mind (whether arising from a condition of arrested or retarded development of mind or any inherent causes or induced by disease or injury) as substantially impaired his mental responsibility for his acts and omissions in doing or being a party to the killing.

The defence is called diminished responsibility in a marginal note to the section. The burden of proof is placed on the defence, as in Scotland and under the McNaghten Rules. In such cases, as in all instances where a legal burden of proof is placed on the defence, the defendant has to establish the defence on a balance of probability, or in more homely language that it is more likely than not that his responsibility is diminished. If so proved, murder is reduced to manslaughter, just as in Scotland it is reduced to culpable homicide. It applies only to murder, following the predominant Scottish view. A successful defence of insanity leads to a verdict of 'not guilty by reason of insanity'.

The introduction of this new defence, coupled with the abolition of capital punishment for murder by Parliament in 1965, has led to the virtual disappearance of the defence of insanity.

From the outset difficulties were found in directing the jury on the question of fact they had to determine under section 2 (1). In *R.* v. *Spriggs* 1958 1 QB 270, the trial judge read the section to the jury, reviewed in detail the evidence relevant to the defence, made no attempt to explain the various medical terms that had figured in the evidence, and gave the jury copies of the section as they retired. The Court of Criminal Appeal quoted the charge to the jury from a Scottish case, which consisted largely of a quotation from the charge to the jury in *Savage* mentioned above as a *locus classicus*. The court considered that the case had been put to the jury in the only way it could be put, and affirmed the conviction.

In *R.* v. *Walden* 1959 43 Cr. App. R. 201, the trial judge construed the section as meaning: 'Poor fellow, he is not insane, but not far from it; his mental condition is one which is bordering on, but not amounting to insanity.' He gave the jury copies of the section. The Court of Criminal Appeal refused leave to appeal. Parliament had not defined 'abnormality of mind' or 'mental responsibility'. The reference to substantial impairment connoted a question of degree, and questions of degree are questions of fact in each case.

At this stage English juries were not receiving the necessary guidance: Charles Doe, while insisting that the question of mental disease was one of fact for the jury, had also stressed that the jury must be given some help. Help was forthcoming from the Court of Criminal Appeal in *R.* v. *Byrne* 1960 2 QB 396. The court gave a definition of two important concepts in the section. 'Abnormality of mind' meant a state of mind so different from that of ordinary human beings that the reasonable man would term it abnormal. It covered the mind's activities in all its aspects—not only the perception of physical acts and matters and the ability to form a rational judgement whether an act is right or wrong, but also the ability to exercise will power to control physical acts. 'Mental responsibility' pointed to a consideration of the extent to which the accused's mind is answerable for his physical acts; this must include a consideration of the extent of his ability to exercise will power to control his physical acts. Inability to exercise will power to control such acts entitles the accused to the benefit of the section; difficulty in controlling such acts may do so, if great enough to amount to substantial impairment. The jury must decide, though there is no scientific certainty to guide them. Thus the court in *Byrne* clearly decided that an irresistible impulse falls within the concept of diminished responsibility, a status it never achieved under the McNaghten Rules.

The effect of *Byrne* was soon apparent. In *Rose* v. *Reginam* 1961 45 Cr. App. R. 102, a summing-up that had passed muster in *Walden* now led to a successful appeal. In *R.* v. *Terry* 1961 2 QB 314, a summing-up that failed to explain section 2 (1) on the lines laid down in *Byrne* was held deficient. Further, the jury had been handed a transcript of volumes of medical evidence without explanation. It is of course the duty of the trial judge to take the jury through the evidence, trying to synthesize it and render it easier to digest. The conviction was in fact upheld as the crucial question was held to be whether the accused was shamming, and on this matter the summing-up was adequate. In *R. v. Gomez* 1964 48 Cr. App. R. 310, a summing-up to the jury by Judge Paull on similar lines to that in *Walden* was again held inadequate: the proper course was to tell the jury what in law the section means, and what are the ingredients in the section, and then direct them on the evidence. The conviction was reduced to manslaughter. In *Walton v. R.* 1978 AC 788, the Privy Council put the clock back to *Walden* by indicating that the main question before the jury was whether the state of mind of the defendant was bordering on but not amounting to insanity, supporting this view by a quotation from *Byrne* itself. It is submitted that this is oversimplified, and regard should be had to the more thorough examination of the question demanded by *Byrne* rather than to an isolated passage taken out of context.

Although the question is one that the jury must decide, if they ignore unchallenged medical evidence that all points to substantial impairment, an appellate court may reduce the conviction to manslaughter, on the ground that the verdict of murder is unsafe or unsatisfactory, as in *R. v. Matheson* 1958 42 Cr. App. R. 145. The verdict may, however, be allowed to stand if the medical evidence was challenged in cross-examination, as in *R. v. Latham* 1965 Cr. LR 434, or the solitary expert witness in the case, who considers the impairment to have been substantial, is unsupported by objective evidence of any history of mental disorder, as in *Walton* (above).

An issue of considerable importance is the position of one diagnosed as *psychopathic personality as defined by the Mental Health Act 1959. In the case of Fenton (1975, 61 Cr. App. R. 261) it was concluded that psychopathic personality was no defence under the terms of the Homicide Act 1957, regardless of whether the accused was affected by alcohol at the time of his offence. Furthermore, as intoxication with drink or drugs cannot be regarded as an 'inherent cause' of mental abnormality, an attempt to reduce the verdict to manslaughter in place of murder on the ground that the accused was drunk at the time of the killing will not succeed.

Nevertheless, the introduction of the defence of diminished responsibility has undoubtedly had beneficial effects. This is because psychiatrists have adapted themselves to giving opinions in accordance with the legal formula, vague and unscientific as it undoubtedly is.

5. Proposals for reform

The Butler Committee on Mentally Abnormal Offenders, in their report of 1975, Cmnd. 6244, recognizing the difficulties under which experts were labouring, proposed an alteration in the wording of section 2 (1), substituting after the word 'murder', 'if there is medical or other evidence that he was suffering from a form of mental disorder as defined in section 4 of the Mental Health Act 1959, and if, in the opinion of the jury, the mental disorder was such as to be an extenuating circumstance which ought to reduce the offence to manslaughter'. The Committee claims that this amendment would provide a firm base for testifying psychiatrists to diagnose mental state. The claim is justified. The Mental Health Act 1959 contains definitions of mental disorder, psychopathic disorder, subnormality, and severe subnormality, so that the expert is now operating in a familiar field; and the Mental Health Act 1983 does not materially alter this situation. Although mental disorder includes psychopathic disorder as one of the defined components, as already mentioned, it is unlikely that this diagnosis will be admissible as a defence of diminished responsibility under the Homicide Act 1957.

The Criminal Law Revision Committee in its Fourteenth Report of 1980 (Cmnd. 7844) recommends that the Butler wording should be changed so that instead of the need for the jury to seek 'an extenuating circumstance' their quest should be for 'a substantial enough reason'.

The Fourteenth Report recommends, as the Committee had recommended in its Eleventh Report of 1972, and the Butler Committee in 1975, that there should be no burden of proof on a defendant raising a plea of insanity or diminished responsibility: the burden of proof should be on the prosecution to disprove the defence beyond reasonable doubt.

See also CRIMINOLOGY.

RNG

diopter. Unit for the power of a lens or prism. For a 'positive' (convex) lens, 1 diopter brings parallel light to a focus at a distance of 1 metre from the centre of the lens; a 2-diopter lens a focal length of 0.5 metre; and so on.

diplopia. Double vision, resulting from failure to combine or 'fuse' the images from the two eyes. This often, though not always, gives total loss of stereoscopic depth perception. It may be due to squint (strabismus), or, temporarily, to tiredness, or to temporary or permanent disturbance of the central neural processes.

displacement activity. During courtship a male three-spined stickleback (*Gasterosteus aculeatus*) is often observed to break off his display to the female. He swims to his empty nest on the substrate and fans water through it. He may also creep through the nest before returning to display to the female. These nest-directed activities are normally associated with the parental care of eggs (carried out by the male in this species) and as such are considered 'out of context' or 'irrelevant' to courtship. Behaviour of this kind is called a displacement activity.

Displacement activities often occur when an animal has a tendency for more than one incompatible behaviour, such as approach and avoidance (motivational conflict), or when it is prevented from reaching a goal such as an anticipated food reward (thwarting). In stickleback courtship it is thought that the female represents a stimulus for both aggression and for mating. Other examples are ground pecking (feeding) during fights by red junglefowl (*Gallus gallus*), bill wiping during fights by great tits (*Parus major*), and preening during approach–avoidance conflict by the common chaffinch (*Fringilla coelebs*). Many human actions, such as excessive drinking, nibbling food, or manipulation of the face in stressful social contexts, seem to be similar to the displacement activities seen in other animals. There is an extensive ethological literature on displacement activities because of the clues they are thought to provide about mechanisms of motivation, and because of their possible importance in communication displays (see also ETHOLOGY).

In many cases displacement activities have been found to have a function related to their context. For example, it has been shown that stickleback courtship does not proceed to a normal completion if displacement fanning is prevented. Similarly ground pecking by red jungle fowl has an important influence on the outcome of a fight. In other cases the activity has a function even if not relevant to the context: for example, bill wiping by great tits removes sloughed material from the beak, although this is not relevant to a territorial dispute. But our judgement of irrelevance may simply indicate ignorance of the true situation.

While the time of occurrence and duration of displacement activities are mainly dependent on causal factors relevant to the context (conflict or thwarting) in which they occur, their form and intensity are dictated largely by causal factors related to the displacement activities themselves. Thus displacement preening in chaffinches is more vigorous when the feathers are made dirty, but the timing of preening bouts is hardly affected. One explanation for this is that displacement activities are disinhibited, and it is based on the idea that during normal behaviour the current activity inhibits other incompatible activities for which the causal factors are also present. During a motivational conflict the incompatible tendencies suppress one another, leaving the displacement activity to occur by default, governed in performance by its usual causal factors but delimited in time by the context. An empirical test of this explanation involves showing that the amount of displacement activity seen depends on the ratio of the conflicting tendencies rather than on their absolute value. This has been demonstrated in terns (*Sterna hirundo*), sticklebacks, chaffinches, and great tits, but there are other attributes of displacement activities which are not accounted for by this explanation. In chaffinches the precise preening movements seen during approach–avoidance conflict depend on the context as well as on

causal factors relevant to preening. In great tits displacement activities during fights are affected by the absolute levels of competing tendencies as well as by the ratio.

Displacement activities often appear hurried, stereotyped, or incomplete when compared with similar behaviour occurring in its normal context. They share some of the characteristics of a variety of other behavioural effects seen when animals are thwarted. With rats, the omission of an expected food reward may lead to increased motivated behaviour towards the absent goal (e.g. increased running speed to the goal box of a runway), excessive performance of an alternative activity such as drinking or wood gnawing, or a generalized increase in the rate of activities normally seen between deliveries of food. Such phenomena are sometimes attributed to a generalized state, frustration, caused by thwarting. The excessive behaviour induced by certain intermittent reward schedules (adjunctive behaviour) may also be a related phenomenon, though such schedule-induced activities differ in some respects from frustration effects: for example, they are not abolished by minor tranquillizing drugs. Displacement activities and frustration effects may represent a class of 'coping behaviour', enabling an animal to resolve a situation in which it is unable, due to inadequate or contradictory information, to decide what to do next.

Apart from intention movements and compromise postures, many of the displays seen in social behaviour, especially in the courtship or agonistic behaviour of vertebrates, appear to incorporate movements which are derived from activities not relevant to the context of the display. For example, in birds many threat displays are very similar to preening movements. This has given rise to the idea that displacement activities may have been important in the evolutionary origin of social communication. Because of what they can reveal about the motivational state of the performer, it has been thought probable that displacement activities are attended to by other individuals to whom such information might be useful, and that it is often advantageous to the performer to inform others of its motivational state. It has been argued that this 'tell-tale' of internal state has become established as a means of communication, with natural selection leading to emphasis of the original signal (ritualization) and probably to the emancipation of the activity from its original motivational mechanism. More recently it has been pointed out by those interested in the game-theoretical analysis of social transactions between animals that the contestants often need to conceal their true motivational state (e.g. not show fear to an opponent) or to mislead others (e.g. threaten to attack while contemplating flight). The highly redundant nature of derived displays, which are usually stereotyped, rhythmic, and repetitive, is characteristic of persuasive rather than informative signals. Persuasive signals are to be expected where it is advantageous to the sender to manipulate recipients of the message, but advantageous to the recipients to avoid manipulation. Animals that cooperate in the exchange of reliable information to their mutual advantage might be expected to communicate in 'conspiratorial whispers', rather than by means of conspicuous announcements, since signals are likely to be intercepted by animals other than the intended recipient, to the disadvantage of the sender. For example, some predators make use of the courtship displays of their prey in order to locate them. This currently controversial area is discussed in detail by Krebs and Dawkins (1984). Whatever the explanation, any animal signals are, apparently, derived from other actions in the repertoire which have no connection with the motivational context of the display.

RHM

Krebs, J. R., and Dawkins, R. (1984). 'Animal signals: mind-reading and manipulation'. In Krebs, J. R., and Davies, N. B. (eds.), *Behavioural Ecology* (2nd edn.).

dissociation of the personality. Two—or more—mental processes can be said to be dissociated if they coexist or alternate without becoming connected or influencing one another. Prior to Sigmund *Freud and to the discovery of the *unconscious, dissociation was a term much used by psychiatrists to describe and, by implication, to explain many neurotic symptoms, the underlying assumption having been that neurotics suffered from some inherent or constitutional weakness of the integrative function, as a result of which they were liable to perform actions, think thoughts, dream day and night dreams, which were unconnected with and dissociated from their usual, real, or true personalities. However, since Freud and the general abandonment of the assumption that the neuroses are the result of a 'functional', constitutional defect, the concept of dissociation has, with one exception, fallen into disuse, terms like 'repression', 'isolation', 'splitting' being preferred to describe those defence mechanisms by which a person, for specific though usually unconscious reasons, keeps wishes, actions, images, memories, etc., outside his self-image or *ego.

The exception consists of a group of phenomena which have it in common that the subject maintains for a considerable length of time some line or course of action in which he appears not to be actuated by his usual self—or, alternatively, his usual self seems not to have access to the recent memories that one would normally expect him to have. Contemporary psychiatry categorizes such phenomena as 'hysterical dissociations', the best-known examples being sleepwalking (see SOMNAMBULISM), trances, post-hypnotic suggestions, fugues (in which the subject wanders off, not knowing who or where he is), loss of memory (hysterical *amnesia), in which the subject has a gap in his memory for some finite, recent period of time, and split, dual, or multiple personality, in which the subject appears to change from one person to another.

The last of these, dissociation of the personality, is a puzzling and, indeed, disturbing phenomenon, since it calls into question a basic assumption we all make about human nature, namely that for every body there is but one person; that each of us, despite the passage of time and changes in mood and activity, remains the same person, with a single biography and store of memories. Given the fact that all social relations and contracts presume consistency and unity of personality, it is hardly surprising that the occasional person who claims or appears to change into someone else becomes an object of concern to the police, of curiosity to the psychiatric profession, and of fascination to the general public.

Dissociation of the personality is not only bizarre but also extremely rare—so rare, indeed, that one has to take seriously the possibility that it may be a social and psychiatric artefact: i.e. that it can only occur if (i) prevailing views on the nature of personality make it conceivable that two personalities can occupy the same bodily frame, and (ii) the potential case of split or multiple personality encounters a psychiatrist who believes in, or is already interested in, dissociation of the personality.

In fact, the great majority of reported cases of multiple personality date from between 1840 and 1910—that is, from after demoniacal possession had ceased to be a plausible, scientifically respectable explanation of sudden, extraordinary changes in personality until the time at which psychoanalytical ideas began to have an impact. During this period two conditions existed which, it seems likely, must have facilitated the diagnosis of multiple personality. First, the prevailing Victorian conventions of reticence must have made it unthinkable that patients should tell, or that their doctors should enquire into, those intimate physical details of their lives which would have established continuity of bodily feeling despite massive changes in mental feeling; if *cogito, ergo sum* were the basis of identity, then indeed personality and identity could change if thought changed, in a way that could not happen if patient and physician believed that the ground of being is located in the body.

Secondly, there was obliviousness to what is nowadays called *transference and counter-transference and, in particular, to the fact that patients can and will produce symptoms to please their physicians. The great majority of the physicians reporting cases of multiple personality have been men, and the cases they have reported have been women younger than themselves. For instance, Dr Morton Prince of Boston, Massachusetts, was 44 when, in 1898, he was consulted by Sally Beauchamp, a young, single woman aged 23, who suffered from various nervous disorders. During the next seven years, three further personalities emerged in or from her, two of them while Dr Prince was hypnotizing her, and in 1908 he described his treatment of the foursome, whom he called collectively 'the family', in his classic *The Dissociation of a Personality*. In view of the fact that Dr Prince had already published papers on double personality and was widely known to be interested in the subject, and that Miss Beauchamp is on record as pleading to be hypnotized by him—'And I do want you, please, please, to hypnotize me again. You know it is the only thing that has ever helped me . . .' —it is hard to resist the conclusion that Miss Beauchamp was obliging Dr Prince by formulating her experiences in terms that accorded with his known enthusiasms, and that both were erotically more attached to one another than the proprieties of New England at the turn of the century allowed either to realize. 'There was over her spine a "hypnogenetic point", pressure upon which always caused a thrill to run through her that weakened her will and induced hypnotic sleep.'

Rather similarly, most of the work done on multiple personality by the French neurologist Pierre *Janet was with women—notably Lucie, Léonie, and Rose—who regularly produced new or subpersonalities during hypnotic sessions. Janet, incidentally, distinguished clearly between 'roles' played by hypnotic subjects in order to please their hypnotist and new, unknown personalities which emerge spontaneously during hypnosis, particularly as a return to childhood. Presumably Janet was describing as dissociated personalities what contemporary psychiatrists and analysts would call revivals of repressed memories. Janet believed that the new personality emerging during hypnosis was more nearly the real person than the one that the patient originally presented, and that it was therapeutically helpful to name an emergent personality.

Both Prince and Janet believed that the self is not a pristine unity but an entity achieved by integration of 'simultaneous psychological existences', and that, therefore, multiple personalities and dissociated states generally were due to failures in integration. Contemporary psychoanalysis and psychiatry tend to take the opposite view: that the self is a pristine unity but uses defence mechanisms, notably repression, which make it unconscious of much of its total activity. As a result, many of the phenomena which Janet, Prince, and other 19th-century physicians described in terms of dissociation of the personality are nowadays described in terms of repression, splitting of the ego, etc.

This change seems to have occurred around 1910 and must presumably have been due to the impact of Freud's more dynamic, more biological, more sexual view of human nature. According to H. F. Ellenberger (1970), 'after 1910 there was a wave of reaction against the concept of multiple personality. It was alleged that the investigators, from Despine to Prince, had been duped by mythomaniac patients and that they had involuntarily shaped the manifestations they were observing.' And, although Ellenberger reports a slight revival of interest in the subject, contemporary textbooks of psychiatry are notably cautious and uncertain in their approach to dissociation of personality and to hysterical dissociation states generally. Henderson and Gillespie, in their *Textbook of Psychiatry* (9th edn. 1962), give only two paragraphs to multiple personality and the only two clinical examples they give date from the 19th century, while the emphasis in their paragraphs on hysterical dissociation states generally is on their rarity, on their purposiveness, which is usually transparent to observers but not to the subject himself, and on their dependence on gullibility. Explaining their rarity, Henderson and Gillespie remark, 'Both the public and their doctors have become more sophisticated'. Hysterical dissociation states, including dissociation of the personality, seem indeed to have more to do with the psychology of deception and self-deception than with any innate or acquired incapacity for integration. In the second half of the 19th century it seems to have been possible, in some circles at least, to evoke concern among friends and family and earn attention, if not effective treatment, from physicians by having trances, fugues, losing one's memory, or being taken over by another personality; but in the second half of the 20th century less dramatic and more subtle signals of distress became the order of the day.

CR

Ellenberger, H. F. (1970). *The Discovery of the Unconscious*.
Prince, M. (1905). *The Dissociation of a Personality* (repr. 1978).
Sizemore, C. (1978). *Eve*.

diver performance. The professional diver has probably the most hostile working environment on earth—or indeed off it, according to Scott Carpenter, who has been both an astronaut and an aquanaut and rates the underwater environment as the more hostile. Not only must the diver take along his own breathing mixture, but if he breathes air he is likely to suffer the dangerous intoxication of nitrogen narcosis at depths below 30 metres (100 feet); if he breathes pure oxygen he is likely to suffer from convulsions at depths exceeding 9–12 metres; and even breathing oxyhelium he is liable to have problems in voice communication and to find his performance impaired if he goes much deeper than 300 metres. He must either carry his supply of breathing mixture with him on his back, and risk it running out, or must be attached by an umbilical cord to some more generous source, with all the attendant risks of snagging and tangling and the dangers resulting from having the umbilical cord cut.

He will be relatively weightless, which might seem to be an advantage when it comes to moving about, but this presents real problems. If he is required to exert any great physical pressure to turn a wrench or wield a hammer, it is all too likely that he will turn, the wrench remaining where it is. Underwater vision is severely restricted by the tunnelling effect of refraction through his face mask, if indeed he is fortunate enough to be working under conditions that allow him to see anything. He is often required to work under conditions of zero visibility, operating by touch alone.

A commercial diver will expect to have to work under very cold conditions. While suits heated by a constant flow of warm water may be available, they are by no means the rule. Similarly, although a wide range of diving gloves exists, none appears to be really adequate under near-freezing conditions. Communication presents a further problem. The diver's voice is likely to be distorted by pressure and even further distorted if he is breathing an oxyhelium mixture. Helium unscramblers help, but are very far from perfect.

Having successfully completed a job under water, the problems are far from over. As the diver breathes air or oxyhelium at pressure, the nitrogen from the air or the helium from the oxyhelium is absorbed by his blood and body tissue. If he surfaces too rapidly, the gas forms bubbles in his tissue and bloodstream, leading to decompression sickness, otherwise known as 'the bends'. These may range from relatively minor joint pains (the niggles) to symptoms associated with breathing (the chokes), and to impairment of the central nervous system, producing motor disability (the staggers), pain, and possibly death. The bends can be avoided provided the diver surfaces slowly enough, but if he has been working at a depth of several hundred metres, decompression is likely to take a matter of days. In order to cope with this problem it is common for divers having a major job to do at depth to live at pressure in a decompression chamber, being transported to and from the job every day by means of a submersible decompression chamber that can be locked onto or detached from the main chamber on board the ship or rig. After a week of living at pressure the diver will spend the next week or so decompressing before taking some well-earned leave.

Socially, a diver's life is likely to be a rather curious one: unless he limits himself to inshore harbour work, periods out on an oil rig or pipe-laying barge are likely to alternate with periods of leave. If he is working on a rig, he may have long periods of inactivity followed by an emergency and a requirement suddenly to dive to a considerable depth. If he is working on a barge, he may be required to operate under saturation for many days. Under these conditions it is essential to be able to maintain good relations with fellow divers.

Diving is a dangerous occupation even if the diver takes good care to breathe the right gas mixture and maintain

the right working temperatures and the appropriate decompression schedule. He is working in an environment in which accidents are all too common, even out of the water. Under water, a minor accident can be fatal. Divers are very well paid—and so they should be. See also NITROGEN NARCOSIS.

ADB

Godden, D., and Baddeley, A. D. (1979). 'The commercial diver'. In Singleton, W. T. (ed.), *The Study of Real Skills: Compliance and Excellence*, vol. ii.

Dodge, Raymond (1871–1942). American experimental psychologist, born in Wobern, Massachusetts, the son of a physician. He was educated at Williams College, where he obtained his degree, but failed to gain admission to Harvard. He then spent several years in Germany working with Benno Erdmann in Halle, where he obtained his doctorate and jointly with Erdmann published a book on the experimental psychology of reading (1898), which was a classic in its day. He returned to America in 1898 and became a professor at the Wesleyan University in Middletown, Connecticut, where he became well known among psychologists for his originality and skill in psychological instrumentation and research. (Erdmann told him that he should have become an engineer!)

Dodge saw service in the First World War and invented an instrument for testing, selecting, and training gun pointers, which found wide application. He also worked on the psychological effects of alcohol. He later became chairman of the division of anthropology and psychology of the National Research Council in Washington.

After the war, Dodge became a professor at the Institute of Psychology at Yale and continued to pursue his early interests on the relation of eye movements to perception and on the conditions of human variability, about which he published several books, the best known of which is *Conditions and Consequences of Human Variability* (1931).

OLZ

Dodgson, Charles Lutwidge. See CARROLL, LEWIS.

dominance, hand. See HANDEDNESS.

dopamine neurons in the brain. Dopamine neurons are one type of a class of neurons all of which use biogenic amines as *neurotransmitters. These have been identified as *adrenaline (epinephrine), noradrenaline (norepinephrine), dopamine, and serotonin. A common feature of these groups is that a comparatively small number of neurons of each type in the brain stem give rise to a highly branched network of ascending and descending fibres of very fine calibre. These fibres carry action potentials of low frequency and slow conduction velocity. The post-

synaptic effects of their transmitters are slowly mediated by chemical reactions, in contrast to more 'classical' neurotransmitters such as *acetylcholine, which act extremely rapidly by means of the opening of specific ionic channels to carry current. Anatomically there appears to be a high degree of connections between some of these neuron groups, allowing for mutual interaction of function. The noradrenaline and serotonin neurons innervate a vast area of tissue throughout the brain and spinal cord. The adrenaline and dopamine groups on the other hand are somewhat more restricted in their anatomical distribution and their functions are likely to be correspondingly more specific.

The entire dopamine projection system arises from only a few thousand neurons located in the midbrain. One subgroup, the substantia nigra, innervates chiefly the caudate nucleus and putamen which lie in the basal ganglia—a brain region that controls movement. The substantia nigra also contains a non-dopamine neuron population by means of which it is brought into close relation to other sensory and motor brain regions. Degeneration of the dopamine neurons of the substantia nigra has been found to occur in *Parkinson's disease, a condition characterized by poverty of movement (hypokinesia), tremor, and rigidity. It seems likely, then, that these symptoms are related to disturbance in the coordination of neural activity in these circuits. Several observations strongly suggest that in Parkinson's disease both the basal ganglia and thalamus are concerned with the appearance of tremor and rigidity. It is probable that the globus pallidus (a subregion of the basal ganglia) is more concerned with the production of rigidity, while the thalamus is concerned with tremor. Successful neurosurgical treatment of these symptoms can be achieved by destroying small areas of these parts of the brain. On the other hand, it seems that the hypokinesia of Parkinsonism is due to degeneration of dopaminergic neurons. Thus it seems that there is a distinction between those symptoms in the Parkinsonian syndrome which are due to dopamine, and those due to non-dopamine neurons. Indeed, symptoms of hypokinesia can occur independently of rigidity and tremor. Hypokinesia can be successfully treated by giving the patient levodopa, an amino acid that is taken up in the brain and converted to the neurotransmitter dopamine in those dopamine neurons not affected by the disease.

The other main dopamine subgroup of neurons innervates various nuclei in the limbic system, including the amygdala. They are likely to be closely involved in the organism's emotional response to the environment. The same dopamine group also provides an innervation to important areas of the cerebral cortex—the frontal and temporal lobe cortices. Both these areas (particularly the latter) are targets for convergence of association fibres from extremely wide expanses of neocortex. They therefore provide potential anatomical structures in which the highest of cortical functions can be carried out. In man they are likely to be involved in the functions of memory, intellect, and personality. Dopamine neurons innervating these cortical regions also receive inputs from hypothalamic areas and the basal forebrain. These regions appear to be closely involved in motivation, learning, and rewarding mechanisms. *Schizophrenia is a condition which appears to be sensitive to the action of drugs that act on brain areas innervated by dopamine neurons. Drugs which act more selectively on only the limbic and cortical dopamine systems are also antipsychotic. Thus it may be that disturbance of these neurons, particularly those related to the amygdala and the temporal lobe cortex, may play an important part in the development of this condition.

OTP

doppelgänger (or autoscopy). The term given to the experience of meeting one's own 'double'. The apparition takes the form of a mirror image of the viewer (see MIRROR REVERSAL), facing him and just beyond arm's reach. It is life-sized and may move. Indeed, it usually replicates the viewer's posture, facial expressions, and movements as though it were his reflection. But beyond these features, reported experiences show several differences from the stereotype of popular imagination. First, the image is usually transparent: it has been described as being 'like jelly', or like a film projected on glass. (But it is not blurred or misty—its details are quite clear.) Secondly, it is generally monochromatic; if colour is observed, it is described as dull or 'washed out'. And thirdly, although the apparition may be inferred to include the whole figure, only the face, or head and trunk, are commonly 'seen'.

As reported by normal people, doppelgänger experiences occur most often late at night or at dawn. They are rare, occurring during periods of *stress or fatigue and in conjunction with disturbed *consciousness. (However, the first recorded account, which is attributed to Aristotle, describes a man who could not go out for a walk without meeting his 'double'.) A doppelgänger episode is usually of very short duration with normal people, lasting only a few seconds. The experience is more common among delirious patients, among those with brain lesions in the parieto-occipital regions, or, most notably, among epileptics, where it may be part of a complex partial seizure. Autoscopy can occasionally be a feature of an attack of migraine, sometimes in association with a sense of distortion of a part of the body. The doppelgänger experience, when the subject sees himself standing behind his back or in another room, is referred to as an extracampine *hallucination.

The fact that an apparition is presumed in most cultures to be a visitor from the grave, a spirit of the dead, may well account for the morbid response accorded the doppelgänger experience. After all, the subject is apparently being accosted by his own ghost, which not only raises some knotty questions about the nature of time, but bears the distinct implication that the subject's own time is up. Indeed, the German folk belief was that the doppelgänger was a harbinger of death. Like many old wives' tales, this superstitious belief may have had a factual basis, for in those cases where doppelgänger is associated with severe brain injury or cerebral thrombosis, the illness is often fatal.

The idea of a phantom 'double' has existed throughout recorded history, and still flourishes in superstitions, fairy tales, and folklore throughout the world. It is taken seriously by some parapsychologists as an example of an *out-of-body experience. It figures in many primitive religions, where the 'double' is assumed to be the person's soul. Witches and shamans put their 'doubles' to good use, sending them on occult errands or as representatives or intermediaries. But the doppelgänger concept has also intrigued sophisticated people, and induced in them a dread of the unknown and a morbid assumption of doom akin to the responses of primitive groups. Autoscopic phenomena have frequently been described in the literature of the Western world, always in terms of sinister foreboding or impending tragedy. Descriptions have figured in the works of Dostoevsky, Kafka, de Maupassant, Edgar Allan Poe, Steinbeck, and Oscar Wilde. It is of interest that several of these suffered from epilepsy or cerebral disorder.

Doppelgänger experiences have attracted little medical or psychological study, despite widespread interest. Traditionally, the phenomenon has been classified as a visual hallucination, and its form can be examined in the same terms as other hallucinations. But an added dimension is that the experience is not limited to the visual modality; many subjects have reported that they could 'hear' and 'feel' their doubles. This multi-modality suggests the intriguing possibility that doppelgänger may in some way represent an externalization or displacement of Sir Henry *Head's 'body schema'. However, why should the apparition appear as a mirror image? GFR

double vision. See DIPLOPIA.

doubting. The questioning of accepted beliefs or opinions. In Greek philosophy such doubting was erected into a philosophical system by the sceptics, such as Pyrrho of Elis (fl. c.300 BC), who argued that all truth is unknowable and that the only appropriate attitude for life is one of total suspension of belief. In the 17th century, *Descartes's famous 'method of doubt' involved withholding assent from all matters that allow even the smallest possibility of doubt. Thus all information derived from the senses is potentially unreliable; further, we cannot know whether

we are awake or asleep, so that even such a simple statement as 'I am holding this piece of paper' is open to doubt; and, finally, there may be a malicious all-powerful demon who is bent on deceiving us, and so 'the earth, sky, and all external things' may be merely delusions. Cartesian doubt is not, however, an end in itself, but it is designed to clear the way for the establishment of a secure system of knowledge built on indubitable foundations.

The questioning of accepted beliefs and preconceived opinions can be a valuable exercise both in philosophy and in science generally (see COMMON SENSE). It seems, however, that to insist on indubitability as a criterion of the acceptability of beliefs is to insist on an impossibly high standard. Immunity to all conceivable doubt is something that belongs to only a handful of very simple and relatively unexciting propositions, such as (perhaps) 'two and two make four', or Descartes's famous 'cogito' ('I am thinking'), and it does not seem possible to construct any worthwhile system of knowledge on such meagre foundations.

The difficulty of seriously maintaining a position of philosophical scepticism was highlighted by G. E. *Moore in the 20th century, and earlier by David *Hume. Hume observed that 'Nature is always too strong for principle, and though a Pyrrhonian may throw himself and others into a momentary . . . confusion by his profound reasonings, the first and most trivial event in life will put to flight all his doubts' (Enquiry Concerning Human Understanding, 1748). JGC

Down's syndrome. The most common genetic cause of learning disability, which is believed to occur during the early stages of embryological development due to the presence of an extra chromosome 21. The human body usually has 46 chromosomes in each cell, half from the mother, half from the father. A person with Down's syndrome has an extra chromosome, making 47 in all, which causes disruption in growth of the developing baby. There are three different types of Down's syndrome: standard trisomy 21, which is found in 95 per cent of people with Down's syndrome and is not inherited. The second type occurs in approximately 1 in 100 people with Down's syndrome who have inherited the condition from their mother or father because of a genetic anomaly called a translocation. The third type, mosaic Down's syndrome, is also rare.

The characteristics of Down's syndrome include: a flattened face, a thick tongue which may be too large for the mouth, extra folds for eyelids, hands that are broad with short fingers, a deep cleft between the first and second toe extending as a crease on the side of the foot, and a much lower than average IQ. Certain medical problems are more common in people with Down's syndrome: for example, heart disease and problems with vision and hearing. Increasing evidence has also shown that almost all individuals with Down's syndrome show neuropathological changes similar to those seen in Alzheimer's disease, if they survive into their 40s. This has been attributed to excess production of beta-amyloid protein, which is encoded by the *APP* gene on chromosome 21 (see Petronis 1999 for a recent review).

It is now more common for people with Down's syndrome to enjoy longer lifespans of 40–60 years. This is a massive increase in life expectancy (which, for example, in 1983 was estimated at 25 years) resulting from better treatment for frequent causes of death, a shift in attitudes towards Down's syndrome, and accompanying changes in medical practice (Yang, Rasmussen, and Friedman 2002). Although increasing life expectancy in people with Down's syndrome does have implications for the primary carers, such as the parents, it is increasingly being recognized that people with Down's syndrome are capable of living fulfilled and relatively independent lives (e.g. Alderson 2001). The social issues surrounding increased life expectancy and attitudes towards people with Down's syndrome have huge implications for prenatal screening policies. It is important that potential parents of Down's syndrome children have access to realistic, unprejudiced knowledge about the condition, which should come from a variety of psychological, medical, and personal sources.

Prenatal tests for Down's syndrome include, for example, amniocentesis. Amniocentesis, the most common diagnostic test of Down's syndrome, is usually carried out at around 15–16 weeks of pregnancy and involves taking a sample of the amniotic fluid in the womb. The test is almost 100 per cent accurate but carries a risk of miscarriage of around 1 in 100. Screening tests such as the triple test are also available that provide an estimate of the probability of the baby having the condition rather than a categorical decision. A blood sample is taken at around 16 weeks and an individualized risk value is calculated. For reasons not understood, the incidence of Down's syndrome is higher in children born of older parents, especially of an older mother.

For further information or support concerning Down's syndrome visit: www.dsa-uk.com (The Down's Syndrome Association, UK). RLG

Alderson, P. (2001). 'Down's syndrome: cost, quality and value of life'. *Social Science and Medicine*, 53.

Epstein C. J. (1995). 'Down syndrome (Trisomy 21)'. In Scriver, C. R., Beaudet, A. L., Sly, W. S., and Valle, D. (eds.), *The Metabolic and Molecular Bases of Inherited Disease*, vol i.

Petronis, A. (1999). 'Alzheimer's disease and Down syndrome: from meiosis to dementia'. *Experimental Neurology*, 158.

Yang, Q., Rasmussen, S. A., and Friedman, J. M. (2002). 'Mortality associated with Down's syndrome in the USA from 1983 to 1997: a population based study'. *Lancet*, 359.

drama.

1. Some characteristics of drama
2. Drama and society
3. Drama as a composite art
4. Connections with religion
5. Rules of drama

The word 'drama' is used in at least four distinct though overlapping meanings. It may loosely describe any uncommon event—say, a 'dramatic encounter'. More properly, it means a play script destined either for the theatre or for more recent media such as television or radio. More specifically still, it denotes a particular *kind* of play—one that, occupying the middle ground, slips through conventional categories such as tragedy, melodrama, farce, or whatever. In its widest meaning 'drama' stands for playwriting as such, a distinct form of literary production. This has inherent advantages as well as drawbacks One of the main advantages of drama in the general sense is the presence of the public watching (as 'spectators') as well as listening (as the 'audience') to a performance of the text. The drawbacks are the reverse of this. Fortuitous events (the weather, the casting, capricious reviews) may colour the reception of plays regardless of their intrinsic quality. What is more, some aspects of the human condition do not readily lend themselves to dramatization. Subtle shifts in relationships that result in a minimal outer action may be hard to portray on the stage. Emotions left unuttered, thoughts left concealed can indeed be expressed by such—now unfashionable—devices as the soliloquy and the aside, but the novel can handle them far more adequately. In contrast to music, which is a universal human activity, drama is not in fact encountered everywhere and at all times. At its heart there are certain ambiguities.

1. Some characteristics of drama

Let us remember that drama as a vehicle just for the spoken word only, unaccompanied by song, instrumental music, dance, and stylized gesture, is a relatively new phenomenon in the long history of theatre. Ancient Greek drama was what Wagner called a 'Gesamtkunstwerk'—a total work of art—in which the role of the verse-speaking, singing, and dancing chorus was crucial. In Europe, opera and ballet split off as distinct genres only in the late 16th century as the spoken drama was itself becoming an autonomous vehicle for new and challenging ideas. A purely verbal drama deprived of music and dance is to this day alien to traditional forms of Asian theatre.

Like other forms of narrative literature, drama is a time-based art. But—unlike, say, the novel that tends to use the narrative past—drama works in the *present* tense. An action performed on stage takes on a palpable immediacy, amplified by the reactions of the audience. This power has often anatagonized the powers that be who have tended to view with suspicion any entertainments capable of challenging their social, moral, or political hegemony. Hence censorship has left its greasy finger mark on many pages of stage history, from the French Crown issuing edicts against satirical plays in the 15th century to Glavrepertkom controlling the repertoire of Soviet theatres or the Lord Chamberlain blue-pencilling play scripts in Britain between 1737 and 1968.

For all its pitfalls, the art of drama has at various times enjoyed the highest literary prestige. In the last chapter of his *Poetics* the philosopher *Aristotle (4th century BC) placed tragedy (admittedly only one aspect of drama) above the parallel literary art of the epic. And it is true that drama has furnished the world's imagination with such figures as Oedipus, Electra, Hamlet, Falstaff, Tartuffe, and Faust—no less recognizable as recurrent types of humanity than their counterparts in narrative fiction – e.g. Don Quixote, Robinson Crusoe, and Emma Bovary.

2. Drama and society

As a medium depending on collective responses, drama cements the cohesion of social groups. In the Athens of the 5th century BC the City Dionysia, where new plays were premiered, was the expression of a self-confident democracy presenting itself to its citizens. Medieval mystery plays brought together entire Christian communities under the aegis of guilds, municipalities, and confraternities. Drama may also crystallize class allegiances. Whereas Ben Jonson and Inigo Jones's masques (1605–34) appealed to an aristocratic elite at the Stuart court, trade union audiences cheering the plays at London's Unity Theatre (1936–75) were bonded by a common anti-Establishment stance. Drama has at times strengthened a sense of national identity: Shakespeare's histories are notable examples of this. At other times it has served the interests of the autocratic state. The setting up of the Comédie-Française by Louis XVI (1680) consecrated the cultural–political importance of what was then the dominant power on the Continent. The theatres of imperial countries, from Rome to Great Britain, have imposed metropolitan values on the colonies by cultural means. Conversely, in countries late in achieving political independence, drama has often helped to fire popular aspirations. Thus, the National Theatre in Prague was built out of the Czech people's voluntary contributions and opened in 1881—only to be burnt down and rebuilt two years later with yet further popular support; above its proscenium arch it was to bear the proud legend: 'A Nation's Gift to Itself.'

3. Drama as a composite art

Drama is not always text based. Indeed the more popular and/or comic in its form, the more likely it is to depend on non-literary devices. Chinese theatre has always been intimately linked with music. The actors of the centuries-old Italian *commedia dell'arte* often used a scenario, i.e. a plot outline, instead of a fully written-out text; much of its humour was physical rather than verbal. Two still current forms of improvisatory theatre of the Middle East, *ruhowzi* and *orta-oyunu*, adjust the duration of performances to the given occasion: in other words, the play text is kept flexible as required.

So one could say that dramatic texts are menus rather than meals complete in themselves. In this they differ from forms of literature autonomous from their inception like the essay, as well as from those—like lyric and epic poetry—that have long since retreated from song and recitation to the printed page. Play scripts in concept and practice are linked with a wide range of sister arts: dynamic ones such as speech, movement, gesture, acrobatics, singing, instrumental music, or dance, as well as static ones such as architecture or stage and costume design. This hybridity applies even to so-called closet drama aimed at a mental rather than a physical stage. True, Aristotle conceded that tragedy could be *read* as easily as it could be enjoyed in the theatre. The classical canon of Greek tragedians, of Plautus, Terence, and Seneca, of Shakespeare, Corneille, Racine, and Molière, as well as other national authors like Schiller and Goethe, has long been and still is taught at schools and colleges—though more often than not with a fine disregard of its theatrical context. Nowadays the publication of plays is indeed a lively business. But the fact remains that drama demands to be read in a special way, i.e. empathetically. In the theatre of the mind, the unheard voices and unseen gestures of the agents are a vital part of the reading experience.

4. Connections with religion

The origins of drama are usually held to go back to religious beliefs and practices. But ritual, which may well be a universal factor in man's evolution, is not quite the same thing as drama, however closely related the two may be. Unlike ritual, a dramatic performance bears an 'as if' character that invites the onlooker's detachment which Coleridge called a 'willing suspension of disbelief'. Drama's emancipation from pure ritual is hard to pin down in time. Egyptian texts going back as far as 2500 BC are thought to represent something like the dialogue and stage action for rituals unfolding in a temple setting. Ancient Chinese and Korean theatre may well have originated in shamanistic rituals. The *Natya-shastra*, the Indian classic on drama compiled some time between the 2nd and the 8th centuries AD, ascribed the beginnings of the art to a heavenly performance arranged by Brahma for an audience of gods and demons. The *kagura*, a type of Japanese play performed as an offering to the gods at Shinto shrines from the Yamato (3rd to 6th century AD) period onwards until the present day, is traditionally linked with the myth of the goddess Ame no Uzume who tempted the sun goddess Amaterasu out of her cave by dancing for her. Attic tragedy, the oldest form of high drama in the European tradition, grew according to Aristotle out of the dithyramb, a choric hymn addressed to Dionysus, god of wine, wild nature, and ecstatic possession. And indeed, when the great tragedies of 5th-century Athens were performed at the City Dionysia—celebrations partly religious, partly civic, and partly competitive—an altar to the god occupied a prominent place in the acting area. Aristotle claimed that comedy, too, derived from improvised phallic songs, celebrations of fertility linked with the god.

However, there have been long periods when some religions—notably the three monotheistic faiths—set their faces sternly against any performance art. Judaism in ancient times disapproved of the theatre as an expression of Hellenistic, i.e. pagan, culture. Early Christianity was fiercely opposed to the public spectacles of imperial Rome. Tertullian condemned the theatre as the devil's church; the hostility of many later Fathers of the Church opened a wide gulf for hundreds of years between the new faith and the ancient art of theatrical representation. It is of course the case that much later, long after the theatre of antiquity had perished in the 6th century AD, the Church itself was to use dramatic means to preach its message. This Christian drama, which depicted scriptural history as well as the lives of saints and which allegorized everyman's moral dilemmas, flourished in many parts of Western and Central Europe for centuries in the latter part of the Middle Ages. A distant echo of this is still to be found in the Oberammergau Passion Play. Even so, the Church maintained its reservations concerning profane drama. As late as 1673 the great actor/playwright Molière was refused a Christian burial. The Reformation, which proved even more hostile to theatre than the Catholic Church, brought about the total demise of scriptural drama in England and elsewhere in the 16th century. Puritan revulsion against the theatre reached its climax in England when all theatres were kept closed under the Commonwealth from 1648 to 1660.

Islam did not favour dramatic performances for a great part of its history either; it saw them as attempts to create an alternative reality to God's creation. To be sure, fundamentalism has not stifled religious drama in the Islamic world altogether. In Iran the *taziyeh*, a kind of Passion Play, has been developing since the 18th century as an annual commemoration of the martyrdom in 680 of Husayn ibn 'Ali', the third Imam of the Shiite faith.

But a fuller development of drama has arguably come about precisely when it cut itself adrift from its otherworldly origins. Not that religious impulses would have been the sole motivation for performance even in the earliest times. Other motives of a more profane kind must have come into play as well: the sense of a joyous public occasion, of being taken 'out of oneself', and—last but not least—open-mouthed admiration for the skills of performers. The satiric impulse, too, is an ancient one; the pleasure of poking fun at men of power had long been familiar by the time of Aristophanes.

5. Rules of drama

Aristotle's *Poetics*, looking back on the great period of Greek playwriting which in his day had passed its prime, was to have a long-term effect on the Western conception of drama. Intended as a philosophical approach to criticism, this brief work laid down some ground rules, particularly for tragedy. It recognized drama as a composite art but placed the playwright's skill in devising the plot above other aspects such as character, diction, thought, spectacle, and song. It insisted on unity of action, i.e. a well-articulated plot complete in itself, but it did *not* mention the other two unities—those of time and place (except for a passing reference to the latter)—which Renaissance critics some eighteen centuries later were to consider mandatory in 'regular drama'. Practising playwrights from Lope de Vega in the early 17th century to Victor Hugo over 200 years later held out against the tyranny of these supposed 'rules'. Even as recently as the 20th century, Brecht proclaimed an anti-Aristotelian dramaturgy, objecting as he did to the philosopher's conservative view of the impact of theatre on the spectator. Dramatic theory has been in a state of flux for centuries. Many have seen conflict as being the soul of plot, and broadly speaking that is correct. But even this claim may be open to question. Some of Beckett's plays—*Waiting for Godot*, *Endgame*, or *Happy Days*—run counter to this conventional assumption.

The confrontation of one character with another takes place even in puppetry, employing—in place of the human actor—creatures made of wood, papier-mâché, cloth, leather, or whatever, which are operated by gloves, strings, or rods. Minuscule or huge, three-dimensional or flat shadow figures, these substitute persons represent dramatic dilemmas fully as much as 'real' actors do, albeit in a distanced, frequently caricatural form. The interrelationship between live theatre and the puppet show is a complex one. In Japan, the popular *kabuki* borrowed texts and even acting techniques from the *bunraku* (puppet) theatre. In Europe, the Punch-and-Judy show is a miniaturized offshoot of the *commedia dell'arte*.

It has been said that today we live in a dramatized society. The rules of the game may have changed over time, altering the function and the very shape of the playhouse. The media of the moving image have evolved new rules with their ability to incorporate large segments of external reality into their narrative. But some play-wrights—Euripides, Shakespeare, Molière, to name but a few—have proved immune to the ravages of time, made freshly relevant by constant reinterpretations on the stage. Drama in some shape or form is all around us—perhaps to the extent of enveloping us in a virtual reality. It continues to be of the first importance as an outlet for creative energies as well as a key to understanding the human condition, and we are—as always—left with the critical task of sorting out ephemeral dross from works of enduring value.   GWB

Banham, M. (ed.) (1995). *The Cambridge Guide to Theatre.*

Brandt, G. W. (ed.) (1998). *Modern Theories of Drama.*

Chambers, C. (ed.) (2002). *The Continuum Companion to Twentieth Century Theatre.*

Dorsch, T. S. (trans.) (1965). *Classical Literary Criticism: Aristotle/Horace/Longinus.*

Elam, K. (1980). *The Semiotics of Theatre and Drama.*

Kennedy, D. (ed.) (2003). *The Oxford Encyclopedia of Theatre and Performance.* 2 vols.

dreaming (1). Dreaming can be defined as the images and thoughts that are experienced during sleep. The scientific study of dreaming relates these images and thoughts to the physiology of the brain during sleep, and to the waking life events and personality of the dreamer (Hobson 2003). There are two major aspects of brain physiology that relate to dreaming. First, sleep in humans is divided into light sleep (stages 1 and 2), deep sleep (stages 3 and 4), and rapid eye movement sleep (REM sleep). REM sleep occurs approximately every 90 minutes, each REM period becoming longer across the night; the last one can be as long as 40 minutes, the first as short as 5 minutes. Brainwaves during REM sleep have some similarity to waking brainwaves, and parts of the brain are very active, while muscle tone is very low; because of the brain being very active while the body is asleep REM sleep has been termed paradoxical sleep. REM sleep has usually been identified by the use of the electroencephalograph to measure brainwaves, with *eye movements detected as a result of their electromagnetic field. These eye movements can also be visible to a person watching. In 1953 Aserinsky and Kleitman found that dream recall was more likely if people were woken from REM sleep than from sleep stages 1 to 4. In 1962 Foulkes investigated dreams in non-REM sleep, showing that dreams can occur in non-REM sleep but that they were usually shorter and less dramatic and vivid than REM dreams. It is currently a matter of dispute whether differences between REM and non-REM dreams are just due to non-REM dreams being shorter on average than REM dreams, or whether there are fundamental differences between them, such as REM dreams being more bizarre, with these differences possibly being physiologically based.

On the latter, Hobson has proposed a cholinergic neuro-chemical difference between REM sleep and both being awake and non-REM sleep, to explain the amnesic and irrational nature of REM dreams. The second relevant aspect of brain physiology is that whereas the brain becomes very much less active during non-REM sleep compared with being awake, during REM sleep the brain becomes very active, including activation of areas of the parietal lobe related to visual imagery, and of the amygdala and paralimbic cortex which are related to emotional processing. In his reviews of the neuropsychological literature Solms shows that lesions to the ventral–mesial quadrant of the frontal lobe (at the front of the brain, and involved with emotional motivation and wishes), or to the parietotemporo-occipital junction (the sensory areas of the brain nearer the back at the side), result in the loss of dream recall, but with REM sleep preserved. These brain areas thus seem to be important for creating dreams.

The relationship of REM dreaming to the limbic system provides a basis to findings that there are dream content changes and altered frequency of dream recall following emotional waking experiences. However, although dream content can be related to waking life experiences, this seems to account for no more than a minority of the entire dream content, leading to the claim by Hobson (1999) that much of dream content is delirium-like, rather than motivated or meaningful.

This leads to the empirical work on whether individual differences in dream content can be related to individual differences in waking life experiences or personality. Domhoff proposes a methodology for quantifying samples of dreams, taken either from one person over time, or from a group of people, who are then compared with another group, or with a population mean. Many variables can be derived, for example the percentage of characters who are aggressive, the percentage of negative emotions, the number of dreams that contain a misfortune, or the number that contain a success. Domhoff shows that these variables can be stable across time in people. The methodology of scientific studies on dream content, and their related statistics, is described on the website www.dreamresearch.net, and in Domhoff (2003).

Given that some of the dream content can be related to waking life cognition and emotions the next question is whether dream content provides information about waking cognition and emotions that are not within conscious awareness, that is, whether studying dreams can provide therapeutic insight. Clara Hill (2003) has developed a cognitive method for obtaining insight from dreams and initiating altered cognition and action, and Hartmann (1998) provides evidence that dreams can provide a form of therapy without a therapist. There have been claims that dreams can provide the inspiration for inventions and discoveries, such as the structure of the benzene molecule by Kekulé, but some of these claims are disputed: accounts of the claims have been collated in works by Deirdre Barrett.

It was a claim of Freud that dreams provide a 'royal road to the unconscious', because during sleep we censor thoughts less than when awake. His method of dream interpretation required the person undergoing analysis to free-associate to each component of the dream, the theory being that this would lead from the manifest dream content (the dream that was remembered) to the latent dream thoughts (the wishes and other factors, often unconscious, that was the source of the dream). Clearly this method can result in confabulation of links between the dream content and waking cognition and memories; however, a similar free-association method is now used by Cavallero and many others to distinguish whether items in dreams have as their source a waking episodic memory, a semantic memory, or abstract memory or knowledge about the self. The claim of Cavallero and colleagues has been that REM dreams have less reliance on episodic sources than do non-REM dreams or sleep-onset dreams, but as with most claimed differences between REM and non-REM dreams, the differences are small, especially when dreams of similar length are compared.

Although dreams can be very vivid and dramatic they are easily forgotten if effort is not made to recall or write them down immediately upon waking. Whereas Freud claimed that dreams were easily forgotten because of repression, it is now thought that a lack of memory consolidation during sleep causes this forgetting, although the fact that delayed dream recall can suddenly occur hours after waking due to cues later in the day indicates that some memory consolidation of dreams does occur prior to waking. People who are more creative have been found to have more dreams, and dreams that are more bizarre, although it is not clear if their dreams are different from less creative people or if this is a reporting effect, in that they may have a greater interest in, or a more favourable attitude towards, dreams than less creative people. In favour of it being a reporting effect, people who never recall dreams usually do recall them frequently if woken in the sleep laboratory during REM sleep.

The widely held continuity theory of dreams holds that individual differences in waking cognition and personality correlate with formal and content characteristics of dreams. Notwithstanding this continuity there is also another widely held view that highlights the deficiencies of cognition in dreams, such as of memory, rationality, and volition. This has led to Rechtschaffen's view of dreams being 'single-minded', that is, it is rare to have critical thoughts during a dream about the events of the dream, such as noticing bizarre instances, or deliberating about what to do next in the dream, or even realizing that

it is a dream. It has been claimed that deficiencies in volition during dreams occur due to the lack of activity of the dorsolateral prefrontal cortex during sleep. However, there is evidence from Kahan and LaBerge that volition, choice, and deliberation can be shown to occur in dreams if the dreamer is asked about it soon after waking, rather than the usual method of having an independent judge rating written dream reports for the presence of these characteristics. This then raises the issue of the rare occurrence of lucid dreams, defined as dreams in which one knows one is dreaming, and can decide to alter the plot of the dream. Their rarity—approximately just 10 per cent of the population will have them at least once per month—reinforces the deficiency view of dreaming, but levels of self-awareness and lucidity in dreams can be increased by cognitive training methods, and Blagrove and Hartnell in 2000 found lucid dreamers have a greater internal locus of control and need for cognition than non-lucid dreamers, which is evidence for the continuity hypothesis.

More common than lucid dreams but equally of theoretical importance are nightmares. Some studies have shown that people with frequent nightmares have lower well-being or anxiety in their waking lives. However, many other studies have not found a relationship between nightmare frequency and current waking life psychopathology, leading to the possibilities that it is the degree of suffering from nightmares, rather than the number of them, that is related to psychopathology, or that nightmares and bad dreams are common in all people, or that nightmares are related to trauma. The last possibility is explored in Barrett (1996), but may only hold for some nightmares, especially those early in the night.

The work of David Foulkes shows that dreaming develops with age from simple scenes with no plot and no participation by the dreamer in children aged 3–5, social interaction in dreams developing at ages 5–7, and self-participation at ages 7–9, and diverse emotions and novel characters at ages 9–13. That dreaming is a complex symbolic activity that thus develops in parallel with cognitive development may mean that animals do not dream, or that, if they do, their dreams are simpler copies of the waking environment than are the dreams of humans.

Whether dreams have a function is disputed. There is much evidence that REM sleep is needed for forming memories, and so it may be that the dreams that occur during REM sleep have a function in forming novel connections between memories. That dreams are themselves so easy to forget may count against this theory, or some say in its favour, and there are of course many dreams, called impactful dreams, that surprise and intrigue us and remain strong in our memory throughout life. Others claim that dreams help us adapt to stress, but disputed then is whether we need to be able to remember a dream for its function to occur, or whether the 2–3 hours of dreams that we may have each night have a function even if we do not wake during them and hence never remember them.   MB

Barrett, D. (ed.) (1996). *Trauma and Dreams.*

Domhoff, G. W. (2003). *The Scientific Study of Dreams: Neural Networks, Cognitive Development, and Content Analysis.*

Hartmann, E. (1998). *Dreams and Nightmares: The Origin and Meaning of Dreams.*

Hill, C. E. (ed.) (2003). *Dream Work in Therapy: Facilitating Exploration, Insight, and Action.*

Hobson, J. A. (1999). *Dreaming as Delirium: How the Brain Goes out of its Mind.*

—— (2003). *Dreaming: An Introduction to the Science of Sleep.*

Pace-Schott, E. F., Solms, M., Blagrove, M., and Harnad, S. (eds.) (2003). *Sleep and Dreaming: Scientific Advances and Reconsiderations.*

dreaming (2). In our *sleep we all intermittently experience insanity. Some of our dreams differ so from normal awareness that they have often been attributed to the departure of the soul to another world, or to the visitation of alien beings, such as angels. Since earliest history, dreams have been interpreted in order to give guidance for the future, up to the dream books of the 19th century and punters' guides of the 20th. In the 1950s Nathaniel Kleitman of Chicago, with E. Aserinsky and W. Dement, opened an era of laboratory techniques for studying dreams.

Dreams are often misleadingly defined as successions of visual images, but these are merely common accompaniments. A dream is an experience of living in a fantasy world in which things happen, emotions are felt, actions are carried out, people are present, with all the waking sensations coming and going. The congenitally blind have dreams of their touch world, without brightness or colour, that are no less vivid even though they see nothing. Visual images in dreams are as often in colour as in real life.

Dement and Kleitman (1957) introduced the technique of awakening and questioning volunteers about possible dreams at critically sensitive moments during sleep, and found that during periods of sleep accompanied by rapid eye movements (REM) detailed dream reports could usually be elicited, whereas recall from other times during sleep was meagre. Dement wakened some further volunteers repeatedly as soon as their REM began, and later found a compensatory increase of sleep with REM. He proposed that he had deprived them of dreams, that they needed to dream, and that if they did not they might become insane. This notion achieved wide circulation but has not since been supported. We may need to dream, but no one has yet devised an experiment to see whether we have such psychological needs at night.

There are two kinds of sleep; they came to be called non-rapid eye movement (NREM or orthodox) and rapid eye movement (REM or paradoxical) sleep. In 1962 David Foulkes of Chicago asked of his subjects not the leading question, 'Have you been dreaming?' but instead, 'What was passing through your mind?' He found that NREM sleep allowed recall almost as often as REM sleep, but its less colourful content was more often characterized as 'thinking' and, despite considerable overlap, it was possible to distinguish between the 'dream' reports from REM sleep and those from NREM sleep. Typical dreams can be elicited especially easily from NREM sleep at the end of the night and when first falling asleep. The brief dreamlets that come as we drowsily drift to sleep are known as *hypnagogic hallucinations or images.

In subsequent research Molinari and Foulkes made awakenings from REM sleep both just after one of the intermittent bursts of REM and when over 30 seconds of ocular quiescence had elapsed during REM sleep, and sought details of mental life just prior to waking. The first type of awakenings elicited many 'primary' visual and other experiences (for example, a little brother suddenly vomiting 'on my shoulder'), the second elicited 'secondary cognitive elaborations' resembling the thinking characteristic of NREM sleep. Jerky eye movements, limb twitches, face twitches, middle-ear muscle twitches, and sudden respiratory changes are all *phasic* components of REM sleep, whereas muscle relaxation and penile erections are *tonic* features. It seems that the special 'dream' elements are injected intermittently in company with the phasic components of REM sleep.

As the night progresses, the REM periods contain a higher rate of phasic components, and dreams are more active and less passive in quality. Sleeping pills diminish the phasic elements and dreams become more passive. There has been a lot of controversy about such relations between bodily events and the contents of a dream. While the majority of the REM certainly cannot be ascribed to scanning the visual field of a dream-world, there are occasional large eye movements that do seem to bear a relation to described dream content. Closer correspondence has been found for movements of the limbs: Jouvet made lesions in the lower brains of cats so that they were no longer paralysed during REM sleep, and they rose up and appeared to the observer to be acting out their dreams. There is certainly a strong correlation between dream emotionality and heart-rate fluctuations or skin-potential fluctuations, while in anxiety-ridden dreams there is loss of the usual penile erections.

The intensified dreaming qualities to the mental life that accompanies each REM sleep period about every 90–100 minutes led to findings that, while awake and in unchanging environments, people engage in intensified oral activity and have more daydreaming qualities to their thoughts according to a daytime cycle of 90–100 minutes. Daydreaming and night-dreaming are both associated with a 90- to 100-minute rhythm.

The term 'nightmare' is today used for dreams that occur during REM sleep, usually in the later night, and in which a series of events is associated with *anxiety. As the sleeper awakens from his nightmare, he is often aware of the inability to move that characterizes REM sleep. On the other hand, night terrors arise in the early night, from NREM sleep with large slow electrical brainwaves. They involve brief and less elaborately detailed experiences of entrapment, of being choked or attacked, often with shrieking, sitting up, or sleepwalking (see SOMNAMBULISM), and tremendous acceleration of the heart. Both night-mares and night terrors occur unpredictably in even the most emotionally stable people, but become more frequent when there is greater daytime anxiety; they are frequent among wartime battle evacuees and night ter-rors are commonly experienced by children aged 10–14. Likewise, those who are depressed by day have dreams by night that contain themes of failure and loss.

Environmental circumstances influence dream con-tent. Dreams reported after awakenings by investigators in the home have more aggressive, friendly, sexual, or success-and-failure elements than those reported in the laboratory, but in both cases most are duller than would be supposed. Anxiety-provoking films seen prior to sleep can lead to dreams containing related themes. Events occurring around the sleeper during dreams are often in-corporated, so that, for example, the words 'Robert, Rob-ert, Robert' spoken to a sleeper led to his reporting a dream about a 'distorted rabbit'.

Dream reports from successive periods of REM sleep in a single night can be distinguished from those of other nights, and the dreams of one individual are different from those of another: dreams thus reflect both day-to-day psy-chological variations and enduring individual traits. Sigmund Freud (see FREUD ON DREAMS), C. G. *Jung, and many others since have sought hidden features of person-ality and understanding of an individual's emotional con-flicts, through examination of, or *free association from, dreams described by day. Whatever the clinical value of such dream recollections, they hardly compare with the rich reports that can be elicited by awakenings at night. Despite the symbolism and fascinating condensation of ideas to be found in dreams, there is no evidence that a more useful understanding of personality can be gained from them than can be divined from the realities of wak-ing behaviour.   IO

Dement, W., and Kleitman, N. (1957). 'The relation of eye move-ments during sleep to dream activity, an objective method for the study of dreaming'. *Journal of Experimental Psychology*, 53.
Foulkes, D. (1966). *The Psychology of Sleep*.
Hall, C. S. (1953). *The Meaning of Dreams*.
Kramer, M. (ed.) (1969). *Dream Psychology and the New Biology of Dreaming*.
MacKenzie, N. (1965). *Dreams and Dreaming*. London.

dreams in ancient Greece. Belief in the dream as a revelation was widespread in the ancient Near East, and is present in our earliest Greek documents, the poems of Homer. Dreams may contain prophecy or bind-ing instructions, because they come 'from Zeus'; but they are a mixed blessing, because they may be sent to deceive. Later authors distinguish between significant and non-significant dreams; a dream that simply reflects the anx-ieties or desires felt by the dreamer during the previous day is non-prophetic. This distinction does not imply a weakening of belief; anthropologists report that no soci-ety treats all dreams as significant, and evidence of the most diverse kinds shows that some dreams were widely regarded as god-sent or otherwise revelatory up to and beyond the end of the pagan Greek world. Of classical authors, the dream is noticeably absent only from Thu-cydides. *Plato describes *Socrates as composing poetry in obedience to a dream while in prison awaiting execu-tion; the practical Xenophon twice records significant dreams of his own in the *Anabasis*; and the politician De-mosthenes could claim to have received messages from the gods in sleep. Incubation, the practice of seeking sig-nificant dreams by sleeping in a sacred area, was a wide-spread oracular technique, and the incubation healing cult of Asclepius at Epidaurus became a centre of pilgrim-age from all Greece. Dream interpreters are already men-tioned in Homer, and from the 5th century BC there grew up an extensive literature on dream interpretation; this is represented for us by Artemidorus (2nd century AD), whose approach is, given his premises, cautious and prac-tical, and shows that specialists in this sphere were not necessarily wild, marginal figures. It should be noted that Greek dream interpretation, though it operated with symbols, was prophetic in aim, and thus has little in com-mon with the system of Sigmund Freud (see FREUD ON DREAMS). Any dream that could be explained by the ex-periences or desires of the dreamer was dismissed as in-significant; many dreams, however, that would now be seen as psychologically revealing were regarded as exter-nally motivated and therefore prophetic. For instance, the frequently reported dreams of incest (many men have dreamt of sleeping with their mothers, says Sophocles) were generally interpreted symbolically as auspicious, and Plato (*Republic*, 571–2) is unusual in censuring them as wish fulfilment. Only a few passing remarks by Artemidorus on symbolic wish fulfilment (*Onirocritica*, preface to Book IV) and the role of puns in dreaming sug-gest modern ideas.

Scientific theories of the dream were strongly influ-enced by these traditional beliefs in its veridical nature. For Democritus (5th century BC), images emanating from distant persons and objects, somewhat distorted in trans-mission, impinge on the sleeper: images of people reflect their thought as well as their external shape. Aristotle in his early works spoke of the soul exercising special clairvoyant powers, in accord with its divine nature, when freed from the body's constraint in sleep. Later, much more sceptically, he denied the divine origin of dreams (the gods would not care to communicate with the animals, or lower classes) and suggested that veridical dreams, if they really occurred, should be explained by a modified version of Democritus' theory. Of later philosophical schools, the *Epicureans went still further in scepticism, but others much less far. Traditional belief in dreams of good and evil omen reappears, under a rather thin scientific disguise, in an anonymous medical treatise, perhaps of the 4th century. This distinguishes from 'divine' and wish-fulfilment dreams a third category, in which the soul, being 'master of its own house' in sleep, indicates symbolically the condition of the body, thus providing a valuable aid to medical diagnosis.

Though numerous Greek dreams, real and literary, are recorded, comparatively few strike the modern mind as very dreamlike, presumably because reported dreams tend to fall into stylized, culturally determined types. In one typical dream, familiar also from the Old Testament, a god, parent, or figure of authority stands over the dreamer's head and issues prophecy or instructions; when the god is Asclepius in an incubation dream, he performs an act of healing that on waking proves to have been effective. The fullest account of an individual's dreams is post-classical, the 'sacred discourses' in which the hypochondriac orator Aelius Aristides (2nd century AD) describes Asclepius' revelations to himself, and his own extraordinary obedience to the god's commands.

RCTP

Aristotle (1931). *On Dreams*, and *On Divination in Sleep*. In Ross, W. D. (ed.), *The Works of Aristotle translated into English*, vol. iii.

Artemidorus (1975). *The Interpretation of Dreams*. Trans. R. J. White.

Behr, C. A. (1968). *Aelius Aristides and the Sacred Tales*.

Dodds, E. R. (1951). *The Greeks and the Irrational*.

——(1965). *Pagan and Christian in an Age of Anxiety*.

Hippocrates (1978). *On Dreams*. In Lloyd, G. E. R. (ed.), *Hippocratic Writings*.

Driesch, Hans Adolf Eduard (1867–1941). German developmental biologist, and a vitalist, born in Bad Kreuznach, Prussia. Educated at Frieburg and Munich, he received his doctorate in Jena in 1889 under Ernst *Haeckel. Driesch travelled extensively in Europe and the Far East, working at the International Zoological Station in Naples between 1891 and 1900. During this time he performed a renowned series of experiments on sea urchin embryos that conclusively demonstrated that the fate of a cell is not determined in the early developmental stages. In 1896, he became the first to demonstrate embryonic induction. After serving as the Gifford

lecturer at Aberdeen in 1907–8, Driesch was appointed professor of philosophy at Heidelberg (1911–20), and subsequently at Cologne and Leipzig.

Driesch's early interest in biology was gradually overshadowed by his involvement in philosophy. The discovery, in sea urchins, that a portion of an early embryo could develop into a complete, though smaller than normal, organism contradicted then-current mechanistic theories and led Driesch to develop a theory of vitalism that life is directed by a unique principle and cannot be explained solely in terms of chemical and physical processes. His main work on the subject of vitalism is *The History and Theory of Vitalism* (1905). Driesch came to believe that living activities, especially development, were controlled by an indefinable vital principle, which he called *entelechy.

Driesch's pacifism and philosophical beliefs made him anathema to the Nazi regime. He was forced to retire in 1933. He died in Leipzig on 16 April 1941.

Key publications include *The Science and Philosophy of the Organism* (1908) compiled from the Gifford lectures at Aberdeen in 1907, *Theory of Order* (1912), *Logic as a Task* (1913), and *Theory of Reality* (1917). RLG

drugs, recreational. The commonest recreational drugs in our society are alcohol and nicotine. More than 80 per cent of adults admit to using alcohol occasionally, and despite the health hazards associated with tobacco more than a third continue to smoke. Third in popularity (although illegal) is cannabis (known as marijuana in the USA). Cannabis is tried at least once by most teenagers and used regularly by millions of young people. Much smaller numbers of people are regular users of the so-called 'hard drugs', cocaine, heroin, and amphetamines.

People take recreational drugs because they find their effects on the brain pleasurable. The various drugs differ in their primary actions in the brain. Some drugs act because they mimic the actions of naturally occurring chemicals associated with normal physiological brain mechanisms. Thus, heroin is recognized in the brain by specific receptor proteins that normally recognize and react to the endorphins—a series of naturally occurring chemicals in the brain that play roles in signalling pain and pleasure. The active chemical in cannabis, delta-9-tetrahydrocannabinol (THC), is recognized by a cannabinoid receptor which is normally targeted by the naturally occurring cannabis-like chemical anandamide in the brain. Cocaine acts by blocking the inactivation of the brain chemical dopamine after its release in the brain—thus enhancing the effects of dopamine—and amphetamines act similarly to increase the availability of dopamine in the brain by stimulating its release. The intoxicants alcohol and THC act by both enhancing the actions of the inhibitory chemical messenger GABA (gamma-amino butyric acid) in the brain, and simultaneously dampening the actions of a key excitatory chemical, l-glutamate. The psychedelics (d-LSD, mescaline, psilocin, 'magic mushroom') have very different actions. These are not drugs of addiction, and the sensations they induce represent highly unusual states of consciousness. Much less is known about the precise circuits that are activated by these drugs, although a common mechanism of action appears to be activation of receptors that normally recognize the brain chemical messenger serotonin.

Neuroscientists have found in recent years that although the various individual drugs act on different primary mechanisms in the brain there are certain final common pathways that are triggered by many of the recreational drugs. In particular pathways that use the brain chemical dopamine in the forebrain are activated in a similar way by alcohol, nicotine, heroin, amphetamines, cocaine, and THC. These are brain mechanisms involved in pleasure and reward that are important for the normal functioning of the brain in, for example, learning and memory—in which reward for correct responses plays a key role. In effect drugs of abuse 'hijack' these brain mechanisms, i.e. drug-induced activation of the brain mechanisms normally associated with learning and memory triggers drug-seeking behaviour, dependence, and addiction. In establishing addiction it seems to be important that the taking of the drug is associated with an immediately pleasurable sensation if addiction is to be learned rapidly. Thus, drugs that can be injected or smoked, which deliver the active chemical to the brain very rapidly, tend to be most addictive. For example, injected or smoked heroin, insufflated or smoked cocaine, smoked cannabis, and smoked or injected methamphetamine ('speed') are all readily addictive, whereas the same drugs taken by mouth are absorbed much more slowly and are less likely to lead to addiction. Children treated with amphetamines (e.g. Ritalin) for 'attention deficit hyperactivity disorder' (ADHD), for example, rarely become addicted—but injected or smoked amphetamines can be highly addictive.

Addiction to alcohol, heroin, and cocaine is often associated with physical signs of withdrawal if the drug is removed. These include severe gastrointestinal disruption, pain, insomnia, and possibly life-threatening convulsions. Addiction to nicotine or THC is not associated with physical signs of withdrawal but there may be intense psychological distress if the drug is withdrawn. Addiction is also associated with a craving for the drug, which together with the desire to avoid unpleasant withdrawal effects motivates continuing drug-taking behaviour. Addiction per se is not necessarily harmful—many coffee drinkers are mildly addicted to caffeine but it does them no personal harm and does not damage society. But addiction to recreational drugs can damage both the addicts and society. The long-term consumption of alcohol and tobacco is associated with the risk of life-threatening illnesses (e.g. cirrhosis of the liver, lung cancer)—and these represent some of the largest preventable causes of death. Smoking cannabis carries health risks—particularly to the lungs— and the heavy use of cannabis by young people also appears to be associated with an increased risk of developing schizophrenia-like illness later in life. Addiction to 'hard drugs' is frequently associated with criminality, as both addicts and suppliers operate in a criminal underworld in which addicts may be driven to crime to fund their drug habit. Not all recreational drugs are equally addictive. Although a proportion (perhaps as high as 10 per cent) of regular cannabis users become psychologically dependent on the drug, most are able to stop using cannabis by the time they reach their 30s. In contrast most cigarette smokers find it very difficult to quit. Although it is difficult to measure the 'addictiveness' of drugs, most pharmacologists have a mental list ranking the recreational drugs in this way. At the top of my list would be nicotine, followed by cocaine, heroin, amphetamines, cannabis, alcohol, and caffeine.

Attempts to control the abuse of recreational drugs by punishing the users as criminals have not been successful in curbing the increasing problem that drug abuse poses. More emphasis is increasingly being placed on the medical model, which attempts to treat addiction as a medical problem. Unfortunately few treatments have been found to be effective—although a combination of behavioural therapy and medicines shows most promise. In terms of medicines, the most effective approach that has been found so far is to replace the addictive drug with a less harmful form of the same type of chemical. Thus, cigarette smokers use nicotine-containing chewing gum or a skin patch loaded with nicotine to obtain nicotine rather then inhaling harmful tobacco smoke. Heroin addicts may be treated with methadone—a drug that targets the same brain receptors but is taken by mouth and acts slowly to reduce craving. New approaches to the treatment of drug addiction are badly needed but so far progress has been slow. LLI

Everitt, B. J., and Dickinson, A. (2001). 'The neuropsychological basis of addiction behaviour'. *Brain Research Review*, 36.

Iversen, L. L. (2001). *A Very Short Introduction to Drugs*.

Koob, G. F. (2000). 'Neurobiology of addiction: towards the development of new therapies'. *Annals of the New York Academy of Science*, 909.

Lingford-Hughes, A. R. et al. (2003). 'Addiction'. *British Medical Bulletin*, 65.

Nestler, E. J. (2002). 'From neurobiology to treatment: progress against addiction'. *Nature Neuroscience*, Suppl. (Nov.).

dualism. The philosophical theory that supposes that mind is essentially independent of the brain, though mental events run parallel with physical brain events. This leads to several suggested (usually causal) relations: (i) mental and brain events run in parallel without causal interaction (epiphenomenalism). (ii) The brain 'secretes' mental events, rather as glands secrete substances. (iii) Brain and behaviour are controlled by an essentially autonomous mind. (iv) The mind is an *emergent property of brain processes, rather as the properties of water emerge from the combined atoms of oxygen and hydrogen, which in isolation have very different properties. (v) Mind and brain are essentially separate but have some mutual interaction (interactive dualism). This last was the view of *Descartes. (vi) Mind is like 'software' of the brain 'hardware'.

An account of the mind–brain relation which is not dualistic is the identity theory, of which there are various versions. These suppose that what we take to be mind and brain are different aspects of the same thing. See also MIND AND BODY; MIND–BODY PROBLEM: PHILOSOPHICAL THEORIES.

RLG

Du Bois-Reymond, Emil Heinrich (1818–96). German physiologist. The son of a Swiss father and Huguenot mother, he was born and lived in Berlin. He was assistant to Johannes *Müller, and succeeded to his chair as professor of physiology at the University of Berlin in 1858, becoming head of the new institute of physiology there in 1877.

His work was of fundamental importance. It began with the investigation of electrical discharge in certain fish; his discoveries related especially to electrical activity and chemical changes in the nerves and muscles generally. In 1845 he discovered the existence of a resting current in the nerve. The value of this work was recognized early, and in 1851 he was elected to the Berlin Academy of Sciences. Later, in 1877, he suggested that nerve impulses might be transmitted chemically. His major published work was *Untersuchungen über thierische Elektricität* (Researches on Animal Electricity, 2 vols., 1848 and 1860).

DDH

Duncker, Karl (1903–40). German psychologist with strong affiliations to the *Gestalt school. He worked for several years in Berlin as an assistant to Wolfgang *Köhler but spent a year at Clark University in 1928–9. He then went back to Berlin, but returned to America in 1938 after a short interlude in the department of experimental psychology at Cambridge. He committed suicide in America in 1940.

Duncker reported an important study on induced motion, in part translated by W. D. Ellis (*A Source Book of Gestalt Psychology* (1938), pp. 161–73). Perhaps his best-known work was a monograph on the psychology of productive thinking (German, 1935; English translation, 1945).

OLZ

Dunne, John William (1875–1949). British inventor and philosopher of time. He designed the first aerodynamically stable aeroplane (1906–7), but he is best known for his philosophical–psychological books *An Experiment with Time* (1927) and *The Serial Universe* (1934). These inspired many people to record their dreams, looking for dream predictions, the notion being that time is an unfolding of preordained events. Dunne's views are not now taken seriously, and there seems no substantive evidence for predictive dreaming.

dyslexia. At the end of the 19th century (1896), a case study of a boy with congenital word-blindness was reported in the *British Medical Journal* by W. Pringle Morgan. Percy F was described as a bright, intelligent boy, quick at games, as good as others of his age except for an inability to learn to read. In spite of laborious and persistent training, he could only spell out words of one syllable with great difficulty. This report served as a stimulus for research and debate on word-blindness. Half a century later, the term 'dyslexia' was adopted for the condition. 'Dyslexia' is derived from the Greek 'dys' (difficulty) and 'lexicos' (words). Today, developmental dyslexia is seen as a complex neurological condition occurring in about 4 per cent of the population and is a legally recognized disability.

The criteria for recognizing the existence of a condition are that it should have a distinct aetiology, identifying characteristics, and a prognosis, and should respond to intervention. There has been a lot of controversy about the extent to which dyslexia meets these requirements and in the UK the term 'specific learning difficulties' was preferred for use in legislation ('specific learning disabilities' in the USA). The word 'dyslexia', however, has continued to be used in cognitive research and has entered everyday parlance to such an extent that the legal term in the UK has been changed to 'specific learning difficulties (for example, dyslexia)'. The definition of dyslexia and its subtypes, and programmes for remediation, continue to evolve with developments in research and understanding of the condition.

In the 1980s and 1990s, the dominant theoretical framework for dyslexia research focused on phonological deficits. These include difficulty segmenting words into phonemes, in keeping strings of sounds or letters in short-term memory, in repeating long non-words and in reading and writing short ones, and slowness in naming colours, numbers, letters, or objects in pictures. The association between poor phonological awareness and later reading difficulty has been demonstrated across different languages, ages, and tasks. The emphasis on phonological difficulty is seen in the Orton Society (now the International Dyslexia Association) Research Committee's definition of 1994. In this, dyslexia is seen as a specific language-based disorder of constitutional origin characterized by difficulties in single word coding, usually reflecting insufficient phonological processing abilities. Such difficulties are unexpected in relation to age and other cognitive and academic abilities and are not the result of generalized developmental disability or sensory impairment. Dyslexia is seen not only as a problem with learning to read but also in acquiring proficiency in writing and spelling.

Much remedial help for dyslexic children has focused largely on the provision of multisensory phonic programmes involving the systematic teaching of letter–sound correspondences. Many dyslexic children learn to read fairly accurately but they read slowly. The positive effects of phonological support are largely on reading accuracy with relatively little effect on reading fluency. Research on speed of processing has shown a strong relationship between early letter-naming speed and later reading fluency. A 'double deficit' hypothesis for dyslexia led to the suggestion that effective remedial programmes should contain not only phonologically based instruction but also a systematic and comprehensive support directed at developing reading fluency and comprehension.

Over the last two decades, there has been a growing interest in visual processing problems in relation to text. In 1980, Olive Meares, a teacher in New Zealand, described the difficulties reported by some children of dealing with glare from the printed page when reading. At about the same time, Helen Irlen, in California, was exploring the use of tinted lenses to alleviate a problem which she called scotopic sensitivity syndrome. Irlen centres were set up in several countries to supply tinted lenses using her techniques. This triggered a great deal of interest in visual processing difficulties and poor reading, particularly as only some dyslexic children appear to benefit from using coloured overlays or tinted lenses.

In the early 1970s, Arnold Wilkins was interested in the 4 per cent of people with epilepsy who experience visually induced seizures. He noted that susceptibility to visual discomfort is most pronounced in people who suffer from frequent severe headaches. He went on to argue that reading can provoke 'pattern glare' which can result in eyestrain and headaches, and even visual illusions and seizures. Electric lighting changes in brightness twice during each cycle of the alternating electricity supply and fluorescent lighting pulsates even faster. Wilkins suggested that, although the pulsations from such lights are too fast to be seen as flicker, they affect the firing of the visual neurons in the eye. In 1991, he examined twenty volunteers with a history of reading difficulty who had been selected by the Irlen Centre in London as having benefited from the use of tinted glasses. Seventeen of them had a history of migraine in the family; nearly all of them reported a reduction in headaches when wearing their tinted glasses. To investigate this finding systematically, he built a colorimeter for the intuitive manipulation of colour (hue) and depth of colour (saturation), and developed a Rate of Reading Test to identify the poor readers who would benefit from using coloured overlays on the printed page. There is now good research evidence that some poor readers, particularly those with a family history of migraine, can be helped in this way, and that this is due neither to a *placebo nor a *Hawthorne effect (Wilkins 1995).

Poor readers sometimes display erratic eye movements which appear to be associated with blurring of print, letters jumping over other letters, and letter reversals. Stein and Fowler (1985) reported a study on the effect of monocular occlusion on reading in dyslexic children. They suggested that the experience of an unstable visual world when reading could be attributed to unstable vergence control of the eyes and that this could be improved by the occlusion of one eye. This was open to the objection, however, that a relationship between vergence control and the experiences reported had not been shown to be causal. In 2000, they attempted to set up a double-blind randomized controlled trial to test this. One hundred and forty-three children were selected as dyslexic with unstable binocular control from a sample of 300 7- to 11-years-olds who had been referred to a learning disabilities clinic. The children were randomly assigned to wear spectacles with pale yellow lenses with or without the left eye occluded for all reading and writing activities for nine months. They were tested without their spectacles every three months by researchers who did not know whether they belonged to the occluded or non-occluded group. At the end of nine months, there was no difference in the number of children who achieved stable binocular control but the occluded group achieved it earlier and had gained an advantage in reading performance which was maintained throughout the study. It was of course impossible for the children, parents, or teachers to be unaware of whether a child was in the occluded or non-occluded group.

Evidence has accumulated about differences in the symmetry of the cerebral hemispheres in dyslexics and controls and on the predominant location of language processing in the left hemisphere. Much detailed research has been done on the visual system and its responses to different types of visual stimuli.

In 1980, Bill Lovegrove and his colleagues suggested that dyslexic readers have low-level impairments of the transient visual system. The transient (magnocellular) visual system carries fast low-contrast information and is responsible for detecting moving stimuli but does so with poor acuity. The sustained (parvocellular) system transmits information more slowly but with high acuity. In 1991, Margaret Livingstone and her co-workers examined the functioning of the magnocellular and parvocellular divisions of the visual system by recording visually evoked potentials in response to high- and low-contrast stimuli in dyslexic and non-dyslexic people. There were no differences between the groups for the high-contrast stimuli but there were for the low. With Albert Galaburda, she and their co-workers went on to carry out a series of histological postmortem studies of the brains of people known to have been dyslexic and to compare them with non-dyslexic controls. They found that whilst the magnocellular and parvocellular layers of the lateral geniculate nucleus were clearly separated in the controls they were more merged together in the brains of the dyslexics. Moreover, the magnocellular neurons in the dyslexics were about 30 per cent smaller than in the controls. Both the magnocellular and parvocellular layers receive neuronal projections from the ganglion cells of the retina at the back of the eye. Ninety per cent of these are parvocells which signal fine detail and colour and the remainder are larger magnocells which signal the timing of visual events. Differences have since been found between dyslexics and controls in the magnocells of the auditory thalamic relay associated with the processing of sounds.

The critical factor behind fluent word reading appears to be the ability to recognize letters, spelling patterns, and whole words effortlessly and automatically. Rod Nicolson and Angela Fawcett (1990) explored the idea of automaticity suggesting that dyslexic children have difficulties in making some cognitive and motor skills automatic in spite of intensive practice. A conscious compensation hypothesis was invoked to explain why in spite of more limited automaticity many dyslexic children are able to perform at apparently normal levels in most areas, most of the time. There is growing evidence that there are differences between dyslexics and controls in motor coordination and balance. Motor skills training can improve performance on motor tasks and it was suggested in the early 1970s that motor skills intervention could help learning-disabled children. A longitudinal evaluation of a balance remediation exercise training programme for dyslexic children and matched controls is currently under way in the UK.

It has been shown recently, using positron emission tomography (PET), that in comparison with controls, dyslexics showed less activation of the cerebellum during a motor learning task. In addition, the metabolism of the cerebellum has been shown to be lower in dyslexics than controls. Research using magnetic resonance imaging (MRI) in the USA has provided evidence of the involvement and integration of seventeen regions in the brain, including the cerebellum, in reading. The cerebellum contains and receives considerable inputs from the magnocells and recent histological study of the cerebellum has confirmed cerebellar differences between dyslexics and controls.

John Stein, Joel Talcott, and Caroline Whitton (2001) suggested that the influence of polyunsaturated fatty acids (PUFAs) on the magnocell membrane may be under the control of a particular enzyme that is higher in dyslexics than controls. They think that the decline of eating fish in modern diets has led to lower levels of PUFAs. Research is under way on supplementing the diets of dyslexic children with particular omega-3 fatty acids found in some fish oils and on a breath test to identify children who may benefit from this. They also suggested that individual differences in magnocellular sensitivity may be under genetic control.

Familial clustering of dyslexia is well documented. Strong support for genetic influences rather than a shared family environment comes from studies which have found twice the rate of dyslexia in monozygotic twins who have almost identical genetic make-up, compared with dizygotic twins who have about half their genes in common. Techniques in molecular genetics have so far identified loci on chromosomes 2, 4, 6, 13, and 18 as being implicated in dyslexia. Several authors have pointed out that some of these genetic markers occur in the same regions as genes involved in some autoimmune diseases which have an increased prevalence in dyslexics. Although considerable advances have been made, understanding the biological basis of dyslexia is still at a relatively early stage, and significant questions remain about its genetic basis and the brain mechanisms involved.

Since the identification of pre-reading correlates of dyslexia, considerable efforts have been made to develop early screening programmes; this is difficult because early childhood development is so variable but a recent study compared the literacy skills of children at genetic risk of dyslexia with those with no such family history. The children at genetic risk were more likely to have slower speech and language development at 4 years of age and literacy problems at age 6. It appears that early childhood screening should be sequential to allow for differences in rates of development and treated as probabilistic. Developments in screening and assessing the difficulties of school children and adults now include work on computerized screening and assessment.

In describing the pattern of difficulties in dyslexia, Tim Miles (1993) pointed out that dyslexia involves more than a language and literacy problem. Certainly there can be considerable individual differences in schoolchildren and adults with dyslexia, not least because many develop individual coping and compensatory strategies. For some, the extent to which their dyslexic difficulties will impair performance at work will be minimal but for others it may result in working in occupations which do not make full use of their real abilities and potential. The stress of coping with dyslexia at school, college or university, and work is well documented (e.g. Miles and Varma 1995). Information on screening, assessment, intervention, and current legislation affecting children and adults is available on the websites of the British Dyslexia Association, the Dyslexia Institute, and the International Dyslexia Association.

MNH

Bradley, L., and Bryant, P. (1983). 'Categorizing sounds and learning to read'. *Nature.*

Livingstone, M. S., Rosen, G. D., Drislane, F. W., and Galaburda, A. M. (1991). 'Physiological and anatomical evidence for a magnocellular defect in developmental dyslexia'. *Proceedings of the National Academy of Sciences of the USA,* 88.

Lovegrove, W. J., Martin, F., Blackwood, M., and Badock, D. (1980). 'Specific reading difficulty: differences in contrast sensitivity as a function of spatial frequency'. *Science,* 210.

Miles, T. R. (1993). *Dyslexia: The Pattern of Difficulties* (2nd edn.).

—— and Varma, V. (1995). *Dyslexia and Stress.*

Morgan, W. P. (1896). 'A case study of congenital word blindness'. *British Medical Journal,* 2.

Nicolson, R. I., and Fawcett, A. J. (1990). 'Automaticity: a new framework for dyslexia research'. *Cognition,* 35/2.

Orton Society Research Committee (1994). 'Dyslexia'. *Perspectives,* 20.

Stein, J. F., and Fowler, S. (1985). 'Effect of monocular occlusion on reading in dyslexic children'. *Lancet,* 13 July.

—— Talcott, J., and Whitton, C. (2001). 'The senorimotor basis of developmental dyslexia'. In Fawcett, A. J. (ed.), *Dyslexia Theory and Good Practice.*

Wilkins, A. (1995). *Visual Stress.*

Websites:

www.bda-dyslexia.org.uk

www.dyslexia-inst.org.uk

www.interdys.org

E

Ebbinghaus, Hermann (1850–1909). German experimental psychologist, born at Barmen, near Bonn, and educated at the University of Bonn. He obtained his doctorate in 1873 but thereafter worked for a number of years on his own. After a brief sojourn in Berlin, he travelled in France and England for three years, in the course of which he unearthed in a second-hand bookstall a copy of G. T. *Fechner's *Elemente der Psychophysik*, which evidently impressed him deeply and gave him the idea of applying Fechner's quantitative methods to the study of the higher mental processes.

Ebbinghaus thereupon embarked on a prolonged series of experiments designed to formulate the fundamental laws of human memory. As his experimental material, he laid great store on nonsense syllables in the belief that only by ridding his stimuli of conventional meaning could he treat them as constant and interchangeable units. Somewhat as Fechner had treated just noticeable differences in sensation as equivalent units of sensation, he carried out numerous, and—for the time—surprisingly well-controlled, experiments to establish learning curves under a variety of conditions. He hoped that this work would not only lead to advances in our understanding of the nature of learning and forgetting but also be of practical value in the field of education. His results were embodied in *Über das Gedächtniss* (1885), much of which was replicated and in certain respects amplified by, among others, G. E. Müller of Göttingen; and it was introduced to English psychologists by C. S. *Myers (1909). See RE-MEMBERING.

In more recent years, Ebbinghaus's methods have come under considerable criticism on the grounds that he was concerned with the acquisition of verbal repetition habits rather than with memory as it operates under the conditions of everyday life. In particular, the artificiality of nonsense syllables has been repeatedly stressed. F. C. *Bartlett, for instance, pointed out long ago that it is impossible to rid stimuli of meaning so long as they remain capable of eliciting any human response. He further insisted that the Ebbinghaus methods totally ignore those important conditions of recall which relate to pre-existing attitudes and response tendencies. None the less, the work of Ebbinghaus did much to convince the sceptical that quantitative methods were applicable to the higher mental processes. OLZ

Ebbinghaus, H. (1885). *Über das Gedächtniss*. Trans. as *Memory*, 1913.
—— (1897). *The Intelligence of School Children*.
—— (1902–8). *Textbook of Experimental Psychology*, vols. i and ii.
Myers, C. S. (1909). *Textbook of Experimental Psychology* (reissued 1980).

ECT (electroconvulsive therapy). Applying a voltage, with surface electrodes on the head, across the brain. This is done under anaesthesia or muscle relaxant, as it produces convulsions which can be dangerous. ECT is extensively used as a convenient and quick treatment for depression, though there is no theoretical basis to justify it. There is considerable criticism of its extensive use because it may produce permanent brain damage, especially losses of memory and intelligence, though the evidence is not entirely clear.

Geddes, J. (2003). 'Efficacy and safety of electroconvulsive therapy in depressive disorders: a systematic review and meta-analysis'. *Lancet*, 361/9360.

education: theory and practice. The true nature of education, its goals, proper methods, and effects have long been a matter of argument; certainly since the time of *Plato (4th century BC, see *Republic, passim*) and probably before, education has been a matter of concern, not only to the individual child who is to be educated, and to his parents, but to the whole society responsible for its provision. Though people sometimes urge that politics should be kept out of education (and they are right to hope that the extremes of party dogma may be avoided), the fact is that education is necessarily a political issue. For one thing, education itself is an expression of values, moral and political as well as academic. Moreover, what subjects children are taught, how and where they are taught, how many of them are taught and for how long, whether all are equally provided with education—all these questions are of interest to the whole of society, and the answers to them will determine the character of that society. No wonder, then, that politicians interest themselves in education, and if they are wise they will try to formulate a coherent theory, to justify the provision they decide to make.

In the 18th century the philosopher Jean-Jacques *Rousseau (1712–78) thought of education as child centred. In *Émile* he propounded the theory that a child would flourish if allowed to grow freely in his own way and his own time, not forced or stunted by too much teaching. He was not concerned with who should be educated, but only with how a child, any child, should or should not be taught. He thought of education in the 'true' sense as a natural process, and therefore believed that all children, regardless of class or status, could benefit from it. His back-to-nature philosophy has had a considerable effect on later theories, if in nothing else then in the proliferation of all kinds of horticultural metaphors, according to which children, like plants, will flourish in the right soil, but may wilt or wither if either forced or neglected. In the early 20th century this Rousseauesque philosophy was taken up and adapted by John *Dewey (1859–1952), who held that to educate a child was to provide him with experiences, out of which his thoughts and interpretations would flow; experience, and especially shared experience, was infinitely more educative than books. This anti-intellectual kind of educational theory had considerable effects in the development of British education in the 1960s.

However, at the time when Rousseau wrote, education was narrowly spread. It was a luxury to which by no means everyone could aspire. Though there had long existed charity schools and the provision for poor scholars, the beneficiaries were comparatively few. In the 19th century education came to seem more and more desirable, and therefore the question to be faced was not what education was, or what its best form was, but rather who should have it. The Utilitarians in particular valued education extremely highly, for they believed that people could, all of them, be taught to take pleasure in the right things, that is in things which would spread social advantages widely in society, and would in general raise the standards of life, both morally and materially. A man of education, John Stuart *Mill (1806–73) thought, would never wish to return to the enjoyment of the pleasures of the uneducated. Once introduce a child to the infinite resources of reading and learning, and his taste, his sensibility, and his understanding of true political goals would all inevitably be elevated. He needs must pursue the higher. This being so, Mill thought that it did not so very much matter what was taught, provided that education of some kind was universally available. Therefore in *On Liberty* (1859) he argued that the state should require all children to be educated, at least so that they could read, write, and calculate, but should not itself provide that education. If it were illegal to allow a child to go uneducated, demand would produce schools which could be inspected for efficiency by government servants, and the pupils of which could be publicly examined. Government could also subsidize those too poor to pay the fees. In this way he thought universal literacy at least would be ensured, while freedom to conduct educational experiments would also be preserved.

Mill's arguments were not accepted. But the goal of universal education gained ground, along with the conviction that the state must make provision for those whom it insisted should be educated. And at last, in the Education Act of 1944, all children in the United Kingdom became entitled to primary education, and to secondary education up to the age of 15: such education as was, in the words of the Act, suited to their aptitude and ability. Only those children deemed to be too severely mentally handicapped to be able to benefit from education were excluded. Education was thus conceived as a right for everyone, but it was acknowledged that some kinds of education were better than others, not only in duration but in actual content. Success in life, in salaries, and the exercise of power all followed upon *good* education. What democracy demanded was that all children should have, not the same education, but the same chance of the best. So, in an admittedly competitive field, competition at the age of 11 for entry to the best schools, from which a child could proceed to university, was thought to be just, and also to be the best way of distributing an amenity which, by a marvellous natural harmony, was seen to be in short supply but also something from which only some members of the population would benefit.

But two things went wrong. First, the 11-plus selection became suspect. It selected too many of the middle classes. Secondly, it became clear that the mere *chance* to enter the lists for selection was not sufficient. Those children who were not selected for the best education at 11 had virtually no further chances, and it began to be thought that one chance was not enough. And so gradually, during the 1950s and 1960s, it began to seem that what was wanted was not equality of opportunity to be educated, but something more like equality of education for all. Even the universities were not exempt from the demand that they should open their doors to literally everybody. (Financial considerations and a certain realism, however, prevailed.) But at school things were different. The comprehensive school, which had started as a convenient and often excellent way of educating a large number of children of very different abilities under one roof, began to be identified with a demand that all children should be given the very same education, so that neither their social nor their intellectual differences would distinguish one from another. During the 1960s, educational theory was predominantly concerned with such issues as these. The comparative affluence of the country, which allowed the establishment of new universities, also made it seem feasible to take the competitiveness out of education. Especially in the primary schools, the voice of Rousseau spoke again. Children must not be taught; they must discover things for themselves at their own pace. So an innate love of learning would find expression, and the old authoritarian style of education, which insisted that children be marked, graded, put in order of merit so that the best could get to the top, would finally disappear off the face of the earth. This was the kind of ideal incorporated in the Plowden Report (*Children and their Primary Schools*, HMSO, 1967). But it spread into the sphere of secondary education as well. In particular, it was linked with a Marxist view of the role of teachers (that the very concept of 'teaching' entailed the domination of one class over another, the perpetuation of a bourgeois value system, embodied in an insistence, for example, on reading, when books were predominantly middle-class productions). The very word 'teach' became suspect in the 1960s and early 1970s, and educational theory itself was difficult to separate from Marxist-dominated sociology.

However, while these influences were certainly important, in that they had a considerable effect on young teachers, and therefore on the actual educational provision within the comprehensive system, there was another element in educational theory which persisted from the 1950s onwards, and this was what may be called the Anglo-Saxon philosophical school. The theories of education that may be called, loosely, Marxist naturally linked theory with practice, and equally naturally were quite overtly political in their aims. Education is and ought to be a part of the armoury of the class war. The philosophers, on the other hand, believed (I think wrongly) that education could be treated as a 'pure' subject—that it need have no connection with politics, and that, insofar as educational theory led to a change in practice, this would be practice based on totally rational considerations, concerned with the nature of knowledge and thus with the process of passing on knowledge from one person to another.

P. H. Phenix in America and P. H. Hirst and R. S. Peters in the United Kingdom were the most influential philosophers of education in the 1960s. They believed that there is a finite number of forms or kinds of knowledge, separable from each other by a process of logical analysis, and that no human being could be a full 'person' without some acquaintance with all these forms of knowledge. A school curriculum, therefore, must be so constructed that all of the forms have their place. Sometimes the august name of *Wittgenstein (1889–1951) was invoked in favour of this kind of theory, with the suggestion that each form of knowledge was naturally incorporated in its own 'language' or 'language game', and this was sometimes taken to prove that, if the forms of knowledge were confused with each other, the result would be nonsense (but it can never have been taken to show that everyone ought to be able to speak in each of the different languages). This stipulation was, and must always have been, an independent judgement of value. The list of the forms of knowledge was intended to provide a value-free schema, arrived at a priori, within which education could be organized. The difficulty was that there exists no Platonic world of

forms of knowledge. The list of forms, mathematical, historical, moral, literary, artistic, and so on, looked suspiciously like something derived from the timetable of an old-fashioned grammar school. And some of the items on the list could only very dubiously be counted as knowledge at all. Is it really the case that the moral education of children, for example, consists in teaching them to know certain things? And how about religion? The difficulties were manifold, and the practical effect of such philosophical theories was not as great as the proponents hoped, for the very good reason that it is quite impossible, by the analysis of the concept of education, to derive any satisfactory or agreed guide to action.

Nevertheless the influence of this kind of exercise was not absolutely negligible. Especially in the contentious sphere of moral education, held, ever since the days of J. S. Mill, to be one of the most important aspects of education, and even to constitute a justification for increasing the spread of education among people in general, the analytic approach has had some consequences, in the kind of curricular material thought appropriate for school. It has been widely argued that, particularly in a multicultural society, it is impossible, and in any case undesirable, to lay down any actual moral principles for children to adopt. What must be done is to teach children to conduct moral arguments, so that they will be able both to determine what is and what is not a moral matter, and to make their own decisions rationally. Thus the analytic value-free educational philosophy at this point coincided with the anti-authoritarian theory of the neo-Marxists, and the result has been a considerable increase in some relativism among teachers. Nothing must be declared right or wrong; children must construct their own values, and are entitled to value anything high or low, provided they can argue on a rational basis to defend their evaluation.

Roughly, then, these two types of theory, the one overtly political and at first concerned with the distribution of education, the other supposedly value free and concerned with curriculum content, dominated the field of educational theory and consequential practice until the late 1970s. Then a change came about. The affluent 1960s had passed; the financial climate was threatening; unemployment was beginning to be alarming. The days of student revolt, of permissiveness, of the excesses of the youth cult seemed to be over. Employers in industry were beginning to complain that young people coming out of school were ill prepared for employment. Parents were becoming increasingly disenchanted with some of the educational theories of young teachers. In 1977, the prime minister, James Callaghan, instituted what was known as 'the Great Debate'. Everyone was encouraged to think about the proper goals and purposes of education, what should be taught, and in what state of preparedness for life children should leave school. A reform of the school curriculum, as well as of the public examination system which dominated the curriculum in most schools, began to be universally expected.

It had been clear for a long time that, despite the greater spread of education since the beginning of the century, in many ways the structure of the school curriculum had remained remarkably unchanged. Some schools, it is true, had invented interdisciplinary subjects to replace the old subjects of 'geography' or 'history'. But as long as universities demanded competence in classical languages, or even the ability to translate modern foreign languages though not to speak them, the old standards, according to which knowing Latin and Greek brought the highest prizes, were not wholly overthrown. Even when the universities relaxed their demands, the old domination of the classics remained to bedevil the teaching of modern languages, taught traditionally as if they were a kind of dialect of Latin; and the notion that a child must choose between language learning and science, that if he was doing well with languages he could drop mathematics as early as possible . . . all these factors remained unchanged, and were ossified in the examination system and hence in the school timetable. Moreover, the children who did not take, or did not succeed in passing, public examinations had very little that was structurally different in their curriculum. A school devoted to the egalitarian ideal of the 1960s could not discriminate too blatantly between the curricula of different children.

Meanwhile in the early 1970s another quiet reform had come about which had a significant effect. It was then that those very severely mentally retarded children, hitherto deemed ineducable, and therefore left as the responsibility of the health services, were brought under the educational umbrella. At last it became the duty of local authorities to provide education for all children without exception. It was inevitable that the notion of education itself should be re-examined now that it was supposed to be available for children of such totally different capabilities. The fact that these newly educable children had to have a curriculum, with curricular aims which could be achieved slowly and step by step, cast fresh light on the practical nature of teaching itself. Successful education depends on teachers who know what they are doing and what they are doing it *for*.

In the context, then, of economic recession and the widening scope of education, together with the general assumption of the 1970s and 1980s that government should be open, and provision or lack of it publicly justified, a new way of looking at education as a whole can gradually be seen to emerge. It is a mixture of pragmatism and idealism. All children are now legally entitled to education, not merely so that they may get better jobs (for some of them may get no jobs at all) but so that their lives may be of a decent quality. The old utilitarian belief in education is perhaps returning, but in a different form. Education is seen to have certain quite general goals, to increase the understanding, the independence, and the pleasure of the child who receives it; and if these aims are not to be frustrated, then as many obstacles to education as possible must be removed from the path of the child. The dominant question has become 'What does this child *need*, if he is to get from his education what he is entitled to?'.

Of course, part of what a child needs is a sensible, useful, enjoyable curriculum. But the question of needs goes further. For a curriculum is futile, however well devised, if the particular child has no access to it, either because he cannot understand what he is being taught, or because the environment of the school where he is taught it is inimical to learning. Thus one of a child's essential educational needs is a good school, in the simple sense of a school where learning is possible. It has been increasingly recognized in the last few years that what has been called the 'hidden curriculum' is as important as the curriculum itself—the system of values, that is, which the school by its very existence as an institution hands on to its pupils.

Once the philosophy of educational needs is accepted, the criteria by which education is judged to be good or bad become immediately extremely wide and varied. It is no longer adequate to raise either the simple political question 'Is education justly distributed?' or the supposedly more philosophical question 'Is the curriculum appropriate to the common epistemological framework?'. On the contrary, the first question must be 'Does this kind of education *work*? Is this child or that child actually learning anything?', and then the second question is the value-laden one: 'If he is learning something, what do we hope will come of it—exactly how will he benefit?' Increasingly, schools, and teachers themselves, are taking responsibility for answering these questions, with the more and more active cooperation of parents. There has never, perhaps, been any time when theory and practice have been so closely interrelated. The philosophy and the action can hardly any longer be separated.   MW

Frankens, W. (1965). *Three Historical Philosophies of Education.*
Hartnell, A., and Naish, M. (eds.) (1976). *Theory and the Practice of Education,* 2 vols.
Peters, R. S. (ed.) (1967). *The Concept of Education.*
Rutter, M. et al. (1979). *15,000 Hours.*
Young, M. (ed.) (1971). *Knowledge and Control.*

EEG. See ELECTROENCEPHALOGRAPHY.

efferent. Pertaining to the motor nerves innervating the muscles. Efferent neural signals produce muscle contraction. (Afferent neural signals provide the brain with signals from the senses.)

ego and superego. Sigmund *Freud supposed that three components make up the psychic structure: the id, the ego, and the superego. The id represents instincts and innate needs. The superego, manifest in conscience, shame, and guilt, is the agency by which the influence of parents and others is prolonged. Their judgements and prohibitions are internalized by the process of introjection in early childhood before the child is able to question them. The ego has been differentiated from the id through the influence of the external world, to whose demands it adapts. In so adapting it has to reconcile the forces of the id and superego in such a way as to maximize pleasure and minimize unpleasure. The development of ego psychology as a branch as psychoanalysis, which reflected a shift of interest from the earlier instinct theory to the adaptive functions of the ego, in relation to other persons especially, facilitated some rapprochement between psychoanalysis and psychology. DRD

Freud, A. (1937). *The Ego and the Mechanisms of Defence.*
Hartmann, H. (1964). *Essays on Ego Psychology.*

Egyptian concepts of mind. Although Egyptian civilization was described by Greek and Roman travellers in antiquity, the written language was unknown before the hieroglyphs were 'decoded' early in the 19th century. The physician–physicist–physiologist Thomas *Young (1773–1829) played a major role in this decoding, which became possible when a stone—the Rosetta Stone—engraved with the same passage in three languages: Greek, Demotic, and Egyptian hieroglyphs, was discovered by one of Napoleon's soldiers. It was finally transcribed by the French archaeologist Jean Champollion (1790–1832). Egyptian literature is surprisingly unphilosophical (and gives away little about their almost incredible engineering skills), perhaps because unlike the Greeks their society was dominated by priests. But Egyptian scholarship has done much to interpret their strange (to us) ideas on the universe and mind.

Whereas the people of other ancient civilizations believed that they were created by gods from matter, the ancient Egyptians saw themselves as created directly out of nothing by the god who created the universe. They saw themselves as a divine nation, and their king as a god, though with a mortal body. They were uniquely religious. They had far more gods than any other country or civilization, their many gods reflecting their extremely animistic way of looking at nature—the heavens and everything on earth being seen as under the control of a great variety of often hostile beings. The most hostile spirits were often represented by dangerous animals: wolves, crocodiles, and venomous snakes, which overran Egypt in predynastic times. The more powerful the threat, such as inundation of the Nile, the more powerful the responsible god; so the sun god was more powerful than the god of the moon.

Many of the gods, however, were benevolent, or at least their goodwill might be sought by prayer or bought or bribed by gifts or offerings; or they might be made to help through the powers of magic and prayer. They might be persuaded to challenge the evil gods—so there were battles of good and evil in heaven, where the gods lived. Heaven was at first thought of as a rectangular ceiling, the earth (the land they knew) being this shape; later, it was thought of as the arched body of the goddess Nut, the stars being her jewels.

Many of the gods or spirits were occupied with carrying out the routine processes of nature, for everything in nature depended on the intentions of the gods, but as even these guardians, of what to us are natural laws, were open to suggestion or propitiation, magic was seen as immensely powerful. Perhaps this is why science was less developed in Egypt than in the contemporary Babylonia. Egyptian science lacked imagination and was essentially practical. From their experience of embalming the ancient Egyptians had considerable knowledge of anatomy, and also of surgery and dentistry (their teeth were ground away by the sand in their food), but their knowledge of mathematics and physics was not sophisticated and their literature lacked incisive questioning or thoughtful discussion. Their knowledge and application of mechanical principles, for handling and carving stone and constructing vast buildings from blocks weighing several tonnes, is however uniquely impressive, and they did achieve much in the measurement of time, if again for practical purposes. For arithmetic, multiplication was done with a two-times table (much as with present-day *digital computers) and their geometry was simple and practical, without a system of proof. There were, nevertheless, a few enquiring minds: Imhotep, for example, wrote the mathematical treatise known now as the Rhind Papyrus (c.2600 BC); but even this lacks abstract notions or any concept of proof, which was the invention of the Greeks.

The gods of both Egypt and Babylonia were credited with speech, and with at least human intelligence, and human passions, and morality. The Egyptian judgement at death was not, however, entrusted either to gods or to men—but to a great mechanical balance on which the heart was weighed against the feather of truth. This balance in the hall of judgement was served by many gods, including the god of wisdom, learning, language, and number—the ibis-headed god Thoth (who was sometimes baboon-headed, baboons being seen as highly intelligent).

Egyptian hieroglyphic writing was fully developed by 3000 BC. It is a wonderful record of the use of pictures as formal symbols to represent meaning. Although pictures cannot at all directly convey opinions, beliefs, commands or requests, or logical or other relations, they were given such powers by referring to animal characteristics—such as the power and fecundity of the bull associated with the sun and controlling the Nile—and by representing human gestures. Thus 'not' was written as arms flung out, the hands later being left out, to become our negation sign '—'. It seems strange that little or no attention has been paid by psycholinguists to ancient picture writings, for, surely, here lies invaluable 'fossil' evidence of the development of human communication and mind. (See, for example, CHINESE EVIDENCE ON THE EVOLUTION OF LANGUAGE.)

The flowering of Egyptian literature occurred in the eighteenth dynasty (1570–1293 BC). In the writings of this period, especially in its second half, are to be found many references to complex though not always consistent notions of mind, soul, personality, and their relations to the body. Throughout, there is a consistent and indeed dominating belief in eternal life. Man was believed to consist of several entities, each separate but each necessary for his welfare. These were the natural body, the spiritual body, the heart, the double, the soul, the shadow, the intangible casing of the body, the form, and the name.

The body as whole, the *khat*, is associated with things that decay. In early times the bodies of the dead were buried in the dry sand, beyond the agricultural land watered by the Nile, and they were preserved for thousands of years. But when the dead were placed in stone coffins, the flesh disappeared—supposedly eaten by the stone. Hence the Greek 'sarcophagus', meaning 'flesh eating', which reflects the prehistoric notion of the body and soul of the dead entering and being preserved in stone.

For the Egyptians, the brain (being bloodless in death) was not important and was generally ignored; the heart was the power of life, and the source of good and evil. Thus, in their funerary literature, the *Book of the Dead*, the heart was weighed, against feathers, to determine the balance of good and ill at death. According to the Egyptologist Sir Wallace Budge (1895, in a most lucid account of this complicated psychology of gods and men, p. lxiii):

In close connection with the natural and spiritual bodies stood the heart, or rather that part of it which was the power of life and the fountain of good and evil thoughts. And in addition to the natural and spiritual bodies, man also had an abstract individuality or personality endowed with all his characteristic attributes. This abstract personality had an absolutely independent existence. It could move freely from place to place, separating itself from, or uniting itself to, the body at will, and also enjoying life with the gods in heaven. This was the *ka*, a word which conveys at times the meanings . . . image, genius, double, character, disposition, and mental attributes. The funeral offerings of meat, cakes, ale, wine, unguents, etc., were intended for the *ka*; the scent of the burnt incense was grateful to it. The *ka* dwelt in the man's statue just as the *ka* of a god inhabited the statue of the god. In this respect the *ka* seems to be identical with the *sekhem* or image. In the remotest times the tombs had special chambers wherein the *ka* was worshipped and received offerings . . .

The *ka* . . . could eat food, and it was necessary to provide food for it. In the twelfth dynasty and in later periods the gods are entreated to grant meat and drink to the *ka* of the deceased; and it seems as if the Egyptians thought that the future welfare of the spiritual body depended upon the maintenance of a constant supply of sepulchral offerings. When circumstances rendered it impossible to continue the material supply of food, the *ka* fed upon the offerings painted on the walls of the tomb, which were transformed into suitable nourishment by means of the prayers of the living. When there were neither material offerings nor painted similitudes to feed upon, it seems as if the *ka* must have perished; but the texts are not definite on this point.

The *sekhem* was also thought of as the power, or vitality, of a man, but evidently it is very difficult to establish just what *sekhem* meant.

The Egyptians also accepted a more refined 'soul' named the *ba*. Again according to Wallace Budge (1895: p. lxiv):

To that part of man which beyond all doubt was believed to enjoy eternal existence in heaven in a state of glory, the Egyptians gave the name *ba*, a word which means something like 'sublime', 'noble', and which has always hitherto been translated by 'soul'. The *ba* is not incorporeal, for although it dwells in the *ka*, and is in some respects, like the heart, the principle of life in man, still it possesses both substance and form: in form it is depicted as a human-headed hawk, and in nature it is stated to be exceedingly refined or ethereal. It revisited the body in the tomb and re-animated it, and conversed with it; it could take upon itself any shape it pleased; and it had the power of passing into heaven and of dwelling with the perfected soul there. It was eternal.

There is more: the shadow, or shade of a man—the *khaibit*—which may be compared with the *umbra* of the Romans. The *khaibit* is not so frequently mentioned as the *ka* and *ba*. Wallace Budge (1895: p. lxvi):

It (the *khaibit*) was supposed to have an entirely independent existence and to be able to separate itself from the body; it was free to move wherever it pleased, and, like the *ka* and *ba*, it partook of the funeral offerings in the tomb, which it visited at will . . . in later times at least the shadow was always associated with the soul and was believed to be always near it.

Little seems to be known, though, of the life of the shadow.

Now we come to human intelligence. The *khu* of a man could journey to heaven as soon as the prayers said over his dead body allowed it. Wallace Budge again (1895: p. lxvii):

Another and most important and apparently eternal part of man was the *khu*, which . . . may be defined as a 'shining' or translucent, intangible casing or covering of the body, which is frequently depicted in the form of a mummy. For want of a better word *khu* has often been translated 'shining one', 'glorious', 'intelligence', and the like, but in certain cases it may be tolerably well rendered by 'spirit'.

Finally, there is the *ren* of a man—his name. This too had its own existence and could live in heaven among the gods. It has been suggested (Bauval and Gilbert 1994), intriguingly though controversially, that gods were believed to live in certain bright stars and could be visited at least by the Pharoah, via carefully constructed narrow shafts in the Great Pyramid. These were aimed at that time (2600 BC) at the Belt of Orion, associated with the god Osiris, and at the star Thurban in the constellation of Draco. Elaborate rituals to this effect are described in the Pyramid Texts.

The scholarship of Egyptologists tells us of past minds, and modes of thought and understanding. But clearly there are limits to modern understanding of what dead words such as 'ka', 'ba', and 'khaibit' meant for there may be no anologies from our experience to read the past. Even now a word like 'soul'—or for that matter 'mind'—is exceedingly hard to define, and different writers may use words differently. Evidently the Egyptians saw *khaibit* as more than we see in the shadow of a man, for theirs could walk away and be its own self. Is it possible for scholarship to become so immersed in ancient ideas that such thoughts of long-lost minds can, through their dead language, enter our present understanding? Even though this is sometimes doubtful, journeys of such scholarship are wonderfully rewarding, extending our vision through space and time and even into how long-departed minds saw, questioned, and often falsely believed.

RLG

Bauvel, R. and Gilbert, A. (1994). *The Orion Mystery: Unlocking the Secrets of the Pyramids.*

Budge, E. A. Wallace (1891). *Egyptian Magic* (repr. 1971).

——(1895). *The Egyptian Book of the Dead: The Papyrus of Ani* (repr. 1967).

Gardiner, A. (1957). *Egyptian Grammar: Being an Introduction to the Study of Hieroglyphs* (3rd edn.).

Katan, N. J. (1985). *Hieroglyphs: The Writing of Ancient Egypt.*

Kramer, S. N. (1963). *The Sumerians: Their History, Culture, and Character.*

Simpson, W. K. (ed.) (1973). *The Literature of Ancient Egypt: An Anthology of Stories, Instructions, and Poetry.*

Ehrenfels, Christian von (1859–1933). Austrian philosopher and psychologist, who was a student of Franz *Brentano in Vienna and is remembered as a precursor of *Gestalt psychology. His important paper *Über Gestalt Qualitäten* (On Gestalt Qualities) appeared in 1891. Although influenced to some extent by Mach's *Analysis of Sensations* (1886), this was an original and timely contribution to the psychology of *perception. Ehrenfels introduced the term 'Gestalt qualities' to denote the perception of form or melody which, though based on sensory stimulation, can in no sense be regarded as inherent in the pattern of stimulation. In his view, Gestalt qualities represent novel elements in the field of perception, and this is well brought out in the phenomena of transposition. For example, a form such as a square or circle is

recognized as such even after changes in its size or colour. Similarly, a melody is recognized even when played in a different key. Indeed object constancy, whether spatial or temporal, is perhaps the most basic property of a Gestalt quality.

Ehrenfels, and after him Alexius Meinong (1853–1920), elaborated the system further, pointing out for instance that a particular direction of change might be a potent source of Gestalt qualities, as when one observes a slowly spreading blush. Gestalt qualities may also combine with one another to produce superordinate Gestalt qualities, as commonly found in music. Although no precise theory was put forward to explain Gestalt qualities, Ehrenfels came very close to formulating the principle of isomorphism, which is usually attributed to Max *Wertheimer and Wolfgang *Köhler, and which played so important a role in the Gestalt theory.

The idea of Gestalt qualities was then little known outside Austria, but it seems to have inspired the English philosopher and psychologist George Frederick Stout to write his two-volume *Analytic Psychology* (1896).

OLZ

eidetic imagery. See MENTAL IMAGES; HALLUCINATION.

Electra complex. A son's hostility towards the parent of the same sex and sexual impulses towards the parent of the opposite sex make up the *Oedipus complex. Usually the same term is applied to the corresponding feelings of a girl; less often, but following C. G. *Jung, the term applied is the Electra complex. In the plays of ancient Greece, Electra, unmarried and still grieving for her father Agamemnon, who has been killed long before by her mother Clytemnestra and Clytemnestra's paramour, encourages her brother Orestes to kill them in retribution. Versions of Electra's story have been used by modern playwrights, notably T. S. Eliot, Jean Giraudoux, Eugene O'Neill, and Jean-Paul *Sartre.

DRD

electroconvulsive therapy. See ECT.

electroencephalography. A common aim of research of the normal brain and of clinical diagnosis of its disorders is to build a complete image of the living tissue and its activity. All practical techniques allow one to view only one aspect of it. The electroencephalogram (EEG) registers potential differences on the scalp which arise as a result of 'feeble currents' of the brain. Electrical activity of the brain was first reported in 1875 by Richard Caton, a British physiologist who studied it in monkeys, cats, and rabbits. Human EEG was first described by Hans *Berger, a German psychiatrist, in 1929, but not until E. D. Adrian (later Lord *Adrian) and B. H. C. Matthews in England published their work in 1934 did human EEG become a routine diagnostic test in neurology and psychiatry. It also became one of the widely used tools of brain research in humans.

For clinical purposes, most modern EEG machines register as many as sixteen '*channels' of brain activity. Many channels are used in order to be able to detect if there are different types of electrical activity in neighbouring brain areas. However, as will be explained later, spatial resolution of abnormal brain activity is not one of the strong points of clinical electroencephalograms. A 'channel' refers simply to the amplified record of the potential difference between two points on the skull and its changes. Since brain potentials change in time and do not usually measure more than 100 microvolts, the tiny signals need to be amplified and registered, usually with the help of an ink pen recorder. In most clinical EEG studies, small metal discs pasted on the skull, or fine needles inserted

into the scalp, will pick up the electrical activity of the brain. They are called electrodes, and each is connected to a powerful amplifier. A number of amplifiers, each with its pen recorder, constitutes the essence of an electro-encephalographic machine. When the brain is alive, the potential difference between two recording electrodes changes 'spontaneously' as time goes on. When written out by the pen recorder, this is seen on the EEG record as undulations. By inspecting these one gains the impression that the brain produces waves. In fact, 'brainwave test' is a term used in the United States for the EEG. The wavy appearance provides a simple way of describing and classifying the EEG by sheer visual inspection. The Greek letters alpha, beta, delta, and theta are commonly used for the different periodicities or wave frequencies apparent in the EEG. Alpha stands for brainwaves with a periodicity of about 9–11 per second. Beta is a higher-frequency

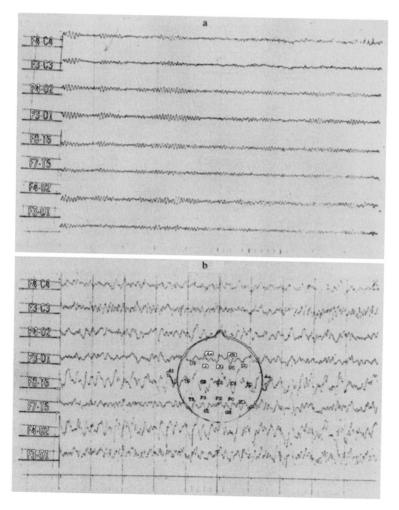

Fig. 1. a. Eight simultaneously recorded channels of normal EEG. Letters to the left of each trace represent electrode locations referring to a schematized drawing of a head. Notice on the right side of the figure the spindling of normal alpha range activity in several channels.

b. Abnormal EEG of a patient with right cerebral lesion. Notice large-amplitude, slow-wave activity in the even-numbered right-sided channels, especially in the frontotemporal (F_8–T_6) derivation. There was clinical evidence of focal seizure manifested by jerking of the left leg of the patient.

'component' of the EEG, while delta and theta are slower-changing brain potentials, or low-frequency waves.

Much interest has accompanied the nature of the alpha rhythm since it was shown by Berger that it appears when a human is resting quietly, but disappears when he opens his eyes. This disappearance is called 'alpha blocking'. Some people produce alpha waves even with eyes open, and in these people a flash of light is needed to block them. The presence of alpha is thought to be associated with a meditative, quiescent state, while its disappearance in the normal human is thought to be due to *attention and *arousal. Because of the relation of the alpha rhythm to vision, several investigators studied its presence or absence when patients suffer from abnormalities of their visual system. It has been reported that if a person has reduced vision due to some ocular abnormality but can see flashes of light, these are not enough to block his alpha rhythm. Apparently, not all visual activities block alpha rhythm. However, mental imagery, such as occurs when playing blindfold chess, can block alpha rhythm. Another pertinent observation has been that most patients who lose the ability to see as a result of a *stroke of the visual cortex on both sides of the brain do not have alpha rhythm. Stroke results from depriving a part of the brain of its blood supply, such as occurs when one of its supplying arteries is completely or partially occluded. Bilateral stroke of the visual cortex occurs when the so-called basilar artery or its branches receives diminished blood supply.

The slow waves of the EEG occur for short periods only in normal *sleep, but commonly when there is pathology of the brain—such as a stroke or a tumour. The electroencephalographer can sometimes diagnose the size and nature of brain pathology by comparing the simultaneous activity of many channels of the EEG. In some patients brainwaves paroxysmally change their characteristics: they no longer appear as gentle waves of the sea, but become very sharp and spiky. (The appearance of such a 'brainstorm' unfortunately does not represent the occurrence of some sharp thought.) These abnormalities are seen in seizure disorders, called epilepsies. The EEG provides a major contribution to the diagnosis of *epilepsy. Clinically different types of epilepsies have their individual EEG fingerprints, and these different types respond to different medications. Sometimes a medication which is good for one type of seizure disorder may be harmful in another. Thus for these patients EEG recording is indispensable.

The understanding of potential changes of the human brain has been helped by experimental recordings done in other animals. While their surface skull potential EEG is recorded, simultaneously an electrode is being advanced into the depth of the cortex and a third electrode may be held at a constant depth near to or within a single cortical cell. Thus surface EEG, intracellular potential changes, and extracellular spike activity can be recorded in the same animal at the same time. Studies by D. A. Pollen showed that slow surface potential changes (one of the main components of the EEG) are not influenced by spike generation of individual neurons; rather waves represent changes of potential differences between the bodies and processes of single neurons.

Using the electroencephalogram to reveal abnormal or even normal cognitive processes of the brain has been very disappointing. The attempt has been likened to trying to diagnose the problems of a computer by holding a voltmeter up to it. The EEG reveals the pathology of the human brain, but little about abnormal thinking. One reason may be that the EEG scalp electrode samples potential changes which arise in a large volume of the brain, and deficiencies of specific nerve cells which may not all be in the same volume of tissue cannot be detected. The situation is different when, under surgery, the electrical activity of the brain can be directly recorded. With some patients there are medical reasons for putting electrodes on the surface or in the depth of the cortex, and exploring connections between distant areas of the brain. Surprisingly, under this condition, even a relatively large surface electrode samples only the activity of a small volume of tissue. Two intracranial surface electrodes, when spaced only 1 millimetre apart, can show different EEGs.

Resolution of brain pathology by EEG methods is limited by the organization of the human cerebral cortex itself. Sensory stimuli such as light through the eyes, tones through the ears, temperature and pressures, and other sensations, are first transduced and then transmitted to the cortex as changes in electrical activity along nerve fibres as a series of pulses. Often, as the nerves enter the cortex they branch like a tree and connect to many different cells (neurons) of the brain. In addition there are connections between various neurons in the immediate vicinity of each other, as well as long fibres connecting different parts of the brain. Consequently distant cells may register identical changes.

Modern diagnosis in clinical neurology relies less and less on registering spontaneous activity of the brain. Rather, one attempts to induce changes in specific brain areas devoted to one or another sensory modality, such as vision and hearing. Induced activity is of much smaller amplitude than the 'spontaneously' arising potential change and, to detect it, the averaging and summation of a large number of tiny signals is required. The technique is called '*evoked' (as opposed to spontaneous) potentials.

The conventional EEG is obtained through an alternating current (AC) coupled recording. Usually only changes in potentials that occur in less than 1 second are registered. Recordings that show the slower changes of so-called 'standing' potentials of the brain were made as long ago as the 19th century. 'Slow' in this context means a DC shift noticeable only over many seconds. Beck, a Polish investigator, was remarkably successful using the then available technique to record DC potentials. DC recording became clinically useful only with the development of transistorized amplifiers and better electrodes. DC potential changes of the brain may reveal more about cognitive processing than classical EEG does. For example, W. Grey *Walter, one of the pioneers of modern electroencephalography, has been able to show that DC potential shifts occur and may relate to *anticipation and decision making by the human. A potential shift measured at the top of the head and called the contingent negative variation or CNV is the best-known example of a 'slow' potential change.   IBW

Cooper, R., Osselton, J. W., and Shaw, J. C. (1974). *EEG Technology*.
Pollen, D. A. (1969). *Basic Mechanisms of the Epilepsies*.
Walter, W. G. (1953). *The Living Brain* (repr. 1968).

embarrassment. See BLUSHING.

'emergence' and 'reduction' in explanations. A classical question of philosophy is the one/many problem: is everything in the universe ultimately one thing—or are there, as it certainly appears, many things? In another and more interesting form the question becomes: are there many *kinds* of things—or could there be a single unifying account of all the apparently various kinds of events and phenomena?

It is sometimes raised as an objection to science, especially to medicine, that reducing complex issues to simpler terms produces loss of significance of the whole, which like Humpty Dumpty cannot be put together again. This is the 'holistic' criticism of science's reduction of complex issues into simpler parts or concepts. The converse of reduction is that when parts are combined, surprising or mysterious 'emergent' properties may appear—mysterious because reduction-descriptions are inadequate. A familiar example is the creation of water by the combination of the gases oxygen and hydrogen.

Just as the properties of water are different from those of its constituent gases, so, it is sometimes suggested, mind may be similarly emergent upon physical brain structure or activity. Douglas Hofstadter (1979) makes effective use of an analogy—originating from a paper (1911) by William Morton Wheeler—that though ants build their nests they cannot reconstitute them when they have been disturbed and the structure has been destroyed. To conceive that the functioning ants' nest is more than the sum of the ants is helpful when thinking about brain cells (which, also, individually do not understand, or see, etc.), and it is helpful to conceive of the cooperative functioning of brain cells in the process of understanding the mind. Knowledge of individual ants cannot explain nest behaviour and knowledge of individual brain cells cannot explain the mind, even though the nest is no more than ants and the mind depends entirely on brain cells.

Vitalist biologists such as Hans *Driesch (1867–1941) have held that the functioning of organisms can never be explained from knowledge, however complete, of their parts because of a vital principle which relates to the whole but not the isolated parts. This doctrine precludes 'reductive' explanations drawn from analyses of the whole into parts that may be separately investigated and described. It implies that the biological and medical sciences are essentially outside the kinds of explanation by reductive analyses that have proved so powerful in the natural sciences. If this is so, biology (and psychology even more so) would seem to be essentially different in kind from physics. Is this holistic view of biology and mind justified? To consider this it is useful to look at simple *machines* and ask: do we find emergence when parts of a construction set, such as Meccano, are combined to make a simple working model? Putting the parts together in various ways creates very different mechanisms: cars, cranes, clocks, and so on. It is indeed remarkable that the same differently arranged parts may move as a car, lift things as a crane, or keep time as a clock. This can look like emergence beyond explanation—much as for organisms—though here we clearly have simple mechanisms with just a few parts.

The Oxford philosopher Gilbert *Ryle tried (1949) to exorcize common concepts of mind that, implicitly or explicitly, dubbed the mind 'the Ghost in the Machine'. But even the simplest of Meccano mechanisms can look quite ghostly! Is this because they have emergent properties? If so, do they still appear ghostly in this way when they are fully understood? Or could it be that we do not yet completely understand simple machines reductively—though we may come to understand machines and organisms so fully that appearance of emergence vanishes, as analysis of the functions of their parts becomes complete?

A machine is assembled from component parts, yet how it functions may be explained by more or less abstract general concepts rather than in terms of its parts. Thus, how a clock keeps time is explained less by describing the parts and their mechanical interactions than from general principles, such as those stating why pendulums swing at a constant rate. We have to look beyond the parts of a mechanism to explain what the parts do. Moreover, there is no simple relation between a machine's structure and its function. A single part, such as the anchor of the clock's escapement, may have several functions, or several parts may combine to provide a single function. Similarly there is no simple correspondence of parts to functions in an organism. (Insights to relations between structures and functions of machines are powerfully expressed by Robert M. Pirsig (1974).)

It is tempting to believe that the high-level properties of organic systems must somehow be present in a rudimentary or dormant form in their parts. But such belief does little to explain how organisms function, and can lead (as with inorganic mechanisms) to notions of molecules, atoms, or even fundamental particles such as electrons having *intention, or *consciousness. Such notions are without verification, however, and must surely be dismissed (see FALSIFICATION). We should prefer to say that mind emerges from brain function—if only because there is some hope of finding out what is so special about the brain. But it is hard enough to understand how organisms can be intelligent or conscious, even with all their interacting complexity, and to say that individual brain cells (or, even more extreme, that the individual molecules, atoms, or electrons of which we are composed) have intelligence or consciousness merely pushes the question further beyond answer.

The Cambridge philosopher C. D. *Broad argued (1929) that the universe is inherently 'layered', to give emergences with increasing complexity that can never be predicted or explained from any knowledge of lower (generally simpler) 'layers' of reality. On this account, mind may remain beyond understanding despite knowledge of brain or other function—even though mind is causally given by physical functions. Moreover, most neurophysiologists, at least until recently, have held that brain and mind are essentially different—irreducibly two kinds of things—the causal connection (denied by *Leibniz) notwithstanding. (See also MIND AND BODY; MIND–BODY PROBLEM: PHILOSOPHICAL THEORIES.)

This duality may be criticized on the principle of Occam's razor, as postulating entities unnecessarily, though one might follow the physiologist Sir Charles *Sherrington's (1906, 1940) opinion: 'That our being should consist of two fundamental elements offers, I suppose, no greater inherent improbability than that it should rest on one only.' By contrast the neurologist Wilder *Penfield (1975) came to the view that the mind is the emergent characteristic of brain function and depends on physical processes of the brain. This is probably the prevailing view, though Broad's 'layers', limiting reductionist explanations, are largely ignored or denied.

Whether these dualist and emergent accounts of mind are so different, and just what each implies, depends on extremely difficult issues of what should be accepted as causal and what as emergent, and how emergence may be seen in causal terms. The answer seems to be that causal explanations require general concepts, or 'meta'-accounts, and that these can remove the mysteries of emergence, though not simply by 'reduction' to the parts. But so far an adequate meta-account for linking brain function to mind is lacking.

These issues have significance not only in science but also for anyone who wishes or needs to understand or apply scientific concepts, for the language, ideas, and aims of scientists differ according to the level of reduction in which they think and work. Thus a fundamental particle physicist or a cell biologist may find the concepts and aims of the neurologist alien and hard to appreciate— while the cognitive psychologist might as well be living in a different universe. And yet such universes of discourse have to be bridged for adequate understanding, and in many cases for effective research and action. Art and science have been described as 'two cultures'; but science is also divided within itself, with prestige accorded to the 'deeper', more 'fundamental' concepts—even though they may be inadequate to explain the way things are higher up the tree. And it is not clear even that this tree is rooted in the 'fundamental' sciences—for its 'levels' of explanation depend on the observations and intelligence of our minds at the treetop.   RLG

Broad, C. D. (1929). *The Mind and its Place in Nature.*
Hofstadter, D. R. (1979). *Godel, Escher, Bach: An Eternal Golden Braid.*
Morgan, C. Lloyd (1923). *Emergent Evolution.*
Penfield, W. (1975). *The Mystery of the Mind.*
Pirsig, R. M. (1974). *Zen and the Art of Motorcycle Maintenance: An Enquiry into Values.*
Ryle, G. (1949). *The Concept of Mind.*
Sherrington, C. S. (1906). *The Integrative Action of the Nervous System.*
—— (1940). *Man on his Nature.*
Wheeler, W. M. (1911). 'The ant-colony as an organism'. *Journal of Morphology*, 22/2.

Emmert's law. It was reported by E. Emmert in 1881 that a visual *after-image appears to change in size, according to whether it is seen as lying nearby or far away. This is easy to demonstrate by looking for a few seconds at a bright light, or a camera's flashlight, and then viewing the after-image as seen on a nearby surface (say a book held in the hand) and then on a distant screen or wall. The after-image is perceptually 'projected' on to the viewed surface, so that it appears near on the book and more distant on the wall. When near it looks small, and the more distant it is seen to be the larger it appears. Its apparent size—though it is actually a fixed-size 'photograph' on the retina of the eye—increases roughly linearly with its apparent distance. This linear increase of apparent size with increasing distance is Emmert's law.

Consider now a normal retinal image, of some object, rather than the local fatigue of a region of retina of an after-image. As the object increases in distance its image in the eye will correspondingly shrink—just as for a camera. But (and this is easily checked for oneself) as the viewed object recedes it does not appear to shrink anything like as much as the optical halving of the retinal image with each doubling of the object's distance. It normally *looks* almost the same size over a wide range of distances. This is due to a perceptual compensation called 'size constancy scaling'.

After-images are odd because they do not change in size at the retina. What we see in the *apparent* changes of size noted by Emmert is a compensation at work. It is compensating for what would normally be changes of size of the retinal image, but as the after-image remains unchanging, size constancy gives illusory changes of size.

Constancy scaling is set by several 'distance cues': convergence of the eyes, geometrical perspective, and the graded texture and falling of sharpness ('aerial perspective'), which are all associated with increasing distance of a viewed object. Correspondingly, after-images change their size with changes of convergence angles of the eyes, or with perspective—many *illusion figures having converging lines. Any cue to distance can set the compensatory size-scaling mechanism, and when mis-set there is a corresponding size or shape distortion illusion.

Emmert himself thought that a visible screen, on which after-images are 'projected', is necessary for the size changes he described. This is not so, however, for these changes occur in the dark, if the observer moves backwards or forwards from an imaginary screen. This observation is important for it shows that Emmert's law is not due merely to relative size changes of the fixed after-image and the changing image of the screen, or its texture, but is indeed due to the brain's perceptual compensatory size constancy scaling, which, when inappropriate, produces illusions of size or shape. But Emmert's law holds over a huge range of distance—seemingly far beyond what size scaling can explain—so it is not fully understood.

Boring, E. G. (1942). *Sensation and Perception in the History of Experimental Psychology*.

Emmert, E. (1881). 'Grossen verhalnisse der Nachbidder'. *Klinische Monatsblätter für Augenheilkunde*, 19.

Gregory, R. L., Wallace, J. G., and Campbell, F. W. C. (1959). 'Changes in the size and shape of visual after-images observed in complete darkness during changes of position in space'. *Quarterly Journal of Experimental Psychology*, 2/1.

Thouless, R. H. (1931). 'Phenomenal regression to the real object, I'. *British Journal of Psychology*, 21.

——(1932). 'Individual differences in phenomenal regression'. *British Journal of Psychology*, 22.

emotion. Emotion is central to human life and intimately connected with *consciousness. Historically, the link with consciousness has led to a relative neglect of emotion as a subject of systematic scientific enquiry in comparison with other fields, such as *cognition. However, the last few decades have seen a significant increase in research on emotion, leading to important new discoveries of the brain mechanisms involved.

The concept of emotion can usefully be subdivided into two components: (i) the *emotional state* that can be measured through physiological changes such as autonomic response, and (ii) *feelings*, seen as the subjective experience of emotion. The latter is linked with *qualia and the hard problem of consciousness, that is to say, what it is *like* subjectively to experience an emotional state. How the brain gives rise to consciousness remains an unsolved problem, but it is becoming increasingly clear which brain areas are involved in producing and representing emotional states.

Ancient Greek and later Western philosophers have always discussed emotion, although the emphasis has almost exclusively been on its cognitive evaluation. Cognition and emotion have been regarded as separate areas, and subsequently, for the larger part of the 20th century, most scientific research focused on cognition at the expense of emotion. Notwithstanding, important theoretical advances were made by pioneering individuals such as Charles *Darwin (1872) who examined the evolution of emotional responses and *facial expressions. Emotions allow an organism to make adaptive responses to salient stimuli in the environment, thus enhancing its chances of survival.

In the 1880s William *James and Carl *Lange independently proposed the idea that, rather than emotional experience being a response to a stimulus, it is the perception of the ensuing physiological bodily changes. The James–Lange theory suggests that we do not run from the bear because we are afraid but that we *become* afraid because we run.

Walter *Cannon (1929) offered a detailed critique of the James–Lange theory showing that surgical disruption of the peripheral nervous system in dogs did not eliminate emotional responses as would have been predicted by the theory. Further investigations by Schacter and Singer (1962) suggested that bodily states must be accompanied by cognitive appraisal for an emotion to occur. However, this research did not fully resolve the basic question of the extent to which bodily states influence emotion. Recently, the James–Lange theory was resurrected by Antonio Damasio (1994) in the form of his somatic marker hypothesis, in which feedback from the peripheral nervous system controls the *decision* about the correct behavioural response rather than the *emotional feelings* as postulated in the James–Lange theory.

An alternative to such bodily theories of emotions has been proposed by Larry Weiskrantz (1968), Jeffrey Gray (1975), and Edmund Rolls (1999) who instead regard emotions as states elicited by rewards and punishments. Emotional stimuli are evaluated and mediated by specific brain structures which subsequently give rise to feelings and to changes in bodily response.

Although the theoretical debate over the nature of emotion has been very important, the development of

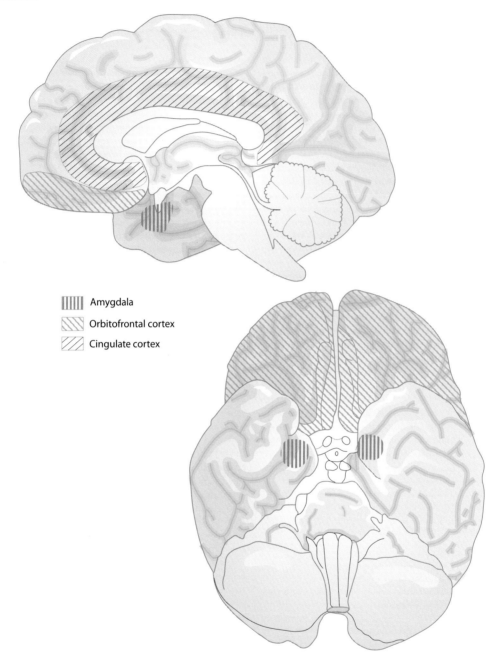

||||| Amygdala

▨ Orbitofrontal cortex

▧ Cingulate cortex

Fig. 1. Key brain structures underlying emotion shown on a midsagittal view (top) and on a ventral view (bottom) of the human brain.

experimental paradigms for the reliable testing of emotion in animals and humans has had just as much influence on the field of emotion research. Given that consciousness in animals remains controversial, the presence of feelings in animals is also a contentious issue. Animals do, however, show the characteristic behavioural, autonomic, and hormonal responses associated with emotional states when confronted with emotionally salient stimuli. Building on this insight, one of the most successful paradigms in emotion research has been fear *conditioning where an auditory conditioned stimulus is paired with a foot shock. LeDoux (1996) and others have shown that for rats to learn the appropriate fear response depends crucially on a brain structure in the temporal lobes, the amygdala (Latin for 'almond'). Subsequently, much neuroscientific research has concentrated on elucidating the full role of the amygdala in fear, so that it has become popularly known as the fear centre in the brain. However, the amygdala is not a homogeneous brain structure but rather a collection of at least thirteen anatomically distinct nuclei. In addition, other research using appetitive conditioning has also implicated the amygdala, indicating that it can be activated by both positive and negative stimuli. It is therefore unlikely that the amygdala is concerned only with fear. Nevertheless, the fear-conditioning paradigm has been very successful in creating an adequate scientific model of emotion and firmly establishing the field of emotion research.

Paul Ekman's cross-cultural studies of human *facial expression have been another influential paradigm which has strongly suggested an innate, biological basis for emotional experience. In the primate brain a dedicated neural circuitry for recognizing faces has been found in the fusiform gyrus, and in social animals such as humans and higher primates facial expressions act as highly significant social signals communicating the state of the individual to others. Ekman's research on universally recognized facial emotions and analyses of emotion terms in all the world's major languages have led to discussions on the existence and enumeration of the fundamental emotions that can act as basic building blocks of our entire emotional repertoire. Based on such research up to seven emotions have been proposed: anger, disgust, fear, sadness, joy, shame, and guilt. It remains an open question whether these emotions are really distinct or whether they are found on a continuum produced by shared brain mechanisms.

The question of what brain structures represent and mediate emotions can now be addressed more fully with *neuroimaging, which allows a unique window on the living human brain. Experimental paradigms with emotionally salient stimuli have also allowed researchers to probe the nature of emotion. Negative emotions such as fear and disgust have already been the subject of much research, while positive emotions such as joy have been found much harder to induce experimentally. Consequently only a few studies to date have dealt with this important subject. Many neuroimaging studies build on the findings from animal studies using conditioning paradigms and primary reinforcers such as taste and smell, while other studies have begun to probe the brain mechanisms involved in more complex human activities such as gambling.

The findings from neuroimaging and anatomical evidence from lesions in humans and other higher primates have pointed to the role of several interconnected brain structures in emotion. An early attempt to synthesize the emotion literature was the theory proposed by James Papez (1937) where the cingulate cortex was seen as important for the *experience* of emotion, whereas emotional *expression* was governed by the hypothalamus, and these two structures were linked by the thalamus and the hippocampus.

This theory was further elaborated by Paul MacLean (1952) with his proposal for the evolution of the triune primate brain with three functionally distinct systems, of which the limbic system was the one mediating emotion. The term limbic lobe (Latin *limbus*, border) was proposed by Paul *Broca in 1878 who coined the name for those structures surrounding the brain stem and corpus callosum on the medial walls of the brain. Broca did not specify a role for the limbic lobe in emotion, and indeed subsequent research has found that the concept of emotion mediated by a unifying limbic system is too simplistic.

These early pioneering theories were built on a paucity of experimental data, and with the recent flourishing of emotion research, and especially given the ever-increasing amount of human neuroimaging data, we are now in a much better position to evaluate which brain structures are crucial to emotion. The evidence points to the amygdala and the cingulate cortex as necessary for the proper emotional functioning of the primate brain. Furthermore, it has also become clear that in humans and other higher primates a very significant role is played by the orbitofrontal cortex (the part of the frontal lobes just above the eyeballs). Some of the first evidence for this came from the case of the young railway engineer Phineas *Gage whose frontal lobes were completely penetrated by a metal rod in 1848. Miraculously, he survived but his personality and emotional processing were changed completely. Recent studies have shed further light on the functioning of the orbitofrontal cortex, and shown that the reward value of primary reinforcers such as taste, smell, and visual stimuli can be found there. Strong reciprocal connections are also found with the amygdala, and the scientific evidence suggests a similar role for the two brain areas, although the orbitofrontal cortex appears to be the more important for emotion in humans and higher primates.

Mood is the longer-lasting continuation of an emotional state and mood disorders such as depression and anxiety affect a large proportion of the population. Some statistics suggest that as much as a third of the population will experience a major depression during their lifetime. A very important goal in understanding the neural basis of emotion is to develop better treatments for these disorders. *Neurotransmitters acting on the frontal lobes such as serotonin, dopamine, and other catecholamines have all been implicated in mood disorders. This has led to the development of antidepressants that have helped many sufferers, but the efficacy of these drugs has not yet been matched by a better understanding of the underlying brain mechanisms.

There are many interesting and important issues in emotion research which are not yet fully understood. It is clear that personality plays a significant role in shaping emotions, but we are a long way from understanding personality in neural terms. Studies in *split-brain patients seems to suggest a hemispheric specialization of emotional processing, but the issue of lateralization is still much debated among researchers. It also clear that, although conscious appraisal of emotion is important for emotional expression, many emotional stimuli appear to be processed on a non-conscious level, only later to become available for conscious introspection (or, as in the case of *blindsight, not at all). Emotion helps to facilitate learning and memory adaptively, and so there are strong links between emotion, learning, and memory, but the exact relationship between these are is yet fully understood.

The most difficult question facing emotion research is the question of where qualia are created in the brain. Science has not yet found the neural basis for our subjective experience of emotion, and some researchers have even raised doubts about whether this will ever happen. Nevertheless, it is clear that emotions are evolutionarily important for animals in preparing for appropriate actions. The evolution of conscious feelings could be adaptive, because they allow us to consciously appraise our emotions and actions, and subsequently to learn to manipulate these appropriately. Emotion may be one of evolution's most productive breakthroughs, constantly reminding us that we are still animals at heart, but endowed with the possibility of conscious appraisal and enhanced control of our subjective experience that comes with it.   MK

Cannon, W. B. (1927). 'The James–Lange theory of emotion'. *American Journal of Psychology*, 39.

Damasio, A. (1994). *Descartes' Error*.

Darwin, C. (1872). *The Expression of the Emotions in Man and Animals*.

Ekman, P., and Davidson, R. J. (eds.) (1994). *The Nature of Emotion: Fundamental Questions*.

Frijda, N. (1987). *The Emotions*.

Gray, J. (1975). *Elements of a two-process theory of learning*.

James, W. (1890). *The Principles of Psychology*.

Lange, C. G. (1887). *Über Gemustsbewegungen*.

LeDoux, J. E. (1996). *The Emotional Brain*.

MacLean, P. D. (1952). 'Some psychiatric implications of physiological on the frontotemporal portion of limbic system (visceral brain)'. *Electroencephalography and Clinical Neurophysiology*, 4.

Panksepp, J. (1999). *Affective Neuroscience*.

Papez, J. W. (1937). 'A proposed mechanism of emotion'. *Arch. Neurol. Psychiat.* 38.

Rolls, E. T. (1999). *Brain and Emotion*.

Schacter, S., and Singer, J. (1962). 'Cognitive, social and physiological determinants of emotional state'. *Psych. Rev.* 69.

Weiskrantz, L. (1968). 'Emotion'. In Weiskrantz, L. (ed.), *Analysis of Behavioural Change*.

emotional brain. In the last few years there has been an explosion of interest in the brain mechanisms of emotion. Not so long ago, though, this was a topic that few brain scientists felt was worth pursuing. This state of affairs was due in large part to the fact that emotions did not figure prominently in the cognitive approach to psychology, which strongly influenced the direction of research on the relation of brain and mind. And, besides, and there seemed to be a perfectly good explanation of how the brain makes emotions—the *limbic system does it.

It is now widely recognized that a purely cognitive approach to mental function that ignores emotions is at best incomplete. And the limbic system theory of emotion no longer carries the explanatory weight it once did. With these hindrances now in the background, emotions are being avidly pursued across the spectrum of neuroscience, occupying the interests of researchers who study genes and their molecular products, cellular physiological properties of neurons in dishes as well as in living brains, pharmacology of synaptic transmission, behavioural processes, computer simulations of brain function, and imaging of normal subjects and neurological and psychiatric patients. Emotions, in short, are hot.

1. The credibility problem
2. Emotions, one at a time
3. Defence
4. Conscious feelings
5. The future of the brain

1. The credibility problem

As with any other psychological process, the pursuit of emotions in the brain is only as good as our understanding of the process itself. In order for interest in emotions to be sustained, it is thus important that we develop rigorous ways of thinking about the underlying processes in a way that will make it possible to relate specific aspects of emotion to detailed brain mechanisms. Fortunately, such an approach has recently begun to emerge.

In the late 19th century, William *James and other psychologists came to think of emotions as having two components: a subjective or conscious manifestation, typically referred to as an *emotional feeling*, and a set of behavioural and physiological body alterations called *emotional responses*. Following this lead, researchers interested in the brain mechanisms of emotion often proposed different systems for conscious feelings and emotional responses.

Problems quickly arose. The partition between the conscious and bodily components of emotion was nothing more than a scientific restatement of the philosophical *mind–body problem in the realm of emotion. And to make matters worse, most brain research was, and still is, conducted in non-human species, organisms in which there is little scientific evidence (as opposed to anecdotal stories and hard-felt beliefs) for the existence of subjective conscious states. In spite of this, most theorists discussing the brain mechanisms of emotion—from James to Cannon to Papez and MacLean, to name some of the key historical figures—used this research on non-human organisms to generate theories of how emotional experiences are mediated by the brain. This has created a credibility gap between the research itself and its application, a gap that must be overcome in order for emotion research to progress.

We readily make the leap about consciousness from our own mind to minds of other humans—life as we know it would be impossible otherwise. So why shouldn't we do the same for other animals? All we really have on which to base our conclusion about mental states in either case is overt behaviour. If another person or another animal acts the same as we do, shouldn't we assume they have the same internal states? Other humans, yes; other creatures, no. All humans have pretty much the same kind of brain, but there are important differences between the brains of humans and other animals, including other primates. And the parts of the brain that are most different (the prefrontal areas) are just the ones that are key to higher mental processes, and possibly to consciousness. This anatomical fact alone forces us to be extremely cautious in drawing conclusions about an animal's mental states on the basis of the similarity of its behaviour to ours. A cockroach runs away under the shadow of a descending human foot, just as we run if we notice something falling towards us. But it is unlikely that the roach feels the fear that a human does when doing essentially the same thing under similar circumstances. So where do we draw the line as to conclusions about whether different organisms have different mental states? Vertebrates vs. invertebrates? Reptiles vs. mammals? Primates vs. other mammals? I would say that the safest conclusion on scientific grounds is to assume that organisms with similar brains (same neural systems) have similar kinds of mental states, and organisms with brains that have verifiably

different neural systems are likely to have different kinds of mental states. This does not mean that a monkey, cat, dog, rat, frog, lizard, or pigeon has no feelings. It means that if they do have feelings the feelings they have are likely to be different from the ones we have since our brains differ from theirs.

In all fairness, researchers in other areas of psychology were, for quite some time, really no better off than emotion researchers when it came to relating mental states to brain mechanisms. There is nothing less subjective about a conscious perception or a conscious memory than a conscious emotion. But a way emerged for closing the credibility gap for cognitive processes like perception and memory. With the rise of cognitive science came a way of studying how the brain systems process information independent of whether, and if so how, that information enters conscious awareness. For example, much has been learned about how the brain processes colour while little is still known about how the brain experiences colour. Presumably, the mechanisms that process colour are involved in the experience of colour, but the experience of colour is the end result rather than primary subject of interest. One important consequence of this view is the conclusion that we are not conscious of the processing that leads to an experience—information processing is by default unconscious. This point was made by Karl *Lashley many years ago but has since become a cornerstone of the cognitive approach to the mind.

Emotion, though, was not part of the cognitive revolution in psychology and the processing approach was not applied to this topic. But there is no real reason why emotion cannot, like cognition, be thought of in terms of processing functions. Indeed, in recent years, the processing logic can and has been fruitfully applied to the study of emotion, thus overcoming the credibility problem. That is, it is possible to study how the brain of a human or other animal detects and responds to danger, food, sexual partners, and so forth without first understanding how we consciously experience fear, gustatory delight, or sexual pleasure. The relevant stimuli, in other words, are processed unconsciously, and on the basis of this processing appropriate responses are initiated and controlled. This point of view offers a great advantage in the study of other creatures. Given that animal research is key to understanding brain mechanisms at a detailed level, and that we cannot inspect the inside of an animal's mind, the ability to close the credibility gap is not only useful, it is essential to progress in understanding the emotional brain.

2. Emotions, one at a time
In providing a way of thinking of emotions as processing functions of the brain, the processing logic gave a great boost to modern studies of the emotional brain. But there was another important development. In the

past, researchers treated 'emotion' as a brain function. The limbic system, for example, was said to be the seat of 'emotion', in the general sense of the term. But in trying to be everything to all emotions, the limbic system theory failed to provide an adequate explanation of how any particular emotion process is represented in the brain. This convinced many researchers to turn to a different approach, one that assumes that there are different systems in the brain for different emotions.

This approach would seem to overlap considerably with the psychological notion of 'basic emotions', which assumes the existence of a set of biologically determined primary emotions, such as fear, anger, joy, disgust, and so forth. However, the brain approach is fundamentally different. The psychological basic emotions are defined on the basis of human subjective experience, and thus take us back to consciousness and the credibility problem. The brain science approach, in contrast, starts with an animal behaviour system, like the defence system, and tries to understand how this system detects and responds to danger. For convenience, the defence system is often called the fear system. But when this is done, it is with the understanding that fear responses, not fearful experiences, are the topic of investigation. This understandably sometimes leads to confusion outside the field.

3. Defence
The defence system is the most extensively studied emotion system of the brain. While there are a number of different approaches to studying defensive behaviour, much of our current understanding comes from studies of a particular behavioural paradigm called classical fear (or defensive) conditioning. This is a variant on Pavlovian conditioning in which an aversive stimulus, such as an electric shock, occurs in association with an emotionally neutral stimulus, such as pure tone. After only a few pairings (one is enough) a long-lasting memory of the experience is established such that the next time the subject encounters the tone it will express defence responses—freezing behaviour, changes in blood pressure and heart rate, stress hormone release, and so on. The sound serves as a warning signal that danger may be imminent, and bodily resources are mobilized to deal with the impending threat.

The neural system underlying this form of emotional learning is well characterized in studies of rats. It involves the transmission of sensory information to the amygdala, and the control of defence responses by way of output connections of the amygdala (see EMOTION). Within the amygdala two nuclei are especially important—the lateral (input region) and central (output region). Connections between these allow the stimulus to elicit the responses after the sound has been paired with the shock. Neurons in the lateral nucleus receive information about the sound

and the shock and appear to be crucially involved in the learning process. Recent studies on a number of different fronts have begun to pinpoint the exact cellular and molecular changes that underlie the learning, implicating specific neurotransmitters and specific intracellular pathways leading to gene induction and protein synthesis.

One interesting feature of the defence system is that it can be activated by information from either the thalamus or the cortex. Given that the cortex is likely to be involved in the conscious awareness of the stimulus, in the case of thalamic activation, the amygdala can begin to respond before we 'know' what we are responding to. This has implications for understanding psychiatric conditions characterized by uncontrolled and unexplained fear—perhaps the amygdala is being rapidly triggered by stimulus elements that are processed differently at the cortical level.

Recent studies of patients with amygdala lesions, or damage to the temporal lobe that includes the amygdala, have verified that this region is also necessary for defence conditioning in people. Further, functional imaging studies have shown that the amygdala is activated during defence conditioning. Interestingly, one study found evidence for thalamic as opposed to cortical activation of the human amygdala, confirming the rat work.

4. Conscious feelings
There is a growing consensus in cognitive neuroscience that consciousness in humans critically depends on working memory functions distributed across several regions of the prefrontal cortex. This notion is readily extended to account for emotional feelings. When an emotion-unconscious processing system, like the defence system involving the amygdala, is activated, it calls into play a variety of other brain systems, including memory systems that function implicitly (unconsciously) and explicitly (consciously accessible), arousal systems in the brain stem that activate forebrain regions, and bodily responses that feed back to the brain. When the activity of these various systems is represented in working memory, conscious states become conscious emotional states, that is, emotional feelings. Because of the widespread and diverse activation of brain and body systems during emotional states, the experience tends to be more intense and longer lasting. Intensity and duration, in fact, distinguish emotional from non-emotional experiences. An alternative view of conscious emotional feelings is that they are defined by bodily states. This view, which overlaps considerably with William James's theory, mainly differs from the working memory view in emphasis.

5. The future of the brain
While considerable progress has been made in understanding the emotional brain, much work remains. In particular, future work needs to account more thoroughly for the organization of fear in the brain and to explore other

emotions in comparable detail. In addition, the manner in which emotional and non-emotional, especially cognitive, systems, interact needs to be unravelled. This will allow research on the brain to move beyond an emphasis on either cognition or emotion and towards broader questions, especially questions about how the brain creates the self, which is neither cognitive nor emotional, but both, and more.   JEL

Andreson, A. K., and Phelp, E. A. (2000). 'Perceiving emotion: there's more than meets the eye'. *Current Biology*, 10.

Buchel, C., and Dolan, R. J. (2000). 'Classical fear conditioning in functional neuroimaging'. *Current Opinion in Neurobiology*, 10.

Damasio, A. (1994). *Descartes' Error*.

Davidson, R., and Erwin, W. (1999). 'The functional neuroanatomy of emotion and affective style'. *Trends in Cognitive Science*, 3.

LeDoux, J. E. (1996). *The Emotional Brain*.

—— (2002). *Synaptic Self*.

Panksepp, J. (1998). *Affective Neuroscience*.

Rolls, E. (1999). *The Brain and Emotion*.

empathy. The feeling of 'belonging to', associating ourselves with, or 'being carried along' with something. Thus a golfer may feel that he is almost soaring into the air with the ball when he hits a good drive. It has been suggested that when we look at the columns of buildings, such as Greek temples, we identify ourselves with the columns: if they are very thin, we feel uncomfortable as though they, like us, must be inadequate to take the weight they support, and if they are very fat, we feel uncomfortable as some people do when large and clumsy. This application of the notion of empathy is a theory of *aesthetics due to the German philosopher and psychologist Theodore Lipps (1851–1914), professor at Bonn, Breslau, and Munich. 'Empathy' in this sense is a rough translation from the German *Einfuhlung*. The theory has been stated as: 'Aesthetic pleasure is an enjoyment of *our own* activity *in an* object.' This idea was developed by Vernon Lee (pen-name Violet Paget, 1856–1935), who applied it especially to studies of Renaissance architecture.

Carritt, E. F. (1949). *The Theory of Beauty* (5th edn.)

Lee, V. (1913). *The Beautiful*.

Lipps, T. (1907). *Ästhetik*.

encounter group. During the Second World War and immediately after it, there were several initiatives intended to help individuals to become, through participation in groups, more sensitive to their own and other people's attitudes and emotions and more spontaneous in expressing feelings. The focus of 'T-groups' (training groups) was on issues of leadership and authority and the dynamics of change in organizations. 'Sensitivity' groups aimed at producing change by promoting 'interpersonal awareness'. Encounter groups, which became popular in the 1960s and 1970s, first in California and later in Britain, developed from Carl Rogers's 'client-centred' therapy, which emphasizes personal growth and communication. Encounter groups provide the conditions in which participants can be freed from a sense of isolation and alienation through self-discovery in a supportive, permissive, non-authoritarian group setting. The qualities to be induced are openness, authenticity, honesty in the physical, non-verbal expression of feeling, and 'actualization' as a person. Those who advocate them have resisted any attempt at scientific formulation and investigation of the processes involved, and claim that they are 'theory-free'. Nevertheless, several assumptions seem to be made—for example, that the physical expression of feeling in an unstructured setting is cathartic and beneficial. Participants probably do acquire certain social skills, which are transferable outside the groups. Whether the persona revealed in the group, although more congenial to the other participants, is more real or true than the one it replaces is open to question. A few participants are more confused than liberated, and there is a small risk of more serious ill effects, especially if, despite the claim that groups are 'threat free', a participant is confronted aggressively.   DRD

Cheshire, N. M. (1973). 'Review of Carl Rogers's *Encounter Groups*'. *British Journal of Educational Psychology*, 43.

Rogers, C. R. (1971). *Encounter Groups*.

endorphins. One of the major classes of peptides that occur in the brain. They appear to take part in the transmission of chemical messages between nerve cells by acting on receptors which have the characteristic property of binding opiate compounds such as morphine.

It has been known for a very long time that certain plant extracts contain opiates and that these compounds have powerful effects on behaviour, mood, and pain (see OPIUM). Only recently, however, was the question asked whether the presence of opiate receptor sites indicated the existence of naturally occurring opiate-like compounds in the nervous system itself. In 1975 the first successful extraction of such endogenous compounds was achieved. They were called encephalins (literally: in the brain). Originally two distinct forms were found. Both were peptides with five amino acid constituents in the sequence, differing from each other only at one site and named methionine–encephalin and leucine–encephalin.

Following this breakthrough, many more active endogenous compounds were found. They all contain the same opioid core of five amino acids found in encephalin. It is now clear that they can be grouped into three genetically different peptide families with different distributions in the nervous system. The situation appears to be similar to that found for another family of *neurotransmitter substances—the monoamines, where modification in the basic chemical structure is associated with their distribution in several anatomically distinct groups of neurons.

endorphins

1. Three opioid peptide families
2. Functions

1. Three opioid peptide families

It has been known for some time that hormones secreted into the gut are synthesized initially as high-molecular-weight precursors, and that the active hormones are produced by cleavage of a fragment or several fragments from the precursor before they act at receptor sites. This same principle appears to hold true for hormones secreted from the pituitary gland and for the opioids in the brain and pituitary. The three precursors for the opioids are called pro-opiomelanocortin (POMC), proencephalin, and prodynorphin. The POMC molecule, in addition to containing the encephalin sequence, contains another opioid peptide of very high potency, and two other hormone sequences, one for adrenocorticotrophic hormone (which stimulates the adrenal cortex) and one for melanocyte-stimulating hormone (which regulates skin pigmentation). Proencephalin contains several peptides all of which have opioid activity, while prodynorphin is a simpler precursor than the other two and produces three main opioids.

As is the case for many other neurotransmitters, there appear to be several types of receptor for the opioids. This may reflect differing mechanisms for translating opioid effects into different responses or the presence of several types of opioid compound within a given synaptic terminal, or the different anatomical distribution of the three main opioid families (see below), or all these possibilities together. For example, slight variations in the structure of the peptide sequence may result in subtly differing effects at the opiate receptor, particularly when these variations occur in the amino acids adjacent to the central encephalin sequence. It is possible to imagine a wide range of activity at receptors resulting from such modifications, which, when they act at different receptor subtypes, confer an enormous dynamic range of responsiveness. In addition, receptor super- or subsensitivity resulting from long-term functional adaptation may add further to the complexity of effects. The picture becomes even more complicated by the discovery that transmitters may coexist in the same synaptic terminal. It was thought that neurons used only one transmitter to exert their effects at chemical synapses, but this assumption collapsed. Many examples are now described where a low-molecular-weight transmitter such as acetylcholine or noradrenaline (norepinephrine) coexists with a peptide. One example is the co-presence of encephalin and noradrenaline in the adrenal medulla, an endocrine gland. The significance of the phenomenon of coexistence is unknown, but it may be related to the slow time course of action of many neuropeptides. Thus the peptide may modulate the responsiveness of a neuron to its partner transmitter in some way, perhaps to sharpen or broaden the time resolution of the synaptic message. These properties may confer further subtlety on neuronal events, which may allow us to transcend the simple idea that excitation or inhibition in a neural network is the only information subject to coding, translation, and transformation.

Anatomy of the opioid systems. In the brain the main POMC cell group lies in the arcuate nucleus of the hypothalamus and it sends axons to innervate many limbic and brain-stem regions. Another small group of neurons lies in the brain-stem centres that regulate autonomic functions (such as cardiovascular control). In the pituitary gland POMC is synthesized mainly in the intermediate lobe and in a few anterior lobe cells.

The most abundant type are neurons which synthesize proencephalin. They are distributed widely in the brain from the highest cortical to the lowest spinal levels, as both long axon and short axon pathways. In the peripheral neuroendocrine system, proencephalin-derived peptides are also found in the adrenal medulla, the gut, and many other structures.

Prodynorphin is found in the gut, posterior pituitary, and brain, where it is located chiefly in the hypothalamus, basal ganglia, and brain stem.

2. Functions

The distribution of opioids indicates that they participate in many different brain functions and (in a broad sense) probably in every brain function. For technical reasons, however, some areas have received more attention than others. These are mechanisms of *pain sensation, cardiovascular regulation, hypotensive *shock, and endocrine activity. More complex systems controlling feeding, drinking, movement, motivation, reinforcement, memory, mood, and affect are also influenced by opioids but little is known of their effects in these difficult areas.

Pain and stress. The experimental finding that brain stimulation of specific sites produces a reduction in pain responses, which can be reversed by the specific opiate antagonist naloxone, suggests that endogenous opiates are involved in analgesic mechanisms (see ANAESTHESIA). Furthermore, pain relief is accompanied by increased opioid levels in the cerebrospinal fluid which circulates around the brain.

Analgesia may also be produced by repeated stressful stimuli. This is accompanied by a reduction in hypothalamic opioids, perhaps because the material is released by the stimulus. Stress-induced analgesia may also be counteracted by opiate receptor-blocking drugs. The sites of action and neural circuits involved are far from clear, however, and they must involve non-opiate as well as opiate pathways. In addition, stress-induced analgesia may depend partly on opioids released from the pituitary gland or peripheral organs such as the adrenal glands. Thus the adrenal medulla stores and releases both the catecholamines and encephalin together in responses to stress.

An interesting finding has been obtained in relation to the phenomenon of *placebo analgesia. Here subjects may report relief of pain even when given a dummy tablet. Those reporting analgesia following an inactive placebo show raised opioid concentrations in the circulation. No matter where the opioid is generated, the result suggests that physiological processes may be influenced by the belief of the subject that an analgesic substance has been given. The implications of this finding would appear to be quite far reaching.

Circulation and endocrine control. The anatomical distribution of the three opioid families suggests that they all play a role in the central regulation of cardiovascular functions. Thus, all three are present in neurons of the brain-stem cardiovascular regulatory centres. The POMC family is present in the anterior pituitary which influences the adrenal cortex and hence blood pressure, and the prodynorphin group acts on posterior pituitary hormones to control blood volume. Furthermore, the encephalins of the sympathetic nervous system, via their control of the vascular bed, are well placed to regulate regional blood flow and hence blood pressure.

These fundamental discoveries feed through to applications of importance to medical treatment. For example, the state of shock resulting from loss of blood is a dangerous condition which is difficult to treat. Since naloxone, by blocking opiate receptors probably located in the brain, can reverse shock-induced reduction in blood volume, it is possible that more effective management of this condition will soon be available.

See also BRAIN FUNCTION AND AWARENESS; NEURONAL CONNECTIVITY AND BRAIN FUNCTION; PSYCHOPHARMACOLOGY.   OTP

engram. A physical brain change, supposed to take place as a result of experience, and to represent memories. The physical basis of *memory is not, however, known.

entailment. The relation that holds between one or more propositions $P_1 \ldots P_n$ and each proposition C which follows logically from them. Thus $P_1 \ldots P_n$ entail C (frequently symbolized $P_1 \ldots P_n C$) if, and only if, the inference from $P_1 \ldots P_n$ to C is logically valid. The further analysis of this relation has been extensively discussed and disputed both by logicians and by philosophers. It is generally agreed that whenever A entails B it must be impossible for A to be true without B also being true, in which case, according to the definition introduced by C. I. Lewis, A strictly implies B. The further analysis of entailment has thus come to be linked to the account given of the logic of

the modal notions of possibility and necessity which is supplied in works on modal logic. Lewis, who produced the first axiomatized modal logic, proposed that the relation of strict implication should be regarded as the correct formal counterpart of the informal notion of entailment. Others, however, for example Anderson and Belnap, have argued that for A to entail B it is not sufficient merely that it be impossible for A to be true without B being true. On their view there must also be some connection between the meanings of A and B, and the truth of A must be relevant to the truth of B (giving rise to the idea of developing what has been called a relevance logic). This would mean, for example, insisting that although a contradiction strictly implies any proposition whatsoever ('Grass is green and grass is not green' strictly implies 'The earth is flat') it only entails those propositions to which it is relevant ('Grass is green and grass is not green' entails 'Grass is not red').   MET

Anderson, A. R., and Belnap, N. D. Jr. (1975). *Entailment*, vol. i.
Hughes, G. E., and Cresswell, M. J. (1968). *An Introduction to Modal Logic.*
Lewis, C. I. (1922). 'Implication and the algebra of logic'. *Mind* 21.

entelechy. The term *entelecheia* is first used in Greek philosophy to mean the actualization of something as opposed to its mere potentiality. Thus Aristotle in the *De anima* (Concerning the Soul) defines *psyche (soul) as the 'entelechy of an organic body', namely that which makes a body actually alive and functioning. Aristotle did not, however, regard the *psyche* as a separate non-material entity, but merely as the 'form' or organizing principle of the body.

In the philosophy of *Leibniz, 'entelechy' is used to refer to the active principle present in all created substances which makes them complete, self-sufficient, and changing only as a result of internal action. Later the term was used by vitalists (e.g. *Driesch) to refer to the (alleged) active principle responsible for organic life.   JGC

Epicurus (341–270 BC). Greek philosopher, who was born in Samos, and died in Athens. He founded a school in Athens whose members secluded themselves from the city and lived austerely, and included (most surprisingly) slaves and women. The second head of the school was a slave called Mys.

Of Epicurus' enormous literary output (about 300 rolls) most is lost, including his 37 books *On Nature*. Although he lived frugally, his moral precept was: 'We say that pleasure is the beginning and end of living happily.' He argued that the pleasures of the soul—contemplation, and the expectation of bodily pleasures—are more valuable than bodily pleasures alone. The ideal is freedom from distraction, and the study of philosophy is the best way to achieve this ideal. Natural (physical) explanations of mind and soul free us from being distracted by the fear of the supernatural.

Epicurus maintained the notion of unchanging and indestructible atoms, from Leucippus and Democritus. He was unusual in holding an atomistic philosophy, which was revived only in the early 19th century, by John *Dalton, though in a rather different form. Most Greek philosophers thought that it could be made to explain anything, and therefore explained nothing. Epicurus also denied the power of gods, holding that natural motions explain all phenomena. He held a view of evolution that anticipates in some respects Charles *Darwin's theory of natural selection by survival of the fittest.

Panichas, G. A. (1983). *Epicurus*.

epilepsy. A person is said to suffer from epilepsy if he is prone to recurrent epileptic seizures. The epileptic seizure is a transient episode of altered consciousness and/or perception, and/or loss of control of the muscles, which arises because of abnormal electrical discharges generated by groups of brain cells. Many varieties of seizure are recognized. Most last for no more than a few minutes, but occasionally they are prolonged beyond 30 minutes or else recur so rapidly that full recovery is not achieved between successive attacks—these conditions are labelled status epilepticus.

It has been estimated that 6–7 per cent of the population suffer at least one epileptic seizure at some time in their lives and that 4 per cent have a phase when they are prone to recurrent seizures (i.e. can be said to suffer from epilepsy). Between 0.05 and 0.1 per cent of the population suffer from 'active epilepsy'—that is, they have had a recurrent seizure within the previous five years or are taking regular medication to prevent the occurrence of seizures. Seizures are particularly liable to occur in early childhood, during adolescence, and in old age.

The history of epilepsy is probably as long as that of the human race. The definition of the condition as a clinical entity is generally attributed to *Hippocrates. He recognized that it arises from physical disease of the brain. He also took the first step towards unravelling the intricacies of cerebral *localization of function with his realization that damage on one side of the brain can cause convulsions which commence on the opposite side of the body. Further significant advances in this direction, based on observations of seizures, were delayed more than 2,000 years until the 19th century, and in particular until the observations and deductions of Hughlings *Jackson.

William Gowers, writing towards the end of the 19th century in the same era as Hughlings Jackson, proposed a dichotomy with his suggestion that some people have epileptic seizures because of overt cerebral pathology whereas others have them because of some factor in their brain's innate constitution unaccompanied by any detectable abnormality of structure. To some extent this is reflected in the current classification which divides epileptic seizures into the two main categories: 'primary generalized' and 'focal' (or 'partial' in the current terminology). However, further advance lay beyond simple clinical observation and was delayed until the technique for recording the electrical activity of the human brain (the electroencephalogram, EEG—see ELECTROENCEPHALOGRAPHY) was developed, first in the 1920s by the German psychiatrist Hans *Berger and then in the 1930s by the Cambridge physiologists E. D. *Adrian and B. H. C. Matthews. The technique was rapidly applied to the analysis of epilepsy, especially by E. L. and F. A. Gibbs, W. G. Lennox, H. Jasper, and H. Gastaut. Their findings, and the findings of those who followed them, have supported the view that seizures can be broadly divided into the two main categories mentioned above. Primary generalized seizures are those in which the symptoms of the seizure, and the EEG if it is being recorded at the onset, indicate that the whole of the brain becomes electrically abnormal synchronously at the moment when the seizure commences. In contrast, focal (partial) seizures are those in which the symptoms, and the EEG if it is being recorded at the onset, suggest that the electrical abnormality commences in a restricted area, usually a part of the cerebral cortex, even though the electrical abnormality may then spread more or less widely.

The commonest forms of primary generalized seizure are the tonic–clonic convulsion without aura (the *grand-mal* convulsion), the *petit-mal* absence, and the myoclonic jerk. The convulsion commences with the tonic phase in which the muscles stiffen symmetrically on both sides of the body and this is followed by the clonic phase of muscle jerking. Consciousness is lost from the outset and the person falls to the ground if he was standing. There may be an epileptic cry at the outset, a blue coloration may develop around the lips (cyanosis) and the facial skin, especially in the tonic phase when breathing is interrupted, the bladder and/or the bowels may be emptied, and the tongue may be bitten. When consciousness is regained the person may be confused and may act in an automatic fashion; a period of sleep may follow. The *petit-mal* absence lasts only a few seconds. There is loss of awareness but the person does not fall to the ground; he stares blankly and any movement is confined to flickering of the eyelids and/or very slight twitching of the facial and/or arm muscles. There are several varieties of absence seizure, but the true *petit-mal* absence is characterized by an EEG pattern consisting of spike-wave activity occurring at the rate of 3 cycles per second. The myoclonic jerk consists of a very rapid symmetrical upward jerk of the arms accompanied by a nod of the head and a forward bend of the trunk.

The true *petit-mal* seizure occurs very predominantly in childhood and adolescence. It is almost invariably a manifestation of constitutional epilepsy rather than due to cerebral pathology, and it is strongly associated with a hereditary factor. Children who are prone to *petit-mal* seizures may also have myoclonic jerks and tonic–clonic convulsions. *Petit-mal* absence seizures and myoclonic jerks tend to become much less frequent after adolescence but convulsions may continue. Primary generalized convulsions and myoclonic jerks are most often seen in childhood and adolescence when the epilepsy is usually due to a constitutional predisposition—idiopathic epilepsy—but they can be due to diffuse cerebral pathology.

Focal (partial) seizures commence with electrical discharges in a restricted area of the brain. The initial symptom of the attack depends upon the location of the focal discharges. Thus, when the focus is in the motor cortex the seizure usually begins with jerking in a restricted group of muscles on the opposite side of the body, especially those of the face, hand, or foot, since these are represented by the largest areas within the motor cortex. As the electrical discharges spread to other parts of the motor cortex, so more and more muscles on the opposite side of the body are incorporated into the convulsion. This spread in a pattern corresponding to the homunculus mapped on the motor cortex is known as the Jacksonian seizure and indeed enabled Jackson to predict such a map. When the electrical discharges extend beyond the motor cortex, and especially when they pass through the *corpus callosum to the opposite cerebral hemisphere, conciousness is lost and the convulsion may become generalized involving both sides of the body.

A particularly common variety of focal seizure originates from discharges in the structures of one or other temporal lobe—temporal lobe epilepsy. The demonstration, particularly by the Montreal school under the leadership of Wilder *Penfield, that some cases of temporal lobe epilepsy can be cured by surgery has been an enormous stimulus to detailed study of many of its facets. The seizures often commence with a visceral sensation or an alteration of thought processes and perception which can be remembered afterwards. This is the aura. Those who experience an aura often find the content very difficult to describe, partly because their awareness and memory systems are distorted by the seizure and partly because the appropriate words to convey the quality of these abnormal sensations do not exist. Common visceral sensations include a feeling of nausea in the stomach or chest which may rise to the throat or head, nausea felt elsewhere in the body, hallucinations of smell or taste, giddiness, and palpitations. The alterations of thought process and perception often have an emotional content and frequently involve a distortion of memory. Brief feelings of extreme fear, anxiety, or depression are common. Feelings of elation are much less so. The aura may contain a feeling of familiarity as if everything has happened before (*déjà vu*),

there may be a feeling of intense unreality, sensations of perceptual illusion such as macropsia or micropsia may occur, and occasionally a complex visual or auditory hallucination is experienced. The aura may be followed by an automatism (referred to as a complex partial seizure in the current terminology). That is a period of altered behaviour for which the person is subsequently amnesic and during which he appears to have only limited awareness of his environment, if any at all. The behaviour in an automatism is usually primitive and stereotyped consisting of, for instance, lip smacking, chewing, grimacing, and gesturing, but sometimes much more complex behavioural acts are performed. Very occasionally an automatism continues for a prolonged period—a state known as an epileptic fugue (see DISSOCIATION OF THE PERSONALITY).

Whereas primary generalized seizures are characteristic of epilepsy due to a constitutional predisposition (idiopathic epilepsy) focal seizures are attributed to a focus of pathology. It is usually impossible to define the precise nature of this pathology, but occasionally it is a tumour or an area of brain damage due to head injury. Some cases of the most severe temporal lobe epilepsy are due to loss of neurons in the hippocampus (a structure situated in the medial part of the temporal lobe) caused by a prolonged convulsion occurring in early childhood, and when this abnormality is restricted to one side of the brain there is a good chance that surgery will effect a cure. Regular medication can suppress the seizures of many people prone to epilepsy but unfortunately by no means all.

Lastly, mention must be made of the concept of an epileptic personality. It has been claimed that a particular personality type is associated with epilepsy. The matter is complicated because epilepsy is associated with many factors which themselves may affect not only personality but many other aspects of mental function. These include cerebral pathology, anti-epileptic medication, the depression to which many people with epilepsy are prone, and the restrictions which society imposes on them. It is difficult to find any evidence that a particular personality is associated with epilepsy *per se* after due allowance has been made for these factors.   JMO

Hippocrates. 'The sacred disease'. In *Hippocrates. Medical Works*, vol. ii (Loeb Classical Library, no. 148).

Hopkins, A. (1981). *Epilepsy: The Facts.*

Kaneko, S., Okada, M., Iwasa, H., Yamakawa, K., and Hirose, S. (2002). 'Genetics of epilepsy: current status and perspectives'. *Neuroscience Research*, 44/1.

Kuzniecky, R. I., and Knowlton, R. C. (2002). 'Neuroimaging of epilepsy'. *Seminars in Neurology*, 22/3.

Penfield, W., and Jasper, H. (1954). *Epilepsy and the Functional Anatomy of the Human Brain.*

Schmidt, D. (2002). 'The clinical impact of new antiepileptic drugs after a decade of use in epilepsy'. *Epilepsy Research*, 50/1–2.

Villalobos, R. (2002). 'Advances in the diagnosis of epilepsy'. *Revista de neurologia*, 34/2.

epiphenomena. Phenomena that occur in association with, or are supervenient upon, a given set of events, yet supposedly are not caused by those events. The term is applied particularly to the mind–brain problem. An epiphenomenal account of mind is that mental events, and especially *consciousness, occur during physical brain activity but are not caused by physical activity. They are supposed, rather, to run in parallel but to be autonomous. This, of course, leaves the mind totally inexplicable and mysterious from the point of view of physiology and everything we know of the physical world.

René *Descartes narrowly avoided epiphenomenalism, holding that the bodies and brains of organisms are 'mere' machines and supposing that mind is causally linked to the brain at the pineal gland. Mind and brain were, for Descartes, largely independent, and this is also so for many more modern psychologists, philosophers, and neurophysiologists—such as William *James and Sir John Eccles (Popper and Eccles 1977)—who hold forms of interactive parallelism. These are almost statements of epiphenomenalism, except for limited causal interaction between mind and brain. It is indeed often thought that mind (especially awareness of pain, colours, emotions, etc.) is more affected by physical brain states than it, considered as a largely separate entity, itself affects the brain. The common-sense view is that most behaviour is automatic (in physiological terms, controlled largely by *reflexes) without corresponding mental events, and that only when there is deliberate or conscious volition does mind affect behaviour.

Milner, A. D., and Goodale, M. A. (1995). *The Visual Brain in Action*. Popper, K., and Eccles, J. (1977). *The Self and its Brain*.

epistemology. The branch of philosophy concerned with the theory of *knowledge. One of the oldest of philosophical debates concerns the origin of human knowledge. Empiricists traditionally maintain that all knowledge is ultimately derived from sensory experience. According to John *Locke the mind at birth is a blank sheet, or *tabula rasa*: 'how then comes it to be furnished with that vast store which the busy and boundless fancy of man has painted on it? To this I answer in one word, from *experience*' (*Essay Concerning Human Understanding*, 1690). Rationalist philosophers such as René *Descartes, by contrast, insist on the doctrine of innate ideas—that the mind is furnished from birth with certain fundamental concepts which enable it to arrive at knowledge a priori, independently of the senses (see INNATE IDEAS). The question of whether human knowledge can transcend the senses, and of whether, and in what sense, a priori knowledge is possible, is one of the major themes

of the philosophy of Immanuel Kant (see KANT'S PHILOSOPHY OF MIND).

A central epistemological issue that goes right back to *Plato is the question of what is the difference between knowledge and mere belief. In what sense does the person who has knowledge differ from one who has a belief that may happen to be true? Much recent work in epistemology has been concerned with answering this question by analysing the concept of knowledge, and attempting to formulate a precise set of necessary and sufficient conditions for the truth of statements such as S knows that P. (See ESSENCE; KNOWLEDGE.)   JGC

ergonomics. The study of efficiency of persons in their working environment, sometimes called 'human engineering'. It received its first impetus during the First World War, when the problem was to increase the productivity of semi-skilled munitions workers. This led to work by the British Medical Research Council's Industrial Health Research Board in the 1920s and 1930s on the effect of fatigue and boredom in repetitive tasks, and on the effect of the environment at work: lighting, heat and humidity, and noise. The main thrust came during the Second World War, when men in the fighting services had to handle equipment which was a lot more complex than they were used to. The obvious alternative to long and difficult training was to make the work easier.

1. Design of displays
2. Design of controls
3. Control–display compatibility
4. Layout of equipment
5. The environment at work
6. Interface between user and computer

1. Design of displays

Late in 1945, as soon as the war was over, Paul Fitts of the US Aero Medical Laboratory at Dayton, Ohio, started a comprehensive investigation of the problems facing people using the new complex equipment. He and his colleagues asked wartime pilots to describe actual experiences in which errors were made in reading and interpreting aircraft instruments. Of the 270 critical incidents reported, 40 involved a misreading of a three-handed altimeter by 1,000 feet (300 metres) or more.

An altimeter tells the pilot how high he is flying. Its three hands are covered with luminous paint. One hand is for the 10,000s, one for the 1,000s, and the third for the 100s. A bedside clock has only two luminous hands; even so, when waking up at night it is possible to confuse the minute hand and the hour hand, when the minute hand is pointing to a likely hour like 2 or 4 a.m. With three hands to confuse, the altimeter provides still greater opportunities for error. On a clear day, an error in reading the height will be realized because the pilot can see the ground below; but on a dark night, and when flying in or above cloud, the pilot has no external means of telling that he has misread his height. An investigation in the laboratory compared reading the three-handed altimeter with reading the same heights from a digital counter, like the counter showing mileage in a car. The three-handed altimeter took longer to read, an average of seven seconds, compared with about one second for the counter. It caused more errors of 1,000 feet or more, which could be fatal in an aircraft—10 per cent compared with less than 1 per cent for the counter. Three-handed altimeters were used by the commercial airlines for another twenty years and continued to result in accidents. But they are not used now.

2. Design of controls

Fitts and his colleagues also asked the wartime pilots about errors in operating the controls of aircraft. Practically all the pilots of the US Army Air Force who were questioned reported that they sometimes made errors. Of the 460 errors reported, 89 involved confusing the three engine controls which alter the throttle, the propeller speed, and the fuel mixture. This was because the three controls were located in three different orders in three of the standard aircraft in use at the time. A pilot who was used to flying one type of aircraft was particularly likely to make an error when he changed to flying one of the other two types. As Fitts remarked: 'Imagine the difficulty most car drivers would experience in learning to brake with the left foot and to use the clutch pedal with the right.' In aircraft the error can be serious if just after take-off the pilot inadvertently reduces the throttle or mixture, when he intends to reduce the propeller speed. Yet pilots are trained not to look at the controls they are operating: they have to look at their instruments, and at the world outside the aircraft. They should not need to look to see if they are operating the correct control.

These and other reports of confusion between the controls of aircraft also led to laboratory investigations. One question investigated was the distance between controls needed to prevent a person from operating the wrong control. Another was the shape of control knobs needed, so that each could easily be identified and distinguished by touch. Following this work, the controls in aircraft are now separated and shaped to avoid confusion, and they are located in approximately the same position in each new type of aircraft. (See also TRANSFER.)

3. Control–display compatibility

Of the 460 pilot errors reported in operating controls, 27 involved moving the control in the direction opposite to that required to produce the desired result. Some of these moves would have been in the correct direction if the pilot had been in his accustomed type of aircraft, and they are avoided by standardizing controls between aircraft. But other errors involved moving the control in the

'natural' or 'expected' direction, which happened to be wrong.

This finding led Fitts to his principle of 'control–display compatibility'. The most compatible control is the display marker itself. In setting the minute hand of a clock, the minute hand is clasped directly with the fingers and rotated to the desired time. The nearer the control–display relationship can approximate to this, the easier it will be for the person operating the control. If the clock hand is controlled by a knob or key, the control should rotate in the same direction as the clock hand, not in the reverse direction. Where a number of instrument displays and their controls are located on a single panel, each control should be next to its display. The controls should not be mounted on a separate panel far away from their displays, or the person may operate the wrong control in error.

4. Layout of equipment

The investigations of displays and controls led naturally to investigations of the optimal layout for a set of displays and their related controls. People have to be able to see the displays and to reach the controls. Yet people come in different sizes: from anthropometry, the systematic measurement of body heights and lengths of limb segments, it became clear that seats must be adjustable, both in height and in the distance from the working surfaces. With adjustable seats, most displays and controls are now located in positions suited to the people who use them. The strength of the limbs operating controls in various positions has also been measured, to ensure that a control in a particular position is not too stiff to operate.

The layout of individual workplaces is now often part of the overall layout of a control room or factory department. Since equipment has to be maintained as well as operated, it is necessary to leave space behind the consoles for the maintenance engineers. The time spent maintaining equipment may be small compared with that during which it is operated but, when equipment breaks down, it is inconvenient, expensive, or in the case of military equipment unacceptable if repairs cannot be carried out quickly. Thus maintenance needs to be considered in design, as well as the needs of operatives.

In planning a factory department, the ergonomist now usually considers the organization of the work to be done. Some functions can be performed automatically, while others require people. The layout of the machines and work stations is made to follow the sequence of operations to be carried out.

5. The environment at work

Equipment sometimes needs to be designed especially for the environment in which it is to be used. Driving farm tractors and harvesters over rough fields subjects both the driver and the equipment to vertical vibration and jolting. The vibration blurs the numbers on the instrument scales, and so they have to be larger than usual if they are to be read easily. The jolting may make the driver move a control accidentally: the chances of this happening may be reduced if the controls move horizontally—that is, at right angles to the vertical jolting.

It is particularly important for the equipment which a person is using in a noisy environment to be designed ergonomically. In quiet surroundings a person can usually hear when he is operating equipment correctly: switches may produce audible clicks when they are pressed, and the tap of a hammer has a higher pitch when it hits a nail or rivet than when it misses and hits wood or canvas. In noisy surroundings such cues may not be audible, or may be difficult to distinguish one from another. If in operating equipment a person has to use his eyes, or sense of touch, instead of his ears, and if these senses are already heavily engaged, he may fail to notice mistakes.

The medical problems of the environment at work are now giving ergonomics a new impetus. Loud noise causes industrial deafness, as well as masking sounds, and calls for noise control and hearing protection. Vehicles and aircraft crashing at speed cause injuries that call for better designs of safety harness and seat belts. Work under water, say on oil and gas installations, is carried out at pressures several times greater than atmospheric pressure, and requires foolproof equipment (see also DIVER PERFORMANCE). Industrial processes produce dusts, vapours, and gases which may cause cancer or other illnesses. Ionizing radiation, and electromagnetic radiation of short wavelength, like gamma rays, X-rays, ultraviolet light, and the microwaves used in cooking, can also damage the human organism. Dosimeters have to be designed and worn. The more generally harmful effects of atmospheric pollution need to be reduced by changes in industrial activity. Ergonomists today require knowledge of chemistry and physics in addition to their traditional knowledge of displays and controls.

6. Interface between user and computer

Research has now expanded to study the interface between people and computers. At first a computer system was considered acceptable as long as it worked. To use the system, the operator had to learn to think like the computer engineers who designed the system. The few full-time computer operators learnt to do this, but it was too difficult for many of the non-specialists who wanted to use a computer to help them with their job. Research is now directed towards designing 'user-friendly' interfaces, which are easy for the part-time and casual user to learn and use (Card, Moran, and Newell 1983).   ECP

Card, S. K., Moran, T. P., and Newell, A. (1983). *The Psychology of Human–Computer Interaction.*

Fitts, P. M., and Jones, R. E. (1947). '(i) Analysis of factors contributing to 460 "pilot-error" experiences in operating aircraft controls; (ii) Psychological aspects of instrument display: analysis of 270 "pilot-error" experiences in reading and interpreting aircraft instruments'. Reprinted in Sinaiko, H. W. (ed.), *Selected Papers on Human Factors in the Design and Use of Control Systems* (1961).

Parker, J. F., Jr., and West, V. R. (eds.) (1973). *Bioastronautics Data Book* (2nd edn.).

Poulton, E. C. (1979). *The Environment at Work.*

Van Cott, H. P., and Kinkade, R. G. (eds.) (1972). *Human Engineering Guide to Equipment Design* (rev. edn.).

erotic. Evocative of sexual passion, from the name of the god of love in Greek mythology. Eros is not personified in Homer, although the word is used to describe the sexual desire that drives Paris to Helen, and Zeus to Hera. Hesiod describes Eros as the god who 'loosens the limbs and damages the mind', and makes him (together with Earth and Tartarus) the oldest of the gods and all powerful.

The Greek philosopher Parmenides makes Eros (the power of love) that which joins contrasting things together. In fact, it is no exaggeration to say that love for the Greeks was a binding force in their physics. Magnets (lodestones) were described as male and female; according to Pliny (*Natural History*, 36. 126–30) strong magnets are male and weak magnets female. *Plato discourses upon Eros in the *Symposium* and *Phaedrus*. See also APHRODISIACS.

essence. The essence of something is what it is to be that thing as opposed to something else. Thus the essence of a triangle is three-sidedness. In *Aristotelian philosophy, a thing's essence is given by specifying its defining characteristics—its 'essential' as opposed to 'accidental' features. Thus, being a malleable metal would be an essential characteristic of gold, but being mined in South Africa would be an accidental characteristic (since if gold ceased to be mined in South Africa it would still be gold).

There is a celebrated philosophical debate about whether statements about essence reflect the real nature of things or merely human linguistic conventions. The former view is known as 'essentialism' or 'realism', the latter as 'nominalism'. Recently the American philosopher Saul Kripke has revived a version of essentialism according to which natural kinds (gold, water) possess real essences: that is, certain characteristics are necessarily true of these substances, and this is not a matter of linguistic convention but is a matter of the real structure that these substances necessarily possess.

Questions about essence ('what is X?', 'what is it to be X?') have traditionally been distinguished from questions about existence ('does X exist?'), and questions of the former sort have been supposed to be prior to the latter (thus we can raise questions about the essential characteristics of triangles without having to concern ourselves about whether triangles really exist). Existentialists such as

*Sartre, however, maintain that, in the case of human beings, 'existence precedes essence'. On this view, the first truth of which a human is aware is simply that he exists; his freedom to choose how to live is not constrained by any predetermined 'nature' or essence.   JGC

Kripke, S. (1980). *Naming and Necessity.*

ethology. Modern ethology abuts on so many different disciplines that it defies simple definition in terms of a common problem or a shared literature. The subject started out as the biological study of behaviour. However, as Robert Hinde (1982) noted, those who *call* themselves ethologists are now to be found working with neurobiologists, social and developmental psychologists, anthropologists, and psychiatrists, among many others. Even classical ethology gave itself a wide remit. Niko Tinbergen (1963) pointed to four broad but separate problems raised by the biological study of behaviour, namely: evolutionary history, individual development, short-term control, and current function. Moreover, it was plain that he and the other grandmasters of the subject, such as Konrad Lorenz, were not only aware of these different problems, but were actively interested in all of them.

Inasmuch as ethology still has a distinctive flavour, much of it derives from this breadth of interest. For that reason it is worthwhile taking a closer look at the four central problems identified by Tinbergen. (i) *Evolution*. What is the ancestral history? What can be deduced about the ways in which the behaviour evolved and the pressures that gave rise to it? (ii) *Development*. How is the behaviour assembled? What internal and external factors influence the way it develops in the lifetime of the individual, and how does the developmental process work? (iii) *Control*. How is the behaviour controlled? What internal and external factors regulate its occurrence, and how does the control process work? (iv) *Function*. What is the current use of the behaviour? In what way does the behaviour help to keep the animal alive or propagate its genes into the next generation?

Many ethologists had strong childhood interests in natural history and subsequently received a training in zoology. This aspect of their personal histories explains their interests in the evolution and survival value of behaviour. Impregnated as their thinking has been with the Darwinian theory of evolution, they repeatedly speculate on the adaptive significance of the differences between species. Indeed, many ethologists are primarily interested in biological function. Others are wary of proceeding far in laboratory studies without first relating their findings to the context in which the behaviour naturally occurs. The functional approach has certainly helped those who are interested in the study of mechanism.

Understanding what behaviour patterns are for provides the scientist with an important way of distinguishing between different types of behaviour. Equally valuable, the background knowledge obtained in functional studies has been fruitful in guiding investigators to the principal variables controlling a behaviour pattern. Being able to distinguish the important causal factors is extremely useful when designing experiments—in which, inevitably, only a small number of independent variables are actually manipulated while the others are held constant or are randomized. While looking at animals in an unrestricted environment, the observer becomes aware of the context in which each pattern of behaviour occurs. This suggests some of the conditions necessary for its occurrence and the events that bring it to an end.

The preoccupation of many ethologists with function has led to excellent studies of animals in natural conditions. The justification for fieldwork is that an animal's behaviour is usually adapted to the environment in which it normally lives, in the same way that its anatomical or physiological characteristics are adapted. A captive animal is usually too constrained by its artificial environment to provide a complete understanding of the functions of the great variety of activities which most animals are capable of performing. To observe the full richness of its repertoire and understand the conditions to which its behaviour is adapted, the animal must usually be studied in the field. The patient observer notices the circumstances in which an activity is performed and those in which it never occurs, thereby obtaining clues as to what the behaviour pattern might be for (that is, its function). Field studies also relate behaviour patterns to the social and ecological conditions in which they normally occur. This led to the development of an area of research known as behavioural ecology. Another subdiscipline, sociobiology, brought to the study of behaviour important concepts and methods from population biology and stimulated further interest in field studies of animal behaviour. As commonly happens, the announcements that a new discipline had been founded were accompanied by strenuous efforts to distance the newcomer from its roots (see Wilson 1975). However, the eclectic wisdom of the classical ethologists seems to have prevailed, and the various subdisciplines are showing signs of merging into a unified approach to the study of the biology of behaviour.

Studies in unconstrained conditions of animals, and increasingly of humans, have been an important feature of ethology and have played a major role in developing the distinctive and powerful methods for observing and measuring behaviour. Even so, it would be a mistake to represent ethologists as non-experimental and merely concerned with description. The point of doing an experiment is to distinguish between alternative explanations of hypotheses. Field observation can also achieve this goal if, for example, naturally occurring events demonstrate associations between variables that previously seemed unrelated, or break associations between variables that previously seemed bound together. Moreover, many simple, well-designed experiments have been performed outside the laboratory.

For example, Tinbergen wanted to explain why the ground-nesting black-headed gull removes the eggshell from its nest site after a chick has hatched. A number of different functional explanations initially seemed possible —the chick might injure itself on the sharp edges of the shell; the shell might be a source of disease by harbouring micro-organisms; the chick might get trapped under a shell and suffocate; the white inner surfaces of the shell fragments might attract predators visually; or the smell might attract predators by olfactory means. Tinbergen and colleagues were able to exclude a number of these candidates at the outset, using comparative evidence. Another gull, the kittiwake, nests on cliffs where it is not vulnerable to predators and does not remove the eggshell from its nest. This suggested that the first three possibilities were unlikely to be of major importance. A simple test, which involved placing shells at different distances from the nest, was then used to show that the broken eggshell does indeed attract predators to the black-headed gull's nest. The egg is cryptically coloured on the outside, but the inside is white and therefore easy for an airborne predator, such as a crow, to spot. The study confirmed that nests with open shells lying near them were more likely to be raided.

Field experiments have also been used to understand how an animal's behaviour is controlled. For example, tape recordings of predators or conspecifics (such as offspring or potential mates) have been played to free-living animals in order to discover how they respond (see DANGER RECOGNITION). Dummies of different designs have similarly been used to gauge responsiveness to a particular shape or colour, such as the pecking of gull chicks at different objects more or less resembling the bills of their parents. These and many other examples make the point that even core ethology involves a great deal more than passive observation. Moreover, many people who call themselves ethologists have devoted much of their professional lives to laboratory studies of the control and development of behaviour.

At a certain stage in the history of ethology, certain key concepts and theories were associated with it. They no longer form a central part of ethological thought, although they were important in its development. Two basic concepts were the 'sign stimulus' and the 'fixed action pattern'. The notion of the sign stimulus, such as the red breast of a robin releasing an attack from an opponent, was productive in leading to the analysis of stimulus characters that selectively elicit particular bits of behaviour. Fixed action patterns (or modal action patterns as they are sometimes more appropriately called) provided useful units for description and comparison between species. Behavioural characters were used in taxonomy, and the zoological concern with evolution led to attempts to formulate principles for the derivation and ritualization of signal movements.

Both the concept of sign stimulus, or releaser, and that of the fixed action pattern played important roles in the early ethological attempts to develop systems models of behaviour. Lorenz's lavatory cistern model was a flow diagram in more than one sense and provided a generation of ethologists with a way of integrating their thinking about the multiple causation of behaviour, from both within and without. Needless to say, the model was seriously misleading; and in some systems of behaviour, notably *aggression, performance of behaviour makes repetition *more* likely, not less as the model predicts. Another systems model has stood the test of time rather better. It was developed by Tinbergen and was concerned with the hierarchical organization of behaviour. Here again, though, its major role lay not so much in its predictive power but in helping ethologists to bring together evidence that would otherwise have seemed unrelated.

Another classic ethological concern was with the inborn character of much behaviour (see INSTINCT). Indeed, Lorenz saw adult behaviour as involving the intercalation of separate and recognizable 'learned' and 'instinctive' elements. Very few people share this view any longer, and the work by the developmentally minded ethologists on such phenomena as song learning and imprinting in birds has been important in illustrating how the processes of development involve an interplay between internal and external factors (see IMPRINTING). After the early abortive attempts to classify behaviour in terms of instincts, attention has increasingly focused on faculties or properties of behaviour that bridge the conventional functional categories, such as feeding, courtship, caring for young, and so forth. Consequently, more and more emphasis is being placed on shared mechanisms of perception, storage of information, and control of output. As this happens the interests of many ethologists are coinciding to a greater and greater extent with the traditional concerns of psychology.

The modern work has also eroded another belief of the classical ethologists: that all members of the same species of the same age and sex will behave in the same way. The days are over when a fieldworker could confidently suppose that a good description of a species obtained from one habitat could be generalized to the same species in another set of environmental conditions. The variations in behaviour within a species may, of course, reflect the pervasiveness of learning processes (see CONDITIONING). However, as in a jukebox, some alternative modes of behaviour may be *selected* rather than informed by prevailing environmental conditions. For instance, many adult male gelada baboons are very much bigger than the females and, once they have taken over a group of females, defend them from the attentions of other males. Other males, who are the same size as a female, sneak copulations when a big male is not looking. The offsetting benefit for the small males is that they have much longer reproductive lives than the big ones. It seems likely that any young male can grow either way, and the particular way in which it develops depends on conditions. Examples such as this are leading to a growing interest in alternative tactics, their functional significance, and the nature of the developmental principles involved.

In describing and analysing behaviour, it makes good sense to start by obeying the canon of Conwy Lloyd *Morgan and treat animals in the simplest possible way until there is good reason to think otherwise. Nevertheless, as in other fields, many ethologists have come to feel that slavish obedience to a methodological maxim tends to sterilize imagination. A person who studies behaviour and *never* treats the animal as though it were human is liable to miss some of the richness and complexity of what it does. Many experienced ethologists have found how much they are helped if they put themselves in the animal's place and consider how they would deal with the situation. They notice important influences on the animal's behaviour which they would otherwise have overlooked, and are led to perform experiments which they would not otherwise have done. For these reasons, terms such as 'intention', 'awareness', and 'reasoning' are being used with increasing frequency in studies of animal behaviour, despite the well-known pitfalls of anthropomorphism and teleological argument. It seems likely that cognitive ethology will expand and, as it does so, start contributing to the study of mind.   PPGB

Hinde, R. A. (1982). *Ethology*.
Tinbergen, N. (1963). 'On aims and methods of ethology'. *Zeitschrift für Tierpsychologie*, 20.
Wilson, E. O. (1975). *Sociobiology*.

Euclid (*c*.300 BC). Famous for his work on geometry, known as Euclid's *Elements* (modern English translation by T. L. Heath, 1956), Euclid was a Greek whose birthplace is not known. (In the Middle Ages he was known as Euclid of Megara, but this was the result of a confusion between him and a philosopher who lived around 400 BC.) It is thought probable that he received his mathematical training in Athens from pupils of *Plato. What is known is that he taught in Alexandria and founded a school there. From the writings of Greek commentators we learn that he wrote about a dozen works other than the *Elements*. Only a few of these, among them the *Data*, the *Division of Figures*, the *Phaenomena*, and the *Optics*, have survived.

Aristotle described as elements of *geometry those propositions whose proofs are contained in proofs of most other geometrical propositions. In a similar vein Proclus (*c.* AD 412–85) likened the relation the elements of geometry bear to the rest of geometry to the relation the letters of an alphabet bear to a language. Euclid's was not the first exposition of the elements of geometry; we know of at least three earlier versions, including one by Hippocrates of Chios. But Euclid's seems to have so outclassed these that it alone has survived. His achievement was to have imposed a thorough systematic organization on geometry, one in which, starting from *axioms, definitions, and postulates, each proposition is proved either directly from these or from these together with propositions already proved. It thus provides an early example of a deductively organized body of knowledge, and it has functioned as a paradigm for all other sciences for at least 2,000 years.

The *Elements* is divided into thirteen books of which the first four concern basic plane geometry. Books V and VI develop a theory of proportions, generally credited to Eudoxus of Cnidos (*c*.390–340 BC), which overcomes the problem of incommensurable magnitudes, which are explicitly tackled in Book X. Books VII–IX deal with numbers and ratios between numbers, and Books XI–XIII are chiefly devoted to solid geometry.   MET

Artmann, B. (1999). *Euclid: The Creation of Mathematics*.

evoked potentials. The study of evoked brain potentials arose as an extension of the interest in the spontaneous electrical activity of the brain, recorded in *electroencephalography. It was recognized even by Richard Caton, who first recorded the electrical activity of the brains of animals in 1875, that the voltages recorded from the brain's surface could be influenced by external events impinging on the senses.

Hans *Berger, who discovered the resting alpha rhythm of the electroencephalogram (*electroencephalography) in man some 50 years later, noted the disappearance of this oscillation, which had a characteristic frequency between 8 and 12 hertz, when the subject was stimulated by stroking the back of the hand (Fig. 1) or alerted by an auditory stimulus. He noted that the alpha rhythm could also be blocked by voluntary movement or mental arithmetic. This alpha-blocking reaction could be said to be the first of the evoked responses of the human brain to become the subject of scientific study.

Lord *Adrian in Cambridge demonstrated that the alpha rhythm arose particularly from the occipital areas of the brain and that its appearance was associated especially with visual inattention. Visual stimuli were much more effective in blocking the alpha rhythm than those of other modalities (Fig. 2). He also showed that a train of evoked potentials could be recorded from electrodes situated over the occipital lobe in response to a series of bright flash stimuli presented to the eyes. These photically evoked potentials were the first of the 'specific' sensory evoked potentials to be recorded in man.

The two decades following Berger's discovery of the alpha rhythm were marked by an increasing pace of advance in knowledge of the electrical activity of the brain. The potentials evoked by sensory stimulation in the specific visual, auditory, and somatosensory receiving areas in the cortex were studied in the exposed brains of animals, and became accessible to study in man when methods of separating out the small potentials from the larger oscillations of the spontaneous background EEG were developed in the 1940s by George D. Dawson. Recorded from electrodes on the intact scalp, he was able to show that consistent responses of around 10 μV in amplitude could be recorded following electrical stimulation of peripheral nerve trunks through the skin in the conscious, intact human subject. The technique used depended on giving a large number of similar stimuli and adding the responses together, either by photographic superimposition or (in a later development) with an electronic averager. In this way, the consistent features of the response are reinforced, while the random variation in the background (noise) is minimized.

Small laboratory averagers became commercially available in the 1960s, enabling many centres to begin work on the clinical and scientific applications of evoked potential recording. As well as much further work with the types of stimulation used in the earlier studies, such as electrical stimulation of the limb nerves and stroboscopic flash stimuli, the responses to more 'natural' forms of stimulation were investigated, including tactile stimulation of the fingers and the visual responses evoked by sudden reversal of a black-and-white chequerboard pattern, which the subject viewed on an illuminated screen. The latter type of stimulus proved particularly successful in clinical work, as it transpired that marked abnormalities of the response were found in association with demyelinating lesions of the visual pathways in multiple sclerosis and in other disorders of vision associated with ocular or neurological disorders.

At about the same time, the scope of evoked potential research was greatly widened by an awakening interest in other event-related brain potentials associated, for instance, with preparing to make a response (readiness potential, *Bereitschaftspotential*, and motor potential) or expecting a stimulus to which one is to respond (contingent negative variation, CNV, or expectancy wave, E-wave).

The motor potential studies required the development of a new technique of opisthochronic averaging, 'averaging backwards in time', since interest was here focused on the events preceding an event, the response, whose exact time could not be predicted in advance. The latter

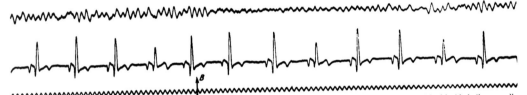

Dr. V., 30 year old physician. Double-coil galvanometer. Condenser inserted. Recording from forehead and occiput with chlorided silver needle electrodes. Electrocardiogram with silver foil electrodes from the left arm and the left leg. At the top: the electroencephalogram; in the middle: the electrocardiogram; at the bottom: time in 1/10ths sec. B: time at which the dorsum of the right hand was touched and stroking with a glass rod along the latter began.

Fig. 1. Figure from one of Hans Berger's original papers on the electroencephalogram, published in 1930, showing the blocking of the alpha rhythm in response to touching the back of the right hand with a glass rod, together with Berger's original legend.

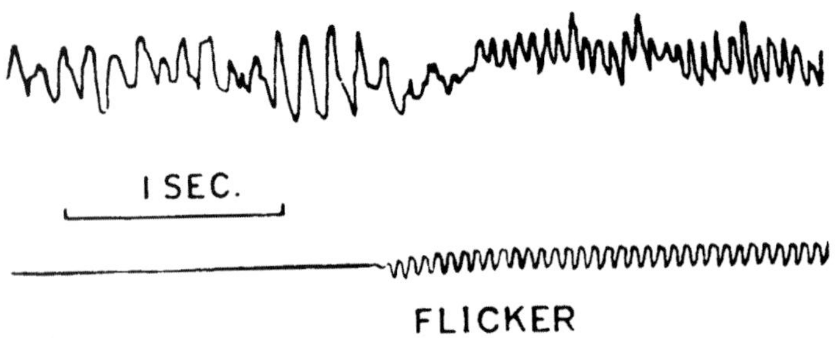

Fig. 2. An early recording of the visual evoked potential to flicker stimulation, from a paper by Adrian, published in 1944.

I SEC.

FLICKER

Electroencephalogram from the occipital region, showing the change from the α rhythm to the flicker rhythm when the eyes are opened and the subject looks at a screen lit by a flickering light. The rate of flicker (17 a second) is shown by the photo-electric cell record below.

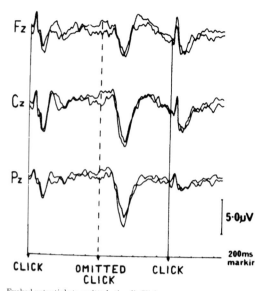

Evoked potentials to omitted stimuli. Clicks were presented regularly every 1.1 sec and occasionally a click was omitted; the subject was asked to count the number of omissions. The averaging computer was triggered by the click immediately preceding the omission. Evoked potentials are shown for three different scalp positions. Each tracing represents the average of 64 responses. Subject T.P.

Fig. 3. P300 evoked by a non-event, viz. the unexpected omission of one of a regular train of clicks. Note the large P300 wave, occurring with each scalp position.

is an example of a so-called endogenous potential as distinct from the exogenous sensory evoked potentials, whose occurrence and timing depended upon an external event, the sensory stimulus.

The *Bereitschaftspotential*, or readiness potential, which consisted of a slow build-up in negativity over the central regions of the cortex during the 1–2 seconds preceding a response, depended for its occurrence on the probability and predictability of the motor act, whether this was self-paced or made in response to an expected stimulus.

An even more interesting family of event-related potentials (ERPs) can be recorded when a stimulus is sufficiently *improbable and yet significant*. These are the so-called P300 waves, which depend for their incidence on the unexpectedness of the relevant event. They were first described in two papers by Sutton and colleagues in 1965 and 1967 and have been extensively studied since that time. Even the unlooked-for absence of an expected event (Fig. 3) can elicit a P300, as in the case of a single missing stimulus in a long train of repeated tones.

Semantic improbability is associated with an N400 wave, a negativity occurring about 0.4 of a second following the unexpected word (e.g. when the sentence 'He spread the warm bread with socks' is presented, one word

at a time, on a visual display, a large N400 wave occurs only in respect of the unexpected word 'socks'). No such response occurs to the sentences 'It was his first day at work' or 'She put on her high-heeled shoes'. These language-related ERPs were first described by Kutas and Hillyard from San Diego in 1980. Work on linguistically related ERPs has also been carried out by Goto in Japan, who has studied the brain responses associated with the resolution of linguistic ambiguities.

New developments in evoked potential research have demonstrated their ability to serve clinical assessment of a variety of cognitive problems and neurological deficits, including, for example, head injury, cerebral palsy dyslexia, language impairments associated with stroke, and other language deficits (see Connolly and D'Arcy 2000 for a review). This technique of assessment not only combines existing standard neuropsychological tests (e.g. Peabody Picture Vocabulary Test—Revised) and ERP recordings to establish level of functioning but allows accurate diagnoses to be made independent of the patient's current communicative ability. A recent case study (Connolly et al. 1999) of a 21-year-old man, H.F., highlights the importance of development in this area with regard to diagnostic techniques and subsequent rehabilitative help.

H.F. suffered traumatic brain injury as a result of being stabbed though the head with a knife. On admission to hospital the patient displayed global aphasia and showed no reliable movements of any type. Rehabilitation was not recommended, as he appeared to have no cognitive functioning abilities. However, using ERP testing and sentences varying in semantic appropriateness, H.F. was found to have intact speech comprehension abilities and subsequently received successful rehabilitation.

Further developments in evoked potential research follow from the discovery of P300 waves (see Picton 1992 for a review) and N400 waves (Kutas and Hillyard 1980). Although work has continued with these ERPs a more recent discovery, the phonological mismatch negativity (PMN), has also been extremely promising (Connolly and Phillips 1994). This component occurs in response to violations in expectations when someone is listening to speech and a word they expected to hear given a context (e.g. sentence) is, in fact, not presented but instead something else. This response, which occurs in an interval between 250 and 350 ms, precedes the semantic processing response (N400) and is independent of it (Connolly and D'Arcy 2000). Recent evidence indicates that it is generated in language areas of the brain and is linked directly to phonological processing of speech. Recent data has found that the PMN is not observed in dyslexic individuals but does appear after reading remediation.

Finally, another important ERP component, discovered by Näätänen and colleagues (for a review see Näätänen 1992) is the mismatch negativity (MMN). The MMN is an auditory component that relates to echoic memory traces and is now viewed as a 'pre-attentive' response linked to very low-level attentional mechanisms. The MMN has demonstrated the exquisite sensitivity of ERP components and has wide basic and applied relevance.

AMH

Connolly, J. F., Mate-Cole, C. C., (1999). 'Global aphasia: an innovative assessment approach'. Med. Rehabil., 80, 1309–15.

—— and D'Arcy, R. C. N. (2000). 'Innovations in neuropsychological assessment using event related potentials'. International Journal of Psychophysiology, 37.

—— and Phillips, N. A. (1994). 'Event-related potential components reflect phonological and semantic processing of the terminal word of spoken sentences'. Journal of Cognitive Neuroscience, 6.

Kutas, M., and Hillyard, S. A. (1980). 'Event related potentials to semantically inappropriate and surprisingly large words'. Biological Psychology, 11.

Näätänen, R. (1992). 'The mismatch negativity: a powerful tool for cognitive neuroscience'. Ear Hear, 16.

Picton, T. W. (1992). 'The P300 wave of the human event-related potential'. Journal of Clinical Neurophysiology, 9.

evolution: has it a purpose? If we agree that all organisms show something that may reasonably be called choice, it implies that their actions are at least partly directed towards an end. Of course, if one reserves the words 'aim' and 'end' for something that is sought 'consciously' then they cannot be used for the 'teleonomic' actions of all living things. The biologist's plea should surely be that we seek for enlightenment from the similarities between species, as well as from their differences, and not allow terminology to interfere. It is amazing that many biologists should have so strongly maintained that they did not wish to consider aims, in the face of the obvious fact that organisms act so as to stay alive. Equally surprising is the unwillingness to admit that it is possible to see any sign of progress in evolution. Of course there are difficulties, but we can now put measures on the degree of complexity of organisms and can give a precise meaning to such statements as that man is the summit of an increasing process of collection of information. It is still conventional to say that questions of value cannot be decided by facts, and indeed everyone will agree that the meaning of 'good' is difficult to determine. Following G. E. *Moore, we are usually asked to hold that the only things that possess intrinsic value are human states of mind. The biologist can hardly accept that this is the last word. Surely our decisions about value are not wholly 'intuitive'. Whether we like it or not they are guided by the influences that have imposed themselves upon us, many of them biological, others social. Of course, to insist that it is nonsense to claim that judgements are wholly intuitive does not actually provide us with criteria for the meanings of 'good' and 'bad', still less for making ethical judgements and recommendations. Yet the general biologist can contribute marginally even to the characteristically human discussion of ultimates.

We do not know yet for certain how, when, or why life began or whether and when it will end. On such things indeed biologists are gaining some knowledge but can still only speculate. The anthropomorphic guesses of theologians have led people to hope for a certainty that we now realize to be unobtainable. But this does not mean that there are no signs of direction in human life. We can see that we have a long and wonderful history, involving an increasing collection of information and its use to allow life to invade regions not habitable before (Young 1938).

Life probably began over 3,000 million years ago, perhaps in a probiotic soup of organic molecules. We are uncertain what originally determined the ordering of specific nucleotides and proteins, but the subsequent course of evolution has certainly involved an increase of order. For perhaps the first 2,000 million years, life remained very simple. The few fossil remains that we have are of bacteria or algae. The evidence of the sedimentary rocks shows that by 500 million years ago there were already many complex invertebrates. Then came the first fish and after them the amphibians, reptiles, birds, and mammals. The point of this now familiar story is that the whole sequence indubitably involves an increase of complexity of organization and of the information transmitted to ensure it. Under the pressure of natural selection, organisms have invaded ever new niches, made habitable by the development of special mechanisms. The examples are endless—to colonize fresh water an organism needs to pump out the excess that flows in. To colonize the land involves preventing loss of water and developing mechanisms for finding it. The skin, which in fish is a relatively homogeneous tissue, becomes differentiated in mammals into perhaps 100 different sorts, all coded for in the DNA. And so on, through all the adaptions that pervade organisms. Of course the progressive increase of order is notoriously irregular. But the numbers of pairs of nucleotides give us a means of quantifying it. In a virus there are about 2×10^5 pairs, equivalent to 100 pages of 2,000 letters to the page. In a bacterium there are 5×10^6 pairs (2,500 pages) and in man 3.5×10^9 (1,700 books of 1,000 pages each). There are many difficulties—for instance we cannot yet properly qualify the differences in complexity among mammals. But we do know that man has developed entirely novel methods of gathering information and storing and transmitting it outside the body.

These facts show that life has had a direction in the past and that man in the last million years has speeded it along its course. We cannot see direction or purpose when we look at the heavens, but we can see them in the progress of life on earth. Perhaps one day we shall be wise enough to see them in the stars too.

Meanwhile we can see that our wants and needs and ambitions are not in vain. They are there to guide us and we should not deny them. They tell us truly what is worthwhile to do for ourselves and for our species. If we look wider still we can see the implications of our very special place in nature. This shows the biological ethic, the imperative to increase variety and to collect further information with which to conserve life and even to create new ways in which it can continue. JZY

Young, J. Z. (1938). 'The evolution of the nervous system and of the relationship of organism and environment'. In de Beer, G. R. (ed.), *Evolution*.

evolution: neo-Darwinian theory.

1. History
2. Classification
3. Variation
4. Natural selection
5. Origin of species
6. Embryology
7. Behaviour
8. Current status of neo-Darwinism

1. History

Charles *Darwin was by no means the first evolutionist. Ideas of transformation of species can be found in the classics ('It's all in Lucretius' was Matthew Arnold's comment on Darwin) and in the writings of 18th-century thinkers such as Buffon, Diderot, Goethe, and Charles's grandfather Erasmus *Darwin. But all those ideas are vague or covert. The French biologist (he coined that word) Jean Baptiste de *Lamarck was the first to present an articulate and explicit theory of biological evolution in his *Philosophie zoölogique* (1809). Other notable precursors of Darwin were the Scottish publisher Robert Chambers (1802–71) with his anonymous *Vestiges of the Natural History of Creation* (1844), and Alfred Russel *Wallace, whose independent discovery of the mechanism of natural selection prompted Darwin to abridge a vast, unfinished manuscript as *On the Origin of Species by Means of Natural Selection, or the Preservation of Favoured Races in the Struggle for Life* (1859). Natural selection, a materialistic explanation for adaptation and the diversity of life, was Darwin's main contribution. Coupled with a candid and persuasive argument, it was enough to convince most scientists of the truth of evolution, and to capture the imagination of most late 19th-century thinkers.

The latter part of the 19th century was a period of exploration of evolutionary theory. Its biological ramifications formed the mainspring of much late Victorian science, and Darwin's theory soon became influential in many other fields, notably anthropology, sociology, politics, philosophy, and psychology. As this list implies, Darwinism was seen by many as a coherent world-view.

In 1900, Gregor Mendel's work on inheritance, originally published in 1866, was rediscovered, and the science of genetics was born. Mutation theory soon replaced natural selection as the most promising field of research into mechanisms of change, and for a while Darwinism was at a low ebb. But towards the end of the 1920s, mathematicians and geneticists—chiefly R. A. *Fisher, J. B. S. Haldane, and Sewall Wright—showed that genetic theory and natural selection were fully compatible, so founding population genetics, which became the central area of evolutionary research. The integration of population genetics with more traditional fields of evolutionary interest such as anatomy, palaeontology, and systematics (classification) was pushed forward in the late 1930s and early 1940s in books by T. Dobzhansky (a geneticist), E. Mayr (a systematist), and G. G. Simpson (a palaeontologist). Julian Huxley's *Evolution: The Modern Synthesis* (1942) gave an alternative name—the synthetic theory—for neo-Darwinism.

In 1953 Francis Crick and James Watson transferred interest to the molecular level with their model of the structure of deoxyribonucleic acid (DNA), the material basis of heredity. Exploration of the implications of the Watson–Crick model soon resulted in the breaking of the genetic code, unravelling of the mode of translation of the genetic message, and development of other branches of molecular biology. Ideas from molecular biology, though broadly consistent with neo-Darwinism, are one of many sources of a new ferment in evolutionary thought. Darwinism and its modern descendant are by no means fossilized theories, embedded as true foundations by scientific progress. Where the current ferment will lead, or end, is impossible to guess. But the ingredients of the brew can be matched with some of the main headings of Darwin's argument as presented in *The Origin*: variation, natural selection, instinct (behaviour), fossils, classification, embryology—and the origin of species, the title of his book, but a topic that he hardly tackled.

2. Classification

The basic unit in biological classification is the species. Attempts to define species have been made for centuries and no definition has yet been found to cover every case. Virtually all definitions emphasize reproduction—species are those aggregations of organisms within which mating and reproduction are normal and successful. The modern abstraction covering this concept is 'gene pool': a species is a set of organisms sharing a set of genes, and the sharing is manifested in the mixing of the genes of two parents in the fertilized egg. Genes of one species are not mixed with those of another, because mating is not attempted, or is unsuccessful through the sperm failing to fertilize the egg,

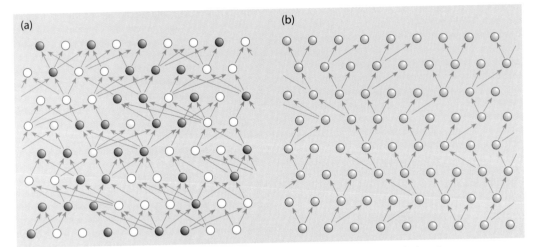

Fig. 1. Population structure in sexual and asexual species. **a.** A sexual species, like our own, in which each individual has two parents of different sexes (dark or light blobs). **b.** An asexual species in which the parent reproduces by dividing into two, as in simple plants and animals like amoeba; each individual has only one parent. According to the theory of evolution, the history of life is a pattern like this, in which blobs are species, not individuals. If the population is to remain constant from generation to generation, only half the individuals in **b** may reproduce. In **a**, a parent produces more than two offspring only at the expense of others.

or through failure in development of the embryo, or through sterility of the hybrid offspring. The molecular basis for success or failure in reproduction is the exact matching of maternal and paternal chromosomes which is necessary in the cell division producing egg or sperm cells.

These criteria are broadly applicable in all sexual plants and animals. In asexual organisms, reproducing by simple fission, for example, it is difficult to form a rational concept of species, since the only link between organisms is a historical one of more or less remote common parentage (see Fig. 1). We recognize this by resemblance between the descendants.

The basic tenet of a theory of evolution is that the relation between species is also historical and due to past common ancestry, manifested in resemblances between species. To evolutionists, the distinct gene pools of today's species are selected and modified fractions of the gene pools of more or less distant common ancestral species. One central task of a theory of evolution is to explain how discontinuities in gene exchange may arise—how a species may split (see section 5 below).

Above the species level, it is common experience that there are groups of species which seem to go together: birds, for example, or beetles or cats. Biological classification formalizes this fact of life by giving these groups Latin or Latinized proper names (birds are Aves, beetles are Coleoptera, cats are Felidae), and by ranking those names in a hierarchy of more or less inclusive categories

(Aves is a class—category—within the phylum Vertebrata; Coleoptera is an order in the class Insecta; Felidae is a family in the order Carnivora and class Mammalia). These names and ranks are conventions, but from *Aristotle to Linnaeus (18th century) to today, those who propose classifications usually believe that they express something real, an order in nature. Before Darwin, that order was commonly rationalized as 'the plan of the Creator' or the imperfect reflection of unchanging and ideal *essence. According to Darwin and his followers, the relation between birds, or between beetles, or between birds and cats is not abstract but historical or genealogical, due to common descent (see CLADISTICS).

The central concept of classification is *homology*. When a child learns to recognize birds, the criteria used are, at root, the same as those used by the scientist: the feathers, beak, wings, and so on are 'the same' in a sparrow and a swan, whereas the wings of a beetle or the beak of a turtle do not make those creatures birds—the 'sameness' is different or inessential; technically, it is analogy rather than homology. The task of biological classification is thus to distinguish homology (informative sameness) from analogy (misleading sameness). And the interest of classification to the evolutionist is that homologies, the characters of groups, are seen as evidence of common ancestry, so that the hierarchy reflects real historical relations. A research programme is implicit here, to reconstruct the history of life through the common ancestry inferred from homologies. Since Darwin first proposed that 'Our classifications will come to be, as far as they can be so made, genealogies', this programme has been followed with enthusiasm. The programme concerns the main outlines of life's history; it integrates classification with morphology, palaeontology, and embryology. This work is an extrapolation from evolutionary theory, and the fact that the work can be carried out does not materially affect the theory itself. The theory depends on more basic matters, an explanation of how species originate. Darwin approached that problem first through his study of variation.

3. Variation

Lacking a sound theory of inheritance, Darwin studied it through the experience of those with a practical interest in it: animal and plant breeders. Of the manuscript from which *The Origin* was abridged, the only part that Darwin actually published was the two-volume *Variation of Animals and Plants under Domestication* (1868). In *The Origin* Darwin argued by analogy. Under domestication, breeders observed variations and were often able to perpetuate them by selective mating. Over many generations, the breeds or varieties of dogs, cabbages, pigeons (Darwin's pets), and so on are the result. Darwin's opinions on the causes and inheritance of variation are chiefly of historical interest now. He wrestled with the problem of whether variation is spontaneous, or is provoked by the 'conditions of life' (i.e. the environment), and favoured the environment. And he tried to analyse the mode of inheritance, whether or not it is 'blending', offspring being intermediate between the parents. Blending seemed empirically true for many characteristics, and it has the consequence that a new variation would be swamped or diluted over the generations. These problems, of the origin of variation and its inheritance, were not solved until the 20th century, with the development of genetics and, later, molecular genetics.

There is no space here to go into genetic theory, and its outlines must be baldly stated. The material basis of heredity is DNA, a ladder-like molecule which carries a message in the form of a 'four-letter' code, the letters being four chemical bases, each of which may occupy any rung in the ladder. The message is read in triplets, or 'three-letter words', and the words are of two kinds, 'stop' or 'amino acid X'. Twenty different amino acids are encoded by triplets, some by a single triplet, others by up to six different ones (see Table 1). Thus the genetic message specifies sequences of amino acids terminated by stop signs, and, when translated and acted upon, the result is proteins, which are chains of amino acids. Genes are sections of DNA which specify a discrete amino acid chain.

DNA is carried in chromosomes, in the nucleus of every cell. When sex cells (eggs or sperm) are produced, the chromosomes pair off very precisely, each pair containing one chromosome from each of the two parents, and within each pair parts are exchanged at random (crossing-over). The newly mixed chromosomes then separate in a cell division which produces sex cells containing one member of each pair, so that the number of chromosomes is halved. The number characteristic of the species is restored when the egg and sperm nuclei, each carrying a half-set, unite in the fertilized egg. Inheritance is not blending: genes are passed on unchanged from generation to generation.

Table 1. The genetic code

					SECOND LETTER					
			A		**G**		**T**		**C**	
FIRST LETTER	A	AAA	Phenylalanine	AGA	Serine	ATA	Tyrosine	ACA	Cysteine	A
		AAG	Phenylalanine	AGG	Serine	ATG	Tyrosine	ACG	Cysteine	G
		AAT	Leucine	AGT	Serine	ATT	Stop	ACT	Stop	T
		AAC	Leucine	AGC	Serine	ATC	Stop	ACC	Tryptophan	C
	G	GAA	Leucine	GGA	Proline	GTA	Histidine	GCA	Arginine	A
		GAG	Leucine	GGG	Proline	GTG	Histidine	GCG	Arginine	G
		GAT	Leucine	GGT	Proline	GTT	Glutamine	GCT	Arginine	T
		GAC	Leucine	GGC	Proline	GTC	Glutamine	GCC	Arginine	C
	T	TAA	Isoleucine	TGA	Threonine	TTA	Asparagine	TCA	Serine	A
		TAG	Isoleucine	TGG	Threonine	TTG	Asparagine	TCG	Serine	G
		TAT	Isoleucine	TGT	Threonine	TTT	Lysine	TCT	Arginine	T
		TAC	Methionine	TGC	Threonine	TTC	Lysine	TCC	Arginine	C
	C	CAA	Valine	CGA	Alanine	CTA	Aspartic Acid	CCA	Glycine	A
		CAG	Valine	CGG	Alanine	CTG	Aspartic Acid	CCG	Glycine	G
		CAT	Valine	CGT	Alanine	CTT	Glutamine Acid	CCT	Glycine	T
		CAC	Valine	CGC	Alanine	CTC	Glutamine Acid	CCC	Glycine	C

With that background, the sources of heritable variation can be specified. First, the genes of each new individual are a new assortment, because they combine two half-sets (from egg and sperm) each shuffled in the crossing-over between chromosome pairs in the parental cell divisions that produced them. This is a form of variation generated by shuffling existing material, as each deal of a shuffled pack of several thousand cards would be unique. Secondly, new variation may be introduced by mutations: accidents or mistakes in replication and repair of DNA or mishaps in cell division. Mistakes in DNA can alter one or more bases in the molecule (letters in the code), and may alter one or more amino acids in the protein specified. Mishaps in cell division may alter parts of chromosomes—lengths of DNA—which may be inverted, deleted, duplicated, or transferred to another chromosome. The effect of mutations on individual organisms ranges from negligible or undetectable to lethal. The effect of mutations on the reproductive capacity of an individual (i.e. the formation of viable eggs or sperm) also varies from undetectable to sterility. Known mutations in DNA turn up with frequencies from about 1 in 10^4 to 1 in 10^8: they are rare, but frequent enough for every human individual to carry several mutations which have arisen during his or her life. Most of these will be in somatic (body) cells, not in eggs or sperm, and so cannot be passed on to the next generation.

That statement recalls the other question that bothered Darwin—whether variations acquired during life can be inherited. The question refers to what is now called Lamarckian inheritance, for Lamarck proposed that the effects of use and disuse and other changes during life are heritable, and are a cause of evolutionary change. In fact, Darwin held much the same belief. The orthodox answer to the question is no—acquired characters are not inherited. One reason for this is that offspring inherit only an egg or sperm from each parent, and at least in animals those cells are sequestered very early in embryonic life, before the environment takes its effect. A second reason is that translation of DNA into protein—construction of the organism—is held to be a one-way process, with no feedback from the organism to the DNA. This notion is the 'central dogma' of molecular genetics. The one known exception to that dogma is reverse transcriptase, an enzyme that transcribes RNA, the messenger nucleic acid, into DNA, the message store. But to get environmentally induced information into DNA requires more, a way of getting such information into RNA (reverse translation rather than transcription). No such mechanism is yet known. But there has been support for a neo-Lamarckian model of evolution, and various ways in which the environment might direct or influence the genes have been suggested.

Ideas on variation have gained impetus from techniques for separating variant protein molecules, and so estimating the proportion of variant genes in individuals and species. The result is surprising: there is much more hidden variation than was expected. Hidden genetic variation in one individual is due to different forms of homologous genes in the half-set of chromosomes inherited from each parent. In humans, if the few that have been tested are a fair sample of the whole, the proportion of variant genes in each individual is at least 6 per cent, about normal for vertebrate species; in plants and invertebrates variation is often higher, 15 per cent or more. With the discovery that the genes of species are less uniform than expected, the problem has shifted from Darwin's—where does variation come from?—to a new one—why is there so much variation? Orthodox neo-Darwinism demands that it be due to natural selection.

4. Natural selection

Darwin's main contribution was natural selection, the survival of the fittest, a materialist explanation for evolutionary change. There have been several presentations of natural selection theory as a deductive argument. Here are three: (i) all organisms produce far more offspring than are necessary to replace them, yet numbers of each species remain roughly constant. Therefore, there is differential mortality, a struggle for existence. (ii) All organisms manifest hereditary variations. Therefore, those organisms inheriting variations useful in the struggle for existence will be more likely to survive to pass on those variations. (iii) The environment is not constant. Therefore, those hereditary variations advantageous in a changing environment will be selected, and species will change to remain in harmony with the environment. This is adapted from an 1870 formalization by A. R. Wallace. It emphasizes the effect of changing environments, and the observed constancy in numbers of individuals.

A briefer form, due to the philosopher A. G. N. Flew, is: (i) geometrical rate of increase + limited resources → struggle for existence. (ii) Struggle for existence + variation → natural selection. (iii) Natural selection + time → biological improvement. This emphasizes the theoretical limits on environmental resources rather than constant populations and changing environments, and introduces the notion of 'improvement'. What is improved is not specified.

Another brief form: (i) all organisms must reproduce. (ii) All organisms exhibit genetic variation. (iii) Genetic variations differ in their effect on reproduction. (iv) Therefore, variant genes with favourable effects on reproduction will succeed, those with unfavourable effects will fail, and gene proportions will change. This emphasizes variant genes, and reproductive success rather than environmental factors.

If natural selection can be presented as a deductive

argument in which the conclusion follows logically from the premises, then it must be true if the premises are true. If the premises in one, or all three, of these formulations are empirically true, natural selection must occur.

But we have to be clear about what is selected. Natural selection concerns differential survival or, the other side of the coin, differential extinction. What are the units that survive or become extinct: are they genes, or fragments of genes (e.g. triplets or single nucleotides), or chromosomes, or genotypes (genetic constitutions of individuals), or phenotypes (individual organisms, each expressing its own genotype), or groups of organisms, or species? Wallace's formulation of selection refers to species, Flew's perhaps to individuals, and the third form to genes: are they all correct? All descriptions of natural selection invoke interactions, of individual organisms with the inorganic environment, with other individuals in reproduction, with individuals of other species in predator–prey interactions, and so on. Descriptions of natural selection also invoke replication or multiplication, of genes, or of individuals carrying favourable mutations. DNA and chromosomes mutate and replicate, but since they do not interact with the environment, selection cannot act on them directly. It is individual organisms or phenotypes —life histories—that interact with the environment, but the genotype of every successful organism, the set of chromosomes, is broken up and reshuffled by crossing-over when it produces eggs or sperm, so that individuals (genotype + phenotype) do not reproduce themselves exactly.

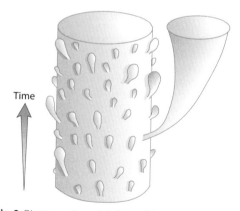

Time

Fig. 2. Diagrammatic model of part of the history of a species, as envisaged by advocates of quantum speciation. The parent species is more or less stable through time, and is continually budding off potential new species in the form of small, inbreeding populations, which may be isolated by geography or by genetic accidents such as chromosome mutations. Most of these incipient species soon become extinct, but a few (one in this example) may succeed.

In the network of ancestor–descendant relations over the generations (Fig. 2), the units that survive differentially, or are selected, are bits of DNA of unspecifiable length. If there is selective change over a number of generations, some bits of DNA in the original population will be represented by many copies in the final population, and others will not be represented at all, because they became extinct when the organisms carrying them failed to reproduce. In order to summarize the change, we have to use the abstraction 'gene pool'. Over the generations, there is a change in the gene pool of the population or species. Of course, no one has ever seen a gene pool or dipped a finger in one, and the tangible effect of the change will be a change in the phenotypes in the population.

One definition of 'gene' is 'a portion of chromosome which survives enough generations to act as a unit of natural selection'. That definition may sound vacuously circular, as if we have to understand natural selection before we can understand genes, yet understanding natural selection depends on understanding genes. But it at least emphasizes the point that, because chromosomes are randomly broken up in each generation by crossing-over, there is no particular unit that survives intact over many generations. Indeed, there is a theory of 'hitch-hiking' natural selection; a neutral or disadvantageous mutation may spread because it happens to be adjacent to an advantageous one, so that the two survive as a unit without being separated by the chances of crossing-over.

Because some organisms exhibit parental care, or social organization in which more or less extensive kinship groups take part, the family or kin group may have sufficient cohesion to act as a unit of natural selection, kin selection as it is called. Beyond kin groups, the next steps up the genealogical hierarchy are populations and species. Like kin groups, they are linked by descent, by a shared gene pool, and might act as units of selection, or of differential survival. It is doubtful whether populations of the same species ever interact so that one gene pool becomes extinct: mixing of the gene pools through interbreeding is the likely outcome (though some interactions between human populations may have resulted in extinction, by genocide without interbreeding). But different species do seem to interact in this way. One thinks of the extermination of native species in the Galápagos and other closed habitats after the introduction of animals like pigs and goats. In such cases, one speaks of species selection (see section 5 below). This, on its own, can only decrease diversity, not generate it.

The observation explained by natural selection is adaptation, the apparent design of organisms for the environments in which they live. The 'argument from design' was one of the chief pre-Darwinian props for natural theology —evidence for a wise and benign Creator. Darwin's theory of natural selection cut the ground from that argument (see also HUME, DAVID). In essence, neo-Darwinian selection theory is that mutations arise at random, with no feedback from the environment to direct or influence the type of mutation that is 'needed', and interaction between the environment and organisms bearing the mutation determines success or failure. Wallace's formalization of natural selection emphasizes changing environments as the driving force, but an alternative view is possible, of a static inorganic world which is explored by life through natural selection, so that the environment is in a sense created by organisms. For instance, it is difficult to conceive of environmental change which would lead originally aquatic plants first to colonize the land, or terrestrial animals to take to the air: the land and air were there, but not part of the habitable environment until organisms made them so. Of course, once there are plants on land, or insects in the air, we can easily conceive of the advantage of becoming a cow or a swallow.

But talk of cows and swallows introduces the problem with natural selection. Two entirely distinct aspects of the theory must be distinguished. One is concerned with things like cows, swallows, and giraffes' necks. The other is concerned with selection in populations, the bread and butter of population genetics. As for this latter sort, there is no doubt that it works. The deductive form of the argument for it proves that it ought to work, and there is experimental and observational evidence that it does. Classic instances of natural selection in populations include bird predation of light and dark forms of the peppered moth in industrial and rural Britain; the development of resistance to antibiotics in bacteria, to insecticides in insects, and to rat poison in rats; and the relation between human sickle-cell trait and malaria in Africa. These instances cover two sorts of selection. In antibiotic or insecticide resistance, the gene pool of the population is altered: genotypes to which the agent is lethal are eliminated, and those that can survive it increase. This is *directional* selection, where there is a shift from one state to another. Melanism in moths and sickle-cell trait are instances of *stabilizing* or *normalizing* selection, which results not in a shift, but in maintenance of the norm by elimination of variants. In both instances it happens that the norm maintained is a polymorphic population, and this is sometimes called *balancing* selection. Another type of selection is so obvious that it almost escapes attention; instances are the poor reproductive success of people suffering genetic defects which place them far outside the norm. Those defects are eliminated by *purifying* selection. The terminology seems varied and complex, but in general we can think of selection as either eliminating variation (purifying, directional) or maintaining it (balancing, stabilizing), and also as either promoting change (directional) or maintaining the status quo (purifying, stabilizing).

To neo-Darwinians, the important types of natural selection are directional selection (an explanation of inferred change) and balancing selection as an explanation of observed variation. The basis of change is the replacement of one form of a gene, or portion of chromosome, by a new (mutant) form. This will take place when the mutant form confers a relative advantage, and spreads through the population. The rate of spread depends on the degree of advantage or selection pressure (roughly the proportion of selective deaths per generation), and on whether the mutation is recessive (expressed only in those inheriting it from both parents—homozygous for it), dominant (expressed if inherited from only one parent—heterozygous), or intermediate (expressed more strongly if inherited from both parents rather than one). Change is irreversible only when the original form of the gene has disappeared; that is, the mutant becomes fixed, or universal in the population. Fixation is achieved most rapidly when the mutation is neither dominant nor recessive but intermediate, which is probably true for most mutations considered at the molecular or protein-producing level.

Balancing selection will occur when heterozygotes, inheriting different forms of a gene from each parent, are more successful than homozygotes. Here, selection will eliminate homozygotes in each generation, but will not alter the equilibrium proportions of the two (or more) forms of the gene. Balancing selection is the neo-Darwinian explanation for the high incidence (averaging 6–15 per cent of sampled proteins—see above) of heterozygosity observed in natural populations. The assumption is that heterozygotes are fitter than homozygotes because they have a wider array of resources to meet variations in the environment. An alternative explanation is the 'non-Darwinian' proposal that the observed protein variants are selectively neutral; they confer no real advantage or disadvantage and are maintained purely by chance, by random genetic drift. On this neutralist theory, harmless or even slightly deleterious mutations may spread and become fixed (or eliminated) purely by chance. As with natural selection, experiments show that genetic drift occurs, especially in small populations where biased samples are more likely, and there is a highly developed mathematical theory of how quasi-neutral mutations may behave in populations.

So far, it has proved impossible to discriminate between these two mechanisms, neo-Darwinian selection and neutralist drift, as general explanations, though neutralism has had remarkable recent successes. In essence, the neo-Darwinian expects that a given variation is correlated with some environmental variable, and the neutralist expects that it is not. When one such environmental variable is identified with one genetic variant, as malaria has been with sickle-cell trait (abnormal red blood cells) in humans, this may seem a triumph for neo-Darwinism, but a myriad protein polymorphisms remain to comfort the neutralist. The generality of balancing selection as an explanation for genetic variation took a sharp knock when it was found that bacteria, which lack sex and so cannot be heterozygous, are just as polymorphic as sexual organisms. At least the neo-Darwinist seems to have a task, or a research programme: to dissect the environment into factors correlated with variations in organisms. Neutralists have no such programme, and instead neutralism comes into its own in explaining evolution that is invisible to selection by the environment, changes in stretches of DNA which are not translated into the phenotype (see section 5 below).

Natural selection, the idea that organisms are moulded or 'designed' by the environment, is also used as an explanation in quite a different sense, when applied to cows, or swallows, or giraffes' necks. Here, explanations are under virtually no empirical control, because the environmental factors invoked are necessarily in the past. In this mode, explanations take the form of conjectures or narratives, in which organisms are analysed in terms of function, and demonstration that one design is more efficient than another is sufficient to explain its origin by natural selection, or environmental conditions under which particular features could be advantageous are postulated or imagined. Critics argue that such exercises of the imagination demonstrate the emptiness of selection theory. In explaining everything, it explains too much; as an explanation of design in nature it seems hard to distinguish from the all-seeing Creator of *Paley and other natural theologians. On this view, natural selection is equated with a vacuous Panglossian optimism—'all is for the best in this best of all possible worlds'—or with the explanation of the action of opium by its content of 'dormitive principle'. One response to these critics is that they do not touch the status of natural selection: it could still be as effective in the global sense as it is in the experiments of population geneticists. Nevertheless, no one has yet reported the origin of a new species by means of natural selection.

5. Origin of species

Although this was the title of his book, Darwin scarcely addressed the problem of how new species arise. His mechanism, natural selection, concerns change or transformation of species through time, but this alone will not produce new species; it will merely modify and preserve old ones. New species appear only if the number of species increases, if a species splits into two or more. Darwin proposed what he called the principle of divergence: by analogy with artificial selection, and by appealing to 'many and widely different places in the economy of nature', he argued that the most divergent members of a species tend to be preserved, and gradually diverge into varieties, subspecies, and eventually into distinct species. The kernel of his explanation was gradual adaptive divergence.

The neo-Darwinian theory of the origin of species—of *speciation*—differs from Darwin's chiefly in the emphasis placed on geographical isolation as a necessary precursor of species formation, and in emphasis on genetic isolating mechanisms. Neo-Darwinian speciation theory is by no means monolithic, and there are arguments for speciation without geographical isolation, and without Darwinian gradualism.

That species can arise at one stroke there is no doubt. Doubling of chromosome number in a cell is a fairly common accident: it happens if the chromosomes divide, as before normal cell division, but the cell then fails to divide. Such cells are unable to give rise to normal eggs or sperm, because the chromosomes will associate in fours, not in pairs as is necessary in production of sex cells. But in a hybrid between two species, itself sterile because of incompatibility between the two sets of chromosomes, chromosome doubling will restore fertility (each chromosome now has a partner to pair with), and self-fertilization can then initiate a new species intermediate between the two parents of the hybrid. Many species of plants and a few of animals have evidently appeared in this way, and some have been created or recreated in the laboratory.

Speciation by multiplication of chromosome number (*polyploidy*) is instantaneous; the new species is descended from a single self-fertilizing individual; accident—macromutation—is the cause; and geographical isolation is unnecessary. In all these four ways, it differs from the classic neo-Darwinian model of speciation, which demands geographical isolation, gradual selective change over long periods of time, and involves populations, not individuals. Between these two extremes, there is a third model of speciation which has received much recent support and interest. This model is inelegantly called 'punctuated equilibrium'—'quantum speciation' is an alternative. One group with evidence bearing on this model includes geneticists who have found that similar or closely related species usually differ in chromosome arrangement, implying fixation of chromosome mutations during their history. For instance, human chromosomes differ from those of chimpanzees by inversions of parts of nine chromosomes, and fusion of two. Whereas identical point mutations in DNA recur at measurable rates, each chromosome mutation is virtually unique, for each depends on the coincidence of at least two accidental breaks in a chromosome, followed by rearrangement and fusion. Organisms heterozygous for a chromosome mutation (inheriting it only from one parent) usually show reduced fertility, but those inheriting it from both parents (homozygous) are potentially fully fertile. Chromosome mutations can therefore act as genetic isolating mechanisms, favouring mating among carriers of the mutation (hence homozygous offspring) and so initiating speciation. But since chromosome mutations are each virtually unique, the only way homozygotes can be produced is by inbreeding among the offspring of the individual in which the mutation originally occurred. This model—'chromosomal speciation'—resembles the chromosome doubling mode of speciation in several ways: no geographical isolation is necessary, accident rather than natural selection is the cause, inbreeding among the descendants of a single individual is necessary, and a new species may arise in a few generations, with the establishment of a population homozygous for the mutation.

A second set of arguments in favour of quantum speciation comes from palaeontologists, who generally fail to find evidence of gradual transformation in the fossil record. Instead, fossil species appear suddenly, persist unchanged over more or less long periods, and disappear as abruptly as they came. Data of the same sort was available to Darwin and his geological mentor Charles Lyell (1797–1875). Lyell built a theory on them, of piecemeal creation of species by 'a power above nature'. Darwin, who believed natural selection was the power in question, appealed instead to imperfections in the fossil record, and hoped that future discoveries would show the gradual transitions he expected. Today, some palaeontologists have at last given up that hope and taken the fossils at face value, as a true record of the mode of evolution. They infer that speciation occurs rapidly, in small populations, so that transitions between species are evanescent. For if change does not occur during the recorded history of species, it must occur elsewhere, in the unrecorded history of small founder populations. From these ideas comes a theory of species continually and randomly throwing off small offshoots, of which most perish but a few succeed as new species (see Fig. 2). As in the chromosomal theory of speciation, natural selection is not responsible for the appearance of these offshoots, but operates at a higher level in selecting among them. In populations, random mutations throw up material on which selection acts; in just the same way, it is argued that random speciation throws up material—species—on which selection acts. Major evolutionary changes are not due to the action of selection on mutations of genes or chromosomes, but of species selection on a mass of species, thrown up by a random process.

A third group of scientists whose ideas fit in here are molecular biologists. Techniques recently developed make it possible to work out the sequence of nucleotides in DNA and in the messenger nucleic acid, RNA. The letters of the genetic code may then be compared with the amino acid sequence in the protein synthesized on the message in the messenger RNA. The genetic code has a lot of redundancy. In eight of the sixteen boxes in Table 1 the third letter of the triplet makes no difference; the amino acid is specified by the first two letters alone. This means that mutations in the third position of many triplets will be 'silent' and will not alter the amino acid. Amino acids specified by triplets with different first (arginine, leucine) or first and second (serine) letters may also sustain silent mutations in the first and second positions. When the RNA and amino acid sequences are compared for human and rabbit beta-haemoglobin genes, for instance, two-thirds of the differences between the RNAs are silent, not reflected in the protein; the same comparison between mouse and rabbit alpha-haemoglobins gives virtually the same proportion of silent and non-silent changes. If all these differences represent mutations fixed during the history of the species compared, two conclusions can be drawn. First, the rate of 'silent evolution' must be greater than the rate of phenotypic change (we come back to this point later); second, the silent mutations must have been fixed by random drift, not by selection, since a change in DNA which is not reflected in the organism cannot be selected. If the majority of inferred change in DNA is due to mutations drifting randomly to fixation, then small populations should be frequent in the history of species, since drift is more effective in small populations, and most effective in inbreeding.

Thus three independent lines of enquiry—chromosomes, fossils, and molecular sequences—converge in a view of speciation which differs profoundly from neo-Darwinian orthodoxy. The nature of this difference or disagreement is interesting. It concerns three main things: time, or number of generations; number of individuals; and natural selection. But these three things, the first two in quantity, are the staples of population genetics. Neo-Darwinism depends on the synthesis of natural selection with experimental and mathematical population genetics, which themselves depend on avoiding random effects by considering many generations and many individuals. Population genetics can explain stability, or variety, or gradual change within species. The thrust of the above ideas on speciation is that those factors may all be irrelevant to the origin of species. In other words, the principles of population genetics are directed at the wrong level in the hierarchy: they explain the behaviour of genes in populations, but are inappropriate when extrapolated as an explanation of the history of life. It is, after all, a fairly fundamental criticism of neo-Darwinism to propose that natural selection is not relevant to the origin of species.

6. Embryology

Before Darwin, the word 'evolution' had a different meaning in biology. It referred to the unfolding of form in the development of the embryo, and in particular to the notion of preformation—that the adult organism is preformed in the fertilized egg. One complaint among Darwin's critics was that he and his followers misused and misappropriated the word 'evolution'. But in the neo-Darwinian theory, something approaching the doctrine of preformation seems to have reappeared. The theory is concerned almost exclusively with genes, but what interests most biologists is organisms and the form of organisms. Neo-Darwinism has, as yet, little to say on how form is generated; it is assumed simply to be programmed in the genes, as if the adult and its development are preformed in the DNA, or the four dimensions of a life history are mapped in the two dimensions of the linear information store.

Darwinism and neo-Darwinism are concerned with historical transformation of organisms. Despite more than a century of work in evolutionary biology, it remains true that the only transformations of which we have empirical knowledge are those observed in the life histories of organisms—the acorn into the oak tree, or the egg into the caterpillar, pupa, and then butterfly. It is remarkable that these transformations remain almost as mysterious today as they were in Darwin's time. The orthodox, genetic explanation of the genesis of form invokes control genes, which are thought of as switching on and off one or more structural (protein-specifying) genes. A hierarchy of control genes is envisaged, with 'master genes' which switch on batteries of lower-level control genes. Mutations in such control genes could obviously produce relatively large changes in the adult organism. But these control genes remain theoretical, and theoretical entities can, in theory, accomplish anything. Indeed, an immediate inference from the reductionist viewpoint of randomly mutating genes is that anything is possible, and it is natural selection that sorts out the actual from the possible.

Yet the regularity and uniformity of embryonic development in animals and plants seem to demonstrate that anything is not possible. One symptom of a reaction against the reductionist programme of neo-Darwinism and molecular biology is the insistence of some biologists that the transformations of embryology demand 'something more' than proteins and interactions between proteins: the miracle that demands explanation is not necessarily how the eye (for example) evolved in the ancestors of vertebrates, but how it evolves from nothing in every vertebrate today. The embryologists and others who take this stand have produced no fully coherent alternative to neo-Darwinism, but appeal to non-genic inheritance (through the cytoplasm of the egg, inherited from the mother), to possible neo-Lamarckian modes of change, or to the self-organizing and self-regulating powers of the developing organism. This revolt against the tyranny of the genes may be summed up as an interest

in epigenetics (the sequence of events that happens in the embryo after fertilization).

A neo-Darwinian response is that these complaints are nothing new, smack of vitalism, and demonstrate a confusion between proximate causes, the embryologist's proper domain, and ultimate causes, the domain of evolutionary theory. Epigenesists might reply that neo-Darwinian theory offers no better explanation of the self-organizing capacity of the organism than contingency, a lucky chapter of irretrievable historical accidents. Like so much else in neo-Darwinism, the argument degenerates here into incommensurables, the conflict between chance and apparent necessity.

7. Behaviour

One of the modern growth areas within neo-Darwinism is sociobiology. It is concerned with evolutionary interpretation of behaviour, especially in social interactions within species. Darwin initiated work on these lines with explanations, in terms of natural selection, of insect societies (ants, bees) which entail self-sacrifice or altruistic behaviour by individuals or castes. Modern sociobiology is a fusion of population genetics, *ethology (study of behaviour), and game theory (see VON NEUMANN, JOHN), interpreting behaviour in terms of strategies which will have selective advantage if they increase the chance of survival of individuals or their kin, who share their genes. Though relatively uncontroversial when applied to birds or butterflies, these ideas have raised a storm when, as was inevitable, they are extrapolated to human societies. The controversy, which has marked political overtones, centres over the extent to which behaviour is genetically determined, a topic on which agreement seems no more likely than in the argument over the relative contributions of heredity and environment to intelligence.

In order to be subject to natural selection, traits—whether behavioural or structural—must be heritable, or under genetic control. To bring some behavioural trait within neo-Darwinism, all that is necessary is to argue that it is adaptive under certain circumstances (few traits resist ingenuity), and to postulate a gene for it. There is little harm in theoretical genes for altruism or homosexuality, but critics of sociobiology see such exercises as examples of the reductionist tyranny of the genes, or of the emptiness of a theory that can explain anything.

8. Current status of neo-Darwinism

In the preceding sections, various new directions in, and criticisms of, neo-Darwinism have been outlined. The basics of neo-Darwinism, as of Darwinism, are heritable variation and natural selection. Molecular and population genetics have supplied much insight into the source of variation and the mechanism of selection. There is no doubt that generation of genetic variation is an intrinsic property of sexually reproducing organisms as we know them. Nor can one doubt that natural selection censors variation, and maintains organisms in harmony with their environments. That might seem to be the end of the matter. Nevertheless, there have been persistent arguments over the status of neo-Darwinism, both as legitimate science and as a comprehensive explanation of life.

In considering these arguments, it is essential to distinguish the two disparate aspects of neo-Darwinian theory. The first is that evolution has occurred: relations between species are material, not immaterial, and historical, due to common ancestry. This aspect is more general than Darwinism or neo-Darwinism. The particular contribution of those systems is a mechanism—natural selection—to account for evolution.

The general aspect of the theory, that evolution has occurred, has a curious philosophical corollary: acceptance of it entails a revolutionary change in the ontological status of its subject matter. Concepts such as 'ravens' and 'swans' are traditionally considered classes or universals ('all swans are white' and 'all ravens are black' are classic statements about universals in logic). Evolution changes that. Biological species, and groups of species related in a closed system of descent, become individuals, and names like *Homo sapiens* or Mammalia become proper names, the names of individuals, or 'chunks of the genealogical nexus', a nexus that is necessarily unique. If evolution has occurred, it follows that there can be no real laws of evolution, for laws concern classes or universals, and evolution implies that all of life is one individual system, like the solar system. In other words, one consequence of evolutionary theory is that comparative biology becomes historical science, and there can no more be evolutionary laws than there are historical laws.

The general scientific method is to propose hypotheses about nature, and to test them by deducing what each hypothesis forbids, turning to nature to see if the forbidden consequence actually occurs. Then the question is what forbidden consequences, or potential tests, may be deduced from the proposition that evolution has occurred. Various possible observations have been suggested, such as the discovery of human fossils in Cambrian rocks, which could falsify evolution and so demonstrate its testability. But none of the potential tests that have been proposed appears to be directed exclusively at evolution. For instance, Cambrian human bones would falsify not evolutionary theory but the general comparative method in biology, codified before Darwin as the theory of 'threefold parallelism'—between the succession of fossils in the stratigraphic record, the transformations of embryonic development, and the hierarchy of natural classification, based on homologies. Evolution may seem to be an inescapable deduction from that theory, but the

biologists who proposed and upheld it in the 19th century would not agree. Those who argue that evolution is falsifiable seem to demonstrate the weakness of that position by the conviction, which shines through their prose, that they know the truth. The only thing forbidden by evolution is that there should be species unrelated to others by descent, and since we have no access to unambiguous records of descent, no decisive test is forthcoming. Nevertheless, evolution explains important discoveries unforeseen by Darwin, such as the universality of the genetic code, and comparisons of nucleic acid and protein sequences.

One may reject testability as a criterion, and appeal instead to the fruitfulness of evolutionary theory as a research programme. That criterion has no necessary connection with *truth, for phlogiston chemistry and Ptolemaic astronomy were fruitful research programmes. Or one can point to the explanatory power of the theory, the quantity of disparate areas of knowledge it unites. Darwin used this argument: 'It can hardly be supposed that a false theory would explain in so satisfactory a manner . . . several large classes of facts.' A different strategy for evolutionists is not to analyse or defend their own theory, but to attack the opposition, alternative explanations of life. Only two seem to be on offer. The first is spontaneous generation or creation, necessarily on multiple occasions and locations rather than the one required by evolution. The second is the notion that the earth has been seeded from space, and again seeding on multiple occasions is required to distinguish this from evolution. The difference between the three explanations, when considered in terms of testable predictions, explanatory power, fruitfulness, or whatever, seems to come down to the principle of parsimony, or Occam's razor: evolution is superior because it does not multiply entities unnecessarily. For creation and seeding both imply repeated intervention (intelligent or not), whereas evolution implies no more than one such intervention. When treated as a criterion of truth, this has been called the 'best-in-field fallacy'. Fallacious it may be, yet evolution has no real competitors. (See FALSIFICATION.)

Turning to mechanism, the specifically Darwinian aspect of neo-Darwinism, we are on surer ground with natural selection. Darwin offered several potential tests of the mechanism: for example, 'If it could be proved that any part of the structure of any one species had been formed for the exclusive good of another species, it would annihilate my theory.' But he also wrote: 'I am convinced that natural selection has been the main but not the exclusive means of modification.' That is also the stance of modern neo-Darwinians, who allow genetic drift and other non-Darwinian means of modification such as polyploidy and less radical chromosomal saltations. In these terms, natural selection is clearly beyond criticism, for it is expected to explain only that which is explicable by it. Cases which are beyond the most ingenious selective explanation have another cause at hand, in random effects due to drift or inbreeding. Comparison of DNA sequences indicates that 'silent' substitutions are about four times as frequent as non-silent ones (with an effect on the phenotype): in other words, the majority of evolutionary change is immune to natural selection. This important conclusion is summed up in 'Kimura's rule' (Motoo Kimura is the father of the neutral theory of molecular evolution): molecular changes that are less likely to be subject to natural selection occur more rapidly in evolution. One corollary of this is the 'molecular clock', the inference that in each lineage DNA evolves at a roughly constant rate. This contrasts with evolution of form or phenotype, which seems to occur in jerks in some lineages, hardly at all in others (so-called 'living fossils'), and never at a constant rate. If, at the molecular level, the majority of evolutionary change takes place in spite of natural selection rather than because of it, natural selection seems to be false as the general explanation of evolutionary change.

The effect of Darwin's theory was to give a mechanistic explanation of apparent intelligent design: the appearance was illusory, for the creative power was in natural selection. The effect of the large neutral or 'non-Darwinian' component discovered in molecular evolution is further to downgrade the role of design: the apparent creative power of natural selection was illusory, if it is outweighed by chance effects. In other words, the role of chance increases. It is this that seems to be the nub of the matter. The reductionist line of neo-Darwinism, aiming to reduce the diversity of life to the laws of chemistry and physics, leads to randomness. Instead of the relentless mill of natural selection, 'daily and hourly scrutinising, throughout the world, the slightest variations . . . silently and insensibly working . . . at the improvement of each organic being' (Darwin's words), buttressed by the equations of population genetics, modern neo-Darwinians seem to be turning on the one hand to pure randomness (neutral theory and the molecular clock), and on the other to explanations which approach the miraculous (to use a provocative word), unique events perpetuated by inbreeding. The latter has echoes in the biblical account of the genesis of mankind. Natural selection has been called a mechanism for generating the improbable and, if the role of natural selection is diluted, the improbability of the results increases. The ultimate in reduction is a recently fashionable idea, that the whole of life is an accidental excrescence, a by-product of selfish DNA, whose structure is such that it survives, multiplies, and diversifies. That view seems to lead nowhere, but there are two lines of research that might lead out of the impasse. One is into the structure of the genome (the genetic equipment of the indi-

vidual), where surprising things like 'jumping genes' and spontaneous amplification of bits of DNA are being discovered. Perhaps the permanence we attribute to DNA is also illusory. The other line is in epigenetics, the link between the genes and the organism. It is here that the mystery of transformation can be approached most directly.   CP

Bowler, P. J. (1984). *Evolution: The History of an Idea.*
Dawkins, R. (1996). *The Blind Watchmaker.*
Dennett, D. C. (1995). *Darwin's Dangerous Idea.*
Gould, S. J. (1977). *Ever Since Darwin.*
——(1980). *The Panda's Thumb: More Reflections on Natural History.*
Mayr, E., and Provine, W. B. (eds.) (1980). *The Evolutionary Synthesis: Perspectives on the Unification of Biology.*
Ridley, M. (1985). *The Problems of Evolution.*
——(1995). *The Red Queen: Sex and the Evolution of Human Nature.*
——(2003). *Nature vs Nurture: Genes, Experience, and What Makes Us Human.*

evolutionary psychology. A hybrid discipline that draws insights from modern evolutionary theory, cognitive psychology, anthropology, economics, and palaeoarcheology. The discipline rests on a foundation of core premises: (1) manifest behaviour depends on underlying psychological mechanisms, information-processing devices housed in the brain, in conjunction with the external and internal inputs that trigger their activation; (2) evolution by selection is the only known causal process capable of creating such complex organic mechanisms; (3) evolved psychological mechanisms are functionally specialized to solve adaptive problems that recurred for humans over deep evolutionary time; (4) human psychology consists of a large number of these functionally specialized evolved mechanisms, each sensitive to particular forms of contextual input, that get combined, coordinated, and integrated with each other to produce manifest behaviour.

1. Behaviour requires underlying psychological mechanisms
2. Evolution by selection is the causal process that creates psychological adaptations
3. Evolved psychological mechanisms are functionally specialized
4. The human mind contains a large number of evolved psychological mechanisms
5. Strategies for generating and testing evolutionary psychological hypotheses
6. Evolutionary psychological science

1. Behaviour requires underlying psychological mechanisms

Behaviour cannot be produced without psychological mechanisms, and all theories within psychology imply the existence of such mechanisms. If a man responds to a public insult with violence, but a woman does not; if a child cries to get its way, but an adult does not; and if a human gossips and a chimpanzee does not, it is because these different beings possess somewhat different psychological mechanisms. All psychological theories, even the most strongly environmental ones, imply the existence of psychological mechanisms.

2. Evolution by selection is the causal process that creates psychological adaptations

Only two theories retain currency for the origins of complex organic mechanisms: evolution by selection and creationism. Creationism, the idea that a supreme deity fashioned current organic mechanisms in all their glorious diversity, is regarded as a matter of religious belief. It leads to no specific scientific predictions and cannot predict or explain in a principled manner the organic forms that science has documented and discovered. Evolution by selection, in contrast, is a powerful and well-articulated theory of the dynamics of replicating entities that has successfully organized and explained thousands of diverse facts in a principled way. This theory unites all living forms into one grand tree of descent, accounts for the origin of new species, explains the modification in organic structures over time, and explains the functional quality of the component parts of those structures. Other causal processes in evolution, such as mutation and genetic drift, do not produce complex functional mechanisms in the absence of selection.

3. Evolved psychological mechanisms are functionally specialized

A central premise of evolutionary psychology is that the main non-arbitrary way to identify, describe, and understand psychological mechanisms is to articulate their functions—the specific adaptive problems they were designed to solve. Anatomists identify the liver, heart, and lungs as separate, although connected and integrated, mechanisms because they perform different functions—filter toxins, pump blood, and uptake oxygen, respectively. Understanding the nature of these mechanisms requires understanding their functions, the adaptive problems they were designed to solve. The concept of *function* has a rigorous definition that does not correspond to folk intuitions—it refers solely to the specific manner in which a mechanism or design feature contributed to its own propagation during the period in which it evolved. This ultimately reduces to the manner in which the mechanism or design feature contributed to fitness—the reproduction of the individual bearing the trait, or the reproduction of the individual's genetic relatives (Hamilton 1964). Evolutionary psychologists propose that the human mind consists primarily of functionally specialized psychological mechanisms, each designed to solve a specific adaptive problem. Cheater-detection

mechanisms function to solve the problem of free-riders in social exchange; mate preference mechanisms function to solve the problem of selecting reproductively valuable mates; kin-identification mechanisms function in part to solve the adaptive problem of allocating acts of altruism; and parental investment mechanisms function as devices to allocate resources to offspring (Buss 2004).

The adaptive problems that psychological mechanisms are designed to solve have several key features. First, they must have recurred over the long course of human evolutionary history. Evolution is a slow and iterative process, resulting in the gradual accumulation of adaptations design feature by design feature. Second, the past is the key to the present, so our current psychological adaptations were designed to solve problems in the ancestral past. There is no expectation that humans have evolved mechanisms to solve modern adaptive problems, such as avoiding dangerous electrical outlets or fast food that currently clogs arteries. Third, adaptive problems are those problems whose solution contributed to successful reproduction, either directly or indirectly. If successfully climbing a status hierarchy eventually leads to success in mating, which in turn leads to success in reproduction, adaptations for status striving can be selected, even though their contribution to reproduction is distal and occurs through intermediary routes. Since differential reproduction is the engine of evolution by selection, only those solutions that lead to an increment in reproduction, relative to alternative variants that exist in the population at that time, can evolve.

4. The human mind contains a large number of evolved psychological mechanisms

Detailed task analyses of adaptive problems have led to the empirical discovery of evolved psychological mechanisms in many domains, such as predator avoidance, food aversions, habitat selection, mate choice criteria, mate retention devices, reciprocal altruism, parental investment, kin altruism, coalition formation, and many others. Thus, the theory of the human mind depicted by evolutionary psychologists tends to be far more complex, containing many more mechanisms, than more traditional non-evolutionary theories of the mind. Although the criticism of lack of parsimony is sometimes levelled at this view of the mind, the criticism is misplaced. An adequate theory of the body requires postulating the existence of many anatomical and physiological mechanisms, and empirical evidence supports that view of the body. Evolutionary psychologists propose that the mind is no less complex, and have amassed considerable empirical evidence for many functional specializations that cannot be explained on any other view. Contrary to folk intuitions, the exquisite flexibility and context-sensitivity of human behaviour comes from having a large number of these functionally specialized mechanisms that are coordinated and integrated with each other, not from having a small number of general or 'plastic' psychological mechanisms.

5. Strategies for generating and testing evolutionary psychological hypotheses

Evolutionary psychologists use two basic strategies for generating and testing hypotheses about evolved psychological mechanisms. The first method starts with an adaptive problem, and generates hypotheses about an evolved psychological solution. As an example of this 'top-down' method, consider the adaptive problem of 'paternity uncertainty'. Because fertilization occurs internally within women, they are 100 per cent 'certain' that they are the mothers of their children. Putative fathers can never be sure, because another man might have inseminated his mate and hence fathered 'his' child. Evolutionary psychologists have hypothesized that male sexual jealousy is a psychological mechanism that has evolved as one possible solution to the adaptive problem of paternity uncertainty (Daly, Wilson, and Weghorst 1982). The prediction is that men's jealousy should focus heavily on cues to *sexual* infidelity. Women are also predicted to get jealous, but no woman has ever faced the adaptive problem of 'maternity uncertainty'. From an ancestral woman's perspective, however, if her mate committed an infidelity, she stood to lose her mate's investment, commitment, and resources—all of which could get channelled to rival women. The prediction, therefore, is that women's jealousy will focus more heavily on cues to the long-term diversion of her partner's commitments, such as the partner becoming emotionally involved with another woman. Although jealousy had been studied extensively prior to this sex-linked prediction, no previous social science theories had ever predicted that the sexes would differ in the weighting given to the triggers of jealousy. Although evolutionary psychologists are sometimes criticized for telling ad hoc just-so stories, this accusation cannot be reconciled with the actual scientific practice of evolutionary psychology, in which the theoretically anchored predictions precede the actual empirical tests of them, as in this example of jealousy.

After the predictions were generated, a variety of empirical studies were subsequently conducted to test the evolutionary psychological hypothesis. Consider the following scenario: *Imagine that your romantic partner became interested in someone else. What would upset or distress you more? (A) Imagining your partner having sexual intercourse with that other person, or (B) Imagining your partner becoming emotionally involved with that other person.* In contrast to the dozens of previous studies that had yielded no sex differences in jealousy, this dilemma produced large sex differences. Whereas both events are upsetting to both

sexes, the majority of men (roughly 60 per cent) indicated that they would be more distressed by the sexual infidelity. Only 15 per cent of the women, in contrast, indicated that they would be more distressed by the sexual infidelity, with the overwhelming majority declaring greater distress about the emotional infidelity (Buss 2003).

These sex differences have been replicated using physiological measures. When imagining a partner's sexual infidelity, men show greater distress as measured by increased electrodermal activity, electromyographic activity, and heart rate. These sex differences have been replicated across cultures as diverse as Germany, the Netherlands, Korea, and Japan. They have survived well when pitted against competing non-evolutionary hypotheses designed post hoc to account for the sex difference. And many independent researchers have replicated the findings using a variety of physiological and psychological methods (Pietrzak et al. 2002). In sum, sex differences in the activators of jealousy circuits were discovered using the first method of evolutionary hypothesis generation—starting with an adaptive problem and making predictions about a possible evolved solution.

The second method consists of starting with observed psychological phenomena, and generating hypotheses about what adaptive problem they might have evolved to solve. As an example, evolutionary psychologists started with the observation that women and men seemed to be very selective in their choice of marriage partners (Ridley 1995). Mainstream non-evolutionary psychologists, of course, had also observed this phenomenon, but none had developed hypotheses about what functions they might have evolved to solve. Evolutionary psychologists predicted that women's mate preferences might have evolved to solve the problem of securing resourceful mates to invest in their children, whereas men's mate preferences might have evolved to solve the problem of selecting fertile mates. These predictions were then tested in a study involving 37 different cultures, ranging from the Zulu tribe in South Africa to coastal-dwelling Australians (Buss 2003). The results confirmed predictions generated from these hypotheses—across cultures, women expressed a greater preference for mates who were high in status, ambition, industriousness, and financial prospects, whereas men expressed a greater preference for mates who were young and physically attractive, two known cues to a woman's fertility. No prior non-evolutionary theories of mating had predicted either the sex differences or their cross-cultural universality.

These two methods have been used to discover a host of interesting psychological phenomena, including: patterns of fears and phobia, particular mechanisms of colour vision, universal adaptations to terrestrial living, beliefs and desires about the minds of other people, patterns of step-child abuse, causes of marital dissolution, shifts in mate preferences depending on temporal context, sex differences in sexual fantasy, patterns of mate guarding and mate retention, sex differences in risk taking, superior spatial location memory in women, mechanisms of cheater detection in social exchange, patterns of sexual harassment, patterns of altruism and cooperation, and cross-cultural variations in patterns of food sharing (see Barkow et al. 1992 and Buss 2004 for extensive summaries).

6. Evolutionary psychological science

Scientific success in uncovering the mysteries of life has been based on three critical foundations—mechanism, natural selection, and historicity (Williams 1992). Since the cognitive revolution, psychologists have moved away from behaviourism's unworkable anti-mentalism, making it respectable to study information-processing mechanisms inside the head. Evolutionary psychology integrates natural selection and historicity with modern cognitive formulations of information-processing mechanisms. The previous neglect of evolution by natural selection has led psychologists to ignore the adaptive functions of mechanisms and hence has impeded the quest to unravel the mysteries of why these mechanisms exist at all and why they exist in the particular forms that they do.

A critical task for this new psychological science will be the identification of the key adaptive problems that humans confronted repeatedly over evolutionary history. We have barely scratched the surface by identifying some of the problems most obviously and plausibly linked with survival and reproduction. Most adaptive problems remain unexplored, most psychological solutions undiscovered. Evolutionary psychology provides the conceptual tools for emerging from the fragmented state of current psychological science. It provides the keys to unlocking the mysteries of where we came from, how we arrived at out current state, and the mechanisms of mind that define what it means to be human.

Charles Darwin (1859) ended his classic book, *On the Origin of Species*, with this prediction: 'In the distant future I see open fields for far more important researches. Psychology will be based on a new foundation, that of the necessary acquirement of each mental power and capacity by gradation.' Evolutionary psychology, emerging more than 130 years after *Origin*, represents the fulfilment of Darwin's vision.   DMB

Barkow, J., Cosmides, L., and Tooby, J. (eds.) (1992). *The Adapted Mind: Evolutionary Psychology and the Generation of Culture.*

Buss, D. M. (2003). *The Evolution of Desire: Strategies of Human Mating* (rev. edn.).

——(2004). *Evolutionary Psychology: The New Science of the Mind*, (2nd edn.).

Daly, M., Wilson, M., and Weghorst, S. J. (1982). 'Male sexual jealousy'. *Ethology and Sociobiology*, 3.

Darwin, C. (1859). *On the Origin of Species by Means of Natural Selection.*

Hamilton, W. D. (1964). 'The genetical evolution of social behavior. I and II'. *Journal of Theoretical Biology*, 7.

Pietrzak, R., Laird, J. D., Stevens, D. A., and Thompson, N. S. (2002). 'Sex differences in human jealousy: a coordinated study of forced-choice, continuous rating-scale, and physiological responses on the same subjects'. *Evolution and Human Behavior*, 23.

Ridley, M. (1995). *The Red Queen: Sex and the Evolution of Human Nature.*

Williams, G. C. (1992). *Natural Selection.*

evolution of the ear. There are several different designs of vertebrate ears. The evolution of hearing organs has progressed along at least three parallel evolutionary pathways, with convergent functional results. Three hundred and fifty million years of terrestrial evolution have produced hearing architectures that include mammals as one of the many examples. What can be seen in the structure of the human inner ear is a consequence of selective pressures throughout mammalian and pre-mammalian evolution. The hearing mechanisms used by birds, by reptiles, and by placental mammals differ but how such differences have arisen is a matter of reconstructing the fossil record and observing the physiology of hearing in living mammalian and non-mammalian species. The fossil traces can only provide information about the imprint that the soft structures leave in the bone. The forking evolutionary path that documents the development of subtle structural changes in the tissues within the hearing organs has perished.

Since the beginning of the great mammalian radiation over 70 million years ago, it is clear that there must have been further significant improvements in the design and abilities of hearing function. This has led to the astonishing ultrasonic hearing abilities of bats and whales, the spectacular hearing sensitivity of the cat family, and, in primates, the evolution of an inner ear that allows the resolution of complex patterning of frequency and timing information that underlies human language.

The mammalian hearing organ, the cochlea, is a fluid-filled tube divided down its length by a membrane (the basilar membrane) which vibrates in a pattern uniquely determined by the frequencies in the incoming sound. Sound vibration entering through the ear canal is communicated to the cochlea by a cluster of three delicate bony ossicles in the middle ear. This arrangement is an elaboration of structures found in pre-mammalian species where evolution of yet more primitive structures has led to inner ears designed to detect sounds carried through the ground. In living species of amphibia a structure in the inner ear, the saccule, acts like an auditory organ. Frogs, for example, use the saccules to detect the source of a sound by positioning their front legs to triangulate from where the sound is coming. In the fossil traces of the middle ear, many of the larger reptiles had massive ossicular stapes; it seems likely that the dinosaurs also heard by detecting their own body movements. In other vertebrates, including mammals, the saccule has been relegated to a vestibular organ associated with maintaining balance.

With a few exceptions, the hearing of non-mammalian species is optimized to detect acoustic frequencies below about 2 kHz. The neural mechanism by which this comes about is known in some reptiles, birds, and amphibia. The mechanism depends upon the individual hair cells (see HAIR CELLS) in the hearing organs acting as selective filters, each of which relays information about different frequencies to the brain. In these hair cells, conducting ion channels are built into the cell membrane to ensure that the hair cells resonate electrically at only one frequency. In mammalian species, and in those animals where high frequency hearing is critical, frequencies are selected not by the electrical properties of the individual hair cells but by the intrinsic mechanical properties of the whole cochlea. In these cases, the mechanical excitation pattern activates appropriate subpopulations of hair cells (see HEARING). In the mammalian cochlea it is believed that the separation of frequency information is carried out only by the mechanics of the cochlea fluids and the basilar membrane. This is similar to the mechanism proposed by *Helmholtz in 1862 and subsequently elaborated by *Békésy in the 1930s.

The earliest mammals, coexisting with dinosaurs, probably occupied and exploited nocturnal niches. This places great emphasis on good olfaction and the ability to identify the source of a sound accurately with no visual cues. Animals with small heads also need to detect sounds at higher frequencies for only then will the acoustic shadow of the head produce a detectable interaural difference in sound intensity. Directional clues can also be enhanced by skin folds around the ear canal and these must have become the outer ear (pinna).

Another evolutionary change that favoured the direct detection of airborne sound was the reorganization of the body plan to gain mobility. As the animal develops longer legs less sound conduction passes through the limbs. The compensating factor was the evolution of an efficient transmission pathway between the outer and inner ears. The emergence of effective middle-ear structures, coupling sound to the cochlear fluids, facilitated the sensing of airborne sound. In the fossil record there is evidence that the middle-ear bones have indeed changed, evolving out of the jaw bones as the jaws themselves became smaller, lighter, and more loosely coupled to the skull.

Reduction in body size and an efficient temperature regulation system to match a nocturnal lifestyle seem also likely to have favoured the conserved mechanical design of cochlea that we find in mammals. The coiled structure of the cochlear duct is a uniquely mammalian development. In the nearest mammalian relatives (e.g. in monotremes) and in non-mammals the cochlea is straight. The coiling is not important for the physics of sound propagation in the cochlear fluids, but it does provide for an efficient and compact packing of the duct in the skull.

Surprisingly, the size of the mammalian cochlea does not vary as much between different species as would be naively expected. The basic structure of the cochlea has not changed with the diversity of modern mammals nor does the cochlea scale change significantly with brain size or body mass. Excluding specialized hearing (in bats, for example), the acoustic range in modern mammals extends over four to nine octaves when measured as in the range of a musical instrument. Although the lowest frequencies detectable by the mammalian ear do vary between species, the biophysics of cochlear mechanics requires, very approximately, a fixed length of basilar membrane per octave analysed. Thus, this membrane in a mouse is about 10 mm long and occupies the volume of a small lentil, yet in an elephant, the membrane is only six times longer. In the human inner ear the basilar membrane is 34 mm long and is coiled into a cochlea the size of a baked bean. JA

existentialism. Several central themes characterize the principal writings of the existentialists from the 1920s to the 1940s. (i) The very name existentialism indicates that existence, properly speaking, *belongs only to human beings*; in Heidegger's famous phrase, human being is the only being for whom being is an issue. (ii) There are various 'states' in which humans' attunement to their world is manifest, such as anxiety, boredom, and joyousness. (iii) In *Sartre's famous phrase, 'human existence precedes essence', that is, an individual's essence, his 'real' nature, is not fixed in advance; rather, it is established through his or her own non-trivial choices. (iv) An individual can 'fall away' from the difficult task of choosing him- or herself and become lost in the public, the herd, or the 'they'. (v) Only human beings are always in the process of becoming, they are always ahead of themselves, and oriented towards the future.

Conscious being is not itself given as just another part of the natural world, one that must be made sense of; it is the being who *gives sense* to its experiences of the world and other subjects. As conscious beings humans are different from other (sentient) beings in that some things *make a difference for them*. Humans' unique mode of being is signalled by the term 'existence' which literally means 'to stand out from'; humans stand out from everything else, and their interest in things makes these things stand out from the background. Their forward-directed projects drive their yet-to-be-filled lives. Only through this temporal dimension, the horizon of one's projects, can possible options become one's own actualities.

The existentialists were devoted to the demolition of dualist oppositions, such as that between the mind and body. On their view, experience of the 'outer' world is mediated by a unique kind of body, the living body or flesh; this is not itself reducible to purely physical properties. Mindful behaviour is exhibited by the whole body's actions, i.e. speech and gestures which show sense-giving and sense-making activities. Also, the opposition between 'inside' and 'outside': it is *one* thing that has an inside and an outside, not one thing on *this* side and another thing on *that* side. My mind is not located inside my body, nor my thoughts in my mind, in the way that water fills a bucket. My skin surface is a fleshy membrane through which my encounter with the world takes place. Things and persons and values become parts of me through my comportment towards them; not real object-like parts, but vital moments of my own self-chosen life. Merleau-Ponty said, 'Our own body is in the world as the heart is in the organism; it keeps the visible spectacle constantly alive, it breathes life into it and sustains it inwardly, and with it forms a system.' Prior to the existentialists the subject was constituted by a unique point of view: one that is private, privileged, and incorrigible; objects are 'over-against' the subject. For the existentialists subjective features permeate the objective world; subject-endowed meanings are found everywhere. In 'falling away' subjects turn themselves and others into objects and hence reinforce the philosophical notion of a basic opposition between mind and world. PSM

Cooper, D. E. (1999). *Existentialism: A Reconstruction* (2nd edn.).
Guignon, C., and Pereboom, D. (eds.) (1996). *Existentialism: Basic Writings*.
MacDonald, P. S. (ed.) (2001). *The Existentialist Reader*.

external world. The very use of the phrase 'the *external* world' suggests that there may be something problematic about the existence and nature of the reality 'out there', beyond what is immediately given in subjective experience. This way of viewing the matter is probably due to *Descartes, whose philosophical starting point was his conscious awareness of his own existence as a thinking thing; he was then faced with the difficulty of moving on from this subjective starting point to conclusions about the existence and nature of the physical universe. Another source of the idea of the external world as problematic is the notion of a 'veil of perception' between our subjective experience and the world: if we are directly aware only of our own impressions (*Hume) or sense data (*Russell and others), then the problem seems to arise of how we know that these immediate objects-of-experience resemble anything in the 'real world' outside us.

Twentieth-century philosophers became increasingly dubious about the genuineness of many of these supposed problems about the 'external world'. First it was argued that the idea of a 'veil of perception' rests on a philosophical confusion: the fact that we do not always see things as they are does not license the inference that all we ever see are subjective appearances. Second, the arguments of *Wittgenstein suggested that the traditional, solipsistic presentation of these problems ('How do I, the lone isolated conscious subject, know that an external world exists?') may be incoherent. According to Wittgenstein's celebrated 'private language' argument (see WITTGENSTEIN'S PHILOSOPHY OF LANGUAGE), the use of the very linguistic concepts necessary for the raising of such questions already presupposes the existence of an objective world of public rules, and public criteria for the application of terms.

See also APPARENT; BERKELEY ON PERCEPTION.

extrasensory perception (ESP). The term extrasensory perception, or ESP, was coined in 1934 by J. B. Rhine, who, with his wife Louisa, founded the first parapsychology laboratory in the world at Duke University in North Carolina. His definitions of terms are still used today. Paranormal (or psi) phenomena are divided into two classes: ESP and PK (*psychokinesis). ESP is defined as the ability to acquire information without the use of the recognized senses, and includes telepathy (the information comes from another person), clairvoyance (the information comes from a distant object or event), and precognition (the information is about the future).

1. The history of ESP research
2. Modern parapsychology

1. The history of ESP research
Scientific study of paranormal communication began in the late 19th century. In 1882 the Society for Psychical Research was founded 'to examine without prejudice or prepossession and in a scientific spirit those faculties of man, real or supposed, which appear to be inexplicable on any generally recognized hypothesis'. The founders established committees to investigate thought transference (i.e. telepathy), mesmerism (or hypnosis), apparitions and haunted houses, and the physical phenomena of mediumship.

In 1886 the 'Census of Hallucinations' was published. Seventeen thousand people were asked whether they had ever seen or felt something, or heard a voice, that was not due to any physical cause. Of special interest were hallucinations of people occurring within twelve hours either way of that person's death. These occurred far more often than expected by chance and seemed to be evidence for telepathic communication with the dying.

In experiments on thought transference an 'agent' typically drew a picture and a 'percipient' tried to reproduce it. Although impressive results were obtained, many important factors were not controlled. For example, the agent chose the target. This meant that if the agent and percipient knew each other, or were affected by the same cues around them, they might easily think of similar things. With an effectively infinite number of possible targets, differences in popularity of targets could also bias the results. Later experiments used playing cards or numbers as targets, with random selection of targets. This meant that statistical methods for evaluating the results could be developed, laying the foundation for Rhine's work and modern experiments in parapsychology.

At the start of parapsychology, Louisa Rhine concentrated on collecting accounts of spontaneous cases, while J. B. worked largely in the laboratory. A simple set of cards was developed, originally called Zener cards (after their designer) but now called ESP cards, bearing the symbols circle, square, wavy lines, cross, and star—with five of each in a pack of 25. In a typical telepathy experiment the 'sender' looked at a series of cards while the 'receiver' guessed the symbols. For clairvoyance the pack of cards was hidden from everyone while the receiver guessed. For precognition the order of the cards was determined only after the guesses were made. Rhine used ordinary people as subjects and claimed that, on average, they did significantly better than chance expectation.

In all such experiments the order of the cards must be random so that hits are not obtained through systematic biases or prior knowledge. In Rhine's early experiments the cards were shuffled by hand, then by machine. Later, random number tables were used and nowadays computers or truly random sources such as radioactive decay are used for randomization.

Rhine's controversial 1934 book, *Extrasensory Perception*, led others to criticize his methods and try to repeat his findings. Most failed, including the London mathematician Samuel Soal, who tried unsuccessfully for five years. Then, after a reanalysis, he found that one subject was apparently performing precognition. In the early 1950s, further tests with this subject, under tightly controlled conditions, gave astronomically significant results, convincing many people that Rhine was right after all. Accusations and counter-claims abounded until, in 1978, it was finally proved that Soal had cheated. However, many people had been convinced by these results for nearly 30 years.

Meanwhile, other parapsychologists found that some subjects scored below chance (psi-missing), scores tended to decline during testing (the 'decline effect'), and people who believed in psi, called 'sheep', scored better than those who did not, or 'goats' (the sheep–goat effect). However, none of these effects proved easy to replicate and

card-guessing experiments are extremely tedious to do. In recent years, therefore, parapsychologists have turned to other methods, notably free-response ESP tests.

2. Modern parapsychology

In free response ESP tests the receiver can respond as they like, for example by describing their guesses, or writing or drawing pictures, but then they are shown a pool of possible targets and must, on the basis of their guesses, select which they think was the target. This method has the advantage of providing rich responses while keeping randomized target selection and statistical validity.

One of the most commonly reported forms of spontaneous ESP is precognitive or telepathic dreams and in the 1960s parapsychologists began testing dream telepathy with free-response methods. The receiver slept in a laboratory while a sender looked at a randomly chosen target picture or series of pictures. However, the experiments were very time consuming and other methods were soon developed, including the 'ganzfeld' technique. In a psi-ganzfeld experiment the receiver relaxes for half an hour or more with white noise playing through headphones, and halved ping-pong balls taped over their eyes to provide a uniform visual field (the ganzfeld). Meanwhile a sender looks at one of four pictures or videotapes in a distant room. After emerging from the ganzfeld the receiver is shown the four possible targets and asked which one most closely matches the ganzfeld experiences.

By 1985 many such experiments had been done and, in a much publicized debate, parapsychologists used 'meta-analysis', which pools the results of many experiments, to claim a consistent effect and a repeatable experiment. However the critics pointed to experimental error, fraud, selective reporting of data, and non-random selection of targets as explanations. In an attempt to settle the dispute critics and parapsychologists came together to decide on criteria for valid experimental designs and developed the autoganzfeld—an automated technique for running experiments. Autoganzfeld studies were initially carried out by Charles Honorton at Princeton, and then at Edinburgh University. The results seemed to confirm the findings of the original meta-analysis and also suggested better results with subjects who knew each other, had previous ganzfeld experience or experience with meditation, and were artists or musicians. Scores were higher with dynamic targets, such as video clips, than with static targets. These results were published with a new meta-analysis in 1994. Once again critics found serious faults with many of the experiments and with the meta-analysis itself. It remains unclear whether the ganzfeld method really can provide evidence for ESP or not.

Another free-response method is remote viewing. In early studies one person travelled to a randomly chosen distant location while another stayed in the laboratory, trying to visualize the location. As with ganzfeld, the subject, or an independent judge, then matched up the reported experiences with several possible locations. Early experiments, although successful, were criticized for allowing clues such as the weather to influence the results. In 1995 the American CIA released reports of more than twenty years of government research into remote viewing. They concluded that a small effect had been demonstrated in the laboratory but that it was not useful for intelligence purposes.

Other ESP research includes telepathy in twins, ESP in young children, the use of hypnosis or relaxation to improve ESP, detection of physiological changes, correlations with geomagnetic variations, and tests of psychic claimants. After more than a century of research many of the most basic questions about ESP remain unanswered. There is no good evidence that ESP ability reliably correlates with age, sex, imagery ability, fantasy proneness, childhood history, or personality variables. There is no consensus about which kinds of target are most effective, what state the participants should be in, or which experimental methods work best.

Meanwhile, ostensibly paranormal experiences and belief in ESP are widespread. Surveys in many countries show that over 50 per cent of the population believes in the paranormal, especially telepathy. Believers are more often female, have higher scores on tests of temporal lobe epileptic signs, have poorer reasoning skills, and show certain kinds of cognitive bias more than non-believers. Some psychologists suggest that such biases lead people to misinterpret normal events as paranormal.

Scientists are sometimes accused of rejecting paranormal claims out of hand or even conspiring to suppress them. In fact, if ESP really existed it would be of enormous importance to science. Thousands of experiments have therefore been carried out and many scientists involved. However, it has proved extremely hard to get positive results, let alone develop and test theories, and very little progress has been made. ESP is either extremely rare and elusive, or it does not exist.   SJB

Bem, D. J., and Honorton, C. (1994). 'Does psi exist? Replicable evidence for an anomalous process of information transfer'. *Psychological Bulletin*, 115.

Irwin, H. J. (1999). *An Introduction to Parapsychology* (3rd edn.).

Marks, D. (2000). *The Psychology of the Psychic*. (2nd edn.).

Stein, G. (ed.) (1996). *The Encyclopedia of the Paranormal*.

extraterrestrial intelligence. It was once believed that the earth lay in the centre of the universe, with the entire sky revolving round it. We know better today. The earth is an ordinary planet, the sun is an ordinary star, and our galaxy, with its hundred thousand million stars, is an ordinary galaxy. It has been found that many stars are attended by planets, and it is therefore logical to assume that 'other earths' must be common; it follows that life is likely to be widespread. This view is not accepted by all authorities, however, and at the moment we have no proof that life exists anywhere except on the earth. If it does exist, does this indicate that there may be intelligent civilizations—and, if so, will they resemble our own?

The solar system. In the solar system, only the earth is suitable for advanced life of the kind we can understand. It is just possible that primitive organisms may exist on Mars or the large satellites of Jupiter, but certainly there can be nothing more. We cannot rule out the possibility that life appeared on Mars, only to die out when conditions there became hostile, but again there is no proof, and we will not find out one way or the other until we can obtain samples from the planet and analyse them in our laboratories. It has been said that if the earth were not suitable for us, we would not be here—we would be somewhere else.

However, if we consider an earthlike planet orbiting a solar-type star—and there must be many of these—it is not unreasonable to suggest that life may have appeared and evolved just as it has done on our own world. Our civilization is only a few thousand years old; a civilization that is older than this may well be far more advanced than ours. On the other hand, there is always the possibility that a civilization may have destroyed itself by warfare, as we have been in danger of doing: in fact the threat is still with us at the present time.

Alien life? All the evidence indicates that life, wherever it appears, must be carbon based. If this is wrong, then much of our modern science is also wrong, which is hard to believe. Extraterrestrial intelligence may therefore not be wildly different from ours, though there will certainly be important variations—particularly with civilizations on planets which are markedly more massive or less massive than the earth, or which have more extreme climates. But when we consider totally alien life forms, we are entering the realm of science fiction, so that speculations are not only endless but also pointless. We can at once discount all claims of 'alien contact' and UFOs. If there are many advanced civilizations in the galaxy it is not impossible that they could visit earth, but there is not the slightest evidence that they have done so as yet.

Possibilities of contact. There is no prospect of achieving interstellar travel by any methods available to us at the moment. Even if we could travel at 99.9 per cent of the speed of light, a journey would last for years; the nearest stars which are of solar type, and which may well be planetary centres, are more than ten light years away. Exotic methods of travel, such as space warps, time warps, wormholes, and thought travel, may become practicable in the future, but again there is no point in speculating. We need a fundamental 'breakthrough', which may come this year, next year, in 100 years, 1,000 years—or never.

Remember, however, that science fiction does often turn into science fact, and television would have been regarded as sheer science fiction not so very long ago.

SETI. By now SETI, the Search for Extra-Terrestrial Intelligence, is being taken very seriously indeed. The only hope lies in picking up a radio message from afar. Obviously any message would have to be based upon mathematics (and after all, we did not invent mathematics; we merely discovered it). The procedure is to 'listen out' at various selected wavelengths which will be familiar to any other civilizations in the galaxy. As long ago as 1991 the International Astronomical Union laid down the official procedures to be followed by any researcher who does manage to establish contact, and at least it is reasonable to assume that a civilization of our type will be able to interpret a mathematical message.

Dangers of contact. It has been claimed that attempts to contact extraterrestrial civilizations are unwise, because of the fear that we might attract unwelcome attention from hostile beings. Yet this seems unreasonable, for two reasons. First, our presence will be known already. If we agree that full-scale broadcasting began around 1920, we are 'radio noisy' to any civilizations within about 80 light years of us (the various spacecraft now on their way out of the solar system will not be within range of any other star for an immensely long period, and moreover the chances of their being identified are vanishingly small). Secondly, any civilization capable of achieving interstellar travel will be far more rational than we are. As was said by the American astronomer Percival Lowell almost a century ago, 'War is the survival among us from savage times, and affects now the boyish and unthinking element of the nation. It is something a people outgrow'.

Effects on ourselves. If we could contact an extraterrestrial civilization, the effects upon our thinking would indeed be profound; we would have to adjust to different characteristics, different philosophies, and different religions. One day it may happen, and all in all it would be strange if we were unable to recognize any form of extraterrestrial intelligence that we might encounter.   PM

Boss, A. (1998). *Looking for Earths.*

Crosswell, K. (1997). *Planet Quest.*

Drake, F., and Sobel, D. (1993). *Is Anyone Out There?*

McDonough, T. (1987). *The Search for Extraterrestrial Intelligence.*

Moore, P. (2000). *The Data Book of Astronomy.*

Swift, D. (ed.) (1990). *SETI Pioneers.*

extroversion/introversion. The terms 'extroversion' and 'introversion' entered popular use in England, with pretty much their current meaning, during the 19th century; they can be found in several popular novels, referring respectively to sociable, impulsive, carefree behaviour, and unsociable, responsible, thoughtful behaviour. C. G. *Jung popularized the terms on the continent, and linked

them with a very complex and difficult psychoanalytic set of theories; these theories are not now widely entertained, and the Jungian meaning of the terms is only accepted by a few followers of his. Jung suggested that there were links, in neurosis, between extroversion and hysterical symptomatology, and introversion and depressive/*anxiety symptomatology; this connection has been verified by later workers. The behavioural patterns which underlie the notion of extroversion/introversion were of course observed long before the 19th century; they go back at least to *Hippocrates and *Galen, the Greek physician who elaborated the earlier system of the four temperaments (choleric, melancholic, phlegmatic, sanguine) which has lasted in some form or other for 2,000 years, and is still popularly used by many people.

The relation of this system to modern conceptions of personality was first suggested by Wilhelm *Wundt, the founder of modern psychology, just before the turn of the century. The four temperaments, until then, had been conceived of as qualitatively different types; you belonged to one or the other of these groups, and you could not show traits and qualities belonging to more than one group. This is patently untrue; many people do seem to belong to one or other of these types (otherwise the system would not have survived), but equally obviously others do not. Wundt pointed out that the melancholic and the choleric types had something in common that set them off against the phlegmatic and the sanguine types, namely a strong emotional reaction; this suggests a dimension of personality ranging from high to low emotional reactivity, or 'emotionality' (also often called 'neuroticism' or 'anxiety' by modern psychologists). Equally, the choleric and sanguine types have something in common which sets them off from the melancholic and phlegmatic types. Wundt called this quality 'changeableness', but we would nowadays call it extroversion, as opposed to introversion. Wundt was very perceptive: changeableness is indeed one of the most characteristic traits of the extrovert—but it is not the only one, and consequently a less specific name for this personality dimension was required.

With this important change from four entirely discrete personality types to two separate dimensions of personality, with individuals located at any point on each scale, Wundt rescued the ancient scheme from oblivion and made it capable of reflecting the complexity of real life. The four Greek temperaments lie in the four quadrants generated by these two intersecting dimensions of personality. Melancholics are introverted and emotional (Jung's anxious and depressed neurotics), while cholerics are extroverted and emotional (Jung's hysterics, and, as modern research has shown, psychopaths and criminals as well). Phlegmatics are introverted and stable, while sanguinics are extroverted and stable. We can now measure the degree of emotionality/stability a person shows, or the degree of extroversion or introversion, and we can show that on both these scales the distribution of people is roughly in line with the Gaussian probability curve, i.e. most in the middle, with fewer and fewer towards the extremes. We do not, then, divide the population into extroverts and introverts: we measure the degree of extroversion or introversion shown, and allocate the person in question to some place along the continuum—very much as we would do if we measured his height, or weight, or *intelligence. When in what follows we speak of extroverts or introverts, we mean people falling towards one or the other end of this distribution; those in the middle are usually referred to as ambiverts.

Two problems are raised by the postulation of a concept such as extroversion/introversion. The first is a *descriptive* one: is it in fact true that the traits postulated to characterize the extrovert, or the introvert, actually occur together? This is fundamentally a statistical problem, concerned with correlations. We can rate the degree of sociability, impulsiveness, changeableness, talkativeness, outgoingness, activity, liveliness, excitability, optimism, etc. of a few hundred persons, chosen at random, and determine whether all these traits are positively correlated—i.e. whether a person showing one of these traits is also likely to show the others. We would not expect perfect agreement, of course, but we should expect reasonable correlation between these traits if the concept of extroversion were to have much meaning. Hundreds of empirical studies have shown that these various traits do indeed hang together to a degree that exceeds chance by a large amount; furthermore, these studies have demonstrated this general cohesion between traits for adults and children, men and women, different social classes, and different nations (including Japanese, Indian, European, and American). There is little doubt that descriptively the personality dimension of extroversion/introversion is amply supported by relevant research.

The second problem is the *causal* one—given that some people are extroverted, others introverted, others ambivert, can we say why these personality differences occur? The evidence suggests that genetic causes are very strongly implicated: something like two-thirds of the total variation in extroversion/introversion is probably due to heredity, with only one-third left for environmental causes. There is no evidence of dominance in the hereditary determination; this suggests that from the evolutionary point of view neither extroversion nor introversion is more successful in adapting to environmental *stress. But this answer is unsatisfactory: heredity cannot determine behaviour, only structure. Underlying extroverted or introverted behaviour there must be some physiologico-anatomical structure, presumably in the central nervous system, which mediates these personality differences.

Recent experimental work has suggested that this is indeed so, and that extroversion is linked with resting states of low cortical *arousal, introversion with resting states of high cortical arousal. At first sight this would seem to be the wrong way round; one would have thought that the active, uninhibited extrovert would be the person with high cortical arousal. However, the main function of the cortex is one of inhibiting lower centres; effective functioning of the cortex, due to high arousal, produces inhibited (introverted) behaviour. In the same way alcohol, a depressant drug which lowers the arousal of the cortical centres, produces extroverted, uninhibited behaviour; it frees the lower centres from cortical control. Cortical arousal in turn is determined by the so-called ascending reticular activating system, a group of cells lying in the brain stem and responsible for reacting to incoming sensory messages by alerting the cortex so that it may be better able to deal with these messages. Here, theory suggests, is the causal locus of extroverted and introverted behaviour.

The evidence for this theory is by now quite strong. Part of it is direct, based on electroencephalographic measurement of resting level brainwaves and other psychophysiological measurements of arousal (see ELECTROENCEPHALOGRAPHY). Part of it is indirect, based on laboratory investigations of certain psychological functions which are known to be determined in part by arousal level (conditioning, sensory thresholds, habituation, etc.). These studies are as yet not conclusive, but they do on the whole suggest that this theory is along the right lines. Unfortunately it is still impossible to record directly from the ascending reticular activating system in humans, so that the part played by this system must rest on work done on cats and other animal preparations in the laboratory; the evidence for the cortical part of the theory is much stronger. Certainly no other aspect of personality is as widely studied, or has given rise to such clear-cut theories and experimental investigation, as has extroversion/introversion; we probably know more about this trait (or system of traits) than about any other.   HJE

A general survey of the field is offered in Eysenck, H. J. (ed.), *Readings in Extraversion–Introversion*, 3 vols. (1970). The genetic and physiological theories of extroversion are discussed in detail, together with the evidence, in Eysenck, H. J., *Biological Basis of Personality* (1967). Alternative theories are considered in Nebylitsyn, V. D., and Gray, J. A. (eds.), *Biological Bases of Individual Behavior* (1972). A more general approach will be found in Brody, N., *Personality: Research and Theory* (1972). Jung's theory is described in detail by Hall, C. S., and Lindzey, G., *Theories of Personality* (1968). For the most recent summary of the evidence, see Eysenck, H. J., and Eysenck, M. W., *Personality and Individual Differences* (1985).

eye contact (or 'mutual gaze'). Eye contact occurs when two people look each other in the area of the eyes simultaneously. During conversation, two people seated 2 metres apart will each look at each other for about 60 per cent of the time (with wide individual differences), and there will be eye contact for about 30 per cent of the time. This other-directed gaze consists of glances of 1–5 seconds in length, with mutual glances of about 1 second. Each glance in turn consists of a number of fixations of 0.3 of a second on different parts of the other's face, especially eyes and mouth, linked by saccadic movements; there are repeated cycles of such fixations. Eye contact and glances can be recorded by observers who activate an interaction recorder, either observing directly or using a video recording. The sequence of fixations requires an eye-movement recorder.

Eyes are responded to as a social signal by animals, some of whom have developed eye spots as a threat signal. Human infants respond to their mother's eyes and establish eye contact by the fourth week of life—which may be partly an innate response—and gaze plays a central role in the earliest sequences of social behaviour with the mother (see INFANCY, MIND IN). These gaze phenomena occur in all cultures, though they vary in the levels of gaze which are regarded as appropriate, and gaze may acquire special meanings, as in the case of the Evil Eye.

Gaze acts as a social signal: for example, if A likes B he will look at B a lot, and B correctly decodes this in terms of liking. In this situation, gaze is rewarding, and results in favourable evaluation of the person gazing. The basic effect of gaze is to show attention and to increase arousal, but the meaning can vary with the situation and facial expression—from threat to sexual attraction. Eye contact is experienced as a special form of intimacy. Gaze is used and received as a signal for sexual attraction; couples who are in love have a high level of mutual gaze; girls enhance the stimulus properties of their eyes by cosmetics and dark glasses. Pupil dilatation acts in a similar way, and can be produced artificially by drops of belladonna. The eyebrow flash is used in courting in many parts of the world.

The pattern of glances is closely coordinated with speech. Interactors look nearly twice as much while listening as when talking; they look during grammatical breaks and at the ends of utterances, and look away at the beginning of utterances. Glances act as signals of attention or emphasis, help to indicate the grammatical structure, and as 'terminal gazes' are one of the signals announcing the ends of utterances, but the same glances are also used to collect visual information. When relevant objects of mutual interest are present, a lot of gaze is deflected to them; there is more gaze at others when they are further away, less when intimate topics are discussed. Gaze plays an important role in greetings, farewells, and other ritualized social sequences.

There are large individual differences in amount of gaze. Autistic children scarcely gaze at all, for reasons not yet understood; *schizophrenics have a low level of gaze when talking to psychologists but not when talking to each other; depressives look little and look downwards; some neurotics avert gaze and some stare; extroverts gaze more than introverts (see EXTROVERSION/INTROVERSION), females more than males, children and adults more than adolescents. Assertive or powerful people look as much while speaking as while listening. These findings help to explain the reasons behind gaze—it is a product of affiliative and other motivations—and various kinds of gaze aversion.

It is now realized that gaze plays a central part in social behaviour: the perception of others' reactions is essential, and gaze is necessary for this to occur. While the primary purpose of gaze is to collect visual information, it has acquired meaning as a social signal—in the course of evolution for animals, but mainly by learning for humans. While gaze is important for animals as well as humans, in human social behaviour it forms part of an intricate sequence in which it is closely coordinated with speech.

See also BODY LANGUAGE; FACE-TO-FACE COMMUNICATION; FACIAL EXPRESSIONS: ORIGINS. MA

Argyle, M., and Cook, M. (1975). *Gaze and Mutual Gaze.*
Emery, N. J. (2000). 'The eyes have it: the neuroethology, function and evolution of social gaze'. *Neuroscience and Biobehavioral Reviews*, 24.

eye movements. The eyes move incessantly throughout our lives. These eye movements reflect our active exploration and monitoring of the visual environment.

While looking at a picture, the eyes make fast ballistic movements, called *saccades*. Saccades are followed by *fixations* when the eyes are stationary. Fixations stay at one location for only a short time, somewhere between one-tenth and three-tenths of a second, before another saccade is generated to a new location. The eyes gather little useful visual information during a saccade, so patterns of fixation over time indicate the way the eyes are sampling the visual environment. Saccades are required to sample the visual world because our visual ability is not the same across the visual field. Vision is better in the centre (or *fovea*) than out in the peripheral part of the visual field.

Saccade and fixation behaviour is one of the fundamental ways in which visual information is gathered. This is an active process and depends on both the person's goal and the visual information that is present. For example, consider the task of looking for your car keys. If you know your car keys have a red fob your eyes are more likely to be directed to red items rather than green ones. This is an example of the observer's goal directing the eyes. However, if during the search a sudden event occurs such as a door opening or the phone ringing then your eyes are immediately drawn to this new, abrupt, event. In this case the environment directs the eyes. This example illustrates how the eyes can be goal directed as well as being captured by sudden visual events that may prove to be a danger or a threat (see Ludwig and Gilchrist 2002).

Fixating a location in space is paying attention to that location. Movements of the eyes are referred to as movements of *overt* attention. However, it is also possible to pay attention to a location in space that is not being fixated. For example, if you look straight ahead at the full stop at the end of this sentence it is still possible to see the colour of your watchstrap. Paying attention to a location that is away from the fovea is called *covert* attention. Of course in normal visual behaviour paying covert attention to something is normally followed by a shift of overt attention: something catches our attention and then we move our eye to take a look at it (see Findlay and Gilchrist 2003).

While reading our eyes also move along the text using saccades. Saccades in reading typically move between seven and nine characters along the line of text before a large saccade is generated back to the beginning of the next line. However, the eyes do occasionally move backwards in the text. These *regressive* saccades occur when the reader has failed to understand the text. For example while reading the sentence 'Although Chris had won the prize money would never bring him happiness' you may have made a regressive saccade to reparse the sentence. This is an example of the processes of interpretation influencing where the eyes go next (see Rayner 1998). The nature of the text can also influence how long the fixation is maintained on a word; more difficult words are fixated for longer, and some short words are even skipped altogether. The durations of all the individual fixations ultimately add up to the time it takes to read a page or even a whole book. In reading, as elsewhere, the nature of the visual material, in this case the text, determines both when and where the eyes move.

The eyes do not only make saccadic eye movements; there is a range of types of eye movement that serve different functions (see Carpenter 1988). For example, *smooth pursuit* eye movements track moving objects to keep the object of interest on the fovea. Smooth pursuit movements differ from saccades in that they are slower and vision of the object is maintained during tracking.

Humans have two eyes that normally move together so that the fovea in each eye points at the same object in space. However, because the two eyes are separated they have two slightly different views of the world. As a result, to point both eyes at objects that are different distances away requires the eyes to move different amounts. Specifically, as an object moves towards the face both eyes have to move, in a coordinated manner, towards the nose. This type of movement is called a *vergence* movement. Vergence movements keep the fovea in each eye pointing at an object as it moves in depth. The amount of vergence that the eyes generate also gives a clue as to how far away the object is.

The repertoire of different eye movements, some of which are discussed above, carries out two distinct functions. First, objects of interest in the visual environment can be kept static on the fovea, for example by fixation or smooth pursuit. Second, eye movements move the fovea onto objects of interest, for example by saccades, and vergence movements.

When, where, and how the eyes are moved is determined by the nature of the visual environment. However, eye movements are also controlled by the goal or task we are carrying out. Eye movements are at the interface between the mind and the visual world. As a result where our eyes are looking at any one time provides a real insight into what is currently on our minds.　　　IDG

Carpenter, R. H. S. (1988). *Movements of the Eyes* (2nd edn.).

Findlay, J. M., and Gilchrist, I. D. (2003). *Active Vision: The Psychology of Looking and Seeing*.

Ludwig, C. J. H., and Gilchrist, I. D. (2002). 'Stimulus-driven and goal-driven control over visual selection'. *Journal of Experimental Psychology: Human Perception and Performance*, 28.

Rayner, K. (1998). 'Eye movements in reading and information processing: 20 years of research'. *Psychological Bulletin*, 124.

eye movements for pictures. When an observer views a scene or a picture, he or she fixates on a point of regard, and then makes a *saccadic eye movement to shift the fixation. This pattern of saccade-fixation eye movements, often referred to as a *scanpath*, necessarily results from the physiological properties of the retina: fixations allow the image projected from the scene to fall onto the two foveae, retinal areas that can process fine detail and colour information. As the series of fixations continue, the corresponding retinal images are processed over time. The rationale for studying saccade-fixation patterns is based on an underlying assumption of predominant theories of visual perception (cf. Gregory 1997): sequential retinal images are processed to develop an internal representation of the information in the stimulus; therefore, understanding what determines eye movements may partially explain perceptual processes.

The questions of where and why one fixates on certain aspects of a stimulus remain unanswered. Empirical studies done in laboratory settings have shown that salient features in a picture, such as a saturated colour (e.g. Itti and Koch 2000), can 'drive' the eye, thereby inducing *bottom-up* processes. However, other studies (e.g. Buswell 1935; Yarbus 1967) of recorded eye movements have suggested that cognitive factors, such as the viewer's motivation and previous experience, can affect fixations by inducing *top-down* processes.

To examine the degree to which stimulus characteristics or cognitive factors influence viewing artwork under natural conditions, Heidenreich and Turano (2004) asked observers to regard paintings displayed in a museum, while wearing a portable eyetracker. The eye-movement patterns were used to test several hypotheses. First, if fixations are drawn to salient features in the stimulus, then eye-movement patterns should differ for two distinct genres of art (i.e. representational vs. abstract paintings). Second, if cognitive factors dominate, then saccades and fixations should follow aspects of a painting that suggest the narrative; that is, fixations should land on portions of a painting that contain the most relative information (i.e. areas in the painting defined in a prior experiment as 'most informative'). Third, if aesthetic judgements are linked to eye-movement patterns, then viewing times and fixation durations should increase for paintings judged to be beautiful or interesting.

To conduct the study, four observers, unaware of the hypotheses being tested, viewed fourteen paintings displayed in the Baltimore Museum of Art. The representational genre comprised nine works in an exhibition of French Neoclassical to Post-Impressionist work, from artists such as Cézanne, Ingres, and Van Gogh. The pieces varied in degree of representation; however, all had easily identifiable elements and recognizable narratives. The abstract genre comprised five paintings, including pieces from Albers and Rothko, that were selected because they lacked recognizable features and narrative content.

Observers wore a battery-operated, headband-mounted eyetracker (ISCAN), containing two cameras that simultaneously videotaped the eye and the scene (with an 88×60 degree field of view). The videotapes were digitized, synchronized, and analysed off-line; specialized hardware and software produced an eye-on-the-scene video, with a graphic character superimposed on each frame, to indicate eye position. Fixations were determined by using a velocity threshold ($< 24°/$sec) relative to a scene landmark. The video was used to plot the x and y coordinates for each fixation-saccade sequence made for every painting.

Each recording session began with an initial calibration procedure, followed by instructions to the observer to regard each painting as one would normally when visiting a museum, moving freely and viewing for an unlimited time. The viewer was given the title of each piece, but no accompanying narrative. After seeing the entire set of paintings, the observer judged six aesthetic properties of each piece, using semantic-differential scales adopted from several studies of aesthetics (e.g. Berlyne, 1974, 1976). Each scale contained a numbered continuum, with endpoints labelled by antonyms: uninteresting–interesting, displeasing–pleasing, ugly–beautiful, weak–powerful, indefinite–clear, and disorderly–orderly.

The most salient finding was that saccade-fixation patterns made for representational and abstract paintings were idiosyncratic. Qualitative comparisons, across the four observers, indicated that no one eye-movement pattern emerged for any painting, and no distinguishable differences were evident for the two genres. Quantitative analyses showed that fixations may have been determined by a motivation to derive narrative information, in that some fixations predictably fell on areas of the painting previously judged to be informative. Surprisingly, some fixations fell on homogeneous patches of colour, or on the blank, white walls. Together, these findings suggest that stimulus features alone are not sufficient to 'drive' the eye, or to produce a replicable scanpath when observers look at paintings in a natural setting. The discrepancy with other studies, which have reported effects for conspicuous features in the stimulus, can be explained by the fact that the Heidenreich and Turano study was conducted with observers viewing actual artwork in a gallery, rather than photographic images in a laboratory setting.

Other quantitative analyses showed that mean viewing times and fixation durations were significantly different for the four observers, pointing again to strikingly idiosyncratic results. However, neither viewing times nor fixation durations differed for the two genres of art. Eye-movement patterns did not appear to change in an obvious diverse-to-specific mode of exploration; however, mean fixation durations did increase over the course of viewing, but only for the abstract art.

Contrary to predictions, viewing durations for representational artwork were negatively correlated to judgements of 'beautiful' and 'powerful'. Therefore, simple measures of eye movements are not likely to produce reliable predictions of how the observer would rate the aesthetic properties of a work of art. The search for ways to quantify emotional responses, which characterize aesthetic experiences, continues.   SMH/KAT

Berlyne, D. E. (1974). *Studies in the New Experimental Aesthetics.*

Buswell, G. T. (1935). *How People Look at Pictures.*

Gregory, R. L. (1997). *Eye and Brain: The Psychology of Seeing* (5th edn.).

Heidenreich, S. M., and Turano, K. (2004). 'Where does one look when viewing artwork?' *Perception.*

Itti, L., and Koch, C. (2000). 'A saliency-based search mechanism for overt and covert shifts of visual attention'. *Vision Research.*

Yarbus, A. (1967). *Eye Movements and Vision.*

eye position signals in active visual processing.

Active vision plays an important role in many primate behaviours, and was critical to the success of early primates in their ecological role as visual predators in the fine branch niche. Eye movements are one of the most important means through which information from the environment is actively selected to enter the visual system. The cortical processing of this information may be controlled as actively as the eyes themselves, and may therefore constitute a 'covert' component of active vision.

eye position signals in active visual processing

The active coordination of cortical processing with the selection of information entering the visual processing stream can be mediated by eye position signals present in the visual cortex.

Eye position signals were among the first non-visual (extra-retinal) signals found to influence the responses of neurons in the visual cortex. Almost 30 years ago, they were sought for and found in the posterior parietal cortex. There was strong evidence that eye position signals were required in this area for performing coordinate transformations supporting visuospatial localization. The role of eye position signals has since become strongly associated with the dorsal visual processing stream and with coordinate transformation theory. Subsequent research has, however, found eye position signals to be present in many other visual cortical areas. Recently strong eye position modulation effects have been found in area V4 along the ventral processing stream.

Significant modulatory effect with respect to point of regard (point in three-dimensional space that is being fixated) is both common, affecting 85 per cent of cells, and strong, frequently producing changes in the mean firing rate of neurons by a factor of 10. Anatomical tracing experiments have demonstrated an input to V4 from the small saccade part of frontal eye fields, an important component of the cerebropontocerebellar pathway involved in governing voluntary eye movements. This data suggests that the eye position modulation seen in V4 may arise from efference copies of commands arising in the frontal eye fields.

The presence of eye position signals in visual areas of the ventral visual processing stream raises the possibility that these signals might facilitate identifying objects. The locations of objects in the visual field provide important clues to their identity. Object distance together with its retinal subtense reveals the size of an animal and whether it is a possible food item or a potential predator. Some threatening animals, like raptors, tend to be located in the upper visual field while others, like snakes, tend to creep in the lower visual field. The experience with their probable location will facilitate their identification and speed the initiation of life-saving protective responses. Similarly, different types of food sources tend to be located in different parts of visual space, and this knowledge will facilitate efficient foraging. There is also a close association between the near response, consisting of convergence, accommodation, and pupillary constriction, and the behaviour of scrutinizing during object recognition. The prevalence of neurons in area V4 showing a preference for near distances may be indicative of the involvement of this area in close scrutiny during object recognition.

In addition to the eye position-related signals relayed from frontal eye fields, penalty-related signals from the

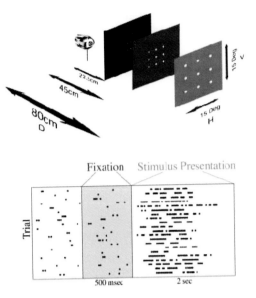

Fig. 1. The top part of Figure 1 shows a schematic the experimental apparatus used in testing for modulation of neurons in V4 with respect to changes in point of regard. A fixation spot presented on a monitor can appear at any one of 27 possible different spatial positions: 3 possible horizontal positions; 3 possible vertical positions; and 3 distances from the eye. The monitor is viewed through an aperture which masks off all visual stimuli but those on the monitor. Fixation spot's size and position are scaled with distance so as to keep retinal stimulus and position constant with respect to distance.

The bottom part of figure one shows the experimental paradigm. After the fixation spot appears at one of the 27 possible positions, the subject acquires the fixation spot for a fixation period, after which a visual stimulus (typically a white bar on a black background) is presented to the receptive field of the V4 neuron that has been isolated prior to the start of the experiment. The stimulus presented on the monitor is scaled and translated with respect to the point of regard so as to keep the retinal stimulus constant throughout the experiment, regardless of experimental condition. This figure shows the spiking behavior of the neuron during ten repetitions of the same experimental conditions, each horizontal line representing a single trial. It is this data that is used to compute the mean firing rate of the neuron (computed separately for the fixation only (FO) period and for the stimulation (S) period). These two values are computed for each of the 27 experimental conditions. An example is shown in Figure 2.

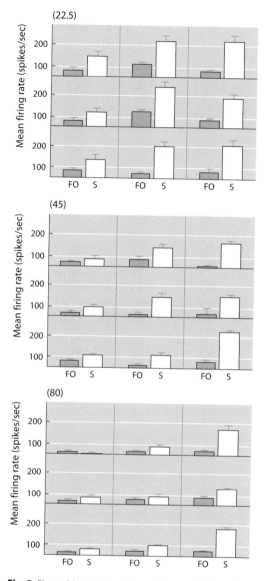

Fig. 2. Figure 2 is a representation of the modulation of the mean firing rate of a single V4 neuron with respect to point of regard. The three rows represent the three possible viewing distances. Each panel is divided into nine bar graphs representing the nine (h,v) pairs. FO is the mean firing rate during the Fixation Only period of the trial. S is the mean firing rate during the Stimulation period of the trial. This cell is significantly modulated with respect to horizontal eye position, and appears to have a slight preference for near distances. The bars represent the mean of the mean firing rates over 10 repetitions of the experimental condition, and the error bars represent standard error of the mean.

amygdala, and reward-related dopaminergic signals which serve a critical role in learning, are present in early visual cortical areas. All three of these extra-retinal signals converge on layer 1 of V4 and the frontal eye field and dopaminergic inputs also converge on layers 5 and 6 of V4. Such extra-retinal signals are often important indicators of a change in behavioural or sensory context and often precede these changes of context. As a result of learning mechanisms present in visual cortex, such predictive signals would tend to influence neuronal responses.

Because modulatory eye position signals exist in the visual cortex prior to visual stimulation, they might function as conditioning stimuli. Retinal stimulus characteristics (unconditioned stimulus) produce sensory responses in visual cortical neurons (unconditioned response). Learning would result from repeated pairing of eye position signals (conditioned stimulus) with retinal stimulus characteristics (unconditioned stimulus) resulting in the eye position signal alone potentiating those neurons sensitive to the stimulus characteristics (conditioned response), prior to stimulus presentation, thus preparing visual processing for the expected stimulus. A functional linkage between point of regard (conditioned stimulus) and the responses of visual cortical neurons (unconditioned response) learned in this way could result in perceptual learning of systematic relationships between point of regard and statistical characteristics of the visual environment. Ivo Kohler's studies with prism glasses have demonstrated psychophysically that the visual system is indeed capable of adapting in an eye position-dependent manner, a phenomenon that he termed 'situational or conditioned aftereffects'. There are circumstances in which strong correspondences exist between eye position and stimulus characteristics, and in these circumstances the visual system is capable of adapting to the eye position signal alone. In natural behaviour it is more likely that eye position signals are but one of an array of extra-retinal signals that, when taken together, are very informative about the current sensory and behavioural demands, and strongly predictive of future sensory inputs.

'What we see depends on where we look.' This is obvious as a statement about the non-uniformity of our external visual environment. But it is also true, in a much less obvious sense, as a statement about the internal neurophysiology of the visual system.

What we see depends on where we look in the neurophysiological sense that eye position signals have a dramatic effect on the responsiveness of visual cortical neurons. These two different ways in which 'What we see depends on where we look' may be bound together through the learning of associations between eye position and statistics of the visual environment. Devices for human use as simple as rear view mirrors or bifocals, and as complex as a virtual cockpit explicitly based on a 'what-you-see-depends-on-where-you-look' concept, create correspondences between point of regard and distinctive information sources, and may be implicitly exploiting the natural talent humans have for learning such associations.

DR/JAl

Ahissar, E., et. al. (1992). 'Dependence of cortical plasticity on correlated activity of single neurons and on behavioral context'. *Science*, 257.

Allman, J. (1998). *Evolving Brains*.

Amaral, D., and Price, J. (1984). 'Amygdalo-cortical projections in the monkey (*Macaca fascicularis*)'. *Journal of Comparative Neurology*, 230.

Andersen, R. (1994). 'Coordinate transformations and motor planning in posterior parietal cortex'. In Gazzaniga, M. (ed.), *The Cognitive Neurosciences*.

Hollerman, J. R., and Schultz, W. (1998). 'Dopamine neurons report an error in the temporal prediction of reward during learning'. *Nature Neuroscience*, 1.

Kohler, I. (1964). *The Formation and Transformation of the Perceptual World*.

Maunsell, J. H. R. (1990). 'The brain's visual world: representation of visual targets in cerebral cortex'. *Science*, 255.

Rosenbluth, D., and Allman, J. (2002). 'The effect of gaze angle and fixation distance on the responses of neurons in V1, V2, and V4'. *Neuron*, 33.

Sejnowski, T. J. (1999). 'The book of Hebb'. *Neuron*, 24.

Stanton, B., Bruce, C., and Goldberg, M. (1995). 'Topography of projections to posterior cortical areas from the macaque frontal eye fields'. *Journal of Comparative Neurology*, 353.

Eysenck, Hans Jürgen (1916–87). H. J. Eysenck was born in Germany, but moved permanently to England in the mid-1930s shortly after the Nazis took power. His first book, *Dimensions of Personality* (1947), was an influential early attempt to identify the structure of personality. The emphasis of this book was on the orthogonal personality dimensions of extroversion and neuroticism, which are still regarded as being of central importance.

In subsequent work, he added the dimension of psychoticism, which was orthogonal to the other two. The key insight underlying this work was that personality is more fruitfully conceptualized as consisting of a small number of orthogonal traits than as a large number of correlated traits. Another distinguishing characteristic of Eysenck's approach to personality was his notion that individual differences in personality depend to a large extent on genetic factors, a notion which has received much empirical support (see *Personality and Individual Differences*, 1985).

Eysenck's other two main scientific contributions were in the area of clinical psychology. The first of these contributions was based on the assumption that there are close links between extremes of normal personality and mental disorders. This theme was pursued in *The Dynamics of Anxiety and Hysteria* (1957), in which he argued that vulnerability to anxiety and hysteria depends on an individual's level of extroversion. This general approach has since been adopted by others, especially in connection with attempts to understand the factors related to susceptibility to the various personality disorders.

His second contribution to clinical psychology was forthright championing of behaviour therapy in the late 1950s and early 1960s. Even though he was not a clinical psychologist, Eysenck was very influential in establishing behaviour therapy as a major approach to the treatment of mental disorders, and as a serious rival to the psychodynamic approach initiated by Sigmund Freud. The gradual replacement of the psychodynamic approach with the approach of behaviour therapy (later cognitive-behaviour therapy) probably also owes something to Eysenck's frequent trenchant attacks on Freud.   RLG

Eysenck, H. J. (1947). *Dimensions of Personality*.

—— (1957). *The Dynamics of Anxiety and Hysteria*.

—— and Eysenck, M. W. (1985). *Personality and Individual Differences: A Natural Science Approach*.

F

Fabre, Jean Henri (1823–1915). French entomologist, born at St Leon, Aveyron. Fabre taught at Carpentras and Avignon before retiring to Sérignan, where he carried out remarkable investigations on the behaviour and sensory capacities of insects. He carried out controlled experiments: for example, by putting cotton wool, on which a female butterfly had spent some time, in a jar in one part of the room and the female herself in full view under a glass dome in another part of the room. He found that the males would fly straight to the jar, ignoring the female. This showed that the males were guided by a remarkable sense of *smell, dependent upon their antennae. Fabre is also celebrated for his work on the behaviour of the praying mantis and the hunting wasp, which he believed incapacitated larvae without killing them so that they remained available as food over long periods.

His fullest work is *Souvenirs entomologiques* (10 vols., 1879–1907, collected edn. 1925, with a *Life* by Lenoir).

face-to-face communication. The face conveys a bewildering variety of different messages to the human mind. Babies are attentive to facelike patterns as soon as they are born, and learn about their parents' faces within days. As adults, we use faces to identify individuals, and even for unfamiliar people we can categorize their sex, approximate age, and racial group from their face, and deduce other things about social grouping from style of hair or facial ornament or make-up. The face is also central in judgements of attractiveness, and there is strong agreement across cultures about which faces are more or less attractive. Bruce and Young (1998) provide an introduction to the field of face perception.

Judgements of identity or attractiveness depend on relatively enduring features of an individual's face. But important messages are also contained in the momentary configuration of the face as it speaks and expresses. It is these signals upon which we focus here.

1. Facial speech
2. Face gaze
3. Facial expressions
4. Non-verbal communication

1. Facial speech

Everyone lip-reads, not just those who are hard of hearing. We are much better at deciphering speech in a noisy environment if we can see as well as hear the speaker. Phonemic distinctions which are difficult to hear may easily be visible. For example, the difference between an 'F' and an 'S' in a postal or zip code may need spelling out when we give an address by telephone, but when the speaker is present the difference is easy to see—the lips close for an 'F' but not for an 'S'. Lip-reading is well demonstrated by the illusion first reported by McGurk and MacDonald (1976). If a face is shown mouthing one speech sound, but simultaneously the soundtrack plays a different sound, in some circumstances the perceiver hears a phoneme which is neither that seen nor heard, but a blend of the two. For example, an auditory 'ba' with a visual 'ga' will result in the perception of a 'da'. The brain appears to do the best job it can of reconciling the auditory information (for 'ba', that the vocal tract has been closed at the lips), with the visual signal (for 'ga' that the lips are open), and comes up with a compromise perception (the vocal tract must be closed further back—perhaps just behind the teeth, as in 'da'). However, the precise rules of combining these signals remain unclear (Summerfield 1987). Neuroimaging has shown that silent lip-read speech activates areas of the cortex which otherwise respond only to auditory signals, suggesting that the integration of visual with heard speech sounds occurs at a very early level of cortical analysis (Calvert et al. 1997).

Lip-reading skills dissociate from other aspects of face perception. Campbell, Landis, and Regard (1986) studied two patients, one of whom had impaired face perception but intact lip-reading, while the other was proficient at all face processing tasks except lip-reading. So, the first patient could tell that pursed lips sounded 'p', but not that downturned ones signalled sadness, while the second showed the opposite pattern. Such patterns of dissociation are strongly suggestive that the neural structures which allow us to lip-read do not overlap with those that are used to derive other kinds of facial meaning. Research with non-brain-injured volunteers has also shown that the McGurk 'blend' illusion is unaffected by whether or not the face and voice match in gender. The brain will combine a male spoken 'ba' with a female mouthing 'ga', suggesting that the visual analysis of face gender and the use of visual speech are kept quite distinct (Green et al. 1991). However, when the faces and voices are of familiar individuals this blending is suppressed (Walker, Bruce, and O'Malley 1995), suggesting that audio-visual speech perception is not completely immune from other aspects of person perception.

2. Face gaze

The direction and timing of movements of the eyes provide important cues which regulate conversation and can convey a sense of intimacy or dominance (see Kleinke 1986 for a review). We may stare directly at people if we wish to intimidate them, and look down when embarrassed or ashamed. People look away from their conversational partners when they are speaking but look at the other person when it is their turn to speak. Our gaze patterns are also informative about the locus of our attention. We look away or upwards when we are thinking, and look at an object that captures our attention. Recent work on gaze and perception has shown how other people's gaze patterns have cognitive consequences for the observer. A shift in gaze triggers a shift in direction of attention by the observer, who finds it easier to detect targets in the direction indicated by the gaze shift. For example, if a face is seen to gaze to the left, an observer will spot targets to the left more easily than those to the right—showing that the perceived gaze shift has had an effect on the observer's attentional focus. Such observations demonstrate how gaze can mediate shared attention between people. Such shifts appear to occur automatically, and at an early age. Some models of social attention suggest that it is the eyes that are the main key to other minds, and that people suffering from autism may be impaired in their use of such signals from gaze. However, developmentally, and evolutionarily, manual pointing seems to be the most salient cue, followed by head direction, with eye gaze cues being used later in the developmental sequence and only by higher primates (Langton, Watt, and Bruce 2000 provide a recent review). (See also EYE CONTACT.)

3. Facial expressions

The extensive facial musculature pulls the face into distinctive postures which reveal different emotional states. According to Ekman (e.g. 1992) there is a small number of expressive categories which are universally perceived by people of all cultures (though cultures may differ in the 'display rules' which dictate when certain emotions are appropriate to display). The universal basic emotions include happiness, sadness, anger, fear, disgust, and surprise. Recent research into the neuropsychological underpinnings of emotion has revealed that part of the brain called the amygdala is strongly involved in the perception and expression of negative emotions, particularly fear. Patients with damage to the amygdala are poor at recognizing fear, from voices as well as from faces, and in normal people the amygdala becomes active when faces are more fearful or less happy. Work with patients with Huntington's

disease has implicated different brain areas, including the insula, in the perception of disgust (Calder, Lawrence, and Young 2001 review these findings). However, other psychologists have been critical of the idea that there is a small number of discrete expression categories which are perceived universally (e.g. see Russell 1994).

Much work on the perception of emotions from faces has examined the perception of static images, whereas in everyday life we perceive faces in continuous change. Accuracy and intensity of expression perception seem affected by the timing as well as the spatial pattern of the facial gesture (Kamachi et al. 2001). Kamachi and colleagues used image sequences in which a neutral face transformed into an expressive one at different speeds. Sadness was seen more intensely when sequences unfolded slowly, while happiness appeared more intense when changes occurred quickly.

4. Non-verbal communication

Given the important information conveyed by the face, in association with other gestures, it is perhaps not surprising that communication can suffer when people cannot see each other. Speech is harder to hear when faces are not visible, but conversational structure may also be affected more subtly when adults communicate by telephone. For example, nodding the head can signal to a speaker that the listener is still attending, and vocalizations such as 'uh-huh' may be needed to substitute when speakers rely on voice alone. Video-mediated communication does not necessarily substitute simply for face to face, and considerable research is being conducted to try to optimize the design of remote VMC systems to capture the best aspects of face-to-face communication (e.g. Doherty-Sneddon et al. 1997).

While adults can adapt well to different communication media, young children may not. Young children depend more upon non-verbal cues than do adults, and this dependence can have both positive and negative effects. Children are generally better at communicating when they can see as well as hear each other, since they can use gestures to supplement speech, particularly for things that may be difficult to express in words.

However, the social presence of an adult can have an intimidating effect on a child. Recent research has shown that children may be more resistant to leading questions when they communicate via a live video link rather than face to face—perhaps because the link removes some of the social pressure (Doherty-Sneddon and McAuley 2000).

VB

Bruce, V., and Young, A. (1998). *In the Eye of the Beholder: The Science of Face Perception.*

Calder, A. J., Lawrence, A. D., and Young, A. W. (2001). 'Neuropsychology of fear and loathing'. *Nature Reviews Neuroscience*, 2.

Calvert, G. A., Bullmore, E. T., Brammer, M. J., et al. (1997). 'Activation of auditory cortex during silent lipreading'. *Science*, 276.

Campbell, R., Landis, T., and Regard, M. (1986). 'Face recognition and lipreading: a neurological dissociation'. *Brain*, 109.

Doherty-Sneddon G., and McAuley, S. (2000). 'Influence of video-mediation on adult–child interviews: Implications for the use of the live link with child witnesses'. *Applied Cognitive Psychology*, 14.

——Anderson, A., O'Malley, C., Langton, S., Garrod, S., and Bruce, V. (1997). 'Face-to-face and video-mediated communication: a comparison of dialogue structure and task performance'. *Journal of Experimental Psychology: Applied*, 3.

Ekman, P. (1992). 'Facial expressions of emotion: an old controversy and new findings'. *Philosophical Transactions of the Royal Society of London*, B, 335.

Green, K. P., Kuhl, P. K., Meltzoff, A. N., and Stevens, E. B. (1991). 'Integrating speech information across talkers, gender and sensory modality: female faces and male voices in the McGurk effect'. *Perception & Psychophysics*, 50.

Kamachi, M., Bruce, V., Mukaida, S., Gyoba, J., Yoshikawa S., and Akamatsu, S. (2001). 'Dynamic properties influence the perception of facial expressions'. *Perception*, 30.

Kleinke, C. L. (1986). 'Gaze and eye contact: a research review'. *Psychological Bulletin*, 100.

Langton, S.R.H., Watt, R.J., and Bruce, V. (2000), 'Do the eyes have it? Cues to the direction of social attention'. *Trends in Cognitive Sciences*, 4/2.

McGurk, H., and MacDonald, J. (1976). 'Hearing lips and seeing voices'. *Nature*, 264.

Russell, J. A. (1994). 'Is there universal recognition of emotion from facial expression? A review of the cross-cultural studies'. *Psychological Bulletin*, 115.

Summerfield, Q. (1987). 'Some preliminaries to a comprehensive account of audio-visual speech perception'. In Dodd, B., and Campbell, R. (eds.), *Hearing by Eye: The Psychology of Lip-Reading*.

Walker, S., Bruce, V., and O'Malley, C. (1995). 'Facial identity and facial speech processing: familiar faces and voices in the McGurk effect'. *Perception & Psychophysics*, 57.

facial expressions: origins.

A primary source of information for judging another's mood, and even his or her character. The human head has the most advanced set of facial expression muscles to be found anywhere in the animal kingdom. Monkeys and apes have highly expressive faces, but even they cannot reach the level of subtlety and complexity found in the human face. We read these facial signals with great sensitivity and employ the information we gain from them when assessing the intentions, moods, and emotions of our companions. It is much easier for us to lie with our words than with our faces, which makes face-to-face encounters such a vital part of social interaction. While listening dutifully to the words being spoken, we unconsciously absorb a great deal of information concerning the feelings of the speakers from facial expressions. An attempt to classify expressions and facial types was first made by the *physiognomists. *Essays on Physiognomy* by John Lavater (1741–1801) appeared in many versions and editions from 1775 and throughout the 19th century. Much of it is based on comparisons of human faces and expressions with those of animals, as well as on Lavater's wide experience with people. It has little, if any, scientific validity, but the fact remains—we do, all the time, 'read faces'.

Charles *Darwin's *The Expression of the Emotions in Man and Animals* (1872) is a companion to, and was originally conceived to be part of, his *The Descent of Man* (1871). Both works are concerned with drawing conclusions from the hypothesis, startling at the time, that man as a species is derived by processes of natural selection from other species, and especially from his near relations, the great apes. Darwin argues that the facial expressions of man, which are now important as social *symbols*, were originally *functionally* important—often in ancient and even extinct species. For example, frowning shaded the eyes; drooping of the mouth rejected bitter or poisonous fruit; widening of the eyes improved vision for emergencies, and so on. His studies were meticulous, leading him to consider the development of particular muscles, and identifying reactions in his own children—sometimes even making them cry for experimental purposes, though he was the kindest of men and most deeply attached to his family. In the 20th century it became fashionable to deny any genetic influence on human behaviour and it was claimed that all behaviour patterns, including facial expressions, were purely the result of cultural learning. Darwin's earlier ideas were rejected and in the 1930s psychologist Otto Klineberg's conclusions were summarized by the phrase: 'what is shown on the face is written there by culture'. In the second half of the 20th century this school of thought was discredited and new research demonstrated that Darwin had been correct. The major facial expressions displaying such emotions as fear, disgust, anger, happiness, and sadness are common to all cultures and are found in remote tribal societies that have previously known no contact with the outside world. It is, however, true that each culture slightly modifies its genetically inherited set of expressions, according to local display rules. In one culture, for example, it might have become socially unacceptable to laugh out loud, while in another it was equally unacceptable *not* to laugh out loud, when amused. The basic expression of a 'happy face' would therefore suffer suppressions or exaggerations as one moved from one location to another. In some cultures a new expression, such as a 'wink' or a 'tongue-in-cheek' would be invented and added to the facial repertoire. In this way, the primary, evolved set of human facial expressions would become modified or expanded by minor cultural influences.

A popular treatment of the subject is found in the writing of Desmond Morris (*Manwatching*, 1977; *Bodywatching*, 1985; *Body Talk*, 1994; and *Peoplewatching*, 2002) which brings out subtle and sometimes clear-cut regional differences. These are interesting in their own right and provide evidence of racial migrations.

A curious logical point was raised by the philosopher C. D. *Broad (in *Mind and its Place in Nature*, 1925). He points out (p. 325) that we could hardly learn by association to read moods in others from their facial expressions by analogy with our own expressions and moods, because we only see our own faces and expressions in mirrors. He considers the possibility of some kind of telepathic association, or link, from which we know other people's moods from their expressions. An alternative and surely more plausible explanation is that expressions are largely innate (which would be Darwin's view), though, as Desmond Morris and others have shown, they are modified by social interaction. See also GESTURES.   RLG

Darwin, C. (1998). *The Expression of the Emotions in Man and Animals*. Ed. P. Ekman (3rd edn.).

Ekman, P. (1997). *Darwin and Facial Expression: A Century of Research in Review*.

faculty psychology. The brain-child of the Scottish philosopher Thomas *Reid (1710–96), central to the 'Scottish School' through the 18th and 19th centuries, with implications for *phrenology (which gave it physical though dubious realization), and into modern ideas of *localization of brain function, with implications for interpreting *brain imaging. Reid's notion was that the mind is innately structured to see objects from sensations (categories of objects being the structure of reality in which we survive and live), though he generally denied innate knowledge, and is divided up into separate inherent powers of 'faculties' such as *memory, *learning, *intelligence, *perception, and will. The faculties might be contrasted with those other powers which the individual could acquire through use, exercise, or study, and which were generally known as 'habits'. The theory was associated with *phrenology, which supposed that the various faculties were more or less represented in each individual according to the size of bumps which could be seen or felt on the skull. Similar divisions are still made in textbooks of psychology, but the notion that they are strictly distinct and localized individually in different regions of the brain has very largely been abandoned.

It is now held that abilities and skills result from the interplay of very many brain mechanisms and that these do not show up as 'bumps'. Even if they did, it would be necessary to know a great deal about the organization of the brain to 'read bumps'. It is, however, the case that through the evolution of species some functional brain regions have grown and others have shrunk—with a general development of the cerebral cortex in mammals. (See PRIMATES, EVOLUTION OF THE BRAIN IN.)

A related objection to the notion of faculties is that, for example, perception involves memory and no doubt various kinds of intelligence. For convenience we separate perception, memory, and intelligence, even though each is involved with the others and it is hardly possible to see any one in isolation.

There has recently, however, been some return to the old notion of 'faculties', as the brain is now seen to be organized with many 'modules' of cells in small regions, each responsible for a particular ability (such as face recognition) though of course many other parts of the brain must also be involved. The modules are seen as relatively separate systems (presumably switched in or out as needed), each module being clusters of cells cooperating in operations that may be very different from classifications of psychological faculties. To draw an analogy from electronic circuits: a television has specialized circuits of interacting components, generally grouped spatially as 'modules'. But their operations—what they do—are not apparent in the output, sound or pictures, and their functions can only be understood by knowing how the system works. For example, there is an internal oscillator which beats with the received carrier to produce a fixed intermediate frequency, for efficient amplification; but neither the generated oscillations nor the intermediate frequency they produce are present in the output. (And the oscillators giving line and frame rasters are not present in the TV picture, though are essential for producing it.) Considerations like these have implications for localizing brain functions. In general there is no simple one-to-one relation between the parts or components of complex systems, and what each part does to produce the output (Gregory 1958). The implication is that general, if not detailed, theoretical understanding of the system is needed for specifying functions. An understanding of this is necessary when interpreting brain-localization experiments. Thus for a radio:

the removal of any of several widely spaced resistors may cause a radio set to emit howls, but it does not follow that howls are immediately associated with these resistors, or indeed that the causal relation is anything but the most indirect. In particular, we should not say that the function of the resistors in the normal circuit is to inhibit howling. Neurologists, when faced with a comparable situation, have postulated 'suppressor regions'. (Gregory 1961)

This may or may not be the right interpretation. These issues are most evident within a 'module', but also apply whenever modules are not entirely separate. For example, overloading a power supply will affect circuits most sensitive to voltage changes: the effects may be far-removed causally, and produce 'symptoms' that puzzle and mislead expert engineers—even its designer—especially as *any* cause of voltage change will produce very similar symptoms. Doesn't this apply to neurology?

How far should such arguments be considered for interpreting fMRI brain imaging? Are brain modules given innately (as Thomas Reid thought) or by learning? All this may seem far-removed from faculty psychology, but this is a sign of the general importance of its ideas and questions, only touched on here. The 19th-century neurologist Hughlings *Jackson was well aware of these issues.

RLG

Fodor, J. A. (1983). *The Modularity of Mind.*

Gregory, R. L. (1958). 'Models and the localisation of function in the central nervous system'. National Physical Laboratory Symposium 10, *Mechanisation of Thought Processes.* Vol. 2.

Gregory, R. L. (1961). 'The brain as an engineering problem'. In Thorpe, W. H., and Zangwill, O. L. (eds.), *Current Problems in Animal Behaviour.*

Klein, D. B. (1970). *A History of Scientific Psychology.*

falsification. Scientists have generally been more concerned to justify their theories than run the risk of falsifying them with counter-evidence. This is a criticism of science which has been argued most powerfully by Sir Karl Popper (1902–94). Unusually for a philosopher of science, Popper with his comments and criticisms actually changed the way science is carried out, establishing especially that hypotheses should be formulated in such a way as to be falsifiable. Popper based his ideas on examples in early 20th-century physics, especially on how Einstein's ideas challenged Newtonian physics, but his strictures are also applicable to biology and clinical hypotheses, as Sir Peter Medawar has discussed most cogently (1967, 1969).

One usually thinks of science as producing new truths by observation and experiment, and the more secure the better—so Popper's idea that it should be possible to falsify a hypothesis, if it is to be acceptable as a 'good' hypothesis, came as a considerable shock. The point is not that a hypothesis cannot be good unless it is likely to be false; rather it is that a hypothesis should be conceived and formulated in such terms that experiments or observations could deal it a mortal blow. The hypothesis thus attacked might die or might be merely wounded, to recover in a changed form, but Popper prefers sudden death to hanging on to life. For him a hypothesis that staggers on, mutilated, generally does so because it was not formulated with sufficient vulnerability to die cleanly and be forgotten.

As an example of a hypothesis which refuses to die because inadequately formulated, we may consider Freud's notion of trauma at birth having significant effects in adult life. Suppose to test this we looked at adults who were born by Caesarean section, and suppose we found that they had, as adults, the characteristics that Freud attributed to birth trauma. If the post-Freudians accepted this as falsifying evidence for the birth trauma hypothesis, then in Popper's terms well and good—for the hypothesis was evidently set up in such a way as to be falsifiable. And in showing it to be false something has been learned: that these characteristics are not due to birth trauma. But the post-Freudians would have lost their hypothesis, and losing hypotheses can itself be traumatic. Popper would object to the post-Freudians responding by redefining 'birth trauma'—so that, let's say, it is not the birth itself but the shock of coming into the world that produces the trauma—for then the hypothesis would have changed, rather than decently died, and it is hard to see how any evidence could count against it.

Popper would probably prefer that the whole idea be abandoned at this point, but it might be that such forced redefining is a way in which science can work well, cumbersome though it seems. For could not some hypotheses be refined and improved in this way? There is surely a danger of throwing out the baby with the bathwater.

Popper has compared falsification as a way of gaining knowledge (and for him it is the *only* way, as he completely rejects *inductive generalizations) with the deaths of individuals leading to improved species in evolution by natural selection of the fittest to survive. There is now, based on this analogy, an active school of epistemology led by Donald Campbell (1974) and Stephen Toulmin (1972). It goes back at least to the American philosopher Charles Sanders *Peirce (1839–1914) with the view that hypotheses die by competition, much as species die out when they are inadequate, for the cumulative good of life and science. There are objections, however, to saying that it is *only* by falsifying hypotheses that we gain new knowledge. It is very hard to believe that animals, including ourselves, with all the evidence of learning curves and so on, never learn by induction (Gregory 1981).

It seems clear that strictly speaking hypotheses cannot be falsified by observational or experimental evidence alone, for all evidence has to be interpreted according to subjective background knowledge or assumptions which may be wrong. Thus, we take it as obvious that the stars appear to move across the sky because the earth is rotating daily on its axis; but, before this was accepted, the stellar observation was differently described. Aristotle thought he had falsified the hypothesis of daily rotation of the earth by jumping up and then finding that he landed on the same spot, when according to his assumption of earthly rotation he should have come down west of where he took off, and there should have been a continuous easterly wind.

Is there a fundamental difference between *falsifying* and *predicting* as a means of testing hypotheses? Isn't a successful *surprising prediction* excellent evidence for the hypothesis suggesting it? Perhaps there is no asymmetry between falsifying and predicting (logically, the failure of a prediction is no different from any other discordant evidence), except that dramatic true predictions may be rarer than equally surprising falsifications. Falsifications of the stationary and the flat earth hypotheses were extremely surprising—and so conveyed a very great deal of information. But there are comparably surprising predictions, such as the apparent shift of positions of the stars near the sun, photographed during its eclipse in 1919, which *supported* Einstein's ideas against Newton.   RLG

Campbell, T. D. (1974). 'Evolutionary epistemology'. In Shilpp, P. A. (ed.), *The Philosophy of Karl Popper.*

Gregory, R. L. (1981). *Mind in Science.*

Medawar, P. (1967). *The Art of the Soluble.*

——(1969). *Induction and Intuition in Scientific Thought.*

Popper, K. R. (1959). *The Logic of Scientific Discovery.*

——(1970). 'Logic of discovery or psychology of research?' In Lakatos, I., and Musgrave, A. (eds.), *Criticism and the Growth of Knowledge.*

——(1972). *Objective Knowledge: An Evolutionary Approach.*

Toulmin, S. E. (1972). *Human Understanding.*

Farabi, Al-. See AL-FARABI.

fatigue. In living beings fatigue refers to deterioration of their performance with the passage of time. It is associated with feelings of tiredness, slowing down, and making simple errors. More severe effects include disturbance of reasoning and judgement, depression, and disturbances in perception (mainly visual) leading to florid *hallucinations. A broad view of fatigue in people involves consideration of the extremes of physical and psychological hardship, when they are trying to accomplish some task.

Fatigue most commonly occurs from lack of sleep. A deterioration in the performance of (albeit dull) laboratory tests after one night with only two hours of sleep, or after two consecutive nights with only five hours of sleep each, can be reliably demonstrated. Highly motivated people—such as doctors on duty, soldiers in battle, adventurers in hostile environments—are able to keep going longer, but after one night without sleep most of them will be functioning inefficiently, although they may not realize it themselves.

1. The effects of fatigue
2. Lessening of effects

1. The effects of fatigue

The effects are increased by adverse conditions such as cold, excessive heat, hunger and thirst, noise and vibration, isolation, lack of oxygen, being wet or seasick, or being under the influence of alcohol or drugs. They may also be increased by anxiety, which can occur in people who doubt their ability to perform a task in hand, or who have worries about separate matters such as money, employment, or relationships. The effects include the following:

Simple errors, poor concentration, and forgetfulness. The initial slowing down is not usually noticed by the individual, though it is plain to observers who are rested. Later on, tasks are started but not completed, things are put down and cannot be found afterwards, a cup of coffee is made and the fatigued person forgets to drink it. Doctors who have to work excessive hours can be shown, for example, to make errors in their interpretation of laboratory reports and electrocardiograph tracings.

Faulty judgements and perceptions. In practice it is not possible to determine whether an error of judgement exists directly as a result of, say, tiredness, or whether it is the consequence of a faulty perception. At a traffic junction where there are tired and frustrated motorists about, a driver wants to go straight ahead but the light is red. A green arrow lights up, permitting traffic to filter off to one side. The tired driver very much wants to see a green light, and so misperceives the filtering light as the signal for going straight ahead, and drives off. He will correct the error in a shorter or a greater time according to the degree of fatigue. Other such circumstances are the overhead railway gantries that carry signals for several adjacent tracks, and harbour lights with many opportunities for 'seeing' the lights a ship's navigator wants to see, indicating a particular channel.

As a second example, a driver when rested and relaxed takes in all relevant information—his car's speed and position in the road relative to other traffic, the condition of the road, proximity to junctions and other hazards, the mechanical state of the car, and weather conditions and visibility—and then responds in a logical manner, having evaluated the relative importance of the different factors; but the fatigued driver may instead concentrate exclusively on one aspect—such as his position in the middle lane—to the neglect of the other factors, and drive remorselessly along the middle lane without regard for speed, visibility, or other vehicles.

Either poor or extremely good visibility, moonlight, high vantage points (with nothing intervening)—all can lead to perceptual errors, especially among the fatigued, so that distances are overestimated or underestimated. Small objects seem to move in the distance, rocks high up on mountains appearing as people.

Ordinary phenomena can be misinterpreted by fatigued people. For instance, a very tired sailor thought the bow wave of his yacht was a flat fish, like a ray; another sailor, in mid-Atlantic, thought he saw a Ford car which later he realized was a small whale; another thought a sleeping-bag laid out on a bunk to be his wife.

A severely fatigued person will not be able (or try) to correct the initial impression. A dramatic example of an uncorrected illusion concerned Shackleton and his two companions as they struggled across South Georgia. All three felt there was a fourth person with them, a presence that was felt to be friendly and supportive. Such experiences are indicative of the limits of endurance.

Ecstasy, depression, and frustration. These are states which can afflict those who are fatigued, and increase the risk of danger. Ecstatic states of mastery over, or of oneness with, all things are to be treasured, but they can lead to overconfidence if experienced, say, while climbing a mountain or piloting an aircraft. Depression is part of ordinary experience and commonly accompanies fatigue, especially if the person is isolated at the time, and can lead to lethargy and carelessness. Frustration, like depression, can be induced by inactivity, especially among the normally energetic. People accustomed to solving problems by increased effort can become very disturbed when no amount of physical effort is of any avail, as when becalmed in a small boat on the ocean or marooned in a tent in a blizzard. Then the ability to relax and go with events, rather than try to combat nature, has great survival value; the art is to cultivate a kind of alert inactivity.

Disorganization and psychological breakdown. Deprivation of 50 hours or more of sleep at one stretch is likely to lead to visual hallucinations and paranoid delusions, and to render the deprived person incapable of effective action. Experiments in which subjects are given impossible tasks—such as trying to fly a particular course in a trainer cockpit programmed to make the course impossible to steer—bring most subjects, eventually, to a state of complete incapacity.

A traumatic event such as seeing a relative or companion killed may lead to a period of shock-induced inactivity followed by acute distress or engagement in some activity which is useful only in that it distracts. Another response to traumatic crisis is denial of its happening at all: a ship may be sinking but the distressed person simply denies that he is at sea at all. These are instances of the psychological process compensating for circumstances to which the individual cannot adapt.

Panic is not a common reaction to a crisis unless there is imminent danger, as in the case of risk of escape routes closing in the event of fire or flood, or there is repetition of a crisis that has occurred.

2. Lessening of effects

Exceptional people (such as Shackleton) and ordinary people at times of extreme need can accomplish quite extraordinary physical feats. Most people on most occasions—say, those who have to make accurate observations, exercise rational judgements, or carry out complicated tasks over prolonged periods—can do something to maintain their efficiency. It helps to observe strict routines for rest and eating, especially when any prolonged activity is called for, and when in the middle of intense activity, to take every opportunity to rest and eat, rather than make a kind of virtue of keeping going. It is also useful for people to monitor themselves—to remain aware of how tense, tired, frightened, or hungry they are—and to make due allowances by taking extra care with observations and decisions.

See also STRESS.
                                                                GBE

Bennet, G. (1983). *Beyond Endurance: Survival at the Extremes.*

Gawron, V. J., French, J., and Funke, D. (2001). 'An overview of fatigue'. In Hancock, P. A. (ed.), *Stress, Workload and Fatigue: Human Factors in Transportation.*

fear and courage. Although the word 'fear' is used without difficulty in everyday language to mean the experience of apprehension, problems arise when it is used as a scientific term. It cannot be assumed that people are always able, or even willing, to recognize and then describe their fears. In wartime, admissions of fear are discouraged. Similarly, boys are discouraged from expressing fear. In surveys carried out on student populations, it has been found that the admission of certain fears by men is felt to be socially undesirable.

The social influences that obscure the accurate expression of fear complicate the intrinsic difficulties in recognizing and describing our own experiences or predicted experiences. For instance, it is regularly found that some people who state that they are fearful of a particular situation or object are later seen to display comparatively fearless behaviour when confronting the specified fear stimulus. Subjective reports of fear tend to be of limited value in assessing the intensity of the experience because of the difficulties involved in translating phrases such as 'extremely frightened', 'terrified', and 'slightly anxious' into degrees on a quantitative scale with stable properties.

For these reasons among others, psychologists have extended the study of fear beyond an exclusive reliance on subjective reports by including indices of physiological change and measures of overt behaviour. It is helpful to think of fear as comprising four main components: the subjective experience of apprehension, associated physiological changes, outward expressions of fear, and attempts to avoid or escape certain situations. When these four components fail to correspond, as they commonly do, problems arise. People can experience subjective fear but remain outwardly calm and, if tested, show none of the expected psychophysiological reactions. There can also be subjective fear in the absence of any attempt at avoidance. The fact that the four components do not always correspond makes it helpful in speaking of fear to specify which component one is referring to.

In our everyday exchanges we rely for the most part on people *telling* us of their fears and then supplementing this information by interpreting their *facial and other bodily expressions. Unfortunately this kind of interpretation, when made in the absence of supporting contextual cues, can be misleading. Moreover, facial and related expressions register only certain kinds of fear, particularly those of an acute and episodic nature; diffuse and chronic fears are less visible. We may easily observe signs of fear in an anxious passenger as an aircraft descends, but fail to recognize it in a person who is intensely apprehensive about ageing.

While there are many types of fear, certain of them, such as neurotic fears, have understandably been studied more intensively than others. Among the many types, a major division can be made between acute and chronic fears. Acute fears are generally provoked by tangible stimuli or situations and subside quite readily when the frightening stimulus is removed or avoided (SEE PHOBIAS): the fear of snakes is an example. (A less common type of acute fear is the sudden onset of panic which seems to have no tangible source, can last for as long as an hour or more, and often leaves a residue of discomfort.) Chronic fears tend to be more complex but are like the acute types in that they may or may not be tied to tangible sources of provocation. The fear of being alone is an example of a chronic, tangible fear. Examples of chronic, intangible fears are by their very nature difficult to specify; one simply feels persistently uneasy and anxious for unidentified reasons—a chronic state of aching fear that has been better described by novelists than by psychologists.

Repeated or prolonged exposure to fearsome stimulation can give rise to enduring changes in behaviour, feelings, and psychophysiological functioning. Clear examples of such changes are encountered during war conditions and after. Adverse reactions can be classified in two broad categories: *combat neuroses*, which are persisting fear and related disturbances, and *combat fatigue* (far more common), which is a temporary disturbance readily reversed by rest and sedation. Wartime observations and research on animal subjects suggest that the fear and *anxiety experienced by many patients with psychological troubles may well give rise to enduring psychophysiological changes, as well as to the more obvious behavioural changes such as marked and persistent avoidance of the frightening stimuli. However, given the nature of chronic anxiety, it can be difficult to confirm causal connections between it and specific psychological and physiological changes (a major problem, incidentally, in studying *psychosomatic disorders).

A distinction is sometimes made between fear and anxiety: fear is taken to refer to feelings of apprehension about tangible and predominantly realistic dangers, whereas anxiety is sometimes taken to refer to feelings of apprehension which are difficult to relate to tangible sources of stimulation. Inability to identify the source of a fear is often regarded as the hallmark of anxiety, and, in psychodynamic theories such as psychoanalysis, is said to be a result of repression.

A clinically useful distinction can be made between focal and diffuse fears. Generally speaking, focal fears are more easily modified, despite the fact that they are often of long standing.

The distinction between innate and acquired fears is an interesting one, although it may be of little practical value. The impact of early *behaviourism, with its massive emphasis on the importance of acquired behaviour, led to the demise of the notion that some fears may be innately determined. Even the possibility of such fears existing in animals was only reluctantly conceded. In recent years, however, the possible occurrence of innately determined fears in human beings has once again come under serious consideration. See Dolan and Morris (2000) for recent neuroimaging perspectives on innate and acquired fear.

The major causes of fear include exposure to traumatic stimulation, repeated exposure to subtraumatic (sensitizing) situations, observations (direct or indirect) of people exhibiting fear, and the receipt of fear-provoking information. Fears usually diminish with repeated exposure to a mild or toned-down version of the frightening situation. This decline in fear as a consequence of repetition can be facilitated by superimposing on the fearful reactions a counteracting influence, such as relaxation.

Fears can be thought of as existing in a state of balance, in which repeated exposures to a fear-evoking situation may lead to an increase in fear (sensitization) or, at other times and in other circumstances, to a decrease (desensitization). The balance tilts in the direction of increased or decreased fear according to the type of exposure, intensity of stimulation, the person's state of alertness, and other factors.

Fear and its first cousin, anxiety, play a major part in most neurotic disorders, and clinicians and their research colleagues have explored the effects of a variety of therapeutic means. Leaving aside the pharmacological methods which are often capable of dampening fear (but seldom of removing it), we are left with psychological methods. These can be divided into two main types: those that attempt to reduce the fear or anxiety directly (as in *behaviour therapy) and those that attempt to modify its putative underlying causes (as in *psychoanalysis and related techniques). The direct methods are comparatively new and are largely products of experimental psychology. The best-established and most extensively used, desensitization, has been joined recently by *flooding* and by *modelling*, methods that involve repeated practice in confronting the frightening situation. Of the indirect methods, psychoanalysis is of course the most famous and influential, and it has spawned many derivations. Most of them, like psychoanalysis itself, were developed by psychiatrists or psychologists. The most widely practised is psychotherapy (a confusingly wide term covering many types of activity), and not psychoanalysis, which is a comparatively rare form of therapy. Although there are many different techniques, the indirect methods share the assumption that a thorough exploration of matters seemingly unrelated to the pertinent fear is a prerequisite for its reduction.

There is no generally accepted theory to account for the genesis and persistence of fears. The psychoanalytic theory, originally proposed by *Freud, has undergone little revision, despite a great deal of criticism. The *conditioning theory, derived from the work of *Pavlov, appears incapable of providing a comprehensive account. The conditioning theory postulates that any neutral object or situation which is associated with painful or fearful experiences will acquire fear-evoking properties. Although there is some evidence to support this theory, there remain important observations that cannot be accommodated by it, such as the non-random distribution of human fears, and the non-appearance of fears in predicted circumstances.

Although fearlessness is often regarded as synonymous with courage, there is some value in distinguishing it from a particular view of courage: the occurrence of perseverance despite fear, which is perhaps the purest form of courage—it certainly requires greater endurance and effort. Despite frequent exposure to dangerous and stressful situations, most people acquire few lasting fears. Wartime surveys testify to the resilience of people subjected to air raids. Experimental analysis of programmes designed to train people in such dangerous tasks as parachute jumping provides further information about the nature of courage. Although fear during or immediately after exposure to danger is a common reaction, we apparently have the capacity to recover quickly. And our capacity to persevere and adapt when faced by fear and stress is remarkable.

Training for courage plays an important part in preparing people to undertake dangerous jobs, such as fire fighting or parachuting. One element of such training, gradual and graduated practice in the tasks likely to be encountered, seems to be of particular importance. This aspect of courage training is strikingly similar to the clinical method of reducing fear known as desensitization.

In the early stages of courage training, the probability of success is improved if the subject's motivation is raised appropriately, encouraging perseverance despite subjective apprehension. The successful practice of courageous behaviour should lead to a decrease in subjective fear and finally to a state of fearlessness. Novice parachute jumpers display courage when they persevere with their jumps despite subjective fear; veteran jumpers, having successfully adapted to the situation, no longer experience fear when jumping: they have moved from courage to fearlessness.

SR

Dolan, R. J., and Morris, J. S. (2000). 'The functional anatomy of innate and acquired fear: perspectives from neuroimaging'. In Lane, R. D. and Nadel, L. (eds.), *Cognitive Neuroscience of Emotion*.

Freud, S. (1905). 'The analysis of a phobia in a five-year-old boy'. In *Collected Papers*, vol. iii.

Gray, J. A. (1971). *The Psychology of Fear and Stress*.

Marks, I. (1969). *Fears and Phobias*.

Rachman, S. (1978). *Fear and Courage*.

Fechner, Gustav Theodor (1801–87). German philosopher and physicist, the son of a village pastor. He took his degree in medicine in the University of Leipzig, where he remained for the rest of his life. Fechner's interests soon turned to mathematics and physics, and for a time he earned his living by translating scientific texts from French into German. He also undertook some research on electricity which won him the chair of physics at Leipzig at the early age of 33. Owing to a serious nervous breakdown, he resigned from his chair after a few years and, on recovering, with a deepened religious consciousness, he became a convinced pantheist.

Fechner's fame rests largely on his two-volume work *Elemente der Psychophysik* (1860). Basing his argument on E. H. *Weber's work on differential sensitivity, Fechner argued that, in a series of sensations of increasing magnitude, say brightness or pressure, the intensity of the stimulus must increase in geometrical proportion if a just noticeable difference (j.n.d.) in sensation is to result. Further, if such just noticeable differences could be regarded as units each greater by one than its predecessor, it follows that the intensity of sensation is proportional to the logarithm of the stimulus. This is known as the Weber–Fechner law (also known as Weber's law), which Fechner regarded as basic to our understanding of the relationship between body and mind. It is the first formulation of this relationship in quantitative terms (see PSYCHOPHYSICS for further discussion).

Fechner insisted that what he called 'outer psychophysics', i.e. the correlation of sensory magnitude with the intensity of physical stimulation, would eventually be replaced by 'inner psychophysics', i.e. the correlation of subjective magnitude with the intensity of the central excitatory process. He thought that ultimately it would make possible a quantitative treatment not only of sensory magnitude but also of images, feelings, and indeed states of consciousness generally. Unfortunately, techniques were not available in his time to achieve this aim, but developments in contemporary neuropsychology might at least suggest that such an aim is not wholly fanciful.

OLZ

Fechner, G. T. (1860). *Elemente der Psychophysik*, vols. i and ii (vol. i trans. H. E. Adler, and eds. D. H. Howes and E. G. Boring, 1967).

Ross, H. E., and Murray, D. J. (trans.) (1978). *E. H. Weber: The Sense of Touch. De Tactu and Der Tastinn*.

feedback and feedforward. When we move to catch a ball, we must interpret our view of the ball's movement to estimate its future trajectory. Our attempt to catch the ball incorporates this anticipation of the ball's movement in determining our own movement. As the ball gets closer, or exhibits spin, we may find it departing from the expected trajectory, and we must adjust our movements accordingly. This is an example of the visual system providing inputs to a controller (our brain) which must generate control signals to cause some system (our musculature) to behave in some desired way (to catch the ball). *Feedforward* anticipates the relation between system and environment to determine a course of action; *feedback* monitors discrepancies which can be used to refine the actions. In general terms, therefore, a *control problem* is to choose the input to some system in such a way as to cause its output to behave in some desired way, whether to stay near a set reference value (the regulator problem), or to follow close upon some desired trajectory (the tracking problem). A control signal defined by its intended effect may not achieve that effect either because of the effect of disturbances upon the system, or because of inaccuracy in the controller's knowledge of the controlled system. Feedback is then required to compare actual and intended performance, so that a compensatory change in the input may be determined. Overcompensation yields instability; undercompensation yields poor adjustment to '*noise'. Thus, not only is feedback necessary, but it must be properly apportioned if the controller is to obtain smooth coordinated behaviour.

It is important to note that feedback can only be used effectively if the controller is 'in the right ballpark' in his (or its) model of the controlled system. However, in the real world the exact values of the parameters describing a

system are seldom available to the controller, and may actually change (compare short-term loading effects on muscles and longer-term ageing effects and weight changes). To adapt to such changes, the outer, feedback, loop of Fig. 1 must be augmented by an *identification* *algorithm*. The job of this algorithm is to monitor the output of the controlled system continually and to compare it with the output that would be expected on the basis of the current estimated state, the current estimated parameters, and the current control signals. On the basis of this data, the identification algorithm can identify more and more accurate estimates of the parameters that define the controlled system, and these updated parameters can then be supplied to the controller as the basis for his (or its) state estimation and control computations.

If the controlled system, or the disturbances to it, are sufficiently slowly time-varying for the identification procedure to make accurate estimates of the (system plus disturbance) parameters more quickly than they actually change, the controller will be able to act efficiently, despite the fluctuations in the system dynamics. The controller, when coupled to an identification procedure, is precisely what is often referred to as an 'adaptive controller': it adapts its control strategy to changing estimates of the dynamics of the controlled system.

Marvin Minsky (1961) has observed that it may also be necessary for the identification procedure to generate some of the input to the controlled system—in other words, to apply test signals to try out various hypotheses about the parameters of the controlled system—trading off the loss of control caused by an inaccurate estimate of the parameters against the degradation resulting from the controller intermittently relinquishing control.

Note that the identification algorithm can only do its job if the controller is of the right general class. It is unlikely that a controller adapted for guiding the arm during ball catching will be able, simply as a result of parameter adjustment, properly to control the legs in the performance of a waltz. Thus the adaptive control system of Fig. 1 (controller plus identification procedure) is not to be thought of as a model of the brain; rather each such control system is a model of a brain 'unit' which can be activated when appropriate. We may think of it as a *synergy. An important problem in analysing human movement is that of the coordinated phasing in and out of the brain's various synergies (control systems).

Feedforward is that strategy whereby a controller monitors a system's environment directly, and applies appropriate compensatory signals to the controlled system —rather than waiting for feedback on how changes in the environment have affected the system before giving compensatory signals. The advantage is speed—such changes may be compensated before they have any noticeable effect on the system—but the cost is paid in controller

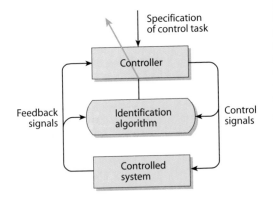

Specification of control task

Controller

Feedback signals

Identification algorithm

Control signals

Controlled system

Fig. 1. To render a controller adaptive, an identification algorithm monitors control signals and feedback signals to provide the controller with updated estimates of the parameters that describe the controlled system.

complexity: for the controller must have an accurate model of the effect of all such disturbances upon the system, if it is to compute controls which will indeed effect the necessary compensations.

Feedforward generates large control signals which rapidly correct large discrepancies from the desired output. The resultant change in output may be too fast for long-latency feedback paths to play a major effect.

Feedback and feedforward are separate control strategies and thus *may* have separate structural embodiments, as shown in Fig. 2 (which does not show the identification algorithms that may provide the adaptive components for each strategy). Note that feedforward is 'pulse activated' in the hypothetical scheme of Fig. 2. It is activated when the error is not small. If well calibrated, the feedforward controller will, with a single brief time pattern of control,

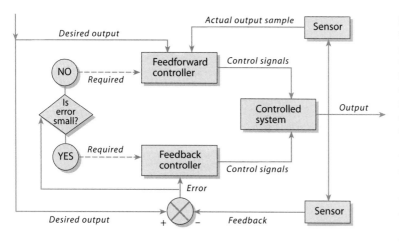

Fig. 2. Discrete-activation feedforward—one of various possible configurations in which feedback and feedforward controls are explicitly separated. Here feedforward is active for large errors to get the controlled system 'into the right ball-park', while feedback provides 'fine-tuning' in the presence of small errors. The dashed lines marked 'required' indicate the supply of necessary activation if the system supplied is to function. Non-dashed lines indicate 'data flow'.

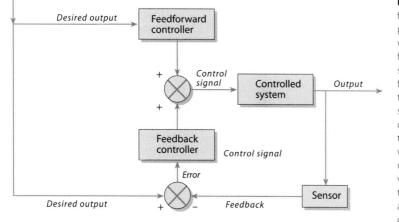

Fig. 3. Co-activation feedforward—one of various possible configurations in which feedback and feedforward are explicitly separated. Here the feedforward controller continually supplies a control signal which can maintain the output of the controlled system 'in the right ballpark', while the feedback controller utilizes error feedback to provide the necessary fine-tuning to compensate for inaccuracy in the feedforward controller's model of the controlled system, as well as for disturbances. Such a mode of control is appropriate only when the controlled system has a functional relation between maintained input and maintained output.

return the system to the 'right ballpark', i.e. making the error small enough for feedback control to function effectively. The system should thus have a 'refractory period' based on the time constants of the controlled system—it should not generate a second control signal before the control system has had time to respond fully to the first control signal. The reader should note what at first appears to be a semantic trick. The sample of the system's output is called 'feedback' when fed to the feedback controller, yet is called 'actual output sample' when fed to the feedforward controller. This looks like a way of avoiding the admission that feedforward requires feedback! But the difference is, in fact, a genuine one. A feedforward controller will, in general, need to know the actual state of the controlled system before generating its control signal, but need not monitor that output while the control signal is actually emitted. By contrast, the feedback controller continually monitors the error signal in generating its controls. As suggested by our ball-catching example, the situation in Fig. 2 might be refined so as to have the feedforward controller monitor the relation between the actual trajectory and a predicted trajectory, changing strategy if the discrepancy or error exceeds a threshold. But, again, we have a discrete-activation form of feedforward.

Fig. 3 shows a different strategy, which appears to describe better the control of muscle. Here, the control neuron must maintain a specific level of firing to hold a limb in a desired position—there is a functional relation between a desired output (e.g. muscle length) and a necessary input (e.g. maintained tension). In this case, the feedforward would be *co-activated* with the feedback system, so that feedforward sets and maintains the control level specified by the functional relationship, while feedback compensates for minor departures.

See also BIOFEEDBACK; CYBERNETICS, THE HISTORY OF.

MAA

Feldman, A. G. (1966). 'Functional tuning of the nervous system with control of movement or maintenance of a steady posture—II. Controllable parameters of the muscles'. *Biophysics*, 11.

Greene, P. H. (1969). 'Seeking mathematical models of skilled actions'. In Brodsky, R. (ed.), *Biomechanics*.

MacKay, D. M. (1966). 'Cerebral organization and the conscious control of action'. In Eccles, J. C. (ed.), *Brain and Conscious Experience*.

Minsky, M. L. (1961). 'Steps towards artificial intelligence'. *Proceedings of the Institute of Radio Engineers*, 49.

Ferrier, Sir David (1843–1928). British physician, who was born near Aberdeen and went to university there. He graduated in classics and philosophy in 1863, having studied under Alexander *Bain, and went on to study medicine at Edinburgh in 1865–8. He was appointed physiology lecturer at the Middlesex Hospital in 1870 and in 1871 moved to King's College, London, where he spent the rest of his working life. The post of professor of neuropathology was created specially for him.

In 1873, Ferrier became interested in electrical excitation of the brain. He devised a method of faradic stimulation whereby he could explore the brains of various types of vertebrates including the monkey. The results confirmed his belief that cerebral functions were localized and enabled him to establish their areas. He noticed that, if certain areas of a monkey's brain were destroyed, symptoms similar to those of a '*stroke' in humans were produced. He was now convinced that operations to treat brain injuries and diseases could be undertaken—if Lister's precautions against sepsis were observed—and these began to be successfully performed, thus changing the outlook in this field totally.

Ferrier was elected a Fellow of the Royal Society in 1876 and a lecture named after him was endowed.

See also LOCALIZATION OF BRAIN FUNCTION AND CORTICAL MAPS.

DDH

figural after-effects. These are changes in the appearance of a visual display consequent upon relatively prolonged fixation. These changes may affect size, shape, brightness, and location in space.

Figural after-effects were first described in 1933 by J. J. *Gibson, who observed that after fixating a curved line for several minutes it appeared to be curved in the opposite direction. Somewhat similar after-effects were studied in greater detail by the *Gestalt psychologists Wolfgang *Köhler and Hans Wallach in 1944, and their work attracted considerable interest. Although these effects are often striking, unfortunately it cannot be said that their nature and mechanisms are fully understood.

Köhler's method of inducing figural after-effects in two dimensions may be briefly described. Two identical rectangles separated by about 25 cm (10 inches) are displayed on a white ground and a fixation point provided midway between them. After the subject has satisfied himself that, when viewed from a distance of a few metres, the figures look identical, one rectangle, known as the Test or T-figure, is concealed by a screen, and the subject is instructed to fixate the remaining rectangle, known as the Inspection or I-figure, for three minutes. The screen is then swiftly removed and the subject is required to describe the appearance of the two figures. The typical response is to say that the I-figure appears smaller, dimmer, and lying further back in space than the T-figure. Although these effects vary appreciably as between subjects, very few fail to report them in whole or in part. Furthermore, they may persist for a short period after the T-figure has been exposed.

Köhler satisfied himself that these after-effects are of central rather than peripheral origin. In particular, he claimed that, if the I-figure is viewed with one eye and the T-figure with the other, the outcome is the same as with binocular vision throughout.

Köhler and Wallach attempted to explain figural after-effects in terms of an electrical field theory, often referred to as the 'satiation' theory. This theory is based in part on classical physics and in part on the tenets of Gestalt theory, in particular the concept of *isomorphism. Although ingenious, it can hardly be said that this theory carries conviction. An alternative theory, put forward by C. E. Osgood and A. W. Heyer, and owing much to W. M. Marshall and S. A. Talbot's excellent work on the mechanism of vision, is altogether more plausible than Köhler's theory though not perhaps without difficulties of its own.

Köhler and his colleagues subsequently recorded some other varieties of figural after-effects, the most striking of which are figural after-effects in the third dimension, as described by Köhler and Emery in 1947. According to Osgood, these find ready explanation if we assume that size changes are interpreted in terms of changes in distance. More perplexing are the accounts of figural after-effects in kinaesthesia reported by Köhler and Dinnerstein, also in 1947. These appear to continue very much longer than those reported in the visual experiments and may, it seems, persist for several days. Even Köhler was obliged to conclude that after-effects in the third dimension of visual space and those in kinaesthesis 'appear at present almost inaccessible to the theorist'! Indeed we are driven to conclude that whereas figural after-effects merit recognition as convincing perceptual phenomena, they still evade convincing psychological explanation.   OLZ

Köhler, W. (1940). *Dynamics in Psychology*.

McEwan, P. 'Figural after-effects'. *British Journal of Psychology*, Monograph Supplement no. 31.

Osgood, C. E. (1944). *Method and Theory in Experimental Psychology*.

figure–ground. A term used in technical discussions on visual perception. In 'ambiguous figures', the *figure* alternates with the *ground* (Fig. 1) or with alternative figures or objects (see ILLUSIONS, Fig. 8). 'Figure' corresponds roughly to seeing *objects*. These important phenomena were investigated by the Danish psychologist Edgar *Rubin, among others, and may be thought of as changing perceptual hypotheses. See also GESTALT THEORY.

Gregory, R. L. (1970). *The Intelligent Eye*.

filling in scotomas. Gaps in vision, and also of hearing, can it would seem be 'filled in' and so not noticed. Yet of course we can see gaps. In music pauses are very important. A written or a printed C is different from an O because of the gap. The Landolt Ring test for visual acuity has a gap, which may be in any of four positions in the ring; but

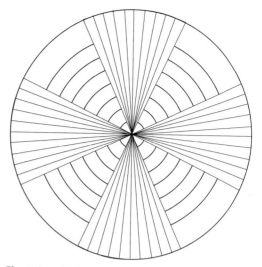

Fig. 1. One of Rubin's figure–ground reversing figures. Here there are two equally held figures, which in turn are relegated to ground. Regions accepted as figures are subtly changed perceptually in the process: if the concentric cross is seen as a figure after the radial one, it is possible to note a characteristic change in the concentric markings, which depends on whether they belong to the figure or the ground. When they are part of the ground, they do not appear interrupted but seem to continue behind the figure. This is not noticed when the concentric cross is seen as the figure.

it would be a useless test of acuity if the gap is perceptually filled in.

Filling in may repair loss of information, or it may remove distracting illusory holes. The most dramatic visual hole is the blind spot of each eye where the optic nerve leaves the retina for the brain. This blind region is as large as twenty moons packed together; yet normally it is not seen, even when the other eye is closed. Looking now at this page, it is remarkable that one does not see a great black blob moving with the eyes. Yet the blind region in each eye is easily demonstrated with an isolated feature:

    &   *

Look at the asterisk with the left eye, the right eye being closed. Move the book slowly towards and away from the eye. At about 6 inches—when the & falls on the blind region—it will disappear. This also works with a background pattern, including written or printed words; yet even when one eye is shut this local blindness in the visual field of each eye is hardly ever experienced. The surrounding colour and pattern is seen in the blind region.

How is this possible? If this process were 'low-level', and not occupying consciousness, it would avoid our being distracted by a black blob hovering (like an after-image) before the eyes. But is it actively filled in? A perhaps simpler alternative has been suggested by the American philosopher Daniel C. Dennett (2002): that the blind spot is *ignored*. This would be like a boring guest at a party, failing to attract attention as he offers nothing worth hearing. Not seeing or noticing a familiar ornament or picture, and not hearing the ticking of a familiar clock, could be similar. These are filled in or ignored for lack of information of a too-familiar signal, rather than total lack of information from a region. There could be different processes for various situations. There could be filling in and ignoring.

Phenomena of the blind spot are hard to investigate as this region is far out in peripheral vision. For an experiment, Ramachandran and Gregory (1991) induced artificial scotomas in the human eye, which could have almost any position or size. This was done with a kind of adaptation that is not fully understood, the Troxler Effect, which is a curious kind of cortical effect. The subject of the experiment stared fixedly at a pattern, which had a blank region of about the average brightness and similar colour. When this display was viewed with a fixed eye, by staring at a fixation mark somewhat displaced from the blank region, or 'hole' in the pattern, the hole faded away, and after about ten seconds disappeared. Then the pattern appears to be complete. Is this artificial scotoma actively filled in, or is it ignored?

A computer display was used to present the pattern, with a square hole. When after about ten seconds the hole disappeared, this display was switched off—and immediately replaced with a blank screen, of about the same brightness and colour. (The fixation spot remained in the same place so the eye(s) could continue looking, without moving). What was seen on the blank screen? Amazingly, a small part of the original pattern—looking rather degenerated, like a poor Xerox—where the hole had been in the adapting pattern.

This is quite unlike a normal after-image. Even more different, the experiment also worked with dynamic visual noise, or 'twinkle', looking like a swarm of busy ants. Similar twinkle was seen on the blank screen, in the region of the hole in the previous twinkling display.

This seems evidence for active filling in. For we seem to be seeing what the brain creates, to fill in the hole in the static or the dynamic twinkling display.

This interpretation has led to an interesting debate. Dan Dennett has written (Dennett 2002): 'In this new perceptual illusion, the illusory *content* is that *there is twinkling in the square*. But, one is tempted to ask, how is this content *rendered*? Is it a matter of the representation being composed of hundreds or thousands of individual illusory twinkles or is it a matter of there being, in effect, a label that just says "twinkling" . . . Can the brain represent twinkling, perceptually, without representing individual twinkles?' Dennet generalizes this to normal

perception: 'It does not follow from the fact that *we see the twinkling* that the individual twinkles are represented.' This is an important general issue for perception, as perceptions may be largely fictional, even when they are not false. It is also important for artists; they do not have to represent each leaf of a tree, a 'leafy pattern' will serve, though it has no individual leaves. Although this experiment supports the notion that scotomas can be filled in neurally, just what is filled in may be questioned.

Short-term artificial scotomas may be different from lifelong scotomas, including the blind spots where the optic nerves leave the retinas. As these never provide information, they are more likely to be ignored. It seems, though, that they also are filled in (Ramachandran 1992). There is physiological evidence of rapid neural changes associated with 'filling in', including long-term cortical remapping (Pessoa and de Weerd 2003). But different processes could apply for various situations. It does seem unlikely that we create the silence that fills the unheard ticking of the familiar clock; yet much of perception is created, rather than simply received from the world around us.
VR/RLG

Dennet, D. C. (2002). 'Seeing is Believing—Or is It?' In Noe, A., and Thompson, E. (eds.), *Vision and Mind: Selected Readings in the Philosophy of Perception*.

Pessoa, L., and de Weerd, P. (2003) (eds.), 'Filling-in'. In *From Perceptual Completion to Cortical Reorganization*.

Ramachandran, V. S. (1992). 'Blind spots'. *Scientific American*, 266.

—— and Gregory R. L. (1991). 'Perceptual filling in of artificially induced scotomas in human vision'. *Nature*, 350.

films, perception of. The explanatory power of perceptual theories and the generality of perceptual research findings are both strongly challenged by the sensory phenomena on which motion pictures and television are based, and by the perceptual devices that they employ.

Motion pictures are possible because we perceive continuous movement in response to a rapid succession of static views. The phenomenon is often called *apparent movement* (or stroboscopic movement). Writers about cinema routinely appeal to 'visual persistence' to explain this fundamental phenomenon. Such persistence, however, although real enough (see AFTER-IMAGE) simply cannot explain apparent movement. At best, it names the fact that we do not detect the brief periods (*c*.0.0125 sec.) during which the motion picture screen is dark. At worst, persistence would result in the superposition of the successive views. In fact, we have only begun to explore the sensory mechanisms (including direct motion detectors, retrograde masking, and fast and slow neural channels) that must contribute to the phenomenon of apparent movement by eliminating the superposition of successive disparate views that mere visual persistence would provide, and to consider the cognitive processes that fit

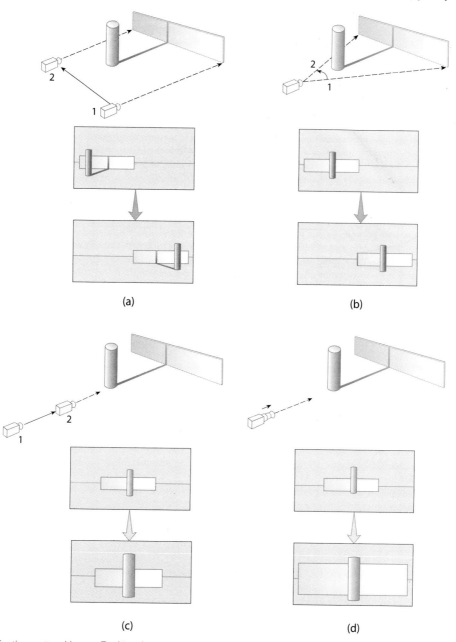

Fig. 1. Continuous transitions. **a.** Tracking shot: at top, the camera moves from station 1 to station 2 (solid arrow); the dotted arrows show the camera's line of sight at beginning and end of section. Below: view from point 1 over view from point 2. Note effects of parallax. **b.** Pan shot: camera rotates (solid arrow) around stationary point. Note absence of parallax in resulting views. **c.** Dolly shot: camera approaches from station 1 to 2. Note parallax (i.e. change in relative size of nearer and further objects). **d.** Zoom shot: camera remains stationary, but focal length is increased. Note that magnification, but no parallax, is obtained.

compelling perceptual meaning to those views (Hochberg and Brooks 1978).

Some of these mechanisms and processes must also be engaged when we build up a continuous percept of our physical environment by taking successive discrete and discontinuous glances at it. Motion pictures and television differ in significant ways, however, from the information provided by glances taken at the real world. When the viewer looks over his environment, his knowledge of where in space his eye is directed during each successive glance is at least potentially informative about how the separate glimpses fit together into a single coherent object or scene. Considerable thought and research have been devoted to this matter of 'taking eye direction into account', but motion picture and television usage assures us that more elaborate integrative processes are available to the viewer than have been the subject of such research. When different camera shots of an object or scene are projected successively on the screen, the viewer's knowledge of where his eye is directed could not possibly tell him how the successive views are to be put together. At best, by taking his eye direction into account, the viewer could learn only that all of the partial views of the scene have been presented at the same place in space, i.e. on the viewing screen.

Changes in camera viewpoint are made for many purposes, and in several distinct ways. Such view changes serve to direct the flow of thought, emphasizing specific objects or events; to provide visual rhythms analogous to those of poetry and music; to recapture visual attention once a view's content has been identified and the viewer's visual interest wanes; and to provide narrative economy by 'skimming' lengthy events and presenting only the essential features. Most importantly, by changing camera viewpoints, the film-maker can present a scene that is vastly larger than each view on the screen, and can present scenes that do not really exist in any one place, or that are too large to display all at once on the screen in sufficient detail.

View changes can be continuous or discontinuous. That is, the camera may move continuously, as shown by the solid arrow in Fig. 1, from one station (1) to another (2), moving perpendicular to the line of sight (as in the *tracking shot*, Fig. 1a), or moving in the direction of the line of sight (as in the *dolly shot*, Fig. 1c). These movements, or their combinations, usually offer visual information about the depth relationships within the scene (for example, *motion parallax*; note the different displacements of near and far objects between the first and last shots as shown in Figs. 1a and 1c). Keeping the camera stationary, but changing the direction in which it is pointed from (1) to (2) in the *pan shot* of Fig. 1b, or changing its focal length in a *zoom* which merely imposes a uniform magnification on the field of view (Fig. 1d), achieves changes in view that are

superficially similar to the track and dolly shots respectively, but provide no motion parallax and therefore no depth information.

Theoretically, because they lack depth information, pans and zooms should look very different from dolly and track shots, but for reasons of convenience and economy film-makers often use the former instead of the latter, with results that appear to be acceptable to the viewer. Although our ability to detect motion parallax in the laboratory is astonishingly good, how much we actually use it in motion pictures or in real life is an unexplored question of some importance to film-makers and of considerable theoretical interest to psychologists.

Part of its theoretical interest rests on the following issue: in recent years, several perceptual theorists have proposed that our visual systems are *directly* sensitive to the spatial information that is provided by transformations over time within the light that reaches the eye of a viewer who is in motion relative to a scene. In the case of track and dolly shots, this includes the three-dimensional relationships within the scene; in all of the transformations, the overlap between successive views provides information about the loci of objects in the scene and the order in which the successive views were obtained. This is true of *discontinuous* sequences of overlapping views, as well: the sequence in Fig. 2 specifies that W is to the left of Z even though the two are never shown at the same time.

It is proposed that both in normal saccadic glances (rapid changes of regard between which the eye remains static for about 200 milliseconds), and in motion picture transitions, we respond directly to the visual information about spatial layout that the view sequences contain. At least in the case of discontinuous motion picture cuts, however, the perceptual process appears not to be as

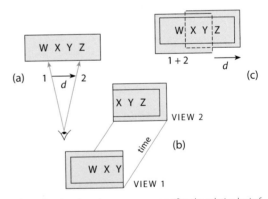

(a)

(b)

(c)

Fig. 2. Overlapping view sequence specifies the relative loci of parts of the scene (W, Z) that are not on the screen at the same time, and also specifies the direction of change in view (d) of eye or camera. **a.** Scene. **b.** Successive views. **c.** Information theoretically available in the view sequence at **b.**

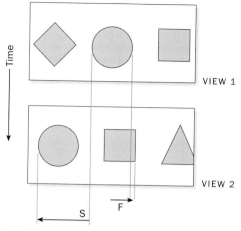

Fig. 3. Bad cut, 1.

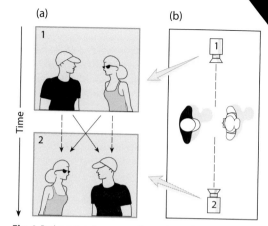

Fig. 4. Bad cut, 2. **a.** Sequence of two views taken from camera positions 1 and 2 in **b**.

automatic, direct, or veridical as the preceding analysis implies. The relationship between successive views may be grossly misperceived, even though those views overlap substantially. In Fig. 3, for example, although successive views 1 and 2 are in fact displaced leftward (vector S), rightward movement (F) is perceived (except at very slow presentation rates) because objects in one view have been incorrectly 'identified' by the viewer's perceptual system as being quite different objects in the preceding view. There is a great deal of laboratory work showing that apparent motion occurs, in this way, even between unlike but contiguous shapes or parts of shapes (Orlansky 1940, Kolers 1972, Hochberg and Brooks 1978). And these are not merely laboratory phenomena: film-makers distinguish good and bad cuts, and most examples of the latter result from an unwanted apparent movement that may be completely independent of the actual displacement between views (Vorkapich 1972), or indeed result from an apparent absence of displacement where a large displacement in fact exists. For example, when the camera direction changes by approximately 180 degrees ('crossing the camera axis', as in Fig. 4), there is a brief but upsetting impression that the people remain on the same places on the screen, but change their shape (as signified by the dotted arrows in that figure). Similarly changes in focal length in the traditional sequence of Fig. 5a should be large ones, for if they are small, as in Fig. 5b, the apparent movement between contours in successive views is perceived as a rapid expansion or approach, rather than as the changes in the field of attention that we discuss below.

Successive views of different objects or people are often aligned deliberately in order to avoid the apparent 'jump' that occurs between successive non-aligned contours, and thereby to achieve a cut that is smooth and unaccented. Such cuts probably take longer to comprehend, however,

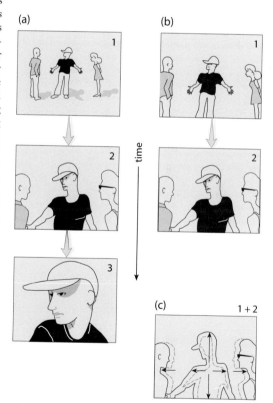

Fig. 5. Good and bad changes in focal length. **a.** Good sequence of long shot, medium shot, and close-up. **b.** Cut from 1 to 2 is bad because with small change in focal length, unintended movement occurs between successive views. **c.** Perceptual consequence of the sequence in **b.**

because no adequate signal has been given to the eye that the view has been changed.

The factor of apparent movement between unrelated but contiguous successive shapes is of practical importance in that its various cinematic manifestations are evidently used by film-makers (through rules of thumb, and by trial and error in film editing) to achieve comprehensibility, and to control the accents in the cutting rhythm (or montage). It is theoretically important in showing that the overall relationship between discontinuous overlapping views is not directly and automatically perceived. Where the local factors do not change to provide apparent movement that conveys the intended spatial relationship, the film-maker must allow the viewer sufficient time to construct the spatial relationship using other sources of information. Those responses (i.e. 'readings' of any sequence) that depend on factors that are relatively local, but undetailed, like the phenomena in Fig. 3, seem to be rapid, effortless, and transient, and tend therefore to determine how sequences of brief views are perceived. Responses that depend on more detailed identification, or on more involved 'visual inferences', as discussed below, are slower, and perhaps more sustained. The same sequence of views may therefore be differently comprehended at different cutting rates. For instance, Fig. 3 appears to move rightward at rapid rates (less than a second per view) and leftward at slow rates (such as three seconds per view).

Why don't these local factors cause noticeable confusions in the course of normal saccadic glances as they do in cinematic view sequences? Several factors may account for this difference. In saccades, the entire field of view (well over 100 degrees) is translated as a whole, as compared to the relatively small regions (c.45 degrees) within which translation occurs on the motion picture or television screen; a brief but significant period of partial visual suppression accompanies each saccade, and this may prevent the local apparent movements that afflict cinematic cuts, and may perhaps thereby permit invariant information in overlapping saccadic glimpses to be correctly used. Furthermore, we know that the viewer can take some account of the direction in which his or her eyes have been ordered to move. Perhaps most important of all, in the case of saccadic glances, the viewer has asked the visual question that motivated the eye movement, and to which the resulting glimpse comes as an answer.

Such perceptual question asking or 'hypothesis testing' (a central feature in current perceptual theories: see Gregory 1974, Hochberg 1979) cannot readily be studied in the course of normal saccades, nor even with motion picture cuts that overlap substantially (e.g. Fig. 2), because of the purely visual information such events contain, and the possibility of the direct use of such information. But the fact is that *many or even most motion picture cuts occur between views that do not overlap at all*. It is these that allow the film-maker to construct scenes and events that never existed. No purely sensory information within such transformations could provide the basis for their combination in the mind's eye of the viewer, nor make the view sequence comprehensible. The film-maker connects such non-overlapping shots either by leading the viewer to ask the visual question, to which the next view is an answer, or by providing a context that identifies the relative locations of subsequently presented views. Fig. 6a is an example of the former: an actor looking leftward in one view naturally leads the viewer to expect that the next shot shows the object of the actor's regard, i.e. to the viewer's left. Fig. 6b is an example of the latter: in the sequence of a long shot followed by a medium shot and close-ups (views 1–4, respectively), the long shot acts as an *establishing shot* within which the non-overlapping close-ups take their appropriate places. (Note that the factor at work in Fig. 6a would reverse the relative locations of views 3 and 4, were the latter presented without the first two shots in their

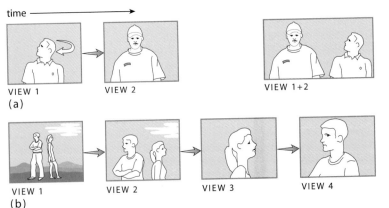

time ⟶

VIEW 1   VIEW 2   VIEW 1+2
(a)

VIEW 1   VIEW 2   VIEW 3   VIEW 4
(b)

Fig. 6. Typical devices for providing meaning to successive views.

sequence.) After a sequence of non-overlapping close-ups has gone on for a while, or after a *cutaway shot* has shown *parallel action* going on elsewhere, *re-establishing shots* (like view 1) may again be needed.

Some of the film-makers' devices are clearly mere conventions (for instance: dissolves, indicating parallel action; calendar leaves, indicating elapsed time); some are simply logical inferences that follow from the viewer's legitimate assumption that the film sequence was created with a coherent narrative or expositional purpose (recent attempts to analyse the maxims of spoken discourse, notably by Grice 1968 and Searle 1969, may suggest ways to study such inferences). Some methods probably tap more general cognitive processes: for example, in the sequence from long shot to close-ups in Figs. 5 and 6, the viewer's attention is directed first to a general survey of the scene and then constrained to smaller regions and details that take their meaning from the preceding context.

Research in this area has barely begun. The cognitive skills by which the information from successive glances is integrated—skills that are of the utmost importance to any perceptual theory that aspires to apply beyond the momentary glance—are open to study through the medium of motion picture cutting. Since *Leonardo da Vinci, perceptual research and theory have been primarily concerned with the still picture. For both practical and theoretical reasons, we should turn our attention to motion pictures.   JH

Gregory, R. L. (1974). 'Choosing a paradigm for perception'. In Carterette, E. C., and Friedman, M. P. (eds.), *Handbook of Perception*, vol. i.

Grice, H. (1968). 'Utterer's meaning, sentence-meaning and word-meaning'. *Foundations of Language*, 4.

Hochberg, J. (1978). *Perception* (2nd edn.).

——(1979). 'Sensation and perception'. In Hearst, E. (ed.), *The First Century of Experimental Psychology*.

—— and Brooks, V. (1978). 'The perception of motion pictures'. In Carterette, E. C., and Friedman, M. P. (eds.), *Handbook of Perception*, vol. x.

Kolers, P. A. (1972). *Aspects of Motion Perception*.

Orlansky, J. (1940). 'The effect of similarity and difference in form on apparent visual movement'. *Archives of Psychology*, 246.

Reisz, K., and Millar, G. (1968). *The Technique of Film Editing*.

Searle, J. R. (1969). *Speech Acts: An Essay in the Philosophy of Language*.

Vorkapich, S. (1972). 'A fresh look at the dynamics of film-making'. *American Cinematographer* (Feb.).

Fisher, Sir Ronald Aylmer

Fisher, Sir Ronald Aylmer (1890–1962). British statistician and geneticist, born in London and educated at Cambridge. While working on experimental methods in agricultural research at the Rothamsted Experimental Station, he developed the analysis of variance and the now standard methods of assessing statistical significance. He summarized this work in *Statistical Methods for Research Workers* (1925), a book whose many editions have been very influential. While at Rothamsted he also published *The Genetical Theory of Natural Selection* (1930), which became a classic of population genetics. In 1933 he became Galton Professor of eugenics at University College London and in 1943 professor of genetics at Cambridge. His continued interest in statistics and experimental design led to two further important books, *The Design of Experiments* (1935) and *Statistical Tables for Biological, Agricultural, and Medical Research* (1938), the latter written jointly with F. Yates.

Flourens, (Marie Jean) Pierre

Flourens, (Marie Jean) Pierre (1794–1867). French physiologist, born at Maureilhan, Hérault, and who studied medicine at Montpellier, qualifying in 1813. He moved to Paris, where he was helped by the anatomist Georges Cuvier. He became a member of the Académie des Sciences in 1828, professor of comparative anatomy at the Collège de France in 1835, and a member of the Académie Française in 1840. He was a pioneer in techniques of ablation for investigating brain function.

An accomplished experimentalist, his findings led him to conclude that there is considerable diversification of function in the central nervous system: 'All sensory and volitional faculties exist in the cerebral hemispheres and must be regarded as occupying concurrently the same seat in these structures.' He likewise concluded that 'feeling, willing, and perceiving are but a single and essentially unitary faculty residing in a single organ (i.e. the cerebral hemispheres)'. These findings have been widely taken to imply that the various categories of psychological function are not discretely localized in the cerebral cortex—a view that held sway for some 60 years until Paul *Broca's claim that articulate speech in man is localized in a small area of the left cerebral hemisphere.

As might be anticipated, Flourens was a convinced opponent of phrenology and his work did much to discredit the standing of F. J. *Gall. And he is often held, not wholly with justice, to have anticipated the views of Karl *Lashley on the cerebral localization of psychological function. His important work on the effects of cerebral ablation in animals is *Recherches expérimentales sur les propriétés et les fonctions du système nerveux dans les animaux vertébrés* (1824).

forgetting

forgetting. There are three possible causes of forgetting. First, relevant information may have been lost from the storage system of the brain—'storage loss'. Second, there may be failure to retrieve or to use stored information—'retrieval failure'. Third, insufficient information may have been put into storage to permit of differentiation between wanted and unwanted information—'encoding deficiency'. (Strictly, this is only one form of encoding deficiency. *How* information is encoded can also affect retrieval, as the success of *mnemonic systems testifies.)

Storage loss can occur in several ways. There may be decay of the physical representation of the information. Decay is a plausible explanation for the very rapid forgetting which takes place in the first second or so after an experience has occurred—for example, the fading perception of the visual world that occurs if you close your eyes. Another possibility is that information is displaced from storage by new information; the idea of displacement is used, for example, in the 'slot' theory of the memory span (see SHORT-TERM MEMORY). Or information may be modified by new information rather than be displaced by it, as in *Bartlett's '*schemas' theory. Modification of schema may underlie the way our memory for a changing feature of the environment is updated, whether the feature is transient, such as our own location in space, or one that changes only slowly, such as the face of a friend. Schemas provide a basis for recording abstractions from events without recording the events as such.

There is no direct evidence for storage loss. If such evidence is obtained it will be physiological. However, the total absence of storage loss would mean that, in a sense, nothing is ever really forgotten. This view was popularized by Freud but it is doubtful whether he meant that every trivial detail of every trivial experience remains stored. There is suggestive evidence of storage loss in postencephalytic amnesia, since the *amnesia is characterized by unusually rapid forgetting. (Typically, amnesia is characterized by poor learning rather than rapid forgetting.) Suggestive evidence for storage loss, without any association with disease, comes from an extensive investigation of memory for school-learned Spanish: there was forgetting for the first five years after study, no forgetting for the next 25 years, and additional forgetting with the onset of middle age. The interpretation of such evidence is, however, controversial.

Without physiological evidence it is impossible to be sure that storage loss occurs, for retrieval failure can never be excluded as a reason for forgetting. There is plenty of everyday evidence for retrieval failure: for example, we all forget names we know that we know and which we can later recall (the tip-of-the-tongue phenomenon). The likelihood of successful retrieval is greatly affected by the presence or absence of relevant cues—stimuli, logically or associatively related to the information to be retrieved —especially if they were present at the time of learning. Mood, which provides internal cues, has been shown to have quite a powerful effect on retrieval. It is easier to remember happy events when we are happy than when we are unhappy and vice versa (thus reinforcing a current mood state). Hypnosis can be used to alter mood state and can thereby affect retrieval. However, the common belief that hypnosis produces a dramatic increase in

retrieval (thereby supporting the notion that there is no true forgetting) has been shown to be false, and the memories produced under hypnosis have proved to be highly unreliable.

An event is difficult to remember if it is one of a number of similar events (What did you have for lunch on Tuesday last week?)—a difficulty which has been extensively studied under the heading of proactive and retroactive interference. The difficulty probably arises partly because insufficient information has been stored to enable differentiation of one event from another—that is, from encoding deficiency. Immediately after an event has occurred, its recency is a sufficient basis for its identification, but later it can be distinguished from similar events only by some form of stored code of adequate precision. The difficulty also arises because retrieval failure becomes more likely; according to cue-overload theory, this is because retrieval of similar memories tends to depend on the same cues, and the effectiveness of a cue falls as the number of memories associated with it rises.

We think of forgetting as undesirable. However, the difficulty of remembering similar events suggests that there is a positive advantage in forgetting, through storage loss, the great majority of our moment-to-moment experiences: such forgetting should reduce retrieval loss for information of importance to us. Can we, then, voluntarily discard information? Experiments suggest that the extent to which we can is very limited and probably confined to ceasing active maintenance of recently acquired information. Sadly, the mind does not seem to have at its disposal anything corresponding to the erase button of a tape recorder or computer.

See also MEMORY: BIOLOGICAL BASIS.   JB

Baddeley, A. D. (1976). *The Psychology of Memory*.

Bahrick, H. P. (1984). 'Semantic memory content in permastore: fifty years of memory for Spanish learned in school'. *Journal of Experimental Psychology: General*, 113.

Fourier analysis. A method of analysing into simpler components any complex sound or other waveform (whether it describes fluctuations over time or over place). The analysis uses the Fourier theorem, which states that any function or waveform can be described as a series of sine waves of multiple frequencies and various amplitudes. Conversely, the characteristic timbre of musical instruments can be produced by combining separate sine wave oscillations (Fourier synthesis).

Fourier analysis is useful for studies of electroencephalography and *speech recognition by machine. The notion that visual *pattern recognition may employ Fourier analysis is due largely to the work of F. W. Campbell at the University of Cambridge.

The Fourier theorem was formulated in 1826 by the French mathematician and physicist Jean Baptiste Joseph de Fourier (1768–1830), who was a professor at the École Polytechnique in Paris from 1795 to 1798; he accompanied Napoleon to Egypt as scientific adviser and was for a time governor of Lower Egypt. He was created baron in 1808 and in 1827 became president of the council of the École Polytechnique.

Campbell, F. W., and Robson, J. G. (1968). 'Application of Fourier analysis to the visibility of gratings'. *Journal of Physiology*, 197.
Herivel, J. (1975). *Joseph Fourier: The Man and the Physicist*.

Frankenstein. The creator of a monster in a story, suggested in a dream, written by Mary Wollstonecraft Shelley (1797–1851) for her future husband, the poet Shelley, and their friend Lord Byron during a wet holiday on Lake Geneva in August 1816. The monster, created from parts of dead men, represented the fearful power of science to create uncontrollable beings and forces that threaten and might destroy us. The titlepage of the novel (published in 1818) reads:

FRANKENSTEIN

or,

THE MODERN PROMETHEUS.

in Three volumes.

Did I request thee, Maker, from my clay
To mould me man? Did I solicit thee
From darkness to promote me?—

Paradise Lost

Mary Shelley gives the full story of how it came to be written in the 1831 preface to the novel.

Frankenstein has been reborn in many films (Daniels 1975), the first made in 1910 by the American inventor Thomas Alva Edison; sadly, this is lost, though there remain photographs of the first film monster: Charles Ogle. Boris Karloff played the monster in Universal Pictures' classic *Frankenstein* of 1931; his creator, Dr Frankenstein, vitalizes the monster most impressively by harnessing the powers of lightning with a wonderful apparatus. The same studio made seven sequels, while many other Frankenstein monsters appeared from other studios, demonstrating the power of a myth that represents the fears of our time. RLG

Daniels, L. (1975). *Living in Fear*. (Reissued in 1977 as *Fear: A History of Horror in the Mass Media*.)
Grylls, R. G. (1938). *Mary Shelley: A Biography*.

Frazer, Sir James George (1854–1941). British social anthropologist and scholar of myths and comparative religions. Born in Glasgow, he graduated at Cambridge in 1878 and became a Fellow of Trinity College. His major work is *The Golden Bough* (1890; 3rd edn., rewritten in twelve volumes, 1911–15; abridged 1922). He also wrote *Folklore in the Old Testament* (1918), *Belief in Immortality* (1913–24), *Fear of the Dead* (1933–6), and *Magic and Religion*

(1944). He became professor of social anthropology at Liverpool in 1907, was knighted in 1914, and was awarded the Order of Merit in 1925. Strangely, although his scholarship extended to the mythology of many countries, his sources were entirely from books, as he never travelled.

Ackerman, R. (1990). *J. G. Frazer: His Life and Work*.

free association. Sigmund *Freud gave a new direction to the study of the association of ideas as he developed his therapeutic techniques in clinical practice. He came to claim that the unforced remarks made by patients during treatment unwittingly revealed their wishes and motives, and thereby enabled the therapist to circumvent resistance to personal disclosure. In 1912, in *The Dynamics of Transference*, he described his fundamental principle of *psychoanalysis as the requirement that the patient repeats whatever comes into his or her head without criticizing it.

Interest in applying principles of organization to the headlong abundance of thoughts, images, memories, and *perceptions that distinguish mental life had previously overlooked the possible importance of personal experiences and preoccupations. *Aristotle's description of the formal (similarity, contrast) and accidental properties (contiguity in time or place) that linked thoughts, had been taken up by *Locke and *Hume to provide a detailed but highly abstract explanation of the contents of the stream of consciousness. No attempt to account for the individual colouring of associations was made by the British empiricists, even after an experimental approach had been introduced by Francis *Galton. Of course Freud's clinical findings had been intuitively anticipated by dramatists and novelists, and perhaps most powerfully realized in their depictions of suffering so great as to effect disintegration of syntax. Hamlet's wordplay though dark is not impenetrable, and it has the effect of drawing the anxious listeners into the drama of his distress.

*Jung, who in so many of his researches followed where Freud led, had in fact begun to study free association before they met. He approached the subject from a different angle but also came to focus on the personal significance of associations. His interest had been aroused by his application, as an instrument of clinical investigation, of the word-association test invented by Galton. This test had provided a technique for putting the mechanism of association under scrutiny, although it suffered the limitation of being so atomistic as to produce highly artificial results. The procedure was very simple: the experimenter worked through a list of prepared words, perhaps 50 or 60, calling out each one in turn. The subject was required to respond as quickly as possible with the first word that came into his or her mind, and the experimenter recorded this together with the time lapse between stimulus and response. The early work looked at formal relations between word pairs and attempted a variety of classifications of responses. The vast amount of data collected, particularly by Wilhelm *Wundt and his associates, attracts little interest now, being regarded as a recalcitrant body of facts without practical application. Jung temporarily breathed new life into the procedure by noticing that the responses of psychiatric patients often revealed their most intimate concerns. He described a group of responses bound together by a pervasive feeling as a *complex, and transformed the test into a diagnostic tool. He also used it to make interesting observations on speech disturbances in psychotic states, regarding intense emotional preoccupation as a handicap to rational thought. In extreme disturbance, the Aristotelian principles of association became stronger than the influence of any particular directing idea, leading to a loosening of logical associations, and sometimes to a loss of any unifying feeling tone. Even so, beneath the fractured surface of psychotic communication, it was possible to find evidence of profound hurt and compensatory aggrandizement. That this early work made him receptive to the more sophisticated innovations of Freud is clearly indicated in the conclusion to his paper 'Association, Dream and Hysterical Symptom', published in 1906, a year before he met Freud. He wrote there that 'the interferences that the complex causes in the association experiment are none other than the resistances in psychoanalysis as described by Freud'.

Freud's approach to the treatment of neurotic disorders evolved over many years. In its final form, after he had abandoned the use of *hypnosis, he would sit behind his patient who lay on a couch. There was no agenda of problems or topics to be discussed, and the session would be facilitated by Freud's non-emotive promptings. Although the therapeutic alliance required that the conscious attitude of the patient should be desire for change, Freud recognized that there would inevitably be unconscious resistance, as the abandoning of neurotic defences involved the renunciation of cherished illusions. The degree of resistance was a principal factor determining the length of therapy. The method of free association enabled him to capitalize on the unintended candour of the patient and make interpretations which could then be reflected on. Central to this endeavour was the examination of dream material, which provided a 'royal road to the unconscious' and a privileged glimpse of primary process thinking (see DREAMING). In this primitive style of thinking, the categories of space and time were said to be ignored and images tended to become fused and distorted by condensation and displacement. The key to understanding unconscious mental activity was the pleasure principle, which determined that all frustration of instinctual drives was repaired by hallucinatory wish-fulfilment. Freud regarded his longest book, *The Interpretation of Dreams* (1900), as his seminal work, and 30 years after its first publication

described it as containing the most valuable of all his discoveries. So it was that dreams, supplemented by recollections and anecdotes, provided the raw material which through interpretation revealed the motives and wishes of the patient. At first these were ill discerned but later became clearer through the lessening of resistance and the resolving of transference feelings for the analyst. It was not uncommon for a powerfully charged and unusually lucid dream to coincide with a therapeutic breakthrough. Freud insisted on the objectivity of the method, contrasting his approach, in which the interpretation of associations is drawn from the patient by gentle probing, with the classical account of Artemidorus (2nd century AD), in which the adept authoritatively imposed his view on the dreamer.

Nowhere more clearly than in *The Interpretation of Dreams* does Freud display his extreme rationalism. It is as though he employs a psychological principle of sufficient reason, as every feature of a dream is explained in terms that illuminate the conflicts of the dreamer. While the sheer analytical power of his thinking is impressively demonstrated, there are perhaps few therapists today who would interpret with such complete confidence or not allow for undecidable or meaningless elements. Moreover, it is difficult not to feel that Freud's strength of personality imposed itself both on the material he analysed and on the patients themselves. Accounts by patients of their therapy with him tend to confirm this impression and contradict his own description of assumed emotional detachment during therapy. Perhaps Freud's patients tended to have Freudian dreams, as later Jung's patients had Jungian dreams. Nevertheless, the points of agreement between Freud and Jung seem much more profound than the points of difference. Jung subsequently developed his own therapeutic style to suit his temperament, and one of his innovations was to invite the patient to fantasize in the therapeutic sessions and thereby actively promote free association.

As psychotherapeutic practice has proliferated, so ways of conducting therapy have multiplied. The most important general feature of newer therapies has been the attempt to reduce the length of the procedure, from years to months, or even to a fixed number of sessions agreed in advance. In order to abbreviate therapy, various devices have been employed for breaking down resistance. Some examples of this trend are: structuring the therapy sessions, strategic focusing on specific problems, concentrating on patient–therapist interactions in the here and now, and more aggressive styles of interpretation. However, the common denominator in all these approaches is the use of the free associations of the patient to point up contradictions between unconscious attitudes, wishes and motives, and the self-image which unintentionally announces alienation from fundamental impulses.   DAGC

Freud, S. (1900). *The Interpretation of Dreams*, standard edition, iv–v.

—— (1912). *The Dynamics of Transference*, standard edition, xii.

Galton, F. (1897). 'Psychometric experiments'. *Brain*, 2.

H.D. (Hilda Doolittle) (1956). *Tribute to Freud*.

Jung, C. G. (1906). 'Association, dream and hysterical symptom'. *Collection Works*, ii.

free will. Some freedom or other in our choices and actions is a prerequisite of our being held morally responsible for them and getting moral credit for them. It is necessary, we occasionally hear, to our general standing as humans or as individuals. It is also a prerequisite for a good deal else, including our confidence in our enquiries and conclusions, and our large hopes for our futures. This freedom, whatever it is, is sometimes referred to as free will. But the latter term is also used for something more particular: the power of acting without the constraints of necessity or fate. The term is used as well, maybe in the same dictionary entry—see *The New Oxford Dictionary of English*, 2001—for something else more particular: the ability to act at one's own discretion. There are two questions. What does this important freedom really amount to? Do we really have it?

To the first question, one answer given by philosophers is that this freedom is partly choosing and acting without the choices and actions being *determined*—without their being just effects of certain long causal sequences. This seems pretty close to the power of acting mentioned by the dictionary. Notice, however, that the absence of determinism—the concept that our actions are causally determined—or necessity is not necessarily an absence of constraints or compulsions as usually understood. A choice of mine might be quite other than just an effect of a certain causal sequence, other than determined, even if I made it because of a threat by the man with the gun.

The other main answer given by philosophers to the question of what the important freedom comes to is indeed that it is no more than not being constrained or compelled in the sense just noticed. That is, to have the freedom is to be able to act in accordance with your own desires and nature, rather than somehow against them because of something else. This may be what is intended by the second idea in the dictionary entry.

If dictionaries were really to help us be clear-headed about the whole subject, they might speak of the main question as a question of our *freedom*. They might use the term 'free will' just in connection with undetermined choices. It is relevant that, as used to be said and as still is conveyed by other terms, such choices are somehow owed to our wills, or indeed a faculty called 'the Will'. It could usefully be added that such choices can be spoken of as *originated*, since they come about without being certain effects and yet are definitely not understood as chance or random events. Finally, it would be useful to speak of choices that do not go against our desires and natures as being *voluntary*.

The main questions, then, can be made more explicit. Is the important freedom we want origination or is it voluntariness? Have we actually got whichever it is?

It is difficult to proceed with the questions without noticing a crucial difference between origination and voluntariness—although noticing it may bring into operation a prejudice or two. Origination is inconsistent or incompatible with determinism as well understood. An originated choice, whatever else is to be said of it, is by definition somehow not determined. Voluntariness, on the other hand, is perfectly consistent with determinism. The point is well made by saying that for a choice to be voluntary is not for it to be causeless, but for it to have a certain kind of cause. It has, we can say, the cause that is the chooser's own desires or nature, not a cause going against them.

The tradition in philosophy known as incompatibilism (in which freedom is considered to be incompatible with determinism) has offered many persuasions, often called proofs, of the supposed fact that our conception of freedom, our conception of the great prerequisite, is of origination. We are told that what we think about and want, or certainly mainly think about and want, is origination. The tradition of compatibilism (in which freedom is considered to be compatible with determinism), as you will anticipate, has offered many persuasions of the other supposed fact. We are told that at least our fundamental thought and desire with respect to freedom is for no more than voluntariness. Incompatibilists, as defined, do not have to take a view on whether determinism is true. But, as you may also anticipate, almost all of them have denied or been inclined to deny determinism. They say we have actually got the freedom that matters because our choices in fact are not effects of certain causal sequences. Compatibilists, on the other hand, have either supported determinism or been agnostic about it.

Perhaps it is true that the main impetus to or ground for compatibilism has been a belief in determinism or an inclination to it. If you do believe in determinism, and also believe that the fact or reasonableness of responsibility and hope and so on in our lives presupposes *some* freedom—well then, the freedom must be voluntariness. The main impetus to incompatibilism, although this is not so clear, is perhaps that we or most of us want to hold others responsible for things, and have responsibility ourselves, in a way that requires origination and thus is inconsistent with determinism.

Partly on account of what may be the main impetus to compatibilism, it is a good idea to start on the whole problem with the matter of the formulation and truth of determinism. Formulating it, formulating a determinist philosophy of mind, indeed getting clear about causation itself, is no easy matter. Such a philosophy of mind is easiest for those very few philosophers who believe that the mind is only the brain, that choices have only neural properties. But such materialism is in fact not the position even of most so-called physicalists or mind–brain identity theorists.

As for the truth of a formulated determinism, a persistent but irrelevant kind of resistance to it consists in pointing to events that are in fact or practice unpredictable—Brownian motion, electronic noise, or events in Chaos Theory. What would defeat determinism is unpredictability in theory or principle—as a result of events actually not being effects, there actually being no causal circumstances for them to be discovered by God or ultimate and complete science or anything else.

The main relevant resistance to determinism, now a lesser resistance than before, is the interpretation or group of interpretations of the mathematics that is quantum theory. The interpretation is that there are events down in the microworld that are not effects. Certainly such interpretations of quantum theory have been and still are influential.

Still, it is or should be notorious that, nearly a century after they were announced, there has been no direct and univocal evidence of the existence of chance events of the given kind. There is also the question of whether such microevents, if they exist, do issue in random macroevents—including events that are our choices or are bound up with them. There is also the possibility of arguing that random microevents would issue in random macroevents, and since there are none of the latter, there are none of the former. Plainly these materials can be argued to result in a certain dilemma. If any microevents would, so to speak, translate upwards into the brain and world we know, there are none, since there are no random macroevents. Or, if microevents would not or do not translate upwards, they do not matter to our subject at all.

Compatibilists, in addition to being moved by determinism, have provided a string of supposed proofs of their position. They have insisted, for example, that it is just clear to all who think about it that the freedom we think of and want is paradigmatically what is lacked by a man in jail. That freedom is evidently voluntariness. Further, the freedom that matters to us has been taken as our being able to *choose and do otherwise than we do*, and this is rightly analysed in a way consistent with determinism. Lately there has been much reliance on the contention that there are cases where we hold a person morally responsible for an action to which he or she had no alternative because of some background feature.

Incompatibilists have also made a direct appeal to clear truth—to what we are all said to know. We know, it is said, that someone who acts freely has more than one

possibility open to him or her. What that means, it is said, is that he or she is not caused to do one thing. We are said to be convinced of this, for example, when we are in the process of deciding what to do, whether that action is wagging a finger to the right or something more significant.

Latterly it has been argued again that a free action of mine is one that is *up to me*, and that something crucial follows from this. If determinism is true, my choice is the effect of long-past events of a causal sequence, events before my birth. My action can be up to me only if those past events are up to me, which they cannot be. Thus a free action, being one that is up to me, cannot possibly be something consistent with determinism.

Perhaps the philosophical debate is changing, however. Both compatibilists and incompatibilists agree and assume or assert that we have *one* important conception of freedom, one that at least stands above another. The whole debate depends on this. Is it true? To speak for myself, I am sure it is not, and can be as good as proved false. There is more agreement about this than there used to be.

Also, if you think about your past life from the inside, you can take it to have been determined, but also to feel something like a responsibility for it that has seemed to go with origination or free will. Can it be that the freedom that is important to you, or anyway whatever it is that is important to you, has a source in something wholly different from origination? Maybe something to do with the very nature of your consciousness, its subjective and constructive nature?   TH

The best anthology on free will is *The Oxford Handbook of Free Will* (2002), edited by Robert Kane. For incompatibilism, see in particular Peter van Inwagen, *An Essay on Free Will* (1983). Daniel Dennett's *Freedom Evolves* (2003) is a recent defence of compatibilism. For scepticism about both, there is Ted Honderich's *How Free Are You? The Determinism Problem* (2nd edn., 2002).

Freud, Anna (1895–1982). Born in Vienna, the sixth child of Sigmund *Freud, Anna was the only member of the family to follow in her father's footsteps and make her career in psychoanalysis. She was admitted to membership of the Vienna Psychoanalytical Society in 1922 and for a time became its chairman. After the Nazis occupied Vienna, she emigrated to England with her parents, and after the outbreak of the Second World War organized the Hampstead War Nurseries in cooperation with her close friend and admirer Dorothy Burlingham. In 1945, this enterprising venture was succeeded by the Hampstead Child Therapy Course and Clinic, which for long led the field in the training of child psychotherapists in the London area. Anna Freud's work, like that of her contemporary Melanie *Klein, was based not on the earlier Freudian ideas about child development, which derive largely from the analysis of adults, but on the direct observation of the behaviour of young children. This approach did much to make possible the remedial treatment of psychologically disturbed children.

Although she never held a formal medical or psychological qualification, Anna Freud's significant contribution to child psychology and psychiatry was acknowledged by her election to an Honorary Fellowship of the Royal College of Psychiatrists and the conferment of honorary degrees from a number of well-known universities, including Harvard, Yale, Sheffield, and Vienna.

Anna Freud is best remembered for her book on *The Ego and the Mechanisms of Defence* (German 1936; English translation 1937), which carried further some of the ideas developed by her father in his book on *The Ego and the Id* (1923) and played a very real part in the genesis of what later came to be known as 'ego-psychology'.

OLZ

Freud, Sigmund (1856–1939). Sigmund Freud, who was born of Jewish ancestry at Freiberg in Moravia, was educated in Vienna, in which city he spent almost the whole of his long life. Here he enrolled at the university as a student of biology and medicine in 1873 and while still a medical student embarked on some research under the distinguished physiologist Ernst Brücke, whose interests lay predominantly in the vertebrate nervous system. In 1878, this work resulted in Freud's first published scientific paper, on the histology of the spinal cord in a primitive fish. He qualified in medicine in 1881 at the age of 26, somewhat tardily, and after working for a time in Theodor Meynert's Institute of Cerebral Neurology, decided to specialize in clinical neurology. He was appointed to a lectureship in neuropathology in 1885 and, soon after, was awarded a travelling fellowship to enable him to study in Paris with the world-famous neurologist J. M. *Charcot. This proved to be the turning point in Freud's career; from it can be dated his metamorphosis from a clinical neurologist into a medical psychologist in the modern sense of the term.

While still active in neurology, Freud published several papers and two books. One of the latter, on disorders of speech (*aphasia) resulting from lesions of the brain, attracted considerable interest and has since been regarded as well in advance of its time. It has also been argued that his ideas about aphasia provided some basis for his later psychological thinking. It may be added that, as a young doctor, Freud only narrowly missed becoming the first to recognize the anaesthetic properties of cocaine.

In 1885, he arrived at the Salpêtrière in Paris, which then enjoyed a worldwide reputation as the Mecca of clinical neurologists. At this period, Charcot had become much preoccupied with the so-called functional nervous diseases, in particular *hysteria, in which no clear-cut somatic basis had been established. This protean disease was at that time widely treated by hypnosis, upon which Charcot held strong views. First, he maintained that only those of innate hysterical disposition are amenable to hypnosis; and, secondly, that hypnosis provides a kind of laboratory for the induction and modification of hysterical symptoms. But whereas Charcot still believed that hypnosis had a physical basis, Freud became increasingly convinced of its psychological origin. It is not without interest that some years later he paid a special visit to M. Bernheim, of Nancy, who was perhaps the first to insist upon the overriding role of suggestion in bringing about hypnosis, and to stress its applicability to a wide range of individuals who sought his aid as a physician. Although Freud later repudiated hypnosis as a clinical tool, it is most improbable that, had it not been for Charcot's influence, he would have been led to collaborate with Joseph *Breuer and ultimately to evolve the psychoanalytical method.

This work with Breuer began soon after Freud's return to Vienna. Breuer had been interested for some time in using hypnosis in the treatment of hysterical illness, and came to place great reliance on the therapeutic benefit of what came to be called abreaction. This was essentially a kind of re-enactment, during hypnosis, of stressful and disturbing experiences which appeared to have precipitated the illness, and the free and uninhibited expression of emotion was actively encouraged. While seeing some benefit in abreaction, Freud quickly came to realize not only that the structure of neurosis was much more complex than Breuer, at least, was prepared to admit, but also that it involved active processes of defence (repression) against the reproduction, or even the mere acknowledgement, of painful, distressing, or otherwise emotionally disturbing memories. He surmised that many of these had to do with sexual life, a conclusion which Breuer appears to have been ill disposed to concede. Freud also came to appreciate that the understanding and disarming of these defences could often be achieved more effectively in the waking than in the hypnotic state. In consequence, hypnosis was replaced by the so-called method of *free association, from which psychoanalysis as a technical psychotherapeutic procedure gradually evolved.

Over the next few years, Freud was essentially concerned in developing his brilliantly original, if to many people extremely disconcerting, ideas about the causation and treatment of neurotic illness. He was led increasingly into study of the sexual life of his patients, at first believing that much neurosis is attributable to distressing sexual experiences in early adult life. Soon, however, he discovered that many of these supposed experiences existed only in imagination and were the products of fantasies evolved at a very much earlier age, often in quite early infancy. Analysis of these fantasies led him to believe not only that psychosexual life has its origins in early infancy but also that it involves intense and often complicated emotional relationships, both positive and negative, with the parents. These ideas were brought together in his *Three Contributions to the Theory of Sex* (1906), a book which shocked many people but which nevertheless had wide influence on modern conceptions of personality and its development. It also marks the transition from psychoanalysis conceived as a special theory of neurosis to psychoanalysis as a general theory of human personality.

This period, too, was marked by Freud's Herculean attempt at self-analysis, using many of his own dreams to furnish clues as to his own early development and emotional relations with his parents. It further provided the occasion for the writing of what is often regarded as his greatest book, *The Interpretation of Dreams* (1900). As Freud's views on dreams are considered in a separate article, *Freud on dreams, it is unnecessary to say more here than that dreams, in his view, have meaning and are largely the product of infantile wishes and thought processes, and that their personal significance can be assessed if their language can be understood and translated into the currency of adult, waking thought.

Although Freud's ideas incurred much odium in medical circles, his work none the less attracted a small but devoted band of followers, many of them neurologists who, like Freud himself, had felt challenged by the ubiquity of neurosis among their patients. Among them were Karl Abraham, Sandor Ferenczi, Alfred *Adler, Carl Gustav *Jung, Otto Rank, and the Welsh physician Ernest Jones, who became for many years Britain's foremost Freudian. Shortly before the outbreak of the First World War, this group was weakened by two major defections, those of Adler and Jung. Adler's defection was less important, as it is doubtful whether he was ever a committed Freudian, and Freud himself thought little of his ideas. (None the less, after Adler's death, some of his views, in particular those associated with the nature of aggression, came to exert considerable influence on neo-Freudian theory.) Jung, on the other hand, was a man of real distinction of mind and impressive literary productivity. As a psychiatrist, he did much in his early days to extend Freudian thinking to the psychoses, in particular *schizophrenia, and is remembered as the originator of the word-association test at one time much in vogue as a 'lie detector'. There can be no question that Freud thought of Jung as his eventual successor in the leadership of the psychoanalytical movement, and his defection caused him very real chagrin. Subsequently, Jung wrote widely (if somewhat obscurely) on individual development, psychological types, and the cultural frontiers of psychology.

In his later writings, Freud displayed an admittedly speculative turn of mind, and though some of his ideas are of great interest, their empirical foundation became decidedly weaker. Among them are *Beyond the Pleasure Principle* (1922), *The Ego and the Id* (1923), *Inhibitions, Symptoms and Anxiety* (1936), and, finally, the work of his old age, *Moses and Monotheism*, published a year before his death.

Freud's work came to be widely known to the general reader, particularly through such works as *The Psychopathology of Everyday Life* (1904), *Wit and its Relation to the Unconscious* (1905), *Introductory Lectures on Psychoanalysis* (1922), and *New Introductory Lecures on Psychoanalysis* (1933). In America, the five lectures which he delivered at Clark University in 1910 (at the invitation of the veteran psychologist G. Stanley *Hall, then president of the university) subsequently appeared in English and enjoyed a certain vogue. But Freudian thinking did not seriously penetrate American psychiatry until after the end of the Second World War, when it came to dominate psychiatric practice for some years, possibly to the detriment of other and less doctrinaire approaches. It has also had wide influence on literature, particularly on biography, on some aspects of painting (for example, Surrealism), and on much contemporary thinking in anthropology and the social sciences. Indeed many people nowadays regard psychoanalysis in the light of a social rather than a biological or medical discipline. Even so, its roots, like those of Freud himself, are wholly within the biological domain.

Following the Nazi invasion of Austria, Freud, by then a very sick man, fled from Vienna and lived quietly in London for the last year of his life. Shortly before his death, he was made a Foreign Fellow of the Royal Society, a belated though none the less imaginative tribute to his world stature and influence on modern thought. His daughter, Anna *Freud, a pioneer in the psychoanalytical study of children, became a leading member of the British psychoanalytical community. As a person, Freud is remembered by those who knew him as a man of some austerity but unchallenged personal integrity.   OLZ

Freud, S. (1935). *An Autobiographical Study*. Trans. J. Strachey.
Jones, E. (1953–7). *Sigmund Freud: Life and Work*, 3 vols.

Freud on dreams. 'Find out all about dreams and you will find out all about insanity.' This prophetic remark was made by the English neurologist John Hughlings *Jackson, whose main contribution to its truth lay in establishing that certain curious alterations in *consciousness, in some respects akin to dreaming, might occur in a particular variety of epilepsy. But we owe almost entirely to Freud such little as we know regarding the relationship between dreams and the history and development of personality, normal no less than abnormal. Although Freud became interested in dreams largely in connection with psychoanalytical techniques, and more particularly in relation to his own self-analysis, it may be said that his work has given rise to the only theory of dreams which has so far won general acceptance (Freud 1900).

Freud's approach to the interpretation of dreams was by way of the method of *free association he had evolved in the course of his early studies of neurosis as a substitute for hypnosis, with which he had become increasingly dissatisfied. As in psychoanalysis proper, the subject is required to relax and allow his mind to wander freely from elements in the dream to related ideas, recollections, or emotional reactions which they may chance to suggest. By this route, he is gradually led from the dream as recollected, which Freud termed the *manifest content*, to the underlying thoughts and wishes, called by Freud the *latent content*—this, he believed, is typically based upon wishes, recollections, and fantasies related to the deeper emotional reactions of early infancy. In short, the dream is a heavily disguised form of infantile wish-fulfilment expressed as a hallucinatory experience in the course of sleep.

The activity which transforms the latent into the manifest content is known as the *dream work*. This makes use of three principal mechanisms, known respectively as *condensation*, *displacement*, and *dramatization* (also known as *representation*). To these is sometimes added a fourth, *secondary elaboration*, or *revision*. The major function of the dream work is to evade what Freud picturesquely calls the *dream censorship*. This is envisaged as the continued operation of the mechanisms of repression which serve in waking life to protect the individual from the effects of potentially disturbing wishes and fantasies originating in early life. In spite of its name, the censorship was not envisaged as primarily of social or cultural origin, i.e. as an instrument of society. As Freud saw it, repression, whether operating during sleep or during wakefulness, is an essentially biological process, supervening after the age of 5 or thereabouts with the onset of the so-called latency period. *Inter alia*, it is responsible for the onset and maintenance of childhood amnesia, as a result of which very little can be recalled of the experiences or emotions of earlier infancy. At the same time, repression can of course be reinforced as a result of identification and social learning in childhood and after, and its derivative, the dream censorship, may in consequence be in some degree acquired.

Of the activities constituting the dream work, the most familiar is almost certainly condensation, which few people fail to notice on occasions when recalling their own dreams. For example, a visual image in the dream may embody the features or manner of two or more quite distinct people, being evidently a composite figure. The same may also occur with places, buildings, and the like. Condensation also affects words; some neologisms in dreams are produced by condensing parts of two or more words or phrases. In a more general way, condensation of ideas may frequently be traced in dreams, often indicating that more than one theme or motive is being expressed in the same dream situation ('overdetermination'). In view of the drastic ideational compression brought about by condensation, it is not surprising that Freud referred to the manifest content as 'meagre, paltry and laconic' as compared with the richness and variety of the latent dream content.

Whereas Freud regarded condensation as, in part at least, intrinsic to the dream process, displacement he attributed wholly to the effects of the censorship. It consists in attributing emotional significance to some element in the dream that, on analysis, turns out to be essentially trivial. For example, a dream image may recur for some hours after awakening and seem to possess a disturbingly haunting quality. Yet analysis may reveal that it is operating essentially as a decoy to lure the attention of the dreamer from more dangerous themes. In Freud's view, a great deal of the disguise making the memory of the dream so obscure originates from the vicissitudes of displacement.

The term 'dramatization' refers to the transposition of thoughts into imagery, largely, though not exclusively, visual. Inevitably, this mode of representation of thought is highly concrete, and it has therefore been disputed whether abstract ideas can feature in dreams. While dream thinking is certainly concrete in much the same sense as the thinking of the young child or the brain-damaged adult, this does not mean that abstract ideas may not be represented metaphorically in the dream by concrete images. At the same time, it seems unlikely that genuinely creative abstract thinking can take place in dreams.

Secondary elaboration refers to the further distortion or elaboration of the dream that occurs after awakening. As much of this proceeds by rapid and often progressive omission of elements in the manifest content, 'secondary revision' is probably a better term for it. Although it is often held that the power of *memory is intrinsically weaker in dreaming than in the waking state, the rapidity and completeness with which many dreams are forgotten only a few moments after awakening undoubtedly suggest that its basis is in part at least psychogenic. It would be interesting to compare the repeated reproduction of dreams with that of stories or pictures in the manner described by F. C. *Bartlett (1932). Insofar as the writer is aware, such an experiment has not been attempted.

Although Freud relied for the most part on free association to 'undisguise' dreams, i.e. to provide clues to the nature of the persisting wish or motive behind the dream, he noted that on occasion no relevant associations were forthcoming. In some cases, Freud considered it legitimate to appeal to what he called 'primal symbolism', i.e. modes of representation which occurred so consistently in dreams that he could attribute a meaning to them independently of associative context. Among these are the familiar symbols of the male and female genitalia, based quite evidently on association by similarity. But Freud, unlike Jung, always supposed that such symbolic devices were acquired through individual experiences and should not be regarded as inborn modes of symbolic representation, independent of history and culture. The Jungian universal symbols, or 'archetypes', found no place in his theory.

Freud's hypothesis of the dream as wish-fulfilment and as representing the 'primary process' of human thinking, unaffected by realities of space, time, and logic, underwent some modification in his later thinking. In particular, he came to accept the existence of a class of dreams which in no sense embody the fulfilment of infantile wishes. These are the repetitive dreams in which the dreamer re-enacts a traumatic episode in his recent experience. Freud was obliged to concede that dreams of this character, not infrequently associated with war neuroses, do not accord with the 'pleasure principle' and merit explanation in other terms. It is also of interest that W. H. R. *Rivers (1923), likewise on the basis of experience of war neuroses, was led to the view that many dreams could be interpreted in terms of an attempt in fantasy to resolve current emotional problems.

Although the respective parts played by infantile and adult experiences in the motivation of dreams remain controversial, and the concept of dream symbolism is undoubtedly treacherous, it is probably true to say that the dream is a mode of symbolic expression that has certain affinities with language. As Richard Wollheim (1985) has pointed out, however, the dream lacks what is most characteristic of language: a grammar or structure. Moreover, it lacks any real communicative function. None the less, as a form of personal expression it merits attention as a modest manifestation of human *creativity.

See also DREAMING.   OLZ

Bartlett, F. C. (1932). *Remembering: A Study in Experimental and Social Psychology.*
Freud, S. (1900). *The Interpretation of Dreams.* In Strachey, J. (ed.), *Complete Psychological Works* (1900–1), vol. v.
Rivers, W. H. R. (1923). *Conflict and Dream.*
Wollheim, R. (1985). *Freud* (2nd edn.).

Frey, Max von (1852–1932). German physiologist, best known for his investigations into the sensations of pain and touch. In 1882 he became a university lecturer in physiology at Leipzig, eventually being appointed to a professorship there, which he held from 1891 to 1898. He later taught for a year at Zurich, and then at Würzburg. Developing the earlier studies of Blix (1882) and Goldscheider (1884), who had established that the skin has separate spots for cold, warmth, and touch, von Frey showed that pain is a special skin modality, separate from these sensa-

tions and also from pressure. He went on to map out 'pain spots'.

The set of hairs, carefully graded from soft to stiff (and including human hair), which he used in experiments investigating tactile senses became known as 'von Frey's hairs'.

Boring, E. G. (1942). *Sensation and Perception in the History of Experimental Psychology,* ch. 13.

Frisch, Karl Ritter von (1886–1983). Austrian ethologist. Born of an academic family in Vienna, Karl von Frisch worked at several universities, in particular Breslau and Munich. His research was on the light sensitivity of sea anemones. He collaborated with his uncle Sigmund Exner (1846–1926), who became professor of physiology in Vienna and worked on both reaction times and cerebral localization. Von Frisch went on to show by behavioural experiments that fish are not, as had been thought, colour-blind. In more detail, he found that in dim light using 'rod' vision they are, like us, colour-blind, but with brighter light stimulating the retinal 'cone' cells, they do have *colour vision. He went on to demonstrate, by whistling to catfish, that fish are not deaf.

Having established unexpected sensory capacities in many animals, von Frisch carried out his celebrated experiments on how scout honey bees convey information of where they have found nectar. He started by assuming that the other bees recognized the successful scout by odour, but he found evidence that the scout could convey information of direction and distance of the food source, which was surprising. Following experiments to discount the odour theory, he arrived at the wild conjecture that they signal by a symbolic dance, which he learned to interpret. Direction was normally signalled by reference to the sun, but on cloudy days it was established by the polarization angle of the light of the overcast sky, which the bee's compound eye can detect. Distance of the food source was signalled by different kinds of dance—a 'round' dance when near, and a 'waggle' dance when distant—and the speed of the dance was greater for greater distances. The direction of the food source with respect to the sun was signalled by taking the vertical of the honeycomb as, symbolically, the direction of the sun. This discovery (which has been independently confirmed) that bees use a symbolic language was wholly unexpected, and it forces us to accept that man is not unique in organizing society by means of language.

Von Frisch shared the Nobel Prize with Konrad Lorenz and Nikolaas Tinbergen in 1973. His books include: *You and Life* (1940), *Animal Architecture* (1974), and the celebrated *Dancing Bees* (1954).   OLZ

Froebel, Friedrich Wilhelm August (1782–1852). Friedrich Froebel was born in Oberweissbuch, Thuringia.

His father was a busy pastor, and his mother died soon after his birth, an event he regarded as crucial to his development. His early childhood was unhappy and he was thrown on his own resources, developing the passion for self-contemplation and self-education which he thought essential for all. Though he was moved by the mystical language of his father's hymns and sermons, he was critical of his schooling with its reliance on memorization of facts inculcated by stern teachers. At 15 he was apprenticed to a forester, and he wrote later of his religious communion with Nature at this period: 'I looked within myself and to Nature for help.' He began to develop his personal philosophy: a belief in the organic unity of man, God, and Nature. At the University of Jena he eagerly embraced the idealist philosophy of the time. He believed that all living things had an inherent form and purpose, not predetermined but developing through a kind of creative struggle with the environment. He studied the transcendental biology of the period, and was deeply impressed by the underlying pattern which seemed to unite all living things and by their growth from simple to complex structures. He had a romantic and mystical belief in universal harmony: 'Everything has a purpose, which is to realize its essence, the divine nature developing within it, and so to reveal God in the transitory world.'

Froebel early demonstrated an interest in education and in 1805 began in Frankfurt the work as schoolmaster and private tutor which was to occupy the rest of his life. Like *Rousseau he regarded man as essentially good, and his pedagogy starts from perceptive observation of children's behaviour. 'Educators', he wrote, 'must understand their impulse to make things and to be freely and personally active; they must encourage their desire to instruct themselves as they create, observe and experiment.' The teacher was to guide the child in his self-discovery, not direct him. Each stage of development was critical and had to be fully experienced. Play was the young child's 'spontaneous expression of thought and feeling' and was central to learning. For this reason Froebel established the kindergarten, which provided the activities and materials needed by the pre-school child. He invented toys and exercises which became the basis of a pedagogic system whose formalism was curiously at odds with the permissiveness of his philosophy. He laid great emphasis on the relationship between teacher and pupil and on the need for continuity and connectedness in the school curriculum. The child had naturally a sense of the unity of life: it was the business of the school to make him conscious of it. Starting from the child's own experience, the study of religion, nature, mathematics, and language would encourage his awareness of self, the world, and God. The arts would enable him to express his inner life, and physical work teach him the dignity of labour. At all times the school was to maintain close contact with family and community; only so could it remain relevant and vital.

Froebel was a visionary as well as a gifted teacher. He had great ambitions for his educational programme, believing it would unify Germany as well as mankind generally. In fact his influence in his lifetime was limited—a year before his death in 1852, Prussia banned the kindergarten for its 'revolutionary' tendencies. Devoted disciples in Europe and America continued his work, however, and from the 1870s it profoundly influenced the training of teachers and the education of young children. The importance of play, the unified curriculum, links with home and community, and non-directive rather than authoritarian teaching remain live issues. But Froebel's 'organic' theory of human development led him seriously to underestimate social influences in individual lives. When he was asked to plan the education of the poor in Bern, he was at pains to point out that 'there need be no fear that individual pupils will want to improve their position and leave their own class. On the contrary, this system will produce educated men, each true to his calling, each in his own position.'   NS

Froebel, F. (1825). *Menschenerziehung* (Eng. trans. 1877, *The Education of Man*).

Lilley, I. M. (1967). *Friedrich Froebel: A Selection from his Writings*.

Weston, P. (1998). *Friedrich Froebel: His Life, Times and Significance*.

functionalism. An American school of psychology based principally on the University of Chicago at the turn of the 19th century. It owes something to William *James but a great deal more to John *Dewey, who has been described by E. G. *Boring as the 'organizing principle' behind its emergence. Apart from Dewey, its principal advocate was James Rowland *Angell, for many years professor of psychology at Chicago, who stressed the functional significance of adaptive behaviour and viewed mind as mediating between the environment and the needs of the organism. As E. G. Boring wittily put it: 'Functionalism represented the Philosopher's approach to a science that had rebelled against Philosophy'; it was often contrasted with Wilhelm *Wundt's structuralism.

As an outcome of functionalism, experimental work on animal behaviour and its neurological foundations developed rapidly at Chicago, particularly at the hands of C. M. Child, G. E. Coghill, and J. B. *Watson before he became a doctrinaire behaviourist. Indeed functionalism did much to lay the foundations of biological psychology as we know it today. The term functionalism is now more often used to denote functionalist theories of mind.

Functionalism emphasized learning by adapting to situations, and incorporating skills from largely unconscious learned behaviour. It introduced some evolutionary ideas into psychology because innate behaviour could be included. Consciousness was introduced when behaviour was not sufficiently functional to perform tasks unconsciously. Functionalism became swamped by *behaviourism, which quite recently gave way to *cognitive psychology.   OLZ

functionalist theories of mind. Recent functionalist theories of the mind, though they may be characterized broadly as 'materialist', can be seen as a reaction against the physicalist theories that baldly identified mental states with physically characterizable types of brain state. A difficulty with such theories is that there seems no reason to suppose that a particular type of mental state, such as being in pain, or having a given belief, will always be realized by a specific type of neurophysiological structure. Indeed, it is a well-attested fact that, if a certain brain structure is damaged, resulting in mental impairment (e.g. after a stroke), the brain is often, after a period of time, able to utilize alternative neurological networks so that the relevant mental activity is eventually restored. These and other difficulties with straightforward mind–brain identity theories led to the suggestion that mental states should be identified not with the brain's physical states, but with its *functional* states. Such states, the functionalist argues, can be specified in purely formal terms—in terms of the logical and computational processes involved—and so are neutral with respect to the actual way in which the processes are physically realized. In computer terminology, functional descriptions are 'software' descriptions, and these can be given in a fairly abstract way, using logical symbols, transformation rules, organizational principles, and so on, without any need to be specific as to the precise design of the hardware needed to realize the functions involved. Many researchers into *artificial intelligence (AI) have adopted what may broadly be called a functionalist approach to the mind, which can encompass a variety of positions, from the radical thesis that mental states are nothing more than functional states of *Turing machines, to the weaker claim that the computational states of such machines may at least be used as helpful models or analogies to illuminate our understanding of the phenomena of mind.

Two difficulties for functionalism may be mentioned here. (i) First, since a functional system could be instantiated by a wide variety of physical systems, e.g. a computerized robot, or perhaps even a complex telephone exchange, it seems that the functionalist would be committed to ascribing mental states to such systems, provided that they exhibited the relevant organizational complexity. Yet (the objection runs) there is obviously no human parallel to being a robot; robots have no inner mental life. Hence mental states must be more than mere functional states. Against this, functionalists have argued that if we could build a robot that was complex enough to instantiate the kind of enormously complicated program needed to model human mental states, and if, moreover, the robot was able to interact causally with the environment in all the appropriate ways, then the assumption that the robot could not possibly have a 'mental life' might begin to lose much of its plausibility. (ii) A second objection concerns the phenomenon of *intentionality. Mental states have intentionality: they have representational content, or are 'about something'. Yet opponents of the strong AI programme (such as John Searle) have argued that functional specifications, being couched in terms of purely formal or syntactic operations, cannot possibly exhibit intentionality. A system might perform impeccably in manipulating symbols in accordance with complex operational rules, yet, for all that, it might be quite unaware of the meaning of the symbols, what they were 'about'; and hence (the argument runs) it could not be considered as having a 'mind' in the sense in which humans have minds. These matters are currently the subject of vigorous debate among philosophers and AI theorists.

See also HOMUNCULUS.   JGC

Biro, J. I., and Shahan, R. W. (eds.) (1982). *Mind, Brain and Function: Essays in Philosophy of Mind.*

Boden, M. A. (1981). *Minds and Mechanisms.*

Dennett, D. C. (1979). *Brainstorms.*

Searle, J. (1982). 'Minds, brains and programs'. In Hofstadter, D., and Dennett, D. C. (eds.), *The Mind's Eye.*

future shock. Term coined by the American writer Alvin Toffler, to mean the trauma experienced by rapid changes—for example, to the environment, especially destruction of familiar buildings, or customs of childhood. The trauma is similar to that often experienced by *émigrés*, but is even less reversible as it is in time.

Toffler, A. (1970). *Future Shock.*

G

Gage, Phineas (1813–60). Survivor of a horrific injury to the frontal lobes in an industrial accident in 1848. His subsequent personality change provides some of the earliest evidence for the role of the frontal cortex in mental activity.

Gage was working as a construction foreman for the Rutland and Burlington Railroad, rock blasting for a new railway line in Vermont. An accidental explosion drove a tamping iron, 3 cm (1¼ in) in diameter and 109 cm (45 in) long, through Gage's head. It entered at the left cheek, passed upwards through the brain and exited the skull through the frontal bone close to the midline. Reconstruction of the injury from damage to the skull using modern neuroimaging techniques suggests that the ventral and medial areas of the prefrontal cortex, including the anterior cingulate gyri, were extensively damaged in both cerebral hemispheres (Damasio et al. 1994). Gage regained consciousness almost immediately and although he was debilitated for a time by infection he eventually recovered his physical health. Before the accident he had been conscientious, well socialized, and was said to have a shrewd business sense. His employers considered him the 'most efficient and capable' of their workers. The injury left him with no impairment of movement or speech, and his learning, memory, and natural intelligence seemed to be only partially impaired. However, his personality and mood had undergone severe changes. He had become irreverent, impatient, profane, irresponsible, insensitive to others, and unable to stick to plans he made for himself (Macmillan 2000). From 1851 until 1859 he worked in a relatively menial capacity in livery stables, looking after horses and driving coaches. He died after developing epilepsy in 1860 and was buried without a post-mortem examination of his brain.

Soon after the accident, news of Gage's personality change reached American phrenologists who had a ready explanation for it: the 'organs of benevolence and veneration' situated in the frontal lobes had been destroyed. However, orthodox medicine was in the process of rejecting phrenology and with it, for a time, the concept of localization of function in the cerebral cortex. Influential clinicians like Henry Bigelow played down Gage's antisocial behaviour and its possible significance (Barker 1995). Seven years after Gage's death, John Harlow, the railway physician who had treated him at the time

of the accident, arranged for the body to be exhumed so that he could study the skull. He published an account of his findings which revealed to the medical community for the first time the selective effect of the brain damage on Gage's character, sparing movement and language (Harlow 1868). The appearance of this report within a few years of the discoveries of Broca, Wernicke, Ferrier, Fritsch, and Hitzig undoubtedly contributed to the renewal of interest in functional localization in the second half of the 19th century. A detailed theory of the functions of the frontal cortex in terms of its role in attention, planning, decision making, socialization and the control of emotional expression had to await the 20th century, for the behavioural effects of frontal lobotomy and the advent of neuropsychological and neuroimaging techniques. Although his behaviour could not be understood in his own time, Phineas Gage has become the classical example of the psychological effects of damage to the ventromedial frontal cortex.   SBu

Barker, F. G., II (1995). 'Phineas among the phrenologists: the American crowbar case and nineteenth-century theories of cerebral localisation'. *Journal of Neurosurgery*, 82.

Damasio, H., Grabowski, T., Frank, R., Galaburda, A. M. and Damasio, A. R. (1994). 'The return of Phineas Gage: clues about the brain from the skull of a famous patient'. *Science*, 264.

Harlow, J. M. (1868). 'Recovery from the passage of an iron bar through the head'. *Publication of Massachusetts Medical Society*, 2.

Macmillan, M. (2000). 'Restoring Phineas Gage: a 150th retrospective'. *Journal of the History of Neuroscience*, 9.

Galen (or Claudius Galenus, 2nd century AD). Greek physician, born at Pergamum in Mysia. He studied medicine there, and also at S.nyrna, Corinth, and Alexandria, and became physician to Marcus Aurelius. He probably died in Sicily.

Galen wrote extensively on medical and on philosophical subjects and his extant works consist of 83 treatises on medicine and 15 commentaries on *Hippocrates. He dissected animals and developed, to our minds, somewhat fanciful physiological theories. His clinical discoveries include diagnosing by the pulse. He was the authority from whom all later Greek and Roman medical writers quoted, with more or less accuracy.

Galen considered that the body worked by three types of spirit: natural spirit (located in the liver), vital spirit (located in the left ventricle of the heart), and animal spirit (located in the brain). He postulated several anatomical features, such as the *rete mirabile* (wonderful network) on the undersurface of the brain, which is found in some animals (especially those with hooves) but not in man, although on Galen's authority it was accepted as present in the human brain for over thirteen centuries. It was also believed on his authority that the septum of the heart contained minute pores—these were essential for Galen's physiological system as he believed that blood passes from the heart to the body from both the arteries and the veins, new blood being manufactured in the liver and supposedly burnt up in the tissues. The exhalation of breath, when concentrated, was known to be asphyxiating, and was compared to the smoke of fire. Galen made considerable discoveries in neurology and especially the kinds of paralysis associated with damage at various places to the spinal cord (see GREEK INVESTIGATIONS OF THE MIND AND SENSES).   RLG

Galen (1821–33). *Opera omnia*. Ed. C. G. Kühn (the only complete edition of Galen's surviving works).
Green, R. M. (1982). *Claudius Galenus*.

Galileo (or Galileo Galilei, 1564–1642). Italian physicist, astronomer, and inventor, born at Pisa. He preferred to be known by his first name, rather than by his surname Galilei. When a student of medicine at the University of Pisa, in 1583, Galileo noticed that the oscillations of a suspended lamp in the cathedral kept the same rate whatever the amplitude of its swing. This at once suggested a timekeeper for the pulse, and much later (dictated on his deathbed to his son) the invention of the pendulum clock. He greatly improved the refracting telescope (which was invented in the Netherlands in 1608) and discovered the four 'Galilean' moons of Jupiter (1610), lunar craters, and sunspots, and he described the Milky Way as made up of countless stars. He was probably the inventor of the compound microscope (1610), and he was the first to see the seven photoreceptors in each optical element of the compound eye.

Much of his work challenged *Aristotle, initially by establishing that heavy and light weights fall at the same rate—though the story of dropping weights from the Leaning Tower of Pisa is most likely apocryphal, as the experiment would have been very difficult to perform reliably. He pointed out that if heavy and light weights were attached to each other with a string, it would not stretch or break during the fall, as one would expect if their rate of fall differed. For his experiments, he effectively slowed down gravitational fall by rolling balls down sloping tracks, and little bells placed at intervals along the tracks, told him of the speed of the balls by intervals between

tinkling, so in various ways he made laws of nature observable. Some of his apparatus, including his telescope, can be seen at the Laurentian Library in Florence.

Galileo's challenge of Aristotle provoked such a reaction that as early as 1591 he was forced to leave Pisa and retire to Florence. A year later, however, he gained a professorship in mathematics at the University of Padua, where his lectures attracted immense attention, with pupils from all over Europe, and where he remained for eighteen years (1592–1610). It was his book on sunspots (1613) that gave the explicit account of the earth moving round the sun, initiating the long tiring trial that cost him his freedom. This was a powerful defence of the Copernican view that the earth is not the centre of the universe, a view denounced in 1616 as a danger to the Catholic faith. Galileo's insistence on it was probably not intended as a deliberate attack on the Church, but rather as a defence of the right to make scientific observations and reasoned arguments, and so saving the Church from errors that science revealed. After a long trial by the Inquisition he was imprisoned, and forced to recant his views, though probably he was not tortured.

Although Galileo wrote mainly on physics and astronomy (especially the work translated as *The Starry Messenger*, 1610) he also considered *sensation and *perception. His *The Assayer* (1623) has this passage:

To excite in us tastes, odours, and sounds I believe that nothing is required in external bodies except shapes, numbers, and slow or rapid movements. I think that if ears, tongues, and noses were removed, shapes and numbers and motions would remain, but not odours or tastes or sounds. The latter, I believe, are nothing more than names when separated from living beings, just as tickling and titillation are nothing but names in the absence of such things as noses and armpits. And as these four senses are related to the four elements, so I believe that vision, the sense eminent above all others in the proportion of the finite to the infinite, the temporal to the instantaneous, the quantitative to the indivisible, the illuminated to the obscure— that vision, I say, is related to light itself. But of this sensation and the things pertaining to it I pretend to understand but little; and since even a long time would not suffice to explain that trifle, or even to hint at an explanation, I pass this over in silence.

Having damaged his eyes with his telescopic studies of sunspots, in 1637 Galileo lost his sight. Five years later he died, blind, in the year Newton was born.   RLG

Drake, S. (trans. and ed.) (1957). *Discoveries and Opinions of Galileo*.
Reston, J. (2000). *Galileo: A Life*.

Gall, Franz Joseph (1758–1828). German anatomist and founder of phrenology, who was born in Baden and settled in Vienna (1785) as a physician. He was an anatomist of some distinction and the man to whom we are really indebted for the ideas we now hold on the relations which the constituent parts of the nervous system bear to one another. He was the first to distinguish clearly between the white matter of the brain, which consists of nerve fibres, and the gelatinous grey matter, which forms the cortex of the brain, and the ganglia. For the speculative ideas as to the cortical localization of human faculties, see *phrenology and *faculty psychology. Gall's most important work, written jointly with J. C. Spurzheim (1776–1832) is *Anatomie et physiologie du système nerveux en général, et du cerveau en particulier, avec observations sur la possibilité de reconnaître plusieurs dispositions intellectuelles et morales de l'homme et des animaux par la configuration de leurs têtes*, 2 vols. (1810, 1819).   OLZ

Wegner, P. C. (1991). *Franz Joseph Gall (1758–1828)*.

Galton, Sir Francis (1822–1911). Francis Galton pioneered the application of measurement and statistics to the study of human individual differences, and introduced several specific methods of enquiry which are now standard. Association of ideas, for example, had been discussed for centuries, but he was the first to devise an experimental approach. Again, in asking people to fill in questionnaires about their *mental imagery, he not only inaugurated the scientific study of imagery but also the systematic use of psychological questionnaires. In attempting to tease out the contributions of nature and nurture, he became the first to gather systematic data about the life histories of *twins, and about the family and educational backgrounds of people with exceptional talents in, say, literature or science or sport. He collected fingerprints, devised a method of classifying them, and introduced the fingerprint system into police work. He invented the statistic known as 'the correlation coefficient', which is now a basic tool in education, biology, and psychology.

Born near Birmingham, Galton was the youngest of a large family which was wealthy, talented, and energetically involved with practical science and statistics. His intellectual precocity is shown by one of his early letters:

My dear Adèle, I am four years old, and I can read any English book. I can say all the Latin substantives, adjectives and active verbs, besides fifty-two lines of Latin poetry. I can cast up any sum in addition and multiply by 2, 3, 4, 5, 6, 7, 8, 9, 10, 11. I read French a little and I know the clock. Francis Galton. February 15th, 1827.

He attended private schools in England and France, studied medicine in Birmingham and London, and studied chemistry in Germany before entering Cambridge University in 1840 to read mathematics. During those early years, he developed strong interests in doing independent-minded scientific experiments, constructing gadgets, and keeping orderly records of numerical data. These interests foreshadowed his adult preoccupations and the guiding maxim of his mature years: whenever you can, measure or count.

In 1844, the year Galton graduated from Cambridge, his father died and he found himself, at the age of 22, with a substantial financial inheritance and no clear plans. For six restless years he engaged in various enterprises, including a tour of the Middle East and an attempt to settle as a sporting English country gentleman. Then in 1850 he organized, financed, and led a scientific exploration of an unexplored part of Africa. When he returned from this two-year journey, he married Louisa Butler, and wrote reports of his travels which gained him, in his own words, 'an established position in the scientific world'. He now entered upon a settled way of life as a London-based scientist-at-large.

From 1854 until his death, Galton contributed to the scientific life of London. Although he never had or sought paid employment, he held various responsible posts in the Royal Society, the Royal Geographical Society, the Anthropological Institute, the Royal Institution, and the British Association for the Advancement of Science. At the same time, he privately undertook miscellaneous investigations of a characteristic style. He sought some issue which might lend itself to quantitative treatment; accumulated relevant data, often with single-handed ingenuity; systematized the data to extract their implications; and promptly reported his findings in a memoir to one of his scientific societies. He produced hundreds of these memoirs, and his several books were mostly edited collections of them.

Throughout his long and industrious life, Galton maintained interest in many branches of science: for example, in meteorology he invented the idea and the name of 'anticyclone' and devised the now-familiar weather map which first appeared in *The Times* in 1875. In studying the threshold for high-pitched notes, he invented the calibrated whistle which later bore his name and became a standard piece of equipment in psychological laboratories until it was replaced by electronic equipment. However, after 1859, when his cousin Charles *Darwin published *The Origin of Species*, Galton's dominant interest was to study, by measurement, the influences of heredity upon the mental and physical characteristics of human beings. He accepted Darwin's view that evolution was a trial-and-error process involving the inheritance, variation, and natural selection of organic characteristics. He applied this view to man, and conceived the enterprise of collecting the data necessary to understand human evolution. (See his books *Hereditary Genius*, 1869; *English Men of Science*, 1874; and *Inquiries into Human Faculty*, 1883.)

This ambitious enterprise raised a host of challenging questions. What were the characteristics in terms of which people resembled, and differed from, each other? How might they be specified and measured? How far did they arise from genetic inheritance (nature) or environment (nurture)? What were the cumulative, generation-by-generation effects of the fact that individuals contributed differing numbers of offspring to the next generation? How did different environments and social practices exert natural selection by affecting fertility and breeding patterns and, thereby, affect the composition of what, nowadays, would be called the 'genetic pool' of human populations? (See GENETICS OF BEHAVIOUR.)

Such questions inspired Galton to conduct many enquiries which, if viewed out of context, seem unrelated and even eccentric. He examined, for example, the number of children in different families, and he related these numbers to the age at which the parents married, the migration of families from rural to urban environments, and the social tendency for the eldest sons of aristocratic families to marry wealthy heiresses. He accumulated data about the tendency for outstanding talents to run in families (his own family tree, and that of his wife, were cases in point). (See GENIUS.) He devised gadgets and methods for recording any mental or physical characteristic that seemed measurable: for example, bodily proportions, fingerprints, strength of grip, sensory acuity, and mental imagery. He used unconventional photographic techniques (composite portraits) to record facial resemblances among different members of the same family, among criminals, tubercular patients, and various national groups. Some of his enquiries led nowhere. Some led to findings which have not been confirmed by later studies. Some led to findings that have been confirmed and extended, but given varying theoretical interpretations.

Galton hoped that human evolution would, one day, be understood in terms that were strictly materialistic, deterministic, and unaffected by unaccountables such as 'divine intervention' or 'free will'. In order to discount divine intervention, he conducted ingenious but controversial studies which showed, to his own satisfaction, that prayer was ineffective in bringing about the events that were prayed for. His experiments about association of ideas were aimed at discovering whether people may 'freely' choose what they think. He concluded against the intervention of 'free will'. Psychologists, who are nowadays familiar with the tradition of experiments about word association and idea association (see FREE ASSOCIATION), are usually unaware of the motive that led Galton to found the tradition.

Galton was imbued with 19th-century ideas about human progress and about science as the chief practical instrument of such progress. He envisaged his ambitious enterprise as leading, in the fullness of time, to nothing less than a body of scientific knowledge by which men could rationally direct the future course of human evolution. He invented the word 'eugenics' for this science which would provide such far-reaching practical applications. He was, like many Victorians, deeply interested in, but ambivalent about, religion, and he supposed that eugenics would supply a new, universal religion to supersede those that men had devised hitherto. In his autobiography, published in 1908, he wrote with high-minded passion about this elevating new religion, and he bequeathed £45,000 to establish the study of eugenics at London University.

As a person, Galton was socially reserved, preoccupied by scientific labours, and inclined to be aloof. Yet his courtesy, generosity, and gentle good humour endeared him to the few people who knew him closely. He was widely respected, and honoured by, scientific circles, even though many scientists regarded him as crankish. He was knighted in 1909. Since his death, his eugenic ideals have remained deeply controversial and liable to misunderstanding. But his stature as a pioneering scientist has steadily increased. Modern genetics, mental measurement, and statistics owe much to the innovations that Galton introduced while pursuing his solitary enquiries into the human condition.   IMLH

Forrest, D. W. (1974). *Francis Galton: The Life and Work of a Victorian Genius*.

Gillham, N. W. (2001). *A Life of Sir Francis Galton: From African Exploration to the Birth of the Eugenics*.

Pearson, K. (1914–30). *Life, Letters and Labours of Francis Galton*, 3 vols.

galvanic stimulation. Named after Luigi Galvani (1737–98), Italian physiologist born at Bologna who became professor of anatomy there in 1762. Galvani thought he had demonstrated animal electricity by showing that frog muscles twitch when touched by wires. He believed that the electricity flowed from the muscles to the nerve. We now know that the stimulation is produced by small currents applied to the nerve: the electricity in Galvani's experiment was produced by chemical reaction from acids present on the frog's skin. His work led, however, to the modern understanding of the electrical basis of neural activity.

game theory. The most famous of *Von Neumann's many contributions to mathematics was embodied in *The Theory of Games and Economic Behavior* (1944; rev. edn. 1953), which he wrote in collaboration with the American economist Oskar Morgenstern. It was concerned to develop a general theory of the rational behaviour of two or more people in what are basically conflicting or competing situations, although coalitions are also considered. First he developed the theory of two-person, zero-sum games, in which one player's gain is the other player's loss; he then suggested the concept of equilibrium, known as the *minimax* solution, in which one player minimizes the maximum loss the other player can impose on him. The solution of a game depended on the players using mixed strategies where the actual moves are chosen at random. Later, games for many players were devised, not necessarily zero-sum; here coalitions were possible, and a number of solution concepts were developed. The special case of 'the prisoner's dilemma' was made explicit, where neither player would wish to change his move given the strategy of the other—a pair of strategies that is worse for both players than any alternative. The development of the theory of games since Von Neumann has been considerable and involves decision making (especially under conditions of uncertainty), games against nature, and the very important interpretation of the theory known as linear programming.   FHG

generalizing. The deriving of general statements from individual instances. Generalizing occurs in learning, and is essential for deriving knowledge from experiences and experiments. It is the basis of empiricism, although it can be dangerous. See also INDUCTION.

genetics of behaviour. Behaviour genetics is the study of the genetic basis of behaviour and of psychological characteristics such as *intelligence, temperament, *learning, and *perception. Long before the emergence of behaviour genetics as a science, man practised selective breeding for behavioural characters. The domestication of animals involved changing their behaviour in a number of respects by manipulating their genetic constitution (genotype) through selective breeding. The various breeds of dogs provide an interesting example, in that many breeds were produced for behavioural characteristics—for example, hunting dogs such as the spaniel and working dogs such as the sheepdog. The ancient world was also concerned with the relationship between heredity and behaviour. The Greeks anticipated eugenics with their belief that young men who distinguished themselves in war or other socially valued activities should be encouraged to breed, whereas depraved persons should not.

The importance of hereditary components of behaviour was the subject of much dispute and theorizing in psychology during the first part of the 20th century, but little sound empirical work was undertaken. The arguments centred around the nature vs. nurture controversy (see GALTON, SIR FRANCIS), or in other words whether the characteristic patterns of behaviour shown by an individual were learned or innate. Some believed with the eminent geneticist William Bateson that the natural genetic distinctions differentiated men into types—artists, actors, farmers, musicians, poets, scientists, servants, etc. At the other extreme J. B. *Watson, the founder of *behaviourism, made the proud boast that given a dozen healthy infants and the freedom to shape their environment he could train anyone to become any kind of specialist—doctor, lawyer, merchant, artist, etc. These sharply opposing viewpoints delayed a proper appreciation of the essential interdependence of genetic *and* environmental factors

in the determination of behavioural and psychological characters. Both are essential, though the degree of contribution made by each depends on the character in question.

The effects of genes vary with differences in the environment in which the organism develops and lives. This can be appreciated by a gastronomic analogy. The taste, texture, and quality of a cake can be modified by changing both the ingredients and the way it is cooked, but it is not always easy to tell what has been changed by eating the cake. Both the ingredients and the cooking are essential to producing the cake, for without both there would be no cake. Much recent research in behaviour genetics has sought to identify the contributions of genetic and environmental factors in order to determine the causes of differences in behaviour, and to explore the mechanisms of behavioural development.

There are two broad areas of interest. The first involves tracing the pathways that link the genome (a set of chromosomes) with behaviour, and is consequently concerned with issues about how genes specify the properties and functioning of nervous systems. The second is about the genetic organization of behaviour itself, in the individual and in the population, and how genetically controlled differences in behaviour lead to population changes and ultimately to evolutionary change.

While the genetic constitution of an organism is called its genotype, the organism's form as perceived (or the character to be measured, such as height, personality, or intelligence) is called its phenotype. Genetics is concerned largely with examining the relationship between genotypes and phenotypes. A distinction is drawn between major genes (a single gene having a measurable effect on a phenotype) and polygenes (where many genes interact to produce phenotypic effects). Most of the known genetic effects on behaviour are due to polygenes: continuously variable characters such as intelligence or emotionality result from the effects of polygenes which individually have tiny effects but which cumulate.

Quantitative or biometrical genetics is concerned with studying the effects of polygenes in populations. In respect of a given phenotype, the amount of variability in a population that is due to genetic factors is called the heritability. It is a characteristic of polygenes that their phenotypic expression—for example, measured intelligence—is subject to environmental modification. The interaction of genetic and environmental factors during development leads to the enormous variability observed in populations. A few examples of the effects of a single gene on behaviour have been described in man. About 30 per cent of the population are unable to taste a substance called phenylthiocarbamide in very low concentrations. Now the ability to taste this substance is known to be due to the action of a pair of genes designated

TT, which are carried on homologous chromosomes. In people who cannot taste the compound, the genes exist in another form, *tt*. A heterozygote, having the genetic constitution *Tt* at the relevant locus (address of a gene on a chromosome), can taste the compound. Thus in this case the effect of a single *T* gene is said to be dominant over *t*, which is recessive.

Various methods have been used to study the genetics of behaviour. Broadly speaking, they may be divided into the phenotypic and the genotypic. In the case of the phenotypic approach the investigators begin with a behavioural character and attempt to find a relationship between it and genetic variation. In the genotypic approach the investigator starts with a standard genotype and examines the effects on behaviour of changing the components of the genotype. The principal methods are as follows.

Selective breeding. The aim here is to change the population in specified directions, usually for 'high' or 'low' expression of the chosen phenotype. The method is based upon an assumption of correlation between phenotype and genotype and entails breeding together high/low-scoring males and females. The method has been used extensively with animals, and lines showing divergences in behavioural characters such as learning or emotionality in rats have been produced. The existence of such lines allows further genetic and behavioural analysis of the phenotype.

Inbred lines. Long-continued inbreeding results in lines in which individuals are in effect genetically identical. Highly inbred lines, in which the members are genetically alike, but genetically different between lines, may be reared in identical environments and compared in respect of given behaviours. Observed differences between lines reared in identical environments will be genetic in origin. Many highly inbred lines of animals, particularly mice and fruit flies, have been produced and provide valuable material for behavioural study. Certain inbred strains of mice drink a solution of alcohol in preference to water when offered a choice, whereas other strains take only water. Crosses between such lines enable analyses of the genetic architecture to be undertaken.

Mutations. These offer a way of changing the genetic instructions at a single locus. Comparisons are made between normal genotypes and genotypes carrying the mutant gene. If the experimental and control animals are genetically identical except for the mutant gene, and if they are reared in identical environments, then any differences will be a consequence of the mutation. The effects of gene mutation can sometimes be highly specific, but more often they are part of a cascade of developmental effects, some of which have consequences for an animal's behaviour. A number of single gene mutations which have behavioural consequences have been identified. In man the best known of these results in a condition called

phenylketonuria (PKU). Individuals who carry two abnormal PKU genes are unable to metabolize the amino acid phenylalanine because they congenitally lack the necessary enzyme phenylalanine hydroxylase. Babies carrying two PKU genes are of low intelligence, though the extent of the disability can be reduced by rearing the children on a diet lacking phenylalanine. Mutations can also be used to create animals with various abnormalities of the nervous system which provide another means of examining the relationship between genes, nervous system, and behaviour. By using, genetically, mosaic flies (individuals having male and female tissues where male tissues carry a mutant gene) and a technique called fate mapping, it is possible to locate sites in the nervous system for particular behavioural components.

Family pedigree studies. This approach provides the most direct way of studying the mode of inheritance of a character in man, and tracing the incidence of a trait down a family line provides a means of determining genetic dominance and recessiveness. Colour-blindness is a phenotype which has been studied in this way. (See COLOUR VISION: EYE MECHANISMS.)

Twin studies. This is probably the best-known method of studying the genetical basis of behaviour in man. Twins are either identical (monozygotic, MZ) or fraternal (dizygotic, DZ). MZ twins are derived from the splitting of a single fertilized egg, whereas DZ twins derive from the fertilization of two eggs by two sperm. DZ twins are no more genetically alike than ordinary siblings, but since they share a common prenatal environment and usually grow up together they tend to be more alike than siblings born at different times. Differences within MZ pairs arise only from environmental origins, whereas within-pair differences between DZ pairs are a consequence of genetic and environmental factors. Observations on MZ twins reared apart and hence in dissimilar environments provide information on the differentiating effects of the environment. In general the results of such investigations show that family environments can vary greatly without obscuring the basic similarities between MZ twins, though the importance of genotype varies for different psychological characters.

A very wide range of behavioural and psychological phenotypes is subject to genetic variation. In man, data from investigations of MZ twins, reared together and apart, and from DZ twins shows that the higher the degree of relationship between individuals the higher the correlation of intelligence-test scores. Thus the correlation for DZ twins reared together is 0.53, for MZ twins reared together 0.87, and for MZ twins reared apart 0.75. While this indicates that genetic factors play a major part in determining intelligence, there is also plainly an important environmental component. Studies with adopted children and their adopted and biological parents also provide support for this, since the correlation between children and their biological parents is higher and rises through early childhood. Measured intelligence is thought to be an aggregate of a number of primary mental abilities: verbal, spatial, number, reasoning, word fluency, and *memory. The available evidence indicates that genetic loadings on these vary, with verbal and spatial abilities having high loading, whereas memory has a lower loading. Many sensory and perceptual motor tasks show evidence of a substantial genetic component in man.

Evidence from multifactorial studies of twins indicates that the personality dimensions of *extroversion and introversion are both influenced by polygenic systems. There is also evidence which indicates that many psychiatric conditions have a substantial genetic component. Manic–depressive illness, for example, shows a concordance (agreement) rate of 95.7 per cent in MZ twins and 26.3 per cent in DZ twins. For *schizophrenia, one model has been put forward for a major gene effect, but the case for a polygenic constellation that leads some individuals to be prone to the condition when subjected to too stressful an environment is stronger: thus both genes and environment contribute in a significant way to its manifestation.   KJC

Abeelen, J. H. F. (1974). *The Genetics of Behaviour*.

Burnet, B., and Connolly, K. J. (1981). 'Gene action and the analysis of behaviour'. *British Medical Bulletin*, 37.

Hay, D. A. (1985). *Essentials of Behaviour Genetics*.

genetics of mental illness. The belief that some aspects of human behaviour are innately determined is an ancient one. For example, *Plato postulated that humans were born with certain kinds of knowledge carried in reincarnated immortal souls. Modern science points to genes rather than immortal souls as the carriers of such information. Genes not only program molecular functioning but also, in turn, complex behaviours and, remarkably, knowledge of the environment. This has led some to conclude that given a complete genetic code it should be possible to predict the behaviour of the resultant organism. However, living organisms are systems influenced by their environments, and the differences between genetically identical twins demonstrate that non-genetic factors can influence both form and function.

It is well known that certain personality characteristics and mental illnesses tend to aggregate in families. However, not everything that runs in families is necessarily genetic. For example, career choice or what political party people vote for is often familial. Twin and adoption studies have been used to distinguish between the effects of genes and family culture, and to estimate heritability. Such heritability estimates—the proportion of variation in a particular characteristic accounted for by genes— indicate that genes contribute substantially to the liability

to many mental illnesses (e.g. autism about 80–90 per cent; schizophrenia and bipolar affective disorder 70–80 per cent; major depression 40–70 per cent; alcohol dependence 40–50 per cent). Recent advances in molecular genetics have given us the ability to directly search for genes predisposing to mental illness. Two strategies have been employed to find these genes: linkage and association studies.

Linkage studies look for DNA regions that co-segregate with the illness within families with several affected members. These studies do not require the disease process to be understood, which is fortunate given the shortfall in our knowledge of the biological basis of mental illnesses. Clues to the location of predisposing genes can be used to narrow the search down to a particular region of a particular chromosome, and eventually to a specific gene—a process referred to as 'positional cloning'. For example, the increased frequency of early onset *Alzheimer's disease (AD) in people with *Down's syndrome—who have an extra chromosome 21—led researchers to search for a gene predisposing to AD on that chromosome. At around the same time, the gene coding for a protein of crucial importance in AD was located in chromosome 21. Mutations in this gene were subsequently identified. Although these mutations have been found in only a small percentage of those with the illness, these findings greatly furthered our understanding of the disease process, and allowed the development of transgenic animals (rodents genetically engineered to carry the mutated gene) in which new studies could be conducted.

The positional cloning approach has successfully identified two other genes causing early onset AD, as well as the gene causing *Huntington's disease, and a number of conditions that cause learning disabilities. All of the above are disorders caused by a single gene whereas it appears likely that many different genes contribute to late-onset AD and other common psychiatric disorders. Positional cloning approaches have proved much more difficult in these disorders, in that initial reports of promising positive linkages have often not been confirmed. Although linkages have been reported for illnesses such as *schizophrenia, bipolar affective disorder, and alcoholism, and even for characteristics such as intelligence and homosexuality, none has yet been definitely confirmed.

A complementary approach is provided by association studies. These compare the genetic code of those who have a particular trait or illness (cases) to those who do not (controls). Association studies have greater power than linkage studies to identify genes of very small effect. Until recently these studies have been limited to searching small regions of DNA which contained a gene believed to be involved in the disorder being investigated. For example, association studies of schizophrenia have examined genes involved in the dopamine pathway on the basis that most anti-schizophrenic drugs block dopamine. Studies of depression have often focused on genes in the serotonin pathway since drugs that increase brain serotonin are often antidepressant. Technological advances combined with the automation of laboratory techniques have provided the means by which association studies can now search large tracts of DNA with the sensitivity and specificity needed to find genes predisposing to mental illness.

The spectacular success of the Human Genome Project meant that a draft of the entire human sequence was available well ahead of schedule in February 2001. There are thought to be around 32,000 genes of which about half are expressed in the brain. Roughly a third of these genes are 'housekeeping' genes that are present in every tissue and not, therefore, likely to contribute to individual differences. This means that there are approximately 11,000 genes that may contribute to variation in brain structure and function. Searching through all of these for the gene variants that affect liability to psychiatric disorders is a large but feasible task.

Meanwhile whole new branches of biology have been developing in the wake of the genome project. These include functional genomics—the study of how genes work —and the allied field of proteomics, the study of the properties of the proteins made by genes. Both of these are increasingly dependent on the exploding field of bioinformatics—which combines mathematics and computing to manage, annotate, and make sense of the vast amounts of information generated. These developments have major implications for the study of mind and brain and herald a new era of post-genomic psychiatry.

HW/PMcG/RMM

Andreasen, N. C. (2001). *Brave New Brain: Conquering Mental Illness in the Era of the Genome*.
Bishop, T., and Sham, P. (eds.) (2000). *Analysis of Multifactorial Disease*.
Gottesman, I. I., Alkinson, R. C., Lindzey, G., and Thompson, R. F. (eds.) (1991). *Schizophrenia Genesis: The Origins of Madness*.
McGuffin, P., and Murray, R. (1991). *The New Genetics of Mental Illness*.
——Owen, M. J., O'Donovan, M. C., Thapar, A., and Gottesman, I. I. (1994). *Seminars in Psychiatric Genetics*.
———— Gottesman, I. I (eds.) (2000). *Psychiatric Genetics and Genomics*.

genius. The word comes from the Latin *genius*, the male spirit of a household existing, during his lifetime, in the head of the family and subsequently in the divine or spiritual part of each individual; the English word 'genial' has the same root since the spirit was thought to be propitiated by festivities.

The notion that special gifts run in families was explored by the 19th-century polymath Sir Francis *Galton in *Hereditary Genius* (1896). Galton was a grandson of Erasmus *Darwin, and a cousin of Charles *Darwin. Extreme ability does run in some families—for example, the Bachs, the Darwins and their relations, including the Wedgwoods, the Huxleys, and the Barlows; and in a few political families, such as the Cecils (William, Lord Burghley, 1520–98; Robert, Earl of Salisbury, c.1563–1612; and successive generations in high positions of government in England until the present day), though this might just be chance. It is of course extremely difficult to distinguish heredity from effects of family tradition and upbringing, yet there does seem some evidence for genetic transmission of special abilities.

The genius of, for example, *Newton (whose ancestry was undistinguished) seems in part to lie in the ability to concentrate on particular problems for very long periods of time. The genius of Mozart seems different, in that his music seemed to pour from him almost without effort, and, compared to Beethoven, with remarkably little correction or rethinking.

Since geniuses are rare and there are very marked differences between each, it is extremely difficult to make generalizations or to explain genius beyond saying that there are wide individual biological differences on almost all dimensions, including such obvious ones as height. An important question is whether genius is a fortunate *combination* of characteristics, or whether there are 'genius genes'.

See also CALCULATING GENIUSES; CREATIVITY; GENETICS OF BEHAVIOUR.

RLG

Lykken, D. T. (1998). 'The genetics of genius'. In Steptoe, A. (ed.), *Genius and Mind: Studies of Creativity and Temperament*.

geometry. Even the earliest history of geometry as a theoretical study of spatial relationships and spatial structures reveals that it had, in addition, a powerful symbolic role in both imaginative and theoretically speculative thought. Thus, although the history of geometry can be told in purely mathematical terms, it is also, from another point of view, a history of forms of representation, of ways of thinking about the world and of views on the nature of thought itself.

We can never recapture the origins of geometry. Certainly there were in ancient cultures, such as those of the Babylonians and Egyptians, systematically codified empirical procedures relating to land measurement, the construction of temples, and astronomical observation which could be regarded as antecedents. But it is only with the Greeks that a sophisticated theoretical and demonstrative geometry of the kind we find in *Euclid's *Elements* emerges. It would be difficult to overestimate the impact of the emergence of geometry as a *deductively organized discipline, one in which it is shown that, for example, the internal angles of a triangle *must* equal two right angles, given the apparently undeniable truth of the kind of propositions which Euclid adopts as *axioms and postulates and the definition of a triangle. Such a demonstration provides knowledge not merely that something happens to be the case, but also an understanding of why it *must* be so, given the nature of the things concerned. Geometry thus provided, and to some extent continues to provide, the paradigm of what it is to have scientific knowledge or understanding, moulding, for example, *Aristotle's discussion in the *Posterior Analytics* of the demonstration of *causes.

But the very feature of geometry that singles it out as providing a conception of the ideal at which all other putative sciences should aim was also, from the outset, the source of philosophical problems concerning the status of geometrical knowledge and its relation to the ever-changing physical world. Many sketches of the history of geometry suggest that the Greeks regarded geometry as a theory of *physical* space and that they thus thought they had found a way of discovering truths about the *physical* world by mere contemplation. But this is to project onto the Greeks a way of thinking about geometry, physical space, and their relation, which is a product of the Renaissance and of the new scientific outlook that emerged from it. For while geometry did provide the Greeks and subsequent generations of Western thinkers with their ideal of what it is to have scientific understanding (theoretical knowledge involving demonstrations from accounts of *essence), it is clear that geometry itself was not regarded as yielding a scientific understanding of the ever-changing *physical* world, even though it finds application in that world, especially in the applied mathematical disciplines of astronomy, optics, and harmony; geometry deals with a timeless, unchanging world of pure shapes and sizes (forms).

From this point of view, the problems raised by geometry concern the relation between forms and items in the physical world, how knowledge of forms is possible, and how this knowledge can be so useful in everyday dealings with the physical world. To the Pythagoreans and to *Plato the example of mathematics suggested that the knowable, intelligible reality, must be an unchanging realm behind that of changing appearances. Aristotle, on the other hand, insisted that shapes and sizes have no existence except as aspects of physical, changeable things which are the things that have primary reality. The mathematician then deals with the possible shapes and sizes of physical things but *qua* measurable, not *qua* changeable, whereas the physicist, being primarily concerned with change and its explanation, seeks an understanding of natural objects *qua* changeable. Geometry is the science not just of spatial magnitudes but of all continuous magnitudes which, being represented by lines, can then be handled geometrically. Arithmetic is the science of discrete magnitudes.

Thus, far from taking geometry to be the science of physical space, the Greeks tended to see it as the science of continuous magnitudes, essentially concerned with ratios and proportions and with methods of construction enabling these to be determined. The physical space of the Aristotelian universe is not the infinite, homogeneous space of Euclidean geometry, but the highly structured bounded set of nested spheres centred on the earth. It was the cumulative effect of a number of diverse factors operating from the beginning of the Renaissance that led, by the 18th century, to that identification of physical with geometric space which is most clearly apparent in the works of Isaac *Newton when he talks of absolute space. Perhaps the two most important of these factors were the coordinate development of geometrical theories of perspective and of geometrical optics. The work of Italian artists such as *Leonardo da Vinci gave geometry a role in accounts of the mechanisms of visual perception. The geometrical treatment of problems of perspective, involving two-dimensional representations of three-dimensional spatial relationships, brings with it (*a*) a tendency to treat geometry as descriptive of both perceptual and physical space, and (*b*) the development of the methods of projective geometry (needed to handle the various possible projections of three-dimensional solids into two dimensions). In projective geometry there is a shift of emphasis away from figures and their fixed shapes and sizes towards descriptions of the possible types of projections, the behaviour of shapes under such transformations, and a move towards a consideration of the more global, structural properties of spaces. The adoption of the Copernican, sun-centred view of the universe shattered once and for all the crystalline spheres, leaving the earth spinning through an infinite, homogeneous three-dimensional Euclidean space.

But if geometry is to be a theory of physical space then its axioms must be true of this space, and there is a problem of just how it is that we can come to recognize truths about physical space, the space of the world of experience, as necessary truths. To account for this necessity, it would seem that they must be knowable *a priori, but without proof, for they are first principles. But then how can any truths about the world of experience be knowable prior to, or independently of, experience? There are two problems to be separated here. First there is a psychological problem of how we come by our grasp of spatial relations and spatial concepts, and of what exactly we do acquire simply by experience. Secondly there is a philosophical problem which concerns not how we in the first instance come by our beliefs about space, but how, if at all, these beliefs can be proved or justified.

So long as geometry was synonymous with Euclidean geometry it was possible to think that we have some innate knowledge, or a faculty of geometric intuition which makes it possible for us to recognize the Euclidean axioms as necessarily and self-evidently true. But Euclid's fifth postulate (which says, in effect, that parallel lines never meet however far they are extended) had never seemed entirely self-evident, and there is a long history of unsuccessful attempts to prove this postulate from the other four. In a work published in 1733, the Italian mathematician Girolamo Saccheri adopted a new strategy which was that of combining the first four of Euclid's postulates with the negation of the fifth, with the aim of deriving a contradiction and thus showing indirectly that the fifth postulate is a logical consequence of the remaining four. Although he thought he had succeeded in doing this, his proofs were faulty, as was shown by Bolyai, Lobachevski, Riemann, and others who almost simultaneously demonstrated the existence of non-Euclidean geometries, ones in which the fifth postulate is false. These were shown to be consistent if Euclidean geometry is consistent, by interpreting them as the geometries of curved surfaces of various kinds (e.g. the surface of a sphere). When Einstein made use of non-Euclidean geometries in his theories of Special and General Relativity, treating space–time as a non-Euclidean four-dimensional space, it was no longer possible to regard the Euclidean axioms as self-evident, necessary truths concerning physical reality. This opened up once again questions concerning the nature and status of geometry and its role in physical theories. Some have argued that the choice of geometry is merely a matter of convention; it is just a question of the form of representation we want to use. Others argue that it is an empirical matter, a question of seeking empirically to determine a correct account of physical space.

It is possible, however, to articulate more sophisticated intermediate positions as a result of the work carried out in pursuit of Felix Klein's Erlangen programme (1872). Klein proposed that every geometry can be defined by specifying its group of transformations, and thereby its invariants. This leads to a hierarchy of geometrical theories of increasing generality: metrical geometry, affine geometry, projective geometry, topology (roughly speaking). Given these distinctions it is possible to ask more precise questions about which parts of the full metrical geometry we use could be regarded as factually constrained and which are a matter of convention. MET

Boyer, C. B. (1968). *A History of Mathematics*.
Koyré, A. (1957). *From the Closed World to the Infinite Universe*.
Lanczos, C. (1970). *Space through the Ages: The Evolution of Geometrical Ideas from Pythagoras to Hilbert and Einstein*.
Nerlich, G. (1976). *The Shape of Space*.

Gestalt theory. A theory developed in opposition to the classical theory of psychology best represented by J. S. *Mill and H. von *Helmholtz. In the classical account of *perception, our sensory receptors analyse the

energies provided by the physical world into independent, simple, but *unnoticeable* sensations, and the world teaches us to perceive those objects and events that would, under normal conditions, most probably have produced any given set of sensations. Many perceptual phenomena, however, seem at first to defy analysis in terms of such 'atomistic' independent sensations. As an object moves laterally or sagittally in the field of view, its apparent shape and size remain unchanged (i.e. they display perceptual *constancy*) even though its projected image stimulates a changing set of visual receptors; a melody sounds the same although transposed to a new key and therefore to different auditory receptors; and the form depicted by any pattern can be completely changed by changing its context.

The most important example of this last point is the 'figure–ground phenomenon', i.e. that the same outline can be perceived as different alternative figures, with very different shapes. As Edgar *Rubin, a phenomenologist, noted in 1921, the region that is perceived as 'figure' appears to have a hard surface, with a recognizable shape and definite boundaries; the 'ground' is usually less surface-like, and without definite boundary, extending indefinitely behind the figure's contour. In Fig. 1a, either the vase (Fig. 1b) or the pair of faces (Fig. 1c) can readily be perceived as figure, with the other possibility then relegated to ground. For a shape to be perceived or recognized, it must be figure. The perception of objects, of depth, and of scenes rests, in each case, on shape perception (for instance, on the shapes that comprise the *depth cues* of linear perspective). Yet the classical theory seemed unable to account for the figure–ground phenomenon and, therefore, for shape perception.

Such phenomena implicate a *Gestalt* (configurational) quality in addition to, or in place of, the individual elements composing the pattern of stimulating energies.

To Gestalt psychologists, notably Max *Wertheimer, Kurt *Koffka, and Wolfgang *Köhler, *form* is the primitive unit of perception, taking its properties from underlying configured brain processes ('fields'). These brain processes were thought to be direct responses to the patterned energies acting on the sensory nervous system. The latter was variously conceived as an electrical network or a colloidal bioelectric medium. Brain fields might be studied indirectly by their effects on perceptual organization, an attempt pursued most concertedly by Köhler and H. Wallach (1944) through the study of the *'figural after-effect'. After staring at the fixation point, x, in an 'inspection figure' (Fig. 2a), a 'test figure' (Fig. 2b) appears distorted to subsequent viewing, as exaggerated in Fig. 2c; presumably the latter's contours are 'repelled' from regions previously 'satiated' by the brain fields (direct currents) involved in the perception of the inspection figure.

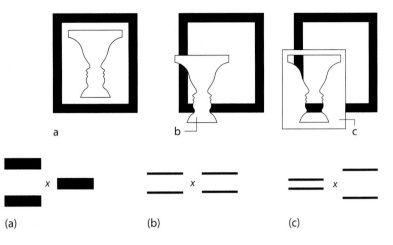

Fig. 1. Figure and ground. The figure perceived in **a** can be either a vase **(b)** or a pair of faces **(c)**.

a

b

c

Fig. 2. Figural after-effects. **a.** Inspection figure. **b.** Test figure. **c.** Exaggerated sketch of appearance of **b** after staring at point x in **a**.

(a)

x

(b)

x

(c)

x

In point of fact, however, although there is ample evidence of organization in the nervous system (in that nerve fibres are arranged in patterns that constrain their function), there is no evidence for the direct-current, steady-state, whole-figure process models of the Gestalt theories. Indeed, such steady-state brain fields seem inappropriate even as metaphors, because in order to perceive any extended object or scene, the eye must direct the very narrow region of detailed vision (the fovea) at different places, so that different parts of the object are seen in succession by the same part of the eye at a rate of about four discrete glances per second. This basic fact would result in a superimposition of different fragments of the stimulus configuration in rapid succession on any hypothesized brain field. It is hard to see how this process could be represented by the holistic steady-state models of the Gestalt psychologists.

With no viable physiological model, the Gestalt theory consists primarily of the so-called 'laws of organization'. The figure–ground method for studying these 'laws' uses ambiguous patterns of either dots (Fig. 3a) or lines (Figs. 3b and 4c) which can be perceived as forming one shape or another, reversible pictures in which the contour that separates two regions gives only one of them recognizable shape as figure at any moment in time (Figs. 1, 4a and 4b), or reversible-perspective outline drawings (such as 'wire' cubes) which can be perceived as either flat or three-dimensional objects (Fig. 5). Configuration is varied to discover what factors lead one or another figure–ground organization to predominate.

One such factor is the 'law of good continuation', i.e. we perceive the organization that interrupts the fewest lines (for example, Figs. 3a and 3b are perceived as a square wave and a sine wave, not as the set of truncated squares in Fig. 3c). Another is the 'law of enclosedness', i.e. the enclosed region tends to be figure (for example, Fig. 4a is perceived as a set of convex shapes, Fig. 4b as concave

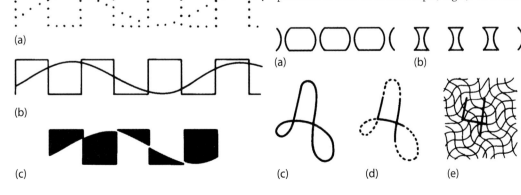

(a)

(b)

(c)

Fig. 3. Laws of organization, **I**.

(a)

(b)

(c)

(d)

(e)

Fig. 4. Laws of organization, **II**.

ones). It is not merely that we perceive familiar as opposed to unfamiliar shapes: letters and numbers (surely familiar) can be concealed by embedding them in a completely unfamiliar set of squiggles, if the latter provide good continuation, as they do in Fig. 4c but not in Fig. 4e.

Many such 'laws' were proposed. They are potentially of practical importance because they seem to determine whether any shape that is presented (by artist, photographer, cartographer, architect, or computer) will in fact be perceived. They seemed potentially of the greatest theoretical importance, because they were taken to show that we perceive objects and events not by learning to interpret our sensations, but because evolution has provided nervous systems that yield three-dimensional perceptual organizations under appropriate conditions. In Fig. 5a the good continuation of the line i–ii would have to be broken in order to perceive the pattern as a three-dimensional cube; in Fig. 5b, the edge i–ii must be broken to see the figure as flat.

For the most part, unfortunately, these 'laws' remain subjective demonstrations of unknown reliability. They can conflict: in Figs. 3a and 3b good continuation is in conflict with enclosedness. Because their relative strengths are unknown, they cannot be applied predictively. Many of them can, however, be subsumed under a single *minimum principle*, i.e. that we perceive the simplest or most homogeneous organization that will fit the pattern of sensory excitation. Fig. 5a, for example, is simpler (in terms of the number of different lines and angles that have to be specified) as a flat figure than is Fig. 5b, whereas they are equally simple as cubes (cf. Hochberg and Brooks 1960). This formulation offered a unifying thread to Gestalt theory that the 'laws' themselves did not. Because the Gestalt demonstrations seem visually compelling, as far as they go, and because of their potential importance, various objective and quantitative treatments of the minimum principle continued to be attempted (notably by F. Attneave, J. Hochberg, P. C. Vitz, and E . Leeuwenberg), all of them quite dissociated from the Gestalt theory and its brain fields.

What was new about Gestalt theory is almost surely not true: aside from the speculations about brain fields,

the main Gestalt notion was that the whole of any perceptual organization determines the appearance of its parts. Although the limits of this principle were never fully spelt out, both the individual laws of organization and the minimum principle were clearly intended to be applied to an entire figure. Thus, whether any intersection in a reversible-perspective figure looks like a flat pattern or like a solid corner in space is presumably a function of the whole configuration. Such anti-elementarism surely goes too far. This point is *suggested* by the 'impossible pictures' devised by Penrose and Penrose in 1958, in which inconsistently oriented parts of objects combine in a single picture that is physically impossible as a three-dimensional organization yet nevertheless looks three dimensional. Fig. 6a is such a picture. The same point is *proven* by making a single intersection in the cube irreversible, and observing that the other intersection continues to reverse spontaneously (Hochberg 1978). Overall simplicity simply will not serve as even a vague and unquantitative explanatory principle.

What is true about Gestalt theory was not new. Not only were the Gestalt 'laws' never systematized or quantified: they were never explained by Gestalt theory, nor were the perceptual constancies, nor was the figure–ground phenomenon itself. In fact, the figure–ground phenomenon is most plausibly explained within the Helmholtzian framework, i.e. that we fit our perceptual expectations about objects and their edges to the relatively unusual situation of viewing lines on paper. If an outline is taken as an object's edge, even slight changes in viewpoint (such as head movements) from 2 to 1 in Fig. 7a would be expected to cause parts of the further surface (such as point i) to disappear behind the nearer surface; so that the definite shape of figure and the indefinite shape of ground, described in connection with Fig. 1, are characteristic of the expectations associated with the edges of objects. In this view, as Brunswik implied in 1956, the 'laws of organization' are merely assumptions about what parts of the visual field are most likely to belong to what object, under normal conditions. For example, because it is very

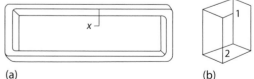

(a)   (b)

Fig. 6. Relative independence of wholes and parts. Object **a** looks three-dimensional even though the corners are inconsistently oriented and connected by an unbroken line (x). In cube **b**, the orientation is fixed at intersection 1, but perceived orientation reversals occur spontaneously at intersection 2 when the gaze is kept directed there.

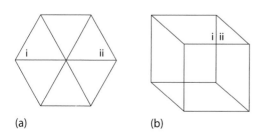

(a)   (b)

Fig. 5. Organization and tridimensionality.

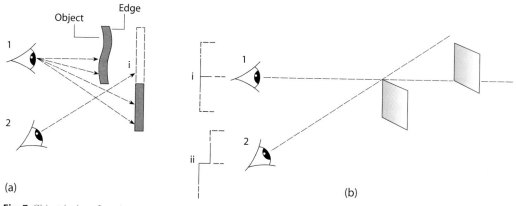

Fig. 7. Objects' edges, figural properties, and 'good continuation'.

unlikely that the viewer would be standing at that one precise point in space (point 1 in Fig. 7b) from which the edges of objects at different distances would be aligned (i) rather than offset (ii), the 'law of good continuation' simply reflects the probability that aligned edges belong to the same object.

The Helmholtzian theory that we perceive whatever most probably would produce the stimulation we receive, and that psychological structure therefore generally reflects physical structure not only still accounts best for the perceptual constancies and illusions (Gregory 1974) but it may account as well for Gestalt organization. The fact that we perceive impossible figures as three dimensional, however, and that figures which are made non-reversible at one corner are free to reverse elsewhere (Figs. 6a and 6b respectively) surely does not reflect the constraints of physical structure, and therefore is not accounted for by Helmholtzian principles without more specific amendments and extensions than have yet been undertaken.   JH

Attneave, F. (1954). 'Some informational aspects of visual perception'. *Psychological Review*, 61.
Brunswik, E. (1956). *Perception and the Representative Design of Psychological Experiments*.
Ellis, W. D. (ed.) (1938). *Source Book of Gestalt Psychology*.
Gregory, R. L. (1970). *The Intelligent Eye*.
——(1974). 'Choosing a paradigm for perception'. In Carterette, E. C., and Friedman, M. P. (eds.), *Handbook of Perception*, vol. i.
Hochberg, J. (1974). 'Organization and the Gestalt tradition'. In Carterette, E. C., and Friedman, M. P. (eds.), *Handbook of Perception*, vol. i.
——(1978). *Perception* (2nd edn.).
——and Brooks, V. (1960). 'The psychophysics of form: reversible-perspective drawings of spatial objects'. *American Journal of Psychology*, 73.
Koffka, K. (1935). *Principles of Gestalt Psychology*.
Köhler, W. (1929). *Gestalt Psychology*.

Gestalt therapy. A non-interpretative psychotherapy which emphasizes awareness and personal responsibility and adopts a holistic approach, giving equal emphasis to mind and body. It began to achieve prominence towards the end of the 1960s. It is one of the several alternative therapies that comprise the Humanistic Psychologies of the Human Potential Movement. Existing more as a style of practice than as a theoretical framework, its ideas are drawn from many sources; the precise boundary between Gestalt therapy and its neighbours is not always clear, and many practitioners use it in conjunction with other approaches.

Gestalt is a German word taken from the psychology of perception. A Gestalt is a figure or pattern which can be distinguished against the background or field of perception (see GESTALT THEORY). But the term has a wider meaning than the nearest English equivalents, 'shape' and 'form', and carries stronger connotations of significance and meaning. Moreover, its use extends over the whole range of perception: shapes and tunes are *Gestalten*, and so are aesthetic and causal phenomena. The term applies whenever a significant pattern or construct (the 'figure') emerges against the background scene or noise (the 'ground').

Fritz Perls (1893–1970), German-born psychoanalyst, was one of the main founders of Gestalt therapy. His inspiration was to give the concept relevance to psychotherapy and use it as a hook on which to hang a number of therapeutic concerns. He saw the task of psychotherapy as one of enhancing the figure–ground differentiation of those Gestalten that reflect the patient's needs. The needs of a healthy person organize the field of experience into well-differentiated Gestalten which command appropriate response. So, for example, a fluid-depleted person experiences the complex of perceptions which emerge into awareness as the Gestalt of thirst, and he gets himself a drink. An affronted person who is aware of his anger has a choice of responses; a person who is unaware or incompletely aware, on the other hand, may repress his anger and get a headache instead. The neurotic is continually interfering with the process of Gestalt formation. He is unable to deal effectively with certain needs because he interrupts and avoids the formation of the relevant Gestalten.

Much of Gestalt therapy is a training in awareness, in improving the individual's contact with himself and his environment. A commonly used exercise is to produce a series of observations, starting with 'Now I am aware that . . .'. Other exercises direct attention to specific experiences, and a distinction is drawn between observation and inference. 'I observe that you are smiling. I infer that you are happy.' Perls described Gestalt therapy as the psychology of the obvious, and he trained people to use what was immediately available by asking such basic questions as 'What are you feeling now?', 'What are you doing?'. An important strategy to increase the immediacy and completeness of any material used in therapy by bringing it into the here-and-now. This means that the patient describes his *dreams, *memories, and preoccupations in the present tense and, where possible, enacts them. 'Shuttling' is another method of increasing figure–ground differentiation. The subject moves his attention between different focuses. For example, if he shows confluence—i.e. lack of differentiation—between an emotion such as resentment and an associated symptom such as a headache, he might be asked to shuttle between his pain and his awareness of resentment.

Clarifying the splits and polarities within the personality is another important area, and for this Perls used one of the most famous of Gestalt props, an empty chair. The subject may put feelings or a fantasy or a part of himself into the empty chair and begin a dialogue; in due course he moves into the empty chair and speaks as the other partner in the dialogue. It is a technique that illustrates a characteristic feature of much Gestalt work, which is to dramatize problems, thereby externalizing them and making them more accessible to the client.

According to one of its leading exponents, Irma Lee Shepherd, Gestalt is at its most effective with 'overly socialized, restrained, constricted individuals', and she points out the dangers involved when inexperienced therapists use the powerfully confronting techniques of Gestalt to 'open up' unstable people with vulnerable personalities. Such people need time, support, and long-term commitment from their therapists. This warning is necessary because much of the public image of Gestalt therapy derives from Perls's dramatic performances, many of which were filmed and video-taped. His clients must have been fairly tough and self-secure to risk public exposure at the hands of a charismatic figure with an almost magical ability to penetrate defences.

Perls dominated Gestalt therapy during his lifetime. His years of experience and training and his extraordinary skill as a therapist made the work look deceptively easy, and it is this that was probably responsible for the overselling of both the theory and his particular model of its application to people lacking in experience. His mistrust of authority matched the anti-authoritarian spirit prevailing in the 1960s. Thus Gestalt therapy has a great deal to say about the harmful effects of the superego but says little about the positive value of discipline, and there is little emphasis on the steady, unremitting work between sessions that must be maintained by patients wishing to make significant changes in their lives. The Gestalt view —which is that of humanistic psychology in general—is that the organism has an innate tendency towards health and wholeness and the full expression of its potential, but in Perls's work there is more emphasis on removing obstacles to growth than there is on working to acquire and strengthen desirable traits.

Research into psychotherapy has not yet reached a point where useful comparisons can be made between the effectiveness of different schools. It is therefore not possible to answer the question 'How effective is Gestalt therapy?'. Even so, there are several indications of the worth of the Gestalt approach. (i) It has survived and expanded over a period which has seen the emergence, stasis, and collapse of many other therapies. (ii) It has survived the death of its charismatic founder. (iii) Most important, it is widely acceptable to many therapists, who apparently find Gestalt ideas valid and useful in their work. FGR

Passons, W. R. (1975). *Gestalt Approaches in Counselling.*

Perls, F. S. (1947). *Ego, Hunger and Aggression.*

——(1969). *In and out the Garbage Pail.*

——(1969). *Gestalt Therapy Verbation.*

——(1973). *The Gestalt Approach and Eye Witness to Therapy.*

Shepherd, I. L. (1970). 'Limitations and caution in the Gestalt approach'. In Fagan, J., and Shepherd, I. L. (eds.), *Gestalt Therapy Now.*

gestures. Movements of the body that signal intentions, commands, or comments—or suggestions, which may be rude or crude. Human gestures form a rich *body language. Some are innate, and probably derive from purely functional movements, such as picking something up, turning the head to look in a different direction, or hitting something hard. No doubt these functional movements were read by other members in a social group as indicating states and needs, and then they became developed as more or less conventional signs for conveying emotional states, intentions, commands, and so on. Although there is a genetic basis, the role of learning is clear because some gestures are specific to geographical regions, or to particular groups or families. People moving into a new area or marrying into a family will pick up some of their characteristic gestures.

The biological basis of gesture was pointed out in Charles *Darwin's masterpiece, *The Expression of the Emotions in Man and Animals* (1872), which suggests that many symbolic gestures are derived from functional behaviour. Their development may sometimes be traced through the use of individual or groups of muscles for purposes which changed in the evolution of species.

It is remarkable that artists, and especially cartoonists, can convey so much by recording a gesture even with just a few lines. It follows that gestures can be signalled and read from small changes of position of the limbs or body; some gestures may be recognized even at night or with the corner of the eye. Evidently we are well attuned in reading and responding to human gestures, which sometimes indicate vitally important intentions, sometimes a state of hope or fear, and sometimes doubt or confidence in those around us. It is necessary that it should be so, for the well-being and survival of any group.

Human gestures have been described and classified in considerable detail; for various regions, social classes and occupations, especially by Desmond Morris (1977, Morris et al. 1979). The range of social gestures is vast: 'the nose thumb', 'the eyelid pull', the vertical and horizontal 'horn sign', the 'palmback V-sign' and many more. It has also been shown how some of them have spread geographically, sometimes over several centuries.

See also BODY LANGUAGE; FACIAL EXPRESSIONS: ORIGINS; MIRROR CELLS.   RLG

Darwin, C. (1872). *Expressions of the Emotions in Man and Animals*.
Morris, D. (1977). *Manwatching: A Field Guide to Human Behaviour*.
—— Collett, P., Marsh, P., and O'Shaughnessy, M. (1979). *Gestures*.

Ghazzali, Al-. See AL-GHAZZALI.

ghost.
A manifestation of a dead person in human form, usually partially transparent and sometimes speaking (like Banquo's ghost in *Macbeth*). Ghosts, of various guises, are believed in to some degree in all societies.

Evidence from photography is dubious (if only because double exposures look remarkably the way ghosts are supposed to appear), and there are plenty of possible explanations in terms of visual illusions. For example, *after-images of, say, candle flames or keyholes will appear very much larger when the gaze is transferred to a distant wall (see EMMERT'S LAW). There is a tendency to 'see' faces and human forms in even quite random shapes (such as 'faces in the fire') which, indeed, is a very great help to artists, and especially cartoonists, who can represent the human face complete with expression with a very few lines. It is possible that perceptual creations of this kind are occasionally elicited in states of *fear, and there do seem to be social factors determining to some degree the forms that ghosts take. There are, of course, less sceptical views, but lack of consistent evidence prevents general acceptance of ghosts. It is suggestive that ghosts and 'appearances' of, for example, the Loch Ness monster are transitory, yet only occasional observations would be needed to justify the existence of such objects. A ghostly perception of a house would be very different—as it should persist day after day. They are notably absent as ghostly perceptions.   RLG

Myers, F. W. H. (1903). *Human Personality and its Survival after Bodily Death*.

Gibson, James Jerome
(1904–79). Distinguished American experimental psychologist, whose work on visual perception was and remains unusually influential. Following an appointment at Smith College, Northampton, Massachusetts, where as a young professor he was considerably influenced by Kurt *Koffka, who had recently emigrated from Germany, Gibson for many years ran a major department at Cornell University. His life work was investigating visual perception of form and motion, his early work including the discovery that distorting lenses produce negative (reversed) adaptation to curvature even with free eye movements. But his main work was to challenge the approach of *Helmholtz and suggest a very different account of perception.

Gibson first of all moved away from the traditional experiments with pictures, and what is seen with a single static eye, towards the observer moving around freely and viewing moving objects in natural conditions. He was led to this by considering pilots landing on fields, where the 'flow lines' of motion are important for seeing the landing point and estimating height and speed. From such considerations of 'visual flow', and texture gradients, he developed what he called 'Ecological Optics'. This almost ignored retinal images, and active brain processes, in favour of regarding perception as 'picking up information from the ambient array of light'. This is very different from the Helmholtzian notion of perceptions as Unconscious Inferences from sensory data and knowledge of objects. Gibson tried to explain object perception by supposing that some 'higher-order' features are invariant with motion and rotation and are 'picked up' with no perceptual computing or processing being required. His search for such invariances, and for just what the visual system uses under various conditions has proved useful for developing computer vision. His general philosophy, however, that perception is passive pick-up of information, present in the world, is hard for Helmholtzians, who stress the importance of knowledge of objects to provide information enhancing sensory signals, to follow. His important books are: *The Perception of the Visual World* (1950) and *The Senses Considered as Perceptual Systems*

(1966). Much of his work was done with his wife Eleanor, a distinguished developmental psychologist.　　　　RLG

Reed, E. S. (1988). *James J. Gibson and the Psychology of Perception*.

gnostic. Relating to knowledge, from the Greek *gnosis* (knowledge or investigation), which is also the root for 'cognitive' and 'cognition'. Gnosticism in general is a variety of religious belief, assuming privileged knowledge of the spiritual world—knowledge considered superior to the science of the day—and bringing with it the promise of salvation. It has taken many forms, having its origins in a variety of pagan sources, including Greek philosophy, Hellenistic mystery cults, and Babylonian and Egyptian mythology, and persisting into modern times in movements such as theosophy.

The best-known adherents are the Christian Gnostics, active during the 2nd century AD. They appeared first as schools of thought within the Church, eventually mostly becoming separate sects; indeed much of early Church doctrine was formulated to counteract their heresies. The various groups widely differed in their teachings and practices but in common made a distinction between a remote and unknowable Divine Being and an inferior deity (the Demiurge) who was the immediate source of creation which was necessarily imperfect since he was held to be antagonistic to the truly spiritual. Some men, however, were thought to contain a divine spark and, through gnosis and the (often secret) rites associated with it, this spiritual element could be rescued from its evil material environment. Gnosis came from the Divine Being through the medium of Christ bringing redemption.

goals in learning. A technical term in *learning theories and experiments in animal learning. Goals are set up by rewards (usually food) to establish learning through consistent (goal-directed) performance. In 'latent learning' (especially associated with Karl *Lashley) animals are allowed to explore mazes before goals are set up. It is then found, when food is provided at a particular place, that the goal is reached with fewer trials than for a control group which has not had previous access to the maze. It follows that learning can occur without goal seeking (or drive reduction), but it is difficult to establish or measure this since specific goals for scoring the successes and failures of performance cannot be used. For further discussion, see PURPOSE.

Gödel, Kurt (1906–78). A mathematical logician, born in Czechoslovakia, who emigrated to the United States and held a position at the Princeton Institute for Advanced Study from 1940 until retirement. In the 1930s he proved three major theorems. The first of these, presented in his doctoral dissertation to the University of Vienna in 1930, was a proof of the completeness of first-order predicate calculus. The second, published in 1931, was a proof of the incompleteness of formal systems of arithmetic, and the third, presented in lectures given during 1938–9, was a proof of the consistency of the continuum hypothesis with the basic axioms of set theory. Each of these results had a profound influence on all subsequent work in the fields of formal logic, number theory, and set theory. But it is the second result that has had the greatest impact outside mathematical circles. This is often known simply as Gödel's theorem (more precisely his first incompleteness theorem) and states that, given any formal system S capable of expressing arithmetic, if S is consistent then there exists a proposition A of arithmetic which is not formally decidable within S, i.e. neither A nor its negation is provable in S.

There are two aspects of this result which mean that its implications extend well beyond the domain of pure mathematical logic. (i) The theorem concerns formal systems capable of expressing arithmetic, but the notion of a formal (logical) system is closely associated with the idea of reducing reasoning to a mechanical, computational process. In preparing the ground for the actual proof of his theorem, Gödel did much to clarify the relation between a formal logical system and the notion of a recursive, and hence effectively computable, function. He showed, loosely speaking, that the functions representable in a formal system of arithmetic coincide with the recursively definable functions. This means that his result applies to all computer implementations of arithmetical reasoning based on recursive processes. Thus each such system will be incomplete in the sense that there will be sentences on which it can produce no decision. (ii) The proof works by providing a numerical coding (Gödel numbering) of formulae and sequences of formulae of the formal language which, since the sentences of the formal system were intended to be interpreted as statements about numbers, means that the system can also be interpreted as talking about its own formulae. This makes it possible to show that there must, for any such system S, be a sentence P of S which can be interpreted as saying 'P is not provable' or, more loosely, 'I am not provable'. It is then shown that, if S is consistent, neither P nor its negation can be provable in S. Thus, it is frequently argued, since P says 'P is not provable', P must be true. On the basis of this last step it has then been claimed that Gödel's theorem shows that the human capacity to recognize arithmetic truths can never be fully captured in a formal system and hence, in view of (i), that men are superior to machines in that given any machine there will be an arithmetical proposition which men can prove but which the machine cannot. But this argument overlooks the fact that the proof of Gödel's theorem only allows one to conclude that *if S is consistent*, neither P nor its negation is provable in S. To go on to conclude that P is not provable, and hence is true, requires that one show S to be consistent. Because the proof methods Gödel used are, via Gödel numbering, themselves formalizable in S, one can argue that one machine T *could* prove of another machine, or even of itself, that *if* it is consistent there exists a sentence which it cannot decide. What a machine cannot do is prove its own consistency. To this extent the proof of Gödel's theorem does not of itself establish the superiority of minds over machines, but it shows that the issue here must be pushed back to the kinds of ground we have, or could have, for believing either a system of arithmetic or ourselves to be consistent.   MET

Dawson, J. W. (1996). *Logical Dilemmas: The Life and Work of Kurt Gödel*.

Depauli, W., and Casti, J. L. (2001). *Gödel: A Life of Logic*.

Gödel, K. (1962). *On Formally Undecidable Propositions*.

Hofstadter, D. R. (1979). *Gödel, Escher, Bach*.

Lucas, J. R. (1961). 'Minds, machines and Gödel'. *Philosophy*, 36.

Goethe, Johann Wolfgang von (1749–1832). Germany's most distinguished poet and a scientist, Goethe was born in Frankfurt am Main. He made discoveries in comparative anatomy, especially on the skull, and in botany showing that leaves are the characteristic form of which all other parts of plants are variations. He vigorously attacked Newton's theory of light and colour, and although here he was incorrect he did point out important colour contrast effects—'Goethe's shadows'. These are shadows cast by coloured lights, and they appear the complementary colour of the light. This is a starting point of Edwin Land's *retinex theory of colour vision.

Goethe is best known for his *Faust* (Part I, 1808; Part II, 1832). It is based on the medieval legend of a man who sells his soul to the Devil. This became linked with the name and adventures of a 16th-century conjuror, Johann Faust. According to Goethe, Faust sold his soul to the Devil in exchange for superhuman powers of intellect and wisdom, and the Devil finally failed to claim his part of the bargain—Faust's soul. This story greatly affected *Freud in his early years, and it has passed into psychoanalytical folklore.   RLG

Matthaei, R. (ed.) (1971). *Goethe's Colour Theory*.

Williams, J. R. (2001). *The Life of Goethe: A Critical Biography*.

Golgi, Camillo (1843–1926). Born at Corteno, Lombardy, he became professor of pathology at Pavia. In 1873 he described his method of using chromate of silver to impregnate neural tissue, so that a proportion of neurons show up in high contrast, enabling microscopic examination. Golgi used this method on normal and pathological material. The method was developed by Santiago *Ramón y Cajal (1852–1934) to study the fine structure of the brain. The two men were awarded the Nobel prize jointly in 1926. See NEUROANATOMICAL TECHNIQUES.

Mazzarello, P. (1999). *The Hidden Structure: A Scientific Biography of Camillo Golgi*. Trans. H. A. Butchel and A. Badiani.

Gombrich, Ernst (1909–2001). The art historian Sir Ernst Hans Joseph Gombrich was a scholar of the highest distinction, combining deep understanding of painting with appreciation of the science of visual perception. Born in Vienna, and settling in London, he was professor of the history of the classical tradition at the University of London and director of the Warburg Institute (1959–76). It was his wartime experience in the BBC's overseas listening service that set him thinking about the nature of perception. Listening to German messages, hard to hear through static and irrelevant interfering signals, he came to realize the significance of *meaning*. His most accessible books, which capture the two aspects of his work in art and *perception, are *The Story of Art* (1950), *Art and Illusion* (1956), and some twenty further books including *Illusion in Nature and Art* (1973) with R. L. Gregory, based on an exhibition at the Institute of Contemporary Arts. Gombrich concluded that no artist can, 'paint what he sees', asking: 'Why is it that different ages and different nations have represented the visible world in such different ways?' This takes the reader through adventurous journeys in the history of art and the psychology of perception. Social factors are not absent. He wrote: 'If art were only, or mainly, an expression of personal vision, there would be no history of art'.

The power and magic of image-making was not revealed to Gombrich by a great painting, but rather by a child's drawing game for representing a cat. A circle representing a loaf of bread was transformed into a shopping bag, adding a curve at the top, and two squiggles on its handle, shrunk into a purse—another squiggle for the tail—and here is the cat. He said: 'What intrigued me, as I learned of the trick, was the power of metamorphosis: the tail destroyed the purse and created the cat; you cannot see one without obliterating the other. Far as we are from completely understanding this process, how can we hope to approach Velázquez?' His many honours included the highest his adopted country could bestow: the Order of Merit (1988).   RLG

graphology. The 'science' of making inferences about personality from handwriting. Graphologists see writing as illuminating underlying mental states the writer would prefer not to disclose, or is perhaps not even conscious of.

Over 200 objective scientific studies into graphology have claimed associations between personality and handwriting that are not above the purely chance level. Any weak ability of graphology to predict personality could be merely based on gender and social status information naturally implicit in most handwriting. Yet in countries like

France, the estimate is that 38–93 per cent of companies still use graphology in personnel selection, while in the UK and the USA the figure is probably closer to around 5–10 per cent.

In seventeen studies investigating the use of graphology in personnel selection, where it seems to have gained the strongest foothold, the evidence is that graphologists cannot accurately predict job performance from handwriting. One theory for the persistence of graphology in the absence of empirical support is the surprisingly high level of agreement between ordinary members of the public about what different aspects of handwriting reveal about personality. For example, the population at large seem to agree that untidy handwriting is linked with depression—though there is no scientific support for this conclusion.

In graphology size of handwriting, for example, is believed to be diagnostic with respect to the personality dimension of modesty–egotism. Small handwriting implies modesty while large handwriting suggests egotism. Also graphology seems to associate words used to describe handwriting features (e.g. regular rhythm) with personality traits (e.g. reliable). This suggests the real way graphology 'works', and why it seems to have such a strong hold with the public, is that meaning of the words attached to handwriting descriptions, such as 'regular rhythm', is linked to a similar meaning in personality, i.e. reliable. This seems to make intuitive sense to most people, although there is no scientific basis to this whatsoever.

Perhaps the problem is that graphology seems to have the right kind of properties for reflecting personality—in that both personality and handwriting do indeed vary between people. Though you could replace handwriting with bumps on the skull to illustrate the reason natural variation between people should not mean personality is associated with such features.   RP

King, R. N., and Koehler, D. J. (2000). 'Illusory correlations in graphological inference'. *Journal of Experimental Psychology: Applied*, 6/4.

Stein, D. J. (2001). 'Handwriting and obsessive-compulsive disorder'. *Lancet*, 358.

Greek investigations of the mind and senses.

At what stage did the ancient Greek thinkers begin to realize the possibilities of carrying out empirical investigations in connection with their psychological theories, and at what stage did they actually do so?

Most of the terms used in Homer to refer to the seats of cognitive and emotional activity have strong concrete associations. Thus one of the words for a part of the body with which men think and feel is *phrenes*. Although this later came to be used of the diaphragm, it originally signified the lungs, as we can tell from a passage in the *Iliad* (16. 504) where, when a spear is withdrawn from a dead warrior's chest, his *phrenes* are described as prolapsing. But if we try to reconstruct in detail what was believed about the physical events corresponding to thoughts and feelings—about, for example, the movements of the blood and the breath and the changes taking place in parts of the body—much of the picture remains vague and unclear.

It has often been maintained that the first thinker who can be claimed to have undertaken dissections in connection with a theory of sensation is the pre-Socratic natural philosopher Alcmaeon (whose precise dates cannot be fixed but who appears to have been active some time around the middle of the 5th century BC). But that claim is probably unfounded. The chief evidence cited to support it is a reference to an investigation of the eye in the commentary on *Plato's Timaeus* written by Calcidius in the 4th century AD. But even if—as Calcidius may suggest—Alcmaeon used the knife in this connection, it was almost certainly not to carry out a dissection of the eye, let alone to cut open the skull to study the structures communicating with the eye within the skull itself, but merely to excise the eyeball to show that the back of the eye is linked to the brain.

The admittedly very meagre fragments of other natural philosophers of the 5th and early 4th centuries BC (see PRE-SOCRATIC PHILOSOPHERS) show that they were interested in such questions as the constitution or substance of the soul (where we find such suggestions that it consists of water or air or fire, or of all the elements or of atoms of a particular shape), in the seat of life and *consciousness (the heart and the brain were the favourite candidates), in whether sensation is by like apprehending like or by unlikes, and, sometimes, in the workings of the individual senses. They frequently cite analogies with objects outside the body to illustrate or suggest theories about its internal functioning, and some philosophers (Empedocles and Democritus especially) had some idea of the complexity of the structure of the eye, for instance. But our sources fail to yield clear and definite evidence that any of the natural philosophers employed dissection.

The possibility of opening the bodies of animals for investigative purposes is, however, occasionally mentioned in isolated texts from the 5th century BC. Herodotus (4. 58) remarks that the fact that the grass in Scythia is exceptionally bilious may be judged by opening the bodies of cattle who have fed on it. Similarly the author of the Hippocratic treatise *On the Sacred Disease* (ch. 11) claims that his view that the sacred disease is due to the flooding of the brain with phlegm can be confirmed by inspecting the brains of goats who have suffered from the disease.

These texts establish that the idea of post-mortem animal dissection had begun to be mooted long before *Aristotle. Yet the occasions when this possibility was suggested were restricted, and the dissections that were actually carried out were cursory and confined to a narrow range of questions. Our chief evidence for this negative conclusion comes from the Hippocratic corpus, a collection of some seventy medical treatises dating mostly from the 5th and early 4th centuries BC. With the exception of one much later treatise (*On the Heart*, now generally thought to belong to the 3rd century BC), these works mostly ignore the method entirely. Their anatomical and physiological theories, when not purely speculative or traditional, were based on the evidence obtainable from the observation of lesions, or on what their authors discovered in surgical operations, or on what they believed could be inferred from such clinical practices as venesection.

Passages in Aristotle indicate, however, that some dissections had been undertaken by his predecessors, although the contexts in which they did so were limited (they included, especially, the investigation of the courses of the blood vessels) and even in those contexts the method was still far from being generally accepted or employed. We have, in fact, to wait until Aristotle himself for good evidence of more than merely occasional use of dissection. His zoological treatises refer frequently to the method, and sometimes do so in sufficient circumstantial detail to make it clear that what is reported is, in part at least, the result of first-hand observation.

It may, therefore, reasonably be claimed that Aristotle and his associates were the first to begin to exploit the possibilities of animal (though not of human) dissection for the purposes of research—with beneficial results in many areas of anatomy especially. The extent to which he did so in connection with his complex and intricate doctrines concerning the soul and the activities 'common to soul and body' is, however, problematic. His view that the heart is the seat of life is supported by what he claims to have observed in embryos, notably in his comparatively detailed researches on the growth of the embryo chick, namely that the heart is the first part to develop and become distinct. On the other hand on many topics in psychology his discussion is, in parts, quite imprecise. Thus, although he claims (for example, in *De juventute*, 469a 12 ff.) that the senses of touch and taste 'clearly' extend to the heart, he makes no attempt to identify and trace the connections. The various descriptions of the anatomy of the pores or channels leading off from the back of the eye to the brain are vague, and are evidently based in part on inferences from lesions. His account of the movement of substances between the brain and the heart (on which depends his explanation of the mechanisms of sleeping and waking) is also largely unclear, as also is his description of the structure of the brain. His anatomical and some of his physiological theories are supported by much more systematic empirical research than those of his predecessors had been. Yet in the particular context of psychology, where the starting point of many of

his speculations lies in certain traditional ideas and problems, it is often the case that his empirical investigations are not pursued beyond the point where he has satisfied himself that he has cited *some* evidence in favour of his own doctrine, or *some* to undermine those of his opponents.

The limitations of Aristotle's work in this area are evident when we compare it with what we know of that of the major Alexandrian biologists of the 3rd century BC, Herophilus and Erasistratus. Although the evidence that they dissected—and indeed vivisected—humans as well as animals has often been doubted, there is no good reason to reject it. The results they obtained, insofar as these can be judged from the reports in Rufus and *Galen especially, were, in any event, impressive. They were responsible for the first detailed accounts of the structure of the brain (including its ventricles) and of the heart (including its valves); and they distinguished four main membranes in the eye, corresponding to (i) the cornea and sclera, (ii) the choroid, (iii) the retina, and (iv) the capsular sheath of the lens. Most importantly, from the point of view of psychology, they discovered the nervous system. Whereas earlier theorists had spoken vaguely of channels or pores as the routes by which sensation and movement were transmitted, and the term *neuron* itself had been applied indiscriminately to what we should call sinews and tendons as well as to the nerves, Herophilus and Erasistratus identified the nerves as such and began to classify them, distinguishing, for example, between the sensory and the motor nerves.

By the 2nd century AD, as we learn from Rufus and Galen, human dissection had almost entirely ceased, and even the value of animal dissection was contested by different medical schools. Nevertheless, that did not stop Galen himself from engaging in extensive animal dissections and vivisections in connection with his physiological and psychological doctrines. Disclaiming any definite theory concerning the substance of the soul, he concentrated his efforts on an account of its faculties, and his work on the nervous system, particularly, goes appreciably beyond that of Herophilus and Erasistratus. Apart from many specific discoveries (such as that of the recurrent laryngeal nerves), he undertook a masterly series of investigations of the nerves of the spinal column. In *On Anatomical Procedures* (Book IX, chs. 13 f.) he reports the results of systematic animal vivisections, where he made incisions either right through the spinal cord or through one side of it, beginning with the vertebra next to the sacrum and working his way up the spinal column in order to reveal the effect that incision at each level had on the animal's faculties—the gradually increasing loss of movement, sensation, respiration, and voice. Although many of his own physiological theories, such as the doctrine of the various kinds of breath or *pneuma*, are highly speculative, these sustained investigations of the nervous system are the supreme example from the ancient world of the application of empirical methods to the understanding of vital functions. Although many of the disputes on the nature of the soul were not susceptible to resolution by such methods, from the Hellenistic period Greek theorists had available quite detailed information concerning many aspects of the functioning of the nervous system.

GERL

Hippocrates (1978). *On the Sacred Disease* and *On the Heart*, in Lloyd, G. E. R. (ed.), *Hippocratic Writings*. Aristotle's psychological and zoological treatises are in Ross, W. D. (ed.) (1910–31), *The Works of Aristotle translated into English*, vols. iii, iv, v. There are no adequate collections and translations of Herophilus and Erasistratus, but Celsus, *On Medicine*, ed. Spencer, W. G., 3 vols. (1935–8), and the works of Galen provide much of our most important information. Three of the most important treatises of Galen are: *On Anatomical Procedures*, trans. C. Singer (1956), together with *Galen, On Anatomical Procedures, The Later Books*, trans. W. L. H. Duckworth and eds. M. C. Lyons and B. Towers (1962); *On the Natural Faculties*, ed. A. J. Brock (1916); and *On the Usefulness of the Parts of the Body*, trans. M. T. May, 2 vols. (1968).

grief. Distress through loss. Especially by bereavement but also loss of youth, possessions, innocence or love. See also BEREAVEMENT.

guessing and intelligence

1. Background
2. Detecting new, non-chance associations
3. Insight from the information sciences
4. Three aspects of intelligence
5. Summary

1. Background

Intelligence is a quality easily recognizable in other people's actions, talk, or writing, yet the current trend among psychologists is to deny that it can be accurately defined or described. This has mainly resulted from the many ways in which intelligence manifests itself, but there is also concern at the arrogance of regarding the IQ as the only adequate measure of an individual's mind, and at the degradation and insult to racial groups that resulted from the intelligence-testing movement. Furthermore the early discussions of the topic were singularly inconclusive and unproductive (Thorndike et al. 1921), so many wished to draw a line under them and pursue the topic no further. Some even accepted the infamous definition given by Boring (1923)—intelligence is what the tests test—but to let the matter rest there surely belittles the status of psychology as a science. Heat, like intelligence, shows itself in many ways, but where would physics be if it had simply been accepted that heat was what thermometers respond to and that its theoretical nature was not a problem worth

tackling? There have been great theoretical advances in the information sciences since the early days of intelligence tests; because intelligence is something to do with the way the brain handles information, it is time for another look at the problem.

The suggestion pursued in this article is that intelligence is the art of guessing right. 'Guessing' is sometimes used as a pejorative term, and of course it is not intelligent to guess blindly when sound knowledge is available. But only bad guesswork ignores sound knowledge; good guesswork uses all the knowledge and evidence that are available, and it is the science behind the art of guessing *right* that illuminates the nature of intelligence.

2. Detecting new, non-chance, associations

We can start with the suggestion that intelligence is the capacity to detect new, non-chance, associations (see Barlow 1970, Fatmi and Young 1970). Consider the hungry dog that leaps from its comfortable rug in front of the fire when it hears the sound of the refrigerator door being opened. That sound has often been experienced as the precursor of food, and the recognition of this association by the dog deservedly earns it some reputation for intelligence. This is not, however, an easy task: first the sound of a refrigerator door opening is not a simple sound like a whistle or a bird's alarm call, with much acoustic energy concentrated in easily defined frequency bands; it is a series of sounds spread over a wide bandwidth, and it is likely to vary greatly according to the vigour with which the door is pulled open and the rattling of objects inside and on top of the fridge. Furthermore it is heard against a background of other complex sounds that are in some ways similar—the opening and closing of other doors, the pad of feet along corridors, and perhaps the sounds of traffic from outside the house.

Communication engineers now know exactly how to design an optimal detector for such a sound, but to do so they would need a great deal of information about the sounds produced by the fridge door and the other sounds from which it must be discriminated, as well as the technical knowledge about how to use this information to construct the detector. It would be hard work to provide this information to the engineers, but the dog's behaviour shows that it has automatically acquired the necessary information about the acoustic environment, and that its brain has the technical means to produce some approximation to an optimal filter for the detection task.

3. Insight from the information sciences

Initially the dog's feat seemed a simple example of learning a new association, but the modern statistical viewpoint tells us something quite different. It says that the environment is complicated and uncertain, but that knowledge of the complexity (in this case statistical aspects of the sounds produced by the fridge door and of other sounds in the acoustic environment) can be used to reduce uncertainty about likely sources of food and thus help the dog to guess right. One can see immediately that, if the general role of intelligence is to master similar complexity in all other aspects of the environment, it faces a truly stupendous task. It should assess the frequencies of all the sensory messages from the environment, the ways they are associated with each other, and the ways they fail to behave as random, independent elements. That may seem a tall order, but a dog *does* have considerable knowledge of its environment and can detect many other acoustic patterns that have significance for it, such as that of the postman opening the garden gate or of its mistress's car returning home. For humans the task is even more stupendous, for no one can doubt that through language, books, libraries, academies, and now the internet, the world we are in touch with is truly complex.

Those familiar with the rudiments of information theory will appreciate that it defines two quantities in a collection of messages such as those a dog or a person receives about the environment—*information* and *redundancy*. Our hypothesis about the art of guessing right could be restated thus: *intelligence exploits redundancy to make predictions more certain*. This relation between redundancy and intelligence was appreciated early in the history of information theory (Barlow 1959, Watanabe 1960) and an account, updated with the benefit of hindsight, can be found elsewhere (Barlow 2001). The importance of the statistical structure of natural stimuli in problems of perception is now widely recognized (Simoncelli and Olshausen 2001). Macphail (1982) reviewed evidence on the learning abilities of many species of animal, and was surprised to find that there was apparently no correlation with their supposed intelligence. He concluded that intelligence was not closely linked to learning, but this is just as the current hypothesis predicts; most learning tests are carefully designed to prevent test animals benefiting from knowledge of the associative structure of their environment—precisely the knowledge intelligence is thought to exploit to improve guesswork.

4. Three aspects of intelligence

What do these insights from the information sciences tell us about its measurement? In order to guess right there are three conceptually distinct tasks, namely formulating possible guesses (i.e. hypotheses about new association), testing them to find if they are acceptable, and working out the implications of those that escape disproof.

Associative efficiency. Of these three, it is easiest to imagine an objective measure of the testing process, because the theory and practice of statistical tests for associations are well developed, and in principle this makes it possible to compare an individual's performance at an associative task with an 'ideal statistician's'. The ideal statistician

will devise tests that make the best possible use of all the evidence, and a measure of 'associative efficiency' is obtainable from the ratio of the amounts of evidence required for these tests and for the individual being tested, when each performs at the same level of reliability. This is an absolute measure of how well the subject utilizes the information available—how well he guesses in fact. This concept of statistical efficiency (Fisher 1925) has been used to measure human perceptual tasks (Rose 1942, Tanner and Birdsall 1958, Barlow and Reeves 1979, Barlow and Tripathy 1997), but has not yet been applied to the associative tasks that underlie intelligence (nor to learning for that matter).

It is satisfying that the definition enables one to specify one aspect of intelligence that could in principle be measured objectively and in absolute terms, knowing precisely what one was measuring. The idea that there is an absolute zero of intelligence, where none of the available information about a new association is used, or 100 per cent intelligence, where all of it is used, may be new to some people, as will be the idea that one aspect of intelligence is in principle measurable on an absolute scale, free of reference to population norms.

Imaginative intelligence. The next question is; 'How does the possibility of a particular association enter someone's mind?' One naturally attributes intelligence to a mind that generates its own array of plausible possibilities, and stupidity to a mind that produces inappropriate ones or has to be fed with suggestions in every new circumstance. Seeing possible solutions is an essential part of good guesswork, and the nature of this imaginative ability may be a more interesting question than that of assessing statistically whether a given association is present or not. The main difficulty here is the astronomical number of possible associations: it is certainly *not* intelligent to point to any or all of them for testing, whereas it would, for instance, show a glimmer of intelligence to start looking for associations between events that occur with approximately the same frequency. It seems likely that numeric measures of imaginative inventiveness would have to depend upon comparisons with population norms, as with the standard IQ. One must also pay attention to the third distinctive part of intelligence.

Deductive intelligence. It is not intelligent to claim as a new association something that can readily be deduced from associations that are already known. Every moment we see sights and hear sounds that can be predicted from associations already established by our own minds, or implanted in them by others. To distinguish what is new, knowledge of these pre-existing associations must be organized so that they are taken into account. Thus the deductive reasoning required to use a background of general knowledge is a necessary part of intelligence on the current definition.

5. Summary

The suggestion that intelligence is complex and requires imagination, judgement, and reasoning will surprise no one. But insight from the information sciences leads to two novel conclusions: first, the part concerned with statistical judgement can in principle be measured on an absolute scale, using theoretical limits as references rather than population norms; and second, the basis for efficient use of information in guessing right comes from processes that are part of perception, rather than learning. The diversity of minds and their aptitudes should not conceal the fact that there is a recognizable unity behind all manifestations of intelligence, namely the goal of improving the reliability of predictions by exploiting the redundancy of sensory messages—in other words, intelligence helps us to guess right.   HBB

Barlow, H. B. (1959). 'Sensory mechanisms, the reduction of redundancy, and intelligence'. In *The Mechanisation of Thought Processes*.

—— (1970). 'Definition of intelligence'. *Nature*, 228.

—— (2001). 'Redundancy reduction revisited'. *Network: Computation in Neural Systems*, 12.

—— and Reeves, B. C. (1979). 'The versatility and absolute efficiency of detecting mirror symmetry in random dot displays'. *Vision Research*, 19.

—— and Tripathy, S. P. (1997). 'Correspondence noise and signal pooling in the detection of coherent visual motion'. *Journal of Neuroscience*, 17.

Boring, E. G. (1923). 'Intelligence as the tests test it'. *New Republic*, 35.

Fatmi, H. A., and Young, R. W. (1970). 'A definition of intelligence'. *Nature*, 228.

Fisher, R. A. (1925). *Statistical Methods for Research Workers*.

Macphail, E. (1982). *Brain and Intelligence in Vertebrates*.

Rose, A. (1942). 'The relative sensitivities of television pick-up tubes, photographic film, and the human eye'. *Proceedings of the Institute of Radiation Engineers*, 30.

Simoncelli, E. P., and Olshausen, B. A. (2001). 'Statistical properties of natural images'. *Annual Review of Neurosciences*, 25.

Tanner, W. P., Jr., and Birdsall, T. G. (1958). 'Definitions of "d" and "n" as psychophysical measures'. *Journal of the Acoustical Society of America*, 30.

Thorndike, E. L., et al. (1921). 'Intelligence and its measurement: a symposium'. *Journal of Educational Psychology*, 12.

Watanabe, S. (1960). 'Information-theoretical aspects of inductive and deductive inference'. *I.B.M. Journal of Research and Development*, 4.

H

habituation (adaptation). In general, an aspect of learning whereby an animal becomes accustomed to a situation that persists. In a narrower sense, habituation is the gradual loss of a *reflex behaviour by repetition of a stimulus without reinforcement—for example, continual tapping on the shell of a snail; after a few taps, it ceases to emerge from its shell. Habituation, or adaptation, allows animals to disregard irrelevant stimuli. (If the snail came out every time its shell got tapped, it would get worn out!) Some reflexes are highly resistant to habituation—such as blinking at loud sounds, or at air blown on the eye. This may be because these reflexes are particularly necessary to the survival of the organism, disregard of the stimuli being highly dangerous. See also INVERTEBRATE LEARNING AND INTELLIGENCE.

Hilgard, E. R., and Marquis, D. G. (1940). *Conditioning and Learning*.

Haeckel, Ernst (1834–1919). German zoologist, biologist, and philosopher who was born in Potsdam, Prussia. He studied medicine at the universities of Würzburg, Vienna, and Berlin, obtaining his doctorate in medicine in 1858. He was a lecturer in comparative anatomy (1861–5), then professor of zoology at Jena (1865–1909). He was a member of more than 90 learned societies and scientific associations, ranging from the Imperial Academy of Sciences of Vienna (1872) to the American Philosophical Society (1885).

Haeckel's works included descriptions of approximately 4,000 new species of lower marine animals, mainly radiolarians, medusae, and sponges. He was immediately converted to Darwinism upon reading *On the Origin of Species*, and became one of the most prolific and enthusiastic advocates of *evolution. He developed Haeckel's law of recapitulation where 'ontogeny recapitulates phylogeny'. Haeckel was one of many thinkers who believed that all species were historical entities (lineages) but did not share *Darwin's enthusiasm for natural selection as the main mechanism for generating the diversity of the biological world. Haeckel believed that the environment acted directly on organisms, producing new races (a version of *Lamarckism). The survival of the races did depend on their interaction with the environment, a weak form of natural selection. Haeckel's mechanism of change required that formation of new characters diagnostic of new species occurred through progressive addition to the developmental trajectory. For example, most metazoans go through a developmental stage called a gastrula: a ball of cells with an infolding that later forms the gut. Haeckel thought that at one time an organism called a 'gastraea' existed that looked much like the gastrula stage of ontogeny, this hypothesized an ancestral metazoan giving rise to the rest of the multicelled animals.

The 'law of recapitulation' is largely discredited. Experimental morphologists and biologists have shown that there is not a complete correspondence between phylogeny and ontogeny. Although a strong form of recapitulation is not correct, there are remarkable similarities between all vertebrate embryos at early stages of development, and the concept may serve as a guiding principle for human embryology and the role of reflexes in later life.

Although best known for the famous statement 'ontogeny recapitulates phylogeny', Haeckel also coined many words commonly used by biologists today, such as *phylum, phylogeny,* and *ecology.* Haeckel also stated that 'politics is applied biology', a quote used by Nazi propagandists. The Nazi party, rather unfortunately, used not only Haeckel's quotes, but also Haeckel's biology for justifying racism and nationalism. Haeckel was a freethinker who went beyond biology, into anthropology, psychology, philosophy, and cosmology. Haeckel's speculative ideas and lack of empirical support for many of his ideas tarnished his scientific credentials.

Among Haeckel's books are his *General Morphology* (1866), *Natural History of Creation* (1867), and *Die Weltraetsel* (1899), English title *The Riddle of the Universe*.   RLG

Bowler, P. J. (1989). *Evolution: The History of an Idea.*
Haeckel, E. (1899). *The Riddle of the Universe at the Close of the Nineteenth Century.*
Milner, R. (1990). *The Encyclopaedia of Evolution.*

hair cells. The sensory cells of the inner ear are called hair cells. When sound enters through the ear canal, these cells detect small movements of fluid in the cochlea. As part of many balancing reflexes, hair cells are also found in the inner ear's vestibular organs. Hair cells are named after the short cellular processes which project from one end and which resemble hairs when viewed with a microscope; there is no connection with the cells from which hair grows on the head. Within both the cochlea and the

hair cells

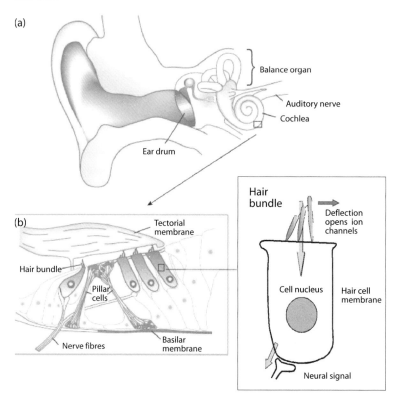

(a)

Balance organ

Auditory nerve

Cochlea

Ear drum

(b)

Tectorial membrane

Hair bundle

Pillar cells

Nerve fibres

Basilar membrane

Hair bundle

Deflection opens ion channels

Cell nucleus

Hair cell membrane

Neural signal

Fig. 1. The organization of hair cells in the ear. **a**, section of head showing the site of the cochlea and balance organs. **b** shows the organ of Corti in a cross-section of the cochlear duct and the position of the hair cells. The hair cell is a mechanically sensitive cell that signals to the brain when its hair bundle is deflected.

vestibular organs, hair cells form synaptic contacts with the auditory and vestibular nerves respectively, and information about inner ear displacements can then be relayed from the periphery to the brain (see Fig. 1).

When the projecting bundles of hairs (stereocilia) are deflected, an electrical signal is generated in the cell. The cells are very sensitive: deflection of the stereocilia by no more than a nanometre (10^{-9} m, the width of a molecule) can be detected. Since the hairs are relatively stiff and pivoted around their base like small levers, the relative slippage between neighbouring pairs of stereocilia causes protein pores to open in the surrounding cell membrane. Charged ions entering through the pores create a potential within the hair cell. The potential controls the release of neurotransmitter from the hair cell and this influences the rate at which action potentials are sent along the (post-synaptic) *afferent nerve fibre to higher brain centres. Although hair cell stereocilia are deflected at acoustic frequencies (up to 20 kHz in humans), the electrical properties of the hair cell membrane smooth the rapidly changing potential to a slower rate which can be transmitted by the nerve axons to the brain. Thus information about which hair cell has been stimulated is carried by a specific set of nerve axons.

In each human cochlea there are two distinct types of hair cell. About 3,500 inner hair cells form a population of sensory hair cells with each cell contacting about twenty auditory axons. The remaining population of 12,000 hair cells are known as outer hair cells. These cells have an additional function that contributes to the sensitivity of hearing. Outer hair cells are both sensory cells, like inner hair cells, and are also able to function as fast motor cells that control the mechanics of the vibration pattern of the cochlea. Outer hair cells can generate forces at acoustic rates and therefore work much faster than conventional muscles. The mechanism is based on a protein motor expressed in the lateral surface of the cell. This protein (named 'prestin' because of its ability to confer rapid motor movements on the cells) was discovered only recently and appears to be unique to the cochlea.

Outer hair cells enhance the sensitivity of the cochlea by about 40 dB (or 100 times). The progressive loss of outer hair cells with age and particularly from the high-frequency end of the cochlea leads to deafness. At present there is no known biological mechanism to rebuild cochlea cells once they are lost. Hearing aids, although improving dramatically, only compensate imperfectly for the loss of intrinsic cochlea amplification. JA

Hall, Granville Stanley (1844–1924). American psychologist who became Wilhelm *Wundt's first American student—and eventually president of Clark University, Worcester, Massachusetts. He was born at Ashfield, Massachusetts, and educated in New York and at Harvard. He obtained his doctorate under William *James with a dissertation on space perception. As president of Clark University, he was largely instrumental in inviting Sigmund *Freud and Carl *Jung to visit in 1909 and deliver a course of lectures. His best-known book is *Adolescence* (1904).

hallucination. Briefly defined as sensory perception in the absence of external stimuli, hallucination has three characteristics: thoughts or memory images, perhaps when they are as vivid and immediate as perceptions, are experienced as if they were perceptions; they are externalized, or projected, being experienced as if they came from outside the person; and the mistaking of imagery for perception is not corrected in the light of the other information available. The term pseudohallucination has been used to describe imagery as vivid and immediate as perception but not mistaken as such. Pseudohallucinations are more likely to be perceived in response to isolation or an intense emotional need: for example, shipwrecked sailors may visualize boats coming to their rescue. The fanciful elaboration of perception of external stimuli—for example, faces seen in the fire—is *illusion. The imagery of a vision is experienced as if it came from outside, although not from ordinary reality as perception does.

Young children often fail to distinguish between imagery and perception and suppose that what they imagine is external and perceptible to others. Adults sometimes fail to make the distinction, especially at a time of high expectation or *arousal. A widow mourning her husband may see him or hear his voice or footsteps repeatedly after his death, resulting in a 'sense of presence' which fades with the passage of time. In a wood at night, dark shadows are seen as lurking beasts. Waking from a frightening dream, a person feels that what he has experienced has happened in reality.

Mistakes like these are corrected when the person recognizes that they conflict with other information or the views of others. Normally imagery is continually reappraised in the light of further information becoming available, and further information is sought by testing reality. Hearing a noise, a person makes a small head movement and tests whether the change in the strength and character of the noise conforms to his expectation. Perceiving someone in a crowd as an acquaintance, a person looks again or asks a companion for confirmation. Macbeth in Shakespeare's play, while planning to murder Duncan, hallucinates a dagger, and asks: 'Art thou not, fatal vision, sensible to feeling as to sight? Or art thou but a dagger of the mind, a false creation, proceeding from the heat-oppressed brain?'

After a long period of wakefulness or busyness, attention tends to be withdrawn from the outside world, and the testing of reality to be impaired and reduced. Hallucination is relatively common under these conditions and remains uncorrected for longer. Sufficient information is available but is not used. On the other hand, the subjects of experiments on the effects of sensory deprivation, who are put into a darkened and soundproofed room, do not get sufficient information to enable them to test reality and to reappraise their hallucinatory experiences. (See ISOLATION EXPERIMENTS.) Also, a person on his own is less able to test reality and to reappraise what he has experienced.

Hallucinations tend to be disowned, the person feeling that he has no control over the imagery, which he feels is imposed on him by an outside agency. They are often reported as distressing, threatening, or tormenting, only occasionally, for example by a widow, as reassuring. There are other distressing phenomena that are not hallucinations, although akin to them in some respects. Thus, some recurring images obtrude and cannot be stopped, but are accepted as belonging to the individual. Such images are termed *obsessions. Ringing in the ear ('tinnitus'), resulting, for instance, from disease of the ear, is sometimes described by a fanciful simile, e.g. as being like sea flowing over shingle, or as if there were nearby a machine crushing stones. What is being described may be thought mistakenly to be hallucination if the explicit comparison of the 'like' or the 'as if' fails to be noted.

Hallucination is common in patients who have suffered damage to the brain as a result of trauma, infection, or intoxication by drugs or alcohol. The association of hallucination, fearfulness, and agitation in these cases may be described as *delirium. A patient who suffers from delirium tremens as a result of alcoholism may see such frightening things as red spiders or pink elephants, or he may feel that lice are crawling over his skin, because hallucination although usually visual may be experienced through any of the senses. Indeed, hallucinations in functional psychoses are more often auditory than visual. *Schizophrenic patients may hear the voices of their persecutors, conversations about themselves between third parties, or their own thoughts spoken aloud (*echo de pensée*). Severely depressed patients may hear voices making derogatory remarks or threatening them with punishment or torture. Some schizophrenic patients even experience tactile hallucinations which give rise to delusional beliefs that they are being sexually assaulted. Olfactory hallucinations are sometimes perceived by severely melancholic patients who come to believe that they are giving off revolting odours from their bodies causing people to avoid them. Patients mistake hallucinations of all these kinds for perceptions coming from outside themselves, and attribute to others what they experience, usually without any testing of reality.

Explanations of hallucination refer to several processes. In delirium there tends to be a high level of arousal and at the same time a lowering of vigilance, impairment of perception, and impairment and reduction of reality testing. Enhancement of imagery as a direct effect of drugs or toxins on nervous tissue is similar to that of electrical stimulation of the temporal lobes of the brain when it produces, in a conscious patient whose brain has been exposed during surgery, intense visual, auditory, or other imagery as 'strips' of experience. Poisoning by drugs may also, more importantly, increase the random activity of nervous tissue. Sensations then become blurred, to produce background noise, which is then elaborated into illusion. A person poisoned by LSD may see visual patterns like lace curtains, usually coloured. In some illnesses in which there is hallucination, the functioning of peripheral nerves is affected by neuritis, and as a result the patient may experience numbness, pins and needles, or itching, which is elaborated into the illusion of lice. Similarly, the result of neuritis of the retina may be spiders dangling in front of the eyes, brain-elaborations of phosphenes. In schizophrenia, the patient has typically disengaged from social activities, and the testing of reality is reduced as a result, but this does not account for his disowning of what he experiences. It has to be supposed that thoughts and feelings have been dissociated as a psychological defence in order to reduce the *anxiety which would otherwise arise. The patient positively resists any reappraisal of what he has experienced. DRD

Galton, F. (1907). *Inquiries into Human Faculty and its Development*.
Harris, J. P., and Gregory, R. L. (1981). 'Tests of hallucinations of Ruth'. *Perception*, 10.
Siegel, R. K. (1993). *Fire in the Brain: Clinical Tales of Hallucination*.
—— and West, J. L. (eds., 1975). *Hallucinations*.

halo effect. A powerful social phenomenon, that reputation or belief affects judgement. For example, we may regard people wearing spectacles as especially intelligent. People distinguished in one field are often regarded—by the halo effect, and sometimes dangerously—as wise and learned in others. For example, the great inventor Thomas Alva Edison was consulted on political and philosophical matters. Wealth and fashionable clothes, and even opinions, can similarly confer unjustified prestige. The converse phenomenon is 'Give a dog a bad name . . .'.

hand. The anatomist Wood Jones (1879–1954) proposed that 'man's place in nature is largely writ upon the hand'. There is a great deal of evidence that human *perception and the way in which we classify objects are very much determined by how we handle them, not only in infancy but also in the later development of perceptual and motor skills. So mind may depend as much upon the hands as it depends upon the senses for gaining knowledge, and so developing.

See BLINDNESS, RECOVERY FROM; HANDEDNESS; SPATIAL COORDINATION; TOUCH.

handedness. A characteristic peculiar to man. Only in man do individuals have a consistently preferred (and more skilful) hand for manual actions, and only man is predominantly right-handed. Other animals show paw preferences when freely picking things up, reaching into small spaces, pressing bars, or opening boxes, but they are less consistent within and across these activities, and are easily influenced by environmental variables such as training and object position. Moreover, in subhuman species tested (including mice, rats, cats, dogs, monkeys, and apes), one finds an even distribution of left and right preferences, without the typically human tendency to right-handedness. Man, by contrast, is predominantly dextral in all races and cultures, with most individuals' preferences remaining constant from an early age.

The inconsistency and lability of preferences in lower animals probably reflect their lack of an upper-limb dexterity comparable to man's. That is, the range of actions available to them—pushing, reaching for, or picking things up—usually involves whole-limb movements which require an accompanying postural body adjustment. Such movements are often stereotyped and appear to be controlled by lower centres in the brain. In man and the higher primates, an individual's handedness becomes more marked the greater the manipulative skill required in an action, where movements independent of bodily position are controlled by higher cortical brain circuits.

Human handedness, therefore, appears to have developed along with, and to be a feature of, man's uniquely high level of finger dexterity and capacity to make and use tools. Anthropological evidence, although necessarily indirect, suggests that handedness first appeared in the lower Stone Age when tool making became common. Some tools, for example, appear to have been made by right-handers for right-hand use.

By historical times the predominance of right-handedness was well enough known for its origin to be discussed and for sinistrality to be noted as exceptional. *Aristotle discusses ambidexterity as a problem for contemporary ideas of the inherent superiority of the right side of the body. The Old Testament notes two cases of left-handedness: a group of 700 sinistral sling shooters in the tribe of Benjamin, and Ehud the Benjamite who stabbed an enemy king with his left hand.

Once established, manual asymmetry quickly attracted a potent mythology associating the right side of the body and the right hand with things that are good, strong, pure, and honourable, while the left in contrast was equated with evil of all kinds. This symbolism has pervaded nearly all cultures (except the Chinese) throughout the ages. Ancient Greeks and Romans regarded the left side as inferior and profane, and in medieval times use of the left hand was associated with witchcraft. Arabs still regard the left as the 'unclean' hand and forbid its use in normal human contact. The odium of the left remains today in terms such as sinister, gauche, and cack-handed.

Right-handedness is of interest to psychology and neurology in that the development of a consistent hand preference in relation to fine motor skills may be linked to the development of hemispheric specialization in the human brain for certain cognitive functions. It is known that in 95 per cent of dextrals language is mediated exclusively by the left hemisphere, that is, by the hemisphere controlling the right side of the body, including the preferred hand. Originally this 'cerebral dominance' for speech was thought to imply that the left hemisphere was the vehicle for all man's highest mental functions. Subsequently, however, it was established that the right hemisphere plays its own dominant role in tasks requiring spatial perception, reasoning, or memory, as in map reading and the recognition of faces, patterns, and melodies. This complementary specialization of the two sides of the brain is, like strong right-handedness, peculiar to man, so they may have evolved together.

Handedness may, however, reflect more directly the cerebral basis of sensorimotor function. Clinical and physiological evidence suggests that in right-handers the left hemisphere has sensory and motor connections to both sides of the body, whereas the right hemisphere is almost exclusively unilaterally connected. The former may thus have a dominant role in integrating activity of the two sides of the body to make a coordinated behavioural unit. If so, voluntary control of the right hand may be easier, and a preference for its use in delicate manipulative skills may emerge as a result.

In accordance with this idea, although it is not yet known exactly what the difference is between the hands in terms of skill, the evidence to date suggests that it centres on timing and the coordination of movements into sequences. Single-finger contractions can be made as precisely or as fast with the left as with the right hand, and with practice either hand may run off pre-programmed sequences of movement (as in typing or piano playing) equally well, provided they do not require adjustment during their execution. But tasks involving visual aiming (such as peg placing or threading a needle) or serial adjustment (as in turning a crank handle or threading a nut on to a bolt) yield consistent differences in performance between the hands. Current theories of the basis of handedness include: (i) increased variability in the left arm's execution of movements, so that they require more fre-

quent correction; (ii) longer time lag in the correction of inaccurate movements when they occur, especially using vision; (iii) greater irregularity in timing of movements by the left hand; and (iv) a greater repertoire of movements available to the right hand because it has had more practice (this last being a rather circular argument).

Another explanation of dextrality is based on the predominant use of the right hand for gesturing, that is, for movements of communication rather than manipulation. This again links it with the development of speech, itself seen as man's most sophisticated form of communication. Certainly the neural motor systems of speech and the right hand are adjacent, and motor activity in the latter is strongly associated with speech generation. Talking in dextrals is accompanied by gestures mainly of the right hand and arm (whereas arm movements in other situations are not specifically dextral), and talking interferes with a concurrent motor activity in the right hand, such as balancing a rod on one finger, more than in the left. Musicians report that conducting rather than finger-work is the most difficult action to perform with the non-preferred hand, implying that handedness consists of a 'closer, more immediate availability of the right hand as the instrument of the individual's conceptions and intentions'.

Any theory of handedness has to account for the minority of left-handers found in all human societies, a proportion variously reported as from 4 to 36 per cent. The classification of subjects is itself a problem, because most sinistrals are less well lateralized than dextrals. Their preferences and usage are weaker and more changeable both within and across tasks, that is, they may prefer to use the right hand for any actions occasionally or for some tasks regularly. There seems, moreover, to be no hierarchy of preferences, nor any activity common to all sinistrals suitable for selecting them as such (although writing, throwing, shooting, and using scissors have been used for the purpose).

Nor is it clear whether handedness is a continuum (albeit an unusual J-shaped one) ranging from total dextrality to total sinistrality or comprises discrete categories and, if so, whether there are two groups (left and right) or a third 'ambilateral' (mixed-handed) group as well. Much variability in results between different studies of handedness stems from this ambiguity. The great variety of laterality measures used—including grip strength, touch sensitivity, eyedness, and writing hand—also adds to the confusion, especially as many have little relation to dexterity and do not intercorrelate.

On tests of manual speed, accuracy, and steadiness, the performance of pure sinistrals mirrors and equals that of dextrals, both showing a distinct superiority of the preferred hand. In ambilaterals of all kinds (including most self-professed left- and some right-handers) the two hands are more equal in skill, and neither performs quite as well as the preferred hand of the strongly lateralized.

Cerebral specialization and dominance in sinistrals is less clear cut than in dextrals. Speech is still represented in the left hemisphere in 70 per cent of left- and mixed-handers, but 15 per cent have right-hemisphere language and 15 per cent bilateral representation. Sinistrals may suffer *aphasia from damage to either hemisphere, but recover from it better than do dextrals. Similarly equivocal results are found for other skills, suggesting a bilateral brain involvement in all mental functions. Some investigators claim pure left-handers are the mirror opposites of dextrals while ambilaterals are a separate group. Others distinguish 'familial' left-handers (with sinistral relatives) from 'non-familials'. Others again classify all sinistral brains as 'imperfectly developed' or 'undifferentiated'.

Theories of the origins and distribution of handedness are of three kinds. (i) Learning-cultural theories claim that it is produced by social pressures or early experience, especially of tools designed for right-hand use. These (mostly older) theories are too imprecise to predict accurately the handedness of any individual or the distribution of handedness in any group. (ii) Genetic models (see GENETICS OF BEHAVIOUR) suggest handedness is inherited, although the exact mechanism is as yet unknown. Theories include a two-gene model and a right-shift model in which pure right-handedness may be inherited from a dominant gene but, if not, the degree of laterality to either side is determined randomly by environmental factors. (iii) Brain-damage theories hold that neonatal injury shifts cerebral dominance and handedness or prevents normal hemispheric specialization. They explain thereby the higher incidence of sinistrality found in such pathological states as learning disability and epilepsy. Whether they account for left-handedness in the population generally is debatable.   KAF

Annett, M. (2002). *Handedness and Brain Asymmetry: The Right Shift Theory* (2nd edn.).

Barsley, M. (1966). *The Left-Handed Book.*

Geschwind, N., and Galadurda, A. M. (1987). *Cerebral Lateralization.*

Hardyck, C., and Petrinovich, L. F. (1977). 'Left-handedness'. *Psychological Bulletin*, 84.

McManus, I. C. (1999). 'Handedness, cerebral lateralization, and the evolution of language'. In Corballis, M. C., and Lea, S. E. G. (eds.), *The Descent of Mind: Psychological Perspectives on Hominoid Evolution.*

Springer, S. P., and Deutsch, G. (1981). *Left Brain, Right Brain.*

Zangwill, O. L. (1962). 'Handedness and dominance'. In Money, J. (ed.), *Reading Disabilities.*

handicap. A term sometimes applied to a person suffering from a physical or mental disability (as opposed to illness). The word probably comes from the phrase 'hand i' (in) cap', referring to a 17th-century sporting lottery in which the contestants deposited forfeit money in a cap or hat. Later, in horse racing, it referred to the extra weight which various horses were required by the umpire to carry in order to penalize the superior animals and so even out the contest. Since the 19th century the term has been applied to any disability in a contest.

See also MENTAL HANDICAP; SUBNORMALITY.

Hartley, David (1705–57). British philosopher and physician, born in Halifax and educated at Jesus College, Cambridge. While a medical practitioner in Newark, London, and Bath he developed an account of mind based on soundlike vibrations, which he used not only to explain transmission of messages in the nervous system but also association of ideas by a kind of resonance, as when one vibrating string activates another by sympathy. His associationism is important in the history of psychology. *Observations on Man* appeared in 1749.

Hawthorne effect. A kind of experimenter effect which has been found in industrial research. There may be changes in productivity etc. simply in response to attention from the investigators, rather than as the effect of any particular experimental treatments. It is so named because of a study at the Hawthorne plant of the Western Electric Company in Chicago in 1927–9 in which five girls were moved into a test room and subjected to various changes in rest periods and refreshments; it was found that output increased by about 30 per cent, this being unrelated to any particular experimental conditions. It was generally concluded that the increase was due to social factors within the group, although it could be accounted for by the change in group piecework which was shared among a group of five instead of a larger group, the smaller variety of work done, the replacement of two of the girls by faster ones, the enthusiasm of the penurious operative number two, and the general expectation throughout the works that the experiment would be a 'success'.

Whether the result was correctly interpreted or not, this study had a profound effect on the subsequent development of research in industrial *social psychology. It was concluded that physical conditions of work might be less important than factors like the structure of groups and the style of supervision, and the study thus led to the 'human relations' movement. It also led to greater care in later work to avoid errors of this kind.   MA

Parson, H. M. (1974). 'What happened at Hawthorne?' *Science*, 193.

Adair, J. G. (1984). 'The Hawthorne effect: a reconsideration of the methodological artefact'. *Journal of Applied Psychology*, 69/2.

Head, Sir Henry (1861–1940). British neurologist, born in London and educated at Charterhouse School and Trinity

College, Cambridge. As a young man, he studied with Ewald *Hering in Prague. Later he joined the London Hospital, becoming consulting physician. He is best known for his work with W. H. R. *Rivers, Gordon *Holmes, and others on sensation and the cerebral cortex and for his studies on *aphasia, in which he cast doubt on the prevailing ideas regarding the cortical localization of speech. His concept of the *schema—a flexible representation of past experience in memory—greatly influenced the British psychologist F. C. *Bartlett. His books include *Studies in Neurology*, 2 vols. (1920) and *Aphasia and Kindred Disorders of Speech*, 2 vols. (1926).

hearing. When an object vibrates, pressure changes are set up in the surrounding medium, usually air, and these pressure changes are transmitted through the medium and may be perceived as sound. Sounds can be categorized into two main classes. Those for which the pressure changes have a random or irregular quality are perceived as noiselike: examples are the sound of a waterfall, or the consonants 's' or 'f'. Those that repeat regularly as a function of time are called periodic sounds, and generally have a well-defined tone or pitch: for example, a note played on a musical instrument. The size of the pressure change is related to the perceived loudness of a sound: the greater the pressure variation the greater the loudness. However, it is inconvenient to express the magnitude of sounds in terms of pressure changes, because the ear can perceive sounds over a huge range of pressures. Hence a logarithmic measure called the decibel (abbreviated dB) is used to express sound magnitude, or level; o dB corresponds roughly to the quietest sound that can be heard by a healthy young adult, normal conversation has a level of 60–70 dB, while sounds above about 100 dB tend to be uncomfortably loud and can damage our ears if heard for a long time. Sounds with a level above 120 dB can damage our ears within quite a short time, perhaps only a few minutes. When the level of a sound is increased by 10 dB, the subjective loudness roughly doubles, whereas the sound power actually increases by a factor of 10. The smallest detectable change in level is about 1 dB.

Periodic sounds can also be described in terms of their repetition rate and the complexity of the pressure variation. The repetition rate is related to the subjective pitch: the higher the rate the higher the pitch. Complexity is related to the subjective timbre or tone quality: differences in timbre distinguish between the same note played on, say, the violin and the organ. The simplest pressure wave has the form of a sinusoid: pressure plotted against time varies as the sine of time (see the lower part of Fig. 3). A sine wave may also be called a pure tone or simple tone, since it has a very 'pure' or 'clean' quality, like that of a tuning fork or the Greenwich time signal. For a pure tone the repetition rate, the number of complete cycles per second, is the frequency. The unit of one cycle per second is called the hertz (abbreviated Hz). The Greenwich time signal has a frequency of 1,000 Hz. The highest frequency we can hear varies from 16,000 to 20,000 Hz in young adults, but tends to decrease with increasing age. The lowest frequency which is heard as sound is about 20 Hz. Below that the pressure changes are felt as a vibration rather than heard as sound. We are most sensitive to frequencies around 1,800 Hz.

Sine waves, or pure tones, are particularly important in the study of hearing. Joseph Fourier showed that any periodic complex sound can be considered as composed of a sum of sine waves with different frequencies and levels. Conversely, any periodic sound can be synthesized by adding together sine waves with appropriate frequencies and levels. This is very useful if we are investigating how some part of the auditory system works, as it is often sufficient to measure only the way it responds to sine waves of different frequencies. The response to any complex sound can then be predicted from the response to the sine waves. The same philosophy lies behind the specification of amplifiers or loudspeakers in terms of their frequency response. It is assumed that, if an amplifier faithfully reproduces any sine wave within the audible range, and amplifies each sine wave by the same amount, then it will also faithfully reproduce any complex sound composed of those sine waves.

A further reason why sine waves are important in the study of hearing is that the ear behaves as though it carries out a *Fourier analysis, although it does not do this analysis perfectly, and is therefore said to have limited resolution. Thus when we are presented with two sine waves which are sufficiently separated in frequency, we are able to hear two separate tones, each with its own pitch. This contrasts with the eye, where a mixture of two different colours (frequencies of light) is perceived as a single colour. The process by which the different frequencies in a complex sound are separated in the ear is known as frequency analysis or frequency resolution.

If we subject a complex sound to Fourier analysis, and then plot the level of each sine wave component as a function of frequency, the resulting plot is known as the spectrum of the sound. The spectrum is related to the complexity of the pressure variation: the simple sine wave has a spectrum composed of a single point, or vertical line, whereas musical instrument tones generally contain many sinusoidal components, and have a spectrum composed of many lines. The subjective timbre of sounds is more easily explained in terms of the spectrum than in terms of the pressure variation as a function of time. Sounds with many high-frequency components will seem sharp or strident, while those with mainly low-frequency components will seem dull or mellow. This correspondence between spectrum and timbre provides another example of the action of the ear as a frequency analyser. In the following sections we will discuss the physiological basis of this frequency analysis, and some of its perceptual consequences. We will also discuss the perception of pitch. Finally we will describe the major types of hearing impairments, and their perceptual consequences.

1. The anatomy and physiology of the ear
2. Theories of pitch perception
3. The ear as frequency analyser
4. Hearing impairments
5. Labyrinths of the ear

1. The anatomy and physiology of the ear

Fig. 1 illustrates the basic structure of the outer, middle, and inner ear. The outer ear consists of the pinna and the ear canal. The pinna is thought to play an important role in our ability to locate complex sounds. The spectrum of such sounds is modified by the pinna in a way that depends upon the direction of the sound source relative to the head. These spectral modifications are not perceived as changes in timbre, but rather determine the perceived direction of the sound source. They are particularly important in allowing us to distinguish whether a sound comes from behind or in front, and above or below.

Sounds impinging upon the eardrum are transferred by means of three small bones in the middle ear (the smallest bones in the body, called the malleus, the incus, and the stapes) to a membrane-covered opening (the oval window) in the inner ear or cochlea. The main function of the middle ear is to improve the efficiency of transfer of energy from the air to the fluids inside the cochlea. Small muscles attached to the bones contract when we are exposed to intense sounds, reducing sound transmission to the cochlea, particularly at low frequencies. This may serve to protect the cochlea, and it may also help to stop intense low frequencies, occurring in the environment or in our own voices, making higher frequencies inaudible.

The cochlea is filled with fluids, and running along its length is a membrane called the basilar membrane. This membrane is stiff and narrow close to the oval window (called the base), while at the other end (the apex) it is wider and less stiff. In response to sine wave stimulation a wave appears on the basilar membrane travelling from the base towards the apex, at first increasing in amplitude and then decreasing. The position of the maximum in the pattern of vibration along the basilar membrane varies with frequency: high frequencies produce peaks towards the base, and low frequencies towards the apex. This is illustrated in Fig. 2. Thus the basilar membrane acts as a

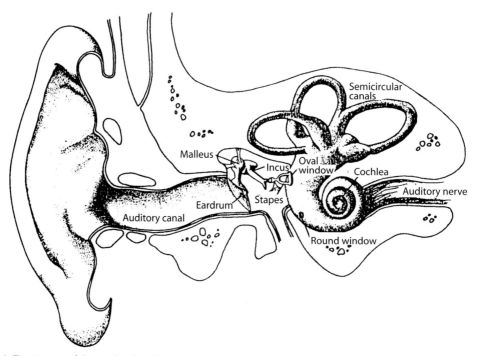

Fig. 1. The structure of the peripheral auditory system, showing the outer, middle, and inner ear.

frequency analyser, different frequencies producing activity at different places along the basilar membrane.

The patterns shown in Fig. 2 are rather broad to account for the frequency resolution which is actually observed in human subjects (see below). However, recent work has indicated that many of the early measurements may have been in error. The basilar membrane appears to be extremely vulnerable, so that even small impairments in the physiological condition of the animal being studied alter the responses and produce broader 'tuning'.

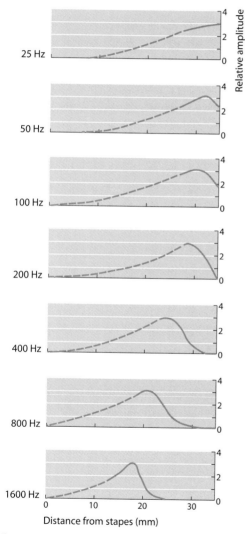

Fig. 2. Envelopes or outlines of patterns of vibration on the basilar membrane for low-frequency sine waves of different frequencies. Solid lines indicate the results of actual experiments, whereas the dashed lines are extrapolations.

It has recently been shown that the 'tuning' on the basilar membrane, i.e. its frequency resolution, can be extremely sharp if the animal and its cochlea are in good condition.

The information which is contained in the patterns of vibration on the basilar membrane has to be transmitted to the brain in some way in order for us to perceive sound. This transmission is achieved by an electrical 'code' carried in the auditory nerve. Each auditory nerve contains the axons or 'fibres' of about 30,000 individual nerves, or neurons, and information is transmitted in each of these in the form of brief electrical impulses, called spikes or action potentials. Thus transmission takes place in an all-or-none fashion; the size of the spikes does not vary, and only the presence or absence of a spike is important. (See ADRIAN, EDGAR DOUGLAS.)

The vibrations on the basilar membrane are transformed to spikes by rows of special cells, called *hair cells, which rest on the basilar membrane. The hair cells are among the most delicate structures in the cochlea, and they can be destroyed by intense sound, lack of oxygen, metabolic disturbance, infection, or drugs. They also tend to be lost with increasing age. Once lost they do not regenerate, and loss of hair cells is a common cause of hearing impairment.

The exact way in which information is 'coded' in the auditory nerve is not clear. However, we know that any single neuron is activated only by vibration on a limited part of the basilar membrane. Each neuron is 'tuned' and responds to only a limited range of frequencies. Thus information about frequency can be coded in terms of which neurons are active or 'firing' with spikes. This form of coding is called 'place' coding. Information about sound level may be carried both in the rate of firing (i.e. the number of spikes per second) and in terms of the number of neurons that are firing. Finally, information may also be carried in the exact timing of the spikes. For stimulating frequencies below about 5 kHz (1 kHz = 1,000 Hz), the time pattern of neural spikes reflects the time structure of the stimulus. Nerve spikes tend to occur at a particular point or phase of the stimulating waveform, a process called phase locking, although a spike will not

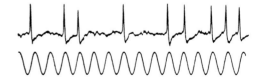

Fig. 3. The lower trace shows the waveform of a sine wave with frequency 300 Hz. The upper trace shows the response of a single auditory nerve fibre. Note that each impulse occurs at the same phase of the waveform, although an impulse does not occur on every cycle.

necessarily occur on every cycle. This is illustrated in Fig. 3. For a sine wave stimulus with a frequency of, say, 1 kHz, the time for one complete cycle will be 1 millisecond (ms), and the time intervals between successive nerve impulses will be integral multiples of this, namely 1, 2, 3, 4, 5, . . . ms. Thus phase locking provides another way in which the frequency of a sound may be coded. Notice that a given neuron cannot 'fire' more than a few hundred times per second. It used to be thought that the frequency of the stimulus at higher frequencies could be coded by cooperation between groups of neurons firing in volleys, the so-called 'volley' theory. In fact, the time pattern of response in a single neuron is sufficient to define the frequency of the input, provided that time *intervals* between firings are analysed, rather than overall firing rate.

2. Theories of pitch perception

The pitch of a sound is defined as that attribute of sensation in terms of which sounds may be ordered on a musical scale; variations in pitch give rise to the percept of a melody. For sine wave stimuli the pitch is related to the frequency, and for other periodic sounds it is usually related to the overall repetition rate. Classically there have been two theories of how pitch is determined. The *place* theory suggests that pitch is related to the distribution of activity across nerve fibres. A pure tone will produce maximum activity in a small group of neurons connected to the place on the basilar membrane which is vibrating most strongly, and the 'position' of this maximum is assumed to determine pitch. The *temporal* theory suggests that pitch is determined from the time pattern of neural impulses, specifically from the time intervals between successive impulses (this used to be called the volley theory, but, as discussed above, volleying is no longer considered necessary).

It is generally agreed that the place theory works best at high frequencies, where the timing information is lost, and the temporal theory works best at low frequencies, where resolution on the basilar membrane is poorest (see Fig. 2). However, the frequency at which the change from one to the other occurs is still a matter of debate. We can get some clues from studies of frequency discrimination, the ability to detect a small difference in frequency between two successive tones. For low and middle frequencies a change of about 0.3 per cent is detectable, but above about 5 kHz the smallest detectable change increases markedly. Furthermore, above 5 kHz our sense of musical pitch appears to be lost, so that a sequence of different frequencies does not produce a clear sense of melody. Since 5 kHz is the highest frequency at which phase locking occurs, these results suggest that our sense of musical pitch and our ability to detect small changes in frequency depend upon the use of temporal information. Place

information allows the detection of relatively large frequency changes, but it does not give rise to a sense of musical pitch.

We do not have space to deal with the pitch of complex sounds, but it is thought that relatively complex pattern-recognition processes are involved which depend upon both place and temporal information. For a review see Moore (1982).

3. The ear as a frequency analyser

We initially described how the auditory system functions as a limited-resolution frequency analyser, splitting complex sounds into their sine wave components. Although we have argued that place information is not the most important determinant of pitch, it seems almost certain that the place analysis which takes place on the basilar membrane provides the initial basis for the ear's frequency analysing abilities. We will now describe briefly some perceptual consequences of this analysis.

We are all familiar with the fact that sounds we wish to hear are sometimes rendered inaudible by other sounds, a process known as masking. Fig. 4 shows masking patterns produced by a masker containing only a small range of frequencies: a narrow-band noise. The threshold elevation of the sinusoidal signal (the amount by which the masker raises the threshold) is plotted as a function of signal frequency for several different masker levels. The figure illustrates two basic points. First, the greater the masker level, the more masking there is. Secondly, more masking occurs for signal frequencies close to the masker frequency than for those farther away. This makes sense if we assume that masking will be most effective when the pattern of vibration evoked by the masker on the basilar membrane overlaps that of the signal. If the place analysis on the basilar membrane is sufficient to separate completely masker and signal, then no masking will occur. (See also AUDITORY ILLUSIONS.)

As was described earlier, the subjective timbre of a sound depends primarily on the spectrum of the sound—the level of sound at each frequency. Presumably timbre is perceived in this way because the different frequencies excite different places on the basilar membrane. The distribution of activity as a function of place determines the timbre. Obviously, this distribution can be quite complex, but each different complex tone will produce its own distribution, and hence will have its own tone colour. This helps us to distinguish between different musical instruments, and to distinguish between the different vowel sounds in human speech.

4. Hearing impairments

Hearing impairments can be classified into two broad types. *Conductive* hearing loss occurs when the passage of sound through to the inner ear is impeded in some way, for example by wax in the ears, or by some problem

Fig. 4. Masking patterns for a narrow-band noise masker centred at 410 Hz. The threshold elevation of the sine-wave signal is plotted as a function of signal frequency, with masker level as parameter.

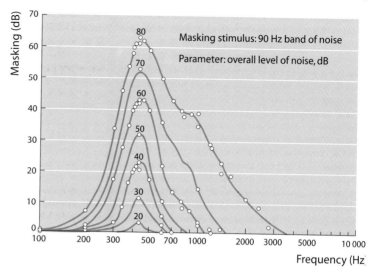

with the bones in the middle ear. It can often be cured by simple medical treatment, or by surgery, and when this is not possible a simple hearing aid can effectively alleviate the problem. *Sensorineural* hearing losses arise in the inner ear, or at some point 'higher up' in the auditory system. Cochlea hearing losses are often produced by damage to the hair cells and they are common in the elderly. Sensorineural hearing losses are not usually helped by surgery, and simple hearing aids are of only limited use, since the percepts of the listener are 'distorted' in various ways.

One common problem in cochlea hearing loss is *recruitment*, an abnormally rapid growth of loudness with increasing sound level. Faint sounds may be inaudible to the sufferer, but high-level sounds are as loud to him or her as to a normal listener. A hearing aid that amplifies all sounds will overamplify intense sounds, and these will be uncomfortably loud. One way round this problem is to use hearing aids that 'compress' the dynamic range of sounds, by amplifying low-level sounds more than high-level sounds. Such aids are currently being evaluated, and have met with some success.

A second common problem in cases of cochlea hearing loss is an impairment in frequency selectivity. This has a number of consequences. First, the sufferer will be more susceptible to the effects of masking. Secondly, the ability to identify the timbre of different sounds, including speech, will be impaired. These two effects mean that the sufferer will have great difficulty in understanding speech whenever there is more than one person talking at once, or when there is background noise. Hearing aids at present cannot compensate for this problem, and as a result many people with cochlea hearing losses never go to pubs or to parties.

Further research may clarify the nature of the defects in

impaired ears, and suggest ways in which those problems can be alleviated. In the meantime we should remember that for most impaired people a hearing aid does not restore normal hearing; it may make sounds louder but it does not bring them into focus. See also EVOLUTION OF THE EAR.

5. Labyrinths of the ear

The labyrinths of the ear are a complex organ for attaining balance, provided by a fluid in three orthogonal circular tubes (the semicircular canals), which move beads of calcium carbonate suspended on hairs, and so activate special nerves sending signals to the brain of movement of the head. In Ménière's disease these signals occur inappropriately, through damage of the hair cells, to produce dangerous unpleasant dizziness. The condition is most frequent in middle life and it generally subsides of its own accord.   BCJM

Békésy, G. von (1960). *Experiments in Hearing.* Trans. and ed. E. G. Wever.

Moore, B. C. J. (1982). *Introduction to the Psychology of Hearing* (2nd edn.).

—— (1997). *Introduction to the Psychology of Hearing* (4th edn.).

Hebb, Donald Olding (1904–85). A lifelong loyal Canadian, Hebb's theory that the brain is a multitude of nets reconciled the mass action ideas of Lashley and the holistic phenomena beloved of *Gestalt psychologists with specific functional locations. He gave learning a physical basis in modified conductivities with use of synapses, and generally promoted a strongly physiology-based empiricist theorizing. His book *The Organisation of Behaviour* (1949) was among the most influential books on brain and mind in the 20th century. It is both a clear account of the power of interactive neural nets to learn and generalize, and recognize or remember complex scenes or situations from small samples, but also to form concepts with 'cell assemblies'. Hebb's work is the basis and direct inspiration of modern connectionism. This radical departure from digital serial processing is steering the brain sciences and artificial intelligence on a course that promises many more dramatic theoretical and practical successes.   RLG

Hebb, D. O. (1949). The Organisation of Behaviour.

Valentine, E. R. (1989). 'Neural nets: from Hartley and Hebb to Hinton'. Journal of Mathematical Psychology, 33.

hedonism. Name for (i) the ethical doctrine that pleasure is the only good, and (ii) the psychological thesis that all actions are in fact directed towards the pursuit of pleasure in some form or another. Hedonism in both its forms has a long philosophical ancestry, but was especially prominent in the work of the utilitarians of the late 18th and 19th centuries. Jeremy *Bentham argued that 'nature has placed mankind under the governance of two sovereign masters, *pain* and *pleasure*. It is for them alone to determine what we ought to do as well as what we shall do' (*Introduction to the Principles of Morals and Legislation*, 1789). For Bentham, pleasure was a purely quantitative notion, and the utility of an act could be calculated by measuring the amount of pleasure it produced in terms of intensity, duration, etc. J. S. *Mill, by contrast, distinguished between higher and lower pleasures, and argued that certain types of pleasure (notably those of the intellect) are qualitatively superior, irrespective of the actual amount of pleasure they produce (*Utilitarianism*, 1861). It seems, however, that this manoeuvre involves a radical departure from hedonism, since it suggests that the value of an activity is not solely a function of the pleasure involved.

The psychological thesis that people pursue only pleasure seems false. It is a matter of common sense that people pursue a wide variety of goals in life (e.g. scientific truth, justice, religious enlightenment), and it does not appear that the pursuit of these differing goals can be exhibited as being 'really' the pursuit of pleasure—unless the concept of pleasure is defined so widely that the claim that only pleasure is pursued becomes trivially true. Ethical hedonism also seems untenable. The value of goods such as liberty and autonomy cannot, it seems, be explained solely in terms of the amount of pleasure that may be produced by securing them.   JGC

Hegel, Georg Wilhelm Friedrich (1770–1831). German philosopher born at Stuttgart. He studied theology at Tübingen, and became *privat-docent* at Jena and then headmaster of a school at Nuremberg, where he instructed the boys in his own, highly obscure, philosophy, which is a modification of *Kant's. He became professor of philosophy at Heidelberg in 1816 and finally at Berlin in 1818, where he dominated German philosophy.

Hegel is essentially mystical; he rejects the reality of separate objects, and of minds in space and time, and holds, rather, an all-embracing unity: the *absolute* which is rational, real, and true. To draw attention to a particular is to separate this from the whole, and so the particular is only partially true. Greater unity and truth are achieved by the dialectic of positing something (*thesis*), denying it (*antithesis*), and combining the two half-truths in a *synthesis*. It has been said that Karl Marx 'stood Hegel on his head' by making matter, and not reason, the ultimate reality. Hegel is the contrary of an empiricist, for he held that the whole has a greater claim to reality than the parts that may be observed, and (in societies) that the group has more reality than the individuals composing it. This came to justify extreme authoritarian political philosophies, from Fascism to Communism. It is also the mainspring of *idealist philosophies such as *Bradley's, which were finally abandoned with the impact of *pragmatism and *logical positivism, and the linguistic analysis and emphasis on 'atomic statements' of G. E. *Moore, Bertrand *Russell, and Ludwig *Wittgenstein.

Hegel's main philosophical work is *Phänomenologie des Geistes* (1807; English trans. *The Phenomenology of the Mind*, 1844).   RLG

Heidegger, Martin (1889–1976) German philosopher, lecturer at Freiburg University (1917–23), professor at Marburg University (1923–8), professor at Freiburg University (1928–45, emeritus from 1952). After reading *Husserl's *Logical Investigations* (1900), Heidegger decided to pursue phenomenology as the best avenue towards his own radical reconception of human being. He cultivated Husserl's mentorship and was made his assistant at Freiburg where he read many of his teacher's unpublished texts; some of these influenced his thinking in his landmark work *Being and Time* (1927) (English trans. 1962). In this work he adjured Husserl's approach with its over-reliance on theoretical cognition, the reduction to a pure intentional domain, and the detached status of the transcendental spectator. Instead Heidegger focused his attention on the meaning of Being, specifically to the kind of being for whom this question has meaning, which he called *Dasein* ('being-there'). *Dasein* does not exist like an object lying around, nor is *Dasein* merely a subject of conscious awareness, for whom objects appear. Rather, it finds itself already out there in the world, in a referential totality of meanings, equipment, and possibilities. *Dasein* finds some things already invested with meaning, such as tools, which are available as things-to-be-used. Other things are merely lying around, they are occurrent, though sometimes they too can be turned into tools; *Dasein* is neither kind of object. Moreover, *Dasein* does not have its essence in advance, rather it is aware of the many possibilities which it can make its own, since its being lies ahead of itself; this is one of the core tenets of *existentialism. *Dasein*'s comportment towards things, other humans, and its own future reveals a mode of understanding which cannot be reduced to rational insight; he calls this 'circumspective concern'. Insofar as *Dasein* is resolute in its decisions to carry out its own projects, it manifests the temporal structure of 'care'. The fact that *Dasein* cares for the possibilities which it attempts to actualize means that *Dasein* is aware that death brings about the non-being of the self which it has thrown ahead. This awareness of future severance from the ground of its being is the source of the basic attunement of anxiety. Conscience is the call or summons to face squarely the null basis of our being, he said, to recognize our lostness in an everyday, average self and to live instead in an authentic manner the own-ness of our own choices.   PSM

Guignon, C. (ed.) (1992). *The Cambridge Companion to Heidegger.*

Helmholtz, Hermann Ludwig Ferdinand von (1821–

94). German physiologist and physicist, born at Potsdam. He was the son of Ferdinand Helmholtz, a teacher of philology and philosophy in the gymnasium. His mother's maiden name was Penne; she was descended from the Quaker founder of Philadelphia, William Penn. Hermann Helmholtz became the founder of the science of perceptual physiology. He carried out a vast number of observational experiments, often with himself as observer, as well as physiological experiments for explanations. He also formulated psychological concepts which have lasting significance. His immense range—he was one of the greatest physicists of the 19th century— even includes ideas on *aesthetics and art. He was also a director of research, and with his *Popular Lectures* a lucid presenter of science: by following a suggestion of his, his student Heinrich Hertz (1857–94) discovered how to confirm James Clerk Maxwell's theoretical prediction of radio waves. Helmholtz was professor of physiology at Königsberg (1849), Bonn (1855), and Heidelberg (1858). Then in 1871 he became professor of physics at Berlin, and from 1888 to 1894 was president of the Physikalisch-Technische Reichsanstalt, which he designed as 'an institute for the experimental promotion of exact science and the *technique* of precision'. It is, however, for his earlier work on the nervous system and especially on vision and hearing, and as the founder of the experimental study of *perception, that he concerns us here.

His first great achievement, in 1850, was to measure the rate of conduction of signals in nerves. It had been thought that sensory signals arrive at the brain immediately. Indeed, the founder of modern physiology, Johannes *Müller (1801–58) considered it to be beyond experimental possibility to measure the neural conduction rate, because nerves are so short, in comparison with the astronomical distances over which the velocity of light had

been estimated, that no instrument could measure the very short time differences. But Helmholtz's friend Emil *Du Bois-Reymond (1816–96), the originator of electrophysiology, suggested that there might be a molecular basis for neural conduction, so it could be a great deal slower than the velocity of light. Further, a new instrument, the chronograph, was invented in 1849, making it possible to record short durations and rapid changes with an electrically operated pen on a revolving drum. Helmholtz used this with frog preparations, and then on humans. The method with humans was to find the difference between *reaction times to a stimulus at, say, the ankle and the calf of the leg. Since the muscle action time (which he also succeeded in measuring) would be the same in either case, a longer reaction time from the ankle must be due to conduction time in the nerve of the leg. Helmholtz found it to be comparable to the speed of sound, rather than of light. His father commented in a letter to him: 'the results at first appeared to me surprising, since I regard the idea and its bodily expression not as successive, but as simultaneous, a single living act, that only becomes bodily and mental on reflection; and I could as little reconcile myself to your view, as I could admit that a star that had disappeared in Abraham's time should still be visible.' This was, however, a misunderstanding which was for some time shared by the older physiologists, for as Helmholtz immediately pointed out to his father: 'the interaction of mental and physical processes is initiated in the brain, and consciousness, intellectual activity, has nothing to do with the transmission of the message from the skin, from the retina, or from the ear, to the brain. In relation to intelligence this transmission within the body is as external as the propagation of sound from the place at which it takes origin, to the ear.' The measurements did however lead Helmholtz to appreciate that the brain is quite slow, for reaction times are much longer than they should be from the speed of signals in peripheral nerves, and so he came to appreciate that a great deal of routeing and switching of signals must be going on during perception, and for decisions for muscle movement. This led to analogies between brain function and telephone exchange switching, and then computers.

Helmholtz was philosophically a thoroughgoing empiricist, believing that sensory signals only have significance as the result of associations built up by learning. We are essentially separate from the world of objects, and isolated from external physical events, except for neural signals which, somewhat like language, must be learned and read according to various assumptions, which may or may not be appropriate. This is the basis of Helmholtz's interest in perceptual and especially visual *illusions. More generally, it is the basis also of his notion, at that time disturbing, that perceptions are 'unconscious inferences'. This challenged the prevailing view that responsibility, and just blame and praise, depend on consciously held reasons and motivations. Sigmund *Freud's slightly later notion of an active unconscious mind is a rather different idea, though equally shocking to the Victorians. For Helmholtz it was simply that most of what goes on in the nervous system is not represented in consciousness. Physiological and psychological experiments are important, and often surprising in their findings, because we cannot experience or discover by introspection how we see or think, or even know on what data our perceptions and beliefs are based. Thus Helmholtz wrote of visual illusions, in his last paper on perception (1894):

Knowledge gained through daily experience, with all its accidents, does not usually have the range and completeness which it is possible to obtain with experiments. . . . We usually refer to incorrect inductive inferences concerning the meaning of our perceptions as *illusions of the senses*. For the most part they are the result of incomplete inductive inferences. Their occurrence is largely related to the fact that we tend to favour certain ways of using our sense organs—those ways which provide us with the most reliable and most consistent judgements about the forms, spatial relations, and properties of the objects we observe. . . . Unusual perceptions, concerning whose meaning we have no trained knowledge, occur with unusual positions and movements of our sense organs, and incorrect interpretations of these perceptions may result. We can, in fact, lay down the general rule that with abnormal positions and movements of the eyes, the intuitions which occur are those of the objects which would naturally have to exist in order to produce the same perceptions under the conditions of normal vision.

Then, after pointing out that ordinary plane mirrors produce illusions of this kind, though we are seldom actually misled, he adds: 'most observers know how to change an unusual kind of observation into one that is common and normal, thus causing the illusion to be recognized and to disappear.' Thus *after-images impressed on the retina by a flash of light are seen as external objects, even though we may realize they are illusory, as we move our eyes and find part of the visual world moving with them. The illusion persists but we are not fooled by it.

Helmholtz was remarkable in combining shrewd psychological accounts with extraordinarily powerful physical insights, as in his work on the conservation of energy. His experimental and inventive skills were also remarkable. They led to the ophthalmoscope (1851) for examining the retina; the ophthalmometer for measuring the curvature of the optical surface of the eye; and the Young–Helmholtz trichromatic theory of *colour vision, which is the basis of current theories. In *hearing, he introduced the resonance theory of pitch discrimination. That he achieved his results before there were stable sources of light, or electronic instruments for producing and measuring sound waves, humbles the present-day investigator.

Helmholtz's *Treatise on Physiological Optics* (3 vols., 1856–67; trans. 1924–5, reprinted 1962, 2000) is the foundation of the science of visual perception and well worth reading today by the serious student. His *On the Sensations of Tone* (1863; 4th edn. 1877, trans. 1954) was his main work on perception in hearing, and his *Popular Lectures* (1881; 1962) range from painting through perception to physics and the basis of geometry.
RLG

Kahl, R. (ed.) (1971). *Selected Writings of Hermann von Helmholtz.*

Koenigsberger, L. (1906). *Hermann von Helmholtz.* The fullest and best biography, with a good account of the development of most of his ideas.

McKendrick, J. G. (1899). *Hermann von Helmholtz.* More concerned with his work in physics than on perception or the mind.

Wade, N. (2000). *Helmholtz's Treatise on Physiological Optics* (5th edn.). Trans. J. Southall.

Warren, R. M., and Warren, R. P. (1968). *Helmholtz on Perception: Its Physiology and Development.* A selection of Helmholtz's writings on perception, with a short life and excellent comments on his work and ideas.

Helvétius, Claude-Adrien

Helvétius, Claude-Adrien (1715–71). French encyclopedist philosopher. In *De l'esprit* (1758) he set out to prove that sensation is the source of all intellectual activity. This work was denounced by the Sorbonne and condemned by the French parliament to be publicly burned. It was, however, translated into several European languages. His posthumous *De l'homme* (1772) is supposed to have influenced Jeremy *Bentham.

Heraclitus (c.540–c.480 BC). Greek *Pre-Socratic philosopher, born at Ephesus; he founded a school in the Ionian tradition. Fragments exist of his *On Nature*, which is divided into 'On the Universe', 'Politics', and 'Theology'. It was placed in the Temple of Artemis, and it has been suggested that it was deliberately written so obscurely as to be intelligible only to aristocrats and scholars. Heraclitus' philosophy is based on unity in change; hence the famous remark of his follower Cratylus that 'you cannot step twice into the same river'. Apparent permanence of objects is attributed to conflicting movements or flows; the essential element is fire, out of which all else comes and perishes. In modern times this emphasis on change, and on permanence as illusion, is expounded by A. N. *Whitehead.
RLG

Barnes, J. (1982). *The Presocratic Philosophers* (2nd edn.).

Kirk, G. S., and Raven, J. E. (1957). *The Presocratic Philosophers.*

Herbart, Johann Friedrich (1776–1841). German philosopher and educator, born at Oldenburg. He was professor of philosophy at Königsberg and Göttingen. His account of mind essentially followed the philosophy of *Leibniz. For Herbart the universe consisted of independent elements, called reals, though these were different from the Leibnizian monads, as the reals were not necessarily conscious. They were, rather, units of a causally interacting machine—which is very different from Leibniz's conception of pre-established harmony. Herbart defined psychology as the 'mechanics of the mind', but at the same time he emphasized the importance of *consciousness, explaining mental states and thinking as interactions of ideas. They were supposed to interact somewhat as physical particles obey and represent or manifest the laws of physics.

Herbart believed that experimentation is impossible for psychology. He maintained that for psychology to be a science it must be mathematical. To this end he set up equations: for example, for how ideas are suppressed. He attempted to show how the mind could be atomic—with ideas as atoms, displaying attraction and repulsion as in Newtonian physics. Some ideas (such as a musical tone and a visible colour) would, however, not interact, except presumably in special cases of *synaesthesia.

For Herbart ideas were in themselves active, and could struggle with one another to cross the threshold into consciousness, rather as the most active molecules of water escape through the boundary of surface tension. His philosophy of mind may appear absurd, but it did introduce concepts of suppression which reappear in *Freud's account of the unconscious, and also, if more mundanely, in current theories of memory and forgetting by interactive inhibition.

His *Textbook in Psychology* was translated into English by M. K. Smith (2nd edn. 1891) and *The Science of Education* by H. M. and E. Felkin (1892).   RLG

Garmo, C. de (1896). *Herbart and the Herbartians.*
Stout, G. F. (1930). *Studies in Philosophy and Psychology.*

Hering, Ewald (1834–1918). German physiologist, born and raised near the Bohemian border; the son of a pastor. He studied medicine in Leipzig in the 1850s. His contributions to sensory physiology contrast distinctly with the main current of German science of his time. The outstanding representative of the latter was Hermann von *Helmholtz, a thorough physicalist and empiricist. By careful attention to the findings in more basic sciences, coupled with thoughtful but still simple experiments, and rigorous application of mathematics, Helmholtz managed to place physiological optics and acoustics as well as thermodynamics on the solid foundations so magnificently utilized by 20th-century science. But Helmholtz had strayed a long distance from the two giants of the German intellectual scene, *Goethe and *Kant. Their much more direct descendant was the physiologist Ewald Hering, who claimed also to have been influenced, as a student, by *Schopenhauer and *Fechner.

After gaining his MD, Hering stayed in Leipzig for several years, and before he was 30 had written a series of short monographs on *visual space and eye movement. They are slightly querulous in tone and do not now make the same impact as his contribution during the following decades, but they obviously marked the author as a rising young scientist of significance. His first major academic post, as physiology lecturer in the Vienna military medical academy (the Josephinum), brought him into contact with Josef Breuer, who was later to work with Sigmund *Freud on the foundation of psychoanalysis. Together Hering and Breuer showed that respiration was in part controlled by receptors in the lung, which signal excessive distension and cause cessation of inspiration: the Hering–Breuer reflex. The Josephinum was about to be dissolved, and in 1870 Hering accepted a call to be professor of physiology at the Charles University in Prague, where he stayed for 25 years, until returning to Leipzig as head of the physiology department in 1895.

In his physiological researches Hering sought a synthesis of physics and psychology. He epitomized his attitude to purely physical analysis in sensory physiology in his analogy of those who might understand a timepiece by dissecting it into component gears: would not a glance at its face and hands yield an indispensable insight into its function? Accordingly, Hering made the subjective phenomena of sensation fully fledged ingredients when assembling the bases for a physiological theory, most successfully in his theories of brightness perception and *colour vision. In this he broke ranks with almost the entire materialist natural philosophy of his time, except indeed with *Mach, a colleague in Prague. Hering did not follow Fechner, who stressed a rather simple form of psychophysical parallelism. Nor was he entirely in the tradition of Goethe and Schopenhauer, who, while sponsoring opponent theories of colour vision, placed almost all the emphasis on the subjective elements. Hering's theories of light and colour postulated substances and neural processes that could go in two directions from their neutral point—anabolic and catabolic. To arrive at these formulations, he used not only the available data on colour mixture that had been basic to previous theories, but also the observations that subjectively yellow did not *appear* to be a mixture of green and red, that yellow was a stable hue with changes in intensity, and that *after-images and complementary colours fitted best into an opponent-colour scheme. It took 75 years before electrophysiologists demonstrated the existence at the cellular level of Hering's mechanisms: centre-surround organization of retinal ganglion cells, and opponent, i.e. excitatory *and* inhibitory, coding of colour. However, Hering was still very much a creature of the science of the middle of the 19th century. His postulated sensory and neural processing may have been more advanced and more encompassing than that of his contemporaries, yet he also believed it to reside in the cells of the organism. Its universality and presence at an early stage of development (in the case of perfect conjugacy of the eye movements even at or shortly after birth) led him to conclude that the mechanism for this kind of processing (i.e. of eye movements, of colour and brightness detection) was inborn.

In his most widely read essay (1870), Hering dealt with 'Memory as a general function of organized matter'. Because memory survives periods of unconsciousness (see MEMORY: EXPERIMENTAL APPROACHES) and *sleep, it cannot be merely associated with our *consciousness but must be regarded as a capacity inherent in brain substance and hence must follow the rules of purely material processes.

Hering's acceptance of compelling perceptual impressions as pointers of how the organism processes sensory inputs, and his willingness to postulate for them physiological, i.e. to him material, channels, at one time had great influence. A whole generation of researchers in perception followed Hering's lead by basing their theories on rules derived from (to them) persuasive sensory judgements: *Gestalt psychology was a major force until well into the 1930s. While never popular with the physicalist researchers who have dominated sensory physiology and psychology from the 1930s to this day, Hering's theories had more unity of design and less of a dualistic component than those of, say, Helmholtz. The latter relegated certain visual phenomena, such as apparent contrast, to 'errors of judgement', whereas Hering looked at them as inevitable concomitants of the physiological organization that gives us good discrimination of colour or contrast or space. As the diversity and richness of neural connectivity of the mammalian brain are being displayed by modern neuroanatomy and neurophysiology, and the untold variety of possible pathways becomes evident, many scientists are turning again to Hering and his characteristically synthetic way of making theories. GW

Herophilus (*fl.* 300 BC). Greek anatomist, and founder of the medical school of Alexandria. He was the first person who is known to have dissected a human body and compared it with other animals. He described many bodily organs and was the first to distinguish between sensory (*afferent) and motor (*efferent) nerves. See GREEK INVESTIGATIONS OF THE MIND AND SENSES.

heuristics. Serving to discover or solve problems, even when no *algorithms or rules exist, using rules which involve essentially a process of trial and error. An item of information or a rule used in the process is sometimes known as a heuristic for that problem. The term is important in *artificial intelligence and *cybernetics.

hippocampus. A region of the brain, in the lower part of the cerebrum. The old anatomists thought it looked like a sea horse, hence its name. There are two parts:

hippocampus major (or horn of Ammon) and hippocampus minor. It is especially associated with memory.

Hippocrates (*c.*470–*c.*370 BC). Greek physician born on the island of Cos. He practised medicine in Thrace, Thessaly, and Macedonia, before returning to Cos, where a school of medicine gathered around him. It is not known how much of the Hippocratic collection, consisting of some 70 books in the form of notes, is his own work. Some is known to be much later and indeed the collection may have been the library of Cos. Like his contemporaries, Hippocrates believed that disease was the result of an imbalance of the humours (see, for example, INSANITY: HISTORY), but his emphasis on objective observation and critical deductive reasoning was enormously influential in separating medicine from superstition. He and his followers were the first to record case histories—some of the descriptions of disease contained in their writings are so vivid that a modern diagnosis can be made. Of particular interest among the works is the treatise entitled 'On Wounds of the Head', which describes trephining—making holes in the skull. This is known to have been a prehistoric practice, probably usually intended as a means of releasing evil spirits from the heads of the afflicted, though Hippocrates describes trephining for what we would regard as rational medical usage. His ethical standards, largely embodied in the much later Hippocratic oath, have offered inspiration to the medical profession over the centuries and largely account for his reputation as the 'father of medicine'.

See also GREEK INVESTIGATIONS OF THE MIND AND SENSES.

Singer, C., and Underwood, E. A. (1962). *A Short History of Medicine* (2nd edn.).

Hobbes, Thomas (1588–1679). British philosopher, born prematurely at Malmesbury, Wiltshire, when his mother 'fell into labour upon the fright of the invasion of the Spaniards'; Hobbes was later to say that his life was dominated by a constitutional timorousness. Foreseeing the impending civil war he went over to France in 1640— the 'first of all that fled'; in Paris he met Mersenne, friend and principal correspondent of *Descartes, who persuaded him to contribute the Third Set of Objections to Descartes's forthcoming *Meditations* (published 1641). Hobbes's masterpiece, the *Leviathan*, appeared in 1651. This work is famous for its investigation of the basis of political authority. The authority of the sovereign (whether an assembly or, as Hobbes preferred, a monarch) depends on the fact that supreme power is used to provide for the citizens that stability and physical security without which life would be 'a war of every man against every man' and the condition of humanity 'nasty brutish and short'. Hobbes's other works include the *De cive* (1642), *De corpore* (1655), and *De homine* (1658), dealing respectively with political theory, the nature of matter, and human nature.

Though Hobbes is best known as a political theorist, he made a major contribution to the philosophy of mind. He may be regarded as an early exponent of a physicalist or materialist approach to mental phenomena. First, the universe is purely material, and contains none but physical things: 'the universe, that is the whole mass of things that are, is corporeal, that is to say body' (*Leviathan*, ch. 46). Second, talk of the soul as an independent substance that could be separated from the body is absurd: to say that something possesses a 'soul' is simply to say that it is alive (ch. 42). Third, statements about mental or psychological properties can ultimately refer only to the motions of matter in the body: 'all qualities called sensible are in the object that causeth them but so many motions of the matter that presseth our organs diversely. Neither in us that are pressed are they anything else but diverse motions, for motion produceth nothing but motion' (ch. 1).

JGC

Martinich, A. P. (1999). *Hobbes: A Biography.*

Holmes, Sir Gordon Morgan (1876–1965). Irish neurologist. He was born in Dublin and studied medicine there at Trinity College. He was awarded a scholarship which gave him two years' study abroad after qualifying and went to Germany to work under Karl Weigert and Ludwig Edinger, the neuroanatomist. In 1901 he was appointed house physician at the National Hospital for Nervous Diseases in London, where he stayed until his retirement in 1941, and later in his career also held consultancies at the Royal London Ophthalmic and Charing Cross hospitals. In 1914 he became consulting neurologist to the British army, and from 1922 to 1937 was editor of *Brain.*

For about ten years from 1901, Holmes was concerned mainly with improving the accuracy of neurological examination, and this he accomplished through research and stringent clinical observation. It led him to investigate the neurophysiology of sensory perception in the cerebral cortex and the location of sensations with (later Sir) Henry *Head. During the First World War, especially, his work on spinal and head injuries was of great importance.

Holmes was revered as a teacher and he inspired the many postgraduates who came to work under him. His *Selected Papers* (edited by Sir F. M. R. Walshe) were published in 1956.

DDH

homeostasis. The main concept of homeostasis is the principle of negative *feedback control, which was developed for military purposes in the Second World War. It is the basis of *cybernetics, whose founding fathers were Norbert *Wiener, Ross Ashby, and Grey *Walter. Producing stability in dynamic systems by negative feed-

back has, however, a history back to James Watt's governor for the automatic regulation of steam engines as their load varies, and the still earlier controls for windmills. There are even hints of the notion of feeding the output of a system back to its input for maintaining stability in some ancient Greek devices, described by Hero in the 1st century AD, especially for maintaining constant supply for water-clocks by a float and needle valve, as in modern carburettors.

The term 'homeostasis' was coined some years before cybernetics, by the American physician Walter B. *Cannon, in his germinal book *Wisdom of the Body*, 1932. It is interesting that Cannon stated the basic idea of feedback as a fundamental physiological principle before it was properly recognized by engineers, though it had been used as it were implicitly, without recognition or understanding. Cannon explained the regulation of body temperature by mechanisms such as perspiring when the body is too hot and shivering when it is too cold, as maintaining the body's equilibrium by feedback signals from *what* is needed to *how* what is needed can be attained. It is now clear that this is an extremely important principle for almost all physiological processes, and also for the guiding of skilled behaviour.

See also CYBERNETICS, HISTORY OF; FEEDBACK AND FEEDFORWARD.

Ashby, W. R. (1952). *Design for a Brain.*
Cannon, W. B. (1932). *Wisdom of the Body.*
Walter, W. G. (1953). *The Living Brain.*
Wiener, N. (1948). *Cybernetics.*

homunculus. Literally a 'manikin' or 'little man'. The term 'homunculus fallacy' is often used to condemn accounts of psychological processes which are vacuous or circular, because they ascribe to some internal device the very psychological properties that were being investigated in the first place. Consider, for example, a theory of vision which says that there is within the brain a 'soul' or 'sensorium', or whatever, that 'views' or 'inspects' images on the retina: such a theory is vacuous, since 'viewing' and 'inspecting' are both instances of the very visual processes that the theory was supposed to be illuminating in the first place. At the crudest level such explanations invite us to imagine a 'little man' sitting inside the skull inspecting some neurological equivalent of a television screen on which images of the outside world are displayed. Such theories arguably commit the 'category mistake' of trying to locate, within the structure of the brain, events and processes that belong to a higher level of description.

The term 'homunculus' is also commonly used in *artificial intelligence theory to refer to a subsystem which executes functions specified entirely in formal terms. Whether reference to such homunculi is fallacious or circular hinges on the complexity of the functions they are supposed to perform. If the operations involved can be specified ultimately in terms of very elementary devices (e.g. very simple switching devices), then the role of homunculi in this context seems relatively benign. Thus D. Dennett: 'homunculi are only bogeymen if they duplicate entirely the talents they are rung in to explain. . . . If one can get a team of relatively ignorant, narrow-minded, blind homunculi to produce the intelligent behaviour of the whole, this is progress' (1979: 123).

See also FUNCTIONALISM. JGC

Dennett, D. C. (1979). *Brain Storms.*
Kenny, A. (1971). 'The homunculus fallacy'. In Grene, M. (ed.), *Interpretations of Life and Mind.*

Hull, Clark Leonard. (1884–1952). American psychologist, born at Akron, New York. He originally intended to become an engineer but contracted poliomyelitis, and this obliged him to pursue a less taxing career. In consequence, he turned to psychology, obtaining his doctorate at the University of Wisconsin and eventually becoming a professor at Yale. His early work was concerned with the measurement of attitudes and with an important study of hypnosis—almost certainly the first in which the experimental procedures were fully controlled and the results submitted to statistical analysis (see HYPNOSIS, EXPERIMENTAL). His major work, however, lay in the field of systematic *behaviour theory, in which he won considerable renown, though his attempt to evolve a hypothetico-deductive model of the learning process in animals and man has not stood the test of time (see BEHAVIOURISM; REASONING: DEVELOPMENT IN CHILDREN). None the less, he brought much-needed rigour and control into research in experimental psychology. His books include *Hypnosis and Suggestibility* (1933), *Mathematico-Deductive Theory of Rote Learning* (1940), *Principles of Behaviour* (1943), and *A Behaviour System* (1952).

human growth. A term which covers both the increase in size of individuals with increasing age, and change in shape during the same time. In considering either aspect it is fundamental to recognize the effects of sexual dimorphism in determining both change in size and differential change in shape between the sexes. See also SEX DIFFERENCES IN CHILDHOOD.

1. Growth in size
2. Sex differences
3. Differences between individuals of the same sex
4. Prediction of adult height
5. Environmental factors

1. Growth in size

It is convenient to use growth in height as an example. Our knowledge of the pattern of growth can come only

from repeated measurements on individual children as they grow. Fig. 1 shows the growth in height of a boy from 0 to 18 years of age, measured by his father every six months (see Tanner 1978). The upper panel shows the actual height measurements at each age, and the lower panel shows the rate of growth at the various ages. Growth is a form of motion, and the former can be considered as distance travelled while the latter shows velocity. Two principal facts are shown by this figure: first the marked regularity of growth, and secondly the existence of three important epochs. From birth to about 4 years of age the child is growing very rapidly, but slowing steadily from growth rates of 20 cm (8 in) per year to nearer 6 cm per year. Over the next 6–8 years the growth rate slows still further, but gently, so that the average velocity is about 5 cm per year. At 10–12 years of age the rate increases rapidly before finally slowing down to cessation of growth between 17 and 19 years. This general pattern

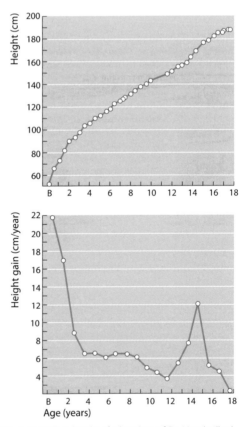

Fig. 1. Growth in height of a boy (son of De Montbeillard, during the years 1759–77): (above) distance curve, height attained at each age; (below) velocity curve, increments in height from year to year.

holds for all muscular and skeletal measurements and for the more composite variables such as weight, but not for all body organs. Growth of the reproductive organs is quiescent for many years and does not start properly until the onset of puberty. Then there is very rapid growth to adult size over five or six years. Growth of the lymphatic organs, such as the tonsils and lymph nodes, is considerable in early childhood, so that between 8 and 12 years their size is actually greater than in the adult, although at puberty these organs regress to adult size. Lastly, brain growth occurs very much earlier than general body growth, achieving some 95 per cent of mature size by the age of 6 years. (The growth and development of the human brain is discussed separately, under BRAIN DEVELOPMENT.)

2. Sex differences

On average, growth in height is little different between boys and girls until the onset of adolescence in girls, on average at about 10 years of age. Then the average girl starts her adolescent growth spurt and for one or two years she is taller than the average boy, who is still continuing to grow at a pre-pubertal rate. At about 12 years of age, by which time the average girl is at the peak of her growth spurt and starting to slow down again, the average boy starts his adolescent growth spurt. This is greater in intensity than in the average girl, so that not only does he reach equal height again but he goes further, to attain a greater adult height by some 12 cm. The excess of adult height in the male has two components. First there is the extra two years of growth at the pre-adolescent rate, and secondly there is the more intense growth spurt once adolescence begins.

A similar pattern is seen in other body dimensions, such as leg length, trunk length, and shoulder width. There are, however, some interesting sexual differences in timing and intensity. The growth spurt in shoulder width is more intense in the male than in the female, whereas that of pelvic breadth is rather similar between the sexes. The net effect of this is the greater shoulder breadth relative to pelvic width of the male. Thus the differential growth of these few simple dimensions is already beginning to produce differences in the characteristic shapes of the average male and female adult. Added to this are differences in the growth of subcutaneous fat. During adolescence the average male actually loses subcutaneous fat and increases muscle bulk under the influence of male sex hormones. In contrast, although the rate of gain of subcutaneous fat slows down in girls, they do not actually lose it. The effects of female hormones on the distribution of body fat produce the softer female profile, compared with that of the male.

3. Differences between individuals of the same sex

There are two principal differences: first, in size at a given age, and, secondly, in tempo—the timing with which each individual reaches the various stages of physical growth.

The range of variation in size at any age is surprisingly large. The height of a perfectly normal 10-year-old boy at the lower end of the range might be 124 cm (4 feet 4 in), which is the same as that of an equally normal 6-year-old at the upper end of his range. This variation increases with age, so that the normal range of height for 2-year-old boys is about 14 cm (6 in), whereas for 10-year-old boys it is about 26 cm.

With tempo—the differences in speed with which a child passes through the various stages of development—it is slightly more complicated. Thus a child with a fast tempo, who is always advanced in his growth, seems large compared with his peers, goes through an early adolescence, and finishes growing early. This is in contrast with the so-called 'late developer', who passes each of the stages late compared with the average, and finishes growing much later. Such differences are most apparent in adolescence, and so are important when assessing individuals or groups of individuals at or after the onset of puberty: it is possible to find among boys of identical chronological age one who is pre-adolescent and another who is nearly mature. Clearly in such cases comparison is invidious and to be avoided; usually it is possible to relate growth to a maturity index, such as the stage of pubertal development.

Size at birth is generally related to maternal size; large women tend to have large babies. The size of the father is relatively unimportant, except insofar as, due to assortative mating, there is a tendency for large mothers also to have large husbands. It is believed that the dominant maternal influence is due to the environment within the uterus determining the intra-uterine growth of the child. After birth, the influence of the father's size gradually increases, until, from about the age of 2, the child's growth is related principally to the average of its parents' heights, both exerting an equal influence. This association between the child's and the parents' heights remains fairly constant from then until maturity, although during adolescence it becomes distorted unless the child matures at an absolutely average rate.

4. Prediction of adult height

Without knowledge of a child's tempo, it is very difficult to make any sort of prediction of his final height from heights at earlier ages. Given a measure of his skeletal maturity obtained from studies of X-rays, the possibility of prediction improves considerably, though there is still room for quite considerable error. For example, a prediction of the final height of a child of 9, with known skeletal maturity, is subject to a range of 14 cm in possible error. This range becomes progressively smaller the older the child is at the time of the prediction, but unless he is very near maturity it is always quite significant. A large part of scope for error arises from the great unpredictability of the size and the timing of the adolescent growth spurt.

5. Environmental factors

Thus far, genetic factors have been our main consideration. Chronic illness of any sort may affect growth, usually to reduce and very rarely to increase it, and there are some diseases, such as deficiency of growth hormone, which have highly specific effects. Disease apart, nutrition is the most obvious environmental influence, and it varies from extreme, starvation situations, where children's growth may be grossly stunted, to less severe, suboptimal situations. With suboptimal nutrition there is a tendency for growth in size to be reduced overall, but relative to reduced weight and reduced body fat. Tempo is usually affected first. Minor differences in diet, as between a child who is just rather 'faddy' about his food and one who eats heartily, do not produce significant effects on growth.

Socio-economic class has long been considered to be a significant determinant of physical size. Generally, children from families of higher socio-economic groups are taller than others. Part of the reason is nutrition, but it is probably due also to the general circumstance of the environment: children from better-off families are, for example, less exposed to recurrent infection. The fact that in the West such differences between socio-economic groups are getting smaller, and in Scandinavia have almost disappeared, presumably relates to family income and size. The more children there are in a family, in general, the smaller they are, but again these differences are tending to decrease.

Allied to the socio-economic effects are certain psychological problems. Without doubt, severe psychological stress may affect a child's growth. The condition may mimic organic disease, and severe growth failure may be apparent before it becomes clear that there are emotional difficulties. In such a situation resolution of the emotional problems leads to a prompt improvement in growth and usually to complete, or near complete, normality.

Although in general children appear to grow evenly over a span of years, in some cases there are quite marked variations within any one year. In about one-third of children there is a seasonal variation, most commonly with fast growth in the spring, and slower growth during the rest of the year. In a rather larger number there are less regular cycles, with the fast time not necessarily occurring at a fixed time of year, while in some children there is no variation at all. A child's growth should be considered over a whole period of one year; indeed, all growth standards are constructed on this criterion.

The most striking environmental effect of the last 150 years, called the secular trend, is the tendency for all children to grow to greater adult height and to mature earlier. Adult height has increased by approximately 1 cm per decade, while the first menstrual period has advanced from an average age in Norway of about 16½ in 1840 to about 13 at the present time. The cause of this secular trend is still obscure, but certainly includes improved nutrition (perhaps especially in infancy) and social circumstances.

Growth is the result of a continuing interaction between environmental and hereditary factors. It is a matter not of a simple additive effect of environment upon heredity, but of a complex interaction between the two that determines the timing of events and the degree to which various changes occur at different ages. The timing and degree vary between groups of individuals—between sexes, for example, or between ethnic groups—and in turn determine the final size and physical characteristics of the adult. But they do not materially alter the fundamental physique of an individual from that seen at a very early age. Thus it is that a child's ultimate adult appearance can largely be predicted from about the age of 5.

MAP

Falkner, F., and Tanner, J. M. (1985). *Human Growth* (2nd edn.). Tanner, J. M. (1978). *Foetus into Man.*

humanism. How does *humanism* connect with *humanity*? The dictionary doesn't help, both words have a cluster of meanings. The Renaissance humanists (for example, Petrarch and Erasmus) were so called because they felt that Christianity should be as much concerned with human affairs here on earth as with the afterlife in heaven and hell, and also because they were learned in the newly discovered literature of classical Greece and Rome, which was rated as 'the humanities' because it was the secular work of man whereas the Bible and the patristic commentaries were treated as the divinely inspired works of God.

Contemporary humanism is a morally concerned style of intellectual atheism openly avowed by only a small minority of individuals (for example, those who are members of the British Humanist Association) but tacitly accepted by a wide spectrum of educated people in all parts of the Western world. The essence of this modern humanism is summed up in the following quotation from Vico (Giovanni Battista Vico, 1668–1744, professor of rhetoric at Naples), who was an 18th-century Italian, though he wrote in the manner of the Renaissance humanists: '[it is] a truth beyond all question that the world of civil society has certainly been made by man and that its principles are therefore to be rediscovered within the modifications of our own human mind.'

Vico considered himself a Christian, but 20th-century humanists had no use for God either as an external force which interferes in the processes of nature and the affairs of men or as an arbiter of moral judgements. Many things that happen are the consequence of pure chance, but there is no point in deifying chance and treating it as a disembodied mind which might respond intentionally to prayer. The only intentional force in the world is our own human mind.

But although modern humanists reject supernaturalism, they are not *behaviourists in any simple sense. They do not claim that all human action can be explained in terms of triggered responses to external stimuli. Humanists believe that we are capable of making choices, changing our minds, and telling lies. Men are therefore responsible for what they do. But this formula is less straightforward than it seems. Where is this 'I' located that can assume responsibility for what I do?

Let us go back to Vico, who was a thinker of great subtlety. Vico contrasted certainty (*certum*), which is what we learn from empirical observation, and truth (*verum*), which he thought of as a kind of structural model in the mind which we use to interpret the 'certainties' of our sensory experience. Hence history, that which we know as certain, is constantly transformed by the developing modifications of the mind through which alone we come to know what is true. Putting the same argument in a different way, Vico insisted that an external observer can never understand a product of human craft in the way that the craftsman himself understands it. Comparably we can understand human history not only because men made it but because our understanding comes from the truths which we hold in our mind rather than from the certainties which we obtain as external observers.

The relevance of all this to humanism is that it bears on what we might mean by the concept *humanity*. In what sense is this creature 'man', who makes his own history as a carpenter makes a chair, 'other than' just an animal caught up in the accidents of fate? How is man different? What makes him a human being?

The religious answer to this question is that man has a soul; the atheist–humanist answer is that man has a mind. But what do we mean by that? Significantly, both in German (*Geist*) and in French (*esprit*) soul and mind are covered by the same word.

Let us try to be more specific. Humanity is that which differentiates man from other animals. Where does that get us to? What can we do that they cannot do?

All animals have a limited capacity to discriminate and categorize other animals. They can recognize members of their own species and discriminate as to sex; they can distinguish food from not-food; they can recognize potential predators; some highly social species (for example, various insects, birds, rodents, baboons) can learn to discriminate neighbours from strangers. In man this last capability has been greatly elaborated. In the human case the development of a self-conscious 'I' which is contrasted with 'other' is closely linked with the formation of verbal concepts. The structure of speech, which is linear and segmented, encourages us to perceive our environment as consisting of separable 'things' and 'events' and 'categories' each of which can be described by a name. The discriminations which are indicated by such contrasts as 'I'/'other', 'we'/'they' are a part of this very general process.

But our thinking is not limited to this linear form in which we distinguish polarities, one thing after another. We also think by analogy (*metaphor), one thing superimposed upon another. Thus, while polarity may lead us to distinguish 'I'/'other', 'we'/'they', 'man'/'animal', 'tame'/'wild', 'cultivated'/'natural', analogy may lead us to feel that these pairs somehow resemble one another, so that 'we' are to 'they' is as 'man' is to 'animal', as 'tame' is to 'wild', and as 'culture' is to 'nature'.

The way we make discriminations and the way we make metaphoric associations seems to be largely arbitrary so that, overall, there are many degrees of freedom built into the way we perceive the environment in which we live. A great deal of this 'freedom' (arbitrariness) derives from our use of language in category formation; hence we may infer that other animals, which do not possess language, have a much more constricted perception of the world. To put it differently, because we have language we are able to convert sensory inputs into 'concepts in the mind' and we can play with these concepts in the imagination without reference to operations in the external world. We have persuaded ourselves that this is a human characteristic which is not shared by other animals.

The concepts which have been listed above all represent categories that derive from our experience of the external world, but language allows us to form other concepts which are wholly products of the imagination and which have no objective counterpart in the world out there. We can then use polarity to distinguish things in the world from products of the imagination, thus: 'man'/'God', 'mortal'/'immortal', 'imperfection'/'perfection', 'impotence'/'omnipotence'—and then, by the use of analogy, we may come to polarize 'impotent–imperfect–mortal–man' against 'omnipotent–perfect–immortal–God'. But this is precisely the dichotomy that modern humanists reject as superstition!

In some ways this is paradoxical since it is one of the peculiarities of our humanity that we should be capable of inventing such religious concepts at all. The point is, however, that whereas religion insists that God created man in his own image, humanist scepticism maintains that man created God in his own (mirror) image and that it is only self-deception that leads us to credit this mirror image with a potency which we ourselves lack. Humanists hold that religious faith is undesirable first because it encourages belief in what is false, namely that the human individual survives after death, and secondly because, by attributing omnipotence to God, it undervalues both the limited potency of man and the final responsibility that goes with it.

But God is more than a magnified non-natural man; he is also the source of moral judgement and here the humanists run into difficulty.

During the 19th century atheistical moralists believed that they could dispense with God the Moral Arbiter and substitute an equally metaphysical concept, Human Reason. At this stage in its development rationalist humanism was simply a variation of 18th-century deism and was itself a form of religion which even developed a church hierarchy. Modern humanism has largely abandoned ideas of this sort, though the central humanist thesis that human beings are what they are because of their education rather than because they were created to be that way by God has persisted right through. But 'education' must here be understood in the broad sense of socialization. The individual is created by the whole social milieu into which he was born; my consciousness of myself is coloured by my class consciousness, by my community consciousness, and by my national consciousness of what 'we' are as against the 'others'.

When it comes to morality, humanists now recognize that each individual's conceptions of what is right and wrong will depend upon the circumstances of his upbringing. And since humanists reject the idea that there can be any absolute criteria for making such distinctions they are led to put an unusually high valuation on the virtue of tolerance.

Many religions preach tolerance, but they do not practise it. The divine commandment 'Love thy neighbour as thyself' has never inhibited Christians from inflicting every imaginable barbarity upon their neighbours in the name of true religion. But it was a 16th-century humanist, Montaigne (1533–92), who first complained that the contemporary treatment of heretics was far more horrible than anything that had been reliably reported of South American cannibals.

In this context the unique feature of humanism is that not only does it proclaim the virtue of tolerance but at the same time it denounces all forms of religious zeal, including zeal for humanism itself. In short, humanism is an intellectual attitude rather than the creed of a religious sect or political party; it provides us with a sceptical base from which to criticize the prejudiced certainties with which other people are prepared to proclaim the Will of God and the Destiny of Mankind, but it is not in itself a guidebook to any new kind of Utopia.   ERL

Blackburn, S. (2003). *Being Good*.
Hinde, R. (1997). *Religion and Darwinism*.
Holloway, R. (1999). *Godless Morality*.

Hume, David (1711–76). The second son of a minor Scottish landowner, Hume was educated at Edinburgh University, and after unsuccessful attempts at business and law he left Britain to live cheaply in rural France, where from 1734 to 1739 he composed his greatest philosophical work, *A Treatise of Human Nature*. He returned to see this through the press (1739), and settled into a literary life in Edinburgh. His *Essays, Moral and Political* was published in 1742, followed by *An Enquiry Concerning Human Understanding* (1748) and *An Enquiry Concerning the Principles of Morals* (1751). His *History of England* was published in six volumes between 1754 and 1762. His *Four Dissertations* of 1757 included *The Natural History of Religion*, and his final, posthumous philosophical text, the groundbreaking *Dialogues Concerning Natural Religion*, was published by his nephew in 1779. His philosophical and literary life was punctuated by occasional forays into the wider world, notably as secretary to the Embassy in Paris from 1763 to 1766, where he was lionized as a leading figure of the Enlightenment.

Hume is celebrated philosophically as the first great naturalistic philosopher of the modern age. He was the first to step aside completely from a religious dimension in his approach to human nature. The human mind had to be theorized about not in terms of a small replica of the mind of God, nor as a specially favoured device for knowledge of things, but as a piece of nature subject to natural laws. Hume's distinction lies in the rigour with which he pursues the aim.

There is no God-given guarantee that our minds are tuned to the truth about nature, and for this reason Hume has often been dubbed a sceptic, although that needs careful qualification. His aim was not general scepticism, about which he is often scornful. It is to bring the experimental and empirical method into the study of the mind. Just as the Newtonian scientist looks for the patterns exhibited in natural events, so the scientist of the mind finds the patterns underlying the superficial jumble of contents of the mind.

For Hume, the inhabitants of the mind are all 'perceptions'. These include impressions of the senses, ideas of memory, reflection, and imagination, but also the passions. Hume makes distinctions between simple and complex ideas, and between impressions, or the vivid and powerful delivery of the senses, and subsequent ideas in which impressions are in some way copied or rehearsed before the mind. At the beginning of the *Treatise* Hume tends to think of perceptions as individual atoms of consciousness, and it is the principles associating these together that are his first concern. For this reason Hume is often regarded as a father of associationist psychology, optimistically expecting to find some laws whereby one perception gives rise to another. However, if this was ever his aim it was quickly superseded by a far more searching interest. A purely perceptual model of the mind, in which it is filled with impressions and ideas occurring in some alleged order, does no justice to the active, conceptual powers exhibited by the mind. Hume's topic rapidly becomes the concepts that structure our thought and the complex relationship these bear to the perceptual basis.

Important concepts for Hume are those governing our idea of the external world, extended away from ourselves in space and time, the concept of the self as a perceiver of that world and an agent within it, and the concept of the causal connection between events. In each case Hume offers a sceptical starting point, followed by a reconstruction, or account of the processes whereby the conceptual ability arises. The sceptical starting point is the realization that these concepts are not simply manifested in experience. They are the result of interpreting experience in a certain way, rather than a passive piece of data that is simply presented to us. So the external world is not a given, but rather the result of supposing that our perceptions have a life of their own, a continuity in time beyond that which is given in experience. Unfortunately this is also a continuity beyond any that, on reflection, we can defensibly suppose them to have, so that, as far as the external world goes, it seems as if we are condemned to having a world-view that cannot possibly be true. True to his naturalism, however, Hume regards this not as a criticism of the way we conduct ourselves, naturally confident of our place in an external order of things, but as a criticism of the power of reason to untangle the rationale of that belief. It is useless to kick against the belief itself, since nature compels us to think in terms of it.

The continuing self is not given to us in our kaleidoscopic experience either, but is the result of an imaginative or fictive process, rather as a commonwealth or club is a kind of fiction. Hume's reason for suggesting imagination and fiction here is not just that we have no impression of the self, but also that the various considerations that determine our judgements of personal identity through time are arbitrary and unsettled. They are unlikely indicators of any real or substantial truth about a definite subject matter—such as the self is supposed to be. But we do think and talk in terms of such a thing. Here too it is important to notice that Hume abandons the strict empiricist doctrine that an idea must be preceded by some suitably related impression. We have no impression of the abiding self, but again must work in terms of an imaginative sense of our continuing existence through time.

Finally the causal connections between things are never the direct object of perception, for regularities may be differently interpreted in causal terms. Rather, after experiencing regularities in the ways events fall out, we ourselves acquire habits of prediction and control. When we have done so we express ourselves by attributing causal powers and causal relations to those same events. Hume here applies a lesson he takes himself to have learned from Francis Hutcheson in the very different domain of moral philosophy. Interpreting events in causal terms, just like interpreting them in moral terms, shows the mind 'gilding and staining' the world with the 'colours borrowed from internal sentiment'. In other words, a functional change in the mind, such as the occurrence of a passion or the arrival of a habit of expectation, leads us to talk in the one case of ethical properties, and in the other case of causal powers.

A salient part of Hume's picture in all such cases is that it is not reason that performs this constructive role. According to Hume no kind of reasoning could give us the result we want. There is no principle either of logical or mathematical or probabilistic reasoning that justifies talk of an external world (indeed, reason here strenuously opposes such talk), or of a continuing self, or of a causal order of things. In each case custom, or habit, or principles of imagination, step in to fill the void left by reason. Hume's account of our conceptual powers is in this sense a sceptical one, but the target of the scepticism is reason itself, rather than the end products of custom and imagination. Nevertheless, the end of the first, metaphysical part of the *Treatise* is gloomy enough about the powers of enquiry ever to make sense of the basic nature of the world, and of us ourselves and our relationship to it.

Hume's moral psychology is again entirely antirationalistic. There are no logical or quasi-mathematical 'proofs' of our basic moral principles, and neither, of course, is there any knowledge of them as an expression of God's will. Rather, we must once more investigate the moral psychologies of human beings. Here we find neither the confined self-interest of a *Hobbes or a Mandeville, nor the sunny benevolence of a Hutcheson. We find a confined generosity, whereby people are naturally concerned not only for themselves but to a limited extent for those around them. However, Hume also discovers an artificial or conventional source of much moral motivation. Even if I hold no concern for you, nor you for me, nevertheless the benefit of mutual cooperation can, in favourable circumstances, motivate us to act together, replacing competition with cooperation. The favourable circumstances will be those in which trust is cautiously extended beyond immediate social groupings, notably the family, and then through repeated reciprocation builds into a pattern the agents can rely upon in future transactions. Hume here gives the first game-theoretic or evolutionary reconstruction of the emergence of cooperation in action and motivation. If all goes well, then in the end the process of coordination can give rise to the psychologies of those who 'belong to the party of mankind'. Hume is clear that this is an achievement of civilization rather than the gift of an Aristotelian telos or naturally benevolent human nature. The resulting moral system is nearer to what is now called 'virtue ethics' than utilitarianism or its *Kantian rivals. The primary foci of moral appraisal, for Hume, are the character traits manifested in action, according to whether they are 'useful or agreeable to ourselves or others'. The system is funded by the same elements as utilitarianism—the pleasures and pains of individuals—but the space between those elements in the basement and fully fledged ethical judgements in the superstructure is much greater, and much more subtly traversed, than in subsequent utilitarian theories.

Although Hume gave an entirely naturalistic picture of the mind, he left himself space for normative reflections upon its workings. In both philosophy and history he had a strong interest in reasonings gone wrong, or the causes of error and bias in human judgement. Possibly the most famous example of this is the chapter on miracles in the *Enquiry Concerning Human Understanding*, one of the most explosive texts of the 18th century. In this Hume considers the proper response of one hearing human beings testifying to miraculous occurrences. Resolutely regarding testimony, as a naturalist should, as just one effect of causes among others, Hume would have us ask which constitutes the greatest miracle: on the one hand the alleged event occurred, and the testimony is truthful, or on the other hand the alleged event did not occur, and the testimony is delusive. And then the trouble is that, although delusive testimony may be quite uncommon, it is not so very uncommon, whereas if the event to which it testifies is extraordinary enough to count as miraculous, that has to be of a quite different order of improbability. Hence (either by Bayesian or other statistical reasonings) the rational stance can never be to accept the miracle on the basis of the testimony.

Psychologically, Hume goes on to diagnose the mechanisms that nevertheless lead people to prefer the wrong hypothesis. He gives a seminal account of the influence of the passions (wonder, surprise, enjoyment) on belief. In this and other writings he extends his diagnosis to many areas where there are 'moral causes' shunting people into many cul-de-sacs of thought and sentiment (a particularly interesting section is that on 'unphilosophical probability' in part iii of Book I of the *Treatise*, in which Hume notices the disproportionate influence of anecdotal evidence on belief, where it is usually given a priority above abstract statistical and scientific proof). All this opens the way to his sociological and psychological investigations of the causes of religious belief, with its associated superstitions and enthusiasms. Interestingly, when we follow his diagnoses, we understand them because our own minds share sufficient of the frailties of those of others to reflect their workings (we can ourselves feel fear of the unknown as motivating the desire to assuage the gods, for example).

Importantly, it is not that we rationally endorse the defective reasonings, but that we recognize the temptationztowards them. In this Hume may be said to have anticipated but also to have gone one better than subsequent 'verstehen' accounts of interpretation, based solely upon our own capacity to replicate the reasonings of other agents. We can understand the mechanisms of credulity and superstition without in any sense reliving the thought processes of those who are credulous and gullible. However, we do rely upon a uniformity of human nature, whereby we can take our own minds to be 'mirrors' of the minds of those we seek to understand. Hume has been much criticized for his belief in a uniform human nature, constant across cultures and times. But in fact his interest, as both a philosopher and a historian, lay in diversity as much as uniformity, and he implies no more uniformity in human beings than whatever is needed for processes of interpretation and understanding to take place. See also CAUSE.   SB

Ayer, A. J. (1980). *Hume*.

humour. Most popular dictionaries when defining 'humour' include the psychologist's three usages—stimulus, response, and disposition. Hence, for example, the *Concise Oxford Dictionary of Current English* refers to 'comicality', the 'faculty of perceiving', and 'state of mind'. It is extraordinary, therefore, that Drever's *Penguin Dictionary of Psychology* (the best-known specialist dictionary for psychologists) provides a much narrower definition of humour and a provocative definition of laughter. Humour is defined as the 'character of a complex situation exciting joyful, and in the main quiet, laughter, either directly, through sympathy, or through empathy'; and laughter is said to be an 'emotional response, expressive normally of joy, in the child and the unsophisticated adult'. Drever's dictionary was published by Penguin in 1952, and it was revised in 1964. Today few psychologists, and perhaps no one currently researching humour and laughter, would endorse his definitions without substantial qualification. The psychological literature has burgeoned since the early 1970s, and we now know considerably more about humour, that ubiquitous phenomenon which most of us cherish so dearly.

Drever's reference to the 'unsophisticated adult' might startle many of us. Some would find it quaint, even amusing. It reflects a long period of history, finishing not so far back, when laughing was not so universally prized. In the 18th century, Lord Chesterfield, writing to his son, said, 'there is nothing so illiberal, and so ill-bred, as audible laughter'; and others have said of laughter that it is 'the mind sneezing' (Wyndham Lewis), 'the hiccup of a fool' (John Ray), and that it '[speaks] the vacant mind' (Oliver Goldsmith). In the 1930s Ludovici argued that humour was a principal cause of the decadence of the times, and, for him, laughter was a sinister behaviour. More recently a number of writers have inferred from systematic analysis that it is only in contemporary times that humour and laughter have been regarded as important; and they point, for example, to the Bible, where there is scant mention of laughter, and such laughter as there is tends to be of a scornful kind.

Surveys indicate that these days nearly all of us believe that we have an above-average sense of humour. That statistical impossibility might merely illustrate that 'sense of humour' has many shades of meaning, but in part at least it stems from the high value that society now places on humour. The possession of a good 'sense of humour', or the capacity to laugh frequently at pleasurable and amusing events, is regarded as thoroughly desirable by almost all of us. Far from being base and degenerate, fit solely for the trivial and ignorant, the appreciation of humour is now taken as a sign of health and well-being. Humour is valued as a way of preserving order, changing group esteem and cohesion, expressing allegiances and revealing attitudes with relative impunity, testing the standing of a relationship, maintaining or undermining a status hierarchy, and so forth. The quality of our exchanges with other people can be greatly enhanced by the use of humour, whether or not it is injected as a deliberate ploy. Across a wide variety of everyday encounters, humour can be a crucial tool in our social armoury, conscripted for attack and defence. Humour can be used by protagonists to precipitate an absorbing and pacifying digression: with little danger of rebuke, they can use it to defuse the threats of others by engendering a debilitating discomfort, and through it they can easily make light, or pretend to make light, of their own misfortunes and predicaments.

Beginning with Plato's *Philebus* in 355 BC, philosophers, essayists, and others have provided a broad array of earnest and challenging statements concerning the nature of humour and laughter. Plato saw the weak as a justifiably prime target for humour. For Aristotle (in *Poetics*) the ludicrous was based in deformities, defects, and ugliness which are neither destructive nor painful. Notions such as these were revived in *Hobbes's superiority theory: in *Leviathan* and *Human Nature* Hobbes presented laughter as a self-glorifying, triumphant gesture emanating from comparisons made with inferiors. The origins of incongruity theories can be traced back through Schopenhauer (1819) and beyond to *Kant (1790), who talked of 'an affection arising from the sudden transformation of strained expectation into nothing'. According to Schopenhauer, laughter is the expression of our recognizing an incongruity, and Spencer (1860) limited it to descending incongruity: laughter naturally occurs when 'the conscious is unawares transferred from great things to small'.

There are various other forms of theory, the most influential of which has been *Freud's (1905, 1928). His was a synthesis of incongruity, relief, and conflict theories. A sharp distinction was drawn between 'the comic',

'wit', and 'humour'; and humour was said to grant relief through diverting energy from unpleasant emotion. In 'joke-work' (i.e. making jokes) there is said to be a number of techniques each of which is also to be found in 'dream work', and the principal two of which are 'condensation' and 'displacement'. Both of these techniques require deviations from normal thought and representation, and both entail an economy of thought and expression. It was Freud's contention that the ludicrous always results in a saving in the expenditure of psychic energy: not only is the joke expressed with brevity, but amusement is taken to be the most economical response to the joke. Freud also maintained that both forms of economy could be false: energy can be liberated unnecessarily and then dissipated in expressing amusement. However, through techniques analogous to those of dreaming, humour can lift repressions, and in Freudian theory humour is among the most important defences.

The pervasive view of the classic Greek and Roman scholars that humour and laughter are rooted in shabbiness and deformity persisted in various guises for many centuries, but it has been largely discarded in recent years as empirical researchers, particularly psychologists, have begun to contribute significantly to knowledge. There has been a genesis and development of substantial strands of experimentation, and at the same time the quest for a grand theory has been generally abandoned. No one seems sanguine about there ever being a grand theory of humour which is capable of embracing adequately all aspects of creation, imitation, and reaction. Instead the new literature abounds with 'mini-theories' which, typically, address stimulus issues (e.g. content, structure, complexity), *or* individual differences (e.g. personality, cognitions, physiology), *or* overt expression (e.g. verbal and non-verbal reactions), *or* social influences (e.g. effects of companions and audiences), etc.

The mini-theories differ from the older, global theories in a number of salient respects (cf. Keith-Spiegel 1972). For example, the older accounts, with few exceptions, were in effect statements of function or properties; they were little more than taxonomies of laughter-provoking stimuli, or descriptions of conditions under which laughter is sometimes evoked. The modern-day accounts draw more on general principles in psychology, and most of them tacitly or explicitly acknowledge that laughter can find expression when there is a total absence of humour. They recognize that it may not be possible to delineate any set of circumstances under which laughter is never to be found. It can prosper under conditions of deprivation, pain, and oppression: seemingly it can be observed in persons experiencing any of mankind's diverse emotional states. In his book *The Sense of Humour* (1954) the English humorist Stephen Potter summed up laughter's ubiquity as follows:

We laugh when the sea touches our navel. . . . We laugh at something because it is familiar and something else because it is unfamiliar. . . . We laugh at misfortunes if they do not incur danger. . . . We laugh because other people are laughing. . . . Then there is the laugh which fills up a blank in the conversation. . . . The laugh of the older man talking to a girl, which can suggest: 'You are charming, but I am charming too.' The laugh to attract attention. . . . The laugh . . . which we hear in the hall from the new arrival not sure of himself, who wishes to appear sure of himself, and it makes us sure we are not sure of him. The laugh of the lone man at the theatre, who wishes to show that he understands the play or understands the foreign language which is being spoken, or gets the point of the joke quickest, or has seen the play. The laugh of creative pleasure. . . . The laugh of relief from physical danger. . . . We laugh at funny hats . . . we laugh at sex jokes. We do not laugh at sex jokes if they are not funny unless other people are present.

While it is important to be aware that any particular instance of laughter need not have been triggered by humour, it is disturbing to find that the vast majority of humour researchers opt to exclude laughter and other behavioural measures from their indices of humour appreciation. It seems that humour loses much of its splendour, infectiousness, and power under laboratory scrutiny, to such an extent that exuberant laughter is rarely elicited from experimental subjects. There is a need for more trenchant empirical work, and particularly research in 'the field', rather than for any continuation in the escalation of asocial, laboratory studies. As far as theoretical progress is concerned, no one has made noticeable headway in answering questions of the sort, 'Why does humour produce laughter, rather than, say, a more quiescent form of behaviour?' and 'Why should the enjoyment of humour climax in any overt response whatsoever?'. Then there are other questions, barely more tractable, to do with the conditions necessary for laughter to feature in the repertoire of behavioural responses. The label 'humorous laughter' is to some extent a misnomer because research indicates that the quality and quantity of laughter which, temporally, follows a joke are primarily governed by social aspects of the prevailing situation in which the joke is presented.

It is generally thought that in the early stages of an individual's development a 'safe' or 'playful' mood has to be generated for the infant to engage in 'humorous laughter'. Laughter maturationally precedes humour appreciation and first appears at about 4 months of age. An inevitable consequence of definitional disagreements is that distinguished scientific scholars dispute when humour is first experienced. Those who say that symbolism is an essential ingredient in humour (e.g. McGhee 1979) report that humour does not occur until the second year of the child's life: only then does the child have sufficient capacity for fantasy and pretend activities. Others report that humour is experienced by children as young as 4

months (e.g. Pien and Rothbart 1980). At that age they laugh when incongruous events are presented in safe situations, but then the cognitive resolution does not entail symbolic capacities. Rothbart (1976) observes that, for children this young, incongruity is limited as an explanatory principle: while the perception of an unexpected event may lead to laughter, it may instead lead to curiosity, fear, problem solving, or concept learning. For laughter, the incongruous event must be safe or playful, and resolution, or partial resolution, of the incongruity must be feasible.

Incongruity is defined in terms of a disparity between what was perceived and what was expected, and such a disparity is usually taken to be a necessary but not a sufficient condition for humour. Resolution refers to the rendering of the disparity as meaningful or appropriate, or to the discovery of a rule which renders the incongruity explicable within the context of the joke. We still have no model that satisfactorily embraces both the perception and resolution aspects of incongruities. However, we do know from empirical work as well as from everyday experiences that incongruities can be too trivial or they can be too complex for humour to be experienced, and, independent of complexity, some themes (e.g. sex and aggression) are generally more comic than others.

A notable exception to the modern-day brand of mini-theory is that propounded by D. E. Berlyne. His was an 'arousal' theory which enjoyed considerable support in the 1970s. Like Freudian theory, however, it has been gradually discarded by empirical researchers as they have increasingly dedicated their investigations to cognitive dimensions of humour. Berlyne's analysis was founded upon the view that moderate levels of arousal ('nonspecific drive') and changes in arousal are pleasurable, whereas high and low levels of arousal are not pleasurable. Humour was said to boost the individual's arousal to an unusual level until resolution of incongruity caused a sharp decline. Hence pleasure can result from the change *per se* and from the raising of arousal from an uncomfortably low level. It is not clear from Berlyne's writings whether arousal changes and humour appreciation are related in a linear, inverted U, or U-shaped fashion. Since it is possible to argue for any of these three possibilities, the theory is inherently untestable.

The superiority theories of yesterday were precursors of contemporary disposition theory (Zillmann 1983), and that theory posits that humour emanating from disparagement depends upon a balance of affective dispositions towards the disparaged and non-disparaged parties. The theory predicts that humour appreciation will be strong when one is negatively disposed towards the disparaged party, and it will also be strong when one is positively disposed to the person purveying the disparagement. A principal difference between disposition theory and superiority theories (e.g. La Fave 1977) is that the latter highlight both the debasement of an inferior and the enhancement of a superior, whereas in disposition theory the enhancement of the superior is a by-product and is not essential to humour appreciation. Disposition theory is especially useful when accounting for the success of jokes aimed at minority groups, such as the physically handicapped and psychiatrically disturbed. It is similarly useful when accounting for the pervasiveness of jokes aimed at demographic, political, and ethnic minorities.

It has been claimed that women find jokes funnier when heard by the left ear, with the suggestion that this ear routes to the right hemisphere of the brain, which processes information more holistically than the left hemisphere, which is analytical. Could this be the basis for a biological explanation of sex differences in humour appreciation? Unfortunately, each ear is represented in both hemispheres (though with some contralateral preference) so this is hardly a serious suggestion. Clinical studies of patients with damage to the right hemisphere have identified correlated deficits in humour comprehension and appreciation. However, it cannot be assumed that a cerebral 'centre for humour' is located in the right hemisphere. The operation of the left hemisphere is crucial in providing and organizing relevant information necessary to resolve perceived incongruity.

The bias of psychological theory and investigation has been towards a characterization of *responses* to humour. We know little about factors bearing on the creation and initiation of humour. Also, researchers tend to neglect fundamental conceptual and measurement questions, and they are too often insular in their approaches and objectives. None the less there is now much evidence to the effect that humour reflects basic underlying trends in emotional, social, and cognitive development.

AJC/NPS

Critchley, S. (2002). On Humour (Thinking in Action).
Freud, S. (1905). Der Witz und seine Beziehung zum Ubewussten.
——(1928). 'Humour'. International Journal of Psychoanalysis, 9.
Kant, I. (1790). Kritik der Urteilskraft.
Keith-Spiegel, P. (1972). 'Early conceptions of humor: varieties and issues'. In Goldstein, J. H., and McGhee, P. E. (eds.), The Psychology of Humor: Theoretical Perspectives and Empirical Issues.
La Fave, L. (1977). 'Ethnic humour: from paradoxes towards principles'. In Chapman, A. J., and Foot, H. C. (eds.), It's a Funny Thing, Humour.
Ludovici, A. M. (1932). The Secret of Laughter.
McGhee, P. E. (1979). Humor: Its Origin and Development.
Pien, D., and Rothbart, M. K. (1980). 'Incongruity humour, play, and self-regulation of arousal in young children'. In McGhee, P. E., and Chapman, A. J. (eds.), Children's Humour.
Ramachandran, V. S. (1998). 'The neurology and evolution of humour, laughter and smiling: the false alarm theory'. Medical Hypotheses, 51/4.
Rothbart, M. K. (1976). 'Incongruity, problem-solving and laughter'. In Chapman, A. J., and Foot, H. C. (eds.), Humour and Laughter: Theory, Research and Applications.
Schopenhauer, A. (1819). Die Welt als Wille und Vorstellung.
Spencer, H. (1860). 'The physiology of laughter'. Macmillan's Magazine, I.
Vaid, J. (1999). 'The evolution of humour: do those who laugh last?' In Rosen, D., and Lluebbert, M. (eds.), Evolution of the Psyche.
Zillmann, D. (1983). 'Disparagement humor'. In McGhee, P. E., and Goldstein, J. H. (eds.), Handbook of Humor Research.

humours, classical. See INSANITY: HISTORY.

hunger and food intake regulation. That organisms need to ingest nutrient is obvious, but what the mechanism is that controls such ingestion is not, and that is a question of more than academic interest. Disorders of the hunger mechanism, of which obesity is the most common, are cosmetically disfiguring and pose a very considerable danger to health, curtailing the lifespan significantly. Because of the threat that obesity poses, a large dieting industry has sprung up, which, as a result of misconceptions and ignorance of the normal hunger mechanism, is almost totally ineffective.

Normal humans and normal rats (and we know much more about rats) regulate their caloric intake so as to maintain their weight within close limits. Further, they are able to select various dietary constituents so as to maintain themselves in good health. Infants given a choice of a variety of foodstuffs at each meal thrive better than those whose diet is prescribed by a dietician, and so do rats. There are two questions posed by these observations. The first is how do organisms manage to regulate the amount of food eaten and the second is how do they know which dietary constituents to choose? Let us start with the first question. To regulate the amount eaten there must be an internal signal which initiates eating, the introspectible counterpart of which we call hunger, and another signal which terminates eating, which we call satiety. It is sad to report that we do not know what these signals are.

We have found that it is possible to induce eating through various interventions. Peripheral injections of insulin produce hunger, and injections of noradrenaline (norepinephrine) into the brain ventricles produce some increase in food intake. However, rats and people that do not secrete insulin still feel hungry and eat, and noradrenaline produces a drop in body temperature which itself will increase food intake. Secondly we have believed that we know where the biochemical change that produces hunger acts in the brain. Small lesions in the lateral hypothalamus in rats produce an animal that starves in the midst of plenty, and electric stimulation of the same area through chronically implanted electrodes induces vigorous eating in an already satiated animal. These experiments might seem fairly conclusive, but there are problems. A rat with a lateral hypothalamic lesion is a very sick animal, and a number of peripheral mechanisms are disrupted by the operation: the effect on eating might therefore be indirect. Similarly, stimulation of the lateral hypothalamic area may stimulate other mechanisms which then induce eating. But the most devastating objection is that it is also possible to induce eating simply by a sustained pinching of the rat's tail!

Although the exact identity of satiety signals still eludes us, some progress has been made in their discovery. The simplest idea was that termination of eating occurs when the changes that produce hunger are reversed. But such an idea must be incorrect because eating stops when the digestion of a meal has barely begun. Another idea has been that we learn to eat a certain amount of a particular food because such an amount has in the past eventually led to the reduction of hunger. Though there is some evidence that this can be a minor factor under some circumstances, it cannot by any means be the whole story, because when an animal eats and the food does not either reach or stay in the stomach, the animal may continue to eat until exhausted. This suggests that satiety signals are generated somewhere in the upper gastrointestinal tract, either in the stomach or in the upper part of the gut. Such a conclusion is supported by experiments in which food is placed directly in the stomach: great reductions in subsequent feeding are observed. Unfortunately, however, the reason for this result could be wholly artefactual, for it has been recently found that placement of food in the stomach causes nausea, which by itself could produce a reduction in eating.

As we have just seen, when food is not allowed to stay in the stomach, animals eat abnormally large amounts. One popular hypothesis for this has been that the nutrient does not reach the duodenum; and experiment has shown that if food is pumped into the duodenum and not allowed to stay in the stomach, then overeating does not take place. But this experiment also is not conclusive, for it has subsequently been shown that pumping of food into the duodenum causes discomfort or nausea. Secondly, the duodenum is sometimes considered to be the origin of satiety messages because it secretes the gastrointestinal hormone cholecystokinin, injections of which have been shown to reduce eating. But although this has been taken to indicate that cholecystokinin is a satiety hormone, subsequent research has shown that the same dose also causes nausea. Thus there is no compelling evidence that the duodenum or its hormones are involved in satiety.

There is now clear evidence, however, that satiety signals emanate from the stomach. It is possible to implant a pyloric cuff round the exit from the stomach of a rat, a cuff which, when inflated, prevents the escape of stomach contents into the duodenum, without causing distress to the rat. (The gut may be squeezed, cut, or cauterized without producing pain or distress, while distension is aversive.) Also implanted in the stomach is a tube for the overflow when pressure in the stomach reaches the normal limit. Under these circumstances rats do not overeat, as they would if it was signals from the duodenum that produced satiety. A further experiment makes the same point in another way. A rat is allowed to drink nutrient to satiety and, after the pyloric cuff has been inflated, a certain amount of nutrient is drawn off through the stomach tube. The rat then begins to drink again, even though the content of the duodenum is unchanged. Moreover, if a rat drinks nutrient to satiety while the pylorus is occluded, and then nutrient is allowed to escape from the stomach to the duodenum, the rat will drink more nutrient, when it is presented, even though the cuff is inflated.

These experiments demonstrate that signals of satiety emanate from the stomach. However, we are not yet sure what such signals are. There are various possibilities. It may be that satiety arises when the stomach has been distended past a certain point. Or it could be that the stomach senses the total amount of nutrient in the volume ingested, and that it is this that signals satiety. We now have evidence that both may be true. Rats are allowed to drink under two conditions: in the first they simply drink nutrient to satiety; in the second they also drink to satiety but as the nutrient is drunk the same volume of saline is pumped into the stomach. If the stomach-distension hypothesis is correct, the rats in the second condition should on average drink only one-half the volume of nutrient. If the theory of absolute amount of nutrient is correct, on the other hand, the same volume should be drunk in both conditions. The truth is complex. Rats that drink very large volumes to satiety support the distension hypothesis, but those that drink small amounts behave as if the absolute amount of nutrient theory is true. So it seems that satiety at small volumes is regulated by nutrient. However, past a certain point distension becomes an important cue in causing a rat to stop eating.

There is other evidence that the stomach can sense nutrient when volume is kept constant. A hungry rat is given a choice between the contents of two tubes, each containing a different non-nutritive flavour. When it drinks from one of the tubes, nutrient made non-aversive by predigestion is placed in the stomach. When it drinks from the other, an equal volume of saline is placed in the stomach. Each training session lasts only ten minutes and a pyloric cuff is inflated during this period. The rat quickly learns to drink from the tube that produces nutrient in the stomach. We do not know as yet whether this sensitivity to nutrient is due to early absorption of small amounts of this nutrient or whether it is due to sense organs within the stomach. We do know, however, that the partial digestion is necessary for the nutrient to produce satiety signals. The rat secretes an enzyme at the back of its tongue which splits a portion of the fat or oil into its constituents. When a rat drinks oil and we place some of the same oil directly in the stomach, thus bypassing that part of the early digestive process due to the enzyme secreted by the tongue (lingual lipase), there is little or no reduction in the amount that the rat chooses to drink. On the other hand, an amount of predigested oil, drawn from the stomach of a donor rat, when placed in the stomach reduces the volume drunk by the same amount.

If, as seems likely, the sense organs are in the stomach, we do not know how they relay their messages to the brain. It is known that the stomach produces hormones which could affect the brain via the bloodstream, and it is also known that a large number of nerve fibres carry messages to the brain via the vagus and splanchnic nerves. But it has been found that sectioning of the vagus does not affect a rat's ability to monitor nutrients in the stomach: a rat with its vagus nerve cut still compensates accurately for any nutrient removed from the stomach during a meal. On the other hand, it no longer stops eating in response to overdistension of the stomach.

So far we have spoken of hunger as if it was a single phenomenon. However, in order to obtain an adequate diet most organisms must select a balanced mixture of foods, because they must satisfy not only their caloric needs, but their protein, vitamin, and mineral requirements as well. The mechanism of selection varies from one requirement to another. For instance, the appetite for common salt is 'wired in' or built in: when a shortage of sodium occurs, whether it be through dietary insufficiency or malfunction of the adrenal cortex, the shortage is directly translated into a craving for a particular *taste—the taste of salt—and the rat does not have to learn that the ingestion of salty tastes has beneficial consequences. There are other types of deficiency, on the other hand, where the rat has to learn what food will relieve the deficiency. The way this happens is rather curious. The deficient rat begins to prefer any novel foodstuff; it seems to develop an aversion to its normal diet. If the novel diet relieves the symptoms of deficiency the rat will then learn to consume it even if the relief is not immediate.

Generally learning occurs only if a few seconds at the most separate an act, or a signal, from its consequences, but this is not true in the case of eating. If a rat eats poison, it will learn to avoid its taste even if sickness due to the poison occurs between 10 and 24 hours later. Similar taste avoidance has been noted in children who have eaten ice-cream of a certain flavour before undergoing chemotherapy. Clearly organisms must learn what foods are good for them, although learning is not necessary in every case. In the same way as the example of salt, aversions

can also be 'wired in'—and that is as true of sweet as of bitter substances.

'Wired in' aversions and preferences have consequences for weight control. It has been shown that rats fed palatable diets maintain much higher body weights than those whose diets are unattractive. Another finding is that rats fed diets low in calories compensate by eating more. Now the stock-in-trade of the diet food industry seems to consist of two main items. The first is the substitution of sugar as a sweetener by non-nutrient substances such as saccharin. The second is the sale of food that has a lower number of calories per unit weight or volume than normal food. Now, if calories per unit volume are reduced and there is no restriction on the volume that can be eaten we would expect from the results of research that the volume eaten would increase to compensate. And as for saccharin, when it was shown that it was carcinogenic, the major argument for its retention as a food additive was that it made dieting easier; but as we have seen above, making a food palatable, or less aversive, increases its intake. One of the major aims of food production and preparation is to make food more attractive both by the addition of substances which are palatable and by removing tastes and textures which are aversive. Such gastronomic practices have almost certainly led to much ill health and a curtailment of lifespan through a general increase in obesity and other disorders.

See also ANOREXIA NERVOSA AND BULIMIA NERVOSA.

JAD

De Castro, J. M. (1996). 'How can eating behaviour be regulated in the complex environments of free-living humans?' *Neuroscience and Biobehavioural Reviews*, 20.

Mela, D. J., and Rogers, P. J. (1998). *Food, Eating and Obesity: The Psychobiological Basis of Appetite and Weight Control*.

Rogers, P. J. (1999). 'Eating habits and appetite control: a psychobiological perspective'. *Proceedings of the Nutrition Society*, 58.

Huntington's disease. Several types of cerebral degeneration occur which lead to loss of mental powers in middle age. All are rare. One type is Huntington's 'chorea', which owes its name to George Huntington (1850–1916), an American physician, who first described the disease. Among its cardinal features Huntington mentioned 'a tendency to insanity and suicide'. In the early stages spontaneous movements give the impression of clumsiness and fidgetiness, but, as the disease progresses, the characteristic jerking and writhing movements become more prominent, particularly affecting the face, tongue, and upper limbs, although, ultimately, all parts of the body musculature may be involved. The disease runs in families, and its pattern of distribution within families shows it to be due to a single autosomal dominant gene. It survives because the average age of onset is in the middle thirties, late enough for most carriers of the gene to have begotten children. The patients described by Huntington were said all to be descendants of a family of three brothers who had emigrated from England.

Two expectations have to be met before a disease is attributed to a dominant gene. One parent must have been affected, and the proportion of children affected must not depart significantly from one-half. Cases of Huntington's disease do occur occasionally in which neither parent seems to have been affected. In some of these, a parent has died young; in others, there is doubt about the identity of the father. The proportion of children affected has usually been found to be about one in three. The probable reason why this falls short of one-half is that a relatively high proportion of the sibship have died young; some of those affected die before birth.

The course is progressive, with increasing disability due to the loss of neurons leading to *dementia. The cerebrum atrophies and loses weight. The ventricles enlarge. The caudate nucleus and putamen of the midbrain are especially affected. Severe *depression is a common complication which may end in suicide attempts or actual suicide, which is the cause of death of 7 per cent of non-hospitalized patients.

Numerous attempts have been made to identify carriers of the gene before they enter the reproductive period of life but, so far, none has been of proven validity. In any case, predicting a progressive, incapacitating neuro-psychiatric illness in somebody who may at the time be relatively healthy raises ethical problems which may outweigh the potential eugenic advantages.

The first polymorphic DNA marker linked to Huntington's disease (HD) gene locus was discovered in 1983 and was cloned in 1993. The HD gene (*IT15*) is on the short arm of chromosome 4 (4p16.3) and regulates, controls, or encodes production of the protein huntingtin. The exact function of huntingtin is unknown but it has been suggested that it may be involved in cytoskeletal transport. The *IT15* gene in healthy individuals contains an expanded trinucleotide repeat (CAG) that ranges from 9 to 35. In contrast, those with the disorder may have about 36 to 180 repeats. The length of the expanded CAG repeats is thought to have some relation to the age at symptom onset where those with a large number of repeats tend to develop symptoms at an earlier age. Extremely large CAG repeats (of 80 or more) are often associated with a disease onset during childhood (juvenile HD or the 'Westphal variant'). It must be recognized that age of onset is variable in individuals and does not always correlate with repeat size.

With the discovery of the *IT15* gene, genetic testing for Huntington's disease has become available, which can be pre-symptomatic (i.e. at-risk individuals can have a blood test and find out if they carry the gene), or prenatal (parents having a child can find out if the fetus has inherited

the gene). Pre-implantation genetic diagnosis also exists where the genotype of an oocyte can be determined before fertilization and only non-carrier embryos are implanted. Pre-implantation genetic diagnosis became possible due to simultaneously developing in vitro fertilization techniques (IVF). IVF treatment, however, can be both psychologically and physically demanding and does not necessarily result in success. Genetic testing raises all sorts of ethical issues (see Evers-Kiebooms and Decruyenaere 1998 for a review) and has actually proved much less popular than predicted, with the number of people taking the test at about 2–16 per cent compared with the anticipated 60 per cent.   DRD

Evers-Kiebooms, G., and Decruyenaere, M. (1998). 'Predictive testing for Huntington's disease: a challenge for persons at risk and for professionals'. *Patient Education and Counselling*, 37.

Georgiou-Karistianis, N., Smith, E., Bradshaw, J. L., Chua, P., Lloyd, J., Churchyard, A., and Chiu, E. (2003). 'Future directions in research with presymptomatic individuals carrying the gene for Huntington's disease'. *Brain Research Bulletin*, 59/5.

Myrianthopoulos, N. C. (1966). 'Huntington's chorea'. *Journal of Medical Genetics*, 3.

Ross, C. A., and Margolis, R. L. (2001). 'Huntington's disease'. *Clinical Neuroscience Research*, 1.

Husserl, Edmund Gustav Albert (1859–1938). Husserl's investigations began with his *Philosophy of Arithmetic* (1891), which was intended to lay the foundations of a philosophy of mathematics. In this initial phase, Husserl analyses the concept of number from both the psychological and the logical points of view. From the psychological point of view, numbers do not only correspond to sets of elements liable to be counted, they constitute wholes beyond the capacities of immediate perception as soon as they include a large quantity of units. From this moment on, they only exist for consciousness as wholes expressed by symbols. This theory of symbolic wholes foreshadowed the basic principle which was to be fully developed by *Gestalt theorists in later years.

The second phase of Husserl's work began with the *Logical Investigations* (1900–1). His main concern was then to establish the foundations of logic outside psychology, namely against the empiricists' contention that the basic principles of logic could be ultimately referred to psychological laws. As a result, the main effort of Husserl's philosophy centred for many years on a fundamental criticism of *psychologism*, i.e. the conviction that not only logic, but every field of knowledge, would be rooted in psychology, being the science dealing with consciousness. The reasons for rejecting psychology as the fundamental science are twofold. First, from the point of view of logic and of mathematics, the psychologistic postulate leads to internal contradictions within the theoretical systems because it can be established that psychology, *as a science*, is necessarily a subsystem of a more extensive one comprising at the outset the minimal postulates which psychology needs to proceed as an organized field of knowledge. Secondly, in Husserl's time, scientific psychology, then mainly represented by early psychophysics and experimental psychology, was not in a position to furnish sufficiently rigorous proofs of its supposed founding role within the general framework of the theory of knowledge.

Consequently, the *Logical Investigations* stressed the fact that the logical structures exist independently of their psychological correlates and that the search for the psychological aspects of the logical acts as subjective experiences must itself be conducted beyond the realm of psychological science. In other words, if we want to study adequately such experiences, we are bound to turn to a descriptive science of psychic acts. Such an enterprise needs a science of phenomena, i.e. a *phenomenology*. It is, however, clear that if phenomenology is to be such a basic 'descriptive psychology' it has to cope with the *essences* of our subjective experience and not with the concrete scientific facts as evidenced in experimental psychology.

We see, thus, that in his attempt to situate the phenomena of experience in their proper subjective perspective, Husserl broadens *Brentano's theory of *intentionality up to a general epistemology, amounting finally to a radical theory of subjectivity. This implies that the descriptive dimension of phenomenology should evolve towards a *transcendental* mode of analysis, in which the point of view of natural science is 'bracketed', i.e. left out of consideration, but not eliminated because every act of consciousness is intentionally directed towards some object. This is the sense of his so-called 'reduction'.

Husserl's search for an adequate science of phenomena, as outlined in the second part of his *Logical Investigations*, was further developed in his *Ideas* (1913). In the period between 1901 and 1913 he produced two major works: *Die Idee der Phänomenologie* (1907) and *Die Philosophie als strenge Wissenschaft* (1911), in which the philosophical dimension of his epistemological strivings is thoroughly developed.   GT

Giorgi, A. (1970). *Psychology as a Human Science*.
Kockelmans, J. J. (1967). *Edmund Husserl's Phenomenological Psychology*.
Spiegelberg, H. (1960). *The Phenomenological Movement: A Historical Introduction*.
Thinès, G. (1977). *Phenomenology and the Science of Behaviour*.

Huxley, Thomas Henry (1825–95). English biologist and palaeontologist, born in London. He studied medicine but did not complete his degree. He served on the four-year cruise of HMS *Rattlesnake* (1846–50) and undertook detailed studies of marine life, for which he was elected a Fellow of the Royal Society. In 1854 he was appointed lecturer of natural history at the Royal School of Mines (now Imperial College) in London. Huxley explicitly rejected the possibility of evolution until he read Charles *Darwin's *Origin of Species* (1859), upon which he became 'Darwin's bulldog', propounding the theory in public on many critically important occasions and thus protecting Darwin from the public appearances which he found onerous and tiring. Huxley was in his own right a first-rate scientist, and he also supported popular education. His essays *Man's Place in Nature* (1863) contain his philosophy. He coined the term 'agnostic', following *Hume in his theological questioning.

White, P. (2002). *Thomas Huxley. Making the 'Man of Science'*.

hypnagogic hallucination. An extremely vivid image, usually visual, which is often experienced when one is dropping off to *sleep, or, less commonly, immediately on awakening. Unlike fully fledged *dreams, hypnagogic states are to a large extent under the control of the will and can be described to a second person on, or immediately after, their occurrence. Hypnagogic images are often said to possess an overwhelming sense of reality, with much detail and supersaturated colour.

An interpretation of hypnagogic phenomena along the lines of Freud's celebrated theory of dreams (see FREUD ON DREAMS) has been put forward by a Belgian psychologist, J. Varendonck, to whose book on *The Psychology of Day Dreams* Freud himself contributed an introduction. Varendonck places much emphasis on the role of preconscious thought and wishful thinking in hypnagogic phenomena, but it might seem more probable that these possess a physiological basis related to the incipient onset of sleep or partial awakening.   OLZ

hypnosis.
1. Background and history to the mid-20th century
2. Later developments
3. What is 'hypnosis'?
4. Hypnosis in entertainment
5. Hypnosis in treatment

1. Background and history to the mid-20th century
Modern accounts of hypnosis normally commence with the ideas of an Austrian doctor, Franz Anton *Mesmer (1735–1815), who proposed that illness was due to a disturbance of a natural force he called 'animal magnetism'. Initially using magnets, but later with 'passes' of his hands over the bodies of the afflicted, he attempted to normalize the flow of animal magnetism and so to produce a cure. Many seemed to be relieved of their symptoms, often after a 'crisis' that included fainting and convulsions. Mesmer's claims were investigated experimentally in 1784 by a team of experts led by Benjamin Franklin. The Franklin

Inquiry concluded against the existence of a 'magnetic fluid' and dismissed the whole spectacle as the potentially dangerous product of 'imagination' and 'involuntary imitation'. Nevertheless, others continued to work in the Mesmeric tradition. The Marquis de Puységur (1751–1825) developed an approach, without the need for dramatic crises, that he called 'artificial somnambulism', and the Abbé de Faria (1756–1819) described a procedure for 'lucid sleep'.

Mesmerism in England was promoted by John Elliotson (1791–1852), a professor of medicine in the University of London, but the failure of 'magnetism' once more to stand up to experimental investigation led eventually to his resignation from his post at University College Hospital. In India, James Esdaile (1808–59) used mesmeric procedures as a form of anaesthesia to carry out surgical operations. Whilst many of these 'mesmerizers' recognized the importance of psychological processes it was with James Braid (1795–1860), a Scottish doctor working in England, that the mantle of Mesmer finally slipped away. Braid initially emphasized the similarities between some mesmeric states and sleep and promoted the new term 'hypnosis'. He also described a novel way of producing this state in which the individual stared at an object, creating 'visual fatigue' and 'nervous sleep'. His later, more psychological view was that the crucial factor was not eye fixation or neural fatigue but the concentration by the individual on a single thought or idea, a process he labelled 'monoideism'.

Braid's ideas had little impact in England but in Europe they were taken up by E. Azam (1822–99), a French physician and surgeon, from whom they spread to the Salpêtrière Institute in Paris where Jean Martin *Charcot was an influential neurologist and surgeon. Charcot noted the similarity between symptoms such as paralysis and amnesia shown by hysterics and phenomena produced by hypnosis. He concluded that the two were pathological conditions with similar neurological mechanisms. Recent brain-imaging evidence supports the belief that hypnosis and hysteria involve similar brain processes, though not the view that both are pathological states (Halligan et al. 2000). Charcot's views were challenged within France by Hippolyte Bernheim (1837–1919), a professor of medicine in Nancy, who argued that hypnosis is based on normal psychological processes underlying suggestion and suggestibility. In the longer term it is the views of Bernheim that have prevailed. Charcot nevertheless had a considerable impact on influential contemporaries such as Pierre *Janet, who developed the idea that hypnosis might depend on dissociation, and Sigmund *Freud, who abandoned his early use of hypnosis in favour of free association.

With the development of chemical anaesthetics in surgery, Freud's move away from hypnosis in therapy and the rise in psychology of *behaviourism, interest in hypnosis had waned by the end of the 19th century and was not effectively revived for 50 or so years. One important exception to this trend was the publication of *Hypnosis and Suggestibility* in 1933 by an American psychologist, Clark *Hull, who showed experimentally that, whilst hypnosis did not convey extraordinary physical or mental powers, the classical phenomena of hypnosis such as anaesthesia, analgesia, and amnesia were valid and reproducible. Another significant contribution in this low period came via Milton Erickson (1901–80), a former student of Hull's, who adopted a less formal and more person-centred approach to hypnosis. Erickson's methods have been very influential in developing a particular form of hypnosis used in therapy, though they have remained outside the mainstream of clinical and academic research.

2. Later developments

In 1955 the British Medical Association produced a favourable report on the use of hypnosis in medical and therapeutic settings and in the United Kingdom more recently university-based training courses have been established in the use of hypnosis for doctors, dentists, and psychologists (Heap and Aravind 2002). The revival of academic and research interest in the mid-1950s, however, took place primarily in America and found hypnosis placed firmly in the domain of psychology. Even so, theoretical debate continued to reflect the dispute between Charcot and Bernheim. That is, does hypnosis depend on a fundamentally altered state of consciousness or is it a product of normal, everyday psychological processes? This has been characterized as the 'state/non-state debate' (see Kirsch and Lynn 1995). On the 'state', or special-process, side Ernest Hilgard, Kenneth Bowers, Frederick Evans, and others developed Janet's view that hypnosis involved the dissociation or division of some mental activities away from the main flow of conscious mental processing. The state view typically sees hypnosis as something that happens to the individual as a consequence of the hypnotic induction procedure. Others, notably Theodore Barber, emphasized a 'non-state', or sociocognitive, approach based on normal psychological factors such as role play (Theodore Sarbin), compliance (Graham Wagstaff), and expectancy (Irving Kirsch). The sociocognitive view portrays the hypnotized individual as being actively engaged in strategies (consciously or unconsciously) to achieve the appropriate effects without the need to assume the presence of an altered state of consciousness created by a hypnotic induction. With very few exceptions, however, the proponents of both views agree that hypnotic phenomena are not the product of deliberate faking—they are experienced as 'real' and involuntary. In hypnotic reliving ('age regression'), for example, the individual has the clear experience of being younger and of producing childlike drawings. However, research has shown that this is not a literal return to an earlier developmental stage and the drawings do not correspond to those actually produced by the individual at that age (Nash 1987). In this sense the 'reliving' is a role play or enactment, but it is a wholly believed-in enactment with an 'as-real' quality.

A major practical concern for hypnosis researchers in the mid-20th century was the construction of scales to measure susceptibility to hypnotic suggestions. The best known are the Harvard Group Scale of Hypnotic Susceptibility (devised by Ronald Shor and Emily Orne in 1962) and the Stanford Hypnotic Susceptibility Scales (constructed by Andre Weitzenhoffer and Hilgard between 1959 and 1962), which were also produced in shortened clinical and child versions. All of these commence with a hypnotic induction procedure and consist of a number of test suggestions, such as an arm feeling heavier, the inability to open one's eyes when challenged to do so, and amnesia. Researchers working from the non-state perspective produced scales such as the Creative Imagination Scale (Sheryl Wilson and Barber, 1978) and the Barber Suggestibility Scale (Barber, 1969), using similar sets of test suggestions but with the hypnotic induction procedures omitted or optional. More recently devised scales are the Carleton University Responsiveness to Suggestion Scale (Nicholas Spanos and his colleagues, 1981) and the Waterloo–Stanford Group Scale of Hypnotic Susceptibility (Kenneth Bowers, 1998). All these scales are scored in terms of the number of test suggestions that the participant responds to and in general they correlate reasonably well with each other. Individuals vary very widely in their hypnotic suggestibility as measured by these scales, with approximately one-quarter of the population being classed as 'low in hypnotic suggestibility', a similar number as 'high', and the majority somewhere between the two. The scales show very good test–retest reliability over up to twenty years. This suggests that hypnotic suggestibility is a stable personality trait, though Spanos and the Carleton University group have devised a training programme to increase an individual's scores on hypnotizability tests. There is a general tendency for hypnotic suggestibility scores to peak between the ages of 9 and 12 years. Consequently hypnotic procedures have been seen as especially suitable for use with children (Olness and Kohen 1996). Hypnotic suggestibility tends to be higher in groups and professions with creative and artistic backgrounds and also in professional sports people, but no reliable differences have been found in hypnotic suggestibility between males and females.

The work on hypnotic suggestibility scales has demonstrated that people can respond to the test suggestions without first receiving a formal hypnotic induction procedure. This indicates that individuals vary naturally in their responsiveness to this sort of suggestion. Wayne Braffman and Kirsch have identified this natural capacity as 'imaginative suggestibility', which may then be influenced by the use of hypnotic induction procedures (Kirsch and Braffman 1999). The ways in which suggestibility can be altered by a hypnotic induction is currently under investigation. Overall, it appears that 'hypnotic suggestibility' is an extension of a natural ability that we all possess to a varying degree and does not depend on an unusual state of mind.

3. What is 'hypnosis'?

Hypnosis has two major components. One is 'trance', the mental state of focused attention, disattention to extraneous stimuli, and absorption in some central thought, image or idea that is produced by instructions given during the hypnosis induction period. Hypnosis scripts typically include phrases such as, 'look steadily at the spot on the wall' (focusing of attention), 'let other sounds and sensation slip to the back of your mind' (disattention to extraneous stimuli), and 'bring to mind a garden, just imagine yourself there, notice the flowers' (absorption in imagery). In this sense 'trance' is similar to other everyday 'entranced' states such as when we are daydreaming or become absorbed in a film, a book, or a physical activity and lose track of time. Similar time distortions also occur spontaneously in hypnosis. Trance in this account does of course correspond to a particular 'state', but it is a familiar state of mind not the uniquely altered state of consciousness proposed by traditional state theory.

It is assumed that the establishment of trance facilitates responsiveness to suggestion, which is the other component of hypnosis. 'Suggestion' refers to the, usually verbal, input from the hypnotist that is intended to produce a change in the way individuals perceive themselves or the world. A typical suggestion might be: 'Your left hand is beginning to feel lighter and wanting to float upwards all by itself.' In the majority of people this will eventually result in their hand beginning to rise effortlessly upwards without any intention on their part to move it. In this way suggestion can produce specific, and sometimes very unusual, effects such as relaxation, analgesia, anaesthesia, limb paralysis, involuntary movement, amnesia, changes in blood flow, visual hallucinations, or the feeling of having changed sex. Whilst the hypnotic trance itself is neither unusual nor dangerous, suggestions given in hypnosis without due care could lead to unwanted consequences. The suggested reliving of a traumatic incident without appropriate psychological support could result in the individual being retraumatized, for example, or suggestions in the form of leading questions might contribute to the development of false memories.

Many suggestions in hypnosis are intended to act at the time they are presented. Post-hypnotic suggestions, however, are given in hypnosis but have their effect afterwards.

In the Harvard scale one item involves a tapping sound accompanied by the suggestion that when that sound is heard again the participant will touch their ankle but will forget having been given the suggestion. If this post-hypnotic suggestion is successful the participant will carry out the suggested action when the tapping sound is repeated after hypnosis without knowing why they have done so.

The examples so far have implied that another person, 'the hypnotist', delivers the induction instructions and the suggestions in hypnosis. However, individuals can take themselves through hypnosis procedures, using their own inner speech to give themselves suggestions This procedure is self-hypnosis. There are some differences in the subjective experience of self-hypnosis and hypnosis conducted with another person but it is usually assumed that the underlying processes are essentially the same.

There are at present no convincing studies to show what neurophysiological changes, if any, uniquely accompany the hypnotic trance state. However, a number of neuroimaging studies have demonstrated changes in activity in appropriate brain areas in response to a variety of suggestions in hypnosis, supporting the view that such suggestions produce genuine changes in perceptual experience or voluntary motor function. As a result hypnosis is increasingly used as a tool in psychological and neuropsychological research to explore normal processes such as those involved in memory, pain experience, and control of movement. The changes it produces are reliable and reversible. Formal assessments of experimental hypnosis procedures have found that after-effects such as headache, drowsiness, or dizziness are no more frequent than after attending a lecture or taking part in a non-hypnotic psychological experiment.

4. Hypnosis in entertainment
From the time of Mesmer onwards, hypnotic phenomena have been used for entertainment and this continues in the form of hypnosis acts in theatres and on television. Though some hypnotic shows may have used stooges, the majority appear to depend on genuine hypnotic phenomena produced in highly hypnotically suggestible volunteers. Hypnosis shows typically commence with the selection of suitable individuals from the audience through simple suggestibility tests—such as the hand-lock (one of the tests on the Harvard scale). The success of the stage show then depends on dramatic presentation coupled with rapid induction techniques, suggestions of amnesia (adding to the feeling of mystery for the volunteers afterwards), and the use of suggestions with comic potential, such as that the individual is a prize fighter who will adopt a boxing pose every time a bell is rung (McGill 1996). The volunteers may also bring with them from previous shows, films, books, and so on, expectations that

hypnosis is very rapid, that the hypnotized individual appears to be deeply asleep, that they will be out of control when hypnotized, and so forth. All of these serve as self-suggestions and affect the experience the hypnotized person has on stage. In contrast to the absence of statutory controls in the United Kingdom over other uses of hypnosis, stage hypnosis is regulated by Parliament through the Hypnotism Act 1952 supplemented by a series of Model Conditions issued by the Home Office that restrict the way in which stage hypnosis shows can be advertised and conducted. The current consensus is that, provided the statutory restrictions are observed, there is no greater danger to the general public from taking part in stage hypnosis than there is from other legitimate forms of entertainment. The possibility remains that some vulnerable individuals could be harmed by their experiences on stage, but this appears to be extremely rare.

5. Hypnosis in treatment
Hypnosis is not a form of treatment in its own right. The induction of trance combined with appropriate suggestions, however, is increasingly used as an adjunct in medical, dental, and psychological settings to facilitate and support other forms of treatment (Lynn, Kirsch, and Rhue 1996, Heap and Aravind 2002). It does this in a number of ways, including the alteration of sensory experiences and motor responses, promoting physiological and immune system changes, facilitating the use of imagery, enhancing relaxation, controlling stress responses, and supporting the safe recall of earlier experiences. Post-hypnotic suggestions can be used to ensure that helpful responses, such as relaxation, learned during hypnosis sessions, also occur outside hypnosis in response to cues in everyday situations. An important aspect of the use of hypnosis in therapy is that patients and clients are taught self-hypnosis techniques so that they can practise them for themselves and can repeat helpful therapeutic suggestions in their self-hypnosis sessions. In dentistry, uses for hypnosis include the control of pain, anxiety, salivation, bleeding, gagging (retching), and bruxism (teeth grinding). Medical applications include the management of gastrointestinal disorders (such as irritable bowel syndrome), skin disorders (such as eczema, psoriasis, and warts), respiratory disorders (such as asthma), childbirth, surgical procedures (controlling pain, reducing anaesthetic use and blood loss, and speeding recovery), and in alleviating the unpleasant side effects of cancer treatments (such as nausea and vomiting). Clinical and counselling psychologists use hypnosis to facilitate their own therapeutic techniques in the treatment of a wide range of conditions such as phobias, post-traumatic stress disorder, social anxiety, eating disorders (obesity, bulimia, and anorexia), stuttering, depression, chronic pain, smoking, and other habit disorders (such as nail biting, bedwetting, and hair

pulling). In addition hypnosis is used by educational and sports psychologists, speech therapists, nurses, and others in their respective professional areas. Much of the evidence for the effectiveness of hypnosis as an adjunct to treatment is based on clinical case studies, though there are growing numbers of controlled clinical trials and experimental studies that support the efficacy of hypnosis —especially in the areas of pain control and as an adjunct to cognitive–behavioural therapy (Kirsch, Montomery, and Sapirstein 1995, Montgomery, DuHamel, and Redd 2000). An important advantage of using hypnosis in this way is that the benefits of the combined approach appear to increase over time. It seems likely that this is because the participants are taught self-hypnosis procedures that they continue to practise.

As a final note on terminology, it is misleading to bundle these very varied adjunctive uses of hypnosis under the umbrella term 'hypnotherapy', or to refer to the practitioners themselves as 'hypnotherapists'. They remain doctors, dentists, psychologists, etc. who use hypnosis alongside their other profession skills in pursuit of their different objectives. As such their work with hypnosis is carried out within the ethical and practical boundaries set by their own professional bodies. The terms 'hypnotherapy' and 'hypnotherapist' are more appropriately applied to the use of hypnosis procedures as a form of alternative therapy and to the lay practitioners who carry it out. At present there are no statutory regulations in the United Kingdom concerning training in hypnotherapy or who may call themselves a hypnotherapist, though some countries have imposed legal restrictions.   DAO

Gauld, A. (1992). *A History of Hypnotism*.

Halligan, P. W., Athwal, B. S., Oakley, D. A., and Frackowiack, R. S. J. (2000). 'Imaging hypnotic paralysis: implications for conversion hysteria'. *Lancet*, 355.

Heap, N., and Aravind, K. K. (2002). *Hartland's Medical and Dental Hypnosis* (4th edn.).

Kirsch, I., and Braffman, W. (1999). 'Correlates of hypnotisability: the first empirical study'. *Contemporary Hypnosis*, 16.

——and Lynn, S. J. (1995). 'The altered state of hypnosis: changes in the theoretical landscape'. *American Psychologist*, 50.

——Montgomery, G., and Sapirstein, G. (1995). 'Hypnosis as an adjunct to Cognitive Behavioural Psychotherapy: a meta-analysis'. *Journal of Counselling and Clinical Psychology*, 63.

Lynn, S. J., Kirsch, I., and Rhue, J. W. (eds.) (1996). *Casebook of Clinical Hypnosis*.

McGill, O. (1996). *The New Encyclopaedia of Stage Hypnotism*.

Montgomery, G. H., DuHamel, K. N., and Redd, W. H. (2000). 'A meta-analysis of hypnotically induced analgesia: how effective is hypnosis?' *Journal of Clinical and Experimental Hypnosis*, 48.

Nash, M. (1987). 'What, if anything, is regressed about hypnotic age regression? A review of the empirical literature'. *Psychological Bulletin*, 102.

Olness, K., and Kohen, D. P. (1996). *Hypnosis and Hypnotherapy with Children* (3rd edn.).

hypnosis, experimental. In the course of the 20th century, interest in hypnosis largely passed from the physician to the experimental psychologist, whose concern is with its nature and mechanisms rather than with its therapeutic efficacy. While a few scattered experiments, such as those of D. R. L. Delboeuf, were reported towards the end of the 19th century, the modern era in the study of hypnotism may be said to have been ushered in by the work of Clark L.*Hull and his co-workers at Yale University in the early 1930s. While militantly disowning hypnotism's murky past, Hull insisted that hypnosis is an essentially normal phenomenon that can be studied in precisely the same way as any other mental capacity which varies from one individual to another. His book published in 1933 represents the first systematic attempt to apply the experimental and statistical methods of modern psychology to the study of hypnosis and suggestibility.

Hull's work was to a considerable extent designed to cast doubt on the extravagant claims current in some quarters that individual capacity in the hypnotic state might transcend the limits of the normal. Thus it has been argued that exceptional feats of sensory discrimination, of muscular strength, or of *memory might be performed in the hypnotic state, suggesting that hypnosis *per se* enhanced many aspects of human capacity. Hull and his co-workers were able to show that, whereas hypnosis as such does not appear to confer any obvious advantages, it is none the less possible to influence human performance, sometimes dramatically, by hypnotic suggestion. For example, he produced evidence of some increase in muscular capacity, more especially in sustained resistance to fatigue, and alterations in threshold of a variety of sensory stimuli, whereby the lower limits of intensity of stimulation necessary to produce a conscious sensation were appreciably raised. As regards memory, whereas no improvement in the reproduction of recently memorized material under hypnosis could be demonstrated, there was some evidence that memories of childhood might become more readily accessible. Hull's work, while producing no real evidence of the transcendence of normal capacity in hypnosis, did undoubtedly demonstrate the reality of many classical hypnotic phenomena (for example, hypnotic anaesthesia or analgesia and post-hypnotic amnesia) under reasonably well-controlled experimental conditions. His work also served to bring out the essential continuity between the effects of suggestion in the waking and the hypnotic states.

Experimental hypnosis rapidly expanded in the 1950s and 1960s, some of its foremost representatives being T. X. Barber, E. R. Hilgard, M. T. Orne, and T. R. Sarbin. One of the main preoccupations at this period was the construction of standardized scales of hypnotic susceptibility, of which the best known and most widely used were the Stanford scales devised by A. M. Weitzenhoffer and

E. R. Hilgard in 1961. The rationale of their construction and use was well described by Hilgard (1965) and one need only comment here on some of the more interesting findings. In the first place, contrary to traditional belief, there is no real evidence that women are more readily hypnotizable than men, or are capable of greater depth of hypnosis. In the second place, a critical period seems to exist as regards hypnotic susceptibility. While it has long been known that children are in general more easily hypnotized than adults, it has been found that children between the ages of 8 and 12 are more easily hypnotized than either older or younger children. The advantage may lie in part in the fact that whereas children of 8 and below find sustained concentration difficult and are readily distracted, children above the age of 12 or so have developed greater powers of self-criticism and are consequently less suggestible. Although changes in hypnotic susceptibility over the adult lifespan do not appear to be striking, the natural history of hypnosis is certainly deserving of closer study.

From Hull onwards, experimental methods have been widely used to study such classical phenomena of hypnosis as hypnotic anaesthesia or analgesia (Hilgard and Hilgard 1975) and sensory deceptions or *hallucinations. In some ingenious experiments, Hilgard has shown that it is not difficult to induce selective deafness for sounds of weak intensity—for example, the ticking of a watch—without interfering with the subject's perception of the experimenter's voice. In susceptible subjects, it may even prove possible to effect profound attenuation of sensation within a particular sensory modality, such as touch or pain. Experiments by A. M. Halliday and A. A. Mason (1964) have, however, shown that, in such cases, the nervous messages from the sense organs do reach the relevant areas of the cerebral cortex, where they give rise to electrical responses ('*evoked potentials') of normal amplitude. It therefore seems that the conscious sensory responses with which these electrical activities are ordinarily correlated must undergo some form of suppression or dissociation. That this is so is strongly indicated by a dramatic experiment of Hilgard's, in which he showed that a hypnotized subject in whom a profound loss of pain sense had been induced by suggestion, and who entirely denied feeling pain when appropriately stimulated, did in fact admit to doing so when tested by automatic writing, the content of which was ostensibly unknown to him. This is a classical example of hypnotic dissociation of the kind much discussed by Pierre *Janet (see HYPNOSIS) and other early expositors of the relations between hypnosis and *hysteria. It strongly suggests that hypnotic anaesthesia and analgesia are true dissociative phenomena rather than mere exaggerations of ordinary suggestibility.

Sensory deceptions (illusions) and even hallucinations induced by suggestion have also been demonstrated on occasion, using healthy, volunteer subjects in an experimental situation, but only in those whose susceptibility to hypnosis is unusually high (Weitzenhoffer 1947, Hilgard 1965). In such cases, a distinction should be made between the generation of behaviour appropriate to an imagined object, which is not difficult to induce, and the production of what is described by the subject as a true perceptual experience (hallucination proper). For example, Hilgard has shown that many subjects will react positively to the suggestion that a fly has alighted, say, on their face, by grimacing or brushing it off. This might almost be regarded as play-acting in the sense of Sarbin and others who stress the 'role-playing' element in hypnosis. Even so, a few such subjects will say when asked that the experience was very real and lifelike, suggesting a true positive hallucination. Further experiments, in which it is suggested that the subject will perceive two dim lights, when only one is shown, likewise on occasion elicit surprisingly convincing reports of a hallucinated experience. It is possible in such cases that suggestion in alliance with the artificial hypnotic state has produced a condition akin to *dreaming, in which a visual image can assume the vividness and reality of an actual external object. At all events, such phenomena seem to magnify, if not transcend, the effects of suggestion in the ordinary waking state.

Similar considerations also arise in connection with so-called age regression, in which a subject aged perhaps 20 is told that he will experience himself as he was when, say, 10 years old (Hilgard 1965, Gill and Brenman 1966). He will thereupon comport himself, superficially at least, in accordance with his suggested age. Without further or more specific suggestions being given, he will commonly write or draw in a strikingly more juvenile manner and may even develop an apparent disorientation, stating, for example, that he is in the school he attended at the age of 10 and that the experimenter is a schoolmaster at that time known to him. In such cases it is often difficult to decide whether the subject is an accomplished, if unintentional, actor or whether there is a genuine reactivation of long superseded attitudes and modes of behaviour, i.e. a true regression to an earlier state of the person and genuine re-enaction of the past. One simple test might be to suggest to him that he should progress rather than regress in age, and see to what extent he can duplicate the presumed behaviour of a very much older person. It is also entirely conjectural whether regression, as some believe, can be pursued into earliest infancy.

As might be expected, experimentalists have given much attention to the relationship between hypnosis and ordinary *sleep (see Hull 1933). Although subjects often refer to lethargy, drowsiness, and diminished contact with reality as characteristic of hypnosis, it seems clear that this state, whatever its nature, differs categorically from normal sleep, with or without dreaming. As James Braid observed in the 19th century, the muscles do not relax as in ordinary sleep and the subject does not drop an object held in the hand as he becomes hypnotized. Further, *reflexes which disappear in sleep can be elicited normally in the hypnotic state. Finally, study of the electrical rhythms of the brain (*electroencephalography) shows that the electroencephalogram (EEG) in hypnosis in no way resembles that in any of the recognized states of sleep but is essentially identical with that of ordinary wakefulness. From the electrophysiological point of view, therefore, the hypnotized person is awake.

Let us now turn briefly to theories of hypnosis. William *James wrote in 1890 that the suggestion theory of hypnosis may be approved, provided that we regard the trance state as its essential prerequisite. Although the term 'hypnotic trance' is seldom used today, most people regard the hypnotic state as something *sui generis* with its own peculiar properties. In addition to greatly enhanced suggestibility, these are commonly said to consist in voluntary suspension of initiative, restriction of attention to a narrow field, and marked reduction in self-consciousness and critical appraisal. Some would add that the hypnotized person, much like the dreamer, is not fully in contact with reality and exhibits a facile mode of reasoning ('trance logic') in some respects characteristic of childhood. Although the state of hypnosis lacks definite physiological or biochemical criteria of an altered state of consciousness, it does not of course necessarily follow that no such criteria will ever be discovered. Indeed, it is only in comparatively recent years that firm physiological correlates of ordinary dreaming have been securely established.

None the less, this lack of physiological criteria of the hypnotic state, together with its resemblances to many phenomena in ordinary waking life involving the effects of suggestion, has induced some recent workers, in particular Barber, who has published much useful work in experimental hypnosis, to argue that the concept of a trance state is an unnecessary assumption (Barber 1969). As he sees it, hypnosis is to be viewed as an essentially normal state of waking consciousness in which a voluntary compact between experimenter and subject enables each to exercise his respective role, which is, so to speak, enshrined in traditional expectation. Although such a view has the merits of parsimony, it fails to account for many features of the hypnotic state, such as spontaneous post-hypnotic amnesia in highly susceptible subjects, loss or diminution of pain sense, and the operation of post-hypnotic suggestion. Further, the production of sense deceptions and hallucinations is more reminiscent of the effects brought about in indisputably altered states of consciousness, such as may be produced by drugs or toxic agencies, than the ordinary operations of waking suggestibility.

To say this is not of course to deny that there are important psychogenic factors in hypnosis which are closely related to suggestion and fantasy in daily life. Josephine Hilgard, in particular, has emphasized the links between susceptibility to hypnosis and the propensity to become immersed in novels, plays, and films and to participate in the fictional existence of the characters. She likewise stresses the element of identification with parents or other emotionally significant features in early life, and indeed calls attention to many aspects of hypnosis, among them the blurring of fantasy and reality, the ready involvement in games of pretence, and the tendency to believe uncritically in the pronouncement of others, which may be viewed as 'part and parcel of childhood' (Hilgard 1965: 343–74). But just as dreaming, in itself essentially psychogenic, presupposes the altered state of consciousness characteristic of a certain stage of sleep, so it may be argued that hypnosis, likewise essentially psychogenic, presupposes the less dramatic alteration of consciousness formerly known as the hypnotic trance.

In conclusion, one may ask whether experimental hypnosis presents any hazards. By and large, the procedure seems harmless enough, though medical men rightly warn that it can be dangerous if the subjects should happen to include emotionally disturbed individuals or those with a history of psychiatric illness. In such cases, the experimenter may well lack both the knowledge and the experience to handle the emotional relationships, positive or negative, which may unwittingly be generated in the process. A related question is whether experimental hypnosis calls for ethical guidelines. We know, for example, that certain types of psychological experiment involve calculated deceit, as in the work of Stanley Milgram on obedience. Milgram explained to his subjects that it was necessary for the purposes of his experiment to deliver shocks of potentially lethal intensity to other human beings, and he found, somewhat to his surprise, that many subjects were prepared to undertake this in spite of their ignorance of the deceit that was being practised upon them. (See OBEDIENCE, MILGRAM ON.) If such an experiment were repeated under conditions of hypnosis, it is entirely possible that even greater conformity with the instructions of the experimenter would be forthcoming. While it remains true that, in general, hypnotized subjects cannot be induced to perform actions that are morally repugnant to them, and that the danger of crimes being committed as a result of hypnotic suggestion appears to be extremely small, there is no doubt that any form of experiment on the effects of suggestion, with or without hypnosis, must be regarded as open to potential abuse. It is to be hoped that the psychological fraternity will take due notice of these hazards and introduce appropriate ethical guidelines for the conduct of human experiments, in particular those making use of hypnosis.   OLZ

Barber, T. X. (1969). *Hypnosis: A Scientific Approach.*

Gill, M. M., and Brenman, M. (1966). *Hypnosis and Related States.*

Halliday, A. M., and Mason, A. A. (1964). 'The effect of hypnotic anaesthesia on cortical responses'. *Journal of Neurology, Neurosurgery and Psychology*, 27.

Hilgard, E. R. (1965). *Hypnotic Susceptibility.*

——and Hilgard, J. R. (1975). *Hypnotism and the Relief of Pain.*

Hull, C. L. (1933). *Hypnosis and Suggestibility: An Experimental Approach.*

Milgram, S. (1974). *Obedience to Authority.*

Weitzenhoffer, A. M. (1947). *Hypnotism: An Objective Study in Suggestibility.*

hysteria. Long-supposed a disease of women, hysteria was attributed by *Hippocrates to the movement of the womb (*hystera*) from its normal anatomical site into other parts of the body. The feelings of constriction in the throat, so typical of hysteria (*The Suffocation of the Mother*, by Edward Jorden, 1603), were thought to be caused by the uterus becoming lodged in that region. It followed, therefore, that men, since they do not have a womb, would not be affected by this disease, although Thomas Sydenham (1682) maintained that they were able to suffer from the symptoms experienced by the opposite sex. The belief that hysteria was a disorder confined to women had a long innings, and *Freud's report to the Vienna Medical Society in 1886 that men too could be affected by it was not well received. As an elderly surgeon remarked, 'But my dear sir, how can you talk such nonsense? Hysteria means the uterus. So how can men be hysterical?' (Stafford Clark 1967).

Like many other words used in psychiatry, hysteria has been given many meanings. The following list shows how a disease that was once considered to be a single entity has been given different interpretations according to the nature of the symptoms and the theories proposed to explain them. (i) Hysteria as a personality disorder: for example, histrionic personality, or attention-seeking personality. (ii) Conversion hysteria, presenting a variety of neurological disturbances such as paralysis, convulsions, losses of sensation, blindness, speech abnormalities, and ataxic gait. (iii) Hysteria as a dissociation phenomenon manifested as fugues, twilight states, amnesias, and multiple personality. (iv) Hysteria as a disease entity affecting women. There is also (v) hysteria as a term of abuse.

(i) *Hysteria as a personality disorder.* Hysterical personality is one of those misnomers that bedevils the subject, largely because it is often assumed that individuals showing the features of it are liable to develop other forms of hysteria. On the whole, the evidence does not favour this belief, and the term should be discarded in favour of one of the synonyms. The dominant characteristics are shallow, labile emotions, manipulative behaviour, a tendency to overdramatize situations, a lack of self-criticism, and a fickle flirtatiousness with little capacity for sustained sexual relationships. It has been said that these qualities add up to a caricature of femininity; and as men are rarely labelled hysterical personalities it is likely that the old association of hysteria with uterine disturbance is responsible for the transformation of hysteria as a disease into an adjectival description of a constellation of certain behavioural characteristics.

(ii) *Conversion hysteria.* Freud's theory of hysteria, based largely on his treatment of female patients in late 19th-century Vienna, proposed that repressed sexual conflicts, which, if brought to consciousness, would arouse anxiety and distress, were converted into physical symptoms that symbolized the repressed wish and permitted the anxiety to be dispelled—the so-called primary gain. As Fenichel (1955) wrote, 'In conversion, symptomatic changes of physical function occur which, unconsciously and in a distorted form, give expression to instinctual impulses that previously had been repressed.' The lack of emotional response of the patient to her symptoms, for example a paralysed limb, was referred to by *Janet as 'la belle indifference des hystériques'. In fact hysterics are by no means as free from *anxiety as they might appear to be. Understandably, considering the time and place of Freud's original communications on hysteria, his emphasis on repressed sexuality in the female as a cause of neurosis aroused a good deal of hostility. But *Charcot once remarked, 'Hystérie, c'est toujours la chose sexuelle' —a point re-emphasized by Freud when he wrote, 'I do not think I am exaggerating when I insist that the great majority of severe neuroses in women have their origin in the marriage bed'.

As time has gone by this emphasis on repressed sexual drives as a cause of conversion hysteria has declined. Some writers have considered the roles of anxiety and *depression in the genesis of hysterical symptoms, and others have stressed the importance of secondary gain, particularly when symptoms persist in compensation cases following accidental injury. The hysteric is nothing if not suggestible, and susceptibility to suggestion, especially in those of a relatively unsophisticated nature, could be an important determinant of the site and type of a conversion symptom.

(iii) *Hysteria as a dissociation phenomenon.* Janet considered *dissociation to be an important component of some hysterical symptoms. These include fugues (wandering away from one's usual environment, with subsequent amnesia), trances, multiple personality, and twilight states. The individual who enters into a fugue state is sometimes escaping from an intolerable situation or suffering from a severe depression. This wandering behaviour has been equated with an act of suicide, with the patient seeking some state of nirvana which will free him from his worldly cares and responsibilities.

Much attention has been given to the phenomenon of *multiple personality, and the famous case of Sally

Beauchamp, described by Morton Prince (1854–1929), has been succeeded by other well-publicized examples. There is reason to think that the subject's suggestibility and the amount of attention focused on the alleged change of personality to some extent perpetuate and elaborate the phenomenon. Multiple personality can sometimes be of forensic interest when the defendant blames her alter ego for the offences of which she is accused. Obviously it is difficult to prove beyond reasonable doubt claims of this kind. In any case, multiple personality is a rare condition, and only its dramatic and bizarre nature is reason for the disproportionate interest in it. (See DISSOCIATION OF THE PERSONALITY.)

(iv) *Hysteria as a disease entity.* The old concept of hysteria as a disease peculiar to women was gradually abandoned in the face of evidence that a great variety of hysterical symptoms affect men as well as women. The revival of the disease entity concept by psychiatrists in St Louis, USA, under the label Briquet's syndrome—the name derives from a French author who published a monograph on hysteria in 1859—has been criticized on the grounds that it appears to be resurrecting the ancient myth of a sexually determined illness confined to women. Indeed, many of its symptoms are functional disorders of the female reproductive system. Multiple surgery to treat such symptoms, and a variety of other abdominal complaints of a psychogenic nature, result in what is known in some hospitals as 'the thick file syndrome'. This is largely because of the sheer number of the patient's records and reports on multiple investigations that accumulate over the years. It could be argued that 'thick files' could not develop in a society which did not have well-developed medical and surgical technology, but all the same such patients are not the most welcome in busy outpatient departments, not only because of the time required to unravel their histories but also because of the sense of therapeutic and diagnostic hopelessness that overcomes the examining physician.

(v) *Hysteria as a term of abuse.* The layman—and sometimes the medical practitioner—faced by tiresome, noisy, and overdramatic behaviour may be inclined to react with 'Pull yourself together and don't be so d— hysterical'. As the behaviour that provokes this kind of response has

much in common with the chief characteristics of the hysterical personality, it is more likely to arouse antipathy when the subject is a woman. An 'attack of the vapours' is an older term used to describe such 'hysterical' behaviour by women; when the 'wandering womb' hypothesis of hysteria was discarded, it was replaced by the notion that noxious vapours could rise up from the womb to the brain and produce symptoms which today would be called conversion hysteria, especially hysterical convulsions.

Although there can be no doubt that psychological disturbances play a considerable part in the genesis of hysterical symptoms, it is important to realize that, in nearly two-thirds of patients presenting to hospital with such symptoms, there will be some evidence of pre-existing or developing brain injury or disease (Slater 1965, Whitlock 1967, Merskey and Buhrich 1975). It has been suggested that the capacity for manifesting acute hysterical illness is something which is built into the central nervous system to protect it from overwhelming stress. If the brain is damaged or diseased, there is an increased possibility for this innate mechanism to spring into action, especially if an added psychological stress serves as a trigger. Thus hysterical symptoms may be the first indication that some hitherto unsuspected brain disease is developing. Conversion hysteria in older patients with no previous evidence of psychiatric morbidity should alert the physician to this possibility. Indeed, given the high incidence of brain disease in patients with hysteria, it has been suggested that the time has come for the word as a noun signifying a disease entity to be relegated to psychiatric history. But this is unlikely to happen for, as Lewis (1975) has written, 'A tough old word like hysteria dies very hard. It tends to outlive its obituarists'.   FAW

Fenichel, O. (1955). *The Psychoanalytic Theory of Neurosis.*

Lewis, A. (1975). 'The survival of hysteria'. *Psychological Medicine,* 5.

Merskey, H., and Buhrich, N. A. (1975). 'Hysteria and organic brain disease'. *British Journal of Medical Psychology,* 48.

Slater, E. (1965). 'The diagnosis of hysteria'. *British Medical Journal,* 1.

Stafford Clark, D. (1967). *What Freud Really Said.*

Whitlock, F. A. (1967). 'The aetiology of hysteria'. *Acta psychologica Scandinavica,* 43.

I

Ibn 'Arabi (Ibn Al-'Arabi, Sheikh Abu-Bakr Muhammad ibn-'Ali Muhyiuddin, called the Greatest Sheikh/Sheikh Al-Akbar/Doctor Maximus, 1164–1240). He was born in Murcia, Spain, a descendant of the illustrious Arabian family of Hatim Tai, and died in Damascus. His work influenced Western thought and literature: for example, Asín Palacios and others have argued for textual copying by Dante in the *Divine Comedy*. He was a most influential *Sufi teacher who wrote, according to *Jami, over 500 works, mostly in Mecca and Damascus; in 1234 he himself reckoned them at 298 volumes. About 90 are extant, mostly in manuscript. Ibn 'Arabi's *Tadbirat* (Managements) is an important manual of Sufi training. The *Fusus al-Hikam* (Bezels, or Phases, of Wisdom), written in 1230, is his best-known work. Each of its 27 chapters is named after a prophet or teacher and deals with the Sufi principles which that teacher is said to represent. He is associated with the doctrine of Unity of Being (*Wahdat al-Wujud*), which is characterized by his critics as pantheism. Although he claimed to have no master and to have been initiated into Sufism by Khidr, a spiritual being, A. E. Affifi (1939) places him firmly in the context of the Spanish Sufi thought of his time. His work constantly appeals to the Koran and traditions of Muhammad, though his interpretations are idiosyncratic. Two other major works are *The Meccan Revelations* and *The Interpreter of Desires*, both attacked by pietists as mere love poetry but successfully defended by the author as mystical allegories. By a curious tradition in the East, pious men sporadically assemble groups of students and charge them with the literary study of Ibn 'Arabi's works. The intention is either to exhaust their capacity for research, or for them to discover the authorities who state that Ibn 'Arabi's works are not meant to be understood but to produce bafflement. This realization, according to these Sufis, drives the students to seek the current living exemplar of the teaching who alone can explain the writings.   IS

Affifi, A. E. (1939). *The Mystical Philosophy of Muhiyid Din Ibnul Arabi*.

Ibn Bajjah (Abu-Bakr Muhammad ibn-Yahya ibn-al-Sa'igh, *c*.1106–38) A major *Islamic thinker, poet and musician, scientist, and mathematician, Ibn Bajjah was a forerunner of Averroes. Known to the Latin Schoolmen as Avempace, or Avenpace, he was born in Saragossa, Spain, and known in his lifetime as the prime exponent of Aristotelian thought after *Avicenna. He follows *Al-Farabi and his work greatly influenced Ibn Tufail. Averroës himself states that his own ideas of mind are derived from Ibn Bajjah. His *'Ilm al-Nafs* (Science of the Soul) is the earliest text hitherto known that gives the gist of all the three books of the *De anima* of *Aristotle, and he is known, among other things, to Western scholars for his theory of separate substances, which they adopted from him. In his *Guide to the Solitary* he deals with the soul's return to reality by detaching itself from matter.   IS

Leff, G. (1958). *Medieval Thought*.

Ibn Hazm ('Ali ibn-Hazm, 994–1064). A native of Córdoba, Spain, he was the first scholar of comparative religion, and Hitti (1951) characterizes him as anticipating theological problems only arising in Christian Europe in the 16th century. Guillaume (1949), in referring to this author of over 400 books, accepted in the West as the greatest scholar and the most original thinker of Spanish Islam (see ISLAMIC PHILOSOPHY), notes that he composed 'Europe's first *Religions-geschichte* and the first systematic higher critical study of the Old and New Testaments'. This is his *Al-Fasl fi'l-Milal w'al-Ahwa' w'al-Nihal* (the Decisive Word on Sects, Heterodoxies, and Denominations), but he also wrote love poems. In *The Necklace of the Dove* he extols platonic love, and his romanticism is regarded as related to the Spanish–Arabian influence on the formation of the troubadour mentality.   IS

Guillaume, A. (1949). 'Philosophy and theology'. In Arnold, T. (ed.), *The Legacy of Islam*.

Hitti, P. K. (1951). *History of the Arabs*.

Ibn Khaldun (Abu-Zaid Abd-al-Rahman ibn-Khaldun, 1332–1406). Born in Tunis, he was one of the greatest *Islamic scholars of Moorish Spain, Arab ambassador to Pedro the Cruel, judge, and professor of jurisprudence at Cairo. Author of the *Muqaddima* (Introduction), the first analysis of history by political and social pattern, Ibn Khaldun is regarded as the 'father of the science of history' and one of the founders of sociology. A *Sufi by persuasion, he is buried in the Sufi cemetery near Cairo where he died.

Ibn Khaldun was an historian, politician, sociologist, economist, a deep student of human affairs, anxious to analyse the past of mankind in order to understand its present and future . . . one of the first philosophers of history, a forerunner of Machiavelli, Bodin, Vico, Comte and Cournot (Sarton 1927–48: iii. 1262).

IS

Dawood, N. J. (ed.) (1967). *The Muqaddimah: An Introduction to History*. Trans. F. Rosenthal.

Gellner, E. A. (1981). *Muslim Society*.

Sarton, G. (1927–48). *Introduction to the History of Science* (repr. 1975).

Ibn Sina. See AVICENNA.

iconic image. If a visual pattern is presented only very briefly (for example, by flashing a light on it in a dark chamber) an image of that pattern will persist in experience beyond its physical termination. Such an image is called an iconic image (or, alternatively, the information is said to be in a 'sensory register') and, unlike the after-effects produced by very strong lighting, will appear very much like the pattern itself, though faded. Indeed, careful measurements have shown that observers often believe that the stimulus is still physically present when, in fact, it has been terminated a fraction of a second previously.

One implication of the latter point is that this record is remarkably complete (contains all or most of the detail of the original) especially as compared to the contents of other memory systems. George Sperling demonstrated this point directly by signalling his subjects immediately after stimulus offset to report to him the contents of one of a set of rows of letters which he had presented on a screen for 50 milliseconds. No matter which row was randomly requested, the level of accuracy was quite high.

Interestingly, however, a slight variation on this procedure drastically reduces performance. That is, if a mixture of letters and numbers is presented and the observer is requested immediately thereafter to report, for example, the letters but not the numbers, fewer successes are achieved. The implication is that, although all of the items are available, they have not yet been identified, and so, in order to perform the task, the subject must identify each item whether called for or not. This is time consuming and the image disappears before the task can be completed. Thus, while iconic images may be remarkably complete, they apparently exist in a sensory, rather than properly perceptual, form.

The very 'unprocessed' nature of such records of stimulation may provide a key to their importance. It may be that such records hold information so that further, relatively time-consuming, processes such as segmentation, *figure–ground organization, and identification can occur. However, such a proposal must be developed cautiously. In nature the conditions under which these images have been studied are extremely rare, the rule in nature being relatively long-lasting scenes which we tend to explore with our eyes by fixating upon first one place and then another. This latter point is especially significant since it is also known that any part of an iconic image can be destroyed if new contours appear. For example, in an experiment such as Sperling's, if a particular letter on the screen is followed very quickly by another, an observer will not be able to report the former and may even indicate that it did not occur at all. The potential problem is, then, that in ordinary viewing the image produced by one fixation would be destroyed by the next, so that it would not be available for further processing. For example, what is now in the centre of the eye would destroy the image of what had been there just before the eyes moved.

Actually, the strength of this objection depends upon two assumptions: first, an assumption that the image is located in a fixed position in the retinas, and, secondly, an assumption that the specific part of an image, which will be destroyed when new information arrives, will be that part which used to occupy that same place on the retina, even if the eyes have moved in the meantime.

As to the first assumption, while it is clear that some component of iconic images might be within the retinas, there is also ample evidence of a non-retinal component. For example, if these images were retinal, then they ought to appear to move around the environment when the eyes move. On the contrary, however, Douglas Hall observed that when his subjects were requested to report a particular row of letters, they moved their eyes so as to scan the (now blank) area of the screen where those letters had been. This would hardly make sense if the image, too, had moved. Instead, those things 'seen' in the image seem to stay in their proper environmental locales. If it is further assumed that various parts of an iconic image will be destroyed only by new stimulation that occurs in the same environmental locales as those parts, then it will be appreciated that such destruction does not occur unless the scene itself changes in whole or in part. That being the case, several such images (each produced by a different fixation of the eyes) are perfectly free to coexist and may well add together in normal everyday viewing.

Whether such additivity actually occurs or not, the fact that not only do iconic images stay in place when they should, but also may appear to move when induced by moving stimulation (anorthoscopic visual perception), suggests the involvement of some exceedingly sophisticated mechanisms.

TEP

Averbach, E., and Sperling, G. (1961). 'Short-term storage of information in vision'. In Cherry, C. (ed.), *Fourth London Symposium on Information Theory*.

Hall, D. C. (1974). 'Eye movements in scanning iconic imagery'. *Journal of Experimental Psychology*, 103.

id. According to Freud, the unconscious reservoir of primitive instincts from which spring the forces of behaviour and the conflicts and guilts of neurosis.

ideal. The concept of an ideal seems to come from extrapolating from that which is seen as inadequate to some relatively perfect state. There are thus 'ideals of manhood' and general 'ideals worth striving for'. In *metaphysics, ideals can be supposed to exist, in some kind of heaven. This holds for *Plato's ideal forms of objects, including mathematical fictions such as the ideal triangle.

For Plato, mathematical and indeed all significant knowledge is of ideal unchanging forms, of which we see only transitory and imperfect replicas paraded before the senses. (See PLATONIC FORMS.) It is likely that this Platonic view has deeply affected ethics, and set up moral standards directed towards static, unchanging ideals which, in practice, cannot be realized, and, if they were, would be death. RLG

idealism. Name given to a group of philosophical doctrines which suggest that what we know as the '*external world or the 'material universe' is in some important sense created by the mind or mind dependent. (i) According to the Berkeleian version of this view, nothing exists outside the mind. To exist (*esse*) is to be perceived (*percipi*), and what we perceive can be nothing but our own ideas or sensations (see BERKELEY ON THE MIND). Subsequent 'phenomenalist' theories, which maintain that physical objects are merely 'permanent possibilities of sensation' (in J. S. *Mill's phrase), have something in common with Berkeley's view. (ii) Kantian or 'transcendental' idealism maintains that the fundamental categories in terms of which we characterize the world are not objective features of things in themselves but are structures imposed by the mind; without such organizing structures experience would not be possible (see KANT'S PHILOSOPHY OF MIND). (iii) According to *Hegelian idealism, the whole of history consists in the progressive realization of a single 'self-positing' mind or spirit (*Geist*). JC

ideas. Ideas might be called 'the sentences of thought'. They are expressed by language, but underlie language—for the idea comes before its expression. (Though it is sometimes said that one knows what one thinks only after one has said it!)

Philosophers have traditionally distinguished between 'simple' ideas and 'complex' ideas. Simple ideas are supposed to be directly derived from sensation. When combined, they can produce complex and abstract ideas far removed from sensory experience and expressed in shared language. Simple ideas are the 'atoms' of associationist accounts of the mind. In common speech, 'one idea leads to another': and it is this which was formalized by the 18th- and 19th-century associationists such as John *Locke, David *Hume, James *Mill, J. S. *Mill, and Alexander *Bain. But how does one have a new idea, if ideas can only follow from others, or from sensations? Is it by

the *emergence—as in chemistry—of new and surprising properties of combined elements? This leads to considerations of *intelligence, *creativity, and *genius. RLG

illusions.

1. What are illusions?
2. Phenomenal phenomena
3. Illusions and behaviour
4. Illusions in science and art
5. Explaining illusions
6. Some principles, with examples

1. What are illusions?

Illusions are discrepancies from truths. All kinds of perceptions are subject to illusions; but generally they pass unnoticed, except when there are marked internal inconsistencies, or clear departures from what is believed to be true. As beliefs largely determine what is accepted as true, so beliefs can dismiss or affirm appearances as illusory. A ghost-hunter may accept an appearance, such as an after-image, as truly a ghost which a sceptic would reject as illusory. Believers in UFOs have seen lampshades reflected in windowpanes as flying saucers. But here we will not simply reject illusions, for many kinds will be accepted as significant phenomena of mind. Not natural phenomena of physics, but *phenomenal phenomena* of physiology and cognitive processes of the brain.

Although they are often called 'optical illusions' most are physiologically or psychologically caused. Optical phenomena can produce weird and wonderful visual effects—distortions of fairground mirrors, changes of size or distance with telescopes, repeated patterns with a kaleidoscope—but are these illusions? Is a rainbow an illusion? This is a phenomenon of optics, studied and explained with concepts of optics. Isn't it an illusion, only when not understood, so evoking misleading expectations? Rainbows mislead when one thinks it possible to walk under the heavenly arch, as though it were made of stone or brick, though the rainbow recedes and is always beyond touch. This is a conceptual error, perhaps best called 'delusion'. Illusions of perceptions and delusions of conceptions are linked in complex ways not fully understood.

The sun is seen as sinking to the horizon at dusk, yet we know this is due to the earth rotating under our feet. This takes us to the notion that neural signals from the eyes and other senses must be interpreted, or 'read' by the brain for meaning. There is nothing odd with the optical images in our eyes, or with the neural signals to the brain, when we see the sun setting; but they are misread. They are misread visually, even when conceptually we know what is going on. Conceptual understanding seldom destroys perceptual illusions. Perceptions and conceptions are remarkably separate in the brain, and so we continue to experience illusions though they are recognized as such, and even explained. As illusions are such robust phenomena they are easy to investigate, for they do not disappear before our eyes when we start to understand them. But 'seeing is believing' should be taken with a large pinch of salt.

All the senses can suffer illusion, but as most research has been done on vision its illusions are most fully understood, though many have controversial explanations, or even none. Here we shall make our best guess at explaining various phenomena of illusions, and attempt to classify them by *kinds* and *causes*. As we have said: some have physical *optical* causes (such as mirages), some are *physiological* (such as after-images), others are *cognitive* (such as the moon appearing huge when low on the horizon—see MOON ILLUSION). It seems important to put these strange phenomena into categories, because their significance, as surely for all phenomena of science, depends on explanations. Here there is something of a paradox: phenomena suggest explanations—yet explanations give meaning to phenomena. So science is ping-pong played with phenomena and explanations. As a general principle, *phenomena cannot speak for themselves*. Explanations are essential for giving phenomena significance, and with changes of understanding a phenomenon may appear very different. Thus, as thunder moved from theological accounts of wrath of the gods, to moving charges in physics, its meaning and implications were transformed. One might say that this to-and-fro between phenomena and explanations is the game of science, applying to illusions as to any other phenomena.

Illusions are explained by various sciences with a variety of concepts, but artists are intuitive experts, in some ways knowing more of illusions than does science. Science and art have met for centuries in technologies of painting and architecture. Now cinema and television depend on fooling eyes and brains with processes of illusion—especially the Phi phenomenon of continuous movement seen from displaced pictures switched in sequence—giving realistic smoothly moving objects from flat intermittent shadows. In painting, cinema, and television, processes of illusion are used to produce surrogate realities, and evoke wonderful fictions. Illusions of the various senses have important parts to play in music, in cooking, and of course for conjuring. They enrich life.

It is sometimes said that illusions occur only in laboratory or other artificial conditions, but this is far from true. Illusions of all the senses are frequent in normal conditions, and may be dramatic even with familiar objects in full lighting. The mast of a sailing boat looks far longer when vertical than when lying horizontal on the ground. Light regions look larger than darker areas, which can affect women's choice of dress. (Hence perhaps the popularity of the 'little black number'.) Illusions are used by gardeners and architects to improve proportions, and make properties look more spacious. Illusions occurring in everyday situations can be disastrous, as in playing golf or driving a car, or flying, and illusions can fool scientists into serious errors. Illusions deserve to be studied and understood for very practical reasons, as well as for their philosophical significance.

Although illusions are prevalent in normal conditions, admittedly the best known are seen in pictures, in children's books, and psychology texts. It is important to compare pictures—which are very special objects for vision—with normal objects we can interact with. Experiments on vision and illusion should not be limited to computer screens! Pictures would make little or no sense without years of experience of interacting with objects. Seeing what the patterns of pictures represent depends on knowledge from primary experience with touchable, tastable objects, including emotional ties with people, for appreciating portraits. Yet, curiously, the brain's perceptual knowledge is not the same as, and does not always agree with, its conceptual understanding.

2. Phenomenal phenomena

For the physical sciences illusions are nothing much more than threats to be avoided; but these out-of-this-world phenomena are important for suggesting and testing theories of how we perceive things. That there are illusions shows that at least some perceptions are not tied to the object world, as they float free of physical reality. Does the fact that some perceptions take off from object reality indicate that *all* perceptions are essentially separate from the physical world? This is a central question for theories of perception.

The Greeks generally thought of vision as intimately associated with objects; but with the discovery of intervening *retinal images, and neural channels with long chains of synapses, some sort of indirect relation became far more plausible. Perhaps curiously, 'direct' theories are not wholly abandoned today by some philosophers and psychologists, though these accounts do seem hard to defend against what we know of physiology and cognitive processing. Illusions are embarrassing and generally ignored by 'direct pick-up' theorists. The view taken here is that perceptions are indirectly related to the object world: they are predictive, based on neural signals from the senses, and depending on knowledge derived from the past, to make sense of present signals (Gregory 1968, 1980). As accepted knowledge may be wrong, or not appropriate to the present, there is a great wealth of cognitive illusions due to signals from the senses being misread. These are cognitive rather than physiological, but are genuine phenomena, that can be studied to illuminate principles of brain and mind.

3. Illusions and behaviour

Illusions affect behaviour, yet behaviour does not always correspond to the illusion experienced. With other evidence, this has suggested there are two kinds of perception: full-blown experience of the present surroundings, essentially for planning behaviour; and an ancient far simpler system giving rapid behaviour with minimal cognitive processing, for simple actions but without *consciousness. It is suggested that these have different brain pathways (dorsal and ventral), though how separate these are functionally is at present controversial (Milner and Goodale 1995). Cognitive illusions can be used to investigate this notion, and see how the pathways are functionally separate. Only the ventral system should be affected by cognitive illusions—rapid touch should not be affected by the visual illusion. Present evidence is somewhat conflicting. Only some experiments find that touch is not affected by the Titchener illusion (Fig. 5), but this may be because rapid snatch movement is difficult here. As dramatic reversal of cognitive space is given by the Hollow Face illusion (Fig. 9), we may ask: is fast touch not reversed (to agree with appearance) when the hollow mask is seen as convex? This seems to be true, as the two streams notion would predict.

Illusions of behaviour can of course be measured objectively. Illusions of subjective experience can be measured, though with more difficulty, with so-called 'psycho-physics', by comparing illusory with non-illusory perceptions. The choice of these is not always easy, because to establish an illusion we must have some reference truth; but what should be accepted as truths for comparisons? Sometimes this may seem obvious, but what for example of colours? What is an illusory colour is particularly hard to say, because we may not be able to specify any *non*-illusory colour for comparison.

Although such deep questions are usually avoided or ignored, there is the ever-present question of how far *any* perceptual experiences match physical realities. The philosopher John *Locke (1632–1704) drew an interesting analogy with language (in 1690). Locke asked whether sensations (such as white or red, loud or soft) are at all like physical properties of objects and events, or rather whether they *stand for* very different physical characteristics, much as words stand for things that are very different from their shapes and sounds. For example, the word CAT is very different in form from the animal, yet it stands for the physically very different living pet, and calls it to mind. The physical blue of the sky is undoubtedly different from the sensation of blue, yet the experience stands for the very different physical reality, and serves us much like the word 'blue', which is totally unlike the sky or its colour, but brings it to mind.

Locke realized that neither objects nor light are coloured. Colours are created in the brain, as we now know, from various wavelengths of the electromagnetic spectrum activating 'cone' receptor cells in the retina. Locke appreciated that without eyes and suitable brains, there would be no colours in the universe.

4. Illusions in science and art

We generally *see* objects as very different from how science *describes* them—with invisible electrons and so on—so are *all* perceptions illusory? There is no point in saying this any more than 'everything is a dream', as such words lose meaning when there are no accepted contrasting reference 'truths'. This makes defining 'illusion' difficult, as what is accepted as illusory changes with accepted non-illusory references. These could hardly be from fundamental physics, even though we accept physics as providing the deepest truths, because its accounts are so different from how things appear that using them as reference would make all perceptions illusory.

We might say that the references we accept for non-illusions are from simple commonsense 'kitchen' physics. We check for illusion with simple measures, with kitchen-type instruments, such as rulers and scales, thermometers, and clocks. This is very different from taking fundamental physics as reference truths for perceptions. Paradoxically, we cannot use our deepest beliefs as hallmarks for true perceptions.

Illusions are important for artists who, with great skill, make use of many kinds. Should we call all pictures illusions? Pictures seldom look just the same as the scene they represent, but if they do not mislead there seems little point calling them illusory. Again, like words, they stand for reality, which is good enough for 'truth' when they are not seriously misleading.

Pictures can, however, very easily upset the visual system to produce a wealth of phenomenal phenomena: jazzing instability, systematic distortions, even impossible or paradoxical objects, as well as fictions. Representational pictures are curious objects that stand for other objects or abstractions though not by exact copying.

5. Explaining illusions

So many processes contribute to perception, it is often difficult to know which is responsible for an error or illusion, and no doubt there are more processes going on we know nothing about. Some illusions, such as the bright or dark *after-images that hover around after one looks at a bright light, are clearly due to physiological adaptations of receptors in the retina.

But illusions can be caused not by systems *misbehaving*, but very differently, by normal functioning being *inappropriate* to the situation. This distinction implies that there is more to life than physiological functions; it matters what they are *doing* in particular circumstances. For example, the brain effectively scales up retinal images optically shrunk by object distance (as in a camera) giving 'size constancy', but this scaling may not be appropriate. Then a distortion of size or shape occurs though the physiology is working normally.

There is a danger of postulating special mechanisms, or processes, when none is needed. It is well known that the images in the eyes are optically reversed—upside down and switched left–right—yet the world looks upright, and visual right and left agree with touch. It is generally accepted that this does not need a special compensating mechanism because retinal images are not seen, as objects are seen—or they would need another eye to see them—with another picture in the brain, a regress, going on forever without getting anywhere. A compensating mechanism is not needed as they are not objects of perception but rather one stage of processing lying between objects and vision. But is this all there is to it? When the head is tilted, the world remains upright. This extends to standing on one's head, when the retinal image is reversed and yet up and down remain normal. Does head-tilt need a compensating mechanism, or does perception *ignore* the tilt of the head, as the brain knows it is irrelevant? Perhaps we don't really know whether there is a special mechanism here, but dizziness, and various kinds of instability, suggest there is. Nature does not always adopt neat solutions, such as simply ignoring tilts of the head, or the blind regions of the eyes. We need experiments to settle such issues and there can be surprising answers.

It was shown at the end of the 19th century, by G. M. Stratton, that after days of wearing inverting goggles the world comes to look more or less normally upright. Yet just how normal it becomes—and whether this is behavioural rather than perceptual learning—remains unclear. Another example of doubt over the need for a special mechanism is Emmert's Law—after-images appearing larger when seen as more distant—because though this seems so simple it is not fully understood.

Physiologists and psychologists often disagree when trying to explain illusions. For example, physiologists have generally explained the well-known Müller-Lyer distortion illusion (Fig. 10b) as due to neural signalling in the eyes being upset, as through 'lateral inhibition', by the angles of the 'arrowheads'. But, as already hinted, very different explanations lie in the domain of cognitive psychology. The arrowheads are perspective depth cues and may set size constancy scaling inappropriately.

These are extremely different kinds of causes. As the implications of symptoms and the phenomena of science depend on kinds of explanations—classifications are very important in medicine and science—we will now try to classify illusions by 'kinds' and 'causes'. This will lead to a tentative—this is certainly not engraved on stone—'Peeriodic Table' of elements of perception and illusion.

A classification with causes needs some theoretical account or model of what is going on. We may start with a simple scheme like Fig. 1, 'Ins-and-outs of vision'. The central notion is that perceptions are hypotheses, rather like the predictive hypotheses of science. As in science, the process starts with signals from the (ultimately mysterious) world of physics, signalled *bottom-up*. The signals are interpreted, or read, with *top-down* knowledge. Then there are *sideways* general rules, such as perspective for seeing depth, and the *Gestalt laws of organization or grouping *output*, for behaviour with feedback of errors, is essential for perceptual learning.

So, with apologies to the great Russian chemist, Dmitri Ivanovich Mendeleyev, we have the Peeriodic Table.

6. Some principles, with examples

Table 1 suggests ten main kinds of phenomena, with four main kinds of cause. The four causes have already been hinted at: *optical*; *physiological*; and two kinds of psychological or *cognitive* causes: misleading *rules*; and misleading *knowledge*.

The ten suggested *kinds* of phenomena are selected somewhat intuitively, though there are 'litmus tests' for assigning phenomena to the various categories.

The suggested kinds of perceptual phenomena are: *non-sense* (various kinds of blindness—from no signals from the eyes to inability to make sense of the signals); *context* (over space or time); *grouping* (generally of features organized into likely objects); *instability* (perceptual stability being hard to achieve); *confounded ambiguity* (confusing different stimuli or objects); *flipping ambiguity* (creating alternative perceptions for one stimulus or object); *distortion* (as of size or shape); *unlikely* (perception is greatly affected by probabilities: the more unlikely, the more the information; but if too unlikely will be rejected); *paradoxical* (generally from conflicting rules); *fiction* (going beyond the available information).

A word is needed on the two kinds of ambiguity, 'confounded' and 'flipping'. 'Ambiguity' is used in two very different senses, so the word 'ambiguity' is itself ambiguous! It may mean *failing to distinguish differences* ('confounded'), or, very differently, *creating different perceptions* from one stimulus or object ('flipping').

Non-sense   Total Blindness. Our lives depend on reliably *not* seeing—so that not seeing corresponds to *nothing there*. The driver moves off when *not* seeing another car, or person, in the way. Much of driving depends on not seeing, yet *no* evidence is different from evidence of *nothing*. As uncertainty increases with age, it is right for older drivers to be slower and more cautious, to ensure that seeing nothing corresponds with nothing to be seen.

The long-term blind do not see blackness—they see *nothing*. The nearest sighted people can get to this is imagining what is behind the head. One does not see black (which is a colour), one simply sees nothing. Though one may of course guess what is behind one's head, and this is

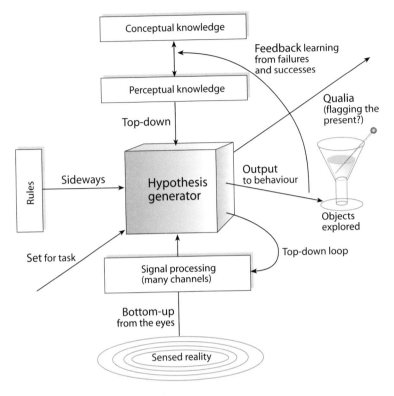

Fig. 1. Ins-and-outs of vision: simple tentative scheme for how vision may be organized.

important. The rare cases of adult recovery from infant *blindness are theoretically interesting as well as remarkable human stories. There are many kinds of blindness, or non-sense, the most familiar being *colour-blindness. There are also cognitive blindnesses.

Inattention blindness. Conjurors (magicians) are expert at producing selective blindness by directing attention away from what is going on. A coin passes invisibly from one hand to the other by dropping it from a stationary into a moving hand, for the drop is not seen, and the coin appears magically in the moving hand. Also, conjurors direct their audience's eyes by looking away from where the action is. Attention is vital for seeing and inattention gives blindness.

Agnosia. The most interesting kind of non-sense is inability to read meanings into perceptions, even failure to recognize common objects: *agnosia. A famous account is Oliver Sacks's book *The Man Who Mistook his Wife for a Hat* (1985). Failures of perception when knowledge is not available, as in brain-damaged subjects, shows how important available knowledge is for perception.

Neglect. There can be neglect of regions of space (Fig. 2). Most often the left visual field is missing, with a parietal lesion. Amazingly, the left halves of objects are missing wherever the eyes are looking.

Perhaps stranger still is:

Blindsight. *Blindsight is some visual ability, such as pointing to objects, though without consciousness. There may be an alternative more primitive pathway for simple perception without consciousness. This throws light on the evolution of the visual brain, and perhaps on the role of consciousness.

Retinal rivalry. Red presented to one eye and green to the other gives the alternating blindness in each eye of 'rivalry'. This occurs for different shapes. So why do red–green anaglyph stereo pictures work? Common contours for the eyes prevent colour rivalry. Movement presented to one eye almost always brings sight to this eye, the other being effectively blind.

Instability Jazzing. Repeated patterns of high-contrast lines produce jazzing effects, as in Op Art. Some authorities believe they stimulate movement areas of the brain directly; but it seems to be mainly due to small eye movements and 'hunting' of the lens for focus, or accommodation as it is misleadingly called. The repeated lines may stimulate on/off receptors normally signalling movement, and they may 'beat' with their immediate after-image to produce flower-like moving patterns (Fig. 3).

A major miracle of perception is achieving stability of sensory experience though we move. This applies to

Table 1. Peeriodic table of the elements of Perception and Illusion

Kinds of PHENOMENA	Kinds of CAUSES			
	PHYSICAL		COGNITIVE	
	[Kitchen physics] 1 OPTICS	[Bottom-up] 2 SIGNALS	[Side-ways] 3 RULES	[Top-down] 4 KNOWLEDGE
I NONSENSE	**General blindness from lack of retinal images**, as by cataract or corneal opacity. Long-term blindness–no qualia–is not blackness–but NOTHING–like behind one's head. For any phenomenon to have meaning it must be interpreted, by knowledge or assumptions.	**Retinal failure.** Mainly 'central' loss of form vision. **Sensory adaptation:** Loss of sensation from maintained stimuli. **Saccadic suppression:** Rejection of foveal signals during saccades. **Misdirected or inattention.** As in conjuring, and disappearance of small objects with background motion.	**Change blindness. (Perceptual hypotheses tend to stay until challenged, so bridge data-gaps).** Failing to see differences following a short delay.	**Mind-blind–agnosia.** Objects seen as mere patterns. **Ignoring familiar (so low-information) objects:** Not seeing familiar ornaments or pictures. Not hearing a ticking clock.
II CONTEXT	**Context gives meaning.** Important for conceptual and statistical significance. But context can mislead into illusion, especially as the senses signal relative not absolute values.	**Thresholds limited by statistical significance of action potentials and signal-noise ratio.** Weber's Law = constant ratio. **Lateral inhibition:** Brightness and colour illusions–from space and time 'references'.	**Relative size:** Titchener circles. Induced movement: (stationary train seeming to move). The Haunted Swing. **Stick-and-Frame:** Tilt and size-change illusions.	**Emmert's Law (not fully understood). Size-distance partly set by object knowledge.** After-images expand linearly with increased seen distance. **Tilted room.** Upsets balance and produces bizarre phenomena such as water flowing upwards. (Especially with typical room features.)
III GROUPING	**Photons arrive in patterns,** especially when focused by the eye, related to events and objects, and sometimes related to other senses.	**Signals are structured into messages.** 'Chunking' increases powers of memory, and may be a basis of object perception.	**Dots grouping by Gestalt Law (or mis-grouping).** Fraser spiral. **Auto-correlation.** Glass effect.	**Small features grouped by object knowledge.** Dalmatian dog. Martian canals ('seen' by Percival Lowell).
IV INSTABILITY	**By atmospheric turbulence,** especially for astronomy. **Illumination varies**–yet perception is usually stable. Largely achieved with active constancy mechanisms.	**Upset eye movement stability–cancellation.** Autokinetic effect. **Lack of 'border-locking'.** Ouchi illusion. **Chaotic brain instability.** Epilepsy.	**Competing Gestalt Laws:** Shifting organizations. **Pseudo parallax.** Perspective scene in picture follows viewer's movements.	Jazzing of duplicated eyes. Portrait's eyes following viewer.
V CONFOUNDED AMBIGUITY	**Same stimulus from different objects**–e.g. small and near = large and distant giving the same retinal image. So must look the same. The reversed-perspective Ames Room = a rectangular room.	**Overlapping reponse curves.** Red+green = yellow light. **For shape distortion**–when the distortion = a matching object (Useful for measuring the illusion).	**Gestalt Laws concealing objects.** Camouflage. **Unusual angles of view.** Failure to recognize familiar objects.	**Lack of object knowledge.** Different kinds of objects confounded. E.g. fossils, or makes of cars which are hardly distinguishable, except by experts.
VI FLIPPING AMBIGUITY	**Quantal photon jumps.**	**Multi-stable patterns.** Retinal rivalry.	**Equally probable, rule-based perceptual hypotheses.** Figure-ground reversals. Parallax motion reversals.	**Equally probable knowledge-based alternative objects.** Necker Cube? Duck-Rabbit; Boring's Old Lady-Mistress figure; Rubin's faces.
VII DISTORTION	**Deviations from 'kitchen sink' reality.** As by refraction: Astigmatism. Bent-stick-in-water. Mirage. **Strobing flashing light:** Change apparent speed; reversed motion.	**Sensory signals disturbed (as by lateral inhibition):** Café Wall. **Adaptation of spatial fequency channels, or 'feature detectors'** Tilt, curvature, size, colour, motion, etc. **Delay of one eye with dark-adaptation** Pulfrich Pendulum.	**Depth cues mis-setting size-scaling:** Ponzo; Müller-Lyer; Hering; Poggendorff; Horizontal-Vertical; Harvest Moon illusion.	**False expectation:** Size-weight illusion (smaller objects feel heavier than larger objects of the same scale weight, as muscles set for expected weight). Moving staircase–when stationary seems to move backwards.
VIII UNLIKELY	**The more improbable an event, or object, the more information it may convey.**	**If too improbable it may be rejected, as when bottom-up sensory evidence is not adequate for selecting very unlikely alternative.** Hollow Head Illusion.	**Depth from probable (like the sun) or improbable (from below) lighting.** Shape-from-shading.	**Depth seen from rule that images shrink with objects distance.** Perspective depth in scenes and pictures.
IX IMPOSSIBLE	**In a mirror:** Seeing oneself in two places at once. **Pepper's Ghost.** Objects superimposed, transparent.	**Conflicting signals from parallel channels:** Spiral after-effect–expands or shrinks without changing size.	**Conflicting Rules.** Corners of Impossible Triangle appear the same distance, because optically they touch–paradoxical for the perspective depth.	**Escher pictures.** Spatial paradoxes.
X FICTION	**Physical phenomena can appear fictional when not understood.** Rainbows are seen as fictional arches one might walk through, when misunderstood.	**False neural signals, 'noise':** After-images. Hermann's grid. Mach bands. Phi movement.	**Ghostly contours and surfaces:** Kanizsa figures. Neon spreading.	**Perceptions that take off from stimulus control:** Inkblots. Faces-in-the-fire. Hypnogogic and psychedelic dreams. Scrying.

touch as to vision. When we handle an object it remains constant in form, though the touch signals change as we explore different parts. A room full of furniture looks stable though we move around. It is stability that needs explaining.

All movement is relative, yet normally we know from vision whether we are moving or objects are moving around us. Proprioception from the limbs helps but,

remarkably, stability is achieved by vision alone when our feet are off the ground, as in a car. There are rules, originally suggested by the *Gestalt psychologists, such as large distant objects tending to be accepted as stationary 'references' for seeing smaller nearer objects as moving.

There is recent evidence that decisions about what is moving can be taken early on, without complicated

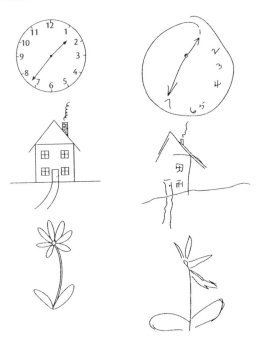

Fig. 2. Neglect: with cortical damage to the visual brain there can be blindness generally in the left field, but this is not simply loss of sight, and half an object may be invisible wherever the eyes are looking (from Thompson 2000).

Fig. 3. Op Art Jazz (after Bridget Riley).

cognitive processing. But object knowledge comes into play—which is useful for film animators, who have to show what is supposed to be moving. Illusions of self-movement can occur thus: moving large objects can appear stationary, while smaller fixed objects seem to move—known as induced motion. This is dramatic in the fairground Haunted Swing oscillating room, where the stationary observer seems to move, even to be turning upside-down.

The world normally appears stable when we move our eyes, as the movement signal at the retina is cancelled by the command signal to move the eyes. So after-images move with the eyes, as there are no retinal motion signals cancelling them. But is this all there is to it? Various illusions suggest complexities.

Auto-kinetic effect. This is apparent motion of a small fixed light viewed in darkness. It occurs though the eyes are not moving. It is generally explained as due to the system that normally compensates eye movements—so giving stability to the world when the eyes are moved—but sending small fluctuating signals when the eyes are held still. If the eyes are held hard over to one side for a few seconds, the light usually swings round violently in the opposite direction, as the compensating system is unbalanced (Gregory 1966/97). But why does the auto-kinetic

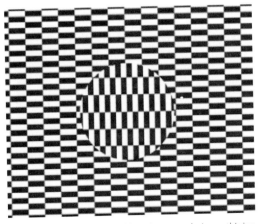

Fig. 4. Ouchi illusion: created by a Japanese designer, this is a powerful example of instability perhaps due to lack of border locking, as there are different spatial frequencies and orthogonal eyes.

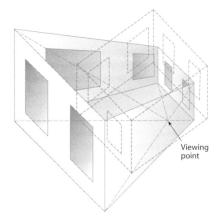

Viewing point

Fig. 5. The Titchener illusion: the inner disks are the same size, but look different in contrast to the surrounding larger and smaller disks.

effect work only for a small light in darkness? Why doesn't a whole room look as unstable? This takes us back to the *cognitive assumption* of stability; a rich familiar world is assumed to be stable, so small imbalances are ignored.

Tilted Room. A *tilted room is very disturbing, as it violates basic assumptions. The assumption of horizontal for a floor is so strong, water can seem to run up hill in a tilted room.

Pseudo-parallax. Curious instabilities are associated with one's own motion. Normally when we move, the world looks stable—which is remarkable as there are very complex changes of the retinal image. With lateral motion, everything rotates, counter to one's movements, around the fixation point of the eyes. This is *motion

Fig. 6a. The Ames Room: the odd-shaped room gives the same retinal image to the eye (placed at the right distance) as a normal rectangular room. So it must appear the same—and does—until there are objects, such as people, inside it. Then they look odd sizes while the room continues to look (falsely) like a normal rectangular room.

parallax, which is optical but partially compensated perceptually. One sees the compensation when there are *apparently* different distances but not true depth—as in a perspective picture. Moving across the picture gives the extraordinary illusion of the entire scene swinging round, following one as one moves, though it is a flat picture. It appears to rotate in the opposite direction to true parallax.

Fig. 6b. The Ames Room: this is what it looks like.

We may call this strange effect, of apparent but not true depth, 'pseudo-parallax'. It is most easily investigated with 3-D projected images. Another way of seeing the brain's compensation to one's own motion uses a flash after-image of a dark room: though fixed like a photograph in the eyes, features such as corners are seen to change shape as one walks around the invisible dark room, with the fixed after-image stuck in one's eyes.

Portrait eyes. The eyes of a portrait following one's movements is similar to the pseudo-parallax of perspective pictures, except that the portrait effect is due to object knowledge rather than general perspective rules. The knowledge is that eyes keep looking at one as they rotate; but evidently the visual brain is not clever enough to realize that these eyes are fixed and flat. They give the same fixed image of normal eyes looking at one, so this is how they are accepted and seen.

'Border locking'. Given the essential physiological fact that vision works with many parallel neural channels, and they can have different delays and other different characteristics, it is surprising that moving regions of brightness and colour remain registered. There can, however, be discrepancies, especially with large brightness differences and in dim light. For example, the instrument lights of a car can appear to move around in their dials, especially in dim light. (This was dramatic in the old Morris Minor, at least one owner stripped down the instruments looking for where they were loose!)

Registration at borders with colour printing is hard to achieve. Is there a special mechanism for visual channels? The notion of 'border locking' has been proposed, luminance normally locking colours at edges, though this can fail, as when colours have equal luminance. It has been suggested that the Café Wall distortion (Fig. 11) is due to inappropriate border locking, causing distortion in this special case (Gregory and Heard 1979).

A dramatic, recently discovered example of instability is the Ouchi illusion (Fig. 4). With small movements, the central region shifts separately from the surrounding pattern. Is this due to lack of border locking?

Context Perception works very much with contrasts. It is contrasts at edges that provide visual *information. So even a simple line figure can be very effective, as in cartoons. Surrounding brightness and colours affect neighbouring regions, and so does size (Fig. 5).

Contrasts at borders are extrapolated into plain regions, which saves information transmission but can result in illusions, including perhaps Mach Bands. Colour regions with high-contrast edges appear more saturated, and there are many contrast illusions where contrast at an edge spreads to the surrounding regions, including beautiful 'neon-spreading', when colours wonderfully leak out of gaps, surely useful for painters.

Confounded ambiguity This is failure to distinguish differences. It may be due to neurological noise—limited physiological discrimination, or to lack of higher level cognitive categorizing.

A clear case of sensory confounding though there is high contrast is red light mixed with green, which looks

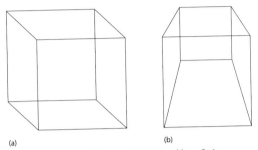

(a)   (b)

Fig. 7a. The Necker Cube was discovered by a Swiss crystallographer L. A. Necker in 1832 while he was drawing crystals. When one flipped, they suddenly looked different! **b.** The Necker Cube with perspective is more stable.

Fig. 8a. The Danish psychologist Edgar Ruben made faces alternate with vases in fascinating ways.

yellow though this mixture yellow cannot be distinguished from monochromatic (single-wavelength) yellow light. This is the basis of an important test for red–green colour blindness, or 'anomaly'.

It is not surprising that different-shaped objects are confounded when they present the same or very similar stimuli to the senses. The most famous example is the Ames Room (Fig. 6).

This illusion presents the brain with a question: are the people the same size, or is the room an odd shape? Generally the room 'wins'—looking normal though it is not, and the people look different sizes even though they are the same size. Here the brain has to assess probabilities, and may guess wrongly. It may be noted that *Emmert's law for after-images follows the *apparent* distances of the walls of the Ames Room, not the true distances. So, like any other perception, it is not directly attached to reality. *Stereoscopic vision is useful as it can break through visual assumptions, which may be—and here are—wrong.

Flipping ambiguity Perception can spontaneously flip between alternatives, especially with pictures or objects having equally likely alternative 'perceptual hypotheses'.

There are many well-known figures that change spontaneously, flipping from one alternative to another. These phenomena reveal most clearly the dynamic nature of object perception. Related brain processes are beginning to be discovered. We may say that rival perceptual hypotheses are entertained in turn, when the brain can't make up its mind.

The most famous is the *Necker Cube (Fig. 7a). A Necker Cube drawn with perspective (Fig. 7b) will stay longer in the orientation of its perspective depth.

A three-dimensional wire cube is a fascinating and most revealing ambiguous object. (The wires should be black, to minimize the occlusion cue of the nearer wires hiding the further.) When it reverses in depth, it seems to stand up on a corner and rotate to follow one as one moves around it. This is because the motion parallax is misread when the apparent distances of the nearer and further

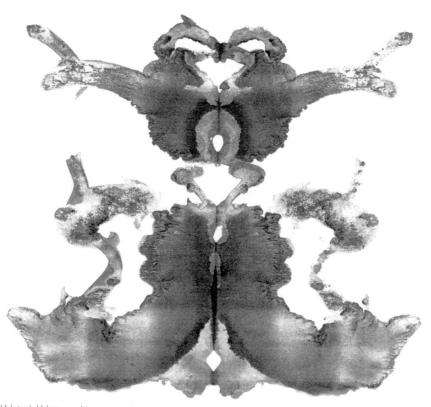

Fig. 8b. Inkblots. Inkblots can be seen as almost anything, with slowly changing perceptual hypotheses projecting meaning. Perhaps these are truly minimal art—where the viewer does more work than the artist.

illusions

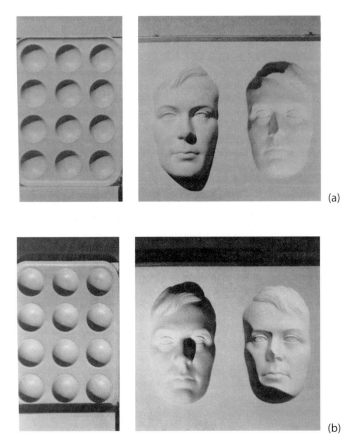

(a)

(b)

Fig. 9a and b. The Hollow Face illusion: a hollow mask (the back of a 'joke' face) looks convex, until seen close up with both eyes. This is evidently knowledge driven, from our immense experience of convex faces. Rotating it is fascinating (www.richardgregory.org). Here we compare what happens to the 'top-down' knowledge-based face illusion, with depth seen 'bottom-up' from shape-from-shadows with neutral objects—lighting from above in (**a**) below in (**b**)—that could be concave or convex. They switch in depth, but the face doesn't. This separates a rule (shape-from-shading) from knowledge (that faces are convex and noses stick out).

faces are perceptually reversed. Also, the cube *changes shape*. When flipped, the apparently further face looks too large. So instead of appearing as a cube, it looks like a truncated pyramid. This is strong evidence that Constancy Scaling can work 'downwards' from the prevailing perceptual hypothesis (Gregory 1963).

Flipping can occur against evidence from other senses. Holding a small wire cube in the hand while seeing it depth reversed is weird. When the hand is gently rotated, the cube seems to rotate against the hand's movement. This feels (though painlessly!) as though one's wrist is broken. Recent experiments with fMRI are beginning to show where this flipping—where this perceptual decision-taking—is processed in the brain.

When there are only two accepted possibilities, flipping is between a pair of alternatives, which is dramatic, as for the Necker Cube (Fig. 7) and Rubin's Faces (Fig. 8a).

On the other hand, inkblots (Fig. 8b) may provide hundreds of slowly changing perceptions, used in psychological 'projection' tests.

Distortion These are perhaps the best-known illusions, especially systematic errors of length, or curvature, of lines. Even after a century of intensive investigation by physiologists and opticians, neurologists and psychologists, explanations for some of these effects remain controversial. Curiously, many of the well-known distortion illusions were discovered by astronomers trying to reduce errors by placing guide wires in eye-pieces for accurate measurements. It turned out that these guide wires upset the eye in dramatic, lawful ways. It was found that converging lines produce distortions such as those of (Fig. 10a) the Ponzo illusion, and (Fig. 10b) the Müller-Lyer illusion.

These are large, repeatable phenomena, which are easy to measure, and are favourites for experiments. But what causes these distortions? There are *optical* distortions such as astigmatism. There are *physiological* distortions such as the Café Wall illusion (Fig. 11). And it has been suggested there are *cognitive* distortions, especially associated with size scaling normally giving constancy. We

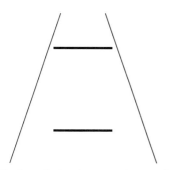

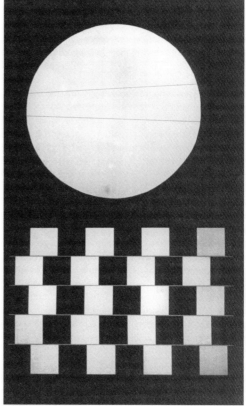

Fig. 10a. The Ponzo illusion: the converging outer lines make one of the inner lines look longer than the other, though they are the same length. Is this a physiological distortion of signals from the eyes, or is it cognitive, the perspective convergence (like receding railway lines) setting size scaling to correct what should, in the object world, be different distances?

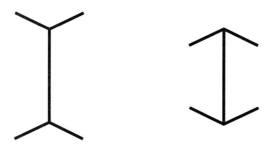

Fig. 10b. The Müller-Lyer illusion: a line terminated at each end with inward-pointing arrowheads (**a**) appears longer than a line with outward-pointing arrowheads (**b**).

Fig. 11. The Café Wall illusion: found on a 19th-century café (originally a butcher's shop) in Bristol, the parallel mortar lines appear as long wedges. When originally built, the illusion would hardly have been present—for the brightness of the mortar must be between the brightnesses of the tiles. New mortar would be too bright! This seems to be a physiological error of retinal signalling. The adjustable lines on the screen above show how the illusory wedges can be measured, by matching.

will look at these in some detail as some basic principles emerge.

'Physiological' distortions. A reason for believing that the Café Wall distortion is 'simply' physiological, and near the start of visual processing, is that it is strongly affected by brightness differences. It occurs only when the brightness of the narrow mortar lines lies between the brightnesses of the dark-and-light tiles. When the mortar is darker, or lighter, the wedge distortion is lost. When the 'tiles' are alternately coloured (for example red and green) with no brightness difference, there is no distortion (Gregory and Heard 1979). It may be noted that this figure has parallel lines, and lines at right angles, but no converging lines, as of perspective or any other depth cues. This makes the Café Wall illusion different from the classical 'geometrical illusions' (Fig. 11).

The Café Wall is conceptually puzzling as it seems to contradict a principle of physics—Curie's Principle—that symmetry cannot produce asymmetry. Yet the repeated pattern of tiles is symmetrically repeated across the figure. So how can these long wedges be produced? There are two processes.

There are small-scale asymmetries in this figure for each pair of dark and light tiles. These produce local distortions, small wedges (which can be seen individually with smaller tiles). These little wedges are integrated along the figure—the second process—to give the long wedges in the figure, as also in the original wall.

What causes the small-scale 'primary' distortion? Opposite-contrast tiles seem to suck together across the neutral mortar. This effect (which we have named the 'phenomenal phenomenon') can be isolated and studied in detail. It is striking with light or dark shapes having

437

narrow neutral edges: the rectangular or other shape expands or shrinks in lawful ways when made brighter or darker than the surround (Gregory and Heard 1983). Are these movements and distortions symptoms of 'border locking', normally serving to keep neighbouring regions together at edges, but in the Café Wall producing distortions that become dramatic when adding across the figure? This does suppose a relatively unknown process, which is dangerous; but postulating processes can give new knowledge.

'Cognitive' distortions. Cognitive explanations can be complicated and speculative, so it is wise to treat them with caution. But as the human brain clearly is cognitive, with memory, intelligence, planning, and so on, no great step is involved. The question here is how much *perception* is cognitive. Illusion phenomena help to provide an answer. However, we have suggested that 'phenomena cannot speak for themselves'. We meet the to-and-fro ping-pong game played between phenomena and theories. Here the art of science is to be a fair umpire.

A phenomenon almost impossible to consider without cognitive concepts is the *size-weight illusion*. A smaller object feels heavier than a larger object of the same scale weight. This can be a kitchen experiment, with tins of different sizes filled with sugar to be the same measured weight. The smaller tin feels 20–30 per cent heavier than

the larger tin of the same weight. For explanation: one anticipates a greater weight for the larger tin as larger objects are usually heavier—setting an expectation of the muscle power needed to lift them. Similarly, an empty suitcase flies up into the air (making one feel foolish!) when lifted with the expectation it will be heavy. The same kind of principle—misleading knowledge or assumptions—applies to many well-known illusions. Although they have, of course, a physiological basis. This is not relevant for the explanation when the error is due to the *misapplication* of the physiology, through inappropriate knowledge or false assumptions.

Misleading depth cues. The well-known, often called geometrical, illusions have perspective depth features. It is suggestive that all these distortion illusions represent *distance* (by perspective) associated with *expansion*. This is the opposite of the normal shrinking of retinal images with increasing distance. Normally, this shrinking with distance is largely compensated by size scaling, giving constancy, so objects appear much the same size at different distances. This is an active scaling process that may be set wrongly. The suggestion is that perspective, or other depth cues in pictures, set the scaling inappropriately to the lines in the picture. As the picture is flat, though it represents objects in three-dimensional space, something must go wrong!

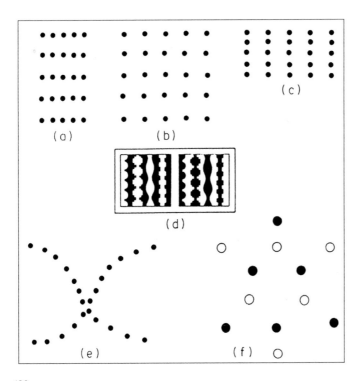

Fig. 12. Gestalt grouping laws.

Fig. 13. Fraser Spiral: the circular pattern (this can be checked with a compass, or by placing a circular object over it) appears as a spiral—not because edges are shifted, but because the features are grouped to form the spiral pattern.

It turns out that scaling may be set either 'upwards', from depth cues, or 'downwards', from seen distance. We can use flipping ambiguity to separate 'bottom-up' from 'top-down' effects. A convenient example is a wire cube. As we have said (pages 435–6), when flipped in depth the further face looks too large, though there is no change of stimulus. When not flipped it looks like a cube, though the nearer face gives a larger retinal image. So here constancy scaling is following *seen* distance (Gregory 1963, 1970, 1997).

But scaling can also be set 'upwards', from depth cues. The simplest and the clearest example is the Ponzo illusion (Fig. 10*a*). The converging lines represent depth by perspective, and the cross line signalled as more distant is expanded. A similar, though less 'obvious' example, is the Müller-Lyer illusion, which is a perspective drawing of corners (Gregory 1963, 1968). What happens for these figures when they are truly three-dimensional? The distortions are destroyed when scaling is appropriate (Gregory and Harris 1975). It should be noted that scaling can be set 'upwards' by depth cues even when seen depth is countermanded by the texture of the

Fig. 14. This famous photograph is of a dalmatian dog on a beach. But it is hard to see which features belong to the dog and which to the beach. When viewed at first upside down, the dog is essentially invisible. Once seen it is easier to see again. The knowledge it is a dog helps to group the features.

picture's flat surface. This is evidently a simple-minded process.

It was pointed out of the Café Wall illusion (Fig. 11) that it challenges Curie's Law, that symmetry cannot produce systematic asymmetry. This chess board-like pattern repeats across the figure and yet produces long asymmetrical wedges. It was suggested that a second process integrates little wedges (produced by local asymmetries) across the figure. Asymmetries occur in some higher level distortions, such as the Zöllner. Here there is a further possibility for what is going on. When perceptions are somewhat removed from the stimulus pattern, and from the initial signals, they may be modified downwards by scaling processes imposing large-scale distortions on symmetrical patterns. To recognize such differences depends on how the phenomena are classified, requiring experiments. In general, there are more possibilities for the 'higher' processes—such as inappropriate size scaling. So the Peeriodic Table has implications.

Grouping   The *Gestalt psychologists of the first half of the 20th century stressed the importance of grouping with their Laws of Organization. Working mainly with patterns of dots, they showed that there are strong tendencies to group dots according to 'proximity', 'continuity', 'closure', and with movement, 'common fate' (Fig. 12). These principles can be used in nature and art to conceal and confuse. Camouflage is a good example.

Fig. 15. Hogarth's engraving *The Fisherman* (1754). This is perhaps the earliest example of an artist deliberately playing with rules of perspective, and other cues to distance, producing wonderful paradoxes.

Grouping features into patterns and objects occurs at all levels of perceptual processing, from simple rules, to high level cognitive processing based on knowledge of objects. A well-known grouping illusion is the Fraser Spiral (Fig. 13).

This is easily mistaken for a distortion illusion, such as the Café Wall (Fig. 11), but it is different as edges are not shifted, but are organized into more or less appropriate patterns. The Dalmatian Dog picture (Fig. 14) is an example of object knowledge giving grouping 'downwards'.

Unlikely   It is significant that, although we tend to see what is likely, we *can* see things so unlikely they appear impossible, or even paradoxical. To be totally blind to unlikely objects or events would be dangerous—as they do occur, and may be hazardous, or useful. If we could see only expected things and events there could hardly be perceptual learning.

Impossible   Impossibility may be *paradoxical* or *too unlikely*. The first of these generally falls under cognitive rules, the second under knowledge. But there can be physiological paradoxes, for stimuli may conflict with other stimuli, especially when one of several parallel channels is adapted differently. The after-effect of motion from a rotating spiral appears as shrinking or expanding though without changing size, which is 'physiologically' paradoxical, movement and position being represented in parallel channels.

Pictures can present objects in paradoxical space. Perhaps the first example is Hogarth's engraving *The Fisherman* (1754) (Fig. 15). Striking examples are the Impossible Triangle, and the Impossible Staircase figures of Lionel and Roger Penrose (Penrose and Penrose 1958) (Fig. 16a). These are the basis of many of Maurits Escher's wonderful paradoxical pictures. It is strange that we can experience a paradox perceptually while knowing its solution conceptually, as with the Impossible Triangle model (Fig. 16b). This paradoxical perception occurs because the visual system assumes that the sides meet and touch at all three corners. At one corner they are separated in depth, though they touch optically in the eye.

Fiction   Perceptions are far richer than the available sensory data, as perceptions are enhanced by knowledge, from previous interactions with objects. As sensory signals are almost absurdly limited, perceptions must be largely fictional—at least have fictional features—though this does not necessarily mean they are wrong. Fictions can be importantly true, though not based on current data. Such leaps beyond sensed data or measurements are common in science, often justified by verified predictions. As our sensations (or '*qualia*') may be very different from physical reality, we should concede that all perception may be largely fictional.

Fig. 16a. Impossible Triangle Model: created as a drawing by Lionel and Roger Penrose in 1958, this is an early and the most famous Impossible figure. Here is a model, appearing impossible from critical positions—when two sides separated in depth at a corner touch at the eye, and are seen falsely as the

Fig. 16b. Impossible Triangle revealed: here the same object appears possible. (Hiding a corner of Figure 16a will make this, also, appear possible.)

It is useful for perception to be able to take off from stimuli—and to fill gaps—even though this can be misleading, even to creating apparent objects that are not there. The Italian artist-psychologist Gaetano Kanizsa (Kanizsa 1979) produced such superb examples of illusory contours and surfaces, he put such visual fictions on the map (Fig. 17). Though known to psychologists from the beginning of the 20th century, they had been ignored, though known in art for thousands of years, back to cave paintings. Fictional contours do not stimulate brain cells in the first stage of processing (V1). They seem to be quite low-level cognitive phenomena, obeying simple rules. They can give just about every effect of true contours, including inducing distortion illusions, and may come and go with flipping ambiguity.

These ghostly effects include 'neon-spreading' of colours, leaking through gaps in contours, which should be useful for artists. To modify a Dan Dennett remark: these mental figments extend pigments available to painters.

'Filling-in' scotomas. There is a huge blind region of each retina where the optic nerve leaves for the brain, yet we do not normally see a great black cloud hovering before the eyes. Why do we not normally see this local blindness, even though it can easily be demonstrated (Fig. 18)?

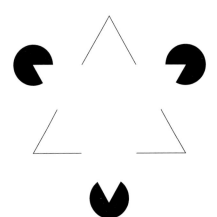

Fig. 17. The Kanizsa Triangle: this is the most famous of Gaetano Kanizsa's 'fictional' figures.

    &   *

Fig. 18. Filling-in (or ignoring?) a scotoma: with the left eye only, look at the dot from about 1 foot away. Move the page around a bit and the '&' will disappear, when it falls on the blind spot. As the '&' is replaced with the colour of the surrounding paper (or a pattern), is the blind region filled in or ignored?

Dennett (1991) has suggested that the blind spot may not be seen not from filling-in, but rather because the brain *ignores* this region, as it never gives useful information (like ignoring a boring person at a party). Yet there is evidence that the blind region is made invisible by active *filling-in from copying the surrounding retinal pattern (Ramachandran and Gregory 1991). It will complete patterns, but will not add missing noses, so this is hardly cognitive. Ignoring is a neat idea, and may occur often, but nature does not always adopt the neatest solutions— and does not always please philosophers.   RLG

Block, R. J., and Yuker, H. E. (1992). *Can You Believe Your Eyes.* (Eclectic collection: black and white only.)

Dennet, D. C. (1991). *Consciousness Explained.*

Gibson, J. J. (1950). *The Perception of the Visual World.*

—— (1966). *The Senses Considered as Perceptual Systems.* (This, and the previous work listed, give a 'direct' account of perception that is very different from the account accepted here.)

Gombrich, E. H. (1956). *Art and Illusion.*

Gregory, R. L. (1963). 'Distortion of visual space as inappropriate constancy scaling'. *Nature*, 199.

—— (1966). *Eye and Brain* (5th edn. 1977). (Based on the notion of perceptions as hypotheses, with discussions of illusions.)

—— (1968). 'Perceptual illusions and brain models'. *Proceedings of the Royal Society*, 171.

—— (1970). *The Intelligent Eye.*

—— (1980). 'Perceptions as Hypotheses'. *Philosophical Transactions of the Royal Society*, 290.

—— and Harris, J. P. (1975). 'Illusion-destruction by appropriate scaling'. *Perception*, 4.

—— and Heard, P. (1979). 'Border-locking and the cafe wall illusion'. *Perception*, 8.

—— —— (1983). 'Visual dissociations of movement, position, and stereo depth: some phenomenal phenomena'. *Quarterly Journal of Experimental Psychology*, 35A.

Hoffman, D. (1998). *Visual Intelligence: How We Create What We See.* (Very good on perceptual rules.)

Kanizsa, G. (1979). *Organisation of Vision: Essays on Gestalt Perception.*

Milner, P., and Goodale M. A. (1995). *The Visual Brain in Action.*

Penrose, L. S., and Penrose, R. (1958). 'Impossible objects: a special type of illusion'. *British Journal of Psychology*, 49.

Ramachandran, V. S., and Gregory R. L. (1991). 'Perceptual filling in of artificially induced scomata in human vision'. *Nature*, 350.

Robinson, J. O. (1972). *The Psychology of Visual Illusion.* (A comprehensive collection of illusion figures, with names and dates of discoveries.)

Sacks, O. (1985). *The Man who Mistook his Wife for a Hat.*

Seckel, A. (2002). *More Optical Illusions.* (Delightful collection.)

Thompson, R. F. (2000) *The Brain: A Neuroscience Primer* (3rd edn.). (Clear general account.)

image rotation. Experiments by Roger Shepard, at Stanford, have shown that at least most people can 'rotate' mental images of fairly simple objects and that this rotation can take place only at a limited rate, which varies between individuals. Remarkably, there is a precise linear relationship between the angle at which the mental image is rotated and the time required. What is rotating may perhaps be some kind of analogue representation, as Shepard believes, or it may be changing parameters of a *digital description. This distinction between analogue and digital representations is a fundamental one, which is one reason why these experiments are so important. See also MENTAL IMAGERY.

Shepard, R. N., and Chipman, S. (1970). 'Second-order isomorphism of internal representations: shapes of states'. *Cognitive Psychology*, 1.
—— and Metzler, J. (1971). 'Mental rotation of three-dimensional objects'. *Science*, 171.

imagination. The word imagination covers a spectrum of meanings in everyday language, from the experiencing of vivid images in different modalities, to states of mind such as daydreaming, characterized by fantasy and fluidity of thought, to the generation of novel ideas and outputs. Though imagination is typically associated with artistic spheres, scientific investigation also involves intuitive 'leaps in the dark' and other hallmarks of imaginative thought. The chemist Mendeleev is reputed to have woken from a dream in which the elements of the Periodic Table were laid out as patience cards, thus solving in imagination the problem that had eluded him during many weeks of effortful reasoning.

1. Imagination and psychological theory
2. Components of imagination
3. Evolution of imagination
4. Development of imagination in children
5. Impairment of imagination
6. Imagination and mental disorder
7. Imagination and the brain

1. Imagination and psychological theory
Contemporary child-rearing and educational practices stress the importance of fostering children's imagination, and in adult life a high premium is placed on activities and outputs which demonstrate imagination. Evolutionary theorists see it as a crucial feature of the cognitive apparatus which sets humans apart from other animals. Yet studies of imagination have played a comparatively small part in mainstream psychology—reflecting theoretical influences which have acted in combination to downgrade its importance. Behaviourists deemed imagination, along with consciousness and other complex attributes of mind, a meaningless construct, because it was impossible to operationalize or measure. Psychodynamic perspectives have recognized its significance, but presented it as 'primary process thinking'—a primitive, associative, non-rational form of thought linked to both dreaming and pathology. In reaction to this, cognitive psychology has either ignored imagination, or sought to explain it

within the framework of conscious, logical reasoning processes—'secondary process thinking'—which is its central subject matter. The theoretical hiatus between psychodynamic and other accounts, which obscures the probable role of both associative and logical processes (Martindale 1999), has stunted the development of a satisfactory psychology of imagination. Where the term features (for instance, in research on pretence), the imaginative content of the activity is rarely clearly defined.

The first task for a psychology of imagination is therefore to identify a configuration of characteristics which epitomize imaginative processes and distinguish them, albeit in degree, from other forms of thought.

2. Components of imagination
*Mental imagery—the capacity to 'see things in the mind's eye', or indeed 'hear them in the mind's ear'—is the most obvious concomitant of imagination. If we ask someone to imagine themselves on holiday, they may report sights, smells, sounds, and tastes from an actual holiday, that is, memories of past experiences stored or accessed in the form of images (see MENTAL IMAGERY for a discussion of the representations involved). However, imagination is not necessarily or exclusively image based. The processes outlined below are likely to involve verbal as well as non-verbal or imaginal thinking.

Counterfactual thinking—the capacity to disengage from reality in order to think about events and experiences which have not actually occurred and might never occur—is a crucial feature of much imaginative thought. Thus the holiday which a person sees in his mind's eye may be one he has never had. Counterfactual imagining is also involved in contemplating potential courses of action, fantasy and pretence, and understanding other people's thoughts, beliefs, and desires (so-called Theory of Mind), all of which are likely to involve verbal as well as non-verbal processes.

A third characteristic of imagination is *symbolic representation, the use of concepts and images to evoke or represent real-world entities, or the use of one set of real-world entities to evoke others (e.g. as when a child uses a stick as a gun in pretend play). It is hard to conceive of any form of thought which does not involve such symbolism. However, imagination appears distinctive in the quality and scope of the symbolism involved. An artist or poet may use paint on paper or words on a page to evoke imaginative ideas which transcend regular references or meanings. Mithen (1998) describes the basis for this as cognitive fluidity—the exchange of concepts between different cognitive domains, such that laws applying in one domain can be broken in another. Thus a sequence of notes may be 'heard' as a mountain stream; a child engaged in a pretend fight readily accepts that an ordinary twig 'is' a sword; an adult may believe in life after death, or that supernatural beings can travel through solid objects.

Cognitive fluidity also underpins the capacity, crucial for imagination, to operate on familiar symbolic representations generating novel ones. This manifests itself most obviously in the works of creative artists. A composer, for instance, may work with the same set of notes or harmonies to generate entirely new compositions. This raises the difficult question of how, if at all, imagination differs from *creativity. According to one contemporary approach imagination is a basic and universal characteristic of human cognition, while true creativity is the attribute of an exceptional, talented minority. Thus Boden (1990) points out that, while all humans possess the imagination necessary to generate new combinations of thoughts or words, true creativity transcends such routine generativity. However, other researchers see creativity as a universal human attribute, and, as such, perhaps indistinguishable from imagination.

An alternative criterion for distinguishing imagination and creativity revolves around the production of outputs. While the act of imagining something can be an entirely personal experience, the concept of creativity is closely associated with the generation of social and cultural products such as music and works of art. Such outputs originate in the imagination of one individual, and have the power to evoke imaginative responses in others. But some recent theories emphasize that both imaginative thought and creative outputs have their sources in social interactions between individuals, once again questioning the idea that creativity is an individual and special talent. It may be soundest to adopt an intermediate position—that imagination reflects universal human processes which are particularly enhanced in those individuals or those interactions that generate creative outputs.

Finally, it seems likely that certain states of mind, accompanied by modifications in brain activity, are particularly conducive to imaginative thought. Martindale (1999) notes that the imagination-rich thinking involved in discovery, creation, and problem solving reflects distinct cognitive phases. The initial phase is typically dominated by the conscious, logical, reality-oriented reasoning referred to earlier as secondary process thinking. Following this is an 'incubation phase'—a 'fallow period' in which no apparent progress on the task is made, and the person may experience a powerful sense of frustration and block. Eventually there is an illumination, or solution, typically when the individual's mind has not been consciously 'focused' on the problem for a time. Both the incubation and illumination phases are thought to be characterized by free-associative, non-logical, or primary process thinking.

The emotional euphoria which often accompanies illumination is epitomized in the apocryphal tale of Archimedes shouting 'Eureka' as he jumped from the bath.

A sustained form of euphoria, the hypomanic mood, typically preceding manic breakdown, in which many great composers and artists have been most prolific, is believed to involve atypical functioning of neurotransmitters and brain circuits (Nettle 2001). Further ideas about brain activity are considered later on.

3. Evolution of imagination

Studies within cognitive archaeology and evolutionary psychology suggest that fully fledged imagination may have emerged only in the last 100,000 years, as a unique characteristic of Homo sapiens sapiens. As much as 2 million years ago, members of the first species of the genus Homo (Homo habilis) displayed a limited capacity to 'imagine' a future outcome, in their ability to fashion stones into simple tools. Since they transported these tools to distant sources of food, these hominids could also perhaps 'see' in their mind's eye locations they had visited earlier. But these embryonic forms of imagination were practised imitatively and inflexibly for a further 1.5 million years, with only gradual changes in technological and behavioural complexity and, by implication, cognitive sophistication. According to Foley (1995), the capacity for counterfactual thinking was a later and crucial evolutionary stage, which coincided with the significant increase in hominid brain size some 300,000 years ago. A hominid capable of imagining the possible outcomes of different actions, or the possible responses of its peers, would have the selective advantage of control over its physical and social environment, uncompromised by expenditure of energy in physically enacting and evaluating alternative outcomes.

From 50,000 years ago, there was a so-called 'symbolic explosion', a proliferation of creative activity including cave art depicting scenes as much imaginary as real, and decorative artefacts, such as the 30,000-year-old Hohlenstein–Stadel statuette of a fantastic creature, half lion and half man (see Fig. 1). Since all the different elements of imagination—imagery, symbolism, counterfactual thinking, novelty, and creative output—are evident during this period, it seems plausible to locate the full flowering of modern imagination here. According to some researchers (Clottes and Lewis-Williams 1998), the humans of this era even understood the role of altered state of mind in promoting imagination, using trance states and hallucinogens to enhance their own powers.

However, we cannot rule out that earlier peoples engaged in rituals, told stories, or fashioned fanciful objects from materials which have perished. Moreover, since modern humans (Homo sapiens sapiens) appeared approximately 150,000 years ago, the reasons for a 'watershed' in imaginative behaviour at around 50,000 years are unclear. Mithen (1998) has argued that the symbolic explosion represents the culmination of evolutionary changes

Fig. 1. Imagining the impossible: a 30,000 year-old statuette of a 'lion-man'.

occurring *beyond* the first appearance of humans, in which a strictly modular cognitive architecture (see COGNITIVE MODULARITY), adapted to deal entirely independently with domains such as the natural world, technology, and social relations, was superseded. A system of flexibly interacting modules, permitting cross-talk between different domains, might confer greater capacity not only for technological innovation, but also for anticipating future actions, and for cooperation in complex social groups, with, as a

by-product, the ability to pretend that a banana is a telephone, or to create (and believe in) a mythical creature. In contrast, Foley and others have suggested that the cognitive capacity for such imagination was fully in place when the first members of *Homo sapiens sapiens* started to think in 'what if?' terms. Accordingly, the later 'symbolic explosion' may reflect behavioural and cultural changes, motivated by population pressures and the need to demarcate one social group from another.

4. Development of imagination in children

Current theories of the development of imagination in children echo evolutionary approaches in stressing the link between imaginative thinking and advanced social and cognitive skills. Much of this work focuses on observational and experimental studies of pretence. Typically developing children display simple forms of pretence, such as using one object to represent another, from as early as 12 months. More elaborate forms of pretence unfold thereafter, in which isolated pretend acts become incorporated into complex scripts (such as making a cup of tea), and children adopt pretend roles (such as Batman or 'mothers and fathers') in social interactions. Leslie (1987) described pretence as an ontogenetically early form of meta-representation. The representation 'this is a banana' is decoupled from reality to allow acceptance of the proposition, in pretence, that 'this is a telephone'. This, he argues, 'kick starts' the general capacity for counterfactual thinking. By contrast, Harris (2000) argues that children employ pretence partly in order to learn *about* reality. His claim that elements of reality are imported into pretence in order to 'run through' their consequences may explain why a pretend episode such as a fight can generate genuine emotional responses. Both theories give pretence a central role in developing the child's theory of mind, and hence their capacity to enter the social world of other people.

Harris's model encompasses a wide range of childhood phenomena including imaginary companions, belief in magic, and fairy stories. His view of imagination as a sophisticated and logically coherent mode of cognition, which reinforces rather than disrupts the developing child's grasp of social and physical reality, clearly links it with the notion of secondary process thinking. As such, Harris's account provides no obvious sources for the inventive juxtapositions of startlingly disparate ideas which we may see in the work of artists and poets. A complete theory of the imagination needs to address how, if at all, the normal, well-regulated fantasy world of children pretending relates to the exceptional 'zany' imagination which we find, for instance, in surrealist paintings or James Joyce's stream of consciousness. As Martindale (1999) suggests, the capacity for creative imagination may depend upon the facility with which an individual can alternate between primary process and secondary process thought.

5. Impairment of imagination

The extensive imaginative impairments documented in people with *autistic spectrum disorders* (ASDs), and the usually profound consequences for how such people engage with the human world, serve as a 'test case' for the importance of imagination in human cognition and social behaviour. Yet if imagination is such a crucial human adaptation, why should genes conferring susceptibility to a condition marked by imagination deficit persist in human populations? Baron-Cohen et al. (2002) have speculated that the presence in early human societies of some individuals with a typically autistic cognitive style, combining diminished imaginative capacity with an enhanced grasp of physical and mechanical systems, might have had certain selective advantages. These would be the individuals who, while the shamans contacted the spirit world, or dealt with social disputes among kin, and while the artists embellished cave walls, would be fulfilling other functions such as predicting the path of an oncoming storm, or building a robust dwelling.

The paucity of pretend play in children with ASDs is such a robust finding that it now forms part of a clinical tool for the early detection of autism (Baron-Cohen et al. 1996). A child with autism given a pile of toy bricks is likely to arrange them obsessively in patterns or colours, but unlikely to use them for a 'tea party' or a make-believe train. Difficulties in imagining other people's thoughts (Theory of Mind) have been extensively documented using tasks such as false belief (Baron-Cohen, Leslie, and Frith 1985) which require an understanding that another person's belief about a situation might be different from one's own.

Of particular interest in this context are studies by Craig and colleagues. One study, based on the Torrence tests for creativity, highlighted the inability of children with ASDs to generate a range of novel interpretations for a junk object. Another (Craig, Baron-Cohen, and Scott 2001) showed that these children lack precisely the imaginative capacity which enabled our ancestors to fashion a lion man. The children were unable to produce drawings of fantastical creatures combining, say, the top half of a fish with the body and legs of a mouse. Yet their drawings of real-world creatures were unimpaired, reinforcing the notion that full-blown imagination requires not just the ability to 'see in the mind's eye', but also to manipulate and combine mental images fluently and in defiance of domain-specific constraints.

Yet any interpretation of imaginative impairments in ASDs must accommodate substantial variations in their severity across the spectrum. For instance, some people with Asperger syndrome or high functioning *autism have a measure of social imagination in the form of partial Theory of Mind skills. The recent case of an autistic child with exceptional poetic and literary skills (Mukhopadhyay 2000) and the claim that geniuses such as Beckett and Wittgenstein suffered from Asperger syndrome (Glastonbury 1997) argue for a complex relationship between imaginative impairment and ASDs.

6. Imagination and mental disorder

We find a mirror image for imaginative impairment in the wild, uncontrolled imagination that accompanies mental disorders such as manic depression and psychosis. Some research (see Jamison 1993) suggests that composers and artists such as Schumann and Van Gogh have been particularly prolific during hypomania or borderline psychosis, states that precede actual breakdown, when thought and behaviour become too disorganized for creative output. The gradual onset of schizophrenic illness in the painter Louis Wain is precisely charted in his series of cat paintings, first animated and intriguing, then developing an increasingly nightmarish, demonic, and fragmented quality as the disorder took hold.

Studies of the family trees of exceptional people suggest the presence of traits which, depending on genetic loading and environmental circumstances, may be expressed as an outstanding imaginative talent, or mental disorder, or a combination of the two. Nettle (2001) concludes that the same brain processes which promote originality and mental fluidity as key components of imagination can also, depending on environmental circumstances, lead to mental disorder. Like Baron-Cohen, Nettle sets this, speculatively, in evolutionary context: genes which promote the adaptive attributes comprising exceptional imagination carry with them the cost of susceptibility to mental disorder.

Atypical functioning of brain processes and circuits is implicated both in the 'strong imagination' described by Nettle, and contrastingly, in autism, with its impairments in social and creative imagination. This returns us to the intriguing question of how imaginative processes generally are instantiated in the structure and activity of the brain.

7. Imagination and the brain

The notion that we could identify brain specific correlates for imaginary thoughts, such as that of a lion man, seems far fetched. However, both PET and fMRI studies have begun to reveal some of the areas of the brain involved in imagery, which as we saw earlier is a basic, though not universal, feature of imagination. As Damasio observes, cortical brain circuits involved in creative imagination are shaped by each individual's activities and experiences.

Of particular interest are PET studies indicating that imagining oneself involved in a particular action may activate the same areas of the brain as actually performing the action (see Robertson 2002). Moreover when such imaginary movements are mentally practised repeatedly, the relevant motor areas of the brain exhibit sustained changes similar to those which occur when the movements are practised physically. This fascinating finding explains the efficacy of the 'mind game', the technique of imaginary practice used by many top sports people and musicians.

Similar results occur in visual imagery tasks. When a participant is asked to imagine a particular object, the primary visual cortex is activated, as it would be on actually viewing such an object. However, when a person mentally accesses familiar images—whether of movements or objects—he or she must also be using those brain regions where the relevant memories are laid down. This is effectively highlighted in a study by Maguire, Frackowiack, and Frith (1997). London taxi drivers, famed for completing 'the knowledge'—the intensive training in negotiating the highways and byways of London—were PET scanned while imagining the routes they would take to familiar locations. The scans indicated intense activity in the right *hippocampus, where, it seems, the spatial memories of the routes had been laid down.

Studies of the brain activity involved in imagining familiar objects or routine movements unfortunately tell us little about what brain activity underpins more complex forms of imagination. What happens, for instance, when we think about an event which has never occurred, pretend to be a train, or create an entirely novel object in the mind's eye? The relevant experiments have never been done. However, as many researchers have noted, such activities require mental fluidity—the combination and transformation of images or thoughts from the same or different domains. Damasio may therefore be correct in proposing a key role for the frontal lobes, which are involved in organizing and coordinating information from different parts of the brain. Yet frontal lobe activity also operates to inhibit 'irrelevant' thoughts and actions. Since this could potentially suppress precisely those eccentric connections that mark creative imagination, perhaps imaginative thought involves, at different phases, both upward and downward modulation of frontal lobe activity. *Electroencephalography (EEG) studies (see Martindale 1999) support the idea that fluctuating levels of cortical (and particularly frontal) arousal are related to imaginative thought.

Studies of the relation of brain activity to imaginative thought are clearly in their infancy, but one final study merits inclusion here. Gruzelier et al. (2002) have made EEG recordings of brain activity during a controlled trial of biofeedback training designed to enhance the imaginative performance of musicians. The performance of young musicians at the Royal College of Music was evaluated before and after they had learned to control their own brain rhythms. The learned capacity to evoke theta-wave activity over other frequencies was found to be correlated with the musicians' imaginative involvement in their performance, as evaluated by independent experts. The idea that brain activity might eventually be harnessed to enhance imaginative thought provides a suitably optimistic conclusion to this discussion.   IR

Baron-Cohen, S., Leslie, A. M., and Frith, U. (1985). 'Does the autistic child have a theory of mind?' Cognition, 21.
—— Cox, A., Baird, G., et al. (1996). 'Psychological markers in the detection of autism in infancy in a large population'. British Journal of Psychiatry, 168.
—— Wheelwright, S., Lawson, J., Griffin, R., and Hill, J. (2002). 'The exact mind: empathising and systemising in autism spectrum conditions'. In Goswami, U. (ed.), Handbook of Cognitive Development.
Boden, M. (1990). The Creative Mind.
Clottes, J., and Lewis-Williams, D. (1998). The Shamans of Prehistory: Trance and Magic in the Painted Caves.
Craig, J., Baron-Cohen, S., and Scott, F. (2001). 'Drawing ability in autism: a window into imagination'. Israel Journal of Psychiatry and Related Sciences, 38.
Damasio, A. R. (2001). 'Some notes on imagination and creativity'. In Pfenninger, K. H., and Shubik, V., The Origins of Creativity.
Foley, R. (1995). Humans before Humanity.
Glastonbury, M. (1997). 'I'll teach you differences: on the cultural presence of autistic lives', Changing English, 4.
Gruzelier, J. H., Egner, T., Valentine, E., and Williamson, A. (2002). 'Comparing learned EEG self-regulation and the Alexander technique as a means of enhancing musical performance'. In Stevens, C. et al. (eds.), Proceedings of the 7th International Conference on Music Perception and Cognition, Sydney 2002.
Harris, P. L. (2000). The Work of the Imagination.
Jamison, K. R. (1993). Touched with Fire: Manic-Depressive Illness and the Artistic Temperament.
Leslie, A. M. (1987). 'Pretense and representation: the origins of "theory of mind"'. Psychological Review, 94.
Maguire, E. A., Frackowiack, R. S. J., and Frith., C. D. (1997). 'Recalling routes around London: activation of the right hippocampus in taxi drivers'. Journal of Neuroscience, 17.
Martindale, C. (1999). 'Biological bases of creativity'. In Sternberg, R. J. (ed.), Handbook of Creativity.
Mithen, S. (1998). 'A creative explosion? Theory of Mind, language, and the disembodied mind of the Upper Palaeolithic'. In Mithen, S. (ed.), Creativity in Human Evolution and Prehistory.
Mukhopadhyay, T. (2000). Beyond the Silence: My Life, the World and Autism.
Nettle, D. (2001). Strong Imagination.
Robertson, I. (2002). The Mind's Eye.

impression. This term reflects the ancient notion that experiences are impressed on the 'wax' of the mind by the 'seal' of experience in *memory. This implies that memory is essentially passive, but modern work, following F. C. *Bartlett (Remembering, 1932), strongly suggests that memories are active constructions, and are often distorted towards the familiar or the wanted. So this notion of memories as impressions like seals on wax is not an appropriate model.

imprinting. When recently hatched birds such as ducklings are hand reared for a few days, they strongly prefer the company of their human keeper to that of their own species. This remarkable process, which can so dramatically influence the development of social relationships, is called 'filial imprinting'. A bird's experience later in life can also strikingly influence its sexual preferences. When exposed to another species at a certain stage in development, it may subsequently prefer to mate with that species. The process influencing mate choice is known as 'sexual imprinting'.

In many ways the term 'imprinting' is a misnomer since it implies an instantaneous stamping into the bird's memory of information that will determine its social preferences. In fact, the process is more gradual and is better likened to the painting of a portrait in which the broad outlines are first sketched and fine details are filled in by degrees. Furthermore, despite the remarkable distortions of social preferences that can occur under artificial conditions, some stimulus objects are much more effective than others. In general, objects that are most like the animal's own species are most effective in influencing its subsequent preferences.

The procedures used for studying imprinting are not associative. The experimenter merely exposes the bird at the right age to a single conspicuous object and subsequently shows that its preferences have become restricted to that object. Even so, the underlying process might be associative. If this were the case, initially significant and attractive features of the stimulus object would be linked to initially neutral features in the course of learning. Deciding whether or not this is really what happens is not easy. Even if the imprinting process that leads to the identification of parents (or future mates) is not associative, it operates simultaneously with both classical and operant *conditioning. What is more, the objects that work best for purposes of imprinting can be used with the associative procedures as rewards. Thus, the imprinting stimulus is highly effective as a reinforcer, and a young duckling can easily be trained to press a pedal that switches on a motor and brings an object into motion. However, enough is now known about the neural mechanisms to dissociate by lesions in the brain the operant conditioning which involves learning to press a pedal from the imprinting which involves the narrowing of preferences to a familiar object.

As it happens, filial imprinting in domestic chicks has proved to be a useful model for studying the neural basis of *learning. Using biochemical measures of neural activity and autoradiography, a site in the intermediate part of the medial hyperstriatum ventrale (IMHV) has been found to be intimately involved in filial imprinting. When the neurons in this area are destroyed before imprinting, a chick fails to identify the object with which it has been trained; furthermore, when they are destroyed immediately after imprinting, a chick no longer responds preferentially to the object with which it was trained. Nevertheless, lesioned birds are just as capable as intact animals of learning discriminations in which reward is involved, and will work just as readily for an imprinting object—even though they do not learn its characteristics.

Some other discoveries of the work on the neural mechanisms involved in imprinting are also striking. Storage only remains localized in the IMHV on the left side of the brain. On the right side, information is stored initially in the IMHV but within 24 hours it has dispersed to other, and as yet unknown, sites in the brain. In the left IMHV, where information about the imprinting object remains stored, the dendritic synapses increase in size. It would be an exciting as well as demanding task to discover whether the pattern of synaptic enlargement codes the information stored in the course of imprinting.

One of the striking features of filial imprinting is that it is easiest to get birds to learn about an object at a particular stage early in life. This stage is referred to as a 'sensitive period' in development. However, it is important not to confuse the descriptive evidence for such a period with explanations for how the evidence has been generated. The nature of the timing mechanisms has proved to be subtle, and the image of a clock, opening a window onto the external world and then shutting it again, is not good enough.

Generally, the onset of sensitivity is measured in terms of time after hatching. However, birds can differ by as much as 30 hours in the stage of development at which they hatch. In other words, when eggs have been incubated under identical conditions, the time from the beginning of incubation to hatching varies greatly. It is possible, therefore, to have birds of the same post-hatch age which are at different stages of development, and birds which are at the same stage of development but of different post-hatch ages. The influence on imprinting of the general stage of development can be separated from the influence of experience occurring at hatching and after it. It turns out that both the age from beginning of embryonic development and the age from hatching influence the results. In other words, it looks as though the general stage of development of the bird plays a part in the onset of sensitivity, but that the events associated with hatching, or experiences subsequent to it, also play their part. Part of the increase in sensitivity is attributable to the changes in the efficiency of the visual system. This being the case, the interaction between internal and external influences is particularly easy to understand. Visual experience with patterned light has a general facilitating effect on the development of visually guided behaviour. It also serves to strengthen connections in neural pathways. Thus, it is probable that the development of the visual pathways, on which filial imprinting must depend, can be accelerated by early hatching if this means that the bird receives more experience from patterned light than the bird that is still inside the egg.

The end of sensitivity to novel objects arises from a property of the imprinting process. When a bird has formed a preference for an object, as a consequence it ignores or even escapes from other objects. Therefore, imprinting with one object prevents further imprinting with other objects from taking place. While some objects are much more effective than others in eliciting social behaviour from naive birds, domestic chicks can form social preferences for suboptimal stimuli such as the static cages in which they were isolated, although this takes several days. It follows, that if some birds are reared with near-optimal stimuli, such as their siblings, and some are reared in isolation, it should be possible to imprint the isolated birds with a novel object at an age when the socially reared birds escape from, or are indifferent to, new things. This is clearly the case with both domestic chicks and mallard ducklings. Investigators find it difficult to get older birds to respond socially to an object, because the birds have already developed a preference for something else.

It seems, then, that the end of sensitivity of a bird to a wide range of objects is generated by a runaway process in which the consequences of an initial change in state generate the conditions for further and more rapid changes. When the bird is poised to learn, all that is required is the presence of a suitable external stimulus to trigger the process. As a result of learning about a particular object, the bird escapes from those it can detect as being different. This escape from strange objects intensifies the young bird's contact with a familiar object, and the range of acceptable companions rapidly contracts so that in the natural world the bird ends up with a distinct preference for its own mother. Enforced contact with something other than the preferred familiar object may wear down the behavioural constraints to the point where the bird does form a new preference. Escape from novel objects can be habituated, and domestic chicks that have developed a preference for object *A* can be induced to prefer object *B* to object *A* by sufficiently long exposure to the second object. It turns out that the early preference is not forgotten and may resurface after isolation from both types of object. So, it would seem, the protection of preferences from subsequent disruption is accomplished not only by behavioural means, but also by internal processes as well.

For many years it was thought that imprinting enabled an animal to learn about its species. However, it is becoming apparent that imprinting serves a more subtle but equally important purpose, enabling the young to recognize one or both of their parents as individuals. The species that are feathered and active at hatching must learn the parental characteristics quickly because, on leaving the place where it was hatched, the young bird must stay near a parent. If it approaches another adult of its own species, it may be attacked or even killed. For this reason, as soon as the young animal is able to recognize its parent (or a substitute parent in an experiment), it escapes from anything that is noticeably different. The rapid attachment to the first conspicuous objects encountered after hatching is characteristic of the precocial species. In birds like the swallow, which are hatched naked and helpless, learning occurs later in development, and the young respond selectively to their parents only when they have left the nest about two weeks after hatching. Sexual imprinting probably occurs later in development because birds need to know the characteristics of their siblings' adult appearance when they come to choose a mate. The ideal mate must be a bit different but not too different from close relatives in order to avoid the dangers of inbreeding and, at the other extreme, the dangers of mating with a genetically incompatible partner such as a member of another species. Some animals are so careful in their choice of sexual partner that, having been reared with their siblings, they then choose first cousins as mates. This has been discovered in Japanese quail and also in mice. Indeed, it is becoming apparent that processes similar to those first described in birds are equally important in mammals. The biological need to recognize close kin, both early in life and when adult, is a general one.

PPGB

Bateson, P. (2000). 'What must be known in order to understand imprinting?' In Heyes, C., and Huber, L. (eds.), *The Evolution of Cognition.*

Horn, G. (1986). *Memory, Imprinting and the Brain: An Inquiry into Mechanisms.*

——(1991). 'Cerebral function and behaviour investigated through a study of filial imprinting'. In Bateson, P. (ed.), *The Development and Integration of Behaviour: Essays in Honour of Robert Hinde.*

Indian ideas of the mind. A short survey cannot do justice to the enormous range of ideas of the mind produced in India. In an unbroken cultural tradition of some 3,000 years, which has given birth to Hinduism (itself the name not of a single religion but of a family of religions), Buddhism, and Jainism, one of the main topics of conceptual interest has been in philosophical psychology: how the mind is to be analysed, trained, and developed, in order to explain and obtain the religious goal of enlightenment and release from rebirth. Here it is possible only to indicate some of the main structures and attitudes of Indian thought, and certainly exceptions to everything said here have existed.

Indian ideas of the mind

Among the many words which can be translated as 'mind' are: *manas*, from *man*, to think; *citta* or *cetas*, from *cit*, to perceive or attend to (these latter two are often better translated as 'heart', the Western term for the affective and intentional centre of personality; indeed the word usually translated as heart, *hṛdaya*, itself is often used to refer to cognitive acts); *buddhi*, from *budh*, to be awake or aware; *vijñāna*, from *jñā*, to know or be conscious; and, finally, in many philosophical contexts the term *antahkarana*, literally inner activity or inner organ, is used to refer collectively to a variety of perceptual, intentional, and cognitive functions or agencies. Often some or all of these terms are to be regarded as synonymous; in particular systems they can also be taken to refer to different things. In no case can we assume anything simply comparable to Western *mind–body dualism; nor has much attention been paid to the specific mind–brain problem. Insofar as mind or *consciousness has been given a physical location, or at least been associated with particular locations in the body, it has been in terms of the mystical physiology of *chakras*, circles or centres of energy, twelve of which are thought to be located in various parts of the body; different kinds of consciousness are then associated with different *chakras*.

The first and most general point to make about Indian ideas of the mind is that they have been elaborated in a conceptual context derived from, or at least constantly in interaction with, religious concerns. The basic structure of the religious world-view is given by the following three terms. (i) *Saṃsāra*—'the round of rebirth'—is the idea that each person (however that is conceived) lives through a series of lives, which can occur in various forms both in this world and elsewhere. (ii) *Karma*—'action', 'moral retribution'—is the belief that it is action that causes this process of rebirth, and experience within it; the moral quality of actions performed previously—usually but not necessarily in past lives—determines the happiness or suffering experienced thereafter. This gives both one type of explanation of suffering and evil, and a possible rubric for religious and moral behaviour which tries to improve one's lot in the future. One may hope for rebirth in better circumstances, or for an escape from rebirth entirely. (iii) *Mokṣa*—'release', 'liberation' (in Buddhism usually called nirvana)—refers to the escape from rebirth, to an ultimate state variously conceived, but usually involving some or all of the qualities of freedom, bliss, transcendental knowledge, and power.

This conceptual system is understood in at least two main ways. First, in a literal or mythological sense it can be taken straightforwardly to refer to a sequence of births, lives, and deaths, and to escape from them. Secondly, it can be interpreted in a psychological or 'demythologized' sense—that is, as referring to different ways of perceiving and evaluating the temporal world, rather than to differ-

ent life histories or destinies within it or beyond it. In this sense, *saṃsāra* is best taken as something like 'differentiated perception', or 'unenlightened understanding'—that is, seeing the multiform and in itself unreal ordinary world as ultimately real and desirable, in contrast with *mokṣa*, which is seeing the world in its eternally true light (a true light, of course, very differently described by different systems). Here, instead of the religious goal of enlightenment being taken in a horizontal perspective—as something awaiting the holy man at the end of his earthly life—it is taken in a vertical perspective, as a possibility of moral–mystical experience *now*. (Of course, these two perspectives are not mutually exclusive; the symbolic, psychological sense can be, and is regularly taken to be, the means of operation of the literal, religious-destiny sense.) A very fine expression of the vertical, demythologized interpretation of these concepts is given by the 10th–11th-century theologian Abhinavagupta, for whom the ultimate subjective reality of the self and the objective reality of the experienced universe are both God, known as Siva or Bhairava. It is God's essential nature, as pure consciousness, constantly to manifest or emanate the individual selves and objects of the ordinary world (*saṃsāra*) as both its efficient and its material cause. Thus we read that:

[Liberation *is* knowledge; it is not a separate phenomenon which knowledge produces], for liberation *is* the revelation of one's true identity; and the identity of the self is consciousness. . . . When one has established oneself in the sphere of prediscursive intuition one may become supreme Siva, through any of the levels of manifestation, from the grossest impenetrable matter to the subtlest Siva. One's awareness becomes supreme Siva by these [various inroads, by centredness] in the light which manifests itself as these ordered aspects as they shine in their primal brilliance. . . . One becomes Bhairava by the revelation that within one's own identity as the void of consciousness one is oneself causing the universe to appear and that as one creates it one is it. This entire system of the six parts of the cosmos is reflected in me alone and it is I that sustain its existence. Thus shines forth one's identity with everything. This universe is dissolving into me as I roar with the fire of absolute awareness beyond time. With this vision he comes to rest. The realization that one is Siva [is] the surging holocaust [which] burns to nothingness the dream-palace of *saṃsāra*, with its infinite, diverse and beautiful chambers. (*Tantrāloka*, i. 156; i. 211–12; iii. 283–6, trans. A. Sanderson)

In this general religious context, ideas of the mind depend on different notions of the enlightening realization, and specifically on different notions of what is the soul or self that is realized and liberated. Answers to this latter question vary greatly: there is the view, as we have just seen, that the single and ultimately real self is (a personal) god; the real self can be seen as the impersonal cosmic spirit or essence, usually called *brahman* (as in the *Vedānta*); it can be a separate, eternally monadic soul or person (as in Jainism and *Sāṃkhya*. These two systems are atheistic: elsewhere such a monadic soul is also related, devotionally, to a god); and finally, as in Buddhism, the ultimate realization is that there is no self at all.

In all these systems, what we call the human mind is *not* part of what is released; it is in itself either an obstacle to, or at most merely an instrument of, release, on a par with the physical senses. One system which exemplifies this, and which was used in various developed forms by many later traditions, is the classical *Sāṃkhya* (Discrimination). It is a dualism, but not at all in the Cartesian sense. On the one hand, the real self is called *puruṣa*, 'person'; it is eternally inactive, a mere spectator at the show of existence. On the other hand, *prakṛti*, 'matter' or 'nature', evolves from within itself the whole drama of rebirth and release. From an undifferentiated state of equilibrium, at the start of each cosmic aeon, there evolves first something called *mahat*, the great, or *buddhi*, will, or determinative awareness, then *ahaṃkāra*, 'I-maker' or ego, and then *manas*, mind, conceived as a *sensus communis*, a cognitive organization and recognition of sensory activity and experience. (Subsequently there evolve five sense organs, five organs of action—these, together with *manas*, in fact evolve together and are called the eleven faculties—five subtle elements, the 'sense data' perceived by the senses, and five gross elements, the external substances thus perceived.) The first three evolutes are together termed *antaḥkaraṇa*, inner organ, or in a general sense 'mind'. This mind is constantly changing, moving and being moved in the ordinary world of action and experience. In itself it is unconscious and inanimate; it is only the presence of the static and inactive *puruṣa* which, as an animating catalyst, transforms mental activity into conscious experience. This conjunction of the *puruṣa* and the 'material' mental/sensory apparatus is likened to that of a lame man and a blind man: separately incapable of movement and sight, respectively, but together capable of progress (towards enlightenment) (*Sāṃkhya Kārikā*, XXI). Another image conveys the notion of a release which comes to the 'witnessing' person, entirely without activity on its part, but rather from the material mind's own cessation of action: a dancer, whose dancing show, beautiful but temporary, is finished, gracefully withdraws from the stage, leaving the spectator free (ibid., LXV–LXVI).

Thus the religious context of Indian thought puts ideas of the mind into this sort of conceptual structure. Equally, it influences these ideas by its overriding moral and spiritual attitudes. Generally speaking, the senses and mind are regarded as appetitive, as desiring, grasping, and relishing their objects, in the very act of sensing or knowing them. In the unenlightened, this rapaciousness is wayward and uncontrolled; enlightenment requires the imposition of control on it, either to stop

ordinary experience entirely, or to let it proceed seen in its true light, seen as it really is. The *Kaṭha Upaniṣad* (c.6th–5th century BC) uses an image familiar in the West, and widely used in India:

Know the self as the chariot-owner (i.e. he who is carried, inactively, by it), the body as the chariot. Know awareness (*buddhi*) as the driver, the mind (*manas*) as the reins. The senses, they say, are the horses, sense-objects the path they range over. The self joined to mind and senses, wise men say, is the experiencer. He who is without understanding, whose mind is ever unharnessed, his senses are out of control, as bad horses are for a charioteer. (*Kaṭha Upaniṣad*, i. 3–5)

In the *Bhagavad Gītā* (c.3rd century BC), India's most popular religious text, we read of the unenlightened that 'when a man's mind follows after the wandering senses, his wisdom is carried away, as the wind [carries away] a ship on water'. Contrastingly, 'when everywhere a man withdraws his senses from their objects like a tortoise [withdrawing] its limbs, then his wisdom is firmly established' (ii. 67; ii. 58). The Buddha taught that 'just as a monkey in a big forest seizes one branch, lets it go and seizes another, so too that which is called mind (*citta*), thought (*manas*), or consciousness (*vijñāna*) by night and by day at one moment arises as one thing, [the next moment] ceases as another' (*Saṃyutta Nikāya*, ii. 94–5).

This last text embodies the Buddhist idea that the mind itself changes as rapidly as do its objects, and this points to a very general fact about Indian ideas of the mind. Whereas the true self, or whatever lies behind the ordinary experienced world (in Buddhism not a self or an 'absolute' of any sort, but the fact of emptiness), is unchanging and timeless, the mind and its temporal experiences are constantly changing; but, further, the mind changes *together with* its objects, because the mind and the senses conform to the nature of what they cognize or perceive. A regular idea of perception, for example, is that a ray of light goes out from the eye, makes contact with, and takes on the form of, its object, and then carries vision of the object back to the eye (see, for example, the 3rd-century BC *Nyāya Sūtras*, iii. 32 f.). In a medieval *Vedānta* text (cited from *Panchadasi: A Treatise on Advaita Metaphysics*, trans. H. P. Shastri, 1956) it is said that 'the mind, which is the illuminator of all objects, assumes the forms of the objects it perceives, as sunlight assumes the forms of the objects which it illumines' (iv. 29).

From this notion that the mind assumes the form of its object arise various other Indian ideas. In certain devotional schools of Hinduism, since intense mental concentration of any sort on God will transform the mind into God, even intense hatred will produce God-realization and thus liberation in the hater's mind. Similarly, in certain meditation traditions in Buddhism and Hinduism, when the mind concentrates on a certain level of the psychological–cosmological hierarchy, it 'becomes' that level, and (particularly if the mind is in this state at death) the meditator will be reborn in the corresponding heaven. If, in contrast, an ordinary man's mind is regularly characterized by a predominant emotion, he will be reborn in an appropriate sphere—greed, for example, might produce rebirth as a dog. In the traditions of religious thought and practice known as the *tantra*, this pattern of ideas explains the attainment both of this-worldly pleasure and powers (*bhukti*) and of final release (*mukti*). In order to achieve a particular good (or, in what we call black magic, a harm), the religious specialist will concentrate his mind on the particular deity who controls the desired object, usually in that god's *mantra* form. (A *mantra* is a hymn, sound, or 'spell'. Language—that is, Sanskrit—is regularly thought to be the ground of all thought and consciousness, so particular gods, and the supreme God, have two forms of representation, one visual and iconographic, the other sonic and 'bodied forth' in *mantras*.) In this way, the mind concentrates on and becomes the *mantra*, and thus becomes the god, and so gains control over the god's domain. When this technique is applied to lower-level gods, for this-worldly goods or harms, we tend to see it as magic; it becomes more recognizably religious when final release is sought, when the human microcosmic mind seeks identification with (or, as it is expressed, 'possession by') the macrocosmic supreme divinity. In both these contexts, an image regularly used is that of the god's seal, *mudrā*, impressing itself on the wax of the disciple's mind.

In all contexts, magical, religious, and philosophical, the simple description of the workings of the mind is embedded in their moral evaluation. This can be seen in (though not proved by) the terminology used: the standard terms for the functioning of consciousness, regardless of its ultimate subject (or lack of one), are *grāhaka*, *grāhya*, and *grahaṇa*, grasper, grasped, and grasping, subject, object, and (act of) knowing or perceiving. These three elements of consciousness may or may not be thought of as arising simultaneously or in one or other causal sequence. It is true that in most uses of these terms there is as little concentration on their etymologically literal meaning as there is in the case of their English translation; equally, the fact that Indian thought regularly uses concepts which do not distinguish factual description from moral evaluation does not show (what would be false) that it cannot do so. Nevertheless, these terms are used in systems where the unenlightened mind's 'grasping' its objects *is* seen as intrinsically connected with, or a function of, the foolish desire mistakenly to take the ordinary world for true reality, by grabbing hold of the pleasure and illusory permanence of the experience of the ordinary world. The earliest text of the *Vedānta* school, Gaudapāda's *Māndūkyopaniṣad-kārikā* (c.7th–8th century AD?), demonstrates this:

It is consciousness (*vijñāna*), birthless, motionless and immaterial, [eternally] at peace and non-dual, which seems to be born, move and perceive substance. . . . Just as the movement of a firebrand produces the appearance of straight and crooked [lines], so the vibration of consciousness produces the appearance of perception and perceiver. . . . This duality of subject and object is just a vibration of mind (*citta*). . . . [This] is the craving for what is [ultimately] non-existent, but in truth no [real] duality is found; he who realizes the absence of duality, beyond qualifications is not reborn. (iv. 4s, 47, 72a, 75)

Just as description and evaluation are conflated in these accounts of the mind, so too moral and religious explanations of character and destiny derived from the idea of karma enter into the account of other kinds of mental activity. The key concept here is that of 'traces' or 'impressions' (the term is usually, but not always, *vāsanā*, 'perfuming'), and the notion is that each act, mental or physical, leaves behind it a trace which 'perfumes' or conditions the individual series of mental events which is the mind of the agent/experiencer, just as a sesame seed retains the smell of the flower after the flower has died. These traces in the mind can be representational—that is, a trace can be reactivated as a memory, a dream, or in some systems a perception—or they can be moral and psychological conditioning factors—that is, they may operate in the future as one of the various kinds of determining influence on an individual's character and behaviour in a particular lifetime. The location of these traces is differently described; it is often seen as a particular kind or level of the mind, for which the translation 'the unconscious' is tempting. The metaphor of depth, however, usual in (at least popular versions of) Western psychoanalysis, is not much stressed in India, even in the other image used to picture the mind's operation here, that of 'seeds' sown by action and experience, which ripen later into the 'fruits' of memory, character disposition, and so on.

In the case of the traces being representational, the realist *Vaiśeṣika* system holds that 'memory, dreams and dream-consciousness arise from a particular contact between the self and the inner organ, along with traces' (*Vaiśeṣika Sūtras*, ix. 22–3). In the idealist school of Buddhism, the *Vijñānavāda*, a comparable mechanism, produces perception of a world mistakenly thought to be external, but in fact arising, just as do memory and dreams, from the traces kept in the 'store-' or 'base-consciousness' (*ālaya-vijñāna*) (e.g. in Vasubandhu's *Viṃśaik ā*). When the traces act as moral and psychological conditions, the overall effect of such 'perfuming' by previous unenlightened acts is to predispose the mind habitually to perform further desire-based and ignorant deeds. The general predisposition is specified in various ways. When rebirth at one of the various levels in the cosmic hierarchy takes place, particular kinds of trace in the mind are activated, so as to produce the appropriate mental dispositions for that kind of being (e.g. *Yoga Sūtras*, iv. 8–11, and Commentaries). These dispositions in each life are both general, as species-specific characteristics and instincts, and particular, as those patterns of motivation and behaviour which give rise to individual personality. These individual characteristics are usually described as the predominance of one or more kinds of emotion and attitude; often they are expressed in terms of the 'humours' of traditional Indian Ayurvedic medicine, which resemble the humours of ancient and medieval Western thought. Sometimes, individual character as a man is derived from the predominance of traces derived from species-specific characteristics in former lives, and this individual character can continue even after enlightenment (for although the enlightened man creates no new karma, he may well still have old karma to work off). Étienne Lamotte (in Cousins 1974) recounts the following story:

In Vaisali, a monkey met his death after having filled the Buddha's bowl with honey. He was reborn into a brahman family and as in recompense for his good deed he had as much honey as he needed, he received the name Madhuvasistha, 'Excellent-Honey'. As soon as age allowed he took up the robe [became a monk] and attained holiness. Nevertheless he retained his monkey habits and was often seen perching on walls and climbing trees.

Indian ideas of the mind, then, are influenced by their cultural context, both by the kind of conceptual structure in which they are cast, and by the kinds of moral and religious attitude which arise from the various ways of construing the belief system of rebirth and release. What happens to the mind when release is achieved is variously imagined. The opening lines of the *Yoga Sūtras* declare uncompromisingly that 'Yoga is the cessation of mental activity', and frequently the religious training of the mind consists in an ever-deepening meditative absorption and implosion, in what Mircea Eliade (1958) has called ecstasy. The difference between this kind of quietistic vision of the enlightened mind and more activist conceptions can be illustrated by the following two examples of ocean imagery. In the *Vijñānavāda* school of Buddhism, objects of thought and perception, as well as the illusion of a real subject, are said to arise from within the mind, from the 'store' (*ālaya*). Thus we read that 'just as on the ocean, waves stirred up by the wind dance and roll unceasingly, so the (*ālaya-*) mind-sea, constantly stirred up by sense-objects, dances and rolls with its multiform consciousness-waves' (*Lankāvatāra Sūtra*, 46). The attainment of enlightenment here is then conceived as a calming of the storms of ordinary consciousness; and the mind-ocean finally stops at the 'further shore' of nirvana. In non-dualistic Saivism, contrastingly, while God (Siva) is the only reality, subjectively and objectively, he is not conceived as a quiescent and transcendent divinity, but as the radically immanent and active event of consciousness. Enlightenment consists then not in calming the mind to an absolute stillness, but in the full realization of God's nature in all its self-manifestation. Thus we read (*Tantrāloka*, i. 116; i. 5–6, trans. A. Sanderson) of Siva, whose nature is nothing other than self-transformation through the energies of consciousness (expressed mythologically as goddesses):

The undivided lord, consciousness, has creative awareness as his innermost nature; [thus] the totality of the waves of this consciousness is contemplated and worshipped in various specific conformations, mild or wrathful. . . . [His] power of freedom, the impulse to project himself as order [in space and time] and his embodiment as this order: may this triad of goddesses, the all-inclusive glory of the all-pervading lord, shine within me revealing my ultimate nature. May Ganeśa, son of Siva's consort, the unique ego which controls the faculties of cognition and action, and whose inner nature is as the lord of the great rays which are the fullness of those three [great] goddesses— may Ganeśa, offspring of absolute awareness, radiant full moon, swell the tide of the ocean of my consciousness.   SC

Cousins, L. et al. (eds.) (1974). *Buddhist Studies in Honour of I. B. Horner.*

Eliade, M. (1958). *Yoga, Immortality and Freedom.*

induction. A term encompassing a variety of forms of inference, commonly, but not always, in contrast to *de-duction. If 'proposition' is defined as a thought expressible by a grammatical sentence having either prescriptive or descriptive force, 'inference' may be defined as a transition in thought between one or more propositions (premisses) and a further proposition (conclusion), where the premisses purport to be reasons for the conclusion. The conclusions of deductive inferences cannot be rejected without contradicting the thoughts contained in the premisses, and in this sense are already contained in the premisses. Deductive inferences were consequently classified by C. S. *Peirce as 'explicative', while inferences whose conclusions were not already implicit in their premisses were called 'ampliative'. 'Induction' is sometimes used in the sense of 'ampliative inference'. Classically, however, following *Aristotle's use of '*epagōgē*' (from the Latin translation of which we have 'induction'), the term applies to a subclass of ampliative inferences, namely those in which the conclusion is more general (applies to a wider range of instances) than the premisses.

The root idea of a movement in thought from particular to general has given rise to the practice of applying the term 'induction' to two forms of inference which are in fact deductive. The first of these is complete induction (in Aristotle, 'deduction from induction, *ex epagōgēs sullogismos*'), where the premisses are all less general than the conclusion, but collectively exhaust the instances covered by the conclusion. If chimpanzees, gorillas, humans, etc.

are found species by species to react in a certain way to a certain virus, and these species exhaust the class of primates, one may conclude that all primates react in this way to the given virus. The second is the large family of proof procedures used by mathematicians on a variety of order structures, the simplest example of which is numerical induction: if (1) F is a property of the number one and (2) if F is a property of the number n, then it is a property of n+1, then (1) and (2) together *entail that F is a property of all (natural) numbers.

The narrower classical idea of induction as inference from particular to general excludes certain ampliative inferences involving probability, e.g. inferring that x is F from the high probability that a member of a class, C, to which x belongs, will be F. It also excludes ampliative inference from one or more descriptions of an individual case to some further descriptions of that case. (Where the further description stands as the best explanation of why the first descriptions apply to that case, Peirce distinguished what he regarded as a scientifically vital form of inference, and which he called 'hypothesis' or 'abduction'.)

It is clear from this account that ampliative inferences are by definition not deductions and hence not deductively valid. Where, in other words, an induction is not complete—that is, the cases covered in the premises do not exhaust those referred to in the conclusion (e.g. when concluding that all chimpanzees react in a certain way to a certain virus on the basis of having examined any number, n, of chimpanzees)—the premises may all be true and the conclusion false, and the inference may be reasonable but unfortunately misleading. This gives rise to the so-called problem of induction, but from a purely logical standpoint it can appear to be a matter of lamenting the fact that not all of the inferences which we make have the rigour and compulsion of deductions, coupled, perhaps, with the insinuation that only deductive inferences are rationally grounded. But, against the insinuation, it is far from obvious why good reasons for a conclusion must preclude its negation on pain of contradiction. It is clearly possible to distinguish good from bad reasoning which is not in this way absolutely compelling.

From the standpoint of certain epistemological presuppositions, however, the problem is acute. If we assume, as is done in traditional empiricism, that all our knowledge is founded on (sensory) observations of individual instances, inductive inference presents itself as the only, however doubtful, means at our disposal for building on this modest foundation the vast edifice of our beliefs about the natural world. Unless there are general statements whose truth can be known *a priori, all premises of our deductions must be reached by induction; and every attempt to infer what holds for some unobserved

or unobservable case on the basis of what has been observed must explicitly or implicitly appeal to a general proposition, which can only rest on induction from observed cases.

But the most, it is held, we are able to observe in individual cases are certain similarities among them, and it seems reckless in the extreme to expect such similarities to appear elsewhere unless we can identify some *cause or constraint which ensures that a pattern we have observed will occur elsewhere. However, in seeking such a causal constraint in what we observe, all we will find are further patterns of similarities in the features of what we observe which are constantly conjoined. We can find, in other words, no basis for a causal constraint which is not itself in need of the very justification that we are seeking to provide.

David *Hume, who is the classic source for this problem (although he did not formulate it using the word 'induction'), considered whether a global principle such as the uniformity of nature could underwrite our inferences from observed to unobserved cases. But such a global principle seems a non-starter: nature is uniform only in certain respects, and in other respects is highly variable. This is reflected in our practice of making inductive inferences. In some cases it is reasonable to generalize on the basis of very few instances; in others a very large number of observed instances is no basis at all for a generalization. Traditional empiricism tends to obscure this difference because it presents all inductive inferences as ultimately proceeding by 'simple enumerations', which have to be assessed in the absence of any background of established beliefs and experimental techniques. Popular and oversimplified views of Karl Popper's response to Hume, namely that science does not rely on induction but on finding exceptions to its generalizations, are likewise based on the notion that induction is simply a matter of projecting a similarity in our experience of part of a class of cases onto the whole of that class (e.g. of expecting what we have observed in some chimpanzees to hold of all chimpanzees which have yet to be observed). In fact we move no closer to real science by saying that the aim is rather to find exceptions to such attempts at superficial generalization.

Francis *Bacon rejected the procedure of applying a global principle as 'childish', insisting that induction must proceed 'by proper rejections and exclusions'. The underlying principle of this genuine Baconian induction (known as 'eliminative induction') is the control we exercise over the circumstances of our observations. We must, in other words, move beyond simply projecting our observations to cases not yet observed and project in the form of experimental hypotheses, which ascribe a network of links between circumstances, which can be varied, and phenomena, which we can observe. We have observed a link between heavy smoking and lung cancer, but do not yet know how the circumstances may be varied so as to interfere with the link (and therefore cannot yet explain why many heavy smokers do not get lung cancer). In this spirit Peirce defined induction as 'the operation of testing a hypothesis by experiment'.

J. S. *Mill's 'four methods of experimental inquiry' were designed to help identify the laws and causal factors governing phenomena. We need (i) to find what is common among the differences in the instances that we have observed ('method of agreement') and (ii) to compare the instances in which the phenomena occur with those in which they do not ('method of difference'). We can (iii) 'subduct' from the phenomena all portions which we can assign to known causes and the remainder will be the effects of causes still to be determined ('method of residues'). And we can (iv) look for functional relations between variations in phenomena ('method of concomitant variations'). The application of such methods and the testing of the hypotheses which they yield evidently involve a procedure of thought which goes well beyond the projection of superficial similarities (expecting future crows to be black because all observed crows have been black); it requires an account of the causal mechanism, which we can then test by creating circumstances which would very likely not occur in nature without our intervention.

Arguably, traditional empiricism generalized inadequately on the procedures by which all humans learn about their environment. Some things are learned by simple *habituation, developing a uniform response to similar stimuli, but a great deal of human learning involves interfering with the environment.

Such a response to traditional empiricism and the problem it has with induction will, however, appear to beg the question unless at the same time one calls into question the assumptions that observation consists in the passive reception of sensory qualities and that the concepts we apply to what we observe derive wholly from this source rather than, in a large and important part, from the control we are able to exercise over what we observe. Bacon, for one, saw that induction properly conducted (i.e. as experimental inquiry) needed to be used not only 'to discover axioms but also in the formation of notions'. If we allow that induction is a procedure through which we develop our concepts of what is or is not a (natural) possibility the traditional problem of induction appears in a quite different light.   JET

Bacon, F. (1620). *The New Organon* (1960 edn.), esp. Bk. I.
Hume, D. (1739–40). *A Treatise of Human Nature* (1888 edn.), Bk. I, pt. iii.
Mill, J. S. (1843). *A System of Logic* (1879 edn.), Bk. III.
Peirce, C. S. (1955). *Philosophical Writings of Peirce*. Ed. J. Buchler, chs. 11–15.
Swinburne, R. (ed.) (1974). *The Justification of Induction*.

infancy, mind in.

1. The baby and philosophers
2. Newborn intelligence
3. Imitating to share
4. Protoconversions in 'primary intersubjectivity'
5. Chasing and manipulating objects; playing games; sharing songs
6. Gaining a sense of self, and awareness of meaning in cooperation
7. The pride and shame of a social identity
8. Beginning to speak: the end of infancy
9. A mind adapted for human society and for cultural learning

1. The baby and philosophers
Theories of human mental life offer very different descriptions of the *intelligence of infants. Empiricists, who tend to be materialists and rationalists, see *consciousness coming into existence through learning—by a material brain remembering experiences. They claim the infant to be a reflex organism, making adaptive responses to stimuli and possessing drives for survival, but inert mentally and amoral, synthesizing representations of objects in the world and building up new motivations. A child gains thinking, intentions, perception of meanings, and appreciation of social values entirely through imitative learning and training—from parents and then from a wider society of peers and elders. Thus are collective knowledge, consciousness of meanings and purposes, and principles of morality and justice acquired and passed on from generation to generation. Individualities arise from each subject's unique voyage of experience.

Romantic nativists assume a quite different view. They assert that the infant is born with unspoken wisdom: a human spirit with mind and feelings, who has simply to grow in strength and skill and in knowledge of the specifics of reality while acting on inherent human impulses. All humans, they believe, have the same basic forms of consciousness, the same instinctive motives, and the same intuitive awareness of one another's consciousness and emotions. In health, human minds grow on the same overall specifications. The characters of individuals differ in their particular natural gifts, and weaknesses, as well as in the opportunities these have had to grow and develop.

Contemporary theories of the infant's mind are 'interactionist', combining elements of the extreme empiricist and nativist philosophies. Psychoanalysis, by focusing on unconscious organizing processes of the individual, created a new interest in the development of the child's separate mental identity: a 'self' whose motivation and awareness grow within the protective mother–child relationship. John Bowlby's *attachment theory takes up this view and interprets the emotional strength of the mature self as a product of the sensitivity and responsiveness of maternal care in the first years. Cognitivists emphasize the novelty-seeking and problem-solving tendencies of infants as active and aware individuals, and they explain development as a construction of increasingly complex 'cognitive representations' for mastery of physical reality and its patterns of change. The Swiss educational psychologist Jean *Piaget, who made systematic observations of infants solving problems that he designed to test developing powers of thought, was the 20th century's great rationalist among developmental psychologists. He portrayed the child as an autonomous experimenter, a 'little scientist', who constructs concepts of objects in the world and who gains rational awareness through an obligatory sequence of stages of concept formation, by 'assimilating' the effects of his acts in 'circular reactions'. For both Sigmund *Freud and Piaget, however, the newborn infant has little beyond reflex powers of integration. This was the prevailing view a century ago. Separation of 'self' from 'outside world' and from 'the other' who shares life with one was thought to be achieved by the learning of distinctions and forms of relationship that arise in interaction of the sensitive subject with the environment. This is called the 'object concept', and the formation of an 'object relation'.

Laboratory experiments to measure what infants can attend to have provided evidence that a baby is born with coherent intentions and a capacity to adapt body actions in one field of awareness. Information is taken in from many senses about the location, motion, and changes of certain nearby objects, integrating 'core concepts'. Tests of infants' perceptual preferences have established that Piaget underestimated the awareness of very young infants for the categories and qualities of objects and events in the world around them. It is important to note, however, that most tests of infant intelligence are still, like those of Piaget, of *visual* cognition. Vision develops, of necessity, after birth. New evidence from observing the infant's use of hearing and proprioceptive (body-sensing) modalities, especially for detection of the presence of persons and their vocal expressions, enriches the developmental picture. A conscious experience of human company may be active from birth. Indeed, it has been shown that an infant a few days old can see, and remember for a short time at least, subtle differences between the faces of different women. Even the undeveloped visual system is serving consciousness of people, and learning.

Thus recent knowledge supports a more nativist position in opposition to a physiological empiricism that dates from Ivan *Pavlov. The increased detail of our knowledge also makes a self-controlled process of differentiation in the child's mind more obvious. An infant's consciousness is neither simple nor incoherent.

2. Newborn intelligence

Experimental tests of infants' acts of exploration and choice prove that they experience in one mental time–space frame, and do so with a measure of foresightfulness or 'future sense'. Their consciousness creates measures of time in movement, and a space that is defined by the form of the body and by inherent capacities for directed action of its parts. For example, a baby no more than a few minutes old may turn as one whole person to anticipate the path of motion of an object seen (Fig. 1). Newborns can detect patterns in the recurrence of particular things—they make perceptual distinctions, and record the timing and location of recent happenings. Babies adapt, by co-ordinated movements, to the time, place, and nature of events that have importance for them. They demonstrate 'subjectivity', the awareness and purposefulness of a motivated self.

Habituation tests, in which infants are subjected to repeated similar events, show that they may generate predictive strategies. They learn new 'rules', or 'habits', for keeping track of a changing world near them, and become avoidant of events that repeat with no interesting consequences. These tests count the infant's looking and listening behaviours, or record heart rate, breathing, or sucking on a pressure-sensitive nipple. The physiological measures detect fluctuations in attending, since visual or auditory focusing is preceded by changes in the pulse of the heart, and interruption of sucking and breathing. Evidence for complex emotional reactions to events also comes from video and film studies of the facial and vocal expressions and hand movements, and how these change in reponse to another person's behaviour. Expressions of concentrated puzzlement, surprise, pleasure, and displeasure are clearly delineated, and infant arms and hands make movements that vary systematically with the other signs of attending. Evidently babies are ready to signal a subtle variety of feelings.

Of course, the neonate period, to about 3 weeks old, is highly specialized. It is true that survival and adapting to a new environment is the baby's main preoccupation then. Functions of suckling for milk, breathing, and protective action against threatening variations of temperature or injurious contact with hard objects or dangerous animals are all of top priority, and babies adjust quickly to the events of an entirely new human environment. The quick and effective movements of newborns to gasp air, to find the nipple, and to seek comfort and protection from a mother's body are remarkable. They are classically described as *reflexes and assumed to be due to thoughtless neural links from sensory receptive tissues of the brain stem and spinal cord to motor nerve centres. But a healthy baby born without complications is immediately capable of more than mere fixed responses to physical stimuli, and

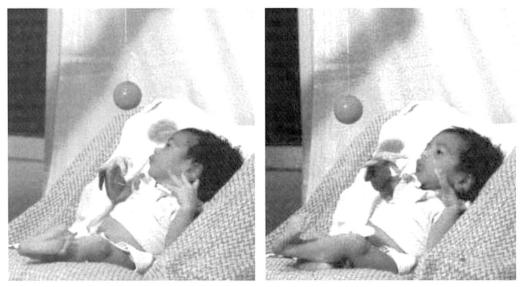

Fig. 1. A newborn infant turns to follow the path of motion of an object seen.

much of the behaviour is spontaneous, curious, and adaptable.

Neonatal suckling, which involves both drawing milk and swallowing it, has been demonstrated to be a well-coordinated, intentional skill that is guided by perceptual anticipation or 'prospective control'. Even the true reflex responses to artificial stimulation with pricks, sounds, or flashing lights that the baby cannot anticipate are powerfully modulated by central physiological processes (called 'state variables') that arouse the brain's activities to alertness, or quiet them down in sleep. Experiments with supposedly 'simple' events—simple, that is, in physical dimensions—produce highly variable and complex results, because the infant's state of motivation is changing. Stimuli that do not engage the infant's expectations cause confusion and avoidance.

There are, in fact, many innate, non-reflex, investigative or seeking behaviours. Given quiet and gentle attention, a baby born without trauma or sedation may be strikingly alert within minutes of birth to the new world of sights and sounds. Wide-open eyes make finely coordinated stepping movements (see SACCADES) aimed in different directions round the body. They may stop or change direction to fixate bright places, or track stimuli in motion (see Fig. 1). They orient to the face of a person who approaches close and speaks gently in a tone of greeting. The eye movements are coupled to small pulsating rotations of the head. Films of newborns orienting to and tracking objects with their eyes reveal that a reach-and-grasp movement of arm and hand is inherently coordinated within the visual space–time field of awareness.

The movements are a well-formed prototype of the movement an adult makes to take hold of an object. This automatic *prereaching*, linked to perception of the changing reality outside the body, is a necessary basis for the eventual exploration of objects and intentional command of actions. If a higher mental command is to work, it must eventually decide about goals in a richly patterned world, and the lower-level problems of perceptual locating and motor patterning must be solved speedily, without reflection. Apparently some of the required solutions have been formulated in outline during fetal stages of brain growth. They are ready for adjustment to perceptions of certain goals very soon after birth. Critical tests show that the newborn has almost no capacity to modulate the form of the basic reach-and-grasp automatism once it is triggered, by changing its duration or size in relation to different kinds of object with different kinds of motion, but the old idea that visual field and aiming of the hand have to be linked together by experience to build a reach-and-grasp movement is disproved.

Most remarkable of all are the infant's reactions to persons. Newborns will turn in the direction of a voice from a loudspeaker behind a curtain, orienting not only the head and ears but the eyes as well, searching to see the person who calls. Simultaneously, hands and face move in ways that indicate a total involvement of a coordinated expressive brain. At birth a baby prefers to hear its own mother's voice—her particular vocal characteristics have been learned *in utero*. In the first few days the sounds of different syllables in speech, as well as their emotional tone, are discriminated by the baby. Observations of face

457

movements of both premature babies and full-term neonates prove that the nerve centres exciting the muscles are organized, so that a wide repertoire of well-formed expressions is present before the baby has had an opportunity to learn from adult exemplars of these human movements. Paediatricians and mothers sense the infant's facial expressions, hand activity, and body posturings to appraise a baby's state and needs. These subtle expressive movements, which may be small and fleeting, are only now being accurately charted by developmental scientists.

After the initial hormonally triggered excitement of birth, the first weeks of a neonate's life are mostly spent in asleep. Infants are usually wide awake and active just after birth, but for two or three weeks thereafter the most common state is either one of sleep with eyes closed, or a vague open-eyed condition in which awareness of the outside world appears weak and fluctuating. The routine cycle of sleep and wakefulness is unstable at birth. It responds to shaping by the consistent routine of responsive care. Often a wakeful newborn is actively avoidant of experiences, and this is particularly noticeable in noisy, highly stimulating circumstances. The tissues of the brain undergo enormous developments in these few weeks and need protecting (see BRAIN DEVELOPMENT). Intercellular connections are rapidly multiplying. There is evidence that nerve circuits in this condition powerfully limit their own excitation by controlling the movements that direct sensory pathways away from stimuli.

In spite of this avoidant state, which is comparable with the dark-seeking, closed-eyed condition of a nestling kitten, controlled observations show that newborns are capable, like other newly born mammals, of rapid conditioning. With the assistance of a mother's routine, a newborn's sleep cycles become adjusted to time of day and night. The opinion of many mothers that a baby learns in a couple of feeds to find the breast with more skill, and that her baby soon knows her and the father as particular individuals, different from others, is confirmed. Olfactory, gustatory, visual, auditory, and body-contact senses have all been implicated in this recognition by familiar caregivers. The mother is known by her smell and ways of moving even when she takes the baby up silently in the dark. The individual appearance of her face is learned immediately.

3. Imitating to share

Psychologists are astonished, and mothers and fathers are delighted, by demonstrations that babies can *imitate* many expressions. Indeed, with some babies, it is easy for a mother to see for herself that her newborn, just minutes old, may watch her mouth intently if she protrudes her tongue or opens her mouth wide; then the baby's mouth opens and the tongue pokes out or the mouth opens wide. The model is accurately copied. Exaggerated expressions of happiness, sadness, or surprise, extensions of the fingers, blinking, looking up are also imitated. Even more remarkable are demonstrations that a newborn infant only hours old may repeat an action he or she has just imitated to 'provoke' an imitative reply from the adult, thus setting up a two-way 'conversation' of gestures. Concurrent changes in the infant's heart rate—acceleration with excitement before the imitation, and slowing with attentive expectation before the 'provocation'—prove that the imitations are intended as signals or requests in reciprocal communication. They anticipate responses. When calling vocalizations are offered, a similarly prompt imitation of the voice can be obtained when the baby is a few weeks older. Imitation of movements of the hands opening or coming together and index finger extension have also been documented.

All these movements, like the expressions of smiling, knitting of the brows, etc., and hand movements of gesture, including making a fist, extending all fingers, or pointing with the index finger, may occur also without a model—but prompt and well-differentiated imitation of some of them is confirmed by well-controlled experiments. At the very least, this phenomenon proves that the infant has made a reasonably well-differentiated awareness of what the mother's face, vocal apparatus, or hands are expressing. This image of her must be formed in close relation to the appropriate motor command which sets off the right imitative response shortly after the baby's focused attending to the model the first time it is presented. Denials of the newborn's ability to imitate, and industrious tests expecting to show it is an artefact or a misinterpretation of the data, reflect a historical–cultural belief that a newborn cannot have awareness of persons. The more sympathetic acceptance that a baby is ready to communicate is increasingly confirmed by psychologists' research, and by the latest data from recording activity in babies' brains when they see or hear persons. Parents are certainly made happy by a simple imitation test that shows their babies 'know' them. Clinically, systematic use of such relatively complex natural social behaviours has value for diagnosis of sensory or motivational differences and abnormalities of young infants.

4. Protoconversations in 'primary intersubjectivity'

Besides imitating, neonates can smile and coo and make hand gestures when spoken to, and a newborn infant can enter into a conversational exchange of coo vocalizations with a parent who is imitating the baby's sounds. These *expressive signs* to persons become much more evident in the second month, after the perceptual systems of the cerebral cortex have developed, especially those for vision. A majority of 2-month-olds raise the right hand more than the left when they are making an expressive

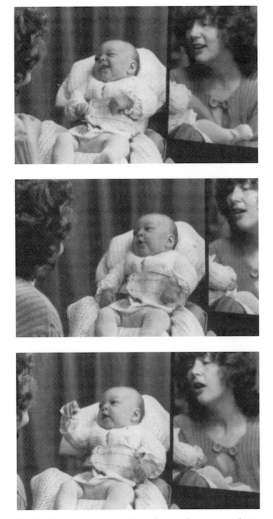

Fig. 2. A 6-week-old girl smiles at her mother, coos and gestures, raising her right hand more than her left. Her mother is speaking gentle 'baby talk' on a steady beat and watching closely.

response when looking at a person speaking to them (Fig. 2). Their brains already have asymmetry of control for making messages of communication. Contented facial expressions of a baby may be stimulated by soft handling and gentle speech or singing; quite different patterns are evoked by loud, impatient, or aggressive speech and abrupt movements. The split-second timing of exchanges of expression between the infant and the mother has been analysed, and proves that both of them are actively controlling the exchange. The baby is wanting someone to 'talk' to.

A highly significant series of experiments has examined infants' responses, in the second and third month and later, to broken or unreal communication, or to the confused expressions of a distressed mother. Threatening expressions or inconsistencies in a partner's behaviour cause the baby to show sadness or fear. When being spoken to in the normal way, babies show quickly changing patterns of face movement, alternating between the appearance of puzzled attending, with knit brows and mouth depressed, and a face full of pleasure and greeting with raising of the eyebrows and a smile (see Fig. 2). The subtlety of these positive expressions of interest and enjoyment, and the speed of their disappearance when a mother holds her face artifically still on a prearranged signal, proves that the baby is highly perceptive that 'something has gone wrong with mother'. A similar effect on the infant's mood and orientation to the mother has been seen in an experiment where infant and mother first engage in 'protoconversation' via a video link, and then a taped portion of the mother's happy communication is replayed to the baby—this 'unresponsive' mother, who does not react appropriately or 'contingently', is distressing for the baby.

It has been found that a mother who is emotionally depressed, anxious, and inattentive to her infant will have difficulty holding her baby's attention, and the baby may be avoidant and even become depressed as well. This work has helped determine how the baby is normally eager to enter into control of the communication of moods and levels of awareness with support from the other person. But we have much description to do before we can give a full account of early intersubjectivity, how the baby perceives people, or how parents and the infant 'co-create' their communication.

Microanalysis of ordinary face-to-face play between mothers and their 2-month-old babies reveals a precise *timing* in the way they address one another and reply. Babies stimulate an adult to use a gentle and questioning *infant-directed speech*, 'motherese', or 'baby talk', which has a regular beat and characteristic expression of mood in its changing intonation, rhythm, and in the accompaniment of movements of head, eyebrows, eyes, and so forth. The infant watches the affectionate and playful display intently, and then makes a reply—on the beat, with a smile, and with head and body movements, cooing, hand movements, and lip-and-tongue movements that have been called *pre-speech*. Photographic records suggest that the last are developmental precursors of actual speech. The attempts at vocal expression are synchronized with hand gestures, as in adult conversation.

It is not claimed that babies have things to say, or that they can hear words as such, but they are certainly perceptive of identifying features in the sight and sound of human speech. They appear to want to make rudimentary 'utterances' themselves when persons excite them by friendly greetings. The outbursts of infant expressive movement form *phrases* that last two or three seconds, and that are organized in *narratives* of expressed excitement with characteristic beginning, climax, and end. Sometimes they contain coos or calls—but often there is no vocalization at this age, merely activity of mouth and hands. Their regularly repeated form helps the mother give the right support and encouragement in her well-timed movements and speech (see Fig. 2). The enjoyment parent and child have in extended 'protoconversations' is taken to demonstrate a state of 'primary intersubjectivity' or dynamic interpersonal awareness that allows mutual regulation of feelings and motives.

Analysis of vocal exchanges in protoconversation by acoustic techniques that allow the timing, rhythms, pitch modulations, and quality of sound expressions to be accurately defined has led to the hypothesis that human beings are born with a 'communicative *musicality'. Tests of young infants' preferences and capacities to discriminate sounds show that they perceive many musical parameters, such as melodies, harmonies, rhythms, accents, in both vocal and instrumental sound, and that their sensibilities are particularly adapted to hear the melody of emotions and states of animation in the human voice, especially the mother's.

The intensity of interest and the delicacy of response of young babies to persons who speak to them reinforces an affectionate personal relationship, which has great importance in the baby's well-being and mental development. In the 'bond' (in the sense of a compact of mutual trust) that develops between them, infant and favourite companion begin to develop a shared repertoire of expressive tricks and exchanges of feeling (see ATTACHMENT).

5. Chasing and manipulating objects; playing games; sharing songs

As the babies' cognitive powers increase by selective retention of mental rules that work better and better to control objects, and after actions have become stronger, more alert and discriminating, around 3 or 4 months, mutual interest with the mother undergoes a subtle but pervasive change. There develops a conflict between pursuit of purpose in subjugation of objects and ways of exploring them, on the one hand (i.e. development of an 'object concept'), and the sharing of sympathy or interpersonal interest with people, on the other (see Fig. 4). But out of this complication, or 'conflict of interests', appears a new *playfulness* that offers a crucial bridge for sharing motives, and for learning arbitrary cultural knowledge. The baby begins to enjoy and contribute to games.

The nature of *humour and play has long baffled philosophers and psychologists. Whatever it is for, play certainly has a key role in the taking of this major developmental step in infancy. As soon as infants gain the ability to

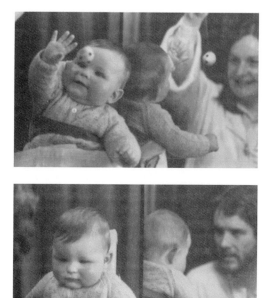

Fig. 3. Paul, at 36 weeks, plays happily with his mother trying to 'catch' a ball, but he is shy then sad with a friendly stranger.

reach and grasp objects, they also respond to gentle teasing about their gropings after a changing target, and to a playmate's emotional attunement to everything the baby does (Fig. 3). An affectionate parent of a blind baby will tease the infant's gropings after an object heard or felt, with much lively vocal attunement, and cause the baby to laugh. Frequently, a 6-month-old will try to grasp the mother's face or her hand. This leads to many games in which the mother moves the attractive part of her about, tempting and dodging the infant's interest. Games of 'peek-a-boo', 'pop goes the weasel', and creeping of the hands up the baby's body ('round and round the garden') will come to mind. Such games, with their well-marked patterns in time, all tease the infant's growing curiosity and expectations, and they reinforce companionship.

Traditional musical formulae in *nursery songs*, *chants*, and *rhymes*, found in all cultures, are purpose built to entertain a baby at this age. They show that all babies gain a sense of fun and appreciation of musical forms of

Fig. 4. Emma, at 28 weeks, has learned to play a traditional hand game ('clappa, clappa handies') with her mother. Songs for infants have similar musical form in different cultures. Emma is a genetic left-hander; already she claps left hand over right. Esme, 40 weeks, enjoys playing with and exploring wooden dolls and a truck, but has to be physically 'persuaded' to obey the instruction 'Put the man in the truck'. She does not understand her mother's gestures and spoken instructions.

communication long before they speak (Fig. 4). Research on spontaneous vocal games and baby songs confirms and extends the theory of 'communicative musicality' developed for protoconversations with younger infants. A typical baby song has a predictable narrative of feeling, a mini-drama in which the changes in excitement are portrayed in expressive timing and in the pitch and tonality shifts of melody and quality of sounds, with repetition of rhythmic forms and extended rhyming vowel sounds that can be anticipated and learned by the infant.

6. Gaining a sense of self, and awareness of meaning in cooperation

Out of the interacting developments of object perceiving and communicating with persons emerge powerful mental functions that open the way for language and other symbolic communications, effective logical formulae for systematic reasoning, and other key artefacts of human culture. Before a baby is 9 months old, he or she has become clever at handling and mouthing objects, very alert to the sight and sound of happenings, including effects of their own manipulations transforming and combining objects, and clear about the distinctions between the familiar and the strange. Life with others is enlivened by humorous games and clowning, created mutually. Sometimes there are conflicts of purpose, and the baby learns to adjust to these with strong and unambiguous expressions of refusal or acquiescence. But there is rarely any sign before the baby is 9 months old of specific interest in taking up another's wishes or intentions in regard to the shared reality (see Fig. 4).

Then, within two or three weeks, this phase of self-directedness or self-absorption (called 'egocentricity' by some psychologists who see it as a limitation of immaturity, rather than a necessary process of development in purposeful autonomy) changes fundamentally. By 1 year a baby starts both to express and to respond to a new kind of mental relationship, a *cooperative awareness* in which the purposes and experiences of another in relation to the world outside both of them become of primary interest (Fig. 5). Both joint and mutual attention draw the infant into cooperative tasks. The 1-year-old is interested in what others intend, what interests others, and how others feel about what they are doing. He or she is beginning to take up other persons' responsible purposes and concerns. The way this consciousness develops gives a fascinating account of a specifically human way of being.

Towards the end of the first year, the infant develops a clear awareness of the persistence of objects in their own right. A short-term 'episodic' memory for identified things and a new more curious searching impulse can direct the baby to find a toy when it has been hidden by someone in view of the infant. But there are other developments, too, that change the infant's communication

Fig. 5. Basilie, one year old, co-operates. When her mother hands her the doll, saying, 'Put the man in the truck', Basilie does so immediately, then looks at her mother and grins. She understands her mother's wishes, and can use 'protolanguage' of gesture and vocal expression to influence others. Basilie is a right-hander.

and awareness of what things mean, how they can be categorized. Before 9 months, babies do not 'offer to give to' or seek 'to have help from' or 'point to direct the attention of' the person with whom they play. They gesture and babble in a highly expressive way, obviously playing with the postures and sounds, and with effects on others, but they do not make utterances about their experiences that are addressed to others as comments or enquiries that seek an affirmation or complement. They do not make

baby words to specify objects to others. Nor do they appear to recognize the mother's names for objects. But by the end of the first year most babies everywhere do all of these things. They quickly learn intricate reciprocal or cooperative games where they purposefully share the effort to build something, look at a book, create an amusing effect. They become aware of and are interested in the changing focus of another person's interest. They retain impressions of interesting events shared with others, and can show 'deferred imitation' of meaningful acts, reproducing ideas or tricks as offerings to interested others several days after first learning them. The motivation for this kind of cooperative play is strong, and people who know the baby well become aware of an intense companionship in it. It leads to a sharing of experiences and of symbols that is uniquely human. It has been called 'secondary intersubjectivity' or cooperative awareness.

7. The pride and shame of a social identity

As an infant is gaining in clever awareness of how others know the world, he or she is also changing emotionally and becoming more subtle in personality and temperament. Through the last six months of the first year babies show strong selective affection for their principal caretakers, usually mothers, and they become highly sensitive to approaches from strangers—often acting afraid or distressed (see Fig. 3). This sign of trust in the familiar 'friend', with matching anxiety about unfamiliar company, seems to relate to the great increase, at 9 months, in complexity of the baby's interest in the knowledge and skills that can be shared best with steady and trusted companions. The familiar playmate is an integral and necessary part of the baby's developing consciousness—a friend. One-year-olds are beginning cultural learning and they show powerful feelings of joyful pride at sharing what they know with appreciative company, and fearful 'shame' when their expressive games are not appreciated, or not comprehended by a stranger, who, too, is naturally sensitive to the mistrust. The infant is showing the early signs of 'basic complex emotions' that will be so important in regulating social relationships and moral attitudes later in life.

8. Beginning to speak: the end of infancy

There is much attention in contemporary developmental psychology to the start of spoken language when, by definition, a child ceases to be an infant (the Latin *infans* means 'unable to speak'). (See LANGUAGE DEVELOPMENT IN CHILDREN; LANGUAGE: LEARNING WORD MEANINGS.) Language, and the symbolic understanding of moods, purposes, and meanings, is central in human nature. Evidence from the interpersonal skills of infants strongly supports the idea that language skills are built on a communicative but non-linguistic sharing of motives that begins soon after a baby is born. The speedy and rich exchange of thoughts that is made possible when insubstantial words stand for all manner of actions and physical objects and events is preceded by the infant's ability to enter into the minds of others, first by their direct expression of interest and mood in affectionate relationship, then by their playful teasing, and finally by their willingness to share significant moments in the experience of surroundings and what may be done inside this evolving joint experience.

The time patterns of speech in a particular language can be discriminated even by a baby a few weeks old. Infants listen to talk from birth. They start to imitate speech sounds more accurately and to play with babbling of repeated syllables at about 6 months of age. At the same age a deaf baby in a home where hand sign language is used to share ideas will begin practising and showing expressive hand movements or 'sign babble'. This shows that the impulse to communicate in artful ways—by means of learned signs—is not confined to the vocal–auditory channel. In fact, during the first eighteen months, vocalizing and making hand gestures develop synchronously as complementary ways of communicative expression, responding to the usage in the family from six months. Humans can 'see' language as well as hear it, as long as the meaning is defined in consistent, mutually accepted forms. A 1-year-old does not merely want to keep close to mother. He or she wants to take note of comments, give and take, share the looking and handling of things, and try to follow the words or signs that seem to be given special emphasis in these interactions. The baby will make vocalizations with gestures in order to mean something, or to give a deliberate message: a demand, a request, a refusal, etc. This *protolanguage* shows to other people what interests the baby, or what he or she intends (see Fig. 5). At 2 years the same baby is not only walking about, but also speaking.

For speaking, objects of interest have to become significant, with conventional meaning and symbolic value. No regimen of conditioning can explain these transformations of a child's mind. Nor are they explained by attachment theory concerned with a need for care and protection. They must be motivated within the child by growth of mental processes that are ready for the instructions and examples that come from older friendly acquaintances, from a seeking for 'companionship'. And in this companionship the toddler is increasingly taking active part in imaginative games and discoveries with siblings and peers, extending the social world.

9. A mind adapted for human society and for cultural learning

It would appear that, from infancy research, we are beginning to appreciate the fundamental form of human motives. We are gaining detailed evidence on how social understandings emerge in infancy, from the sensitivity of the neonate to human care and human emotions to the intelligent, talkative cooperativeness of a 2-year-old. In the process, we seem to be learning a new philosophy of mind that does not set the empiricist against the nativist, and that does not wholly segregate the material from the mental. How else can we attempt to conceptualize an inherent set of motives to share experience with others and to learn ways of communicating cultural meanings in community and through history? And, finally, we are setting a new challenge for brain science. Clearly we have to develop a theory of neural systems that seek, recognize, and learn human company, and that acquire consciousness of human-created meaning by cooperating in purposeful activity and imagination and by sympathizing with the emotions and moral feelings that evaluate a common experience and mutually supportive relationships.   CT

Carpenter, M., Nagell, K., and Tomasello, M. (1998). 'Social cognition, joint attention, and communicative competence from 9 to 15 months of age'. *Monographs of the Society for Research in Child Development*, 63.

Custodero, L., and Fenichel, E. (2002). 'The musical lives of babies and families'. *Zero to Three*, 23/1.

Dissanayake, E. (2000). *Art and Intimacy: How the Arts Began*.

Draghi-Lorenz, R., Reddy, V., and Costall, A. (2001). 'Re-thinking the development of "non-basic" emotions: a critical review of existing theories'. *Developmental Review*, 21/3.

Hobson, P. (2002). *The Cradle of Thought: Exploring the Origins of Thinking*.

Lacerda, F., von Hofsten, C., and Heimann, M. (eds.) (2001). *Emerging Cognitive Abilities in Early Infancy*.

Locke, J. L. (1993). *The Child's Path to Spoken Language*.

Malloch, S. (1999). 'Mother and infants and communicative musicality'. In *Rhythms, Musical Narrative, and the Origins of Human Communication*. Musicae Scientiae, Special Issue, 1999–2000.

Nadel, J., and Butterworth, G. (eds.) (1999). *Imitation in Infancy*.

Papousek, H., and Papousek, M. (1987). 'Intuitive parenting: a dialectic counterpart to the infant's integrative competence'. In Osofsky, J. D. (ed.), *Handbook of Infant Development* (2nd edn.).

Reddy, V. (2000). 'Coyness in early infancy'. *Developmental Science*, 3/2.

Spelke, E. (1991). 'Physical knowledge in infancy: reflections on Piaget's theory'. In Carey, S., and Gelman, R. (eds.), *The Epigenesis of Mind: Essays on Biology and Cognition*.

Trehub, S. E. (1990). 'The perception of musical patterns by human infants: the provision of similar patterns by their parents'. In Berkley, M. A., and Stebbins, W. C. (eds.), *Comparative Perception*, i: *Mechanisms*.

Trevarthen, C. (1998). 'The concept and foundations of infant intersubjectivity'. In Bråten, S. (ed.), *Intersubjective Communication and Emotion in Early Ontogeny*.

—— (2001). 'Intrinsic motives for companionship in understanding: their origin, development and significance for infant mental health'. *Infant Mental Health Journal*, 22/1–2.

—— (2002a). 'Proof of sympathy: scientific evidence on the cooperative personality of the infant, and evaluation of John

Macmurray's "Mother and Child"'. In Fergusson, D. and Dower, N. (eds.), *John Macmurray: Critical Perspectives*.

——(2002*b*). 'Learning in companionship'. *Education in the North: The Journal of Scottish Education*, NS 10/2002.

——and Hubley, P. (1978). 'Secondary intersubjectivity: confidence, confiding and acts of meaning in the first year'. In Lock, A. (ed.), *Action, Gesture and Symbol*.

Tronick, E. Z., and Weinberg, M. K. (1997). 'Depressed mothers and infants: failure to form dyadic states of consciousness'. In Murray, L., and Cooper, P. J. (eds.), *Postpartum Depression and Child Development*.

Uzgiris, I. (1999). 'Imitation as activity: its developmental aspects'. In Nadel, J. and Butterworth, G. (eds.), *Imitation in Infancy*.

von Hofsten, C. (2001). 'On the early development of action, perception, and cognition'. In Lacerda, F., von Hofsten, C., and Heimann, M. (eds.), *Emerging Cognitive Abilities in Early Infancy*.

inferiority complex. His view that *Freud had put too much emphasis on sexuality in the genesis of neurosis and too little on the 'will to power' was one of the reasons why Alfred *Adler broke away from psychoanalysis in 1911 and formed the more or less independent school of 'individual psychology'. According to Adler's theory an individual adopts a style of life which tends to relieve feelings of inferiority. Thus a boy feeling himself to be inferior in sports devotes himself to his studies. Demosthenes, finding a way to overcome his stammer by speaking on the seashore with pebbles in his mouth, became the greatest orator in Greece. Or a person may hold to conceited fantasies which falsify a discouraging reality. Striving for success, self-assertion, and self-aggrandizement thus reflect both the will to power and its obverse, a sense of inferiority. This has its roots in the circumstances of childhood. A child feels inferior if he lacks affection, acceptance, and approval. Physical or 'organ' inferiority may play an important part. Position in order of birth, in particular, as Adler pointed out, moulds a child's style in competitive situations.

Inferiority and *complex were put together to make a portmanteau phrase. This soon became popular because it offered an explanation, albeit a simplified one, of inappropriate or neurotic behaviour in terms of underlying ideas and feelings which are part of most people's experience. DRD

Ansbacher, H. L., and Ansbacher, R. (1956). *The Individual Psychology of Alfred Adler*.

information rate of vision. Let us first estimate the information capacity of the visual system, then see how much of this capacity is used in a decision based solely on visual information, and finally discuss what are the factors that determine the capacity. Accurate data is available only for the central region of the retina (a circle whose diameter is 2 degrees in the visual field) and this area is considered below. The total information capacity of the visual system is about ten times that of this central circle, the fovea.

The number of points that can be resolved within the central 2-degree circle is about 10^4. When the eye is working near the limit of resolution, contrast discrimination is poor. Jacobson (1951) assumed that, at the limit of resolution, a person could distinguish black from white but not discriminate any intermediate shades of grey. He thus associated one bit of information with each small area surrounding one of the resolved points. (One bit is the amount of information required to decide between two equally probable alternatives: see BIT; INFORMATION THEORY.) For the central region the flicker–fusion frequency is about 50 cycles per second, so that the information capacity is $50 \times 10^4 = 5 \times 10^5$ bits per second.

Ditchburn and Drysdale (1973) calculated the information capacity from measurements of the variation of contrast sensitivity with number of lines per degree of visual angle for targets which were sinusoidal gratings. This calculation also yields a value of 5×10^5 bits per second, though their method includes capacity in terms of targets with different shades of grey. Neither of these estimates includes colour information, but it is unlikely that the additional information due to colour is more than about 20 per cent, making 6×10^5 bits per second in all.

Jacobson estimated the capacity for the ear at about 10^4 bits per second. Thus the central region of the retina has about 50 times the capacity of the ear and the whole visual system has about 500 or 600 times the aural capacity.

Vernier acuity judgements are probably the most precise decisions based on visual information. Foley-Fisher found that 4–5 bits of visual information were used in this judgement. For other visual tasks, values of 3 and less have been found (Crossman 1969). Experiments on rates of response have yielded values of up to 50 bits per second (Klemmer 1957). Some allowance must be made for unutilized spare capacity—for instance, when a subject makes a vernier acuity judgement on whether two lines are correctly aligned he could simultaneously make judgements on the width, length, and colour of the lines. When considerations like this are taken into account, the information used may rise to between 10 and 20 bits in a single judgement and the rate to about 200 bits per second, but even these values are very small compared with a capacity of 10^4 bits for a single judgement or 6×10^5 bits per second for the rate.

Ditchburn and Drysdale calculated that, for the lower illuminances at which foveal vision operates, nearly one bit of information was obtained for every photon absorbed by the cone detectors. This was true both for steady illumination and for brief flashes of light. At higher luminances the efficiency (measured in bits per photon absorbed) fell so that at daylight level about 10^4 photons must be absorbed to yield one bit. Thus at the lower luminances purely physical considerations determine the efficiency, but at higher levels it is determined by properties of the visual system. The relevant properties are (i) the aperture and quality of the lens of the eye, (ii) the number, and hence the spacing, of the photon detectors, (iii) the number of associated nerve fibres, and (iv) the neural processes by which information is transformed so that it is most readily appreciated by the higher centres of the brain.

The first three of these properties are matched in such a way that each by itself would give a limit of about 10^4 resolved points in the central 2 degrees. The neural processes include an edge-sharpening device (lateral inhibition), an arrangement by which an object appears to be about the same size over a range of distances (size constancy scaling), and many similar manipulations of the basic information. Some loss of information in these processes is inevitable, but the system is very economical and the loss may only be about 20 per cent.

In the situation involved in the evolution of the higher animals, decisions vital to survival had to be made mainly or solely on visual information. A wide variety of situations was encountered, so a vast information capacity was needed. Yet the amount used in making a decision had to be limited to the minimum required for a correct decision. This limited amount had to be processed to yield an action as rapidly as possible. If too little information was processed so that there was a considerable chance of a wrong decision, or if too much was processed so that the decision came too late, the animal did not survive. Those species which did survive usually had a large visual information capacity but were able to select a small number of bits for processing towards an action decision.

The amount of information actually used in a decision is determined by limitations of *short-term memory and other aspects of brain processing which are not strictly part of the visual system. See also INFORMATION THEORY.

RWD

Crossman, R. H. S. (1969). In Meetham, A. R., and Hudson, R. A. (eds.), *Encyclopaedia of Linguistics, Information and Control.*
Ditchburn, R. W., and Drysdale, A. E. (1973). *Vision Research*, 13.
Jacobson, H. (1951). *Science*, 113.
Klemmer, E. T. (1957). *Journal of Experimental Psychology*, 49.

information theory. The idea of measuring information might at first seem as senseless as that of weighing the theorem of Pythagoras, but it was in fact among hard-headed communication engineers that the need to do so was first recognized. A communication channel exists (and is paid for) in order to 'transmit information'. In order to compare the efficiencies of alternative methods we must be able to estimate the 'capacity' of each to do the job.

In ordinary language we say we have received information when *what we know* has changed. The bigger the change in what we know, the more information we have received. Information, then, like energy, does *work*, but whereas energy does physical work, information does logical work. There are various ways of measuring the size of the logical job done when a communication signal is received. Different measures are relevant in different contexts. The main consideration is whether the output of the communication channel has to be *constructed* by the signal, or merely *selected* (identified) by it from a range of prefabricated forms. Some examples will make this clear.

1. Construction
2. Selection

1. Construction
When a camera shutter is opened, we say that 'information' is transmitted from the scene to the film. By this we mean that the image on the film is constructed by the action of the light signal received. In comparing results from two cameras, two quite different criteria may be relevant. (i) We might compare the number of distinguishable picture elements, which is called the *structural information content* of each picture. A picture taken with poor optical resolution would have a low structural information content. (The unit of structural information content, 1 *logon*, specifies one independent element or 'degree of freedom' of a signal.) (ii) Alternatively, or additionally, we might compare the statistical weight of evidence gathered by the two films, or their *metrical information content*. A picture taken with too short an exposure, for example, would be deficient in metrical information content. (The unit of metrical information content, 1 *metron*, represents a certain minimum weight of statistical evidence.)

2. Selection
Although in many telecommunication systems (such as domestic telephones, radio, and TV) the signal has to construct the output, in other cases (such as telegraphy and teleprinting), where the range of possible outputs is small and is known in advance, a much more economical approach is possible. This is known as encoding. Instead of transmitting a complete description of the output required, a code system transmits only instructions to select (identify) that output from a range of prefabricated outputs (for example, letters of the alphabet) available at the receiving end. Thus, whereas the construction of a television picture of a page of type might require several million independent signals, the same page of type can be specified by only a few thousand selective code signals controlling a teleprinter.

In this context, the size of the selective job done by a signal depends not on the size or complexity of the output as such, but on the number of alternative forms that it might have taken, and on the relative likelihood of each. The simplest selective operation is the identification of one out of two equally likely possibilities—as in the game of 'Twenty Questions'. This, in the jargon of communication engineers, has a *selective information content* of one '*bit' or *binary digit*. Selection of one out of four equally likely possibilities requires 2 bits; one out of eight requires 3; and so on. In general, then, selective information content measures the statistical unexpectedness of the event in question. The precise form of the event is irrelevant, except as it may affect its prior probability. The more improbable an event, the larger its selective information content. This way of measuring information flow was developed chiefly by the American engineer C. E. *Shannon (Shannon and Weaver 1949) and the mathematician Norbert *Wiener (1948). (Mathematically, the number of bits per event is $\log_2(1/pi)$. Where events 1, 2 . . . i have prior probabilities pi_1, pi_2 . . . pi_i, the average selective information content or 'entropy'

$$H = \sum_{pi} \log_2(1/pi).)$$

The average unexpectedness or selective information content per event is greatest when all possible events are equally probable. The communication channel is then being used with full 'informational efficiency'. If some events are much more or much less probable than others, the average number of bits per event is correspondingly reduced, and the sequence is said to have 'redundancy'. (Redundancy is defined as $1 - H/H_{max}$, where H_{max} is the value of H when all pi are equal.) A redundancy of 50 per cent values means that the average number of bits per event is only half what it could be if all events were equally probable.

Despite its pejorative label, redundancy has one great merit. It allows a communication system in principle to tolerate a corresponding amount of random transmission error or 'noise'. If the right kind of code is used, it is even possible to achieve almost error-free transmission up to a certain rate, despite the presence of 'noise', by building in redundancy in such a way that errors can be identified and corrected. Although this may sound almost magical, it is similar in principle to what a human reader does when spotting and correcting printers' errors. The detection of misprints in an unfamiliar passage is possible only because the sequence of letters in typical English text is about 50 per cent redundant. With a table of random numbers, it would be impossible! Saying the same thing several times in different ways (a device familiar to teachers and public speakers) is another sensible way of building in redundancy, so as to make a message more resistant to distortion, either by noise in the communication channel or through misperception by the recipient.

By analogous reasoning, it has been proved that networks of computing elements can be constructed with redundant connections in such a way as to perform without errors, even if individual elements were to break down at random. Here again, the amount of malfunctioning that can be tolerated depends directly on the amount of redundancy built in. There is reason to believe that the amazing reliability of the human brain (despite a steady loss of nerve cells throughout life) depends on a sophisticated use of redundancy on these lines.

Since the theory of information embraces communication processes of all kinds, whether in human societies, in nervous systems, or in machines, it inspired at first some exaggerated expectations. Early efforts to measure the flow of information through sense organs, or through human operators controlling machines, were sometimes frustrated because the probabilities attached to events by the experimenter were not the same as those represented in the subject's nervous system. In other cases, where there was no reason to believe that the neural systems concerned worked on a selective principle, the use of Shannon's measure gave irrelevant or trivial results.

On the other hand, the development and spread of information-theoretical ideas has made notable contributions to brain research by suggesting new ways of looking at the function of the nervous system and new kinds of experimental questions. To take one of the earliest examples, Hick (1952) found that the *reaction time of human subjects to a stimulus depended in a particularly simple way on its selective information content. In other words, what mattered in his experiment was not the form of the stimulus *per se*, but rather the number of alternative forms that it might have taken but did not. The idea that the range of forms *not* taken by the input might be an important part of its specification is typical of the shift in emphasis brought to psychology by information theory.

Again, both physiologists and psychologists now make extensive use of test signals originally developed by communication engineers to measure the performance of TV and radio channels. Both highly redundant signals such as regularly repetitive patterns (Fig. 1a–c), and completely non-redundant patterns of 'noise' (Fig. 1d), can induce the nervous system to reveal characteristics that might have remained unsuspected without their use.

It is now commonplace to regard the impulses that flow along nerve fibres as 'conveying information', but just how information about the world is represented in the brain remains an unresolved question. Although nerve impulses do not function like the code signals in a *digital computer, the general ideas of information engineering are proving increasingly useful in suggesting experiments to throw light on the way they do operate. One of the chief advantages of these ideas is that they

(a)

(c)

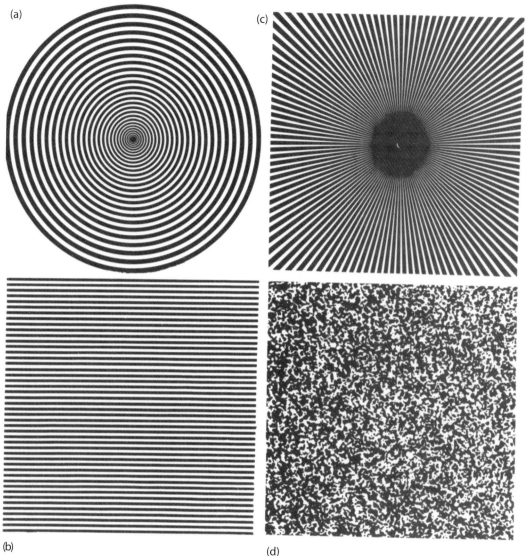

(b)

(d)

Fig. 1. a to **c.** Examples of visual stimuli incorporating a high degree of structural redundancy. **d.** A sample of 'visual noise' with minimal redundancy.

belong in a sense to both the psychological and the physiological levels. They thus offer an invaluable working link or 'conceptual bridge' by which data and questions at either level can be brought to bear on hypotheses at the other.

For the application of information theory to the visual system, see INFORMATION RATE OF VISION.   DMM

Attneave, F. (1959). *Applications of Information Theory to Psychology: A Summary of Basic Concepts, Methods and Results.*

Hick, W. E. (1952). 'On the rate of gain of information'. *Quarterly Journal of Experimental Psychology*, 4.
MacKay, D. M. (1969). *Information, Mechanism and Meaning.*
——(1970). 'Perception and brain function'. In Schmitt, F. O. (ed.), *The Neurosciences: Second Study Program.*
Shannon, C. E., and Weaver, W. (1949). *The Mathematical Theory of Communication.*
Wiener, N. (1948). *Cybernetics.*

ink-blot test. See RORSCHACH, HERMANN.

innate ideas. The philosophical theory of innate ideas has its roots in *Plato. In *Meno*, Socrates manages to get a slave boy to recognize certain mathematical truths (the example concerns the properties of a square) simply by asking the right questions. The conclusion drawn is that the boy already has the knowledge within him; Socrates was merely 'drawing it out'. Innate ideas play a crucial role in the metaphysical systems of the 17th-century rationalists. For *Descartes, the mind possesses innate awareness of certain fundamental concepts (God, triangle, mind, body), as well as of certain elementary propositions of logic (such as 'it is impossible for the same thing to be and not to be'). The infant may be distracted by bodily stimuli from reflecting on these truths but 'nonetheless it has them in itself, and does not acquire them later on; if it were taken out of the prison of the body, it would find them within itself' (letter of 1641). Such theories receive short shrift from empiricist philosophers—notably John *Locke in the *Essay Concerning Human Understanding* (1690). According to Locke, talk of innate knowledge must imply conscious awareness, yet many people are obviously unaware of many of the allegedly innate principles: children, for example, 'have not the least apprehension or thought of them'. To this *Leibniz replies (in the *New Essays on Human Understanding*, written 1705) that 'we must not expect that we can read the eternal laws of reason in the soul as in an open book'. The ideas are present not in a fully developed form but as dispositions or *virtualités*.

In recent years the debate between rationalists and empiricists over innate ideas has aroused fresh interest in the context of the linguistic theories of Noam Chomsky. According to Chomsky, the ability of children to become language users, i.e. to acquire a set of highly complex and creative skills on the basis of very meagre sensory data, suggests that the child has innate knowledge of the principles of 'universal grammar' (see LANGUAGE: CHOMSKY'S THEORY). However, while the human ability to master language does suggest the presence of innate, genetically determined structures and predispositions in our brains, it is doubtful whether such structures should be said to amount to 'knowledge' of concepts or principles in anything like the sense supposed by the traditional theory of innate ideas. JGC

Hook, S. (ed.) (1969). *Philosophy and Language*.
Stich, S. (ed.) (1975). *Innate Ideas*.

insanity: history. Although attempts to find logically satisfactory definitions of insanity have been dogged with failure, their construction has given much scope to the imagination. Two broad and irreconcilable traditions can be discerned: the Galenic and the Aristotelian views of madness. *Aristotle is alleged to have asked, 'Why is it that all those who have become eminent in philosophy or

politics or poetry or the arts are clearly of an atrabilious temperament and some of them to such an extent as to be affected by diseases caused by black bile?'. Robert *Burton is firmly within this tradition when in *The Anatomy of Melancholy* (1621) he describes melancholy men as 'of a deep reach, excellent apprehension, judicious, wise and witty'. On the other hand, the tradition which stems from *Galen sees madness as due to an imbalance of the four humours. According to Galen the four bodily humours were blood, phlegm, choler, and black bile, and they were endowed with the elementary qualities of heat and moisture. The preponderance of a particular humour determined a person's temperament, thus providing an early schema of psychosomatic or constitutional types. The theory was a comprehensive one in that it was able to account for health, temperament, and the type of illness to which a person was likely to succumb. In the essential characteristics of their outlook these two traditions have persisted to the present day, and can be recognized in the writings of contemporary psychiatrists.

Humour	Temperament
Blood (warm and moist)	Sanguine
Phlegm (cold and moist)	Phlegmatic
Choler (hot and dry)	Choleric
Black bile (cold and dry)	Melancholic

Although it is possible to construct elaborate and exhaustive typologies of psychiatric terminology for each particular age—and, indeed, this has been done (see, for example, Karl Menninger's appendix to *The Vital Balance*)—at any one given period one diagnosis predominates and serves to describe a variety of ills. Alternatively, several terms are used interchangeably. For example, in 16th- and 17th-century England all varieties of psychological distress were described as melancholy. Renaissance psychopathology could be dealt with under a single rubric. No wonder that melancholy had many aspects! Robert Burton wrote: 'Proteus himself is not so diverse; you may as well make the *moon* a new coat, as a true character of a melancholy man; as soon find the motion of a bird in the air as the heart of a melancholy man.'

By the 18th century a new term, 'the spleen', had become fashionable. The spleen referred not only to the bodily organ of that name, but also to disease associated with it. The spleen, being the source of black bile and hence of the melancholy temperament, is clearly a development of earlier Elizabethan melancholy and also a reaffirmation of links with the Galenic pathology of the humours. During the course of the century the spleen acquired a number of additional names: the vapours, hypochondriasis, hysteria, and the English malady. William Stukeley in his book *Of the Spleen* (1723) enumerates a long list of symptoms of the spleen:

When the head is attack'd, coma's, epilepsy, apoplexy, or the numbness of a part ensue, or talkativeness, tremors, spasms, head-ach; when the heart, palpitation, swooning, anxiety; when the breast, sighing, short-breath, cough; when the diaphragm, laughing; when the belly (and more frequently being the seat of the morbid minera) rugitus, cardialgia, colic, iliac passions, etc.

Thus the spleen could strike the unwary in myriad unsuspected forms. According to the 18th-century physician, Thomas Dover, the difficulty of detecting the spleen was accentuated by the fact that it could mimic the symptoms of other illnesses. Thus the accounts of many of these early concepts somewhat resemble the *Freudian view of hysteria. In view of the diversity of its symptoms, it is not surprising that preoccupation with the spleen spread rapidly throughout England and encouraged both a growth in the number of physicians and diversity of opinion. Both in England and abroad the spleen earned the title of the English disease.

The fashionable and well-known physician George Cheyne (1671–1743) regarded the corrosive and viscid humour associated with splenetic disorders as being caused by 'the English climate, the richness and heaviness of our food, the quality of the soil, the wealth and abundance of the inhabitants, the inactivity and sedentary occupations of the better Sort and the Humour of living in great, populous and unhealthy towns'. However, he attached prime importance to diet and in his *Essay on Health and Long Life* (1724) he advocated a milk and seed diet. Nevertheless, madness continued to be associated with inner excellence and social quality. Cheyne himself suffered from depression and claimed that 'those of the liveliest and quickest natural Parts . . . whose genius is most keen and penetrating', were most prone to such disorders. First, the spleen, unlike lowness of spirits, was an indicator of high social rank. Secondly, it also implied a degree of intelligence, imagination, and sensitivity in the sufferer. As a youth, David *Hume was in correspondence with Cheyne. After describing his symptoms, Hume was flattered and reassured to learn that his was no ordinary complaint, but 'a disease of the learned'. Thus, even a rank order in illnesses was acknowledged. Eighteenth-century writers on the spleen were also concerned with the relationship between imagination and the spleen and, in particular, with the possible dangers of too much imagination. The fear of imagination developed from and is related to the fear of passion. Thomas Wright was able to voice these fears most clearly and forcefully (*The Passions of the Minde in Generall*, 1620). He described the evil effects of unrestrained passions as: 'blindness of understanding, persuasion of will, alteration of humours; and by them maladies and diseases and troublesomeness and disquietness of the soul.' The paradoxical demands of reason and imagination and the precariousness of their relationships were recognized well in advance of Freud's discussion of the dilemmas of civilized man. Foremost among the 18th-century distrusters of imagination was Samuel Johnson, who waged a lifelong battle against melancholy. Idleness and solitude were both to be avoided on the grounds that they provided a fertile breeding ground for the imagination. Solitude 'is dangerous to reason, without being favourable to virtue. . . . Remember . . . that the solitary mortal is certainly luxurious, probably superstitious and probably mad: the mind stagnates for want of employment, grows morbid and is extinguished like a candle in foul air.' Idleness was condemned not because of its later associations with poverty, but because it promotes inner stagnation and decay.

Early 19th-century writing on insanity was dominated by the work of the moral managers. Their ideas developed from faculty psychology, according to which man possessed three souls: the rational, the sensitive, and the vegetative. The rational soul is concerned with understanding and the will; the sensitive soul is concerned with the imagination, memory, and perception; and the vegetative soul is concerned with growth, nutrition, and reproduction. Health depends upon the right relationship between the rational and the sensitive soul, namely one of dominance and control. The moral managers held that insanity was a 'lesion of understanding' and that the will could be trained to cope with the possibility of madness. John *Locke had first put forward the view that madness was a self-contained defect of reason and thus left open the possibility that other parts of the self could be enlisted to combat this weakness. In *An Essay Concerning Human Understanding*, Locke wrote that:

madmen do not appear to have lost the faculty of reasoning, but having joined together some ideas very wrongly they mistake them for truths . . . as though incoherent ideas have been cemented together so powerfully as to remain united. But there are degrees of madness as of folly; the disorderly jumbling ideas together in some more, in some, less. In short, herein seems to lie the difference between idiots and madmen. That madmen put wrong ideas together, and so make wrong propositions, but argue and reason right from them. But idiots make very few or no propositions, but argue and reason scarce at all.

Now that the seat of madness had been isolated, optimism and cure became possible. In fact, much of the writing on insanity in the first half of the 19th century was concerned with delineating the strategic role played by the will. One such book which crystallizes the early 19th-century outlook is called *Man's Power over Himself to Prevent or Control Insanity*, published anonymously in 1843. The author assigns the following role to the will:

The affection of the brain which causes delusions is not madness, but the want of power or will to examine them, is. Nothing then but an extent of disease which destroys at once all possibility of reasoning, by annihilating, or entirely changing the structure of the organ, can make a man necessarily mad. In all other cases, the being sane or otherwise, not withstanding considerable disease of brain, depends on the individual himself. He who has given a proper direction to the intellectual force and thus obtained an early command over the bodily organ by habituating it to processes of calm reasoning, remains sane amid all the vagaries of sense.

Within asylums treatment consisted of the cultivation of character and the rediscovery and strengthening of will power.

During this period there was one important change of emphasis in the accounts of madness. James Cowles Prichard, ethnologist and physician, first introduced the term 'moral insanity' in 1833, and defined it as follows: 'This form of mental disease . . . consists of a morbid perversion of the feelings, affections, habits, without any hallucination or erroneous conviction impressed upon the understanding; it sometimes coexists with an apparently unimpaired state of the intellectual faculties.' Thus the will was no longer the impenetrable stronghold against insanity, and madness had shifted from defective reasoning to the emotions. Given that the will in man was seen to be like a pilot in a ship, this reappraisal constituted a far more serious threat to man's supremacy over madness. Incidentally, the term 'moral insanity' is often, but erroneously, claimed to be the forebear of the modern '*psychopathic personality', whose cause still remains a matter for debate.

The theme of moral decline which lunacy represented was developed in a more systematic way and on a larger scale in the last third of the 19th century. Henry Maudsley published *Responsibility in Mental Disease* in 1873. Misleadingly titled, it was in fact a claim for non-responsibility in mental disease (although not in any indulgent sense) and was largely an argument against the claims of the moral managers. Maudsley was not concerned with cure so much as with identifying and segregating the morally degenerate. Man's life is governed by *genetic laws, and thought and volition are determined by them as much as are all other aspects of human life. Maudsley called this genetic determinism 'the tyranny of organisation'. He writes:

Individuals are born with such a flaw or warp of nature that all the care in the world will not prevent them from being vicious or criminal, or becoming insane. . . . No one can escape the tyranny of his organisation; no one can elude the destiny that is innate in him, and which unconsciously and irresistibly shapes his ends, even when he thinks he is determining them with consummate foresight and skill.

Whatever the complex intellectual and social changes that contributed towards this position (see ASYLUMS: A HISTORICAL SURVEY), it is a startling reversal of earlier accounts. Maudsley brings the dialogue with the irrational to a bleak and abrupt close. His concept of the 'tyranny of organ-

ization' seems to have been taken to its logical conclusion by Johannes Lange in his book *Crime and Destiny* (1930). Later studies of twins involved in crime have given as much emphasis to environmental as to hereditary factors as causes of felony.   VS

inspiration. The use of this word both for 'breathing' and for 'a bright idea' is not accidental. It derives from the notion of the ancient Greeks that mind pervades the universe, and is a subtle vapour—the pneuma. (Pneumatic bliss is, indeed, a state of mind!)

instinct. St Thomas *Aquinas wrote that animal judgement is not free but implanted by nature. Thus, from an early time, instinctive behaviour was regarded as the counterpart to voluntary behaviour. In everyday, though not in scientific, speech the term 'instinct' is still used to imply 'without thought'. For example, if I heard a taxi driver say, 'I instinctively stamped on the brakes', I would assume that he meant that his behaviour was *reflex or involuntary, and not that he was born with an innate ability to apply the brakes in motor cars.

The associationists believed that human behaviour is maintained by the knowledge of, and desire for, particular consequences of behaviour, and they looked upon notions of instinct with disfavour. However, John *Locke did concede that there was 'an uneasiness of the mind for want of some absent good. . . . God has put into man the uneasiness of hunger and thirst, and other natural desires . . . to move and determine their wills for the preservation of themselves and the continuation of the species' (*An Essay Concerning Human Understanding*, 1690). Francis Hutcheson argued that instinct produces action prior to any thought of the consequences (*An Essay on the Nature and Conduct of Passions and Affections*, 1728). Thus Hutcheson made instinct into a kind of motivational force, and this concept was taken up by the 19th-century rationalists, such as William *James, who conceived of human nature as a combination of blind instinct and rational thought.

The irrational forces in man's nature were emphasized by *Freud, but the ideas of William *McDougall (1871–1938) probably had a greater influence upon the scientific development of the concept of instinct. McDougall regarded instincts as irrational and compelling motivational forces. He enumerated particular instincts, each of which was accompanied by an *emotion. Examples are: pugnacity and the emotion of anger; flight and the emotion of fear; repulsion and the emotion of disgust (*Instincts and their Vicissitudes: Collected Papers*, 1915). McDougall's views do not find favour with modern psychologists because they are derived from subjective experience and are therefore hard to verify. There is inevitable disagreement among psychologists as to the number of instincts that should be allowed.

A different line of thought was initiated by Charles *Darwin. In his *Origin of Species* (1859), Darwin treated instincts as complex reflexes that were made up of inherited units and therefore subject to natural selection. Such instincts would evolve together with other aspects of the animal's morphology and behaviour. Darwin laid the foundations of the classical ethological view propounded by Konrad Lorenz and Niko Tinbergen. See ETHOLOGY.

Lorenz maintained that animal behaviour included a number of fixed-action patterns that were characteristic of species and largely genetically determined. He subsequently postulated that each fixed-action pattern or instinct was motivated by action-specific energy. The action-specific energy was likened to liquid in a reservoir. Each instinct corresponded to a separate reservoir, and when an appropriate releasing stimulus was presented the liquid was discharged in the form of an instinctive drive which gave rise to the appropriate behaviour. Tinbergen proposed that the reservoirs, or instinct centres, were arranged in a hierarchy so that the energy responsible for one class of activity, such as reproduction, would drive a number of subordinate activities, such as nest building, courting, and parental care.

The concept of instinct that is identified with classical ethology does not find favour with the majority of present-day behavioural scientists, for two main reasons. The first reason is connected with the idea that there are instinctive forces, or drives, that determine certain aspects of behaviour. Although the notion of drive as an energizer has been very influential in psychology, it involves a misuse of the concept of energy. In the physical sciences, energy is not a causal agent but a descriptive term arising from mathematically formulated laws. Analogous laws can be formulated for animal behaviour, but they do not lead to a concept of energy that corresponds to the notions of drive popular with the early psychologists and ethologists. Although the idea of drive as an energizer of behaviour has intuitive appeal, this is not nowadays regarded as sufficient justification for a scientific concept. In addition there are empirical problems. Early psychologists sought to identify a drive for every aspect of behaviour: a hunger drive responsible for feeding, a thirst drive, a sex drive, etc. It proved impossible to classify animal behaviour in this way without resorting to a *reductio ad absurdum* involving drives for thumb sucking, nail biting, and other minutiae of behaviour. A more modern view is that animals choose from among the set of alternative courses of action that is available at a particular time, in accordance with certain precisely formulated principles of decision making. This approach obviates the view that animals are driven by instinctive forces to perform particular behaviour patterns.

The second reason for abandoning the classical concepts of instinct is an objection to the implication that certain aspects of behaviour are innate in the sense that they develop independently of environmental influences. Most scientists now recognize that all behaviour is influenced both by the animal's genetic make-up and by the environmental conditions that exist during development. The extent to which the influences of nature and nurture determine behaviour varies greatly from activity to activity and from species to species. For example, the vocalizations of pigeons and doves are relatively stereotyped and characteristic of each species, and are not influenced by auditory experience after hatching. The vocalizations of other birds, however, may depend heavily upon such experience, as in the strongly imitative birds, or they may be partly influenced by experience. For example, chaffinches will learn the song they hear during a particular sensitive period of early life, provided it is similar to the normal song.

While the influence of particular genes may be necessary for the development of a behaviour pattern, it is never a sufficient condition. All types of behaviour require a suitable embryonic environment for the correct nervous connections etc. to develop. Normally, the physiological medium provided by the parent is designed to ensure that normal embryonic development occurs. Just as the parent provides an environment suitable for the development of the embryo, so it may provide an environment suitable for the development of a juvenile. Thus a chaffinch is normally reared in an environment in which it inevitably hears the song of other chaffinches, and so it develops the song that is characteristic of its own species.

Even apparently stereotyped activities may, upon closer examination, be shown to be influenced by the environment. For example, the newly hatched chicks of herring gulls peck at the tip of the parent's bill, which bears a characteristic red spot on a yellow background. The chick's behaviour induces the parent to regurgitate food. The behaviour is typical of all newly hatched chicks, is performed in an apparently stereotyped manner, and would appear to be a classic example of instinctive behaviour. Upon closer examination, however, it can be seen that the initial behaviour of individual chicks varies considerably in force and rapidity of pecking, angle of approach, and accuracy. As the chicks gain experience their pecking accuracy improves, and the pecking movements become more stereotyped. Some of these changes are due to maturation. The chicks become more stable on their feet as their muscles develop, and their pecking coordination improves. Some of the changes are due to learning. Initially the chicks peck at any elongated object of a suitable size. Although the red spot on the parent's bill is attractive to them, it is not their only target. Once the chicks begin to receive food they learn to exercise greater discrimination. It is not surprising that the behaviour of different chicks develops along similar lines, because in the natural environment they are all confronted with a similar situation. Practice and experience in similar situations lead to similar results, and the behaviour of the older chick consequently becomes more and more like that of its peers.

The concept of instinct has undergone many changes over the years. Whereas, at one time, instinctive behaviour was seen as inborn, stereotyped, and driven from within, the modern approach is to treat the innate, the reflex, and the motivational aspects as separate issues. While much animal and human behaviour is innate in the sense that it inevitably appears as part of the repertoire under natural conditions, this does not mean that genetic factors are solely responsible. Modes of learning that are characteristic of the species may be just as important. Much of the nature–nurture controversy, particularly that associated with sexual and racial differences among humans, results from a failure to recognize the vast complexity of developmental processes.   DJM

Hinde, R. A., Hinde, J. S., and Head, J. J. (1987). *Instinct and Intelligence*.

intellect. Mental abilities, usually distinguished from feelings, *emotions, and also *perception—though perception, we now generally believe (following Hermann von *Helmholtz), in fact depends upon unconscious inferences. The word is seldom applied to animals, and an 'intellectual' person means someone concerned with problems requiring high *intelligence and much learning. The intellect is associated with cortical brain function.

intelligence. Innumerable tests are available for measuring intelligence (see INTELLIGENCE: MEASUREMENT), yet no one is quite certain of what intelligence is, or even of just what it is that the available tests are measuring. There have been any number of attempts to resolve these uncertainties, attempts that have differed in their approach to the problem, and in the outcome of applying each given approach.

One time-honoured approach to discovering the meaning of a construct is to seek expert opinion regarding its definition. This is exactly what the editors of a major psychological journal did in 1921, when they sought the opinions of experts in the field of intelligence regarding what they 'conceive "intelligence" to be, and by what means it can best be measured by group tests' (*Intelligence and its Measurement*, 1921, p. 123). Fourteen experts replied, with definitions of intelligence such as the following: (i) the power of good responses from the point of view of truth or fact (E. L. *Thorndike); (ii) the ability to carry on abstract thinking (L. M. *Terman); (iii) having learned

or having the ability to learn to adjust oneself to the environment (S. S. Colvin); (iv) the ability to adapt oneself adequately to relatively new situations in life (R. Pintner); (v) the capacity for knowledge, and knowledge possessed (V. A. C. Henmon); (vi) a biological mechanism by which the effects of a complexity of stimuli are brought together and given a somewhat unified effect in behaviour (J. Peterson); (vii) the capacity to inhibit an instinctive adjustment, the capacity to redefine the inhibited instinctive adjustment in the light of imaginally experienced trial and error, and the volitional capacity to realize the modified instinctive adjustment into overt behaviour to the advantage of the individual as a social animal (L. L. *Thurstone); (viii) the capacity to acquire capacity (H. Woodrow); and (ix) the capacity to learn or to profit by experience (W. F. Dearborn). The other experts did not answer the question directly.

Viewed narrowly, there seem to be almost as many definitions of intelligence as there were experts asked to define it. Viewed broadly, however, two themes seem to run through at least several of these definitions: the capacity to learn from experience and adaptation to one's environment. Indeed, an earlier definition often cited by these experts viewed intelligence as general adaptability to new problems and conditions of life. (For an update of the 1921 symposium, see Sternberg and Detterman 1986.)

If one is dissatisfied with the heterogeneity in these definitions, one can attempt to answer the question of what intelligence is by begging the question. Edwin *Boring (1923) did just that when he defined intelligence as whatever it is that the tests measure. This definition tells us no more than we knew when we started, and it may tell us less: no two tests measure exactly the same thing, so that one is left with as many definitions of intelligence as there are tests (which is certainly a number greater even than that of experts in the field!).

A more recent and sophisticated version of the definitional approach to discovering what intelligence is has been suggested by Ulric Neisser (1979). According to Neisser, the concept of intelligence is organized around a 'prototype', or ideal case. One is intelligent to the extent that one resembles this ideal case:

There are no definitive criteria of intelligence, just as there are none for chairness; it is a fuzzy-edged concept to which many features are relevant. Two people may both be quite intelligent and yet have very few traits in common—they resemble the prototype along different dimensions. . . . [Intelligence] is a resemblance between two individuals, one real and the other prototypical. (p. 185)

If there is a single prototype, or ideal case, Neisser's notion will give us a concept of intelligence validated by consensus, if not a concrete definition. There are at least two problems with Neisser's approach, however. First, there exist multiple prototypes, or ideal cases, not just a single one. Different groups of people have somewhat different prototypes. Which one do we use? If we use all of them, including those of various groups of experts and laymen, we end up with as many ideal concepts of intelligence as there are different prototypes, and we are no better off than we were when appealing to experts' definitions. Secondly, the 'ideal case' approach seems to be an excellent way of discovering what people mean by 'intelligence', but not of discovering what 'intelligence' means. Neisser would argue that the two are indistinguishable, but I suspect they are not. Suppose, for example, that people in some culture view their ideal case as able to harmonize with Kron, the god of nature. This description tells us what these people think intelligence is, but it does not tell us much about the nature of intelligence: we still have to find out what it means to harmonize with Kron. In our culture, an analogous notion might be the ability to adapt to natural events. Again, we still need to find out what kinds of mental events and physical behaviours result in the ability to adapt. What is it that people who are able to adapt well do that people who are not able to adapt well do not do?

Questions such as this have led some theorists of intelligence to seek the nature of intelligence by the analysis of individual differences. The question asked here, as above, is what aspects of mental functioning distinguish more intelligent people from less intelligent ones. The nub of this individual-differences approach is to have people perform a large number of tasks that seem to predict intelligent performance (in school, on the job, or wherever), and to analyse patterns of individual differences in task performance. These patterns of individual differences have usually been analysed through the use of a method of statistical analysis called 'factor analysis'. The idea is to identify the 'factors' of human intellect.

The earliest factorial theory of the nature of intelligence was formulated by the inventor of factor analysis, Charles *Spearman. Spearman's (1927) analysis of relations among the kinds of mental tests he and other psychologists had been administering led him to propose a 'two-factor' theory of intelligence. According to this theory, intelligence comprises two kinds of factors—a general factor and specific factors. General ability, or g, as measured by the general factor, is required for performance of mental tests of all kinds. Each specific ability, as measured by each specific factor, is required for performance of just one kind of mental test. Thus, there are as many specific factors as there are tests, but only a single general factor. Spearman suggested that the ability underlying the general factor could best be understood as a kind of 'mental energy'.

Godfrey Thomson's (1939) reassessment of Spearman's individual-differences data led him to accept Spearman's hypothesis of a general factor running through the range of mental ability tests; however, it led him to reject Spearman's interpretation of this factor. Thomson disputed Spearman's claim that the general factor represented a single underlying source of individual differences. Instead, he proposed that the appearance of a general factor was due to the workings of a multitude of mental 'bonds', including reflexes, learned associations between stimuli, and the like. Performance of any particular task activates large numbers of these bonds. Some bonds will be required for the performance of virtually any task requiring mental effort, and these bonds will in combination give rise to the appearance of a general factor.

L. L. Thurstone (1938), like Thomson, accepted Spearman's hypothesis of a general factor. But he disputed the importance of this factor. He argued that it is a 'second-order' factor or phenomenon, one which arises only because the primary or 'first-order' factors are related to each other. What are these primary factors, or, as Thurstone called them, 'primary mental abilities'? Thurstone suggested that they include verbal comprehension (measured by tests such as knowledge of vocabulary), word fluency (measured by tests requiring rapid word production—for example, a listing of as many words as a person can think of that have c as their third letter), number (measured by tests of arithmetical reasoning and computation), spatial visualization (measured by tests requiring mental manipulation of geometric forms), perceptual speed (measured by tests requiring rapid visual scanning, for example, proofreading), *memory (measured by tests of recall and recognition of previously presented information), and reasoning (measured by tests such as number series, which require people to say which of several numbers should come next in a given series).

J. P. Guilford (1967) parted company with the majority of factorial theorists by refusing to acknowledge the existence of any general factor at all in human intelligence. Instead, he proposed that intelligence comprises 120 elementary abilities, each of which involves the action of some operation upon some content to produce some product. An example of an ability in Guilford's system is 'cognition of verbal relations'. This ability involves recognition of a conceptual connection between two words: for example, recognition that a *caboose* is often the last car in a *train*.

Probably the most widely accepted factorial description of intelligence is a hierarchical one. A good example of this class of descriptions was proposed by P. E. Vernon (1971). He proposed that intelligence can be described as comprising abilities at varying levels of generality: at the highest level of generality (the top of the hierarchy) is general ability as identified by Spearman; at the next level are 'major group' factors, such as verbal–educational ability (the kind of ability needed for successful performance in courses such as English, history, and social studies) and practical–mechanical ability (the kind of ability needed for successful performance in courses such as draughtsmanship and car mechanics); at the next level are 'minor group' factors, which can be obtained by subdividing the major group factors; and at the lowest level (the bottom of the hierarchy) are specific factors, again of the kind identified by Spearman. This description of intelligence may be viewed as filling in the gaps between the two extreme kinds of factors proposed by Spearman: in between the general and specific factors are group factors of intermediate levels of generality.

The factorial views of intelligence are unlike the definitional ones in that they are based on the analysis of intelligent functioning (on ability tests), rather than merely on the speculations of one or more psychologists or laymen. The factorial views are like the definitional ones, however, in their potential number and diversity. Is it the case that one of the factorial descriptions is right and the others wrong, or is it possible that a single entity or complex of entities, intelligence, can conform to all of these different descriptions? In other words, is there some level, or common denominator, at which these various descriptions all reduce to the same thing? It is here suggested that such a level of description exists, and that it can be found by analysing the ways in which people process information when solving problems of the kind found both on intelligence tests and in everyday life.

Information-processing psychologists have sought to understand general intelligence in terms of elementary components (or processes) used in the solution of various kinds of problems (Sternberg, 1979a, 1979b). Let us distinguish five kinds of components that people use in the processing of information. *Metacomponents* are higher-order control processes that are used for planning how a problem should be solved, for making decisions regarding alternative courses of action during *problem solving, and for monitoring one's progress during the course of problem solution. *Performance components* are processes that are used in the actual execution of a problem-solving strategy. *Acquisition components* are processes used in learning, that is, in the acquisition of knowledge. *Retention components* are processes used in *remembering—that is, in the retrieval of previously acquired information. *Transfer components* are used in generalization—that is, in the transfer of knowledge from one task, or task context, to another.

Consider, for example, how each of these five kinds of components might be applied in the solution of an arithmetical problem.

Mrs Smith decided to impress Mrs Jones. She went to a costume jewellery shop and bought three imitation diamonds of equal

value. She received £4 in change from the £10 note she gave the assistant. (But as Mrs Smith was receiving her change, Mrs Jones walked into the shop!) How much did each imitation diamond cost?

Metacomponents would be used in setting up the equations for solving the problem, for example, in deciding that the problem can be solved by subtracting £4 from £10 and dividing the difference by three; the metacomponents must also decide what information is relevant to the problem at hand, and what information is irrelevant. Performance components would be used in the actual solution of these equations to obtain, first, £6 as the price of the three imitation diamonds and, then, £2 as the price of each item. Acquisition components were used in the problem solver's past to learn how to set up the equations, how to subtract, how to divide, and so on. Retention components are used to retrieve this information from memory at the time that it is needed. Transfer components are used to draw an analogy between this problem and previous ones: the problem solver has never learned how to solve this particular problem, and must generalize his or her learning from similar problems previously encountered to the problem presently being encountered.

How can this scheme account for the various factorial views of intelligence described earlier? According to this view, the general factor that appears in various theories of intelligence results from the operations of components that are general across the range of tasks represented on intelligence tests. For the most part, these are metacomponents—mental activities such as deciding upon the particular components to be used in the solution of problems, deciding upon a strategy for problem solution, monitoring whether the strategy that has been chosen is leading to a solution, deciding upon how quickly the strategy can be executed and still lead to a satisfactory result, and so on. Major group factors of the kind found in Vernon's theory, and primary factors of the kind found in Thurstone's theory, are obtained in factor analyses primarily as a result of the operations of performance, acquisition, retention, and transfer components. For example, verbal comprehension, as tested by vocabulary, is the product of past executions of acquisition components to learn new words, and of present executions of retention components to retrieve the meanings of these words. If vocabulary is tested by presenting the words in unfamiliar contexts, transfer components may also be involved in applying previously acquired information to the new contexts that are presented. Reasoning, as tested by problems such as numerical series completions (say, 3, 7, 12, 18, 25, . . .), requires the execution of various performance components, such as encoding the terms of the problem, inferring the relations between the given pairs of numbers, applying these relations to the last given number to obtain the next number, and the production of a response.

This information-processing view of intelligence seems to unify what were formerly a number of disparate views regarding the nature of intelligence. A number of important questions still need to be answered, however, and it is possible to consider only a small number of them here.

First, is the meaning of intelligence the same across different societal and cultural groups? On the view proposed, the answer is both yes and no. On the one hand, the components that would be applied to the solution of a given problem in one culture or society probably overlap to a large degree, although perhaps not completely, those that would be applied to the solution of the same problem in a different culture or society. On the other hand, the kinds of problems that need to be solved may differ widely from one culture or society to another. The mental (and physical) processes needed to corner game in a hunt are very different from those needed to balance accounts. Hence, the kinds of persons who are considered intelligent may vary widely from one culture to another, as a function of the components that are important for adaptation to the requirements of living in the various cultures.

Secondly, if intelligence tests measure, in greater or lesser degree, the components of information processing, why are they so imperfectly predictive of real-world performance? One reason is that they are fallible as measuring instruments: they measure only imperfectly what they are supposed to measure. Another reason is that they do not necessarily weigh most heavily those aspects of intellectual functioning that are most important for intelligent functioning in a given environment. Metacomponential functioning is probably underemphasized, for example, in the measurements made by most of these tests. Yet another reason, and probably the most important one, is that there is a great deal more to everyday living than what the intelligence tests measure, or even than what can reasonably be called intelligence. The tests fail to take into account such important aspects of functioning as motivation, social skills, persistence in the face of adversity, and ability to set and achieve goals. The tests provide reasonably good measures of limited aspects of functioning for most people. But even here a qualification is necessary, since there are some people whose anxieties, or inability to take tests, render their test scores meaningless or even deceptive.

Finally, is intelligence largely inherited, as has been claimed by some (for example, Jensen 1969), or is it largely or exclusively determined by environment, as has been claimed by others (for example, Kamin 1974)? Few bodies of evidence are more confused and confusing than that

dealing with the heritability of intelligence. The probability is that heredity, environment, and the interaction between heredity and environment in intelligence as it has traditionally been measured all play some role in intelligence, but it is not at all clear what the relative extents of these roles are. Nor is it clear what it means, in practical terms, to assign proportional values to the influence of each. No matter what the proportions are, there is good evidence that at least some aspects of intelligence are trainable, and theoretical interest in the heritability of intelligence should not divert attention from questions about how intelligence can be modified in individuals of all levels of measured intelligence.

See also ARTIFICIAL INTELLIGENCE; GUESSING AND INTELLIGENCE.

RJS

Boring, E. G. (1923). 'Intelligence as the tests test it'. *New Republic*, 6 June.

Gardner, H. (1999). *Intelligence Reframed: Multiple Intelligences for the 21st Century*.

Guilford, J. P. (1967). *The Nature of Human Intelligence*.

Jensen, A. R. (1969). 'How much can we boost IQ and scholastic achievement?' *Harvard Educational Review*, 39.

Kamin, L. J. (1974). *The Science and Politics of IQ*.

Neisser, U. (1979). 'The concept of intelligence'. In Sternberg, R. J., and Detterman, D. K. (eds.), *Human Intelligence: Perspectives on its Theory and Measurement*.

Spearman, C. (1927). *The Abilities of Man*.

Sternberg, R. J. (1979a). 'The nature of mental abilities'. *American Psychologist*, 34.

—— (1979b). 'Stalking the I.Q. quark'. *Psychology Today*, 13.

—— (2000). *Handbook of Intelligence*.

—— and Detterman, D. K. (eds.) (1986). *What is Intelligence? Contemporary Viewpoints on its Nature and Definition*.

Thomson, G. H. (1939). *The Factorial Analysis of Human Ability*.

Thurstone, L. L. (1938). *Primary Mental Abilities*.

Vernon, P. E. (1971). *The Structure of Human Abilities*.

intelligence: measurement. Definitions of 'intelligence' vary with the theoretical position (and also the political persuasion) of the definer. The biologist tends to stress concepts such as healthy adaptation, capacity for adjustment to the environment, and learning to learn. The more philosophically minded intellectual is liable to emphasize the element of abstraction: indeed, 'the capacity for abstract thought' was the definition offered by Lewis *Terman. But many would reject the implicit value judgement that abstract thinking is in some way superior to—or, in any case, more intelligent than—concrete or practical thinking. (See INTELLIGENCE for a fuller discussion.)

'Intelligence' has sometimes been contrasted with '*instinct', the latter posited as being a feature of the lower animals, common to all members of a species and relatively immutable because unlearned, i.e. performed almost perfectly at its first manifestation. Intelligence, on the other hand, was assumed to be an attribute unique to mankind and evincing wide individual differences. Of recent years, however, such distinctions between man and beast have become blurred (as, in certain quarters, have those between man and machine). The concept of instinct has both increased in flexibility and diminished in scientific respectability, since it is held to encourage mere naming and to lack explanatory or predictive power.

The stature of 'intelligence' has, for several reasons, also declined recently. First, the assertions made by certain psychometrists as to its degree of innateness (cf. Cyril Burt's (1955) 'innate, general, cognitive ability') and the alleged constancy of its nature/nurture ratio (cf. Hans Eysenck's '4 : 1') are now largely discredited, as are claims for the existence of 'culture-fair' intelligence tests. Secondly, the identification of tested intelligence with everyday intelligence is questionable, especially in view of the many so-called intelligence tests which lack cogency. Thirdly, the whole climate of opinion during the 1960s and early 1970s among 'progressives' was anti-assessment; and while this attitude persisted, intelligence testing was bound, rightly or wrongly, to be a target for attack.

The word 'intelligence' is indeed likely to give rise to misconceptions, owing partly to the above overtones and partly to the suggestion implicit in an abstract noun that the word refers to 'something'—perhaps to something which one either possesses or lacks. This is, of course, a gross oversimplification of the issue. To avoid perpetuating such reification of intelligence (or any other factor) let us consider a *description* of *intelligent activity* rather than a definition of intelligence: that intelligent activity consists of grasping the essentials in a given situation and responding appropriately to them. This purposely leaves open such questions as speed versus accuracy or abstract versus practical; as to whether the most intelligent is he who can solve the most diverse problems or he who can answer the $64,000 question; as to the existence of people who grasp the essentials but fail to react, and of others who respond appropriately but cannot explain their action. This open-endedness is deliberate in order to stress the flexibility of the term 'intelligent activity' and to cover intelligence both as tested and as manifested in everyday life.

How then is this elusive quality appraised? And what are the purposes of such appraisal? The agreement on what an intelligence test actually assesses is far greater than that found among the definitions and the theories in this realm. An intelligence test is essentially a test of deductive reasoning. In fact, since 'intelligence' has become a dirty word, many psychologists prefer to talk of 'tests of reasoning'. More specifically, the phrases 'verbal reasoning' or 'numerical reasoning' or 'perceptual reasoning' may be used. Two examples of each of these are given in Fig. 1.

It may be seen from these examples that some element of acquired knowledge is assumed—i.e. the understanding of everyday words and of simple arithmetical concepts, the capacity to recognize certain features of formal shapes and to interpret representational pictures. A test which makes no such assumptions would be both impracticable and valueless. But, insofar as is possible, all the information required to solve each problem is contained within it, and the items are unambiguous in the sense that only one of the proffered responses is defensible.

Such problems can be devised that are appropriate for people of almost every level of ability: for the 7-year-old (e.g. no. 5), for the young adolescent (e.g. no. 1), or for the sixth-former or older (e.g. no. 3). These tests are often good predictors of academic or vocational success but they differ from examinations in that they are less dependent on memory, diligence, and congenial teaching, as they are not primarily concerned with assimilated knowledge, and they are clearly more objective than *interviews or other methods involving direct personal judgement.

The purposes of assessing intelligence are manifold. Let us consider four of the uses to which such tests are put: selection, vocational guidance, clinical work, and research. First, selection: whenever the number of applicants exceeds the number of places—whether in education, or industry, or the civil service—some form of assessment is necessary, in order to determine which candidates to accept. Intelligence is only one of the factors to consider, but it is nearly always relevant and it is easier to assess than such traits as conscientiousness, sense of responsibility, and the ability to get on with people. The test scores, unlike interviews, are not liable to be influenced by such factors as the applicant's clothing or accent, or his willingness to appreciate his interviewer's sense of humour (though the *ability* to do this may well be related to intelligence!).

So much for selection. Vocational guidance is the other face of the same coin: here the psychologist advises the individual as to what kind of job is likely to give him most satisfaction and to make the best use of his talents. Advice is especially helpful in those cases where people have no idea what work would suit them or where, for one reason or another, they are in a state of conflict on the matter. Tests of aptitudes and of interests may also be helpful in vocational guidance.

Tests are used in clinical situations as an aid, sometimes to diagnoses and sometimes to assess the progress of a patient. They can help in determining whether brain damage has occurred, and also in deciding whether one particular course of treatment is more appropriate than another.

In research, the intelligence test may be a valuable instrument either in its own right—in a study of 'slow developers', for example, or of the effects of environmental change, or of male/female intellectual differences (if such

1. Which one of six lower words means **either** the same as **or** the opposite of the top word ?

   probable

sure	likely	impossible	convenient	profitable	certainly
1	2	3	4	5	6

---

2. **seed** is to **plant** as **egg** is to ...

tree	root	pollen	oats	potato	bird
1	2	3	4	5	6

---

3. In the following series, the fifth member is omitted. Which is it ?

   56   35   20   10   ...   1

   | 2 | 3 | 4 | 5 | 6 | 7 |

---

4. 42 people work in four shops. Half the people work in the big shop and the rest are divided equally among the smaller shops. How many work in each small shop ?

   | 7 | 5 | 21 | 6 | 4 | none of these |

---

5.  ⬅   ⬆   ➡   Which one comes next ?

    1    2   ⬅ 3    4   ⬇ 5   6

---

6. Which one of the lower pictures is like the top two but unlike the other five ?

1   2   3   4   5   6

Fig. 1.

study is still within the law!)—or as a means to an end. Since it is rarely the case in human psychology that 'other things are equal', techniques such as matching members of pairs on intelligence-test performance may be usefully employed in the investigation of other psychological or social variables.

Equality of opportunity is as important as ever it was, and it is gradually becoming more of a reality—partly owing to the use of intelligence tests, since they often facilitate the recognition of an able child from an under-privileged background. But to insist, as some education-ists do nowadays, that equality *of ability* is the rule—and to decry assessment of any kind, since if some are designated as brighter it follows that some must be designated as duller—is unhelpful to the individuals concerned as well as to their subsequent employers or instructors.

The intelligence test can yield valuable data, provided that it is devised with critical care, interpreted with under-standing, and used always in conjunction with other pro-cedures. Indeed, intelligence testing is most informative in those somewhat rare cases when its results are at vari-ance with other relevant criteria.   AWH

Burt, C. (1955). *The Subnormal Mind* (3rd edn.).
Butcher, H. J. (1968). *Human Intelligence: Its Nature and Assessment.*
Heim, A. W. (1970). *Intelligence and Personality.*
—— (1975). *Psychological Testing.*
Hinde, R. A., and Hinde, J. S. (1976). *Instinct and Intelligence.*
Sternberg, R. J., and Kaufman, J. C. (1997). 'Innovation and intel-ligence testing'. *European Journal of Psychological Assessment*, 123.
Vernon, P. E. (1969). *Intelligence and Cultural Environment.*

intelligence differences. In one sense humans are equally intelligent. The modal cognitive apparatus of all humans affords perception, memory, reasoning, and so forth. Discovering the structure and functional bases of what the average person can do with their brain is the province of cognitive psychology and evolutionary biol-ogy, allied with neuropsychology and neuroscience. Within the discipline of differential psychology (the psych-ology of individual differences) the interest is in what makes people different. The dialogue between these modal and differential approaches to mental functions is surprisingly sparse (Novartis Foundation 2000).

Differences are about the most obvious feature of human intelligence, and have been recognized since an-tiquity. The study of cognitive differences among humans can be seen as three main topics: the structure and meas-urement of human intelligence; the predictive power of mental ability tests; and the causes of human intelligence differences. These topics are usefully and accessibly re-viewed by Neisser et al. (1996) and Deary (2001).

1. Structure and measurement of human intelligence differences

2. What do intelligence differences predict?
3. The causes of intelligence differences

1. Structure and measurement of human intelligence differences

In 1904 the English ex-army officer Charles *Spearman made one of the most important discoveries in the history of psychology. Taking their school examination scores, and testing schoolchildren on various assessments of sens-ory acuity, he found that all assessments of mental per-formance showed positive correlations. Those who were good at one test of mental function tended to be good at all the others. Moreover, he thought the correlations showed a particular pattern of positive associations, al-lowing him to conclude that what was common to the tests was just one underlying trait, which he famously called 'general intelligence,' usually denoted g. His 'two-factor theory' of intelligence stated that, when we per-form a mental test, we employ just two abilities: general intelligence and a highly specific ability applicable only to the test being performed. Because g was a part of all men-tal performances, Spearman suggested that, to measure it, one need not worry what basket of mental tests was used, so long as they were varied, because the general elem-ent would be g. This is Spearman's dictum, 'the indiffer-ence of the indicator'. Spearman's ideas about the bases of g were articulated in cognitive, sensory, and physiological terms. Thus, respectively, he suggested that differences in g might be accounted for by 'eductive' cognitive skills, fineness of sensory discrimination, and differences in mental energy. All of these ideas find a place in modern research on intelligence differences (Deary 2000).

Spearman's breakthrough happened without the aid of a single mental test as we would know it today. The first mental test appeared a year after, when the Frenchman Alfred Binet (1857–1911) devised a series of tests to help in finding those children who would not progress in normal school circumstances. *Sans* theory, Binet put together a series of high-level mental tasks and found that the aver-age child at any given chronological age could perform certain tasks but not others. That the Binet tests took off around the world was largely due to the evangelizing of the Americans Henry Goddard and Lewis Terman. From these 'hotch pots' (Spearman's term) of mental tasks emerged the idea of a child's mental age: the mental tasks he or she could manage compared with other children— as compared with a chronological age. Divide mental age by chronological age and multiply by 100 and we have the well-known 'intelligence quotient' or IQ. These tests were so successful because they identified children with learning difficulties more accurately and in a much shorter time than did extensive observations and medical examinations. The next step in the massive expansion of mental testing came with the application of mental tests to American recruits in the First World War. By the end of the war millions of Americans had been tested using the first group tests of mental abilities (see Zenderland 1998 for a history of mental testing in this period).

Ever since Spearman's seminal paper in 1904 there are two aspects of human intelligence differences that have caused tension in research. First, from then until now, there have been arguments about the number of concepts one needs to understand human intelligence differences. Second, there has been a tension between those researchers who, like Binet, proceeded, apparently successfully, to measure intelligence differences and those, like Spearman, who tried to understand the bases of intelligence differences. The former question is addressed now, and the latter is addressed in the last section.

How many dimensions of intelligence are there along which humans differ? The standard method of answering this question has been to devise multifarious mental tasks, apply them to a group of people, and employ statistical techniques like factor analysis to find how many underlying traits are needed to account for the associations among the test scores. Over the 20th century the suggestions ranged as follows: one (Spearman), a huge number (Thomson), about seven unrelated intelligences (Thurstone), perhaps 120 distinct abilities (Guilford), seven to nine-and-a-half (Gardner) (Neisser et al. 1996). The answer that most researchers accept today was available in the first half of the 20th century, from the British psychologists Philip E. Vernon and Sir Cyril Burt. Both suggested that human intelligences formed a hierarchy, and that it was not necessary to conceive human intelligences exclusively in terms of general or specific abilities.

The accuracy of the Burt–Vernon view was established when, in 1993, John Carroll published his reanalysis of hundreds of the most impressive and best-known studies of human intelligence conducted throughout the 20th century. He gathered data from the laboratories of many famous researchers, often those with disparate views about the structure of human intelligence, and submitted them to a common mode of factor analysis. He found that almost all studies found a general intelligence factor, often accounting for 40–50 per cent of the variance in test battery scores. Next, he found that there were separable, but correlated, 'group factors' of intelligence. These are mental capabilities less general than g, such as reasoning, verbal ability, memory, mental speed, and so forth. Finally, he found that there were separable, but correlated, highly specific mental abilities. Therefore, a partial consensus exists in the century-long debate about the number and type of human intelligence differences. There is a general intelligence factor; there are correlated but separable abilities that are broad in scope but are more specific than g; and there is a large number of correlated but distinct specific mental abilities.

There are still dissenters to this workable but imperfect descriptive scheme. The best known is Howard Gardner (1999) who has found large audiences, largely outside academic psychology, for his theory of multiple intelligences. His proposal is that the following separate intelligences exist: linguistic, logical–mathematical, musical, spatial, bodily kinaesthetic, interpersonal, intrapersonal, and naturalistic. Gardner is criticized for having done relatively little empirical work to validate these ideas. The first four of his intelligences are well known to be correlated, physical abilities are not usually considered to be a type of intelligence, and the personal skills are usually viewed as aspects of personality.

Returning to the hierarchy of intelligence, it is clear that this is a descriptive scheme for mental test performances. It may be asked whether these test scores can predict anything and whether we understand the bases of intelligence differences in terms of brain function.

2. What do intelligence differences predict?

The results of a brief encounter with an intelligence test have some predictive power in education, in work, and in life more generally. This area is vast, but three examples make these points.

Intelligence test scores correlate positively with educational outcomes: people who score higher on mental tests do better in school and college examinations. The typical correlation is in the region of 0.5 (Neisser et al. 1996). A large-scale example of this is the intelligence testing in English schools (Smith, Fernandes, and Strand 2001). In the 1990s, over 20,000 pupils took the Cognitive Abilities Test (CAT) at entry to secondary school. They were from six education authorities and 176 schools, and were representative of pupils nationwide. The CAT has verbal, quantitative, and non-verbal sections. The mean score on the CAT at entry to secondary school correlated highly with GCSE scores five years later, as follows (with correlations in parentheses): total GCSE performance score (0.74), art and design (0.45), business studies (0.56), creative arts (0.53), design and technology (0.51), English language (0.68), English literature (0.63), French (0.66), geography (0.68), German (0.59), history (0.65), information technology (0.47), mathematics (0.76), physical education (0.54), science (0.72), Spanish (0.61). The correlations with the non-verbal section for the CAT test, which involves neither verbal nor numerical skills, were still high, typically being about 0.1 lower for each subject. Therefore, in this massive, representative, and longitudinal study it is clear that performance on a relative brief test of intelligence has impressive associations with school performance several years later. This applies to everything from art to physical education, in addition to the more traditional academic subjects.

In the world of work it is important for an employer to

make some assessment of how effectively a new worker will perform. Over the past 80 years thousands of studies of this type of question have involved various assessments of potential new recruits: interviews, references, personality tests, *graphology, intelligence tests, and so forth. The field's thousands of studies were reviewed by Schmidt and Hunter (1998). They found that a psychometric test of general intelligence had an average correlation of 0.51 with work performance. Work performance is assessed in various ways, but one common method is ratings by supervisors. The only assessment that did better was a 'work sample' test, where people carry out some of the work they will be doing in the job. This type of assessment is expensive and not suitable to many situations, whereas a mental test is cheap and can be given to all applicants. By comparison with mental tests, the following correlated more poorly with job performance: unstructured interview (0.38), conscientiousness test (0.31), reference checks (0.26), job experience (0.18), years of education (0.10), and graphology (0.02). Thus a cheap and fast mental test is almost universally applicable in recruitment for employment and has surprisingly high utility.

In medical settings, tests of mental abilities are used to assess people's cognitive functions in response to illness and to treatments. By comparison with the fields of education and work their application here attracts little controversy: they are merely useful tools for assessing outcomes. Here, though, two unusual medical applications of intelligence tests are mentioned. First, cognitive impairment with ageing, especially dementia, is a common clinical problem. It is important to assess a potential sufferer's mental capabilities. However, these are interpretable only against an assessment of the person's previous mental function, something that is rarely available. A British invention, the National Adult Reading Test (NART), provides an assessment of 'premorbid IQ'. The test involves reading a series of English words that do not follow normal pronunciation rules. The ability to pronounce these words correlates very highly with long tests of intelligence in healthy people and, more importantly, the ability is preserved while others fade in early dementia. Therefore, the NART provides an invaluable archaeological record of the person's prior ability even in the face of cognitive decline associated with dementia. Another surprising finding using IQ tests is that people with higher IQ scores at age 11 are significantly more likely to be alive at age 77 (Whalley and Deary 2001).

3. The causes of intelligence differences

Intelligence test scores from tests assessing disparate-seeming abilities co-vary and form a hierarchy, and the scores are useful in various fields of human endeavour and problems. However, there is still the question of the origins of intelligence. Family, adoption, and twin studies demonstrate beyond doubt that intelligence differences are substantially heritable. Across all studies, the contribution of genes to human cognitive ability differences in the population is about 40–50 per cent, though the actual figure is not considered important (Plomin et al. 2001). The small print of this finding is of more interest. Heritability probably changes with age, from as low as 20 per cent in childhood to over 60 per cent and even as high as 80 per cent in very old age. Given that the remainder of the 100 per cent must come from environmental influences and error, the main source of environmental influence is a person's individual experience, not the environment shared with the rest of the family. Most of the heritability of specific mental tests (such as verbal ability, spatial ability, and memory, say) arises from the genetic contribution to general intelligence. Though it is still in its infancy, the main enterprise of the coming years will be the search for the individual genes that contribute to intelligence differences, using molecular genetic techniques.

Other research on the origins of intelligence differences seeks a more mechanistic account (Deary 2000 reviewed this research). Thus, echoing ideas that came from the Victorian polymath Sir Francis *Galton and from Spearman, researchers have found associations between intelligence test scores and several types of assessment. It is now well established that, in healthy adults, the correlation between intelligence and brain size is about 0.4. Intelligence test scores correlate significantly with speed of reaction and with the efficiency of processing visual and auditory information. And people with better scores on mental tests are notable for having more efficient working memory. Though there are many such associations, the main limitation of this type of research is that the fields of cognitive science and neuroscience have not provided validated models of mental function that afford an understanding of the brain-processing measures that are used to correlate with test scores.   ID

Carroll, J. B. (1993). *Human Cognitive Abilities: A Survey of Factor Analytic Studies*.

Deary, I. J. (2000). *Looking down on Human Intelligence: From Psychometrics to the Brain*.

—— (2001). *Intelligence: A Very Short Introduction*.

Gardner, H. (1999). *Intelligence Reframed: Multiple Intelligences for the 21st Century*.

Neisser, U., Boodoo, G., Bouchard, T. J., et al. (1996). 'Intelligence: knowns and unknowns'. *American Psychologist*, 51.

Novartis Foundation (2000). *The Nature of Intelligence: Novartis Foundation Symposium 233*.

Plomin, R., DeFries, J. C., McClearn, G. E., and McGuffin, P. (2001). *Behavioral Genetics* (4th edn.).

Schmidt, F. L., and Hunter, J. E. (1998). 'The validity and utility of selection methods in personnel psychology: practical and theoretical implications of 85 years of research findings'. *Psychological Bulletin*, 124.

Smith, P., Fernandes, C., and Strand, S. (2001). *Cognitive Abilities Test 3: Technical Manual.*

Whalley, L. J., and Deary, I. J. (2001). 'Longitudinal cohort study of childhood IQ and survival up to age 76'. *British Medical Journal*, 322.

Zenderland, L. (1998). *Measuring Minds.*

intention. Intention—deliberate, purposive behaviour —is one of the most difficult concepts to understand or discuss in academic psychology, although most 'common-sense' psychological explanations are in terms of intentions. Behaviour is commonly explained by intentions (such as: 'Why did the chicken cross the road . . . ?'), but just what an intention is, in terms of brain processes or anything else, is exceedingly hard to say.

Intention seems to characterize mind, for we can hardly say that natural objects (atoms, molecules, tables and chairs, or planets or stars) have intentions. They are controlled, rather, according to natural laws. The forming of an intention seems to imply free will and the ability to choose. Whether such an ability is compatible with the operation of strictly causal laws at the physical level is a matter of philosophical debate. Neurophysiological experiments show that activity in the relevant part of the motor cortex starts before the person is consciously aware of forming the intention to move. Some people take this as evidence that intentions have no causal effects, and are mere epiphenomena.

Can a machine show intention? It has been argued, for example, by the philosopher Margaret Boden (1972) that *artificial intelligence machines can exhibit *purpose and intention.

RLG

Boden, M. (1972). *Purposive Explanation in Psychology.*

Dennett, D. C. (1984). *Elbow Room: The Varieties of Free Will Worth Wanting.*

——(1991). *Consciousness Explained.*

intentionality. Intentionality is *aboutness.* Some things are about other things: a belief can be about icebergs, but an iceberg is not about anything; an idea can be about the number 7, but the number 7 is not about anything; a book or a film can be about Paris, but Paris is not about anything. Philosophers have long been concerned with the analysis of the phenomenon of intentionality, which has seemed to many to be a fundamental feature of mental states and events. It should be clear that this use of 'intentionality' and 'intentional' is a technical use, and should not be confused with the more familiar sense (discussed in the entry INTENTION) of doing something deliberately or on purpose. Hopes and fears, for instance, are not things we *do*, not intentional *acts* in the latter, familiar sense, but they are intentional phenomena in the technical sense, for they are *about* or *of* something.

The term was coined by the Scholastics in the Middle Ages (see, for example, AQUINAS, ST THOMAS), and derives from the Latin verb *intendo*, meaning to point (at) or aim (at) or extend (toward). Phenomena with intentionality point outside themselves, in effect to something else: whatever they are *of* or *about.* The term was revived in the 19th century by the philosopher and psychologist Franz *Brentano, one of the most important predecessors of the school of *phenomenology. Brentano claimed that intentionality is the defining distinction between the mental and the physical; all and only mental phenomena exhibit intentionality. Since intentionality is, he claimed, an irreducible feature of mental phenomena, and since no physical phenomena could exhibit it, mental phenomena could not be a species of physical phenomena. This claim, often called the Brentano thesis, or Brentano's irreducibility thesis, has often been cited to support the view that the mind cannot be the brain, but this is by no means generally accepted today.

There was a second revival of the term in the 1960s and 1970s by English and American philosophers in the analytic tradition. In response to seminal work by R. Chisholm and W. V. Quine, a vigorous attempt was made to develop an account of intentionality in harmony with the canons of modern logic and semantics. Since the phenomenological tradition, mainly on the Continent, has continued to exploit the concept of intentionality along rather different lines, the problem of intentionality is one of the best points of convergent concern in these two largely separate—and often antagonistic—research traditions.

In spite of the attention currently devoted to the concept, there is a striking lack of received wisdom about the proper analysis of intentionality. What agreement there is concerns the nature of the problems raised, and, while some of the proposed solutions are forbiddingly technical, the problems themselves readily emerge on a little reflection.

If we make an initial rough catalogue of the things that can be about things, it will include a great variety of *mental* states and events (ideas, beliefs, desires, thoughts, hopes, *fears, *perceptions, *dreams, *hallucinations, etc.), also various *linguistic* items (sentences, questions, poems, headlines, instructions, etc.), and perhaps other sorts of *representations* as well (pictures, charts, films, symphonic tone poems, computer programs, etc.). Many have thought that these linguistic and non-linguistic representations are only derivatively about anything. They depend for their intentionality on their being the creations and tools of creatures with minds, and particular representations derive their specific aboutness from the specific aboutness of the ideas, beliefs, and intentions of their creators. What makes the particular sequence of ink marks on the next line:

Napoleon was exiled to Elba

about Napoleon is its role as a sentence in a language used by people who know about Napoleon, or at least have beliefs about Napoleon, and wish to communicate about Napoleon. What *representations* mean depends on what *people* mean by using them. This suggests that the primary or underived intentionality of mental states and events is a very special feature indeed—the source of all meaning in the world. On this view, sentences, pictures, diagrams, and the like are in effect prosthetic extensions of the minds of those who use them, having no intrinsic meaning but only the meaning they derive from their utilization.

With regard to conventional representational artefacts, this is surely a plausible view, but it is not so plausible to claim that *all* intentionality is either the underived intentionality of (purely) mental phenomena or the derived intentionality of such artefacts. An exposed cliff-face might be said by a geologist to store information *about* the Triassic period; impulse trains in nerve bundles might be said by a neuroscientist to carry information *about* state changes in the inner ear. How is this sort of aboutness related to the aboutness discussed by philosophers under the rubric of intentionality? It is tempting to suppose that some concept of *information* underlies all these phenomena, and could serve eventually to unify mind, matter, and meaning in a single theory.

Identifying intentionality with aboutness nicely locates the concept, but hardly clarifies it, for the ordinary word 'about' is perplexing on its own. A belief can be about Paris, but a belief can also apparently be about phlogiston —and there is no phlogiston for it to be about. This curious fact, the possible non-existence of the *object* of an intentional item, may seem to be an idle puzzle, but in fact it has proved extraordinarily resistant to either solution or dismissal. Brentano called this the *intentional inexistence* of the intentional objects of mental states and events, and it has many manifestations. I cannot want without wanting something, but what I want need not exist for me to want it. It can be true that I now want a 2-ton diamond even if there is not now and never has been or will be such a thing. People have believed in Poseidon, and children often believe in Santa Claus, and, while in one sense we can say these believers all believe in *nothing, their beliefs are quite different states of mind—they have different *objects*—and both are to be distinguished from the state of mind of the sceptic or agnostic who can be said in quite a different sense to believe in nothing.

It might seem that there is a simple and straightforward solution to these problems: although Poseidon does not exist, an idea of Poseidon surely exists in each of the believers' minds, and this idea is the object of their belief. This will not do, however, for it is one thing to believe in the existence of the *idea* of Poseidon—we can all believe in the existence of that mental item—and quite another to

believe in Poseidon. Similarly, what I might want could hardly be the idea in my mind of a 2-ton diamond, for that I already have. Moreover, when, as normally happens, the object of an intentional state does exist—for example, when I believe that London is crowded—that very object, London, the city itself and not my idea of it in my mind, is what my belief is about.

The relation, then, between a state of mind—or for that matter a sentence or picture—and its intentional object or objects is a very peculiar relation in three ways.

First, for ordinary relations, like *x is sitting on y* or *x is employed by y*, *x* and *y* are identifiable entities quite apart from whether they happen to be thus related to each other. The thing which is *x* would be the same *x* whether or not it were sitting on *y* or employed by *y*. But the same is not true of intentional 'relations'. One and the same belief cannot at one moment be about a frog (that it is green, say) and at another moment be about a house (that *it* is green). The latter is a *different* belief. What a belief is supposed to be about is crucial to which belief it is.

Second, for ordinary relations, each of the things related must exist (or have existed), but, as we have seen, intentional 'relations' can be to non-existents.

Third, ordinary relations obtain between things regardless of how they might be specified. If I am sitting next to Jones and Jones is the Mad Strangler, then it follows that I am sitting next to the Mad Strangler, whatever anybody may think. But if I believe that Jones is harmless, or hope that he will marry my sister, it does not at all follow that I believe that the Mad Strangler is harmless or hope that the Mad Strangler will marry my sister. Even if one is tempted to object that, in this case *in one sense* I *do* hope the Mad Strangler will marry her, there is clearly another sense in which I *might* hope this and *do* not.

For these reasons the normal logic of relations cannot accommodate the presumed relation between an intentional state and its intentional object or objects, but it has also not proved comfortable for theorists to deny on these grounds that there are such things as intentional relations —to hold that mental states, for instance, are only *apparently* relational. This, then, is the unsolved problem of intentionality.

Faced with this problem, the Anglo-American tradition, characteristically, has tended to favour a tactical retreat, to a logical analysis of the language we use to talk about intentional states, events, and other items. This move, from the direct analysis of the phenomena to the analysis of our ways of talking about the phenomena, has been aptly called 'semantic ascent' by Quine, and its immediate advantages are twofold. First, we set aside epistemological and metaphysical distractions such as: 'How can we ever know another person's mental state anyway?' and 'Are mental states a variety of *physical* state, or are they somehow *immaterial* or *spiritual*?' The *things people say* about mental states are in any event out in the public world where we can get at them and study them directly. Second, switching to language puts at our disposal a number of sophisticated techniques and theories developed by philosophers, logicians, and linguists. Semantic ascent is not guaranteed to solve any problems, of course, but it may permit them to be reformulated in ways more accessible to ultimate solution.

In its new guise, the problem of intentionality concerns the semantics of the so-called *intentional idioms*—'. . . believes that *p*', '. . . desires that *q*', '. . . dreams that *r*', etc. (where *p*, *q*, and *r* are replaced by clauses, such as 'frogs are green' or 'Labour is returned to power'). Linguistically and logically, intentional idioms are a subset of those that Quine calls 'referentially opaque'. What this means is that many normally valid logical moves are not valid for the clauses 'within the scope' of intentional idioms. For instance, normally, if two words happen to be words for the same thing, then one can freely substitute one for the other without affecting the *truth* of the whole sentence (although one may change its meaning, or effectiveness, or style). Thus, since 'Cicero' and 'Tully' are names for the same man, from the truth of 'Cicero was an orator' we can infer the truth of 'Tully was an orator'. By contrast, however, the same substitution is not always allowable in 'Tom believes that Cicero denounced Catiline', for Tom may believe that Cicero denounced Catiline but not believe that Tully did. So '. . . believes that *p*' is an opaque idiom.

Clearly this is just another (and more precise) way of putting the point made earlier, that intentional relations depend on how their objects are specified. The other points have analogues too. Thus, normally, a relational statement is false if one of the alleged *relata* does not exist; not so within the scope of opaque idioms. And, of course, the fact that the identity of a particular belief depends on the object or objects it is supposed to be about emerges on this treatment as the fact that the ascription of a particular belief depends crucially on the words used in the clause expressing it. We can see now that this condition is essentially the same as the first, and that the second condition (possible non-existence of the object) is also just a special case of opacity: believing that Santa Claus is generous and believing that Poseidon is generous are different beliefs, in spite of the fact that 'Santa Claus' and 'Poseidon' refer to 'the same thing', i.e. to nothing.

Seeing this unity in the various conditions of intentionality is one of the benefits of semantic ascent. Another is that it thus provides us with a relatively formal and uncontroversial test for the intentionality of idioms, and hence a test for appeals to intentionality in a theory. This is an interesting test, for theories relying on intentional idioms—such as classical 'rational agent' economics and cognitive psychology—cannot be formulated in any non-

controversial way within standard logic, while it seems that other theories, pre-eminently in the physical sciences, can be so formulated. The logical oddity of intentional idioms, and their resistance to regimentation, led Quine and several other theorists to declare the bankruptcy of all intentional theories, on grounds of logical incoherence. The only sound alternatives within the social sciences, then, would have to be theories making no appeal to meaning or intentionality at all: purely *behaviouristic or purely physiological theories. This claim strikes a familiar note: many psychologists and brain scientists have expressed great scepticism about the utility or permissibility of 'mentalistic' formulations in their fields —while others of course have held them to be indispensable. The philosophical analysis of intentionality yields a clear logical characterization of this fundamental theoretical division in the social sciences and biology: 'mentalistic' theories are all and only those making ineliminable use of intentional idioms, and hence inheriting the *logical* problems of construing those idioms coherently.

Dispensing with intentional theories is not an attractive option, however, for the abstemious behaviourisms and physiological theories so far proposed have signally failed to exhibit the predictive and explanatory power needed to account for the intelligent activities of human beings and other animals. A close examination of the most powerful of these theories reveals intentional idioms inexorably creeping in—for instance in the definition of the stimulus as the 'perceived' stimulus and the response as the 'intended' effect, or in the reliance on the imputation of 'information-bearing' properties to physiological constructs. Moreover, the apparent soundness of information-processing theories, and their utility in practice, has strengthened the conviction that somehow we *must* be able to make sense of the ineliminable intentional formulations they contain without compromising thoroughgoing materialism.

One avenue currently being explored apparently challenges the thesis that the intentionality of linguistic entities is derivative, and, turning that idea on its head, attempts to explain the intentionality of minds by analysing minds as systems of 'mental representations'; our thoughts and beliefs exhibit intentionality *because* they are couched somehow in a 'language of thought' physically embodied in our brains. The intentionality of 'expressions' in the language of thought is held to be primary— the intentionality of expressions in natural language, for instance, is supposed to be derived from it—but the hope of this research strategy is that the impressive resources of formal theories of semantics in logic, computation theory, and linguistics can render the puzzles about aboutness more tractable, and lead to their eventual solution in cognitivistic or information-theoretic theories of the mind. If, for instance, the *theory of reference* for expressions in *public* (natural or formal) languages can be exploited to produce a theory of reference for expressions in the language of thought, the problem of what mental states are about might be solved.

It is far from clear, however, that this is not a fundamental error, leading, for instance, to a vicious regress of languages and language users within the mind or brain, in spite of the beguiling constructions already devised and to some degree tested by the enthusiasts of this persuasion. It is too early to say, then, whether the semantic ascent of the analytic tradition in philosophy, and its ideological cousin, cognitive or computational psychology, will provide more durable solutions to the problems of intentionality than the more frankly metaphysical investigations of the phenomenologists.   DCD/JCH

Aquila, R. E. (1977). *Intentionality: A Study of Mental Acts.*
Brentano, F. (1874). *Psychologie vom empirischen Standpunkt* (rev. edn. 1925). (An English translation of excerpts can be found in Chisholm 1960.)
Chisholm, R. (1957). *Perceiving: A Philosophical Study.*
——(1960). *Realism and the Background of Phenomenology.*
Dennett, D. C. (1978). *Brainstorms: Philosophical Essays on Mind and Psychology*, chs. 1 and 4.
——(2003). *Freedom Evolves.*
Field, H. (1978). 'Mental representation'. *Erkenntnis*, 13.
Fodor, J. (1975). *The Language of Thought.*
Quine, W. V. O. (1960). *Word and Object.*
Searle, J. (1983). *Intentionality.*

intention tremor. A neurological term meaning an increase in tremor, especially of the arms and hands, when close to picking up or manipulating objects. It is associated with various neurological disturbances, and is probably due (in engineering terms) to increasing the gain of the servo-control systems of the limbs, mediated by the gamma-efferent system: a small error in position (for example, when picking something up with the hand) produces an over-correction so that the hand overshoots; this is over-corrected in its turn to produce an oscillation, or tremor. It is common, though not inevitable, in *Parkinson's disease.

internal models. This term was coined by the Cambridge psychologist Kenneth *Craik, in his important book *The Nature of Explanation* (1943). Internal models are the supposed brain representations of reality (or imagination) as accepted for perception and for setting behaviour appropriate to the world. Craik thought of internal models as analogue representations—similar to F. C. *Bartlett's 'schemas', and Donald *Hebb's later 'phase sequences'. His notion was an important break from the prevailing emphasis on stimulus–response mechanisms of behaviour: it was a step towards psychological accounts based on the importance of stored knowledge; and it drew attention to the importance of control engineering, and

later computers, for understanding brain function. Craik wrote when analogue computers were in vogue, and just before the impact of *digital computing. His internal models are analogues rather than digital programs. There is a return to this for *brain function.

Bartlett, F. C. (1932). *Remembering.*
Craik, K. J. W. (1943). *The Nature of Explanation.*
Gregory, R. L. (1986). 'Kenneth Craik's *The Nature of Explanation*: forty years on'. In *Odd Perceptions.*
Hebb, D. (1949). *Organisation of Behaviour.*

interviews. People seek interviews with their bank manager or their doctor, they are interviewed for a job or for promotion, and at work they may have an annual 'appraisal interview'. Some are interviewed as they apply for Social Security or other benefits, and others may be interviewed by a journalist or a market researcher.

These different encounters all have as defining characteristics a certain formality and an asymmetry. Participants' roles are specified, in that one person is the interviewer and the other is the interviewee (although in practice more than two people may be involved) and each has a fairly clear idea of the type of behaviour which is expected. The objective is for the interviewer to obtain and interpret information from the interviewee in order to make a decision or take some action.

Let us look particularly at interviews in personnel selection, where an official of an organization has to decide which candidate to select for a job from among a number of applicants. Such interviews are often criticized on the grounds that different interviewers can reach different conclusions about the same candidate, and a number of experiments have examined the ways in which interviewers can be 'calibrated' so that they reliably form similar impressions. One approach has varied the degree of structure imposed upon the interview, in terms of the requirement to obtain certain kinds of information and to draw inferences only about pre-specified attributes or likely behaviours. Results indicate that increased structure yields significantly greater uniformity between interviewers. Similar outcomes can be achieved through training schemes which aim to make interviewers aware of possible biases and which stress the need to identify goals and important issues in advance. For example, the 'seven-point plan' encourages interviewers to define job requirements carefully and to obtain information about candidates in terms of physique, intelligence, aptitude, attainments, interests, disposition, and circumstances.

Although reliability can be enhanced in these ways, there remains the question whether interviewers can validly predict subsequent work behaviour. A major research problem is the difficulty of establishing acceptable measures of 'good' or 'bad' behaviour in an occupational role. Limited measures of skilled performance or of output levels may be available for some manual jobs, but professional and managerial work is much less open to quantification, and it is in those areas that interviews are particularly widespread. This problem, of adequately measuring the behaviour we wish to predict, is endemic in all areas of personnel selection, and is often referred to as 'the criterion problem'.

However, despite the commonly expressed doubts, selection interviews are here to stay, if for no other reason than that they provide an opportunity for the candidate to ask his own questions and to reach his own conclusions about a potential employer. The interpersonal processes at work during an interview are subtle, complex, and fascinating. Consider the ways in which an interviewer will search for and integrate information about the applicant. Research has established clearly that people form impressions of each other through the application of previously established expectancies or 'inference rules'. Evidence that a person has a certain characteristic (anxiousness in the interview situation, for example) sets up a network of inferences about other characteristics. These networks are sometimes referred to as 'implicit theories of personality', and perceivers apply their own implicit theories to even the most limited pieces of evidence. Indeed, some people take pride in 'summing him up as soon as he comes through the door', whereas others may devote their energies to fighting a similar form of stereotyped perception, where extensive inferences are drawn from single cues such as 'black', 'female', or 'handicapped'. In general terms, manifested features have been found to make their greatest impact during short encounters, when other evidence is meagre. Thus many perceivers initially take the wearing of spectacles to imply intelligence and thoughtfulness (see HALO EFFECT). Conventional wisdom has it that 'first impressions count', and research has looked in detail at this question. It seems that the initial impression is tested through subsequent investigation. However, there is often a predisposition in an interviewer to obtain *negative* information, material which suggests that the candidate should not be selected. This is understandable in the light of the interviewer's regular need to reject most of the applicants, but it is important for the 'first impressions count' thesis. This needs to be refined to suggest that an early negative impression is readily reached and is difficult to change, whereas an early positive impression is less easily made and is liable to be overridden if negative evidence becomes available subsequently.

One interesting research finding bears upon this issue. There is typically a significant positive correlation between the proportion of time during which the *interviewer* talks and the probability that a candidate will be offered the job. This may be interpreted in terms of an early implicit decision by an interviewer which tends to make later questioning redundant and perhaps suggests that the

desirable candidate should be encouraged through conversation to maintain his interest in the vacancy.

The skills of interviewing extend to coordinating the interaction through verbal and non-verbal cues at the same time as gaining and integrating a variety of items of information. Recent research has placed emphasis on the non-verbal cues which contribute to impression formation and management: they may be relatively unchanging—as with general appearance, clothes, *facial expression, and so on—or they may be dynamic—as in *eye contact, bodily movements, or loudness of speech.

How can people learn to be good interviewers? We all have relevant experience, talking with and acquiring information from others, and there is a tendency to feel that we are quite competent. But experience without detailed feedback is often of limited value: we need to learn with some precision about the effects of our actions and impressions so that we can improve upon them. This requirement has been the basis of recent experiments in interviewer training, and powerful procedures are now available. These have as their core the use of feedback about performance, often through the replay of video-taped practice sessions. In this way, trainees are able to chart and improve their performance over a series of practice interviews, assisted both by their tutors and by their fellow trainees. Behaviour category systems are often applied to generate profiles of an interviewer's style in a way that points up strong and weak points, providing in a striking manner the feedback that is necessary for learning.

PBW

Anstey, E. (1977). *An Introduction to Selection Interviewing.*
Argyle, M. (1973). *Social Encounters: Readings in Social Interaction.*
Mackensie D. D., and McDonnell, P. (1975). *How to Interview.*
Sidney, E., Brown, M., and Argyle, M. (1973). *Skills with People: A Guide for Managers.*

introspection. Looking into one's own mind. Used as a psychological technique it has great dangers of misinterpretation, even though introspections may seem to provide the most direct knowledge of ourselves that we have. It has, however, become clear that very little that goes on in the brain associated with the mind is accessible to conscious introspection, and we regard the mind as a much broader concept than awareness, conciousness, or what is known by introspection.

introversion. See EXTROVERSION/INTROVERSION.

intuition. This is, essentially, arriving at decisions or conclusions without explicit or conscious processes of reasoned thinking. It is sometimes thought that intuitions are reliable, and indeed we do act most of the time without knowing why or what our reasons may be. It is certainly rare to set out an argument in formal terms, and go through the steps as prescribed by logicians. In this sense, almost all judgements and behaviour are 'intuitive'.

The term is used in philosophy to denote the alleged power of the mind to perceive or 'see' certain self-evident truths (Latin *intueor*, to see). The status of intuition has, however, declined over the last century, perhaps with the increasing emphasis on formal logic and explicit data and methods of science.

'Woman's intuition' is, perhaps, largely the subtle use of almost subliminal cues in social situations from gestures, casual remarks, and knowledge of behaviour patterns and motives. Psychologists find these important matters for living almost impossible to formulate.   RLG

invention. Inventions may be old ideas or techniques applied in new ways: they are very often combinations of old, and even highly familiar, ideas. To some degree almost all human behaviour is inventive, for it is seldom strictly repetitive and is aimed at contingencies which, though small and trivial, nevertheless require invention even if of a humble kind. The outstanding inventions, such as the phonograph of Thomas Alva Edison, represent the extension of abilities to some degree possessed by us all. Edison had remarkable perseverance towards imaginative goals; indeed he described invention as '99 per cent perspiration and 1 per cent inspiration'. The motivations, methods, and travails of inventors are described with case histories in *The Sources of Invention*, by J. Jewkes, D. Sawers, and R. Stillerman (1958). Most important is realizing what is needed; most difficult is attracting support for development.   RLG

invertebrate learning and intelligence. There are some signals to which an animal must respond, if it is to remain alive. It must pull back if it is hurt, and it must respond to extremes of hunger or thirst, heat or cold. One might add that it must, sooner or later, respond to the opposite sex and reproduce if the species is to survive.

Response to all other signals is optional. The fact that animals respond to a much wider range of events than those that immediately affect their physical well-being is a reflection of the non-random nature of the natural world. Stimuli of whatever sort may have predictive value, and a creature that responds appropriately can often avoid future unpleasantness and ensure the regular enjoyment of the better things in life, to the immediate benefit of itself and the ultimate survival of its species.

Learning is largely concerned with establishing the predictive value of stimuli that do not of themselves demand responses. We recognize other animals as intelligent when they predict effectively from these stimuli, and as highly intelligent when they begin to predict by analogy, gener-

alizing to the point where they can take appropriate preemptive action without prior experience of the particular sequence of events to which they are reacting.

All invertebrate animals learn, many show glimmerings of *intelligence, and some would qualify as highly intelligent by the definitions employed above. A major problem, as we shall see below, is that we are often ourselves insufficiently intelligent to devise situations that will fairly test their performance. This problem becomes particularly acute when an invertebrate is making an elaborate response in an apparently complex situation, so it is perhaps most appropriate to begin by considering 'simple' forms of learning in which it does seem to be possible (i) to define the stimuli to which the animals are responding and (ii) to recognize the likely advantage of the behaviour in question.

One such category is *habituation*. Animals, in general, soon cease to respond to stimuli that prove to have no predictive value. A shadow passes. It could signal the approach of a would-be predator. In the past, individuals that played safe and ducked, or froze, lived to breed. Their offspring are liable to do the same; caution is genetically determined, natural selection having eliminated the unwary over countless generations in the past history of the species. But a shadow is not invariably dangerous. It may signal no more than a passing cloud, or the waving of a frond of seaweed. An animal that reacts to every moving shadow is doomed to a restless and economically hopeless existence, and cannot effectively compete with its less wary neighbours; in the long run the overcautious are eliminated as surely as the foolhardy. Animals must habituate if they are to remain in business, and the best assumption with which genetics can equip them is that the immediate future is likely to resemble the immediate past. If a stimulus recurs regularly, unaccompanied by consequences of importance to the animal, it is well to ignore it. Rates of habituation vary, as we might expect, because the degree of built-in caution will vary from one sort of stimulus to the next, but caution is always present.

In an opposite direction, we find that nearly all animals will *sensitize*, becoming more rather than less responsive in circumstances where anything that happens *is* likely to have predictive value. If recent experience has revealed that something of importance is going on, it is well for the animal to remain more than usually alert, so that it responds to stimuli that it might otherwise have ignored. An animal that has just been hurt will flinch at stimuli that have nothing to do with the damage, and an animal that has just engulfed a tasty mouthful is more than usually attentive; any event could be a signal that more of the same is in the offing. It should be noticed that such effects can be quite unspecific: if things are going badly for the animal it will sensitize in the direction of caution, and take no chances over stimuli that would normally evoke a positive reaction; and if events are proving favourable, it becomes particularly responsive to stimuli that may indicate desirable objectives, like food, or sex. The animal, in either case, is responding to the sum of events (good and bad) in its recent past, and adjusting its response levels accordingly.

Taken together, habituation and sensitization will ensure that an animal behaves economically and opportunistically, cashing in when the going is good and lying low when conditions are unfavourable. The two interact: *dishabituation*, where a sudden change in circumstances re-establishes responses to a repeated stimulus that the animal has come to ignore, is a special case of sensitization. Between them the twin processes of habituation and sensitization will ensure better-than-even odds on an animal's responding appropriately, even under conditions where the creature is quite incapable of determining the precise nature of the stimulus to which it is responding. The system works, provided only that events occur in a non-random sequence—provided, in short, that the future is likely to resemble the recent past. Inside the laboratory it may, for various reasons, be desirable to randomize trial sequences so that an animal cannot predict what is going to happen without precise identification of the stimuli offered to it, but in the wild the animal is never likely to encounter a random sequence of events. Predators hang about, or go away; food comes in patches, scattered in time and space but never quite at random.

It is relevant to an understanding of invertebrate learning and behaviour to realize that cold-blooded animals in general can afford to be opportunists to an extent unthinkable in a homoiotherm. We poor warm-blooded creatures consume fuel so fast that we tend to discuss motivation in terms of imperatives: hunger must be satisfied or we die. We get thirsty because we live above the temperature of our surroundings and evaporate our body water; the need to replenish the water becomes an imperative because we overheat and die if we fail to do so. This personal experience distorts our thinking about invertebrates; we tend to assume that a starved snail or a thirsty cockroach will take risks to satisfy its needs as we would, becoming increasingly desperate as time passes. There is no evidence for this, at least on the sort of time scales that one would expect from an experience of rats and people. A fed octopus is more, rather than less, liable to attack a strange but potentially edible object lowered into its tank; it cashes in while the going is good, and can starve for weeks if conditions suggest that it is unprofitable or even dangerous to respond to the unfamiliar. Sensitization is relatively unimportant in ourselves, because we can rarely afford to accept its dictates for very long; invertebrates can lie low for months, then stuff themselves, mate, and multiply when conditions improve.

One consequence of this is that it may be difficult to investigate invertebrate learning by conventional methods, forcing the animal to become active and solve problems because it is hungry or thirsty.

A further difficulty that confronts any biologist rash enough to examine learning in the lower animals is that most of them depend predominantly upon chemical stimuli, which we find awkward to classify and almost impossible to measure in the laboratory, let alone in the wild. Experimenters tend, in consequence, to set problems based on visual and spatial cues, so that their unfortunate subjects are more often than not tested with learning problems based on our sensory capabilities rather than theirs, a situation that can only lead to persistent underestimation of their learning abilities.

At a somewhat more subtle level, it is easy to forget that the bodily construction of animals may itself preclude certain forms of learning. Many of the things that we do, and believe simple, are based on an awareness of bodily position that is probably lacking in most invertebrates. When we move, we know how the position of our limbs is changing. If I pick up and examine an object, I am continually moving my fingers; each time I change my grip I know about the new positions adopted and, putting this information together with the feel of the contacts made, I can build up a mental picture of the shape of the thing I am holding. An octopus, for example, apparently cannot. It is quite as capable as I am of feeling over an object that it touches, and there is no doubt whatever that the animal can learn by touch, since it can be taught by simple reward and punishment techniques to distinguish between a wide variety of different textures and tastes (chemoreception again!), learning to perform such discriminations with great accuracy after a dozen or so trials. But it cannot manage shapes. A cube and a sphere are alike to it, apparently because the animal has no means of assessing the relative positions of its equivalent of our fingers, the many suckers arrayed along its flexible arms.

On reflection this is perhaps not very surprising. It is the animal's very flexibility that defeats it. We can compute the precise position of our hands because the human body only bends in a few places and is even there restricted to movement in a few directions. Sense organs in and around our joints can tell us about the angle adopted at each. No such easy computation is possible in a soft-bodied animal, where the position of each part depends upon the degree of contraction or relaxation of muscles all over the rest of the body. Muscle stretch receptors, which all have, are useless in this respect since they can only signal tension in the muscle concerned, not the position achieved as a result. The jointless animal perforce lacks any equivalent of our proprioceptive sense of position.

This divides the animal kingdom rather abruptly into two groups. On the one hand, there are the jointed animals, the vertebrates and the arthropods, which seem to have a double (muscle and joint) set of proprioceptors. These creatures are potentially able to learn to manipulate; they can discover by trial and error precisely which movements it pays to repeat; they can monitor the number of steps they have taken and the angle of any turns that they have made. On the other hand, there is the world of the soft-bodied, forever debarred from learning to make skilled movements, and faced with learning to find their way about entirely from exteroceptive cues. Arthropods, like vertebrates, can readily learn to run mazes, while many of the other things that they do or make (such as honeycombs and spiders' webs) necessitate accurate measurement of lengths and angles. A hermit crab, investigating the inside of an empty shell with its claw, plainly learns about the size and the shape of the hole it is examining before risking exposure of its soft abdomen as it quits its old home in favour of the new. In marked contrast to all this, the soft-bodied snails and worms (and octopuses) rarely succeed in mastering any maze more complex than a T or Y, they never seem to create patterned structures, and they never, so far as we can assess the matter, learn to carry out a skilled movement. As a result we tend to assess their learning capabilities and their intelligence generally as exceedingly limited compared with arthropods and our fellow vertebrates, which find easy the same sorts of tasks as we do ourselves. It may well be, indeed it seems very likely, that the individual adaptive capacity of worms and snails *is* very limited; but it is well to remember that most of our present evidence comes from tests appropriate to ourselves rather than the creatures we have studied.

Granted, then, that we are almost certainly underestimating the capacities of most invertebrate animals, what generalities can be made in comparing higher forms of learning in vertebrates and invertebrates? Can we, for example, detect signs of *latent learning* ('the association of indifferent stimuli in situations without patent reward') or *insight learning* ('the production of a new adaptive response as a result of the apprehension of relations') among invertebrates, as we can among the higher vertebrates?

The answer appears to be 'yes', if one searches. Many invertebrates, inevitably, show little sign of these more complex forms of learning. Any animal that lives a highly specialized existence (an aphid on a rose bush or a lugworm in the mud of a saltmarsh) is unlikely to show conspicuous signs of intelligence. It does not need to: the same very limited range of problems has cropped up generation after generation for so long that almost the totality of its behaviour has come to be programmed genetically. Wherever this is possible, because the future

has always rather precisely resembled the past, learning, with its inherent capacity for errors that could be dangerous or even fatal, is plainly a luxury that will be eliminated in the course of natural selection.

To discover what invertebrates can really do, one is obliged to examine cases where the animals live in complex environments. In general, also, it is necessary to look at predators, because predators must always be a little brighter than the prey they feed upon. Two such animals will be considered below, one soft-bodied (a cephalopod, of course), the other a jointed animal, an insect.

The octopus can be taught to make a wide variety of visual and tactile discriminations in the laboratory and it learns rapidly in these trial-and-error situations. It is also plain, from its lifestyle in the sea (where it returns to a home in the rocks after foraging expeditions that may carry it quite far afield) that it is capable of learning its way about a complex landscape, despite the restrictions already considered in relation to the consequences of flexibility. Observations of octopuses in the sea suggest that they can return home from any point in their range without retracing their outgoing steps, and this suggests a capacity for latent learning. In the laboratory octopuses will readily make detours to get at prey that they cannot approach directly; in a typical apparatus the animal was obliged to run out of sight of a crab, down an opaque corridor, and turn appropriately to reach its food. Even untrained octopuses manage this quite readily and will reach their goal with considerable reliability even if delayed for a minute or more by shutting them into the corridor. Plainly the animals are in some manner aware of the spatial relations of the crab and the various baffles that prevent them from reaching it—they show *insight*. (It is surprising how few vertebrates will detour successfully in similar circumstances.)

Performances that are in some ways even more impressive are shown by some of the hunting wasps. *Ammophila*, for example, hunts, paralyses, and stores caterpillars. Each mated female operates alone. She digs a hole in sand, covers it over, and, after a brief orientation flight in the vicinity of the nest, departs to search for caterpillars. A caterpillar is paralysed by a sting in the central nervous system and is thus preserved as a living food supply for the egg, which is subsequently deposited with it in the hole that the wasp has dug. The wasp's first problem, however, is to get the caterpillar home. Often the prey is too heavy to fly with, and the wasp sets off to drag it, often for many tens of metres, across the ground and round obstacles to the nest site. This performance is in itself remarkable because it implies a considerable knowledge of the geography of the district round the nest, apparently derived from the brief orientation flight carried out before setting out to hunt down a caterpillar—another nice example of latent learning. Extensive tests show that the cues used are entirely visual and more often than not precisely the sort of landmarks, skyline patterns and the like, that we would choose in the same circumstances.

More impressive still, however, is the discovery that *Ammophila* will run as many as three nests, in different stages of construction, at one and the same time. After the first egg and caterpillar have been deposited, she begins and provisions a new nest. A day or two later she returns to the first nest, checks whether the egg has hatched, and if it has, begins to stuff further caterpillars down the hole to feed her grub. Any spare time is spent digging out nest three, with a visit to nest two after a couple of days to see whether that egg has now begun to develop. Quite clearly the wasp not only remembers the precise position of each separate hole, but also recalls the state of play at each site, often delaying the response that she makes as a result of an inspection visit for two or three days on end.

Performances like those of *Ammophila* and the octopus leave no reason to doubt that learning by invertebrate animals can be every bit as complex as that found in vertebrates, which have been far more extensively studied. Whether one regards such creatures as 'intelligent' is largely a matter of taste, that is to say the precise definition of that somewhat elusive property one chooses to employ. We have come a long way from the proposition that the lower forms of life are automata, bereft of the ability to adapt and determine their individual destinies.   MJW

Corning, W. C., et al. (eds.) (1973–5). *Invertebrate Learning*, 3 vols.
Hinde, R. A. (1970). *Animal Behaviour: A Synthesis of Ethology and Comparative Psychology* (2nd edn.).
Wells, M. J. (1978). *Octopus: Physiology and Behaviour of an Advanced Invertebrate*.

iris. The coloured (usually blue or brown in man) ring round the pupil of the eye, named from the Greek for rainbow. It partially closes in bright light, and opens in dim light as a result of the action of light on the retina—including a reflex from one eye to the other. The small pupil in bright light reduces the optical aberrations of the eye, and gives maximal depth of field (focus over a wide range of distances). These qualities are sacrificed in dim light to give greater light-gathering power. Albinos, who lack pigment in their irises, have severe visual problems. The word 'pupil' was suggested to Aristotle from the tiny images of people seen reflected in eyes.

In mammals, the pupil is controlled involuntarily, with 'smooth' muscles, by the autonomic nervous system. In birds this is quite different: the pupils of their eyes are controlled by striate muscle and at least in some parrots the pupils respond to their level of arousal. Remarkably, the pupils of talking parrots open and close in apparent relation to their attention when producing, or listening to, sounds meaningful for them. The human pupil is affected, though far less markedly than the parrot's, by emotional changes, increasing in size with autonomic emotional arousal. This increase in size in women is seen as attractive. The drug belladonna (pretty woman) has been used to enlarge the pupils by applying it to the eye as a turn-on.
                                                                RLG

Davson, H. (1984). *The Eye: Vegetative Physiology and Biochemistry*, vol. i (3rd edn.).
Gregory, R. L., and Hopkins, P. (1974). 'Pupils of a talking parrot'. *Nature*, 252.

irradiation. In vision, the apparently greater size of a white area than a corresponding darker area. Described in detail by *Helmholtz, it is still not fully understood.

irritability. As a technical term in biology, the triggering of responses from small stimuli, such as gentle *touch. It is a defining property of living organisms—as through their 'irritability' they do not obey Newtonian mechanics—for they are active and wholly or partly autonomous, in a way that non-living objects (apart perhaps from some machines) are not.
                                                                RLG

Islamic philosophy. A traditional occidental theme is that the thinkers of Islam were mere synthesizers of Greek and other traditions (such as those of India and Persia) and made no original contribution to human thought. This simplistic view originates with the assumption that such work as that of *Avicenna was the totality of Islam's philosophy: which in turn is understandable when it is realized what a profound effect Avicenna had upon the Schoolmen.

The importance of Avicenna's thought for the West cannot be overestimated. Both in its negative aspect, such as the necessity of everything, and its more sympathetic notions, it offered a stimulus to the West. It was *par excellence* a combination of Neoplatonism and Aristotle, transforming the One into a first mover from whom all existence ultimately sprang. For Christian thinkers it offered especial attraction in distinguishing God from His creatures in terms of being; in holding essence to be the foundation of all existence; in making the effect dependent for both its being and its movement on what was prior to it; and in regarding all knowledge as the result of illumination. (Leff 1958: 154 f.)

Characteristically, T. P. Hughes's massive *Dictionary of Islam* of 1885 (1964 edn., p. 452) baldly repeats: 'The whole philosophy of the Arabians was only a form of Aristotelianism tempered more or less with Neo-Platonic conceptions.' More recently this generalization has been challenged with great vigour by both Muslim and Western scholars.

The Arab conquest and occupation of eastern and western lands from the early 8th century produced intense intellectual activity in centres of learning as widely dispersed as Baghdad and Spain, Bukhara and Egypt. The study and exercise of traditional knowledge were directly linked to the Prophet's dictum, accepted with the force of law: 'Seek knowledge even unto China.' During much of the thousand years of the period known as the Dark Ages in Europe, the Islamic centres of learning were major agents for the preservation and transmission of accumulated knowledge, those of Spain especially being a magnet for Christian scholars. 'The Christian West became acquainted with Aristotle by way of Avicenna, *Al-Farabi, and Algazel (*Al-Ghazzali). Gundisalvus' own encyclopedia of knowledge relies in the main on the information he had drawn from Arabian sources' (Guillaume 1949: s.v. 'Philosophy and theology', p. 246).

Many Islamic theorists, including Al-Ghazzali, were even believed by European scholars of the time to be Christian divines. The widespread belief that the Arabian schools were the great source of wisdom was later replaced, particularly in Victorian thought, by the thesis that they were merely run by copyists of the Greeks. More comprehensive study from a wider perspective has indicated that original contributions began to appear as the period of translation of classics and the absorption of ancient teaching advanced, after the 8th century. Work published during the 20th century has increasingly asserted unexpected anticipations of relatively modern Western thought by the major Islamic philosophers, especially from the 9th to the 15th centuries.

Typically, M. S. Sheikh (1982: p. x and *passim*) has propounded themes in the systems of Al-Farabi, Avicenna, Al-Ghazzali, Ibn Khaldun, and others as prefigurings of the ideas of *Descartes (methodological doubt and *cogito, ergo sum*) and *Spinoza (*idealism), of Cartesian occasionalism, of *Leibnizian pre-established harmony, of *Kant (antinomies of pure reason and metaphysical agnosticism), *Hegel (panlogism and the notion of the absolute), and *Hume (denial of causality), of *Bergson's creative evolutionism, and even of logicism and positivism. The Indian Muslim poet and thinker Sir Muhammad Iqbal (1876–1938) is the best-known Islamic philosopher of modern times.

In the Islamic world, in addition to the many customary preoccupations of philosophy as expressed in logic, ethics, method, knowledge, and political thought, there were also a vast number of exponents and schools of religious philosophy and *metaphysics (seen as mysticism). Among the most important were the Islamic theologians and the *Sufis. The works of the latter are today increasingly studied by both East and West in newer disciplines such as psychology and sociology.

From the comparative point of view, the picture of the Islamic contribution that emerges indicates the relative freedom of speculation within the culture, as contrasted with the somewhat more restricted categories of the West in the same epoch. This may be because Islam has never had a central ideological disciplinary institution which could succeed in imposing dogmatic authority over large populations for long periods of time, and because the door of reinterpretation of the limits of philosophical speculation has remained open, being the responsibility of the courts, in the absence of a priesthood.   IS

De Boer, T. J. (1961). *The History of Philosophy in Islam*. Trans. E. R. Jones.

Guillaume, A. (1949). *The Legacy of Islam*.

Hashimi, A. Al- (1973). *Islamic Philosophy and Western Thinkers*.

Hitti, P. K. (1951). *History of the Arabs*.

Houtsma, W. T., et al. (eds.) (1908–38). *The Encyclopedia of Islam and Supplement*.

Leff, G. (1958). *Medieval Thought: St Augustine to Ockham*.

Nicholson, R. A. (1966). *A Literary History of the Arabs*.

O'Leary, D. (1954). *Arabic Thought and its Place in History*.

Schacht, J., and Bosworth, C. E. (eds.) (1974). *The Legacy of Islam* (2nd edn.).

Sheikh, M. S. (1982). *Islamic Philosophy*.

isolation experiments. When people are cut off from communication with other people, or, in even more extreme cases, from almost all sensory stimulation, there is a strong tendency to develop *hallucinations and hallucinogenic druglike experiences not altogether dissimilar to those of *schizophrenia. There are many accounts of delusions and loss of reality and personal identity in, for example, single-handed voyages, and many experiments have been conducted in isolation chambers in which subjects have only diffused lighting and a minimum of auditory or tactile stimulation. Many of these experiments have been carried out on students, of an age group that is perhaps less stable than later adult life, and the effects may be less for older people; but nevertheless there is good evidence that loss of sensory inputs seems to free the active mind to generate fantasies which may be overwhelming. Also, upon re-entering the normal world there may be dramatic visual and other *illusions (which makes these experiments dangerous unless carefully controlled), suggesting that fairly continuous inputs are required to maintain the sensory system in calibration. The results strongly suggest that, for example, space flights should be made by several crew members and not individually, and that there may be isolation problems for divers and others working and living alone (see DIVER PERFORMANCE).

Similar principles may apply to all levels of neural activity—hence the beneficial stimulation of companionship and competition in sport and academic activities. There seem to be important implications for education, and generally for a satisfying and productive way of life (the rich introspections of mystics and monks may be due to being cut off from stimulation they see as irrelevant and trivial).

The first experimental studies were by W. H. Bexton, W. Heron, and T. H. Scott in 1954, in Donald Hebb's laboratory at McGill. J. C. Lilly in 1956 increased the sensory isolation of his subjects by immersing them in a tank of water maintained at body temperature. Apart from a mask which covered the head, they were naked and so deprived of the sensations produced by pressure from clothing. After variable periods of time, thinking became less directed, and was eventually replaced by highly personal fantasies and hallucinations which were usually visual. Subjects were unable to distinguish between sleeping and waking—a finding of some importance as, regardless of the psychological explanations, there is evidence that episodes of microsleep occurred in which there was an early onset of REM *dreaming sleep. None the less, hallucinations of a similar kind may be experienced by other persons deprived of sensory stimulation, examples being prisoners in solitary confinement. Although *sensory* isolation may not be a prominent feature, being cut off from normal human intercourse when coupled with a fair measure of intense anxiety seems to produce both real hallucinations and pseudohallucinations. OLZ

Zulley, J. (2000). 'The influence of isolation on psychological and physiological variables'. *Aviation Space and Environmental Medicine*, 71/9.

isomorphism. Literally 'equal form'. Used by the Gestalt writers to refer to supposed electrical brain states, or 'fields', of the same shape as perceived objects. This notion has now been abandoned. See GESTALT THEORY.

iterative procedures. A computing term meaning successive approximations to a good, or the best, solution.

J

Jackson, John Hughlings (1835–1911). Widely known as the 'father' of British neurology. He was born in Yorkshire and spent the greatest part of his life in London, where he was for many years consultant physician to the then newly founded National Hospital for Nervous Diseases, Queen Square. His conception of nervous and mental disease, which owed much to the writings of Herbert *Spencer, was formulated in terms of the evolution and dissolution of the nervous system and is perhaps the most thoroughgoing attempt to explain the breakdown of neurological functions along evolutionary lines.

Jackson's most important contributions were to the study of *epilepsy and *aphasia. As regards the former, he was the first to appreciate that the sequence of involuntary movements which characterizes focal epilepsy indicates the spatial layout of excitable foci in the motor cortex. This brilliant inference was confirmed soon after by the experiments of David *Ferrier and others, who demonstrated in animals that electrical stimulation of individual cortical foci elicits discrete bodily movements. Jackson was also the first to describe perceptual illusions and other dreamlike states of consciousness evoked by focal epileptic discharges in the temporal lobes. These have since been fully studied by Wilder *Penfield.

In his work on aphasia, Jackson laid great stress on the fact that the disorder is an affection of language rather than merely one of speech. In his view, aphasia is essentially an intellectual deficit marked by inability to formulate propositions, rather than by failure to recall individual words. He further pointed out that words or phrases may on occasion be uttered under stress of emotion when they cannot be spoken voluntarily. (See also LANGUAGE: NEUROPSYCHOLOGY.)

Although in agreement with Paul *Broca that aphasia almost invariably results from damage to the left cerebral hemisphere, Jackson suggested that visual and spatial disabilities might bear a comparable relation to the right cerebral hemisphere. Though long ignored, this idea of cerebral asymmetry of function has been widely accepted in contemporary neuropsychology.

Jackson's *Selected Papers* (2 vols., ed. J. Taylor, 1931) is an indispensable source of his writings. His papers on aphasia were republished by Sir Henry Head in *Brain*, 38 (1915).

OLZ

Critchley, M., and Critchley, E. A. (1998). *John Hughlings Jackson: Father of English Neurology.*

James, William (1842–1910). A towering scholar, talented communicator, individualist, celebrity in his day, and a warmly empathic man who inspired genuine affection and respect. His personal charm shows through his writings, most of which follow closely the spoken lectures he gave to students and intelligent non-specialists. His greatest work, the two-volume *Principles of Psychology* (1890), is still fresh and informative. Probably the best-known book in all psychology, it is a treasure house of ideas and finely turned phrases which psychologists continue to plunder with profit.

James was an American who, for most of his adult life, was associated with Harvard, where he graduated in medicine and taught successively physiology, psychology, and philosophy. He was also very much a European. He first visited Europe before his second birthday, and almost every year of his life spent some time there, occasionally staying for a year or two at a stretch. He was fluent in German and French, competent in Italian, and personally acquainted with most of the leading intellectuals of his time, ranging from Ralph Waldo Emerson to Sigmund *Freud and Bertrand *Russell. His brother, the novelist Henry James (1843–1916), settled in England, where he, the novelist who wrote like a psychologist, often received William, the psychologist who wrote like a novelist. Both brothers were fascinated by the problem of expressing in words the phenomena of individual consciousness. Henry approached the problem through novels which exhibited the subtle uniqueness and partiality of individual people's perspectives. William approached the problem through psychology.

James was born in New York, the eldest of five children whose education was unconventional. His father, a brilliant conversationalist and writer on theology, enjoyed a large inherited fortune which enabled him to devote his time to travelling, meeting interesting people, and educating his children. Wherever father went, his wife and children went also, accompanied by a variable entourage of relatives, friends, and servants. The children were actively encouraged to absorb their surroundings, talk about their experiences, read, write, and paint. This lively nomadic troupe lodged in hotels and rented houses on both sides of the Atlantic. They everlastingly engaged in wide-ranging, self-analytic discussions which, often shared by visiting celebrities, dominated Jamesian life and education.

James was educated by short-stay tutors and brief attendances at private schools, but mainly by his father and family. The upshot was that he developed a formidably heterogeneous repertoire of academic, social, linguistic, and artistic talents. Between the ages of 18 and 30 he continued further studies and intensive programmes of private reading. He also became increasingly perturbed about what to do with his life. He was torn among so many possibilities. He suffered bouts of depression and neurotic malady, and family letters spoke of his 'ill health', 'the choice of a profession', and 'the awful responsibility of such a choice'.

At 18 he started training as a painter. He later switched to the study of science, then to medicine. Even after deciding on medicine he had doubts, and interrupted his studies to go on a geological expedition to Brazil, and again to spend a year in Germany. He travelled in Europe in 1867–8, graduated MD from Harvard in 1869, and thereafter entered a period of black despair and took a decisive step towards resolving his existential crisis. This step averted suicide and began to heal what he later called his 'sick soul'; it also contained themes which he explored for the rest of his life and which dominated his mature work. On 30 April 1870, he wrote as follows in his private diary.

Yesterday was a crisis in my life. I finished the first part of Renouvier's 2nd Essay and saw no reason why his definition of free will—'the sustaining of a thought *because I choose to* when I might have other thoughts'—need be the definition of an illusion. My first act of free will shall be to believe in free will. For the remainder of the year, I will abstain from mere speculation and contemplative *Grübelei* [musing] in which my nature takes most delight, and voluntarily cultivate the feeling of moral freedom. . . . Today has furnished the exceptionally passionate initiative which Bain posits as needful for the acquisition of habits. . . . Now, I will go a step further with my will, not only act with it, but believe as well; believe in my individual reality and creative power. My belief to be sure can't be optimistic—but I will posit life, (the real, the good) in the self-governing resistance of the ego to the world.

Once his self-administered, existentialist cure began to work, he returned to Harvard, where he was offered a post as a teacher of physiology. He accepted and, at the age of 30, began his career as a university teacher. In 1878 he married, happily, and subsequently children were born in whom he and his wife took delight. Also in 1878, he contracted to write a book based on the lectures he was giving on psychology. The book took twelve years to write but, when *Principles of Psychology* appeared, it established James as the foremost psychologist of the day. The

opening pages plunged into the recurrent Jamesian themes of individuality, *choice, and *purpose. Each of us is, within the limits of our biological potential and environmental circumstances, forever pursuing purposes, long term and short term, by making choices, great and small, which cumulatively shape every aspect of our individual being. As James said elsewhere, 'Sow an action, and you reap a habit; sow a habit, and you reap a character; sow a character, and you reap a destiny'.

These themes ran through all James's work. In *The Varieties of Religious Experience* (1902), he examined the biographies of people who reported a belief 'that there is an unseen order, and that our supreme good lies in harmoniously adjusting ourselves thereto'. Such beliefs were subjective, but none the less real to the experiencer, and they had manifest effects on the individual's conduct. When such effects were 'good', he argued, the individual was right to exercise the 'will to believe', although not to insist that others share the same belief. James's contributions to the philosophy of pragmatism were in the same vein. In brief, any hypothesis was true if the consequences of holding it were satisfactory to the individual concerned. The truth of which he spoke was not absolute but relative to each individual. The 'pluralistic and unfinished universe' had undiscovered potentialities which different individuals might make actual through the hypotheses they held, the choices they made, and the purposes they pursued.

Between 1878 and 1899, James vigorously enjoyed work, family life, and social life. He travelled, attended conferences, lectured, kept up a massive correspondence, and took unassuming pleasure in his growing international fame. In 1899 he suffered the first of many attacks of angina, which progressively impeded his vigour even though he still continued a formidable round of activities. On 11 August 1910, he and his wife left Henry James's home at Rye in England and made what William knew to be his last Atlantic crossing. He died in America fifteen days later.

During his life, James fostered much psychological discussion and enquiry, but he was precluded, by his artistic sensitivity to the many-sidedness of the human condition, from adopting any one view as final. His popular lectures inspired many people with a new sense of human worth and dignity, but he himself was never entirely free from bouts of depression. In 1875 he established at Harvard a laboratory for psychological experiment (see LABORATORIES OF PSYCHOLOGY), but he himself had insufficient patience to conduct experiments, make measurements, or use statistics. He was consistently protean.

His pluralistic vision is evident in the brilliant perceptiveness, intuitiveness, and inconsistency of the *Principles*. The book presents, in masterly language, a wealth of naturalistic observation about human behaviour and conscious experience, culled partly at first hand and partly from wide reading. It contains sharp intellectual analyses in which issues are turned over critically and open-mindedly. It makes clear that psychology concerns, and is of concern to, the lives of individual people. It is exploratory, not consistently scientific in spirit, and arrives at no coherent theory of psychology. However, it widens horizons and raises issues that were, in the 20th century, approached scientifically. It raises many issues that still challenge scientific enquiry.

See also EMOTION.   IMLH

Allen, G. W. (1967). *William James: A Biography.*
James, W. (1890). *Principles of Psychology*, 2 vols.
—— (1907). *Pragmatism: A New Name for Some Old Ways of Thinking.*
Myers, G. E. (2001). *William James: His Life and Thought.*

James–Lange theory of emotion. See EMOTION.

Jami (Mulla Nuruddin 'Abdurrahman ibn-Ahmad, 1414–92). Jami, who was born in Jam, Khurasan, and died in Herat, modern Afghanistan, is often called the last great classical poet of the Persian language. He was a most prolific writer and a great scholar, as well as being a mystic of the Naqshbandiyya (Designers) School of *Sufis. For him, God alone is absolute truth, and human duty is to reach this truth through love. In his *Lawa'ih* (Flashes) are the short utterances which encapsulate his teaching, while *Nahfat al-Uns* (Fragrances of Companionship) is a considerable work treating the lives of 611 male and female Sufi sages. His *Silsilat al-Dhahab* (Chain of Gold) resembles *Sanai's *Walled Garden*, and his *Baharistan* (Land of Spring) may have been suggested by Saadi's *Rose Garden*. In personality he was remarkably straightforward and free from cant, and he expected this behaviour in others: the traditional Naqshbandi attitude. His sense of humour was remarkable. When he was on his deathbed and Koran readers had been brought in, he exclaimed: 'What is all this commotion—can't you see that I am dying?'   IS

Browne, E. G. (1964). *A Literary History of Persia.*
Davis, F. H. (1967). *Jami, the Persian Mystic.*

Janet, Pierre (1859–1947). Pierre Janet must rank with the handful of thinkers, including William *James and Wilhelm *Wundt, who established psychology as a discipline. Yet nowadays in Britain and America he is acknowledged merely as a contributor to early psychiatric studies of *hysteria. Remarkably little is known of his ideas, although many of them have passed into common usage. His systematic theorizing is ignored, and none of the current standard English-language textbooks in experimental, clinical, cognitive, or personality psychology makes more than a passing reference to his work. Even histories of psychology and medicine refer to him only as a 'pupil' of J. M. *Charcot who studied hypnotism in relation to hysterical phenomena (see HYPNOSIS). Such accounts fail to recognize Janet's work in many other fields, his encyclopedic scholarship, his meticulous and subtle clinical observations, his intellectual stature, and the originality of his theorizing.

In 1894 Janet published his textbook on philosophy. By the turn of the century he had published papers on a variety of psychological topics, and had established his reputation as a clinical teacher and outstanding expert on the neuroses. By then his interest had shifted from hysterical states to 'psychasthenia', a term he coined to cover what we would now call *anxiety states, *phobias, and *obsessional disorders. In 1898 he published *Névroses et idées fixes*, to be followed by *Les Obsessions et la psychasthénie* in 1903. Each of these was a massive work in which he developed a classification of the neuroses, together with an integrative theory which encompassed both hysteria and psychasthenia. These two books introduced, for the first time, terms and concepts such as 'dissociation', and 'narrowing of the field of consciousness', which are now in general use. Janet's distinction between hysteria and psychasthenia was directly responsible for the concepts of extroversion and introversion introduced by C. J. *Jung (who attended Janet's lectures in 1902–3 and made many references to him). Similarly, Alfred *Adler's emphasis on inferiority feelings was directly derived from Janet's *Sentiment d'incomplétude*.

In his old age, Janet continued to be active and, after the completion of his vast reconceptualization, he applied himself to the study of belief and the development of a theory of conduct. He devoted much time to the revision and preparation for publication of his lectures at the Collège de France. The lectures appeared in the form of six major books between 1928 and 1937; none of them, unfortunately, was translated into English.

Unless the English student can read French with ease, it is very difficult for him to familiarize himself with Janet's thought or even capture the flavour of his writing. The small number of Janet's works which have been translated into English are not at all representative, and in any case they, like all his books, have long been out of print. His best-known books are *L'Automatisme psychologique* (1892), *Les Névroses* (1905), *The Major Symptoms of Hysteria* (fifteen lectures delivered at the Harvard Medical School, 1907), *Psychological Healing* (trans. Eden and Cedar Paul, 2 vols., 1925), and *L'Évolution de la mémoire et de la notion du temps* (1929).   GFR

Ellenberger, H. F. (1970). *The Discovery of the Unconscious.* (An excellent biography of Janet with a scholarly summary of his theories appears as chapter 6.)
Ey, H. (1968). In Wolman, B. B. (ed.), *Historical Roots of Contemporary Psychology.* (A brief biographical note, with a good account of Janet's work from the psychiatric viewpoint.)
May, E. (1952). *The Psychology of Pierre Janet.* (An introduction to some of Janet's ideas.)

Japanese concepts of the mind: the new religions.

Although it is sometimes asserted that the Japanese lack religious instinct, the facts would suggest otherwise. Such apparent indifference as there is may be due to the absence in their lives of any fixed boundary between the sacred and the secular; it is to this distinction that they are indifferent. The success of the new cults is an indication of a permanent need to 'lean on' a *guru* in the 'dependency attitude' defined by the hardly translatable word *amaeru* (noun, *amae*: see JAPANESE CONCEPTS OF THE MIND: TRADITIONAL VIEWS). The shaman (originally a Sanskrit word) or the sibyl (*miko*) fulfilled this function in ancient society, beginning perhaps with the mysterious virgin queen, Pimiko or Himiko, who is spoken of in the ancient chronicles. And it is a role which, still openly played in certain remote regions of Japan, may be exercised under various guises in more 'civilized' regions (cf. Blacker 1975: ch. 6). If spiritual leadership were wielded by more than one empress (for example, the 8th-century Empress Jingo), the sacred female role—surprising perhaps in a country otherwise male dominated—could be assumed by far humbler individuals. Of these the most remarkable was undoubtedly Mrs Nakayama Miki (note that in Japanese the family name comes first), founder of the enormously successful cult of Tenrikyo (*tenri* = 'divine wisdom'). Born in poor circumstances in 1797, Miki acquired her first sense of mission in 1838 in a state of trancelike possession, during which she believed that her body had been 'occupied' by Ten-no-Shogun, god and saviour of mankind. Thenceforward so extraordinary were her actions and vatic declarations that a number of disciples, beginning with her bewildered husband, gathered round her and began to promote her teaching. Despite official persecution, her cult grew until, when she died in 1887 at the age of 90, it was recognized as a new and flourishing religion, though classified as a branch of Shinto. Her followers maintain that she is in the world as the 'parent' of mankind, and she is ceremonially put to bed every night in the huge temple at Tenri.

Tenrikyo remains the largest and one of the most active of the Japanese new cults, with many adherents among the Japanese overseas communities and with some foreign disciples. Not long after Miki embarked upon her mission, another poverty-stricken woman, Deguchi Nao (1837–1918), falling into a trance and declaring herself to be possessed by the god Ushitora-no-Konjin, received a similar summons to lead mankind to salvation. Out of this experience grew the Omoto ('teaching of the great origin') cult. Both Nao and Miki produced extensive 'scriptures', some of them apparently by automatic writing. Although many religious leaders were women (who nevertheless often attracted to their side a capable male administrator), the leader of the powerful Sekai Meshiakyo or 'World Messianity' sect, now about 700,000 strong, was Okada Mokichi, born in 1882. This strange man, who was at first a failure as well as a chronic invalid, announced that he was 'possessed' by Kannon, the goddess of mercy: thereafter he developed extraordinary psychic powers as well as the gift of healing.

Another more recent claimant to divine status was Kitamura Sayo (b. 1900), foundress of the so-called 'Dancing Religion' (Tensho Kotai Jingukyo), who declared in 1944 that her body was inhabited by a snake. This creature not merely gave her commands, but inspired the homilies and songs which, without her bidding, poured from her lips and also the dance which her followers still perform. These followers today number something like 350,000, and they regard Kitamura Sayo as a true successor of the Buddha and of Christ.

Many of the cults place emphasis upon happiness and contentment in this world. To that extent they diverge from 'pessimistic' religions such as Buddhism, even in the case of cults with Buddhist affiliations, such as the well-known Soka Gakkai, with its political wing of Komeito, and also Reiyukai, another cult founded by a woman, Kotani Kimi. Most of the others betray blends of all the higher religions, particularly Christianity. All stress the need for ritual purity. Indeed, the general aim seems to be to effect in their disciples a kind of psychic spring-clean, by expelling evil forces from the unconscious in order to achieve 'peace of mind'. In Japan, the extraordinary phenomenon called 'fox possession' was formerly an indication of the presence of some psychic obstruction, and just as in the field of psychiatry the patient can sometimes produce precisely the symptoms—such as dreaming the dreams—expected of him, what was formerly considered to be 'possession' by an animal might today be interpreted in terms more in keeping with psychoanalytic thinking. But even so, the Japanese psyche seems to have resisted psychoanalytic investigation more than that of the West, possibly owing to the strength of the 'dependency relationship', which would otherwise be undermined. The fact remains that psychic 'possession' of some kind, whether by another creature or by 'voices', seems a good deal commoner in Japan than in Western countries. Consequently, in the rural areas, the shaman or the ascetic is still much in demand, whereas these figures have no equivalent in the West save in the few ecclesiastically licensed exorcists or freelance faith healers.

We may sum up the significance of the *Shinkō-shūkyō* by reaffirming that the Japanese have traditionally regarded the mind not as an engine of perception and cognition, but as the psychospiritual part of the person which seeks identification with ultimate reality. If some of the new cults strive to achieve this identification by rather superficial means—for example, by the emotional and to some extent hypnotic appeal of mass gatherings—this may be due to their simplistic view of 'the end of life'. As with Aristotle—in the *Metaphysics* at least, and in that part of the *Metaphysics* which is concerned with 'being as such'—knowledge is an experience, not the accumulation of information. Granted, there are Japanese philosophers who, following the Western empiricists in their early and latterly in their linguistic form, believe in the identity of the mind and the brain—the one being an epiphenomenon of the other—and who consider philosophy not as an experience, leading to enlightenment, but as 'linguistic analysis' (not that some analytic thinking would come amiss on occasion). But this is mainly due to the tendency for the academic world in Japan to assume an attitude of excessive veneration for whatever happens in the West, and particularly in the Anglo-Saxon countries. Meanwhile, the cults undoubtedly meet a psychospiritual need which the decline of the higher religions has rendered all the more compelling. The persistence of such cults also raises for the student of mind the unsettled question of the nature of hypnotic and trance states, and of 'possession' by another 'self'—divine, daemonic, or animal. (See DISSOCIATION OF THE PERSONALITY; HYPNOSIS; HYPNOSIS, EXPERIMENTAL; MESMERISM.)   EWFT

Blacker, C. (1975). *The Catalpa Bow: A Study of Shamanistic Practices in Japan.* (Includes extensive bibliography.)
McFarland, N. (1967). *The Rush Hour of the Gods.*
Thomson, H. (1963). *The New Religions of Japan.*

Japanese concepts of the mind: traditional views.

An important clue to the Japanese understanding of the mind is the fact that in Japan there has been, until modern times, no tradition of thought comparable to the Western philosophical tradition from the time of *Socrates and *Plato. The Japanese tradition is mythico-religious. Although the origin of the Japanese as a race is still a matter of dispute, it is reasonable to suppose that Shinto developed in the Japanese archipelago, possibly from the 4th century. But during the 6th century—the key date is considered to be either AD 534 or 552—the influence of a 'higher religion', Buddhism, began to make itself felt. Buddhism was disseminated by missionary effort and by sponsored delegations from China and Korea. Despite the multiplication of Buddhist sects and a gradual accommodation with Shinto (the founder of the Shingon sect, Kukai or Kobo Daishi, maintained that the more exalted Shinto gods were incarnations of Buddhas), this faith of Indian origin influenced the Japanese character no less profoundly than did Shinto itself. For many centuries, most works of religious exegesis were written in Chinese, which, like Greek in the Occident, was pre-eminently the 'classic' language. Of Chinese origin likewise were Taoism and the *ethic* of Confucius, the impact of which should not be underestimated. Finally, the Christianizing work of the remarkable Spaniard Francis Xavier (1506–52), though later subject to pitiless persecution, proved in many respects so durable that, with the provision of a measure of freedom of belief after the Meiji Restoration of 1868 (Muraoka 1964), many 'underground' Christians emerged into the open, especially in the Nagasaki area. Behind the Japanese tradition, therefore, lies China, and behind that India, with a distinct Christian influence first felt in the 17th century and renewed in the 19th.

It is not uncommon for a Japanese to profess several faiths at once. And even a Japanese who declares himself a total unbeliever—as a great many do today—may merely be displaying reluctance to subscribe to a particular creed or set of dogmas, for in any case he prefers non-verbal modes of communication. Indeed, his intense cult of aesthetic values, which has probably gained strength in an industrial society, may be his way of honouring the 'sacred' in another form. The holiness of beauty is for him a substitute for the beauty of holiness.

Interpreted philosophically, Shinto, though the least philosophical or theological of religions, implied a form of pantheism or panpsychism. Although the world of the gods (*kami*) was an invisible world outside the spatiotemporal dimension, it had 'ingression'—to employ A. N. Whitehead's term—in terrestrial affairs. Of individuality, the human being enjoyed little: there is a Japanese proverb, 'A nail that sticks out will be hit hard'. The community, possessing a kind of group mind, took precedence, and the group mind, animated by *tatemae* or 'consensus', submitted at every moment to the influence and intervention of the countless divinities of the celestial hierarchy.

By contrast, Buddhism and Christianity tended to make a direct appeal to the individual conscience, where *ura* reigned, and Buddhism presupposed the existence of some kind of awareness at every level of creation. Among the voluminous Buddhist writings, one of the most attractive is that entitled *The Buddha's Law among the Birds* (trans. Edward Conze, 1955); according to Kukai, even trees and plants could attain to Buddhahood—the processes of budding, growing, yielding, and dying corresponded to aspiration, training, enlightenment, and nirvana. (See Sakamoto 1960.) In preaching the need to extinguish the blind life instinct—sometimes called craving or attachment—and to discharge the accumulated burden of karma (a Sanskrit word meaning 'action' or 'fate') which had 'fed' that instinct, the Buddha was presupposing the traditional Hindu doctrine of rebirth, for only after the shedding of the karmic load was entry into nirvana possible. Where the Buddha's teaching differed from that of the tradition, and also from Western conceptions, was in his view of the mind or soul. (It is important to stress that the Buddha's sayings, as reported, are highly and no doubt deliberately ambiguous on this as on many other fundamental matters—see Bahm 1958, ch. 10.) The so-called Wheel of Becoming started from ignorance, which gave rise to desire attachment, but although that which moved through this cycle was endowed with consciousness (*vijnāna*), it was not an ego entity, or indeed an entity at all, but rather a psychic process (see Allen 1959); so the succession of rebirths was intended to lead to that form of enlightenment which entailed a total awakening from psychic sleep, with its tormenting dreams. Indeed, the word Buddha means the 'Enlightened' or 'Awakened' One. At the same time, this condition of spiritual awareness, which certain sects held to be attainable in a single lifetime, represented a final liberation from individuality and the merging in nirvana. It is often stressed that the doctrine or *dharma* preached by the Buddha was practical rather than metaphysical: 'Buddhism teaches the practical means of remolding the mind' (Kishimoto 1959). But in due course Buddhist teaching, especially as elaborated in the Mahayana or 'Great Vehicle', came to erect a system of metaphysical ideas of extreme refinement. No longer an atheistic creed, Mahayana theology elaborated the idea of the three bodies of the Buddha: the *Nirmānakāya*, or historical body of Gautama that existed on earth; the *Sambhogakāya*, or the transfigured body existing in paradise; and the *Dharmakāya*, or the transcendent, cosmic Buddha body, which was identical with ultimate reality itself (Eliot 1935: 113–14). (Certain sects, e.g. the Kegon, distinguished ten bodies of the Buddha.) Being above or outside all categories, this Buddha of Essence was apprehensible not by reason but by intuition (Eliot 1935: 45). Such a faculty, in fact, was higher than that of reason—not supplementary or inferior to it, as in Western notions. Indeed, intuitive knowledge in this sense was identical with intellectual knowledge in the traditional sense. Another name for it might be 'unitive' knowledge or what J. H. Newman seems to have been striving to convey by his idea of the 'illative' sense (*An Essay in Aid of a Grammar of Assent*, 1870, ch. 9). Now such knowledge, the attainment of which presupposed prolonged meditation, involved, at its highest reach, 'oneness' with its object, that is to say, identification with the Buddha nature, the concept of which is common to all the Mahayana sects except the Amidist ones.

This conception of the structure of the mind as composed of (i) psyche, (ii) reason, and (iii) (intellectual) intuition was similar at base to that of the Hindu tradition, in the context of which Buddhist theology was of course elaborated; and as scholars such as René Guénon (1954) have pointed out, it was a view expounded by *Aristotle in the *Posterior Analytics* and part of the *Metaphysics*. And Aristotle too believed in the final identification of knower and known. Indeed, such identification was abandoned in the West only with the disintegration of Scholastic philosophy, the exaltation of *ratio* as the highest mental faculty—the instrument of mathematico-physical science —and the loss of the concept of intellect as a spiritual faculty.

Admittedly, such considerations on the nature of mind entered hardly at all into the everyday thoughts of the ordinary man. Nor were they entertained by most Buddhist priests, who concerned themselves chiefly with the performance of ritual, including the highly stylized reading of the *sutras*, and the doing of good works. Similarly, the visitor to an Indian temple, with its milling devotees and animal sacrifices, will see no obvious connection between what is going on and the recondite doctrines of the Upanishads. And in Amidism—a simple theism in which the devotee needed merely to call upon the name of Amida for salvation—the ordinary man and woman found a non-intellectual faith which they could easily grasp. (This was *Jōdo*, or Pure Land Buddhism, which began to flourish in Japan towards the end of the 12th century.) But this is precisely where the oriental distinction between esoteric and exoteric—inner and outer, *shruti* and *smriti*—knowledge applies. To speak of the philosophy, still less the theology, of Buddhism is misleading, since, as already implied, 'the purpose of Buddhist doctrine is to release beings from suffering, and speculations concerning the origin of the universe are held to be immaterial to that task' (Conze 1951: 39). Nevertheless, the Mahayana is a metaphysical teaching of such comprehensiveness as to stand to Hinduism much as Christianity stands to Judaism, and its dependence for its basic metaphysical principles on Hinduism makes it easy to understand why many Hindus regard the historical Buddha as an *Avatara*, i.e. a divine manifestation, the ninth incarnation of Vishnu.

The Christian missions of the 16th and early 17th centuries introduced Christian theology to many Japanese, and even to some of the Ainu aborigines of the northern island of Hokkaido, but the Meiji Restoration of 1868 opened the floodgates of Western thought. True to form, the intellectually curious Japanese seized on what was novel, iconoclastic, and supposedly scientific. Thus the French positivists and the British utilitarians were greatly in demand, and later the German idealists. To the Japanese intelligentsia, Herbert *Spencer became as much a hero as he did to the 'interpreter' of Japan to the West, Lafcadio Hearn. (Spencer had in fact expressed the hope, in a letter to a Japanese baron, that Japan would continue its 200-year isolation, or *sakoku*—see the appendix of Hearn's *Japan: An Interpretation*, 1904.) Consequently, the philosophy taught in Japanese universities is now largely Western, and some Japanese have mastered this so successfully as to be able to teach it in Europe and America. On the other hand, there have been philosophers such as Nishida Kitaro (1870–1945) who have sought to combine schools of Buddhism such as *Zen (virtually a blend of the Mahayana and Taoism) with Western thought, though this has resulted in some obscurity, not least because of the inherent ambiguity of the Japanese language. (See Nishida 1904.) The Japanese founder of Zen was Eisai (1141–1215), who also originated the mind-calming tea ceremony.

Through concentrating on paradoxes or *kōans*, Zen forms a technique for disciplining the mind for the purpose of attaining *satori*, or sudden illumination, and its apparent use of irrational means has endeared it to Westerners in revolt against rationalism. What its vogue seems to reflect, however, is that philosophy in the Orient is at heart not a matter of abstract speculation or analysis, but an experience, designed to bring with it enlightenment and knowledge. Whereas in the Occident the mind is treated primarily as an engine of perception and cognition, the Oriental regards his mental faculties as in need of training for the purpose of achieving, at best, a condition of what the Buddhists call 'self-luminous thought'. This condition is sometimes rather unhelpfully called 'emptiness', because the word nirvana literally means 'the extinction of breath or of disturbance'; but we should treat such a description as on a par with St John of the Cross's paradoxical 'ray of darkness': in short, nirvana is a condition of supra-individual 'fullness'. See Guénon's remarks on Buddhism in his *Man and his Becoming According to the Vedanta* (1945), 173.

See also JAPANESE CONCEPTS OF THE MIND: THE NEW RELIGIONS.   EWFT

The literature of Buddhism is so extensive and in many instances so recondite that a short reading list is extremely difficult to compile. The following works are recommended for their comprehensive character:

Allen, G. F. (1959). *The Buddhist Philosophy*.
Bahm, A. J. (1958). *Philosophy of the Buddha*.
Conze, E. (1951). *Buddhism, its Essence and Development*.
Eliot, Sir C. (1935). *Japanese Buddhism*.
Guénon, R. (1954). *Introduction to the Hindu Scriptures*.
Kishimoto Hideo (1959). 'The meaning of religion to the Japanese people'. In Japanese Association for Religious Studies (ed.), *Religious Studies in Japan*.
Muraoka Tsunetsugu (1964). *Studies in Shintō Thought*.
Murti, T. R. V. (1959). *The Central Philosophy of Buddhism*.
Nishida Kitaro (1904). *A Study of Good*.
Sakamoto Yukio (1960). 'On the attainment of Buddhahood by trees and plants'. *Proceedings of the Ninth International Congress for the History of Religions*.
Suzuki, D. T. (1948). *Introduction to Zen Buddhism*.

For Shinto, understood in its relation to Japanese culture, Tomlin, E. W. F. (1973), *Japan* may be consulted.

For a general study and analysis of the Japanese character and mentality, Hajime, N. (1960), *Ways of Thinking of Eastern Peoples* may be recommended.

Jaspers, Karl (1883–1969). German psychiatrist and philosopher, Professor of Philosophy at Heidelberg University (1921–37), Professor of Philosophy at Basel University (1948–69). Jaspers began his academic career as a psych-

iatrist in a hospital where his philosophical orientation drove him to consider the various competing accounts of the origin and meaning of schizophrenia and manic–depressive disorders. In his *General Psychopathology* (1913) (English trans. of the 7th edn. 1963), he argued that all normal and abnormal thoughts and behaviour were manifestations of human intentional orientation to its world and that only an accurate description of conscious and semi-conscious states would rehabilitate psycho-pathology. Jaspers credited *Husserl with key ideas about the intentional structures of consciousness, the constitution of meaning, and the elaboration of complex objectivities. These provided Jaspers with a precise, deductive model for the description of hallucinations, delusions, and affective disorders. Jaspers considered his *Psychology of Worldviews* (1919) one of the earliest works in *existentialism, since his book concerned the human significance of a world imbued with meaning; boundary situations (death, suffering, chance, guilt, and struggle); the multi-dimensional nature of the meaning of time; the movement of freedom in the process of creating one's self; and the concept of *Existenz*, the uniquely human manner of existence (similar to *Heidegger's *Dasein*). In his lengthy three-volume work *Philosophy* (1932) (English trans. 1969–71), he developed an elaborate account of *Existenz* and its relation to transcendence. In questioning its existence *Existenz* can bring about a constructive conversion to a more intrinsic mode of being-in-the-world and a heightened level of thinking about the 'gift' of its unique mode of being. He developed a language of *Existenz* that mediates between subjectivity and objectivity, and elucidates the limit-like character of boundary situations. These inescapable events disclose an ineffable dimension of human experience in which the outer and the inner coincide; the language of subject and object is inadequate to communicate the depth of this experience. The experience of transcendence depends on its rupture into immanence and this occurrence is manifest through what Jaspers called 'ciphers'. Through the existential encounter with such ciphers as Nature, History, Evil, God, and the Soul, humans can experience a sense of 'hovering', where subject and object are suspended in mysterious indefiniteness.   PSM

Jastrow, Joseph (1863–1944). Polish perceptual psychologist. He was born in Warsaw, studied at Johns Hopkins University, and became professor of psychology at Wisconsin (1888–1927). He contributed to psychophysical methods, and wrote *Fact and Fable in Psychology* (1900), but he is remembered for his visually ambiguous figure the duck-rabbit.

Jennings, Herbert Spencer (1868–1947). American zoologist, born at Tonica, Illinois. His studies of the behaviour of lower organisms, such as protozoa, convinced him that their reactions are too variable to find explanation in terms of mechanistic principles. He therefore promulgated the unfashionable view that mind extends to all levels of the evolutionary scale. His best-known book is *Contribution to the Study of the Lower Organisms* (1904). Jennings's views were strongly contested by the German–American zoologist Jacques *Loeb, who advocated a strictly mechanistic explanation of animal behaviour.

jet lag. Jet lag refers to a group of symptoms that affect travellers following rapid transition across multiple time zones. The syndrome includes feelings of fatigue and inertia, difficulties in concentrating and in sleeping, gastrointestinal problems, and a general malaise. It is distinct from travel fatigue which is associated with tiredness after the hassles of a long journey, and which occurs after flying north or south. Jet lag is therefore a relatively modern phenomenon, associated exclusively with long-haul flights.

The cause of jet lag is disturbance of the normal circadian rhythms, referring to biological cycles that recur over the solar day. These rhythms are controlled by the body 'clock' located in the suprachiasmatic nucleus cells of the hypothalamus. Nerve connections with the pineal gland (which secretes melatonin) and the retina allow the body clock to react to light in the external environment. Consequently, the body responds rhythmically to the alternations of light and darkness. The hormone melatonin is secreted as darkness falls, causing peripheral vasodilation, a drop in body temperature, and promoting sleep. Melatonin is inhibited by light and so alertness and wakefulness are associated with daytime light. The alternation of light and darkness in the environment locks the timing of the internal body clock into a 24-hour cycle.

The synchronization of the human circadian rhythm with external local time is disrupted after travelling across different time zones. It takes some days for the body clock to adjust to the new environment, depending on the direction of flight and the number of time zones crossed. Jet lag is more severe and lasts longer, the greater the number of time zone transitions. It takes longer to adjust going eastwards compared with westward travel, the body clock coping more easily with a phase delay. Physical fitness helps combat the effects of jet lag, whilst ageing individuals compensate for any reduced capability to cope by using their previous experience. Generally it takes on average one day for each time zone traversed for symptoms to disappear totally.

Various means have been promoted to help cope with jet lag. These include pharmacological, dietary, and behavioural methods. Effective treatments are based on influencing the body clock directly or manipulating the sleeping or wakefulness phases of the day. Behavioural methods attempt to accelerate the phase advance or phase delay of the body clock, according to requirements of the trip.

The influence of a drug on jet lag symptoms depends on its mode of action. A chronobiotic refers to a direct effect on the body clock whereas a hypnotic initiates the drug's sleep-promoting characteristics. This explains why sleeping pills have been used as antidotes to jet lag. In particular the benzodiazepines have been adopted for use. Temazepam has been the minor tranquillizer of choice, although it may have hangover effects in some individuals. Shorter-acting hypnotics such as zolpidem are preferable for individuals severely affected.

Synthetic versions of melatonin may benefit travellers, but there are cautions. Timing of administration is crucial and should fit the phase–response curve of the drug. Administration of the drug in the hours before the trough of the body temperature rhythm is likely to advance the body clock, whilst administration of melatonin in the hours after this nadir should delay it. Melatonin is available only by prescription in most European countries, although it can be accessed in any drugstore in the USA. The British Olympic Association has not recommended use of melatonin or sleeping pills as a means of coping with jet lag.

Light visors have been suggested for promoting adjustment to the new time zone. Light inhibits melatonin secretion and constitutes a major environmental signal for the brain's timekeeping function. Bright light is necessary to fulfil this role and its phase–response curve is the opposite of melatonin's. Travellers should seek natural daylight early in the morning after travelling westwards, but would benefit from a lie-in for two days or so after travelling east.

The macronutrients in diet have been proposed for promoting alertness and drowsiness as required while the body's rhythms are desynchronized. The theory is that carbohydrates contain tryptophan, a precursor of serotonin, and so would increase drowsiness. By contrast, a protein diet would increase tyrosine levels, a substrate for noradrenaline (norepinephrine), thereby promoting alertness during the day. As yet there is no convincing evidence that dietary manipulation relieves jet lag: the timing rather than the type of meals seems to be the key.

Caffeine can help maintain wakefulness during the day but should be avoided before retiring to bed owing to its effect in stimulating the central nervous system. Alcohol too is a poor nightcap as its promotion of diuresis is likely to disrupt sleep. It is important to drink more than the normal daily intake, since the body may be dehydrated after the long time in the aircraft's dry air.

Indeed attention to fluids should start during flight. Fruit juices are preferable to tea, coffee, and alcohol which have diuretic effects. Light exercise—such as isometric contractions while seated, or gentle stretching at the back of the plane—will help to avoid joint stiffness and risk of deep vein thrombosis. The latter refers to blood clotting due to staying in a restricted seated posture for too long. Use of elasticated stockings to avoid blood pooling in the lower limbs has also been advocated.

Behavioural approaches to dealing with jet lag cover activity prior to embarkation, on the plane, and for days after arrival. Being well prepared for the journey and keeping refreshed during it do seem to be beneficial. Adjusting the normal sleep–wakefulness cycle for days prior to departure is too disruptive but an adjustment of bedtime by 1–2 hours can help prior to taking an eastward-bound flight. Strategies for the first few days after arrival will depend on the direction of the flight. After the first day, it should be possible to fit in closely with habitual activity of local residents. Effects of jet lag are transient, periodic, and should not entail avoidance of activity. Nevertheless, business people should allow time to adjust and should not schedule important meetings for the evening (or morning after travelling eastwards) until they have had the time to overcome the worst symptoms. Napping in the afternoons during the period of resynchronization is not advised since it may anchor circadian rhythms in the time zone of departure. For brief visits (a few hours) it is possible to maintain the body clock in its unadjusted state but the strategy required is outside the reach of the vast majority of travellers. For those a positive mindset helps to shrug off transient symptoms when they are at their most severe. Experience of previous personal strategies for coping with travel stress can reduce symptoms to subliminal levels. Travellers can therefore learn some tips on what works best for them when exposed to jet lag.   TR

Waterhouse, J. M., Minors, D. S., Waterhouse, M. E., Reilly, T., and Atkinson, G. (2002). *Keeping in Time with your Body Clock*.

Jung, Carl Gustav (1875–1961). Swiss psychologist, born at Kesswil, the son of a pastor of the Swiss Reformed Church; his paternal grandfather and great-grandfather were physicians. He enrolled at the University of Basel in 1895, where he took a degree in medicine, and then decided to specialize in psychiatry. In 1900 he went to the Burgholzli, the mental hospital and university psychiatric clinic in Zurich, where he studied under Eugen Bleuler. It was while working at the Burgholzli that he published his first papers on clinical topics, and also a number of papers on the use of word-association tests, which he pioneered (see FREE ASSOCIATION). Jung concluded that through word association one can uncover constellations of ideas that are emotionally charged and give rise to morbid symptoms. The test worked by evaluating the patient in terms of the delay between the stimulus and his response, the appropriateness of the response word, and the behaviour exhibited. A significant deviation from normal indicated the presence of unconscious affect-laden ideas, and Jung coined the term '*complex' to describe this combination of the idea with the strong emotion it aroused.

In 1906, Jung published a study on dementia praecox, and this work was to influence Bleuler when he proposed the name *schizophrenia for the illness five years later. Jung hypothesized that a complex was responsible for the production of a toxin which impaired mental functioning and acted directly to release the contents of the complex into consciousness. Thus, the delusional ideas, hallucinatory experiences, and affective changes of the psychosis were to be understood as more or less distorted manifestations of the originally repressed complex. This, in effect, was the first psychosomatic theory of schizophrenia, and although Jung gradually abandoned the toxin hypothesis and thought more in terms of disturbed neurochemical processes, he never relinquished his belief in the primacy of psychogenic factors in the origin of schizophrenia.

By the time (1907) that Jung first met Sigmund *Freud in Vienna, he was well acquainted with Freud's writings, and from the success of this meeting there followed a close association until 1912. In the early years of their collaboration Jung defended Freudian theories, and Freud responded to this support from an unexpected quarter with enthusiasm and encouragement. In fact, at that time Freud felt the psychoanalytic movement to be isolated and under attack, and in 1908 wrote to another colleague: 'It is only his [Jung's] arrival on the scene that has removed the danger of psychoanalysis becoming a Jewish national affair.'

In 1910 Jung left his post at the Burgholzli to concentrate on his growing private practice and also began his investigations into myths, legends, and fairy tales and the light that their contents threw onto psychopathology. His first writings on this theme were published in 1911 and indicated both an area of interest which was to be sustained for the rest of his life and an assertion of independence from Freud in their criticism of his classification of instincts as either self-preservative or sexual. Although Jung's dislike of the conceiving of the libido as essentially sexual was already apparent at this early stage, the significance became clear only much later, when he wrote about individuation. However, it was not only intellectual differences that led to the breach between Freud and Jung. Jung has recorded that he found Freud unduly concerned to preserve the tenets of psychoanalysis as articles of faith, immune from attack, and that this attitude diminished his respect for him. In fact, Jung's writings reveal that he too was prone to dogmatic assertions, but his fundamental assumptions run counter to those of Freud. Thus, while Freud, characteristically, established causal links stretching back to childhood, Jung was concerned to place man in a historical context which gave his life meaning and dignity and ultimately implied a place in a purposeful universe. In their later writings, both men became more concerned with social questions and also more metaphysical in the way they expressed their ideas. Thus Freud balanced the life instinct against the death wish, and Jung discussed the split in the individual between the ego and the shadow.

Whatever the factors involved, Jung records that after breaking with Freud he underwent a prolonged period of inner uncertainty. Although we are given glimpses of this episode in his writings, we do not have a detailed chronological account. It is clear, however, that the inner images, which he felt almost overwhelmed him, became the major inspiration both for his writings and for his clinical practice throughout the rest of his life.

The theme which unifies the large number of writings that Jung subsequently published is individuation, a process that he saw as taking place in certain gifted individuals in the second half of life. While he felt that Freud and Alfred *Adler had many valuable insights, he saw their field of interest as restricted to the problems that might be encountered during maturation. His particular concern was with those people who have achieved separation from their parents, an adult sexual identity, and independence through work, who may yet undergo a crisis in middle life. Jung conceived of individuation as being directed towards the achievement of psychic wholeness or integration, and in characterizing this developmental journey he used illustrations from alchemy, mythology, literature, and Western and Eastern religions, as well as from his own clinical findings. Particular signposts on the journey are provided by the archetypal images and symbols which are experienced, often with great emotional intensity, in *dreams and visions, and which as well as connecting the individual with the rest of mankind also point towards his own peculiar destiny. In his writings on the collective unconscious and the archetypal images which are its manifestation, it is clear that Jung feels that cultural spread cannot wholly account for the dissemination of mythological themes in dreams and visions. He writes of many patients who, while completely unsophisticated in such matters, describe dreams that exhibit striking parallels with myths from many different traditions. Indeed, Jung records an example from the time of the resolution of his own mid-life crisis. He had taken to painting representational pictures of his experiences, but under a new impulse began to paint abstract circular designs often divided into four or multiples of four. It was only later that he discovered that similar designs were found throughout the East, and under the name 'mandala' were used as instruments of contemplation in tantric yoga. He came to see the mandala as an archetypal symbol of the self, the totality of which embraces not only the conscious but also the unconscious psyche. The appearance of the mandala symbol as a spontaneous psychic event is associated with the attempt to integrate the discordant elements within the personality at a time when disintegration is threatened.

However, there does seem to be a basic ambiguity in Jung's various descriptions of the collective unconscious. Sometimes he seems to regard the predisposition to experience certain images as understandable in terms of some genetic model. In effect he is doing no more than pass a normative judgement about the way human beings experience the world. But he is also at pains to emphasize the numinous quality of these experiences, and there can be no doubt that he was attracted to the idea that the archetypes afford evidence of communion with some divine or world mind. It is interesting to find that T. S. Eliot, who might himself be described as having experienced a mid-life crisis, wrote, 'We take it for granted that our dreams spring from below: possibly the quality of our dreams suffers in consequence'.

The latter part of Jung's life was relatively uneventful. He lived in Zurich, where he pursued private practice and also studied and wrote. It has been regretted that he left no detailed accounts of his clinical activities, although throughout his works there are scattered anecdotes from his professional experience as a psychotherapist. His great interest in religious questions is often treated as an embarrassment by practising psychotherapists, and certainly the problems with which he wrestles seem esoteric when compared with those encountered in a psychiatric outpatient clinic. Nevertheless, his popularity as a thinker derives from precisely this subject matter and from his assurance that life is a meaningful adventure. He studied Eastern religions and philosophy, but saw himself as inescapably belonging to the Christian tradition although he was in no sense an orthodox believer. In a late work, *Answer to Job* (1952), he pictures Job appealing to God against God, and concludes that any split in the moral nature of man must be referred back to a split in the Godhead. The book is often obscure, and there is no easy solution to this problem, but in a letter he wrote subsequently about the book he said: 'I had to wrench myself free of God, so to speak, in order to find that unity in myself which God seeks through man. It is rather like that vision of Symeon, the Theologian, who sought God in vain everywhere in the world, until God rose like a little sun in his own heart.' Whereas Freud said, 'I have not the courage to rise up before my fellow men as a prophet and I bow to the reproach that I can offer them no consolation', Jung in contemplating the future found himself able to view the division in man as an expression of divine conflict. 'The outcome', he wrote, 'may well be the revelation of the Holy Ghost out of man himself. Just as man was once revealed out of God, so, when the circle closes, God may be revealed out of man.'

Such darkly impressive statements are common in Jung's writings. However, in his memoirs, which were written shortly before he died, he is more detached and agnostic and denies having any definite convictions. He concludes the book: 'The more uncertain I have felt about myself, the more there has grown up in me a feeling of kinship with all things. In fact, it seems to me as if that alienation which so long separated me from the world has become transferred into my own inner world, and has revealed to me an unexpected unfamiliarity with myself.'

DAGC

Adler, G. (ed.) (1973). *C. G. Jung: Letters*.
Casement, A. (2001). *Carl Gustav Jung*.
Jung, C. G. (1953–71). *Collected Works*.
McGuire, W. (ed.) (1974). *The Freud/Jung Letters*.
Storr, A. (1973). *Jung*.

just-noticeable differences. Small changes of stimulus intensity (such as an increase in light or sound intensity) may go unnoticed, and in general will not be noticed unless the increase is greater than about 2 per cent. The critical intensity change that is discriminated is known as the 'just-noticeable difference' (or 'j.n.d.'), and it may be called the 'threshold' of sensation. It was discovered by Ernst Heinrich *Weber that the just-noticeable difference increases in direct proportion with the stimulus intensity. Gustav *Fechner, having become interested in galvanism (see GALVANIC STIMULATION), turned to philosophy, and tried to relate physiology to psychology (in his *Elemente der Psychophysik*, 1860) by assuming just-noticeable differences to be equal units of sensations, over the entire intensity range, and so quantifying sensations as integrations of j.n.d.s. His arguments for measuring sensation, though ultimately unsound, essentially founded psychology as an experimental science.

See PSYCHOPHYSICS.

RLG

K

Kant, Immanuel (1724–1804). German philosopher. Born in Königsberg, Prussia (since annexed by the USSR and renamed Kaliningrad), Kant never left the town and taught at the university there, where he became professor of logic and metaphysics in 1770. His earliest works were concerned with astronomy, and his great philosophical masterpiece, the *Critique of Pure Reason* (*Kritik der reinen Vernunft*) did not appear until 1781. This was followed by the *Critique of Practical Reason* (1788) and the *Critique of Judgement* (1790).

Kant gave the name 'transcendental idealism' to his philosophy (see IDEALISM), but in fact it is a brilliant and complex synthesis of rationalism and empiricism. On the one hand, he condemns the aspirations of the rationalists to ascend to a world of pure *a priori knowledge independently of the senses; on the other hand, he rejects the empiricist notion that knowledge can be founded purely on sensory data. Kant argues that in order to experience the world at all the mind necessarily interprets it in terms of a certain structure; it is already armed with certain concepts of the understanding (*Verstandesbegriffe*). These concepts are derived from certain fundamental 'categories' (such as the category of substance and the category of causality), and the categories are a priori, not in the sense that they are independent of experience, but in the sense that they are presupposed by experience. In a complex chain of arguments called the 'Transcendental Deduction', Kant attempts to demonstrate the 'objective validity' of the categories. (See KANT'S PHILOSOPHY OF MIND).

In addition to his crucial and enduring contribution to the theory of knowledge, Kant was also highly influential in the field of ethics. In the *Groundwork of the Metaphysic of Morals* (1785), he puts forward his famous doctrine of the 'categorical imperative': 'Act only on that maxim through which you can at the same time will that it become a universal law.'   JGC

Bennett, J. (1966). *Kant's Analytic.*
Korner, S. (1990). *Kant.*
Kuehn, M. (2001). *Kant: A Biography.*
Scruton, R. (1982). *Kant.*
Zweig, A. (1999). *Correspondence.*

Kant's philosophy of mind. It is a commonplace that the character of our experience of the world, and hence the character of the world *as experienced by us*, while dependent in part on the nature of the objects we perceive, is also in part dependent on our own cognitive constitution, our physiological and psychological make-up. Experience is the causal outcome of objects affecting our constitution, and the causal mechanisms involved are matter for empirical investigation and discovery: the discovery of what it is about objects and about ourselves that makes them appear to us as they do. The distinctive feature of Kant's 'transcendental' philosophy is his transposition or transformation of this commonplace in such a way as to lift it out of the sphere of empirical investigation altogether.

Any empirical researcher, any natural scientist, takes as his field of investigation some aspect or selection of natural objects and events, located in space and occurring or persisting in time. Among these natural objects, of particular concern to biologists, psychologists, and physiologists, are our human selves. The scientist's business is to discover the laws of working which govern the behaviour and account for the characteristics of his selected objects. But those general features that constitute the very framework of such enquiries—the spatio-temporality of nature and the existence of discoverable law—are alike attributed by Kant to the constitution of the human mind, whence he contentedly draws the conclusion that empirical enquiry can yield us knowledge *only* of appearances—of the appearances that things present to beings constituted as we are. Of things as they are in themselves (including ourselves as we are in ourselves) experience and scientific investigation can yield no knowledge at all. The field of empirical enquiry is nature: but all the characteristics of natural things (including ourselves as natural objects) are thoroughly conditioned by features which have their source in the human subject.

Kant distinguishes two primary subjective sources of these features: the *sensibility* and the *understanding*. Sensibility is passive or receptive: it is the mind's capacity so to be affected by things as they are in themselves that mental contents or representations which Kant calls 'intuitions' or 'perceptions' are thereby generated. Within this receptive faculty of sensibility Kant distinguishes between 'inner' and 'outer' sense, saying that time is nothing but the form of the one and space nothing but the form of the other. The doctrine is that the temporal character of experience in general, and of its objects, and the possession by some intuitions of the character of spatiality which allows of their being so ordered as to count as perceptions of objects in space are due to the constitution of inner and outer sense respectively; and that, in particular, time, the form of inner sense, is the mode of ordering which results from the self-affection of ourselves as we are in ourselves. For, in addition to the passive or merely receptive faculty of sensibility, we have the active, affecting faculty of understanding. Understanding is the faculty which, acting on the sensibility, enables us to conceptualize our intuitions, and, more, it is the subjective source of those general principles of conceptualization (the categories) which enable and require us so to conceptualize our intuitions as to give them the character of perceptions of a law-governed world of objects of which the governing laws are open to investigation by the methods of empirical science.

For this theory, as elaborated in the *Critique of Pure Reason*, Kant made great claims. He claimed that it provided the unique explanation of certain features of our empirical knowledge of nature (i.e. of the world of appearances), features which were necessary conditions of the very possibility of any such knowledge; that it supplied a salutary demonstration of the impossibility of theoretical knowledge of the supersensible realm of things as they are in themselves; and that, at the same time, it left room, not for theoretical knowledge, but for the morally based conviction that the requirements of moral responsibility and moral justice were somehow fulfilled in that realm inaccessible to our knowledge.

These claims we need not consider here. From the brief sketch given above, it seems hardly to be expected that Kant's transcendental theory of mind should have much in common with the firmly empirical theories current among psychologists and physiologists who concern themselves with the mind as a naturally given phenomenon, or, indeed, with the views of those philosophers of mind who concern themselves with the analysis or elucidation of the mental concepts which men and women employ in thinking about themselves and their fellows. When Kant speaks of the 'human mind' or of 'ourselves' as the subjective source of time, space, and the categories, it seems that it must be of those mysteries, ourselves as we are in ourselves, that he is speaking and not of ourselves as we know ourselves; and when he distinguishes sensibility and understanding, we cannot take him as referring to such familiar objects of empirical study as sensory receptors and the day-to-day workings of human intelligence.

Kant distinguishes further faculties: notably that of imagination, which serves sense and understanding as their indispensable go-between, synthesizing the manifold and discrete data of sense in such a way as to make possible recognition of objects as falling under empirical concepts. In this doctrine of synthesis we may be tempted to find a near or remote analogue of some findings of empirical

(including physiological) psychology. But the qualification 'transcendental' standing before the phrase 'synthesis of imagination' should warn us to tread warily. The transcendental synthesis of imagination is not to be conceived as any kind of occurrent process which could be empirically studied. The doctrine is more intelligibly seen as reflecting an inescapable feature of sense perception of a world of objects: the fact that we cannot, in general, veridically characterize even a momentary perception except by acknowledging that, for example, we see what we see *as* a dog, say, or *as* a tree—thus uniting, as it were, the instantaneous impression with other past or possible impressions (of the same object or of different objects of the same kind) which would similarly require, for *their* characterization, employment of the same general concept. This infusion or penetration of momentary sense impressions by object concepts which extend beyond (and 'combine') them, Kant saw as a necessary condition of experience of a world of objects; and thus he saw imagination as a necessary ('transcendental') mediator between sense, as merely receptive, and understanding as the faculty of concepts in general and in particular as the source of those very general a priori concepts (the categories) which necessarily found a footing in experience in the use we make of our merely empirical concepts of types of object and event. (There are instructive parallels and contrasts to be drawn between Kant's doctrine of imagination and that of *Hume.)

To the faculty of 'reason' Kant assigns a role which includes, but goes beyond, those merely conceptualizing, judging, and generalizing operations of the understanding whereby empirical knowledge of nature is gained and extended. Reason typically demands more than this limited knowledge which always leaves room for further questions and thus is knowledge, as Kant puts it, only of the 'conditioned', for reason sets before itself the ideal of ultimate explanations, of final and complete knowledge which would leave no room for further questions. Insofar as this 'demand of reason for the unconditioned' encourages us to push our empirical researches in the direction of more and more comprehensive theories or into ever-remoter regions of the physical universe or of past time, its effect is wholly beneficial. But insofar as we are encouraged to believe that the demand can be met, that we can, by pure reasoning, attain knowledge of objects answering to reason's 'ideas' of the unconditioned, its effect is simply to generate illusion, for our knowledge is necessarily confined to the realm of experience, the realm of appearances, in which no such objects are to be found.

Rather less convincingly, Kant finds for pure reason a 'practical' role as the essential source and end of morality. He further suggests that, though we are denied theoretical knowledge of the supersensible realm of things as they are in themselves, yet reason in its practical role may yield moral certainties, falling short of knowledge, regarding that realm. He argues that our recognition of the unconditional binding force of the moral law carries with it both a belief in freedom of the will—a power of free choice which we do not possess as natural beings subject to causal determination but may possess as we supersensibly are in ourselves—and a belief in the supersensible fulfilment of the demands of moral justice and hence in a supersensible divinity capable of securing the moral ideal.

A question naturally arises regarding the internal consistency of the 'critical' philosophy and in particular of the doctrines of 'transcendental idealism'. If the spatio-temporality and law-likeness of nature and all that is in it are to be attributed to a subjective source in the human mind, this source cannot be identified with the human mind as a part of nature, the topic of empirical psychology —a discipline that Kant rather dismissively describes as a kind of 'physiology of inner sense'. So when Kant speaks of *our* sensibility and *our* understanding as the source of space, time, and the categories, it must be to ourselves as we (supersensibly) are in ourselves that he is referring. But this conclusion appears to be in direct contradiction to the doctrine that nothing can be known of things (including ourselves) as they are in themselves: a doctrine he is at pains to emphasize in his criticism of 'rational psychology' which seeks to argue from the bare fact of self-consciousness to the conclusion that the soul is a simple, immaterial, indestructible substance. The fallacies of 'rational psychology' Kant declares to be among those to which pure reason is prone in its search for the unconditioned which cannot be found in experience. It is not clear why Kant's own brand of what might be called 'transcendental psychology'—which is clearly distinguished from the empirical—does not fall under the same interdict that he places on 'rational psychology'.

These (and other) difficulties may tempt us to reconstrue, or reconstruct, the central doctrines of the critical philosophy, by (i) eliminating all reference to ourselves other than those natural selves which can be empirically studied and (ii) interpreting Kant's doctrine of the mind as concerned with certain powers and properties which we ordinary human beings (objects in nature) innately possess, and our possession of which is a necessary condition of our enjoyment of the type of experience that we do enjoy and of attainment of such knowledge of nature, including our own nature, as we do attain. Such a radically reinterpreted, such a *domesticated*, Kant would perhaps be more intellectually acceptable to us, but he would not be the great and difficult philosopher that he is in himself.

A final note may be added concerning Kant's treatment of *aesthetics in The Critique of Judgement, where he turns his philosophy of mind to strikingly good account. The judgement of taste, the judgement that an object of art or nature is beautiful, is subjective insofar as it necessarily involves, and rests on, a subjective feeling of pleasure; and yet it claims universal or objective validity. This claim Kant declares justified insofar as the feeling of pleasure results from the fact that the formal properties of the object are such as to excite the harmonious free play of the faculties of understanding and imagination, for these faculties are common to all men. The functioning of these faculties in this connection is described as 'free play' just because it is not under the governance of concepts such as we employ in ordinary non-aesthetic empirical judgements; i.e. our aesthetic response is not to the object *as* being of some general kind, but rather to it as the unique individual that it is.
                                                                    PFS

Katz, David (1884–1953). German psychologist, born in Kassel of Jewish extraction. He was educated at Göttingen, where he worked under G. E. Müller, though he was also much influenced by Edmund *Husserl's phenomenology. He obtained his doctorate in 1906 and in the following year became a *privat-docent* at Göttingen. In 1911 he published his first and best-known book, *Die Erscheinungsweisen der Farben*, abridged in English translation as *The World of Colour*. He served in the German army in the First World War and in 1919 became professor of psychology at Rostock, where he remained until 1933, when he went to England. He worked first in Manchester and later in London until he was offered and accepted the chair of pedagogy at Stockholm, where he died.

Katz was a man with wide and, on occasion, somewhat bizarre interests. After the First World War he wrote a monograph on *phantom limbs, and while a refugee in Manchester he undertook research on the tongue as a primitive sense organ and on the feeding habits of captive monkeys.

His most important books were *The World of Colour* (1935) and its companion volume *Der Aufbau der Tastwelt*, 1925 (The World of Touch). Other books are *Animals and Men* (1937) and *Gestalt Psychology* (1950).   OLZ

Keller, Helen Adams (1880–1968). Born in Alabama, at 19 months she became deaf and blind. Educated by Anne M. Sullivan (Mrs Macy), she gradually learned to speak. She obtained a university degree in 1904, and achieved worldwide fame as a writer—a unique case of international recognition of a person with this double handicap. The story of how she discovered channels of communication and powers of expression is remarkable: see *Story of my Life* (1903, 1959, 1966).

Keller, H. A. (1969). *Midstream: My Later Life.*

Kepler, Johannes (1571–1630). A key figure in the history of ideas, Johannes Kepler was both astronomer and astrologer to the Holy Roman Emperor Rudolf II, and later to Wallenstein, duke of Friedland. Kepler combined medieval mysticism with the analytical power of a great scientist whose achievements encompass laws of planetary motion and the optics and visual functions of the eye—that it provides optical images.

In his *Mysterium cosmographicum* of 1596 he attempted a geometrical theory of the motions of the five known planets: that the five types of regular polyhedra control the planets. He was disappointed over this essentially Platonic notion, for the new highly accurate observations of Tycho Brahe did not fit this notion any better than much earlier observations. Kepler reconsidered his static geometrical models, to take into account and emphasize the importance of times and speeds. This new idea of relative speeds led to his *Harmonie mundi* (Harmony of the Universe) in 1619, which included the mathematical statement known as his third law: that the square of a planet's periodic time is proportional to the cube of its mean distance from the sun. Here by heroic arithmetic from the new data he discovered, with no prior hypothesis, an entirely surprising key to the universe, and he justified his astronomy with the aesthetics of music, believing that the harmony of the universe, which we may appreciate by science and by art, is in God's mind. Kepler in his account recognized seven good chords: the octave, major and minor sixths, the fifth, the fourth, and the major and minor thirds. These musical ratios he conceived in terms of a vibrating string, thought of as bent round the sides of a polygon, so that each polygon is a musical conception based on Pythagoras' discovery that musical pitch is inversely related to the length of a vibrating string. Enjoyment of music is not just pleasurable stimulation of the ear, for 'the souls of men rejoice in those very proportions that God employed (in the Creation), wherever we find them, whether by pure reflection, or by the intervention of the senses . . . (or exercise of reason) by an occult, innate instinct'. So the astronomer should learn to match the harmony of the heavens with the harmony within his mind. Kepler applied this also to astrology, holding that the earth is an animated being. How the soul of the body perceives planetary influences was for him no more mysterious than how retinal images in our eyes give us conscious perceptions. And yet he wrote (in a letter to Herwart): 'My aim is to show that the heavenly machine is not a kind of divine, live being, but a kind of clockwork (and he who believes that a clock has a soul, attributes the maker's glory to the work), in so far as nearly all the manifold motions are caused by a most simple, magnetic, and material force, just as all motions of the clock are caused by a simple weight.'

Kepler's first law, that planets move in ellipses, and his second law, that planets describe equal areas in equal times, were both published in 1609. The notion that planets move in ellipses took a great deal of working out, and it was not intuitively likely or aesthetically acceptable. The ellipse was seen as inelegant, as only one focus is filled—by the sun—the other being empty. Kepler could not even be sure that the planets revolve with constant angular (or rather swept area) velocity round the sun-filled focus, rather than the empty focus, and indeed there were rival claims that the empty focus was the key to planetary movements, rather than the massive sun. It still seems amazing that *conic sections* provide a master key to the heavens!

In his strange book, which is fanciful science fiction while also providing thinking tools, *Somnium* (A Dream, or astronomy of the moon; first draft 1611), Kepler wrote an allegory in which he protected himself against attack for holding the Copernican notion of the earth moving round the sun. He described what things would look like from the moon, which was well known to be in motion. He was able to point out that the stars would seem to move from a moving base, and thus to imply that, against appearances, the earth may be moving and so produce the movements of the 'fixed' stars. He had heard of Galileo's discoveries with the telescope in 1610, of lunar craters and the four bright moons of Jupiter, and he very soon had the use of a telescope to which he added optical improvements. He supposed that, as the lunar craters are circular, they must have been made by intelligent moon dwellers, to shield them from the heat of the sun, but he also supposed that, as the lunar mountains are irregular, they are natural and not constructed by intelligence. This criterion for extraterrestrial intelligence was also accepted by NASA in the early years of space exploration with planetary probes; they looked for circular or straight-line structures as evidence of intelligence. It was the reason also for the American astronomer Percival Lowell believing there to be intelligent life on Mars, as he saw straight 'canals'; these turned out to be a visual illusion.

The *Somnium* portrayed Kepler's own mother as an enchantress; it may have contributed to the calamity of her being prosecuted for witchcraft. (She died a year after being released from custody.) Be that as it may, he describes, in this first science fiction, how to get to the moon and suggests that the best space travellers would be 'dried up old crones who since childhood have ridden over great stretches of the earth at night in tattered cloaks on goats or pitchforks'. To avoid being shrivelled by the great heat of the sun, they must travel during the four brief hours of a lunar eclipse, in the shadow of the earth, and be pulled up to the moon by the sun's power that raises the tides of the sea. From prehistoric times tides had been seen as evidence of the harmony of the universe with life on earth. This strange work has been translated by Edward Rosen as *Somnium: The Dream, or Posthumous Work on Lunar Astronomy* (1967).

RLG

Armitage, A. (1966). *John Kepler*.

Caspar, M. (1958). *Johannes Kepler* (3rd edn.). (Trans. C. D. Hellman, 1959).

Koestler, A. (1959). *The Sleepwalkers*.

—— (1961). 'Kepler and the psychology of discovery'. In *The Logic of Personal Knowledge: Essays Presented to Michael Polanyi*.

Kierkegaard, Søren Aaby (1813–55). Danish philosopher, founder of existentialism. He read theology but did not take orders. Suffering ill-defined guilt, he broke off his engagement to Regina Olsen and lived as an obsessive bachelor, on capital that was exhausted the day he died. Rejecting philosophical systems, he argued that subjectivity is truth. He attacked official Christianity; he also attacked his own books in anonymous reviews. His principal works are *Either/Or* (1843), *Philosophical Fragments* (1844), and *The Concluding Unscientific Postscript* (1846).

RLG

Allen, E. L. (1935). *Kierkegaard: His Life and Thought*.

Collins, J. D. (1953). *The Mind of Kierkegaard*.

kinaesthesis. See SPATIAL COORDINATION.

knowledge. Knowledge may be described as representations of facts (including generalizations) and concepts organized for future use, including *problem solving. There is 'useless' knowledge, such as which is the third, or the thirteenth, longest river in the world; on the other hand, there is also knowledge that far transcends even what is necessary for immediate survival. It is on this latter that civilization's future depends, and in our possession of it we are, surely, outside the biological stream of natural selection.

It is useful also to distinguish 'knowing how' from 'knowing what', for knowledge includes the skills of knowing how to make effective use of individual facts and generalizations. When appropriately organized, it allows us to transfer experience from the past to the future, to predict and control events, and to invent new futures. It is, thus, a crucial component of *intelligence.

knowledge by acquaintance, and knowledge by description. This distinction was made by Bertrand *Russell (see especially Russell 1914: 151). Knowledge by acquaintance is 'what we derive from sense', which does not imply 'even the smallest "knowledge about" ', i.e. it does not imply knowledge of any proposition concerning the object with which we are acquainted. For Russell knowledge is primarily—and all knowledge depends upon—the 'knowledge by acquaintance of sensations', but when this is expressed in language, and organized by common sense or science, we have knowledge by description. It is a deep question how we learn to name objects of common experience (stones, tables and chairs, etc.) from our private 'knowledge by acquaintance'.

More recently, theories of *perception have blurred Russell's distinction by suggesting that there is no *direct* knowledge by the senses, but that perceptions are essentially descriptions (though by brain states rather than language) of the object world. This follows from the view that perception is knowledge based and depends upon (unconscious) inference, as suggested in the 19th century by Hermann von *Helmholtz and now very generally, if not quite always, accepted.

RLG

Russell, B. (1914). *Our Knowledge of the External World*.

Koffka, Kurt (1886–1941). *Gestalt psychologist, born Max in Berlin. With Max *Wertheimer and Wolfgang *Köhler, Kurt Goldstein, and Hans Gruhle, he founded the journal *Psychologische Forschung*. This survived for 22 volumes, until 1938 and the rise of Hitler. Koffka spent much of his academic life after 1924 in America. His main works are *The Growth of the Mind* (1924), and many important papers on *perception.

RLG

Köhler, Wolfgang (1887–1967). Co-founder and leading member of the Gestalt school of psychology, Köhler was born in Reval on the Baltic and educated at Tübingen, Frankfurt, and Berlin. While at Frankfurt, he became acquainted with Max *Wertheimer, and both he and Kurt *Koffka acted as subjects in Wertheimer's classical experiments on apparent visual motion. Between them, they evolved what became known as *Gestalt theory.

In 1913, Köhler went to Tenerife to study the behaviour of anthropoid apes and was perforce obliged to remain there for the duration of the First World War. His celebrated book describing his observations and experiments appeared in German as *Intelligenzprüfungen am Menschenaffen* (English translation *The Mentality of Apes*, 1925). In this book, Köhler developed the important thesis that *problem solving involving detours or simple tool using comes about through sudden insight, and does not depend on fortuitous trial and error as E. L. *Thorndike had contended. (This controversy was further reviewed by Koffka, who strongly defended Köhler's standpoint.)

Although the Gestalt view of problem solving as due to sudden insight has often been questioned, the idea of a 'restructuring' of the field of perception to enable key features previously hidden or unnoticed to be literally 'seen' undoubtedly describes aptly some types of problem solving—in particular visual–spatial—in both higher animals and man. Köhler further laid stress on the ways in which differences of size or brightness might apparently be perceived directly, irrespective of the actual value of the differences themselves.

Köhler was appointed to the chair of psychology at Berlin in 1921, largely on the strength of an important work on aspects of modern physics which he held to be relevant to psychological issues (*Die physische Gestalten in*

Rühe und stationären Zustand; translated in abridged form by W. D. Ellis, *A Source Book of Gestalt Psychology*, 1938, pp. 17–55). Though exhibiting high intellectual quality, this work is often dismissed as a *synthèse manquée*; none the less, Köhler believed implicitly that the road to scientific advance in psychology is by way of physics, and he attempted to justify this view in many of his later books and papers (cf. *The Selected Papers of Wolfgang Köhler*, ed. Mary Henle (1971)). All his books are essentially inspired by Gestalt thinking. The most important are: *Gestalt Psychology* (1929; rev. edn. 1947); *The Place of Value in a World of Facts* (1938); *Dynamics in Psychology* (1940 and 1960).

Köhler felt obliged for reasons of conscience to abandon Hitler's Germany in 1934 and emigrated to the United States, where he found a congenial home at Swarthmore College, where he remained for nearly all the rest of his long life.   OLZ

Konorski, Jerzy (1903–73). Polish neurophysiologist and behavioural scientist, born in Lodz. After studying medicine at the University of Warsaw, he visited Ivan *Pavlov's laboratory before returning to Poland to work at the Nencki Institute of Experimental Biology. At the time of his death he was both the director of the Nencki Institute and head of its department of neurophysiology.

Konorski's studies of the relationship and interaction between classical and instrumental *conditioning in the 1930s antedated comparable research in the West by more than a decade. Unfortunately, even the belated English publication of his first monograph, *Conditioned Reflexes and Neuron Organization* (1948), was largely ignored in the West at the time. This book attempted to provide an interpretation of Pavlovian and instrumental conditioning in terms of *Sherringtonian neurophysiology. Although his second book, *Integrative Activity of the Brain* (1969), in which he extended his ideas to cover perception and motivation, received more attention, Konorski's full influence on Western psychology became apparent only after his death. The influence of his work and ideas on current research on conditioning and related areas is secondary only to that of Pavlov himself.   AD

Korsakoff syndrome. Sergei Korsakoff (1854–1900), a Russian neuropsychiatrist, published in 1887 the first of several papers on a special form of psychic disorder which occurs in conjunction with peripheral neuritis. He mentioned as characteristic such symptoms as irritable weakness, rapid fatiguing, sleeplessness, *memory disturbance, preoccupation with fantasy, and fearfulness. In its modern use the term 'Korsakoff syndrome' refers to a group of symptoms—known alternatively as the amnesic syndrome—which includes inattentiveness, memory defect for recent events, retrograde *amnesia

and other disorders of recall and recognition, and disorientation in time, place, and situation. Confabulation, grandiose ideas, and an inappropriate cheerfulness are prominent symptoms in some cases. The syndrome can occur without peripheral neuritis, for example as a stage in recovery after trauma to the brain. When it is combined with peripheral neuritis, the term 'Korsakoff psychosis' tends to be used.

The Korsakoff syndrome develops most often in chronic alcoholics who fail to take an adequate diet. This may cause an acute deficiency of thiamine (vitamin B_1), which produces an acute delirious illness known as *Wernicke's encephalopathy. When or if the patient recovers he will probably be left with the typical features of the Korsakoff syndrome.

The syndrome has seized the interest of neurologists and psychologists because it throws light on normal processes of recall and recognition, although many of the questions it raises have yet to be given precise answers. The memory defect is revealed in the difficulty the patient shows in finding his way about, his forgetfulness in simple matters, and especially his failure to retain information. Also, presented with an object he has been shown a few minutes before, he tends to respond to it as not identical or as in some manner changed. A learning disability can readily be demonstrated in such tests as 'paired associates' and in the delayed recall of pictures of everyday objects. There is a tendency to persist in giving wrong answers, and to fail to 'unlearn'. The deficiency in recalling recent events has been attributed to partial or total derangement of the consolidation of sensory impressions as a permanent memory trace, or engram, or, to put it another way, to a failure to transfer information from a short-term to a long-term memory store. Explanation along these lines has to be qualified by the observation that the patient sometimes recalls after a few hours what he has not recalled after a few minutes.

Some of the symptoms have been attributed to lack of insight or lack of self-critique. A patient with severe memory loss will generally confabulate when questioned about recent activities. That is to say, he will answer incorrectly by describing events that could not possibly have happened. This may give the impression that he is fabricating replies to cover the gaps in his memory. In fact he is doing nothing of the kind. His replies are often accounts of occasions in his more distant past life which are now transposed into the immediate past. He is unaware of the absurd nature of his replies as he is unconscious of the fact that he is answering incorrectly. As Barbizet so neatly put it, 'Confabulation is due to the patient's inability to remember that he can't remember'. If his memory improves he ceases to confabulate and merely replies that he does not know the correct answer to the question that has been put to him.

The lack of self-critique is shown too when he 'entertains incompatible propositions'. He says, for instance: 'I am 52 years old. I was born in 1920. It is now 1975.' The item most likely to be correct is the year of birth. He does not apply tests to check the correctness of what he has said, as a healthy person tends to do. One reason may be indolence or passivity. However, by insisting on the incompatibility of the propositions the observer may provoke a 'catastrophic reaction', and this suggests that false propositions are held to as a defence against *anxiety.

Neuropathological studies of patients who have shown the syndrome have contributed to knowledge of the brain structures concerned in memory processes. The floor of the third ventricle is usually affected. The lesion tends to be localized in subcortical structures. The hippocampal region and the mamillary bodies are involved, it has been claimed, in all cases. Recent work has shown that damage is not confined to these structures. There is also evidence of atrophy of the frontal lobes and dilatations of the cerebral ventricles. This structural damage of the brain has been reported not only in chronic alcoholics but also in young heavy drinkers and may help to explain why it is so difficult for these subjects to learn new ways of dealing with their drinking problems.   DRD

Kopleman, M. D. (1995). 'The Korsakoff syndrome'. *British Journal of Psychiatry*, 166/2.

Paller, K. A., Acharya, A., and Richardson, B. (1997). 'Functional neuroimaging of cortical dysfunction in alcoholic Korsakoff syndrome'. *Journal of Cognitive Neuroscience*, 9.

Victor, M., and Yakovlev, P. I. (1955). 'S. S. Korsakoff's psychic disorder in conjunction with peripheral neuritis'. *Neurology*, 5. (A translation of Korsakoff's original article.)

Korte's laws. A. Korte was a student of the *Gestalt psychologist Kurt *Koffka, who with Max *Wertheimer and others described various kinds of 'apparent movement' elicited by lights switched alternately. The following kinds of movement were distinguished.

φ-movement: pure movement from pairs of flashing lights.

β-movement: movement of an object from one position to another.

α-movement: change of size with successive presentation (e.g. of the two arrow figures in the *Müller-Lyer illusion).

γ-movement: expansion or contraction with, respectively, increasing or decreasing illumination.

δ-movement: 'reversed' movement occurring when the later stimulus is much brighter than the earlier. This movement is in the opposite direction to the order of presentation.

Korte's laws refer to the time interval and separation of alternating pairs of stimuli for giving optimal apparent movement. Perhaps, though, 'laws' is too strong a word for such variable effects.   RLG

Boring, E. G. (1942). *Sensation and Perception in the History of Experimental Psychology*.

Kraepelin, Emil (1856–1926). German psychiatrist, educated at Würzburg, who became professor of psychiatry at Dorpat (1886), Heidelberg (1890), and Munich (1903). He was probably the only psychiatrist of his day to study with Wilhelm *Wundt, thereby acquiring considerable understanding of experimental methods. This he passed on to many of his early students of psychiatry, some of whom carried out experiments with their patients, in particular, studies of *reaction times and *mental disorders. Kraepelin is best known for the fundamental distinction which he drew between manic–depressive psychosis and *schizophrenia (then known as dementia praecox). His textbook of psychiatry, which went into several editions, was for many years the standard text.   OLZ

Krafft-Ebing, Richard von, Baron (1840–1902). German neurologist, born at Mannheim and educated at Prague; he became professor of psychiatry at Strasburg in 1872, at Vienna in 1889. He established that general paralysis of the insane can be a late manifestation of syphilitic infection. This was one of the first clear examples of severe personality change and, finally, loss of mental abilities and behaviour from a specified organic brain disease. It led to identifying the effects of chronic intoxication with alcohol, lead, and other such substances.

Kretschmer, Ernst (1888–1964). German psychiatrist, educated at the University of Munich, where he studied under Emil *Kraepelin. He worked at Tübingen and then at Marburg, where he was appointed professor of psychiatry and neurology. He is best known for his books *Körperbau und Charakter* (1921; English trans. *Physique and Character*, 1925) and *Geniale Menschen* (1929; English trans. *The Psychology of Men of Genius*, 1931). Although his attempts to correlate body build with types of psychosis proved to have little importance in psychiatric diagnosis, Kretschmer's work did much to reawaken interest in the relations between body build and qualities of temperament or personality.   OLZ

laboratories of psychology. The first laboratories for carrying out experiments under controlled and isolated conditions were devised by the alchemists, and much of their apparatus is to be found almost unmodified in modern chemical laboratories. The first laboratory of experimental psychology was founded by Wilhelm *Wundt at Leipzig in 1879, in an old building which has not been preserved. Many celebrated psychologists received their training at this first laboratory: A. Lehmann and O. Külpe; and from America G. Stanley *Hall, J. *Cattell, E. W. Scripture, Frank *Angell, E. B. *Titchener, G. M. Stratton (famous for his inverting spectacles experiment), and C. H. Judd, also a pioneer in the study of visual *perception.

In America, William *James, although not himself much of an experimenter, introduced physiological psychology to Harvard in 1875. He persuaded Harvard to spend $300 on 'physiological' apparatus and to set aside two rooms in the Lawrence Scientific School, where he held a class on 'the relations between physiology and psychology'. In 1877 he added space in Harvard's Museum of Comparative Zoology.

In Russia, Vladimir Bekherev (1857–1927) founded a laboratory at Kazan, where learning, psychopathology, and alcoholism were investigated. The first officially recognized institute of psychology, at Moscow University, was not, however, founded until 1911, and this was based on German psychological theory of the 1880s.

The first psychological laboratory in Britain was founded at Cambridge in 1879, under the direction of W. H. R. *Rivers. It became effective under C. S. *Myers from 1913, and was directed by Sir Frederic *Bartlett from 1931 to 1952. The Oxford Institute of Experimental Psychology was founded in 1936. It is now the largest psychological laboratory and teaching department of psychology in Britain. Only three years before its foundation, William Brown (then the Wilde Reader in mental philosophy) wrote, in the *Oxford Magazine* of 11 May 1933: 'Psychology has encountered more difficulty breaking away and finding its own level in Oxford than in any other university. . . . Oxford is the only great university in the world which still has no laboratory in experimental psychology.'

The post of Wilde Reader in mental philosophy was founded by Henry Wilde in 1898. It was first held by G. F. Stout, then by William *McDougall—who violated the original stricture that no experiments were to be

undertaken. It has been suggested that this bizarre restraint reflected the comment of a Cambridge mathematician, that it 'would insult religion by putting the human soul in a pair of scales'. However this may be, Wilde's bequest required that: 'The Reader shall from time to time lecture on illusions and delusions which are incident to the human mind. He shall also lecture, as far as may be practicable, on the psychology of the lower races of mankind . . .' This statute has since been changed.

The present laboratory owes its creation to a student of McDougall's, Mrs Hugh Watts, who in 1935 donated £10,000 to the university for this purpose, thus inspiring the university to action. The second chair of psychology is named after Mrs Watts.   RLG

Lamarck, Jean-Baptiste de (1744–1829). Born at Bazantin, he joined the French army in Germany at the age of 17, and while stationed at Toulon and Monaco became interested in Mediterranean flora. He resigned after an injury and worked on botany, publishing a *Flore française* in 1778. He became Keeper of the Royal Garden —the nucleus of the Jardin des Plantes—where he lectured for a quarter of a century on invertebrate zoology. He began to consider the origin of species about 1800; the result was his *Philosophie zoölogique* (1809), and his *Histoire naturelle des animaux sans vertèbres* (1815–22). By stressing the variation of species he was a pioneer, before *Darwin, of an evolutionary account. His view that characteristics acquired by individual experience can be inherited was popular politically, and educationally, even though variation of species was opposed to religious belief in special creation. Darwin accepted *Lamarckianism (inheritance of acquired characteristics), but apart from occasional claims it has now been abandoned. Lamarck's evolutionary views were opposed particularly by the French geologist and zoologist, Georges Cuvier (1769–1832), who effectively destroyed him. Lamarck became blind, and died in poverty. Shortly after his death he was honoured by a vast monument, which still stands.   RLG

Lamarckianism. The doctrine that what is learned by individual experience can be inherited by the offspring. It is named after the French anatomist Jean-Baptiste de *Lamarck. Charles *Darwin accepted the Lamarckian thesis, even to the extent of advising young women to learn as much as they could (including manly skills!) before starting their families (in *The Descent of Man*, 1888).

Inheritance of acquired characteristics appeared highly unlikely following the acceptance of Mendel's laws of inheritance, first appreciated in 1900, and with the development of the gene theory of inheritance in the 1920s. Many experiments have been conducted to test the issue, but none has convincingly shown inheritance of memories or learned skills. The collapse of Lamarckianism has consequences for accounts of ethics which may be upsetting—for, however hard one struggles to be good or wise, one's virtue and knowledge as acquired by one's own efforts die with one. Possibly the neo-Darwinianism which rejected inheritance of acquired characteristics—arguing that evolution depended entirely upon random genetic variation and selection of the fittest to survive and procreate—was resisted largely because of its moral implications: it might reduce motivations towards good behaviour. (See EVOLUTION: NEO-DARWINIAN THEORY.)

Lamarckianism was the basis of Russian agricultural policy under Lysenko, though with unfortunate results. It is still not dead: every few years claims are still made of inheritance of acquired characteristics, and to a limited extent it just might be possible.   RLG

Balter, M. (2000). 'Was Lamarck just a little bit right?' *Science*, 288.
Burkhardt, R.W. (1995). *The Spirit of System: Lamarck and Evolutionary Biology*.

La Mettrie, Julien Offray de (1709–51). French philosopher and surgeon. His courageously expressed mechanistic ideas became so unpopular in France that he lived in exile in Leiden, where he published the first clear account of man as a machine: *L'Homme machine* (1748; English trans., Gertrude C. Bussey, *Man a Machine*, 1953) an important and liberating description.   RLG

Thompson, A. (1996). *La Mettrie: Machine Man and Other Writings*.

Land colours. The American inventive genius Edwin Land (inventor of 'instant' photography and polaroid filters) discovered (following some early experiments by C. H. Judd) that although, as Thomas *Young showed in 1801, three spectral colours are required to match any spectral hue (see COLOUR VISION), a remarkable range of colours is produced by only two colours, for patterned or picture displays. Thus, a pair of photographs taken one with a red and the other with, say, a yellow or a green filter, or even white with no colour, give almost perfect colour pictures when combined with a pair of slide projectors each fitted with its appropriate filter. This led Land to develop his retinex theory of colour vision, which suggests that colours are seen by ratios of different intensity regions, which may be quite widely separated, rather than only from the relative stimulation of neighbouring 'red', 'green', and 'blue' cone receptor cells. These Land effects are related to the well-known colour contrast phenomena, which were investigated by *Goethe, but they are gradually forcing a revision of understanding of colour vision. See RETINEX THEORY AND COLOUR CONSTANCY.
RLG

Land, E. H. (1977). 'The Retinex theory of color vision'. *Scientific American*, 237/6.
Matthaei, R. (ed.) (1971). *Goethe's Colour Theory*.

Lange, Carl Georg (1834–1900). Danish psychologist and materialist philosopher working in Copenhagen. Independently of William *James, he arrived at an almost identical theory of *emotion, i.e. that emotion consists of the bodily changes evoked by the perception of external circumstances. Lange, however, placed far greater stress on the role of the cerebrovascular system in the genesis of emotion than did James. None the less, their views are so similar that the theory has always been known as the James–Lange theory of emotion. Lange's principal work first published in Denmark in 1885 became widely known in German translation as *Über Gemustsbewegungen* (1887). The respective contributions of James and Lange were brought together in a book entitled *The Emotions* (ed. K. Dunlap, 1922).   OLZ

language: Chomsky's theory. In undertaking the study of mind, it is useful to consider the less controversial question of how we study a complex physical system such as the human body. We assume that the species is characterized by a certain biological endowment. The embryo grows to the adult as its genetic programme unfolds, under the triggering and controlling effect of the environment. The organism does not 'learn' to grow arms or reach puberty. Rather, the general course of maturation is genetically determined, though the realization of the genetic plan depends in part on external factors. The result is a system of interacting organs—the heart, the visual system, etc.—each with its structure and functions, interacting in largely predetermined ways.

It is fortunate that we have such a refined and specific innate endowment. Were this not so, each individual would grow into some kind of amoeboid creature, merely reflecting external contingencies, utterly impoverished, and lacking the special structures that make a human existence possible. Naturally, the same innate factors permit the organism to transcend environmental factors, reaching a remarkable level of complexity of organization that does not 'mirror' the limited environment, rule out many possible courses of development and limit drastically the final states that can be reached in physical growth.

Little is known about how any of this happens, but no one seriously doubts that something of roughly this sort is true. Why? Because of the vast qualitative difference between the impoverished and unstructured environment, on the one hand, and the highly specific and intricate structures that uniformly develop, on the other.

Turning to the human mind, we also find structures of marvellous intricacy developing in a uniform way with limited and unstructured experience. Language is a case in point, but not the only one. Think of the capacity to deal with abstract properties of the number system, common to all humans apart from gross pathology, and, it seems, unique to humans. The essence of this system is the concept of adding one, indefinitely. The capacity is not 'approached' by the ability of some birds to match patterns of n objects for some finite (and small) n, just as human language with its discrete infinity of meaningful expressions constructed by abstract rules crucially involving operations on phrases is not simply 'more' than some finite system of symbols imposed on other organisms—or, for that matter, just as the ability of a bird to fly, though finite, is not simply an extension of the human ability to jump; whatever the evolutionary history may have been, quite different mechanisms are involved. The capacity to deal with the number system or with abstract properties of space—capacities that lie at the core of what we might call the human 'science-forming faculty'—are no doubt unlearned in their essentials, deriving from our biological endowment. One can think of many other examples.

These systems have many of the relevant properties of physical organs. We might think of them as 'mental organs'. Thus the human language faculty might well be regarded on the analogy of the heart or the visual system. It develops in the individual under the triggering effect of experience, but the mature system that grows in the mind (that is, 'learned', to use the standard but misleading term) does not 'mirror' the contingencies of experience, but vastly transcends that experience. True, there are differences among individuals contingent on experience; some know English, others Japanese. Similarly, onset of puberty varies over some range, as does body size, or the ability to pole vault, or the distribution of cells of the visual cortex specialized to respond to lines of particular orientation in the visual field. But the pole vaulter will never fly like a bird (even a chicken), and the human language faculty will never grow anything but one of the possible human languages, a narrowly constrained set.

In brief, our genetic endowment provides for the growth and maturation of special mental organs, the language faculty being one. The development of these systems is essentially uniform among individuals. Two people from the same speech community can converse freely on some topic new to them despite substantially different experience, despite the fact that the sentences they produce and understand bear no direct analogy to anything that they have heard. Their minds contain roughly comparable rule systems of highly specific structure determined in general character by some property of the human species. These rule systems cannot be derived from the data of experience by 'induction', 'abstraction', 'analogy', or 'generalization', in any reasonable sense of these terms, any more than the basic structure of the mammalian visual system is inductively derived from experience.

As in the case of the physical body, we are fortunate to have this rich innate endowment. Otherwise, we would grow into 'mental amoeboids', unlike one another, merely reflecting properties of the impoverished environment, lacking the finely articulated structures that make possible the rich and creative mental life that is characteristic of all humans who are not severely impaired by individual or social pathology. These same innate factors provide the basis for a social existence in common with others whose capacities are not unlike our own despite accidents of individual history. We live in a world of shared understanding that extends far beyond the limited experience that evokes cognitive structures in the mind.

Again, the very same innate factors that provide for the richness and variety of mental life, shared with others comparably endowed, impose severe bounds on what the mind can achieve. Scope and limits are intimately related. Our inability to fly like birds derives from the same innate properties that enable us to become humans rather than amoeboid creatures. Comparably, the fact that there are many imaginable languages that we could not develop through the exercise of the language faculty is a consequence of the innate endowment that made it possible for us to attain our knowledge of English or some other human language. Similarly, the fact that there are no doubt many systems of musical organization that we simply could not comprehend or enjoy should be a source of satisfaction, because it reflects the same innate endowment that enables us to appreciate Bach and Beethoven. And the fact that many possible branches of science lie beyond our cognitive reach should cause no dismay when we realize that it results from that innate science-forming capacity that permits the construction of intelligible explanatory theories on weak and limited evidence in at least some domains of thought. And so on.

This talk of 'mental organs' should not mislead. We can discuss a physical organ—say the visual system—in terms of its abstract properties, knowing little about its physical realization. Nothing more than this is implied when one speaks of the mind as a system of mental organs, or when one studies these organs and their interaction as systems of mental representation and mental computation.

How can we proceed to gain insight into the specific properties of particular mental organs? Consider the case of language. There are three basic questions that arise: (i) What do we know when we are said to know a language? (ii) What is the basis for the growth of this knowledge? (iii) How is this knowledge put to use?

The answer to the first question seems to be that knowledge of a language is mentally represented as a 'grammar'—that is, a finite system of rules and principles that interact to determine ('generate') an infinite class of expressions, each with a phonetic form, meaning, and associated structural properties (for example, an organization into words and phrases). As for (ii), it seems that many of the fundamental properties of these grammars are part of innate endowment, so that the child in effect knows in advance what kind of grammar he must construct and then must determine which of the possible languages is the one to which he is exposed. Study of (iii) leads to the construction of 'performance models' that have access to the grammar—the knowledge of language—represented in the mind.

To illustrate with a simple example, consider the reciprocal construction in English: such sentences as 'The men saw each other', 'I asked them about each other', 'We shot arrows at each other', etc. The rule of grammar governing these constructions specifies that the expression 'each other' requires a plural antecedent. Once the antecedent is found, we apply the dictionary rule of interpretation to fix the meaning: roughly, that each of the men saw the other men (or man), etc. However, it is not always so easy to select an antecedent. Sometimes it lies in a different clause, as in 'The candidates wanted [each other to win]' or 'The candidates believed [each other to be dishonest]'. In these sentences the bracketed expression is a subordinate clause with 'each other' as its subject, just as in 'John wants [Bill to be successful]' 'Bill' is the subject of 'be successful' in the bracketed subordinate clause. The antecedent of 'each other' lies outside the clause. But we cannot always select an antecedent outside of the subordinate clause. Consider 'The candidates believed [each other were dishonest]' (compare 'The candidates believed [their opponents were dishonest]') or 'The candidates wanted [me to vote for each other]' (compare 'The candidates wanted [me to vote for them]').

Such facts as these are known to all speakers of English, and analogues appear to hold in all other languages. The facts are known without experience, let alone training. The child must learn that 'each other' is a reciprocal expression, but nothing more, so it seems. No pedagogic grammar would mention such facts as those described above; the student can be expected to know them without instruction. The principles that determine selection of an antecedent, it seems reasonable to assume, belong to 'universal grammar', that is, to the biological endowment that determines the general structure of the language faculty. From another point of view, these principles form part of a deductive, explanatory theory of human language.

Proceeding in this way, we can attempt to construct grammars that answer question (i), a theory of universal grammar that in part answers question (ii), and performance models that incorporate grammars, answering question (iii). Insofar as it succeeds, this quest provides the theory of a particular mental organ. Others can be studied in the same way, and in principle we should be able to proceed to the study of the interaction of such systems—a central topic as soon as we turn to the study of word meaning, for example.

This seems to be a reasonable paradigm for the study of mind, one that has achieved a certain measure of success and holds much promise for the future. NC

Chomsky, N. (1965). *Knowledge of Language: Its Nature, Origin and Use.*

Jackendoff, R. (1985). *Semantics and Cognition.*

Lightfoot, D. (1982). *The Language Lottery.*

language: learning word meanings.

It may seem at first sight easy to tell when a child knows what a word means. When a little girl of 13 months sees a ball, says 'ball', and then at once goes to pick it up, the obvious conclusion may appear to be that the meaning of the word is now known to her. But if, during the next month or so, she is heard to say 'ball' on seeing a balloon, an Easter egg, a small round stone, and so on, doubts must begin to arise, and it may then seem wiser to replace the first conclusion by the more guarded one that the word 'ball' has now entered her lexicon and that her knowledge of its meaning has begun to grow.

The above example is not invented. It is provided by Bowerman (1978) from a study of her daughter Eva. And many similar instances have been recorded by Bowerman and others. So it is clear that, even in the case of 'simple' words like 'ball', the acquisition of word meaning is not an all-or-none affair. Word meanings grow and change—a fact stressed by *Vygotsky (1962), who regarded it as central to an understanding of the development of thought and language. Thus it is by no means so easy as one might suppose to give a straightforward answer to the question: how large is a child's vocabulary, on average, at different ages? Differences in the manner of collecting and handling the data (whether, for instance, the past tense of a verb is to be treated as a separate word or not) have led to widely differing estimates. However, normal children certainly have several thousands of words which are in some sense in their vocabulary by the age of 5. This means that some very rapid and efficient learning must go on.

Although nouns that name familiar objects—or people—are frequently among the earliest words that a child produces, the vocabulary, even in the beginning, need not be limited to words of this kind. Expressions such as 'all gone', 'more', and 'bye-bye' are common. Nelson (1974) reports marked individual differences in this respect among the children she studied: some used many object names, others were more inclined to use words expressing feelings and needs. However, some later studies (e.g. Benedict 1979) suggest that children have early vocabularies that represent all word classes. It is in any case a problem to know how to classify words in this stage of a child's development, since even a common noun, when used by a very young child, appears to function not just as a label but rather as a substitute for some more complex utterance (expressing a limited range of communicative acts such as interest, desire, intention, etc.) of which the child is not yet capable.

Commonly, when a young child begins to use a word, the meaning is 'overextended', as in Eva's use of 'ball': that is, the range of referents to which the child applies the word is wider than in normal adult usage. Sometimes the extension is to objects all of which share with the original referent some common perceptual feature. All Eva's 'balls' have rounded contours. But the rule that governs extensions need not be of this straightforward kind. Vygotsky (1962) reports a principle of grouping known as a 'chain complex', where each new referent has a feature in common with some other, but where no single feature is common to them all. Thus the word 'quah' may be used first of a duck in a pond; then of any liquid; then of a coin with an eagle on it; then of any round object resembling the coin.

Bowerman did not find that chaining was common in the speech of her daughters, but she reports frequent occurrence of a kind of extension, also noted by Vygotsky, where the first referent serves as a nucleus or 'prototype', so that later referents all have some feature in common with it; though, as in 'chaining', they may not have any feature in common with one another. Thus for Eva the word 'close' had as its nucleus the act of closing a drawer or a box and was later used for the act of folding a towel (shared feature: bringing two parts into close contact) and of turning the knob on the TV set till the picture darkens (shared feature: hiding or concealing something).

Some theorists have suggested that a prototype or central exemplar may function as a kind of unanalysed image or '*schema'. But, as Bowerman and others have pointed out, there is no reason to think that the existence of prototypes makes featural analysis unnecessary, and there is every reason to think that such an analysis must actually occur on some level even at very early stages in language acquisition.

A second kind of departure from Eva's overextension of 'ball' involves extension to objects that share with the original referent not some perceptual feature but some function. Thus the word 'ball' might be applied not to other round objects but to other objects able to be bounced or thrown. Nelson (1974) argues that, when the children are developing their first word meanings, function is more important than form. But this claim has been disputed and is certainly not proven. What is clear is that, from

a very early stage, a child may use either perception of similar form or knowledge of common function (or both) as the basis for a generalization of word meaning—a generalization which may go beyond the limits of the accepted adult norm.

There is nothing surprising in the fact that children initially make such mistakes. It would indeed be astonishing if they were to arrive at a knowledge of the limits of adult usage by one simple assimilative move. It is much more reasonable to think of them as entertaining hypotheses—though these are unlikely to be consciously articulated—and modifying them progressively as more evidence is obtained.

So far we have considered only evidence that comes from observation of a child's *use* of language. However, knowledge of word meanings must also manifest itself in understanding. The problem is that when one considers both the evidence of how young children use language and the evidence of how they understand it, there is often a lack of accord between the two.

For instance, though children are apt to overextend meanings when they produce words, they do not consistently do the same thing when they interpret the words of others. If anything, a child may initially interpret a word more narrowly than an adult would do. Thus Reich (1976) reports that his son Adam in response to 'Where's the shoes?' would crawl only to the shoes in his mother's shoe cupboard, bypassing shoes on the floor to get there. Later he would also crawl to shoes in his father's cupboard; then to shoes on the floor, but not to shoes on someone's feet; and finally to shoes wherever they happened to be.

The assumption that there is a single 'word store' drawn on in the same way for comprehension and for production is thus called in question, and a related challenge arises when one considers evidence about the interpretation of words in longer utterances by older children. If a child understands an utterance, it may seem obvious that the words which compose it are 'known' and that, in the process of making sense of the utterance, each of these words is given 'its meaning'. But this is to suppose that a child interprets the language in isolation from its immediate context, which is not what typically happens. Macnamara (1972) argues that it is only to the extent that children understand *situations* that they are able to begin to work out the meaning of the language that is used in them, and this view is now widely accepted. Thus a child can begin to learn the meaning of 'Do you want some milk?' because when someone picks up a jug and holds it over a cup the intention to offer milk is understood. On this view it is to be expected that for a long time the interpretation of language should remain, for the child, embedded in, and powerfully dependent on, the context of occurrence.

There is now clear experimental evidence that this is so. What a child takes an utterance to mean is liable to be determined not just by knowledge of the language but also by an assessment of what the speaker intends (as indicated by non-linguistic behaviour) and by the context in which the language is being used. In one study, Donaldson and McGarrigle (1974) found that children aged between 3 and 5 who correctly judged that a row of five cars contained more cars than a row of four might reverse this judgement a moment later when the four cars were enclosed in a row of four garages (so that this row was 'full') while the five cars were enclosed in a row of six garages (so that one garage was left empty). One is tempted to say, then, that these children gave 'more' a different meaning on the two occasions, and yet to put it this way is probably to suggest a more analytic, word-by-word, interpretation than actually occurs, at any rate at the level of the child's conscious awareness. (It seems that children have only a limited awareness that the flow of language is broken up into words at all, and yet of course if they did not break it up this way, at some level, how could they produce, in their turn, words organized into new utterances which they have never heard before? Much that goes on in language learning is clearly not conscious.)

Attempts have been made to study children's ability to arrive at word meanings by giving them 'nonsense words' in linguistic contexts so devised that inferences as to meaning are possible. A classic study by Werner and Kaplan (1950) used such sentences as:

A corplum may be used for support.

A wet corplum does not burn.

You can make a corplum smooth with sandpaper. Children proved to be very bad at deriving the meanings of isolated words from a series of examples of this kind.

It seems clear, then, that non-linguistic contexts are essential for the early stages of the growth of word meaning. And recent work has emphasized also the early importance of *conversational* contexts, within which the child's use of single-word utterances gradually shifts from a limited to a wider range of communicative acts, and eventually to the *predicative* function (as in uttering a comment on an adult-introduced topic) that appears to mark the threshold into early word combinations (Dore 1985, Griffiths 1985). But it is perhaps only with the advent of literacy that language starts to become sufficiently 'disembedded' to be considered and reflected upon as a system in its own right (cf. Donaldson 1978 and Perera 1984), so that linguistic contexts alone can begin to provide the basis for additions to the mental lexicon.

See also LANGUAGE DEVELOPMENT IN CHILDREN.   MD

Benedict, H. (1979). 'Early lexical development: comprehension and production'. *Journal of Child Language*, 6.

Bowerman, M. (1978). 'The acquisition of word meaning: an investigation of some current conflicts'. In Waterson, N. and Snow, C. (eds.), *Development of Communication: Social and Pragmatic Factors in Language Acquisition*.

Donaldson, M. (1978). *Children's Minds*.

—— and McGarrigle, J. (1974). 'Some clues to the nature of semantic development'. *Journal of Child Language*, 1.

Griffiths, P. D. (1985). 'The communicative functions of children's single-word speech'. In Barrett, M. D. (ed.), *Children's Single-Word Speech*.

Macnamara, J. (1972). 'Cognitive basis of language learning in infants'. *Psychological Review*, 79.

Nelson, K. (1974). 'Concept, word and sentence: interrelations in acquisition and development'. *Psychological Review*, 81.

Reich, P. A. (1976). 'The early acquistion of word meaning'. *Journal of Child Language*, 3.

Vygotsky, L. S. (1962). *Thought and Language*.

Werner, H., and Kaplan, E. (1950). 'Development of word meaning through verbal context: an experimental study'. *Journal of Psychology*, 29.

language: neuropsychology. Language is a complex structure and it is used in many ways – to communicate, as part of thinking, to encode facts in memory, and so on. The scientific study of the neuropsychology of language is mostly focused on identifying the location and internal organization of the areas of the brain responsible for the everyday processes of speaking, understanding spoken language, reading, and writing.

Speaking, understanding spoken language, reading, and writing can be seen as mapping meanings onto linguistic forms and vice versa. Speaking and writing use those forms to activate the motor system, and auditory comprehension and reading activate these forms from sensory stimuli. Language consists of several types of forms. For instance, words consist of sound segments (called phonemes) organized into syllables, with stress patterns or tones; sentences consist of syntactic structures. Each level of the language system is associated with certain types of meanings. Words, for instance, are associated with items, actions, and properties; sentences express events and states of affairs. Each level of language is quite complex, with respect to both its form and meaning. Speaking, understanding spoken language, reading, and writing involve activating all these levels of language simultaneously.

Speaking, understanding spoken language, reading, and writing also involve activating these forms and meanings in sequence. In addition, speaking and so on take into account the non-linguistic, situational context. For instance, we select our words as a function of what we think the person we are speaking to will understand, using very different vocabulary items when we talk to a child or to a colleague. There is evidence that there is feedback from ongoing computations on the processes of speaking, understanding spoken language, reading, and writing. Finally, speaking, understanding spoken language, reading, and writing are controlled through the exercise of attentional and other executive systems. For instance, a person may decide to take notes on a lecture, thereby engaging the writing system, and decisions have to be made about what type of notes to take—everything from verbatim recording to an occasional noun is possible. These higher-level decisions are not linguistic, but affect the functioning of the language-processing system.

All these aspects of speaking, understanding, reading, and writing make these processes highly complex functions, and studying their neural basis presents a challenge.

Data bearing on the neural basis of language processing—including the operations involved in speaking, understanding, reading, and writing—includes deficit-lesion correlational analyses, originally based on post-mortem material and today largely on computed tomography (CT), magnetic resonance imaging (MRI), positron emission tomography (PET), and other imaging techniques; recording electrophysiological responses using event-related potentials (ERPs) and magnetoencephalography (MEG) in normals and intraoperative and preoperative recordings from single cells and subdural electrodes in patients; intraoperative and preoperative local cortical stimulation in patients and transcranial magnetic stimulation in normals; and recording vascular responses to language using PET and functional MRI (fMRI). The development of many of these techniques has been extremely rapid in the past decade. As a consequence, the field is flooded with information. Some new concepts have been introduced, and some old ideas have been supported and others disconfirmed, and, overall, views of the functional neuroanatomy of language are controversial and evolving.

With respect to the inventory of brain regions that support language, over a century of deficit-lesion correlational studies has shown that the association cortex in the lateral portion of the left cerebral hemisphere plays a crucial role. This cortex surrounds the sylvian fissure and runs from the pars triangularis and opercularis of the inferior frontal gyrus (Brodman's areas (BA) 45, 44: Broca's area), through the angular and supramarginal gyri (BA 39 and 40), into the superior temporal gyrus (BA 22: Wernicke's area) in the dominant hemisphere (Fig. 1).

There is increasing evidence that cortex outside the perisylvian association cortex also supports language processing. Written language appears to involve cortex closer to the visual areas of the brain (Petersen et al. 1988) and sign language brain regions closer to those involved in movements of the hands than movements of the oral cavity (Bellugi et al. 1990). Some ERP components related to processing language are maximal over high parietal and central scalp electrodes (Osterhout and Holcomb 1992), suggesting that these regions may be involved. Both lesion studies in stroke patients and functional neuroimaging studies suggest that the inferior and anterior temporal lobes are involved in aspects of language processing (Damasio et al. 1996). Injury to the supplementary motor cortex can lead to speech initiation disturbances (Masdeu, Schoene, and Funkenstein 1978); this region may be important in activating the language-processing system, at least in production tasks. Activation studies have shown increased activity in the cingulate gyrus in association with many language tasks (Cabeza and Nyberg 2000). Though this activation occurs in many non-linguistic tasks as well and may be non-specifically

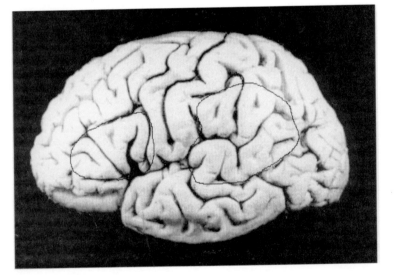

Fig. 1. View of the left hemisphere of the brain illustrating the location of the principal language-processing areas.

due to increased arousal and deployment of attention, it may reflect language processing.

Subcortical structures may also be involved in language processing. Several studies report aphasic disturbances following strokes in the deep grey matter nuclei (the caudate, putamen, and parts of the thalamus: Naeser et al. 1982). In general, subcortical lesions cause language impairments when the overlying cortex is abnormal (often the abnormality can be seen only with metabolic scanning techniques) and the degree of language impairment is better correlated with measures of cortical than subcortical hypometabolism (Metter et al. 1988). It may be that subcortical structures serve to activate a cortically based language-processing system but do not themselves process language. Lesions in the cerebellum affect language and the cerebellum has shown increased rCBF in some activation studies involving both language and other cognitive functions (Schmahmann and Sherman 1998). This may be a result of the role of this part of the brain in processes involved in timing and temporal ordering of events, or in its being directly involved in language and other cognitive functions.

Lesions of white matter tracts disconnect regions of the brain from others and make the operations performed in one region unavailable to others. This can cause language disorders (Geschwind 1965). The fact that multiple language-processing disturbances occur following subcortical strokes affecting white matter is consistent with the existence of many information transfers carried out by white matter fibres, suggesting that many of the areas of cortex and/or subcortical nuclei that carry out sequential language-processing operations are not contiguous.

Language processing differs in the two hemispheres. Most essential aspects of language processing go on in one hemisphere, usually the left, called the 'dominant' hemisphere. The non-dominant hemisphere understands many words, especially concrete nouns (Beeman and Chiarello 1997), and is involved in processing at the discourse level of language, such as revising inferences, interpreting non-literal language, and appreciating humour (Joanette and Brownell 1990). Hemispheric dominance for language bears a systematic relationship to handedness. The neural basis for lateralization is probably in part related to asymmetries in size of key parts of the perisylvian cortex (Geschwind and Levitsky 1968).

Because the perisylvian cortex is essential to the representation and processing of language, the way it is organized to support these functions has been the subject of much investigation. There is overwhelming evidence that language-processing components are localized in specific parts of this cortex, but exactly how this occurs is still under investigation. Three aspects of language processing reveal possible different patterns of localization.

The first is the perception of the sounds of language (phonemes). In many studies, contrasts between simply listening to speech and listening to a low-level auditory baseline (such as white noise) activate both left and right temporal lobe, while more complex tasks involving phonological representations, such as rehearsal, making rhyme judgments, and recognizing specific sequences of phonemes, have activated parts of a larger area that includes the left inferior parietal lobe and Broca's area (Binder 2000). To account for these results, it has been suggested that perceiving phonemes in an unconscious, automatic fashion as part of the process of recognizing words is uniquely localized in the superior temporal lobe (though in both hemispheres), and that parietal and frontal areas, particularly in the left hemisphere, are involved in the conscious use of these representations (Hickok and Poeppel 2000).

A second pattern may be revealed by the study of word meaning. Word meaning is affected by lesions in the inferior temporal lobe, notably by a degenerative disease (a form of Pick's disease) that results in 'semantic dementia' and by herpes encephalitis. Activation studies using PET and fMRI have also associated semantic processing with the inferior temporal lobe (Beauregard et al. 1997) but have shown activity elsewhere, notably the inferior frontal area (Peterson et al. 1988). The picture that is currently emerging about lexical semantics is that it is represented multifocally.

A third mode of organization is suggested by the facts regarding syntactic processing in comprehension. Deficits in this function occur after lesions throughout the perisylvian cortex (Caplan, Baker, and Dehaut 1985, Caplan 1996), and, conversely, patients of all types and with all lesion locations have been described with normal syntactic comprehension (Caplan, Baker and Dehaut 1985, Caplan 1987). All regions of the perisylvian cortex have been activated by syntactic tasks in functional neuroimaging studies, with differences in localization of activation perhaps being related to individual differences in performance levels (Caplan, Waters and Alpert 2003, Waters et al. 2003). This data suggests variation in the localization of syntactic processing within the language area across the adult population.

In summary, data from many sources converges on the view that one area of the brain—the left perisylvian association cortex—is especially important in representing and processing language, though other regions are likely to be involved as well. Within this area, particular language operations are localized in specific regions. The exact details of these localizations are just beginning to be studied, as the modern tools of cognitive neuroscience are applied to this problem.   DNC

Beauregard, M., Chertkow, H., Bub, D., Murtha, S., Dixon, R., and Evans A. (1997). 'The neural substrate for concrete, abstract, and emotional word lexica: a positron emission tomography study'. *Journal of Cognitive Neuroscience*, 9/4.

Beeman, M., and Chiarello, C. (eds.) (1997). *Right Hemisphere Language Comprehension: Perspectives from Cognitive Neuroscience.*

Bellugi, U., Poizner, H., et al. (1990). 'Mapping brain function for language: evidence from sign language'. In Edelman, G., Gall, W., and Cowan, W. (eds.), *Signal and Sense: Local and Global Order in Perceptual Maps.*

Binder, J. (2000). 'The new neuroanatomy of speech perception', *Brain*, 123.

Cabeza, R., and Nyberg, L. (2000). 'Imaging cognition II: an empirical review of 275 PET and studies with normal subjects'. *Journal of Cognitive Neuroscience*, 12.

Caplan, D. (1987). 'Discrimination of normal and aphasic subjects on a test of syntactic comprehension'. *Neuropsychologia*, 25.

—— Baker, C., and Dehaut, F. (1985). 'Syntactic determinants of sentence comprehension in aphasia'. *Cognition*, 21.

—— Hildebrandt, H., and Makris, N. (1996). 'Location of lesions in stroke patients with deficits in syntactic processing in sentence comprehension'. *Brain*, 119.

—— Waters, G., and Alpert, N. (2003). 'Effects of age and speed of processing on rCBF correlates of syntactic processing in sentence comprehension'. *Human Brain Mapping*, 19.

Damasio, H., Grabowski, T. J., Tranel, D., Hichwa, R. D., and Damasio, A. R. (1996). 'A neural basis for lexical retrieval'. *Nature*, 380.

Geschwind, N. (1965). 'Disconnection syndromes in animals and man'. *Brain*, 88.

—— and Levitsky, W. (1968). 'Human brain: left–right asymmetries in temporal speech region'. *Science*, 161.

Hickok, G., and Poeppel, D. (2000). 'Towards a functional neuroanatomy of speech perception'. *Trends in Cognitive Science*, 4.

Joanette, Y., and Brownell, H. H. (eds.) (1990). *Discourse Ability and Brain Damage: Theoretical and Empirical Perspectives.*

Just, M. A., Carpenter, P. A., Keller, T. A., Eddy, W. F., and Thulborn, K. R. (1996). 'Brain activation modulated by sentence comprehension'. *Science*, 274.

Masdeu, J. C., Schoene, W. C., and Funkenstein, H. (1978). 'Aphasia following infarction of the left supplementary motor area: a clinicopathological study'. *Neurology*, 28.

Metter, E. J., Riege, W. H., Hanson, W. R., Jackson, C. A., Kempler, D., and VanLancker, D. (1988). 'Subcortical structures in aphasia: an analysis based on (F-18)-fluorodoxyglucose positron emission tomography, and computed tomography'. *Archives of Neurology*, 45.

Naeser, M. A., Alexander, M. P., Helm-Estabrooks, N., Levine, H. L., Laughlin, S., and Geschwind, N. (1982). 'Aphasia with predominantly subcortical lesion sites: description of three capsular/putaminal aphasia syndromes'. *Archives of Neurology*, 39.

Osterhout, L., and Holcomb, P. (1992). 'Event-related brain potentials elicited by syntactic anomaly'. *Journal of Memory and Language*, 31.

Petersen, S. E., Fox, P. T., et al. (1988). 'Positron emission tomographic studies of the cortical anatomy of single-word processing'. *Nature*, 331.

Posner, M. I., Inhoff, A. W., et al. (1987). 'Isolating attentional systems: a cognitive-anatomical analysis'. *Psychobiology*, 15/2.

Schmahmann, J. D., and Sherman, J. C. (1998). 'The cerebellar cognitive affective syndrome'. *Brain*, 121.

Waters, G. S., Caplan, D., Stanzcak, L., and Alpert, N. (2003). 'Individual differences in rCBF correlates of syntactic processing in sentence comprehension: effects of working memory and speed of processing'. *Neuroimage*, 18.

language areas in the brain. The study of the neurological basis of language began in 1861 when Paul *Broca published his findings from the brain of a patient who had suffered from one form of *aphasia. The superiority of one side of the brain for a particular function is called *cerebral dominance*. Each half of the brain is dominant for several functions—for example, the left side is usually dominant for language, the right side for certain musical and spatial abilities (see also NEUROPSYCHOLOGY). Dominance has usually been regarded as a unique biological feature of humans, but it is now known to be present in other species. Thus birdsong is much more severely affected after damage to one side of the brain.

The basis of dominance was unclear for many years. It has recently been established that certain areas of the cortex are much larger on one side of the brain. In particular, one of the major speech areas has been found to be usually of greater extent on the left than on the right. This anatomical asymmetry is found in the fetus at 31 weeks of intra-uterine life, suggesting that dominance is genetically determined. Left-handers show less anatomical asymmetry than right-handers, a finding concordant with other data showing that functional dominance is less marked in left-handers. (See HANDEDNESS.) Asymmetries have also been observed in the brains of great apes, a finding of interest since recent studies support the thesis that chimpanzees have certain capacities for language. (See PRIMATE LANGUAGE.)

The human skull is also asymmetrical since its shape is moulded to that of the underlying brain. The long-rejected ideas of the *phrenologists are thus partially justified. Skulls of ancient humans (dating back as much as 300,000 years) exhibit similar asymmetries, so that cerebral dominance for language was probably present early in human evolution.

Our knowledge of the speech areas and their functions has been based on several techniques: post-mortem study of brains of aphasic patients; electrical stimulation of the exposed brain during neurosurgical operations; recording of changes in the electrical activity of the brain during language activities; and injection of radioactive substances into the bloodstream which permits measurements of changes in blood flow in localized brain regions during speech.

The major language areas, named after two of the great pioneers in the study of aphasia, lie along the lateral (or sylvian) fissure of the left side of the brain. We do not know the full extent of these areas. Broca's area lies in the frontal lobe above the lateral fissure. It is just in front of the region of the cortex, stimulation of which leads to movements of the muscles involved in speech. Broca's area may be thought of, as a simple first approximation, as the region that contains the learned programmes for control of the musculature of speech. After destruction of this region, speech is slow and hesitant and the sounds of language are badly produced. In addition the speech is agrammatical, i.e. prepositions, conjunctions, and auxiliary verbs are often omitted, and incorrect endings may be used in verbs or nouns (for example, 'President live Washington'). These findings suggest that Broca's area has a major role in the production of grammatically correct language. The Broca's aphasic also produces defective writing which is agrammatical. His comprehension of spoken and written language may be excellent. Although the Broca's aphasic produces defective speech, he usually sings melodies well. The programmes for production of musical sounds appear to lie elsewhere in the brain, probably on the right side. In a few cases, singing actually facilitates the production of words and this has been used as the basis of an experimental method of speech therapy.

The second major speech area lies in the left temporal lobe below the lateral fissure and is named after Carl *Wernicke. This area lies adjacent to the primary auditory cortex, which is the end station for auditory input to the brain. The speech of the Wernicke's aphasic is quite different from that of the Broca type. The patient may speak very rapidly, with good articulation and melody and a normal grammatical structure. He has, however, great difficulty in finding the correct word and uses imprecise words (such as 'it' or 'thing') and circumlocutions. He may use words incorrectly. Such improperly used words are called paraphasias and may bear a close relation in meaning to the desired word (for example, 'knife' for 'fork') or no obvious relation at all (for example, 'Argentinian rifle' for 'coin'). He may use non-existent words, which are called neologisms (for example, 'flieber').

There are other areas involved in language functions, damage to which may lead to other distinctive language disorders. Furthermore, there are bundles of nerve fibres (tracts) which connect the language areas to each other and to other parts of the cerebral cortex on the same or the opposite side of the brain. The corpus callosum is the largest and most obvious collection of such tracts. Destruction of a group of connecting fibres may prevent intact portions of the brain from communicating with each other. The resulting disorders are called disconnection syndromes. They demonstrate the fact that different regions of the brain may carry on complex functions without the awareness of activities in other regions.

A great variety of other aphasic syndromes can result from damage to the language areas or their connections.

'Pure alexia', 'pure word-blindness', and 'alexia without agraphia' are synonyms for a nearly isolated loss of the ability to understand written language while other language capacities are intact. 'Pure word-deafness' is an isolated loss of the ability to comprehend spoken language. 'Pure agraphia' is the isolated loss of the ability to write correct language (in the absence of paralysis). 'Apraxia' is loss of ability to carry out movements to verbal command despite good comprehension, and despite preservation in most cases of correct movements in response to non-verbal stimuli. Some remarkable patterns of loss of function are often seen. Thus, the pure alexic may fail to read words and to name colours, but he may read numerals and name objects without difficulty. A patient with callosal damage may write correct language with the right hand, but with the left hand he may produce legible but aphasic, i.e. linguistically incorrect, language. The mechanisms of many of these dissociations of function are well understood, but others still remain obscure. They are of course important clues to the intellectual processes of the brain.

In the adult, extensive damage to one of the primary language areas leads in most instances to permanent disability. However, children who sustain gross damage to the left hemisphere before the usual age of language acquisition will go on to acquire language. The right hemisphere thus has the potential to become the major seat of language. Similar findings are found in birds who sustain unilateral damage on the dominant side before song appears.

If the left hemisphere is damaged after the appearance of language but before the age of 8 or 9, the child nearly always recovers language in a period ranging from a few months to three years. The mechanisms of this plasticity or recovery by means of the right hemisphere are not clearly understood. Their elucidation may help to lead to more effective means of therapy for that majority of older patients who do not recover adequate function spontaneously.
NG

Joanette, Y., and Brownell, H. H. (eds.) (1989). *Discourse Ability and Brain Damage: Theoretical and Empirical Perspectives*.

language development in children. How does a child acquire his native language? Perhaps this question presupposes a more basic one: what is it that a child has to know in order to be said to have acquired his native language? All the current answers to this question suggest that the child has to have competence. Some claim he needs linguistic competence, others that he needs cognitive as well as linguistic competence, and others again that he needs communicative competence, which adds a strong social component to the other two. Before we discuss these three alternative theoretical approaches, we must first clarify the notion of competence.

What does it mean when we say a person has competence? The first aspect of competence is that it is abstract knowledge. An example of linguistic competence is the general rule that to form a plural in English you add an 's' to the noun. Of course, you do not need to be consciously aware of this rule in order to use it—children aged 2 or 3 use it reliably, but cannot describe it. The fact that they *are* using a general rule is, however, clear from their errors. They are highly unlikely to have heard of 'sheeps' or 'mans' from someone else, so it is clear they are constructing these words themselves from a rule they have overgeneralized.

This brings us to the second feature of competence— it is generative. That is, knowledge of general rules means that we can generate new examples, new instances of those rules. 'Sheeps' and 'mans' are, for the child who spoke them, completely new instances, his own creations. The sentence I am writing now is a completely novel one, based on my knowledge of the rules whereby one constructs sentences.

But when we consider a child speaking, or, for that matter, an adult writing a sentence for *The Oxford Companion to the Mind*, we are unwilling to attribute these performances simply to linguistic competence. Putting it crudely, we know that the child has to have something to say before he expresses it, and that, hopefully, so does the adult. In other words, a certain cognitive competence as well as a linguistic competence is a necessary condition for successful linguistic performance; we have to mean something when we speak, and we have to go some way towards understanding what the other person means when he speaks to us.

This feature was somewhat underemphasized until the late 1960s and early 1970s. During the early 1960s, Noam Chomsky's account of generative linguistics dominated the research scene (see LANGUAGE: CHOMSKY'S THEORY). Investigators audiotaped young children in dialogue with their parents, transcribed the tapes, and analysed the transcripts linguistically. That is, they performed a *structural* analysis, whereby they treated the child's utterances as though they were a novel language. This analysis resulted in a description in terms of classes of words which did not correspond to adult-form classes (such as noun, verb). Children might say 'car gone', 'Daddy gone', 'lettuce gone', 'that red', 'that bow-wow', 'that man', demonstrating use of a class of pivot words (gone, that), which each occur frequently in one position only in a two-word sentence, and upon which other, open-class words are hung. Generative psycholinguists tried to extend these findings both back- and forwards in the child's development. First, they suggested that these two-word utterances embodied the linguistic universals with the knowledge of which the child had been innately endowed. That is, every infant is pre-programmed, they maintained, with the capacity for using features that are common to all languages, such as the distinction between subject and object or that between qualifier and noun. The generative psycholinguists also tried to trace the ways in which the early two-word sentences subsequently develop into full linguistic performance. They attributed this development to the acquisition of more and more complex transformation rules—that is, rules that transform the deep underlying structure into the surface structure.

Soon dissatisfied with a purely linguistic approach, investigators started to videotape as well as audiotape the child's conversations with his mother. When they did so, they found that a *functional* analysis was appropriate for the data collected. It is only from a videotape that one can discover whether, when a child said 'Mummy shoes', he was meaning 'Those are mummy's shoes' (possessive) or 'Mummy, put my shoes on' (actor, action, object). Clearly, the child has meanings he wishes to express, and functional analysis soon revealed a corpus of about a dozen or fifteen other such relationships which were expressed in the utterances of children aged 2. From this point of view, language development lags behind cognitive development—the child has to understand what he wants to say before he can say it. Or, as Dan Slobin has put it more elegantly, 'New forms first express old functions, and new functions are first expressed by old forms'.

In some cases, though, linguistic development lags far, far behind cognitive development. The 4-year-old child has long since acquired the notion of himself as an individual. Yet the linguistic forms he uses to refer to himself develop painfully slowly. He may use his own name all the time to begin with—'Adam go hill', 'Pick Adam up'. Next he uses 'I' in the initial sentence position only, 'me' in all other positions—'I Adam do that', 'Why me spilled it?' Finally, he grasps the subject and object functions of I and me—'That what I do' and 'You want me help you?'. This example shows that, while a certain level of cognitive development is a necessary condition for linguistic performance, it is not a sufficient condition: there are certain specifically linguistic competences which also have to be acquired. What is more, some languages make it very hard to be linguistically competent—how does the French child acquire the right gender for all his nouns?

The mechanisms by which linguistic competence develops, and the nature of its dependence on cognitive development, have been the subject of much speculation; little, however, is really known. *Piaget and his followers suggest that the grammatical expression of such structures as action–object and actor–action is dependent upon the sensorimotor development of the child. The child has to act upon his own environment before he can conceive of the notions of actor, action, and object and subsequently express them.

More recently, psychologists have stressed the social context of the precursors to language. At a very early stage of his life indeed the child can direct his mother's attention to something in his environment simply by focusing his gaze upon it. Subsequently in his development he may make grasping movements towards it, and later still gesture or point towards it. Jerome Bruner suggests that it is by this manipulation of his *social* environments that the child is laying the foundations for competence. And it is *communicative* competence that is being acquired; he is acquiring the rules relating to how we refer.

See also LANGUAGE: LEARNING WORD MEANINGS.   PH

Cromer, R. (1974). 'The development of language and cognition: the cognition hypothesis'. In Foss, B. M. (ed.), *New Perspectives in Child Development*.

Fletcher, P., and Garman, M. (1986). *Language Acquisition: Studies in First Language Development* (2nd edn.).

Greene, J. (1975). *Thinking and Language*.

Slobin, D. I. (1972). 'Seven questions about language development'. In Dodwell, P. C. (ed.), *New Horizons in Psychology, II*.

Wanner, E., and Gleitman, L. R. (eds.) (1982). *Language Acquisition: The State of the Art*.

Lashley, Karl Spencer (1890–1958). American neuropsychologist, educated at Johns Hopkins University, Baltimore. While still relatively junior he began to work with Shepherd Ivery Franz, a pioneer in the application of physiological methods to the study of brain mechanisms and intelligence in animals. Lashley later worked closely with J. B. *Watson and may be regarded as a co-founder of *behaviourism. Indeed his understanding of neurology was a good deal more sophisticated than that of Watson and he soon abandoned Watson's reliance on *reflexes and conditioned reflexes (see CONDITIONING) as the building blocks of behaviour. At the same time, he held strongly to Watson's insistence on objective methods and the abandonment of consciousness in the explanation of behaviour.

Lashley's best-known work involved study of the effects of lesions of the cerebral cortex on intelligence and learning in the rat and monkey. He was a most competent experimenter and the first to apply statistical methods to the analysis of the results of brain lesions and to ascertain their locus and extent by post-mortem anatomical study. He published two influential groups of studies, the first concerned with cerebral function in learning (1920–35) and the second on the neural mechanisms of vision (1930–48). His monograph *Brain Mechanisms and Intelligence* appeared in 1930.

Lashley's work convinced him that, although sensory and motor functions are in some sense localized, the effects of cerebral lesions involving the so-called association areas do not indicate clear-cut functional *localization, but rather as he thought 'mass action' such that loss of complex skills was a function of the volume of excised brain rather than its location. With later, more sophisticated experiments, this view is greatly modified in favour of specific regions of specialized functions. Lashley was a figure of high standing in the field of physiological psychology and although, unlike his early colleague Franz, he never extended his studies to brain injury in man, he had great influence on the evolution of contemporary *neuropsychology. Among his students were Donald O. *Hebb and Karl Pribram. He was a Foreign Fellow of the Royal Society of London.   OLZ/RLG

Beach, F. A., Hebb, D. O., and Morgan, C. T. (eds.) (1960). *The Neuropsychology of Lashley*.

Orbach, J. (1982). *Neuropsychology after Lashley*.

lateral thinking. There may not be a reason for saying something until after you have said it. That statement does not make sense in the world of logic, where each step has to rest securely on the preceding step: reason must come before a conclusion, not after it. Yet the statement makes perfect sense in the world of lateral thinking, of perception, of patterning systems, of poetry, and of hypothesis. Philosophers and scientists have always complained that we have no logical way of generating hypotheses. We do have such a way, but it cannot be logical for logic involves analysis of what we know. Instead of analysis we need provocation, and that is what lateral thinking is about.

Suppose we are looking for a new idea for a cigarette product. We use one of the more provocative lateral thinking techniques and we bring in a random word as provocation. The word can be picked from a dictionary with a table of random numbers so that no unconscious selection takes place. Does this mean that any word whatsoever may be used as a provocation with any problem whatsoever? It does. There is no connection at all between the random word and the problem. The word is 'soap', and from this comes the idea of freshness, and of spring, and of putting flower seeds in the butt of cigarettes so that when the butts are thrown away a flower will grow from each one and beautify the surroundings instead of polluting them. It is very difficult to see how such an idea could ever come purely from *analysis* of a cigarette since there is no part of it which would suggest this type of idea. Another time the provocation is 'traffic lights' and from this comes the idea of putting a red band round the cigarette about two centimetres from the butt end to indicate a danger zone and so give the smoker a decision point. Now this idea is very logical in hindsight and could possibly have come through analysis. In hindsight it is often difficult to tell how an idea actually came about since the aim of lateral thinking is to produce ideas that are logical in hindsight.

The first stage of thinking is the perception stage: how we look at the world; the concepts and perceptions we form. The second stage of thinking is the processing stage: what we do with the perceptions that have been set up in the first stage. Logic can only be used in the second stage since it requires concepts and perceptions to work upon. So what can we do about the first or perception stage? We can rely on chance, circumstance, experiment, or mistake to change our perceptions, or we can try to do something more deliberate. That is where lateral thinking comes in.

A perception is a particular way of looking at some part of the world. It is the grouping together of certain features or the isolation of a certain relationship. Perceptions are the patterns which form in our minds after exposure to the world at first or second hand. These patterns are only some among the *many possible patterns* that could have formed. Moreover, because of the nature of patterning systems, we may be unable to use one perception because we are led away along another. So the type of processing we want to do in the first stage of thinking is concerned with *changing perceptions*. It is concerned with forming new perceptions and with uncovering the perceptions we have but are unable to use.

If we accept that the mind is a pattern-making and pattern-using system, at least in the perception stage (and all the evidence suggests it is), then we need to develop some deliberate habits of provocation if we are to move from established patterns to open up new ones. Our usual mode of thinking is, quite properly, based on judgement. But judgement serves only to reinforce existing patterns, not to change them. Instead of judgement we need something more provocative. Instead of judgement we need movement, and that is what lateral thinking is about.

There is nothing mystical or magical about lateral thinking. As soon as we accept that perception is based on patterns (rather like the streets in a town) then we need some method for getting out of the familiar patterns—some jolting or provoking system. If our ideas are only a summary of what we already know, then how are we to get new ideas? Certainly we can get some by analysing more fully the implications of what we do know, but the really new ideas depend on new hypotheses, on new conceptual jumps. In a patterning system it is perfectly logical to be illogical. In the example given earlier there is no connection between a cigarette and soap, but one quickly forms along one of the many association pathways we have. Our ideas about cigarettes can now start to move out along this track—and it is a different track from the one they would otherwise have moved along. So the reason for juxtaposing cigarette and soap only appears after the juxtaposition has been made and has proved useful.

We need some indicator to show that we are not operating in the usual judgement system. Otherwise, if we made a statement like 'The hands of a watch should move backwards', we would be judged as unhinged. So from

*poetry, hypothesis, and suppose we extract the syllable *po* which indicates that we are using an idea in a provocative manner in order to open up new ideas. So we now say, 'Po the hands of a watch should move backwards', and using that as a stepping stone we might come to consider the idea of having the numbering of the hours running from twelve down to one so that by glancing at our watch we can tell how many hours are *left* to the day rather than how many have passed.

The use of random juxtapositions and provocative stepping stones is only part of the process of lateral thinking—there are many other techniques, some of which are more analytical than provocative. With all the techniques the aim remains the same: the changing of concepts and perceptions. Occasionally the changed perception gives a solution or a valuable new idea. More often lateral thinking gives only a new starting point which has then to be developed in the usual logical manner. For instance, in a fish-processing plant the starting point that it might make more sense to take the bones away from the flesh instead of the more usual method of taking the flesh away from the bones led to a new process which saved a great deal of money.

In general our mental tools for judging and processing and analysing are very good. But we have been very poor at generating new ideas and hypotheses because we have failed to realize that in a patterning system provocative methods are required. It was necessary to invent the term 'lateral thinking' because creativity is too vague a word, simply meaning the production of something new. Lateral thinking is concerned with changing concepts and perceptions. Some of artistic creativity has to do with lateral thinking but much of it does not. The term 'divergent thinking' covers only a small part of lateral thinking: that is to say the generation of alternatives as a method for changing perceptions. Indeed some of the lateral thinking processes are not divergent at all. Lateral thinking is concerned with the changing of concepts and perceptions by provocative and other means.

A young toddler is upsetting granny's knitting by playing with the ball of wool. One suggestion is to put the child into the playpen. Another suggestion is to leave the child outside and put granny into the playpen.

See also CREATIVITY; PROBLEM SOLVING.   EdeB

de Bono, E. (1970). *The Dog Exercising Machine.*
—— (1971). *Lateral Thinking for Management.*
—— (1977). *Lateral Thinking* (2nd edn.).
—— (1990). *Six Thinking Hats: An Essential Approach to Business Management from the Creator of Lateral Thinking.*
—— (1996). *Lateral Thinking.*

laughing gas (nitrous oxide). The effects of breathing nitrous oxide were first investigated by the distinguished chemist Sir Humphry Davy (1778–1829). In Bristol, as a young man, Davy joined the Pneumatic Institute, which was run by Dr Thomas Beddoes (1760–1808). Here experiments were undertaken on the effects of breathing gases. They were frequently dangerous, but were an important step towards the discovery of *anaesthetics. The 'subjects' included some of the most famous men of letters of the day, for example Robert Southey and Samuel Taylor Coleridge, who wrote:

The first time I inspired the nitrous oxide, I felt a highly pleasurable sensation of warmth over my whole frame, resembling that which I remember once to have experienced after returning from a walk in the snow into a warm room. The only motion which I felt inclined to make, was that of laughing at those who were looking at me.

Davy first tried the experiment on 11 April 1799, when he obtained nitrous oxide in a pure state. He describes a later experiment in these words:

A thrilling, extending from the chest to the extremities, was almost immediately produced. I felt a sense of tangible extension highly pleasurable in every limb; my visible impressions were dazzling, and apparently magnified, I heard distinctly every sound in the room, and was perfectly aware of my situation. By degrees, as the pleasurable sensations increased, I lost all connection with external things; trains of vivid visible images rapidly passed through my mind, and were connected with words in such a manner, as to produce perceptions perfectly novel. I existed in a world of newly connected and newly modified ideas: I theorized, I imagined that I made discoveries. When I was awakened from this semi-delirious trance by Dr Kinglake, who took the bag from my mouth, indignation and pride were the first feelings produced by the sight of the persons about me. My emotions were enthusiastic and sublime, and for a minute I walked round the room perfectly regardless of what was said to me. As I recovered my former state of mind I felt an inclination to communicate the discoveries I had made during the experiment. I endeavoured to recall the ideas: they were feeble and indistinct; one collection of terms, however, presented itself; and with a most intense belief and prophetic manner, I exclaimed to Dr Kinglake, 'Nothing exists but thoughts! The universe is composed of impressions, ideas, pleasures and pains!' (Kendall 1954: 44–5).

Davy realized that the gas might be useful as an anaesthetic, for he wrote in 1800: 'As nitrous oxide in its extensive operation appears capable of destroying physical pain, it may probably be used with advantage during surgical operations in which no great effusion of blood takes place.' He tried it for toothache, but unfortunately the pain returned worse than before—so he missed a great discovery by not continuing. It was not until 1844 that Horace Wells, an American dentist, first employed nitrous oxide successfully for this purpose—for the extraction of one of his own teeth. (See ANAESTHESIA.)   RLG

Kendall, J. (1954). *Humphry Davy, Pilot of Penzance.*

law of effect. The law of effect is a kind of hedonism of the past: actions that lead immediately to pleasure are

learned, remembered, and repeated as habits, whereas actions leading to pain are not remembered, or are suppressed so that later painful behaviour is avoided. This is a reversal of the moralist's hedonism which suggests that we seek pleasure in the future. The concept of the law of effect is a basic tenet of *behaviourism, which eschews *purpose or *intention. It is now held to be correct, although not to be accepted as accounting for all learning and behaviour.

The concept derived from E. L. *Thorndike's experiments with cats placed in puzzle boxes, from which they escaped by trial-and-error behaviour. The escape was the reward that produced the learning, though without understanding.   RLG

Thorndike, E. L. (1898). *Animal Intelligence.*

laws of nature. Perhaps the most mysterious issue in the whole of science is the origin and logical status of the laws of physics. Why do they continue to hold without change? Did physical laws 'exist' before matter? Do they change, through the history of the universe? Are they, even, derived by a kind of natural selection of the inorganic world—as suggested by the American philosopher Charles Sanders *Peirce? These impossibly deep questions are discussed in the works listed below.   RLG

Feynman, R. (1965). *The Character of Physical Law.*
Hawking, S. W. (1988). *A Brief History of Time: From the Big Bang to Black Holes.*
Peirce, C. S. (1931–58). *The Collected Papers of Charles Sanders Peirce.* Eds. C. Hartshorne and P. Weiss.
——(1958). *Values in a Universe of Chance.* (Selected writings.)
Rees, M. (1998). *Before the Beginning: Our Universe and Others.*

laws of thought. These have traditionally been linked with, and sometimes identified with, laws of logic. (This tradition was challenged by, among others, Sigmund *Freud, who held that there are highly irrational, powerful laws determining behaviour and how we perceive the world and ourselves.) The English mathematical logician George *Boole was perhaps the first, since *Aristotle, to develop the idea that laws of logic are rules by which the mind works. Thus,

that which renders Logic possible, is the existence in our mind of general notions—our ability to conceive of a class, and to designate its individual members by a common name. The theory of Logic is thus intimately connected with that of language. A successful attempt to express logical propositions by symbols, the laws of whose combinations should be founded upon the laws of mental processes which they represent, would, so far, be a step toward a philosophical language. (Boole 1847: introd.)

For Boole, it seemed possible to discover how the mind works by looking at rules of logic. This idea is remarkably similar to Ludwig *Wittgenstein's account of the procedures of language as generating concepts according to the chosen 'language games'. Language, for Wittgenstein, is a kind of machine which by operating generates understanding—and sometimes confusions, which need to be made explicit and sorted out by philosophers. (See WITTGENSTEIN'S PHILOSOPHY OF LANGUAGE.)

A deep question is how far laws of thought are *innate (and, together with this, how far the structures of language are innate, as Noam Chomsky holds with his deep structure theory of language: see LANGUAGE: CHOMSKY'S THEORY) and how far they are learned, and are products of particular cultures, societies, and technologies. Here there is an enormous range of opinion, from Immanuel *Kant's notion that our ideas of space and time are innately given, to the extreme empiricism of *Helmholtz, for perception, and the earlier empiricist philosophers, who believed, following *Locke, that all we have to start with is the ability to associate sensations to generate ideas and understanding.

At present, it seems that we shall not be able to specify effective laws of thought in detail before there are adequate computer programs for solving problems—including problem solving that is not strictly and explicitly logical. (See ARTIFICIAL INTELLIGENCE.)   RLG

Boole, G. (1847). *The Mathematical Analysis of Logic: Being an Essay towards a Calculus of Deductive Reasoning* (repr. 1998).

learning theories. The study of learning has been prominent in psychology for more than 80 years. Since the pioneering work of Ivan *Pavlov and E. L. *Thorndike, its importance has consistently been reflected empirically through experimental investigations and conceptually through interpretative theories.

Pavlov demonstrated empirically the ways in which dogs develop acquired *reflexes, and thus identified the basic phenomena of what is now termed classical *conditioning. As the result of a temporal association with a stimulus which already elicits a response, a previously neutral stimulus comes to elicit a similar, conditioned, response. Thus, for example, a bell paired with food elicits conditioned salivation. At an empirical level, Pavlov's extensive research was remarkably effective in producing robust data relating to a psychological phenomenon. At a theoretical level, Pavlov introduced an important element of plasticity into the Russian reflexological tradition which interpreted all behaviour, including that of humans, as the result of environmental stimuli. Pavlov regarded conditioned behaviour as a reflection of higher nervous activity set in train by stimuli.

Thorndike also used experimental methods and animal subjects, studying 'intelligence' by investigating, for example, how cats learned to escape from a puzzle box to obtain food. He too obtained pleasingly orderly behavioural data which indicated gradual changes in behaviour rather than sudden 'insightful' changes. Thorndike

argued that the gradual changes occurred because the 'satisfying state of affairs' which followed the correct response made it progressively stronger or more probable. Through his *law of effect Thorndike emphasized that patterns of behaviour can be selected by their consequences, rather as advantageous taxonomic form is selected by evolutionary pressures on species. In both cases, apparent purpose can be reinterpreted in terms of the effects of consequences. Thorndike originally believed that behaviour followed by an 'annoying state of affairs' became weaker, but his own research, here largely with human subjects, did not demonstrate this. Thorndike therefore retained a truncated form of his law of effect which emphasized the selective strengthening effects of what are now termed reinforcers in instrumental conditioning.

The impact of subsequent empirical studies of learning was for some time largely reflected by theories which were in effect general theories in psychology. This is illustrated in J. B. *Watson's writing. He exploited his familiarity with early empirical studies which related changes in behaviour to environmental conditions in order to advocate that psychology as a whole should be reformulated as the science of behaviour rather than of mental life and experience. Watson's *behaviourism has contributed to the widespread adoption of behavioural studies in psychology, but his more negative views about the relevance of mental life to the refocused discipline of psychology have been less influential. Like subsequent theorists, Watson used the empirical data of studies of learning as a platform for his approach to psychology in general. In particular, he extended the principles of classical conditioning to emotions in humans through his famous studies with 'little Albert', and emphasized environmental influences on behaviour to the neglect of inherited differences.

Edward *Tolman carried out ingenious experiments on learning in animals, and demonstrated patterns of behavioural change which were not so readily interpreted in simple stimulus–response terms. For example, he showed that rats learned to run to a particular place for food rather than to make a stereotyped response such as turning right at a choice point. He also investigated latent learning, shown through savings when animals were allowed simply to explore a maze before being required to run through it to a specific goal box. Tolman used the methods of behavioural investigations, but extended the complexity of the environmental arrangements whose effects on behaviour were studied. He was drawn to use intervening concepts, such as expectancies or cognitive maps, to deal with the relationships he observed between environment and behaviour. In this regard, Tolman was a precursor of contemporary cognitive psychology.

The most detailed and systematic account of learning yet developed was that of Clark *Hull. Yet again based on controlled experiments with animals, Hull's theory was presented in formal terms, with postulates giving rise to precise behavioural predictions expressed in quantitative terms through equations with intervening variables. These variables, which in Hull's theory were such concepts as drive, habit strength, and reaction potential, were more tightly tied to empirical measurements than were Tolman's more cognitive terms. Hull's theory is often cited as the best example in psychology of the hypothetico-deductive method of scientific enquiry, and in this sense it is a further example of a learning theory which has implications for psychology reaching far beyond the empirical studies of learning on which it is based. The theory also strove for a general explication of learning, emphasizing similarities between classical and instrumental conditioning and across species, though incorporating quantitative differences.

In the 30 years 1950–80 the emphasis on formal global theories of learning diminished. Empirical research on conditioning and learning has continued to flourish, however. The methods of free-operant conditioning developed by Skinner have been extremely beneficial in this respect, making it possible to study more effectively the effects of intermittent reinforcement, discriminative control, punishment, and so on. Indeed operant conditioning has become a technology for the experimental analysis of behaviour. One systematic use of the data of operant conditioning has been to support the general behaviouristic approach to psychology favoured by Skinner, with its emphasis on explanations of behaviour couched in terms of its relationships with environmental events in applied contexts with humans as well as with animals in the laboratory (functional analysis of behaviour). (See BEHAVIOURISM, SKINNER ON.) However, the behavioural data obtained from operant conditioning may be evaluated in terms of other theories.

In recent years a number of trends have emerged from empirical studies of conditioning. First, conventional distinctions between classical and instrumental conditioning have been further challenged. One important factor here has been the suggestion that activities of the autonomic nervous system such as heart rate and blood pressure, previously thought to be affected only by classical conditioning procedures, can be modulated by instrumental reinforcement, a possibility that encouraged the use of so-called biofeedback techniques with patients in clinical practice. Secondly, greater interest has been shown in biological or phylogenetic influences on conditioning and learning. It seems that some patterns of behaviour are more readily affected by conditioning procedures than others: animals appear, for example, to be biologically prepared to associate novel tastes and nausea, no doubt because of the implications of such preparedness for survival. Similarly, species-characteristic patterns of

behaviour may intrude even in the controlled environment of the conditioning laboratory. These findings have raised some doubts about the generality of the laws of learning established thus far, but they emphasize that behaviour must be interpreted in terms of interactions between inheritance and experience. Thirdly, the increasingly complex relationships between environment and behaviour studied in conditioning experiments have led some contemporary learning theorists (e.g. Mackintosh 1983) to reintroduce cognitive explanations even of animal behaviour.

The field of learning has consistently been one of the most active areas of experimental psychology. The empirical data which has been produced has consistently demonstrated the power of experimental and comparative methods in psychology. In turn it has given rise to theories which, though designed primarily to accommodate the phenomena of animal learning, have implications for psychology in general, in terms of human as well as of animal behaviour. These theories have therefore reflected (or perhaps led) changing perspectives in psychological science. Learning and learning theory can be said to offer an insight into the empirical and theoretical development of psychology as a whole.

See also MEMORY: BIOLOGICAL BASIS.   DEB

Mackintosh, N. J. (1983). *Conditioning and Associative Learning.*
—— and Colman, A. M. (1995). *Learning and Skills.*

least effort, principle of. This asserts that minimal energy will be expended, sufficient for survival. As a 'complacent cow' description of behaviour, this is not true even for complacent cows! Some degree of more or less random searching—apparently having a basis of curiosity—is characteristic of virtually all organisms, and is exceedingly highly developed in man. We by no means take least effort as our maxim for behaviour: hence the ziggurats of Babylon, the pyramids of Egypt, the temples, statues, and paintings as well as the philosophy of Greece, and the science that has come to mould Western civilization. The effort involved in building a city—be it Athens or New York—is truly remarkable. It provides the clearest evidence that behaviour is not passive, initiated by stimuli, and that we are not organisms content to exist with least effort. On the other hand, least effort *is* a criterion for the intelligent planning of an enterprise: we set up goals difficult to achieve, and with intelligence try to reach them without wasted effort.   RLG

left-handedness. See HANDEDNESS.

Leibniz, Gottfried Wilhelm, Freiherr von (1646–1716). Born in Leipzig and trained as a lawyer, Leibniz depended for his livelihood on the patronage of German princes, for whom he worked as a counsellor, diplomatist, and historian. Much of his life was spent as librarian to the electors of Hanover; George I, who disappointed him by not taking him to England when he became king in 1714, called him a 'living encyclopedia'. There were few areas of learning to which he did not make important contributions.

He is best known as a philosopher and mathematician. He shares with *Newton the honour of discovering the calculus; their discoveries were effectively independent, though Leibniz was bitterly attacked by Newton's followers, who accused him of plagiarism. He attempted to apply the mathematical type of reasoning as widely as possible, and in so doing can be said to have invented symbolic logic, though because he did not publish his work it had to be invented again 150 years later. He wanted to create a perfect language, which would reflect in its grammar and word structure the full logical complexity of what we say; this idea has been very fruitful in recent philosophy, especially through the work of Bertrand *Russell, who was much influenced by Leibniz. But Leibniz was also interested in how actual languages worked, and was a pioneer of systematic philology. He invented the first gear-wheeled calculating machine, for his father, to do his accounts, in 1642.

He was a leading critic of the physics of *Descartes, which left no place for the force he considered to be inherent in matter; this was one of the things that led to his remarkable philosophical theory of matter as built up out of little minds (monads). He was heavily influenced by Descartes and *Spinoza, who are usually classed with him as rationalists; he in turn was to be a major influence on *Kant. Popularly he was perhaps best known for maintaining that this is the best of all possible worlds, a view Voltaire satirized in *Candide*. But Voltaire was unjust in treating him as a shallow optimist: he did not believe this world is obviously perfect, but only that because a good God exists this *must* be the best world possible, however evil it may seem.

See also LEIBNIZ'S PHILOSOPHY OF MIND.   RCSW

Leibniz's philosophy of mind. Although he never published it in complete form, *Leibniz's philosophy is a closely knit system of speculative metaphysics, with a neatness and story-book attractiveness which led *Kant to say that Leibniz had built 'a kind of enchanted world'. Subsequent philosophers have generally found the system as a whole too strange to be taken seriously, but some of the individual ideas have been extremely influential.

It could all be described as philosophy of mind, for it is Leibniz's opinion that only minds exist. There are endlessly many of them, all different, and what we take to be inert matter is made up of nothing but minds of a rather stupid variety. There is no difference of kind between

them and ourselves, only a difference of degree. They can be thought of as coming low on a scale of gradually increasing intelligence, with microbes and insects and animals and men above them. Above men come angels, and right at the top, God. God is rather a special case, being infinite and the creator of everything else; all other minds are finite minds, of more or less intelligence. Leibniz calls them 'monads'.

Monads have perceptions and desires; according to Leibniz, when mental states are analysed it turns out that fundamentally they all come down to these two kinds. Each monad continually seeks its own improvement, which consists in coming to perceive things more clearly and distinctly. The awareness that one's perceptions have become more clear and distinct is called pleasure, while the awareness that the opposite has occurred is called pain. This leads to so implausibly intellectual a view of the feelings and emotions that only a philosopher could have adopted it. Leibniz probably derived it largely from *Spinoza, and does not work it out in much detail, but he does provide a few analyses—love, for example, is pleasure at the pleasure of another, pleasure itself being defined as above.

Perceptions may be more, or less, clear and distinct; it is in respect of the clarity and distinctness of their perceptions that minds differ. What makes one mind more intelligent than another is just that it can perceive things better. Leibniz includes as perceptions both thoughts and sense experiences, for he sees no essential difference between them; sense experiences are one variety of clear but not very distinct perception. A perception is clear when one understands what one is perceiving, but distinct only to the extent that one can analyse the concepts involved. Many of our thoughts are obscure and confused perceptions, but a few are clear and distinct: the thought that 2+2=4, for example, and our apprehension of the two principles Leibniz thinks fundamental to all reasoning: the principle of contradiction ('No proposition can be both true and false at once') and the principle of sufficient reason ('Nothing occurs without adequate reason'). These things are not learned from sense experience, as *Locke and the empiricists maintain; our knowledge of them is innate, though experience is required to bring them to consciousness. Leibniz also rejects Locke's claim that all our concepts are acquired from experience by abstraction. No experience could give us concepts like those of God or of mathematical equality, and these must be inborn in us in the same way. Recently the defence of *innate knowledge has been taken up by Noam Chomsky (see LANGUAGE: CHOMSKY'S THEORY), but it is one of the things that mark Leibniz off as a rationalist, and it leaves him with the perennial problem of rationalist philosophers: why should an inborn propensity to believe certain things be any guarantee of their truth?

Leibniz was the first to introduce the idea of the *unconscious*. He points out that one can often recall having perceived something—some detail of a familiar scene, perhaps—although one did not notice it at the time: clearly one must have perceived it without being aware of doing so. And in listening to the sea breaking, one is conscious only of the sea and not of each individual drop of water; yet the sound of the sea is made up of the sounds of the drops, so that one must in some way be perceiving each of them. Such unconscious perceptions he calls 'little perceptions'; they differ from conscious perceptions only in degree—degree of clarity and distinctness. Unconscious perceptions are highly obscure and confused, and Leibniz thinks we have far more of them than we might ever suspect; for each monad continually perceives the entire universe, though we are never conscious of more than a small part. Those monads which come very low on the scale, so low that we normally fail to recognize them as minds at all, have only unconscious perceptions, and there are times when we are in this state ourselves—in *sleep, for example, and in death. For when someone dies his mind loses its clearer and more distinct perceptions, but does not cease to exist or lose its identity; it sinks down, temporarily at least, to a lower position on the scale.

No monad wants its perceptions to become less clear and distinct; on the contrary, all its actions are directed towards moving further up the scale. Leibniz regards an action as an event directly caused by the will of a monad, and this is much too crude an account of action. But it is over freedom that Leibniz gets into particular difficulties; he is anxious to defend free will against the determinism of Spinoza, yet it is hard to see how he can. Since every monad must will its own improvement, it can exercise choice only over how to achieve this. But it is bound to choose whatever means seem the best available—the principle of sufficient reason guarantees that no choice can be made without adequate grounds. So the choice is completely determined by the monad's beliefs about what the best means are. Leibniz ties himself up in knots over this, and attempts various solutions, but he usually says that its beliefs *incline* it, without *necessitating* it, to make the choice it does. Since they incline it quite irresistibly this constitutes a memorable attempt to have your cake and eat it.

The difficulty is made even more acute by a further part of his theory, for he holds that God programmed into every monad at the creation the whole course of its future development, including every action and every thought. We would hardly describe as free a robot all of whose behaviour had been determined in advance by its designer.

Leibniz actually holds that created monads never produce effects in one another. They only appear to. They are like different clocks which strike the hours together. God has so designed them that whenever an event we regard as a cause occurs in the career of one monad, the events we think of as its effects will occur in the histories of the others. So the monads keep time with one another, and appear to act on one another, but really do not: there is a 'pre-established harmony' between them. In virtue of the harmony there is a correspondence between each monad's perceptual states and how things are outside it, so that it can be said to 'mirror' the universe even though its perceptions are not caused by the things outside.

Leibniz's reason for this remarkable theory is that if monads could act on one another he thinks they would not be genuinely independent things, substances. Indeed, he goes so far as to maintain that monads cannot really stand in any relations to one another at all. This leads him to deny the reality of space, for he thinks that space can only be a system of relations between things. Things do appear to be spatially related, but really there are no relations between them and therefore no space. Nevertheless, the appearance is 'well founded' in the perceptual states of the individual monads, for they each differ in the clarity with which they mirror different parts of the universe, and our idea that they have positions in space is a confused awareness of these differences. Roughly speaking, I appear closest to those things I most clearly perceive. But one cannot do other than speak roughly here, for the theory is not properly worked out, and could not be. I can perceive the Pleiades, after all, more clearly than the back of my head.

Clarity and distinctness are being given too much work to do. They cannot provide the reality behind our awareness of spatial relationships, nor is it really our sole aim in life to get more of them. Leibniz's overvaluation of them is characteristic of an age intoxicated with the recent successes of rational thought and its apparent capacity to solve every problem; it does not detract from the brilliance and originality of many of his ideas.   RCSW

Broad, C. D. (1975). *Leibniz: An Introduction*.

Joseph, H. W. B. (1949). *Lectures on the Philosophy of Leibniz* (repr. 1974).

Leibniz, G. W. (1965). *Logical Papers*. Trans. and ed. G. H. R. Parkinson.

Morris, M., and Parkinson, G. H. R. (eds.) (1973). *Leibniz: Philosophical Writings*.

Leonardo da Vinci (1452–1519). Italian sculptor, painter, architect, and engineer–inventor, born at Vinci near Florence, the natural son of a notary. He was apprenticed to Verrocchio (about 1470) in Florence and in 1482 settled in Milan, working with Lodovico Sforza. In 1502 Leonardo entered the service of Cesare Borgia, as architect and engineer. The *Mona Lisa* was painted about 1504.

Leonardo's *Notebooks* are of great interest in describing his work and ideas on hydraulics, the casting of statues, and many inventions, as well as in giving his advice to painters and clear accounts of perspective and the use of shadow. He did not, however, appreciate that the two eyes give perception of depth (by stereopsis), and he wrongly thought that light must cross twice in the eye to produce a right-way-up retinal image, for perception to be non-inverted. He was also confused on why *mirrors normally reverse left and right but not up and down—see MacCurdy (1938: vol. i, ch. 9). Leonardo recognized, however, many properties of the eye, such as 'irradiation'—bright objects appearing larger than dark ones—and his anatomical drawings are masterpieces, even though they sometimes incorporate features which he believed present when in fact they are not. Leonardo is generally recognized as the most universal genius of all time.

A feature of Leonardo's *Notebooks* of particular psychological interest is that these manuscripts were consistently written in mirror script. As is well known, mirror writing is not an altogether uncommon accomplishment, particularly among the left-handed. Although Leonardo's handedness is not reliably known, some experts have claimed that careful study of the detail and shading of his marginal sketches indicates that—at all events before he sustained a partial left-sided paralysis in later life—the pen was held in his left hand. It appears probable, therefore, that Leonardo was naturally left-handed and, like some other left-handed individuals, had a particular facility in mirror writing.   OLZ

Critchley, M. (1928). *Mirror-Writing*.
MacCurdy, E. (1938). *The Notebooks of Leonardo da Vinci*.

leucotomy. The removal of small regions of the frontal lobes of the brain, for extreme depression. The operation is now seldom, if ever, performed. See also PSYCHOSURGERY.

levitation. A *paranormal phenomenon which has been claimed to occur in the open air (at a garden party and witnessed by perhaps 100 guests), and, by the 19th-century medium Daniel Dunglas Home, at a party when he was reported as gliding out of an upstairs window and into another without material support. There appear to be no recent reports of levitation.

An interesting party game is to press down on the head and shoulders of someone blindfolded and seated in a chair, and then to release the pressure. He will then (with some added verbal suggestion) feel that he is floating up to the ceiling. The experience can be extremely convincing, and frightening, though of course he remains seated in the chair.   RLG

libido. For Sigmund *Freud, the libido was essentially the sexual drive, which could be sublimated into the great variety of human creative expressions. The evidence that all *creativity beyond *least effort is sexual in origin is now generally regarded as too narrow, and Freud probably exaggerated the sexual basis of creativity.

lie detector. The test most widely used for lie detection is known as 'the polygraph'. It does not detect lying directly but monitors physiological changes which usually accompany heightened states of emotion. For the test, a polygraph is used to provide a continuous write-out of blood pressure, heart rate, respiratory movements, and skin conductance (a measure of sweating) while an examiner asks a series of questions intended to evoke emotional responses which distinguish the guilty from the innocent. In the control question technique the examiner asks a mixture of 'relevant' and 'control' questions. These are designed with the expectation that a guilty person will experience more emotion when answering the relevant questions ('Did you murder your wife?') while an innocent person is likely to find the control questions more disturbing ('As a child, did you ever steal anything?'). The guilty knowledge technique requires the subject to answer questions or listen to a list of facts which include items only a guilty individual would recognize as connected with the investigation.

In laboratory studies, the accuracy of the polygraph has been found to be highly variable. Reports vary between 40 per cent and 88 per cent for the successful detection of lying and between 7 and 25 per cent for falsely categorizing truthful people as liars. Its accuracy is thought to vary according to the technique employed, the skill of the examiner, how much the examiner knows about the truth from other sources of information, and whether the individual being investigated uses 'countermeasures'. The purpose of countermeasures is either to obscure the pattern of emotional response (this can be achieved, for example, by periodically biting the tongue, pressing the toes down on a pin in the shoe, or having painful thoughts) or to block emotional responses by neutral thinking (e.g. counting backwards). Countermeasures significantly decrease the number of successful detections in laboratory simulations.

It is not known how accurately the polygraph detects lying in real-life situations where the individual's liberty or employment may be at stake and where the emotional reactions of some offenders may be abnormal. Polygraph examiners claim a success rate of 87–95 per cent but, on the basis of the scientific evidence available in 1983, the Polygraph Validity Advisory Panel of the US Congress concluded that the polygraph's ability to detect lies was only slightly better than chance. It has been estimated that when the polygraph is used to screen large numbers of people most of whom have nothing to hide (e.g. potential employees), only a small minority of those identified as lying about their past are actually untruthful (Brett,

Phillips, and Beary 1986). Injustice which results from the high proportion of false positives has provoked vigorous opposition to the polygraph from civil liberties groups (ACLU 1996, Maschke and Scalabrini 2002). The majority of psychologists and psychophysiologists believe that polygraphic lie detection is not theoretically sound and that claims for its high validity are not supported by evidence (Iacono and Lykken 1997).

Other physiological responses have been proposed as possible markers of lying. These include changes in pupil diameter, tremor in the vocal muscles, and measurements of brain activity (*evoked potentials). There is no evidence that they are any more effective than the polygraph.

SBu

ACLU (American Civil Liberties Union) (1996). *Lie Detector Testing: Briefing Paper No.4.*

Brett, A. S., Phillips, M., and Beary, J. F. (1986). 'Predictive power of the polygraph: can the "lie detector" really detect liars?' *Lancet*, 1/8480.

Iacono, W. G., and Lykken, D. T. (1997). 'The validity of the lie detector: two surveys of scientific opinion'. *Journal of Applied Psychology*, 82.

Maschke, G. W., and Scalabrini, G. T. (2002). *The Lie behind the Lie Detector.*

limbic system. The term 'limbic system' derives from the concept of the 'limbic lobe'. It was first used by the French anatomist Paul *Broca in 1878 to describe that part of the brain surrounding the brain stem and lying beneath the neocortex. A generally accepted modern definition of the 'limbic system' has, however, never been given. Some neuroanatomists believe that the term should be abandoned. Nevertheless it is a widely used 'shorthand' term and most authors would include the following structures within its definition: the hippocampal formation, olfactory regions, hypothalamus, and amygdala.

Functionally, the limbic system is generally said to be concerned with visceral processes, particularly those associated with the emotional status of the organism. Both experimental and clinical data indicate that the amygdala is involved in emotional experiences and reactions, particularly those associated with fear and anger, flight and defence. Stimulation of the amygdala in conscious animals can give rise to quite integrated response patterns evolving over time and involving a wide variety of motor and autonomic responses which are integral parts of the overall behaviour pattern. Although the amygdala would therefore appear to be involved in these responses, it may not be the only such area. Thus changes in aggressiveness can be obtained by stimulation or ablation of septum, certain areas of cerebral cortex, and the grey matter of the mesencephalon. This emphasizes the importance of considering the interaction of connected brain areas, rather than the activity within particular 'centres', as effectors of functions.

The hippocampus has been the object of much experimental work, and theories about the nature of its function have multiplied. One possibility which has attracted attention from *behaviourists is that it may be involved in *memory. However, at present no clearly formulated results can be stated. This is in consequence partly of the anatomical complexity of the region and partly of the semantic difficulties surrounding the words 'memory' and 'learning'. Since the hippocampus is richly connected to many other brain regions, it is, as in the case of the amygdala, probably misleading to think of such a structure as a 'centre' of such a function. Physiologically one of its most striking properties is seen in relation to activity in the cerebral neocortex. When the neocortex is 'desynchronized' (i.e. shows low-voltage rapid potentials) the hippocampus becomes 'synchronized' and shows rhythmic sinusoidal waves of 4–7 per second ('theta waves': see ELECTROENCEPHALOGRAPHY). When the neocortex is synchronized, on the other hand, the hippocampus is desynchronized. The functions of this reciprocal relationship are not understood, but it appears to be related to the activity of the reticular formation and the state of attentiveness of the subject. Recent work strongly suggests that serotonin and noradrenaline (norepinephrine) are closely involved in the switching of mechanisms between these two states.

Another division of the 'limbic system', the entorhinal area, is closely related anatomically to the hippocampus, providing its main cortical source of afferent fibres. Recent anatomical work has shown that it also receives fibres from the frontal, temporal, and cingulate neocortex as well as the olfactory cortex, indicating that it is the final cortical link between the sensory systems of the neo- and transitional cortex, on the one hand, and the hippocampus and dentate gyrus, on the other. It would seem from an anatomical point of view that the sensory information arriving at the entorhinal area is probably highly refined (see DOPAMINE NEURONS IN THE BRAIN).

The information derived from the entorhinal area interacts with hippocampus and amygdala. These structures deliver further messages both directly (from amygdala) and via septum and nucleus accumbens to regions of the hypothalamus concerned with motivational and rewarding mechanisms.

Thus interaction of all the structures in the complex, from the entorhinal area to hypothalamus, is probably of great importance in deciding the final actions of an organism in a particular environment, and in the formation of adaptive behaviour patterns. See also EMOTIONAL BRAIN.

OTP

Lobachevski, Nikolai Ivanovich (1793–1856). Russian mathematician, founder of non-Euclidian *geometry. This was extremely important in epistemology as it showed that *Euclid's axioms are not known with certainty, a priori, but are hypotheses which may or may not correspond to physical space. His work is published in *Über die Principien der Geometrie* (1829–30).

localization of brain function and cortical maps.

One of the oldest controversies in psychology and neurology concerns localization of function, the notion that different aspects of behaviour are mediated by different parts of the brain. The issue of mental localization was debated by classical thinkers from 400 BC to AD 200 and Aristotle even argued that the soul (i.e. the mind) occupied the heart. Only after several hundred years did Greek writers such as Alcmaeon finally prevail in their arguments that the faculties of the mind lay in the watery ventricles of the brain. The emphasis then shifted to the number of mental faculties and by AD 400 the Church Fathers, including St Augustine, proposed the cell doctrine of the mind, the cells being the ventricles and the faculties of sensation, imagination, reasoning, movement, and memory residing in separate cells, with some sharing since there were only three cells. Although the number of faculties eventually rose to seven or eight, little then changed for another thousand years—making the cell doctrine easily the most enduring theory of the physical basis of mind. But 18th-century anatomists like Sylvius were busy undermining it, convincing their contemporaries that the convolutions of the cerebral cortex were far too complex to be mere cooling pipes for the blood. However, the idea of cortical localization of function had to wait for Franz Joseph *Gall in the early 19th century. From first observing that the mental characteristics of his school friends appeared to be related to the shape of their heads, Gall believed that traits like cautiousness and mirthfulness—he announced 27 in all—were localized and that their magnitude was reflected in the size of a particular region, which in turn was indicated by the size of the overlying skull. Gall's *phrenology enjoyed a brief ascendancy until about 1820 when *Flourens, noting that damage to different parts of the brain often had similar and diffuse effects on behaviour, concluded that the brain acts as a whole. It was much later that localization of function acquired scientific respectability when *Broca showed in 1861 that speech impairment followed damage to a restricted part of the left frontal lobe, and Gustav Fritsch and J. L. Hitzig reported their observations on the effects of electrically stimulating different parts of the exposed brain, first in soldiers with head injuries and then in animals. They found that stimulating discrete parts of what is now known as the motor cortex produced movements of different regions of the body. Interestingly, the doyen of Scottish phrenology George Coombe had observed similar patients in the 1830s and noted that the exposed brain swelled and reddened when the patient became excited. Coombe had stumbled on changes in cerebral blood flow in relation to particular mental activity, which formed the basis of late 20th-century functional neuroimaging, whereby the localized changes in blood flow that correlate with particular mental events can be registered and pinpointed from outside the head. Much later, in 1950, W. G. *Penfield and Theodore Rasmussen published the results of similar observations made on fully conscious patients awaiting brain surgery under local anaesthetic. By electrically stimulating small regions along the central fissure, they showed that there was a map of bodily movements in front of the fissure and a map of sensation behind it (see Fig. 1). Meanwhile Gordon *Holmes had discovered that the eye is mapped onto the back of the brain. By charting small areas of blindness in the visual field of patients with gunshot wounds at the back of the head he found that the part of the eye that was blind depended on the part of the visual cortex that was damaged. Thus were sensory and motor maps established.

Despite this apparently irrefutable evidence of regional specialization in the brain in connection with speech, movement, seeing, and touch, the American psychologist Karl *Lashley produced evidence that Flourens' position remained tenable with respect to some forms of behaviour. By studying maze learning in rats, Lashley showed that the deleterious effects of removing parts of the cerebral cortex depended on the amount of tissue removed rather than on its exact location, a finding enshrined in the principles of mass action and equipotentiality. Lashley's views struck a sympathetic chord with many psychologists of the mid-20th century, who likened the brain to a complex electronic device which can become increasingly unreliable as more of its components are damaged, but which rarely suffers a severe breakdown when a small number of specific localized components are removed.

With hindsight, the often bitter controversy was unnecessary. The view that the brain acts as a whole stems from investigation of complex phenomena, such as learning and remembering complicated tasks involving several of the senses. It is small wonder that a good deal of the brain is involved in such behaviour and, therefore, that damage to any part of it has some effect. The evidence for regional specificity stemmed, by contrast, from investigations of relatively simple actions such as moving a finger, seeing a light in one part of space, or detecting that a particular part of the skin had been touched. The latter are all examples of simple perception or voluntary movements, the former of higher-level cognitive and intellectual behaviour. Even so, the mediation of some complex cognitive abilities can be surprisingly localized. For example, the modern techniques of functional neuroimaging by positron emission tomography (PET) or magnetic resonance imaging (MRI) (see BRAIN IMAGING), both depending

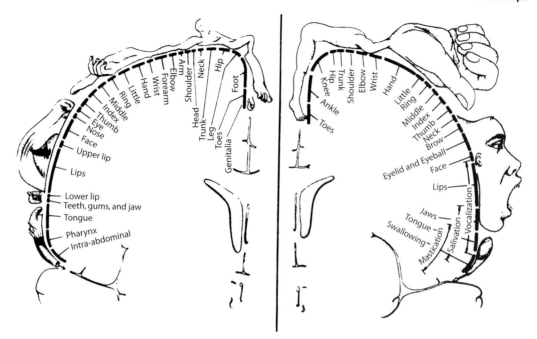

Fig. 1. The diagram on the left shows a slice through one side of the brain, roughly between the ears and through what is called the somatosensory cortex. There is a map of the body surface here. Note that some areas, like face and fingers, have a much larger cortical representation than others, i.e. the map is distorted. The diagram on the right shows the map of the muscles in the motor cortex on a slice of the other side of the brain and at a more anterior portion.

on changes in regional cerebral blood flow, have shown that spatial memory is concentrated in the hippocampus and the recognition of faces in the fusiform gyrus. But let us not forget that this simple view of localization conceals the fact, stressed by Hughlings *Jackson in 1879, that localizing the lesion that leads to a 'selective' disturbance of behaviour is not the same as understanding how that bit of the brain works. Jackson's logical argument is just as true today with respect to focal changes in blood flow revealed by functional brain imaging.

The acceptance of the idea of localization of function had one unfortunate effect. It came to be taken for granted that the senses of touch and vision and hearing were mapped on the surface of the brain and that there was a similarly orderly representation of the muscles, as shown in Fig. 1. But why there is a map at all was not recognized as a question of fundamental importance, despite the fact that nature went to enormous trouble to evolve genetic instructions which ensured that the retina of the eye and the surface of the body are represented on the surface of the brain in an orderly map and not higgledy-piggledy. Furthermore, a computer programmed to recognize

patterns does not need within its components anything like a geographical map of the original scene. So why does the brain have one?

It became increasingly difficult to sidestep this question with the demonstration from 1970 onwards of multiple maps of the eye in the brain. A map is demonstrated by recording the electrical activity of clusters of nerve cells, determining where a visual stimulus must lie on the retina for it to excite these particular cells, and then moving the recording electrode to another group of cells. Using this procedure in anaesthetized animals, it was shown that the retina is mapped not once but many times in the cortex. The macaque monkey has at least ten mapped representations of the retina, and about twenty others where it is the nature of the stimulus rather than its position that is computed. At least a third of the cerebral cortex in the owl monkey is concerned with the multiple mapped representations of visual space (see PRIMATES, EVOLUTION OF THE BRAIN IN, Fig. 8).

What is the purpose of such an arrangement, which is not confined to vision, for there are now known to be several topological representations of the surface of the

531

body and the musculature in monkeys? A plausible explanation concerns a well-known physiological phenomenon called lateral inhibition. In the eye itself, adjacent differences in the brightness of colour of the image are given prominence in the nerve signals that leave the eye. This is accomplished by a system of lateral inhibitory connections in the retina which ensure that nerve cells tend to inhibit their immediate neighbours. In an area of uniform illumination or colour, all cells are equally excited by the light and equally inhibited by their neighbours. But where there is a sharp difference in illumination, as at the image of a contour, the highly illuminated cells exert a powerful inhibition on their neighbours in the shade, and the difference in signals sent by the two groups of cells is enhanced. Lateral inhibition cannot create something out of nothing, but it can enhance one feature of the visual image at the expense of another. Lateral inhibition of this kind ensures that edges and contours are prominently coded in the signals from the eye.

There is now incontrovertible evidence from physiology and anatomy that lateral inhibition works in the brain as well as in the eye, and this provides the major reason for the existence of a map of the eye on the cortex of the brain. If the differences in illumination of adjacent parts of the eye are to be accentuated in the cortex, the sensory connections between the nerve cells concerned with the two adjacent parts of the image should be close together. In a map they are as close together as possible, and lateral interactions will be maximally efficient. If there were no map, so that nerve cells concerned with adjacent parts of the image were often far apart in the relevant cortical area, the problem of interconnecting the cells becomes formidable and the average length of a connection would be much greater, about 20 to 30 times greater in visual area 1 of man and monkey. In a map of the sensory surface the lateral interconnections between cells can all be local, and anatomy has shown this to be so.

But why are there many maps for each of the senses rather than just one? The answer is really the same. Inhibitory connections between neighbouring nerve cells of the cortex are now believed to be involved in coding many attributes of the visual image, such as colour, movement, disparity, orientation, size, and spatial periodicity. If all of these were to be attempted within one map, the local interconnections would again have to be longer and the problem of interconnecting the right cells would increase. By having many maps, each small and containing nerve cells concerned only with one or a few of the stimulus attributes just mentioned, the lateral interconnections can be kept as short as possible and the problem of interconnecting the right type of cell is minimized.

This simple idea has much to support it. First, although there are long fibre connections from one part of the brain to another, microscopy has shown that the connections within a particular map are short and predominantly inhibitory. Second, physiology has shown that nerve cells within a particular cortical representation of the eye tend to be concerned with a restricted range of stimulus qualities, such as orientation, distance, size, colour, or movement. Different maps deal with different stimulus qualities. Third, the human corpus callosum contains about 600 million nerve fibres connecting the two sides of the brain. They are grouped from front to back according to destination and function; if they were not, their average length would have to be longer. Fourth, there are many examples of very selective effects on visual perception of localized brain damage. Although they are rare, some patients suffer a highly selective disturbance of the perception of colour or position or depth or motion, as would be expected when the damage is occasionally restricted to one of the visual maps. Functional maps keep connections short and, therefore, keep the brain (and skull) small enough to be born through a narrow birth canal.

Although the different sensory qualities of the visual scene are initially coded in separate visual areas, our visual perception is unitary not fragmented, which means that the timing of the activity of cells in different visual areas must be precisely coordinated. If we look at a moving, spinning, coloured object and the nervous signals in one visual area are out of phase with all the others, some distortion should occur in what is seen. Indeed, fever, toxicosis, and brain damage can all lead to temporary visual perceptual dislocations. For example, in one part of the visual field objects may appear too large or too small, smooth movement may look jerky, contours may be multiplied, position and orientation be greatly misperceived.

Multiple brain maps of sensory and motor systems are now established. They permit the maximum efficiency and economy in the myriad interconnections between nerve cells responsible for analysing sensory signals. Their existence also throws light on what is now seen as an unwarranted controversy about localization of function. The cortical representations of the sensory attributes of stimuli, such as colour, may be confined to a few areas. The cortical events underlying certain complex and cognitive actions are probably so widely dispersed that no brain damage, however great, can either destroy them entirely or leave them wholly unimpaired. See also NEUROPSYCHOLOGY.
AC

Cowey, A. (2001). 'Functional localisation in the brain: from ancient to modern'. *Psychologist*, 14.

Locke, John (1632–1704). Born at Wrington, Somerset, the first son of a lawyer whose father was a clothier, he was educated at Westminster School, where he was a King's Scholar, and Christ Church, Oxford, where he obtained a scholarship in 1652. His first published work was a complimentary poem for Oliver Cromwell, written while he was an undergraduate.

He took degree courses in logic, metaphysics, and classical languages, but he was dissatisfied with the peripatetic philosophy he was taught. Even so, he developed an interest in experimental philosophy which led him to the study of medicine and the foundations of empirical philosophy. Through this he met Robert Boyle, probably the strongest influence on him, and became his close friend, student, and unofficial assistant. He graduated as an MA in 1658 and was elected a Senior Student of Christ Church and then a lecturer in Greek.

After a brief excursion into diplomacy in 1665–6 he returned to Oxford to study medicine and collaborated with the great physician Thomas Sydenham. In 1667 he left Oxford to become personal physician to Lord Ashley, later first earl of Shaftesbury, whose life he was credited with saving by an operation. He was elected Fellow of the Royal Society in 1668. On the third attempt he gained a doctorate in medicine in 1674 and was appointed to a medical studentship at Christ Church. In the 1670s he spent periods in France and drafted his first *Letter Concerning Toleration* and *Essay Concerning Human Understanding*.

Under the influence of Ashley and his friends, Locke's political views became more liberal and he was involved in Whig and Protestant struggles against the power of the king. The first of his *Two Treatises of Government*, probably written in 1681, may be seen as a justification of Shaftesbury's revolutionary movement for a Protestant succession. Shaftesbury fled to Holland in 1682 and, after the Rye House Plot to kidnap the king in which a number of his friends were implicated, Locke followed in 1683. A year later, at the command of Charles II, he was deprived of his studentship at Christ Church.

While in Holland Locke worked at his *Essay*, sending it for publication in 1686. He also wrote letters, later published as *Thoughts Concerning Education*, to his cousin Mary Clarke, wife of Edward Clarke, about the upbringing of her son. He also had contact with William Penn, of whose constitution for Pennsylvania he had criticisms. In 1688 Penn secured a pardon for Locke from James II, which Locke rejected, but he returned to London on the accession of William III in 1689. William offered him more than one ambassadorship, which he refused partly because of his inability to drink as deeply as such a post demanded. Instead he became a commissioner of appeals. His *Essay* was published in 1689 (dated 1690) by Thomas Bassett, who paid him £29 for the privilege. Locke met Isaac *Newton in 1689 and corresponded with him for the rest of his life, mainly on theological matters.

Perhaps Locke's greatest mistake was to dismiss *Leibniz's criticisms as trivial.   PA

Cranston, M. W. (1985). *John Locke: A Biography.*

Locke on the mind. In an early scholarly book on Locke, James Gibson (1917: v) said that it is too often assumed that the *Essay Concerning Human Understanding* 'can be understood without being studied and that its full significance can be summed up in a small number of simple propositions'. This assumption is still made in spite of recent efforts by scholars. Locke is often spoken of as a precursor of modern psychology, but his view of the mind and its influence is seldom studied in detail. It is said that for Locke the mind was a mere passive receptor of sensations, that he espoused a crude *faculty psychology, and that he was an important initiator of associationist psychology. When these allegations are not plainly false they are seriously misleading.

Locke begins by saying (*Essay*, I. i. 1, 2) that the understanding, like the eye, makes us 'see and perceive all other things' but takes no notice of itself; 'Art and Pains' are required to discover its nature. However, he says that he does not intend to enquire into the physical concomitants of the mind or to 'examine wherein its Essence consists'. What he does propose to examine is the relations between the mind and its objects.

A central conception of Locke's philosophy is that of *ideas*. This word is used to refer to various different things, including sensations or sense data, memories, and concepts: when I see a yellow daffodil I am having, *inter alia*, an idea of yellow, when I remember the colour I am having a memory idea of it, and when I think about democracy I am operating with an idea (i.e. concept) of democracy. None of these ideas should be thought of as mental *images*, but an idea *may* be an image. It is usually clear from the context which of these meanings is intended. The term 'idea', Locke says, stands for 'whatsoever is the Object of the Understanding when a Man thinks' or 'whatever it is which the Mind can be employ'd about in thinking' (*Essay*, I. i. 8).

All ideas originate in experience. Locke devotes the whole of Book I to arguing directly against the conception of *innate ideas, and then says that the whole of the rest of the *Essay*, based as it is on the hypothesis that there are no innate ideas, shows that we can do without this conception.

There are two sources of ideas: sensation and reflection. Ideas of sensation occur when we observe external objects, and ideas of reflection when we observe the operations of our minds. Thus we come by ideas of yellow, cold, square, sweet, and of perceiving, believing, willing (II. i. 2–4).

Ideas may be simple or complex. Complex ideas are analysable into, or constructed out of, simple ideas, but simple ideas are unanalysable and unconstructed. The mind is passive in its reception of simple ideas; it cannot prevent simple ideas from being impressed on the mind, or alter them, or choose to have a particular simple idea in the absence of the appropriate stimulus. However, this passivity is limited, and in the reception of simple ideas the mind may be active in attending to, or noticing, different things. The reception of simple ideas is not regarded by Locke as a purely physical process but involves also a mental element, logically distinct from the physical elements. He says that 'in bare naked *Perception*, the *Mind* is, for the most part only passive' (II. ix. 1), but he also says that 'whatever impressions are made on the outward parts, if they are not taken notice of within, there is no Perception' (II. ix. 3). If we are concentrating on a difficult book we may fail to notice even a loud noise and so not receive the idea even though our sense organs are stimulated (II. ix. 4). It is similar with simple ideas of reflection (II. ix. 7, 8).

However, the mind is active in operating upon its ideas as it does in remembering, discriminating, comparing, combining and enlarging, and abstracting them. By *combining* simple ideas the mind makes complex ideas, by *comparing* the mind arrives at ideas of relations, and by *abstracting* them from other ideas with which they occur it makes general ideas (II. xii. 1).

Locke refers to thinking and willing, 'the two great and principal Actions of the Mind', as 'faculties' (II. vi. 2), but he warns us against thinking of them as 'real Beings in the Soul, that perform[ed] those Actions of Understanding and Volition'. They are not separate mental agents each with its own task to perform; it is *the mind* that performs all these actions (II. xxxi. 6).

Locke devotes a whole chapter to 'the association of ideas'. If it is true that this chapter was an important influence on the creators of associationist psychology then it is likely that those creators were among the many who have misunderstood Locke. This chapter, the last in Book II, was included only in the fourth and fifth editions of the *Essay* and the central conception is put to a very limited use: that of explaining one of the ways of going wrong in thinking, which Locke describes as 'a sort of madness'.

The sort of unreasonableness shown by a person who argues obstinately for his view in the face of all the 'evidence of reason' is often thought to result from education, presumably faulty, and prejudice. Locke says,

Education is often rightly assigned for the Cause, and Prejudice is a good general Name for the thing it self: But yet, I think, he ought to look a little farther who would trace this sort of Madness to the root it springs from, and so explain it, as to show whence this flaw has its Original in very sober and rational Minds, and wherein it consists. (II. xxxiii. 3).

Locke calls this 'Madness' because it is 'opposition to reason', which he sees as one, but not the only, form of madness. What particularly concerns him includes arguing from false premises provided by the association of ideas.

Some ideas are 'naturally' connected. An example that he might have given is the ideas of shape and size, which are essential properties of matter. However, besides this 'natural connexion',

there is another Connexion of Ideas wholly owing to Chance or Custom; Ideas that in themselves are not at all of kin, come to be so united in Mens Minds, that 'tis very hard to separate them . . . and the one no sooner at any time comes into the Understanding but its Associate appears with it . . . (II. xxxiii. 5)

Locke then proposes a possible explanation for this which resembles a 'brain-trace' theory (see ENGRAM). Custom may 'settle' trains of motion in the 'animal spirits', 'which once set a going continue on in the same steps they have been used to, which by often treading are worn into a smooth path, and the Motion in it becomes easy and as it were Natural' (II. xxxiii. 6). Thus two ideas may be connected by accident and then, by the strength of the original impression or frequent repetition, appear to be necessarily connected. If an adult is surfeited with honey, the very idea of honey may call up the ideas of dislike and vomiting. He can trace this association to its origin. However, if this happens to a very small child the cause may not be noticed and the child may be thought to have a 'natural antipathy' to honey (II. xxxiii. 7). We should, in educating children, strive to prevent the undue connection of ideas that are in themselves 'loose and independent' of one another. Children may, for example, become afraid of the dark because goblins are, unnaturally, associated with darkness.

Associationism, seen primarily as the attempt to reduce all mental activity, including rational thinking, to the association of ideas, or sensations, is very far from Locke's conception of association. However, other aspects of Locke's philosophy of mind, and matter, might be more plausibly related to one idea of 'mental chemistry' espoused by some associationists. He was greatly influenced in his discussion of physical phenomena by chemistry and the corpuscular hypothesis of Robert Boyle. Locke accepted that physical objects are composed of minute corpuscles having just a few simple, intrinsic, 'primary' qualities, and that the more complex 'secondary' qualities of the physical objects may be explainable in terms of the primary qualities of the constituent corpuscles in their many different arrangements. There are suggestions in Locke's works that if he had gone on to consider mental phenomena in more detail he would have arrived at a view similar to his view about physical phenomena, namely that complex mental states or activities could be analysed into, or explained in terms of, simple mental entities. He does appear to have supposed that there is mental as well as material substance, and he might well have distinguished between primary *mental* qualities (simple) and secondary *mental* qualities (complex). There is a parallelism between the concepts of simple physical corpuscles combined to form complex physical bodies—primary qualities so arranged as to produce secondary qualities—and simple ideas combined to form complex ideas. Applied to mental as well as physical phenomena, this suggests a form of 'mental chemistry', according to which mental compounds may be analysed into simple mental elements, such as sensations (Woodworth 1931). Locke does not, however, show any signs of attributing the combining of ideas involved to *his* conception of the association of ideas; he reserved that for the explanation of the involuntary connecting of ideas and held that the *reliable* connections of ideas were the result of natural or chosen connections (*Essay*, II. xii. 2). There are, of course, problems about what 'natural' means, about how the ideas of natural connections and voluntary connections would relate to one another and to the combining of primary mental qualities to give secondary mental qualities, and how far the analogy with the corresponding physical combinings would hold.   PA

Aaron, R. I. (1971). *John Locke* (3rd edn.).

Alexander, P. (1985). *Ideas, Qualities, and Corpuscles.*

Gibson, J. (1917). *Locke's Theory of Knowledge.*

Locke, J. (1690). *An Essay Concerning Human Understanding* (5th edn. 1706; references in the text above are to the edition of P. H. Nidditch, 1975).

Woodworth, R. S. (1931). *Contemporary Schools of Psychology.*

Loeb, Jacques (1859–1924). German biologist, born in Mayen. Educated in Berlin, Loeb emigrated to America in 1891, and finally became head of the general physiology division of the Rockefeller Institute for Medical Research (1910–24). He worked on comparative physiology, and on artificial parthenogenesis, but he is perhaps best known for his elegant experiments on the 'forced movements' of tropisms in simple animals and for his 'tonus hypothesis' to explain this highly ordered behaviour. The tonus hypothesis is that paired receptors, such as the eyes, send signals to paired muscles which when in balanced tension make the animal move in a straight line either towards the source of the stimulus (positive tropism) or away (negative tropism). Loeb's work on quantifying tropisms, and combining and opposing them to find their relative strengths and interactions, is important in its own right, and it is historically a basis of *behaviourism, as it suggested that there might be simple laws for the behaviour even of higher animals. The tonus hypothesis is now abandoned for even simple animals, and the behaviour of higher animals is not stimulus determined.

Loeb's books include *Dynamics of Living Matter* (1906); *Artificial Parthenogenesis and Fertilisation* (1913); and *Forced Movements, Tropisms, and Animal Conduct* (1918).   RLG

logical positivism. Philosophical school, based on linguistic analysis (to clarify the meanings of statements and questions) and on demands for criteria and procedures of empirical verification (for establishing at least in-principle truth or falsity of statements, by observation or experiment). Logical positivism is essentially a systematic attack on *metaphysics by demanding observations for conferring meaning. Metaphysics is rejected as nonsense. Many positivists (such as Bertrand *Russell) were influenced by the doctrines of 'logical atomism', which claimed that the world is a collection of atomic facts describable by simple propositions, the truth of which is independent of the truth of all other propositions. The positivist analogue of this doctrine is the idea that every basic statement must, in order to be meaningful, be verifiable in isolation. This argument has, however, largely been abandoned, as many clearly important statements in science are not individually verifiable; and it has proved impossible to formulate consistent criteria of verification which are not either too 'weak' (failing to reject metaphysics) or too 'strong' (rejecting important statements in science or other knowledge).

The book which introduced and most clearly formulated logical positivism in the English language is A. J. Ayer, *Language, Truth and Logic* (1936).   RLG

lunacy. The term was originally used to denote an individual subject to intermittent bouts of insanity thought to be influenced by the phases of the moon. According to Hugh Farmer in 1775, in Greek and Roman times it was synonymous with epilepsy, and the evangelist St Matthew also appears to have considered lunacy and epilepsy as one and the same condition (Matthew 17: 15).

In English law, lunacy implied such mental unsoundness as interfered with civil rights and transactions. The word was used in Britain throughout the 19th century in titles of the numerous Bills and Acts brought into Parliament for the regulation of persons suffering from mental illness. The general currency of lunacy and lunatic is shown in the title of a book published in 1850, *Familiar Views of Lunacy and the Lunatic Life*. If, as is probable, the author was Dr John Conolly of Hanwell Asylum, a man with the deepest concern for the welfare of patients committed to his care, evidently he did not consider the book's title to be derogatory but simply an apt description of conditions in his hospital. As time has gone by the words 'lunacy' and 'lunatic' have dropped out of medical parlance, to be replaced by 'mental illness' and 'mental disorder' in the last two 'Lunacy' Acts, the Mental Health Acts of 1959 and 1983.

Luria, Alexander Romanovich (1902–77). Soviet psychologist, probably the only one to become generally known outside the USSR after the Second World War. Born in Kazan of Jewish extraction, Luria was educated at the University of Kazan and graduated in social sciences in spite of his father's wish that he should qualify in medicine, which in fact he did several years later when his career in psychology underwent an unexpected check. His interest in psychology developed rapidly and while still a student he had the temerity to found a psychoanalytic circle in Kazan which he brought to the attention of Sigmund *Freud himself—though later he repudiated psychoanalysis.

In 1925 Luria was appointed to a junior post at the Moscow Institute of Psychology, where, under the direction of N. K. Kornalov, he carried through an ambitious research programme on the effects of emotional stress on human motor reactions recorded under experimental conditions. This work owed something to Ivan *Pavlov's work on experimental neurosis in dogs, though it should be stressed that, while Luria had the highest regard for Pavlov as a physiologist, he never accepted his view that complex human behaviour could ever be satisfactorily explained in terms of reflexes and conditioned reflexes. (His adherence to this view caused him great difficulty in later life and nearly brought his career to an untimely end.) Luria wrote up his experimental findings in a massive book which was published in English translation as *The Nature of Human Conflicts* (1932).

In 1924, Luria had made the acquaintance of Leo Semionovich *Vygotsky, originally a language teacher who deviated to psychology and came to exert a remarkable influence on the younger generation of Soviet psychologists. Although a convinced Marxist, Vygotsky was far from doctrinaire and had wide interests in human development and the role of education and culture in shaping it. Also he developed a lively interest in the effects of nervous disease on human intellectual capacities and was almost certainly responsible for redirecting Luria's interests towards *neuropsychology. He agreed strongly with Luria in deploring Pavlov's rejection of mind and consciousness in the human sciences.

Partly as a result of Vygotsky's influence, Luria successfully qualified in medicine, and in 1941 he was pressed into service as a medical officer with special responsibilities for the assessment and rehabilitation of brain-injured servicemen. His background in psychology, together with a more recently acquired knowledge of linguistics, enabled him to devise some simple, yet effective, methods of assessing deficits in higher psychological capacities and of retraining the patients whenever possible. This work was later transferred to the Institute of Neurosurgery in Moscow, and Luria continued to work there until 1950, when he was summarily dismissed from his post, apparently for ideological reasons, in particular his somewhat feeble enthusiasm for Pavlovian methods and theory. Fortunately, he was restored to his post some years later and was able to return to his neuropsychological studies virtually until his death.

Luria was a prolific writer, many of whose books and scientific papers were translated into English. He visited Britain and the United States on many occasions in the 1950s and 1960s to attend conferences and give lectures, and he made numerous friends in psychological and neurological circles, many of whom visited him in Moscow on occasion and came to know him well. His posthumous autobiography, *The Making of Mind: A Personal Account of Soviet Psychology*, edited by Michael and Sheila Cole (1979), provides a brief but evocative account of his life and work.

Luria's principal books in English translation are *The Nature of Human Conflicts* (trans. W. H. Gantt, 1932), *The Role of Speech in the Regulation of Normal and Abnormal Behaviour* (1961), *Traumatic Aphasia* (trans. B. Haigh, 1970), *Basic Problems in Neurolinguistics* (trans. B. Haigh, 1976), and *Higher Nervous Functions in Man* (2nd edn. trans. B. Haigh, 1980).   OLZ

Homskaya, E. D. (2000). *Alexander Romanovich Luria: A Scientific Biography*. Ed. D. E. Tupper.

Luria on mind and brain. The relation between brain and mind has been for many centuries one of the most difficult problems, both of philosophy and of science. Two approaches to the problem have been proposed—and both have failed. The first was a mentalistic, the second a naturalistic approach.

For many centuries philosophers and other scholars supposed that the brain was a *detector* of mind, which itself was seen as an inner, subjective state of *consciousness. It was supposed that mind was a primary quality of the inner life whereas all external experience could be thought of as a secondary kind, consciousness of self being treated as the immediate existence of the soul. According to this spiritual approach, the brain was merely a device connecting a man's existence with his inner subjective experience, or—as some other scholars thought—with the objective spiritual reality. This theory—now out of date, it seems—persisted in some modern studies: Sir Charles *Sherrington and Sir John Eccles postulated brain units as special kinds of detectors of the spiritual life. It is easy to see, however, that such a theory was not amenable to proof.

The second approach was of a naturalistic kind. Brain was supposed to be the highest product of the natural history of evolution, during which special forms of apparatus of great complexity emerged, resulting in the appearance of internal sensations, memory, and—last but not least—a series of associations that gave rise to the appearance of the most complicated forms of subjective experience. So, it was supposed, very specific groups of nerve cells (neurons) existed, each having some special function, each serving a special purpose to evoke sensations, images, ideas, motives, and voluntary actions. The hope of this group of scholars was to find *special* mechanisms serving to create *special* mental states.

Unfortunately this is not the case: the oversimplified naturalistic hypothesis of cerebral units creating complex subjective images could no more be verified than could the oversimplified mentalistic hypotheses—and all attempts to postulate that sensations, or images, or ideas, could be found in single units of the brain were as unrealistic as trying to find an image inside a mirror or behind it. They originated in archaic notions of mental functions as elementary, primary properties or 'capacities' of the brain. Whereas two or three centuries ago it seemed obvious that sensations and images, thoughts and voluntary impulses were kinds of 'capacities', or immediate functions of specific brain organs—thinking of the brain as a system of specialized 'micro-organs'—such a concept is no longer acceptable. It is better to suppose that mental processes are complex information-processing activities, reflecting reality. Instead, mind is now considered to be a product of active processing of the flow of information working through elementary drives, or complex motives, set to single out important information about reality, relating bits of information and synthesizing them, and constructing plans and programmes of behaviour, which are expressed through speech.

In other words it is implausible to think of the brain as a 'generator of mind'. Quite a different approach to the brain–mind problem is needed. The human brain can be supposed to be a complex working system which consists of different functional blocks or units, every one of which plays a part in reflecting the external world, in complex information processing, in establishing plans and programmes of behaviour, and in conscious control of actions.

It is now known that the deep structures of the brain (the higher brain stem, the old cortex of the *limbic system) have a decisive role in the active state of the cerebral cortex. When this functional system is deranged the activity of the cortex is reduced. A dreamy state is observed, selectivity of the cortical processes is no longer possible, and the first and most important condition for the normal working of the brain—its vigilance—breaks down.

A second functional system, associated with the posterior parts of the cerebral hemispheres, can be considered as the system receiving, preserving, and elaborating information the brain accepts from the external world. This system consists of a series of highly specialized ('modality-specific') units: the occipital lobes dealing with visual, the temporal lobes with acoustic, and the post-central lobes with cutaneous information processing. Each of these parts of the cortex has a clearly organized hierarchical structure. The primary parts are believed to be central receptor devices consisting of highly specialized neurons, which are activated by particular signals (for example, in the primary visual cortex some neurons react to lines of specific orientation, others react to specifically oriented

movement in certain directions, and so on). The combination of single excitations, with the creation of complex patterns reflecting complex features of images, only becomes possible by transition to the secondary parts. Transition to the tertiary parts (which are seen only in the human brain) allows the separate, modality-specific areas of the cortex to work together; a cooperative functioning of different modalities is provided, and successive series of excitations are reorganized into simultaneous spatial (or quasi-spatial) schemes.

A third functional system includes the anterior parts of the human brain—the frontal and prefrontal areas, which are responsible for the retention of stable motives, the establishing of complex plans and programmes of actions, and control of their execution. It is the pinnacle of cerebral organization: when it is deranged, elementary forms of activity can be preserved but there are no stable motives, no goal-directed plans or programmes can be executed, and no higher forms of action control, including language, are possible.

Thus the cooperative working of the different systems of the brain supplies humans with information processing, provides active and plastic adaptation to the immediate environment, and links human conduct to particular goals. It is a complex of functional systems, organized according to plans and programmes created by man's social history. As an alternative to both mentalistic and naturalistic theories, such a concept provides a significant step towards analysis of the intimate mechanisms of the brain as an organ of mind.   ARL

Luria, A. R. (1966). *Higher Cortical Functions in Man.*
——(1972). *The Working Brain.*
——(1976). *Basic Problems of Neurolinguistics.*
Magoun, M. H. (1963). *The Waking Brain.*
Walter, W. G. (1953). *The Living Brain.*
Young, J. Z. (1978). *Programs of the Brain.*

Luria on reductionism. For a very long time reductionism remained the generally accepted philosophical aim of the natural sciences as well as of psychology. It was supposed that the basic goal of science is to reduce complex phenomena to separate simple parts, and that such reduction provides significant explanations of phenomena.

Reductionism had its origin in the middle of the 19th century, and in biology it was closely associated with Rudolf Virchow's cellular anatomy and pathology, which supposed that the organism is a complex of organs—and the organs a complex of cells. So to explain basic laws of the living organism we have to study as carefully as possible the features of separate cells.

The same principle of reductionism was seen in psychology. It was supposed that the basic goal of the behavioural sciences is to reduce the whole wealth of human behaviour to associations of separate elementary events.

This was the aim of *Pavlovian physiology and also the direction of *behaviourism, which tried to reduce behaviour to the simple laws of conditioning.

Although the philosophy of reductionism was accepted as a general principle in the natural sciences and psychology, there are grounds to suppose it may be false.

To study a phenomenon, or an event, and to explain it, one has to preserve all its basic features: one must be able to describe their rules and their mechanisms without the loss of any individual characteristics. It can easily be seen that reductionism may very soon conflict with this goal. One can reduce water (H_2O) into H and O, but—as is well known—H (hydrogen) burns and O (oxygen) is necessary for burning, whereas water (H_2O) has neither the first nor the second quality. This is why the outstanding Soviet psychologist Leo *Vygotsky stated that reduction can only be done up to certain limits. In order not to lose the basic features of water, one must split it into *units* (H_2O), not into *elements* (H and O). The same is true for the psychological analysis of human conscious behaviour.

Although this may seem obvious, psychology as a science followed, for many decades, a different line. During the period of associationist psychology, it was supposed that all forms of mental processes could be reduced to simple sensations (or ideas) and their associations. Even after *Gestalt psychology had made its well-known criticisms of the associationist point of view, the basic tenets of reductionism did not change: the only difference was that the Gestalt group of psychologists continued their attempts to reduce complex mental phenomena to physical or quasi-physical Gestalts, which were larger elements than single sensations or associations. It remained evident that the wealth and diversity of mental events was being lost through expression in the too-generalized terms of Gestalt psychology, just as it had been in the former associationist theory. This situation remained unchanged in the 20th century, when attempts were made to reduce complex forms of man's conscious behaviour to conditioned reflexes (see CONDITIONING), or to overgeneralized laws of conditioning.

Of course, human behaviour can be reduced to reflexes and their combinations; and general rules of conditioning are often supposed to be the most elementary rules for establishing new forms of connection. But it is evident as well that a reduction of human conscious behaviour to these 'elements' does not preserve the whole wealth of conscious behaviour. This means that the procedure of such kinds of reductionism is futile, and that real 'units' of conscious behaviour have to be found, which can preserve all the richness of the behaviour while at the same time pointing out models for it which can be the subject of an accurate study. Now we come to the basic question: what can serve as a real *model* of human conscious behaviour, as the 'unit' that includes all its essential qualities?

Vygotsky supposed that higher mental processes are of a social origin, and that the basic unit of human conscious behaviour is not to be found in unconditional or conditional reflexes (the latter being rather general physiological 'elements', not psychological 'units' which preserve all the essential features of conscious actions). He suggested that the simplest form of such behaviour can be found in tool or sign using, where a tool (or a sign) can be used to reach a certain goal. Instead of the elementary scheme of $S \rightarrow R$ ('S' for stimulus, 'R' for reflex), he proposed a new scheme, $S \downarrow x \uparrow R$, where S stands for stimulus or situation, x for means (tool or sign), and R for reaction. Some decades later this scheme was improved, and a new component—that of feedback (see CYBERNETICS, HISTORY OF)—was added. This provides the formula $S \downarrow x \uparrow R$, essential for a self-regulating system.

This assumption changed significantly the general philosophy of reductionism. New components were added. Instead of attempting to reduce complex psychological phenomena to biological (or physiological) 'elements', a new method was proposed—to step outside the organism itself and to try to find the basic units of human conscious behaviour in the relation of the subject with the social environment, treating these *relations* as an essential feature of human mental processes.

Such an attempt radically altered the classical attitude of reductionist philosophy. The goal of psychology became not to try to explain the essence of complex phenomena by reducing them to elementary parts, but rather to find *new relations* in which the organism is involved. This became the ultimate goal of science. The more of these essential relations that can be found, the closer we come to the whole wealth of the phenomenon, and to its explanation. *The explanation of the phenomenon is supposed to lie not in its reduction to single elements but rather in its inclusion in a rich net of essential relations.*

This attitude has basic significance for every science, and for psychology especially. It is the way Marx calls 'ascending to the concrete', as opposed to the classical way of 'ascending to the abstract', based on singling out definite features and progressing to more and more general categories, such as 'dog' (opposed to 'cat')→'tame animal' ('wild animal')→'animal' ('plant')→'living being' ('inanimate nature')→'natural' ('unnatural')→'something' (as opposed to 'nothing'). Such a way of 'ascending to abstractness', a kind of inverted reductionism, inevitably leads to an overgeneralized nullity, in which the whole richness of concrete events is lost. The way of 'ascending to the concrete', i.e. the inclusion of the event in a rich net of relations, preserves the whole complexity of events, while at the same time revealing new and essential relations and thus providing the most important steps to the discovery of the *essence* of the phenomenon or the event, as opposed to its scientific explanation.

It may be supposed that such a method can serve as an alternative to dry reductionism, and that it can open new and productive ways for the scientific analysis of human conscious behaviour.   ARL

Leontiev, A. N. (1959). *Problems of Mental Development*. (In Russian.)
—— (1979). *Activity; Consciousness; Personality*. (In Russian.)
Vygotsky, L. S. (1956). *Selected Psychological Studies*. (In Russian.)
—— (1960). *Development of the Higher Mental Functions*. (In Russian.)
—— (1962). *Thought and Language*.

Luria on speech and brain processes. Natural speech is a communication of information by means of the codes of language. This means that, to communicate, man has to have a definite motive or intention (knowing what and why he has to communicate) and to use for his purposes a particular language, its phonemic, lexical, and syntactic codes (the last relating to the question of *how* to communicate).

Systems of language can have different complexities. It was the Swedish linguist Svedelins (1897) who described two basically different classes of verbal communication: *communication of events* ('The house is burning', 'The boy hit a dog') and *communication of relations* ('Socrates is a man', 'That is the father's brother', 'Mary is fairer than Cathy', 'The triangle under the circle', etc.). These basic kinds of verbal communication are different both in content and in linguistic structure. Communication of events can be represented in concrete images; communication of relations cannot. Communication of events can use comparatively simple forms of linguistic codes; for the communication of relations, more complex linguistic codes are required, including complex case markers and auxiliary words that express relations ('on', 'under', 'before', 'after', etc.). In the communication of relations, special grammatical codes (incorporation of one phrase into another, relational means, inversion, etc.) can be used as well.

These basic linguistic differences in the two forms of verbal communication are related to different psychological structures. The first class of constructions (which is most typical for the communication of events) is associated with an (immediate) sequence of words which constitutes a phrase. This kind of construction can be considered as a *syntagmatic* type, which is sometimes quite simple, and does not necessarily require any transformation for understanding. Communication of relations generally requires more complex grammatical rules and includes a kind of *paradigmatic* organization (Jakobson 1971). The process of decoding these structures (or their understanding) very often requires a certain transformation, and the meaning of this form of logico-grammatical communication often becomes clear only after such transformations have been performed. So, the understanding of the construction 'brother's father' requires a chain of transformations and a series of additional grammatical or semantic markers, such as: 'That is my brother. He has a father. His father is my father too'; while the understanding of the construction 'Mary is fairer than Cathy' requires analogous transformations: 'Cathy is fair; but Mary is even more fair; so she is fairer than Cathy', etc. The loading with these additional transformations is much greater for communicating relations than events.

The most important fact observed in *neuropsychology (i.e. in the analysis of the changes of psychological processes associated with local brain lesions) is that the two kinds of verbal communication require different cortical mechanisms, and are based on different cortical systems. In cases where the lesion is situated in posterior ('gnostic') parts of the brain, acquisition of the language codes suffers: both the production and the understanding of paradigmatically organized verbal utterances become difficult, sometimes even impossible, whereas fluent, syntagmatically organized speech remains preserved. This is why patients who are unable consciously to make all the transformations needed for the understanding of complex linguistic structures remain able to use these forms in practice. They are unable to decode the construction 'father's brother' but are still able to include it in a practically preserved syntagmatic system, saying: 'Oh, well, that's my father's brother.' The breakdown of one of the levels (phonemic, lexical, or logico-grammatical) of paradigmatically organized language codes is typical of verbal disorders associated with lesions of the posterior parts of the speech regions of the left hemisphere; in all these cases, practical fluent speech, expressing communication of events or well-imprinted syntagmatic structures, remains basically preserved; that is why these forms of language impairment are called 'fluent aphasias' (see APHASIA).

Conversely, damage to the anterior parts of the 'speech areas' of the left hemisphere results in the opposite kind of deterioration of language. The performance needed for the acquisition of language codes (phonemic, lexical, logico-grammatical) and the systems of opposition these codes include remains basically intact, but the combination of words into fluent sequential (syntagmatic) structures, as well as all kinds of 'kinetic melodies' included in skilled movements, breaks down. This is why patients of this group can easily grasp phonemic oppositions, lexical meanings, and even paradigmatically organized structures—while fluent speech becomes impossible, and may be replaced by separate naming of objects, taking the form of 'telegraphic style'.

The basic brain mechanisms underlying these two forms of verbal utterance are not sufficiently clear, but it seems very probable that the posterior parts of the human brain are associated with the process of transformation of successively arriving information in simultaneous (spatial or quasi-spatial) schemes, whereas the anterior parts of the brain deal with the 'serial organization' of the processes providing skilled movements or successively organized 'kinetic melodies'. This is why a breakdown of the posterior, 'gnostic' regions of the cortex results in a derangement of the acquisition of complex, paradigmatically organized codes of language, while a breakdown of the anterior parts of the cortex (in both cases, of the major hemisphere) results in disturbance of 'serial organization' of the processes, and in a breakdown of syntagmatic organization of verbal utterances.   ARL

Jakobson, R. (1971). *Kindersprache und Aphasie.*

Luria, A. R. (1966). *Higher Cortical Functions in Man.*

——(1970). *Traumatic Aphasia.*

——(1972). *The Working Brain.*

——(1976). *Basic Problems of Neurolinguistics.*

Svedelins, C. (1897). *L'Analyse du langage.*

Lyceum. The name of the gymnasium and covered garden adjacent to the temple of Apollo Lyceus in Athens where Aristotle taught his students.

lying and deception. Three criteria are commonly cited as being relevant to a statement being classified as a lie: the statement is false, its producer believes it to be false, and it is intended that others believe it to be true. When all three conditions are met, there is near consensus among adults, but the label is also applied by some people when fewer criteria are met. Further, and as is frequent with words, metaphorical extensions and other rhetorical devices permit it to be used informatively even where no words are uttered, but deception is present. There are of course a multitude of ways in which statements can depart from informative cooperative truthfulness without them becoming lies, and often these evasions are designed to avoid the condemnation that is associated with accusations of telling lies. A lie by any other name can smell much sweeter; a clever deception can be an occasion for praise. This is but one of the paradoxes and myths that render lying and deceit such fascinating psychological and sociological activities to study.

Language is used directly by people for controlling and signalling many states and social activities in which questions of truth and falsity do not arise, but in its representational function truthfulness is the *raison d'être* of a language-based communication system. Conveying useful information from one person to another about 'facts' is the essence of this extraordinary human invention. Lying is therefore parasitic upon general truthfulness, and if its incidence becomes too high the system becomes useless. At the sociological level, governments of the so-called Western democracies seem to be ignoring the fable about the little boy calling 'Wolf!' when none was present in their concern to 'spin' appearances about the realities within and beyond their countries (see below), but then their priorities may be to survive and win rather than to inform.

In the wider Darwinian struggle for survival and reproduction, not becoming the food of other creatures too soon is a crucial achievement, and one of the protective devices that has developed is camouflage. In turn, successful predators have also been selected for characteristics that keep them hidden from their prey. The other common form of deception is the polar opposite of appearing to be much more dangerous than is the case. Not all black and yellow wasps and flies are armed with stings, and in inter-male conflicts for mating with females, what is only apparently powerful weaponry may see off the competition. Whilst these forms of deception lack the agentive and linguistic components of lying, they serve as a reminder that living is a competitive activity and that deception is a ubiquitous feature of inter- and intra-species activities.

Throughout human history the same rules have applied. Both camouflage and apparent strength have served to facilitate survival and to gain power, wealth, and status within human groups. In intergroup conflicts and especially fighting, being able to hide from or bluff the enemy has always been useful, whilst the additional human capacities for deceiving the enemy as to one's intentions, strategies, and tactics have often been the basis for victory. With the invention of new modes and media of communication in recent centuries, lies under the title of 'disinformation' have become a major adjunct to military operations.

The same principles apply to competitive activities within societies (Robinson 1996). Successful commercial negotiations may well be underpinned by bluffing, and certainly successful marketing relies on buyers paying greater attention to the strengths and desirability of products than to their weaknesses and disadvantages. Advertisements are rightly notorious for their product-favouring biases and falsification. Caveat emptor. Government-appointed regulatory bodies seemingly do little to ensure honesty of wordings, but then governments themselves are perceived as among the worst offenders. In both the UK and the USA national surveys have shown dramatic declines over the last twenty years in the perceived trustworthiness of many institutional authorities and their personnel: governments, politicians, civil servants, 'big business', the media, the police, and lawyers, among others. Lying by some members of these categories is seen as being frequent, while particular types of recent examples of such falsifications have been judged as wrong by upwards of 85 per cent of people surveyed. 'Sleaze' and 'spin' are two words that have been added to notions of cover-ups to refer to such activities.

Granted that lying by some other name appears to be endemic among authorities in several social orders, and that the public condemns this, it does little if anything to change the norms, and is itself not immune to deceiving authorities. If all pleas of 'Not guilty' in courts of law were true, then prisons would be less overcrowded. There is a sense that, in the course of trials, jury members have to weigh the relative dishonesty of witnesses for the prosecution and defence. People may not use the word 'lie' to refer to false insurance claims, dishonest Inland Revenue returns, phoney benefit claims, unjustified paid sickness leave, or trading in the 'black economy', but estimates of the incidence of losses to society from these add up to billions of pounds per year. Ironically, of those listed, lying to obtain benefits fraudulently attracts the most publicity and condemnation, whilst probably being the least costly to the taxpayers.

Neither the conduct of authorities nor that of the public can be construed as anything other than displaying a propensity to lying and deception as soon as threats to power, wealth, or status or opportunities for advancing these occur, and similar tendencies, along with justificatory biases and rationalizations, appear in interpersonal behaviour as well. Valid empirical evidence is difficult to collect, but lying is almost certainly a daily act for most people. People generally believe that others lie more than they do, and that strangers lie more than their friends and relatives do. Most of the lies are told within close relationships, and many are classed by the tellers as trivial. Estimates from diary-type recordings depend heavily on the honesty and conscientiousness of the participants, as do the reasons they may give during debriefings (Tornqvist, et al. 2001). Results are also confounded by the varieties of definitions of lying used; lies to avoid punishment or loss of face or to gain advantages can be mixed in with 'white lies', told out of consideration for the feelings of others. Our societies have invented social norms of politeness which require falsification to preserve or enhance the 'face' of others. No deception may be intended and none experienced. A more sinister variant, however, is when powerful persons lie to or about subordinates, who can be accused of rudeness or even libel, if they challenge the lies. False claims of credit for the successes of subordinates and false blaming of them for failures are a major concern of junior staff in organizations. Although the idea of lying to oneself might be treated as a rational impossibility,

under the title of 'delusions' self-deception is a widespread practice as evidenced in Taylor's (1989) review of the extent to which people exaggerate the positive features of themselves and their lives.

In evolutionary and developmental terms there is some evidence of intentional deception among chimpanzees and young children learn to deceive before they learn to lie. Pretend play is cited as one likely context for the beginnings of deception and lying, and lying itself may well arise accidentally in the first instance with its success being the occasion for children to learn its value. Although socialized into the rule to tell the truth, they subsequently have to learn when this rule should not be followed if they are to fit into the social norms of their culture. They are also told that their lies can be detected, but learn that this is not so. To date little has been done to find out precisely how lying itself comes into the child's repertoire of skills or how learning to lie affects other developments; both issues could prove to be fascinating and informative (Robinson 1996).

Lie detection has its mythology. The USA has over 10,000 people trained to interpret the recordings of the polygraph—the lie detector. Unfortunately this faith in technology has little empirical support; rates of false positives and of false negatives show the validity to be much too low for accurate individual assessment. The success of liars in court and elsewhere, and the difficulties of uncovering enemy agents, show that both amateurs and professionals can outwit current technology. The latest ideas are that lying may be shown up by microanalysis or heat sensors of muscle movements below the eyes (Vrij 2001). Ordinary people have beliefs about symptoms of lying, but, as Ekman (1992) has shown, the cultural stereotypes are a mix of invalid cues and weak indicators. Statistically, there are combinations of cues that may be indicative of lying, but they are too weak to permit judgements in individual cases.

The *Penguin Book of Lies* (Kerr 1990) offers an excellent Cook's tour of issues of definition and morality, along with accounts of some of the more famous historical examples.

PRo

Ekman, P. (1992). *Telling Lies*.

Kerr, A. (ed.) (1990). *The Penguin Book of Lies*.

Robinson, W. P. (1996). *Deceit, Delusion and Detection*.

Taylor, S. (1989). *Positive Illusions*.

Tornqvist, J. S., Anderson, E., and DePaulo, B. M. (2001). 'Deceiving'. In Robinson, W. P., and Giles, H. (eds.), *New Handbook of Language and Social Psychology*.

Vrij. A. (2001). *Detecting Lies and Deceit*.

M

McCulloch, Warren Sturgis (1898–1968). As a young man, Warren McCulloch set himself the goal of developing an *experimental epistemology*, to understand the mind in terms of the brain. More particularly, he sought to discover the logical calculus immanent in nervous activity. When America joined the First World War McCulloch moved as an undergraduate to Yale University where he joined the navy's Officers' Training Program. From the First World War navy he learned of what he refers to as *redundancy of potential command*. In a naval battle, there are many ships widely separated at sea and normally command rests in the ship with the admiral. But, if some fighting breaks out or some crucial information becomes available locally, then temporarily the ship that has that information is the one with command.

The study of philosophy was especially important for the young McCulloch. In his study of Descartes, McCulloch found examples of feedback in the nervous system and temporal coding of impulses. Kant's notion of the synthetic a priori got McCulloch thinking about how to connect a priori with knowledge the senses provide about everyday experience. Given this background, McCulloch determined to equip himself to understand the physical nature of perception and thought, and obtained his MD in 1927. Ideas about reflexes dominated analysis of the nervous system at that time but he came upon various neurological conditions, such as the constant pain of causalgia, for which he felt reverberating loops of neurons provided the best explanation. In 1934, McCulloch moved to Yale to do functional neuroanatomy with Dusser de Barenne but he continued to ask 'What could be the logic of the brain?'. Given *Whitehead and *Russell's attempt in *Principia mathematica* to reduce all the complexity of number down to logical propositions, McCulloch wondered if one could then see how to map logical propositions into the brain. He was stymied by loops of neurons—if you negate something as you go around the loop then the input must equal its negation, and how can that be? The solution that eventually came to him was to introduce a delay between the input and output of each neuron.

In 1941 McCulloch moved to Chicago, and then to Massachusetts Institute of Technology (MIT) in 1952, where he remained until his death in 1968. In Chicago he met an amazing young man named Walter Pitts who worked with the mathematical logician Rudolf Carnap and so saw how to apply Carnap's formalism to McCulloch's ideas about the logic of the nervous system. The result was 'A logical calculus of the ideas immanent in nervous activity' (McCulloch and Pitts 1943). The paper presented nets of formal neurons, showing how different patterns of excitatory and inhibitory connections forming neurons into loops could realize a great variety of different functions. Basically, McCulloch and Pitts proved that any finite-state control box for a Turing machine could be replaced by a network of their formalized neurons. And so, in a way, one can say that Turing provided the 'Psychology of the Computable' whereas McCulloch and Pitts provided the 'Physiology of the Computable'.

Pitts and McCulloch (1947) studied 'How we know universals: the perception of auditory and visual forms' and is a classic in the study of pattern recognition. This paper extends in three ways the 1943 ideas of building networks: one was to go back to the neuroanatomy and see that the brain is not a random network, but is structured and layered; the second was to think more subtly about perception; while the third was to show how visual input could control motor output via the distributed activity of a layered neural network without the intervention of executive control, perhaps the earliest example of 'cooperative computation'.

One of the classics of single-cell neurophysiology, 'What the frog's eye tells the frog's brain' (Lettvin et al. 1959), is acknowledged to be an outgrowth of 'How we know universals', even though the processes found in frog tectum are not those predicted for mammalian cortex. What the latter paper did confirm, however, were the notions that (*a*) an important method of coding information in the brain is by topographically organized activity distributed over layers of neurons, and (*b*) computation may be carried out in a distributed way by a collection of neurons without the intervention of a central executive, while adding the finding that (*c*) the retina begins the process of transformation that extracts from the visual input information that is relevant to the action of the organism (in this case, the frog's need to get food and evade predators).

More specifically, the physiologist Lettvin and the anatomist Maturana showed that if you measure activity of frog retinal ganglion cells, then there will be basically four kinds of feature detectors—dimming detectors, small moving object detectors, and so on—and that their axons end in four different layers of the optic tectum of the midbrain. We see here a prime example of the importance of distributed computation mediated by topographically organized activity distributed over layers. Their work also shows that the retina processes information in a species-specific way relevant to specific jobs like turning to catch flies and avoid enemies. We now know that the story is not that simple—the frog needs the rest of its brain, too!—but this paper does add tremendously important ideas to our thinking about the brain. Moreover, the work tied to McCulloch's interest in Kant's synthetic a priori by showing that in some sense the frog's retina demonstrated a 'biological a priori' adapted to the frog's ecological niche.

In the 1960s, McCulloch worked with Bill Kilmer to model the reticular formation, inspired by the findings that: (i) you can transform a person from sleep to wakefulness by appropriate patterns of activity in the reticular core of the brain stem; (ii) the anatomy of the reticular system could be approximated by a stack of 'poker chips' each comprising neurons with overlapping or adjacent dendrites sampling, hopefully, roughly the same information. These ideas grounded a computational model, RETIC, which contains an array of modules corresponding to the poker chips, with each getting a different sample of the sensory input, with some communication up and down the neuraxis (Kilmer, McCulloch, and Blum 1969). Each module, with its limited sample of sensory input, makes a tentative initial 'vote', setting a confidence level for each mode. The modules then communicate in such a way that, if the votes that a particular module has for the different modes of behaviour are roughly similar, they have relatively little effect on the neighbours. But if, on the other hand, one module had a much stronger vote for one mode than another, then the neighbours it talked to would accept that as meaningful information and would shift their votes in that direction. The idea goes back to that First World War form of naval command: the module (or ship or person) which has the crucial current information temporarily has command. We are thus encouraged to think of the brain not as a hierarchy but rather as a heterarchy in which many different modules communicate with each other, such that temporary coalitions dominate the overall behaviour as appropriate.

The 1943 paper is the most famous paper by McCulloch and Pitts, and has been incredibly influential, due to its basic idea that, not to get too technical, any 'finite enough' specification of what is to be done can be realized by some McCulloch–Pitts network. One line of influence was through its shaping effect on John *Von Neumann who developed the stored-program logic of the computing machines that emerged as one of the new technologies of the Second World War. In the Von Neumann tradition, techniques of switching theory were developed to design

explicitly as needed a McCulloch–Pitts network that would do a particular job as part of a computer. Here, the framework is one of 'logical design'. The other line of influence stems from the challenge which was met by Frank Rosenblatt building on ideas of Donald Hebb and laying the basis for the modern topic of 'connectionism'. In this approach, given some 'finite enough' job, rather than just simply saying there is a logical circuit to do it, the connections between the formal neurons change automatically by some learning rule on the basis of experience, so that a sufficiently large network can be trained to perform the given job increasingly well over time. Here, notions of 'approximation' and 'optimization' seem more important than whether or not neurons can be described by a logical calculus.

However, although the 1943 paper has been incredibly influential in the history of computation and the development of connectionism, many a computational neuroscientist may lament the paper's simplicities. Neurons have complex dendrites and neuromodulation and calcium channels and many other properties. But McCulloch knew that. He never claimed that the 1943 model exhausted the richness of individual neurons, and even our brief sample above shows that much of his later work was devoted to coming up with more subtle (but certainly not biophysical or neurochemical) models of the neuron. None the less, he and Pitts had shown that 'anything finite enough' that could be logically conceived could be done by a neural network. They had killed dualism! Until then, there was no convincing argument for the idea that logical thought could be done by a brain since the working out of neurophysiological detail was mostly at the level of reflexes and things of this kind. Theirs is a tremendous achievement.

In this sense, Warren McCulloch's search for the logic of the nervous system was successful. Yet, in some sense, the 1943 paper was the apogee of that search, expressing neural activity in a logical calculus. In such contributions as 'How we know universals', 'What the frog's eye tells the frog's brain', and 'A model of the vertebrate central command system' the ability of neural networks to solve the organism's problems in interacting with a complex and ambiguous world are elucidated using a variety of concepts—feature detectors, averaging, decision making without executive control, etc.—which are not directly rooted in a specific logical calculus. In my opinion, these 'alogical' contributions have the most to say for the development of computational neuroscience, while the 'logical calculus' has the greater philosophical importance but has contributed more to computer science than to neuroscience.   MAA

Arbib, M. A. (2000). 'Warren McCulloch's search for the logic of the nervous system'. *Perspectives in Biology and Medicine*, 43.
Heims, S. J. (1991). *The Cybernetics Group*.

McCulloch's contributions to brain theory

Kilmer, W. L., McCulloch, W. S., and Blum, J. (1969). 'A model of the vertebrate central command system'. *International Journal of Man–Machine Studies*, I.

Lettvin, J. Y. (1989). 'McCulloch and Walter'. In McCulloch, R. (ed.), *Collected Works of Warren S. McCulloch*.

——Maturana, H., McCulloch, W. S., and Pitts, W. H. (1959). 'What the frog's eye tells the frog's brain'. *Proceedings of the IRE*, 47.

McCulloch, R. (1989). 'Foreword'. In McCulloch, R. (ed.), *Collected Works of Warren S. McCulloch*.

McCulloch, W. S. (1974). 'Recollections of the many sources of cybernetics'. *ASC Forum*, 6/2.

——and Pitts, W. H. (1943). 'A logical calculus of the ideas immanent in nervous activity'. *Bulletin of Mathematical Biophysics*, 5.

Pitts, W. H., and McCulloch, W. S. (1947). 'How we know universals: the perception of auditory and visual forms'. *Bulletin of Mathematical Biophysics*, 9.

McCulloch's contributions to brain theory. Warren *McCulloch was a central pioneer figure of cybernetic and computational models of brain function. The year 1943 saw the publication of 'A logical calculus of the ideas immanent in nervous activity' by McCulloch and Walter Pitts, in which they offered their formal model of the neuron as a threshold logic unit, building on the neuron doctrine of *Ramón y Cajal and the excitatory and inhibitory synapses of *Sherrington.

A major stimulus for their work was the *Turing machine, an imagined device which could read, write, and move upon an indefinitely extendable tape each square of which bore a symbol from some finite alphabet. Alan Turing (1936) had made plausible the claim that any effectively definable computation (i.e. anything that a human could do in the way of symbolic manipulation by following a finite and completely explicit set of rules (in 1936 the referent of 'computer' was still a human!)) could be carried out by such a machine equipped with a suitable program. What McCulloch and Pitts demonstrated was that each such program could be implemented using a finite network, with loops, of their formal neurons.

In another classic paper, 'How we know universals: the perception of auditory and visual forms', Pitts and McCulloch (1947) sought 'general methods for designing nervous nets which recognize figures in such a way as to produce the same output for every input belonging to the figure'—just as we recognize a figure such as a square, despite changes in position or size.

Thus they sought to explain how we know universals. Lettvin et al. (1959) turned to the frog for experimental answers to the questions set by the earlier paper, noting that the frog is normally motionless, and that its visually guided behaviour can be adequately described in terms of recognition of two universals, *prey* and *enemy*. (Subsequent research has complicated this picture considerably —Fite 1976.) Lettvin et al. (1959) found that the majority of the axons of the frog's retinal ganglion cells could be classified into one of four groups, on the basis of their response to visual stimuli, and that moreover the axons of the four groups ended in four distinct layers of the tectum (part of the frog's midbrain), with the four layers being in registration, in that vertically arranged cells in the tectum would signal the presence or absence of the four features in the same region of the visual field. The four feature detectors described in this celebrated paper, 'What the frog's eye tells the frog's brain', were:

(i) *Sustained contrast detectors* yield a prompt and prolonged discharge whenever the sharp edge of an object, either lighter or darker than the background, moves into its receptive field and stops there (or appears there when light is turned on).

(ii) *Net convexity detectors* respond to a small or convex edge of a large dark object passed through the visual field; the response does not outlast the passage; a smooth motion across the visual field has less effect than a jerky one.

(iii) *Moving-edge detectors* respond to any distinguishable edge moving through its receptive field.

(iv) *Net dimming detectors* respond to sudden reduction of illumination by a prolonged and regular discharge.

The essential point of this is that 'the eye speaks to the brain in a language already highly organized and interpreted, instead of transmitting some more or less accurate copy of the distribution of light on the receptor' (Lettvin et al. 1959: 1950). Further, the encoding is such as to aid the frog in finding food and evading predators—in recognizing the universals *prey* and *enemy*.

We now turn to McCulloch's consideration of the question 'How is the central nervous system structured to allow coordinated action of the whole animal when different regions receive contradictory local information?'. McCulloch suggested that the answer lay in the *principle of redundancy of potential command*, which states, essentially, that command should pass to the region with the most important information. He cited the example of a naval fleet, where the behaviour of the whole (First World War) naval fleet is controlled at least temporarily by signals from whichever ship first sights the enemy— the point being that this ship need not be the flagship, in which command normally resides. McCulloch suggested that this redundancy of potential command in vertebrates would find its clearest expression in the reticular formation (RF) of the brain stem. W. L. Kilmer and McCulloch then made the following contributions toward building a model of RF. First, they noted that at any one time an animal is in only one of some twenty or so gross *modes* of behaviour (e.g. sleeping, eating, grooming, mating), and they suggested that the main role of the core of the RF (or at least the role they sought to model) was to commit the organism to one of these modes. Secondly they noted that anatomical data (of the Scheibels, 1958) suggested that RF need not be modelled neuron by neuron, but could instead be considered as a stack of 'poker chips', each containing tens of thousands of neurons, and each with its own nexus of sensory information. Thirdly they posited that each module ('poker chip') could decide which mode was most appropriate to its own nexus of information, and then asked: 'How can the modules be coupled so that, in real time, a consensus can be reached as to the mode appropriate to the overall sensory input, despite conflicting mode indications from local inputs to different modules?'

In this framework, Kilmer, McCulloch, and Blum (1969) designed and simulated a model, called S-RETIC, of a system to compute mode changes, comprising a column of modules that differed only in their input array, and that were interconnected in a way suggested by RF anatomy, as the anatomy was at that time described.

The overall effect of the scheme is to decouple the modules initially, after an input change, in order to accentuate each 'poker chip's' evaluation of what the next mode should be, and then through successive iterations to couple them back together, in order to reach a global consensus. Computer simulation showed that S-RETIC, at least with the coupling patterns they studied, would converge for every input in less than 25 cycles, and that once it had converged it would stay converged for a given input. When the inputs strongly indicate one mode, convergence is fast, but when the indication is weak, initial conditions and circuit characteristics play an important role. Although the anatomical picture of S-RETIC has now changed, this is the start of the important concept of 'cooperative computation' for brain function.

Let us now briefly examine the general implications of these papers for brain theory. For Pitts and McCulloch, the point of their model of the superior colliculus (the mammalian analogue of the frog's tectum) was that it gave an implementation of their conceptual scheme that did justice to neurophysiological data. However, the scheme has far greater significance than this, for it shows how to design a *somatotopically organized network in which there is no 'executive neuron' that decrees which way the overall system behaves; rather, the dynamics of the effectors, with assistance from neuronal interactions, extracts the output trajectory from a population of neurons, none of which has more than local information as to which way the system should behave. In other words, the Pitts and McCulloch model of the superior colliculus showed how 'the organism can be committed to an overall action by a population of neurones none of which had global information as to which action is appropriate'. This is the organization (and sometimes disorganization!) of a democracy. The study of cooperative computation in

somatotopically organized networks now provides a central paradigm of brain function.   MAA/RLG

Apter, J. (1945). 'The projection of the retina on the superior colliculus of cats'. *Journal of Neurophysiology*, 8.
——(1946). 'Eye movements following strychninization of the superior colliculus of cats'. *Journal of Neurophysiology*, 9.
Fite, K. V. (1976). *The Amphibian Visual System*.
Kilmer, W. L., McCulloch, W. S., and Blum, J. (1969). 'A model of the vertebrate central command system'. *International Journal of Man–Machine Studies*, 1.
Lettvin, J. Y., Maturana, H., McCulloch, W. S., and Pitts, W. H. (1959). 'What the frog's eye tells the frog's brain'. *Proceedings of the Institute of Radio Engineers*, 47.
Pitts, W. H., and McCulloch, W. S. (1947). 'How we know universals: the perception of auditory and visual forms'. *Bulletin of Mathematical Biophysics*, 9.
Scheibel, A. B., and Scheibel, M. E. (1958). 'Structural substrates for integrative patterns in the brain stem reticular core'. In Jasper, H., et al. (eds.), *Reticular Formation of the Brain*.
Turing, A. M. (1936). 'On computable numbers with an application to the Entscheidungs-problem'. *Proceedings of the London Mathematical Society*, ser. 2, 42.

McDougall, William (1871–1938). British psychologist, born in Lancashire. After studying at Weimar, Manchester, and Cambridge, he became a medical student at St Thomas's Hospital, London. In 1898 he accompanied an important anthropological expedition to the Torres Strait. Having held the Wilde readership in mental philosophy at Oxford from 1904 to 1920, he emigrated to America, going first to Harvard, and then, in 1927, to Duke University, North Carolina.

McDougall rejected *behaviourism and made *purpose the centre of his philosophy of psychology. He wrote extensively and was very widely read. Of particular interest are *Body and Mind* (1911), *Outlines of Psychology* (1923), *The Energies of Man* (1933), and *An Outline of Abnormal Psychology* (1926), which has an account of hypnosis. McDougall held a theory of mind involving monads, somewhat similar to *Spinoza and *Leibniz (see LEIBNIZ'S PHILOSOPHY OF MIND). He suggested that the mind is a kind of interacting network of monads linked by telepathy, and that brain damage can have little effect provided these links remain. His hydraulic analogies of purpose were taken over by the early ethologists. Late in life, McDougall espoused *Lamarckianism, carrying out with an assistant (who probably falsified the results) experiments in which rats' tails were cut off to demonstrate inheritance of an acquired characteristic. These experiments damaged his reputation, but his books remain worth reading today for their clarity and verve. The significance of some of his concepts for current thinking is well brought out by Margaret Boden in *Purposive Explanation in Psychology* (1972). In particular, his account of *emotions as the experience of thwarted drives remains important, as, more generally, does his attempt to use purpose as an explanatory concept in psychology.

Mach, Ernst (1838–1916). Austrian physicist and philosopher of science. Born in Moravia, he studied at Vienna, and became professor of mathematics at Graz in 1864, of physics at Prague in 1867, and of physics at Vienna in 1895. His experimental work was largely on the flow of gases. His philosophical writings both laid the foundations for *logical positivism and were a basis for Einstein's theory of relativity. (Mach's principle suggests that effects of accelerated motion, including rotation, are absolutely related to the mean mass of the universe; in practice, to the 'fixed' stars.)

Mach contributed to knowledge of *perception, especially in his *Beiträge zur Analyse der Empfindungen* (1897; trans. C. M. Williams, *The Analysis of Sensations; and the Relation of the Physical to the Psychical*, 1959). He was among the first to use visually ambiguous figures as research tools, for separating what we now call 'bottom-up' and 'top-down' processing. (See ILLUSIONS.)

He tried to base the whole of physics on the observer's sensations. This was important philosophically, as it is an extreme form of operationalism which led to logical positivism and criteria of verification (as set out in A. J. Ayer's *Language, Truth and Logic*, 1936). The attempt has, however, turned out to be unsuccessful—unless, at least, we allow very large gaps with many unverified steps between observations (and especially sensations) and accepted facts of the world. Further, the relation between sensation and perception remains far from clear, for—as Mach himself showed—how we perceive objects affects sensations, such as surface colour and brightness. So, though important, sensations can hardly be the building blocks of perception or of physics.

Other works by Mach available in English are: *Space and Geometry: In the Light of Physiological, Psychological and Physical Inquiry*, trans. T. J. McCormack (1960); *The Principles of Physical Optics: An Historical and Philosophical Treatment*, trans. J. S. Anderson and A. F. A. Young (1926); and *The Science of Mechanics: A Critical and Historical Account of its Development*, trans. T. J. McCormack (1960).

'mad as a hatter'. This expression probably derives from the fact that mercury, used in the manufacture of felt, which in turn was used to make hats, produces loss of memory and other symptoms of the *Korsakoff syndrome when absorbed by the skin. The idea is immortalized in the Mad Hatter in Lewis *Carroll's *Alice's Adventures in Wonderland*.

Magendie, François (1783–1855). French physiologist, who was born at Bordeaux and died at Sannois. He studied and practised medicine in Paris, researching in many fields and lecturing on experimental physiology; he was appointed professor of medicine at the Collège de France in 1831.

In 1809 he demonstrated that poison from the plant *Strychnos* was carried in the bloodstream and not by the lymphatics. This led to the isolation of strychnine in 1818, and he introduced it, as well as emetine, morphine, iodides, and bromides, into medical usage. He also studied nutrition scientifically, and realized the importance of proteins.

Magendie's discovery in 1822 that the dorsal root of a spinal nerve was sensory and the ventral root motor was also claimed by Sir Charles *Bell: it is generally accepted that Magendie gave the final proof and description to work originated by Bell. His wide interests included research on the cerebellum, on olfaction, and on the circulation.

See also REFLEX ACTION.   DDH

Maine de Biran (Pierre-François Gonthier de Biran, 1766–1824). French philosopher. The son of a doctor from Bergerac, he held public office after the Revolution, under the Consulate and the Empire, and after the Restoration. For most of his mature life, he pursued the project of producing a single major work devoted to the Science of Man. Though he wrote extensively, this central project was never fulfilled, and he published very little during his lifetime. Most of the works subsequently published are (sometimes misleading) editorial reconstitutions and compilations. However, the historical place of his work and the main lines of development of his thought can readily be seen.

Biran marks an important transition in man's attempt to explore and understand his own mind. We must place him, on the one hand, in the introspective tradition of those like Montaigne and *Pascal who gave prominence to the analysis and exposure of the intimacies of their own souls and, on the other hand, in the empiricist tradition stemming from *Bacon, especially as it emerged through *Locke and the British empiricists in the sensationalism of the 18th century propounded by authors like David Hartley, *Condillac, and Charles Bonnet. He represents not only an intersection of these traditions, but also a source of later very divergent approaches to the mind, in experimental psychology, in psychoanalysis, and in *phenomenology.   FCTM

Moore, F. C. T. (1970). *The Psychology of Maine de Biran*.
Tisserand, P. (ed.) (1920–49). *Œuvres de Maine de Biran*, 14 vols.

male and female brain. A new theory claims that the female brain is predominantly hard-wired for empathy, and that the male brain is predominantly hard-wired for understanding and building systems. It is known as the empathizing–systemizing (E-S) theory.

Empathizing is the drive to identify another person's emotions and thoughts, and to respond to these with an appropriate emotion. The empathizer intuitively figures out how people are feeling, and how to treat people with care and sensitivity. Systemizing is the drive to analyse and explore a system, to extract underlying rules that govern the behaviour of a system, and the drive to construct systems. The systemizer intuitively figures out how things work, or what the underlying rules are controlling a system. Systems can be as varied as a pond, a vehicle, a computer, a plant, a library catalogue, a musical instrument, a maths equation, or even an army unit. They all operate on inputs and deliver outputs, using rules.

According to this new theory, a person (whether male or female) has a particular 'brain type'. There are three common brain types. For some individuals, empathizing is stronger than systemizing. This is called a brain of type E, but we can also call it the female brain, because more females than males show this profile. For other individuals, systemizing is stronger than empathizing. This is called the a brain of type S, but we can also call it the male brain, because more males than females show this profile. Yet other individuals are equally strong in their systemizing and empathizing. This is called the 'balanced brain', or a brain of type B.

1. Are females better at empathizing?
2. Are males better at systematizing?
3. Testosterone on the mind
4. The extreme male brain: autism
5. Other sex differences in mind

1. Are females better at empathizing?

The evidence for a female advantage in empathizing comes from many different directions. For example, given a free choice of which toys to play with, more girls than boys will play with dolls, enacting social and emotional themes. When children are put together to play with a little movie player that has only one eyepiece, overall boys tend to get more of their fair share of looking down the eyepiece. They just shoulder the other boys out of the way. Or if you leave out those big plastic cars that children can ride on, what you see is that more little boys play the 'ramming' game. They deliberately drive the vehicle into another child. The little girls ride around more carefully, avoiding the other children more often. This suggests the girls are being more sensitive to others.

Baby girls, as young as 12 months old, respond more empathically to the distress of other people, showing greater concern through more sad looks, sympathetic vocalizations, and comforting. This echoes what you find in adulthood: more women report frequently sharing the emotional distress of their friends. Women also show more comforting than men do. When asked to judge

when someone might have said something potentially hurtful – a *faux pas* – girls score higher from at least 7 years old. Women are also more sensitive to facial expressions. They are better at decoding non-verbal communication, picking up subtle nuances from tone of voice or facial expression, or judging a person's character.

There is also a sex difference in aggression. Males tend to show far more 'direct' aggression (pushing, hitting, punching, etc.). Females tend to show more 'indirect' (or 'relational', covert) aggression. This includes things like gossip, exclusion, and bitchy remarks. It could be said that to punch someone in the face or to wound them physically requires an even lower level of empathy than a verbal snipe.

Two other ways to reveal a person's empathizing skill are to see how they (as a newcomer) join a group of strangers, and to see how they (as a host) react to a new person joining their group. This has been cleverly investigated in children by introducing a new boy or girl to a group who are already playing together. If the newcomer is female, she is more likely to stand and watch for a while, to check out what's going on, and then try to fit in with the ongoing activity. This usually leads to the newcomer being readily accepted into the group. If the newcomer is a boy, he is more likely to hijack the game by trying to change it, directing everyone's attention onto him. And even by the age of 6, girls are better at being a host. They are more attentive to the newcomer. Boys often just ignore the newcomer's attempt to join in. They are more likely to carry on with what they were already doing, perhaps preoccupied by their own interests.

How early are such sex differences in empathy evident? Certainly, by 12 months of age, girls make more eye contact than boys. But a study from Cambridge University shows that at birth, girls look longer at a face, and boys look longer at a suspended mechanical mobile. Furthermore, the Cambridge team found that how much eye contact children make is in part determined by a biological factor, prenatal testosterone. This has been demonstrated by measuring this hormone in amniotic fluid.

2. Are males better at systemizing?

Boys, from toddlerhood onwards, are more interested in cars, trucks, planes, guns and swords, building blocks, constructional toys, and mechanical toys—systems. They seem to love putting things together, to build toy towers or towns or vehicles. Boys also enjoy playing with toys that have clear functions—buttons to press, things that will light up, or devices that will cause another object to move.

The same sort of pattern is seen in the adult workplace. Some occupations are almost entirely male: metalworking, weapon making, crafting musical instruments, or the construction industries, such as boat-building. The focus of these occupations is on constructing systems. Professions such as maths, physics, and engineering, which require high systemizing, are also largely male-chosen disciplines.

Some psychological tests also show the male advantage in systemizing. For example, in the mental rotation test, you are shown two shapes, and asked if one is a rotation or a mirror image of the other. Males are quicker and more accurate on this test. Reading maps has been used as another test of systemizing. Men can learn a route in fewer trials, just from looking at a map, correctly recalling more details about direction and distance. If you ask boys to make a map of an area that they have only visited once, their maps have a more accurate layout of the features in the environment, e.g. showing which landmark is south-east of another.

If you ask people to put together a three-dimensional mechanical apparatus in an assembly task, on average men score higher. Boys are also better at constructing block buildings from two-dimensional blueprints. These are constructional systems. The male preference for focusing on systems again is evident very early. The Cambridge study found that at 1 year old, little boys showed a stronger preference for watching a film of cars (mechanical systems), rather than a film of a person's face (with lots of emotional expression). Little girls showed the opposite preference. And at 1 day old, little boys look for longer at a mechanical mobile.

Culture and socialization play a role in determining whether you develop a male brain (stronger interest in systems) or a female brain (stronger interest in empathy). But these studies of infancy strongly suggest that biology also partly determines this.

3. Testosterone on the mind
Some of the most convincing evidence for biological causes comes from studies of the effects of hormones. There was a time when women were prescribed a synthetic female hormone (diesthylstilbestrol), in an attempt to prevent repeated spontaneous miscarriages. Boys born to such women are likely to show more female-typical, empathizing behaviours, such as caring for dolls. And if a female rat is injected at birth with testosterone, she shows faster, more accurate maze learning, compared with a female rat who has not been given such an injection. So masculinizing the rat hormonally improves her spatial systemizing.

Some important lessons have been learnt from studies of clinical conditions. Male babies born with IHH (idiopathic hypogonadotrophic hypogonadism) have very small testes (and therefore very low levels of testosterone) and they are worse at spatial aspects of systemizing, relative to normal males. Other male babies born with androgen insensitivity (AI) syndrome (testosterone is an

androgen) are also worse at systemizing. Compare these to female babies born with CAH (congenital adrenal hyperplasia), who have unusually high levels of androgens and who have enhanced spatial systemizing.

But even leaving aside these clinical conditions, there is evidence for the effects of hormones on the mind in the typical child: a Cambridge study found that toddlers who had lower fetal testosterone had higher levels of eye contact. Eye contact may be related to sociability and empathizing. And a group of Canadian researchers found that the higher your prenatal testosterone the better you do on the mental rotation (systemizing) test.

4. The extreme male brain: autism
The E-S theory does not stereotype. Rather, it may help us explain why individuals are typical or atypical for their sex. It may help us understand the childhood neurological conditions of *autism and Asperger syndrome, which appear to be an extreme of the male brain. Such individuals may have impairments in empathizing alongside normal or even talented systemizing.

5. Other sex differences in mind
Earlier studies of psychological sex differences focused on what is sometimes called 'the holy trinity': spatial ability, mathematical ability, and verbal ability. The first two of these are areas where males perform at a higher level, and the last of these typically shows a female advantage. However, spatial and mathematical abilities involve systemizing, and so may simply be further evidence for the E-S theory. Verbal ability may have nothing to do with empathy, in which case this will need to be regarded as an additional dimension along which the sexes differ psychologically. However, good empathizing and good verbal skills both facilitate communication, so that verbal and empathy skills may not be truly independent.   SBC

Baron-Cohen, S. (2003). *The Essential Difference: Men, Women and the Extreme Male Brain*

Kimura, D. (1997). *Sex and Cognition*.

Malthus, Thomas Robert (1766–1834). English economist and mathematician, born at Dorking, Surrey, and educated at Jesus College, Cambridge. His *Essay on the Principle of Population* (published anonymously in 1798; enlarged, 1803) inspired, or triggered, both Charles *Darwin and Alfred Russel *Wallace to develop the theory of evolution of species by natural selection. The key idea was struggle for survival with limited resources.

mania. A form of mental disorder manifested by uncontrolled excitement, overactivity, and obsessive behaviour.

manic depressive. A personality oscillating between overactivity and inability to summon up energy or make decisions. In extreme form, it is *manic–depressive* *psychosis.* In a controlled form it can be useful for creativity. The writer Samuel Johnson was supposed to be manic–depressive, using the manic phase for writing and the depressed phase for self-criticism. See DEPRESSION.

manners. Rules of manners can be found in every culture. They are meant to regulate the behaviour of the individual in everyday life and social intercourse. There are rules for walking, sitting, laughing, eating, speaking, greeting, etc. Manners are not identical (though closely related) to either rites or morals. Although some of them are very refined and change with fashion, manners probably reflect a more primitive level of behaviour than rites such as sacrifice, or moral commandments such as the Ten Commandments. In general, rules of manners focus either on neatness (which may have hygienic origins) or respect: two examples of the latter are elaborate systems of salutation, and a rule not to stare into another person's eyes. Francis *Bacon has given one of the best definitions: 'The whole of decorum and elegance of manners, seem to rest in weighing and maintaining, with an even balance, the dignity betwixt ourselves and others' (*The Advancement of Learning*, 1605).

Many of these aspects of behaviour can also be found in higher animals. Dogs and cats have elaborate rules of greeting which also determine the order of rank. Many animals—for example, rhesus monkeys—interpret fixating the eyes as aggressive behaviour. A subordinate animal would instantly turn away with some submissive gesture, while an animal with a higher rank might start an attack. Monkeys display such behaviour not only towards other monkeys but also towards man. The existence of certain basic modes of behaviour which can be instantly understood by man and by some higher animals suggests genetic determination. However, one should not conclude that manners are genetically fixed; rather, the potential that manners develop seems to be genetically fixed in man. The individual rules are determined by tradition and can differ widely. Also, rules of manners for men usually focus on ideals, which may be very different from actual behaviour.

1. History
2. Manners at table and in conversation

1. History
European antiquity does not have special books on manners. There are, however, several hints in the Bible as well as in writings on morals by Plutarch, Epictetus, and Cicero. Two concepts characterize the ancient ideal of the good-mannered man: the concept of propriety and the concept of urbanity.

Acting 'properly'—that is, with propriety—means doing the right thing at the right time in the right place.

The Greek idea of propriety belongs to the ideal of universal harmony; the rule itself seems to arise from the more primitive rules of obeisance and submission to society. That the definition of 'proper' could be a matter of public opinion and therefore be changed is a discovery of later times. Urbanity may be defined as the courteous and elegant and therefore charming behaviour of (educated) citizens. The frequent social intercourse of those who live closely together might have made it a necessity that people should not only respect but also please each other. The aim to please is reflected in the ancient art of rhetoric, which acquired so much importance during the urban democracies of ancient Greece and Rome. It was a work by Cicero, *De oratore* (On the Orator), which inspired the Renaissance author Baldassare Castiglione to write one of the first widespread books on manners: *Il libro del cortegiano* (The Courtier, 1528), stressing the courtier's duty not only to submit to the rules of propriety but to do so gracefully. Indeed, in most of the conduct books following *Il libro del cortegiano* the art of good behaviour has been reduced more or less to an 'art of pleasing'. At court the meaning of propriety sometimes changed to simple conformity, and, since the decisions of the monarchs were often influenced by sudden humours or moods, the art of pleasing degenerated to open flattery. Consequently the art of compliments—which forms an important part of the older books on manners—was later heavily criticized, and even banned, during the ages of bourgeois democracy.

Life at court also for the first time set forth rules to respect and even worship women, an idea unknown to ancient moralists. From the Middle Ages women had an increasing influence on the refinement of manners, though there can also be observed a strong tradition of misogyny, especially in England.

The first important books on manners for the bourgeoisie were written by Erasmus, *De civilitate morum puerilium* (On the Civility of Boys' Manners, 1528), and Giovanni della Casa, *Il Galateo* (1558). Both books were translated into the main European languages and often imitated. Rather detailed rules were given, such as: comb your hair, clean your ears and nose, wash your hands, lift your hat. In the English tradition of conduct books of the 16th and 17th centuries, a puritanical attitude towards 'pleasing' manners predominated; the books mostly taught moralistic and religious maxims or principles, and the first American books on manners were based on this tradition. In the age of Louis XIV (1638–1715), France became the leading nation on questions of conduct. Several treatises were translated into most of the European languages, for example the *Art de plaire dans la conversation* (The Art of Pleasing in Conversation, 1688) by Pierre d'Ortigue. The moral pressure of court life 'to please' was even apparent in the famous *Letters* by Lord

Chesterfield (1694–1773), who wrote to his son: 'By *manière* I do not mean bare civility; everybody must have that, who would not be kicked out of company: but I mean engaging, insinuating, shining manners: a distinguished politeness, an almost irresistible address' (19 April 1747). Since the 19th century, books on etiquette, which were simply guides in how to conform to the rules of society, have enjoyed a wide distribution. Good manners were no longer considered to be an 'art'.

2. Manners at table and in conversation

To select two of the many possible aspects of manners, *table* and *conversational manners* will be described: two forms of civilized behaviour which were closely connected in the ancient institution of the symposium. From the 15th century the upper class developed highly restrictive rules, not only for the more natural needs but also for the use of napkins, handkerchiefs, and cutlery. Many table-books were published, in which detailed instructions for the use of spoons and especially of knives were given. By the end of the 18th century the use of individual plates and cutlery (knife, spoon, and for the first time also fork) was general. Until then it had been quite usual to eat communally from the same plate. Similarly the manner of how meat was served changed considerably. In the Middle Ages the entire animal (often decorated with its own fur or feathers to suggest the illusion that it had been hunted down on the spot) was presented and carved in front of the family or the guests, either by the host or by somebody especially trained. Whole books on the art of carving were written —strangely enough sometimes combined with the 'Art of Compliments', as if hungry people could have been calmed down only by compliments while waiting. Then, later, the carving of the meat was largely banned from the table and delegated to the cook in the kitchen or even to the butcher himself.

Conversational manners also have a well-documented history. Characteristic human behaviour has been described by types: the chatterer, the flatterer, the silent man, all of whom are familiar in all societies. One of the most influential works in antiquity was Cicero's book *De officiis* (On Duties). Cicero reprimands those who speak too long, too loud, or too aggressively, and those who praise themselves or criticize others. He also stresses an important point of good conversational manners: respecting the right of everybody to take part. Interest in the *theory* of conversation awoke only in the Renaissance, i.e. around 1500. Castiglione in *Il libro del cortegiano* differentiates between conversation with monarchs and with equals. Conversation with monarchs should consist mainly of information, flattery, or respectful silence—witticisms are allowed only in conversation with equals. The bourgeois conduct books give Ciceronian rules and prescriptions: do not interrupt other people, do not speak in riddles, do not

hurt anybody with jokes (the last-mentioned rule became a typical bourgeois taboo). At the time of Louis XIV, conversation meant the opposite of 'talking on serious matters'; in the drawing rooms of French gentlewomen, it degenerated to more or less brilliant chat. Since the rules of conversation have always aimed at the protection of mutual respect, conversation theory consequently tends to demand not only social but also intellectual equality in those who converse with each other. In fact in the 18th century the ideal of Henry Fielding gained increasing influence: 'Certain it is, that the highest Pleasure which we are capable of enjoying in Conversation is to be met with only in the Society of Persons whose Understanding is pretty near on an Equality with our own' (*Essay on Conversation*, 1742). Real development of conversational ideals in the 19th century seems to have taken place only in so-called intellectual circles. At least in America and Germany a certain distrust of conversation began to prevail: 'Good as is discourse, silence is better, and shames it,' wrote Ralph Waldo Emerson (*Circles*, 1841). On the other hand, there was a tendency to confine conversation not only to equals but to the privacy and intimacy of dialogue: 'The best conversation probably takes place between two persons' (Emerson, *Clubs*, 1847).

Conversation in all its possible forms has never ceased. Books on conversational manners are written nowadays as never before. The concentration of theoretical interest towards the end of the 19th and the beginning of the 20th centuries on the most private dialogue (and even the soliloquy) may have been due to the development of a democratic society, in which conversation between equals, i.e. public discussion, is now taken for granted.

CSC

Marr, David Courtenay (1945–80). British psychologist, born at Woodford in Essex. In his short life, David Marr made a contribution to the psychology of vision that could be regarded as more important than that of anyone since Hermann von *Helmholtz. He was educated at Rugby School and Trinity College, Cambridge. He put his mathematics to use in the construction of a model of the function of the cerebellum. Despite its ingenuity, it was at best oversimplified and he himself became dissatisfied with it. After a junior research fellowship at Trinity College, he moved to a senior research fellowship at King's College, which he held from 1972 to 1976. He became increasingly aware of the promise of computer simulation for modelling brain function, and while still a Fellow at King's made a protracted visit to the artificial intelligence laboratory at the Massachusetts Institute of Technology (MIT) in order to learn the techniques of computer modelling. In 1975 he again visited MIT and decided to remain there permanently. The last five years of his life were marked by an outburst of creative energy that culminated in a book entitled *Vision*, which was posthumously published in 1982.

Marr's main work was on three topics: first, the method by which the visual system recovers lines and edges, which, although they look so clean to the viewer, are extremely hard to reconstruct from the messy retinal image; second, stereopsis, particularly the correspondence problem, that is the method by which the brain matches a point in the image on one eye with the equivalent point in the other eye's image; and, third, the problem of how objects are represented in the brain in such a way as to facilitate recognition. Although he made highly original and important contributions to all three problems, he will probably be remembered less for the details of his research than for the style of his approach. Before Marr, most computer programs in vision dealt only with very restricted 'toy' worlds, for example plane-sided blocks. Marr set out to model vision as it operates in the real world in all its complexity. Moreover, he was the first person to construct computer models that took account of neurophysiological and psychological findings. He did not want to produce just any model—he wanted to uncover the way the human visual system actually works. Finally, he saw more clearly than almost any of his contemporaries that, in order to build an adequate model of how the brain executes a certain task, it is first necessary to obtain a clear understanding of that task: his mathematical ability helped him to achieve this kind of understanding. In addition to carrying out his own research, Marr through his intelligence, charm, and liveliness attracted around him a group of outstanding research workers drawn from all over the world. Inspired by him, they made important contributions of their own, many of which are recorded in his book.

David Marr's move to MIT seemed to lead to a remarkable flowering of his imagination and personality. Part of his vitality over the last few years of his life may have come from the fact that he knew he had not long to live. Three years before he died he contracted leukaemia, a disease that necessitated repeated and painful stays in hospital. He faced his illness with quiet courage and, no matter how weak he felt, he went on working: his fascination with his work was so great that however ill he was he never had to force himself to do it. His attempt to grapple with the deepest problems of vision was for him a source of spontaneous enjoyment. As he writes at the beginning of his book, 'This book is meant to be enjoyed'. One can be sure he enjoyed writing it.

See also PERCEPTION.   NSS

masochism. Pleasure (especially sexual) from being subjected to pain or cruelty. It is named after Leopold von Sacher-Masoch (1835–95), an Austrian writer and lawyer who wrote *Der Don Juan von Kolomea* (1866) and other books describing sexual pleasure derived from pain. The converse is *sadism—sexual pleasure from inflicting pain.

A curious problem arises as to whether one could say that an animal is motivated by masochism—for normally motivations for behaviour are supposed to be pleasurable. Pleasure might, of course, be deferred, but how far these subtle and important distinctions can be made on purely behavioural grounds, as in animal experiments and observations of animal behaviour, is an open and difficult question.

materialism. See MIND–BODY PROBLEM: PHILOSOPHICAL THEORIES.

matter. The distinction between mind and matter is as old as philosophy and as controversial. Both are ultimately mysterious. On the view known as *dualism (developed by *Descartes), matter has spatial extension and non-mental properties such as divisibility, while mind is not extended in space and does not obey the laws of physics. According to the *idealism of *Berkeley, the notion of matter existing independently of mind is incoherent. As physics has advanced, its accounts of matter have grown even further from the 'common-sense' knowledge given by perception. This has given rise to 'two worlds' of physical reality and perceived experience. With this development matter seems to be more and more different from mind, whereas in mythology and early science mind and matter are hardly separated, and matter is seen as alive and intelligent. See also MIND AND BODY.

ME. Myalgic encephalomyelitis (ME) was a term originally given to a distinctive post-viral clinical syndrome characterized by fatigue, post-exertional malaise, muscle pain, altered skin sensations (allodynia), and neuropsychiatric features. These symptoms were uniformly recorded in many epidemic outbreaks of ME during the 1960s. Morbidity was significant, relapses were common, and recovery was slow and gradual. In the later years, sporadic cases of an identical syndrome became recognized after Epstein–Barr virus and Coxsackie virus infections (post-viral fatigue syndrome or PVFS). ME or PVFS is qualitatively similar to a number of fatigue syndromes known as a sequel of systemic infections (poliomyelitis, Lyme disease, Q fever, sepsis) and post-infective neurological diseases (multiple sclerosis, Guillain–Barré syndrome).

1. Definition and nomenclature
2. Differential diagnosis
3. Pathophysiology
4. Treatment
5. Prognosis
6. Conclusions

1. Definition and nomenclature

Chronic fatigue syndrome (CFS) was introduced in 1988 as a broad term for persistent and relapsing fatigue of over six months' duration for which there was no known medical explanation. ME/PVFS was subsumed within this new designation of CFS. The diagnosis of CFS is clinical. However, not all known psychiatric causes of chronic fatigue are reliably excluded by the present diagnostic criteria of CFS. As a result, it is difficult to know what proportion of patients receiving a diagnosis of CFS will have ME/PVFS as opposed to the cases with medically unexplained chronic fatigue due to anxiety and depression where fatigue is considered to be a physical symptom of psychiatric disorders (somatization). This problem is also central to the interpretation of the research studies and therapeutic trials in CFS that have used different sets of criteria for the selection of patients. It appears that a strict application of the revised Centers for Disease Control (CDC) criteria (Fukuda et al. 1994) with exclusion of major psychiatric and somatization disorders is the best possible way to identify ME patients (CFS/ME) at present (Report of the Scottish Short Life Working Group 2002). When appropriately defined, CFS/ME has a much lower prevalence (0.2–0.4 per cent in adults and 0.07 per cent in the paediatric age group of 5–15 years) as compared with the cases with medically unexplained chronic fatigue more commonly seen in the primary care (prevalence rate of 2 per cent and above).

The use of ME as a diagnostic term has been criticized because there is inadequate pathological evidence of inflammatory changes in the brain and spinal cord of patients. The conjoint term CFS/ME is preferred at present.

2. Differential diagnosis

There is no specific or sensitive 'test' or diagnostic marker for CFS/ME. While making a diagnosis of CFS/ME, it is essential to exclude other medical and psychiatric causes of chronic fatigue not the least because therapeutic approaches may differ. A thorough clinical evaluation based on history and physical examination and appropriate screening investigations are necessary before the diagnosis of CFS/ME is offered. It is important not to make assumptions in the presence of diagnostic uncertainties. As in other chronic medical conditions, prevalence of depression and anxiety is higher in CFS/ME patients as compared to the general population. However, presence of depression (or anxiety) in CFS/ME patients does not imply its causation. Despite an overlap, CFS/ME is distinct from depression. Unlike many depressed patients, CFS/ME patients retain normal motivation, are eager to maintain social contacts, and do not experience inappropriate guilt at the onset of their symptoms. Somatization is not a specific problem in CFS/ME (Johnson, DeLuca, and Natelson 1996) and is similar to the prevalence figure

in the general population. The descriptions of the major psychiatric disorders have been fairly well characterized in the Diagnostical Statistical Manual of Mental Disorders, 4th edn. (DSM-IV) (American Psychiatric Association 1994) and, when a patient with chronic fatigue fits the criteria outlined in the DSM-IV perfectly, a psychiatric diagnosis can be made with confidence. However, when the patient's symptoms or clinical course do not fit these criteria well, it is inappropriate to attribute the diagnosis to a primary psychiatric disorder. Specialist referral may be necessary, particularly in severely affected children, before a final diagnosis is made.

3. Pathophysiology

The precise cause of CFS/ME is *unknown* as is the exact pathogenesis of this disorder. This point needs to be emphasized as there is a recurring statement in the psychiatric literature that CFS/ME is essentially an abnormal illness behaviour or a functional somatic syndrome (somatization). The concordance rate of chronic fatigue in monozygotic twins is around 50 per cent (Buchwald et al. 2001), indicating that both genetic predisposition and environmental factors play an equal role in CFS/ME. Typically, CFS/ME is seen in previously healthy and, often, physically active individuals (MacDonald et al. 1996). In over a third of all the cases, the onset is abrupt. Life events, stress, and viral infections are common triggers and, in many cases, a combination of these co-factors (e.g. stress and infection) over a short period of time precipitates symptoms. The core symptoms of CFS/ME are fatigue, pain, and post-exertional malaise. Fatigue in CFS/ME is characterized by an increased perception of effort and reduced levels of endurance to sustained physical or mental activities. It is best understood as an amplified sense of fatigue experienced in normal life. An underactive hypothalamic–pituitary–adrenal axis in CFS/ME is considered to be relevant to the symptoms of weight disturbance, altered temperature perception, sleep disorder, and subtle immunological changes (recurrent lymph node swellings and new-onset asthma) seen in this condition. However, there is an emerging view that relatively low levels of cortisol, a hormone released by the adrenals, may itself be the predisposing factor for the development of a chronic fatigue state after serious infections or stressful life events (Yehuda 2002). Autonomic function in CFS/ME is impaired, although the degree of impairment may vary between patients. As a result, patients may experience symptoms of light-headedness or fainting and an abnormal blood pressure response to postural changes or head tilt (orthostatic intolerance) is particularly common in younger patients. Pain in CFS/ME is poorly localized, diffuse, and, like fatigue, worsens after unaccustomed physical exertion. A reduced threshold for pain perception due to an altered central 'gating' is a possible explanation.

In chronic sufferers, low levels of physical activity imposed by persistent fatigue lead to muscle and cardiac deconditioning. Depression in CFS/ME is generally encountered as a consequence of its chronicity, poor recovery, and related socio-economic problems. Early studies of proton magnetic resonance spectroscopy of selected brain regions have shown increased levels of choline (derived from cell membrane phosphocholine) in CFS/ME patients and appear promising as a future research tool in this area (Chaudhuri et al. 2003).

4. Treatment

There is no specific treatment for CFS/ME. Therapeutic interventions are symptomatic and rehabilitative. Pharmacological treatment for pain, sleep disorder, and depression should be advised where appropriate. Opioids and long-acting benzodiazepines are not usually recommended because of the risk of dependence. Low-dose tricyclic antidepressants like amitriptyline are widely used for pain and poor night-time sleep. Gabapentin is also an effective treatment for pain control. Sertraline and cipramil (both selective serotonin reuptake inhibitors) are particularly useful in patients with low mood and anxiety. Among non-pharmacological interventions, pacing is considered to be a simple and effective coping strategy. Early results of graded physical exercise and cognitive–behaviour therapy appear encouraging but very little is known about the role of any treatment in severely affected CFS/ME patients (Whiting et al. 2001). Antioxidants, essential fatty acids, and dietary manipulation may help a few. Alcohol worsens symptoms of fatigue and alcohol intolerance is common in CFS/ME. There is no knowledge of any effective treatment in paediatric CFS/ME. It is likely that children with CFS/ME will require educational support for part-time or home tuitions.

5. Prognosis

A proportion of adults with CFS/ME will make a slow recovery. This usually begins in the first year or two and in some cases the time to recovery may take between 3 and 5 years from the initial symptoms. Prognosis for adults who do not make any progress to recovery after two years is poor and those with over five years of symptoms are unlikely to experience a complete remission. Overall, about 40 per cent of adults and 60 per cent of children make a good recovery and another third of patients remain largely independent for their daily activities despite experiencing some symptoms. Severe disability with needs for personal assistance is seen in approximately 25 per cent of adult cases. Female sex, longer duration of symptoms, muscle wasting, and exercise intolerance indicate poor prognosis.

6. Conclusions

Many clinicians prefer to invoke a psychiatric diagnosis when the patient's symptoms do not match an established neurological diagnostic category. The opposite also occurs and as a general rule, when a patient's symptoms do not quite fit the criteria of a psychiatric diagnosis, a neurological condition is a possible cause (Pincus and Tucker 2003). CFS/ME is an example of a disorder that overlaps the traditional boundaries of neurology and psychiatry. It will take some time before its cause is understood and more effective and specific treatments are developed. However, CFS/ME should be recognized and diagnosed clinically, and many patients disabled with fatigue and pain will be helped by empathy and understanding, rather than rejection and scepticism, from their physicians.

ACha

American Psychiatric Association (1994). *Diagnostic and Statistical Manual of Mental Disorders* DSM-IV (4th edn.).

Buchwald, D., Herrell, R., Ashton, S., et al. (2001). 'A twin study of chronic fatigue'. *Psychosomatic Medicine*, 63.

Chaudhuri, A., Condon, B. R., Gow, J. W., Brennan D., and Hadley D. M. (2003). 'Proton magnetic resonance spectroscopy of basal ganglia in chronic fatigue syndrome'. *Neuro-Report*, 14.

Fukuda, K., Strauss, S. E., Hickie, I., et al. (1994). 'The chronic fatigue syndrome: a comprehensive approach to case definition and study'. *Annals of Internal Medicine*, 121.

Johnson, S. K., DeLuca, J., and Natelson, B. H. (1996). 'Assessing somatization disorder in the chronic fatigue syndrome'. *Psychosomatic Medicine*, 58.

MacDonald, K. L., Osterholm M. T., LeDell, K. H., et al. (1996). 'A case control study to assess possible triggers and cofactors in chronic fatigue syndrome'. *American Journal of Medicine*, 100.

Pincus, J. H., and Tucker G. J. (2003). *Behavioral Neurology* (4th edn.).

Report of the Scottish Short Life Working Group (2002). 'Chronic fatigue syndrome/myalgic encephalomyelitis (CFS/ME). Outline for development of services for CFS/ME in Scotland'. Edinburgh: Health Department, Scottish Executive.

Whiting, P., Bagnall, A. M., Sowden, A. J., Cornell, J. E., and Mulrow, C. D. (2001). 'Intervention for the treatment and management of chronic fatigue syndrome'. *Journal of the American Medical Association*, 284.

Yehuda, R. (2002). 'Current status of cortisol findings in post-traumatic stress disorder'. *Psychiatric Clinics of North America*, 25.

meaning. The concept of meaning is every bit as problematic as the concept of mind, and for related reasons. For it seems to be the case that it is only *for a mind* that some things (gestures, sounds, marks, or natural phenomena) can *mean* other things. The difficulties that we have understanding the place of mind in nature spill over into, and create problems for, our understanding of the phenomena of meaning. Anyone who conceives of science as objective, and of objectivity as requiring the study of phenomena (objects and relations between objects) that exist and have their character independently of human thought, will face a problem with the scientific study of meaning.

One might attempt to overcome this problem by finding a natural relation holding between things that have meanings (i.e. signs) and the things they mean (or signify). The idea that meaning is, or needs to be, founded upon a natural relation is responsible for the lure of causal, picture, and onomatopoeic theories. Cause and effect and similarity of shape are thought to be relations which hold independently of being recognized by a mind.

*Plato (*Cratylus*, 432–5) argued against the idea that the meaning relation could be founded purely on a natural relation of similarity. No signs, he observed, can be exactly similar to the thing signified without duplicating that thing in all respects. What counts as sufficiently similar is governed by convention (*nomos*) and there must, therefore, be an element of convention in every use of a thing as sign.

But while it appears unavoidable that meaning should have some component of convention, it does not seem unreasonable to seek a theoretical account of the general conditions under which such conventions, established for a relatively small number of linguistic elements (a basic vocabulary), would fix the meanings of complex terms and sentences constructed out of these elements. It would be the work of that branch of the science of logic known as compositional (or recursive) semantics to determine these general conditions, and the result would constitute an objective account of how parts of a language can mean something. If one added assumptions about how it is proper to fix the meanings of the basic elements—say they had to be tied in some way to sense experience—one could test any piece of discourse for meaningfulness by applying the principles of logic to analyse the discourse until it became clear whether its elements had been properly constituted or legitimized by experience, and hence whether it was a meaningful piece of discourse.

Early efforts in this direction were made by the classical British empiricists (*Hobbes and *Hume), but the important advances in logical technique at the turn of the 19th century gave those attracted to this approach a new self-consciousness and self-confidence, and they emerged as 'logical empiricists' (or 'logical positivists'). These were the philosophers (A. J. Ayer, Rudolf Carnap, and Moritz Schlick) who challenged the 'cognitive meaningfulness' of metaphysics, theology, and ethics, and whose slogan was 'the meaning of a sentence is its method of verification', for the analysis of a sentence would, if carried out, also show how one could go about verifying the sentence. (See FALSIFICATION.)

The logical empiricists, however, differed over the way basic elements should be tied to sense experience. One group (including Ayer, Schlick, *Mach, and Bertrand *Russell) saw basic elements as grounded in subjective experience; another (including Otto Neurath and Carl Hempel) did not regard it as proper to anchor scientific discourse in subjective experience, and urged instead publicly accessible outcomes of publicly accessible (e.g. laboratory) procedures as the proper foundation for cognitive meaningfulness. The approach of this second group underwent a development as a result of the realization that what constitutes a test of something in science is not independent of the constellation of theories which scientists accept. The result was the abandoning of the idea that some elements of a language can be treated as basic with regard to the verification of all other sentences of that language. Hempel proposed instead a 'translatability criterion' according to which a whole body of discourse would be regarded as cognitively (i.e. scientifically) meaningful if it could be translated into a logically regimented language whose primitive vocabulary consisted of either 'logical locutions' or 'observation predicates'. None of the sentences, however, was to be regarded as basic for the purposes of verifying the sentences of the body of discourse thus translated. Instead of individual sentences confronting experience, the body of discourse as a whole stood or fell in the face of experience.

W. V. Quine and Donald Davidson developed further the line of this second group of positivists, by shifting attention from the attempt to say what it is to be cognitively meaningful to what is involved in one person understanding another person's (or culture's) language. In each case, they maintained, the interpreter has to work as a scientist works. The interpreter has to collect data, which consists in observations of the conditions under which the people whose discourse is to be interpreted will assent to, and dissent from, certain sentences. The interpreter also has to select basic elements (by proposing 'analytic hypotheses') and has to construct a theory which assigns truth conditions to basic elements and, through this, truth conditions to all the sentences of the language in such a way as to conform to the data. (Since the development of the logical apparatus, the compositional semantics, thought to be needed for this theory building, is due to Alfred Tarski; his name is often mentioned in this context.) As in Hempel's account, which is supposed to reflect the actual practice of natural scientists, the theory constructed stands or falls by its ability to accommodate the data taken *as a whole*.

As Quine and Davidson acknowledged, indeed urged, this approach to interpretation in an important sense undermines the idea that sentences or fragments of sentences have a meaning, or that names have a reference. The body of data is never adequate to determine uniquely one system of interpreting a language. There is no sense to the question what a noun *really* refers to, or what a speaker *really* means. In effect we should, in order to treat language as a natural phenomenon, abandon the notions of meaning and reference, and make use only of the concept of truth.

It was in the context of this challenge to the conceptions of meaning and reference that the 'causal theory of reference' was advanced by Saul Kripke and Hilary Putnam. According to this theory, A refers, for example, to a liquid chemical composed of two parts hydrogen and one part oxygen as 'water', because A heard B, C, D, etc. refer to it by that name, and they did so because they heard others do so; and so on back to an 'initial baptism' of that stuff with the name 'water'.

Although the phrase 'initial baptism' suggests a conscious attempt to establish a conventional pattern of linguistic response (as in a genuine christening), the initial baptism need not be regarded in this way. It could be treated as an unspecified natural occurrence, which under the circumstances holding at that time established a pattern of response to all essentially similar features of the environment. The similarity of feature, which is the basis of the pattern of response, need not be understood by those conforming to the pattern, although understanding could be achieved later by scientific investigation. This account thus underwrites the possibility of saying that what Aristotle *meant* by 'to hudor' was H_2O, even though it is obvious that Aristotle did not possess our understanding of the composition of water. It is clear from this illustration how the notion of meaning can be conceived as a relation which obtains independently of what humans think.

To its critics, the causal theory failed to provide a historically plausible account of the mechanisms by which reference is secured and maintained. But to those sympathetic to it, it offered an alternative to abandoning the use of these notions and accepting the conclusion drawn by Quine and Davidson that meaning and reference are too indeterminate for scientific study. (A corollary of this conclusion, to the effect that mind is insufficiently determinate for proper scientific study, was subsequently drawn by Bernard Williams.)

One might also try to escape Quine's conclusions by calling into question the positivist conception of science which underpins them. Those prone to read the theoretical pronouncements of scientists literally, i.e. 'realists', brush aside the possibility, which is frequently stressed by Quine, that any body of scientific evidence, e.g. electrical phenomena, can be accounted for in a variety of incompatible ways, not just by postulating the existence of electrons. They insist that we are often justified in selecting one of the competing accounts as *the best explanation*, and this outlook can be applied to the phenomena of language to endorse, as perfectly respectable scientific reasoning, the idea that the best explanation of linguistic phenomena will postulate mental states as the causes of those phenomena.

Although the word 'idea' no longer figures prominently, this approach in effect returns to the position of John *Locke, who held that 'words, in their primary or immediate signification, stand for nothing but the ideas in the mind of him that uses them' (*Essay*, III. ii. 2). Instead of ideas, the internal states most commonly appealed to are beliefs and desires, but the approach would still fall under the strictures of those philosophers and logicians who, since Frege, have indicted such theories on a charge of 'psychologism', for such theories do indeed shift the attention of those studying meaning away from the relationship between signs and the things they signify to the relationship between the (minds of) sign users and the things they signify.

Recent developments along these lines begin with an analysis of speaker's meaning advanced by H. P. Grice. We do quite often use the word 'meaning' to label what a speaker intended or was trying to do with his words. Thus Spooner's audience recognized that he *meant* to refer affectionately to the monarch when he used the words 'our queer dean'. This complex intention was analysed by Grice in terms of an intention to modify the beliefs or behaviour of the audience via the audience's recognition of that intention; and the presence of such intentions, Grice held, was what distinguished the ('nonnatural') meaning of linguistic phenomena from the ('natural') meaning of natural phenomena (such as in 'those spots mean measles').

Criticisms of Grice's analysis focused on the difficulty of bridging the gap between this notion of (speaker's) meaning and the notion of word (or linguistic) meaning, for which we still need an account. Spooner's *words* after all *meant* something quite at variance with his intention; his words referred slurringly to a college official. Jonathan Bennett attempted to bridge the gap by integrating Grice's analysis with a sophisticated account of convention, which was devised by David Lewis. Under Lewis's analysis, a convention need not be established by conscious agreement (something which would presuppose, and hence could not explain, the existence of language) but is nevertheless more than a mere regularity because, however it was established, it is maintained by the recognition on the part of those who conform to it that conformity to it solves a 'coordination problem', i.e. eliminates certain disadvantages which would occur unless activities were coordinated. Bennett's account in effect rested linguistic meanings on the hardening into convention of speakers' meanings.

Bennett's approach has been criticized for not providing a convincing account of how what are essentially unstructured and unrelated primitive signalling acts (acts that express communication intention without presupposing a language) come to have the structure evident in all languages, namely that by which each speech act is composed of elements which make a similar contribution to a variety of different speech acts. A second criticism called into question the sense of crediting non-language users with intentions sufficiently complex to count as (Gricean) communication intentions. The first of these criticisms rests on an important feature of meaning, its systematic nature. Different theoretical traditions give different accounts of this essential structure, but agree at least on the principle of systematic relatedness. (In the controversy over whether chimpanzees in acquiring the use of Ameslan signs had achieved *linguistic* mastery, a crucial point was whether they had the ability to form signs of sufficient complexity.) (See PRIMATE LANGUAGE.)

Compositional semantics offers an account of this structure based on the principle that the meanings of complex expression are functions of the meanings of elementary components. In fashioning the central concepts of this approach Frege had insisted that a sentential (or propositional) unit is primary to language, that singular terms and predicate expressions made radically dissimilar contributions to sentences, and that one must not ask for the meaning (*Bedeutung*) of a word outside the context of a sentence. Bennett's account seems in particular to lack resources to explain how a set of internally unstructured and logically homogeneous signalling acts could yield expressions with the different logical functions of subject and predicate. Frege's ideas were transmogrified in the hands of Quine, and, as the importance Frege attached to reference decayed, Quine replaced Frege's maxim about looking for the meaning outside the context of a sentence by a stricture against seeking the meaning of an expression outside the context of a whole language.

A radically different account derives from the work of the linguist Ferdinand de Saussure, who saw as relevant to meaning not only the relation between sign and thing signified, but also the 'value' of the sign (word). The value of a word is a function of the words that can in some contexts be exchanged for the word ('strike' and 'hit' are interchangeable only in some contexts) and the words that stand in contrast to it. 'Sheep' and 'mutton' are used for the animal and its meat in English, where the French use 'mouton' for both. Thus the latter could have the value of neither of the former words.

Saussure's work provided an important inspiration for the movement known as structuralism. In the hands of the structuralists the relation between signified and signifier was virtually discarded, leaving the meaning of a sign resting on the structure of values constituted by the language as a whole. Coming from a different direction, the structuralists arrived at a linguistic holism which bore a number of striking similarities to that advanced by Quine and Davidson. In neither case could one look to some definite aspect of the world outside of discourse for what an expression meant or signified. If it made any

sense to ask for the meaning of an expression, one had to look for it in its connections to other expressions.

Were this a viable account of linguistic meaning, it would support the idea that linguistic mastery (the ability thought by many to be essential to the possession of a mind) can be modelled in computer programs. A program, if it has the power to generate the right syntactic structure and vocabulary, could represent the way expressions interact with each other to constrain the formation of expressions and the assent to or dissent from sentences. Computer modelling along these lines has tended to draw more on the tradition which Frege founded than on that which Saussure founded. Such computer modelling leads to a second application of the 'realist' strategy mentioned above. Instead of postulating beliefs and intentions (in the head) to account for linguistic acts, what is postulated is an internal configuration formally isomorphic to a computer program (one we have yet to write) which accounts for what is conceived of as human linguistic 'printout'. Many cognitive scientists see their task as the writing of such a program, or possibly working in conjunction with physiologists to determine which of several possible programs the human mind actually runs. (See also ARTIFICIAL INTELLIGENCE.)

There are, however, several doubts about the aspirations of such cognitive scientists. If these aspirations are based on a thoroughgoing holism, it is difficult to see how language mastery can be acquired (as humans evidently acquired it) in stages, for the whole of language would have to be mastered in order to have mastered any part of it. It is difficult also to see how two adult human beings could communicate with one another, so long as their vocabularies did not precisely coincide. For it would be impossible to determine whether a difference of opinion was based on one person being misinformed or the two speakers at cross purposes because they in effect spoke different languages.

Computer modelling need not rest on a holistic approach, but if there is thought to be some component of the meaning of an expression which is independent of its relationships to other expressions in the language, this component would seem to have to be sought in the relation that the expression bears to things outside the language. Computer models can be extended by connecting the machinery and software to 'external sensors', so that the printout bears an appropriate relation to the world. But this expedient leaves open the possibility that different sensors responding to different external features (or even direct interference from the programmer) could produce the same internal states and the same printout; insofar as this is possible, the computer fails to model the meaning of the words on the printout. Those, such as Jerry A. Fodor, who are convinced of the adequacy of computer models have tried to make a virtue of this difficulty and have advanced 'methodological solipsism . . . as a research strategy in cognitive psychology'. Others, such as John Searle, have turned these difficulties into an a priori argument against the possibility of computer modelling of human languages and against the claim that the human mind is in all essential respects a computer.

So far we have considered approaches to meaning which look either to the relation between language and the world or to the relation between language and mind. (The latter may seek to preserve the meaning relation as a fit subject for scientific study by treating mental structures or intentions as natural, possibly purely physical, phenomena.) A third approach would argue that the difficulties of the first two arise from not recognizing that meaning must be studied in the context of a (three-term) relation between mind and the world and language, where the last of these is conceived of as a social phenomenon. This was an important feature of Saussure's theory, for he insisted that 'language never exists apart from social fact', but it is also an important principle of the outlook of such diverse thinkers as *Hegel, Marx, *Dewey, Mead, *Vygotsky, and *Wittgenstein.

It is from this perspective that Bennett's programme would be criticized for assuming that non-language users could have, and recognize in others, intentions as complex as required for Grice's analysis of (even) a simple act of signalling. Thought, from this perspective, cannot exist without (or prior to) language.

According to the social behaviourists, George Herbert Mead for example, it would be acceptable to regard social animals as affecting the behaviour of one another in the following complex way: the beginning of a pattern of behaviour (a gesture) on the part of one animal elicits from another a pattern of behaviour which modifies the development of that pattern as it unfolds in the behaviour of the first animal. But to behave as a human does in such a social interaction, the second animal would have to respond not only to the gesture, but to the relationship between the gesture and the object that had acted as stimulus to the gesture, *and to do so from the standpoint of the first animal.* This is what is required for the second animal to respond to something as meaningful, the concept of meaning implied here being 'an individual reaction which an object may call out'. For the meaning of an object to be 'ours' we must have adapted ourselves to a comprehensive set of reactions toward it, which we can not only adopt ourselves but do so also in the role of others who can respond in that way. Meaning is not, on this account, primarily a property of objects, John Dewey observed, it must be primarily a property of behavioural responses and derivatively of the objects that enter into those patterns.

Another development of an essentially social approach to meaning will be found in the later work of Wittgenstein. Wittgenstein interpreted Frege's suggestion that a word has a meaning only as part of a sentence, as a way of saying that things cannot have names except in a 'language game' (*Investigations*, I. 49), a label which Wittgenstein applied to social contexts in which words are used in structured ways of interacting with the world. All three, language, language users, and the world, are bound up in this concept, and its implications were spelled out in the advice, 'Don't ask for the meaning, ask for the use.' Wittgenstein, moreover, mounted controversial and much debated arguments against the possibility of a person assigning a meaning to a word on the basis of an intention to use that word to apply to something experienced privately. The use of language to describe subjective experience is dependent on and derivative from linguistic practices in which several people coordinate their interactions with each other. (See also WITTGENSTEIN'S PHILOSOPHY OF LANGUAGE.)

Whether one treats this third approach as conforming to or repudiating the demand for a scientific approach to language depends on whether one conceives the study of human social interaction as (at least potentially) continuous with the scientific study of nature. A tradition going back to Giambattista Vico in the early 18th century regards the study of human institutions and artefacts as the province of a study which, if scientific, involves methods quite discontinuous with the natural sciences. More recent developments in this tradition insist upon the need for the imaginative re-creation of the experience of other human beings, of the need for empathy or sympathy in grasping the meaning of a text, and generally refer to their methodology under the rubric 'hermeneutics'. Not all those, however, who insist on the importance of the social in the study of meaning adopt this methodological dualism. Whether or not one does adopt a dualist approach is related in an important way to the conception one has of scientific knowledge. This in turn rests on the way one conceives the relationship between human beings (in particular their minds) and the rest of nature.　　　JET

Ayer, A. J. (ed.) (1959). *Logical Positivism.*

Bennett, J. (1976). *Linguistic Behaviour.*

Davidson, D. (1984). *Inquiries into Truth and Interpretation.*

Fodor, J. A. (1981). *Representations.*

Frege, G. (1952). *Philosophical Writings.* Eds. and trans. P. T. Geach and M. Black.

Kripke, S. (1980). *Naming and Necessity.*

Mead, G. H. (1964). *Selected Writings.* Ed. A. J. Reck.

Quine, W. V. (1960). *Word and Object.*

Saussure, F. de (1960). *Course in General Linguistics.* Trans. W. Baskin.

Wittgenstein, L. (1958). *Philosophical Investigations.* Trans. G. E. M. Anscombe.

medulla. The inner part of an organ, or the abbreviation for 'medulla oblongata' (or 'bulb') at the top of the spinal cord. The medulla functions primarily as a relay station between the spinal cord and the brain. It also contains the respiratory, vasomotor, and cardiac centres, as well as many mechanisms for controlling reflex activities such as coughing and vomiting.

memes. Memes are skills, habits, songs, stories, or any other kind of information that is copied from person to person. The term was coined by Richard Dawkins in his 1976 book *The Selfish Gene*. Memes, like genes, are replicators. That is, they are information that is copied with variation and selection. Because only some of the variants survive, memes (and hence culture) evolve. Memes are copied by imitation and teaching, and they compete for space in our memories and for the chance to be copied again.

On this view our minds and culture are designed by memetic selection, just as organisms are designed by natural selection acting on genes. Many memes succeed because they are useful to us, while others use a variety of tricks to get copied, regardless of their effect on either us or our genes. A central question for memetics is therefore 'why has this meme survived?', remembering that advantage to the human carrier is only one survival strategy a selfish meme might use.

Among the most virus-like of memes are chain letters and e-mail viruses. Their basic structure is a copy-me instruction (pass this message to all your friends) backed up with threats and promises, and they can be highly virulent. Dawkins pointed out that many religions have essentially the same structure and hence called them 'viruses of the mind'. Such religions use threats (hell and damnation), promises (heaven, salvation, and God's love), and instructions to pass them on (teach your children, read the texts, and sing hymns). Some use tricks such as promoting faith over doubt to reduce any sceptical enquiry into dubious claims. This approach makes sense of otherwise puzzling behaviours, such as celibacy. A truly celibate priest cannot pass on his genes, but having no children means he can devote his time and resources to spreading the memes of his religion, including celibacy. So the meme for celibacy succeeds.

Apart from religions, other viral memes include alternative therapies that do not work, new-age fads and cults, and astrology, which is immensely popular even though most of its claims have been shown to be false. Children's games, jokes, and urban legends also spread infectiously, and epidemiological methods can be used to study them.

The vast majority of memes are not viruses but are the very foundations of our lives, including all of the arts and sports, transport and communications systems, political and monetary systems, and science. Note that the memeplexes of science have a different structure from those of religion. Science certainly contains some viral memes, such as false theories and fraudulent claims, but it encourages critical enquiry and experimental testing as criteria for accepting or rejecting its memes. There are several mysteries about human nature that might potentially yield to a memetic explanation. Humans are extraordinarily cooperative and altruistic, often at great cost to themselves or their genes. Indeed, in those cultures with the best communications—and hence the most memes—many altruistic activities thrive, such as pacifism, vegetarianism, recycling, charity work, and the caring professions. People put enormous efforts into helping others who are not their relatives and who are unlikely or unable to reciprocate in the future. In other words these behaviours are hard to explain biologically. The memetic approach explains how these particular memes are able to spread and provides a very different view on the origins of morality.

A process that Susan Blackmore (1999) calls 'memetic drive' may also explain our exceptionally large brains and unique capacity for language. The turning point came when our early ancestors first began to imitate (a skill that is otherwise rare in the animal kingdom). This let loose the new replicator, the memes, which then began to spread. People who could copy the latest memes were at an advantage and so genes for the ability to imitate those memes also spread. As imitation got better and better this meant increasing brain size, and more memes. As the memes evolved in one particular direction, the genes were forced to follow. This explains why we are so good at dancing, music, and religious ritual—abilities that seem hard to explain in biological terms. Finally, since some memes are dangerous or even deadly, the coevolution of genes and memes forced us to copy memes selectively. In other words, unlike other species, we evolved as selective imitators.

This same process might account for the origins of language. On this view competing sounds were copied from person to person, and those of higher fidelity spread more than others. Human brains then evolved to become better and better at copying those winning sounds.

In early human evolution memes spread very slowly, and often vertically from parent to child. Today most memes are spread horizontally, and the machinery for copying them has moved on from human brains to books and newspapers, broadcasting, computers, and the internet. Communication is faster and more extensive all the time, and the internet is a vast playground for memes, supporting the next stage of memetic evolution.

Finally memetics has implications for the mystery of human consciousness. According to Daniel Dennett (1995), humans are a particular sort of ape infested with memes, human consciousness is itself a huge complex of memes, and the self is a 'benign user illusion'. Blackmore suggests that this illusory self is a collection of memes that have come together for their own mutual protection and propagation, regardless of their effects on the organism that sustains them, and is far from benign. Ordinary human consciousness is distorted by the false idea of a self which has consciousness and free will. Practices like meditation can penetrate the illusion.

Memetics has many critics and is still in its early stages, but it provides testable predictions. Only future research will show whether the meme should be rejected as a useless virus or welcomed as a new idea with real scientific power.   SJB

Aunger, R. A. (ed) (2000). *Darwinizing Culture: The Status of Memetics as a Science.*
Blackmore, S. J. (1999). *The Meme Machine.*
Dennett, D. (1995). *Darwin's Dangerous Idea.*

memories, false. False memories arise when an individual 'remembers' details or events from the past that did not actually occur. Most of the time memory serves us well. However, memory is inherently a constructive process prone to elaboration, omission, and distortion (Bartlett 1932). Although we usually remember the gist of past experience, we often forget the details. Sometimes, we incorrectly recall parts of experiences, and sometimes we 'remember' entire events that never occurred. Knowledge of memory's vagaries can help us reduce errors, both harmless and harmful.

1. Memory for the past
2. Cultivating false memories
3. Imagination and false beliefs
4. Auto-suggestion
5. Applications of false memory research

1. Memory for the past
How do people remember significant events from the past? Memory is affected by a variety of factors, from the quality and quantity of the sensory experiences that are encoded to the retrieval of those details. One way in which researchers study these factors is by simulating real events, such as accidents or crimes.

A witness's initial perception of a crime can be divided broadly into three categories: (1) event characteristics (e.g. quality of lighting, duration of event, presence of a weapon); (2) witness characteristics (e.g. age, whether the witness was under the influence of alcohol or other drugs); and (3) how the event affects the witness (e.g. presence of weapon can cause witness to fixate on weapon instead of on the face of the weapon holder).

The memory associated with a witnessed event does not simply lie idle in the mind awaiting retrieval. Instead, the memory may be supplemented, distorted, or perhaps even altered by new information that somehow contradicts the original memory. People exposed to new, misleading information often erroneously report details absent from the original event.

Researchers use a straightforward procedure to demonstrate the impact of post-event information. For example, witnesses view a simulated accident in which a car passes a stop sign. Later, half the witnesses receive new misleading information about the event: it was a yield sign. Others receive no misinformation. Finally, all participants try to recall the original event. When asked about the key detail, misinformed participants often say they saw a yield sign (Loftus 1996).

There is considerable debate over the permanence of the original memory after exposure to misinformation (Loftus and Loftus 1980, Ayers and Reder 1998). Namely, is memory altered, or does misinformation co-exist with the original memory? In the former case the original memory is unrecoverable, whereas in the latter case proper cueing may potentially elicit the memory. Despite this controversy, most scientists agree that misinformation can significantly change people's reports of their past.

The manner in which eyewitnesses are interrogated influences their reports. Biased or leading questions (e.g. 'Did you see the flat tyre?') can distort people's recollections. Definite articles like 'the' suggest the existence of a flat tyre, and often cause people to misreport details. It is also possible to increase eyewitness confidence simply by providing feedback. Statements like 'You chose our prime suspect' can enhance confidence. Unfortunately, this feedback may be inaccurate. Thus, leading questions and feedback may increase confidence in memory details that are false.

2. Cultivating false memories
The details surrounding witnessed events and past experiences can undergo many changes from their initial viewing to their final report. It is also possible to create entirely new memories about the past, 'memories' that are false. Research demonstrates that not only can you tinker with a true memory, making it partially false, but you can also plant complex false events in memory. For instance, people can be convinced that they had been lost in a shopping mall as children or that they had knocked over a punchbowl at a family wedding and spilled punch over the bride's parents (Hyman, Husband, and Billings 1995, Loftus 1997). These studies often use a blatant form of suggestion: participants are told that their parents or older relatives recalled the experience, and the participants are encouraged to remember.

Another technique that utilizes the power of suggestion to create false memories is that of dream interpretation. In such research, a dream 'expert' tells participants that their dreams reveal some critical event that occurred before the age of 3, e.g. that they had been lost in a public place or had their lives threatened and had to be rescued. Typically, this suggestion is sufficient to make participants believe that the event actually occurred to them (Mazzoni et al. 1999).

Real memories and false planted memories are, unfortunately, quite difficult to distinguish. Although some group differences have been found (e.g. real memories have more sensory detail), with repeated rehearsal false memories assume the qualities of true memories. Sadly, there is at present no reliable way to differentiate real from suggested memories without some form of independent corroboration.

3. Imagination and false beliefs

There are also more subtle means by which false beliefs and memories can be induced. Simply imagining a false event, like breaking a window with one's hand as a child and bloodying the glass, increases confidence that this personally occurred. Imagination can also influence memory for a complex event occurring only minutes before the imagination.

Why does imagination affect our memory for the past? One possibility is that a source-confusion error has occurred. When people imagine that they had an experience, they may later remember the content of the imagination but fail to realize the source of that content— they attribute the experience to their own life rather than to the imagination. Related to this explanation is the idea that imagination makes the information seem more familiar. People may fail to realize the source of this familiarity, resulting in a misattribution to prior history rather than to the imagination.

4. Auto-suggestion

Sometimes a false memory can be internally generated without external suggestion or misinformation. For example, Roediger and McDermott (1995) modified a technique, originally developed by James Deese, in which participants see lists of related words (e.g. bed, pillow, dream, tired) that are all associated with a critical lure word that is not presented (e.g. sleep). Later, when people try to remember the words that were presented, they typically recall the critical lures. False memory for the critical lure word occurs frequently —sometimes at a rate that is even greater than the recall of actual words that were presented on the list. Because many lists can be presented to experimental subjects, and so many false 'memories' can be obtained from a single subject, this paradigm is useful for studying the processes involved in creating false memories. However, because these studies involve memory for isolated words, some scientists have questioned whether the processes involved in false word memory apply to more detailed, complex types of false memories.

Auto-suggestion can also be seen in a recent study conducted by Hannigan and Reinitz (2001). Participants were asked to view a series of slides depicting ordinary routines. In one series, a woman is shown grocery shopping. When participants initially viewed a slide depicting oranges strewn across the floor, they later mistakenly claimed to have seen a slide showing the woman taking an orange from the bottom of a pile of oranges. Apparently these false memories arise from a causal inference that people naturally make in the process of trying to reconstruct their memories.

5. Applications of false memory research

Memory can fail us for many reasons. Factors affecting encoding, retention, and retrieval can distort memory. Additionally, leading questions, suggestion, dream interpretation, imagination, and inferential reconstruction powerfully sculpt memories. These findings reveal that memory is imperfect, at times relying on questionable strategies to plug the holes left by myriad details that cannot be remembered.

Memory distortion research has practical relevance. Police interrogations often supply information purportedly offered by other witnesses. 'Our other witness, Mr Banks, says the culprit was limping?' Such statements can distort the content of a person's memory, or the confidence with which a memory is expressed. Judges and juries are influenced by the detail and confidence of witness testimony; therefore, these tactics can skew verdicts.

The fact that memories can be distorted and created suggests that controversial 'repressed memories'—memories that have been forgotten for some time and then suddenly 'remembered'—may be subject to the same vagaries that affect ordinary memories. Therefore, it is imperative that therapists treating such cases be aware that common techniques such as hypnosis, guided imagery, and dream interpretation used to unearth unpleasant memories may, inadvertently, be planting false 'memories'.
DMBe / EFL

Ayers, M. S., and Reder, L. M. (1998). 'A theoretical review of the misinformation effect: predictions from an activation-based memory model'. *Psychonomic Bulletin and Review*, 5.

Bartlett, F. C. (1932). *Remembering: A Study in Experimental and Social Psychology*.

Hannigan, S. L., and Reinitz, M. T. (2001). 'A demonstration and comparison of two types of inference-based memory errors'. *Journal of Experimental Psychology: Learning, Memory, and Cognition*, 27.

Hyman, I. E., Husband, T. H., and Billings, F. J. (1995). 'False memories of childhood experiences'. *Applied Cognitive Psychology*, 9.

Loftus, E. F. (1996). *Eyewitness Testimony* (1st edn. 1979).

——(1997). 'Creating false memories'. *Scientific American*, 277.

—— and Loftus, G. R. (1980). 'On the permanence of stored information in the human brain'. *American Psychologist*, 35.

Mazzoni, G. A. L., Loftus, E. F., Seitz, A., and Lynn, S. J. (1999). 'Creating a new childhood'. *Applied Cognitive Psychology*, 13.

Roediger, H. L., and McDermott, K. B. (1995). 'Creating false memories: remembering words not presented in lists'. *Journal of Experimental Psychology: Learning, Memory, and Cognition*, 21.

memory. When we learn something there must be a change in the brain, but no one knows what the change is. Until quite recently the concept of memory was used only in mentalistic contexts. Few dictionaries contain any reference to memory as a feature of a physical system, though we now have the language of computer scientists to help us in thinking about our own memories, as physical records in the brain. In computer language the memory is an instrument in which is placed a store of whatever information is to be used for calculation. This information is thus a representation of some set of events, embodied in a code. How does the nervous system come to contain useful representations of its environment?

The code of the nervous system is provided basically by the fact that each nerve fibre carries only one sort of information. In such a system learning must consist of a change in the connection pattern of the pathways from input (say the eyes) to output (say movement). The initial basis of the nervous memory is thus provided by heredity (the genetic memory), which establishes the nervous pathways of the newborn. Natural selection has ensured that at birth each individual is provided with potentialities suitable for its future type of environment. A young kitten already has the connections which ensure that each cell of its visual cortex responds mainly when a particular contour moves in front of its eyes, though the responses are less vigorous than they are in an adult. If the kitten is only allowed to see vertical lines then it will later be found to lack the power to respond to horizontal (or other) lines. Meanwhile the response to vertical contours has become much stronger. (See VISUAL SYSTEM: ENVIRONMENTAL INFLUENCES). Memory thus depends upon selection from the original multiplicity of possible actions of those that represent useful responses to the environment. Other work with kittens shows that normal capacities only develop if there is appropriate input at certain short *critical periods. (See SPATIAL COORDINATION.)

A human child similarly is born with a range of capacities, and given the right stimulus he then learns to take those actions that are appropriate (see INFANCY, MIND IN). Thus from 12 months onwards he learns to speak whatever language he hears, making certain vocal movements and rejecting others. All skills involve such selection. As development proceeds we thus build a model in the brain that ensures appropriate behaviour. The problem of memory is to find the mechanism that increases the probability of use of some pathways and decreases that of others.

The decision as to whether a nerve cell is to send a signal depends upon the synapses that it receives from other nerve fibres. It was early suggested by the histologist *Ramón y Cajal that memory depends upon forming synapses. By contrast, Ivan *Pavlov, who pioneered the physiological study of learning, attributed the 'conditioned reflexes' in his dogs to vague processes of spread of excitation and inhibition in the cortex. These two types of theory persist to the present. The majority of neuroscientists probably believe in a synaptic change, but there is little direct evidence of the details of it.

The nervous system contains many pathways that re-excite themselves, and it was suggested that these might serve for memory in the brain, as in some computers. This is not likely to be true for long-term memories, which must surely be physically embodied, since they can endure for up to 100 years, in spite of shocks and anaesthetics and (in rats) even freezing. But it frequently happens that immediately after a shock there is no memory, say of an accident (see AMNESIA). It is therefore postulated that memory is recorded on two or more time scales. The *short-term memory is transient and easily interrupted. Perhaps it is carried by the chains that re-excite themselves. It must endure for long enough to allow a record to be 'printed' in the long-term memory. This may involve synaptic change, perhaps by some sort of growth process. Parts of the brain concerned with memory contain many very small nerve cells ('amacrine cells' or 'micro-neurons'). One suggestion is that these serve to produce an inhibitory substance whose action closes the unwanted pathway. This would allow the other one to be used: its synapses would then become more effective and those of the other pathway would wither away. All such changes would involve synthesis of new protein, and there is evidence that, if a substance inhibiting protein synthesis is given shortly after a learning occasion, no memory is established. This does not mean that the new protein carries the memory. It alters the probability of use of one set of channels rather than another. Information in the brain is coded by channels not molecules. Not appreciating this, biochemists have sought for a memory molecule, on the mistaken analogy of DNA. They have even claimed that memory can be transferred by injecting extracts from a trained brain, or even by the cannibalism of worms. Many injected substances will indeed change brains, but the claims of transfer of specific memories have not been substantiated. The attraction of the idea of cannibalism tells more about human psychology than about the biology of memory.

The capacity to change nervous pathways, that is to learn, is quite widespread. A cockroach without its head will learn not to dip its leg into water from which it gets a shock. From such simple learning systems it has been discovered that various changes in the electrical and chemical properties of the nerve cells are involved. But memories like our own usually store more complicated information, and this involves special nervous equipment. In each species the brain has a memory system suitable to its special way of life. Memories are not parts of a generalized computer system but specific analogue devices. In octopuses we have been able to find two anatomically distinct memory mechanisms. In one are stored records of objects seen and in the other records of objects touched or tasted. The decisions that an octopus makes are rather simple—whether to attack a particular object or to draw in an object touched with its arms. It can learn to attack a horizontal rectangle and avoid a vertical one or to discriminate between rough and smooth spheres. (See INVERTEBRATE LEARNING AND INTELLIGENCE.) Such choices are typical of the selections between alternatives that are the essential features of recording in memory. The animal or man must be provided with feature detectors that can allow the performance of two or more actions. Learning which action to perform must depend upon a system that allows for information about past results to alter the probabilities of the use of the pathways in the future. We believe that this is done by initially reducing the effectiveness of the wrong pathway and then increasing the right one—perhaps by new synaptic growth. Many special features are required to make such a system effective, and it is not surprising that neuroscientists have not yet fully unravelled the secret of the memory mechanism. And, of course, in mammals memory does not depend upon switching single neurons, say in the visual cortex, but somewhere the pathways are changed when we learn.

There must be nervous tracts that bring information such as that of *taste or *pain together with signals from the outside world. In mammals there is evidence that these come through the reinforcement pathways, which can be activated by self-stimulation for reward. These lead through the hypothalamus to the hippocampus, which is a part of the brain particularly concerned with memory.

Another special need is for mechanisms of generalization in the memory, and here the octopus has proved most helpful. It does not have to learn everything eight times over. Martin Wells was able to show that what is learned by one arm can be performed by the others—but not if a particular piece of the brain is removed. This piece, the median inferior frontal, has a weblike structure that allows signals from the different arms to interact. This is one small example of how study of parts of the brain can tell us about the memory mechanism. Again, in an octopus the visual memory can be removed without damaging the touch memory, and vice versa. So the memory record in the octopus brain is localized. In mammals it has proved difficult to find where the record is, so that the psychologist Karl *Lashley, after his lifelong 'search for the *engram', could not decide whether it was nowhere in the brain or everywhere.

The model of the mnemon, or unit of memory, can be considered either as an anatomical reality, as I believe it to be in the octopus, or as a logical schema representing the much more complex situation in man. The essence of it is that establishing a permanent memory record involves

selection from an initial set of possible pathways. Selection is made on a basis of the rewards that follow from different actions. The particular type of memory of each species depends upon modification of the connections of an inborn feature-detector system. In man these detectors are particularly tuned to respond to features of human behaviour. The child is specially sensitive to human speech sounds even at 2 months, long before he can talk or understand speech (see BRAIN DEVELOPMENT). By learning to react in appropriate ways to particular features he then builds a model in his brain that allows him to live in his human environment. See MEMORY, AUTOBIOGRAPHICAL.

JZY

Baddeley, A. D. (1976). *The Psychology of Memory*. (For a comprehensive bibliography.)
Bartlett, F. C. (1932). *Remembering*.
Young, J. Z. (1978). *Programs of the Brain*.

memory: autobiographical. Autobiographical memory refers to our ability to recall knowledge of our past and to form detailed specific memories of single experiences. Because of this our conceptions of ourselves are grounded in experience and constrained by it. Autobiographical memory limits what we can be. For instance, if one can remember going to university, becoming a parent, talking a holiday in France, etc., then the goal of achieving these things (for the first time) can no longer be held. Autobiographical memory constrains the goals we can hold and delimits what aims the self can adopt. It is notable that in certain psychiatric illnesses, e.g. schizophrenic delusions, and following brain damage, an impairment that is often observed is that of a breakdown of the relationship between the self and memory. When autobiographical memory no longer constrains the self to (remembered) reality the result is distortion and fragmentation of the self. Autobiographical memory is then central to an integrated and functioning self-system and, as might be expected with such a central form of cognition, engages neural processing networks that topographically are widely distributed within the brain. In what follows we will take a brief look at the nature of autobiographical memory, its relation to personality, and how it can be disrupted by illness and brain injury.

1. The nature of autobiographical knowledge
2. Autobiographical memory and personality
3. Autobiographical memory following brain damage and in psychiatric illnesses
4. Summary: autobiographical memory and the self—a uniquely human memory system?

1. The nature of autobiographical knowledge
Autobiographical information frequently comes to mind not in the form of memories but rather in the form of statements, propositions, declarations, and beliefs about

the self, often accompanied by generic and/or specific images of details of prior experience: we refer to this information as *autobiographical knowledge*. Autobiographical knowledge is distinct from *sensory perceptual episodic memories* which represent specific details derived from actual experience (Conway 2001). In the formation of a specific autobiographical memory, autobiographical knowledge becomes linked to episodic memories and a stable pattern of activation forms over the indices of autobiographical knowledge structures and associated episodic memories (Conway and Pleydell-Pearce 2000). When this occurs the remember has *recollective experience*—a sense or feeling of the self in the past (Tulving 1985, Wheeler, Stuss, and Tulving 1997)—attention is directed inwards to the autobiographical memory, and at the same time other episodic memories and autobiographical knowledge may also come to mind. Of course, full autobiographical memory formation does not have to take place and autobiographical knowledge can be processed independently of memory formation—although when autobiographical knowledge is accessed autobiographical memory formation is never very far away. Thus, personal knowledge can be accessed and used independently of episodic memories and full memory formation.

Conway and Pleydell-Pearce (2000) propose that this whole system of autobiographical memory formation—the dynamic combining of autobiographical knowledge and episodic memories—is modulated by a control structure they term *the working self*. The working self consists of a currently active goal hierarchy (only parts of which are consciously accessible), abstract knowledge of the self, and other knowledge that facilitates access to autobiographical knowledge structures. It is through the working self that new autobiographical knowledge and episodic memories are formed (encoded) and the working self also influences memory construction by controlling input to the knowledge base and in evaluating output (activated autobiographical knowledge). The working self may even exercise inhibitory control over the knowledge base (cf. Conway and Pleydell-Pearce 2000).

2. Autobiographical memory and personality

In general the working self operates to increase the accessibility of goal-related autobiographical knowledge. Markus (1977) found preferential access to memories of experiences congruent with central self-schema, i.e. how independent or dependent a person was. McAdams (1982) identified individuals with a strong intimacy motivation or with a distinctive power motivation and found that in memories of 'peak' or 'self-defining' experiences the intimacy motivation group recalled peak experiences with a preponderance of intimacy themes compared to individuals who scored lower on this motivation, who showed no memory bias. Similarly, the power motivation group

recalled peak experiences with strong themes of power and satisfaction. Subsequently, McAdams et al. (1997) examined the influence of the Eriksonian notion of *generativity* (Erikson 1963) on the life stories of middle-aged adults. Generativity refers to nurturing and caring for those things, products, and people that have the potential to outlast the self. Those individuals who were judged high in generativity, i.e. who had a *commitment story*, were found to recall a preponderance of events highly related to aspects of generativity. In contrast, those participants who were not identified as holding a commitment story showed no such bias. In a similar way work by Woike and her colleagues has further established the connection between personality and memory (Woike 1995, Woike et al. 1999). Woike et al. (1999) investigated groups of individuals classified as 'agentic' (concerned with personal power, achievement, and independence) or as 'communion' (concerned with relationships, interdependence, and others). Across a series of studies agentic types were found consistently to recall emotional memories of events that involved issues of agency (mastery, humiliation). In contrast, communal types recalled emotional memories featuring others, often significant others, in acts of love and friendship. These and a range of findings from other studies (see McAdams 2001) all show a powerful relationship between memory and the self in which the dominant motives or goals of the self make memories of goal-relevant experiences highly accessible.

3. Autobiographical memory following brain damage and in psychiatric illnesses

Autobiographical memory can become impaired in many different ways following brain injury (see Conway and Fthenaki 2000 for a review). Injuries to regions of the frontal lobes often lead to a 'clouding' of memory and patients with these types of injuries cannot recall detailed memories. In more extreme cases patients may 'confabulate' and construct autobiographical knowledge into plausible but false memories. Patients with damage to the temporal lobes and underlying structures in the limbic system, i.e. hippocampal formation, may lose the ability to form new memories while retaining access to at least some memories from the period before their brain injury. Yet other patients with damage to posterior regions of the brain, regions involved in visual processing (occipital lobes), may lose the ability to generate visual images of the past and because of this become amnesic. Their amnesia occurs because episodic content of autobiographical memories is predominantly encoded in the form of visual images. When the ability to generate visual images is compromised or lost as a consequence of brain damage then access to specific details of the past held in episodic images is also lost and an amnesia for details of the past is the result. In psychiatric illness a common occurrence is that of a severe clouding of autobiographical memory resulting in *overgeneral memories*. For instance, in clinical depression patients recall many memories that lack detail and are much more schematic than typical autobiographical memories. Thus, a patient asked to recall specific memories of his father could only recall general events such as 'walks in the park after Sunday lunch' and was unable to generate a single specific memory of a single walk (see Williams 1996 for review). Clouded overgeneral memories have also been observed in schizophrenic patients and in patients suffering from obsessional–compulsive disorder. One possibility is that the complex control processes that modulate memory construction (working self) become attenuated in psychiatric illnesses in general, and also following damage to the frontal lobes, and so can no longer form fully detailed memories.

4. Summary: autobiographical memory and the self—a uniquely human memory system?

Autobiographical memory is a complex form of higher-order cognition that is intricately bound up with the self and personal identity. As such it may well be an exclusively human form of memory, one not shared with other species. Aspects of it, such as episodic memory, may be common across species and, of course, many species show obvious signs of retention of spatio-temporal information (a hallmark of episodic memory). Whether non-human species also have the capacity to form more abstract autobiographical knowledge and so contextualize their episodic memories is not known. Selves with complex personal histories, histories that can be shared and used to form the basis of social interactions and social groupings, require autobiographical memory—a memory system that is, perhaps, uniquely human. **MC**

Conway, M. A. (2001). 'Sensory perceptual episodic memory and its context: autobiographical memory'. *Philosophical Transactions of the Royal Society of London*, 356.

——and Fthenaki, A. (2000). 'Disruption and loss of autobiographical memory'. In Cermak, L. S. (ed.), *Handbook of Neuropsychology* (2nd edn.): *Memory and Its Disorders*.

——and Pleydell-Pearce, C. W. (2000). 'The construction of autobiographical memories in the self memory system'. *Psychological Review*, 107.

Erikson, E. H. (1963). *Childhood and Society* (1st edn. 1950).

McAdams, D. P. (1982). 'Experiences of intimacy and power: relationships between social motives and autobiographical memory'. *Journal of Personality and Social Psychology*, 42/2.

——(2001). 'The psychology of life stories'. *Review of General Psychology*, 5.

——Diamond, A., de Aubin, E., and Mansfield, E. (1997). 'Stories of commitment: the psychosocial construction of generative lives'. *Journal of Personality and Social Psychology*, 72/3.

Markus, H. (1977). 'Self-schemata and processing information about the self'. *Journal of Personality and Social Psychology*, 35/2.

Tulving, E. (1985). 'Memory and consciousness'. *Canadian Psychologist*, 26.

Wheeler, M. A., Stuss, D. T., and Tulving, E. (1997). 'Towards a theory of episodic memory: the frontal lobes and autonoetic consciousness'. *Psychological Bulletin*, 121.

Williams, J. M. G. (1996). 'Depression and the specificity of autobiographical memory'. In Rubin, D. C. (ed.), *Remembering our Past: Studies in Autobiographical Memory*.

Woike, B. (1995). 'Most-memorable experiences: evidence for a link between implicit and explicit motives and social cognitive processes in everyday life'. *Journal of Personality and Social Psychology*, 68/6.

——Gershkovich, I., Piorkowski, R., and Polo, M. (1999). 'The role of motives in the content and structure of autobiographical memory'. *Journal of Personality and Social Psychology*, 76/4.

memory: biological basis. For materialist theories of the mind, it is axiomatic that in some way there must be brain representations of memory. This may not be intuitively obvious when we consider our own individual memories, for we can clearly rehearse in our minds the histories of past experience (the memories of a childhood birthday party, the image of an absent friend's face, the opening notes of a Beethoven symphony, or the taste of a roast dinner) without these rehearsals affecting our external behaviour in any obvious way. However, for an experimenter studying memory in others, whether human or non-human animal subjects, what is observed is a change in behaviour—a human showing a new skill, or an animal traversing a maze correctly and thereby finding food or avoiding electric shock—and it is from this change that memory is inferred. Indeed memory is a portmanteau expression which includes within itself two processes and, by hypothesis, a thing. The processes are the *learning of some new skill, behaviour pattern, or piece of information (sometimes called the *acquisition* of the memory) and, at some later time, the recall and re-expression of the skill or information (sometimes called *retrieval*). The thing that connects the two processes of learning and recall is a change in the properties of the brain system so as to store the new information which the learning represents, in such a form that it can subsequently, in response to appropriate cues, be searched for and retrieved. This change is known as the memory trace, or *engram. The relationship between the language used to discuss these phenomena in the brain and that used in the description of the properties of computers and their memory stores is not accidental, for much of our present-day thinking about biological memory is directed—and constrained—by a framework of analogies from computer technology and *information theory.

For experimental science, the question is how far memory and its brain representation are amenable to experimental analysis rather than to logical and philosophical enquiry. Over recent decades, this has been one of the central problem areas for psychology and neurobiology. However, the nature of experimental method in these disciplines is such that most attention has been focused on a study of the processes of learning and recall; the engram which links them has been inferred rather than demonstrated. Research has concentrated on asking questions concerning the strategies and temporal processes involved in learning and recall—what and how much can be learned, how fast, and over what period—and concerning the brain systems, at the biochemical, cellular, and physiological levels, that subserve these processes. This research may be conducted either by a direct comparison of the brains of experimental animals which have learned, with those of controls which have not, or by examining, in humans or other animals, the effects of procedures which enhance or retard learning or recall.

The major obstacles to advance in this area are, on the one hand, conceptual—the need to develop clear and testable alternative models—and, on the other, experimental —the development of appropriate control procedures. As will become apparent shortly, it is relatively easy to perform experiments which show that in experimental animals particular drugs and treatments prevent learning or recall from occurring, or that, when learning occurs, particular changes in brain-cell properties accompany it. The problem is to be sure that observed biochemical, anatomical, and physiological changes which accompany learning form the necessary, sufficient, and exclusive representations of that learning at the biological level, rather than being merely the correlates of other phenomena which occur at the same time as the learning. For example, in order to motivate experimental animals to learn it may be necessary to subject them to mild stress (hunger, electric shock); in order to learn, the animals may need to be rather active in the exploration of a particular environment. The challenge is to design experiments which eliminate the possibility that any observed change to be studied is a correlate or consequence of stress, activity, sensory stimulation, or whatever, rather than of the learning itself. Rigorous control of all alternative possibilities is virtually impossible to achieve in a single experiment; rather, the goal must be a balance of probabilities on the basis of a number of separate approaches.

There is ample evidence that the learning process is not a simple one-step process. The most popular hypothesis is that there are at least two separate stages, involving different physiological mechanisms and in all probability different brain regions. The first process is short-lived, the second slower but of longer duration, and they are conventionally referred to as *short-term (STM) and long-term (LTM) memory respectively, though some would claim that short-term memory itself embraces more than one process. The distinction between STM and LTM is illustrated by an experiment in which a list of

seven numbers is read out to a subject, who is asked to repeat them back. Most people can repeat the numbers with accuracy if asked to do so within a few minutes of hearing them, but will fail if asked an hour or so later. However, if the numbers are of importance to the subject (for example, if they form a telephone number) they can generally be recalled days or even years later. Many items are placed in short-term store—numbers, names, this morning's breakfast menu—but only a few find their way into the permanent memory system. This is obviously functionally desirable from the biological viewpoint, as the utility of recalling most short-term stored items for more than a brief while is very limited, and there must be a finite capacity to any store and to the retrieval mechanism.

STM, then, is labile and, in the normal course of events, decays over a period of minutes to hours. If the item to be recalled is not, over this period, transferred from STM to LTM, it is irretrievably lost as STM decays. A variety of drugs and other treatments can affect the memory while it is in STM. Substances which interfere with the brain's electrical activity, or treatments like electroconvulsive shock or the infliction of injury, such as a blow to the head resulting in concussion, will effectively obliterate all items in STM at the time, so that the individual on recovery will have no recall for the events leading up to the injury (see AMNESIA). Certain drugs also appear to enhance STM or facilitate transfer from STM to LTM. These include strychnine and amphetamine (the former having even more considerable and undesirable effects than the latter!). We are led to the hypothesis that the form in which STM is held within the brain involves transient changes in the electrical properties of the brain as a system, very likely a result of a reversible modulation of the firing properties of particular neurons or their *synapses. There is suggestive evidence, based on studies utilizing microinjection of drugs, electrical stimulation or recording, and ablation techniques, as well as the study of human patients with STM deficits, that the hippocampal region of the brain is closely involved in the mechanism of STM and its transfer to LTM. Yet this is a relatively simple model of the relationship between STM and LTM, and the situation is probably a good deal more complex. Not every item which cannot be retrieved from LTM has been lost for ever by STM decay: it may have been overlaid or suppressed, and can be recovered under appropriate circumstances, sometimes by recreating the context in which the memory was first formed. Such observations have led some psychologists to argue that the terms STM and LTM be replaced by new concepts of 'active' and 'labile' memories. However, for the purpose of studying the cellular mechanisms of memory formation, the exact phenomenological features at the behavioural level are of relatively minor importance.

What matters here is that memories, when fixed, are notoriously difficult to erase (indeed they are the most durable features—other, perhaps, than scar tissue—acquired during a person's lifetime). Their durability has led to the widely shared hypothesis that they must be coded for in terms of some equally lasting change in brain structure, with a consequent effect on physiological processes. There is good evidence that LTM is a cortical function in mammals generally, and that in humans the temporal lobes are likely to be involved in memory processes, but what sort of changes in brain structure might one envisage as being able to code for memory? Since at least the 1940s there has been a long-running controversy among physiological psychologists over the localizability or non-localizability of the memory trace. Localized models essentially suggest that particular memories are coded for in terms of particular pathways, or neuronal circuits, and were given theoretical substance by Donald *Hebb, who postulated the existence of a class of neurons whose connections were in the form of synapses which could be modified by experience, thus opening or closing unique pathways. Particular circuits or pathways could correspond to particular memory traces; learning resulted in the modification of synapses and recall from the passage of impulses along the particular pathway concerned. Hebb's modifiable synapse theory found support in the clinical studies of the neurosurgeon Wilder *Penfield, who observed, in human patients being treated for *epilepsy, that electrical stimulation of particular regions of the temporal lobe of the cortex regularly caused the patient to recall specific, if fragmentary, memory sequences.

The rival memory model suggests that, rather than there being localization of memory circuits, the storage of information is a molar property of the mass of cortical cells, a 'field' rather than a 'point' representation being involved. Experiments which lead in this direction derive from the studies of Karl *Lashley, who, also in the 1940s, showed that when rats had been trained to particular maze-running skills, these skills could not be obliterated by removal of particular cortical areas; rather the results of such ablations were generalized deficits proportional to the amount, but not the region, of cortex removed. The theoretical rationale for this model was not available until more recently, in the form of analogies with the non-localized storage of information on a photographic plate provided by the hologram. (See also LOCALIZATION OF BRAIN FUNCTION.)

It is probably true that holographic memory theories have found more favour with mathematical theorists than with experimental neurobiologists, most of whom favour a modifiable synapse/neuronal circuit model, with the proviso that it is likely that any individual memory will have multiple representations in the brain, involving numerous different circuits. Could a neuronal circuit model account for the information storage capacity of the human brain? The number of neurons of the human cortex is often quoted as 10^{10}, and direct counts of synapses would suggest upwards of 10^4 synapses for each neuron; 10^{14} synapses would seem to give ample storage potential for the information acquired in a human lifetime.

How about the direct demonstration of synapses or neuronal circuitry being modified by experience and during learning? Physiological, biochemical, and anatomical evidence on this score has accumulated over the last two decades, though it is fair to say that no fully systematic model exists and rigorous proof that observed changes are the necessary, sufficient, *and* exclusive correlates of learning is lacking; we have to make do with indicative rather than conclusive demonstrations.

At the anatomical and physiological levels, most of the evidence concerns long-term changes in the structure and properties of particular neurons or their synapses in response to experience. For instance, the visual cortex of experimental animals responds to the input of new visual information by lasting changes in the number and dimensions of synapses, including changes in the contact areas between pre- and post-synaptic sides of the synapse and of the storage vesicles which contain transmitter substances. The physiological response properties of visual cortex neurons are modulated in a predictable manner by the environment in which the animal, for example a cat, is reared (see VISUAL SYSTEM: ENVIRONMENTAL INFLUENCES). The neurons are thus 'learning' to recognize and respond to characteristic features of the environment.

Such plastic brain responses to environmental change are regarded as analogies of what happens, on a much more precise scale, during learning. But they are only analogies. To move to greater precision a learning 'model' is required. This is not as easy as it sounds. Psychologists explore memory in rats learning to run mazes, or pigeons pressing levers for reward. Such tasks often require training animals over a long period, and encouraging them to learn by keeping them either hungry or thirsty so that they may be rewarded with food or drink for correct responses, or by punishing them—for instance, by mild electric shocks—when they make mistakes. In such situations, if one trains an animal and finds a subsequent biochemical or cellular change, how can one be sure that the change is not the result of the shocks, or the motor activity involved in the running of the maze, or the sensory stimulation, or the stress?

Although biochemists could and did know in the 1960s and in the 1970s that training animals under these conditions affected the rate of protein synthesis in particular brain regions, the interpretation of such experiments was open to doubt. Other experiments used drugs which affected the rate of protein synthesis in the brain. In general, drugs that speed protein synthesis enhance the rate of learning of complex tasks, whereas those that inhibit protein synthesis are without effect on STM or the recall of acquired memories, but prevent the development of LTM. None the less it was argued that the effects of these drugs on memory formation and on protein synthesis were independent, both being the consequence of other types of central effect of the drugs concerned. More precise models and methods, at both behavioural and biochemical levels, were required.

In more recent years, three types of experimental system have begun to yield particularly revealing information about the cellular mechanisms involved in learning processes. In the first, the learning 'model' is the young chick. Day-old chicks readily learn a number of tasks—for instance, they become '*imprinted'—learning to distinguish their mother (or, in the experiments, a mother substitute) from all other objects in their environment, and following her subsequently. The chicks also continually explore their environment by pecking, and learn to distinguish food objects from inedible or distasteful items. For Pat Bateson and Gabriel Horn in Cambridge and Steven Rose's group at the Open University, these spontaneous forms of learning proved particularly amenable to cellular study. When a bird pecks at a distasteful object which it learns to avoid, there results a series of biochemical changes in very specific regions of the forebrain. The changes involve first the mobilization of certain key enzyme systems which modulate synaptic transmission, and then, as part of a longer-term process, the synthesis of new glycoproteins, which are transported from the nerve-cell bodies in which they are made to the synapses, where they become incorporated into the synaptic membranes. As a consequence of these biochemical modifications, synapses in at least three separate but connected left-hemisphere regions of the brain of the chick change in their structure in ways which can be detected at high magnification in the electron microscope; in particular, the number of synaptic vesicles—the transmitter-containing bodies at the synapse—increases and the region of the synapse that directly apposes the pre- and post-synaptic cell changes in length. All this looks uncommonly like what might be expected if synaptic connectivity were being modulated and new pathways being formed. Over the period of hours following learning, the electrical properties of the cells in at least one of these forebrain regions also change dramatically, with large increases in the rate of neuronal firing. Such changes occur only in birds which remember the aversive stimulus. If they are trained but made to forget, the changes in physiology and biochemistry do not occur. Moreover, as Gabriel Horn has shown, using imprinting, these regions of synaptic change are *necessary* for memory formation to occur; if one particular region is excised from the chick brain before training,

learning the imprinting task becomes impossible. If the bird is trained and then the region is immediately excised, the chick behaves as if it is naive and has no recall for the task. In other respects it behaves normally, and sham operations do not produce the memory deficits.

The young chick may seem a simpler organism in which to study memory than the psychologists' traditional beasts, but the other two recent types of experimental system have even greater simplicity. For Eric Kandel and his colleagues in New York, the organism of choice was the seemingly unpromising sea slug, *Aplysia californica*. These large molluscs have a limited repertoire of behaviour, and do not even have brains in the vertebrate sense—their nerve cells are distributed through their body in a variety of groups of cells known as ganglia. What makes them attractive to the neurobiologist is that, whereas vertebrate brains have many thousands of millions of smaller cells, *Aplysia* has fewer than a million neurons, and many of them are large—up to a millimetre in diameter as opposed to the vertebrate size of 10–100 micrometres. Individual nerve cells are thus amenable to physiological study: the 'same' cell can be located in many different individuals; it can be dissected out, and its connections studied. The entire ganglion plus its inputs and outputs can be isolated from the rest of the organism and maintained in physiologically functional condition for several days. Kandel studied in particular the nerve cells involved in a number of cellular systems active in the processes of *habituation and sensitization of reflexes. When they are lightly touched, regions of the surface of the animal around its gill contract vigorously, as part of an escape and withdrawal reflex. This response diminishes if the same region is repeatedly touched (habituation) but may be extended to form a reaction to previously neutral stimuli if they are coupled with potentially noxious ones (sensitization). Kandel has mapped in some detail the neural pathways involved in these processes and has been able to record physiologically, from the pre- and post-synaptic cells involved in the responses, the changes that occur as habituation or sensitization takes place. He has been able to show the direct involvement of transmitters such as serotonin in the process, and has followed a number of key biochemical steps in the synapse—especially the role played by a combination of a synaptic membrane protein, capable of being reversibly phosphorylated in response to external stimuli, and the intracellular 'second messenger' substance cyclic AMP. These molecular processes are involved in regulating the entry of calcium ions into the cells; the calcium ions alter the membrane potentials and directly modulate synaptic connectivity. Kandel argues that such changes in the electrical properties of individual synapses as a result of experience both occur and underlie at least relatively short-duration memory processes.

The third experimental approach has been to abandon living organisms altogether in searching for a system in which to study the molecular biology of neuronal plasticity. It is well known that, if thin slices of brain tissue—no more than a third of a millimetre in thickness—are cut and placed in a warm, oxygenated, glucose-containing medium, they retain their biochemical properties and some physiological properties for a period of several hours. If the slices are cut appropriately they can be made to retain at least some of their nerve inputs. Recording electrodes can be placed among the cells of the slice, and the effect on the cells of electrically stimulating the inputs can be followed. A particularly interesting brain region to study in this way is the mammalian hippocampus, for long considered to be involved in aspects of the process of transfer of short- to long-term memory. Gary Lynch and his colleagues at Irvine, California, among others, have shown that, if hippocampal slices are electrically stimulated from their appropriate nerve inputs, there can be long-lasting (up to an hour or more) changes in the electrical outputs from these cells—the so-called hippocampal potentiation. This phenomenon *in vitro* is known to mimic the *in vivo* properties of the cells of this brain region, which were found to show such potentiation by Bliss and others in the early 1970s. *In vitro* the biochemical mechanisms involved can be studied in detail, and shown to involve, as in *Aplysia*, phosphorylated membrane proteins, cyclic AMP, glutamate receptors, and calcium ion channels in the membrane. Lynch argues that hippocampal potentiation is an *in vitro* analogue of memory processes.

All this may seem a long way from Marcel Proust's evocation of youthful memory, À *la recherche du temps perdu*, with its sense imagery. Are young chicks, sea slugs, or slices of brain tissue really going to reveal the molecular mechanisms of such a durable if elusive property of the human brain? It is an act of faith, perhaps, to claim that they are. Complex phenomena are not merely the result of the additive properties of simpler ones, because as systems increase in complexity their properties change qualitatively (which is why we may speak of human consciousness, but are much more doubtful about animal consciousness despite the similarities in basic brain structure). Nevertheless, the general principles of organization that underlie these brain systems are similar. Biochemically, nervous and hormonal systems of body regulation involve similar chemical processes subserving different ends. The organization of nervous transmission is almost identical over a range of living organisms from insects and molluscs to humans. There seems no reason to doubt that the mechanisms involved in nervous system plasticity will turn out also to be related, even though the complexity and richness of the plastic response will vary qualitatively as we move from small-brained and rather 'hard-wired'

organisms into the immensely plastic and flexible brain of the human.

However, it is important to emphasize what it is that such studies will not reveal. Some years ago there was wide publicity for experiments which purported to show that particular memories were encoded in particular molecular structures—substances which could be extracted from a trained animal and then injected into a naive one, carrying the memories with them. This type of experiment, always theoretically dubious, has since been largely discredited in practice as well, as being based on fallacious and artefactual errors of experimental design. What the biochemical and anatomical studies show is *not* specific 'memory molecules', but general cellular systems which underlie all plastic responses of the brain to experience. Although it is not known whether such mechanisms occur in all types of neurons in all organisms, a general parsimony principle which does not multiply processes needlessly would suggest that this is likely to be the case. If it is so, then the specificity of a memory—as when the brain distinguishes among remembering a telephone number, a friend's face, and a childhood recollection—does not lie in the particularity of the biochemical substances concerned. Rather it depends on which cells are involved in the circuits, where in the brain they are located, and with which other cells they are connected.

In this respect, analysing the biochemistry and anatomy of memory is like studying the chemistry and design of the recording head of a tape recorder and a cassette of magnetic tape. To know how a tape recorder works, these things must be studied. But no amount of information revealed by such study will enable one to predict the message on the tape. For that, one has to play the machine. This is likely to remain true for analysis of the cell biology of memory as well. See MEMORY, AUTOBIOGRAPHICAL.

SPRR

Hebb, D. O. (1961). *Organisation of Behavior* (2nd edn.).
Horn, G. (1985). *Memory, Imprinting, and the Brain.*
Kandel, E. R., and Schwartz, J. H. (1982). 'Molecular biology of learning: modulation of transmitter release'. *Science*, 248.
Lashley, K. S. (1963). *Brain Mechanisms and Intelligence.*
Luria, A. R. (1969). *The Mind of a Mnemonist.*
Rose, S. P. R. (1976). *The Conscious Brain.*
—— (1981). 'What should a biochemistry of learning and memory be about?' *Neuroscience*, 6.
—— (ed.) (1982). *Towards a Liberatory Biology.*
Squire, L. R., and Butlers, N. (eds.) (1984). *Neuropsychology of Memory.*

memory: experimental approaches. One of the problems in the study of psychology is that it deals with the familiar. And the familiar, being taken for granted, provokes little curiosity. It is therefore often easier to perceive scientific problems when we are confronted with unexpected malfunction. The study of memory is a case in point. The failure of memory, or *amnesia, not only excites interest but also reveals unsuspected facets of the memory process. The form of amnesia which we will first discuss often occurs after blows to the head have produced unconsciousness. Upon recovery the subject cannot remember certain events that occurred in the past. However, it is not the events in the distant past, the memory of which is normally dim, that are most severely affected. It is precisely those events whose memory would be sharpest at the time of the accident that cannot be recalled—the events that occurred closest in time to the accident. For instance, in car accidents the injured person cannot remember the accident itself. The last thing he may remember is being at a place many miles from where the accident occurred. In severe cases the memory of weeks before the accident is unavailable. However, with the passage of time the blank in the memory shrinks, those episodes furthest away in time from the accident returning first. The extent of recovery is variable but a short period of about one second before the accident seems always to remain inaccessible to memory.

From this quite common type of amnesia (retrograde amnesia) some surprising consequences follow. It is obvious that some change occurs at the moment of the registration of a memory. Not so obvious is the observation that such a change is more vulnerable to trauma the more recent the change is. Apart from anything else, this 'age dependence' indicates that the physiological change underlying memory is not all-or-none but alters in a continuous manner with time. The remarkable length of time over which such alterations occur can be most clearly seen in *Korsakoff's syndrome, a condition which sometimes occurs in association with alcoholism. The patient here also suffers from retrograde amnesia. However, the memory blank may be very extensive, perhaps extending over many years and often spreading further and further back until the patient can remember only events in his early youth or childhood. This indicates that the changes in memory we spoke of above must continue over decades.

Unfortunately the physiological changes that occur to produce amnesia clinically are somewhat obscure. A blow on the head can hardly be considered to be a delicate biochemical or anatomical dissecting tool. Consequently scientists have attempted to produce amnesia in animals using more controlled methods. One such method produces amnesia through the use of electroconvulsive shock. A brief surge of current is passed through the nervous system of a rat so as to produce unconsciousness. Twenty-four hours later the rat appears not to recall habits it learned just before the application of such a shock. However, other habits acquired a little while before the shock survive unscathed. These results encouraged theorists to postulate that memory existed in two stages —a labile short-lived stage, disruptible by electric shock,

and a permanent stage invulnerable to such interference. Two main problems with such an interpretation are that slightly different experimental circumstances produce widely varying estimates of the duration of the time during which a memory is vulnerable. The second and more severe difficulty emerged when rats were tested at other times besides the traditional 24 hours after learning. It emerged that if rats were tested four hours later they did remember, though matched animals would not remember 24 hours later. Further rats, given electroconvulsive shock five minutes after training, would remember well 24 hours later, but remember nothing a week later, when untreated rats showed good retention. Such findings are difficult to square with a two-stage theory of memory, but suggest instead that electroconvulsive shock causes an acceleration of forgetting. However, such forgetting may not be permanent because there exist well-authenticated cases of recovery of memory after such amnesia. In any case it turns out that passing a large current across the head is hardly more sophisticated as a research tool than a sharp blow to the skull.

In an effort to increase the specificity of physiological interference, various chemical agents have been administered after a learning task, and some of these, such as potassium chloride, flurothyl, and barbiturates, were found to have effects qualitatively similar to electroconvulsive shock. Nevertheless, no specific process in the central nervous system could be pinpointed, and the conclusion seems to be that almost any agent capable of producing a profound interruption in the working of the brain will also induce retrograde amnesia.

Because of advances in the understanding of the storage of genetic information, attention became focused on the possibility that some analogous processes carried information in memory, and attempts were made to affect memory by administering RNA, DNA, and protein synthesis-inhibiting drugs. While there is no doubt that these drugs do have effects similar to electroconvulsive shock, interpretation of the way they achieve those effects is in doubt. Even if we accept the premiss that amnesia is caused as a result of protein, RNA, or DNA synthesis inhibition by the drug and not by one of its side effects, this does not necessarily mean that memory itself is coded by what the drug inhibits. Protein synthesis inhibition might very well interfere with some other changes that underlie memory. Suspicious also are the facts that the amnesic consequences of the above treatments may be countered by the administration of stimulants and that the memories that should lack a physiological substrate have in several experiments been shown to return. In any case the idea that the information stored in memory is encoded in a large molecule seems rather unlikely. While such a molecular hypothesis would solve the problem of storage, it fails when it comes to an equally important characteristic of the memory system—namely fast access. It is difficult to see how the nervous system would find the information once it was stored.

A more likely hypothesis than the molecular, concerning memory storage, which was put forward as early as the end of the 19th century, is that the change underlying memory consists of synaptic modification. Synapses are the gaps across which neurons communicate with each other, and it is easy to envisage how changes in the facility of transmission across such gaps could be used to store easily accessible information. Even so, in spite of its plausibility, such a hypothesis has received no experimental support till recently. The test that was made utilized a fact already mentioned above, that of a rather slow change in the substrate of memory. If this change is in the transmission capacity of a synapse, or a group of synapses, then pharmacological tools are available to show the existence of such changes. Poorly conducting synapses react differently to the same dose of drug from normally conducting synapses. A good example of this occurs in myasthenia gravis. In this condition the patient has great difficulty in contracting skeletal muscles. The neural pathways to the muscles are intact and so are the muscles themselves. What is impaired is the junction between the neuron and the muscle. This junction is a type of synapse. For reasons that need not concern us here, the transmitter substance, acetylcholine, which is ejected from the neuron, has a much smaller effect on the muscle than normal. When the patient is given a certain dose of the anticholinesterase group of drugs, the destruction of acetylcholine which normally occurs is slowed, and so more acetylcholine becomes available to cause muscle contraction. As a result, movement is facilitated and normal functioning is made possible. However, the same dose of drug administered to a normal person produces paralysis instead, as a consequence of too much transmitter. In a similar manner, we might expect new or weak memories to be facilitated and older or strong memories to be blocked, if the substrate of memory was a synapse that varied in efficiency. As a test of this, rats were trained to perform a habit. The rats were then divided into a large number of groups and made to wait different lengths of time before being retested. They were injected with anticholinesterase in the same dose at the same time, before being tested on their memory of the habit. Any effect of the drug on performance should therefore have been the same. However, the memory of the task was strongly affected by the age of such memory. Little effect of the drug was seen on memories of up to three days. Almost complete forgetting was manifest when the habit was 7–14 days old. However, when the habit was 21–28 days old and almost forgotten by rats not treated with the drug just before retest, the treated rats showed very good retention. It was thus possible in a simple experiment to show both block and facilitation of a habit using a synaptically active drug.

These experiments strongly suggest that memory is based on a change in synaptic function. As a result of learning, a synapse begins to transmit, then transmits more strongly, and eventually such transmission attenuates to express itself as *forgetting. Because of the changes in susceptibility to drugs, it became important to look for changes in the strength of memory that these changes in susceptibility suggested. As a result it has now been found that when the memory for a habit is tested at various times after learning, such memory does get progressively stronger before forgetting sets in. For instance, rats are placed in a box consisting of two compartments, one lit and the other dark. These are connected by a hole in a partition. When rats are placed in the lit compartment they invariably, after a certain average time, enter the dark compartment. Upon entering the dark compartment they are given an electric shock. On being placed in the lit compartment again, the time it takes the rats to enter the dark compartment is greatly increased. It is the magnitude of this increase that gives us an index of the strength of memory. It has been shown that the time that rats stay out of the dark compartment increases with the time since they were shocked in it. Interestingly enough, the longer the time that rats stay out of the dark compartment the greater the effect of anticholinesterase in reducing memory strength, again as measured by the time that rats choose to stay out of the dark compartment. So that, as memory improves, so does its susceptibility to anticholinesterase, confirming the notion that the physical change in memory occurs at a cholinergic synapse.

Separate from the question of what the change is that underlies memory is the problem of where in the nervous system the change occurs. Is there a place in the nervous system whose destruction abolishes memory? The answer is complex. During operations for removal of epileptogenic foci it is necessary for the surgeon to stimulate the brain while the patient is conscious. Such a procedure, while it may seem extreme, is actually quite innocuous and quite painless. During stimulation of the temporal lobe, complex memory-like imagery arises. However, while such local stimulation triggers recall, the memory does not reside within this locus, because surgical removal of the locus does not abolish later recall of the same memory. Bilateral lesions in the same general area do produce memory disorders, but again these are not due to the destruction of existing memories. Rather, the disorder closely resembles Korsakoff's syndrome, mentioned above, in which old memories survive while new memories are strangely transitory.

There seems to be no particular area in the nervous system that functions as a memory store, as no lesion so far has abolished all memory. There has been an assumption, now shown to be false, that the cortex somehow mediates memory and learning. However, totally decorticate animals, while diminished in the capacity to discriminate, show good learning and retention. This of course does not mean that each particular memory is diffusely stored all over the brain. It probably implies that the specialized capacity to change is a characteristic of most neural tissue. There is also suggestive evidence that memories are stored in those parts of the brain that mediate the perceptions on which those particular memories are based. For instance, patients with lesions of the visual cortex are blind, but unlike people whose blindness is due to an injury to more peripheral organs of sight they cannot even remember what it was like to see. Further, it has been shown by experiments on how items in memory inhibit each other that it is those items that are represented as neighbours in the sensory part of the brain which interfere with each other most. Such a pattern of interference would be expected if memory storage occurred in the parts of the brain devoted to perceptual processing.

JAD

Rose, S. (2003). *The Making of Memory: From Molecules to Mind*.

memory and context. A popular standby of writers of detective stories over the years has been the witness who is unable to recall some crucial piece of information until the cunning detective hits on the idea of reconstructing the exact situation in which the incident occurred, whereupon all comes flooding back. Such a device did indeed play a central role in the first ever detective novel, *The Moonstone* by Wilkie Collins. But is there any foundation to the belief that context may have such powerful effect? In fact there is.

A number of studies have been carried out in which subjects learn material, typically lists of words, in one environment and attempt to recall it in either the same or a different environmental context. There is usually a tendency for recall to be better when it takes place under conditions identical to those in which the material was learnt. The effect is, however, typically rather small, and certainly not enough to suggest—for example—that examinees should do all their revision in the examination hall. With really dramatic shifts in environment, however, quite large effects can be obtained.

Godden and Baddeley (1975) used divers as subjects and had them learn a list of words either on the shore or on the ocean bed at a depth of about 6 metres (20 feet). The divers then attempted to recall either in the same environment or in the other one. A drop of about 40 per cent occurred when divers who had learnt under water were required to recall on land, or vice versa, indicating that it was crucial to reinstate the context if good recall was required. A subsequent experiment showed that if, instead of asking the subjects to recall the words, they were given a recognition

task in which they simply picked out the words they had seen before from a list comprising both presented and non-presented words, no such decrement occurred. This seems to suggest that context dependency is a retrieval effect, with context helping the subject to locate the relevant information in his memory store. Under recognition conditions, the presentation of the word itself acts as an excellent retrieval cue which dispenses with the need for environmental context to assist in locating the relevant memory trace.

A phenomenon which is closely related to that of context-dependent memory is that of state-dependent memory in which, instead of varying the environmental context, the internal state of the organism is manipulated, for example by means of drugs (Kumar, Stolerman, and Steinberg 1970). Goodwin et al. studied the role of state dependency in alcoholics. They cite clinical evidence of heavy drinkers who, when sober, are unable to find alcohol and money which they hid while drunk, but who remember the hiding places once they are drunk again. They attempted to test this, using a group of heavy drinkers and studying the learning and recall of a series of tasks, including memory for words and for pictures, which included both neutral pictures taken from a mail-order catalogue and 'emotional' pictures from a nudist magazine. They found clear evidence of context dependency in all the tasks involving recall, but no effect for picture recognition. A similar lack of effect has subsequently been shown for word recognition. As in the case of environmental context, an effect occurs for recall, but disappears when the retrieval component is diminished by using recognition testing.

One very powerful source of context effects is that of mood. In one series of experiments, subjects were hypnotically induced to feel either happy or sad during the learning of a list of words, and to be either happy or sad during recall. Words that were learnt when sad were recalled best when sad and vice versa (Bower 1981). Similarly, quite powerful effects have been observed in the case of depressed patients who have great difficulty accessing memory for pleasant and happy events during periods of depression, while they are well able to recall sad incidents. This tendency of course tends to reinforce their depression, locking them into a vicious circle of increasing sadness and increasing difficulty in remembering anything not associated with sadness. Breaking away from this cycle has obvious therapeutic potential, and forms one component of the cognitive treatment of depression.

We have so far been concerned with the role of *extrinsic* or environmental context in memory. As we have seen, this typically occurs in the case of recall but not of recognition. Much more dramatic contextual effects can be obtained by means of *intrinsic* context, that is contextual cues which change the interpretation of the material to be remembered. To take an extreme example, suppose I ask you to remember the word 'jam'. I can bias the way in which you encode and remember the word by preceding it with the word 'traffic' or with 'strawberry'. If I have initially biased your interpretation of the word in the direction of traffic jam, you are much less likely to recognize the word subsequently if it is accompanied by the word 'raspberry', which biases you towards the other meaning of jam. This effect occurs even though the subject knows full well that he is only supposed to remember the word 'jam' and not the contextual or biasing words. As Tulving and Osler have shown, this effect is not limited to words that have more than one meaning. If one takes a word like 'city', and presents it alongside a weakly associated word such as 'dirty', then recognition is substantially impaired if the test item is accompanied by another but different weakly associated word such as 'village'. This suggests that the subject is not remembering the word 'city' in and of itself, but is creating some representation which is biased by the context. For example, he may be thinking in terms of the dirt and litter associated with a busy city. When 'city' is subsequently presented with another biasing word such as 'village', he may well be thinking of some secluded district within a city, a district which has many of the neighbourhood characteristics of a village, and which would therefore be very different from the original encoding of a busy, dirty city. Note that this intrinsic context effect differs from that of the environmental context effect in that the intrinsic context determines what is learnt by the subject during the initial presentation, whereas the extrinsic or environmental context merely assists the subject in accessing a particular memory trace. Since the effect of intrinsic context is on learning rather than simply retrieval, it shows up with both recall and recognition.

Most of the instances we have discussed have been concerned with remembering words. However, there are clear and important examples of the role of intrinsic context in other areas, and in particular in the recognition performance of witnesses. The Australian psychologist Donald Thomson has extended the original verbal studies into this particular area, and has shown that the probability of a witness falsely identifying someone in an identification parade, as the person observed at the scene of a crime, can be dramatically increased by changing irrelevant contextual features, such as having the suspect wear similar clothes or showing him in a similar contextual environment. He has shown that even careful and experienced witnesses such as police or lawyers are very subject to bias of this type. His work adds to the considerable evidence that eyewitness identification is very much less reliable than juries typically realize. We do not perceive or remember in a vacuum. The context within which we experience an event will determine how that event is encoded and hence retained. What we *have* learned, we are not always able to call to mind, particularly if we try to recall it when our internal or external environment is dramatically different from the conditions during learning. See MEMORIES, FALSE. ADB

Bower, G. H. (1981). 'Mood and memory'. *American Psychologist*, 3b.

Godden, D. R., and Baddeley, A. D. (1975). 'Context-dependent memory in two natural environments: on land and underwater'. *British Journal of Psychology*, 66.

Kumar, R., Stolerman, I. P., and Steinberg, H. (1970). 'Psychopharmacology'. *Annual Review of Psychology*, 21.

mental concepts: causal analysis. In recent years analytical philosophers have become increasingly aware of the importance of causality (see CAUSES) in the logical analysis of mental concepts. Consider, for instance, what it is for somebody to *infer* one proposition from another. A person, A, believes that p is the case and, on that basis, infers q is true (whether reasonably or unreasonably is of no concern), so acquiring the belief that q is true. It seems clear that A's believing that p is true brings about, that is causes, the acquiring of the belief that q is true. For consider the case where A, believing that p is true, later acquires the belief that q is true, though the original state of belief is in no way causally responsible for acquiring the belief that q is true. In such a case we should not allow the possibility that A had inferred q from p. It is a necessary condition of A's making such an inference that the belief that p is true give rise to the belief that q is true.

Similar considerations may be adduced in the case of other mental concepts. When we *remember* an event, that event must play a part in bringing about the later recall. When we *perceive* an object, that object must play a part in bringing about the perception of it.

Awareness of the ubiquity of causal conditions in analyses of mental concepts has led some philosophers to make a more ambitious, though more speculative, proposal. They suggest that a logical analysis can be given of all the mental concepts in purely causal terms. This proposal, or research programme, in logical analysis constitutes the causal theory of the mental concepts.

As models for the proposed undertaking, consider the ordinary language concept of 'brittleness' and the scientific notion of 'gene'. To say that something is brittle is to say that it is in a certain state. If, in addition, the object is struck sharply, then the combined influence of the two factors, the state and the blow, brings it about (generally) that the object shatters. The state of brittleness is defined simply in terms of what it causes. The concrete nature of the state cannot be elicited simply from its definition, but may be established by further scientific research.

Genes were originally conceived of simply as a set of causal factors at work within the organism. These factors, acting and interacting in a certain way, bring it about that the organism has certain hereditary characteristics (the notion of a hereditary characteristic being itself causally definable). The further nature of genes cannot be elicited simply from the notion as originally introduced. It is a later scientific discovery that genes are in fact DNA molecules. The original concept of the gene is simply the concept of that, whatever it may be, which brings about certain effects.

The causal analysis of the mental concepts asserts that all mental concepts are of the same general sort as the concepts of 'brittleness' and 'gene'. The mental concepts are concepts of states, events, processes, etc. which are definable purely in terms of their *causal role* (the phrase is due to D. K. Lewis). The casual role of brittleness is constituted by the fact that, in conjunction with striking, it produces shattering. The causal role of the gene is constituted by its production of hereditary characteristics. The causal role assigned to mental processes etc. by this analysis is primarily the production of certain sorts of physical behaviour by the organism. As a rough characterization of that behaviour, it is the most flexible and sophisticated behaviour exhibited by the organism. An account of *purposes, for instance, is sought for along the following lines. The purpose to do *X* is a state of the organism, whatever that state may be, which initiates and sustains those trains of physical activity which, in favourable circumstances, bring *X* to be.

Minds are the most complex and sophisticated systems known to exist. It is to be expected, therefore, that the concepts which we have evolved for dealing with mental processes should be among the most complex and sophisticated concepts that we possess. Given that the causal theory is correct, it is quite certain that the causal roles involved will be exceedingly complex and correspondingly difficult to spell out. What was just said about purposes, for instance, can be no more than the crudest first sketch for an analysis. It turns out, in particular, that the different causal roles which constitute different mental processes are of an interlocking sort, so that it is not possible to give an account of one sort without giving an account of others, and vice versa. For instance, purposes and beliefs involve a package deal so that, although their causal roles in the production of behaviour are different, the one causal role cannot be described without reference to the other. This reflects the familiar point that actual behaviour is always a joint product of purposes and beliefs.

Those who have actually proposed the causal analysis have been materialists. They wished to give a purely physicalist account of mental processes. The causal analysis makes it easy to do this, because the nature of that which plays these complex roles is not determined by the analysis. The causal theorist can then go on to maintain, on grounds of general scientific plausibility, that mental processes are in fact ordinary physical processes in the brain. This yields the doctrine of *central-state* (as opposed to *behaviouristic) materialism. However, it may prove possible to uphold a materialist view of the mind without accepting the causal analysis of the mental concepts.

Furthermore, the causal analysis is entirely compatible with an anti-materialist view of the mind. A causal theorist could maintain without contradiction, for instance, that mental processes are, in their own nature, processes in a spiritual substance, processes that produce certain bodily effects.

The causal analysis of the mental concepts is far from having been completed. It remains a research programme. How promising a programme it is is a matter for controversy among those philosophers who seek a general view of the mind. No full-scale critique of the causal theory has yet been developed, but various difficulties have been raised.

First, a property such as brittleness or an object such as a gene is a *theoretical* entity. It is something which is postulated as an explainer of certain phenomena: shattering after being hit; the recurrent patterns of characteristics in organisms related by descent. To give an account of mental concepts in terms of the causal role of the entities involved seems therefore to assimilate mental entities to theoretical postulations. Yet, unlike the case of brittleness or the gene, when we introspect we are directly, though no doubt not infallibly, aware of some of our own mental processes. We observe them. But could the content of our introspective observation be confined simply to this: the presence of something playing a certain causal role?

Secondly, all or almost all mental processes have the property of pointing beyond themselves to something which, nevertheless, need not exist. We may desire and pursue that which is unattainable, we may think of and believe in that which does not exist. Franz *Brentano spoke of this phenomenon as the *intentionality of mental processes. Can mere causal role, however complex and sophisticated, fully explain the intentionality of mental processes? If this objection can be made good, it may pose a threat to a materialist doctrine of the mind as well as to the causal analysis of the mental concepts.

Thirdly, by introspection we appear to become aware of certain mental *qualities*. Having an itch is introspectively different from having a pain, having a sensation of something green is introspectively different from having a sensation of something red, being angry is introspectively different from being afraid. In all these cases, it is quite plausible to assert, we are introspectively aware of a difference in the qualities of the mental processes involved. But it is difficult to see how a purely causal analysis of the mental concepts could account for such an awareness of qualitative difference. This objection is attractive to many philosophers working within what may be called the 'British empiricist' tradition.

It is an interesting question whether this objection, supposing it well taken, refutes not only the causal analysis but also a materialist account of mental processes. Such introspected qualities are in prima facie conflict with materialism, but perhaps the conflict is prima facie only.

DMA

Armstrong, D. M. (1968). *A Materialist Theory of the Mind*, Part II.
Campbell, K. K. (1970). *Body and Mind*, chs. 5 and 6.
Lewis, D. K. (1966). 'An argument for the identity theory'. *Journal of Philosophy*, 63 (repr. in Rosenthal, D. M. (ed.) (1971), *Materialism and the Mind–Body Problem*).

mental handicap. It is estimated that about one in every 1,000 children in the United Kingdom and the United States of America is mentally handicapped. It is not easy to judge the total number because of the various definitions of mental handicap. The American Association on Mental Deficiency (AAMD) describes retardation as 'sub-average general intellectual functioning which originates during the developmental period and is associated with impaired adaptive behaviour'. 'Sub-average' means more than one standard deviation below the normal average level of intelligence commonly accepted (in the UK, 100; in the USA, 90–100); 'developmental period' means from birth to about 16 years of age; and 'impaired adaptive behaviour' means failure to mature, to learn, or to adjust socially.

This definition has been challenged because it does not take account of environmental and social factors, both of which may have an important influence on retardation. The lack of a clear definition has significance, for failure to diagnose may lead to failure to treat.

The problem of mental handicap emerged in the 19th century. Before that time, the handicapped were assimilated into the general background of rural societies or they did not survive at all. The percentage of children who were mildly mentally handicapped increased with the growth of towns, because of poor housing, lack of care before, during, and after birth, malnutrition, poverty, and poor working conditions for mothers. These causes remain, but, with the improvement of general standards of living and literacy, children handicapped in this way are now among the 'ablest' of the mentally handicapped. As societies become more complex and technologically oriented, the number of people unable to cope with life increases, and the burden on the working population is correspondingly increased.

In the 19th century many schemes to train and educate the mentally handicapped were begun and found to be successful. Possibly the first attempts at education were made by Jean-Marc-Gaspard Itard, who described his work with a wild boy found in the woods of Aveyron. Truffaut's film *L'Enfant sauvage* is an account of Itard's attempts to socialize and educate the boy Victor, who was, however, probably already handicapped when he was found.

Since the success of treatment depends very much on the cause of the illness, improved skills in diagnosing mental handicap have also meant improved chances of rehabilitation. The aetiology of mental handicap is divided into two parts: intrinsic and extrinsic causes.

1. Intrinsic causes
2. Extrinsic causes
3. Treatment and provisions

1. Intrinsic causes

These are biological, mainly genetic. One of the commonest is *Down's syndrome (mongolism), which results from a chromosome abnormality. One birth in 250 will have a chromosome abnormality, which can be diagnosed by counting the chromosomes taken in smears. Unfortunately the cause of the damage to the chromosome structure that produces Down's syndrome has not yet been identified, although a connection with infective hepatitis has been suggested. Genetic counselling may reduce the incidence of one type of Down's syndrome, for if one or both parents have an abnormal chromosome structure there is a greater likelihood that their child will have an abnormality. The chances of an abnormal birth increase with the age of the mother, and after the age of 35 special attention should be paid to the chromosomal compatibility of the parents.

Other intrinsic causes are metabolic. In phenylketonuria (PKU), which occurs in one in 10,000 births, failure to metabolize the amino acid phenylalanine results in a toxic condition which affects the brain and causes retardation unless a phenylalanine-free diet is given to the child. In the United Kingdom, every newborn baby is now tested for PKU, and so a dangerous condition is prevented by early intervention. Osteogenesis imperfecta ('brittle bones'), Tay–Sachs disease, and Duchenne's muscular dystrophy (both degenerative killing diseases) are other intrinsic causes of mental retardation. The causes of many intrinsic diseases are not yet known. The American Association on Mental Deficiency (AAMD) and the American Psychiatric Association maintain lists of most of the categories of intrinsic causes of retardation, and these lists are updated as knowledge extends.

2. Extrinsic causes

These are mental handicaps that result from infections, accidents, poisoning, or other brain damage. Difficult or premature births may cause brain damage because of anoxia (shortage of oxygen supply to the brain). Babies may be born blind and/or mentally retarded if the mother is infected with rubella (German measles) before the fourth month of pregnancy. Congenital syphilis can also damage the child. (It used to be thought that this disease was the cause of Down's syndrome. The misery and anxiety such a mistaken belief must have caused parents whose children suffered from Down's syndrome can hardly be imagined.) Smoking, excessive use of alcoholic drinks, poor prenatal care, malnutrition, infection, or poisoning from environmental pollution (such as mercury or lead) may lead to immature or damaged babies.

During the neonatal period, factors such as high fever, jaundice, failure to breathe properly, or inadequate or unsuitable nutrition may cause retardation. The child's brain may be damaged by poisoning from sucking toys painted with paint containing lead monoxide or cadmium, or by baby battering (see CHILD ABUSE), or by falls. One category in the AAMD list should be looked at with particular attention: diseases and conditions due to unknown or uncertain factors with structural reaction alone manifest—a category into which the 'wild boy' of Aveyron might well fit. It is known that a child deprived of tender loving care will grow up with deficient sensory and social ability. If the impoverishment and lack of stimulus in a child's upbringing are not remedied early, he will grow up with reduced social and intellectual capacity and may be diagnosed as a case of 'mild' (category I) retardation. *Autism is a condition which may fit into any of the categories of retardation, from I to V, and which causes great distress —particularly, perhaps, as at first sight the child may seem to be quite normal. There continues to be much debate about the nature and causes of autism.

3. Treatment and provisions

The amount of handicap in individual cases varies as much as intelligence does among 'normal' people, and this range makes management and discussion complex and difficult. Diseases caused by poisoning (intoxication) may be halted or even cured by removing the source of the poison, and eliminating the poison already in the child, before there is irreversible brain damage. Diseases caused by social factors—such as malnutrition, lack of care before, during, or after birth, poor stimulus, or infection of the mother—could be eliminated or at least reduced by social welfare programmes (for example, inoculation against measles and rubella) and by the education of parents to help counter retardation of this kind.

Treatment of intrinsic causes is more difficult because the damage is irreversible. However, prevention is beginning to be possible. Amniocentesis can be used to detect chromosome abnormalities while the child is still in the womb. The technique cannot be used until the fourth month of pregnancy, and, as the fluid has to be taken out of the uterus, there is the possibility of damage to a normal fetus and the risk of natural abortion; also it must be practicable to offer induced abortion as an alternative. Once a child is born with irreversible brain damage, drugs

can help to prevent fits and special programmes can help to develop existing intelligence and mobility. The Doman–Delacato course of treatment may improve the abilities of some children, although it demands tremendous dedication and energy on the part of the parents, while the cost to the family as a whole should not be disregarded. More usually, brain-damaged children go to nursery schools and then to special schools where attention is paid to individual differences and needs. If this sort of help is given from birth onwards it may be possible to educate the child and support the family who look after him. In the United Kingdom such programmes have been devised by Mr R. Brinkworth, the founder of the Down's Babies Association.

In some parts of the world there are excellent provisions, while in others they are sadly lacking or even non-existent. At best the mentally handicapped may be helped to lead relatively normal lives, to do some sort of work, and to live in sheltered housing with some support. Whether the work is in workshops or on the land, it will give the moderately handicapped a sense of individual dignity and purpose. The severely handicapped will have to spend their lives in hospitals and will need dedicated nursing as well as support from all the other social services. It is important to distinguish here between the mentally handicapped and the mentally ill (see MENTAL ILLNESS). In the popular mind these two conditions are often confused, leading to much ill-informed fear and prejudice. None the less, there is good evidence that the mentally handicapped do have a higher incidence of neurotic and psychotic disorders.

Wherever adequate provision is made for the mentally handicapped, it will be found that the cost is great. Against this cost must be set the cost of *not* providing. The incidence of broken marriages is ten times higher where there is a mentally handicapped child. There are risks to physical and mental health—mothers typically suffer more than fathers, while the normal children in the family are also under pressure. Widows and deserted wives figure prominently in surveys.

In the past the mentally handicapped often died at birth or in early childhood. They survive into mature adulthood with the help of care before and after birth and the widespread use of antibiotics. Should doctors perhaps not strive 'officiously to keep alive' if spina bifida has been diagnosed and the child, and later the adult, is condemned to a crippled and handicapped life after operations which may relieve the symptoms but cannot cure the condition? How can we balance, for instance, the cost of keeping a mentally handicapped child against the cost of a kidney machine for a working man who supports a family? In a sensitive and civilized society, euthanasia is an emotive and difficult subject. Doctors need guidelines and support to avoid accusations of murder when they must make decisions which affect not only the individual family but society as a whole.

See also SUBNORMALITY. PMH

Adams, M. (1971). *Mental Retardation and its Social Dimensions*.

Cuckle, H. S., and Wald, N. J. (1984). 'Maternal serum alpha-fetoprotein measurement: a screening test for Down's syndrome'. *Lancet*, 28 Apr.

Grossman, H. J. (ed.) (1983). *Classification in Mental Retardation*.

Heston, L. L. (1982). 'Alzheimer's dementia and Down's syndrome: genetic evidence suggesting an association'. *Annals of the New York Academy of Sciences*, 396.

Kemp, R., and Henry, C. (1978). *Child Abuse*.

Kurtz, R. (1977). *Social Aspects of Mental Retardation*.

McNamara, J., and McNamara, B. (1977). *The Special Child Handbook*.

Stone, J., and Taylor, F. (1977). *A Handbook for Parents with a Handicapped Child*.

Warnock, M. (1978). *Meeting Special Educational Needs*.

mental health. Answers given nowadays to the question 'What are the characteristics of a mentally healthy person?' are likely to refer to such signs as the capacity to cooperate with others and sustain a close, loving relationship, and the ability to make a sensitive, critical appraisal of oneself and the world about one and to cope with the everyday problems of living. At other times or places, different qualities would have been mentioned, according to the values prevailing in the culture. For the English middle class at the turn of the 19th century, *mens sana in corpore sano*—a sound mind in a sound body—would have included a disciplined intelligence, a well-stocked memory, qualities of leadership appropriate to the person's station, a respect for morality, and a sense of what life means. There was at that time an absolute refusal, as Clouston (1906) put it, 'to admit the possibility of a healthy mind in an unsound body, or at all events in an unsound brain'. Nowadays we regard mental health as attainable by even the severely crippled. Brain injury may put limits on the degree to which social capacities can be developed, but it does not prevent their development altogether; the influence of the milieu may be as strong as that of the severity of the injury. For a vigorous critique of the concept of mental health one can hardly do better than turn to Barbara Wootton's review (1960) in which, after commenting on a number of proposed definitions, she concluded that 'whichever way, therefore, the problem may be approached, no solid foundation appears to be discoverable on which to establish the propositions [as] formulated'.

The shift in emphasis from intellectual ability to harmonious relationships as the criterion of mental health can be partly attributed to the recognition that, whatever part physical inheritance plays in determining intelligence, intellectual development depends largely on learning in the setting of a relationship. The publication in 1951 by the World Health Organization of John *Bowlby's monograph *Maternal Care and Mental Health* was a landmark because it made it widely known that an essential condition for the mental health and development of the child is 'a warm, intimate, and continuous relationship with his mother in which both find satisfaction and enjoyment'. 'Sound cognitive development', it has been said, 'occurs in a context of communication.' The abilities which enable the child to play the roles appropriate to a boy or girl are acquired through the learning engendered by the expectations of the family. Interruption, or disturbance, during early childhood in the relationship with the mother has been shown to retard or distort the development of language and the skills related to it, and to lead in some circumstances to an impairment in social relationships which lasts into adult life. The effects depend on the character of the 'support' or 'security' system, of which the mother is usually the chief member. The father, the grandparents, older siblings, and family friends contribute to the system. The young child is vulnerable if the system is weak or fragile.

The young child tends to attach himself to one person especially, usually the one who mothers him, and this relationship, established in the second half of the first year of life, prepares him for a monogamous relationship when sexual maturity is reached, and influences then his choice of partner. (See ATTACHMENT.) Social training of other kinds, in the family and outside it, prepares him for the several roles he is to play in adult life. A boy tends to take his father as a model, and a girl, her mother. Of importance too is membership of a peer group in the early teenage years. From his experience in relationships with his mother and father, peers of the same sex, and then a peer of opposite sex, the young person discovers what sort of person he is—i.e. he forms a conception of himself, or establishes his 'identity', especially his sexual identity. His education and early experience in a job establish his occupational identity. This conception of himself is tested out by further experience which confirms or modifies it. The first *affaire* confirms or, if it goes badly, confuses his sexual identity. He becomes emancipated in greater or lesser degree from his parents, and free to form relationships outside the family. The rapid intellectual development at the time of puberty helps the young person to understand, and in some degree gain control over, the world around him.

The social training he has had during childhood is put to the test at turning points in circumstances, or 'crises', which require old habits to be abandoned, new habits to be developed. Crises are conveniently divided, following Erikson (1968), into 'developmental' and 'accidental'. By developmental crises are meant those decisive changes in circumstances ordinarily expected to occur in the life cycle—for example, being born, going to school, leaving school, getting married, becoming a parent, or retiring from work. Examples of accidental crises are the untimely loss of a member of the family, a spouse or other loved person, the loss of a job, or illness. If he is prepared for the new circumstances, as is usual when the crisis is developmental, a person acquires new habits quickly through the processes of learning. If not prepared, because the crisis is untimely, or social training has been lacking or inappropriate, a person may go through a period of instability and distress while he works out new ways of coping.

In studies of *bereavement—for example, by C. M. Parkes—are to be found illustrations of the differences between mental health and illness. After the loss of a loved one, one person mourns for a time. While doing so, he is able to express to others his grief and distress openly and authentically, and thus to review his relationship with the person lost. He soon re-engages in relationships with others, which change and develop. Another person becomes preoccupied by his fantasies about the person lost. These may be out of keeping with the realities, which are denied. He withdraws from other relationships, and shows a general contraction of activities and interests. He feels diminished and depreciated. Withdrawing from relationships, and unable to communicate his distress, his conception of himself remains uncorrected, and he does not work out a new pattern of relationships. This kind of severe reaction to bereavement occurs especially when the loss has been sudden or unexpected, or there have been distressing circumstances: for instance, if the death was due to *suicide, or to the negligence or misconduct of others. Such a reaction may also reflect the personality of the bereaved person and his relationship with the person lost. He may have been unaccustomed to taking decisions for himself, or have had limited personal resources, or have been unduly dependent, or the relationship may have been discordant and fraught with unresolved difficulties.

The features of the reaction of this person are the antithesis of mental health, and amount to mental illness if he also claims exemption from normal social responsibilities. Yet they reflect psychological processes which are part of the organism's normal reactive equipment, and which are adaptive in that they serve to reduce *anxiety. They can be described as due to 'the renunciation of functions which give rise to anxiety' (which Sigmund *Freud said was the essence of neurosis). The psychological processes are maladaptive in the particular circumstances in that they do nothing to remove the sources of the anxiety. There is thus a deadlock. By avoiding a situation or staying out of relationships in which he has experienced pain or anxiety, a person does not explore and re-evaluate the situation, or learn to cope with it in more effective ways. Other characteristics of behaviour in mental illness are persistence or repetitiveness and resistance to modifica-

tion by experience, whereas behaviour in mental health tends to be flexible and modifiable.

To break the deadlock, and to restore mental health, a therapist creates conditions in which the testing of reality and learning can be resumed. New habits can then be acquired which are more appropriate to the circumstances. The person's conception of himself can be corrected by further experience. He is encouraged to re-enter into relationships. In other words, the therapist intervenes or mediates in order to bring about reconciliation, and to enable communication with others to be reopened.

DRD

Clouston, T. C. (1906). *The Hygiene of Mind.*
Erikson, E. H. (1968). *Identity: Youth and Crisis.*
Goodwin, I. (2003). 'The relevance of attachment theory to the philosophy, organization, and practice of adult mental health care'. *Clinical Psychology Review*, 23 / 1.
Parkes, C. M. (2001). *Bereavement* (3rd edn.).
Wootton, B. (1960). *Social Science and Social Pathology.*

mental illness. Most people think of mental illnesses as strange and frightening conditions, which can affect other people but not themselves or their families. But in the average family doctor's surgery psychological symptoms are surpassed in frequency only by common colds, bronchitis, and rheumatism. In the course of a year, about one in every eight people in Britain consults their general practitioner for problems which are predominantly or completely psychological in nature. General practitioners refer about 10 per cent of such patients to a psychiatrist; most of these will be treated as outpatients but some will need admission to hospital, which in Britain is nearly always on a voluntary basis. Thus, out of all those who seek medical help with psychological problems, only a small minority become psychiatric in-patients. It is then a striking indicator of the extent of such problems that psychiatric patients occupy nearly a quarter of all the hospital beds in Britain and in most other industrialized nations.

Arguments continually rage over the exact limits of mental illness. Some authorities regard the concept of mental illness as a myth while others, by contrast, consider that the majority of seemingly normal people suffer, often unknowingly, from psychiatric abnormalities amenable to treatment. Furthermore, some believe that psychiatric disorders are simply mental equivalents of physical diseases, while others argue that there are as many sorts of psychological problems as there are individuals who suffer from them.

In practice it is possible to discern certain recurring patterns of complaints and disabilities that can be regarded as reasonably discrete entities. These disorders can be divided into two broad groups: organic disorders, in which some demonstrable physical illness including brain disease underlies the psychological symptoms, and functional disorders, where no definite physical abnormality has yet been reliably demonstrated. Since most forms of mental illness fall into the latter category, the classification of psychiatric disorders is generally based on the clinical distinction between different clusters of symptoms, each with a characteristic outcome. (See CLASSIFICATION OF PSYCHIATRIC DISORDERS.) In general medicine, advances in classification occurred when technological progress allowed the elucidation of the underlying causes of illnesses. Unlike their colleagues practising general medicine or surgery, however, psychiatrists are unable to rely on laboratory or other tests to refute or confirm their clinical diagnoses. Recent attempts to develop specific diagnostic investigations, such as the dexamethasone suppression test for depressive illness, have yet to produce a procedure of proven value. Unfortunately other mental illnesses show the same response that was found with a proportion of depressed patients, but the search for laboratory tests to aid with the diagnosis of affective disorders and other conditions continues.

In the meantime it is useful to distinguish between the neuroses and the psychoses. Neurotic symptoms correspond to what is commonly called 'nerves' and comprise feelings and thoughts that most normal people have experienced at some time or other, albeit in a relatively minor form. However, if they become persistent and severe, such symptoms can become markedly disabling, and result in a frank neurotic illness or 'nervous breakdown'. Psychotic symptoms, on the other hand, are not part of normal experience and are almost invariably severe. The picture of psychotic illness is quite distinct from normality and corresponds to what in popular usage is called 'madness' or 'insanity'. Women outnumber men among neurotics by about two to one, but psychosis is equally frequent in the two sexes.

Neurotic problems account for about two-thirds of those consulting family doctors because of psychological symptoms, the remainder being made up by a variety of conditions including *psychosomatic complaints, abnormalities of personality, alcoholism, and the psychoses. Most neurotics are treated by their general practitioners,

but individuals with psychotic illnesses are almost always referred on to psychiatrists. Thus, while those with psychoses form only about 4 per cent of patients consulting GPs because of psychological problems, 25 per cent of psychiatric outpatients and more than half of all psychiatric inpatients suffer from psychotic illnesses.

Table I lists the expectancies of being affected at some time during life by the different psychiatric conditions for (i) a member of the general population and (ii) someone who has a first-degree relative (i.e. parent, sibling, or child) with one of the disorders.

1. Neuroses
2. Organic psychoses
3. Functional psychoses

1. Neuroses

Anxiety states are among the most common of all psychiatric disorders and are characterized by persistent apprehension and fear, at times amounting to panic. They are often accompanied by sensations caused by overactivity of the *autonomic nervous system: these include excessive sweating, tremor, faintness, choking or breathlessness, and 'butterflies' in the stomach. (See ANXIETY for further discussion).

Phobic neuroses have much in common with anxiety states in that the predominant symptoms are again of fear or panic together with autonomic overactivity. But in phobic neuroses the symptoms are provoked by certain specific stimuli, such as dogs, spiders, the sight of blood, or having to talk to strangers. The most common variety is agoraphobia, which means fear of open spaces. The agoraphobic is afraid of leaving home and subject to panic attacks in crowded public places such as supermarkets. He or she often dreads travelling on public transport, especially underground trains, and has great difficulty in tolerating lifts or rooms from which there is no ready exit. Since these symptoms considerably limit normal life, agoraphobic patients may become totally housebound. (See PHOBIAS for further discussion.)

Obsessive–compulsive neurosis is much rarer, but nevertheless the symptoms that form its core are

Table 1. Lifetime risk of developing the disorder

	In the general population		In the first-degree relatives of individuals affected (per cent)
	Males (per cent)	Females (per cent)	
Schizophrenia	1	1	10
Manic-depressive psychosis	2	3	15
Neurotic depression	6	12	11
Anxiety states	3	6	15
Obsessive-compulsive neurosis	0.05	0.05	10
Alcoholism	7	2	15

phenomena with which, in milder form, most people will be familiar. There can be few people who have not at some time been unable to stop a song going round in their head, or had an irrational urge to avoid stepping on cracks in the pavement, or rechecked windows and doors which they know they have already secured. In obsessive–compulsive neurosis, such thoughts or practices become pathologically exaggerated. Fears of having been contaminated by dirt, or of having harmed someone, may preoccupy the sufferer for most of the day even though he recognizes that they are silly. Similarly, he may wash his hands or check taps a hundred times a day, while all the time trying to convince himself that his behaviour is ridiculous. Such repetitive thoughts and compulsive acts become so intrusive that productive activity becomes impossible. (See OBSESSIVE–COMPULSIVE DISORDER for further discussion.)

The predominant features of depressive neurosis are gloom and despondency. Bouts of weeping are common, as are edginess, irritability, and a tendency to tire easily. There is a general loss of ability to concentrate and in particular a lack of interest in things that were previously enjoyed. The symptoms tend to vary in intensity, but often cause difficulty in getting off to sleep. (See DEPRESSION for further discussion.)

A variety of neurosis which was formerly common but is now much less so is hysteria, which in its classical forms beguiled 19th-century physicians such as J. M. *Charcot and Sigmund *Freud. Indeed, it was while studying a hysterical patient, the celebrated 'Anna O', that Freud and *Breuer developed many of the concepts upon which psychoanalysis came to be based. The essence of hysteria is that, in the face of intolerable stress, symptoms develop which provide a defence against the stressful circumstances. Characteristic symptoms include a paralysed limb, loss of speech, convulsions, or blindness, and are often called conversion hysteria because the psychological trauma has figuratively been 'converted' into a bodily form. Some forms of hysteria involve a different mechanism called dissociation, in which an individual may forget even his own identity. He may wander off in a 'fugue state' that carries him many miles from home, or he may take on some new identity or switch from one identity to another—the 'split personality' of popular films, such as *The Three Faces of Eve*. (This phenomenon is discussed under DISSOCIATION OF THE PERSONALITY.) Although hysterical mechanisms are usually unconscious, many psychiatrists doubt the genuineness of some of the more theatrical forms. Indeed one of the problems confronting psychiatrists in legal work is where to draw the dividing line between hysteria and conscious simulation or malingering. Fortunately, hysterical symptoms are becoming less common due to improved education and awareness of psychological matters; this allows the expression of emotional difficulties for what they are, and renders the communication of suffering via hysterical symbolism redundant. None the less, it is important to remember that conversion hysteria can develop against a background of serious organic brain disease, either pre-existing or unsuspected, in a considerable percentage of cases. (See HYSTERIA for further discussion.)

In contrast to hysteria, anorexia nervosa appears to be on the increase, particularly among adolescent girls and young women. The central feature is self-imposed starvation, which frequently starts with a slimming diet and occasionally ends with complete inanition and death. Weight loss, physical overactivity, cessation of menstrual periods, and the growth of downy hair on the face and back are the cardinal symptoms. Surprisingly, most patients shun treatment and instead show considerable ingenuity in avoiding weight gain. Thus they hide food or secretly throw it away, and abuse laxatives. Like the obsessive–compulsive, the anorexic often recognizes the pointless irrationality of her behaviour but nevertheless feels bound to continue. Psychoanalysts have suggested that anorexia is a desperate unconscious attempt to stave off imminent sexual maturity, but a simpler explanation is that the anorexic has a distorted perception of her body that causes her consistently to overestimate her own size. The rise in anorexia has been attributed to increasing pressure on women to diet, as over the past 30 years or so the ideal female shape has become thinner and less buxom. Although the environment is of obvious importance, genetic factors have also been implicated in causing anorexia. (See ANOREXIA NERVOSA AND BULIMIA NERVOSA; GENETICS OF MENTAL ILLNESS, for further discussion.)

Two neurotic disorders that have received increased recognition over the past decade are neurasthenia and post-traumatic stress disorder. Neurasthenia, commonly termed chronic fatigue or myalgic encephalomyelitis (ME), is characterized by substantial physical and mental fatigue that significantly impairs daily activities. Although the diagnosis requires the exclusion of detectable organic disorders, neurasthenia may be triggered by physical illness—most commonly viral infection. Through advice and support, the sufferer is encouraged to return to preonset functioning. For the severely affected a formalized behavioural approach, including cognitive–behavioural therapy, may be required. To date, no pharmacological treatment of neurasthenia has been established.

Post-traumatic stress disorder arises as a delayed and protracted response to an exceptionally stressful event which is likely to cause pervasive distress in almost any individual. This disorder is characterized by repetitive, intrusive recollection or re-enactment of the event in memories, daytime imagery, or dreams. Antidepressants and behavioural and cognitive therapy are often combined in the treatment of this disorder.

Causes and treatment of neurosis. Everyone is probably capable of experiencing neurotic symptoms in some form or degree, but individuals differ in their susceptibility to *stress. Some neurotic patients develop their symptoms without obvious precipitating factors, whereas others only become ill after major tragedies, such as the loss of a husband or child. Vulnerability to anxiety states and to phobic and obsessional neuroses appears to be partly influenced by genes. But it is generally agreed that life experiences play a major role. What is not generally agreed is which life events are crucial, and how they produce their effects. According to psychoanalytic theory, neurosis is an outward manifestation of deep-seated intrapsychic conflicts which were set up in early life. Treatment, which is necessarily prolonged and intensive, aims to make this unconscious material accessible to consciousness, and the resultant insight is expected to produce resolution and relief. The *behaviourists, however, think that the symptom is the neurosis and that it is the result of faulty learning processes. Theoretical assumptions concerning unconscious mechanisms and insight are regarded as irrelevant. Instead the aberrant behaviour and/or cognitions are examined closely and broken down into their component parts, and the goal is then to persuade or educate the patient into adopting more appropriate and adaptive cognitions and/or patterns of behaviour. This approach is particularly useful with phobias and obsessive–compulsive neurosis. (See BEHAVIOUR THERAPY.)

Most patients with milder neuroses never see a psychiatrist, but are instead treated by their general practitioner with a combination of simple support and antidepressants. Cognitive–behavioural therapy is the treatment of choice for the majority of neurotic disorders that require more expert clinical management. Over the past two decades new types of antidepressants, such as the selective serotonin reuptake inhibitor Prozac, have been developed. These newer antidepressants are no better than the older antidepressants in treating depressive symptoms. However, they are less dangerous when taken in overdosage and have been found to be effective in treating most neurotic disorders. Cognitive–behavioural therapy is therefore often augmented with a selective serotonin reuptake inhibitor. Previously tranquillizers such as the benzodiazepine Valium were universally prescribed for all forms of neuroses. However, recognition of their time-limited efficacy in treating symptoms, potential for abuse, and addictive properties have made their role very limited—if not contraindicated.

2. Organic psychoses

Acute. A variety of physical illnesses may produce an acute reversible mental disorder called delirium; the causes include fever or disturbance in body chemistry as well as infections of the brain. Delirium may also follow intoxication with drugs or withdrawal from heroin or alcohol ('DTs'). The most striking feature is the rapid onset of confusion. The patient has no idea where he is or what day it is, and only the most tenuous grasp of what is going on around him. He may see or hear things that are not really there (*hallucinations), or experience distorted perception of things that are there (*illusions). He is often very fearful and may believe he is being attacked or persecuted. Evelyn Waugh's *The Ordeal of Gilbert Pinfold* is an excellent, presumably first-hand, account of an acute organic psychosis that could possibly have been an example of alcoholic hallucinosis complicated by the taking of other drugs. Most delirious patients recover completely when the cause of the insult to the brain is corrected.

Chronic. By contrast, dementia refers to chronic insidious organic psychoses that are usually progressive. Loss of memory for recent events is often the first symptom. Thus, an elderly woman may be able to describe vividly the days of her childhood, but be unable to recall what she has just eaten for breakfast. She then begins to forget the faces of friends and relatives, and may be unaware of where she is or what year it is. Deterioration in intellect and personality may show itself as a lack of propriety, lack of attention to personal appearance, and loss of normal social niceties and inhibitions. In about 10 per cent of cases dementia in later life is caused by remediable conditions such as benign brain tumours and hypothyroidism, but the great majority of cases are due to degenerative disease of the brain or its blood vessels. The ageing of Britain's population has rendered these disorders, senile and so-called multi-infarct dementia, so common that the increase has been called 'the quiet epidemic'. Sadly, there are at present no effective cures. (For further discussion see DEMENTIA.)

3. Functional psychoses

In 1898 Emil *Kraepelin made the now classical distinction between the two major types of functional psychosis. He contrasted manic–depressive psychosis with its recurrent gross swings in mood with a more severe and progressive illness starting in young adulthood that he termed dementia praecox. Dementia praecox and manic–depressive psychosis are now termed schizophrenia and bipolar affective disorder, respectively. The distinction between these two disorders still holds; however, recent research has suggested that they may in part share the same genetic causes.

Schizophrenia. Most schizophrenics suffer at some point from hallucinations that usually take the form of voices talking to or about them. Occasionally these voices are friendly but in the main they are disparaging and abusive. The schizophrenic is beset with strange beliefs (*delusions). He may think, for example, that he is the victim of a plot, that everyone can read his thoughts, or that alien forces are inserting or removing thoughts from his head or controlling his body.

Schizophrenia is correctly diagnosed only when these beliefs are unshakeable and totally out of keeping with the ideas and philosophies of the sufferer's own class and culture. Thus, a rural West African who believes he is a victim of a witch doctor's spell, or a member of a spiritualist congregation receiving instructions from the dead, is unlikely to be schizophrenic. But an Englishwoman who is absolutely convinced that her every action is personally controlled by a famous pop singer through a radio receiver he has installed in her brain may well be.

About 80 per cent of schizophrenic patients make a good recovery from their first attack. Unfortunately, many patients later relapse and require further admission to hospital, and in the long term only about 50 per cent remain quite free of any disability. More severely affected people become so preoccupied with their delusions and hallucinations that they tend to withdraw from social contact, and lose touch with reality. As a result their social and occupational functioning deteriorates, and about 10 per cent of all those initially affected become long-term hospital inpatients. In spite of the disorganized and irrelevant speech and disintegration of personality of such severe schizophrenics, their basic intelligence is usually unaffected and improvement can still occur after many years of hospitalization.

If, as some claim, schizophrenia is a myth, then it is a myth with a strong hereditary component! The risk of the identical twin of a schizophrenic also developing the disorder is about 50 per cent, whereas the risk for a non-identical twin is less than 15 per cent; this difference presumably reflects the greater genetic similarity of identical twins. Similarly, children of schizophrenic parents who were adopted and raised by normal families still have an increased risk of schizophrenia, whereas children born to normal parents and by mischance raised by a schizophrenic do not. The precise way in which liability to schizophrenia is transmitted is not known, but biochemical factors may be important. Some drugs, such as amphetamines, can in excess produce a mental state mimicking schizophrenia; this has led to the suggestion that schizophrenics could be endogenously producing some aberrant chemical.

Once fashionable psychodynamic theories that abnormal parenting and childhood experiences could by themselves induce schizophrenia are now discounted. The importance of both the environment and neurodevelopment in the aetiology of schizophrenia is still recognized; however, a scientific biological perspective is taken. For example, fetal viral infection and obstetric complications have been implicated in causing abnormal neurodevelopment that may in part increase the susceptibility of an individual to schizophrenia, and traumatic life experiences or intense intrafamilial pressures have been shown to precipitate breakdown in susceptible individuals.

In treating schizophrenia, the two essential elements are antipsychotic drugs and social rehabilitation. Intrusive therapies such as psychoanalysis are harmful, but a long-term supportive relationship with a concerned psychiatrist, community psychiatric nurse, or social worker can be invaluable. Antipsychotic drugs are effective in treating and preventing florid symptoms, such as delusions and hallucinations, in 70 per cent of patients. Recent advances have resulted in the production of atypical antipsychotics —so named primarily because of their reduced propensity to cause side effects such as stiffness. Only clozapine, an atypical antipsychotic, has been found to be effective in treating the more insidious schizophrenic symptoms such as emotional flattening and poverty of thought. Clozapine has also been found to be effective in treating two-thirds of the 30 per cent of patients for whom treatment with other antipsychotics has been unsuccessful. A variety of social measures provide social and work environments to suit each patient's individual need. Rehabilitation may involve occupational therapy, attendance at a day hospital, or residence in a halfway hostel. The aim of such measures is, of course, to help the patient to find a satisfying role in the community and to stop him becoming institutionalized in hospital. Voluntary organizations such as the Schizophrenia Fellowship often play a major role in this. See also SCHIZOPHRENIA.

Bipolar affective disorder. In its full-blown form, this is a cyclical disorder in which opposite extremes of mood are successively shown—mania and depression. Mania is characterized by an extraordinary sense of well-being, overactivity, and elation and is usually accompanied by a conviction of great self-importance which causes the individual affected to make grandiose pronouncements —for example, that he is the most talented and intelligent person in the world. He may consequently enter into wild and ruinous business ventures, or indulge in other unaccustomed excesses of spending, eating, drinking, or sex. His talk is profuse and prolix, flitting from topic to topic with an unstoppable stream of ideas interspersed with puns and feeble witticisms. His jollity may initially be infectious, but before long he becomes overbearing and tiresome. Not surprisingly most sufferers eventually dissipate their energy and return to normal, but an unfortunate minority descend straight into depression with no intermediate period of normality.

Bipolar affective disorder is much less common than depressive psychosis, the predominant symptoms of which are profound gloom and despair. Life appears futile and hopeless and suicidal ideas are usually entertained, and, not infrequently, successfully acted upon. Depression produces a marked depletion in self-confidence and self-regard and the depressive may see himself as the most evil and wicked individual who ever lived. Racked with guilt, the previously blameless character becomes convinced that he has committed some grave infamy or that he is to blame for all the sin and misery that exists in the world. Less commonly he may believe that he has been stripped of all his possessions, or that his body has become hideously diseased and is rotting and decayed. Real bodily disturbance of a less bizarre nature does usually occur. Appetite is poor, weight loss ensues, and there is often constipation and loss of sex drive. Some depressed patients physically slow down, and their talk may decrease or altogether cease, a condition known as psychomotor retardation: occasionally such a patient develops a state of mute, immobile stupor. In others restlessness and edginess may culminate in severe agitation.

Bipolar affective disorder, like schizophrenia, is partly determined by genetic factors. Again there is evidence that biochemical factors are important: for example, drugs which deplete the brain of chemical messenger substances called monoamines can induce depression, while drugs which raise the level of monoamines relieve depression and can precipitate mania. Despite the importance of these biological components, the part played by psychological factors can in no way be discounted. Adverse life circumstances or *bereavement or other forms of loss are known to result frequently in depression, and psychoanalytic theory considers that it is the turning-in on the self of the consequent feelings of hostility and annoyance that produces the illness. Some behaviourists on the other hand have stressed the importance of learning experiences, such as exposure to inescapable mental trauma that produces a feeling of helplessness. This, they believe, forms the basis of the depressed state.

Bipolar affective disorder is a serious condition, not just because of the misery and the disruption it causes, but because about 15 per cent of sufferers eventually die by suicide. Fortunately, treatment is effective. Antidepressant drugs are of proven efficacy in the majority of typical cases and, although the manner in which it works remains obscure, *electroconvulsive therapy can often relieve depression that has proved resistant to other treatments. Hospital admission, which is the general rule for cases of mania, provides a temporary sanctuary for those suffering depression, and is essential when the risk of suicide seems great. Psychotherapeutic help is invaluable and, in people who have recurrent episodes of illness, mood stabilizers such as lithium and carbamazepine may be used on a long-term basis to prevent further relapses.

HW/PMcG/RMM

Berrios, G., and Porter, R. (eds.) (1999). *A History of Clinical Psychiatry: The Origin and History of Psychiatric Disorders.*

Clare, A. (1980). *Psychiatry in Dissent* (2nd edn.).

Gelder, M. G., Gath, D., Mayou, R., and Cowen, P. (1996). *Oxford Textbook of Psychiatry* (3rd edn.).

Marks, I. M. (2003). *Living with Fear* (2nd edn.).

Murray, R., Hill, P., and McGuffin, P. (eds.) (1997). *The Essentials of Postgraduate Psychiatry* (3rd edn.).

Stefan, M., Travis, M., and Murray, R. (2002). *An Atlas of Schizophrenia.*

mental imagery. The idea that mental imagery may have a role in reasoning goes back a long way—one of the earliest attempts to study empirically the role that such imagery played in thinking was carried out by Sir Francis *Galton in 1883, when he surveyed a large number of people for their use of mental imagery, using his 'breakfast table' visualization test. He was surprised to find that many people disavowed having any visual imagery and that scientists generally played down the role of imagery in their thinking. But the study of such mentalistic concepts soon fell on hard times under *behaviourism. When behaviourist ideology began to lose its grip on psychology, about two-thirds of the way through the 20th century, mental imagery was one of the first mentalistic concepts to emerge into prominence. Initially this emergence showed up in the use of 'imagery ratings', which overtook the venerable frequency-of-occurrence index as an 'intervening variable' in traditional studies of associative learning and memory. Soon after the rehabilitation of mental imagery began, a large number of experiments were performed to explore the form and function of mental images in reasoning. These experiments showed that images could be 'rotated', and examined in the 'mind's eye' in order to judge their size, shape, or other visual properties. Other studies also showed that examining mental images 'projected' onto perceived scenes exhibited many properties associated with vision. Such images could lead to interference with perceptual tasks, to visuomotor adaptation, and even to visual illusions of the sort that might be expected if the imagined forms were actually part of the stimulus. This persuaded many people that mental images themselves had many of the properties of visual stimuli—and in particular that they possessed metrical spatial properties, such as size and inter-object distances.

The consensus that soon emerged was that mental images were very similar to real visual stimuli, except that they were generated by the mind instead of by stimulation of the retina. One influential view took the form of a 'cathode ray tube' (or CRT) metaphor, in which an image was assumed to be projected onto a mental 'display' that was then perceived by the visual system (Kosslyn et al. 1979). Another view suggested that imaginal memory could 'feed into' the visual system at various levels—from the earliest stages of vision to later conceptual stages (Finke 1980). Yet a third suggested that, because imagery and vision use some of the same mechanisms, imaging bears a 'second-order isomorphism' to the similarity of patterns arising from vision (Shepard and Chipman 1970). A common recurring theme is that cognition can draw a 'picture' that it can then 'reperceive'—a notion that clearly leads to a regress, especially since it is assumed that imagery and vision use the same inner display. That this obvious regress is not generally recognized is a tribute to how strong a grip our subjective impression of imagery, as something that an inner observer examines, has on us.

As claims of the similarity between vision and imagery multiplied, it became clear to some writers that something was amiss. It was beginning to look more and more as if the peripheral visual apparatus as well as the visible world itself were being moved inside the mind. For example, experiments showed that 'small' mental images were harder to see (and took longer to report details from) than 'large' images, that the mind's eye could 'squint', that it exhibited the 'oblique effect' (in which oblique lines were harder to distinguish than similarly spaced horizontal or vertical lines), that it showed an acuity profile similar to that of the real eye, and so on. Since many of these properties arise in vision because of the neuroanatomy of the eye and its connections to the visual cortex, it appeared that the 'mind's eye' might share all these properties (presumably it had a blind spot and in some cases might even need corrective glasses)! What was happening was that the pull of our subjective experience of 'seeing with our mind's eye' was blinding us to the fact that our experience of imagery is an experience of *seeing a possible world*, not of examining causal information-processing mechanisms within the brain. Even more importantly, it was blinding us to alternative (and in most cases rather obvious) explanations of many of the empirical phenomena.

The alternative that was being overlooked is that when one is asked to 'imagine' something, the natural interpretation of this task is that one should try to recreate as many aspects as one can, or as one believes to be relevant, of a situation in which one is actually viewing the imagined situation unfold. Thus if asked to imagine shifting attention across a mental map, one attempts to create (or simulate) a sequence of mental states in which one is attending to a sequence of places one knows to be along the route, (or, more likely, one computes time-to-contact durations to landmarks that we can see while imagining; Pylyshyn 2003*b*): the entire route need not be represented in detail anywhere, just the thought that one is looking 'here' and then one is looking 'there' and so on. The demonstratives *this* and *that* in this case can refer to objects that are actually perceived, perhaps visually if the eyes are open, or through audition or proprioception if the eyes are closed. Similarly, if asked to imagine a 'small' thing one takes into account that small things are harder to see, have fewer visible details, and so on, and then one simulates, in terms of whatever responses one is required to make, what

one believes would happen in such a situation. In the case of 'mental searching' experiments, we have demonstrated that if the experimental demands are removed (for example, when subjects are not invited to imagine that they are shifting their attention across the scene) no 'scanning effect' relating time to distance ensues (Pylyshyn 1981). This 'simulation based on tacit knowledge' explanation seems to fit the great majority of mental imagery findings reported in the literature. It also fits the following obvious fact about images: they are *our* images and we can make them have very nearly any property we wish—and we generally make them have the properties we believe would actually obtain if we were to see the real situation. (Cases not covered by this simple explanation are discussed in detail elsewhere—Pylyshyn 2002, 2003*b*).

If this were the entire story of research on the picture theory of mental imagery, cognitive scientists might well have lost interest in the topic. What has kept it alive is that the intuitively appealing picture theory has been given new life by recent research in neuroscience. Although the facts are not uncontested, even within neuroscience, the research has been taken to show that even the most peripheral part of the visual cortex (area V1) is active during episodes of mental imagery. Combined with the fact that activity in the visual cortex in primates is known to be retinotopic (i.e. it maps patterns of retinal activity in a continuously transformed, or locally affine, manner), these findings suggest a possible neural implementation of the elusive internal display long favoured by picture theorists. Many writers jumped to the conclusion that these results showed the existence of spatial patterns in the brain that underwrite a pictorial form of mental images (indeed some have referred to this evidence as finally providing 'the resolution of the imagery debate'—Kosslyn 1994). But this is far from being the case. Even if the neuroscience evidence were not problematic, the arguments against a picture theory that had been discussed over the past 30 years (not to mention *Locke's argument against *Berkeley's claim that ideas are images) remain unanswered. The interpretation placed on the neuroscience evidence by picture theorists is *highly* problematic and when the evidence is examined even cursorily it is found to provide no support at all for the picture theory of mental imagery.

While the finding that some part of the visual system is active in mental imagery is (if sustained) itself quite interesting, it tells us nothing about the *nature* and *form* of the representation underlying mental images; representations in vision and imagery could have exactly the same form without either being pictorial (they could, for example, both take the form of symbol structures). But more importantly, the argument from activity in the visual cortex during imagery ignores the very significant (indeed, decisive) differences between retinal/cortical 'images' and mental images, a few of which are summarized below.

1. The pattern of activity in the visual cortex is in retinal coordinates and, like vision, is limited to a field of view not much more than a few degrees of visual angle. In contrast, mental images (as shown by both phenomenological and experimental observations) are in allocentric or environmental coordinates and are panoramic or even cycloramic (360 degrees) in breadth. Consequently, the retinotopically mapped pattern of activity in the visual cortex is totally inappropriate for underwriting mental imagery.

2. The only topographical mappings of perceived space found in the visual cortex are two dimensional. Yet mental images are clearly three dimensional, and indeed all imagery phenomena (e.g. mental searching, mental rotation) occur as readily in three dimensions as in two. This means that explaining the three-dimensional versions of these phenomena would require postulating a different mechanism and a different form of representation—one that itself could not take the form of a neural display since there are no known three-dimensional neural displays that map space.

3. Information in cortical patterns and in mental images is accessed and interpreted very differently. If you construct a mental image, the result, however much it might feel like a picture, does not have the signature properties of visual perception. For example, imagined patterns of lines in two dimensions do not automatically lead to a three-dimensional interpretation or to reversals between ambiguous interpretations. Try the following example. Imagine a parallelogram. Now imagine an identical parallelogram directly below it. Connect each vertex of the top figure to the corresponding vertex of the bottom figure. What does it look like? The striking difference between an image and a display can be made clear if you now draw the figure and look at it.

Accessing information from a mental image is different in many other ways from accessing information from a visual scene. If you were to write a word on the board you could easily read the letters in any order. But you cannot do that with an image of the word. Mental images are also not like retinal images in that they are not subject to *Emmert's law. If you have an image on your retina (e.g. an after-image), and you look at some surface in the distance, the apparent size of the image varies with the distance of the surface: the further away it is the larger the apparent size of the retinal image. This is not true of a mental image, as it should be if the image were actually a retinotopic pattern of cortical activity (in fact our informal observations suggest that an image projected onto a surface appears to get smaller, rather than larger, as the surface is moved away).

4. If the same cortical display provides input to both vision and imagery, both should connect with the motor system in the same way. Yet they do not: reaching for an imagined object does not exhibit the signature properties that characterize reaching for a perceived object (Milner and Goodale 1995), and many visuomotor phenomena, such as smooth pursuit, do not occur with imagined motion.

5. Even more important is the fact that retinotopic patterns in the visual cortex have yet to be interpreted, while mental images *are* the interpretation; there is every reason to believe that images cannot be further reinterpreted *visually*. Of course one can think about them and figure out what would happen if we did things to them, such as rotate them or combine them with other patterns, but we can do so only when the combinations are easy to infer (e.g. from fragmental cues), not when they involve a clearly visual (re)perception.

6. Clinical neurological findings, often cited by adherents of picture theory, provide little support for the claim that the pattern of cortical activation corresponds to the mental image. If mental imagery and vision use the same cortical display, it is hard to see why vision and imagery capacities are so radically dissociated: there are many reports of normal imagery in people who have a variety of visual deficits, and there are many reports of normal vision in people with little or no mental imagery. Indeed, virtually all the experimental results cited in support of the picture theory have been obtained with blind people, though they may not be accompanied by the experience of 'seeing', except in the recently blinded.

The recent interest in mental imagery has not clarified the puzzles that have been around since the time when Locke and Berkeley argued about them 300 years ago. Moreover, the new picture theories have not dealt with the recent empirical arguments (as outlined in Pylyshyn 2003b). Yet despite the problematic state of theoretical understanding of mental imagery, most psychologists continue to assume that representations underlying mental imagery are very different from ones underlying other forms of thought, and in particular that such representations are in some important sense 'spatial' (for an alternative interpretation of the apparent 'spatial' nature of mental images that does not attribute this character to properties of an inner display, see the discussion in chapter 7 of Pylyshyn 2003a). This refractoriness of theorizing about mental imagery to counter-arguments is no doubt attributable to the almost irresistible grip that our subjective impressions have on our inclination to accept certain kinds of theories, a grip that in earlier years had burdened theorizing about the physical world as well.   ZP

Finke, R. A. (1980). 'Levels of equivalence in imagery and perception'. *Psychological Review*, 87.

Galton, F. (1883). *Inquiries into Human Faculty and its Development*.

Kosslyn, S. M. (1994). *Image and Brain: The Resolution of the Imagery Debate*.

——Pinker, S., Smith, G., and Shwartz, S. P. (1979). 'On the demystification of mental imagery'. *Behavioral and Brain Science*, 2.

Milner, A. D., and Goodale, M. A. (1995). *The Visual Brain in Action*.

Pylyshyn, Z. W. (1981). 'The imagery debate: analogue media versus tacit knowledge'. *Psychological Review*, 88.

——(2002). 'Mental imagery: in search of a theory'. *Behavioral and Brain Sciences*, 25/2.

——(2003a). 'Return of the mental image: are there really pictures in the brain?' *Trends in Cognitive Sciences*, 7/3.

——(2003b). *Seeing and Visualizing: It's Not What you Think*.

Shepard, R. N., and Chipman, S. (1970). 'Second-order isomorphism of internal representations: shapes of states'. *Cognitive Psychology*, 1.

mental imagery: depictive accounts. When we gaze in front of us, we see objects and their properties arrayed in space. We do not have direct contact with these objects, but become aware of them only because our brains have constructed internal representations. According to the depictive view of imagery, mental images arise from representations like those created during the early phases of *perception, but these representations are based on information stored in *memory (rather than on sensory input, as occurs during perception). Specifically, depictive views of imagery claim that the phenomenology of mental imagery—such as the experience of 'seeing with the mind's eye' reflects key properties of the underlying representations. According to this view, image representations *depict* information about the way an object or scene would appear when viewed from a particular perspective. In a depictive representation, each point corresponds to a point on the represented object or scene, such that the distances in an internal space among the points in the representation correspond to the distances among the represented points on the object or scene. In this context, we refer to depictive representations in the brain, where points on the cortex are used to represent specific locations on the object or scene being depicted. Although pictures are one form of depiction, neither perceptions nor mental images are pictures—they are internal representations, whereas pictures are objects in the world (which can be hung on walls, and so on). Pictures have additional properties that no depictive theorist has attributed to mental images; for example, actual pictures have unlimited complexity, can be rotated without portions becoming scrambled, and usually can be easily reinterpreted—but mental images are subject to the limits of human information processing capacity, like all representations in short-term memory. The fact that pictures, percepts, and mental images all depict does not imply that they must behave the same way in every respect.

The depictive form of representation limits the types of images we can experience (e.g. all shapes must also have a size and orientation), but depictive theories do not claim that *all* properties of imagery arise from the depictive characteristics of the representation. Only properties related to the geometric layout of shapes are governed by depictive representation. In particular, one's knowledge can alter many properties of imagery (such as changing movement or colour)—which is one reason why imagery is useful in reasoning. However, if non-depictive knowledge governs how our images behave, why do we need to posit a depictive form of representation at all? Why can't we treat image representations in the same way as those that underlie language?

Initial evidence for depictive representations came from *behavioural studies, which typically measured the time participants required to perform certain tasks. One line of research demonstrated that people require more time to scan farther distances across visualized objects. However, such findings proved ambiguous. For example, the time to scan over an object in an image initially was used as a kind of 'mental tape measure', to demonstrate that the underlying representation embodied spatial extent. Thus, participants were asked explicitly to scan objects in their images. However, Pylyshyn (1981) argued that participants have tacit knowledge about how perception works, and interpret the task as requiring them to mimic what they would do in perception—and thus simply wait longer to respond when they were supposed to scan longer distances. If so, then the data would not reflect properties of image representations. However, such findings have been obtained even when no explicit scanning instructions were given, but it is possible that participants somehow unconsciously fathom the purpose of the study.

Thus, the most compelling evidence for depictive representation during imagery comes from studies in which brain activity is directly examined during mental imagery: participants cannot intentionally alter their brain states, nor are they even aware of how their brains are functioning during imagery tasks.

Mental images in the brain

We will focus on visual mental imagery, which is the best understood type of imagery. Depictive theories of how imagery is implemented in the brain are grounded in three sets of facts: first, the occipital lobe contains numerous *topographically organized areas* (TOA, starting with Area 17, the first cortical area receiving input from the eyes); physically nearby neurons in TOAs represent physically nearby portions of the visual field. The topographic organization is important during perception because it makes explicit and accessible information that is needed to organize the input into coherent shapes. In fact, most of the connections among neurons in these areas are short and inhibitory; this arrangement helps edges to be specified (because neurons activated by light inhibit nearby neurons that are less activated, thereby exaggerating the change from light to dark). We stress the following: patterns of activity in TOAs function to represent shape depictively; the signals sent deeper into the brain from these areas depict shapes—they use space on the cortex to represent space on the depicted object. How do we know this? For example, a small hole in a TOA produces a scotoma (a 'blind spot') (see FILLING-IN SCOTOMAS) in the corresponding part of the visual field—and holes that are farther apart in a TOA produce blind spots that are correspondingly farther apart in the visual field. In addition, stimulation of TOA sites produces phosphenes or scotomas at corresponding locations in the visual field. Furthermore, studies of Area 17 in monkeys have provided especially compelling evidence that TOAs actually use depictive representation. For example, Roelfsema and Spekreijse (2001) recorded from multiple neurons simultaneously while monkeys mentally traced a pair of lines (without moving their eyes) to decide which one was connected to a starting dot. Neurons that represented adjacent points of the target line were activated in an orderly manner, literally laying out an image of the line. Furthermore, when the animal made an error, the activation indicated where the line was visualized incorrectly! The precise spatial layout of these effects is strong evidence that TOAs support depictive representations.

Second, what about the concern that depictive representations require a 'little man' (a *homunculus) to 'look at' them? This concern is dispelled by the fact that TOAs in the occipital lobe are part of a larger system. These areas send input to a set of areas in the temporal lobes that store visual memories, and also send input to a set of areas in the parietal lobes that specify spatial relations. The physical 'wiring' from occipital TOAs to later areas is designed in effect to 'read' the depictive aspects of the representation in the early visual cortex; the interpretive processes are tailor-made for the representation. Without question, TOAs support depictive representations that are actually used in information processing.

Third, how could mental images arise? During perception, activity in TOAs is engendered by stimulation from the eyes; what about during imagery? The temporal-lobe areas that store visual memories have many connections that run *backwards* to the TOAs of the occipital lobe. Visual memories are apparently stored in a compressed, abstract code, and these connections are used to reconstruct the local geometry of a surface by evoking patterns of activation in TOAs—that is, to create a mental image. For example, we can visualize a cat's head and notice the shape of its ears, even though we have never described their shape. Moreover, during image generation the two-dimensional representations in TOAs are linked to representations in other brain regions, allowing them to represent additional properties; for instance, images of

shape are linked to representations of spatial relations in the parietal lobe, specifying three-dimensional properties, and to colour representations in the fusiform gyrus. In some ways, the TOAs can function like a corkboard with notes pinned on it (where the notes specify colour, depth, and other properties); the board depicts the layout of space, and organizes the values specified for local regions.

Neuroscientific evidence

Four classes of neuroimaging findings provide strong support for depictive theories. First, TOAs are activated when participants form visual images of shapes (Kosslyn and Thompson 2003); these depictive areas do not store language-like descriptions—they are tailor-made to represent shape depictively. These areas are not activated if the task can be accomplished using spatial relations (such as 'X is above Y'), during verbal tasks or during auditory imagery. Moreover, the nature of the image affects how the representation depicts shape. For example, when participants visualized line drawings of objects at different sizes (as if they fit into boxes memorized before the scan), the locus of activation depends on the size of the imaged object as in perception.

Second, there is evidence that depictive representations in Area 17 play a functional role in imagery. When transcranial magnetic stimulation (TMS) was applied repeatedly to Area 17 prior to an imagery task, until the neurons became relatively unresponsive, every participant subsequently required more time to perform this task than when TMS did not target Area 17 (Kosslyn et al. 1999).

Third, another study used statistical methods to remove the influence of other brain areas, which may have been affected incidentally by the TMS. Participants closed their eyes and visualized letters of the alphabet. After forming the image, they judged whether the letter had a specific characteristic (e.g. an enclosed space). Not only were variations in the level of activation in Area 17 significantly correlated with the response times, but this correlation was present even after all other correlations between variations in regional cerebral blood flow (in other brain regions) and response time were statistically removed.

Finally, the claim that depictive representations in TOAs during imagery in effect are 'read' by other parts of the visual system has also been supported: most brain areas activated during perception are also activated during like-modality imagery (Ganis et al. in press). Images in fact do occur in the context of a processing system used in perception.

Partially overlapping mechanisms

If imagery relies on TOAs in the occipital lobe, why do some neurological patients continue to have some use of imagery in spite of the fact that these areas have been severely damaged? The answer is clear: the occipital lobe is not necessary for all forms of imagery. For example, images of spatial relations rely on TOAs in the parietal cortex; such images sometimes may rely on how attention is allocated (such as occurs when one forms an image of a letter on a tile floor by attending to specific arrangements of tiles). But such 'spatial indexing' cannot explain all imagery findings. For example, the finding that occipital TOAs are activated only when tasks do not require spatial processing—and parietal cortex is activated when they do (Kosslyn and Thompson 2003). To make fine shape variations accessible to later processes, one apparently needs to reconstruct the local geometry in occipital TOAs.

If imagery and perception draw on the same systems, why does brain damage sometimes disrupt imagery without affecting perception or vice versa? Neuroimaging (see BRAIN IMAGING) and neuropsychological research have confirmed that visual mental imagery and visual perception do not draw on identical processes. Imagery activates approximately two-thirds of the same areas as perception. Imagery does not require as much low-level organizational processing as perception does, whereas perception does not require activating information in memory when the stimulus is not present. Thus, when shared areas are damaged in neurological patients, one should observe both functions impaired—but when non-shared areas are damaged, imagery and perception should be dissociated (Ganis et al. 2003). Finally, this partial overlap in mechanisms also illuminates why imagery and perception sometimes operate differently. For instance, unlike percepts, images fade quickly, are created with an internal organization, and rely on limited working memory capacity; they are created on the basis of organized units, and preserve that organization. Thus, it is not surprising that it is more difficult to reinterpret patterns in visual images (e.g. to see alternative interpretations of ambiguous figures) than to reinterpret perceptions. Furthermore, low-level visual phenomena that are stimulus-driven are not expected in imagery because visual mental images are not driven by input from the eyes. For instance, colour mixing, motor tracking, and similar visuomotor phenomena emerge from bottom-up processing, which should be mimicked in imagery only with difficulty.

A final word on tacit knowledge

Tacit knowledge theories claim that there is no evidence for depictive representations; instead, the data merely indicate ways in which participants can alter their performance in accordance with their knowledge about what they would do during perception. However, even the most knowledgeable among us does not know how the brain responds during imagery, and does not know how to modify that response to mimic how it responds during perception. In contrast, depictive theories focus on the mechanisms that give rise to information processing

and—ultimately—to conscious experience. The properties of depictive representations do not necessarily have to be evident in consciousness, but many of them are. Knowing this opens new vistas for understanding the relationship between mind, brain, and conscious experience.
SMK/GG/WLT

Ganis, G., Thompson, W. L., Mast, F., and Kosslyn, S. M. (2003). 'Visual imagery in cerebral visual dysfunction'. *Neurologic Clinics*, 21, 631–46.
——, and Kosslyn, S. M. (2004). 'Brain areas underlying visual imagery and visual perception: an fMRI study'. *Cognitive Brain Research*, 20, 226–41.
Kosslyn, S. M., Pascual-Leone, A., Felician, O., Camposano, S., Keenan, J. P., Thompson, W. L., Ganis, G., Sukel, K. E., and Alpert, N. M. (1999). 'The role of Area 17 in visual imagery: convergent evidence from PET and rTMS'. *Science*, 284, 167–70.
——, and Thompson, W. L. (2003). 'When is early visual cortex activated during visual mental imagery?' *Psychological Bulletin*, 129, 723–46.
Pylyshyn, Z. W. (1981). 'The imagery debate: analogue media versus tacit knowledge'. *Psychological Review*, 87, 16–45.
Roelfsema, P. R. and Spekreijse, H. (2001). 'The representation of erroneously perceived stimuli in the primary visual cortex'. *Neuron*, 31, 853–63.

mentally ill, services for the. The provision of proper care for the mentally ill has been a problem for centuries (see ASYLUMS: A HISTORICAL SURVEY). There is no right solution, for the size and nature of the problem changes according to society's definition of mental illness and its tolerance of unusual behaviour among its members. Therefore, before embarking on detailed planning of services for the mentally ill, it is necessary to establish the need for such services.

It is traditional in Britain to adopt the medical model of *mental illness. This means that the disability is seen in terms of symptoms and signs arising from a pathological process (which may be undefined) for which medical diagnosis and treatment are appropriate. This model has been challenged by those who consider that much mental illness is related to adverse social or environmental factors. Doctors have not rejected this view, but have tended to extend their areas of interest to incorporate such fields as marital disharmony for which a purely medical model is inappropriate. This extension of medical activity into fields which would previously have been the province of other groups such as priests, with its implied extension of the range of 'mental illness', has to be taken into account when planning medical services.

The development of psychoactive drugs has had a major effect on the need for services for the mentally ill. The ability to control pharmacologically some of the symptoms of severe illnesses such as *schizophrenia and *manic–depressive psychosis has reduced the need for long-term residential care. On the other hand, there has been a massive increase in consultations with general practitioners on account of some form of *mental illness. This is partly associated with the ready availability and comparative safety of drugs that affect mood. People have learned that they can be relieved of the discomfort of *anxiety or *depression by means of tablets, and acknowledgement of these conditions is no longer associated with social stigma. The evidence that some drugs which were initially considered 'safe' can in fact be addictive has not reduced the demands for treatment, but has increased the need for non-drug approaches, such as counselling and *psychotherapy. These changes at both ends of the mental illness spectrum, which appear likely to continue, have to be taken into account when planning, so as to develop the appropriate balance of facilities for care.

The demand for medical services for the mentally ill is not determined entirely by the activities of doctors and the opportunities for medical treatment. Society itself contributes to the equation by setting the somewhat arbitrary line which distinguishes between abnormal, though tolerable, behaviour and mental illness. The position of this line varies, both with time and between nations. In Britain at present, people are still relatively intolerant of even mild psychotic symptoms, whereas there is increased acceptance of sexual deviance, especially homosexuality. In some countries, disagreement with the governing regime is considered so deviant as to merit the label 'mental illness'. These differences predominantly affect the requirement for residential care, since the demand is usually for the deviant to be removed from the community at large, and there is indeed an overlap between those labelled mentally ill who are sent to hospital and those who contravene the law and receive prison sentences. Another influence on the way mental illness is viewed stems from changes in mental health legislation.

The needs of the elderly have to be considered separately because of the different nature of their illnesses. It is, of course, not unusual for people over 65 years of age to suffer from the common psychiatric disorders for which the generally available treatment is appropriate; but with advancing years, the incidence of *dementia increases, and it is often accompanied by physical illness or handicap. Special account of the needs of such patients must be taken in planning services, both for assessment in order to ensure that remediable complicating factors are dealt with and for their long-term care. Greater longevity has increased the need for psychogeriatric facilities, and governments in most Western developed nations have become concerned over the need to provide care for increasing numbers of aged patients, many of whom are suffering from irreversible dementia. How to relieve the strain on existing facilities is one of the problems to be faced in the future.

The planning of medical services demands quantification of future needs and knowledge of the resources that will be available to meet them. However, whereas the size of the population to be served can be calculated with reasonable accuracy on an actuarial basis, the proportion who will be suffering from mental illness is much more difficult to estimate. It depends on guesses about future patterns of designation of mental disorder and future therapeutic developments. Moreover, assessment of the treatment requirements of the mentally ill, upon which provision must be based, is dependent on further guesses about future social attitudes and about opportunities for care in the family when increasing numbers of women work outside the home.

Having reached an estimate of the quantity of service which will be needed, the way in which it will be provided has to be determined. The balance of care between medical and non-medical agencies, between psychiatrists and general practitioners, between large psychiatric hospitals and units in general hospitals, and between residential and non-residential facilities has all to be decided. Decisions cannot be reached entirely rationally: in many cases, there is little evidence to support one view or another. The enthusiasms of local practitioners, current government policy, and the necessity of modifying rather than replacing existing facilities may all take precedence over projections of future needs and opportunities, which in any case will be somewhat theoretical. It is important, however, that the factors which are taken into account are recognized and recorded, so that planning decisions taken now can be properly evaluated in the future and the quality of decision making thus improved. In addition, it is essential that the full implications of each option are explored before a decision is reached. For example, expansion of care for the mentally ill in the community inevitably means that the most ill patients with the least likelihood of improvement in their condition will remain in the large hospitals. Realistic proposals for the maintenance of standards and for the recruitment of staff at these hospitals, by such means as rotation of posts with other units, in-service training programmes, and research projects, must be put forward before plans are implemented, in order to prevent serious problems of morale and an unacceptable fall in the standards of patient care.

The change in the balance of care poses problems in the community as well as in the institution. It is difficult to provide mentally ill people living in small groups with the range of supporting staff and activities that can be offered in institutions. When it is practical to offer such facilities in the community, the dispersal of the patients means that the cost of the services is much higher than the cost of an equivalent level of care in a hospital. The policy of transfer from hospital to community care is based on clinical and humanitarian arguments, but much support for it derives from the assumed financial savings. It is now clear that mentally ill people based in the community, receiving services funded at a lower level than hospital services, are at grave risk of 'community neglect' rather than 'community care'.

The prevention of mental illness is a complicated issue to which little attention has been paid in the past. It is unlikely that simple methods like vaccination will ever be appropriate in this field. Like other common non-communicable diseases such as coronary heart disease, any advances in the prevention of mental illness are likely to require changes in patterns of behaviour, which are extremely difficult to achieve and may raise ethical problems. Epidemiological evidence on topics such as suicide (see SUICIDAL BEHAVIOUR) and *bereavement and on the effect of important life events on the development of mental illness do, however, give clues about possible future activity in this field.

The rehabilitation of the mentally ill is of major importance and has also been somewhat neglected in the past. If, in general, the objective of treatment is to maximize the patient's independence, it is clear that exclusively medical services are inadequate, and must be complemented by help with social and employment problems. It is highly desirable that all the agencies which patients may need should be involved in the preparation of service plans.

The detailed planning of services must take place at a local level if they are to meet the needs of the local community. In Britain, however, the money for healthcare is not raised locally but comes from central government. The local planning therefore has to be undertaken within the framework of national policy. This determines what proportion of the gross national product will be allocated to health and, within that, the apportionment between services. At present, mental illness is a priority service and can expect an increased proportion of the health budget to be allocated to it. It is not, however, always possible to achieve such transfers of resources, especially in a time of economic stringency, because of the difficulties of making cuts in other services.

Planning has also to take account of government policy with regard to medical manpower. In Britain the aim at present is to remove the inequalities in staffing levels across the country and between specialities. Current initiatives to expand the consultant grade and to control entry of junior doctors into training posts in the popular acute specialities may attract more doctors into psychiatry, which has not historically been a popular career of first choice among medical graduates.

Planning of services for the mentally ill is an activity dependent on estimates of future medical, pharmacological, and social changes, but the range of such estimates is inevitably wide, and the interaction between the different factors imprecisely defined. It is not possible to predict with any accuracy the level of the financial or manpower resources that will be available in the next decade. Even so, it is important that planning should continue on as rational a basis as possible and that facts, assumptions, and arguments should be recorded. It is only in this way that planning can move from meeting vocal demands to meeting true needs. Meanwhile, all service plans should maintain the maximum flexibility, so as to minimize constraints on future developments.

See also ASYLUMS: ARE THEY REALLY NECESSARY?   JMC

For extra information or help for those affected by mental illness contact SANE (UK): SANELINE: 0845 767 8000 or visit their website at **www.sane.org.uk**.

mental rehearsal. Mental rehearsal, sometimes known as mental or imaginary practice, has long been familiar to athletes and musicians as a partial substitute for physical practice. Richardson (1967) defined it as 'the symbolic rehearsal of a physical activity in the absence of any gross muscular movements'. It can take a variety of forms, including visualizing the performance of a skill such as a tennis serve or a gymnastic leap (*the external view*), or feeling what it is like to perform the skill (*the internal view*). The former is characterized by predominantly visual imagery and the latter by kinaesthetic imagery. Sometime both internal and external views are experienced. Both visual and kinaesthetic imagery have been reported to be effective in enhancing performance, although there is considerable variation between studies of different groups of athletes and types of sport. Some have found that elite athletes are more likely to use the internal view. Another study found that Olympic athletes are more likely than trialists to use the external view, whilst also reporting stronger physical sensations accompanying their visual imagery.

In the late 19th century Sir Francis *Galton and William *James both described varieties of imagery, including images of muscular sensations and movement. However, the subject attracted little research activity until the revival of interest in cognitive components of motor skills and the psychology of sport in the 1960s. Among psychological approaches to sporting success, the idea of the 'inner game' in which visualization and imagery played a major role was adopted by many coaches. In the 1980s the National Research Council, prompted by the US army, set up a committee to report on a variety of popular techniques for the enhancement of human performance. The committee found a number of studies which confirmed the effectiveness of mental practice as a means of maintaining and improving physical skills. Meta-analyses (statistical summaries of the results of a number of empirical studies) by Feltz and Landers (1983) and by Driskell, Copper, and Moran (1994) reached the general conclusion that mental rehearsal was more effective in acquiring and maintaining skill than not practising at all, but generally less effective than fully overt physical practice. Mental rehearsal does, however, have the positive advantage that it can be used when opportunities for physical practice are limited, or would be physically exhausting or dangerous.

A long-standing belief of *behaviourism is that no learning can occur without feedback, or positive reinforcement. Evidence that performance can be maintained and even improved by mental rehearsal—which involves no feedback from the external world—challenges this belief. A number of theories have been advanced to account for the effectiveness of mental practice. The first is that mental rehearsal enhances the motivation to perform well, and thus has an indirect effect on the level of performance without necessarily affecting learning as such. Imagery of success and 'positive thinking' is often recommended by sports coaches, such as Orlick (1986), and there is no doubt that elite athletes are typically highly motivated and may spend more time thinking about their performance than those who are less skilled. However, the association between the use of imagery and high motivation is not necessarily causal. Alternative theories are based on the general hypothesis that imagery and perception, and perhaps also imagery and action, have some brain processes in common, and that these can be influenced by rehearsal alone.

William James proposed that 'All consciousness is motor'. By this he meant that a stimulus to the nervous system always produces some response as activity flows through the organism from sensation to action. Consciousness was associated with what he called 'the middle part' of this flow of neural activity. It follows that conscious imagery of movement, whatever its initial 'stimulus', would have an effect on motor activity. The tendency to make small muscle movements when imagining actions appears to support this view. Some people find it difficult to imagine movement without engaging in some muscular activity. Try to mentally rehearse the sentence 'Peter Piper picked a peck of pickled peppers' and then again with the lips and tongue held immobile by clenching a pencil between the teeth. Most people report that the clear auditory image becomes blurred and indistinct when overt movement is suppressed. This phenomenon is claimed as support for James's theory that motor imagery is suppressed action. The 'psychoneuromuscular' theory proposes that imaginary actions, of the kind involved in mental rehearsal, are essentially partially suppressed actions, and can appeal to evidence of neural and muscular activity during imaginary movement in support of this theory.

A variation on the general theme of processes shared between imaginary and actual perception and action is sometimes referred to as the symbolic theory. This theory was originally proposed to account for enhanced retention of a maze habit through mental rehearsal. Its central feature is that all overt activities have a cognitive or symbolic component, which may be rehearsed independently of the overt or muscular components. These symbolic

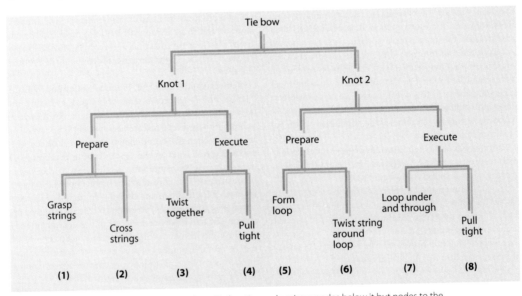

Fig. 1. A putative control hierarchy for tying a bow. Each active node primes nodes below it but nodes to the right are inhibited while those to the left remain active. The upper nodes are 'mental' and those at the bottom are 'muscle' nodes. Only the mental nodes are active during imaginary practice.

features might include a mental plan which specifies the order and timing of actions, or which allows the performer to chunk information in an efficient way. D. G. Mackay (1981) showed how a theory of this kind can be applied to serial skills. Many skills involved in both sport and music require a precisely timed sequence of actions. Mackay's theory describes how such behaviour might be controlled by excitation and inhibition flowing through a hierarchy of nodes from high-level, or mental, nodes down to motor nodes which control detailed muscular activity.

The theory can be illustrated as in Fig. 1 by the serial skill of tying a bow. At the top of the hierarchy is a node 'tie a bow', which may itself have been activated as part of some higher-level plan such as wrapping a parcel. The two subordinate nodes comprise two partial knots, and each of these in turn comprises a preparation and an execution phase, which in turn devolve into specific actions such as grasping the free ends, twisting them together, and pulling them tight. The key to the process is that each node is primed when its superior node is activated, and that when nodes to the left are activated those to the right are inhibited—thus ensuring that the actions are run off in the correct order. Primed nodes are not activated until triggered, and the triggering of muscle nodes is under voluntary control. During mental rehearsal motor nodes are inhibited, but the triggering of mental nodes has an effect, such that the more frequently a node has been activated by another, the faster it will be primed by activation in the nodes connected to it. Practising the sequence increases priming rates and the whole sequence will then be run off faster. An important feature of the higher-level nodes is that the sequences in which they are involved occur less frequently than the lower-level or muscular nodes—we make grasping movements much more frequently than we tie bows—and thus mental rehearsal will increase the priming rates of serial skills. Mackay's theory fits the mental rehearsal of speech production and has received partial support in a study of typing (Annett 1995). Both speech production and typing of scrambled sentences were shown to benefit from mental practice, but a prediction that skilled typists should benefit relatively more than the unskilled from mental practice was not confirmed.

Advances in non-invasive techniques for studying brain activity, including EEG, PET, and MRI during physical and mental practice (see BRAIN IMAGING), show some interesting similarities and differences between the two (see Annett 1995). Areas in the frontal lobes which support planning, and the parietal lobes which support spatial representations and working memory, tend to be active equally during physical and mental practice—whilst in purely mental rehearsal there is reduced activity in the primary motor cortex, which exerts direct control over voluntary muscle movement. There is also some evidence that sufferers from Parkinson's disease, which affects the basal ganglia by restricting motor outflow, have relatively less difficulty in imagining movement than its physical execution. Studies with monkeys have demonstrated the existence of groups of cells in the premotor cortex which respond to both the execution and perception of specific movements. This finding is consistent with the symbolic theory of mental rehearsal.   JAn

Annett, J. (1995). 'Motor imagery: perception or action?' *Neuropsychologia*, 33/11.

Driskell, J. E., Copper, C., and Moran, A. (1994). 'Does mental practice enhance performance?' *Journal of Applied Psychology*, 79.

Feltz, D. L., and Landers, D. M. (1983). 'The effects of mental practice on motor skill learning and performance: a meta-analysis'. *Journal of Sport Psychology*, 5.

Mackay, D. G. (1981). 'The problem of rehearsal or mental practice'. *Journal of Motor Behavior*, 13.

Orlick, T. (1986). *Psyching for Sport: Mental Training for Athletes.*

Richardson, A. (1967). 'Mental practice: a review and discussion'. *Research Quarterly*, 38.

Merleau-Ponty, Maurice (1908–61). French existentialist philosopher, professor of child psychology at the Sorbonne University (1949–52), professor of philosophy at the College de France (1952–61). In his early work in the 1930s, Merleau-Ponty employed *Gestalt theory, abnormal psychology, and ethnological studies of 'primitive' mentality to develop the idea that there was a primordial dimension of human being, below the level of conscious awareness, and hence prior to reflection, judgement formation, and explicit calculation. His use of *Husserl's unpublished manuscripts on the life-world, the living body, and intersubjectivity helped to shape his *The Phenomenology of Perception* (1945; English trans. 1962). Here he strove to articulate a third way between the first-person cognitive perspective and the third-person behavioural perspective. This third way takes form through the basic concept of structural shape or schemata, modes of organizing reality itself, matched by a correlative self-organization of human being. Perception is primary in conscious formation since the openness and indeterminacy of perception are found throughout cognitive and sensuous operations. Perception is also basic since it makes an original contact with reality at the level of the life-world and forms the background against which all actions are seen. He shows that there is a pre-objective view of humans being-in-the-world which effects the union of the mental and physical; it is through actions that the human body and external space form a practical system. He extended Husserl's concept of *intentionality into the corporeal dimension: the whole human body works with an intentional agency. Things in the world are given to me along with the parts of my living body in an organic connection comparable with that existing between the parts of my body itself. My living body is the fabric into which all objects are woven and it is the general instrument of human comprehension. Conscious acts outstrip themselves in the generation of *meaning and the achievement of their goals; hence, conscious being is an active transcendence towards the world of its concerns. A unique mode of human comportment is speech which does not translate ready-made thought but accomplishes the cognitive process. Cognitive neuroscience has recently begun to take an active interest in Merleau-Ponty's basic ideas about conscious embodiment.   PSM

Langer, M. (1989). *Merleau-Ponty's Phenomenology of Perception.*

mesmerism. It is often said that *hypnosis was discovered by the controversial Viennese physician Franz Anton Mesmer (1734–1815), whose name gave the word 'mesmerism' to the English language. While it seems certain that some of Mesmer's patients indeed became hypnotized, it must be borne in mind that no formal concept of hypnotism existed at the time, and Mesmer attributed his therapeutic successes to a hitherto unknown physical agency to which he gave the name 'animal magnetism'. Greatly influenced by Newtonian physics—which he evidently misunderstood completely—Mesmer envisaged animal magnetism as a physical force or 'fluid', somewhat akin to gravity, which permeates the universe and to which the human nervous system is somehow attuned (Mesmer 1779). Nervous illness, he believed, results from an imbalance between the animal magnetism in the patient's body and that in the external world at large, which can be redressed by human agency. This Mesmer sought to achieve by channelling animal magnetism through his own body to that of the patient, either directly by applying his hands to the affected part ('passes') or indirectly by requiring the patient to grasp an iron bar or other object which he had previously 'magnetized' by direct contact. Although magnets or magnetized iron filings were sometimes used as intermediaries, Mesmer insisted that animal magnetism is quite different from physical magnetism and in itself possesses no curative properties. None the less, the term 'magnetizer' long persisted as the popular designation of those who made use of Mesmer's methods for therapeutic ends.

Although Mesmer's theory of animal magnetism was rejected by scientists even in his own lifetime, there can be no doubt that he won many disciples and not a few grateful patients. Indeed his colourful personality and robust self-confidence created a distinct stir, first in court circles in imperial Vienna and later in the fashionable salons of pre-revolutionary Paris. Inevitably, perhaps, he incurred the odium of the medical establishment, and the French government was eventually led to appoint a royal commission to conduct an enquiry into animal magnetism under the chairmanship of Benjamin Franklin. Among its members were Lavoisier, the famous chemist, and Guillotin, who gave his name to the instrument of decapitation that a few years later claimed the head of Lavoisier himself. This commission examined exhaustively not only the alleged medical benefits of mesmerism but also the evidence for the existence of animal magnetism itself, to which it quite properly adopted an experimental attitude. Although Mesmer did not give personal evidence to the commission (the brunt of cross-examination falling on one of his followers, Dr Deslon), there can be no doubt that it was in effect Mesmer himself who was on trial.

The commission published its report in 1784 and came out strongly against the existence of animal magnetism as a physical force. It did not, however, deny that in some cases mesmeric treatment brought therapeutic benefit. This the commissioners had no hesitation in attributing solely to the powers of imagination, which is hardly surprising when it is borne in mind that Mesmer, in his Paris days, made his patients sit in groups round a large barrel-like object known as a *baquet*, each grasping an iron rod protruding from the interior (which contained water and iron filings, sometimes magnetized), while he himself, splendidly attired, treated them by magnetism to the accompaniment of soft music. Also it is interesting that, in a section of the report apparently suppressed at the time but published over a century later by *Binet and Féré (1887), the commissioners directed special attention to the moral dangers attendant on mesmeric treatment, evidently reminding the reader that a high proportion of those seeking it were of the female sex. This provides a striking anticipation of Sigmund *Freud's contention that sexual factors are of great importance for our understanding of the hypnotic state.

In consequence of the royal commission's findings, mesmerism was officially discredited for many years and Mesmer himself disappeared into obscurity. None the less, a small number of 'magnetizers' continued to ply their trade. One of these was the Marquis de Puységur, who is credited with the first account of a case of *somnambulism evoked by mesmerism, with the subject showing a complete loss of memory for the events of the trance after being awakened. This would nowadays be called posthypnotic *amnesia. Among other magnetizers, several of whom visited England and America, was Dupotet, who first introduced John Elliotson (1791–1868), professor of the practice of medicine at University College London, to the phenomenon of mesmerism (see Bramwell 1913). Elliotson soon became convinced of its value in medical practice, particularly in the treatment of what were then (as now) called functional nervous disorders, i.e. disturbances of bodily or mental functions for which no physical pathology can be established. Like Mesmer before him, Elliotson was to suffer greatly from the hostility of the medical establishment, but he had the courage to resign from his professorship rather than comply with the ruling of the college council forbidding the practice of mesmerism in the hospital. His temerity was also shown by the fact that, when invited by the Royal College of Physicians to deliver the Herveian Oration, he chose mesmerism as his subject. Whereupon the *Lancet* dubbed him a professional pariah and asserted that his lecture would strike a vital blow at legitimate medicine. None the less, Elliotson duly delivered his lecture, which was received in stony silence, and did much thereafter—if in slightly eccentric ways—to advance the cause of what is nowadays known as psychological medicine.

Thereafter, the history of mesmerism merges into that of hypnotism and, more broadly, into that of psychological medicine. Indirectly, however, it is linked with a number of broader issues in social history, not least that of faith healing and Christian Science. Mary Baker Eddy, the founder of Christian Science, is thought to have first conceived its tenets through being cured of a hysterical paralysis when a girl, by a faith healer who had been inspired by a visiting French magnetizer.   OLZ

Binet, A. and Féré, C. (1887). *Le Magnétisme animal.*

Bramwell, J. M. (1913). *Hypnotism: Its History, Practice and Theory* (3rd edn.)

Mesmer, F. A. (1779). *Le Magnétisme animal* (repr. 1971).

Walmsley, D. M. (1967). *Anton Mesmer.*

mesopic vision. Twilight vision. Vision is poor in the 'half-light' between the scotopic black–white vision given by the retinal rods and the *colour vision given by the cones (photopic vision). It is important to know for driving that mesopic conditions are essentially dangerous and require extra care.

metaphor. The topic of metaphor has a history dating back at least to *Aristotle, but not until the 20th century did it come to be regarded seriously as a problem relevant to the general study of language and thought.

Aristotle took the use of metaphors to be evidence of a superior intellect. At the same time, he seemed to believe that their use was primarily the prerogative of poets and politicians. For philosophers and scientists, they were potentially too misleading. In limiting the use of metaphors to the ornamental, rather than concentrating on their communicative value, Aristotle essentially elevated metaphor from the prosaic to the esoteric. The unfortunate result was that attention to the topic came to be largely restricted to rhetoricians. Indeed, during the 19th century, the principal activity of rhetoricians became the interpretation of particular metaphors (and other tropes) in literary texts—an obsession that was largely responsible for the demise of rhetoric as a serious discipline.

In spite of limiting what he presumably considered to be the legitimate uses of metaphor, Aristotle's analysis of the underlying logic of metaphor has always dominated thinking on the topic. He believed metaphors to be implicit comparisons based on the principles of analogy. It can be argued that this view has had the undesirable effect of blurring the distinctions of metaphor, analogy, and similarity—more will be said of this later.

Around the turn of the century there appeared an English translation of Michel Bréal's *Essay de sémantique*. In this influential work, Bréal claimed that metaphor was a linguistic device, widespread in its use, and of great importance in linguistic change. Then, in 1936, metaphor was revitalized in the study of the language of literature by I. A. Richards. Richards introduced useful terminology for talking about metaphors (topic/tenor, vehicle, ground, and tension)—terminology that has come to be fairly standard.

In 1962 Max Black's book *Models and Metaphors* appeared. In it, Black rejected the Aristotelian 'comparison' view wherein metaphors are merely elliptical comparisons, and he questioned the generality of the 'substitution' view wherein metaphors are merely ornamental substitutes for literal language. Instead, elaborating on the views of Richards, he proposed an 'interaction' view. On this view, the *tenor* (or topic, or subject) of a metaphor is seen as interacting with the metaphorical *vehicle* to produce a kind of emergent meaning for the entire sentence —one that could not have resulted from the combination of the tenor with some other predicate, literal or metaphorical. Thus, in the metaphor 'man is a wolf', 'man' is viewed, as it were, through a 'wolf' filter. Our interpretation of both terms is altered.

By the mid-1970s, an active interest in the topic had spread to all sorts of disciplines, most relevant of which, in the present context, was cognitive psychology. Psychologists became interested in questions such as: does the comprehension of metaphors involve special processes not normally involved in the comprehension of literal language? Do metaphors play a role in the development of language? Why do people use metaphors? What is the interrelationship of metaphor, analogy, and similarity? Many of these questions have their counterparts in philosophy, but the empirical techniques that psychology brings to bear may throw more light on them.

The principal dispute over comprehension mechanisms is about whether or not metaphors are understood by first unsuccessfully attempting to impose a literal interpretation. According to one view, when people encounter metaphors they recognize that a literal interpretation is incompatible with the context and then proceed to reinterpret the metaphor figuratively. According to the other view, ordinarily people interpret the metaphorical meaning directly, without even entertaining a literal interpretation. Flatly stated in this way, each view has its problems. One problem with the reinterpretation account is that it does not specify the basis upon which a reinterpretation is made. Many linguistic forms require 'reinterpretation': sarcasm ('That was a clever thing to do,' said of an obviously foolish act), hyperbole ('There were millions of people at the party,' said to indicate that there were many—but obviously not millions), and indirect speech acts, such as indirect requests ('Do you know what time it is?', meant as a request to be told the hour of the day), are just some of the many examples. Reinterpretation theories need to be able to characterize the differences between these (and other) kinds of non-literal uses of language. They need both to specify the different rules that underlie the comprehension of different types, and to offer an account of how people are supposed to know in advance which rules to employ on a particular occasion: it hardly seems likely, for example, that the rules for reinterpreting sarcasm are applied, or even considered, in the ordinary interpretation of a metaphor.

The direct comprehension view finesses this last question. However, as stated, it suffers from underspecification. It amounts to little more than a statement to the effect that, when people encounter metaphors, they understand them; on its own, it has no answer to the question, how? A more general theory of language comprehension is needed to answer this question. The theory (or theoretical framework) that is most often appealed to is one based on the notion of *schemas (or scripts, or frames). The idea is that comprehension in general proceeds by finding a schema that 'fits' the input. Then, the argument goes, the difference between understanding literal and metaphorical language turns out to be simply one of quality of fit.

Data from experiments suggests that elements of both views are correct. Experiments measuring (for example) the time taken by people to indicate that they have understood a sentence (either metaphorical or literal) show that, with sufficient preceding context, subjects do not require the additional time to process metaphors that the reinterpretation theory predicts. On the other hand, when a metaphor is encountered with very little prior context, the predicted increase in *reaction time is found. In such cases, it seems, people have to 'work out' what the sentence means, whereas in other cases what they do seems more like confirming contextually generated expectations. Of course, 'working out the meaning' is something that is often required for literal uses of language too. Furthermore, there are many 'frozen' metaphors in the language, often idioms, that, once known, never require special processing. Thus, the evidence suggests that extra processing is required by language that is not well integrated into the context, be it literal or metaphorical, and that under appropriate circumstances metaphorical language is processed as quickly and easily as literal language.

Observant parents, as well as developmental psychologists, have often noticed that quite young children (2–3 years of age) appear to be very creative in their use of language. When the young child tries to express something for which he has not learned the conventional word, he often uses some other word that succeeds in realizing his communicative intentions, even though the choice may not be literally appropriate. This activity is described by developmental psychologists as 'semantic overextension' (see LANGUAGE: LEARNING WORD MEANINGS), but some have claimed that this behaviour in fact reflects the use of metaphor by young children, and that the use of metaphor is a fundamental ingredient in language development.

Attractive though this view might be, it seems to suffer from some rather serious drawbacks. First among these is the evidence that such young children are unable to understand metaphors. Estimates of the age at which children begin to understand metaphors properly vary considerably. Some investigators claim that it is not until early adolescence, while others claim that by the age of 7 or 8 many children can deal with metaphors. The variations in these estimates are the result of several factors, the principal ones being fluctuating and often rather atheoretical criteria for what is to count as a metaphor, and for what is to count as evidence of its comprehension. However, most investigators agree that 3-year-old children cannot understand metaphors. Since it is well established that children's language comprehension is far ahead of their language production, if 2- and 3-year-old children were producing metaphors it would be the only known example of behaviour contrary to the comprehension-before-production rule. A second problem is that the claim that such young children produce metaphors fails to recognize that an utterance could be metaphorical from an adult's perspective, but not from that of the child who produces it. In other words, the claim may be excessively 'adultocentric'.

Doubtless, part of the attractiveness of claiming that very young children produce metaphors is that an important function of metaphors is to permit the expression of ideas that might otherwise be (literally) inexpressible for a particular speaker in a particular language. In some cases the lack of words in the language has resulted in entire domains being mapped into other domains so that the language itself incorporates now unnoticed metaphorical means of description—this is one of the ways in which, as Bréal pointed out, metaphors are important in linguistic change. A familiar example of such a mapping is the use of temperature terms to describe personality characteristics —we talk of people in terms of their being warm, or cool, cold, or icy. When such metaphors are embedded in the language to fill systematic gaps in the lexicon, they often go unnoticed. But the same principle operates at the level of the individual speaker, except that, if the language does not supply conventional resources (be they literal or metaphorical), the speaker may have to create his own. In such cases he uses a novel metaphor.

The expression of the otherwise inexpressible is not the only communicative function that metaphors serve. They also achieve a certain communicative compactness, since all the applicable predicates belonging to the metaphorical vehicle are implied succinctly through the vehicle itself. Thus, even if what a metaphor expresses may have been more or less expressible without the metaphor, its use may be more economical and hence more effective than the long list of predicates that it entails.

The relationship between metaphors and similarity is a complex one. Without having to commit oneself to one of the various theories about how metaphors work, it is apparent that at some level, and in some way, metaphors capitalize on a similarity between the term used metaphorically (the vehicle) and the thing that the metaphor is a metaphor for. Thus, even though it may be incorrect to claim, as some have, that a metaphor is *merely* a statement of similarity, it is probably not incorrect to say that a metaphor is *largely* a statement of similarity. Clearly, if one says of jogging that it is a religion, the metaphor would not work if jogging and religion were not in some way similar. On the other hand, it is obvious that in many ways jogging is not in the least bit like a religion. It could be argued, in fact, that jogging is not really like a religion at all; if we want something that is really like a religion, a cult is. The interesting thing is that if one now considers the two similarity statements 'Jogging is like a religion' and 'A cult is like a religion', the latter, while appearing to be really true, has no metaphorical potential. This suggests that, if metaphors are based on similarity statements, only some similarity statements can fulfil the required role. The similarity statements that seem to fit the bill are those that themselves seem to be metaphorical. According to this view, that is why one can say 'Metaphorically speaking, jogging is like a religion', but not 'Metaphorically speaking, a cult is like a religion'. Now, if the only similarity statements that can form the basis of metaphors are metaphorical similarity statements, two important consequences follow. The first is that it is futile to attempt to *explain* metaphors by reducing them to similarity statements because the statements to which they get reduced still have the characteristic of being metaphorical. The second is that, as a research strategy, the examination of similarity statements may be the best way to uncover the difference between the literal and the metaphorical.

Psychological discussions about the nature of metaphor often seem to use the terms 'similarity' and 'analogy' as though they were interchangeable. It is possible, however, to be more precise about the relationship between the two by arguing that an analogy is a similarity between relations rather than between single-place predicates. On this view, an analogy is a particular kind of similarity statement and, from a psychological perspective, whether a particular comparison is or is not an analogy may depend on the way in which the entities being compared are conceptualized or represented at the time. A simple example will illustrate the point. Suppose we are told that cigarettes are like time bombs. If we entertain this proposition in terms of a simple similarity statement, we might say that both cigarettes and time bombs share the property of (potentially) causing death after a delay. In other words, considered in this way we would have something to the effect: 'Being a cigarette is like being a time bomb.' On the other hand, suppose one conceptualizes the statement in the following way: 'People smoking cigarettes are like people exposed to time bombs.' Now what we have is something roughly equivalent in meaning, except that it is stated as a similarity between two relations—it is an analogy. Again, from a psychological perspective, how the terms in a similarity statement will be represented is likely to depend on the context, it is not fixed by the linguistic structure of the statement itself. Thus, again, the point is not whether metaphors are built on similarity or on analogy, since both are forms of comparison. The point is that metaphors are built on comparisons which are themselves metaphorical, be they analogical or not.

AO

Black, M. (1962). 'Metaphor'. In Black, M. (ed.), *Models and Metaphors*.

Blasko, D. G. (1999). 'Only the tip of the iceberg: who understands what about metaphor?' *Journal of Pragmatics*, 31.

Glucksberg, S. (2003). 'The psycholinguistics of metaphor'. *Trends in Cognitive Sciences*, 7/2.

Lakoff, G., and Johnson, M. (1980). *Metaphors we Live by*.

Ortony, A. (ed.) (1979). *Metaphor and Thought*.

metaphysics. Metaphysics is generally taken to mean philosophical speculation beyond the current or even seemingly possible limits of science or technology to test, the development of systems intended to explain origins and purpose, and the place of man in the universe. The word 'metaphysics' has its origin simply from those books of *Aristotle which were placed in sequence after his *Physics*. The pejorative sense of 'obscure' and 'over-speculative' is recent, especially following attempts by A. J. Ayer and others to show that metaphysics is strictly nonsense.

It is a moot point how far science is, or can be, free of metaphysics. There may always be untested and even forever untestable theoretical assumptions, which are necessary for interpreting experiments.

Metaphysics is associated especially with idealist and rationalist philosophers, chief among whom is Immanuel *Kant. Kant argued, for example, most clearly in his

Prolegomena to Any Future Metaphysics (1783), that time and space are categories of mind, and that it is impossible to conceive the physical world without such *a priori categories. Empiricism, on the other hand, is often thought to be free of metaphysical assumptions—at any rate for operationalist philosophers, who hold that all knowledge is derived from observation, and especially from observed matches and mismatches against test procedures and measurements.

A very different current view, which is developed especially by the American philosophers Norwood Russell Hanson and Thomas Kuhn, is that there is no such thing as a neutral theory-free observation language which simply records 'the facts'; even the simplest observations and experiments must be made within the context of theoretical assumptions (see PARADIGM). Given that these assumptions cannot be objectively verified or tested operationally, they may be said to be metaphysical, which this leads to a more or less extreme relativism, which rejects the notion of 'brute facts' and 'objective' observational data.   RLG

Ayer, A. J. (1936). *Language, Truth and Logic.*
Hanson, N. R. (1972). *Patterns of Discovery: An Inquiry into the Conceptual Foundations of Science.*
Kuhn, T. S. (1970). *The Structure of Scientific Revolutions* (2nd edn.).

metempsychosis. When a living thing dies, its 'soul' or *psyche takes up a new residence in some other body, which it thereby vivifies: for the psyche, bodily death means emigration, bodily birth immigration. That is the ancient doctrine of 'metempsychosis' or the transmigration of the soul.

Among the Greeks, the followers of *Pythagoras were particularly associated with the doctrine—indeed it is one of the few beliefs that can confidently be ascribed to Pythagoras himself. (In *Twelfth Night*, 'Sir Topas' asks the imprisoned Malvolio: 'What is the opinion of Pythagoras concerning wild fowl?' And Malvolio rightly answers: 'That the soul of our grandam might haply inhabit a bird.') Empedocles, too, subscribed to the doctrine; one of his poems contained the following couplet:

For already have I once been a boy, and a girl,
and a bush, and a fish that jumps from the sea as it swims.

(Bushes are living things, and therefore have a psyche. The jumping fish is the dolphin.)

Note that the psyche is a principle of individuality for living things: since Empedocles' psyche once inhabited a fish, Empedocles himself once was a fish—metempsychosis is about the personal survival of bodily death. We are told that Pythagoras 'passed a dog that was being whipped; he took pity on it and said: "Stop! don't beat it—it is the psyche of a friend of mine; I recognize him by his voice."'

Different thinkers composed variations on the metempsychotic theme: for some, the process of transmigration went on for ever; some imagined a cycle of incarnations; some spoke of a hierarchy of lives; in some versions of the theory, incarnations are separated by periods of non-corporeal existence, during which divine judgement may take place. The doctrine was sometimes associated with a theology or with a quasi-religious way of life; and Empedocles based a moral theory upon it: if one and the same psyche may animate now a man, now a lion, now an eagle, then living creatures are all akin; and we should have moral scruples about maltreating our psychic kinsmen. Empedocles denounced all bloodshed and advocated a form of vegetarianism, for if you kill and eat a sheep, you may be killing and eating your own father. ('Sir Topas' counsels Malvolio to 'fear to kill a woodcock, lest thou dispossess the soul of thy grandam'.) Strictly speaking, if you eat a parsnip, you may be eating your father, but Empedocles did not have the strength of character to insist upon a wholly inanimate diet.

Metempsychosis may seem at best an irrational form of mysticism, at worst a risible piece of nonsense. To some Greeks, at least, it appeared to be an empirical theory; and its empirical basis lay in memory. Thus, according to Heraclides Ponticus, a pupil of *Plato's, Pythagoras

says about himself that he was once Aithalides, and was deemed a son of Hermes; and Hermes told him to choose whatever he wanted except immortality: so he asked that, both alive and dead, he should remember what happened. Thus in his life he remembered everything, and when he died he retained the same memory. Some time later, he passed into Euphorbus, and was wounded by Menelaus. . . . And when Euphorbus died, his psyche passed into Hermotimus. . . . And when Hermotimus died, he became Pyrrhus the Delian diver; and again, he remembered everything—how he had first been Aithalides, then Euphorbus, then Hermotimus, then Pyrrhus. And when Pyrrhus died, he became Pythagoras, and he remembered all the events I have mentioned.

Pythagoras claimed to have memories of his earlier lives, and those memories supported the theory of metempsychosis—or at least, they constituted evidence that Pythagoras himself was a migratory psyche. Sceptical Greeks dared to doubt Pythagoras' claim to remember being wounded under the walls of Troy, but Pythagoras was prepared to back up his claim:

They say that, while staying at Argos, he saw a shield from the spoils of Troy nailed up, and burst into tears. When the Argives asked him the reason for his emotion, he said that he himself had carried that shield in Troy when he was Euphorbus. They didn't believe him, and thought he was mad; but he said he could provide a true sign that this was the case: on the inside of the shield they would find written in archaic letters: EUPHORBUS'. Because of the extraordinary nature of his claim, they all urged him to take down the offering. And the inscription was found on it.

Thus transmigratory claims are supported by an appeal to memory, and memory claims are supported in their turn by practical demonstration. The stories about Pythagoras' abilities are doubtless apocryphal, but the moral they point is not: even in their most extravagant moments, the ancient Greek psychologists did not lose all touch with reason and empirical reality.   JBA

Michotte, Albert (1881–1965). Belgian experimental psychologist of high reputation. He is best known for his investigations of perceptual causality. By combining with remarkable ingenuity various types of real object movements (such as coloured rectangles moving on a screen and visible through a slit), he was able to demonstrate that, in certain spatial and temporal conditions, the subjects reported a causal action of one moving object on another, such as 'launching', 'entraining', and the like. These perceptual effects were described by Michotte with a wealth of detail and framed within an overall theory of dynamic relationships between objects. If we were to confine ourselves to the historical developments of Michotte's ideas, we should refer to this aspect of his work only at the end of our analysis; however, his extensive investigations of perceptual causality are too typical of his conception of experimental psychology to be mentioned solely as the last productive moment of his exceptionally creative career.

From 1905 to 1908, Michotte was active in experimental psychology under *Wundt and Külpe and tackled various experimental problems ranging from the study of tactile sensitivity to that of so-called superior functions, namely thought and will processes. There is no doubt that Külpe's *Denkpsychologie* (thought psychology) exerted a considerable influence on him, namely by introducing him to the descriptive techniques of subjective impressions, a major feature of the early German laboratories of experimental psychology. In addition to this, Michotte was exceptionally gifted mechanically. His great skill in designing and even building laboratory devices specially conceived in view of particular effects greatly helped him in realizing numerous original experiments.

In 1906 Michotte became a lecturer at the University of Louvain and was entrusted with the task of developing the laboratory of experimental psychology which had been founded in 1892 by Cardinal Mercier and whose first director was A. Thiéry, himself a direct collaborator of Wundt at Leipzig (1892–4). Through the work of Külpe on thought processes, Michotte became acquainted with act psychology (the school of Graz), especially with the work of Carl Stumpf and Ernst *Mach. Stumpf was the founder of a new kind of psychology, partly descriptive and partly experimental, which he called *experimental phenomenology*. According to his theory, experiments in psychology should be elaborated on the basis of a descrip-

tion of subjective phenomena as related to objects, *phenomenology proper being supplemented by a theory of contents (eidology) and a theory of relations between contents (logology).

In view of these influences, it may be said that Michotte's theoretical and experimental position was the joint result of the teachings of Wundt and of Stumpf. To this should be added the fact that, from 1912 on, Michotte became influenced by *Gestalt theory, which itself was greatly indebted to the theories of the school of Graz. However, to the end of his life he resented being called a Gestaltist, because he rejected generalized isomorphic theory, preferring to call himself an experimental phenomenologist. Summarizing the main trends of his research work, he wrote in 1962:

When *The Perception of Causality* was published, I used the language which was then used by numerous psychologists and by Gestalt psychologists in particular. It seems however that in spite of precautions which may have seemed sufficient at the time, certain expressions and certain wordings are liable to cause some misunderstandings concerning our theoretical standpoint in the study of perception. I therefore consider it necessary to state exactly here the point of view of psychological (or experimental) phenomenology as I conceive it. (Michotte 1962: 10)

This kind of experimental phenomenology rests on two methodological hypotheses. (i) The verbal reports of experimental subjects may be considered as the dependent variable of the stimulation systems. If the latter change in their spatio-temporal organization, changes will be observed in the categories of responses (for instance, causal against non-causal ones). (ii) The changes observed in the responses are not only quantitative (as expressed by frequencies), but also qualitative (as referring to contents). As a consequence, a theory of subjective impressions may be established on the basis of the descriptive properties of verbal responses. It is this second hypothesis alone that qualifies this type of analysis as belonging to experimental phenomenology, and that explains, among other things, why Michotte reflected unceasingly on the role of language in the analysis of perceptual phenomena. He may be best characterized by saying that he was an experimentalist who succeeded in studying with great accuracy the dynamic organization of the perceiver's phenomenal world. In this sense, he is more akin to Gestalt teachings than to phenomenological issues as expounded by *Husserl, i.e. within the framework of transcendental philosophy. The Graz school, which emerged from *Brentano's *intentional theory of *consciousness, split at the beginning of the 20th century into Gestaltism and transcendental phenomenology.

As a laboratory researcher deeply concerned with the analysis of subjective phenomena, Michotte is one of the few psychologists of the time who were able to bring Stumpf's experimental phenomenology to a high level of scientific accomplishment. Because of his early training in scholastic philosophy, Michotte did not develop the epistemological implications of his researches on perception, a task that would have required a comparative analysis of Stumpf's and Husserl's respective phenomenologies. In Michotte's conception, the phenomenological is always equated with the phenomenal. However, it was his achievement to demonstrate that an accurate experimental analysis of the perceptual world is a kind of phenomenological research which leads in some cases to more fruitful theoretical constructs than mere phenomenological descriptions in the classical sense. His outstanding contribution appears therefore as a strong argument in favour of the fairly recent idea that phenomenological psychology may include controlled scientific work.   GT

Michotte, A. (1946). *The Perception of Causality* (trans. T. R. and E. Miles, 1963).

—— (1959). 'Réflexions sur le rôle du langage dans l'analyse des organisations perceptives'. *Acta Psychologica*, 15.

—— (1962). *Causalité, permanence et réalité phénoménales*.

Thinès, G. (1968). *La problématique de la psychologie*, esp. ch. 2.

migraine. Migraine (from a French word derived from the Greek 'hemi' meaning half and 'kranion' meaning skull) is a transient disorder of brain function which is commonly associated with headache. The diagnosis is usually made when discrete headaches are accompanied by two or more of the following features: unilateral *pain, nausea or vomiting, focal cerebral symptoms (e.g. visual phenomena), and a family history of the condition. Attacks usually start to occur before the age of 30 and decrease in frequency with advancing age. Sixty per cent of sufferers are women.

The headache is often preceded by a variety of warnings. Days or hours before its onset there may be a change of mood (usually elation), or an alteration in behaviour, in wakefulness, appetite, bowel activity, or fluid balance. In 'common migraine' these are the only warnings but in 10–15 per cent of patients (those who suffer 'classic migraine') the headache is immediately preceded by disturbances of sensation. These disturbances are usually visual in character, taking the form of flashing coloured lights, zigzag lines, or distortions of visual perception, with or without areas of blindness that begin near the centre of gaze or at the periphery, and then move, usually expanding in size. Less commonly sensations of tingling or numbness occur, usually on one side of the body, particularly in the arm, and even less frequently there can be disturbances of speech and language. In rare forms of migraine other focal neurological deficits may precede the headache: for example, when vertigo, slurred speech, and unsteadiness of gait suggest brain stem dysfunction ('vertebrobasilar migraine'), when there is dysfunction of the nerves that control eye movements ('ophthalmoplegic

migraine'), or when there is a unilateral weakness of the limbs (familial 'hemiplegic migraine').

The disturbances, sensory or otherwise, usually last for 20–30 minutes and are followed by a headache which, although often unilateral, may involve both sides of the head, and which is often severe and pulsating in character. When both the sensory disturbances and the pain are unilateral they can involve the same or opposite sides of the body. The pain is often accompanied by nausea (occasionally leading to vomiting) and by an aversion to light and noise. Recovery is almost invariably complete within hours, but can take days. Very rarely an acute attack may result in a permanent neurological disturbance, for example a defect of vision.

Attacks can be precipitated in a number of ways. Perhaps the most common cause is *stress of a non-specific kind, as in the case of loss of sleep or overwork, and in some people attacks tend to occur in the period of relaxation that immediately follows the stress. There are many visual triggers, such as glare, flashing lights, and striped patterns. Attacks may also occur in relation to the menstrual cycle and sexual activity. In about 20 per cent of sufferers certain foods, especially chocolate, cheese, and citrus fruit, can precipitate attacks. The agents responsible may include biogenic amines and, when attacks are precipitated by red wine, complex phenols.

The origin and nature of the brain disorder are not known with any certainty. Changes in cerebral blood flow, alterations in *neurotransmitter levels, and electrophysiological disturbances found before, during, and after attacks have led to a variety of hypotheses. The fact that attacks are often precipitated by a strong sensory input suggests that a neurological disturbance leads to the development of the attack (and the role of non-specific stress would be consistent with such a viewpoint). The onset and progression of visual disturbances in classical migraine suggest the propagation of a wave through the visual cortex of the brain, at a velocity of 3 mm/min with abnormal excitation at the front of the wave, followed by a depression of activity. It is not clear whether this neurological dysfunction is due to a progressive loss of cortical blood supply or to a disturbance of the neurochemical composition of the environment that surrounds nerve cells (as in the spreading depression of Leao). These two alternatives are not mutually exclusive, but any possible relationship between them is unclear. Specific changes in neurotransmitters have been found during migraine attacks, particularly with regard to serotonin (5-hydroxytryptamine), a vasoactive monoamine. Although these changes relate mainly to reduced levels in circulating plasma, it has been suggested that there is also depletion within the brain, which is of interest in view of the role of serotonin-producing neurons in the perception of pain. Nevertheless it goes without saying that many other neurotransmitters (known and as yet unknown) are undoubtedly involved.

The mechanisms of pain in migraine may involve dilatation of the meningeal and scalp blood vessels, which are known to be pain sensitive. This dilatation is associated with a sterile inflammatory response in and around the vessels and with the release of a number of pain-producing substances such as the neurokines. There are persistent abnormalities in the pulse of scalp arteries in between attacks of unilateral pain on the affected side.

Treatment of migraine is twofold: medication for relief of the acute attack and, for those individuals who suffer frequent attacks, daily treatment to prevent their occurrence. The pain of an acute attack can be reduced by common analgesics or paracetamol, and the nausea by metoclopramide. In addition, it has been common in the past to use the ergot alkaloid derivatives (e.g. ergotamine) which cause constriction of blood vessels and may alleviate pain for this reason. Frequent attacks can be prevented with a variety of drugs, some of which antagonize serotonin (among other neurotransmitters). These drugs include methysergide, pizotifen, amitriptyline, and propranolol. Relaxation therapy and biofeedback may have a role in treatment and claims have been made that the herb feverfew may help prevent attacks.   CK/AJW

Olesen, J. (1985). 'Migraine and regional cerebral blood flow'. *Trends in Neurosciences*, 8.

Pearce, J. M. S. (1984). 'Migraine: a cerebral disorder'. *Lancet*, 2.

Peatfield, R. (1986). *Headache*.

Sacks, O. W. (1999). *Migraine*.

military incompetence. An apparently inescapable feature of human progress is the toll in lives and money that occurs through our imperfect management of the institutions and technologies which we develop. The histories of railways, flying, bridge building, communications, and political institutions, to name but a few of man's inventions, are replete with examples of costly disasters and harrowing chapters of human misery—part of the price for growing complexity. If an increasing ability to wage war— to kill more people at a greater distance more quickly— can be considered as a manifestation of human progress, then we have here what is probably the best and certainly the most expensive illustration of this principle. Judging from the recent spate of books that have been devoted to martial mishaps, the military case is also probably the most interesting, for three reasons.

First, despite the fact that the professionalizing of human intra-specific aggression has a longer history than most other human enterprises, the record of incompetence in this sphere is far the worst. As T. E. Lawrence said in criticism of British military endeavour: 'With 2,000 years of examples behind us we have no excuse when fighting for not fighting well.' Secondly, an explanation of the psychological causes of faulty generalship is usually in terms of a single factor—stupidity. (In the writer's opinion this so-called 'bloody fool' theory of military incompetence reflects no more than a natural preference for simple explanations of what are in fact very complex phenomena. If the phenomena are unpleasant and the simple explanation abusive then so much the better.) Thirdly, a feature of military incompetence which, incidentally, belies the 'bloody fool' theory is the recurrent and relatively unchanging pattern of military ineptitude.

If incompetent generalship resulted from stupidity (i.e. low intelligence) then we might expect to find the history of war revealing a random miscellany of errors. This is not the case. Indeed, it is just because military incompetence constitutes a syndrome that it is necessary to seek an alternative theory of underlying causation.

As a first attempt towards providing a viable theory, a study was made of military disasters occurring between the 'imbecilic' Walcheren expedition of 1809 and the Vietnam War. They included the retreat from Kabul in the first Afghan War; episodes in the Crimean War; the Franco-Prussian War, the Indian Mutiny and Boer Wars; the siege of Kut, Verdun, and the third battle of Ypres in the First World War; the events leading up to Dunkirk, the attack on Pearl Harbor, the losses of Tobruk and Singapore, and the abortive attempt to capture the road bridge at Arnhem in the Second World War; the siege of Dien Bien Phu and the Tet offensive in the Indo-China and Vietnam wars; and the Bay of Pigs fiasco. While all these episodes share the distinction of being classed as costly military disasters, the question arises as to whether they reveal a common pattern of errors. The following summary of frequently recurring factors suggests that they do:

1. A serious wastage of human resources and failure to observe one of the first principles of war—economy of force. This failure derives in part from an inability to make war swiftly. It also derives from certain attitudes of mind which we shall consider presently.
2. A fundamental conservatism and clinging to outworn tradition, with an inability to profit from past experience (owing in part to a refusal to admit past mistakes). This also involves a failure to use, or a tendency to misuse, available technology.
3. A tendency to reject or ignore information which is unpalatable or which conflicts with preconceptions.
4. A tendency to underestimate the enemy and overestimate the capabilities of one's own side.
5. Indecisiveness and a tendency to abdicate from the role of decision maker.
6. An obstinate persistence in a given task despite strong contrary evidence.
7. A failure to exploit a situation gained and a tendency to 'pull punches' rather than push home an attack.

8. A failure to make adequate reconnaissance.
9. A predilection for frontal assaults, often against the enemy's strongest point.
10. A belief in brute force rather than the clever ruse.
11. A failure to make use of surprise or deception.
12. An undue readiness to find scapegoats for military setbacks.
13. A suppression or distortion of news from the front, usually rationalized as necessary for morale or security.
14. A belief in mystical forces—fate, bad luck, etc.

Contemplation of these 'symptoms' suggests that, far from being a product of ordinary stupidity, military incompetence stems from complex interactions of three things—the hazards of professionalizing violence, the nature of military organizations, and the personalities of some of those who are attracted to, and then for a time prosper in, a military career.

The theory which attempts to outline and explain these interactions starts from the premiss that in professionalizing violence man set himself the task of legitimizing and then controlling patterns of behaviour which are normally taboo in a civilized society. To achieve this difficult contortion there gradually evolved that system of rules, conventions, incentives, and punishments which constitutes militarism, a subculture of controls and constraints which may be likened to those precautionary measures adopted by any imaginative explosives expert to ensure that his particular stock-in-trade goes off only when and where he wants it to. Now, since many of the components of militarism bear more than a superficial resemblance to those personal defences which some people erect against their own anxieties and aggressive impulses, it is hardly surprising that a minority of men are attracted to joining organizations which not only provide legitimate outlets for controlled aggression but also have perfected an elaborate set of rules for maintaining order and discipline within their ranks. On the one hand, as I. L. Janis (1963) remarks: 'The military group provides powerful incentives for releasing forbidden impulses, inducing the soldier to try out formerly inhibited acts which he originally regarded as morally repugnant.' On the other hand, in so doing, militarism provides a therapeutic gain for some of its members. Thus, according to Robert Holt (1971):

It was a common clinical observation during the war that military service was an unusually good environment for men who lacked inner controls. . . . The combination of absolute security, a strong institutional parent-substitute on which one could lean unobtrusively, and socially approved outlets for aggression provided a form of social control that allowed impulses to be expressed in acceptable ways.

Some confirmation of this relationship between personality and liking of a military career has been forth-coming from those recent researches that have found a relationship between authoritarianism and liking of a military ideology. When it is considered that authoritarianism, as measured by the Californian F (Fascist) scale, correlates positively with rigidity and the possession of obsessive traits, a personality type emerges which is remarkably similar to traditional descriptions of the military mind. (The F scale measures anti-Semitism, ethnocentrism, political and economic conservatism, and implicit anti-democratic trends or potentiality for Fascism.) In its most extreme form such a person would be conventional, conforming, rigid, and possessed of a closed mind. He would also be one who is orderly, obstinate, and unimaginative. Finally he would be the sort of individual who believes in force and toughness, is lacking in compassion, and is prone to stereotype out groups (i.e. the enemy) as less gifted than himself. Obviously there are, among this miscellany of characteristics, traits which are no handicap to those seeking advancement in their military career. Such a person would do well because in many ways he fitted in so well.

Unfortunately, however, those very traits that would facilitate his promotion up the military hierarchy are not conducive to competence at the highest levels. Being inflexible and unimaginative, predisposed to 'bull', excessively obedient and having a mind closed to unpalatable information, conservative and conformist, are not the characteristics for handling, let alone fathoming, the great uncertainties of war. Needless to say, attempts at applying this theory of incompetence to actual military disasters, and particular military commanders, encountered the difficulty that we have no personality measures of the characters concerned. However, a comparison between the best and the worst of military commanders, in terms of their military performance and what is known of their personalities and childhood, strongly suggests that failure of leadership and decision making are due less to stupidity than to the fact that militarism attracts a proportion of people whose personalities are ill suited to warring behaviour.

See also MILITARY MIND. NFD

Dixon, N. F. (1976). *On the Psychology of Military Incompetence*.
Holt, R. R. (1971). *Assessing Personality*.
Janis, I. L. (1963). 'Group identification under conditions of external danger'. *British Journal of Medical Psychology*, 36.

military mind. Consideration of whether human beings as a species have an innate tendency towards aggression among themselves has generated a massive literature and negligible evidence: the question remains completely open. Whatever the answer, it is certain that few people lack the qualities required to make at least an adequate member of an armed force: during the wars of the last hundred years, tens of millions of men, and many millions of women, have been taken into the forces of many nations; and very few—for good reasons or bad—have proved wholly unsuitable. Thus virtually any mind is more or less 'military' on the lower level, and consequently, when discussing the 'military mind' *per se*, it is usual to refer to the qualities needed for, or associated with, high command.

Any serious examination of the commanders of history (see, for example, Windrow and Mason 1975) reveals at once that the range of character and personality, even among the successful, is very wide, and this is the case even if we look only at those traits loosely called 'aggression' in individuals: the humane Wellington, the callous Bonaparte, and the sadistic Chingis (Genghis Khan) immediately spring to mind. Can either history or modern experimental studies cast any light, then, on the main qualities of the military mind?

Every successful commander—every great commander, even more—has had to take decisions of grave consequence upon partial and more or less uncertain information, in circumstances of great psychological pressure and often of great physical danger. Small wonder, then, that Wavell (1941) considered 'the first essential of a general [to be the possession of] the quality of robustness, the ability to withstand the shocks of war . . . a high margin over the normal breaking strain'. High intelligence, professional competence, and imagination are naturally desirable, but those who sneer at the failure of commanders to grasp *at the time* solutions which seem simple and obvious in the quiet of a study (see, for example, Dixon 1976), should ever remind themselves of the circumstances in which the problems were faced. Very often, what was wanting when they failed was a sufficiently 'high margin over the normal breaking strain'.

In modern times all major armed forces have attempted to set up rational selection and training procedures for potential commanders, but difficulties stem from the fact that much has to depend on theory. Whereas the young doctor or engineer can practise under guidance on real patients or bridges, the young officer cannot train in real battle. The solutions adopted differ in detail from one nation to another.

Validation presents considerable problems (Reeve 1972), but that used by the British army appears to be at least as successful as any. Psychological tests are used first in the process of elimination: for example, with the prospect of combat there is good theoretical reason for rejecting candidates who appear introverted (Corcoran 1965). Then there is an ingenious technique invented by Major R. Bion and known as the 'Leaderless Group Test' (Bidwell 1973: esp. ch. 8). Candidates are randomly assigned to groups of about ten, and a fairly difficult practical task, whose solution is not obvious and which requires cooperation within the group, is set ostensibly as a test for the group as a whole. No instructions are given, and no leader appointed: the testing officers simply stand and watch. It is set in as reasonably a stressful a situation as can readily be set up, and no importance at all is attached to whether or not the group actually succeeds: the real object is to observe how the several members respond to the situation—who can cooperate, who can induce cooperation, who 'puts people's backs up', and who simply follows along. Such tests select those who become junior officers.

At a later stage, after some years of experience with their units, officers are given training for higher command at staff college or equivalent institution. The techniques now generally known as 'management gaming' were invented for this purpose and are intensively used. Trainees are placed in groups of eight to ten, known as 'syndicates'. Sometimes these are 'leaderless groups', as described above, and sometimes roles (such as commander-in-chief, divisional commanders, and so on) are allotted to the members. The syndicates tackle a succession of exercises based on carefully prepared (and often very entertaining) 'scenarios' produced by the directing staff. In British staff training there are no predetermined 'best solutions' to these exercises—as there are, for example, in both the American and Russian equivalents; instead, the general virtues of simplicity and flexibility are sought. Solutions produced by syndicates or by individuals within them are subject to thorough and uninhibited criticism by both teaching staff and peers.

As with the selection of junior officers, this training for the higher ranks involves a considerable degree of pressure and stress. Not only are the problems faced difficult in themselves, and to be solved in limited time, but those taking part know that their careers are at stake, and that every word they write or utter is likely to be 'shot down' by rivals or tutors. It is thus a selective as well as an instructive mechanism, and, as far as can be discerned, a highly successful one. The students emerge not only with the vast amount of procedural knowledge that any modern officer needs but also with practical experience of solving difficult command problems under harassing conditions. They gain experience, too, in leading teams of equals without being able to rely upon the formal compulsions of military discipline.

Thus, by the time an officer is appointed to senior command he has passed through, first, a rigorous and well-validated selection procedure, and, second, a rigorous and highly competitive 'higher education' in his profession. There is thereby as much certainty that he possesses the necessary abilities and skills and as much evidence that he possesses the 'quality of robustness' under stress as can reasonably be obtained. Since the 'mind' of any profession requires a combination of general ability, special skills, and particular aptitudes, it seems difficult, in the present 'state of the art' to go much further than this.

See also MILITARY INCOMPETENCE.   MH

Bidwell, R. G. S. (1973). *Modern Warfare*.

Corcoran, D. W. J. (1965). 'Personality and the inverted-U relation'. *British Journal of Psychology*, 56.

Dixon, N. (1976). *On The Psychology of Military Incompetence*.

Reeve, E. G. (1972). *Validation of Selection Boards*.

Wavell, A. (1941). *Generals and Generalship*.

Windrow, M., and Mason, F. K. (1975). *A Concise Dictionary of Military Biography*.

Mill, James (1773–1836). British writer and political economist, born near Forfar, Scotland, and educated for the ministry at Edinburgh. In 1802 he moved to London to start a literary career, editing and writing for various periodicals. He also worked for the East India Company after writing a *History of British India* (1818). Having written *Elements of Political Economy* (1821–2) he produced *Analysis of the Phenomena of the Human Mind* in 1829 and *A Fragment on Mackintosh* (1835).

He was closely associated with Jeremy *Bentham and was one of the founders of utilitarianism. His remarkable personality is recorded with rare insight by his son, John Stuart *Mill, in his *Autobiography* (1873).   RLG

Mill, John Stuart (1806–73). British philosopher and political economist, born in London, the son of James *Mill. He was brought up by his father to be a genius— which indeed he became—being taught Greek at the age of 3, Latin and arithmetic at 8, logic at 12, and political economy at 13. His only recreation was a daily walk with his father, and during this he was given oral examinations. Perhaps not surprisingly he suffered a severe mental crisis, but he recovered to become one of the outstanding intellects of his generation. In his *System of Logic* (1843) he provided, among other things, a systematic account of inductive reasoning (see INDUCTION, and, for Mill's predecessors on this matter, ARISTOTLE and BACON, FRANCIS).

Mill also wrote extensively on political economy, and morals and ethics, developing his father's and Jeremy *Bentham's utilitarianism. His essays on *Representative Government* and *Utilitarianism* both appeared in 1861. He disagrees with the earlier authors by admitting qualitative differences between pleasures, and so raising doubts as to whether pleasure can be equated with right action. In his *On Liberty* (1859) he provides a famous principle (the 'harm' principle) which severely limits the extent to which individuals may be coerced by government. He was an early supporter of liberal campaigns for women's suffrage, and his *The Subjection of Women* (1869) provoked antagonism at the time, but heralded justice and equality.

RLG

mind and body. Until quite recently most philosophers have held a *dualistic view of the relation between mind and body. This dualism has, however, taken several different forms. There have been those, like *Descartes, who ascribe mental attributes to spiritual substances which are supposed to be logically independent of anything physical but to inhabit particular bodies in a way that it has not proved easy to define. Others, like *Hobbes, have admitted only a duality of properties, ascribing both mental and physical attributes to human bodies. Others again have recognized an ultimate category of persons, differentiating them from physical objects just on the ground that they possess mental as well as physical attributes. Exactly what constitutes a mental attribute is itself not easy to define, but it can perhaps be sufficiently illustrated by examples, which may be chosen so as to cover the different varieties of sensation, perception, imagination, feeling, and thought.

For the most part, those who have subscribed to one or other form of dualism have also held that there is causal interaction between mental and physical events. The main opposition to this view has come from those who conceive of the physical world as a closed system, in the sense that every physical event must be explicable in purely physical terms, if it is explicable at all. If they also accept the existence of irreducibly mental occurrences, they regard them as accompanying and perhaps being causally dependent on physical events, but as not themselves making any causal intrusion into the physical world.

This refusal to admit psychophysical interaction does not seem justified, especially if one takes a *Humean view of causation as consisting basically in nothing more than regular concomitance. Even if there were a physical explanation for every physical event, this would not preclude there being alternative forms of explanation which relied at least in part on mental factors. It is, however, unlikely that such psychophysical correlations would be nearly so stringent as the laws of physics, and the same would apply to any generalizations that were couched in purely mental terms.

The difference in the type of causal laws to which they are subject is one of the ways in which mental and physical events are distinguished in the theory of neutral monism, which was advanced by William *James and subsequently by Bertrand *Russell. According to this theory, the elements of our experience consisted of actual or possible sense data out of which the physical world was supposed to be constructible. These elements were also regarded as entering into the constitution of minds so that one and the same sense datum might as a member of one group be a constituent of some physical object and as a member of another group be a constituent of a mind in whose biography a perception of the object occurred. Apart from the fact that there were also images and feelings, which entered only into the constitution of minds, the difference between mind and matter was represented not as a difference of substance, or content, but as a difference in the arrangement of common elements, involving their participation in different forms of causality. This was in many ways an attractive theory, but it met with serious difficulties. Though there may be a sense in which physical objects can be generated out of the immediate data of perception, an outright reduction of one to the other seems not to be feasible. Nor did the exponents of the theory succeed in giving a satisfactory account of *personal identity or of the special relation in which the elements that make up a person's mind stand to the particular physical object that is that person's body.

Similar difficulties beset the attempt made by *Berkeley to eliminate matter in favour of mind, by representing physical objects as collections of sensible qualities, which he termed ideas. In Berkeley's case, the want of a criterion of personal identity is especially flagrant, since he followed Descartes in treating minds as spiritual substances. It is, indeed, one of the principal objections to this view of the mind that it is incapable of furnishing any such criterion.

In recent times, monistic theories have mainly taken the other direction. They have gone beyond the older forms of materialism in that they not only ascribe mental attributes to certain physical objects, but also treat these attributes themselves as physical. The strongest theory of this type is that in which it is maintained that propositions which would ordinarily be construed as referring to mental states or processes are logically equivalent to propositions which refer only to people's overt behaviour. This theory may be allied to a verificational theory of meaning. Since the only way in which we can test the truth of the propositions in which we attribute experiences to others is through observation of the ways in which these other persons behave, it is deduced that this is all that such propositions can legitimately be taken to refer to. Then, since it can be shown that one cannot consistently combine a behaviouristic treatment of propositions about the experiences of others with a mentalistic treatment of propositions about one's own experiences, the conclusion is drawn that all references to one's own experiences are to be construed behaviouristically, even when they are made by oneself.

This argument can, however, be turned on its head. One can start with the premiss that the knowledge which one has of one's own experiences cannot be fully set out in any series of propositions which refer only to one's overt behaviour and then use the fact that the analysis of propositions about a person's experiences must be the same, whoever asserts them, as a ground for rejecting a purely behavioural account of propositions that refer to the experiences of others. And, indeed, unless one is prepared to feign anaesthesia, it would seem undeniable that this premiss is true. The advocates of logical behaviourism were indeed able to show that references to behaviour are often comprised in the use of what are classified as mentalistic terms. They were even justified in claiming that intelligent thought and action do not necessarily require the occurrence of inner processes. Nevertheless we do very often have thoughts that we keep to ourselves, and the existence of such thoughts cannot be logically equated with any disposition to report them. Nor, on the face of it, is there any logical equivalence between a person's having such and such sensations or perceptions and his dispositions to engage in any form of overt action.

In recent years logical behaviourism has given way to the less radical theory in which mental occurrences are held to be not logically but only factually identical with states of the central nervous system. On this view, for a person to have such and such an experience *is* for his brain to be in such and such a state, in the way in which lightning *is* an electrical discharge or temperature *is* the mean kinetic energy of molecules. As in those other cases, the suggested identity is supposed to be established not through the analysis of concepts but on the basis of empirical research. It rests on the assumption that there is a perfect correlation between a person's experiences and events which take place in his brain. In fact, this assumption goes further than the evidence yet warrants. There is, indeed, very strong evidence of a general dependence of mental occurrences on the functioning of the brain, but it has still to be shown that the correspondence is so exact that from observation of a person's brain one could arrive at a knowledge of his experiences in every detail.

Even if we make this assumption, it is not clear that it justifies the postulation of identity. If events which appear from their descriptions to belong to different categories are capable of being empirically correlated, the implication is rather that they are distinct. It is only on the basis of some theory that we can proceed to identify them. In this case the theory seems to be linguistic. It is thought that a general acceptance of the hypothesis that mental events are causally dependent upon events in the brain will lead to the denial of their separate existence. It has even been suggested that the use of psychological terms will be given up altogether.

This does not seem probable. Even if we were aware of what was going on in people's central nervous systems, it is unlikely that we should cease to find a use for explaining their behaviour in terms of their conscious thoughts and feelings. Nor is it likely, in a case in which an inference drawn from one's physical condition conflicted with one's awareness of one's own experience, that one should not continue to treat this awareness as the better authority.

If we have to adhere to dualism, the most defensible form of it would seem to be that in which we admit only a duality of properties. Unhappily, the problem of showing how these predicates combine to characterize one and the same subject has not yet been adequately solved.

See also MIND–BODY PROBLEM: PHILOSOPHICAL THEORIES.

AJA

mind–body problem: philosophical theories. Classifications of theories are bad masters, but may be useful servants. In the following classification of the main theories of the mind–body relationship upheld by philosophers, it is to be understood that the positions sketched are 'ideal types' to which actually held positions may approximate in different degrees.

If we think of mind and body as two opponents in a tug-of-war, then we can distinguish among theories that try to drag body, and matter generally, over into the camp of mind; those that try to drag mind over into the camp of body; and those theories where an equal balance is maintained. This yields a division into mentalist, materialist (physicalist), and dualist theories.

It is convenient to begin by considering *dualism. The major position here is *Cartesian dualism*, named after *Descartes, the central figure in post-medieval philosophical discussion of the mind–body problem. For a Cartesian dualist the mind and body are both substances; but while the body is an extended, and so a material, substance, the mind is an unextended, or spiritual, substance, subject to completely different principles of operation from the body. It was this doctrine that Gilbert *Ryle caricatured as the myth of the ghost in the machine. It is in fact a serious and important theory.

Dualist theories are also to be found in a more sceptical form, which may be called *bundle dualism*. The word 'bundle' springs from David *Hume's insistence that, when he turned his mental gaze upon his own mind, he could discern no unitary substance but simply a 'bundle of perceptions', a succession or stream of individual mental items or happenings. Hume thought of these items as non-physical. A bundle dualist is one who dissolves the mind in this general way, while leaving the body and other material things intact.

Besides dividing dualism into Cartesian and bundle theories, it may also be divided according to a different principle. *Interactionist* theories hold, what common sense asserts, that the body can act upon the mind and the mind can act upon the body. For *parallelist* theories, however, mind and body are incapable of acting upon each other. Their processes run parallel, like two synchronized clocks, but neither influences the other. There is an intermediate view according to which, although the body (in particular, the brain) acts upon and controls the mind, the mind is completely impotent to affect the body. This intermediate view, especially when combined with a bundle theory of mind, is the doctrine of *epiphenomenalism*. It allows the neurophysiologist, in particular, to recognize the independent reality of the mental, yet acknowledge the controlling role of the brain in our mental life and give a completely physicalist account of the brain and the factors which act upon it.

Mentalist theories arise naturally out of dualist theories, particularly where the dualist position is combined with Descartes' own view that the mind is more immediately and certainly known than anything material. If this view is taken, as it was by many of the greatest philosophers who succeeded Descartes, it is natural to begin by becoming sceptical of the existence of material things. The problem that this raises was then usually solved by readmitting the material world in a dematerialized or mentalized form. *Berkeley, for instance, solved the sceptical problem by reducing material things to our sensations 'of' them. Berkeley thus reaches a mentalism where the mind is conceived of as a spiritual substance, but bodies are reduced to sensations of these minds.

It is possible to combine Berkeley's reduction of matter to sensations with a bundle account of the mind. In this way is reached the doctrine of *neutral monism*, according to which mind and matter are simply different ways of organizing and marking off overlapping bundles of the same constituents. This view is to be found in Ernst *Mach and William *James, and was adopted at one stage by Bertrand *Russell. The 'neutral' constituents of mind and body are, however, only dubiously neutral, and the theory is best classified as a form of mentalism.

Just as Cartesian dualism may move towards mentalism, so it may also move towards materialism. Surprisingly, Descartes' own particular form of the theory lends itself to this development also. Descartes was one of the pioneers in arguing for an anti-Aristotelian view of the material world generally and the body in particular. First, this involved the rejection of all teleological principles of explanation in the non-mental sphere. Second, it involved taking the then revolutionary, now scientifically orthodox, view that organic nature involves no principles of operation that are not already to be found operative in non-organic nature. Human and animal bodies are simply machines (today we might say physicochemical mechanisms) working according to physical principles.

A view of this sort naturally leads on to the suggestion that it may be possible to give an account of the mind also along the same principles. In this way, a completely materialist account of nature is reached, and so a materialist account of the mind.

The word 'materialism' sometimes misleads. The materialist is not committed to a Newtonian 'billiard-ball' account of matter. Keith Campbell has spoken of the 'relativity of materialism'—its relativity to the physics of the day. Materialism is best interpreted as the doctrine that the fundamental laws and principles of nature are exhausted by the laws and principles of physics, however 'unmaterialistic' the latter laws and principles may be. Instead of speaking of 'materialism' some writers use the term 'physicalism'.

Materialist accounts of the mind may be subdivided into *peripheralist* and *centralist* views. A more familiar name for the peripheralist view is *behaviourism*: the view that possession of a mind is constituted by nothing more than the engaging in of especially sophisticated types of overt behaviour, or being disposed to engage in such behaviour in suitable circumstances. Behaviourism as a philosophical doctrine must be distinguished from the mere methodological behaviourism of many psychologists who do not wish to base scientific findings upon introspective reports of processes that are not publicly observable.

Very much more fashionable at the present time among philosophers inclined to materialism is the centralist view, which identifies mental processes with purely physical processes in the central nervous system. This view is sometimes called *central-state materialism* or, even more frequently, the *identity* view. Unlike behaviourism, it allows the existence of 'inner' mental processes which interact causally with the rest of the body.

It remains to call attention to one important variety of theory intermediate between orthodox dualism and orthodox materialism. It is a 'one-substance' view, denying that minds are things or collections of things set over against the material substance which is the brain. But it does involve a dualism of properties, because brain processes, besides their physical properties, are conceived of as having further non-physical properties which are supposed to make the brain processes into *mental* processes. Such views may be called *attribute* or *dual-attribute* theories of the mind–body relationship. A theory of this sort could be said to be a variety of identity view, since it also holds that mental processes are identical with certain brain processes.

According to the doctrine of *panpsychism*, not simply brain processes but all physical things have a mental side, aspect, or properties, even if in a primitive and undeveloped form.

Although the dual-attribute view is important, it inherits the considerable difficulty and confusion which surrounds the philosophical theory of properties. There are many difficulties in giving a satisfactory account of what it is for a thing to have a property, and these difficulties transmit themselves to this sort of theory of the mind–body relationship. **DMA**

Armstrong, D. M. (1968). *A Materialist Theory of the Mind*, ch. 1.
Broad, C. D. (1925). *The Mind and its Place in Nature*, chs. 1–3.
Campbell, K. K. (1970). *Body and Mind*.

mind in science fiction. Science fiction (sf) is a literary genre which eludes precise definition. It is often classed with fantasy, though many sf readers reject this. Although usually set in some future date, it is not coextensive with the story of the future: most of the 'future war' stories which proliferated in the early years of the 20th century had no sf element. I will here adopt a fairly strict definition: sf is the branch of fiction which deals with the effects of supposed future advances in science or technology and which pays at least outward respect to currently accepted science (cf. Amis 1961).

Within sf, we find speculations on 'mental' questions—the word is used with no Cartesian commitment—in three main areas. These are future developments in human minds, the possible characteristics of alien minds, and those of artificial minds. Although no man can claim to have read more than a fraction of the field (and the present writer certainly makes no such claim) a conclusion hard to avoid is that it is much easier to imagine very different bodies than convincingly different minds.

In Wells's deeply pessimistic 8028th century (Wells 1895), the human race has bifurcated into two distinct species: a feeble surface-dwelling type which is maintained as cattle by an owl-eyed, white-skinned race of subterranean machine minders. The minds of the former are imbecilic; those of the latter are just about able to maintain and repair the world's crumbling infrastructure.

Very different are the minds foreseen in Bernal's almost forgotten masterpiece *The World, the Flesh, and the Devil* (1929). Perhaps not strictly sf, this speculation has been so shamelessly quarried by sf writers (Stapledon and Heinlein, to name but two) that it deserves consideration here. He proposes that eventually human brains will be maintained, without our present bodies, in strong containers. Although without our effectors and senses, they will manage even better by having the appropriate nerve endings linked to the world via a wide range of sensors and apparatus. Further, they will be linked to one another so that 'the multiple individual would be . . . immortal . . . the individual brain will feel itself part of the whole'. He concedes that it is 'difficult to imagine this state of affairs effectively. It would be a state of ecstasy in the literal sense . . .'.

Between these extreme visions, most writers appear strangely pedestrian. Future humans are depicted as very like us—perhaps a bit brighter, but entirely recognizable. Such are the people of Clarke's future City of Diaspar (1956), although it is set hundreds of millions of years hence. Occasionally writers have speculated upon the qualities of minds connected to computers, usually seeing them as enhanced in some useful way. Bujold's chief of security, for example, has an implant which gives him an infallible eidetic memory. Less inhibited writers have allowed human personalities to be 'downloaded' onto computers in a way that achieves a kind of surrogate immortality—an idea which is mere hand waving as yet.

The depiction of alien minds is often disappointingly human-like. It may be argued that evolution within roughly comparable environments, subject to universal physical laws, must produce broadly convergent results. Nevertheless, the majority of 'aliens' in sf are really humans in fancy dress. 'Adzell the Wodenite' may be a 6-metre (20-foot) crocodilian centauroid who is almost bulletproof, but 'inside' he is that stock figure, the gentle giant.

Sometimes writers take a known human characteristic and endow aliens with it in an exaggerated form. Niven's 'Puppeteers' carry caution to the point where abject cowardice is regarded as sanity: no human has ever met a sane member of the species because no sane one would ever travel in space! The title of their head of state is translated as 'Hindmost'. The members of one of Forward's alien species, by contrast, have only two serious interests in life: pure mathematics and water sports.

Artificial brains have decreased in size since they first appeared during the late 1940s. (I do not count Čapek's original robots, which were allegorical rather than sf.) Whilst early specimens would occupy a city block, they are now portable or self-propelled. Many of their characteristics seem to have remained constant, however. They tend to take statements very literally and to display little initiative or originality. They command vast knowledge but want common sense. They work to rules. Although many use the first person, this is not always taken to imply a sense of 'self'.

The sort of assumptions which writers tend to make are well exemplified in a tale in which the hero has to determine which of two sources of messages he is receiving is human and which artificial: in effect to make *Turing's test. He finds evidence that one source has used a mnemonic, and concludes that that is the human one. (Saberhagen 1974).

A number of writers have accepted that artificial intelligences (AIs) may at last exceed humans in ability. This is usually associated with a certain Olympian detachment. In one tale, the superior AI left in charge of the abandoned earth continues to communicate with humans by radio, but eventually its lucubrations become so abstract and elevated that its messages cannot be understood. This, indeed, is not unreasonable: the thoughts of a more powerful brain must always be more or less incommunicable to a weaker one. How much of his interests could Einstein have conveyed to Joe Soap (cf. Housman 1922)?

It is clearly difficult to imagine a superior mind, be it alien or artificial. Medieval theologians tried to imagine the mind of God, and their efforts are neither convincing nor agreeable. Sf writers may not have been much more successful, but their fabulations, if no more convincing, are at least usually more fun.   MH

Amis, K. (1961). New Maps of Hell.

Bernal, (1929). The World, the Flesh, and the Devil. Repr. 1970.

Clarke, A. C. (1956). The City and the Stars.

Housman, A. E. (1922) 'The application of thought to textual criticism'. Proc. Classic. Assn., 18.

Saberhagen, F. (1974). 'Inhuman error'. Analog, Oct.

Wells, H. G. (1895). The Time Machine.

mirror cells.

1. The basic findings
2. Imitation
3. Understanding
4. Language evolution

1. The basic findings

The neurophysiological findings of the Sakata group on parietal cortex and the Rizzolatti group on premotor cortex indicate that parietal area AIP (the anterior intraparietal sulcus) and ventral premotor area F5 in monkey form key elements in a cortical circuit, which transforms visual information on intrinsic properties of objects into hand movements that allow the animal to grasp the objects appropriately. Further study revealed a class of F5 neurons that discharge not only when the monkey grasped objects in a certain way, but also when the *monkey observed the experimenter* make a similar action (Gallese et al. 1996). Neurons with this property are called 'mirror neurons'. We distinguish mirror neurons, which are active both when the monkey performs certain actions and when the monkey observes them performed by others, from *canonical neurons* which are active when the monkey performs certain actions but not when the monkey observes actions performed by others. In summary, area F5 is endowed with an *observation/execution matching system*.

Positron emission tomography (PET) experiments were then designed to seek 'mirror systems' in humans (Rizzolatti et al. 1996). There were three conditions: subjects grasped a three-dimensional object; subjects observed the experimenter grasping the object; and (control) subjects simply observed the object. A mirror region was then defined as one that was activity for grasping and observation of grasping, but not for object observation alone. Intriguingly, the only mirror region found in the part of the human brain corresponding to monkey premotor cortex was Broca's area, a major component of the human brain's language mechanisms. More about language later.

2. Imitation

Imitation seems a natural extension of mirror system capability—not just recognizing an observed action, but playing out the mirror system's neural code to yield a replica of that action. Surprisingly, however, monkeys seem not to have this 'playback' feature. The key point

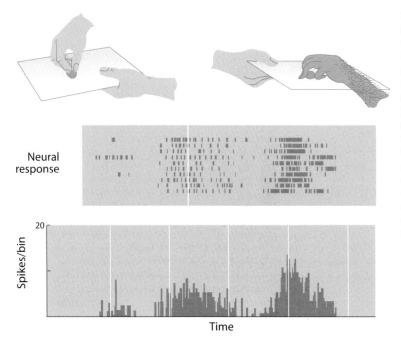

Neural response

Spikes/bin

20

Time

Fig. 1. Upper row: behavioural situations. Lower rows: the firing pattern of the neuron on each of a series of consecutive trials is shown above the histogram which sums response from each trial. Left: the experimenter grasps a piece of food, then moves it towards the monkey, who then grasps it. The neuron discharges during observation of the experimenter's grasp, ceases to fire when the food is given to the monkey, and discharges again when the monkey grasps it.

seems to be that monkeys and chimps can recognize how actions bring hand, object, and body in relation to each other, rather than being able to tease out the specific motions involved in an instance of that action.

The monkey's F5 mirror neurons will fire when the experimenter grasps a block even if it is hidden from view, so long as the monkey has recently seen that the block is there. The monkey has to know about the goal to recognize the action. By contrast, humans can recognize an action from pantomime, without needing the prompt of seeing the object toward which the hand is directed. Indeed, human imitation can be more abstract still—not only can we freely imitate hand movements, but we can use hand movements to signal actions of a very different kind, such as the flapping of wings of a flying bird. Thus, there is much interest in understanding not only what the mirror systems of monkeys and humans have in common, but also the evolutionary changes that must have occurred. There is little imitation exhibited by monkeys, while chimpanzees exhibit 'simple' imitation, a process which is long and laborious compared to the rapidity with which humans can acquire novel sequences. When the chimpanzee imitates a human behaviour, the focus is on moving objects in relation to other objects or the chimpanzee's body. By contrast, we may say that humans have 'complex' imitation: they can acquire (longer) novel sequences in a single trial if the sequences are not too long and the components are relatively familiar. Moreover, the actions need no longer be directed at specific actors or

objects. Indeed, brain imaging directed at linking neural correlates of imitation to the mirror system in humans is now an active area of research.

3. Understanding

Much attention has been drawn to the idea that the mirror system may provide the basis for one monkey to 'understand' the activity—even the intentions—of another, since the mirror system's neural activity is similar whether the monkey is performing an action or observing a related action. However, if one probes the nature of 'understanding', this seems to be only part of the story. New findings on the monkey begin to fill this in. Rizzolatti's group extended its search beyond F5, and found mirror neurons in some other areas, including region PF of parietal cortex. In one study of PF, 61 cells were responsive when the monkey observed biological actions, and two-thirds of these were also active during the monkey's own actions. However, about a quarter of these 'PF mirror neurons' do *not* match observed actions to congruent executed actions. For example, a cell active for observation of downward motion of the hand when grasping an object may also be active during execution of grasping by *mouth*. At first this may seem counter to the notion of a mirror neuron but for us it sets the stage for exploring the notion that understanding will in general involve more than the recognition of an action in isolation, and may also involve some notion of 'meaning', e.g. the context in which the action is appropriate and the expectations that such a behaviour evokes. This opens the door to extending the study of mirror neurons to include the recognition of context and expectations. For example, recognition of one action may be seen as a preliminary for either doing something or predicting what the observed primate will do next (e.g. bringing food to the mouth to eat). The context and expectations set the stage for action recognition, action recognition modifies the context and expectations, and so on. This will let us explore the notion that mirror neurons can act as the basis for 'understanding' if a given action can be placed in the context of its observed (in self and/or others) consequences.

4. Language evolution

Rizzolatti and Arbib (1998) argued that the homology between the monkey F5 mirror system and Broca's area provides a neurobiological 'missing link' for the long-argued hypothesis that primitive forms of communication based on manual gesture preceded speech in the evolution of language (Stokoe 2001). Their 'Mirror System Hypothesis' states that the matching of neural code for execution and observation of hand movements in the monkey is present in the common ancestor of monkey and human, and is the precursor of the crucial language property of parity, namely that an utterance usually carries similar meaning for speaker and hearer

Developing this theme, Arbib (2002) hypothesized seven stages in the evolution of human language: (1) grasping, (2) a mirror system for grasping, (3) a 'simple' imitation system, (4) a 'complex' imitation system, (5) a manual-based communication system, (6) speech, and (7) language. Turning to stage (5), our hypothetical sequence for the evolution of manual-based communication involves: (i) observation of pragmatic action directed towards a goal object; (ii) pantomime in which similar actions are produced away from the goal object; and (iii) abstract gestures divorced from their pragmatic origins (if such existed) and available as elements for the formation of compounds which can be paired with meanings in more or less arbitrary fashion. Imitation is the generic attempt to reproduce movements performed by another, whether to master a skill or simply as part of a social interaction. By contrast, pantomime is performed with the intention of getting the observer to think of a specific action or event. It is essentially communicative in its nature. The imitator observes; the pantomimic intends to be observed. Note that there are two roles for imitation in the evolution of manual-based communication. The first extends imitation to pantomime to provide ad hoc gestures that may convey a situation to the observer. The second extends the mirror system from the grasping repertoire to mediate imitation of gestures to support the transition from ad hoc gestures to conventional signs which can reduce ambiguity and extend the semantic range.

On this view, the 'speech' area of early hominids, i.e. the area somewhat homologous to monkey F5 and human Broca's area, is not yet even a proto-speech area. Instead, it mediated orofacial and manuobrachial communication. The 'generativity' which some see as the hallmark of language is present in manual behaviour. Combinatorial properties are inherent in the manuobrachial system. This provided the evolutionary opportunity for stage (6): the manual–orofacial symbolic system 'recruits' vocalization as association of vocalization with manual gestures allowed them to assume a more open referential character. This explains why F5, rather than the primate call area, provides the evolutionary substrate for speech. Locating phonology in a speech–manual–orofacial gesture complex we see that language acquisition takes various forms: a hearing person shifts the major information load of language—but by no means all of it—into the speech domain, whereas for a deaf person the major information load is removed from speech and taken over by hand and orofacial gestures. Even blind humans accompany speech with hand movements.

Finally, we note that some authors (e.g. Chomsky 1980) have postulated that the framework for the rich variety of human languages is encoded in the genome, a sort of universal grammar. By contrast, I would argue that the six biological stages described above bring us to a human brain that is 'language ready' in that it has the following properties supporting pre-language communication: (i) symbolization: the ability to associate an arbitrary symbol with a class of episodes, objects, or actions. (At first, these symbols may not have been words in the modern sense nor need they have been vocalized.) (ii) Intentionality: extension of communication to be intended by the utterer to have a particular effect on the recipient. (iii) Parity (the mirror property): what counts for the speaker must count for the listener. In addition it has other properties not specific to communication, including (iv) hierarchical structuring: perception and action involving components with sub-parts; (v) temporal ordering: coding hierarchical structures 'of the mind'; (v) the ability to recall past events or imagine future ones; and (vi) paedomorphy and sociality: conditions for complex social learning. This language readiness involved major evolution of the mirror system to include a rich ability for imitation. I would then claim that, once we have groups of people with language-ready brains in this sense, biology need do no more. Rich processes of cultural evolution and diffusion can, I claim, then bring us to the current range of human languages without any recourse to a genetically inscribed universal grammar. The proof or disproof of this claim is one of the most exciting challenges for our study of the mind.

MAA

Arbib, M. A. (2002). 'The mirror system, imitation, and the evolution of language'. In Nehaniv, C., and Dautenhahn, K. (eds.), *Imitation in Animals and Artifacts*.

—— (2004). 'From monkey-like action recognition to human language: an evolutionary framework for neurolinguistics'. *Behavioral and Brain Sciences* (in press).

Chomsky, N. (1980). *Rules and Representations*.

Gallese, V., Fadiga, L., Fogassi, L., and Rizzolatti, G. (1996). 'Action recognition in the premotor cortex'. *Brain*, 119.

Rizzolatti, G., and Arbib, M. A. (1998). 'Language within our grasp'. *Trends in Neurosciences*, 21/5.

—— Fadiga, L., Matelli, M., Bettinardi, V., Perani, D., and Fazio, F. (1996). 'Localization of grasp representations in humans by positron emission tomography: I. Observation versus execution'. *Experimental Brain Research*, 111.

Stokoe, W. C. (2001). *Language in Hand: Why Sign Came before Speech*.

mirror reversal. It is surprising how few people can give an intelligible answer to the question: 'Why are mirror images reversed sideways, but not up and down?' Even physicists, and experts in visual *perception, can be shaken by this apparently simple question, and find no ready answer; though 'mirror writing', and lateral reversal of objects—including oneself—seen in mirrors is an everyday experience.

This is best seen with writing. For example, ʏɿoǫɘɿ⅁ is quite difficult to read. It is inverted laterally—as in a mirror. Vertical inversion is: ⅁ʁɘƃoʏʎ. Double inversion looks like this: ʎɿoƃɘʁ⅁.

Distinguishing left from right has been held, especially by *Kant, to depend upon an observer, and not to be a physical distinction of the world. Kant uses this as evidence for his mental categories of knowledge (*Prolegomena to any future Metaphysics*, 1783).

The mirror reflects top as top, bottom as bottom, right as right, and left as left: the mirror does not reverse right to left or up to down. All this is entirely symmetrical, so where does the asymmetry come from? That there is no asymmetry of the mirror round the line of sight may be demonstrated by rotating the mirror (or rotating it in imagination) in its plane. Clearly it is optically the same for any angle of rotation: there is no asymmetry here. To explain horizontal but not vertical reversal with optical ray diagrams is doomed to failure, for they cannot distinguish horizontal from vertical, as they are symmetrical and equally valid when held in any orientation.

Is the asymmetry of 'mirror reversal' related to the fact that we have a pair of horizontally separated eyes? This is sometimes suggested; but close one eye, and the 'reversal' is unchanged. Consider also a man born blind in one eye: would he not suffer 'mirror reversal' as we do? Yes, he does. The reversals (both upside-down and right–left) of the *retinal image by the optics of the eye cannot be relevant either; for this would affect *all* vision. (The inversion

produced by the eye's image-forming optics is of no consequence, for the retinal image is not seen by the brain as a picture by some internal eye. Provided its—doubly inverted—relation of external objects remains unchanged, the inversions have no effect, and do not present any special difficulty for babies during perceptual learning. Experiments with inverting spectacles show that we can *adapt* to changed touch–vision relationships even when we are adult, which is remarkable, but this is not relevant here.)

It is sometimes said of 'mirror reversal' that it is 'merely verbal—how we *speak* of right and left' (Bennett 1970). But 'mirror writing' is difficult to read: it *looks* very different from 'normal' writing. If the difference is difficult to express, it is present before we attempt to describe it; so it cannot be due to the way we use words, such as 'left' and 'right'.

If 'mirror reversal' is not in the mirror, not in the eyes, and not due to how we use words—can it be some *cognitive* perceptual effect? This kind of explanation has been put forward (Gardner 1964). It is suggested that since we appear behind the mirror, facing ourselves, we make a cognitive rotation—as a mental perceptual act—selecting rotation around the vertical axis because our bodies are nearly symmetrical left–right but not vertically, so this is the easier mental operation to perform. It is remarkable that this explanation appears to have gone unchallenged. If true, it would be of the greatest interest as a dramatic perceptual phenomenon, somehow specifically associated with mirrors. Mental *image rotation is possible, though it is slow and often inaccurate. It is very different from mirror rotation.

If mirror inversion were a cognitive rotation it would have to depend on knowledge that a mirror is involved. Suppose we hide from the observer the fact that he is looking in a mirror. He is shown a large, very clean, wall-to-wall mirror with no frame, so there is no information or knowledge that he is looking in a mirror—but the usual 'mirror reversal' still occurs. Consider, further, a photograph taken by reflection from a frameless mirror: the lateral 'reversal' still occurs in the photograph, and yet there is certainly no information here that a mirror was involved. We may also consider introducing false information that there is a mirror when in fact there is not—a typical mirror frame but with no reflecting glass. Does the world reverse when we look through what *appears* to be a mirror but is not? There is no reversal. Since absence of knowledge that there is a mirror does not remove mirror reversal, and introduction of 'false' knowledge that there is a mirror when in fact there is no mirror does not produce it, we may rule out such cognitive explanations. What then is the answer?

It is remarkably easy to forget that the reflected object has to be rotated, to face the mirror, for us to see it in the mirror. Now we generally rotate objects, including ourselves, around a *vertical* axis. This produces the right–left reversal. The 'mirror reversal' is not in the mirror; or in the optics; or in ourselves as a cognitive reversal: it is the rotation of the object from our direct view of it, to face the mirror, which produces 'mirror rotation'. What is odd about mirrors is that they allow us to get a front view of objects though we are behind them. But for this, the object must be rotated from facing us to face the mirror. The reversal of the mirror image is right–left only when the object is rotated around a *vertical* axis. It is entirely possible (though often less convenient) to rotate objects around their *horizontal* axis. When, for example, a book is rotated around its horizontal axis to face a mirror, it appears upside-down, and not in 'mirror writing'.

If we stand on our head before a mirror, then we are upside-down and not right–left reversed. But this is a confusing case because, quite apart from mirrors, the world continues to look its normal way up though we are upside-down. Here there is indeed a perceptual phenomenon; but this is quite different from mirror reversal, though it may be confused with it. In the case of a room seen laterally inverted in a wall mirror, we see the room from the point of view of the mirror, though we stand opposite to it. The inversion occurs as we walk round the room and so rotate to face the mirror.

It is worth pointing out that if we place a transparent glass sheet with writing on it in front of a mirror, we see the writing on the front of the sheet, and its reflection from its back from the mirror, and they both look the same. This is because we have not had to rotate the transparent sheet for the writing to be reflected from the mirror, as we do have to rotate writing on opaque paper for it to be visible in the mirror. In all cases, it is *object* rotation that produces these mirror reversals in plane mirrors. Mirrors are not even required: the same considerations apply to lateral reversal of type in printing, as the paper is rotated when removed from the type—so type is made left–right reversed.

There is another kind of reversal of mirror images. We see objects *behind* the mirror though we are *in front* of it. This does have an immediate optical explanation; though this is not quite the whole story. Optically, the light path is from the object to the mirror and back to the eye, so we see reflected objects (and ourselves) according to the total length of the light path, which is always longer than the distance of the mirror from the eyes. So it is not surprising that we see objects *through* the mirror: except that we continue to see this though we know intellectually that the objects (and ourselves) are in front of the mirror. So here our knowledge does not affect what we see. This is an interesting limitation of our cognition, which allows us to *see* ourselves through the mirror, as we are optically, though we *know* we are in front of it. Knowledge of the

situation does not correct perception of where we are or which way round we are.

While driving, looking at the cars behind reflected in the mirror, their number plates appear right–left reversed; but what is physically rotated to cause this? It cannot be the cars, or the entire scene. What is rotated is the observer's head. The cars behind are seen with the eyes looking forward, into the mirror; so the head is rotated from direct view of the cars and their number plates. This is the cause. It is puzzling when we forget that we are looking forward but seeing backward!

Although we see ourselves in a different place from where we know ourselves to be, we seldom mistake our image for that of another person. This appears not to be true for animals, other than the higher primates and human infants in their first year of life (Gallup 1977). Almost all animals respond to their own images as to another individual of the same species. Gordon Gallup placed marks on one side of animals' faces, and did the same for infants, and found that even after lengthy experience with the mirror there was no tendency for the subjects to refer the mark to their own face. He suggests that this is an objective criterion for testing for awareness of self.

Somewhat similarly, tactile writing on the forehead may be read as from the *outside* or from the *inside*. It has been suggested that women tend to 'see' touch writing on their forehead from the point of view of an observer in front of them, while men generally 'see' the touch writing laterally inverted as though from inside their own head. Possibly this difference, if real, is because women spend rather more time concerned with their own faces and with how others see them while men look out.   RLG

Bennett, J. (1970). 'The difference between right and left'. *American Philosophical Quarterly*, 7, 3.

Gallup, G. G. (1977). 'Self-recognition in primates'. *American Journal of Psychology*, 32, 329–38.

Gardner, M. (1964). *The Ambidextrous Universe*.

mnemonics. Consider the mnemonic sometimes given to a right-handed child who has difficulty in remembering which hand is called 'right' and which 'left'. 'When you write, you write with your right hand, and the hand that is left over is left.' The puns appropriately link the confused items of knowledge, and the whole is anchored to the act of writing, which the child can readily carry out or imagine (even if he or she can only draw!). The mnemonic organizes the information in a way the child can grasp, and provides a procedure for working out, when in doubt, which is 'right' and which 'left'.

In general terms, mnemonics are mental techniques aimed at helping us to learn and remember specific items of information. They provide organization in terms of which we can more easily comprehend and remember information that has, as we say, little rhyme or reason for us. Mnemonics contrive meaning, sometimes of a quixotic sort, for information we find relatively meaningless and, because of this, they are sometimes called 'artificial memory'.

To illustrate further, consider the problem of remembering the number of days in each month of the year. A commonly used mnemonic runs, 'Thirty days hath September; April, June, and November; all the rest have thirty-one; excepting February alone; which has twenty-eight days clear; and twenty-nine in each leap year.' This jingle helps by rearranging the information, categorizing it, compressing it, and introducing rhythm and rhyme. A less widely used mnemonic consists of counting each successive month on our knuckles. Long months fall on the knuckles, short months on the hollows between. Once more, organization makes the information easier to grasp and remember.

The mnemonics just mentioned achieve organizations which are relatively conventional and publicly comprehensible. But many mnemonics devised by individuals for private use achieve an idiosyncratic organization involving the person's unique background of experiences, visual imagery, and other features that are not readily communicable. Sir Donald Tovey, for example, was a highly accomplished musician who happened to assign a number to each location on the musical stave. When he wanted to memorize any telephone number, he translated each successive digit into the correspondingly numbered location on the stave, and remembered the resulting tune. Idiosyncratic mnemonics may work well for the individual concerned, but if he tries to explain them publicly they seem tortuous, arbitrary, and even laughable. They also imply that he cannot easily comprehend the information. Because of this, mnemonics are discussed less than they are used, and there is a lack of systematic data on their uses and abuses in everyday life.

The most familiar mnemonics are ad hoc, opportunistic, and contrived by or for an individual who is having difficulty with some specific information. However, throughout history, mnemonic *systems* have been devised to provide standard, generalizable techniques for memorizing such things as random lists of words or historical dates. Each of these systems is paradoxical: it enables anyone who masters it to carry out impressive feats of memory, but of a kind that is rarely useful in everyday life. Such systems have been used mainly for entertainment, and their strengths and weaknesses are best illustrated by the Method of Loci.

The Method of Loci was known in classical Greece, described by Cicero in 55 BC, and discussed critically by Quintilian a century later. Used by stage performers into the present day, it has, in recent years, been studied experimentally by psychologists. It enables us to accomplish

the kind of memory feat in which a randomly chosen list of nouns is read out one at a time, memorized at a single hearing, and later recalled in exact sequence. Under appropriate conditions, the Method works spectacularly well. But it is useless for most practical purposes.

The Method has two main ingredients, *loci* (places) and *imagines* (images). The *loci* are mentally pictured places arranged in a strict sequence with which we make ourselves familiar—for example, distinctive landmarks on a journey. The first landmark might be a particular church, the second a baker's shop, etc. These *loci* provide the pre-arranged topography into which the list of nouns will be pigeon-holed, one at a time. When we hear the first noun, we mentally picture the thing it represents and relate this, by interactive imagery, to the first landmark.

Suppose the first noun is 'tiger'. We might visualize a huge tiger scrambling over the façade of the church and ripping off the roof with its powerful claws. The many perceptual-like attributes of the imaged tiger and the imaged church facilitate our bringing the two together into lively interaction. We are free to devise whatever interactive imagery best suits us, but the more animated and distinctive the better. Having thus associated the first noun and its *locus*, we dismiss the scene from our mind, and deal likewise with the second noun and the second *locus*. And so on.

Memorizing is thus broken down into a succession of small subtasks. Each subtask involves interactive imagery which associates a presented noun with its *locus*, and the several subtasks are held in sequence by the prearranged *loci*. When the time comes for recall, we revisit each landmark in turn. When we mentally picture the church, this brings to mind the tiger which is attacking it. When we move to the baker's shop, this prompts recall of the second image, and hence the second noun. The entire procedure may seem absurd. But its efficacy has been repeatedly demonstrated, not only by stage performers but also by ordinary people who have been instructed in the Method and given a little practice in applying it.

The Method has limited utility because it requires certain task conditions, of which three deserve mention. The presented words must be readily translatable into mentally pictured objects. The words must be presented slowly, not faster than one every three or four seconds. The Method breaks down if we depart from considering, at any one time, only one imaged object and its corresponding *locus*—for example, if we allow ourselves to notice relationships among the presented words. Now, such task conditions rarely arise in real life—for instance, the Method cannot be used in the word-by-word memorization of naturally spoken speech. In brief, the Method is an exhibition piece which, as Francis *Bacon observed in 1605, is 'not dexterous to be applied to the serious use of business and occasions'.

The Method is of psychological interest on two main counts. First, it shows that mental imagery is a powerfully effective means of learning and remembering, at least under certain conditions which have not yet been fully explored. Second, it sheds light on how people handle information. It shows that intellectual skills may be re-deployed so as to accomplish unfamiliar feats: the Method does not require us to master any new component pro-cesses, but merely to select existing processes and se-quence them in a new way. Again, if the Method is modified, new accomplishments become possible, such as our being able to recall instantly the noun which oc-cupied any given location in the list. It is also surprising that an individual can, without confusion, use the same set of *loci* to memorize different lists; but, although such has been demonstrated to be the case, the explanation is not yet known.

In general, mnemonics take many forms, all aimed at contriving some comprehensibility for information that is relatively incomprehensible to the individual concerned. On a theoretical level, the chief importance of mnemon-ics is that they illumine, almost in caricature, what is in-volved when someone is said to 'comprehend' something, or find it 'meaningful', or 'understandable'. On a practical level, mnemonics clearly have both uses and limitations. Some of these are highlighted by the abilities and inabil-ities of S. V. Shereshevskii; he was a skilled professional mnemonist who tended to use the Method of Loci off-stage as well as on it (see Luria 1969).

The best way to learn and remember information is to 'understand' it. Most people appreciate this fact. But they may sometimes want to have in their head information which is not readily 'understandable'. When this happens, the trick is to recognize that a mnemonic is indeed a sub-stitute form of comprehension, and to deploy and devise our mnemonics intelligently, with due regard for what they enable us, and do not enable us, to achieve. Unfor-tunately, but not surprisingly, it is generally the case that the people with most need of mnemonics tend also to be the least able to devise them intelligently and evaluate their advantages and disadvantages.

See also REMEMBERING.   IMLH

Ericsson, K. A. (1985). 'Memory skill'. *Canadian Journal of Psych-ology*, 39.

Hunter, I. M. L. (1964). *Memory*.

Luria, A. R. (1969). *The Mind of a Mnemonist*.

Yates, F. A. (1967). *The Art of Memory*.

models, explanatory. Essentially analogies, drawn from engineering or other physical systems, to explain, for example, behaviour and brain function. The prevail-ing technology has throughout history been drawn upon to provide explanatory models of mind. For *Descartes it was hydraulics (fluid in the supposed nerve tubes). For the ancient Greeks, marionettes controlled by strings (*neuron* is the Greek word for 'string') provided the model.

Recently the complex switching of telephone ex-changes has served as a (too passive) model of brain function. The evident power and flexibility of digital com-puters have inspired models of brain function where soft-ware represents mind. More recently, explicit analogies with digital circuits have given way to analogue neurol-ogy (especially with neural nets), but the hardware–software distinction remains as a model for the brain–mind relationship.   RLG

monad. See LEIBNIZ'S PHILOSOPHY OF MIND.

Montessori, Maria (1870–1952). Italian educationist, born at Chiaravalle, Ancona. Maria Montessori can take much credit for the things that are best in primary schools and in pre-school education. When the creative energies of children are allowed free expression, when classrooms are no longer full of the cast-iron-framed desks in which children were once confined, when the teacher is a helper and an enabler rather than a dictator of notes and pur-veyor of inert knowledge, credit must be given to the Montessori method and the influence of her work which has pervaded our thinking about children and their *edu-cation. Like the man who discovered to his great surprise that he had been talking 'prose' all his life, most workers in the education field have been advancing the ideas of the Montessori method without being fully aware of the debt due to her. By the same token, much of the criticism lev-elled against modern teaching methods—that children work only when they want to, that they are *supposed* to enjoy themselves in school nowadays, that there are no punishments, no rewards—is in essence criticism of Mon-tessori principles.

Maria Montessori became the first woman in Italy to receive a medical degree. She was a doctor in medicine at the University of Rome at a time when the education of women was still unusual, and she excelled in a field which had been a male preserve. Had she simply continued to work as a doctor her life would have been remarkable enough. Her early work was with mentally-retarded chil-dren. Between 1898 and 1901 she ran a special school, trained teachers, and lectured internationally on her methods of achieving results with her charges. She came to the conclusion that the same transformation she had been able to achieve with the mentally retarded was needed, and possible, in ordinary schools. Her work with the 'idiots' had been thought to be miraculously effective: they had learnt to read and they passed examinations. She wrote: 'While everyone was admiring the progress of my idiots, I was searching for the reasons which could keep the happy, healthy children of the common schools on so low a plane that they could be equalled in tests of intelligence by my unfortunate pupils.'

With her medical and scientific training, Dr Montessori observed children rather as an anthropologist watches the customs of a tribe, and free from the limiting views of childhood held by the traditional educators. Her approach was democratic, and it is interesting to note that in Russia after the Revolution and in Italy and Germany during the totalitarian regimes, Montessori schools were closed down. Her method was to treat children not as adults in miniature or as objects to be moulded in some 'correct way' but as individuals in their own right. She maintained that she had 'discovered' the child. This was not a just claim, because the child had already been seen in his own right by *Rousseau, Blake, and the Romantics—though, as Aries has shown us, *childhood itself is a relatively new concept (Aries 1973).

Discovering the child also means acceptance of his relative helplessness, and in Montessori schools the apparatus and whole environment of the classroom are structured with the child's needs in mind. The role of the teacher is based both on respect and on confidence that learning will take place without formally set tasks; the child is assumed to want to learn because he has a creative spirit and wishes to discover the world for himself. Like the Freudian psychoanalyst, the teacher should not intervene unless the moment is right. Parallels between psychoanalysis and teaching were recognized by Dr Montessori.

There are limits to her methods. They demand particularly well-trained and sensitive teachers, for authoritarian personalities cannot flourish in a Montessori environment. Middle-class children will probably do better than others, as will children of parents more interested in individuality than in the corporate state. A society that values skill and conformity more highly than creativity and sensitivity is likely to reject or modify the Montessori principles.   CH

Aries, P. (1973). *Centuries of Childhood*.
Kramer, R. (2000). *Maria Montessori: A Biography*.
Montessori, M. (1936). *The Secret of Childhood*.
——(1976). *Education for Human Development*. (The publishers, Schocken, have produced a wide range of books on her work and her own writings.)

moon illusion. The moon (or sun) *illusion refers to the fact that the celestial bodies appear larger when low on the horizon than when higher in the sky. The effect is not caused by atmospheric refraction, which reduces the vertical diameter of the image, making the image slightly oval. It is unlikely that any relevant factors cause an appreciable change of image size within the eye. Most authors agree that the scaling takes place within the brain, and that the mechanisms are the same as for size constancy. Here the agreement ends. The oldest explanation

(dating back at least to *Cleomedes, c.1st–3rd century AD) is that observers take distance into account, and scale the image size in a geometrical manner (*Emmert's law). However, the moon is usually reported to appear nearer when on the horizon, and not further as theoretically required. A rival explanation (dating back to Castelli in 1639) is that size is scaled in relation to other sizes in the visual scene. Alternatively, *Berkeley proposed that size scaling became conditioned to various perceptual cues, including bodily posture. Modern experiments show that the sight of the terrain is the most important factor, though postural and other factors may contribute a little. It remains controversial whether these factors are effective through perceived distance or automatic size scaling. Some authors propose that the moon is automatically 'registered' as far on the horizon, but consciously 'judged' as near because it appears enlarged. Others describe the illusion as an automatic misperception of angular size, with the enlarged angular size making the horizon moon appear close and also large in linear size. Others maintain that size and distance are computed independently.

See also ILLUSIONS.   HER

Hershenson, M. (ed.) (1989). *The Moon Illusion*.
Kaufman, L., and Kaufman, J. H. (2000). 'Explaining the moon illusion'. *Proceedings of the National Academy of Sciences of the USA*, 97.
McCready, D. (1986). 'Moon illusions redescribed'. *Perception and Psychophysics*, 39.
Plug, C., and Ross, H. E. (1994). 'The natural moon illusion: a multi-factor angular account'. *Perception*, 23.

Moore, George Edward (1873–1958). British philosopher, born in London. He was educated at Dulwich College, and read classics at Trinity College, Cambridge, where he became a Fellow in 1898 and was professor of mental philosophy and logic from 1925 to 1939. He was editor of the philosophical journal *Mind* from 1921 to 1947. He was awarded the Order of Merit in 1951.

As a philosopher Moore was extremely important for attacking *Hegelianism with common sense. For example, in a famous lecture he raised his arm and said, 'I *know* this is a hand'—meaning that no conceivable evidence or argument could be brought effectively to challenge the statement. The key essay is 'The nature of judgment' (1899), which served to emancipate Bertrand *Russell from his early philosophical *idealism. Moore's writing now appears overdetailed and somewhat fussy, but this was an essential palliative to the windy metaphysics of Hegelianism, represented in England—with commendable clarity—by John McTaggart (1866–1925). Indeed McTaggart, who was also at Trinity College, provoked Moore and Russell to counter Hegelianism by developing and demanding criteria for meaning, which in its extreme form became 'logical atomism', in which no statement is allowed that cannot be individually justified by some kind of test. This is the basis of *logical positivism.

Moore's *Ethics* (1912) was a key work which pointed out that moral philosophers, and particularly the utilitarians, were logically confused: for the word 'good' cannot be defined in terms of natural qualities, as it always makes sense to ask whether anything possessing natural qualities is good. Moore accepted that goodness is a simple, unanalysable, non-natural quality.   RLG

Morgan, Conwy Lloyd (1852–1936). British psychologist, born in London. He first intended to make a career as a mining engineer, and entered the School of Mines and Royal College of Science in London. There he came under the influence of T. H. *Huxley, who encouraged his interest in biology and put him to study the instinctive behaviour of animals. After five years in South Africa as a college lecturer, he returned to England and became professor of geology and zoology in the University College of Bristol in 1884, and then principal of the college. He was elected a Fellow of the Royal Society in 1899, the first Fellow to be elected for psychological research. This was in recognition of the distinction of two books—*Animal Life and Intelligence* (1890) and *An Introduction to Comparative Psychology* (1894)—as well as numerous papers in scientific journals. When in 1909 the college became the University of Bristol, he served for a short time as vice-chancellor. In 1910 his chair was renamed the chair of psychology and ethics, and he continued to hold it until his retirement in 1919.

Modern animal psychology grew out of the work of Lloyd Morgan in England and the early work of E. L. *Thorndike in America. Lloyd Morgan established a tradition of careful observation of behaviour in natural settings, with systematic variation of the conditions. He enumerated some of his findings, for example when he showed that the proportion of limpets accomplishing a return home is in inverse ratio to the distance they have been removed. His caution in theorizing is exemplified in the canon named after him—the law of parsimony—which was a corrective to the anecdotalism and anthropomorphism of G. J. Romanes (1848–94): 'In no case may we interpret an action as the outcome of a higher psychical faculty, if it can be interpreted as the outcome of one which stands lower in the psychological scale.'

In 1894 Morgan introduced the term 'trial-and-error learning' to describe what he had observed while his fox terrier, Tony, learnt to carry a stick with a heavy knob at one end, and to open a gate by putting his head under the latch. Trial and error, which constitute the method of *intelligence, he remarked, continue until a happy effect is reached. In order to understand a clever performance, one must have observed how it has developed. With this purpose he observed the development of the behaviour of birds after they were hatched—for example, the effect of practice on instinctive pecking, and of experience on the choice of object.

The term 'trial-and-error learning' came into general use when Thorndike put forward in 1911 the *law of effect, which explains the selection or rejection of responses as due to the retroactive strengthening or weakening of connections by the effects. However, one of the neatest experiments, and the first in a fully controlled laboratory setting, on the strengthening of responses by reward—instrumental conditioning—was made in 1932 by G. C. Grindley, a pupil of Morgan's who had moved from Bristol to F. C. *Bartlett's laboratory in Cambridge. By this time, research into detour behaviour and maze learning, prepared for by Morgan's work, was in full flood.
                                                        DRD

Grindley, G. C. (1932). 'The formation of a simple habit in guinea-pigs'. *British Journal of Psychology*, 23.
Morgan, C. L. (1900). *Animal Behaviour*.
Thorndike, E. L. (1911). *Animal Intelligence*.

motion perception. Motion has been called the most ancient and primitive form of vision. Lions have little use for colour vision because gazelles are the same colour as their surrounding; but lions see motion very well in order to see their prey running away. For similar reasons, gazelles also see motion far better than colour. A hungry frog will starve to death on a pile of dead flies, but will instantly snap up an insect in flight; the frog seems to respond *only* to moving objects. We humans have excellent motion perception, both to see moving objects and to steer our own movements by sensing the 'optic flow' of the visual world.

Moving images scan across the retina and stimulate receptors to fire in sequence. This sequential firing is converted into a motion signal by neural motion detectors, first described by Werner Reichardt (1957, 1961).

1. Models of motion perception
2. First- versus second-order motion
3. The correspondence problem
4. Biological motion
5. Physiology of motion perception
6. Motion blindness

1. Models of motion perception
Reichardt's motion model for insect vision was applied to human vision by van Santen and George Sperling and others.

If a spot moves across the retina from region A to region B (Fig. 1) the signal from A is internally delayed and reaches the comparator at the same time as the non-delayed signal from B, provided that the spot's transit time is equal to the internal delay. The resulting large output

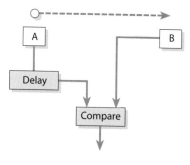

Fig. 1.

2. First- versus second-order motion

Moving contours defined by luminance can stimulate Reichardt detectors and exhibit first-order motion. Moving contours that are defined solely by texture are incapable of stimulating such neurons, yet are seen to move. This is called second-order motion. Fig. 2 shows a random-dot example, in which the first, then the second, third . . . row reverse their polarity in sequence. An observer sees a ripple running downwards. It is not yet agreed whether first- and second-order motion have separate neural pathways, or whether a non-linear process such as rectification converts second- into first-order motion.

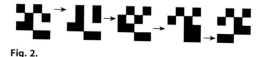

Fig. 2.

from the comparator indicates motion from A to B. If a spot moves from B to A, the delayed signal from A arrives too late to combine with the earlier signal from B; however, this leftward motion is seen by a mirror-image unit (not shown) that compares the delayed output of B with the non-delayed output from A. The preferred speed of this unit depends on the spatial separation between A and B, and the duration of the internal delay. It is not yet clear whether the comparator multiplies (that is, correlates) its two inputs, which would explain how we can see motion when the stimuli at A and B have different contrasts, or whether it subtracts them, which would explain why such a model responds to a single flash.

Motion adaptation and inhibition   After gazing steadily at continuous motion, say by fixing the gaze on a rock halfway down a waterfall, and then turning one's gaze toward the bank, the bank appears to flow back in the opposite direction to the waterfall. This is the negative after-effect of motion, first noted by *Aristotle—although his description is not clear and he may have got the direction wrong. The after-effect is almost certainly caused by adaptation of Reichardt motion detectors, producing an imbalance between opposed motion detectors. Functional magnetic resonance imaging (fMRI) studies show that most of the adaptation occurs in cortical area MT. Adaptation to second-order motion can give an after-effect that is visible on a dynamic or twinkling test field, but never on a static test field.

Sekuler found directionally selective adaptation; following adaptation to upward motion, sensitivity to upward motion is lower than to downward motion. In directional repulsion, two fields of sparse random dots move transparently over each other, towards 2 o'clock and 4 o'clock. They are perceived as if moving towards 1 o'clock and 5 o'clock. This results from mutual inhibition between neurons whose overlapping, petal-shaped directional tuning curves are about 90 degrees wide. *Induced movement*, as when the stationary moon appears to be sailing against the clouds that drift across it, may have a similar explanation.

Motion thresholds   Seeing motion is crucial to our survival. Visual optic flow helps us to steer ourselves through the world, and we watch for motion to help us find the three most interesting things in the universe: predators, prey, and mates.

The slowest motion that we can just see is 2–3 minutes of angular velocity per second. Adding stationary landmarks, which provide relative motion cues, improves motion sensitivity tenfold, and the smallest visible distance travelled is only a 10 second arc (1/360 degrees). In fact we can almost see the moon moving!

The fastest motion that we can see, before motion blurs out completely, is 1000 to 10,000 times faster for a light-adapted eye. It is slower for the more sluggish dark-adapted eye, which like a slow camera shutter sacrifices temporal resolution in order to gain sensitivity. So at dusk, moving objects are hard to see and light stops play for cricket and baseball.

Relative thresholds.   The Weber fraction, or just-noticeable difference (j.n.d.) in the speed of two moving targets presented successively, is in the order of 7–8 per cent. This is worse than the j.n.d. for light intensity or length of lines (2 per cent). However, it is better than the ability to judge the components of motion such as the temporal frequency, or rate at which the bars of a drifting grating appear at the edge of a window, or the time it takes for a target to move through a given distance. This suggests that motion is judged directly, not by calculating the ratio of time/distance or the like. Surprisingly, observers are insensitive to the changes in speed of an accelerating target, and the j.n.d. is about 15 per cent, probably because the visual system integrates the motion over a period of 0.1–0.2 second, which tends to blur out any speed differences that occur within this time window.

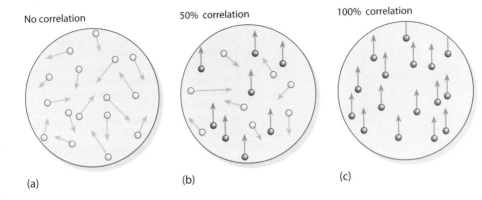

No correlation   50% correlation   100% correlation

(a)   (b)   (c)

Fig. 3.

Motion coherence has been studied with the random-dot kinematograms shown in Fig. 3. Because the correlated dots all move in the same direction, the fraction of correlated dots controls the net motion of the display. A typical human observer can detect the direction of motion when only 6 per cent are moving in one direction.

The fovea is more sensitive to motion than the periphery, yet the periphery is much better at detecting moving than stationary objects: one waves at a friend in a crowded airport in order to stimulate his or her peripheral motion detectors and elicit a *saccadic eye movement that turns the gaze towards the target.

Apparent motion In 1875, Hermann Exner presented his observer with two successive, spatially separated electric sparks. The time order of the sparks could be seen correctly when the time interval was 45 milliseconds or longer. He then put the sparks closer together and got, not succession, but the stroboscopic appearance of movement of a single spark from the earlier position to the later. The threshold for the correct perception of this moving spark was only 14 msec. In other words, movement caused by the displacement of position in time could be sensed correctly when the time interval itself was too small to be perceived as such. Exner concluded that movement must involve a special process, which he claimed was a sensation and not a complex like a perception.

3. The correspondence problem

When two movie frames are presented in rapid succession, how do we match up items in the first frame with corresponding items in the second frame? This is the correspondence problem. A single flying ball presents no problem. But how do we pair up the leg of a somersaulting acrobat with the correct leg in the next frame (Fig. 4)?

We tend to pair up 'nearest neighbours', since this proximity algorithm reduces total motion path length. However, we also use motion heuristics based on the fact that

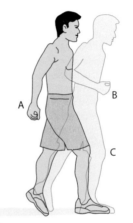

Fig. 4.

objects usually move in predictable ways in the real world. In the ambiguous motion display used by Ternus, three dots at positions *a*, *b*, *c* alternate over time with three dots presented at positions *b'*, *c'*, *d*. This can be perceived in two different ways. Sometimes a single dot appears to jump back and forth between positions *a* and *d*, while the dots at positions *b* and *c* remain stationary (element motion). Sometimes the trio of dots appears to translate back and forth en masse (group motion). Element motion is favoured when the time interval between frames is short and the same eye sees both frames. Group motion is favoured when the time interval is long, or when the two frames are seen by different eyes, or when the dots are lighter than the surround in one frame and darker than the other; these operations reduce the perceptual 'glue' between frames.

In another ambiguous display, two dots at the opposite corners of an imaginary square are abruptly replaced by two dots at the other two corners (Fig. 5). Horizontal or vertical apparent motion is seen, alternating at irregular

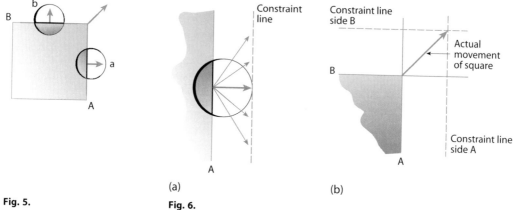

Fig. 5.   **Fig. 6.**

(a)   (b)

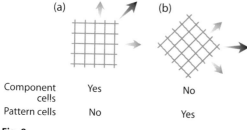

Fig. 7.

Fig. 8.

	(a)	(b)
Component cells	Yes	No
Pattern cells	No	Yes

right (Fig. 6*a*). In the same way, upward motion of a horizontal line behind an aperture is ambiguous.

But when a square moves up to the right (Fig. 6*b*), we see it unambiguously. How? By computing the intersection of the two constraints, giving a percept of motion up to the right. Adelson and Movshon (1982) showed observers sets of overlapping horizontal and vertical gratings moving (say) up and to the right. This is called a plaid (Fig. 7).

Experiments have varied the contrast, orientation, and spatial frequencies of the two gratings, and observers generally saw coherent motion of a single plaid, consistent with the intersection of constraints. Sometimes, however, they saw transparent motion, in which the two gratings appeared to slide over each other. It is believed that motion of the component gratings is sensed by component-selective neurons in V1, whilst motion of the single plaid is sensed by pattern-selective neurons in area MT (Fig. 8).

In the *chopstick illusion*, a vertical and a horizontal rod, overlapping at their centres, each move along a clockwise circular path without changing their orientation. Their sliding intersection actually moves counter-clockwise, but it is perceived as moving clockwise because the clockwise motion of the tips propagates along the lines and is blindly assigned to the centre. Observers cannot track the sliding centre well, showing that pursuit eye movements depend upon object perception.

4. Biological motion

We are good at analysing complex motion displays. When a friend waves from a moving train, we see the motion of the train plus the vertical motion of the hand—we do not see the hand as tracing out a sinusoid. Johansson (1975) attached 10–12 lights to the joints of a person walking in the dark (Fig. 9). Observers can immediately identify this as a walking person, even within one second. They can even tell the gender of the walker, or infer how heavy a

time intervals. If a dozen ambiguous quartets are viewed at once, they all flip between horizontal and vertical motions at the same instant. Adding 'priming' dots can constrain the motion to be horizontal, showing that objects in motion tend to continue along the same path ('visual inertia'). Rapid presentation of the two dots creates ambiguous motion, either clockwise or counter-clockwise, but preceding them by the initial dot causes the motion to be clockwise.

The aperture problem If a straight vertical line moves to the right behind a circular aperture, there is no way of knowing whether it moves up right, or down right, or just to the right, because motion of the line along its own length generates no motion signal. The more oblique the motion is to the contour orientation, the faster it seems to move. The set of possible motions is shown as arrows, and is called a velocity constraint. Usually one defaults to seeing the slowest motion, directly to the

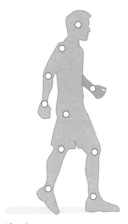

Fig. 9.

weight she or he is lifting. If a rotating glass cylinder is spattered with black paint and viewed in silhouette with one eye, one immediately perceives a three-dimensional cylinder ('structure from motion').

5. Physiology of motion perception

In humans, lesions in some brain areas degrade the ability to perceive motion coherence but do not affect the ability to see motion-defined edges, where dense fields of dots moving in different directions abut. Lesions in other areas degrade the ability to see motion-defined edges without affecting motion coherence thresholds. This dissociation shows that different brain areas govern these different motion tasks.

Some motion sensitivity is found in the eyes of insects and the retinas of pigeons or rabbits, but not until the cortex in primates. The most important primate motion pathway begins with the parasol cells in the retina and continues through magno cells in the LGN and cortical areas VI, MT (also known as V5), and MST (medial superior temporal area). In VI, only about a quarter of all cells are direction selective, but nearly all cells in MT are, and their receptive fields are far bigger than in VI. Whereas VI cells are tuned to one direction, some cells in MST are tuned to expansion or to contraction, or else to a central region moving in one direction surrounded by a region of motion in the opposite direction.

Newsome and Pare studied motion coherence (Fig. 3) and found that an ibotenic acid lesion in area MT of a macaque raised the coherence threshold fourfold. This deficit heals itself within a week or two, but other motion tasks such as speed discrimination can be affected permanently. Newsome et al. found that, averaged over many trials, a single directionally selective cell in MT was as good at detecting coherence as the whole macaque was! Furthermore, when this MT cell was stimulated electrically, the macaque was more likely to behave as if the stimulus moved in the direction preferred by this neuron.

6. Motion blindness

Zihl et al. studied a patient L.M. who lost most of her ability to see motion following a stroke. She cannot see coffee flowing into a cup, but instead the liquid appears to be frozen. She adopts a trick used by the blind, putting her finger over the edge of the cup and pouring until her finger feels hot and wet. She cannot cross the street for fear of being struck by a moving car. She has difficulty in segregating moving dots from a background of stationary dots, or of randomly moving dots; but her ability to see form, colour and stereo depth seem unimpaired. Her lesions cover a large area of the visual cortex, so it is hard to be sure which areas are important for motion perception. Her problems reveal graphically how important the perception of movement is to us.   SA

Adelson, E. H. and Movshon, J. A. (1982). 'Phenomenal coherence of moving visual patterns'. *Nature*, 300.

Johansson, G. (1975). 'Visual motion perception'. *Scientific American*, 232.

Mather, G., Verstraten, F., and Anstis, S. M. (1998). *The Motion Aftereffect: A Modern Perspective*.

Nakayama, K. (1985). 'Biological image motion processing: a review'. *Vision Research*, 25.

Ramachandran, V. S., and Anstis, S. M. (1986). 'The perception of apparent motion'. *Scientific American*.

Smith, A. T., and Snowden, R. J. (1994). *Visual Detection of Motion*.

Watanabe, T. (1998). *High Level Motion Processing: Computational, Neurobiological and Psychophysical Perspectives*.

Zanker, J. M., and Zeil, J. (2001). *Motion Vision: Computational, Neural and Ecological Constraints*.

Müller, Johannes Peter (1801–58). German physiologist and anatomist, widely regarded as the founder of modern physiology. Born and educated in Koblenz, he studied medicine at Bonn (1819–22), where he became professor of anatomy and physiology (1830), before moving to take up a similar chair in Berlin (1833). He remained in Berlin for the rest of his life. As rector of the university there in 1838–9 and again in 1847–8, he was inevitably involved in the serious student disturbances during the 1848 revolution, events which troubled him deeply and caused a serious breakdown of his health.

He taught human and comparative anatomy, embryology, physiology, and pathological anatomy, and made important contributions in all these fields. His work included an explanation of the colour sensations produced by pressure on the eye, confirmation of the *Bell–Magendie law, and studies of *reflex action; he was also one of the first to use the microscope in pathology. His *Handbuch der Physiologie des Menschen* (2 vols., 1833–40; English trans. 1840–9) became the standard text in physiology. Among a generation of brilliant physiologists taught by Müller are *Helmholtz and *Du Bois-Reymond, the latter of whom succeeded him in the chair of physiology at Berlin after his premature death in 1858.

Müller-Lyer, Franz Carl (1857–1916). Discoverer of the most famous of all the visual *illusions—the Müller-Lyer illusion: that a line terminated at each end with inward-pointing arrowheads appears longer, and a line with outward-pointing arrowheads appears shorter, than a 'neutral' comparison line (Fig. 1). He reported and described this distortion and many related examples, with detailed experiments, in two papers dated 1889 and 1896. Müller-Lyer is not a well-known psychologist, in spite of the enormous literature and the many attempts to explain the illusion that bears his name.

Born in Baden-Baden, he studied medicine at Strasburg, and at the age of 24 became assistant director of the Strasburg Psychiatric Clinic, where he remained until 1883. He visited and worked with E. *Du Bois-Reymond and J. M. *Charcot. He ended his career in private practice in Munich. His major work, in extent though not in fame, was in sociology, in which he wrote a seven-volume book, arguing a somewhat Marxist thesis of direction and inevitable development of societies (Salomon 1959).

Müller-Lyer offered as the explanation of his distortion illusion that 'the judgement not only takes the lines themselves into consideration, but also, unintentionally, some part of the space on either side'. This is known as the principle of confluxion. So, for him, it is not the angles of the figure, but rather the spaces bounded by the lines (or by dots corresponding to the ends of the lines) that produce the distortion. He counters some rival theories in his second paper (1896). See also ILLUSIONS.

Müller-Lyer's two papers 'Optical illusions' (1889) and 'Concerning the theory of optical illusions: on contrast and confluxion' (1896) are translated by R. H. Day and H. Knuth, *Perception* (1981), 126–49. For his sociology, see entry by F. Salomon in *Encyclopaedia of the Social Sciences*, ed. R. A. Seligman and A. Johnson, ii (1959), 83–4.

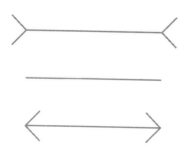

Fig. 1.

multiple personalities. See DISSOCIATION OF THE PERSONALITY.

Munchausen syndrome. Towards the end of the 19th century a publication appeared from the pen of Baron Munchausen giving an account of his worldwide travels and experiences. This included long and eloquent observations of cases of the disease and of the hospitals where they were treated. There were many medical critics who regarded the case descriptions as implausible and ridiculous. Others regarded them as crude and incompetent accounts of real organic illnesses.

Some decades later, Dr Richard Asher (1951), director of the casualty department of the Central Middlesex Hospital, published a paper in which it was plain to large numbers of medical readers that he had captured the essential features of a hitherto unrecognized acute and dramatic 'illness'. These patients had a record of presentation to a large number of casualty departments and frequent admissions to medical and surgical wards. Here the judgement made was that the symptoms and signs had been fabricated and that individuals, who were often homeless, were seeking shelter and protection rather than requiring treatment, and suffering from what was now regarded as some form of 'personality disorder'.

Within a short time observations of such disorders began to appear from all parts of the world. This paper, from an observant and imaginative writer, made it clear that the existence of medical, psychological, and social phenomena in these patients was relatively common in all countries and the high prevalence had escaped notice until attention had been drawn to it.

Until the 19th century novelists and writers had neglected its social and familial repercussions when the danger of death transfigures the perception of the outer and inner worlds of experience and their fate shaped by their illness.

1. Literature and illness
2. Some social and historical associations
3. Case histories
4. Psychopathology of the Munchausen and related forms of personality disorder
5. Concluding remarks

1. Literature and illness
During the period since the middle of the 19th century an increasing number of novels and other writings have included sick or disabled persons and their vicissitudes, often emanating from the life history of the author, and playing an important part in the action and its relationship to the inner life of the central characters.

The attitudes of those in the community to the progress of disease and its treatment to an increasing extent brought the medical profession into contact with their potential patients by inviting them to participate in the medical programme. These early contributions to the lives of ill persons and their carers tended to be over-dramatized but they improved in authenticity in later decades.

An early contributor, Virginia Woolf, brought to bear a delicate and insightful sensibility to her representations and her own experiences of disease. In her case this eventually led to her suicide by drowning.

Considering how common illness is, how tremendous the spiritual change that it brings, how astonishing when the lights of health go down, the undiscovered countries that are then disclosed, what wastes and deserts of the soul a slight attack of influenza brings to view, what precipices and lawns sprinkled with bright flowers a little rise of temperature reveals, what ancient and obdurate oaks are uprooted in us by the act of sickness, how we go down into the pit of death and feel the waters of annihilation close above our heads and wake thinking to find ourselves in the presence of the angels and the harpers; when we have a tooth out and come to the surface in the dentist's armchair and confuse his 'rinse the mouth—rinse the mouth' with the greeting of the Deity, stooping from the floor of Heaven to welcome us—when we think of this as we are so frequently forced to think of it, it becomes strange indeed that illness has not taken its place with love and battle and jealousy among the prime themes of literature. Novels, one would have thought, would have been devoted to influenza, epic poems to typhoid: odes to pneumonia; lyrics to toothache.

It will be apparent that some of the effect of these representations can enrich the personality and help in the healing of illness. But in some vulnerable individuals it may generate neurotic or personality disease; what used to be called 'hysterical personality' has now been changed to 'narcissistic personality' or 'borderline personality disorder'.

Characters afflicted with disease have usually been described from the outside in literature, and distance has tended to lend enchantment to the view. For the manner in which they have been depicted has often given to illness an aura of sentiment and romance, and established fashions that have been widely emulated. In the 19th century tuberculosis was a common cause of disease and death: the literature of this love-shackled period endowed the disease with a tragic and spiritual beauty. The heroines of *La Dame aux camélias* and *La Bohème* die of tuberculosis on the stage. They had been based upon the characters of women loved by the younger Alexandre Dumas and Henri Murger, who had suffered from phthisis. This was the time when Keats wrote 'Youth grows pale and spectre thin and dies', and the imperishable sonnet 'Bright star would I were steadfast as thou art' was composed four months before his death from consumption in Rome. Byron said, 'I should like to die of a consumption because the ladies would all say "look at that poor Byron, how interesting he looks in dying".'

In this manner tuberculosis came to be incorporated into the ideal conception of beauty and artistic sensibility, and good health was almost equated with bourgeois coarseness, materialism, and vulgarity.

Half a century earlier the publication of Goethe's *Werther*, whose romantic hero took his own life, let loose an epidemic of yearning and melancholy in Germany and made suicide a fashionable pastime among those who wished to cut a poetic figure. Heroines and high-born ladies swooned and fainted in the reign of Queen Victoria.

Florence Nightingale dominated the worlds of public health, nursing, and social welfare and exerted a powerful political influence from her sickbed, while Elizabeth Barrett languished for many years in a state of romantic fragility, suffering from a spinal injury, delicate lungs, and threatened consumption. Medical science was unfortunately insufficiently advanced for anyone to be able to remove a prolapsed intervertebral disc. However, she managed to survive long enough to make her celebrated escape from 50 Wimpole Street and consummate her epic love affair with Robert Browning, whom she married.

The role of helpless invalid, or indeed of affliction with specific disease, is therefore not always repugnant or unwelcome. It may provide an avenue of escape from the turmoils and conflicts of active life. Or it may be conceived as adding an appealing lustre and significance to the personality and ego of the unloved, depressed, and rejected. Here we approach close to the essence of the condition which is a vicarious attempt to resolve conflict that has become insupportable or reached a critical stage, by flight into disease.

The typical neurotic subject is insensible of the true nature of his malady and by a convenient dissociation of mental processes into separate, uncommunicating departments (a device for which the narcissistic personality is specially gifted), the problems from which he has taken refuge are also shelved in some hidden corner of the mind. The narcissistic personality assumes illness for a specific and understandable purpose which may be uncovered by psychological enquiry and is largely unconscious of the escape that disease provides and of the psychological processes that motivate it.

Special interest attaches, however, to those subjects who appear, in full consciousness, to choose disease, mutilation, and physical suffering as a way of life for its own sake. These are the individuals who manage to feign soaring temperatures, or who are brought into hospital with seeming haemorrhages of alarming proportions from a bewildering variety of orifices, who succeed in getting their abdominal walls covered with an intricate pattern of surgical scars, who may get their limbs amputated and their cranial cavities explored. The phenomenon has become notorious under the eponym 'Munchausen syndrome' coined by Asher (1951). The description was unfortunate for it helped to establish a strong hostile bias towards individuals, often endowed with valuable qualities, who are set on a course of self-destruction and whose condition reflects a distorted state of mind that requires early and sustained treatment.

2. Some social and historical associations

It is perhaps relevant that the self-inflicted injuries by patients with Munchausen syndrome figure to some extent in the periods of fasting or self-inflicted pain and deprivation in the practices of many religions in the rituals prescribed for atoning for sin or achieving a higher spiritual tendency.

It would be superficial, as William *James pointed out, simply to explain all such phenomena in terms of an egotistical craving for sympathy and notoriety, but one cannot but suspect that in many instances some important relationship to an inherent personality disorder exists. Some of the early religious activities recorded in ancient history were dominated by services where some shaman or priest engaged in heroic activities such as crossing mountains and rivers, wars with demons and ghosts, acted out in front of an audience who participated in these activities. These were among the earliest religious group activities. In the rites of Dionysus in ancient Greece, the participants enacted the birth, death, and resurrection of a god. The death of the god sometimes took the form of human sacrifice, either of a priest or some substitute. The rites were enacted mainly by women led by a male priest, a description perhaps reminiscent of the wards of a modern hospital.

So when we attempt to use the term 'narcissistic personality' in a pejorative sense, let us remember the ancient lineage and ubiquity of the phenomenon. If we were to dispense with the deviation from the norm that is narcissism, we should have to do without great actresses and actors, opera singers, many executant musicians, journalists, salesmen and women who carry their beauty with panache, and some of the best teachers in medicine.

Nowhere is it more difficult to hold condemnation in check than in the face of the persistent, tale-spinning deceit and exhibitionism of the chronic hospital addict. Nowhere is it more important to maintain a spirit of objectivity, tolerance, and detachment.

3. Case histories

Case 1 This case exemplifies both the characteristic natural history and the psychological background of the phenomenon particularly well. It is that of a nun aged 41 who joined an Anglican order at the age of 24 and, when not afflicted with some physical complaint, had been described as serving it with dedication. She was admitted to hospital with a suspected diagnosis of hyperthyroidism,

owing to loss of weight and a raised pulse rate. Perplexity and later suspicion were aroused by the fact that although her basal metabolic rate (BMR) was raised, the uptake of radioactive iodine by the thyroid was negligible, a finding thought to be sufficiently bizarre for a psychiatrist to be consulted in the matter. After having noted the thickness of the case records and the combination of reserve and icy hostility with which the psychiatric consultation was greeted, it was thought advisable to survey the history of past disabilities.

Her medical history had begun at the age of 16 with bilateral, middle-ear infection which rapidly became chronic. After a number of periods in hospital, a mastoidectomy was carried out followed by a second operation two years later. The purulent discharge from both ears continued. She then developed a thick nasal discharge and pain over the sinuses. Several operations were carried out, including submucus section of the septum.

Some time later, while working as a probationer nurse, she was diagnosed as having scarlet fever and to have tachycardia and swollen ankles. She was kept for four months on her back and after dental extractions she suffered a recurrence of the sinus infection. She then developed an infection of the left thumb, resistant to treatment, necessitating amputation. She was thereafter given short-wave therapy for a period. A further flare-up of infection in the stump was treated by penicillin but the responsible organism proved extremely resistant and, following infections in several fingers, a number of nails were removed. However, the monotonous recurrence in her case records of the words 'a pure culture of *E. coli*' in the bacteriological reports provided an important clue.

She suffered further sinus troubles and a massive epistaxis which required blood transfusion. She then went abroad where frequent epistaxes, often necessitating blood transfusion, gave rise to considerable perplexity. There followed a recurrence of *E. coli* infection, this time in the left knee joint, followed by a further admission for tachycardia, sweating, and loss of weight. It is of interest that she was carrying out nursing duties at this time and had responsibility for dispensing a wide range of drugs. Some years later there was a recurrence of septic arthritis and also a rectal fissure for which she was admitted to hospital for the eighteenth time.

After completion of the psychiatric interview it was felt advisable to carry out a careful inspection of the patient's locker. In it were found two syringes, numerous needles, two catheters, Price's *Textbook of Medicine*, a textbook of nursing, and several hundred tablets of various kinds, including thyroid extract. Marked thermometers failed to return, indicating that she was secreting one or more of them on her person. This provided an apparently logical explanation for the swinging temperature which had meanwhile appeared, until this was traced to a number of gluteal abscesses subsequently admitted to have been self-induced by injections of bath water. Study of the bacteria of the contents of the abscesses made it certain that the fluid which had been injected by her had been contaminated.

Subsequently the patient admitted to having simulated many of the disabilities of recent years. It was not possible to get her to admit that the early haemorrhages, sinus infections, and the chronic infection of the left thumb had been self-inflicted. As her cooperation in treatment had been obtained it became clear that further confessions would have proved humiliating, and there did not seem any purpose in eliciting them.

Her father was a general practitioner working in private practice, and during the patient's childhood the family lived in close proximity to a nursing home owned by him. Able, energetic, but cantankerous, impatient, and prone to bursts of explosive temper, the children were terrified of him. The mother was an efficient and conscientious woman, but poorly gifted in expressing affection or tenderness and most of her energies, like those of her husband, seemed to be absorbed in the management of the nursing home. The patients were, in other words, highly privileged members of the community in which our nun had grown up. Noise or high spirits tended to be discouraged and at an early age the patient was sent to a convent school.

One can perhaps best convey what conclusions were eventually reached in respect of the most likely psychological starting point for the patient's disabilities by recounting the story of a man and wife, both working in the medical profession. They had only one child. All day long the father and mother would be busy working in the same private hospital and nursing home. When the little child was asked one day what she would like to do when she grew up, she replied without hesitation, 'I would like to be a patient'.

Case 2 This man was a highly capable, charming, widely respected citizen, successful in life, a devoted husband and father. His many commercial contacts had led him to an early stage of his life into increasingly heavy drinking and, as alcohol was for him a social lubricant, he found himself, in his early 30s, getting drunk before the usual boost to wit and eloquence could take effect, and this was happening in the middle of the day. He had, in other words, become a chronic alcoholic. He dealt with the situation with unusual courage and energy, sought treatment, went off alcohol, and became a teetotaller and a leading light in Alcoholics Anonymous.

Seven or eight years later he suffered a mysterious malady which led to numerous admissions to hospital in a state of profound coma. Detailed neurological and metabolic studies proved largely negative and it was eventually decided that he was suffering from some slowly developing, diffuse neoplasm of the midbrain on account of the recurrent attacks of prolonged coma and the intermittent abnormality in his *EEG, which took the form of high-voltage, bilaterally synchronous, slow activity. Before this conclusion had been reached, however, he had had several lumbar punctures, some twelve EEGs, an air encephalogram, and, in the course of a severe depressive episode between admissions for coma, a course of electroconvulsive treatment. All these measures he endured with a resignation and good humour which everyone regarded as stoical and astonishing.

After eighteen months of fruitless investigations, he suddenly developed a state of acute confusion, becoming disoriented in hospital and insisting that he was being criticized, accused, and insulted by a number of people shouting at him from an adjoining room. He was voluble, excited, and aggressive and was restrained with great difficulty from leaving hospital to seek the help of the police. It was decided that his condition could be due only to an acute toxic state or some toxin he had been taking regularly and had been suddenly withdrawn. He was admitted to a mental hospital where, after the clearing of his confusion, he was allowed to go freely into town. Twenty-four hours later he was, as anticipated, lying comatose on his bed. Underneath his mattress was found a litre bottle half full of chloral, which had been prescribed for his insomnia some five years previously and to which he had become increasingly addicted.

A certain superficiality of emotion and a capacity for dissociation of consciousness had no doubt helped him to hoodwink himself and others about what was happening, to the point where he permitted ventriculography to be carried out. Why had he not behaved with the determination and forthrightness that had enabled him to achieve the rare feat of an effective and lasting cure from alcoholism some years previously? To some extent probably because chloral provided oblivion for him, and possibly he obtained a certain satisfaction from the high drama his admission to hospital had provided. However, perhaps his chronic intoxication, which was far worse than anything he had suffered during the period of alcoholism, made it impossible for him to hold his tendencies to self-display in check. There is evidence that hospital addiction and self-mutilation sometimes appear for the first time after brain injury or disease. Hence, even in the oddities of conduct which look so like wilful misdemeanours, we cannot get completely away from the brain and its preformed patterns of response. That there may be something in this explanation is suggested by the fact that this patient made an excellent response to treatment and has, over a period of five years, remained a successful, respected, and valuable member of the community.

4. Psychopathology of the Munchausen and related forms of personality disorder

From the facts outlined is it possible to infer any explanations for the deliberate simulation of illness or disability? Clearly any complete explanation would require much more knowledge than we possess at present and the field is worthy of research by the psychiatrist, the physician, and the social scientist. But there are certain consistent themes which run through the lives of their patients and it is on these themes that attention should be focused.

The craving for the special care and attention, the concern and the high drama that are all available in the medical or surgical ward and at home seems commonly to have been the starting point in the early stages of childhood when the affection and tenderness which are indispensable for healthy development appear often to have been lacking, or when conditioning to a role of extreme helplessness and dependence has occurred.

The condition is commoner in women than men, and some of the phenomena under the heading of the syndrome Munchausen-by-proxy, in which the mother or female care person is responsible for imitating the syndrome or inflicting a serious feeding disorder, such as anorexia nervosa, has some factitious element. In this condition the transfusion of blood or some other fluid being injected into the child is contaminated by the addition to it of some toxic or poisonous substance. Those who undertake these dangerous and illicit acts prove, in most cases, to be mothers or carers of the child.

Young persons with personality disorder engaged in antisocial behaviour such as burglary, violence, and antisocial conduct in a setting of drug dependence are mainly male. These are, of course, two completely different populations.

The phenomenon of hospital addiction appears therefore to be an escape into illness for a specific purpose: to achieve vicariously the love, pity, or sense of significance of which the familial and social background has, for one reason or another, deprived these individuals in their formative years. If this is correct the condition must, despite the distinction drawn earlier, be related to underlying *borderline* personality disorder (DSM-IV).

For persons whose life history and presenting features reveal some positive assets of emotional strength, stability, intelligence, and achievements in personal relationships, it is possible for psychotherapy to achieve considerable success. Treatment in such cases is quite often rewarding, particularly after one has succeeded in bringing the patient to the point where he admits to his deceptions and prevarications.

5. Concluding remarks

The desire to be ill is a relatively common human failing and possibly connected with that willingness to undergo or to exhibit physical suffering that has played an important part in the history of some cultures and religions. In cultures where the fakir excites admiration and miracles are considered everyday events, there are perhaps outlets which our society provides only within the confines of the hospital. Yet in seeking for explanations one is in danger of explaining them away. It would be naive and shallow to overlook the fact that those who have been prepared to accept martyrdom in a cause have written some of the noblest chapters in history. It would be just as unfortunate if the doctor were to be too ready to suspect a breach of the contract of mutual trust and candour by his patient as if he failed to be alive to the possibility that illness might be exaggerated or feigned in an appeal for compassion or understanding.

Bringing the law into the situation is contraindicated and can make matters worse. It would be most tragic of all if we failed to react to a diagnosis of a 'desire to be ill' with sympathy and imagination.

In Molière's *Le Malade imaginaire* Béralde remonstrated with his hypochondrical brother for his foolish infatuation with doctors and medicines. 'Doctors', he insisted, 'know their classics, talk Latin freely, can give the Greek names of all the diseases, define them and classify them, but as for curing them, that is a thing they know nothing about.' And again, 'all that their art consists of is a farrago of high sounding gibberish, specious babbling which offers words in place of sound reasons and promises instead of results'. The words you will agree have a contemporary ring. The only thing that has altered is that it is not to general medicine that they are commonly applied nowadays. Ironically enough, Molière collapsed and died after taking part in his play: for some years his enemies had been ridiculing him as a hypochondriac.   MaR

Asher, R. (1951). 'Munchausen's syndrome'. *Lancet.*
American Psychiatric Association (1994). *Diagnostic and Statistical Manual of Mental Disorders DSM-IV* (4th edn.).

muscular action. Muscle power has served man's needs for far longer than more recent, and apparently more abundant, sources of power. And even with those additional sources, doing work with muscles remains essential to most human activity. But it is so commonplace that we easily forget how complex are the processes which make chemical energy from food available to us as mechanical energy. Not only has the energy derived from the oxidation of food to be stored so that it can be released when needed as mechanical energy, but the release must be precisely controlled in order to make movements coordinated and purposeful.

The contractile properties of a muscle reside in the cells (muscle fibres) of which it is composed. Each muscle fibre is a long cylindrical cell which may be several centimetres long and is nearly a tenth of a millimetre in diameter. As cells go it is very large, and it is almost wholly specialized as a generator of mechanical force. By far the greater part of the constituents (apart from water) of each muscle fibre are two proteins, actin and myosin, whose interactions provide a means of generating a force. Actin is a moderately sized protein (molecular weight 60,000); myosin is substantially larger (molecular weight about 250,000), but both molecules have the property of aggregating with themselves into rods between 1 and 2 micrometres in length. These rods of actin and myosin are arranged within the muscle fibre in a very highly ordered array: transverse bands of actin rods and myosin rods alternating in the length of the fibre, and overlapping in such a way that each type of rod can slide along rods of the other kind. Small quantities of additional proteins are incorporated into the arrays of actin and myosin rods; their functions are to give order to the arrays of rods and to regulate the interactions of actin and myosin.

When a muscle is relaxed, the protein rods slide without hindrance past each other, allowing easy stretching of the muscle fibre by an applied force. When a muscle is contracting, the actin rods are pulled towards the centre of each myosin rod, and if the force generated by the pulls of all the myosin rods exceeds the external force the fibre will shorten.

How do the myosin rods move the actin rods and, in so doing, do work? From the sides of the myosin rods short flexible arms (about 200 on each myosin rod) can swing out and form cross-bridges between the myosin rod and an adjacent actin rod. Provided calcium ions and adenosine triphosphate (ATP) are present, a cyclical process occurs, triggered by calcium ions and powered by the hydrolysis of ATP to adenine diphosphate and inorganic phosphates, a reaction which is well known as an immediate source of energy in living systems. The ATP is synthesized in the muscle fibre with energy derived from the oxidation of food. The cycle of events appears to involve a myosin cross-bridge attachment to a site on an actin rod; a multi-stage and progressive change in the cross-bridge attachment which results in a small but finite movement of the actin site past the myosin rod; and finally cross-bridge detachment. The cycle may be repeated and the actin rod moved on by another small distance. Hydrolysis of ATP is involved at each turn of the cycle because, however small the movement of the actin rod, if it is achieved against an external load mechanical work is done, and even if no net movement is achieved there will still be some stretching of elastic structures in the muscle. In any actual muscle fibre there are, of course, very many cross-bridges (approximately 5×10^{12}), and in any short time interval many will become detached from, and many will become attached to, actin: the net result is a smooth movement of the actin rods along the myosin rods and a smooth shortening of the fibre. If movement is prevented by an external

force, the repeated attaching and detaching exerts a steady tension which is proportional to the degree of overlap of the actin and myosin rods, that is to the number of the myosin side-arms which find an actin site for attachment.

In each fibre, contraction depends on the presence of azsufficient concentration of calcium ions (about 10^{-6} molar), and it is turned on and off by the release of calcium from, and uptake of calcium ions into, an intracellular compartment, which is separate from the main part of the cell containing the contractile proteins. This special compartment for calcium storage is called the sarcoplasmic reticulum, and it is bounded by a membrane containing a special protein capable of transporting calcium ions from the sarcoplasm—which is the main part of the fibre and contains the actin and myosin rods—to the interior of the sarcoplasmic reticulum, from which the calcium ions cannot normally escape.

This calcium-pumping protein does work by scavenging calcium ions from the sarcoplasm and concentrating them within the sarcoplasmic reticulum. It therefore also requires an energy source. As with contraction, the energy is provided by the hydrolysis of ATP. The calcium pumping by the membrane of the sarcoplasmic reticulum can account for the normally relaxed state of a muscle fibre and for relaxation following a contraction. What events lead to a release of calcium ions into the sarcoplasm and thereby to a contraction?

Muscles (with the important exception of the heart and visceral muscles) contract only when there are nerve impulses in the nerve fibres which run from the spinal cord to the muscle. Skeletal muscle contraction is initiated and controlled entirely by the brain and spinal cord by impulses in these motor nerve fibres. All movements, whether skilled and voluntary or postural and apparently automatic, are organized and initiated in the central nervous system, and a nerve going to a muscle is the pathway by which executive instructions for contraction are passed to the muscle fibres and by which sense organs in the muscle (muscle spindles) signal information to the central nervous system about the results of the contraction and the effects of external loads on the muscle. The nerve contains many nerve fibres carrying impulses to the muscle and a separate set of fibres carrying nerve impulses from the muscle spindle to the spinal cord. The nature of these nerve impulses is the same, but the directions and fibres in which they travel as well as their purposes differ.

Impulses in nerve fibres going to a muscle produce from the end of each nerve fibre, where it is in close contact with a muscle fibre (at the neuromuscular junction), the release of a small molecule, acetylcholine. The release of acetylcholine is brought about by a small entry of calcium ions into the nerve terminal, resulting from the propagation of the nerve impulse into the terminal.

Acetylcholine has the role of a chemical transmitter because it is released by the nerve terminal and reacts with a special receptor protein in the membrane of the muscle fibre. As a result of this transmitter–receptor interaction, a propagated electrical change occurs in the entire surface membrane of the muscle fibre, and this action potential in the muscle fibre is very much akin to the nerve impulse in the nerve fibre. The acetylcholine has served to bridge the gap at the neuromuscular junction between the propagating electrochemical changes in the nerve fibre and the very similar propagating electrochemical changes in the surface of muscle fibre. In the case of the muscle fibre, its surface includes a network of very fine tubules which are invaginated from the outer surface of the fibre and ramify in the entire cross-section and length of the fibre interior. By means of this transverse tubular system the electrical changes initiated at the neuromuscular junction spread rapidly to all parts of the volume of the fibre; the transverse tubular system enables contraction to be started more or less synchronously in the entire muscle fibre. Not only do the transverse tubules extend throughout the fibres, but they also make special and intimate contact with parts of the sarcoplasmic reticulum. Just as the nerve fibre contacts the muscle fibre at a special neuromuscular junction, so the transverse tubule comes very close to the sarcoplasmic reticulum at a recognizable structure called a triad junction.

We know in some detail about the release and role of acetylcholine at the neuromuscular junction; our knowledge of the physiological events at the triad is as yet sketchy. But we do know that an appropriate electrical change at the wall of the transverse tubule at the triad results in the rapid release of stored calcium ions from the sarcoplasmic reticulum and therefore triggers a contraction of the fibre.

We have traced the sequence of events between the spinal cord and the contraction of a muscle fibre, but this tells us nothing about the organization of a coordinated movement. We can say that any voluntary movement has its origin in the cerebral cortex. Such a statement begs many questions. One can, however, within the central nervous system trace pathways of nerve fibres in which impulses give rise to muscular movements. In a very general way there are two kinds of pathway in the spinal cord which can cause muscles to contract. Descending impulses from the brain may directly excite the nerve cell (motor neuron) in the spinal cord whose main process is the nerve fibre going to a group of muscle fibres in a muscle. Alternatively, descending impulses may excite the motor neurons whose fibres go to special muscle fibres which form part of the muscle spindles. In a normal muscle there are so few of these spindle muscle fibres that they themselves generate no detectable tension in the muscle, but their contraction increases the frequency of

nerve impulses going from the spindle to the spinal cord. These impulses in turn may be able to excite the main motor neurons and make the muscle contract. Stretching a muscle also increases the frequency of impulses from a muscle spindle in that muscle and can produce a contraction which resists the stretch. It is possible, too, that the sensitivity of the motor neurons to the incoming signals from the muscle spindles may be under the control of the higher parts of the central nervous system, providing a variable gain to the feedback pathway made up of the muscle spindle and its sensory nerve fibre.

Any actual muscular movement probably results from complicated temporal sequences of descending impulses; these play with varying intensities on the neurons which send fibres to the ordinary muscle fibres and to the spindle muscle fibres. Many parts of the brain interact and cooperate in the generation of any particular movement or sequence of movements. Interference with the functioning of the cerebral cortex, the basal ganglia and internal capsule, and the cerebellum diminishes motor performance in varying but characteristic ways; however, the precise roles of each part are still matters of speculation. One can describe in some detail the cellular and even molecular events associated with muscular action, but gaps in the account are more obvious when it concerns the role of the mind, or even of the brain, in originating and organizing movement.   RHA

Walsh, E. G. (1992). *Muscles, Masses and Motion.*

music, psychology of. Music has existed in all human cultures, as far as we know, and all scale systems are based on the octave, which suggests a neurological factor. This suggestion is supported by the fact that animals conditioned to respond to a certain pitch will do so almost equally to its octave, whereas the intervening notes will evoke either much less response or none at all. However, only the Western tonal system originated in the Pythagorean division of the octave into intervals according to the frequency ratios of small whole numbers by which the harmonic series of overtones in a complex tone are related. This ratio basis of the 'chord in nature' was given theological significance and determined the early history of concerted music, which developed from octave ensemble (ratio 2 : 1), to perfect fifth (3 : 2), perfect fourth (4 : 3), and major third (5 : 4). These intervals occur in the first four overtones of the series and were deemed consonant. After the great development of polyphonic music their ratios were adjusted to very complex ones in the 18th-century compromise of equal temperament tuning, yet our experience of the tension of dissonance and the repose of consonance survives in these newer complex interval ratios. Moreover, people prefer an octave tuned slightly larger than the exact 2 : 1 ratio, whether of pure tones (Ward 1954) or complex tones (Sundberg and

Lindquist 1973), and this applies whether they are trained in the Western tonal system or in the Indian system of twenty-two *śrutis* (microtones) to the octave (Burns 1974). Sensory theories of consonance, which attribute it to the ear's special sensitivity to the harmonic series, must reckon with these anomalies, and also with all the non-harmonic, complex ratio scale systems of other cultures. Thus, psychologists recognize that ultimately they must span the chasm between psychoacoustics and ethnomusicology. They must also endeavour to account for the whole response to music, not only sensory and cognitive, but also emotional and aesthetic. This latter task is beset with difficulties of method, and at present the main concern is with perception and memory in the Western tonal system, and its later development (using the same intervals) towards atonality.

In seeking to understand how the listener makes sense of music, should psychologists treat it as a set of arbitrary conventions (as David Hilbert views mathematics), or as a description of reality (as *Plato sees both mathematics and music), or as a property of mind (as Chomsky regards language)? All three approaches are essential, since all three characteristics—pattern-structural, acoustic, and grammatical—play their part; moreover they function interdependently in musical perception. Though a musical grammar may have been culturally evolved, acoustic characteristics and the constraints of performance will have contributed to its formation. That we perceive music phrase by phrase is not only because of repeated practice in hearing conventional design, but also because phrase length, as in sentence structure, has been historically constrained by what can be managed in one breath. The human auditory system evolved not only to be receptive (as are those of other species) to the sounds of nature, but also apparently to be 'wired for speech'. Vowel perception, like that of musical pitch and timbre, depends on the spectral characteristics of the complex waveform. Even so, perception phoneme by phoneme is not totally an acoustic process, for it also depends on knowledge of phonological constraints. In both speech and music, this 'wiring' for sequential processing of meaningful acoustic events must form the basis for the subsequent, more specialized expansion of perceptual skill through experience.

1. Music as pattern
2. Music and psychoacoustics
3. Music as language
4. Music and performance

1. Music as pattern

The Hilbertian approach is relevant here, since the brain is biased towards detecting regularities, the non-random organization of pattern, irrespective of sense modality. Experiments on auditory temporal pattern (Garner 1974, Jones 1978) treat music as arbitrary design, evoking perception of features such as symmetry, repetition, and imitation, which occur also in other non-musical symbolic or visual design. The span of short-term memory sets a limit to the perception of auditory pattern; musical palindromes are difficult to perceive for this reason, whereas visual perception of bilateral symmetry is immediate. Listeners tend to impose structure and to discover or unconsciously apply the rule by which a pattern is defined. Formal transformations of melodies used in serial music are perceptible (depending on their length) in an ascending order of difficulty from exact repetition to inversion, retrograde, and retrograde inversion. Perceiving retrograde tunes is a particular tax upon short-term memory, and the strong salience of forward temporal order is apparent if one plays backwards the tape of a well-known piece, even one of equal note values, where rhythm plays no part. In experiments where subjects are asked to identify the starting point and the segmentation pattern of a sequence which is continually recurring, like auditory wallpaper, their perception tends to conform to *Gestalt principles of organization. Patterns of eight or ten recurring events, composed of only two pitch elements, seem to evoke a *figure-ground perception, sometimes reversible, as in an Escher picture. A slow tempo of presentation affords active coding into memory, whereas a fast one yields a more passively received Gestalt. The formal devices of composition are amenable to this approach, often presented by psychologists in terms of *information theory. But such an approach can give only an inadequate account of musical perception where it disregards the listener's use of an implicit tonal grammar in perceiving even quite simple melodies.

2. Music and psychoacoustics

The second approach, the acoustic one, is the study of constraints imposed upon the perceptibility of musical phrases by psychoacoustic factors. Throughout musical history these constraints have been intuitively respected or exploited by composers, even when not yet scientifically defined. For instance, tonal proximity in melodic steps is an important perceptual organizing principle. The ear requires some milliseconds of extra processing time to monitor large pitch intervals in melody. This need has been explained as due either to the 'critical band' (the theory that the ear functions neurally as a series of band-pass filters), or to the brain's momentary conflict between integrating the frequency change as one of pitch or of timbre (this also is a neurological theory). Palestrina and other 16th-century composers observed the rule that, after a melodic leap in polyphonic music, voice must return by stepwise motion within the compass of the leap—an intuitive recognition of the ear's need of extra steadying time. Even a well-known tune, when transposed note by note into disparate octave registers, becomes unrecognizable. Yet this very widely spaced layout is a character-istic device of 20th-century serial music, and either of the two psychoacoustic theories mentioned would suggest why it is notoriously difficult to perceive. The salience of tonal proximity in perceptual organization is also apparent when two tunes, each consisting of large ascending and descending leaps, are presented one to each ear (Deutsch 1975). They are heard as consecutive by the tonal proximity of the notes arriving alternately at each ear, and not, as might be expected, as a left ear tune and a right ear tune. A similar perception by tonal proximity which overrides that by separate sources occurs with the layout between violin parts in Tchaikovsky's Sixth Symphony (see Fig. 1).

J. S. Bach, in his solo violin partitas, exploits a related phenomenon now called 'auditory stream segregation' (McAdams and Bregman 1979), where alternating notes will appear to separate into two coexistent tunes, depending on the tempo and on the pitch separation between the alternate notes. An eight-note tune, continually recurring, will perceptually separate into more than two streams of ever more restricted frequency ranges: the faster the tempo, the more streams are heard. Prestissimo gives the experience of eight coexistent streams forming a continuous chord or an inharmonic timbre (see Fig. 2). However, streaming does depend on what is being

listened for, whether streaming itself or coherence, so it cannot be entirely attributed to neural factors. In some sequences, one of the eight notes may be 'captured' by either of two adjacent streams; the brain makes the best bet on the basis either of tonal proximity or of harmonic pleasingness. This latter criterion, however unconsciously it is used, reflects the listener's internalized musical grammar, derived from past experience, which will affect his performance in all experimental tasks, however musically neutral they may be. In general, the validity of explaining perception as due to acoustic rather than attentional processes rests on the experimenter's selection of subjects, how rigorously he distinguishes among non-musicians, musicians, those with absolute pitch, and acoustic engineers, for experience endows each group with demonstrably different coding processes.

The drawback of many psychoacoustic experiments hitherto has been their endeavour to regard perception as context free. Furthermore, the functions—amplitude, duration, frequency, and spectral complexity of the waveform—of the four main attributes of music—loudness, rhythm, pitch, and timbre—have often been treated independently of each other. This has perpetuated the philosophical notion of 'raw sense data'. For music the notion originated in the Pythagorean naive realism concerning sensory coding, which assumed that sensory

Fig. 1. A section of the violin parts of Tchaikovsky's Sixth Symphony, showing **a** the music as it is actually played, and **b** how it is perceived by the listener.

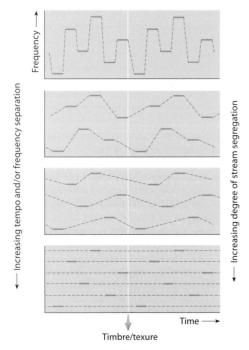

Increasing tempo and/or frequency separation →

Frequency →

Time →

Timbre/texure

Increasing degree of stream segregation →

Fig. 2. The decomposition of an acoustic sequence into smaller and smaller perceptual streams as the frequency separation between the tones or the tempo of the sequence increases. In the latter case, a point is ultimately reached where one can no longer perceive individual tonal events; a texture or timbre is heard instead.

processes exactly matched physical events in the world. It survived in the assumptions of classical music theory (e.g. that of Rameau and Tartini) and in *Helmholtz's model of the ear as a frequency analyser which coded each discriminable pitch by its specific nerve. Combination or difference tones were thought to be manufactured in the waveform in the ear, rather than neurally. But the four attributes are by no means independent; loudness also depends on frequency, pitch is affected by amplitude, and timbre by frequency. Paul Divenyi (1971) shows that perception of time intervals is affected by the frequency separation between notes, and this has obvious importance for rhythm. Then also, there is no clear distinction between pitch and timbre, but rather a continuous dimension from the unequivocal pitch of pure tones to the spectral inharmonicity of church bells (though their fundamental pitch is distinguishable), to the vague 'pitchiness' of noise within a narrow band of wavelength (Erickson 1975). Timbre is of course multidimensional, being also affected by fluctuations of harmonics or of pitch (in vibrato), and by the non-pitched starting noises of instruments, or 'transients'. A similar continuous

dimension can be traced from the single complex tone to the chord, for if a single harmonic of a complex tone is sufficiently amplified it separates from the fundamental, and a chord is heard. This property is exploited in the chant of a Tibetan monk when he sings alone in two-part harmony (Smith et al. 1965).

The fact that the fundamental may be perceived when no energy is present at its frequency level, and that the three or four adjacent harmonics which best give rise to this percept fall within a certain middle frequency range (the 'existence region'), whatever the fundamental involved, totally alters the picture of sensory coding inherited from Helmholtz. He held that we have to learn to combine the separately received harmonics of a complex tone, yet most people are unable to regain Helmholtz's supposed primal state of hearing even the first five harmonics separately (the rest of the higher ones, the 'residue', are not separately distinguishable in any case). The problem is to explain how we hear the components of sound as 'belonging' together, whether in hearing the harmonics of a complex tone as fused, or in hearing distinctly each separate stream of all the orchestral instruments in single waveform from a mono loudspeaker. How far does this ability depend on innate neural mechanisms which fuse the spectral components, and how far on mechanisms which have been built up by repeated experience? The limited resolution power of the ear is a psychoacoustic factor which is particularly important to the perception of rhythm. Although hearing is the most accurate temporal sense, there are nevertheless limits (in milliseconds) to the perceptibility of synchrony, successiveness, and 'flutter', i.e. rapid repetition.

The rise of computer and electronically synthesized music has greatly expanded the vocabulary of music so that, as the American composer Milton Babbitt has remarked, the limits are no longer those of sound production, but rather those of the human auditory system. Rapid changes of timbre are difficult to follow, just as speech recorded syllable by syllable in different voices is incomprehensible. Richard Warren and his colleagues (Warren and Obusek 1972, Warren 1974) have shown that subjects have great difficulty in identifying the order of recurring sequences of sounds which are unrelated in timbre (for instance, a high tone, a hiss, a lower tone, and a buzz) although they are presented at a slower speed than that necessary for auditory temporal resolution. Yet if the two tones are placed adjacently within the four-event sequence, performance is improved. That continuity of timbre is important to perceptual organization is also apparent where a single, pure tone is interrupted by noise, the cessation of the tone being exactly synchronized with the start of the noise, and vice versa (see Fig. 3). The pure tone is heard as continuing through the noise, much as in vision one object is seen as existing

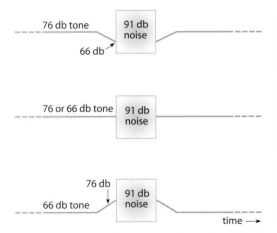

Fig. 3. The stimuli used by Bregman and Dannenbring (1977) consisted of a pure tone interrupted by noise. The level of the tone leading into and coming out of the noise burst was varied as shown. The greatest degree of continuity was found in the centre case where there was no change in level.

behind another by which it is occluded. (See ILLUSIONS.) Computer music is easily perceived in the degree to which the sounds resemble or are systematic near distortions of natural sounds. Composers of computer music not only are able to use these parameters of sound from experience but, in collaboration with psychologists, are also able to assess the reasons for the limits to the listeners' perceptual skills (IRCAM Reports).

3. Music as language

The third approach, the grammatical one, treats music as analogous to language, since music also is hierarchically organized and makes selective use of the same neurally close-knit system of voice, ear, and brain, though without denotative meaning, music is both syntactic and communicative (of subjective states). Its two linguistic elements, melodic phrasing, which reflects the intonations of speech, and the formal, syntactic devices of composition, imply that the listener understands both the expressiveness of contour and the 'argument' of musical form. Even the musically untutored listener acquires a musical grammar, a system of rules unconsciously applied, by which he makes sense of music and would detect 'wrong notes' in an unfamiliar work in the tonal idiom, though unable to name the notes or to state the rules. This grammar implies that the single note is characterized not only by its tone height, and its chroma (all B flats sound alike), but also by its grammatic function (e.g. whether it is, at a particular point, functioning as a tonic, leading note, or unaccented passing note). As a word in a sentence is defined by its context, even more so is a note in music.

Formal theories of music and artificial intelligence models seek to define how the listener correctly perceives rhythm, key, tonal modulations, and thematic organization. Some models are based on traditional music theory and linguistics (Winograd 1968, Longuet-Higgins 1971), or on Gestalt principles (Tenney and Polansky 1980). A more recent theory (Lerdahl and Jackendoff 1981) covers formal, acoustic, and quasi-linguistic aspects, and accommodates the fact that a musical phrase might admit of more than one correct parsing by distinguishing 'well-formedness' rules from those 'preference' rules which can account for conscious and unconscious organizing principles of musical perception. Its emphasis on the interactions between rhythmic and tonal aspects provides a useful antidote to some research where such interactions have hitherto been disregarded.

Experiments show that, as with language, salience of originally perceived or imposed rhythmic groupings is very strong in subsequent recognition memory, and tunes ending in cadence are easier to remember than those which are harmonically inconclusive. Most musicians would agree that tonal grammar is dominant, that it is not easy to eradicate entirely one's tonal habits of listening when hearing non-tonal idioms.

However, the swiftly moving innovations in the history of tonal music, particularly of the last two centuries, undermine the analogy of its grammar with that of language, which is anchored by semantic meaning. Any ancient Greek who conversed with Socrates could equally well have done so with Wittgenstein, but having heard only the musical grammar of the Delphic hymns he would not naturally make sense of Boulez, Beethoven, or even Byrd. Musical style and comprehensibility have increasingly depended upon the listener's developing tolerance of protracted dissonance through his grammatical understanding of its possible resolution in consonance, implicit in his familiarity with past and present idioms. That his long-term memory store, upon which present comprehension depends, is more idiosyncratic than it could ever be for language presents a difficulty to the psychologist in testing general theories of musical grammar.

In psycholinguistics the experimenter tests a linguistic theory which treats grammaticality as paramount (i.e. whether a string of words constitutes a sentence), whereas ambiguity plays a much lesser role in the whole theory (i.e. whether a sentence is susceptible of more than one meaning and consequently of more than one structural description). But phrases in music frequently admit of differing interpretations and may be ambiguous. Indeed, the performing musician's enduring task is to choose, between the various possibilities of phrasing, the one that to him seems to represent the composer's message most faithfully and eloquently, and his interpretation is to a large extent judged by its internal coherence. Thus the psychologist of music must work with a grammar which can accommodate the latitude of perhaps many equally 'correct' parsings of a musical structure.

The three approaches outlined here, each concerned with an essential factor operative in musical cognition, remain at present more experimentally distinct than is warranted by their interrelation in the perception of musical structure. In making sense of music, its attributes of contour, interval, tonality, modulation, rhythm, symmetry, repetition, inversion, imitation, and the like must in turn and at different moments assume different shares of the total cognitive process, and must influence the nature of perceptual grouping or coding processes. Exactly how this fluctuating process operates remains the fundamental question.

4. Music and performance

Musical perception and performance are both dependent on short-term memory and expectancy. 'The practically cognised present is no knife-edge but a saddleback, with a certain breadth of its own, on which we sit perched, and from which we look in two directions into time' (William *James, 1890). From this perch the performer monitors and constantly corrects the flow, shape, and tone quality as it occurs, by a highly integrated system of coexistent codes: auditory, visual, and kinaesthetic. Implicit vocalizing may underlie musical perception, much as Liberman holds that we perceive speech by 'internal generation' at some neural level below that of overt response. But the acquired codes of the musician instrumentalist are more complex, including visual ones for musical notation and instrumental fingering, and kinaesthetic ones for fingering and more general muscular movement. Kinaesthetic imagery for one's own instrument can also underlie one's perception while only listening. Karl *Lashley (1951) cites the musician's performance when he emphasizes that all human serial behaviour (speech, gesture, and perceptual motor skill) is grammatically structured, on hierarchically ordered levels of organization. Well-practised sequences occurring too fast for monitoring at the level of individual events are perceived and executed at a higher level of pre-planned groups. In music (unlike, for instance, Morse code) the flow of 'information' to be monitored or executed is not constant. Not only the number of consecutive events but also the denseness of harmonic texture may vary from moment to moment, yet the performer maintains a steady flow of action and perception through these variations in information load. The basis here is principally the intrinsic feedback of the nervous system, amplified by the extrinsic feedback of sight and sound, e.g. of the conductor's beat and the sound of other instruments.

Although the appropriate model for research on performance may well be the cybernetic one, it is not surprising that little has yet been done to tease out the components and interactions in this very complex skill. Seashore's research (1938) on intonation and vibrato anticipated the present experimental technique of wiring up musical instruments to computers which record the infinitesimal variations in tone and rhythm that distinguish live performance from computer deadpan accuracy, and one artist from another. Analysis of these recordings shows the variation to be consistent in respect of some general principles of rhythmic displacement, or differences of intonation according to the function of a particular note within a tonality. Some experiments on sight-reading indicate that good sight-readers take in and hold in short-term memory (the eye–hand span) phrase-length chunks (see CHUNKING), rather than a steady bar-by-bar succession of chunks at the rate of their performance.

A promising source of evidence as to how the components of musical skill may be integrated is the clinical evidence on amusia, the breakdown of a previously established capability for music due to brain pathology. Although there are strong indications that in right-handed people music is stored in the non-dominant hemisphere of the brain, this is by no means invariably so, nor are musical and linguistic functions entirely lateralized. There are many mental abilities common to both speech and language, for instance perception of rhythm and of temporal order, and these seem to be processed in the dominant hemisphere. In left-handers, either hemisphere can mediate many musical functions, and in some professional musicians a dominant life work may be stored in the dominant hemisphere. The distinctions between the roles of each hemisphere have been oversimplified in investigations hitherto, although broadly they are apparent. Nevertheless, research which correlates a patient's performance with damage to a particular brain structure is gradually building up a picture which illuminates our understanding of the nature of musical skill.

An equally promising area is that of developmental psychology, an area that has been largely centred on aptitude tests. The early acquisition of the unconscious ability to operate the rules of musical grammar can be as rich a source of psychological theory as that of the child's acquisition of language. Teplov (1966) finds that children will complete half-finished musical phrases presented to them, with a fine sense of their tonality, rhythmic character, and implied harmonic cadence. The special aptitude of absolute pitch, the possession of which correlates with the early age at which the names of the notes were learned, illustrates the power of category systems in expanding musical intelligence. If more parents were equipped to teach note names as easily as colour names, it is possible that music might more easily resemble an artistic lingua franca.

5. Music and aesthetics

Most musicians would agree that, as well as the sensory and cognitive aspects we have discussed, aesthetic and emotional factors also play a part in perceiving and remembering music, but it is less easy to see how these can be approached experimentally. The belief that memory for melodic contour and implicit harmony is allied to its affective character is well described by Deryck Cooke (1958), whose theory gives general principles why, for instance, we all experience, with Browning, 'those minor thirds so plaintive, Sixths diminished sigh on sigh'. This characterization is, of course, dependent not on pitch intervals alone, but also on rhythm, phrasing, and tempo (for instance, descending couplet phrasing is a particularly plaintive use of minor thirds). The music of non-Western cultures, based on quite different scale systems, no doubt has different aesthetic and emotional significances which are nevertheless experienced to similar degrees in those cultures. In Western music, the factor of musical imagery is partly understood universally by musical people, and is partly idiosyncratic to each composer and listener. Composers have self-consistent mood associations with key colour and timbre. Bach's use of the brazen timbre of the D major trumpet associated that key, for him, with jubilance, and the D major open string basis of tone colour enhances this characterization for most composers and hence for most listeners.

Hitherto experiments on aesthetic aspects have centred largely on subjects' ratings for a certain attribute, or for the more general 'pleasingness'; they were often directed to whole works, or to very large segments of them, rather than to phrases (Schoen 1927). There are also correlations of measures of autonomic arousal with hearing or performing certain music, including one such study with the conductor Herbert von Karajan as subject (Harrer and Harrer 1977). Sometimes responses are related to a measure of the information content of a work (Berlyne 1974). Psychologists may well feel that judgements of whole works do not yield data that is specific enough, and they may be daunted by the great number of confounding variables, such as social, cultural, or fashion determinants of taste.

As yet no systematic experimental study of Cooke's theory has emerged relating it to musical education, though a pilot study (Gabriel 1978) showed that, for 22 non-musician students, Cooke's characterizations of musical phrases were not experienced. This evoked a music theorist's objection to the theory itself (Cazden 1979), and another to the validity of using 'deadpan' sine wave sequences as an experimental test of a theory concerning real live music (Nettheim 1979). To these one must add an objection to the restricted choice of subjects. A study using real live music, and musician subjects, to test Leonard Meyer's theory of the perception of certain melodic characteristics which he calls 'archetypes' attributes the variability of response to the degree of complexity in the underlying hierarchic phrase structure (Rosner and Meyer 1981). It would seem that experimental musical aesthetics may have to await further progress in the rapprochement between experimental psychology and the theories of musical grammar discussed earlier.

Is it possible for the analytic methods of science to contribute a comprehensive account of the flexible, living performance and enjoyment of music? At the sensory and cognitive levels there has been substantial and illuminating progress. On the other hand, at present the aesthetic level of the musician's use of imagery, particularly with contour, key colour, tone quality, and emotional association, seems, like the painter's idiosyncratic choice of palette, to be outside the realm of experimental psychology.

NSP

Berlyne, D. (1974). *Studies in the New Experimental Aesthetics.*

Bregman, A., and Dannenbring, G. (1977). 'Auditory continuity and amplitude edges'. *Canadian Journal of Psychology*, 31.

Burns, E. (1974). 'Octave adjustment by non-Western musicians'. *Journal of the Acoustical Society of America*, 56.

Cazden, N. (1979). 'Can verbal meanings inhere in fragments of music?' *Psychology of Music*, 7/2.

Cooke, D. (1958). *The Language of Music.*

Deutsch, D. (1975). 'Musical illusions'. *Scientific American*, 233/4.

Divenyi, P. (1971). 'The rhythmic perception of micromelodies'. In Gordon, R. (ed.), *Research in the Psychology of Music.*

Erickson, R. (1975). *Sound Structure in Music.*

Gabriel, C. (1978). 'An experimental study of Deryck Cooke's theory of music and meaning'. *Psychology of Music*, 16/1.

Garner, W. (1974). *The Processing of Information and Structure.*

Harrer, G., and Harrer, H. (1977). 'Music, emotion and autonomic function'. In Critchley, M., and Henson, J. (eds.), *Music and the Brain.*

Helmholtz, H. (1863). *On the Sensations of Tone* (trans. 1954).

IRCAM Reports, Pompidou Centre, Paris.

James, W. (1890). *Principles of Psychology.*

Jones, M. Reiss (1978). 'Auditory patterns: studies in the perception of structure'. In Cartarette and Friedman, *Handbook of Perception*, 8.

Lashley, K. (1951). 'The problem of serial order in behavior'. In Jeffries, L. (ed.), *Cerebral Mechanisms in Behavior.*

Lerdahl, F., and Jackendoff, R. (1981). *A Generative Theory of Tonal Music.*

Longuet-Higgins, C. (1971). 'On interpreting Bach'. *Machine Intelligence*, 16.

McAdams, S., and Bregman, A. (1979). 'Hearing musical streams'. *Computer Music Journal*, 3/4.

Nettheim, N. (1979). 'Comment on a paper by Gabriel on Cooke's theory'. *Psychology of Music*, 17/2.

Rameau, J. P. (1750). *Treatise on Harmony* (trans. 1971).

Rosner, B., and Meyer, L. (1981). *Melodic Processes and the Perception of Music.*

Schoen, M. (1927). *The Effects of Music.*

Seashore, C. (1938). *The Psychology of Music* (repr. 1967).

Smith, H., Stevens, K., and Tomlinson, R. (1965). 'On an unusual mode of chanting by certain Tibetan lamas'. *Journal of the Acoustical Society of America*, 61/5.

Sundberg, J., and Lindquist, J. (1973). 'Musical octaves and pitch'. *Journal of the Acoustical Society of America*, 54.

Tenney, J., and Polansky, L. (1980). 'Temporal Gestalt perception in music'. *Journal of Music Theory*.

Teplov, B. (1966). *Psychologie des aptitudes musicales*.

Tobias, J. (1970, 1972). *Foundations of Modern Auditory Theory*, 2 vols.

Ward, W. D. (1954). 'Subjective musical pitch'. *Journal of the Acoustical Society of America*, 26.

Warren, R. (1974). 'Auditory temporal discrimination by trained listeners'. *Cognitive Psychology*, 6.

—— and Obusek, C. (1972). 'Identification of temporal order within auditory sequences'. *Perception and Psychophysics*, 12.

Winograd, T. (1968). 'Linguistics and the computer analysis of tonal harmony'. *Journal of Music Theory*, 12.

music perception: history of thought. The study of music perception has a fascinating history. From the time of Pythagoras in the 6th century BC, thinking on the subject was heavily influenced by two factors. One was a profound distrust in the evidence of our senses (particularly our sense of *hearing), and the other was an obsession with numerology. As Boethius, the leading music theorist of the Middle Ages and a strong follower of Pythagoras, wrote: 'For what need is there of speaking further concerning the error of the senses when this same faculty of sensing is neither equal in all men, nor at all times equal within the same man? Therefore anyone vainly puts his trust in a changing judgement since he aspires to seek the truth.'

Matters were made even worse by the strong theoretical link, also stemming from the Pythagoreans, between music and astronomy. It was argued that the planets as they moved must surely produce sounds which would vary with their speeds and their distances from the earth. It was further argued that the distances between the earth and the different planets were such that the combination of sounds emitted must form a harmony. Fig. 1 shows the Pythagorean view of the distances of the planets relative to each other, and the musical intervals formed thereby. (This was the prevailing view in ancient and medieval times.) The distance from the earth to the moon formed a whole tone, from the moon to Mercury a semitone, from Mercury to Venus another semitone, from Venus to the sun a tone and a half, from the sun to Mars a tone, from Mars to Jupiter a semitone, from Jupiter to Saturn a semitone, and finally from Saturn to the Supreme Heaven a semitone.

Considerable discussion centred on the issue of why, if the heavenly bodies do indeed produce this harmony, we cannot hear it. One suggestion, fielded by Censorinus (*fl.* c.238), was that the loudness of this sound is so great as to cause deafness. Another, more sophisticated view was that since this sound is present at all times, and since sound is perceived only in contrast to silence, we are not aware of its presence (perhaps this was one of the first suggestions concerning auditory adaptation).

At all events, the link between music and astronomy in ancient and medieval times was so great that the scientific half of the programme of higher education developed into the Quadrivium: the related studies of geometry, arithmetic, astronomy, and music. And even very recently Paul Hindemith in his book *A Composer's World* endorsed this association, writing that Johannes Kepler's 'three basic laws of planetary motion, expounded at the beginning of the seventeenth century, could perhaps not have been discovered, without a serious backing of music theory'.

The Copernican revolution did, however, weaken the link between music and astronomy, since it became clear that the planets did not in fact form a harmony. Nevertheless, the strong rationalistic and numerological approach to musical issues persisted. A few enlightened thinkers pleaded for empiricism (notable among these was Galileo's father Vicenzo Galilei). However, their writings had little impact; and Hermann von *Helmholtz in 1862 felt impelled to express his concern on this matter in his book *On the Sensations of Tone*. He wrote: 'Up to the present time, the apparent *connection* of acoustics and music has been wholly external, and may be regarded as an expression given to the feeling that such a connection must exist, rather than its actual formulation.' And yet, despite Helmholtz's writings, the numerological approach has prevailed right up to very recent times.

However, we are now witnessing a most interesting phenomenon. The advent of electronic music and the increasing use of the computer as a compositional tool has caused a profound change in the thinking of many music theorists, particularly those who are also composers. If they are to make effective use of this new technology they need to obtain answers to various questions in perceptual psychology. For instance, they need to know the characteristics of a complex sound spectrum that result in a single sound image, and those that result in several simultaneous but distinct sound images. Given that sounds of any spectral composition can now be generated, they

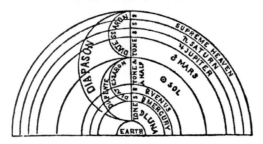

Fig. 1. Pythagorean view of the universe, in musical intervals.

wish to characterize the dimensions underlying the perception of timbre, so that they can create sounds that vary systematically along these dimensions. Given the potential to generate any sequence of sounds, they need to develop an understanding of the perceptual and mnemonic constraints of the listener, so that their music will not fall on uncomprehending ears.

This same technological development has provided psychologists with the tools with which to explore the mechanisms underlying our processing of music. Such studies, apart from their implications for music, are of considerable value to our understanding of perceptual systems, mechanisms of memory and attention, and even abstract cognitive activity. Music is unique in that it involves an elaborate and highly organized processing system where verbal labelling plays a very minor role.

Given this new interest on the part of both psychologists and musicians, we are at present witnessing an explosion of collaborative work between the two disciplines. This type of interaction is quite recent, but already it has considerably advanced our understanding of the brain mechanisms underlying music perception.

See also MUSIC, PSYCHOLOGY OF.   DD

Boethius. *De institutione musica.* Trans. C. M. Bower (1967), *Boethius' The Principles of Music.*

Hawkins, Sir J. (1853). *A General History of the Science and Practice of Music* (repr. 1963).

Helmholtz, H. von (1862). *On the Sensations of Tone* (4th edn., 1877; trans. A. J. Ellis, 1885; repr. 1954).

Hindemith, P. (1961). *A Composer's World.*

Hunt, F. V. (1978). *Origins in Acoustics.*

Myers, Charles Samuel (1873–1946). British psychologist, born in London. He qualified in medicine at Cambridge but his interests lay in the natural sciences. After a brief period as professor of psychology at King's College,

London, he returned to Cambridge, where he took over the lectureship in experimental psychology from W. H. R. *Rivers. With the assistance of members of his family, he founded the Cambridge psychological laboratory, of which he became director in 1913. His *Text Book of Experimental Psychology* (1909; 3rd edn. 1925) was for long the standard introduction for students of psychology at Cambridge, though it was criticized in some quarters for the perhaps excessive weight which the author placed on the special senses, psychophysics, and the work of Hermann *Ebbinghaus.

During the First World War, Myers served as a physician in the army. Many years later, in 1940, he published *Shell-Shock in France, 1914–18* based upon his wartime experiences. After the war he moved to London and founded the National Institute of Industrial Psychology, of which he was the first director.

Myers's books include *Mind and Work* (1920), *Industrial Psychology in Great Britain* (1926), and *In the Realm of Mind* (1937).   OLZ

Myers, Frederic William Henry (1843–1901). British writer, born at Keswick. He was a Fellow of Trinity College, Cambridge, where he became friendly with Edmund Gurney and Henry Sidgwick, who became the first president of the Society for Psychical Research (SPR) in 1882. Myers was interested in *spiritualism several years before the SPR was founded. Professionally, he was a school inspector, and a prolific if not particularly good poet. His magnum opus is the remarkable *Human Personality and its Survival of Bodily Death* (2 vols., 1903). Here he discusses hundreds of cases of phenomena such as 'fantasms of the dead', 'automatism', 'trance states', 'possession', and 'disintegrations of personality', as well as hypnotism.   RLG

Hall, T. H. (1964). *The Strange Case of Edmund Gurney.*

N

nativism. The doctrine that certain capacities or abilities, especially of sense perception, are inherited rather than acquired by learning.

It can be surprisingly difficult to establish what is inherited and what learned, for much that is inherited develops, sometimes over several years, by maturation, and this is hard to distinguish from development by experience and learning. Often there is a mixture of maturation from inheritance and learning from experience—as in the infant's development of crawling and walking. Even for *language development in children there may be innateness, gradual maturing, and—as obviously there is—learning from experience of adult speech. As is well known, Noam Chomsky has suggested that natural human languages are based on a common 'deep structure', which is inherited and makes the infant's learning task possible (see LANGUAGE: CHOMSKY'S THEORY). Part of the evidence for inherited deep structure is indeed the apparent impossibility of the task with which the infant is faced, that of discovering the structure of language.

There is a similar controversy over how much visual and other *perception develops in the individual by maturation from inherited brain structures and how far (if at all) the physiology is developed or modified by early experience. It has been suggested that linguistic deep structure might be a pre-human, pre-language, perceptual classifying system developed by natural selection, over hundreds of millions of years, for perceiving and behaving appropriately to various kinds of objects. If that is so, it would explain how the deep structure could have developed so rapidly, on the biological time scale, for human language.

See also INNATE IDEAS.   RLG

Necker cube. A drawing of a wire cube (drawn without perspective) which spontaneously reverses in depth (Fig. 1). It was first described by the Swiss naturalist and crystallographer L. A. Necker in a letter to Sir David *Brewster in 1832. Necker discovered it while looking at rhomboid crystals with a microscope and drawing them: the drawings switched in depth and no longer seemed to compare with the crystals as seen with the microscope. There are many other depth-ambiguous figures.

A true wire cube will also reverse in depth, when it will stand up bizarrely on a corner, and rotate as the observer

moves—following every movement, though at twice the speed. It also changes in shape.

Necker's drawing was not quite the familiar cube (Fig. 1). As Boring (1942) points out, his original figure is reversed more easily than the cube: 'for the rhomboid stands upon an edge and is prejudiced by neither perspective, whereas that cube is seen more easily flat upon the ground ("M near") than in the alternative peculiar uplifted position ("N near")'. John Harris (1979) found this for the Schröder staircase—tending to remain stable when drawn in perspective—though perspective Necker cubes will still sometimes reverse. Evidently the perceptual system dynamically seeks alternatives against considerable evidence for one 'hypothesis'.

Try holding a skeleton cube (made of wire, or matches glued together) in the hand, and wait for it to reverse (viewed with one eye if necessary) and slowly rotate it. As it rotates, the cube swings round visually in the opposite direction. It moves counter to touch and proprioception. This feels as though one's wrist has broken, though with no pain (Shopland and Gregory 1964). The counterrotation shows that vision is not essentially tied to touch, though it can be affected by touch. Why does the flip-reversed cube appear to rotate backwards to its real motion, and backwards also to the observer moving around it? Depth-reversed vision effectively reverses motion-parallax, as near and far are perceptually switched.

The reason for the shape-change of a flipped cube is significant. We may ask first: why *normally* does a skeleton cube look like a true cube—its near and far faces appear-

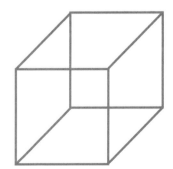

Fig. 1. Necker cube. This can be seen as switching spontaneously in depth, the front face reversing with the back face.

ing practically the same size, though they are very different on the retina? (One can see this by viewing the cube as a shadow, from a small source of light such as a candle. The shadow is a perfect perspective projection, and is precisely the form of the retinal image (whether reversed or not) given by the cube, yet it looks very different.) It is surprising that the unreversed wire cube appears with its near and further faces the same size, as there are no 'bottom up' cues for setting size constancy. The perspective *drawing* of the cube does not have these effects. What is the crucial difference between the *wire cube object* and the *drawing*? The difference is: the cube object is seen in realistic *depth*—the drawing is seen as flat, or in the curious pseudo-depth of pictures. We can show that this is a crucial difference by making the drawing appear in true depth, by removing the paper background. This can be done by drawing it in luminous paint, and viewing in the dark with one eye. Then it appears as strikingly three-dimensional, like a true cube, and will change shape when it flips in depth.

Such ambiguous objects are wonderfully useful as demonstrations for separating 'bottom-up' from 'top-down' visual processing. When the perception changes though there is no change of the sensory input, the change of appearance cannot be due to bottom-up processing. It must be set downwards by the prevailing perceptual hypothesis of what is near and what is far. This shows that size constancy can operate 'downwards' from the prevailing perception of depth, which is important for explaining many distortions, such as the *moon illusion.

See also ILLUSIONS. RLG

Boring, E. G. (1942). *Sensation and Perception in the History of Experimental Psychology*.

Gregory, R. L. (1963). 'Distortion of visual space as inappropriate constancy scaling'. *Nature*, 119.

——(1968). 'Perceptual illusions and brain models'. *Proceedings of the Royal Society of London*, 171.

——(1997). *Eye and Brain* (5th edn.).

Harris, J. P. (1979). 'The Schröder Staircase: a new perspective'. *Perception and Psychophysics*, 26.

Necker, L. A. (1832). 'Observations on some remarkable phaenomena seen in Switzerland; and an optical phaenomenon which occurs on viewing of a crystal or geometrical solid'. *Philsophical Magazine*, series 3 1.

Shopland, C., and Gregory, R. L. (1964). 'The effects of touch on a visually ambiguous three-dimensional figure'. *Quarterly Journal of Experimental Psychology*, 16.

negotiation. Negotiation, or bargaining, happens when two or more parties communicate in order to reach an agreement on a mutually acceptable outcome in a situation where they need jointly to achieve a goal that is not available to either party alone and their preferences for outcomes are usually negatively related, i.e. one party's gain is often the other party's loss. It is a complex, competitive, and interactive activity that is influenced by a variety of factors, including cognition, perception, emotion, motivation, and interpersonal skills, and the context in which the negotiation occurs.

The dominant framework for understanding fundamental negotiation strategy is the dual concerns model (Rubin, Pruitt, and Kim 1994). An early version of the dual concerns model was proposed as the Managerial Grid (Blake and Mouton 1964), and was reinterpreted by Thomas (1976). The model postulates that individuals in negotiation have two somewhat independent concerns: a concern for realizing one's own substantive outcomes in the negotiation, and a concern for helping the other party achieve their outcomes, usually in order to strengthen a positive working relationship with the other party. The strength of one's concerns on each of these two dimensions dictates one of five major strategies. *Contending* (i.e. competing or dominating) is the strategy to consider when one has a strong concern for one's own outcome and has little concern about the other's outcomes. Negotiators employing a contending strategy try to obtain the best outcome possible only for themselves. Negotiators using a *yielding* (i.e. accommodating or obliging) strategy show little interest in attaining their own outcomes but strongly care that the other party achieves their goals, possibly in order to build a stronger *future* relationship with the other party. The third strategy, *inaction* (i.e. avoiding), occurs when negotiators have little interest in achieving either their own outcomes or the other's outcomes and is equal to retreating or withdrawing from the negotiation. When negotiators show high concern for attaining their own outcomes and a high concern for whether the other party attains his or her outcomes, they pursue a *collaborative* or *problem-solving* strategy, in order to maximize their joint outcome and to reach a 'win–win' situation. Finally, negotiators pursue a *compromising* strategy when they display a moderate effort to pursue their own outcomes and a similarly moderate amount of effort to help the other party achieve his or her outcomes and strengthen the relationship (Lewicki et al. 2003).

Since parties negotiate largely to enhance their own outcomes, the two most common strategic approaches are competing (contending) and collaborating (problem solving). Thus, the dominant choice confronting the negotiator is whether the relationship with the other party is important or not. These two negotiation approaches are also called distributive (competitive or claiming value) vs. integrative (collaborative, problem solving, or creating value). In distributive bargaining, negotiators believe that there is a limited, controlled amount of key resources to be distributed—a 'fixed-pie' situation. One party's gain is anticipated to be at the cost of the other's. Moreover, each negotiator attempts to maximize his or her outcome at the expense of the other party, and assumes that no long-term relationship with the other party is desired. A classic prototype for a distributive bargaining process is the sale of a used automobile, where the seller tries to persuade the buyer to purchase the auto at the highest possible price and the buyer attempts to buy the auto at the lowest possible price. In order effectively to execute a distributive bargain, it is recommended that each party identify three key points. First, the party should have a target point (or a 'goal'), the point at which a negotiator would like to conclude negotiations. Second, negotiators should identify a resistance point or bottom line—the least acceptable deal he or she would accept and still consummate the negotiation. Finally, negotiators should set an opening offer, where they intend to begin the negotiation, and what they would consider to be the most optimistic settlement. As the process unfolds, parties exchange their initial offers, and then engage in a process of concessions as each moves towards their target, but go no further than their resistance point. The spread between the parties' resistance points is called the 'bargaining range' or 'settlement range'. When the buyer's resistance point is above the seller's (i.e. the lowest price the seller will accept is within the range of what the buyer will pay), any price in that bargaining range is acceptable to both parties and agreement can be reached. A fourth point that is important to parties in a distributive negotiation is their *alternative*—that is, another deal they could do away from the table with another party. Thus, a buyer probably has an alternative used car he can buy from another seller and the seller hopefully has an alternative buyer. Alternatives are important because they give the negotiator power to walk away from a negotiation when the emerging deal is not likely to be acceptable. Thus in distributive bargaining, the fundamental strategy for a negotiator is to push for a settlement close to the other party's resistance point, to persuade the other party to change his or her resistance point, to get the other party to think that this settlement is the best that is possible, and/or to convince the other party that one has a strong alternative available. Many books and articles have been written on the tactics and execution of this approach (see Lewicki et al. 2003).

When negotiators expect a future relationship with the other party, or wish to maximize the joint outcome between the parties, they are more likely to employ a collaborative negotiating approach. Because the parties have had a history of past interaction and expect to work with the other in the future, they should be less willing to act competitively, because this approach is likely to harm the relationship with the other. Instead, a collaborative (integrative) approach allows both parties to achieve their goals. The tactics of integrative negotiation include: a focus on needs and interests rather than positions; an effort to discover the interests of both sides; an open exchange of information and ideas; an effort to brainstorm and find creative ways to meet as many interests as possible; and a use of independent standards to determine whether the proposed settlement is fair (see Fisher, Ury, and Patton 1991, Lewicki et al. 2003). In an integrative bargaining situation, it is critical to generate mutual trust between parties to assure adequate information sharing and collaboration.

In either negotiation process, how negotiators perceive and frame a situation and an outcome has a huge influence on the negotiation process and reaction to the final outcome. The most scrutinized and understood framing effect is the gain–loss frame (Tversky and Kahneman 1981), in which an outcome can be perceived as a gain or loss compared to a reference outcome that is judged neutral. Decision theorists have found that people are more loss averse, i.e. the pain of losing the same amount of value exceeds the pleasure of gaining the same. Furthermore, in any given situation, there are almost always multiple possible reference points to compare to, therefore the same problem and outcome can be framed differently. Negotiations in which the outcomes are framed as losses tend to produce fewer concessions, reach fewer agreements, and perceive outcomes as less fair than negotiations in which the outcomes are framed as gains. Hence a successful negotiator should be able to understand both positive and negative framing of the situation and present it strategically to their opponent and at the same time avoid being framed by the opponent. There are other cognitive biases that influence negotiators' success. For example, many negotiators assume that all negotiations only involve a fixed pie and pit their own gain against the opponent's benefit. Consequently, many negotiators fail to explore integrative negotiation opportunities because of this 'fixed-pie belief'. Another bias is called the 'winner's curse'. When a negotiator makes an offer that is immediately accepted by the opponent, this response signals that the negotiator may have offered too much, which makes the negotiator feel discomfort about a negotiation victory that came too easily (Thompson 1998).

The outcome of a negotiation is also influenced greatly by each party's real or perceived power, which is the ability to influence the other party or bring about outcomes they desire. Common sources of power for a negotiator come from the information and expertise that may change the other party's point of view, the amount of control over resources, and the negotiator's legitimate power (rank or title of office). Another source of power derives from the negotiator's alternative (BATNA—best alternative to a negotiated agreement). Negotiators with attractive BATNAs can set higher reservation prices for themselves and have the power to walk away from the negotiation table when the offers are too low.

As in many other social interactions, negotiators should pay close attention to ethical standards. Ethics are rules or standards for what kind of behaviour is right or wrong in a negotiation situation. Ethics in negotiation are mostly about truth telling—how honest, candid, and disclosing a negotiator should be. Arriving at a clear, precise, effective negotiated agreement depends on the willingness of the parties to share accurate information about their own true preferences, priorities, and interests. At the same time, because negotiators may also be interested in maximizing their self-interest, they may want to disclose as little as possible about their positions. RJL/ChW

Blake, R. R., and Mouton, J. S. (1964). *The Managerial Grid: Key Orientations for Achieving Production through People.*

Fisher, R., Ury, W. L., and Patton, B. (1991). *Getting to Yes: Negotiating Agreement without Giving in* (2nd edn.).

Lewicki, R. J., Barry, B., Saunder, D. M., and Minton, J. W. (2003). *Negotiation* (4th edn.).

Rubin, J. Z., Pruitt, D. G., and Kim, S. H. (1994). *Social Conflict: Escalation, Stalemate, and Settlement.*

Thomas, K. W. (1976). 'Conflict and conflict management'. In Dunnette, M. D. (ed.), *Handbook of Industrial and Organizational Psychology.*

Thompson, L. (1998). *The Mind and Heart of the Negotiator.*

Tversky, A., and Kahneman, D. (1981). 'The framing of decisions and the psychology of choice'. *Science,* 211.

neo-haptic touch.

1. Diverse aspects of 'touch'
2. Being touched
3. Touching one's self
4. Neo-haptic touch

1. Diverse aspects of 'touch'

Touch is commonly regarded as the contact of some object with the body, together with the accompanying sensations aroused through receptors in the skin. Touch, however, is not to be seen as a unitary phenomenon but as a complex group of cutaneous senses which include responses to pressure, pain, temperature, and tickle. Moreover the many facets of touch and touching have led to experimental psychology offering another perspective, which is particularly important to neonatal (health) psychology, and requires sharp differentiation between being touched, touching one's self, and touching an object.

2. Being touched

An example is the effects of systematic gentle/light touch (stroking only) on the physical and psychological well-being of both ventilated and non-ventilated pre-term neonates of 24–36 weeks' gestational age. These effects included babies' behavioural responses to touch therapy (TAC-TIC therapy), and the information processing of pre-term babies who had been so 'touched' compared with their control counterparts who had been matched for socio-economic status, ethnic origin, and variables at birth. As this work had proceeded, babies' behaviours when lying alone in their incubators or cots were closely observed, and the patterns of activities led to questioning the assumption that babies only sleep, whimper, or cry when left alone.

Current evidence suggests that being touched facilitates self-touching by babies in ways described below.

3. Touching one's self

Recent systematic analyses of video films of ventilated pre-term neonates who were engaging in spontaneous activities (defined as any gross or fine movements of head, face, or upper and lower limbs) have demonstrated their possession of a very rich behaviour repertoire.

Pre-term ventilated babies when alone in their incubators, albeit among tubes and wires, touch both themselves and items in their particular environments. Moreover their type of touch changes as a function of the surface that is being encountered. Corresponding analyses of video recorded observations of hospitalized but non-ventilated pre-term babies show them also to be engaged in exploration of face, body, and local environment. Although not exclusive, such spontaneous and rudimentary proto-play is characteristic of pre-term neonates and the term 'neo-play' has been coined accordingly.

Touching the mouth (Fig. 1), lips (Fig. 2), or face is organizing/self-comforting behaviour; pre-term neonates display them in accordance to their age. Practices in some neonatal units, which encourage the baby to touch him- or herself (Fig. 3), are likely to facilitate behaviours as mentioned above. An interesting example is that of a pre-term baby of 33 weeks' gestational age filmed, in his incubator, for 33 minutes. When the baby was awake and active he touched the face 16 times, the lips 4 times and the mouth 7 times; after 16 minutes of filming, the baby started crying and water in a bottle was given. After contacts of the water/bottle on his mouth, the results reversed, the baby now touching the mouth 16 times, and the lips and face each 10 times. Such observations suggest a tactile working

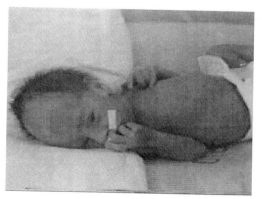

Fig. 1.

memory by which the bottle in his mouth has 'reminded' him of the locations of mouth and lips.

Touching the mouth/lips/face may well be the precursors of *hand-to-mouth facility*, which is the ability of the baby to bring hands to his mouth, insert thumb or finger, and maintain it there long enough to establish a strong suck; this motoric capacity is included in Brazelton's 'newborn assessment', and is absent, incomplete, or weak in pre-term neonates.

Being touched and touching themselves, as above, in turn, is likely to enhance babies' capabilities to touch objects.

4. Neo-haptic touch

Neo-play occurs in the manual mode, without toys, but is also manifested through the use of age-appropriate 'tools' in order to decode/process information. Assump-

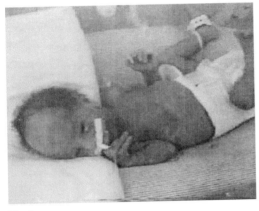

Fig. 2.

tions abound regarding the abilities of newborns to encode and retain sensory information when specific stimuli are introduced. Two examples are the stereotyping of infant palm grasps, characterized by a 'clutching' action which does not decode/process information, and fingers simply open and close synergistically. In consequence, because the infants lack the more intricate hand movements which yield information, they are not expected to perceive texture, weight, shape, etc. with precision. Such questionable expectations imply that manipulation/exploration of an object with fingers is not present before 3–4 months, and that fingering is needed to decode/process information and perform haptic (active) touch.

Based upon the assumption that perception is predictive hypotheses of whatever may be external, and that behaviour depends largely on stored knowledge, original work is providing evidence that tactile sensitivity indeed exists in neonates: fingering occurs before 3 months, in full-term babies if the environment can provide them with the appropriate 'tools', so that their intelligent hands can explore (haptically) an object.

Original and ongoing (personal) research is showing that full-term healthy newborn babies, before the age of 4 months, are capable of different types of grasping, quite distinct from 'clutching', and also different types of fingering whenever an appropriate specially designed object is placed in the palms; for this form of haptic touch the term 'neo-haptic touch' has been coined. With healthy full-term babies, it is generally asserted that the hands gradually take over as the primary sources of discovery for both shape and texture; such propositions are questionable, and rest on classic amodal experiment(s) which were designed to investigate decoding, processing, and retention of information but based on the mouthing/sucking

Fig. 3.

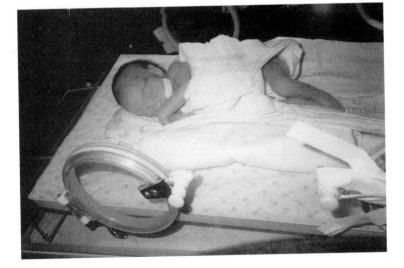

of objects. Employing the manual mode for similar objectives, but using an age-appropriate 'tool', has hitherto been neglected. Thus far, the evidence derived from using a new 'preferential touching' paradigm is that the hands may well be the primary source of discovery of, for example, texture during the first 3–4 months of post-natal life.

It has been established that babies use their hands intelligently, as a perceptual system; they are able to use haptic touch, that their 'fingering' varies according to the texture they encounter. To discriminate texture a baby must be able to perform a stroking action, and this has recently been shown to be a recognizable behaviour of both full-term and pre-term neonates. 'Clutching' however is not a recognizable behaviour of the pre-term neonate.   ENAM

Adamson-Macedo, E. N. (1998). 'The mind and body of the preterm neonate'. *International Journal of Prenatal and Perinatal Psychology and Medicine*, 10/4.

Connolly, K. J. (ed.) (1998). *The Psychobiology of the Hand*.

Gregory, R. L. (1981). *Mind in Science.*.

Kruger, L. (ed.) (1996). *Pain and Touch*.

Walker, J., Adamson-Macedo, E. N., Myers, J., and Henley, D. (2000). 'Towards a new theory of play with particular reference to the preterm babies'. *International Journal of Prenatal and Perinatal Psychology and Medicine*, 12/1.

Neumann, John Von. See VON NEUMANN, JOHN.

neural networks in the brain. In order to understand how the brain actually works, it is necessary to know what information is being exchanged between the computing elements of the brain, the neurons. Recordings from single neurons (and from several single neurons simultaneously) show not only what is represented at each stage of processing, but also how the information is represented, and how the information is transformed from stage to stage. To understand how large numbers of neurons can collectively have interesting computational properties, theories of the properties of networks of neurons, and indeed of neural computation, are needed. Many of the properties of the mind can now be understood in the context of neural networks. These properties include the ability of the mind to associate from one idea to another, to complete a thought or memory from just a fragment, to continue to operate reasonably even when some of its neurons are damaged, and for its final functionality to emerge from a relatively small number of connection rules specified in the genome operating in concert with self-organization resulting from interaction with the environment. The theory of neural networks, when combined with knowledge of neuronal activity and complemented by evidence from other techniques in neuroscience, enables not just a qualitative, but also a quantitative, understanding of how the brain works,

enables predictions to be made, and also has spin-off into the area of the application of artificial devices which mimic some useful aspects of the processing that is performed by the brain.

1. Neurons and learning in network models of brain function
2. Three neuronal network architectures

1. Neurons and learning in network models of brain function

In simple but biologically plausible models, the computing elements, the neurons, sum the inputs received from a large number of axons each of which has its own synapse or connection. The synapse weights the strength of the effects of the input spike activity being received via each axon from other neurons. The number of synaptic inputs received by each neuron is large, typically in the range 10,000–50,000, and this large number of inputs is crucial because it sets the memory capacity (the number of different memories that can be correctly retrieved) of networks in the brain. The synaptically weighted sum of inputs is then transformed by a non-linear function with a threshold into the spike train of the neuron. The threshold non-linearity of the neurons is important, for it enables the network to retrieve an individual memory correctly with little interference, to control positive feedback which otherwise might cause epilepsy, and more generally to perform useful computation, which almost always requires non-linearity.

To enable the network to learn, and to self-organize under environmental influence, a simple synaptic learning rule is used that was originally presaged by Donald *Hebb in 1949, and specifies that synapses increase in strength when there is conjunctive presynaptic and postsynaptic activity. The Hebb rule can be expressed more formally as follows:

$$\delta w_{ij} = k \, r_i \, r'_j$$

where δw_{ij} is the change of the synaptic weight w_{ij} which results from the simultaneous (or conjunctive) presence of presynaptic firing r'_j and postsynaptic firing r_i (or strong depolarization), and k is a learning rate constant which specifies how much the synapses alter on any one pairing. The presynaptic and postsynaptic activity must be present approximately simultaneously (to within perhaps 100–500 milliseconds in the real brain).

The Hebb rule is expressed in this multiplicative form to reflect the idea that *both* presynaptic and postsynaptic activity must be present for the synapses to increase in strength. The multiplicative form also reflects the idea that strong pre- and postsynaptic firing will produce a larger change of synaptic weight than smaller firing rates. The Hebb rule thus captures what is typically found in studies of associative synaptic long-term potentiation (LTP) in the brain.

With an associative learning rule of the type described above, three neuronal network architectures arise which appear to be used in many different brain regions.

2. Three neuronal network architectures

In the first architecture (see Fig. 1a, b), pattern associations can be learned. The output neurons are driven by an unconditioned stimulus. A conditioned stimulus reaches the output neurons by associatively modifiable synapses w_{ij}. If the conditioned stimulus is paired during learning with activation of the output neurons produced by the unconditioned stimulus, then later, after learning, due to the associative synaptic modification, the conditioned stimulus alone will produce the same output as the conditioned stimulus. This architecture is used in general to learn associations between events, for example between the sight of food and the taste of food, and insofar as associations between previously neutral stimuli such as a visual stimulus and a reward or punisher (such as the taste of palatable food) are crucial to emotional learning, this type of pat-

tern association learning is very important in emotion. Pattern association learning also appears to implement top-down processes important in perception, attention, and memory, via corticocortical back-projection synapses. For the 'emergent' properties of these and other networks such as generalization to similar stimuli to arise, the representation of each stimulus must be distributed across many different neurons (with a different set of neurons firing for each stimulus), and this is the type of representation found in the brain.

In the second architecture, the output neurons have recurrent associatively modifiable synaptic connections w_{ij} to other neurons in the network (see Fig. 1c). When an external input causes the output neurons to fire, then associative links are formed through the modifiable synapses that connect the set of neurons that is active. Later, if only a fraction of the original input pattern is presented, then the associative synaptic connections or weights allow the whole of the memory to be retrieved. This is called completion. Because the components of the pattern are associated with each other as a result of the associatively modifiable recurrent connections, this is

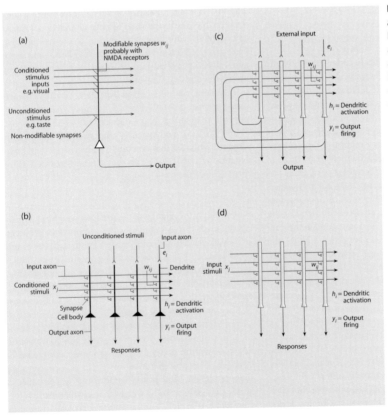

Fig. 1. Three network architectures that use local learning rules: **a.** Pattern association introduced with a single output neuron. **b.** Pattern association network. **c.** Autoassociation network. **d.** Competitive network.

called an autoassociative memory. It is believed to be used in the brain for many purposes, including episodic memory in which the parts of a memory of an episode are associated together, and helping to define the response properties of cortical neurons, both by the recurrent collateral connections within an area, and by the reciprocated forward and backward connections that are typical of cortical areas which are connected.

In the third architecture, the main input to the output neurons is received through associatively modifiable synapses w_{ij} (see Fig. 1d). Because of the initial values of the synaptic strengths, or because every axon does not contact every output neuron, different patterns tend to activate different output neurons. When one pattern is being presented, the most strongly activated neurons tend via lateral inhibition to inhibit the other neurons. For this reason the network is called competitive. During the presentation of that pattern, associative modification of the active axons onto the active postsynaptic neuron takes place. Later, that or similar patterns will have a greater chance of activating that neuron or set of neurons. Other neurons learn to respond to other input patterns. In this way, a network is built which can categorize patterns, placing similar patterns into the same category. This is useful as a pre-processor for sensory information, and finds use in many other parts of the brain too.

The operation of many brain areas involved in processes such as perception, attention, and memory are starting to become understood in terms of the operation of sets of interconnected neural networks (Rolls and Deco 2002). A major issue for future research is how some of the very complex aspects of brain function, such as language, can be implemented in networks which utilize local synaptic learning rules such as the associative rule described above (in which the information to modify the synapse is available locally in the presynaptic spike activity and the activation of the postsynaptic neuron), or whether non-local synaptic modification rules (see McLeod, Plunkett, and Rolls 1998) must be introduced.   ETR

Dayan, P., and Abbott, L. F. (2002). *Theoretical Neuroscience*.

Hertz, J., Krogh, A., and Palmer, R. G. (1991). *Introduction to the Theory of Neural Computation*.

Koch, C. (1999). *Biophysics of Computation: Information Processing in Single Neurons*.

McLeod, P., Plunkett, K., and Rolls, E. T. (1998). *Introduction to Connectionist Modelling of Cognitive Processes*.

Rolls, E. T. (1999). *The Brain and Emotion*.

—— and Deco, G. (2002). *Computational Neuroscience of Vision*.

—— and Stringer, S. M. (2000). 'On the design of neural networks in the brain by genetic evolution'. *Progress in Neurobiology*, 61.

—— and Treves, A. (1998). *Neural Networks and Brain Function*.

neuroanatomical techniques. Although one can study the mind knowing nothing about the structure of the brain, rather as one can drive well and be knowledgeable about the performance of motor vehicles without understanding the internal combustion engine, few doubt that mental events are related to the activity of the brain and that the structure can give clues about how the brain works. However, the brain is so complex that its detailed structure is only beginning to be understood. For example, in humans it contains about 10,000,000,000 nerve cells, some of which make and receive several thousand contacts with other cells. The following describes the principal methods of obtaining information about the most complex circuit in existence.

Even before the invention of the microscope it was possible to say something about gross brain structure by postmortem dissection. The nerve bundles carrying information from the eyes, ears, nose, and skin can all be followed to their first major destination in the thalamus of the brain. But from here we are lost, and in any case dissection has never revealed the course and connections of individual nerve fibres, which are often less than one-thousandth of a millimetre thick. The first leap forward came in 1873 when Camillo *Golgi discovered that a small proportion of nerve cells could be stained black with silver chromate, rendering them readily visible against the background of unstained, transparent cells. Why the Golgi method selects a few cells apparently at random is still unknown, but for over a 100 years it was the principal tool in revealing their precise shape. It was the only method that let us see the trees instead of the wood (Fig. 1), and showed that most nerve cells, or neurons, consist of a cell body, dendrites, and an axon (fibre) which may have a length from less than a millimetre to several metres in large mammals.

Although the Golgi method is unsurpassed for revealing local details, it is unsuitable for showing whether two widely separated areas of the brain are directly connected by nerve fibres. A solution to this problem was that of 1870 by Gudden, who observed that when axons are cut their cell bodies often die. When the tissue is sectioned and stained, the cells that gave rise to the cut axons are conspicuous by their absence (Fig. 2). Retrograde cell degeneration, as the method is called, was widely used in the first half of the 20th century to show which parts of the thalamus in the centre of the brain send axons to particular parts of the cerebral cortex on the surface of the brain. The resulting map is shown as Fig. 3. But the method produces too many false-negative results. Some cell bodies do not die when their axon is cut, perhaps because of regrowth of the axon. Other axons branch, and only if all branches are cut does the cell die. Therefore the absence of cell degeneration following axon cutting does not prove that two regions lack connections. Nerve cells may also degenerate in the opposite direction, that is when the cell body is destroyed the axon and its terminal connections swiftly degenerate. In the 1950s Walle Nauta and his

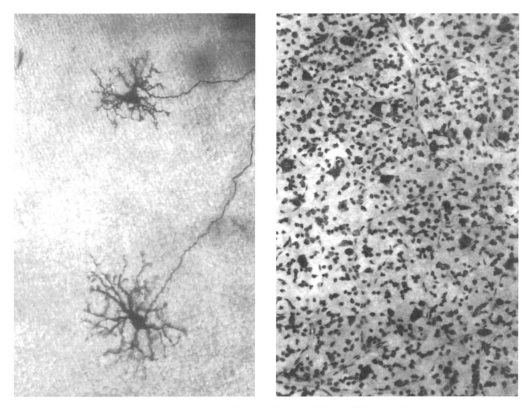

Fig. 1. *Left.* Two Golgi-stained nerve cells in the retina of the eye of a rat. Each has a cell body with branching dendrites that make connections with other cells. The long thin process is the cell's axon. The hundreds of other cells are unstained and therefore invisible. *Right.* A photograph of a similar region of the eye using a conventional stain, which shows up all the cell bodies but none of the dendrites or axons.

colleagues developed what are known as the Nauta techniques for selectively staining degenerating axons and their terminal branches with silver, and an entirely new set of nerve connections was discovered. For example, the visual cortex at the back of the brain is now known to send axons to at least eight different regions of the cerebral cortex and subcortex (Fig. 4). None of these pathways is demonstrable by retrograde degeneration.

So far we have mentioned only histological methods. But nerve cells can be stimulated by a natural agent such as light in the eye, or by brief pulses of electricity delivered through electrodes in the tissue. The electrical activity evoked in the nerve cells can then be recorded as it is propagated in the brain along axons. For more than 50 years this method was used to map pathways in the brains of animals. One advantage of it is that the induced activity is neurochemically transmitted across the junctions (synapses) between cells, so that the entire route can in principle be revealed. For example, the impulses from the eye travel to the dorsal lateral geniculate nucleus of the

thalamus, thence to the primary visual cortex, and from there to several other so-called secondary visual areas, all traceable by electrophysiological recordings.

Such methods reveal a great deal about the route followed by axons of a particular sensory system and about the areas where the axons terminate, but they reveal nothing about the connections of individual cells. One way of overcoming this limitation is to record the activity of a cell body with a micropipette and then inject the cell with a dye. When the tissue is then sectioned the dyed cells and all their processes are visible microscopically. This method is tedious and can never reveal more than a few cells at a time, but it has shown, for example, which of the millions of cells in the visual cortex are the first to receive impulses from the eye, and how many brain cells an incoming fibre can contact.

The methods described above had reached their peak by the early 1970s, and radically new discoveries about the connections of the brain seemed impossible. How wrong this was! Neuroanatomy was on the threshold of major

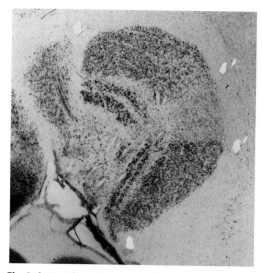

Fig. 2. Section through part of the thalamus in a monkey's brain showing the lateral geniculate body, whose cells send axons to the visual cortex. The cells in the centre have disappeared because a small part of the cortex was damaged. This method of retrograde degeneration shows which thalamic cells send axons to the damaged area.

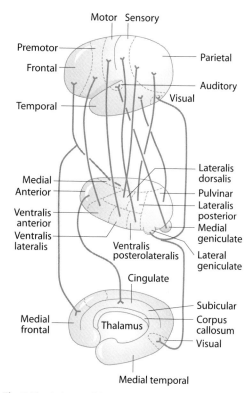

Fig. 3. The thalamus of the brain (shown much enlarged in the centre of the figure) consists of discrete groups of cells. By the method of retrograde degeneration the parts of the cerebral cortex to which they send their axons have been discovered. The lines show these pathways from the thalamus to the lateral surface of the brain (*top*) and to the medial surface of the brain (*bottom*).

advances. Since 1948 it had been known that the axoplasm inside a nerve fibre flows along the fibre. By injecting radioactive amino acids into the eye of a mouse it was shown, in 1965, that the amino acid was absorbed by nerve cell bodies and incorporated into proteins, which were then passed along the axons. In 1968 it was shown that if the brain tissue was sectioned and the sections coated with photographic emulsion, the radioactivity that had reached the axon terminals could be detected by its blackening of the photographic film. Since then, this technique of autoradiography has been widely used to study the course of axons from groups of cells that have been bathed in minute injections of radioactive chemicals, which can be delivered through a micropipette to any part of an animal's brain. Not only does the technique take advantage of a normal biological process without damaging the injected cells, it is far more sensitive than degeneration techniques. For example, autoradiography has shown that the nerve cells in the eye send fibres to at least ten different parts of the brain, whereas only four were known previously (Fig. 5). If the radioactive sections are kept for several months in contact with the film it is even possible to reveal the next link in the pathway by anterograde transneuronal transport.

When a nerve fibre is squeezed tight, axoplasm accumulates on *both* sides of the ligature, implying that there is active transport in both directions. If that is the

case, it should also be possible to apply chemicals to the terminals of axons and trace them back to the parent cell bodies elsewhere in the brain. Such a technique, called retrograde marking, has been in use since 1970. The commonest tracer is horseradish peroxidase, which is rapidly conveyed from nerve axon terminals back to the cell body, where its presence can be revealed by histochemical treatment of thin slices of the tissue (Fig. 6). However, a variety of materials can be used so long as they can be chemically attached to a transportable substance. For example, colloidal particles of gold, which show up well in light and electron microscopes, can be attached (conjugated) to transportable wheatgerm agglutin. Some tracers will even cross the junctions between cells retrogradely and transneuronal retrograde transport has shown which parts of the visual cortex connect with which parts of the eye.

New transportable substances are continually being discovered, and one class has already proved to be especially

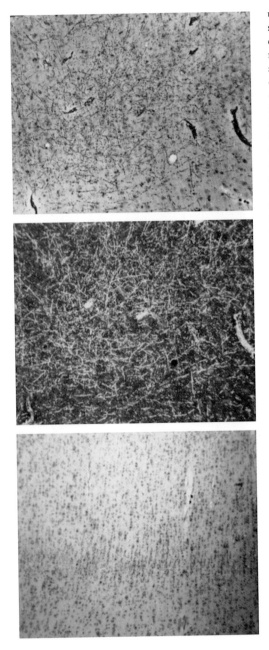

Fig. 4. *Top.* Degenerating axon terminals revealed by the Nauta technique in the cortex of the temporal lobe after damaging cells in a distant part of the occipital lobe. *Centre.* The same slide with the contrast reversed so that the degenerating fibres are even more conspicuous. *Bottom.* The same region of cortex stained conventionally. Only cell bodies are visible.

useful. When bathed in light of a particular wavelength some chemicals absorb the light and emit light of a very different colour, i.e. they fluoresce. It is now known that many fluorescent dyes are transported in the axoplasm. If such labelled nerve cells are observed under a fluorescence microscope where they are illuminated by light of one wavelength (which, like ultraviolet, may be invisible to the human eye), they fluoresce at visible wavelengths, for example blue, and stand out against a dark background. By injecting two different fluorescent tracers in separate parts of the brain it was first shown in 1978 that some cell bodies accumulated both tracers because they glowed red or blue according to the wavelength of the illuminating light. This proved conclusively that some cells give rise to an axon which branches and reaches different areas of the brain. A few fluorescent dyes, e.g. DiI, will passively diffuse along fibre bundles in dead brains, especially if the brain was young and the fatty sheath around axons is therefore thin. This method, still in its infancy, could show how the brain's connections develop by making use of post-mortem tissue.

Although nerve cells transmit information as electrical impulses along their axons, the communication between cells at their points of contact, or synapses, is chiefly chemical. The terminals of an axon release minute quantities of the chemical, or transmitter, which then stimulates the membrane of adjacent cell bodies. Although many different transmitters exist, any cell releases predominantly only one type. If that type can be selectively stained in some way it should be possible to display all the pathways that use that particular transmitter. This was achieved in 1962 by the discovery that nerve terminals secreting catecholamines fluoresced with a greenish hue after the tissue was treated with formaldehyde vapour (Fig. 7). Since then several other transmitter-specific pathways have been demonstrated, but the most precise and exciting development is immunostaining. When cells producing a particular transmitter are injected into another animal of a different species, the host develops antibodies to the transmitter. These antibodies can be isolated from blood serum taken from the host. A fluorescent or other marker is now chemically attached to the antibodies, which are then applied to fresh sections of brain tissue or even injected into living brains, where they attach themselves to the type of cell producing the original transmitter (Fig. 8). In this way several cell groups and their fibres have been shown to act by secreting specific neurotransmitters e.g. dopamine or gamma-aminobutyric acid (GABA), a discovery that could not be made by studying their structure or electrical activity. Nor is the discovery of mere academic interest. Disturbances in the metabolism of specific transmitters have been implicated in several neurological and psychiatric conditions, for example dopamine in *Parkinson's disease, acetylcholine in senile *dementia, and GABA

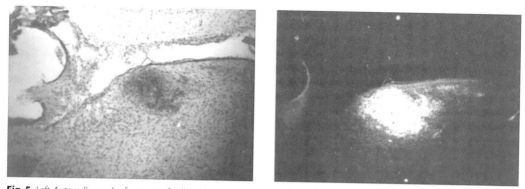

Fig. 5. *Left.* Autoradiograph of a group of cells in the midbrain of a rat after radioactive amino acids have been absorbed by the eye and transported to the brain. The dark patch shows the radioactivity. *Right.* The radio-activity is even clearer when the contrast is reversed.

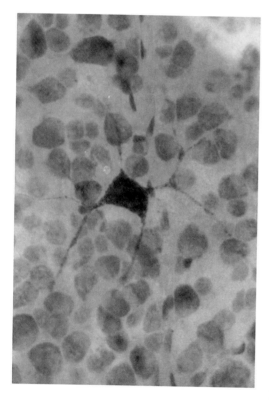

Fig. 6. Photograph of part of the retina of the eye of a rat. The dark cell in the centre has accumulated horseradish peroxidase tracer injected in minute amount into a small part of the brain, showing that this and other similarly labelled cells send their axons to this part of the brain.

in *epilepsy. To pinpoint such pathways is therefore of great potential value to medicine. (For further discussion see DOPAMINE NEURONS IN THE BRAIN.)

So the connections within the brain may be discovered by a variety of means, but what do they do and under what behavioural circumstances are they active? If only the brain were semi-transparent with pathways that lit up when they were in use, we might more easily relate structure to mind. This idea is not preposterous, as two examples show. Nerve cells need glucose, and the more active they are the more glucose they use. The glucose is normally metabolized rapidly but, if an injection of a closely related radioactive chemical, carbon-14 2-deoxyglucose, is given to an animal, the brain cells absorb it as if it were glucose, but they fail to metabolize it. The chemical sticks in the cells and can be demonstrated by the autoradiographic method described earlier. By these means it has been shown which cells in an animal's brain are the most active when it looks through one eye, gazes at vertical lines, moves about, or listens to sounds (Fig. 9). But this is a drastic procedure, because the brain has to be sectioned. However, regional activity can now be demonstrated in the living brain without harming it. If a subject inhales radioactive xenon, the gas enters the bloodstream, where it circulates for a few minutes before gradually being lost again in the breath. As those parts of the brain that are most active at any particular time receive the greatest blood supply, they contain the most radioactivity, which can be detected by sensors outside the skull. The method was used clinically in the 1980s to pinpoint brain abnormalities that may require surgery, but it also successfully shows which regions are most active when we are looking, listening, talking, moving a limb, problem solving, or just daydreaming. Since then it has been replaced by positron emission tomography (PET) and, in the last decade, by functional magnetic resonance

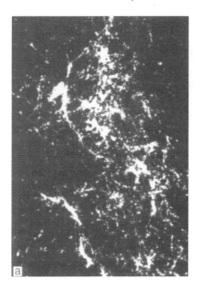
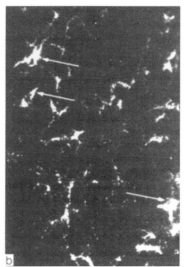

Fig. 7. a. Fluorescence in the septum of the rat brain after treating the tissue with formaldehyde. Both adrenaline and noradrenaline fluoresce. **b.** The same region from a different brain treated to make the fluorescence specific for a different transmitter, dopamine. The arrows show that the transmitter is concentrated round cell bodies.

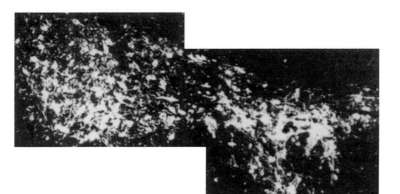

Fig. 8. Immunofluorescence in the substantia nigra of a rat brain after incubating the tissue with fluorescent antibodies to an enzyme which controls the metabolism of the transmitter tyrosine.

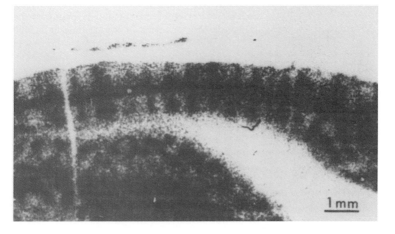

Fig. 9. Deoxyglucose autoradiograph of a section through the visual cortex of a monkey after the animal was looking at a pattern of stripes. The array of vertical stripes in the cortex shows which groups of cells were activated by the stimulus.

1 mm

imaging (fMRI). Both depend on task-specific changes in regional cerebral blood flow, detected by increased emission of radioactivity (PET) or decreased signal from deoxygenated haemoglobin (fMRI), detected and pinpointed from outside the head. They are the modern window on the mind at work.

To describe the bare bones of some of the techniques now available for studying the structure and connections of the brain seems a far cry from understanding the mind. But we are certainly much closer to saying something about the physical counterparts of perception, action, and mood than was St Thomas *Aquinas, who saw mind as those faculties that in their operation dispense entirely with matter. See BRAIN IMAGING.   AC

Bolam, J. P. (1992). *Experimental Neuroanatomy: A Practical Approach.*

Carter, R. (1998). *Mapping the Mind.*

Walsh, V., and Cowey, A. (2000). 'Transcranial magnetic stimulation and cognitive neuroscience'. *Nature Reviews, Neuroscience*, 1.

neurolinguistics. This term is used mainly in Europe, and in some centres in the USA, to describe the application of linguistic theories to the classification and analysis of acquired disorders of language or speech in patients with brain damage (for example, *aphasia). Some work has also considered the corresponding development disorders of speech, reading, and writing in children (see LANGUAGE DEVELOPMENT IN CHILDREN), as well as the dissolution of language in dementing diseases.

While ideas from linguistic theories have been applied to aphasia for many years (e.g. Steinthal 1871, Pick 1913, Isserlin 1922, Jakobson 1956), the term neurolinguistics and more systematic application of linguistic ideas have only become widespread since 1970.

In 1969, the neurologist Henri Hécaen and the linguist Armand Dubois declared the object of neurolinguistics to be, first, the establishment of 'a purely linguistic typology' of neurologically caused verbal disorders, and, second, the achievement of an experimentally verifiable correlation of lesion sites with the linguistic types. In practice, however, it has proved difficult to use solely linguistic criteria of classification, and Hécaen's own 1972 scheme classifies patients on the basis of clinical and psychological, as well as linguistic, features: 'sensory aphasia', for example, has three aspects—a disorder of semantic relations, a failure of auditory decoding at a phonemic level, and a disorganization of attention.

Neurolinguistic researchers have used various types of linguistic theory, for example *Luria's (1947) linguistic theories come from the structuralism of the Prague school (see NEUROLINGUISTICS, LURIA ON); Lecours and Lhermitte (1979) use Martinet's theories, while Weigl (1981), Whitaker (1971), and others adopt the perspectives

of transformational generative grammar (see LANGUAGE: CHOMSKY'S THEORY).

Progress towards the secondary aim of discovering the anatomical substrates of various functions has not proved impressive, partly because of the lack of agreement on what constitutes a proper classification of aphasia in linguistic terms. It is becoming clear that the relationship between linguistic theories and brain structures will not be simple; many workers would now see the development of a neuropsychology of language as a prerequisite for the further advance of neurolinguistics.

See LANGUAGE: NEUROPSYCHOLOGY; LURIA ON SPEECH AND BRAIN PROCESSES.   DH/BLB

Hécaen, H. (1972). *Introduction à la neuropsychologie.*

——and Dubois, A. (1971). 'La neurolinguistique'. In Perren, G. E., and Trim, J. L. M. (eds.), *Applications of Linguistics.*

Isserlin, M. (1922). 'Über Agrammatismus'. *Zeitschrift für die gesamte Neurologie und Psychiatrie*, 75.

Jakobson, R. (1956). 'Two aspects of language and two types of aphasic disturbances'. In Jakobson, R., and Halle, M. (eds.), *Fundamentals of Language.*

Lecours, A. R., and Lhermitte, F. (1979). *L'Aphasie.* (English edn. 1983, *Aphasia.*)

Luria, A. R. (1947). *Traumatic Aphasia.* (English trans. D. Bowden, 1970.)

Pick, A. (1913). *Die agrammatischen Sprachstoerungen.*

Steinthal, H. (1871). *Einleitung in die Psychologie und Sprachenwissenschaft.*

Weigl, E. (1981). *Neuropsychology and Neurolinguistics: Selected Papers.*

Whitaker, H. A. (1971). *On the Representation of Language in the Human Brain: Problems in the Neurology of Language and the Linguistic Analysis of Aphasia.*

neurolinguistics, Luria on. During the last few decades the sciences of language and speech have undergone a remarkable development.

A few decades ago linguistics was supposed to be a science concerned with general laws of the formal codes employed by language—its phonetic (or phonemic), lexical, syntactical structures. The goal of comparative and structural linguistics was to describe ideal codes of the language, their interrelations, and their formal organization. During the 1950s and 1960s the development of transformational grammar converted linguistics into a very precise science using systems of basic rules which could be expressed by mathematical means.

The discovery of these rules brought linguistics very close to basic psychological questions. The way in which initial motives and thoughts lead to inner speech, abbreviated in its structure and predicative in its function, and then towards extended speech utterances, appeared as a fundamental problem. The process of encoding the initial thought (generation of the speech utterance) and of decoding it (understanding of the speech utterance, its general meaning, and its deep sense) became the most important area for investigation. Leo *Vygotsky's classic work *Thought and Language* appeared, and started the development of a new branch of language science—that of psycholinguistics, which abandoned the formal description of the basic laws of the language and began to follow up carefully the steps of the semantic rules of speech, the conversion of the thought into a verbal intention. Problems associated with the actual psychological generation of verbal utterances, of dialogue and monologue, and of verbal and written speech (as well as their decoding) appeared, and a group of gifted scholars (among them G. Miller, D. E. Broadbent, J. Mehlez, T. Bever, R. Brown, T. Fodor, D. McNeill, and D. Slobin) made a series of really important contributions to this field.

In spite of the considerable progress associated with psycholinguistics, one important question remained unsolved. Psycholinguistics was scarcely able to single out basic factors in speech; nor was it able to analyse basic forms of speech composed of separate units, each dealing with a different factor underlying the form. To solve this problem a new step was needed, and this step was provided by a new branch of linguistic science—that of neurolinguistics.

The general method of neurolinguistics is to follow all changes in language and speech that are associated with local lesions of the brain, and to describe as carefully as possible the different forms of breakdown of the processes of encoding of verbal utterances and of their decoding which appear in cases of differently localized brain lesions.

It is thought that speech, as well as other kinds of mental activity, is really a functional system based on the co-operation of many cortical and subcortical regions, each contributing its own part to the whole processing of information or the establishing of plans and programmes of behaviour. This is why analysis of the derangement of speech processes associated with separately localized brain lesions provides a unique opportunity to single out factors included in language and speech, and to describe different kinds of language disorders each involving different factors in its manifestation.

Observations have shown that the process of speech, which includes mastering language codes and processing their encoding and decoding, can be impaired differently with lesions of different parts of the brain. As a rule, in lesions of posterior ('gnostic') regions of the major (left) hemisphere the process of acquisition of language codes can be disturbed. Lesions of the verbal–acoustic areas of the left temporal lobe evoke a derangement of phonemic organization of the sounds perceived, and as a secondary result considerable disturbance of the lexical units of the language is seen: words which are acoustically similar can be confused, and 'alienation of word meaning' takes place. This can result in marked difficulty in understanding single words, while the whole prosodic and partly syntactic structure of the phrase is preserved, and the patient remains able to understand the sense of the whole phrase in spite of lacking stable recognition of single lexical units.

It was found that lesions of the most complex 'tertiary' regions of the left hemisphere (inferoparietal or parieto-occipital regions of the cortex) are associated with different forms of impairment of language. Phonemic organization of language remains intact and the understanding of separate lexical units is preserved. Trouble appears when separate lexical parts are related in simultaneous 'paradigmatically' organized structures which require processes of simultaneous synthesis and perception of logico-grammatical relations. This is why in patients with lesions of these regions, fluent 'syntagmatically' organized verbal utterance, or simple 'communications of events' (such as: 'The house is burning', 'The boy hit a dog', 'Mother went to a movie and the children remained at home'), are preserved, while complex 'communications of relations' resulting in logico-grammatical structures (such as: 'Brother's father', 'The triangle under the circle', 'Mary is fairer than Ann'), phrases, or complex distant constructions that need a series of additional transformations for their understanding, are severely deranged.

A careful description of these disturbances makes it possible to divide all utterances into two basic groups—one that is 'syntagmatically' organized and remains intact, and a second that is 'paradigmatically' organized and breaks down.

The general statement of neurolinguistics is that in differently localized brain lesions, verbal utterances can be broken down into different links (phonemic, lexical, logico-grammatical, etc.). This is of great importance for increased knowledge of the basic rules involved in language acquisition and linguistic performance, and is the reason why neurolinguistic studies can contribute to a better understanding of the basic structure of language. What we have described here are new ways of studying some linguistic structures, their components, and the basic types of their breakdown.

But speech comprises more than the mastering of the codes of the language. The generation of speech utterances, as well as their understanding, requires a long journey, starting from motives and intentions, including inner speech, and ending with extended verbal utterances—or, in the case of understanding, starting with perception of extended utterances and finally arriving at an understanding of the basic sense. Last, but not least, there is the motive of the whole verbal communication. This complex journey includes some important psychological, extra-linguistic factors, such as: retention of motives and intentions; constructing plans and programmes of verbal constructions ('realizations') of these plans; and building a 'closed semantic system' which has to remain stable and which can resist distracting factors.

This requires an adequate 'tone' of the cortex (it is impossible to retain goal-linked programmes in dreamy states) and an active participation of the frontal lobes of the brain, which should be considered as a special apparatus for retaining stable programmes and for permanent control of the information processing. If the mechanisms ('apparatuses') of the brain stem are deranged and the 'tone' of the cortex becomes low, or if the frontal lobes are injured and do not provide the control needed, 'closed semantic systems' are broken down and replaced by 'open semantic systems', i.e. by systems open to every distraction, or to inert stereotypes (perseverations). These extra-linguistic conditions result in a special kind of pathology, in which the subject becomes unable to use syntactical codes of language, or to generate extended verbal programmes, or to single out the meaning of complicated verbal constructions, which easily become deranged by external influences of immediate impressions, fixed stereotypes, etc.

The application of neuropsychological methods (i.e. the careful study of change in behavioural processes associated with local brain lesions) opens up new techniques both for linguistics and for the psychology of speech. This new field of science can be used with success to improve our knowledge of the inner mechanisms of language.

See also LANGUAGE: NEUROPSYCHOLOGY.   ARL

Luria, A. R. (1960). *Traumatic Aphasia*.
——(1976). *Basic Problems of Neurolinguistics*.

neuronal connectivity and brain function. The nervous system is made up largely of nerve cells (neurons), with their associated neuronal processes, and glial cells. The role of the glial cells in the mature brain is believed to be supportive to the neurons, but in development their involvement in establishing organized connections, and in the formation of differentiated brain structures, appears to be most important. Here we concentrate on the neurons, which, with their axons and dendrites interconnecting the cells in a formidably complex fashion, are thought to carry out the main business of the nervous system. This business, the primary function of the nervous system, is information processing in the most comprehensive sense of the term. For many years there has been discussion on the relationship between the structure (here meaning connectivity) of the nervous system and its function. If this discussion is to be more than a series of guesses and counter-guesses, we need to have a clear idea of what the structure and function of the system actually are; and here, because of recent advances in neuroanatomical techniques, we are in a much stronger position in relation to neural structure than to function.

We have a fairly extensive, though far from complete, knowledge of the connections that exist within both the vertebrate and the invertebrate nervous systems. About parts of the system in various vertebrates (the main sensory pathways, the main motor pathways, the cerebellum, the hippocampus, and certain regions of the spinal cord) our knowledge of connectivity is pretty comprehensive; about other parts of the system (many cortical regions of the cerebrum, the reticular core of the brain stem, and numerous other parts) our knowledge of the patterns of connectivity, although increasing rapidly, is still very limited.

Many invertebrate nervous systems have a relative simplicity, in which not only are the classes of neurons fewer, but also the total numbers of cells, and concomitantly of connections, are less than in vertebrates. In such invertebrate systems this reduced complexity has enabled a fuller picture of connectivity to be obtained. As a result of technical advances in recent years investigators are now in a relatively strong position to start examining how connectivity in small circuits, in which the identities of the individual constituent neurons are known, is related to their function. The extent to which such systems model the circuitry of the more complex vertebrate nervous system awaits clarification.

In contrast to these 'simple' nervous systems, those of the vertebrates are impressively complicated. The brain of man is often quoted as comprising some 10^{12} neurons. Since, at any given time, an unknown number of these are probably altering their connections, and may be altering their basic characteristics, our attempts to obtain any sort of complete description of neural connectivity are fraught with practical and also theoretical difficulties. The numbers being dealt with are so large and so uncertain that, as was pointed out by Horridge (1968), no statement of the complete structure of the nervous system can ever be correct; by the time the statement is made, it will be out of date.

This gloomy thought need not deter us, however. In practice, we can get a long way by concentrating on *classes* of connections. When we do this, a most significant fact emerges. To the extent that we are able to demonstrate patterns of neural connections from one part of the nervous system to another, or to the rest of the body, we find that these patterns are closely similar from one animal to another within the same species, and in some instances are found to be remarkably similar in animals of widely different species.

These similarities in neural connection patterns between different animals indicate two things. First, they tell us that neural connections are not random but are formed in a controlled fashion. Second, they suggest that orderly connections have relevance for the function of the system. Teleologically speaking (and teleology is, after all, essential in any meaningful consideration of the nervous system), it would seem pointless for evolutionary mechanisms to perpetuate and refine the vastly complicated and highly ordered networks of neural connectivity, if these were purely decorative, so to speak.

When we consider neural function we find ourselves beset with far greater difficulties than in the study of neural structure. This is because, except for its most obvious roles, we do not really know what the function of the nervous system actually *is*. The above definition of neural function as 'information processing' merely hides our ignorance behind a term which is currently popular without explaining anything. With man-made information-processing machines we know what the mechanism is and the nature of the operations performed by it, because we construct the machines in a particular way and for a particular purpose. With the nervous system we did not construct the mechanism, and we have not been able, so far, even to define some of its operations.

There are multiple levels of function in the nervous system and the only ones we know much about are those at the bottom. Some of the simpler spinal *reflexes we can both understand in terms of function and account for (almost) in terms of the connectivity underlying this function. At a higher level of complexity, we also have a fairly good understanding of many of the connection patterns that underlie the arrangement of sensory inputs and motor outputs. It is readily demonstrable at these levels of the nervous system that there is a close relationship between structure and function.

In the adult nervous system it is customary to consider that function is highly dependent upon structure. However, there is now good evidence that it also works the other way round, that structure may depend upon function, particularly during development. Experiments have shown that the refinement of the connection patterns formed between arrays of neurons is dependent upon normal stimulation of the system. If the normal pattern of stimulation is altered during crucial stages of development, the connection pattern can be modified, which in turn changes the functional capabilities of the circuitry.

The existence of a relationship between structure and function in the formed nervous system is readily demonstrated experimentally. Thus one can alter spinal reflexes in an accurately predictable fashion by switching nerve pathways; one can cause people to feel bodily sensations, to hear or see things by electrical stimulation of the appropriate parts of the brain; and one can alter the position of the apparent external stimulus by altering the point of stimulation in the brain. Observations such as these tell us that there are maps of the outside world, as perceived by our various sensory apparatuses, which extend across specific parts of the brain. The visual world, the auditory world, the sensitive surface of the body, are all represented

in particular areas of the *cerebral cortex. All this is common knowledge and has been for many years; yet to a large extent the central mechanisms which are responsible for the motor outputs we associate with these sensory inputs remain unknown.

Even at the relatively low organizational level of sensory inputs and motor outputs, however, things are only fairly straightforward as long as we confine our attention to the three-dimensional geometry of the nervous system; as soon as we try to include the fourth dimension, taking into consideration the effects of such things as *learning, *memory, and previous experience, the study of sensory inputs moves into another class of complexity.

The main difficulties we find in attempting to relate high-level neural functions to neural structure are tied up with the problems we have in defining these functions. *Pattern recognition is an easy one and we can almost see how it could work. *Intelligent behaviour is more difficult. We all know what we mean by the term intelligent, but there are almost as many definitions as there are people prepared to define it. Perhaps the most difficult function is language, since it may be very closely related to the very mechanisms of thought. What indeed *is* thought?

The brain is the organ of the mind. There can no longer be any doubt about this in the light of recent neurosurgical observations. The intimacy of the relationship between the brain and the mind is very clearly brought out by the personality changes that occur following surgical lesions of the frontal parts of the brain, and perhaps even more dramatically by the occurrence of two separate minds, or spheres of consciousness, one related to each side of the brain, in patients who have undergone '*split-brain' surgery (Sperry 1966).

What we do not yet know is whether a form of inbuilt connectionist mechanism exists to underlie the highest neural functions. Here, the mind boggles (and we would indeed be far advanced if we knew what we meant by mind and if we could usefully define the term '*boggle'). However, while it is in no sense explanatory, a computer analogy may be useful. Simple computers can be wired up to do specific jobs. The larger the computer, and the wider the variety of tasks it can perform, the smaller is the emphasis placed upon specific patterns of wiring and the greater the emphasis on the programming. In the most powerful machines the wiring is in essence relatively simple, whereas the programs are highly complex. We may look on the brain as a form of computer, extensively hybrid, and containing many more elements, more complexly interconnected, than any man-made machine. It seems likely that, in the brain, connections are not pre-specified for the highest orders of function. Perhaps these latter depend upon programs which may themselves be either built in or, maybe more likely, acquired during the development of the individual, through the interaction of environmental factors on a genetically transmitted potential.

Although we do not know the nature of the relationship between neural connections and, for instance, intellectual and linguistic activities, we do know that such a relationship exists. It seems likely that many of the intractable difficulties we encounter in attempting to find out about the relationship between the brain and the highest neural functions, follow from the self-referential nature of the enquiry. The brain is the organ of the mind, of intelligence, and yet we use the brain to investigate its own activity in these fields. Since modes of thought (including modes of *perception) are conditioned by the structure of the brain, it is hardly surprising, in principle, that we find that our thoughts on these matters tend to run in tight philosophical circles.

See also LOCALIZATION OF BRAIN FUNCTION AND COR-
TICAL MAPS. RMG/JSHT

Horridge, G. A. (1968). *Interneurons*.

Sperry, R. W. (1966). 'Brain bisection and mechanisms of consciousness'. In Eccles, J. C. (ed.), *Brain and Conscious Experience*.

neuropeptides. The study of neuropeptides, i.e. peptides occurring in the nervous system, is one of the fastest-growing areas in neurobiology today. Novel peptides from the brain with actions related to functions such as *pain, analgesia, *sleep, etc. are being discovered at an increasing rate. There are probably two reasons for this neuropeptide 'explosion'. One is that methods for the identification of peptides in very small amounts, such as are present in the brain, have been developed and greatly improved in recent years. The other is the growing realization by neuroscientists of the importance of peptides in brain function, based on the ability of neuropeptides to relay messages selectively between particular groups of cells.

Peptides are made of amino acids joined together to form a chain, and since eighteen different amino acids are found in animals there are 306 ways of putting these together to make a dipeptide and, theoretically, there is an astronomical number of different decapeptides (with ten amino acids). Different peptides can be distinguished because many brain cells, and cells elsewhere in the body, have receptors on their surface which can 'recognize' a particular peptide. Thus each peptide used by the brain can carry a particular message if it can travel to a nearby or distant site to interact with its receptor. The combination of the peptide with its receptor will induce a change in the cell: for example a nerve cell may be excited or inhibited. In this way a peptide can be used by one group of cells to influence or control another group. There are several types of control. A peptide which is released into the bloodstream and acts on distant cells is a hormone: this

type of action tends to be slow and long lasting. A peptide released from the fibre terminal of one neuron into the synaptic cleft to act on the membrane of another neuron is a neurotransmitter: this type of action is relatively fast and short lasting.

The first important neuropeptide to be identified chemically was the hormone vasopressin, shown by Vincent Du Vigneaud and his colleagues at Cornell Medical School in 1953 to be a peptide with nine amino acids. Vasopressin is made by a particular group of neurons in the hypothalamus and is transported to their terminals in the posterior pituitary gland, or neurohypophysis. When these hypothalamic neurons are activated, vasopressin is released from their terminals into the bloodstream and is carried all round the body. Reaching the kidney it recognizes receptors and acts on them and, in effect, commands the kidney to conserve fluid. Thus its function is to act as a messenger between the brain and the kidney in the control of water balance in the body.

Following this discovery, it was some years before it was realized that there are peptides that can relay messages within the brain. Evidence is now accumulating that some peptides act as neurotransmitters at synaptic junctions. It is also possible, though by no means established, that some peptides are released into the cerebrospinal fluid to act at a variety of distant neuronal sites. Research into these possibilities is being eagerly pursued.

The strongest evidence for a neurotransmitter role for a peptide comes from the study of substance P, which was known to be a biologically active peptide, present in brain extracts, as long ago as 1936, although its chemical identity was not established until 1970. Substance P is present in fine sensory fibres which inform the nervous system of painful stimuli, for example it is found in fibres from the tooth pulp. There is a body of evidence to suggest that it is released from the terminals of such fibres at synapses, where it excites sensory neurons which transmit the message that noxious stimulation has occurred to higher parts of the brain concerned in pain sensation and in behavioural responses to pain.

There are also peptides that can produce analgesia. These are the enkephalins and β-endorphin, which are known as opioid peptides because their action resembles that of morphine and other derivatives of opium. Their discovery in 1975–6 was a major advance in our knowledge of brain function. These peptides occur in particular groups of neurons and their best-known action is to produce analgesia by inhibiting neurons which are attempting to transmit the message that pain-producing stimulation has occurred.

Is there a sleep peptide? This intriguing possibility has spurred the activity of several research groups. Certainly a substance of peptide composition with sleep-inducing activity can be extracted from the brain, or cerebrospinal fluid, or cerebral venous blood, of sleeping or sleep-deprived animals. However, different groups of workers are not yet in agreement on the identity of this peptide, and identification is necessary before its role in sleep can be determined.

One group of peptides made in hypothalamic neurons is transported via local vascular channels to influence the release of hormones from the anterior pituitary gland. These include thyroid hormone-releasing factor (THRF), luteinizing hormone-releasing factor (LHRF), and growth hormone release-inhibiting factor (somatostatin). These three peptides are also found in neurons in many other areas of the central nervous system, where their functions are as yet unknown.

Peptides that occur in the alimentary canal and various other naturally occurring peptides have been found to be distributed in particular groups of neurons in the central nervous system, but little is known about their possible functions. Some peptides have been shown to influence behaviour, and a recently discovered tripeptide, containing pyroglutamate, histidine, and glycine, has been obtained from the urine of patients with one type of anorexia nervosa: given to mice it acts to reduce food intake, but it is likely that this peptide is present only under pathological conditions.

How are neuropeptides made? Nerve cells are different from other cells in that they possess large amounts of RNA (Nissl substance) in the cytoplasm. The RNA makes proteins with a sequence of amino acids that depends on the sequence of bases in the RNA in each cell; these proteins are then cleaved at particular points by peptidases. The short-chain peptides thus produced can be transported to the fibre terminals of the neuron and released when required. During evolution, mutations occur which change the base sequence in the DNA in the genes, and therefore in the RNA, and this results in changes in the amino acid sequence in the proteins and peptides. These changes may be unimportant, resulting in minor differences between species in closely related peptides with the same function. Alternatively the changes may be more significant, resulting in the development of different peptides which, although related to their ancestral peptide, have become specialized for different functions. Thus vasopressin has the same function in different mammals even though in some species a particular amino acid in the sequence has been changed. On the other hand, vasopressin and another hypothalamic peptide, oxytocin, are related in that they both have nine amino acids, seven of which are identical, but the difference is sufficient for them to have different actions. Some mutations may throw a spanner in the works by preventing the formation of a particular peptide or by producing a peptide that interferes with normal function. In this way some pathological defects of genetic origin may arise.

For the future, we know that there are many peptides in the brain and spinal cord whose chemical identity and actions remain to be determined. Since some peptides have been shown to have actions related to specific functions we can speculate that this may be true also for many other peptides. Does each peptide supply the chemical code for particular types of activity? Within the next decade we can expect to know much more about the role of peptides in brain function. For better—it is hoped—or for worse, this work will lead eventually to the development of important new drugs with effects on brain and behaviour. One might also hope that better understanding of the functions of neuropeptides in the brain will yet produce a non-addictive analgesic. For example, β-endorphin, when injected, has effects similar to those of morphine. Unfortunately tolerance to and physical dependence upon both β-endorphin and metenkephalin have been demonstrated as well as cross-tolerance between these peptides and exogenous opioids.

See also NEUROTRANSMITTERS AND NEUROMODULATORS.

JHW

Barker, J. L. (1976). 'Peptides: roles in neuronal excitability'. *Physiological Reviews*, 56.

Copper, J. R., Bloom, F. E., and Roth, R. H. (1978). *The Biochemical Basis of Neuropharmacology* (3rd edn.).

Gainer, H. (ed.) (1977). *Peptides in Neurobiology*.

Pappenheimer, J. R. (1976). 'The sleep factor'. *Scientific American*, 235.

Sandman, C. A., Beckwith, B., Chronwall, B. M., Flynn, F. W., Nachman, R. J., and Strand, F. L. (1999). *Neuropeptides: Structure and Function in Biology and Behavior*.

Wolstencroft, J. H. (1978). 'The neurophysiology of transmitters in relation to pain and analgesia'. In Taylor, A., and Jones, M. T. (eds.), *Chemical Communication within the Nervous System and its Disturbance in Disease*.

neuropsychology. The first issue of the international journal *Neuropsychologia*, in January 1963, contained an editorial which defined the term 'neuropsychology' as 'a particular area of neurology of common interest to neurologists, psychiatrists, psychologists and neurophysiologists'. It added that 'this interest is focused mainly, though not exclusively, on the cerebral cortex', that 'topics of particular concern are disorders of language, perception and action', and that 'although certain of these disorders can, of course, be studied only in man, we are none the less convinced that information of great value to human pathology is to be obtained from animal experiment, which may be expected to throw valuable light on the basic mechanisms of cerebral organization'. An editorial in the same journal nearly twenty years later commented that 'there is still no better definition available'. The developments which led up to the emergence of an autonomous discipline of neuropsychology have a long and chequered history and provide insights into the perennial issues which still occupy neuropsychologists.

Attempts to localize mental processes to particular bodily structures can be traced back at least to the 5th century BC, when Hippocrates of Cos identified the brain as the organ of intellect, and the heart as the organ of the senses. Empedocles (about 490–430 BC), concerned with the same central and enduring philosophical problem of the relationship of mind to body, located mental processes in the heart. For the next 2,000 years, the relative merits of what have been called 'the brain hypothesis' and the 'cardiac hypothesis' were debated. The natural successor to Hippocrates was the anatomist *Galen, who, in describing aspects of brain anatomy, argued for the brain hypothesis. There is little doubt that both Hippocrates and Galen drew heavily upon their experiences as physicians. Galen as a surgeon tending gladiators was doubtless well aware of some of the consequences of brain damage. His views contrast with those of *Aristotle, who, having decided that the heart was warm and active, saw it as the source of mental processes, whereas the brain was relegated to the minor role of serving as a mechanism cooling the blood of the heart. Galen believed that the mind was located in the fluid found in the large ventricles of the brain, a view which continued to be canvassed until it was refuted by Vesalius (1511–64). *Descartes, continuing the debate, adopted a quite explicit dualist position, seeing the body and the mind as separate but nevertheless able to interact. By the 18th century, some of the issues that were to represent major viewpoints in what was to become neuropsychology were already being identified—the principal one being whether, and to what extent, particular mental functions could be localized in particular parts of the brain.

The detailed argument for localization of function is usually associated with the phrenological theory of *Gall and with his contemporary J. C. Spurzheim (1776–1832). Both Gall and Spurzheim were anatomists and made important contributions to their discipline by which they were assured a place in the history of science. Regrettably, once they went beyond anatomy and attempted to locate functions in different parts of the brain, they indulged in speculation which led them wildly astray. From their observations of the external structure of the skull, they developed the view that such external features might correlate with important aspects of behaviour. Despite the conceptual ingenuity of their views, they failed to produce evidence which was even reasonably objectively based and could be regarded as convincing support for their main hypothesis. The demolition of their views was brought about by the work of the French anatomist Pierre *Flourens, who ablated parts of the brains of pigeons and studied the changes that occurred postoperatively in their behaviour. He concluded that there was no evidence for localization of function within the cerebrum but that any loss that was observed simply reflected the extent of damage to brain tissue.

The possibility of demonstrating localization of function, however, took a decisive step forward on 21 February 1825, when J. Bouillaud (1796–1881) read a paper to a scientific meeting in France in which he argued from his clinical studies that speech was localized in the frontal lobes, a view already suggested by Gall. Shortly afterwards, in 1836, Marc Dax read a paper in Montpellier, also reporting a series of clinical cases; these he believed demonstrated that speech disorders were linked with lesions of the left hemisphere. It was not, however, until 1865 that Dax's manuscript was published, by his son. Meanwhile, in 1861, Paul *Broca, founder of the Anthropological Society of Paris, heard Bouillaud's son-in-law report the case of a patient who had ceased to speak when pressure was applied to his exposed anterior lobes. Soon afterwards, he saw a patient who had lost his speech and could say only one word, 'Tan', and utter oaths. Results of the post-mortem on this patient indicated left frontal pathology. It is usual to credit Broca with describing this syndrome, which consisted of the inability to speak despite normal understanding of language, and also as the person who elaborated the concept of cerebral dominance of language in the left hemisphere. The other outstanding figure at this time was *Wernicke. To him is attributed the discovery that there is more than one language area in the brain.

The history of thought on *aphasia over the past 150 years and more illustrates the continuing debate about how mental functions are related to brain structure. Thus, one group of workers on aphasia, taking their lead from the early phrenologists, maintained that specific mental functions were subserved by separate areas of the brain. Those who opposed this 'localizationist' view believed that mental capability reflected total intact brain volume. While Broca and Wernicke lie in the localizationist tradition, Hughlings *Jackson and Kurt Goldstein represent the so-called holistic approach to aphasia.

In view of these early observations on the relations between brain and behaviour, it remains something of a puzzle why a separate discipline of neuropsychology did not develop by 1900 rather than by 1949. Perhaps part of the reason was the intervention of the world wars, part was the suspicion of any views that seemed to indicate a retreat to the localizationist views of the phrenologists, and part was the strong presence of the so-called *Gestalt theories in psychology. All of these, it would seem, led to the localizationist approach being abandoned in favour of a more holistic approach. Henry *Head, during the First World War, was dissatisfied with the classical neurologists' attempts to deduce schemes from clinical observations, believing that they were, as he put it, 'compelled to lop and twist their cases to fit the procrustean bed of their hypothetical conceptions'. He attempted to bring some order to the field by devising a standard list of tests to be used in the study of aphasia, an idea developed by Weisenberg and McBride (1935). Earlier (1933), Weisenberg and McBride had made the important discovery that individuals who do not understand spoken language, although their hearing is intact and they can identify non-verbal sounds (e.g. a telephone ringing), may have damage in two different locations. Around the same time, the influence of Karl *Lashley, who published his paper 'In search of the engram' in 1938, is usually seen as significant. Lashley proposed a theory of mass action, contending that the behavioural result of a lesion depends on the amount of brain removed more than on the location of the lesion.

During the second half of the 20th century and, in particular, immediately after the Second World War, there was a reawakening of interest in the brain–behaviour relationship, and, as often happens in science, it was not so much the discovery of new ideas but the rediscovery of old ones. In this case it was the views of some of the classical neurologists, combined with the development of the new behavioural techniques of the experimental psychologists, which were to give the necessary impetus to lead to the development of neuropsychology as such. Recent research (Bruce 1985) suggests that the term 'neuropsychology' was first used in 1913 by Sir William Osler in an address he gave at the opening of the Phipps Clinic at the Johns Hopkins Hospital. In his address entitled 'Specialism in the General Hospital' Osler expressed the hope that 'time may be found for general instruction of the senior class in the elements of neuropsychology'. Bruce speculates that Lashley, who was appointed research professor of neuropsychology at Harvard in 1937, may have heard Osler give his address at the Phipps Clinic, since Lashley was a graduate and postdoctoral student at Johns Hopkins from 1911 to 1917. Subsequently in 1949 the term 'neuropsychology' was given wide publicity when Donald Hebb published *The Organization of Behaviour: A Neuropsychological Theory*. Nine years later, Heinrich Klüver, in the preface to his book *Behaviour Mechanisms in Monkeys*, suggested that it would be of interest to 'neuropsychologists'. In 1960, Lashley's collected writings were published under the title *The Neuropsychology of Lashley*. At no point, however, thus far, was the term 'neuropsychology' used systematically, nor was it carefully defined in the text. Hans-Lukas *Teuber, one of the early pioneers in neuropsychology, argued that the task of neuropsychology is twofold. First, to help the patient with the damaged brain to understand his disease and, secondly, by carefully studying such experiments of nature, to provide essential insights into the physiological basis of normal brain function. Although such study draws information from several disciplines, including anatomy, biophysics, ethology, pharmacology,

and physiology, nevertheless its central focus continues to be the development of a science of human behaviour based upon the study of the function of the human brain. Teuber showed elegantly and convincingly how the precise methods traditionally used by experimental psychologists in the study of psychophysics could be applied to problems in neuropsychology. His monograph *Visual Field Defects after Penetrating Missile Wounds of the Brain*, published in 1960 and written jointly with Battersby and Bender, illustrates the success of such methods.

Thus by 1963 the time seemed ripe for the launching of *Neuropsychologia*. The editorial of the first issue traced its background to regular meetings of a small group of European neurologists and psychologists who had first gathered in Austria in 1951 to discuss disorders of higher mental functions associated with injury or disease of the brain.

Today there are several different approaches to the study of the brain–behaviour relationships, but the method which has figured most prominently is the one that is the natural successor or complement to the work of the early neurologists, namely study of the effects of lesions in specific areas of the brain by carefully observing associated changes in behaviour. It is noteworthy that the results of carefully controlled animal studies have been very important in the development of neuropsychology. In studying patients, one must, for obvious ethical reasons, take what comes and thus accept that the limits of any brain damage are not precisely known. By contrast, in animal studies, the locus and extent of lesions can be precisely defined and pre- and postoperative behaviour carefully studied and measured. In human studies, experimental psychologists have contributed significantly by devising ingenious techniques to be used under controlled conditions and by proposing theoretical concepts to account for the deficits in behaviour observed in brain-damaged patients: for example, the distinction between short-term memory and long-term memory and models of their interrelationships.

Neuropsychologists study our awareness of the world in which we move. What we see, hear, and touch are dependent upon the proper functioning of the intact central nervous system. Likewise, how we respond by taking action is dependent on the intactness of those parts of the nervous system concerned with initiating and sustaining coordinated motor activity. But it is not only sensory and motor processes that may be altered by changes in the nervous system: higher functions such as language, thought, and memory may also be changed. The human brain is well endowed with so-called association cortex, i.e. regions of neocortex not specialized as primary sensory or motor regions. Thus, *memory, for long a topic of interest to philosophers, was a central concern of Lashley, who, after years of animal experimentation, concluded that 'it is not possible to demonstrate the isolated localization of a memory trace anywhere in the nervous system'. Only three years after Lashley reached this conclusion, a neurosurgeon, William Scoville, in 1953 operated on a patient known as H.M. and left him unable to remember virtually anything that occurred after his operation. It appeared that the surgical bilateral removal of the hippocampus and adjacent structures had not touched H.M.'s stored memories but had made it impossible for him to store or retrieve new memories. The detailed study of H.M. changed the emphasis in the study of memory from searching for a location for memories to analysing how memories are stored and retrieved. Today, the roles of the temporal, frontal, and parietal lobes in memory form part of a wider study of the complementary specializations of the left and right hemispheres, to which we now turn. Since studies of cerebral asymmetries have been a major part of research in neuropsychology for several decades, they illustrate well the methods used by neuropsychologists, how their results are presented, and the controversies and uncertainties that remain.

Cerebral asymmetries. The discovery by Dax and Broca in the 19th century that damage to the left hemisphere resulted in inability to talk, whereas damage to the right hemisphere did not affect speech production, led to the general acceptance of the view that the left hemisphere plays a special role in language which is not shared by the right hemisphere. Language, however, is not the only special function of the left hemisphere. At the beginning of the 20th century, H. Liepmann demonstrated that the left hemisphere has a special role in controlling complex movements. Nevertheless, the special functions of the right hemisphere remained a comparative mystery until the early 1950s when, following the work of *Zangwill, Hécaen, and Milner, it became clear that it was more involved in the analysis of visual and spatial dimensions of the world than was the left hemisphere.

The potential for some behaviours, it would seem, is virtually wired into the structure of the nervous system. These include not only reflex and instinctive behaviours, but also behaviour as complex as language. In this sense, psychological asymmetry is based upon microanatomical asymmetry. In 1968, Geschwind and Levitsky reported gross anatomical asymmetries following their study of a large series of human brains. They reported that the part called the 'planum temporale' was larger on the left-hand side of 65 per cent of the brains they studied and that it was larger by nearly 1 cm than on the right. Subsequent studies have confirmed Geschwind and Levitsky's findings and have shown, moreover, that these structural differences are in evidence very early in life.

In addition to those studies of neurological patients with lesions on one side or other of the brain, there are studies of those who have had the brain stimulated during surgery and of those receiving temporary anaesthetization of one side of the brain before surgery. Most recently, studies of regional blood flow have added another technique for the study of functional asymmetry. Studies of healthy people have also added significantly to neuropsychological knowledge. One widely used technique is to present sensory information selectively to one or other cerebral hemisphere and to ask for some kind of verbal or non-verbal response. Electrical recordings from the two hemispheres have also been studied. Even so, the method that has proved most powerful in demonstrating lateralization is that called, by Teuber, 'double dissociation'. Having demonstrated that lesions in the left hemisphere of right-handed patients produce difficulties in language, including speech, writing, and reading, and that such difficulties do not follow from lesions in the right hemisphere, we may say that the functions of the two hemispheres are dissociated. By contrast, difficulties which follow right-hemisphere damage are found with spatial tasks, with singing, and with playing musical instruments; such abilities are thus more disrupted by damage to the right than the left hemisphere. It is then said that the two hemispheres are doubly dissociated.

Another approach which has proved important in identifying cerebral asymmetries has been study of the results of an operation carried out on a small number of patients to whom *epilepsy had become a problem unresponsive to other forms of therapy. In some such cases, neurosurgeons resorted to cutting through the major fibres which interconnect the two cerebral hemispheres, known as the neocortical commissures. These include the corpus callosum and the anterior commissure. Their complete sectioning is known as 'total commissurotomy'. After the operation, the two hemispheres behave as if they are virtually independent. Because of the particular way in which sensory inputs are connected to the cerebral hemispheres, we know that information coming from the left visual field or the left hand is directed to the right hemisphere, and vice versa for the right visual field and the right hand. From numerous studies of such so-called 'split-brain' patients, it is now acknowledged that when the left hemisphere has access to information it can initiate speech, and thus talk about the information, whereas the disconnected right hemisphere cannot. The right hemisphere apparently is good at recognizing things but is unable to initiate speech because it cannot get access to the speech mechanisms in the left hemisphere. By presenting stimuli such as pictures or words to the left visual field, and thus the right hemisphere (or the right visual field and left hemisphere) and asking the patients to name or otherwise act upon what is seen, it has been possible to carry out careful studies of the functions of the isolated right and left hemispheres (see SPLIT-BRAIN AND THE MIND).

The technique of selectively presenting information to one or the other hemisphere, whether through the eyes or through the ears, or through the sense of touch, has also been applied to normal people. The results indicate relative differences between the two cerebral hemispheres; but it is difficult to repeat such experiments and get the same results each time.

Another approach to the study of brain function arises at times in the course of major brain surgery when a neurosurgeon may briefly stimulate the exposed surface of the brain electrically in order to ascertain which part of the brain he is treating, and also to establish with as much certainty as possible on which side of the brain speech is lateralized. Using such stimulation and asking the conscious patient to report what he feels or to answer questions, further information is gained about the functions of particular areas of the brain.

There is yet another source of neuropsychological knowledge associated with the study of neurological patients. To discover as precisely as possible in which hemisphere speech and language are lateralized, a neurosurgeon may temporarily inactivate one or the other hemisphere by injecting sodium amylobarbitone selectively into the carotid artery supplying one or other side of the brain. In this way, it is possible to study what one side of the brain is able to do in the temporary absence of help from the other side. The flow of blood to the neocortex increases in areas where the neurons are particularly active; by injecting a solution of a radioactive substance into the blood, it is possible to examine where it accumulates when particular cognitive activities are taking place.

The auditory system (see HEARING) is not completely crossed, as both hemispheres receive projections from both ears. It appears that the connections from each ear have a preferred access to the opposite hemisphere, so that sounds to the right ear are principally handled by the left hemisphere and vice versa. Kimura (1973) showed that when words are presented simultaneously to the two ears through headphones, the material that is entering through the right ear is more easily analysed than that coming in through the left ear. The converse seems to be true with musical material similarly simultaneously presented. Observing this difference, it has been inferred that the left hemisphere specializes in the analysis of language and the right hemisphere in music. A similar technique can be used to study sensation through *touch. For example, two flat stimuli can be represented simultaneously, one to each hand, and the subject is asked to identify the objects that are being palpated. In all such experiments the results show that, in normal subjects, hemispheric asymmetry is relative rather than absolute. In the normal subject, since the two hemispheres are intimately interrelated through the corpus callosum, any information that is put into one hemisphere can rapidly be transferred to the other hemisphere. Thus, the most likely reason for the observed asymmetries is that the direct route into the left hemisphere is much more efficient than the indirect interhemispheric route.

Neuropsychologists recognize that such talk about lateralization of function begs a number of important questions. What, for example, is it that is lateralized? On this issue there are a number of competing theoretical arguments. For example, there are those who take the view that the two hemispheres are organized differently. Thus, Josephine Semmes suggested that the left hemisphere functions as if there is a collection of discrete regions, whereas the right hemisphere functions in a much more holistic and diffuse manner. Others take the view that the two hemispheres have distinct ways of processing information, and they argue that the left hemisphere works in a much more analytical way, as it processes information sequentially and abstracts out the relevant details, whereas the right hemisphere synthesizes what comes in. The possibility of different forms of cerebral organization is well illustrated by the continuing debate about how speech and language are organized in the brains of left-handers. Thus some (e.g. Zangwill 1960), noting the higher incidence of aphasia in unilaterally brain-injured left-handers, have postulated an incomplete functional lateralization of speech in the vast majority of left-handers, resulting in greater sensitivity to brain lesions.

As the young science of neuropsychology has grown up in different parts of the world, so it has developed its own distinctive emphases and techniques. In the USA, the emphasis has been on quantitative and psychometric techniques. In some cases batteries of tests have been applied to large groups of patients in an attempt to analyse quantitatively the patterns of deficits that emerge between the different brain-damaged groups. In the UK, the approach has been more qualitative and less psychometric and has paid more attention to the in-depth study of crucial single cases, from which a great deal can be learned and any one of which may, properly studied, call into question an existing neuropsychological hypothesis. The case of H.M. cited earlier is a prime example of work in this tradition, including the work that has been done in Canada. In the former USSR also, under the leadership of *Luria, qualitative and non-psychometric techniques have had pre-eminence. For Luria, the preferred techniques were simple, often using only pencil and paper, which could be administered at the bedside and not requiring the full panoply of the experimental psychologist's laboratory. Commenting on Luria's contributions to neuropsychology, Teuber described them as 'monumental', noting that they spanned a third of a century and, in addition to being concerned with the major syndrome of man's left cerebral hemisphere, encompassed 'a detailed and brilliant analysis of the syndrome of massive frontal-lobe involvement'. The publication in 1965 of an English translation of his book, *The Higher Cortical Functions in Man*, made available to the West a wealth of neuropsychological theory and practice.

Each of these distinctive approaches to neuropsychology has contributed significantly to its development and will continue to do so. From time to time, excessive claims have been made for the young discipline, and simplistic accounts have been given of results. In the case of cerebral asymmetries, wide generalizations have been made, speculation going far beyond the relatively limited data and not always helping the development of the subject. See also BRAIN IMAGING. MAJ

Bruce, D. (1985). 'On the origin of the term "neuropsychology"'. *Neuropsychologia*, 23.

Gazzaniga, M. S. (1970). *The Bisected Brain*.

—— and Le Doux, J. E. (1978). *The Integrated Mind*.

Geschwind, N. (1972). 'Language and the brain'. *Scientific American*, 226.

Hécaen, H., and Lateri-Laura, G. (1977). *Évolution des connaissances et des doctrines sur les localisations cérébrales*.

Kimura, D. I. (1973). 'The asymmetry of the human brain'. *Scientific American*, 228.

Kolb, B., and Whishaw, I. Q. (1980). *Fundamentals of Human Neuropsychology*.

Luria, A. R. (1968). *The Mind of a Mnemonist*.

—— (1972). *The Man with the Shattered World*.

—— (1973). *The Working Brain*.

Milner, B. (1971). 'Interhemispheric differences in the localisation of psychological processes in man'. *British Medical Bulletin*, 27.

Osler, W. (1913). 'Specialism in the general hospital'. *Bulletin of Johns Hopkins Hospital*, 24.

Pribram, K. H. (1971). *Languages of the Brain*.

Sperry, R. W. (1964). 'The great cerebral commissure'. *Scientific American*, 210.

Zangwill, O. L. (1960). *Cerebral Dominance and its Relation to Psychological Function*.

neurosis. A habit that is either maladaptive in some obvious respect and/or distressing, yet more or less fixed and resistant to modification through the normal processes of learning. Its original meaning was a circumscribed disorder or loss of function of a bodily organ that was attributed, mistakenly, to disorder in the function of peripheral nerves or nervous tissue. It is diagnosed nowadays only when any disease or disorder in the nervous system seems improbable. Examples of neurotic habits are persistent anxiety out of keeping with the immediate circumstances, *phobias, obsessive thoughts, compulsions, and such losses of function as the paralysis of a limb or erectile impotence. (See OBSESSIVE–COMPULSIVE DISORDER.)

Therapeutic investigation of a neurosis turns on the mental mechanisms involved, its origins in past experience, and the current circumstances determining its persistence. These tend to lie in the benefits, often hidden, that the habit confers. Thus the essence of the neurosis may be, as Sigmund *Freud argued, the renunciation of a function whose exercise would give rise to anxiety. The neurosis then persists because, keeping away from a situation that would arouse anxiety, the patient is denied opportunities to learn more constructive ways of dealing with the sources of the anxiety.

See PSYCHOSIS. DRD

neurotransmitters and neuromodulators. The soft warm living substance of the brain and nervous system stands in stark contrast to the rigid metal and plastic hardware of a modern day computer, but at the fundamental level there are clear similarities between these two apparently disparate organizational systems and, of course, one is a product of the other. Not only are the nerve cell units (neurons) self-repairing and self-wiring under the grand design built into our genes, but they can also promote, amplify, block, inhibit, or attenuate the micro-electric signals which are passed to them, and through them. In this way they give rise to signalling patterns of myriad complexity between networks of cerebral neurons, and this provides the physical substrate of mind.

These key processes of signalling by one group, or family, of neurons to another is achieved largely by the secretion of tiny quantities of potent chemical substances by neuronal fibre terminals. These neurotransmitters stimulate selected neighbours, with whom they junction, into producing electrical responses which both qualitatively (i.e. by excitation or inhibition) and quantitatively (i.e. by frequency of neurotransmitter release) reflect the patterns of presynaptic stimulation.

In this way, the nerve impulses are passed on from cell to cell. This continuous alternation between electrical and chemical conveyance of signals on their journeys through the pathways of the brain and nervous system provides a special opportunity for the traffic of electrical impulses to be modulated or blocked as they attempt to jump the gap between one neurone and the next at their junctions, transposed into pulses of chemical substances. This is the point where selected constellations of neurons from the vast array of neuronal populations can effectively interact, one with another, to filter, edit, integrate, and add precise direction to their interplay of communication. Thus, neurotransmitters and their functional partners, the *neuromodulators*, play a cardinal role in controlling the flow of information through the nervous system.

1. Neurons as information receivers and transmitters
2. How many neurotransmitters are there?
3. How do neurotransmitters work?
4. Neuromodulators

5. Coexistence and co-release of neurotransmitters
6. Postsynaptic and presynaptic neuroreceptors
7. How are neurotransmitters released?
8. Why are there so many neurotransmitters?

1. Neurons as information receivers and transmitters
The extensive web of branching *dendrites which characterizes so many neurons in the brain is primarily an adaptation to provide maximal surface area for receiving inputs from other nerve cells with which they make contact. *Interaction* is very much the principle theme which underlies the shape and cellular anatomy of neurons. Each pyramidal neuron in the vertebrate brain is likely to be receiving up to some 100,000 contacts from the neurons to which they are wired, and the dazzlingly complex and extensive multi-branched dendritic tree of the Purkinje cells of the *cerebellum, concerned with learning coordination tasks, probably extends to some 300,000 neuronal contacts. The *axons, the single output line of the neuron, can be rather short (e.g. in so-called *interneurons*) or very long, perhaps 12 metres in cortical pyramidal cells of the giant blue whale, which course from brain to lower spinal cord. At various points along its length, the axon may branch to make contact with local neuronal communities, though most of its contacts are made towards its terminal region. Thus, it is not surprising that the cell-body region of the neuron is estimated to take up only 5 per cent or less of the cellular volume of the brain, the greater part comprising the dense fibrous feltwork of dendrites and axons (Fig. 1).

Sometimes the neuron-to-neuron contacts or *synapses, as they are termed, are highly organized junctions allowing an extremely close approach between the two cells so that they are separated only by a very narrow gap or *cleft* (typically 20 nanometres wide) (Figs. 2 and 3). In this case, neurotransmitters are delivered at a very precise location when their secretion is triggered by the incoming nerve-terminal. In other cases, the axon produces long chains of swellings (so-called *varicosities*) towards its terminal branching regions, and these provide multiple sites for neurotransmitter release as the nerve-impulse courses through them on its passage towards the distal regions of the neuron (Fig. 4).

These varicosities, while containing synaptic vesicles and granules of the type characteristic of the 'tight-junction' synapses described above, do not exist in highly organized apposition to other neurons, and the highly structured synaptic cleft (gap between neurons) or post-synaptic thickenings typical of 'tight-junction' synapses are rarely present (compare Figs. 3 and 4). The neurotransmitter is probably released from the whole bulbous surface of the varicosity as a miniature cloud which will diffuse away, diminishing in concentration, until it encounters the appropriate neurotransmitter neuroreceptors at which it can bind and act. These varicose modifications of nerve axons were first discovered in the peripheral nervous system, but in the past decade they have become established as a common feature of the synaptic organization of the brain itself, and provide a semi-localized form of neurotransmitter release called *paracrine* neurosecretion.

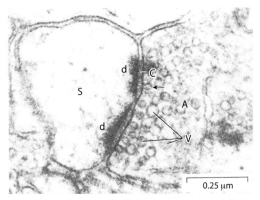

Fig. 2. Electron micrograph of a nerve axon ending making a synapse of the 'tight-junction' variety in a rat brain. These synapses are identical in the human brain. The presynaptic nerve axon ending (axon A) makes synaptic contact with a dendrite spine (S) of the dendrite of the next (postsynaptic) neuron. Note the synaptic cleft (C), 20 nm wide, which is the narrow space separating the two neurones, synaptic vesicles (V), and postsynaptic densities (d). Also note the synaptic vesicles emptying their neurotransmitter content into the cleft by exocytosis (compare with Fig. 3)

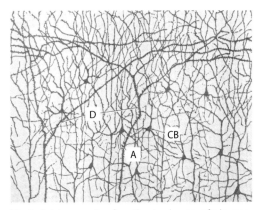

Fig. 1. Golgi preparation from the visual cortex of a human infant, showing the vertical orientation of many neuronal processes. Dendrites (D) can be identified by the dendrite 'spine' processes which give their surface a rough, granular appearance (see also Figs. 2 and 3). In contrast, axons (A) and neuron cell bodies (CB) are smooth-surfaced.

Fig. 3. Diagrammatic version of an axon terminal forming a synapse on a dendrite spine. The structures shown are only approximately to relative scale. Endocytosis produces coated vesicles consisting of a hexagonal basketwork of fibres (cytonet) which form part of the inner surface of the nerve terminal membrane at regions called 'coated pits'. In this diagram, vesicles are shown which contain monoamines, neuropeptides (in granules), or other neurotransmitters, are shown. A vesicle is shown expelling a neurotransmitter into the synaptic cleft by exocytosis. Compare with Fig. 2.

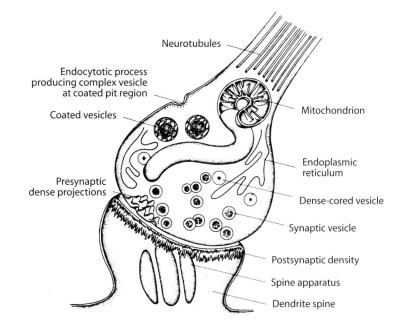

Neurotubules

Endocytotic process producing complex vesicle at coated pit region

Coated vesicles

Presynaptic dense projections

Mitochondrion

Endoplasmic reticulum

Dense-cored vesicle

Synaptic vesicle

Postsynaptic density

Spine apparatus

Dendrite spine

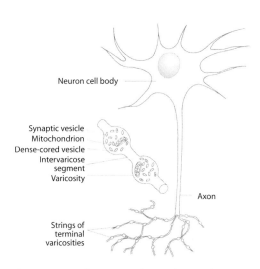

Neuron cell body

Synaptic vesicle
Mitochondrion
Dense-cored vesicle
Intervaricose segment
Varicosity

Axon

Strings of terminal varicosities

Fig. 4. Diagram of a neuron with axonal terminal varicosities.

2. How many neurotransmitters are there?
The search for chemical agents which could transmit the activity of peripheral nerves onto their target organs began early in the 20th century. In the 1920s and early 1930s, after a long trail of research *acetylcholine was un-equivocally demonstrated to be mediating the inhibitory influence of the vagus nerve on the heart, as well as the excitatory action of motor nerve terminals on voluntary muscle. At that point, acetylcholine became the first chemically identified neurotransmitter substance. *Adrenaline, too, was an early candidate as neurotransmitter in the peripheral nervous system at ganglionic sites, but after long accumulation of evidence its unmethylated derivative, noradrenaline, was finally shown in the mid-1940s to be the actual agent responsible. *Dopamine, a closely related amine (monoamines), followed a similar history, with doubt and then certainty following its progress to acceptance as a neurotransmitter in the 1950s (see CATECHOLAMINES). In the 1940s another neuroactive monoamine, serotonin, first isolated from blood was accepted as a neurotransmitter in the brain and peripheral nervous system.

Thus, in the 1950s only four compounds, together with a few other unlikely candidates, including a peptide (substance P), were the full armoury of agents known to be acting as neurotransmitters. They were found to be localized to the neurons from which they were released. These substances seemed to be specialized for their task as neurotransmitters and were not involved in other biochemical activities. At that time, it seemed likely that, together, they provided the principal means of chemical neurotransmission throughout the nervous system. However, it was also in the 1950s and later in the 1960s that four amino acids (glutamate and aspartate as excitatory agents, and GABA and glycine as inhibitory agents), also amines (but carrying an acidic group as well), were being considered as new and important contenders as neurotransmitters in the brain and spinal cord. They were most unlikely candidates, being found ubiquitously in all cells and organs in high concentrations, and being involved in a wide range of metabolic pathways and biosyntheses in the general biochemical economy of the cell.

The first members of yet another entirely different biochemical category of neurotransmitters became serious contenders in the 1970s, namely the *neuropeptides (2 to 50 residue oligopeptides). Unlike the amino acids, the neuropeptides are mostly present in extremely small quantities in localized regions of the nervous system. The earliest candidates proved to be already operating in the brain as local neurohormones in the hypothalamus and anterior pituitary gland. One example is thyrotropin-releasing hormone (TRH, a tripeptide). During the 1970s and 1980s many or most of the peptides known to be serving an endocrine or neurotransmitter role in the gastrointestinal system were found to be also serving as neurotransmitters in the brain. The significance of the dual existence and bioactivity of these peptides is not clear, but specific neuroreceptors for them exist in both brain and gastrointestinal systems, allowing the possibility of brain–gut interactions at the neurohormone level, and giving rise to the concept of the 'brain–gut axis'.

Many of these neuropeptides seem to evoke rather more complex responses than simple physiological synaptic excitation or inhibition (both of which they also mediate). This includes evocation of behavioural and emotional responses. For example, very small quantities of TRH can induce euphoric states, and it can act as an antidepressant drug for the treatment of affective disorders. Another neuropeptide, β-endorphin, causes muscular rigidity and immobility (catatonia), whilst luteinizing-hormone-releasing hormone (LHRH) is reputed to stimulate the libido, and has been used to cure oligospermy. Cholecystokinin (CCK) and Gastrin promote feelings of appetitive satiety and cause cessation of feeding in animals via the brain–gut axis of communication. Bombesin dramatically lowers body temperatures, controls many aspects of gastric secretion, and stimulates appetite by actions at sites within the brain. The *endorphins and encephalins not only produce fairly complex and sophisticated behavioural effects, they also induce analgaesia, behaving like endogenous 'morphine-like compounds'. Unfortunately, they (and their active synthetic derivatives) are also addictive when given in quantity as analgesic drugs. The endorphins seem to serve a neurohumoral role as well as that of neurotransmitter (see PSYCHOPHARMACOLOGY).

Peptide-releasing neurons show certain special features in their organization. Thus, cholinergic (i.e. 'worked' by acetylcholine), monoaminergic, and amino acidergic neurons synthesize neurotransmitter principally in their nerve terminals, by simple enzymatic processes. Peptidergic cells, in contrast, synthesize their peptide neurotransmitters as subcomponents of large 'mother' proteins by

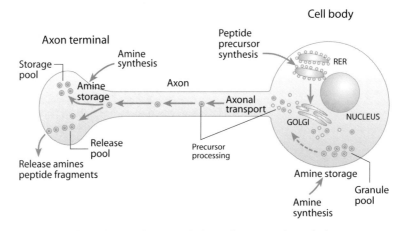

Fig. 5. Diagram illustrating the biosynthesis, packaging, and release of neuropeptides, and other neurotransmitters, in neurons. The peptides are generated from very large precursor molecules (pre-proteins) produced in the rough endoplasmic reticulum (RER) of the neuronal body. These are packaged into secretory granules or vesicles in the Golgi membrane stacks. The granules are then transported out of the cell body (by axonal transport) to the terminals. Here they release their contents by exocytosis by incoming nerve impulses. Other neurotransmitters are produced in the cytosol of the cell body, axon, and principally in the nerve terminal. They are then packaged into synaptic vesicles by specific uptake processes.

protein synthesis processes occurring in the cell body. These are then loaded into large granules and transported down the length of the axon to the terminal regions of the neurone. During this journey, the active neuropeptides are 'snipped' off the mother protein by specific enzymes (proteases), and the peptide neurotransmitters are then ready for release on arrival (Fig. 5). Inactivation of the released peptide neurotransmitter is by enzymatic hydrolysis, as for acetylcholine, and unlike most other neurotransmitters, which are rapidly reabsorbed back into the terminals, and into surrounding glial cells.

When one surveys the current (2003) list of neurotransmitters (Table 1), it can be seen that apart from the simple amines and amino acids discovered during the first 70 years of the last century, some fifty neuropeptides must be included. The latter serve in hybrid capacities as neurotransmitters-neurohormones-neuromodulators, and in this way trigger off complex patterns of behaviour.

Table 1. Neurotransmitters, putative neurotransmitters, and neuroactive peptides.

System	Compound
Amino acidergic	γ-Aminobutyrate (GABA) Aspartate Glutamate Glycine Taurine
Cholinergic	Acetylcholine
Histaminergic	Histamine
Monoaminergic	Adrenaline Dopamine Noradrenaline Serotonin Tryptamine
Peptidergic	Angiotensin Bombesin family (2 members) Bradykinin Calcitonin gene related peptide (CGRP) Carnosine *Caerulein Cholecystokinin family (5 members) Corticotropin Corticotropin releasing hormone (CRF) Dynorphin family (5 members) *Eledoisin Endorphin family (2) Encephalin family (2) Gastrin family (2 members) Luteinizing-hormone-releasing-hormone (LHRH) Melatonin Motilin Neurokinins (2 peptides) Neuromedin family (4 members) Neuropeptide K Neuropeptide Y Neurotensin Oxytocin Peptide Histidine Isoleucine (PHI) *Physalaemin Sleep-inducing peptides (4 peptides) Somatostatin Substance K Substance P Thyroid hormone releasing hormone (TRH) Vasoactive intestinal peptide (VIP) Vasopressin
Purinergic	Adenosine ADP AMP ATP
Gaseous neurotransmitters	Carbon monoxide Nitric oxide

*found mainly in lower vertebrates.

neurotransmitters and neuromodulators

In order to be accepted as a neurotransmitter, the substance must satisfy some eight key criteria. Until they satisfy all criteria, they are called *putative* neurotransmitters. Most of the compounds listed in Table 1 have satisfied these criteria and are fully-fledged neurotransmitters. There are usually several highly qualified putative neurotransmitters awaiting final acceptance or rejection, e.g. currently, agamatine, 3-,4-dihydroxyphenylalanine. Many of the neuropeptides listed (Table 1) are still of putative neurotransmitter/neurohormone status. In recent years, other, atypical, neurotransmitters have been discovered which have been accepted as serving the neurotransmitter function, even though they do not satify all the criteria referred to above. These include the gaseous substances nitric oxide and carbon monoxide. Like monosodium glutamate, viewed prospectively, these gases were most unlikely candidates as neurotransmitters, but now their case is proven (see below). Monosodium glutamate is now a well established excitatory neurotransmitter, which is known to operate far more synapses in the human and animal brain and spinal cord than any other known neurotransmitter!

3. How do neurotransmitters work?

These highly potent substances are released from their storage sites in the close apposition synapses, or in terminal varicosities (or dendrites—see below), and diffuse shorter or longer distances until they encounter neurotransmitter receptors with which they are designed to specifically interact. Once bound to the neurotransmitter in question, the neuroreceptor, which is a large glycoprotein molecule, spanning the membrane thickness (10 nanometres), undergoes conformational or other structural change, and this results in one of two known categories of response. The first of these is called an *ionotropic* response, and results in the appearance of a 'hole' or 'passage' right through the neuroreceptor protein molecule from outside to inside the membrane, through which only a particular charged ion can pass (Na^+, K^+, or Cl). The specific ion in question proceeds to move through the neuroreceptor molecule either into or out of the cell interior, driven down its concentration gradient, and attracted or repulsed by the prevailing electric field across the membrane, according to the nature of its own net charge (Figs. 6 and 7). Each neuroreceptor channel may be open for only a very brief period (e.g. 1 microsecond) as the neurotransmitter rapidly dissociates and is inactivated, or may remain open for much longer periods (e.g. 1 sec.) depending on the ion channel concerned. As the postsynaptic membrane is densely packed with these structures, the net effect is a substantial movement of charged ions across the membrane. This movement generates excitatory or inhibitory synaptic potentials and, from this pattern of impingement of electrical signals (information) onto its dendrites and cell body (inhibitory inputs), the target neuron will be triggered to fire its own action potential, or remain quiescent, as appropriate according to the intensity of the excitatory and

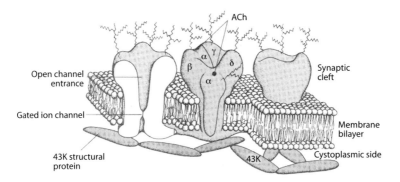

Fig. 6. Three-dimensional models of the nicotinic acetylcholine receptor from the electric ray fish *Torpedo californica* depicted as membrane proteins in the postsynaptic membrane of the synapse between the nerve and electric organ. This organ works essentially like a neuromuscular junction, and employs acetylcholine as a neurotransmitter. Note the subunit arrangement around the central channel which conducts ions into, or out of, the electric organ. Small black spots indicate the sites on the two alpha subunits which bind acetylcholine, and other neurotransmitters. This binding leads to the opening of the ion channel. The proposed shape of the central ion channel can be seen in the vertical section. Also shown is the membrane structural protein, of mol. wt. 43,000, often found in association with the receptor in the *Torpedo* electric organ.

inhibitory signals received. Individual neuroreceptor channel-opening and -closing events can now be distinguished by so-called 'single channel recordings' by 'patch clamping' electrophysiological recording techniques where the neurotransmitter is perfused onto the postsynaptic membrane and the properties of small patches of membrane are studied.

The second category of neuroreceptor response is known as *metabotropic* because enzymes are involved. These enzymes are buried in the lipid membrane close to, and linked permanently or temporarily (depending on the cellular location) to, the neuroreceptor protein molecule. Following neurotransmitter-receptor activation there are conformational changes in the neuroreceptor-enzyme complex, which cause activation of the enzyme. The latter consequently acts upon its substrate, which is situated on the inner surface of the membrane, to produce a soluble product which diffuses into the neuronal cytoplasm and evokes responses which mostly lead on to produce a change in local membrane potential, usually resulting in the generation of a synaptic potential. These soluble enzyme products are called *second messengers*, as they produce actions which are secondary to the primary action of the neurotransmitter. Examples of such metabotropic, second-messenger, neuroreceptor-enzyme systems would be (1) the cyclic nucleotide system and (2) the phosphoinositide system:

1. The key enzyme here is adenylate cyclase which produces the soluble product cyclic AMP (adenosine monophosphate) inside the postsynaptic neurone. This catalyses a cascade of protein phosphorylations and dephosphorylations resulting in the secondary opening of particular ion channels with accompanying generation of synaptic potentials (Fig. 8). In this system coupling of neuroreceptor to adenylate cyclase is via a so-called G-protein (because it requires guanylate-triphosphate for its activation) which can convey either a stimulatory (N_s) or inhibitory (N_i) influence from the neuroreceptor to adenylate cyclase (Fig. 9). There is a parallel system which employs guanylate cyclase linked to neuroreceptors, which is particularly prominent in the cerebellum.

2. The key enzyme in the phosphoinositide system is a particular molecular subtype of phospholipase C (phosphoinositidase C) which is buried in the lipid membrane in close association with particular neurotransmitter receptors (Fig. 10). When this enzyme is activated indirectly via a G-protein following binding of neurotransmitter to neuroreceptor, its substrate, triphosphoinositide (actually, phosphatidylinositol (4,5) diphosphate), is hydrolysed to release water-soluble inositol triphosphate (IP, Inositol (1,4,5)-triphosphate) (Fig. 10). This IP molecule has the ability to release calcium from intracellular stores, and the calcium (which can be regarded as a *third* messenger in this case) then initiates a series of other biochemical events, particularly phosphorylations of key proteins in the cell. Such phosphorylations can switch on various ionic movements into the cell through channels (e.g. potassium ions) and thereby cause synaptic potential changes by this delayed and indirect route (Fig. 10).

The other product of phosphoinositidase C hydrolysis is a special neutral fat (diglyceride, containing arachidonic acid, a rather long fatty acid), which, in concert with calcium and a phospholipid, activates another enzyme, protein kinase C. This enzyme initiates a series of protein phosphorylations. These can result in the opening of local ion channels, and can therefore generate membrane or synaptic potentials (Fig. 10) on a par with those initiated by adenylate cyclase activation (see (1) above and Fig. 8). Close control of these two systems is provided by inactivating phosphatase enzymes, which work by rapidly removing the phosphate groups, from the key proteins involved, as fast as they are inserted to activate them (Fig. 10).

These metabotropic responses to neurotransmitter–neuroreceptor activation are necessarily much slower (10 to 30 times) than their ionotropic counterparts, because they involve enzyme activation and subsequent cascades of biochemical responses before inflow/outflow of charged ions. This is an intrinsically slower pathway than the ionotropic response which involves initiation of ion flow through membrane channels following their instant opening.

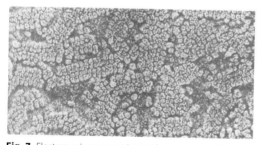

Fig. 7. Electron microscope picture showing acetylcholine-activated neurotransmitter receptors densely packed in the postsynaptic membrane of a cell in the electric organ of *Torpedo californica*, the electric ray fish. Note the central channel, or hole, through the centre of the neuroreceptor. The scale bar is 100 nanometres, showing that each neurotransmitter receptor is 8.5 nm wide.

4. Neuromodulators

It is now well established that the synaptic action of a neurotransmitter may be modulated (i.e. made more or less efficient) by a third party, a neuromodulator substance, thereby amplifying or attenuating the action of the neurotransmitter. This seems to be achieved by more

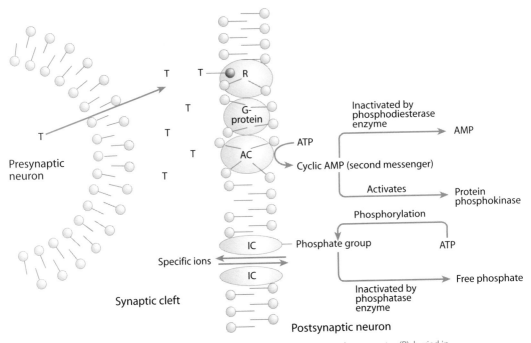

Fig. 8. The second-messenger concept: the adenylate cyclase system. Neurotransmitter receptor (R), buried in the postsynaptic membrane, interacts with neurotransmitter (T) and initiates cyclic nucleotide formation via the adenylcylase enzyme (AC), which is also in the membrane. The cyclic nucleotide (cyclic AMP) is the second messenger, the first messenger being the neurotransmitter released from the nerve-ending of the presynaptic neuron. The cyclic AMP stimulates phosphorylation of a postsynaptic membrane ion channel protein (IC) via a protein phosphokinase enzyme. This event opens the ion channel, allowing ions to move in or out of the cell, resulting in the generation of electrical signals, finally producing a new nerve impulse. The effect is reversed first by a phosphoprotein phosphatase, which de-phosphorylates the ion channel, and secondly by a phosphodiesterase which inactivates the cyclic AMP. Coupling between R and AC is known to involve guanylnucleotide-binding protein (G-protein). See Fig. 9 for details.

than one mechanism. Thus, the neuromodulator has the capacity to enhance or decrease the extent of release of the neurotransmitter following action potential invasion of the nerve terminal. For example, adenosinetriphosphate (ATP), secreted together with the neurotransmitter, will decrease noradrenaline or acetylcholine release from some adrenergic or cholinergic nerves, respectively. In other cases, the neuromodulator will alter the *efficiency* with which the neurotransmitter interacts with its neuroreceptor so as to allow the inward, or outward, flux of more ions per unit time by: (*a*) lengthening the opening period, (*b*) causing a greater frequency of channel opening, or (*c*) causing a greater activation of neuroreceptor-linked enzymes (e.g. adenyl cyclase).

Another, rather curious, neuromodulator substance is of considerable interest because of its links with benzodiazepine anxiolytic (anxiety-reducing) drugs. In fact, the existence of this naturally occurring neuromodulator has

been *inferred* from the potent facilitatory actions of anxiolytic benzodiazepines, such as diazepam (Valium), on the most widespread inhibitory neurotransmitter system in the nervous system, namely the GABA (γ-aminobutyric acid) system. These benzodiazepine drugs both increase the affinity of GABA for GABA neuroreceptors located on synaptic membranes, and enhance GABA-mediated behavioural responses and synaptic potential generation. Moreover, there are neuroreceptors naturally present in the brain which very specifically bind to the drugs. The endogenous benzodiazepine receptor protein (or binding site) is thought to form part of the GABA receptor complex. When released from its nerve endings (or co-released with GABA from GABAergic nerve endings) it works by increasing the extent, or time period, of opening of GABA-operated chloride ion channels (Fig. 11). There has been a thorough hunt in the brain over the past fifteen years for the indwelling Valium-like endogenous

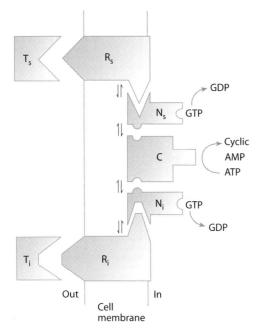

Fig. 9. Scheme showing the coupling inside the postsynaptic membrane between neurotransmitters and adenylate kinase (C) via guanidine nucleotide-binding protein (G-protein). Key: T, neurotransmitter; R, receptor protein; N, guanidine-binding protein; C, catalytic subunit of adenylate cyclase. Subscript 's' to N indicates a stimulatory action; subscript 'i' to N indicates inhibitory action. The coupling between the three membrane components is shown as being reversible. The binding of GTP by N enhances the interaction, which can result in either stimulation or inhibition of adenylate kinase, as shown, depending on the category of N involved. GTP is removed by its hydrolysis. See also Fig. 8.

benzodiazepine, but with little firm success. Various candidates have been found, but as yet no endogenous substance has been isolated which completely mirrors the properties of the endogenous neuromodulator, or endozepine, as it has now been termed. The latest front runner is ODN (octadecaneuropeptide), an 18 amino acid neuropeptide which has most of the properties of Valium. A specific blocking agent for ODN has been developed, called Flumazenil, which prevents the actions of both Valium and ODN supporting the case for ODN as the endogenous benzodiazepine.

A precise definition of a neuromodulator is difficult to produce, since the same substance may act as a neurotransmitter in one synapse, and a neuroregulator at another synapse. Therefore, a definition must represent the category of neuroactivity at a particular site, rather than the identity of the substance itself. For instance, ATP, ADP,

AMP (adenosine tri-, di-, and mono-phosphates), or adenosine itself, may function as a neurotransmitter or as a neuromodulator according to the nature of the neuroreceptors with which it interacts.

5. Coexistence and co-release of neurotransmitters

The long-held dictum, enunciated by H. H. Dale (1935) and later developed by J. C. Eccles in the 1950s, that 'only one and the same neurotransmitter is released by each neuron at all of its nerve terminals, at each of its terminals' (Dale's principle), is no longer universally tenable. We now have many examples where neuroactive peptides coexist with longer-standing ('classical') neurotransmitters, such as acetylcholine, noradrenaline, serotonin, and GABA. The coexistence of other, relatively newly established, neurotransmitters, such as ATP within cholinergic and adrenergic neurones is also now well founded. For the most part, the different neurotransmitters appear to be contained in different categories of storage vesicle or granule within the nerve terminals concerned, and can be released independently of one another. Thus, Vasoactive Intestinal Peptide (VIP) coexists with acetylcholine in parasympathetic nerves supplying the cat salivary gland, each being contained in its own vesicle type. High-frequency stimulation of the nerve releases VIP, whilst low frequencies release acetylcholine. Each neurotransmitter can act as a neuromodulator to influence the extent of release or post-synaptic actions of the other (Fig. 12).

6. Postsynaptic and presynaptic neuroreceptors

Postsynaptic neuroreceptors represent the longer established category of neuroreceptor, and provide the conventional feed-forward of electrical and trophic influences of neurone on neurone. The past three decades have seen the discovery of *presynaptic* neuroreceptors which serve a modulatory function in neurotransmission, being primarily concerned with controlling the *extent* of neurotransmitter release. These neuroreceptors respond to the principal neurotransmitter released by the nerve-ending concerned (so-called autoregulation), or to the actions of co-released, or extraneous, neurotransmitters or neuromodulators of different identity (so-called heteroregulation), by reducing or 'shutting down' the release of that neurotransmitter. This negative-feedback action is the more common consequence of presynaptic neuroreceptor activation (e.g. noradrenaline release from heart, spleen, vas deferens, and also centrally in the brain). A minor category of presynaptic neuroreceptors actually mediate enhancement (positive-feedback) of neurotransmitter release. It seems that both negative- and positive-feedback control can be exercised in the same synapse at a few particular central and peripheral axonal endings, particularly of adrenergic nerves. In this case, integration

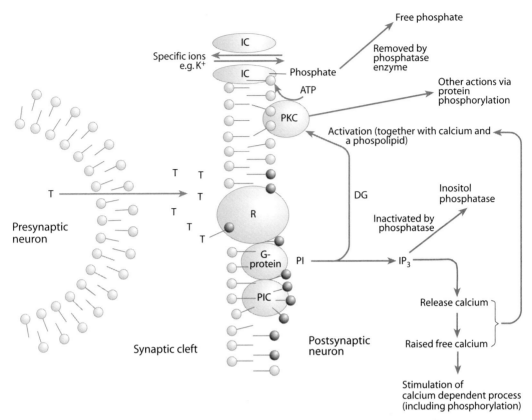

Fig. 10. The second-messenger concept. The phosphoinositide-inositol system. Neurotransmitter receptor (R), buried in the post-synaptic membrane, interacts with neurotransmitter (T) and initiates formation of inositol (1,4,5) triphosphate (IP_3), the second messenger (the first messenger is the neurotransmitter). This is achieved by activation of the enzyme phosphoinositidase C (PIC, also in the membrane) via G-proteins with the consequent hydrolysis of a membrane phospholipid (PI, phosphatidyl inositol (4,5) diphosphate) which is located close to the enzyme and is indicated by the black heads. The second messenger, IP_3, releases calcium from intracellular stores and thereby raises the level of free calcium in the cytoplasm of that neuron. This second messenger is inactivated by another enzyme, inositol phosphatase. The other product of PI hydrolysis is diglyceride (DG). This activates the enzyme protein kinase C (PKC), which begins to phosphorylate various proteins, including specific ion channels, causing them to open and generate synaptic potentials and eventually to produce, or block, nerve impulses. PKC activity can also influence rates of neurotransmitter release, as well as produce profound effects on cell growth and development by influencing gene expression.

of their actions is achieved as follows: when low levels of neurotransmitter (e.g. noradrenaline) are present in the synaptic cleft, the facilitatory (usually beta-type) neuroreceptors are activated, leading to increased release of neurotransmitters. When higher concentrations are reached in the cleft, the inhibitory (usually alpha-type) adrenoreceptors come into play, resulting in a reduction in the level of noradrenaline release. Thus, differential sensitivity to neurotransmitter concentration allows a delicate balance to be maintained between the opposing actions of the two categories of pre-synaptic neuroreceptor.

7. How are neurotransmitters released?
Calcium ions are the critical factors in triggering neurotransmitter release from the nerve terminal onto adjoining neurons, muscles, or glands. Normally these calcium ions are at almost undetectable levels in nerve terminal cytoplasm (10M), but rapidly flood into the terminals from the surrounding fluid through special voltage-dependent

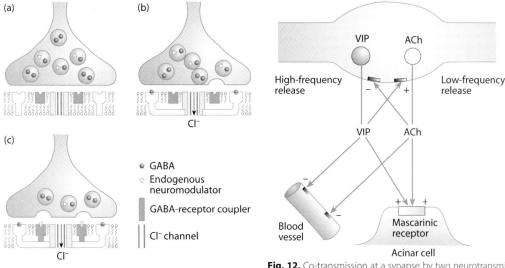

(a)

(b)

Cl⁻

(c)

Cl⁻

- • GABA
- ▽ Endogenous neuromodulator
- ▮ GABA-receptor coupler
- ‖ Cl⁻ channel

Fig. 11. Neurotransmitter and neuromodulator action.
a. Model of GABAergic synapse functioning with a double signal generation, that is GABA and a neuromodulator whose actions are mimicked by benzodiazepine anxiolytic drugs such as Librium and Valium. The coupler for the GABA recognition site and chloride ion (Cl) channel is shown as a postsynaptic membrane protein. In **b.** the GABA, when released alone, is seen to operate the chloride ion channel at normal levels of opening, allowing standard rates of Cl influx. In **c.** the released neuromodulator works through the receptor, along with GABA, to increase the influx of Cl through the channel by interacting with the GABA receptor, and changing its protein shape.

channels during nerve-terminal depolarization caused by invasion by the action potential. Equally rapidly, the raised cytosolic levels of calcium are reduced to very low, ineffective, concentrations by fast absorption into mitochondria and endoplasmic reticulum within the terminal, and neurotransmitter release therefore ceases.

It has been demonstrated that in neuron-to-neuron communication, neurotransmitters can also be released, in the reverse direction, i.e. from the dendritic tree of the post-synaptic neurone, onto the incoming pre-synaptic axon terminal, as well as from the axon terminals onto this tree, as classically conceived. They can therefore act as retrograde neurotransmitters, providing feedback of information (see below).

It may be that neurotransmitters can be released from other regions of the neuronal cell surface, including the unmyelinated regions of axons, and from the cell bodies themselves, though the greater proportion of neurotransmitter is released from the nerve terminals, where it is mostly to be found.

Fig. 12. Co-transmission at a synapse by two neurotransmitters. This is the saliva secreting submaxillary gland in which acetylcholine (ACh), and a neuropeptide neurotransmitter, VIP (vasoactive intestinal peptide), coexist in the parasympathetic nerve terminals supplying this gland. Note that the ACh and VIP are stored in separate vesicles and can therefore be released at different rates at different nerve impulse frequencies to act on the saliva-secreting acinar cells to either increase (+), or decrease (−), saliva secretion. They also act on the blood vessels supplying the gland relaxing (−) the smooth muscles of the blood vessel walls to allow a greater flow of blood carrying precursors to the gland for saliva synthesis. Cooperation between the two neurotransmitters is achieved by selective release of ACh at low nerve impulse frequencies, and of VIP at high nerve impulse frequencies. The two neurotransmitters are also seen acting as neuromodulators mutually influencing the extent of one another's release and postsynaptic action. Key: (+), increased effect; (−), decreased effect.

Whether neurotransmitter is actually released from these various sites by a single process remains unclear. Certainly the traditional view envisages an exocytotic process involving the calcium-triggered fusion of the neurotransmitter-filled synaptic vesicles with the inner side of the nerve terminal wall, resulting in the expulsion of about 1,000 molecules (one quantum) of neurotransmitter into the synaptic cleft from each vesicle. Many multiples of such quanta are released as the nerve impulse invades the nerve terminal, and this involves fusion with the nerve terminal membrane and exocytosis by equivalent multiples of vesicles. However, the synaptic vesicles involved must already be in contact with the terminal membrane, and ready to release their content, as there

667

is less than 200 microseconds between first entry of calcium through its voltage-dependent channel, and first detectable appearance of neurotransmitter in the cleft. The synaptic vesicles which release the neurotransmitters are positioned on the inside face of the membrane close to the point of influx of calcium through its channels, which span the membrane (Fig 13).

The balance of evidence is in favour of the vesicular release hypothesis, though this may not be exclusive, and vesicular release, and release by controlled outward diffusion through membrane channels, could be occurring, according to the neurotransmitter in question. The structure and function of the protein molecules present in the membrane or the vesicle, and which are involved in the exocytosis of synaptic vesicles, have been well defined over the past decade. At least eight of these have been isolated (Fig 13). First, synaptic vesicles attached, via proteins called neurophysins, to structural cytoskeleton scaffolding (microtubules and microfilaments) to limit their migration, are dissociated from this linkage by the addition of phosphate groups to the neurophysins by a calcium-stimulated phosphorylating enzyme. The vesicles can now move, slowly, but freely. Then, synaptic vesicles, full of neurotransmitter, are recruited, from those in the immediate vicinity of the pre-synaptic membrane, transported to this membrane, and then docked by attachment close to where an N-type voltage-dependent calcium channel protrudes through the membrane. Then the vesicle is 'primed' by addition of a molecule of magnesium-ATP salt complex, to enable it to exocytose to the outside and expel its 1,000 molecules of neurotransmitter into the synaptic cleft. The proteins involved here are known to include syntaxin and snap-25 (in the nerve terminal membrane), and synaptotagmin (a calcium-sensing protein), Rab3a and synaptobrevin (VAMP) (in the synaptic vesicle membrane). The next, and critical step, is the coming together and fusion of the vesicle-associated proteins with the membrane-associate proteins, rather like the fingers of two hands being closely intermeshed (Fig 13). This formation is known as the SNARE complex (i.e. Soluble N-sensitive factor Attachment protein REceptor), which is the last stage before neurotransmitter release. It drives vesicle fusion with the terminal membrane and immediate exocytosis by a process called *zippering*, in which calcium ions, flooding into the terminal through their membrane channels, bind to synaptotagmin and neurexin to change their conformations. This enables the latter to form the SNARE, and the former to bind it closer to the calcium channel. Other proteins, including alpha-snap, Rop, Rab3a, and NSF (Fig. 13) are necessary for docking of the vesicle at the terminal membrane before triggering of tight zippering of the SNARE proteins. This is followed immediately by exocytosis, with consequent neurotransmitter release. Spontaneous exocytosis in the absence of

nerve impulse traffic is limited in rate by the vesicle membrane protein, synaptotagmin, whose block is neutralized when it binds to the calcium influxing during nerve impulse traffic. It is interesting that many of these proteins are also found in to be involved in membrane fusion and exocytosis which occurs in invertebrates and even yeasts, indicating their conservation throughout evolution due to their efficacy in these processes.

Most excitatory glutamate receptors are silent most of the time. Glutamate is the most widely used excitatory neurotransmitter in the central nervous system, and operates far more synapses in the brain and spinal cord than any other neurotransmitter. Yet, its most common form, the NMDA ionotropic receptor, is paradoxically silent most of the time and glutamate cannot work as a neurotransmitter via these majority receptors! This is due to its ion channel, which runs across the post-synaptic membrane, being physically blocked by the entry of positively charged magnesium ions which are drawn into the ion channel from the extracellular fluid by the attracting influence of the negative interior of the neurone. This is established by the prevailing negative membrane potential across the neuronal membrane (approx. -70mV). Until this magnesium block is removed by a fall in membrane potential to -40mV or less, the NMDA receptor remains inactive. Membrane potential depolarization, and therefore activation of the NMDA receptor, is achieved by an unusual arrangement in the post-synaptic membrane. This involves the close juxtaposition of the NMDA receptor proteins with other types of glutamate receptors which are not blocked, such as ionotropic AMPA receptors or metabotropic glutamate receptors (mGluRs). Thus, when glutamate is released into the synaptic cleft from the pre-synaptic terminal, it cannot activate the NMDA receptors, but can activate the other, neighbouring, glutamate receptors. As a result, the post-synaptic membrane potential is locally depolarized by excitatory-postsynaptic potentials (EPSPs: usually due to sodium and calcium influx through the AMPA receptor ion channel). This depolarization causes efflux of the magnesium ions blocking the NMDA receptor channel, and this NMDA glutamate receptor can then respond to the synaptically released glutamate neurotransmitter, alongside the AMPA receptors in the same membrane, once sufficient membrane depolarization has occurred (Fig. 14). This functional arrangement means that NMDA receptors will only be recruited during periods of high and persistent neural activity, when glutamate release into the synaptic cleft occurs at a high rate. Once recruited, NMDA receptor activity, which has a large excitatory impact due to the high rate of entry of sodium / calcium ions, will massively boost the effect of the glutamatergic excitatory pathway. This occurs as part of the normal way of providing the upper range of intensity of normal nerve impulse traffic,

Fig. 13. Neurotransmitter release by exocytosis of synaptic vesicles. **a.** Protein domain structure of synaptotagmin and the other proteins involved in docking the synaptic vesicles at the presynaptic nerve terminal membrane. **b.** The interrelations of the proteins shown in (**a**) after docking and before the final exocytosis stage which releases the neurotransmitter into the synaptic cleft. Adapted from Fig. 1 in Littleton and Bellen (1995).

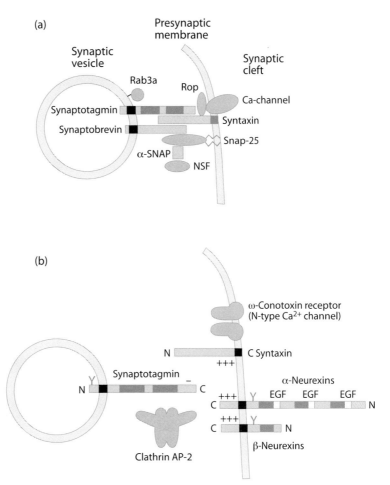

and it is also involved in abnormal situations such as the initiation and propagation of epileptic fits.

Retrograde and gaseous neurotransmitters, and synapses working backwards to establish memory stores. Among the interesting new discoveries in recent years has been the discovery that communication between nerve cells across a synapse can be two-way, i.e. forward directed (anterograde), and also retrograde in direction, back across the synapse. It was long thought that nerve impulses, when they invaded the nerve terminal, released neurotransmitter by causing influx of calcium ions, and the released neurotransmitter then activated specific postsynaptic receptors on the next neurone in the chain, causing postsynaptic electrical impulses which stimulated this receiving neurone. It was not conceived that events could take place inside this receiving (postsynaptic) neuron which could result in a retrograde action on the presynaptic neuron which had released the neurotransmitter. It did

not seem possible, as no mechanisms for such retrograde action were known. This has turned out to be wrong; it is possible, and indeed, common. The thinking began to change when two observations were brought together. The first finding, in the 1970s, was that glutamate-operated synapses, in particular, can somehow learn when they receive an invasion, via the incoming axon, of high-frequency (tetanic) nerve impulses—a kind of intensive bout of neural activity, i.e. strong synaptic stimulation. This was shown by making simple electrical recordings from glutamate-operated pathways in isolated slices of the hippocampus, a brain region much involved in memory processes. It has subsequently been demonstrated to occur in synapses located in other brain regions concerned with memory, e.g. the cerebral cortex. Thus, after strong, high-frequency, tetanic stimulation, the postsynaptic response to a subsequent low/normal frequency stimulation was greatly enhanced. This enhancement of postsynaptic response lasted for at least several hours, and has been shown to last weeks. Indeed, the phenomenon was appropriately called Long-Term Potentiation of the postsynaptic response (LTP, Fig. 14). There is also Long-Term Depression (LDP) of the EPSP which can occur in other synapses under similar circumstances. The question was, how could the postsynaptic part of the synapse which was part of the next neurone in the chain apparently influence the presynapse to release more transmitter on all subsequent occasions that it received a low-frequency nerve impulse volley, i.e. how could it *learn*? After all, there was no known method of communication *backwards* from the second neuron to the first, i.e. from the postsynapse to the presynapse. The synaptic pathway was thought to be a rectifier, and allow only one-way traffic of the stimulus. It has since been established that there is a parallel increase in the pre-synaptic release of the excitatory neurotransmitter, glutamate, which occurs during the establishment of the LTP. Moreover, LTP was prevented by agents (antagonists) which blocked the synaptic action of glutamate at its post-synaptic receptors, showing that these receptors were somehow involved in LTP.

The second observation, in the 1980s and 1990s, which was to throw light on the mechanism of retrograde synaptic action, and the mechanism of LTP, was the finding that at least two gases are working as neurotransmitters, namely nitric oxide and carbon monoxide. The latter is, of course, a very poisonous gas when inhaled, and excess nitric oxide will also kill neurons! These surprisingly atypical neurotransmitters have properties which would allow them to work in a synaptically retrograde fashion, because, as gases, they are able to diffuse in all 3-D spherical directions, once synthesized and released. Unlike most other neurotransmitters, there are no storage pools for these gases. They must be synthesized and released when needed. Nitric oxide synthesis occurs both in the pre- and postsynapse. It readily dissolves in, and passes through, cell membranes, which do not, therefore, provide a barrier to its movement in any direction. It turns out that nitric oxide gas is made in significant amounts for a short time in the postsynaptic dendrite by the enzyme nitric oxide synthase (NOS) following the action of glutamate jointly at its postsynaptic AMPA and NMDA receptors (see 'silent glutamate receptors', above). This is because the ionotropic NMDA receptor channel, once activated following sufficient AMPA-glutamate receptor induced membrane depolarization, allows a large influx of calcium ions into the postsynapse, where it stimulates NOS to produce nitric oxide (Fig. 14). The NOS-enzyme is attached to the postsynaptic density (Figs. 2 and 3), close to the NMDA glutamate receptor. The released nitric oxide gas then diffuses rapidly and reaches the presynaptic nerve terminal where it stimulates the formation

of the activating agent cyclic-GMP, by the enzyme Guanylate cyclase. The amount of glutamate neurotransmitter release is then increased via the action of this cyclic GMP (Fig. 14). Either the postsynaptic production of nitric oxide (or carbon monoxide; see below) must be constant to maintain the LTP, once established, or another, as yet unidentified mechanism is responsible for maintenance of the synapse in a potentiated state which persists for a lengthy period of time that greatly outlasts the period of application of the inducing stimulus.

Thus, nitric oxide gas is indeed likely to be one of the retrograde chemical signals that stimulate the persistent increased release of glutamate by the presynapse which characterizes LTP. Other candidates include carbon monoxide, which is produced by the enzyme haem oxygenase, which cleaves haem into carbon monoxide and the protein biliverdin. There are many parallels in the range of neuroactivity and the organization of the carbon monoxide and nitric oxide neurotransmitter systems, both in relation to NMDA receptor activation and to calcium influx. The long chain polyunsaturated fatty acid arachidonic acid is another front-running candidate as a retrograde signalling agent initiating LTP. These retrograde messengers, and LTP, are likely to be involved in the early phase of memory, lasting ten or twenty minutes, and involving acquisition and consolidation of the memory. This is where, immediately after acquisition, the memory is transformed from an initially unstable state into a stabilized store.

The calcium-dependent protein kinase enzyme, known as calcium calmodulin-dependent kinase (CaM kinase II) may be also be part of the mechanism which allows persistence and consolidation of the synaptic LTP (i.e. the memory store) triggered by NMDA-receptor activation. Thus, this CaM kinase protein is located postsynaptically, in particularly high concentrations (20–40 per cent) in the postsynaptic densities of glutamatergic synapses (Figs. 2 and 3). It is therefore in a good location to respond immediately to the cytoplasmic calcium ions flooding in through the activated postsynaptic NMDA receptor channels, following high-frequency (tetanic) synaptic stimulation. Furthermore, CaM kinase remains active, phosphorylating its own protein structure (autophosphorylation), as well as that of the juxtaposed NMDA and AMPA glutamate receptors, which further increases the rate of calcium and sodium ion entry through these receptor channels during subsequent nerve impulse invasion and synaptic activation. Metabotropic glutamate receptors and their second messengers such as IP (see Figs. 10 and 14) are also involved in LTP, though this is not so well understood. This activated synaptic state continues long after the calcium levels have dropped back to basal levels. Moreover, the CaM kinase enzyme protein has been reported to increase in amount in the postsynaptic dendrite during the tetanic stimulation which establishes

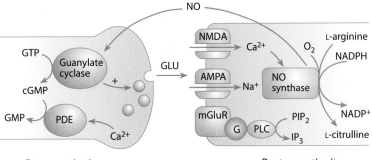

Presynaptic site   Postsynaptic site

Fig. 14. Theories of how the retrograde gaseous neurotransmitter nitric oxide could be involved in Long-Term Potentiation (LTP) of a glutamatergic hippocampal synapse. The excitatory neurotransmitter glutamate first activates AMPA and metabotropic glutamate receptors which leads to recruitment of NMDA receptor activity. Calcium ion entry, via NMDA receptor channels, into the postsynaptic site activates nitric oxide synthase (NOS). The nitric oxide gas (NO) produced diffuses to the presynaptic site where it is absorbed by the haem group of an NO-sensitive guanylate kinase enzyme which triggers the production of cyclic GMP which increases neurotransmitter glutamate release. Key: mGluR, metabotropic glutamate receptors; IP, inositol triphosphate second messenger; PDE, phosphodiesterase, which inactivates cyclic GMP. Adapted from Fig 2 in Holscher (1997).

LTP of the hippocampal synapse. Also, more synapses have been reported to develop, i.e. there is remodelling of the post-synaptic dendrite spine. The CaM kinase II enzyme can therefore 'remember' that the juxtaposed NMDA receptors have been activated, and the resulting calcium influx has produce phosphorylated CaM kinase II in the post-synaptic density. The stimulation has also stimulated increased gene-expression of the CaM kinase II protein of the postsynaptic density, dendrite, and cell body of the postsynaptic neurone over the subsequent 30 minutes (Fig. 15). These changes could partly explain why there is persistence of an enhanced postsynaptic response to subsequent pre-synaptic invasion of this potentiated synapse by nerve impulses, i.e. a key part of a the molecular mechanism of establishing memory traces in the brain.

The dendritic tree and retrograde neurotransmission. It has been demonstrated that neurotransmitters can also be released from the *dendritic tree* of the neuron as well as from *axon terminals* as classically conceived. Indeed, the dendrites show localized accumulations of synaptic vesicles which are characteristic of all neurotransmitter release sites (e.g. synapses, terminal varicosities). Both long-established neurotransmitters (e.g. dopamine, ATP), and neuropeptide neurotransmitters, such as vasopressin and oxytocin (normally known only as neurohormones), can be released from the dendrites of neurons at many sites within the CNS, to act as retrograde signals to modulate incoming synaptic transmission, electrical activity, and, in some cases, to modify the morphology of the surrounding presynaptic neurons. Such dopamine release has been

unequivocally demonstrated to occur from the dendrites of dopaminergic neurones of the substantia nigra of the brain (see BASAL GANGLIA).

The neurotransmitters glutamate and GABA act as retrograde dendritic synaptic signals for the mitral cells and GABAergic axonless granule cells of the olfactory bulb. The dendrites can support an invasion of action potentials spreading, backward and upwards, from the cell body where they are generated. It is these invading action potentials which trigger dendritic neurotransmitter release. Through this mechanism, the neuron cell body can transmit information back, from its dendrites, to its neighbouring presynaptic neurons, through the actions of dendritically released neuroactive substances. The gaseous neurotransmitters nitric oxide and carbon monoxide and the long, polyunsaturated fatty acid arachidonic acid are other membrane-permeable neuroactive compounds that are released from neuronal dendrites onto synaptic inputs where they have a major role in synapse formation, and memory establishment.

8. Why are there so many neurotransmitters?

The answer to this question is far from resolved. Certainly, subgroups of the 50 or so neurotransmitters (Table I) produce different categories of effect in both qualitative and quantitative respects, and many will coexist in different neuronal populations. First, there is the differential speed of response following receptor activation, with ionotropic being some 10- to 30-fold faster than metabotropic responses. Another dimension is provided in the *variety* of second-messenger activation of *different* cascades

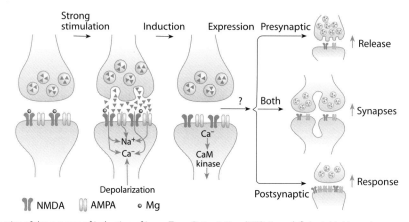

Fig. 15. Theories of the process of induction of Long-Term Potentiation (LTP). From left to right: Normal stimulation of the presynaptic (upper) nerve terminal activates only the postsynaptically positioned glutamate-AMPA receptors, the juxtaposed glutamate-NMDA receptors being sterically blocked by magnesium ion binding to and occupying their ion channels. Strong repetitive (tetanic) stimulation, or high-frequency nerve-impulse invasion, of the presynapse activates first AMPA receptors sufficiently to cause a large depolarization (EPSP) of the postsynaptic membrane, and consequent activation of NMDA receptors by outflow of the blocking magnesium channels ions. As a result, sodium ions enter through the channel of the AMPA receptors, and sodium and calcium ions enter through the NMDA channel, into the cytoplasm of the postsynaptic dendrite, close to the postsynaptic density. This calcium ion influx induces LTP by activating nitric oxide synthase and CaM kinase II (see text). There is evidence that LTP involves, in the long term: increased presynaptic release of glutamate neurotransmitter, permanent increase in the expression and state of activation of CaM kinase II, phosphorylation to activate NMDA and AMPA receptors, as well as the increased synaptic response (e.g. 10-fold) to subsequent normal levels of synaptic stimulation by nerve impulses. Adapted from Sanes and Lichtman (1999), Fig. 1 in *Trends in Neuroscience*, 2/7.

of biochemical sequelae, with particular metabotropic neurotransmitter actions being mediated by one or other second messenger system. Further possibilities for adding to the qualitative features of the response could come through the range of distances through which the neuroactive compounds exert their influence once released, if they can survive the inactivation processes. This may be 20 nanometres within the synaptic cleft but several millimetres from axonal varicosities or unstructured release points, and of course the concentration of neurotransmitter diminishes rapidly with the distance travelled, and some neuroactive substances will be less efficiently inactivated than others. Actions ranging over a greater volume of tissue would activate specific neuroreceptors sited on a larger variety of neurone types, producing complex sequences of neuronal triggering, and therefore a greater spectrum of overall responses (so-called trophic or paracrine actions). Continuous (tonic) release of neurotransmitter (e.g. from axonal varicosities or dendrites), as opposed to discrete and occasional release, would also provide a basis for variation in the patterns of activation of targeted neurons due to changes in sensitivity, accommo-

dation, and desensitization of neuroreceptors which ensues during continuous neuroreceptor stimulation.

Thus, the large number and the chemical variety of neurotransmitters, together with their tendency to activate anatomically distinct neuronal pathways, often in pairs, and the evidence that they provide many palpable possibilities for variation in response, can be seen to provide a chorus of informational voices, each adding tonal colour or timbre to the final output of the brain and nervous system.   HFB

Bajjalieh, S. (2001). 'SNARES takes the stage: a prime time to trigger neurotransmitter secretion'. *Trends in Neurosciences*, 24/12.

Baranano, D. E., Ferris, C. D., and Snyder S. H. (2001). 'Atypical neural messengers'. *Trends in Neurosciences*, 24/2.

Bradford, H. F. (1986). *Chemical Neurobiology*.

Hampton, L. L. et al. (1998). 'Loss of Bombesin-induced feeding suppression in gastrin-releasing peptide receptor deficient mice'. *Proceedings of the National Academy of Sciences of the United States of America*, 95/6.

Holscher, C. (1997). 'Nitric oxide, the enigmatic neuronal messenger: its role in synaptic plasticity'. *Trends in Neuroscience*, 20/7.

Kandel, E. R., Schwartz, J. H., and Jessell, T. M. (2000). *Principles of Neuroscience* (4th edn.).

Kennedy, M. B. (1998). 'Signal transduction molecules at the glutamatergic postsynaptic membrane'. *Brain Research Reviews*, 26/2–3.

Kiss, J. P., and Vizi, E. S. (2001). 'Nitric oxide: a novel link between synaptic and non-synaptic transmission'. *Trends in Neuroscience*, 24/3.

Lamacz, M., et al. (1996). 'The endogenous benzodiazepine receptor ligand ODN increases cytosolic calcium in cultured rat astrocytes'. *Molecular Brain Research*, 37.

Littleton, J. T., and Bellen, H. J. (1995). 'Synaptotagmin controls and modulates synaptic-vesicle fusion in a calcium-dependent way'. *Trends in Neuroscience*, 18/4.

Ludwig, M., and Pittman, Q. P. (2003). 'Talking back: dendritic neurotransmitter release'. *Trends in Neurosciences*, 26/5.

Medina, J. H., and Izquierdo, I. (1995). 'Retrograde messengers, long-term potentiation and memory'. *Brain Research Reviews*, 21/2.

Nichols, J. G. (2001). *From Neuron to Brain*.

Ojima, K., Matsumoto, K., and Watnabe, H. (1997). 'Flumazenil and endogenous benzodizepines'. *Brain Research*, 747/1–2.

Siegel, G. J., Agranoff, B., Albers, R. W., Fisher, S. K., and Uhler, M. D. (1999). *Basic Neurochemistry: Molecular, Cellular and Medical Aspects* (6th edn.).

Snyder, S. H., Jaffrey, S. R., and Zakhary, R. (1998). 'Nitric oxide and carbon monoxide: parallel roles as neural messengers'. *Brain Research Reviews*, 26/2–3.

neutral monism. See RUSSELL'S PHILOSOPHY OF MIND: NEUTRAL MONISM.

Newton on mind. Although Newton is celebrated mainly for his discoveries and theories of physics and astronomy, he made significant discoveries in *colour vision—realizing, as did *Locke, that objects and light are not themselves coloured; but that colour depends on suitable eyes and brains. He experimented with colour mixture, not only with the famous prisms—which showed that white light is made up of all the colours of the spectrum—but also with pigments. He recognized the importance of the optic nerves and the large-scale structure of the visual system. He described after-images (after looking at the sun and going to bed with an after-image for two weeks!), and persistence of vision from a burning coal swung in a circle on the end of a rope. He made with his own hands the first reflecting telescope (to avoid chromatic aberration) which is now in the Royal Society, in London.

His *Opticks* (1704) is written in beautiful English (his other works being in Latin) and is a delight to read today. The experiments are models of science, and the *Queries* are windows to his strange, unique mind. He wrote more (though never published) on alchemy, and Biblical dating, than he wrote on the science that, with his genius, he transformed. RLG

Brewster, Sir D. (1831). *Life of Sir Isaac Newton*.

More, L. T. (1934). *Isaac Newton* (repr. 1962).

Newton, I. (1959–77). *The Correspondence of Isaac Newton*. Eds. H. W. Turnbull and J. F. Scott.

Westfall, R. S. (1973). *Science and Religion in Seventeenth-Century England* (2nd edn.).

—— (1980) *Never at Rest: A Biography of Isaac Newton*.

Nietzsche, Friedrich Wilhelm (1844–1900). Born at Röcken, Saxony, and brought up the son of a Lutheran pastor, he was a brilliant undergraduate at Bonn and Leipzig; and accepted the professorship of classical philology at Basel before graduating. He was a disciple of *Schopenhauer, and Schopenhauer's 'will to power' was a basis of his philosophy that only the strong ought to survive, while sympathy perpetuates the unfit. His magnum opus is *Also Sprach Zarathustra* (1883–91; Eng. trans. *Thus Spake Zarathustra*). It develops the idea of the 'superman', which was taken up by George Bernard Shaw in his play *Man and Superman* (1903). Nietzsche died insane at Weimar.

Safranski, R. (2003). *Nietzsche: A Philosophical Biography*. Trans. S. Frisch.

nitrogen narcosis (the bends). The term used to describe the apparent drunkenness experienced by deep-sea divers. Jacques Cousteau has termed it 'l'ivresse des grands profondeurs' (rapture of the deep), while divers typically use the rather more prosaic term 'the narks'. As its name implies, the primary source of intoxication in air breathed at pressure comes from nitrogen. One might expect therefore that breathing pure oxygen would alleviate the problem. Unfortunately, however, when the partial pressure of oxygen exceeds that obtained at a depth of 9–12 metres (30–40 feet) it produces oxygen poisoning, resulting in convulsions and loss of consciousness.

Nitrogen narcosis first becomes detectable at a depth of about 30 metres (100 feet), while below a depth of 60 metres the effects are sufficiently marked to make working risky even for an experienced diver. The symptoms are not unlike drunkenness: the diver may become euphoric, his ability to reason reduced, and his manual skill impaired, with a tendency to make errors of judgement that can be disastrous at depth. For example, a diver taking part in an open-sea experiment at 60 metres noticed that he had insufficient air to complete the dive; he reasoned that he had enough air left either to do a decent job and complete the experiment or to get to the surface, but not both. He opted to complete the experiment. Fortunately, being a strong swimmer with a clear head, and having a good life-jacket, he managed to make the surface and was able to collect a fresh supply of air without suffering from 'the bends'—compressed air illness which may occur on return to normal atmospheric pressure, nitrogen dissolved in the bloodstream expanding to form bubbles which lead to pain, and possibly paralysis and death.

Most research on nitrogen narcosis has been carried out in dry pressure chambers, which are safer and allow better control over conditions than open-sea studies. Do they, however, provide an adequate simulation of the real thing? An experiment conducted by Baddeley (1966) suggests that they may not. He studied the manual dexterity of divers using a simple brass plate containing 32 holes and 16 nuts and bolts. The diver simply had to transfer the nuts and bolts from the holes at one end of the plate to the other, and was timed as he did so. Subjects performing this task in a dry pressure chamber showed a small but reliable decrement in performance (5 per cent) when they were performing under an air pressure equivalent to pressure at a depth of 30 metres of sea water. A parallel experiment tested the performance of subjects at a depth of 3 metres, and at a depth of 30 metres, in the open sea. The experiment was carried out in the Mediterranean, ensuring good visibility and with no problems of cold. Simply testing a subject under water slowed him down by approximately 28 per cent, while testing him at a depth of 30 metres caused a drop of 49 per cent as compared to dry-land performance.

Note that the decrement in performance observed at 30 metres is greater than would have been predicted by simply adding the effects of water (16 per cent) and pressure (5 per cent). Why should this be? A clue was given by a later experiment which used the same task, and again tested at a depth of 30 metres, but on this occasion resulted in a decrement of only 5 per cent. The difference between the two studies was as follows: the first was carried out in the open sea from a ship, the divers being required to go straight down. The second was carried out close inshore, where the diver could swim straight down from the jetty to a site populated by many other divers. It seems reasonable to suppose that the divers in the first experiment were much more anxious than those in the second, and subsequent studies have supported this conclusion. They reveal relatively small decrements when divers are tested in the relatively safe conditions of a 'wet' pressure chamber, and under open-sea conditions with divers who show little evidence of anxiety, while much greater decrements are shown by anxious divers and under relatively threatening open-sea conditions.

The nature of the anxiety effect is still far from clear. Performance on a reasoning task does not show the interaction with anxiety, suggesting that the anxiety effect may result from some factor such as muscular tension, impairing motor rather than cognitive skills. The point remains, however, that while initial work is best done in the pressure chamber, generalization to open-sea performance must proceed with caution.

How can nitrogen narcosis be prevented? The standard procedure at present is to have the diver breathe a mixture of oxygen and helium (Heliox). Using this, dives have been made to as much as 600 metres (2,000 feet) without the diver losing consciousness. For a while it seemed as though there might be no psychological decrement. Although a tendency to tremor and nausea, which was termed HPNS (high-pressure nervous syndrome), did occur, it was thought to result from compressing the diver too rapidly so that it could be avoided provided the rise in pressure was gradual. It has, however, subsequently become clear that more general intellectual and performance decrements do occur and are detectable at depths in excess of 300 metres. The effect observed is almost certainly different from that obtained with nitrogen, and it is possible that some more complex mix of gases may allow greater depths to be achieved. Heliox has two further disadvantages: it conducts heat very efficiently, making it harder to keep the diver warm, and it distorts the voice. If you take a lungful of helium at normal pressure and speak, you sound like Donald Duck, while at pressure the effect is even further exaggerated. A number of helium speech unscramblers have been designed, and do improve communication. However, the existing commercial models still leave a great deal to be desired.

In recent years there has been increasing interest in operating with Trimix, a mixture of oxygen, helium, and nitrogen. Such a mixture has a possible advantage in terms of narcotic potency. However, this is still a controversial issue. At a pharmacological level we still seem to be some distance from understanding the mechanism of inert gas narcosis; theories exist, but it is probably true to say that no theory has yet won broad acceptance.

See also DIVER PERFORMANCE.   ADB

Baddeley, A. D. (1966). 'Influence of depth on the manual dexterity of free divers'. *Journal of Applied Psychology*, 50.

nothingness. Nature abhors a vacuum—and so do we. The idea of a void—of emptiness, nothingness, spacelessness, placelessness, all such 'lessness'—is at once abhorrent and inconceivable, and yet it haunts us in the strangest, most paradoxical way: 'Nothing is more real than nothing.'

For *Descartes there was no such thing as empty space. For Einstein there was no space without field. For *Kant our ideas of space and extension were the forms our 'reason' gives to experience, through the operation of a universal 'synthetic a priori'. The nervous system, intact and active—*Leibniz's stream of 'minute perceptions'—was envisaged by Kant as a sort of transformer, forming ideality from reality, reality from ideality. Such a notion has the virtue—very rare in metaphysical formulations—that it can instantly be tested in practice—specifically, in neurological and neurophysiological practice.

Let us proceed at once to examples. If one is given a spinal anaesthetic that brings to a halt neural traffic in the lower half of the body, one cannot feel merely that this is paralysed and senseless; one feels that it is wholly, impossibly, 'non-existent', that one has been cut in half, and that the lower half is absolutely missing—not in the familiar sense of being somewhere, elsewhere, but in the uncanny sense of *not-being*, or being nowhere. The terms that patients use communicate something of this incommunicable nothing. They may say that part of them is 'missing', 'evacuated', 'gone': that it seems like dead flesh, or sand, or paste; devoid of life, of activity, of 'will'; devoid of the organic, of structure, of coherence—without materiality or imaginable reality; cut off or alienated from the living flesh (with which, none the less, it forms an impossible continuity). One such patient, trying to formulate the unformulable, finally said that his lost limbs were 'nowhere to be found', and that they were 'like nothing on earth'. Hearing such phrases, as one will hear from every patient who finds himself in such a situation—or, more properly, 'situationless'—and from every patient who can articulate this ultimate abhorrence, one is irresistibly reminded of the words of *Hobbes: 'That which is not Body . . . is no part of the Universe: and since the Universe is all, that which is not Body . . . is Nothing, and Nowhere.'

Spinal anaesthesia is common—perhaps a million women have had it for painless childbirth—but descriptions are most rare, partly because the experience is so abhorrent that it is instantly banished from the memory and mind, and partly because the experience (or nonexperience) is an experience of *nothing*. How can one describe nothingness, not-being, nonentity, when there is, literally, nothing to describe? This paradox is pungently expressed by *Berkeley, in his denunciations of the nothingness of 'matter': 'It neither acts, nor perceives, nor is perceived . . . it is *inert, senseless*, unknown . . . a definition entirely made up of negatives.' Spinal anaesthesia provides a striking and dramatic example of a *transient* 'annihilation' (although it does not seem transient, but endless, when it occurs—a part of its peculiar horror).

But there are many simpler examples of annihilation in everyday life: all of us have sometimes slept on an arm, crushing its nerves and briefly extinguishing neural traffic; the experience, though very brief, is a terrifying one because (it seems to us) our arm is no longer 'our arm', but an inert, senseless nothing which is not part of ourselves. *Wittgenstein (following *Moore) grounds 'certainty' in the certainty of the body: 'If you can say, *here is one hand*, we'll grant you all the rest.' When you wake up, after nerve crushing your arm, you cannot say 'This is my hand,' or even 'This is *a* hand,' except in a purely formal sense. What has always been taken for granted, or axiomatic, is revealed as radically precarious and contingent; having a body, having *anything*, depends on one's nerves.

Yawning is the abyss of nothing. It is only 'by favour of nature' that there are countless other situations—physiological and pathological, common or uncommon —in which there is brief, or prolonged, or permanent annihilation. Strokes, tumours, injuries, especially to the right half of the brain, tend to cause a partial or total annihilation of the left side—a condition variously known as 'imperception', 'inattention', 'neglect', 'agnosia', 'anosognosia', 'extinction', or 'alienation'. All of these are experiences of nothingness (or, more precisely, privations of the experience of somethingness).

Blockage to the spinal cord or the great limb plexus can produce an identical situation, even though the brain is intact but deprived of the information from which it might form an image (or a Kantian 'intuition'). Indeed it can be shown by measuring potentials in the brain during spinal or regional blocks that there is a dying away of activity in the corresponding part of the cerebral representation of the 'body image'—the empirical reality required for Kantian ideality. Similar annihilations may be brought out peripherally, either through nerve or muscle damage in a limb, or by simply enclosing the limb in a cast, which by its mixture of immobilization and encasement may temporarily bring neural traffic and impulses to a halt.

To conclude. Nothingness, annihilation, is a reality in this ultimately paradoxical sense. There is, indeed, no space without field, but there are conditions in which the 'field' may be lost—a perceptual-ideal 'Kantian' field which is closely analogous to an Einsteinian field. One's sense of *being* is entirely contingent upon, coextensive with, and contained in such a field. And anything that produces 'fieldlessness' (or field defect, or scotoma) is certain to produce a corresponding nothingness.

Clinical descriptions of this neuropsychological nothingness may be found in Oliver Sacks's books *A Leg to Stand on* (1984) and *The Man who Mistook his Wife for a Hat* (1985). While nothingness has long been a central concept in mathematics ('zero'), and in philosophy and theology (the 'Void' of the Gnostics, the 'Tsimtsum' of the Kabbalists), it has recently become a central topic in physics and cosmology too, so that the 'Vacuum' is no longer seen as empty, but as filled, charged, with potential existence and 'vacuum energy', as the very cradle and origin of everything. The concepts are discussed by K. C. Cole in *The Hole in the Universe* (2001). Many further references may be found in Cole's bibliography. OS

Cole, K. C. (2001). *The Hole in the Universe: How Scientists Peered over the Edge of Emptiness and Found Everything.*
Sacks, O. (1984). *A Leg to Stand on.*
——(1985). *The Man Who Mistook his Wife for a Hat.*

nulling. An important technique for precise measurement, by cancelling an unknown against a known standard. When the unknown and the opposed standard cancel, or 'null', then they are equal. The most familiar example is weighing with a balance: when the known mass balances the unknown mass they must be equal, so the unknown mass has been established by a simple nulling technique. A Wheatstone bridge determines electrical resistances with great precision and over a wide range in a similar way. Nulling methods are particularly useful for instruments as they do not require precise linearity of the apparatus, though the results can be extremely accurate over a wide range.

It has been suggested (Gregory 1968) that the nervous system may employ nulling for sensory discrimination (especially for weight), by comparing an *expected* against a *sensed* value. This could help to explain how discrimination can be so good over a very wide range, from a few grams to 10 or even 100 kilograms, though neural components are far less stable than the components available for electronic weighing devices, which would probably have to adopt a nulling method to do as well. There is some evidence from the *size–weight illusion that mass discrimination works by nulling, and this might, possibly, explain the *Weber–Fechner law.

Gregory, R. L. (1968). 'Perceptual illusions and brain models'. *Proceedings of the Royal Society*, 171.

O

obedience, Milgram on. Among the more perplexing problems of human nature is this: how is it possible that a decent, kindly person may, in a short time, find himself killing others with ease? Preposterous? No, the transformation occurs routinely in society as young men are inducted into the armed services and are sent to kill the young men of another society. This is not intended as a moralistic statement against war, but as a source of genuine scientific puzzlement. How is such a transformation possible? The answer would seem to lie in an understanding of the psychology of obedience.

For the psychologist, obedience is neither a good nor an evil, but a neutral mechanism whose moral and adaptive aspects depend on the circumstances in which it occurs. Failure to obey the law in order to satisfy selfish interests is the hallmark of criminality, yet an excess of obedience may also present grave moral problems.

To the parents of small children obedience is, no doubt, perceived as a good thing. And indeed, much energy is expended teaching children to do as they are told. This process of socialization is indispensable to producing persons who can function in the everyday world; and humans are born into an overwhelmingly social world, which possesses a structure and order to which they must adapt. Indeed, human society as we know it could not exist unless a capacity for obedience were present in its members.

Obedience is often rational. It makes good sense to follow the doctor's orders, to obey traffic signs, and to clear the building when the police inform us of a bomb threat. But the habit of obedience may be so deeply ingrained that it overrides rationality. Indeed, for the fully socialized adult there is a readiness to defer to authority that is astonishingly powerful.

Obedience is not limited to human beings. Dominance hierarchies are found in many species. But its expression in human beings occurs in a uniquely symbolic field. We recognize a general category of individuals who, by virtue of status, have a right to direct our behaviour, i.e. we recognize authority. And people respond to abstract designations of authority such as insignia, rank, and title. Frequently, the transaction with authority benefits the person and the larger society. But this is not always the case.

In recent times, the widespread acceptance by the German people of a system of death camps that destroyed millions of innocent people has raised some profound questions about the way human nature is conditioned by obedience. Most heinous deeds were carried out by people who asserted they were merely obeying orders. What is the implication for our picture of human nature? Did their behaviour reveal a potential that is present in all of us? An experiment was set up to explore the response of ordinary people to immoral orders.

The experiment was relatively simple: a person comes to the laboratory and, in the context of a learning experiment, he is told to give increasingly severe electric shocks to another person—who, unknown to the subject, is a confederate, and does not actually receive the shocks. This arrangement provided an opportunity to see how far people would go before they refused to follow the experimenter's orders.

A scenario is needed to grasp the flavour of the experiment. Imagine you have answered an advertisement to take part in a study of memory and learning, and are arriving at the university at a time agreed upon. First, you are greeted by a man in a grey technician's coat, and he introduces you to a second volunteer, and says you are both about to take part in a scientific experiment. He says it is to test whether the use of punishment improves the ability to learn. You draw lots to see who is to be the teacher and who the learner. You turn out to be the teacher, the other fellow the learner. Then you see the learner strapped into a chair and electrodes are placed on his wrist (Fig. 1). The experimenter says that when the learner makes a mistake in the lesson his punishment will be an electric shock.

As teacher you are seated in front of an impressive-looking instrument, a shock generator (Fig. 2). Its essential feature is a line of switches that range from 15 volts to 450 volts, and a set of verbal designations that goes from slight shock to moderate shock, strong shock, very strong shock, and so on to XXX—danger, severe shock. Your job, the experimenter explains to you, is to teach the learner a simple word-pair test. You read a list of words to him, such as 'blue day', 'nice girl', 'fat neck', etc., and he has to indicate by means of an answer box which words were originally paired together. If he gets a correct answer you move on to the next pair, but if he makes a mistake, you are instructed to give him an electric shock, starting with 15 volts (Fig. 3). And you are told to increase the shock one step each time he makes an error. In the course of the

Fig. 1. Learner is strapped into chair and electrodes are attached to his wrist. Electrode paste is applied by the experimenter. Learner provides answers by depressing switches that light up numbers on an answer box.

Fig. 2. Shock generator used in the experiments. Fifteen of the thirty switches have already been depressed.

Fig. 3. Teacher receives sample shock from the generator.

experiment the 'victim' emits cries of pain and demands to be set free, but the experimenter orders you to continue. The question is: how far will you proceed on the generator before you turn to the experimenter and refuse to go any further?

Before the experiment was carried out, people were asked to predict their own performance. The question was put to several groups: psychiatrists, psychologists, and ordinary workers. They all said virtually the same thing: almost no one would go to the end.

But in reality the results were very different. Despite the fact that many subjects experienced stress, despite the fact that many protested to the experimenter, a substantial proportion continued to the last shock on the generator. Many subjects obeyed the experimenter no matter how vehement the pleading of the person being shocked, no matter how painful the shocks seemed to be, and no matter how much the victim pleaded to be let out. This was seen time and again, and has been observed in several universities where the experiment has been repeated.

But there is more to the experiment than this simple demonstration of obedience. Most of the energy went into systematically changing the factors to see which increased obedience, and which led to greater defiance: the effects of the closeness of the victim were studied, as was the importance of the sponsoring institution, and how the sight of other people obeying or defying an authority affected obedience. All of these factors had a powerful effect on whether subjects obeyed or defied the malevolent authority, showing that how a person behaves depends not only on his 'character' but also on the precise situational pressures acting on him.

A person who obeys authority does not see himself as responsible for his own actions, but rather as an agent executing the wishes of another person. In the experiment subjects frequently turned to the experimenter, saying: 'Am I responsible?' And as soon as he said they were not, they could proceed more easily.

Even if the conflict between conscience and duty gives rise to strain, there are psychological mechanisms that come into play that help to alleviate this strain. For example, some subjects complied only minimally: they touched the switch of the generator very lightly; they had the feeling that this really showed that they were good people, whereas in fact they were obeying. Sometimes they would argue with the experimenter, but argumentation did not necessarily lead to disobedience; rather it served as a psychological mechanism, defining the subject in his own eyes as a person who opposed the experimenter's callous orders, yet reducing tension and allowing the person to obey. Often the person became involved in the minute details of the experimental procedure; becoming engrossed, he would lose all sight of the broader consequences of his action.

Fig. 4. Teacher breaks off experiment. On right, event recorder wired into generator automatically records switches used by the subject.

When the results of the original experiments were published, opinion about them was sharply divided. On the one hand, the American Association for the Advancement of Science awarded the work its annual sociopsychological prize. At the same time the experiments attracted fierce criticism, centring mainly on the ethical issues of carrying out the research. The experiments that it was hoped would deepen our understanding of how people yield to malevolent authority themselves became the focus of controversy.

But the problem of authority remains. We cannot have society without some structure of authority, and every society must inculcate a habit of obedience in its citizens. Yet this research showed that many people do not have the resources to resist authority, even when they are directed to act callously and inhumanely against an innocent victim. The experiments posed an age-old problem anew: what is the correct balance between individual initiative and social authority? They illuminated in a concrete and specific way what happens when obedience is unrestrained by conscience.   SM

Arendt, H. (1963). *Eichmann in Jerusalem: A Report on the Banality of Evil*.

Blass, T. (2000). *Obedience to Authority: Current Perspectives on the Milgram Paradigm*.

Comfort, A. (1950). *Authority and Delinquency in the Modern State: A Criminological Approach to the Problem of Power*.

Fromm, E. (1941). *Escape from Freedom*.

Koestler, A. (1967). *The Ghost in the Machine*.

Milgram, S. (1974a). *Obedience to Authority*.

—— (1974b). *Obedience* (a filmed experiment).

object perception. Although, for convenience, physiologists and psychologists tend to study *perception with controlled stimuli presented to the sense organs, man and the higher animals are adapted to recognize and behave in ways generally appropriate to complex objects of the external world. To understand how objects are perceived it is necessary to appreciate how the sensory inputs of stimuli are 'read' as evidence of objects and where they lie in surrounding space. This ability is in many ways the most remarkable that the higher organisms ever accomplish. The fact that we perceive objects from stimuli without even seeming to try is extremely misleading—for in fact it requires computations by neural mechanisms which at present can only be carried out very inadequately by the most powerful available computers.

When objects change in position, or rotate to present a different view, they provide very different stimulus patterns—yet, remarkably, they are still seen as the same object. This is accomplished visually in part by perceptual selection of invariant features, such as corners, whose retinal images do not change much with changes of orientation. More important (almost certainly) is the brain's ability to use typical features of objects as cues for building up hypotheses. Objects as perceived are generally richer than the available sensory inputs or stimuli—evidently through 'projection' of knowledge derived from interacting with objects in the past. So objects are seen as solid and hard, though the images in the eyes are but fleeting ghosts. The details of how the brain generates object perception remain essentially unknown.

An interesting approach is to ask how a computer might recognize objects. Following significant early artificial intelligence ideas by Terry Winograd in 1972 and David Marr (1982), the most promising current development is Irving Beiderman's (1985) 'geons'—unit shapes of objects, which combine like words of sentences to give descriptions that computers can use and create. Is this how our brains see objects?   RLG

Beiderman, I. (1985). 'Recognition-by-components: A theory of human image understanding'. Repr. in: Yantis, S. (ed.) (2001). *Visual Perception: Essential Readings*.

Marr, D. (1982). *Vision*.

obsessive–compulsive disorder. The central feature of the obsessive–compulsive form of neurotic disorder consists of repetitive thoughts and urges to act. The 'obsession' refers to the ideas, and 'compulsion' to the actions urged. The themes of the compulsions are usually concerned with fear of dirt and contamination (which enforces cleansing rituals), improper sexual conduct, and violent action or are often obscene or sacrilegious. The theme of the obsession may, however, be some anxiety-laden idea, a religious thought, or preoccupation with fear of religious faith. The patient is disturbed by it for a number of reasons. Although he is aware that the thoughts and urges to action emanate from his own mind, he finds them strange, irrational, and morbid. By applying his own will he can bring them under control for a while but he is unable to prevent their recurrence. Any attempt to expunge them in their entirety generates anxiety. He has therefore to settle for a compromise which results in periodic relief interrupted by inevitable recurrence of painful ideas.

A common symptom consists of a persistent urge to voice some obscene idea during a church service. This and other ideas which arouse guilt and shame are not acted out or permitted to continue unchallenged in the mind. Alternative rituals, such as repeating lines from a favourite poem or walking six steps forwards and backwards before crossing a threshold, may serve to suppress them in part. But such defences are regularly overpowered until the illness has been brought under control.

Obsessional ruminations may cause preoccupation with religious or quasi-philosophical themes around questions such as 'Who created God?' or 'Was there a world before God created the universe?'. The patient is engaged in long periods of speculation in which he moves from logical reasoning towards a disbelief in the existence of God, but he is tormented at the same time that he might be punished for indulging in such faithless deviations in his mental activity.

It is common for doubt to enter as an obstructive element in all the patient's mental activities and conduct. For instance, while driving a car he may feel compelled to retrace his journey to banish the doubt that he may have injured or killed someone and left a blood-stained body on the road.

The themes from which obsessions and compulsions are derived include the danger of dirt and contamination, contact with strangers, or specific articles of clothing or other articles which may have been in contact with the bodies of others. There may be a preoccupation with numbers, leading the patient to a ritual assembly of a sequence of numbers derived from a chosen starting number expanded until figures cover all the pages of a large exercise book. Books, papers, pictures, and furniture may have to be in a special position, generally of a geometrical regularity or symmetry, and bouts of anger may be provoked if they are moved from a selected site. Bizarre and imaginary dangers may form the theme. The patient may be afraid of handling any piece of string, however short, lest he strangle himself with it. A girl may be unable to travel in a public conveyance lest when she casts her gaze at male travellers she be judged to be focusing on their genital organs.

Many of the compulsions associated with this disorder are derived directly from the patient's obsessions. Cleansing rituals and multiple baths are determined by an overall ritual in several stages which are all precisely defined. Dressing in the morning has to be undertaken in a specific manner from the feet upwards, and similar checks must be made to supervise each step before retiring for the night. There may be a compulsory round of the house to ensure that all windows and doors are closed and locked. The accountant or bookkeeper may have to check and recheck each column of figures, and repeated cleansing procedures may have to be undertaken after each excretory function.

The inability to feel certainty that any of the ritualistic routines have been undertaken thoroughly, and his endless recheckings which may occupy most of the day, are partly responsible for the slowness of the obsessive–compulsive person in getting anything done. The expression 'folie à doute' has emerged in the French language to describe these activities.

There is evidence of hereditary factors and also environmental exposure as causal factors. A minority of those with obsessive–compulsive disorder have a family history of this condition, affecting some first-degree relatives, and also exposure to the influence of parents, one or both of whom may suffer from this form of neurotic disorder. It has not been determined what proportion of this hazard in the patient's life stems from hereditary factors. No single gene has been isolated as being responsible, but evidence that parental traits play a part in shaping the obsessive–compulsive condition, or obsessive personality in patients, is more firmly established. Stress over many years often damages the self-esteem of these patients. Obsessive illness can cause considerable impediment in the patient's life and depression is associated with a proportion of cases. Affective disorder is a causal agent in some attacks of obsessive–compulsive disorder. But well-defined and severe obsessional symptoms may continue unchanged after antidepressant treatment, and in these cases the obsessional illness has to be judged as the primary cause.

Obsessive–compulsive illness, and the obsessive–compulsive personality disorder often associated with it, may generate defeatism and suffering over long periods and limit the achievement of distinguished intellects and artists. The composer Bruckner, now widely regarded as a musician of genius deserving to be classed with those of the highest merit such as Brahms and Wagner, was never able to achieve satisfaction in the musical compositions he first set down. He subjected them all to laborious and repeated revisions in an emotional state that brought him at times close to breakdown—perhaps an indication that he suffered from obsessive–compulsive disorder. Yet in association with a powerful will, suffering may be surmounted, enabling the patient to sustain his social position and affectionate friendships and support. Dr Samuel Johnson was a very capable example of this. An account given by the daughter of Sir Joshua Reynolds of Dr Johnson's obsessive–compulsive episodes was as follows:

His extraordinary gestures or anticks with his hands and feet, particularly when passing over the threshold of a Door, or rather before he would venture to pass through any door-way. On entering Sir Joshua's [Reynolds] house with poor Mrs. Williams, a blind lady who lived with him, he would quit her hand, or else whirl her about on the steps as he whirled and twisted about to perform his gesticulations; and as soon as he had finished, he would give a sudden spring, and make such an extensive stride over the threshold, as if he was trying for a wager how far he could stride, Mrs. Williams standing groping about outside the door, unless the servant or the mistress of the House more commonly took hold of her hand to conduct her in, leaving Dr. Johnson to perform at the Parlour Door much the same exercise over again. (Brain 1960)

This provides an account of the compelling force of obsessional ideas and behaviour in this case by a leading figure, writer, lexicographer, poet, and personality with a wide-ranging influence on his intellectual contemporaries. Samuel Johnson's disability would have confined and crippled most. But his personality and distinction of mind created a seminal influence upon a whole generation. Johnson was fully aware of the irrational character of his compulsions but powerless to control them. He had also thought about their possible origins and judged them to have originated in sensuous preoccupations and fantasies in which he had been engaged for some years, and which had aroused profound guilt.

Treatment with drugs now plays an important part and has been shown to be effective in some 50–60 per cent of cases, providing considerable relief and in many cases a complete remission from the attack. However, additional measures may be required. Supportive psychotherapy, derived from exploration of the historical development of the patient and understanding of his personality and special needs, relieves symptoms and improves compliance. Behavioural therapy is of particular value in patients who cannot tolerate drugs and those who require treatment over long periods.

The efficacy of a range of recently introduced drugs, such as fluoxetine, fluvoxamine, paroxetine, which augment serotoninergic activity in the brain has been attributed to their effectiveness in reducing obsessive–compulsive symptoms due to reuptake inhibition of 5-hydroxytryptamine (5-HT, or serotonin). This explanation is not entirely satisfactory, although reuptake inhibition of 5-HT commences early and augments rapidly in patients treated. Therapeutic improvement does not begin until 2–3 weeks have passed and does not reach optimal levels until 6–8 weeks.

The view that the new drugs act through their influence on concomitant depression, which is present in a proportion of cases, is not consistent with the absence of any significant correlation between measures of improvement and the score of patients on depression scales.

Further enquiries may lead to more cogent explanations of drug action. Other studies of the brain may provide insight into the significance of the anomalies

identified with the aid of *positron emission tomography (PET)—(a method of imaging the activity of functional systems in the brain) of the left frontal gyri and caudate nuclei in patients with obsessive–compulsive disorder (Luxenberg et al. 1988).

Advances on a wide front may pave the way for better treatments and a deeper understanding of the functional pathways in the brain, whose abnormal activity causes great emotional distress but which, in its normal functioning, plays an important part in the promotion of a healthy mental life and the quality of personal relationships and creative activities.   MaR

Brain, W. R. (1960). *Some Reflections on Genius, and Other Essays.*
Luxenberg, J. S., Swedo, S. E., Flament, M. F., et al. (1988). 'Neuroanatomical abnormalities in obsessive-compulsive disorder detected with quantitative X-ray computed tomography'. *American Journal of Psychiatry*, 145.
Slater, E., and Roth, M. (1969). *Clinical Psychiatry.*

Oedipus complex. Sigmund *Freud's first mention of the Oedipus complex was in a letter written in 1897, while he was reviewing his relationship with his father, who had died six months before. In *The Interpretation of Dreams*, written at about the same time, he referred to 'being in love with one parent and hating the other' as being 'among the essential constituents of the stock of psychical impulses' formed in childhood, and as important in determining the symptoms of later neurosis. These psychical impulses, which he called the Oedipus complex, retain their power to determine neurotic symptoms, he supposed, only when there is fixation at the Oedipal level of development. This happens when rivalry with the parent of the same sex is not resolved through identification with this parent or when sexual feelings for the parent of the opposite sex are not transferred to a sexual partner outside the family. In Jung's theory, the essential process in neurosis is not the fixation of the complex, but its revival when a new adaptation is required. Modern theories of neurosis attach more importance to the quality of the relationship between mother and child before Oedipal impulses develop (see ATTACHMENT).

Freud claimed some confirmation of his theory in the universal appeal of the legend of Oedipus Rex in Sophocles' play. The Thebans are told by an oracle that the plague will cease when the murderer of Laius, the former king, has been driven from the land. The play gradually reveals, in the manner of psychoanalysis, Freud remarked, that Oedipus is the murderer, and that he is the son of Laius and Jocasta, whom he married after Laius' death. Freud's formula, which is based, as is usual in psychoanalysis, on the child's feelings towards his parents, gives a one-sided and too simple account of the complex interactions in a family. The son is the transgressor whereas in the legend the father, feeling threatened because he has been told by the oracle that he will perish at the hands of his son, instructs the mother to destroy him at birth. Instead she abandons him. The father later starts the quarrel which ends in his death. In the story of Hamlet, in Shakespeare's play, which psychoanalysts regard as similar to that of Oedipus, the stepfather, not the son, is the aggressor. DRD

Freud, S. (1974). *Introductory Lectures on Psychoanalysis*. Trans. J. Strachey.

Jones, E. (1949). *Hamlet and Oedipus*.

Olds, James (1922–76). American psychologist who received his degree in 1947 from Amherst College and his doctorate from the laboratory of social relations at Harvard in 1952, working with Richard Solomon. At Harvard he attempted to combine the neurological views of Donald *Hebb with E. C. *Tolman's model of learning.

In 1953 he went to McGill as a postdoctoral Fellow to learn physiological techniques and to work more closely with Hebb. It was during this time that he discovered that electrical stimulation of the septal area, lateral hypothalamus, and some other brain areas could act as a reward, one of the most significant physiological contributions to learning, and one that turned the attention of students of the neural bases of learning from the cortex to the brain as a whole. See also MEMORY: BIOLOGICAL BASIS.

After a further two years' postdoctoral research at the Brain Research Institute of the University of California at Los Angeles, Olds became a member of the psychology department of the University of Michigan, where he continued to explore the anatomy, pharmacology, and behavioural features of brain-stimulation reward.

In 1967 he moved to the California Institute of Technology, where he remained until his death in 1976 of a heart attack. Here his main energy was devoted to the study of learning by recording the activity of cells in different areas of the brain during conditioning. PMM

opium. The word is derived from the Greek for poppy juice. Opium is obtained by incising the fruit and collecting the exudate from the opium poppy, *Papaver somniferum*. The plant appears to have originated in the lands bordering the eastern Mediterranean, whence it spread both eastwards and westwards. The psychological effects of opium may have been known to the Sumerians, but the first clear reference to poppy juice is found in the writings of Theophrastus in the 3rd century BC, and Discorides in the 1st century BC gave the first description of modern opium.

During the subsequent centuries opium appears to have enjoyed both medicinal and recreational uses. Medically it was known to relieve pain and suppress dry coughing, and it was given for a wide variety of other complaints, including epilepsy and colic. Its sleep-inducing properties were well known to Greek and Roman writers; the Greeks appear to have taken opium cakes and sweetmeats for relaxation and recreation. Whereas opium smoking has been most widespread in the Far East, consumption of the drug in the form of its tincture—laudanum—became fairly commonplace in Western Europe. Its addictive properties were well recognized and described in England at the end of the 17th century by John Jones, a physician in Windsor, who, in his book *The Mysteries of Opium Reveal'd* (1700), gave a clear account of the effects of intoxication and sudden withdrawal of the drug in one habituated to it. None the less, regardless of its recreational use, it was as a sovereign remedy for pain that it was most widely prescribed. As Thomas *Sydenham wrote, 'Among the remedies which it has pleased Almighty God to give to man to relieve his sufferings, none is so universal and efficacious as opium'. In the 19th century many patent medicines, freely available to the public both in Britain and in the USA, contained opium. Virginia Berridge (1977) has described how easily opium was obtained in the Fenland area of England. Opium pills were sold openly in Cambridge on market day and many a person bought 'a ha'pennard o'elevation' to last for the week. Although opium was mainly imported in the 19th century from Turkey, the medical profession showed a preference for opium from poppies grown in fields near to the village of Winslow in Buckinghamshire.

Opium is a crude preparation containing at least twenty different alkaloids of which the best known are morphine, first isolated by F. W. A. Sertürner in 1803, and codeine, identified by Robiquet in 1832. Heroin is not a naturally occurring alkaloid but is derived from morphine by acetylation (the addition of an acetyl group). It is at least three times as effective as morphine for the control of pain, and when first synthesized in 1898 it was hoped that it would be less addictive than the parent drug. In fact, as the history of heroin has shown, it has proved to be the most addictive of all the opiates, both natural and synthetic, although none is free from this potential.

In spite of the free availability of opium medicines to the public in the 19th century, there is little evidence to show that addiction to the drug was particularly widespread. None the less, the giving of opium to small children as a sedative was a pernicious practice and a not infrequent cause of wasting and premature death. Although somewhat conflicting opinions were expressed by the medical profession, eventually restrictions were placed on the sale of opium to the public. In the 20th century these restrictions were tightened, the main impetus for strict control of the sale of opium and its derivatives coming from the USA, at first through the Harrison Narcotic Act of 1914 and later through the League of Nations and the United Nations Commission on Narcotic Drugs. It was hoped that international control of opium and heroin production would reverse the steady increase in the number of persons addicted to these substances. Unfortunately there is very little evidence that intense legal and law enforcement activity has made much difference, as the use of these drugs has become more extensive both in the USA and elsewhere.

Statements about opium and its derivatives tend to be overshadowed by the problem of addiction to such a degree that concern over this single issue has led to restrictions on their medical use. As a result some doctors avoid their use even for the control of severe *pain in terminal illness, lest the patient become addicted. Fortunately, however, their medical use is not a common cause of addiction. Even so, if a patient is dying from cancer it is hardly a matter of importance if the drug that ensures freedom from pain also makes him addicted to its continued administration.

Although those who misuse opiates and other types of drugs are generally referred to as addicts, the term 'drug addiction' was replaced by 'drug dependence' by a WHO expert committee report in 1970. Dependence can be both physical and psychological. Opiates, like some other drugs of dependence, can, if taken repeatedly, result in the development of tolerance, so that some drug-dependent persons can build up a tolerance which allows them to take massive doses of the drug without immediate harm. De Quincey was well aware of this phenomenon, describing it in his *Confessions of an English Opium-Eater* (1821). Sudden withdrawal of the drug will cause an abstinence syndrome: the 'cold turkey' in the slang jargon of the junkie's world. To a high degree of physical dependence will usually be added a compulsion to use the drug on a 'continuous or periodic basis in order to experience its psychic effects' (WHO 1970).

See also ADDICTION.   FAW

Berridge, V. (1977). 'Fenland opium eating in the 19th century'. *British Journal of Addiction*, 72.
Goodman, L. S., and Gilman, A. G. (1980). *The Pharmacological Basis of Therapeutics* (6th edn.).
Jones, J. (1700). *The Mysteries of Opium Reveal'd*. In Hunter, R., and Macalpine, I. (1963). *Three Hundred Years of Psychiatry*.
WHO Expert Committee on Drug Dependence (1970). *Technical Report*, Series 460.

other minds. The classical problem of why we believe that other people (and perhaps at least the higher animals) have sensations, thoughts, and so on, essentially similar to our own. It seems that we draw a widespread analogy from our own behaviour, and related internal affective states, to the internal states of other people (and sometimes animals), especially when their behaviour is similar to ours. Some clinical states, especially coma, are very difficult to interpret or 'read', as behaviour is no longer typical or at all like our own.

Given that computers are developing some abilities until recently thought specifically human, the question of whether computers can have minds is rapidly becoming a significant issue. As Alan *Turing suggested, we may say that a computer is as 'intelligent' as a human if it answers questions as a human does; but would we say that the computer is *conscious*, or *aware*, as we are? Has it a mind? Such questions may give *behaviourism its prima facie scientific validity—though behaviourism rejects what we take to be the most important fact of at least *our* minds: *consciousness.   RLG

Dennett, D. C. (1978). *Brain Storms*.
Wisdom, J. (1952). *Other Minds*.

out-of-body experience. An out-of-body experience (or OBE) is an experience in which a person seems to perceive the world from a location outside their physical body. In other words, when you have an OBE you feel as though you have left the body and are able to see, feel, and move around without it. Note that this definition treats the OBE as an experience or state of consciousness, not as a psychic phenomenon. So if someone feels as though they are out of the body then they are—by definition—having an OBE, whether or not anything has left the body. This neutral definition allows researchers to study the experience without committing themselves to any particular theory of the OBE.

Some of the most dramatic OBEs have been reported as part of the near-death experience, for example in those who are resuscitated from cardiac arrests or survive life-threatening accidents. However, similar experiences can occur under less traumatic conditions. Surveys in several countries show that about 15–20 per cent of the population have had an OBE at some time during their life. Most of these people have only one, or a very few OBEs, although a few have many. Spontaneous OBEs most often occur during resting, just before sleep, or when meditating. However, they can occur at almost any time and occasionally the person carries on with what they were doing (such as walking, driving, or even speaking) apparently without interruption. Common factors include relaxation, loss or disruption of the body image, and reduced sensory input. Most spontaneous OBEs last only a few seconds. Some begin with the experience of travelling down a dark tunnel, often with a bright white or golden light at the end. Others begin with rushing or whirring noises, odd vibrations, or simply a brief period of blackout. Returning is usually gradual but occasionally there is a sensation of shock or disorientation.

People who have OBEs (OBErs) often feel as though they can travel anywhere and see anything they wish. Some seem to have another body or double, sometimes referred to as the 'astral body'. This is usually something like a replica of the physical body, though less distinct.

Sometimes it is ghostly or transparent and described as whitish or pale grey. In rare cases this double is connected to the physical body by a silver cord. More commonly no double is experienced and the person feels as though they are a disembodied awareness or point of view.

Vision and hearing are reportedly clearer and more vivid than normal. Some people even get the impression that they could see all round at once or hear anything anywhere if they wished to—a sense of limitlessness. OBEs are like *dreams in some ways—for example, the scenery and lighting can be very strange, and the ordinary physical constraints of the physical world do not seem to apply. However, unlike ordinary dreams, OBEs feel very real, consciousness is clear, and the experience is usually remembered vividly afterwards—often for years. In some ways OBEs are more like lucid dreams, that is dreams in which you know *during the dream* that you are dreaming. OBEs sometimes merge into mystical or transcendent experiences. Many people claim that OBEs cause positive changes in their attitudes and beliefs. An analysis of hundreds of cases of OBEs showed that fear of death was reduced and belief in life after death increased.

OBErs frequently interpret their experiences as psychic, paranormal, or mystical. They sometimes claim that they could see not only their own bodies, but distant scenes, although the experimental evidence to support these claims is extremely weak. More rarely they also claim to be able to influence distant events, although the frustration of being unable to speak to people or touch objects is more common.

Techniques for inducing the experience mostly use imagery and relaxation exercises. Experimental techniques have also used special sounds and visual displays and, from the early days of psychical research, *hypnosis has been used to induce OBEs or 'travelling clairvoyance'. Drugs associated with OBEs include the psychedelics LSD, psilocybin, DMT, and mescaline, and the dissociative anaesthetic ketamine which often induces feelings of body separation, floating, and even dying. However, there is no known drug that reliably induces OBEs.

The occurrence of OBEs is not related to age, sex, educational level, or religion. However, OBErs score higher on measures of hypnotizability and absorption—that is, they can more easily become absorbed in films, books, or fantasies. OBErs are also more likely to believe in the paranormal, to have various kinds of psychic experiences, and to report frequent dream recall and lucid dreams. They are not more likely to be mentally ill. Indeed Gabbard and Twemlow's (1984) study of over 300 OBErs found that they were generally well adjusted with low levels of alcohol and drug abuse. Other studies found no differences in various measures of psychopathology between people who do and do not have OBEs. Some OBErs fear that they are ill or going mad, or that they will leave their body and not be able to get back. This fear is not well founded and most OBEs end spontaneously after only a few seconds or minutes with no ill effects.

1. Experiments on the OBE
2. Theories of the OBE

1. Experiments on the OBE

Experiments on OBEs have been of three types. Attempts to detect the double began early in the 20th century using spiritualist mediums who claimed to be able to project their double at a distance. Photographs were taken and attempts made to weigh the soul as it left the body of people dying of tuberculosis, but the studies were not well controlled and the effects disappeared when better methods were developed. More recent studies used magnetometers, thermistors, ultraviolet and infrared detectors, as well as humans and animals, but no reliable detector of an out-of-body presence has ever been discovered.

The second type tests perception during OBEs. In early experiments mediums were asked to exteriorize their double, smell scents, or view the actions of people at a distance, but usually the medium herself could have seen what was going on, invalidating the results. More recently, target letters, numbers, or objects have been concealed from view in the laboratory and people who can have OBEs at will asked to try to see them. In a well-known experiment one subject correctly saw a five-digit number, but this success has never been repeated, and most other experiments have had equivocal results. There are many claims from case studies that people can really see at a distance during OBEs but the experimental evidence does not generally substantiate them.

The third type of experiment involves physiological monitoring of OBErs. No unique physiological state seems to be involved and OBErs are usually found to be in a very relaxed waking state or on the verge of sleep. There is no evidence that they are in REM (rapid eye movement), or dreaming, sleep. So OBEs cannot be equated with dreams.

2. Theories of the OBE

There are three main types of theory. First is the idea that something leaves the body. Most OBErs find the experience so compelling and realistic that they assume that their consciousness has separated from their physical body. Many conclude that this proves the existence of a soul or spirit that is independent of the physical body and can continue after physical death, although this does not necessarily follow since the physical body was always functioning at the time.

The idea of a double can be traced back to ancient Egypt and to Greek philosophy, and can be found in folklore, mythology, and religious doctrines from many cultures. A popular modern version is the theory of 'astral projection' derived from the teachings of theosophy. The astral body is said to be one of several energy bodies and can travel about on the astral plane.

There are numerous problems with this and all related theories. For example, it cannot specify what the astral body is made of, in what sense it is conscious, or how this consciousness is related to the obvious sensory and memory functions of the brain. It cannot explain how the double perceives the world without using any sensory apparatus and without being detected, nor why the astral world appears the way it does.

The second kind of theory is that OBEs are imagination plus extrasensory perception (ESP). In principle this might account for the claims of paranormal perception during OBEs without involving all the problems of other worlds and other bodies. However, this is the weakest possible kind of theory since imagination is such a broad term, and there is little evidence for the existence of ESP. In addition it is not easy to see how this theory could be tested.

Finally, there are psychological theories which involve no self, soul, spirit, or astral body that leaves.

Psychoanalytic interpretations treat the OBE as a dramatization of the fear of death, an uncoupling of the bodily ego from the mental ego, regression of the ego, or a reliving of the trauma of birth. One such theory suggests that a loss of, or change in, the body image threatens the self-image, with the OBE being an unconscious attempt to re-establish personal identity. Others liken the OBE to birth. Superficially there may be similarities between the tunnel and the birth canal, or the silver cord and the umbilicus, but the birth canal would look nothing like a tunnel to a fetus being born. Birth theories predict that people born by Caesarean section should not have either tunnel experiences or OBEs but one study showed that they have just as many of these experiences as people born normally.

Irwin (1995) suggested that, the OBE begins with a disruption of the normal body sense leading to somaesthetic sensations of floating or flying. This is then translated, by synaesthesia, into a complete experience of leaving the body, with visual, tactile, auditory, and other senses all being transformed. The process requires attention to, or absorption in, the new experience and loss of contact with somatic sensations. This explains not only the conditions under which the OBE occurs, but the tendency for OBErs to score higher in tests of absorption.

Blackmore (1992) suggested that, when sensory input is inadequate or disrupted, the normal impression that we are inside our own head is replaced with a bird's-eye view from memory and imagination—much like bird's-eye views in dreams. When such an image takes over as the current 'model of reality' an OBE occurs. Sounds can be incorporated relatively easily into the bird's-eye view, making many OBEs quite realistic. On this theory the OBE is entirely imagined but, because the new viewpoint has taken over completely, the experience feels real.

These psychological theories account for the conditions under which OBEs occur and explain why the out-of-body world is rather like the world of imagination, with transparent walls, the ability to move around at will and to see in all directions. They also explain why apparently correct details are often mixed with false ones since the brain has simply put together the best information it has. Experiments have confirmed that OBErs are better able to manipulate spatial images and more frequently experience bird's-eye views during dreams.

These three types of theory differ in their implications for life after death but we should be clear that the occurrence of the experience itself is not proof of survival. On balance the evidence suggests that nothing leaves the body during an OBE and that paranormal phenomena do not occur during OBEs. Nevertheless the experience is dramatic, interesting, and can have profound effects on people's lives.

SJB

Alvarado, C. S. (1992). 'The psychological approach to out-of-body experiences: a review of early and modern developments'. *Journal of Psychology*, 126.

Blackmore, S. J. (1992). *Beyond the Body*.

Gabbard, G. O., and Twemlow, S. W. (1984). *With the Eyes of the Mind*.

Irwin, H. J. (1985). *Flight of Mind: A Psychological Study of the Out-of-Body Experience*.

Owen, Sir Richard (1804–92). British physician and naturalist. Born at Lancaster, he studied medicine at Edinburgh and at St Bartholomew's Hospital, London, and became curator in the museum of the Royal College of Surgeons, producing splendid catalogues. In 1856 he became superintendent of the natural history department of the British Museum. He accepted evolution before *Darwin but maintained a lengthy dispute, especially with T. H. *Huxley, criticizing Darwin's principle of natural selection. They finally made up the quarrel. Owen is well known for creating the word dinosaur from two Greek words 'deinos' and 'sauros' meaning 'fearfully great' and 'lizard' respectively.

An important essay is *On Parthenogenesis* (1849). There is a splendid statue of Owen in the British Museum (Natural History), South Kensington, London.

Rupke, N. (1994). *Richard Owen: Victorian Naturalist*.

P

pain. Pain research and therapy have long been dominated by specificity theory which proposes that pain is a specific sensation subserved by a straight-through transmission system, and that the intensity of pain is proportional to the extent of tissue damage. Recent evidence, however, shows that pain is not simply a function of the amount of bodily damage alone, but is influenced by attention, anxiety, suggestion, prior experience, and other psychological variables (Melzack and Wall 1982). Moreover, the natural outcome of the specificity concept of pain has been the development of neurosurgical techniques to cut the so-called pain pathway, and the results of such operations have been disappointing, particularly for chronic pain syndromes. Not only does the pain tend to return in a substantial proportion of patients, but new pains may appear. The psychological and neurological data, then, forces us to reject the concept of a single straight-through sensory transmission system.

In recent years the evidence on pain has moved in the direction of recognizing the plasticity and modifiability of events in the central nervous system. Pain is a complex perceptual and affective experience determined by the unique past history of the individual, by the meaning to him of the injurious agent or situation, and by his 'state of mind' at the moment, as well as by the sensory nerve patterns evoked by physical stimulation.

In the light of this understanding of pain processes, Melzack and Wall (1965) proposed the gate control theory of pain. Basically, the theory states that neural mechanisms in the dorsal horn of the spinal cord act like a gate which can increase or decrease the flow of nerve impulses from peripheral fibres to the spinal cord cells that project to the brain. Somatic input is therefore subjected to the modulating influence of the gate *before* it evokes pain perception and response. The theory suggests that large-fibre inputs (such as gentle rubbing) tend to close the gate while small-fibre inputs (such as pinching) generally open it, and that the gate is also profoundly influenced by descending influences from the brain. It further proposes that the sensory input is modulated at successive synapses throughout its projection from the spinal cord to the brain areas responsible for pain experience and response. Pain occurs when the number of nerve impulses that arrive at these areas exceeds a critical level.

Melzack and Wall (1982) have recently assessed the present-day status of the gate control theory in the light of new physiological research. It is apparent that the theory is alive and well despite considerable controversy and conflicting evidence. Although some of the physiological details may need revision, the evidence supporting the concept of gating (or input modulation) is stronger than ever.

The subjective experience of pain clearly has sensory qualities, such as are described by the words throbbing, burning, or sharp. In addition, it has distinctly unpleasant, affective qualities which are described by words such as exhausting, wretched, and punishing. Pain becomes overwhelming, demands immediate attention, and disrupts ongoing behaviour and thought. It motivates or drives the organism into activity aimed at stopping the pain as quickly as possible. On the basis of these considerations, Melzack and Casey (1968) have proposed that there are three major psychological dimensions of pain experience: sensory–discriminative, motivational–affective, and cognitive–evaluative. Psychophysiological evidence suggests that each is subserved by specialized systems in the brain which interact to produce the multidimensional qualities of pain experience.

Recent recognition of the complexity of pain experience has led to the development of a paper-and-pencil questionnaire (the 'McGill Pain Questionnaire') to obtain numerical measures of the intensity and qualities of pain (Melzack 1975). The questionnaire consists of twenty sets of words that people use to describe pain. Ten sets describe sensory qualities, five describe affective qualities, and one is an evaluative group. Four sets consist of miscellaneous words. Since each word has a numerical value, patients asked to check those words that best describe their pain provide quantitative measures for each of the major dimensions of pain. The power of the questionnaire has been demonstrated in many quantitative, controlled studies of the effects of different forms of pain therapy (Melzack 1983). In addition, the questionnaire has been shown to discriminate among different types of pain. Distinctive patterns of words discriminate between migraine and tension headaches, between low-back pain of organic and that of functional origin, and between dysmenorrhoea and pain caused by an intra-uterine device.

Drugs, especially *opium and its derivatives, are among the oldest methods for controlling pain. Thomas

*Sydenham in 1680 wrote: 'Among the remedies which it has pleased Almighty God to give to man to relieve his sufferings, none is so universal and efficacious as opium.' Since then, more effective derivatives of opium, notably morphine and heroin, have been discovered. The invention of the hypodermic needle and syringe not only stimulated the search for pure, injectable analgesics but also, unfortunately, increased the risk of drug dependence. The quest for preparations free from addictive properties has proved to be fruitless, but withholding such pain-relieving drugs from the terminally ill lest they become 'addicted' is as ridiculous as it is inhumane. Other drugs said to have analgesic properties include the antidepressants, but it does not appear that relief of depression is their mode of action. Possibly this may be by blocking the reuptake of serotonin and so potentiating the effect of enkephalins in the brain (see NEUROPEPTIDES).

Many new methods to control pain have been developed in recent years (Melzack and Wall 1982). Sensory modulation techniques such as transcutaneous electrical nerve stimulation (TENS) and ice massage are widely used in the attempt to activate inhibitory neural mechanisms to suppress pain. These techniques have a long history but were not understood until recently. Acupuncture, for example, is an ancient Chinese medical procedure in which long needles are inserted into specific points at the skin. The traditional Chinese explanation is that the needles bring yin and yang (which flow through hypothetical tubules called meridians) into harmony with each other. It has been discovered, however, that the sites of insertion correspond to myofascial 'trigger points' which are well known in Western medicine. It has also been found that acupuncture and electrical stimulation through electrodes placed on the skin (TENS) are equally effective in relieving low-back pain and several other forms of pain, including pains due to peripheral nerve injury. The neural mechanisms which underlie the relief produced by these forms of stimulation are not entirely understood, but evidence suggests that the intense stimulation produced by acupuncture or TENS activates an area in the brain which exerts a powerful inhibitory control over pathways that transmit pain signals.

Psychological techniques that allow patients to achieve some degree of control over their pain have also been developed. These techniques include biofeedback, hypnosis, distraction, and the use of imagery and other cognitive activities to modulate the transmission of the nerve-impulse patterns that subserve pain. Psychological techniques are being used increasingly and provide relatively simple, safe approaches to pain control. They represent a significant advance over the earlier tendency to treat pain by neurosurgical operations intended to cut the 'pain pathway' and which so frequently ended in failure.

The techniques of sensory modulation and psycho-logical control work well in conjunction with each other. A large body of research demonstrates that several of these procedures employed at the same time—'multiple convergent therapy'—are often highly effective for the control of chronic pain states, particularly those such as low-back pain which have prominent elements of tension, depression, and anxiety.

While great strides have been made in the control of pain, there are still many pain syndromes which are beyond our comprehension and our control. Back pains, especially of the lower back, are the most common kind of pain, and literally millions of sufferers are continually seeking help. Sometimes they obtain temporary relief, but most continue to suffer. *Migraine and tension headaches similarly plague millions of people. Perhaps the most terrible of all pains are those suffered by some cancer patients in the terminal phases of the disease. In recent years, specialized medical units have been developed to cope with these problems. Their major feature is that physicians and other health professionals from many different disciplines work together in the attempt to alleviate the pain of each individual patient. Pain clinics have been set up in every major Western city to cope with benign chronic pain, and hospices or palliative care units in hospitals have been developed to control pain (and other miseries) of patients who are terminally ill with cancer.

The development of pain clinics and hospices represents a breakthrough of the highest importance in the clinical control of pain. They are radical, new approaches to old problems. Chronic pain and terminal pain are major challenges to the scientist and clinician. But the giant step has been the recognition that they are special problems. The challenges ahead are clear: to conquer pain and suffering in all their forms.

See also ANAESTHESIA.   RME

Dickenson, A. H. (2002). 'Gate Control Theory of pain stands the test of time'. *British Journal of Anaesthesia*, 88/6.

Melzack, R. (1975). 'The McGill Pain Questionnaire: major properties and scoring methods'. *Pain*, 1.

——(ed.) (1983). *Pain Measurement and Assessment*.

——and Casey, K. L. (1968). 'Sensory, motivational and central control determinants of pain: a new conceptual model'. In Kenshalo, D. (ed.), *The Skin Senses*.

——and Wall, P. D. (1965). 'Pain mechanisms: a new theory'. *Science*, 150.

—— —— (1982). *The Challenge of Pain*.

Wall, P. (1999). *Pain, the Science of Suffering*.

Paley, William (1743–1805). British philosopher, born at Peterborough. He was a Fellow of Christ's College, Cambridge, from 1766 to 1776. His *Principles of Moral and Political Philosophy* (1785) propounded a form of utilitarianism, while *Evidences of Christianity* (1794) was required reading for entrance to Cambridge University for many years. Paley is celebrated for his formulations of the argument from *design for the existence of God, and his arguments (especially in *Horae Paulinae*, 1790) that the New Testament is not myth.

Dawkins, R. (1986). *The Blind Watchmaker*.

panpsychism. See ANIMISM.

paradigm. 'Paradigm' has become an important technical term in the philosophy of science following the publication of *The Structure of Scientific Revolutions* by Thomas Kuhn (1962). Kuhn's thesis is that 'normal science' operates within a largely unquestioned framework governed by fundamental theoretical models, or 'paradigms'. These ruling paradigms determine the way in which experiments are designed and observational results are interpreted. Once a theory gains the status of a paradigm (an example is Darwin's principle of natural selection by the survival of the fittest) it remains unchallenged until a scientific 'revolution' occurs and it is overthrown in favour of a new paradigm (cf. the switch from Newtonian to Einsteinian physics); when this happens even old-established observations and experiments change their significance. This has been likened to a *Gestalt switch in perception of an ambiguous figure. An important part of Kuhn's view is the assertion that different scientific paradigms are 'incommensurable': there is no common body of neutral observation which can be used to decide between two competing theories—a notion that may be thought to cast doubt on the claims of science to objectivity and rationality.

Kuhn's view of paradigms has been criticized in detail by Margaret Masterman (1970), but it has proved of great importance by emphasizing the role of general conceptual models in science and thinking. Psychology may be a somewhat unsatisfactory science because it lacks effective unifying paradigms. Although the great theorists, such as Sigmund *Freud and B. F. *Skinner (following the lead of J. B. *Watson), are important partly because they did provide paradigms found to be useful clinically and by experimenters, these paradigms have never gained the degree of general acceptance achieved by paradigms in the physical sciences. RLG

Kuhn, T. S. (1962). *The Structure of Scientific Revolutions*.
Masterman, M. (1970). 'The nature of a paradigm'. In Lakatos, I., and Musgrave, A. (eds.), *Criticism and the Growth of Knowledge*.

paralysis. Loss of motor function. Thought processes and *perception may be subtly modified or impaired. It is an interesting question whether perception (which almost certainly depends primarily on active learning in infancy) and *emotion (which may largely be sensations of bodily changes, for example to perceived danger) can remain normal with extensive paralysis. William *James described the case of a woman paralysed almost from the neck down following a hunting accident, who yet experienced emotions when visited by her family. This has been used as evidence against the James–Lange theory of emotion, which is essentially that emotions are visceral sensations, and should therefore cease with sufficiently general paralysis. It was the observation, in classical times, that head wounds are associated with paralysis on the opposite side of the body that led to concepts of *localization of brain function, with the left hemisphere controlling the right side of the body, and vice versa.

Paralysis is usually organic, due to brain damage or loss of peripheral nerve function, but it can occur as a functional symptom of *hysteria. See NOTHINGNESS.

paranoia. Although paranoia today is a diagnosis used to describe patients who exhibit systematized delusions of grandeur and persecution, its original meaning, as the etymology of the word indicates, was 'being out of one's mind'. Heinroth in 1818 appears to have equated paranoia with *Verrücktheit* (madness); Kahlbaum in 1863 was the first psychiatrist to give it its modern meaning, and although he regarded paranoia as a persistent, chronic condition, he believed that paranoid patients suffered from a disorder of intellect. The term survives as the name given to one type of functional *psychosis, namely that in which the patient holds a coherent, internally consistent, delusional system of beliefs, centring round the conviction that he (or, more rarely, she) is a person of great importance and is on that account being persecuted, despised, and rejected. As Henderson and Gillespie's *Textbook of Psychiatry* (9th edn. 1962) puts it: 'A person so affected believes that he is right, that he is justified in his beliefs, and that anyone who opposes his point of view is behaving maliciously or at least non-understandingly towards him.' Such a person does not subscribe to the view that he is ill, does not accept treatment, does not enter hospital voluntarily, and may do great harm to himself and others: to himself by coming into active collision with a world that does not subscribe to his own exalted view of himself, and to others by attacking those he conceives to be persecuting him. Paranoiacs on occasion commit murders, not infrequently engage in futile litigation, and generally make an infernal nuisance of themselves, quarrelling incessantly with their neighbours and falsely accusing people of trespass or their spouses of infidelity.

True paranoia is, fortunately, rare; it has a bad prognosis and is not amenable to any known treatment. However, despite its rarity, it is for a variety of reasons of considerable interest and importance.

First, incoherent, internally consistent delusions of grandeur and persecution occur in other psychoses, notably in *schizophrenia, where they form part of a clinical picture that includes *hallucinations, emotional withdrawal, and autistic thinking (in which syntax is disrupted).

These are three classes of symptoms which are conspicuous by their absence in true paranoia. Most but not all textbooks of psychiatry list 'paranoid schizophrenia' as one of three varieties of schizophrenia, the other two being hebephrenic schizophrenia, which is characterized by withdrawal, bizarre mannerisms, and neglect of the person; and catatonic schizophrenia, characterized by periods of excitement and stupor.

Secondly, many people who are not regarded as mentally ill, and who do not come under the care of psychiatrists, display a cluster of personality traits which can be, and nowadays often are, described as paranoid. These people are opinionated, touchy, and have an idea of their own importance which the rest of the world does not endorse. Such people patently suffer from a disorder of self-esteem, not of intellect—their opinions must be correct because they hold them; their families, their careers, their lives must be especially important because they are *their* families, *their* careers, *their* lives—and the same must presumably be so for true paranoia. According to classical psychoanalytic theory, paranoia and paranoid traits generally are narcissistic disorders, the implication being that they indicate fixation at some infantile stage of development during which the self is its own love object; but many contemporary analysts hold that narcissistic self-overestimation is a compensatory reaction to humiliation in infancy and childhood. Later research (Schatzman 1973) has shown that Daniel Paul Schreber (1842–1911), the subject of *Freud's classic paper 'Psycho-analytical notes on an autobiographical account of paranoia (dementia paranoides)' (1911), was from birth subject to gross mechanical restraints by his father, who was determined to nip in the bud all signs of self-will and 'innate barbarity' in his infant son. Freud, however, made no enquiries into his subject's childhood, took his expressed devotion to his father at its face value, and interpreted his delusions of being persecuted by God as a reversal and projection of repressed homosexual longings for his father.

Thirdly, paranoiac delusions bear a disconcerting, embarrassing resemblance to the beliefs held and propagated by founders of religions, by political leaders, and by some artists. Such people often make claims on behalf of themselves, their religious ideas, their country, their art, which would be regarded as grandiose and delusional if their ideas did not harmonize with the needs of their contemporaries and thereby achieve recognition and endorsement. Nowadays anyone who claimed to be the Messiah, who addressed God as his personal father, and asserted that 'he who is not for me is against me' would be at risk of being referred to a psychiatrist and diagnosed a paranoiac. But presumably in the 1st century AD his Word spoke to many—as indeed it continues to this day to do. Similarly, any politician who asserted the innate superiority of his own race and claimed that his country was the

victim of an international conspiracy would today raise doubts as to his sanity, but in Germany in the 1930s Hitler found all too many people prepared to agree with him. There must, it seems, be some as yet unformulated relationship between the psychology of paranoia and that of prophets and leaders. See OBEDIENCE.

Fourthly, the adjective 'paranoid' is sometimes used by psychoanalysts to describe anxiety and ideas that are inferred to be projections of the subject's own impulses, so that, for instance, a person who is unaware of his own hostility may suffer 'paranoid anxiety', imagining that everyone else is hostile towards him, or a person who is unaware of his own homosexual tendencies may have the 'paranoid idea' that other men are always about to make a pass at him. This usage derives historically from Freud's idea that the psychology of paranoia hinges on reversal and projection of unconscious homosexual impulses.

Finally, it must be mentioned that the word 'paranoid' has slipped into general use to refer to enhanced suspiciousness, often with the implication that such suspiciousness is evidence of unusual sensitivity and perceptiveness. Hence the catch-phrases 'Paranoia is total awareness' and 'The fact that you're paranoid doesn't mean that you aren't being followed'.   CR

Freud, S. (1911). 'Psycho-analytical notes on an autobiographical account of paranoia (dementia paranoides)'. In *Complete Psychological Works*, vol. xii.

Schatzman, M. (1973). *Soul Murder*.

paranormal. The adjective used for phenomena lying outside the range of normal scientific investigations. Among other things it includes communication without physical links, telepathy, clairvoyance, movements of objects without known causes, and extrasensory perception (ESP). What these phenomena have in common is not only lack of accepted explanations but the much stronger claim—essentially difficult to justify—that there never will be acceptable explanations, even for any future science.

It is said of paranormal phenomena (and it is these suggestions that seem to lie outside science) that they demonstrate powers of disembodied minds, are associated with some kind of consciousness, and occur without physical force or material stimulus. They thus have implications for psychology, and for our views of the mind and its relation to the physical world. Many of the claimed phenomena are commonplace events, such as objects falling off shelves, for which no natural cause can be established. If any explicable reason can be supposed, then the claim vanishes, however bizarre the event, for the onus is always to show that the event *is* paranormal. Paranormal intervention is nowadays seldom accepted as the reason for any other than very unusual events, except perhaps in *astrology. This has not always been so: 'primitive' explanations of everyday events were often in terms of the direct action of mind on matter, or on other minds.

Research on claims of paranormal phenomena has been and still is active in many countries, but the most influential body organizing experiments and examining such claims is the British Society for Psychical Research. After a century of work, by many highly distinguished people, including scientists of the first rank, there is probably less confidence now in the existence of paranormal phenomena than when the society was founded. As experiments designed to test for extrasensory perception, telepathy, telekinesis, 'fork bending', and so on are tightened up, the phenomena tend to disappear or turn out to be clearly fraudulent. Of course one cannot say that every case is mistaken or fraudulent, but it is hardly to be taken lightly that, for example, the conjuror James Randi is able by conjuring methods to duplicate Uri Geller's fork bending and other phenomena which only recently were widely accepted as paranormal. There are, however, a few cases of dramatic demonstrations of claimed paranormal abilities which have never been explained in terms of known or conceivable physics, or as cheating: especially those of Daniel Douglas Home (1833–86) who, among other inexplicable reported events, was 'seen' by many people at a party in London to levitate—passing out of one window and through another into a different room—and to perform many other dramatic 'paranormal' feats over many years without ever being 'found out'. On the other hand, there have been several accepted conjurors whose methods, though never ascertained, are assumed not to be paranormal abilities. In any case, it has come as a shock to discover how easily even the best observers and experimenters can suffer *illusions and be mistaken and misled into errors of observation and reporting. Even if all claims of paranormal phenomena are totally rejected, as they have been by such sceptics as David *Hume in his famous 'Essay on miracles' (1748) and more recently C. E. M. Hansel (1966), it is interesting nevertheless to consider such claims, as they do highlight weaknesses of observation and experiment (for science depends on the reliability and honesty of its practitioners). They may also highlight some extremely difficult questions concerning the relation of mind to matter, and suggest what kinds of evidence might be useful for settling philosophical questions by scientific means, as discussed, for example, by S. E. Braude (1978).

The Cambridge philosopher Charlie Dunbar *Broad (1887–1971) suggested that we have beliefs which are deeper and more general than scientific theories, and that it is when these 'basic limiting principles', as Broad called them, of acceptable belief are violated that we move into the domain of the paranormal. Broad did not attempt to give an exhaustive list of these limiting principles, beyond which acceptable science cannot go, nor did he say

how the limits of scientific acceptance might be determined. No doubt some people do believe that the paranormal is somehow 'beyond' science, and that science is blind to paranormal truths. This may, however, be difficult to maintain when we consider that many 'paranormal' phenomena are simple and well-known kinds of events— apart from their explanation. So, whether they appear to be within the bounds of science or beyond it depends on showing that they cannot be explained in normal terms in those particular conditions. The difficulty is to establish that some kind of 'trick' conditions are not in operation, such as a child pushing objects off a shelf with a knitting needle poked through the wall from the next room. For example, there is the famous case of the 'telepathic' boys, who communicated with supersonic whistles hidden in their pockets—with air bulbs which they squeezed according to a code. The high-pitched signals were inaudible to the elderly investigators, who assumed that a paranormal explanation was necessary—until the trick, for trick it was, was found out. But suppose that telepathy can occur by some kind of scientifically acceptable though at present unknown radiation, analogous to radio. (And, after all, radio must seem magical to people with no understanding of its principles—it is amazing enough to those who do!) Telepathy would, then, no longer be regarded as paranormal as it could be explained by science. This brings out the difficulty in defining 'paranormal' as lying outside accepted science—for with new discoveries and theories science often changes dramatically and unpredictably—so what once seemed mysterious or 'paranormal' may become accepted science, as science changes to take account of it. This is so for several past mysteries, which have moved from being regarded as occult or paranormal to being accepted by and even to becoming central in science: such as thunder and lightning being once considered to be the wrath of the gods, but now understood as the same electricity that we generate and use for wonders of our technology.

While electricity was seen as an occult life fluid—which it appeared to be with its ability to shock and convulse, its frenzied sparks, and its sinuous ethereal glow in discharge tubes responding wonderfully to magnets and to a nearby human hand—both electricity and magnetism were supposed to effect cures, and produce trances and other mental states. Franz *Mesmer (1734–1815) convinced many highly intelligent people with his demonstrations of such vital powers of magnetism, seeming to act directly upon mind. As we see it now, Mesmer was demonstrating hypnotism. He worked with histrionic skill, and most effectively. He made wooden pretend magnets, which worked as well as the real steel magnets—provided they *looked* like steel magnets. Mesmer attributed this to some far more general, and indeed all-pervading, spiritual magnetism, acting on mind, though obeying laws of physics (such as being reflected from mirrors). The curious trance states and other phenomena which Mesmer demonstrated were gradually distinguished from 'spirit' or 'animal magnetism'—especially after the clinical demonstrations of the French neurologist Jean Martin *Charcot (1825–93)—when hypnotism was finally seen to be a psychological phenomenon, and it was used as a tool for probing the unconscious mind by Sigmund *Freud, who was a pupil of Charcot's.

However all this may be, we remain uncertain about the powers and limits of mind; so claims of paranormal powers can hardly be dismissed out of hand. What seems to underlie accounts of the paranormal is the notion of mind affecting matter, or other minds—but this is exactly what most of us believe happens whenever we do anything at all, even just waggling a finger. This is part of the deep problem of dualistic accounts of 'mental' mind and 'material' brain (see DUALISM). A way out for psychology is to suppose that minds are not entities which control behaviour, or brains, but are generated by brain activity. Hence the significance of the various kinds of mind–brain identity theories, which deny a causal relationship between mind and brain; it should be recognized, however, that mind –brain identity accounts are controversial and hard to formulate. Clear-cut paranormal phenomena demonstrating disembodied mind might conceivably show identity theories to be untenable. So paranormal accounts do have empirical consequences, even though—in spite of the immense work of controlled experiments, especially on telepathy, and the collections of accounts of bizarre phenomena by Frederic *Myers (1903) and later writers—we may seriously doubt whether there are any such phenomena.

For further discussion of the paranormal see EXTRA-SENSORY PERCEPTION; PARAPSYCHOLOGY: A HISTORY OF RESEARCH. RLG

Braude, S. E. (1978). 'On the meaning of "paranormal" '. In Ludwig, J. (ed.), *Philosophy and Parapsychology*.

Broad, C. D. (1962). *Lectures on Psychical Research*.

Hansel, C. E. M. (1966). *ESP: A Scientific Evaluation*.

Hume, D. (1748). 'Of miracles'. In *Enquiry Concerning Human Understanding*, section X.

Ludwig, J. (ed.) (1978). *Philosophy and Parapsychology*.

Myers, F. W. H. (1903). *Human Personality and its Survival after Bodily Death*.

parapsychology: a history of research. The term 'parapsychology' was introduced in the 1930s to refer to the scientific investigation of *paranormal phenomena—in particular the allegedly extrasensory powers of the mind (see EXTRASENSORY PERCEPTION). Previously this interesting but highly questionable area of science had generally been described as 'psychical research'.

Man has always been fascinated by the possibility that his mind may be capable of exercising unusual powers not apparently linked to the physical senses—telepathy, the capacity to see the future, etc.—and it has to be admitted that mythology, religion, and much of art and literature are on his side in this respect. Furthermore there exists a great body of anecdotal evidence and personal testimony to the effect that such powers exist—almost everyone has had an experience which could be interpreted as having been telepathic, and most people have listened to friends or relations giving superficially convincing accounts of precognitive dreams they have had or of paranormal occurrences that have changed their lives. The history of psychical research or parapsychology in fact reflects the attempts of three or four generations of scientists to convert this intriguing anecdotal material into something more tangible—specifically to trap it in the laboratory. Throughout the course of this history, there has been a continuing shift of emphasis in the focus of research, but for the sake of simplicity it can be conveniently divided into three overlapping phases or periods.

1. Spiritualistic research
2. Psychical research
3. Modern parapsychology

1. Spiritualistic research
The great achievements of 19th-century science seemed to be unfolding a picture of a universe of a depressingly materialistic kind, a vast and rather pointless cosmos made up of tiny billiard balls known as atoms and with no trace of souls or spirits. But most Victorian scientists brought up in the ethos of orthodox Christianity were expected to believe in the reality of an immortal, non-physical soul. For this reason a substantial body of them became involved in the minority religion of spiritualism, taking the line that if souls or spirits survived the death of the physical body then these spirits must exist *somewhere* in the universe, and should, in principle, be contactable. This remarkable period of science saw some of the outstanding brains of the time—the physicists Sir Oliver Lodge and Sir William Crookes, the Nobel Prize-winning biologist Charles Richet, the materialist and anthropologist Alfred Russel *Wallace, and numerous others of equivalent calibre—solemnly attempting to induce spirit forms to materialize in their laboratories. No better testimony could be offered of the simple logic and unbounded optimism of Victorian scientists, but their unbridled enthusiasm for their findings led other, more critical and sceptical colleagues to conduct their own experiments. The result was that medium after medium was exposed as fraudulent, the pioneers were shown up to be gullible, incompetent, or both, and this phase of psychical research, which had fleetingly looked as though it might have almost revolutionary importance, came to an inglorious end. Crookes, Lodge, Wallace, and others, having committed themselves to spiritualism, not

unnaturally remained steadfastly loyal to it, but by 1900 scientific interest was moving away from seances and was concentrating on 'more plausible' aspects of the paranormal. (See also SPIRITUALISM.)

2. Psychical research

Put quite simply, the second phase was the era of the 'ghost hunter', a period when scientists and affluent amateurs turned their attention to such phenomena as manifestations in haunted houses, poltergeist activity, demonic possession, apparitions, premonitions, and other such spectacular and supposedly paranormal events. It also included a large number of casual studies of telepathy and precognitive dreams. The open-minded, amateurish, and 'gentleman scientist' approach of the time is epitomized perhaps by J. W. *Dunne's book *An Experiment with Time*, an influential work, which plotted the author's ad hoc investigation into his own dream-life and its supposedly precognitive content. Almost equally representative were the popularized investigations and writings of Mr Harry Price, who made a decrepit Suffolk rectory world famous as 'The Most Haunted House in England'. Price's research findings, and indeed those of all amateur, non-quantifiable psychic investigations, took a heavy blow when he was exposed by members of the Society for Psychical Research for faking phenomena at Borley. Since then (he was exposed in 1955) it is probably true to say that 'ghost hunting' is no longer considered to be anything much more than crank or fringe science.

3. Modern parapsychology

The third phase was ushered in by the opening of a special university department devoted to the investigation of ESP at Duke University in North Carolina. The department was headed by a young biologist, Dr Joseph Banks Rhine, who, much influenced by the British psychologist William *McDougall, was convinced that the supposedly paranormal powers of the mind were essentially psychological phenomena, and should thus be investigated with the tools of traditional psychological research. The failure of the pioneers of psychical research to achieve anything concrete he assumed to be not because they were investigating ephemera, but because they had not attempted to quantify the phenomena they were supposed to be studying. Throughout the 1930s, therefore, Rhine and his co-workers embarked on a lengthy series of quantifiable experiments, mainly using decks of specially designed cards (Zener cards) for the ESP tests, and automatically thrown dice for the psychokinesis (PK) tests. The admirable rationale for these studies was that they allowed the experimenter to compare the results achieved with what would have been expected by chance. For example, in a deck of 25 cards containing five each of five distinct symbols, one would expect, on average, five to be guessed

right 'by chance'; persistent deviations above chance over a long series of trials would suggest that the guesser was receiving some information about the test cards. This in turn would imply that if the experiments had been so rigorously controlled as to exclude all normal or known sensory cues, then the information must be coming via 'extrasensory perception'.

Rhine's early results in fact yielded just such sustained 'above-chance' scores and he swiftly claimed that he had established ESP as a legitimate phenomenon, or set of phenomena. As might be expected, however, his claims were met with considerable opposition from the psychological establishment. Were his subjects physically completely isolated from the experimenter so that information could not be passed over unwittingly— for example, by unconscious whispering or other non-deliberate cues? Were checks on the data and records precise enough to ensure that minor errors were not made, either unconsciously or deliberately, to bias the results in a pro-ESP direction? To do him justice, Rhine tightened up his procedures on both these accounts—separating subject and experimenter in different buildings, for example, and arranging independent verification and analysis of the results. As a consequence, the above-chance results became rarer, but still remained sufficiently common for them to constitute apparently inarguable evidence for ESP. But then came another, and more fundamental, criticism. When psychologists not committed to a belief in ESP attempted to repeat the Duke findings in their own laboratories, they simply failed to come up with any positive results. The Duke team replied with more sets of positive findings, but the critics again failed to replicate them. Aware that this non-repeatability was a cardinal weakness in their armour, the parapsychologists came up with the ingenious argument that a significant factor in ESP might be the attitude of the experimenter to the phenomena; if he was inclined to be unduly sceptical or dismissive, he might have a 'negative effect' on the results. This is a plausible but also a glib argument which seems to imply that only those who believe in ESP are fitted to investigate it—a point of view that cuts across the main spirit of scientific research. More recently, however, parapsychology received a severe blow when the director of research at Rhine's laboratory (Rhine had himself retired) was caught flagrantly modifying experimental results to provide pro-ESP data, thus offering up to the critics of parapsychology evidence for an argument they had frequently advanced in the past—that no researcher, however distinguished, can be exempted from suspicion of fraud, minor or major, in this controversial field. Since this rather cataclysmic exposure, new evidence has appeared which seems to imply that one of the most distinguished British parapsychologists, Dr S. G. Soal, was also guilty of falsifying data in a key experiment.

At the time of writing, it looks as though the third phase of research in this area is coming to a close without parapsychology having demonstrated ESP to the general satisfaction of science. Indeed there appears to be a swing back to the study of poltergeist phenomena, paranormal healing, and the spectacular claims of Uri Geller and others, almost as though the failure of the strictly experimental approach has been implicitly recognized and agreed upon by all workers in the field. In sum, while it is true that many feel that parapsychology or psychical research is still a legitimate area of study, most scientists who have studied the topic in any depth are inclined to the view that 100 years of fairly dedicated research has yielded disappointingly little in an area which should have offered great riches. See also PSYCHOKINESIS.

CE

Parkinson's disease. The name given to a syndrome, or characteristic set of symptoms, shown by patients with lesions to certain subcortical areas of the brain. From the patient's point of view the main complaints are of involuntary tremor in the limbs together with a difficulty in initiating and controlling voluntary movements, and some general changes in posture, mood, and level of activity. There is no pain, little loss of sensation or awareness, and the mental state often remains well preserved. From the scientific point of view Parkinsonism is of interest because of the insight it gives into the processes involved in translating thoughts and intentions into the appropriate actions for their overt expression. It produces a number of behavioural changes stemming from a disruption of the brain mechanisms that mediate these processes.

Originally called the 'shaking palsy', the syndrome was first described by the surgeon James Parkinson in 1817. Nowadays it is termed 'idiopathic paralysis agitans' in recognition of its status as a naturally occurring degenerative disease of the nervous system of late middle or old age, and of its main features of impaired voluntary movement and a noticeable, continuous, induced shaking of the limbs at rest. The disease has an insidious onset, and there is a tendency for the patient's condition to deteriorate slowly, but it may remain stable for long periods. This is Parkinson's disease proper, for which no cause is yet definitely known—it is almost certainly not hereditary, but no definite link has been established with any slow virus, dietary deficiency, chemical toxin, or other suggested environmental cause.

The characteristic features, however, may occur as 'symptomatic Parkinsonism' in adults of any age as a result of a wide range of damage to the brain, including metal poisoning, anoxia (oxygen deficiency), strokes, certain drug overdoses, and infections. One special instance of the last category was the epidemic viral disease of the 1920s called 'encephalitis lethargica', which is often held to be the cause of a certain kind of Parkinsonism in that generation. In the 1980s a dramatic series of cases occurred in California in young heroin addicts who injected themselves with a designer drug containing the toxic side product MPTP, which destroys the same cells in the brain as are affected in idiopathic Parkinsonism.

The main defining features of Parkinsonism involve the motor system, and comprise *tremor* of the limbs at rest, a relatively slow repetitive oscillation which disappears during sleep or deliberate movement; *increased rigidity* of the limbs to passive movement; and *akinesia*, an impairment of the voluntary control of movement. Other symptoms which may be associated with these include difficulties in maintaining or adjusting posture; difficulties in walking steadily or with normal-size steps; an immobile facial expression; loss of strength in and modulation of the voice; eye movement abnormalities; and an inability to get up out of a bed or low chair without help. The disease in fact affects all the forms of action, communication, and expression by which we interact with the environment and with each other.

In all Parkinsonian disorders the parts of the brain affected are groups of cells lying in the centre and at the base of the forebrain—the *basal ganglia. These nuclei have extensive and complex connections, and form part of several circuits through different levels of the brain. Neural activity in these circuits involves the neurotransmitter dopamine, whose progressive depletion underlies the disease, at first disrupting, and ultimately blocking, transmission through the pathways. A number of drug therapies are now available to patients to help them regain biochemical balance in the system and restore normal movement.

Pathways through the basal ganglia include some to and from the *autonomic nervous system (which controls bodily functions), the cortex, and the limbic system. So it is not surprising that other symptoms often associated with the disease include: autonomic changes such as excessive sweating or trouble with digestion; cognitive changes, with impaired memory and thinking ability; and personality changes, most notably depression and lethargy or increased irritability. Although the last may be a reflection of the patients' reaction to their impaired movement or embarrassing tremor, some observers think that they stem directly from the effects of the disease on the working of those circuits in the brain concerned with an individual's cognitive and emotional state. On this view Parkinsonism has a widespread effect on behaviour, and may be seen as a neuropsychological and neuropsychiatric disease.

1. Motor symptoms: the role of the basal ganglia in movement

2. Cognitive and personality changes: the role of the basal ganglia in general behaviour

1. Motor symptoms: the role of the basal ganglia in movement

While tremor is obvious and embarrassing, the impairment of voluntary movement is the disabling symptom of Parkinsonism. In its extreme form, untreated, it results in an immobile 'frozen' state where the patient remains fixed in a catatonic, typically crouching, posture. Even mild cases sometimes experience 'freezing' when walking or shifting posture.

More often, however, the mild form results in a subtle disturbance of movement, involving both a retardation in initiating movements (akinesia) and slowness and clumsiness in carrying them out (bradykinesia). There is an obvious lack of control, with patients complaining that their hands and fingers 'won't do what I tell them to'. Movements are slow and appear uncoordinated, as if the patient has lost the art of automatically performing familiar skills and has to think about and monitor his actions all the time as he carries them out. But the limbs are not numb, nor paralysed, although the grip may be weak and writing become small and spidery. When doing things slowly movements may be reasonably accurate, and visual control is still precise enough to allow fine adjustments of the fingers—patients who continue (on a good day) to mend watches or carve wood have been known. Moreover the muscles themselves and their immediate control from the motor cortex (see Fig. 1) are still intact, because they respond normally to direct stimulation.

Thus the components of movement appear to be intact in Parkinsonism, but patients have difficulty in coordinating them so as to produce effective actions. There is a dissociation of some kind between thought and action, suggesting that the basal ganglia play a crucial role in the neurological systems that underlie perceptual motor coordination. Parkinsonism disrupts the process at the very centre where the orders for movement are formulated; the patient's difficulty stems from faulty instructions being sent to the motor system, rather than from the motor system responding inaccurately.

Recently, anatomical studies have shown that the basal ganglia provide a connecting link between those areas of the brain mediating thought and those directly initiating movement. They receive inputs from the association cortex of the forebrain (frontal and parietal areas especially) and send their main outputs to the motor cortex and the red nucleus which innervate spinal motor neurons. In this respect they are similar to the *cerebellum, another structure known to be concerned with the control of movement. The two subcortical areas are in fact connected in parallel between association and motor cortex (see Fig. 1).

On this model it may be postulated that the idea or initial plan for a movement takes place in the cortex, that this is passed on to the basal ganglia and cerebellum where some kind of 'programming' of orders for the contraction of muscles takes place, and that these are then passed on to the motor cortex for transmission to the muscles. The subcortical structures may thus be a kind of 'general staff' of the motor system, organizing the

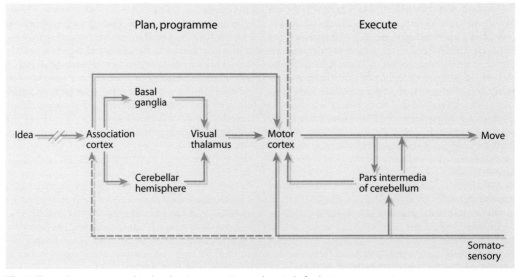

Fig. 1. The pathways concerned in the planning, execution, and control of voluntary movement.

force, duration, timing, and coordination of various kinds of movement.

This physiological model reinforces the notion of the basal ganglia and cerebellum as interface mechanisms between cognitive and motor systems of the brain, providing the means by which general intentions and ideas for action are translated into specific programmes of movement for their fulfilment. If either is damaged, therefore, connections through one pathway will be impaired, but those through the other will still be intact. So patients will not be paralysed, but will lose some aspect of control according to the function disrupted by the lesion. Exactly how the two structures divide control is not known, but there are several possibilities. Some workers have suggested that each is concerned with a different kind of movement (the cerebellum generating visually controlled and the basal ganglia proprioceptively controlled movements), others that each controls a different parameter of movement (for example, the basal ganglia determining the strength to be put into a muscle contraction while the cerebellum regulates its spatial position or timing). These, and other, possibilities are open to experimental test—showing that the disturbed nervous system may be a good proving ground for theories of how the normal system works.

Experimental investigations of Parkinsonian movement, by the author and others, have found that Parkinsonian patients asked to hit a visual target with hand or arm movements from a stationary starting point have difficulty executing quick, large-amplitude aiming movements which are pre-programmed and executed as discrete units (ballistic movements). They can, however, perform small or slow movements under continuous visual correction reasonably well. Patients with cerebellar action tremor show just the reverse. Parkinsonian subjects tend not to increase the amount of force they put into large-amplitude ballistic movements appropriately, so that their movements undershoot the target point (hypokinesia) and are more erratic. Similar dissociable effects between 'ballistic' and visually guided movements have been found in monkeys who, in an experiment, track a target while output from either the basal ganglia or cerebellum is temporarily experimentally inactivated by cooling. These features may underlie the slowness and clumsiness in executing movements which characterize bradykinesia in Parkinson's disease.

If bradykinesia reflects a difficulty in programming individual muscle actions appropriately to achieve an intended movement, akinesia reflects a difficulty in the accurate selection and initiation of responses, that is, in the formation and implementation of 'motor plans'. This is the point at which a general decision or intention is specified as a particular set of actions to achieve it—in computer terms an 'algorithm' for movement. Often it involves switching in a repertoire of well-learnt sequences of movement (as in playing scales or chords on a piano) but it may involve assembling new patterns and sequences for the immediate task in hand. It also involves timing (when to start and stop movements) and whether to control movements through vision, touch, or proprioception—or without *feedback—in short, what strategy to adopt to achieve the goal originally set.

There is some evidence that Parkinsonian patients lose their facility in such higher-level aspects of a motor plan. They are slow in initiating movements of any kind, even when not aiming at a target but just responding to a signal as quickly as possible. They take longer to switch from one movement or movement sequence to another, even when using different limbs where there is no overlap of musculature involved. They have difficulty doing two things at once, and in running off rapid sequences where they cannot monitor each movement separately. They sometimes 'freeze' while walking or getting up out of a chair, as if unable to coordinate and synchronize an action involving several groups of muscles. They have difficulty tracking a continuously moving target on a screen if the target disappears for even short periods, as if they need continual visual information to initiate successive actions. (Tremor patients carry on through such gaps in visual data quite well.) And they tend not to make use of any available advance information about impending movements to reduce their reaction time or events, as normals do, as if the initiation of movements has to be done from an external trigger signal, Parkinsonian subjects being unable to begin them spontaneously.

Such rather curious Parkinsonian characteristics suggest that the basal ganglia are especially involved in assembly, selection, and triggering sequences of action, which explains why Parkinsonian subjects may tire quickly with repeated movement, be unable to do two things at once, or find difficulty in switching from one action to another. The functions disrupted are at the transition point between cognition and action, and are central to the control of behaviour. It is not surprising, therefore, that Parkinson's disease affects other aspects of behaviour as well, both mental and social.

2. Cognitive and personality changes: the role of the basal ganglia in general behaviour

In his original definition of the disease, Parkinson specifically excluded mental changes, declaring 'the senses and intellect being uninjured'. Since then, many observers have disagreed with him, and associated Parkinsonism with dementia or other psychological disturbances. In this they possibly mistake the outward appearance of the untreated advanced stage, with its profound motor immobility and unresponsiveness, for an inner mental deterioration. Nowadays it is generally agreed that Parkinsonian patients may show impairments on a range of cognitive activities, and personality changes too. But their nature is not certain, nor what are the crucial underlying changes in the brain.

Some studies emphasize certain subtle perceptual–motor difficulties in Parkinsonism. The only sensory deficit reported is a slight blurring of vision, possibly due to a retinal dopamine deficiency; otherwise there seems to be little disturbance of the ability to register and identify sensory information. But patients are reported as showing perceptual difficulties in the ability to use sensory information to guide their actions, especially where this involves orientation in space. Thus they have been reported as showing deficits in locating parts of the body correctly from diagrams; in following a given route round a room from a map; in setting a tilted rod to the vertical with the body itself tilted; and in correctly copying or making up gestures with the arms. In all these cases, the difficulty appears to lie in keeping track of one's own movements so as to maintain one's orientation in space, and results from a loss of the reafferent information that one gets from one's own movements. But perceptual judgements of external objects and space are still intact.

Thus the Parkinsonian difficulty is not a cognitive deficit *per se*, but rather a deficit in the use of knowledge for action. It raises the intriguing possibility that motor and behavioural systems use a different sensory input from that, through the cortex, which underlies our conscious perception, so that one's actions may be initiated by signals and controlled by systems not directly amenable to awareness, which is a dissociation commonly found in motor-skills learning and performance.

On standardized tests of intellectual function, Parkinsonian patients often do badly, but this is probably at least partly due to motor difficulties on timed tasks which require manipulation of materials. On many tasks of perception, memory, and reasoning, Parkinsonian patients show little deficit. Or they may have lower scores than normal without showing any qualitative differences typical of *dementia, indicating rather a slowness in thinking (bradyphrenia). Where there is often a specific impairment is in what is termed mental 'set' (that is, the ability to choose one behavioural or mental strategy when several alternatives are available, and then either to maintain it or to switch to another strategy, as appropriate). This deficit in mental control parallels some of the motor difficulties described above, implying that the mental and motor effects of Parkinsonism are similar.

Some years ago, attention was drawn to the existence of ascending dopamine pathways through the basal ganglia from cell bodies in the reticular core of the brain to forebrain areas, especially the prefrontal cortex and the limbic system of the temporal lobes (Fig. 2). Disturbance of these diffuse projections might well interfere with the activity of the innervated structures, producing cognitive impairments or emotional changes respectively. There are several theories of this kind.

Parkinsonism and dementia as diseases of a common core. According to this theory, a loss of neurons in the reticular core of the brain will at first produce symptoms appropriate to whichever structure first loses its input. As neuronal losses increase, symptoms typical of other diseases of old age (dementia, depression, and Parkinsonism) will appear as all three systems are affected. This theory is supported by a number of anatomical and biochemical studies showing similar neuronal changes in Parkinsonism and dementia, and clinically there is often overlap of symptoms too. But not all advanced Parkinsonian patients show signs of dementia, so the overlap may be coincidental.

Loss of arousal. On this theory, ascending projections through the basal ganglia are necessary to activate or initiate cortical activity. Loss of this facility means that patients show lethargic thinking and behaviour because they lack arousal, resulting in inefficient mental activity, although the mechanisms of thought, memory, and thinking are themselves still intact. Undoubtedly lethargy and a lack of spontaneous activity are often observed in Parkinsonism, particularly in the advanced stages, and increasing motivation can improve performance (although it does not always do so).

In the past, advanced cases deteriorated into a 'frozen' state of rigid immobility and unresponsiveness to external stimuli. The discovery in the 1960s of drugs which rectified the biochemical deficiency of Parkinsonism led to dramatic increases in the level of spontaneous activity, even in long-standing catatonic cases. The effect has been appropriately described as 'awakening' by Oliver Sacks (1973) in a vivid and moving account.

Frontal syndrome. This theory proposes that Parkinsonian patients show behavioural effects similar to those of frontal cortical damage, that is, personality and behavioural symptoms rather than loss of intellectual capacity and awareness. The mental set effects described above would fit this description, as would other observations of such frontal signs as perseveration—being unable to change an adopted strategy or sequence of behaviour if conditions change during a task, as, for example, in perceptual adaptation or on tasks where the requirements or rules change on different trials. The theory emphasizes the close mutual interconnections of parts of the basal ganglia with prefrontal cortical areas, and it is likely that cortical and subcortical areas of the brain work together as an integrated unit, such that disruption at any point in the circuit impairs the function of the whole.

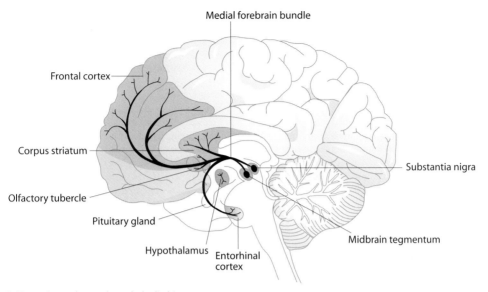

Medial forebrain bundle

Frontal cortex

Corpus striatum

Olfactory tubercle

Pituitary gland

Hypothalamus   Entorhinal
cortex

Substantia nigra

Midbrain tegmentum

Fig. 2. Dopamine pathways through the limbic system.

An extension of this theory attributes the personality changes often found in the disease (notably depression and irritability), as well as the autonomic changes, to basal ganglia connections with the *limbic system. The limbic system is a complex circuit of pathways connecting structures on the inside borders of the cortex with central structures in the brain stem and cerebrum, and is often described as the cerebral mechanism of emotional behaviour. Parts of the frontal lobes form an important link in this circuit, so frontal symptoms might well be accompanied by disturbances of mood and personality. Some authorities, therefore, describe Parkinsonian behavioural changes as frontal–limbic dementia, or subcortical dementia, to distinguish them from senile dementia (Alzheimer's disease) with its global deterioration in memory, thought, and language.

Of particular interest is the finding that while a deficiency of dopamine is associated with Parkinsonism, overactivity in the dopamine system produces schizophrenia-like behavioural effects (see DOPAMINE NEURONS IN THE BRAIN). This opens up the possibility that it is the biochemical status of the nervous system that underlies psychological and psychiatric changes in Parkinsonian patients and schizophrenics. It also holds out hope for the continued development of effective treatment, but, as with studies of the biochemical basis of *schizophrenia, the exact relation of the mechanisms of the nervous system to the characteristics of the mind remains elusive. Progress in this problem may well depend as much on advances in our understanding of the latter as of the former.   KAF

Divac, I., and Öberg, R. G. E. (eds.) (1979). *The Neostriatum.*

Flowers, K. (1976). 'Visual "closed-loop" and "open-loop" characteristics of voluntary movement in patients with Parkinson's disease and intention tremor'. *Brain*, 99.

—— (1978). 'Lack of prediction in the motor behaviour of Parkinsonism'. *Brain*, 101.

—— and Robertson, C. (1985). 'The effect of Parkinson's disease on the ability to maintain a mental set'. *Journal of Neurology, Neurosurgery, and Psychiatry*, 48.

Hallett, M. (1979). 'Physiology and pathophysiology of voluntary movement'. In Tyler, H. R., and Dawson, D. M. (eds.), *Current Neurology*, vol. ii.

Sacks, O. W. (1973). *Awakenings.*

Siegfried, J. (ed.) (1973). *Parkinson's Disease: Rigidity, Akinesia, Behaviour*, 2 vols.

Yahr, M. D. (1975). 'The extrapyramidal disorders'. In Beeson, P. B., and McDermott, W. (eds.), *Textbook of Medicine* (14th edn.)

—— (ed.) (1976). *The Basal Ganglia.*

Pascal, Blaise (1623–62). French mathematician and philosopher. Brought up in Paris by his father to be a mathematician, he worked out for himself when 11 years old the first 23 propositions of *Euclid, and at 16 published a paper on solid geometry that *Descartes refused to believe had been written by one so young. With his father he confirmed Torricelli's theory that nature does not abhor a vacuum—by carrying mercury barometers up a mountain and showing that the column of mercury varied in length. This finally disposed of Greek notions of air, pneuma, and the void. In 1642 he built the first metal-tooth-wheeled calculating machine, later to be developed by *Leibniz.

Pascal was also an influential Christian thinker. He contested the view of Descartes that human reason reigns supreme, arguing that it is unable to deal with ultimate *metaphysical problems. 'The heart has its reasons of which reason knows not.' His religious writings were published after his death as *Pensées* (1670; Eng. trans. A. Krailsheimer, 1966).   RLG

pattern recognition. Informally, a pattern is defined by the common denominator among the multiple instances of an entity. For example, commonality in all fingerprint images defines the fingerprint pattern; the commonality in fingerprint images of John Doe's left index finger defines the John-Doe-left-index-fingerprint pattern (see Fig. 1—showing a bunch of fingerprints of the same finger; and a bunch of impressions of arbitrary fingers in Fig. 2). Thus, a pattern could be a fingerprint image, a handwritten cursive word, a human face, a speech signal, a bar code, or a web page on the internet (see Fig. 3). Often, individual patterns may be grouped into a category based on their common properties; the resultant group is also a pattern and is often called a pattern class. Pattern recognition is the science of observing (sensing) the environment, learning to distinguish patterns of interest (e.g. animals) from their background (e.g. sky, trees, ground), and making sound decisions about the patterns (e.g. Fido) or pattern classes (e.g. a dog, a mammal, an animal).

1. Introduction

Since our early childhood, we have been observing patterns in the objects around us (e.g. toys, flowers, pets, and faces). Learning patterns also reinforces, and is reinforced by, the acquisition of language. By the time children are 5 years old, most can recognize digits and letters. Small and large characters, handwritten and machine-printed characters, characters of different colours and orientations, and partially occluded letters— all are easily recognized by the young. We take this ability for granted until we face the task of teaching a machine how to recognize the characters. In spite of almost 50 years of research, design of general-purpose machines for pattern recognition remains an elusive goal.

Humans are the best pattern recognizers in most scenarios, yet we do not fully understand how we recognize patterns. Ross (1998) emphasizes the work of Nobel laureate Herbert Simon whose central finding is that pattern recognition is critical in most human decision-making tasks: 'The more relevant patterns at your disposal, the better your decisions will be. This is hopeful news to proponents of artificial intelligence, since computers can

Fig. 1. Examples of patterns: six fingerprints from the same finger of the same person.

Fig. 2. Examples of patterns: Fingerprints of different persons.

Fig. 3. Examples of patterns: sound wave, fingerprint, trees, face, bar code, and character images.

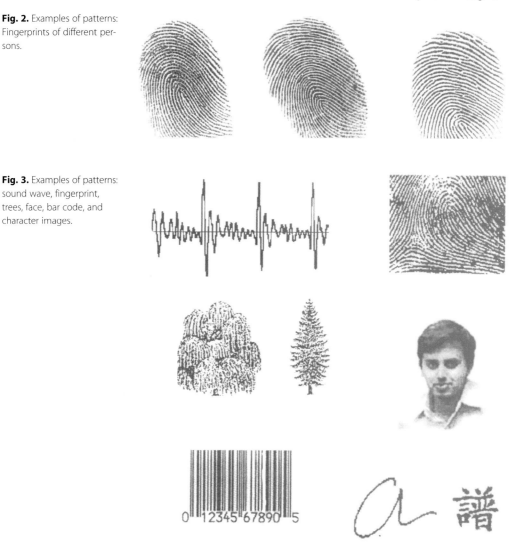

surely be taught to recognize patterns. Indeed, successful computer programs that help banks score credit applicants, help doctors diagnose diseases and help pilots land airplanes depend in some way on pattern recognition.'

We will first describe the area of pattern recognition in detail and relate it to the more restricted problem of pattern classification. This is followed by systems for automatic pattern recognition. In particular, we describe some methods for generalization, i.e. how the derived decision rules can be applied to new observations. Next, some aspects of pattern learning are discussed that may play a role in human learning as well. Finally, some applications are

described that are already in use in various sectors of our society.

2. Pattern recognition and classification

Pattern recognition aims to make the process of learning and detection of patterns explicit, such that it can be partially or entirely implemented on computers. Automatic (machine) recognition, description, and classification (grouping of patterns into pattern classes) have become important problems in a variety of engineering and scientific disciplines such as biology, psychology, medicine, marketing, computer vision, artificial intelligence, and remote sensing. In almost any area of science in which

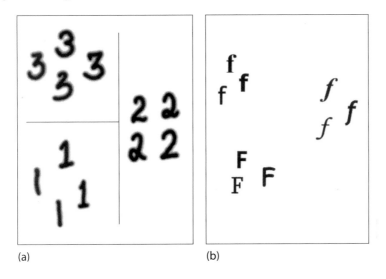

(a) (b)

Fig. 4. a. Supervised pattern recognition deals with classifying objects with (known) different labels. **b.** In unsupervised pattern recognition, classes or subclasses have to be derived from the data.

observations are studied but the underlying mathematical or statistical models are not available, pattern recognition can be used to support human concept acquisition or decision making. Given a group of objects, there are two ways to build a classification or recognition system (Watanabe 1985): supervised, i.e. with a teacher, or unsupervised, without the help of a teacher (see Fig. 4).

Interest in pattern recognition has been renewed recently due to emerging applications which are not only challenging but also computationally more demanding, such as data mining, document classification, organization and retrieval of multimedia databases, and biometric authentication (i.e. face recognition and fingerprint matching).

3. Systems for automatic pattern recognition
Rapid advances in computing technology not only enable us to process huge amounts of data, but also facilitate the use of elaborate and diverse methods for data analysis and classification. At the same time, demands on automatic pattern recognition systems are rising enormously due to the availability of large databases and stringent performance requirements (faster recognition speed and higher accuracy at a lower cost). In many emerging applications, it is clear that no single approach for classification is 'optimal' and multiple methods and approaches have to be used. Consequently, combining several sensing modalities and classifiers is now a common practice in pattern recognition.

The design of a pattern recognition system essentially involves the following four aspects: (i) data acquisition and pre-processing, e.g. taking a picture of an object and removing the irrelevant background; (ii) data representation, e.g. deriving *relevant* object properties (like its size,

shape, and colour) which efficiently offer pertinent information needed for pattern recognition; (iii) training, e.g. imparting pattern class definition into the system, often by showing a few typical examples of the pattern; and (iv) decision making that involves finding the pattern class or pattern description of new, unseen objects based on a training set of examples. The application domain dictates the choice of sensor(s), pre-processing technique, representation scheme, and decision-making model. It is generally agreed that a well-defined and sufficiently constrained classification problem will lead to a compact pattern representation and a simple decision-making strategy. Learning from a set of examples (training set) is an important and desired characteristic of most pattern recognition systems, in contrast with systems consisting of handcrafted decision rules only.

The five major approaches for pattern recognition are summarized below (Jain, Duin, and Mao 2000).

Template matching. Objects are directly compared with a few stored examples or prototypes that are representative of the underlying classes. Because of the large variations often encountered in these examples, template matching is not the most effective approach to pattern recognition.

Geometrical classification. Classes are represented by regions in the representation space (e.g. a feature space as in Fig. 5) defined by simple functions such that the training examples are classified as correctly as possible. Suppose the average value of (height, weight) of women is (1.6 m, 57 kg) (5'5", 125 lb) and that of men is (1.7 m, 71 kg) (5'11", 157 lb). A simple geometric woman vs. man classifier using (height, weight) as a two-dimensional representation may simplistically divide the representation space into two triangular regions (similar to Fig. 4a). So, a person with

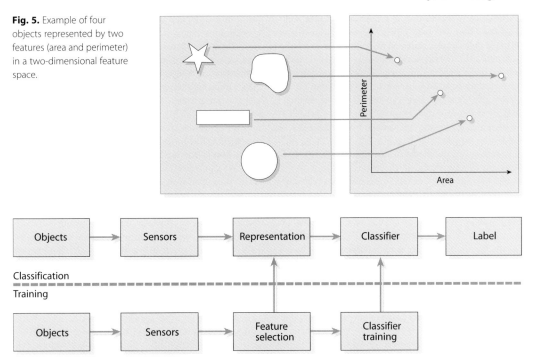

Fig. 5. Example of four objects represented by two features (area and perimeter) in a two-dimensional feature space.

Fig. 6. Design of a pattern recognition system.

(height, weight) = (1.5 m, 55 kg) will be classified by this classifier as a woman.

Statistical classification. Continuing with the foregoing example, a statistical classifier may estimate the statistical distribution of the two features, namely height and weight of the two classes of interest (women and men), from known samples. At any coordinate or point in the representation space, one could estimate the likelihood of it being a man or a woman; depending upon which likelihood is higher, one could determine the class of an entity. This method differs from the geometrical method in that the classes are not (pre)defined in terms of any regular shapes in the representation space.

Syntactic or structural matching. The height and weight representation space is too simplistic and it is conceivable that a person's body shape is a better representation for determining his or her gender. One could decompose the shape of a person into component *parts* and describe the shape in terms of component parts and their relationships (e.g. how they are attached to each other). Now, the determination of gender could be performed based on either the shapes of the individual body parts or their relationships, or both. In a syntactic or structural approach, a complex pattern (e.g. animal) is described in terms of component patterns (e.g. hair and head, or torso and limbs) and their relationship (e.g. articulated

joints). Strategies for learning such a language (defining the structure) from examples are problematic, as it is essentially difficult to compensate for noise (see Fu 1983, also Perlovsky 1998).

Artificial neural networks. These networks attempt to apply the models of biological neural systems to solve practical pattern recognition problems. This approach has become so popular that the use of neural networks for solving pattern recognition problems has become an area on its own, and is often studied outside the biological context, e.g. see the books by Bishop (1995) and Ripley (1996).

It is interesting to compare these approaches for automatic pattern recognition with the various ways the human learning process may be modelled: simulation of the neural system itself, or simulation of the processes in that system, based either on direct information from the senses (as in the statistical and the geometrical approaches) or on higher-level symbolic information (as in the structural approach). The template-matching procedure can be compared with learning by storing all facts without understanding them.

4. Some challenges in pattern and class learning

Selection of training sets. If we want to learn from examples, care should be paid to the way the examples are selected.

For instance, a system for the recognition of electrocardiograms (say, into normal heart vs. diseased heart) can be based on examples collected in hospitals, on examples collected in a general screening test, on typical cardiograms that are clear examples of particular classes of heart problems, or on selected cardiograms that are the border cases between these classes. The choice of such a strategy is strongly related to the learning approach to be used and to the way the recognition system can be used.

Representation of objects. There are various ways to represent objects: raw data measurements (e.g. overall height, overall weight), derived measurements or features (e.g. ratio of height to weight), a structural description (e.g. height to weight ratios of parts of bodies and spatial relationship of the body parts), etc. In the statistical approach, the feature representation is the most common. For the recognition of simple real-world objects, the features can be their sizes, shapes, colours, etc. More features do not necessarily imply a better classification performance. Given a representation scheme, an objective measure (e.g. 'distance' or 'score') needs to be defined to quantify the (dis)similarity between any two representations.

Inter- and intra-class distances. A direct and intuitive way to see whether a feature representation is good for a classification problem is to compare the inter-class distances (e.g. between the two sets of pictures of two different persons) with the intra-class distances (e.g. between all pictures of a single person). If the inter-class distances are much larger than the intra-class distances, the classification problem is easy. If they are of similar orders, either the classes overlap, or a more advanced procedure is needed to separate the classes. Obviously, a representation with large inter-class variability and small intra-class variability is desirable. See Fig. 7 for an illustration on inter- and intra-class distances.

Invariance of representation. Some object variations may not be important for the classification task, e.g. the size of a character, the angle (pose) at which a face is observed, the speed by which a word is spoken. These variations may influence the representation so that the position of the object in feature space is changed. An important problem is how to identify and extract these so-called invariants. We can collect objects under all possible variations, which is expensive. A preferred approach is to use invariant features.

The problem of overtraining. An overly complex pattern recognition system may learn unnecessary details of training samples of a pattern and, consequently, will be unable to recognize the essential commonality defining the pattern. It is necessary to adapt the complexity of the recognition system to the complexity and size of the data set under consideration.

5. Pattern recognition applications

Pattern recognition is used in any area of science and engineering that studies the structure of observations. It is now frequently used in many applications in manufacturing industry, healthcare, and the military. Examples include the following.

Optical character recognition (OCR) is becoming an integral part of document scanners, and is also used frequently in banking and postal applications. Printed characters can now be accurately recognized, and the improving performance of automatic recognition of

(a)   (b)

Fig. 7. Different faces of the same person, or different persons? **a.** Faces belonging to two different people. **b.** Multiple faces of the same person.

handwritten cursive characters has diminished significantly the need of human interaction for OCR tasks.

Automatic speech recognition is very important for user interaction with machines. Commercial systems for automatic response to flight queries, telephone directory assistance, and telebanking are available. Often the systems are tuned to a specific speaker for better recognition accuracy.

Computer vision deals with the recognition of objects as well as the identification and localization of their three-dimensional environments. This capability is required, for example, by robots to operate in dynamic or unknown environments. This can be useful for applications ranging from manufacturing to household cleaning, and even for rescue missions.

Personal identification systems that use biometrics are very important for security applications in airports, ATMs, shops, hotels, and secure computer access. Recognition can be based on face, fingerprint, iris, or voice, and can be combined with the automatic verification of signatures and PIN codes.

Recognition of objects on earth from the sky (by satellites) or from the air (by aeroplanes and cruise missiles) is called remote sensing. It is important for cartography, agricultural inspection, detection of minerals and pollution, and target recognition.

Many tests for medical diagnosis utilize pattern recognition systems, from counting blood cells and recognition of cell tissues through microscopes to the detection of tumours in magnetic resonance scans and the inspection of bones and joints in X-ray images.

Many large databases are stored on the repositories accessible via the internet or otherwise in local computers. They may have a clear structure such as bank accounts, a weak structure such as consumer behaviour, or no obvious structure such as a collection of images. Procedures for finding desired items (database retrieval) as well as learning or discovering structures in databases (data mining) are becoming more and more important. Web search engines and recommender systems are two example applications.   AKJ/RPWD

Bishop, C. M. (1995). *Neural Networks for Pattern Recognition*.

Duda, R. O., Hart, P. E., and Stork, D. G. (2001). *Pattern Classification and Scene Analysis* (2nd edn.).

Fu, K. S. (1983). 'A step towards unification of syntactic and statistical pattern recognition'. *IEEE Transactions on Pattern Analysis and Machine Intelligence*, 5/2.

Jain, A. K., Duin, R. P. W., and Mao, J. (2000). 'Statistical pattern recognition: a review'. *IEEE Transactions on Pattern Analysis and Machine Intelligence*, 22/1.

Perlovsky, L. I. (1998). 'Conundrum of combinatorial complexity'. *IEEE Transactions on Pattern Analysis and Machine Intelligence*, 20/6.

Picard, R. (1997). *Affective Computing*.

Ripley, B. (1996). *Pattern Recognition and Neural Networks*.

Ross, P. E. (1998). *Flash of Genius*.

Watanabe, S. (1985). *Pattern Recognition: Human and Mechanical*.

Pavlov, Ivan Petrovich

Pavlov, Ivan Petrovich (1849–1936). Russian physiologist. His importance for the study of animal behaviour is mainly due to his work on conditional reflexes; this work provided the basis for much of the subsequent research on *learning. Pavlov also conducted significant research on the physiology of digestion and on neurosis.

1. Brief life
2. Physiology of circulation and digestion
3. Conditional reflexes
4. Experimental neurosis and personality

1. Brief life

Pavlov was born in Ryazan, Russia, and attended the religious school and seminary there, where he studied natural science. He did not complete his studies, but entered St Petersburg University in 1870, where he continued to study natural science, and decided to make his career as a physiologist. After graduation in 1875, he went to the Military Medical Academy to pursue his research. He completed his doctorate there in 1883, and then went to Germany (1884–6), where he studied in Leipzig with Carl Ludwig, and in Breslau. In 1890 he was appointed professor in the department of pharmacology in the Military Medical Academy, and in 1895 he moved to the department of physiology. In 1904 he received the Nobel Prize for his work on the physiology of digestion. He remained professor of physiology until 1925, when he resigned in protest against the expulsion of sons of priests from the Academy (he himself was the son of a priest, but would not have been expelled). Initially Pavlov was outspokenly opposed to the Bolsheviks, even though they supported his research. In 1922 he asked Lenin's permission to transfer his research abroad, but was refused: Lenin wanted prestigious scientists. However, during the last few years before his death (in Leningrad) Pavlov increasingly accepted and approved of the Bolsheviks. From 1925 to 1936 he worked mainly in three laboratories: the Institute of Physiology of the Soviet Academy of Sciences (which is now named after him), the Institute of Experimental Medicine, and the biological laboratory at Koltushy (now Pavlovo), near St Petersburg.

2. Physiology of circulation and digestion

Pavlov held that physiologists should study 'the actual course of particular physiological processes in a whole and normal organism'. He also held that the main problems for experimental research were the mutual interactions of organs within the body, and the relation of the organism to its environment. The method of working on the whole, healthy body of an animal contrasted with the mainstream of physiology in the latter half of the 19th century; most investigations then were on isolated organs and prepared specimens.

Pavlov's work on the physiology of circulation (*c.*1874–88) was mainly concerned with the mechanisms that regulate blood pressure. His experimental animal for this, and for most subsequent research, was the dog. He was mainly interested in nervous mechanisms. He discovered, for instance, that the vagus nerve controls blood pressure, and that there are four nerves controlling the heartbeat, which can vary the heartbeat's rhythm and intensity (work on the nervous control of the heart had formed his doctorate).

Pavlov's work on the physiology of digestion began in about 1879, and culminated in his book *The Work of the Digestive Glands* (1902, a translation of *Lektsii o rabotie glavnych pishchevaritel'nykh zhelez*, 1897). He investigated the nervous mechanisms controlling the secretions of the various digestive glands, and how these nervous mechanisms were stimulated by food. He had to expose the structures of interest surgically, and work on them in a healthy animal, so it was crucial to his success that he was also a brilliant surgeon. (Similar experiments had been attempted in the laboratory in Breslau that he visited in the mid-1880s, but had failed because the experimenters lacked Pavlov's surgical skill.) Once he had exposed part of the gut, Pavlov could directly insert food or chemicals, and observe the effects on the activity of the digestive glands. The method of sham feeding was a related development. A slit is made in the animal's throat so that food entering through the mouth falls out through the neck before reaching the stomach. The animal can be fed through a second opening made into the stomach. By sham feeding, Pavlov could observe the effect of food in the mouth on the secretion of digestive juices elsewhere in the gut; he found that the *taste of food in the mouth causes the release of gastric juices in the stomach. A smaller quantity of juice is released if food is put directly into the stomach. Sham feeding has been used and developed extensively by later workers.

Pavlov's own theory for the control of digestive secretions postulated control exclusively by nervous mechanisms. Subsequent research has shown this theory to be incomplete: control by hormones also occurs. He made many other important discoveries while working on digestion. Two of the most important were the enzyme *enterokinase*, which controls the activity of another digestive enzyme, and the connection between the properties of the saliva and the type of food being eaten (the Pavlovian curves of salivary secretion). N. P. Shepovalnikov and Pavlov were co-discoverers of enterokinase.

Pavlov's work on the physiology of digestion is important for understanding his work on animal behaviour, for his explanations of animal behaviour are similar to those

of the control of digestion. In addition, his methods were similar in all his studies.

3. Conditional reflexes

While at the seminary in Ryazan, Pavlov had read I. M. Sechenov's *Refleksy golovnago mozga* (Reflexes of the Brain), which argued that mental events were reflexes. Then, while working on the physiology of digestion, he had noticed 'psychic' salivation: when the dog was confronted by a *stimulus that customarily preceded feeding, it salivated even before being fed. This psychic salivation could be induced, for example, by the animal's food container, or by the presence of the attendant who normally fed the animal, or even by the sound of the attendant's approach. Armed with these incidental observations and with the reflexology of Sechenov, and stimulated by Charles *Darwin's evolutionary arguments about animal behaviour (which encouraged materialistic analyses of mental events), Pavlov set out to investigate the psychic salivation of dogs. This was a simple extension of his earlier studies on the control of digestive secretions, and once again it was the nervous reflex that he looked to for his explanation. He worked on conditional reflexes from about 1902 until his death.

A typical Pavlovian experiment on psychic salivation would be as follows. On several occasions a bell is rung just before the dog is fed, and the dog salivates on receiving its food. Then the bell is rung without presentation of food. It is observed that the dog salivates in response to the bell's ringing. Pavlov termed the food the *unconditional stimulus*, the sound of the bell the *conditional stimulus*, the salivation to the food the *unconditional reflex*, and the salivation to the bell alone the *conditional reflex*. ('Conditional' is what Pavlov actually wrote, but the early mistranslation of 'conditioned' is now widespread in the psychological literature.)

Many of the fine details of the conditional reflex were studied by Pavlov and his collaborators. First, there is the temporal sequence of stimuli. Pavlov found that it is much easier to form a conditional reflex if the unconditional stimulus (food) follows the conditional one (bell) than if they are simultaneous, or if the conditional stimulus follows the unconditional. Second, there is the time delay between stimuli. Here he found that a discrete conditional stimulus is more effective in forming a conditional reflex if it occurs near in time to the food than if it occurs a long time before. However, if the conditional stimulus starts a long time before, but continues right up to when the unconditional stimulus is presented, then it is as effective as a conditional stimulus which starts just before the food is given. Third, there is the intensity of the stimuli. A dog salivates more if it is trained on bigger pieces of food, and similarly, it salivates more to a louder bell. Fourth, Pavlov studied generalization of the conditional stimulus. If the animal has been trained on a stimulus of one pitch, it can then be tested for a response to a stimulus of another pitch. This leads to a method of investigating the animal's powers of sensory discrimination, which again was originated and developed by Pavlov.

Pavlov was not only interested in how conditional reflexes were gained; he also studied how they were lost. He classified factors causing loss of a conditional reflex into cases of either *external inhibition* or *internal inhibition*. If an animal, conditioned in one way, is moved into a new environment, or is exposed to new stimuli before being fed, it loses its original conditional reflex; this is called external inhibition. There are several forms of internal inhibition. The most straightforward is the gradual loss of the conditional reflex if the food is withheld after the conditional stimulus; the conditional reflex requires regular reinforcement (to use Pavlov's term) by the unconditional stimulus.

Pavlov thought of the conditional reflex as similar to any other kind of reflex. The flow of digestive juices is stimulated by the mechanical and chemical properties of food, through the mediation of a nervous (unconditional) reflex. Similarly, salivation could be induced by some environmental indicator of food, again by a nervous (conditional, in this case) reflex. The conditional reflex, however, is easily modifiable by the environment, according to whatever the local indicators of food happen to be. So, Pavlov regarded the formation of conditional reflexes as an adaptation whereby the animal could survive better in a changing environment.

Pavlov also speculated on the fine details of the formation of a conditional reflex. He suggested that the cells of the central nervous system must change structurally and chemically when a conditional reflex is formed: 'the locking in, the formation of new connections, we attribute to the functioning of the separating membrane, should it exist, or simply to the branching between neurones.' This idea has subsequently been confirmed.

Although nearly all his research was on dogs, Pavlov also showed that conditional reflexes can be formed in mice and monkeys, and he was in no doubt that they occur in man, and in all other animals. He wrote: 'A temporary nervous connection is a universal physiological phenomenon in the animal world and exists in us ourselves.' He also showed that more or less any environmental factor can act as a conditional stimulus (though this conclusion has been slightly modified by later research). Pavlov was aiming at truly universal laws of learning, and that is why his discoveries are so fundamental to modern theories of associative learning. One branch of psychology—*behaviourism*—went so far as to attribute all human behaviour to *conditioning and reinforcement. Pavlov, however, made no such extravagant claims for the conditional reflex, and ridiculed the claims of behaviour-

ism to scientific status. The most famous expression in English of Pavlov's work on conditioning is his book *Conditioned Reflexes* (1927). In psychiatry, conditioning is used in *behaviour therapy.

4. Experimental neurosis and personality

In a famous experiment (1921) by Shenger-Krestovnika a circle was used as a conditional stimulus before feeding, and the dog was also trained to associate an ellipse with not being fed. By small steps the ellipse was then made more and more like a circle. When the ellipse was almost round, initially the dog could usually distinguish it from a circle. But after a few weeks the dog became neurotic: it ceased to be able to recognize obvious ellipses and circles, became very excited, and was no longer calm during experiments. Pavlov termed the animal's abnormal condition experimental *neurosis, and he attributed it to a disturbance of the balance between excitatory and inhibitory processes in the nervous system. This explanation of experimental neurosis is grounded in Pavlov's theory of personality. He explained personality by variation in the excitation of the nervous system. He did not, however, attribute neurosis solely to external factors, such as contradictory stimuli. His experiments on experimental neuroses showed that dogs with different 'personalities' were differentially susceptible to the treatment: the same treatment on different dogs could produce quite different neuroses. In the 1930s Pavlov decided to work on the *genetics of behaviour, and his government built him the biological station at Koltushy for this research.

There is an underlying unity to all Pavlov's work. In his earliest work on blood circulation he established his method (intervention in unanaesthetized, whole dogs) and his paradigm explanation: nervous control. The same procedure was used in his work on the control of digestive secretion, and he started research on conditional reflexes as just another kind of nervous control of digestion. Late in his life, he saw how conditioning could be used to analyse personality and neurosis, and once again he was able to carry over his theoretical framework into a new field.

MR

Babkin, B. P. (1951). *Pavlov: A Biography*.

Gray, J. A. (1979). *Pavlov*.

Grigorian, N. A. (1974). *Pavlov, Ivan Petrovich*.

Peirce, Charles Sanders (1839–1914). Considered by many to be the most original of American philosophers, Peirce is remembered principally for his teleological account of truth, for founding *pragmatism, for contributions to formal logic, and for pioneering work in the theory of signs (semiotics). His early published work attacked the idea, dominant in the nominalist tradition from William of Occam onward, that a proposition is true if it corresponds to a reality which is the efficient cause of our sensations. In place of this Peirce gave an account based on the idea of 'a final conclusion, to which the opinion of every man is constantly gravitating'. Peirce, however, understood this gravitational attraction strictly in terms of the operation of rigorous scientific method, and as a practising experimental scientist he was impressed by the way a scientific concept is made precise by being tied to observable consequences of concrete operations. It was along these lines that he formulated a general maxim for achieving clear ideas, which he later came to identify as the core of his pragmatism. From the outset the centre of Peirce's philosophical concerns was logic, and he made important contributions to the logic of relations and devised, a few years after, but independently of, Gottlob Frege, the theory of quantification. Both his pragmatism and his work on logic were embedded in a theory of signs based on the idea that the *meaning of a sign is its power to determine observers of it to interpret it in a determinate fashion.

Peirce had mixed feelings when in 1898 William *James drew attention to him as the founder of pragmatism but at the same time advanced under this label a doctrine of truth (seen by many as the crude idea that truth is what works or what is useful) to which Peirce was quite antipathetic. As a result Peirce tried (in vain) to change the name of his approach to 'pragmaticism'.

Peirce's father, a professor at Harvard, was the leading American mathematician of his generation, but the son, largely through an inability to get on with people, failed to secure a permanent academic appointment. Apart from five years teaching at Johns Hopkins University, Peirce was employed as a scientist by the US Coast Survey. He published voluminously (estimated total of 24 volumes) on science, mathematics, and philosophy but never succeeded in giving his logical and philosophical ideas a systematic treatment in book form.

One extensive selection of Peirce's work is *Collected Papers* (vols. i–vi eds. C. Hartshorn and P. Weiss, and vols. vii and viii by A. W. Burks) (1931–58). Another selection, *Writings of Charles S. Peirce: A Chronological Edition* (eds. M. H. Fisch et al.), began to appear in 1982. Two one-volume selections are available: *Charles S. Peirce: Selected Writings* (ed. P. P. Weiner) (1966), and *Philosophical Writings of Peirce* (ed. J. Buchler), (1955). Two useful introductions to his thought are *Peirce and Pragmatism* by W. B. Gallie, (1952), and *Peirce* by C. Hookway, (1985).   JET

Penfield, Wilder Graves (1891–1976). American neurosurgeon, born in Spokane, Washington, and educated at Princeton and Oxford, where he held a Rhodes scholarship. At Oxford he came to know C. S. *Sherrington, and returned to work with him for two years after qualifying in medicine at Johns Hopkins University, Baltimore. He also made contact with Gordon *Holmes and other neurologists at the National Hospital for Nervous Diseases in London, where David *Ferrier had pioneered brain surgery. On his return to America, Penfield specialized in neurosurgery and worked in both New York and Baltimore before moving to Montreal, where he was largely responsible for setting up the Montreal Neurological Institute, erected with the support of the Rockefeller Foundation and of which he became the first director. It has since led the world in the field of neurosurgery.

Penfield was remarkable not only for his high surgical accomplishment but also for his belief that neurosurgery made possible important advances in our scientific understanding of the functions of the brain. This, in its turn, made possible important progress in surgical treatment and rehabilitation. He made extensive use of advances in neurophysiology, in particular *electroencephalography, and later of techniques in experimental *neuropsychology, in ascertaining the *localization and extent of brain lesions. He also undertook important work on the surgical treatment of focal *epilepsy.

Penfield was a man of varied accomplishments, who wrote several novels in addition to an informative autobiography, *No Man Alone: A Neurosurgeon's Life* (1977). Of particular interest is his book with Theodore Rasmussen on *The Cerebral Cortex of Man* (1950).   OLZ

Lewis, J. (1982). *Something Hidden: A Biography of Wilder Penfield.*

Penrose, Lionel Sharples (1898–1972). British physician, born in London. Penrose's father was a portrait painter and both his parents were members of the Society of Friends. After serving in the Friends' Ambulance Train of the British Red Cross during the First World War, he went in 1919 to St John's College, Cambridge, where he wanted to study mathematical logic with Bertrand *Russell. He obtained his degree in 1921, and then studied with F. C. *Bartlett and at the University of Vienna, where he did work on *memory and *perception in E. Buhler's laboratory and met Sigmund *Freud. At this time, Penrose was very interested in the problems of abnormal psychology and mental disorder and realized that he would be advised to qualify in medicine in order to pursue this interest. He therefore went to Cambridge in 1925 and subsequently to St Thomas' Hospital in London. He presented his MD thesis on the subject of *schizophrenia in 1930 and the following year applied for, and ultimately obtained, an appointment as research medical officer at the Royal Eastern Counties Institution at Colchester.

From this time on, the chief interest of his life, namely the study of mental deficiency, began to dominate his work, and when he left Colchester in 1939 to go to Canada, as director of psychiatric research for Ontario, he had already produced his classic *A Clinical and Genetic Study of 1,280 Cases of Mental Defect* (1938). This work alone would have established him as a leader in the subject, and at the time it advanced the study of mental deficiency very considerably. In addition, before leaving for Ontario he had developed a test which he believed might aid the diagnosis of *schizophrenia, and had been instrumental, according to his own statement, in proposing the idea and outline of the *intelligence test that subsequently became generally known as Raven's progressive matrices (1936).

In 1945 Penrose was appointed to the Galton Professorship of eugenics at University College London. He retired in 1965 but continued to work at the Kennedy-Galton Centre, which he set up at Harperbury Hospital, St Albans. He remained a leader in the field of subnormality and genetics, especially in relation to *Down's syndrome.

NOC

Penrose, L. S. (1938). *A Clinical and Genetic Study of 1,280 Cases of Mental Defect*.
—— (1959). *Problems of Intelligence and Heredity*.
—— with Raven, J. C. (1936). 'A new series of perceptual tests: a preliminary communication'. *British Journal of Medical Psychology*, 16.

Pepper's ghost. A simple optical effect which is used for stage ghosts and in optical instruments, such as the *camera lucida* for drawing from the microscope, and the tachistoscope, which presents pictures for controlled duration in visual experiments. A part-reflecting mirror superimposes one picture (or object) which is *reflected* on another seen *through* the glass. By brightening one while dimming the other, one is seen to appear as the other disappears—and when roughly equally illuminated both are seen, superimposed, as transparent ghosts. The effect often occurs in window-panes, especially at night, though curiously it is seldom noticed unless attention is drawn to reflected lampshades etc. floating outside. This effect may produce 'flying saucers'. RLG

perception. Our senses probe the external world. They also tell us about ourselves, as they monitor positions of the limbs and the balance of our bodies, and through pain they signal injury and illness. More subtly, there are innumerable internal signals monitoring everyday physiological activities, and conveying and maintaining our well-being; though little of this enters our *consciousness. In perception of objects and pictures, as Sir Ernst *Gombrich (1950) realized to such good effect, art and science meet.

Just how we know things through sensory experience is a question that was discussed by the Greek philosophers and has continued to be discussed ever since. But, perhaps curiously, planned experiments in the spirit of the physical sciences were hardly attempted much earlier than the mid-19th century. Since then, the experimental study of perception has yielded fundamental knowledge

for physiology and psychology, especially from the outstanding work of Hermann von *Helmholtz (1867). It has revealed many surprises in the form of processes of which we are unaware, though they can often be demonstrated simply and dramatically as by the phenomena of *illusions. The study of perception, especially of vision and hearing and touch, has allowed psychology to grow from its philosophical roots into an experimental science; yet deeply puzzling philosophical questions remain, especially over the role of consciousness. It is puzzling, both that we are aware of so *little* of perception, and that we have *any* awareness or consciousness.

There is a long-standing tradition in philosophy that perception gives undeniably true knowledge. Philosophers have traditionally sought certainty, and often claimed it, whereas scientists—who are used to their theories being modified and upset by new data—generally settle for today's best bet. Philosophers have a heavy investment in the reliability of perception, for they stake their all on the certainty of knowledge from the senses to provide secure premises for their arguments based on experience. Scientists, on the other hand, who are used to errors in measurement and observations, have found it necessary to check, and compare, and repeat observations as they do not expect reliability from the senses. Indeed, many scientific instruments have been developed precisely because of the limitations or the unreliability of perception: for it is easy to produce and demonstrate all manner of dramatic illusions, which could hardly occur if perception were direct reliable knowledge. Yet although illusions of object perception have been discussed by philosophers from *Aristotle to *Berkeley and more recently, philosophy generally has paid more attention to errors of logic and ambiguity of language, than to fallibilities of perception.

Philosophers are traditionally impressed by the undeniability of the 'raw experience' of *sensations. The sensation of toothache may be undeniable; but are perceptions of objects, and things happening, similarly infallible? One would think so if one believed that perceptions are simply sensations; but we now regard perceptions as giving us knowledge, albeit surprisingly indirectly, of the *causes* or *sources* of sensations—such as the states of our bodies, and especially objects in the environment—rather than of sensations themselves. It is now clear that there are vast, still largely mysterious perceptual jumps, intelligent leaps of the mind, which may land on error. One can, indeed, be wrong about the cause of toothache!

It is worth asking why we have both *perceptions* and *conceptions* of the world. Why is perception somehow separate, and in several ways different from our conceptual understanding? Very likely it is because perception, in order to be useful, must work very fast; whereas we may take minutes, hours, or years, forming concepts.

Perception is not traditionally thought of as an intelligent activity, though the power, especially of vision, to probe distance gains time needed for intelligent reactions to on-going events. It can be argued (see STIMULUS) that the development of distance perception freed organisms from the tyranny of reflexes, and allowed perception to be intelligent.

Are perceptions *picked up* by the senses, or are they *created* internally by the perceiver? This question about the passivity or activity of perception is long-standing, and still debated. If sensations are created by the brain, a notion that receives strong support from physiology (see VISUAL BRAIN IN ACTION; VISUAL SYSTEM: ENVIRONMENTAL INFLUENCES; VISUAL SYSTEM: ORGANIZATION), we should expect to find, as we do, a vast amount of brain activity for perception. Whereas, if perceptions are simply 'picked up' (*Gibson 1950, 1966), the brain would have little to do. But a very great deal goes on, physiologically and cognitively.

This raises the old question: what is 'objective' and what is 'subjective'? The philosopher John *Locke (1690), who was well aware of the new science of his time, suggested that there are two kinds of characteristics: *primary* characteristics, such as hardness, mass, and extension of objects in space and time—being in the world before life, and quite apart from mind—and *secondary* characteristics, which are created by brain–mind. Thus colours are not in the world, but are created within us, though they are related in complex ways to light and the surfaces of objects.

It is generally accepted that Locke's 'primary' characteristics are present independently of mind and perception, and it is clear that 'secondary' characteristics are affected by states of the sensing organism; because colours change with adaptation, and everything appears tinged with yellow if we have jaundice. Isaac *Newton, writing on sensations of colour in *Opticks* (1704), agreed with his friend Locke, saying that red light is not itself red, but is 'red-making'. Spelling this out, he said of light rays: 'there is nothing else than a certain power and disposition to stir up the sensation of this or that colour. For as sound in a bell or musical string . . . is nothing but a trembling motion.' Then (in Query 23), he specifies something of the neural mechanism of vision that leads to the mysterious seat of sensation: 'Is not vision perform'd chiefly by the Vibrations of this (Eatherial) Medium, excited in the bottom of the eye by Rays of Light, and propagated through the solid, pellucid and uniform Capillamenta of the optic Nerves in the place (the "Sensorium") of Sensation?'

The empiricist school, of which Locke and Newton were founders, rejected the notion that had been the basis of much philosophy, that minds can receive knowledge by direct intuition, quite apart from perception. Mind was now regarded as essentially isolated from the physical world, linked by tenuous threads of nerve, sending signals to the brain, which has to make sense of sensations. At the same time, there were attempts to discover 'laws' of mind, corresponding in some ways to the laws of physics, though seldom if ever seen as being in quite the same category. Newton did, however, write (in a letter to Henry Oldenburg, secretary of the Royal Society): 'I suppose the *Science of colours* will be granted *Mathematicall* and as certain as any part of Optiques'. Laws of colour mixture were developed later, especially following the work of Thomas *Young, who made the important discovery in 1801 that all the spectral colours can be produced by mixture of various intensities of only three spectral lights. This took the sensations of colour somewhat outside the realm of physics, and yet they were seen as bound by certain laws. So evidently there could be a lawful science of sensation and of mind (see COLOUR VISION: BRAIN MECHANISMS; COLOUR VISION: EYE MECHANISMS). Newton fully appreciated that colour sensations are not always given by light, as he said (*Opticks*, Query 16): 'When a Man in the dark presses either corner of his Eye with his finger, he will see a Circle of Colours like those of a Peacock's Tail.' At the same time, much like Pythagoras linking music with the physics of vibrating strings, Newton tried to describe aesthetics according to physical principles (Query 14):

May not the harmony and discord of Colours arise from the proportions of the Vibrations propagated through the Fibres of the optick Nerves into the Brain, as the harmony and discord of Sounds arise from the proportions of the Vibrations of the Air? For some Colours, if they are view'd together, are agreeablezto one another, as those of Gold and Indigo, and others disagree.

So we find long-standing attempts to explain perceptual experience—from sensations to aesthetics—by physical principles of the natural sciences. But though, for example colour mixture, is linked to the physics of light, it is not derivable from optical principles. As the direct realism of immediate experience of the object world has been (almost universally) abandoned, we are left with having to devise bridging theories of perception to relate mind to the matter of the universe.

It is now generally accepted that perception depends on active physiologically based processes; but this notion is non-intuitive, for we know nothing of such processes or mechanisms by introspection, by consciousness. Moreover, perceiving objects around us seems so simple and easy! It happens so fast, and so effortlessly it is hard to conceive the complexity of the processes that we now know are involved.

This takes us to concepts familiar to engineers. It is not misleading to describe the organs of the senses—the eyes, ears, touch receptors, and so on—as 'transducers' that accept and signal patterns of energy from the external world, as coded messages, read by the brain to infer the state-of-play of the surrounding world. Another useful engineering concept is that of 'channels'. The various senses: touch and vision and hearing, and so on, are each subdivided into channels which generally can only be discovered by experiment. Thus, for example, though this was not at all realized before Young's (1801) colour mixture experiment, colour vision works with just three channels, responding to long-wavelength red, medium-wavelength green, and short-wavelength blue, light, respectively. All the hundreds of colours we see are, neurally, mixtures from these three colour channels (see YELLOW.) Then there are channels representing the orientation of lines and edges, and channels for movement, as shown by direct physiological recording from the visual cortex, demonstrated dramatically by David Hubel and Torstin Wiesel (1962), who received the Nobel Prize for this outstanding work. By less physiologically direct methods, such as selective adaptation, it has been found that there are more or less independent channels for spatial frequency and many other visual characteristics. The ear has many frequency channels (see HEARING), and there is a score of channels for *touch, various kinds of pain, tickle, and for monitoring the positions of the limbs and setting muscle tensions for moving them appropriately (see PAIN; TICKLING). Small discrepancies, such as delay in sound between seeing a ball hit by a bat and hearing the impact, are rejected or pulled into place, to maintain a consistent world. Here, the constancies (see COLOUR PERCEPTION: CONSTANCY AND CONTRAST) are very important; they modify sensations and perceptions to fit what should be there!

For signalling by the senses, as from instruments, it is important to appreciate the range of likely or possible objects that may be present (see INFORMATION RATE OF VISION; INFORMATION THEORY). The eye receives all sorts of irrelevant stimuli, which are mainly disregarded, just as unwanted data and random disturbances are rejected whenever possible by scientific instruments, and in computer signal-processing. Sometimes, though, what is rejected turns out to be just what is needed. The immense difficulties encountered in current attempts to program computers to recognize objects from signals provided by television cameras indicate the incredible complexity and subtlety of animal and human perception (see OBJECT PERCEPTION). A key, surely, is the vast knowledge needed for sophisticated perception; but as yet this is inadequate, and hard to access as needed, in computers (see ARTIFICIAL INTELLIGENCE).

David *Marr (1980) suggested that object shapes are derived from images via three essential stages: (i) the 'primal sketch'(es), describing intensity changes, locations of critical features such as terminal points, and local geometrical relations; (ii) the '2-D sketch', giving a preliminary analysis of depth, surface discontinuities, and so on, in a frame that is centred on the viewer; (iii) the '3-D model representation', in an object-centred coordinate system, so that we see objects much as they are in three-dimensional space though they are presented from just one viewpoint. Marr supposed that this last stage is aided by restraints on the range of likely solutions to the problem of what is 'out there', the information-processing restraints being set by assuming typical object shapes, for example that many objects such as human beings, are modified cylinders, spheres, and cones. Interestingly, the painter Paul Cezanne came close to this notion in 1904: 'Treat nature by the cylinder, the sphere, the cone, everything in proper perspective so that each side of an object or a plane is directed towards a central point . . . nature for us men is more depth than surface'.

The limited variety of typical objects may set restraints that are useful both for brains for perceiving, and for the artist to represent objects, and for the artificial intelligence endeavour to program computers to see. But although it can be difficult to represent or see some atypical objects (or even familiar objects from atypical viewpoints), perhaps it is not clear that these difficulties reflect perceptual restraints based on assuming cylinders, spheres, or cones, etc., for very different shapes can generally be seen without special difficulty.

Looking 'inwards' by introspection, we *seem* to know that perceptions are made of *sensations, although from physiological and psychological experiments, as well as from the engineering approach, it has to be denied that sensations are the data for perceptions. The data are neural *signals*, from the transducer senses, transmitted by many parallel channels—we may say to generate predictive hypotheses, which are our perceptual reality of the object world (see PERCEPTIONS AS UNCONSCIOUS INFLUENCES).

It was generally thought that perception occurs *passively* from inputs from the senses. It is now, however, generally accepted that stored knowledge and assumptions *actively* affect even the simplest perceptions. The relative importance of what are called passive 'bottom-up' processes to active 'top-down' processes, is a central controversy among those who study perception. There is more and more evidence for top-down knowledge, carried to lower-level perceptual mechanisms, some of this evidence being physiological. Psychological evidence, bearing on this, is discussed in the entry on *illusions. The changes of shape of wire cubes which reverse spontaneously in depth (see NECKER CUBES) is clear evidence of top-down processes affecting what used to be regarded as simple sensory characteristics, such as shape and brightness. This is an example of how illusory phenomena can reveal processes of perception far removed from the world we perceive. Yet the brain is a physical system, the most wonderful machine we know.   RLG

Cezanne, P. (1904). Letter from Aix-en-Provence. In Rewald, J. (ed.) (1941), *Letters*, and in Goldwater, R., and Treves, M. (eds.) (1976). *Artists on Art*.

Gibson, J. J. (1950). *Perception of the Visual World*.

—— (1966). *The Senses Considered as Perceptual Systems*.

Gombrich, E. (1960). *Art and Illusion*.

Gregory, R. L. (1966, 5th edn. 1997). *Eye and Brain*.

Helmholtz, H. von (1867). *Handbuch der Physiologischen Optic*. Hamburg. (3rd edn. 1909; trans. 1924 by Southall, J. P. C., with additions, as *Helmholtz's Treatise on Physiological Optics*, repr. 1962).

Hubel, D. H., and Wiesel, T. N. (1962). 'Receptive field, binocular interaction and functional architecture in the cat's visual cortex'. *Journal of Physiology*, 160.

Locke, J. (1690). *Essay Concerning Human Understanding*.

Marr, D. (1982). *Vision: A Computational Investigation into the Human Representation and Processing of Visual Information*.

Newton, I. (1704). *Opticks*. (4th edn. 1730).

perception: cultural differences. Cross-cultural studies in perception arose from speculations on whether different patterns of behaviour and linguistic usage indicated differences in perception. For example, the difficulty of translating colour terms suggested that the ancient Greeks perceived colours differently from present-day observers, and reports from travellers and missionaries suggested that there might be differences in perception between Western and non-Western populations.

The growth of anthropology as an empirical discipline, and the development of psychological techniques modelled on those of physics (sometimes by scientists whose interests spanned both disciplines, such as G. T. *Fechner and E. *Mach), encouraged systematic research and led to several research projects, of which the Torres Straits expedition (1899) is probably the most significant. The object of this expedition was in part to assess the perceptual characteristics of remote groups. The scope of its investigations included acuity of vision, colour vision, visual *illusions, and visual *perception in general, which were studied by W. H. R. *Rivers; cutaneous sensation and discrimination of weight, studied by W. *McDougall, and hearing, smell, taste, and reaction times, studied by C. S. *Myers.

The effects that have been investigated subsume forms of social usage (for example, the economic structure of a group, child-rearing practices, and nutritional habits), purely environmental influences such as the topology of the terrain, the effect of cultural artefacts such as architectural style, and even genetic factors. Such is the plethora of factors which may influence perception that an entirely convincing isolation of one of them and a demonstration of its effects is not generally achieved. The results to hand strongly suggest, however, that although isolation of causes of the observed cross-cultural differences may be difficult or even impossible, such differences probably do exist.

1. Visual perception
2. Other perceptual modalities
3. Theoretical approaches
4. Problems

1. Visual perception

The differences seem to be most pronounced in the visual modality. For example, an extensive study of simple illusions conducted by Segall, Campbell, and Herskovits showed that certain illusion figures, such as the *Müller-Lyer illusion and the Sander parallelogram, did not evoke such strong effects in the cultures where rectangular objects and arrangements of objects were rare as in those more 'carpentered' cultures where such phenomena abounded. The more carpentered the culture in which the observers lived, the higher was their susceptibility to these illusions. Another influence was found to affect the magnitude of the horizontal–vertical illusion. Observers living in open vistas, such as savannah, experienced the illusion more strongly than those living in more visually confined environments, such as tropical rainforests.

Cross-cultural differences have also been noted in the ability to perceive shape and the orientation of simple geometrical patterns and in the magnitude of shape constancy scores. The latter issue is thought by some to be related to the characteristics of art styles, since these differ in the manner in which they employ constancies. Similarly the ability to *interpret* pictorial material is found to differ with culture. This finding is of some practical consequence, since such materials are used as primary means of communication in illiterate cultures. Specifically it was found that pictures which to a Westerner appear unambiguous are often misunderstood in non-pictorial cultures. However, detailed, but unfortunately sparse, follow-up investigations offer no evidence to sustain the claim that single clearly depicted objects are likely to be consistently misperceived in these cultures. Even in a culture entirely devoid of graphic art, when large drawings of familiar objects printed on cloth were displayed, these were recognized, albeit with difficulty and rather slowly. There is, on the other hand, sufficient evidence to show that *relationships* between various items in the same picture are likely to be misperceived. Thus an observer may maintain that an elephant is nearer to a man than an antelope simply because the elephant is drawn nearer to the man (by perspective) in the plane of the picture, notwithstanding the fact that the elephant is drawn smaller than the antelope and hence, if the implied depth cue is taken into account, should be seen as being further away.

Such failures in correct interpretation of pictorial depth cues were first investigated systematically by W. Hudson, whose work has proved seminal to a large number of studies which confirm the existence of cross-cultural differences. The likelihood of such a misinterpretation varies with both the characteristics of the observer and the nature of the picture. Neither a correct interpretation nor a misinterpretation of any particular picture can therefore be regarded as an index of the observer's ability to perceive pictorial depth.

Considerations of such basic phenomena as the implicit-shape constancy in abstract figures show that the differences observed are not confined to depictions of lifelike scenes. A drawing of a square on a face of a drawn cube, both of which are, in a strictly geometrical sense, diamonds, leads to an impression of a figure whose 'squareness' appears to vary with culture, being greater, for example, in Scottish than in African observers.

Consistent with the above observations, the extent to which pictures can be regarded as object substitutes varies with culture. For example, the ability to categorize objects does not predicate an ability to categorize pictures of these objects equally well.

Perception of colour has traditionally formed a testing ground for linguistic hypotheses, such as the Sapir–Whorf hypothesis which argues that any grouping of colours is entirely determined by linguistic labels extant in any given culture. However, studies of grouping of colours by people drawn from a variety of linguistic communities have put such an interpretation in question. It seems that the same colours are regarded as *focal* (or archetypal) whether a language has a very rudimentary or a sophisticated colour vocabulary. Yet the linguistic cause cannot be said to be entirely routed, for language may exercise influence within the valleys between such focal peaks.

Another issue which has been studied is the perceptual outcome of binocular rivalry, when two different stimuli are presented separately to the two eyes. When the stimuli used were derived from two different cultures, it was observed that the subjects tended to describe the stimuli derived from their culture and ignore the alien stimuli. Ambitious but unfortunately inconclusive studies of eidetic imagery have also been carried out.

2. Other perceptual modalities

Perceptual modalities other than the visual one have received but scanty and unsystematic attention in cross-cultural studies. Of the more complex issues, perception of time has been studied; but here, too, the effects observed can be more readily attributed to the social values that are attached to activities occupying time rather than to time itself.

3. Theoretical approaches

Two theoretical frameworks, deriving from the work of *Piaget and from that of H. A. Witkin, dominate the research. The former is concerned with the stages through which a child passes as it gradually acquires cognitive concepts needed for the effective handling of perceptual information. Such stages as defined by Piaget have also been reported in other cultures and are said to occur in similar sequence. The age ranges within which they occur are, however, said to differ between cultures. Witkin links the style of child rearing and therefore of general social structure and ecological conditions with the extent to which members of a culture show field dependence. The effects of dependence are apparent not only in perception of social relationships but also in perception in general. Subjects with higher dependence find it more difficult to perceive parts of the perceptual field as discrete from the field as a whole than do subjects with lower dependence. This distinction in ability greatly affects performance on such tasks as reproduction of simple geometric designs (block design test), detection of a figure embedded in a matrix of irrelevant lines (embedded figure test), or adjustment to the true vertical of a luminous rod presented within a tilted luminous frame in a darkened room. In addition, there are a number of more ad hoc hypotheses attempting to interpret the way in which various factors combine to affect perception. One group of these, whose popularity owes more to their appeal to the sense of charity or justice than to empirical evidence, is the 'compensatory hypotheses'. These suggest that rather poor performance by a cultural group in one perceptual modality (such as vision) is likely to be compensated by (generally as the result of ecological or cultural adaptation) a relatively superior performance in another modality (such as hearing or touch).

4. Problems

Although cross-cultural comparisons provide an excellent ground for testing the universality of postulated theories or of observed phenomena, they also present the experimenter with greater than usual methodological obstacles. The main problems are the difficulty of 'distinguishing differences of perception from failures of communication' (D. T. Campbell), and the lack of adequate control groups, since generally populations not only differ in culture but also live in different ecological conditions and are of different genetic stock. Indeed so intertwined are these three variables that many of the studies which are now classified as cross-cultural would, in the not-so-distant past, have been seen as studies of differences in racial characteristics.

JBD

Deregowski, J. B. (1980). *Illusions, Patterns and Pictures: A Cross-cultural Perspective.*

Jahoda, G. (1982). *Psychology and Anthropology.*

Segall, M. H., Campbell, D. T., and Herskovits, M. (1966). *Influence of Culture on Visual Perception.*

Triandis, H., et al. (eds.) (1980). *Handbook of Cross-cultural Psychology*, vol. iii.

perception: early Greek theories. The *Pre-Socratic philosophers attempted to explain the phenomena of perception, and to show how sensory interactions with the external world differ from non-sensory interactions. Of the several theories they produced, that of Empedocles may stand as typical. Empedocles' views are summarized for us by *Plato in his dialogue the *Meno*:

SOCRATES. Do you agree with Empedocles that existing things give off a sort of effluence?
MENO. Certainly.
SOC. And that they have pores into which and through which the effluences travel?
MENO. Yes.
SOC. And of the effluences, some fit some of the pores, while others are too small or too big?
MENO. That's right.
SOC. And there's something you call sight?
MENO. There is.
SOC. From this, then, 'grasp what I say to you', as Pindar puts it: colour is an effluence from things which is fitted to sight and perceptible.

The book in front of you is constantly emitting 'effluences' (streams of minute particles) differing one from another in kind; as they strike your body, some fit snugly into various of its 'pores' or openings, others do not; one kind of effluence (call it 'colour') fits precisely into the pores of your eyes—and thus you see the book. To see the book is simply for your eyes to receive colour effluences sent out by the book. Similarly with the other senses; so that, in general, to perceive an object is to receive from it effluences of a kind to fit the organs of perception.

This theory is thoroughly 'materialistic': it makes no mention of non-physical objects of perception (immaterial 'sense data'), and it does not invoke a peculiarly 'mental' relation of 'experiencing' or 'being aware of' an object; rather, one physical object reacts with another. The theory was criticized for just this reason: Theophrastus observes that 'one might wonder . . . how inanimate objects differ from the rest with regard to perception; for things fit into the pores of inanimate objects too'. Empedocles himself used the mechanics of pores and effluences to explain various non-perceptual phenomena (reflection, magnetism, deciduousness): how, then, can his theory distinguish between perception and other, non-sensory, pore-and-effluence interactions with the world? (Suppose a modern psychologist were to say that perception was a discriminatory capacity, nothing more; then we might ask him how he proposed to distinguish genuinely perceptual activity from, say, the performance of a potato-sorting machine which discriminates among potatoes according to their size.)

Theophrastus remarks that, in Empedocles' view, perception comes about 'by likes', and a surviving fragment from Empedocles' own pen confirms the point:

> For by earth we see earth, by water water,
> by air bright air, and by fire brilliant fire.

Thus for perception to take place, the effluence must not only 'fit' the appropriate pore: it must also be 'like' or homogeneous with (some parts of the walls of) the pore. I see red when a red effluence slots neatly into a red-edged pore in my eye. Perceptual interactions differ from non-perceptual interactions just because they require homogeneity, as well as a good fit between effluence and pores.

There are two points to note about this suggestion. First, it is pretty crude: as a physical theory of perception, it will not do; and Theophrastus tells us that Empedocles himself, in his detailed accounts of the modes of perception, did not in fact assign much work to the notion of 'likeness' or homogeneity. But secondly, and more importantly, the notion of homogeneity is thoroughly materialistic: in order to distinguish perceiving from other, non-perceptual, activities, Empedocles does not leave the hard land of matter. He does not appeal to some soft 'mental' or 'experiential' aspect of perceivers to mark them off as beings of a unique kind; rather, he supposes that the crucial difference between perceiving and non-perceptual activity can be characterized in physical terms: biology and physiology (we might now add: neurophysiology) will suffice to give a complete account of the phenomena of perception.   JBA

perceptions as unconscious influences. Philosophers have generally considered *visual* perceptions to be closely related to, or even to be samples of, surfaces of surrounding objects. Thus, vision was thought to be rather like *smell, and as direct and immediate as *touch. However, with the invention of the camera obscura, and the related discovery that the object world is imaged optically in the eyes, it became clear that patterns of light in the eyes (retinal images) are transmitted to the brain by coded electrical signals (action potentials), which are then, somehow, read as objects having very different and far richer properties than the optical pictures in the eyes. It became clear, at least to physiologists, that there must be a great deal going on in the brain in order to produce perceptions from sensory signals: that our perceptions are created in us, and that they may be very different from the corresponding objects of the external world, as described by physicists. Furthermore, there are *illusions, of many kinds, which are hard to reconcile with a 'direct' or 'immediate knowledge' account of *perception.

An alternative account—very largely due to Hermann von *Helmholtz (1821–94), is that perceptions are *conclusions of unconscious inductive inferences*. Introducing this idea, he compared visual perception from images with the arbitrary signs of language, and how we learn language. Thus, Helmholtz (1866) points out that, as with meanings of words, 'the concept of the normal meaning of frequently repeated perceptions can come about with immutable certainty, lightning speed and without the slightest meditation'. Helmholtz continues:

The example of language is instructive in another respect, for it affords an explanation for the problem of how such a certain and conventional understanding of a system of signs may be obtained, considering that these signs can have only a quite arbitrarily selected effect upon the individual observer. . . . The child hears the usual name of an object pronounced again and again when it is shown or given to him, with the same word. Thus the word becomes attached to the thing in his memory more firmly the more frequently it is repeated. . . . The same name may become attached to a class of objects similar to each other, or to a class of similar processes. . . . I conclude from these observations that by frequent repetition of similar experiences we can attain the production and continual strengthening of a continually recurring connection between two very different perceptions, or ideas, e.g. between the sound of a word and visible and tactual perceptual images, which originally need not have had any natural connection; and that when this has happened we are no longer able to report in detail how we have arrived at this knowledge and on what individual observations it is based.

Helmholtz stresses that the association of word with meaning, and of sensation with meaning in perception, comes from regular experiences of the connection with no (or few) exceptions. In this way, meanings are built up *inductively* (from many instances to a conclusion that is not logically necessary), both for language and for perceptions. These associations are, presumably, built up largely by interaction with objects—so that, for example, the patterns of the grain of wood become associated with a hard substance which can be dropped without breaking, and which can be cut with a saw; and the transparency of glass becomes associated with potentially dangerous brittleness; in consequence, we behave very differently with wooden as opposed to glass objects. Helmholtz suggested that we come to our ideas of the physical form of objects inductively, by combining visual experiences from many viewpoints, following the rules of perspective. Comparing these 'inductive conclusions' with the scientific method, Helmholtz says: 'Inductive conclusions are never so reliable as well-tested conclusions of conscious thought. . . . False inductions in the interpretation of our perceptions we tend to label as illusions.' Of these he says: 'Obviously, in these cases there is nothing wrong with the activity of the organ of sense and its corresponding nervous mechanism which produces the illusion. . . . It is, rather, simply an illusion of the judgement of the material presented to the senses, resulting in a false idea of it.' He goes on to say: 'These unconscious conclusions derived from sensation are equivalent . . . to [his italics] *conclusions from analogy*.' He attaches a lot of weight to active structuring of perception, which is especially evident in conditions of dim illumination, or when complex crystals or other structures are viewed stereoscopically:

a visual impression may be misunderstood at first, by not knowing how to attribute the correct depth-dimensions; as when a distant light, for example, is taken to be a near one, or *vice versa*. Suddenly it dawns on us what it is, and immediately, under the influence of the correct comprehension, the correct perceptual image also is developed in its full intensity. . . . Similar experiences have happened to everybody, proving that the elements in sense-perceptions that are derived from experience are just as powerful as those that are derived from present sensations.

In this connection, phenomena of *ambiguity* (which occur especially with vision and hearing) are clearly very important: 'Without any change of the retinal images, the same observer may see in front of him various perceptual images in succession, in which case the variation is easy to recognize.' For these and other reasons, Helmholtz thinks of perception as given by learning, and as *empirical*. It is not passive acceptance of stimulus patterns, but rather *projection* (though not merely geometrical projection) from internally organized knowledge of objects and processes. In current terminology, this may be termed use of stored knowledge 'top down', for interpreting or reading sensory signals, as originating from particular objects. Similarly, we project our meanings of words on what we describe. (The emphasis on processes searching for the best reading, or interpretation, on the available evidence, we call 'active', in comparison with 'passive' accounts, such as that of J. J. *Gibson.)

It seems a natural development to extend Helmholtz's account by calling perceptions (which, not altogether happily, he called 'perceptual images'), *perceptual hypotheses* (Gregory 1970, 1981). This suggests useful analogy with hypotheses in science and the ways they are developed, used, and tested. That is not to say that perceptual hypotheses and scientific hypotheses are formed or used or tested identically, but they do seem to share striking similarities. Since the methods of science are open to inspection, they may provide a basis for considering processes of perception, which (as Helmholtz realized) are exceedingly hard to discover by direct methods, because they are hidden in brain processes that are only beginning to be understood, and also because they are unconscious.

RLG

Helmholtz, H. von (1866). *Treatise on Physiological Optics*, vol. iii (3rd edn.). Trans. and ed. J. P. C. Southall, 1925, section 26. (Repr. 1962.) (Also given in Warren, R. M., and Warren, R. P. (1968), *Helmholtz on Perception: Its Physiology and Development*.)
——(1896). 'The origin of the correct interpretation of our sensory impressions'. In *Treatise on Physiological Optics* (2nd edn.).

personal equation. Several important characteristics of the human observer have been discovered by astronomers. Most celebrated is the 'personal equation': corrections applied to individual differences in response time in observing stars crossing graticule lines in transit telescopes. This was extremely important as clocks were set by these measures; in 1799 the Astronomer Royal at Greenwich, Nevil Maskelyne, dismissed his assistant, D. Kinnebrook, because Kinnebrook recorded stellar transit time almost a second later than Maskelyne did. The method used was James Bradley's (1693–1762) 'eye and ear' method. The observer looked at the clock, noting the time to the nearest second, and then counted seconds as he heard the beats of a pendulum while watching the star cross the telescope field. As it crossed the field, he noted the position of the star in relation to each of a series of parallel threads in the eyepiece. This task involved co-ordination between eye and ear, and judgement of the position of each thread. The method was supposed to be accurate to one- or at least to two-tenths of a second—so Kinnebrook's difference of eight-tenths of a second appeared as such a gross error that Maskelyne concluded he had fallen into 'some irregular and confused method of his own'. However, the German astronomer Friedrich Bessel (1784–1846), at Königsberg, eventually heard of the incident and realized that there may be large personal differences. In 1820 Bessel compared himself with a colleague, Walbeck, by taking observations of ten stars on alternate nights, for five nights. Bessel observed them earlier than Walbeck, there being an average difference of 1.041 seconds between them. This difference was so large that there may have been an error of method — but nevertheless it stimulated research. When the chronograph was invented in 1859 absolute response times could be made, and observations were corrected accordingly.

It seems clear that, in this complicated task at least, there is a major element of *anticipation in response to a stimulus. If the importance of anticipation had been generally realized, the history of experimental psychology would have been very different—for the immensely (indeed seductively) powerful stimulus-response paradigm would surely not have been accepted as the basis of perception and behaviour. See also REACTION TIMES.   RLG

Boring, E. G. (1929). *A History of Experimental Psychology*, ch. 8 (repr. 1950).

Gregory, R. L. (1981). *Mind in Science*.

personal identity. In ordinary everyday affairs we are sometimes concerned with questions of personal identity. The police, for example, may want to know whether the man they have detained is the man who broke into the cricket pavilion. It may be a difficult question to answer. Perhaps the fingerprints on the door jamb were smudged. But the difficulty is not of a sort which calls for reflection on what is meant by 'personal identity'. For the police, questions like 'Is this the same person?' are practical

questions, not conceptual ones. The questions and answers involve the criteria of personal identity, but they are not about the criteria.

Conceptual questions about personal identity may arise either from philosophizing which throws in doubt our ordinary practice with the 'Is this the same person?' question, or from extraordinary cases, real or imaginary, where the 'Is this the same person?' question cannot be answered on the basis of our ordinary practice. It is not unusual for philosophers writing on personal identity to refer to extraordinary cases with a view to persuading their readers that one sort of consideration should be treated as decisive. The contrast is usually between a mental criterion, such as *memory, and a bodily criterion.

The philosophizing which pre-eminently throws in doubt our ordinary practice with the 'Is this the same person?' question is that of *Descartes, though the questions about personal identity to which his philosophy gave rise came to the fore only in the writings of his successors, in particular John *Locke (*Essay Concerning Human Understanding*, Bk. II, ch. xxvii) and David *Hume (*Treatise of Human Nature*, Bk. I, pt. iv, sect. 6). To understand how Descartes came to set the scene for Locke, Hume, and subsequent philosophers writing on personal identity, it is necessary to sketch, very briefly, the relevant part of his philosophy.

Descartes was concerned, among other things, to replace the medieval, largely Aristotelian, conception of the world as inhabited by a multitude of things programmed teleologically according to their various fixed intelligible essences. For *Aristotle, as for *Plato, the paradigm of explanation was mathematical. The relations of numbers are necessary relations, and knowledge is of what is necessarily, and therefore unchangingly, the case. But despite their efforts, possibly inspired by the *Pythagorean discovery of the numerical basis of musical concordances, to bring numbers and nature together conceptually, they remained distinct, with the result that science was not proof against scepticism. Descartes saw a way of reading the necessity of number relations into nature. He had invented analytical geometry, which shows how every geometrical object or relation can be given numerical expression. It follows that if the extension of spatial, i.e. physical, objects is the extension of geometrical objects, and if 'matter' is defined in terms of this extension, then matter is thereby brought into the domain of what is necessarily true. Nature, *qua* matter, becomes through and through numerical. There were problems—such as how one bit of matter can exclude another bit of matter from the same place if there is no more to matter than extension—but Descartes thought they could be dealt with without having to add something non-numerical to the definition, such as solidity. But one major problem remained. It does not follow from the truths of arithmetic and geometry being necessary that science is proof against scepticism. There is still a gap between justified subjective certainty and objective necessity. Descartes needed to find a criterion whereby he could recognize those things of which he could justifiably claim to be certain. He found it via the intuition 'I think, therefore I am'. This, he thought, is true without a shadow of doubt. What assures me of its truth is my clear and distinct perception of it. Provided there is not an all-powerful malicious demon who makes things appear clear and distinct to me which are not, I can therefore adopt this as my criterion.

Now, Descartes thought that someone who thinks 'I think, therefore I am' is certain not only that this thought is occurring but also that there is a being which thinks the thought. He went on to consider whether there is more, essentially, to this being than that it is capable of thought. Specifically, is it essentially a being with a body? He argued (fallaciously, according to many critics both contemporary and present day) that it is not. Accordingly, he dismissed, as philosophically naive, what he described as 'that notion of the union of soul and body which everybody always has in himself without doing philosophy— viz., that there is one single person who has at once body and consciousness'. His own notion of a person was that of a particular thinking being which happens to be, but could equally well not be, united with a particular body. The significance of his replacement of our ordinary notion of a person with that of a thinking being which just happens to be united with a body is that it allows for the question 'How are such beings to be identified, and reidentified, if not by reference to the bodies they happen to occupy?'.

Our ordinary practice with the 'Is this the same person?' question is geared to the notion everybody always has of themselves, the notion that there is one single person who has at once body and *consciousness. It is not geared to the notion of a person as a being for whom a body is not conceptually necessary. Assuming that the question still makes sense, we need a new practice with 'Is this the same person?' to go with the new notion. Obviously it will be a very different practice. Given the origin in Descartes' philosophy of both questions, we may expect it to be rather like trying to find a meaning for 'Is this the same bit of matter, or has another, of exactly the same shape and size, taken its place?', with 'matter' defined solely in terms of extension.

Probably the most revealing attempt to find a meaning for 'Is this the same person?', with 'person' defined in the new, non-body-implying way, is that by Hume. He reformulates the personal identity question as the question 'whether in pronouncing concerning the identity of a person, we observe some real bond among his perceptions, or only feel one among the ideas we form of them'. This is revealing precisely because the question has been trans-

formed into one a person can ask only about himself. Only he is aware of 'his perceptions'. So it is no longer the sort of question that could, on occasion, truthfully be answered with 'No; it is somebody else'. The sort of answer now catered for is 'There is a real bond among my perceptions' or 'There is no real bond, only a felt one'. It has become a question about the unity of a person's consciousness rather than what we ordinarily understand as a question about someone's identity.

Hume opts for there being only a felt bond. There is felt to be a bond because causal relations exist between a person's experiences. 'The true idea of the human mind, is to consider it as a system of different perceptions or different existences, which are linked together by the relation of cause and effect, and mutually produce, destroy, influence, and modify each other.'

Ordinarily we would think of any causal relations between different experiences as following from their being the same person's experiences, with telepathy as a possible exception to the rule. Hume, if the question about the unity of consciousness is regarded as being one about personal identity, tries to reverse that conceptual order. It is hardly surprising that (in the appendix to the *Treatise*) he should write: 'Upon a more strict review of the section concerning personal identity, I find myself involved in such a labyrinth, that, I must confess, I neither know how to correct my former opinions, nor how to render them consistent.' He has reaped the harvest sown by Descartes.

Locke says that 'personal identity consists . . . in the identity of consciousness'. By 'consciousness' he means something that can be 'interrupted by forgetfulness', but also something that can be 'extended back' to actions done by people long since dead and buried. Locke says that a person who extends his consciousness back to actions done by someone in the distant past 'finds himself the same person' as the person who performed the actions. Exactly what he means by this is debatable, and has been debated at considerable length, but there is no doubt what question is most frequently raised by what Locke says on the subject. It is: 'Could memory be the sole criterion of personal identity?'

The standard argument against an affirmative answer is one which draws attention to the conceptual grammar of the word 'remember'. If a child says he 'remembers' being in a certain place at a certain time, and he was seen to be somewhere else at that time, we say he is wrong. It is part of the concept of remembering that we take what can be seen, the physical presence or absence of a person, as relevant to whether or not he really remembers something. Hence memory could not be the sole criterion of personal identity.

Given that our talk of personal identity is against the background of using a bodily criterion, what should we say if someone claimed to remember having been at some place before he was born, and his memories of it proved to be uncannily accurate? Can there be exceptions to the rule? We can have exceptions to the rule that promises are kept, and still understand what it is to make a promise. Is it the same with personal identity? Is reincarnation conceivable? This is only one of many extraordinary cases, real or imaginary, which may be said to call for decisions that are not implicit in our ordinary practice with 'Is this the same person?' questions. Another whole range of such cases arises if we consider the possibility of transplanting brains, and, especially, of bisecting a brain and performing a dual transplant, so that two people claim to remember doing what one person did. Are they both identical with the earlier person, and so with one another?

Two distinct approaches to such extraordinary cases are possible. We can regard the concept of personal identity as being like an Aristotelian essence, that is, such that if only we had sufficient intellectual insight into it we could see what the answer should be. Or we can say that the concept of personal identity we have is one which goes with the criteria we employ, coinciding in the vast majority of cases, and that if they were to start failing to coincide then the concept we have would become incoherent. Whether the conditions would exist for us to have a new concept, perhaps 'psychological continuity', which took over some of the uses of the old one, is debatable. There are lessons to be learnt from Hume in this regard.

GNAV

Perry, J. R. (ed.) (1975). *Personal Identity*.
Shoemaker, S., and Swinburne, R. (1984). *Personal Identity*.
Williams, B. (1973). *Problems of the Self*.

personality disorder. Personality disorder is present when a persistent trait of personality, possessed by the individual to an abnormal extent, causes that person or others to suffer over time. Personality, in this context, implies the unique quality of the individual, his feelings and personal goals; this leads to a characteristic pattern of behaviour which allows us, to some extent, to predict his future actions and which makes this individual different from other people.

This clinical description of personality is purely descriptive, based upon persistent traits of normal personality such as ambition, anxiety, assertiveness, conventionality, dutifulness, energy, and so on; these tend to conglomerate in *personality types*, clusters of traits that frequently occur together. When one or more of these clinically significant features of personality are present to an extent that is statistically deviant from the expected or normal range (significantly more or less), then the individual may be considered to have abnormality of personality. Only when this abnormality causes suffering to the individual himself or to other people is personality disorder present.

Personality disorder is an important concept for psychiatry, and hence for medicine, and is recognized as a generic category of mental and behavioural disorders. In the internationally used *International Classification of Diseases*, 10th revision (ICD-10) (WHO 1992), these conditions are considered to be clinically significant, persistent, and the expression of an individual's characteristic lifestyle and mode of relating to self and to others. The generic category of 'Disorders of adult personality and behaviour' includes specific personality disorders, enduring personality change after catastrophic experience or psychiatric illness, habit and impulse disorder, gender identity disorder such as transsexualism, disorders of sexual preference, and psychological and behavioural disorders associated with sexual development and orientation. These are varied groups, but they all have abnormality of personality and its expression in common.

Both of the psychiatric classifications currently in regular use are based upon a categorical rather than a dimensional model for the description of personality disorder. That is, personality is classified according to the presence or absence of items from a list of criteria rather than being measured according to the amount of a quality demonstrated. The latter, dimensional, method for assessment of personality has been used by Hans Eysenck, and others, with a quantitative measure of such lifelong qualities as extroversion and neuroticism. The categorical method is used both in ICD-10 and in the American *Diagnostic and Statistical Manual of Mental Disorders*, 4th edn. (DSM-IV—APA 1994), with general diagnostic criteria for personality disorder, and specific diagnostic criteria for each type of personality disorder. There is a detailed list of criteria, all of which are described as enduring or persistent, that must be fulfilled for the diagnosis to be made.

DSM-IV makes an important distinction between personality disorders and other categories of mental disorder with its application of multi-axial diagnosis. In this scheme, with five axes for clinical and research use, Axis I refers to clinical disorders and conditions that may be a focus of clinical attention. The implication is that the condition has an onset that interferes with the otherwise healthy mental state of the individual. Axis II refers to personality disorders or mental retardation, conditions that are considered to have no distinct onset and are innate to the individual.

In the same way that personality characteristics tend to occur together to form the commonly described personality types, so DSM-IV considers that the different types of personality disorder tend to occur in three distinct clusters. Cluster A includes paranoid, schizoid, and schizotypal personality disorders; Cluster B, antisocial, borderline, histrionic, and narcissistic personality disorders; and Cluster C avoidant, dependent, and obsessive–compulsive personality disorders. However, many mixed types of personality disorder are found, and many mixtures of personality types from different clusters also occur.

There has been considerable confusion in the United Kingdom, especially at the interface between the law and psychiatry, concerning the meaning and the use of the term 'personality disorder', as two senses of the term have been used with significantly different meanings. Most psychiatrists use it, as above, to include those cases where persistent abnormality of personality causes suffering to the individual or to others. However, some people have used the term solely to refer to the antisocial consequences of abnormal personality. This latter dates back to Prichard's concept (1835) of 'moral insanity', denoting the loss of feeling, of control and of ethical sense in certain criminals. This was the forerunner of the term 'psychopathic personality', included as a condition meriting detention in hospital in the 1959 and 1983 England and Wales Mental Health Acts.

Psychopathic personality is there defined as 'a persistent disorder or disability of the mind . . . which results in abnormally aggressive or seriously irresponsible conduct on the part of the patient and requires or is susceptible to medical treatment'. Thus, if the condition of the patient is considered, in the view of the treating psychiatrist, to require and be amenable to treatment, the patient may be admitted under the Act. As most psychiatrists working in general psychiatric, as opposed to specialist forensic, units regard most of those with psychopathic personality as not being treatable, this clause has often been a reason for excluding these people from admission to psychiatric hospital or unit.

Whereas, according to correct psychiatric classification, psychopathic personality should be regarded as synonymous with dissocial personality disorder (ICD-10), the term *personality disorder* has been used interchangeably with psychopathic personality by some people, and the stigma of psychopathy has been attached thereby to all those suffering from personality disorders. A precise use of terms is recommended, so that those with the features of psychopathic personality should be diagnosed as suffering from dissocial personality disorder. The generic term personality disorder should also include those, such as those suffering from anankastic personality disorder, whose abnormalities of personality cause themselves to suffer but in no way predispose them to criminality.

This area of confusion has been further compounded over recent years with discussion, initiated by government, concerning 'dangerous people with severe personality disorder' (DSPD), and whether such people should be placed compulsorily in hospital even if they have not committed an offence. Again, the type of personality disorder is not stipulated, but whilst only those with certain types of personality disorder are ever likely to be 'danger-

ous', any of the types described below may be 'severe'. Because a few of those suffering from certain categories of personality disorder may be dangerous, the reputation of all those with the condition has been unjustifiably tarnished as having a propensity for violence with consequent stigmatization.

Personality types are the landmarks scattered across the map of human variation. Real people, with real personalities, approximate more or less closely to one or more type, so those with personality disorder may show the classical features of one type or mixed features of two or more different personality disorders. Simply stating that an individual has a disorder of personality is not enough; the features of his personality, the type of personality disorder must always be described. Personality type predicts, to some extent, behaviour and cognition, and is thus always significant.

For diagnosing type of personality disorder, a recognized scheme or classification should be used and, because of its widespread, international application, ICD-10 is recommended. This lists eight specific personality disorders and allows for the recording of 'mixed', 'other', and 'unspecified' personality disorders. Although the specific types described below appear to be discrete and differentiated from each other, the description is only a guide and individuals are likely to show mixtures of different types.

With *paranoid personality disorder* there is a pattern of mistrust and suspiciousness so that other people's motives are interpreted as malevolent. Personality characteristics may be 'active', resulting in hostility, quarrels, litigation, and even violence or destructive behaviour on occasions, or 'passive', with the individual facing the world from a position of submission and humiliation. He believes that others dislike him and will do him down but is not able to do much about it.

There is enduring detachment from social relationships and a restricted range of emotional expression with *schizoid personality disorder*. Such individuals are disinclined to mix—'loners' who hold themselves aloof from others, more interested in things than humans. They are emotionally cool and detached and indifferent to the feelings of other people.

In *dissocial personality disorder* there is a defect in the capacity to appreciate the feelings of others, especially how others feel about the consequences of their behaviour. There is disregard for and violation of the rights of other people. Synonyms are antisocial, psychopathic, and sociopathic personality disorder.

Emotionally unstable personality disorder has two types—impulsive and borderline. With impulsive personality there is liability to intemperate and uncontrolled outbursts of mood—violent anger, inconsolable grief, and so on. Borderline personality shows a pattern of instability in personal relationships, self-image, and mood with marked impulsivity.

Theatrical behaviour, craving for attention and excitement, excessive reaction to minor events, and outbursts of mood characterizes *histrionic*, previously known as hysterical, *personality disorder*. There is a shallowness of feelings and relationships, seen by others as lack in genuineness, and producing difficulty in long-term partnership.

Perfectionism, rigidity, sensitivity, indecisiveness, a lack of capacity to express deeply felt emotion, and conscientiousness occur with *anankastic* (obsessive–compulsive) *personality disorder*. There is preoccupation with orderliness, control, and excessive attention to detail. This personality characteristic within normal limits is socially useful, but causes distress to the sufferer in excess.

Those considered to be 'born worriers', anxious in public situations, as at work, but comfortable at home may suffer from *anxious (avoidant) personality disorder*. There are persistent, pervasive feelings of apprehension, a belief that one is inept or inferior, and a consequent restriction of lifestyle, avoiding those situations that might provoke disapproval.

In *dependent personality disorder* there are feelings of inadequacy concerning oneself and emotional dependence upon others. This clinging, submissive stance may become manifest when the object of dependence is removed through death, divorce, or loss of job.

The causes of personality disorder may lie either in heredity or in the environment. In practice, there is good evidence for both. There is a consistent finding of a genetic contribution to antisocial, anxious/avoidant, and cschizoid personality. However, environmental causes are usually given for most personality disorders and these are particularly related to early upbringing within the family.

For management or treatment of personality disorder, personality type entirely dictates the nature of treatment and differs for each type. Thus, for anankastic personality disorder, for example, pharmacological treatment may be used for the component of anxiety associated with doubts, indecisiveness, and scruples. Psychological treatment, especially cognitive–behavioural treatment, concentrates upon perfectionism, rigidity, scrupulousness, and intolerance of failure. Psychodynamic psychotherapy was formerly extensively used.

For dissocial personality disorder, drugs have been used to control impulsivity and aggression. In-patient small self-help groups and the larger group therapeutic community have proved beneficial to a limited extent. Personality is regarded as relatively fixed during adult life and the aim of treatment is to enable patients to live more comfortably and safely with themselves.

Frequently personality disorder overlaps with other psychiatric disorder and this makes the other condition more difficult to treat and exacerbates the prognosis. Co-morbidity is especially frequent with substance misuse but also quite often occurs with schizophrenia, depressive illness, and neurotic disorders such as anxiety, dissociative, and obsessive–compulsive disorders.

AS

American Psychiatric Association (1994). *Diagnostic and Statistical Manual of Mental Disorders* (4th edn.).

Gelder, M., López-Ibor, J.J., and Andreasen, N.C. (2000). *New Oxford Textbook of Psychiatry*.

Sims, A. (2002). *Symptoms in the Mind: An Introduction to Descriptive Psychopathology* (3rd edn.).

Tyrer, P., and Stein, G. (1993). *Personality Disorder Reviewed*.

World Health Organization (1992). *International Classification of Diseases* (10th revision).

perspective. Our perception of space is dominated by perspective, in the sense of a reduction of the projected size of objects with distance. One of the key jobs of the visual brain is to decode this size diminution as distance in the third dimension, or egocentric distance. If the eye were a pinhole camera, the projection of the world onto the back plane would be in perfect linear perspective (and in perfect focus). The succession of images projects on the curved retina within the eye in what *Leonardo da Vinci termed *natural perspective*, a series of distorted projections that need to be integrated over time in a representation in the brain as the eye moves around the scene. How the brain decodes the information in natural perspective into an accurate appreciation of the spatial layout has yet to be resolved.

Incorporating lens optics into the projection system introduces the potential for curvature in the projected image. Such internal curvature may consequently be a property of human perception at the extremes of the field, but this curvature would apply equally to the original scene and to its projection from the picture plane to the eye, so does not affect the external projection rules of geometric perspective. The key simplification in perspective construction is that the pictorial image is governed by linear projection through the point where the pupil is located, regardless of any optical distortions beyond that point.

Historically, space representation through perspective has engendered great conceptual effort. Perspective scene painting was a springboard of mathematical geometry even at the time of Plato and remained influential through the Hellenistic era, but did not re-emerge as an artistic technique until the 1300s. However, full mastery of analytic perspective took another six centuries to evolve. Accurate one-point perspective dominated the 1400s, being first used by Masolino da Panicale and his pupil Masaccio. Two-point perspective was initially described by Viator in 1505, although the two-point construction remained unknown throughout the Renaissance until 1650, becoming widely used in the 1700 and 1800s. Three-point and multi-point construction diagrams for mathematical treatises were attempted unsuccessfully by Piero della Francesca and Leonardo da Vinci in the late 1400s, but none appeared in art works until an isolated example by Tiepolo in 1744. The three-point construction seems to have been first introduced into 20th-century art by Georgia O'Keeffe in her New York Series in the mid-1920s. Far from springing into force during the early Renaissance, therefore, a full understanding of linear perspective was not achieved for 600 years. Interestingly, most of the conceptual advances in perspective construction were made by artists rather than geometers.

Linear perspective is the geometry of projection of the lines in a scene through a picture plane to a point in space (or centre of projection) corresponding to the pupil of the viewing eye (Fig. 1). The picture plane would be the canvas on which the painter wishes to depict the scene. For correct perspective, the picture will generate the same arrangement of light rays at the eye as did the scene behind it. When viewed from this point in space, therefore, the picture will form exactly the same image on the retina as did the original scene. The different forms of perspective construction concern the rules that apply to specific structures, but all are subcases of the same optical transform.

Principles of perspective 1. In geometric perspective, all straight lines in space project to straight lines (or points, if end on) in the picture plane. Rotating the line within the

Fig. 1. *Projection of parallel lines in space.* Three parallel lines in the *scene* at left are projected through a rectangular *picture plane* to the point where the observer's *eye* is located. The light rays projecting to the eye are shown by dashed lines. The three parallel lines project as straight lines in the picture, but not as parallel because their orientation is not parallel to the picture plane. The point in the picture where the projected lines converge is termed the vanishing point (VP).

Fig. 2. *Binocular perspective.* **a.** The different left (l) and right (r) eye views of the three parallel lines projecting onto the picture plane. The two straight lines from each eye are combined in the brain by binocular fusion into the straight lines of fused image, **b.** whatever their geometric relationships.

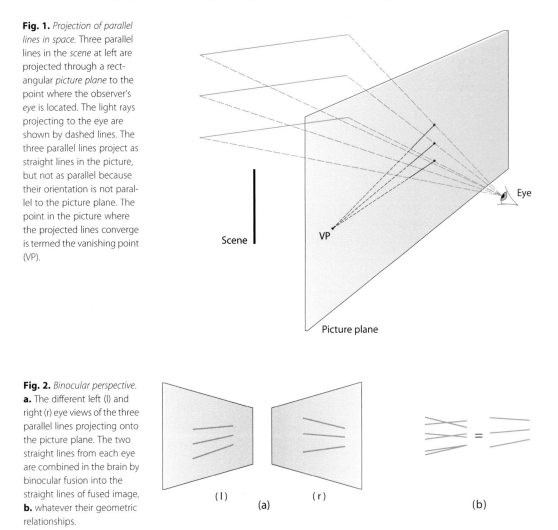

719

plane of projection will not introduce any curvature, just a change in its extent within the line of projection. In the limit when the line is viewed head on, the projected line will contract to a point in the picture plane.

Humans actually view scenes with two eyes, but the straight-line projections for each eye are both straight lines (Fig. 2a left and right). The average, or binocularly fused, projection is the combination of two straight lines and is therefore also a straight line (see Fig. 2b). No curvature is introduced by the geometry of binocular combination.

2. The projections of all lines that are parallel in space either remain parallel in the picture plane or intersect at a single vanishing point (see Fig. 1). Although the lines run to infinity in space, their projection to a picture plane has a vanishing point at a specific location. Each different set of parallel lines intersects at a different vanishing point. Thus, the first job in perspective projection is to identify all the lines in the scene that are parallel to each other, then make sure that they are drawn so as to project to a common vanishing point.

In the particular case of *central perspective*, all the lines on the scene are either parallel with the line of sight or at right angles to it, parallel with the picture plane (Fig. 3). There is thus only one vanishing point, which is directly in front of the viewer's eye for any viewing position (a requirement widely violated by Renaissance painters). When the eye is at this centre of projection, the perspective geometry in the picture plane is independent of the direction in which the eye is looking.

Central perspective is illustrated by the earliest exponent of accurate perspective, Masolino da Panicale, in his *Herod's Feast* (Fig. 4). The primary set of parallels is those horizontal and receding from a viewer toward the central vanishing point. The other sets of parallels consist of any lines at right angles to the first set, at any angle within the

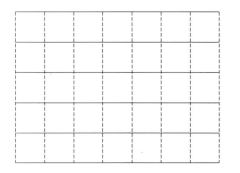
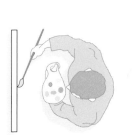

(a)

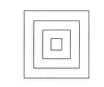

Fig. 3. a. *A painter at his canvas painting a scene of a rectangular grid with ziggurat.* Dashed lines in the grid are parallel to the canvas (transversals), solid lines are perpendicular to it. **b.** Depiction of the scene as projecting to the plane of the canvas, with the perpendicular lines converging at the central vanishing point, while the transversals remain parallel to it.

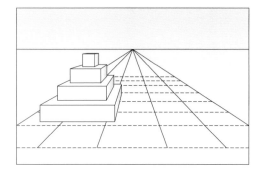

(b)

Fig. 4. *Early example of central perspective. Herod's Feast* by Masolino (1435), where many receding horizontal lines project to a single central vanishing point. This is one-point perspective because the horizontal (black) and vertical (white) sets of parallel lines project as parallel in the picture.

Fig. 5. *Viewing geometry for perspective constructions.* The viewer's angle to the vanishing points is 90 degrees, matching the angle between the edges of the cube that generated the vanishing points.

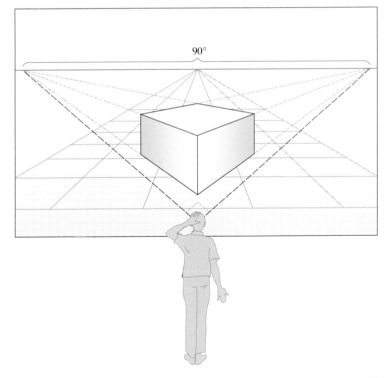

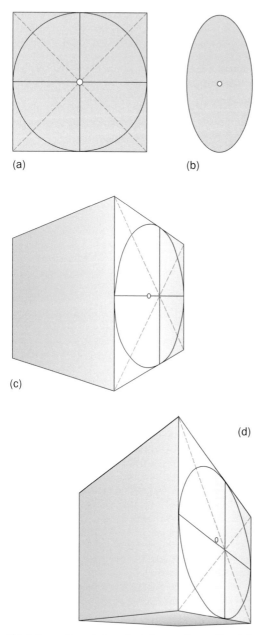

(a)

(b)

(c)

(d)

picture plane. These parallels, such as the verticals of the sides of buildings, will all remain parallel within the picture plane.

A particular case of the lack of distortion in central projection is the case of circles, and circular arches (such as those at right in Fig. 4). When they are facing us, i.e. parallel to the picture plane, circles and parts of circles remain circular in the projection to the picture. The projection to the retina distorts them to ellipses, but they should be shown as circular in the picture.

3. The viewer's angle to any pair of vanishing points is the same as the angle between the generating parallels in space. In particular, the vanishing points for any 90-degree angle in space form a 90-degree angle at the viewer's eye (Fig. 5). However the angle is rotated in space (even to complete foreshortening), the vanishing points will none the less hold to a 90-degree angle at the viewer's eye. The physical distance between the vanishing points depends on the intended viewing distance, but a good rule of thumb is at least twice the width of the picture. Leonardo da Vinci recommended 10–20 times the height of the largest objects depicted.

4. All sets of parallel lines lying within a particular plane in space have vanishing points that fall on the horizon line defined by that plane. In Fig. 5, three sets of converging parallels are shown converging on the same horizon. The fourth set, the transversals, may be said to converge at the horizon at infinity to the left and right.

5. Although perspective distorts rectangles to asymmetrical trapezoids in general, the properties of circles are such that they always project to an ellipse of some orientation, with the centre of the resulting ellipse generally displaced forward from the centre of the projected circle (Fig. 6). Geometrically, ellipses may be drawn by attaching

Fig. 6. *Perspective projection of a circle to an ellipse.* **a.** The circle inscribed on the face of a cube. **b.** The simple ellipse, with its centre marked. **c.** The projection when the cube is on the visual axis forms an ellipse whose centre (and vertical axis) is displaced from that of the projected circle. **d.** For a circle above the visual axis, the major axis of the ellipse is rotated from the vertical, making its construction a challenging geometric problem with no known geometric solution.

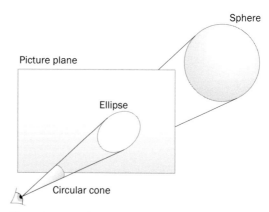

Fig. 7. *Projection of spheres.* Spherical objects always form a circular cone projecting to the eye whatever the angle of view. Unless this cone is perpendicular to the picture plane, the sphere will project as an ellipse in the picture plane.

a string to the foci and drawing a perimeter by keeping the string fully stretched. However, there is no known geometric method for placing the foci for a required ellipse in the perspective construction.

6. Spheres in space also project to ellipses in the picture plane, although generally with much less distortion than for circles (Fig. 7). Spheres always project to circles when at the centre of projection. The elongation arises only because of marginal distortion, the stretching of the image as the picture plane itself recedes from the viewer at increasing angles of view.

In conclusion, perspective proves to be a rich paradigm for revealing the interplay of the mind with the space that it inhabits. Its problems posed in Greek antiquity have challenged the human intellect into the 21st century. Some issues, indeed, still resist a geometric solution. Moreover, virtually nothing is known about the representation of perspective in the brain itself. It will be fascinating to follow the investigation of the neural processing structure and dynamics of this profound modality of space representation by present and future brain-imaging techniques.   ChT

phantom limbs. There are many things about yourself that you take for granted and yet can be called into question. Are you sure your parents are your real parents? Or that you are not dreaming right now? But one thing you feel certain of is your own body, which you can control, whose pains and tickles you feel, which has a name and a bank account and for whose funeral you may eventually prepare. Yet even this axiomatic foundation of your existence—your 'body image'—is called into question by the curious clinical syndrome of phantom limbs.

Phantoms have been known since antiquity. In the last century Lord Nelson used his phantom arm as a basis for logically deducing the existence of an immortal, imperishable soul, and therefore of God. His reasoning was ingenious but dubious; if an arm can survive physical annihilation, he asked, why not the entire body?

Ninety to 98 per cent of patients experience a vivid phantom limb after loss of an arm or leg. It appears immediately in three-quarters of cases and after a delay of a few days or weeks in the rest. After it has emerged, it can persist for years or even decades (Melzack 1992).

The phantom usually adopts a 'habitual' position, e.g. partially flexed at the elbow with the forearm pronated, but involuntary changes in posture are common. The extent to which movements—both voluntary and involuntary—occur in the phantom varies from patient to patient.

Phantoms can occur for almost any body part, e.g. face, breast, penis, jaw, or even for internal viscera such as the rectum. Patients can experience the pain of appendicitis after appendectomy, ulcer pains after gastrectomy,

phantom erections (S. Anstis, personal communication) after the penis is removed, and even phantom menstrual cramps after hysterectomy. (It would be interesting to see whether they still get phantom PMS!)

The term was originally coined by Silas Weir-Mitchell in 1872. Since then, an extensive clinical literature has emerged on the topic and there are hundreds of case studies. But a systematic scientific study of them began only a decade ago, inspired mainly by the demonstration of striking changes in somatosensory maps in animals following denervation or amputation. These animal studies, combined with brain imaging in amputees and systematic psychophysical testing, has allowed the study of phantom limbs to move from the era of vague clinical phenomenology to the era of experimental research (Ramachandran and Hirstein 1998).

The vividness of the phantom is enhanced by the presence of referred sensations: stimuli applied to other parts of the body that are experienced as arising from the phantom. For example, after arm amputation, touching the face will often evoke precisely localized sensations in the phantom fingers, hand, and arm. The points that evoke such sensations are topographically organized and the referral is modality specific: ice on the face will elicit cold in the phantom digits and vibration is felt as vibration. Even water trickling down the face is felt, sometimes, as water trickling along the phantom arm. Such referred sensations probably arise because there is a complete map of the skin surface on the somatosensory cortex (SI in the post-central gyrus) and, in this map, the face is right next to the hand. The sensory input from the face skin ordinarily activates only the face area of the cortex, but if the adjacent hand cortex is denervated—by amputation—then the input from the face skin starts 'invading' and activating the original hand area of the cortex as well—a striking demonstration of plasticity in the adult human brain. Intriguingly even though the hand area is now being activated by face skin, higher brain centres continue to interpret the signals as arising from the missing hand. The changes in somatosensory cortex topography—occurring over distances of two to three centimetres—has also been shown using functional brain-imaging techniques (MEG) in the same patients (allowing researchers to correlate perceptual phenomena such as referred sensations with anatomy). These striking demonstrations of 'plasticity' in the adult brain can also be seen in monkeys in which one arm has been deafferented (Pons et al. 1991). In humans, referred sensations also occur after the trigeminal nerve—supplying the face—is cut: the patient then has a map of the face on the hand Also, after leg amputation stimuli are referred from the genitals to a phantom foot. This is consistent with the fact that in *Penfield's original maps the foot representation is next to the genitals. One wonders whether this anatomical proximity might provide a basis for foot fetishes even in normal people (Ramachandran and Blakeslee 1998).

Some patients can voluntarily 'move' the phantom but a majority cannot do so. These sensations are very 'real' to the patient—so much so that volitional movements of the phantom hand can interfere with a dissimilar movement performed by the normal hand in a manner identical to the inter-manual interference that occurs in normal people (e.g. the patient cannot rub his belly with his real hand while tapping his head simultaneously with the phantom). These sensations probably arise from 'feed forward' or corollary discharge: when the patient's motor or supplementary motor area (SMA) sends a command to the (missing) arm, a copy of the command is simultaneously sent to the cerebellum and parietal lobes so that intention can be compared with action. These commands may initially be experienced as movements but the prolonged absence of 'confirming' visual and proprioceptive feedback from the missing arm leads eventually to a subjectively 'paralysed' phantom that the patient cannot move.

In some patients, the phantom will develop a painful clenching spasm and he cannot voluntarily 'unclench' his fist even with intense effort. If a mirror is propped up vertically on the table parallel to the nose and if the patient views the reflection of his normal hand in the mirror, the reflection of the hand is seen superimposed on the felt position of the phantom—giving the visual illusion that the phantom has been resurrected. If he now moves the normal hand, the phantom is suddenly 'animated' and is felt to move vividly. Sometimes this can lead to the unclenching of a previously clenched, painful phantom, suggesting a promising new therapeutic approach for phantom pain. The clinical usefulness of the procedure requires detailed evaluation, but the illusion suggests that a great deal of interaction can occur between visual and haptic sensations.

Phantom limbs are also seen in a small percentage of patients who are congenitally missing arms or legs, suggesting that at least the basic scaffolding for one's body image may be innately specified. Indeed the phenomenon provides a valuable probe for investigating how nature and nurture interact to generate body image; for instance, the 'gesticulations' felt in such phantom arms might be sustained at least partly by 'mirror neurons' (see MIRROR CELLS) that are activated by watching other people's movements. Patients with leprosy whose hand gets whittled away gradually with progressive sensory loss and trophic changes do *not* have a phantom hand, but if the stump is then amputated, what is seen is not a phantom stump but a whole phantom hand. It is as though the original image of the hand had survived but was inhibited by the stump, only to be resurrected when the stump is amputated.

Memories of sensations in the original arm sometimes resurface in the phantom. A painful blister in the arm prior to amputation can survive and get passed on into the phantom as a phantom blister. Remarkably even long-forgotten or 'repressed' sensory memories may emerge in the phantom, e.g. chilblains experienced in early childhood in a snowstorm may suddenly re-emerge in the phantom any time the weather turns cold. We have also seen a patient whose phantom hand sometimes became involuntarily clenched with the phantom thumb usually extended and abducted. But sometimes the thumb was involuntarily adducted and flexed and this caused the excruciating sensation of the thumbnail digging into the palm. Whether such phenomena might lend credibility to the otherwise discredited phenomenon of 'repressed memories' of emotional trauma remains to be seen.

In summary, five factors seem to contribute to the phantom:

(1) stump neuromas (scar tissue and curled-up nerve endings);
(2) remapping of somatosensory areas in the brain leading to referred sensations;
(3) genetically specified scaffolding for your body image that partially survives limb loss;
(4) monitoring of corollary discharge associated with motor commands sent to the phantom. Such 'command' neurons could also be activated when the patient watches the movements of others ('mirror neurons');
(5) survival of pre-amputation sensory memories in the phantom.

In the last decade the combined use of systematic psychophysical testing with neuroimaging in human amputees, together with animal studies on somatosensory remapping, has allowed the study of phantom limbs to progress very rapidly. Doing such experiments will allow researchers to investigate not only how the brain remodels itself continuously in response to injury but also how the activity of somatosensory brain maps leads to conscious experience sensations and to the construction of a body image that endures in space and time, forming the anchor for your 'self'. Many parts of the brain must be involved in the construction of this image but the parietal lobes play a key role; a stroke in this area can cause the sudden loss of a phantom.   VR/DRR

Melzack, R. (1992). 'Phantom limbs'. *Scientific American*, 266.

Pons, T. P., Garraghty, P. E., Ommaya, A. K., Kaas, J., Taub, E., and Mishkin, M. (1991). 'Massive cortical reorganization after sensory deafferentation in adult macaques'. *Science*, 252.

Ramachandran, V. S., and Blakeslee, S. (1998). *Phantoms in the Brain*.

—— and Hirstein, W. (1998). 'The perception of phantom limbs: the D. O. Hebb lecture'. *Brain*, 121.

phenomenology. A term used in philosophy to denote enquiry into one's conscious and particularly intellectual processes, any preconceptions about external causes and consequences being excluded. It is a method of investigation into the mind that is associated with the name of Edmund *Husserl, as it was he who did most to develop it, although when Husserl's system appeared on the philosophical scene, the word already had a long history and had undergone a conspicuous semantic evolution.

The first use of it goes back to Johann Heinrich Lambert (1728–77), a disciple of Christian Wolff (1679–1754). Lambert published in 1764 a treatise on epistemology dealing with the problem of truth and illusion, under the rather pedantic title of *Neues Organon oder Gedanken über die Erforschung des Wahren und der Unterscheidung von Irrtum und Schein* (New Organon, or Thoughts on the Search for Truth and the Distinction between Error and Appearance), in the fourth part of which he outlines a theory of illusion that he calls 'phenomenology or theory of appearance'. Although he belongs to a period in the history of philosophy in which the question of the intuition of essences had not yet been raised, his implicit definition of phenomenology, taken literally, does not sound odd to the post-Husserlian reader, except that to him, Lambert, an appearance (or phenomenon) is necessarily an illusion. More important, Lambert was acquainted with *Kant, and Kant in 1770 was writing to him about the need for a 'general phenomenology' which he conceived as a preparatory step to the metaphysical analysis of natural science. According to Spiegelberg (1960), what Kant called phenomenology was in fact synonymous with his idea of the critique of pure reason, though nothing allows us to suppose that he specifically used the term forged by Lambert to qualify phenomena as antithetic to noumena or things in themselves.

It is, however, with *Hegel's *Die Phänomenologie des Geistes* (Phenomenology of the Mind), published in 1807, that the term is used explicitly for the first time to label a philosophical work of fundamental importance. A significant step in its evolution from Lambert to Hegel may be found in J. G. Fichte's *Wissenschaftslehre* (Theory of Science), in which its role is to establish the origin of phenomena as they exist for *consciousness; and in Hegel's elaborate system, its basic task is primarily historical since it aims at discovering the successive steps of realization of self-consciousness from elementary individual sensations up to the stage of absolute knowledge through dialectic processes.

The few authors worth mentioning who dealt with phenomenological problems between Hegel and Husserl are William Hamilton (1788–1856), who in fact equates phenomenology with psychology as opposed to logic, Eduard von Hartmann (1842–1906), whose studies on religious, ethical, and aesthetic consciousness were greatly inspired by Hegel's phenomenology, and, to some extent, Charles Sanders *Peirce, though his work on the classification of phenomena belongs more to *metaphysics than to an actual phenomenology of subjective experience. Except in the case of Hegel, phenomenology was not a major field of reflection until Husserl's monumental work.

Since Husserl's transcendental phenomenology is discussed in some detail in the entry under his name, it will suffice here to underline its distinctive features. In contrast with pre-existing philosophies, it is no mere, closed, abstract construct that theoretically allows the philosopher to pronounce on the conditions of principles of experience; it is rather an endless attempt to stick to the reality of experienced phenomena in order to exhibit their universal character. In order to succeed in the endeavour, Husserl has to discard the classic dualistic view, according to which the knowing subject reaches the world only through representation—a position typical of rationalistic and idealistic systems. Hence he refers, after *Brentano, to the *intentional* character of consciousness, and condemns psychologism (the theory that psychology is the foundation of philosophy) in view of the contradiction it brings about: that the supposedly universal laws of logic and mathematics would be dependent on the concrete functioning of psychological mechanisms.

The Husserlian standpoint is thus a radical one, since it aims at 'going back to the things themselves' by claiming that there is no reason to suppose that phenomenon and being are not identical. In other words, the *noema* (object content) and the *noesis* (knowing act) are directly related by the *intentionality of consciousness, so that every phenomenon is intuitively present to the subject. However, phenomena, as they are grasped by the subject, are always given under a particular *profile*. No object whatsoever is given in its totality as a simultaneous exhaustible whole, but every profile *conveys* its essence under the form of meaning for consciousness. In order to reach the essence of any object, one is bound to proceed to unceasing variations around the object as thematic reality, i.e. to discover the essence through the multiplicity of possible profiles. This procedure applies to all phenomena, ranging from current perceptual experience to the highly intricate constructs characterizing the various fields of knowledge, such as physics and psychology.

Every phenomenon belongs to a regional ontology by virtue of its essence, as revealed by the so-called *eidetic intuition*, the essence (*eidos*) being the sum of all possible profiles. In the course of this process, consciousness operates as a *constitutive* moment, i.e. its activity in grasping the essence of phenomena is, perforce, part of the process of their emergence. Thus Husserl overcomes the classic dualism of subject and object. Reaching the universal essence of an object through eidetic intuition, i.e. discovering the basic structure implied by its very existence, is a process which Husserl calls *eidetic reduction*. This being granted, the next step consists in referring phenomena to subjectivity without falling back into psychologism, since the empirical subject, as referred to psychology's own regional ontology (or *Descartes' res cogitans*), belongs to a realm of contingent being, which cannot furnish by itself the necessary foundation for the organization of the absolute principles governing universal essences. Husserl is therefore bound to exclude belief in the natural world as the ultimate reference of all our intentional acts. This process is termed *phenomenological reduction*. It presupposes, in Husserl's terms, a provisional 'bracketing' (*Einklammerung*) of the natural and a description or explication of our intentional acts as referred to pure noematic structures. The final accomplishment of this process is the transcendental reduction, by which the fundamental conditions of every possible meaningful intentional relation must be elucidated. This is the core of Husserl's theory of transcendental subjectivity or *transcendental ego*.

Thus Husserl's phenomenology reconsidered the philosophical problem of consciousness in a radical fashion and contributed thereby to the placing of psychology —and the human sciences in general—within a new epistemological framework. Criticism of the one-sidedness of both empiricist and idealistic standpoints could be developed so that the shortcomings of dualistic views, with all their derivatives such as mechanism, parallelism, and phenomenalism, became more apparent. As a fundamental theory of phenomena ranging from *perception to creative thinking, it has provided a firm starting point for the integration of concepts of the subject at different levels: hence phenomenologically inspired hypotheses such as those that guided F. J. J. Buytendijk and V. von Weiszäcker in anthropological physiology. The French philosopher Maurice Merleau-Ponty's analyses of the experienced body (1942) and perception (1945) were phenomenological works that contributed to the transforming of the classical standpoints in psychology.   GT

Farber, M. (1943). *The Foundations of Phenomenology*.

Kockelmans, J. J. (1967). *Edmund Husserl's Phenomenological Psychology: A Historico-critical Study*.

Misiak, H., and Sexton, V. S. (1973). *Phenomenological, Existential and Humanistic Psychologies*.

Spiegelberg, H. (1960). *The Phenomenological Movement: A Historical Introduction*, 2 vols.

Strasser, S. (1963). *Phenomenology and the Human Sciences*.

Thinès, G. (1977). *Phenomenology and the Science of Behaviour*.

phobias. When fear in response to a particular object or situation is excessive and seemingly irrational it is a phobia. Fear is helpful when it stops us entering or remaining in dangerous situations or when it prompts us to weigh up the risks that face us. However, about one in nine people at some point in their lives are restricted by phobic anxiety falling into three broad categories.

1. Clinical features
2. Aetiology
3. Onset and treatment

1. Clinical features

Agoraphobics (from the Greek root *agora* meaning assembly or market place) fear and avoid crowded shops, public transport, lifts, travelling far from home, or any situation where escape is difficult. Sudden overwhelming bouts of extreme anxiety called 'panics' or 'panic attacks' often accompany this phobia and lead sufferers to the understandable but misguided belief that they could suddenly die, collapse, or become mad if they do not escape. Sufferers' lives become increasingly restricted as they panic in more and more situations.

Social phobics fear the scrutiny and negative judgements of others. They worry that others will notice them blushing, trembling, or sweating or 'making a fool of themselves'. For some the fear is confined to specific situations (e.g. public speaking), for others it is pervasive. Sufferers compensate by not speaking up, avoiding eye contact, or consuming alcohol, but such manoeuvres are counter-productive.

Specific phobias occur in many forms. Common 'triggers' include animals (spiders, snakes, cats), heights, air travel, confined spaces, injections or blood (the only phobia associated with fainting), vomiting, and storms. In each case the fear attached to the trigger is extreme (raised heart rate, rapid breathing, trembling, and subjective terror), results in a powerful desire to escape, and cannot simply be reasoned away.

Agoraphobia and social phobia sometimes result from another illness such as depression or alcoholism and resolve when these conditions are treated. More often phobias arise independently. Agoraphobia and social phobia generally develop or become prominent in early adulthood whereas specific phobias emanate from childhood and usually cannot be traced to a traumatic encounter with the trigger. Childhood fears of monsters, the dark, or animals are very common and usually resolve before adulthood.

2. Aetiology

From an evolutionary perspective phobic fear may have evolved as a strategy for coping with the potentially catastrophic situations prevalent in the environment of early mammals. To be effective at averting disaster this strategy needed to be triggered by relevant environmental cues and result in a powerful automatic response—fight, flight, or freeze. Phobias are more likely to be of events and situations that threatened the survival of our distant ancestors (snakes, spiders, open spaces, heights, strangers) than modern-day threats such as weapons or motorcycles. Phobic responses appear to be mediated by the amygdala, an older (in evolutionary terms) brain structure, and do not require, nor are they greatly influenced by, more recently evolved higher (conscious) thought. (Conversely phobic anxiety often leads to distorted thinking and an overestimation of threat—see below.)

However, genetic 'preparedness' is not a complete explanation. Phobias (apart from blood/injury phobia) are not strongly inherited and most people do not develop them even when exposed to snakes, spiders, etc. Some phobias defy any evolutionary explanation (e.g. feather phobia). Phobias must be 'learned', with evolutionary genetic influences making certain phobias more likely. Extensive experiments on humans and animals since the mid-20th century have drawn on theories of classical (Pavlovian) and operant *conditioning and social learning to shed light on how this learning occurs. The process in real life is complex and may be influenced by the emotional state, stage of development, and expectation of the individual, how the stimulus is presented, and cultural factors. Sigmund *Freud's assertion that phobias are a manifestation of an unresolved unconscious conflict has not been consistently borne out, nor has the prediction that if treated behaviourally (see below) a phobia will re-emerge in another form.

3. Onset and treatment
By a process that is often unclear, anxiety or panic becomes associated with a particular trigger, be it a crowded bus or a spider. (Brain mechanisms involved in generating spontaneous panic almost certainly play a role in agoraphobia with panic, where fear is of panic itself.) The individual then avoids or escapes fear by subsequently avoiding or running away (often literally) from the trigger or from situations linked with it (e.g. a crowded train or a dusty window ledge). In this way a hierarchy of feared situations develops around a central fear. This avoidance is counter-productive in the longer term and maintains the problem. Allowing anxiety to subside ('habituate') through gradual and prolonged exposure to the trigger (usually by working back through the hierarchy) is a highly effective treatment particularly for specific phobias. In cases of panic and social phobia complementary strategies are used with the aim of rationalizing fear-maintaining beliefs ('I will have a heart attack if I panic', 'when I go into a room everyone stares at me') and eradicating subtle behavioural components (such as avoiding eye contact in social phobia).

Such cognitive–behaviour therapy (CBT) is widely considered the first-choice treatment for all phobias, though certain antidepressants (e.g. selective serotonin reuptake inhibitors) can be effective for agoraphobia with panic and social phobia. CBT can be therapist delivered or guided by self-help books or computer programs. Hypnosis is used by some practitioners to facilitate exposure treatment though its additional benefit is uncertain.   MMcD

Ballenger, J. C. (2000). 'Clinical syndrome of adult psychiatry: anxiety disorders'. In Gelder, M. G., Lopez-Ibor, J. J., and Andreasen, N. C. (eds.), *New Oxford Textbook of Psychiatry*.

Kenwright, M., Liness, S., and Marks, I. (2001). 'Reducing demands on clinicians by offering computer-aided self-help for phobia/panic: feasibility study'. *British Journal of Psychiatry*, Nov.

Marks, I. M. (1987). *Fears, Phobias and Rituals*.

——(2001), *Living with Fear*.

Morris, J., Öhman, A., and Dolan, R. J. (1998). 'Modulation of human amygdala activity by emotional learning and conscious awareness'. *Nature*, 393.

Öhman, A., and Mineka S. (2001). 'Fears, phobias and preparedness: toward an evolved module of fear and fear learning'. *Psychological Review*, 108/3.

phonetics. Phonetics, the science of speech sounds, is traditionally divided into two branches: *acoustic*, concerned with the structure of the acoustic signal itself, and *articulatory*, concerned with the way these sounds are produced. The most important initial impetus was to develop a standard means for the accurate and convenient transcription of the sounds of various languages and dialects. Proper transcription was regarded as an essential tool for field linguists and missionaries dealing with new languages, and for recording dialectal variations of known languages (and 'correcting' them—e.g. Henry Sweet 1908). The idea of an International Phonetic Alphabet (IPA), suitable for all languages, was first suggested by Otto Jespersen in 1886; the International Phonetic Association (which included Paul Passy and Sweet, as well as Jespersen) published the first IPA in 1888. This was based on the articulatory features of the sounds: the place of maximum constriction of the vocal tract, the manner of the constriction (completely closed for consonants like /p/; with the nasal passage open for consonants like /m/, etc.) and the onset of voicing (immediate in the case of /b/, but delayed for /p/). Daniel Jones's classification of the 'cardinal vowels' was similarly based on articulatory features, the height of the tongue, front or back of the mouth, with lips rounded or unrounded. The IPA system enables the transcription of sound distinctions which have no significance for the speaker of one language, though they do for the speaker of another. Thus the initial consonants in 'key' and 'cool' can be heard, and felt, to be different but do not, in English, constitute different phonemes (units of significant sound); in Arabic they do.

Although methods of analysing the frequency components of the acoustic signal had been known since *Helmholtz in 1862, no convenient way of plotting frequency, energy, and time was available until the development of the 'sonograph' in the 1940s by R. K. Potter and others. The analysis of the movement of the vocal organs during speech has in recent years been advanced by the use of high-speed film to record the opening and closing of the vocal folds during phonation (though the earliest use of this technique can be traced back to 1913) and by cineradiography. Two surprising and paradoxical results have emerged from these methods of acoustic and articulatory analysis: first, there is no simple correspondence between acoustic parameters and the phenomenological sound. The English phoneme /d/, for example, has a quite different sound depending on the vowel that follows it. Second, there is no simple correspondence between the sound and vocal action used to produce it. These fundamental puzzles have motivated the growth of experimental phonetics, which combines sophisticated analysis and synthesis of speechlike sounds with the investigative procedures of experimental psychology, with the aim of discovering which abstract characterizations of acoustic dimensions are critical in determining the sound contrasts meaningful in language. That is to say, what kinds of representation underlie the perception and production of spoken language? BLB

Collins, B., and Mees, I. (1999). *The Real Professor Higgins: The Life and Career of Daniel Jones*.

MacMahon, M. K. C. (1986). 'The International Phonetic Association: the first 100 years'. *Journal of the International Phonetic Association*, 16.

phrenology. Phrenology, from the Greek words for 'mind' and 'discourse', is about reading character from the shape and especially from the 'bumps' of the skull. This has also been called 'cranioscopy', 'craniology', 'zoonomy', and '*physiognomy', though the last usually refers to reading character from faces. Phrenology was popular from the middle of the 18th to the middle of the 19th centuries; its principal proponents were Franz Joseph *Gall (1758–1828), who was a physician in Vienna and a more than competent anatomist (he was the first to distinguish the functions of the 'white' and the 'grey' matter of the brain), and Gall's student, Johann Kaspar Spurzheim (1776–1832), who with the controversial Scottish moral philosopher George Combe (1788–1858) spread the doctrine to England and America. It had such a vogue that by 1832 there were 29 phrenological societies in Britain, and many journals in Britain and America, including the *Phrenological Journal*, a quarterly edited by Combe at Edinburgh from 1823 to 1847. There was, however, much criticism, such as from the philosopher, and early proponent of associative psychology, Thomas Brown (1778–1820), and phrenology was often lampooned in verse and on the stage.

Gall claimed to have discovered his phrenological principles inductively from people (and animals) of his acquaintance who had marked character traits associated with distinctive skull shapes, or 'bumps' that could be felt with the fingers. For example, the region he numbered as 1—Amativeness (*Instinct de la génération*), at the back of the head below the inion—he identified from its heat in a hysterical widow. Just above this region is No. 2—Philoprogenitiveness (*Amour de la progéniture*)—which Gall selected as the organ for the love of children because this occipital part of the skull is prominent in women and apes, in whom the love of infants is supposedly stronger than in men. To take an intellectual example: No. 22 (Individuality), immediately above the nose, was named as the organ for recognizing external objects and for forming ideas from being large in Michelangelo and small in the Scots.

The 26 regions identified as personality organs by Gall (increased to as many as 43 by later phrenologists) were based on very few instances. Implausible excuses were made for exceptions, and for such matters as inability to distinguish the skulls of saints from those of sinners. Phrenology does, however, have considerable importance in the history of psychology and brain studies. Even its obvious failures are revealing.

Phrenology is based on the notion that mind is intimately related to physical brain function. It is thus opposed to Cartesian mind–brain dualism, and is in line with much modern neurological thinking, and with 'identity' accounts, which suppose that mind is an aspect of brain structure and function. Phrenology implies some kind of *localization of brain function, though what are thought to be localized in the brain, as read from the 'bumps', are *complete traits* of ability and character, rather than *processes* generating characteristics of behaviour and intellect. The implied notion of brain 'organs', such as Veneration, Wonder, Wit, Tune, Language, Memory, Vanity, Cautiousness, and so on, is misleading, because these depend on many underlying processes which, as we now know, are widely separated and in many cases never appear in the 'output' of the brain. Nevertheless, we do still speak of 'speech centres' (SEE LANGUAGE AREAS IN THE BRAIN), and evidence for speech in pre-human and early human skulls is sought from bumps in casts corresponding to those anatomical features associated with language in modern man.

Phrenology made psychological classifications which still survive. Spurzheim grouped human faculties in the following way:

I. *Feelings*, divided into:
  1. Propensities (internal impulses to certain actions).
  2. Sentiments (impulses prompting emotions as well as action).
     (i) Lower: those common to man and the lower animals.
     (ii) Higher: those proper to man.

II. *Intellectual faculties*, divided into:
 1. Perceptive faculties (knowledge by observation and through language).
 2. Reflective faculties (knowledge by intuition and reasoning, especially by noting comparisons).

Although the phrenologists accepted and formulated *faculty psychology, they did not contribute to brain anatomy. This, in part, was because they did not say, simply, that the larger the 'bump' the greater the characteristic. Thus Spurzheim writes, in *Phrenology: In Connexion with the Study of Physiognomy* (1824), under the heading 'Of the heads of the sexes':

The body and face vary in the two sexes. Do their brains differ likewise? The talents and feelings of the male and female are commonly considered as dissimilar; indeed it is proverbially said that women feel and men think. The majority of modern authors, however, have attributed the phenomenon to the modified education which the sexes receive. The female head is smaller than that of the male; it is commonly narrower laterally. The female cerebral fibre is slender and long rather than thick.

He continues:

Lastly, and in particular, the organs of philoprogenitiveness, of attachment, love of approbation, circumspection, secretiveness, ideality, and benevolence, are for the most part proportionately larger in the female; while in the male those of amativeness, combativeness, destructiveness, constructiveness, self-esteem, and firmness predominate.

But he then argues:

I say that the heads of men are wider than those of women, and then I state that I consider circumspection and secretiveness, whose organs lie laterally, as more generally active in the female than in the male. They who make this objection do not understand the phrenological principle, according to which the organs which are most largely developed in every individual display the greatest energy, and take the lead of all the other powers. Now, although the female head be so commonly narrower than the male, the organs of secretiveness and circumspection are still the most prominent, and thus contribute essentially to the formation of the female character.

Spurzheim concludes that phrenologists examining innate dispositions 'do not compare the heads of the sexes together, nor even those of the same sex; they judge of every head individually, and form conclusions in regard to the dispositions generally, according as the respective faculties are developed'.

The phrenologists generally stressed innateness of faculties. Spurzheim, while admitting that the education of the girls of his time was inferior to that of boys, argues that 'girls are more commonly instructed in drawing, painting, and music than boys', and often spend much time at these occupations; 'nevertheless, no woman has hitherto produced such works as those of Handel, Mozart, Haydn, Titian, Rubens, Paul Veronese, Canova, and so

many others'. He adds: 'The female sex appears to greater advantage in actions which result from feeling.' Now this argument depends on the assumption of faculty psychology, that skills such as painting are developed simply by practising that particular skill. But it is possible that other, and perhaps traditionally male, activities transfer knowledge and abilities to give males an advantage even for skills such as painting which are frequently practised by girls. This possibility could hardly have been considered by proponents of a faculty psychology based on localized organs of behaviour and personality.

Phrenology seemed to give promise of objective assessments and judgements of people; it was even proposed to select Members of Parliament from candidates having propitious bumps. It was suggested, as a joke, by the distinguished editor of *Blackwood's Magazine* and professor of moral philosophy at Edinburgh, John Wilson ('Christopher North'), that children's heads should be moulded —to accentuate their good qualities and remove evil. The suggestion was taken up by several practising phrenologists.

With the advent of experiments in which small regions of brain were removed, by careful operations pioneered by the French physiologist Pierre *Flourens, and by electrical stimulation with fine wires, electrodes, pioneered by Gustav Theodor Fritsch (1838–97) and Julius Eduard

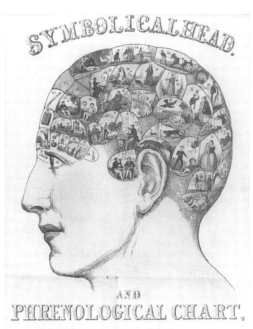

Fig. 1.

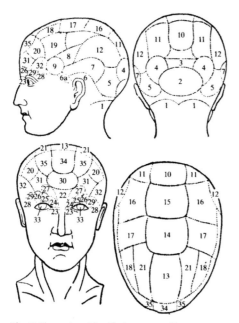

Fig. 2. The regions identified as personality organs, according to the classification of Gall, with additions by Spurzheim and Combe, were:

1. Amativeness	18. Wonder
2. Philoprogenitiveness	19. Ideality
3. Concentrativeness	20. Wit
4. Adhesiveness	21. Imitation
5. Combativeness	22. Individuality
6. Destructiveness	23. Form
6a. Alimentiveness	24. Size
7. Secretiveness	25. Weight
8. Acquisitiveness	26. Colour
9. Constructiveness	27. Locality
10. Self-esteem	28. Number
11. Love of approbation	29. Order
12. Cautiousness	30. Eventuality
13. Benevolence	31. Time
14. Veneration	32. Tune
15. Conscientiousness	33. Language
16. Firmness	34. Comparison
17. Hope	35. Causality

Hitzig (1838–1907) on the 'motor cortex' of dogs (1870), it at last became obvious that functions are localized, but that localized functions are not simply related to behavioural skills, or to mental attributes or abilities. However, although this became clear to many physiologists towards the end of the 19th century, it was resisted by some, and especially by the members of the *Gestalt school of psychology, who held that the brain works holistically, with perception given by perceived objects represented

'isomorphically' as brain traces like pictures, so that circles are represented by circular traces, houses by house-shaped traces, and so on. This was a rejection of functionally interacting processes of analysis and of inference-generating perceptions, in favour of notions more like those of the phrenologists. And such ideas die hard. One might say that the current interest in 'cerebral dominance', with the left hemisphere of the cortex supposedly 'analytic' (responsible for skills such as arithmetic and logical thinking) and the right hemisphere 'synthetic' or 'analogue' (responsible for intuitive and artistic skills), is the dying kick of phrenology. (See SPLIT-BRAIN AND THE MIND.) Physiological experiments on localizing functions give very different functional maps from those of the phrenologists (Figs. 1 and 2) and are highly revealing and of great use in brain surgery; yet they too are subject to logical difficulties of interpretation. For ablation especially, there are difficulties in inferring from loss, or change in behaviour, what the missing region does in the normal intact brain. It is extremely difficult to isolate functions in interactive systems, and in systems where parts can take over the functions of other parts when these are overloaded or damaged. Moreover, it is logically necessary to appreciate what the functions are before they can be named or localized. Physiological functions are not units of behaviour, and so are not to be discovered simply from observation. What is required is an adequate theoretical understanding—an adequate conceptual model—of brain function, which is something very different from the localized mental faculties of the phrenologists.

Recently, however, the brain has been seen to be organized in 'modules' carrying out complex functions, such as face recognition (Fodor 1983). This is something of a return to phrenological ideas. RLG

Fodor, J. A. (1983). *The Modularity of Mind.*
Karmiloff-Smith, A. (1992). *Beyond Modularity.*
Van Wyhe, J. (2004). *Phrenology and the Origins of Victorian Scientific Naturalism.*

physiognomy. The word 'physiognomy' is a compound of two Greek words meaning 'nature', and 'an interpreter'. Francis *Bacon described it as 'discovery of the disposition of the mind by the lineaments of the body'; and indeed this is the aim of portrait painting. *Aristotle wrote extensively on physiognomy, with many comparisons between human and animal characteristics, and many Latin authors discuss it as a descriptive science; but in medieval writings, physiognomy becomes linked with *astrology and necromancy. It was made illegal by George II, in 1743, and earlier Queen Elizabeth had decreed that 'all persons fayning to have knowledge of phisiognomic or like Fantasticall Ymaginacions' were liable to be 'stripped naked from the middle upwards and openly whipped until his body be bloudye'. Nevertheless,

Elizabeth set much store on delineation of character in paintings. Our own view, now, is surely as paradoxical, for we generally hold that physiognomy as a science is unfounded and yet we spend a great deal of time reading character from faces and pictures.

There are many examples, from Aristotle onwards, of people looking dull but being bright (and Aristotle admitted it of himself, saying that it was the practice of philosophy that brightened his native dullness), while the converse can also be true. But there are good grounds for associating expression with character traits and habits of thought. The point is that groups of muscles are associated with emotions, moods, and activities, and the use of facial muscles both modifies the countenance and produces permanent changes, such as lines and wrinkles. The first scientific study of this notion was by the distinguished Scottish anatomist–surgeon and neurologist Sir Charles *Bell, whose *Essay on the Anatomy of the Expressions* (1806) related specific muscles to *facial expressions.

The idea was developed, with strong evolutionary implications, by Charles *Darwin in his still highly important book *The Expression of the Emotions in Man and Animals* (1872). Darwin dismisses earlier writers on expression and physiognomy, such as the French painter Charles Le Brun (1619–90), who wrote *Conférence sur l'expression des différents caractères des passions* in 1667, and the Dutch anatomist Peter Camper (1722–89), but he does give full and just praise to the work of Bell. He also refers to the best known of the physiognomists, Johann Kaspar Lavater (1741–1801), born in Zurich, whose *Physiognomische Fragmente* (1775–8; translated by Thomas Holcroft as *Essays on Physiognomy* in 1793) went into many editions and was widely read. Lavater is interesting for his many drawings of faces, and his astute comments on the characters and lives of his examples, but there is a total absence of system or theory. Darwin refers also to Burgess's *The Physiology or Mechanism of Blushing* (1839), which points out that *blushing cannot be caused 'by any physical means', but that it must be the mind that is affected, 'for if we try to restrain blushing, this increases it'. Finally, Darwin refers to the French pioneer in electrophysiology, Guillaume Duchenne (1806–75), who was the first to describe locomotor ataxia, and was the founder of techniques using electrical stimulation for therapy. Darwin refers to Duchenne's *Mécanisme de la physionomie humaine* (1862), in which he 'analyses by means of electricity, and illustrates by magnificent photographs, the movements of the facial muscles'. Duchenne lent and allowed Darwin to copy his photographs, many of which appear in *The Expression of the Emotions*. He succeeded in showing the effects of contraction of individual muscles of the hand, and their effects in producing creases in the skin, and, perhaps most significant, in showing which muscles are and which are not under voluntary control. Both he and Darwin were

well aware of the problem of how it is that groups of muscles are innervated for behaviour, gesture, and expressions. This could not be investigated experimentally before techniques of cortical stimulation were developed.

The philosopher Herbert *Spencer contributed an account of facial expression and emotion somewhat similar to Darwin's (in *Principles of Psychology*, 1855), and Darwin quotes from it with approval:

Fear, when strong, expresses itself in cries, in efforts to hide or escape, in palpitations and tremblings; and these are just the manifestations that would accompany an actual experience of the evil feared. The destructive passions are shown in a general tension of the muscular system, in gnashing of the teeth and protrusion of the claws, in dilated eyes and nostrils, in growls; and these are weaker forms of the actions that accompany the killing of prey.

Darwin's essential point is that the facial muscles of monkeys are similar to ours, but, as he puts it, 'no one, I presume, would be inclined to admit that monkeys have been endowed with special muscles solely for exhibiting their hideous grimaces'. Rather the 'grimaces' were originally of functional importance—and in many cases still are in us—as when muscles surrounding the eyes contract to protect the eyes from increased blood pressure or from the blow of an assailant. Frequent use of such sets of muscles, either in action or in the simulation of imagination and emotion, will produce, gradually, permanent changes of expression. So there is strong evidence and a consistent theory for a biological basis to physiognomy. It is, however, very far from clear how accurately it is possible to read the subtleties of human character from facial forms and expressions having pre-human functional origins.

It is most curious that expressions of extremely different emotions can be so similar that they are indistinguishable in photographs—unless the context of the situation is available. Pictures of reactions of horror and uncontrollable laughter are easily confused when presented out of context. In normal life, no doubt, it is facial and verbal reactions to events—speed and appropriateness—that are crucially important signals for evaluating character and ability. This is the power of the cinema, for it presents the context of situations, and the timing of responses. There remains a considerable mystery just why and how static portraits convey so much of the character of individuals by their physiognomy. Perhaps sometimes it happens in reverse—a person one knows to be interesting *looking* interesting in the picture by association. This might apply for good, evil, or foolishness, or genius. No doubt the '*halo effect' applies to pictures as to people.   RLG

Piaget, Jean (1896–1980). Swiss psychologist born at Neuchâtel, Switzerland, who became professor of child psychology at the University of Geneva, and director of the Centre d'Épistémologie Génétique; he was also a director of the Institut des Sciences de l'Éducation. He was the great pioneer of the study of cognitive development through childhood, and he virtually founded *epistemology as an experimental science. He wrote a vast number of books, using writing as his principal aid to thought and inspiration for new experiments. The best are highly important, and are clearly written to be read, but some are clumsy vehicles of his thinking, though no doubt useful for the author and immediate colleagues at the time of writing.

J. H. Flavell (1963) describes how Piaget worked on and published some 25 papers on molluscs, of which about 20 were in print before he was 21. Piaget's early studies in zoology and the behaviour of simple organisms evidently gave rise to his interest in comparing external with internal organizational principles, and in the nature of *intelligence, which crystallized as he worked in *Binet's laboratory in Paris on standardizing intelligence tests for children.

Although Piaget became one of the most famous psychologists of his time, psychology was not his main aim or interest; rather this was to unify biology and logic. To this end he investigated the development of concepts and language, and interactive behaviour with objects in children, and their internal mental manipulations of symbols. He saw knowledge as providing 'self-regulating' symbolic structures, developed by processes of 'assimilation' and 'accommodation'. There is something of *Hegel in his manner of discussion and thinking, which he calls 'dialectical constructivism': passing from *thesis* to its contradictory *antithesis* to the next step, the *synthesis*. This in its turn might serve as a new thesis, so his thinking climbs in a kind of staircase. It is however a spiral staircase, for the contextual premises are re-examined each time the 'spiral' sweeps round, from successively higher levels of consideration. Piaget sees psychological development as this kind of spiral, with interacting antitheses generating new knowledge, rather than as an unfolding of innate properties by maturation, triggered or released by experiences, which is perhaps a more usual view. He thus adds empiricism to Hegel's a priori idealism for cognitive development.

'Assimilation' is the modification of perceptual inputs by existing knowledge structures, while 'accommodation' is modification of the knowledge structures to adapt to the input. The result is a lifelong quasi-stable equilibrium which is maintained by climbing to new generalizations along the spiral of the growth of mind. This is, essentially, a dynamic model of mind, with active exploration seen as the basis for learning and understanding and discovery.

The child goes through various stages of learning and development, and he is unable to proceed to later stages before critically important earlier stages have been passed,

or lessons learned, or discoveries created by new syntheses. Piaget sets specific ages to some of these stages, but it appears that these tend to be somewhat late for most children. Paradigm experiments include the famous 'mountain' test, in which the child is asked to describe a model of mountains from the point of view not of himself but of someone in a different location—the tester, or a model person placed in the scene. He found that young children find this impossible. Equally celebrated experiments concern predicting what will happen to the levels or slopes of liquids, as glass jars are tilted or liquid is poured into jars of various diameters. These are extremely interesting tests of understanding, and may be pre-verbal. There are, however, difficulties in ensuring that very young children understand exactly what is asked of them, and later experimenters have sometimes found that inability to perform the tests is due to lack of understanding of the instructions. (See REASONING: DEVELOPMENT IN CHILDREN.)

Broadly, children seem to go through a phase of *Aristotelian physics before they understand acceleration, inertia, and so on, as these are now understood by scientifically educated adults.

Piaget's work is important for considering *education, communication of ideas, and epistemology. By applying *cybernetic concepts of dynamic stability it may have implications and applications at several levels, for programming computers to be intelligent (see ARTIFICIAL INTELLIGENCE) as well as for teaching children.

Among Piaget's main works are *The Language and Thought of the Child* (1923; Eng. trans. 1926); *The Child's Conception of the World* (1926; Eng. trans. 1929); *The Child's Conception of Physical Reality* (1926; Eng. trans. 1960). His theory of visual illusions based on his notion of assimilation is described in *The Mechanisms of Perception* (1961; Eng. trans. 1969).   RLG

Boden, M. (1979). *Piaget*.
Flavell, J. H. (1963). *The Developmental Psychology of Jean Piaget*.

Piaget and education. Piaget's work on children's intellectual development owed much to his early studies of water snails. *Limnaea stagnalis* spends its early life in stagnant conditions. On transfer to tidal waters and in order to remain on the rocks the snail is forced to engage in motor activity, and this activity directly influences the development of the size and shape of its shell. This model of development through active adaptation has become the prototype for learning. Inherited patterns of motor activity (such as sucking, grasping) enable the infant to interact with the world but are themselves transformed as a result of this interaction. So too with knowledge. The complementary processes of 'assimilation' and 'accommodation' (see PIAGET, JEAN) are invoked by Piaget to describe the course of adaptation and the stagelike nature of the development of understanding as the child strives for stability between new learning and old at successively higher levels ('equilibration').

Piaget insists on the fundamental importance of the child as agent of his own learning throughout development. In the early years knowledge of the outside world is assimilated to the structure of elementary actions, and later involves the reconstruction in thought of operations performed in action. This restricts the child's ability to think logically. By middle childhood (the junior school period) greater coordination of thought is achieved but is limited in its sphere of application to objects rather than to verbal propositions. According to Piaget's theory of stages, it is not until early adolescence that children become capable of formal reasoning and hypothetico-deductive thinking.

Although Piaget did not systematically apply his theory to teaching, his account of intellectual development has been used to reinforce and provide theoretical justification for aspects of earlier theories of education and practices, such as those advocated by *Montessori and *Dewey. His theory stresses that knowledge and understanding are derived from the active adaptation of children to their environment and not through direct instruction, and consequently that schools should provide children with opportunities to invent and to discover; it recommends a sequence of intellectual demands compatible with the forms of thought which define the stages of development described. Direct application of the theory has proved difficult, partly because Piaget's interest was in skills not normally taught and partly because of lack of clarity or inconsistency on certain fundamental points. There is, for example, no empirical support for equilibration as a mechanism of learning, and Piaget was generally indifferent to more parsimonious accounts of the phenomena he described. Recent research to train children on various concepts has been more successful than the theory would predict. Piaget's account also underestimates social interaction and cultural transmission as constituents of education.

Nevertheless, some specific curricula derived from Piaget's work have been devised, notably by Lavatelli in the USA for children aged 4–7, by Weikart and others at Ypsilanti in Michigan, by Kamii and De Vries for preschool children, and in the Schools Council science 5–13 project in Britain. Stage theory has also been used to develop techniques to assess intellectual capacity (as in the British Ability Scales) in skills that are, according to Piaget, only minimally influenced by teaching, if at all. Although Piaget's theory provides possible guidelines as to reasonable demands for children at different age levels, to ascribe to his influence alone the idea that children learn by manipulation, comparison, and reconciliation of discrepant events (proceeding from the equilibration concept) is mistaken. Despite the conscious extension of

Piaget's ideas into education by the few mentioned above, many more have employed his theory to justify practices already in vogue with educationists seeking to emphasize discovery learning.   DS

Meadows, S. A. C. (ed.) (1983). *Developing Thinking.*

Pieron, Henri (1881–1964). Founder of French experimental psychology. He was trained in philosophy and physiology, and became a leader in physiological studies of sensation and perception. He designed several ingenious optical and other instruments, and was also influential in personnel selection, vocational guidance, and animal psychology, as well as in psychophysics. His important works include *Thought and the Brain* (reprint 1999) and *Vocabulaire de la psychologie* (1951; reprint 1990).   RLG

placebo. A placebo is a medical treatment that works (i.e. relieves symptoms or cures disease) because the patient *believes* it works.

1. The placebo response as a process
2. Therapeutic potential of the placebo response
3. Mechanisms of the placebo response

1. The placebo response as a process
A placebo response (or placebo effect) is a process that typically consists of several steps. The first step occurs when a patient receives some medical treatment. Next, the patient forms a belief that the treatment just received will help relieve or cure the condition that he or she is suffering from. The next step involves a cascade of chemical messengers that translate this belief (a neural process) into a physiological and/or immune response. Finally, this physiological or immune response must effect some measurable clinical improvement. Each of these steps will now be discussed briefly.

The first step in a typical placebo response involves the application of some medical treatment. If this medical treatment is one that can work *only* because a patient believes it works, such as a sugar pill or an injection of salt water, it should be called a *pure* placebo. Even medical treatments that work independently of belief can, however, also produce placebo effects; such treatments may be called *impure* placebos, since they work both by means of the belief effect and by other routes that do not depend on belief. Thus potentially any treatment modality can function as a placebo, including surgical procedures and the various kinds of psychotherapy and alternative medicine.

The next step in a typical placebo response is the activation of some psychological process. Not everyone would concur with the description of this psychological process in terms of 'belief'. Some describe the psychological process in terms of 'expectancies', whereas others prefer to speak of *conditioning. Despite these disagreements, all agree that some psychological or neural process must mediate the effects of a medical treatment for it to be regarded as a placebo.

Next, the neural process must trigger the release of chemical messengers which, in turn, activate or suppress physiological and/or immune processes.

Finally, the activation or suppression of these physiological or immune processes must result in some measurable clinical improvement. This final step is essential; if a treatment has no clinical effect, it cannot be called a placebo, and no placebo effect can be said to occur. Suppression of immune processes may lead merely to symptomatic relief, since many common symptoms are in fact produced by the immune system to protect the body and enhance recovery, but it may also result in clinical improvement if the preceding pathology involved overactivation of an immune response.

2. Therapeutic potential of the placebo response

There is still substantial disagreement among medical scientists as to the range of medical conditions and symptoms that can be affected by placebos. An influential paper by the American anaesthetist Henry Beecher gave rise to the view that placebos could affect virtually any medical condition. This view was largely accepted by medical scientists until the late 1990s, when a number of critical studies began to appear arguing that placebos were virtually useless. These studies pointed out that Beecher had based his claims on clinical trials that simply compared a group of patients receiving an active treatment with another group who received a pure placebo. As the critics noted, such studies tell us nothing about the placebo effect. To get relevant data on that question, it is necessary to compare patients receiving placebos with those who receive no treatment. Yet very few clinical trials include a no-treatment group, so good data is hard to come by.

Rather than asking whether or not placebos work, which carries the absurd implication that placebos must either work for all medical conditions or none, researchers are now beginning to ask the much more sensible question of which medical conditions placebos work for. There is already substantial evidence that placebos can have powerful analgesic effects. Placebos have also been shown to relieve other symptoms and signs such as trismus and swelling, but debate still rages as to whether placebos can cure diseases as well as relieving symptoms. There is some evidence that placebos can cure stomach ulcers and relieve depression, but not everyone finds this evidence convincing. Contrary to popular opinion, there is no evidence that placebos can cure cancer.

3. Mechanisms of the placebo response

The debate about which conditions are placebo responsive has had a profound impact on thinking about the mechanisms by which placebos work—i.e. on theories about the chemical messengers and biological pathways that translate the relevant beliefs into measurable clinical benefits. When scientists believed that placebos could affect any and every medical condition, they assumed that placebo responses must therefore involve a wide variety of biological mechanisms, since the idea that a single type of mechanism could alleviate so many different medical conditions would have been totally implausible. Now that scientists reject the earlier grand claims made for placebos, and it is increasingly plausible that the class of placebo-responsive conditions will turn out to be quite restricted, it is more tenable that a single biological pathway, or a small group of such pathways, may be activated in all placebo responses. With a few exceptions, scientists have so far been generally unwilling to speculate about which pathways are involved, although current research in psychoneuroimmunology (which studies the interaction between the nervous system and the immune system) will no doubt throw light on this question.

The first breakthrough in elucidating the biological pathways involved in the placebo response came in 1978, when Jon Levine, N. C. Gordon, and Howard Fields showed that endorphins played a crucial role in placebo analgesia. Endorphins (short for 'endogenous morphine') are the body's natural painkillers, and their release is highly sensitive to psychological input. It is not yet known whether endorphins mediate placebo responses for symptoms other than pain.

Just how the release of endorphins comes to be associated with medical treatments (even ones that are otherwise useless) remains the subject of debate. One influential model is based on the theory of *conditioning. According to this view, drugs and other kinds of medical treatment that work even if you do not believe in them function as unconditioned stimuli, while the improvement that ensues after receiving such treatments is the unconditioned response. The conditioned stimuli are all the things that are repeatedly paired with taking the drug. Suppose, for example, that you notice that the pill is always pink and round, and is always prescribed by a man in a white coat. After being prescribed this pill several times, you will come to associate these things with the feeling of getting better. Then, if the doctor gives you a pink pill with no medication in it, you will respond by feeling better, just as *Pavlov's dogs salivated in response to a bell that was not accompanied by food.

It is now known that various immune processes can be conditioned, so conditioning may also explain how other kinds of chemical messenger, apart from endorphins, may be triggered by placebos. Although much research into the process of conditioning was conducted by behaviourists, who deny the existence of mental states such as beliefs, the conditioning theory of placebos does not in fact rule out a role for belief as the crucial psychological variable that mediates all placebo responses.   DE

Beecher, H. K. (1955). 'The powerful placebo'. *Journal of the American Medical Association*, 159.

Evans, D. (2003). *Placebo: The Belief Effect*.

Harrington, A., (ed.) (1997). *The Placebo Effect: An Interdisciplinary Exploration*.

Humphrey, N. (2002). 'Great expectations: the evolutionary psychology of faith healing and the placebo response'. In *The Mind Made Flesh: Essays from the Frontiers of Psychology and Evolution*.

Levine, J. D., Gordon, N. C., et al. (1978). 'The mechanism of placebo analgesia'. *Lancet*, 2.

placebo effect. When people are unwell, they will often begin to recover just as soon as they receive medical attention, but before the treatment could have any direct effect and even when the treatment is a sham. Mere belief that recovery is coming can by itself bring the recovery about.

This is the *placebo* effect (named in the Middle Ages after the professional mourners at a funeral who were paid to sing vespers for the dead, beginning 'Placebo Domino . . .'). The essayist Michel de Montaigne, writing in 1572, noted that 'there are men on whom the mere sight of medicine is operative', and he went on to describe what would now be considered a textbook case:

[There was] a man who was sickly and subject to [kidney] stone who often resorted to enemas, which he had made up for him by physicians, and none of the usual formalities were omitted. . . . Imagine him then, lying on his stomach, with all the motions gone through except that no application has been made! This ceremonial over, the apothecary would retire, and the patient would be treated just as if he had taken the enema; the effect was the same as if he actually had. . . . When, to save the expense, the patient's wife tried sometimes to make do with warm water, the result betrayed the fraud; this method was found useless and they had to return to the first.

Recent scientific studies, comparing placebo with no-placebo, as Montaigne did here, have confirmed the reality of the phenomenon. The effects appear to be strongest and most reliable in the treatment of pain, where in both clinical and laboratory settings placebos of all kinds—sugar pills, cold creams, saline injections, fake ultrasound, even mere words, *when convincingly presented as medical painkillers*—have been found to bring significant relief. But placebos can also be effective in the treatment of a range of other illnesses, including stomach ulcers, heart disease, depression, and Parkinson's disease. As Robert Buckman has summed it up: 'Placebos are extraordinary drugs. They seem to have some effect on almost every symptom known to mankind, and work in at least a third of patients and sometimes in up to 60 per cent. They have no serious side-effects and cannot be given in overdose. In short they hold the prize for the most adaptable, protean, effective, safe and cheap drugs in the world's pharmacopoeia.'

Still, much remains to be discovered about how and why placebos work. What exactly is the message the placebo gives the patient, and by what perceptual routes does it arrive? How does this message and the meaning that is attached to it affect the patient's specific expectations and/or general mood? How do these changes in what the patient thinks (particularly) or feels (more generally) about his ailment activate the physiological mechanisms that lead to recovery? And, then, the deeper question about evolutionary design: what biological advantage can there be in having the *mind* control the *body's* healing systems in this way?

People rely on a variety of sources of information for foretelling the future. It is clear that the placebo's message—to the effect that 'this treatment will soon make you better'—can be conveyed by any or all of them: learned associations, explicit instruction, rational argument, magical reasoning, trust in authority, and, of particular importance, subtle social cues of the kind called 'bedside manner' (so that, for example, the same placebo pill may work consistently better when administered by one doctor than another). But, by whatever route the message comes, the patient must have the right mind-set to receive it. There are large cross-cultural differences in placebo responsiveness, which, though little understood, promise to throw light on how local attitudes to medicine and the symbolism of the body may enable or disable the 'meaning response'(Moerman 2002). For example, placebo medicine works powerfully for the treatment of stomach ulcers in Germany (60 per cent healing rate), but hardly at all in Brazil (7 per cent); yet for the treatment of hypertension, placebo medicine is less effective in Germany than elsewhere.

Placebo treatments tend to have results specific to the particular ailment and the part of the body to which they are applied (for example, placebo pain-relieving cream applied to the left hand does not relieve pain on the right). So the effects cannot be being mediated entirely through changes in the patient's general mood. Rather, the patient's expectations that the treatment will work (like a real medicine) to help with the particular problem it addresses must be being channelled into a relatively narrow and 'appropriate' response.

How does the mind talk to the body's healing systems in such specific ways? Recent research in neuroimmunology has uncovered intimate links between the central nervous system and the immune system, with several kinds of neurotransmitters doubling as signallers for immune activation and vice versa (Evans 2003). There is therefore plenty of scope for cross-talk. However, one chemical pathway in particular—the endogenous opiates—very likely plays a central role: for it has been found that placebo treatments for pain become completely ineffective if the patient is also given the drug naloxone, which blocks endogenous opiates from working. What is more, endogenous opiates are known also to be involved in the regulation of inflammation, nausea, wound healing, and antibody production. So it is possible —but as yet unproved—that endogenous opiates are responsible for mediating placebo effects across the board: indeed that they provide a kind of lingua franca for mind–body interaction in relation to healing.

No doubt we shall soon have answers to these questions about *how* placebos work, but there will remain the larger question: *why*.

When people recover from illness as a result of placebo treatments, it is of course their own healing systems that are doing the job. Placebo cure is *self-cure*. But if the capacity for self-cure is latent, then why is it not used immediately? If people can get better by their own efforts, why don't they just get on with it as soon as they get sick—without having to wait, as it were, for outside permission? Why should the mind be allowed to have such influence, when the net result is, if anything, to *put a brake* on healing?

This paradox has to be resolved by considering the placebo effect in a broader evolutionary context (Humphrey 2002).

Long before medicines or doctors came on the scene, human beings had already developed a fine capacity for looking after their own health: by mounting defences such as pain and fever, by actively attacking infections, by repairing bone and tissue damage, by indulging in sickness behaviours, and so on. However none of these measures is free of cost (immune resources are expensive, pain is debilitating, acting sick is time wasting, etc.). So it has been essential to have some kind of internal 'health management system' in place, to ensure that the way the body responds to any particular threat is nearly optimal.

Sometimes, for example, it would be best for a sick person to get well as rapidly as possible, throwing off defences such as pain and mounting a full-scale immune response, but at other times it might be more prudent to remain unwell and out of action and to conserve resources for later use. As a general rule (and of crucial importance for the story of placebos): *the brighter the prospects for a rapid recovery, the less to be gained from playing safe and remaining sick.*

But this has meant that the health management system has needed to take account, so far as possible, of any intelligence available to the sick person about what the future holds. Relevant information would include the nature of the threat, the costs of the defensive measure, the prospects for spontaneous remission, evidence of how other people are faring, the presence of social support,

and so on. The mind therefore has had to become an adjunct to the healing system—precisely so as to gather this intelligence.

In the past all kinds of environmental information would be brought to bear. And no doubt they still are. But today, the medicalization of sickness has changed the picture. For it means there will often be a novel and even overriding piece of information to take into account. People have learned—their culture has taught them—that nothing is a better predictor of how things will turn out when they are sick (whether the pain will ease, whether the infection will abate, whether they will be nursed back to health, etc.) than the presence of doctors, medicines, and so on.

Yet human beings remain tied to their evolutionary heritage. And so, today, the very prospect of medical attention—the patient's belief in it—works its magic for the simple reason, stemming from the general rule above, that for most of human history, once a sick person has had cause to *think* that he will soon be safe and well, he has had just the excuse he needs to bring on his own recovery as fast as possible.   NKH

Buckman, R., and Sabbagh, K. (1993). *Magic or Medicine: An Investigation of Healing and Healers.*

Evans, D. (2003). *The Belief Effect.*

Humphrey, N. (2002). 'Great expectations: the evolutionary psychology of faith healing and the placebo response'. In *The Mind Made Flesh: Essays from the Frontiers of Psychology and Evolution.*

Moerman, D. (2002). *The Meaning Response: Rethinking the Placebo Effect.*

Montaigne, M. de (1572). *Essays.* (Trans. J. M. Cohen, 1958.)

plasticity in the nervous system. We now describe three situations in which parts of the nervous system show forms of plastic alteration: changes in eye–brain connections (i) induced experimentally in adult fish and (ii) during the initial development of the visual system, and also (iii) changes in the connections between the left and right optical tectum. These examples all come from the visual system in lower vertebrates and illustrate some of the changes that may occur in different situations.

1. Changes in eye–brain connections induced experimentally in adult fish
2. Changes in eye–brain connections during the initial development of the visual system
3. Changes in the connections between the left and right optic tectum, associated with the development of binocular vision in xenopus frogs

1. Changes in eye–brain connections induced experimentally in adult fish
The ganglion cells of the retina are distributed in a two-dimensional array across the back of the eye. In lower vertebrates (including fish) optic nerve fibres from these

ganglion cells form the optic nerve connecting the retina to the main visual centre of the brain, the optic tectum. Here, the fibres distribute their endings across the surface of the tectum in such a way that neighbourhood relationships between adjacent ganglion cells in the retina are reproduced in the relationships between the endings of their fibres on the tectum (Fig. 1). The entire sheet of retinal ganglion cells thus forms, through the distribution of its nerve fibres on the tectum, a neighbourhood-

preserving 'map' of the retina across the entire extent of the tectal surface.

If half the retina is removed and the optic nerve is cut in a fish, when the retinal fibres regenerate (as they do, in lower vertebrates, within a few weeks) back to the tectum, they form a map of the remaining half of the retina across the appropriate half of the tectum (Fig. 2). The regenerating fibres will even ignore available, but inappropriate, termination sites left unoccupied by the

Fig. 1. Diagram showing the right eye (A) and the brain (B) of a *Xenopus* frog. Ganglion cells in the retina of the eye send their nerve fibres via the optic nerve (C) to the main visual centre, the optic tectum (D). These fibres form a 'map' of the retina on the surface of the optic tectum, and the way the retinal surface is represented on the tectum is indicated by the relative orientation of the flies. Ganglion cells underlying each particular part of the fly on the retina send their fibres to terminate at the corresponding part of the fly on the tectum.

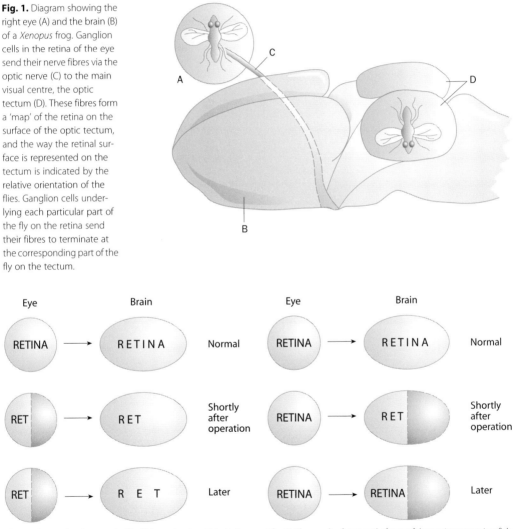

Fig. 2. The result of removal of half the retina in a fish. At first, fibres from the remaining half retina form a partial map over the corresponding half of the tectum. Later, fibres from the remaining half retina spread out to form an expanded, but still properly ordered, map across the whole of the tectum.

Fig. 3. The result of removal of part of the optic tectum in a fish. Initially, fibres from half the retina form a partial map over the remaining half of the tectum. Later, fibres from the whole of the retina form a compressed, but properly ordered, map over the remaining half tectum.

part of the retina that has been removed (Attardi and Sperry 1963). A similar phenomenon of the precise re-establishment of connections is demonstrated when half the tectum is removed (Gaze and Sharma 1970). In this case, it is again only fibres from the appropriate half of the retina that are found to have re-established connections (Fig. 3). This shows, therefore, that the factors controlling the initial re-establishment of the nerve connections are acting in a quite unplastic way; no change results other than that directly attributable to the surgical treatment. Removal of part of the retina or tectum always produces a corresponding gap in the retinotectal map.

If, however, one examines the result some considerable time (several months) later, one finds that the connection pattern between retina and tectum has now changed. Where only half a retina innervates a whole tectum, fibres from the half-retina are found to have spread their terminals, in an orderly fashion (see Fig. 2), across the whole of the tectum (Schmidt, Cicerone, and Easter 1978). In similar fashion, where half the tectum has been removed (Gaze and Sharma 1970), it is found that ganglion cells from the entire extent of the retina now form an organized but compressed map across the available tectal surface (see Fig. 3).

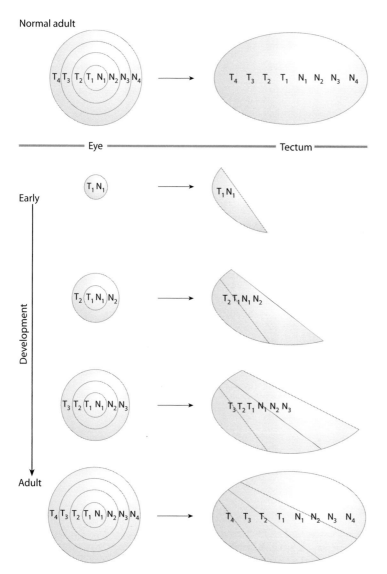

Fig. 4. The relationship between the growing eye and the growing optic tectum in *Xenopus* frogs. The top diagram shows how the horizontal (temporo-nasal) axis of the retina maps on to the antero-posterior axis of the tectum in a normal adult animal. The most temporal ganglion cells in the retina (T_4) send their fibres to the front of the tectum and the most nasal ganglion cells (N_4) send their fibres to the back of the tectum. When the retina first forms, it has very few cells (T_1, N_1) and these connect with the small tectum then existing. The *order* of the map is correct (i.e. similar to that in the adult) from very early stages of development. Next, a further ring of retinal ganglion cells develops (T_2, N_2) and these connect with tectum in the same relative order: most temporal fibres (T_2) to the front, most nasal fibres (N_2) to the back. And so on. The result of the different modes of growth of eye and tectum is that there occurs a continual shift of fibre connections across the tectum as the system grows.

2. Changes in eye–brain connections during the initial development of the visual system

In amphibia and fish the retinotectal system continues to grow for much of (in some cases, all of) the animal's life. The retina grows by the addition of rings of cells at its periphery, so that the oldest part is at the centre of the eye, close to where the optic nerve fibres leave the retina, and the youngest part is at the edge of the retina. The optic tectum, on the other hand, grows from front to back.

In the earliest stages of development, when both the retina and the tectum are very small, the few optic nerve fibres that then exist connect the early retina to the early tectum and make a 'map' which is properly ordered and properly oriented on the tectum. The orientation of the map formed by the retinal fibres on the tectum is such that fibres coming from ganglion cells at the temporal margin of the retina (i.e. furthest away from the nose) connect to the frontmost part of the tectum, while those at the nasal edge of the retina (nearest to the nose) connect towards the back edge of the tectum. This orientation persists throughout life, despite the continuing growth of the system (Fig. 4).

This would present no problems if the retina and the tectum were growing in a similar fashion. However, the fact that the retina grows in rings while the tectum grows from front to back in bands means that, during development of the visual system, there has to be not merely the addition of new fibres between the eye and the tectum,

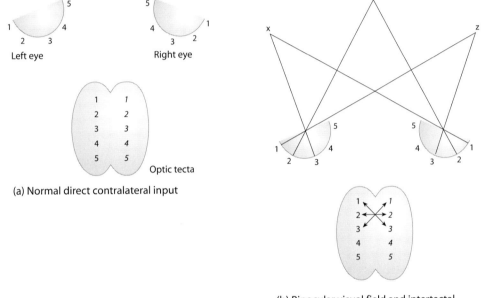

(a) Normal direct contralateral input

(b) Binocular visual field and intertectal connections—normal

Fig. 5. a. In a normal adult *Xenopus* frog fibres from ganglion cells distributed along the horizontal (temporo-nasal) axis of the retina send their fibres to the opposite (contralateral) optic tectum, as shown. Most temporal retinal cells (*1* and 1) connect to most anterior tectum, while most nasal retinal cells (*5* and 5) send their fibres to posterior tectum.
b. *Xenopus* frogs can see part of the visual field with both eyes. Except for parts of the visual field along the midline of the animal, each point in visual space that can be seen by both eyes will be represented at a relatively different position on each optic tectum. For instance, point X in the visual field is 'seen' by ganglion cells at position *3* in the left retina and position 1 in the right retina. These ganglion cells send fibres respectively to position *3* on the right tectum and position 1 on the left tectum. *Experiment shows that these positions, on right and left tecta, are interconnected.* This means that, in addition to the direct contralateral connection of each eye to its opposite tectum, there is also an *indirect* connection from each eye to the tectum on the same side (ipsilateral). Position *3* in the left retina, for example, sends fibres directly to position *3* on the right tectum. But position *3* on the right tectum itself connects, through other nerve fibres, with position 1 on the left tectum. The pattern of intertectal connections is as shown by the arrows.

but also a continual shift of those fibre connections already existing on the tectum (see Fig. 4). Thus during growth of the eye there is a continual addition of new ganglion cells round the retinal margin, including the temporal edge. Fibres from these new temporal ganglion cells must connect with the frontmost part of the tectum, which is where the problem arises. The front of the tectum is the oldest part and already holds connections from the preceding group of temporal fibres. Fibres from the nasal edge of the retina have no such problem. They grow to the back of the tectum where new cells are being added and so have plenty of room to connect. Obviously, as the system grows, something has to give; and what happens is that, on the arrival of new temporal fibres, all the previous fibres shift backwards across the tectum to make room for the newcomers (Gaze, Chung, and Keating 1972). This type of shift of nerve connections during development has been demonstrated both in amphibians and in fish.

3. Changes in the connections between the left and right optic tectum, associated with the development of binocular vision in xenopus frogs

In adult *Xenopus* species there is a binocular visual input to the optic tectum on each side of the brain. From each eye the retinal ganglion cell axons send fibres directly to the tectal lobe on the other (the contralateral) side of the brain (Fig. 5a). The input to the tectal lobe on the same side, the ipsilateral visual input, is indirect, involving some form of second-order nerve connections between the two lobes of the tectum (Fig. 5b). This intertectal connection system itself shows topographic order, such that terminations of retinal ganglion cell axons which arise in complementary positions in each eye (i.e. look out at the

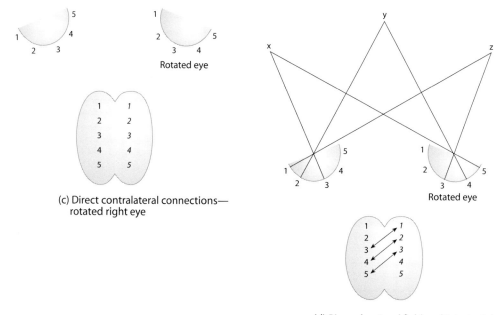

(c) Direct contralateral connections—
rotated right eye

Rotated eye

(d) Binocular visual field and intertectal connections—rotated right eye

c. When one eye is rotated by 180° in embryonic life, each part of the *retina* still connects, later in development, with the proper part of the tectum. Thus retinal position 1 still connects with anterior tectum, although the position of the eye has been altered. But, since the eye is rotated, the map of the *visual field* on the tectum is back-to-front and upside-down.

d. When one eye has been rotated in embryonic life, experiment shows that, later, the representation of the visual field seen through the *rotated eye* is rotated on the contralateral tectum. Thus point X in the visual field is *seen* by ganglion cells at position 3 in the left retina, but is now seen by ganglion cells at position 5 in the rotated retina. However, the map of the visual field on the ipsilateral tectum, as seen through the rotated eye, is *normal*. Conversely, the visual field-map seen through the *normal eye* is normal on its contralateral tectum but *rotated* on the ipsilateral tectum. Any point in the binocular visual field maps, through each eye, to one position only on each tectum. This means that the pattern of intertectal connections is different from normal, as shown here.

same point in visual space) are interlinked. The development of this intertectal fibre system occurs at a later stage than the direct contralateral visual input, and appears to be linked to the onset of metamorphosis, during which the initially laterally projecting eyes migrate dorsally and rostrally, providing partial binocular vision in the adult frog.

If, in embryonic life, one eye is surgically rotated by 180 degrees, the connections that it forms with the contralateral tectal lobe are unaltered (Fig. 5c), but since the eye is now upside down and back to front the visual information coming from the outside world through that eye will be inverted along both axes. If one examines the ipsilateral intertectal fibre pathway at around the time of metamorphosis in such an animal, one finds that, while the visual field map established through the *rotated* eye on its contralateral tectum is rotated as expected, the ipsilateral map from that eye is *normal*; conversely, the contralateral map from the *normal* eye is normal while the ipsilateral map from the *normal* eye is rotated (Fig. 5d). This remarkable phenomenon has the effect (which could be closely related to its cause) that, after rotation of a larval eye, the binocular inputs to each tectum remain congruent. The result is that we obtain a plastic alteration in the intertectal connections underlying the ipsilateral visual input, and this change in connectivity is dependent upon the existence of binocular visual input during a formative period. In this case, therefore, we have a change in functional connections initiated by a *functional* interaction following a *structural* alteration to the eye (Gaze et al. 1970).

In contrast to these observations in the lower vertebrates, observations concerning structural plasticity in the mammalian central nervous system have mainly been made during embryonic and neonatal life. In the mammalian central nervous system there appears to be a loss, at a specific time period in development, of the ability of axons to grossly alter their connections. This time limit for structural plasticity may be related to changes in the ability of axons to regenerate, believed to be caused by changes not in the neurons themselves but in the surrounding glial cells. Technical advances have made it possible to demonstrate that more subtle changes in the fine details of the connection pattern are occurring even in young adult animals. These changes involve the production and retraction of dendritic arbors, altering the morphology of the neuron and, in consequence, its synaptic relationships to those cells which have made functional connections with it. This ability for subtle alteration of what has generally been considered an apparently rigid structural connectivity pattern adds even further complexity to the study of the formation of nerve connections.

Even more elusive are functional changes occurring in the 'established' nervous system. These may include changes in synaptic type, thereby altering the signal communicated to contacted neurons, or alteration in the 'strength' of synapse—which in turn may profoundly change the relative effect of one neuron on another. It is perhaps these latter mechanisms that are more important in the vastly more complex nervous systems of the higher vertebrates. Such functional plasticity may be a form of evolutionary trade-off, where the smaller degree of variable 'wiring' is exchanged for a greater flexibility in the 'programming' of the system.   RMG/JSHT

Attardi, D. G., and Sperry, R. W. (1963). 'Preferential selection of central pathways by regenerating optic fibers'. *Experimental Neurology*, 7.

Gaze, R. M., and Sharma, S. C. (1970). 'Axial differences in the reinnervation of the goldfish optic tectum by regenerating optic nerve fibres'. *Experiments in Brain Research*, 10.

—— Chung, S. H., and Keating, M. J. (1972). 'Development of the retinotectal projection in *Xenopus*'. *Nature*, 236.

—— Keating, M. J., Szekely, G., and Beazley, L. (1970). 'Binocular interaction in the formation of specific intertectal neuronal connections'. *Proceedings of the Royal Society of London, Series B*, 175.

Schmidt, J. T., Cicerone, C. M., and Easter, S. S. (1978). 'Expansion of the half retinal projection to the tectum in goldfish: an electrophysiological and anatomical study'. *Journal of Comparative Neurology*, 177.

Plato (427–347 BC). Plato was born into a distinguished family whose members played a prominent part in the political life of Athens. It is probable that he himself expected to follow a political career, but at some point he came under the influence of that charismatic talker, *Socrates: Socrates was put to death in 399 BC, and it may have been this which changed the course of Plato's life and turned him to philosophy. He did not give up all political aspirations—indeed, he later meddled with unhappy results in the affairs of Sicily—but he seems to have had little to do with the politics of his native city.

His celebrated school, the Academy, probably opened its doors in about 385 BC; and it soon attracted the brightest ornaments of intellectual Greece, among them *Aristotle. Little is known of the structure and nature of Plato's Academy; but it is not implausible to think of it as an institute for advanced research. A comic poet portrays the young academicians as attempting to classify the pumpkin: is it a species of tree? a kind of grass? a vegetable? The caricature suggests that the natural sciences were studied in the Academy; there is good evidence for the study of mathematics; and of course philosophy, in all its branches, was the centrepiece. Plato himself doubtless spent much of his time in teaching and lecturing to his disciples and colleagues, and there are stories of a public lecture in which he managed to bemuse most of his lay audience.

Plato left behind him a body of philosophical writings, in dialogue form, unsurpassed for their literary elegance and their profundity. The notion of the *psyche exercised him throughout his life, and reflections upon one aspect or another of psychology can be found in most of his works; but the primary sources for his psychological theories are the *Phaedo*, *Republic*, *Phaedrus*, and *Timaeus*.

Two topics concerned him especially: the question of the immortality of the psyche, and the problem of its unity. The two questions are closely linked; for Plato, like many thinkers after him, believed that only a unitary and indivisible item could be eternal—anything divisible would at some time actually be divided and hence destroyed. A psyche with parts cannot be immortal; and since Plato held both that the psyche has parts and that it is immortal, he found himself in a perplexity from which he never really escaped.

The *Phaedo* represents Socrates, on the day of his death, talking to his friends about the nature of the psyche: he is determined to discover whether the psyche survives death, or whether, as certain theories dictate, it perishes when the body perishes. The dialogue produces a battery of arguments, developed with great sophistication, to show that the psyche is indeed immortal. The arguments —together with subsidiary reflections produced in the *Republic* and the *Phaedrus*—repay close study. They are none of them cogent, and they are too complex to be profitably summarized, but one point about them is worth mentioning: in arguing for the immortality of the psyche, Socrates is arguing for his own immortality—in the *Phaedo* he believes that he has proved that *he* will survive his death. In other words, Socrates' psyche is the very same thing as Socrates: the one survives if and only if the other does. That is thoroughly consistent with the general Greek notion of psyche, and it shows that Plato, unlike many Christian thinkers, did not regard the person as a compound of body and soul, only one component of which can achieve immortality. My soul may be a *part* of me; my psyche *is* me.

The doctrine that the psyche has 'parts' is expounded in the *Republic*, the *Phaedrus*, and the *Timaeus*. According to the *Republic*, the psyche is composed of an appetitive, an emotional, and a rational part. Plato argues for this tripartite division from the existence of certain types of psychological conflict; for example, a desert traveller may feel thirsty and experience a strong desire to drink from a well, while at the same time his reason (observing that the well is insanitary) urges him not to drink. Since one and the same thing cannot at one and the same time possess opposite properties (a single and undivided psyche cannot at the same time both urge the traveller to the well and hold him back from the water), it follows that the psyche contains at least two distinct parts.

Plato's tripartition of the psyche has been compared to *Freud's distinction among the id, the ego, and the superego, and certainly it is very different in style from Aristotle's division of the various psychological faculties.

Moreover, the basis of Plato's tripartition is logically dubious, and it is not clear if the tripartition is meant to be exhaustive or even exclusive. (Plato himself hints at a more refined and numerous partition, and elsewhere in the *Republic* he assigns appetites to the rational part of the psyche itself.) The fact is that Plato is not primarily concerned, as Aristotle was, with analytical psychology: his interest in the psyche centres on its role as a source of human behaviour, and in particular of moral action. The 'rational part' of the psyche is the morally superior part— the part that ought to govern our actions; and Plato singles it out, not from a desire to develop a detailed psychological theory, but because he wants to attend to the place of reason in the ethics of human action.

In the *Timaeus* (and also in a short passage in the *Theaetetus*) Plato offers accounts of the psychological faculties which are similar in style and motivation to those of the *Pre-Socratics and of Aristotle. But those contributions to analytical psychology are not particularly original: *moral* psychology—the study of the psychological conditions of moral activity—was the focal point for Plato's interest in the affairs of the psyche.

Plato's dialogues have often been translated into English. The best complete translation is still the Victorian masterpiece of Benjamin Jowett (now available, in a revised and more accurate form, in paperback).   JBA

Hare, R. M. (1982). *Plato*.

Platonic Forms. The so-called 'theory' of Forms or Ideas is the name given to a group of Platonic doctrines found in the *Republic* (*c*.380 BC) and elsewhere. The central notion is that, over and above the particular objects that are, for example, beautiful, there is a separate Form—'the beautiful itself'. And in general, wherever a single term is applied to a group of particulars (e.g. beds, tables) there is a corresponding Form. Unlike particulars, which are subject to change and decay, the Forms are eternal and unchanging, and possess their properties in an absolute unqualified way. *Plato argued that true knowledge or understanding relates to the Forms alone, and the Forms must be apprehended not by the senses but by the intellect. Hence, the mind must be drawn away from the senses if it is to apprehend ultimate reality (a doctrine that had considerable influence on subsequent philosophy). *Aristotle criticizes the theory of Forms, arguing that what makes a man a man, for example, is a set of essential characteristics which do not have a separate existence, but must always be instantiated or embodied in particular individuals. Commentators sympathetic to Plato have suggested that the doctrine of Forms contains an important insight: that true scientific understanding must always attempt to go beyond particular observation and ascend to the more universal realm of theoretical models and mathematical laws.   JGC

Annas, J. (1980). *An Introduction to Plato's Republic*.

Plato (1941). *The Republic*. Trans. F. M. Cornford.

pleasure centres. See OLDS, JAMES.

Poincaré, Jules Henri (1854–1912). French mathematician and philosopher, born at Nancy. The range of Poincaré's work was so great that the obituary number of the *Revue de métaphysique et de morale* (September 1913) devoted 130 pages—written by a philosopher, a mathematician, an astronomer, and a physicist—to outline his contributions. Bertrand *Russell, in his introduction to the English translation of Poincaré's collected essays *Science and Method* (1908), contrasts Poincaré's writings on science with most professional philosophers as having 'the freshness of actual experience, of vivid contact with what he is describing', which shows, for example, in his vivid account of mathematical invention. As Poincaré says in his essay 'Mathematical discovery': 'This is a process in which the human mind seems to borrow least from the exterior world, in which it acts, or appears to act, only by itself and on itself, so that by studying the process of geometric thought we may hope to arrive at what is most essential in the human mind.' This leads him to ask how it is that many people do not understand mathematics, as it is founded on logic and principles common to us all. For his own discoveries Poincaré describes 'appearances of sudden illumination, obvious indications of a long course of previous unconscious work', and he gives interesting first-hand examples. He holds that most creative work consists of unconscious selection of possibilities, the selection being guided by subtle rules for rejection which may be worked out during conscious activity. The result is direction and purpose, with a minimum of thinking time wasted on dead ends. Analogies are important for guiding (conscious or unconscious) thinking, but Poincaré holds that the ultimate guide for creative mathematics is a sense of aesthetic elegance. This, however, does have the snag that it can bias thinking towards errors when the truth is less than elegant.

Poincaré was concerned with how sensation and perception relate to physics, or, rather, how physics is *derived* from our experience. Here his thinking in some ways paralleled that of Einstein, who derived some of his ideas from these deep questions of how knowledge can be gained, and how observations can suggest and test theories. Poincaré stressed the importance of hypotheses in science, and he was content to see truth as the unattainable end of a convergence.

Poincaré, H. (1905). *Science and Hypothesis*.

——(1908). *Science and Method*.

pragmatism. A largely American philosophical tradition, too divergent in doctrine to constitute a school, which stresses the purposive nature of cognition and seeks in practical consequences the key to the meanings of concepts, or the correctness of belief. The term was coined by the philosopher C. S. *Peirce, who applied it to a method, first published in 1878, for determining the meanings of 'intellectual concepts'. This method counselled us to consider the effects likely to have practical bearings which 'we conceive the object of our concept to have', for in those lie 'the whole of our conception of the object'. (Peirce thus anticipated verificationist themes which were to be prominent in quite different forms in logical positivism.) Peirce's method attracted the ready sympathy of his close friend William *James, who wrote in 1879 that a conception 'is a *teleological instrument* . . . a partial aspect of a thing which *for our purpose* we regard as its essential aspect, as the representative of the entire thing' (*Principles of Psychology*, ii. 335 n.).

Peirce, however, resisted the way James widened pragmatism to incorporate a theory of truth. This theory, which provoked intense controversy in the decades prior to the First World War, appeared to suggest that truth is nothing more than what works in practice. Doubtless James's vivid way of expressing his views (speaking of 'cash value' and of truths as having in common only the quality 'that they *pay*') contributed to the tendency of his opponents to father on him hopelessly crude views; but it remains exceedingly difficult to extract a coherent theory of truth from James's writings. The reason may be that truth as we commonly use the notion points to a divorce of cognition from purposive activity, so that a pragmatic spirit is best developed by leaving the notion of truth behind. This was the path taken by John *Dewey (e.g. in his *Logic* of 1938), who abandoned the notion of truth in favour of 'warranted assertibility'. JET

Thayer, H. S. (1968). *Meaning and Action: A Critical History of Pragmatism*.

Pre-Socratic philosophers. The term 'Pre-Socratic' is conventionally applied to a heterogeneous collection of Greek thinkers who lived and worked in the period from *c.*600 to *c.*400 BC. These men in no sense formed a single sect or school, but they wrestled, each in his own way, with a common set of problems— problems that we would now classify as scientific or philosophical.

None of their writings (some of which were in verse, some in prose) has survived intact: what we know about them is gleaned from the reports of later authors, and from the short quotations contained in those reports. Our knowledge of Pre-Socratic philosophy is thus fragmentary, and the interpretation of those fragments is generally subject to scholarly controversy. Moreover, many Pre-Socratic opinions and theories were certainly primitive, ill informed, and simple minded. For all that, the Pre-Socratics are of primary importance to any student of Western intellectual progress: they first posed the questions which *Plato and *Aristotle later attempted to answer; and they thereby determined, indirectly, the whole course of Western science and philosophy. Above all, they began the tradition of rational enquiry which disdains any appeal to authority (whether human or divine) and which insists that observation and inference are the twin pillars of knowledge.

The Pre-Socratics were all polymaths, and their studies left few fields of human knowledge unsurveyed. They made precocious investigations into most of the issues which now fall under the heading of psychology or philosophy of mind: thus they discussed the nature of the 'soul' or *psyche and of the various psychological faculties; they developed theories of perception (see PERCEPTION: EARLY GREEK THEORIES) and of thought; they pored over the related phenomena of memory, dreaming, and sleep. Aristotle's pupil Theophrastus wrote a critical appreciation of Pre-Socratic theories of the mind: a large part of his book has survived, and it gives us some idea of the scope and detail of those early intellectual adventures.

The main Pre-Socratic thinkers were these (the dates are at best approximate): *Thales (620–550 BC), Anaximander (610–550), and Anaximenes (570–500)—all from Miletus in Asia Minor; *Pythagoras (570–500); *Heraclitus (540–480); Parmenides (520–430), and Melissus (480–420)—the 'Eleatics'; Anaxagoras (500–430); Empedocles (490–430); Democritus (460–370). Thales, the founder of Western thought, reflected on the nature of psyche, and argued that the magnet has a psyche (since it can initiate motion). Pythagoras advocated the doctrine of *metempsychosis. Heraclitus, an enigmatic thinker, avowed that the psyche was too profound to be fathomed by human thought—but he nevertheless offered certain speculations on its fiery nature. Empedocles and Democritus, the atomist, produced detailed theories of perception and of other psychological activities. Two minor figures deserve mention: Alcmaeon (510–440), a doctor, taught that the various sense modalities are unified in the brain, and he produced an argument, which Plato later adopted, for the immortality of the psyche. Philolaus (470–390), a follower of Pythagoras, suggested that the psyche is nothing more than an attunement or harmony of the body: a creature has a psyche (or: is alive) just so long as his physical constituents are harmoniously interrelated.

The fragments of the Pre-Socratics are translated in Jonathan Barnes's *Early Greek Philosophy* (1986); for discussion see Jonathan Barnes, *The Presocratic Philosophers* (2nd edn. 1982).   JBA

primate language. There are several historical attempts to teach our fellow animals human language, but until 1966 no such attempts yielded positive results. Then R. A. and B. T. Gardner, in extensive studies carried out in America, considered the possibility that, although primates might be unable to produce voluntary speech, perhaps they could learn to communicate by a human sign language. So they set out to teach an 11-month-old female chimpanzee—Washoe—the signs of American Sign Language (ASL).

After 51 months, Washoe had acquired 132 signs of ASL, being able to use them for indicating general classes as well as specific objects or events. Thus the sign for *dog* was used to refer to live dogs and pictures of dogs of many sizes, breeds, and colours, and for the sound of barking (Gardner and Gardner 1978: 38). She would use the signs spontaneously, and it was estimated that her use of combinations of signs was comparable to that of the early word combinations of human children. Washoe was brought up as nearly as possible in a child's environment, as the Gardners assumed that this would be conducive to human-like development and learning. So her days were like a child's, with baths, play, schooling, and outings to interesting places. She had furniture, toys, tools, a kitchen, a bedroom, and a bathroom. It should, however, be noted that ASL is constructed differently from spoken or written language—generally having larger 'units' of meaning, so direct comparison with a language such as English is not easy.

In 1972 the Gardners added four more young chimpanzees—Moja, Peli, Tatu, and Dar, who were only a few days old—to study signing *between* the chimpanzees. Washoe was nearly a year old at the beginning of her language learning, but the newcomers started a few days after birth: 'After seven months of exposure to the conditions of the project, her [Washoe's] vocabulary consisted of the signs, *come-gimme, more, up,* and *sweet.* By contrast, both Moja and Peli started to make recognizable signs when they were about three months old.'

For example, Moja's first four signs (*come-gimme, more, go,* and *drink*) appeared during her thirteenth week. The Gardners (1978) comment that though the acquisition of first signs for chimpanzees may seem early compared with children's first speech, this is not so for deaf children exposed to sign language from birth, for parents report that these deaf children's first signs appear between the fifth and sixth months.

The Gardners (1978) compared the five chimpanzees' 10-sign and 50-sign vocabulary acquisition with reports in the literature of hearing children's 10-word and 50-word acquisition: 'The age for ten-sign vocabulary was five months for Moja, Peli, and Tatu, and six months for Dar, but 25 months for Washoe; in the case of children, the age at ten words ranged from 13 to 19 months, with a mean of 15 months' (p. 50).

The Gardners report that the chimpanzees modified or extended their sign language, such as signing *tickle* on the hand of another chimpanzee, or a human, and sometimes giving an object to a human who is then expected to tickle the chimpanzee with the object. Eye gaze and facial expression are also important adjuncts to the signs, and may be used to distinguish between a declaration and an interrogation. Repetition is also used, for example when a sign is ignored.

A question had remained with regard to the Gardner project as to whether a chimpanzee could acquire ASL from another chimpanzee. The author's experiments, with Loulis, answered this question. The signs used by the humans were limited to seven: *who, what, where, want, which, name,* and *sign*. Apart from these, vocal English was used to communicate with Loulis, to ensure that he could not acquire extra signs from humans. These experiments found that the chimpanzees will communicate with each other, for not only had Loulis acquired signs from Washoe and the other signing chimpanzees with whom he lived, but Washoe and the other chimpanzees had acquired new signs from each other in their chimpanzee-to-chimpanzee signing conversations. Teaching was observed when Washoe demonstrated the chair sit to Loulis using a toy chair. Fouts (1994) made remote video recordings of the chimpanzees' conversations with no human present whatsoever. In randomly selected twenty-minute periods, she recorded 612 signs used in the chimpanzees' conversations with each other. The remote video recording technique is very effective at removing any possibility of the humans cueing or encouraging the chimpanzees to sign. In addition to conversations, Bodamer et al. (1994) used remote video recording to study private signing among the chimpanzees, when they sign to themselves, and Jensvold and Fouts (1993) used the technique to examine the imaginative use of signs during play by the chimpanzees.

Jensvold and Gardner (2000) tested the chimpanzees' conversational skills with an interlocutor responding to a chimpanzee signed utterance with one of four types of probes. When the interlocutor asked a general question, the chimpanzees frequently expanded their utterances across turns showing persistence in their original topic and giving the interlocutor more information. When the interlocutor asked a relevant on-topic question, the chimpanzees responded with many incorporations and expansions. These responses are indicators of topic maintenance. When the interlocutor asked an off-topic question, the chimpanzees often failed to respond and when they did respond they used few incorporations and expansions. When the interlocutor replied with a negative statement, Washoe and Dar often did not respond. The chimpanzees' responses were contingent and appropriate to the interlocutor's rejoinders and resembled patterns of conversation found in similar studies of human children.

Bodamer and Gardner (2002) systematically studied how the chimpanzees initiated conversations. The interlocutor sat in the workroom with his back toward the chimpanzees' enclosure. When the chimpanzee made a noise he turned and faced the chimpanzee immediately or after a 30-second delay. When the interlocutor was not facing the chimpanzees, they made noises, such as raspberries, and rarely signed. The few times the chimpanzees signed they used signs that made noise, such as DIRTY where the back of the hand hits the bottom of the jaw making a 'clacking' sound. In the delay condition the noises became louder and faster. Once the interlocutor faced the chimpanzees, they signed and stopped making sounds. Using a naturally occurring situation this experiment showed that chimpanzees initiate interactions and sign spontaneously.

Regardless of the continuity of the linguistic behaviours reported between chimpanzee and human language use, Cartesian linguists continue to insist that language is a uniquely human behaviour. Cartesian language theorists build their foundations on Chomsky's notion of the language 'organ', which is essentially a metaphor for the structures within the brain that facilitate speech (Chomsky 1975, Pinker 1994). By utilizing the concept of an organ, Cartesian linguists evoke an image of innateness for human language that has consequences as to how one views both the ontogeny and phylogeny of language development. For example, by viewing language as the function of an imagined organ, one can postulate that humans are born with language. This view eliminates the need for intermediate stages of grammar and proposes a distinct gap between lexical and grammatical aspects of language. A child according to this model only has to be exposed to language in order to acquire language and it leaves little room for diachronic language change between categories. There is no room in this view for interaction between language use and language form (Bybee, Perkins, and Pagliuca 1994) or for the social interaction between the child and her linguistic environment, which is necessary for language acquisition outside an idealized theoretical situation (Stokoe 1983).

The closest there is to a language organ that can currently be identified is a loose collection of areas within the brain which when damaged in adults result in similar language deficits. These structures have been synthesized into a neurological language-processing model by Geschwind (1970) that includes Broca's area in the frontal lobe, Wernicke's area in the temporal lobe, and the angular gyrus which acts as an intermediate between the visual cortex and Wernicke's area. Cartesian theories of language evolution predict that these areas are the result of a mutation that either produced or transformed them from a previous non-language function into a uniquely human language organ. However, far from being neuroanatomical adaptations exclusive to humans the components of Geschwind's model have been found in non-human primates.

Gannon et al. (1998) found asymmetries in the planum temporale part of Wernicke's area in the left hemisphere in seventeen of eighteen chimpanzee cadaver brains. These results and reports of asymmetries in the angular gyrus were later confirmed with the use of magnetic resonance imaging (MRI) (Hopkins et al. 1998). The comprehension of human speech by chimpanzees (Fouts, Chown, and Goodin 1976) suggests that these areas may also have a homologous function.

The functions of Wernicke's area are better examined when one removes the belief that language is a modular behaviour with language-specific structures. An early example of non-language functions within Geschwind's model came from research involving patients with left-hemisphere brain injuries specific to areas associated with language production. The injuries examined were similar to those that generated the proposed model. Besides language and speech production disabilities, difficulties consistent with sequential movements in general were found such as turning a knob followed by flipping a switch. They could however do repetitive hand movements and repeat single syllables (Kimura 1976). Bischoff-Grethe et al. (2000) found an effect of sequential predictability on the neural activity in Wernicke's area when subjects were presented with non-linguistic, sequential, visual patterns. These results were found whether the subject was made aware of the pattern or not. Thus the function of Wernicke's area is most likely not specific to language but is utilized for general pattern recognition and prediction as well. Both pattern recognition and prediction are traits central to the survival of most individuals regardless of their species.

The Cartesian linguists propose a hierarchical structure of language with discrete syntactic categories of lexicon and grammar, often represented by the familiar sentence tree. Empirical evidence on actual language use suggests otherwise and actually is more congruent with the functions of Wernicke's area. During language acquisition infants utilize predictive frequency of use to segment word boundaries. Predictive frequency also appears to be important when infants learn the grammar of artificial languages in experimental conditions (Gomez and Gerken 2000). Likewise similar transitional probability is proposed to be responsible for the phonetic reduction of frequent word constructions (Gregory et al. 1999). Such phonetic reduction in frequently occurring constructions often accompanies the semantic reduction that serves as a mechanism for the emergence of grammatical morphemes from lexical items (Bybee, Perkins, and Pagliuca 1994).

The importance of the cortical area homologous to Broca's area in non-human primates would not have been found if the importance of gesture to the evolution of language had not been recognized. Rizzolatti and Arbib

(1998) have reported that the rostral part of the ventral premotor cortex, area F5, in monkeys is active when they observe the motor behaviour of another monkey. Area F5 in monkeys is proposed to be homologous to Broca's area in humans and is also active when the monkeys perform manual actions. The neurons in area F5, *mirror neurons, appear to map the motor neurons that are active when one produces similar actions. In other words, neural activity in the mirror system fires in a way that is sympathetic to the action observed. This system is a neurological bridge between the receiver's perceptions and the sender's actions. What is remarkable about the mirror system is that different patterns of neural activity are observed for different actions. For example, the pattern of neural discharge in a monkey grasping a raisin or observing another grasp a raisin will be different from when observing or grasping a larger item or grasping at nothing at all.

Armstrong, Stokoe, and Wilcox (1994) illustrate how arm movements involved in visible gesture contain the framework on which grammar can be built. Since a gesture occurs in three-dimensional space, observation of directionality of a single sign can contain the syntax of an entire sentence. For example, the sign for 'catch' where the fist of one arm moves across the body and is caught by the other hand includes subject, verb, and direct object within a single icon.

Most of the natural gestures observed in chimpanzees and gorillas are representative of actions rather than objects (Tanner and Byrne 1996), and a gesture that represents an action carries with it an inherent actor. In addition, while most gestures can occur as simultaneous signals, gestures that include the serial motion mentioned above have an inherent sequential component (Wilcox 1997). Given the proposed function of Wernicke's area this sequentiality could be parsed into its components of the actor, the action, and the recipient of that action. In addition, the representation of movement in area F5 is more segmented into the component parts of grip, action, and object than the more global representations in other areas (Jeannerod et al. 1995).

Of the identified natural gestures of apes, many have the possibility of the standard noun/verb or actor/action sentence. One can also find an example of this theory in action, as well as its presence in our closest relatives. Rimpau, Gardner, and Gardner (1989) noted that the cross-fostered chimpanzee Dar placed signs such as BRUSH on himself and on another person to show who was to receive the action. Here we see a noun, a verb, and a direct object within the same gesture. It may be the case that language is indeed the function of a language organ, but one based on the social interaction of an actor and an observer—a 'language organ' that is not hardwired in humans alone for the purpose of a universal grammar, but rather in many other social animals for the adaptive purpose of understanding and predicting the actions of one another.   RSF/DF

Armstrong, D. F., Stokoe, W. C., and Wilcox, S. E. (1994). 'Signs of the origin of syntax'. *Current Anthropology*.

Bischoff-Grethe, A., Proper, S. M., Mao, H., Daniels, K. A., and Berns, G. S. (2000). 'Conscious and unconscious processing of nonverbal predictability in Wernicke's area'. *Journal of Neuroscience*.

Bodamer, M. D., and Gardner, R. A. (2002). 'How cross-fostered chimpanzees (*Pan troglodytes*) initiate and maintain conversations'. *Journal of Comparative Psychology*.

——Fouts, D. H., Fouts, R. S., and Jensvold, M. L. A. (1994). 'Functional analysis of chimpanzee (*Pan troglodytes*) private signing'. *Human Evolution*.

Bybee, J., Perkins, R., and Pagliuca, W. (1994). *The Evolution of Grammar: Tense, Aspect, and Modality in the Languages of the World*.

Chomsky, N. (1975). *Reflections on Language*.

Fouts, D. H. (1994). 'The use of remote video recording to study the use of American Sign by chimpanzees when no humans are present'. In Gardner, R. A., Gardner, B. T., Chiarelli, B., and Plooji, F. X. (eds.), *The Ethological Roots of Culture*.

——Chown, B., and Goodin, L. (1976). 'Transfer of signed responses in American Sign Language from vocal English stimuli to physical object stimuli by a chimpanzee (*Pan*)'. *Learning and Motivation*.

Gannon, P. J., Holloway, R. L., Broadfield, D. C., and Braun, A. R. (1998). 'Asymmetry of chimpanzee planum temporale: humanlike pattern of Wernicke's brain language area homologue'. *Science*.

Gardner, R. A., and Gardner, B. T. (1978). 'Comparative psychology and language acquisition'. *Annals of the New York Academy of Sciences*.

Geschwind, N. (1970). 'Organization of language and the brain'. *Science*.

Gomez, R. L., and Gerken, L. A. (2000). 'Infant artificial language learning and language acquisition'. *Trends in Cognitive Sciences*.

Gregory, M., Raymond, W. D., Bell, A., Fosler-Lussier, E., and Jurafsky, D. (1999). 'The effects of collocation strength and contextual predictability in lexical production'. *Proceedings of the Chicago Linguistic Society*.

Hopkins, W. D., Marino, L., Rilling, J. K., and MacGregor, L. A. (1998). 'Panum temporale asymmetries in great apes as revealed by magnetic resonance imaging (MRI)'. *NeuroReport*.

Jeannerod, M., Arbib, M. A., Rizzolatti, G., and Sakata, H. (1995). 'Grasping objects: the cortical mechanisms of visuomotor transformation'. *Trends in Neuroscience*.

Jensvold, M. L. A., and Fouts, R. S. (1993). 'Imaginary play in chimpanzees (*Pan troglodytes*)'. *Human Evolution*.

——and Gardner, R. A. (2000). 'Interactive use of sign language by cross-fostered chimpanzees (*Pan troglodytes*)'. *Journal of Comparative Psychology*.

Kimura, D. (1976). 'Neuromotor mechanisms in the evolution of human communication'. In Steklis, H. D., and Raleigh, M. J. (eds.), *Neurobiology of Social Communication in Primates*.

Pinker, S. (1994). *The Language Instinct: How the Mind Creates Language*.

Rimpau, J. B., Gardner, R. A., and Gardner, B. T. (1989). 'Expression of person, place, and instrument in ASL utterances of children and chimpanzees'. In Gardner, R. A., Gardner, B. T., and Van Cantfort, T. E. (eds.), *Teaching Sign Language to Chimpanzees*.

Rizzolatti, G., and Arbib, M. A. (1998). 'Language within our grasp'. *Trends in Neuroscience*.

Stokoe, W. C. (1983). 'Apes who sign and critics who don't'. In de Luce, J., and Wilder, H. (eds.), *Language in Primates: Perspectives and Implications*.

Tanner, J. E., and Byrne, R. W. (1996). 'Representation of action through iconic gesture in captive lowland gorilla'. *Current Anthropology*.

Wilcox, P. P. (1997). 'GIVE: Acts of giving in American Sign Language'. In Newman, J. (ed.), *The Linguistics of Giving*.

primates, evolution of the brain in. The earliest placental mammals were small, nocturnal, insectivorous animals that lived in the Cretaceous period more than 100 million years ago (Fig. 1). They possessed acute senses of smell and hearing and long, sensitive snouts bearing vibrissae. Their eyes were small, laterally directed, and possessed very limited acuity. Their brains were somewhat larger than those of similarly sized reptiles, but the neocortex, which was to become the great focus of mammalian brain evolution, had undergone only very limited development (Fig. 2). The telencephalon was largely devoted to the olfactory bulbs and olfactory cortex. The early placental mammals lived in a landscape dominated by reptiles, but this was to change radically with the massive extinctions that devastated the ranks of the reptiles at the end of the Cretaceous period. A host of theories has been advanced to explain the sudden extinctions. Perhaps the most compelling, because of its strong support from geophysical data, is the theory advanced by L. W.

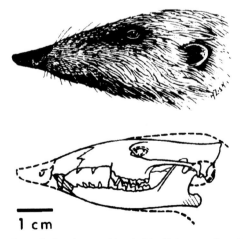

Fig. 1. Skull and restored head of the Cretaceous placental mammal *Zalambdalestes lechei*.

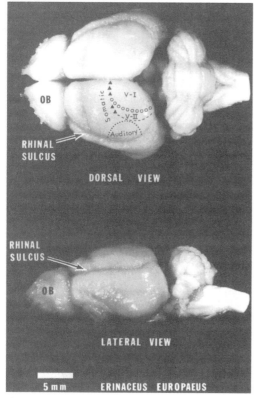

Fig. 2. Dorsal and lateral views of the brain of the European hedgehog (*Erinaceus europaeus*), a modern insectivore that has retained many features characteristic of the primitive placental mammals. The neocortex lies dorsal and medial to the rhinal sulcus. V-I, first visual area; V-II, second visual area. The circles indicate the representation of the vertical meridian (mid-line) of the visual field; the triangles indicate the representation of the far periphery of the contralateral half of the visual field. Note the large olfactory bulbs (OB). The cortex ventral to the rhinal sulcus is largely devoted to the processing of olfactory input.

Alvarez and his collaborators that a large asteroid struck the earth, resulting in the release of enormous quantities of dust into the atmosphere and thus a great reduction in sunlight reaching the earth's surface. The nocturnal, warm-blooded mammals would have been much better equipped for survival during a period of sudden climatic cooling than were their reptilian contemporaries. Whatever the cause, 65 million years ago at the beginning of the Cainozoic era, the 'age of mammals', a large number of ecological niches lay vacant that formerly had been occupied by reptiles.

During the next 10 million years the basal stock of placental mammals began to differentiate into the various orders of mammals. The fossil remains of the earliest primates that bear a close resemblance to living primates have been recovered from early Eocene deposits approximately 55 million years old. The skull and cranial endocast of one of these early primates, *Tetonius homunculus*, is illustrated in Fig. 3. *Tetonius* possessed large bony orbits that completely encircled its eyes, and a cranium containing a large brain compared with its similarly sized contemporaries. The relative size and position of the orbits in *Tetonius* closely resemble living nocturnal prosimians such as *Galago* (Fig. 4). As can be seen in Fig. 5, *Galago* possesses large, frontally directed eyes with virtually as much binocular overlap, in the order of 120–140 degrees, as is present in monkeys, apes, and man. The great similarity in the size and position of the orbits in *Galago* and *Tetonius* suggests that *Tetonius* also possessed large, frontally directed eyes and was crepuscular or nocturnal. The cranial endocasts of *Tetonius* and other Eocene primates show that their brains possessed a conspicuous enlargement of the neocortex in the occipital and temporal lobes, which in modern primates are known to be devoted mainly to the cortical processing of visual information (Fig. 4). Thus, by the early Eocene, there appeared in primates the concomitant development of large, frontally directed eyes with improved acuity and an expanded visual cortex. The sensitive snout of the primitive placental mammals was greatly reduced in the early primates. The functions of the snout as a tactile probe and an apprehender of insect prey were taken over by the hands. The olfactory system in the early primates retained a comparable degree of development to that present in the early placental mammals. The size of the olfactory bulbs did not diminish relative to body size, but the occipital and temporal neocortex expanded so greatly that the olfactory bulbs became small by comparison (see Figs. 2, 3, and 4).

These developments must reflect fundamental changes in ecological specialization that occurred in the evolutionary progression from the earliest placental mammals to the early primates. Two theories have recently been advanced to explain the basic adaptations that served to differentiate primates from the early placental mammals. In the first, R. D. Martin has suggested that the early primates, like the smaller living prosimians they closely resemble and the small arboreal marsupials of Australia and South America, adapted to a 'fine branch niche'; the prehensile hands and feet found in these animals developed to grasp the fine terminal branches of trees. Most arboreal mammals, such as squirrels, run on the trunk and larger branches but are unable to grasp the finer branches. The second theory is based on the observation that, outside the order Primates, animals with large frontally directed eyes (owls and felids) are nocturnal, visually directed predators, which has led M. Cartmill to propose that visually

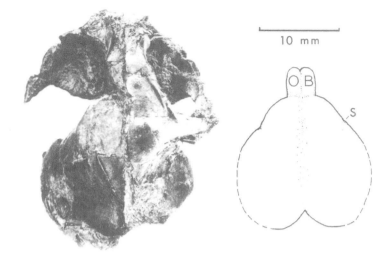

Fig. 3. *Left.* Dorsal view of the skull of *Tetonius homunculus*. (A.M.N.H. No. 4194.) *Right.* Dorsal view of L. B. Radinsky's cranial endocast of *Tetonius*. OB: olfactory bulbs. S: sylvian sulcus.

10 mm

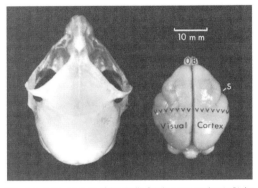

Fig. 4. *Left.* Dorsal view of the skull of *Galago senegalensis*. *Right.* Dorsal view of the brain of *Galago senegalensis*. The visual cortex corresponds to approximately the posterior half of the neocortex. The Vs demarcate the anterior border of visual cortex. OB: olfactory bulbs. S: sylvian sulcus.

Fig. 5. Close-up of the face of *Galago senegalensis*. Note the mid-line cleft in the upper lip, which is a feature present in all strepsirhine primates but absent in haplorhine primates.

directed predation was the ecological specialization responsible for the developments in the early primates. Cartmill's visual predation hypothesis is supported by the fact that the tarsier, the living primate that most resembles the early primates of the Eocene, is exclusively a predator (Fig. 6). It appears that both hypotheses have considerable merit. It seems probable that the early primates did invade the 'fine branch niche', where they gained access to a rich array of insect and small vertebrate prey.

What are the advantages that frontally directed eyes afford nocturnal, visually directed predators? Predators generally orient so that the prey is located in front of them so that they can propel themselves forward rapidly and carry out a coordinated attack with forelimbs and jaws, and it is likely that frontally directed eyes provide

maximal retinal image quality, for the central part of the visual field where the prey is located, in the crucial moments before the final strike is made. Image distortion tends to increase the further an object is located off the optical axis of the lens system, and thus it is advantageous to a visually directed predator to have frontally directed eyes in which the optical axes are directed toward the central part of the visual field, so that the predator can utilize the maximum-quality retinal image in the crucial moments before the strike, when it is evaluating the prey's movements, the prey's suitability as food, and the prey's ability to defend itself. The dimly illuminated nocturnal environment makes these optical factors particularly important, and rules out other mechanisms for improving retinal image quality such as stopping down lens aperture.

Fig. 6. Tarsier seizing a lizard. The tarsier is exclusively a predator; it eats no fruit or vegetable matter. Of the living primates, the tarsier most closely resembles the early primates living in the Eocene.

Frontally directed eyes also provide a large binocular field over which binocular summation can be achieved, which may be of particular value in conditions of low illumination. The binocular input is also used to reconstruct a *stereoscopic view of a large portion of the visual field. The advantages of stereoscopy to a predator are that it provides information about the distance of prey, and, as Bela Julesz has pointed out, it helps the predator to discriminate camouflaged prey from background.

Almost all of the distinctive features of the primate visual system relate to the frontal direction of the eyes and binocular integration and, since these features are present in all primates, it is likely that they developed in the early primates. These features include: (i) a high concentration of retinal ganglion cells in the central retina, and the greatly expanded representation of the central retina in the neural maps of the visual field in the brain; (ii) the representation restricted to the contralateral half of the visual field in each side of the optic tectum, differing from complete representation of the field of view of the contralateral retina found in each side of the optic tectum in all other vertebrates that have been investigated (Fig. 7); (iii) a relatively large retinotectal projection, which, together with the unique visuotopic organization found in the primate tectum, suggests that the optic tectum in the early primates developed capacities related to the integration of binocular input; (iv) a distinctly laminated dorsolateral geniculate nucleus in which inputs from the two retinae are brought into precise visuotopic register before being relayed to the primary visual cortex (VI); and (v) a greatly expanded visual cortex containing a number of neural maps of the visual field (see LOCALIZATION OF BRAIN FUNCTION AND CORTICAL MAPS).

Why does the visual cortex contain a series of separate representations of the visual field rather than a single map? In attempting to develop computer analogues of

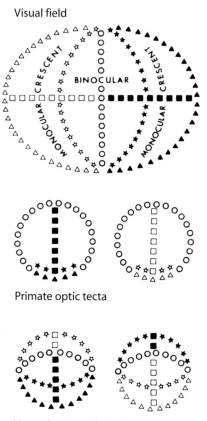

Fig. 7. Schematic plan of the representation of the visual field in the optic tectum of primates and non-primates. Circles indicate the vertical meridian (mid-line) dividing the two halves of the visual field; squares, the horizontal mid-line; triangles, the extreme periphery of the visual field; stars, the division between binocular and monocular portions of the visual field.

visual perception, David Marr elaborated the principle of modular design. Marr stated that any large computation should be broken into a collection of smaller modules as independent as possible from one another, otherwise, 'the process as a whole becomes extremely difficult to debug or improve, whether by a human designer or in the course of natural evolution, because a small change to improve one part has to be accompanied by many simultaneous changes elsewhere'. This modular principle has many counterparts in other biological systems. The palaeontologist W. K. Gregory noted that a common mechanism of evolution is the replication of body parts due to genetic mutation in a single generation which is then followed in subsequent generations by the gradual divergence of structure and functions of the duplicated parts. An analogous idea has been advanced by a number of geneticists. They have theorized that replicated genes escape the pressures of natural selection operating on the original gene, and thereby can accumulate mutations which enable the new gene, through changes in its DNA sequence, to encode for a novel protein capable of assuming new functions. Many clear-cut examples of gene replication have been discovered, and DNA sequence homologies in replicated genes have recently been established. Using this analogy, the author and J. H. Kaas have proposed that the replication of cortical sensory representations has provided the structures upon which new information-processing capabilities have developed in the course of evolution. Specifically, it has been argued that existing cortical areas, like genes, can undergo only limited changes and still perform the functions necessary for the animal's survival, but if a mutation occurs that results in the replication of a cortical area, then in subsequent generations the new area can eventually assume new functions through the mechanisms of natural selection while the original area continues to perform its functions.

The primary visual cortex (VI) and the adjacent second visual area (VII) are present in all mammalian species that have been investigated. Thus, VI and VII were probably present in the early placental mammals that were the common ancestors of the various living mammalian orders. The full complement of cortical visual areas varies in different mammals from a minimum of two in a basal insectivore, the hedgehog (see Fig. 2), to a maximum of twelve found in cats by Palmer, Tusa, and Rosenquist. At least nine cortical visual areas are present in the owl monkey, the primate that has been mapped most completely (Fig. 8). Beyond VI and VII it is very difficult to establish homologies among the visual areas present in mammals belonging to different orders. The last common ancestor of the different mammalian orders lived no more recently than the late Cretaceous period more than 65 million years ago, and this ancestral mammal had only a very limited development of its neocortex. In addition, the adaptive radiation of mammals into different ecological niches with widely divergent behavioural specializations serves to make very difficult the discovery of diagnostic similarities among potentially homologous cortical areas in different mammalian orders.

Within the order Primates, it is easier to determine homologous areas in different species. The highly distinctive middle temporal visual area (MT) is present in prosimians and in both New and Old World monkeys and thus probably existed in the early primates. MT neurons are selective for the direction of movement of visual stimuli and often are particularly responsive to moving fields of visual texture. MT may have developed as a specialized mechanism for detecting and tracking moving prey. MT may also participate in visuomotor coordination by analysing the visual flow patterns that the animal sees as it moves through its environment; MT projects via the pontine nuclei to the cerebellum, a major centre for the control of body and eye movements. The evolutionary development of this system may be related to the special demands of locomotion in the 'fine branch niche'.

The dorsolateral visual area (DL) lies adjacent to MT and also appears to be part of the basic complement of visual areas common to all living primates and thus probably existing in the early primates. In DL about 70 per cent of the neurons are selective for the spatial dimensions (length and width) of visual stimuli within excitatory receptive fields that generally are much larger than the preferred stimulus dimensions. The dimensional selectivity of DL neurons is independent of the sign of contrast in the receptive field, as they are equally selective to both light-on-dark and dark-on-light stimuli, the amount of contrast, and the position of the stimulus within the excitatory receptive field. It suggests that DL contributes to *form perception*. This hypothesis is consistent with the fact that DL, of all the visual areas, has the most expanded representation of the central visual field where the most acute recognition of form takes place, and with the discovery (by Weller and Kaas) that DL is the main source of input to the inferotemporal cortex (IT) has been strongly implicated in the analysis of complex visual stimuli and the learning of visual form discriminations.

The small amount of neocortex possessed by the early placental mammals and the great variation in the number of corticovisual areas reported for different mammalian species suggest that some of the areas beyond VI and VII developed at different stages in evolution and independently in different lines of descent. One clear example of variation within the order Primates is among the areas immediately anterior to VII. In the prosimian *Galago*, only one map of the visual field, the dorsal area (D), is located in the position occupied by three separate maps, M, DM, and DI, in the owl monkey (see Fig. 8). The existing data suggests that there exists a core of areas including VI, VII, MT, and DL and possibly one or two others that are common to all primates, but that there also exist areas present in some species but not in others. It is probable that each area performs a distinct set of functions in visual perception and visuomotor coordination, and that an area possessed by one species (or larger taxon) and not by another will endow its possessor with behavioural capacities not present in the other. A major task for the future will be to determine what are the distinctive functions of these cortical areas and how they relate to the behavioural and ecological specializations of their possessors.

The early primates probably were small nocturnal predators living in the fine branches; some primates

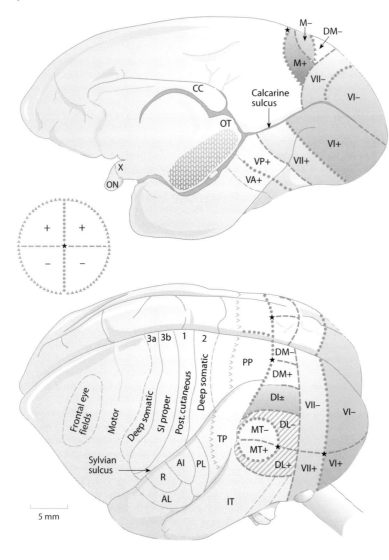

Fig. 8. The representations of the sensory domains in the cerebral cortex of the owl monkey. Above is a ventromedial view of the right hemisphere, below is a dorsolateral view of both hemispheres. On the left is a perimeter chart of the visual field. The symbols in this chart are superimposed on the surface of the visual cortex. Pluses indicate upper quadrant representations; minuses, lower quadrants. The row of Vs indicates the approximate border of visually responsive cortex. AI, first auditory area; AL, antero-lateral auditory area; CC, corpus callosum; DI, dorsointermediate visual area; DL, dorsolateral crescent visual area; DM, dorsomedial visual area; IT, inferotemporal cortex; M, medial visual area; MT, middle temporal visual area; ON, optic nerve; OT, optic tectum; PL, posterolateral auditory area; PP, posterior parietal cortex; R, rostral auditory area; VI, first visual area; VII, second visual area; VA, ventral anterior visual area; VP, ventral posterior visual area; X, optic chiasm. The main connections of the visual areas are as follows. VI projects to VII and MT. VII projects to DL, which in turn projects to IT. MT projects to all visual areas except VII and IT. MT and PP project to the frontal eye fields.

have retained this mode of life, but most have become larger, diurnal folivores or frugivores. Frugivorous diet is correlated positively with brain size and the amount of neocortex relative to body size in primates. This association between frugivorous diet and enlarged brain and neocortex may be related to the special demands imposed because a fruit eater's food supply is not constant, since different plants bear fruit at different times and at different locations in the complex matrix of the tropical forest. It is clear that an animal guided by memory of the locations of fruit-bearing trees can more efficiently exploit the available fruit resources than would be possible otherwise. Thus natural selection would have favoured the development in frugivorous primates of capacities for visuospatial memory, which may be localized in a particular area or set of areas.

Another, even more significant behavioural specialization is the development of complex systems of social organization in many primate species. The neural substrate for the mediation of social communication is bound to be an important focus of evolutionary change in the brains of primates. The order Primates is divided into the strepsirhines (lorises, lemurs, galagos), which tend to have relatively simple forms of social organization, and the haplorhines (tarsiers, monkeys, apes, and humans), in which social organization tends to be much more complex. In strepsirhines, as in most mammals, the rhinarium, the space between the upper lip and the nostrils, is furless, moist mucosal tissue that is tightly bound to the underlying maxillary bone and is divided along the midline by a deep cleft (see Fig. 5). Since strepsirhines share this type of rhinarium with most other mammals, it is very likely to have been the primitive condition in primates. By contrast, haplorhines possess a furry rhinarium and a mobile upper lip that is capable of participating in *facial expression. Strepsirhines, like most primitive mammals, have scent glands and scent-marking behaviours that play a very important role in their social communication, and, while haplorhines also use olfactory cues to some extent, they rely much more heavily on the use of visually perceived facial expressions and gestures, which allow much more rapid and subtle communication. Strepsirhines also tend to have much larger olfactory bulbs than do haplorhines. Thus it appears that, as complex systems of social organization evolved in haplorhine primates, social communication was increasingly mediated by the visual channel at the expense of the olfactory. One expression of this evolutionary development is the sensory input to the amygdala, which controls the neuroendocrine functions of the hypothalamus and thus emotion. Primitively, the main input to the amygdala was from the olfactory bulb, but in haplorhines the main input is from the temporal lobe and particularly from the inferotemporal cortex, which is a high-level processor of visual information. Neurons responsive to the specific configurations of faces have been recorded in the amygdala and temporal cortex. The clinical condition prosopagnosia, the inability to recognize familiar faces with relatively little impairment of other visual functions, which is usually associated with lesions located near the occipital temporal junction (see SPLIT-BRAIN AND THE MIND), suggests the development of a specialized system for processing the information in faces. Finally, in man, another system of social communication, language, has developed along with specialized cortical regions in the temporal and frontal lobes (see LANGUAGE AREAS IN THE BRAIN). JMA

Allman, J. M. (1977). 'Evolution of the visual system in the early primates'. In Sprague, J. M., and Epstein, A. M. (eds.), *Progress in Psychobiology and Physiological Psychology*, vol. vii.
—— (1998). *Evolving Brains*.

Cartmill, M. (1974). 'Rethinking primate origins'. *Science*, 184.
Clutton-Brock, T. H., and Harvey, P. H. (1980). 'Primates, brains and ecology'. *Journal of Zoology*, 190.
Gregory, W. K. (1951). *Evolution Emerging*.
Jerison, H. J. (1973). *Evolution of the Brain and Intelligence*.
Julesz, B. (1971). *Foundations of Cyclopean Perception*.
Martin, R. D. (1979). 'Phylogenetic aspects of prosimian behavior'. In Doyle, G. A., and Martin, R. D. (eds.), *The Study of Prosimian Behavior*.
Penfield, W., and Roberts, L. A. (1959). *Speech and Brain Mechanisms*.
Polyak, S. (1957). *Vertebrate Visual System*.
Radinsky, L. (1979). *The Fossil Record of Primate Brain Evolution*.

priming. In reacting to an object or stimulus we often benefit from previous exposure to the same or a related object. It is easier to identify a face, for instance, when that face has been encountered in the recent past. Such benefits in their various forms are referred to as manifestations of priming. The major distinction is between cases in which the same event is repeated (repetition priming) and ones in which benefits are induced by a different but related object or stimulus (e.g. semantic priming, phonological priming).

Repetition priming was first discovered in the context of measurements of the threshold for identifying visually presented words. If a word has been read a few minutes previously its threshold is markedly lowered. Hence repetition priming is a memory phenomenon whereby an initial encounter with an object leaves behind some influence on later performance. It is now known that priming effects can last for very long periods of time. It has been shown, for example, that a passage of typographically inverted text will be read faster if reading similarly inverted text was practised a year earlier, and moreover that this benefit is greatest when the same passage is repeated. Thus memory under these conditions seems to maintain a record of a far remote episode in which a particular passage was read in an unusual (inverted) type. Parallel results have been observed with other materials such as faces and pictures. When a person studies a picture on two separate occasions separated by several days, the pattern of their eye movements is characteristically different on the second compared to the first occasion.

Priming is detected even when the earlier exposure is not recollected. This observation suggests that priming and explicit recollection are distinct processes and there is indeed much evidence in support of this proposal. Numerous variables affect priming and explicit memory (e.g. recall, recognition) differently. As an example, depth of processing (thinking about an object's meaning versus making judgements about its perceptual qualities) has a substantial effect on measures of explicit memory but little effect on priming, whereas changes in modality between study and test have a substantial impact on priming but little effect on explicit memory. Even more striking is the fact that amnesic individuals whose ability to recall prior events is impaired may often show entirely normal levels of priming. This has suggested to some that different neural structures mediate priming and episodic memory, and consistent with this is the fact that brain-imaging and lesion studies have localized them to different brain systems: while episodic memory depends crucially on the medial temporal lobes, (visual) priming is often associated with more posterior sites such as the fusiform gyrus. However, there exists some controversy over whether distinct computational mechanisms are required to account for priming and other types of memory or whether they instead emerge from a unitary memory system which can be probed in different ways (see Schooler, Shiffrin, and Raaijmakers 2001).

What is the basis of the enduring influence of repetition in a priming task? One idea is that priming is simply the temporary activation of existing mental representations (e.g. word nodes) but the fact that priming can last over periods of months or even years and that it can occur for novel stimuli argues against such an explanation. More plausible is the notion that the initial presentation of a stimulus is encoded in long-term memory, for instance as a set of tiny weight changes in the connections in a distributed system, and that these changes can influence later processing of the same stimulus in a small but none the less detectable way. Brain-imaging and electrophysiological studies have revealed a phenomenon called *repetition suppression* whereby the second occurrence of a stimulus evokes less brain activation than the first. This suppression, which is especially marked for familiar as opposed to unfamiliar stimuli, appears to be the functional basis of priming and is consistent with an enduring facilitation in processing a stimulus as a result of long-term learning.

In contrast to repetition priming, which can be very long-lasting, semantic priming is usually much more short-lived. In a typical procedure, a person reads a pair of words such as *rake–leaf* which appear in succession with a brief interval between them. The first word does not require any response but the second requires a lexical decision (i.e. is it a word or a non-word?) or has to be named. Numerous experiments have shown that such decisions are speeded up if the first, prime, word is semantically related to the second, target, word. However this form of priming is disrupted or even abolished when the interval between the words is longer than one or two seconds or if other events intervene. Semantic priming can be observed when the prime–target interval is very brief (e.g. 250 milliseconds), suggesting that the effect can be automatic and outside voluntary control. When the interval is longer (e.g. 500 milliseconds) patterns of priming effects

are somewhat different from those observed at shorter intervals and suggest a role for a second mechanism based on conscious expectancies.

Semantic priming has been used extensively as a means of drawing inferences about the way in which semantic and conceptual knowledge is organized. For example, it has been used to monitor the longitudinal loss of semantic knowledge in people developing dementia. Much of this work is driven by the assumption that semantic priming is attributable to the automatic spreading of activation between concepts, but this view has been questioned. There is little direct evidence of spreading activation. More recent models have viewed semantic priming, like repetition priming, as being based on long-term learning.

Both semantic and repetition priming appear to occur subliminally, that is, when the initial event is too brief to be consciously perceived, although few issues in experimental psychology have proven so controversial. In one example, Dehaene et al. (1998) flashed number words (e.g. six) very briefly prior to digits (e.g. 3) and participants were simply asked to decide whether the digit was greater or less than 5. Dehaene et al. found that these decisions were speeded if the number word fell on the same side of 5 as the digit and were slowed if it fell on the opposite side, even when the number word prime was not consciously visible. The neural basis of this unconscious priming effect was in the motor cortex, suggesting that the prime activated a motor response which could either facilitate or inhibit responding to the digit depending on whether it fell on the same side of 5 or not. Hence the subliminal prime triggered essentially the same stream of perceptual, semantic, and motor processes as a consciously perceived stimulus.   DRS

Dehaene, S., et al. (1998). 'Imaging unconscious semantic priming'. *Nature*, 395.

Schooler, L. J., Shiffrin, R. M., and Raaijmakers, J. G. W. (2001). 'A Bayesian model for implicit effects in perceptual identification'. *Psychological Review*, 108.

problems: their appeal. People enjoy the mental stimulation of a good problem, and for some it becomes a powerful need—a cerebral restlessness epitomized in fiction by Sherlock Holmes. It makes little odds whether the problem is trivial or profound, vague or precise, so long as it tempts us to resolve a state of puzzlement or contradiction. Harlow, Harlow, and Meyer (1950) have shown that even monkeys spend considerable time in the manipulation of puzzles, without any extrinsic reward, when left to their own devices. Does curiosity constitute a biological need? White (1959) and Berlyne (1971) have developed the theory that one reason for seeking the stimulation of novelty is to ward off boredom. The challenge of the problematic is manifested in a wide variety of forms, and here we contrast the response to two problem situations of a very different kind in order to see what they have in common.

The solution to a formal problem generally demands the postulation of a hypothesis, the assumption that something is true without knowing whether it is true. Its consequences can then be tested to see whether they fit the facts. The following is a very precise problem which critically requires this ability (Wason 1977). (For a fascinating development of this problem, see Smyth and Clark 1986.) If the individual does not think about it hypothetically he finds himself in a looking-glass world where everything seems the wrong way round.

In front of you imagine four designs made up of two colours and two shapes:

Blue diamond
Red diamond
Blue circle
Red circle

The problem is this: 'In these designs there is a particular shape and a particular colour such that any of the designs which has one, and only one, of these features is called a THOG. If the *blue diamond* is a THOG, could any of the other designs be a THOG?'

The problem hardly seems difficult. The *red circle* obviously could not be a THOG, and the other two could be THOGS because each has one feature of the *blue diamond*. That is the common-sense solution and it is wrong; it is the mirror image of the correct solution. If the *blue diamond* is a THOG, then the *red circle* is a THOG, and neither the *blue circle* nor the *red diamond* could be a THOG.

There is more than one path to the solution, but the following one is probably the clearest. Postulate a hypothesis about the pairs of features consistent with the *blue diamond* being a THOG. It could not be ['blue' and 'diamond'] and it could not be ['red' and 'circle']. These hypotheses have both, or neither, of the features contained in the *blue diamond*, and the problem states that a THOG has just one. Try ['blue' and 'circle'] as a candidate. It would stop the *blue circle* being a THOG (it has both features) and also the *red diamond* (it has neither feature), but it would make the *red circle* a THOG because 'circle' is one of its features. The only other hypothesis compatible with the blue diamond being a THOG is ['red' and 'diamond']. By the same argument it would rule out both the *red diamond* and the *blue circle* but it also would make the *red circle* a THOG because 'red' is one of its features. The solution is rather elusive because the reasoner has to keep clear the distinction between the designs and the features that constitute them.

Elsie Mimikos showed that students with a science education do better on this problem than students with an arts education. A subsequent experiment convincingly replicated this result. Twenty-five out of 32 science graduates solved it compared with only three out of 32 arts graduates. It would seem that the precise hypothetical thinking which is involved may be alien for the latter group, although there is no imputation that the problem is in any way a test of intelligence.

The formal elegance of the 'thog problem' prevents it from resembling most of the problems we encounter in daily life. It tests a highly specific skill—that is all. Problems do not generally come like this, in neatly packaged form. They have to be discovered, and it is difficult to investigate this process experimentally. Moreover, the problems used by the psychologist to study thinking usually have one right answer. In real life problems are seldom like this; they have many different grades of adequate answer. Art, furthermore, provides a realm in which problems do not have right answers at all. It may be objected that this is to stretch the meaning of the word 'problem' metaphorically, but artists (and poets) do often discuss their work in these terms.

In a unique longitudinal study of artistic creativity, Getzels and Csikszentmihalyi (1976) were struck by the fact that students of fine art seemed primarily motivated by self-discovery. It might be expected that they would discuss the rewards of the artist in aesthetic terms, in terms of 'beauty', 'harmony', or the creation of 'order'. Instead they talked about them much more in terms of 'discovery' and 'understanding', and this suggested that their work was structured around 'discovered problem situations'. The investigators developed an ingenious technique to test this idea. Thirty-one fine-art students were asked to compose a still-life drawing based on a selection from a number of objects which were placed on an adjacent table. The first task of each student was to choose some of these objects, and arrange them on another table to form the subject of his composition. The investigators made the assumption that the choice of objects corresponded to a 'problem-finding' stage. They observed the number of objects chosen, the way in which the student explored and handled them, and their uniqueness, i.e. the extent to which each had been chosen by the other students. These indices were assumed to reflect the characteristic ways in which a person approaches an unstructured aesthetic task. They were used to test the hypothesis that individuals who considered more problematic elements, explored problematic elements more thoroughly, and selected the less common among them would formulate a visual problem which would result in a more original drawing. Five art critics, who knew nothing about the experiment, then independently rated each drawing for originality, aesthetic value, and craftsmanship. The main result confirmed the prediction. The problem-finding process results in drawings which are judged to be more original, but not necessarily of higher craftsmanship. In fact, the correlation between the problem-finding scores and 'originality' was highly significant.

This result is really surprising: the quality of the final product is related to behaviour *before* the drawing started. It was corroborated by subsequent interviews. Those artists who stated that when they started to work they had no clear idea about what they would do produced drawings which were highly rated for aesthetic value and originality; those who stated they already had a problem in mind when they approached the task were rated low on the same dimensions. It was corroborated by measures of time taken during the experiment. The only such measure significantly related to the quality of the drawings was time spent in choosing objects, as opposed to time spent in arranging or drawing them.

In science the result would hardly be surprising because its theories are based on explicitly formulated problems, while the products of art are based on the attempt to come to grips with unformulated private problems. Copernicus's questioning of the common-sense observation that the sun revolves around the earth was also highly original. But in the long run his doubts would have had no more value than a delusion had they not also been shown to be true. After problems have been discovered in science the testing of possible solutions can proceed deductively in order to see whether they can be falsified. It is precisely this ability which the 'thog problem' attempts to catch in a small way. A scientist would probably regard it as trivial because skill in solving it involves no imagination. And yet this skill involves an analysis of the structure behind the surface of things. Without it, a person finds the solution incredible in its outrageous assault on common sense—the *red circle* has *nothing* in common with the *blue diamond*. How different it is from the production of a work of art subject only to aesthetic appraisal! We should not allow the difference to conceal a more fundamental similarity. In both science and art the individual is driven by an insatiable curiosity which refuses to accept things as they are, and which forces us to think about them in a new way. The origin of this curiosity is manifest in the appeal which artificial problems exert upon us. PCW

Berlyne, D. E. (1971). *Aesthetics and Psychobiology*.

Getzels, J. W., and Csikszentmihalyi, M. (1976). *The Creative Vision: A Longitudinal Study of Problem-Finding in Art*.

Harlow, H. F., Harlow, M. K., and Meyer, D. R. (1950). 'Learning motivated by a manipulation drive'. *Journal of Experimental Psychology*, 40.

Smyth, M. M., and Clark, S. E. (1986). 'My half-sister is a THOG: strategic processes in a reasoning task'. *British Journal of Psychology*, 77.

Wason, P. C. (1977). 'Self-contradictions'. In Johnson-Laird, P. N., and Wason, P. C. (eds.), *Thinking: Readings in Cognitive Science*.

White, R. W. (1959). 'Motivation reconsidered: the concept of competence'. *Psychological Review*, 66.

problem solving. A great deal of the art of problem solving is to understand the kind of question that is posed and the kind of answer that is demanded. It is for this reason that psychologists prefer problems with unique solutions, and that they try to ensure that individuals understand what they have to solve.

There are several theoretical points of view about problem solving, but none is really complete because each tends to be restricted to different problem domains, and there is little definitive agreement about what constitutes a problem. The *Gestalt theorists (e.g. Wertheimer 1969) believed that a problem occurs because of the way in which a situation is initially perceived, and that its solution emerges suddenly from reorganizing it in such a way that its real structure becomes apparent. On the other hand, many contemporary psychologists have been impressed by ideas borrowed from research on *artificial intelligence. They conceive of the mind as analogous to a computer program which operates in discrete steps ('information processing') to reduce the difference between existing states and 'subgoals'. Their pioneering efforts were devoted mainly to a small number of computable games and puzzles, and they were not deterred by the fact that early computer programs played poor chess. See Newell and Simon (1972), and, for criticism, Dreyfus (1972) and Weizenbaum (1976); and COMPUTER CHESS for recent improvements. For an account of the fundamental difficulties of computer chess, see Hartson and Wason (1983: ch. 6). My own interest has been to devise problems in which the initial response may ensnare the capacity to see the point.

The difficulty of writing about problem solving is that one may either insult the reader's intelligence, or create states of frustration. Hence I shall not report the solution to my first problem. Instead I shall take the reader by the hand (if he will pardon the condescension) and ask him to solve with me two related, simplified problems. These may alter the way in which he conceived the original problem. Of course, he may find the first problem trivial, but then I hope his boredom will be alleviated by the knowledge that others find it rather puzzling. I could say a lot more at this point, but that would be to lay all my cards on the table. Consider the first problem.

Problem 1 I formulated this problem in 1966, and the present version was devised for the 1977 Science Museum Explorations Exhibition in London. Earlier versions contained some confusing features. The problem is generally known as 'the selection task'.

You are shown a panel of four cards, A, B, C, D (Fig. 1), together with the following instructions:

Which of the hidden parts of these cards do you *need* to see in order to answer the following question decisively? FOR THESE CARDS IS IT TRUE THAT IF THERE IS A CIRCLE ON THE LEFT THERE

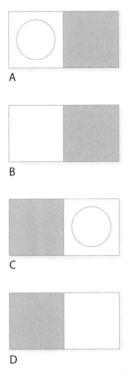

A

B

C

D

Fig. 1. Problem 1: the Science Museum Problem.

Fig. 2. Problem 2.

IS A CIRCLE ON THE RIGHT? You have only *one* opportunity to make this decision; you must not assume that you can inspect cards one at a time. Name those cards which it is absolutely necessary to see.

Please record your solution, and then consider the next problem.

Problem 2 This problem is based on Johnson-Laird and Wason (1970). A more recent, intensive investigation of the issues may be found in Wason and Green (1984). In front of you are two boxes, one labelled 'white' and the other labelled 'black' (Fig. 2). There are fifteen white shapes in the white box and fifteen black shapes in the black box, and the only shapes are triangles and circles. Your problem is to prove the following sentence true, as economically as possible, by requesting to inspect shapes from either box: IF THEY ARE TRIANGLES, THEN THEY ARE BLACK.

The students who were tested in this experiment tended to ask first of all for a black shape—they were handed a black triangle. The task turned out to be fairly easy; on average only six black shapes were requested. Of course, when individuals asked for a white shape they were always handed a white circle. Somebody in my class said recently: 'The best strategy is to alternate your

choices between the two boxes.' This would have been a perverse strategy, especially if one were to apply it consistently by exhausting the contents of both boxes. In fact, insight came rapidly, and all the individuals exhausted the supply of fifteen white circles, and requested no more than nine black shapes. Moreover, they tended to do so with a broad grin, as if they had penetrated a secret, or seen the point of a joke. In order to prove the truth of the sentence 'If they are triangles, then they are black', it is merely necessary to establish the absence of a white triangle. The contents of the black box are gratuitous.

What is the connection between problems 1 and 2? In the first place, problem 2 is concerned only with half the amount of information in problem 1. In problem 2 no decision has to be made about 'triangles' and 'circles' which corresponds to the presence and absence of a 'circle on the left'. Secondly, problem 1 involves a single and ultimate decision for its solution, but problem 2 involves a series of decisions so that an earlier error can be corrected. Thirdly, problem 2 involves a number of concrete objects rather than the consideration of symbols positioned on cards.

Are you still satisfied with your solution to problem 1?

Problem 3 This problem is based on Wason and Shapiro (1971). There are four cards on the table in front of you, showing (respectively) 'Manchester', 'Leeds', 'Train', 'Car' (Fig. 3). The students who were tested in this experiment had first of all examined a larger set of cards (from which these four had been selected), each of which had on one side a town (e.g. Chicago), and on the other side a mode of transport (e.g. aeroplane). They had been asked to satisfy themselves that this condition obtained on every card. The four cards were then placed on the table, and the individuals were instructed to imagine that each represented a journey made by the experimenter. They were then presented with the experimenter's claim about her journeys: EVERY TIME I GO TO MANCHESTER I TRAVEL BY TRAIN.

The problem is to state which cards need to be turned over in order to determine whether this claim is true or false. The solution is 'Manchester' and 'Car' because only 'Manchester' associated with a transport other than 'Train', or 'Car' associated with 'Manchester', would disprove the claim. This thematic problem proved much easier than a standard, abstract version which was structurally equivalent to problem 1. However, later attempts to replicate this effect have not been at all clear. For a general discussion, see Griggs (1983).

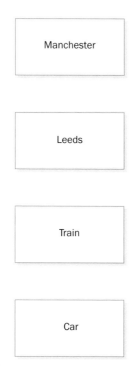

Fig. 3. Problem 3.

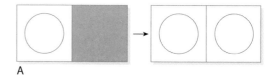

A

'What does this tell you about the answer to the question?' ('For these cards is it true that if there is a circle on the left there is a circle on the right?') Everybody said that this told them the answer is 'yes'.

Then the card, corresponding to D, which nearly everyone had (wrongly) omitted, would have been revealed thus:

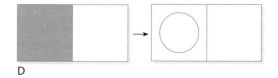

D

Conflict: a card which had been chosen allowed the answer 'yes', but now a card which had been ignored indubitably forces the answer 'no'. The majority of individuals remained unmoved—they refused at this point to incorporate D into their solution. When prompted, they made remarks like, 'It's got nothing to do with it', and 'It doesn't matter'. All the available evidence is present, but the correction tends not to be made.

We went on informally to discuss the potential consequences of B and C which were never fully revealed. B had nearly always been omitted (rightly) and C selected (wrongly).

'Can you say anything about the answer from this card [B]?':

'It's got nothing to do with it because there's no circle [on the left].'

'Can you say anything about the answer from this card [C]?':

'There has to be a circle under it for the answer to be "yes".'

What is the connection between problems 1 and 3? In both a single decision has to be made about four cards, so in this sense they are both unlike problem 2. But in problem 3 the cards are not simply cards. They represent four different journeys and their two sides are connected intrinsically in this respect. This means that the material of the problem is intimately related to experience, and the solution can be guided by it. For a more detailed account of these, and similar, experiments see Wason and Johnson-Laird (1972).

Still happy about the solution to problem 1? If it did cause any difficulties, it seems fairly likely that any error will now have been corrected because that particular problem has been broken down into two much simpler ones, each of which eases the original burden of thought. But suppose, just for the sake of argument, that the solution to problem 1 is still wrong—for instance, it might be cards A and C. In the original experiments based on it I devised therapies which induced contradictions between the first attempted solution and a subsequent evaluation of the material. The card, corresponding to A, which everybody had (rightly) selected, would have been revealed thus:

'What if there is no circle?'

'Then the answer would be "no".'

What could be the selfsame card has a different meaning according to whether it had been selected initially. The individual is confronted with the possibility of both cards being like this:

But only when this contingency derives from C is it assumed (wrongly) to be informative. It is evidently the individual's intention to select a card which confers meaning on it.

Reality, for the individuals who made these kinds of error, is determined by their own thought. That is not, perhaps, surprising. What is very surprising is that this reality is so recalcitrant to correction. See Wason (1977) for further discussion. For a recent and much more comprehensive account of the issues raised by this problem, see Wason (1983). It is as if the attention mobilized in the initial decision is divided from their subsequent attention to facts, or possibilities. The solution, cards A and D, is systematically evaded in ways which are not yet properly understood. There is even the finding that the origin of the difficulty might arise through differences in the functioning of the two hemispheres of the normal brain. When corrective feedback is induced in the left ('analytic') hemisphere it is more effective than when it is induced in the right ('synthetic') hemisphere.

Our basic paradigm (problem 1) has the enormous advantage of being artificial and novel; in these studies we are not interested in everyday thought, but in the kind of thinking which occurs when there is minimal meaning in the things around us. On a much smaller scale, what do our students' remarks remind us of in real life? They are like saying 'Of course, the earth is flat', 'Of course, we are descended from Adam and Eve', 'Of course, space has nothing to do with time'. The old ways of seeing things now look like absurd prejudices, but our highly intelligent student volunteers display analogous miniature prejudices when their premature conclusions are challenged by the facts. As Kuhn (1962) has shown, the old paradigms do not yield in the face of a few counter-examples. In the same way, our volunteers do not often accommodate their thought to new observations, even those governed by logical necessity, in a deceptive problem situation. They will frequently deny the facts, or contradict themselves, rather than shift their frame of reference.

Other treatments and interpretations of problem solving could have been cited. For instance, most problems studied by psychologists create a sense of perplexity rather than a specious answer. But the present interpretation, in terms of the development of dogma and its resistance to truth, reveals the interest and excitement generated by research in this area.　　　　PCW

Dreyfus, H. L. (1972). *What Computers Can't Do*.

Griggs, R. A. (1983). 'The role of problem content in the selection task and in the THOG problem'. In Evans, J. St B. T. (ed.), *Thinking and Reasoning: Psychological Approaches*.

Hartston, W. R., and Wason, P. C. (1983). *The Psychology of Chess*.

Johnson-Laird, P. N., and Wason, P. C. (1970). 'Insight into a logical relation'. *Quarterly Journal of Experimental Psychology*, 22.

Kuhn, T. S. (1962). *The Structure of Scientific Revolutions*.

Newell, A., and Simon, H. A. (1972). *Human Problem Solving*.

Wason, P. C. (1977). 'Self-contradictions'. In Johnson-Laird, P. N., and Wason, P. C. (eds.), *Thinking: Readings in Cognitive Science*.

——(1983). 'Realism and rationality in the selection task'. In Evans, J. St B. T. (ed.), *Thinking and Reasoning: Psychological Approaches*.

——and Green, D. W. (1984). 'Reasoning and mental representation'. *Quarterly Journal of Experimental Psychology*, 36.

——and Johnson-Laird, P. N. (1972). *Psychology of Reasoning: Structure and Content*.

——and Shapiro, D. (1971). 'Natural and contrived experience in a reasoning problem'. *Quarterly Journal of Experimental Psychology*, 23.

Weizenbaum, J. (1976). *Computer Power and Human Reason*.

Wertheimer, M. (1969). *Productive Thinking*.

programs and planning. It is safe to predict that concepts of computation will play an increasing role in the articulation of theories of the mind. Here we introduce the basic notion of a 'program' which underlies computation and relates it to the mental activity of planning. It is emphasized that computer science is an evolving subject, and that the analysis of mental activity is feeding back into computer science to yield notions of programs of increasing subtlety and flexibility.

A program for an ordinary electronic computer executes one instruction at a time: to transfer inputs to memory, to combine pieces of data, to control output devices, and—crucially—to choose the next instruction on the basis of a test. Because of these tests, the 'overt behaviour' of the program—the temporal sequence of reading of inputs and emission of output values—will depend on both the input values and data values already stored internally. This dependence yields the basic logical property of *algorithms: a program can be specified in a form shorter than any normal execution upon particular data.

By contrast, normal English usage often takes 'preprogrammed' as a synonym for 'stereotyped', and for many people, the word 'program' is synonymous with the notion of a 'fixed sequence', so that each fixed behavioural sequence is a different program. However, for the computer scientist, it is the program that provides the formal description of the process which generates different output sequences on the basis of differing values of inputs and internal parameters. To take a simple example, consider a man walking to the door. Depending on where he starts, his overt behaviour might require three steps or 30—and each such sequence would constitute a 'program' in the fixed-sequence sense. But it seems more insightful to hypothesize that a single program in the computer scientist's sense underlies all these behaviours. In one formalism, we might represent it as:

do *advance one step* until *door is reached*.

(This can be recognized as a notational variant of the TOTE unit—test–operate–test–exit—of Miller, Galanter, and Pribram 1960: 26.) Here we explain all behaviours of the class in terms of a program with one action, *advance one step*, whose execution is repeated under the control of a single test, *is door reached?*

If we regard this program as a hypothesis about human behaviour, we turn attention from the release of patterns with fixed numbers of steps to the study of ways in which perceptual mechanisms testing *is door reached?* may 'gate' motor mechanisms. At a simple level, such 'gating' differs little from negative *feedback, but when we move to planning behaviour in a complex environment, the loops within loops seem to call for the richer vocabulary that computer science can help to provide. We turn then to a look at this vocabulary.

For certain motor tasks, a sufficiently high-level choice of strategy need not involve specification of the details of execution at the muscular level. For example, *Lashley (1929: 137) notes that animals which have learned a maze prior to injuries to the motor system continue to traverse it, although muscular activity may be changed completely—one animal had to roll over completely in making each turn, yet made no errors in traversing the maze. Again, in writing a word, we use a completely different set of muscles, depending on whether the instrument available is a pencil or whether it is a paintbrush on the end of a long pole. How is it that we can still produce our characteristic mode of writing with these two different systems? Computer scientists find it expedient to program a computer not in the machine language that directly controls the basic operations of its machinery but rather in terms of some high-level language. They provide the computer with a translation program called an 'interpreter' that will enable the computer to translate each instruction from the high-level program and then execute it. In much computing, the process of translation is relatively straightforward—multiplication of matrices, or sorting a sequence of numbers into a histogram, can be carried out by standard procedures which (once the size of the matrices or the length of the sequence is given) do not depend on the idiosyncrasies of the situation. However, the study within AI (*artificial intelligence) of *planning*—

programming a computer to go from goal specifications to a plan for achieving the goals—may be viewed as the study of *context-dependent* translation. Consider, for example, our program above as one way of compiling the higher-level instruction *go to the door*. Such a compilation is appropriate only if the system is facing the door and there are no obstacles en route. Otherwise, the position of the 'organism' and the layout of obstacles within the room must be taken into account in determining a path.

We shall illustrate the AI approach to high-level planning of movement by considering a mobile robot equipped with a television camera and wheels. The planning problem for this robot enables it to respond to a command such as 'Push the large cube to the door' by (i) forming a plan that will take it to the cube without bumping into obstacles, and then will allow it to push the cube to the door without bumping into obstacles; and, then, (ii) executing the plan. A separate problem, then, is the design of a visual system to locate the obstacles.

To simplify the planning problem for the mobile robot, we may schematize its task as that of selecting a number of intermediate points (called nodes) to pass through in sequence, en route to its goal. A path is then a trajectory that links up these nodes in order. Clearly, the nodes must be so chosen that, in moving from one point to the next, the robot does not bump into any obstacle. When given a task specified in a high-level language, the robot must find a path that achieves the task and that is also, ideally, as short as possible.

The simplest form of this problem is to find the shortest path from one specified place to another. What makes the problem interesting is that the space may be so complicated that it is impossible to consider all alternatives. Instead, workers in AI have sought ways to 'grow' paths, considering for each point along a possible trajectory a limited number of candidates for the next segment. It should be emphasized that this process of path growing is made within the computer during the *planning* stage. At the completion of this path-growing process, a single path results, and it is this that directs the actual movement of the robot. In most AI research projects, all relevant details about the 'search space' are represented in the 'internal model' within the computer. In biological organisms, the internal model is only approximate, and sensory input must be used in model updating and, where necessary, replanning. In building on such AI approaches to model the neural control of movement in animals and to build more adaptable robots, we study the extent to which planning and execution would be interwoven within the action—perception cycle (see SCHEMAS).

In 1966 Doran and Michie proposed a path-growing program that used the idea of a *heuristic distance*, which is defined as an indication, rather than a guaranteed measure, of distance to the goal. For example, the straight-line distance is a heuristic distance for the real distance when one avoids the obstacles. The Doran–Michie approach proceeds by exploring alternative paths, giving first preference to the exploration of paths whose next node has the least heuristic distance to the goal node. However, while this algorithm always yields a path from the start node (which represents where the system is) to the goal node (which represents where the system is to be), it cannot be guaranteed that the path obtained is the shortest. This problem was overcome in 1968 by Hart, Nilsson, and Raphael, who developed an algorithm that gave first preference to the exploration of paths whose next node had a minimal sum of distance already traversed from the start node plus heuristic distance to the goal node.

In later work, Fikes, Hart, and Nilsson studied generalized robot plans. Very briefly, the idea is to store information about the changes in the relationship between the robot and the environment brought about by a sequence of actions that are part of a successful plan. As time goes by, and other plans are made, various constants within both the sequence of operations and the prescription of its effects are replaced by variables, in such a way that the robot has available a number of MACROPs: high-level operations that will let it meet many familiar planning problems. Sacerdoti has built on this study to define a problem solver called ABSTRIPS, which uses planning in a hierarchy of abstraction spaces. It usually proves far more efficient to plan the overall stages of a series of movements, and then refine the plan with greater and greater detail, making modifications only when necessary, than to grow the overall plan step by step, with each step defined at the lowest level. The importance of these studies is clear. The first shows how AI provides techniques which we may refine into a theory of 'learning from experience'. The second gives us a clue as to how to analyse the relation between a 'plan' in its colloquial sense of a high-level 'strategic' specification of a course of action, and the detailed step-by-step unfolding of that action when the plan is executed.

With those programs written by AI researchers to explicitly embody aspects of the planning process, we are well on our way to an even more abstract type of program —a *program synthesizer*, which takes as its input samples of behaviour (e.g. input–output relations) and generates programs that can yield this type of behaviour. In fact, we may regard the generation of MACROPs as an example of program synthesis. To summarize, then, we have the following levels of program sophistication. (i) Straight-line program: executing a fixed predetermined sequence. (ii) Program: executing a sequence of actions whose composition may depend on on-line testing of internal and external values. (iii) Planning (= context-dependent interpretation): knowing what to do, in general terms, to find a solution tailored to the current situation. (iv) Program synthesis from examples: starts by finding out what is the problem to be solved.

Yet another style of programming comes with the study of *concurrent programming*, stimulated by the technological concern with playing out computation over a network of concurrently active, communicating computers. In brain theory and AI we speak of *cooperative computation*. A classic example in brain theory is the Kilmer–McCulloch model (1968) of the reticular formation of the brain as a set of interacting modules that could reach a global consensus without any single module having executive control. To put the AI problem in picturesque terms, consider that you have a library of books, and need to get the references to solve a problem. The cooperative computation approach is the analogue of having each book become an *active* process, with the books responding to user questions, and 'talking' to each other, until they agree on what is required. Arbib and Caplan (1979) have analysed the relevance of such techniques to the study of language mechanisms in the human brain.

And this is only the beginning of the evolution of computing concepts relevant to the construction of theories of mind and brain.   MAA

Arbib, M. A., and Caplan, D. (1979). 'Neurolinguistics must be computational'. *Behavioral and Brain Sciences*, 2.

Kilmer, W. L., McCulloch, W. S., and Blum, J. (1968). 'Some mechanisms for a theory of the reticular formation'. In Mesarovic, M. (ed.), *Systems Theory and Biology*.

Lashley, K. S. (1929). *Brain Mechanisms and Intelligence*.

Miller, G. A., Galanter, E., and Pribram, K. H. (1960). *Plans and the Structure of Behavior*.

projective techniques. These derive their name from the psychoanalytic concept of *projection*, the mechanism whereby psychological states or processes in the self are seen as pertaining to an object in the outside world. Projection is most commonly regarded as a defence mechanism, a means whereby the *ego protects itself from anxiety, associated with unpleasant or unacceptable thoughts and feelings, by attributing them to others. This aspect of projection, however, is not part of the rationale of projective techniques, which can be used without necessarily accepting the tenets of psychoanalytic theory. A more helpful definition of projection in this context is the process whereby the individual 'projects' something of himself or herself into everything he or she does, in line with Gordon Allport's concept of expressive behaviour. The aim of projective techniques is, then, to provide stimuli or situations, to which variations in response may be interpreted in accordance with a set of rules.

The two best-known projective techniques are the *Rorschach ink-blots and the thematic apperception test (TAT).

The Rorschach test consists of a series of ten symmetrical ink-blots, five in black and white, and five introducing colour. The subject is asked to report what he or she sees in each blot in turn; at the end of the series an 'enquiry' allows for clarification of the responses. Responses are classified within each of three 'scoring' categories: *location*, *determinants*, and *content*. *Location* refers to how much and which part of the blot area has been used; *determinants* to the structural qualities, namely form (shape), colour, shading, and inferred movement; *content* to the types of object seen, with particular emphasis on human, animal, and anatomical percepts. Total incidence of each type of response is noted, and various ratios and percentages calculated. Traditionally considerable importance is attached to scoring, but recently there has been a move towards increased interest in content, treated in the same way as other material obtained in clinical interview.

Material for the TAT, devised by the American psychologist H. A. Murray as an adjunct to his 'need-press' theory of motivation, consists of black-and-white pictures representing personal and interpersonal situations, the subject being required to make up a story about each in turn. In its original form the test is administered individually, in two series of ten pictures each; the response is given orally, with provision for prompting, if required. More recently there has been a trend towards a single shorter series and group administration with written response; non-standard pictures are also sometimes used. Since relatively little importance is attached to formal scoring, such flexibility is permissible, and indeed thematic apperception is probably best regarded as designating a group of procedures rather than a specific test.

Murray's own system of analysis rests on his concepts of *need*, a hypothetical force or process in the organism, and *press*, a force or other element in the environment which activates a need in the perceiver. Incidence of the expression of need and press variables, as well as others, such as 'outcome', in the subject's TAT material may be compared with norms, which will obviously vary with populations and circumstances of testing. For this reason, among others, many users of the TAT prefer to use systems of analysis which they consider better suited to the purpose in hand.

Other projective methods include word association (in which the subject speaks or writes the first word that comes to mind in response to a stimulus word), sentence completion, and various 'activity' methods, principally drawing (most commonly of the human figure) and structured play, as in the sand-tray procedures familiar in child guidance and child psychiatry settings.

In all of these, as well as in the Rorschach and the TAT, it is possible to achieve some measure of quantification of the data, and so to claim that measurement has taken place. Measurement, however, is not a primary concern of projective psychology, a fact reflected in the choice of the term 'techniques' rather than 'tests' in the title of this entry. Interpretative hypotheses are, of course, attached to Rorschach variables, and to other projective 'indicators'. In some cases, as in the formulation of a set of 'signs' of brain damage, criteria for validation are available, and would appear, in that particular case, to have been met. In others, particularly when a form of response relates to experience rather than to behaviour, demonstration of validity presents more serious problems. In the cognate field of reliability, test–retest reliability presupposes personality to be static, and in statistical terms can be applied only to single-category scores, whereas the projective standpoint has always been that a protocol must be interpreted as a whole.

Attempts to make projective testing conform to psychometric standards have in general met with relatively little success; many projectivists indeed believe that such an aim is illusory. Projective techniques are properly regarded as an aid to, rather than an instrument of, diagnosis or other decision-making process. They may be found useful in counselling, in psychotherapy, particularly of the type known as client centred, and in some forms of personnel selection—in short, in any situation in which 'understanding' is regarded as relevant.   BSE

Gregory, R. L. (2000). 'Reversing Rorschach'. *Nature*, 6773.

Leichtman, M. (1996). *The Rorschach: A Developmental Perspective*.

Rorschach, H. (1921). 'Psychodiagnostics: a diagnostic test based on perception'. In *Hermann Rorschach Psychodiagnostics* (2nd edn.). Trans. P. Lamkau and B. Kronenberg.

proprioception. Positions of the limbs are continuously signalled to the central nervous system, angles of the joints, and tension of the muscles, by specialized receptors. All this vitally important 'internal perception'—called proprioception—goes on without consciousness.

psyche. The Greek word *psyche*, from which our terms 'the psyche' and 'psychology' derive, is generally translated as 'soul', but the translation is in several respects misleading. *Psyche* is intimately connected to the notion of life: all and only living things possess a psyche; and to have a psyche is to be alive. (To have a psyche is to be *empsuchos*, and *empsuchos* is appropriately translated by 'animate'. Note that 'animate' derives from the Latin *anima*, which, like *psyche*, is conventionally Englished as 'soul'.) Thus a psyche is a principle of life, or an 'animator'. In addition, a psyche is a principle of individuality for living things; that is to say, anything that possesses my psyche is the very same living thing as I am—Socrates and Socrates' psyche are identical. The psyche, in sum, is the living self.

Different Greek thinkers offered different accounts of the nature of *psyche*: most of the *Pre-Socratic philosophers were materialists, primitive or sophisticated—they held that psyche was a special portion of air or fire, or perhaps a special parcel of particles or atoms. *Plato supposed that the psyche was an entity quite distinct from such crass corporeal stuffs: his view of the nature of *psyche* is comparable to *Descartes' notion of the soul as a separate spiritual substance.

Of all Greek theories, that of *Aristotle is the most refined (though some of its features are anticipated in Philolaus' doctrine that the psyche is an attunement). Aristotle offers two connected definitions of *psyche*. The first, couched in the terminology of his metaphysics, runs thus: 'If we are to say something which applies in common to every psyche, it will be the first actuality of a natural organic body.' (Roughly speaking, he means that to have a psyche is to be a natural body, equipped with the organs of life, and capable of functioning.) His second definition reads as follows: 'A psyche is a principle of the aforesaid things [i.e. of the various faculties of living things] and is defined by them—by the faculties of nutrition, perception, thought, and motion.' (Roughly: to have a psyche is to be capable of self-nourishment—including growth and reproduction—of perception, of thought, and of independent motion; or, rather, to have a psyche is to have at least some of those capacities.)

Aristotle's first definition emphasizes the connection between *psyche* and the body; his second definition indicates the existence of interdependent psychic 'parts' or faculties—and those faculties, in Aristotle's view, turn out to be hierarchically ordered. Both definitions fit well with Aristotle's predominantly biological and physiological approach to the notion of *psyche* (though it is a celebrated and perplexing aspect of his psychology that thinking, or some special type of thinking, is to some extent untouched by corporeal contamination).

In one important respect at least, the Greek notion of 'psychology' is strikingly different from the modern notion. For the Greeks, all living things, including plants and the lower animals, have, by definition, a psyche, so that the general study of 'psychology' will aspire to give a unified account of all that distinguishes animate from inanimate objects. Modern psychologists may be said, at the risk of oversimplification, to deal with 'the mind': for the Greeks, the primary distinction is between what is alive and what is not alive (and the primary problem is the connection between living and non-living matter); for the moderns, the primary distinction is between what possesses mind and what does not (and the primary problem is the connection between 'the mental' and 'the physical'). Despite that fundamental difference, the particular problems discussed by ancient psychologists frequently overlap with those of their modern successors; but the difference is significant—and it prompts an intriguing question: did the ancient Greeks hit upon a more fruitful

and unitary way than ours for tackling the problems of the mind? JBA

psychiatry. Psychiatry applies knowledge from the biological and social sciences, e.g. genetics, pharmacology, and psychology, to the care and treatment of patients suffering from disorders of mental activity and behaviour. It emerged as a branch of medicine in the first half of the 19th century when some of those kept under social control for the protection of society in workhouses and other institutions were recognized as curable, i.e. susceptible to moral treatment, or requiring the firm although therapeutic use of restraint, and as lying therefore within the province of medicine. One of its first tasks was to classify mental disorders. After the First World War its practice, hitherto based in Britain on the county *asylums, was extended, although still based on the hospital services, to provide treatment for those living in the community and suffering from disorders not requiring admission to hospital. The term, usually restricted in Britain to the work of suitably qualified medical practitioners, is used more widely in North America to cover the work of other mental-health professions such as clinical psychology and psychotherapy. DRD

Bynum, W. F., Porter, R., and Shepherd, M. (eds.) (1985). *The Anatomy of Madness: Essays in the History of Psychiatry*, 2 vols.
Doerner, K. (1981). *Madmen and the Bourgeoisie: A Social History of Insanity and Psychiatry*.

psychoanalysis. During the last years of the 19th century *Freud gave up the use of hypnotism, because its effects proved capricious and encouraged dependency, and developed a new method, which he referred to at first as psychical analysis. This method, which relies on the interpretation, or analysis, of what a patient says or omits to say, while freely associating under instruction to report his thoughts without reservation, is the essence of what became the specialized form of psychotherapy known as psychoanalysis (see also FREE ASSOCIATION). The first volume of papers on psychoanalysis, *Studies in Hysteria*, published in 1895, brought together a series of case histories, including that of Fräulein Anna O., which have subsequently been much discussed, an account of a new method of examining and treating hysterical phenomena and of the 'cathartic method', and some 'theoretical reflections', which introduced the concepts of unconscious ideas, ideas inadmissible to consciousness, and splitting of the mind. (For a discussion of the Anna O. case history, see BREUER, JOSEPH.)

Freud immediately applied his new method to the study of dreams, and published in 1900 an account of his analysis of his own dreams in *The Interpretation of Dreams*, which he came to regard as his most important book. 'Insight such as this', he remarked, 'falls to one's lot but once in a lifetime.' It presented the concepts that became the essence of a comprehensive theory of mental life: the meaningfulness of seemingly chaotic and absurd mental activity, wish-fulfilment, the *Oedipus complex, infantile sexuality, regression, the *unconscious, resistance, *repression, defence, projection, and symbolism, as well as the similarities of dreams and mental disorders. The decisive step lay in the demonstration that phenomena which might be dismissed as accidental, capricious, or meaningless products of disorder in the brain can be explained by reference to past experience and the motives revealed by psychoanalysis. He elaborated on the essential concepts in *Introductory Lectures on Psychoanalysis* (1922).

Freud gathered round him in Vienna a group of colleagues who shared his views and who published accounts of their own experiences in psychoanalytic practice. There were notable defections: Alfred *Adler in 1911, who led the development of 'individual psychology', and Carl Gustav *Jung in 1913, who led the development of 'analytic psychology'. The Clark Lectures in 1909 in America by Freud and Jung brought psychoanalysis to the notice of the English-speaking world, but psychoanalysis did not become widely known in England until the 1920s. It then aroused as much interest among scholars in the humanities as among physicians. In the 1920s and 1930s Freud examined civilization, religion, and literature in the light of the findings of psychoanalysis.

Psychoanalysis was dominated in its early development by the biological ideas of the time, e.g. the derivation of energy from instincts. The shift in emphasis, starting in the 1930s, from biological or intrapsychic, to social or interpersonal, processes and object relations, and from the origins of symptoms to those circumstances of the 'here-and-now' determining their persistence, reduced greatly the differences in method and theory from other schools of psychotherapy, from which, however, psychoanalysts still maintain their independence.

Since it requires several sessions a week over two or three years with a trained therapist, psychoanalysis is a lengthy and therefore expensive form of treatment that is available to few patients. Its effectiveness is open to question. Its original purpose was to circumvent the resistances to the recall of the painful experiences thought to underlie *neurosis. Later, greater importance was attached to the transference of feelings into the relationship with the therapist. There has been little systematic research to evaluate the benefits achieved in these ways. Comparisons made of the effects on symptoms and attitudes produced by psychoanalysis with those produced in other ways have so far proved controversial and inconclusive.   DRD

Clark, R. W. (1980). *Freud: The Man and the Cause.*
Eysenck, H. J. (1985). *Decline and Fall of the Freudian Empire.*
Fisher, S. (1978). *The Scientific Evaluation of Freud's Theories and Therapy: A Book of Readings.*
Freud, S. (1973–85). Pelican Freud Library: *1. Introductory Lectures on Psychoanalysis; 3. Studies on Hysteria; 4. The Interpretation of Dreams; 12. Civilisation, Society and Religion; 14. Art and Literature.*
—— and Young-Bruehl, E. (1990). *Freud on Women: A Reader.*
Jones, E. (1961). *The Life and Work of Sigmund Freud* (abridged edn.).
—— (1964). *The Life and Work of Sigmund Freud.*
Roazen, P. (1974). *Freud and his Followers.*
Wyss, D. (1966). *Depth Psychology: A Critical History, Development, Problems, Crises.*

psychokinesis (PK). Psychokinesis refers to the possibility that a person may be able to affect a physical event or situation by mental influence alone. Research into the possible existence of such 'mind over matter' has employed a wide range of methods and generated a huge amount of controversy. One strand of the work has examined individuals claiming to be able to produce directly observable PK effects, such as levitation, materializations, and the movement of large objects (often referred to as 'macro-PK'). Many of these demonstrations were popular around the turn of the last century, and often produced by mediums during seances. However, many argued that the conditions associated with seances (e.g. semi- or complete darkness, expectation) rendered it impossible to know whether the phenomena were genuine, or were the result of self-deception, misreporting, and trickery (Brandon 1983). More recent macro-PK claims have included metal bending and 'thoughtography' (wherein an individual's thoughts allegedly appear as images on photographic film). However, the conditions under which these phenomena have been demonstrated have again been questioned by many sceptics (including several well-known magicians), and are thus frequently the subject of fierce debate (see Beloff 1993 for a review). Some researchers have also examined the possible existence of much weaker effects that are demonstrable only via statistical analyses. This type of work, typically referred to as 'micro-PK', might involve asking participants to will dice to land with certain numbers facing upwards, or to influence an electronic random event generator (REG) to produce a certain type of output. This work has shifted the study of PK away from the seance room and into the scientific laboratory. As a result, the findings are not open to many of the criticisms that have been aimed at demonstrations of alleged macro-PK. Proponents of micro-PK argue that the combined results of many well-controlled studies support the existence of some form of anomalous, paranormal, effect (see, e.g. Radin 1997). However, critics have argued against this conclusion, often questioning the validity of the research on grounds of procedure, statistics and replication rates (see, e.g. Alcock 1990). A final strand of work has examined the possible effect of mental intention on various forms of biological systems, including, for example, plants, insects, and humans. Again, proponents of this work argue that the research suggests the existence of a genuine paranormal effect, and sometimes use the work to support the efficacy of distant healing and prayer. However, sceptics have noted that this form of PK research is relatively recent, and thus has not been subjected to sufficiently rigorous examination to allow firm conclusions to be drawn from the existing database.

RW

Alcock, J. E. (1990). *Science and Supernature: A Critical Appraisal of Parapsychology*.
Beloff, J. (1993). *Parapsychology: A Concise History*.
Brandon, R. (1983). *The Spiritualists*.
Radin, D. (1997). *The Conscious Universe*.

psychology. *Psyche, personified by the ancient Greeks as the goddess loved by Eros, means breath and hence soul or mind. Psychology, when introduced as a term in the 18th century, described the branch of philosophy covering the study of the phenomena of mental life, i.e. what is perceived, through *introspection, as taking place in the mind, and of such activities as perceiving (see PERCEP-TION), *remembering, *thinking, and reasoning.

'The science of mental life, both of its phenomena and their conditions' was William *James's definition. The strength of his classic *The Principles of Psychology*, published in 1890, lies in its descriptions, as the result of 'looking into our minds and reporting what we there discover', of 'feelings, desires, cognitions, reasonings, decisions and the like'. For half a century *The Principles* provided much of the material for textbooks such as R. S. *Woodworth's *Psychology: The Study of Mental Life*, which went on into the 1950s as a standard text. The main chapters of contemporary texts are still about perceiving, remembering, thinking and language, and concepts and reasoning, as well as emotions, needs, and motives, learning, coping behaviour, and conflicts, skills, and attitudes and beliefs in relation to social and cultural factors.

Herbert *Spencer had given in 1874 a wider definition of 'objective psychology', which he said forms with physiology the two subdivisions of zoology, this and botany being the two divisions of biology. Objective psychology 'deals with those functions of the neuromuscular apparatus by which organisms are enabled to adjust inner to outer relations' and includes 'the study of the same functions as externally manifested in conduct'. 'Subjective' psychology 'deals with the sensations, perceptions, ideas, emotions, and volitions that are the direct or indirect concomitants of this visible adjustment of inner to outer relations'.

Spencer and James both struggled with the ancient problem of the relation between *mind and body. James accepted dualism as a stratagem, not as a conviction. Certain mental processes cannot be reduced to physical processes, he insisted, otherwise there would be no science of psychology. 'When the brain acts a thought occurs.' 'Mental phenomena lead to bodily processes.' 'No mental modification ever occurs that is not accompanied or followed by a bodily change.' Contemporary explanations in psychology sometimes reduce the phenomenon or the behaviour to what is regarded as the essential physiological or biochemical process; more often they relate it to the conditions or the contexts in which it occurs or to the system of which it is a part.

In James's time there were turning points in the development of several branches of psychology. Wilhelm *Wundt had founded in 1875 the first laboratory devoted to the experimental study of sensation, memory, and learning. Francis *Galton's *Inquiries into Human Faculty*, first published in 1883, had opened up the study of individual differences in mental functions. Lloyd *Morgan's *Animal Life and Intelligence*, published in 1890, and E. L. *Thorndike's *Animal Intelligence*, published in 1911, pioneered comparative studies of learning. Studies of the effects of lesions of the brain on mental functions were being pioneered by David *Ferrier, Herman Munk, and Hughlings *Jackson. *Psychoanalysis with its concept of the unconscious was just over the horizon.

Soon after James's death in 1910, attention was drawn away from his work by the emergence of several confident schools, particularly *behaviourism, physiological psychology, *Gestalt psychology, psychoanalysis, purposivism (see MCDOUGALL, WILLIAM; PURPOSE), factor analysis (see SPEARMAN, CHARLES EDWARD), and *ethology. Behaviourism especially narrowed the definition of psychology so as to exclude subjective psychology, on the grounds, based on a narrow definition of science, that the phenomena of mental life are not susceptible to scientific study—that is, psychology should restrict itself to the study of those aspects of behaviour that can be directly observed and measured or graded.

For nearly half a century few scholars, except in the older universities in Britain, engaged with the formidable problems of method in psychology, which James had admitted could be no more than the hope of a science. Interest in mental phenomena revived again in the 1960s, partly as a result of the emergence of schools of *phenomenology, such as *Husserl's.

The meaning given to the term psychology changed gradually, first to insist that the study should be systematic, observations being made under prearranged conditions that allow reliable conclusions to be drawn, and, secondly, to include the responses of the subject to external events or stimuli, whether these occur naturally or are manipulated by an experimenter. Interest grew, under the influence of Kenneth *Craik, in an interactional approach, in which behaviour is seen as exchanges between man and machine or man and man (see CYBERNETICS,

HISTORY OF). The dividing line between objective and subjective psychology became blurred.

In most universities there is now a department of psychology, in which an assortment of research methods is applied in the study of the behaviour, including the mental activity, of intact organisms, humankind especially. Comparative studies of the behaviour of animals (see ETHOLOGY) are shared with the department of zoology. The psychology department is likely to have a place in the faculty of science, with links with other departments of biology, with which it shares work on the physiological mechanisms of behaviour, in the faculty of social sciences, in which it shares work on the behaviour of individuals in social groups, in the faculty of education, in which it shares work on mental development and learning processes in childhood, and in the faculty of medicine, in which its work lies in applications in the diagnosis and care and treatment of the sick.

It is one of several branches of science applied in *psychiatry to the care and treatment of the mentally disordered. Psychopathology is the branch of psychology that seeks to explain disorders of mental activity and behaviour in terms of psychological processes, whereas neurology and *neuropsychology relate them to the site, extent, and character of faults in the structure or function of the central *nervous system. Psychology contributes to many other branches of knowledge, among them, in the faculty of engineering, to *ergonomics, and especially AI (*artificial intelligence). Also, in the faculty of law, *criminology. Since the 1920s, students of the humanities, such as literary critics and historians, have increasingly turned for their interpretations to psychological and, especially, psychoanalytic theories. DRD

psychometric testing. Psychometrics is the science of psychological assessment. The scientific testing of human abilities and characteristics began with the Chan dynasty in ancient China when the emperor introduced a system of assessment for the promotion of civil servants (Wainer 2000). It was recognized that a few measures taken over a short period of time were able to predict future behaviour. Subsequent influences arose from the development of psychiatry and psychophysics in the 19th century, culminating in the seminal work of Francis *Galton, often considered the father of psychometrics. Galton initiated psychometric testing as we know it today, and with his colleagues Karl Pearson, James McKeen *Cattell, and Charles *Spearman, developed the statistical techniques of correlation and factor analysis that form the backbone of psychometric procedures. A major influence in the 20th century was the growth of compulsory education. Alfred *Binet developed the first intelligence tests in Paris in 1904 to identify learning difficulties in French schoolchildren.

Today the Binet scales still play an important role in the work of educational psychologists.

Psychometric tests can be divided into two broad categories: knowledge based and person based (Rust and Golombok 1999). Tests of ability, aptitude, attainment, competence, and achievement are examples of the former, while tests of personality, clinical symptoms, mood, integrity, interests, and attitude typify the latter. A major difference between the two is that knowledge-based tests have right and wrong answers, while person-based tests differentiate different types of individual. Within knowledge-based testing, tests of general intelligence have largely given way to tests of specific abilities. For example, occupational psychologists use tests of clerical aptitude, computing skills, and numerical and verbal reasoning, all of which assess particular abilities that have relevance to different types of work. Educational psychologists and speech and language therapists use tests that assess dyslexia, language impairment, and other forms of educational underachievement. Clinical psychologists have a special interest in neuropsychological tests of cognitive functioning such as memory and abstract thinking that affect our ability to carry out everyday tasks.

Psychometric personality testing began in earnest when factor analytic techniques were applied to Galton's lexical hypothesis, i.e. the view that all varieties of human personality can be found in everyday speech. Examples include words such as lively, anxious, conventional, conscientious, and kind. Today, this approach is epitomized by the Five Factor Model, which has established through factor analysis that the five traits of extroversion, neuroticism, openness-to-experience, agreeableness, and conscientiousness underlie individual differences in personality (McCrae and Costa 2003). Some psychometric models of personality are more theory driven than others. H. J. Eysenck's approach, for example, was based on the classical theory of *Galen who believed that there were four types of individual: the phlegmatic, the choleric, the sanguine, and the melancholic. Eysenck recast these four types as two independent dimensions of extroversion and neuroticism. Other psychometric tests take their inspiration from the work of psychoanalysts such as Sigmund *Freud and Karl *Jung. One problem for all personality tests is that of lying or 'faking good', and much effort is put into test construction today to circumvent this tendency.

There are four basic scientific principles that underpin psychometric testing and psychometric test development. These are reliability, validity, standardization, and bias (Anastasi and Urbina 1997). Reliability is the extent to which an assessment is free from error. The reliability of a rating scale, for example, can be assessed by looking at the correlation between the ratings given by two independent raters, or the same test may be given to the same set of individuals on two separate occasions and their scores correlated. Reliable tests should generally have a correlation of about 0.70 or higher. Validity is the degree to which an assessment is able to achieve its purpose. Thus, if the purpose of a test is to select high-performing computer programmers for an IT company, we would need some independent verification that those individuals who achieve high scores on the test actually do demonstrate superior programming skills once they are employed. Standardization provides the benchmark against which an individual may be assessed and can be either criterion or norm based. In a criterion-referenced test, the scores should relate directly to the individual's competencies, for example, whether or not a child has reached a particular standard of reading. Criterion referencing is the form of standardization favoured within educational settings. A norm-referenced test compares the score of an individual on a test with the scores of other individuals who have taken the test. This other group of individuals is called the norm group, and has to be specifically chosen to be appropriate to the situation. For example, when using a critical reasoning test to select managers, the norms should be derived from the scores of other managerial candidates on the same test. Sometimes the norm group may be a whole population, as, for example, with the Wechsler Intelligence Scale for Children (WISC), where the score of a particular 7-year-old child can be compared with the scores of a representative sample of the whole population of 7-year-olds in the country. Identification and reduction of bias in assessment, particularly in terms of gender, race, and disability, are a legal requirement within an equal opportunities society. The reduction of such bias is an important part of psychometric test development, although it is often found that differences between groups in test scores, when they occur, are a result of inequalities in society rather than of bias in the tests themselves.

Today, psychometric testing is arguably the area of psychology that has the widest application. Over 70 per cent of human resource departments in leading companies use psychometric testing, and most of us can expect to be tested at least once in our working lives. Because psychometrics is such a powerful tool it is essential that it is applied responsibly. Today, the British Psychological Society and the American Psychological Association, as well as psychometric test publishers, lay down specific guidelines for the development of psychometric tests and their application.   JR

Anastasi, A., and Urbina, S. (1997). *Psychological Testing* (7th edn.).
McCrae, R., and Costa, P. (2003). *Personality in Adulthood: A Five-Factor Theory Perspective.*
Rust, J., and Golombok, S. (1999). *Modern Psychometrics* (2nd edn.).
Wainer, H. (2000). *Computer Adaptive Testing: A Primer* (2nd edn.).

psychopathic personality. Strictly speaking, this term should be applied to all varieties of abnormal personality (see PERSONALITY DISORDER). Schneider (1958) defined the psychopathic personality as an abnormal personality who either suffers because of his abnormality or makes the community suffer because of it. In the UK and the USA greater emphasis has been placed on the second part of this definition, mainly because of the frequent involvement of such persons in breaches of the law. American authors prefer the terms 'sociopath' and 'antisocial psychopath' which more clearly define the individual by virtue of his criminal propensities. In the UK, before the Mental Health Act of 1959 the psychopath was an entity unrecognized by law, but the Act defined psychopathic disorder as 'a persistent disorder or disability of mind (whether or not including subnormality of intelligence) which results in abnormally aggressive or seriously irresponsible conduct on the part of the patient, and requires or is susceptible to medical treatment'. Although a good deal of controversy surrounds the last seven words of this definition, quite clearly the Act considered psychopathic disorder to be a form of mental illness. If such a person is 'ill'—and he would be the last person so to regard himself—it is up to the medical profession to treat him. The Mental Health Act of 1983 apparently recognizes the questionable value of medical treatment, as the phrase is omitted from its definition of psychopathic disorder. None the less, the term stays under the general heading of mental disorder.

Numerous attempts have been made to identify the principal characteristics of the psychopath. The term in a general sense is often applied to adolescent or young adult males who appear unable to conform to the rules of society. The qualities of this sort of person's psychological make-up include an inability to tolerate minor frustrations, an incapacity for forming stable human relationships, a failure to learn from past experiences, however unpleasant they might have been, and a tendency to act impulsively or recklessly. Henderson (1939), in a well-known essay on the subject, divided psychopathic personalities into three categories: the predominantly inadequate, the predominantly aggressive, and the creative. They are by no means mutually exclusive but, whereas the first two have gained general acceptance and receive more psychiatric attention, far less has been heard about the creative psychopath, whose sometimes erratic behaviour may seem less significant than the creations of his fertile imagination. He is less likely to come before the courts or to the attention of the mental health services, for his eccentricities are not usually regarded as indicative of mental disorder.

The question of whether, in the long run, psychopaths do learn from experience was considered in a follow-up study of children who showed persistent antisocial behaviour in St Louis (Robins 1966). Of those who survived—there was a high mortality from accidents, suicide, and alcoholism—a significant number appeared to be keeping out of trouble by middle life, finding that relative conformity was preferable to constant conflict with society and the law. Whether maturation or learning from experience was the more responsible for this beneficial change is uncertain, but it does appear that some so-called antisocial psychopaths do ultimately learn to mend their ways. There was little evidence that medical treatment had made much contribution to this outcome.

It is often said—erroneously as it happens—that our present-day concept of psychopathic personality originates from the introduction of the diagnosis of moral insanity into English medical and legal theory and practice by J. C. Prichard, a Bristol physician, in 1835. At the time, Prichard and many others were considerably influenced by *Gall's writings on *phrenology which localized human propensities to specific parts of the brain. Among these propensities was included the moral faculty, and it was widely assumed that moral insanity was caused by a derangement of that part of the brain concerned with making a choice between good and evil. Prichard, however, was using the term 'moral insanity' to denote emotional disturbances—delusions and hallucinations—that were devoid of the usual hallmarks of insanity. None of his cases bore the remotest resemblance to the present-day psychopath, but because he used the word 'moral' it was widely believed that this form of insanity was responsible for the actions of individuals who exhibited a persistent tendency to indulge in criminal behaviour—hence the plea of moral insanity in the courts in attempting to exculpate the offender from the full penalties of the law. Understandably, it was not an excuse that found much favour with the judges of the day. As they reasonably pointed out—and it has continued to be pointed out—it was impossible to decide whether a crime had been caused by the innate wickedness of the offender, or whether it resulted from a fit of moral insanity.

The Mental Deficiency Act of 1927 softened the term 'moral imbecile'—incorporated in the earlier Act of 1913—to 'moral defective', but retained in its definition the words 'mental defectiveness coupled with strongly vicious or criminal propensities', and added 'who require care, supervision and control for the protection of others'. This was the forerunner of the psychopathic disorder definition in the Mental Health Act of 1959. Because many of those so constrained were not devoid of normal intelligence, placing them in hospitals for the mentally defective was neither appropriate nor beneficial.

Why *psychopathic* personality? As already mentioned, Schneider used the term to denote all varieties of abnormal personality, but his subgroups of explosive, affectionless, and weak willed come close to Henderson's

categories of aggressive and inadequate psychopaths. Koch in Germany in 1891 introduced the term 'psychopathic inferiority' as a catch-all phrase implying a constitutional predisposition not only to neurosis but also to abnormalities and eccentricities of behaviour. At the time of his writing, psychiatric thought was dominated by concepts of degeneration and the hereditary transmission of 'the taint of insanity'. As such degeneration was often attributed to parental excesses, particularly alcoholism and sexual profligacy, it is understandable that what at first sight appeared to be persistent immoral or criminal behaviour became linked with the prevailing notions about psychopathic inferiority and moral insanity. Although in Britain the Royal Commission on the Law Relating to Mental Illness, 1954–7, repeatedly used the word 'psychopath', it avoided making any precise definition of what the word meant. Baroness Wootton (1959) considered that the modern psychopath is the linguistic descendant of the moral defective, which takes us back to 19th-century writings on moral insanity. Whatever word is used, it has to be admitted that making clear distinction between the mentally healthy offender and the presumably mentally abnormal one is not an easy task.

The question thus arises whether psychopathic personality should be classed as a form of mental disorder. Opinions differ widely, but as the psychopath now has legal status the existence of such a condition has understandably been put forward in criminal proceedings as a plea for mitigation of sentence. In some cases of homicide, the verdict has been reduced from murder to manslaughter on the basis of *diminished responsibility as defined in the Homicide Act of 1959. But many psychiatrists would have reservations about claims that psychopathic disorder is a mental illness on a par with neurosis or psychosis. While it could be argued that it amounts to an abnormality of mind which could seriously impair the responsibility of an offender for his alleged homicidal act, what is 'abnormality of mind' in this context? The subject was clarified by Lord Chief Justice Parker, who said that it meant 'a state of mind so different from that of ordinary human beings that the reasonable man would term it abnormal'. He went on to indicate that such an opinion applied to a person's acts, his ability to decide whether they were right or wrong, and his capacity for exercising will power to control such behaviour in accordance with rational judgement. None the less, as Nigel Walker (1965) comments, 'It is clear . . . that while a diagnosis of psychopathy is now recognized by English courts as an acceptable basis for a defence of diminished responsibility, the psychopath's chances of succeeding in this defence are by no means high'.

The causes and treatment of psychopathic disorder are as contentious as its legal implications. Theories of aetiology have included brain damage in childhood, late maturation of the central nervous system, and adverse circumstances of upbringing, particularly difficult relationships with parents and those in authority. As far as treatment is concerned, there is little evidence that a purely psychiatric approach to the problem has been successful. Controlled studies are hard to come by, but one such investigation found that firm but sympathetic handling in a disciplined environment was better than a more permissive approach based on group therapy and a self-governing type of regime. As the psychopath appears to lack the inner controls normally developed during childhood and adolescence, this result is hardly surprising. Time, however, seems to be a significant factor in treatment, an observation which could be interpreted as favouring the late maturation theory of psychopathic disorder. But in all probability learning over a period of years may also play a part in this process of maturation.

FAW

Craft, M. J. (1965). *Ten Studies into Psychopathic Personality.*

Henderson, D. (1939). *Psychopathic States.*

Robins, L. N. (1966). *Deviant Children Grown Up.*

Schneider, K. (1958). *Psychopathic Personalities.* Trans. M. W. Hamilton.

Walker, N. (1965). 'Liberty, liability and culpability'. *Medicine, Science and the Law,* Jan.

Whitlock, F. A. (1967). 'Prichard and the concept of moral insanity'. *Australian and New Zealand Journal of Psychiatry,* 2.

Wootton, B. (1959). *Social Science and Social Pathology.*

psychopharmacology. The use of drugs that act on the mind is as old as the recorded history of man. Alcohol in the form of fermented beverages such as mead was probably already popular in the palaeolithic age, about 8000 BC, and grape wine from about 400–300 BC. *Opium is referred to in Sumerian tablets of around 4000 BC, and marijuana was known in China at 2737 BC. The hallucinogenic properties of the magic mushroom (teonanacatl) were known from 1000 BC in Mexico, while in northern Europe and Asia the inebriant properties of the fly agaric mushroom, *Amanita muscaria*, feature in Norse legends. The concept that drugs can be used medically to restore mental health is, in contrast, the result of a very recent revolution in pharmacology, following the discovery in the 1950s of new classes of drugs, the tranquillizers and antidepressants, and their widespread use in the treatment of mental illness.

Staggering quantities of psychoactive drugs are now consumed for medical purposes. About half of the female population of the United Kingdom over the age of 60 regularly uses sedative drugs to put them to sleep each night. Benzodiazepines in the form of Valium (diazepam) and related substances by day, and Mogadon (nitrazepam) and Dalmane (flurazepam) for night sedation, have largely replaced barbiturate sedatives and hypnotics. The success of these 'tranquillizers' can be gauged by the astonishing quantity consumed, amounting to tens of billions of doses throughout the world each year. These substances have a definite although mild calming effect, they relieve anxiety and diminish aggression, and they are relatively safe—in contrast to the barbiturates, which all too commonly lead to death from overdose. Because these newer drugs are relatively safe, and since almost all of us feel anxious from time to time, the extravagant success of the benzodiazepines during the 1960s and 1970s is not hard to understand. More recently, with the recognition that prolonged use of benzodiazepines can lead to addiction, there has been a growing reaction to their widespread use.

The most remarkable modern development in this field, however, is the discovery of drugs that are successful in the treatment of some of the fundamental symptoms of psychosis and depression. The first drug found to have such effects in schizophrenic patients was chlorpromazine (Largactil, Thorazine), and from this a large number of other so-called 'major tranquillizers' with similar effects have been developed. Since the first favourable reports on chlorpromazine appeared in France in 1952, such drugs have been adopted widely for the treatment of schizophrenia. More than 100 million schizophrenic patients have been treated with chlorpromazine since 1953. The major tranquillizers have definite beneficial effects on some of the most fundamental symptoms of schizophrenia: patients show less disordered thinking, suffer from fewer delusions and hallucinations, exhibit more appropriate emotional behaviour. They are not simply quietened or sedated, and indeed other sedative drugs such as the 'minor' tranquillizers (benzodiazepines) do not exhibit these effects. It is not surprising that the massive use of chlorpromazine and similar drugs has had an enormous impact on the treatment of schizophrenia. (For further discussion, see SCHIZOPHRENIA: EVIDENCE FOR A NEUROCHEMICAL BASIS.) The mental institutions have been transformed from sombre places with a largely custodial function to hospitals with open doors in which community therapy and rehabilitation techniques have been introduced. The number of patients so severely ill as to need more or less permanent hospitalization has also diminished strikingly—to the extent that separate psychiatric hospitals may no longer be necessary in future.

Other groups of drugs have been discovered to have beneficial effects in treating the melancholia of depressed patients. Two major classes of antidepressants have been introduced since the late 1950s—one derived from the substance iproniazid and the other from imipramine. Both groups of compounds have beneficial effects in depression, although these actions are usually less dramatic than those seen with the antipsychotic drugs. A remarkable discovery, made by Dr John Cade in Australia in 1949, has been that the symptoms of mania can often be treated very effectively by administration of small doses of an inorganic salt—lithium carbonate. Continued treatment with lithium carbonate reduces the frequency of recurrence of manic episodes in individuals who would otherwise show a regular cycle of such illness.

The problems of madness have not been solved by the drugs—we still do not understand what causes schizophrenia or depression, or even the nature of these illnesses. The idea that abnormalities in brain chemistry may underlie mental illness has, however, derived strong support from the finding that psychosis can be treated with simple chemicals. Much research effort is currently directed towards discovering precisely how the antipsychotic and antidepressant drugs alter brain chemistry. It is now widely accepted that antipsychotic drugs act by blocking the effects of one of the chemical transmitter substances used by brain cells to transmit signals to one another. The transmitter blocked by chlorpromazine and related drugs is dopamine, and this finding has suggested the possibility that in schizophrenia excessive amounts of dopamine secreted in the brain might represent an immediate causative factor for the psychotic state. (See DOPAMINE NEURONS IN THE BRAIN.) On the other hand, antidepressant drugs seem to act by enhancing the effects of other chemical transmitter substances, noradrenaline (norepinephrine) and serotonin, in the brain—suggesting that these chemicals may be available in abnormally low amounts in the brains of depressed people.

In general, however, our knowledge of the mode of action of many psychoactive drugs is limited. This applies particularly to nicotine, cannabis, and the hallucinogens, but both barbiturates and alcohol act as central nervous system depressants. With respect to barbiturates and benzodiazepines it is likely that their depressant effects on neural activity are mediated by the *neurotransmitter gamma-aminobutyric acid (GABA), but other neurotransmitters may also be involved. Rather surprisingly, less is known about the precise mode of action of alcohol on the brain beyond the fact that it appears to depress synaptic transmission.

The fact that simple chemical substances can have such profound influences on the state of the mind, as between madness and sanity, between depression and euphoria, between normal perception and the vivid hallucinations induced by lysergic acid diethylamide (LSD), has obvious philosophical implications for the relation between the mind and the chemistry of the brain. It is clear that subtle changes in brain chemistry can have profound effects on the state of consciousness, and it behoves us to understand more of such subtleties.

Drugs are also consumed very widely for non-medical reasons. Of these alcohol, nicotine, and caffeine are relatively universal—others, whose use is strictly controlled by legislation, such as the hallucinogens, barbiturates, amphetamines, marijuana, phencyclidine, cocaine, and

opiates, are, nevertheless, also quite widely taken. These compounds have a bewildering variety of different psychic effects. Alcohol and barbiturates are depressants, leading to a feeling of relaxation, loss of inhibition, and to inebriation and sleep. Others are stimulants, such as nicotine and the more powerful amphetamines; these are performance-enhancing drugs. LSD, mescaline, phencyclidine, and the many other hallucinogens are in a class apart because these compounds can produce bizarre changes in perception—they replace the present world with another that is equally real but different, often with vivid sensory hallucinations. There are other drugs whose actions are primarily euphoriant, notably cocaine, morphine, heroin and other opiate drugs, and—in a milder form—marijuana. They replace the present world with one in which the individual experiences no problems, and often intense pleasure. The most powerful euphoriants, the opiates and cocaine, are medically dangerous drugs—largely because their continued use leads inevitably to tolerance and *addiction, i.e. larger and larger doses become necessary to achieve the desired effects, and the organism becomes physically dependent on continued drug use, so that stopping the drug may precipitate very unpleasant withdrawal symptoms. It should be remembered, however, that morphine and related opiates still have important medical uses in the control of pain. Opium has long been regarded as a sovereign remedy for the relief of pain and other symptoms. As Thomas *Sydenham, the English physician, wrote at the end of the 17th century, 'I cannot forbear mentioning with gratitude the goodness of the Supreme Being who has supplied afflicted mankind with opiates for their relief'. Almost certainly it is the insanitary habits and unsterile modes of use as well as the actions of the drugs as such that make opiates such a hazard to the life and health of the addict today.

We may one day discover how to eliminate the problem of addiction, and we will then be faced with the difficult decision as to whether 'safe' euphoriant drugs should be allowed widespread availability and use. Several millennia of experience with alcohol suggests that strict control of the availability of such substances would inevitably be needed. The 'soma' of Aldous Huxley's *Brave New World* may be nearer than is generally realized. There is little doubt that legislation controlling the use of marijuana will gradually become less prohibitive, and that modern plant breeding could work wonders with the Indian hemp plant to produce 'super-pot'. It is also clear that society has not yet decided what its attitudes should be to the general availability of chemically induced pleasure.   LLI

Iversen, L. L., Iversen, S. D., and Snyder, S. H. (eds.) (1975–84). *Handbook of Psychopharmacology*, vols. i–xviii.
Iversen, S. D., and Iversen, L. L. (1981). *Behavioral Pharmacology* (2nd edn.).
Ray, O. S. (1972). *Drugs, Society and Human Behavior*.

psychophysics. Psychophysics originally meant the study of the *sensations evoked by physical stimuli. As an example to illustrate the distinction between a stimulus and a sensation, the amount of light reflected by this page is its luminance, and can be measured with a light meter such as photographers use; the sensation evoked by that reflected light is the experienced brightness of the page, and may be deceptively related to the luminance, as photographers know well. Psychophysics is concerned with the *brightness* of the stimulus, and its other subjective qualities, and, secondly, with the relation of that brightness to the physical luminance.

The term 'psychophysics' was introduced by Gustav *Fechner in his *Elemente der Psychophysik* (1860), in which he conceived an indirect method of measuring sensations. If a luminance L_2 can just be distinguished as greater than L_1, then, to a close approximation, L_2/L_1 is constant; this is Weber's law (formulated as the Weber–Fechner law). If one supposes that all *just-noticeable differences (e.g. between L_1 and L_2) are subjectively equivalent, then the *sensation* (in this case, of brightness) must increase as the logarithm of the physical stimulus magnitude, for if L_2/L_1, is constant, so also is $\log L_2 - \log L_1$.

Fechner's logarithmic measure was universally accepted until the 1930s, at which time it was questioned for a purely practical reason. At that time the decibel scale for the measurement of auditory intensity was newly developed. On this scale 20 dB represents a tenfold increase in the amplitude of modulation of sound pressure, or a hundredfold increase in acoustic power, and, since the range of acoustic powers to which the ear may be exposed is typically $1 : 10^{12}$, a logarithmic scale is convenient. Decibel measurements are always relative to a reference point, which is usually taken as about equal to the faintest sound that the ear can detect. So, a naive application of Fechner's law would suggest that 50 dB should sound half as loud as 100 dB, but it is generally agreed that 50 dB sounds much quieter than that. To enable acoustic engineers to communicate meaningfully with their customers, the 1930s saw some research on how people assign numbers to ratios of sound levels and this research led to the development of the sone scale by S. S. *Stevens in 1936. Loudness in sones grows as the 0.3 power of the physical sound power.

Subsequently, in the 1950s, S. S. Stevens and his collaborators developed the methods and ideas of the 1930s to devise power law scales of the sensations, evoked by more than 30 different sensory attributes, substantially those for which Weber's law holds. When subjects judge the ratios of stimuli, the numbers assigned vary as $N = aX^\beta$, where X is the magnitude of the stimulus being judged and β is an exponent characteristic of the attribute. This exponent varies from 0.33 for luminance to 3.5 for electric shock.

Inspired by Fechner's use of the just-noticeable difference as a unit of sensation, there has evolved a very great body of experimental work and practical knowledge about human discrimination of all kinds of sensory attributes, and following from Stevens's power law, there has developed a comparable body of facts and figures about human judgement. For practical purposes, psychophysics has come to refer to these two large accumulations of data and models. But, notwithstanding its long history, basic theoretical principles are only just beginning to emerge.

On mature consideration it can be seen that sensation is not, in fact, measurable independently of the physical stimulus from which it is derived. Fechner's logarithmic transform exists only as a mathematical construction, having no operational validity, and conformity to Stevens's power law depends on getting the experiment 'right'. These two assertions can be supported by a demonstration and a simple experiment.

Panel *a* of Fig. 1 shows a black-and-white sectored disc which, when spun rapidly, appears as in panel *b*. Intermittent illumination interrupted at a sufficiently rapid rate is not distinguishable from uniform illumination of the same time-average illuminance. So the centre and periphery of the rotating disc must have the same luminance—but their brightnesses are manifestly different. Now if the boundary between the centre and periphery of the rotating disc is covered with an opaque annulus (panel *c*), the brightnesses of the centre and the periphery are immediately seen to be equal. Remove the annulus (panel *b*) and they are again different. This phenomenon is known as the Craik–Cornsweet illusion. It depends on the kinky profile of luminance at the boundary of the figure, which may be appreciated from the shape of the black sector on the stationary disc. There is an abrupt step in luminance which is easily perceived, and two ramps which are not. And so the centre appears darker than the periphery. When this profile is obscured by the annulus, centre and periphery appear equally bright. It follows that we do not see relative brightness only from a comparison of the two luminances in question, but from the *perceived change* in luminance at the boundary. That is, the sensation of brightness is obtained by a differential process from the physical stimulus. This idea was first proposed as long ago as 1865, by Ernst *Mach.

The Craik–Cornsweet illusion is known to have analogues in the attributes of sound intensity and frequency, and in the length and spacing of lines. It is probably a general feature of human sensory perception. And the differential process which it reveals explains Weber's law, why the just-noticeable difference increases in direct proportion to the stimulus magnitude. The logarithmic transform is a matter of the imagination only.

If our sensory experience is differentially coupled to the physical world, what of Stevens's power law? An elegant

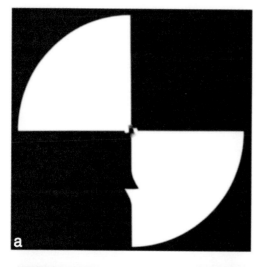
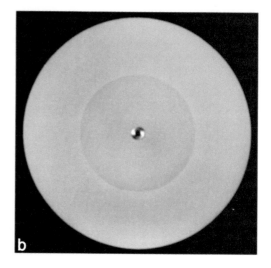
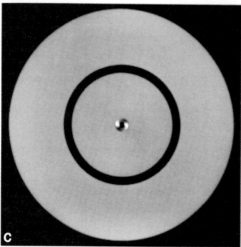

Fig. 1. The Craik–Cornsweet illusion. Plates **b** and **c** have been made from the same photographic negative which was taken while the sectored disc was rotated at high speed. The inner disc has the same average luminance as the outer annulus, but in plate **b** it appears darker because only the sharp step in luminance at the boundary is perceptible.

experiment by W. R. Garner addresses this point. Thirty subjects listened to a standard tone at 90 dB and then a comparison tone. The comparison tone was to be judged 'more' or 'less' than half as loud as the standard, and from each subject's judgements of a series of such comparisons was estimated that intensity of tone that would have been judged 'more' and 'less' equally often—a subjective half-loudness value. One group of subjects listened to comparison tones varying between 75 and 85 dB, and having half-loudness values within that range. Another group listened to comparison tones between 65 and 75 dB which all had

half-loudness values within *that* range; and likewise for a third group listening to tones between 55 and 65 dB. Only one subject complained that the comparison tones presented did not straddle the half-loudness value, and she was happily reassigned to the third group.

It is apparent that most people have no idea what 'half as loud' means. Not wishing to appear foolish, the subjects in Garner's experiment assumed that some comparison tones must be more, and some less, than half as loud as the standard (else the experiment made no sense) and adjusted their criteria of judgement accordingly. They were conned. Their judgements depended on the immediate context rather than on the loudness of the stimulus. In experiments on the estimation of sensations the influence of context is very powerful and the accuracy of judgement is typically poorer by one to two orders of magnitude compared to that accuracy revealed in the measurement of just-noticeable differences. The accuracy of judgement of single stimuli has been found, with many different attributes, to be equivalent to the identification of no more than five different stimulus levels.

In conclusion, there is no way to measure sensation that is distinct from measurement of the physical stimulus. Sometimes we are deceived—Fig. 1 presents an example—and such examples present intriguing problems to the experimental psychologist. Attempts to 'measure' sensation have taught us that judgements of quantity are astonishingly poor. For this reason photographers use exposure meters, and cars are fitted with speedometers, so that the driver merely has to judge that the needle is adjacent to the mark representing 30 mph, rather than 25 or 35—a 'yes or no' kind of judgement that is reliable. We habitually make our judgements of quantity with the aid of a measuring instrument, a ruler or scale pan, and, in practice, problems arise only with those attributes which we feel intuitively ought to admit a continuum of values, but for which no measuring instrument exists—attributes like the merit of essays written in an examination or the aesthetic value of a painting. Such problems are nicely illustrated by the auction prices of Old Master paintings. The authenticity of such a painting can often be determined with great reliability, but sometimes the provenance is reappraised and the market value of the painting, physically the same, with its aesthetic qualities entirely unchanged, can vary at least thirtyfold in consequence. In the auction room aesthetic merit is of very little account, precisely because it cannot be accurately assessed; in its stead, provenance, a 'yes and no' matter, is almost everything.   DRJL

Gescheider, G. A. (1985). *Psychophysics: Method, Theory, and Application* (2nd edn.).

Laming, D. (1986). *Sensory Analysis.*

psychosis. The word 'psychosis' seems to have been coined in the mid-19th century and to have meant originally any kind of mental disturbance arising from whatever cause. But after the turn of the century its meaning was restricted by excluding both the mental consequences of familiar physical illnesses (such as *delirium associated with fever) and the neuroses. In contemporary psychiatric terminology, 'psychosis' is a classificatory and descriptive term, referring to a specific range of illnesses and symptoms, the illnesses being those in which the patient's basic competence as a person is called into question, the symptoms being those which seem to indicate some gross

disorder of perception and thought (such as *hallucinations and *delusions). A psychosis is, therefore, any mental illness which is liable to render its victim *non compos mentis*, and unfit to plead in a court of law; and a symptom is 'psychotic' if it betrays misapprehension and misinterpretation of the nature of reality.

If, for instance, someone asserts that he is Napoleon, or emperor of Canada, or has had sexual intercourse with God, he is psychotic, since such assertions are by common consent untrue and anyone making them seriously must be misapprehending the nature of reality and failing to distinguish between his fantasies and the facts of the case. In contrast, if someone asserts that he spends time imagining that he is Napoleon, or day dreaming that he has established an empire in Canada, or that he has dreamt he was emperor of Canada or has had intercourse with God, he is not psychotic, for he has correctly distinguished between his own imaginings and the nature of the external world. Similarly, if someone asserts that he has committed terrible crimes (when he has not) and deserves lifelong imprisonment for having done so, he is psychotic, but someone who complains of feeling irrationally guilty is not; nor is a religious person who has a lively sense of original sin.

The *International Classification of Diseases* (see CLASSIFICATION OF PSYCHIATRIC DISORDERS), published by the World Health Organization and used by the National Health Service in Britain, lists eight specific psychoses. Four of these, the so-called organic psychoses (senile, pre-senile, arteriosclerotic, and alcoholic), are generally agreed to be the result of degenerative changes in the brain. They excite little interest within the psychiatric profession and practically none at all with the general public. The other four, the so-called functional psychoses—*schizophrenia, manic–depressive psychosis (see DEPRESSION), involutional melancholia, and *paranoia—arouse considerable controversy within the profession and great interest with the general public, partly because their symptoms are dramatic, but more importantly because research has (as yet) failed to discover any convincing, as opposed to plausible, causes for them—and in the absence of any specifiable physical causes it is possible and legitimate to question even whether the medical model is the appropriate one to apply to psychosis.

However, the majority of psychiatrists do seem to believe that the functional psychoses are true medical diseases and that, one day, physical causes will be found for them—and that as a result, rational, effective treatments will become available. If they are right, not only will an enormous amount of suffering be relieved, but the claims of the medical profession to be the appropriate people to care for and treat the mentally disturbed will finally be vindicated. In fact, the advent of effective drugs for the treatment of schizophrenia and manic–depressive psychoses has given considerable support to the possibility that biochemical rather than structural changes in thezbrain could be causes of these diseases. The medical model therefore gains some plausibility from these discoveries.

But, it must be stressed, at least two non-organic, non-medical conceptions of psychosis are also in circulation. One, held by some but not all psychoanalysts, argues that the functional psychoses are not in principle all that different from the neuroses; it is merely that the fixation points are earlier, the regressions deeper, the infantile traumas more massive, the defence mechanisms more primitive. If the analysts who hold this view are right, the functional psychoses are psychogenic, not organic, illnesses, and their symptoms require interpretation in terms of their concealed meanings, not explanations in terms of cerebral dysfunction.

The other, non-organic conception, held by anti-psychiatrists, 'family process' therapists, and the post-Laingian counter-culture generally, explains the functional psychosis of any single individual as the end result of complex and skew interactions within his family that have driven him into bizarre and incomprehensible behaviour, which is then 'disauthenticated' by being labelled 'mad' or 'psychotic'. This theory exists in more than one form. In one the psychotic patient is the victim of a villainous schizophrenogenic parent, usually the mother; in another he is the overt casualty of a deeply concealed family tragedy. This last is a socio-political theory which locates pathology not in the body or the mind of the individual patient but in the power politics of society and the family.   CR

Bateson, G. (1956). 'Towards a theory of schizophrenia'. In *Steps to an Ecology of Mind*.

Fairbairn, W. R. D. (1952). 'A revised psychopathology of the psychoses and psychoneuroses'. In *Psychoanalytic Studies of the Personality*.

Laing, R. D. (1971). *The Politics of the Family*.

—— and Esterson, A. (1964). *Sanity, Madness and the Family*.

psychosomatic disease: a medical view. The successes achieved in the 1920s and 1930s in the treatment of diabetes mellitus with insulin, of pernicious anaemia with liver extract, of malnutrition with vitamins, and of infectious diseases with antitoxin and their prevention by immunization, all encouraged the reductionist view that the objective of scientific medicine should be the discovery of the essential internal disorder underlying the symptoms, and the specific treatment for it. However, this model was soon recognized to be too simple. For many diseases the causes appear to be multiple and complex, some lying in internal and some in external conditions and others being, in a loosely defined sense, psychological. The interest in psychological processes grew in the 1930s,

as the psychodynamic theories derived from psycho-analysis became more widely known. The term 'psychosomatic' was then applied to diseases in which disorder in the function of an organ was thought to be due to, or associated with, psychological factors. A definition of psychosomatic medicine was given in 1939 in the editorial introducing the first number of the journal *Psychosomatic Medicine*. Its object was 'to study in their interrelation the psychological and physiological aspects of all normal and abnormal bodily functions and thus to integrate somatic therapy and psychotherapy'. The journal's intention was to promote an approach to causes and treatment, rather than to make distinctions between classes of disease. Nevertheless, certain diseases were identified as psychosomatic—for example, atopic dermatitis, anorexia nervosa, bronchial asthma, essential hypertension, gastric and duodenal ulcer, myocardial infarction, and ulcerative colitis. It should be said, however, that the inclusion of some of these conditions under the rubric of psychosomatic disorders has been questioned.

The stress/strain analogy became popular. Just as stress, an external force, produces strain in a material, so forces in the physical, biological, or social environment produce strain in the mental and physical functions and behaviour of organisms. The strain effects are potentially adaptive, the form taken by the adaptation depending on the organism's constitution and past experience, and hence they are idiosyncratic. The analogy is, however, misleading in one respect at least, for whereas the effects constituting strain in a material cease as soon as the stress ceases, there is no return in the organism to the status quo, because stress causes reorganization or 'reprogramming' of the adaptive mechanisms. The organism acquires new habits, for instance, or a new immunity.

Support for the psychosomatic approach comes from epidemiological studies of the incidence of diseases among those subjected to more or less defined stresses. Gastric ulcer, for instance, was noted in the First World War to be unduly common among soldiers who had recently been in action in the trenches. Recorded deaths from gastric and duodenal ulcer rose in the Second World War during the period of heavy air raids. When stocks go down in New York, diabetes goes up, it was remarked. The survivors of fires and floods and of imprisonment, and the *bereaved, among others, have been shown to have rates of morbidity and mortality greater than those in comparable populations. Many diseases not directly related to the known effects of the stress are then unduly common—for example, heart disease, cancer, disease of the gastrointestinal tract, and pulmonary tuberculosis, as well as suicide and accidents. So many diseases have now been included in such lists as to discourage any inclination to distinguish between those diseases that are psychosomatic and those that are not.

Experiments on mammals have shown that such stresses as confinement, restraint, and frustration affect the function of almost every organ. The temporary separation of newborn mammals from their mothers results in high rates of morbidity and mortality. It is well known that in man emotions such as anger, *fear, and *anxiety tend to be accompanied by changes throughout the body in almost every function. The effects of various stresses on functions of the stomach, colon, skin, and cardiovascular system in particular have been studied experimentally in healthy human subjects. Some of the effects are mediated by the autonomic nervous system, some by the endocrine system, and others through behaviour such as refusing food or eating to excess. Some create the conditions in which the disease arises—for example, by affecting the resistance to infection—while others form an inherent part of the disease. Research has tried to give some definition to the psychological factors, although this has proved difficult, and to elucidate the processes involved in each pattern of disease. There is no distinctive psychosomatic process, but rather a wide variety of processes. For this reason the use of the term 'psychosomatic' has declined.

The pattern of responses has been shown in experiments on mammals to vary with the character of the stress. In human patients, on the other hand, there tends to be a remarkable consistency in the psychosomatic disease, which tends to recur in a stereotyped form. The pattern is peculiar to each patient and more or less fixed. It could be argued that a genetic predisposition, as, for example, in the asthma–eczema syndrome, to some extent determines the type of psychosomatic disorder that is likely to recur. Evidence from studies of children suggests that the pattern is laid down before the child is 6, 'organ vulnerability' being decided by this age. From time to time there may be a 'syndrome shift'. Thus a patient who has had several attacks of atopic dermatitis develops bronchial asthma, or perhaps, later in life, rheumatoid arthritis. A sufferer over many years from migraine develops ulcerative colitis, or a patient who has had a recurrent peptic ulcer develops essential hypertension. It has often been suggested that each pattern of disease is associated with particular traits of personality, but systematic studies have largely failed to show correlations. However, recurrent diseases like asthma and ulcerative colitis may be held to influence the style of life a person adopts and so indirectly affect his medical state.

See also PSYCHOSOMATIC DISEASE: PHILOSOPHICAL AND PSYCHOLOGICAL ASPECTS; STRESS. DRD

Alexander, F. (1950). *Psychosomatic Medicine*.
Fava, G. A., and Freyberger, H. (1998). *Handbook of Psychosomatic Medicine*.
Hill, O. W. (ed.) (1976). *Modern Trends in Psychosomatic Medicine—3*.
Tanner, J. M. (ed.) (1960). *Stress and Psychiatric Disorder*.

psychosomatic disease: philosophical and psychological aspects. Diseases are designated as psychosomatic if two conditions are fulfilled: if (i) the symptoms are accompanied by demonstrable physiological disturbances of function and (ii) the illness as a whole can be interpreted as a manifestation or function of the patient's personality, conflicts, life history, etc. The first condition distinguishes psychosomatic illness from psychoneurosis, particularly conversion hysteria, in which, by definition, the physical symptoms are not accompanied by demonstrable physiological disturbances. The second condition distinguishes psychosomatic illness from physical diseases pure and simple, which are explicable solely in terms of bodily dysfunction without reference to the psyche of the patient.

Although the word 'psychosomatic' was used by Coleridge, and its reversed form 'somapsyche' occurs in the original Greek of the New Testament, the concept of psychosomatic disease dates properly from the first half of the 20th century, when it became necessary to have a concept that cut across the division of diseases into physical (somatic) and mental (psychical) which had been established by *Freud and *Breuer's demonstration that the psychoneuroses were not functional disturbances of the central nervous system but symbolic expressions of psychical conflict. Given the resulting tendency to assume that illnesses were either physical and all in the body, or mental and all in the mind, the term 'psychosomatic disease' became necessary to categorize illnesses resembling psychoneuroses in being expressions of psychical conflict but yet having solid, demonstrable physical signs and symptoms.

As the preceding two paragraphs perhaps reveal, psychosomatic disease is logically and philosophically speaking a most tricky concept, since its meaning and precise implications necessarily depend on each particular user's basic assumptions about the relationship between body and mind. Presumably a materialist must hold that all diseases, including so-called mental ones, are ultimately somatic, and an idealist must hold that all physical illnesses are ultimately mental, while those who hold that physical and mental events belong to different causal sequences have to explain, if they believe in the possibility of psychosomatic disease, how the leap from one to the other is effected. However, in actual practice, the term is used only to categorize illnesses which present with physical signs and symptoms but none the less require the clinician to explore the patient's biography and state of mind. It is never used to refer to illnesses which present with mental symptoms but are none the less due to physical causes such as, for example, depression caused by a brain tumour.

Georg Groddeck (1866–1934), the maverick German psychoanalyst, is often regarded as the father of psychosomatic medicine. His way of formulating the relationship of body and mind was to assume that both are the creations of a third, impersonal force, *das Es*, the It:

the body and mind are a joint thing which harbours an It, a power by which we are lived, while we think we live. . . . The It, which is mysteriously connected with sexuality, Eros, or whatever you choose to call it, shapes the nose as well as the hand of the human, just as it shapes his thoughts and emotions. . . . And just as the symptomatic activity of the It in hysteria and neurosis calls for psychoanalytical treatment, so does heart trouble and cancer.

Rather similarly, another maverick psychoanalyst, Wilhelm Reich (1897–1957), held that all illnesses were the result of imprisonment of spontaneous bioenergy within character armour imposed by a repressive, authoritarian society. More soberly but less imaginatively, many workers during the last 50 years have produced evidence, much of it statistical, suggesting that many physical illnesses occur predominantly in individuals who have rigid personalities, who are subject to stress, who have recently experienced upheavals in their lifestyle, or who have lost all connection with other people. Psychoanalysts such as Franz Alexander and Flanders Dunbar in the USA attempted to relate specific psychosomatic disorders to specific emotional conflicts and personality patterns. This theory of psychosomatic illness has not been generally supported by recent work, although there is some evidence that coronary artery disease occurs more often in individuals with a particular personality make-up—the so-called type A personality. This concept is still controversial and the mode of interaction between personality and cardiac disease is not fully understood.

However, psychosomatic disease remains an elusive concept. Many, perhaps most, clinicians feel that there is something in it, but the problem of formulating correctly the nature of the relationship between body and mind implicit in it has proved recalcitrant.

See also PSYCHOSOMATIC DISEASE: A MEDICAL VIEW.　　CR

Bakan, D. (1968). *Disease, Pain, and Sacrifice.*
Dunbar, F. (1954). *Emotions and Bodily Changes.*
Groddeck, G. (1923). *Das Buch vom Es.* (Eng. trans., *The Book of the It*, 1935).
Grossman, C. M., and Grossman, S. (1965). *The Wild Analyst.*
Reich, W. (1960). *Wilhelm Reich: Selected Writings.* Ed. M. B. Higgins.
Strube, M. J. (1991). *Type A Behaviour.*
Totman, R. G. (1979). *Social Causes of Illness.*

psychosurgery. This term is used to denote operative procedures on the brain specifically designed to relieve severe mental symptoms that have been unresponsive to other forms of treatment. Although surgery for mental illness had been attempted sporadically—mostly in the form of trephining—since early times, it was not until

1935 that the Portuguese neurologist Egas Moniz, in association with the surgeon Almeida Lima, performed the first systematic series of operations known as prefrontal leucotomy, severing the connections between the prefrontal cortex and the rest of the brain. Although the operation was crude, of the first twenty cases seven recovered and seven improved. The best results were obtained in cases of agitated *depression, a finding which has been repeatedly confirmed by later workers. Unfortunately, some patients developed adverse personality changes, an effect which could have been predicted from the case of Phineas Gage, a competent worker in the USA who, in 1847, had the misfortune during a rock-blasting operation to have an iron bar blown through the front part of his head. He survived this extremely violent form of prefrontal leucotomy but, on recovery, was found to have undergone a profound change in personality. He swore in the grossest manner, behaviour not previously indulged in, and his overall qualities as a likeable individual were severely impaired. Despite these changes to his character he did not show any decline in intelligence or memory. Although patients treated by prefrontal leucotomy did not usually show such severe impairment of personality as Gage did, it is undeniable that adverse alterations in behaviour occurred sufficiently often to arouse opposition to the operation.

None the less, it was taken up enthusiastically in the USA by Freeman and Watts in 1942 and with rather less vigour in the UK, where it was carried out on 10,365 patients suffering from mental illnesses between 1942 and 1954 (Tooth and Newton 1961). It was stated that only 3 per cent showed undesirable side effects and that more than 40 per cent had been ill for at least six years. The operation was performed in only a few centres, a fact which seems to imply that, regardless of its alleged usefulness, attitudes opposing it were strongly held by medical staff in many hospitals. By 1961 the annual frequency of leucotomy had fallen substantially.

As time has gone by there have been many modifications of the original operation, and today it has been almost entirely replaced by exact stereotactic procedures which allow very small lesions to be placed in certain key areas of the brain. Such methods are designed to alleviate symptoms without causing undesirable changes in personality. Comparatively few patients are treated each year by psychosurgery, largely because of the development of more effective drugs (see PSYCHOPHARMACOLOGY) and behavioural (see BEHAVIOUR THERAPY) methods for the treatment of mental illness.

What kinds of symptoms are most susceptible to surgical intervention? The phrase 'tortured self-concern' is often quoted to indicate the degree of distress which has failed to respond to less drastic treatments. The best results have been obtained from patients suffering from severe chronic *anxiety, agitated depression carrying a high risk of suicide, and those afflicted with incapacitating *obsessive–compulsive disorders.

Although there is every indication that, with careful selection and post-operative management, many patients with these apparently intractable symptoms have benefited from the more precise forms of psychosurgery, very strong opposition has been mobilized in some quarters against any form of surgery for the relief of psychiatric symptoms. Such opposition has been most vigorously expressed in the USA, where in some states these operations are forbidden by law. Peter Breggin, a psychiatrist in Washington, has claimed that there is no scientific justification for the operation and that the price paid in terms of blunted emotions and other personality changes is too high. Furthermore he has argued that psychosurgery could be used as a means for controlling antisocial behaviour and the activities of political dissidents. While there may be too few skilled in stereotactic surgery to permit its extensive use for political and social reasons, in India and Japan operations on the amygdaloid nucleus of the brain have been performed to control 'hyperactivity' in children. Although there is no doubt that outbursts of unbridled violence can be caused by diseases of the limbic brain, there is very little evidence that psychosurgery has been systematically applied to control such symptoms in the UK. And at present the requirements of section 57 of the Mental Health Act of 1983 would almost certainly prevent any form of brain surgery being carried out expressly for the purpose of controlling antisocial, aggressive, or politically dissident behaviour.

Others have been concerned not only about the irreversible nature of the operation and permanent alteration of the personality, but also that in some way the patient's immortal soul would be damaged. Perhaps such considerations are best left to the theologians and the Almighty. A charitable view might be taken of man's efforts to relieve his fellow creatures of suffering. Be that as it may, given the safeguards that limit psychosurgery to the alleviation of distress, there seems to be a place for it as one form of effective treatment.

Although psychosurgery has been used for the treatment of deviant sexual behaviour, drug dependence, and alcoholism such methods can only be condemned, partly because they are unlikely to be effective but also because of uncertainty over whether such kinds of behaviour fall within the ambit of psychiatric illness. In any case they are unlikely to cause 'tortured self-concern' to those who are so afflicted although the disturbing effects of these behaviours upon relatives cannot be denied. But psychosurgery to allay the anxieties of relatives has not yet achieved whole-hearted support even from its most enthusiastic practitioners.   FAW

Clare, A. (1976). 'Psychosurgery'. In *Psychiatry in Dissent*.
Smith, S. J., and Kiloh, L. G. (1977). *Psychosurgery and Society*.
Tooth, G. C., and Newton, M. P. (1961). *Leucotomy in England and Wales, 1942–1954*.

psychotherapy, assessment of.

1. What happens to untreated patients?
2. The assessment of psychotherapy
3. Are some patients made worse by treatment?

1. What happens to untreated patients?

It must surely always have been true that a proportion of neurotic difficulties eased, or resolved, or were adapted to, in relation to the happenings of everyday life. Paradoxically, an issue only arose because, following Sigmund *Freud, a group of persons claimed special expertise in the curative role and this expertise tended to be somewhat uncritically accepted, especially in the USA. However, it was the English psychologist H. J. Eysenck who in 1952 turned the issue into a challenge.

Eysenck suggested that psychoneurotic difficulties tended to resolve 'spontaneously', i.e. regardless of treatment. Backed by an analysis of data such as the discharge rates of neurotics from mental hospitals and the outcome of insurance claims for psychological disability, he suggested that approximately two-thirds of neurotics recovered without treatment. Both his statistics and his basic analysis of data were challenged. An influential paper (Bergin and Lambert 1978) suggested that, while spontaneous recovery certainly takes place, the likely figure was nearer 46 per cent. The exact figure is intrinsically unknowable because it depends on the type of patients considered, the disorders from which they suffer, the length of follow-up, the criteria of recovery used, and the objectivity of their assessment. Considering only severe hospitalized neurosis, for instance, Simms (1978) made a careful twelve-year follow-up of 146 neurotic former in-patients and compared their symptomatic and social status (work, marital, sexual) with a matched control group of patients operated upon for varicose veins. A satisfactory outcome was achieved by only 42 per cent of the neurotics compared to 90 per cent of the surgical group. Thus the figure for neurotics is not dissimilar to that of Bergin. Malan et al. (1975) developed this trend further, being concerned to assess in detail the *quality* of recovery of untreated patients. Forty-five untreated neurotic patients were followed up and carefully assessed symptomatically and psychodynamically. Fifty-one per cent were judged improved symptomatically and 24 per cent showed at least partial psychodynamic improvement.

It seems probable, therefore, that one-third to one-half of neurotic patients who have no systematic psychotherapy improve symptomatically. A smaller percentage, perhaps one-quarter, show constructive personality changes.

In any case, the outcome of this debate has been wholly constructive. Psychotherapists of all allegiances now tend to look more critically at their therapeutic results. In particular, from a research point of view, the necessity of including adequate control groups, either untreated or treated by another type of therapy, is accepted.

2. The assessment of psychotherapy

Psychotherapy and psychotherapists faced up to, and recovered from, the crisis of identity induced by Eysenck's challenge. Comprehensive examination of available objective data by Bergin (1971), Malan (1973), and Luborsky, Singer, and Luborsky (1975) suggests that the results of psychotherapy, even if not as outstanding as enthusiasts would hope, demonstrate that it is effective and has a valued place among psychiatric treatments. It is also now clear how complex and difficult is the assessment of psychotherapeutic outcome.

Bergin contrasted the spontaneous remission rate of 30 per cent with 65 per cent for all forms of psychotherapy other than psychoanalysis and with the 83 per cent which is the overall rate for psychoanalysis. But these were, admittedly, rough figures. Others attempted the double task of assessing outcome studies for the adequacy of their design, and noting the therapeutic results, particularly from controlled trials. Malan, discussing these reviews of control studies, concluded that the evidence for the effectiveness of psychotherapy was relatively strong, especially for *psychosomatic conditions. However, for the neuroses and personality disorders—for which this form of therapy was developed—the evidence was weak. His own careful studies at the Tavistock Clinic in London over a period of many years, and repeated on two groups of patients, established the effectiveness of brief psychodynamic psychotherapy. He also made explicit a number of the criteria for selection of patients, as well as points of therapeutic technique.

Luborsky et al. critically reviewed comparative studies of psychotherapy. When comparisons were made between different psychotherapies, most studies failed to show significant differences in the proportion of patients who improved. However, controlled comparative studies indicate that a high percentage of patients who go through any of the psychotherapies do gain from them. From both individual and group psychotherapy, about 80 per cent of the studies show positive results. In addition, combined treatments (for psychosomatic conditions such as peptic ulcer or asthma) often did better than single treatments— a further plea for eclecticism rather than rigid ideology in psychotherapeutic practice. Luborsky et al. emphasized, as Frank et al. (1978) had for many years, the components common to psychotherapies, especially the helping relationship with the therapist. Luborsky et al. also stressed that the quality of outcome from therapy to therapy is im-

portant, as well as the amount of improvement. Again, this is an area for further careful consideration in the future.

It seems clear that research into psychotherapy needs to become more analytic, and must try to assess the multiple and interacting factors involved, such as the therapist, the patient, their relationship, the social situation, the type of treatment, the type of disorder, and the experience of the therapist.

A study by Sloane et al. marks a significant advance. Ninety-four persons suffering from moderately severe neuroses and personality disorders were carefully assessed clinically, using structured rating scales, and also on psychological tests. A close friend or relative was also interviewed, for an outside informant's view. Patients were randomly assigned to a waiting list or to one of three experienced behaviour therapists (see BEHAVIOUR THERAPY) or analytically oriented psychotherapists. The controls were promised therapy in four months and were kept in touch. Patients were treated for four months (an average of fourteen sessions) and then reinterviewed and tested. Two measures of psychological change were used, one aimed at symptom assessment and the other at work and social adjustment. The assessors who had originally seen the patients reassessed them, and were 'blind' as to which treatment had been used. Informants were also interviewed, and reassessed the patients. Further follow-up was done one and two years after the original assessment. Major trends were: symptomatic improvement in the control group and the two experimental groups at four months showed the treatment groups to be significantly more improved, but there was no difference between psychotherapy and behaviour therapy. On work and social adjustment, there was no significant difference in amount of improvement between the three groups. Assessment of overall improvement showed 93 per cent of the behaviour therapy group, compared to 77 per cent of the waiting list, or psychotherapy groups, improved or recovered. After one year, improvements were maintained or continued in most patients. Sixty-one patients were seen at the two-year follow-up; the great majority in all groups increased or maintained symptomatic improvement and personality adjustment. Special interest attached to the control group which had contact and interest maintained but no formal therapy. Both of the formal therapies were, however, more effective than this minimal therapy.

The conclusion of this study was that psychotherapy, in general, works, and its effects are not entirely due to nonspecific effects such as arousal of hope or to spontaneous recovery. The general effectiveness of psychotherapy has been confirmed by a new statistical research technique, meta-analysis, in which the outcome from active psychotherapy is compared to the variation in a control treatment (Shapiro and Shapiro 1982).

3. Are some patients made worse by treatment?

When critical attention first began to be paid to outcome studies, especially to those which reported no difference in average outcome between patients and waiting-list controls, it was noted that there was significantly greater variation of outcome among treated patients. It became apparent that some patients were actually being made worse by psychotherapy.

Any practising psychotherapist must recognize the truth of this observation—we do make some patients worse. A systematic attempt was made, therefore, to note the incidence of deterioration effects and also possible causes. Strupp, Hadley, and Gomes-Schwartz (1978) systematically reviewed the problem of negative effects. The best quantitative estimate of deterioration effects, both from dynamic and from behavioural psychotherapy, is 3–6 per cent. Possible sources of these negative effects include: poor preliminary assessment; personality factors in the patient, the therapist, or their interaction; inadequate training of therapists, leading to clumsy or rigid therapeutic techniques; and misguided or erroneous choice of therapy or of treatment goals. This is an area of current interest and importance: further investigation is necessary.   SCR

Bergin, A. E., and Lambert, M. J. (1978). 'The evaluation of therapeutic outcome'. In Bergin, A. E., and Garfield, S. L. (eds.), *Handbook of Psychotherapy and Behaviour Change*.

Eysenck, H. J. (1952). 'The effects of psychotherapy: an evaluation'. *Journal of Consulting Psychology*, 16.

Frank, J. D., Hoehn-Saric, R., Imber, S. D., Liberman, B. L., and Stone, A. R. (1978). *Effective Ingredients of Successful Psychotherapy*.

Lambert, M. J. (2003). *Bergin and Garfield's Handbook of Psychotherapy and Behavior Change* (5th edn.).

Luborsky, L., Singer, L., and Luborsky, L. (1975). 'Comparative studies of psychotherapies'. *Archives of General Psychiatry*, 32.

Malan, D. (1973). 'The outcome problem in psychotherapy research'. *Archives of General Psychiatry*, 29.

——Heath, E. S., Bacal, H. A., and Balfour, F. H. G. (1975). 'Psychodynamic changes in untreated neurotic patients'. *Archives of General Psychiatry*, 32.

Mohr, D. C. (1995). 'Negative outcome in psychotherapy: a critical review'. *Clinical Psychology: Science and Practice*, 2/1.

Shapiro, D. A., and Shapiro, D. (1982). 'Meta-analysis of comparative therapy outcome studies: a replication and refinement'. *Psychology Bulletin*, 92.

Simms, A. C. P. (1978). 'Prognosis in severe neurosis'. *Current Themes in Psychiatry*, 1.

Strupp, H. H., Hadley, S. W., and Gomes-Schwartz, B. (1978). *Psychotherapy for Better or Worse: The Problem of Negative Effects*.

Ptolemy (Claudius Ptolemaeus, *c*.AD 100–80). A Graeco-Egyptian scholar in Alexandria, who wrote astronomical and other texts, including the *Optics* (*c*.170), which contained his views on *perception.

His account of an earth-centred universe with eight concentric crystal spheres, each of the first seven carrying an independently moving heavenly body, the outermost the 'fixed' stars—with an elaborate system of epicycles to explain the various motions, including reversals of motion of Mars—dominated scientific thinking until the 16th century. It was described in his *Algamist* ('the greatest'). His ideas stem from Hypparchus (fl. 160–125 BC) who discovered the precession of the equinoxes, estimated the distances of the sun and moon from measurements, and is credited with inventing trigonometry. Ptolomy is far better remembered because the *Algamist* and other writings remained in print and were accepted 'bibles of belief' for many centuries. They affected how music was conceived, from the Ptolomaic 'music of the spheres', modified much later by Kepler, when the sun was seen as dominating the planetary system with earth a minor player. His *Optics* influenced the more famous work by *Alhazen. Ptolemy combined the mathematical, philosophical, and physiological traditions. He held an extramission–intromission visual theory: the rays from the eye formed a cone, the vertex being within the eye, and the base defining the visual field. The rays knew their own length, and thus conveyed information about the distance and orientation of surfaces. Size and shape were determined by the visual angle combined with perceived distance and orientation (this being one of the earliest statements of size and shape constancy). Ptolemy used these principles to explain many objective and subjective phenomena connected with illumination and colour, size, shape, movement, and binocular vision. He also divided *illusions into those caused by physical, optical, or judgemental factors. He gave an obscure explanation of the *moon illusion based on the difficulty of looking upwards.   HER/RLG

Smith, A. M. (1996). *Ptolemy's Theory of Visual Perception: An English Translation of the Optics with Introduction and Commentary*.

Pulfrich's pendulum. This famous stereophenomenon, first described by Carl Pulfrich (1858–1927), is easily observed, by those with normal binocular vision, with the help of a pair of sunglasses and a length of string with a weight such as a teacup attached to one end. The string and weight are used to make a pendulum attached to a convenient point on the ceiling, and oscillating slowly from side to side. If the pendulum is viewed with the sunglasses covering one eye, the other eye remaining open, it will appear to move through an elliptical path in depth (Fig. 1). The direction of movement in depth is clockwise (as viewed from above) when the sunglass filter is covering the left eye, and counter-clockwise if the dark glass covers the right eye. The function of the sunglass is simply to reduce the amount of light reaching the eye. The depth illusion applies not just to a pendulum but

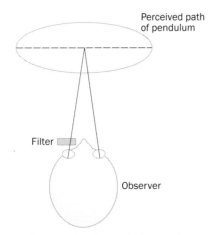

Fig. 1. A plan view of an observer looking at a horizontally oscillated pendulum, the actual path of which is shown by the dotted line. When the observer's left eye is covered by a sun-glass filter, the pendulum appears to move in depth along the trajectory represented by the solid line. The direction of movement is opposite if the right eye is covered.

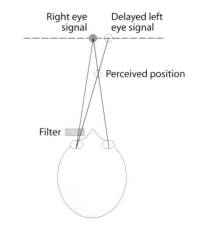

Fig. 2. Fertsch's 'delay line' explanation of Pulfrich's effect. The signals from the covered eye are effectively delayed so that the eye signals an earlier point on the target's trajectory; the delay therefore produces a stereoscopic disparity, and the target is seen as shifted in depth.

to any object in horizontal movement with respect to the eyes. In an ordinary television picture, for example, objects moving from left to right will appear displaced in front of the screen if the right eye is covered by a filter.

In his 1922 paper Pulfrich (who was blind in his left eye and never saw the phenomenon himself) describes previous observations of the effect by astronomers using stereo-comparators. He attributes to Fertsch, an optical engineer with the Zeiss company in Jena, the now generally accepted 'delay line' explanation. Fertsch proposed that the filter causes a delay in the transmission of signals from the retina to the brain. Since the target is moving, a temporal delay corresponds to a spatial displacement: the covered eye is seeing the target with a delay in time, and thus at a spatially lagging point on its trajectory. The lag produces a stereoscopic disparity, and therefore a shift in depth (Fig. 2). Fertsch's hypothesis is now well established by direct electrical recording of the latency of the retinal response to light, and the geometrical reasoning can be verified by using a haploscopic display in which one eye's target is subjected to an actual delay. The cause of the delay is that the filter induces the covered eye to adapt to a reduced general level of illumination, which is a visual mechanism (like increasing photographic exposure time) for gaining sensitivity in dim light. The converse effect can be achieved by shining a bright pen torch into the corner of one eye: this eye now adapts to a higher level of illumination and thus responds more quickly, with a consequent depth shift in the reverse direction to the normal

Pulfrich effect (i.e. if the left eye is illuminated depth shift is anticlockwise).

Technical interest in the phenomenon was rekindled by the finding that Pulfrich's effect can be observed with stroboscopically lit targets, and even when viewing an 'electronic snowstorm' on a detuned television set. In the latter case the snowstorm appears to rotate horizontally in depth when one eye is filtered. Since there is no real motion in the display, the delay line explanation needs to be supplemented by spatio-temporal averaging of the target position.

A clinical use of Pulfrich's phenomenon has several times been suggested, on the basis of the finding that it may arise spontaneously, without the use of a filter, as a result of demyelinating disease of the optic nerve. **MJM**

Christianson, S., and Hofstetter, H. W. (1972). 'Some historical notes on Carl Pulfrich'. *American Journal of Optometry*, 570.

Morgan, M. J., and Thompson, P. (1975). 'Apparent motion and the Pulfrich effect'. *Perception*, 4.

Sachs, E. (1946). 'Abnormal delay of visual perception'. *Archives of Neurology and Psychiatry*, 56.

Tyler, C. W. (1974). 'Stereopsis in dynamic visual noise'. *Nature*, 250.

purpose. We commonly explain what people (and perhaps animals) do by assuming they have some purpose in doing it, some idea in mind which guides their activity towards their goal in an intelligently flexible fashion.

We say, for instance: Why is Mary buying arsenic? Maybe she intends to poison Martha, but more likely she needs it to get rid of the rats. Why did the chicken cross the road? To get to the corn on the other side. What made Jill insult Joan? I don't know, but she must have had some reason. As these examples suggest, we rarely use the word 'purpose' itself; perhaps this is why the Mock Turtle got the word wrong when assuring Alice that 'No wise fish would go anywhere without a porpoise. . . . Why, if a fish came to *me*, and told me he was going a journey, I should say "With what porpoise?" '. But we assume that we can explain or make sense of what people do by referring to their intentions, goals, aims, interests, ambitions, desires, wants, motives, needs, in a word, to their purposes.

Despite this universal acceptance of the concept of purpose in our everyday thinking about why people do what they do, it is not universally accepted by theoretical psychologists. On the contrary, throughout the history of psychology this concept has been, and remains, one of the most controversial of all. (It follows that the position argued in this article would not be endorsed by all current psychologists, although it is an increasingly accepted view. Examples of more 'reductive' approaches are given by the neurophilosopher Paul Churchland and the ethologist David Macfarland.) People do not merely disagree about purpose, but get more than usually heated in discussing it, often ascribing gross irresponsibility of one sort or another to their opponents in debate.

Some psychologists refuse point-blank to admit the concept of purpose into their theories, regarding it as not merely unhelpful but positively mystifying. Others are content to use it as a convenient shorthand, but believe that purposive explanations of behaviour could in principle be replaced by complicated stimulus–response or neurophysiological explanations in which the concept of purpose would not appear. Yet others insist that psychology must give a central role to purpose, that action and experience cannot possibly be explained without it; usually, they add that what it is to be a *human* being cannot be understood without this notion, so that to reject it is to adopt an essentially dehumanizing image of mankind.

Theoretical resistance to purpose arises primarily from its close connection with the *mind–body problem. It is difficult to understand how purposes can function as guiding factors in behaviour, for how can an idea affect bodily action? (There is no help in identifying the purpose with the actual goal state, rather than with the subject's idea of the goal; for the goal state is always in the future until the action has been completed, and is often not achieved at all. How can a not-yet-existent state, which may in fact never exist, cause anything to happen here and now?) The *behaviourists, with the exception of *Tolman, rejected purposive explanation, because they avoided all reference to *consciousness, subjectivity, ideas, or mind. And neurophysiology, at least at first sight, seems to leave no place for purpose, since it deals with brain cells and brain functions whose physical description does not involve reference to ideas.

However, with the work of Kenneth *Craik, neurophysiology gained the concept of a cerebral model, or inner representation of the world. According to Craik, we possess physical mechanisms in the brain that function as inner models of the world by which we perceive, think about, and act upon the environment. Explanations of psychological phenomena must refer to these models, since it is only via these internal representations that action and experience can take place. But inner models may sometimes be misleading: the fact that there are no unicorns does not prevent people from developing internal representations of such mythical beasts. Similarly, an inner model may represent a state of affairs that does not yet exist, or a plan of action that cannot be fully carried out; the person can nevertheless use this model to guide present behaviour in various ways. So there is no radical difficulty in understanding how it can be that a person acts with the purpose, or goal, of finding a unicorn even though this purpose can never be achieved.

Cerebral models correspond to the *'schemas' described by the psychologist F. C. *Bartlett. They are essentially subjective, in that they constitute the psychological subject's view of the world—and of itself. This is why action and experience possess what *Brentano and *phenomenologists call *intentionality. Many psychologists and philosophers have claimed that intentionality could not possibly be explained in terms of a physical system, so that physiology is in principle incapable of helping us understand how psychological phenomena arise. In any case since very little is known about the detailed physiological basis of cerebral models, neurophysiologists cannot yet offer precise explanations of specific psychological characteristics.

But the concept of internal representation has entered *artificial intelligence, the science of writing computer programs which enable computers to do the sort of things that are done by human minds. Programs using different inner models of cubes, for instance, recognize (and misrecognize) cubes in different ways and on different occasions. (See OBJECT PERCEPTION; PATTERN RECOGNITION.) Each program has its own view of the world, and its behaviour (saying that *this* is a cube whereas *that* is not) can be fully understood and explained only by reference to its inner schemata or models. Even though electronic engineers know precisely how the underlying mechanism works, it is the representational functions of the program which explain the 'psychological' characteristics of the programmed computer. Whether or not every aspect of human psychology could in principle be simulated on a computer is irrelevant here. The important point is that, even though the computer's 'physiology' is fully understood, its 'psychology' can be explained only in terms of its subjective (internal) models of the world.

By analogy, then, even if neurophysiologists knew

everything there is to know about the brain, *psychological* explanations would still be required to understand psychological phenomena. So psychology is not reducible to physiology, if by that is meant the claim that with sufficient physiological knowledge we could stop talking about purposes, ideas, beliefs, mistakes, and the like. Psychology is reducible to physiology only in the quite different sense that psychological features like purposes are generated by cerebral mechanisms, rather than being mysteriously inexplicable features outside the scope of science. A faith in the second kind of reducibility need not entail a faith in the first kind. It follows that the concepts in terms of which we express everything specifically *human* about human beings would still be needed, even if we understood in detail how purposes are embodied in brain mechanisms. MAB

Boden, M. A. (1972). *Purposive Explanation in Psychology.*
Churchland, P. M. (1989). *A Neurocomputational Perspective.*
McFarland, D. J. (1996). 'Animals as cost-based robots'. In Boden, M. A., (ed.), *The Philosophy of Artificial Life.*
Woodfield, A. (1976). *Teleology.*

puzzles. A puzzle is a problem having one or more specific objectives, contrived for the principal purpose of exercising one's ingenuity and/or patience. This definition, whilst separating the recreational aspects of puzzles from the undesirable features of problems, in no way explains why humans find them so necessary or enjoyable. A random survey will usually show that nearly everyone has recently played with a jigsaw, a crossword, or a mechanical puzzle and that they have answered a riddle or composed a pun. One might have anticipated that, with lives full of worries about the unavoidable problems of survival, mankind would studiously avoid volunteering to solve any unnecessary puzzles. The reality is different. Puzzles are found in every culture from their early myths and religions through to their airport shops and internet websites. It seems that evolution has identified the didactic value of puzzles and now they are a part of what makes us a successful species.

In the past when most people could not read, pub signs and coats of arms often incorporated visual puns. In much early art there is imagery that appears puzzling to us today only because we have forgotten either the meaning of the symbols or the function of the object depicted. Many word puzzles were produced combining the visual and riddling context into anagrams and acrostics. There is a book (*Anagrammata regia*) published in 1626 which contains anagrams, chronograms (where the capitalized letters are added together to produce the date of publication), and a triple acrostic. Rebuses, in which pictures replace some or all of the words, were very popular in the 18th century; some are more puzzling today than when they were produced—from looking at a tiny picture, would

you recognize a porter's knot? The porter's knot could be used to represent 'not'. Some were very silly: a 'snake' might be used to represent 'Hiss' or 'His' as in 'His Royal Highness'.

Riddles, like crossword clues and rebus picture puzzles, usually rely on special, often culturally exclusive, knowledge whereas mechanical puzzles transcend cultural and language barriers. A mechanical puzzle is a physical object that incorporates the definition given at the beginning of this article. The mechanical puzzle contains all that is required for its solution within itself.

Legend tells that Gordius, a minor king in Anatolia *c*.300 BC, had tied his ox cart to the temple gate with an intricate knot. As it was prophesied that whoever untied the Gordian Knot would rule all Asia, it may be considered as early example of both a topological puzzle and a puzzle competition. Alexander the Great arrived and promptly cut the knot. This has been held up as an example of lateral thinking, of decisiveness, and of tackling problems in novel ways; however, what succeeding generations have generally failed to notice is that this was cheating and, just as validly, it may be reasoned that this is why Alexander never did rule the whole of Asia.

Archimedes is reputed to have played with a dissected square puzzle; did this perhaps start with the accidental breaking of a tile? If you drop a china plate, have you just invented an assembly puzzle? Tangle a ball of wool—is it a topological puzzle? Even these accidental problems can become puzzles if approached in a recreational way.

'Cup and ball' is one of the earliest dexterity puzzles and together with its variants, where you have to try and stab a stick through bone rings, has probably been popular since neolithic times, to develop stabbing skills.

Two thousand years ago, Hero of Alexandria wrote in his work about pneumatics of various 'trick' vessels, among others for pouring wine and water from the same jug, and for producing 'magic' fountains. The Exeter Museum in England has a magnificent puzzle jug made *c*.1300 in France. This is a true puzzle jug with the challenge of drinking from the jug without spilling any liquid through the many holes below the rim.

Before the existence of local banks, one concealed one's valuables in secret compartments, which were the precursors of puzzle boxes. Before the technical sophistication of the 1800s, many locks relied on puzzling mechanisms in addition to, or instead of, a key. The so-called 'Chinese rings puzzle' was used in many parts of the world as a lock (Fig. 1), and, though it was probably more of a delayer than a real deterrent to a thief, it certainly qualifies as an early tanglement puzzle. The mathematician Cardan wrote about it in 1550.

A six-piece burr puzzle is illustrated in Sebastien Leclerc's engraving of *The Academy of Science and Arts* in 1698. However objects manufactured solely as puzzles did

Fig. 1. Ivory cup and ball, Chinese rings, tangram, and six-piece burr.

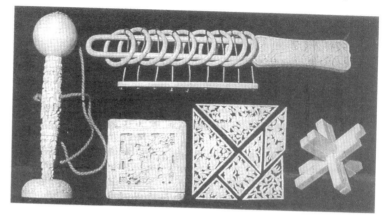

not really manifest themselves until the start of the Industrial Revolution and the advent of a relatively wealthy middle class and a wider number of people seeking and able to afford an education for their children. Initially puzzles were produced as paper or wood versions of problems that were appearing in books of recreational mathematics and 'natural philosophy', as Science was called. The jigsaw was initially invented to teach geography, but history, religion, and other subjects soon followed and finally they were developed for purely recreational purposes.

Around 1810 tangrams (a puzzle in which seven geometric pieces are used to create many pictures) and other ivory puzzles began to arrive in Europe and the USA from China. However there is no evidence, other than hearsay, that any puzzles, other than the tangram, were made in China for the Chinese prior to this date. Of the ivory puzzles that came from China apart from the tangram, most had been documented as existing in Europe beforehand and so it is not unreasonable that they were originally made exclusively to the order of Westerners for the export trade. The most significant feature of these puzzles is that, apart from jigsaws, they were the only puzzles that most people ever saw; thus 'Chinese puzzle' became the generic term for any mechanical puzzle other than jigsaws or dissected maps. To Europeans the Chinese were an enigmatic race full of mystery and secrets and so it would be natural, albeit maybe incorrectly, to credit them with the invention of such devious objects.

As industrial society developed, both leisure time and the number of puzzles being manufactured increased. William Jones's *Catalogue of Optical, Mathematical, and Philosophical Instruments* (1788) lists only a few puzzles among his scientific apparatus. In the 1840s a Mr Crambrook was producing a catalogue with over 100 puzzles and holding what is believed to be the first ever puzzle exhibition. In 1893 Hoffmann published his *Puzzles Old and New* listing several hundred puzzles in then current production, but even he was only scratching the surface of what had become available.

Puzzle crazes probably started with a tangram craze in the 1820s, followed by the 'fifteen-puzzle' craze in the 1870s. There was a well-known puzzle of arranging the numbers 1 to 16 on a four by four grid so that each line adds up to 34. Sam Loyd removed the number 16 and arranged the remaining numbers in order apart from the numbers 14 and 15. He then offered the huge prize of $1,000 to anyone who could put the puzzle in order by only sliding the pieces. Today it does not take us long to understand that a solution only exists for half the possible starting arrangements of the fifteen blocks, and that an arrangement with only 14 and 15 in the wrong order is one with no solution. However at that time most people could not comprehend why, having randomly put the pieces in the tray, sometimes they could find the solution and sometimes not. This lack of comprehension led to a craze, which spread from the USA to Europe. Loyd never actually claimed to have invented the fifteens puzzle, but he certainly started a craze the like of which was not seen again until the Rubik's cube of the 1980s which generated similar hysteria, with possibly up to 160 million being sold worldwide. It raises the interesting thought that perhaps in 2100 people will look at the cube and wonder why in the 1980s we found it so difficult to solve.

Before the computer and communications revolution the same puzzle ideas were reinvented again and again. Today there are more different types of puzzle than ever before. The exchange of ideas and information on the internet is reducing the duplication of effort and enabling the creation of ever more baffling puzzles. There is now a continuous and entertaining struggle between metagrobologists (people who are puzzled or puzzling): some use computers to solve puzzles, some use computers to make puzzles more difficult, and some search for puzzles that cannot be solved on a computer at all. Craftsmen who could never have made a living by making such exclusive items twenty years ago can now find customers for highly complex puzzles anywhere in the world. Thus the latest technology is enabling a revival of traditional crafts applied to new ideas. Computers are also enabling the modelling of puzzles in virtual reality that cannot exist in our physical three-dimensional world; for example, assembly puzzles where pieces are composed of cubes joined by their corners, and mazes in non-Euclidian space where taking three right turns on a square grid does not bring you back to your starting point.

When playing with a puzzle we are having too much fun to notice that we are exercising our brains. Puzzles play tricks with the way we think and teach us to think in new ways.   JD

Pythagoras (*c*.570–*c*.500 BC). Born in Samos, he founded a school at Croton in Magna Graecia, which combined asceticism, strict traditional rules of conduct and taboos (such as smoothing out the imprint of the body upon leav-

ing the bed, and not eating beans), and an emphasis on reason and mathematics. Although *Plato wrote a book on Pythagoras (lost in antiquity), all that has come down to us are a few doctrines, including that of the transmigration of souls (see METEMPSYCHOSIS); a list of ethical rules; and some mathematics, including his famous theorem (which has Babylonian origins), and especially number theory, which, so far as is known, he founded. Pythagoras linked the motions of the stars and planets with the mind, through music. The 'music of the spheres' was a notion continuing through the Middle Ages based on the cycles of the heavenly bodies. This doctrine was challenged by Newton's 'clockwork heaven'.

See also PRE-SOCRATIC PHILOSOPHERS.

Guthrie, K. S (comp. and trans.), and Fideler, D. R. (introd. and ed.) (1987). *The Pythagorean Sourcebook and Library: An Anthology of Ancient Writings Which Relate to Pythagoras and Pythagorean Philosophy.*

Strohmeier, J., and Westbrook, P. (2002). *Divine Harmony: The Life and Teachings of Pythagoras.*

Q

qualia. What it is like to have an experience. Qualia include the ways things look, sound, and smell, the way it feels to have a pain, and, more generally, what it is like to have experiential mental states. ('Qualia' is the plural of 'quale'.) Qualia are experiential properties of sensations, feelings, perceptions, and, more controversially, thoughts and desires as well. But, so defined, who could deny that qualia exist?

Although the existence of subjective experience is not (or anyway should not be) controversial, 'quale'—which is more clearly a technical term than 'subjective experience'—is more often used by those who are inclined to reject the common-sense conception of subjective experience. Here is a first approximation to a statement of what is controversial: whether the phenomenology of experience can be exhaustively analysed in intentional, functional, or purely cognitive terms. Opponents of qualia think that the phenomenology of an experience can be exhaustively analysed in terms of its representational or intentional content ('representationism'); or that the phenomenology of experience can be exhaustively analysed in terms of its causal role ('functionalism'), or that having a subjective experiential state can be exhaustively analysed in terms of having a state that is cognitively monitored in a certain way or accompanied by a thought to the effect that I have that state. If we include in the definition of 'qualia' the idea that the phenomenology of experience outruns such intentional, functional, and cognitive analyses, then it is controversial whether there are qualia.

This definition of 'qualia' is controversial in a respect that is familiar in philosophy. A technical term is often a locus of disagreement, and the warring parties will often disagree about what the important parameters of disagreement are. Dennett (1988), for example, assumes that it is of the essence of qualia to be intrinsic (in the sense of atomic, unanalysable, and non-relational), private (in the sense that any objective test would miss the target), incorrigible (to believe one has one is to have one), and non-physical. Dennett says there are no qualia. Hence the title of his paper, 'Quining qualia'. ('To Quine', according to the tongue-in-cheek Philosophical Lexicon, www.blackwellpublishing.com/lexicon/, is 'to deny resolutely the existence or importance of something real or significant'.) Of course, Dennett is free to use 'qualia' as

he likes, but a defender of a scientific approach to qualia (the point of view of the author of this entry) will prefer a definition of 'qualia' that allows that science can investigate qualia, that qualia may turn out to be physical, and even that we may discover aspects of introspective beliefs about one's qualia can be mistaken. Indeed, I do not see that a scientific approach can rule out in advance that we could discover, empirically, that qualia are intentional, functional, or cognitive. So I prefer to define 'quale' as an aspect of subjective experience that cannot be shown by a priori or other armchair means to be intentional, functional, or cognitive. This is an epistemic rather than a metaphysical conception of a quale (see Block 2002). Importantly, there is nothing in the conception of qualia that I am advocating that is incompatible with the claim that a quale is a physical state, just as heat is molecular kinetic energy and light is electromagnetic radiation. An empirical reductionist thesis about qualia is legitimate—what is not legitimate is an armchair reductive analysis of qualia (e.g. in functional, representational, or cognitive terms).

1. Absent qualia
2. The inverted spectrum
3. Inverted Earth
4. The knowledge argument
5. The function of qualia

1. Absent qualia
Qualia are often discussed with respect to certain thought experiments that purport to demonstrate the falsity of representationism, functionalism, and cognitivist approaches.

One of these thought experiments involves 'absent qualia'. If human beings can be described computationally, as is assumed by the research programme of cognitive science, a robot could in principle be built that was computationally identical to a human. But would there be anything it was like to be that robot? Would it have qualia? (See Block 2002, Shoemaker 1975, 1981, and White 1986.) If it had no qualia, the claim that the nature of qualia is to be found in their computational or functional role is mistaken, and functionalism is false. Further, if a zombie robot could have states that represent the properties of the world that our experiences represent (shape, size, colour, etc.) then representationism is false. (Representationism is the view that the qualitative character of an experience is identical to its representational content.) Some thought experiments (Block 1980) have appealed to oddball realizations of our functional organization, e.g. the economy of a country. If an economy can share our functional organization, then our functional organization cannot be sufficient for qualia. Many critics simply bite the bullet at this point, saying that the oddball realizations do have qualia. Lycan (1996) suggests thinking of these roles as requiring evolution and as involving the details of human physiology. Economies do not have states with the right sort of evolutionary 'purpose', and their states are not physiological. But the evolution stipulation is incompatible with the very plausible doctrine that qualia supervene on the brain: that is, no difference in qualia without a neural difference. If we are ever able to manufacture a brain like ours, it will also lack evolutionary 'purpose', but to the extent that it is physically just like our brains, it will serve as the neural basis of similar experience. On the idea of including physiological roles in our functional characterization of mental states, note that this will make the definitions so specific to humans that they will not apply to other creatures that have mental states. (Block (1980) calls this the chauvinism problem.) Further, this idea violates the spirit of the functionalist proposal, which, being based on the computer analogy, abstracts from hardware realization.

2. The inverted spectrum

Imagine that we could 'invert' colour processing in the visual system in one of two twins at birth. (See Palmer (1999) for a discussion of a variety of kinds of 'inversion', some of which are more likely to be possible than others.) If the twins grow up using colour terms normally, we might hypothesize that things they both call 'red' look to one the way things they both call 'green' look to other, even though they are functionally (and therefore behaviourally) identical. This inverted spectrum hypothesis would be further confirmed if the brain state that one twin has on seeing red things is the same as the brain state that the other has on seeing green things (and the same for other complementary colours)—assuming supervenience of qualia on the physiological properties of the brain. The relevance of this version of the inverted spectrum hypothesis to qualia is that a physicalist view of qualia can be used to challenge functionalism (qualia are causal roles) and representationism (qualia are representational contents).

For when one twin is looking at a red thing and the other is looking at a green thing, they can have two states that are physically and qualitatively the same, but are functionally and representationally different, one representing red and the other green. And if both twins are looking at the same object, they may have states that are functionally

and representationally the same but qualitatively different. (I assume that all parties can agree on which things are green, which things are red, etc.)

There is a natural reply. Notice that it is not possible that the brain state that I get when I see things we both call 'red' is *exactly* the same as the brain state that you get when you see things we both call 'green'. At least, the *total* brain states cannot be the same, since mine causes me to say 'It's red', and to classify what I am seeing as the same colour as blood and fire hydrants, whereas yours causes you to say 'It's green', and to classify what you are seeing with grass and Granny Smith apples. Suppose that the brain state that I get when I see red and that you get when you see green is X-oscillations in brain area V4, whereas what I get when I see green and you get when you see red are Y-oscillations in area V4. The functionalist says that phenomenal properties should not be linked to brain states quite so 'localized' as X-oscillations or Y-oscillations, but rather to more holistic brain states that include tendencies to classify objects together as the same colour. Thus the functionalist will want to say that my holistic brain state that includes X-oscillations and your holistic brain state that includes Y-oscillations are just *alternative realizations* of the same experiential state. So the fact that red things give me X-oscillations but they give you Y-oscillations does not show that our experiences are inverted. The defender of the claim that inverted spectra are possible can point out that when something looks red to me, I get X-oscillations, whereas when something looks green to me, I get Y-oscillations, and so the difference in the phenomenal aspect of experience corresponds to a local brain state difference. But the functionalist can parry by pointing out that this difference has only been demonstrated intrapersonally, keeping the larger brain state that specifies the roles of X-oscillations in classifying things constant. He can insist on typing brain states for *inter*personal comparisons holistically. And most friends of the inverted spectrum are in a poor position to insist on typing experiential states locally rather than holistically, given that they normally emphasize the 'explanatory gap' (Levine 1993), the fact that no one has the faintest idea how to explain why the neural basis of an experience is the neural basis of that experience rather than some other experience or no experience at all. So the friend of the inverted spectrum is in no position to insist on local physiological individuation of qualia. At this stage, the defender of the inverted spectrum is stymied.

One move the defender of the possibility of the inverted spectrum can make is to move to an intrapersonal inverted spectrum example. Think of this as a four-stage process. (1) You have normal colour vision. (2) You have colour signal inverting devices inserted in your retinas or in the lateral geniculate nucleus, the first way-station behind the retina, and red things look the way green things used to look, blue things look the way yellow things used to look, etc. (3) You have adapted, so that you naturally and spontaneously call red things 'red', etc., but when reminded, you recall the days long ago when ripe tomatoes looked to you, colourwise, the way Granny Smith apples do now. (4) You get amnesia about the days before the lenses were inserted. Stage 1 is functionally equivalent to stage 4 in the relevant respects, but they are arguably qualia inverted. And we can add that the subject starts off with X-oscillations when he sees green but the shift induced by the inverters makes green things produce Y-oscillations. So we have an inverted spectrum over time. The advantages of this thought experiment are two. First, the argument profits from the force of the subject's testimony at stages 2 and 3 for qualia inversion. The critic of the intersubjective inverted spectrum says X-oscillations and Y-oscillations are alternative realizations of the same quale, but that is a less plausible move here, since the subject himself says at stage 3 that the state he has now when he sees grass (Y-oscillations) is quite different from the state he used to have on seeing grass (X-oscillations), and there is no reason to suppose this changes at stage 4. Second, the four-stage set-up forces the opponents to say which stage is the one where the inversionist argument goes wrong (see Shoemaker 1981, Block 1990). Rey (1993) attacks stage (3) and White (1995) attacks stage (4).

Nida-Rümelin (1996) notes that, in one kind of genetic colour-blindness, the pigment of the long-wave sensitive cones (L-cones) replaces the normal pigment of the medium-wave sensitive cones (M-cones). Another kind of colour-blindness is the converse: the normal M pigment replaces the L pigment. If a person were to have both kinds of genetic abnormality, they would have the M pigment in the L cones and the L pigment in the M cones. (No such person has been found, but we can predict that there are 14 such persons for every 10,000 males.) Nida-Rümelin argues that such a person might be a natural case of spectrum inversion.

Why, an opponent might ask, is the inverted qualia argument against functionalism any more powerful than a corresponding inverted qualia argument against physicalism? After all, it might be said, one can imagine particle-for-particle duplicates who have spectra that are inverted with respect to one another (Chalmers 1996). But though particle-for-particle duplicates with inverted spectra are in some sense imaginable, they are ruled out by the highly plausible principle, mentioned above, that qualia supervene on physical constitution (i.e. no difference in qualia without a physical difference). By contrast, the form of the inverted spectrum that I have been describing does not flout supervenience: two people can be functionally identical while yet having different physical realizers of those functional states (your red-induced state is realized the same way my green-induced state is).

3. Inverted Earth

In discussing the inverted spectrum, I emphasized its relevance to functionalism. There is an interesting variant that is more relevant to representationism. The variant depends on a thought experiment, Inverted Earth (Harman 1982, Block 1990). Inverted Earth is a planet that differs from earth in two relevant ways. First, everything is the complementary colour of the corresponding earth thing. The sky is yellow, the grasslike stuff is red, etc. (To avoid impossibility, we could imagine, instead, two people raised in rooms in which everything in one room is the complementary colour of the corresponding item in the other room.) Second, people on Inverted Earth speak an inverted language. They use 'red' to mean green, 'blue' to mean yellow, etc. If you order paint from Inverted Earth, and you want yellow paint, you fax an order for 'blue paint'. The effect of both inversions is that if you are drugged and kidnapped in the middle of the night, and colour inverters are inserted behind your eyes (and your body pigments are changed), you will notice no difference if you are switched with your counterpart on Inverted Earth.

Now consider the comparison between you and your counterpart on Inverted Earth. We could run the story with the counterpart being your identical twin who was fitted with an inverter at birth and raised on Inverted Earth, or we could think of the counterpart as you after you have been fitted with the inverter and switched with your twin and have been living there for a long while. Imagine you and your counterpart gazing at your respective skies, saying 'How blue!'. Your brains can be stipulated to be molecular duplicates, *not just locally speaking but holistically speaking*. You are looking at different colours, but because of the inverter you have the same overall brain state. So very plausibly, your experiences are exactly the same. And this is plausible independently, since, as the story goes, you notice no difference when you are fitted with the inverter and placed in a niche on Inverted Earth. But the representational content of those experiences is different: your experience represents blue, the colour of the earth sky, whereas your counterpart's experience represents yellow, the colour of the Inverted Earth sky, the colour that they all call 'blue' (meaning yellow). Same qualia but different representational content. And the same set-up argues for the converse case as well. If you are looking at the blue sky on earth while your counterpart is looking at an Inverted Earth lemon (which, you will recall, is actually blue), you will have experiences that represent the same colour, blue, but are phenomenally different. Same representational content, different qualia. And both cases are challenges for representationism.

There are two major advantages of this case over the inverted spectrum thought experiment: (1) the twins' brains are *total* replicas (when they gaze at their respective skies), so there is no potential conflict of holism vs. localism, (2) in the version in which your twin is just you after emigration, there is no need for the adaptation that was required in the intrasubjective inverted spectrum thought experiment.

However, there is a compensating difficulty that derives from the fact that there is a kind of adaptation in the environment rather than in the head. Let me explain. Consider the intrasubjective case. The strength of the intrasubjective inverted spectrum case lies in the personal testimony in stage 3 that grass looks the way blood used to look colourwise. The weakness lies in the fact that the subject has undergone a strange adaptation process that perhaps impugns his judgements. In the case of the subject being moved from earth to a niche on Inverted Earth, when the subject says things look the same now as they always did, he is believable because he undergoes no phenomenal adaptation process. However, we can reasonably wonder whether his experience on Inverted Earth really does represent the sky as yellow. We can agree that the natives all around him represent the sky as it really is, that is, as yellow, but our subject after all grew up (and evolved) using *that very experience* to represent blue. This is one of the objections made in Tye (2000).

One response is that the representational content of experience is not fixed by evolution or early experience. If we find out that your grandparents were 'swamp-people' who came together from particles in the swamp and did not evolve at all, we would not thereby have shown that your experience does not have the normal representational and qualitative content. Also, if I come to develop a Bush recognitional capacity but then move to a place where Bush's twin brother is the president, I don't misrecognize twin Bush forever. Eventually, my recognitional capacity readjusts. My visual experience represents Bush as Bush. So why should we suppose that the colour represented by the subject's early experience on earth makes it forever misrepresent the colour of the sky on Inverted Earth? (I have only been able to touch on issues that are discussed in much more detail in Lycan 1996 and Tye 2000.)

4. The knowledge argument

The inverted spectrum, Inverted Earth, and absent qualia arguments are critiques of functionalist and representationist views of qualia. The final thought experiment to be discussed here is directed as much at physicalism as at functionalism. Jackson's (1986) Mary is raised in a black-and-white environment in which she learns all the functional and physical facts about colour vision. None the less, when she ventures outside for the first time, she learns a new fact: what it is like to see red. So, the argument goes, what it is like to see red cannot be a functional or physical fact. Dennett (1991) objects that perhaps she

could have 'figured out' which things are red; but that is beside the point for two reasons. The question is whether she knows what it is like to see red, not which things are red. And does she know it simply in virtue of knowing all the functional and physical facts about colour vision?

A natural objection is that physicalism is not concerned with what Mary knows, but rather what qualia are, what their metaphysical nature is. Someone could know all the physical facts about molecular kinetic energy changes but not know about heat changes—if the person does not know that heat is molecular kinetic energy. But the analogy does not apply, since we can suppose that Mary *does* know that what it is like to see red is something physical and even exactly what state of the brain it is. That will not keep her from learning a new fact when she learns what it is like to see red.

Lewis (1990) denies that Mary acquires any new knowledge-*that*, insisting that she only acquires knowledge-*how*, abilities to imagine and recognize. But others have emphasized that what Mary learns seems very propositional: she could even express it as: 'What I learned is that *this* is what it is like to see red.' Further, as Loar (1990) points out, the knowledge she acquires can be expressed in embedded contexts. For example, she may reason that, if this is what it is like to see red, then what it is like to see red is more enjoyable than what it is like to be slapped in the belly with a wet fish.

Here is a different (and in my view more successful) objection to Jackson (Horgan 1984, Peacocke 1989, Loar 1990, Papineau 1993, van Gulick 1993, Sturgeon 1994, Perry 2001): what Mary acquires when she sees red for the first time is a new phenomenal *concept*. This new phenomenal concept is a constituent of genuinely new knowledge— knowledge of what it is like to see red. But the new phenomenal concept picks out *old* properties, properties picked out by physical or functional concepts that she already had in the black-and-white room. So the new knowledge is just a new way of knowing old facts. Before leaving the room, she knew what it is like to see red in a third-person way; after leaving the room, she acquires a new way of knowing the same fact. If so, what she acquires does not rule out any possible worlds that were not already ruled out by the facts that she already knew, and the thought experiment poses no danger to physicalism.

5. The function of qualia

It is often supposed that qualitative character has all sorts of wonderful functions, promoting flexibility, creativity, and even making recursive models. Block (1995) suggests that the main function of qualitative character is promoting access to mechanisms of short-term memory, perceptual categorization, reasoning, and decision making. Qualia are red flags that representations wave at intelligent processors. The intelligent processing that results is a product of three things: the preconscious mechanisms that determine what representations are to acquire qualitative character, the post-conscious mechanisms that actually do the intelligent processing, and finally, the qualitative character that helps to make the representations accessible to the intelligent mechanisms. To give the qualitative character *itself* the credit for creativity, flexibility, etc. is like giving the printing press the credit for the ideas that are printed.   NB

Block, N. (1980). 'Troubles with functionalism'. Reprinted in Block N. (ed.), *Readings in the Philosophy of Psychology*, Vol i.
—— (1990). 'Inverted earth'. In Tomberlin, J. (ed.), *Philosophical Perspectives*, 4.
—— (1995). 'On a Confusion about the Function of Consciousness'. *Behavioral and Brain Sciences*, 18.
—— (2002). 'The harder problem of consciousness'. *Journal of Philosophy*, 99/8.
Byrne, A. (2001). 'Intentionalism defended'. *Philosophical Review*, 110.
Chalmers, D. (1996). *The Conscious Mind*.
Dennett, D. (1988). 'Quining qualia'. In Marcel A., and Bisiach, E. (eds.), *Consciousness in Contemporary Society*.
—— (1991). *Consciousness Explained*.
Davies, M., and Humphreys, C. (1993). *Consciousness*.
Harman, G. (1982). 'Conceptual role semantics'. *Notre Dame Journal of Formal Logic*, 23/2.
Horgan, T. (1984). 'Jackson on physical information and qualia'. *Philosophical Quarterly*, 34.
Jackson, F. (1986). 'What Mary didn't know'. *Journal of Philosophy*, 83.
—— (1993). 'Armchair metaphysics'. In O'Leary-Hawthorne, J., and Michael, M. (eds.), *Philosophy in Mind*.
Levine, J. (1993). 'On leaving out what it is like.' In Davies and Humphreys (1993)
Lewis, D. (1990). 'What experience teaches'. In Lycan, W. (ed.), *Mind and Cognition*.
Loar, B. (1990). 'Phenomenal properties'. In Tomberlin J. (ed.), *Philosophical Perspectives: Action Theory and Philosophy of Mind*.
Lycan, W. (1996). *Consciousness and Experience*.
McGinn, C. (1991). *The Problem of Consciousness*.
Nida-Rümelin, M. (1996). 'Pseudonormal vision: an actual case of qualia inversion?' *Philosophical Studies*, 82.
Palmer, S. (1999). 'Color, consciousness, and the isomorphism constraint'. *Behavioral and Brain Sciences*, 22/6.
Papineau, D. (1993). 'Physicalism, consciousness and the antipathetic fallacy'. *Australian Journal of Philosophy*, 71.
—— (2002). *Thinking about Consciousness*.
Peacocke, C. (1989). 'No resting place: a critical notice of *The View from Nowhere*'. *Philosophical Review*, 98.
Perry, J. (2001). *Knowledge, Possibility and Consciousness*.
Rey, G. (1993). 'Sensational sentences switched'. *Philosophical Studies*, 70/1.
Shoemaker, S. (1975). 'Functionalism and qualia'. *Philosophical Studies*, 27.
—— (1981). 'Absent qualia are impossible: a reply to Block'. *Philosophical Review*, 90/4.
Sturgeon, S. (1994). 'The epistemic view of subjectivity'. *Journal of Philosophy*, 91/5.
Tye, M. (2000). *Consciousness, Color and Content*.
Van Gulick, R. (1993). 'Understanding the phenomenal mind: are we all just armadillos?' In Davies and Humphreys (1993)
White, S. L. (1986). 'Curse of the qualia'. *Synthese*, 68.
—— (1995). 'Color and the narrow contents of experience'. *Philosophical Topics*, 23.

qualities. The universe, as described by modern science, is conceived largely in quantitative terms. Mass, energy, velocity, length, breadth, and height are all expressible as mathematical quantities or amounts—as answers to the question *Quantum?* or 'How much?'. But it is striking that most of the ordinary ways in which we describe our environment are not quantitative but qualitative: the descriptions involved answer the question *Quale?*, 'What is it like?'. Such *qualia, or qualities, include redness, softness, sweetness, rankness, shrillness (of the five types of so-called 'sensible qualities' of sight, touch, taste, smell, and hearing, respectively). There is a long-standing philosophical debate about whether such qualities really inhere in objects or whether they are simply subjective effects in the mind of the observer. John *Locke systematized (though he did not invent) a distinction between primary and secondary qualities. Primary qualities (roughly corresponding to the scientifically measurable *quanta* mentioned above) include shape, magnitude, and number, and are supposed to inhere in objects, so that our ideas of size etc. actually resemble genuine features of the objects in question. But secondary qualities, such as redness, sweetness, etc., are rather different: our ideas of them do not, according to Locke, directly resemble anything in the object themselves, but are merely the result of the way objects affect our senses by means of their primary qualities.

Some philosophers have been suspicious of the primary/secondary distinction, pointing out that our attributions of colour, no less than our attributions of size, are a function of perfectly straightforward and objective rules of language, so that it is as correct to say that the sun is 'really' yellow as it is to say that it is 'really' spherical. But there remains a special subjective or phenomenological character to our sensation of qualities like yellowness which seems to depend in part on the particular sensory apparatus with which our species is equipped—and it is not the same for all individuals. Thus it is possible to imagine that aliens equipped with different kinds of organs would perceive light of a certain wavelength in radically different ways from us, to the point where the human notion of 'yellowness' would be inaccessible to them. This line of thought lends support to the idea that there is indeed something 'subjective' about sensory qualities such as redness and sweetness; the notions of squareness or sphericity, by contrast, do not seem similarly tied to the particular sensory 'mode' in terms of which they are experienced.

Apart from questions of subjectivity, there is a problem about whether *qualia* such as redness or sweetness can usefully figure in scientific explanations. Robert Boyle, writing in the 1650s, pointed out that if you want to know why snow dazzles the eyes it is no help to be told that it has the 'quality of whiteness'. Similar charges of explanatory vacuity were levelled against the scholastic theory that bodies fall because of an inherent quality of *gravitas* or heaviness. It was for this kind of reason that we find *Descartes insisting that scientific explanations should invoke 'nothing apart from that which the geometricians call quantity, and take as the object of their demonstrations, i.e. that to which every kind of division, shape and motion is applicable' (*Principles of Philosophy*, 1644). Nevertheless, while this quantitative approach has undoubtedly been fruitful for physics, its application to psychology is more controversial. Sensible qualities are, after all, an inescapable part of the psychological landscape; any understanding of our mental life must, it seems, include some account of *what it is like* for us to see colours, smell smells, and so on. JGC

quantifying judgements. Human judgement is so fallible that, in assessing magnitudes, objective physical measures need to be used wherever they are available. There are cases, however, where physical measures are not available: some magnitudes lack them. The loudness of noises, for example, cannot be measured directly in physical units because loudness is a subjective quantity which depends on the ear and the brain. A noise is likely to sound less loud to a partially deaf person than to a person with normal hearing. Similarly, the likableness of people cannot be measured directly. In these and comparable cases it is necessary to resort to quantitative subjective judgements.

1. Theoretical issues
2. Avoiding biases

1. Theoretical issues

Two kinds of stimulus magnitude It is important to distinguish between stimulus magnitudes with familiar physical units and those without. Lengths, weights, and durations can be measured in physical units learned at school. In judging differences in magnitude or ratios between different magnitudes measured in familiar units, observers have merely to perform the appropriate arithmetical operations. Such judged differences and ratios are thus related by the rules of arithmetic, and the average of the findings of, say, several people in a group will be a reasonably accurate one.

Here we will consider only stimulus magnitudes which observers are unable to measure in familiar physical units and for which they have to develop and use their own, subjective units. Such units of discriminability do not

have, at the sensory threshold, an obvious zero from which absolute magnitudes can be judged; and therefore they cannot be used to judge ratios of magnitude. Even so, they can be used to judge differences between magnitudes, because where two magnitudes are the same size the difference between them is zero.

Two kinds of quantitative judgement There are two ways of quantifying subjective judgements. One method uses a restricted range of responses with specified upper and lower limits: category ratings are the most frequently used examples. In contrast, the other method uses direct numerical magnitude judgements, which can provide the judge with a potentially infinite range of numbers.

Category ratings characteristically give a logarithmic relation between stimulus magnitude and subjective magnitude:

$$R = k + n \log S \tag{1}$$

where R is the response, S is the stimulus, and k and n are constants. By contrast, direct numerical magnitude judgements characteristically give a loglog relation (Stevens 1975):

$$\log R = \log k + n \log S \tag{2}$$

Taking antilogs, Equation (2) becomes a power function:
$$R = kS^n$$
where n is the exponent.

S. S. *Stevens (1906–73) was the main protagonist of direct numerical magnitude judgements. Most technologists or others who need to quantify subjective judgements use category ratings, on the other hand, because their restricted range makes judging easier and provides less variable averages.

Logarithmic response bias There has been controversy over whether Equation (1) or Equation (2) better represents the observers' perceptions of magnitude. It is now tacitly accepted that Equation (1) is correct. Stevens's Equation (2) incorporates a logarithmic response bias which occurs when observers use for responses a range of numbers containing a change in the number of allowed digits. After responding with numbers up to 10, observers have two alternative ways of proceeding. They can continue 11, 12, 13, 14 . . ., using numbers linearly. Or they can go more logarithmic and continue 20, 30, 40 . . . The average of a group of observers is likely to be a compromise between a pure linear and a pure logarithmic use of numbers, but closer to logarithmic.

Once Stevens had obtained his loglog relation, he instructed his student observers to use for responses a scale of numbers calibrated in ratios, like a slide rule. But this ensures that a loglog relation will be found, because it changes the R on the left side of Equation (1) to the log R on the left side of Equation (2).

There are two main lines of evidence that support the linear relation of Equation (1). In providing the first,

Poulton (1986) asked separate groups of uninitiated observers to judge the difference between the loudnesses of two noises. The less intense noise he called 1·0. The observers were told to respond with a higher number that represented the loudness of the more intense noise. When the medians of the very first judgements were numbers less than 10, they were linear in decibels.

The medians of the very first judgements showed a logarithmic response bias only when they were greater than 10, and so median responses were taken from a range of responses that contained both single-digit and two-digit numbers. A logarithmic response bias was found, also, when observers made a series of judgements of different loudnesses, but this was because the logarithmic response bias from using a range of responses which contained both one-digit and two-digit numbers transferred to the responses using only single digits.

Judged differences and ratios of magnitude have the same underlying relation The second main line of evidence comes from several comparable investigations using different stimulus dimensions, which are summarized by Birnbaum (1980). In an investigation of the likeableness of people, described by single adjectives, Hagerty and Birnbaum (1978) compared judgements of differences, $(A-B)$, with judgements of ratios, A/B. The median difference judgements (of their 23 undergraduates) showed a linear relation to the stimulus magnitudes, following Equation (1). The median ratio judgements showed a logarithmic relation, following Equation (2).

Yet the rank orders of the sizes of the median difference judgements can be compared with the rank order of the sizes of the median ratio judgements, using Kruskal and Carmone's computer program Monanova. This program maximizes the fit of all the rank orders to the linear model, without changing the orders. When this is done, the two rank orders are found to fit almost exactly the same subtractive model. This should not happen if the difference and ratio judgements represent genuine differences in perception because, for example, $(7-3)$ is greater than $(4-1)$, yet $7/3$ is less than $4/1$. Clearly the subjects' difference and ratio judgements are simply two ways of describing the same perceptual relation between the stimuli of a pair.

Judged ratios of magnitude are simply judged differences with a logarithmic response bias In the Hagerty and Birnbaum investigation, the relation perceived and judged must be a difference, not a ratio, because there are no familiar physical units of likeableness. The experimental subjects could use only their own improvised subjective units of discriminability. But these have no zero corresponding to a sensory threshold, which would have enabled ratios to be perceived and judged. When they were instructed to judge ratios, they were given a scale described in ratios, but it

turned out that they could not perceive and judge the ratios. However, they could use their subjective units of discriminability to judge the differences, because differences become zero when the two members are equal. Thus, differences were judged, but by using a scale of ratios.

In confirmation of this, Hagerty and Birnbaum presented adjectives representing pairs of people. The undergraduates were instructed to judge the ratios of the two differences in likeableness, $(A-B)/(C-D)$. Both differences having obvious zeros, the undergraduates could judge their ratio. For the differences $(A-B)$ in the numerator, the median judgements changed from positive to negative as A changed from being more likeable than B to being less likeable than B. This indicates that the median of the subjects perceived the difference in likeableness between A and B. For the ratios, reducing the size of the difference $(C-D)$ in the denominator magnifies the median differences $(A-B)$ in the numerator. This indicates that the median of the subjects judged the ratio of the perceived differences.

Since the ratios of the differences in likeableness bear the appropriate arithmetic relation to the magnitudes of the differences, the Monanova program cannot fit a simple model to all the medians taken together. To produce a simple acceptable linear fit, the ratios have to be excluded. The medians for each size of difference in the denominator have to be fitted separately. For the same reason, when all the medians are taken together, a non-metric scaling program cannot fit a simple multiplicative relation either.

The important point is that it is the *differences* in likeableness that are perceived and their *ratios* that are judged, not vice versa. There is no corresponding condition where ratios are perceived and their differences are judged. In a crucial control condition, the undergraduates were instructed to judge the differences of the ratios, $(A/B) - (C/D)$, and their median judgements showed a linear relation to the stimulus magnitudes. When subjected to the Monanova program, these median judgements fit almost exactly the same subtractive model as do the median judgements of a *differences* of *differences* condition $(A-B) - (C-D)$. Thus, the subjects must have judged the differences of the differences, not the differences of the *ratios* as they were instructed to do.

Theoretical conclusions The general rule is that in dealing with stimulus magnitudes that do not have familiar physical units, people perceive only differences in magnitude. People can judge the ratios of the perceived *differences*, because they can use their improvised units of discriminability. But they cannot perceive the *ratios* of the magnitudes directly, because this requires an obvious zero at the sensory threshold, which units of discriminability do not have.

quantifying judgements

By contrast, in dealing with stimulus magnitudes that do have familiar physical units, observers can calculate both differences and ratios. The differences and ratios are related by the rules of arithmetic. Thus it is not possible to tell whether the observers actually perceive the differences and ratios, or simply calculate them. Presumably they perceive differences as they do in dealing with stimulus magnitudes that do not have familiar physical units. But they may or may not perceive ratios as well.

2. Avoiding biases

Biases found in quantifying judgements are illustrated in Fig. 1. The biases are considerably larger when stimulus magnitudes cannot be judged directly in familiar physical units. The centring bias, a, and the stimulus spacing and stimulus frequency biases, e, are most often recognized in judgements using category ratings. The logarithmic response bias, f, and the stimulus and response range equalizing bias, b, occur most frequently in direct numerical magnitude judgements (see below). The contraction bias, c, and transfer bias (not shown) occur with all kinds of quantitative judgements. The local contraction bias, d, is seldom reported.

Centring bias or adaptation level in rating In rating, people tend to use a symmetrical distribution of responses. This centres their range of response ratings on the midpoint of the range of stimuli, as is illustrated in Fig. 1a. Thus, in judging a series of road vehicle or aircraft noises, the just acceptable noise level in the centre of the rating scale is found to lie close to the middle of the range of noises—at whatever intensity level that happens to be. This means that in a quiet residential area the loudest noises will continue to be judged too loud, however much they are reduced in intensity.

In designing an investigation, this bias is avoided by presenting a range of stimuli with an unbiased midpoint which corresponds to the centre of the rating scale. The unbiased midpoint can be determined by presenting separate groups of people with ranges of stimuli that bias the centre of the rating scale in one direction. Other groups of people are presented with ranges which bias the centre of

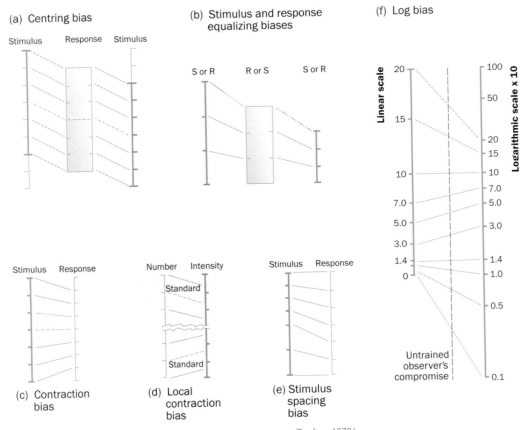

Fig. 1. Biases in quantitative judgements. S = stimulus. R = response. (Poulton 1979.)

the rating scale in the opposite direction. The stimulus range with the unbiased midpoint can then be determined, by interpolation.

The centring bias affects most kinds of judgement. In judging how hard up they are, people are likely to judge their present income against what they are used to spending, or what their neighbours spend. The relatively unstressful events in a relaxed period of people's lives are likely to appear at the time almost as stressful to them as the most stressful events in a stressful period of their lives.

Stimulus spacing and stimulus frequency biases The stimulus spacing and stimulus frequency biases are produced by using all parts of the response scale about equally often. In the stimulus spacing bias, people judge a set of stimuli to be more equally spaced subjectively than they really are, as is illustrated in Fig. 1e. The stimulus frequency bias can be treated as a special case of the stimulus spacing bias. The observers behave as if all the stimuli were equally probable. When one stimulus is presented more frequently than the others, the observers treat the more frequent stimuli as if they had almost, though not exactly, the same magnitude. Thus three identical stimuli one-quarter of the way from the top of the stimulus range are treated as three closely spaced stimuli of slightly different size, as is illustrated on the left of Fig. 1e. This bias increases the amount of the observers' response range that is allocated to the identical stimuli. In designing an investigation, the *stimulus spacing* bias is avoided by spacing the stimuli at subjectively equal intervals. The *stimulus frequency* bias is avoided by presenting all the stimuli equally often.

The stimulus spacing bias may influence the choice of the candidate for a job. There may be a few very good candidates who are all close together in order of merit, like the stimuli at the top on the left of Fig. 1e. Yet, owing to the stimulus spacing bias, all the candidates are judged to be about equally spaced. As a result, the candidate who is only marginally the best may be selected, whereas if all the very good candidates were known to be almost equally good, the choice between them could be made in part on other criteria that are important.

The stimulus frequency bias may influence the interpretation of a situation or object represented as a branching tree, which is sometimes used to help make decisions, or to find faults in equipment. People assume that all the branches represent equal frequencies or probabilities and so are equally important, whereas some branches may be much more important than others.

Logarithmic response bias The logarithmic response bias is the cause of the theoretical controversy discussed above. The bias is avoided by taking two precautions: (i) do not provide for responses a range of numbers that includes a change in the number of digits; (ii) do not instruct the judges to use a scale of numbers calibrated in ratios.

Stimulus and response range equalizing bias When judged magnitudes are plotted on the ordinate of a graph against physical magnitudes on the abscissa, smaller stimulus ranges give steeper slopes. People start their judgements with what they believe to be a sensible range of responses. They distribute these responses over the range of stimuli presented to them. With a smaller range of stimuli, the responses are spaced more closely, as is illustrated on the right of Fig. 1b. Thus the slope is steeper. This bias is usually unavoidable.

Contraction bias People underestimate large sizes and differences, and they overestimate small sizes and differences. Once they know the range of responses that is available, they select a response that lies too close to the middle of the range, as is illustrated in Fig. 1c. The figure shows that the range of responses is contracted when compared with the range of stimuli. Hence the name 'contraction bias'. Stevens (1975) calls it the regression effect.

The contraction bias can be counterbalanced by reversing stimuli and responses. The dimension previously used for the stimuli is now used for the responses, and so has the contracted range. Averaging the results of the two investigations should counterbalance the contractions.

The contraction bias occurs in every kind of judgement. In giving people references, exceptional people do not usually receive as good references as they should do. Dreadful people do not usually receive as bad references as they should do. At universities, the bias is likely to result in too many students being awarded second- or third-class degrees, while too few students are awarded first classes or failed. Small risks are usually overestimated, whereas large risks are underestimated. When respondents specify the range of confidence within which a statement is judged to lie, the extent of the range is likely to be underestimated at both ends, as in Fig. 1c.

Transfer bias This is the influence of a condition on the performance of subsequent conditions. Transfer biases are likely to occur in any investigation where people perform more than one condition, especially if they are free to choose their strategies. Transfer biases are particularly common and powerful when uninitiated people have to judge several magnitudes in turn. Once a person uses a particular range of numbers in direct magnitude estimation, he or she is likely to use a similar range in subsequent investigations. If the instructions mention a range of possible numbers or ratios, they are likely to influence the numerical magnitude judgements of uninitiated people. Transfer bias occurs both between successive judgements within an investigation and between successive investigations.

Investigators who use balanced Latin square designs assume that transfer is symmetrical, but it may be asymmetrical. The effect of performing condition *A* on the subsequent performance of condition B may be different from the effect of performing condition B on condition A. If so, comparing the average of the two A conditions with the average of the two B conditions does not remove the transfer bias.

Worse still, adding conditions C and D to the Latin square may reverse the differences found between conditions A and B. This happens when conditions C and D require a new strategy. The strategy may transfer to conditions A and B, and change the way in which the observers approach the task. Transfer bias can be avoided for certain only by using separate groups of uninitiated people for each investigation or judgement.   ECP

Birnbaum, M. H. (1980). 'Comparison of two theories of "ratio" and "difference" judgments'. *Journal of Experimental Psychology: General*, 109.

Hagerty, M., and Birnbaum, M. H. (1978). 'Nonmetric tests of ratio vs. subtractive theories of stimulus comparisons'. *Perception and Psychophysics*, 24.

Poulton, E. C. (1979). 'Models for biases in judging sensory magnitude'. *Psychological Bulletin*, 86.

——(1986). 'Why unbiased numerical magnitude judgments of the loudness of noise are linear in decibels: a rejoinder to the Teghtsoonians'. *Perception and Psychophysics*, 39.

Stevens, S. S. (1975). *Psychophysics: Introduction to its Perceptual, Neural, and Social Prospects.*

Quetelet, Lambert Adolphe Jacques (1796–1874). Belgian statistician and astronomer, born at Ghent. He was a pioneer in developing and applying statistics to social and human characteristics, especially in relation to the average man. His works include *Sur l'homme* (1835) and *L'Anthropométrie* (1871).

R

Ramón y Cajal, Santiago (1852–1934). Spanish neuro-anatomist, born at Petilla, Navarra, in the Pyrenees. He studied medicine, and after army service in Cuba he returned to Spain to teach, becoming professor of anatomy at Valencia (1883), of histology at Barcelona (1887), and of histology and pathological anatomy at Madrid (1892–1922). He improved Camillo *Golgi's method for staining nervous tissue with silver and undertook a systematic study of the microscopic structure of the brain. He established that adjacent nerve cells did not join each other however close their fibres might be and suggested that nerve impulses passed from the axon of one neuron to the dendrite of the next, and not in the opposite direction (see BRAIN DEVELOPMENT). In 1906 he shared a Nobel Prize with Golgi for their work on the structure of nervous tissue.

rapid eye movement (REM). See DREAMING.

reaction times. Like all other animals, humans can only *experience* the immediate past. Many scores of milliseconds must pass before any change in the world can be registered by a sense organ or interpreted by a brain. This perpetual lag behind the world, measured from the moments at which changes actually occur and the moments at which we can apprehend them, has become known as 'reaction time'.

Philosophies that attributed human consciousness to incorporeal entities whose rates of apprehension were infinitely fast ('the speed of thought') delayed recognition of this simple fact until very late in human history. In 1799, Nevil Maskelyne, then British Astronomer Royal, sacked his assistant Kinnebrook because their timings of stellar transits always disagreed. Friedrich Bessel (1784–1846), a more considering scientist, noted that discrepancies between measurements made by individual astronomers were widespread and substantial. For the first time someone saw the necessity of calibrating human observers, as well as the equipment that they used. Each astronomer, thenceforth, determined his personal, characteristic lag and used it as a corrective constant in his work.

By 1858 *Helmholtz had recognized a further implication of this lag, seeing that one factor limiting human reaction time must be the speed with which electrical impulses travel along nerve fibres. To measure this speed he asked a human observer to bite on a contact switch as soon as he felt an electric shock, which might be delivered either to his foot or to his face. Responses to foot shocks were slower. Assuming that this difference occurred because impulses from the foot have further to travel before they reach the brain, Helmholtz measured the difference to obtain the first estimate for the velocity of transmission of nerve impulses. The phrase 'swift as thought' took on a potentially exact, if rather humble, value.

Helmholtz's brilliant insight, that measurements of human reaction times may be used to make deductions about the nature of otherwise unobservable neural processes, provided impetus for a next step. In 1868, F. C. Donders, a Dutch ophthalmologist, reasoned that a human must recognize a new stimulus before he can begin to organize a response to it. As we shall see, this is not quite true. However, Donders argued that, since a stimulus must be recognized before a response to it can be chosen and executed, lags for these two processes must seem to give overall observed reaction times. By appropriate techniques reaction times may therefore be decomposed to give independent estimates for times taken to recognize signals and for times required to choose responses to them.

To obtain such estimates Donders required his observers to carry out each of three different tasks. In the *a* task (simple reaction time task) they always had to make the same response as fast as possible every time a single signal occurred. In the *b* task (choice reaction task) any one of five different signals might occur in unpredictable order and the observer made a different response to each. In the *c* task (Go/No Go task) any one of the same five stimuli might occur, unpredictably, but the observer responded only to occurrences of one of them and ignored the others. Donders argued that differences in observed reaction times $c-a$ would provide estimates of how much longer a person needed in order to distinguish among five different signals than to make a response without having to discriminate which signal had occurred. Similarly, the difference $b-c$ would give an estimate of how long an observer needed to select among five different responses, rather than merely always to choose whether or not to make a particular response, after making the same discrimination. Donders's experiment gave him estimates for perceptual discrimination times (less than 50 milliseconds) which were far shorter than his estimates for response selection times (over 150 milliseconds), and he began to hope that his technique would allow independent estimates for other, more complex 'unobservable internal mental processes'.

Donders's results were reasonable in principle, but the logic of his experiment was flawed in two ways: first, in his *c* task his observer never had to discriminate each of five signals from all of four others, as in the *b* task. In the *c* task the observer merely had to discriminate one 'Go' signal from all of another set of four 'No Go' signals. There was thus no requirement to discriminate any 'No Go' signal from any other 'No Go' signal. Thus the *b* task involved both a more complex perceptual discrimination and a more complex response choice than the *c* task, and the *b*−*c* estimate for discrimination time confounded these factors.

A more interesting weakness of Donders's experiment was that, like all other successful animals, human beings overcome their temporal lag behind events in the external world by learning to predict what will happen next. When they can do this they can have reaction times of zero milliseconds, responding to events just as soon as they occur, or they can even take leaps into the future, gaining an edge over a rapidly changing environment, or over rapidly moving adversaries, by anticipating events which have not yet occurred. In Donders's *a* task his observer could set himself, in advance, to identify the same, recurrent, signal on every trial, and on every trial he could also safely prepare to make the same response to it. Thus the neural processes timed in the *a* task have much more to do with anticipation and expectancy than with the processes of discrimination and choice that underlie the *b* and *c* tasks, in which observers must always wait until after something happens before their sense organs and brains can begin to work out what has occurred.

It is now widely recognized that reaction-time measurements make little sense unless we bear in mind that, although all living things can *experience* only the past, animals like ourselves have gained our success in the world by continuously, and accurately, predicting the very immediate future. A good cricketer has to predict, before the ball leaves the bowler's hand, the precise point in space at which it will be intercepted by his bat. A squash player who could not anticipate would founder hopelessly behind the game. Reaction times do not provide us with measurements of the time necessary for sets of nerve impulses generated in the sense organs to activate those parts of the brain that, in turn, activate our muscles. They rather measure the duration of operation of processes of active, predictive control, by means of which we organize responses that anticipate, and pre-empt, very fast changes in the world.

This point was only very slowly recognized. In Leipzig, in 1879, *Wundt set up the first laboratory of experimen-

tal psychology. His research programme was largely concerned with criticisms and extensions of Donders's work. It is sad that his many years of heroically dull experimentation now merely provide a textbook moral that conscious introspection can tell us little about the nature of decisions that may take us less than a fifth of a second to make.

As is often the case in experimental psychology, unpretentious calibrational studies proved the most fruitful in the long run. In 1892, von Merkle showed that an observer's reaction times increase regularly with the number of signals among which he has to discriminate, and with the number of responses among which he must, consequently, choose. In 1931 Henmon showed that, as pairs of signals become more similar to each other, people take longer to discriminate between them. Observations such as these are very simple, and unsurprising, but their consequences are not at all trivial. From experiments based on von Merkle's results, Hick (1952) developed models for human reaction times that were the first, and the most influential, demonstrations that the new sciences of *cybernetics and *information theory, which had been developed during the 1940s, have very fruitful applications as abstract descriptions of the way in which the human brain arrives at decisions. From data similar to those gathered by Henmon, later workers such as Audley, Crossman, Falmagne, Laming, Luce, and Vickers have shown how reaction-time measurements may be incorporated into a new *psychophysics of signal detection (see BIT). Non-specialists may capture something of the importance of this endeavour if they reflect that human experimental psychologists can only measure two things about human performance: how accurately people do things and how long they take to do them. Metrics and models that allow us to discuss speed and errors as complementary indices are basic tools of research.   PR

Hick, W. E. (1952). 'On the rate of gain of information'. *Quart. J. Exp. Psychol.*, 4.

reading speed and colour. Some people experience distortions when they look at striped patterns, provided the stripes have certain characteristics. The characteristics are those of *strong* patterns—patterns that can be seen most easily, that interfere with the perception of other stimuli most readily, that evoke the greatest electrical or blood-flow changes in the brain, and that can provoke headaches or even seizures in those who are susceptible. Text provides a strong striped pattern. The distortions of text may involve blurring, movement of letters, words doubling, shadowy lines, shapes or colours on the page, and flickering. The distortions are at their most confusing in small, closely spaced printed text, but they also occur to a lesser extent in handwriting. The distortions are characteristic of a condition that some have called

Meares–Irlen syndrome and others visual stress. The cause of the distortions is not known with any certainty. Some authors have hypothesized that the distortions are due to a dysfunction, perhaps a hyperexcitability, of nerve cells in the visual cortex of the brain. Individuals with migraine are particularly susceptible to the distortions in strong patterns, and there is other evidence that in migraine the cortex can be hyperexcitable.

The perceptual distortions may occur quite independently of any refractive error, although they are often, but not invariably, associated with a mild binocular vision difficulty. The binocular difficulties do not appear to be the basis for the distortions, and indeed the reverse may in fact be the case: the distortions may interfere with binocular control.

A substantial proportion of children in mainstream primary education (perhaps as many as 20 per cent) will report distortions of text. It is difficult to elicit reports of these subjective phenomena without bias, but children who report distortions differ from others in that they read faster and for longer without discomfort when the text is coloured, either by covering the page with a coloured sheet of plastic (an overlay) or when coloured glasses (spectral filters) are worn. The children report that the colour reduces the distortions. Children with reading difficulty are slightly more likely than others to report distortion, and to benefit from coloured overlays. The susceptibility to distortions runs in families. The children who benefit from colour are twice as likely to have migraine in the family as those who do not.

Each individual benefits from a different colour, and the precision of colour required to optimize reading speed is remarkable. Departures from optimum of two *just-noticeable differences are sufficient to reduce reading speed appreciably. The possible long-term effects of wearing coloured glasses for reading are unknown at present. It seems that children benefit most from colour if treatment is offered as soon as any reading difficulty is suspected, before the cycle of failure has begun. Many 7-year-olds use coloured overlays for a year or two and then discard them as unnecessary. This is usually because reading fluency without the overlay has improved.

The British College of Optometrists recommends that children use and demonstrate benefit from a coloured overlay before treatment with coloured glasses is considered. The therapeutic colour in glasses is *not the same* as that in overlays. When you use an overlay only part of the visual scene is coloured and the eyes are adapted to white light. When you wear glasses the entire visual scene is coloured and the eyes are adapted to the coloured light. (Usually you are quite unaware of this adaptation. For example, the colour of light from a normal household light bulb is very yellow in comparison to daylight, but you are rarely aware of this.) The neurological processes involved when the entire scene is coloured are very different from those when only part of the scene is coloured. The optimal colour of a pair of lenses can be assessed only under conditions in which a sufficiently large range of colours is assessed while the eyes are fully adapted to each colour in turn.

The distortions may be less pronounced when reading becomes fluent and text ceases to be a meaningless collection of confusing shapes. Although some people seem to grow out of the distortions, many do not. Visuoperceptual distortion still remains undetected in many children, and many enter adulthood without ever having been treated. AJW

Wilkins, A. (2002). 'Coloured overlays and their effects on reading speed: a review'. *Ophthalmic and Physiological Optics*, 22.

realism. Realism as a philosophical term generally refers to the doctrine that objects exist independently of sensory experience. The essential problem of *perception is to account for how we experience things which exist in the time and space of the real world. 'Naive' or 'direct' realism suggests that we experience objects as they are by a kind of direct awareness comparable with intuitive understanding of mathematics. This is very different from theories which suppose that perceptions are hypotheses. Realism may be contrasted with *idealism.

reasoning: development in children. It is commonly claimed that, until the age of 6 or 7, children are very limited in their capacity for deductive reasoning. This claim is made largely on the basis of research carried out within two main traditions: that based on the thinking of Jean *Piaget in Geneva, and that based on the thinking of Clark *Hull in the United States.

The theories of Piaget and of Hull are in most respects opposed, and their conceptions of the nature of inference are very different. It is all the more striking that their work has led to agreement about young children's lack of competence, and indeed this agreement has seemed to many to be conclusive. More recent research, however, makes it necessary to reopen the debate.

Piaget's claims may best be illustrated by his studies of 'class inclusion'. These have demonstrated that, if young children are shown a group of, say, six flowers, comprising four red ones and two yellow ones, and are then asked whether there are more red flowers or more flowers, they are likely to answer: 'More red ones.' And they will probably justify the answer by pointing out that there are 'only two yellow ones'.

Piaget's explanation is that at this stage a child's mind is lacking in a certain kind of flexibility, a kind crucial for reasoning. Piaget points out that the child who replies 'more red flowers' will normally have no difficulty in recognizing that if you take away the yellow flowers the red ones will be left, and further that if you take away all the flowers none will be left. To reach these conclusions, however, children need only think of the class and the subclasses successively. What they cannot do, according to Piaget, is think of them *simultaneously* (as they must, of course, if they are to reason as to the relations between them), for when they 'centre' on the whole class they mentally lose the subdivisions, and when they centre on the subdivisions they mentally lose the totality. So the seemingly simple comparison of whole with part is impossible for them. They have no mental structure representing a hierarchy of classes, with some included in others and these again included in still broader groupings, this being of course precisely the kind of structure with which logicians have traditionally been much concerned.

The deficiency in thought that is manifested by young children in the class inclusion task is held by Piaget to be quite general. Until it is overcome children's thinking is said to consist largely of a succession of separate 'moments', poorly coordinated with one another, so that the current one is too dominant. According to this argument, young children are not good at seeing their own momentary 'point of view' as one of a set of possible points of view coordinated into a single coherent system within which reasoning as to relationships can freely take place.

Piaget claims that the process of overcoming this deficiency is one of building 'cognitive structures', for which the original 'building blocks' are overt actions—acts of combining, ordering, etc. carried out on the real world. According to him, such actions, once they have been internalized (so that they can be performed 'in the mind') and organized into systems, are the very stuff of reasoning. It is then interesting to find that, in the other major tradition within which experimental studies of children's reasoning have been carried out—namely, the *behaviourist tradition, as exemplified in the thinking of Hull—there appears the same emphasis on actions that are initially overt and subsequently internalized. Beyond this, however, the theories of Hull and Piaget have little in common.

For Hull and his followers, the essence of reasoning lies in putting together two 'behaviour segments' in some novel way, never actually performed before, so as to reach a goal. For instance, one 'behaviour segment' might consist in pressing a button, which act would release a marble from a little slot; a second might consist in putting a marble in a hole, which act would open a little door and allow access to a toy. An act of inference would consist in combining these (separately learned) acts in order to get the toy. Such an inference would obviously have the form: if A leads to B and if B leads to C, then A leads to C.

Work by Kendler and Kendler (1967) has shown that young children who have learned these separate 'behaviour segments' do not readily integrate or combine them.

So these investigators, like Piaget, conclude that children under the age of 7 are very limited in their capacity for inference.

There is now reason to think, however, that this conclusion needs to be modified. Simon Hewson has shown that if the apparatus and the procedure used by the Kendlers are changed in certain ways that do not alter the basic structure of the problem, then 5-year-old children can perform as well as did the college students in the original studies.

Hewson replaced the button-pressing mechanism in the first 'segment' by a drawer which the child could open. Also he played a 'swapping game' with the children to help them to understand the functional equivalence of different marbles as means of opening the little door (so that they would realize there had been nothing special or 'magic' about the marble used in their original learning of the second 'segment'). These two modifications produced a jump in the 5-year-old success rates from 30 per cent to 90 per cent.

It seems then that, whatever was the nature of the children's difficulty with the original task, it did not consist in a radical inability to make the inferential link. The conclusion that there is no such radical inability is supported by Peter Bryant (1974). Bryant argues that, in their perception of the world, young children continually make comparisons which depend on reasoning in the form: if A = B and if B = C then A = C. Thus they combine two separate pieces of information to reach an inferred conclusion.

Hewson's demonstration that the difficulty of the Kendlers' task can be greatly altered by inessential modifications has its parallel in studies of class inclusion. These have established that very slight changes in Piaget's class inclusion task can enable many young children to perform it successfully (see, for instance, McGarrigle, Grieve, and Hughes 1978). It now appears that much of the difficulty with this and other similar Piagetian tasks lies in the fact that children are powerfully influenced by context, so that they do not interpret the experimenter's words alone with the strictness and rigour which—by adult standards—a reasoning task demands. It should also be noted that evidence obtained from observation rather than experiment suggests the presence of considerable reasoning skills in children as young as 3 or 4. An example is provided by a comment from a 4-year-old who was listening to the story of Cinderella and looking at a picture of Cinderella marrying the prince. In the picture the prince looked effeminate, and the child thought it was a picture of two women. He called out, 'But how can it be (that they are getting married)? You have to have a man too!'. He appears to have been using two premises:

1. If there is a wedding there must be a man.
2. There is no man.

And he concludes validly:

So there is no wedding.

The general conclusion which we are now justified in drawing seems to be that young children have a considerable capacity for reasoning deductively about topics related to ongoing activities in which they are spontaneously engaged. What is hard for them is to accept verbal premisses which are 'set' for them by someone else in the absence of a meaningful, supportive context. Young children do not readily constrain their thinking in this way. Cross-cultural studies (for instance, Cole et al. 1971) indicate that the same tends to be true of unsophisticated, illiterate adults.

With increasing age, and especially with the advent of literacy, people tend to become better able to turn their minds deliberately to a reasoning task and respect its constraints. But at all ages this kind of rigorous, disciplined inference is difficult for the human mind (see Henle 1962).

MD

Bryant, P. (1974). *Perception and Understanding in Young Children*.

Cole, M., Gay, J., Glick, J. A., and Sharp, D. W. (1971). *The Cultural Context of Learning and Thinking*.

Henle, M. (1962). 'The relationship between logic and thinking'. *Psychological Review*, 69.

Hewson, S. N. P. (1977). 'Inferential problem solving in young children'. Oxford University: unpublished doctoral dissertation.

Kendler, T. S., and Kendler, H. H. (1967). 'Experimental analysis of inferential behavior in children'. In Lipsitt, L. P., and Spiker, C. C. (eds.), *Advances in Child Development and Behavior*, vol. iii.

McGarrigle, J., Grieve, R., and Hughes, M. (1978). 'Interpreting inclusion: a contribution to study of the child's cognitive and linguistic development'. *Journal of Experimental Child Psychology*, 26.

Mitchell, P., and Riggs, K. (2000). *Children's Reasoning and the Mind*.

reflex action. Reflexes are the automatic reactions of the nervous system to stimuli impinging on the body or arising within it. They are more easily described than further defined. The knee jerk (one of the 'tendon jerks') is a familiar instance. The tendon below the kneecap is struck sharply with a rubber hammer and the muscles of the kneecap in the thigh are caused to give a brief twitchlike contraction which extends the knee joint and causes a little kick of the foot. The latency, the time between the blow and the first sign of muscular contraction, is about a fiftieth of a second, not much longer than is required for nerve impulses to travel from the sense endings excited by the blow to the central nervous system (here the spinal cord) and back down to the muscle.

The word 'reflex' comes from the idea that nerve impulses are 'reflected' in the central nervous system. *Descartes instances the constriction of the pupil when a light is shone in the eye. In the 18th century, Robert Whytt and Stephen Hales showed that the integrity of the central nervous system is, indeed, essential for 'reflection' to occur. In the next century the subject was greatly clarified by the discovery of *Magendie and *Bell that the nervous system uses separate *channels (nerve fibres) for input and output so that 'reflection' must occur centrally. With minor exceptions ('axon reflexes') the dorsal spinal nerve roots are exclusively sensory and the ventral roots exclusively motor in function. Detailed knowledge of the connections between the sensory and motor nerves in the grey matter of the spinal cord dates only from 1951, when Eccles obtained records from a microelectrode inside a motor nerve cell—the first time this had been achieved with any central neuron.

The tendon jerk is the simplest and fastest mammalian reflex known and its neuronal mechanism (although not its function in everyday life) is still the best understood. Endless other reflexes exist of greater complexity and longer latency. Commonly instanced are responses to injury or irritation: sneezing and coughing, the withdrawal of a foot in a frog or quadruped, the scratching of a dog. There are very many reflexes concerned in the vital functions: blood pressure is reflexly affected by pressure receptors in the walls of the aorta, breathing by reflexes from stretch receptors in the diaphragm, and so forth. Reflexes from receptors in the muscles of the limbs and trunk (of which the knee jerk is one) are a large class, of still controversial function in the control of bodily movement.

Although the experimental investigation of reflexes in animals is traditionally carried out on the spinal cord after severing it from the brain, or on the lower parts of the nervous axis after removing the cerebral hemispheres (decerebrate preparation), there are many reflexes whose pathway is through the cerebral cortex. The involuntary blink to a threatening gesture is one. And the elaborate learned responses called 'conditioned reflexes' (see CONDITIONING) are cortical or usually so.

C. S. *Sherrington, to whom we owe much of our knowledge of reflex action, regarded the reflex as the unit of nervous action and suspected that complex sequential acts, such as walking, were in the nature of chain reflexes, in which one element reflexly caused the next: in walking, for example, the movement of the leg forward excited receptors in the leg which reflexly caused it to move back again, and so on. There is now evidence that the nervous mechanism for performing such acts as walking or breathing exists in the central nervous system and can function, after a fashion, without reflex inputs, but that, normally, reflexes modify and regulate these actions and adapt them to changing circumstances.

The point at which an animal's responses to stimuli cease to be regarded as reflex and are called deliberate or voluntary, or by some similar term, is ill defined. A mild cough can be suppressed by an effort of will during a concert, but such coughing would be regarded as reflex. A similar suppression of the urge to pass water is more easily achieved and passing water is normally to be considered a deliberate act; the underlying reflex element is dominant only in infancy or when self-control is impaired.   PAM

Eccles, J. C. (1957). *The Physiology of Nerve Cells*.

Liddell, E. G. T. (1960). *The Discovery of Reflexes*.

Merton, P. A. (1979). 'The central nervous system'. In Lippold, O. C. J., and Winton, F. R. (eds.), *Human Physiology*.

Sherrington, C. S. (1900). 'The spinal cord'. In Schäfer, E. A., *Textbook of Physiology*, vol. ii.

—— (1906). *The Integrative Action of the Nervous System* (new edn. 1947).

Reid, Thomas (1710–96). Scottish philosopher, born at Strachan Manse, Kincardineshire. He succeeded Adam Smith as professor of moral philosophy at Glasgow (1764–80). He reacted sharply to the scepticism of David *Hume's *Treatise of Human Nature* (1739), and defended intuitive common-sense knowledge and belief. His principal work is *Inquiry into the Human Mind on the Principles of Common Sense* (1764); also important are his essays on the *Intellectual Powers* (1785) and *Active Powers* (1788) of man.

Reid was influential in developing *faculty psychology, which supposed that human abilities can be considered in separate units, probably localized in specific brain regions. This is a basis of *phrenology—which on the whole had unfortunate consequences for 19th-century neurology.

There is a strong orthodox theological streak in Reid, who argued that our perception of the existence of external objects is given directly though with help from God, whereas sensation, as the raw data of experience, is given directly by physical objects. Reid's distinction between sensation and perception is still frequently used (though with God left out), but recent accounts of perception tend to blur this distinction, as sensation can be affected by processes of object perception, and it is far from clear that sensations are given at all directly by neurally peripheral or simple physiological processes (see PERCEPTION).
RLG

Cuneo, T., and van Woudenberg, R. (2004). *The Cambridge Companion to Thomas Reid*.

Lehrer, K. (1999). *Thomas Reid*.

religion. John Macmurray used to say that the obvious difference between science on the one hand and art and religion on the other is that science is intellectual, while art and religion are peculiarly bound up with the emotional side of human life. Failure to make this distinction has led to much confusion. Some have simply dropped religion as no longer worthy of a thinking man's attention. Others, in extreme contrast, have turned a blind eye on contemporary doubts, and entrenched themselves in traditional dogma. But the 20th century was essentially the age of the half-believer—the person who is not without intuitions about the meaning of life, but is baffled by the dead weight of theology which has been accumulated.

The so-called five proofs of God's existence have never carried as much conviction as the personal encounters with God which religious people have claimed to have. 'Dieu d'Abraham, Dieu d'Isaac, Dieu de Jacob, non des philosophes et des savants.' So said *Pascal. And it is significant that all the great religions do appear to stem from some shattering personal experience. The Buddha achieved enlightenment as he sat in meditation beneath the Bodhi tree. As a result, he believed that he had found the cure for all human sufferings and dissatisfactions. The Old Testament prophets had experiences which, they alleged, told them profoundly important things about God—even suggesting that what passes for religion can be a bar to finding him. There is always this gap between the religious founder and what the faith has become. We see it in Jesus's denunciation of the religion of *his* day, in contrast with his own sense of intimate closeness to the Father. One cannot read the Upanishads, the main source of Hindu doctrine, without feeling the writer's sense of union between the self and the Holy Power. And it was alone in the desert that Muhammad received his call to preach. True, these key figures quickly gathered round them a band of disciples, and other elements, such as a sense of common purpose and a sense of fellowship, accrued. Religion ministers to the group mind as well as to the individual. For all that, what has been said about literature may equally be said about religion in its essence: 'The best in each kind comes first, comes suddenly, and never comes again.'

Is it the *same* basic experience that all religions are seeking to interpret? Making every allowance for the divergencies of time and place, it would seem a strong possibility. A study of so-called primitive people may offer useful clues. Their world is alive and shot through with elemental unseen power. This power is thought to take possession of certain of their chieftains, priests, and medicine men. One group of special interest are the shamans. In Siberia an aspiring shaman has to pass many hours in a cabin of snow, contemplating his own skeleton. He ends, we are told, by obtaining the 'flash' or 'illumination'—'a mysterious light that the shaman suddenly feels in the interior of his head'. He is now able to discern things hidden from other human beings.

Is the experience of conversion, as we know it in the West, so very different? Problems of language make it hard to judge. Here is a witness, quoted by Rudolf Otto: 'The more I seek words to express this intimate intercourse, the more I feel the impossibility of describing it by any of the usual images.' However, William *James analysed it as consisting of two elements—an uneasiness and its solution. Carl *Jung said that 'it gives a human being that sense of wholeness, which he had as a child, but loses when he leaves his parents'. And its common characteristic is a sense of something not earned, or even asked for—a sense of something 'given'. This led men naturally to infer a Giver, and therefore the postulation of a 'Someone', not ourselves, wholly other, out there in the void, and may be directly connected with the origin of religion.

The human race, on the whole, has found no difficulty in filling that void with an endless variety of deities. Considering that no one could really have supposed that they had been *seen* by anybody, it is amazing the number of forms these gods have taken—from Rongo, the Polynesian god of agriculture, to Shiva, the Hindu lord of the dance, and from the Zeus of Greek mythology to the Jehovah of Michelangelo. From earliest times man has sought to establish some sort of working relationship with these powers that be—some enlistment of their aid against the evil all round him. The many and bloody sacrifices which the Hebrew prophets denounced were believed to open up communication between the sacred and the profane, and the idea of sacrifice has not yet ceased to be an important element in religion. Men have also believed that 'mercy and *not* sacrifice' was what was required: that personal values count, when it comes to being right with God. Religion has always been closely linked with morality—even though it has given rise to some curious anomalies. Today the questions are still being asked. Is celibacy, or virginity, really demanded of us, if we are to be numbered among the saints? Are there absolute standards of conduct, applicable at all times and in all places? Or is everything relative?

As to our ultimate chances and the possibility of judgement after death, these remain beyond our logical apprehension. But Jung has suggested that our unconscious, which is free from the categories of space and time, may be the part of our make-up that 'knows' about these matters. Responses are set up in the unconscious by the use of certain symbols. Rituals give a sense of 'timeless moments', and myths of flight and ascension suggest escape from one mode of being to another. The rites of spring around the world celebrate the rhythm of rebirth. Jung has furthermore maintained that the crisis of the West is in part due to the fact that the Christian myths and symbols are no longer lived by. They have become fossilized and irrelevant to most of the population. To some extent this must be true of Eastern religions as well—despite all their genuine holy men and all their various techniques for quieting the mind. A recent traveller to Bodh Gaya, where the Buddha was enlightened, was disheartened to see so many Buddhists, in his opinion, missing the point. If the truth lies within the self, why so much noisy ceremonial?

What then of the future? The 20th century was certainly a crisis for mankind. The sheer achievement of science has caused modern man to claim that 'what no God did for his worshippers in thousands of years, he has by his own efforts succeeded in bringing about'. For authentic existence from now on, so the existentialists say, we shall have to face up to the absence of God. Nobody can give us directions. We are alone in the cosmos. But the history of religions shows that they have an uncanny capacity for revival, even when they have seemed to be most dead.

Hinduism was at a low ebb at the time of the establishment of the British Raj, and it was thought that the educated Indian would soon reject it. But far from rejecting it, he has done much to reinstate it. Its strength lies in the recognition of different levels of spiritual development, and it has a special attraction for men alienated from the religion of their own society. One of the great texts of the Upanishads is: 'God does not proclaim himself. He is everybody's secret.' An old prophecy says that after 2,500 years Buddhism will either fade away or enjoy a renaissance. It does not involve belief in God, over which many Westerners today have intellectual difficulties, and is undogmatic and experimental. One day a Zen master may deliver a sermon. Another day, if a bird begins to sing, the master will say nothing, and everyone will listen to the bird. Islam has been steadily increasing in influence and numbers, till there are over 817,065,200 Muslims at the latest count. In Christendom, the Roman Catholic Church is by far the largest, with 872,104,700 members. Its discipline is stricter than that of the Protestant Churches, and its appeal lies in its unbroken tradition. Protestants, by comparison, have broadened their outlook, yet they continue to preach to an anxiety-ridden world that 'sin' means separation from the ground of one's being, and that, as a matter of urgency, wholeness must be restored.

It is hard to be objective where religion is concerned. Objectivity suggests lukewarmness. It is easy for the agnostic to be objective, for there is nothing much at stake for him. It is very difficult for the man who claims that he has been vouchsafed a vision of the truth. 'Woe *is* me! for I am undone . . . for mine eyes have seen the King, the Lord of hosts.'

See also HUMANISM.   OJWH

Eliade, M. (1960). *Myths, Dreams, and Mysteries*.
James, W. (1902). *The Varieties of Religious Experience*.
Jung, C. G. (1933). *Modern Man in Search of a Soul*.
Macmurray, J. (1961). *Reason and Emotion*.
Otto, R. (1923). *The Idea of the Holy*.
Pascal, B. (1670). *Pensées*.
Smart, N. (1971). *The Religious Experience of Mankind*.

remembering. If one asks teachers, students, or the proverbial man or woman in the street for the best available techniques for remembering something, the answers will be quite varied. However, one recurrent theme is sure to be: 'Repeat it!' A psychologist is likely to comment: 'Yes, but . . . repetition by itself, mere repetition, does not help.' Yet the history of experimental investigations of *memory is to a large extent concerned with mere repetition. In fact, the father of the experimental psychology of memory, Hermann *Ebbinghaus, started his investigations in Germany in the last quarter of the 19th century by focusing almost exclusively on the effect of repetition. How many repetitions did it take to learn a list of words (or nonsense syllables)? How many trials were saved in relearning some list as a function of its prior repetition?

Both the common lore about repetition and the influence of Ebbinghaus dictated a preoccupation with the effect of repeated rehearsals. After all, it is well known that repeating a telephone number between looking it up and dialling it protects it from disappearance. And handsome, negatively accelerated learning curves resulted from numerous experiments that studied the effect of repetition on retention. But repetitive activities do not lead to effortless retrieval. Actually, when we try to remember an address, a name, the title of a book, or the plot of a play, we seem to engage in rather complicated search operations. The success of these operations depends not so much on how often we have repeated the required information in the past as on the proper embedding (the organization) of the target information within the larger flux of our knowledges and memories. When shopping for the weekend meals, we might retrieve the meats to be bought as a single memorial 'chunk', and liquid refreshments in another. Or another shopper might organize a mental shopping list by remembering what to buy in terms of what is where in the local supermarket. Both of these schema are kinds of organizations of the to-be-remembered things, and both require effort. Trying to recall the plot of a play, the rememberer might first recall vaguely the gist ('It was about a family who were always arguing') and then more and more details within coherent subdivisions ('Yes, there was the unhappy daughter and her pitiful suitor').

The notion that organization and structure are essential for memory retrieval is not novel. Extensive *mnemonic techniques date at least to ancient Greece, where orators constructed complex spatial and temporal schema as an aid in rehearsing and properly presenting their speeches (see Yates 1966). In modern times the associationism of British empiricism and German experimentalism was seriously questioned during the first half of the 20th century by the *Gestalt psychologists in general and by the British psychologist F. C. *Bartlett in particular. Today we know in some detail what it is that repetition makes possible, what it is that is needed in addition to *mere* repetition.

A set of objects, events, or mental representations is said to be organized when consistent relations among the members of the set can be identified and specified. The result of such organization is called a structure. Structures may exist among events in the world as well as among mental events. A special kind of structure is the *schema, which is a mental structure, specifically an organized representation of a body of knowledge. Thus, schema determine the expectations people have about events to be encountered, and about the spatial and temporal structure of those events.

The organization of to-be-remembered material takes time and conscious capacity. If we are told to remember a luncheon appointment while reading a book or watching our favourite television programme, conscious capacity is taken up by these primary activities and little organizational action will result. In order to remember the luncheon appointment we need to retrieve other plans (schema) about the specific day and 'fit in' the appointment. For example, we need to store such things as 'After the dentist, go to work, but go to the luncheon an hour later'. In the temporal organization of that day's plan, dentist, work, and luncheon will form an appropriate mental schema. And thinking about these plans (repeating them) will make their proper retrieval on the appointed day more likely. But again it is not mere repetition that provides a better schema, rather it is the anchoring of the relevant events within better, richer, and more accessible events that provides the more effective schema. Thus, each repetition provides an opportunity to relate the target event (the luncheon) to other events and thoughts. We may store the fact that our best friend will be at the luncheon, that it is held at a favourite restaurant, etc., etc. Each of these additions produces a more elaborate structure, and the more elaborate the retrieval opportunities for a target event the more likely it is that it will be recalled. Repetition provides opportunities for the organization of the to-be-remembered events.

While it is the case that most events are stored in long-term memory in complex, multistructured forms, certain frequently used structures can be identified. First there is the categorical or subordinate kind of structure in which a list of instances is stored under a general concept or label. To recall all the animals we know requires the use of such subordinate structures within a hierarchy of categories. Typically we gain access to some general animal category and then generate its subcategories such as domestic animals and catlike animals. Second there are coordinate structures of a few, usually less than five, events or things that are related to one another. Spatial structures, such as the directions of the compass, are one good example; another is the set of things called a table setting. Whereas in the categorical structure the higher-order label or node retrieves the lower instances, in the coordinate structure the members of the set act as retrieval points for one another. The third kind of structure is a serial or pro-ordinate structure in which a string of events is organized, usually in a temporal or spatial form. An excellent example is the way we retrieve the alphabet; another is the structure that represents the route we take to work from home. Parts of the serial string act as retrieval cues for subsequent things or events.

These idealized structures usually interact within any complex memorial event. More important, they are incorporated within the more general spatio-temporal schema mentioned earlier. Thus the understanding of a conversation involves the kinds of expectation inherent in our schema for social conversations, story schema tell us to look for crucial aspects and themes of a story, restaurants require that we have the proper schema for ordering from menus, talking to waiters, and so forth. The episodes of our daily lives are organized within such schema, which in turn incorporate the three kinds of structures described above.

Up to now the description of memory systems has focused on the recall of information. Another important kind of memory feat involves the recognition of previously encountered events. We are able to determine that people, rooms, foods, tunes are events that we have previously met, seen, tasted, heard. Not only do we know that we have encountered them before but we usually also know who or what they are. Conversely we sometimes know only that the event is familiar without knowing exactly who that person is, where we have seen that room before, what kind of food it is, what the name of a tune is. It is the latter phenomenon that has generally been studied by psychologists under the rubric of recognition.

The recognition of prior occurrence is a two-stage process involving two distinct mechanisms. One of them is a judgement of familiarity, the other a retrieval process essentially identical to that discussed for the recall of information. The judgement of familiarity is an automatic process, requiring no conscious effort and occurring as an immediate response to the event. However, the familiarity of information available of the event may be inadequate to make a confident judgement of prior occurrence. In that case a search process queries the long-term memory system whether the event in question is in fact retrievable. If such an attempt is successful then the event is considered to be 'old', i.e. having been previously encountered. Thus, recognition involves a judgement of familiarity which is supplemented by a retrieval attempt. For example, we meet someone who looks vaguely familiar, but the definite judgement that we 'know' that person is not made until we can recapture the place or context where we have previously encountered him or her.

The process of judging familiarity brings us back to the problem of repetition, because mere repetition does affect familiarity. The more frequently an event has been observed the more likely it is to be recognized on the basis of familiarity alone. Thus, repetition does have a function, but not for the retrieval of information. Repetition affects the process of integrating the representation of an event; it establishes its familiarity independent of its context or its relations to other mental contents.

Finally, errors of memory can obviously be of two kinds: retrieval errors and, less frequently, errors of familiarity judgements. Given the structural, schematic organization of memory storage, it is obvious that some events that 'fit' into the appropriate schema are likely to be retrieved even though they were not originally encountered. One might remember having witnessed an argument in a play because the structure of the play is stored under some general schema of 'family conflict', or one might 'recall' having seen a particular red armchair before, because it was stored as 'striking-looking furniture'. Thus, errors of memory are often even more instructive about the nature of mental structure than the normal recovery of information. See also DÉJÀ VU.   GM

Baddeley, A. D. (1976). *The Psychology of Memory*.
Bartlett, F. C. (1932). *Remembering*.
Mandler, G. (1985). *Cognitive Psychology*.
Norman, D. A. (1976). *Memory and Attention* (2nd edn.).
Yates, F. A. (1966). *The Art of Memory*.

repression. Repression, a key concept of *psychoanalysis, is a defence mechanism that ensures that what is unacceptable to the conscious mind, and would if recalled arouse anxiety, is prevented from entering into it. Akin to denial, which tends to refer to current events, it was invoked to account for a patient's failure to recall, in the course of *free association, events of significance in the past. Painful memories, being kept out of consciousness by repression, achieve 'psychic autonomy' and become fixed. Derivatives of what has been repressed may evade the censorship and enter into consciousness in a disguised form as strange or seemingly irrational thoughts. Or they may be recalled in dreams or in other states, e.g. those due to alcohol or drugs, or hypnosis, with what *Freud described as 'the undiminished vividness of recent events'.

The method of psychoanalysis creates conditions for the undoing of repression, i.e. making conscious what has been repressed. Painful experiences when so recalled are ranged alongside other related experiences which perhaps contradict them; they then undergo correction by means of other ideas.   DRD

Freud, S., and Breuer, J. (1974). *Studies on Hysteria* (Pelican Freud Library, vol. iii).

responsibility. In ordinary discourse some people are spoken of as 'not responsible' for acts or omissions, but there are several uses of the term 'responsible'. For example, not only people but things or events also are spoken of as 'responsible' for occurrences or non-occurrences, when all that is meant is that they had a part in the physical causation of them. Again, people are said to be 'responsible' for other people—such as their children—or for organizations, in the sense that they are morally or legally culpable if the latter misbehave. In the sense, however, with which we here are concerned, 'responsible' means 'to some extent culpable (either morally or in law, according to the context) for *one's own* acts or omissions'. The ascription of responsibility in this sense depends on what we believe to have been the person's mental state at or before the time of the act or omission. 'Premeditation' usually makes an objectionable act seem more culpable. If the actor foresaw a real possibility of his causing harm—for example, by his way of driving—his act or omission will be called 'reckless', and blamed accordingly. If he did not foresee it, but we think that he should have, he may be called 'negligent', and blamed accordingly—usually less than for 'recklessness'. The law, too, makes distinctions of this sort, although with more subtlety (for example, civil law takes into account 'contributory negligence' by the person harmed).

More often it is the actor's state of mind at the time of the act—or more precisely what it is believed to have been—that determines the degree to which he is regarded as blameworthy. If the act seems to have been quite accidental—if for instance he knocks over a child whom he did not see in his path—he is not blamed, unless we think that he should have been aware of this as a real possibility. Again, if his physical movements that did the harm were of a kind which are not willed, then he is not blamed: examples are the movements of a sleepwalker, or of a man who is sneezing. This excuse is called 'automatism' by English lawyers. Criminal courts usually demand medical evidence before accepting it, since it is usually based on abnormal cerebral conditions, such as an epileptic fit, or a hypoglycaemic state (which may occur in diabetics).

In certain situations, however, lawyers—and ordinary people—regard intentional actions as excused. Violence may be excused by the belief that one is about to be killed by the other person and that there is no alternative (such as escape). 'Necessity' is an excuse in the US Model Penal Code, although English judicial decisions are hostile to it. 'Duress'—acting under threats of death to oneself or one's family—is sometimes accepted. About 'superior orders' there is even more disagreement. An official executioner who carries out a lawful sentence of death is not legally culpable, but is morally condemned by many people for accepting the task. Carrying out an order which one knows to be unlawful usually incurs moral—and sometimes legal—blame, unless one does so in the knowledge that one would suffer death or a severe penalty for disobedience.

Even uncoerced intentional acts, however, may be excused, or at least mitigated, by other explanations. Provocation, if sufficient, is accepted by English law as lessening culpability rather than excusing the act completely, although courts are sometimes persuaded by it not to penalize the convicted person. Less transient mental states may also mitigate or even excuse. An example is an abnormal inability to control desires or impulses, especially if given a psychiatric label such as '*psychopathic'. Other mental states, such as *depression, frequently persuade courts to forgo penalties, and, if a hospital or clinic is willing to accept the sufferer, to entrust him to psychiatric care and treatment. The extent to which such states protect the sufferer against moral censure varies with the circumstances and the viewpoint of the censurer. The English Homicide Act of 1957 (following Scots common law) allows a person charged with murder (but paradoxically not attempted murder) to offer a plea of '*diminished responsibility': if successful this reduces the crime to manslaughter, and allows the judge freedom to impose a less severe sentence than life imprisonment. (The Infanticide Act of 1938 allows a somewhat similar plea of 'disturbed balance of mind' to a mother who kills a baby to whom she has given birth within the previous twelve months.)

Some kinds and degrees of mental disorder are regarded as excusing offenders completely. English law recognizes an 'insanity defence'. To qualify, the offender must, at the time of his act or omission, have been suffering from a 'disease of the mind' (in more modern language 'mental disorder') such that he did not 'know the nature and quality' of the act, or alternatively know that it was 'wrong' (which is now interpreted in England as meaning 'against the law'). A third qualifying possibility is that he was suffering from a *delusion which, if true, would have legally justified what he did: for example, a deluded belief that his life was threatened. In other common-law countries which have adopted and adapted this defence the exact definitions of the sufficient conditions vary, so that, for instance, 'wrong' can mean 'morally wrong'. In countries which follow the Code Napoléon the rule is simpler: no crime has been committed if the accused was suffering from *démence* at the time; but *démence*—or its equivalent—is defined very restrictively in practice. Most such countries also recognize 'partial insanity' or its equivalent as grounds for reducing the severity of the penalty; definitions of states which amount to this vary greatly.

Moral or political convictions are often regarded—especially by those who share them—as excusing behaviour which would normally be condemned, such as assassinations, violent demonstrations, or even genocide. Few legal codes allow for such a defence, although it has been proposed, for example by Moran (1981).

NDW

Hart, H. L. A. (1968). *Punishment and Responsibility*.

—— and Honoré, A. M. (eds.) (1985). *Causation in the Law* (2nd edn.).

Homicide Act 1957 (UK), s. 2.

Moran, R. (1981). *Knowing Right From Wrong*.

Report of the Committee on Mentally Abnormal Offenders (1975, Cmnd. 6244), chs. 18, 19.

Walker, N. D. (1984). 'Psychiatric explanations as excuses'. In Roth, M. (ed.), *Psychiatry, Human Rights and the Law*.

retina. The screen at the back of the eye on which *ret-inal images are projected. The word derives from the medieval Latin *rēte*, meaning 'net'. In human and many other eyes there are closely packed 'rod' light receptors which signal levels of brightness (giving scotopic vision), and considerably fewer 'cones' which allow colours to be identified: photopic vision. Photopic vision occurs only in fairly bright light. The evidence suggests that mammals have very little *colour vision, and that most almost certainly have none—except for primates including man. In the human eye there are about 100 million rods and about 5 million cones. Curiously, they lie at the back of the ret-ina, so light has to pass through the vascular system, a mesh of nerve fibres, and three layers of cell bodies, before it reaches the light-sensitive cells. It is possible to see the arterial system in another person's eye with an ophthal-moscope. It is also possible to see one's own retina by holding a torch bulb close to the closed eye and waggling it about—a tree of blood vessels becomes visible as their shadow image moves across the underlying receptors. The central, foveal region of best vision can be seen in one's own eye by waggling, in front of the pupil, a piece of cardboard containing a small hole, and looking at a blank screen—a faint pattern of nerve fibres (the blood vessels do not cover the fovea but pass round it) is revealed.

RLG

retinal images, stabilization of. The eye is continu-ally moving—even when a person tries to fixate a well-marked point as steadily as he can. The small residual movements of the eyeball cause irregular oscillations of the retinal image across the *retina and fluctuations in the light falling on retinal receptors near to boundaries (Fig. 1). W. H. Marshall and S. A. Talbot in the early 1940s worked out a detailed theory of the visual process based on the hypothesis that the receptors respond primarily to *fluctu-ations* of illumination and little, or not at all, to steady illumination—as indicated in the 1920s by the neuro-physiological experiments of E. D. *Adrian and R. Mat-thews, and of H. K. Hartline and R. Granit and their co-workers. According to this theory, the retinal-image movements are essential to vision. An opposed view was that the eye movements were an unavoidable imper-fection of the neural control of the eye muscles and that the retinal-image movements effectively blurred the boundaries, causing a loss of visual acuity—so that vision would be better if the retinal-image movements were stopped.

A crucial experiment to decide between these views is to make the eye movements control the movements of a target so that its image remains on the same part of the retina even when the eye moves, i.e. to produce a stabil-ized retinal image. A way to do this is to attach the target (and a lens which focuses it) onto a tightly fitting contact lens (Fig. 2). The whole system then moves with the eye and the retinal image is fixed on the retina. A more elab-orate apparatus (Fig. 3) enables a wider range of targets to be used. The target is in the projection system P. The beam from P is reflected from the mirror M, which is attached to a contact lens worn by the subject. It enters the eye after passing through the telescope T. When the eye rotates through an angle θ, the beam from the mirror M rotates through an angle 2θ. If the telescope T has an angular magnification of ½, the beam which enters the eye rotates through θ and its image falls on the same part of the retina even when the eye moves.

When a person views a stabilized image, the structure of the target fades out in two or three seconds and the field appears dark grey or black. If the target has no sharp boundaries between areas of high contrast, the field re-mains black so long as stabilization is maintained. Thus the retinal-image movements are essential to normal vi-sion, as was suggested by Marshall and Talbot.

If the target does contain sharp boundaries between areas of strong contrast, it reappears intermittently. These reappearances are usually hazy and sometimes fragmen-tary. There has been some controversy whether these reappearances are due to imperfect stabilization or to a weak visual signal which remains even when the image is stationary on the retina. Sharp *after-images may be imprinted when a target with sharp boundaries is illumin-ated with a brief, but strong, flash of light. These after-images, which are certainly stationary on the retina, exhibit the same hazy, fragmentary, and intermittent

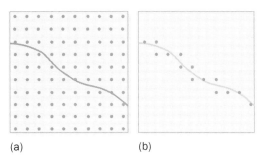

(a) (b)

Fig. 1. a. Light–dark boundary superimposed on a schematic regular array of retinal receptors. **b.** Receptors that receive fluctuating signals when boundary is given a small oscillation.

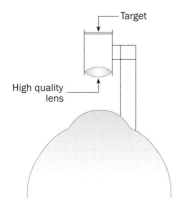

Fig. 2. Direct attachment apparatus with external contact lens mounted on a stalk.

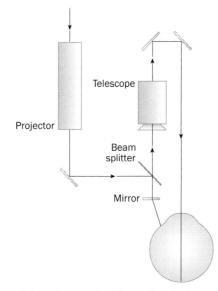

Fig. 3. Telescopic system involving a mirror that is caused to rotate by the eye.

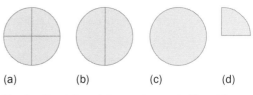

Fig. 4. a. Target. **b, c, d.** Fragments seen at different times when the retinal image is stabilized.

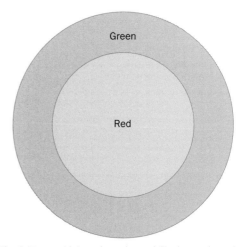

Fig. 5. Target with inner boundary stabilized, outer boundary unstabilized.

reappearances. This strengthens the view that a weak secondary signal remains even when the retinal image is accurately stabilized.

When a target consists of a line pattern (Fig. 4*a*), fragmentation of the stabilized image is observed (Fig. 4*b, c, d*). Fragmentation is not purely random, but the factors which determine what part of a pattern is seen at a given moment are not understood. Pattern units which are seen—or not seen—as a whole can be identified. The circle is one such unit and a complete circle may be seen even when the target is an incomplete circle. Fragmentation supports the ideas of those who have postulated the existence of pattern units (including the *Gestalt school) but does not support any previously proposed scheme in detail. It seems probable that the human visual cortex contains cells which respond to particular pattern elements. The signals which reach these cells when the image is stabilized are very weak and difficult to distinguish from a background discharge of 'noise'. From time to time the signal in one cell is recognized as greater than the noise, and the corresponding pattern element is 'seen'. Only very rarely do sufficient of these cells have signals above threshold simultaneously so that the whole target is seen.

Suppose that a target consists of a red centre surrounded by a green annulus (Fig. 5), with the outer boundary unstabilized and the inner boundary stabilized. Then the whole field appears green. The signals from the outer boundary give information that immediately within this boundary the field is green. Little or no information is received from the inner boundary, so the logical deduction is that the whole field is green. The target is 'completed', as happens in normal vision with a target which extends over the blind spot.

A more subtle example of the same process is obtained when a subject views a stabilized image of a large circle—

38 cm (15 in) or more—divided by a diameter into two parts, light and dark. The boundary may fade first in the outer region while it is still seen in the central region. The available information cannot then logically be reconciled, because it is possible to go from a light to a dark region without crossing any perceived boundary. In this situation, the brain struggles to reconcile the irreconcilable. Various shapes of hazy boundaries appear briefly. Finally the whole field goes grey—and a 'logical', but useless, picture is obtained.

If eye movements operate in the way indicated by the experiments we have described, then the main visual information accepted by the visual system comes from receptors near to boundaries between strong contrasts of illumination or of colour—if there are any such boundaries. This may account for the extent to which an artist can convey both form and sensuous feeling by means of a drawing in which just a few lines indicate the boundaries (see ART AND VISUAL ABSTRACTION).

An animal, in order to survive in a natural situation, needs to keep in mind prominent features of the area in which it is placed and to give instant attention to any movement in the visual field which may reveal predator or prey. The visual receptors that respond mainly to *changes* of illumination filter the visual information so as to retain the permanent background but to give great prominence to any change, even in the periphery of the field. There is thus an inbuilt bias in favour of the information that is most important for survival.

See VISUAL SYSTEM: ORGANIZATION.   RWD

Ditchburn, R. W. (1973). *Eye-Movements and Visual Perception.*
Yarbus, A. L. (1967). *Eye-Movements and Vision* (trans.).

retinex theory and colour constancy.

As we view an object from different distances, at different angles, and in different illuminations, there occur vast changes in the physical image on our retina, but our sensations prove much more stable than would be expected from our changeful retinal image. One of the several 'constancies' that characterize our sensory experience is colour constancy. Just as our visual system is built to tell us about the permanent size of objects rather than about the ever-fluctuating size of our *retinal image, so too it is built to tell us about the permanent colours of objects rather than about the spectral composition of the light falling on a local area of retina. The spectral composition of the light, that is, the relative proportions of the different wavelengths it contains, will depend on two factors: (i) the spectral reflectance of the object, its tendency to reflect some wavelengths more than others, and (ii) the spectral composition of the illuminant, the relative proportions of different wavelengths in the light that falls on the object. When we pass from, say, tungsten illumination, which is rich in long wavelengths, to the bluer environment

of daylight, our perception of an object's colour remains dependent on the object's spectral reflectance, and we are aware of little change. To achieve this constancy, the visual system must be taking into account not merely the local absorptions in the three classes of cone cell (see COLOUR VISION: EYE MECHANISMS) but also the pattern of absorptions in other parts of the visual field, for the *local* absorptions can depend only on the local spectral flux, and the latter, being dependent on factors (i) and (ii) above, will vary greatly as the illumination changes.

A particularly impressive and instructive demonstration of colour constancy has been provided by Edwin Land. He performed an experiment in which a single mixture of red, green, and blue light produced many different colour sensations. Observers reported white, pink, green, red, brown, yellow, purple, blue, and black sensations from identical mixtures of red, green, and blue lights. The experiment used a large, complex display that Land called a 'colour Mondrian'. The display had approximately 100 different matt papers arranged arbitrarily so that each colour was surrounded by several others. The display was illuminated with three projectors, each with a different broad-band interference filter. One filter transmitted long-wave, or reddish light; one transmitted middle-wave, or greenish light; and one transmitted short-wave, or bluish light. Each projector had an independent brightness control. The observers picked an image segment—say a white paper—and the experimenter measured the amounts of red, green, and blue light coming from the white paper. Then the observers picked a second paper—say a red one—and the experimenter measured the amounts of red, green, and blue coming to each observer's eyes from the red paper. The measurements showed that roughly the same amount of red light and much less green and blue light are reflected from a red paper. The experimenter then changed the illumination so that the red light from the red paper was exactly equal to the red light from the white paper. This was a small change. The experimenter then substantially increased the brightness of the other two projectors so that exactly the same amounts of green and blue light came from the red paper as had previously come from the white paper. When all three projectors were turned on together, each observer reported the sensation red despite the fact that the physical properties of the light from that image region were the same as that from the white with the previous illumination. In this manner, Land went from paper to paper and showed that nearly the full gamut of colour sensations can be produced from a single mixture of red, green, and blue light.

This experiment led Land to propose that the information from the long-wave receptors is intercompared to compute a biological analogue of reflectance from the long-wave light across the entire image. Similarly, the information from the middle-wave receptors is intercompared to form the biological analogue of middle-wave reflectance, and short-wave information for short-wave reflectance. The information from each of the sets of receptor mechanisms generates a separate lightness image; the comparison of three lightnesses is the determinant of colour. In Land's theory, which he called the retinex theory, these three lightnesses provide the coordinates of a three-dimensional space. Whereas a colour space based on the absolute absorptions in the three classes of receptor will predict only whether or not two physical stimuli will match, a space based on the three lightnesses of retinex theory will predict how colours actually look. For, between them, the three lightnesses give the reflectance of the object in different parts of the spectrum—in other words, its spectral reflectance.

The formation of lightnesses and their comparison could occur in the retina or in the cortex. Land coined the word retinex—a combination of retina and cortex—to designate the mechanism that generates independent long-, middle-, and short-wave lightness images. This system independence does not require that the retinal receptors with the same spectral sensitivity are directly connected to each other. Instead it argues that the retinal–cortical structure acts in total, as if all the colour mechanisms of the same sensitivity form independent lightness images.

McCann, McKee, and Taylor (1976) described a series of quantitative experiments that were patterned after Land's. In these experiments they measured the sensations of each area in a 'Mondrian' using a series of different illuminants. In each situation they measured the sensation by matching each area in the display to a Munsell book of colours in constant illumination. Secondly, they tested how well the sensations correlated with the reflectance of the papers as measured with spectrophotometers. They showed that there was an excellent correlation between sensation and reflectance measured with light meters that had the same spectral sensitivity as the three human cone pigments. (This correlation was particularly good when the reflectance numbers were scaled by Glasser's Munsell lightness function.)

Land and McCann proposed a lightness model that is based on the comparison of receptor-mechanism responses from all parts of the image. This lightness model does not use local averages or global averages, but rather comparisons that are based on the relationships of image segments. Local relationships are calculated by the visual system using the ratio of energies at nearby points, and this information is propagated to other parts of the image by multiplying ratios to form products. These products propagate relationships across the entire image. The mean of many different products is used as the prediction of lightness.

McCann, McKee, and Taylor showed that the ratio-product lightness model combined with retinex colour-mechanism independence accurately predicted the colour sensation reported by the observer in the 'colour Mondrian' experiments.

The rods provide an opportunity to study sets of receptors forming an image in terms of lightness. With the appropriate low-intensity light source it is possible to see, below cone threshold, that the rods interact to form a lightness image—just as above cone threshold, lightness of an image segment is dependent on the relationship of objects in all parts of the image. With a low-intensity light that is very rich in long-wave light, it is possible to see a wide variety of colour sensations from rod and long-wave cone interactions. Colour is determined by the lightness of the image generated by the rods and the lightness generated by the long-wave colour mechanism.

In summary, Land's retinex theory proposed that colour is determined by three lightnesses—each computed from comparisons using intensity information from the entire image. Each lightness is computed independently using intensity information from each spectral region. The Land and McCann lightness model uses the multiplication of ratios to form products that relate each image segment to each of the others. The mean of many different normalized products is used to predict lightness. Quantitative tests have shown that retinex colour-mechanism independence and the ratio-product lightness model can predict colour sensations in experiments with unknown changes in the spectral distribution of the illumination.   JJMcC

Land, E. H. (1964). 'The retinex'. *American Scientist*, 52.

——— (1977). 'The retinex theory of color vision'. *Scientific American*, 237/6.

——— and McCann, J. J. (1971). 'Lightness and retinex theory'. *Journal of the Optical Society of America*, 61.

McCann, J. J. (1973). 'Human color perception'. In *Color Theory and Imaging Systems*.

——— and Houston, K. L. (1983). 'Color sensation, color perception and mathematical models of color vision'. In Mollon, J. D., and Sharpe, L. T., *Colour Vision*.

——— McKee, S., and Taylor, T. H. (1976). 'Quantitative studies in retinex theory'. *Vision Research*, 16.

Ribot, Théodule (1839–1916). French psychologist who did much to advance the subject in both its experimental and its clinical aspects. In 1885, he was made responsible for a course of experimental psychology at the Sorbonne and was later given a chair of experimental and comparative psychology at the Collège de France. His best-known work is *Les Maladies de la mémoire* (1884), translated as *Diseases of Memory* (1885), in which he put forward a theory of the progressive loss of memory brought about by brain disease along the evolutionary lines adumbrated by Hughlings *Jackson.   OLZ

Rivers, William Halse Rivers (1864–1922). British physiologist, psychologist, and ethnologist, born in Luton, Kent. After qualifying in medicine, he was appointed to a lectureship in experimental psychology and the physiology of the senses at Cambridge, but his interests moved increasingly towards ethnology, partly because of the celebrated expedition to the Torres Straits in 1899 in which he took part, along with his fellow psychologists C. S. *Myers and William *McDougall, and the anthropologists C. G. Seligman and A. C. Haddon. As an experimental psychologist to the expedition, Rivers was particularly active in measuring sensory thresholds and visual *illusions in what was probably the first cross-cultural study ever carried out.

Notwithstanding his concern with anthropology, Rivers never wholly forsook his physiological interests, collaborating with the neurologist Henry *Head in an important study of the changes in tactile sensation resulting from the severance of a cutaneous nerve, Head himself being the subject. Their findings led them to the theory that there are two forms of cutaneous sensation, one relatively crude ('protopathic') and the other highly discriminative ('epicritic'). Although raising much interest at the time, this theory has since been wholly discarded.

At the outbreak of the First World War, Rivers's interests were largely centred on medical psychology, and he did important work in the treatment of war neuroses, then known as shell-shock. Among his patients was the writer Siegfried Sassoon, who has painted an unforgettable portrait of Rivers in *The Complete Memoirs of George Sherston* (1937). After the war, Rivers wrote widely on issues in medical psychology and, though he remained eclectic in his views, his ideas were evidently much influenced by *Freud.

Rivers, who died relatively young, was elected a Fellow of the Royal Society in 1908. His books included *Kinship and Social Organization* (1914), *The History of Melanesian Society* (1914), *Instinct and the Unconscious* (1920), and *Conflict and Dream* (1923).   OLZ

Slobodon, R. (1978). *W. H. R. Rivers.*

Rorschach, Hermann (1884–1922). Swiss psychiatrist, born at Zurich, who devised the famous standardized ink-blots (made by placing a blob of ink on paper, then folding the paper to produce symmetrical patterns) that have been widely used as an 'open-ended' test for personality traits and disorders. Though suggestive, the Rorschach test has turned out to be extremely difficult to validate objectively, and its success depends very much on the intuitive grasp of the psychologist who interprets the patient's responses or comments. (See PROJECTIVE TECHNIQUES.)   RLG

Klopfer, B., and Davidson, H. H. (1962). *Rorschach Technique: An Introductory Manual.*

Rousseau, Jean-Jacques (1712–78). Born in Geneva, his mother dying at his birth and his father deserting him when he was 10 years old, he was brought up by relations and had no formal education, except for reading Plutarch's *Lives* and Calvinist sermons. He had an extraordinarily ramshackle early life, taking up with an illiterate maidservant by whom he had five children—whom he committed to the foundling hospital even though he became famous for defending the natural goodness of man while blaming institutionalized life for the ills of the world. His *Confessions* (1781–8) are noted for their frankness. He died insane, and indeed his sanity throughout his life has been questioned in spite of his remarkable achievements and literary fame. See also ROUSSEAU AND EDUCATION.   RLG

Grimsley, R. (1973). *The Philosophy of Rousseau.*

Rousseau and education. In *Émile* (1762) Rousseau presented a view of *childhood and human nature which continues to inform educational thinking. In contrast to the Christian doctrine of original sin, he asserted that human nature was essentially good. He argued that it was the institutions of society that corrupted man. He reacted against the coercive nature of the authoritarian society of his time. 'From the beginning', he writes, 'to the end of life civilized man is a slave. At birth he is sewn up in swaddling bands, and at death nailed down in a coffin.' At a time when many children could not be expected to live for long, he argued powerfully that such life as they did have should be enjoyed. The memory of his own unhappy childhood made him acutely aware of the needs of children and insistent on their right to happiness. He argued for the transformation of child rearing: mothers were to breastfeed their own children, infants were to wear loose clothing and generally to enjoy freedom of movement and a closeness to nature. He viewed the child as a child and not as an inadequate adult, believing that it had the potential within itself to develop almost unlimited talents.

This kind of optimism is central to Rousseau's view of human nature and to his revolutionary ideas about society and education. The role of the teacher was not to restrain or to indoctrinate but so to arrange the child's environment that it could learn for itself. He attacked the education of his time on the grounds of its 'verbalism'; rote learning and textbooks were anathema to him. It was from things that they could actually experience that children best learned. His attitude was not antirational: 'I am far from thinking that children have no kind of reasoning. On the contrary, I notice that they think very well on everything which bears on their present and obvious interest.' From observation and his intuitive sympathy for children he was led to conceive of stages in their development towards adulthood, a notion which Jean *Piaget (another Genevan) later developed more scientifically.

Rousseau did not question contemporary *faculty psychology (the theory that various capacities—moral, aesthetic, reasoning—exist discretely in the human brain and develop separately), but his developmental view led him to recognize that children need to be childish and adolescents adolescent. He notes that the adolescent becomes ever more curious about the world, and eager for knowledge, but stresses that this knowledge must be his own, based on his own experience. Even at this stage he is sceptical of the educative value of books, except for *Robinson Crusoe*, which showed a man learning from nature and hard necessity. Rousseau understood adolescence, the moods and instability associated with the urgency of *sexual development. His views about sex education are still pertinent: 'If your pupil cannot be kept ignorant of sex differences up to 16 make sure he learns about them before 10.' This strength of Rousseau's, his trust in an intuitive understanding of the nature and needs of children, remains a positive stimulus to educational thought and practice. His belief in the essential goodness of human nature may be a myth but it is a more sustaining one than its converse. There are also dangers: a distrust of accumulated human knowledge, an anti-intellectualism that can lead to the worship of unreason, an over-reliance on feeling as a sufficient basis for sane human action. His profound distrust of institutions, however, has proved well justified: we are still struggling to make schools good places for children to learn in. (See EDUCATION: THEORY AND PRACTICE for a discussion of the influence of his views.)

CH/NS

Boyd, W. (1956). Émile for Today.

Rubin, Edgar (1886–1951). Danish psychologist, born and educated in Copenhagen, where he studied with Harold Höffding and Alfred Lehmann. He then worked for three years with G. E. Müller in Göttingen, returning to Copenhagen in 1922 to succeed Lehmann as professor and director of the psychological laboratory. Apart from some early studies of tactile sensitivity, his interests lay mainly in visual perception. His work on 'figure' and 'ground' in the visual perception of form had considerable influence and was viewed by Gestalt psychologists as basic to their treatment of figural organization (see GESTALT THEORY).

OLZ

Beardslee, D. C., and Wertheimer, M. (eds.) (1958). *Readings in Perception*. (This contains a translation of large sections of Rubin's *Visuell Wahrgenomener Figuren*.)

Rumi, Jalaluddin (or Jalaluddin Muhammad Ibn Bahauddin Walad al-Khatibi al-Bakri al-Balkhi, 1207–73). One of the greatest *Sufis and a major Persian poet and thinker. Born of a royal and caliphial line of distinguished

scholars in Balkh (present-day Afghanistan), he taught and died in Iconium (Konya, today Asiatic Turkey). His penname (literally 'of Rome' or 'the (eastern) Roman') was chosen, by poetic substitution cipher, because it represented both the town of his adoption and the Perso-Arabic word *Nur* ('light'). He acknowledges the Sufi masters *Attar and *Sanai as his 'two eyes', and they are undoubtedly his spiritual precursors. His major work is the *Mathnawi-i-Maanawi* (Poem of Inner Meaning), which was something like 40 years in the writing. His theme as a guide to mystical experience is that man in the ordinary state is cut off ('veiled') from higher perceptions by lower, usually emotional, stimuli. This state is often found in both the learned and the emotionalist: addiction to vice or to imagined virtue are both forms of idolatry, which cause 'veiling'. Teaching people to hate evil and covet sanctity is training in hatred and covetousness more than an approach to goodness or holiness. Bad things cannot be avoided, or good ones approached, he insists, by such crude and ignorant methods. The following major themes give an idea of his teaching.

Conventional religious systems are secondary, imitative, and limited: 'Do not attach yourself to the brick of the wall—seek instead the eternal original.' *A teacher is essential*: 'Water needs a medium between it and the fire, if it is to heat correctly.' *Laymen cannot evaluate mystical masters*: ' "This ruin may seem a prosperous place to you: for me, the better place is on the King's wrist," said the Hawk. Some owls cried, "He is lying to steal our home!" ' *Sufi knowledge involves escaping from familiar dimensions*: 'You belong to the world of dimension: but you come from non-dimension. Close the first "shop", open the second.' *Knowledge of Objective Truth (God) is developed through love and self-knowledge*: 'Ultimate Truth is reached by Love, that special love of which worldly love is a crude analogue: HE is within you!'

IS

Nicholson, R. A. (1926). *The Mathnawi of Jalaluddin Rumi*.
Shah, I. (1966). *Special Problems in the Study of Sufi Ideas*.
——(1974). *The Elephant in the Dark*.
——(1978). *The Hundred Tales of Wisdom: Materials from the Life and Teachings of Rumi*.
Whinfield, E. H. (1974). *Teachings of Rumi*.

Russell, Bertrand Arthur William, third Earl Russell (1872–1970). By general consent the most distinguished philosopher of the 20th century, Bertrand Russell made fundamental contributions to logic, and influenced equally academic and popular philosophy, as well as appreciation of psychological issues and social questions. Starting from a broadly *idealist philosophical position (*The Problems of Philosophy*, 1912), he became a thoroughgoing empiricist, after the manner of John *Locke, in later books such as *Human Knowledge: Its Scope and Limits* (1948). His work on the place of the individual in society

included the first of the BBC Reith lectures, *Authority and the Individual* (1949).

Russell also wrote on the philosophy of physics (*The A.B.C. of Relativity*, 1935, 1958). His main works on the basis of logic and mathematics are *The Principles of Mathematics* (1903) and, with A. N. *Whitehead, *Principia mathematica* (1910–13), which attempts to derive mathematics from logic and to resolve Frege's contradictions by means of the celebrated Theory of Types, or Theory of Classes. Among his most important philosophical contributions is his theory of descriptions, given in an article in the philosophical journal *Mind* (1905), 'On denoting'. This distinguished between the logical and grammatical subject of propositions, and developed a theory of meaning which was able to avoid the hitherto widespread view that the grammatical subjects of all meaningful propositions must refer to objects which in some sense exist. This is fundamental for an account of language that does not populate the world with a bizarre zoo of entities, such as glass mountains, female Popes, and all else that we can speak about, whether true or false.

Russell attempted to base physics on sensory—perceptual—experience. For him *sense data (such as sensations of red, hard, extension, and so on) is the basis of all knowledge of the world and the ultimate justification and test for all empirical statements. (It is perhaps unfortunate that he did not consider phenomena of perception in any detail, for if he had, he would surely have concluded that much that we experience perceptually is not given at all directly by the senses of the eyes, the ears, and touch, but is rather itself created, much as we create explanatory concepts.)

Russell will be remembered not only for his own outstanding philosophical achievements but also for the crucially important personal encouragement that he gave to his student Ludwig *Wittgenstein, who might very well have abandoned philosophy had not Russell seen the importance of the *Tractatus logico-philosophicus*, which appeared in 1922 and for which Russell wrote a highly significant introduction. In later life Russell gradually withdrew from his logical studies, and then from his philosophical work, towards political concerns and, especially, dedication to the cause of nuclear disarmament.

Bertrand Russell revelled in and inspired controversy: his *Autobiography* (3 vols., 1967–9) has the frankness one should expect from a man exulting in all aspects of life and intellect, while totally free of humbug. In spite of his unorthodox views and behaviour he received the highest honours: Fellowship of the Royal Society (1908) and the Order of Merit (1949).

Russell's main works include *An Essay on the Foundations of Geometry* (1897); *The Principles of Mathematics* (1903); 'On denoting', *Mind*, NS 14 (1905); with A. N. Whitehead, *Principia mathematica* (vol. i, 1910; 2nd edn. 1935);

'Knowledge by acquaintance and knowledge by description', *Proceedings of the Aristotelian Society*, NS 11 (1910–11); *The Problems of Philosophy* (1912); *Our Knowledge of the External World* (1914); *The Analysis of Mind* (1921); *The Analysis of Matter* (1927); *An Outline of Philosophy* (1927); *An Inquiry into Meaning and Truth* (1940); *The History of Western Philosophy* (1946); *Human Knowledge* (1948); *My Philosophical Development* (1959).

See also RUSSELL'S PHILOSOPHY OF MIND: DUALISM; RUSSELL'S PHILOSOPHY OF MIND: NEUTRAL MONISM. RLG

Ayer, A. J. (1972). *Bertrand Russell as a Philosopher.*
Monk, R. (1996). *Bertrand Russell: The Spirit of Solitude.*
Pears, D. (1967). *Bertrand Russell and the British Tradition in Philosophy.*
——(ed.) (1972). *Bertrand Russell.*

Russell's philosophy of mind: dualism.

When *Russell wrote about the mind, his gaze was also fixed on the physical world beyond it, because he wanted to explain how minds can acquire knowledge of what lies outside them. This gave his philosophy of mind an outward-facing character. He was especially interested in what happens at the point of contact between mind and matter when knowledge is acquired. What he says about the mind's output is less detailed except when the output is language and the language expresses knowledge or belief about the physical world. Emotions, intentions, and actions are treated in a more perfunctory way.

He shared *Hume's view that psychology is the central science, because all the data of physics and physiology is somehow passed into the mind and one of psychology's tasks is to explain how this is done. However, he did not share Hume's tendency to scepticism about the physical world. He believed that science gives us a rich and extensive knowledge of what lies outside minds and that a philosophy of mind which denies, belittles, or jeopardizes that knowledge is unacceptable.

His main contribution to the subject was *The Analysis of Mind*, which he published in 1921. The theory that he there proposes about what happens at the point of contact between mind and matter is not one that appeals to common sense. Common sense might endorse the theory that there is a mysterious interaction between two irreducibly different kinds of things, the mental and the physical (dualism). But the theory proposed in *The Analysis of Mind* is that at the point of contact there occur events which are in themselves neither mental nor physical, but which are the basic components out of which we construct both the mental and the physical world (neutral monism). This is the kind of conclusion that could be reached only at the end of a long philosophical investigation. So perhaps the best way to explain it is to describe its development out of the dualism which Russell espoused first.

Russell's philosophy of mind: dualism

The leading idea in his early, dualistic philosophy of mind is that all knowledge is based on acquaintance. In his philosophical classic *The Problems of Philosophy* (1912) he defines acquaintance as the mind's relation with those objects that directly confront it. He explains that the kind of confrontation that he means occurs in sense perception, introspection, and certain kinds of memory. Sense perception gives us our knowledge of the external world, and the crucial question is whether the direct objects of perceptual acquaintance lie outside the mind. His answer is that they do. However, he does not think that they are the physical objects which the unphilosophical take themselves to perceive. They are *sense data, external to the mind, unlike mental images, but phenomenal, unlike physical objects. Their intermediate status is hard to formulate, and his specification of examples, such things as patches of colour and sounds, does not make it much easier to understand.

The construction of the physical world out of such components does not belong to the philosophy of mind. But the difficult task of specifying the components themselves does belong to it. There was also another difficulty that faced Russell at this point. Sense data, which is by definition appearance presented to minds, does not provide a sufficient basis for constructing the physical world, in which much of what goes on is never presented to any mind. So he had to enrich the basis with unsensed appearances (sensibilia). He could then treat a physical event as a centre from which lines of appearances radiate outwards in physical space and only a small proportion of these appearances would be presented to minds and so become sense data. The introduction of unsensed appearances put a constraint on his philosophy of mind: it had to explain the difference between mere sensibilia and sense data.

At first the distinction did not give him any difficulty. A sense datum was simply distinguished by the fact that it was presented to a mind, or, to put this the other way round, by the fact that a mind was acquainted with it. But later, when this reliance on the mind as the subject of acquaintance (ego) began to strike him as illegitimate, he had to explain the difference between unsensed and sensed appearances in another way.

He finally gave up the ego in 1921, when he was converted to neutral monism, which constructs the mental world out of the very same components as the physical world and, therefore, cannot admit the ego. The construction of the physical world out of these components—the other side of neutral monism—was developed by him eight years earlier in *Our Knowledge of the External World*, and it did not produce a crisis in his philosophy of mind, as the abandonment of the ego did.

Russell's dualism lasted just so long as he refused to construct the mental world out of the same components as the physical world. In that period the main lines of his philosophy of mind were very simple. Acquaintance was a relation connecting the ego with its objects. At that time his main adversary was *idealism, which in its extreme form maintains that we never make any contact with anything outside our own minds. Acquaintance seemed to offer a way of escape from this restriction. It was a relation, and he conceded to the idealists that it was a mental relation. But he rejected their inference that, therefore, its objects must be mental too. His early theory of sense data attempts to exploit the possibility that it is sometimes physical. However, the attempt would succeed only if he could give an acceptable account of sense data, which would not only show that they are the same kind of thing as unsensed appearances but also explain what distinguishes them from unsensed appearances.

If he could do these two things, he would have a realist theory of knowledge and a realist theory of meaning, and he would have thrown off the cramping restrictions of idealism. For though sense data would be the only physical object of acquaintance, all our knowledge of the physical world could start from it and the meanings of all our descriptive words could be derived from it.

This ambitious enterprise ran into two difficulties, one on each of its two main fronts. His reaction was to give up the dualistic theory that mental and physical things are irreducibly different and to take up neutral monism, which reduces both to the same basis.

The first difficulty was that he could rely on acquaintance only so long as he believed that the mind was, or contained, an ego, or subject. In fact, even in 1912, he felt unsure about the ego. It was too vulnerable both to Hume's criticism, endorsed by William *James, that introspection reveals no such thing, and to *Kant's criticism, foreshadowed by Hume, that no empirical meaning can be attached to the hypothesis that there is such a thing. So Russell gave up the ego, and then had to find another explanation of the awareness that distinguishes sense data from mere sensibilia. The new explanation could not be that sense data is related by acquaintance or by any other relation to an ego. It had to be that sense data and other directly presented objects are related in certain ways to one another.

The second difficulty concerned the status of sense data. How could it be the same kind of thing as unsensed appearances? If, as he believed, unsensed appearances exist as actual things at points in physical space, they are unequivocally physical, and the word 'appearance' merely alludes to the possibility that they might acquire a relation with a mind. Sense data, on the other hand, could be physical only if it occurred in the nervous systems of percipients. Now there is no doubt that in his early philosophy of mind he did ascribe this kind of physical existence to them. But that left many mysteries unsolved. How exactly did the mental relation, acquaintance, manage to reach out to them? And how exactly did they themselves manage to represent their causes outside the percipient's body, as he implied that they did, when he specified them as things like patches of colour and sounds?

The neutral monism which he adopted in 1921 was intended to answer these questions. See RUSSELL'S PHILOSOPHY OF MIND: NEUTRAL MONISM.) DFP

Russell's philosophy of mind: neutral monism.

The philosophy of mind adopted by *Russell in his middle period was neutral monism, which denies that there is any irreducible difference between the mental and the physical and tries to construct both the mental world and the physical world out of components which are in themselves neither mental nor physical but neutral. He adopted this theory because he believed that there was no other way of solving the problems that beset his earlier dualism (see RUSSELL'S PHILOSOPHY OF MIND: DUALISM). The book in which he developed the theory, *The Analysis of Mind* (1921), is an unusual one. The version of neutral monism defended in it is qualified in several ways and it is enriched with ideas drawn from his reading of contemporary works on *behaviourism and depth psychology. The result is not entirely consistent, but it is interesting and vital especially where it is least consistent.

The aim of neutral monism is to show that the difference between the physical and the mental is not a difference of components but only a difference in the way in which the components are put together. An analogy can be found in the difference between the division of a country's population into groups living in different areas and its division into the categories used by tax collectors. In both cases the same human material is used, and the difference lies in the method of selection. Similarly, according to neutral monism appearances are grouped in one way to form physical objects and in another way to form minds. In order to get a physical object, you take all the appearances that radiate outwards from its position in physical space. In order to get a mind, you take all the appearances that start from surrounding objects and converge on its position in physical space. The difference is based on the distinction between output and input. However, a physical object is not the separate source of its output of appearances, but only the group of all the appearances sent out, and similarly a mind is not the separate recipient of its input of appearances, but only the group of all the appearances received.

This theory was devised to solve the problems of perception, and its generalization to cover not only sensations (received appearances) but also such things as beliefs and desires was bound to lead to difficulties. But first, did it solve the problems of perception?

There were two such problems which Russell's earlier dualism had failed to solve. First, he had to explain the difference between an unsensed appearance (sensibile) and a sensed appearance (sense datum), and his earlier explanation was that a sense datum is presented to a subject (ego) which is then acquainted with it. But when he ceased to believe in the ego, he was no longer in a position to appeal to its acts, and he could not even use the word 'sense datum', because it implies that something is given to a recipient. So he used the words 'sensation' or 'sensum' instead, and he had to find some other distinguishing mark of sensa. Second, he had to show that sensa really are the same kind of thing as sensibilia, and, what is more, that they are both in themselves neither physical nor mental but neutral.

The neutral monist solution to the first of these two problems was that sensed appearances are distinguished from unsensed appearances by the fact that they are related to other appearances in ways in which unsensed appearances are not related to other appearances. For sensed appearances produce later memories, and at the time they produce beliefs with the help of memories of earlier appearances. These networks of relations cannot be found among unsensed appearances and so they can be taken as the distinguishing mark of sensed appearances. The difference becomes more striking when we add the behavioural effects of memory and belief and all the stratified processes of learning. The details are complicated, but the essential point is that the analysis of *consciousness does not rely on a relation between subject and object, but relies, instead, on distinctive relations between sensed appearances and other appearances.

At this point Russell qualifies his neutral monism. The theory in its pure form would claim that these distinctive relations provide the complete explanation of consciousness. But he avoids this extreme position. In fact, the philosophy of mind of anyone who adopted it would be like *Hamlet* without the Prince of Denmark. More specifically, it would be vulnerable to two objections. Depth psychology shows that the distinctive relations are not always accompanied by consciousness, and common sense suggests that, conversely, consciousness is not always accompanied by the distinctive relations.

The neutral monist response to the second of the two problems amounted to little more than an assertion that sensed appearances really are the same kind of thing as unsensed appearances. But sensed appearances are sensations, and sensations are already mental and do not need any distinctive relations in order to make them constituents of minds, and so their basic neutrality is a pretence. Indeed, the only plausible theory that is at all like neutral monism is the theory that sensations are a special kind of physical occurrence in the nervous systems of observers. It is, therefore, not surprising to find Russell adopting this position in *An Outline of Philosophy* (1927) and in *My Philosophical Development* (1959). However, this is not neutral monism but the kind of materialism that identifies the mental with the physical. In subsequent decades many philosophers subscribed to this identification in the general form that covers everything mental. When Russell suggested the theory in the special case of sensations, he put them in the same category as unsensed appearances only by giving them a physical aspect as well as a mental aspect. In any case, unsensed appearances would have nothing to match the mental aspect of sensations, but only the possibility of becoming sensations. In general, Russell construed the world, in a way that was always *Leibnizian but never *idealist, as a constellation of radiating views each of them something like what would be recorded by a photographic plate at the appropriate point in physical space. But neutral monism is not the right metaphysic to accommodate this idea.

Outside the area of perception it is even harder for a neutral monist to demonstrate that the basis of the mental world is neutral. The two most difficult cases are beliefs and desires. Neither of them can be constructed entirely out of sensa, and Russell's strategy is to call in images. But are images really like sensa? Certainly most images are quite unlike what is recorded on a photographic plate, and the use of an image is often more like drawing a picture than looking at one. In any case, images at best could supply only the content of a belief, and there is also assent to the content. Since Russell was committed to avoiding acts of mind, he adopted *Hume's theory that assent is a feeling. However, such a feeling would be completely unlike a sensum and at this point neutral monism has been left far behind.

Quite apart from neutral monism, it is questionable whether Russell's analysis was on the right lines. Assent may not be an act of mind, but it is directed onto a content and this feature (*intentionality) is not easy to include in a theory that treats assent as a feeling. Intentionality is *Brentano's idea rather than Hume's, and *Wittgenstein put it at the centre of his philosophy of mind. When Russell gave up the ego and its acts, he ought to have retained the essential feature of its acts, intentionality.

In his analysis of desire, his rejection of intentionality is deliberately provocative. His main point, derived from depth psychology, is that people often do not know what they want. Now it is undeniable that people often do not know what they need. So he assimilates desires to needs, and defines desire as a feeling that starts a line of behaviour and defines satisfaction as another feeling that terminates it. The name of the initial feeling is 'discomfort' and the name of the terminal feeling is 'removal of discomfort' or 'pleasure'. However, he is inclined to define these feelings not by their introspectible qualities but by their places in the pattern of behaviour. In fact, his whole analysis is very behaviouristic. The object of a desire is whatever would cure the discomfort, and conscious

desire is merely desire accompanied by a true belief about the cure. If this were correct, it would certainly explain why people do not always know what they want.

The three main theories of *The Analysis of Mind* have had very different fates. Its neutral monism, already heavily qualified, has not survived, and materialism is the only monistic theory that seems to have any hope of replacing it. Russell's rejection of intentionality appears to have been a mistake. On the other hand, his critique of the assumption that all the contents of a mind lie open to inspection has produced an enduring effect. This critique is a characteristic Russellian achievement. It uses ideas taken from behaviourism and depth psychology with panache, and it threatens to destroy the Humean framework in which it is set.   DFP

Borst, C. V. (ed.) (1970). *The Mind/Brain Identity Theory*.

Pears, D. (1967). *Bertrand Russell and the British Tradition in Philosophy*.

Quinton, A. (1972). 'Russell's philosophy of mind'. In Pears, D. (ed.), *Bertrand Russell*.

Wittgenstein, L. (1975). *Philosophical Remarks*. (Eng. trans.)

Ryle, Gilbert (1900–76). British philosopher, commonly characterized as a leading member of the school of 'linguistic philosophy' which was prominent at Oxford in the years following the Second World War. This description of him is questionable, however. He regularly made clear to students that he had no wish to be the founder of any philosophical 'school', and philosophical terms such as 'materialism', 'idealism'—and even perhaps the expression 'linguistic philosophy' itself—were sometimes described by him, almost dismissively, as 'hustings' words.

A central part of his programme was to classify concepts according to their 'category' or 'logical type'. His most famous work, *The Concept of Mind* (1949), is an attempt to show that philosophers have misled themselves by assigning concepts which purport to refer to minds and mental qualities to the wrong category. (One assigns words to categories according to their 'logical behaviour'; thus 'know' does not behave like 'read'—at least in some respects—since one can read carefully or carelessly but one cannot know something carefully or carelessly; similarly one can do some reading for half an hour but one cannot 'do some knowing' for half an hour.) *Descartes, according to Ryle, had correctly recognized that men were different from machines but had mistakenly characterized the difference by suggesting that some human movements were the result of 'non-material' or 'non-mechanical' causes. A second 'world' had therefore to be invented—a 'mental' world—to house such entities; it belonged in the same category as the 'physical' world but contained non-spatial and non-mechanical happenings. The postulation of such a 'world' is scathingly referred to by Ryle as 'the dogma of the Ghost in the Machine'.

He is not saying that there is *no* such world, since this would be to repeat the same category mistake; he is arguing that the counting of 'worlds' is misguided and that we are misleading ourselves if we raise questions couched in 'ghost-in-machine' terms. He argues instead that many mentalistic words are dispositional in character: thus to describe a person as intelligent does not imply that occult events going on 'in the mind' are influencing other events going on 'in the body'; it indicates some of the things which he is disposed to do if particular circumstances arise. Other mentalistic words, such as 'solve', 'detect', and 'see', are 'achievement' words: that is to say, they are used when certain processes or activities have been brought to completion and do not relate to shadowy processes or activities going on 'somewhere else'.

In his later writings (see *Collected Papers*, 1971, and the posthumously published *On Thinking*, 1979) he argues that when a person is described as thinking (like Rodin's *Le Penseur*) it does not follow that there is a single activity, for example operating with words or symbols, that is invariably going on. Other published works include *Dilemmas* (1954) and *Plato's Progress* (1966).

Ryle's views have sometimes been described as 'behaviourist', and they do indeed have a certain amount in common with the radical *behaviourism of B. F. *Skinner. In particular both thinkers are in agreement in their opposition to methodological behaviourism: neither wishes to say that 'mental events' exist *alongside* 'physical events' but are not suitable objects for scientific study. Skinner's attack on 'autonomous man', however, is less sophisticated than Ryle's attack on 'the Ghost in the Machine'; mental-conduct words, for Skinner, are 'perquisites of autonomous man' (1972: 15), and the suggestion that such words are not all of the same logical type is not considered. In addition Skinner writes at times like a traditional determinist, whereas Ryle correctly recognizes that the question, 'Does this action merit praise or blame?' is of a different logical type from the question, 'What were this action's causal antecedents?'. An extension of Skinner's position might be to say that for its own purposes a science of behaviour requires a language without the explanatory superstructures implied by disposition words, and that it is for this reason—not simply for doctrinaire behaviourist reasons—that mentalistic words should not figure in scientific reports on human and animal behaviour. Ryle, however, unlike Skinner, is concerned with the use of mentalistic words for workaday purposes, and, apart from his admonition to philosophers, he is not attempting to argue that our ways of talking require revision.

The final chapter of *The Concept of Mind* offers an account of the subject matter of psychology. Its main thesis is that psychology should not be regarded as though it were a kind of counterpart to Newtonian physics, concerned with 'mental' phenomena as opposed to 'physical' ones.

The Cartesian picture left no place for Mendel or Darwin. The two-worlds legend was also a two-sciences legend, and the recognition that there are many sciences should remove the sting from the suggestion that 'psychology' is not the name of a single homogeneous theory. Few of the names of sciences do denote such unitary theories, or show any promise of doing so.

For those interested in psychology perhaps the most important message from Ryle's work is that insufficient attention to correct categorization can lead to false contrasts, to misleading analogies, and indeed to downright bad theorizing. It is a message which, up to now, not all practising psychologists have fully taken to heart.

TRM

Lyons, W. (1980). *Gilbert Ryle: An Introduction to his Philosophy*.

Skinner, B. F. (1972). *Beyond Freedom and Dignity*.

Wood, O. P., and Pitcher, G. (eds.) (1970). *Ryle: A Collection of Critical Essays*.

S

saccades. Rapid movements, punctuated by brief fixations of the eyes, during searching eye movements. The saccades (or saccadic flicks) of the eyes do not occur when a person is following a moving object with his eyes, or with eye movements due to the head turning as an object is fixated. Thus, there are two kinds of eye movements— 'saccadic' and 'smooth'—given by different neural mechanisms. The world remains fixed only during saccadic movements, and not during smooth eye movements; this is probably because the *efferent commands to move the eyes for searching are cancelled against the movement signals from the retinas: when the eye movement command and retinal-movement signals are equal and opposite, the world remains stable (unlike a panning cine camera) but only while the eyes move saccadically.

The successive fixations between the saccadic jumps refresh the borders of retinal images, as the receptors adapt (fatigue) with constant stimulation, giving rise to *after-images. Visual acuity for resolving fine detail is, however, slightly impaired by the small saccadic movements, as is shown by a slightly improved acuity, for a second or so, in flash after-images, which are 'photographed' fixed on the retinas, although they move.

The word 'saccade' derives from an old French word meaning the sudden flicks of a sail.

See RETINAL IMAGES; STABILIZATION OF. RLG

Alpern, M. (1962). 'Types of movement'. In Davson, H. (ed.), *The Eye*, vol. iii.

sadism. Term first used by *Krafft-Ebing to describe sexual pleasure gained by the infliction of pain or cruelty on others. He derived the word from the name of the Marquis de Sade. De Sade was condemned to death by the *parlement* at Aix-en-Provence for sexual vices, but had his sentence commuted by the king to imprisonment. While in the Bastille he wrote scandalous novels based on fact: *Justine* (1791), *La Philosophie dans le boudoir* (1793), *Juliette* (1797), and *Les Crimes de l'amour* (1800). RLG

Sanai, Hakim (or Khwajah Abu-al-Majd Majdud ibn-Adam Sanai, c.1046–?1141). A native of Ghazna in present-day Afghanistan, he was a major *Sufi teacher and author, acknowledged by *Rumi as one of his inspirers. He wrote an enormous quantity of mystical verse, of which his *Hadiqa* (Walled Garden of Truth,

1131) is his masterwork and the first Persian mystical epic of Sufism. He taught that lust and greed, emotional excitement, stood between humankind and divine knowledge, which was the only true reality. Love and a social conscience are for him the foundation of religion; mankind is asleep, living in what is in fact a desolate world. Religion as commonly understood is only habit and ritual.

IS

Sanai, Hakim (1976). *The Walled Garden of Truth*. Trans. D. Pendlebury.

Sartre, Jean-Paul (1905–80). Sartre's father, a naval officer, died two years after Jean-Paul was born, whereupon he and his mother went to live with her parents. Sartre thus grew up under the supervision of his grandfather Charles Schweitzer (uncle of Albert Schweitzer), who exercised a powerful and not altogether benign influence on the boy's development. He was sequestered at home, and there encouraged in precocious literary aspirations until the age of 10, when he was sent to school, to enjoy for the first time the companionship of other children. Sartre's own account of his childhood in *Les Mots* (1964) is mostly negative, and his grandfather is subjected to extremely unfavourable criticism. In the course of his adolescence he studied at the prestigious École Normale Supérieure, met Simone de Beauvoir, qualified to become a *lycée* philosophy teacher, and did national service in the meteorological section of the army. He nurtured strong literary ambitions and ideals, which came to fruition with the publication (1938) of his first novel, *La Nausée*, the first *existentialist novel. In subsequent years he published several plays and novels, notably *Huis clos* and *L'Âge de raison*, in which his philosophy is given concrete dramatic expression. This work was combined with more purely philosophical productions, dealing with the imagination, the emotions, and *Husserl's notion of the transcendental ego; in this he was much influenced by the works of the German *phenomenological school. These studies culminated in his most systematic and ambitious philosophical work, *L'Être et le néant* (1943), which powerfully integrated his philosophical concerns and his controlling literary themes. In later years he became increasingly occupied with political matters, both practically and intellectually, thus attracting by his outspoken heterodoxy the obloquy of both Church and state.

The subtitle of *L'Être et le néant* is 'an essay on phenomenological ontology', and this aptly describes the method and content of that difficult but rewarding book, for Sartre's aim is to give a systematic descriptive account of the fundamental categories into which reality divides—an architectonic of being—and of their interrelations, by means of a phenomenological enquiry into the structures that *consciousness displays. This is designed to elucidate the basic character of man's existence in the world, and so expose the underlying principles of his various modes of conduct. The starting point and pivot of the enquiry is, in the spirit of the phenomenological tradition, an insistence upon the constitutional *intentionality of consciousness —its directedness onto outer objects—and from this Sartre's whole philosophy ultimately derives. It is first observed that consciousness is, of its very nature, consciousness *of* things other than itself. These things exist independently of consciousness, and are thus transcendent to consciousness, inasmuch as their being is never exhausted by their presentations to consciousness. The objects of consciousness comprise the realm of being Sartre calls the 'in-itself'.

The in-itself, for Sartre, is wholly outside consciousness: intentional objects are not (as they were for Husserl) in any sense constituents of, or in, consciousness. But consciousness itself, by contrast, is a dependent entity in that it cannot be conceived to exist independently of the in-itself, since it is essentially intentional; it is therefore supported in its being, as Sartre puts it, by something other than itself. (His position is thus the reverse of *idealism.) Indeed, consciousness just *consists* in the intentional positing of transcendent objects; it has no other being. Yet— and this is the crucial point—it does not thereby collapse into the in-itself: it remains distinct from its intentional objects, and in a special way. Consciousness is not distinct from its objects in the way the inkwell is distinct from the table, since the being of these things is independent and the relation in which they stand external. Rather, consciousness stands off from the in-itself as a kind of pure emptiness, whose concrete being, such as it is, is exhausted by the objects it cannot but intend. Sartre characterizes the structure of intentionality, and thereby of consciousness itself, by saying that the relation incorporates a kind of negation: consciousness is at a distance from its objects by *not* being those objects, and at the same time what is intended constitutes all that is *positive* in the being of consciousness. Sartre is thus able to conclude that, in virtue of the structure of intentionality, the being of consciousness consists in its unalloyed negativity, i.e. its intrinsic nothingness. The directedness of consciousness is then not the directedness of any *thing*, since that would have to be an in-itself and hence an object for consciousness. So this evacuation of consciousness does not stop at ordinary objects of perception or memory; it includes

one's character, past, body, and even one's ego, which for Sartre (unlike Husserl) is intelligible only as an object of consciousness, not as its immanent unifying and constitutive essence. In general, nothing that is an *object* of consciousness can be *within* consciousness. As a result of this nothingness, says Sartre, we are apt to apprehend small pockets of negativity in the world. This occurs in the attitude of questioning and is revealed in the experience of *lack*, which characterizes human reality; the phenomenon is most famously illustrated by the example of the expectant man apprehending the *absence* of Pierre in the café. Sartre's contention is that consciousness of negation, which is integral to human experience, is possible only on the ground of the nothingness of consciousness itself.

But consciousness is not only engaged in the world by virtue of its intentionality and correlative *nothingness; it is further distinguished from the in-itself by possessing the characteristic of *self*-consciousness. Consciousness is thus a being, as Sartre says, that exists for itself. The primary mode of self-consciousness is what Sartre calls 'prereflective' self-consciousness, i.e. the awareness of its own directedness onto transcendent beings. It is important to Sartre that the structure of this primitive self-consciousness does not recapitulate within consciousness the intentional relation: there is not, between consciousness and itself, the kind of distance that separates consciousness from the in-itself. For if there were, consciousness, in taking itself as object, would be self-transcendent; which is impossible. Pre-reflective consciousness is what Sartre calls 'non-positional' self-awareness. Indeed, if this self-consciousness were positional there would be the threat of an infinite regress, since the positing consciousness must always be transparent to itself. Consciousness is, paradoxically enough, entirely coterminous with itself, yet at a kind of distance from itself: there is, in Sartre's phrase, an 'impalpable fissure' within consciousness. This characteristic of self-consciousness implies that whatever is a property of consciousness is a conscious property of it. Sartre's thesis now is that the properties of consciousness which are thus revealed to consciousness are not tolerable to it, and that we seek, by a variety of stratagems, to conceal these properties from ourselves. (Some of these conditions of consciousness appear also on the reflective plane, which is to say the kind of self-consciousness that is genuinely positional, as when we take up the stance of another with respect to our own being.)

We can now formulate and locate Sartre's conception of freedom: freedom is precisely the nothingness of consciousness as it stands off from its objects. Specifically, one's character or past or body—what Sartre calls one's *facticity*—transcends one's consciousness of it, and is symmetrically transcended *by* consciousness. Choice consists in exploiting this distance in the formation of projects: the for-itself has possibilities because it *is not* its facticity. Imagining and questioning and doubting thus become models of human freedom. But, according to Sartre, consciousness is appalled by its freedom; it is therefore appalled at its own being, which is nothingness. The outcome is that consciousness tries to conceal its own nothingness from itself by denying its freedom: this is the condition of *bad faith*. Bad faith is, however, doomed to failure because of the principle that what is true of consciousness is consciously true of it: there is thus no escaping the anguish that is consciousness of freedom. Moreover, insofar as bad faith represents the aspiration of the for-itself to become an in-itself, it characterizes the attitude of *sincerity* as well as the attitude of refusing to acknowledge to oneself what in fact one is. In both cases bad faith consists in a denial of freedom, either by conceiving of one's choices as externally determined or by trying to collapse the transcendent for-itself into its facticity, as with sincerity. We refuse to acknowledge our actions as our own by trading upon our transcendence from them, or we represent them as inevitable by denying this transcendence. And behind this mode of conduct is the basic structure of *intentionality, now taking facticity as object. Good faith would be an undistorted conception of the relation between free consciousness and all that one *is* in the way of body, character, actions, past, and so forth.

In addition to the in-itself and the for-itself, Sartre discloses, by attending to the structures of consciousness, a third category of being, namely 'being-for-others'. So far, consciousness has been characterized as a pure point of view on the world, rather than as an item within it, but the revealed existence of other consciousness alters this solipsistic picture radically. The body has hitherto been considered as *my* body, as it is lived by me; but it is also the medium through which I exist for the other, and the same is true of other facets of my facticity. According to Sartre, consciousness takes on the structure of being-for-others —it becomes an object *in* the world—when it is subjected, via the body, to the *look* of the other. In experiencing the look I can establish a new relation to myself, as in the attitude of *shame*: I am ashamed of myself as I appear to the other, and my body mediates for me the formation of this attitude. (It is to be noted that, for Sartre, the primary mode of recognition of others is affective, not cognitive: it is not a relation of knowledge.) In being-for-others consciousness presents itself to itself as an object in the field of another subjectivity, and this on the pre-reflective plane. The fundamental character of interpersonal relations is thus a confrontation of freedoms, which Sartre sees as generating relations of *conflict*. As with bad faith, this arises from an inherently unstable oscillation between freedom and facticity. Thus, for Sartre, the basic modes of human relationship embody self-defeating projects. Love, he says, is the wish to possess the other's freedom, for the other to be freely enslaved, but this is not possible, so the project of love is futile. Similarly the conducts of *sadism and *masochism involve, in their different ways, the possession or appropriation of a freedom: but in the end the possession self-defeatingly implies an exercise of freedom. In sex, too, the aim is to induce the identification of the other with his or her body, but the being of the other, as an incarnated consciousness, cannot but transcend the facticity that invades the desiring consciousness.

What is not clear in all this is whether Sartre thinks that his bleak and pessimistic account of human relations is essential to them or whether, like bad faith, they are conditions of consciousness from which we might conceivably be liberated. It does not seem, at any rate, that they issue from the constitutive structure of consciousness as it relates to the subjectivity of others.

It is important to bear in mind, in coming to grips with *L'Être et le néant*, that Sartre's philosophy does not take the form of a series of unconnected but insightful commentaries on the human condition; it consists, rather, of a systematically articulated body of doctrine, ostensibly derived from certain basic tenets of phenomenological ontology, and is to be evaluated as such. In particular, one should be aware that familiar terms—'freedom', 'shame', 'nothingness', 'anguish', etc.—are employed with a specific theoretical content which can be grasped only by coming at the work as an organized whole. Nor should such paradoxical-seeming dicta as 'the being of the for-itself is defined as being what it is not and not being what it is' be taken at face value, but should be construed as dramatic expressions of thoughts whose meaning, often relatively sober, can be grasped only in context.

Next to *L'Être et le néant*, Sartre's main philosophical works are *La Transcendance de l'ego* (1936); *L'Imagination* (1936); *Esquisse d'une théorie des emotions* (1939); *La Critique de la raison dialectique* (1960). Arthur C. Danto, *Jean-Paul Sartre* (1975) contains a bibliography of English translations of Sartre's works. CM

scanning. Used loosely, this word is sometimes used to describe the searching movements of the eyes, but a usefully restricted technical sense is conveying information by movement (as of the flying spot in a television camera and a corresponding electron beam in the receiver) down a single channel. The receptors of the eyes, the ears, and the skin are parallel channels and do not employ scanning in this technical sense. There is, however, a creature with a single channel scanning eye—a copepod, *Copilia quadrata*. RLG

Gregory, R. L., Ross, H. E., and Moray, N. (1964). 'The curious eye of Copilia'. *Nature*, 201/4925.

schemas. In walking down the street with a friend, one simultaneously engages in at least five movement processes: walking (including maintaining posture), breathing, talking, gesticulating, and scanning the shop windows and passers-by. But each of these processes involves the cooperation of multiple processes: for example, stepping is determined *inter alia* by high-level route-selection processes ('turn left at the town hall'), visual *feedback about the location of obstacles, and tactile feedback from the soles of the feet. And each of these in turn requires activity in a neural network linking an array of receptors with an array of motor neurons.

These behaviours involve not only 'externally directed' movement, but also a variety of 'exploratory' movements that help update an 'internal model of the world' (Craik 1943). In a new situation, we can recognize that familiar things are in new relationships, and use our knowledge of those individual things and our perception of those relationships to guide our behaviour on that occasion. It thus seems reasonable to posit that the 'internal model of the world' must be built of units which correspond, roughly, to domains of interaction—a phrase carefully chosen to include objects in the usual sense, but to include many other things besides, from some attention-riveting detail of an object all the way up to some sophisticated domain of social or linguistic interaction for purposeful beings. We may use the word 'schema' to correspond to the unit of knowledge—the internal representation of a domain of interaction—within the brain.

The intelligent organism does not so much respond to stimuli as select information that will help it achieve current goals—though a well-designed or evolved system will certainly need to take appropriate account of unexpected changes in its environment. To a first approximation, then, planning is the process whereby the system combines an array of relevant knowledge, to determine a course of action suited to current goals. In its fullest subtlety, planning can involve the refinement of knowledge structures and goal structures, as well as action *per se*. While an animal may perceive many aspects of its environment, only a few of these can at any time become the primary locus of interaction.

In general, our thesis is that *perception of an object (at least at the pre-verbal level) involves gaining access to routines for interaction with it, but does not necessarily involve execution of even one of these subroutines. Our image for the control of the ensuing behaviour is context-dependent interpretation (in the sense described in PROGRAMS AND PLANNING), in that new inputs (such as coming upon an unexpected obstacle) can alter the elaboration of the high-level structures into lower-level tests and actions which in turn call upon the interaction of motor and sensory systems. We study programs which are part of the internal state of the system prior to action, and which

can flexibly guide that action in terms of internal goals or drives and external circumstances.

To better appreciate the intimate relation between perception and action, consider the *perceptual cycle* (Neisser 1976). The subject actively explores the visual world—for example, by moving eyes, head, or body (or manipulating the environment). Exploration is directed by anticipatory schemas, which Neisser defines as plans for perceptual action as well as readiness for particular kinds of optical structure. The information thus picked up modifies the perceiver's anticipations of certain kinds of information which—thus modified—direct further exploration and become ready for more information. For example, to tell whether or not any coffee is left in a cup we may reach out and tilt the cup to make the interior visible, and keep tilting the cup further and further as we fail to see any coffee, until we either see the coffee at last or conclude that the cup is empty.

Head and Holmes (1911) were perhaps the first to study systematically patients' perceptions of the spatial aspects of their own bodies. They referred to the basis of this perception as the 'postural schema'. This integrated representation of prior movements was held to be updated by each change of position, and to provide a postural model into which all incoming sensations might be integrated. F. C. *Bartlett (1932), who had been much influenced by Henry *Head, introduced the term 'schema' into the psychological literature in the sense of an active organization of past reactions, or of past experiences, which must always be supposed to be operating in any well-adapted organic response. With this, the emphasis shifts from the postural frame to cognitive aspects as revealed in Bartlett's memory experiments.

Workers in *artificial intelligence organize their schema for 'understanding', separating the problem of sensory representation from that of directing action (see Bobrow and Collins 1975 for a sampling of approaches). Minsky (1975) has advanced his concept of 'frames' as a unification of these studies. Here, the stress on recognition of overall contexts which subsume the particularities of the current situation complements the schema-assemblage emphasis on the building up of a representation from familiar subparts.

Neisser (1976), influenced by *Gibson, takes a holistic approach with little concern for mechanism and with the schema usually viewed as corresponding to a total situation rather than some localized element of it. He takes explicit account only of those actions which are directed to sampling sensory data. Neisser's use of schema seems to be that of Bartlett, augmented by the Gibsonian view of information pick-up and the resultant stress on the perceptual cycle discussed above.

Another root of the use of 'schema' in current psychology is found in the work of Jean *Piaget. The Piagetian schema is the internal representation of some generalized class of situations, enabling the organism to act in a coordinated fashion over a whole range of analogous situations. Reviewing his approach to the genesis and development of knowledge, Piaget (1971) relates his schemas to the innate releasing mechanisms of the ethologists and thus, via Konrad Lorenz, to the schema of *Kant in the *Critique of Pure Reason* (1787). Yet Oldfield and *Zangwill (1942–3) assert that the Head–Bartlett concept of schema has no connection with that of Kant!

The concept of schema has also developed a special meaning in the motor skills literature—for instance, in the work of R. A. Schmidt. Schmidt's schemas seem suited to the performance of a single motion in the laboratory or in sports (such as swinging a bat) rather than to a complex manipulation or to goal-oriented performance in a dynamic environment. Each such schema is broken into two parts: the *recall schema* seems akin to feedforward (cf. Fig. 2 in FEEDBACK AND FEEDFORWARD), being responsible for the complete control of a rapid movement, even though environmental feedback may later signal errors. The *recognition schema* is responsible for the evaluation of response-produced feedback that makes possible the generation of error information about the movement. It thus seems to combine on-line feedback and identification procedures which may operate even after a movement is completed to better tune the schema for its next activation.
MAA

Arbib, M. A. (1972). *The Metaphorical Brain.*

Bartlett, F. C. (1932). *Remembering.*

Bobrow, D. G., and Collins, A. (1975). *Representation and Understanding: Studies in Cognitive Science.*

Craik, K. J. W. (1943). *The Nature of Explanation.*

Gibson, J. J. (1977). 'The theory of affordances'. In Shaw, R. E., and Bransford, J. (eds.), *Perceiving, Acting and Knowing: Toward an Ecological Psychology.*

Head, H., and Holmes, G. (1911). 'Sensory disturbances from cerebral lesions'. *Brain,* 34.

Minsky, M. L. (1975). 'A framework for representing knowledge'. In Winston, P. H. (ed.), *The Psychology of Computer Vision.*

Neisser, U. (1976). *Cognition and Reality: Principles and Implications of Cognitive Psychology.*

Oldfield, R. C., and Zangwill, O. L. (1942–3). 'Head's concept of the body schema and its application in contemporary British psychology'. *British Journal of Psychology,* 32–3.

Piaget, J. (1971). *Biology and Knowledge: An Essay on the Relations between Organic Regulations and Cognitive Processes.*

schizophrenia. Schizophrenia is the commonest of the severe mental illnesses, and interferes with the sufferers' thoughts, feelings, and ability to plan and carry out actions. Emil Kraepelin, 19th-century German psychiatrist, carried out work that has led to the current understanding of the illness. Based on meticulous observation of many patients, he suggested that severe mental illness could be differentiated into two major disorders: dementia praecox and manic–depressive insanity. Dementia praecox was a progressive illness that started in adolescence and followed a downhill course, whereas manic–depressive insanity was a phasic illness with periods of full recovery between episodes of the illness. Dementia praecox was rechristened schizophrenia by the Swiss psychiatrist Eugen Bleuler in 1911 to reflect his belief that the illness was due to a splitting between the intellectual and emotional aspects of the individual.

Symptoms of the illness often seem bizarre and difficult to understand. This may be why surveys show that many members of the general public fear people who suffer from schizophrenia. There is a common misconception that it is a 'split personality', and that people with schizophrenia are akin to 'Dr Jekyll and Mr Hyde' characters. Another common myth, fed by a few high-profile cases and sensational media reporting, is that people with schizophrenia are dangerous. In fact, the vast majority are not violent and are much more likely to harm themselves than others. Violence, particularly homicide, has increased in many societies in recent decades, and there is no evidence that schizophrenia has contributed towards this.

People with schizophrenia suffer a range of abnormal experiences, and there is no diagnostic laboratory test. The diagnosis is thus a probabilistic statement and can be difficult to make in some cases. Schizophrenia affects the 'higher'-level functions of the brain, such as the systems controlling thoughts, moods, actions, and perceptions. These functions contribute most to making a person a unique individual, which is why the illness can be so devastating. The symptoms of schizophrenia are classically divided into 'positive' and 'negative' categories.

The positive symptoms include hallucinations, delusions, 'passivity phenomena' (the medical term for the experience that one's actions, feelings, and thoughts are under external control), and disruption of thought processes. People with schizophrenia may experience their thoughts being spoken aloud, or voices that seem to come from an external source although they are internally generated. They may develop unusual or impossible ideas and beliefs (delusions), partly as a response to these experiences. These ideas can take very varied forms with persecutory, grandiose, religious, paranormal, or personal themes, and often reflect the individual's interests. Thinking may be so affected that it becomes disjointed and difficult to follow. At its extreme there may cease to be any discernible connection between ideas so that conversation becomes incomprehensible.

Schizophrenia can diminish motivation, initiative, mood, and emotional expression; these constitute the category of 'negative' symptoms. This may lead sufferers to become slower to talk and act, and increasingly indifferent to social contact and emotional interaction. Over time patients may lose contact with their friends and family, be unable to continue working, and become withdrawn and isolated. At its most extreme, individuals lose the ability to look after themselves.

Infrequently movement disorders, such as fixed postures, repetitive movements, and mutism, are seen. These 'catatonic phenomena' have gradually become less common in Europe and North America but still occur in the developing world

Just fewer than one in 100 people will suffer from schizophrenia at some point in their life. It is more common in those living in urban than rural areas, and in some migrant groups, such as African–Caribbean people living in the UK. It is an illness that affects adults, being rare in children and gradually more common during adolescence. Strikingly, the peak age of onset is earlier in men (early twenties) compared to women (late twenties), and women show a later second peak around the time of the menopause. Nevertheless the lifetime risk for men and women is about equal.

Generally the illness first comes to attention through the acute development of florid positive symptoms. In retrospect it is often apparent that there were gradual changes, such as social withdrawal, before the development of acute symptoms. The course of the illness is very variable. About one in ten people show a good recovery from the first acute episode and go on to have no further episodes and show little or no residual disability. About a third make a good recovery from the initial episode but go on to have further episodes. A further third recover from the first episode but with some residual disability, and experience further episodes. About 20 per cent make a poor recovery from the first episode and have considerable ongoing disability. When assessed over 30 years after illness onset, about half have been found to have a good outcome. Evidence that people in developing countries have a better outcome has generated considerable interest. The likely explanation is that the less complex lifestyle in the developing world enables people who suffer from schizophrenia to integrate back into their community more readily (e.g. it may be easier to cope with continuing symptoms if one is working on the family farm rather than in a computer company). The disability associated with the illness often leads to *depression, and the lifetime *suicide rate among people with schizophrenia is about 1 in 10 (much higher than in the general population). The rates of cardiovascular and respiratory illnesses are also higher, possibly because of the combination of poverty and an unhealthy lifestyle that affects many sufferers. In the past, patients with schizophrenia spent most of their lives in large mental hospitals or 'asylums' but the development of effective treatments in the past 50 years has substantially improved the prognosis.

The disease causes great suffering to patients, their families, and carers. The World Health Organization global burden of disease assessment ranks schizophrenia as the ninth greatest cause of disability in the world. In addition, the health and social care costs for schizophrenia are considerable: about £810 million per year in England alone. It commonly affects individuals in early adulthood and so often prevents them from fulfilling their career and life ambitions. If indirect costs are considered, the financial burden in England is about £2.6 billion per year, even without allowing for lost careers.

The cause or causes of schizophrenia remain elusive despite over 100 years of research. There is evidence for the interplay of genetic and environmental factors. In contrast to Kraepelin's original idea that schizophrenia was a dementia (i.e. a disease characterized by progressive brain degeneration), there is considerable evidence to support the theory that schizophrenia is at least in part a disorder of brain development. This has been termed the neurodevelopmental hypothesis. Brain-imaging scans show that many people with schizophrenia have subtle structural brain abnormalities. In general the temporal lobe volume is smaller, and the fluid-filled parts of the brain (the ventricles) are larger. Studies of brain tissue show differences in the arrangement of cells in the brains of people with severe schizophrenia compared to normal. These findings suggest that early brain development has been impaired.

Children who go on to develop schizophrenia tend to show slight delays in their motor development, poorer educational achievement and social adjustment, and interpersonal difficulties many years before the onset of the symptoms. This supports the neurodevelopmental hypothesis. Home movies of these children show that they have more movement and postural abnormalities than their peers. As they enter adolescence these differences often become more noticeable until they enter the so-called prodrome of the illness, frequently characterized by social withdrawal, and then go on to develop psychotic symptoms.

There is strong evidence of a genetic component to schizophrenia. First-degree relatives of someone with schizophrenia have about a tenfold greater risk of developing the illness compared to the general population. This increases to nearly a 50 per cent lifetime risk of developing the illness among the children of two parents with schizophrenia. Studies of identical twins (who have the same copies of genes as each other) and of children adopted shortly after birth (so they grow up in a different environment to their siblings and parents) show that the increased risk is the result of inherited genes rather than anything to do with the family environment (such as attitudes, culture, or exposure to pathogens). As yet, it has not been possible to identify any of the predisposing genes, and it seems most likely that a number of genes, each with a small effect, are responsible. In this way the genetics of schizophrenia appear similar to those of other chronic medical disorders such as diabetes mellitus or coronary heart disease.

Despite evidence of a major genetic contribution to schizophrenia, other factors must be important. This is highlighted by the fact that among identical twins, where one has schizophrenia, the risk of the second twin developing schizophrenia is slightly less than 50 per cent and not 100 per cent, which would be the case if genes were solely responsible. Early environmental factors, such as medical problems during pregnancy and delivery, play a role. Complications such as pre-eclampsia, bleeding, prolonged labour, and asphyxia during delivery are more likely to have occurred to people who go on to develop schizophrenia compared to the general population. Another curious finding that points to the importance of the early environment for development of the brain in the womb is that people with schizophrenia are more likely to have been born in the late winter/early spring than other times of the year. This seasonal effect is seen in both northern and southern hemispheres. It has been suggested that a maternal viral infection that is more frequent during the winter might be responsible.

The neurodevelopmental hypothesis explains a predisposition to schizophrenia but not the timing of its onset. There is considerable evidence highlighting the role of various precipitating factors. The first psychotic episode often follows a major adverse life event, such as the loss of a relationship. Likewise using dopamine-releasing drugs, such as amphetamine or cocaine, can precipitate the first episode or a relapse of schizophrenia. Prolonged heavy abuse of cannabis also seems to increase the risk.

The acute symptoms appear to result from an excessive release of the neurotransmitter dopamine, while drugs that block dopamine receptors in the brain tend to diminish the symptoms. Consequently, the excess dopamine has been called the 'Wind of Psychotic Fire'. However, there is interest in the role that may be played by other neurotransmitters, particularly serotonin and glutamate. Brain-scanning techniques ('functional imaging') that show the brain working are an exciting recent development, and can show the abnormal neurochemistry (mainly involving dopamine) associated with acute symptoms. These techniques also allow researchers to investigate the abnormal physiology underlying schizophrenic symptoms as they occur. For example, normally when people think to themselves ('inner speech') they show activation of part of the brain responsible for producing speech (Broca's area) and deactivation of the part of the brain involved in processing of speech. Functional imaging scans (see BRAIN IMAGING) of people experiencing auditory hallucinations (voices) show that the parts of the brain responsible for

further processing of sounds are not deactivated. This suggests the illness affects the brain's internal monitoring systems that differentiate between externally and internally generated words and, as a consequence, the mind experiences 'inner speech' as coming from an external source ('inner speech' seems like voices outside the head).

Until 50 years ago, there was little treatment that could be offered to people with schizophrenia, and this led in some cases to desperate therapies. This changed in the 1950s when chlorpromazine was found to have an antipsychotic action. A large number of antipsychotic drugs have been developed subsequently. Numerous high-quality trials have demonstrated the effectiveness of these medications in treating the acute symptoms of schizophrenia. Over two-thirds of sufferers will show a substantial alleviation of the florid positive symptoms, although all the medications take some time to have an antipsychotic effect. The initial action is largely sedative (which led to the old-fashioned name of 'major tranquilizer'). The sedation can be useful to reduce the distress of someone suffering acute symptoms but it takes two to six weeks for the psychotic symptoms to respond to treatment. Gradually the hallucinations and delusions wane in severity and extent. The antipsychotic action is related to the degree to which the drugs block dopamine receptors in the brain, with the clinical effect being most apparent when the D_2 receptors—one type of dopamine receptor—are about 70 per cent blocked. Continuing to take the medication at a lower maintenance dose considerably reduces the likelihood of a further acute episode. People who have suffered two or more episodes are generally advised to continue taking the medication in the long term to reduce the likelihood of further episodes.

Unfortunately, high levels of dopamine blockade can cause abnormal movements, restlessness, and Parkinsonism, as well as unpleasant psychological symptoms (such as loss of enjoyment and enthusiasm). In the 1990s a number of 'atypical antipsychotics' were developed. These antipsychotics do not block dopamine to the same extent, and consequently have fewer side effects on the motor system than the older, 'typical' antipsychotics, making them more 'user-friendly'.

Unfortunately, a proportion of patients show no response to an adequate trial of several different antipsychotic medications, which is often known as 'treatment resistance'. The 1990s saw the recognition that one antipsychotic, clozapine, could be effective in this instance. About two-thirds of people with treatment resistance will show an improvement while taking clozapine. However, clozapine can have severe side effects so its use has to be closely monitored.

Social and psychological interventions are as important as drugs in the treatment and rehabilitation of people with schizophrenia. Research has shown that the environment and social milieu can significantly affect the course of the illness. Understimulation, such as long periods in hospital with nothing to do, has been linked with a poor outcome and, at its extreme, the institutionalization seen in the past among patients confined to asylums for many years. Recognition of institutionalization was a factor behind the moves in many countries towards community care. The opposite extreme, overstimulation (such as high levels of 'expressed emotion' in the form of repeated critical and hostile comments), increases the relapse rate. For patients living in a family with high levels of overstimulation, therapeutic interventions to reduce this have been shown to make relapse less likely.

Increasingly, cognitive–behavioural techniques are being used to treat the symptoms, and to help patients to reinterpret their experiences in a less bizarre way. Behavioural therapy can be effective in improving social skills. Occupational therapy aims to aid independence, for example through developing abilities used in the 'activities of daily living' such as cooking and cleaning. Day centres, employment schemes, and sheltered workshops help maximize an individual's level of function. Other social interventions, such as placement in sheltered housing, hostels, or group homes, contribute to independence, although there will be some who need long-term nursing support: 'asylum' in the sense of safety and provision.

Schizophrenia is a complex and variable condition, and treatment often requires sustained input from a multidisciplinary care team involving psychiatrists, nurses, social workers, occupational therapists, and psychologists. Although there is no 'cure' for schizophrenia, the rapidly increasing understanding of the psychological and neurobiological aspects of the illness is now feeding through into better treatments and an improved outlook. Unfortunately, in most countries the full range of appropriate pharmacological and psychosocial treatments is only available to a minority of sufferers.   OH/RMM

Gelder, M. G., Andreasen, N., and López-Ibor, J. J. (eds.) (2000). *New Oxford Textbook of Psychiatry*.

schizophrenia: evidence for a neurochemical basis.

There are many theories about the abnormal neurochemical systems that may underlie schizophrenia. The main one, the dopamine hypothesis, states that the symptoms result from overactivity of the dopamine neurotransmitter system (either because of increased sensitivity to dopamine and/or an excess of dopamine). This theory grew from research showing that antipsychotic drugs act to block dopamine receptors. Measurements of dopamine metabolism show that all clinically effective drugs act in this way. Chemically related drugs that do not block dopamine receptors are not clinically effective. In addition, the potency of antipsychotics as blockers of dopamine receptors closely parallels their clinical potency.

*Brain-imaging studies that allow the measurement of drug binding to receptors further support the dopamine hypothesis by showing a direct relationship between the extent of D_2 (one type of dopamine receptor) occupancy by the antipsychotic drug and clinical response to the treatment. Other neurotransmitter receptors are not powerfully blocked at the low drug concentrations used clinically, and even closely related receptors (e.g. noradrenaline or norepinephrine receptors) are not sensitive to the drug, indicating that the receptor-blocking action of traditional antipsychotics is specific to dopamine receptors. Thus it seems that brain areas innervated by dopamine neurons are the main sites of the clinically effective action of traditional antipsychotic drugs.

The involvement of dopamine neurons is also suggested by evidence that dopamine-releasing drugs, such as amphetamine and levodopa, may worsen schizophrenic symptoms, and that amphetamine may produce a condition that is indistinguishable from acute paranoid schizophrenia in previously healthy volunteers.

It has proved difficult to find direct evidence for the dopamine hypothesis from studies of brain tissue because of technical difficulties, such as differentiating the effects of treatment from those of the illness. Nevertheless studies of post-mortem brains have found increased D_2 receptors in parts of the temporal lobe, which fits in with other evidence supporting the involvement of this part of the brain in schizophrenia.

Although the dopamine hypothesis has predominated, evidence supports the involvement of other brain chemicals. There has been particular recent interest in serotonin (5-hydroxytryptamine), partly because of the relatively high affinity of the newer antipsychotics for serotonin receptors, and glutamate. The involvement of serotonin was suggested by the observation that drugs that activate serotonin receptors, such as lysergic acid diethylamide (LSD), can cause hallucinations. Further evidence for the involvement of serotonin comes from studies that show reduced levels of serotonin receptors in some parts of the brains of people with schizophrenia. This has also been found for glutamate and gamma-aminobutyric acid (GABA) receptors. Abnormalities have been found in many neurotransmitter systems, which emphasizes the complexity of the alterations seen in schizophrenia.

Evidence supporting the involvement of particular neurotransmitters should be considered carefully in the light of the fact that some of these findings may be artefacts or secondary to other abnormalities in brain function or structure. Although hypotheses have been proposed explaining the interaction of some of the neurotransmitter systems in schizophrenia they are unable to explain all the findings, and it seems unlikely that progress will be made until there is a clearer understanding of how the brain systems involved are interrelated in normal brain function.   OH/RMM

Schopenhauer, Arthur (1788–1860). German philosopher, born at Danzig, now Gdańsk. His father was a banker and his mother a novelist. He was educated at Göttingen and Berlin, where he became *privat-docent*. As a challenge, he held his lectures at the same time as *Hegel, but without success. He retired to Frankfurt am Main as a lonely and unloved bachelor, befriended only by his poodle Atma, 'World Soul'. He was a personal and professional pessimist. He held a subjective idealism that the world is a personal fantasy, while will is primary as creating (subjective) reality. He is thus a kind of solipsist. His main book is *The World as Will and Idea* (1819).   RLG

science and religion. The three Abrahamic faiths believe that God is the ground of all that is and they must, therefore, interact in some appropriate way with science's account of the nature and history of the physical universe. Natural science is concerned with impersonal experience, where reality is treated as an object that can be put to the experimental test; religion is concerned with the encounter with the transpersonal reality of God, an area of human experience in which testing has to give way to trusting. Nevertheless, both science and religion attach importance to the search for truth through motivated belief.

1. History
2. Contemporary ideas
3. Humanity

1. History
Science came into being in a recognizably modern form in the 17th century in Western Europe, following its medieval antecedents. It has been suggested by some scholars that the Judaeo-Christian doctrine of creation played a significant role in encouraging this new development. If the rational God is the Creator, then there will be an order to creation. Yet, since God is totally free, the form of this order has been chosen by the Creator without constraint and it does not have to conform to a prior pattern that could be explored in a Platonic fashion through human thought alone. Hence the need for observation and experiment in order to find out what God has actually chosen to create. Moreover, if the world is God's handiwork, then it is a worthy subject for study. Seventeenth-century authors liked to speak of God's two books, the book of scripture and the book of nature, both of which should be read and which could not contradict each other because they came from the same Author. Whatever the merits of the hypothesis that makes religion the midwife of science (Jaki 1978, Brooke 1991), it is certainly true that the founding figures of modern science were mostly religious people, even if they had trouble with the ecclesiastical authorities (Galileo) or with Christian orthodoxy (Newton). In the 18th century, however, and particularly in France, an increasingly mechanical account of the physical world led many to reject religion and to embrace atheism. In the 19th century, many of the leading physicists (Faraday, Maxwell, Kelvin) were religious believers, but the publication of Darwin's *Origin of Species* in 1859 led to conflicts between biologists and theologians, though there were some religious thinkers who welcomed the insights of evolution, seeing it as the way in which the Creator had allowed creation 'to make itself' (Kingsley).

2. Contemporary ideas
The 20th century, particularly in its second half, saw vigorous activity across the frontier between science and religion, ranging from the outright rejection of religious belief by some scientists to claims for a positive and consonant relationship between these two sources of insight. It has been pointed out that, in the main, both science and theology reject strong postmodernist claims for the relativity of all knowledge. They can, therefore, make common cause in asserting that there is the possibility of a verisimilitudinous understanding of the nature of reality, for in both disciplines there is the belief that truth can be approached through the pursuit of motivated belief.

An important area in which to seek for a fruitful interaction between science and religion has been in connection with the latter's concept of creation. Theologians are anxious to stress that the doctrine of creation is concerned with ontological origin and not with temporal beginning, so that the question it addresses is 'why is there something rather than nothing?' and not 'how did it all begin?'. Therefore, big bang cosmology, though scientifically very interesting, is not particularly theologically significant. Much more important is the deep rational order that physics discerns in the structure of the universe, which can indeed be seen theologically as a pale reflection of the Mind of the Creator. A theological understanding of evolution is also significant, for it offers religion some help as its struggles with the perplexing problem of the evil and suffering in the world. A creation 'making itself' cannot be other than a world with ragged edges (Rolston 1999). If some cells can mutate and give new forms of life, then it is unavoidable that other cells will be able to mutate and become malignant.

The insights of the anthropic principle, recognizing that carbon-based life could evolve only in a universe whose physical laws took a very specific, finely tuned form, raises the question of whether there is an inbuilt design in the ordering of the world. This kind of approach to natural theology is quite different from the old-style arguments of William *Paley and his Cosmic Clockmaker, for it appeals not to those happenings that science can be expected to explain, but to the laws of nature that science by itself has to treat simply as given brute facts. This kind of understanding sees science and religion as being complementary to each other and not in mutual rivalry (Polkinghorne 1998).

The intrinsic unpredictabilities of quantum theory and chaos theory have shown us that whatever the universe may be, it is certainly not merely mechanical. Whether this fact should be interpreted as indicating that cosmic process is sufficiently open and supple to accommodate divine providential interaction within its history remains a contentious issue, under active discussion. Another matter about which there has been much argument is the claims of a strong version of sociobiology to provide the explanation of virtually all forms of human insight, including those of morality and religion (Wilson 1998). Naturally, this scientistic takeover bid is resisted by theologians. At the beginning of the 21st century, an active debate continues on many issues relating to science and religion, approached from a variety of perspectives.

3. Humanity

The question of the nature of the human person is a central issue in the dialogue between science and religion. The claim of a strongly reductionist physicalism that the mind is merely an epiphenomenon of the activity of the brain would be hostile to the theological understanding of the human person as a rational and moral being, open to spiritual contact with the presence of divine reality. It is important to recognize, however, that, although the Western Christian tradition, greatly influenced by Augustine's Platonism, has often tended to take a dualist view of human nature, this is by no means characteristic of all theological thinking, and it is certainly not required by it. In fact, dualism is very much a minority opinion among contemporary theologians. In the Hebrew Bible, and largely in the New Testament, the view taken of humans is that of their being psychosomatic unities. Human persons are considered to be animated bodies rather than incarnated souls. The recoil from a notion of 'the Ghost in the Machine' (see RYLE, GILBERT) does not at all imply that there is no concept of the human soul, but some reconsideration of its nature is required. The soul is not a detachable spiritual component of the person, temporarily housed in the flesh of the body, but it is the immensely complex information-bearing pattern in which the body's matter is at any time organized (Brown, Murphy, and Malony 1998, Polkinghorne 1998). This contemporary concept of the soul has something in common with the ideas of Thomas *Aquinas who, following *Aristotle, considered the soul to be the form of the body. However, modern thought tends to understand this in terms that are more dynamic and relational than would be the case in medieval thinking.

Understood in this contemporary way, the soul does not appear to possess an intrinsic immortality. Its natural destiny is to decay with the death of the body. Yet it is a coherent possibility for theology to claim that this information-bearing pattern will be preserved in the divine memory after death, in order that it may be re-embodied in the life of the world to come through a great final act of the faithful God. This idea corresponds to the Christian concept of death followed by resurrection, rather than to a purely spiritual notion of survival.

Many contemporary theologians are in favour of a metaphysical position that might be called dual-aspect monism. There is only one kind of created 'stuff', but it is experienced in the complementary poles of the mental and the material. It is central to a religious understanding of persons to see them as moral beings, capable of knowing right from wrong and of choosing between these alternatives. This requires the assertion of human free will in the strong form of the liberty of indifference, the ability to choose between genuinely open options and not simply to act in accordance with inner wishes.   JCP

Brooke, J. H. (1991). *Science and Religion.*

Brown, W. S., Murphy, N., and Malony, H. N. (eds.) (1998). *Whatever Happened to the Human Soul?.*

Dawkins, R. (1986). *The Blind Watchmaker.*

Jaki, S. (1978). *The Road of Science and the Paths to God.*

Polkinghorne, J. C. (1998). *Science and Theology.*

Rolston, H. (1999). *Genes, Genesis and God.*

Wilson, E. O. (1998). *Consilience.*

self. See 'BESIDE ONESELF'; CHILDREN'S UNDERSTANDING OF THE MENTAL WORLD; CONSCIOUSNESS; DESCARTES, RENÉ; CHINESE IDEAS OF THE MIND; DEPERSONALIZATION; DISSOCIATION OF THE PERSONALITY; EGYPTIAN CONCEPTS OF THE MIND; HUME, DAVID; INDIAN IDEAS OF THE MIND; MULTIPLE PERSONALITIES; OTHER MINDS; OUT-OF-BODY EXPERIENCE; PERSONAL IDENTITY; PSYCHE; ZEN.

sensations. Traditionally *perceptions have been thought of as made of sensations: sensations such as colours, touches, smells, and sounds being accepted as 'bricks' of which perceptions are made. Hence the now somewhat out-of-date term '*sense data'. But now we generally think of physical *stimuli at the organs of sense (the eyes and ears, and so on) with the neural *signals* from the sense organs as the data of perception. This change of thinking is from regarding sensations such as colours as being in the world of external objects and detected by the senses, rather than as being generated by the brain, or produced in the mind. Sir Isaac *Newton stressed the important notion that light itself is not coloured, but that the sensations of colours are generated in us, according to what sort of light strikes the eyes, discussed fully by *Locke.

Some regions of the brain have been identified as specially important for various sensations; but just how, or indeed why, certain brain activities in critical regions produce sensations remains mysterious. It is not even clear that sensations are necessary for perception, at least as perception is defined behaviourally by recognizing and handling objects. And as an object is differently identified, so sensations of colour or brightness may change. So perception is not simply built up of 'brick'-like sensations—as sensations are modified and even entirely created by what objects are (correctly or not) identified as. Effects of perception on sensation were appreciated by Ernst *Mach, whose book translated as *The Analysis of the Sensations* (1897) remains interesting and important. Mach pointed out that the seen brightness of a surface may change in ambiguous figures, when the surface 'flips' in depth, though there is no change in the stimulus, as is seen in Fig. 1.

This effect appears dramatically with a card bent to this kind of shape. In general, when a region is accepted or is likely to be a shadow, it looks lighter than when seen as a surface. This shows that sensations such as brightness and colour are not simply given by stimulation of the eyes, or the other sense organs, but may be drastically changed and enriched by 'higher-level' perceptual processes. A most dramatic example of this is Edwin *Land's demonstrations of a rich variety of colours given by only two colours, by combining a pair of otherwise identical photographs, one taken, for example, with a green filter and the other with a red filter, and projected with the same filters. This can be done even with one picture unfiltered (white) and the other with a red filter—when greens, blues, and many other colours are seen. Another dramatic example is the appearance of illusory surfaces and contours, which seem to be created perceptually as postulated nearer masking objects, to account for surprising gaps when the gaps are likely object shapes. The best-known examples are due to the Italian psychologist Gaetano Kanizsa (1979). (See ILLUSIONS.)

Fig. 1. Mach figure.

826

Because sensations are essentially private, we have no way of knowing how the world appears to other people. Thus, strictly speaking, we have no way of knowing whether their 'red' is our red—which may bother painters. At least for some colour-blind people, it may well be that sensations are individually different, and surely (if they are conscious) bats must have sensations very different from any of ours when detecting objects by sound ranging. These issues are explored most imaginatively in philosophical papers collected by Hofstadter and Dennett (1981).

Having said that we cannot know another person's sensations, it may seem impossible to *measure* sensations. There have, however, been many attempts to relate stimuli to sensation in quantitative ways, following the pioneer work of *Fechner and *Weber. Fechner measured the smallest difference of stimulus intensities that could be discriminated, and with a mathematical treatment he tried to derive measures of sensations. This involved certain assumptions which are very difficult to justify, but the approach remains of great interest (see PSYCHOPHYSICS). Also interesting are attempts to 'scale' sensory dimensions. Thus, for example, if there were two lights one brighter than the other, how would one set the intensity of a third light to lie halfway between the other two? Or could a picture be said to be twice as beautiful as another? The American psychologist S. S. *Stevens spent many years trying to scale sensations and judgements of various kinds, and claimed that each psychological dimension obeys a power law, with an empirical component that differs for the various senses, or kinds of judgement being made. There are methodological difficulties in this, but again the attempts to measure aspects of mind are interesting. (See QUANTIFYING JUDGEMENTS.) A full discussion of many of these issues is given by Savage (1970).

Although sensation is ultimately mysterious, as *consciousness is mysterious, it is worth pointing out that much the same holds for *matter. If a physicist is asked, 'What is an electron made of?' he has no answer. Indeed he may say that it is nothing but a probability distribution, or some such. In any case he will not say that it is made of matter, for physics is concerned ultimately only with relations and not with substances. Perhaps this is so also for mind—perhaps there is no 'mind stuff'—and in any case sensations should not be thought of in such terms. The trouble is, though, the kinds of relations that have been found and that are so powerful in physics are exceedingly hard to discover or measure in psychology. Although the attempts to measure sensation are intriguing we cannot feel that they are satisfactory, so psychology remains apart from the physical sciences.   RLG

Bradley, I. J. (1971). *Mach's Philosophy of Science*.

Hofstadter, D. R., and Dennett, D. C. (1981). *The Mind's Eye: Fantasies and Reflections on Self and Soul*.

Kanizsa, G. (1979). *Organisation of Vision: Essays on Gestalt Psychology*.

Land, E. H. (1959). 'Experiments in colour vision'. *Scientific American*, 5.

Mach, E. (1886). *The Analysis of Sensation* (Eng. trans. C. M. Williams, 1897).

Savage, C. W. (1970). *The Measurement of Sensation: A Critique of Perceptual Psychophysics*.

sensory deprivation, effects of. See ISOLATION EXPERIMENTS.

sex differences in childhood. Distinctively male and female development begins soon after conception, and the eventual degree of human sexual dimorphism exceeds that in many primate species. The twenty-third pair of chromosomes in females is XX, while in males it is XY. In the presence of the Y chromosome, cell division of the zygote is accelerated, and the medulla of the initially bipotential embryonic gonad differentiates during the seventh week into a testis. The secretion of androgenic hormones from the fetal testis organizes the development of both the genitalia and the brain according to the male pattern. Female differentiation always occurs in the absence of the male hormones. Circulation of androgens *in utero* is known to increase the amount of aggressive behaviour and gross physical activity in primates, and it is likely that these hormones predispose the human male to greater physical activity.

At birth, males are heavier and longer than females, and from the second month their calorie intake is greater; boys have a consistently higher basal metabolism than girls and greater vital capacity. However, in terms of bone age the newborn girl is equivalent to a 4- to 6-week-old boy, and growth velocity in the boy lags about two years behind the girl. Puberty is attained roughly two and a half years later in males than in females. (See HUMAN GROWTH.)

In addition to their relatively retarded post-natal physical development, males are characterized by a greater susceptibility to a variety of adverse conditions. They are more vulnerable to both post-natal and perinatal complications that can lead to death or long-term disability. In developing countries, where infant mortality rises at weaning due to intestinal complications, again it is the male who is more at risk. Throughout life, males remain more prone to a variety of diseases—respiratory, cardiac, infective, and neurological, as well as the sex-linked recessive disorders.

Thus cultural and social pressures that influence sex-typed behaviours act on organisms which, biologically at least, are distinctively male or female. A crucial issue for psychologists is the extent to which these different biological substrata may predispose males and females to different abilities or behaviours. Male and female babies do behave differently—boys are more restless than girls. They are also treated differently by those who care for them; it is therefore difficult to disentangle the relative influences of socialization and biological predisposition. It is none the less illuminating to document cultural influences on behaviour and to speculate upon their possible effects on sex differences.

In the early months of life boys tend to be handled more than girls, but newborn girls are spoken to and smiled at more during feeding sessions. These differences in care-giving behaviour have been attributed to the babies' differential responsiveness, and it is important to stress that any adult–infant interaction is a two-way process, and depends on far more than the adult's perception of the infant's sex. A recent comprehensive review of parental behaviour in laboratory studies concludes that there is 'a remarkable degree of uniformity in the socialization of the two sexes'. Against this finding, though, stands evidence from observations of a more general nature. Consider, for example, a study of 96 middle-class homes—in the 48 boys' rooms there were 375 vehicles, whereas in the 48 girls' rooms there were only 17; over half the girls possessed a baby doll, compared to just 3 of the boys. In general, the boys' rooms contained more educational materials and more sports equipment than the girls' rooms. The agents of socialization are, evidently, insidious.

Books and television are also factors which can strongly influence children's perceptions of sex-appropriate behaviours. In a study of children's literature, it was found that most children's books were about boys, men, and male animals; in nearly one-third of the books which won literature prizes (over a five-year period) there were no women at all. Boys were portrayed as active and adventuresome, girls as passive and immobile. This highly exaggerated presentation of sex stereotypes is repeated in the medium of television, where females are very much in the minority. Males are portrayed as aggressive, constructive, and helpful; females as deferential and passive.

Despite the restricted range of female roles presented by the media, adults appear to tolerate a wider range of behaviour from girls than from boys—thus, whereas it is perfectly acceptable for a girl's behaviour to be tomboyish, a boy who engages in female typical behaviour would be labelled with the more pejorative term 'cissy'. None the less, the preferred play activities of boys and girls are very different: boys play more outside, they are more physically active, and they play less with dolls. Parents tend to allow boys of school age greater freedom to roam the local neighbourhood and are more likely to encourage girls to stay at home. Investigators who have observed young children in playgroups and nursery schools have found that boys initiate more aggression than girls (approximately two-thirds of all aggressive acts are initiated by boys) and their aggressive encounters are more prolonged than those of girls. Even before they reach school age, girls tend to be more nurturant and protective than boys, and this is evident in their increased readiness to comfort a distressed child or to help a younger child in some activity.

The evidence for sex differences in cognitive abilities is equivocal, and this may be partly due to the fact that many tests are specifically designed to ensure that groups of males and females obtain the same mean score. There are, however, two types of tests in which boys do excel: mazes of the kind frequently seen in children's comics, and Koh's blocks (where a set of coloured blocks have to be assembled to match a pattern). Both these are tests of spatial ability and reflect boys' greater facility in understanding concepts of orientation and perceptual configuration. Girls tend to use verbal strategies for solving these types of problems—though this does not affect their accuracy, it slows down their performance relative to boys and accounts for their lower scores. More boys than girls have reading difficulties, and it has been thought that this is due to relatively poor language ability; it is now considered more likely that there is no sex difference in general language abilities, but that boys' greater restlessness at school makes them more difficult to teach! In studies of arithmetical ability, boys have usually achieved slightly better scores than girls; however, it has recently been shown that girls perform better when the problems are phrased in terms of 'female' objects (such as dolls and clothes) than they do when the same arithmetical computations are phrased in terms of 'male' objects (such as rockets and cars).

It is known that in adult males the right hemisphere of the brain is specialized for visuospatial skills, whereas the left hemisphere is specialized for language skills. Thus, if a male adult sustains damage to the left side of the brain his language ability will be impaired. In adult females there appears to be language representation in both hemispheres, and damage to the left hemisphere does not have such a profound effect as it does for the males. These sex differences in lateralization develop during childhood years, and the superior performance of boys on tests of visuospatial skills has been attributed to the earlier specialization of the right hemisphere for these abilities.

The fact that boys show a slight but consistent advantage in visuospatial abilities is insufficient to account for their vastly superior performance in science subjects during adolescence. It is well established that visuospatial ability is correlated with mathematical ability, and it would not be unexpected to find slightly more males than females preferring to study science-based subjects. There is now evidence that girls' reluctance to study science is due less to their lack of ability than to the fact that

they perceive science subjects as 'masculine', and therefore inappropriate to them.

In conclusion, the following four statements summarize our understanding of psychological sex differences in childhood: (i) There are biological sex differences which predispose males and females to some behavioural differences. (ii) Caregivers respond differentially to males and to females, but these responses are to the child's behaviour rather than to his or her sex. (iii) There are sex differences in brain organization, but it is not established beyond doubt that these are related to sex differences in intellectual ability. (iv) Cultural influences act to persuade children to conform to sex-stereotyped expectations.

The overwhelming importance of cultural influences in shaping sex-typed behaviour is evidenced by data from studies of cultures where male and female sex roles are characterized quite differently from those in our own culture. The biological dichotomy of the sexes should not be seen as necessarily implying an equally rigid dichotomy of abilities and behaviour; it would none the less be unhelpful to deny that biological differences will interact with environmental influences. CHU/MHU

Halpern. D. F. (2000), *Sex Differences in Cognitive Abilities*.

Maccoby, E. E., and Jacklin, C. N. (1975). *The Psychology of Sex Differences*.

Wittig, M. A., and Petersen, A. C. (1979). *Sex-Related Differences in Cognitive Functioning*.

sex differences in intelligence 1. The development of intelligence tests has informed us of two important facts about sex differences in intelligence. The first and most significant is that there is no overall difference in general intelligence (or IQ) between the sexes. The second is that there is a different balance between the major groupings of specific abilities, namely, verbal and spatial ability.

In the sense used here, verbal abilities refer to knowledge, or skill, with vocabulary, language-based reasoning, and comprehension. It is well known that females have about one-third of a standard deviation advantage over males (i.e. 60 per cent of females will perform better than the average male). Spatial abilities refer mainly to 'image-based reasoning' and in particular the ability to hold picture-like representations of objects in mind and mentally manipulate them (for example, jigsaw puzzles and maps). Males have an equivalent one-third standard deviation advantage over females in spatial ability. Perhaps any male advantage in chess, and maybe even mathematics, is due to the advantage that this ability can confer in these domains. These sex differences are likely to have multiple causes. It is likely that both experiential and biological differences between the sexes play some role. In the latter category subtle differences in hemispheric lateralization (where the left brain may be more verbal and more developed in girls and vice versa for the right brain, spatial ability, in boys) might have an influence. An interesting possibility is that the balance between verbal and spatial abilities is not sex related per se but a developmental function with children of either sex who reach puberty later having higher spatial ability (Waber 1977). Since, in general, females mature earlier than males this could explain the different profile. However, it has also been argued that any differences might be mediated by experiential differences between the sexes rather than the biological processes related to maturation per se.

The cultural and historical milieu in which the early test developers operated would have predisposed most to believe that women were intellectually inferior to men, yet it is an important finding of intelligence testing that there is no difference between the sexes in average intellectual ability. This is true whether general ability is defined as an IQ score calculated from an 'omnibus' test of intellectual abilities such as the various Wechsler tests, or whether it is defined as a score on a single test of general intelligence, such as Ravens Matrices. There may be a difference in variability, with males over-represented at the highest and lowest abilities. However, this is just as likely to be due to the relative contribution of verbal and spatial abilities at different points of the IQ distribution as it may be due to 'real' differences in variability of general intelligence itself. For example, low verbal ability matters much more than low spatial ability, so there are fewer low IQ girls than boys, but for very high IQ high spatial ability may be a requirement.

Controversially, some researchers have pointed to a difference in brain size to justify the hypothesis that perhaps there is a difference in general intelligence after all. In my view this is idle speculation and I say so for a number of reasons. While there is growing evidence that there is a relationship between brain size and IQ, and it is true that women have smaller brain volumes than men, nobody has any idea what this might mean because (a) there is no difference in IQ between the sexes despite this brain size difference; and if this is not a knockdown argument then consider (b) Neanderthals had a bigger brain than current humans but nobody wants to make the claim that they were more intelligent than modern people; (c) the relationship between brain size and IQ within species is very small; (d) the causal direction is ambiguous (IQ and its environmental consequence may affect brain size rather than the other way round); (e) the brain does far more than generate IQ differences and it may be those other functions that account for any male / female differences in size; (f) although many researchers have attempted to control for confounding variables such as body size, there are likely to be a large number of those, most of which are currently unknown, that could account for the sex difference; (g) some have also tried to explain the 15 or

so IQ point difference between some racial groups on the basis of race differences in brain size, yet race differences in brain size are much smaller than sex differences in brain size while the opposite is true for IQ differences—clearly something does not add up; (h) while there is a consensus that there is a biological basis for general intelligence, nobody knows which property of the nervous system causes that difference—and most contemporary theories would sit more comfortably with properties like neural transmission rather than brain size (Anderson 1992; Jensen 1998).

In conclusion, the psychometric evidence that there is no sex difference in general ability is overwhelming. In other contexts such data are taken to be the final arbiter of debate and the prudent would be advised to ignore counter-claims based on weak speculation about brain size and IQ.   MAn

Anderson, M. (1992). *Intelligence and Development: A Cognitive Theory*.

Jensen, A. R. (1998). *The G Factor: The Science of Mental Ability*.

Newcombe, N., and Dubas, J. S. (1992). 'A longitudinal study of predictors of spatial ability in adolescent females'. *Child Development*, 63.

Waber, D. P. (1977). 'Sex differences in mental abilities, hemispheric lateralization, and rate of physical growth at adolescence'. *Developmental Psychology*, 13.

sex differences in intelligence 2. Sex differences in general intelligence and in specific abilities have been investigated since the early years of the 20th century. By around 1990 a general consensus had emerged that there is no difference between males and females in general intelligence, reasoning ability, and verbal comprehension, but there are differences in a number of specific abilities. Males perform better on average in spatial, visualization, and mathematical ability, and in general knowledge, while females perform better on average on verbal fluency, verbal memory, perceptual speed, spelling, and foreign language acquisition. These differences are present in Europeans, Africans, Chinese, and Japanese. They appear to have some biological basis and are to some degree determined by prenatal and post-natal exposure to testosterone which masculinizes the brain and produces the typical male profile of abilities.

The sex differences in these abilities are of the order of half a standard deviation or 7.5 IQ points. Differences of this magnitude have large effects at the tail end of the distribution. For instance, in Benbow's study of mathematically gifted 12 to 15-year-olds who scored above the mean for college entrance on the maths section of the scholastic aptitude test, boys outnumbered girls by 12 to 1.

The consensus that there is no sex difference in general intelligence was broken in 1992 when Ankney and Rushton showed that the average brain mass of adult males is greater than that of adult females by approximately 100 grams and that this difference is present even when body size and weight are controlled. The sex difference in brain size and weight is about 10 per cent of total brain weight. This raises the problem of the function of the larger male brain. Brain weight and size are known to be associated with intelligence at a magnitude of approximately 0.4, so the expected consequence of the larger male brain would be that males should have higher average intelligence than females.

This logical implication is contrary to the consensus that there is no sex difference in intelligence. Several attempts have been made to resolve this paradox. Jensen has proposed that females may have the same number of brain neurons as males but that these are smaller and more densely packed inside a smaller brain, but the evidence does not support this suggestion. The writer's solution is that among adults males do have higher intelligence than females by about 4 IQ points and this difference is present whether intelligence is defined as reasoning ability or as the sum of the reasoning, verbal, and spatial abilities. The male advantage does not appear until the age of about 16 years because females mature earlier than males and this gives them an advantage that is lost in mid-adolescence. Nyborg (2003) has carried out independent research on this problem in Denmark and obtained similar results, but others such as Jensen (1998) and Mackintosh (1998) have resisted the conclusion that among adults males are on average more intelligent than females.   RL

Ankney, C. D. (1992). 'Sex differences in relative brain size: the mismeasure of woman, too?' *Intelligence*, 16.

Jensen, A. R. (1998). *The G Factor*.

Lynn, R. (1999). 'Sex differences in intelligence and brain size: a developmental theory'. *Intelligence*, 27.

Mackintosh, N. J. (1998). *IQ and Human Intelligence*.

Nyborg, H. (2003). 'Sex differences in g'. In Nyborg, H. (ed.), *The Scientific Study of General Intelligence*.

sexual development. Human sexual development has been described as the last frontier of psychological knowledge. Until quite recently it has been a subject surrounded by myth. Popularized Freudian concepts of the repressed libidinous forces of the id have fuelled the kinds of fantasies that have discouraged serious research. Only the cumulative influence of *Freud (1905), Kinsey and his colleagues (1948, 1953), and Masters and Johnson (1966, 1970), in building up a coherent body of clinical, sociological, and scientific knowledge over the course of the larger part of a century, has at last established a climate of opinion in which sexual function and development have been widely accepted in the scientific community as a proper area of systematic research.

Medical science has traditionally concentrated on the processes connected with birth and the diseases surrounding venery. It is the psychological and sociological sciences that have considered the totality of human sexual experience, and thereby established a core around which physiological and anatomical knowledge about sexual function can be set in its place. Such has been the development in recent years that the mainstream psychiatric view, expressed by Mayer-Gross, Slater, and Roth in 1969 —'a sexual activity is usually regarded as perverse if it has no immediate connection with reproduction, and still more so if it tends to lead to a sexual activity which could replace reproduction'—is no longer supportable. Sexual activity is now seen as a multiply functional part of human potential, in which the intention to reproduce is one among a number of valid intentions, such as pleasure, or the deepening of a bonding relationship, which the sexual act may properly subserve.

As a body of knowledge becomes established, so its operational concepts become increasingly elaborated. What was previously self-evident becomes redefined. That the study of human sexual development has reached this phase is perhaps best exemplified by considering first the biological basis of sexual development and then its psychological basis. It will be seen that the psychological, especially in regard to the development of male and female identity, intrudes continuously upon the biological as the means of making sense of it.

The simple idea that male and female is an unvarying dichotomy, from which much else springs, has been observed by Haeberle (1978, to whose thoughtful writing this contributor is happy to acknowledge an especial debt) to be more complicated than the Latin root of sex (*secare*: to cut, divide, or separate) implies. At least seven different factors have to be taken into account.

In the first place is *chromosomal sex*. The male body cells contain one X and one Y chromosome, whereas female cells contain two X chromosomes. Recently other combinations have been recorded, at least one of which (XYY) may be linked to severe aggressive tendencies. Nevertheless, chromosomal sex appears to be the most basic distinction between male and female.

Secondly, there is *gonadal sex*. The male's testicles and the female's ovaries are their primary anatomical sexual characteristics, but in rare cases tissues of both may occur in the same body.

Thirdly, *hormonal sex*—the balance of the androgens and oestrogens—which starts sex differentiation in the second month of fetal life, and continues through puberty and adult sexual maturity to old age, affecting all stages of growth and differentiation, has a wide range of characteristics of its own. The balance considerably affects essential sex-linked physical features during maturation, such as body shape and hair distribution, as well as controlling the reproductive process.

Fourthly, the *anatomical structures of reproduction* in the male and female may be less than fully developed, giving rise to variations of sexual classification.

Fifthly, the *external sex organs* may in some instances be missing, malformed, or inappropriate to chromosomal sex. Thus a child with the chromosomal structure of a male may be brought up as a female, the absence of a penis at birth giving rise to the assumption that a girl child has been delivered. There is evidence that the presence or absence of a penis is the most marked sign upon which sex is assigned to a child, with considerable social consequences.

Whether or not there is anatomical cause, a child of one sex may be reared as a child of the opposite sex, so that the *gender* or *social role* normally assigned to one sex is transferred, usually by parental influence. Instances are recorded in which early traumatic loss of the penis, through surgical accident for instance, have resulted in a child male by all usual tests being brought up as a female.

Finally, and in seventh place, but by no means least, the individual may assume a *gender identity* other than the gender role assigned during early development. In cases of transsexualism, for instance, the gender identity a person wishes to assume is the opposite of the gender role that has been assigned socially. Sex reassignment surgery may change the anatomical structures very successfully, creating a functioning penis or lubricating vagina, but the individual who encourages psychiatrist and surgeon to cooperate in such a process of elective change cannot change the chromosomal identity of their sex, which has usually been that of their gender role up to the point of reassignment surgery.

For the vast majority of individuals there is no conflict in any of these variables. The XY male has functional testicles, the appropriate hormonal balance of androgen and pituitary hormones, adequate reproductive mechanisms, an apparent penis responsive to sexual stimulation, is raised as a male, and feels himself to be such as he moves through adolescence into adult life. *Per contra* the female. The complexity of that apparent normality, however, and its dependence upon hormone production at the critical time, masterminded, as it were, by the pituitary, is a cause for marvel as hormone assay methods become increasingly refined. It should perhaps be recorded in passing that, embryologically, all human life is female. In the first month of uterine existence the embryo is sexually undifferentiated. Towards the end of the second month testosterone in the potentially male embryo begins to circulate, which causes the gonads that would otherwise have grown into ovaries to become testicles, and the penis and scrotum to form from the tissue that in the woman remains the clitoris, vagina, and labia of the genital structures.

Given this physiochemical developmental process, which by birth is usually responsible for clearly differentiated male and female sexual organs as the *primary sexual characteristics*, two other stages of development can be observed.

Hormonal influences produce the *secondary sexual characteristics* of puberty, confirming the maleness or femaleness of the individual in varying degrees by varying emphasis on anatomical structures. Fifteen secondary sexual characteristics have been noted, ranging from differences between the sexes in body hair distribution, shape of breasts, and muscular size, to the carrying angle of the arm and leg, which in the male is straight and in the female forms an angle at the elbow and the knee.

Finally, *tertiary sexual characteristics* are those gender role qualities of being masculine and feminine that cultural or subcultural conditioning emphasizes as appropriate to one sex or the other. It is clearly in the area of tertiary characteristics that there is most room for change, as the primary and secondary are physiologically determined whereas the tertiary are determined by socio-psychological forces. The feminist movement, which has arisen in part from the separation of the sexual and reproductive processes in consequence of reliable contraception, and advances in medical technology such as artificial insemination, is an excellent example of a social process that has a profound effect upon tertiary sexual characteristics.

Tertiary characteristics are of course always influenced by the family subculture and the larger social context of an individual's growth. It might be assumed that the gender roles of men and women would change only slowly, or, conversely, be changed quickly only by violent or radical means, because of their very fundamental purpose in the identity-stabilizing process of the sequence of the generations. (The psychological theories of *transactional analysis*, as developed by Berne and his followers (e.g. Harris 1970), describe especially the means by which the wisdom, or prejudices, of the generations are transmitted onwards and received.) The involvement of women in the combat forces of many countries is a particular example of a radical process shifting tertiary characteristics suddenly and widely.

As with the gradual and sequential development of the physical sexual characteristics, so the psychological and social tertiary characteristics are established over many years. In reviewing this process, Haeberle (1978) observes that 'the realization that adult human sexual behaviour results from a long, complex, and often hazardous development is relatively new'. While sex may be perfectly natural, it is clear that it is not always naturally perfect. The Freudian challenge of the early 20th century begins this clarification.

In traditional psychoanalytic thinking, the three phases of early and infantile sexual development (oral, anal, and phallic) are more or less successfully passed through and repressed until, after the quiescent period before puberty, puberty itself provokes the awakening of early adolescent sexual urges, which may or may not attach themselves to appropriately mature heterosexual relationships and behaviours. This process of attachment depends upon whether early fixation at one of the infantile stages has taken place, or whether those erotic stages have been integrated, and also upon how the child's attachment to its parent of the opposite sex (the resolution of the so-called *Oedipus or *Electra complex) has been managed.

Cultural variations in these processes, described by anthropologists from Margaret Mead onwards, suggested that the Freudian view was not universally appropriate. In considering the tertiary aspects of sexual development, it is now widely accepted that cultural influences are both significant and variable. The work of Money at Johns Hopkins (Money and Green 1969), as well as that of Kinsey, and Masters and Johnson, can be held to provide firm support for this view.

In the end, it is the sum of the biological processes and the development of gender role and identity, in whatever circumstances that takes place, that results in sexual orientation—whether this be heterosexual, homosexual, bisexual, or object related as in fetishistic behaviours.

In a society that can reconsider long-held aversions to some sexual behaviours—such as admitting that homosexual behaviour can be the basis for both pleasure and long-term relationships—questions of what is normal or abnormal inevitably arise. Such questions have particular relevance for those concerned in an educative or clinical way with the developmental process. As the boundaries alter, so moral and ethical questioning properly arises too. In such circumstances, what are clearly in a developmental sense aberrant behaviours need specifying clearly. In the current state of knowledge it is possible to state without fear of informed contradiction that sexual practices between adults and children (paedophilia) are harmful to the development of children, and that any sexual acts which seek to expose another person unwillingly to the demands of a close aggressor (rape) or more distant aggressor (the *frotteur* or the exhibitionist) do physical and/or psychological violence of a personally intrusive kind that a mature society finds reprehensible. The open sale of pornographic material might come under such a rubric. In addition there are clearly some sexual behaviours, such as the sado-masochistic, which, in their more extreme forms, contain elements of violence that would lead them to be considered symptomatic of a disturbed personality. However, the range of sexual behaviours that are now tolerated and openly advocated (see Comfort 1972) includes mild degrees of fetishism and sado-masochism.

The question of when the normal becomes the abnormal is difficult to resolve in principle, but in specific cases can reasonably easily be determined by a skilled enquiry into the total sexual value system of an individual or partnership. As clinical dependence upon alcohol is considerably distant from the majority of alcohol users, who have personality structures sufficiently robust to be able to enjoy its disinhibiting effects yet control the limits of the experience, so if a person's generally preferred sexual behaviours involve no compulsive quality, and if no manifest physical or psychological harm results to the individuals involved, then such behaviours should be classed as proper and within the realm of private and responsible action.

It is apparent from the above that in considering matters of human sexual development it is not possible to ignore the maturation, or regression, of the society in which the development takes place.

Since Freud drew attention to infantile sexual development, the broad acceptance of such development as natural and proper has become firmly established, even if all the psychoanalytic assumptions deriving from it are not so firmly accepted. Infant boys will have spontaneous erections, and infant girls the equivalent in vaginal lubrication. General body and specifically genital exploration and stimulation is now happily recognized as establishing later adult comfort with sexual matters. The untoward effects of inhibiting such exploration and its consequent discoveries are more strongly acknowledged than was even quite recently the case.

By and large the explorations of the child are sensually diffuse rather than erotically specific, though well before the onset of puberty both boys and girls may masturbate to some kind of orgasmic experience without there being, in the boy, any ejaculatory consequences. Masturbation is itself now recognized as a valid sexual experience throughout the whole lifespan, and the 19th-century horrors with which it was invested are rapidly fading from popular culture. (It might be noted in passing that this statement refers to Western cultures, and even so would not be true of many countries of southern Europe where there is a specifically Catholic cultural tradition. In many developing countries there are often still severe, and perhaps surgical, prohibitions against sexual activities that would be considered a natural part of the developmental process in most of northern Europe and North America.)

Adolescence, started by the hormonal triggers that create the secondary sexual characteristics, is the beginning of sexual fertility. It carries the individual from childhood through to increasing separation from parents and emerging independence in the adult world. Adolescence is a period that is very variable from culture to culture, and where education is extensive it may be considerably prolonged. In the last hundred years or so in Britain, as the period of education has increased and the age of the onset of puberty has decreased, so the time between actual sexual fertility and the opportunity for independent existence in a continuing relationship of adult choice can become surprisingly long. Haeberle observes that there may now be as many as twenty years from the age of puberty to establishing full economic independence, while ten years is very common. In contrast, 'many of the great romances of the world celebrate the passionate love-affairs of the young. . . . Margarethe was a teenager when she fell in love with Faust, Helen was only twelve when she left her husband Menelaus and followed Paris to Troy. Narcissus was sixteen when "many youths and maidens sought his love". Ganymede was even younger when Zeus made him his favourite.' The contentious age of Juliet is well known to generations of schoolchildren.

The prolonged changes of adolescence, which occur at different ages for different individuals, and may take one or several years, begin rather earlier for boys than girls. Heredity, diet, climate, and cultural and emotional influences may all be implicated in the start and duration of this period between the ninth and fourteenth years. The development of adult sexual organs, fertility, the enlargement of breasts in the girl, and the obvious development of male and female body shapes in this period all serve to concentrate adolescent awareness on the increasing differentiation into men and women. The typical same-sex gang behaviour of the early teens begins to give way by the mid-teens to overt sexual awareness of, and increasing interest in, members of the opposite sex. Boys' sexual interest appears to focus on overt sexual activity earlier than girls', a difference in sexual awareness and responsiveness that persists through early adult years. Men are at their most sexually active and interested in the late teens and through the twenties, whereas women's sexual responsiveness and interest appears to increase to a peak in the middle thirties. It is then capable of being sustained for the next 30 years or more, whereas male sexual responsiveness tends to decline from the late twenties onwards. There are of course wide individual variations in this overall pattern. Whether the different rates of growth of interest and responsiveness and decline are physically or socio-psychologically determined is not yet clear. The differences are, however, clearly observed. Changing social roles and expectations may have a particular effect on this tertiary aspect of male and female sexual development.

Homosexual fantasy and/or contact is not at all uncommon among boys and girls in adolescence. In the vast majority of cases it appears to be part of the transition from the sexually undifferentiated responses of childhood to increasingly articulated adult heterosexuality. Characteristically, in the adolescent homosexual phase, boys tend to be sexually attracted to (have crushes on) younger boys, while girls have crushes on older girls. Overt physical contact may or may not be present in these adolescent phases. The presence or absence of overt physical or sexual contact appears to bear no relationship to subsequent adult homosexual or bisexual behaviours.

Adulthood is a period with its own characteristic phases that are only just beginning to receive detailed descriptive attention. In delineating the phases of adult life, Levinson (1978) has remarked that the period from early adulthood to the onset of old age—a span of about 40 years—has been ignored as if it were a tranquil period. Clearly it is not. It is the period sexually when the pleasures and difficulties of the marital and child-bearing years subordinate sexual development into limited expectation and less discovery. It is also the period when sexual difficulties become manifest. The current tendency is to assume that sexual development will have taken place by the early adult years, but that sexual experience and discovery may lag considerably behind physical maturation.

The work of Masters and Johnson has made it quite clear that sexual activity can happily persist well into the seventh and eighth decades of life. The needs and urgencies of a couple may change, yet the reassurance and confirmation of existence that comes from the close physical intimacy of sexual contact can be pleasurable in itself to an advanced age and highly beneficial in the process of adjustment to increasing years. There is a growing though as yet limited professional interest in the relation between poor marital and sexual adjustment and a high incidence of demands for the resources of medicine by way of gynaecological distress, *psychosomatic distress, and psychiatric breakdown, suggesting that much might be prevented by more successful adaptation earlier on.

Quite clearly the doubts, urgencies, and discoveries of adolescent and young adult sexual development give place to sexual function coming more under the influence of increasing life stresses as the thirties and forties merge into the later adult years. In positive caring in relationships, however, sexual development subserves not only the continuation of the species but the most vital existential discovery—that physical encounter with a person of the opposite sex, and perhaps of the same sex too, sustains, supports, and heals in the individual life journey (Dominian 1977).   PTB

Boston Women's Health Book Collective (1976). *Our Bodies, Ourselves*.

Comfort, A. (1972). *The Joy of Sex: A Gourmet Guide to Lovemaking*.

Cousins, J. (1980). *Make it Happy: What Sex is All About*.

Dodson, B. (1974). *Liberating Masturbation*.

Dominian, J. (1977). *Proposals for a New Sexual Ethic*.

Freud, S. (1905). *Three Essays in the Theory of Sexuality* (repr. 1953).

Haeberle, E. J. (1978). *The Sex Atlas*.

Harris, T. A. (1970). *I'm OK—You're OK*.

Hooper, A. (1980). *The Body Electric*.

Kaplan, H. S. (1979). *Making Sense of Sex: The New Facts about Sex and Love for Young People.*

Kinsey, A. C., Pomeroy, W. B., and Martin, C. E. (1948). *Sexual Behaviour in the Human Male.*

———— (1953). *Sexual Behaviour in the Human Female.*

Levinson, D. J. (1978). *Seasons of a Man's Life.*

Masters, W. H., and Johnson, V. (1966). *Human Sexual Response.*

———— (1970). *Human Sexual Inadequacy.*

Mayer-Gross, W., Slater, E., and Roth, M. (1969). *Clinical Psychiatry* (3rd edn.).

Mead, M. (1935). *Sex and Temperament in Three Primitive Societies.*

Money, J., and Green, R. (eds.) (1969). *Transsexualism and Sex Reassignment.*

Stoller, R. J. (1976). *Perversion: The Erotic Form of Hatred.*

sexual problems. Sexual problems in marriage became a matter of particular clinical and popular interest with the publication in 1970 of Masters and Johnson's *Human Sexual Inadequacy.* This was an account of an eleven-year period of clinical work and research, conducted at the Reproductive Biology Research Foundation in St Louis, Missouri, involving the treatment of a group of sexual difficulties that Masters and Johnson classed together as sexual dysfunctions. Over the eleven-year period, 790 instances of sexual difficulty were seen, the majority (733) presenting in 510 marital partnerships where one or both of the partners were experiencing a sexual problem. The treatment of single individuals is referred to later.

This clinical work was itself based upon a research programme into the physiology of human sexual response that Masters and Johnson had started in 1954, and which they had published in 1966 as *Human Sexual Response.* Unlike Kinsey's pioneering work of twenty years previously, which had asked people in considerable detail what they did in their sexual lives, Masters and Johnson established laboratory conditions for observing how people reacted sexually in terms of their physiological mechanisms under specific conditions of stimulation. It was their avowed intention to make the field of sexual function academically and professionally respectable. There is now no doubt that they achieved this aim in a quite signal way, though probably with consequences for the effective use of the knowledge that they supplied which are not yet fully appreciated.

Until the appearance of their works, sexual problems had been seen clinically within the framework of psychopathology, and no distinction was made between difficulties of normal function and variations of normal function. Freudian thinking generally underpinned this view, and there was overall pessimism about the possibility of help for specific sexual problems. Sexual difficulties were themselves seen as symptoms of deeper, underlying problems, and moreover clinicians generally had no clear diagnostic framework within which to consider sexual

difficulties that might not be deeply rooted in psychopathology. The most optimistic views of treatment had been presented by Friedman in *Virgin Wives*, where he reported the work of Balint at the Tavistock Clinic in the mid-1950s. Balint had developed a form of brief psychotherapy, particularly for the disorder of vaginismus, which is a spasm contraction of the outer third of the vaginal barrel that effectively prevents intercourse by presenting such a constricted vaginal entrance that penetration by the male is not possible. Standard psychiatric texts of the 1960s and early 1970s, however, hardly touched sexual difficulties *per se*, beyond the blanket terms 'frigidity' in women and 'impotence' in men, and '*ejaculatio praecox*' also for men who complained of too rapid an ejaculation. In any event, both 'frigidity' and 'impotence' had acquired considerable pejorative overtones in popular usage by the 1960s, and (as had previously happened with such terms as 'idiot' and 'imbecile') required redefinition for clinical usage for that reason if no other.

It was the particular achievement of Masters and Johnson to shift thinking about difficulties of sexual function from considerations of psychopathology to those of learning and the failure to establish effective learning, and it is in this context that sexual difficulties are now first regarded upon presentation at a clinic. It is only when they appear to be unresponsive to treatment based upon educative concepts that considerations of psychopathology and inner psychic conflict are introduced. It is moreover quite possible now to separate sexual difficulties from sexual perversions—which is not to say that the two might not coexist.

Masters and Johnson also made the startling observation, which had previously passed most clinicians by, that sex tends to happen between two people. They concluded therefore that it might be best to see a couple in therapy rather than the single individual, as the focus of treatment is most likely to be upon the couple's pattern of sexual communication—what exactly happens between them—and not so directly upon the specific presenting difficulty of function, which is seen as a consequence of, or as being maintained by, the limitations of the couple's communication. The logic of this observation was also carried through by observing that a male clinician can never fully understand the female sexual experience, nor a female clinician the male. In consequence it might be helpful to have both a male and a female therapist present. This creates the situation of co-therapy—the treatment of a couple by a couple in a therapeutic foursome.

In defining the group of difficulties with which they were concerned, Masters and Johnson also made it possible, as noted briefly above, to distinguish the sexual dysfunctions from the sexual deviations. The sexual dysfunctions are often experienced by the majority of individuals in a transitory fashion, becoming dysfunctions by their persistence or their adverse effect upon the sexual relationship. For instance, most men will experience difficulties of erectile function in their adult life, and most women may have intermittent difficulty establishing a climax, even when these functions are generally satisfactory for the individuals concerned.

The description of the sexual dysfunctions is, briefly, as follows. In the man, primary or secondary impotence, premature ejaculation, and ejaculatory incompetence. That is to say, men who fail to establish and/or maintain an erection of sufficient strength for effective vaginal insertion, either throughout the whole of their adult sexual experience (primary impotence) or temporarily (secondary impotence); and men who ejaculate too quickly for their own and their partner's satisfaction (premature ejaculation), or too slowly, or not at all (ejaculatory incompetence). In the woman, the dysfunctions were classified by Masters and Johnson as being primary orgasmic dysfunction or situational orgasmic dysfunction. The first specified a situation in which the woman had never been orgasmic by any means (intercourse, masturbation, or any other method) throughout the whole of her sexually mature life, while the second described the conditions under which a woman might be orgasmic by coitus but not by masturbation (masturbatory orgasmic dysfunction), by masturbation but not by coitus (coital orgasmic dysfunction), or only occasionally orgasmic and without any feeling of certainty or predictability (random orgasmic dysfunction). Additionally they considered problems of pain upon intercourse in both men and women (dyspareunia) and vaginismus in women. They made a particularly strong case for encouraging physicians to believe in and thoroughly investigate a statement of pain during sexual intercourse, and not simply to dismiss it as 'hysterical' or 'psychogenic' because it was related to the sexual act. They also considered problems of low sexual drive.

In their physiological studies, Masters and Johnson had observed the processes of sexual arousal, from original quiescence through arousal and climax to quiescence (resolution) again, in a total of 694 male and female volunteers in the age range 18–89. In doing so they had made it clear that the sexual physiology of men and women is essentially the same even though the specific sexual anatomy is markedly different—bearing in mind, in regard to this latter statement, that in the embryo eventual male and female both start out as female, and are only differentiated as a consequence of hormonal effects, from about the sixth week of intra-uterine life, so that it is not until the third month of gestation that anatomical differences are apparent.

The first physiological change to arise as a consequence of effective physical or psychological sexual stimulation is that blood begins to flow more rapidly around the body as heart rate increases, so that specific tissues become engorged. This process, called vasocongestion, creates an erection in the male of which the exact equivalent in the female is vaginal lubrication. Both are the early signs of sexual arousal and/or interest. In the female, increasing vasocongestion in the tissues of the vaginal wall creates a type of sweating response on the surface of the walls of the vaginal barrel (the transudorific reaction) which accumulates to form the lubrication of sexual arousal. Masters and Johnson observed this process by the simple expedient of introducing a clear plastic dilator into the excited vagina, illuminating the interior, and filming the process. Not only did they thereby dismiss the assumption that vaginal lubrication came from the glands of Bartholin at the vaginal entrance, or that it was a product seeping through the neck of the womb, but they also observed the continuing process of arousal, which was that after lubrication had established itself the vaginal barrel lengthened and increased its diameter considerably, ballooning in its upper third. The vagina was thus seen to produce changes which were the effective analogue of the male erection. As the limp penis is a potential erection, so the vagina in its unaroused state was seen to be potential space.

One immediate consequence of these observations of vaginal lubrication was that the processes of arousal in the woman began to be seen as equally important to those of the male, if the sexual act was to be mutually satisfying, and that it made as little sense to tell a sexually unresponsive woman to use a cream in order to make male insertion possible as to tell a man without an erection to tie a splint on his penis.

Apart from the vaginal and penile reactions of erection, other marked changes take place in the erectile tissues of the female sexual organs, including the clitoris, and in the breasts, which are all dependent upon vasocongestion. Not only is the sexual response of the body more widespread and complex in the female than in the male, but a wide variety of cultural influences make it possible for the female to value and enjoy the feelings of her body whereas the male is often taught to discount feelings of all kinds. Thus the woman may especially enjoy and value the experience and complexity of feelings in a sexual relationship, while the male may be more concerned with the performance of the act. Difficulties in a sexual relationship frequently arise from this difference, as the man's interest may centre more on achieving climax than upon the pleasure of the encounter. It is also the case that the complexity of the woman's sexual responses is more vulnerable to adverse social conditioning; this may teach her that sexual acts are connected with excretory acts and menstruation which, if they themselves are adversely loaded emotionally, may make it difficult for her to value her sexuality positively and enjoyably.

At a specific point in the process of sexual arousal, involuntary muscular responses are triggered which in the male result in ejaculation of seminal fluid, and in the female in the experience of orgasm. In the male the sites of sexual sensation and orgasm are essentially the same, occurring in both cases around the tip of the penis, the glans. In the female, however, there is relatively little specific sensation inside the vagina, where the muscular spasm of orgasm is experienced. The main site of sexual stimulation on the input side, for the majority of women, is the clitoris, and ineffective clitoral stimulation is one of the main contributors to orgasmic difficulties. The separation of the clitoris and vagina in the sequence of sensory input and orgasmic experience has been a considerable theoretical dilemma in the development of Freudian thinking, giving rise to the now redundant clitoral–vaginal transfer theory of adult female sexuality.

Their physiological observations led Masters and Johnson to conclude that the sexual response cycle of arousal and climax is a natural physiological property of the intact adult human being and responds predictably to adequate stimulation. However, it is also under the potentially inhibitory control of higher centres, and has the singular property for an *autonomic process that its function can be effectively inhibited for the whole of a lifetime. It is therefore distinguished from other autonomic processes, such as respiration, heart rate, digestion, and so on. In consequence, Masters and Johnson's treatment procedures have been developed to aid the establishing of normal function. The goal of therapy is not to teach couples how to function sexually, but to help them discover how to stop stopping their natural functioning.

The therapy format which Masters and Johnson developed was a rapid, fourteen-day programme of intensive, therapist-guided development of effective sexual communication, using all senses but especially touch, the basic source of sexual pleasure. The early stages of treatment involve guided exercises (sensate focus) which the couple build up in discussion with the therapists and then undertake in the privacy of their own lives. Out of the shared experience of sexual responses occurring under the right conditions, specific techniques may become useful for specific difficulties. For instance, in the case of premature ejaculation, the woman in the partnership eventually becomes the therapeutic controller of the ejaculatory experience by applying a specific squeeze upon the glans penis just prior to an ejaculation provoked by masturbation, thus inhibiting the ejaculation and helping the man acquire the kind of reflex arc control that he acquired as a small boy in learning to control the passing of urine by discriminating internal signals.

Not only did Masters and Johnson's therapy proceed upon systematic lines, illuminated by a clear understanding of the expected physiological effects of an increasingly skilled sexual encounter between the couple in treatment, hence commending itself instantly to a planned therapeutic approach previously absent in this field; they also established treatment effects of a very high order. At best, 97.8 per cent of 186 premature ejaculators responded to treatment; at worst, 59.4 per cent of primary impotence cases recovered. Over all disorders, male and female, the initial successful outcome rate was 81.1 per cent, a figure of an extremely high order for any therapy. Five-year follow-up on 313 marital units showed a relapse rate of only 5.1 per cent. In consequence it can be claimed that Masters and Johnson developed not only a very systematic treatment procedure but also a highly effective one, for difficulties not previously responsive to treatment or properly understood.

The publication of their treatment results in 1970 led to a considerable surge of popular and professional interest, occurring as it did at a time when reliable and readily available contraceptive measures in the USA and northern Europe had become established aspects of the sexual life of these cultures. With the separation of the act of intercourse from the act of reproduction, the increasingly discussed concept of sex-for-pleasure *for both partners*, responsibly undertaken, suddenly acquired an authoritative knowledge base. This reached an elegant if early apotheosis in Alex Comfort's *The Joy of Sex* in 1972. Clinics for the treatment of sexual difficulties sprang up throughout the United States, so that within five years of the publication of *Human Sexual Inadequacy* it was reliably rumoured that over 3,000 such clinics had established themselves.

This mushroom development sprang in part from a small amount of work which Masters and Johnson had done with single individuals, where, for 41 males, a female partner, called a 'surrogate', was made available by the therapists to cooperate in providing psychological and physical involvement during therapy. Masters and Johnson themselves abandoned this approach to therapy in view of the considerable administrative and ethical issues which their bold exploration of it raised. It led to a good deal of sexual 'therapeutic' licence in the United States, a process eventually controlled by the development of a professional association for surrogate partners in sex therapy. Reputable schools of practice did also develop using a much more physically involved approach by therapists than Masters and Johnson had advocated, Hartman and Fithian being one example and McIlvenna at the Institute for the Advanced Study of Human Sexuality another. Apart from a treatment series conducted by Dr Martin Cole at Birmingham, the use of surrogates in therapy has not become common in Britain. Therapy for women to explore their own sexuality has become so, however, and there are some accounts of this (e.g. Hooper 1980), though no clinical trials in a formal sense.

Indeed, the whole field of sexual function therapy is notable for its enthusiasm rather than systematization, and it is often difficult to distinguish therapy from sexual enrichment work. Perhaps at times there may be no useful distinction to be drawn. Be that as it may, no systematic replication of Masters and Johnson's work has been attempted, and it is possible that such a task could not now be accomplished. Their work has itself dramatically altered the levels of information available in the population about sexual matters; their personal therapeutic effectiveness as the outstanding pioneer authorities in the field is an element that could not be replicated; the nature of their fourteen-day, vacation-based therapy programme is not one that is easily recreated once a variety of more local centres becomes available; and their criteria for selecting couples for therapy have never been clearly stated.

Despite a flood of literature following their work, of which LoPiccolo and LoPiccolo (1978) is a good summary, the only two studies to have investigated components of their treatment procedures have originated in England, where J. Bancroft and his colleagues at Oxford and P. T. Brown on behalf of the National Marriage Guidance Council at Rugby considered the co-therapy situation, among other aspects, in clinical trials. In both these cases therapy was modified to weekly attendance procedures, and spread out over 10–12 weeks instead of fourteen days. This is now the typical pattern for sexual function therapy in Britain, a development that has in part been systematized through the establishing of a multidisciplinary Association of Sexual and Marital Therapists in 1976.

Kaplan in the United States has been the strongest source of clinical thinking to integrate Masters and Johnson's work into the established psychological therapies, and she has been particularly concerned to distinguish disorders of sexual desire from the dysfunctions, as well as clarifying other aspects of the diagnostic statements of Masters and Johnson. Brown (Brown and Faulder 1977) has summarized Masters and Johnson and Kaplan into a diagnostic schema which lists in a simple fashion the categories of the sexual dysfunctions, and makes it clear that they are now readily distinguishable from those difficulties of sexual expression which were once called 'perversions', then 'deviations', then 'variations', and most recently by the *behaviourists 'excesses', but which Stoller has argued should properly be called 'perversions'. Their characteristic, to distinguish them from the dysfunctions, is that they are not difficulties of sexual expression, but contain choices of sexual object other than the familiar acts associated with heterosexual arousal and response.

Treatment for sexual dysfunction, both for couples and for individuals, is now available throughout the UK, though more so in some areas than others. Both the National Health Service and the National Marriage Guidance Council (Relate) have developed specialist clinic facilities, and there is a limited private field. Therapy typically involves an exploration of not only what the problem is, but why in the particular partnership or individual it has arisen or been maintained; and this is followed, usually on a weekly basis, by guided exploration of effective sexual stimulation. Thus the couple and the individual are helped to become increasingly expert and effective in their own sexual well-being.   PTB

Brown, P. T., and Faulder, C. (1977). *Treat Yourself to Sex.*
Comfort, A. (1972). *The Joy of Sex: A Gourmet Guide to Lovemaking.*
Friedman, L. (1961). *Virgin Wives.*
Hartman, W. E., and Fithian, M. A. (1972). *Treatment of Sexual Dysfunction.*
Hooper, A. (1980). *The Body Electric.*
Kaplan, H. S. (1974). *The New Sex Therapy.*
—— (1979). *Disorders of Sexual Desire.*
Kinsey, A. C., Pomeroy, W. B., and Martin, C. E. (1948). *Sexual Behaviour in the Human Male.*
—— —— —— (1953). *Sexual Behaviour in the Human Female.*
LoPiccolo, J., and LoPiccolo, L. (1978). *Handbook of Sex Therapy.*
Masters, W. H., and Johnson, V. (1966). *Human Sexual Response.*
—— —— (1970). *Human Sexual Inadequacy.*
Matthews, A., Bancroft, J., Whitehead, A., et al. (1976). 'The behavioural treatment of sexual inadequacy'. *Behaviour Research and Therapy*, 14.
Stoller, R. (1976). *Perversion: The Erotic Form of Hatred.*

Shannon, Claude Elwood (1912–2001). American mathematician, engineer, and computer scientist, born in Petoskey, Michigan. Shannon was a graduate of the University of Michigan, being awarded a degree in mathematics and electrical engineering in 1936. He then went to the Massachusetts Institute of Technology where he obtained a master's degree in electrical engineering and his Ph.D. in mathematics in 1940. Shannon wrote a master's thesis 'A symbolic analysis of relay and switching circuits' on the use of *Boole's algebra to analyse and optimize relay switching circuits. In 1940 it was awarded the Alfred Nobel Prize of the combined engineering societies of the United States, an award given each year to a person not over 30 for a paper published in one of the journals of the participating societies. A quarter of a century later H. H. Goldstine, in his book *The Computer from Pascal to Von Neumann*, called this work 'one of the most important master's theses ever written . . . a landmark in that it helped to change digital circuit design from an art to a science'. Shannon's doctoral thesis was on theoretical genetics and was supervised by Professor Frank L. Hitchcock, an algebraist at MIT.

He joined AT&T Bell Telephones in New Jersey in 1941 as a research mathematician and remained there until 1972. During his time at the Bell laboratories, Shannon worked most notably on *information theory, a development that was published in 1948 as 'A mathematical theory of communication'. In this paper it was shown that all information sources, telegraph keys, people speaking, television cameras, and so on, have a 'source rate' associated with them which can be measured in bits per second. Communication channels have a 'capacity' measured in the same units. The information can be transmitted over the channel if and only if the source rate does not exceed the channel capacity. This work on communication is generally considered to be Shannon's most important scientific contribution.

Information theory has now infiltrated fields outside communications, including linguistics, psychology, economics, biology, even the arts. In the early 1950s the *IEEE Transactions on Information Theory* published an editorial, titled 'Information theory, photosynthesis and religion', decrying this trend. Yet Shannon himself suggested that applying information theory to biological systems might not be so far fetched, because he believed common principles underlie mechanical and living things.

In 1952 Shannon devised an experiment illustrating the capabilities of telephone relays. He had held a position as a visiting professor of communication sciences and mathematics at the Massachusetts Institute of Technology in 1956, then from 1957 he was appointed to the faculty there, but remained a consultant with Bell Telephones. In 1958 he became Donner Professor of science.

Shannon's later work looked at ideas in artificial intelligence. He devised chess-playing programs and an electronic mouse, which could solve maze problems. The chess-playing program appeared in the paper 'Programming a computer for playing chess' published in 1950. This proposal led to the first game played by the Los Alamos MANIAC computer in 1956. This was the year that Shannon published a paper showing that a universal Turing machine may be constructed with only two states.

Marvin Minsky described Shannon as follows: 'Whatever came up, he engaged it with joy, and he attacked it with some surprising resource which might be some new kind of technical concept or a hammer and saw with some scraps of wood. For him, the harder a problem might seem, the better the chance to find something new.'

Shannon died on 24 February 2001 in Medford, Massachusetts.

See also INFORMATION THEORY.

McMillan, B. (1994). 'Scientific impact of the work of C. E. Shannon'. In *Proceedings of the Norbert Wiener Centenary Congress, East Lansing, MI.*

Price, R. (1985). 'A conversation with Claude Shannon: one man's approach to problem solving', *Cryptologia, 9.*

Slepian, D. (ed.) (1974). *Key Papers in the Development of Information Theory.*

Sloane, N. J. A., and Wyner, A. D. (1993). *Claude Elwood Shannon: Collected Papers.*

shell-shock. The term 'shell-shock', coined by British soldiers in the autumn of 1914 and first used in print by the Cambridge psychologist C. S. *Myers early the following year, referred to the strange symptoms—such as paralysis, dumbness, deafness, blindness, and disordered gait—which soldiers developed after being exposed to shell-fire at the front. The 'vivid, terse name' was then quickly taken up by the press and 'shell-shock' became reified in the public mind as a specific disorder.

Medical thinking was divided. There were at first those (like Frederick Mott in England and Hermann Oppenheim in Germany) who argued that the aetiology of 'shell-shock' was physical, the result of tiny shell particles causing microscopic lesions in the brain, but by 1916 it was clear that prisoners of war and the wounded did not usually develop its symptoms, however badly shelled, whereas soldiers who had not been to the front—perhaps, even, not left England—quite commonly did. It was therefore concluded that 'shell-shock' was in fact a wartime manifestation of the pre-war maladies known as 'hysteria' and 'neurasthenia', and, after 1916, doctors preferred to speak of 'war neurosis'. But the arguments continued—for example, on the importance of previous vulnerability versus the magnitude of the experience. In 1917, W. H. R. *Rivers argued that 'shell-shock' was born of a mental conflict between the soldier's instinct of self-preservation and his sense of duty; yet, two years later, he gave a 'biological' account influenced by Hughlings *Jackson, which saw 'shell-shock' as a regression to lower 'levels' of the nervous system. Others explained 'war neurasthenia' in terms of Cannon's work on the physiology of emotion—as 'exhaustion or intoxication with the products of the ductless glands'.

The enormous literature on treatment—ranging from Max Nonne's hypnotic cures of 'hysterical' soldiers to Lewis Yealland's 'plain speaking backed up by faradic current' to W. H. R. Rivers's analytic psychotherapy with officers, made famous by Siegfried Sassoon—mostly dealt with chronic cases seen at base hospitals. Much less was written by frontline doctors, who found that the rate of 'shell-shock' could be minimized by effective leadership and that acute cases could usually be treated with simple rest, reassurance, and persuasion administered close to the line.

After 1918, most countries (except France) paid pensions for war neurosis. However, a series of inquests concluded that, next time around, quasi-medical words like 'shell-shock' would not be used, pensions would be kept to a minimum, and 'war neurosis' would not normally be grounds for getting out of the forces. In the Second World War, the Germans carried this policy furthest, but British doctors in the London Blitz also tried not to 'medicalize' the fear and exhaustion of bombed civilians and used social pressure to keep them going. At the same time, attempts were made to exclude from the armed forces those thought vulnerable to breakdown, the British testing recruits for intelligence and aptitude—they had no 'test for courage'—while the Americans, more ambitiously, tested for personality—with doubtful results. The 1940s theoretical literature largely reflects prevailing Freudian fashion, with Ronald Fairbairn finding 'separation anxiety' to be the main cause of war neurosis in British soldiers and Roy R. Grinker attributing American fliers' problems to loss of faith in the 'military superego'. New treatment techniques such as barbiturate abreaction and group psychotherapy were also developed

By the 1950s, military psychiatry had emerged as a separate medical discipline and had reduced the principles of frontline treatment to a formula, PIE—proximity, immediacy, expectancy—which the Americans applied successfully in Korea, and, initially, in Vietnam; psychiatric casualties there were said to be 'lower than in any previous war'. But this narrowly military approach proved unable to withstand new social, political, and intellectual strains in the 1970s. The bitter political divisions of the Vietnam War; the complex role of the Veterans' Administration within the United States healthcare system; the transformation of American psychiatry from the quasi-Freudian formulae of the 1950s to a biological, neo-Kraepelinian nosology, based on symptoms; the rise of feminism; Hollywood's stereotype of the Vietnam veteran as 'Rambo', a bomb waiting to explode—all combined to produce a medico-social campaign which led in 1980 to the creation of the term post-traumatic stress disorder (PTSD).

Intellectually, PTSD was a fusion of Freud, Janet, and Erich Lindemann's writing on trauma, synthesized by Mardi J. Horowitz, with an account of post-traumatic symptoms, which emphasized the triad of 'intrusion, avoidance, and arousal' and derived from Abram Kardiner's observations of war veterans in the 1920s. However, researchers soon migrated away from PTSD's psychoanalytic origins towards more fashionable (and fundable) 'biological' models, drawing on work on the physiology of stress and on modern neuroscience (the role of the amygdala in emotional memory, for example). Advocates of PTSD argued that it had replaced old 'stiff upper lip' denial with a coherent framework which helped patients understand and treat their condition; codified post-traumatic symptoms for the first time; offered a credible hypothesis for the role of traumatic memory in creating symptoms; and was developing distinctive biological indicators of the condition. Opponents claimed that PTSD was a socially constructed diagnosis which shared most of its symptoms with other disorders such as depression, medicalized ordinary human distress, and undermined the capacity of the public (including the emergency services) to withstand traumatic events—

particularly when taken up by the media and the law. The wisdom of 'exporting' PTSD to non-Western cultures was also questioned. By the turn of the century, it was generally agreed that 'debriefing' trauma victims soon after the 'event' was counter-productive and that one of the original planks of PTSD—the assumption that, given a sufficiently powerful stressor, anyone would develop its symptoms—was unsound. Old debates, about the importance of previous vulnerability and the role of intelligence, had resurfaced. But it seemed likely that PTSD was here to stay. BSh

Butler, A. G. (1943). 'Moral and mental disorders . . .'. In *The Australian Army Medical Services in the War of 1914–1918*, vol. iii.

Kardiner, A. (1941). *The Traumatic Neuroses of War*.

Shephard, B. (2000). *A War of Nerves*.

War Office, (1922). *Committee of Enquiry into 'Shell-Shock'*.

Young, A. (1995) *The Harmony of Illusions: Inventing Post-Traumatic Stress Disorder*.

Sherrington, Sir Charles Scott (1857–1952). British physiologist, born in London and educated at Ipswich grammar school and at Cambridge; he qualified at St Thomas' Hospital in London in 1885. As a physiologist he anticipated *Pavlov in attempting to uncover the structure of the nervous system by looking at input and output. Moreover, his discoveries stand up better than Pavlov's because he worked mainly on a comparatively simple aspect of the nervous system, spinal reflexes, whereas Pavlov was attempting to investigate the workings of the brain using the same techniques. This work on nervous integration and brain functions resulted in a neuroanatomical theory of behaviour that prefigures ethological models and, unexpected as it may seem, converges with some basic teachings of *phenomenological psychology. Yet his originality is not limited to his masterwork *The Integrative Action of the Nervous System* (1906; 2nd edn. 1948); it is equally patent in his two late works, *Man on his Nature* (1940; 2nd edn. 1952) and *The Endeavour of Jean Fernel* (1946), which deal with man's place in the world as a living being endowed with *consciousness and reflective power, and involve fundamental issues in the fields of philosophy of science, ethics, and theory of values. To complete the picture, one should remember the great physiologist's interest in the humanities and literature, as evidenced, among other things, by his publication in 1925 of *The Assaying of Brabantius, and Other Verse*.

Sherrington's career was exceptionally brilliant. He was Brown Professor of physiology, London (1891), Fellow of the Royal Society (1893), Holt Professor of physiology, Liverpool (1895), and in 1913 he became Waynflete Professor of physiology at Oxford, a post he held until 1935. In 1932 he shared the Nobel Prize for medicine with E. D. *Adrian. His physiological investigations, which began with the study of nerve degeneration in the decerebrate dog (1884), developed into a manifold and steady production covering a great diversity of topics, ranging from anatomy to perceptual processes. However, the guideline in the vast majority of his works is analysis of the functional properties of the nervous system. Important discoveries within this framework are the reciprocal innervation of antagonistic muscles, decerebrate rigidity, and the basic features of peripheral reflexes. In addition to *The Integrative Action of the Nervous System*, he produced *Mammalian Physiology* (1919; rev. edn. 1929), *Reflex Activity in the Spinal Cord* (1932), and some 300 specialized articles. He opened an era of experimental research and theory by clarifying the functional relations between reflexes and behaviour patterns. This is one of the major objectives, if not *the* major one, of neurophysiology, comparative physiology, physiological psychology, and, most recently, neuroethology. It is therefore necessary to ask where exactly Sherrington's originality lies.

First, his experimental studies of reflexes on decerebrate animals allowed him to discover both the complexity of spinal reflexes and the control effected on them by superior (or 'higher') brain centres. This he could achieve by decerebrating the animal at the mesencephalic level, a technique which proved most appropriate and led him to clear evidence of integrative processes. Secondly, he was able to establish a now classical distinction between different categories of receptors—interoceptors, exteroceptors, and proprioceptors—according to the sites where they gather information as required by the organic processes actually in course. For the connections between neurons, the term *synapses was introduced by Sherrington and Michael Foster in 1897.

These and other important contributions to the systematic and accurate knowlege of the anatomo-physiological structures and functions of the nervous system amounted progressively to a general interpretation of the organism's activity which is present on every page of *The Integrative Action of the Nervous System* and is fully developed in the last two chapters of that work. Sherrington succeeds in explaining the emerging properties of behaviour patterns by referring to the *continuity* that exists between anatomo-physiological substrates and overt behaviour, thus doing away at the outset with classical dualistic views. Moreover, the question of internal causation of behaviour is viewed not in the form of extrinsic mechanical links between acts and supposedly corresponding internal organic events: it is systematically related, rather, to the structural constraints of the body as a spatio-temporal system within the process of evolution.

In brief, physicochemical changes inside the body and bodily changes at the behavioural level occur within subsystems included in overall organic activity. Continuity therefore implies integrative action, for causal factors to be at work between one level and the other in order

to ensure survival. This comprehensive philosophy of the organism is exceptionally well outlined in the penultimate chapter of *The Integrative Action of the Nervous System*. After discussing the main features of the reflex arc, Sherrington goes on to describe the central nervous system as a synaptic network. He then turns to the analysis of *receptive fields, contrasting the richness of the exteroceptive field with the relative poverty of the interoceptive one. This is apparently due to the fact that receptors of a special kind, the distance receptors, initially appeared in relation to locomotion requirements, and are located for this reason in the leading segment of an animal. The distinctive functional advantage of the distance receptors lies in their unique power of dissociating the stimulus from its physical source, thereby enabling the organism to develop around itself peculiar space–time relations in perceptual activity. This may be observed in various degrees in vision, hearing, and smell, as well as in some less widespread mechanical and thermal receptors. The distance receptors are said to be 'precurrent'—i.e. they can gather information about the animal's surroundings without requiring a direct physical contact between the source of a stimulus and the body surface. This important feature is not to be found in the proximal receptors, namely those of touch and taste.

The high survival value of precurrent responses is evident, since it allows for explorative appreciation of, for example, *potential* prey and predators. If food could be detected only by taste, or enemies only by mechanical contact, an organism would be unable to make any preparatory decision as to the positive or negative nature of any biologically important stimulus. In other words, the subjective spatio-temporal field would be practically non-existent and the autonomy of the animal would be drastically limited (as is the case, to some extent, in so-called 'primitive' living forms). Clearly, the product of evolution we call the 'superior' animal is that type of organism which has evolved towards an increasing explorative autonomy, due to the potentialities of the distance receptors and the corresponding development of a highly complicated brain capable of integrating a great diversity of sensory information. Considering the time sequences of behaviour patterns, anticipatory responses, which allow for an extension of subjective space and consequently for an increase in reaction time and duration of response, have the fundamental function of preparing the responses of the immediate receptors, i.e. the reactions triggered by proximal stimuli in contact with the body.

Sherrington's account of these active relations established by the organism with its surroundings converges to a great extent with later ethological teaching, a fact which is still hardly recognized in ethological circles. The expression 'consummatory reaction' appears in *The Integrative Action of the Nervous System* twelve years before

Wallace Craig introduced the term 'consummatory act', to which ethologists refer as the first formulation of the concept. The main difference is that Sherrington's outline of the role of anatomical structures in exteroceptive communication emerged from his neurophysiological experiments, whereas the corresponding topic was developed in ethology on the basis of naturalistic descriptions of behaviour patterns in the social life of animals within the framework of phylogenic studies.

Finally, there exists a definite affinity between Sherrington's analysis of the precurrent receptive fields and the phenomenological descriptions of bodily subjectivity. Phenomenological themes, such as the lived experience of bodiliness in the active constitution of a meaningful world, or even descriptive studies of animal subjectivity referring to the perception of bodily limits in the actualization of observable behaviour patterns, may conveniently be set against Sherrington's theory of the biological significance of the body's 'interface' as meeting point of exteroceptive and interoceptive experiences. His interpretation of the subjective field as a result of his experimental studies on reflex activity also laid the foundations of a physiologically inspired psychology which is in many interesting respects at variance with the Pavlovian model. In Sherrington's view, *behaviour* must be considered as that sector of overall biological activity which is initiated by the precurrent receptors and which ceases to exert itself as soon as the subsequent activity of non-precurrent receptors comes into play. Concerning feeding behaviour, for instance, he writes: 'The morsel vanishes from an experience at the moment when our choice in regard to it becomes inoperative. The psyche does not persist into conditions which would render it ineffective.' In Pavlov's view, on the contrary, behavioural processes are conceived as events resulting from stimuli which impinge on the organism without any previous activity in the behavioural field. Whatever the case may be, the careful reader of Sherrington's writings will readily be convinced of the founding character of his contribution to the biology of behaviour.   GT

Straus, E. (1935). *Vom Sinn der Sinne.* (Eng. trans. J. Needleman (1963), *The Primary World of Senses: A Vindication of Sensory Experience.*)

Thinès, G. (1977). *Phenomenology and the Science of Behaviour.*

shock. This term is sometimes applied to an event of special force or significance that causes disruption or collapse of mental or physical functions or behaviour, and sometimes to the effects of such an event. After the impact, a usually short-lived attempt to restore the position is followed by reduction in activity and in responsiveness to the external world. After a serious accident, for instance, a person becomes apathetic and largely unresponsive to what goes on around him. He lacks initiative and is compliant, sometimes to a degree of childlike dependence on others. These effects protect him from further stimulation. If he has suffered serious physical injury, and his state is one of surgical shock, he is pale, his skin is cold, and his peripheral pulses feeble. These effects reflect the shunting of blood from the skin to organs more essential for survival. The adaptiveness of the effects has not always been recognized: for instance, surgical shock used to be treated by warming the patient in an attempt to restore the circulation to the skin.

short-term memory. *Memory for what happened an hour ago or a year ago fulfils an obvious function in our lives. However, our capacity to store information for periods measured in seconds is equally if not more important to our integrity as human beings. This capacity is referred to as short-term memory (STM). *Descartes asserted, 'I think, therefore I am'. It is equally true to say 'I think, therefore I have short-term memory'. Indeed any mental activity extended in time, including the production and comprehension of language, must involve STM. It is certainly fortunate that STM is robust and, unlike long-term memory, is seldom affected by old age, drugs, or brain damage.

The most familiar fact about STM is the existence of the so-called span of immediate memory. A rough definition of the span is that it is the longest sequence of items that can be reproduced correctly following a single presentation. However, the same individual may manage a sequence of seven items on one occasion and make a mistake with a sequence of only five items on another. Accordingly, the span is in fact defined as that length of sequence for which the chance of correct reproduction is 50–50. The span has a number of interesting properties. Two are as follows. First, for items in random order, the span is about seven, plus or minus two. This is surprising in that the amount of information per item has little effect on the span. For example, the span for binary digits (0, 1) is only slightly longer than for decimal digits (the digits 0 to 9), although the latter contains over three times as much information. Second, within wide limits, the span is almost unaffected by the rate at which items are presented, and is therefore relatively independent of the time elapsing between the presentation of an item and its recall. These two facts are nicely explained by the so-called slot theory. On this theory, the span reflects the capacity of an information store in the brain with about seven 'slots'. Each slot is capable of storing a single item or unit. Once the store is full, new items can be stored only by displacing existing items. Variation in the span is attributed on this theory to the fact that a unit can sometimes comprise more than one item. For example, two or more digits can sometimes be recoded as a familiar number which can then be stored as a unit. Indeed, if an individual has an exceptional familiarity with numbers he may have a digit span of fifteen or more. However, recoding digits into familiar numbers cannot account for the digit span of 80 recently achieved by one individual after extensive practice, who reported using both recoding and a hierarchical grouping strategy. At best, therefore, the slot theory describes the mechanism which *normally* determines the span.

Two other interesting facts force another qualification to the slot theory. The span is reduced if the items of the sequence sound similar. For example, the sequence B V T G P is more difficult than the sequence S K L R N. If reproduction of the sequence involves retrieving the items from separate slots, why should this be so? Similarly, the span is smaller for long words than for short words, which is puzzling if each word is a unit and occupies a separate slot. With visual presentation, the effects of similarity both of sound and of word length vanish if the subject is asked to count aloud during presentation of the sequence. (At the same time, the counting task somewhat reduces the span.) This suggests that normally there is subvocal rehearsal of earlier items during presentation of later items of the sequence and that such rehearsal contributes to the span as normally measured.

Since the slot theory postulates a special store for STM, by implication there must be a different store for long-term memory (LTM). Evidence for a two-store view of memory comes from memory pathology. *Amnesia due to brain damage can take one of two forms. In the common form, STM is intact but LTM, in the sense of the ability to form new permanent memories, is impaired. In a rare form, which has only been identified quite recently, the reverse is found, with LTM intact but STM impaired. Clearly independent impairment of STM and LTM is highly consonant with the two-store theory. However, recent theory tends to postulate not one but several stores for the temporary storage of information. Indeed, evidence from the study of patients with impaired STM suggests that there are separate temporary stores for auditory speech sounds and for non-verbal sounds.

Other evidence has been interpreted as showing that there are also temporary stores associated with touch and vision, although information from the latter fades in less than a second. There is also the possibility that the brain has temporary stores concerned with making responses. In the case of speech, for example, such a store might hold in readiness the codes for articulating several words and would substantially assist the smooth production of speech. Accordingly, the span of immediate memory (and STM generally) may reflect the output of one or more temporary stores, depending on circumstances. The common characteristic of these postulated stores is that each is of limited capacity and new information displaces old information. The slot theory of the span therefore seems

too simple, although the facts it explains need to be accommodated in more complex accounts of the mechanisms underlying STM. If STM depends on specialized stores holding information over short intervals of time, the question arises of how information reaches the store responsible for LTM. One possibility is that there is a process of information transfer from these stores to the LTM store. If so, this process is presumably successful for only a proportion of the information entering the temporary stores, since we forget more than we remember. A second possibility is that information enters the LTM store directly at the time of perception, although at a slower rate than it enters the temporary stores. On this hypothesis, STM as we observe it may depend both on information retrieved from temporary stores and on information retrieved from the LTM store. At present, there is no decisive evidence favouring either possibility. Indeed, some theorists prefer to view memory as a single complex system. For example, the different properties of STM and LTM can be held to reflect, not the operation of different stores, but factors affecting the ease of retrieving stored information. This sort of theory is not implausible in view of the fact that problems associated with the retrieval of information from a storage system often impose major constraints on efficiency. However, the detailed facts about STM do seem to favour the view that specialized temporary stores are involved. Ideally, there would be physiological evidence to show how many stores underlie memory, but at present the evidence is indirect and difficult to interpret.

See CHUNKING; INFORMATION THEORY; MEMORY: BIOLOGICAL BASIS; MEMORY AND CONTEXT. JB

Andrade, J., Baddeley, A. D., and Hitch, G. (2002). *Working Memory in Perspective*.
Baddeley, A. D. (1976). *The Psychology of Memory*.
Ericsson, K. A., Chase, W. G., and Faloon, S. (1980). 'Acquisition of a memory skill'. *Science*, 208/1.
Gathercole, S. (2001). *Short-Term and Working Memory*.

size–weight illusion. Lifting weights was a favourite activity of experimental psychology in its early days, but now, although these experiments involve much of interest, they are unfashionable and are seldom even mentioned in textbooks. This may change, however, as manipulative skills in space at zero *g* give rise to new problems in relation to *perception (see SPACE PSYCHOLOGY). One of the most theoretically significant of perceptual *illusions, which also has practical importance, is the size–weight illusion: when objects are lifted by the hand, a *larger* object feels and is judged to be *lighter* than a smaller object of the same scale weight. This makes a nice kitchen experiment, which can easily be carried out, with a pair of tins of different size, partly filled with sugar or salt (or lead or sand) to have the *same* scale weight.

When lifted a few inches from the table, the *larger* tin will feel *lighter* than the smaller tin—though they both have the same scale weight. Ideally, the tins should be lifted by identical handles or wire loops, so that there are no significant touch signals from the different sizes of the tins—for the whole point is that sensory signals of weight are the same for both tins, though the smaller feels heavier. This illusion is interesting because it shows very clearly that the sensation of the weight—which one might think is directly and simply given from forces on the hand and arm—is markedly affected by the assumption of how heavy it 'should' be. Further, it turns out that it is the *surprise* that the larger weight is not the heavier (as it would usually be) that produces the illusion. (Weight illusion also arises from the colours and shades of objects—darker objects being accepted as probably heavier than lighter ones.)

Even the 'purest' sensory signals must be 'read' or interpreted according to general knowledge or assumptions in order to provide information, sometimes fallible, about the objects handled. Thus, sensed weight is not given simply by skin and muscle receptors, but also from our knowledge that larger objects are usually heavier than smaller objects. Anticipated weight is important when lifting objects, since the muscle force must be set to give a reliable smooth lift and avoid injury. That we do not always correctly anticipate the force required is obvious from the familiar 'empty suitcase' effect: that is, when we pick up an empty suitcase assumed to be full, it flies up in the air! For then our anticipation of its weight was wrong—which shows that we *do* anticipate weight before we lift things.

The size–weight illusion is a large (up to about 30 per cent), stable, and repeatable effect, which offers an opportunity to challenge an assumption of *psychophysics—that our ability to discriminate between small differences depends, simply, on relative stimulus intensities. It is possible to test whether the *Weber–Fechner law depends (as is generally assumed) simply on the weight stimuli, or whether it is related also to our knowledge and assumptions of what objects are like. We can test this by finding out whether it is more difficult to distinguish differences between weights of small objects than it is in the case of larger ones. It turns out that there *is* an effect of size, and so of *apparent* weight, but it is not merely a matter of an increase of the Weber fraction in proportion to apparent weight. Rather, weight discrimination is best—that is, the Weber fraction is smallest—when the density of the lifted weights is about 1, which is roughly the average density of objects. Both lower and higher densities give impaired weight discrimination.

Why should this be so? A possible reason is that the neural signals for weight are compared with expectations, and that the *signalled* and *anticipated* weights are *nulled*— as in delicate measuring instruments such as Wheatstone bridges. Cancelling of received input against anticipated values is useful as a way of gaining sensitivity over a wide range of input values, even when the components (whether electronic or those of the nervous system) have only small dynamic ranges. A *nulling arrangement gives high stability even if the components are liable to 'drift' or fatigue, as neurons are. That our weight-sensing system is labile is obvious—for after carrying a heavy object even for a short time the arm, and even the whole body, feels light when it is released. And the arm may float up, almost out of control. This is the basis of the party 'levitation' trick: after someone's shoulders have been pushed down in the dark, that person may have the impression of rising towards the ceiling, for such is the lability of the nervous system. RLG

Ross, H. E. (1969). 'When is a weight not illusory?' *Quarterly Journal of Experimental Psychology*, 21.

—— and Gregory, R. L. (1964). 'Is the Weber fraction a function of physical or perceived input?' *Quarterly Journal of Experimental Psychology*, 16/2.

—— —— (1970). 'Weight illusions and weight discrimination: a revised hypothesis'. *Quarterly Journal of Experimental Psychology*, 22.

skill, human. In everyday parlance, 'skill' is used to denote expertise developed in the course of training and experience. It includes not only trade and craft skills acquired by apprenticeship, but high-grade performance in many fields such as professional practice, the arts, games, and athletics.

The psychological study of skills came to the fore during the Second World War with the need to match the demands of new equipment such as radar, high-speed aircraft, and various sophisticated weapons to human capacities and limitations. More recently, the growth of sport as highly lucrative entertainment and as a medium of national pride and international diplomacy has raised competitive standards and led to studies of human performance at games and athletics in order to extract maximum physical and mental effectiveness.

The common feature running through all these types of skill is that the performer has to match the demands of a task to his capacities. He does this by applying some *method*, or, as it is often called, 'strategy' of performance. For example, a tradesman will select tools and manipulate them in ways which match his capacities for exerting force and exercising fine motor control to the requirements of the metal, wood, or other material he is using. Similarly, a barrister or negotiator will order the questions he asks in a manner which he judges will best enable his powers of persuasion to secure the outcome he desires. These strategies, it should be noted, are not typically concerned with single responses to stimuli, but with chains or programmes of action which look ahead from the situation that initiates them to a future goal or end result. Some strategies are more efficient than others, in that less capacity, time, or effort has to be deployed to obtain the results required. *Skill consists in choosing and carrying out strategies that are efficient.*

Almost every skilled performance involves the whole chain of central mechanisms lying between the sense organs and the effectors, but different types of skill can be distinguished according to the link in the chain where their main emphasis lies. For this purpose, the central mechanisms can be broadly divided into three functional parts: perception of objects or events; choice of responses to them; and execution of phased and coordinated action giving expression to the choice made. An example of perceptual skill is the ability of musicians to judge 'absolute pitch'. It depends upon the possession of a conceptual scale against which any note heard can be placed. The ability is sometimes claimed to be inborn, but studies have shown that it can be acquired, or at least greatly improved, with practice. Analogous skills occur in other occupations which require the making of fine discriminations, such as dyers distinguishing subtle shades of colour, steel furnacemen deciding when the colour of molten metal indicates that it is ready to pour, wool and other fibre graders assessing thickness by 'feel', cheese graders judging softness by pressure, and wine or tea tasters using a 'sensitive palate'.

Skills in making choices, or, as they are sometimes termed, 'decisional' skills, include the expertise shown in various intellectual pursuits, and also in games such as chess and cards. In all these cases, the perceptual data is usually clear and the precise manner of executing the actions required is unimportant: the essential for success is to decide upon the correct actions to take.

Examples of motor skills include sitting on a horse, riding a bicycle, or manipulating the controls of a car. Their essential characteristics lie in motor coordination and timing. They have attracted somewhat less research than other types of skill, probably because the knacks involved are largely unconscious.

Industrial and athletic skills display the characteristics of all three types. Perceptual factors enter into trades and crafts in the assessment and judgement of materials, and in observing the effects of tools such as drills and lathe cutters. In ball games they are concerned in the observation and assessment of the flight of the ball and of the moves made by other players. Motor skills are obviously involved in the fine manipulation of tools in trade and craft work, and in bowling, catching, or kicking and making strokes with bat, racquet, or club in various games. However, the core of all these skills, especially at higher levels of expertise, lies in processes of choice and decision. Thus high-level skill in craft and trade work lies less in the

ability to execute particular manual operations, such as shaping clay on a potter's wheel or cutting cleanly through a piece of metal with a hacksaw, than in deciding what shape is needed or exactly where the cut should be made. Similarly, high-grade athletic skill lies more in the strategy of the game than in the ability to make accurate individual strokes or in sheer muscular strength. Again, in music, the soloist's skill transcends the mere playing of the instrument to the interpretation of the score.

Strategies are developed and become more efficient in the course of practice, and it is these rather than basic capacities that are amenable to training. Four points should be noted.

1. For improvement to occur with practice, some knowledge of results achieved by previous action (*feedback) is required, and, broadly speaking, the more precise and direct this is the better. Early in practice feedback needs to be detailed, but when comprehension and action become organized into larger units the need for feedback within these is reduced. In extreme cases the units become 'automatic' in the sense that conscious attention to feedback no longer occurs and the performer has little awareness of what he is doing. When this stage is reached two results follow. First, because each decision covers a larger unit of performance, fewer need to be made, so that action becomes smoother and less hurried—the skilled performer 'seems to have all the time in the world'. Secondly, performance becomes highly efficient, but may also become rigid in the sense that it cannot be adjusted to meet changing circumstances. A high-grade yet versatile expertise involves a nice balance between such efficiency and flexibility.

2. Strategies and information acquired in training for one task may *transfer to others: for example, techniques learnt when mastering a foreign language can be applied again when studying another language. Such transfer usually results in the later task being mastered more easily than it would otherwise be, but occasionally the reverse is true: for instance, the coordination between tilt and movement needed to ride a bicycle leads to gross oversteering if applied when riding a tricycle, and must be inhibited before the tricycle can be ridden successfully.

3. Improvement with practice is typically rapid at first, then more gradual but continuing over long periods: for instance, the speed of some repetitive work in factories has been shown to rise with time on the job over several years.

4. Once high levels of skill have been attained, they are usually well preserved over periods of many years. The fine edge of performance may be lost without continual practice, but can usually be regained relatively quickly.

Most discussions of skill have been concerned with men or women interacting with machines, tools, or other objects in their environment. It has recently been recognized that the concepts of skill can be applied also to the interaction of one human being with another. *Social skill* includes all the three types already distinguished. It includes perception of the needs and desires of others and of the effects upon others of one's own actions; decisions about how to react to the behaviour of, and communications from, others to achieve rapport and to influence them in ways desired; and on the motor side it includes the making of gestures, kissing, and modulations of the voice in expressing feelings such as sympathy. Social skill not only applies to relationships between individuals, but is essential for efficient leadership and communication in industry and other organizations, and is indeed necessary for living satisfactorily in any society.   ATW

Argyle, M. (1967). *The Psychology of Interpersonal Behaviour.*

Legge, D. (ed.) (1970). *Skills.*

Singleton, W. T., Spurgeon, P., and Stammers, R. B. (eds.) (1980). *The Analysis of Social Skill.*

Welford, A. T. (1968). *Fundamentals of Skill.*

—— (1976). *Skilled Performance: Perceptual and Motor Skills.*

skills, memory for. One apparently never forgets how to swim or ride a bicycle. Is this really the case? If it is, does it mean *memory for skills is in some fundamental way different from other kinds of memory?

What is the evidence? The fact that one does not immediately fall off a bicycle when remounting after an interval of several years does not necessarily mean that no *forgetting has occurred, it simply means that *something* has been retained. Fortunately we do have an answer to the question, based on studies of specialized skills under relatively controlled conditions.

The answer turns out to depend on the type of skill involved. Here we must distinguish between continuous and discrete skills. A continuous skill involves the performer in continually varying his response to a continuously varying stimulus. An example of this would be the steering response involved in driving a car, or the balancing involved in riding a bicycle, or for that matter simply maintaining an upright posture while walking. Such skills can be contrasted with discrete skills in which a discrete individual response is made; typing or manually changing gear in a car would be examples of such skills.

There was a good deal of interest in the acquisition and retention of continuous skills during the Second World War, since the skill of flying a plane clearly has a continuous component, as indeed does learning to control a missile using a joystick. Over the years, a number of experiments have studied the retention of continuous tracking performance, typically using a task in which the subject is given a joystick and required to control the movement of a spot of light on a cathode ray tube. Usually an analogue computer is used to simulate the control characteristics of the plane or missile, with a movement

of the joystick changing the velocity of the missile or its acceleration, and producing a response that may be immediate or may follow only after a lag.

Fleishman and Parker (1962) studied a very difficult version of such a task. It involved three-dimensional tracking under conditions which simulated the problem of flying a plane on the attack phase of a radar intercept mission. They trained their operators over a six-week period, giving them 357 separate one-minute trials, by which time they were performing the task well. The operators were then split into three groups and given no further access to the apparatus. Retention of the skills was then tested, with one group returning after nine months, one after fourteen months, and one after two years. In all conditions, after a single warm-up trial to refamiliarize the subjects with the situation, performance was virtually as good as it had been immediately after the end of training. A number of subsequent studies have replicated this and shown that even the warm-up decrement shown on the first test trial can be reduced if the subject is sufficiently highly practised.

In the case of discrete motor skills, forgetting does occur. Consider, for example, the study by Baddeley and Longman (1978) in which a large number of postmen were trained to use a typewriter. The purpose was to familiarize them with the typewriter keyboard, which was subsequently to be used as part of a letter-sorting machine. Since the equipment was not ready at the end of the training experiment, it proved possible to study the retention of the skill under conditions where no subsequent practice was occurring, an unusual situation in the case of typing. Even after a warm-up period, clear forgetting occurred, with the average rate of keying dropping from about 80 strokes per minute at the end of the training session to about 70 per minute after one month, and to about 55 per minute after a nine-month delay. At the same time errors increased from about 1 per cent of keystrokes to somewhere in the region of 3 per cent.

Why the difference between the two types of skill? At present we can only speculate, but one possible interpretation is as follows. One source of forgetting is that of retroactive interference. A person learns to associate a particular stimulus with a particular response or action: for example, he learns that a bathroom tap with the letter C on it is likely to produce cold water if turned on. After a while such an association will become relatively automatic. If the situation then changes—for example, if he goes on holiday to Italy where C stands for *caldo*, 'hot'—then he will probably make a number of mistakes before adjusting. On returning to 'English-speaking' bathrooms he is likely to find that, to begin with, the previous habit interferes with his response, causing him to make at least one or two initial errors, although the massive amount of prior learning will mean that it takes very little time to revert. In brief, what has happened is that the person has learned two separate responses to the same stimulus, and at times he will recall the wrong one.

It seems likely that at least some, and some theorists would claim all, forgetting occurs because of interference from other learning (see TRANSFER OF TRAINING). In the case of a discontinuous or discrete skill, the same stimuli probably occur in a range of situations where the relevant motor response cannot or should not be made. For example, our trainee typists would clearly go on being in a situation where they were responding to printed text by reading or writing rather than by hitting the appropriate key. This would be expected to cause some interference and hence some forgetting, although the amount of interference would depend very much on the precise conditions involved in the two interfering tasks. One might contrast this with a continuous skill in which the operator is functioning as if in a closed loop, with his own responses and their interaction with the environment producing the stimulus for further response. In any situation other than that of performing the skill, the essential stimulus situation is simply not evoked, and hence no interference can occur.

Having presented this view, it should be pointed out that there is very little evidence either for or against it, and our knowledge of the detailed operation of interference effects is certainly not sufficiently great to allow one to regard it as more than a speculation. The basic phenomena, however, are reasonably well established, so you can assume with some degree of confidence that you will not forget how to ride a bike, or, perhaps even more importantly, how to swim.   ADB

Baddeley, A. D., and Longman, D. J. A. (1978). 'The influence of length and frequency of training session on rate of learning to type'. *Ergonomics*, 21.

Fleishman, E. A., and Parker, J. F., Jr. (1962). 'Factors in the retention and relearning of perceptual motor skill'. *Journal of Experimental Psychology*, 64.

Skinner, Burrhus Frederic

Skinner, Burrhus Frederic (1904–90). American psychologist, educator, and author, born in the small Pennsylvanian town of Susquehanna. Skinner was educated at Harvard and studied under E. G. *Boring, earning his master's and doctoral degrees in 1930 and 1931 respectively. In 1936 Skinner moved to Minneapolis to teach at the University of Minnesota and in 1945 he took a position as chairman of the psychology department at Indiana University. In 1948 he returned to Harvard where he stayed for the rest of his life.

At Harvard he was heavily influenced by the work of B. John *Watson, the 'Father of Behaviourism'. Stemming from this influence, Skinner became the foremost exponent in the USA of the behaviourist school of psychology, where mental processes do not determine what we do; rather we are a product of our conditioning. For cognitive psychologists, this throws the baby out with the bathwater, as it rejects *consciousness.

Early on in his Harvard career, Skinner invented the cumulative recorder, a mechanical device that recorded every response as an upward movement of a horizontally moving line, where the slope showed the rate of responding. Skinner discovered that the rate at which the rat pressed the bar depended not on any preceding stimulus (as Watson and *Pavlov had insisted), but on the following bar presses. Unlike the reflexes that Pavlov studied and which formed the basis of classical conditioning, this kind of behaviour operated on the environment and was controlled by its effects. Skinner named it 'operant behaviour', and the process of arranging the contingencies of reinforcement responsible for the producing this behaviour 'operant conditioning'.

Throughout his career, Skinner insisted that psychology should be a scientific, empirically driven discipline. The principles of reinforcement that he developed were built upon by clinical psychologists and applied to treatment of mental disorders. The application of behaviourism to clinical psychology was not short-lived, as empirically supported treatments for anxiety disorders (e.g. panic disorder, simple phobia) and child conduct problems are based upon behavioural principles, though may be criticized as ameliorating symptoms without affecting cures.

Among his important works are *Behaviour of Organisms* (1938), *Walden Two* (a novel, 1948), and *The Technology of Teaching* (1968). In *Beyond Freedom and Dignity* (1971) Skinner advocated mass conditioning as a means of social control. Later works include *Particulars of my Life* (1976) and *Reflections on Behaviorism and Society* (1978).

See also BEHAVIOURISM; BEHAVIOURISM, SKINNER ON; CONDITIONING.   RLG

Bjork, D. W. (1997). *B. F. Skinner: A Life*.

Hawkins, R. (2001). 'The life and contributions of Burrhus Frederick Skinner'. *Education and Treatment*.

Skinner box. A type of experimental chamber often used in the laboratory analysis of behaviour, named after the American psychologist B. F. *Skinner. As a graduate student at Harvard in 1929 he invented the first such chamber to facilitate the study of eating behaviour in rats, and he later developed many versions.

The prototypical Skinner box for, say, a rat (Fig. 1) would be cubic in shape, 30 cm (1 foot) long on each edge, and would contain the following elements: (i) an 'operandum', such as a lever that protrudes from one wall, and (ii) an opening in that wall where the rat could obtain a small pellet of food, delivered by a mechanical feeding device. The box would be light- and soundproof to minimize distractions and maximize the effectiveness

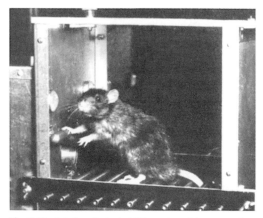

Fig. 1. The interior of a typical Skinner box. A hungry rat is poised over a lever protruding from the front wall. Pressing the lever one or more times will operate a feeder; the rat can retrieve a pellet of food which is dispensed at the small opening in the wall. The rat can easily learn to make discriminations; for example, to press the lever when a light is on and not to press it when the light is off. Chambers for other animals may vary considerably from this one.

of events that occur inside the box. If lever pressing produces a pellet of food in this situation, a hungry rat will typically press the lever repeatedly and thereby eat.

Since its invention, the Skinner box has been adapted to study many organisms besides the rat, behaviours other than bar pressing, and consequences other than food presentation. Behaviour has been studied in the context of auditory and visual stimuli, such as coloured lights and pure tones, as well as more complex stimuli, such as other organisms and slides of the natural environment projected on a screen inside the chamber. In general, the term is now applied to almost any experimental chamber used in the study of the relationships of behaviour, its antecedent stimuli, and its consequences.

The use of the term probably began with Clark *Hull, who made use of what he called a 'modified Skinner box', described in his *Principles of Behavior*. Skinner himself objected to the use of the term and in particular to its erroneous extension to the 'air-crib', an enclosed crib for human infants that he invented in the 1940s.   RE

sleep. A third of our lives is spent in sleep. Of the remainder, some is spent in wishing that our small children would sleep longer, and, during our later years, some is spent wishing that our sleep was less broken. What is sleep? It is a healthy state of inertia and unresponsiveness that is recurrently imposed by unknown mechanismszwithin the nervous system. In most animals the sleep–wakefulness rhythm is coupled to the 24-hour light–dark environment, as are the rest–activity cycles of lower life forms; there is no sharp demarcation between creatures which can be said simply to have rest phases and animals which certainly sleep. In animals possessing developed brains there are electrical rhythms that differ in sleep and in wakefulness, being generally slower during sleep.

The *biological clock that makes us sleepy every 24 hours means that shift workers and those who have just flown to different time zones are often tired and inefficient while they are trying to be alert (see JET LAG). If it is a long time since we last slept then that too makes us sleepy. Monotony, warmth, restricted movement, and a sense of waiting for something that cannot happen yet— all of these make us sleepy. A sleeplike state of 'animal hypnosis' can also follow extreme stimulation.

The amount of sleep each species takes is proportional to the need for restoration, i.e. to the waking metabolic rate, but is in part also determined by predator status: those animals who sleep safely sleep longer. Among human beings there are wide variations. A few are happy and healthy with under three hours' sleep a night; a minority of others will take as many as ten hours. In general those who habitually sleep longer have shorter *reaction times and higher body temperatures by day. Infants sleep a lot, but the sleep of ageing people becomes more and more broken with the years. A person sleeps less if he gets thin and sleeps longer if he gets fat.

There are two kinds of sleep that in man alternate with each other about every 100 minutes. Orthodox sleep (non-rapid eye movement, or NREM, sleep) occupies 80 per cent of the night, and paradoxical sleep (rapid eye movement, or REM, sleep) about 20 per cent. The amount of paradoxical sleep is greater in the newborn, but in adults is proportional to body weight, and among mental defectives to *intelligence. It is diminished by *anxiety and by many drugs.

Neither of the two kinds of sleep should be thought of as deeper than the other: they are different. Mental life continues in both, but whereas awakenings from orthodox sleep and questions about preceding mental life generally lead to reports of 'thinking', awakenings from paradoxical sleep are generally followed by detailed descriptions of '*dreaming'. However, the recall of dreams is much diminished if as little as five minutes of orthodox sleep intervenes prior to awakening. In paradoxical sleep most body muscles are profoundly relaxed and many reflexes are lost, the blood flows faster through the brain than during wakeful rest, and in men the penis is erect.

Talking may also occur in both kinds of sleep, and reports made after prompt awakenings show concordance between the words and what was being thought or dreamt about. Sleepwalking (see SOMNAMBULISM) and 'night terrors' arise from orthodox sleep early in the night, as do most episodes of bedwetting. The shriekings of a night terror often occur with sleepwalking, and liability to them runs in families. They are never remembered in the morning.

Indeed, memory of the events of sleep is always very poor. 'Sleep learning' by means of a tape recorder playing lessons all night is ineffective: although what has been heard while still awake may be remembered, nothing of what was played during sleep will be recalled; to remember we must have paid *attention, and in sleep we do not pay attention. Even so, sleep is important for memory. If a list of nonsense words is learned, and memory of them is tested 8 hours or 24 hours later, more of the list will be remembered after 24 hours, given an intervening period of sleep, than after 8 hours without sleep. It seems that memory traces are strengthened during sleep, maybe especially by paradoxical sleep, and, since they presumably depend upon the durable molecules of brain protein, this can be understood.

Protein synthesis is favoured by sleep and so sleep enhances growth and restoration. Tissues such as the skin are restored by growth of new cells, and this growth proceeds faster during sleep. Throughout the body's tissues there are protein molecules being broken down and being synthesized all the time. There is a 24-hour variation in the rate of synthesis, the rate being fastest during the period of rest and sleep. In the cerebral cortex, and the retina, protein synthesis is faster during sleep, and in the anterior pituitary there are more cell divisions. The fact that the balance shifts away from degradation towards greater net protein synthesis is a consequence of a lower rate of cellular work during sleep.

In higher animals there are hormones that reinforce the more fundamental effect of the lower rate of cellular work. In man, growth hormone is specifically released by orthodox sleep with the largest continuous slow electrical brain rhythms ('slow wave sleep': see ELECTROENCEPHALOGRAPHY). Growth hormone promotes protein synthesis. On the other hand, adrenaline (epinephrine) and corticosteroids are hormones which are plentiful during wakefulness and which increase protein breakdown. In the blood during sleep, these latter hormones are diminished, and that means that the growth hormone is even more effective. Slow wave sleep is not merely the time of growth-hormone release, it is the time when responsiveness to meaningful sounds or to an itchy skin is minimal, when the body's oxygen consumption is lowest, and cellular work is lowest, and therefore slow wave sleep is 'worth more' than lighter (more responsive) stages of orthodox sleep. If there is a greater need for restoration, as after sleep deprivation, or after an athlete has trained hard, then the next night there is a higher proportion of slow wave sleep and extra growth hormone.

Sleep deprivation causes sleepiness. It is difficult to keep awake anyone who has been deprived of sleep for 60 hours. Such a person has frequent 'microsleeps' and recurrently fails to notice things he ought to notice, being unable to sustain a high level of attention. Sometimes visual *illusions or *hallucinations are experienced or the individual becomes *paranoid. After about 240 hours there are signs of adaptation to a more uniform but inert and dulled state.

People who complain of lack of sleep (insomnia) actually sleep more than they suppose. Indeed, the most distinguishing feature of their sleep is the degree to which it exceeds their own estimates—but we cannot yet measure its relative restorative value. Complaints are commonest among women, among those of nervous temperament, and among older people, and it is they who account for most of the sleeping pills consumed. Although most sleeping pills today belong to the benzodiazepine class and are safe and effective, prolonged use leads to dependence, and attempts to stop them are accompanied by heightened anxiety, nightmares, and poor sleep for a week or two. Regular physical exercise, a good-quality, firm mattress, a warm but ventilated room, a malted milk drink, and sexual satisfaction at bedtime—all these promote good sleep, but they will not cure everyone's complaints. It has to be accepted that broken sleep is as normal a part of growing older as are grey hairs or wrinkles, though insomnia of sudden onset can be the result of mental depression, an illness amenable to treatment.

Finally, let it be emphasized that sleep is not a slothful habit. Its study as a necessity encompasses the whole functioning of the body and, with the study of dreams, some of the mind's most intriguing qualities.   IO

Adam, K., and Oswald, I. (1983). 'Protein synthesis, bodily renewal and the sleep–wake cycle'. *Clinical Science*, 65.
Kety, S. S., Evarts, E. V., and Williams, H. L. (eds.) (1967). *Sleep and Altered States of Consciousness*.
Luce, G. G., and Segal, J. (1970). *Insomnia*.
Oram, J., and Barnes, C. D. (eds.) (1980). *Physiology in Sleep*.
Oswald, I. (1980). *Sleep*.

sleepwalking. See SOMNAMBULISM.

smell. Although all living things, both plant and animal, respond selectively to at least some of the chemicals in their environments, what we ordinarily mean by smell is more limited than this. There are really two ways of deciding whether or not we are dealing with smelling rather than some other chemical sense. In the vertebrates—fish, amphibians, reptiles, or mammal—we define smell as involving the stimulation of the first cranial nerve, the olfactory nerve. In the invertebrates, however, we refer to smell when the stimulating substance is airborne. Thus, for example, a moth finds his mate by means of smell.

This inclusion of the invertebrates is important because much of the best controlled (and economically important) study has been and is being done on insects. In man, of course, both these qualifications apply and we speak of smell as involving the first cranial nerve and as having airborne molecules as its stimuli.

In man and other mammals the receptors for smell lie in the mucous membrane at the top or back of the air passages in the nose. These sensitive cells are in a constant state of decline and replacement. They are equipped with hairlike projections, the cilia, which protrude into the mucus and are the probable sites of odorant–receptor interaction. In man, the region of each nostril that they occupy is about the area of a postage stamp—small compared with, say, that in the dog. The cells send their axons directly into the olfactory bulb, which is also relatively small. (Smell is unique among the senses in not having connections through the thalamus to the 'new cortex' or neocortex that has developed in relation to the other sense departments. In fact, the older portion of the forebrain of mammals is called the 'rhinencephalon', or 'smell brain', because of this.) There are many fewer transmission cells in the bulb than there are receptors, and this fact, in addition to the preservation of spatial distribution from receptor surface to bulb, is thought to be important in the perception of odour quality. The system is sensitive and compares well, even in man, with most laboratory methods of analysis: for example, one form of musk can be detected by a 'normal' person at a dilution of less than one ten-millionth of a milligram per litre of air.

Attempts to understand the manner in which odorous molecules affect the receptor cells have led to considerable theorizing without conspicuous success. The problem to be solved is similar to that for any of the senses: how a stimulating agent so alters a cell as to set in play the series of events that result in one or more nerve impulses being transmitted to the central nervous system. In man it is obvious that the molecules either make their way through the mucus and affect the receptor directly in some way, or act at a distance. Both means have been proposed. In explanation of action at a distance, it has been suggested that the characteristic infrared absorption spectrum of a molecule leads it to absorb radiation from certain of the matching receptors. Unfortunately, this is thermodynamically impossible. Other absorption theories, such as the Raman spectrum and ultraviolet, seem aimed more at classifying the molecules than at implying action at a distance.

Theories supposing action directly on the receptor are better supported by modern research. Many have been developed with pharmacological or immunological models in mind. The current conception of the receptor cell membrane as a lipid (fatty) double layer in which protein molecules are embedded in mosaic fashion is compatible both with the suggestion that the molecules actually dissolve in (or 'puncture') the lipid, rather like the anesthetic action of ether, and with the notion that adsorption takes place on the proteins. Evidence of molecules that differ only in being 'right-' or 'left-handed' implies that the proteins are involved, and the theory provides a simple basis for understanding the selectivity of different cells. Precisely what energy transfer is involved is uncertain, but with modern membrane research methodology, including the use of radioactive tracers, resolution of this problem should be forthcoming.

The pervasive role of smell in everyday life is often overlooked. Many unpleasant smells, such as of garbage and offal in the city of not so long ago, have been got rid of. Highly sophisticated methods of washing, filtering, and incinerating odorous discharges have been developed, and there is a host of personal deodorants and air 'purifiers'. On the other side of the coin, the flavours of foods are pretty largely determined by odour—a fact recognized by the international flavour industry. Closely related is perfumery, with its long history.

In the fashions that have surrounded perfumery, sexual attractiveness may be involved. Certainly in many species, particularly the insects, naturally secreted odours, pheromones, play a sexual role. In mammals, pheromones also play an important role in the establishment of territories: the 'marking' activities of dogs are well known, and in other species special glands—for example, the cheek glands of the rabbit—produce marking chemicals. In the mouse the sexual and marking functions come together—the female will ovulate after smelling a male, and will, if pregnant, abort upon smelling a strange male. While some primates—the baboon, for instance—seem to have female pheromones secreted during receptivity, it is not at present clear what role, if any, such secretions might play in man.

One function of smelling is well known: the detection of leaking gas. To non-odorous gases, a warning agent such as ethyl mercaptan is added. In mines, the ventilating system is used to carry the warning. An apparent overrepresentation of older people among the victims of a gas leakage in London led to useful research on the effect of age on sensitivity to smell. (See AGEING: SENSORY AND PERCEPTUAL CHANGES.)

For smell, unlike colour, there is no satisfactory classification scheme. One difficulty is the absence of truly abstract terms such as red or blue; rather, the terms refer to objects (for example, lavender or fruity) or condition (burnt or rotten). Possibly no simple scheme will be found, for the basic scale along which we place odours is from pleasant to unpleasant—a scale that may reflect the approach-avoidance nature of behaviour in evolutionary history. It may be the only way for the organism to classify odours.

Three other topics need mention. First, there are considerable differences between the smell sensitivity of individual persons. Some even, because of disease or trauma, cannot smell anything at all—they are anosmic—while others lack sensitivity for specific odours—they are partially anosmic. Second, adaptation (that is, temporary loss of sensitivity with exposure) proceeds fairly rapidly for smells. This is largely a matter of reduced transmission in the brain, rather than fatigue of the receptors. It makes some jobs tolerable, but sensitivity to warning agents is reduced. Finally, it may be that sensitivity declines with age. If this is in fact so, and it is not certain, then among the important consequences would be diminished stimulation from flavours (see TASTE). Possibly some of the nutritional problems of ageing are ascribable to declining sensitivity.   FNJ

Amerine, M. A., Pangborn, R. M., and Roessler, E. B. (1965). *Principles of Sensory Evaluation of Food.*

Brand, G., Millot, J., and Henquell, D. (2001). 'Complexity of olfactory lateralization processes revealed by functional imaging: a review'. *Neuroscience and Biobehavioral Reviews,* 25/2.

Engen, T. (1982). *The Perception of Odors.*

Proceedings of the Eighth International Symposium on Olfaction and Taste, Melbourne, Victoria (Australia), 23–26 August 1983 (1984). *Chemical Senses,* 8/3.

Voshall, L. B. (2003). 'Putting smell on the map'. *Trends in Neurosciences,* 26/4.

social psychology. Social psychology studies how individuals relate to the societies they live in, particularly insofar as those relations are mediated by face-to-face interaction. Children first learn languages, moralities, and positions in class structures, not by encountering abstract entities labelled 'institutions' or 'social structures' but primarily through everyday intercourse with others. When, as adults, we are in contact with economic, legal, or religious institutions, the contacts in practice are usually with employees or agents of the institutions.

Social psychology should continually be interrelating three levels of analysis: the individual, the interpersonal, and the social structural (which should be taken to include economic and political structures). According to this view, it is something of an interstitial science: it aims to link the study of the individual by general psychology and the biological sciences to that of society by sociology and the other social sciences, and it is thus a very challenging and potentially pivotal social science. Its practitioners, however, have not always fully recognized either the challenge or the potential. To understand why not, a little history is necessary.

The historian of social psychology can manage without difficulty to appropriate as progenitors of social psychology most of the major thinkers of Western civilization from Plato and Aristotle onwards. But the term 'social psychology' did not appear, as the title of a book for instance, until 1908, when it was used twice, by W. *McDougall, a British psychologist, and by E. A. Ross, an American sociologist. Even so, the immediate origins of what has come to be social psychology are apparent for about half a century before then. Many of the originators were European. Le Bon, Tarde, and Durkheim in France, Simmel, *Weber, and *Wundt in Germany, *Freud in Austria, and *Darwin, *Spencer, and McDougall in Britain can all be seen, in part at least, as contributors to the emerging discipline. Had their contributions prevailed, then social psychology would have emerged as a biologically based—or at least 'instinct'-based—theoretically oriented endeavour. But they did not. Whether because a psychologically inclined social analysis was more congenial to the pervasive individualism of American social and political life, or because it proved easier for social psychology to become institutionalized in newer American than in ancient European universities, the subject established itself more readily in the United States, where it rapidly adopted the environmentalism of American sociology and the empiricism of American psychology. The main sociological influences were those of the Chicago school of symbolic interactionism, derived in turn from American pragmatic philosophy. G. H. Mead's (1934) analysis of the social construction of an individual's sense of self must be given pride of place, but other contributors within that tradition have included C. H. Cooley, W. I. Thomas, and, more recently, E. Goffman. American psychologists who exerted influence on the beginnings of social psychology included J. M. Baldwin, G. S. *Hall, and W. *James, but it has been less the ideas of particular psychologists and much more the practices of psychology in general that have proved most influential. A very early—perhaps the first—line of sustained empirical enquiry started from a study by N. Triplett in 1898. In order to examine the impact of the presence of others on the efficiency of individual performance, he had children wind in string on fishing reels on their own and competitively in pairs. From this study there developed a tradition of research on the consequences of the presence of others which today is still actively pursued as 'social facilitation'. This tradition has asked apparently limited questions and has been content with small-scale theories; its questions appear to be readily answerable and lend themselves to experimental studies in laboratories; it takes universality for granted and hence need only study undergraduates in Ann Arbor. Each of these can be regarded as a legacy from American psychology, and the general approach has been and is typical of most social psychology in North America. The approach reached its zenith with the self-conscious creation in the 1960s of a movement towards 'experimental social psychology', whereby prestigious work would be virtually confined to elegant experiments conducted in sophisticated laboratories and interpreted in terms of carefully formulated mini-theories; this latter-day methodological purification would demonstrate that social psychology could be (almost) as rigorous as the asocial parts of experimental psychology.

A decade of such endeavours was enough to provoke numerous criticisms. Two complementary critiques merit mention, those of method and scope. Microsociologists in America, as well as R. Harré in Britain, questioned the appropriateness of laboratory experiments for studying human social experience, because of their artificiality and the mechanistic views of man which, it was claimed, they imply. The main criticisms from resurgent social psychology in Europe, as voiced by S. Moscovici, H. Tajfel, and others, were directed at the narrowness of American experimental social psychology: it studied individuals and sometimes inter-individual influences, but had ceased to be social; society must be brought back into social psychology. Despite some soul-searching, mainly about the ethics of experiments, the critiques had a limited impact in the United States. 'Experimental social psychology' was updated, thinly disguised, and renamed 'cognitive social psychology'; the detailed psychological examination of individual attributions and judgements contrasted with the poverty of social analysis, and technical rigour was far more obvious than social relevance. If for no other reasons than numbers and resources, this narrow view of social psychology became the dominant one, but it has had to compete with a broader, if more diffuse, perspective, derived in part from social psychology in Europe, in part from sociology and other social sciences. This broad view, which has been able to incorporate much of the narrower one, has organized the substance of social psychology around three interlocking sets of issues, each set demanding all three levels of analysis but highlighting one or other of them.

First, there is the social nature of the individual. How has biological inheritance been acted upon so that, within about twenty years, the microscopic egg has become an effective, fully functioning member of society, and over a lifespan the individual personality or self, while maintaining coherence and continuity, has also adapted to changing situations and roles? In part the self emerges through interaction with others. Parents imputing intentions to the infant help purposiveness and intentionality to develop in the child, and the ever-increasing expectations of the child encourage more and more complex, intelligent actions to appear. But the self is, in a sense, a product of social structure as well as of face-to-face interaction. In large part one's personal self is made up of one's views of the salient social categories to which one belongs. As a result, the study of differences and supposed differences between the sexes, classes, ethnic groups, and the like is intrinsic to a properly social conceptualization of the individual.

The second substantive focus is social interaction. Here the social psychologist studies the acquisition and use of language and the non-linguistic communication systems not just as an achievement or skill of an individual but as the means whereby dyads and groups can succeed, or fail, in creating an intersubjectivity, or temporarily shared world which makes possible the transmission of information, the exchange of feelings, and the creation and fulfilment of common tasks. And once some understanding of the details of interaction has been achieved, the details themselves can be used to illuminate the operation of larger-scale social processes. Who is addressed as 'Sir' and who as 'Bill' can quickly tell us much about the operation of status and power within a community; the willingness, or reluctance, of a speaker of one language, or dialect, to switch to another for the benefit of a stranger can be very informative about the relations between communities. In addition to the details and dynamics of interaction, social psychologists increasingly study the sustained interactions that are interpersonal relationships, their initiation and development through dating, mating, and marriage, their maintenance over time, and their dissolution or collapse through, for example, bereavement or divorce.

The third focus consists of representations of the social world. How do we view and think about the social world around us, and what effects do these 'pictures in our heads' have on our actions? Some representations concern individuals and interpersonal processes. Currently a major concern of American social psychology is the attributions to, or inferences about, others that we make—especially whether and how we decide if someone's behaviour is intentional or not. Many complex representations, on the other hand, concern larger-scale social phenomena: ethnic groups, work, unemployment and the unemployed, to mention only a few. Particular representations held by specific individuals may of course be in large part idiosyncratic, but the representations that merit systematic study will usually be those that are socially shared. Whether idiosyncratic or widespread, representations have traditionally been studied in social psychology via the concept of 'attitude'. For the study of shared representations, European social psychologists have recently shown interest in the French conception of 'social representation' (Moscovici and Farr 1983), and even the notion of 'ideology' which hitherto they had largely eschewed (Billig 1976).

The broader, largely European, view of social psychology underlay the definition with which we started, and it is with that view that the best hopes of realizing the potential of the discipline appear to lie.   CF

Allport, G. W. (1968). 'The historical background of modern social psychology'. In Lindzey, G., and Aronson, E. (eds.). *The Handbook of Social Psychology* (2nd edn.).

Billig, M. (1976). *Social Psychology and Intergroup Relations.*

Brown, R. (1986). *Social Psychology: The Second Edition.*

Deaux, K., and Wrightman, L. S. (1984). *Social Psychology in the 80s* (4th edn.).

Lindzey, G., and Aronson, E. (eds.) (1985). *The Handbook of Social Psychology* (3rd edn.).

Mead, G. H. (1934). *Mind, Self and Society.*

Moscovici, S., and Farr, R. (eds.) (1983). *Social Representations.*

Tajfel, H. (ed.) (1983). *The Social Dimension: European Developments in Social Psychology.*

—— and Fraser, C. (eds.) (1978). *Introducing Social Psychology.*

Socrates (469–399 BC). The son of Sophroniscus, a sculptor, and Phaenarete, a midwife, Socrates distinguished himself for bravery in three campaigns at Potidaea, Amphipolis, and Delium. He wrote no books, though the Delphic oracle declared in his own time that he was the wisest man in the world. Physically, he was, as he himself admitted, ugly, with a snub nose. The shrewish temper of his wife Xanthippe is now legend and was probably fact.

Socrates is immortalized in many of *Plato's dialogues, including the *Apology*, which gives his defence when he was charged in 399 BC with corrupting the young, as 'an evil doer and a curious person, searching into things under the earth and above the heaven; and making the worse appear the better cause, and teaching all this to others'. He was condemned to death, by a majority of six in a jury of perhaps 500. His friends planned his escape, but he refused to break the law, and in their company he drank hemlock and, still talking philosophy, died. His last days are most poignantly described in Plato's *Phaedo*.

Socrates is celebrated both for his personal qualities of courage and for maintaining the highest moral standards while yet being susceptible at least to wine and no doubt to the other traditional temptations. He was no recluse, or monastic, but lived to the full the life of a man. Philosophically, he represented, at the highest, values of questioning and discussion without bigotry or preformed conclusions, thus exposing feeble arguments and prejudice.

Guthrie, W. K. C. (1971). *Socrates.*

solipsism. This is the move in the philosophical game of doubting, that only oneself exists. Although there is no strict disproof it is by any common sense absurd—all would be but a dream. Yet we can doubt *other minds.

Bertrand *Russell received a postcard from Christina Ladd-Franklin, the authority on colour vision, saying something like: 'Dear Lord Russell. I am a solipsist. Why are there so few others who think as I do?'.   RLG

somatotopical. A term referring to brain maps or representations of the body surface, especially by signals from the skin receptors indicating touch. The somatotopic maps in the brains of vertebrates, including humans, are upside down—so that the feet are represented at the top and the head at the bottom of the map, which can be

explored with microelectrode recording from the exposed brain surface. This curious arrangement is probably due to the need for rich relations between visual and touch mapping in the brain. As the retinal image is upside down (and laterally reversed) due to the optics of the eye, the touch maps are similarly inverted to simplify and shorten cross-sensory neural connections.

See also LOCALIZATION OF BRAIN FUNCTION AND CORTICAL MAPS.

somnambulism. A sleeper may engage in a variety of more or less coherent activities. He may talk, for instance, or move purposefully, or get up and walk. He then appears dazed, preoccupied, and unresponsive to much that goes on round him. He tends to avoid obstacles, but may incur danger because he is clumsy and unreliable. He may return to bed on his own. After waking he has no memory of the incident. A child may walk half-asleep to the lavatory and return to bed, but usually somnambulism is less purposeful. Sometimes, but not typically, a sleepwalker appears to be acting out, like Lady Macbeth, fragmentary and irrational dream experiences.

Somnambulism is not uncommon among children. It may be repeated several times over a short period and then not occur again. It is said to run in families. It tends to occur early in the night, during 'orthodox' sleep, when large, slow waves are to be seen on the *electroencephalogram. Somnambulism is distinct from the night terrors shown by children. When it is associated with persistent and severe disturbance of behaviour, as in the case of Lady Macbeth, it may be regarded as a manifestation of the 'twilight state' which occurs in some forms of mental illness.

Although it is very unusual for a sleepwalker to harm anyone else, there are cases on record where it has been claimed that acts of homicide have taken place during an episode of sleepwalking. In some of these the accused person had been drinking before falling asleep, only to wake later to find that he had killed his bedmate. It is difficult to believe that sleepwalking in an undrugged state could possibly persist throughout a violent struggle such as would occur if the victim of a homicidal assault made every effort to resist. Furthermore, because sleepwalking takes place during orthodox sleep, and not during dreaming REM sleep, the sleepwalker who acts violently would be unlikely to be acting out a dream in which he might believe that he is defending himself against attack. None the less, pleas of somnambulism have been accepted as defences against charges of murder both in the UK and in the USA.   DRD

Oswald, I. (1980). *Sleep.*

space psychology. The early astronauts were required to be very experienced test pilots, very healthy and resistant to stress, and morally fit to represent the nation. In 1958 the records of 500 qualified men were reviewed, and seven were eventually selected to fly in the *Mercury* programme, after much psychological and medical screening. Some of the early tests—such as keeping the feet in iced water for seven minutes—now seem bizarre. The validity of the early psychological screening is not known, since the 'failures' were not allowed to fly. Orbiting in a capsule sent up by a rocket was thought by some to be rather degrading in comparison with piloting an aircraft. Monkeys had been sent up first, so why send a human? It was soon evident that humans had a vital role in space: they could make observations, report back, make decisions, avert disasters, conduct experiments, and make repairs. And on the ground they were national heroes.

Many more candidates were trained for the *Gemini*, *Apollo*, and *Skylab* programmes. The emphasis shifted towards academic qualifications, and scientists were accepted in addition to pilots. The advent of the space shuttle in the 1980s made space flight almost routine, and civilians were allowed to fly as passengers with relatively little training. Indeed, instead of going to war, the Soviets and Americans vied with each other to offer rides in space to political allies and 'minority' groups. The official route into the space shuttle for civilians is to become a payload specialist (PS), the job being to look after some specialist aspect of the mission, such as a scientific or industrial experiment. The PS initially trains for one mission only, though some individuals continue as career astronauts. Much of the mission training is carried out in the laboratory of the payload developer, and in ground mock-ups of the spacelab and shuttle orbiter. PS applicants go through the screening procedures of their own countries and those of NASA (the National Aeronautics and Space Administration) or ESA (the European Space Agency), a small number then being selected to train for a particular mission. Final selection usually depends partly on performance in training, and partly on political and other considerations. For future long-duration international missions more attention will be paid to the compatibility of crew members.

The number of scientific experiments has increased enormously, several hundred having been carried on *Spacelab* missions (attached to NASA's shuttle) and on *Mir* (the former USSR space station). Civilian scientists have an important role in running space experiments, and they, too, must train to play their part in the complexities of a scientific mission. They have to participate in 'timeline' simulations, and learn how to use the communication systems.

1. The mission
2. The return to earth
3. The future

1. The mission

Many of the difficulties of living in space occur in other confined environments. These include isolation from the normal world and limited communication with it; problems of living in a small space; lack of privacy; social interactions within a small group; artificial day–night cycles, and shift of circadian rhythms (see BIOLOGICAL CLOCK); anxieties about the life-support system and a safe return to the normal world; tiredness due to long work schedules; delays in completing assigned tasks and coping with apparatus failures; and boredom on long missions. All of these difficulties are shared by deep-sea *divers operating from submersible chambers.

The unique aspect of space travel is weightlessness. An orbiting spacecraft is in a state of free fall, because the earth's gravitational acceleration is exactly balanced by the radial acceleration produced by the curved flight path of the spacecraft. The resulting microgravity (near zero gravity) causes various physiological changes, such as a shift of body fluids to the head, loss of calcium in the bones, muscular atrophy, and changes in blood composition. One of the most distressing effects is that of space motion sickness, which affects about half of all astronauts during their first two to four days in space. Motion sickness was not a problem on early NASA missions, but the incidence appears to have increased. One reason for the increase is that crew members move around more in larger spacecraft. The other reason is increased detail in reporting symptoms: for example, a crew member of *Spacelab* 1 gave magnitude estimates of his feelings of discomfort during the first fourteen hours in orbit (Fig. 1).

Space motion sickness—like other forms of motion sickness—is probably due to sensory conflict. The normal correspondence between visual, vestibular, and tactile stimulation breaks down, and the traveller may feel disoriented and nauseated until his brain learns to reintegrate the sensory information (see SPATIAL COORDINATION). It is perhaps remarkable that this learning can occur within two or three days. There is little evidence for a relationship between susceptibility to motion sickness on the ground and in space. This may be because astronauts usually avoid making provocative movements in space, and may not fully report any symptoms. Also, the nature of the sensory conflict is different: passengers on earth are passively subjected to unusual changes in acceleration, whereas astronauts move actively in a constant microgravity environment.

The vestibular system consists of the semi-circular canals (whose sense organs respond mainly to rotary acceleration) and the otolithic organs (which respond mainly to linear acceleration and gravity). Head movements on earth produce a familiar combination of signals from the canals and otoliths. Under weightless conditions the

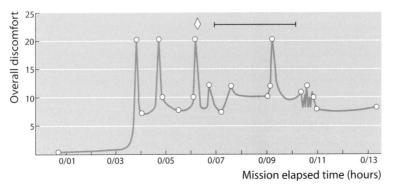

Fig. 1. Magnitude estimate of discomfort for one subject during the first fourteen hours in orbit. A score of 20 indicates vomiting. Curves between data points were interpolated by the subject. The diamond represents medication (scopolamine and Dexedrine), followed by the horizontal bar representing the period of maximal effectiveness.

canals operate normally, but the otoliths do not. They can no longer indicate head orientation with respect to gravity, but only linear acceleration fore–aft or left–right or up–down. The astronaut must therefore learn to reinterpret otolithic information. Pitch and roll head movements are particularly provocative, as are ambiguous visual stimuli such as the view of the spacecraft from an 'inverted' orientation, or seeing another crew member 'upside-down'. Unlike terrestrial travellers, astronauts can remove themselves from provocative stimulation: they can wedge themselves into a corner, close their eyes and keep their head still. Drugs can provide some protection against motion sickness, both on earth and in space, but they may produce unwanted side-effects such as drowsiness or dry throat.

Many investigators have studied how perceptual-motor skills adapt to a microgravity environment. Early in a mission, astronauts rely more heavily on visual than other cues to determine bodily orientation and the direction of gaze. There may be a reduction in the vestibular contribution to reflex eye movements and spinal reflexes. Astronauts learn how to move themselves around in space, using the hands and arms rather than the legs. They learn new patterns of hand–eye coordination, and reprogramme rapid arm movements so as not to over-reach in microgravity. They also partially adapt to their own loss of arm weight, and learn to judge the mass of objects through inertial cues rather than weight. There is some initial rapid improvement in these skills, followed by gradual improvement over a few days; but mass discrimination in space remains poorer than weight discrimination on earth.

Astronauts report good visual acuity for details seen on earth, and current research shows no consistent changes in near vision or the visual contrast sensitivity function.

2. The return to earth

Returning astronauts are rather like swimmers staggering ashore after a long swim. They feel heavy and clumsy. In addition, their vestibular coordination is disturbed, and they may see the world swing round in an unusual manner with head movements. 'I felt like my gyros were caged,' explained one astronaut. It takes a relatively long time for complete readaptation to the earth's gravity. For example, after the ten-day mission of *Spacelab 1* some crew members were still showing neurophysiological and perceptual after-effects a week later. Soviet missions of several months' duration produce more serious and prolonged physiological effects. Astronauts differ in their after-effects, and it is not clear whether prolonged after-effects are correlated with slow or rapid adaptation in space.

Some after-effects may be due to the continued reinterpretation of otolith signals as linear accelerations rather than as head tilt: this causes postural instability with the eyes closed, and an increased reliance on visual orientation

Fig. 2. Dr Ulf Merbold, a European payload specialist, tests himself on return from the Spacelab 1 mission, and shows impaired weight discrimination.

cues. There may also be some changes in sensitivity to linear acceleration in different body axes. Other effects may be due to changes in proprioceptive and tactile sensations, such as feelings of heaviness, impairment of weight discrimination (Fig. 2), under-reaching for objects, and faulty awareness of limb position.

Readaptation to gravity is not the only problem faced by astronauts. They may be short of sleep, or be required to shift their circadian rhythm to local time. They may face several long days of medical, physiological, and psychological tests, debriefing sessions, and press publicity. They must then face the reality of readjustment to normal life, and of difficult career decisions. The life of the astronaut is not quite as rosy as is sometimes pictured.

3. The future

The *Challenger* disaster in January 1986 reduced enthusiasm for manned spaceflight, and made satellites and robotic instruments more desirable. Nevertheless, the usefulness of humans in space had been amply demonstrated, and NASA's shuttle programme continued. The USA and other nations also cooperated with the former USSR in the use of the Soviet space station *Mir*. Helen Sharman became the first British astronaut when she joined *Mir* in 1991, and Michael Foale (NASA, but originally British) helped with on-board repairs to the ageing *Mir* in 1997. *Mir* met its final demise in March 2001. Meanwhile the USA, Canada, Europe, Russia, and Japan are cooperating in building the International Space Station, a new manned orbiting space station, where the crews will include more scientists and technicians, and will stay in space for weeks or months at a time. There is talk of a manned base on the moon, and a manned mission to Mars, in the next fifteen years. Research on space psychology is likely to move away from the causes of motion sickness (which ceases to be a problem after about four days) to the longer-term effects of living in space and returning to earth. Simultaneously, research will go on into the automation of astronauts' tasks, and efforts will be made to replace humans with robots or teleoperators. This is unlikely to be practicable for many tasks, and we can expect to keep the 'human-in-the-loop' for the foreseeable future.   HER

Clement, G., and Reschke, M. F. (1996). 'Neurosensory and sensory-motor functions'. In Moore, D., Bie, P. and Oser, H. (eds.), *Biological and Medical Research in Space*.

Kring, J. P. (2001). 'Multicultural factors for international spaceflight'. *Journal of Human Performance in Extreme Environments*, 5.

Kuroda, I., Young, L. R., and Fitts, D. J. (2000). 'Summary of the International Workshop on Human Factors in Space'. *Aviat. Space Environ. Med.* 71.

Lackner, J. R. (1993). 'Orientation and movement in unusual force environments'. *Psychol. Sci.* 4.

Ross, H. E., Schwartz, E., and Emmerson, P. (1987). 'The nature of sensorimotor adaptation to altered G-levels: evidence from mass discrimination'. *Aviat. Space Environ. Med.* 58.

Young, L. R. (1999). 'Artificial gravity considerations for a Mars exploration mission'. *Annals New York Acad. Sci.* 871.

spatial coordination. Almost everything that a human being does involves the *perception of the spatial locations of objects. The senses used in perceiving spatial locations are known as the spatial senses: they are vision, hearing, touch, and kinaesthesis. Kinaesthesis is the sense which enables us to appreciate the positions and movements of limbs, and depends on receptors in muscles, tendons, and joints, as well as on the sense of muscular effort involved in moving a limb or holding it in a given position. Movements of the head are detected by a set of specialized sense organs in the head, known as the vestibular sense organs.

The task of judging the spatial location of an object is complicated by the fact that sense organs are attached to mobile parts of the body. For instance, the receptive surface of the eye (the *retina) is attached to a mobile eyeball, which in turn is attached to a mobile head. If we wish to know the direction of a seen object with respect to the torso, the position of the eyes and of the head must be taken into account, along with information about the retinal position of the image of the object. This type of process is here referred to as *sensory integration*.

The position of an object is often detected by more than one sense organ at the same time. For instance, we may hold an object which we can also see and hear. Furthermore, we usually see with two eyes and hear with two ears. Spatial information must be coordinated between different sense organs, either two organs of the same type or belonging to different spatial senses. This is the process of *intersensory coordination*.

Finally, after we have located an object we may wish to reach for it. This requires that sensory spatial information be coordinated with the motor commands which control the movements of limbs. This is the process of *sensorimotor coordination*.

Performance of any spatial task has an accuracy and a precision. 'Accuracy' is the extent to which the mean of a set of judgements deviates from the true value. 'Precision' is the extent to which spatial judgements are scattered about their mean position. A darts player is highly accurate, if the throws are evenly distributed about the target, even though the player is very imprecise because the throws are widely scattered. Another player is very inaccurate if the throws are well to one side of the target, even though all the throws land on the same spot.

1. Sensory integration
2. Intersensory coordination
3. Sensorimotor coordination

spatial coordination

1. Sensory integration

As an example of sensory integration, consider the act of estimating the direction of a seen object with reference to the body. Such a task involves estimating where the object is with respect to the eyes, how the eyes are oriented in the head, and how the head is oriented on the body. The visual direction of an object with respect to an eye is indicated by the position of its image on the retina. However, this task is simplified by the fact that we normally direct our gaze towards an object of interest and bring its image onto the centre of the retina (the *fovea*).

Information about the direction of the eyes in the head is provided by motor signals sent to the muscles that move the eyes, or hold them in a given position. An eye never has to move against a variable load, so that the muscular forces, and hence the motor signals, are always the same for a given position of an eye. There is no need for sense organs to indicate the position of the eyes; their position is always indicated by the sense of effort required to move them or hold them in position.

The direction of the head with respect to the body is indicated by sensory receptors in the muscles and joints of the neck; motor signals are unreliable indicators of head position because the effort required to hold the head in a given position on the body depends on the posture of the head with respect to gravity.

For the total task of judging the visual direction of an object, the information from these three components must be summed, or integrated. Since the eye and the head rotate about approximately the same vertical axis, one would expect the algebraic sum of the angular inaccuracies of the three components to equal the inaccuracy of the total task and the sum of the variabilities (precision) of the component tasks to equal the variability of the total task. This is why this case is referred to here as 'sensory integration'.

A similar state of affairs holds when we judge the direction of a hidden object which we touch with the finger. In this case information from the various joints of the arm is summed in estimating the direction of the object relative to the body. An extra factor is involved in this example because, in addition to summing information about the angular positions of the joints, it is also necessary to know the length of each segment of the limb.

Implicit knowledge about the spatial properties of our own body is known as the 'body schema'. This knowledge seems to be stored in the parietal lobes of the brain; damage to these areas results in anomalous experiences of the body (Critchley 1969). A patient with parietal lobe damage may complain that one of his arms does not belong to him, even though he is able to move it and feel with it, or he may feel that his arm is distorted, or not attached to the body. The body schema for a limb changes as the body changes during growth and persists after the limb has

been amputated and this creates the illusion that the limb is still present. An amputee will attempt to use his phantom limb when doing habitual things.

2. Intersensory coordination

In intersensory coordination an object is detected by at least two sense organs and the person is required to coordinate the spatial information derived from these different sources. Consider the act of picking up a small handbell, looking at it, and ringing it. The direction of the bell is sensed by the eyes, by the ears, and by the hand, and yet these separate impressions normally seem to originate from one and the same bell.

Interesting things happen when the spatial information from the various sense organs is not in agreement, that is, when there is a sensory discordance. Such a situation may be induced artificially in several ways. For instance, a person may view a ringing bell through prisms which displace the retinal image to one side. A ventriloquist produces a sensory discordance by moving the lips of his dummy and keeping his own lips still. The same thing happens in the cinema, where the sound that seems to come from the actors actually originates from loudspeakers to one side of the screen. In other words, we misperceive the direction of a sound to make it conform to the direction of a visual object with which the sound is associated—an effect known as ventriloquism or visual dominance. Jackson (1953) did an experiment to determine how far a visual object has to be separated from an associated sound before the discordance becomes noticeable. Subjects reported that a hidden whistle appeared to originate from a silent steaming kettle if the kettle and whistle were separated by less than 30 degrees. A movement of an isolated sound source by this amount is easily detected.

An experiment by Rock and Victor (1964) provides a nice example of the dominance of vision over kinaesthesis. Subjects looked through a lens which caused a square object to appear rectangular. They selected a matching object from among a set of objects they could feel but not see and from a set they could see but not feel. Most subjects selected an object which matched the shape as seen rather than the shape as felt, and few subjects were aware of any conflict.

The conflict between audition and touch kinaesthesis was studied by Pick, Warren, and Hay (1969). Blindfolded subjects pointed with one hand to the felt position of the other hand which touched a loudspeaker that was emitting clicks. At the same time, subjects wore a pseudophone which apparently displaced the clicks by 11 degrees to one side. Subjects pointed to the true position of the other hand and ignored the discordant auditory information.

Thus, in a conflict situation, when the person is convinced that the object detected by one sense organ is

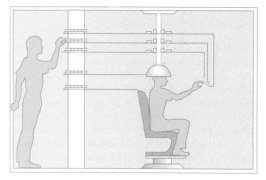

Fig. 1. Schematic representation of an apparatus used to measure the accuracy and precision of intersensory localization.

the same as that detected by another, vision dominates audition and kinaesthesis, and kinaesthesis dominates audition.

If one wishes to determine how precisely a person can bring stimuli detected by different sense organs into coincidence, one must use stimuli that do not evoke a dominance effect. In the procedure shown in Fig. 1 a light, a small loudspeaker, and a small tactile-kinaesthesis 'button' are each mounted on a boom at arm's length. The subject is presented with pairs of stimuli in various positions and reports which member of each pair is to the left of the other. The subject also judges the position of each stimulus presented on its own. In an ideal system—one which makes best use of the available information—the

variability of judgements about the relative positions of two stimuli should equal the sum of variabilities of the judgements about the positions of each stimulus taken separately. Auerbach and Sperling (1974) showed that the performance of human subjects on an auditory–visual localization task, with an apparatus like that shown in Fig. 1, conformed closely to the ideal.

When we direct our gaze towards an object which is straight ahead, it is objectively to the right of the left eye and to the left of the right eye, and yet we experience one object straight ahead. This is because the part of ourselves which we use in making directional judgements is somewhere on a line passing through the bridge of the nose and the centre of the head. This point is known as the visual *egocentre*. Fig. 2 illustrates a simple procedure for demonstrating that lines which extend out from each eye are perceived to lie in a plane midway between the eyes, which is to say that they are referred to a common egocentre in the median plane of the head.

*Stereoscopic vision is a special case of intersensory coordination. In this case objects are seen by the two eyes, but in slightly different directions, because the two eyes are not in the same place. As long as the disparity in the relative positions of the two images is not too large, we experience only one object, but at the same time use the spatial disparity as a clue to the relative distances of objects.

Another interesting case of intersensory coordination is provided by the way we use information from the two ears to judge the direction of sound sources. This is a highly sophisticated mechanism which depends on the detection of relative intensities and times of arrival of sounds at the two ears (see BINAURAL HEARING).

3. Sensorimotor coordination

White, Castle, and Held (1964) described the normal development of visual motor coordination. During the first month the child is able to pursue objects with the eyes and head, and by the second month these movements become more refined and show signs of predicting the future position of moving objects. Arm movements are unrelated to vision at this stage. The grasp reflex is present but is wholly under tactile control. Infants under 1 month of age do not attend to objects within arm's reach, probably because of inadequate accommodation and convergence. In the second and third months the infants visually attend to near objects and begin to take a visual interest in their own arms. The first visually directed swiping movements of the arm develop, but the child grasps an object only if the hand touches it. In the third month the swipe gives way to a more directed arm movement, and the child looks back and forth between object and hand. In the third and fourth months, the child watches the two hands as they contact and manipulate each other, thus producing

Fig. 2. Procedure for demonstrating that visual directions in the two eyes are referred to a common egocentre. Each line must point accurately to the pupil of an eye, and fixation must be maintained on the point where the two lines meet. When this is done a 'fused' image of the two lines is seen extending towards the bridge of the nose.

a double feedback experience. In the fifth month, this double arm action comes under visual control and gradually gives rise to the ability to reach rapidly and grasp an object. White (1970) reported that, for infants nurtured in an environment enriched by a variety of objects hanging within reach, the onset of sustained observation of the hand occurred at a mean age of 50 days, rather than at 60 days as in infants reared in a 'normal' environment.

The spatially coordinated behaviour of adult humans can be adjusted to the changing size and shape of parts of the body during growth, to the demands of novel environments, and to compensate for injury. Because of their intelligence, humans have dispensed with narrowly specialized sense organs and limbs and have instead evolved highly flexible mechanisms that reach their highest expression in learned skills. There are several ways of studying the flexibility of spatially coordinated behaviour. One way is to rotate or transplant sense organs or tendon insertions surgically: a method applicable to humans only when radical surgery is required for medical reasons. A second procedure is to study animals reared in anomalous sensory environments, or people with severe sensory deficits, from an early age. Finally, the flexibility of spatially coordinated behaviour may be studied by temporarily distorting the visual input by placing prisms or lenses in front of the eyes. Some representative experiments of each kind will now be described.

The effects of surgical rotation of the eye As part of a treatment for a detached retina, Barrios, Recalde, and Mendilaharzi (1959) severed each rectus muscle of one eye in several human patients, rotated the eyeball through 90 degrees, and sutured each muscle back onto a stump of tendon which was 90 degrees away from the muscle's normal insertion. The patients were allowed to use both eyes during the six-month recovery period. At the end of this period, when tested using only the rotated eye, the patients reported that the visual scene appeared rotated 90 degrees. Furthermore, pursuit eye movements and visually directed movements made with the unseen hand occurred in a direction at right angles to the movement of the visual targets. The total absence of adaptation in these patients was probably due to suppression in vision in the rotated eye during the recovery period. Human beings are certainly able to compensate behaviourally for the rotation of the visual scene produced by optical means, as the pioneering work of Stratton (1897) demonstrated. When a similar experiment was done on cats, the animals showed accurate visually guided paw placement and obstacle avoidance when seeing with the rotated eye, but only if, during training, the good eye was kept closed. In this experiment, the projection of nerve fibres from the retina of the rotated eye onto the visual cortex was found to be

unchanged. The behavioural compensation was obviously due to changes at a higher level.

The effects of restricted rearing on visual motor coordination One can study the kinds of sensorimotor experience required for the development of visual motor skills by rearing animals in environments which restrict experience in specific ways. In the most famous of these experiments (by Held and Hein 1958) pairs of kittens were reared in darkness, except for a certain period each day when they were placed in an illuminated striped carousel apparatus, as shown in Fig. 3. One kitten of each pair was always placed in the box so that its feet did not touch the ground, and the other kitten was always placed on the other end of the rotating lever so that it could walk and thereby cause itself and its passive partner to be moved round inside the striped drum. Both kittens had the same visual experience, but only for the active kitten was this related to the act of walking. Sensory stimulation which results from self-produced movements is known as reafference, and sensory stimulation which occurs independently of self-produced movements is called exafference. Held and Hein found that only the active kitten developed the ability to avoid a cliff, blink at an approaching object, or extend its paw to a surface. They concluded that reafference is necessary for the development of visual motor skills.

Held, Gower, and Diamond subsequently showed that the paw-placing response developed in immobilized kittens which had experienced only diffuse light. The passive experience in the carousel must have interfered with the maturation of this response, which undermines the claim that reafferent stimulation is necessary for development of visual motor skills.

Held and Hein developed tests for abilities which, they claimed, do not develop without reafferent visual

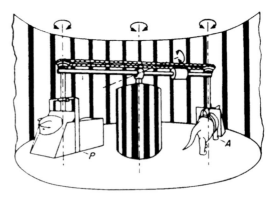

Fig. 3. Apparatus used by Hein and Held for equating motion and consequent visual feedback for an actively moving animal (*A*) and a passively moving animal (*P*).

experience. They reared kittens with opaque collars round their necks which prevented them from seeing their limbs (Fig. 4). These kittens could extend their paws towards prongs (Fig. 5) but could not hit them, except by chance, and they could not strike a ball dangled in front of them. Held and Bauer conducted a very similar experiment with monkeys, who for the first 35 days after birth wore a collar which occluded their arms. When the arms were allowed to come into view the monkeys could not reach accurately towards a bottle. It was concluded that 'an infant Primate initially fails to reach accurately for attractive visible objects with a limb that it has never previously viewed'.

Note that the monkeys were not allowed to touch the bottle before the collar was removed, and therefore had not learned to relate seen objects with anything that the unseen arm did. Walk and Bond repeated the experiment but allowed the monkeys to touch one end of a rod, the

Fig. 4. Kitten wearing a collar that prevents sight of limbs and torso.

other end of which they could see projecting above the edge of the collar which occluded the hand. After this exposure, visually guided reaching was tolerably accurate after the collar was removed. Therefore, sight of the hand is not required for the development of visual motor coordination, only some experience that links its motion to a seen object.

Thus, visual motor skills seem to develop in the presence of any type of information which informs the animal about the accuracy of performance. Certain types of early deprivation have a general debilitating effect, but visual motor learning is usually very specific to the conditions under which it occurs.

The effects of visual distortions on visual motor coordination When stimuli impinging on one sense organ are spatially distorted with respect to those impinging on the other sense organs, there is a sensory discordance. The types of visual distortion that have been studied include sideways displacement, tilt, inversion, left–right reversal, magnification, and curvature.

Anyone with a wedge prism can perform the following simple experiment. A few numbers are marked on the edge of a piece of card which is then placed horizontally under the chin as in Fig. 6. With the prism before one eye and the other eye closed, the finger is directed towards a number on the far side of the card and allowed to come into view. This arm is then returned to the side of the body, after which the aiming movement is repeated several times to each of the numbers in random order. The error in pointing will be very evident for the first few trials, but accuracy is soon restored. When the prism is removed, it will be found that the first few aims will be off target in the opposite direction to the error first experienced when the prism was in place. This after-effect illustrates that adaptation to a visual distortion is not merely a question of deliberate compensation.

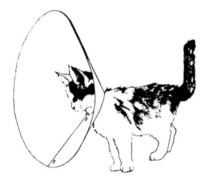

Fig. 5. Apparatus for testing the accuracy of visually guided paw placement in the cat.

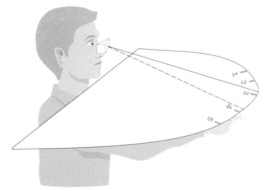

Fig. 6. A simple apparatus for demonstrating adaptation of pointing to displaced vision.

The nature of the changes underlying adaptation to displaced vision It is agreed that visual motor adaptation to distorted vision does not involve changes in the sense organs, or in the muscular system that controls arm movements. The change must be in the way sensory or motor signals are coded in the central nervous system. There is no evidence of a change in the internal calibration of the position of the retinal image. This is not surprising because, when a person points to an object, its image falls on the fovea, which is a very distinctive landmark. Other experiments, reviewed in Howard (1981), have failed to reveal any significant effects of visual motor learning on the apparent directions and shapes of objects, even when the objects are not fixated. It seems that simple visual sensations are insulated from events outside vision. There is an old theory, known as the motor theory of perception, in which it is claimed that the way we see is determined by motor behaviour. It would seem that this theory is wrong with respect to simple visual sensations.

Visual motor adaptation has been found sometimes to involve a change in the sense of eye position. For instance, Craske (1967) found that the objectively determined position of the eyes, when the subject was attempting to look straight ahead in the dark, was shifted after exposure to displacing prisms. Similar experiments have demonstrated that there may also be a change in the felt position of the head on the body.

If training one arm with prisms affects the way the other arm points, the adaptation is said to show *intermanual transfer*. Intermanual transfer indicates that the change must have occurred in the sense of position of the head or the eyes—parts common to both arms. There is general agreement that intermanual transfer is only partial, so that most of the adaptive change to displaced vision must involve a change in the sense of position of the trained arm—a change in the way information from joint receptors is coded, or in the spatial coding of motor commands.

Evidence that motor learning may contribute to adaptation of the visual motor system comes from experiments by Taub and Goldberg on monkeys in whom the sensory roots of the spinal cord had been severed. These monkeys could be trained to reach with the unseen arm towards visual targets and to adapt their pointing when viewing the targets through displacing prisms. This must have been motor learning because the animals lacked sensory inputs from the arm.

Thus it seems that all systems beyond the most peripheral processes in sense organs and muscles are capable of adapting to unusual circumstances, given the correct set of constraints and demands. The one exception seems to be that the central calibration of the position of the retinal image is immutable.

The conditions under which adaptation to displaced vision occurs Held proposed that sensations arising from active movement (i.e. reafferent stimuli) are necessary for visual motor adaptation to displaced vision. In one experiment Hein and Held asked subjects to watch one of their own hands through a displacing prism as the hand was waved from side to side, either actively by the subject or passively by the experimenter. Only after the active condition did subjects show evidence of having adapted to the prisms when they were tested in an aiming test. They concluded that self-produced movement coupled to visual reafferent stimulation (sight of the moving arm) is necessary for a change of visual motor coordination. However, subjects probably paid more attention to what they were doing when moving their own arms and, with this factor controlled, other investigators have demonstrated that self-produced movement is not necessary for visual motor adaptation.

Howard and Templeton (1966) argued that adaptation occurs in response to many forms of discordant information: the important thing is that salient information regarding the discordance (not necessarily consciously perceived) should be available to the subject. The sensory consequences of self-produced movement may be a particularly potent source of information, but the most reasonable general conclusion is that any consistent relationship between stimuli within a given sense or between stimuli in different senses, or any relationship between stimuli and responses, will be learned and the system changed accordingly.

The posterior parietal lobe of the cerebral cortex is well placed to serve as a centre for the higher control of coordination of vision, somaesthesis, eye movements, and limb movements. It has been shown that cells in this region of the monkey's brain respond when the animal sees an object of interest, such as food, towards which it is likely to reach. Many of the visually responsive neurons also respond when the eyes move, and some also respond to stimulation of touch receptors.

Subcortical centres in the brain are also involved in sensorimotor coordination. For instance, it has been shown that cells in the *basal ganglia, which receive highly processed spatial information, probably from the parietal lobes, are active when the animal is tracking a moving visual object. Damage to the basal ganglia in humans, such as is associated with *Parkinsonism, results in *akinesia, or an inability to initiate movements towards a visual object. This disorder is manifest only in certain contexts, which suggests that the basal ganglia are concerned with organizing responses to specific visual information. Our knowledge of the neurology of sensorimotor coordination is very fragmentary. Perhaps the development of artificial automata will help to provide theoretical insights which will guide future work.   IPH

Aldridge, J. W., Anderson, R. J., and Murphy, J. T. (1980). 'The role of the basal ganglia in controlling a movement initiated by a visually presented cue'. *Brain Research*, 192.

Auerbach, E., and Sperling, P. (1974). 'A common auditory-visual space: evidence for its reality'. *Perception and Psychophysics*, 16.

Bailey, J. S. (1972). 'Arm–body adaptation with passive arm movements'. *Perception and Psychophysics*, 12.

Barrios, R. R., Recalde, E. M., and Mendilaharzi, C. (1959). 'Surgical rotation of the eyeball'. *British Journal of Psychology*, 43.

Blakemore, C., van Sluyters, R. C., Peck, C. K., and Hein, A. (1975). 'Development of cat visual cortex following rotation of one eye'. *Nature. New Biology*, 257.

Craske, B. (1967). 'Adaptation to prisms: changes in internally registered eye position'. *British Journal of Psychology*, 58.

Critchley, M. (1969). *The Parietal Lobes*.

Fisher, G. H. (1960). 'Intersensory localization in three modalities'. *Bulletin of the British Psychological Society*, 14.

Held, R., and Hein, A. (1958). 'Adaptation of disarranged hand–eye coordination contingent upon re-afferent stimulation'. *Perceptual Motor Skills*, 8.

Howard, I. P. (1981). *Human Visual Orientation*.

—— and Templeton, W. B. (1966). *Human Spatial Orientation*.

Jackson, C. V. (1953). 'Visual factors in auditory localization'. *Quarterly Journal of Experimental Psychology*, 5.

Pick, H. L., Warren, D. H., and Hay, J. C. (1969). 'Sensory conflicts in judgements of spatial direction'. *Perception and Psychophysics*, 6.

Rock, I., and Victor, J. (1964). 'Vision and touch: an experimentally created conflict between the two senses'. *Science*, 143.

Stratton, G. M. (1897). 'Upright vision and the retinal image'. *Psychological Review*, 4.

Templeton, W. B., Howard, I. P., and Lowman, A. E. (1966). 'Passively generated adaptation to prismatic distortion'. *Perceptual Motor Skills*, 22.

White, B. L. (1970). 'Experience and the development of motor mechanisms in infancy'. In Connolly, K. (ed.), *Mechanisms of Motor Skill Development*.

—— Castle, P., and Held, R. (1964). 'Observations on the development of visually-directed reaching'. *Child Development*, 35.

Spearman, Charles Edward (1863–1945).

Formerly a cavalry officer, Spearman studied psychology in Germany, taking his doctorate at Leipzig. Thereafter he worked in London, becoming Grote Professor of mind and logic at University College, where he remained until his retirement in 1931. He was elected a Fellow of the Royal Society in 1924.

Spearman is remembered as a pioneer in statistical psychology and a convinced believer in the two-factor theory of *intelligence, which he advocated in a paper written jointly with Bernard Hart in 1904. Making use of factorial analysis, Spearman claimed that the correlations between the measurement of different abilities in man tended towards a particular arrangement that could be expressed in a definite mathematical formula. This became known as the tetrad equation. Wherever this equation held throughout any table of correlation, every individual measurement of each ability could be divided into two independent parts, one called by Spearman *g*—i.e. the *general factor*—which, though varying freely from individual to individual, remains the same for any one individual in respect of all the correlated abilities, while the other part—known as the *specific factor*—varies not only from individual to individual, but even in any one individual from one ability to another.

Thus arose what soon became known as the 'two-factor' theory which aroused wide interest but sharp controversy in Britain and further afield. Although Spearman tended to interpret *g* in terms of a vague and unconvincing concept of 'mental energy', most psychological workers in this field who shared Spearman's views preferred to identify it with 'general intelligence'.

Spearman's work attracted much interest but many critics, among them Godfrey (later Sir Godfrey) Thomson, who advocated instead of a general factor a number of overlapping group factors. Later the interpretation of factorial analysis was extended and discussed with much statistical sophistication by Maxwell Garnett, Cyril Burt, William Stephenson, L. L. *Thurstone, and many others on both sides of the Atlantic.

The outcome appears to be that, whereas factorial analysis has evident value in classifying individuals for educational or occupational purposes, it does not materially contribute to our understanding either of the nature of intelligence or of the rationale of individual differences. It is therefore unlikely to make a decisive contribution to psychological theory.

Spearman wrote two major works: *The Nature of 'Intelligence' and the Principles of Cognition* (1923) and *The Abilities of Man* (1927). OLZ

speech recognition by machine.

Until recently, recognition of speech by a machine has seemed impossible—though machines have been talking and singing for the last hundred years. Speech recognition has immense theoretical and practical importance. An example of a now established commercial application for automatic speech recognition is in the sorting of baggage at airports. A human operator reads a destination from a baggage label into a microphone. The spoken destination is automatically recognized and the baggage is routed accordingly. This use of automatic speech recognition has the advantage that it leaves the operator's hands free to handle the baggage.

Speech is a succession of voiced sounds that originate from the vocal cords, interspersed with consonant sounds such as 's' which originates from the hissing of air between teeth and 't' which is produced by an explosive release of air pressure by the tongue. Speech waveforms are often very complicated, and tend to be roughly periodic during short (e.g. 10-millisecond) periods.

Automatic speech recognition is usually a multistage process, in which the first stage is intended to yield a representation of speech that is simpler and less repetitive than the original acoustic waveform. The first stage typically performs various measurements on each successive 10-millisecond portion of the acoustic waveform. For example, in the *Fourier spectrum for each such portion, the energy in various frequency bands spanning 200–6,000 hertz may be measured. Alternatively, linear predictive coding coefficients may be taken as measurements. Zero-crossing rates, glottal frequency, and total energy are further important examples of measurements.

For the simplest kind of automatic speech recognition systems, speakers are required to leave silences before and after isolated words. These isolated-word recognition systems usually work by matching the sequence of measurements, obtained from a spoken word against various sequences of measurements stored in memory. These stored sequences of measurements are known as speech templates, and there is at least one such template for each different word that the machine can recognize. A spoken word is *recognized* as being the same as the template word that it matches best. Preferably the template words are obtained from the same speaker whose speech is to be recognized. A template can be obtained by having this speaker pronounce the word several times, and in some way averaging the resulting sequences of measurements to make a template. The process of obtaining a stored template from several utterances of one word can be regarded as a *learning* process.

A spoken word is generally a sequence of phonemes, and, for example, the third phoneme of a spoken word should be matched against the third phoneme of that word's stored template. The total duration of a spoken word may be different each time the word is uttered, and elongation or compression of the time scale may impair the alignment of phonemic data. For short words this problem can be mitigated by measuring the duration of a spoken word and then elongating or compressing the time scale to standardize the duration of the word before matching it with templates that have been similarly standardized. Speech recognition machines working on these principles became commercially available in the 1970s, and could learn to recognize about 32 words spoken quite carefully by a single speaker.

More sophisticated template-matching technology allows elongation or compression of a word's time scale to vary while the word is being spoken. Time-scale variations can be accommodated by dynamic time warping, which became popular in the 1980s because of the decreasing cost of computation, and because it yields more accurate recognition of larger vocabularies than can be recognized by less sophisticated matching techniques. Dynamic time-warping techniques have been developed to recognize whole sentences composed of words not separated by silences. Templates for whole sentences are composed of single-word templates, and the time-warping technique that time-aligns phoneme-like parts of a single word has been developed to time-align whole-word parts of a single sentence. After matching, it is easy to find which part of the spoken sentence corresponds to which part of a template sentence, and thus find when each spoken word begins and ends.

Except for specialized applications, it is not practical to store or synthesize sentence templates, and radically different techniques are required for automating the work of a typist who types unrestricted text that is dictated without silences between successive words. Instead of attempting to recognize whole words directly by template matching, it is usual to attempt to classify successive subword portions, known as segments. A segment may, for instance, be a portion during which the results of measurements on the acoustic waveform do not change by more than a threshold amount. Alternatively, successive 10-millisecond portions of the utterance may be regarded as segments. Segments may be classified, sometimes erroneously, by means of classical *pattern recognition techniques, which yield one or more plausible labels for each segment. A speech recognition machine contains a dictionary which, for each recognizable word, stores one or more than one combination of segment labels for segments of that word. This stored lexical knowledge is generally not sufficient to cope with erroneous subdivision of speech into segments and erroneous classification of these segments. To bring further order out of this chaos it is usual to employ knowledge of syntax and semantics in addition to lexical knowledge.

JRU

Fallside, F., and Woods, W. A. (1985). *Computer Speech Processing*.

Lea, W. A. (1980). *Trends in Speech Recognition*.

Witten, I. (1982). *Principles of Computer Speech*.

Spencer, Herbert (1820–1903). British philosopher. The influence of Herbert Spencer in his lifetime was immense. It was not only in intellectual circles that his books were read, and their popular appeal in America and Asia, as well as in Britain, was enormous. But since the 19th century his reputation has suffered an uncommonly severe eclipse, and it is necessary to recall the extent of his influence.

Henry Holt, an influential publisher, declared: 'About 1865 I got hold of a copy of Spencer's *First Principles* and had my eyes opened to a new heaven and a new earth.' And

Andrew Carnegie, prototype of the self-made American, publicized Spencer as 'the man to whom I owe most'. For 30 years, from the 1860s, Spencer's thought dominated American universities. The last of those decades, the 1890s, produced the revolution in educational thought and psychology led by William *James and John *Dewey, Stanley *Hall, and E. L. *Thorndike, all influenced by Spencer. In Britain, J. S. *Mill backed financially the subscription scheme that launched Spencer's work, and the scientists supported him too. Charles *Darwin wrote, 'After reading any of his books I generally feel enthusiastic admiration for his transcendental talents', but added that 'his conclusions never convince me'. (He also wrote, somewhat ambiguously: 'I feel rather mean when I read him: I could bear and rather enjoy feeling that he was twice as ingenious and clever as myself, but when I feel that he is about a dozen times my superior, even in the master-art of wriggling, I feel aggrieved.') In 1863 Alfred Russel *Wallace visited Spencer, commenting: 'Our thoughts were full of the great unsolved problem of the origin of life . . . and we looked to Spencer as the one man living who could give us a clue to it.' And as late as 1897 Beatrice Webb noted that: ' "Permanent" men might be classed just above the artisan and skilled mechanic: they read Herbert Spencer and Huxley and are speculative in religious and political thought.'

In the 1880s Spencer was consulted by the Japanese government on education. And in Chekhov's short story 'The Duel' (1891) a female character recalls the beginning of an idyllic relationship: 'to begin with we had kisses, and calm evenings, and vows, and Spencer, and ideals and interests in common.' And, finally, a letter arrived at Spencer's home in the early 1890s addressed to 'Herbt Spencer, England, and if the postman doesn't know where he lives, why he ought to'.

Spencer's fame was based entirely on his books. He rarely appeared in public, save for one triumphant tour of America late in life. He was born in Derby, the only surviving son of a schoolmaster, and he was educated informally at home by his father and later in the family of an uncle. The family was staunchly Nonconformist, with a radical tradition and a keen interest in the social issues of the day. For some years the young Spencer was a railway engineer, but by 1841 he had decided against this career. He became a journalist in London, attended meetings, and was formulating ideas on politics and education. He began to write, and became known for his radical opinions and self-confidence, traits tempered by great honesty. If in old age he became idiosyncratic, in youth he was a shrewd iconoclast who delighted in argument. Perhaps it was these qualities that led him to some influential and lifelong friendships. He got to know the young T. H. *Huxley; they had interests in common and walked together on Hampstead Heath in London. George Eliot

was a fellow journalist who fell in love with him, before he introduced her to G. H. Lewes. It was a remarkably tight-knit intellectual group in which Spencer moved, and it extended into the next generation. In 1877 when William James was attacking Spencer's books at Harvard, William's brother Henry, the novelist, wrote describing his meeting with Spencer at George Eliot's, and comments: 'I often take a nap beside Herbert Spencer at the Athenaeum and feel as if I were robbing you of the privilege.'

Spencer's first books were published in the serene mid-century. His essays on *Education* (1861) remained a standard text in colleges training teachers for many decades. By 1858 he had conceived the plan of writing a major synthetic philosophy, and the prospectus appeared in 1860. Small legacies, publications, and the support of friends enabled him to give up journalism, and for the rest of his life he was an independent author. He never married, and he devoted his life to completing the philosophy as he had originally planned it. The whole massive project, with volumes on biology, psychology, sociology, and ethics, together with the initial *First Principles* (1862), was finally complete in 1896.

Today one point of pursuing Spencer lies precisely in trying to understand something of the reasons for his great appeal in his own time. The social milieu in which he moved is significant. The immense popularity of his work is due to a rather special way in which it reflected some of the preoccupations of his own generation. In his thirties Spencer suffered a severe breakdown in health. He shared the Victorian syndrome, which Darwin and Huxley also endured, of a crisis in health as a young man and thereafter constant hypochondria, insomnia, and headaches; it suggests some of the tensions in their thought and background.

Spencer had no formal education. He believed this to be a great advantage which 'left me free from the bias given by the plexus of traditional ideas and sentiments', and he adds: 'I did not trouble myself with the generalisations of others. And that indeed indicated my general attitude. All along I have looked at things through my own eyes and not through the eyes of others.' In later life he was never able to work for long, and his reading was severely curtailed. In fact he had never read a great deal; he observed, made biological collections and mechanical inventions, and he enjoyed intelligent conversations and his own thoughts much more than reading books. Although he believed this gave him an independent attitude, it in fact left him more than usually open to the influences around him.

When *Darwin's *Origin of Species* was published in November 1859, evolutionary theories were not new—they had been the subject of speculation for half a century. Darwin's achievement was to make the elements of the theory coherent and to demonstrate, by massive evidence, that it must be taken seriously.

One man needed no conversion. Seven years earlier, in 1852, Spencer had published an essay on the 'Development Hypothesis', and coined the term *survival of the fittest*. Years later Huxley recalled that before Darwin's publication, 'The only person known to me whose knowledge and capacity compelled respect, and who was at the same time a thoroughgoing evolutionist, was Mr Herbert Spencer. . .'. Spencer first came across evolution in a secondary work discussing the ideas of *Lamarck, whose theory was partly intuitive and had never convinced professional naturalists (see LAMARCKIANISM). Spencer was won over, before there was convincing evidence, for a characteristically mid-Victorian reason: 'The Special Creation theory had dropped out of my mind many years before, and I could not remain in a suspended state; acceptance of the only conceivable alternative was peremptory.'

An important feature of Spencer's generation of intellectuals is that they had discarded orthodox religion. Spencer himself was never religious, and he enjoyed setting out for Sunday rambles walking provocatively in the opposite direction to the churchgoers. But unconsciously, the agnostic mid-Victorians searched for some other system of thought which could answer their doubts and give them clear first principles. Science was one alternative which was widely seized on, hence the battles over evolution and religion. Evolution offered, it seemed, an alternative conceptual framework, universally operating laws of cause and effect. The 'new heaven and the new earth' which Spencer's philosophy opened up to many of his contemporaries was essentially a systematic metaphysical cosmology: everything from the stars to the embryo, from civilizations to the individual, was in process of development, interaction, change, growth—and progress. For Spencer's conception of universal evolution was optimistic, a view which seemed natural to successful mid-Victorians. 'Progress, therefore, is not an accident but a necessity. Instead of civilisation being artificial, it is a part of the embryo or the unfolding of a flower.' Late 18th-century *laissez-faire* individualism is thus reconciled with the revolutionary changes of 19th-century society.

Naturalistic organic conceptions of society gained a new importance with the addition of evolutionary laws. Spencer was the first to pursue the study of such laws operating in society, and to call his analysis sociology. His book *The Study of Sociology* (1873) was as popular as *Education*. A similar but more dynamic conception was being developed in the same period by Karl Marx.

Fundamentally the reverence for nature which pervades all Spencer's work goes back to *Rousseau. It is romantic, not scientific. Spencer's conception of evolution owes nothing to Darwin. Although greatly impressed by science, Spencer never really grasped scientific method: his method was inductive—he generalizes laws without proof, draws facts haphazardly from his own experience, and is fond of asserting his beliefs as 'obvious'. Spencer understood his own romantic, speculative, and basically unscientific attitude, and recounts against himself the witticism of his friend Huxley that 'Spencer's idea of a tragedy is a deduction killed by a fact'. Not until almost a generation later was it realized that evolutionary theories cannot supply an ethical code for human societies. Spencer's only quarrel with Huxley was in the 1890s, when Huxley first publicly dissented from the view that the law of nature in human society was neither just nor good.

The origins of Spencer's philosophy owe much to the provincial dissenting background of his youth. By the 1880s his individualistic *laissez-faire* views were already anachronistic, though his book *Man versus the State* (1884) had enormous sales. Essentially, Spencer is a Janus figure looking as much backwards as forwards. He only partly understood evolutionary theory and used it considerably to give a systematic framework for the individualistic ethics and organic view of the state prevalent in his youth. John Dewey, in an excellent essay, came to the conclusion that Spencer was essentially a transition figure, preserving the ideals of late 18th-century British liberalism in the only way possible: in 'the organic, the systematic, the universal terms which report the presence of the nineteenth century'.

Yet Spencer really did seize and propagandize the leading idea of his own day. It was Spencer, not Darwin, who opened up the horizons of the evolutionary theory in psychology, sociology, anthropology, and education. He did perhaps more than anyone else to persuade others that the implications of the evolutionary theory were important, and he did it in a thoroughly Victorian manner: energetic, confident, systematic, universal, which a modern scientist, Sir Peter Medawar, salutes with respect:

I think Herbert Spencer was the greatest of those who have attempted to found a metaphysical system on naturalistic principles. It is out of date, of course, this style of thought, it is philosophy for an age of steam. . . . His system of General Evolution does not really work: the evolution of society and of the solar system are different phenomena, and the one teaches us next to nothing about the other. . . . But for all that, I for one can still see Spencer's System as a great adventure.

AL-B

Medawar, P. (1967). *The Art of the Soluble*.
Peel, J. D. Y. (1971). *Herbert Spencer*.

Sperry, Roger Wolcott (1913–94). Roger Sperry is most famous for experimental studies of how brain circuits are formed, and for research on mental activities after the connecting tracts between the cerebral hemispheres have been cut. He worked for his doctorate in close association with the biophysicist Paul Weiss, who had developed surgery to analyse how connections between nerves and muscles are patterned, and had demonstrated that the movement patterns of amphibia develop spontaneously in the embryo. By transplanting limb buds and re-routing motor nerves, Weiss found that salamanders could regain an excellent sequential control of their limb muscles, the nerves making connections that matched, not the locomotor usefulness of the movements, but the embryonic origins of the different muscles. Sperry felt there must be a more specific and refined control of the growth of nerve circuits than any existing theory could explain, and that the intricate networks of the brain must result from a highly differentiated genetic coding for nerve contacts. He transplanted the insertions of extensor and flexor muscles of rats, or cut and re-routed their nerve supply, and then observed their limb movements. He reported that the rats' motor system was almost completely lacking in plasticity: except for some editing out of false moves of the forelimbs, central motor command was inflexible. The rats' wrongly connected nerves or muscles continued to produce maladaptive movements.

In the early 1940s, with Karl *Lashley, Sperry published a paper on the effects of thalamic lesions on olfactory learning in the rat, yet his main endeavour now was to explore the laws that fitted nerves into functional networks in development. He confirmed the finding by Robert Matthey in Switzerland and Leon Stone at Yale that, after a newt's eye had been dissected from the head and replaced, retina and optic nerve would reconnect to the brain and normal vision would return. Sperry observed the behaviour of the animals more closely, and he showed that, when a transplanted eye had been rotated through 180 degrees, movements to catch food after recovery of vision were precisely as predicted by the theory that cells at each retinal point had reconnected themselves to the same place in the brain as before surgery. All orienting reactions were the reverse of correct, like those of a person who has just put on inverting prisms, though for newts adaptive visuomotor coordination was not regained. This proved that the routeing of nerves, beyond a random tangle in the rejoined optic nerve into the brain centres, was precisely guided by some pathfinding principle in which learning played no part.

Later experiments on amphibia showed that regeneration of links from eye to brain, and from brain to the muscles of the eyes and fins—both of which make intricate movements in these species—obeyed the law of innate specification of connections. With Norma Dupree, a fellow biologist, whom he married in 1949, he carried out an important study at the Lerner Marine Laboratory, Bimini, West Indies, which found evidence suggesting that motor nerves preferred to regenerate connections to their own muscles. This suggested that the salamanders Weiss had studied were atypical. Later Richard Mark, working with Sperry in California, showed this to be the case.

In 1950 Sperry reported that fish and newts with one eye removed and the other either inverted or transposed to the opposite side of the head behaved in a peculiar way. They remained quiet, if not caused to swim, but spun in accelerating circles as soon as they moved. This behaviour was affected only by removal of the midbrain, where the optic nerves terminate, and was unchanged by removal of the labyrinths (organs detecting accelerations and gravity) or severance of the oculomotor muscles. Sperry concluded that the midbrain is the site of a predictive adjustment of visual perception triggered by the impulse to turn. The signal on the retina that the external world was displacing relative to the animal's head was now reversed along the front/back axis by surgery. It signalled that the world was receding, and the locomotor system then worked harder to catch up, like a kitten chasing the tail of another kitten running twice as fast. Sperry proposed that there is an internal brain signal, which he termed a 'corollary discharge from efference', that matches visual effects normally consequent on each locomotor displacement for its direction and speed. He pointed out that such a 'central kinetic factor' would help explain both perception of self-movement and the constancy of perception of the spatial layout of the world while in motion. He had independently and simultaneously discovered the integrative principle coordinating perception with movement that von Holst and Mittelstaedt in Germany had found in the reflex optomotor responses of the praying mantis. They called it the 'reafference principle' and explained it, by the same mechanism as Sperry, under the name of 'efference copy'.

Sperry then returned to his old idea that many fundamental laws of perception are reflections of inherent and precisely structured mechanisms for patterning movements. In an essay entitled 'Neurology and the mind–brain problem' (1952) he argued that motor output in free behaviour gave better evidence of the neural basis of integrative behaviour than did the enumeration of simple and unnatural reactions by largely inactive subjects to physical variation in imposed stimuli. He also questioned the anticonnectionist views of Lashley and the *Gestaltists, and indicated that associationist *learning theories are to be attacked by examining how patterns of response are coordinated, rather than by postulating field processes in the sensory cortex. He showed prophetic insight with regard to questions now being tackled by systems engineers and cognitive scientists trying to model *intelligence with computational machines, and also to those questions of interest to psychologists who seek to relate categories of perceptual processing to the problems the brain has to solve if it is to initiate movements that use terrain or objects efficiently. See PROGRAMS AND PLAN-NING.

Lashley, Wolfgang *Köhler, and others believed form recognition to be the result of field effects or interference configurations generated in a random cortical net, or of transitory electrical or magnetic fields arising between nerve cells in the grey matter. To test these ideas, Sperry and his students made minute criss-cross cuts under microscopic control throughout the visual cortex of cats, riddled it with tantalum wires to short circuit any electrical fields, and implanted leaves of mica to interrupt local transverse currents. Then they subjected the cats to extreme tests of visual form discrimination. They found virtually no losses in vision, and concluded that form perception must depend on the passage of information in and out of small cortical territories, presumably by specific neuronal linkage with cells below the grey matter.

A graduate student, Ronald Myers, invented a delicate operation to cut the crossover of visual nerves ('optic chiasm') under a cat's brain, so that each eye would lead to only one cerebral hemisphere. In 1953 Myers and Sperry reported not only transfer of the visual pattern memory between the hemispheres in chiasm-sectioned cats, but also that this transfer did not occur when the huge fibre bridge between the hemispheres, the *corpus callosum, was cut. The term *split-brain, with which Sperry's name is associated, refers to this operation and the research to which it has given rise. The operation proved that specific fibre connections could transmit learning, and further challenged Lashley's 'mass action' theory of brain systems.

Sperry and his associates made many experiments on the divided awareness and learning of split-brain cats, confirming the role of the commissural fibres in memory formation, and he also explored systems by which vision or touch controls voluntary limb movements. The investigations were extended to monkeys: like cats, these showed independent learning in the two brain halves after complete section of the corpus callosum, and experiments found that vision and touch crossed in different parts of the commissure. Colwyn Trevarthen showed that split-brain monkeys could learn two conflicting visual discriminations simultaneously; in other words, they could have double consciousness.

In the cat, each disconnected hemisphere directed movements of the whole body, but the motor system of split-brain monkeys was partly divided. They were both less willing to respond with movements of the hand on the same side as the seeing hemisphere and, if forced into action, were clumsy with this combination, as if they became blind each time they moved. Clearly, when the two halves of the cortex were disconnected, only crossed pathways linking each half of the cortex to the opposite hand could guide the fine exploratory and manipulative movements of a monkey's fingers.

Split-brain animals were used to reveal shifts of attention between the two separated halves of the cortex, and the effects on perception of sets to move in particular ways. Thereby fresh interest was aroused in the global design of the mammalian brain for awareness, learning, and voluntary action. The minimum territory of cortex needed to retain learned control of the hands by touch or vision was determined by progressively removing all other cortex from one hemisphere of a trained split-brain animal around the primary touch or visual area until losses occurred. The other half-brain was left intact, so that behaviour could continue as usual outside the training situation where experiences were confined to the operated side.

Between 1950 and the mid-1970s Sperry continued to direct research on the formation of nerve circuits in lower vertebrates. He published some twenty articles explaining and defending his theory that most cerebral functions are determined genetically by some chemical or physiochemical coding of pathways and connections. New methods for following nerve growth have revealed competitive epigenetic processes involved in sorting out functional connections while they were growing, but so far every attempt to overthrow the chemoaffinity theory by experiment has reached a point where some such selective principle has to be invoked. Sperry has certainly won his battle against the theories of the 1930s that conceived complex psychological functions to be entirely the result of experiences which impose selective influences on random and infinitely plastic nerve nets.

General articles on experiments with cats and monkeys expressed Sperry's belief that learning itself is the consequence of submicroscopic modification in cerebral circuits whose anatomical design is prewired according to genetic instructions. The latter set adaptive goals and give the organism categories of experience as well as intricately coordinated forms of action.

Around 1960, a Los Angeles neurosurgeon, Joseph Bogen, observed with Sperry that the behaviour of split-brain monkeys outside test situations indicated that division of the commissures left motivation, consciousness, and voluntary action virtually unimpaired. Bogen pointed out that the operation offered promise of relief from debilitating epileptic fits which involved reverberation of discharges across the corpus callosum. In 1962 Bogen and Philip Vogel performed a total neocortical commissurotomy on a man who suffered frequent epileptic attacks, and Sperry and a graduate student, Michael Gazzaniga, were able to apply systematic psychological tests. After 1965 a growing team of researchers under Sperry's close direction, including Jerre Levy, Robert Nebes, Harold Gordon, and Dahlia and Eran Zaidel, explored the state of divided and asymmetrical mental activity in a small population of commissurotomy patients. The implications of the findings reached into all areas of human mental life, and excited immense public and scholarly interest. An account of the initial findings was given in P. J. Vinken and G. W. Bruyn (eds.), *Handbook of Clinical Neurology*, vol. iv (1969).

From this research came support for concepts of inherent modes of thought and asymmetrical involvement of the brain in rational/verbal thinking, non-verbalizable imagery, and conceivably also mystical experience (see SPLIT-BRAIN AND THE MIND). It stimulated studies of patients with lateralized injuries of the brain and research on the perceptual, cognitive, and motor asymmetries of function in normal subjects. Sperry's hypothesis that the hemispheres are so constructed as to display unlike psychological functions—genetic variation in *handedness, or the lateralization of language, being but two manifestations of human hereditary regulation—caused a reappraisal of the reasons for differences in intellectual and educational performance of different individuals.

Reflection on inherent mental processes in the human brain led Sperry to publish, in 1965, the first of a series of philosophical papers entitled 'Mind, brain and humanist values'. He proposed a new monist theory of mind in which consciousness is conceived as an emergent, self-regulatory property of neural networks, which enables them to achieve certain built-in goals. These define requirements of the mind and psychological values which are given detailed form and direction by the rituals and symbols of tradition.

Sperry's philosophical ideas have proved somewhat controversial but derive great force from the range and depth of his experience in the field of psychobiology. Among his publications have been his chapter, 'Mechanisms of neural maturation', in S. S. Stevens (ed.), *Handbook of Experimental Psychology* (1951); 'Neurology and the mind–brain problem', *American Scientist*, 40 (1952); 'The eye and the brain', *Scientific American*, 194 (1956); 'The great cerebral commissure', *Scientific American*, 210 (1964); 'Embryogenesis of behavioural nerve nets', in R. L. Dehaan and H. Ursprung (eds.), *Organogenesis* (1965); 'In search of psyche', in F. G. Worden, J. P. Swazey, and G. Adelman (eds.), *The Neurosciences: Paths of Discovery* (1975); 'Forebrain commissurotomy and conscious awareness', *Journal of Medicine and Philosophy*, 2 (1977); and *Science and Moral Priority* (1982).

See also BRAIN DEVELOPMENT.   CT

spindle cells. The spindle cells are large bipolar-shaped neurons located in layer 5 of the anterior cingulate cortex (Fig. 1). They are characterized by an apicial dendrite extending towards the cortical surface and a basal dendrite extending towards the white matter (Fig. 2). Their shape is distinct from the pyramidal and stellate cells that constitute most of the cortical neurons. Their axon exits at a right angle from the cell body. They were described by the classical neuroanatomists such as Von Economo (1929). My colleagues and I (Nimchinsky et al. 1999) have found that the spindle cells are present only in humans and our closest relatives, the great apes. The concentration of spindle cells is greatest in humans. Chimpanzees have more than gorillas, which have more than orang-utans. There was no evidence of spindle cells in 23 other species of primates and 30 non-primate species including representatives of most of the major mammalian orders. Spindle cells probably originated in the common ancestor of humans and great apes about 10–15 million years ago. The spindle cells are thus a unique phylogenetic specialization within the hominoids. Their size scales with relative brain size and their location in layer 5 implies that they relay the processing of the anterior cingulate cortex to other parts of the brain.

Layer 5 of the mid-cingulate cortex also contains a distinctive type of large neuron, the gigantopyramidal cell, described by Braak (1976). These cells are located just posterior to the spindle cell field, buried in the cingulate

Spindle cell   Pyramidal cell

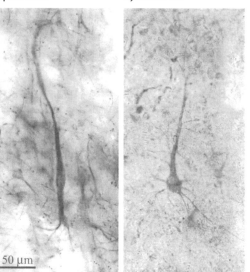

50 μm

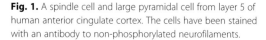

Fig. 1. A spindle cell and large pyramidal cell from layer 5 of human anterior cingulate cortex. The cells have been stained with an antibody to non-phosphorylated neurofilaments.

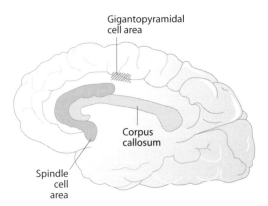

Gigantopyramidal
cell area

Corpus
callosum

Spindle
cell
area

Fig. 2. The location of the cortex containing spindle cells and the gigantopyramidal cells on the medial side of the human brain.

sulcus (see Fig. 2). These cells are motor neurons that control the muscles. Ehrsson, Fagergren, and Forssberg (2001) have studied the cingulate motor area containing the gigantopyramidal neurons in functional magnetic resonance imaging (MRI) experiments. In these experiments, the mid-cingulate motor area is strongly activated when the subject performs the precision grip in which the thumb and index finger grasp an object. Only humans and some monkeys and apes can perform the precision grip, and it is necessary for the fine manipulation of objects. The precision grip produces stronger activation of the mid-cingulate motor cortex than the power grip in which all the fingers wrap around the object to be manipulated. The power grip produces stronger activity in the primary motor cortex. Similarly the mid-cingulate cortex is more strongly activated when the subject makes small, precisely controlled movements, while in the primary motor cortex activity increases with the force exerted by the subject. The mental imagery of hand movements also activates the cingulate motor area. The results imply that the mid-cingulate motor cortex contains phylogenetically specialized circuitry for executing the precise manipulation of objects.

Thus the cingulate cortex contains two phylogenetic specializations characteristic of higher primates. The mid-cingulate motor cortex controls precise, volitional hand movements; the anterior cingulate cortex controls thought and adaptive behaviour. The functions of the anterior cingulate cortex are the analogue of precise manipulation in the realm of thought processes. The anterior cingulate cortex is involved in focused problem solving, the recognition of having committed an error, and the initiation of error-correcting behaviour (see Allman et al. 2001). In a meta-analysis of over 100 functional imaging studies, Paus and his colleagues (1998)

found that the more difficult the cognitive task, the stronger the activation. The dorsal part of the anterior cingulate cortex is strongly activated when subjects sorted out the correct response from conflicting cues (Bush, Luu, and Posner 2000). The anterior cingulate is also activated by a variety of drive states such as hunger and thirst (Liotti et al. 2001) so that it assesses discrepancies between desired states and the current state of an individual and brings about changes in behaviour that will improve the individual's state.

Posner and Rothbart (1998) have proposed that the anterior cingulate cortex is involved in the maturation of self-control as an individual progresses through life from infancy to adulthood. The anterior cingulate cortex is activated when subjects retrieve episodic memories, i.e. when they engage in tasks that require remembering specific events in the past. The capacity to use past experience as a guide as to how to respond to current events in one's life is an important aspect of the process of developing self-control and behavioural maturation. Posner and Rothbart's maturation hypothesis is also supported by the steady increase in the metabolic activity of the anterior cingulate cortex from childhood to young adulthood (Von Bogaert et al. 1998). In the classic condition of lack of self-control, attention-deficit hyperactivity disorder, subjects presented with the conflicting cue task do not exhibit a response in the anterior cingulate cortex, while this task elicits a strong response in normal subjects (Bush et al. 1999). Finally Lane and his colleagues (1997) found increased activation of the anterior cingulate cortex in individuals with greater social insight. The spindle cells, which appear to arise post-natally, may have a role in all of the slowly maturing functions of the anterior cingulate cortex.

The anterior cingulate is strongly implicated in many neurological and psychiatric disorders. The spindle cells degenerate in Alzheimer's disease and may be related to decline in cognitive functioning. The volume and metabolic activity in the dorsal part of the anterior cingulate cortex is reduced in autistic patients (Haznedar et al. 2000). The volume and metabolic activity in the ventral part of the anterior cingulate cortex is reduced in depressed patients (Drevets et al. 1997). The anterior cingulate cortex is activated in obsessive–compulsive disorder (Rauch et al. 1994), a condition characterized by excessive focus on real or imaginary problems.

Just as the gigantopyramidal cells are the output from mid-cingulate motor cortex controlling precise, volitional movements, the spindle cells may relay to other parts of the brain the processing within the anterior cingulate cortex related to focused problem solving and adaptive responses to new conditions. Von Economo (1929) recognized structural similarities between the anterior cingulate cortex and the classic motor cortex including such features as the well-developed layer 5. This analogy might be extended to the functions of these areas. Motor cortical areas control body movements; the anterior cingulate cortex may control thought processes.

AH/JAl

Allman, J. M., Hakeem, A., Erwin, J. M., Nimchinsky, E., and Hof, P. (2001). 'The anterior cingulate cortex: the evolution of an interface between emotion and cognition'. *Annals of the New York Academy of Sciences*, 935.

Braak, H. (1976). 'A primitive gigantopyramidal field buried in the depth of the cingulate sulcus of the human brain'. *Brain Research*, 109.

Bush, G., Luu, P., and Posner, M. (2000). 'Cognitive and emotional influences in anterior cingulate cortex'. *Trends in Cognitive Science*, 4.

——Frazier, J. A., Rauch, S. L., et al. (1999). 'Anterior cingulate cortex dysfunction in attention-deficit/hyperactivity disorder revealed by fMRI and the counting stroop'. *Biological Psychiatry*, 45.

Drevets, W. C., Price, J. L., Thompson, J. R., et al. (1997). 'Subgenual prefrontal cortex abnormalities in mood disorders'. *Nature*, 386.

Ehrsson, H., Fagergren, A., and Forssberg, H. (2001). 'Differential fronto-parietal activation depending of force used in a precision grip task: a fMRI study'. *Journal of Neurophysiology*, 85.

Haznedar, M., Buchsbaum, M., Wei, T.-C., et al. (2000). 'Limbic circuitry in patients with autism spectrum disorders studied with positron emission tomography and magnetic resonance imaging'. *American Journal of Psychiatry*, 157.

Lane, R. D., Reiman, E. M., Axelrod, B., Yun, L. S., Holmes, A., and Schwartz, G. E. (1997). 'Neural correlates of levels of emotional awareness: evidence of an interaction between emotion and attention in the anterior cingulate cortex'. *Journal of Cognitive Neuroscience*, 10.

Lepage, M., Ghaffar, O., Nyberg, L., and Tulving, E. (2000). 'Prefrontal cortex and episodic memory retrieval mode'. *Proceedings of the National Academy of Sciences of the USA*, 97.

Liotti, M., Brannan, S., Egan, G., et al. (2001). 'Brain responses associated with consciousness of breathlessness (air hunger)'. *Proceedings of the National Academy of Sciences of the USA*, 98.

Nimchinsky, E., Gilissen, E., Allman, J. M., Perl, D. P., Erwin, J. M., and Hof, P. R. (1999). 'A neuronal morphologic type unique to humans and great apes'. *Proceedings of the National Academy of Sciences of the USA*, 96.

Paus, T., Koski, L., Caramanos, Z., and Westbury, C. (1998). 'Regional differences in the effects of task difficulty and motor output on blood flow response in the human anterior cingulate cortex: a review of 107 PET activation studies'. *Neuro Report*, 9.

Posner, M., and Rothbart, M. K. (1998). 'Attention, self-regulation and consciousness'. *Philosophical Transactions of the Royal Society, Series B*, 353.

Rauch, S. L., Jenike, M. A., Alpert, N. M., et al. (1994). 'Regional cerebral blood flow measured during symptom provocation in obsessive-compulsive disorder using oxygen 15-labeled carbon dioxide and positron emission tomography'. *Archives of General Psychiatry*, 51.

Van Bogaert, P., Wikler, D., Damhaut, P., Szliwowski, H., and Goldman, S. (1998). 'Regional changes in glucose metabolism during brain development'. *Neuroimage*, 8.

Von Economo, C. (1929). *The Cytoarchitectonics of the Human Cerebral Cortex*.

Spinoza, Benedict (Baruch) de (1632–77). Dutch philosopher, one of the last great metaphysical thinkers of the 'rationalist' period in philosophy. In his major work, *The Ethics*, he starts from supposedly self-evident truths and rigorously develops them through the use of reason and deductive argument. His commitment to the power of reason and to the view that man can gain knowledge of reality through the powers of the mind alone culminates in a profound vision of the world and of man's place within it.

Spinoza was born in Amsterdam of Portuguese Jewish stock. He was educated initially in the Jewish school, but later received Latin lessons from a private tutor, Van Den Ende, who introduced him to the scientific and philosophical developments of the day. Spinoza's growing commitment to secular thought and philosophy brought him into conflict with the Jewish authorities, and in 1656 he was expelled from the synagogue for his 'heretical' views. His Hebrew name, Baruch, he abandoned for its Latin form, Benedictus. The remainder of his life was spent developing his philosophical system while earning a living from polishing and grinding lenses. His reputation as a heretic and atheist did not prevent him carrying on an extensive correspondence with other major thinkers, but only one of his works, the *Theological–Political Treatise*, was published (anonymously) during his lifetime. His other works—*A Short Treatise on God, Man and his Well-Being*, the *Treatise on the Emendation of the Intellect*, *The Ethics*, and the unfinished *Political Treatise*—were collected and published by his friends shortly after his death from consumption.

Spinoza developed his theory of the mind partly in an attempt to solve the problems raised by *Descartes' account of the mind and body as two fundamentally different substances. For Descartes the mind and body are independent and mutually exclusive systems, and it is well known that this strict dualistic theory made it extremely difficult to explain the apparent causal interaction between mental and physical items (see DUALISM).

Spinoza rejected Descartes' dualistic account and replaced it with a theory of 'substance monism'. This may be explained as follows. Substance is that which is self-dependent—needing nothing other than itself in order to exist. So far, both Descartes and Spinoza are in agreement. But where Descartes asserts that there are many such substances (including each finite mind and body), Spinoza argues that there can be only one being which has the character of substance, and this being is

God or nature itself. All finite things, ourselves included, are dependent upon other things for existence. Only God—the being beside whom there *is* nothing else, for he is infinite —has the nature of substance. This being so, all finite things, in particular minds and bodies, are not substances but 'modifications' or 'modes', that is, beings that are manifestations or fragmented expressions of the one reality. Mental and physical items alike have no reality save that which they have as parts of substance.

God or nature (these are synonymous terms for Spinoza) may, however, be viewed in two ways. We may think of the one substance either as a thinking being, or as extended in space. For Descartes, thought and extension constitute the essence of mental and physical substances respectively. In contrast, Spinoza regards thought and extension as two ways of *conceiving* one and the same reality. He is committed not to mental and physical *things* but to things that may be *conceived* in two different ways. He claims that, whether we conceive of God in mental terms or in physical terms, we are thinking of just one being in either case. He then applies this 'conceptual dualism' to all items in the world. Every finite thing or 'mode' can be viewed in two ways, either as mental or as physical. Whatever there is, is fully explicable in either way. But, as in the case of God, there is only one thing that is being described.

When Spinoza came to speak of the human mind and body he said: 'Mind and body are one and the same individual conceived now under the attribute of thought, now under the attribute of extension.' This seems to amount to an identity claim—there is just one thing, which may be viewed and described either as a mind or as a body. This approach to the *mind–body problem has some adherents today. Many accept that a human being can be described in two fundamental ways, attributing to him both psychological and physical properties, while also accepting that there is only one being—the human person—which is being so characterized.

With Spinoza's monistic theory, Descartes' problem—that of explaining causal interaction between disparate items—vanishes, for there are not *two* things at all; the mind and body do not interact, for one thing cannot interact with itself. Anything that occurs in the body can be explained in mental terms and anything that occurs in the mind may be explained and described physically. Spinoza would therefore be sympathetic to those materialist or physicalist philosophers who claim that mental states just *are* physical happenings in the brain. But they would be less happy with Spinoza's reverse claim—that any physical occurrence may be fully explained in mental terms.

Spinoza speaks of the mind as the 'idea' of the body. As such it is aware of the body and of the things that happen to it. When light rays hit the retina of the eye, for example, the physical process may be described in mental terms as an image or sensory idea. But Spinoza thought that such sense perceptions are invariably confused or 'inadequate', because we take them to be the true representations of external objects whereas in reality they are merely reflections of our own bodily processes. (See ILLUSIONS; PERCEPTIONS AS UNCONSCIOUS INFLUENCES; SENSATIONS.)

Spinoza claims that all finite things endeavour or strive to maintain themselves in being and to perfect their existence. Thus the body will try to avoid those things that are harmful to it and will pursue those things that it needs in order to survive. The mind too, in Spinoza's view, exhibits this endeavour (or *conatus*, as he calls it) in its attempt to resist ideas that are inadequate and confused and to grasp those that help it to understand itself, the body, and the external world. Spinoza thinks the mind will be aware that its sense perceptions are inadequate, for they will lack the clarity, distinctness, and self-evident character of all true ideas. This being so, the mind will naturally try to replace sense perceptions with more adequate ideas, through a process of reasoned reflection and the application of self-evident principles. Once this stage is reached the mind is active rather than passive: it pursues and grasps the truth through its innate power of understanding, rather than remaining at the mercy of arbitrary and confused images and sense impressions.

This process of replacing sense impressions with adequate conceptions can also be applied to the emotions. For Spinoza, emotions are merely confused and inadequate ideas which befuddle the mind and which, for the most part, make us extremely unhappy. He thinks that to the extent that we allow our emotions to rule us we are in a state of slavery or bondage: 'When a man is a prey to his emotions, he is not his own master, but lies at the mercy of fortune.' Our emotions can be overcome by replacing the inadequate ideas on which they are grounded with a clear and distinct understanding of their causes. If emotions are confused ideas and if they arise from inadequate understanding, it seems to follow that increased knowledge will change them, and enable us to become free of their power over us. As Spinoza says: 'An emotion therefore becomes more under our control, and the mind is less passive in respect to it, in proportion as it is more known to us.' This account of active self-improvement through the analysis and clarification of ideas has led some commentators to greet Spinoza as an early precursor of Freudian psychoanalysis.

For Spinoza, the mastery of emotions, and the state of improved understanding achieved through the mind's reasoning powers, enables us to become more active and free. But the freedom which Spinoza grants us has seemed to some to be no freedom at all. When the mind understands things adequately it perceives them as necessary, and sees that they could not have been otherwise. Reason, Spinoza tells us, perceives things 'under a certain form of eternity', and we then see that nothing could have been different, because everything results from God, who himself is a necessary and eternal being.

Our freedom consists in recognizing the necessity of our nature, understanding ourselves as expressions and manifestations of God's power and laws, and as having no existence save that which he grants us. Viewed rightly, we see ourselves and all things as in a sense eternal, for we no longer judge things as contingent happenings in time, but as determined by immutable laws. This understanding, which Spinoza calls 'intuition', constitutes the mind's highest achievement and its complete fulfilment. Knowing itself and other things in this manner, the mind achieves a certain immortality, and with true contentment realizes that death, which is a mere temporal event, cannot destroy it.

Spinoza thus ends his *Ethics* on a note of almost religious fervour which has encouraged some in the view that he was a mystic. Although his philosophy has influenced many, and has been hailed by idealists, materialists, atheists, and theists alike, his vision is perhaps most pertinent today to all those who wish to find a place for spiritual fulfilment in a world governed by natural laws.

A translation by R. H. M. Elwes, *Basic Works*, was published in two volumes in New York in 1955, and *The Correspondence of Spinoza*, trans. A. Wolf, appeared also in New York in 1966.   JN

Hampshire, S. (1951). *Spinoza*.
Scruton, R. (1986). *Spinoza*.

spiritualism. Belief in a world of spirits has been a constant feature of all human societies. However, systematic communication with that world through spirit mediumship and possession is a central feature only of certain peripheral cults in primitive societies, and of spiritualism in the Western world since the middle of the 19th century. In preliterate societies, spirit possession cults have been described as deprivation cults, attracting women and other downtrodden and depressed categories of person (Lewis 1971). Through membership of the cult, a measure of lost status and esteem may be regained. In Western society communication with the spirits of the departed has been spasmodic. The voice of God, and intimations of divine presence, though central to the tradition of Christian mysticism, fall outside the province of strictly spiritualist experience.

As an organized movement, spiritualism has a quite precise time and place of origin. Historians of spiritualism trace its beginnings to March 1848, when unaccountable noises were heard by two young sisters in an isolated farmhouse in New York State. The rappings were attributed to the spirit of a travelling salesman murdered there

some years earlier, and were interpreted as his attempts to establish communication with the living. Whatever the significance of the original rappings, within two years of their being heard the Fox sisters and their mother had established themselves as successful mediums with huge followings in New York City. Spiritualist circles and seances mushroomed along the east coast of America, and thence spread in two directions: westwards across the American continent and eastwards across the Atlantic to Europe.

The most striking characteristic of early spiritualist experience is precisely its non-religious quality: messages from spirits are peculiar for their concreteness, triviality, and a certain mundane bizarreness. Conan Doyle, a historian of spiritualism, and himself a spiritualist, was sensitive to the bad impression which such trivial preoccupations might create. He therefore reminded his readers that the first message transmitted by cable across the Atlantic was a commonplace enquiry from a testing engineer. 'So it is that the humble spirit of the murdered pedlar of Hydesville may have opened a gap into which the angels have thronged' (1926: 56).

The movement which developed was quite remarkable in a number of ways. First, it accorded a very special role to women in that mediumship was thought to be primarily, though not exclusively, a feminine art. Secondly, it involved a startling array of events such as *levitations, ectoplasmic apparitions, telekinesis, and apports. Thirdly, it led to an alliance between spiritualists and scientists which is unique in the history of religion. While feminine stereotypes have always attributed greater intuitive and mystical powers to women (as they saw it at the time), their alleged passivity, lack of high intelligence, and lack of education made them seem peculiarly fitted to become mediums. In this connection Conan Doyle wrote: 'Great intellect stands in the way of personal psychic experiences. The clear state is certainly most apt for the writing of a message' (1926: 2). This congruity between stereotypes of femininity and the requirements of mediumship opened up career opportunities for women. The circles or seances were frequently held in the houses of mediums. However, in addition to the domestic setting the concerns of spiritualist messages were also of an intimately domestic and familial kind. The intrusion of scientists into this scene of cosy domesticity seems an unlikely event. The Society for Psychical Research was founded in February 1882 in order to make 'an organized and systematic attempt to investigate that large group of debatable phenomena designated by such terms as mesmeric, psychical and Spiritualistic'. Members of the society included philosophers, scientists, and politicians. Among the famous names are Henry Sidgwick, Lord Balfour, William *James, Sir William Crookes, Andrew Lang, Henri *Bergson, Gilbert Murray, and William *McDougall. Although both science and religion are concerned with the ultimate nature of reality, only in the case of spiritualism were scientific criteria thought to be relevant for the establishment of religious truth and falsehood. This overlap of interests and techniques is perhaps to be accounted for by, on the one hand, the concreteness of spiritualist claims and, on the other hand, the direction of much scientific research during the 1880s, which was concerned with radiation physics.

In contrast to the respectable scientific solidity of the psychical researcher, the mediums tended to be young, vulnerable, beautiful, and possessed of a certain childlike naivety. The relationship between Sir William Crookes and Florence Cook is in many ways typical of the relationship between scientist and medium. Florence Cook's spirit guide was an ectoplasmic apparition called Katie King. It was claimed that this materialization could move and talk quite independently of Florence. However, in 1874 the medium's reputation was dramatically threatened by allegations of fraud and trickery. Florence Cook decided to throw herself on the mercy of Sir William, who was known to have an interest in psychical research, having investigated the Scottish medium Daniel Dunglas Home. The move proved highly prudent since Sir William wasted no time in jumping to Florence Cook's defence. The precondition of his investigating her gifts was that he should remove her from her parents' house to his own, in the north of London. From the very outset he felt it his duty to defend Florence, particularly if he could remove 'an unjust suspicion which is cast upon another. And when this other person is a woman—young, sensitive and innocent—it becomes especially a duty for me to give the weight of my testimony in favour of her whom I believe to be unjustly accused' (quoted in Hall 1962: 35). Hall puts forward the hypothesis that Sir William and Florence became lovers and that he extended scientific respectability to her in return for sexual love. Hall's interpretation appears to be highly plausible but, even if he were proved to be wrong in detail, the alliance is illuminating from a sociological perspective. Whereas most religious roles for women provide an exalted status and liberation for women at the cost of rejecting traditional femininity, spiritual mediumship capitalizes on existing relationships and transfers them to a spiritual plane. Spiritualism enthrones women in their traditional roles and relationships.

Although there have been many charges of fraud and counter-fraud, spiritualist belief has by and large remained impervious to such exposures. The late 19th century was the high point of dramatic apparitions and events. The First World War with its large numbers of bereaved provided yet another peak in the growth of the spiritualist movement. Thereafter, spiritualism gradually reverted to its earlier unassuming concerns. Essentially a domestic religion, it provides women with the opportunity of a religious life without transgressing the norms of traditional femininity. It also provides that much sought-after kind of work, work based at home—and the spiritual attention of circles is directed towards problems associated with marriage, family, and illness.

See also PARANORMAL. VS

Doyle, A. C. (1926). *The History of Spiritualism.*
Hall, T. (1962). *The Spiritualists.*
Lewis, I. (1971). *Ecstatic Religion.*
Nelson, G. K. (1969). *Spiritualism and Society.*
Skultans, V. (1974). *Intimacy and Ritual: A Study of Spiritualism, Mediums and Groups.*

split-brain and the mind. Ever since nerve conduction was understood it has been speculated that the great interhemispheric bridge, the corpus callosum (meaning 'thick-skinned body'), is essential for mental unity (Fig. 1). When it and other smaller interhemispheric connections are cut, communication between the two sides must pass by the stem of the brain, which is normally considered unconscious, or through external relations of the body with the world of stimuli and the effects of actions.

Psychologists, including G. T. *Fechner and William *McDougall, have wondered what would happen to *consciousness if the brain were divided in this way. McDougall, it is said, even tried to persuade the physiologist C. S. *Sherrington to undertake to divide his, McDougall's, corpus callosum if he became incurably ill. Nerve connectionists tended to think conscious experience would be destroyed or divided, but McDougall, a mentalist, believed consciousness would remain unified. It was frustrating that, for a long time, studies of animals, and a few human cases, with corpus callosum sectioned gave no interesting evidence. Consciousness appeared to be slightly depressed and there were transitory lapses in voluntary coordination, but that was all. In irony, Karl *Lashley suggested that the corpus callosum might serve simply to hold the hemispheres together. Warren *McCulloch said its only known function was to spread *epilepsy.

Cerebral commissurotomy, the split-brain operation, has been performed with varying completeness on a small number of human beings since the mid-1940s, always in hopes of checking crippling epilepsy, to stop the non-functional neural discharges reverberating between the hemispheres and severely damaging the cortical tissues. The breakthrough in estimation of the mental effects of this operation came from investigations in Roger Sperry's laboratory at the California Institute of Technology, following the first effective experiments on the consequences of commissurotomy in cats and monkeys. The animal studies had established new methods. They revealed simple explanations for why all previous research had observed only trivial and uninformative consequences

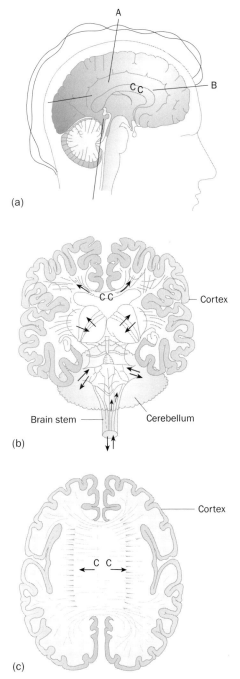

(a)

(b)

Brain stem   Cerebellum

Cortex

C C

(c)

Cortex

Fig. 1. The corpus callosum (CC) is the principal integrator of mental processes which are carried out differently in the two halves of the cortex. It complements connections through the brain stem.

of so great a change in brain structure. With control for orienting, and of information exchange between the hemispheres through transactions with the external world, the split-brain animals were found to have totally divided perception and learning. When free, their movements, alertness, and general motivation were entirely normal.

In Los Angeles, the neurosurgeons Philip Vogel and Joseph Bogen concluded that selected epileptic patients would benefit from the surgery and suffer no serious mental loss. Between 1962 and 1968, nine complete operations were performed with success in reducing fits. Psychological tests performed by Michael Gazzaniga, Sperry, and Bogen at the California Institute soon revealed that, while the general psychological state and behaviour was, in most cases, little affected, there was a profound change in mental activities. Other studies with commissurotomy patients carried out since, in the USA, France, and Australia, have produced similar findings.

For the commissurotomy subject (Fig. 2), direct awareness is no longer whole. An object felt in the left hand out of sight cannot be matched to the same kind of object felt separately and unseen in the right hand. As long as the eyes are stationary, something seen just to the left of the fixation point cannot be compared to something seen on the right side. Comparable divisions in olfactory and auditory awareness may be demonstrated. Furthermore, although sight and touch communicate normally on each side, left visual field to left hand or right visual field to right hand, the crossed two-hemisphere combinations fail, as if experiences of eye and hand were obtained by separate persons. There is no evidence that perceptual information needed to identify an object can cross the midline of the visual field, or between the hands, to unify the patient's awareness. While the division of sight for detail is extremely sharp at the centre of the field, as long as the patient keeps his eyes still, with freedom to look to left and right and to see in both halves of vision what both hands are holding, the division of awareness ceases to be apparent. Indeed, the subject himself seems unaware of anything amiss, except when evidence is presented to him of an inconsistency in his conscious judgement. Then it would appear he feels some lapse of concentration, or absent-mindedness.

With stimuli on arms, legs, face, or trunk, there is some transfer of feeling between the sides. These less discriminatory parts of the body are represented in duplicate, with both sides in each hemisphere of the brain, and their functions, sensory and motor, are cross-integrated at levels of the brain below the hemispheres. Interesting results have been obtained with large, long-lasting stimuli moving in the periphery of vision. Seeing the spatial layout in surroundings at large, called 'ambient vision', is vital in steering on a confined or irregular route or in a

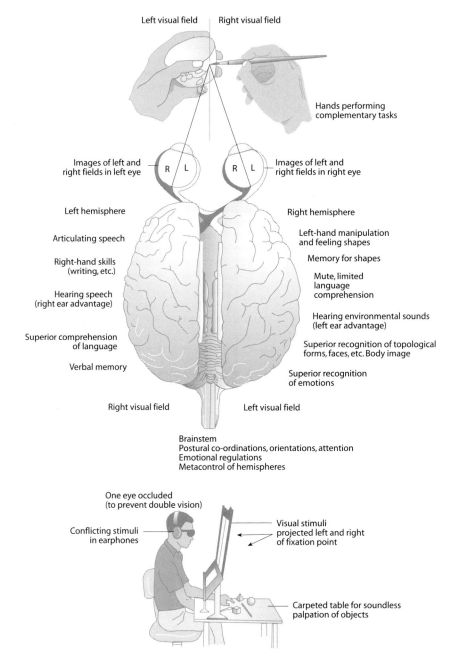

Left visual field | Right visual field

Hands performing
complementary tasks

Images of left and
right fields in left eye

R / L   R \ L

Images of left and
right fields in right eye

Left hemisphere

Right hemisphere

Articulating speech

Left-hand manipulation
and feeling shapes

Right-hand skills
(writing, etc.)

Memory for shapes

Mute, limited
language
comprehension

Hearing speech
(right ear advantage)

Hearing environmental sounds
(left ear advantage)

Superior comprehension
of language

Superior recognition of topological
forms, faces, etc. Body image

Verbal memory

Superior recognition
of emotions

Right visual field

Left visual field

Brainstem
Postural co-ordinations, orientations, attention
Emotional regulations
Metacontrol of hemispheres

One eye occluded
(to prevent double vision)

Conflicting stimuli
in earphones

Visual stimuli
projected left and right
of fixation point

Carpeted table for soundless
palpation of objects

Fig. 2. Commissurotomy, division of the corpus callosum to relieve epilepsy, causes separate awarenesses in left and right halves of the visual field and for objects in left and right hand. Integrations through the brain stem keep the behaviour of the person coherent, but do not permit unification of consciousness. Testing a split-brain patient involves control of orienting movements, with one eye covered and stimuli flashed for $\frac{1}{10}$th second on a screen, or objects felt out of sight on a carpet so no tell-tale sounds are fed back to the subject's ears. Using conflicting auditory stimuli in earphones, division of hearing may be demonstrated.

cluttered environment, and even in maintaining the balance of standing or walking. It also functions to give approximate location to off-centre targets of attention before the eyes move to fixate. Evidently the semi-conscious appreciation of the location and orientation of major features in outside space, mainly picked up from dynamic transformations of the visual image, is not divided by commissurotomy. Indeed, the general background or context of body coordination and orienting must be intact for commissurotomy subjects to retain the freedom of action and coherence of awareness they ordinarily exhibit. To this degree the operation does not divide the agency of the subject, or the experience of whole-body action. The two halves of the neocortex are kept in functional relationship, coordinated through ascending and descending links with the sub-hemispheric regions of the brain stem (see Fig. 1).

By far the most dramatic finding of the early tests was the total failure of the right cerebral cortex on its own to express itself in speech. It could not utter words to explain its awareness or knowledge. In contrast, when stimuli were given to the left cortex the subject could say perfectly normally what the experience had been like. Objects were named, compared, and described, and the occurrence or non-occurrence of stimulus events was correctly reported. Yet similar tests of the right half of the brain, with stimuli in the left visual field or left hand, totally failed. The subjects often gave no response. If urged to reply, they said that there might have been some weak and ill-defined event, or else they confabulated experiences, as if unable to apply a test of truth or falsity to spontaneously imagined answers to questions.

These events not only confirm a division of awareness, but they raise important questions which have been debated in clinical neurology since the discovery, over a century ago, that muteness or disturbance of language comprehension can result from brain injury confined to the left hemisphere. Could the right hemisphere comprehend spoken or written language at all? Could it express itself to any degree in signs, by writing, or by gesture? Could it make any utterance? Could it reason and think? Was it really conscious? The commissurotomy patients offered a wonderfully direct approach to these questions, and ingenious experiments were designed by Sperry and his students Jerre Levy, Robert Nebes, Harold Gordon, and Dahlia and Eran Zaidel to interrogate the unspeaking right hemisphere.

Some comprehension of spoken and written language was certainly present in the mute side of the brain. Information about how the right hemisphere should perform a test could be conveyed by telling it what to do, and if the name of a common object was projected to the right cortex only, the patient could retrieve a correct example by hand, or identify a picture of it by pointing. The right

hemisphere could solve very simple arithmetic problems, giving its answer by arranging plastic digits out of sight with the left hand. Nevertheless, it was clear that both the vocabulary as understood and the powers of calculation of the right hemisphere were distinctly inferior to these abilities in the left hemisphere of the same patient. Rarely, a patient was able to start an utterance or begin to write a word with the right hemisphere, but, in these tests, the vigilance of the more competent left hemisphere blocked all such initiatives after the first syllable or letter. In general only the left hemisphere could speak, write, or calculate.

When Levy applied non-verbal *intelligence tests, the results indicated that there were some functions for which the left hemisphere did not dominate: for some modes of thinking the right hemisphere was superior. All these right brain tasks involved visual or touch perception of difficult configurations, judgements involving exploration of shapes by hand, or manipulative construction of geometric assemblies or patterns. It appeared that the right hemisphere was able to notice the shape of things more completely than the left. Taken with evidence that systematic calculation and forming logical propositions with words were better performed by the left hemisphere, these results favoured the idea that the right hemisphere is better at taking in the structure of things synthetically, without analysis, assimilating all components at once in an ensemble, figure, or *Gestalt. Nebes discovered that the right hemisphere may have a clearer memory of the appearance of things, in the sense that it was better able to recognize familiar objects with incomplete pictorial data, and better able to perceive whole shapes from parts seen or felt in the hand.

The way hands are normally used hints at differences in awareness of the hemispheres. (See HANDEDNESS.) In normal manipulation, a right-hander supports and orients an object in the grasp of the left hand, to facilitate discrete moves of the right fingers that are more finely controlled. Consider such a simple act as taking the last drop of soup from a bowl with a spoon. To grasp, support, and orient objects, the left hand must 'understand' the dimensions and distribution of matter in an object, and usually this kind of judgement does not need visual inspection. In contrast, the discrete and precise acts of the right hand require a succession of decisions that are aimed or guided by a sequence of brief visual fixations. Writing is a cultivated skill that uses the right-hand endowment for rapid repeated cycles of action in the service of language. It may be a learned adaptation of the brain mechanism for gestural communication, the right hand of most persons being dominant for expressive gesticulation. In many tests, the left hand of the commissurotomy patients was more efficient than the right at feeling shapes that resist analysis into highly familiar elements. The left hand palpated complex raised patterns as wholes, as if sensing shape directly. In contrast, the right hand tended to feel the contours, corners, etc. one by one, as if trying to build up an inventory of discrete experiences along a line in time. Recently, experiments with the same subjects have demonstrated that the right hemisphere tends to be superior at metaphorical rather than literal perceptions, and that it perceives the emotions or moods in facial expressions or vocalizations better than the left.

To explore further the processes that direct awareness in the hemispheres, Levy, Trevarthen, and Sperry (1972) gave split-brain subjects a free choice of which hemisphere to use to control responses in tests. Halves of two different pictures were joined together down the vertical midline to make a double picture called a stimulus chimera. When this is presented to the split-brain patient with the join on the fixation point, information about each half is received in a different hemisphere. The tasks are designed so that in every trial the correct choice may be obtained by using the experience of either the left or right hemisphere. Preference for one half of the chimera depends on one-sided mental strategies that arise in response to the test instructions. With this kind of test, preferred modes of understanding of the hemispheres can be sensitively determined, as well as the cerebral functions that allocate attention between the two hemispheres. (See Fig. 3.)

The choices of the commissurotomy patients with chimeric stimuli confirm that thought in words favours the left hemisphere. Single words can be read by the right hemisphere, but the left is always preferred if the meaning of the words must be understood and not just their visual appearance or pattern. Further tests show that the right hemisphere is virtually unable to imagine the sound of a word for an object seen, even a very common one like an 'eye', so it cannot solve a test requiring silent rhyming 'in the head' (for example, 'eye' matches 'pie', 'key' matches 'bee'). It seems as if the habitual, and inherently favoured, dominance of the left hemisphere for speaking is tied in with a one-sided ability to predict how words will sound. The right hemisphere can know the meaning of a word from its sound, but it cannot make a sound image for itself from sight of the word, or from sight of the object the word stands for.

Preference for the right hemisphere in matching things by their appearance becomes strong when meaningless or unanalysable shapes are used, especially if these are not representing familiar objects, with a simple name. An extraordinary superiority of the right hemisphere for knowing a face, especially when it lacks bold distinctive features such as glasses, moustache, hat, or birthmark, relates to a rare consequence of damage to the posterior part of this hemisphere. This inability to recognize even the most familiar faces, called prosopagnosia, can greatly embarrass social life. With split-brain persons and stimuli restricted to the left hemisphere, face recognition is poor and identification is achieved by a laborious checklist of distinctive semantic elements to be memorized and searched for. There is obviously a stark contrast in hemisphere cognitive style, reminiscent of differences described in the way the two hands go about knowing or using objects. In addition to these apparently fixed differences in the organization of hemispheric cognitive structures, commissurotomy patients show a varying activation of the hemispheres under brain-stem control that can favour one or other side independently of task requirements. Sometimes the 'wrong' hemisphere is active in doing a task, and performance suffers. This 'meta-control' may cause differences in the way normal individuals process cognitive problems; i.e. it may determine differences in mental abilities—for example, making one person skilled at visuoconstructive tasks while another is gifted at verbal rationalizations.

Eran Zaidel has developed a method for blocking off half of the visual field of one eye of a commissurotomy patient. He attaches to the eye a contact lens which carries a small optical system and a screen. The patient can cast his eye over a test array in a normal way while picking up visual information by only one hemisphere. The subject has to interpret a story or picture or solve puzzles, many involving choice of the one picture from a group that will identify a concept to which he or she has been cued by a preceding stimulus. These tests prove that both hemispheres have elaborate awareness of the meanings of words and pictures. Metaphorical relationships form an important component of consciousness of meaning in both of them. Objects may be linked in awareness by their abstract properties or customary usefulness and social importance as well as by more obvious features. The usual names, colours, temperatures, and many other properties of things may be correctly identified when each thing is represented by a simple black and white picture. The tests of Zaidel and Sperry have shown that both hemispheres of commissurotomy patients have awareness of themselves as persons and a strong sense of the social and political value, or meaning, of pictures or objects.

Comprehension of words, spoken or written, is surprisingly rich in the right hemisphere, and all grammatical classes of words may be comprehended, but its consciousness does fail with relatively difficult, abstract, or rare words. When words are combined in a proposition, the comprehension of the right hemisphere falls drastically. When simplified items of no particular identity, such as plastic chips of differing size, form, and colour, are used as tokens for arbitrary grouping defined by short descriptions (for example, 'Point to a small red circle and a large yellow triangle'), this too proves difficult for the

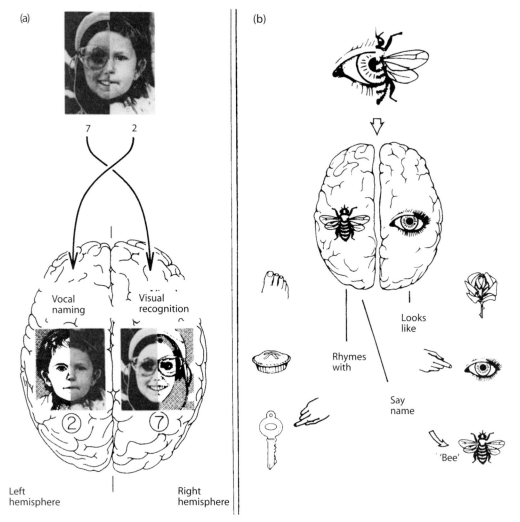

Fig. 3. a. Stimulus chimeras, joining left and right halves of different pictures, permit study of preferences in cognitive processes of the hemispheres. The stimuli are flashed in the precise centre of the visual field in a tachistoscope. If asked to say what was seen, the split-brain subject identifies the right half of the chimera, signifying preferential use of the left hemisphere. If pointing to match the picture that looks most like the stimulus, the left half is selected, indicating that the right hemisphere assumes control of this response.
b. By varying instructions one can obtain three different kinds of response from one stimulus. Saying the name or pointing silently to a picture of an object with a name that rhymes with that of the stimulus causes the left hemisphere to take charge. Visual matching engages the right hemisphere.
Note that in both these diagrams, the awareness of a half stimulus is shown as completed. Indeed experiments indicate that the subject imagines freely over the mid-line, presumably because there is no information at variance with imagined parts in the hemisphere doing the imagining.

right hemisphere. A token test of this description was discovered by the Italian neuropsychologists Di Renzi and Vignolo to be extremely sensitive to left-hemisphere lesions. The linguistic abilities of the right hemisphere thus resemble those of a nursery-school child who understands language best when it is fitted into the world of objects, interpersonal acts, and events, all of which sustain the meaning of what is said. Disembedded or context-free propositions lacking interpersonal force require concentration of the mind on categories, critical formulae, or rules for action. These processes of thought may be developed by transformation of inherent human skills for establishing precise identity or harmony of purpose between thinking agents. Such propositions are difficult alike for young children and the disconnected right hemisphere of an adult.

Commissurotomy patients have helped us understand how consciousness, intention, and feelings are generated in activity at different levels of the brain. Thus separated cortices may experience and learn separately, but each may command coherent activity of the whole body. Feelings of dismay, embarrassment, or amusement, generated in one hemisphere by perceptions of threat, or risk, or teasing, invade the brain stem to cause expressions and *emotions of the whole person, in spite of the operation. Levels of attentiveness and the shifting aim of orientation and purpose are also patterned within brain-stem regions, which can transmit no detailed evidence of experience. The precautions needed to reveal divided awareness after brain bisection emphasize how, in normal active life, information about the world is constantly reflected to all parts of the brain as it and the body engage in changing relations with the external world. It does not appear necessary to imagine that the 'self', which has to maintain a unity, is destroyed when the forebrain commissures are cut, although some of its activities and memories are depleted after the operation.   CT

Levy, J., and Trevarthen, C. (1976). 'Metacontrol of hemispheric function in human split-brain patients'. *Journal of Experimental Psychology: Human Perception and Performance*, 2.

——— and Sperry, R. W. (1972). 'Perception of bilateral chimeric figures following hemispheric deconnexion'. *Brain*, 95.

Sperry, R. W. (1970). 'Perception in absence of the neocortical commissures'. *Research Publications of the Association for Nervous and Mental Diseases*, 48.

——(1974). 'Lateral specialization in the surgically separated hemisphere'. In Schmitt, F. O., and Warden, F. G. (eds.), *The Neurosciences: Third Study Program*.

——(1977). 'Forebrain commissurotomy and conscious awareness'. *Journal of Medicine and Philosophy*, 2.

——Gazzaniga, M. S., and Bogen, J. E. (1969). 'Interhemispheric relations: the neocortical commissures; syndromes of hemispheric disconnection'. In Vinken, P. J., and Bruyn, G. W. (eds.), *Handbook of Clinical Neurology*, vol. iv.

Trevarthen, C. (1974). 'Analysis of cerebral activities that generate and regulate consciousness in commissurotomy patients'. In Dimond, S. J., and Beaumont, J. G. (eds.), *Hemisphere Function in the Human Brain*.

——(1984). 'Hemispheric specialization'. In Darian-Smith, I. (ed.), *Handbook of Physiology*, section I: *The Nervous System*, vol. iii: *Sensory Processes*.

Zangwill, O. L. (1974). 'Consciousness and the cerebral hemispheres'. In Dimond, S. J., and Beaumont, J. G. (eds.), *Hemisphere Function in the Human Brain*.

squint (strabismus). See DIPLOPIA.

stereoscopic vision. 'Stereopsis' (originally) means solid sight and refers to the multitude of sources of information that may be used to determine the structure and layout of the three-dimensional world. Binocular stereopsis refers specifically to the information available from having two eyes (Howard and Rogers 1995). Traditionally, three-dimensional vision has been regarded as a difficult problem for any biological or machine vision system because it is claimed that three-dimensional information is 'lost' in a two-dimensional retinal or camera image (Rock 1984). This view is misleading. A consideration of the geometry shows that there is no information about the depth or distance of an array of infinitely small points in space in the pattern of light reaching a single viewing position (or vantage point). In 1709, the philosopher *Berkeley wrote: 'I think it is agreed by all that distance of itself, and immediately, cannot be seen.' However, the world we live in consists of extended surfaces and it can be shown that these provide three-dimensional information even when there is only a single vantage point. Traditionally, these sources of information have been referred to as painters' 'cues' (such as perspective, interposition, or shading), because they correspond to the techniques that artists have used to represent depth in a two-dimensional painting (Helmholtz 1909). It is important to note that the word 'cue' (a hint or prompt) has the connotation of uncertainty or ambiguity which is consistent with the idea of three-dimensional vision being problematic. Whilst it is true that there are many demonstrations such as the Ames room and Ittelson and Kilpatrick's playing cards (Gregory 1997) which purport to show the unreliability of the pictorial cues, it is important to distinguish between (*a*) the nature and availability of the three-dimensional information (the computational theory of three-dimensional vision) and (*b*) the characteristics of the mechanisms used to extract that information. The unreliability or ambiguity of any particular 'cue' may be due to the intrinsic unreliability of the information or the characteristics of the particular visual system.

The computational theory of perspective, for example, refers to the geometric fact that the angular size of an object or feature varies inversely with the viewing distance—

doubling the viewing distance halves the angular size. It follows that any surface composed of similar-sized texture elements will create a gradient of angular (or image) size—a texture gradient—that provides information about the surface's orientation to the line of sight. Similarly, the amount of light reflected off any matt surface depends on its orientation with respect to the light source and so the spatial changes in light reflected off any surface will depend on the three-dimensional shape of the surface. In both these examples, the information is based on the physics of the situation, just as the particular spectral wavelengths reflected off a surface depend on the physical reflectance characteristics (colour) of the surface. In order to use texture gradient or shading information we have to make certain *assumptions* about the nature of the world, such as the approximate homogeneity of size of the texture elements or the reflectance uniformity of the surface, but as long as these assumptions are overwhelmingly true for the particular world we live in, texture gradients and shading should be regarded as sources of information rather than mere 'cues'.

Accordingly, the Ames room and Ittelson and Kilpatrick's playing card demonstrations can be interpreted as showing that what we perceive is entirely *consistent* with the perspective or interposition information provided, rather than illustrating the poverty of the 'cues'. The fact that the Ames room is actually trapezoidal or Ittelson and Kilpatrick's playing cards are actually arranged in reversed depth order is quite irrelevant (though they show the importance of object assumptions, which here are incorrect, for these strange objects). If the pattern of light—the optic array—reaching the eye from the Ames room peephole is *identical* to that which would be created by a normal rectangular room, then no visual system could ever distinguish between the two and hence this

tell us nothing about the characteristics of our perceptual systems.

So far, we have considered just two of the many sources of three-dimensional information available at a single vantage point. If the visual world can be sampled from two or more vantage points, new sources of information become available. First, simple geometry shows that the *differences* between the optic arrays created at two spatially separated vantage points provide complete information about the structure of the three-dimensional world (Koenderink and van Doorn 1976). In other words, there is three-dimensional information in the small differences or disparities between the two retinal images that we refer to as binocular stereopsis or binocular parallax. In theory, binocular disparities could provide us with complete information about both the local three-dimensional structure (depth) and the absolute distance to objects in the scene. However, because we are able to converge our eyes onto a particular object (which may be at any distance away from us) so that its image falls on corresponding points in the two retinas, binocular disparities only provide information about the local depth structure, in the absence of information about the convergence distance.

Second, geometry also shows that there is three-dimensional information in the *changing* optic array when the vantage point is moved, which we refer to as motion parallax (Koenderink and van Doorn 1975). Rogers and Graham (1979) provided a convincing demonstration that the human visual system is able to use motion parallax information. The invention of the stereoscope (Fig. 1) by Charles Wheatstone in 1838 provided the first evidence that the human visual system is capable of using the disparities between the two retinal images to judge the three-dimensional structure of objects and scenes. The formal similarity between the information available

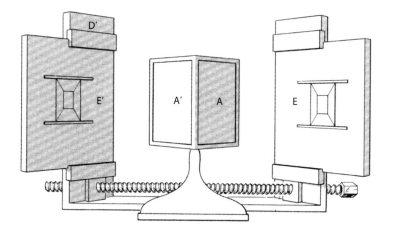

Fig. 1. Diagram of Wheatstone's stereoscopic apparatus. Two mirrors at A',A reflect the drawings at E',E and produce a 'solid' image when viewed simultaneously from very close range. (From *The Stereoscope*, by Sir David Brewster (1856).)

 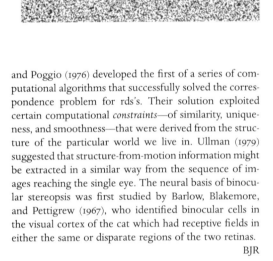

Fig. 2.

from two *simultaneous* retinal images (binocular stereopsis), on the one hand, and the *succession* of retinal images over time (motion parallax), on the other, is reflected in the similarity of our perceptions in the two cases (Rogers and Graham 1979: 82). It could be that the more recently evolved mechanisms of binocular parallax (that depend on the development of forward-facing eyes) utilize similar tricks and strategies to the more ancient mechanisms of motion parallax.

In order to investigate the characteristics and limitations of human binocular stereopsis, it is useful to be able to isolate and manipulate binocular disparities independently of other sources of three-dimensional information. Bela Julesz's invention of random dot stereograms (rds's) in 1959 provided this tool. By using two arrays of random black-and-white dots presented separately to the two eyes, the shape or form of any depicted three-dimensional surface is effectively camouflaged and not visible in either eye's view alone (Fig. 2). Using this technique, Julesz showed conclusively that binocular disparities alone are sufficient to produce a vivid and unambiguous impression of three-dimensional structure and layout. Random dot stereograms were used by Tyler (1974) and Rogers and Graham (1982) to characterize the sensitivity of the human visual system to spatial changes of disparity.

In 1971, Julesz pointed out that the visual system needs to 'know' which features in one eye match with the corresponding features in the other eye's view in order to extract binocular disparities. For a random dot stereogram composed of thousands of identical black-and-white dots, this is not a trivial task and Julesz referred to this as the 'correspondence problem'. To solve the problem, *Marr and Poggio (1976) developed the first of a series of computational algorithms that successfully solved the correspondence problem for rds's. Their solution exploited certain computational *constraints*—of similarity, uniqueness, and smoothness—that were derived from the structure of the particular world we live in. Ullman (1979) suggested that structure-from-motion information might be extracted in a similar way from the sequence of images reaching the single eye. The neural basis of binocular stereopsis was first studied by Barlow, Blakemore, and Pettigrew (1967), who identified binocular cells in the visual cortex of the cat which had receptive fields in either the same or disparate regions of the two retinas.

BJR

Barlow, H. B., Blakemore, C., and Pettigrew, J. D. (1967). 'The neural mechanism of binocular depth discrimination'. *Journal of Physiology*, 193.

Berkeley, G. (1709). *An Essay Towards a New Theory of Vision*. (repr. 1922).

Gregory, R. L. (1997) *Eye and Brain* (5th edn.).

Helmholtz, H. von. (1909). *Physiological Optics*. (Eng. trans. J. P. C. Southall, 1962).

Howard, I. P., and Rogers B.J. (1995). *Binocular Vision and Stereopsis*.

Julesz, B. (1971). *Foundations of Cyclopean Perception*.

Koenderink, J. J., and van Doorn, A. J. (1975). 'Invariant properties of the motion parallax field due to movement of rigid bodies relative to an observer'. *Optica Acta*, 22.

———— (1976). 'Geometry of binocular vision and a model for stereopsis'. *Biological Cybernetics*, 21.

Marr, D., and Poggio, T, (1976). 'Cooperative computation of stereo disparity'. *Science*, 194.

Rock, I. (1984). *Perception*.

Rogers, B. J., and Graham, M. E. (1979). 'Motion parallax as an independent cue for depth perception'. *Perception*, 8.

———— (1982). 'Similarities between motion parallax and stereopsis in human depth perception'. *Vision Research*, 22.

Tyler, C. W. (1974). 'Depth perception in disparity gratings'. *Nature*, 251.

Ullman, S. (1979). *The Interpretation of Visual Motion*.

Stevens, Stanley Smith (1906–73). American psychologist, professor of psychophysics at Harvard University, where he spent all his professional career. He is known, above all else, for the power law which relates physical stimulus magnitudes to the numbers assigned to them in magnitude estimation experiments. During the last twenty years of his life he and his many collaborators replicated this experimental result many times over with more than 30 different stimulus attributes. The same power relation applies when stimulus magnitudes are adjusted to match a given number and to match the magnitude of some other attribute (e.g. matching loudness to brightness). Stevens regarded the numbers uttered by his subjects as direct estimates of the magnitude of the sensation experienced, though this has always been a controversial issue (for technical considerations, see QUANTIFYING JUDGEMENTS).

During the Second World War, Stevens was engaged in studying the effects of intense noise in military aircraft, being then director of the psychoacoustic laboratory at Harvard. About that time he conceived his neural quantum theory, the idea that sensory discrimination is limited by the discrete nature of neural conduction. He also edited the 1,400-page compilation *Handbook of Experimental Psychology*, which appeared in 1951. But his most enduring contribution to science will probably prove to be his early work on measurement. The names he proposed for different kinds of measurement—'nominal', 'ordinal', 'interval', and 'ratio'—have become so universally used that few people are now aware of their origin.

See PSYCHOPHYSICS.   DRJL

Stevens, S. S. (1975). *Psychophysics*. (A posthumous summary of Stevens's work.)

stimulus. Stimuli are patterns of energy received by the senses; they evoke behaviour and are the basis of *perception. Even so, they may not be noticed or experienced, or they may be only part of what we experience and accept as signals or data for behaviour and perception. In particular, *retinal images may be thought of as patterns of energy from the external world, but we do not see them. We see objects, partly as the result of signals from these optical stimuli and partly from our knowledge of what objects are like.

The role of stimuli is rather differently described in various biological and psychological accounts. 'Stimulus–response' theories for behaviour emphasize the importance of received stimuli rather than internal processes—a line of argument most radically worked out in behaviourism (see CONDITIONING). Such an approach, perhaps, had its initial plausibility as a psychological theory from observations of highly predictable tropisms (responses to or away from light, chemical concentrations, etc.) found in many lower organisms. The German-born American physiologist Jacques *Loeb (1859–1924) explained the 'forced movements' in simple animals in terms of the 'tonus hypothesis', namely that the muscular tone on each side of the body is affected by the relative intensity of signals from paired sense organs, especially the eyes, the animal moving towards the side having the strongest muscular tension. This view has been largely abandoned as a theory of tropisms in animals, but a similar explanation *is* accepted for plants as they grow towards the light, or grow upright by geotropisms. It is believed that, whereas stimuli can have quite direct effects on plants, their effects on even simple animals are seldom direct, as they are 'read' or interpreted according to the situation and the needs of the animal.

Stimuli can however evoke *reflexes which may be complex, and were thought by the behaviourists to be the building-blocks of all behaviour (even language). Their role and characteristics were discovered especially by *Pavlov and *Sherrington. Although basic for the internal functions of all animals (with internal stimuli as for *proprioception) and for immediate responses to external events (signalled by the various senses of touch, hearing, vision, etc.), present-day cognitive psychology shows that 'higher' behaviour is not controlled directly by stimuli; but, rather, by what is 'postulated' by the brain as the cause of the stimuli. Stimuli become evidence for what is out there, read from knowledge of objects, and how they interact, and what they might do or be used for. So 'top-down' neural processes modulate effects of stimuli and give them meaning.

See also PSYCHOPHYSICS.   RLG

Jeannerod, M. (1997). *The Cognitive Neuroscience of Action*.
Loeb, J. (1918). *Forced Movements, Tropisms and Animal Conduct*.
Sherrington, C. (1947). *The Integrative Action of the Nervous System*.

stress. Why has the problem of stress become a major issue of our time? Can it really be that life conditions in our society are more stressful, more taxing, than those experienced by our ancestors? From a material standpoint the answer to this question is, of course: no. The conditions in contemporary society are less stressful than those that have been experienced by any previous generation. But our age has its own problems, many of them psychological and social in nature, and we do not need to be starved, or cold, or physically exhausted for stress to occur. Life in technologically advanced societies imposes new demands which trigger the same bodily responses that helped our ancestors to survive by making them fit for fight or flight—responses that may be totally inappropriate for coping with the stresses of life today.

Stress may be regarded as a process of transactions in which the resources of the person are matched against the demands of the environment. The individual's appraisal of the importance of the demands is reflected in the bodily resources mobilized to meet them.

1. Man as a 'stressometer'
2. Underload and overload
3. Helplessness
4. Is stress dangerous to health?

1. Man as a 'stressometer'

One of the notions underlying the use of physiological and chemical techniques in human stress research is that the load that a particular environment places on a person can be estimated by measuring the activity of the body's organ systems. Technological advances, together with progress in the biobehavioural and biomedical sciences, have made new methods available for investigating the interplay between mental and physical processes. Much of what was previously the subject of speculation can now be recorded and measured, and as more of what happens in the different bodily organs becomes accessible to measurement, the effects that mental and physical processes have on one another become increasingly clear. We can record changes in heart rate that accompany changes in the environment. We can show how psychological processes are reflected in the activity of the brain, in cardiovascular functions, in hormonal activity, etc.; and we can see how hormonal changes reflect changes in mood, how blood pressure rises to challenge, and how the alertness of the brain varies with the flow of impressions transmitted by the sense organs.

Since feelings and *perceptions are reflected in the activity of many of the body's organ systems, individuals can themselves be regarded as 'stressometers', instruments that help to identify factors in the environment that tell hard on their mind and body. The environmental factors may be physical or chemical, such as noise or smell; or social and psychological, such as monotonous work, excessive information flow, or interpersonal conflict.

With the development of chemical techniques that permit the determination of small amounts of hormones and transmitter substances in blood and urine, neuroendocrinology has come to play an increasingly important part in stress research. Two neuroendocrine systems, both of which are controlled by the brain, are of particular interest in the study of stress and coping with stressful situations. One is the sympathetic adrenomedullary system, with the secretion of the *catecholamines adrenaline (epinephrine) and noradrenaline (norepinephrine). The other is the pituitary–adrenocortical system, with the secretion

of cortisol. These substances have several important functions: as sensitive indicators of the mismatch between the person and the environment, as regulators of vital bodily functions, and—under some circumstances—as mediators of bodily reactions leading to disease.

What do we know about the environmental conditions that activate these two systems?

2. Underload and overload

Stimulus underload and overload are typical features of modern society, and both of them trigger the adrenomedullary and adrenocortical response. In order to function adequately, the human brain requires an inflow of impulses from the external environment, but both lack and excess of stimulation threaten the *homeostatic mechanisms by which the organism maintains an adequate degree of *arousal. The optimal level of human functioning is located at the midpoint of a scale ranging between very low and very high levels of stimulus input. At the optimal level, the brain is moderately aroused, the individual's resources are mobilized, and full attention is given to the surroundings; he is emotionally balanced and performs to the best of his abilities. At low levels he tends to be inattentive, easily distracted, and bored. Conditions of extreme understimulation, involving both sensory and social deprivation, are accompanied by a state of mental impoverishment with loss of initiative and loss of capacity for involvement. When the brain is over-aroused, on the other hand, the ability to respond selectively to the impinging signals is impaired. Feelings of excitement and tension develop, followed by a gradual fragmentation of thought processes, a loss of ability to integrate the messages into a meaningful whole, impaired judgement, and loss of initiative.

3. Helplessness

Psychological theories of helplessness emphasize the role of learning in the development of active coping strategies. A sense of hopelessness, paired with a reduced motivation to control, is likely to develop when people realize that events and outcomes are independent of their actions. Empirical evidence from many sources, including both animal and human experiments, shows that the organism responds differently to conditions characterized by controllability on the one hand, and lack of control on the other. On the whole it is consistent with the view that increased controllability reduces physiological stress responses, such as adrenaline and cortisol secretion, thus presumably decreasing bodily wear and tear.

4. Is stress dangerous to health?

There is general agreement that mental stress may increase the risk of ill health and affect the course of both somatic and mental disorders. But the biological mechanisms by which stress translates into disease are still obscure. Relationships exist between stress and diseases such as myocardial infarction, high blood pressure, gastrointestinal disorders, asthma, and migraine; however, it is only occasionally that a particular mental factor can be identified as the specific cause of a disease. As a general rule the psychological aspect is merely one thread in a complex fabric in which genetic components, environmental conditions, and learned behaviours are also interwoven.

This lack of a clear picture of the links in the causal chain between stress and disease hampers our efforts to prevent harmful stress responses. However, we know a great deal about the mobilization of stress hormones under conditions of underload and overload, and although it is still not known when such stress responses lead to ill health it is agreed that they should be treated as early warning signals. Moreover, we also know a great deal about how stress that is liable to impair health can be counteracted. Stress responses can be dampened, for instance, by providing opportunities for personal control, which can then serve as buffer, warding off potentially harmful effects of, for example, overload at work.

In short, stress research has already contributed knowledge that can be used to shape the external environment so as to fit human abilities and needs. Such insights are being utilized more and more, particularly in working life, both in the organization of work and in the application of new technology.   MF

Bartlett, D. (1998). *Stress: Perspectives and Processes.*
Frankenhaeuser, M. (1979). 'Psychoneuroendocrine approaches to the study of emotion as related to stress and coping'. In Howe, H. E., and Dienstbier, R. A. (eds.), *Nebraska Symposium on Motivation 1978.*
—— (1980). 'Psychobiological aspects of life stress'. In Levine, S., and Ursin, H. (eds.), *Coping and Health.*
Lazarus, R. S. (1999). *Stress and Emotion: A New Synthesis.*

stroke. Stroke is the third major cause of death in the Western world. It is also the commonest cause of severe physical disability occurring in people living in their own homes. It has major financial implications both for individuals and for nations.

The term 'stroke' is used to describe an acute disturbance of the brain due to an abnormality of blood supply. The onset is usually sudden and, indeed, it is this suddenness which is one of its principal characteristics. The most common initial event is weakness of the arm and leg on one side of the body (hemiplegia). About 15 per cent of 'cases' are accounted for by spontaneous bleeding into the substance of the brain—cerebral haemorrhage—usually the result of rupture of minute aneurysmal weaknesses, on one of the small arteries deep inside the brain. In the remaining 85 per cent, the underlying pathology involves 'infarction' (death of tissue), resulting from partial or complete blockage of an artery, with the resultant cutting-off of arterial blood supply.

The term 'cerebrovascular disease' is used to describe abnormalities of the arteries in the brain. The pathology of cerebral haemorrhage has been mentioned above. In the majority of cases, however, there is infarction due to arterial blockage. The underlying process involves atheroma, in which there is deposition of fatty substances on the wall of the blood vessel. The three principal results of this process are stenosis (narrowing), occlusion (blockage), and embolism, which involves the formation of a blood clot on the damaged arterial wall; this becomes dislodged and may itself produce blockage of an artery 'further on' in the arterial circulation. Cerebrovascular disease is often associated with degeneration of arteries elsewhere—particularly in the heart.

1. Can strokes be avoided?
2. Assessment of neurological deficits
3. How much recovery will occur?

1. Can strokes be avoided?
Much attention has been given in recent years to identifying 'risk factors', with a view to setting up programmes of stroke prevention. The major treatable factor is hypertension (high blood pressure). There is now clear evidence that the effective treatment of hypertension can reduce (although not eliminate) the risk of an acute stroke. This places considerable logistical demands on general practitioners and others who have the responsibility of both detecting and treating the condition.

Other risk factors are of less importance and include diabetes, cardiac disease (particularly disorders of the heart valves and of cardiac rhythm), an increased number of red blood cells (raised haematocrit), and an excessive intake of alcohol.

There has been a steady decline in the death rate from cerebrovascular disease in many parts of the world during the last 30 years. The reason for this, however, is unclear.

2. Assessment of neurological deficits
The patient usually becomes 'medically stable' within the first ten days. At the end of this time, he or she is likely to be fit enough to start the process of 'rehabilitation'. Most patients will have weakness or paralysis of the arm and leg on one side of the body (a hemiplegia). In many instances, this 'motor' loss is accompanied by impairment of sensation in the limbs. The paralysed limbs require careful positioning, and it is essential to avoid excessive pulling and stretching of the affected joints. A variety of other deficits may occur.

Hemianopia. A homonymous hemianopia occurs if the visual pathways in the affected hemisphere have been damaged (see VISUAL SYSTEM: ORGANIZATION). If the disturbance is severe, the patient will not see objects on one side. Thus, a patient with a right homonymous hemianopia may not react to his wife and family, if they are sitting at his bedside on his right side. If mobile, he may walk into door frames and other objects on the right side.

Aphasia (in this context, the terms '*aphasia' and 'dysphasia' are used synonymously) involves a disturbance of *language* function, and usually results from damage to the left cerebral hemisphere. In its mildest form, it may simply involve the inability to name objects such as a table, clock, or pen. In most instances, however, there is a disturbance of comprehension, and reading is impaired. In the worst cases, the patient has almost complete loss of the ability to comprehend language, and cannot speak, though, happily, the problem is rarely so severe.

Visuospatial disorders. Damage to the right cerebral hemisphere often produces disorders of spatial orientation (see SPATIAL COORDINATION) and perception. These can be complicated and difficult to understand, but are of enormous importance to those who are caring for the stroke patient. Some patients neglect one side of the body (usually the left), and may even deny the existence of the left arm. Occasionally, the patient's perception of the arm is distorted so that it appears much longer or shorter than normal, or appears to be covered in hair. Patients with a severe disturbance of spatial function may be, for instance, unable to draw symmetrical objects, such as a house, or a clock-face, the left side of the object being usually less well drawn than the right. Such people are frequently unable to dress because they cannot organize their clothes, and may, for instance, try to don a jacket which is inside out and back to front.

A variety of other deficits may be mentioned. *Apraxia involves a defect of motor programming, so that the person is unable to undertake tasks, although there is no paralysis of the affected part. Thus, the person may be unable to stick out his tongue when asked to do so, although he has no difficulty with licking his lips involuntarily. A patient with visual *agnosia may be unable to recognize common objects, such as a pen or a torch, although his eyesight is satisfactory. The range of scope of cerebral disorders resulting from a stroke is large; their recognition, quantification, and management are discussed in detail in Wade et al. (1985).

Patients with an acute stroke usually remain in hospital for 4–6 weeks and are then allowed home. Their rehabilitation involves physical therapy, designed to help the patient regain lost functions, and to avoid unnecessary complications such as stiff and immobile joints, and fractures (which are often due to falling, associated with premature attempts at walking).

3. How much recovery will occur?

There is now considerable literature on the subject of recovery after stroke (for example, Skilbeck et al. 1983,

Barnett, Stein, and Mohr 1986). The three adverse factors occurring in the first few days are unconsciousness, urinary incontinence, and deviation of the eyes to one side. Only 5–10 per cent of patients who are unconscious in the first week will survive, and those who do survive will usually be left very severely disabled.

About 75 per cent of disabled stroke survivors learn to walk again, though only about 20 per cent can walk at a normal speed. Many cannot, for example, get to the shops or pub. Only 15 per cent of those with a paralysed arm eventually regain normal arm function. Dysphasic patients may be expected to make about a 25 per cent improvement between three weeks and six months. In general, the amount of recovery is largely dependent upon the severity of the initial deficit: those who are severely disabled initially will usually remain with a severe permanent disability, although some recovery usually occurs. Those with a mild initial deficit may eventually make a full recovery. **RLH**

Barnett, H. J. N., Stein, B. M., and Mohr, J. P. (1986). *Stroke: Pathophysiology, Diagnosis and Management.*

Skilbeck, C. E., Wade, D. T., Langton Hewer, R., and Wood, V. A. (1983). 'Recovery after stroke'. *Journal of Neurology, Neurosurgery, and Psychiatry*, 46.

Wade, D. T., Langton Hewer, R., Skilbeck, C. E., Bainton, D., and Burns-Cox, C. (1985). 'Controlled trial of a home-care service for acute stroke patients'. *Lancet*, 9 Feb.

———————— and David, R. M. (1986). *Stroke: A Critical Approach to Diagnosis, Treatment, and Management.*

Stumpf, Carl (1848–1936). German psychologist, born in Wiesenfeld and educated in the University of Würzburg, where he was strongly influenced by Franz *Brentano. After studying with R. H. Lotze (1817–81) at Göttingen, he turned towards psychology, in particular the psychology of tone and music, which, since he was a dedicated musician, remained a lifelong interest. Thereafter he held a number of important academic posts, culminating in the chair of psychology at Berlin, which he held until 1921, when he was succeeded by Wolfgang *Köhler. Among Stumpf's many distinguished students was E. G. *Husserl, the founder of modern phenomenology. Stumpf's best-known work is his *Tonpsychologie* (2 vols., 1883, 1890). **OLZ**

sublimation. The term used in *psychoanalysis for the defence mechanism by which the energy derived from an instinct when it is denied gratification is displaced into a more socially acceptable interest or activity. Aggressive impulses are said to have been sublimated when they are expressed in competitive sports. Dancing may represent the sublimation of sexual impulses. **DRD**

subliminal perception. Few hypotheses in the behavioural sciences have occasioned so much controversy as the suggestion that people may be affected by external *stimuli of which they remain wholly unaware. This notion of *perception without awareness, evidently taken for granted by such philosophers as Democritus, *Socrates, *Aristotle, and *Leibniz but still strenuously resisted by some academic psychologists, concerns a unique and non-commonsensical interrelationship of brain, *consciousness, and behaviour.

As depicted in Fig. 1, it implies that the brain processes underlying conscious experience differ from those that mediate between incoming stimuli and outgoing responses. It implies that information may be transmitted through the organism without ever achieving conscious representation. Three sorts of evidence support this view: that based upon subjective experience, that stemming from neurophysiological studies, and, most specifically, that relying upon the data from behavioural research on subliminal perception. Let us consider these in order of specificity.

The occurrence of *dreams and *hallucinations unrelated to ongoing external stimuli attests to the fact that conscious perceptual experience depends upon brain processes that may operate independently of those subserving the receipt of information from the external world. Conversely, in *skilled behaviour, in situations involving divided attention, in *somnambulism, and in many of the body's involuntary regulatory responses to changes in external stimulation, information may be received, processed, and initiate responses without conscious registration. Taken together these observations suggest that consciousness and information transmission depend upon different systems which may, under certain circumstances, operate independently.

Since 1948 the existence of these two systems, a *sine qua non* of subliminal perception, has been confirmed by neurophysiological research (see Moruzzi and Magoun

1949, Samuels 1959, Dixon 1971, 1981). Whereas the receipt and onward transmission of sensory information, initiated by external stimuli, depends upon the classical sensory pathways linking peripheral receptors with their cortical projections, *awareness* of this sensory traffic—perceptual experience—relies upon sufficient contribution from the ascending fibres of the reticular activating system, that dense network of cells which arises in the brain stem and then spreads upwards and outwards to infiltrate the cortex. If the reticular system is blocked by surgery or drugs, the arrival of sensory information at the cortex still occurs but the owner of the cortex remains oblivious of the fact! This finding, of considerable significance for proponents of subliminal perception, accords with data from research by Libet and his colleagues (1967). Recording from the exposed brains of fully conscious human subjects, they were able to detect electrical potentials initiated by tactile stimuli of which their subjects remained totally unaware. *Pari passu* with intensifying the external stimulus, the recorded waveform became more complex and the subjects reported, 'I can feel something'. It seems reasonable to assume that the additions to the waveform reflected those contributions from the reticular system upon which consciousness depends.

In a subsequent experiment it was found that the amplitude of an electrical response, recorded from the visual receiving area and initiated by a flash of light to one eye, could be reduced by subliminal presentation of an emotional word to the other eye. Since this effect did not occur for emotionally neutral words, we must assume that the brain could analyse and respond to the meaning of words of whose presence the recipient remained unaware. Yet other studies (Dixon 1971, 1981) have shown, by its electrical response, that the human brain will respond to the meaning of words presented to the ears during sleep. It is interesting to note that even in the deepest sleep, and without awakening the subject, such words may also evoke dreams that are relevant to their meaning.

The researches involving human brain responses to subliminal stimuli have their counterpart in studies of lower animals. Thus it has been shown that a monkey's recognition threshold for a meaningful pattern may be significantly altered by direct electrical stimulation of the animal's reticular system. It has also been found that even the surgically isolated forebrain of a cat will respond to a previously learned pattern when this is presented to the preparation's one remaining eye. Since what is left of the animal in this experiment could hardly be capable of consciousness, this finding illustrates a simple and direct instance of subliminal perception.

One of the most extensively researched examples of subliminal perception occurs in connection with the fact that the awareness threshold for threatening words or pictures may be significantly higher or lower than that

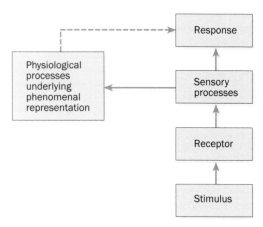

Fig. 1.

for more neutral material. Experiments which involved the simultaneous recording of EEGs (brain rhythms— see ELECTROENCEPHALOGRAPHY), heart rate, and perceptual thresholds suggest that, prior to awareness of a visual stimulus which is gradually increasing in brightness, the brain may analyse the latter's meaning and, as a result, modify its own level of arousal to hasten or retard awareness of the information that it carries.

That the brain monitors and analyses subliminal stimuli receives support from many comparable investigations. Thus, emotional words, presented below threshold to the eye, have been found to change auditory sensitivity, and vice versa. By the same token, during binocular rivalry, in which the subject perceives either with the left eye or with the right but never with the two together, the introduction of a subliminal stimulus to the 'blind' eye produces immediate transfer of perception to that side. Such a mechanism which automatically switches into consciousness a stimulus array that has changed (i.e. one that constitutes a potentially important *new* stimulus) has obvious survival value.

It can be argued that a capacity for subliminal perception came about with the evolution of attentional mechanisms. Since the span of consciousness is severely restricted, selective processes evolved whereby only a limited proportion of available sensory information could be admitted to consciousness. Subliminal stimuli constitute some part of the remainder—stimuli which, though insufficiently strong or important to warrant entry into consciousness, may nevertheless be received, monitored, and reacted to. A number of recent pieces of research attest to this view. In one (Corteen and Wood 1972), people were asked to report a stream of prose presented to one ear while words of which they remained unaware were presented to the other ear. It was found that those 'subliminal' words (on the unattended-to ear), which had previously been associated with electric shock, produced an emotional response (i.e. a change in skin resistance due to sweating) without interfering with the attentional task of 'shadowing' prose on the other ear. In another experiment (Henley and Dixon 1974) imagery evoked by music presented to one ear, above the conscious threshold, was shaped by subliminal words to the other ear. Considered together, these two sets of data suggest that, at a preconscious level of processing, the brain can 'decide' whether or not information on a subsidiary or unattended-to channel should be kept isolated from, or used to facilitate, responses evoked by material to which the recipient is devoting his conscious attention.

That a subliminal stimulus can bypass the moderating, rationalizing effects of consciousness has given rise to a number of useful applications of stimulation below awareness. These include the investigating of processes underlying such psychiatric disorders as *anorexia nervosa and *schizophrenia. Perhaps the most clearly useful application to date has been in the selection of pilots for the Royal Swedish Air Force. In the defence mechanism test (Kragh 1962a, 1962b) the candidate for a flying career has to describe what he sees when flashed a composite picture, consisting of a central human figure which is flanked by a subliminal threatening male face. Numerous applications of this test have shown that those candidates whose responses show characteristic distortions as a result of the subliminal threat are likely to make accident-prone pilots. By using this test to eliminate undesirable trainees, the Air Force has succeeded in making a significant saving in lives and aircraft.

Despite the very great weight of evidence from many disciplines, there are still those who cannot bring themselves to accept the reality of subliminal perception. In the writer's opinion this carefully sustained prejudice is itself a psychological defence against the threat of possible manipulation which is implied by subliminal effects. There is the suggestion here of an unwarranted equation of consciousness with such nebulous properties of mind as will, self-control, and conscience. Evidence of many kinds, including that from studies of behaviour under hypnosis, suggests that this particular conceit is, to say the least, mistaken.

Besides being used in a diagnostic capacity, subliminal stimulation has now been employed in a therapeutic context. For example, by reducing anxiety through the subliminal presentation of reassuring messages it has been found possible to reduce neurotic overeating in cases of obesity (Silverman et al. 1978) and improve performance at mathematics (Ariam 1979). Other techniques involving stimulation below the conscious threshold have proved useful in the treatment of phobias (Tyrer, Lee, and Horn 1978).

From the evidence to date, it seems that all the sensory modalities shown in Fig. 2 have a subliminal range within which excitation can occur without conscious representation. Of particular interest in this connection is the finding (Cowley, Johnson, and Brooksbank 1977, Kirk-Smith et al. 1978) that even subliminal olfactory stimuli—e.g. pheromones—may have a significant effect. Even though unable consciously to detect the smell of female pheromones, their inhalation by male subjects made the latter perceive photographs of women as more attractive than they would otherwise have been.

The subliminal range for each modality is still not clear but probably depends upon the relative importance, from a survival point of view, of the modality in question and the extent to which its response system can function adequately without the aid of consciousness. Thus, while *pain might be expected to have a very short range (i.e. it would be important to be immediately aware of noxious stimuli) the interoceptive senses (i.e. those concerned with

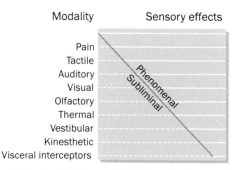

Modality	Sensory effects
Pain	
Tactile	
Auditory	
Visual	
Olfactory	
Thermal	
Vestibular	
Kinesthetic	
Visceral interceptors	

Fig. 2. Hypothetical extents of subliminal and phenomenal effects for different sensory modalities.

internal 'automatic' bodily responses) remain almost entirely subliminal (as indeed we know they are).

Hardly less interesting than the phenomena of subliminal perception has been the resistance to accepting its validity. Since the whole idea of being influenced by things of which one is unaware is repugnant to some people—presumably because it seems to threaten notions of *free will and personal autonomy—various arguments have been put forward to discredit demonstrations of the phenomenon. One of the favourites has been to view subliminal perception as merely a watered-down version of normal conscious perception. According to this argument, so-called subliminal effects have been explained as no more than responses to consciously perceived fragments of the stimulus array. However, a recent study by Groeger (1984) invalidates this suggestion. Subjects were asked to choose either the word 'SMUG' or the word 'COSY' as a completion for the mutilated sentence 'She looked . . . in her new fur coat'. It was found that if they received a liminal (i.e. barely audible) presentation of the word 'SNUG' they chose 'SMUG' as their completion. But if the same cue was given at a *subliminal* level they preferred the completion 'COSY'. In other words, the subliminal response resulted from unconscious semantic analysis while responses to structural features occurred only at or about the threshold of awareness.

See also ATTENTION.   NFD

Ariam, S. (1979). 'The effects of subliminal symbiotic stimuli in Hebrew on academic performance of Israeli high school students' (unpublished Ph.D. diss., New York University).

Corteen, R. S., and Wood, B. (1972). 'Autonomic responses to shock associated words'. *Journal of Experimental Psychology*, 94.

Cowley, J. J., Johnson, A. L., and Brooksbank, B. W. L. (1977). 'The effect of two odorous compounds on performance in an assessment of people test'. *Psychoneuroendocrinology*, 2.

Dixon, N. F. (1971). *Subliminal Perception: The Nature of a Controversy*.

—— (1981). *Preconscious Processing*.

Groeger, J. A. (1984). 'Preconscious influences on language production' (Ph.D. thesis, Belfast).

Henley, S. H. A., and Dixon, N. F. (1974). 'Laterality differences in the effect of incidental stimuli upon evoked imagery'. *British Journal of Psychology*, 65/4.

Kragh, U. (1962a). 'Precognitive defense organisation with threatening and non-threatening peripheral stimuli'. *Scandinavian Journal of Psychology*, 3.

—— (1962b). 'Predictions of success of Danish attack divers by the defence mechanism test'. *Perceptual and Motor Skills*, 15.

Kirk-Smith, M., Booth, D. A., Carroll, D., and Davies, P. (1978). 'Human social attitudes affected by Androstenol', *Res. Commun. Psychol. Psychiat. Behav.*, 3.

Libet, B., Alberts, W. W., Wright, E. W., and Feinstein, B. (1967). 'Responses of human somato-sensory cortex to stimuli below the threshold for conscious sensation'. *Science*, 158/3808.

Moruzzi, S., and Magoun, H. W. (1949). 'Brainstem reticular formation and activation of the EEG'. *Electroencephalography and Clinical Neurophysiology*, 1.

Samuels, I. (1959). 'Reticular mechanisms and behaviour'. *Psychology Bulletin*, 56.

Silverman, L. H. (1975). 'An experimental method for the study of unconscious conflict—a progress report'. *British Journal of Medical Psychology*, 48.

—— Martin, A., Ungaro, R., and Mendelsohn, E. (1978). 'Effect of subliminal stimulation of symbiotic fantasies on behaviour modification treatment of obesity'. *Journal of Consultative Clinical Psychology*, 46/3.

Tyrer, P., Lee, I., and Horn, P. (1978). 'Treatment of agoraphobia by subliminal and supraliminal exposure to phobic cine film'. *Lancet*, 18 Feb.

subnormality. Subnormality and severe subnormality are legal terms which were defined in the UK Mental Health Act of 1959. In the Mental Health Act of 1983 they have been replaced by the words 'mental impairment' and 'severe mental impairment' which are defined as follows. Mental impairment means a state of arrested or incomplete development of mind (not amounting to severe impairment) which includes significant impairment of intelligence and social functioning, and is associated with abnormally aggressive or seriously irresponsible conduct. Severe mental impairment means a state of arrested or incomplete development of mind which includes severe impairment of intelligence and social functioning and is associated with abnormally aggressive or seriously irresponsible conduct.

Incompleteness of the development of the mind has been observed for a very long time, and has been recognized in English law since 1325, whereas subnormality of intelligence is a concept which depends on the meaning given to the word intelligence by Alfred *Binet, in 1909, i.e. ability to learn. Thus the inclusion of the concept of a minimum level of intelligence in the Act of 1959 was meant to complement and limit the definition of subnormality according to social incompetence. Before 1959 social incompetence was the prime definition of subnormality. In addition, in medieval times the legal definition included the idea of incurability, and was distinguished from mental illness insofar as the 'natural fool' was supposed to be incurable, whereas the lunatic was recognized as a person who might perhaps recover from his illness. These legal definitions were of course related to the protection of the property of those involved. They were also the basis for decisions made on the criminal responsibility of persons accused of serious offences.

Subnormality today is regarded as a condition which, when associated with very low intelligence—for example, below IQ 55 or IQ 50—will have a relatively permanent character, whereas when associated with a level of intelligence between 55 and 70 will less frequently be combined with permanent social incompetence. In fact some authors have claimed that in mild subnormality of this kind IQ levels can be considerably increased by early and continuous educational attention. Whether this can be said with certainty or not, a great deal of research has shown that above IQ 55 ability to survive in the community is not very closely related to intelligence. Below this IQ level a relatively small proportion of people will be found to be socially independent, possibly between 10 and 20 per cent.

The prevalence of subnormality

At the beginning of the 20th century, the prevalence of subnormality was thought to be increasing, because the views of Francis *Galton (*Hereditary Genius*, 1869) and Karl Pearson were uncritically applied to the concept of intelligence. It was supposed, therefore, that because of differential fertility more children would be born to those with less intellectual endowment and that, as a result, the average level of intelligence would decline. Few authorities, with the exception of L. S. *Penrose, disagreed with this view, though today few would agree with it. As a result of later studies, the prevalence of severe subnormality is now better understood and we know more about the intelligence level of the children of the mildly subnormal. If we were to define the prevalence of subnormality solely in terms of the level of intelligence, and if all below IQ 70 were assumed to be subnormal, then, further assuming distribution according to Karl Pearson's 'normal' curve, 2.28 per cent of the population would be expected to be subnormal. The great majority of these cases would be between IQs 70 and 55, say 2.14 per cent of the total population. The remaining 0.14 per cent (67,200 in England and Wales) would have IQs in the range of severe subnormality, i.e. lower than IQ 55. When investigations were made, however, fairly firm figures began to emerge for the severely subnormal. These figures were 3.88 per 1,000 (E. O. Lewis), 3.45 per 1,000 (N. Goodman and J. Tizard), for age ranges 7–14 years, and 3.75 per 1,000 (A. Kushlick) for the 15–19 age range. Obviously the actual findings, which for a population of 48 million people would yield a total prevalence of approximately 180,000 severely subnormal cases

on the basis of Kushlick's figures, very much exceed the number which would be expected if the definition were based on intelligence level and the normal curve. The difference was accounted for long ago by Pearson and G. A. Jaederholm (*On the Continuity of Mental Defect*, 1914), the excess of severely subnormal subjects being assumed to be due to the pathological conditions so frequently found at this IQ level.

If we turn our attention to the prevalence of the subnormal as distinct from the severely subnormal we find that, between IQ 70 and 55, 21.4 persons per 1,000 would be predicted on the basis of the normal curve of IQ, which for England and Wales would give an estimate of approximately 1,027,000 cases. In point of fact, the estimates for the mildly subnormal in England have ranged from 1.39 per 1,000 to 6.73 per 1,000. An intervening figure, that obtained by Kushlick in 1961 in Salford, was for an estimate of 2.60 per 1,000. This figure yields a prevalence rate for England and Wales of 124,000 cases. In this instance the discrepancy is in the opposite direction and is easily explained by the fact that the mildly subnormal very often survive in the community despite their relatively low intelligence. As a result they do not attract the attention of the available services, and the actual prevalence rate is found to be much below that which might be expected on the basis of intelligence alone. In this particular group, as was initially pointed out by Penrose (1949), the prevalence is most marked during school years because of the special scholastic demands made at that time. A number of studies since W. R. Baller's initial research in 1936 have shown that, on follow-up, the mildly subnormal are frequently shown to have succeeded very well in social and occupational situations. They often marry and conduct their own businesses, show stability in their job experience, and in normally favourable social circumstances do not fall foul of the law in a serious way or come to represent a social problem in their later years. A variety of theories possibly explaining the relative success of the adult subnormal has been reviewed by Clarke and Clarke (1974).

While the tendency during the early years of the 20th century was to consider that the prevalence of mental subnormality was increasing, N. Goodman and J. Tizard have argued, on the basis of their survey and by comparison with Lewis's earlier survey, that perhaps it is declining so far as the severely subnormal are concerned. The argument rests on two opposite trends, one being the decrease in infant mortality in England and Wales between 1900 and 1959 and the resulting possibility of a decrease in birth injuries, and the other being the likelihood that better birth conditions might lead not only to increasing survival of the fit but also to increasing survival of the unfit. Goodman and Tizard argue that, since many of the severely subnormal, perhaps as many as 25 per cent, suffer from *Down's syndrome (mongolism), and since this group now survive longer than hitherto, an increasing number of the severely subnormal might be Down's syndrome cases. Down's syndrome is of genetic origin and perhaps little influenced by external factors except maternal age. If this were so, then it is possible that the number of the severely subnormal who were not Down's syndrome cases either remained the same or declined slightly between the Lewis survey in 1929 and the Goodman and Tizard survey in 1962.

Obviously, so far as the initial fears that gave rise to the UK Mental Deficiency Act of 1913 are concerned, a decline in national intelligence is no longer thought probable by those who are well informed about the prevalence of mental deficiency. This does not mean, of course, that there is no genetic element contributing to prevalence of subnormality. Perhaps today fewer severely subnormal children are being born, and fewer mildly subnormal adults need care, but of course those severely subnormal children who are born tend to live longer. B. W. Richards found that from 1949 there had been a steady trend towards ageing in the population in a mental deficiency hospital in Surrey. There was an especially great increase in the number and mean age of residents with Down's syndrome, even though the mean age of the Down's syndrome patients was lower than that of their comparable non-Down's-syndrome fellow patients. B. Kirman (in Kirman and Bicknell 1975: 57) presented a table showing the trend of ages in National Health Service hospitals between 1954 and 1969. The main feature of this table is the relative increase in the number of patients aged over 55 as compared with those aged below 14. There is, however, some evidence that Down's syndrome cases continue to die somewhat earlier than non-Down's syndrome cases of the same IQ level. It is interesting to note that practically all Down's syndrome patients over 35 years of age show the same pathological changes in their brains as are seen in the brains of subjects who develop the clinical features of senile *dementia of the Alzheimer type.

Clearly, therefore, the tendency is for fewer severely subnormal children to be born but for more of those who are born to survive over longer periods, and for fewer of the mildly subnormal to come to the notice of social aid services. These trends are probably matched by similar trends in the normal population, and it might be said that the subnormal, like the normal, are profiting from the general increase in the standard of living as well as from the improvement in medical care, especially in relation to birth conditions, since the beginning of the century.

For discussion of the causes of subnormality, and the care of mentally handicapped adults and children, see MENTAL HANDICAP.   NOC

Clarke, A. M., and Clarke, A. D. B. (eds.) (1974). *Mental Deficiency: The Changing Outlook.*

Kirman, B., and Bicknell, J. (1975). *Mental Handicap.*

Penrose, L. S. (1949). *The Biology of Mental Defect.*

Sufism. Sufi individuals and groups became publicly known in Arabia in the 8th century. As mystics, esteemed for religious piety, they were able to exercise the role of mentors of devotion and conduct in the theocratic community of Islam. Observers have been attempting, for 1,000 years, to categorize them, but conventional assessment has proved extremely difficult. Accepting Muhammad the Prophet as the originator of the current phase of Sufi manifestation, they also regard Jesus as a Sufi: while one of the greatest of all Sufis, Jalaluddin *Rumi, openly declared that many non-Muslims understood Sufism better than ordinary Muslims. *Al-Ghazzali, one of the foremost Sufis, is credited with having saved Islamic thought from dissolution by Greek philosophy. From his time (d. 1111) all Islamic thought may be regarded as being indebted to Sufism. Like all gnostic systems, Sufism regards conduct as secondary, and divine illumination as primary. Sufi masters are therefore those who, having experienced the 'path' to such cognition, are able to guide others along it and also to relate it to terrestrial social needs.

There are three distinct ways in which assessment of this powerful and extraordinary movement has been approached. (i) The largely Western, scholarly approach, which has sought to analyse literature, seek origins, and identify affinities. The multiplicity of resemblances between Sufi thought and practices and those of other systems has led many of the followers of this technique to 'proof by selected instances'. According to which expert one reads, therefore, one will find Sufism attributed to Christian, Jewish, Buddhist, animist, or other origins. A listing of the proofs invoked by such students shows that they cancel one another out. (ii) The conclusions reached by Muslim non-Sufis, mainly in the East, over the centuries. Nasrollah Fatemi (1976) provides a summary:

To some it denotes humanitarianism, tolerance, harmony . . . love of mankind and the attempt to achieve spiritual fellowship. To a few, the Sufis are dreamers, rebels and meddlers who interfere with the serious rituals of the church and the business of the state. To others, they are the conscience of society and the antennae of the community, who exhibit in their activities a pronounced concern for humanity [and] the values that lie at the core of society, and who accuse the civil and religious authorities of lacking social conscience. The Sufis felt the need to resist the corrupt, tyrannical and arrogant, to ridicule the cruel rich and merciless might, to exalt the low and to help the helpless.

(iii) The assertions made by the Sufis themselves about what they are and what they do and why they do it.

Although it cannot be expected that the Sufis' contentions about themselves will be accepted by those with different assumptions, it can be seen that the Sufi rationale provides a better explanation than has been offered heretofore by members of the outside observing groups. The Sufis say that they have no history, because Sufism is experience, not recording information. Their goal is attaining knowledge of a higher reality, of which familiar religion is a lower level: that of social and psychological balance. When the goal is attained, the Sufi acquires not only knowledge of the divine (and of extra-dimensional reality) but also functions associated with it which are not to be confused with repetitive observance or emotional stimulus. Those alone who have reached this stage may properly be called 'Sufis'. Anyone else is 'on the Path', or a 'dervish', roughly equivalent to a monk or friar. It is this belief that gnosis commands action of all kinds that explains, according to the Sufis, why they are found in so many branches of literature, philosophy, science, administration, and so on. Their instrumental intervention is directed from beyond conventional limitations and, the doctrine continues, cannot be imprisoned in repetitive activity. Although this assertion is not necessarily acceptable to contemporary Western workers, the rich writings of the Sufis have in recent years interested psychologists and sociologists. Sufism itself was 'named' by August Tholuck, in his *Sufismus, sive Theosophia Persarum pantheistica*, published in Berlin in 1821. Before that it was known as Islamic mysticism and by a number of other names, such as Divine Wisdom (extracted by letter–number substitution cipher from the Arabic).

Sufi 'orders' came into being much later than teachers and schools, and they clearly resemble traditional orders in, for example, Christianity. The orders are therefore regarded as secondary, and few, if any, of their putative founders, famous Sufi masters, were really connected with their establishment. Their practices are mostly of a devotional autohypnotic nature, and produce conditioned states which are much at variance with essential Sufi theory relating to the need for individual and specificzteaching. Most groups which employ the name Sufi in the Middle and Far East and Africa are in fact Islamic prayer congregations of the enthusiast type. Many closely resemble formal churches of whatever religion, and hence have an attraction for people brought up in parallel systems.

The Sufis enjoy, on the whole, a high reputation in the East, and have been extensively appreciated by non-Islamic religionists and scholars, including Western mystics. The numerous extrasensory manifestations which have always been associated with Sufi activity are regarded by the Sufis themselves as undesirable and preliminary (at best) phases; although they continue to excite those who attempt to study such things. At the present time, self-deluded and spurious 'Sufis' abound, in the East and West, as in the case of all enterprises of this nature.

IS

Burke, O. M. (1973). *Among the Dervishes.*

Eastwick, E. B. (1974). *The Rose-Garden of Sheikh Muslihu'd-Din Sadi of Shiraz.*
Fatemi, N. S. (1976). *Sufism.*
Lewin, L. (ed.) (1976). *The Elephant in the Dark.*
Shah, I. (1968, 1971). *The Way of the Sufi.*
Shushtery, A. M. A. (1966). *Outlines of Islamic Culture.*
Subhan, J. A. (1938). *Sufism: Its Saints and Shrines.*
Whinfield, E. H. (trans.) (1975). *Teachings of Rumi.*
Williams, L. F. R. (ed.) (1973). *Sufi Studies: East and West.*

suicidal behaviour. Man's ability to kill himself has been a source of fascination since the beginning of human society. Philosophers from Marcus Aurelius and Seneca to Camus, writers (especially poets) from Virgil to Sylvia Plath, and sociologists from the beginning of the 19th century to the present day have all contributed voluminously to its study. This widespread preoccupation has, if anything, obstructed the scientific investigation of suicide in two distinct ways. First, the long-standing theological taboo against suicide, still discernible in many legal phrases and public attitudes, has tended to make the rational consideration of the subject difficult. Secondly, speculation on the theme has tended to spread over all forms of human activity which are potentially harmful or self-defeating, with a consequence that there is remarkably little that people can do which has not been interpreted as concealing some measure of suicidal intent. Clearly for scientific purposes it is necessary to use a much more precise definition.

In the first place, attention is confined to acts in which self-destruction is the essential component and not simply a hazard incurred in the course of pursuing another goal. Thus the religious martyr, or the soldier who has volunteered for a dangerous mission during which he dies, are not usually considered as suicides. Secondly, suicide is taken to refer to the behaviour of an individual and not a group, so that expressions such as a suicidal policy being pursued by a nation are to be understood as metaphorical. And lastly, present-day usage restricts the term to human beings; the notorious lemmings are firmly excluded.

Though often difficult to assess, intention thus becomes a central issue in categorizing deaths in which the deceased was an active agent. The law in most European countries requires clear demonstration not only that an individual caused his own death, but that he fully intended to do so. Psychiatrists and behavioural scientists would in general assert that this criterion is too narrow and that assessment should be made on the balance of probabilities, recognizing that a certain number of deaths will be unclassifiable. The important practical point is that official statistics tend markedly to underestimate the incidence of suicide according to psychiatric criteria. Additional reasons for under-reporting are a desire by families and general practitioners to conceal suicidal deaths in some cases, and a reluctance of coroners to reach the decision in an open court for fear of causing offence or having their verdicts challenged in, or reversed by, a higher court. Various studies suggest that the order of magnitude of under-reporting is in the region of between 50 and 100 per cent. Nevertheless, official statistics have been widely used and have proved valuable for certain types of enquiry. (For a fuller discussion of the validity of statistics, see SUICIDE: INTERNATIONAL STATISTICS.)

A great deal of literature exists on the epidemiology of suicide. Virtually throughout the world the rate for men exceeds that for women, with the former tending to use more violent methods such as shooting or jumping from heights, and the latter more passive procedures such as taking an excess of drugs. However, these differences are rapidly disappearing in most European countries. Where the rate for males is falling, that for females tends to remain stationary or fall more slowly; conversely, where the rate for males is increasing, that for females increases even more rapidly. Either way the net effect is towards equality, often interpreted in a rather vague way as reflecting the tendency in recent decades for the social roles of the two sexes to become more similar.

The effects of age are complex and interact with those of sex. In the United Kingdom the rates for males rise linearly with age, though in most developed countries, the curve resembles an inverted U, with the peak in the late fifties or sixties. For women, both in the United Kingdom and elsewhere, this latter pattern has always been the one most commonly reported. In general, suicide is very much a phenomenon of later life, suggesting that Shakespeare was correct in asserting that 'men have died . . . and worms have eaten them, but not for love'. Furthermore, old age is often accompanied by painful illness and chronic impairment of health. Such misfortunes may well precipitate a state of severe *depression, when suicidal thoughts and acts commonly occur.

But what is currently true for Europe is not necessarily true for all times at all places. In Japan before the Second World War, for example, there was a distinct peak in the suicide rates for people in their late twenties and early thirties, which then fell away before the rate increased again among the elderly. Commentators ascribed this early peak to the complex and often contradictory social obligations which befell young married Japanese vis-à-vis their respective families. With the Americanization of Japan following the war, this early age peak virtually disappeared, and the general shape of the curve now approximates that of the United States.

In the United Kingdom suicide became increasingly common from 1945 until the early 1960s. There then followed a decline in the rates for all age–sex groups, entirely attributable to the progressive elimination of carbon monoxide from domestic gas, and the virtual disappearance of suicide by this method. This dramatic decline was unexpected. One might have supposed that anyone intent upon killing themselves would use any method to hand and that lack of availability of one particular agent would scarcely make any difference. The facts, however, point in the contrary direction. Extensive research, including for example studies on immigrants from different countries to Australia, has shown that the mode of suicide is strongly influenced by cultural attitudes which appear to favour one method in preference to others. More recently the UK rates have resumed their upward trend.

The role of cultural proscription or prescription has already been hinted at, and a number of sociological theories have been proposed which might account for the differences between societies in their suicide rates, differences which often remain surprisingly stable for sustained periods of time. Of the numerous hypotheses that have been advanced, the social cohesion theory developed by Durkheim and his followers still retains the widest support. On this view social cohesion minimizes the risk of suicide, whereas situations in which individuals are dissociated from their groups (leading to *egoistic* suicides), or live in communities that have no adequate normative values and beliefs to meet current social realities (*anomie*), conduce to suicide. The precise meaning of notions such as social cohesion or anomie is debatable, but it is empirically true that the suicide rates are particularly high among the divorced, among childless women, among those living alone, the retired or unemployed, and where populations are highly mobile or subject to economic uncertainty. Conversely, situations which promote social cohesion tend to lower suicide rates, and of these the classical example is the threat of war. In both world wars suicide rates fell in practically all countries, both belligerent and neutral.

While social factors undoubtedly influence suicide rates, patients with conditions such as severe depression, *alcholism, or *epilepsy all have increased risks of dying by suicide. Reviews of comprehensive series of suicidal deaths have now established that the great majority of such individuals were suffering from a clearly recognizable psychiatric illness at the time of their death. In England and Wales the commonest such disorder is the depressive phase of manic–depressive psychosis (see MENTAL ILLNESS), often triggered by *bereavement. In Scotland and in the United States alcoholism is almost as prominent as depression. It also appears that social factors act as additional determinants *within* groups of depressives or alcoholics. Thus among all depressives those who are socially isolated have an appreciably higher risk of suicide than the remainder. It appears that social and psychological factors are necessary (though not sufficient) causes of suicide.

Such a sweeping statement begs the question of whether there exists such a thing as a rational suicide. The formulation which comes nearest to such a possibility is

Durkheim's description of 'altruistic suicide', which he believed occurred only in communities that had extremely rigid codes of conduct, such as the army in the 19th century. The notion that death was to be preferred to dishonour, a sentiment that goes back at least to Roman times, was not simply an empty phrase. It is also said that elderly Eskimos kill themselves in times of food shortage to help preserve the family. However, it appears that under normal circumstances rational suicide is exceedingly rare, if indeed it exists at all. The nearest approach is possibly the not uncommon phenomenon of an individual who kills himself during the course of a painful terminal illness in order, presumably, to put an end to intolerable suffering. Even so, many such individuals show an impaired ability to adjust to their disorder as compared with the majority of sufferers. Severe depression (or alcoholism) may of course also be a feature of a painful and chronic illness.

Whatever the social and clinical context, the meaning of the suicidal act may vary considerably between individuals. For some, death represents simply a termination. For many others the situation is more complex; suicide notes frequently reflect a theme such as reunion with someone who has already died, or imply that the individual will in some way continue and be able to monitor the activities of his survivors. A desire to inflict revenge on others through their guilt and remorse over the death is often evident. Indeed, a multiplicity of motives which, from a narrow logical point of view, may be mutually incompatible may be displayed. The supremely 'personal' action of suicide may, at the same time, be intensely 'interpersonal' or social. (Some psychologists would aver that ultimately there is no distinction between the two.)

Nothing has been said so far of so-called 'attempted suicide', which in the United Kingdom, at least, is overwhelmingly represented by drug overdoses. The term 'attempted suicide' is profoundly misleading; for the majority of such patients suicide is not what they are attempting. Indeed, advances in the study of the phenomenon have only become possible since it was realized that these individuals do not represent failed suicides, but rather something which, though having a loose behavioural analogy with suicide, should be viewed as a more or less distinct variety of behaviour. To this end the term 'parasuicide' has been introduced.

From the epidemiological point of view suicide and parasuicide are markedly different. Whereas suicides tend to be male, and in the second half of life, the great majority of parasuicides are female and in their teens or twenties. Suicide is prevalent among the widowed and the single, whereas parasuicide tends to be commonest among the married. Suicide is notable among the physically infirm and the socially isolated, whereas parasuicide has no such association with physical illness, and tends to be commoner among those who are living in congested,

overcrowded conditions. Depressive illness and alcoholism certainly figure prominently among parasuicides, but are usually much less severe than among suicides, while lesser emotional disturbance, induced by interpersonal conflicts and other intercurrent events, assumes a much greater significance: an appreciable minority of parasuicides appear to be free of any kind of psychiatric disorder, unless of course the act itself is taken as sufficient evidence of disorder. Whereas, according to the latest figures, suicide shows no obvious social class gradient, parasuicide is very much less common in the upper than in the lower social classes.

Parasuicide is vastly more frequent than completed suicide, and from what has been said it will be appreciated that the magnitude of the ratio varies by age and sex. Thus, among men aged 55 and over, the excess is approximately threefold, while for young women below the age of 35 it is in the region of 200-fold.

From a clinical–descriptive viewpoint, the typical parasuicide tends to have had a disrupted and disadvantaged childhood, often in a broken home. She will be living in a state of conflict with her family of origin, or of procreation, or both; among men a story of trouble with the law and of interpersonal violence is common, as is excessive drinking. In association with these difficulties the patient becomes anxious and depressed, and in response to a crisis or a quarrel takes an overdose of pills (or more rarely deliberately causes self-injury).

The details of the psychological processes involved in the genesis of the act are still unclear, and often the patient herself is confused as to what, if anything, she intended. But certain broad themes can be discerned. A wish for a temporary respite, analogous to getting blind drunk, is one common component. In a minority, a desire to die or an indifference to survival will be reported, or may be inferred. Another very important aspect of parasuicide is its communication function, the much-cited 'cry for help'. Unfortunately the cry so produced may or may not lead to the hoped-for response, since families and friends may as readily pick up the aggressive overtones of the act—the hint of 'I'll die, and then you'll be sorry'.

Parasuicide may, thus, serve a number of purposes, but it is perhaps the communication aspect that is of particular interest. If the act does indeed serve as a means of conveying information, then it can be argued that it is a form of 'language' of a rather special kind. Consequently it could be predicted that the patient would commonly be found among a group of individuals who share a propensity to parasuicide when under stress. This supposition has been empirically confirmed. The concept also points the way to the study of parasuicide as a social institution, and here too the evidence suggests that communities exist in which parasuicide appears to have a more or less standard performed 'meaning'.

Finally, having stressed the numerous differences between completed suicide and parasuicide, it is necessary to point out that there is also an important overlap between the two. About half of all completed suicides are preceded by a parasuicide. Conversely, if a representative sample of parasuicides is followed up, about 1 per cent would be found to die by suicide in the ensuing year (which is about a 100 times greater than would be expected for the general population), and the increased risk of an eventual suicide persists for many years. Subgroups at high and low risk of later suicide can be identified, but no parasuicide should be dismissed a priori as trivial.

NK

Durkheim, E. (1952). *Suicide: A Study in Sociology.*

Kennedy, P., Kreitman, N., and Ovenston, I. (1974). 'The prevalence of suicide and parasuicide in Edinburgh'. *British Journal of Psychiatry*, 124.

Kreitman, N. (ed.) (1977). *Parasuicide.*

Robins, E., Murphy, G., Wilkinson, R., Gassner, S., and Kayes, J. (1959). 'Some clinical considerations in the prevention of suicide based on a study of 134 successful suicides'. *American Journal of Public Health*, 49.

Stengel, E. (1964). *Suicide and Attempted Suicide.*

suicide: international statistics. All civilized countries compile statistics on their suicides; many have done so for over a century. These deaths are usually investigated in detail by legal authorities and forensic medical experts even in the many countries where suicide is no longer a criminal offence, if only to establish the mode of death in people who might have died because of accidents or homicide. A mass of tabulations has resulted, containing details of age, sex, occupation, agent of death, etc., which appears to constitute an invaluable source of firm data, waiting at the student's elbow for employment. Some of the earliest theorists on suicide, such as Durkheim in *Le Suicide* (1892), unhesitatingly drew on this store, and subsequently Hendin (1964) has used such data in rather speculative studies concerning the susceptibility to suicide of the 'national character' of three Scandinavian countries. All the same, the number of studies that have exploited international statistical material has been relatively modest, probably because of lingering uncertainties as to the exact comparability of the figures.

These doubts were forcibly expressed by Douglas (1967) in bold, not to say polemical, tones. His argument, in essence, was that the classification of a death as suicide is effected not by God but by a judicial structure, and a 'verdict' is a social act rather than a scientific observation. Douglas pointed to the pervasive importance of attitudes and stereotypes in the minds of all concerned—families who might suppress or distort the information given to their doctors, who in turn maltreat the information before it is notified to the authorities, the coroner's officer who prepares the material for the inquest according to

informal but powerful normative values, and finally the coroner himself, with his socially given definition of what a suicide ought to be like. He also emphasized the severe social stigma attached to suicide in some countries, which must inhibit coroners, or their equivalents, from making public pronouncements. Douglas concluded that the social scientist seeking confirmation of standard theories of suicide would always find them demonstrated by suicide statistics, since these very theories had determined the manner in which the data was derived. There was, he concluded, no point in using official statistical material.

This attack evoked a dual reaction. On the one hand, it was readily conceded that suicide has always been underreported in official figures, since there must be some instances in which the evidence is more or less suppressed, but few where it is spuriously manufactured. It is also evident that a coroner does not like to upset grieving relatives, and in cases of doubt would incline to some alternative verdict; in the United Kingdom his ruling is also subject to appeal to a higher court. Moreover, the legal definition of suicide is a very narrow one, and requires proof beyond reasonable doubt not only that the deceased caused his own death but that he fully intended to do so, whereas the traditional psychiatric viewpoint would stress, rather, the balance of probabilities. For the United States, Dublin's (1963) investigations suggested to him that nearer 30 per cent of suicides went unrecognized, while in Eire McCarthy and Walsh (1975) thought that a figure of 100 per cent would be more appropriate.

Attempts to correct for under-reporting have taken the form of adding to the official suicide figures all those deaths in adults which are officially classified as 'undetermined', i.e. where the coroner is unable to come to a decision, plus deaths due to self-administered poisoning in adults, irrespective of the declared intent of the individual. The rationale for these procedures is that detailed case studies have shown that according to psychiatric criteria the great majority of such individuals should be regarded as suicides. Interestingly, their aggregation to the official suicide figures makes no difference to trends occurring over time, nor does it materially influence the pattern for age and sex subgroups.

On the other hand, the assertion that official statistical data is of no value at all has been hotly contested. Critics point out that Douglas's attack on the role of ideology in determining the figures was advanced without any empirical evidence. It is a truism, which may be generally accepted, that all data reflects the conceptual organization of the observer as well as the natural world, but this is probably true for all science. More specifically, studies have been carried out to determine whether differences in legal procedures and the like do make any material difference to suicide statistics. One of the best known of these (Sainsbury and Barraclough 1968) showed that, for immigrant groups to the United States, the rank order of their suicide rates closely correlated with that of their home countries, despite the fact that they were being assessed by a completely different set of social agencies. This work has been broadly supported by other studies in Australia. Another study considered the effect of a change in coroner on the suicide rates for his district, arguing that if personal bias played much of a role, then a greater variation in rates should occur at such transitions than in control groups where the same individual remained in office. In fact no differences emerged. Other studies have looked into the training of coroner's officers, with the broad conclusion that this makes virtually no difference to the way in which they prepare information for the coroner's court, or to the final suicide statistics derived from these proceedings.

Another type of investigation has exchanged data between two or more countries and compared the classifications of death that emerge. Evidence was found, in a study comparing Danish and English coroners, of considerable disagreement at the individual case level and, worse, that almost as much disagreement existed between the officers within each country as between the two nations as a whole. This particular series, however, was not meant to be a representative sample, so it is not yet clear how far the results can be generalized. Another investigation, in which records were exchanged between the Scottish Crown Office and a sample of English coroners (the two systems are really very different), again showed that there was appreciable misclassification at an individual level, but that the net effect of this was mutually cancelling and that the final discrepancies were trivial (Ross and Kreitman 1975).

What, then, can be concluded? There is undoubtedly considerable, and variable, under-reporting. Even after allowing for this, however, consistent differences do persist and are not modified to any great extent by alternative statistical classifications or legal procedures. The data, then, is usable, a conclusion much strengthened by its uniformity in certain respects. For example, it is almost universally the case that the rates are higher among men than among women; among the middle-aged and the elderly rather than the young; in urban centres rather than rural regions; among the *bereaved; among the widowed, divorced, and childless; and possibly in populations undergoing rapid industrialization.

It would be wise never to accept international statistical data as *proof* for any particular hypothesis. Its prime role, rather, should be to suggest ideas which could be explored in more closely controlled investigations. This conclusion is particularly relevant when one turns away from the much-belaboured question of validity to the problems attendant on the interpretation of these statistics. Table 1 shows the rates by sex, for a sample of countries, calcu-

Table 1. Standardized sucide rates (ages 15 and over) in thirty selected countries or areas, 1965–9

	Suicides per 100 00	
	Males	Females
Mexico	4.44	1.20
Greece	6.38	2.77
Italy	10.19	4.04
Netherlands	11.78	6.87
Yugoslavia	11.97	4.16
UK: Scotland	12.00	7.44
Israel	12.74	8.42
UK: England and Wales	14.71	9.42
Norway	14.75	4.40
Bulgaria	18.32	8.69
New Zealand	19.11	9.31
Canada	20.63	7.45
Hong Kong	21.40	15.55
Portugal	22.44	5.60
United States	22.98	8.44
Poland	24.51	5.01
Japan	24.71	18.88
Australia	25.43	13.70
Belgium	25.43	10.85
Singapore	27.50	15.22
France	30.20	9.74
Denmark	31.84	17.01
Switzerland	34.69	12.20
Federal Republic of Germany	35.64	16.29
Sweden	36.81	13.84
Austria	41.48	15.87
Czechoslovakia	45.18	16.47
Finland	47.98	12.07
Hungary	58.46	22.34
West Berlin	63.90	31.65

lated after corrections to allow for differences in their age structure. Most published statistics are based on total population figures, but as in most countries suicide by children aged less than 15 years is a rare event, the figures in the table give the suicide rate among adults, with due allowance for age variation between populations.

These figures pose the immediate question of why, within Europe, Hungary should have a (male) rate nine times greater than that of Greece, and thirteen times that of Mexico. Clearly differences between these areas are legion, and, as with any other type of cross-cultural comparison, there are so many discrepancies between pairs of countries or cultures that to propose any one of these as the cause of a difference in suicide rates is a highly hazardous exercise. What are required, rather, are general hypotheses that might explain the overall pattern. Some are mentioned below.

There remains the use of international data analysed for longitudinal trends. Data collected over the years within a particular country is free from many of the hazards already cited; it can reasonably be assumed that such biases as operate will remain reasonably constant. It is thus possible to venture certain generalizations. For example, the effect of war on suicide rates has been studied in some detail, and has invariably been found to be associated with a steep decline, especially at the outbreak of hostilities. This decrease is not due to suicide masquerading as death in combat, as it affects all age groups, to varying degrees, and women as well as men. Interestingly, the decline can also be shown for neutral countries faced with the threat of war but never actually engaged in conflict. A likely cause of the decrease is thought to be an increased sense of national cohesion, coupled with a decrease in unemployment. (Without data of international scope this important conclusion would have been difficult to establish.)

A similar type of analysis has been applied to economic recessions. Sainsbury (1963) showed, by an ingenious series of trend analyses, that economic reverses and unemployment both conduced to higher suicide rates, but that poverty *per se* was not particularly relevant. Again, conclusions of this kind require information from many sources, if the effects of numerous confounding influences are to be dissected out. More recently, similar techniques have begun to be used to elucidate the effects on suicide of improved psychiatric services, the availability of lethal agents, such as guns or toxic domestic gas, the increased deployment of social work services, the role of alcohol abuse, and similar influences.   NK

Douglas, J. (1967). *The Social Meaning of Suicide*.

Dublin, L. (1963). *Suicide: A Sociological and Statistical Study*.

Hawton, K., and van Heeringen, K. (2002). *International Handbook of Suicide and Attempted Suicide*.

Hendin, H. (1964). *Suicide in Scandinavia*.

McCarthy, P., and Walsh, D. (1975). 'Suicide in Dublin: I. The under-reporting of suicide and its consequences for national statistics'. *British Journal of Psychiatry*, 126.

Ross, O., and Kreitman, N. (1975). 'A further investigation of differences in the suicide rate of England and Wales and of Scotland'. *British Journal of Psychiatry*, 127.

Ruzicka, L. T. (1976). *World Health Statistics Report*, 29/7.

Sainsbury, P. (1963). 'The social and epidemiological aspects of suicide, with special reference to the aged'. *Processes of Ageing*, 2.

——— and Barraclough, B. (1968). 'Differences between suicide rates'. *Nature*, 220.

suppression. In psychoanalytic (especially *Freudian) theory, the pushing down of painful memories, so that they are unavailable in *consciousness. It is, however, supposed that they may in some sense persist in the unconscious, sometimes to create psychological havoc.

Sydenham, Sir Thomas (1624–89). British physician. Born at Wynford Eagle, Dorset, he studied medicine at Oxford and Montpellier. He was remarkable in his time for insisting on accurate and detailed descriptions of disease, thereby making important contributions to medical classification. In his Epistolary Dissertation to Dr Cole (1682), entitled 'De affectione hysterica', he made some timely observations on *hysteria, a disorder with protean manifestations which, he believed, affected one-sixth of his patients.

At the time of his writing, two main theories dominated thinking about hysteria. First there was the ancient belief that the condition was confined to the female sex, being caused by a disturbance of the womb, which it was alleged caused symptoms by becoming displaced into the affected part of the body—see Edward Jorden (1603), 'The suffocation of the mother'. A contrary opinion came from Thomas Willis, the anatomist, in 1667 when he denied that the uterus and humours were responsible for hysteria, claiming that the condition arose from disturbances of 'the Brain and Nervous Stock'. He observed similarities between hysteria in women and hypochondriasis in men, conditions which Sydenham likened 'as one egg to another'. Willis emphasized the importance of 'hysterical' convulsions, most of which today would probably be diagnosed as epileptic, but he firmly rejected the wandering womb hypothesis, when he wrote, 'As to the cause of these symptoms, most ancient and indeed Modern Physitians, refer them to the ascent of the womb and vapours elevated from it' and went on to point out that the womb was 'so small in bulk in virgins and widdows, and so strictly tyed by the neighbouring parts round about it, that it can not of itself be moved, or ascend from its place'.

Sydenham, like Willis, repudiated the uterine theory of hysteria, although he considered that women were more prone to the disorder than men; none the less he agreed that men, particularly those 'who lead a sedentary life and study hard, are afflicted by the same'. His other major contribution was his observation that hysteria was more likely to follow 'disturbances of mind which are usual causes of this disease'. He also noted that hysterical symptoms were often accompanied by depression, but could coexist with physical disease.

In making these observations Sydenham placed hysteria firmly in the category of the psychological disorders that could be said to be the forerunners of the psychoneuroses today. No doubt he tended to diagnose hysteria as a psychological disorder far too frequently, and many of the signs and symptoms he described would probably be more indicative of physical than of neurotic illness. None the less, despite his emphasis on psychological causes for hysteria, the ancient uterine hypothesis has continued to influence medical thinking over the past three centuries. Freud faced opposition and ridicule when he described hysteria in men, and the revival of the notion of hysteria as a women's disease, under the title of Briquet's syndrome

(1859), shows that Sydenham's observations have not been so influential as one might have hoped.

When it came to treatment, Sydenham was very much a man of his time, and prescribed bleeding and purging to purify the blood, but he made a point of enquiring whether his patients had suffered from 'fretting, or any disturbances of the mind'. He and his contemporary Dr Thomas Fuller, both of whom had seen service in the cavalry during the Civil War, strongly recommended horse riding as a therapeutic measure for hysteria and hypochondriasis, although probably not for 'slender and weakly women, that seem consumptive, and girls that have the green sickness'. No doubt—unless the patient fell off—horse riding was safer and more beneficial than some of the other widely used remedies of the time. FAW

Dewhurst, K. (1966). *Sir Thomas Sydenham: His Life and Original Writings.*

Hunter, R., and Macalpine, I. (1963). *Three Hundred Years of Psychiatry, 1553–1860.*

symbols. A symbol, broadly speaking, is something that stands for something else. Subordinate questions arise: what sorts of things can stand for things? for what sorts of things? and how do they do so? Also, certain reservations need to be made.

A £5 note once stood for five gold sovereigns, serving the same purposes. Usually a symbol stands for its object in a less robust way: it reminds us of it. It may do so by resembling it, or by standing to it in a known causal relation, or by some conventional connection of whatever origin—hence C. S. *Peirce's trichotomy of 'signs' into 'icons' (e.g. a diagram), 'indices' (e.g. a thermometer), and 'symbols' in a narrower sense (e.g. a name).

Whereas association itself is symmetrical, the relation of symbol to object is not; it is limited to situations in which the object commands more interest than the symbol. The fish symbolizes Jesus, because the Greek ἰχθύς is an acrostic of a five-word description of Jesus, but it does so in churches, not kitchens. The relation is asymmetrical and intermittent.

A physical object, or state, may stand for a physical object or state: a fish for a man, an inscription for a man, a map for a province, a mercury level for a temperature. Often, the symbol is better seen as a whole class, such as that of ichthyomorphic carvings. A name, indeed, may be seen as the class of its inscriptions and utterances. Sometimes, as when gods are said to have symbolized seasons, or Janus to have symbolized wholeness, the symbols are evidently neither physical objects nor states nor classes of such; it is hard to categorize them otherwise than as ideas. A better account might take nominalistic lines, appealing to visual patterns and linguistic expressions.

The heat and wind activate their symbolic indices, the thermometer and weathervane. But primitive peoples have believed, conversely, in an efficacy of symbols upon their objects—thus effigies and the magic of names. Thus also, presumably, the cave paintings of 30,000 years ago.

Fanciful subconscious resemblances must be assumed between symbol and symbolized, if we are to make sense of iconography or of Sigmund *Freud. The flights of creative imagination in our *dreams are undeniable, but their mechanism remains a mystery. Such symbolism must have figured in the origins of language. The surgeon Sir James Paget (1814–99) had an imaginative theory of private gestures within the mouth, private muscular contortions that bore a subjective resemblance to some visible traits of objects. It is in language, at any rate, that symbolism attains the age of discretion. Let us look to its workings.

One way in which a linguistic expression often stands for something is by *designating* it. Designation is the relation that the names 'Plato' and 'Wales' bear to Plato and Wales, and that the phrases 'the author of *Waverley*' and 'Whittington's cat' bear to Sir Walter Scott and Whittington's cat. Symbols that purport to designate are *singular terms*. Some fail—for example, 'Pegasus'—for want of a designatum.

A way in which symbols more commonly stand for things is by *denoting* them. A *general term*, typically a common noun or adjective or intransitive verb, denotes each of the things it is true of. Thus 'horse' denotes each horse, 'green' each green thing, 'swim' everyone who swims.

There has been since antiquity an urge to view general terms as designating. Thus 'horse' was seen as designating some trumped-up abstract object, a universal—the property equinity—besides denoting each horse. This facile positing of universals was deplored by the medieval nominalists, as a confusion.

It was in part a happy confusion. In mathematics, and to some degree elsewhere in science, abstract objects serve theoretical purposes that cannot, evidently, be served by just talking of general terms and denotation. Classes do suffice in lieu of properties, but they are next of kin. Still, there is no need to view the general terms themselves as designating universals in addition to their job of denoting. If properties or classes are to be designated, we do have singular terms for the purpose: 'equinity', 'horsekind'.

General terms are meaningful, surely, and the urge to accord designata to them was due partly to confusing designation with meaning. Meaning is not designation, even among singular terms. The terms 'the Evening Star' and 'the Morning Star' (Frege's example) designate the same thing but differ in meaning. 'Pegasus' is meaningful, though designating nothing.

The notion of meaning is elusive. Jeremy *Bentham appreciated that meaning accrues primarily to whole sentences, and only derivatively to separate words. Setting aside emotive or poetic meaning, and looking only to the cognitive meaning of declarative sentences, we may say that the meaning of a sentence consists in its truth conditions. We know the meaning of a sentence insofar as we know in what circumstances the sentence counts as true. To understand a sentence is to know when to affirm it.

There are sentences, such as 'It's raining', 'This is red', 'That's a rabbit', that count as true only in circumstances observable at the time of utterance. Their meanings can be learned by conditioning, unaided by auxiliary sentences. To proceed from these beginnings to higher levels of language, unaided by translation from another language already known, is an impressive feat, but the child achieves it. He exploits analogies: from the apparent role of a word in one sentence he guesses its role in another. Also, he discovers that people assent to a sentence of some one form only contingently upon assenting to a corresponding sentence of some related form. Exploring, thus, the interrelations of sentences, and corrected by his elders, he learns how to compose innumerable sentences and when to affirm them.

Once he is well started, we could teach him harder sentences by constructing a dictionary along the following lines. Each entry explains some word—for example, 'putative'—by general systematic instructions for paraphrasing all possible sentential contexts of 'putative' into sentences lacking 'putative'. Each word in the paraphrase is either a word of the old sentence or a word more frequently heard than 'putative'. Words very frequently heard are left unexplained. Thus, though meaning belongs to sentences, words serve in generating it. The concept of a dictionary, just presented, shows how.

The sentential contexts of some words can be paraphrased simply by substituting some more frequent word, or some phrase. That word or phrase is then said to have the same meaning as the original word, and thus it is that the notion of word meanings is derivable from that of sentence meanings. Two expressions have the same meaning if substituting one for the other never disturbs truth conditions of sentences.

We saw that singular terms have their designata, when all goes well, and general terms their denotata. Many words claim neither—thus 'or', 'to', 'however', 'which', 'very'. Scholastics called these syncategorematic: lacking in intrinsic meaning, and meaningful only derivatively, through their contribution to the meaning of the containing sentences. There is a trace here of the confusion between meaning and designation, or denotation; words were thought to forfeit intrinsic meaning by not purporting to denote or designate. But let us take it that words generally are meaningful only through their contribution to the meaning of the containing sentences. Then we may keep the term 'syncategorematic' for the words that do not purport to denote or designate, but without thereby imputing any distinctive shortage of meaning.

Consisting, as it does, primarily in the truth conditions of sentences, meaning is pretty thin stuff. In the special case of observation sentences, it can be inculcated by sensory conditioning, or direct demonstration; for the rest, only by other sentences, paraphrases. We give the meaning of a sentence by explaining the sentence, and the meaning of a word by explaining how it works in sentences. Serious confusions could have been avoided if a practice had been made of speaking thus of explanatory activities, rather than of meanings as somehow separable entities that symbols might stand for.

The meaning of a symbol was often confused, we saw, with the designatum. When it was not, it was usually viewed as an idea. This circumstance doubtless delayed the demise of an uncritically mentalistic psychology. Meanings had to be admitted, it seemed, on pain of rendering language meaningless; and it was not easy to see what meanings could be, if not ideas. Hence a dualism of symbol and idea, language and thought.

John Horne Tooke denounced this dualism as early as 1786, protesting that John *Locke would have done well to write 'word' in place of 'idea' throughout his *Essay*. The way was opened for J. B. *Watson to identify thought primarily with language, subvocal speech. The medium becomes, in Marshall McLuhan's phrase, the message. The incipient muscular tugs that constituted the thinking process, according to Watson, were not indeed wholly confined to the speech apparatus; the inarticulate painter or engineer must think partly in his fingers. Without language, however, thought would be meagre.

Mathematics affords the ultimate example of the power of notation as a way of thought. In school, when we did problems about rowing across the current, the hard part was putting them into equations; that was the programming, and algebra was the computer. The boon of arabic numeration goes without saying, and the mere use of brackets to unify a complex expression is a cornerstone of mathematics. It is the use of brackets, together with the variable, that enables us to extrapolate our laws and iterate our operations beyond all finite bounds.   WVQ

Cirlot, J. E. (1962). *A Dictionary of Symbols.*

Frege, G. (1892). 'Über Sinn und Bedeutung' (Eng. trans. 'On sense and reference'). In Frege, *Philosophical Writings*. Eds. P. Geach and M. Black (1952).

Ogden, C. K. (1932). *Bentham's Theory of Fictions.*

Paget, Sir R. (1930). *Human Speech.*

Peirce, C. S. (1932). *Collected Papers*, vol. ii.

Quine, W. V. (1973). *The Roots of Reference.*

Tooke, J. H. (1786). *The Diversions of Purley.*

Watson, J. B. (1919). *Psychology from the Standpoint of a Behaviorist.*

synaesthesia. In the 19th century Francis *Galton, a cousin of Charles Darwin, noticed something peculiar.

He found that a certain proportion of the general population—who were otherwise completely normal—tended to get their senses mixed up. For example, he (or she) might experience the colour red every time he hears the note C sharp played on the piano or the colour blue for F sharp. Or any time he sees the Hindu/Arabic numeral 5 on a sheet of paper he sees it tinged red, whereas a different number might evoke a different colour. The particular colour evoked by a given tone or number is not the same for all synaesthetes but within a given synaesthete the particular associations remain remarkably stable over time (Baron-Cohen et al. 1996).

Several facts about synaesthesia have been known for a long time.

1. As Galton noted, synaesthesia tends to run in families and probably has a genetic basis.

2. It appears to be much more common among drug users, especially those who have used LSD.

3. If you have one type of synaesthesia (e.g. tone–colour) you are also more likely to have another (e.g. number–colour).

4. There is some evidence that it is seven times more common among artists, poets, and novelists than in the general population.

5. Synaesthesia can sometimes be acquired rather than inherited. A patient who became completely blind by the age of 40 suddenly started experiencing both unformed photisms (phosphenes) and clearly formed visual images of simple shapes he palpated—presumably because his tactile sensory input had now 'invaded' (or was indirectly activating) his visual cortex (Armell and Ramachandran 1999).

6. In addition to the common types—number (grapheme)–colour and tone–colour—some exotic variants have also been described, such as a man who tasted shapes (Cytowic 2002) and who palpated tastes (Ramachandran and Hubbard 2002)! We have also encountered synaesthetes who automatically classify all numbers and letters as 'good or bad' and 'masculine or feminine' (as the French do for objects). Perhaps this is a quirky manifestation of the normal human brain's tendency to binarize the world into polar opposites. If so (see below) synaesthesia, far from being bizarre, may represent an extreme version of tendencies that exist in all brains. Perhaps *Aristotle's notion of a 'sensus communis'—a common sense—was not a mere metaphor!

7. Synaesthesia is almost always unidirectional; numbers and letters evoke colours but colours evoking graphemes is very rare (although it does happen).

8. Synaesthesia used to be considered rare (estimates varying from 1 in 10,000 to 1 in 1,000) but we and others have found that it is actually quite common (1 in 200).

This list of observations seems so bewildering that it is hardly surprising that the phenomenon never won general acceptance in mainstream neuroscience; indeed it was sometimes dismissed as confabulatory.

There have been four styles of explanation put forward in the past to account for this curious phenomenon. (1) These people are just crazy or trying to draw attention to themselves. This of course is a common reaction in science towards *Kuhnian 'anomalies'—they tend to get brushed under the carpet if they do not fit the picture, the received wisdom. (2) They are on drugs. This is a reasonable criticism except that it makes the phenomenon more interesting—not less. Why should some chemicals produce this effect—if they do? (3) They are just remembering childhood memory associations, e.g. from having played with coloured refrigerator magnets. But if this is true why is the condition inherited? (4) Maybe they are just being metaphorical. After all ordinary language is replete with sensory metaphors—'loud shirt', 'sharp cheese'—and maybe they are just more gifted in this regard when they say C sharp is red. This explanation is inadequate because it merely substitutes one mystery (metaphor) for another (synaesthesia) but, as we shall see, it probably has more merit than the three preceding explanations.

These explanations have been largely unsatisfactory but the picture has now changed. The combined use of detailed psychophysics and brain-imaging experiments initiated around the turn of the 21st century has allowed the study of this intriguing phenomenon to make the transition from the era of vague phenomenology to the era of systematic empirical research. In particular, four things have happened (Ramachandran and Hubbard 2001a). First, it is clear that synaesthesia is a genuine sensory phenomenon: the subject literally experiences the 'quale' of the evoked sensation. Second, we now have clearly formulated, testable hypotheses about what the underlying neural basis might be and what parts of the brain might be involved. Third, brain-imaging studies by Nunn et al. (2002) and by our group have provided strong hints that our hypotheses about the brain mechanisms involved are correct at least for some synaesthetes. And fourth, it seems likely that far from being an oddity, synaesthesia might help us understand many enigmatic aspects of the mind such as our capacity for metaphor, aspects of language, and even abstract thought. We will also propose a theory to account for why the apparently useless synaesthesia gene(s) (if there is one) might confer a hidden evolutionary advantage.

1. Synaesthesia is a genuine sensory effect
2. The neural mechanism of synaesthesia
3. Different types of synaesthesia

1. Synaesthesia is a genuine sensory effect

Recent experiments suggest strongly that synaesthesia is a sensory phenomenon, not a high-level memory association. If you have a set of 2s embedded among a matrix of randomly placed 5s, normal non-synaesthetes have great difficulty in discerning the 2s since they are mirror images of each other and share the same constituent features (three horizontal lines and two vertical lines). If the 2s are arranged to form a shape such as a triangle or a square, normal subjects take tens of seconds to report the hidden shape accurately. On the other hand synaesthetes who (say) see the 2s as red and 5s as green see the global 'red' triangle or square 'pop out' much more quickly—their reaction time for correctly reporting the shape is much shorter. (And they report seeing a red triangle against a green background.) Since they are *better* than normals at this task, synaesthesia cannot be confabulatory and must be a genuine sensory effect rather than a high-level memory association.

The saturation of the synaesthetic colour also diminishes as the contrast of the number (or letter) is reduced, and below 8 per cent contrast the colour vanishes even though the number is still clearly visible. Alternating two spatially superposed graphemes at higher than 7 Hz also abolishes the colour. Such dependence on elementary physical parameters also suggests an early sensory process.

2. The neural mechanism of synaesthesia

The cortical colour area V4 in the brain and the area representing visual appearance of Hindu/Arabic numbers and letters (graphemes) happen to be right next to each other in the fusiform gyrus. Given that grapheme–colour synaesthesia is the commonest form we suggested that the phenomenon is caused by an abnormal cross-activation between these two areas resulting from a gene mutation(s) that results in defective 'pruning' between brain modules, disinhibition between them, or hyperactivation of ordinarily silent back projections (Armell and Ramachandran 1999; Ramachandran and Hubbard 2002). Preliminary evidence from brain-imaging studies (Nunn et al. 2002) has provided strong hints that this idea might be right.

3. Different types of synaesthesia

There are at least two types of synaesthesia and possibly many 'in-between' categories. We call these 'higher' and 'lower' synaesthesia, depending on the presumed anatomical stage at which the cross-activation occurs.

For example, in many synaesthetes the Hindu/Arabic number (e.g. 5 or 6) evokes colour but not the corresponding Roman number (V or VI), and this is true whether you are Roman or Hindu. This implies that it is not the high-level numerical *concept* or sequence or ordinality that evokes colour, but the visual appearance. This is consist-ent with the cross-activation theory since the fusiform represents appearance not concept.

In certain other synaesthetes, however, even days of the week and months of the year evoke colour, not just number (e.g. Wednesday is pink, Friday is yellow; or December is red and January is green, etc.). In these 'higher synaesthetes' it is the high-level abstract concept of ordinality that seems to drive the colour. Since the next stage in the colour-processing hierarchy is near the temporo-parieto-occipital (TPO) junction and that is where abstract number sequences are represented, it seems plausible that in these people the cross-activation occurs in the vicinity of the angular gyrus/TPO junction.

Analogously, 'lower synaesthetes' tend to see colours evoked by *visually* presented alphabets (represented in the fusiform), whereas in higher synaesthetes it is the heard phoneme (represented near the angular gyrus) that evokes the colour.

We postulate a gene mutation that causes cross-activation between these sensory maps encoding different dimensions. If the gene is selectively expressed in the fusiform you get lower synaesthesia; if expressed near the TPO junction you get higher synaesthesia. If expressed in the vicinity of the insular cortex you may get touch–taste or taste–touch synaesthesia given the proximity of taste maps (in the insula) and the hand/touch region of S1 in the Penfield map. Spatially adjacent maps are more likely to be linked than widely separated maps even in normal brains, and so if the mutations were to strengthen these connections synaesthesia is most likely to involve adjacent brain regions. (But it does not always have to, because sometimes even regions far apart might become abnormally connected.) Even foot fetishes could be regarded as a form of synaesthesia that arises because of the anatomical adjacency of the foot and genitals in the Penfield map.

Although number–colour synaesthesia is probably caused by early sensory cross-activation it can be modulated by top-down influences. If a large 5 is composed of a 'texture' of little 2s the synaesthete can alternatively either pay attention to the global 5 or zoom in on the little 2s, and the colour of the display changes accordingly even though the physical image is constant.

We have even come across a colour-anomalous synaesthete who could see only a limited range of colours in the world because of deficient cone pigments. Yet when he looked at numbers he saw 'Martian colours' that he could not see in the real world. This effect occurs because even though his colour receptors in the eye are deficient he presumably has a normal colour area V4 in the fusiform (specified genetically) that can be indirectly stimulated through cross-activation by numbers! The effect also rules out the memory association hypothesis of synaesthesia; how can you 'remember' colours you have never seen?

Some other facts about synaesthesia that have not been previously noticed include:

1. Letter precedence effect: sometimes the whole word takes on the colour of the first letter. This is true even if the first letter is silent (at least in lower synaesthetes).

2. Font: upper case usually evokes more vivid colour. For lower-case letters the same colour is evoked but it is less saturated, more 'patchy' and 'shiny'—colour 'paraesthesiae', one is tempted to call them.

3. In a rare form of synaesthesia the subject classifies all graphemes (sometimes even objects) as being male or female or good or bad—a quirky manifestation of the universal human tendency to binarize entities in the world into polar opposites (hot/cold; good/evil; big/small; yin/yang, etc.). It is hard to explain this in terms of anatomy.

4. Galton noted that in some synaesthetes each number not only has a colour but occupies a particular location in space with the linear sequence of numbers arranged sequentially in space—a 'number line'. Often the subject claims the number line is convoluted—even doubling back on itself—so that 9 might be (say) nearer to 3 in Cartesian space than to 8. In normal individuals the reaction time for judging which of two numbers is bigger varies inversely with the numerical distance between them, as if they are laid out on a perfectly straight imaginary line in the brain, making it harder to discriminate numerically adjacent numbers. We have found this is not true for synaesthetes with convoluted number lines; their reaction times were some messy compromise between Cartesian distance and numerical distance.

5. When asked to 'imagine' or visualize a number, most lower synaesthetes report, paradoxically, that the colour evoked by the visualized number is actually more vivid than one evoked by a real black or white one. This is because top-down imagery activates the same sensory number areas in the fusiform as real images do—thereby evoking the colours—but in the case of a real number there is contradictory bottom-up information partially vetoing the synaesthetic colours. In the absence of such vetoing the colours are more vivid.

Why is synaesthesia much more common among artists, poets, and novelists? One thing they all have in common is a facility with metaphor, a propensity to link seemingly unrelated concepts (e.g. 'Juliet is the Sun', 'he has a sharp mind'). If the 'hyperconnectivity' gene is expressed more diffusely throughout the brain rather than locally, and if we assume that high-level concepts are also represented in brain maps, then the result would be a

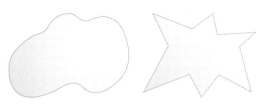

Fig. 1.

greater propensity for metaphor. This would explain the higher incidence of synaesthesia in arty types. This is a speculative idea that is not easy to test. But if correct it would explain why the apparently useless synaesthesia gene (if there is such a thing) has survived; it might confer creativity in some outliers.

Synaesthetic propensities might therefore exist in all of us. Consider the two abstract shapes in Fig. 1. If you ask people which one is 'Bouba' and which one 'Kiki'; more than 95 per cent pick the bulbous amoeboid shape as Bouba and the jagged shape as Kiki. (This is not because the jagged shape resembles K; even Tamil speakers make the same choice.) The effect suggests that we are all closet synaesthetes; the sharp inflections of the sound 'ki ki' mimic the sharp inflections of the jagged visual shapes, and the gentle undulation of contours in the amoeboid shapes corresponds to the sound 'bouba'. Since the subjects have never seen these shapes, or heard the sounds, before, there must be a pre-existing non-arbitrary cross-activation between visual shapes represented in the fusiform and sounds represented in the auditory cortex. Such cross-modal translation probably requires the mediation of the angular gyrus given its strategic anatomical location at the TPO junction—at the crossroads between visual (occipital), auditory (temporal), and parietal (touch) areas of the brain.

Since the visual shape Kiki is composed of photons hitting the eyes in parallel whereas the sound kiki is delivered by sequential stimulation of hair cells of the inner ear, the two have nothing in common except the abstract property of jaggedness in Fourier space. What this ability represents, then, is a primitive form of the process of abstraction that humans excel in (e.g. when we say five rabbits, five tones, five unicorns, they have nothing common except fiveness). There are hints that the Bouba/Kiki effect is compromised when the angular gyrus is damaged.

The angular gyrus became progressively larger in primates, and is disproportionately large in the great apes and humans. Perhaps it was originally an adaptation for arboreal living, allowing the primate brain to match the seen visual orientation of a branch with its position felt through proprioception as the hand rotated to grab it. But once in place it could have been adapted for other more sophisticated types of abstraction of the kind that humans excel at.

Metaphors, too, incorporate synaesthetic elements, as when we say 'loud shirt'. Also, we use the word 'disgusting' and scrunch up our nose when confronting a bad taste or smell, but why do we also use the same word and expression for *moral* disgust? This may occur because olfactory and gustatory disgust are mapped in the orbitofrontal cortex which later became usurped in humans for representing morality and disgust. As Freud said, anatomy is destiny.

Thus synaesthesia, far from being a mere curiosity can provide key insights into some of the most elusive aspects of our mind, such as the emergence of metaphor and abstraction. Once the gene(s) is cloned we can go from the gene to anatomy (fusiform gyrus; angular gyrus) to psychophysics and phenomenology, perhaps all the way to the emergence of metaphor and abstract thought.

VR/RLG

Armel, K. C., and Ramachandran, V. S. (1999). 'Acquired synesthesia in retinitis pigmentosa'. *Neurocase*, 5/4.

Baron-Cohen, S., Burt, L., Smith-Laittan, F., Harrison, J., and Bolton, P. (1996). 'Synaesthesia: prevalence and familiarity'. *Perception*, 25/9.

Cytowic, R. E. (2002). *Synaesthesia: A Union of the Senses.* (2nd edn.).

Dehaene, S. (1997). *The Number Sense: How the Mind Creates Mathematics.*

Domino, G. (1989). 'Synesthesia and creativity in fine arts students: an empirical look'. *Creativity Research Journal*, 2/1–2.

Galton, F. (1997). 'Colour associations'. In Baron-Cohen, S., and Harrison, J. E. (eds.), *Synaesthesia: Classic and Contemporary Readings.*

Merikle, P., Dixon, M. J., and Smilek, D. (2002). 'The role of synaesthetic photisms on perception, conception and memory'. Talk presented at the 12th Annual Meeting of the Cognitive Neuroscience Society, San Francisco, 14–16 Apr.

Nunn, J. A., Gregory, L. J., Brammer, M., et al. (2002). 'Functional magnetic resonance imaging of synesthesia: activation of V4/V8 by spoken words'. *Nature Neuroscience*, 5/4.

Ramachandran, V. S., and Hubbard, E. M. (2001a). 'Psychophysical investigations into the neural basis of synaesthesia'. *Proceedings of the Royal Society of London, Series B*, 268.

——(2001b) 'Synaesthesia: a window into perception, thought and language?' *Journal of Consciousness Studies*, 8/12.

——(2002). 'Synesthetic colors support symmetry perception, apparent motion, and ambiguous crowding'. Talk presented at the 43 Annual Meeting of the Psychonomics Society, 21–24 Nov.

Zeki, S., and Marini, L. (1998). 'Three cortical stages of colour processing in the human brain'. *Brain*, 121.

synapse. A junction between two nerves. Synapses contain 'transmitter substances', of which it is now known there is a remarkable variety. The synapses allow the action potentials in axons to cross in one direction only into contiguous nerves. They are modulated by the activity of many other nerves (up to 2,000) and by chemical signals, especially hormones. See NEUROTRANSMITTERS AND NEUROMODULATORS. RLG

syndrome. In medicine, a typical grouping of features of a physical or mental disease. Thus the syndrome of measles includes spots, a high temperature, and photophobia (dislike or fear of bright light). This raises the question: is a disease more than its symptoms? The symptoms are what are apparent, and used for diagnosis; there is much that is hidden and causative in diseases, beyond the symptoms.

RLG

synergies. There are two related approaches to the 'units of control' employed by the brain in controlling movement. Both are called synergies. The first, formulated by C. S. *Sherrington, posits a reflex unit above that of the motor unit; while the second, formulated by Nikolas Bernstein (1967) suggests that a restricted number of programmes may underlie most of our behaviour.

To understand Sherrington's views we must start with the notion of a reflex. To take two familiar examples: in the knee-jerk reflex, the tap of the physician's hammer stretches a tendon, and this is sensed by a sensor (proprioceptor) which activates a motor neuron which contracts the extensor muscle (which had 'appeared' to be too long) so that the foot kicks out. In the scratch reflex, an irritant localized to part of the skin activates receptors which in turn activate motor neurons which control muscles to bring a foot or hand to the irritated skin and rub back and forth. In each case, we have a reflex loop which mediates direct stimulus–response behaviour: from the external world via receptors to the spinal cord, where motor neurons respond by controlling muscles to yield movement in the external world.

Now consider the scratch reflex more carefully. We may see it as made up of two components. The rubbing component needs the limb movement to ensure that it contacts the (right place on the) skin, the limb movement is guided into contact by feedback from the rubbing movement. The two reflex actions 'synergize', or work together. More generally,

The executant musculature . . . provides a reflex means of supporting or reinforcing the co-operation of flexors with flexors, extensors with extensors, etc. The proprioceptors of reaching muscles operate reflexly upon other muscles of near functional relation to themselves. Active contraction (including active stretch) and passive stretch in the reaching muscles are stimuli for reflexes influencing other muscles, and the reflex influence so exerted is on some muscles excitatory and on others inhibitory; it is largely reciprocally distributed, knitting synergists together. (Creed et al. 1932: 129).

Thus, for Sherrington, the synergy is an anatomically based reflex linkage of a group of muscles.

The Bernstein school is informed by notions of control theory. The brain is to generate control signals which will cause the muscles to contract with just the right timing to bring about some desired behaviour. But there are so many muscles, they suggest, that to control every muscle independently to its optimum would be a computationally unmanageable problem. They thus see the crucial problem in the 'design' of a brain which controls movement to be that of reducing the number of 'degrees of freedom', i.e. the number of independent parameters which must be controlled.

In order for the higher levels of the central nervous system to effectively solve the task of organizing motor acts within a required time, it is necessary that the number of controlled parameters be not too large, and the afferentation, requiring analysis, not too great. [This is achieved] by the so-called synergies. . . . Each synergy is associated with certain peculiar connections imposed on some muscle groups, a subdivision of all the participant muscles into a small number of related groups. Due to this fact, to perform motion it is sufficient to control a small number of independent parameters, even though the number of muscles participating in the movement may be large. (Gel'fand et al. 1973: 162)

So far, the general framework is consonant with Sherrington's synergies. But these are restricted to stimulus–response patterns. Bernstein had a more general concern with dynamic patterns changing over time during some motor act: '[A] complex synergy is involved in walking. . . . "The bio-dynamic tissue" of live movements [appears] to be full of an enormous number of regular and stable details. . . . [In old people] the synergy existing in

normal walking between the action of the arms and legs is destroyed' (Bernstein 1967: 67, 93).

However, this was too global a view of synergy, and later work of the Moscow school came to view synergies as the functional building blocks from which most motions can be composed:

Although synergies are few in number, they make it possible to encompass almost all the diversity of arbitrary motions. One can separate relatively simple synergies of pose control (synergy of stabilization), cyclic locomotive synergies (walking, running, swimming, etc.), synergies of throwing, striking, jumping, and a certain (small) number of others. (Gel'fand et al. 1973: 162)

One thus comes to see a synergy in general as a programme for controlling some distinctive motor performance extended in space and time, built upon synergies of coordinated reflexes as substrate. (The entry FEEDBACK AND FEEDFORWARD places this notion in a control-theoretical perspective.) See also SCHEMAS.   MAA

Bernstein, N. A. (trans.) (1967). *The Coordination and Regulation of Movements*.

Creed, R. S., Denny-Brown, D., Eccles, J. C., Liddell, E. G. T., and Sherrington, C. S. (1932). *Reflex Activity of the Spinal Cord* (repr. 1972).

Gel'fand, I. M., Gurfinkel, V. S., Shik, M. L., and Tsetlin, M. L. (1973). 'Certain problems in the investigation of movement'. In *Automata Theory and Modeling of Biological Systems* (trans. from the Russian *Models of the Structural-Functional Organization of Certain Biological Systems*, 1966).

T

taste. Flavour is usually defined as the overall sensation of taste and *smell. Taste refers to sensations arising from the taste receptors in the mouth and throat while smell arises from receptors in the nose. When a person has a cold or blocks his nose, he will taste but not smell food adequately, so the flavour is reduced. It is unfortunate that in everyday language the words 'taste' and 'flavour' are used interchangeably. Taste and smell, together with texture, visual appearance, and sound, will give the overall sensory percept of the food, which is important in its choice and enjoyment. People who cannot perceive the flavour of food will often not maintain an adequate diet.

There are two main groups of scientists who are interested in understanding taste. The first group consists of food scientists within the food industry, who are interested in discovering the precise mechanisms of flavour perception so as to be able to maintain and control the flavour of the products being manufactured. Furthermore, food scientists use human judges to measure the physical and chemical characteristics of foods that are important for the flavour, texture, appearance, and sound of the food. They exploit the fact that the human senses are often more sensitive than laboratory instruments to the minute quantities of chemicals present in a food that endow it with its characteristic flavour.

The second group of scientists are more interested in the workings of the senses and the brain *per se*. Knowledge of how a taste stimulus reacts with the membrane of a taste receptor would provide information not only about mechanisms of flavour, but also about other similar chemoreceptive functions involved in drug, hormone, brain, and cell mechanisms. Changes in taste perception are beginning to be utilized as diagnostic tools in medicine, while further research is providing insights into areas ranging from genetics to the working of insect and animal attractants and repellants. For this reason, taste, along with smell, is of vital interest to a broad range of scientists.

The behavioural measurement of taste, whether for the sensory evaluation of a food flavour or for elucidating taste mechanisms, can pose problems. People do not pay as much attention to taste as they do to vision and are thus less practised at assessing the taste sensations that they experience. One consequence of this is difficulty with language, for our language is largely concerned with visual stimuli. There are many adjectives available to describe colour but few for taste. Furthermore, parents teach their children to name colours but do not do so for tastes; so that, while young children are fairly skilled at colour naming, even adults can misname common sweet, sour, salty, and bitter stimuli. In particular, the terms 'sour' and 'bitter' are often confused, but this is merely a matter of definition. The confusion can be remedied by giving tasters citric acid and quinine to compare and informing them that the correct descriptions are 'sour' and 'bitter' respectively.

Aside from these common descriptions, there is little agreement on the use of taste adjectives and individuals usually acquire their own sets of definitions or taste concepts. For precise evaluation and communication of the taste or flavour of a foodstuff, however, a precise language has to be invented, for which the breadth of use of the taste adjectives has to be precisely controlled and agreed upon by those using the language. Usually, ad hoc languages are invented for a given food, so that although, say, expert tea tasters may be able to communicate among themselves, their language would be 'foreign' to expert wine or mayonnaise tasters.

The method of language invention generally adopted is to follow the way that children learn colours: words are paired with appropriate sensations. Thus, languages are invented to describe the tastes, odours, and textures of foods, using a set of physical taste standards which are always available to define the adjectives used. These methods fall under the general heading of flavour profiling. There are problems, however, in ensuring that judges have the same breadth of use of the words in their invented language and this is still a subject of research. Without any special training, our command of vocabulary for taste is so poor that the merest suggestion of a word denoting a taste, in the instructions to a person judging a taste, will bias him to use that word. In fact, the power of suggestion is so strong that people have reported experiencing smells that they were told had been transmitted by television. See also SYNAESTHESIA

Different cultures have their own, idiosyncratic languages and confusions about taste, dependent probably on their dietary habits. Just as 'sour' and 'bitter' are confused in English, so it was reported at the beginning of this century that the islanders of the Torres Straits confused 'sour' and 'salty'. Many tribes of North American Indians were unfamiliar with salt until they had contact with Europeans, when they described salt as 'sour'. Some inhabitants of Polynesia and New Guinea had only one word to describe sweet, sour, and bitter. Recent studies have shown a tendency among Malay speakers to qualify taste adjectives. Thus, *masin*, meaning 'salty', is often qualified: *masin ayer laut* (salty like seawater), *masin garam* (salty like salt), or *masin kitchup* (salty like soy sauce). It is not clear why Malay speakers should spontaneously volunteer more detail, though it may be because mothers teach their daughters to cook by telling them to add the various ingredients until the food has a specific taste, rather than to add pre-measured amounts of ingredient according to recipes. The need for precise communication about taste would encourage the development of a precise language. Whatever the reason for such precision, it would be a useful strategy for flavour-profiling techniques.

Interestingly, the idea that there are four primary tastes, sweet, sour, salty, and bitter, is quite arbitrary. In any case, what is meant by the term 'primary taste' has not been defined. It could mean the unit of types of reaction that can take place on the membrane of the taste receptor, or of types of neural code that can communicate sensations to the brain, or even of processes that can take place in the cortex which result ultimately in the sensation of taste. Whichever of these candidates for primacy is adopted, the operative number is not known, for the idea that there are *four* primary tastes came into the taste literature by misunderstanding and accident. In spite of the absence of any firm physiological evidence, some scientists still cling to the idea. The notion is often reflected in the way that taste experiments are designed: the taste stimuli used in research studies being limited to just four, or judges being allowed to use combinations of only four words to describe their whole range of taste experience.

Taste receptors are bathed in saliva, which is secreted from the salivary glands, and contains low concentrations of taste stimuli such as sodium chloride or potassium chloride; these can come from the blood and reflect the physiological state of the organism. The taste receptors adjust so that the zero level for taste (or taste zero) is set at the stimulus level in the saliva. For example, the level of salt in saliva is highest in the morning, drops until the afternoon, and then rises again to the high morning value. The taste zero appears to do the same, so that these salivary changes cause no sensation of taste; rather, the taste zero changes with the slow rise and fall of secreted salivary constituents. This constant adjustment is a useful way of ensuring that tastes are registered only when sudden large changes take place, such as when foods are placed in the mouth. Salivary concentrations can vary tenfold in value and may form the basis for changes in taste sensitivity connected with various diseases; however, they are comparatively unimportant compared to the effect described next.

When, during an experiment, a taste stimulus like salt is tasted, it is sipped and then expelled from the mouth by spitting. However, spitting will not expel all the stimuli and while the person is spitting out the residual stimulus, his taste zero is rising to a higher level to render the residual tasteless. Thus, when the subject believes he has expelled all the residual stimulus, because his mouth feels tasteless, there will still be considerable amounts remaining and these will maintain a higher taste zero. The next stimulus will then be tasted with this new, higher taste zero; the taste system will not be as sensitive. This constant zero drift has caused considerable trouble in taste measurement; the resulting changes in salivary concentration can be a hundredfold and highly significant. If the residual stimulus is continually expelled from the mouth by a regime of water rinses between tastings, a lower average taste zero will be maintained. This confers a greater sensitivity, as well as ensuring that given stimuli taste more intense. Thus, the practice of rinsing between tastings, once thought to be an unimportant experimental detail, can be shown to have a major effect on taste sensitivity, and accounts for major variations in experience reported in the taste literature. One way of circumventing the problem of zero drift in taste measurement is to flow taste stimuli over the tongue. This prevents any residual taste stimuli from remaining in the saliva and affecting taste sensitivity. It also allows the taste receptors to be reset to a constant zero level, between each tasting, by using a standard adapting flow. The taste receptors can adapt to tastelessness in this standard flow, thereby resetting the taste zero to the same level before tasting each new stimulus. The technique is powerful enough to allow tasters to distinguish between once- and twice-distilled water. However, little is yet known about the mechanisms of taste adaptation; even the extent to which taste receptors can 'zero-adjust' has not been explored.

Thus, a stimulus becomes tasteless to the extent that it can resemble saliva. Certainly the osmotic properties of saliva are nearer to those of tap water than to distilled water, so distilled water has more of a taste than tapwater. The flat taste of distilled water is a sub-zero or sub-adapting taste; in fact, pure water can appear to have a whole range of tastes depending on the adaptation state of the taste receptors. Changes in taste zero for a range of receptors during eating or experimentation will lessen or accentuate certain aspects of the taste of other stimuli. This may form the basis for the choice of certain wines with certain foods. A sweet wine may be more suitable for drinking with a sweet dessert because adaptation to one would lessen the sweetness of the other. MOM

Beidler, L. M. (ed.) (1971). *Handbook of Sensory Physiology*, iv: *Chemical Senses*.

Meiselman, H. L., and Rivlin, R. S. (eds.) (1986). *Clinical Measurement of Taste and Smell*.

Miller, G. A., and Johnson-Laird, P. N. (1976). *Language and Perception*.

O'Mahony, M. (1978). 'Smell illusions and suggestion: reports of smells contingent on tones played on television and radio'. *Chemical Senses and Flavor*, 3.

——(1979). 'Salt taste adaptation: the psychophysical effects of adapting solutions and residual stimuli from prior tastings on the taste of sodium chloride'. *Perception*, 8.

——(1984). 'How we perceive flavor'. *Nutrition Today*, 19.

——and Thompson, B. (1977). 'Taste quality descriptions: can the subject's response be affected by mentioning taste words in the instructions?' *Chemical Senses and Flavor*, 2.

tautology. In logic, saying the same thing in a different way, often unwittingly. For example, 'A fair-haired blonde' is tautologous if 'fair-haired' and 'blonde' are taken to have the same meanings. But if 'blonde' means the natural hair colour, then a dark-haired girl who is fair because her hair is dyed fair could be fair but not a blonde, and then 'fair-haired blonde' is *not* a tautology. Tautology always depends on accepted definitions.

When black, swanlike birds were discovered in Australia, there was doubt as to whether they could be 'swans'—for swans were supposed to be white. But it was allowed that though black they were swans—so 'black swan' was no longer contradictory. Conversely, it is not now tautologous to call a swan white—though it would be if the quality of whiteness was part of the *definition* of a swan.

telekinesis. Movement of objects from a distance by supposed *paranormal means. The alleged forces are generally acknowledged to be small, but if they exist at all it is exceedingly hard to understand why it is possible to carry out delicate experiments and operations, with galvanometers and so on: surely eager experimenters would exert their telekinetic powers, though unwittingly, to affect the results of their experiments, and this would produce nonsense in science, and much else. Such negative evidence brings strong weight to the opinion that there is no such thing as telekinesis.   RLG

telepathy. See EXTRASENSORY PERCEPTION.

Terman, Lewis Madison (1877–1956). American experimental psychologist, and professor of psychology at Stanford University (1916). He introduced the Stanford–Binet test and the Terman group *intelligence tests into the US army in 1920. He is particularly known for his studies of gifted children. Perhaps his best-known book is *The Measurement of Intelligence* (1916).

terror. The specific *fear that some evil event or action is going to occur. Its origins go back to the notion of trembling. Strictly speaking, it should be distinguished from horror, in that horror implies something disgusting and negative, whereas terror does not.

In the field of myth, terror has often been associated with visitations from an all-powerful god controlling life and death in a seemingly indiscriminate manner. The Delphic oracle went into a kind of trance or frenzy, during which the awesome god spoke through the prophetess. All this, even the ambiguities of the prophecies themselves, was designed to inspire fear of the god in the onlookers.

Terror appears to fit into the category of instinct response which humans share with most animals. For example, most humans and animals fear the sight of mutilated bodies. Experiments with chimpanzees during which the animals were shown pictures of chimpanzees with their heads or limbs cut off elicited instinctive responses of extreme trepidation. This fear of violence done to the body is at the basis of the terror process.

In the ancient world terror was the basis of tyranny, as in Rome under Marius and Sulla. Historically many political leaders have chosen to rule by terror tactics rather than customary, legal means—that is, by the systematic use of violence to inhibit political opposition. Present-day 'acts of terrorism' bear a different sense, as they are designed to disrupt a given system by violent actions.

While the causes of terror have changed over the centuries, the human mind continues to be highly susceptible to it. Our ancestors gathered round lighted fires not only to keep warm but to ward off 'the terror by night': there were terrifying animals lurking in the darkness. The 'night light' in a child's room reflects this fear of darkness, of the unseen and the unknown. Even so, most humans seem to enjoy the feeling of terror under controlled conditions. Grandmothers have traditionally told tales of terror around the fireplace to countless generations of children, in a role which today has been supplanted by the so-called horror film. Perhaps the monsters who march across the screen are designed to purge the real monsters within the human psyche. (See FRANKENSTEIN.)

Contemporary science and technology have created new sources of terror, such as the threat of nuclear annihilation and highly sophisticated means of electronic surveillance and control of human behaviour. Modern adult human beings may no longer fear the presence of huge animals in the darkness, but most humans experience terror born from technology.   RTM

Teuber, Hans-Lukas (1916–77). German–American psychologist, born in Berlin, who studied in the University of Basel until 1941, when he emigrated to the United States. He took his doctorate at Harvard in the field of social psychology but his interests thereafter deviated to neuropsychology, in which his reputation became firmly established. He was a full professor at Bellvue Medical Center, 1947–51, and thereafter head of the department of psychology at the Massachusetts Institute of Technology, until his untimely death by drowning.

Teuber had a wide scholarship and he was an inspiring leader of research. His own work was mainly concerned with the psychological effects of war wounds of the brain, studied wherever possible through the use of quantitative methods, many of which he devised himself. His most important books were *Somatosensory Changes after Penetrating Brain Wounds in Man* (1960) and *Visual Field Defects after Penetrating Missile Wounds of the Brain* (1960).

OLZ/RLG

Thales (*c.*620–*c.*550 BC). The first named Western philosopher and scientist. Of the Ionian school, he was born at Miletus and travelled widely in Egypt and to Babylon, where he learned techniques of land surveying ('geometry') and astronomy. He is said to have invented formal *geometry as we know it, by formalizing empirical measuring techniques. He is also supposed to have predicted the solar eclipse of 585 BC. He held that all things are made of water; and he investigated magnets (lodestones), suggesting that they were alive, with mind, as they moved each other.

See also PRE-SOCRATIC PHILOSOPHERS.   RLG

Burnet, J. (1955). *Greek Philosophy, Thales to Plato.*
Kirk, G. S., and Raven, J. E. (1957). *The Presocratic Philosophers.* (For Thales' recorded sayings.)

thinkers, independent. On the whole, *Homo sapiens* tends to be conventional: that is, very few people have revolutionary ideas. At an early age, for instance, virtually every child is taught that the earth is a globe, revolving round the sun in a period of one year—and he or she will believe it. Yet a mere 600 years ago, children who were taught at all learned that the sun goes round the earth, and they believed that with equal fervour.

Of course, there have always been rebels who have opposed what may be termed official doctrine. A Greek, Aristarchus, did so, long before the time of Christ, when he maintained that the earth was not the centre of the universe. Nobody persecuted him, but very few people believed him. Some of the later protagonists of the sun-centred theory were not so lucky; one of them, Giordano Bruno, was burned at the stake in Rome as recently as 1600 (though it is true that this was not his only crime in the eyes of the Inquisition, and the Church of those days was not noted for its kindliness).

Obviously, Aristarchus and Bruno were right. Bruno was to all intents and purposes following in the footsteps of Copernicus, a Polish churchman who had scandalized his contemporaries in 1543 by publishing a book in which he rejected the idea of a central earth. One of Copernicus's fiercest critics was Martin Luther, who referred to him as a fool who wanted to turn everything upside down—a comment which cannot have worried Copernicus, who had prudently withheld publication until the last days of his life, but which faithfully reflected official views of the time. It is fair to call Copernicus an 'independent thinker', because he had no respect for orthodox science, and it is equally fair to say that throughout history there have been men of similar calibre who have been responsible for tremendous advances in knowledge. On the other hand, most modern rebels against scientific orthodoxy are not only wrong but so clearly irrational that it is by no means easy (or kind) to argue with them.

Consider, for instance, the Flat Earthers. The belief in a world shaped like a pancake is very old, but the fact that it lingers on is strange. A few decades ago there was a kernel of flat-earth believers in Zion, Illinois, presided over by one Wilbur Glenn Voliva, who believed that the world was disc shaped, with the North Pole in the middle and a wall of ice all round. (To forestall any questions, let it be added that in Voliva's universe there was no South Pole!) Below the earth there was a kind of bargain basement inhabited by the spirits of a race of men who lived on the surface of the world before the arrival of Adam and Eve. Voliva died in 1942, but the International Flat Earth Society is more modern, and was for years controlled by the late Samuel Shenton, whose views were of the same overall type as Voliva's. Even the *Apollo* flights to the moon did not daunt him, and he continued to maintain that the moon is a very small body, while even the sun has a diameter of a mere 32 miles. He also maintained that the space pictures of earth were deliberately faked by those who were intent on suppressing the truth.

This is highly significant. One of the modern hallmarks of the Independent Thinker is that he is convinced that Orthodoxy is persecuting him. Generally, of course, he has no official support—but this is not an invariable rule, and there are a few rebels who have made their mark. Of these, the classic example in recent years has been Academician Lysenko, in the Soviet Union. He was (or claimed to be) a pioneer geneticist, and he produced a whole crop of revolutionary theories, together with experiments which signally failed to work. Yet he remained in favour with the Soviet authorities for an amazingly long time, and to disagree with him was to court official disapproval. All in all, Lysenko managed to put Soviet genetics back at least half a century.

Another case, less extreme but still important, was that of Hans Hörbiger, an eccentric Austrian engineer who believed that the most important material in the universe was, simply, ice. To him almost everything was icy; the stars were gigantic ice blocks, and the moon an ice globe which would eventually spiral down and hit us—as at least six other moons had previously done.

Hörbiger's book *Glazial-Kosmogonie* was published as long ago as 1913, and is regarded as a classic of pseudoscience. It is lengthy, heavy in style, humourless, and entirely without value except as a curiosity, but it led on to what was called WEL (*Welt Eis Lehre*, or Cosmic Ice Theory)—a cult which became popular in Germany between the wars, and continued to be so even after Hörbiger's death. Hörbiger himself was absolutely typical of his type; to him, everyone who disapproved of cosmic ice was to be treated as an enemy.

Most scientists were sceptical, but not all; one near-convert was Philipp Fauth, who had a considerable reputation as an astronomer, and who had compiled a large, albeit rather inaccurate, map of the moon. Some of the politicians were impressed, though they did defer to convention sufficiently to issue a statement that it was still possible to be a good National Socialist without believing in WEL. There is still a Hörbiger Institute with a British branch, though its members cannot have failed to be discouraged when the *Apollo* astronauts landed on the moon and had no need to use skates.

Yet another Independent Thinker who has met with a surprising amount of support is a psychoanalyst, Dr Immanuel Velikovsky, who was born in Russia but made his home in the United States. Velikovsky's book *Worlds in Collision*, published in 1950, is fully up to Hörbiger's standard. He believed that planets can turn into comets, and vice versa, that Venus used to be a comet, and that it made several close approaches to the earth in biblical times, on one occasion stopping the earth's rotation and leaving the Red Sea dry for long enough to allow the Israelites to cross.

Velikovsky's theories, elaborated in subsequent books, are so full of scientific absurdities that it is hard to see how even the most naive reader could take them seriously. None the less, many people did—and still do. The extensive biblical references are quite correct, and the trouble is that one cannot argue—because there is no common scientific ground at all. Anyone who maintains that, for instance, the sun is 193,000,000 miles away instead of 93,000,000 can be challenged and disproved, but Velikovsky's whole theory is based on the possible interchange between planets and comets, which is no more rational than believing the earth to be flat (in fact, rather less on the whole).

There are two cults which are even more widespread: *astrology and flying saucers. Both have not mere hundreds of supporters, but millions. Astrologers are found everywhere, both on seaside piers and in lavish offices. Many are quite sincere, and when asked to explain how the apparent positions of the sun, moon, and planets can affect human destiny generally have the grace to admit that they do not know. Here, too, there is no rational basis for argument. It is useless to point out that a 'constellation'

is merely a line-of-sight effect, and that the patterns are made up of unassociated stars at wildly different distances from us; it is equally useless to comment that the patterns themselves are arbitrary, and that anyone who can see the outline of two fish in Pisces, or a sea-goat in Capricorn, must have a lively imagination by any standards. And now and then, of course, an astrologer makes a correct observation or prediction; it is impossible to be always wrong.

Astrologers are linked with the flying saucer enthusiasts, who now call themselves UFOlogists, and of whom there are two definite types. Type I follows men such as the late George Adamski and the rather mysterious Cedric Allingham, who published books describing their meetings with men from other worlds—a Martian in Allingham's case, and initially a long-haired Venusian in Adamski's. Even more astounding are the members of the Aetherius Society, who believe that they are in constant touch with Mars, Venus, and other worlds, and that messages of vital importance are telepathically relayed. Everything is regulated by the Interplanetary Parliament, which meets on Saturn and whose representatives look like huge ovoids perhaps 40 feet (12 metres) in diameter (one might even describe them as large balls). Among various contactees are Confucius and Jesus Christ. On one occasion the earth was under attack from fish-men living on the far side of the Galaxy, though fortunately the Interplanetary Parliament took prompt action and the oncoming missile was blown to pieces by something equivalent to an Olympian thunderbolt.

The Type II UFO-believers have no faith in the Adamskis, the Allinghams, or even the Interplanetary Parliament, and content themselves with maintaining that various phenomena seen in the atmosphere are due to visiting spacecraft. Unfortunately, no saucer pilot has yet shown himself to the world at large, and most UFO pictures look so strikingly like lampshades that people with critical minds go so far as to suggest that they *are* lampshades (see PEPPER'S GHOST). There is a real problem here, but psychological rather than astronomical. Nobody will deny that there are atmospheric phenomena which are difficult to explain (ball lightning is one), but to suppose alien spacecraft is frankly irrational. Moreover, recently there have been even weirder theories, some UFOlogists believing that the saucers come from inside the earth—popping out from a hole at the North Pole with the intention of keeping a watchful eye on us.

Quite apart from all this, the idea of a hollow earth lingers on—an echo of the episode of 1823 in which an American army officer, Captain John Cleves Symmes, asked Congress for funds to send an expedition to the north polar entrance. (Congress declined, but it is on record that 25 members voted in Symmes's favour.) And in Germany, the present-day Society for Geocosmical

Research believes that the earth is nothing more or less than the inside of a hollow globe; the sun is in the middle, with Australia and Britain on opposite sides, while the solid ground below our feet extends infinitely in all directions.

Such examples of independent thought could be multiplied almost *ad infinitum*. There are those who believe the sun to be cold; those who fear that the accumulation of ice at the North Pole will make the world tilt over, producing disastrous floods; and those who have a profound disbelief in evolution, preferring to think that each species appears fully fledged as if by magic. Few of these people have any scientific qualifications, but most of them are sincere, well-meaning people acting from the best possible motives. Some of the astrologers are less desirable; and there are some cults—mostly quasi-religious—which are to be deplored: they do immense harm by influencing gullible people and breaking up families. But fortunately these are the exceptions, and they are easy to detect.

Generally, the Independent Thinker has one particular theme, and one only. (It was once said that every crank thinks that every other person is a crank.) His exceptional belief does not debar him from accepting all the conventional facts of life: thus President Kruger of South Africa was a Flat Earther, while Gladstone believed so firmly in the lost continent of Atlantis that he asked the Treasury to finance an expedition to the seabed—a request that was turned down. Furthermore, he does not deliberately set out to be different from his fellows; he believes that he has a message, and he will do all he can to propagate it, usually for motives that are entirely altruistic.

What are regarded as erratic ideas are generally greeted with ridicule, but there are occasions when the Independent Thinker has been proved right. Only a few decades ago the concept of flight to the moon was regarded with contempt; some time after the Wright brothers had made their first 'hop' in a heavier-than-air machine, the famous astronomer Simon Newcomb was stating that nothing of the sort could ever be achieved, and that a raft pulled by birds was a more rational idea; and in pre-Stephenson days it was maintained that no human being could possibly stand up to the strain of being carried along at 30 miles per hour. To be dogmatic is always dangerous, and science fiction has the uncanny habit of changing into science fact.   PM

Evans, J. (1975). *Cults of Unreason.*
Moore, P. (1978). *Can You Speak Venusian?*

thinking: how it can be taught. Is thinking simply IQ in action, or is it a separable skill that can be developed just as we develop *skill at cooking, skiing, or riding a bicycle? It seems that, when asked to think about matters within their own experience, children of relatively low IQ do much better than expected when compared with children of high IQ; so the practical operating skills of thinking (decision, judgement, assessment of priorities, breadth of scan) are not the same as the knowledge-absorbing skills (perceiving relationships, attention skills, ordering information, memorizing).

If thinking is a skill, then it seems likely to be a natural skill that we can pick up in the ordinary course of events just as we pick up the skill of walking, talking, or breathing. We may indeed pick up the skill, but as a 'two-finger skill'. The expression comes from the world of typing. Someone who has to pick up the skill of typing as he goes along acquires a fair degree of skill using two fingers, but the skill never develops much beyond this point of coping with immediate needs. Someone else who sets out to train to be a secretary learns touch-typing from the start, and within eight weeks has a greater skill than the two-finger operator. Quite soon the skill of the touch-typist is far ahead. A skill that is built up by coping with the immediate situation may never develop beyond this level. For example, 'prejudice' is an excellent two-finger thinking skill since it allows action without reflection and removes the need for decision. But in a wider field prejudice can be inhibiting.

Twenty-four groups of children, aged 9–10, from six London primary schools with widely differing social backgrounds, were asked to consider the suggestion that 'bread, fish, and milk should be made freely available'. The discussions were tape recorded and analysed. Some of the children came from families that were too poor to afford milk on a regular basis. Yet 23 out of the 24 groups decided that the suggestion was a bad one. Their reasoning went something like this:

'If bread, fish, and milk are free the shops will be overcrowded.'
'So the buses going to the shops will be overcrowded.'
'The drivers will ask for more pay.'
'They won't get more pay so they will go on strike.'
'Other people will join the strike and there will be chaos.'
'So it is a bad idea.'

This is a typical example of 'point-to-point' thinking in which one point becomes the starting point for the next idea and so on. It often occurs with younger children. Teaching some scanning strategy allows the child to broaden his area of attention and to avoid getting pulled along a point-to-point track.

At the other extreme is the highly skilled, highly intelligent, highly articulate thinker. He makes up his mind instantly on an issue and then uses his skill of argument to support the position that he has taken up. The sheer brilliance of this supporting effort makes it unlikely that the thinker will ever feel the need to change his position. And yet at no time has he ever tried to *explore* the subject.

Similarly we put a lot of emphasis on debating skills, with the assumption that if you can prove the other fellow wrong, somehow that proves you right. In terms of thinking skill both these strategies are highly inefficient and indeed dangerously so.

In the past, attempts have been made to teach thinking by teaching the rules of logic or the rules of the syllogism. Taught this way, logic can become an abstract, idealized system with little relevance to everyday life. More importantly, logic can process only the material presented to it by *perception, and it is at the perception stage that most ordinary thinking has to take place. The general approach to teaching thinking is not to teach it directly but to criticize pupils when they make logical errors. Unfortunately, thinking that is free from logical errors is by no means necessarily good thinking. Bad logic makes for bad thinking, but good logic makes for good thinking *only* if the starting perceptions are themselves appropriate. Logic is only a servicing device for perception. It is far too much part of our culture to assume that a logical argument proves a point.

In education we also assume that, from an interested discussion on some subject, pupils will abstract certain habits and skills of thinking and transfer them to new situations. This does not seem to happen. Such discussions increase fluency but seem to provide little transferable skill. If, rather, we create, quite deliberately, various attention-directing tools, these tools can then be practised on a rapidly changing variety of situations. This change is necessary so that attention stays on the tool and does not drift to the content—as it would if the content remained constant.

In the perception stage, much of thinking is concerned with directing attention. After all, a question is only a device for directing attention. The very first lesson might introduce the PMI device. This requires the pupils deliberately to look for the Plus, Minus, and Interesting points in a situation. It is intended to prevent the instant-judgement habit and to encourage exploration before decision rather than after it. Most people would of course claim to carry out this simplistic procedure, and no doubt they do in doubtful situations. But very few people carry out the procedure if they have a firm opinion on the matter. In one experiment two random groups of adults were asked to consider the suggestions 'that marriage should be a five-year contract' and 'that currency should be dated so that at the year end the exchange with the new currency could be altered according to the rate of inflation'. In the first group 23 per cent were in favour of the five-year marriage contract and in the second group 35 per cent were in favour of the dated currency. The questions were then switched over and each group was asked to do a deliberate PMI on the matter. The 23 per cent in favour of the contract marriage now rose to 37 per cent in favour. The 35

per cent in favour of the dated currency now fell to 11 per cent. So asking people to do what they would have claimed to do anyway made a huge difference. A group of 30 children, aged 9–11, was given the suggestion that all children should be paid some money each week for going to school. Each one of them was in favour of the idea. They were then asked to do a PMI on it. Five minutes later 29 out of the 30 had changed their minds and decided it would be a bad idea.

Eight groups of primary-school children were asked to consider the problem of a girl whose parents were being posted abroad. The girl wanted to continue her studies to be a teacher: should she stay behind or go with her parents? The four groups who had had no special training considered the following number of aspects of the situation: 3, 5, 5, and 5. The four groups who had had ten thinking lessons considered 17, 17, 13, and 19 aspects.

It is not really surprising that skill can be developed by direct attention and practice.

See also INTELLIGENCE; PROBLEM SOLVING.   EdeB

Bono, E. de (1977). *Teaching Thinking.*
——(1994). *De Bono's Thinking Course* (rev. edn.).

thinking about feeling. Fashions change. The problem of *consciousness, once banned from serious consideration by psychologists, is again high on the agenda. Yet typically researchers are looking under the lamp that currently shines brightest rather than in the area where the phenomenon went missing. They are identifying consciousness with high-level *thought processes* and seeking to explain it in 'thinking machine' terms, but they are largely ignoring *bodily feeling*.

Yet if we listen to the kinds of questions ordinary people ask—'Are babies conscious?', 'Will I be conscious during the operation?', and so on—it is clear that, again and again, the central issue is not thinking but feeling. People's concern is not with the stream of thoughts that may or may not be running through their heads but with the sense they have of being alive at all—which is to say, alive and *living in the presence of sensation*.

The problem, then, is to explain just what these sensations—conscious sensations—are. We want a theory of why it feels to us as it does to taste salt on our tongue, to look at the blue sky with our eyes, to burn our fingers on the stove. But—and here is what is going to make this problem *hard*—the theory must not beg the question by assuming any prior acquaintance with what is being explained: namely, sensory consciousness as such.

Let's stipulate, then, that the theory has to be comprehensible to a scientist from Mars—an individual in many ways not unlike ourselves, highly intelligent, perceptive, and even capable of self-reflection, but who none the less has never evolved into the kind of being who has sensations. Suppose we could explain to this Martian what happens in the brain of a human being who is engaged, say, in smelling a rose. And suppose he could thereby arrive at the entirely novel (to him) conclusion that it must *be like something to be this human being*, and indeed *like this* : 'I am feeling this thick, sweet, olfactory sensation in my nostrils.' It is a tall order, but, still, it is what the theory ought to do.

Is a theory which could bring this off a possibility even in principle? Since the theory must employ only such concepts as the Martian can make sense of at the outset, we need to consider what kind of pre-theoretical notions he brings with him. Given that as yet he knows nothing about sensations, will he have other essential concepts on which to build?

We want him to understand that the human being is the *subject of sensations*. Can we assume he will at least have, to start with, the idea of what it is to be a 'subject'? I would say we can. For presumably the Martian is already himself a subject in the following crucial sense: an autonomous agent *who acts in the world*. Provided he can take himself as a model, he ought already to have the basic concept of an 'I'. Then, can we assume he also understands the idea of being the 'subject of' something? Again, we can. For, as an 'I' who does things with his body, he himself already has this genitive relationship to his own actions: he is the *author of everything he does*. So, will he even have the idea of being the subject of something with some of the peculiar properties of sensations: especially, that (i) they belong to the subject, (ii) they implicate part of his body, (iii) they are present tense, (iv) they have a qualitative modality, (v) their properties are phenomenally immediate? In fact he will: for analysis shows that *bodily actions already have precisely these characteristics (i)–(v)*.

Now, this may not seem much as a basis for understanding sensory consciousness. But I believe that, with the right theory, it will be enough. Suppose we suggest the following theory to the Martian (it is my own theory, but others like it might also do the trick):

When a person smells a rose, he responds to what is happening at his nostrils with a 'virtual action pattern': one of a set of action patterns that originated far back in evolutionary history as evaluative responses to various kinds of stimulation at the body surface—wriggles of acceptance or rejection. In modern human beings these responses are still directed to the site of stimulation, and still retain vestiges of their original function and hedonic tone, but today, instead of carrying through into overt behaviour, they have become closed off within internal circuits in the brain; in fact the *efferent signals now project only as far as the sensory cortex, where they interact with the incoming signals from the sense organs to create, momentarily, a self-entangling, recursive, loop. The theory is that the person's *sensation*, the way he represents what is happening to him and how he feels about it, *comes through monitoring his own signals for the action pattern*—as extended, by this recursion, into the 'thick moment' of the conscious present.

Then how will the Martian understand this? Presumably nothing in his own direct experience corresponds to what we have just described to him. But, still, he should be able to work it out. He will be able to grasp the key fact that sensation consists in monitoring commands for action in response to stimulation. He will be able to appreciate the peculiar features of the action pattern that has in fact evolved. And so he will be able to work out that, *if a subject like himself were to get involved in doing what the human being is doing, the result would be that he would have just these beliefs about it, these attitudes, these things to say, these that he cannot say, and so on—in short he would experience it *like this*.

But if the Martian can work all this out from the theory, would this mean he actually acquires first-hand experience of sensations in the process? No: no more than someone who works out from physics and chemistry that H_2O constitutes water gets wet. A theory of consciousness is not a way of conferring consciousness; it is a way of understanding why consciousness-generating brain states have the effects on people's minds they do. In fact the Martian himself may have no sense organ with which to smell the rose at all: and yet, if the theory is right, he should still be able to discover *all* that we ourselves can discover by direct acquaintance. (And one day, of course, when *we* get to study Martians, the boot may be on the other foot.)

NKH

Humphrey, N. (1992). *A History of the Mind*.

Thorndike, Edward Lee (1874–1949). Born in Williamsburg, Massachusetts, he is best known for his contributions to the psychology of *learning, and secondarily for his work in educational psychology and mental testing (see INTELLIGENCE). While doing graduate work with William *James at Harvard in the 1890s, he became interested in animal intelligence; he studied the intelligence of chicks in James's own basement. For financial reasons he soon transferred to Columbia University, where he studied under James McKeen *Cattell. His thesis, 'Animal intelligence: an experimental study of the associative processes in animals', became one of the most influential works ever written in American psychology. In it are described the famous 'puzzle-box' experiments with cats, dogs, and chicks. In a typical experiment, a cat could escape from a box by clawing down a rope, lifting a latch, or engaging in a series of different manipulations; and escape would give the cat access to food. From trial to trial, Thorndike plotted the times it took for an animal to escape; over trials, animals were found to require less and less time to make the escape response. This data composed the first 'learning curves', and was said to show something fundamental about the nature of learning.

As formalized in his later works (notably *Animal Intelligence*, 1911), Thorndike's theory of learning may be summarized as follows. Learning occurs 'by trial and error, and accidental success', or, as we have come to simplify this view, by *trial and error*. Correct movements—for example, movements toward a door latch in a puzzle box— will lead to a 'satisfying state of affairs' and be 'stamped in'. Wrong movements will lead to an 'annoying state of affairs' and be 'stamped out'. Over time, only correct movements will survive; a cat at this point would have learned the correct response to the puzzle box and could escape quickly. The learning process could be reduced to a number of 'laws'. The *law of effect* describes the trial-and-success process noted above: a response is more or less likely to occur depending on whether it produces a satisfying or annoying state of affairs. The *law of exercise* states that learning improves with practice. Other laws and sublaws were presented, and occasionally changed, over the course of Thorndike's career.

Thorndike's work on learning was a step away from the earlier psychology of mind and towards the *functionalist and *behaviourist movements that came to dominate American psychology. Prior to Thorndike's work, all learning, even in simple animals, was said to show some sign of *consciousness. But for Thorndike, learning occurred simply as the result of the satisfying or annoying effects of instinctive movements. Though he described the learning process as affecting associative bonds between stimuli and responses, in the tradition of the British associationists, his emphasis on the trial-and-error nature of learning and on observable movement made consciousness seem a less important factor in the learning process.

From 1899 to 1940 Thorndike taught at Teachers College of Columbia University, and his contributions to educational psychology are many. His textbook, *Educational Psychology* (1903, later revised and expanded), became a classic in that field. In 1901 he published a paper with Robert Sessions *Woodworth dispelling the myth that training on one task necessarily transfers to training on a different task (see TRANSFER OF TRAINING); this paper foretold the end of traditional classical education in schools. He also did work on mental measurements and the study of individual differences, applied animal learning theories to human education, constructed a scale to measure children's handwriting, and with I. Lorge compiled an important table of word-frequency counts. By far America's most prolific psychologist, he published more than 450 articles and many books in his lifetime.   RE

Thouless, Robert Henry (1894–1984). British psychologist, born in Norwich and educated at Corpus Christi College, Cambridge. He became a lecturer in psychology at Manchester and later at Glasgow before returning to Cambridge as a lecturer, later reader, in educational psychology, a post which he occupied with distinction for almost 30 years.

Thouless is best known for his experimental work on size and brightness constancy, to which his approach differed substantially from that of the *Gestalt psychologists. He laid the emphasis not on constancy of appearance of objects *per se* but on the element of compromise which he thought to be involved in its genesis. If, for example, a subject is required to match a circular disc placed obliquely so that its retinal image is elliptical, with a series of ellipses placed at right angles to his line of sight, he was found invariably to choose an ellipse that is less elliptical, i.e. more circular, than the retinal image. This Thouless described as phenomenal regression to the 'real' object, and it appeared to indicate that a property of an object, such as its size, shape, or brightness, is intermediate between that of the peripheral stimulus pattern on the one hand and the actual property of the object on the other. At the same time, Thouless insisted that phenomenal regression, although it might show marked individual differences, could not be assigned to learning. Although his work attracted considerable interest, he was not without his critics, in particular Kurt *Koffka.

Thouless had wide interests in general and social psychology, among them psychical research and the psychology of religion. He was for many years a consultant to the National Foundation for Educational Research and was president of both the British Psychological Society and the Society for Psychical Research.   OLZ

Thurstone, Louis Leon (1887–1955). American pioneer in psychometrics (mental measurement). Thurstone was born in Chicago of Swedish ancestry, obtained his doctorate at the University of Chicago, and taught there until he retired to Chapel Hill, North Carolina. Earlier he had studied as an electrical engineer, and worked with Edison on cine projection; but in 1914 he turned to psychology, and became involved in the production of tests for army recruits in the First World War.

The earliest attempts at mental measurement were the so-called *psychophysical methods, developed by German psychologists in the 19th century for studying people's sensitivity to touch, sound, and other sensations. For example, what was the smallest difference in pitch between two tones that people could detect? Thurstone showed that such methods could be extended to much more complex qualities, such as the strength of attitudes, e.g. like or dislike of communism, capital punishment, black people, or the Church. He published a number of such attitude scales, and used them for measuring the effects of propaganda on people's prejudices. Many subsequent research workers in social psychology have constructed, and made use of, Thurstone-type scales.

Another topic was the measurement of progress in learning (i.e. the plotting of learning 'curves'), and in mental development generally. He showed how to express such development in absolute units, comparable to physical measurements. This made it possible to predict the zero point of mental growth, namely around three months before birth.

Thurstone was prolific in the construction of *intelligence tests and, being dissatisfied with current definitions of intelligence, he published a thoughtful book, *The Nature of Intelligence* (1924). This he approached from the biological angle, rather than the logical or statistical. In the 1930s he contested Charles *Spearman's view of intelligence as a unitary, general or 'g' factor. He proposed that it is a combination of several distinctive abilities, e.g. verbal comprehension, reasoning, memory. And he superseded Spearman's statistical technique of measuring g with a much more flexible procedure known as multiple factor analysis, which could handle numerous ability factors simultaneously. With his primary mental abilities tests, constructed for various age groups, he could obtain a profile of each person's strengths and weaknesses (see *Vectors of the Mind*, 1935, and *Multiple Factor Analysis*, 1947). It is for this work on factor analysis that he is most widely known, and it was applied by him, or his numerous followers, to many practical problems: for example, isolating the main distinguishable types of mental illness, analysing human perceptual abilities, or developing new tests of such special aptitudes as mechanical ability.

Thurstone was interested too in the measurement of personality characteristics, and published a widely used test of psychoneurotic tendencies. In each of the many areas that he touched he produced original ideas, and innovative techniques of measurement. He also advanced the study of his subject by founding the outstanding journal *Psychometrika*, and guiding it for nearly twenty years, until his death.   PEV

tickling. Tickling is a common, perhaps universal, experience. Depictions of people engaged in some kind of tickling activity, whether it be between siblings, parents and children, or lovers, can be found in the art of many countries and cultures. Tickling someone often causes them to smile and laugh in a way that is indistinguishable from the laughter caused by being highly amused or pleasured. However, tickling is a curious, paradoxical phenomenon. A ticklish person will often wriggle and writhe in agony as well as laugh hysterically when being tickled. Francis Bacon in 1677 commented that: '[when tickled] men even in a grieved state of mind . . . cannot sometimes forbear laughing.'

Even animals seem to be ticklish. When you tickle the great apes, they react with what is believed to correspond to laughter—a panting sound. Baby rats squeal with pleasure when tickled, although you need a bat detector to hear the sounds because they are at frequencies too high for human ears to detect. They are interpreted as sounds

of joy because they differ markedly from distress calls, and instead are similar to the sounds made by a male while courting females.

Human tickling usually occurs only between people who know each other well: children are likely to be tickled by their parents and siblings, adults are likely to be tickled by their lovers. Normally the tickler is someone who desires to express emotion and affection through their tickle —in other words the source of the tickle is a friendly one. Although there is often an inequality of power during tickling—ticklishness increases if the ticklee feels that they cannot escape from the tickler—ticklishness normally occurs in situations that are entirely non-threatening. Charles *Darwin in 1872 noted that if a stranger tried to tickle a child the child would scream with fear rather than squeal with laughter.

Darwin believed that tickling is an important aspect of social and sexual bonding, and prominent in the development of communication between mothers and babies. Tickle-induced laughter, he argued, is socially induced and results from close physical contact with another person. An alternative claim is that tickle-induced laughter is purely reflexive, something that happens without our voluntary control, similar to the reflex induced when a doctor taps your knee. An experiment carried out at the University of California recently lent some support for this theory. Christine Harris and her colleagues found that people laugh just as much when they believe that a robot is tickling their feet and no one else is around to hear them, as when a human is tickling their feet. So it seems that human social interaction is not necessary for tickling to cause laughter.

What is necessary for tickling, however, is a tickler—it is well known that you cannot tickle yourself. Tickling is a pleasure that 'cannot be reproduced in the absence of another', as psychoanalyst Adam Phillips wrote. The distinction between self-produced and external sensations seems to be physiologically hard-wired in the brain. Studies using brain scanners at University College London have demonstrated that the brain reacts differently when people tickle themselves compared to when someone else does the tickling. The areas of the brain associated with processing the sensation of touch (the somatosensory cortex) and pleasure (the anterior cingulate cortex) react much more strongly to an external tickle than to a self-tickle. The cerebellum, part of the brain that is thought to be involved in predicting the sensory consequences of movement, responds differently to self-generated touch and externally generated touch. In the case of tickling the cerebellum may predict and cancel the sensory consequences of self-produced touch but not those of a touch that is produced externally.

Why have we evolved this inability to tickle ourselves? It probably has something to do with the fact that the sensory results of our own movements are less important for us to notice than sensations that are produced externally. When walking on the ground it is more important to notice bumps and irregularities on the ground (which could be dangerous snakes or insects) than all the sensations that are caused by the movements of our legs and the pressure of our feet on the ground. Natural selection has endowed us with a brain mechanism that cancels the feeling of our own movements and their sensory consequences so that external sensations can be picked out and attended to. Tickling may simply be an accidental consequence of the useful mechanism that heightens our sensitivity to insects and other potentially dangerous elements on our skin.

But why laugh when tickled? Laughing might not be something we necessarily do when happy. Some people have suggested that the components of laughter—convulsion of the abdomen, production of sniggering noises, tears coming out of our eyes—all serve one purpose: they release tension. Nervous laughter often occurs during tense situations, and there are striking similarities between laughing and crying hysterically. Being tickled certainly causes the body to tense. Alternatively, Vilayanur Ramachandran of the University of California, San Diego, claims that we laugh to tell other people that a potentially threatening situation is not serious. 'You approach a child, hand stretched out menacingly. . . . But no, your fingers make light, intermittent contact with her belly,' he writes. As a result of being tickled the child laughs, as if to inform other children, 'He doesn't mean harm. He's only playing.' Some psychologists have suggested that humour evolves from a baby's giggling response to being tickled to an ability to laugh at funny faces and situations and then to jokes, subtle wit, and irony. It all starts, though, with that first tickle. Without tickling, some suggest, there might not be any humour at all.   SBl

Darwin, C. (1872). *The Expressions of the Emotions in Man and Animals.*

Phillips, A. (1994). 'On kissing, tickling, and being bored'. In *Psychoanalytic Essays on the Unexamined Life.*

Ramachandran, V. S. (1998). *Phantoms in the Brain.*

tilted room. A tilted room is extremely disturbing. It is hard to walk, and even to stand up. This happens when the visual sense provides information which does not agree with sensations from gravity. This is disturbing for astronauts living in a zero-gravity environment, and often causes severe disorientation illusions and space sickness. It also happens to pilots executing roll manoeuvres. Their disorientation can be so severe that they lose control and crash. It also happens to old people and people suffering from vertigo.

When we want to know which way is up, we can use any of the following sources of information.

Non-visual information

1. The otolith organs on each side of the head contain small crystals attached to hairs. When the head tilts, the hairs bend and generate nerve impulses that indicate the direction of head tilt.
2. Touch and pressure sense organs in the skin indicate the direction of pressure arising from the support surface.
3. Kinaesthetic sense organs in muscles and joints indicate the direction in which gravity pulls the limbs.
4. The body axis. Normally, the feet are down and the head is up. Astronauts floating in space often feel down to be where the feet are.

Visual information

1. The visual frame. Surfaces such as walls and floors are normally horizontal or vertical. Also, many lines, such as the horizon and the corners of rooms, are horizontal or vertical. Such surfaces and lines are called the visual frame. A simple visual frame indicates horizontal and vertical but does not indicate which way is up.
2. Intrinsic visual polarity. Objects such as houses, people, and trees have a recognizable top and bottom and usually have a consistent orientation to gravity.
3. Extrinsic visual polarity. Spatial relationships between objects can indicate the direction of gravity. For example, an object supported on another object, such as a box on a shelf, a falling object, and an object hanging on a string, possess extrinsic polarity.

Witkin pioneered the study of the effects of tilting the visual frame on the perception of the vertical. He found that a luminous square frame in dark surroundings tilted 28 degrees in the frontal plane causes a vertical rod to appear tilted by 6 degrees on average in the opposite direction (Witkin 1949). This is known as the rod and frame effect. Howard and Childerson (1994) asked observers to set a rod to the apparent vertical as they sat erect in an empty cubic room inclined to various angles about the line of sight (the roll axis). Settings were accurate whenever an axis of symmetry of the room was aligned with the observer's body axis, which occurred at 45-degree intervals. At intermediate angles, the rod was set on average 4 degrees in the direction of tilt of the nearest axis of symmetry. Thus a stationary tilted frame has only a limited effect on the perceived vertical. The non-visual senses restrain the effects produced by a tilted frame.

But what happens when we observe a rotating scene? We measured the pure effects of motion by sitting people at the centre of a 3-metre-diameter sphere lined with dots. Continuous rotation of the sphere at 30 degrees about the roll axis induced an illusion of continuous self-rotation accompanied by a paradoxical sensation of being tilted by up to 20 degrees (Howard and Childerson 1994). Since a sphere contains no visual information about the direction of gravity these illusions must have been induced by visual motion alone. We then added a visual frame by placing people in a rotating cubic room. This also produced illusory self-rotation but people felt upright every time an axis of symmetry became aligned with the subject's body axis.

We then asked what happens when we add visual polarity. Wertheimer (1912) reported that a furnished room seen in a mirror so that it was optically tilted 45 degrees appeared gradually to right itself. Asch and Witkin (1948) had subjects look into a small furnished room tilted 22 degrees about the roll axis. A vertical rod appeared tilted about 15 degrees in the opposite direction. We obtained similar limited illusory tilts of a rod, or of the self, when we placed people in a fully furnished room containing a table, chairs, shelves with objects on them, hanging pictures, and a multitude of other objects with intrinsic and/or extrinsic polarity, as shown in Fig. 1. Thus, a tilted polarized scene induces larger displacements of the vertical than does a simple visual frame.

Finally, we asked what happens when people are placed in a fully furnished room that rotates about the roll or pitch axis. In a fairground device built in Los Angeles towards the end of the last century, observers sat in a stationary gondola suspended in a furnished room. When the room rocked to and fro, the people in the stationary gondola felt that the room was stationary and that they and the gondola had rocked. In Germany in 1937, Kleint placed people in a furnished room that rotated completely about the roll axis. Some subjects reported sensations of total self-rotation but no quantitative data was presented. We found that 80 per cent of observers experienced complete head-over-heels illusory tumbling of the self about

the roll or pitch body axis when sitting upright in our furnished room that rotated completely about the roll or pitch axis (Howard and Hu 2001).

We concluded that the non-visual senses are overwhelmed by vision only when a richly polarized room rotates around the observer. We agreed with other investigators that a stationary tilted visual scene, even when it contains a rich variety of information about the direction of gravity, has only a limited capacity to overcome the non-visual senses. But the experiments we conducted next showed that we were wrong.

In the experiments mentioned so far, the room was tilted with respect to both gravity and the observer's body axis. We asked what happens if the observer and the room are tilted together so that the room remains aligned with the body axis. We slowly rotated the furnished room and the observer through 90 degrees so that the observer ended up supine looking up at the same wall that had been vertically in front before the motion started. For many subjects something remarkable happened. Many observers felt that neither they nor the room had moved. At the end of the rotation, they felt upright in an upright room. When they moved their arms out from the body they felt as if they were weightless. An object hanging down from the wall above them looked as if it were magically suspended in space. We had a professional magician who thought that we had suspended the object by a jet of air! We tested nine NASA astronauts and the five that experienced the illusion reported that it felt just like being in zero gravity. We call this the 'levitation illusion'. We then rotated the room and the observer together through 180 degrees. Many observers reported that they were upright in an upright room when in fact they were

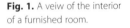

Fig. 1. A veiw of the interior of a furnished room.

Fig. 2. Full-scale replica of NASA'S Space Lab.

upside down in an upside-down room. These effects are due entirely to the presence of familiar polarized objects. There is no motion and the visual frame (the corners and surfaces of the room) is not tilted. Thus, for many people, the visual polarity of a stationary scene can completely overcome conflicting information about the direction of gravity arising from the non-visual senses. This happens when the body axis and the up–down polarity axis of the room are aligned.

We then constructed a full-scale replica of NASA's Space Lab, as shown in Fig. 2. Space Lab is where astronauts conducted experiments in the weightless conditions of space before the advent of Space Station. Space Lab contained virtually no familiar polarized objects. We found that observers did not experience the levitation illusion in this environment. Space Station is also devoid of familiar polarized objects. Thus, the visual environments in which astronauts work do not provide a stable framework for maintaining a consistent sense of orientation. In space, the non-visual senses do not provide information about orientation and the Space Station does not contain a stable visual substitute for gravity. It is no wonder that astronauts experience disorientation.

We found some strong age effects. The illusion of self-tilt in the rotating sphere and the head-over-heels illusion of self-rotation induced by the rotating furnished room were experienced by most subjects of all ages. It is known that the effects of visual motion on the perception of body orientation develop in very young children and are served by primitive postural reflexes. On the other hand, the proportion of observers experiencing the levitation illusion increased with age (Howard, Jenkin, and Hu 2000). Only 20 per cent of a group of 12-year-olds experienced the illusion but 80 per cent of 70-year-olds experienced it. There

are two reasons for these age effects. First, the otolith organs become less sensitive as we get older. Secondly, the levitation illusion depends entirely on our familiarity with the normal orientation of objects (visual polarity). Older people come to rely on this knowledge as their otolith organs lose their sensitivity. Old people are prone to fall and our results predict that they would be especially prone to fall in a place like a stairwell where surfaces are not horizontal and where there is an absence of familiar objects. Our work was funded by NASA and we are recommending that astronaut disorientation would be less severe if the walls of Space Station contained pictures of familiar objects.   IPH

Asch, S. E., and Witkin, H. A. (1948). 'Studies in space orientation: II. Perception of the upright with displaced visual fields and with body tilted'. *Journal of Experimental Psychology*, 38.

Howard, I. P., and Childerson, L. (1994). 'The contribution of motion, the visual frame and visual polarity to sensations of body tilt'. *Perception*, 23.

—— and Hu. G. (2001). 'Visually induced reorientation illusions'. *Perception*, 30.

——Jenkin, H. L., and Hu, G. (2000). 'Visually induced reorientation illusions as a function of age'. *Aviation, Space and Environmental Medicine*, 71.

Kleint, H. (1937). 'Versuche über die Wahrnehmung II. Über Bewegung'. *Zeitschrift für Psychologie*, 141.

Wertheimer, M. (1912). 'Experimentelle Studien über das Sehen von Bewegung'. *Zeitschrift für Psychologie und Physiologie des Sinnesorgane*, 61.

Witkin, H. A. (1949). 'Perception of body position and the position of the visual field'. *Psychological Monographs*, 6 (whole 7).

time-gap experience. Quite frequently, during the course of a long-distance journey, motorists reach some point—a crossroads for instance—and find they have no conscious recollection of covering the miles since the last village. They usually interpret this in terms of time, reporting, for example, 'a lost half-hour'. Having consulted their watches, they may reflect, bemusedly, 'How did it jump to three o'clock?'. For this reason, the term 'time-gap experience' has been coined for discussion of the phenomenon (Reed 1972).

The answer may be found by considering the nature of skilled behaviour (see SKILL, HUMAN). This is hierarchically organized, so that its elementary components become progressively automatized. The skilled driver does not need to pay conscious attention to such basic matters as the position of the controls, or the movements of his hands and feet. He can afford to reserve his attention for the assessment of input at a strategic level. If the situation is relatively undemanding, and external events routine or predictable, he may require only a low level of conscious attention. He will deploy his attentional resources elsewhere—typically, to his own thoughts. In one sense, he has 'switched to automatic pilot'. But any significant change in the situation will involve the processing of new information, the assessment of probabilities, and the making and implementation of decisions. All this requires heightened conscious awareness, a switching back to 'manual control'. The crossroads, for example, introduces a sudden increase in information load, which demands the sharp refocusing of our motorist's attention. And this is the moment when the time-gapper describes himself as 'waking up'. GFR

Reed, G. (1972). *The Psychology of Anomalous Experience.*

Titchener, Edward Bradford (1867–1927). Born at Chichester, Sussex, he studied philosophy at Oxford and took his doctorate under Wilhelm *Wundt at Leipzig. He moved to Cornell in 1892, where he spent the rest of his life. Much influenced by Wundt's psychological outlook, he translated a large part of the fifth edition of his *Physiologische Psychologie*, published in America as *Principles of Physiological Psychology* in 1904. His own work was mainly on sensation and *attention. Although highly respected, he never felt really at home with American psychology, and wholly rejected *behaviourism as irrelevant to psychology as he understood it. (None the less, he liked and respected J. B. *Watson and, unlike his colleagues, supported him warmly after he lost his post at Johns Hopkins University in consequence of a personal indiscretion.)

Titchener's principal works are: *Experimental Psychology: A Manual of Laboratory Practices* (1901, 1905); *Lectures on the Elementary Psychology of Feeling and Attention* (1908); *Lectures on the Experimental Psychology of the Thought Processes* (1909); and *A Text-Book of Psychology* (1909–10). OLZ

Tolman, Edward Chase (1886–1959). American psychologist, born at Newtown, Massachusetts, and educated at the Massachusetts Institute of Technology and at Harvard, where he obtained his doctorate in 1915. He spent almost the whole of his active academic life at the University of California at Berkeley, where he evolved a theory of *learning which, while behaviouristic, owed little to J. B. *Watson; though the theory was formulated in purely behavioural terms, reflexes were not central to his ideas. Tolman, who worked almost exclusively with rats, placed much emphasis on the importance of latent learning, reward expectancy, and the formation of hypotheses in animal learning. He also placed emphasis on spatial orientation and cognitive maps in maze learning.

Tolman's most important book was *Purposive Behavior in Animals and Men* (1932). Jointly with the former Viennese psychologist Egon *Brunswik, he wrote an influential article entitled 'The organism and the causal texture of the environment' (1935).

touch. Objects in contact with the skin can arouse a variety of tactile sensations, of which introspection allows several qualities to be distinguished: for example, vibration, steady pressure, light touch. The sensations can be graded in intensity in a predictable manner in relation to the magnitude of the *stimulus, as described quantitatively by the *Weber–Fechner and *Stevens's power law relations (see PSYCHOPHYSICS). The position of an applied stimulus, both absolute for a single point and relative with respect to two loci of stimulation, can be detected, with varying degrees of accuracy, in different parts of the body surface.

The physiological mechanisms underlying these perceptual properties can be analysed in a systematic manner, starting with the neural receptor elements in the skin. These are at the ends of axons connected with the spinal cord and brain stem. Neural processing occurs at the spinal, brain-stem, and thalamic levels on the pathway from the skin to the cerebral cortex. Further processing in the somatosensory area of the cerebral cortex and in the adjacent association areas of the cortex leads to final elaboration of sensation, where perception is assumed to occur.

The groundwork of knowledge, as of other sensory systems, was laid in experiments on anaesthetized or conscious animals, in which very precise studies of morphology, physiology, and behaviour could be made. This knowledge has recently been extended in a dramatic way, by electrophysiological and correlated psychophysical studies, to conscious human subjects, with a remarkable degree of concordance with the animal studies.

1. Cutaneous sensory tactile receptors
2. Receptive fields

3. Central processing
4. Central control of sensation
5. Recent studies in man
6. Relation to other skin senses
7. Haptic touch

1. Cutaneous sensory tactile receptors

The skin contains several kinds of encapsulated mechano-receptors (tactile receptors) innervated by myelinated dorsal root nerve fibres, and each kind is specialized to detect particular parameters of a mechanical stimulus. The *Pacinian corpuscle*, the first cutaneous receptor to be discovered, is relatively large, up to 2 mm long and 1 mm in diameter, and is present in the deeper layers of both hairy and hairless (glabrous) skin. It is pearl shaped and comprises a lamellated structure, with an outer capsule, outer lamellae, inner lamellae, and in its core the special-ized rodlike nerve terminal. The corpuscle is adapted to respond to vibration, with maximal sensitivity at 20–300 Hz and a range (bandwidth) of 20–1,500 Hz. It is capable of detecting movements smaller than a micrometre (about one-twenty-fifth of one-thousandth of an inch). The la-mellae are high-pass filters that prevent steadily main-tained pressure from penetrating to the nerve terminal in the core, but allow rapidly changing pressures to do so, so that vibrations can be detected, even in the presence of maintained pressure.

Meissner's corpuscles are encapsulated and present in the glabrous skin of primates, including man. They lie in rows just below the epidermis, in dermal papillae. The papillae correspond to the familiar surface ridges of the fingers and toes that form each individual's distinctive fingerprint. Meissner's corpuscles are innervated by myelinated axons and, like Pacinian corpuscles, also detect vibration, but at lower frequencies and with lesser sensitivity. Their maximal sensitivity is at 2–40 Hz and their frequency range from about 1 to 400 Hz. The corresponding recep-tors in non-primates are the Krause end bulbs, which also detect changing stimuli.

In hairy skin, the *hair follicles* are innervated by my-elinated fibres that have terminals arranged in a palisade round the hair shaft. They too respond to changing stim-uli, and can be subdivided into at least three subcategor-ies, with different bandwidths for maximal sensitivity to hair movement and different thresholds of movement sensitivity. All these kinds of mechanoreceptors have one feature in common—they do not respond to a steadily maintained displacement of the skin, and thus are incap-able of detecting steady pressure. On the other hand, they can encode with great precision the magnitude and wave-length of vibratory stimuli of different frequencies, cover-ing a range from less than 1 Hz to greater than 1,500 Hz.

Static or steadily maintained mechanical stimuli are de-tected by two other specialized cutaneous receptors. The first and more numerous are the *Merkel* cells, which occur in small clusters in the lower margin of the epidermis. In hairy skin these clusters are scattered, each innervated by a single myelinated axon, and form Iggo-Pinkus domes visible at the skin surface, especially after depilation of the skin. The receptors form Sa I mechanoreceptors that can sustain a discharge during static deformation, as well as during superimposed vibrations. The mechanical thresh-olds in hairy skin are about 1 μm, and the receptors can fire at rates higher than 1,000 a second when the skin is stroked. The Sa I receptors are also present in glabrous skin, the Merkel cells there lying in the so-called rete pegs of the epidermis.

The other slowly adapting receptor, the Sa II, has the *Ruffini ending* as its receptor. This is present in the dermis. They are spindle shaped, up to 2 mm long, with a distinct capsule, and a densely branched nerve ending in the cen-tral core of the receptor. These receptors are structurally similar to the Golgi tendon organs, and have the similar property of responding with a sustained discharge to maintained displacement of the skin. The mechanical sen-sitivity of the Sa II receptors is less than that of the Sa I.

2. Receptive fields

Each of these receptors occupies a small region of skin, from about 10 to 300 μm in diameter for the Sa I and Meissner's corpuscles in the fingertip, to several centi-metres for hair follicle receptors in the arm and trunk skin. These small spots are the *receptive fields from which a discharge of impulses can be evoked by an appro-priate stimulus. The sizes of individual receptive fields and the density of innervation (the number of receptive fields per unit area) are important factors in determining the location of a stimulus and, for two-point discrimin-ation, the ability to distinguish two stimuli applied sim-ultaneously.

3. Central processing

This array of mechanoreceptors provides the central ner-vous system with a great deal of information about the characteristics of mechanical stimuli (intensity, duration, bandwidth, location) that is further processed at spinal, brain-stem, and thalamic levels before it reaches the cere-bral cortex.

Direct pathways The most direct routes go via the dorsal columns of the spinal cord to the lower end of the brain stem, where the ascending branches of the incoming sens-ory nerve fibres make synaptic connections with neurons that in turn send axons to the ventrobasal thalamus. Thal-amic neurons in their turn send their axons to the somatosensory region of the cerebral cortex. An import-ant feature of this direct system is that it can preserve, to an astonishing degree, the information encoded by the cutaneous receptors—the system has the property of specificity. Individual neurons of the somatosensory cerebral cortex may have characteristics analogous to the different kinds of primary cutaneous sensory receptors, in terms of their responses to mechanical stimuli, encoding parameters such as amplitude, static/dynamic aspects, and frequency response range. This processing is further supplemented by additional properties, such as feature extraction, e.g. location of stimulated skin and direction of a moving object.

Indirect pathways There are several other sensory pathways in addition to those via the dorsal column, medial lemniscus system. These others are more elaborate, since additional neurons are present in them, and may also be non-specific, because an admixture of inputs from different touch receptors, as well as from thermoreceptors and nociceptors, can interact. The ascending information in these pathways (such as the spinothalamic tract) may have lost, to varying degrees, some of the spatial and specific attributes of the dorsal column system. Their role in touch is still open to question, but they provide sensory pathways in parallel with the direct dorsal column routes.

4. Central control of sensation

A further important feature of tactile sensation, also present in other senses, is that not all the stimuli delivered to the skin surface necessarily cause excitation in the somatosensory cortex and an associated sensory awareness. There are very potent control systems, usually originating in the brain, that can modify the transmission of excitation from the skin on its way to the cerebral cortex. This is achieved through descending inhibition that interacts on neurons, at several levels in the sensory pathway, with the incoming excitatory information. This inhibition can totally or partially prevent the onflow of information, and may be used to enhance contrast between a stimulated area and adjacent regions, or to admit only certain inputs to higher levels. In this latter context it is analogous to attention—a familiar capacity to attend to certain stimuli and disregard others. These interactions are based on excitatory and inhibitory synapses playing against each other on individual neurons and, therefore, are accessible to pharmacological manipulation, although this has been little exploited in relation to cutaneous touch.

5. Recent studies in man

In the past there was considerable controversy about the cutaneous sensory mechanisms, including the existence and function of cutaneous receptors. Although experimental evidence from animal studies leads to the conclusion that the general rules of specificity operate, it has only recently become possible to provide direct evidence from studies on conscious man. When a thin insulated tungsten wire electrode is inserted through the human skin and into a peripheral nerve it can, by suitable adjust-

ment, be used to record the impulses in a single axon coming from a cutaneous mechanoreceptor. This technique has been applied most rigorously to analyse cutaneous receptors in the hand, by recording from the median nerve and its branches in the arm and hand. Four principal kinds of mechanoreceptor, with myelinated axons, exist in human glabrous skin, corresponding to: Pacinian corpuscles, Meissner's corpuscles, SA I (Merkel receptors), and Sa II (Ruffini endings). The general characteristics of the receptors closely match those already well known from animal studies, The sensory function of the receptors was assessed by comparing the subject's report of his sensations with the responses of individual afferent fibres recorded at the same time. Criticism of this approach has been directed at the likelihood that a mechanical stimulus, even though controlled with great precision, could excite other receptors in addition to the one recorded from electrically, so that a one-to-one correspondence of sensation and unit receptor activity would be difficult to assert. In a refinement of the technique, electrical stimulation through the recording electrode was used as a means of precise excitation of a single, functionally identified, sensory axon. The exciting, and fundamentally important, result of this approach has been to establish, in a quite convincing way, that the different kinds of receptor can indeed cause perceptually distinct sensation. Thus, the Pacinian corpuscle receptors caused a sense of *tickling or vibration when stimulated at frequencies above 2–50 Hz, with a sensation of vibration related to the actual frequency of stimulation. Meissner corpuscles (FA I) evoked a sense of tapping, flutter, buzzing, or vibration (related to the frequency of stimulation) that did not change its sensory quality if the stimulation continued for several seconds. SA I (Merkel receptor) units did not evoke a sensation if only two or three electrically induced impulses were evoked at frequencies of <10 Hz. For larger numbers of impulses at higher frequencies they evoked a sense of sustained pressure or sustained contact, lacking either the vibratory or tapping quality evoked from the Pacinian and Meissner units. In contrast, activity in Sa II units did not give rise to any sensation, and so may be more concerned with muscle *reflexes and *proprioception which are not in consciousness.

These results brilliantly confirm the suggestions coming from the correlative studies in man and make possible the restatement of *Muller's now ancient law of specific nerve energies. As originally stated, this asserted that excitation of a sense organ, by whatever means, always gave rise to the same modality of sensation, whether—in the case of, say, vision—the stimulus was the normal one of light acting on the retina or was an abnormal one, such as pressure on the eyeball. In late 19th-century elaborations, the law came to be restated as asserting that every kind of sensation required its own kind of nerve fibre, and that each kind of nerve fibre with its end organ had a 'specific energy', giving rise to a certain definite sensation and no other. The experimental results cited above give credence to Muller's original proposal, namely that a given kind of receptor or its nerve fibre, when excited by whatever means, gives rise to a certain sensation. The sensation resulting from the simultaneous excitation of several kinds of receptor, such as mechanoreceptors and thermoreceptors, can, however, yield a sensation that arises from central interactions among the sensory inflow.

A further consequence of this new work is that the old controversy between 'specificity' and 'pattern' theories of cutaneous sensation has been resolved in favour of the 'specificity' theory.

7. Relation to other skin senses

This review of the 'tactile' sensory system has concentrated on the sensory receptors because it is in that area of knowledge that dramatic progress has been made in the last two decades, with the resolution of the long-standing controversy about the nature and role of the sensory receptors. Two other cutaneous sensory systems that coexist with the tactile system provide specific information about nociception (painful stimuli) and thermoreception (temperature sensation). Each is served by its own set of specific sensory receptors. The central processing of sensory information from these receptors is by the indirect route through the dorsal horn of the spinal cord. The three systems, tactile, nociceptive, and thermal, do however interact. A striking example is the reduction in pain that can, in appropriate conditions, be achieved by the concurrent application of a tactile stimulus and a noxious stimulus. A familiar instance is provided by the instinctive act of rubbing a sore place on the skin. Rubbing or stroking excites sensitive tactile receptors that interact on neurons in the spinal cord with an inflow from the nociceptors and block or reduce the excitatory action of the latter. TENS (transcutaneous electrical nerve stimulation) is a method of pain relief, now in clinical use, that is based on this interaction.

Yet another new twist has been given to the cutaneous sensory mechanisms by the discovery of electroreception in monotremes. In this branch of mammals, and especially in the platypus, there is now proof that they can detect electrical fields in water, using electroreceptors in the skin of the bill. The precise mechanism awaits discovery.

7. Haptic touch

Touching by active exploration, especially with the fingers. It is in contrast with 'passive' touch, in which structures are signalled by patterns impressed on the skin. Haptic touch has the advantage that large objects (much larger than any region of skin) can be discerned and identified, but is seldom used, except in the dark, or by blind people,

when it is extremely useful. It is essentially *single-channel* scanning in time, whereas passive touch uses simultaneous *parallel* neural *channels. Since the sensitive nerve endings of the skin adapt with constant stimulation, movement and active touch are important for renewing their signals.   AI

Belmonte, C., and Cervero, F. (eds) (1996). *Neurobiology of Nocoception*.

Euler, C. von, Franzen, O., Lindblom, U., and Ottoson, D. (eds.) (1984). *Somatosensory Mechanisms*.

Handwerker, H. O. H. (1984). 'Nerve fibre discharges and sensation'. *Human Neurobiology*, 3.

Iggo, A. (1982). 'Cutaneous sensory mechanisms'. In Barlow, H. B., and Mollon, J. D. (eds.), *The Senses*.

Proske, U., Gregory, J. E., and Iggo, A. (1998). 'Sensory receptors in monotremes'. *Philosophical Transactions of the Royal Society, Series B*, 353.

transactional analysis (TA). TA can be used as a therapeutic tool in mental health, education, organizational development, and psychometric testing (Temple 2002). Eric Berne, a psychiatrist and psychoanalyst, who developed TA in the late 1950s, suggested that individuals have three ego states: parent, adult, and child, which develop throughout childhood forming an important part of the personality. A *parent ego state* comprises positive and negative introjections from parents and parental figures. As adults, when we react from our parent ego state, our state of mind will correspond to our behaviour in a way copied exactly from a parental figure. The *adult ego state* involves assessing inner and outer current reality and using knowledge and experience to think clearly and respond appropriately. Reacting from our *child ego state* as adults involves feeling, thinking, and behaving in a way we did many years earlier when the situation was very similar. The child ego state is the repository of all childhood experiences, including the decisions we made about ourselves, others, and the world.

Children make decisions based on messages transmitted to them throughout early life. For example, a decision in response to continually disapproving parents might be: 'I am only valid if I please others.' These beliefs become fixated and the child grows up unconsciously seeking out situations that reinforce them, largely through his transactions with others. The way transactions are played out is also determined by each individual's need for strokes or units of recognition. We use strokes to manage our inherent stimulus hunger because strokes provide us with a sense of identity and worth.

Central to TA theory is the notion of *ulterior transactions*. Here, two messages are transmitted simultaneously; one adult to adult, 'Has anyone seen my keys?', the other, carrying the real meaning, between parent and child, 'Look for my keys!' The behavioural outcome is determined by the real meaning. Psychological *games* are unconscious ways of acquiring strokes by the use of repetitive, ulterior transactions. However, the individual's real needs remain unmet.

A Transactional Analyst with a strong adult ego state can support another individual to strengthen their adult ego state by discarding fixated material from the past and updating the content of the parent and child ego states; thus 'I am okay; I don't need to please people to validate my existence.' The content of the ego states can be updated throughout life with new feelings and ideas based on current reality. The 'changed mind' changes the personality structure and is observable in the person's behaviour.   THJ

Berne, E. (1961). *Transactional Analysis in Psychotherapy*.
Stewart, I. (1992). *Eric Berne*.
Temple, S. (2002). 'The development of a transactional analysis psychometric tool for enhancing functional fluency'. Unpublished doctoral thesis, University of Plymouth.

transfer. This essential concept for appreciating learning concerns the benefit of, or impairment from, what has been learned on later performance. When there is resulting improvement, transfer from the past experience is *positive*, when impairment, the transfer is *negative*. The same learned knowledge or components of skill may transfer to be helpful (positive) in some situations, but may impair (be negative transfer) in other situations, or for some other skills. Thus transfer from practising table tennis may impair one's ability to hit a tennis ball with the appropriate arm movements. To understand the concept, it is important to note that the neural mechanisms for positive and negative transfer are exactly the same: the only difference is whether what has transferred is useful or not.

Transfer tends to be thought of in general terms, rather than for particular items of knowledge. Thus the skill of learning Latin is generally supposed to transfer positively to the learning of other languages, although it may transfer negatively to differently constructed languages. A commonly experienced transfer problem occurs when driving in a different country, on the opposite side of the road from that to which one is used. Accidents from negative transfer are particularly likely to occur when starting off in the morning on the wrong side, and when faced with situations such as complicated crossings. It is remarkable that complete reversal of accustomed patterns of behaviour is not more difficult than it generally is.

Precisely what it is that transfers, and why it transfers, are far from understood, though these are essential questions for education. They are also extremely important in appreciating the difficulties a pilot may experience in transferring from one type of aircraft to another, and in designing flight simulators to give as much positive transfer in training, with as little negative transfer as possible.

There may be features of a simulator (such as horizontal raster lines on a video screen) which allow 'flight' with cues that are not available in actual flying, and so may be dangerous.

It is interesting that perceptual abilities and skills can transfer from one part of the body to other parts. Thus, discrimination of two-point touch practised on the back of one hand (with a pair of dividers) can transfer to improved two-point discrimination on the corresponding region of the other hand. See also TRANSFER OF TRAINING.
                                                                 RLG

transference. A patient in psychotherapy tends to transfer into his relationship with the therapist the sometimes intense feelings he experienced at an earlier stage in his life, in his relationship with his mother or father or other important figure. The formation of a transference relationship thus facilitates the overcoming of resistances to the recall of painful experiences from his past. The transference relationship (entirely different from *transfer above) is said to be positive if the patient is compliant, negative if he is defiant. The formation of a positive relationship may by itself relieve symptoms, but this is no more than a false 'transference cure'. If it is strong and persistent, and the patient becomes dependent on the therapist, the relationship amounts to a 'transference neurosis'. By 'counter-transference' is meant the transfer by the therapist of feelings derived from his past into his relationship with the patient: such feelings have to be recognized and overcome.

Sigmund *Freud described transference in 1895 in one of his first papers on psychoanalysis. Seeing the trouble that was caused to his colleague Joseph *Breuer, when he became the object of the erotic feelings of his patient 'Anna O.', he argued that these feelings referred not to his colleague personally but to a fantasy figure. He was later to encourage the development of fantasy about the therapist by his habit of sitting unseen behind the patient lying on a couch. The therapist thus becomes a blank screen onto which the patient projects his feelings. However, the emphasis in psychoanalytic treatment gradually moved from the analysis of dreams (SEE FREUD ON DREAMS) and the overcoming of resistances to the opening up of communication between therapist and patient through the analysis and elucidation of the transference relationship. This was the main therapeutic tool of psychoanalysis, and its hallmark, during the years between the wars. The transference relationship is an inevitable necessity, Freud argued. Psychoanalysis does not create it. It brings it to light so that it can be combated at the appropriate time. It has to be dissolved before treatment ends so that the patient can reassert his or her independence and resume an adult role. Dissolution proves difficult in some cases.

Schools of psychotherapy differ in the balance they seek to achieve between the advantages and disadvantages of the transference relationship. Some modern schools counteract the tendency from the beginning and regard the re-enactment of the conflicts of the past within the relationship with the therapist as inessential. More important is what happens in the patient's relationships with members of his family and others. The relationship with the therapist is then regarded as mediating, and interpretations are concerned with the difficulties the patient experiences outside the treatment sessions, or in his relationships with others in a therapeutic group.   DRD

Freud, S. (1901). 'Fragment of an analysis of a case of hysteria ("Dora")'. Trans. A. and J. Strachey, Pelican Freud Library, viii.
Melan, D. H. (1963). *A Study of Brief Psychotherapy.*

transfer of training. It is often evident in *transfer situations that a very considerable amount of learning has been carried from one task to another. For both theoretical and practical reasons, it is desirable to be able to measure the amount of this transfer.

Let us consider a typical transfer experiment or situation. An experimental group of subjects learns some task or skill A. Initially, as we might expect, their errors are many, but after some time, or number of trials, they reach a satisfactory and stable level of performance characterized by few errors. They then attempt some new task B, and again proceed, more or less rapidly, from making many errors to making only a few. (The mean performance of this group is shown, smoothed for the sake of argument, as the clear line in Fig. 1, whose notation will henceforth be used.) A control group has learned task B ab initio (dark in figure), and it is generally the case that the final error levels of performance of the two groups (S and S^1) are virtually indistinguishable—and may, indeed, be zero.

All the quantities labelled in the figure can be measured. F, C, L, T, S, and S^1 are all measures of performance

in terms of error, while m, n, and r are either numbers of trials or elapsed time. Since all these are available, it is natural to ask how they may best be used and combined to express the amount of learning transferred by the experimental group from task A to task B.

The number of expressions and formulae that have been proposed is very large (Gagne, Foster, and Crowley 1948, Murdock 1957), but they all fall into one of two categories: there are those that measure the saving of training time, or number of trials (i.e. which in some way compare r with n), and those that are concerned with the initial performance of subjects immediately after transfer (i.e. which evaluate T). The former class we may call *savings* measures, the latter we may call *first-shot* measures. Unfortunately, although the contrary was often tacitly assumed, these two classes of measures can give sharply contrasting impressions, for it is quite possible to save a great deal of training time on the second task (r < n) while still finding a marked transient decremental effect of transfer (T > C) (Hammerton 1967, Hammerton and Tickner 1967). The measure selected must answer the question the user wishes to put, and he must always be aware that it may not answer any other question.

The simplest question is: what proportion of training time in task B is saved by prior training on task A? This is clearly and straightforwardly measured by the quantity a, given by:

$$a = (n - r)/n \qquad (1)$$

It is worth pausing to note how difficult it is to apply even the simplest psychological findings in a practical situation. Suppose someone was being trained to use some complex industrial equipment (task B) by practice on a simulator (task A). The proportional saving of time is given by (1), but in practice the following questions arise: what is the running cost per hour of the simulator as compared to that of the real equipment? Does even a poor operator of the real equipment produce some useful output which

Fig. 1. Curves showing form of typical transfer experiment.

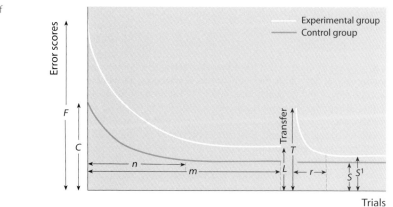

can be set against cost? Is he, on the other hand, likely merely to waste raw materials or damage the equipment itself? Evidently the practical utility of a training programme or device cannot be measured by any simple expression, but is a complex psychological and economic question.

If we recall that there is often a brief but marked impairment in performance immediately after transfer, it will be evident that there are many practical situations in which some measure of first-shot transfer is necessary. Again, more than one question may be asked about this. One is: how does the learning immediately after transfer compare with that required by the control group to reach a stable performance? This comparison may be given by:

$$b = (F - T)/(F - S) \qquad (2)$$

But a user may raise a practical objection to this, for he may not be concerned with the comparative measurement of learning, however interesting that may be theoretically. He generally needs to know whether expensive equipment is liable to be misused when first handled: in other words, how does first-shot transfer performance (T) compare with the stable performance of the control group (S)? The information required may be given as a simple percentage:

$$c = 100 \, (1 - T/S) \qquad (3)$$

Another question which can arise in practice is this. Suppose that you have no control group—i.e. suppose that all trainees start on some simulator device, and that no man is allowed to begin with task B. How much of the skill acquired with the simulator (A) will be retained upon first transfer? This is not the question answered either by (2) or by (3) above, and it is more precisely answered by:

$$d = (F - T)/F - L) \qquad (4)$$

However, in pursuit of understanding, a quite different question may be put, namely: how does the learning shown by the first-shot performance of the experimental group compare with that acquired by the control group? A measure for this is:

$$e = (C - T)/(C - S) \qquad (5)$$

It is by no means claimed that the expressions given here are the only, or necessarily the best, answers to the questions discussed, and certainly many other questions can be put, of both theoretical and economic significance. As we have shown, it is important to be clear about what question is being asked, and especially important to be clear about the extent and limitations of the information obtained from the answer. For example, an answer to a question on saving of training time—such as (1)—gives no information at all about first-shot performance: the one may be excellent and the other deplorable. In one

particular case (Hammerton and Tickner 1967) the several expressions given here yielded values (rendered as percentages) from 92 to *minus* 54. If any one had been taken as 'the' measure of transfer, the oversimple question 'How much learning was transferred?' could have received any answer in the range from 'almost all' to 'less than none'.

Evidently there is no such thing as 'the' measure of transfer, but if a specific question concerning transfer is precisely formulated, expressions exist for answering it, and a useful and informative numerical measure can be obtained.   MH

Gagne, R. M., Foster, H., and Crowley, M. E. (1948). 'The measurement of transfer of training'. *Psychology Bulletin*, 45.

Hammerton, M. (1967). 'Measures for the efficiency of simulators as training devices'. *Ergonomics*, 10.

——and Tickner, A. H. (1967). 'Visual factors affecting transfer of training from a simulated to a real situation'. *Journal of Applied Psychology*, 51.

Murdock, B. B. (1957). 'Transfer designs and formulas'. *Psychology Bulletin*, 54.

truth. There are three main epistemological theories: *correspondence*, that a proposition is true when it corresponds to some kind of reality; *coherence*, that propositions are true when they cohere to form a consistent body of what is taken to be knowledge; and *pragmatism* (or pragmaticism), that propositions are true when useful. Undoubtedly coherence and usefulness are very generally accepted *criteria* for truth, but they are not normally what is *meant* by 'truth'. Some kind of correspondence is what is meant, but it is ultimately impossible to observe correspondences between appearance and reality. It would require a kind of God's eye view to see that the observations of a man, or the understanding of science, correspond to the world. So, although what we generally mean by 'truth' is correspondence with reality, correspondence is not, ultimately, an available criterion for truth.

Most empiricists have supposed that propositions can be individually tested for truth, by suitable observation or experiment. This is a tenet of 'logical atomism'. But the now current view is, rather, that not all can be tested at all directly and that perceptions, observations, and experiments require assumptions (which may be hidden) in order for us to interpret them. The American philosopher Thomas *Kuhn (1962) has put forward the highly influential notion of scientific *paradigms: that there are accepted, though often implicit, assumptions in all 'normal' sciences. For example, *Darwinian natural selection is, or sets, a paradigm for current biology. *Newton's and Einstein's accounts are paradigms for physics and cosmology. One of the problems of modern psychology is the difficulty of making explicit the ruling paradigms and assumptions in terms of which its day-to-day experiments are assessed and interpreted. Where these assumptions are regarded as '*common sense', they may in fact reflect the philosophical and scientific presuppositions of previous centuries, which may change with changes of assumptions or paradigms. But only God knows what the next paradigm will be. RLG

Kuhn, T. (1962). *The Structure of Scientific Revolutions* (enlarged edn. 1970).

Turing, Alan Mathison (1912–54). British mathematician, born in London, and educated at King's College, Cambridge, graduating in mathematics. He was the key figure in the original conception of electronic digital computers and *artificial intelligence (AI), the only other contender being the brilliant American mathematician John *Von Neumann. Working almost entirely independently, they set the stage and wrote the script for the computer revolution, and concepts of mind in terms of artificial intelligence are based on the technology of the electronic digital computer, of which they were the principal inventors.

Turing made a fundamental contribution, shortly after graduating, with his paper 'On computable numbers with an application to the Entscheidungsproblem' (1937). In this he showed that there are classes of mathematical problems that cannot be proved by any fixed definite process or heuristic procedures. At the same time he proposed an automatic problem-solving machine that is the starting point of philosophies, and practical hopes, of digital computer-based AI. The Turing machine, as it is now called, is abstract in the sense that its description defines all possible operations though not all may be realizable in practice. Although the notion in its original form is clumsy, it encapsulates the essentials of modern digital computers.

The Turing machine can be visualized as an indefinitely long tape of squares on which are numbers, or a square may be blank. The machine reads one square at a time, and it can move the tape to read other squares, forwards or backwards. It can print new symbols or erase symbols. Turing showed that his very simple machine (which had as its ancestor Charles *Babbage's 'Analytical Engine' of the 1830s) can specify the steps required for the solution of any problem that can be solved by instructions, explicitly stated rules or procedures.

Turing considered whether a human being, or rather the human mind, can be described by analogy with such a machine, or can be simulated by one with appropriate programs. The essential idea, which he was among the first to see clearly, is that the physical construction of the machine is unimportant. Turing pointed out that Babbage's computer was mechanical, and though in the 20th century electricity could be used, as faster and more reliable, it mattered nothing whether a computer was mech-

anical, electrical, or worked in any other way provided it could carry out the necessary instructions in a given time. It is a short step from this to saying that the biological material of the brain, protoplasm, or the way in which the brain is constructed, is not particularly important for intelligence or perhaps for anything else. If we were constructed differently we would in some ways be different, but we might still be intelligent, perceiving, conscious beings.

'The imitation game'—Turing's Test. Turing suggested how we could recognize whether a simulation of the human mind had succeeded or failed. His paper 'Computing machinery and intelligence' (1950) remains the clearest short account of the philosophy of artificial intelligence, as it came to be called, and 'Turing's test' for judging the adequacy of a simulation of mind remains the best criterion for recognizing intelligence in a machine. The 'test' is the imitation game, which Turing describes in these words: 'It is played with three people, a man (*A*), a woman (*B*), and an interrogator (*C*), who may be of either sex. The interrogator stays in a room apart from the other two. The object of the game for the interrogator is to determine which of the other two is the man and which the woman.' The interrogator is allowed to put questions to *A* and *B*, though not of physical characteristics such as length of hair, and he is not allowed to hear their voices. He is allowed to experience or question only *mental* attributes. The next step of the game is to substitute a machine for one of the humans. The machine communicates with a teletype. The question is whether the interrogator can distinguish the remaining human from the machine. Turing points out that for some questions, such as problems in arithmetic, the humans would show up revealingly poorly, and that this is perhaps an objection to the test, but it seems as good a test as any so far suggested for distinguishing between man and intelligent machines. It is of course behaviouristic, but, as Turing says, we cannot 'get inside' another human being, to know directly whether he or she has conscious experience, such as sensations of colour and emotional state. He leaves it open whether we should assume that the machine which passes the test of the imitation game is conscious.

Turing was the master code breaker who succeeded in reading the German highest-level secret codes during the Second World War. This was not revealed until 30 years after the war, when he was shown to be the originator of the first practical programmed computer—the Colossus (electronic cryptanalytic machine)—which, with human intelligence and a good deal of luck, broke the German codes and demonstrated just how powerful information-handling machines can be. He died tragically at the height of his remarkable powers, as mathematician, biologist, and supreme creative philosopher of computing by machine and brain. RLG

Feigenbaum, E. A., and Feldman, J. (1963). *Computers and Thought.* (Contains a reprint of Turing's Imitation Game paper.)

Hodges, A. (2000). *Alan Turing: The Enigma.* (Foreword by Douglas Hofstadter).

Von Neumann, J. (1958). *The Computer and the Brain.*

twins. Twins have been mentioned since the beginning of recorded history, including ancient stories such as Romulus and Remus, the mythological founders of Rome, who were said to be twins abandoned and raised by a wolf. Although most mammals have large litters, primates including our species tend to have single offspring but occasionally have multiple births. Human twins are more common than people usually realize—about 1 in 85 births are twins. Surprisingly, as many as 20 per cent of all fetuses are twins but because of the hazards associated with twin pregnancies one member of the pair often dies very early in pregnancy.

Twins are of two types. One type, called identical twins, is derived from the same fertilized egg (called a zygote) that splits for unknown reasons to create two (sometimes more) genetically identical individuals. For about a third of identical twins, the zygote splits during the first five days after fertilization as it makes its way down to the womb. In this case, the identical twins have different sacs (called chorions) within the placenta. Two-thirds of the time, the zygote splits after it implants in the placenta and the twins share the same chorion. 'Siamese' twins are identical twins who split after about two weeks, timing that generally results in twins whose bodies are partially fused. Because identical twins come from the same zygote they are usually called monozygotic (MZ) in the scientific literature. The other type of twin involves two separate eggs that are fertilized by different sperm, just like any other brothers or sisters, and are called fraternal, non-identical, or dizygotic (DZ). About one-third of twins are identical twins. The identical twinning rate appears to be similar throughout the world and is not related to any demographic factors such as mother's age. In contrast, the fraternal twinning rate differs in different countries, and increases for older mothers, and may be heritable in some families. Fertility drugs have increased the rate of fraternal twinning by increasing the likelihood that more than one egg will be fertilized, as has *in vitro* fertilization in which several embryos are implanted in the hope that at least one will survive.

Twins are especially interesting today because of concerns about human cloning. Identical twins are more like clones than 'real' clones because identical twins spend their first nine months in the same womb and experience the same family environment and similar generational experiences. In contrast, if you were cloned from one of your cells, although your clone would be genetically identical to you, your clone would be raised in a different womb, different family, and different generation. For this reason, your clone would be less similar to you than if you had an identical twin to the extent that such environmental factors are important. Identical twins are so similar physically that it is often difficult to tell them apart, especially when they are young. For example, identical twins have the same eye colour, hair colour and texture, similar fingerprints, their heights are usually within an inch, and their weight is within a few pounds. In fact, with greater than 95 per cent accuracy, you can tell if twins are identical simply by asking if they are easily confused, because this single question summarizes many physical characteristics that are highly heritable. (DNA is used to assess identical twin status with nearly 100 per cent accuracy—if twins differ for any DNA markers they cannot be identical twins.) Fraternal twins can look similar, as siblings sometimes do, but they do not look identical and are not often confused.

Identical twins are not only similar on the outside. They are also similar physiologically and psychologically. For example, if one identical twin has epilepsy, the chances are greater than 90 per cent that the twin partner also has epilepsy. Identical twin concordances for some other medical illnesses are 70 per cent for ulcers, 60 per cent for Alzheimer's disease, 50 per cent for rheumatoid arthritis, and 30 per cent for ischemic heart disease. For a few diseases, however, identical twins are not very similar, such as chronic obstructive pulmonary disease (15 per cent), breast cancer (15 per cent), and Parkinson's disease (10 per cent), which strongly suggests that susceptibility to these diseases is not much inherited.

Identical twins are at least as similar psychologically. For example, concordance for identical twins is about 60 per cent for autism, 50 per cent for schizophrenia, and 40 per cent for major depressive disorder. This evidence for genetic influence is not limited to disorders but also extends to behavioural differences between people within the normal range of variation. For example, identical twins are nearly as similar to each other in intelligence as measured by IQ tests as are the same individuals tested twice. For personality, identical twins are somewhat less similar than for physical traits and intelligence. The correlation is a statistic describing resemblance that runs from 0.00 indicating no more than chance resemblance within pairs of twins to 1.0 indicating that members of a twin pair are exactly the same. Identical twins correlate about 0.90 for height, about 0.80 for weight, and about 0.80 for IQ scores, but only about 0.40 for most personality traits.

What about your clone? As mentioned above, your clone could be considerably less similar than your identical twin if growing up in the same environment is responsible for making identical twins similar because your clone would not experience so similar an environment. The issue is the extent to which environmental factors are responsible for the similarity of identical twins, which is the long-standing issue of nature (genetics) and nurture (environment). That is, it has long been known that family members resemble each other not just physically but also behaviourally. Do such traits run in families for reasons of nature or nurture? First described by Francis *Galton in England in the late 19th century, the twin method compares similarity for identical and fraternal twins and has been the workhorse for disentangling nature and nurture. The twin method is the main reason why twins are so prominent in the scientific literature. The twin method is like an experiment in which one group (identical twins) are twice as similar genetically as another group (fraternal twins). If this twofold greater genetic similarity of identical twins has no effect on a trait, we would expect that identical twins would be no more similar than fraternal twins for the trait. Because half of fraternal twin pairs are opposite-sex twins, the experiment is better if same-sex fraternal twins are compared to identical twins, who are of course always of the same sex because they are genetically identical.

The twin method confirms, unsurprisingly, that individual differences in height are largely due to genetic differences: identical twins are highly similar for height (0.90) and fraternal twins are also just about as similar as expected on the basis of their genetic relatedness (0.45). You may be more surprised to learn that individual differences in weight are almost as highly heritable as height, with identical twin correlations of about 0.80 and fraternal twin correlations of about 0.40. The reason why the results for weight are more surprising than those for height is that you know that you can do more about your weight than you can do about your height. This raises an important point for interpreting results of twin studies. Finding evidence for genetic influence (often called heritability) does not refer to 'what could be': if you stop eating you will lose weight even though weight is highly heritable. Results of the twin method describe 'what is' in a particular sample rather than predicting what could be. That is, the twin method assesses the relative effects of genetic and environmental differences on observed differences in weight as they exist for a particular sample given that sample's genetic and environmental differences at that time. If you change the genetics of the sample (for example, by studying different ethnic groups) or if you change the environment (for example, by providing fattier foods), you could change the relative effects of genes and environments. This explanation is also relevant to why there is no paradox that twin results show high heritability for height and weight even though height and weight have both increased considerably on average in developed countries in recent generations.

Results of twin studies of physiological and psychological disorders and dimensions also indicate that the resemblance for identical twins discussed above is almost entirely due to genetics, not to environment. The results of the twin method comparing identical and fraternal twins are supported by results from a few hundred pairs of identical twins reared apart which generally suggest that identical twins reared apart are nearly as similar as identical twins reared for psychological as well as physical traits. Thus, we can safely conclude that your clone would be almost as similar to you as would an identical twin. For some traits this means that your clone would be very similar to you – for height and weight and general physical appearance, susceptibility to certain diseases such as epilepsy and ulcers, and intelligence. For a few traits such as Parkinson's disease and breast cancer, there would be little resemblance. For most disorders and dimensions, however, your clone (or identical twin) would be moderately similar to you but would not be just a chip off the same old block. Moreover, research on twins suggests that despite their similarity there is no evidence that identical twins suffer from having a clone either physically or psychologically. For example, identical twins are just as intelligent and as well adjusted as non-twin individuals. Identical twins are clones and they are doing fine.

RPl

Plomin, R., DeFries, J. C., McClearn, G. E., and McGuffin, P. (2001). *Behavioral Genetics* (4th edn.).

Segal, N. (1999). *Entwined Lives: Twins and What they Tell us about Human Behavior.*

U

umami. Fundamental taste in Japanese psychophysics, characteristic of the enhancer monosodium glutamate (MSG). Not reducible to any combination of the traditional four primary tastes of Henning's tetrahedron: sweet, sour, salty, bitter. Means delicious taste.

See TASTE.

unconditioned reflex. Response such as salivation that follows an unconditioned stimulus such as food, naturally, without any prior process of conditioning.

See CONDITIONING; PAVLOV, IVAN PETROVICH.

unconscious, the. According to Sigmund *Freud a large part of the mind is unconscious—though essentially similar to the conscious mind in having wishes and fears and so on. This Freudian theory is very different from the notion which forms a part of many more recent psychological theories, that the brain processes accept and analyse information unconsciously, as one might expect of a computer—lack of *consciousness is not the same as the unconscious.

Opinion is probably moving away from the Freudian view, to something closer to this *artificial intelligence notion that unconscious processing is basic to much behaviour. This view, however, is not that of extreme *behaviourism, which claims that there is no consciousness whatever.

The notion of unconscious inference was developed by Hermann von *Helmholtz, when he considered perception as given by inferences ('Unconscious Inferences') from features of the world as signalled by the senses. This gave rise to a very complex historical controversy, with Helmholtz and Freud as major figures, which even now has not been resolved in detail. At the time, the Helmholtz view was highly unpopular, as it was considered that inference requires consciousness, and this argument was associated with the moral position that consciousness is required for ethical judgement. So the notion of unconscious inference threatened morality and justification of praise, blame, and punishment.

See CONSCIOUSNESS AND CAUSALITY.   RLG

universals. We experience particulars but not universals. Thus we *see* a *particular* triangle, but geometry depends upon generalized concepts of 'triangularity'—which is never seen by the senses. Universals are mental constructs based on inductive inference or hypotheses from the experience of particulars. They are essential for explanations.   RLG

utilitarianism. See BENTHAM, JEREMY; MILL, JOHN STUART.

V

vision-for-action. The specialized visual processes that underlie the programming and control of skilled movements of the body are collectively referred to as vision-for-action.

Vision is so closely identified with visual phenomenology that we sometimes forget that the visual system does more than deliver our experience of the world. It also plays an essential role in the control of our movements, from picking up our morning cup of coffee to playing football. Many traditional accounts of vision, while acknowledging the role of vision in motor control, have simply regarded such control as part of a larger function—that of constructing an internal model of the external world. In most of these accounts there is an implicit assumption that, in the end, vision delivers a single representation of the external world—a kind of simulacrum of the real thing that serves as the perceptual foundation for all visually driven thought and action.

But the idea that vision delivers a single 'general-purpose' representation of the external world is not correct. Instead, nature seems to have given us two different visual systems. One system, *vision-for-perception*, allows us to recognize objects and build up a 'database' about the world. This is the system we are more familiar with, the one that gives us our conscious visual experience—and allows us to see and appreciate objects in the world beyond our bodies. The other system, *vision-for-action*, provides the visual control we need to move about and interact with those objects. Vision-for-action does not have to be conscious, but does have to be quick and accurate.

The division of labour between vision-for-perception and vision-for-action is reflected in the fact that two anatomically distinct 'streams' of visual projections have evolved in the cerebral cortex of primates. One set of projections, called the ventral stream, arises in primary visual cortex at the back of the brain and projects forward to the temporal lobe. Another set of projections, called the dorsal stream, also arises in primary visual cortex but projects instead to the parietal lobe. The ventral stream plays a critical role in transforming incoming visual information into perceptual representations that embody the enduring characteristics of objects and their relations. Such representations enable us to identify objects, to attach meaning and significance to them, and to establish their causal relations—operations that are essential for accumulating knowledge about the world. In contrast, the dorsal stream uses moment-to-moment information about the location and disposition of objects with respect to the observer for the control of goal-directed actions. But even though the two systems transform visual information in quite different ways, they work together in the production of adaptive behaviour. In general terms one could say that the selection of appropriate goal objects depends on the perceptual machinery of the ventral stream, while the visual control of the goal-directed action is carried out by dedicated on-line control systems in the dorsal stream.

Much of the evidence for this distinction between vision-for-action and vision-for-perception comes from work with neurological patients (Goodale and Milner 2003). One of the most compelling cases is that of D.F., a young woman whose ventral stream was selectively damaged as a consequence of hypoxia from carbon monoxide poisoning. D.F. shows no visual awareness of the form and dimensions of objects (visual form *agnosia). Indeed, she cannot discriminate between even simple geometrical shapes such as a triangle and square, and cannot tell a horizontal from a vertical line. Nevertheless, when she reaches out to grasp objects, the posture of her hand and fingers is exquisitely tuned in flight to the size, shape, and orientation of the object in front of her, just as it is in a person with normal vision. For example, when she is presented with a series of rectangular blocks that vary in their dimensions but not in their overall surface area, she is unable to say whether or not any two of these blocks are the same or different. Even when a single block is placed in front of her, she is unable to indicate how wide the block is by opening her index finger and thumb a matching amount. Nevertheless, when she reaches out to pick up the block using a precision grip, the opening between her index finger and thumb is scaled in flight to the width of the block, just as it is in people with normal vision.

Individuals who have suffered selective damage to the dorsal stream show a pattern of deficits and spared abilities that are the mirror image of those seen in D.F. Such patients are unable to use visual information to guide their hand movements as they reach out to grasp objects (optic ataxia), even though they can see the object and can

927

describe where it is and what it looks like. Many patients with dorsal-stream damage are also unable to adjust the posture of their fingers or rotate their hand appropriately when they reach out to pick up an object. It should be pointed out, of course, that these patients typically have no difficulty using input from other sensory systems, such as touch or audition, to guide their movements. As soon as their hand makes contact with an object, for example, they are able to correct their hand posture and grasp it properly. Their deficit is neither 'purely' visual nor 'purely' motor but is instead a visuomotor deficit.

The evidence from neurological patients points to a clear dissociation between the visual pathways supporting perception and action. But why should two separate visual systems have evolved? The answer appears to be that perception and action require quite different operations to be performed on the incoming visual information. The reference frame and the metrics of visual perception, for example, are largely relative. The use of relative or scene-based metrics means that we can construct a detailed representation of the real world without having to compute the absolute size, distance, and geometry of each object in the scene. In fact, computing the absolute metrics of an entire scene would be computationally impossible. It is far more economical to compute just the relational metrics of the scene, and even these computations do not always need to be precise. The reliance on scene-based frames of reference means, for example, that we can watch the same scene unfold on a small television or on a gigantic movie screen without being confused by the changes in scale.

Although we can use our perceptual representations to make inferences about objects in the world, the scene-based metrics of perception are not enough for the control of action directed at those objects. To enable us to pick up the cup of coffee on our breakfast table, for example, our brain has to know more than the fact that the cup is closer to us than the box of cornflakes and further away than the toast. Our brain needs to compute the position of the cup with respect to our hand—and its real size. In other words, it needs to use absolute metrics set within an egocentric frame of reference. Experiments have shown that our brain does indeed carry out such computations—and it does this at the precise moment the action is performed. Moreover, unlike our visual percepts, the visual information that is used to control such actions is not accessible to conscious scrutiny.

The idea of two visual systems in a single brain might seem initially counter-intuitive. Our visual experience of the world is so compelling that it is hard to believe that some other quite independent visual signal—one that we are unaware of—is guiding our movements. After all, it seems obvious that it is the same subjective image that allows us both to recognize the coffee cup on our desk and

to pick it up. But the evidence suggests that this belief is an illusion. The visual signals that give us our experience of the cup are *not* the same ones that guide our hand as we pick it up!   MAG

Goodale, M. A., and Milner, A. D. (2003). *Sight Unseen: An Exploration of Conscious and Unconscious Vision.*

visual brain in action. Evolution has provided primates with a complex patchwork of interconnected visual areas occupying some 50 per cent of the cerebral cortex. These areas fall into two broad 'streams', each emanating from the primary visual area (V1): a ventral stream flowing to the inferior temporal cortex (ITC), and a dorsal stream flowing to the posterior parietal cortex (PPC). Ungerleider and Mishkin (1982) proposed a division of labour between the two streams in dealing with incoming visual information, with the ventral stream signalling information about *objects* and the dorsal stream signalling the *positions* of the objects. More recent evidence, however, favours the idea that the ventral stream provides our conscious *perception*, while the dorsal stream governs the automatic visual *guidance of our actions* (Milner and Goodale 1995, Jeannerod 1997).

Selective brain damage can disrupt these two broad visual functions separately. Patients with PPC damage are often unable to reach accurately towards objects ('optic ataxia'), and also have difficulty orienting their wrist and forming their grasp appropriately to pick up target objects. Instead they grope blindly to grasp the object. Yet, despite this 'visuomotor blindness', these patients often have little difficulty describing the size, orientation, and location of the objects they fail to grasp.

In direct contrast, patients with 'visual form agnosia' are quite unable to tell what they see. For example, patient D.F., whose ventral stream is severely damaged, could not report the orientation of an oriented slot, whether asked to do so verbally or manually. Yet when asked to insert her hand or a card into the slot, she did this skilfully, turning her hand appropriately right from the start of the movement. Similarly D.F. reached out to pick up blocks whose shapes and sizes she could not tell apart, unthinkingly opening her hand, in flight, in proportion to the object's width. Qualitatively similar, though less impressive, results have been found in *'blindsight' patients, perhaps again through the unconscious operation of the dorsal stream, but in this case accessed rather indirectly.

Like D.F., healthy observers too seem to control their actions using visual information that is not present in their perceptual awareness. In providing such automatic guidance the dorsal stream seems to act in isolation, independently of any visual 'knowledge base'. Implicit assumptions based on that database cause us sometimes to misjudge what we see, as when a shift in a large frame makes a stationary spot inside it seem to shift in the

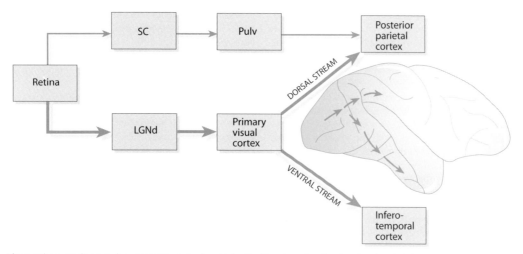

Fig. 1. Schematic diagram showing major routes by which retinal input reaches the dorsal and ventral streams. Inset shows the cortical projections as the right hemisphere of a macaque brain. LGNd: lateral geniculate nucleus, pars dorsalis; Pulv: pulvina nucleus; SC: superior colliculus.

opposite direction. In contrast, the dorsal system is not deceived by such spatial illusions. Instead, it directs our eye and hand movements to where a target really is, instead of where our perceptual experience tells us it is (Bridgeman et al. 2000). Similarly, certain geometric illusions affect visually guided reaching and grasping (Haffenden and Goodale 1998) far less than they affect visual experience. In other words, you may perceive an object as bigger than it really is, but you open your finger–thumb grip correctly when reaching for it. Experienced tennis players presumably use unconscious visuomotor skills like these in guiding their strokes.   ADM

Bridgeman, B., Gemmer, A., Forsman, T. and Huemer, V. (2000). 'Processing spatial information in the sensorimotor branch of the visual system'. *Vision Research*, 40.

Haffenden, A. M., and Goodale, M. A. (1998). 'The effect of pictorial illusion on prehension and perception'. *Journal of Cognitive Neuroscience*, 10.

Jeannerod, M. (1997). *The Cognitive Neuroscience of Action*.

Milner, A. D., and Goodale, M. A. (1995). *The Visual Brain in Action*.

Ungerleider, L. G., and Mishkin, M. (1982). 'Two cortical visual systems'. In Ingle, D. J., Goodale, M. A., and Mansfield, R. J. W. (eds.), *Analysis of Visual Behavior*.

visual system: environmental influences. Experience in early life influences the organization of the visual system. That is, a specific set of environmental conditions seems to modify the properties of the visual system in a way that reflects these conditions. The best-known example of this is the changes produced by 'monocular deprivation'. If in infancy the input to one eye is select-

ively impaired, due to either a severe refractive error or a squint, there is a loss of visual capability in the affected eye, which persists in adult life even after the original disorder has been corrected. This is a type of '*amblyopia' and it has been investigated experimentally by rearing animals (cats or monkeys) from eye-opening time with one eye sutured closed. If after a period of three months or more of this monocular deprivation, the eye is opened, it looks perfectly normal, but the animal appears to be behaviourally blind in it. Examination of the visual cortex of animals reared in this way reveals dramatic changes in the distribution of ocular dominance columns (see VISUAL SYSTEM: ORGANIZATION). Instead of the normal bands of alternating left- and right-eye ocular dominance columns, virtually all the cells outside layer IV are driven only by the non-deprived eye. Within layer IV, the number of cells receiving an input from the deprived eye is greatly reduced, and the number receiving an input from the normal eye greatly increased. In other words, in layer IV the deprived-eye ocular dominance columns appear to shrink, and the non-deprived (normal) columns expand. Moreover, the cells still receiving an input from the deprived eye in layer IV seem to lose the capability to drive the cells in the other layers of the cortex.

1. Critical period and binocular competition
2. Other factors influenced in the critical period
3. Significance of the critical period

1. Critical period and binocular competition
In animals, the marked changes in cortical organization following monocular deprivation are seen only if the

deprivation occurs during the first three months of life. After that age, even extended periods of deprivation seem to have little effect. There is thus a critical period in early life in which the visual system is particularly susceptible to environmental influences. Moreover, within this critical period it is possible to reverse the effects of monocular deprivation. For example, even one week of monocular deprivation can result in the changes described above but, if at this stage the deprived eye is opened and the other closed, after another week or so the situation reverses, and the cortex becomes dominated by the initially deprived eye. A competitive interaction between the inputs from the two eyes therefore seems to be an important factor in producing the changes in cortical organization that can occur within the critical period. If both eyes are closed at eye-opening time, so that there is binocular as opposed to monocular deprivation, both eyes retain equal access to the visual cortex although there is a reduction in the number of binocularly driven cells. It appears that only when the input from one eye is selectively decreased, with respect to the other, does it lose the ability to drive cortical cells. This suggests a competition between the excitatory nerve terminals for synaptic sites on cortical cells. Thus, during monocular deprivation there would be a reorganization of excitatory terminals within the cortex, so that the lateral geniculate neurons and cortical inter-neurons relaying the input from the non-deprived eye take over the synaptic sites normally occupied by terminals from the deprived eye. However, things are not quite this simple. Recent work has shown that it is possible under some conditions to reveal inputs from the deprived eye in monocularly deprived animals, in a way which suggests that at least some synapses are present but ineffective. The cortical changes occurring during monocular deprivation may thus involve a change in synaptic effectiveness, or some form of synaptic suppression, as well as the redistribution of terminals.

2. Other factors influenced in the critical period

So far, a large part of the discussion has been concerned with environmental influences on ocular dominance columns in the cortex. However, other aspects of visual cortical organization also seem to be influenced by the environment. The subset of orientation columns crossing the ocular dominance columns appears to be sensitive to the distribution of the orientation of the contours in the visual world in early life. Thus, rearing an animal in an environment where it only 'sees' vertical stripes results in a population of cortical neurons which, instead of representing all orientations, are biased to orientations in the region of the vertical, and not to others. Precisely organized binocular inputs to cortical cells render them sensitive to retinal image disparity, and form the basis of normal *stereoscopic vision. This is a more subtle level

of organization than that seen in the gross distribution of ocular dominance columns, and it is very sensitive to abnormal environments. Even relatively mild squints seem to be able to upset the formation of these connections, and possibly result in loss of binocular connection altogether.

3. Significance of the critical period

Taken as a whole, it seems that the visual system is set up during early life to match the visual environment. A 'normal' set of connections appears only if the environment is normal. There has been considerable debate as to whether the normal cortical organization is innately determined, but can be distorted by abnormal experience in the critical period, or whether it is mainly experience which determines connections in a system that is 'designed' simply to match the environment. Present evidence suggests that genetic constraints predispose the cortex to a certain pattern of development, whilst the environment determines whether this is fully realized or not. One important reason for the plasticity in binocular connections may be the need to match these to the changing pattern of input as the separation of the eyes increases in the growing head.

This is an exciting area of brain research with a number of important implications. There are many questions to follow up. For example, are other aspects of brain function so dependent on experience in early life? (See, for instance, SPATIAL COORDINATION.) Why is the brain only susceptible in this particular way to its environment in the critical period? Indeed, what factors determine the critical period? Recent evidence has raised the possibility that non-specific inputs to the cortex from the cholinergic and noradrenergic 'neuromodulatory systems' may play an important role in the plasticity seen in the critical period. If this is so, it may be possible to use some type of pharmacological manipulation to regenerate plasticity in the adult brain. The potential clinical implications of this are considerable. We have here an example of how scientific study of fundamental neurobiological problems can produce wide-reaching conclusions of pragmatic value, which strongly influence the way we understand our own development.   AMS

Barlow, H. (1975). 'Visual experience and cortical development'. *Nature*, 258.

Kuffler, S. W., and Nicholls, J. G. (1984). *From Neuron to Brain*.

Lund, R. D. (1978). *Developmental Plasticity of the Brain*.

Sherman, S. M., and Spear, P. D. (1982). 'Organization of visual pathways in normal and visually deprived cats'. *Physiology Review*, 62.

Sillito, A. M. (1986). 'Conflicts in the pharmacology of visual cortical plasticity'. *Trends in Neuroscience*, 9.

Wiesel, T. N., and Hubel, D. H. (1963). 'Single cell responses in striate cortex of kitten deprived of vision in one eye'. *Journal of Neurophysiology*, 26.

visual system: organization. At the simplest level the visual system may be considered as comprising the eyes and a long chain of neural connections extending from the retinal receptors at the back of the eye through the visual pathway to the cerebral cortex. The optics of the eye produce an image of the external world on the *retina. This results in a patterned excitation of retinal receptors which is then processed by the neuronal machinery of the visual system to form a representation of the external world in our brain. The representation does not seem to be formed in any one region but in a series of interacting regions that process different aspects of the input in parallel.

1. Retina

The retinal receptors convert the pattern of light that is the visual image into a neural signal. This is then processed by the neuronal network of the retina and transmitted to the brain by the *axons of the 'retinal ganglion cells'. The retinal receptors make synaptic contact with bipolar cells, which in turn make synaptic contact with the retinal ganglion cells—these are serial connections. At the same time, two other groups of cells, the horizontal cells and amacrine cells, make laterally directed connections that control the transfer of information through the serial connections (see Sterling, Freed, and Smith 1986). The neural organization of the retina is summarized in Fig. 1.

2. Retinal receptors

These fall into two groups: the cones, which are associated with daylight vision and colour vision, and the rods, which are associated with night vision. The cones can be subdivided into three types each responding best to light from a different part of the visible spectrum. These are essential to normal colour vision, and a loss or deficiency in the operation of one of the three categories leads to a corresponding deficiency in colour vision. People referred to as 'protanopes' lack the cones sensitive to the red end of the spectrum, 'deuteranopes' those to the green portion, and 'tritanopes' those sensitive to the blue end of the spectrum.

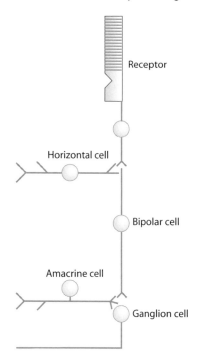

Fig. 1. Interconnections between cells in the retina. The receptors respond to changes in the level of the light falling on them, and synaptically activate bipolar cells which in turn activate the retinal ganglion cells. Lateral connections are made by horizontal cells and amacrine cells. These modify the transmission of information from receptor to ganglion cells and result in the ganglion cell response being influenced in a complex way by the activity of a large number of receptors.

3. Retinal activity

Whilst it is commonly accepted that most nerve cells in the brain generate action potentials, this is not the case in the retina. Only the retinal ganglion cells generate action potentials; the other cells in the retina and the retinal receptors exhibit graded shifts in membrane potential, in response to changing levels of illumination without developing a propagating action potential. If one views an action potential as a mechanism for transmitting information over *long* nerve axons, this is not surprising. The retina is a thin structure, with correspondingly short connections, and the electrotonic spread of potential change is adequate for the length of the neural processes involved. When a retinal receptor is exposed to light the membrane of the receptor 'hyperpolarizes', and the amount of *neurotransmitter released by the synaptic process of the receptor goes down. Receptors depolarize and release more neurotransmitter when the level of light decreases. The potential changes in the receptor are mediated by the action of light on the photopigment contained in the outer segment, and involve a series of chemical interactions leading to a reduction in the level of cyclic guanine monophosphate (GMP), and a consequent decrease in the sodium conductance of the membrane (Lamb 1986). The transmitter released by the retinal receptors produces potential changes in bipolar cells; these can be subdivided into two groups—one is hyperpolarized by the transmitter and the other depolarized. This difference in the response of bipolar cells leads in turn to two categories of retinal ganglion cells.

4. Responses of retinal ganglion cells

The various synaptic interactions occurring in the neural circuits of the retina determine the response of retinal ganglion cells to visual stimuli. Since the retinal ganglion cells provide the output from the eyes to the brain, how they respond to visual stimuli tells us something of the nature of the message the brain is receiving. The visual response properties of retinal ganglion cells can be demonstrated in a very simple experiment. An electrode is implanted into the optic nerve of an eye, which is focused on a projector screen. The electrode records the activity (action potentials) of the axons of retinal ganglion cells in the optic nerve. A spot of light is then shone onto the screen and moved over it. As the image of this spot in turn moves over the retina, a point is reached at which the light excites the receptors providing the input to the ganglion cell under study. This induces an action potential discharge in the ganglion cell, which is detected by the electrode recording from its axon. The area over which responses can be elicited from the ganglion cell constitutes its *receptive field. Although these receptive-field properties can appear quite complex, they can be simply understood if one considers the 'problem' they have to deal with. The retinal image consists of a set of variations in light intensity above and below the background illumination level (this ignores *colour vision). Following from the bipolar cells, retinal ganglion cells exhibit two types of receptive field. In one, the cell is excited by an *increase* in light intensity above background level, and in the other it is excited by a *decrease* in light intensity below the background level. The receptive fields consist of a concentrically organized centre and surround region. Broadly speaking, in each cell's receptive field the amount of light falling on the centre is compared with that falling on the surround, by lateral synaptic interactions, mediated by the horizontal and amacrine cells. For one type of cell, a relative increment in the amount of light falling on the receptive field centre, with respect to the surround, causes an increase in firing, whilst the converse applies to the other type of cell. Obviously, the relative amount of light falling on the centre, with respect to the surround, can be varied by changes in the absolute light level on

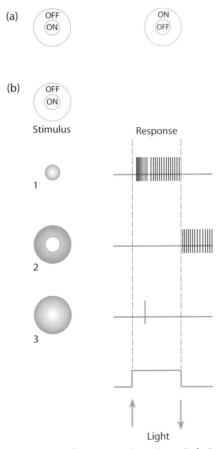

Fig. 2. a. 'On' and 'off' centre retinal ganglion cells. **b.** Responses of 'on' centre retinal ganglion cell to: 1. Spot of light illuminating centre of the receptive field only. 2. Annulus of light illuminating receptive field surround. 3. Large spot of light illuminating both receptive field centre and surround. In each case the light is briefly flashed on and then off as indicated at the bottom of the records. The records show the spikes elicited by each of the three stimuli. In 1 the spot of light elicits a response while it is *on*; in 2 the annulus produces no apparent response while it is on, but a vigorous response when it goes *off*. Illumination of both centre and surround as in 3 produces very little response either while the illumination is on or when it goes off, thus demonstrating the mutual antagonism between the centre and the surround.

either centre or surround. The comparison of illumination levels on the receptive field of centre and surround is important to maintaining optimal sensitivity to change in illumination over a wide range of background illumination levels.

In one type of retinal ganglion cell, an increment in the relative amount of light falling on the centre (light 'on')

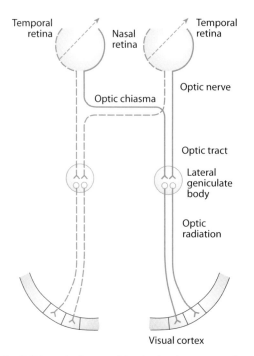

Temporal retina   Nasal retina   Temporal retina

Optic nerve

Optic chiasma

Optic tract

Lateral geniculate body

Optic radiation

Visual cortex

Fig. 3. Schematic diagram of the visual pathway as seen by looking down from above the head. Note that, because of the crossing in the optic chiasma, the right side of the brain 'sees' the left side of the visual world, and vice versa.

causes an increased discharge, whilst in the other a decrement (light 'off') causes a discharge; thus, neurophysiologists describe the two types of cell as 'on' and 'off' centre cells. Because the cells actually compare the light falling on the centre and surround, changes in the surround illumination of the opposite polarity to that exciting the centre cause an increased response; hence 'on' centre cells are said to have 'off' surrounds, and 'off' centre cells have 'on' surrounds. Contrast in the retinal image is defined not only by luminance but also by colour. Thus, the retinal circuitry also processes the input from the three types of cone in a way which allows different classes of retinal ganglion cell to transmit details of the chromatic properties of the image. In some ways, the receptive-field properties of retinal ganglion cells, transmitting information about colour contrast, follow a similar logic to that outlined above for luminance contrast.

5. Types of retinal ganglion cell
Retinal ganglion cells fall into a range of different types. In addition to the 'on' and 'off' centre cells already mentioned, there are further subdivisions in terms of the chromatic sensitivity of the cells and the type of spatial summation shown in the receptive field. With respect to spatial summation, some cells show a linear summation of the components of a distribution of varying luminance across their receptive field, others a non-linear summation (Enroth-Cugell and Robson 1966). These are referred to as X and Y cells respectively, and show distinctions in a range of other properties, including receptive field size, sensitivity to stimulus velocity, and spatial frequency (see PSYCHOPHYSICS) (Sherman 1985). In particular, X cells can resolve finer visual patterns (higher spatial frequencies) than Y cells. They are also distinguished on anatomical grounds; the Y cells correspond to the alpha retinal ganglion cells distinguished by anatomists; they are larger and have thicker axons than the beta cells which correspond to X cells. One important point to note is that the Y cells have faster conducting axons than X cells. These distinctions cut across the broad subdivision into 'on' and 'off' centre types.

6. The visual pathway
The axons of the retinal ganglion cells travel in the optic nerve to the brain. Each retina can be considered as subdivided into two halves in the vertical plane—a nasal half and a temporal half. The axons from the nasal half of each retina, after travelling in the optic nerve, cross over to the other side of the brain in the optic chiasma. They join fibres, from the temporal half of the other retina, which encompass the same half of the visual field, and pass with these to the lateral geniculate body (a group of cells in the thalamus). The lateral geniculate body is a laminated structure with six separate layers, four parvocellular and two magnocellular. The inputs from the two eyes synapse in separate layers. The axons of the lateral geniculate cells project via the optic radiation to the visual cortex. One can view the visual cortex as a folded 'slab' of grey matter containing nerve cells, with an underlying layer of white matter formed by the nerve fibres entering and leaving the grey matter. The grey matter of the cortex is commonly subdivided into six layers. The projection from the lateral geniculate body terminates most densely in the vicinity of layer IV of the visual cortex. In this layer, the input from the two eyes is kept separate (or approximately so). There are thus alternating bands in layer IV of cells dominated respectively by the ipsilateral (same-side) and contralateral (opposite-side) eyes. This forms the basis of the so-called 'ocular dominance' columns in the cortex. In the cortical layers above and below layer IV, there are laterally spreading connections which result in binocularly driven cells. The crossing in the optic chiasma thus ultimately enables the retinal inputs relating to the two views of the same part of the visual world to be brought together.

In the visual projection there is an orderly map of each half-retina on the lateral geniculate body, and then again in the cortex. Each retinal ganglion cell 'looks' at a

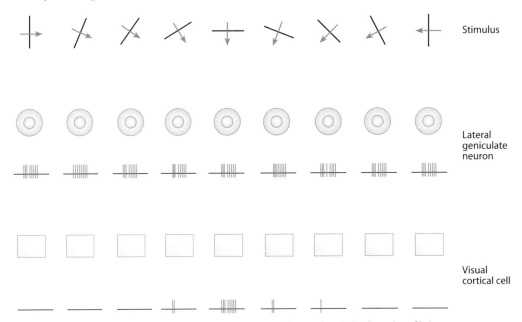

Fig. 4. Comparison of the response of a lateral geniculate neuron and a visual cortical cell to a bar of light moving over their receptive field. The lateral geniculate neuron responds to the bar at all orientations. The visual cortical cell is very selective to the orientation of the stimulus. As visual cortical cells get their excitatory input from lateral geniculate neurons, this implies that there is some specific organization of inhibitory and excitatory interconnections within the cortex generating this orientation selectivity.

particular part of the retinal image, and hence a point in visual space, and its neighbour at an adjacent or overlapping point, and so on. This sequence of sampling of visual space is reflected in the projection to the lateral geniculate nucleus, and from there to the cortex. The inputs from the two half-retinas are in register; thus there is a double mapping of the same view of the visual world, first in the separate geniculate layers, and then again through the ocular dominance columns in the visual cortex. The 'slab' of grey matter forming the left visual cortex is thus a 'map' of the right visual world as seen from two slightly different viewpoints. Moreover, the various categories of retinal ganglion cell all sample the visual field more or less uniformly. They convey different types of information to the central visual system, and the patterns of termination of the inputs relaying this information are distinctive. The input to the visual cortex, thus, reflects not only the visual world seen from two slightly different viewpoints, but also the visual world sampled several times over by elements with differing sensitivity to the properties of the retinal image.

7. Receptor density and the central visual map

The density of retinal receptors is not uniform over the retina, but is highest in the fovea and falls off towards the periphery of the retina. The higher the density of receptors, the smaller their size and the greater the visual acuity. Broadly, one can equate receptor size with the grain size in a photographic emulsion. The proportion of the map in the central visual system devoted to each retinal area reflects the density of receptors, rather than the dimensions of the area. Thus, in terms of the area of the visual field, the visual cortical representation of the fovea is much larger than that for peripheral parts of the retina.

8. Processing of the visual input

Our knowledge of the way in which the visual input is first processed within the brain owes a great deal to the work of Hubel and Wiesel (see VISUAL SYSTEM: PHYSIOLOGY). They studied the response properties of cells in the lateral geniculate nucleus and visual cortex, utilizing the same overall technique as that described for the analysis of retinal ganglion cell response properties. The eyes of an anaesthetized animal were focused on a projector screen and the activity of cells in the lateral geniculate nucleus and visual cortex recorded. Because of the orderly visual projection, as an image moves over the projector screen and hence over the retina, it also moves in a similar fashion over the map of the retina in the lateral geniculate nucleus and visual cortex. When examined this way, cells in the lateral geniculate nucleus were found to have receptive fields that were very similar to those seen in retinal ganglion cells. They were well activated by flashing spots of light, and fell into the same broad categories (e.g. 'on' and 'off' centre X and Y cells). Conversely, the majority of cells in the visual cortex were not best activated by flashing spots of light, but by an elongated stimulus moving over their receptive field at a particular orientation. This selectivity to the orientation of the 'contour' of a stimulus is a characteristic feature of visual cortical cells (Hubel 1963). A retinal ganglion cell, or a cell in the lateral geniculate nucleus, responds to a bar of light moving over its receptive field at all orientations. In the light of this evidence, Hubel and Wiesel proposed that visual cortical cells were concerned with the detection of specific features of the visual environment. The selectivity to stimulus orientation appears to be an important component of the way in which nervous systems throughout the animal kingdom encode the visual input; it is seen, for example, in the higher visual centres of mammals, cephalopods, and birds. Although selectivity to stimulus orientation seems to be a particularly important facet of the neuronal machinery in the visual cortex, cells exhibit selectivity to a range of other properties of the visual input. This includes direction of stimulus motion, the colour, the length, and the depth in visual space. The last property underlies stereopsis (see STEREOSCOPIC VISION) and involves cells that are driven by both eyes, but are sensitive to the disparity of the image location on the two retinas.

9. Columnar organization of the visual cortex

One of the major discoveries made by Hubel and Wiesel was that the visual cortex is divided into a sequence of columns or sheets of neurons, with common functional properties. The ocular dominance columns have been described elsewhere (see VISUAL SYSTEM: PHYSIOLOGY). These run from the surface of the cortex to the white matter, and are themselves subdivided into a further subset of columns, which appear to be concerned with stimulus orientation. These are the 'orientation columns', containing cells with common orientation selectivity. Adjacent orientation columns are sensitive to slightly different orientations and this process repeats as a series of approximately 10-degree steps from one column to the next. The portion of an ocular dominance column, representing one location in visual space, contains a series of orientation columns that, on average, cover an entire 180-degree range. Each location in visual space is thus represented by two ocular dominance columns (for the right and left eye), and their subsets of orientation columns. The orientation and ocular dominance columns can be envisaged as crossing each other at right angles as shown in Fig. 5. However, the true situation is not as orderly as this and it is possibly better to envisage the two sets of columns as intersecting in a pseudo-random fashion, but one which broadly ensures

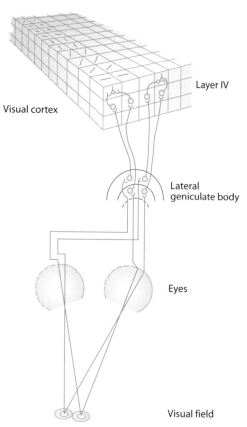

Fig. 5. Detailed view of the organization of the visual perception through the lateral geniculate body to the visual cortex. This shows the projection of two adjacent regions in the visual field on to adjacent groups of neurons in the lateral geniculate body and visual cortex. Note that the input relating to the corresponding points in the two eyes ends on separate layers in the lateral geniculate body and on separate bands (ocular dominance columns) of neurons in layer IV of the cortex. However, there is binocular convergence on to single neurons in the cortex, mainly outside layer IV.

that each location in visual space is represented by a full complement of orientation columns.

10. Laminar organization of the visual cortex

There is a difference between the input and output connections of the cells in each layer of the visual cortex. Consequently, in addition to the columnar organization, there is a differentiation of function in the vertical domain, i.e. within an orientation column. In their early work on this matter, Hubel and Wiesel proposed three types of cell in a column —simple cells, complex cells, and hypercomplex cells. The term 'simple' was applied to the cells in layer IV receiving their input directly from the lateral geniculate body. Orientation selectivity was thought to be set up in this layer by the organization of the geniculate cell connections to simple cells. Each simple cell was conjectured to receive an excitatory input from several geniculate cells, with their receptive fields extending in a row through visual space. Only a bar of the appropriate orientation would simultaneously activate all the input cells, and hence produce a maximal response in the simple cell. A group of simple cells were then thought to provide the drive out of layer IV to complex cells, and complex cells, in turn, to provide a drive to hypercomplex cells. Each of these cell types was considered to have a receptive field organization elaborating successively more complex features of the visual environment.

The strictly hierarchical view of the organization of cells in a column has not been supported by subsequent findings. Present evidence emphasizes parallel processing of different facets of the visual input in the cortex, utilizing a circuitry that is much more complex than originally envisaged (Martin 1984, Rose and Dobson 1985, Sherman 1985). Extensive excitatory and inhibitory connections mediate lateral interactions in the visual cortex, which generate many aspects of the stimulus selectivity of the cells. Indeed, experiments inducing a localized blockade of intracortical inhibitory processes have demonstrated that inhibitory connections play a critical role in the generation of some receptive field properties; these include sensitivity to the direction of stimulus motion and, for some cells, stimulus orientation (Sillito 1984). The direct comparison here is with the retina, where horizontal and amacrine cell connections generate the concentric receptive field of ganglion cells, not just the direct connections from the receptors via the bipolar cells. However, in the central visual system, the heavy reciprocal interconnections between each level in the system suggest that any analysis of its function must take note of the fact that the levels constitute interacting components of a circuit, rather than just a stage in a sequence. For example, the projection from the visual cortex to the lateral geniculate nucleus is as dense as, or even denser than, that from the retina, and yet, remarkably, the function of the former is largely ignored. Obviously the cortex is potentially capable of exerting a powerful control over the response of geniculate cells, and yet at the same time the cortical activity is dependent on the geniculate input. Similar comments apply to the interactions between the cortical laminae and the different cortical areas. Further progress in our understanding, at this level of analysis, requires a hypothesis regarding visual-system function that needs the synaptic complexity we now know to exist.

11. 'Blobs' and colour processing in the visual cortex
Recent evidence in the primate has shown that, in

addition to the columnar organization of the visual cortex, there is a sequence of regularly repeated bloblike structures. These can be distinguished anatomically by virtue of the fact that they stain very densely for the mitochondrial enzyme cytochrome oxidase. They are most conspicuous in layers II and III of the cortex, and are notable in a functional sense because they contain cells that seem to be primarily concerned with processing colour information, and they lack cells sensitive to stimulus orientation. The blobs show a regular distribution in the tangential plane, in relation to the ocular dominance columns, in a way which suggests that there is a blob for each location in visual space as well as a full complement of orientation columns. The pattern of the output from the blobs, and columnar regions of the primary visual cortex, suggests that colour information and orientation are processed in parallel through separate channels.

12. Cortical pathways processing the visual input
The processing of the visual input, after the primary visual cortex, appears to proceed through distinct, although interlinked, groups of cortical areas. The regions of the cortex most strongly dominated by the visual input are often labelled in sequence as V1 (primary visual cortex or area 17), through V2, up to V5. There seem to be two major channels of processing. One passes from V1 to V2, from there to V4, and eventually to the inferotemporal cortex. This seems to be involved in object recognition and colour. The other channel passes from V1 to V2, and from V2 to V5 (V5 is also referred to as 'MT'), and passes the inferior parietal cortex; it seems to be involved in object location and movement in visual space. Within these broad channels, various aspects of the input are likely to be processed in parallel for all, or part, of the sequence of connections, as for example for colour and orientation, in the sequence of connections passing to V4. Neurons in the inferotemporal cortical region can have highly selective response properties; some, for example, seem to respond only to faces. However, it is far from clear that this represents a general case for the sequential elaboration of more and more complex fields dealing with specialized elements of our environment. Many would suggest that in general this level of representation involves ensemble encoding in a matrix of interacting neurons. The presence of face-specific neurons in primates may have more to do with the biological importance of faces than the general rules underlying visual processing.   AMS

Enroth-Cugell, C., and Robson, J. G. (1966). 'The contrast sensitivity of retinal ganglion cells of the cat'. *Journal of Physiology*, 187.

Essen, D. C., and Maunsell, J. H. R. (1983). 'Hierarchical organization and functional streams in the visual cortex'. *Trends in Neuroscience*, 6.

Hubel, D. H. (1963). 'The visual cortex of the brain'. *Scientific American*, Nov.

Kuffler, S. W., and Nicholls, J. G. (1984). *From Neurone to Brain*.

Lamb, T. D. (1986). 'Transduction in vertebrate photo-receptors: the roles of cyclic GMP and calcium'. *Trends in Neuroscience*, 9.

Martin, K. A. C. (1984). 'Neuronal circuits in cat striate cortex'. In Peters, A. A., and Jones, E. G. (eds.), *The Cerebral Cortex*, vol. ii.

Rose, D., and Dobson, V. G. (eds.) (1985). *Models of the Visual Cortex*.

Sherman, S. M. (1985). 'Functional organization of the W-, X-, and Y-cell pathways in the cat: a review and hypothesis'. *Progress in Psychobiology and Physiological Psychology*, vol. ii.

Sillito, A. M. (1984). 'Functional considerations of the operation of GABAergic inhibitory processes in the visual cortex'. In Peters, A. A., and Jones, E. G. (eds.), *The Cerebral Cortex*, vol. ii.

Sterling, P., Freed, M., and Smith, R. G. (1986). 'Microcircuitry and functional architecture of the cat retina'. *Trends in Neuroscience*, 9.

visual system: physiology. David Hubel and Torsten Wiesel's joint work on the visual cortex opened a new chapter in our understanding of the mechanisms of the brain. It started when Hubel joined Wiesel in Steve Kuffler's laboratory at Johns Hopkins University in 1958, and continued for twenty years after Kuffler moved his laboratory to the neurobiology department of the Harvard Medical School. Their outstandingly successful collaboration produced a flow of important new discoveries year after year.

1. Pattern selectivity
2. Binocularity
3. Anatomical arrangement of cortical cells
4. Development

1. Pattern selectivity

The striate cortex (area 17, or the primary visual area) contains some 10^8 cells, and in 1960 many people felt that recording from them just one at a time would not reveal much about how it all worked. But Hubel and Wiesel claimed that for each cell there was a specific pattern of excitation that would reliably excite it, and this obviously had a major impact. They discovered that the most important characteristics of the stimulus were its orientation, size, contrast (darker or brighter than the background), and which eye it was delivered to. The idea of 'feature detectors' was already a familiar one at that time and examples were known in the frog retina and arthropod visual systems, but theirs were the first examples in the mammalian nervous system, and the implications were revolutionary. Instead of thinking of the striate cortex as a structure with myriads of cells, each taking part in the representation of every visual image, one was forced to recognize that each cell had its own specific stimulus requirements, and that consequently when it became active it 'said' something specific about the nature of the image in its own particular part of the visual field. Not all their ideas about the hierarchical connections of cells or the mechanisms whereby pattern selectivity was achieved have stood the test of time, but theirs were the results that put the idea of feature detectors into the psychological literature.

2. Binocularity

Cortical neurons are the first cells in the visual pathway that have access to information from both eyes. Hubel and Wiesel found that many of them could be activated through either eye or both together, and that in such cases the stimulus requirements were nearly the same, regardless of which eye was used. In other cases the cell could be activated only through one eye and not through the other, and there were yet other cells that could be strongly activated by one eye but only weakly by the other. They plotted the numbers of cells of each type as the 'ocular dominance histogram', and this turned out to be a sensitive tool for showing the influence of factors that disturb the normal development of cortical connections. It is, however, a potentially misleading tool, for we now realize that the main significance of the binocular connections of cortical neurons lies in the small differences of alignment of the connections from each eye; this is what makes different cells responsive to different disparities and hence gives information about the distance of objects from the eyes. The ocular dominance histogram tells one nothing about this aspect, and it is therefore wrong to deduce from a normal histogram that the cortex is in a normal functional state. Hubel and Wiesel may possibly have been misled by this when assessing the role of experience in formulating the properties of the mature cortex.

3. Anatomical arrangement of cortical cells

This is the area of their greatest success, for they revealed an orderly arrangement of cortical neurons, constituting a microstructure, that was previously unsuspected. They were fortunate in that many new anatomical methods became available while they were engaged in the task of mapping this microstructure, but they were in the forefront in developing these methods and demonstrating their usefulness. The existence of a map of the visual field on the striate cortex was well known before their work, but this map is accurate only to distances of about 1 mm on the cortical surface. Each square millimetre contains some quarter of a million cells, and Hubel and Wiesel found first that neurons were grouped according to ocular dominance, each eye supplying irregular, alternating strips of cortex about 0.5 mm wide. Orientation was also organized, for the preferred orientation of successively recorded cells tended to shift regularly through a small angle as the recording electrode moved across the cortex, a complete cycle occurring every 0.5–1 mm. It has subsequently been shown that cells preferring a particular spatial frequency (or size) are also clustered, as are those preferring particular colours. The final details of the arrangement of the cells according to their selective properties are still being investigated, but there seems little doubt that Hubel and Wiesel have sketched the skeleton of this microanatomy.

4. Development

The clinical facts of amblyopia (poor sight not caused by defects in the visual system) have long suggested that visual experience has an important effect on the neural development of the visual system. As early as 1963 Hubel and Wiesel published their first results on this problem, showing that depriving a kitten of the use of one eye by closing its eyelids has the effect of permanently disrupting the connections that eye makes to the cortical neurons. This was shown by the bias of the ocular dominance histogram towards the eye that continued in use, and they were also able to modify the histogram by surgically induced strabismus (squint), and by occluding each eye on alternate days; both of these procedures leave many cells connected to each individual eye, but cause a marked reduction in the number of cells that receive connections from both of them, thus showing that these connections require associated use of both eyes to become firmly established. They later showed that these effects of deprivation only occur up to about six weeks of age in the cat, or six months in the monkey.

This was the first demonstration of a critical or sensitive period that has physiologically demonstrable consequences and is caused by changes to normal sensory messages. The results have been obtained consistently by many others and they are among the most robust and well-confirmed findings in a field where not all claims have been substantiated. It is interesting that Hubel and Wiesel have consistently argued that experience does no more than preserve innately formed connections, basing this on the apparently normal responses and ocular dominance histograms found in young, visually inexperienced animals. Later results have shown, however, that immature and inexperienced cortical neurons lack the disparity selectivity and fine spatial resolution of adult cells, and that the cortex is therefore far from normal. Hubel and Wiesel have thus provided some of the best evidence for the effects of experience on the cortex, while making some of the most dogmatic statements on the predominance of ontogenetic factors in determining its properties. (See also VISUAL SYSTEM: ENVIRONMENTAL INFLUENCES.)

Hubel and Wiesel's interpretations of their results have often been replaced by others which they, the pioneers, have vigorously resisted; even so, their results themselves have an enviable record of reliability. Furthermore, they led the field over a twenty-year period during which exceptionally rapid progress was made. It must be added, however, that their contribution cannot be finally assessed, for there is as yet no confident understanding of how the striate cortex helps us to see the world around us.

David Hubel, Torsten Wiesel, and Roger Sperry received the Nobel Prize for their work in neurophysiology, in 1981.   HBB

volley theory. The transmission of sound by the ear to the brain presents a special problem, because sound frequencies greatly exceed the maximum frequency of action potentials in a nerve fibre. The volley theory, based on electrical recordings of action potentials in auditory nerves, states that for frequencies up to perhaps 500 Hz each cycle of a sound wave produces a single neural spike (actually at the zero energy crossover of the wave), but, at frequencies beyond those that a nerve can follow, other nerve fibres are recruited to code higher frequencies by combinations of spikes from cooperating nerves.

For still higher frequencies, the cochlea analyses the various frequencies into different positions along the basilar membrane, so that different hair cells are activated, and different neural channels employed, to transmit each frequency. There are thus three ways, depending on frequency, in which sounds are represented and transmitted by the ear.

See HEARING.

Von Neumann, John (1903–57). A mathematician of international repute, born in Budapest, and later an American citizen. His work touched on most branches of both pure and applied mathematics. During the 1920s and 1930s his work included quantum theory, mathematical logic, ergodic theory, continuous geometry, and abstract algebra; his interest then turned to theoretical hydrodynamics. He became well known as a member of the Atomic Energy Commission, having been professor in the school of mathematics at the Institute for Advanced Study at Princeton from 1933 until 1954.

Von Neumann first became known internationally for his work in developing the digital computer. It was at the Moore School of Electrical Engineering in Philadelphia in 1946 that he led a team that completed ENIAC, the first digital computer. His work gave publicity to the subject under the title *The Theory and Techniques of Electronic Digital Computers*, and set out the design principles that in essentials remain unchanged today. Then, immediately the ENIAC was complete, the design was set out for a smaller and much more powerful computer, with a store of 1,000 words each of ten decimal digits—50 times that of ENIAC. New storage methods were designed and new programming techniques suggested, leading to the present digital computer with a store capacity for millions of words. The work fitted in with that of Alan *Turing. Von Neumann worked primarily from the standpoint of the engineer and was concerned with the hardware realization, while Turing worked on the algorithmic approach to define what was computable. The first four generations of computers are now called Von Neumann machines since they all followed the essential features of Von Neumann's earliest design; as a result nearly all the computer languages in existence are essentially Von Neumann languages.

The most famous of his many contributions to mathematics was embodied in *The Theory of Games and Economic Behavior* (1944; rev. edn. 1953), which he wrote in collaboration with the American economist Oskar Morgenstern. Von Neumann's next major work was *Probabilistic Logics* (1952). In this he was primarily concerned with the role of error in logical nets, which are particular examples of finite automata and designed to be abstract models of the central nervous system. He was interested in the technique of *multiplexing*, which is multiplication of neural connections between neural type elements, so that if a certain number of fibres fail, the system is still operable. The basic element of the Von Neumann automata, unlike the usual use of conjunction and negation, was the Sheffer stroke element. This element fires when either of its two input elements fire, but not when both do, for if they fire together they inhibit the element and stop an output firing. The or-element, and-element, and not-element are then defined in terms of the Sheffer stroke. This in turn leads to the majority organ whose output fires if and only if the majority of the inputs fire. The multiple line trick was used to provide the needed multiplexing. This is done by setting a fiducial level k to the number of lines of the bundle to be stimulated; then, for $0<k<\frac{1}{2}$ at least $(l-k)N$ lines being stimulated are said to be in a positive state—and conversely, when no more than kN are stimulated, it implies a negative state. Building on this multiplexing method, Von Neumann examined in detail the notion of error.

The final phase of Von Neumann's work was represented by the Silliman lectures which he was to have given at Yale in 1956 and which were embodied in his posthumous *The Computer and the Brain* (1958). His terminal illness made the lectures impossible but the book made clear the form they would have taken. The work was that of the mathematician operating in the field of brain studies and emphasized the differences and similarities between brains and computers. The nerve impulse is primarily electrical, apparently digital, and has time characteristics not unlike the pulses in a computer. Overall, computer speeds then were slower at performing the range of functions performed by the brain—a state of affairs that has gradually changed. The languages of the brain involve mathematical, logical, and statistical methods, and Von Neumann foresaw that in describing the brain and the nervous system new forms of mathematics would be developed. This has occurred in the forms of uncertainty logics and empirical logics. The precision of brain operation he thought of as logical, its computational working as arithmetic, and the functional description as statistical.

See also ARTIFICIAL INTELLIGENCE; CRAIK, KENNETH JOHN WILLIAM; MCCULLOCH, WARREN STURGIS; PATTERN RECOGNITION; TURING, ALAN MATHISON; WIENER, NORBERT.   FHG

Vygotsky, Leo (or Lev Semionovich Vygotsky, 1896–1934). The most outstanding Soviet psychologist, and founder of the most influential school of Soviet psychology, Vygotsky was born in Orsha (Belorussia), and began his work in psychology after leaving Moscow University (faculty of letters) in 1919. As a young man he wrote the subsequently well-known pieces that were included in the *Psychology of Art* (1965; Eng. trans. 1971). Psychological analysis of the personality of Hamlet, as well as studies in the psychology of fables, were central to the work of this outstanding young scholar. After a few years in Gomel (Belorussia), where he taught psychology and wrote *Pedagogical Psychology* (1926; in Russian), he moved to Moscow, where his most important work began. He soon became a leading figure of the Institute there, and the central figure in a group of young scholars (including A. N. Leontiev and A. R. *Luria) who became his first co-workers and followers.

At the time of his early studies, psychology was in a state of crisis. It was split into two independent sciences. The first was the *explanatory* or *physiological psychology* of *Wundt and *Ebbinghaus, who tried to explain complex psychological phenomena by reducing them to elementary physiological components. They refused to deal scientifically with the highest, specifically human forms of conscious behaviour—motives, abstract thinking, active memorizing, voluntary actions, etc. The second school attempted a *descriptive psychology* which did consider the highest forms of conscious experiences, treating them as spiritual forms of mental life, and supposing that these phenomena may be described in *phenomenological terms but not explained scientifically.

Vygotsky assumed that the basic goal of scientific psychology was to overcome this division, and to try to explain scientifically not only the elementary but also the highest forms of psychological processes. This—he thought—could be done by reducing the complex psychological phenomena not to physiological 'elements', but rather to more complex psychological 'units', which would preserve all the properties of the complex forms of conscious behaviour and which could serve as its models, making the more complicated forms of mental life accessible for scientific analysis.

Supposing the highest forms of mental life and conscious behaviour to be not of a spiritual nature but a product of social development, Vygotsky saw tool-using and sign-using ('significative') behaviour as essential for all higher forms of psychological processes. He also considered forms of sign-using behaviour, its rules, and the stages of its development. Studies in sign using, as a model of complex active *memory, were his first attempt to approach experimentally the most complicated psychological processes. (The results of these studies were published by A. N. Leontiev.)

His work on simple 'units' of tool- and sign-using behaviour led Vygotsky to investigate the role that language (the most universal system of signs) plays in human behaviour, and to a careful analysis of its development during the life of the individual. The main purpose was to describe the semantic structure of words. His famous experiments with artificial words (the Vygotsky–Sakharov technique) were published later by Hanfman and Kasanin and became known as the Vygotsky–Hanfman–Kasanin tests.

These investigations led Vygotsky to one of his main discoveries—that the meaning of words undergoes a complex development, and that words starting as emotional soon become concrete designations of objects later to acquire abstract meaning. (See LANGUAGE: LEARNING WORD MEANINGS.) This conclusion was followed by the statement that the whole of mental development can be understood as a profound change of psychological systems which mediate the basic forms of activities, and that with each new stage the leading function changes. So, Vygotsky supposed, the child is thinking by memorizing, whereas the adult is memorizing by thinking. This systemic approach to complex psychological functions was one of the most important steps in contemporary psychology.

The idea that the higher psychological processes have a social origin brought Vygotsky to a new approach in the evaluation of the child's mental development, and to the assumption that not only the actual 'mental age' of the child has to be measured, but also its potential capacities—what he called 'the zone of potential development'. This can be done by comparing how the child solves certain problems by itself with a second indicator: how it can solve similar tasks with the help of the teacher—representing here the ability to acquire social prompting. The principles proposed by Vygotsky were of the highest importance for practical educational and clinical psychology.

During his short life in science (he died at the age of 37 from tuberculosis, and worked actively in experimental psychology only for about ten years), Vygotsky was active in many fields of scientific psychology: general psychological problems, child psychology, the problems of retarded and deaf children, the psychological analysis of local brain injuries, and a series of related fields. Although his career was very brief, his influence on Soviet and world psychology has become more and more significant with the passing years. In addition to the two works mentioned, his most important books are *Thought and Language* (1937; Eng. trans. 1962); *Selected Psychological Studies* (1956; in Russian); and *Development of the Higher Mental Processes* (1960; in Russian).   ARL

W

Wallace, Alfred Russel (1823–1913). British naturalist, born at Usk, Monmouthshire. He made extensive natural history collections in the Amazon basin (though a large part of these were lost when the ship he was on caught fire) and later in the Malay Archipelago.

Independently of Charles *Darwin (and, like him, to some extent inspired by reading *Malthus's *Essay on Population*), he conceived the notion of evolution by survival of the fittest. On 18 June 1848 Darwin received a letter from Wallace which expressed the key concept that he had been working on for over twenty years. Darwin wrote to Charles Lyell:

Your words have come true with a vengeance—that I should be forestalled. You said this, when I explained to you here very briefly my views on 'Natural Selection' depending on the struggle for existence. I never saw a more striking coincidence; if Wallace had my MS. sketch written out in 1842, he could not have made a better short abstract! Even his terms now stand as heads of my chapters.

The problem of priority was solved by the two of them in the most gentlemanly fashion, with a joint paper presented to the Linnean Society on 1 July 1858. Nevertheless, Wallace's letter prompted Darwin into writing *The Origin of Species*, which was finished on 19 March 1859.

Though unfortunate in being anticipated by Darwin and overshadowed by him, Wallace was an excellent naturalist and a careful, original thinker. In later life, however, he became an advocate of *spiritualism. He was elected Fellow of the Royal Society in 1893 and appointed to the Order of Merit in 1910.

Among Wallace's main works are *Contributions to the Theory of Natural Selection* (1870); *The Malay Archipelago* (1869); *Darwinism* (1889); *On Miracles and Modern Spiritualism* (1881); and, for solid scientific work, *Geographical Distribution of Animals* (1876) and *Island Life* (1880). See also *Man's Place in the Universe* (1903) and *My Life, an Autobiography*, 2 vols. (1905).   RLG

Shermer, M. (2002). *In Darwin's Shadow: The Life of Alfred Russel Wallace.*

Walter, William Grey (1910–76). Anglo-American physiologist, born in Kansas City and educated at Westminster School, London, and at Cambridge. As a postgraduate student with E. D. *Adrian, he worked on muscle contraction before joining Frederick Lucien Golla at the Maudsley

Hospital in London in 1935, to start his work on the electrical activity of the brain by recording the *electroencephalogram (the EEG) that was to continue for the next 40 years. In 1939 he moved with Golla to Bristol, to open a research laboratory and clinic called the Burden Neurological Institute. In addition to his work on the EEG, Grey Walter was much concerned with the development and use of electroconvulsive therapy (*ECT), and the first shock treatment on patients in Britain was done at the Institute, with apparatus he designed and constructed.

In about 1940 Walter started work on two aspects of the EEG that were to occupy his efforts for many years—frequency analysis, and mental attributes such as imagery (see MENTAL IMAGERY). Then came a period of several years when he turned to the construction of electromechanical models to simulate brain-function behaviour. This was the time of the birth of *cybernetics. The publicity that these fascinating models received tended to distract attention from their scientific value. The famous electromechanical tortoise (*M. speculatrix*) was designed to see how many sensory systems had to interact before interesting complex behaviour patterns were produced. This turned out to require very few active elements, with only two control systems (one light sensitive and the other touch sensitive). The simplicity of the model was the mark of its value: a fact that many imitators did not appreciate, and thus they merely produced elaborate toys. Walter was the first to show that simple control devices could produce lifelike behaviour, with learning.

While all this was going on, the 22-channel toposcope was being made to examine aspects of the rhythmic electrical activity of the brain that the frequency analyser was unable to achieve. The helical scan 'Topsy' was useful for measurement and display of frequency and phase relationships on a short time scale at many electrode sites.

Then, at about this time, two events occurred at the Institute that were to change the course of the work. First was the use of implanted electrodes for investigation of *epilepsy and treatment of psychiatric illness, which allowed recording from local brain regions in conscious humans, and second was the development of a two-channel *evoked potential averager. This gave Walter the chance he had been waiting for—the opportunity of studying the functioning brain in its complexity, particularly interactions between associated stimuli. He had attempted these conditioning experiments on several occasions since the 1930s, probably stimulated in the early days by meeting Ivan *Pavlov. In 1962 a study was undertaken of a group of *autistic children, using scalp electrodes, and it was during this work that Walter first noticed a negative shift between the associated stimuli. The contingent negative variation (CNV)—brain activity occurring just before a decision—was made public at a meeting of the EEG Society in 1964.

His highly productive work on evoked potentials for the rest of that decade was tragically halted in 1970 by a severe head injury from which he never fully recovered. Grey Walter was a pioneer and an intellectual leader of world renown, but he was never fully accepted by the British scientific establishment. He wrote some 200 research papers and a uniquely stimulating book, *The Living Brain* (1953), which attracted many students to follow in his footsteps.   RC

Ward, James (1843–1925). English philosopher, educated at Cambridge and later at the universities of Göttingen and Berlin. While in Germany, he acquired considerable understanding of both physiology and *psychophysics, and after his return to Cambridge published an article on *Fechner's law in the first volume of the neurological journal *Brain*.

Ward's major interest in later life lay almost wholly in philosophy, but this did not deter him from writing a celebrated article on psychology for the ninth edition of the *Encyclopaedia Britannica* in 1886, which he expanded and largely rewrote for the eleventh edition in 1911. His other major contribution to psychology was an impressive, if difficult, treatise on *Psychological Principles* (1918). Although he did not contribute further to experimental psychology, he did much to foster its development in Cambridge through the activities of such men as W. H. R. *Rivers, C. S. *Myers, and F. C. *Bartlett.

A bibliography of Ward's writings by E. B. Titchener and W. S. Foster was published in the *American Journal of Psychology*, 23, and reprinted in 1926, with some extensions to the date of Ward's death, in the *Monist*, 36.   OLZ

Watson, John Broadus (1878–1958). The founder of the American school of psychology known as *behaviourism. The movement was launched in 1913 with his paper 'Psychology as the behaviorist views it', and was bolstered by many subsequent papers and popular articles, as well as by his four influential books: *Behaviour: An Introduction to Comparative Psychology* (1914), *Psychology from the Standpoint of a Behaviorist* (1919), *Behaviorism* (1924), and *The Psychological Care of Infant and Child* (1928). Reacting against the influential introspective psychology of his day,

which even he had practised early in his career, Watson declared that behaviour should be the only subject matter of psychology. Though psychology had long been concerned with the study of mind, Watson believed that such an endeavour had proved fruitless. Psychology could become a productive science like other natural sciences only by being objective and dealing with the observable; the study of mind could never be accomplished objectively, but the study of behaviour could. The goal of psychology would become the prediction and control of behaviour. *Consciousness, mind, and mental states were to be ignored.

Soon after *Pavlov's reflexology became prominent in America, Watson adopted the *reflex as the basic unit by which all behaviour was to be explained. He believed that all complex human behaviour was the sum of simple conditioned reflexes. So powerful did he see the *conditioning process that he eventually promoted a staunch environmentalism, a philosophical belief that all behaviour is learned. In advocating this position, Watson made many extreme statements about the power of conditioning. The best known is:

Give me a dozen healthy infants . . . and my own specified world to bring them up in and I'll guarantee to take any one at random and train him to become any type of specialist I might select— doctor, lawyer, artist, merchant-chief and, yes, even beggar-man and thief, regardless of his talents, penchants, tendencies, abilities, vocations, and race of his ancestors.

Though Watson qualified this statement and others like it, his qualifying statements have often been overlooked and his views simplified. For example, he is usually credited with the simplistic notion that thinking is merely subvocal speech or laryngeal movement, though he repudiated such a view on several occasions (for example, in *The Battle of Behaviorism*, published in 1928 with William *McDougall).

Watson's work had an immeasurable impact on American psychology. The tenets of behaviourism dominated the field until perhaps the 1950s, and psychology is still often known as the science of 'behaviour' rather than the science of 'mind'. It was Watson's behaviourism that inspired B. F. *Skinner's early work in psychology, though Skinner, in developing the modern version of behaviourism, abandoned Watson's environmentalism and his aversion to a consideration of mind (see BEHAVIOURISM, SKINNER ON).

Though his impact was long-lasting, Watson only remained active in academic psychology until 1920, when, as a result of a personal scandal, he was forced to resign from his position at Johns Hopkins University. His subsequent successful career was in advertising.   RE

Bergmann, G. (1956). 'The contributions of John B. Watson'. *Psychological Review*, 63.

Skinner, B. F. (1959). 'John Broadus Watson, behaviorist'. *Science*, 129.

Watson, J. B. (1967). *Behavior: An Introduction to Comparative Psychology*, with an introduction by R. J. Herrnstein.

Woodworth, R. S. (1959). 'John Broadus Watson: 1878–1958'. *American Journal of Psychology*, 72.

Weber, Ernst Heinrich (1795–1878). German physiologist, born at Wittenberg; professor of anatomy and later of physiology at Leipzig. He is celebrated for developing methods of measuring the sensitivity of the skin which, together with the work of Gustav *Fechner, resulted in the Weber–Fechner law ($\Delta I / I$ = constant), where I is the intensity of the sensation and the constant is known as Weber's constant. The constant is different for each sense (for intensity of light, sound, etc.) and tends to increase with ageing, as sensory discrimination becomes impaired. (See AGEING: SENSORY AND PERCEPTUAL CHANGES.) It represents the smallest stimulus intensity difference that can be distinguished, and is a constant proportion (generally about 3 per cent) of the stimulus. This logarithmic relation is basic to almost all sensory discrimination, so that larger differences are required for greater intensities. (For a detailed account of the psychophysics that is the basis of experimental psychology and is still rooted in the work of Weber and Fechner, see PSYCHOPHYSICS; see also SIZE–WEIGHT ILLUSION.)   RLG

Ross, H. (1996). *E. H. Weber on the Tactile Senses*.

Wernicke, Carl (1848–1905). German neurologist and psychiatrist who qualified at the University of Breslau and returned to it many years later as a professor after spending several years in Berlin. He trained under the distinguished neuropathologist Theodor Meynert, who had great influence on Sigmund *Freud. Indeed Freud's early work in neurology betrays an outlook which had much in common with that of Wernicke and he likewise wrote a monograph on *aphasia.

At the early age of 26, Wernicke published the monograph that won him lasting fame. Its title was *Der aphasische Symtomencomplex* (The Aphasic Syndrome) and it appeared in 1874. The syndrome described by Wernicke was quite different from—and in many ways much more interesting than—that described a few years earlier by Paul *Broca and which had become known as *motor aphasia*. Whereas the latter involved essentially a loss or defect in the expression of speech, the form of aphasia described by Wernicke was marked by a severe defect in the understanding of speech, and correspondingly became known as *sensory aphasia*. This term, however, is by no means totally appropriate as expressive disorders undoubtedly occur in Wernicke's aphasia, but they are disorders in word usage and word choice rather than disorders in the articulation or expression of speech. In severe cases,

indeed, the patient's speech approximates to incomprehensible jargon. In such cases it is the phonemic structure of language rather than its formulation and expression that is at fault.

Wernicke was further able to demonstrate that there are important differences between these two forms of aphasia, not only in clinical features but also in the site of the responsible lesions; whereas in Broca's aphasia the lesion as a rule involves the posterior portion of the left frontal lobe, Wernicke's aphasia is typically localized in the left temporal lobe, though bilateral lesions are not uncommon in cases in which the receptive loss is severe.

Wernicke's interest in aphasia was far from limited to its phenomenology and localization. He made a most creditable attempt to tie together anatomical and functional findings in order to produce a general theory of language and its disorders. This approach was well represented in the fact that his monograph bore the subtitle 'A psychological study on an anatomical basis'. By bringing together the cortical localizations of the two major speech areas, namely those of Broca and himself, Wernicke evolved what we should no doubt today describe as a flow diagram for language in the brain, and his theory provided a major stimulus to the discovery and understanding of new syndromes, for example his pupil Hugo Liepmann's work on apraxia and its relation to lesions of the corpus callosum.

Although the type of thinking exemplified by Wernicke and his pupils, with its strong emphasis on brain centres and the connections between them, went out of fashion between the two world wars, in modified form it has once again become a foundation stone in the work of many present-day investigators. (See also LANGUAGE AREAS IN THE BRAIN; LANGUAGE: NEUROPSYCHOLOGY.)

Apart from his papers on aphasia, Wernicke wrote on a variety of neurological issues, and is still remembered for his description of a form of encephalopathy resulting from thiamine deficiency (common among alcoholics), which bears his name. He also wrote a textbook entitled *Foundations of Psychiatry*, which he himself regarded as his most important work, though it failed to achieve the popularity of Emil *Kraepelin's textbook.   NG/OLZ

Eggert, G. H. (1977). *Wernicke's Works on Aphasia: A Sourcebook and Review*.

Wernicke, C. (1895). *Gesommelte Aufsätze und kritische Referate zur Pathologie des Nervensystems*.

Wertheimer, Max (1880–1943). Born in Prague, Wertheimer is conventionally regarded as the founder of *Gestalt psychology. Working under F. Schumann at the University of Frankfurt, he carried out an important study on apparent visual motion, published in 1912 (see KORTE'S LAWS). His colleagues at that time included Wolfgang

*Köhler and Kurt *Koffka, who acted as subjects in his experiments. Wertheimer's report of this work was a seminal paper in the evolution of Gestalt theory: 'Experimentelle Studien über Sehen von Bewegung', *Zeitschrift für Psychologie*, 61 (1912).

Wertheimer later transferred to Berlin and subsequently emigrated to the United States, where he later reported original experimental work on learning, described in a book entitled *Productive Thinking* (1945; enlarged edn. 1959). OLZ

Whitehead, Alfred North (1861–1947). Born in London and educated at Sherborne and Trinity College, Cambridge, Whitehead was both mathematician and philosopher. He was co-author, with Bertrand *Russell, of *Principia mathematica* (1910–13), yet he differed greatly from Russell in his philosophy, as he was an *idealist. His main works are: *Process and Reality* (1929); *Adventures of Ideas* (1933); and *Modes of Thought* (1938). He was elected Fellow of the Royal Society in 1903 and appointed to the Order of Merit in 1945. RLG

Wiener, Norbert (1894–1964). American mathematician of international stature, born at Cambridge, Massachusetts. He joined the faculty of the Massachusetts Institute of Technology at the age of 25, and worked extensively on problems in the mathematics of electrical engineering, and especially on non-linear systems. Much of this work was later published in *Nonlinear Problems in Random Theory* (1958). His exceptional talents as a mathematician were evident very early; he graduated from Tufts University at the age of 14 and won his doctorate from Harvard at 18. His range of activities included work on assemblages, functions of a real variable, mathematical logic, relativity, quantum theory, and the Fourier integral and many of its applications. Late in the 1930s he became increasingly interested in biological and social problems, and formed a group with Arturo Rosenblueth, who was then at the Harvard Medical School. The group included philosophers, anthropologists, sociologists, psychologists, physiologists, mathematicians, and electrical engineers. Their meetings were concerned with scientific method and the unification of science; they continued until 1944, when Rosenblueth went to Mexico, and from them came the concept of *cybernetics. This dates from 1942 but was not named 'cybernetics' until 1947. It was defined generally as 'the science of control and communication in the animal and the machine', but the clear idea was that 'animal' included the human being.

The idea of cybernetics arose not only from the integration of science to include all aspects of scientific activities; it was inspired also by the development of the computer which was taking place at the same time under the influence of *Von Neumann, *Turing, and others.

It was affected too by the development of *information theory, work on which had emanated from the Bell Telephone Company under the influence of C. E. *Shannon and W. Weaver. This work described the principles involved in communication between any 'source' and 'sink'. Meaning was irrelevant to the measurement of information encoded, transmitted, and decoded, in a generally noisy channel. Channel capacity and optimum coding procedures were all considered, and the whole development was incorporated into the cybernetic mode of thought.

Wiener himself made use of time series and other statistical techniques, also involving Gibbsian theory. Information and its processing, in all its aspects, was seen to apply to a wide range of phenomena both organic and inorganic, including human speech, genetics, the nervous system, and the muscular system. Philosophical issues were involved in cybernetics, since vitalism was brought into the cybernetic view and its world was thought of as one of *Bergsonian time rather than *Newtonian. Mathematically, Wiener brought group theory and statistical mechanics into the picture and made it a part of the bulwark of what was primarily an attempt to show that man was a complex 'machine'. The language of the computer (originally binary code) was likened to the language of the nervous system and gave rise to the development of automata known as logical nets. This was carried out by two other members of the cybernetic group, Warren *McCulloch and Walter Pitts.

Yet another component of the cybernetic viewpoint was that of servo-systems. It was recognized that *feedback was essential to learning, and that the sort of adaptive control typified by a thermostat must operate in all animals, and especially human beings. It was recognized too that there were higher-level feedbacks which, as it were, adjusted the thermostat settings. The idea of man being a 'machine' had existed for years before Wiener's cybernetics. Democritus in early Greek times, Diderot, *Helvétius, *La Mettrie, and many others, including Mark Twain, had thought the same, but Wiener was the first person to give genuine evidence to support such a view. He saw human beings as encompassed by the same basic principles as other animals, and this included self-organization and self-reproduction.

Wiener also wrote a number of articles, with Rosenblueth and Julian Bigelow, on the philosophical aspects of cybernetics. The most controversial of these dealt with teleology as purposiveness, and attempts to justify a relatively simple feedback control system as necessary to scientific explanation. That teleological explanation is now widely accepted, as part of scientific explanation, is due mainly to him, even if the precise detail of such a form of explanation is still controversial and goes beyond what he originally envisaged. There are now new subdivisions of cybernetics in which automata theory is more developed mathematically, though the close association with philosophy is maintained. The central core of Wiener's cybernetics has been developed under the label *'artificial intelligence'. This has taken over the concept of 'man as a machine' and, with it, extensive theories of *sensation, *perception, *learning, *thinking, *problem solving, and language have been built up, all in mathematical and 'machine-like' terms. Wiener's most famous book, *Cybernetics* (1947; rev. edn. 1961), started a scientific revolution which has, as he would have wished, evolved and grown, and yet retains the central idea that human beings, however highly complex and sophisticated they might be, are 'machines' in that they can, in principle, be built in the laboratory.

See also MIND–BODY PROBLEM: PHILOSOPHICAL THEORIES.

FHG

Williams syndrome. Williams syndrome takes its name from the cardiologist J. C. P. Williams, who was among the first to describe the condition in the early 1960s.

1. Physical characteristics
2. Early psychological accounts
3. Recent psychological accounts
4. Areas for further research

1. Physical characteristics

Williams and his group described a pattern of physiological characteristics that they consistently observed in a group of patients, including narrowing of the arteries and an 'elflike' facial profile. Subsequent research has shown that Williams syndrome is also associated with raised levels of blood calcium in the early months of life—infantile hypercalcaemia was a common alternative diagnostic label until relatively recently— as well as hypersensitivity to sounds, and that the condition has a genetic basis. Williams syndrome is caused by the deletion of approximately twenty genes on the long arm of chromosome 7. Although there is continuing debate as to which of these genes are necessary and sufficient for a diagnosis of Williams syndrome, and which are responsible for the various different aspects of the condition, genetic testing provides a means of strengthening a diagnosis based on physical features.

2. Early psychological accounts

In addition to these physical characteristics, individuals with Williams syndrome appear to show a particularly unusual psychological or cognitive profile, which has consequently been the focus of considerable research interest. Early accounts of the condition reported marked difficulties in most areas of cognitive functioning, particularly areas of visuospatial cognition, in contrast to strengths in areas of language functioning and face processing. In fact, many of these reports suggested that language and face recognition abilities were entirely spared in Williams syndrome. This raises the possibility that these areas of cognition are encapsulated domains of functioning, probably with distinct underlying neural substrates, which do not depend on general levels of intelligence but can be selectively spared in the face of more general cognitive difficulties. In addition, these accounts highlighted the particularly fluent, empathic, and adult use of language seen in individuals with Williams syndrome, as well as a tendency for individuals to make unusual word choices. For example, when asked to list all the animals that they knew, one child is reported to have included ibex, yak, and chihuahua in their response in preference to more common animals.

3. Recent psychological accounts

Subsequent research has shown that this psychological characterization is slightly oversimplistic. Many of these early studies of cognitive skills compared individuals with Williams syndrome with controls with Down's syndrome. However, Down's syndrome is itself associated with a somewhat uneven pattern of cognitive strengths and weaknesses, which complicates the interpretation of these results. Studies employing more appropriate comparison groups have confirmed that visuospatial abilities tend to be extremely poor in Williams syndrome. For example, individuals have severe difficulties in completing puzzle-like tasks that require the arrangement of parts to form a coherent image, and in drawing. In addition, in many individuals, particularly older and more able individuals, verbal skills are considerably stronger in comparison. However, this discrepancy between strong verbal abilities and much poorer visuospatial skills is not consistently observed in younger and less able individuals, and may even be reversed in infants with Williams syndrome. One therefore needs to take a truly developmental perspective to fully account for the cognitive pattern of strengths and weaknesses associated with the condition. Furthermore, it is increasingly clear that verbal skills are not consistently spared in Williams syndrome—that is, they are rarely at age-appropriate levels. On standardized tests of language functioning individuals tend to receive verbal IQ scores of below 100, and careful comparisons of the language skills of individuals with Williams syndrome and controls have not confirmed the view that language is particularly fluent or that word choices are particularly unusual.

4. Areas for further research

Consequently, Williams syndrome does not provide as strong support for the potential separateness of language and other cognitive domains as was initially thought, although the fact that these skills tend to dissociate in the condition is perhaps consistent with this view. Indeed, it has been argued that one needs to look more carefully within the domain of language to properly determine whether Williams syndrome provides evidence for the distinctiveness of certain language systems. Linguists would argue that one needs to distinguish between the conceptual aspects of language that are necessarily affected by an individual's level of cognitive ability, and computational aspects such as the application of syntactic rules which are arguably innately specified and independent of other cognitive processes. Under this account, individuals with Williams syndrome might be expected to have some language difficulties, but not in the area of syntactic rule application. Recent studies testing this specific hypothesis have provided mixed results, and further work is needed to determine properly whether computational aspects of language are spared in Williams syndrome. The same is true of face-processing skills, which are less impaired than other visual and spatial abilities, but may not be consistently as strong as initial accounts suggested. It is not clear whether apparent strengths in face identity recognition extend to other aspects of face processing such as emotion recognition. Indeed, it may be that individuals with Williams syndrome process face information in a qualitatively different way from other individuals, leading to an unusual pattern of strengths and weaknesses across different types of task.

In fact, although psychologists are primarily interested in Williams syndrome because of the ways in which the condition might shed light on the function and organization of language processes, it seems that Williams syndrome may ultimately tell us more about the nature of visuospatial cognition than it does about language. With the exception of aspects of face processing, visuospatial abilities are consistently and markedly impaired in Williams syndrome. The fact that the condition is caused by the deletion of a limited number of genes raises the possibility of mapping out the links between these genes and the typical development of visuospatial skills. Although this mapping is unlikely to be a simple one, given the complex nature of visuospatial cognition, a better understanding of this relationship would clearly have potential benefits in terms of educational and medical provision for individuals with Williams syndrome.　　　　　CJ

Bellugi, U., and St George, M. (2001). *Journey from Cognition to Brain to Gene: Perspectives from Williams Syndrome.*

Farran, E. K., and Jarrold, C. (2003). 'Visuo-spatial cognition in Williams syndrome: reviewing and accounting for strengths and weaknesses in performance'. *Developmental Neuropsychology*, 23.

Karmiloff-Smith, A. (1998). 'Is atypical development necessarily a window on the normal mind/brain? The case of Williams syndrome'. *Developmental Science*, 1.

Morris, C. A., and Mervis, C. B. (1999). 'Williams syndrome'. In Goldstein, S., and Reynolds, C. R. (eds.), *Handbook of Neurodevelopmental and Genetic Disorders in Children.*

Wittgenstein, Ludwig Josef Johann (1889–1951). Born in Vienna, the son of a wealthy engineer, he studied engineering at Berlin and at Manchester (1908–11), where he designed a propeller. Here he became interested in mathematics and logic, which he studied under Bertrand *Russell at Cambridge from 1912 to 1913. He served in the Austrian artillery during the First World War, was captured, and ended the war in a prisoner-of-war camp near Monte Cassino, where he wrote the *Tractatus logico-philosophicus* (Leipzig, 1921; published with parallel English–German text in 1922 with an introduction by Russell). Wittgenstein taught in a village school in Austria from 1920 to 1926, worked in a monastery garden, and then, after designing a house for his sister, returned to philosophy at Cambridge. He was a Fellow of Trinity College from 1930 to 1936, and professor from 1939 to 1947. For part of this time he did war service as a porter in Guy's Hospital, London. He became a naturalized British subject in 1938.

He lived austerely in his college rooms. It is said that he dined only once in the college hall, finding the conversation dull. His room was furnished with deckchairs for his students and a fireproof safe for his papers. After a lengthy illness, during much of which he lived in Ireland, he died in Cambridge on 29 April 1951.

Wittgenstein's main works are: *Notebooks 1914–16* (repr. 1961); *Tractatus logico-philosophicus* (1922); *Philosophical Remarks* (1930; repr. 1975); *Philosophical Grammar* (1974; compiled in 1933); *The Blue and Brown Books* (1958; compiled from lecture notes of the period 1933–5); *Remarks on the Foundations of Mathematics* (1956; compiled from notes of the period 1937–44); *Philosophical Investigations* (1953).

　　　　　RLG

Anscombe, G. E. M. (1959). *An Introduction to Wittgenstein's Tractatus.*

Bartley, W. W. (1973). *Wittgenstein.*

Kenny, A. (1973). *Wittgenstein.*

Malcolm, N. (1958). *Ludwig Wittgenstein: A Memoir.*

Pears, D. (1970). *Wittgenstein.*

Wittgenstein's philosophy of language. The philosophy of language gives a general account of the nature and function of language. The central question that it tries to answer is, 'What is meaning?'. It is closely connected with the philosophy of mind, because language expresses things that are in the mind, such as thoughts and intentions. More generally, whatever the functions of language, their performance depends on constancy of meaning, and the preservation of this constancy is an intellectual achievement.

*Wittgenstein's philosophy developed in two stages. His first theory of language is set out in *Tractatus logico-philosophicus*, and his second in *Philosophical Investigations*. The first theory is mainly concerned with statements of fact, while the second is equally concerned with other uses of language. The first theory gives a very abstract account of factual discourse and says little about what goes on in the minds of its producers, whereas the second presents language, in all its uses, as part of human life, so that questions about meaning lead inevitably to questions about what goes on in people's minds.

It may seem surprising that Wittgenstein focused his first study on to factual discourse, because he certainly did not regard religion and morality as unimportant, or their statements as meaningless. The explanation is that his interest in the philosophy of language began when he was working on the foundations of logic and mathematics (SEE WITTGENSTEIN'S PHILOSOPHY OF LOGIC AND MATHEMATICS). For anyone who wants to understand how logical formulae achieve necessary truth must first understand how ordinary statements achieve contingent truth. The work already done by Gottlob Frege and Bertrand *Russell on the foundations of logic and mathematics had made that very clear. Now factual statements are the most perspicuous kind, because the conditions under which they achieve truth are most easily understood. So given Wittgenstein's approach, it was natural for him to concentrate on them. He treated them in a very abstract way, because that is what logicians always do to language.

Factual discourse is also the dominant kind, and we tend to construe other kinds of discourse by reference to it, making either an assimilation or a contrast. According to the *Tractatus*, it mirrors the actual world by presenting it as it is, and alternative possible worlds by presenting them as they might be. Since it expresses everything that can be said, it sets a limit to what can be imagined or conceived. Beyond that limit there is nothing—i.e. nothing of the same kind, only better. There are facts and possibilities, and, beyond them, nothing.

This seems to imply that all non-factual discourse is meaningless. But Wittgenstein distinguished two ways of understanding. In order to understand a factual statement, you have to know its sense, i.e. the possibility which, if it were actualized, would make it true. Other kinds of statement lack sense, but they are not, therefore, meaningless, like jumbled factual messages. They achieve meaning by revealing certain features of the world and human life. This is the mystical element in Wittgenstein's early philosophy.

His reconciliation of the competing claims of scientific understanding and other modes of apprehension is *Kantian in spirit. The novelty is that it is presented as part of a theory of language. Factual discourse stretches to the extreme limit of what we can understand, but only on one level. There is also another, deeper level of discourse, which can be construed only by contrast with factual discourse, because assimilation would render it meaningless.

For example, religious statements must not be construed as factual statements of a special kind.

The distinguishing mark of a factual statement is, according to the *Tractatus*, its pictorial character. The words that make up the statement are correlated with things in the world, just as the points on a map are correlated with points on the ground. The arrangement of the words reveals how the things are arranged, if the statement is true, and the statement says that they are so arranged, truly, if they are. The analogy with the kind of picture that is used to convey factual information is obvious. But Wittgenstein generalized the obvious analogy, because he did not think that the words and their arrangement have to be *like* the things and their arrangement. All that he thought necessary is that the statement should have the same form as the fact that it reports. The shared form is spatial in the case of a map, but it need not be spatial, because it could be purely logical. So the analogy between factual statements and informative pictures is a very abstract one.

This theory differs from Frege's, because Wittgenstein takes assertion to be an essential part of a statement, which possesses sense only because it is a shot at the truth. It also differs from Russell's theory, which treated logical forms as things with which we are acquainted, albeit in a Platonic way. The central point of Wittgenstein's theory is that logical form can neither be named nor described. It is inherent in reality, and it can be revealed only in language. So his mysticism touches the centre of his theory of factual discourse.

His later philosophy of language is very different. It does not draw a single line dividing factual discourse from the rest. Language is now presented as something multiply variegated, the nature of each variety being determined by its function. There is no longer any attempt to impose a system on the phenomena. All theorizing is avoided and its place taken by careful description of different uses of language ('language games'). Although the description is untheoretical, it is not undirected, because it is designed to check our endemic tendency to misunderstand the logic of our language. That had been one of the aims of the *Tractatus* too. What is new is the method, which is not to seek a profound, abstract theory, but, rather, to sift the details that lie open to view on the surface of language. So *Philosophical Investigations* is a contribution to *Geisteswissenschaft*. The enquiry traverses some of the territory of psychology, and even sociology, but the purpose is philosophical, namely to understand how we mean what we mean by what we say.

When language is examined in its natural setting, as a part of human life, questions about meaning lead inevitably to questions about what goes on in people's minds. What does someone else mean by those words? How do you know what he means? How do you even know what you yourself meant by a particular word in the past? These questions all lead into the subject that dominates Wittgenstein's later philosophy of language, the preservation of constancy of meaning by individuals and by cultures.

The early account of factual language relied on correlations between words and things. But how were the correlations to be maintained? A natural answer is that the speaker must follow a rule. However, Wittgenstein makes the important point that a rule is not like the mechanism of a clock, which forces the hands to move as they do. You may have internalized a rule governing the use of a particular word, but the internalized rule still needs to be interpreted, and any interpretation will be verbal and so will need to be interpreted in its turn. Perhaps it looks as if we could cut out all problems of interpretation by going straight to your actual applications of the word. But many of them lie in the future, and Wittgenstein argues that nothing that is in your mind now determines exactly how you will apply the word in the future. What you have internalized is not a programme of the kind that can be inserted in a machine.

If what is in your mind now does not rigidly predetermine your use of the word, the same will be true of other people too. But this seems to threaten communication. For how can you be sure that what is in the mind of someone who claims to understand you is the same as what was in your mind when you spoke? Would not improvisation make all communication impossible?

Wittgenstein rejects the theory on which these questions are based. If the meaning of a word, as used by you, had to conform to a kind of template in your mind, communication would indeed be impossible. For when you were using the word, the difference between fidelity and improvisation could not be detected by others. Even you could not be sure of it, because the template might have changed without your noticing the change. So he suggests, instead, that two people agree about the meaning of a word when they agree, and see that they agree, in their applications of it. This may sound like *behaviourism, but in fact there is no repudiation of mental events and processes. The point is only that the contact that keeps the meaning of a word the same for different people is public and part of the life that they live together.

It follows that communication about what occurs in people's minds is possible only if they already share a language for describing what occurs outside their minds. For a vocabulary with the first of these two functions necessarily depends on a vocabulary with the second one (see WITTGENSTEIN'S PHILOSOPHY OF MIND). This argument against the possibility of a 'private language'—i.e. a completely independent language for describing the contents of the mind—is the key to Wittgenstein's later theory of meaning.   DFP

Wittgenstein's philosophy of logic and mathematics. Both logic and mathematics are concerned with connections of thought—for example, the connection between the information that there are two heaps of walnuts on the table, each containing twelve nuts, and the conclusion that there are 24 nuts on the table. This is a necessary connection. It is, perhaps, discovered by experience, but it certainly is not vulnerable to experience. Anyone who claimed to have found that it broke down in certain cases would be told that he did not understand arithmetic. The necessity of a mathematical equation, such as $12 + 12 = 24$, is quite different from the universal truth of the contingent statement that no walnut weighs a pound. The same is true of the necessities of logic. Experience could never upset the hypothetical statement that, if no walnut weighs a pound, and if you have chosen a walnut, then what you have chosen does not weigh a pound.

If a discipline invokes special ideas, or things of a special kind, its philosophy must explain them. Logic and mathematics evidently do introduce new kinds of things, such as numbers and the logical forms of sentences. But the most fundamental idea that is peculiar to these two disciplines is the idea of necessity. What is the nature of the necessity of a mathematical equation or a logical formula? And how do we know about it? Wittgenstein's philosophy of logic and mathematics is mainly a search for answers to these two questions.

Like his other philosophy, it divides into two stages. His first account of logic and mathematics is given in the *Tractatus logico-philosophicus*, and his later ideas are developed in *Philosophical Remarks*, *Philosophical Grammar*, and *Remarks on the Foundations of Mathematics*. The most striking feature of both accounts is his preoccupation with applied logic and mathematics. In the examples used above, a mathematical equation enabled us to answer the question of how many nuts there were on the table without combining the two heaps and counting again, and a logical formula enabled us to answer the question whether a particular nut weighed a pound without actually weighing it. Wittgenstein always kept this kind of application in the centre of the picture. In fact, it is arguable that he did not pay enough attention to pure mathematics or pure logic.

His preoccupation with applied logic and mathematics is most conspicuous in his later work, which treats language as part of human life and investigates it in its natural setting (see WITTGENSTEIN'S PHILOSOPHY OF LANGUAGE). But though his early work is more abstract, and, therefore, less concerned with the actual uses of language, one of its leading ideas already points towards the later developments. Logicians often assume that their job is to prove the formulae that are used in everyday life, but in the *Tractatus* Wittgenstein argues that such proofs achieve nothing, and, anyway, are not needed. This is directed against Gottlob Frege and Bertrand *Russell, who both assumed that applied logic relies on pure logic to ratify its formulae by deducing them from the smallest possible set of axioms.

First, consider what, if anything, such proofs achieve. Suppose that the candidate to be proved is the logical formula used above, namely 'If no A is B, and if this is an A, then this is not B'. You choose a set of axioms and, using them as premises, you set out to prove this particular formula. But even if you are successful, Wittgenstein points out that your achievement will be limited. You will know that, if your axioms are necessary truths, then this formula too is a necessary truth. But how will you know whether your axioms are necessarily true? It is no good saying that they are self-evident, as Russell did. For we have no criterion of self-evidence, and, if we are going to rely on it in the end, we might as well appeal to it immediately and say that the formula itself is self-evident.

Wittgenstein's second thesis, that in any case such proofs are not needed, is based on the idea that the necessary connection between premises and conclusion in an ordinary valid argument, like the one set out above, is guaranteed by their structures. They simply fit together, like the pieces of a jigsaw puzzle, and there is no need for any formula, or instruction for fitting them together, still less for a proof of the formula itself. Such devices seem to be needed only because ordinary language is not perspicuous and does not reveal the structures of the thoughts that it expresses. Consequently, we feel unable to do the jigsaw puzzle without more apparatus. But Wittgenstein regards this as an illusion. If we had a perspicuous language, we would see that 'logic takes care of itself'. If q follows from p, this can be read off from the structures of the two sentences, once they have been made perspicuous.

The idea of a perfectly perspicuous language is one that Wittgenstein borrows from Frege and Russell and uses against them. He also rejects their theory that mathematics is an extension of logic, involving no new ideas and dealing with no new kinds of things (the theory known as 'logicism'). He thinks that mathematics too takes care of itself. For the necessary connection expressed by an equation is guaranteed by the structures of the expressions flanking the sign for equality.

This assignment of an autonomous status to mathematics is another feature that points towards later developments. His hostility to logicism continued, and he came to see mathematics itself as a group of separate, autonomous disciplines, or, to use his word for it, 'a motley'. The new view was a consequence of the general reorientation of his philosophy. He gave up the idea that philosophers should seek systematic theories, and came to think that their task is to describe our modes of thought, or 'language games', in all their variety. In each of them it is possible to distinguish correct from incorrect performances, but the appeal is always to a criterion that is internal to the practice, and never to one that is fixed independently of it.

The new conception of the philosophy of logic and mathematics led to changes that are difficult to assess. His emphasis on application is increased, but there seems to be a complete change in his account of necessity. His early theory was that necessity depends on structure, and we give a sentence its structure by determining its truth conditions, i.e. the contingencies that would make it true. The early theory was that, when we have fixed the semantics of sentences in this way, we have already determined whether they are necessarily connected with one another or not, and there is nothing more that we can do about it. His later view seems to be that there is something more that we can do about it: we can ratify, or refuse to ratify, the connection as a necessary one.

If we really do have this option, proof is not what it seems to be. In the argument about the weight of the nut it seems to trace a necessary connection that is predetermined by the semantics of three sentences. This is, of course, a proof in the application of logic (or of mathematics in the other example). But proofs in the pure disciplines seem to run on equally predetermined lines. However, Wittgenstein appears to be denying predetermination in both kinds of case. If he meant the denial literally, he would be making logic and mathematics completely unsystematic. Every move would be autonomous, and the theory would be extreme conventionalism.

It is difficult to divine the precise meaning of his new, paradoxical view of necessity. This is partly because we try to relate it to other contemporary theories, such as intuitionism or strict finitism. But the chief reason is that he is making a profound suggestion, which is designed to change our whole conception of language and thought without changing the ways in which we actually speak and think. His suggestion is that the concept of following a rule, which is fundamental in the philosophy of language, is not what it seems to be. It seems that there is something in the mind of a person who is following a rule which determines what will count as following it in the future. But Wittgenstein regards this as an illusion. If he is right, we were wrong in thinking that, when we fix the semantics of a sentence, we predetermine everything. On the contrary, there will still be options left open. So the later development of Wittgenstein's philosophy of language is the key to his new philosophy of logic and mathematics. Some problems of interpretation still remain baffling, but it does open many doors.   DFP

Wittgenstein's philosophy of mind. Psychology occupies a central position among the sciences, because everything about which we know anything is filtered through the mind. For the same reason the philosophy of mind stands at the centre of all philosophy. The difference between psychology and the philosophy of mind is that the latter is not concerned with scientific questions but concentrates on questions of the utmost generality. For example, the question why people are aggressive is for psychologists to answer, but the philosopher asks, 'What is a motive?' and, 'What sort of thing is an unconscious motive?'. For his interest is in the general nature of mental phenomena. He also asks how we know what goes on in people's minds, and the history of *behaviourism shows that the two questions are, at least, connected.

Given the central position of the philosophy of mind, it is surprising how little discussion it gets in *Wittgenstein's early works (*Notebooks 1914–16* and *Tractatus logico-philosophicus*). This is because they are concerned mainly with the philosophy of language, approached through logic and mathematics (see WITTGENSTEIN'S PHILOSOPHY OF LANGUAGE; WITTGENSTEIN'S PHILOSOPHY OF LOGIC AND MATHEMATICS). In them Wittgenstein developed a theory of meaning based on an analogy between sentences and pictures. These things mirror the world, but he said very little about what goes on in the minds of people who use them. He believed that their unspoken thoughts must have the same structure as their sentences, but he made no attempt to explain what a thought is. Such details, he supposed, could be left to psychologists. The philosopher only had to produce an abstract model of language and logic, without bothering about the way in which the model is exemplified in real life.

After he had published the *Tractatus* his view of philosophy changed. He came to think that it is impossible to understand the nature of language or of logical necessity without going down into the market place and finding out about people who use sentences and arguments. How do they endow them with meaning? And how do they succeed in understanding what is going on in each other's minds? His later work (*Philosophical Remarks*, *Philosophical Grammar*, *The Blue and Brown Books*, and *Philosophical Investigations*) is mainly an attempt to find answers to these questions.

This may seem surprising, because the questions appear to be for psychologists rather than philosophers. Surely if you want to know what goes on in the minds of people who use language, you should construct a scientific theory about it and test it against the empirical evidence. So how does the philosopher come into it? The short answer, already given, is that he is concerned with very general problems about mental phenomena. But though this is true, it does not tell us about the specific character of Wittgenstein's philosophy of mind. It is equally true of the philosophy of mind of *Spinoza, whose procedure was to define the mental and its various forms.

Wittgenstein's method is completely different. One of the dominant themes of his later philosophy is the futility of definitions. He accepted the fact that the philosopher's interest in mental phenomena is general, but he did not draw the conclusion that his results should be general too. A philosopher who starts investigating meaning or understanding should not expect to be able to pack up his discoveries in neat definitions. On the contrary, he will find the answers to his general questions in individual cases. What he discovers will not be new facts, because he is not a scientist, but, rather, the significance of familiar facts. He will find the essence in its particular exemplifications, like an artist.

This method is well adapted to the philosophy of mind. For the distinctive characteristic of the mental is its infinitely subtle variegation. How else could it hold up a mirror to the world? If someone asks, 'How do people endow sentences with meaning and succeed in understanding one another?' the reaction might well be, 'It depends on what they are talking about'. This simple reaction is a natural one, because there is no reason to expect the same answer when they are talking about objects in their environment and when they are talking about their feelings. The aim of Wittgenstein's new method is to put us back in touch with familiar things—in this case, with the familiar facts of our mental lives—from which we are so often alienated by false analogies.

This introduces two more themes which dominate his later philosophy. One is the variety of different modes of meaning, and the other is the therapeutic character of philosophy, which frees us from the grip of false analogies.

The second theme is especially important in the philosophy of mind. Take, for example, his treatment of the phenomenon of understanding. It is only too easy to be misled by the following piece of analogical reasoning. If *A* uses an ordinary word like 'blue', and *B* understands it, his understanding must be a mental process because it is not a physical one. Now we can often explain a physical process by pointing to some physical event that produces it. So in order to explain understanding, we should look for an introspectible mental event. The most likely candidate is the occurrence of an image of the colour in *B*'s mind. So we are led to conclude that understanding essentially involves mental images.

Wittgenstein's therapeutic treatment of this case starts from the familiar fact, forgotten by this theory, that quite often *B* has no mental image. Then he argues that, even when *B* has one, its occurrence does not explain his understanding. For in order to get the right image and know that he has got it, *B* must already understand the word 'blue', unless, of course, he got the right image by luck. But in that case he might have taken the word 'blue' to mean 'coloured' or anything under the sun.

More generally, Wittgenstein claims that understanding is not really a mental process at all. If you silently run through the dates of the kings of England, that is a mental process. But often there is nothing introspectible to mark the achievement of understanding. What counts is *B*'s ability to operate with the word 'blue'. The idea that at the moment of understanding there must be mental events too quick to be introspected is a myth. It is the false analogy with physical phenomena that generates the myth, and the cure is to remind ourselves of the familiar facts of our mental lives, from which the analogy has alienated us. This is not behaviourism. Wittgenstein's point is not that there are no mental events or processes, but rather that we exaggerate their frequency, because we credit them with more explanatory power than they actually possess.

If philosophy is a kind of therapy designed to free us from bewitchment by false analogies, it will help us to recognize the variety of different modes of meaning, which was the first of the two themes mentioned just now. For we should be misled if we construed sentences about emotions or sensations on the analogy with sentences about physical phenomena. Wittgenstein's explanation of the differences between these two types of sentences is his main contribution to the philosophy of mind.

It begins, characteristically, with a thesis about meaning (see WITTGENSTEIN'S PHILOSOPHY OF LANGUAGE). Meaning must be kept constant, not only in order that *A* should be able to communicate with *B*, but also in order that *A* should be able to communicate with himself across an interval of time—for example, in his diary. But *A*'s use of the word 'blue' cannot be kept constant by reference to anything fixed in his mind, because there are no reliable mental templates. If *A*'s template were a mental image of the colour, it could change without his noticing any change. Even if it did not change, it would not rigidly predetermine his applications of the word 'blue' to other things. It is really the other way round: his public applications of the word to physical objects determine the character of the images that he accepts as 'blue'. So even if he did rely on a private image when he applied the word to a physical object, his appeal to it would not be final, because there would always be the further question whether he had appealed to the right image, namely to a blue one, rather than to one that he was inclined, rightly or wrongly, to call 'blue'.

If the meaning of the word 'blue' is kept constant by its public applications, *B*'s understanding of *A*'s meaning is no longer the unverifiable miracle that it would be on the theory of private mental templates. But what about words like 'pain' and 'anger', which, unlike the word 'blue', are applied exclusively to mental phenomena? Wittgenstein argues that here too constancy of meaning is preserved by

public criteria. But in these cases, which are typical cases of mental phenomena, there is a complication. The words 'pain' and 'anger' are not used to *describe* their public criteria, and yet it is the meanings of *these* words that their public criteria keep constant. Much of Wittgenstein's philosophy of mind is devoted to explaining how this feat is achieved.   DFP

Woodworth, Robert Sessions (1869–1962). American psychologist, born in Belcher Town, Massachusetts, and educated at Amherst College, where he graduated in philosophy. He proceeded to Harvard for his graduate studies, where he worked with William *James, Josiah Royce, and George Santayana, and completed his doctoral thesis 'On the accuracy of voluntary movement'. After working for a time as assistant in physiology at Harvard, Woodworth worked briefly in Sharpey–Schäfer's laboratory in Edinburgh and returned to England two years later as a senior demonstrator in physiology and as an assistant to C. S. *Sherrington at Liverpool, where he published a paper on 'The electrical conductivity of mammalian nerve'.

On his final return to America, Woodworth was appointed to an instructionship in psychology under James McKeen *Cattell at Columbia University, where he collaborated with E. L. *Thorndike, who shared his interest in the measurement of individual differences. He became professor of psychology in 1909 and was elected president of the American Psychological Association in 1914.

Apart from his work on individual differences and his attempt during the First World War to devise objective tests of emotional stability, Woodworth's contributions to research were somewhat meagre. He was, however, a prolific writer, his *Dynamic Psychology* appearing in 1918 and his massive *Experimental Psychology* in 1938 (rev. edn. 1954). His popular, though thoughtful, *Contemporary Schools of Psychology* was first published in 1931 and went into several editions. Woodworth edited a monograph series from Columbia entitled *Archives of Psychology* from 1906 to 1948. He published one book in French, *Le Mouvement*, in 1903.

word-blindness. See ALEXIA.

Wundt, Wilhelm Max (1832–1920). Wilhelm Wundt, the 'father' of experimental psychology, was born at Neckerau in Baden and educated at Tübingen and Heidelberg. He studied physiology at Berlin with Johannes *Müller and *Du Bois-Reymond before qualifying in medicine at Heidelberg, where he became a *docent* in physiology shortly before Hermann von *Helmholtz's arrival as professor and head of the physiology department. Although Wundt held Helmholtz in high esteem, it seems probable that the two men were never close. Whereas Helmholtz did not regard himself explicitly as a psychologist, Wundt became increasingly preoccupied with philosophical and psychological issues and for many years held lectures on psychology directed primarily at students of philosophy.

Wundt's most important book is *Grundzüge der physiologische Psychologie*, which was first published in 1873–4 and went into six editions. It presented psychology as an independent scientific discipline complementary to anatomy and physiology though in no sense reducible to them. The first and largest part of the fifth edition was translated into English by his former doctoral student and great admirer Edward *Titchener, under the title *Principles of Physiological Psychology*. Although it has been said that, in this book, anatomy and physiology were only marginally related to psychology, the book none the less established the principle that experimental psychology will find its future in close alliance with the anatomy and physiology of the central nervous system.

Wundt was appointed professor of physiology at Leipzig in 1875 and, in the same year, established the first laboratory in the world expressly dedicated to the advancement of experimental psychology: the Institute for Experimental Psychology. This laboratory very soon became a focus for those who held a serious interest in psychology, at first mainly for those who had studied philosophy and psychology in other German universities, but soon for graduates of several American and a few British universities. All subsequent psychological laboratories were closely modelled in their early years on the Wundt model.

Understandably, the activities of Wundt's laboratory closely reflected both the physiological background and the more recent philosophical preoccupations of its founder. On the more philosophical side, these were represented by the study of attention and what, following J. F. *Herbart, was termed apperception; on the more psychological side, one might specify the study of sensory processes, psychophysics, and the measurement of reaction times.

In this approach to experiment in psychology, Wundt's subjects were invariably adults who had undergone an intensive training in the technique of introspection (as it was understood by Wundt) in order that the facts of immediately apprehended conscious experience should not be contaminated by previous knowledge or anticipation. Even though this alleged purity of introspective report was taken to extremes, bordering on the ridiculous, there is no doubt that it did provide a genuine training in precise and consistent subjective observation that contrasted strongly with the often haphazard and poorly controlled observations that had characterized much earlier work on sensory thresholds and *psychophysics. Whether, however, such an approach to scientific psychology is truly applicable to the investigation of human personality and its development, or to abnormal states of mind, is an altogether different and far more controversial affair. None the less, it is important to bear in mind that Wundt did not himself believe that experimental method is applicable to all aspects of human psychology. In particular, he had no doubt that our understanding of language and its development must be sought through our understanding of history and culture rather than through experimental analysis. Wundt himself wrote voluminously on such issues in his later years, though very little of this work has appeared in English. It is, however, clear that the 'founder of experimental psychology' was neither a reductionist nor a dualist and that he believed that the field of application of experiment in psychology was distinctly limited.

Wundt's autobiography, *Erlebtes und Erkanntes* (1920), gives a straightforward account of his life and career and describes in some detail the establishment of his Institute for Experimental Psychology. This narrative outlines in a most interesting way Wundt's relations with a number of his contemporaries, not least E. H. *Weber and G. T. *Fechner, both of whom resided in Leipzig and both of whom he came to know well, despite the fact that Weber was a very old man at the time when Wundt first made his acquaintance. Fechner, on the other hand, was still active and directly inspired some of the experimental work in psychophysics that Wundt set in train in his new laboratory.

For a reassessment of Wundt seen through modern eyes, see A. L. Blumenthal, 'A Re-appraisal of Wilhelm Wundt', *American Psychologist* (1975). Also relevant is R. W. Rieber (ed.), *Wilhelm Wundt and the Making of Modern Psychology* (1980); of particular interest is K. Danziger's chapter in this volume on 'Wundt's theory of behaviour and volition'. An older, if possibly unduly fulsome, account of Wundt's psychological system and the work of his laboratory is to be found in E. G. Boring, *History of Experimental Psychology*, 1st edn. (1925), ch. 15.　　OLZ

Rieber, R. W., and Robinson, D. K. (2001). *Wilhelm Wundt in History: The Making of a Scientific Psychology.*

Y

yellow. Yellow appears to be a primary or simple colour, but in fact it is signalled at the retina by a mixture of red- and green-sensitive (cone) receptors having overlapping spectral sensitivity. This is a warning that it is not possible to infer the simplicity of physiological mechanisms from the simplicity or apparent complexity of experience. It shows indeed the fallibility of introspection for understanding functions of the nervous system, if not of the mind.

But, and this is a curious business, it turns out that yellow *is* special neurally, but further along the visual system. *Hering suggested his Opponent Colour theory in 1878—that there are two types of receptor, each having two kinds of response; one kind signalling either red or green, the other signalling either blue or yellow. This seemed to contradict the Young–Helmholtz trichromatic theory; but it now seems that *both* the three-primary colours and the four-primary colours theories are true—though for different stages of colour-processing (see COLOUR VISION: BRAIN MECHANISMS). So, starting from three receptors, in which yellow is a mixture, the later neural coding makes yellow special. We see this system in operation with the 'complementary colours' of after-images.

An excellent test for colour anomaly is matching a mixture of red plus green field with a monochromatic yellow field. This gives what is called the Rayleigh equation. People who are red-weak (protonotes) require more red, and people who are green-weak (deuternopes) require more green, to match the monochromatic yellow. If a normal or colour anomalous person pre-adapts the eye to bright red or green light, both fields are shifted oppositely—though the match is not affected. So this change cannot be detected with an anomalous scope used for measuring colour anomaly.

As the match is unchanged with selective adaptation, why is the match different for colour-anomalous people? Why does the anomaloscope test for 'colour blindness'? For it won't indicate colour-adaptation. It seems that the three response curves are not simply changed for sensitivity in anomaly (as they are with adaptation), but are shifted along the spectrum. Their pigments are under genetic control, so colour anomaly can be inherited. RLG

Gregory, R. L. (1955). 'Colour anomaly, the Rayleigh equation and selective adaptation'. *Nature* 176.

Mollon, J. D., Pokorny, J., and Knoblauch, L. (2003). *Normal and Defective Colour Vision.*

Yoruba concept of the mind. The Yoruba people of West Africa see the 'inner head' as mind—the seat of consciousness, and an arena for achieving mental balance, health, and destiny as goal orientation.

The world begins with one . . . the one that is formed through perfect balance between the powers of expansion and contraction, light and dark, . . . the balance between the masculine and feminine powers . . . and that one is a microcosm of all that is. (Fatunmbi 1992)

In Yoruba psychology, consciousness originated from *lae-lae* (i.e. eternity)—the mystical source of creation. This idea is part of a body of thoughts on the structure of being and of the universe, and these thoughts are referred to as *Awo* (i.e. secrets). These ideas were formulated at the dawn of Yoruba civilization, and were contained in 256 verses each known as an *odu*. Knowledge of these ideas was kept away from the public domain and guarded jealously by the priests of Ifa (the Yoruba religion). They were only passed on via oral tradition from one priest to a descendant priest. It is only recently that some of these ideas have started to be written down by Yoruba scholars.

According to *Awo*, a part of which is paraphrased above, everything in the universe was created from the ontological tension between the opposing forces of expansion and contraction, light and darkness. The contracting forces are centripetal in nature, and therefore absorb light, and the expanding forces are centrifugal and so generate light.

To the Yoruba, light comes from darkness and darkness from light. Both are seen as an expression of *ase*, a spiritual potency sustaining all of creation. In human beings, the seat of *ase* is located within *ori-inu* (i.e. inner head), which is the spiritual consciousness of self and the home of the unconscious mind. The balance of opposing energies in *ase* generates a spherical pattern in consciousness. This is symbolized by the circular format of *opon-ifa*, a divination board used by priests to restore alignment between *ori* (i.e. the physical head, also the seat of the conscious mind) and *ipori* (i.e. the super-soul, imbued with eternal life, which resides in heaven). This board is essentially a map of the polarities of forces in consciousness.

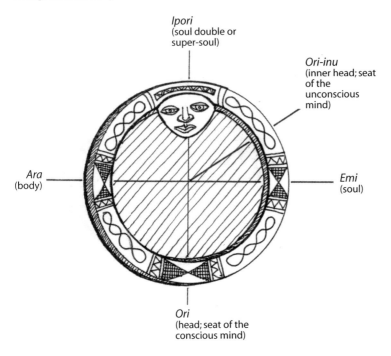

Ipori
(soul double or
super-soul)

Ori-inu
(inner head; seat
of the
unconscious
mind)

Ara
(body)

Emi
(soul)

Ori
(head; seat of the
conscious mind)

Fig. 1. *Opan-ifa* Ifa divination board, showing the map of consciousness.

Referring to the *opon-ifa* model of the structure of consciousness (see Fig. 1), *ori* is to the south, opposite *ipori* in the north. To the east is *ara* (i.e. the body) and to the west is *emi* (i.e. soul). In the centre of these forces is the inner head (*ori-inu*). It is the home of the unconscious mind and the seat of destiny.

It is believed that, just before birth, every *ori* (i.e. consciousness or head) negotiates an agreement with *Olorun* (i.e. God—literal translation is *owner of the sky*), outlining their goals for that lifetime. At birth the details of this agreement are removed from the realm of conscious thought and hidden in the unconscious domain, within the inner head (*ori-inu*) and *ipori* in heaven. One's destiny, therefore, is to remember the original agreement and work towards achieving those goals. Any deviation from these goals creates a misalignment between *ipori* and *ori* and results in disease.

Healing is sought through divination, a process of remembering and of realignment with destiny.   OA

Fatunmbi, F. (1992). *Awo, Ifa and the Theology of Orisha Divination.*

Young, John Zachary (1917–97). English developmental biologist and zoologist, born in Bristol and educated at Oxford University. Young started his research in the late 1920s, in Oxford. He carried out experiments over many summers at the Stazione Zoologica in Naples mainly on cephalopods, and to his great pleasure received the Freedom of Naples. In 1933 Young published the first correct account of the giant axons of the squid, showing that (after thinking they must be blood vessels, from their immense size) they are about 100 times the diameter of mammalian neurons, and have a thin myelin sheath making it easy to record electrical activity. The introduction of the giant axon in neurophysiology opened the way to understanding the physics of nerve conduction. During the war, Young studied axon regeneration, and grafting and nerve injuries in higher vertebrates and man, with the important clinical aim of treating war injuries. In 1945, Young became the first non-medical scientist in Britain to hold a professorship in anatomy, at London, running a first-rate and highly innovative department, with links to cybernetic thinking, and philosophy of brain and mind.

Young showed that octopuses have practically mammalian abilities to learn associations. He demonstrated that they can learn to recognize objects by touch, and can relate touch to vision. He produced highly detailed anatomical descriptions of the octopus brain.

Young combined detailed experimental work with a deep interest in philosophy, especially of mind and brain, relating his stimulating biological ideas to the nature of man and ethical values.

His most important works include *The Life of Vertebrates* (1951; 3rd edn. 1981), *Life of Mammals* (1957), and *Introduction to the Study of Man* (1971).   GGa

Gabella, G. (1998). 'J. Z. Young (1907–1997)'. *International Journal of Systems and Cybernetics*, 27.

Young, Thomas (1773–1829). British physician, physicist, and Egyptologist. Born at Milverton in Somerset he was, as the plaque to his memory in Westminster Abbey says, 'a man alike eminent in almost every branch of human learning, endowed with the faculty of intuitive perception, who, bringing an equal mastery to the most abstruse investigations of letters and science, first established the undulatory theory of light, and first penetrated the obscurity which had veiled for ages the hieroglyphics of Egypt'. This last he accomplished by studying the Rosetta stone in the British Museum.

Young suggested that *colour vision is given by neural mixture from three retinal channels, tuned to different but overlapping spectral bands. The notion was developed by *Helmholtz into the Young–Helmholtz trichromatic theory of colour vision, which is now generally accepted as an account of the first stage of colour analysis. Young also was the first to measure (on his own eyes) astigmatism, which he (wrongly) accounted for by supposing the eye's lens to be tilted. He showed by experiments (correctly) that accommodation to different distances is given by changing curvature of the anterior surface of the lens, and not by changes of curvature of the cornea.

He studied medicine at London, Edinburgh, Göttingen, and Cambridge, and he practised in London, but his main work was in research at the newly founded Royal Institution, where he became professor of natural philosophy in 1801. His optical experiments set the wave theory of light and phenomena of interference on a sound experimental and theoretical basis.

Young's classic paper 'On the theory of light and colours' was delivered to the Royal Society, as the Bakerian lecture, on 12 November 1801, and printed in 1802 (*Philosophical Transactions*, 92). His argument for only a few (three) primary colours is based on the consideration that visual acuity is almost normal in coloured light:

Now, as it is almost impossible to conceive each sensitive point of the retina to contain an infinite number of particles, each capable of vibrating in perfect unison with every possible undulation, it becomes necessary to suppose the number limited, for instance, to the three principal colours, red, yellow, and blue, of which the undulations are related in magnitude nearly as the numbers 8, 7, and 6; and that each of the particles is capable of being put in motion less or more forcibly, by undulations differing less or more from a perfect unison; for instance, the undulations of green light, being nearly in the ratio of 6½, will affect equally the particles in unison with yellow and blue, and produce the same effect as a light composed of those two species: and each sensitive filament of the nerve may consist of three portions, one for each principal colour.

In later papers, Young changed his 'principal' colours to red, green, and violet. The concept of 'principal' or 'primary' colours is a treacherous one, and he never fully grasped its multiple ambiguities. He was not, however, ensnared by one common error, that of supposing that the retinal receptors must have their greatest sensitivities at wavelengths which subjectively appear to us as 'pure' or 'unmixed' hues; but he did fall into a second common error, that of supposing that the three spectral regions that are conveniently used as primaries in colour-mixing experiments are those that produce maximal activity in the three kinds of receptor. We now know that the cone receptors have their peak absorbances in the violet, the green, and the yellow–green parts of the spectrum (see COLOUR VISION). A light that looks red is not a light that optimally excites the last of these three types of cone; rather it is a light that produces the maximum *ratio* of absorptions in the last two of these types, and such a light lies at a wavelength much longer than the wavelength of peak sensitivity of either of them. This realization did not come until the second half of the 19th century, and to this day the term 'primary colour' continues to obstruct the proper understanding of colour among non-specialists.

Young's *A Course of Lectures on Natural Philosophy and the Mechanical Arts* (1807; new edition edited by Kelland in two volumes in 1845) is a useful source. His complete papers were edited in three volumes in 1854 by Peacock and Leitch: *Miscellaneous Works of Dr. Thomas Young*.

RLG

Morse, E. W. (1976). Entry in Gillespie, C. C., *Dictionary of Scientific Biography*, 14.

Wood, A. (1954). *Thomas Young: Natural Philosopher*. (A Life, with a full bibliography of Young's books and papers.)

Z

Zangwill, Oliver (1913–87). A principal founder of neuro-spsychology and professor of experimental psychology in the University of Cambridge from 1952 to retirement. Zangwill might be described as the Disraeli of psychology. Being literary and politically effective, he came from a similarly distinguished, unusually interesting family. His father was the influential novelist and playwright Israel Zangwill (1864–1926), whose writings include *Children of the Ghetto* and *The Master*. A cousin was the artist and writer Michael Ayrton (1920–73), whose bronzes and paintings are powerful statements. A common grandfather was the physicist William Edward Ayrton FRS (1847–1908), remembered especially for his galvanometer, and for introducing electricity to Japan. He explained the curious Japanese and Chinese 'Magic Mirrors' which although appearing perfectly flat project sunlight in the form of a ghostly Buddha on to a distant wall.

Zangwill was born in East Preston in Sussex, the youngest of three. His first recorded experiment was undertaken at the age of 8, at the expense of a lady who claimed to know infallibly when rats were present. Zangwill hid a rat under his collar, and kissed her, but she did not detect that anything was amiss. Could this be the origin of his lifelong sadness at the inconclusiveness of so many psychological experiments?

Zangwill told the writer that the most creative period of his life was at Edinburgh, during the Second World War, assessing brain damage in the Brain Injuries Unit. Records are scarce, but we may quote from his paper 'In defence of clinical psychology' (1966):

In 1940, a Brain Injuries Unity was set up in Edinburgh, under the direction of Mr (later Professor) D. K. (later Sir David) Henderson, Professor of Psychiatry in the University. The Unit was set up under University auspices with the support of the Rockefeller Foundation and its staff held honorary appointments with the Department of Health for Scotland. Professor [Norman] Dott, who is a man of quite exceptional vision and enterprise, had no doubt that psychiatry and psychology could make a worthwhile contribution to the work of his Unit. In consequence, he invited the late Dr. Andrew Paterson to join the Unit as its psychiatrist and Peterson proposed that I should work with him as psychologist. This offer I accepted with alacrity.

Zangwill goes on to describe the aims and work:

My own duties consisted mainly in the study and assessment of psychological defects after injuries to the brain. These were of all kinds and all degrees of severity. At the psychological level, brain injury may be expressed either in intellectual or personality changes of a general kind or in the form of relatively specific defects of a more or less circumscribed nature. Among that latter are defects in various aspects of perception and motor skill, in memory and learning capacity, and in the sphere of language—the aphasias and kindred disorders of speech. It was my job to assess these changes as accurately as I could, where possible by methods somewhat more sophisticated than those of ordinary neurological examination. . . . It will be borne in mind that many of our patients were young Service men and women who could look forward to many years of active life ahead of them.

Later (Zangwill, 1966), assessing the value of this work, Zangwill concludes that they were able to define disabilities, which though mild had importance for resettlement, and began to develop methods of re-education. He believed, justly, that it marked 'the beginning of scientific interest in the re-education of the brain-injured in this country'. Perhaps as significant was the opportunity for research into implication of brain injury for general psychology, with questions such as: is intelligence unitary or composite? Do defects of language imply defect of intelligence? Are intellectual powers discretely localized in the brain? What is the significance of cerebral dominance for psychological activity? Problems of localizing brain function continued to fascinate Zangwill for the rest of his life. He thought that adequate theoretical models of brain function, related to psychology, were needed for classifying psychological problems for diagnosis and therapy. He believed that experimental psychology had an important role to play for clinical advances but was dissatisfied with the current state of understanding, This was an excellent starting point. Zangwill formulated three principles for rehabilitation following brain damage, set out in 'Psychological aspects of rehabilitation in cases of brain damage' (1947): *Compensation*—reorganization of psychological function; *Substitution*—building up a new method of response to replace one damaged irreparably. The final principle—*Direct training*—involves complex and not well-understood issues of how far damaged regions can be taken over by other brain regions, with or without special training. Here animal experiments are important though they do not always correspond to humans. Zangwill's three principles remain the basis of current clinical approaches to rehabilitation.

After the Second World War, Zangwill became assistant director of the Institute of Experimental Psychology (as it was then known) at Oxford, working with its first professor, the Canadian psychologist George Humphrey.

He succeeded Sir Frederic Bartlett as professor of experimental psychology at Cambridge in 1952. He developed important links with physiology and zoology, especially with the subdepartment of animal behaviour at Madingley, through Bill Thorpe and later Robert Hinde. He continued his Edinburgh-inspired work on brain injury at the National Institute of Neurology at Queen Square in London, working especially with George Ettlinger, Michael Humphrey, Clifford Jackson, John McFie, Malcolm Piercy, Moyra Williams, Maria Wyke, Brenda Milner, and Elizabeth Warrington.

His own interests were many. One was handedness (he wrote *Cerebral Dominance and its Relation to Psychological Function*, 1960), and he wrote significant papers on aphasia, cerebral dominance and right-/left-handedness, amnesia, dyslexia, Korsakoff's psychosis, and more. His short book *An Introduction to Modern Psychology* (1950) was widely read.

With the zoologist William Thorpe FRS, Zangwill ran a remarkably successful discussion group from 1953 to 1958, which linked ethologists, physiologists, and psychologists, producing the book *Current Problems of Animal Behaviour* (1961). The introduction, by Thorpe and Zangwill, says (p. ix): 'An interest in animal behaviour had existed in the Cambridge Psychological Laboratory before the war, and given rise to some valuable studies. But work in this field was discontinued in 1940. . . . Zangwill believed that the time was ripe for a revival of interest in comparative psychology.' Meetings were held three or four times a term in Thorpe's room in Jesus College (dominated by the enormous horn of an ancient gramophone), starting with a year-long analysis of the Canadian psychologist Donald *Hebb's seminal book *Organisation of Behaviour* (1969). This introduced what has come to be known as neural nets.

Zangwill's own paper in *Current Problems* is titled 'Lashley's concept of cerebral action'. Karl *Lashley was famous for two principles: mass action and equipotentiality of the cerebral cortex. The danger (though not always recognized) was that *lack* of evidence for specific localized functions may be interpreted as *no* local functions. (This would be like assuming that there are no cars on the road in front when none is visible, in fog.) Zangwill says (p. 67): 'Although Lashley lacked a positive theory, he was convinced that the learning process does not depend upon specific anatomical structures or fixed patterns of neural connections. He adduced over and over again the negative effects of linear (trans-cortical) lesions on behaviour as evidence that the correlations between brain mass and performance level cannot be explained in terms of

reduplication of equivalent neuronal arcs.' So Lashley was 'led to seek some mechanism widely distributed throughout the cortex and able to facilitate a variety of activities by the total mass rather than by "specific mechanisms" '. Zangwill comments (p. 69): 'In spite of the fact that Lashley's principles are certainly not incompatible with concepts of localisation, there can be no doubt that his work served to create a climate of opinion distinctly hostile to the whole idea.' How did this apply to human brain damage? Lashley himself claimed that 'there is . . . little evidence of a finer cortical differentiation in man than in the rat' (1929). Zangwill comments (*Current Problems* 81): 'Although few would nowadays subscribe to the doctrine of localisation of function in its more extreme forms, it is difficult to accept the view that the cerebral cortex in man is in large part equipotential. Although this may perhaps be true of the cortex in early infancy, it certainly does not seem to be so after the development of speech.'

Theoretical issues of localizing function in complex systems, and especially of course the brain, were hotly debated in the department. It was questioned whether it was logically possible to specify local functions in a closely coupled system. Some experimental work, especially by Lashley, suggested that most of the cortex worked as a whole with 'mass action', and the influential *Gestalt school (with good psychological observations though dubious physiology) also argued for this view of brain function. Undoubtedly there are logical problems for localization of functions (especially when for lack of theoretical models we do not know what these functions are), and such difficulties persist with current extremely exciting work on functional brain imaging using magnetic resonance techniques. Although Zangwill was impressed by Lashley's mass action and equipotentiality ideas, he also believed that the brain is organized in hierarchical (following Hughlings *Jackson) functional modules. The brain is now often regarded as modular neural nets: partial destruction of artificial nets causing some typical neural disease symptoms. These issues, which dominated Zangwill's thinking, remain controversial.

Oliver Zangwill was the major founder of the Experimental Psychology Group, which was very influential, though sometimes critically described as an elitist Oxford and Cambridge club. It became the larger, still thriving Experimental Psychology Society with its *Quarterly Journal*, which Zangwill edited from 1958 to 1966. He was president of the EPS 1964–5. He was a member of the influential society, meeting annually in Austria from 1951, which founded the journal *Neuropsychologia*, which Zangwill edited for twenty years. He was elected Fellow of the Royal Society in 1977.

An amusing story is told of Zangwill seeing a *Korsakoff patient weekly. He would take a pen out of his pocket, and ask: 'Have you seen this before?' Every week the patient would say 'No'. At the final session, Zangwill asked: 'Have you seen this before?' The patient replied: 'Are you the man with all those pens?'

His life-long friend was Carolus Oldfield, professor of psychology at Oxford following George Humphrey. They wrote a series of significant papers on the concept of schema.

Oliver Zangwill made major contributions to the first edition of this book, advising especially on clinical psychology. His clinical work is remembered, and continues, in an institute named after him: the Oliver Zangwill Centre for neurological rehabilitation, in the Princess of Wales Hospital, Ely, near Cambridge. The Centre helps brain-injured patients, and it carries out fundamental research in neurology and psychology. Nothing could be more appropriate to the life and memory of Oliver Zangwill.

RLG

Gregory, R. L. (2001). 'Oliver Louis Zangwill'. *Biographical Memoirs of Fellows of the Royal Society*, 47.

Oldfield, R. C. and Zangwill, O. L. (1942*a*). 'Head's concept of the schema and its application in contemporary British psychology'. *British Journal of Psychology*, 32.

———— (1942*b*). 'Head's concept of the schema and its application in contemporary British psychology'. *British Journal of Psychology*, 33.

———— (1943). 'Head's concept of the schema and its application in contemporary British psychology'. *British Journal of Psychology*, 33.

Zangwill, O. L. (1947). 'Psychological aspects of rehabilitation in cases of brain injury'. *British Journal of Psychology*, 37.

——(1966). 'In defence of clinical psychology'. *Bulletin of the British Psychology Society*, 19.

Zeigarnik effect. The psychological tendency to remember an interrupted task more than a completed task, named after the Russian psychologist Bluma Zeigarnik (1900–88), and first reported in 1927.

Zen. The branch of Buddhism that focuses on the real possibility of attaining enlightenment or Buddha-hood, which is the realization of one's true nature, in the present. The term 'Zen' is also used to refer to the state of enlightenment itself. One is said to 'have Zen' when in this state.

1. History
2. What is Zen?
3. Zen tradition and practice
4. Zen and ordinary everyday life

1. History

Buddhism is founded on the teachings of the Buddha, who, in India *c*.500 BC, realized his true nature and attained liberation from illusion. Zen Buddhism emerged as a separate branch where Bodhidharma, the first Zen patriarch,

left India in AD 520 and took his teaching to China, where it took root and flourished. In AD 1100. Zen spread to Japan, where it had its greatest flowering and deeply influenced many aspects of Japanese culture. During the 20th century, perhaps in response to growing spiritual unrest and aided by advances in global communications, an interest in Zen rapidly developed in the West and resulted in the emergence of Western Zen masters and Zen centres.

2. What is Zen?

Whether in the formal setting of a Japanese Zen Buddhist monastery or during the weekly shop at the supermarket, Zen is about directly experiencing one's true nature in the present moment. Zen proclaims that it is possible to wake up to one's true nature right now, and that to put it off, or to work towards it, is to misunderstand what it is.

The experience of realizing one's true nature is enlightenment. This is manifested in a dynamic state of oneness, in contrast to the state generated by the prevailing mode of human consciousness, which is dualistic. This dualism is characterized by a sense of separateness from everything and everyone 'else', and a constant ego-driven manipulation of self and the world. Life is experienced through a fog of attachments and projections, and is reduced to a relentless cycle of desire and disappointment. Enlightenment is living life directly. One is free just to be in the present as it unfolds, carrying no burdens from the past or expectations into the future. This has been described as the great homecoming to the original state of being.

The moment of enlightenment occurs when there is a final, directionless 'letting-go' and all seeking comes to an end, as does the illusory seeker. 'I' is radically changed forever. There is direct perception and spontaneous being. This realization of the absolute self is Zen.

3. Zen tradition and practice

Because Zen is so clearly concerned with the individual's awakening in the now, it has produced few texts, and has no prescriptive rules and only a few practices. The word 'Zen' derives from 'zazen', which means meditation. Zazen is part of the monastic Zen tradition, as is the giving of 'koans': riddle-like questions aimed at bringing the student face to face with what seems to be preventing direct and spontaneous perception. Another part of the living tradition is 'sanzen': a private interview with a Zen master. The master is a totally clear mirror, intrinsically able to show the nature of true being and to reflect the workings of the student's ego. Zen masters all have their own ways, quite unique to them and to the moment, of encouraging students to see into their true nature and resolve the apparent conflict generated by dualism.

4. Zen and ordinary everyday life

Zen has not been confined to monasteries. It spread throughout Japanese culture and found expression in poetry (particularly 'haiku'), calligraphy, painting, Kendo, the Samurai culture, gardens, teahouses, and tea ceremonies. Many Zen masters painted, wrote poems, gardened and cooked, demonstrating that Zen is not divorced from ordinary everyday life. Zen is to be lived—indeed, Zen can *only* be lived.

The qualities inherent in expressions of Zen include spontaneity, simplicity, directness, naturalness, austere sublimity, subtle profundity, freedom from attachment, and tranquillity. Exposure to these qualities can resonate at the profoundest level and provoke an unbearable dissatisfaction at their apparent absence from ordinary everyday life. Yet Zen is fundamentally about ordinary everyday life.

One of the best-known Zen haikus is by Master Basho:

> The old pond, ah!
> A frog jumps in:
> The water's sound!

This is a clear expression of the immediate, simple, and fresh perception of what is, with nothing added or taken away. Life is just as it is. To realize this is to be fully alive. This is the truth of Zen that is manifest everywhere in every moment and can be experienced by anyone.   CSH

Reps, P. (1957). *Zen Flesh, Zen Bones.*
Suzuki, S. (1970). *Zen Mind, Beginner's Mind.*
Suzuki, D. T. (1953). *Essays in Zen Buddhism.*

Zener cards (or ESP cards). Named after the US psychologist Carl E. Zener (1903–64), who invented them at Duke University in 1930. They are used for experiments on telepathy. His brother invented the Zener diode, used to regulate electronic circuits. Carl Zener designed the cards in an afternoon, thought nothing of them, and disliked his name being attached to them. He had no interest in *extrasensory perception (ESP). On the faces of a deck of 25 cards is printed one of five symbols (circle, cross, square, star, or wavy lines). The chance of a hit is one in five for each card, the number of hits expected by chance for the complete pack being five.

See also PARAPSYCHOLOGY.   RLG

Zeno of Elea (5th century BC). Greek philosopher, celebrated for his paradoxes of motion. These are: Achilles and the Tortoise, the Flying Arrow, the Stadium, and the Row of Solids. They are well described by J. Burnet in *Early Greek Philosophy* (4th edn. 1930).

Zeno introduced the philosophical technique of trying to establish characteristics of reality—or at least of what cannot be real—from paradoxes.

The basis of the paradoxes is that if a distance between *A* and *B* can be subdivided an infinite number of times, and an object travels from *A* to *B* by crossing successive points (subdivisions), then it must cross an infinite number of points—which would take an infinite time. Therefore, motion is impossible! The paradoxes derive from the manner of expressing the problem. This is itself interesting, indicating the extreme importance of finding appropriate mathematical and logical kinds of description, as well as appropriate conceptual models for describing or explaining the physical world and mind.   RLG

zero crossings. In hearing and speech, the time intervals at which the wave crosses the zero energy axis, the primary information for speech. Attempts have been made to use this principle for hearing aids, limiting the peak energies and amplifying the zero crossings.

In computational theories of vision, it is the position of sudden changes of contrast, especially used by David *Marr and his followers.   RLG

Gregory, R. L., and Drysdale, A. E. (1976). 'Squeezing speech into the deaf ear'. *Nature*, 264.
Marr, D. (1982). *Vision.*

zoetrope. An optical toy with a sequence of pictures around the inside, viewed through equally spaced slots above the pictures. This gives continuous movement of repeated sequences, which was important in the history of cinema. It was invented in 1834 in Bristol by W. G. Horner (1789–1837). An improvement was invented by Émile Reynaud, the praxinoscope, with mirrors instead of slots, giving a brighter and more continuous picture.

Gregory, R. L. (1990). 'Our forgotten genius: W. G. Horner'. *Perception*, 19.

zombie. Originating in the West Indies, a human capable of only automatic movement and lacking consciousness. Used by philosophers (especially Daniel C. Dennett) in thought experiments for asking: 'What does consciousness do?' What can we do, with free will and consciousness, that a zombie would be incapable of?

Index

Compiled by Susan Leech

Note: The filing order is letter-by-letter. Subjects, authors of initialled articles, and first names to cited articles are listed. Only where an author has contributed two or more articles are the titles given in full. Page numbers in **bold** type refer to main articles.

Index

Index

Index

Index

Index

Index

Index

Index

Index

Index

Index

Index

Index

Index

Index

Index

Index

Acknowledgements

The publishers are grateful to the following for their permission to reproduce illustration material. Although every effort has been made to contact copyright holders, it has not been possible to do so in every case and we apologise to any that may have been omitted. For permission to reproduce figures not listed below, please apply to Oxford University Press.

ADRIAN, EDGAR DOUGLAS: Fig. 1 redrawn from E. D. Adrian, *Basis of Sensation* (Christophers 1928).

AGEING: Fig. 1 redrawn from A. Duane, 'Studies in monocular and binocular accommodation with their clinical applications'. *American Journal of Ophthalmology*, 122. Copyright © by the Ophthalmic Publishing Company. By permission of the *American Journal of Ophthalmology*. Fig. 2 redrawn from C. P. Lebo and R. C. Reddell, 'The presbycusis component in occupational hearing loss'. *Laryngoscope*, 82 (1972). By permission of the *Laryngoscope*.

AGGRESSIVE BEHAVIOUR: Fig. 1 by permission of the author.

ALZHEIMER'S DISEASE: Fig. 1 copyright © The Science Museum. By permission.

BABBAGE, CHARLES: Fig. 1 by permission of the author.

BRAILLE: Fig. 1 redrawn from J. Robin, *Louis Braille* (1960).

BRAIN DEVELOPMENT: Figs 1–3 by permission of the author.

BRAIN IMAGING: ALTERED STATES OF CONSCIOUSNESS: Fig. 1 by permission of the authors.

BRAIN IMAGING: THE METHODS: Fig. 1 redrawn from G. Rees et al., 'Unconscious activation of visual cortex in the damaged right hemisphere of a parietal patient with extinction'. *Brain*, 123 (2000). Figs 2 and 3 by permission of the authors.

CHILDREN'S DRAWINGS: Fig. 5 from *Nature*, 254, 417 (1975). Copyright © 1975 Macmillan Journals Ltd. By permission of the publishers. Fig. 7 from figs 2–4 in N. Freeman, *Strategies of Representation in Young Children* (Academic Press, Inc. 1980). By permission of the publishers.

CHILDREN'S UNDERSTANDING OF THE PHYSICAL WORLD: Fig. 1 by permission of the author.

DELIRIUM: Figs 1 and 2 by permission of the author.

ELECTROENCEPHALOGRAPHY: Fig. 1a by permission of Dr R. Jaffe.

EMOTION: Fig. 1 by permission of the author.

EVOKED POTENTIAL: Fig. 1 from H. Berger, 'On the electroencephalogram of man: 10th report', in P. Gloor (ed.) *Hans Berger on the Electroencephalogram of Man. Electroenceph. Clin. Neurophysiol.* supp. 28: 243 (1935). Fig. 2 from E. D. Adrian, 'Brain rhythms'. *Nature*, 153 (1944). Fig. 3 from T. W. Picton and S. A. Hillyard, 'Human auditory evoked potentials. II: Effects of attention'. *Electroenceph. Clin. Neurophysiol.* 34: 191 (1974). By permission of Elsevier Scientific Publishers, Ireland, Ltd.

EYE POSITION SIGNALS: Figs 1 and 2 by permission of the authors.

FEEDBACK AND FEEDFORWARD: Figs 1–3 redrawn from V. B. Brooks (ed.), 'Handbook of physiology, section on Neurophysiology'. *Motor Control*, Vol. II (Williams & Wilkins), for the American Physiological Society.

HEARING: Fig. 1 redrawn from P. H. Lindsay and D. A. Norman, *Human Information Processing*. Copyright © 1972 by Harcourt Brace Jovanovich, Inc. By permission of the publishers. Fig. 2 redrawn from G. von Békésy, *Experiments in Hearing*, trans. and ed. E. G. Wever (McGraw-Hill 1960). By permission of the publisher. Fig. 3 redrawn from R. M. Arthur et al., 'Properties of "two-tone inhibitions" in primary auditory neurones'. *Journal of Physiology*, 212 (1971). By permission of the Physiological Society. Fig. 4 data from Egan and Hake in *Journal of the Acoustical Society of America*, 22 (1950).

HUMAN GROWTH: Fig. 1 redrawn from J. M. Tanner, *Foetus into Man* (Open Books 1978). By permission of the publishers.

ILLUSIONS: Fig. 2 from R. F. Thompson, *The Brain: A Neuroscience Primer* (W. H. Freeman 2000). Fig. 15 from J. Burke and C. Caldwell, *Hogarth: The Complete Engravings* (Abrams 1968).

LANGUAGE: NEUROPSYCHOLOGY: Fig. 1 by permission of the author.

LOCALIZATION OF BRAIN FUNCTION: Fig. 1 from W. Penfield and T. Rasmussen, *The Cerebral Cortex of Man* (Macmillan, 1950). Copyright © 1950 by Macmillan Publishing Company, renewed 1978 by T. Rasmussen. By permission of the publishers.

MIRROR CELLS: Fig. 1 by permission of the author.

MUSIC PSYCHOLOGY: Figs 2 and 3 redrawn from McAdams and Bregman in *Computer Music Journal*, 3(4).

NEO-HAPTIC TOUCH: Figs 1–3 by permission of the authors.

NEURAL NETWORKS IN THE BRAIN: Fig. 1 by permission of the author.

NEUROANATOMICAL TECHNIQUES: Fig. 3 redrawn from P. Milner, *Physiological Psychology* (Holt, Rinehart and Winston 1970). Fig. 7 from fig. 4 Hokflet and Ljumgdahl, and Fig. 8 from fig. 15, Ljungdahl et al., both in W. M. Cowan and M. Cuenod (eds.), *The Use of Axonal Transport for Studies of Neuronal Connectivity* (Elsevier 1975). By permission of Elsevier Science Publishers, BV, Amsterdam. Fig. 9 from D. H. Hubel et al., 'Anatomical demonstration of orientation columns in Macaque monkey'. *Journal of Comparative Neurology*, 177 (1978). By permission of Alan R. Liss, Inc., publishers.

NEUROTRANSMITTERS AND NEUROMODULATORS: Fig. 1 after a fig. in S. R. Cajal, *Degeneration and Regeneration in the Nervous System*, trans. R. May (OUP 1928). Fig. 2 from A. Peters and I. R. Kaiserman-Abramof in Z. *Zellforsch*, 100 (1969). Fig. 6 redrawn from J. Linstrom et al., *Cold Harbour Symposium on Quantitative*

Acknowledgements

Biology, 48 (1983). By permission of the Cold Spring Harbour Laboratory. Fig. 7 from C. F. Stevens, 'The neuron'. *Scientific American*, 241 (1979). Micrography produced by H. E. Heuser. Used by permission. Fig. 11 redrawn from H. F. Bradford, *Chemical Neurobiology* (W. H. Freeman & Co. 1986). Fig. 12 redrawn from G. Burnstock, *Dale's Principle and Communication between Neurones*, ed. N. N. Osborne (Pergamon Books Ltd. 1983). By permission of Pergamon Press. Fig. 13 adapted from fig. 1 in J. T. Littleton and H. J. Bellen, 'Synaptotagmin controls and modulates synaptic-vesicle fusion in a calcium-dependent way'. *Trends in Neuroscience* (1995) 18(4). Fig. 14 adapted from fig. 2 in C. Holscher, 'Nitric oxide, the enigmatic neuronal messenger: its role in synaptic plasticity'. *Trends in Neuroscience* 20(7) (1995). Fig. 15 adapted from fig. 1 Sanes and Lichtman in *Trends in Neuroscience* 2(7) (1999).

PARKINSON'S DISEASE: Fig. 1 redrawn from figs 4–18 from J. C. Eccles, *The Understanding of the Brain* (McGraw-Hill 1977). By permission of the publishers. Fig. 2 redrawn from A. E. Brotman in L. Iverson, 'The chemistry of the brain'. *Scientific American*, Sept. 1979. Copyright © 1979 Scientific American Inc. All rights reserved. By permission of W. H. Freeman & Co. publishers.

PATTERN RECOGNITION: Figs 1–5 by permission of the authors.

PERSPECTIVE: Fig. 4 from P. Joannides, *Masaccio and Masolino*, (Phaidon Press 1993). Copyright © Scala, Florence.

PRIMATES, EVOLUTION OF THE BRAIN IN: Fig. 1 from W. K. Gregory, 'Mongolian mammals of the "age of reptiles"'. *Scientific Monthly*, 24 (1927). Fig. 2 after J. J. Kaas et al., 'Cortical visual areas I & II in the hedgehog'. *Journal of Neuropsychology*, 33 (1970). Fig. 3 from L. B. Radinsky, 'The oldest primate endocast'. *American Journal of Physical Anthropology*, 27 (1967). By permission of Wistar Press. Figs 4, 5, 6, and 7 (fig. 6 photography by J. Tigges), from J. M. Allman, 'Evolution of the visual system in the early primates'. *Progress in Psychobiology and Physiological Psychology*, 7 (1977). By permission of Academic Press. Fig. 8 redrawn after J. M. Allman and J. H. Kaas, 'Representation of the visual field on the medial wall of occipital-parietal cortex in the owl monkey'. *Science*, 191 (1976); W. T. Newsome and J. M. Allman, 'The interhemispheric connections of visual cortex in the owl monkey (*Aotus trivirgatus*), and the bushbaby (*Galago senegalensis*)'. *Journal of Comparative Neurology*; M. M. Merzenich et al., 'Double representation of the body surface within cytoarchitectoric areas 3G and 1 in SI in the owl monkey (*Aotus trivirgatus*)'. *Journal of Comparative Neurology*, 181 (1978); and T. G. Imig et al., 'Organization of auditory cortex in the owl monkey (*Aotus trivirgatus*)'. *Journal of Comparative Neurology*, 171 (1977).

PROBLEM SOLVING: Fig. 1 from P. C. Wason, 'Self-contradictions' in Johnson-Laird and Wason (eds.), *Thinking: Readings in Cognitive Science* (Cambridge, 1977). By permission of the authors and publishers.

PSYCHOPHYSICS: Fig. 1 from D. Laming, *Sensory Analysis* (Academic Press 1986). By permission of the publisher.

PUZZLES: Fig. 1 with permission The Hordern-Dalgety Collection http://puzzlemuseum.org.

QUANTIFYING JUDGEMENTS: Fig. 1 redrawn from E. C. Poulton, 'Models for biases in judging sensory magnitude'. *Psychological Bulletin*, 86 (1979). Copyright © 1979 by the American Psychological Association. By permission of the author.

RETINAL IMAGES: Fig. 1a and b redrawn from the Thomas Young Oration of the Physical Society, by permission of the Institute of Physics. Fig. 2 after fig. 1 from C. R. Evans, 'Pattern perception using a stabilized retinal image'. *British Journal of Psychology*, 56 (1965). By permission of the author and the British Psychological Society. Fig. 4 after H. Bennett-Clark and C. R. Evans, in *Nature*, 199 1215 (1963). Copyright © 1963 Macmillan Journals Ltd. By permission of the authors and the publisher.

SPACE PSYCHOLOGY: Fig. 1 redrawn from Young et al., 'Spatial orientation in weightlessness and readaptation to Earth's gravity', *Science*, 225 (1984). Copyright © 1984 the AAAS. By permission of the American Association for the Advancement of Science. Fig. 2 by permission of the European Space Technology Centre.

SPATIAL COORDINATION: Fig. 1 redrawn from G. H. Fisher, 'Intersensory localization' (1962). By permission of the author. Figs 2 and 6 redrawn from I. P. Howard, *Human Visual Orientation* (1982). Copyright © 1982 I. P. Howard. By permission of John Wiley and Sons Ltd. Fig. 3 redrawn from R. Held and A. Hein, 'Movement-produced stimulation in the development of visually guided behaviour'. *Journal of Comparative and Physiological Psychology*, 56 (1963). Copyright © 1963 the American Psychological Association. By permission of the authors. Figs 4 and 5 redrawn from A. Hein and R. Held, 'Dislocation of the visual placing response into elicited and guided components'. *Science*, 158 No. 3799 (1967). Copyright © the AAAS. By permission of the American Association for the Advancement of Science.

SPINDLE CELLS: Figs 1 and 2 by permission of the authors.

STEREOSCOPIC VISION: Fig. 1 redrawn from D. Brewster, *The Stereoscope* (1950). Fig. 2 by permission of the author.

TILTED ROOMS: Figs 1 and 2 by permission of the authors.

TRANSFER OF TRAINING: Fig. 1 after a fig. from M. Hammerton, 'Measures for the efficiency of simulators as training devices'. *Ergonomics*, 10 (1967). By permission of the author and the publishers Taylor & Francis Ltd.

VISUAL BRAIN IN ACTION: Fig. 1 by permission of the author.

YORUBA CONCEPTS OF THE MIND: Fig. 1 by permission of the author.